# Law of Torts

**THIRD EDITION**

*To Mary and Alice*

# Law of Torts

**THIRD EDITION**

*by*

**BRYAN M E MCMAHON**

*BCL, LLB, LLM (Harvard), PhD*
*Judge of the Circuit Court*
*formerly Professor of Law*
*University College, Cork and University College, Galway*

*and*

**WILLIAM BINCHY**

*BA, MA, BCL, LLM*
*FTCD, Barrister-at-Law*
*Regius Professor of Laws, Trinity College, Dublin*

Butterworths

**Members of LexisNexis Group worldwide**:

| | |
|---|---|
| Ireland | Butterworth (Ireland) Ltd, 24-26 Upper Ormond Quay, DUBLIN 7 |
| Argentina | Abeledo Perrot, Jurisprudencia Argentina and Depalma, BUENOS AIRES |
| Australia | Butterworths, a Division of Reed International Books Australia Pty Ltd, CHATSWOOD, New South Wales |
| Austria | ARD Betriebsdienst and Verlag Orac, VIENNA |
| Canada | Butterworths Canada Ltd, MARKHAM, Ontario |
| Chile | Publitecsa and Conosur Ltda, SANTIAGO DE CHILE |
| Czech Republic | Orac sro, PRAGUE |
| France | Editions du Juris-Classeur SA, PARIS |
| Hong Kong | Butterworths Asia (Hong Kong), HONG KONG |
| Hungary | Hvg Orac, BUDAPEST |
| India | Butterworths India, NEW DELHI |
| Italy | Giuffré, MILAN |
| Malaysia | Malayan Law Journal Sdn Bhd, KUALA LUMPUR |
| New Zealand | Butterworths of New Zealand, WELLINGTON |
| Poland | Wydawnictwa Prawnicze PWN, WARSAW |
| Singapore | Butterworths Asia, SINGAPORE |
| South Africa | Butterworths Publishers (Pty) Ltd, DURBAN |
| Switzerland | Stämpfli Verlag AG, BERNE |
| United Kingdom | Butterworths Tolley, a Division of Reed Elsevier (UK) Ltd, Halsbury House, 35 Chancery Lane, LONDON, WC2A 1EL, and 4 Hill Street, EDINBURGH EH2 3JZ |
| USA | LexisNexis, DAYTON, Ohio |



A CIP Catalogue record for this book is available from the British Library.

First edition printed 1981
Second edition printed 1990
Third edition printed 2000
Reprinted with revisions 2001
ISBN 1 85475 8314

Typeset by Marlex Editorial Services Ltd, Dublin
Printed and bound by Bookcraft (Bath) Ltd, Midsomer Norton, Avon
***Visit us at our website: http//www.butterworths.ie***

# Foreword to the First Edition

This work has been awaited for more than a generation. The learned authors of this excellent book have very successfully satisfied the long-felt need for a definitive work in this area of Irish law. For most of the sixty years which have elapsed since Ireland became an independent State there has been a total absence of first-class works on Irish law. In recent years a number of excellent works have appeared in the fields of constitutional law, family law and property law. But the law of contracts and the law of torts remained relatively unexplored by writers of legal text-books.

One is moved to ask why the law of torts, one of the main supports of the Irish Bar, should have remained for so long neglected by writers. Perhaps part of the reason may be that for many years our lawyers has not fully appreciated the common law as a system of law rather than as a body of law. Nor had it been recognised that the man on the Crumlin omnibus was not the man on the Clapham omnibus. There appeared to be an unquestioned assumption that English text-books would satisfy all needs. Many practitioners and judges remained unaware of the dimensions of the growing volume of Irish decisions in this field. A good text-book concentrates the mind wonderfully and brings to the practitioner decisions, reported and unreported, whose discovery would require an amount of research for which there is often too little time or too little appetite. In the result the concentration was not on Irish decisions.

In all common law countries, as is most notably demonstrated in the United States, the common law is a system of judge-made law. Judges are expected to reflect the cultural and moral standards which are professed (if not always practised) by the community which has elevated them to their offices. However, a judge does not select the materials with which he works. He must be moved by the action and by the advocate. Therefore it is understandable that for many years after the foundation of the State the judges and advocates, both products of a system of professional training which had conditioned them to seek their criteria outside these shores, should have failed to discern in the Irish context the essential characteristic of the common law system – that it is by definition rooted in the community it serves. Judges and practitioners should always be sensible of the fact that inspiration and new concepts can often be derived from civil law systems as well as from other common law systems and can be built upon in the development of Irish law. Yet there is a depressing lack of evidence of inspiration received and built upon. Why was not the blindingly simple truth underpinning *Donoghue v Stevenson* perceived here? Its inspiration had appeared in case law almost a half century earlier than the great seminal opinion of Lord Atkin. To retort that it had also escaped attention in England would explain much. Even today there are occasional unhappy examples of judicial opinions which appear to indicate a lack of confidence in any reasoning which cannot be vouched by a precedent to be found in another jurisdiction, even to the neglect of Irish authority upon the same point. In view of the great importance of the advocate's role in our Court system the Bar must bear the greater part of the responsibility for that situation.

A new generation of lawyers has appeared. It is better educated in the law and in the philosophy of law than were preceding generations. The authors of this work are brilliant examples of the academics who have emerged from the new generation of lawyers. Their presentation of the very considerable body of Irish tort law should give our practitioners and judges a new stimulus to explore our own legal heritage. It will certainly deprive them of any excuse for not being familiar with it.

It is generally agreed that judges make law. It is inevitable that they should do so. The cases referred to in this book, drawn as they are from the old and the new generations of judges and lawyers, amply illustrate in the Irish context the degree to which the creative function of the judge has been both neglected and exercised. In a common law system a judge does not make a selection from an inexhaustible store of pre-existing readymade legal principles. In dealing with a precedent the judge's function goes beyond perception of what was really intended. He exercises a choice. This is obvious enough when a case is over-ruled. But it is equally true that he also does so when a case is merely distinguished or even when it is followed without qualification. A precedent may be the starting point of a decision for a judge and may more often than not be also the concluding point. Lawyers frequently succumb to the temptation to treat all judicial opinions as being of equal value. They are not. A case must be decided, and the necessity to dispose of the case requires that an opinion be delivered. But the opinion may fail to reflect accurately the state of mind of the judge who delivers it. Happy is the judge to whom complete conviction comes easily. There are some to whom it never comes. Yet uncertainty must be masked. The doctrine of binding precedent has served as a shield for the uncertain and an anchor for the convinced. But it became so intellectually entrenched, even in the courts of final appeal, that for a long time it was thought that it could not possibly be abolished in any common law country. Nowhere was this felt more than in the law of torts. Some of the worst aberrations of the common law, as for example the doctrine of common employment, would not have persisted for so long if freedom had not been abandoned at the judicial summit. Eventually the Oireachtas had to abolish this doctrine by legislation in 1958. Happily the Supreme Court established under the Constitution in 1961 recaptured this freedom a few years later. In the following years, in cases which are referred to in this work, the Supreme Court removed some of the dead wood which old decisions has assembled.

This book reveals a surprising number of unreported cased which can be and have been relied upon and followed. A civilian lawyer would have great difficulty in finding any rational support for this aspect of the doctrine of binding precedent. Professor Goodhart thought that the most important reason for following precedent was to give certainty to the law. But that is scarcely compatible with the fact that the common law permits the use of unreported decisions. It has been said that the doctrine of *ratio decidendi* is the heart of the principle of *stare decisis* but, as one eminent jurist has said, the precise identification and delimitation of *ratio decidendi* 'is the deepest secret of juristic life.'

The law of torts contains much of that 'wilderness of single instances and that codeless myriad of precedent'. Most of these involve the fault principle which dominates the law of torts. It has been argued that in England the reluctance of common law courts openly to recognise their own creative powers by steadfastly maintaining the appearance of the law's inability to surmount difficulties made legislative reform easier and more widesweeping. Thus the English Occupier's Liability Act 1957 came to be enacted. On the other hand, as is illustrated in this book, in recent years the Irish courts by exercising their creative powers achieved the same result without the intervention of any remedial legislation. In England the Evershed Committee almost thirty years ago formed the view that the clarification of law by judicial decision was a swifter and surer process than legislation and one which can go forward at all times without regard to parliamentary time and quite independent of political considerations, thus avoiding the slowness of legislation and the cumbersome process of parliamentary procedure.

A judiciary which too much reminds itself of parliamentary responsibility and abdicates its law-making powers may lose the will to exercise that great historic function which is the basis of the common law system. If there are judges who do not wish to be caught 'engaging in law making' they can at least note statutory provision as a source of analogous decisions. This was done many centuries ago by those judges who evolved the doctrine of 'the equity of the statute' and engaged in creative law making in the courts on the basis of statutes. Our judges have available in addition the concepts and guarantees embodied in the Constitution as a basis for law making.

Common law courts have often shown themselves to be uneasy with statutes and frequently only grudgingly gave legislation its letter and no more. Sir Frederick Pollock in his Essays on Jurisprudence and Ethics thought that this common law attitude 'cannot well be accounted for except upon the theory that Parliament generally changes the law for the worse, that the business of the judges is to keep the mischievous interference within the narrowest possible bounds'. There was a view which regarded statutes as being 'in, but not of, the law.'

In a common law system in modern times there can be no justification for regarding statutes as being less a part of the law than judicial decisions. Judges should welcome these statutes as points of departure in the exercise of the common law technique of law making by analogy. Statutes can also in many cases provide the social data upon which judges may build their law making. The modern approach should be not whether judges should make use of statutes but how they can make the most use of them. That very eminent jurist and law teacher Roger Traynor, former Chief Justice of California, had said 'the well and elevator shaft and the busy intersection aptly illustrate a first grade reader of the mounting interactions of human enterprise, the mounting statutes that govern such enterprise, the mounting use that judges make of statutes that spin in long-travelled orbits of common law'.

The decision in *Rylands v Fletcher* was based upon an analogy drawn from earlier cases which had dealt with the liability of the man who kept wild animals upon his land. The question has been asked if this effect had been achieved by legislation rather than by judicial decision would die-hard judges, resistant to the use of statutes in the formulation of common law rules, have failed to discern the essential similarity between water stored in reservoirs, petroleum stored in tanks and gas and electricity confined or maintained upon the premises. However, there is one area in which in modern times the judges have built upon statutes. That is in the area of industrial welfare legislation. The judicial decisions manifest a desire to afford greater protection to injured workers than the common law of negligence would allow. In 1969 the English Law Commission recommended that there should be a general statute creating a presumption that a breach of statutory duty is intended to be actionable at the suit of a person who suffers or apprehends damage unless a contrary intention is expressly stated. While this recommendation was not implemented by Parliament it was in effect to some extent implemented by the courts in their decisions that a breach of statutory duty could be the ground for an action in damages. The creation of this new type of tort, if indeed it be a tort in the absence of fault, was justified by reference to the presumed intention of Parliament even though the legislative provisions in question were industrial penal provisions. The same results were achieved by Irish decisions. Yet it is noteworthy that breach of statutory duty regarding the use of defective vehicles on the highway contained in penal statutory provisions for the protection of the public has not inspired a similar judicial response giving rise to civil liability.

Can the law of tort in its present form survive without the existence of the fault principle? Many writers think it cannot. Is the case for strict liability dependent on a social value judgment that one undertakes an activity for his own advantage should bear the risk inseparable from it? This was the basis for the decision in *Rylands v Fletcher*. If the EEC draft Directive on Products Liability becomes the law of the land much of what now passes as part of the law of tort will find itself denuded of the fault principle. Yet strict liability as a concept dates from the early middle ages. While some torts require intention, or at least recklessness, most torts can also be committed by inadvertent negligence. The opponents of the abolition of the fault principle sometimes go so far as maintaining that the public interest and morality require, say in a case involving motor cars, that drivers should not be immune from the financial consequences of their negligence. Yet if this were true it would be difficult to justify the existence of compulsory motor insurance. Does not such insurance largely reduce the deterrent effect? Litigation arising out of motor car accidents occupies a great deal of time of the High Court and is a very remunerative type of litigation for many members of the Bar. In reality the defendant is only a nominal party through whom a process of distribution begins to flow. Indeed frequently both parties are in that position. This type of case obscures cases where moral fault and true deterrence may still be sound objectives. In the result the law of negligence is developing in a totally unrealistic setting and the principles so developed may operate in a most bizarre way, or even a most disastrous way, applied to other situations. The chapter which the learned authors have devoted to the tort of negligence provides ample evidence of the very large part which this tort plays in Irish litigation. Surely the time has come when serious thought ought to be given to removing motor car negligence cases and industrial accident negligence cases from the ambit of the fault principle and therefore, strictly speaking, from the law of torts. These are the type of cases where the distribution of loss theory should be openly acknowledged.

This work will reveal to a perhaps surprised common law world the existence of a significant body of Irish tort law. But more importantly it will awaken in Irish lawyers a new awareness of their own law and its separate identity. It is to be hoped that it will stimulate greater efforts to further development in this field of Irish law. We are all greatly indebted to the authors for this outstanding contribution to Irish legal scholarship.

Brian Walsh
The Supreme Court
August 1981

# Preface

In the decade since the previous edition, much has changed in Irish Society. Some of these changes are reflected in the present edition. The law of torts, even in what may seem to be technical and dry areas such as limitation of actions and computation of damages, is never too far removed from social developments.

The abolition of juries in personal injury litigation has had one positive outcome: it has encouraged judges to address a wide range of legal issues relating to such matters as the scope of the duty of care, vicarious liability and breach of statutory duty. Through their judgments reserved and *ex tempore*, we now have a far richer and complex body of tort law than ten years ago.

The outpouring of scholarly commentary by Irish authors, not only from academia but also from the Bench and the practising profession, has eased our task. We have sought to acknowledge their assistance throughout the text but we should express particular thanks to Dr John White, Tony Kerr and Marc MacDonald for their several texts relating to aspects of the law of torts and to Eoin Quill for his textbook on the entire subject.

William Binchy would like to thank his colleagues at Trinity College, Dublin for their help, in particular Eoin O'Dell, Alex Schuster and Clive Symmons. We are very grateful for the assistance given by Elizabeth Gleeson of the Library at Trinity, and the huge support offered by Margaret Byrne, Mary Gaynor, Eddie Mackey, Aoife O'Connor and Ann Marie O'Neill of the Library in the Law Society of Ireland and Joe Donnelly of the Judge's Library.

Finally we wish to thank Ciara Fitzpatrick and Ciarán Toland of Butterworths and Marian Sullivan of Marlex Editorial Services for their encouragement and their patience in seeing this edition into print. We are very grateful to them.

Bryan ME McMahon
William Binchy

20 November 2000

# Contents

*Foreword to the First Edition* ........ v
*Preface* ........ ix
*Contents* ........ xi
*Table of Abbreviations* ........ xxvii
*Table of Cases* ........ xxix
*Table of Statutes* ........ cxxxix

**Chapter 1 Overview of the Law of Torts**

I. Function of the Law of Torts ........ 1
II. Recognised Interests ........ 2
III. Wrongful Interference with Constitutional Rights ........ 4
Introductory Observations ........ 4
Private Individuals as well as the State may be Liable for Infringement of Constitutional Rights ........ 6
The Relationship between Tort Law and Infringements of Constitutional Rights ........ 7
The Hanrahan Resolution ........ 8
Limitation on Right to Damages for Infringement of Constitutional Rights ........ 9
W v Ireland develops Hanrahan Rationale ........ 12
McDonnell Tames the Meskell Principle ........ 17
Some Difficult Questions ........ 20
Are Constitutional Infringements Actionable Sine Damno? ........ 20
When does Infringement occur? ........ 22
The Concept of "Basic Ineffectiveness" of a Tort ........ 23
Interpersonal Infringements of Constitutional Rights ........ 24
Concluding Observations ........ 25
Innominate Torts ........ 25
IV. European Community ........ 26
V. Definition of Tort ........ 30
Tort v Crime ........ 31
Tort v Breach of Contract ........ 32
Restitution and Breach of Trust ........ 36
Unliquidated Damages ........ 36
VI. From Negligence to Strict Liability: from Loss Shifting to Loss Distribution ........ 37
Insurance and Other Schemes of Compensation ........ 39
VII. The Insurance Factor and the Problem of the Uninsured Driver ........ 44
The Operation of Insurance ........ 45
Uninsured Drivers ........ 48
VIII. Features of the Litigation Scene in Ireland ........ 48
IX. Recent Studies and Proposals for Reform ........ 51
County Registrars ........ 54
Tribunals ........ 55

**Chapter 2 Causation**

I. Introduction ..... 59
II. Factual and Legal Causation ..... 60
Factual Causation ..... 60
Legal Causation ..... 64
Legal Cause and Remoteness of Damage ..... 67
III. Novus Actus Interveniens ..... 67
Reasonable Foresight of Intervening Act and Recklessness on the Part of the Intervener ..... 69
Recklessness ..... 72
Summary: Novus Actus Interveniens ..... 77
IV. Proof ..... 78
V. Causation and Medical Negligence ..... 82

**Chapter 3 Remoteness**

I. Introduction ..... 83
II. Direct Consequences ..... 84
Re Polemis ..... 84
III. Reasonable Foreseeability ..... 85
The Wagon Mound (No 1) ..... 85
IV. Types of Damage ..... 90
Intentional Damage ..... 91
Unintentional and Unforeseeable Damage ..... 92
Foreseeability and the Remoteness of Damage ..... 93
The Egg-Shell Skull and the Impecunious Plaintiff ..... 93
Strict Torts ..... 97
V. Conclusion ..... 98

**Chapter 4 Concurrent Wrongdoers: Joint and Several Tortfeasors**

I. Introduction ..... 99
II. Concurrent Wrongdoers ..... 102
Satisfaction, Release and Accord ..... 105
Contribution Between Concurrent Wrongdoers ..... 106

**Chapter 5 Negligence**

I. Introduction ..... 111
II. Elements of the Tort ..... 111

**Chapter 6 The Duty of Care**

I. Introduction ..... 115
II. Concepts and Policy ..... 116
III. The Judicial Development of the Duty of Care ..... 118
British Developments 1932-2000 ..... 118
Irish Developments ..... 123
IV. The Duty of Care in Particular Contexts ..... 128
Physical injury or damage ..... 128
Psychiatric Damage ..... 132

Pure Economic Loss ........ 132
V. Proximity: Levels of Generality ........ 132
VI. Some Troublesome Duty Issues ........ 133
The Defendant must have been in Breach of his or her Duty to the Plaintiff ........ 134
To What Extent is the Duty Concept determined by Objective Criteria? ........ 136
VII. The European Dimension ........ 138

**Chapter 7 The Standard of Care**

I. Introduction ........ 145
II. The Reasonable Person ........ 145
Standard of the Reasonable Person ........ 146
Knowledge ........ 147
III. Physical Capacities ........ 149
IV. Mentally Disordered Persons ........ 153
V. Specific Factors in Assessing Whether Conduct is Negligent ........ 154
The probability of an Accident ........ 155
The gravity of the Threatened Injury ........ 159
The Social Utility of the Defendant's Conduct ........ 160
The Cost of Eliminating the Risk ........ 162

**Chapter 8 Affirmative Duties**

I. Introduction ........ 169
II. Duty to Protect Incapacitated Persons (and their Potential Victims) from Injury 171
III. Duty to Control Others ........ 176

**Chapter 9 Proof of Negligence**

I. Introduction ........ 185
II. Res Ipsa Loquitur ........ 187
Origins of the Doctrine ........ 187
When Will the Principle Apply? ........ 188
The Procedural Effect of Res Ipsa Loquitur ........ 196
III. The Hanrahan Restatement of the Res Ipsa Loquitur Doctrine ........ 199

**Chapter 10 Negligence and Economic Loss**

I. Introduction ........ 203
II. The Contemporary Irish Approach to Pure Economic Loss ........ 206
III. The Contractual Dimension ........ 208
IV. The Hedley Byrne Principle ........ 216
The Old Approach ........ 216
The Hedley Byrne Breakthrough ........ 217
An Irish Harbinger of Hedley Byrne? ........ 218
Hedley Byrne Reaches Ireland ........ 220
Judicial Development of the Hedley Byrne Principle ........ 222
The Scope of the Representation ........ 227

Promissory Estoppel .......... 240
Areas of Competence .......... 242
Statements in a Contractual Setting .......... 243
V. Pure Economic Loss in Products Liability .......... 246

**Chapter 11 Manufacturers' and Producers' Liability for Defective Products**

I. Introduction .......... 249
The Historical Background .......... 251
Abolition of the Privity Requirement .......... 252
II. By Whom is the Duty Owed? .......... 253
Manufacturers .......... 253
Repairers .......... 253
Installers and Assemblers .......... 254
Suppliers .......... 254
Retailers .......... 254
Liability of Manufacturer for Negligence of Supplier of Component Part .......... 256
III. To Whom is the Duty Owed? .......... 257
Intermediate Examination .......... 258
Dangerous Substances .......... 258
Duty to Warn .......... 259
Transfer by way of gift .......... 265
Causation .......... 265
Res Ipsa Loquitur in Products Liability .......... 267
IV. Non-Dangerous Defects .......... 268
The Eclipse of Junior Books in Britain .......... 272
Future Developments .......... 273
V. Strict Liability: The European Regime .......... 274
The Preparation of the Directive .......... 275
The Main Features of the 1991 Act and the Community Directive .......... 275

**Chapter 12 Occupiers' Liability**

I. Introduction .......... 299
II. The Common Law .......... 299
Categories of Entrant .......... 300
III. Trespassers .......... 303
Trespassers Defined .......... 303
A New Approach to Trespassers (and Other Entrants?) 1974-1995 .......... 310
IV. The Hotel Proprietors Act 1963 .......... 314
V. The Occupiers' Liability Act 1995 .......... 315
The Lobby is Marshalled .......... 316
The Main Features of the Act .......... 316

**Chapter 13 Liability of Vendors, Lessors and Builders for Quality and Fitness of Premises**

I. Introduction .......... 337
II. Liability of Vendor and Lessor .......... 337

Defects of Quality: Contract ........ 337
Dangerous Defects: Tort ........ 340
III. Liability of the Builder ........ 350
Defects of Quality: "Contract Builders" ........ 350
Dangerous Defects: "Contract Builders" ........ 350
IV. Liability of Builder/Vendor and Builder/Lessor ........ 353
Qualitative Defects and Dangerous Defects Discovered before Injury or Damage is Caused ........ 357
Voluntary Schemes ........ 358
Proposals for Reform ........ 359
Architects, Engineers, Surveyors, etc ........ 359

**Chapter 14 Professional Negligence**

I. Introduction ........ 361
II. Medical Negligence ........ 363
Courts Should Guard Against Being Wise After the Event ........ 366
Error of Judgment ........ 367
Different Schools of Thought ........ 367
Keeping up-to-date ........ 368
Innovative Treatment ........ 369
Specialists ........ 370
General Practitioners ........ 370
Other Medical Personnel and Hospital Administration ........ 373
Diagnosis ........ 373
Treatment ........ 375
Medical Treatment by Unqualified Persons ........ 378
Informed Consent ........ 379
The "Therapeutic Privilege" ........ 393
Causation and Non-Disclosure ........ 393
Consent in Relation to Medical Research ........ 397
Disclosure of Problems Arising in Medical Treatment ........ 398
Barristers ........ 399
Solicitors ........ 403
The Standard of Care for Solicitors ........ 404

**Chapter 15 Negligence on the Roads**

I. Introduction ........ 419
II. The Duty of the Driver ........ 420
The Presence of Children ........ 420
School Buses ........ 421
III. General Rules of Behaviour on the Highway ........ 424
Failure to Keep a Proper Look Out ........ 424
Negligence Per Se - and Driving When Blinded ........ 426
Pedestrians ........ 427
Cyclists ........ 430
Road junctions ........ 430

Junctions Controlled by Traffic Lights ........ 433
Sounding Horn ........ 434
Emergency Vehicles ........ 435

**Chapter 16 Negligent Care of Children**

I. Introduction ........ 437
II. Parental Negligence ........ 437
Dangerous Things ........ 437
Child's Dangerous Propensities ........ 438
Failure to Control Child Properly ........ 439
III. The Negligence of Schools ........ 441
Negligence in Instruction ........ 442
Supervision in School Playgrounds ........ 444
Supervision Outside Hours ........ 449
Injuries Sustained Off the Premises ........ 454
Other Acts of Negligence ........ 455
Structural Dangers ........ 456

**Chapter 17 Negligently Inflicted Psychiatric Damage**

I. Introduction ........ 461
II. Recent Developments in Irish Law on Nervous Shock ........ 470
III. Primary and Secondary Victims ........ 476

**Chapter 18 Employers' Liability**

I. Introduction ........ 479
II. An Employer's Duty of Care to an Employee ........ 480
The Duty Varies According to the Employee's Circumstances ........ 482
General Guidelines ........ 483
Omissions ........ 485
The Relationship Between Employers' Liability and Claims for Breach of Statutory Duty ........ 487
Employer's Duty to Employees is "Non-Delegable" ........ 490
Does an Employer's Duty of Care Extend Beyond Physical Injury? ........ 495
III. Assessment of Employer's Liability ........ 500
The Provision of Competent Staff ........ 501
The Provision of a Safe Place of Work ........ 503
The Provision of Proper Equipment ........ 507
The Provision of a Safe System of Work ........ 511
Employer's Negligence Must Have Caused the Injury Complained Of ........ 523
Necessary Precautions and Coincidental Injuries ........ 524
Contributory Negligence of Employee ........ 525
IV. Voluntary Assumption of Risk ........ 529

**Chapter 19 Public Authorities**

I. Introduction ........ 533
II. Negligence ........ 535
The Standard of Care Test ........ 538
The Proximity/Policy Approach ........ 539

III. Nuisance ..... 547
IV. Breach of Statutory Duty ..... 547
V. Rylands v Fletcher ..... 547
VI. Misfeasance of Public Office ..... 547
The Irish Cases ..... 548

**Chapter 20 Defences**

I. Introduction ..... 555
II. Contributory Negligence ..... 555
Erosion of the Doctrine ..... 556
The Civil Liability Act 1961 ..... 557
The Nature of Contributory Negligence ..... 559
Contributory Negligence and Particular Risk ..... 560
The "Agony of the Moment" ..... 561
The Dilemma Principle ..... 563
Failure to Mitigate Damage ..... 563
The Seat Belt Defence ..... 566
Degrees of Fault ..... 570
Appeal Regarding Apportionment of Fault ..... 574
Set-Off of Claims ..... 574
Imputed Contributory Negligence ..... 575
III. Volenti Non Fit Injuria ..... 577
Contract ..... 577
Agreement ..... 578
Rescuers ..... 581
IV. Illegality ..... 584

**Chapter 21 Statutory Duties and Rights**

I. Introduction ..... 589
II. Breach of Statutory Duty ..... 589
Benefit of the Public or a Class of Persons ..... 592
Nature of Penalty or Remedy Provided by the Statutory Provision ..... 597
Other Techniques of Statutory Interpretation ..... 597
Limitations on Recovery ..... 598
Nature of Obligation Imposed by Statute ..... 605
Breach of Statutory Duty by Plaintiff not of itself a Bar in Tort Action ..... 607
Contributory Negligence ..... 608
III. Interference with Statutory Rights ..... 612

**Chapter 22 Trespass to the Person**

I. Intoduction ..... 615
Trespass and Negligence ..... 615
Voluntariness, Intention and Motive ..... 616
II. Trespass Against the Person ..... 617
Battery ..... 618
Assault ..... 621

Infliction of Emotional Suffering ..... 624
False Imprisonment ..... 626
Confinement as a Sanction ..... 632
III. Defences to Trespass to the Person ..... 633
Consent ..... 633
Self Defence ..... 641
Defence of Third Persons ..... 642
Necessity ..... 642
Discipline ..... 643
Lawful Authority ..... 646
Defence of Property ..... 650

**Chapter 23 Trespass to Land**

I. Introduction ..... 653
II. Trespass by Entering on Land ..... 653
Constitutional, Common Law and Statutory Rights of Entry ..... 654
Abuse of Right of Entry ..... 659
III. Trespass by Remaining on Land ..... 662
IV. Trespass by Placing Things on Land ..... 664
Nature of Interference ..... 665
Trespass Actionable Per Se ..... 666
Continuing Trespass ..... 667
V. The Defendant's State of Mind ..... 668
Trespass Above and Below the Surface of the Land ..... 668
VI. Interference with Possession ..... 670
Jus Tertii No Defence ..... 671
VII. Defences ..... 672
Consent ..... 672
Lawful authority ..... 672
Necessity ..... 672

**Chapter 24 Nuisance**

I. Introduction ..... 675
II. Public Nuisance ..... 676
What is "Particular" or "Special" Damage? ..... 677
Types of Public Nuisance ..... 680
Public Nuisance on the Highway ..... 681
Extent of Liability for Public Nuisance ..... 684
III. Private Nuisance ..... 685
Physical injury to Land ..... 686
Substantial interference in the Enjoyment of Land ..... 690
Nuisance as a State of Affairs ..... 698
Who may Sue for Private Nuisance? ..... 699
Who may be Sued? ..... 702
Premises Adjoining the Highway ..... 706

IV. Defences ... 709
Legislative Authority ... 709
Prescription ... 710
Contributory Negligence ... 711
Inevitable Accident ... 711
V. Ineffectual Defences ... 711
Coming to the Nuisance ... 711
Acts of Others Combining with Defendant's Act to Make Nuisance ... 713
VI. Highway Authorities ... 714

**Chapter 25 The Rule in Rylands v Fletcher**

I. Introduction ... 717
II. Scope of the Rule ... 719
"Non-Natural" Use ... 719
Defendant Must Have Brought Source of Danger onto Property ... 723
Escape ... 723
Entitlement to Sue ... 726
Status of Defendant ... 727
III. Defences ... 727
Consent of the Plaintiff ... 727
Default or Special Sensitivity of the Plaintiff ... 728
Act of a Stranger ... 729
Act of God ... 730
Statutory Authority ... 731
IV. The Future of the Rule in Irish Law ... 731

**Chapter 26 Liability for Fire**

I. Introduction ... 735
II. Occupiers' Liability for Fire ... 736
Fire and Causation of Damage ... 739
Does "Damage" Include Personal injures? ... 740
The Burden of Proof Under the Act ... 740
Remedies Not Defeated by the Act ... 740
III. Liability of Persons Other than the Occupier ... 741
Contributory Negligence ... 744
Rescuers ... 745

**Chapter 27 Liability for Injuries caused by Animals**

I. Introduction ... 749
II. Liability under the General Principles of Tort ... 750
Negligence ... 750
Nuisance ... 750
Trespass ... 751
Rylands v Fletcher ... 752
Occupier's Liability ... 752

III. Liability under Special Rules ..... 754
The Scienter Principle ..... 754
Dogs ..... 757
Cattle Trespass ..... 762
Animals on the Highway ..... 764
The Control of Horses Act 1996 ..... 767
IV. Law Reform Commission Proposals ..... 768

**Chapter 28 Trespass to Goods**

I. Introduction ..... 769
II. Elements of the Tort of Trespass to Goods ..... 769
Nature of the Interference ..... 769
Is Trespass to Goods Actionable Per Se? ..... 771
The Title of the Plaintiff ..... 772
Defendant's State of Mind ..... 772
Character of Defendant's Conduct ..... 773
Lawful Authority ..... 773

**Chapter 29 Detinue**

I. Introduction ..... 777
II. Adverse Possession ..... 777
III. Bailment and Finding Contrasted ..... 780
IV. Remedies ..... 780
Order for the Value of the Chattel as assessed and Damages for its Detention ..... 781
Order for the Return of the Chattel or its Value as assessed and Damages ..... 781
Order for the Return of the Chattel and Damages for its Detention ..... 782

**Chapter 30 Conversion**

I. Introduction ..... 783
II. Taking Possession ..... 783
III. Abusing Possession ..... 784
IV. Denying Title ..... 786
Bona Fides of Defendant ..... 786
V. Scope of the Tort of Conversion ..... 788
Subject Matter of Conversion ..... 788
Title of Plaintiff ..... 789
Finders ..... 789
Conversion and Contributory Negligence ..... 793
Damages ..... 793

**Chapter 31 Passing Off**

I. Introduction ..... 795
II. Scope of the Tort of Passing Off ..... 797
Intention to Deceive Not Essential ..... 797
Risk of Confusion ..... 798

Survey Evidence ... 801
Shared Goodwill ... 803
Description of Goods ... 804
Packaged Products ... 804
Clothes ... 805
Descriptive Expressions ... 806
The Use of One's Actual Name ... 808
Businesses Not Trading in the State ... 810
III. Interlocutory Injunction Proceedings for Passing Off ... 811
Future Developments ... 815

**Chapter 32 Torts Affecting Business Relations**

I. Introduction ... 817
II. The Action Per Quod Servitium Amisit ... 817
Who is a Servant? ... 818
Contributory Negligence of a Servant ... 820
Damages ... 820
III. Action for Enticement or Harbouring of a Servant ... 820
IV. Interference with Contractual Relations ... 821
Historical Background ... 821
Types of Contract Affected ... 821
Persuasion Distinguished from mere Information or Advice ... 821
Is a Breach of Contract Necessary? ... 823
Degree of Knowledge and Intention Required ... 823
The Wrongful Procurement ... 825
Justification and Malice ... 828
Damages ... 830
V. Intimidation ... 830
The Nature of Intimidation ... 830
The Threat ... 831
Illegal Act or Means ... 831
Submission to the Threat Essential ... 833
Justification ... 834
VI. Conspiracy ... 834
The Traditional View ... 835
Forms of Conspiracy ... 836
VII. Intentional Interference with Economic Interests ... 841
VIII. Trade Disputes ... 842
Introduction ... 842
The Industrial Relations Act 1990 ... 843
Limited Immunity from Liability in Tort for Trade Unions ... 852

**Chapter 33 Torts Affecting Family Relations**

I. Introduction ... 867
II. Damages for Loss of Consortium ... 868
Extent of Recovery ... 869

Effect of Victim's Contributory Negligence or Other Default ..... 872
Reform of the Law Relating to Loss of Consortium ..... 873
III. Seduction ..... 875
IV. Enticement and Harbouring of a Child ..... 875
Reform of the Law ..... 877
V. Action for the Loss of a Child's Services ..... 878

**Chapter 34 Defamation**

I. Introduction ..... 879
II. The Tort of Defamation ..... 882
Publication ..... 883
The Historical Origins of the Libel Slander Distinction ..... 887
Slander Actionable Per Se ..... 889
Special Damages required in all other Slanders ..... 892
Foreign Publications ..... 893
III. What is Defamatory? ..... 894
Vulgar Abuse not Defamatory ..... 905
The Innuendo ..... 906
Functions of Judge and Jury ..... 910
Reference must be to the Plaintiff ..... 912
Reference to a Class ..... 913
Corporate and Personal plaintiffs ..... 914
Unintentional References to the Plaintiff ..... 915
IV. Defences ..... 917
Justification ..... 917
Privilege ..... 920
Fair Comment on Matters of Public Interest ..... 943
Consent ..... 949
Apology ..... 950
Offer of Amends in Unintentional Defamation ..... 951
V. Damages ..... 951
VI. Reform of the Law ..... 961
Abolition of the distinction between Libel and Slander ..... 962
Defaming the Dead ..... 962
Printers and Innocent Distributors ..... 962
Proposal to Abandon Strict Liability in Favour of Fault Based Liability ..... 963
New Definition of Defamation and the Presumption of Falsity ..... 963

**Chapter 35 Deceit and Injurious Falsehood**

I. Deceit ..... 967
Representation of Fact ..... 968
Knowledge of Falsity ..... 971
Intention of Defendant ..... 972
The Plaintiff's Reliance is Essential ..... 973
Damage ..... 975
Lord Tenterden's Act ..... 976
II. Injurious Falsehood ..... 977

**Chapter 36 Misuse of Process**

I. Introduction .................... 981
II. Malicious Prosecution .................... 981
Ingredients of the Tort .................... 981
III. Malicious Abuse of the Civil Process .................... 986

**Chapter 37 The Right to Privacy**

I. Introduction .................... 991
II. Torts relating to Privacy .................... 992
Trespass to Land .................... 992
Torts Affecting Interests in Goods .................... 993
Trespass to the Person .................... 994
Intentional Infliction of Mental Suffering .................... 994
Private Nuisance .................... 995
Injurious Falsehood .................... 996
Negligence .................... 997
Breach of Statutory Duty .................... 998
III. Breach of Confidence .................... 998
The Confidential Nature of the Information .................... 1000
Obligation of Confidence .................... 1002
Remedies .................... 1004
Medical Confidences .................... 1005
IV. Criminal Law .................... 1012
V. Constitutional Aspects of Privacy .................... 1012
Privacy in Marriage, Intimate Conduct (Sexual and Otherwise) and the Termination of Life .................... 1013

**Chapter 38 Liability of the State**

I. Introduction .................... 1025
II. Act of State .................... 1030
III. Diplomatic Immunity .................... 1030
IV. Foreign Sovereigns .................... 1031
V. European Communities .................... 1033

**Chapter 39 Corporations, Partnerships, Unincorporated Bodies and Trade Unions**

I. Corporations .................... 1035
Corporation as Plaintiff .................... 1035
Corporation as Defendant .................... 1037
II. Partnerships .................... 1038
III. Unincorporated Associations .................... 1038
IV. Trade Unions .................... 1042

**Chapter 40 Minors and Mentally Ill Persons**

I. Minors .................... 1045
General Liability in Tort .................... 1045
Negligence and Contributory Negligence .................... 1046

Contributory Negligence ........ 1046
Negligence ........ 1052
Children Performing Adult Activities ........ 1053
Tort and Contract ........ 1054
Proposals for Reform ........ 1055
II. Mentally Ill Persons ........ 1056
Torts of Strict Liability ........ 1056
Torts Involving a Specific Mental Ingredient ........ 1056
Trespass to the Person, Goods or Land ........ 1056
Proposals for Reform ........ 1058

**Chapter 41 Survival of Actions on Death**

I. Historical Introduction ........ 1061
II. The Present Law ........ 1062

**Chapter 42 Fatal Injuries**

I. Introduction ........ 1067
II. The Statutory Right of the Dependants ........ 1069
Who is Entitled to Sue? ........ 1069
When and in What Circumstances Will Liability Arise? ........ 1071
The Injuries Compensatable and the Method of Calculating Damages ........ 1073

**Chapter 43 Vicarious Liability**

I. Introduction ........ 1091
II. The Employer/Employee Relationship ........ 1095
Hired Employees: Who is the Employer? ........ 1095
Personal Liability of Employer ........ 1096
Employer's Liability for the Torts of his or her Employees ........ 1097
III. Liability of Firm for Partner's Wrongs ........ 1112
IV. Liability of the Owners of Mechanically Propelled Vehicles ........ 1114
Road Traffic Act 1961, s 118 ........ 1114
V. Vicarious Liability for Members of One's Family ........ 1116
VI. Doctrine of Common Employment ........ 1117

**Chapter 44 Damages**

I. Introduction ........ 1119
II. Types of Damages Awarded ........ 1119
Nominal Damages ........ 1119
Contemptuous Damages ........ 1119
Special and General Damages ........ 1120
Restitutio in Integrum and Compensatory Damages ........ 1120
Exemplary Damages ........ 1121
III. Appellate Functions Regarding Awards ........ 1136
Uniformity of Awards ........ 1140
IV. Computation of Damages Under Separate Headings ........ 1141
V. Proof of Loss of Earning Capacity ........ 1144
The Physical Condition of the Plaintiff ........ 1144
Claims for "Lost Years" of Earnings ........ 1146

The State of the Labour Market ... 1146
Other Possibilities Affecting Earning Capacity ... 1148
Restriction of Employment Options ... 1149
Moral Obligation to Pay over Earnings to a Third Party Ignored ... 1149
Actuarial Evidence ... 1150
Taxation ... 1152
Hospital Expenses and "Carer" Costs ... 1155
Collateral Benefits ... 1158

VI. Non-Pecuniary Loss ... 1167
Pain and Suffering ... 1167
Loss of Expectation of Life ... 1182

VII. Property Damage ... 1185

**Chapter 45 Injunctions**

I. Introduction ... 1187
II. Prohibitory, Mandatory and Quia Timet Injunctions ... 1187
When Will an Injunction be Ordered? ... 1189
III. Perpetual, Interlocutory and Interim Injunctions ... 1191
A "Serious Question" to be Tried ... 1192
The Balance of Convenience ... 1198
Irreparable Damage ... 1200
IV. Damages in Lieu of an Injunction ... 1201

**Chapter 46 Limitations**

I. Introduction ... 1203
II. The General Rule ... 1204
III. When Does the Cause of Action Accrue? ... 1204
IV. Personal Injuries ... 1209
V. DAte of Knowledge ... 1210
That the Person alleged to have been Injured had been Injured ... 1212
That the Injury was Significant ... 1214
That the Injury was attributable to the Conduct alleged to constitute Negligence, Nuisance or Breach of Duty ... 1216
The Identity of the Defendant ... 1216
The Identity of a Person other than the Defendant (where Appropriate) ... 1217
VI. Undue Delay As a Basis for Dismissal of Proceedings ... 1217
VII. Persons Under a Disability ... 1220
VIII. Fraud ... 1224
IX. Extinction of Title in Conversion and Detinue ... 1225
X. Special Periods of Limitation ... 1225
Actions for Contribution under the Civil Liability Act 1961 ... 1225
Admiralty Actions ... 1226
Causes of Action that Survive Against Estate of Deceased Person ... 1226
Defective Products ... 1227
Claims Relating to Child Abuse ... 1228

**Index** ... 1231

# Table of Abbreviations

| | |
|---|---|
| DPIJ | Doyle's Personal Injury Journal 1990 - 2000 |
| FLEMING | Fleming, The Law of Torts (9th ed, 1998) Sweet & Maxwell |
| LUNNEY & OLIPHANT | Lunney & Oliphant Tort Law: Text and Materials (2000) Oxford University Press |
| MARKESINIS & DEAKIN | Markesinis & Deakin, Tort Law (4th ed, 1999) Oxford University Press |
| PROSSER & KEETON | Prosser & Keeton on the Law of Torts (5th ed, 1984) Keeton, gen ed |
| SALMOND & HEUSTON | Salmond & Heuston on the Law of Torts (21st ed, 1996) ed, by Heuston & Buckley, Sweet & Maxwell |
| STREET | Street, The Law of Torts (10th ed, 1999) by Brazier, Butterworths |
| TRINIDADE & CANE | Trinidade & Cane, The Law of Torts in Australia (3rd ed, 1993) Oxford University Press |
| WILLIAMS | Williams, Joint Torts and Contributory Negligence (1951) Sweet & Maxwell |
| WINFIELD & JOLOWICZ | Winfield & Jolowicz on Tort (15th ed, 1998) by Rogers, Sweet & Maxwell |

# Table of Cases

## A


A & B v Eastern Health Board [1998] 1 ILRM 460 ....................................22.38, 22.84
A & N Pharmacy Ltd v United Drug Wholesale Ltd, [1996] 2 ILRM 42 .................45.02
A & P (Ireland) Ltd v Golden Vale Products Ltd (HC) 7 December 1998 .................4.24
A v United Kingdom [1998] 2 FLR 959 ..........................................................22.96
AB v South West Water Services Ltd [1993] QB 507 ..........................................44.12
ACC Bank plc v Malocco (HC) 7 Febraury 2000 ....................................................4.18
Acton Corporation v Morris [1953] 2 All ER 932 ..................................................23.33
Adam v Ward [1917] AC 309 ..................................................................................34.199
Adams v Ursell [1913] 1 Ch 269 ...........................................................................24.38
Adamson v Jarvis (1827) 4 Bing 66, 130 ER 693 ....................................................4.19
Adamson v Motor Vehicle Insurance Trust (1957) 58 WALR 56 ......... 7.23, 40.41-40.44
Adderley v GN Ry Co [1905] 2 IR 378 ....................................... 7.29, 8.14, 21.20-21.22
..............................................................................................................44.55, 44.84
Addie & Sons v Dumbreck [1929] AC 358 ...................................................12.27, 12.45
Addis v Crocker [1961] 1 QB 11 ...........................................................................34.155
Adidas Sportsschuhfabriken Adi Dassler KA v Charles O'Neill & Co Ltd
[1983] ILRM 112 (SC), affg (HC) 20 May 1980 ................31.11, 31.36, 31.60, 45.05
Admiralty Commissioners v SS Amerika [1917] AC 38 .........................................32.04
Agar v Canning (1965) 54 WWR 302, affd 55 WWR 384 .......................................22.60
Agnesini v Olsen 277 App Div 1006,100 NYS 2d 338 ............................................16.07
Agnew v Independent Newspapers (HC) 29 June 1985 .........................................34.226
Ahearne v Rudd [1945] Ir Jur 45 ......................................................12.13, 24.18, 24.74
Ahearne v Thompson (SC) 26 October 1971 ..........................................................44.92
Ahern v Cork Corporation (1950) 85 ILTR 97 ...........................................................7.44
Ahern v Maguire (1840) Arm Mac & Og 39 .......................................34.14, 44.04
Aherne v Showerlux (Cork) Ltd DPIJ: Hilary and Easter Terms 1992, p 73 ...........18.153
Airedale NHS Trust v Bland [1993] AC 789 ..........................................................22.13
Aitken Agencies Ltd v Richardson [1967] NZLR 65 ...............................................30.02
Aitkenhead v Blades (1813) 5 Taunt 199, 128 ER 663 ...........................................23.24
Akers v P (1986) 42 SASR 30 ......................................................................................7.39
Aksjeselskapet Jotul v Waterford Iron Founders Ltd
(HC) 8 November 1977 .......................................................................31.73, 37.38
Alcoa Minerals of Jamaica Ltd v Broderick [2000] 3 WLR 23 .................................3.37
Alcock v Chief Constable of South Yorkshire Police [1992] 1 AC 310 ..........6.50, 17.08
...................................................................................................... 17.30-17.33, 17.44
...................................................................................... 17.53-17.66, 18.62-18.63
Aldred v Nacanco [1987] IRLR 292 .........................................................................43.33
Aldridge v Van Patter [1952] 4 DLR 93 ..................................................................25.25
Aleksoske v State Rail Authority of New South Wales [2000] NSW CA ................27.30
Alexander v Jenkins [1892] 1 QB 797 ......................................................................34.37
Alexander v North Eastern Ry Co (1865) 6 B & S 340, 122 ER 1221 ..................34.125

Alexandrou v Oxford [1993] 4 All ER 328 .......... 8.04, 8.25
Allan v New Mount Sinai Hospital (1980) 109 DLR (3d) 634 .......... 3.25, 22.73
Allen v Flood [1898] AC 1 .......... 32.48
Allen v Gulf Oil Refining Ltd [1981] AC 1001, [1981] 1 All ER 353 .......... 24.93-24.95
Allen v Ó Súilleabháin (HC) 28 July 1995, (SC) 11 March 1997 .......... 18.23, 18.32
.......... 18.118, 18.156, 20.14
.......... 44.18, 44.103, 44.168
Allen v Sharp (1848) 2 Exch 352, 154 ER 529 .......... 30.19
Alliance & Dublin Consumers Gas Co v Dublin County Council
[1901] 1 IR 492 .......... 7.28, 24.18
Alliance & Leicester Building Society v Edgestop Ltd [1994] 2 All ER 38 .......... 35.15
Allibert SA v O'Connor [1982] ILRM 40 .......... 30.40-30.44
Allied Irish Banks v Murnane, (HC) 21 December 1988 .......... 43.01
Allied Pharmaceutical Distributors Ltd and All-Phar Services Ltd v Walsh
(HC) 14 December 1990 .......... 43.55-43.56
Allsop v Allsop (1860) 5 H & N 534, 157 ER 1292 .......... 34.43
Almonte v New York Medical College (1994) 851 F Supp 34 .......... 37.44
Alsager v Close (1842) 10 M&W 576, 152 ER 600 .......... 30.19
Amalgamated Theatres Ltd v Lumley Ltd [1962] NZLR 226 .......... 24.08
Ambrose v O'Regan (SC) 20 December 1991, rev (HC)
14 November 1990 .......... 43.65-43.66
American Cyanamid Co v Ethicom [1975] AC 396 .......... 31.63, 45.09-45.10
AMF International v Magnet Bowling Ltd [1988] 1 WLR 1028 .......... 12.136
Ancell v McDermott [1993] 4 All ER 355 .......... 8.25
Anchor Brewhouse Developments Ltd v Berkley House
(Docklands Developments) Ltd [1987] 2 EGLR 173 .......... 23.39
Anderson (WB) & Sons Ltd v Rhodes (Liverpool) Ltd [1967] 2 All ER 850 .......... 35.25
Anderson v Minneapolis St Paul & Sault Ste Marie Ry Co 1920 146 Minn LR 430
179 NW 45 .......... 2.14
Andrae v Selfridge [1938] Ch 1 .......... 24.37
Andrews v Grand & Toy Albert Ltd (1978) 83 DLR (3d) 452 .......... 44.74, 44.158, 44.186
Andrews v Hopkinson [1957] 1 QB 229 .......... 11.16
Annaly Hotel Ltd v Bergin (1967) 104 ILTR 65 .......... 24.49
Annaly v Trade Auxiliary Co (1890) 26 LR Ir 394 .......... 34.191
Anns v Merton London Borough Council [1978] AC 728 .......... 1.33, 6.02-6.12,
.......... 6.18, 6.35, 6.40, 6.78, 6.87, 10.09
.......... 10.77, 11.76, 13.17-13.22
.......... 13.66, 19.08, 19.26, 26.24
Anonymous Case 1 Vent 295 .......... 25.17
Anthony v Haney (1832) 8 Bing 186, 131 ER 372 .......... 1.120
Antoniak v Commonwealth (1962) 4 FLR 454. .......... 18.77
Appelbe v The West Cork Board of Health [1929] IR 107 .......... 42.13
Ardmore Studios (Ireland) Ltd v Lynch [1965] IR 1 .......... 24.16, 32.108
Argyll v Argyll [1967] Ch 302, [1969] FSR 415 .......... 37.23, 37.32
Arkwright v Newbold (1881) 17 Ch D 301 .......... 35.16

Armagas Ltd v Mundogas SA [1986] 2 All ER 385 ....43.43
Armagh Union (Guardians of) v Bell [1900] 2 IR 371 ....24.18, 24.104
Armory v Delamirie (1721) 1 Stra 505, 93 ER 644 .... 30.21-30.24
Armstrong (Estate of) v Pennsylvania Bd of Probation and Parole (1979) 46 Pa Commw 33, 405 A 2d 1099 ....8.25
Armstrong v Eastern Health Board (HC) 5 October 1990 ....7.23, 7.29, 14.30 ....20.22, 37.44
Armstrong v Strain [1951] 1 TLR 856 ....35.11
Armstrong v William J Dwan & Sons Ltd (HC) 8 February 1999 .... 18.51-18.55
Arndt v Smith (1997) 148 DLR (4th) 48 ....14.144
Arneil v Paterson [1931] AC 560 ....27.25, 27.38
Arnold v Teno (1978) 83 DLR (3d) 609 ....16.09, 44.158
Article 26 and the Adoption (No 2) Bill 1987, Re [1989] IR 334 ....33.03
Article 26 of the Constitution and the Regulation of Information (Services outside the State for the Termination of Pregnancies) Bill 1995, Re [1995] 1 IR 1 ....22.38
Article 26 and the Employment Equality Bill 1996, Re [1997] 2 IR ....24.03
Ashburton v Pape [1913] 2 Ch 419 ....37.35
Ashby v Tolhurst [1937] 2 KB 242 ....30.07
Ashby v White (1703) 2 Ld Raym 938, 92 ER 126 .... 19.55, 21.66-21.67, 44.06
Ashworth v General Accident Fire and Life Assurance Corporation Ltd [1955] IR 268 ....2.25, 20.46
Askin v Knox [1989] 1 NZLR 248 ....46.10
Askjorn Horgard AlS v GibbslMortac Industries Ltd (1987) 38 DLR (4th) 544 ....31.05
Associated Consolidated Press Ltd v Uren (1966) 117 Comm LR 185 affd [1969] 1 AC 590 ....44.13
Athans v Canadian Adventure Camps Ltd (1977) 80 DLR (3d) 583 ....31.76
Atkinson v Congreve (1857) 7 ICLR 109 ....34.55
Atkinson v Newcastle and Gateshead Waterworks Co (1877) 2 Ex D 441 ....21.19
Atlantic Aviation v Nova Scotia Light & Power Co (19655) 5 DLR (2d) 554 ....24.49
Atlantic Coastline R Co v Daniels (1911) 70 SE 203 (CA) ....2.10
Atlas Tiles v Briers (1978) 52 ALJR 707 ....44.102
Attorney General (Boswell) v Rathmines & Pembroke Joint Hospital Board [1904] 1 IR 161 .... 24.07, 24.37, 45.03-45.05
Attorney General (ex rel McGarry) v Sligo County Council [1991] 1 IR 99 ....24.31
Attorney General v CIE (1956) 90 ILTR 139 ....32.06
Attorney General v Dublin United Tramways Co [1939] IR 590 ....32.06
Attorney General v Hamilton [1993] 3 IR 227 ....34.139
Attorney General v Ireland [1994] 1 IR 369 ....1.136
Attorney General v Mayo County Council [1902] 1 IR 13 .... 23.19, 24.04-24.06 ....24.16, 24.113, 45.02, 45.05
Attorney General v Northern Petroleum Tank Co Ltd [1936] IR 450 ....24.16
Attorney General v Paperlink [1984] ILRM 373 ....1.13, 21.07, 34.08, 37.94
Attorney General v Southern Industrial Trust Ltd (1957) 94 ILTR 161 ....46.80
Attorney General v X [1992] 1 IR 1 ....1.13, 22.38, 37.81

Attorney General for England and Wales v Brandon Book Publishers [1987] ILRM 135 ........ 34.08, 37.21
Attorney General v Copeland [1902] 1 KB 690 ........ 24.99
Attorney General v Corke [1933] Ch 89 ........ 16.15, 25.17
Attorney General v Cory Bros & Co [1921] 1 AC 521 ........ 25.30
Attorney General v Cory Bros (1919) 35 Times LR 570 ........ 25.40
Attorney General v Cox (CCA) 9 April 1929 ........ 22.105
Attorney General v Guardian Newspapers Ltd (No 2) [1990] 1 AC 109 ........ 37.38
Attorney General v Nissan [1970] AC 179 ........ 38.14
Attorney General v Nottingham Corporation [1904] 1 Ch 673 ........ 45.03
Attorney General of Canada v Connolly (1989) 64 DLR (4th) 84 ........ 7.23, 40.41
Attorney General of Canada v Diamond Weatherproofing Ltd (1974) 48 DLR (3d) 353 ........ 25.16
Attorney General for British Columbia v Couillard (1984) 11 DLR (4th) 567 ........ 24.43
Attorney General of Ontario v Dieleman (1994) 117 DLR (4th) 449 ........ 23.20 ........ 24.60, 24.73
Attorney General v Dieleman (1994) 117 DLR (4th) 449 ........ 24.03
Attorney General for Nova Scotia v Beaver (1985) 67 NSR (2d) 281, affg (1985) 66 NSR (2d) 419 ........ 24.43
Attorney General for Ontario v Orange Productions Ltd (1971) 21 DLR (3d) 257 .. 24.12
Attorney General (New South Wales) v Perpetual Trustee Co (1952) 85 CLR 237, affd [1955] AC 457 ........ 32.05
Attorney General v Geothermal Produce (NZ) Ltd [1987] 2 NZLR 348 ........ 3.37
Attorney General v Wilson & Horton Ltd [1973] 2 NZLR 238 ........ 32.09
Attwood v Small (1836) 6 Cl & Fin 232 7 ER 684 ........ 35.15
Auckland Workingmen's Club v Rennie [1976] 1 NZLR 278 ........ 43.39
Australia (Commonwealth of) v Stokes 1996 Aust ACTSC LEXIS 65 BC 9605475 ........ 16.26
Ayles v SE Ry Co (1868) LR 3 Ex 146 ........ 9.13

## B

B & S Ltd v Irish Auto Trader Ltd [1995] 2 ILRM 152 ........ 31.02, 31.07, 31.63, 45.05
B v Arkin (1996) 138 DLR 4th 309 ........ 16.02
B(BR) v B(J) [1968] p 466 ........ 22.77
Backhouse v Bonomi (1861) 9 HLC 503, 11 ER 825 ........ 41.10
Badela v Karpowich (1965) 152 Conn 360, 260 A, 2d 838 ........ 9.21
Badham v Williams [1968] NZLR 728 ........ 44.208
Bailey v Gallagher [1996] 2 ILRM 433 ........ 22.112
Bailey v Warden (1815) 4 M & S 400, 105 ER 882 ........ 46.05
Baker v Alliance & Dublin Consumers' Gas Co [1946] Ir Jur 48 ........ 24.18, 24.93
Baker v Bolton (1808) 1 Camp 493, 170 ER 1033 ........ 42.01-42.03
Baker v Hopkins [1959] 3 All ER 225, affg [1958] 3 All ER 147 ........ 20.80-20.81
Baker v Longhurst & Sons Ltd [1933] 2 KB 461 ........ 15.23
Baker v TE Hopkins & Sons Ltd [1959] 1 WLR 966 ........ 2.47
Baker v Willoughby [1970] AC 467 ........ 2.14

Baldwin v Foy and Forest Way Riding Holidays Ltd (HC) 1 July 1997 .........20.28, 20.72
Balentine v McAleavey DPIJ: Michaelmas 1991, p 114 (HC) ................................44.93
Balfour v Barty-King [1957] I QB 496 ....................................................................26.08
Ballard v NB Ry 1923 SC 43 ..................................................................................9.13
Ballett v Mingay [1943] KB 281 ..........................................................29.01, 29.09, 40.32
Balmain New Ferry Co v Robinson [1910] AC 295, affg
(1906) 4 Comm LR 379 ......................................................................................22.47
Bamford v Turnley 3 B & S 66, 122 ER 27 ...........................................................24.34
Banbury v Bank of Montreal [1918] AC 626 ..........................................................35.25
Banister v Banister cited in 4 Co Rep 17a ............................................................35.26
Bank of Ireland Finance Ltd v McSorley (HC) 24 June 1994 ..................................36.28
Bank of Ireland v Smith [1966] IR 646 .......................................10.65, 10.140, 11.78
Banque Financière v Westgate Insurance Co [1989] 2 All ER 952 .......................10.122
Barber v Houston (1885) 18 LR Ir 475 .............................................35.06, 35.15, 46.82
Barber v Penley [1893] 2 Ch 447 ...........................................................................24.16
Barclay v An Post [1998] 2 ILRM 385 ........................................................7.53, 18.94
Barcock v Brighton Corp [1949] 1 KB 339 .............................................................21.49
Barden v Waterford County Council, DPIJ: Trinity & Michaelmas
Terms 1998, p 6 ...............................................................................................44.90
Barfield v South Highland Infirmary (1915) 191 Ala 553, 68 So 30 ........................22.60
Barker v The Queen (1983) 153 Comm LR 338 .....................................................23.16
Barnes v Hampshire County Council [1969] 3 All ER 746 ,
revs (1968) 67 LGR 53 ......................................................................................16.65
Barnes v Ward (1850) 9 CB 392, 137 ER 945 ........................................................12.40
Barnett v Chelsea and Kensington Hospital Management Committee
[1969] 1 QB 428 .................................................................................................2.12
Barnett v H & J Packer & Co Ltd [1940] 3 All ER 575 ..........................................11.26
Barr v Aetna Insurance Co (1979) 370 So 2d 511 ....................................................7.13
Barrett v Anglo Irish Beef Producers Ltd (HC) 6 March 1989 ......................18.09, 18.77
.................................................................................18.108, 18.152, 34.241
Barrett v Hyndman (1840) Arm Mac & Og 1 ...........................................................35.25
Barrett v Independent Newspapers [1986] ILRM 601, [1986] IR 45 ........................34.51
............................................................ 34.97-34.99, 34.229, 34.234, 34.246
Barrett v London Borough of Enfield [1999] 3 WLR 79, [1999] 3 All ER 193 ..........6.88
.............................................................................................................6.89, 19.12
Barrett v Ministry for Defence [1995] 3 All ER 87 .........................................8.06, 18.127
Barrett v Southern Health Board (HC) 5 December 1988 ......................9.28, 9.38, 14.30
Barrington's Hospital (Governors of) v Minister for Health (HC) 14 March 1988 ...21.22
Barry v Dublin United Tramways Co (1889) 26 LR Ir 150 ......................................43.36
Barry v MacDonald (1966) 110 Sol J 56 .................................................................15.36
Barry v Nitrigin Éireann Teo [1994] 2 ILRM 522 .....................................21.10, 21.25
Barton v Armstrong [1969] 2 NSWR 451 ...............................1.73, 22.22, 32.46
Barton v Harten [1925] 2 IR 37 ...........................................................................32.105
Basebe v Matthews (1867) LR 2 CP 684 ..................................................................36.05
Basely v Clarkson (1682) 3 Lev 37 83 ER 565 .......................................................23.38

Basmajian v Haire (HC) 2 April 1993 .......... 15.18, 44.180
Bateman v Newcourt Credit Group Inc (1995) Ont CJ LEXIS 614 .......... 22.32
Bates v Ireland (HC) 18 May 1995 .......... 7.47
Bates v Minister for Justice (SC) 4 March 1998 .......... 8.37
Bativala v West [1970] 1 QB 716 .......... 27.52
Batty v Metropolitan Property Realizations Ltd [1978] QB 554 .......... 13.70
Baud Corporation NV v Brook (1974) 40 DLR (3d) 418 .......... 29.08
Bauer v Minidoka School District No 331 (1989) 116 Idaho 586, 778 P 2d 336 .......... 16.81-16.83
Baxter v Camden Borough Council [1999] 1 All ER 237 .......... 24.31
BC Electric Ry v Loach [1916] 1 AC 719 .......... 20.06
Beale v Beale (1982) 52 NSR (2d) 550 .......... 40.43
Beale v Gomme Ltd (1949) 65 TLR 543 .......... 21.49
Beals v Hayward [1960] NZLR 131 .......... 22.03, 40.41
Beaman v ARTS Ltd [1949] 1 KB 550 .......... 46.82
Beandesert Shire Council v Smith (1966) 40 ALJR 211 .......... 37.14
Beard v Jevans Furnishings Co Ltd CA (Civil Div), 6 October 1999 .......... 18.60
Beasley v Marshall (1977) 17 SASR 456 .......... 40.26
Beattie v Mair (1882) 10 LR (Ir) 208 .......... 23.02
Beatty v Central Iowa Ry Co 12 NW 332 .......... 7.27
Beatty v Gillbanks (1882) 9 QBD 308 .......... 22.111
Beatty v Illingworth Br Med J 21 Nov 1896, p 1525 .......... 22.60
Beaudesert Shire Council v Smith (1969) 120 CLR 145 .......... 32.84
Beaumont v Surrey County Council (1968) 112 Sol J 704 .......... 16.17
Beaver v Crowe (1974) 49 DLR (3d) 116 .......... 20.34
Bebee v Sales (1916) 32 TLR 413 .......... 16.05
Beckton, Dickinson & Co Ltd v Lee [1973] IR 1 .......... 24.16
Beckwith v Shordyke (1797) 4 Burr 1092, 98 ER 91 .......... 23.29
Becton Dickinson Ltd v Lee [1973] IR 1 .......... 32.20, 32.48-32.56
Bedford v Lane (1991) Prof Neg LR 355 .......... 13.82
Bedford v Minister for Defence DPIJ: Hilary & Easter Terms 1998, p 1 .......... 18.83, 44.90
Beecham Group Ltd v Eirat Pharmaceuticals Ltd (HC) 27 March 1985 .......... 31.34, 45.05
Beecham v Hughes (1988) 45 CCLT 1 .......... 17.34
Beechinor v O'Connor [1939] Ir Jur Rep 5 .......... 43.64
Behan v Bank of Ireland [1998] 2 ILRM 507 (SC), affg (HC) 2 July 1997 ... 46.35, 46.81
Behan v Thornhill (1928) 62 ILTR 65 .......... 40.12
Behrens v Bertram Mills Circus Ltd [1957] 2 QB 1 .......... 27.15, 27.23
Beim v Goyer (1966) 57 DLR (2d) 253 .......... 7.39
Bell Canada v Bannermount Ltd 35 DLR (3d) 267 .......... 28.12
Bell v GN Ry Co (1890) 26 LR (Ir) 428 .......... 6.50, 17.12-17.21, 17.42, 22.34
Bell v Northern Constitution Ltd [1943] NI 108 .......... 34.90
Bell v Pederson (HC) 14 May 1996 .......... 34.193
Bell v Strathairn & Blair (1954) 104 LJ 618 .......... 14.176
Bellaney v Reilly [1945] IR 542 .......... 23.42
Bellew v Cement Ltd [1948] IR 61 .......... 24.31, 24.36-24.37, 45.05, 45.38-45.49

Bellizia v Meares [1971] VR 641 ....................9.20
Benckiser GmbH v Fibrisol Service Ltd (HC) 13 May 1988 ....................31.61, 31.74, 45.05
Bendish v Lindsay (1709) 11 Mod 194, ER ....................34.61
Benham v Gambling [1941] AC 157 ....................44.195
Benjamin v Storr (1874) LR 9 CP 400 ....................24.56
Bennett v Chemical Construction (GB) Ltd [1971] 3 All ER 822 ....................9.39
Bennett v Quane [1948] Ir Jur Rep 28 ....................34.35, 34.54, 34.92
Bennett v Tugwell [1971] 2 QB 267 ....................20.69
Bennett v Walsh (1936) 70 ILTR 252 ....................27.20
Benning v Wong (1969) 122 CLR 249 .................... 25.19, 25.25-25.28, 25.44
Benson v Lee [1972] VR 879 ....................17.22
Berger v Weber (1981) 411 Mich 1, 303 NW 2d 424 ....................33.17
Berkery v Flynn (HC) 10 June 1982 ....................2.11, 2.55
Berkoff v Burdhill and Times Newspapers Ltd [1996] 4 All ER 1008 ....................34.67
Bernina, The (1888) 13 AC 1 ....................20.58
Bernstein (Lord) of Leigh v Skyview & General Ltd [1978] QB 479 ....................23.39,
....................37.06, 37.11
Berry v Brandon Hotel (CC) 7 May 1999 ....................18.61
Berry v British Transport Commission [1962] 1 QB 306 ....................36.18
Berry v Humm & Co [1915] 1 KB 627 ....................42.27
Berry v Irish Times Ltd [1973] IR 368 .................... 34.10-34.12, 34.50
.................... 34.68-34.73, 34.89, 34.102
Best v Samuel Fox & Co Ltd [1952] AC 716 .................... 33.05-33.07, 33.16
Best v Wellcome Foundation Ltd [1992] ILRM 609, [1993] 3 IR 421 ....................11.63, 43.22
Bettel v Yim 20 OR (2d) 617, 88 DLR (3d) 543 Ont Ct 1973 ....................3.25
Betzold v Erickson (1962) 35 Ill Appeal 2d 203, 182 NE 2d 342 ....................40.29
Bexiga v Havir Manufacturing Co (1972) 60 NJ 402, 290, A 2d 281 ....................21.57
Biba Group Ltd v Biba Boutique [1980] RPC 413 ....................31.55
Bielitski v Obadiak (1922) 15 Sask LR 153 ....................22.33
Bigcharles v Merkel (1972) 32 DLR (3d) 511 ....................43.39
Bill v Short Brothers & Harland Ltd [1963] NI 1 ....................21.22
Billings (AC) & Sons Ltd v Riden [1958] AC 240 ....................20.23
Billyack v Leyland Construction Co Ltd [1968] 1 WLR 471 ....................13.49
Birch v Thomas [1972] 1 All ER 705 ....................20.69
Bird v Holbrook (1828) 4 Bing 628, 130 ER 911 ....................12.19, 12.140, 22.34
Bird v Jones (1845) 7 QB 742, 115 ER 668 ....................22.37, 22.43
Birkenhead v Coombs (1983) 143 Vt 167, 465 A 2d 244 ....................22.33
Birmingham v Billing (1875) IR 9 CL 287 ....................29.10, 30.19
Bissett v Heiton & Co (No 2) [1933] IR 242 ....................18.101
Bissett v Thomas Heiton & Co Ltd [1930] IR 17 .................... 18.101, 21.08-21.10, 21.22
Black & Ors v Northern Whig Ltd (1942) 77 ILTR 5 ....................34.59, 34.208
Black v Hunt (1978) 2 LR Ir 10 ....................34.38
Black v Scottish Temperance Life Assurance [1908] 1 IR 541 ....................24.25
Black v Zager (1982) 22 CCLT 231 ....................24.28

Blades v Higgs 10 CB (ns) 713, 142 ER 634 (1861) affd (1865) 11 HL Cas 621 11 ER 1474 .......... 22.114
Blake v Lanyon 6 TR 221 .......... 32.12
Blake v Woolf [1898] 2 QB 426 .......... 25.11
Blanchfield v Murphy (1913) 47 ILTR 24 .......... 44.58, 44.64
Blay v Daly [1997] Ir L Log W 99 .......... 15.40
Blaz v Dickinson 23 MVR (3d) 70, 1996 Ont CJ LEXIS 3410 (1996) .......... 7.39
Blehein v Murphy (SC) 17 January 2000 .......... 22.112
Bliss v Hall (1838) 4 Bing NC 183, 132 ER 758 .......... 24.104
Bliss v Stafford (1573) Owen 37 74 ER 882 .......... 35.26
Bloodsworth v Gray (1844) 7 Man & G 334, 135 ER 140 .......... 34.41
Bloodworth v Cormack [1949] NZLR 1058 .......... 24.106
Bloom v Creed & Consumers' Gas Co [1937] OR 626 .......... 9.18
Blyth v Birmingham Waterworks Co (1856) 11 Ex 781, 156 Eng Rep 1047 .......... 2.49, 7.01
Blyth v Bloomsbury Health Authority [1993] 4 Med LR 151 .......... 14.84
BMTA v Salvadori [1949] Ch 556 .......... 39.30
Board of Education for City of Toronto & Hunt v Hiffs (1959) 22 DLR (2d) 49 .......... 16.26
Boatswain v Crawford [1943] NZLR 109 .......... 26.12
Bognor Regis UDC v Campion [1972] 2 QB 169 .......... 39.03
Bohan v Clements [1920] 2 IR 117 .......... 21.10, 21.19
Bohan v Finn DPIJ: Trinity and Michaelmas Terms 1994, p 61 .......... 20.30
Bohane v Driscoll [1929] IR 428 .......... 12.13, 12.29, 16.70
Boharmor Ltd v Belfast City Council [1987] NILR Bull 1 .......... 25.17
Bolam v Friern Hospital Management Committee [1957] 2 All ER 118 .......... 14.82-14.83 .......... 14.95
Boland v Tara Mines Ltd Irish Times, 3 March 1984 .......... 34.50
Bolands Ltd v Trouw Ireland Ltd (HC) 1 May 1978 .......... 11.30-11.31
Boles v O'Connor (SC) 10 February 1966 .......... 44.63
Bolger v Governor of Mountjoy Prison (SC) 1998 .......... 7.47
Bolger v O'Brien (SC) 16 March 1999 .......... 46.43
Bolger v Queally Pig Slaughtering Ltd, (HC) 8 March 1996 .......... 18.165
Bolitho v Hackney Health Authority [1998] AC 232 .......... 2.63, 14.84
Bollinger v Costa Brava Wine Co [1960] RPC 16, [1961] RPC 116 .......... 31.28
Bolton v Blackrock Clinic Ltd (HC) 20 December 1994, affd by (SC) 23 January 1997 .......... 14.106, 14.119, 37.42, 43.22
Bolton v O'Brien (1885) 16 LR Ir 483 (CA), affg (1885) 16 LR Ir 97 .......... 34.61, 34.124
Bolton v Stone [1951] AC 850 .......... 7.32, 24.18
Bonfield v Tipperary (North Riding) County Council [1941] Ir Jur 76 .......... 21.10
Bonnard v Perryman [1891] 2 Ch 269 .......... 45.30-45.34
Bonnington Castings Ltd v Wardlaw [1956] AC 613 .......... 2.22
Bord Tráchtála v Waterford Foods plc [1994] FSR 316 .......... 31.09, 31.16, 45.05
Borg & Powers Furniture Co v Clark (1935) 194 Minn 305 260, NW 316 .......... 9.21
Borowski v Sacheti (1996) 43 Conn App 294, 682 A 2d 1095 .......... 2.21

Borradaile v Hunter (1843) 5 Man & G 639, 134 ER 715 ....................................... 40.38
Boryszko v Bd of Education of City of Toronto and Bennett-Pratt Ltd
(1962) 33 DLR (2d) 257 ....................................... 16.70
Bottomley v Woolworth & Co (1932) 48 TLR 52 ....................................... 34.19
Boucher v Clyde Shipping Co [1904] 2 IR 129 ....................................... 21.10, 21.32
Boughton v Bray UDC [1964] Ir Jur 57 ....................................... 12.13, 12.29, 44.58
Boulcott Golf Club Inc v Engelbrecht [1945] NZLR 556 ....................................... 26.08
Bourgeault v Board of Education, St Paul's Roman Catholic School
District No 20 (1977) 82 DLR (3d) 701 ....................................... 16.56
Bourgoin SA v Ministry of Agriculture [1986] QB 716 ....................................... 19.81
Bourhill v Young [1943] AC 92 ....................................... 6.58, 17.22
Bouvy v Count de Courte (1901) 20 NZLR 312 ....................................... 36.05
Bow Husky (Bermuda) Ltd v St John Shipbuilding Co Ltd
(1997) 153 DLR (4th) 385 ....................................... 10.14
Bowater v Rowley Regis Corporation [1944] KB 176 ....................................... 18.159
Bowdren v Southern Health Board, DPIJ: Trinity and Michaelmas Terms 1993, p 65
....................................... 18.114
Bowen v Paramount (Builders) Hamilton Ltd [1977] 1 NZLR 394 ....................................... 13.70
Bower v Peate (1876) 1 QBD 321 ....................................... 24.78, 25.05
Bowers v Hardwick (1986) 478 US 186 ....................................... 37.80
Bowes v O'Connor (HC) 21 February 1964 ....................................... 4.10
Box v Jubb (1879) 4 Ex D 76 ....................................... 25.35
Boxins v Goblet Freres [1894] 1 QB 842 ....................................... 34.161
Boyce v Cawley DPIJ: Michaelmas Term 1991, p 144 ....................................... 44.125
Boyd v Great Northern Ry [1895] 2 IR 555 ....................................... 22.37, 24.06, 24.16
Boyd v Ireland (HC) 13 May 1993 ....................................... 7.47, 8.35
Boyhan v Tribunal of Inquiry into the Beef Industry [1992] ILRM 545 ....................................... 45.02
Boylan v Motor Distributors Ltd (HC) 9 June 1993 ....................................... 46.22-46.27
Boylan v Northern Bank Ltd & James Corcoran Ltd (HC) 21 July 1977 ....... 23.02, 43.51
Boyle v An Post [1992] 2 IR 437 ....................................... 45.02
Boyle v Ferguson [1911] 2 IR 489 ....................................... 43.25
Boyle v Holcroft [1905] 1 IR 245 ....................................... 24.48
Boyle v Marathon Petroleum Ireland Ltd (HC) 1 November 1995,
(SC) 12 January 1999 ....................................... 7.39, 18.23, 21.42
Boyne v Commissioner for Public Works in Ireland, DPIJ: Hilary and Easter
Terms 1992 ....................................... 18.108
Boynton v Burglass (1991) 590 So 2d 446 ....................................... 37.44
Brabazon v Morgan (SC) 21 February 1958 ....................................... 44.58-44.60
Bradbury Ltd v Duffy (HC) 26 March 1979 ....................................... 32.92, 32.105
Bradford (Mayor of) v Pickles [1865] AC 587 ....................................... 24.51-24.52
Bradford Third Equitable Benefit Building Society v Borders
[1941] 2 All ER 205 ....................................... 35.06, 35.13
Bradford v Kanellos (1973) 40 DLR (3d) 578 ....................................... 8.14, 20.21
Bradley Center Inc v Wessner (1982) 250 Ga 199, 296 SE 2d 693 ....................................... 8.25
Bradley v Archibald [1899] 2 IR 108 ....................................... 29.10, 30.19

Bradley v Coras Iompair Éireann [1976] IR 217 .................................. 7.41, 7.51, 18.03
........................................................................................ 18.15-18.19, 18.82
Bradley v Wingnut Films Ltd [1993] 1 NZLR 415 .................................................. 22.33
Bradshaw v Grimes [1997] Ir L Log W 332 ........................................................ 15.18
Brady v Beckmann Instruments (Galway) Inc [1986] ILRM 361 ............... 18.07, 18.109
Brady v Doherty (HC) 31 July 1998 ........................................................................ 44.169
Brady v Hopper (1983) 570 F Supp 1333 .................................................................. 37.44
Brady v Igoe [1939] Ir Jur Rep 1 .............................................................................. 43.46
Brady v McCarren & Co Ltd (SC) 6 June 1957 ........................................................ 18.108
Brady v Warren [1900] 2 IR 632 ............................................25.17, 27.06-27.08, 27.42
Braitman v Overlook Terrace Corporation (1975) 68 NJ 368, 346 A d 76 ................ 8.25
Brandon v Osborne Garrett & Co Ltd [1924] 1 KB 548 ............................................ 2.47
Brannigan v Dublin Corporation [1927] IR 513 ................................ 23.07, 23.29, 23.48
Brannon v Guthrie [1988] 5 NIJB 54 ........................................................................ 21.12
Brannon v Wood (1968) 251 Or 349, 444 P 2d 558 .................................................. 9.20
Brasserie du Pêcheur SA v Germany, R v Secretary of State for Transport
ex p Factortame [1991] ECR I-5357 .............................................................. 1.88-1.97
Braund v Henning, 62 ALJR 433 .............................................................................. 15.17
Breen v Tyrone County Council [1905] 2 IR 542 .................................................. 24.113
Breivo v City of Aberdeen (1976) 15 Wn Appeal 520, 550 P 2d 1164 ................. 24.116
Brennan v Bank of Ireland (HC) 23 May 1985 .......................................................... 10.25
Brennan v Gale [1949] NI 178 .................................................................................. 42.38
Brennan v Glennon (SC) 26 November 1975 ............................................................ 45.45
Brennan v Lissadell Towels Ltd, DPIJ: Trinity & Michaelmas Terms 1998, p 272 .. 44.90
Brennan v O'Donnell [1996] Ir L Log W 129 ............................................................ 23.42
Brennan v O'Meara DPIJ: Trinity and Michaelmas Terms 1996, p 45 .................... 15.44
Brennan v Savage Smyth & Co Ltd [1982] ILRM 223 .......... 12.23, 12.31, 40.24, 44.204
Brennan v Teagasc (CC) 30 October 1998 ................................................................ 18.95
Brenner v Toronto Railway Co 13 Ont LR 423 .......................................................... 20.06
Breslin v Brennan [1937] IR 350 ........................................... 7.27, 11.30, 12.21, 12.35
Breslin v Dublin United Tramways Co (1911) 45 ILTR 220 ...................................... 9.21
Bret v Mullarkey (1873) IR 7 CL 120 ........................................................................ 23.42
Breunig v American Family Insurance Co (1970) 45 Wis 2d 536,
173 NW 2d 619 ........................................................................................................ 7.23
Brew Bros Ltd v Snox (Ross) Ltd [1970] 1 QB 612 .................................................. 24.76
Brewer v Dew (1843) 11 M & W 625 152 ER 955 .................................................... 28.04
Bridges Bros Ltd v Forest Protection Ltd (1976) 72 DLR (3d) 335 ........................ 23.32
Bridges v Hawkesworth (1851) 21 LJQB 75 .............................................................. 30.24
Bridlington Relay Ltd v Yorkshire Electricity Board [1965] Ch 436 ...................... 24.106
Brien v McGarry (1928) 62 ILTR 166 ........................................................................ 40.11
Briess v Woolley [1954] AC 333 ................................................................................ 35.06
Brimelow v Casson [1924] 1 Ch 302 .......................................................................... 32.43
Bristow v Cormican (1874) IR 10 CL 398 .................................................................. 23.43
Bristow v Cormican (1878) 3 AC 641 ........................................................................ 30.20

British & Irish Steampacket Co Ltd v Branigan [1958] IR 128 ....................32.01, 32.19, 32.33, 32.45
British Celanese Ltd v AH Hunt (Capacitors) Ltd [1969] 1 WLR 959 .......... 25.25-25.27
British Home Stores Ltd v Mitchell (HC) 18 April 1984 ....................45.05
British Motor Trade Association v Salvadori [1949] Ch 556 ....................32.29
British Railways Board v Herrington [1972] AC 877 .................... 12.42-12.50, 12.101
British Transport Commission v Gourley [1956] AC 185 ..............42.33, 44.101, 44.104
British Wagon Company Ltd v Shortt [1961] IR 164 ....................29.03, 30.09
Broadbent v Ramsbotham (1856) 11 Ex 602, 156 ER 971 ....................24.51
Broadhurst v Millman [1976] Vict R 208 .................... 40.26-40.29
Brock v Richards [1951] I KB 529 ....................27.51
Brogan v Bennett [1955] IR 119 ....................10.50, 10.110, 14.75
Brohan v Crossplan Developments [1985] ILRM 702 ....................13.11
Brooke v Bool [1928] 2 KB 578 ....................8.25
Broome v Agar (1928) 138 LT 698 ....................34.86
Broome v Cassell & Co [1981] ILRM 266 ....................44.22
Broomfield v The Midland Health Board DPIJ: Michaelmas Term 1990 ..............44.178
Brown v Belfast Water Commissioners (1912) 47 ILTR 153 ....................28.06
Brown v Chapman (1762) 1 W Bl 427 ....................36.20
Brown v Cotterill (1934) 51 TLR 21 ....................11.14, 11.26
Brown v Foley [1932] LJ, IFS 205 ....................40.11
Brown v George 294 SE 2d ....................20.12
Brown v Hawkes [1981] 2 QB 718 ....................36.16
Brown v Hubar (1974) 3 OR (2d) 448 ....................17.23
Brown v Norton [1954] IR 34 .................... 13.07-13.09, 13.44
Brown v Raphael [1958] 2 All ER 79 ....................35.08
Brown v Robert Wilkes Ltd DPIJ: Michaelmas Term 1990 p 159 ....................21.55
Brown v Shyne (1926) 242 NY 176, 151 NE 197 ....................21.33
Brown v Swift & Co (1912) 91 Neb 532, 136 NW 726 ....................7.08, 18.10
Brown v The Queen in Right of British Columbia [1994] 1 SCR 420 ....................19.10
Brownbill v Kenworth Sales (1982) 39 ALR 191 ....................42.17
Browne v Barry's Tea Ltd [1996] Ir L Log W 142 ....................15.03
Browne v Dowie (1959) 93 ILTR 179 ....................23.33
Browne v Primark t/a Penneys DPIJ: Michaelmas Term 1990, p 182 .................... 11.16, 11.38-11.40
Browning v The War Office [1963] 1 QB 750 ....................44.118
Bruce v Donaldson and Ors (1918) 53 ILTR 24 ....................39.10
Bruce v Dyer (1966) 58 DLR (2d) 211, affd (1970) 8 DLR (3d) 592n ....................22.14
Bruce v Dyer [1970] 1 OR 482 ....................22.20
Brugh v Bigelow 310 Mich 74, 16 NW 2d 668, 158 ALR 184 ....................20.81
Brunswick (Duke of) v Harmer (1849) 14 QB 185, 117 ER 75 ....................34.18, 46.04
Brushett v Cowan (1987) 40 DLR (4th) 488 ....................22.73
Bruton's Ltd v Milletts' Stores Ltd (1951) 85 ILTR 42 ....................24.85
Bryan v Maloney (1985) 182 CLR 609 ....................13.73
Bryanston Finance Ltd v de Fries [1975] QB 703 ....................34.162

Bryant v Snell (CC) 18 June 1997 .......... 27.59
Bryson v Gardner Merchant Ltd NI CA (Civil Div), 11 October 1996 Lexis transcript NICA 2196 .......... 18.09
Buchan v Ortho Pharmaceuticals (Canada) Ltd (1986) 25 DLR (4th) 658 .......... 11.60
Buckle v Holmes (1925) 42 TLR 147, affd [1926] 2 KB 125 .......... 23.29, 27.23
Buckley v Avonmore Creamery (CC) 7 May 1985 .......... 18.155
Buckley v Farrow (CA (Civil Div) 4 February 1997 .......... 33.19
Buckley v Fitzgerald (1881) 15 ILT Jo 118 .......... 27.42
Buckley v Healy [1965] IR 618 .......... 23.29, 24.31
Buckley v Johnson and Perrott and Woods (HC) 29 July 1992 .......... 43.65
Buckley v Lynch [1978] IR 6 .......... 4.25, 46.87
Buckley v Maloney (SC) 2 July 1996 .......... 15.37
Buckley v Mott (1920) 50 DLR 408 .......... 11.08
Buckley v Musgrave Brook Bond Ltd [1969] IR 440 .......... 43.64
Buckley v National Maternity Hospital (HC) 21 December 1998 .......... 14.30
Buckley v Smith Transport [1946] 4 DLR 721 .......... 7.23
Buckley v Southern Health Board, DPIJ: Hilary and Easter Terms 1994, p 115 .... 18.108
Buckner v Ashby & Horner Ltd [1941] 1 KB 321 .......... 11.27
Bula Ltd v Tara Mines Ltd (No 2) [1987] IR 95, [1988] ILRM 157 .......... 1.06 .......... 12.135, 32.83,45.02
Bula v Flynn, Taxing Master of the High Court (HC) 7 March 2000 .......... 4.18
Bunyan v Jordan (1937) 57 Comm LR 1 .......... 22.33
Burchett v Commissioner for Rys [1958] SR (NSW) 366 .......... 25.36
Burell v Tuohy [1898] 2 IR 271 .......... 7.50
Burgess v City of Woodstock [1955] 4 DLR 615 .......... 24.59
Burgess v Florence Nightingale Hospital for Gentlewomen [1955] 1 QB 349 .......... 42.18
Burgess v M/V Tamanfo (1973) 370 Supp 247 .......... 24.05
Burke & John Paul & Co Ltd [1967] IR 277 .......... 18.95
Burke v Blanch (HC) 28 July 1989 .......... 44.159-44.164
Burke v Burke (SC) 27 July 1971 .......... 44.173
Burke v Central Independent Television plc [1994] 2 IR 61 .......... 34.216
Burke v Dublin Corporation [1991] 1 IR 341 .......... 13.27-13.31
Burke v Good [1997] Ir L Log W 336 .......... 7.47
Burke v John Paul & Co Ltd [1967] IR 277 .......... 2.19, 3.09, 3.22 .......... 3.31-3.36, 18.03, 18.96, 18.148
Burke v McDonald (1989) 17 ILT (ns) 64 .......... 15.42
Burke v Minister for Defence DPIJ: Hilary and Easter Terms 1991, p 234 .......... 18.108
Burkholder v Superior Court (1979) 96 Cal App 3d 421, 158 Cal Rptr 86 .......... 37.11
Burmah Oil Co v Lord Advocate [1965] AC 75 .......... 23.51
Burnard v Haggis (1863) 14 CB (NS) 45, 143 ER 360 .......... 40.32
Burnett & Hallamshire Fuel Ltd v Sheffield Telegraph & Star Ltd [1960] 1 WLR 502, [1960] 2 All ER 157 .......... 34.142
Burnett v George [1992] 1 FLR 525 .......... 22.32
Burnett v The Queen in Right of Canada (1979) 23 OR (2d) 109 .......... 37.02

Burnie Port Authority v General Jones Pty Ltd (1994) 179 CLR 520 ............25.02, 25.10
............ 25.25, 25.42, 25.49-25.53
Burniston v Corporation of Bangor [1932] NI 178 ............24.93
Burns v Cork and Bandon Ry Co 13 Ir CLR 543 ............43.50
Burns v Edman [1970] 2 QB 541 ............20.93, 42.17
Burns v Irish Fibres Ltd (1967) 101 ILTR 172 ............18.102, 18.152
Burns v Johnston [1917] 2 IR 137, affg [1916] 2 IR 444 ............ 22.47-22.50
Burrell v Tuohy [1898] 2 IR 271 ............18.101
Burrows v Rhodes [1899] 1 QB 816 ............35.20
Burton v Davies [1953] QSR 26 ............22.38
Bustos v Hair Transplant pty NSWCA, 15 April 1997 ............14.144
Butler v Acme Markets, Inc (1982) 89 NJ 270 445 A 2d 114 ............8.25
Butler v Standard Telephones & Cables Ltd [1940] 1 KB 299 ............24.28
Butler v Union Pacific RR Co (1995) 68 F 2D 378 ............20.90
Butterfield v Forrester (1809) 11 East 60, 103 ER 926 ............ 20.02-20.04
Butterly v Mayor of Drogheda [1907] 2 IR 134 ............7.44, 15.17
............ 20.02-20.05, 24.17
Bye v Bates (1989) 51 SASR 67 ............40.11
Byrne v Boadle (1863) 2 H & C 722, 159 ER 299 ............ 9.12-9.20, 9.42
Byrne v British & Irish Steampacket Co Ltd (SC) 27 July 1966 ............24.18
Byrne v Corporation of Dun Laoghaire [1940] Ir Jur Rep 40 ............40.18
Byrne v CPI Ltd (HC) 3 February 1993 ............15.04
Byrne v Deane [1937]1 KB 818 ............34.72
Byrne v Duckett (1882) 10 LR (Ir) 24 ............23.23
Byrne v Dun Laoghaire Corporation [1940] Ir Jur 40 ............8.18
Byrne v Grey (HC) 9 October 1987 ............23.06
Byrne v Houlihan [1966] IR 274 ............42.20, 42.25, 42.39, 42.50, 44.10
Byrne v Ireland (CC) 28 January 1985 ............8.16
Byrne v Ireland [1972] IR 241 ............1.06, 1.14, 6.55, 19.01
............21.08, 32.09, 38.01, 38.06, 38.20, 39.13, 43.02
Byrne v ITGWU (HC) 30 November 1995 ............46.65
Byrne v Jefferson Smurfit & Son Ltd [1962-1963] Ir Jur Rep 49 ............18.09, 21.10
............21.43, 21.52
Byrne v Johns (SC) 10 March 1972 ............44.83
Byrne v Kinematograph Renters Society Ltd [1958] 2 All ER 579 ............23.16
Byrne v Londonderry Tramway [1902] 2 IR 457 ............43.32
Byrne v M'Evoy (1871) IR 5 CL 568 ............30.19
Byrne v Martina Investments Ltd (HC) 30 January 1984 ............24.74
Byrne v McDonald (SC) 7 February 1957 ............ 7.07-7.08, 11.30, 40.18
Byrne v Newman Sheeting Centre [1996] Ir L Log W 229 ............18.114
Byrne v Sheedy [1955] IR 1 ............7.04, 15.17, 15.40, 21.22
Byrne v Southern and Western Ry Co (CA) February 1884 ....... 6.50, 17.12-17.21, 17.42
Byrne v Triumph Engineering Ltd [1982] IR 220 ............4.12
Bywell Castle (1879) 4 PD 219 ............20.18

## C

C & A Modes v C & A (Waterford) Ltd [1976] IR 198 .......... 31.06, 31.57, 44.03, 45.03
C v North Western Health Board [1997] Ir L Log W 133 ...................... 7.29, 8.25, 14.30
Cadbury-Schweppes Pty Ltd v Public Squash Co Pty Ltd
[1981] 1 All ER 213 .......... 31.77
Caffrey v North Eastern Health Board (HC) 10 February 1995 .................... 14.30, 14.52
Cagney v Murphy (CC) 13 February 1999 .......... 24.31
Cahill v Kenneally [1955-1956] Ir Jur 15 .......... 7.27, 8.07, 8.18, 11.30
Cahill v Sutton [1980] IR 269 .......... 46.08
Cairns v Canada Refining Co (1914) 6 OWN 562 .......... 25.06
Callaghan v Killarney Race Co Ltd [1958] IR 366 .......... 7.04, 7.28, 7.44
.......... 12.07, 12.102, 18.15
Callinan v Voluntary Health Insurance Board (SC) 28 July 1994 .......... 19.75
Cambridge Water Co v Eastern Counties Leather plc [1994] 2 AC 264 .......... 3.42, 25.02
.......... 25.41-25.42, 25.51
Camden Exhibition & Display Ltd v Lynott [1956] 3 All ER 28 .......... 32.32
Camden Nominees v Forcey [1940] Ch 352 .......... 32.43-32.44
Cameron v Commissioner of Rys [1964] QR 480 .......... 40.26
Caminer v Northern & London Investment Trust Ltd [1951] AC 88 .......... 24.30
Campbell & Cosans v UK (1982) 4 EHRR 293 .......... 22.104
Campbell v Cox (SC) 15 May 1956 .......... 18.09, 18.101, 18.108
Campbell v Irish Press Ltd (1955) 90 ILTR 105 .......... 34.92, 34.124
.......... 34.206-34.207, 44.03
Campbell v John A Best & Co Ltd [1969] NI 123 .......... 21.10, 21.42
Campbell v North Lanarkshire Council 2000 SCLR 373 .......... 17.67
Campbell v O'Donnell [1967] IR 226 .......... 11.30, 11.61, 13.63
Campbell v Paddington Corporation [1911] 1 KB 869 .......... 39.08
Campbell v Spottiswode (1863) 3 B & S 769, 122 ER 288 .......... 34.203, 34.221
Campbell v T & J Farrington Ltd (HC) 3 October 1977 .......... 10.151, 20.28
Campbell v Ward [1981] ILRM 60 .......... 46.80
Campbell v Wilkinson (1909) 43 ILTR 237 .......... 27.26, 27.30
Campbell-Sharp v Magill (HC) 29 June 1985 .......... 34.226
Campion v Chicago Landscape Co (1938) 295 Ill Appeal 225
14 NE 2d 879 .......... 24.18
Campus Oil Ltd v Minister for Industry and Energy (No 2) [1983] IR 88 .......... 31.62
.......... 31.64,45.02, 45.08-45.11, 45.26
Canada Safeway Ltd v Manitoba Food & Commercial Workers Local 832 (1983) 25
CCLTI .......... 31.76
Canadian National Railway Co v Norsk Pacific SS Co (1992) 91 DLR (4th) 289
.......... 6.31
Canadian National Railway v Bakty (1977) 18 OR (2d) 481 .......... 20.80-20.81
Canard v Antifyre Ltd [1933] 1 KB 551 .......... 24.59
Candler v Crane, Christmas & Co [1951] 2 KB 164 .......... 10.51, 10.63, 37.42
Candy v Minch Norton & Co Ltd [1953] IR 192 .......... 15.17
Canning v Cahill, DPIJ: Hilary and Easter Terms 1995, p 42 .......... 18.108, 18.150

Cannon v Midland GW Ry (Ireland) Co (1879) 6 LR Ir 199 ..............................7.44, 8.14
Canterbury v Spence (1972) 464F 2d 772 ..............................14.134, 14.144
Cantrell & Cochrane (Dublin) Ltd v Savage Smythe & Co Ltd
(HC) 1 August 1976 .............................. 31.05-31.10, 31.34
Cantrell & Cochrane Ltd v Neeson [1926] NI 107 ..............................30.20
Caparo Industries plc v Dickman [1989] 1 All ER 798, [1990] 2 AC 605 ..............................6.03
..............................6.21-6.23, 6.29-6.34, 10.09
.............................. 10.64, 10.71, 10.77-10.84, 10.106, 19.11
Capital & Counties plc v Hampshire County Council [1997] QB 1004 ..............................8.04
..............................19.02, 26.24
Carey v Albany Golf Club 4 SR (WA) 168 ..............................7.28
Carey v Cork Consumers Gas Co (SC) 5 March 1958 ..............................3.27, 18.109
Carey v Ireland, DPIJ: Michaelmas Term 1990, p 293 ..............................18.131
Carleton v O'REgan [1997] 1 ILRM 370 ..............................46.88
Carlgarth, The [1927] P 93 ..............................23.16
Carlisle v O'Sheas (Dublin) Ltd (SC) 15 March 1968 ..............................18.96
Carlos v Congested Districts Board [1908] 2 IR 91 ..............................43.69
Carmarthenshire County Council v Lewis [1955] AC 549 ......16.11, 16.66, 20.81, 40.11
Carnahan v Coates 71 DLR (4th) 464 ..............................36.29
Carney v Buyea (1944) 271, Appeal Div 338, 65 NYS 2d 902 ..............................20.81
Carolan v Minister for Defence [1972] IR 62 ..............................38.01
Carrat v Matthews (1921) 59 DLR 505 ..............................7.05
Carriere v Board of Gravelbourg School District No 2244 of Saskatchewan (1977) 79 DLR (3d) 662 ..............................18.81
Carroll Shipping Ltd v Mathews Mulcahy Sutherland (HC) 18 December 1996 ......46.65
Carroll v Clare County Council [1975] IR 221 ..............................7.23, 15.24
.............................. 20.46-20.48, 20.55
Carroll v Kehoe (1927) 61 ILTR 192 ..............................27.26
Carroll v Kildare County Council [1950] IR 258 ..............................7.41, 23.36, 24.58
Carroll v Parkes (1912) 47 ILTR 88 ..............................27.42
Carroll v Post National Lottery Co (HC) 17 April 1996 ..............................43.21
Carroll v Sheridan [1984] ILRM 451 ..............................23.33
Carslake v Mapledoram (1788) 2 TR 473,100 ER 255 ..............................34.40
Carslogie Steamship Co Ltd v Royal Norwegian Government [1952] AC 292
[1952] 1 All ER 20 ..............................2.25, 2.48
Carson v Jeffers [1961] IR 44 ..............................23.22, 23.42, 45.05
Carstairs v Taylor (1871) LR 6 Ex 217 ..............................25.11, 25.31
Cartledge v E Jopling & Sons Ltd [1961] All ER 482 affd [1963] AC 758 ..............................46.19
Casement v London Daily Express Newspapers Ltd (HC) (1933) ..............................34.203
Casey v Automobiles Renault Canada Ltd (1965) 54 DLR (2d) 600 ..............................36.04
Casey v Daughters of Charity of St Vincent de Paul [1996] Ir L Log W 68 ..............................24.31
Casey v Martin (1920) 54 ILTR 185 ..............................15.49
Casey v Tralee UDC DPIJ: Hilary and Easter Terms 1995, p 49 ..............................24.84
Cassell & Co Ltd v Broome [1972] AC 1027 .............................. 44.10-44.12
Cassells v Marks & Spencer plc (HC) 25 March 1999 ..............................7.34, 11.16, 11.54, 25.24

Casserly v CLE (SC) 21 July 1978 .......... 44.145
Cassidy v Clarke DPIJ: Trinity & Michaelmas Terms 1999, p 183 (HC) .... 20.44, 44.176
Cassidy v Daily Mirror Newspapers Ltd [1929] 2 KB 331 .......... 34.96
Cassidy v Kincaid (1865) 10 IJ NS 176 .......... 34.57
Cassidy v Ministry of Health [1951] 2 KB 343 .......... 9.28, 43.22
Cassidy v Wellman International Ltd, DPIJ: Trinity and Michaelmas Terms 1998, p 171 .......... 18.108
Castle v St Augustine's Links (1922) 38 Times LR 615 .......... 24.09, 24.18
Caswell v Powell Duffryn Associated Collieries Ltd [1940] AC 152 .......... 21.54
Cattle Express Shipping Corporation of Liberia v Cheasty (HC) 19 April 1983 .......... 32.29
Cattle v Stockton Waterworks Co (1875) LR 10 QB 453 .......... 10.07, 10.46, 25.27
Caulfield v Bell & Co Ltd [1958] IR 326 .......... 18.126
Caulfield v George Bell & Co Ltd [1958] IR 326 .......... 18.14, 18.106
Cavalier v Pope [1906] AC 428 .......... 13.12
Cavan v Wilcox (1973) 44 DLR (3d) 42 (NBCA) .......... 14.40
Cavanagh v Ulster Weaving Co [1959] NI 109 .......... 18.15
Cazabon v Westinghouse Electrical Irl Ltd t/a ThermoKing (Europe) Ltd DPIJ: Hilary and Easter Terms 1994, p 104 .......... 18.108, 20.30
Cellactite and British Uralite v HH Robertson C [1957] CLY 1980 .......... 34.44
Cellular Clothing v Maxton [1899] AC 326 .......... 31.40
Central & Eastern Trust Co v Rafuse (1986) 31 Dec 31 DLR (4th) 481 .... 10.151, 14.171
Central London Property Trust Ltd v High Trees House Ltd [1947] KB 130 .......... 10.115
Central Ry of Venezuela v Kirch (1867) LR 2 HL 99 .......... 35.15
Chadwick v British Transport Commission [1967] 2 All ER 845 .......... 17.22, 20.80
Challiner v Burgess (1856) 3 Saunders Co Court Cas 147 .......... 29.05
Chambers v Cork Corporation (1958) 93 ILTR 45 .......... 13.09-13.14, 24.59
Champagne v Cummings 1999 Ont Sup CJ LEXIS 12 .......... 22.60
Chan Shin-nin v Tang Kam-ho [1974] HKLR 1 .......... 7.14
Chan v Fong (1973) 5 SASR 1 .......... 40.26
Chaplin of Gray's Inn's Case, YB 2 Hen IV, fo 8, pi 40 .......... 22.89
Chaplin v Hawes (1828) 3 C & P 554, 172 ER 543 .......... 20.58
Chapman v Hearse (1961) 106 CLR 112, affg [1961] SASR 51 .......... 20.80-20.81
Chapman v McDonald [1969] IR 188 .......... 32.09-32.11, 33.04, 33.37
Chappel v Hart (1998) 72 ALJR 1344 .......... 2.22
Charing Cross Electricity Supply Co v Hydraulic Power Co [1914] 3 KB 772 .......... 25.11, 25.19, 25.25
Chariot Inns Ltd v Assicurazioni Generali SPA et al [1981] IR 199 .......... 1.110
Charles v Zadow (1981) 28 SASR 492 .......... 40.26
Chasemore v Richards (1859) 7 HL Cas 349, 11 ER 140 .......... 24.51
Chatterton v Gerson [1981] 1 QB 432 .......... 14.79, 14.144
Chatterton v Secretary of State for India [1895] 2 QB 189 .......... 34.158
Chaytor v London, New York & Paris Assoc of Fashion Ltd (1961) 30 DLR (2d) 527 .......... 22.41

Cherneskey v Armadale Publishers Ltd [1979] ISCR 1067 ....................................34.220
Cherrey v Steinke 13 CCLT 50 ....................................20.70
Chester v Waverley Corporation (1939) 62 Comm LR 1 ....................................17.22
Chesterfield Corporation v Arthur Robinson (Transport) Ltd
(1955) 106 LJ (News) 61 ....................................24.16
Chic Fashions (West Wales) Ltd v Jones [1968] 2 QB 299 ....................................23.26, 28.15
Chilvers v LCC (1916) 32 TLR 363 ....................................16.57
Ching v Surrey County Council [1910] 1 KB 736 ....................................21.10
Chipchase v British Titan Products Co [1956] 1 QB 545 ....................................21.23
Christie v Davey [1893] 1 Ch 316 .................................... 24.48-24.50
Christie v Odeon (Ireland) Ltd (1957) 91 ILTR 25 ....................................7.25, 7.39
....................................12.08, 18.03-18.06, 18.13-18.15, 18.81-18.82
Church of Ireland (Representative Body of the) v Warnock [1898] 2 IR 532 23.29, 23.33
Church of Scientology In v Transmedia Productions Pty Ltd
(1997) NSW LEXIS 7075, BC 8701 359 ....................................22.33
Church of Scientology v Johnson-Smith [1972] 1 QB 522 ....................................34.138
Church Representative Body v M'Loughlin (1896) 31 ILTR 43 ....................................23.33
Churchill v Siggers (1854) 3 E & B 929, 118 ER 1389 ....................................36.19
Ciba-Geigy Canada Ltd v Apotex Inc [1992] 95 DLR 385 ....................................31.02
CIE v Carroll and Wexford County Council [1986] ILRM 312 ....................................2.13, 21.10
....................................21.25, 24.117
Cieplinski v Severn (1929) 269 Mass 261, 168 ER 722 ....................................22.38
Cinnamond v British Airports Authority [1980] 1 WLR 582 ....................................23.26
Clancy v Commissioners of Public Works in Ireland [1988] ILRM 268 ....................................40.18
Clancy v Dublin Corporation (SC) 22 November 1988 ....................................9.09
Clancy v Micro Bio (Irl) Ltd DPIJ: Hilary & Easter Terms 1996, p 67 ........18.61, 44.176
Clancy v Whelan (1957) 92 ILTR 39 ....................................23.02, 23.33
Clark v Chambers (1878) 3 QBD 327 ....................................40.26
Clark v MacLennan [1983] 1 All ER 416 ....................................2.57
Clark v Mincks (1985) 364 NW 2d 226 ....................................8.06
Clark v Monmouthshire County Council (1954) 2 LGR 246 ....................................16.26, 16.57
Clarke v Cooper (1859) 5 Ir Jur (ns) 38 ....................................23.02
Clarke v MGW Ry Co [1895] 2 IR 294 ....................................23.35
Clarke v Molyneaux (1877) 3 QBD 237 ....................................34.193, 34.198
Clarke v O'Gorman (HC) 13 February 1996 ....................................16.42
Clarke v Postan (1834) 6 C & P 423, 172 ER 1304 ....................................36.04
Clarke, Re [1950] IR 235 ....................................22.112
Clayards v Dethick (1848) 12 QB 439, 116 ER 932 ....................................20.23
Clayton v Le Roy [1911] 2 KB 1031 ....................................29.05
Cleary v Coffey (HC) 30 October 1979 ....................................32.162
Clegg v Dearden, (1848) 12 QB 576, 116 ER 986 ....................................23.35
Clements v London & Northwestern Ry [1894] 2 QB 482 ....................................18.02
Clements v Tyrone County Council [1905] 2 IR 415 ....................................24.17, 24.113, 43.52
Clidden v Szybiak (1949) 95 NH 318 63 A 2d 233 ....................................28.08

Clifford v Drug Treatment Centre Board (HC) 7 November 1997 ............................ 24.08
........................................................................................24.38, 24.93, 45.42-45.44
Clinkscales v Carver (1943) 22 Cal 2d, 72 136 p 2d 777 ........................................ 21.24
Clissold v Crotchley [1910] 2 KB 244 ......................................................................... 36.19
Clohessey v Tara Club Ltd Circuit Court, 25 March 1985 .......................................... 8.25
Clooney v Watson (1851) 2 Ir CLR 129 ....................................................................... 30.19
Clough v Bussan [1990] 1 All ER 431 ............................................................................ 8.25
Clunis v Camden and Islington Health Authority [1998] QB 978, [1998] 3 All ER 180 ..........................................................20.94, 20.104-20.105
Coady v Player & Wills (IR) Ltd (1979) 114 ILTR 32 .............................................. 27.53
Cockcroft v Smith (1705) 11 Mod 43, 88 ER 872 ......................................................... 22.86
Coco v AN Clark (Engineers) Ltd [1969] FSR 415, [1969] RPC 41 ............. 37.23, 37.33
Coderre v Ethier (1978) 85 DLR (3d) 621 ...................................................................... 7.39
Cody v Hurley (HC) 20 January 1999 ......................................................................... 44.169
Cody v Player & Wills (Ir) Ltd (1975) 109 ILTR 32 ................................................ 20.14
Coey v Belfast & Co Down Ry Co (1866) IR 2 CL 112 ............................................ 21.10
Coffee v McEvoy [1912] 2 IR 290 ................................................................................ 40.11
Coffey v Burriss (1845) 7 ILR 509 ............................................................................... 23.42
Coffey v Huntenburg DPIJ: Hilary & Easter Terms 1996, p 57 ............................ 44.176
Coffey v McEvoy [1912] 2 IR 95, affd [1912] 2 IR 290 ............................................ 12.18
Cogan v Dublin Motor Co (1914) 49 ILTR 24 .............................................................. 43.32
Colbert v Smithwick (1986) 30 ILT & Sol J 436 .......................................................... 23.43
Coldman v Hill [1919] 1 KB 443 ................................................................................... 29.09
Cole v Turner (1704) 6 Mod 149 at 149, 87 ER 907 .................................................. 22.16
Coleman v Clarke [1991] ILRM 841 ............................................................................ 15.03
Coleman v Dundalk UDC (SC) 17 July 1988 ............................................................... 13.11
Coleman v Keanes Ltd [1946] Ir Jur Rep 5 ..........................................34.38, 34.61-34.61
........................................................................................34.175, 34.194-34.197
Coleman v Kelly (1951) 85 ILTR 48 ............................................................................ 12.07
Coleman v Kilternan Hotel and Golf Club Ltd (SC) 19 July 1996 .......................... 12.58
Coleman v O'Hara (SC) 16 March 1977 ............................................................ 15.03, 15.44
Colgan v Connolly Construction Co (Ireland) Ltd [1980] ILRM 33 ............. 11.29, 11.74
........................................................................................13.53-13.55, 13.76
Colgan v Shannon (SC) 23 October 1958 ........................................................ 15.02, 15.17
Coll v Home & Colonial Stores Ltd [1904] AC 179 .................................................... 45.48
Collen Bros (Dublin) Ltd v Scaffolding Ltd [1959] IR 245 ....................... 4.20, 7.35, 7.50
........................................................................................9.18-9.20, 9.44
Collier v Dublin Wicklow & Wexford Ry Co (1873) IR 8 CL 21 ............................. 33.07
Collier v Earl of Mountcharles (SC) 19 December 1969 ................................ 2.13, 12.08
Collingwood v Home & Colonial Stores Ltd [1936] 1 All ER 74, affd [1936] 3 All ER 200 ........................................................................ 25.16, 26.20
Collins v Bus Atha Cliath/Dublin Bus (SC) 22 October 1999 .................................. 46.65
Collins v Gypsum Industries Ltd [1975] IR 331 .......................................................... 21.08
Collins v Hopkins [1923] 2 KB 617 ............................................................................... 13.11

Collins v Mid-Western Health Board (SC) 12 November 1999
........8.01, 14.30, 14.41, 14.42, 14.56
Collins v Stack [1996] Ir L Log W 427 ........23.33
Collins v Wilcock [1984] 3 All ER 374 ........22.17
Coloca v BP Australia [1992] 2 VR 441 ........44.13
Comerford v Minister for Education [1997] 2 ILRM 134 ........16.69
Commerford v Halifax School Commissioners [1950] 2 DLR 207 (ns) ........21.20
Commissioner for Railways v Quinlan [1964] AC 1054 ........25.48
Commonwealth Life Assurance Society Ltd v Smith (1938) 59 CLR 527 ........36.05
Commonwealth of Australia v McLean (1996) NSW LEXIS 3697, BC 9606-432 ........41.07
Commonwealth v Quince (1944) 68 CLR 227 ........32.05
Components Tube Co Ltd v Naylor [1900] 2 IR 1 ........35.06, 35.11
Comyn v Attorney General [1950] IR 142 ........38.04
Concrete Constructions (NSW) Pty Ltd v Australian Building Construction Employees' and Builders Labourers' Federation (1988) 83 ALR 385 ....23.20, 32.167
Condon v Basi [1985] 1 WLR 866 ........20.77, 22.60
Condon v Coras Iompair Éireann (HC) 4 November 1984 ........3.09, 10.13
Condon v Cork Corporation and An Bord Telecom (HC) 1 February 1991 ...7.13, 24.115
Condon v Mitchelstown RDC [1914] 1 IR 113 ........21.25
Conley v Strain [1988] IR 628 ........ 2.12, 2.27, 14.30, 20.40-20.46
Conlon v Kenney [1996] Ir L Log W 177 ........15.44
Conlon v Times Newspapers Ltd [1995] 2 ILRM 76 ........34.97
Connell v Fahy (SC) 24 June 1959 ........44.58
Connell v Porter (HC) 21 December 1967 ........24.78, 24.106
Connolly (Defendant) v South of Ireland Asphalt Co Ltd (Third Party) [1977] IR 99 ........2.39, 6.58
Connolly v Bus Éireann (HC) 29 January 1996 ........ 15.13, 44.166-44.168
Connolly v Casey (SC) 17 November 1999 ........4.24
Connolly v Congested Districts Board for Ireland 52 ILT & Sol J 52 ........25.12
Connolly v Dundalk UDC [1990] 2 IR 1 ........4.20, 12.138, 18.41, 18.48
........43.22, 43.50, 44.161
Connolly v Loughney (1953) 87 ILTR 49 ........ 32.60-32.70
Connolly v Murphy (SC) 11 October 1971 ........15.33
Connolly v O'Brien (SC) 28 October 1955 ........15.49
Connolly v Radio Telefís Éireann [1991] 2 IR 446 ........45.05, 45.24
Connolly v RTE [1991] 2 IR 446 ........45.05
Connolly v South of Ireland Asphalt Co Ltd [1977] IR 99 ........2.19, 2.34
........2.41, 3.20, 4.20, 7.04, 7.28
........ 7.54, 24.02, 24.09, 24.18-24.19
Connolly v Thorn EMI (Irl) Ltd DPIJ: Trinity and Michaelmas Terms 1992, p 193
........18.40
Connor v Malachy Burke (Contractors) Ltd (SC) 31 March 1955 ........18.12
........18.108, 18.146
Connor v Moran (1894) 29 ILTR 32 ........23.42

Connors v Justice (1862) 13 ICLR 451 ........ 34.34, 34.32
Connors v Pearson [1921] 2 IR 51 ........ 22.112
Conole v Redbank Oyster Co Ltd [1976] IR 191 ........ 2.34-2.38, 11.24-11.27, 13.42
Conroy v Attorney General [1965] IR 411 ........ 24.18
Conroy v McCormack, DPIJ: Trinity Term 1991, p 14 (HC) ........ 44.111
Consorti v Owens v Coring Fiberglass Corp (1995) 86 NY 2d 449, 634 NYS 2d, 18 657 NE 2d 1301 ........ 33.21
Constantine v Imperial Hotels Ltd [1944] KB 693 ........ 1.64, 32.50
Convery v Dublin County Council [1996] 3 IR 153 ........ 13.47, 19.21
........ 19.43, 19.49-19.50, 24.21, 24.94, 43.52
Conway v Archdall (1826) 1 Bat 182 ........ 28.04
Conway v Cniotáil Gaeltarra DPIJ: Michaelmas Term 1990, p 285 ........ 18.32, 21.42
Conway v Ireland (HC) 2 November 1988 ........ 1.16, 1.118
Conway v Irish National Teachers Organisation [1991] 1 ILRM 497, [1991] 2 IR 305 ........ 1.75, 16.69, 32.175, 34.259
........ 34.262, 44.08, 44.31, 44.36, 44.47-44.53
Conway v O'Brien (1940) 111 F 2d 611, 61 S Ct 610, revs 312 US 492, 61 S Ct 634 ........ 7.25
Conway v Tambonni (1966) 68 Ill Appeal 2d 190, 215 NE 2d 303 ........ 40.29
Conway v Wade [1909] AC 506 ........ 32.48, 32.96, 32.119-32.120
Cook v Carroll [1945] IR 515 ........ 37.54
Cook v Lewis [1952] 1 DLR 1 affg [1950 4 DLR 136 ........ 2.60, 22.03
Cook v Swinfen [1967] 1 WLR 457 ........ 1.16
Cooke v McGuigan (1926) 61 ILTR 45 ........ 35.26-35.28
Cooke v Midland GW Ry Co of Ireland [1908] IR 242, [1909] AC 229 7.08, 12.13, 12.26,
........ 12.32, 40.07
Cooke v Walsh [1984] ILRM 208 ........ 44.90, 44.95-44.97, 44.106
........ 44.110, 44.161, 44.187-44.192
Cooney v Browne [1985] IR 185, affd [1985] IR 190 ........ 34.216
Cooney v Cooney (1920) 54 ILTR 60 ........ 23.41, 28.04
Cooney v Dockrell [1965] Ir Jur 31 ........ 12.09
Cooney v Sunday Newspapers Ltd and Terenure Printers Ltd and Computerset Ltd (HC) 7 November 1978 ........ 34.102
Cooney v Thomas Dockrell Sons & Co Ltd [1965] Ir Jur Rep 31 ........ 18.91, 44.64
Cooper v Egan (HC) 20 December 1990 ........ 42.59, 42.66
Cooper v Millea [1938] IR 749 ........ 32.51-32.53, 32.84
Cooper v O'Connell (SC) 5 June 1997 ........ 44.44
Copaz v Louth County Council [1997] Ir L Log W 402 ........ 24.116
Cope v Sharpe (No 2) [1910] KB 168, [1912] 1 KB 496 ........ 1.120, 23.50
Coppinger v Sheehan [1906] 1 IR 519 ........ 24.04, 24.16
Coppinger v Waterford County Council [1996] 2 ILRM 427 ........ 1.101, 20.13
........ 20.41, 33.11, 33.16, 33.20
........ 44.90, 44.110, 44.167-44.168
Corbet v Hill (1870) IR 9 Eq 671 ........ 23.39
Corcoran v Corcoran (1956) 7 ICLR 272 ........ 34.57

Corcoran v Core Electrical [1996] Ir L Log W 228 ........................................ 15.03
Corcoran v W & R Jacob & Co [1945] IR 446 ........................................ 22.11, 22.16, 22.61
........................................ 34.38, 34.61, 34.169-34.171, 34.178, 34.199
Corcoran v West [1933] IR 210 ........................................ 9.17-9.21, 9.44
Cork Corporation v Rooney (1881) 7 LR Ir 191 ........................................ 45.09
Corless and Diggin v Ireland (HC) 23 July 1984 ........................................ 34.20, 34.170
Cornford v Carlton Bank Ltd [1899] 1 QB 392, [1900] 1 QB 22 ........................................ 39.06
Corothers v Slobodian (1974) 2 SCR 633 revg 36 DLR (3d) 597 ........ 7.39, 20.80-20.82
Corporation National del Cobre de Chile v Sogemin Metals Ltd
[1997] 2 All ER 917 ........................................ 35.15
Corry v Lucas (1868) IR 3 CL 208 ........................................ 6.48, 11.06-11.07
Corry v National Union of Vintners, Grocers & Allied Trades Assistants
[1950] IR 315 (SC) ........................................ 45.06
Cosford v Cornwall (1992) 93 DLR (4th) 123 ........................................ 32.03
Cosgrave v National Telephone Co [1901] 2 IR 611 ........................................ 23.44
Cosgrave v Trade Auxiliary Company IR 8 CL 349 ........................................ 34.191
Cosgrove v Ireland [1982] ILRM 48 ........................................ 1.06, 1.16, 21.32, 21.63
........................................ 21.71, 22.84, 33.22, 37.01
Costello v Chief Constable of the Northumbria Police [1999] 1 All ER 550 ............. 8.25
Costello v Orange (HC) Irish Times, 21 June 1986 ........................................ 34.61
Costelloe (Michael B) Ltd v Simek Ltd (HC) 26 February 1981 ........................................ 31.03
Costello-Roberts v United Kingdom (1993) 19 EHRR 112 ........................................ 22.97
Cotter v Ahern (1965) 99 ILTR 45 ........................................ 32.17, 32.24, 32.45, 32.68
Cotter v Minister for Agriculture (SC) April 1993 ........................................ 10.09, 10.141
Cotton v Commr for Road Transport & Tramways (19424) 3 SR (NSW) 66 ........... 40.04
Coughlan v Birr UDC (SC) 22 July 1996 ........................................ 18.108
Coughlan v Marks [1918] 2 IR 306 ........................................ 9.28, 9.44-9.44
Coughlan v Whelton (HC) 22 January 1993 ........................................ 14.48
Council of the Shire of Ballina v Ringland (1994) 33 NSWLR 680 ........................................ 39.05
Countyglen plc v Carway (HC) 10 April 1995 ........................................ 35.13
Court v Wyatt, The Times, 24 June, 1960 ........................................ 16.05
Courtney v Masterson [1949] Ir Jur 6 ........................................ 16.26, 16.70, 40.13
Courtney v Minister for Defence [1996] Ir L Log W 157 ........................................ 7.44
Courtney v Minister for the Marine (HC) 21 December 1988 ........................................ 24.05
Cowper Essex v Local Board of Acton (1889) 14 AC 153 ........................................ 24.07
Cox v Burbridge (1863) 13 CB (ns), 430 143 ER 171 ........................................ 27.47
Cox v Ireland [1992] 2 IR 503 ........................................ 1.48
Cox v Northwest Airlines Inc (1967) 379 F 2d 893 ........................................ 9.25
Coyle v An Post [1993] ILRM 508 ........................................ 2.26, 7.06, 7.54, 18.110
Coyle v GN Ry (1887) 20 LR Ir 409 ........................................ 15.23
Coyne v Tweedy [1898] 2 IR 167 ........................................ 22.111, 23.42-23.43
CPR v Roy [1902] AC 220 ........................................ 25.44
Crawford v Board of Governors of Charing Cross Hospital, The Times,
8 December 1953 ........................................ 14.26
Crawford v Todd (1941) 75 ILTR 233 ........................................ 34.126

Crawford v Vance [1908] 2 IR 521 ........ 34.61
Crean v Nolan (1963) 97 ILTR 125 ........ 23.29, 27.25, 39.11
Creed v Cunningham, [1996] Ir L Log W 404 ........ 15.42
Cregan v ESB (1936) 71 ILTR 62 ........ 24.18, 24.93
Crilly v T & J Farrington Ltd [2000] 1 ILRM 548 ........ 44.108
Crinion v Minister for Justice [1959] Ir Jur 15 ........ 30.36
Crocker v Sundance, Northwest Resorts Ltd [1988] 1 SCR 1186 ........ 8.06
Crofter Handwoven Harris Tweed v Veitch [1942] AC 435 ........ 32.42, 32.58
........ 32.63-32.71
Crofter Harris Tweed Co v Veitch [1942] 1 All ER 142 ........ 32.72
Crofter Properties Ltd v Genport Ltd (HC) 15 March 1996 ........ 32.60, 36.27
Crogate v Morris (1617) 1 Brown & Gold 197, 123 ER 751 ........ 26.08
Croke v Smith (SC) 31 July 1996 ........ 22.112
Cromer v Sullivan (1897) 31 ILT & Sol J 439 ........ 43.12
Cronin v Connor [1913] 2 IR 119 ........ 23.42, 27.01, 27.07, 27.47
Cronin v Cronin DPIJ: Trinity and Michaelmas Terms 1998, p 150 (HC) ........ 44.169
Cronin v Mulligan (SC) 14 May 1999 ........ 20.41
Cronin v O'Shea (1896) 30 ILT & Sol J 436 ........ 24.100
Cropp v Potashville School Unit (1977) No 25, 81 DLR (3d) 115 ........ 16.70
Crosbie v Boland National Car Ltd t/a Euro Dollar Rent-A-Car (HC) 7 July 1995 .. 15.32
Crowe v Brennan [1967] IR 5 ........ 7.28, 8.17, 18.33, 18.40, 18.102
Crowe v Merrion Shopping Centre Ltd (1995) 15 ILT (ns) 302 ........ 12.138, 12.144
Crowhurst v Amersham Burial Board (1878) 4 Ex Div 5 ........ 25.13
Crowley v Allied Irish Banks [1987] IR 287, [1988] ILRM 225 ........ 2.27, 2.36
........ 2.50, 13.42-13.43, 13.82
Crowley v Cleary [1968] IR 261 ........ 24.16, 32.50
Crowley v Ireland [1980] IR 102 ........ 16.69, 32.128, 32.175, 44.36, 45.02
Crowley v Muskerry Co-Operative Society Ltd (SC) 11 December 1972 ........ 44.66
Crowley v Muskery, Lissarda & Balinhassig Co-op Ltd (SC) 11 February 1972 ... 44.179
Crowley v Town Commissioners of Youghal (1986) 30 ILT & Sol J 151 ........ 24.93
Cruise v Burke [1919] 2 IR 182 ........ 36.06-36.16
Crump v Lambert (1867) LR 3 Eq 409 ........ 24.41
Cruzan v Director, Missouri ........ 37.90
Cubbard v Rederij Viribus Unitis and Galway Stevedores Ltd
(1966) 100 ILTR 40 ........ 42.21
Cuckian v Cully (SC) 9 March 1972 ........ 2.11
Cudney v Mid-Continent Airlines (1953) 363 Mo 922, 254 SW 2d 662 ........ 9.25
Culkin v Mcfie & Sons Ltd [1939] 3 All ER 613 ........ 40.26
Cullen v AG [1979] IR 394 ........ 1.107
Cullen v Clein [1970] IR 146 ........ 4.23
Cullen v Cullen [1962] IR 268 ........ 23.36, 45.05, 45.06, 45.49-45.51
Cullen v Dickenson (1913) 33 SD 27, 144 NW 656 ........ 22.37
Cullen v Heagney [1931] LJIFS 149 ........ 40.11
Cullen v Stanley [1926] IR 73 ........ 45.05, 45.34
Cullen v Trappell (1980) 29 ALRI ........ 44.102

Cullen v Williams & Co Ltd [1931] LJ Ir 50 ....................21.10
Cullen, Allen & Co v Barclay (1881) 10 LR Ir 224 ....................29.03
Cullimore v Savage South Africa [1903] 2 IR 589 ....................43.28
Cullin v London Fire and Civil Defence Authority [1999] P 1 QR 314 ....................17.66
Cullinane v Waterford County Council [1997] Ir L Log W 309 ....................8.04, 19.02
....................26.24, 26.33
Cunard v Antifyre Ltd [1933] 1 KB 551 ....................37.12
Cunningham Bros Ltd v Kelly (HC) 18 November 1974 ....................32.104
Cunningham v Blake [1937] Ir Jur 20 ....................7.05, 7.27, 16.04
Cunningham v Frontier SS Co [1906] 2 IR 12 ....................7.01, 21.10, 21.20, 21.42
Cunningham v Harrison [1973] QB 942 ....................44.110
Cunningham v Joe Malone Car Hire Services Ltd (SC) 16 March 1967 ....................44.82
Cunningham v McGrath Bros [1964] IR 209 ....................2.43, 24.14
Cunningham v O'Brien [1982] NI 75 ....................20.80
Cunningham v Whelan (1918) 52 ILTR 67 ....................24.16, 27.05, 27.50
Curley and Dowley v Mulcahy (HC) 21 December 1977 ....................13.81
Curley v Collins [1938] Ir Jur Rep 69 ....................43.65
Curley v Gregan [1895] 2 IR 320 ....................27.23
Curley v Ireland (CC) 2 July 1984 ....................22.38
Curley v Mannion [1965] IR 543 ....................8.20, 16.10, 43.14, 43.68
Curley v Mulcahy (HC) 21 December 1977 ....................10.72
Curling v Walsh (HC) 23 October 1987 ....................13.04
Curneen v Sweeney (1969) 103 ILTR 29 ....................34.35, 34.54, 34.199
Curran v Cadbury Ireland Ltd (CC) 17 December 1999 ....................44.176
Curran v Cadbury Ireland Ltd [2000] 2 ILRM 343 ....................17.67, 18.62, 21.34
Curran v Lapedus (1938) 72 ILTR 246, revd (1939) 73 ILTR 89 ....................40.11
Curran v Mary Gallagher Joseph Gallagher and MIBI (SC) 17 May 1997 ....................1.148
Curran v Northern Ireland Housing Co-ownership Association Ltd
[1987] AC 718 ....................6.18
Currie v Fairy Hill Ltd [1968] IR 232 ....................46.73
Curry v Foster [1960] Ir Jur 33 ....................7.05, 7.44, 24.18
Curry v Moser (1982) 89 Appeal Div 2d 1 454 NYS 2d 311 ....................20.43
Curust Financial Services Ltd v Loewe-Lack-Werk Otto Loewe GmbH
[1994] 1 IR 458 ....................45.05, 45.47
Curwen v James [1963] 1 WLR 748 ....................42.42
Cutler v United Dairies (London) Ltd [1933] 2 KB 297 ....................20.78, 26.34
Cutler v Wandsworth Stadium Ltd [1949] AC 398 ....................21.19
Cutts v Chumley [1967] I WLR 742 ....................33.07
CW Shipping Co Ltd v Limerick Harbour Commissioners
[1989] ILRM 416 ....................1.06, 19.59

## D

D & F Estates Ltd v Church Commissioners for England [1989] AC 177,
[1988] 2 All ER 992, [1988] 2 WLR 368 ....................6.20, 10.75, 10.153
....................10.160, 11.85, 11.124, 13.56, 13.71
D & L Caterers Ltd v D'Ajou [1945] KB 364 ....................34.38, 39.03

D v NSPCC [1978] AC 71 .......... 37.58
D'Amato v Badger [1996] 2 Can SCR 1071 .......... 32.03
D'Amico v Christie (1987) 71 NY 2d 76, 518 NE 2d 890 .......... 8.06
D'Urso v Samson [1939] 4 All ER 26 .......... 26.34
Daborn v Bath Tramways Motor Co Ltd [1946] 2 All ER 333 .......... 7.40, 15.53, 26.36
Dagi v Broken Hill Pty Co Ltd 1995 Vic Lexis 1182 .......... 24.05
Daishowa Inc v Friends of the Lubicon (1998) 41 CCLT (2d) 193 .......... 34.50
Dalepak Foods plc v Frezmet Daily Pack Ltd [1987] NILR, p 1 .......... 31.35, 31.74
Dallison v Caffery [1965] 1 QB 348 .......... 36.09
Dalton v Angus (1881) 6 AC 740 .......... 24.78
Dalton v Frendo (SC) 15 December 1977 .......... 18.03, 18.08-18.12
Dalton v O'Sullivan [1947] Ir Jur 25 .......... 27.08, 27.45
Daly v Avonmore Creameries Ltd [1984] IR 131 .......... 4.20, 11.159, 12.52
.......... 18.05, 20.50, 21.39, 21.60, 27.26
Daly v Ballyclough Co-Operative DPIJ: Trinity Term 1991, p 92 .......... 18.11, 18.108
Daly v Cork Herald Co (1897) 31 ILT & Sol J 165 .......... 34.191
Daly v Cullen (1957) 92 ILTR 127 .......... 23.02, 23.33, 24.25
Daly v General Steam Navigation Co Ltd [1980] 3 All ER 696 .......... 33.09
Daly v Greybridge Co-operative Creamery Ltd [1964] IR 497 .......... 12.09, 21.10, 21.35
Daly v Lawless [1952] Ir Jur 20 .......... 20.07
Daly v McMullan [1997] 2 ILRM 232 .......... 24.79, 25.15
Daly v Murray (1885) 17 LR (Ir) 185 .......... 23.43
Daly v Revenue Commissioners [1995] 3 IR 1 .......... 32.137
Daly v Securicor (Ireland) Ltd DPIJ: Hilary and Easter Terms 1991, p 142 .. 18.84, 18.97
Daly v T & J Macken Ltd (SC) unreported, 6 February 1957 .......... 44.60
Damon v Mc Clelland [1899] 2 IR 486 .......... 4.14
Danaher v Roscommon County Council (SC) 21 December 1973 .......... 24.116, 44.55
Danby v Beardsley (1880) 43 LT 603 .......... 36.04
Daniels v Heskin [1954] IR 73 .......... 9.28-9.34, 14.05-14.08
.......... 14.17-14.22, 14.118, 14.153
Dann v Hamilton [1939] 1 KB 509 .......... 20.70
Darcy v The Minister for Defence DPIJ: Hilary & Easter Terms 1999, p 12 .......... 44.90
Darcy v Torpey DPIJ: Hilary and Easter Terms 1993, p 208 .......... 15.50
Darker v Chief Constable of the West Midlands Polcie [2000] 2 WLR 747 .......... 6.91
Davey v CIE (1968) 103 ILT SJ 164 .......... 43.08
Davey v Harrow Corporation [1958] 1 QB 60 .......... 24.28, 25.14
Davidson v Smyth (1887) 20 LR Ir 326 .......... 36.04, 36.06-36.10
Davie v New Merton Board Mills Ltd [1959] AC 604 .......... 18.35, 18.101
Davies v Mann (1842) 10 M & W 547, 152 ER 588 .......... 20.04
Davies v Powell Duffryn Associated Collieries Ltd (No 2) [1942] AC 601 ... 42.39-42.41
Davies v Solomon (1871) LR 7 QB 112 .......... 34.42
Davies v Sumner [1984] 1 WLR 1301 .......... 11.140
Davis v Radcliffe [1990] 1 WLR 821 .......... 19.66
Davis v Reeves (1855) 45 ICLR 79 .......... 34.50
Davoren v Fitzpatrick [1935] Ir Jur 23 .......... 7.27, 7.44, 8.07, 8.18

Dawkins v Lord Paulet (1869) LR 5 QB 94 ............................................................34.158
Dawkins v Lord Rokeby (1873) LR 8 QB 255, affd (1875) LR 7 HL 744 ..............34.155
Dawson (t/a AE Dawson & Sons) v Irish Brokers Association
(SC) 6 November 1998 ...........................................................................34.177, 34.258
Dawson v M'Clelland (No 2) [1899] 2 IR 503 ............................................................44.04
DB v Minister for Education [1999] 1 IR 29 ................................................................16.69
De Burca v Wicklow County Council (HC) 24 May 2000 ...........................................45.02
De Francesco v Barnum (1890) 45 Ch D 430 .............................................................32.20
De Jager v Payneham & Magill Lodges Hall Inc (1984) 36 SASR 498 ..................24.75
De Rossa v Independent Newspapers plc (SC) 30 July 1999 ..........................34.03, 34.60
................................................................................... 34.231, 34.239-34.243, 34.253
Deatons Pty Ltd v Flew (1949) 79 Comm LR 370 ........................................................43.39
Debtor, Re (1950) 66 Times LR (Pt 1) 313 ....................................................................40.04
Dee Trading Co Pty Ltd v Baldwin [1938] VLR 175 ......................................................28.10
Deegan v Langan [1966] IR 373 ................................ 18.95, 18.151, 44.82-44.84, 44.95
Deegan v Wholey t/a Stonridge Plant Hire DPIJ: Hilary and Easter
Terms 1997, p 121......................................................................................18.23, 43.19
Deering v Mahon (1851) 2 Ir CLR 25 ...........................................................................28.04
Dehn v AGl [1988] I NZLR 564 ......................................................................................23.22
Deighan v Ireland [1995] 2 IR 56, [1995] 1 ILRM 8 .............................1.33, 43.9, 43.12
Deignan v Greene (SC) 21 October 1954 ....................................................................14.169
Delahunty v Croke, (SC) 25 February 1971 ....................................................................44.58
Delancy v Dale (1959) 20 DLR (2d) 12 ..........................................................................36.19
Delaney v Ainsworth (SC) 23 November 1966 .................................................................44.82
Delaney v Dunnes Stores, DPIJ: Hilary & Easter Terms 1992, p 1 ........................44.180
Delaney v Mather & Platt Ltd (HC) 1 December 1976 ................................21.10, 21.37
Delaney v O'Dowd [1997] Ir L Log W 157 ......................................................................16.23
Delaney v Wallis & Son (1884) 15 Cox CC 525 ............................... 30.07-30.12, 30.19
Delany v Dublin United Tramways Co 30 LR Ir 725 ......................................................20.18
Delany v Keogh [1905] 2 IR 267 ........................................................ 35.04-35.06, 35.12
Dellwo v Pearson (1961) 258 Minn 452, 107 NW 2d 859 ............................ 40.29-40.30
Delta Hotels Ltd v Magrum (1975) 59 DLR (3d) 126 ......................................................23.23
Demers v Desrosier [1929] 3 DLR 401 ..........................................................................28.07
Dempsey v Wall & Co Ltd & Philip Ryan 78 ILTR 73 ...................... 34.38, 34.61-34.61
..........................................................................................34.169, 34.175, 34.178
Dennehy v Counter Equipment Ltd DPIJ: Hilary and Easter Terms 1992, p 193
..............................................................................................................18.114, 21.30
Dennehy v Kildare Co Board of Health [1936] IR 384 .........................7.15, 24.07, 43.22
Dennehy v Nordic Cold Storage ......................................................................................44.121
Denniston v McNamara Maxwell & Co (1950) 84 ILTR 168 ................9.08, 9.18, 11.24
Denvir v Taylor [1936] Ir Jur Rep 4 ................................................................................34.169
Department of Health (1990) 110 S Ct 2841 ..................................................................37.90
Department of the Environment v Bates [1991] 1 AC 499 ..........................13.56, 13.71
Depuis v Haulbowline Industries Ltd (SC) 14 February 1962 ..............7.51, 18.09, 18.14
..............................................................................................................18.82, 18.160

Derbyshire County Council v Times Newspapers Ltd [1993] AC 534 ........ 34.110, 39.03
Derry Journal Ltd v Rialto Theatres Ltd (1930) 64 ILTR 87 .......................... 45.05, 45.14
Derry v Handley (1867) 16 LT 263 ........................................................................ 34.44
Derry v Peek (1889) 14 AC 337 ........................................................35.01, 35.10-35.12
Desmond and MCD Management Services Ltd v Riordan (HC) 14 July 1999 ....... 34.148
Devers v Bourke Builders Ltd DPIJ: Trinity and Michaelmas Terms 1991, p 3 ..... 18.108
Devine v Iarnród Éireann [1996] Ir L Log W 419 ...................................................... 7.44
Devine v Keane (1926) 61 ILTR 118 ........................................................................ 34.34
Devine v London & NW Ry Co (1864) 17 ICLR 174 ............................................... 30.19
Devitt v Minister for Education (HC) 13 May 1988 .............................................. 10.146
Devlin v GN Ry Co (Ireland) [1936] Ir Jur 55 ........................................................... 8.14
Devon Lumber Co Ltd v MacNeill (1987) 45 DLR (4th) 300 ...................... 24.60, 24.106
Dewar v City & Suburban Racecourse Co [1899] 1 IR 345 ............... 24.31, 24.42, 45.05
Dewing v St Luke's (Anglican Church in Australia) Association 1999
TAS LEXIS 9, BC 9901351 .................................................................................. 18.118
Dexter v Cole (1858) 6 Wis 319 70 Am Dec 465 ...................................................... 28.13
Deyong v Shenburn [1946] KB 227 ........................................................................... 18.66
DG v Eastern Health Board [1998] 1 ILRM 241 ........................................................ 16.69
Dicenzo v Berg (1940) 340 Pa 305, 16A, 2d 15 ........................................................ 22.60
Dickens v Barnham (1920) 69 Colo 349, 194 P 356 ........................................ ....... 16.03
Dickinson v Del Solar ; Fire Mobile and General Insurance Co Ltd
[1930] 1 KB 376 ........................................................................................................ 38.17
Dickinson v Dickinson (1986) 3 SR (NSW) 233 ......................................................... 16.03
Dickson (Alex) & Sons Ltd v Dickson (Alexander) & Sons
[1909] 1 IR 185 .........................................................31.05, 31.40, 31.51, 45.05-45.05
Dillenkofer v Federal Republic of Germany ................................................................ 1.97
Dillieu v White [1901] 2 QB 669 ................................................................................. 3.32
Dillingham Constructions v Steel Mains Ply (1975) 6 ALR 177 ................................ 4.05
Dillon v Balfour (1887) 20 LR Ir 600 ........................................................................ 34.138
Dillon v Dunnes' Stores Ltd (SC) 20 December 1968 .................... 22.38, 22.105, 22.107
.................................................................................................... 32.58, 32.80, 44.18
Dillon v Irish Industrial Explosives Ltd (HC) 27 October 1998 ................................ 26.24
Dillon v Legg (1968) 68 Cal 2d 728 ............................................................................ 17.23
Dillon v MacGabhann (HC) 24 July 1995 ..................................................................... 4.24
Dillon v O'Brien (1887) 20 LR Ir 300 ..................................................... 28.15, 29.05, 30.19
Dillon v Ryan (SC) 7 April 1960 ................................................................................. 15.02
Director of Public Prosecutions (Dooley) v Lynch [1998] 4 IR 437 ......................... 23.11
Director of Public Prosecutions v Blady [1912] 2 KB 89 .......................................... 32.61
Director of Public Prosecutions v Corrigan [1986] IR 290 ........................................ 23.09
Director of Public Prosecutions v Forbes [1994] 2 IR 542 .............................23.08-23.10
Director of Public Prosecutions v Gaffney [1988] ILRM 39 ...................................... 23.03
Director of Public Prosecutions v McCormack (HC) 8 July 1999 ............................ 22.105
Director of Public Prosecutions v McMahon [1987] ILRM 87 ........................ 23.06, 23.07
.......................................................................................................................23.15-23.16

Diversified Holdings Ltd v The Queen in Right of British Columbia
(1982) 23 CCLT 156 .......................................................................................27.44
Dixon v Bell M & S (1816) 198, 105 ER 1023 ..........................................................16.03
DK v King [1994] 1 IR 166 ........................................................................................43.22
Dockery v Manor Park Homebuilders Ltd (HC) 10 April 1995 ......................25.11, 25.41
Dockery v O'Brien (1975) 109 ILTR 127 .............................................1.106, 2.45, 3.08
Dockrell & Co v Dockrell & Co (1941) 75 ILTR 226 ..............................................31.40
Dodwell v Burford (1670) 1 Mod 24, 86 ER 703 ......................................................22.11
Doern v Phillips (Estate) 43 BCLR (3d) 53 ..................................................................7.39
Doherty Timber Ltd v Drogheda Harbour Commissioners [1993] ILRM 401
[1993] 1 IR 315 ..........................................................6.28, 6.39, 10.09, 21.10, 26.13
Doherty v Bowaters Irish Wallboard Mills Ltd [1968] IR 277 ......................21.10, 21.20
.........................................................21.42, 41.07, 42.37, 44.60, 44.87, 44.110
Doherty v Jas Murland Ltd [1956] NI 34 ................................................................44.197
Doherty v Liddane [1940] Ir Jur Rep 58 ..................................................................22.105
Doherty v McKelvey DPIJ: Trinity and Michaelmas Terms 1994, p 91 .........15.12, 40.11
Dolan v Keohane (SC) 8 February 1994, affg (HC) 14 February 1992 ..........16.61, 16.70
Dominion Rent A Car Ltd v Budget Rent A Car Systems (1970) Ltd
[1987] 2 NZLR 395 ...................................................................................................31.58
Donaghy v Brennan (1900) 19 NZLR 289 ..................................................................40.40
Donahue v Irish Shipping Ltd (SC) 28 November, 1958 .........................................18.108
Donaldson v Irish Motor Racing Club (SC) 1 February 1957 ...................6.10, 6.61, 7.28
...........................................................................................7.47, 12.07, 24.14, 24.18
Donaldson v McNiven [1952] 2 All ER 691 ...............................................................16.05
Donnellan v Dungoyne Ltd [1995] 1 ILRM 388 ........................................................10.151
Donnelly v Browne (SC) 15 May 1972 ............................................................ 44.95-44.97
Donnelly v Cash (SC) 21 February 1958 ......................................................................44.58
Donnelly v Coyne [1901] 2 IR 7 ...........................................................................29.10, 30.19
Donnelly v Donnelly [1899] 2 IR 111 .....................................................................29.10, 30.19
Donnelly v Ingram (1877) 31 ILTR 139 .......................................................................22.19
Donnelly v Joyce [1974] QB 454 ................................................................................44.110
Donnelly v Moloney (1826) Batty's Irish Reports 1825-26 498 ...............................36.05
Donoghue v Burke [1960] IR 314 ...................................................................7.13, 20.55
Donoghue v Morgan DPIJ: Michaelmas Term 1990, p 228 (HC) ...........................44.176
Donoghue v Stevenson [1932] AC 562 ......................................... 1.110-1.111, 6.02-6.12
.................................................................6.35, 6.48, 8.09, 10.07, 10.51, 10.73
................................................................ 10.122, 10.141, 10.154-10.158, 11.02
.................................................................11.08-11.14, 11.23-11.32, 11.71-11.74
................................................................ 11.88, 12.03, 12.53, 13.12-13.17, 13.23
................................................................ 13.45-13.68, 17.63, 18.23, 19.04, 19.28
..........................................................................19.34, 24.20, 32.01, 37.42
Donohue v Bus Éireann (HC) 30 July 1999 ..........................................................32.29, 32.41
Donohue v Coyle [1953-1954] Ir Jur Rep 30 ....................................22.11, 22.23, 40.43
Donovan v Laing, Wharton & Down Construction Syndicate [1893] 1 QB 629
[1964] IR ..........................................................................................................43.11

Donovan v Landy's Ltd [1963] IR 441 ....... 2.37, 6.53, 12.17, 12.28-12.35 ....... 12.45, 15.06, 40.11
Donselaar v Donselaar [1982] 1 NZLR 97 ....... 44.13
Doolan v Murray (HC) 21 December 1993 ....... 10.09, 10.121, 35.09, 35.11
Doona v O'Donoghue [1957] Ir Jur 85 ....... 25.12
Doran v Cosgrove (SC) 12 November 1992 ....... 4.19
Doran v Delaney [1998] 2 ILRM 1, revg [1996] 1 ILRM 490 ....... 3.41, 10.09 ....... 10.129, 14.201
Doran v Dublin Plant Hire Ltd [1990] 1 IR 488 ....... 2.26, 2.33
Doran v Lennon [1945] IR 315 ....... 32.102
Doran v Thompson & Sons Lid [1978] IR 223 ....... 46.93
Dorene Ltd v Suedes (Ireland) Ltd [1981] IR 312 ....... 36.06-36.14, 36.20
Dormont v Furney Ry (1883) 11 QBD 496 ....... 21.19
Dougan v Allen (1912) 46 ILTR 221 ....... 24.06, 24.18
Doughty v Turner Manufacturing Co Ltd [1964] 1 QB 518 ....... 3.20
Douglas Iron Works & Colquhoun v Owen [1951] IR 93 ....... 2.45
Dowdall v Minister for Defence (HC) 23 July 1992 ....... 6.42, 7.52
Dowling v Armour Pharmaceutical Co Inc [1996] 2 ILRM 417 ....... 4.24
Dowling v CIE (SC) 1 March 1956 ....... 18.75, 18.101-18.102
Dowling v ESB DPIJ: Hilary and Easter Terms 1997, p 40 ....... 18.83
Dowling v Great Southern Railways Co [1943] Ir Jur Rep 7 ....... 44.94
Dowling v Jedos Ltd (SC) 30 March 1977 ....... 42.23, 42.38
Dowling v Moore (1897) 31 ILT 367 & Sol J ....... 43.13
Dowman v Ireland [1986] ILRM 111 ....... 38.10
Downey v Limerick Motor Club Ltd (HC) 28 April 1989 ....... 6.66
Dowsett Engineering Construction Ltd v Sloan [1955-1956] Ir Jur 31 ....... 11.27
Doxtator v Burch (1973) 41 DLR (3d) 768 ....... 9.17
Doyle v Atlantic Mills Ltd, DPIJ: Trinity and Michaelmas Terms 1995, p 124 ....... 18.165
Doyle v Flemings Coal Mines Ltd (SC) 29 July 1955 ....... 43.26, 43.46, 43.69
Doyle v Griffin (SC) 21 December 1936 ....... 34.58, 35.26
Doyle v HF Murray Ltd [1967] IR 390 ....... 15.47-15.48
Doyle v Magill [1999] 2 ILRM 66 ....... 12.09-12.11
Doyle v Olby (Ironmongers) Ltd [1969] 2 QB 158 ....... 3.42, 35.21
Doyle v The Economist Newspaper Ltd [1981] NI 171 ....... 34.56
Drane v Evangelou [1978] 2 All ER 437 ....... 44.21
Draper v Trist [1939] 3 All ER 513 ....... 31.07
Drummond-Jackson v British Medical Association [1970] 1 All ER 1094 ....... 34.55
DSG Retail Ltd v PC World Ltd (HC) 13 January 1998 ....... 31.02, 31.60, 45.05
Duane v Barry (1879) 4 LR Ir 742 ....... 36.09
Dubé v Labar (1986) 27 DLR (4th) 653 ....... 20.70
Dublin (South) City Market Co v McCabes Ltd [1953] IR 283 ....... 24.31, 24.75
Dublin Bus v MIBI (CC) 29 October 1999 ....... 1.102, 1.151
Dublin Corporation v Moore [1984] ILRM 339 ....... 24.41
Dublin Plant Hire Ltd [1990] 1 IR 488 ....... 2.46

Dublin Port & Docks Board v Bank of Ireland [1976] IR 118 ........................10.07, 10.97
Dudgeon v United Kingdom (1983) 5 EHRR 373 ..................................................37.80
Duffield v Police [1971] NSLR 381 ..........................................................................23.22
Duffy v Brodigan (1998) 17 ILT (ns) 28 ..................................................................15.32
Duffy v Carnabane Holdings Ltd [1996] 2 ILRM 86 ............................7.45, 12.08, 12.53
Duffy v Fahy [1960] Ir Jur 69 ......................................................7.13, 7.23, 15.06, 40.16
Duffy v NewsGroup Newspapers Ltd [1994] 1 ILRM 364 .........................................34.97
Duffy v North Eastern Health Board, Prof Neg Rep 199 (HC, 1988) .......................14.30
Duffy v Rooney and Dunnes Stores (Dundalk) Ltd (SC) 23 April 1998,
affg (HC) 23 June 1997 ......................................................... 2.16, 7.01, 11.16-11.17
............................................. 11.41, 11.53-11.58, 11.63, 21.22, 25.24, 33.38, 43.07
Duffy v Sutton [1955] IR 248 ...................................................................................35.20
Duggan v An Taoiseach (HC) 11 April 1988 ..........................................................10.146
Duggan v Armstrong [1993] ILRM 222 ...................................................... 12.58, 27.17
Dulieu v White & Sons [1901] 2 KB 669 .................................................................17.10
Dullaghan v Hillen [1957] Ir Jur Rep 10 ................................ 22.10, 22.20-22.23, 22.35
.......................................................................... 22.41, 22.86, 36.03, 36.06-36.15
Dully v North Eastern Health Board (HC) 3 November 1988 ............................9.22, 9.28
Dunbar v Guardians of Ardee Union [1897] 2 IR 76 ....................................................8.06
Duncan Estate v Baddeley (1997) 1450 DLR 4th 708 ..............................................41.07
Duncan v Jones [1936] 1 KB 218 ..............................................................................22.111
Dundalk Urban District Council v Conway (HC) 18 July 1983 ...............................45.05
Dunleavy v Devitt (SC) 19 February 1992 ...............................................................14.30
Dunleavy v Glen Abbey Ltd [1992] ILRM 1 ...........................................18.111, 21.26
Dunlop v Dunlop Rubber Co [1920] 1 IR 280 ................................. 45.05-45.05, 45.14
Dunlop v Kenny (SC) 29 July 1969 ..........................................................................44.92
Dunlop v Selindge [1915] AC 847 ............................................................................32.54
Dunlop v Woollahra Municipal Council [1981] 1 All ER 1212 ...................... 19.60-19.64
Dunn v Birmingham Canal (1872) LR 7 QB 244, affd (1872) LR 8 QB 42 .............25.32
Dunn v Teti (1980) 280 Pa Super 399, 421 A 2d 782 .................................. 40.27-40.28
Dunne (Brendan ) Ltd v Fitzpatrick [1958] IR 29 ........................32.109, 32.146, 32.154
Dunne v Clarke Oil Products Ltd, Irish Times Law Report,
25 November 1996 ........................................................................................................2.19
Dunne v Clinton (SC) 12 December 1931, affg [1930] IR 366 ....................22.38, 22.105
Dunne v Dublin Cargo Handling Ltd (in liq) (SC) 30 August 1997 ..............18.24, 21.22
Dunne v Electricity Board (HC) 19 October 1999 ...................................................46.65
Dunne v Honeywell Control Systems Ltd and Virginia Milk Products
[1991] ILRM 595 ..........................................................................21.10, 21.39, 21.55
Dunne v Lawter Products Ltd, DPIJ: Hilary and Easter Terms 1997, p 66 ..............18.61
.....................................................................................................................44.176
Dunne v National Maternity Hospital [1989] IR 91 ................ 10.09, 14.09, 14.12-14.15
......................................................................... 14.23, 14.51-14.56, 14.95-14.104
............................................................... 14.124-14.128, 14.203, 44.103, 44.192
Dunne v North Western Gas Board [1964] 2 QB 806 .........................24.95, 25.25, 25.44
Dunne v Rattigan [1981] ILRM 365 ............................................................................24.07

Dunphy v Bryan (1963) 97 ILTR 4 .......... 27.01, 27.50
Dunphy v T Carroll & Sons Ltd (HC) 28 June 1984 .......... 44.182
Durham v Public School Bd of Township School area of North Oxford (1960) 23 DLR (2d) 711 .......... 16.57
Durrant v Burke [1993] 4 Med 248 .......... 14.40
Dutton v Bognor Regis UDC [1972] 1 QB 373, [1972] 1 All ER 462 .......... 13.22, 13.64, 13.73
Dwyer Nolan Developments Ltd v Dublin County Council [1986] IR 130 ... 23.29, 45.05
Dwyer v Ascon Ltd (SC) 16 March 1967 .......... 44.84
Dwyer v Esmonde (1878) 2 LR Ir 243 .......... 34.178-34.178
Dwyer v Meehan (1886) 18 LR Ir 138 .......... 34.32, 34.42
Dyer v Dublin Corporation (HC) 10 June 1993 .......... 13.39-13.41
Dymond v Pearce [1972] 1 QB 496 .......... 24.16

**E**

Early v Flood [1953-1954] Ir Jur 65 .......... 24.18
Earp v Nobmann (1981) 175 Cal Rptr 767 .......... 6.03
East Cork Foods v O'Dwyer Steel [1978] IR 103 .......... 4.19
East v Maurer [1991] 2 All ER 733 .......... 35.17
Eastern & South African Telephone Co v Cape Town Tramways Co [1902] AC 381 .......... 24.106, 25.16, 25.33
Eastern Construction Co v National Trust Co [1914] AC 197 .......... 23.46
Eaton v Dineen (SC) 26 July 1971 .......... 15.40
Ebbs v Forkin & Co Ltd (SC) 6 May 1963 .......... 44.60, 44.86, 44.145
EC Commission v United Kingdom Case C-300/95 [1997] 3 CMLR 923 .......... 11.144
Ecock v MF Kent & Co, DPIJ: Hilary and Easter Terms 1994, p 178 (HC) .......... 20.32, 44.91, 44.166
Edgington v Fitzmaurice (1885) 29 Ch D 459 .......... 35.08, 35.15
Educational Co of Ireland Ltd v Craig [1961] IR 345 .......... 24.16
Educational Co of Ireland Ltd v Fitzpatrick [1961] IR 323 .......... 1.12-1.14, 32.50 .......... 32.111, 32.146-32.146, 45.08-45.10
Edwards v Honeywell Incorporated (1995) 50 F 3d 484 .......... 20.90
Edwards v National Coal Board [1949] 1 KB 704 .......... 7.48
Edwards v Sims (1929) 232 Ky 791 at 24 SW 2d 619 .......... 23.39
Edwards v Southern Health Board (SC) 26 July 1994 .......... 14.30, 14.58
Edwards v West Herts Group Hospital Management Committee [1957] 1 WLR 415 .......... 18.66
Effluent Disposal Ltd v Midlands Effluent Disposal Ltd [1970] RPC 238 .......... 31.40
Egan & Sons Ltd v John Sisk & Sons Ltd [1986] ILRM 283 .......... 3.08
Egan v BBC [1973] IR 379-380 .......... 34.74
Egan v Crown Equipment Ltd DPIJ: Trinity and Michaelmas Terms 1995, p 29 .......... 18.09, 18.95
Egan v Dublin Health Authority (SC) 30 July 1965 .......... 21.34, 39.10
Egan v Egan [1975] Ch 218 .......... 45.05, 45.37

Egan v Hibernia National Review Ltd, Mulcahy and Irish Times Ltd (HC) Irish Times 17 July 1980, p. 11 ....................34.226
Egan v Minister for Defence (HC) 24 November 1988 ....................10.146
Egan v Sisk [1986] ILRM 283 ....................3.14
Egger v Chelmsford (Viscount) [1965] 1 QB 248 ....................34.200
EI Co Ltd v Kennedy [1968] IR 69 .................... 24.16, 32.156-32.160
Eilisword and Berni Ni Fhlatharta v Irish Independent, Irish Times, 7 July 1988, p 10 ....................34.92
Eisenstadt v Baird (1972) 405 US 438 ....................37.76
Electrical and Plumbing Union v Times Newspapers [1980] QB 585 ....................39.30
Electricity Supply Board v Gormley [1985] IR 129 ....................23.07
Electricity Supply Board v Hastings & Co Ltd [1965] Ir Jur 51 ....................23.37, 28.11
Electrochrome Ltd v Welsh Plastics Ltd [1968] 2 All ER 205 ....................10.48
Elguzuoli-Daf v Commissioner of Police of the Metropolis [1995] 1 All ER 833 ......1.33
Elias v Pasmore [1934] 2 KB 164 ....................23.25
Ellard v Cade & Son Ltd (SC) 4 November 1959 ....................44.58
Elliotson v Feetham (1865) 2 Bing NC 134 132 ER 53 ....................24.104
Elliott v Alpine Investments Ltd (HC) 11 July 1975 ....................45.46
Elliott v Sir Robert McAlpine & Sun Ltd [1966] 2 Lloyds LR 482 ....................10.48
Ellis v Dun Laoghaire Corporation (CC) 29 January 1982 ....................24.84, 25.17
Ellis v Fullam Borough Council [1938] 1 KB 359 ....................12.13
Ellis v Home Office [1953] 2 All ER 149 ....................8.32
Ellis v Johnstone [1963] 2 QB 8 ....................27.52
Ellis v Wallsend District Hospital (1989) 17 NSWLR 553 ....................14.144
Ellis v Wright [1976] IR 8 (HC) ....................32.162
Ellison v Ministry of Defence (1996) 81 Build LR 101 ....................25.07
Ellison v Rogers (1967) DLR (2d) 21 ....................7.44
Elofson v Davis (1997 )144 DLR (4th) 143 (Alta QB) ....................2.27
Elvin & Powelle Ltd v Plummer Roddis (1933) 50 TLR 158 ....................30.03
Elwes v Brigg Gas Co (1866) 33 Ch D ....................30.24
Emeh v Kensington and Chelsea [1985] 2 WLR 233 ....................2.27
Emerald Construction Co Ltd v Lowthian [1966] 1 WLR 691, [1966] 1 All ER 1013 .................... 32.20-32.29
Emerald Meats Ltd v The Minister for Agriculture (No 2) [1977] 1 ILRM 275 ..........1.98
Emerson v Bailey 156 A 2d 762 ....................15.25
Emery v Knox (1896) 30 ILTR 106 ....................24.18
Empire Jamaica [1957] AC 386 ....................2.12
English v Anglo-lrish Meat Products Ltd (HC) 2 December 1988 ....................18.21
Ennis v Butterly [1997] 1 ILRM 28 ....................35.02, 35.10, 35.20
Eriksen v Clifton [1963] NZLR 705 ....................26.10
Erven Warnick BV v J Townsend & Sons (Hull) Ltd [1979] AC 731 ............31.02, 31.09
Esplanade Pharmacy Ltd v Larkin [1957] IR 285 .................... 32.109, 32.119-32.120 .................... 32.146-32.152
Esso Petroleum Co (Ireland) Ltd v Fogarty [1965] IR 531 ....................45.10
Esso Petroleum Co Ltd v Mardon [1976] QB 801 .................... 10.147-10.152

Esso Petroleum v Southport Corporation [1956] AC 218 .......... 23.50
Estes v Gibson (1953) 257 SW 2d 604 .......... 16.07
Etchingham v Acres & Co Ltd (HC) 24 July 1975 .......... 23.02, 37.04
Euro-Diam Ltd v Bathurst [1990] 1 QB 1 .......... 20.103
Eustace v The Ashtown Tin Box Co Ltd DPIJ: Hilary and Easter Terms 1991, p 31 .......... 18.80
Evans v Doranbrook Services Ltd (t/a The Baggot Inn) [1997] Ir L Log W 389 .... 18.108
Evans v London Hospital Medical College [1981] 1 All ER 715 .......... 36.04
Evans v Walton (1867) LR 2 CP 615 .......... 33.29
Everett v Ribbands [1952] 2 QB 198 .......... 36.05, 36.19
Everitt v Martin [1953] NZLR 298 .......... 28.07
Ewart v Polytechnic Touring Association Ltd [1933] IR 230 .......... 18.81
Ewing v North Western Health Board (HC) 2 December 1998 .......... 14.30
Ewins v Carlton UK Television Ltd [1997] 2 ILRM 223 .......... 34.12, 34.44-34.47
Express Newspapers Ltd v MacShane [1980] AC 672 .......... 32.121

**F**

F v West Berkshire Health Authority [1990] 2 AC 1 .......... 22.13-22.17, 22.73
F v Wirral Metropolitan Borough Council [1991] Fam 69 .......... 33.22
Fagan v Burgess (HC) unrep 25 March 1998 .......... 36.29
Fagan v Cochrane DPIJ: Trinity and Michaelmas Terms 1993, p 112 .......... 15.44
Fagan v Metropolitan Commissioner [1969] 1 QB 439 .......... 22.14
Fahy v Dwan DPIJ: Hilary & Easter Terms 1997, p 71 (HC) .......... 44.110
Fairclough v Whipp [1951] 2 All ER 834 .......... 22.24
Fairman v Ives (1822) 5 B & Aid 642, 106 ER 1325 .......... 34.194
Fairman v Perpetual Investment Building Society [1923] AC 74 .......... 12.50
Falcon Travel Ltd v Owners Abroad Group plc, t/a Falcon Leisure Group [1991] 1 IR 175 .......... 31.02, 45.05
Falcon v Memorial Hosipital (1990) 436 Mich 443, 462 NW 2d 44 .......... 2.21
Fallacies of Simpson v Thomson (1971) 33 MLR 149 .......... 10.07
Fallon v Gannon [1988] ILRM 193 .......... 14.196, 14.213, 43.9
Faranda v Minister for Education [1981] 1 SR (WA) 312 .......... 16.17
Fardon v Harcourt-Rivington (1932) 146 LT 391 .......... 7.32
Farmview Dairies Ltd NI HC (QBD), 18 December 1998 .......... 18.152
Farr v Butters Bros & Co [1932] 2 KB 606 .......... 11.27
Farrall v Stokes (1954) 54 SR (NSW) 294 .......... 40.08
Farrar v Nelson (1885) 15 QB 258 .......... 27.44
Farrell v Alliance & Dublin Consumers' Gas Co [1939] Ir Jur 41 .......... 9.21, 9.44
Farrell v Burke (1953) 87 ILTR 70 .......... 24.77, 24.85
Farrell v Farrelly (HC) 5 February 1988 .......... 23.06
Farrell v Minister for Agriculture and Food (HC) 11 October 1995 .......... 19.58 .......... 28.01-28.04, 28.13
Farrell v Prendergast (SC) 22 May 1958 .......... 15.17
Farrell v Varian (HC) 19 September 1994 .......... 14.106, 14.123
Farrelly v Lynch [1945] Ir Jur Rep 49 .......... 34.32

Farry v GN Rly Co [1898] 2 IR 352 ....................22.38, 43.28
Farwell v Boston & Worcester Railroad (1842) 45 Mass (4 Met) 49 ....................18.02
Fay v Prentice (1845) 1 CB 828, 135 ER 769 ....................24.25, 24.99
Feeney v Ging and Co Council for Laois (HC) 17 December 1982 ....................42.40
Feeney v John Sisk & Sons Ltd DPIJ: Hilary & Easter Terms 1993, p 254 ....................18.152
....................44.93
Felloni v Dublin Corporation [1998] 1 ILRM 133 .................... 13.39-13.41, 20.53
Fels v Hedley (1903) 20 TLR 69 ....................31.40
Fenn v Peterborough (1979) 104 DLR (3d) 174 ....................25.36, 44.158
Fennell v E Stone & Sons Ltd [1967] IR 204 ....................18.03
Fennell v Mulcahy (1845) 8 ILR 434 ....................35.25
Fennell v Stone & Sons Ltd [1967] IR 204 ....................18.10
Fenton v Schofield (1964) 100 ILTR 69 ....................35.03, 35.20
Fenwick v Schmaltz (1868) LR 3 CP 313 ....................25.40
Ferguson v National Life Assurance Co of Canada 1996 Ont CJ LEXIS 1663 ....................2.27
Ferguson v O'Gorman [1937] IR 620 .................... 23.20-23.21, 32.101, 32.166
Ferguson v Welsh [1987] 1 WLR 1553 ....................12.136
Ferriter v Daniel O'Connell's Sons Inc (1980) 413 ALE 2d 690 ....................33.17
Fields v Woodland Products Ltd (SC) 16 July 1999 ....................44.106
Filburn v People's Palace and Aquarium Co Ltd (1890) 25 QBD 258 ....................27.16, 27.23
Findlay v Blaylock 1937 SC 21 ....................32.42
Finlay v Murtagh [1979] IR 249 .................... 1.110, 6.10, 6.55, 10.18-10.20
....................10.72, 10.149, 10.153, 13.51, 13.81
.................... 14.03, 14.171-14.174
Finlay v Price [1932] NI 81 ....................9.07
Finnegan v The Irish Shell Co (1937) 71 ILTR 200 ....................40.11, 40.18
Finucane v Thorton (SC) 31 July 1957 ....................44.58
Fire Manufacturing Co v O'Leary (HC) 29 April 1974 ....................32.51
Firth v South Eastern Health Board (HC) 27 July 1994 ....................18.118
Fisher v Harrods [1966] 1 Lloyd's Rep 500 ....................11.16
Fisher v Nation Newspaper Co Ltd and Rooney [1901] 2 IR 465 ..... 34.85-34.91, 34.194
Fitch v Hyde-Cates (1982) 150 Comm LR 482 ....................41.07
Fitzgerald v Brangan (1905) 39 ILTR 116 ....................12.40, 24.18, 24.85
Fitzgerald v Clancy [1902] 1 IR 207 .................... 45.05-45.05
Fitzgerald v ED & AD Cooke Bourne (Farms) Ltd [1964] 1 QB 249 ....................27.17
Fitzgerald v Firbank [1897] 2 Ch 96 ....................24.25
Fitzgerald v Lane [1987] 2 All ER 455, affd [1988] 2 All ER 961 ....................2.14
Fitzgerald v Northcote (1865) 4 F & F 656, ER ....................22.103
Fitzgerald v Treacy DPIJ: Trinity & Michaelmas Terms 1999, p 85 ....................44.169
Fitzgibbon v Eason & Son Ltd (1910) 45 ILTR 91 ....................34.19
Fitzhenry v Geraghty [1997] Ir L Log W 146 ....................24.115
Fitzpatrick v Dunphy (1851) 1 Ir CLR 366 .................... 30.19-30.20
Fitzpatrick v Furey (HC) 12 June 1998 ....................42.29, 44.106
Fitzpatrick v Midland Health Board (HC) 1 May 1997 ....................14.30, 14.42

Fitzpatrick v Modular Cold Stores Manufacturing Co Ltd
DPIJ: Trinity & Michaelmas Terms 1996, p 240 (HC) ....................................... 44.120
Fitzpatrick v O'Connor (HC) 11 March 1988 ....................................... 24.53, 25.11
Fitzpatrick v The Midland Health Board (HC) 1 May 1997 ....................................... 14.61
Fitzsimmons v Duncan & Kemp & Co [1908] 2 IR 482 ....................................... 34.175, 34.200
Fitzsimons v Bord Telecom Éireann and ESB [1991] ILRM 276 ....................................... 3.20, 7.26
....................................... 42.48-42.51
Flanagan v Griffith (1985) Prof Neg LR 95 ....................................... 13.81
Flanagan v Mulhall [1985] ILRM 134 ....................................... 23.33, 45.05
Flanagan v Robert Usher & Co Ltd, DPIJ: Michaelmas Term 1991, p 84 ....................................... 18.108
Flannery v Dean [1995] 2 ILRM 393 ....................................... 28.07
Flannery v Waterford & Limerick Ry Co (1877) IR 11 CL 30 ....................................... 9.15, 9.44
Fleming v Atkinson [1959] SCR 513 ....................................... 27.51
Fleming v Henry Denny & Sons Ltd (SC) 29 July 1955 ....................................... 9.08, 9.18, 9.44
....................................... 11.21-11.24, 11.71
Fleming v Kerry County Council [1955-1956] Ir Jur Rep 71 ....................................... 7.27, 11.22, 12.36
....................................... 40.06, 40.15-40.20
Fleming v Rathdown School Trust, (HC) 6 April 1993 ....................................... 37.11
Flesk v King DPIJ: Trinity and Michaelmas Terms 1996, p 87 ....................................... 16.26, 16.33
Fletcher v Rylands (1866) LR 1 Ex 265 ....................................... 25.05, 25.50
Flint v Lovell [1935] 1 KB 354 ....................................... 44.195
Flinter v Ryan DPIJ: Hilary and Easter Terms 1993 p 262 ....................................... 27.38
Florida v Riley (1989) 102 LED 2d 835 ....................................... 23.39
Flower v Ebbw Vale Steel Iron & Coal Co [1934] 2 KB 132 ....................................... 21.53
Flynn and Narman's Contract, Re [1948] IR 104 ....................................... 10.152
Flynn v Hibernian Bank Ltd [1938] Ir Jur Rep 34 ....................................... 34.67
Flynn v Irish Sugar Manufacturing Co [1928] IR 525 ....................................... 18.101, 18.108, 18.159
Flynn v O'Reilly DPIJ: Trinity and Michaelmas Terms 1996, p 55,
affd [1999] 1 ILRM 458 ....................................... 16.24, 16.72
Flynn v Ross (HC) 19 February 1974 ....................................... 23.29, 23.48, 24.58
FN v Minister for Ecuation [1995] 1 IR 409 ....................................... 16.69
Fogg v McKnight [1968] NZLR 330 ....................................... 44.13
Folan v Galway County Council DPIJ: Trinity and Michaelmas
Terms 1998, p 99 ....................................... 18.05
Folens v O Dubhghaill [1973] IR 255 ....................................... 44.10
Foley v Berthoud (1903) 37 ILTR 123 ....................................... 27.44
Foley v Independent Newspapers (Ireland) Ltd [1994] 2 ILRM 61 ....................................... 34.05, 34.207
Foley v Irish Land Commission [1952] IR 118 ....................................... 46.80
Foley v Musgrave Cash and Carry Ltd (SC) 20 December 1985 ....................................... 6.01, 12.08, 12.53
Foley v Quinnsworth Ltd (HC) 10 April 1992 ....................................... 7.44, 9.38
Foley v Spain (HC) unrep June 1970 ....................................... 42.22
Foley v Thermocement Products Ltd (1954) 90 ILTR 92 ....................................... 44.07, 44.58-44.60
....................................... 44.145, 44.180
Fontaine v British Columbia (Official Administrator) [1998] 1 SCR 424 ....................................... 9.43, 9.54
Fontaine v Devonis (1975) 14 RI 541, 336 A 2d 847 ....................................... 40.10

Forbes v Cochrane (1824) 2 B & C 448, 107 ER 450 ....................32.12
Forbes v Wandsworth Health Authority [1997] QB 402 ....................46.34, 46.50
Forde v Forde (SC) 20 May 1996 ....................44.65
Forde v Iarnród Éireann - Irish Rail (SC) 4 November 1997 ....................44.65
Forde v Pfizer Chemical Corporation Ltd DPIJ: Hilary & Easter Terms 1991, p 57 ....................44.87, 44.176
Forrester v Tyrrell (1893) 9 TLR 257 ....................34.21
Forshall and Fine Arts and Collections Ltd v Walsh, (HC) 18 June 1997 affd (SC) 31 July 1998 ....................6.28, 6.34, 10.09, 10.78 ....................10.86, 10.106, 35.02, 35.10, 35.25, 43.30
Forster v Donovan, Ireland and the AG (1980) 114 ILTR 104 ....................27.21, 27.29
Forsyth v Roe Quarry Ltd (SC) 2 December 1958 ....................44.58, 44.70, 44.84, 44.145
Forsythe v GN Ry Co (Ireland) [1937] Ir Jur Rep 18 ....................10.50
Fortune v AT Cross Ltd DPIJ: Trinity & Michaelmas Terms 1996, p 78 (HC) ....................44.120
Fortune v Jacob (SC) 22 June 1977 ....................7.44
Fosbroke-Hobbes v Airwork Ltd [1937] 1 All ER 108 ....................9.17, 9.25
Foster v Hood (1873) 7 ILTR 92 ....................35.26
Foster v Warblington UDC [1906] 1 KB 648 ....................24.112
Foth v O'Hara (1959) 15 DLR (2d) 332 ....................36.19
Fouldes v Willoughby (1841) 8 M & W 540, 151 ER 1153 ....................28.04, 30.02
Fowell v National Coal Board, The Times, 21 May 1986 ....................46.27
Fowler v Grace, Times, 20 February 1970 ....................44.07
Fowler v Lanning [1959] 1 QB 426 ....................22.03, 28.11
Fowler v O'Mahoney (SC) 6 February 1973 ....................15.17
Fox v Bord na Mona DPIJ: Hilary & Easter Terms 1991, p 266 (HC) ....................44.176
Fox v Hawkins (1992) 594 NE 2d 493 ....................20.90
Foxcroft v Lacy (1613) Hob 89, 80 ER 239 ....................34.107
France v Gaudet (1871) LR 6 QB 199 ....................29.03
France v Parkinson [1954] 1 All ER 739 ....................15.39
Francovich and Bonifaci v Italy [1991] ECR I–5357 ....................1.85, 1.93, 11.93
Frank v Cox (1956) 54 LGR 142 ....................15.48
Franklin v Giddins [1978] Qd R 72 ....................37.38
Franks v Sanderson (1988) 25 BCLR (2d) 248 ....................26.20
Fraser v Harland & Wolff Ltd [1978] NIJB (Part 2) ....................18.126
Frawley v CIE (1950) 84 ILTR 189 ....................7.39
Freeman v Home Office (No 2) [1984] QB 524 affd [1984] 1 All ER 1036 ....................14.79, 22.67
Freeney v Bray UDC [1982] ILRM 29 ....................46.04
Freese v Lemmon (1973) 210 NW 2d 576 ....................7.15
French v East London & City Health Authority [2000] Lloyds Rep Med 35 ....................46.34
Fricke 'General Practice in Industry' (1960) 23 MLR 653 ....................18.15
Friedel v Castlereagh (1877) IR 11 CL 93 ....................29.10
Friederich v Board of Education (1978) 375 NE 2d 141 ....................16.25
Froom v Butcher [1976] QB 286 ....................20.34, 20.41
Fryer v Salford Corporation [1937] 1 All ER 617 ....................16.70

Fullam v Associated Newspapers Ltd [1953-54] Ir Jur Rep 79 (HC) affd by [1955-56] Ir Jur Rep 45 .... 34.55, 34.92, 34.103
Fullarton v North Melbourne Electric Tramway & Lighting Co (1916) 21 CLR 181 .... 25.16
Fulton v Randall, Gee & Mitchell Ltd [1918] 3 WWR 331 .... 7.08
Furlong v Curran [1959] Ir Jur 30 .... 27.03-27.05
Furmeaux v Willis Oil Tool Ireland Ltd, DPIJ: Trinity and Michaelmas Terms 1993, p 53 .... 18.95, 18.152
Furness v B & S Massey Ltd .... 41.07
Furniss v Fitchett [1958] NZLR 396 .... 37.42
Fusco v O'Dea [1994] 2 IR 93 .... 38.18
FW v British Broadcasting Corporation (HC) 25 March 1999 .... 44.10

## G

G & Crampton Ltd v Building & Allied Trade Union [1998] 1 ILRM 420 .... 32.177, 32.184
G v An Bord Uchtála [1980] IR 32 .... 1.13
G v Attorney General [1994] 1 NZLR 714 .... 37.42
Gabicci v Dunnes Stores Ltd (HC) 31 July 1991 .... 31.13, 45.05
Gaffney v Dublin United Tramways Co [1916] 2 IR 472 .... 7.13
Gagnier v Canadian Forest Products Ltd (1990) 1990 ACW SJ LEXIS 19321 .... 24.05
Gahan v Engineering Products Ltd [1971] IR 30 .... 9.06, 18.97, 44.66, 44.84
Gahan v Maingay Ridg Lap & Scho (1793) 62 .... 28.04
Gala v Preston (1991) CLR 243 .... 20.96
Galashiels Gas Co Ltd v O'Donnell [1949] AC 275 .... 3.42
Galaskey v Stauffer (1994) 112 DLR (4th) 109 .... 16.11
Galbraith v Mitchenall Estates [1965] 2 QB 473 .... 35.06
Gallagher and Shatter v Independent Newspapers Ltd, Irish Times 10 May 1980, p 10 .... 34.103
Gallagher v Barrow Wood School Ltd English CA, 7 October 1999 LEXIS transcript .... 16.69
Gallagher v Concarr DPIJ: Hilary and Easter Terms 1993 .... 15.04
Gallagher v Dorman Long & Co Ltd [1947] 2 All ER 38 .... 21.49
Gallagher v ESB [1933] IR 558 .... 9.02, 42.19, 42.25, 42.42
Gallagher v Leitrim County Council (1955) 89 ILTR 151 .... 24.113
Gallagher v Minister for Defence (HC) 25 February 1998 .... 46.34, 46.46-46.50
Gallagher v Mogul of Ireland Ltd [1975] IR 204 .... 18.81, 21.10, 21.20, 21.42, 21.61
Gallagher v N McDowell Ltd [1961] NI 26 .... 12.03, 13.24, 13.52
Gallagher v Premier Dairies DPIJ: Michaelmas Term 1990, p 316 .... 18.83, 18.106
Gallagher v Tuohy (1924) 58 ILTR 134 .... 45.05, 45.33-45.35
Gallant v Oickle (1982) 53 NSR (2d) 331 .... 20.18
Gambino v Dileo (1970) 17 DLR (3d) 167 .... 16.09
Gambriell v Caparelli (1975) 7 OR (2d) 205 .... 22.91
Gammell v Wilson [1982] AC 27 .... 41.07, 41.12, 42.20, 42.38
Ganly v Ledwidge (1876) IR 10 CL 33 .... 30.07-30.12, 30.19

Gannon v Hughes [1937] IR 284 ....................24.25, 45.50
Gannon v Walsh (HC) 20 June 1996 ....................23.45
Gard v Board of School Trustees of Duncan [1946] 2 DLR 44 ....................16.22
Garda Representative Association v Ireland [1989] ILRM 1 ....................10.146
Gardiner v Miller 1967 SLT 29 ....................27.51
Gardner v Grace (1858) 1 F & F 359, 174 ER 763 ....................40.10
Gargotch v Cohen [1940] OWN 479 ....................40.08
Gariup Construction Co v Foster (1988) 519 NE 2d 1224 ....................8.06
Garnaut v Rowse (1941) 43 WALR 29 ....................35.09
Garrard v AE Southey & Co [1952] 2 QB 174 ....................43.10
Garratt v Dailey (1955) 46 Wash 2d 197, 279 p 2d 109, (1956) 49 Wash 2d 499
304 p 2d 681 .................... 22.06-22.08
Garrett v Attorney General [1997] 2 NZLR 332 ....................19.55
Garry v John Sisk & Son (Dublin) Ltd (SC) 29 January 1973 ....................3.22, 18.96
.................... 18.151-18.154, 44.82
Gartner v Kidman (1962) 108 CLR 12 ....................24.53
Garvey v Ireland [1981] ILRM 266....................1.116, 44.22
Garvey v Walsh DPIJ: Trinity & Michaelmas Terms 1992, p 52 ....................44.176
Garzilli v Howard Johnson's Motor Lodges Inc (1976) 419 F Supp 1210 (EDNY) ....8.25
Gash v Wood (1960) 22 DLR (2d) 625 ....................27.51
Gaunt v Fynney (1872) LR 8 Ch ....................24.106
Gawley v Belfast Corporation [1908] 2 IR 34 ....................42.13
Gaynor v McGinn [1933] LJ Ir 70 ....................26.06, 26.20
Gaysan v Allied Irish Banks plc (HC) 28 January 2000 ....................10.118, 10.148
Geddis v Proprietors of Bann Reservoir (1878) 3 AC 430 ....................24.93
Geier v Kujawa, Weston & Warner Bros (Transport) Ltd
[1970] 1 Lloyds LR 364 ....................20.69
Gello v Brownstone Condominium Association (1980) 82 III Appeal 3d 334
37 Ill Dec 805, 402 NE 2d 807 ....................23.39
General & Finance Facilities Ltd v Cooks Cars (Romford) Ltd [1963] 1 WLR 644
[1963] 2 All ER 314 .................... 29.10-29.11
General Cleaning Contractors v Christmas [1953] AC 180 ....................18.09, 18.85
General Engineering Services Ltd v Kingston and St Andrew Corp
[1988] 2 All ER 867 ....................43.30
Genereux v Peterson Howell & Heather (Canada) Ltd [1973] OR 558
34 DLR (3d) 614 ....................32.03
Gent-Diver v Neville [1953] QSRI ....................20.15
Geoghegan v Harris (HC) 21 June 2000 ....................14.98, 14.106, 14.126
.................... 14.135, 14.139-14.144, 22.82
Geoghegan v Institute of Chartered Accountants [1995] 3 IR 86 ....................38.04
Geraghty v Montgomery [1953] IR 89 ....................12.08
Gerigs v Rose 9 CCLT 222 .................... 40.41-40.43
Gerrard v Crowe [1921] 1 AC 395 ....................24.55
Geyer v Downs (1977) 138 CLR 91, 17 ALR 408 .................... 16.49-16.54
Gibb v Comerford [1942] IR 295 ....................25.17, 27.50

Gibbings v Hungerford [1904] 1 IR 211 ............ 23.29, 24.31-24.32
............ 45.02, 45.05, 45.38
Gibbings v O'Dea & Co Ltd [1948-49] MacGillivray & Le Quesne's Copyright Cases, 31 ............ 34.94
Gibbons v Pepper (1695) 1 Ld Raym 38 ............ 22.05
Gibson v Chief Constable of Strathclyde Police 1999 SC 420 ............ 8.25
Gies v Gunwall (1982) 143 DLR (3d) 126 ............ 18.09
Gilchrist Watt and Sanderson Pty Ltd v York Products Pty Ltd [1970] 1 WLR 1262 ............ 30.24
Gildea v Brien (1821) 10 ICLR 230 ............ 34.152
Gildea v Hipwell [1942] IR 489 ............ 22.38
Gill v McDowell [1903] 2 IR 463 ............ 10.110, 35.06, 35.15
Gill v Wilson 3 ICLR 544 ............ 21.32
Gillen v Fair (1956) 90 ILTR 119 ............ 24.29, 24.85-24.88
Gillespie v Commonwealth (1991) 104 ACTR 1 ............ 18.60
Gillespie v Fitzpatrick [1970] IR 102 ............ 4.19, 20.12, 20.55
Gillick v O'Reilly [1984] ILRM 402 ............ 24.16, 27.05, 27.51
Gillick v Rotunda Hospital (SC) 15 May 1998 ............ 44.65, 44.176
Gillick v West Norfolk and Wisbech Area Health Authority [1986] AC 112 ............ 22.76
Gillingham BC v Medway (Chatham) Dock Co Ltd [1993] QB 343 ............ 24.43
Gillis v M'Donnell (1869) LR 4 CL 342 ............ 34.173
Gilmore v Irish Omnibus Co (1930) 64 ILTR 48 ............ 9.21
Gilmore v Windle [1967] IR 323 ............ 4.24
Gilmour v Belfast Harbour Commrs [1933] NI 114 ............ 5.02
Gilna v Maguire and 3M Ireland (HC) 19 May 1999 ............ 11.13, 18.51, 18.61, 18.101
Gilroy v Ní Cheallaigh [1996] Ir L Log W 310 ............ 16.22
Gilson v Kerrier RDC [1976] 1 WLR 904 ............ 25.31
Gimson v Victorian Work Authority [1995] 1 VR 209 (SC) ............ 22.33
Ginmelli v Johnston (1991) Aust Torts Reps 81-085 ............ 22.60
Ginty v Belmont Building Supplies Ltd [1959] 1 All ER 414 ............ 2.26
GIO Australia Ltd v Robson (1997) NSW LEXIS 1129 ............ 32.09
Glanfield v CIE (1946) 80 ILTR 72 ............ 7.27
Glaser v Schroeder (1929) 269 Mass 337, 168 NE 809 ............ 9.21
Glasgow Corporation v Muir [1943] AC 448 ............ 7.04, 7.24
Glen Ban Ltd v Lefroy (SC) 18 May 1944 ............ 35.27, 45.05
Glencar Exploration plc v Mayo County Council (HC), 20 August 1998 ............ 21.10
Glenwood Lumber Co v Phillips [1904] AC 405 ............ 23.46
Glinski v McIver [1962] AC 726 ............ 36.06-36.16
Glorney v O'Brien (HC) 14 November 1988 ............ 11.15
Glover v BLN Ltd (No 2) [1973] IR 432 ............ 42.34, 44.103
Glynn v Smith (1921) 55 ILTR 67 ............ 21.19
Goddard v Smith (1704) 3 Salk 245, 91 ER 803 ............ 36.05
Gold v Essex County Council [1942] 2 KB 293 ............ 43.22
Gold v Haringey Health Authority, [1987] 2 All ER 888 ............ 14.84
Golden Vale Co-Operative Creameries Ltd v Barrett (HC) 16 March 1987 ............ 10.71

Goldfarb v Williams & Co [1945] IR 433 ....................24.31, 24.75
Goldman v Hargrave [1967] 1 AC 645 ....................24.79, 25.35, 26.12
Goldsmith v Bhoyrul [1997] 4 All ER 268 ....................34.110
Golembe v Blumberg (1941) 262 AD 759, 27 NY 2d 692 ....................16.07
Gomberg v Smith [1963] 1 QB 25, [1962] 1 All ER 725 ....................27.01, 27.51
Good v Callaghan (SC) 25 April 1967 ....................42.30
Good v Collins and Kenna (HC) 4 February 1983 ....................45.05
Goodfellow v Coggburn (1977) 98 Idaho 202, 560 P 2d 873 ....................40.29
Goodman v Minister for Finance [1999] 3 IR 356 ....................4.20
Goodman v Norwalk Jewish Center (1958) 139 A 2d 812 ....................7.13
Good-Wear Treaders Ltd v D & B Holdings Ltd (1979) 8 CCLT 87 ....................16.03
Goody v Odhams Press Ltd [1967] 1 QB 333 ....................34.129
Goonan v Dooley (HC), 23 March, 1994 ....................14.30, 14.44
Gordan v Peerless Transportation Co (1941) 27 NYS 2d 198 ....................20.19
Gorely v Codd [1966] 3 All ER 891 ....................16.07
Gorey v Gorey (HC) 10 June 1993 ....................6.37
Goring v ESB DPIJ: Trinity and Michaelmas Terms 1993, p 169 ....................18.95, 18.152
Gorris v Scott (1874) LR 9 Exch 125 ....................21.34
Goss v Allen (1976) 70 NJ 442, 360 A 2d 388 .................... 40.29-40.30
Gough v Thorne [ 1966] 1 WLR 1387 ....................40.26
Goulding Chemicals Ltd v Bolger [1977] IR 211 .................... 32.88, 32.101-32.104
....................32.146, 32.158
Government Insurance Office of New South Wales v Fredrichberg
(1968) 118 CLR 403 ....................9.43
Government of Canada v Employment Appeals Tribunal [1992] 2 IR 489 ....................38.18
Government v Marine & Trade Insurance Co Ltd 1973 (3) SA 797 ....................7.13
Gow v Glasgow Education Authority 1922 SC 260 ....................16.57
Grace Provision Co v Dortch (1961) 350 SW 2d 409 ....................27.03
Grace v Dwyer Nolan Developments (CC) 9 November 1998 ....................24.31, 24.54
Grace v Fitzsimon and O'Halloran (SC) 14 June 1996 ....................15.45
Gracey v Belfast Tramway Co [1901] 2 IR 322 ....................43.30
Grafstein v Holme (1958) 12 DLR (2d) 727 ....................30.38
Graham v Peat (1801) 1 East 244 ....................23.45
Graham v Saville [1945] OR 301 ....................22.66
Grainger v Cullen (1909) 43 ILTR 132 ....................20.78, 24.18
Grainger v Finlay (1858) 7 ICLR 417 ....................27.06
Grainger v Hill (1838) 4 Bing NC 212, 132 ER 769 ....................36.19
Gramophone Co's Application, Re [1910] 2 Ch 423 ....................31.29
Gran Gelato v Richcliff (Group) Ltd [1992] Ch 560 ....................10.133
Grand Hotel Co of Caledonia Springs v Wilson [1904] AC 103 ....................31.40
Grange Marketing Ltd v M & Q Plastic Products Ltd (HC) 17 June 1976 .....31.05, 31.32
Grant v Australian Knitting Mills Ltd [1936] AC 85 ....................11.24, 11.71
Grassi v WIC Radio Ltd (2000) 49 CCLT (2d) 65 ....................34.66, 34.107, 34.186
Gray v Jones [1939] 1 All ER 798 ....................34.38
Gray v Pullen (1864) 5 B & s 970 122, ER 1091 ....................21.48

Gray v Russell (1993) 853 SW 2d 928 .......... 20.90
Gray v Siev (1949) 83 ILTR 67 .......... 24.77
Grealy v Bank of Nova Scotia, (SC) 11 April 1975 .......... 34.62
Grealy v Casey (1901) 1 NIJR 121 .......... 22.11, 22.23, 44.04
Greaney v Scully [1981 1 ILRM 340 .......... 1.141
Greatorex v Greatorex [2000] 1 WLR 1970 .......... 17.66
Green v Blake [1948] IR 242 .......... 34.58, 34.177, 34.225
Green v Goddard (1798) 2 Salk 641, 91 ER 540 .......... 22.114
Green v Hills, The Times, 22 April 1969 .......... 15.36
Green v Irish Independent Co Ltd [1899] 1 IR 386 , [1899] 1 IR .......... 21.08
Green v Mundow (CC) 20 January 2000 .......... 16.60, 16.76, 27.29
Green v Pickering [1952] IR 274 .......... 15.17, 15.32
Greene v Boyle [1934] Ir Jur Rep 3 .......... 44.58
Greene v Hughes Haulage Ltd [1998] 1 ILRM 34 .......... 44.118-44.121
Greene v London Borough of Hadiney (CA (Civil Div)) 18 February 1992 .......... 20.54
Greene v Lyons & Co (1897) 31 ILT & Sol J 256 .......... 43.13
Greene v Minister for Agriculture [1990] 2 IR 17 .......... 24.71
Greene v Mundow (CC) 20 January 2000 .......... 16.28
Greenock Corporation v Caledonian Ry [1917] AC 556 .......... 25.39
Greenwood v Bennett [1973] QB 195 .......... 29.16
Greer v Belfast & Co Down Ry [1926] NI 68 .......... 21.10
Greers Ltd v Pearman & Corder Ltd (1922) 39 RPC 406 .......... 35.28
Greeson v Gilbert (1783) 3 Dougl 232, 99 ER 629 .......... 22.92
Gregan v Sullivan [1937] Ir Jur Rep 64 .......... 22.87
Gregory v Piper (1829) 9 B & C 591, 109 ER 220 .......... 23.02
Gregory v Protsmouth City Council [2000] 2 WLR 30 .......... 36.28
Grehan v Medical Incorporated [1986] ILRM 627, [1986] IR 528 .......... 11.54
.......... 31.16, 44.142
Greyhill Property Co Ltd v Whitechap Inn Ltd (HC) 5 October 1993 .......... 10.152, 35.17
Griffin v Coleman (1859) 4 H & N 265, 157 ER 533 .......... 22.39
Griffin v Daniels (1952) 86 ILTR 38 .......... 12.21, 12.35
Griffin v Kelly's Strand Hotel (HC) 24 January 1980 .......... 31.40, 45.05
Griffins v Benn (1911) 27 Times LR 346 .......... 35.26
Griffiths v Brown [1999] P 1 QR 131 .......... 8.06
Griffiths v Doolan [1959] Qd R 304 .......... 15.05
Griffiths v Van Raaj [1985] ILRM 582 .......... 42.36, 44.103, 44.149, 44.161
Griggs v Southside Hotel Ltd, [1947] 4 DLR 49 .......... 43.39
Grimm v Arizona Bd of Pardons & Paroles (1977) 115 Ariz 260
564 P 2d 1227 .......... 8.25
Griswold v Connecticut (1965) 381 US 479 .......... 37.76
Gross v Lewis Hillman Ltd [1970] Ch 445 .......... 35.14
Groves v Wimborne (Lord) [1898] 2 QB 402 .......... 21.19, 43.50, 43.69
Guckian v Cully (SC) 9 March 1972 .......... 18.107, 18.152, 20.15
Guerin v Guerin and McGrath [1992] 2 IR 287 .......... 43.66
Guerin v O'Driscoll (SC) 7 February 1966 .......... 15.33

Guilfoyle v Linders (SC) 23 November 1979 ....................2.54
Guille v Swan (1823) 19 Johns 381, 10 AM Dec 234 ....................23.29
Guinness Ireland Group v Kilkenny Brewing Co Ltd [1999] 1 ILRM 531
.................... 31.05-31.10, 45.05
Guldenschuh (1980) 56 Notre Dame L 272 ....................20.44
Gunn v Barr [1926] 1 DLR 855 ....................32.42
Gurliacci v Nayer (1991) 218 Com 531 590 A 2D 914 ....................33.21
Guy v Trizec Equities Ltd (1979) 99 DLR (3d) 243 ....................44.74
Gwinnell v Eamer (1875) LR 10 CP 658 ....................24.76
GWK Ltd v Dunlop Rubber Co Ltd (1926) 42 Times LR 593 ....................28.04
Gwynne v Wairarapa Times-Age [1972] NZLR 586 ....................34.86

**H**

H & N Emanuel Ltd v Greater London Council [1971] 2 All ER 835 ....................26.10
H v H [1966] 3 All ER 560 ....................22.113
H v Pennell (1987) 46 SASR 158 ....................16.57
H v R [1996] 1 NZLR 299 ....................46.99
Hackbart v Cincinnati Bengals Inc (1977) 435 F Supp 352 (D Colo),
revd (1979) 601 F 2d 516 ....................22.60
Hackett v Horan (SC) 14 May 1953 ....................15.06
Hackshaw v Shaw (1984) 155 Comm LR 614 ....................22.03
Hagan v Pasley (1878) 2 LR Ir 573 ....................23.45, 30.02, 30.12
Hagarth v Hall (1998) 166 DLR (45) 193 ....................33.17
Hage v Stade (1981) 304 NW 2d 283 ....................26.24
Haggan v Pasley (1878) 2 LR Ir 573 ....................30.21
Hake v George Wiedemann Brewing Co (1970) 23 Ohio St 65, 262 NE 2d 703 ........9.20
Hale v Jennings Brothers [1938] 1 All ER 579 ....................25.17, 25.25, 25.36
Halford v Brookes [1991] 1 WLR 428 .................... 46.27, 46.47-46.50
Hall (Arthur JJ) & Co (a firm) v Simons [2000] 3 All ER 673 ....................1.33, 6.91
....................14.165,14.167, 14.197
Hall v GN Rly Co of Ireland (1890) 26 LR Ir 289 ....................42.18
Hall v Graham (1795) Ridg Lapp & Schoales 469 ....................36.13
Hall v Hebert (1993) 101 DLR (4th) 129 ....................22.66
Hall v Hollander (1825) 4 B & C 660, 107 ER 1206 ....................32.11, 33.36
Hall v Kennedy (HC) 20 December 1993 ....................8.10, 8.26
Hall v McKone (1968) Ltd [1975] IR 292 ....................2.32, 2.39, 24.18
Hall v Wightman [1926] NI 92 ....................24.16, 27.05, 27.50
Hallett v Nicholson 1979 SC 1 ....................26.24
Halliwell v Venables (1930) 99 LJKB 353 ....................9.17
Halpin v Tara Mines Ltd (HC) 16 February 1976 .................... 24.31, 24.37-24.39
....................24.56, 45.06, 45.49
Halsey v Esso Petroleum Co Ltd [1961] 1 WLR 683 ....................24.06, 24.39
Halushka v University of Saskatchewan 53 DLR (2d) 436 ....................14.150
Hambrook v Stokes Bros [1925] I KB 141 ....................17.22
Hamerton v Green (1863) 16 ICLR 77 .................... 34.165-34.175

Hamill v Oliver [1977] IR 73 ....................20.35-20.44, 21.22
Hamilton v Attorney-General (1881) 9 LR (Ir) 271 .................... 23.43
Hamilton v Donegall (Marquis of) (1795) 3 Ridg PC 267 .................... 23.30
Hamilton v Niblock [1956] NI 109 .................... 21.10, 21.34, 21.42
Hamilton v Nurouf (WA) Pty (1956) 96 Comm LR 18 .................... 18.15
Hamilton v O'Reilly [1951] IR 200 .................... 42.30, 42.38
Hamilton v The Office of Public Works (HC) 22 December 1993 .................... 44.177
Hammersmith Ry v Brand (1869) LR 4 HL 171 .................... 25.44
Hammersmith Skating Rink Co v Dublin Skating Rink Co (1876) IR 10 Eq 235 ....................45.05-45.05
Hamps v Darby [1948] 2 KB 311 .................... 28.06
Hampson v Roddy (DC) 2 March 2000 .................... 24.31
Hanafin v Gaynor, Prof Neg LR 278 .................... 14.201
Hanafin v Minister for the Environment (HC) 24 January 1996 .................... 31.20
Hanahoe v Hussey (HC) 14 November 1994 .................... 6.28, 6.51, 19.68, 37.18
Handley v Moffat (1872) IR 6 CL 104 .................... 21.19
Hanley v Bethell Hotels Ltd (1917) 52 ILTR 10 .................... 26.15
Hanley v ICC Finance Ltd [1996] 1 ILRM 463 ....................29.10-29.10, 30.02, 45.05
Hanley v Minister for Defence [2000] 2 ILRM 276 .................... 1.192
Hanley v Morrissey (SC) 20 December 1974 .................... 15.44, 44.74
Hanley v Randles (1962) 96 ILTR 10 .................... 40.18, 44.58
Hanna v Pollock [1898] 2 IR 532 .................... 44.03
Hannah v Peel [1945] KB 509 .................... 30.24
Hanrahan v Ardnamult Steamship Co (1887) 22 LR Ir 55 .................... 18.101
Hanrahan v Merck Sharp & Dohme (Ireland) Ltd [1988] ILRM 629 ........ 1.18, 1.41-1.43
....................1.52-1.55, 2.11, 2.54-2.58, 7.40
....................9.11-9.16, 9.49-9.53, 11.130, 22.22
....................24.10, 24.24-24.26, 24.31-24.32, 24.39
....................24.56-24.59, 24.106, 25.06, 25.17, 25.25
....................31.82, 32.63, 32.132, 37.12-37.13, 44.51-44.53
Hanratty v Drogheda Web Offset Printers Ltd (SC) (ex temp) 2 June 1994 .................... 18.09
Hanser v Chicago, Rhode Island & Pacific Ry (1928) 205 Iowa 946, 219 NW 60 ..... 7.29
Hanson v Wearmouth Coal Ltd [1939] 3 All ER 47 .................... 25.16
Harberagen v Koppens [1974] 2 NZLR 597 .................... 34.85
Harbinson v Armagh County Council [1902] 2 IR 538 .................... 21.20, 24.113
Harbutts'Plasticine v Wayne Tank & Pump Co Ltd [1970] 1 QB 447 ....... 44.207, 44.208
Hardie (James) & Coy Pty Ltd v Seltsam Pty Ltd .................... 4.19
Harding v Barrett, DPIJ: Trinity and Michaelmas Terms 1993, p 246 .................... 15.36
Hardy v Brooks (1961) 103 Ga App 124, 118 SE 2d 492 .................... 8.03
Hardy v Ryle (1829) 9 B & C 603, 109 ER 224 .................... 46.05
Hare v BTC [1956] 1 WLR 250 .................... 33.07
Harfani & Co Ltd v Midland Bank Ltd [1968] 2 All ER 573 .................... 30.14
Hargreaves v Bretherton [1959] 1 QB 45 .................... 36.29
Hargreaves v Meade 10 ICLR 117 .................... 23.50
Harland v Fancsali (1993) 102 DLR (4th) 577 .................... 35.05

Harley v Imokelly Co-Operative Creamery Ltd (SC) 29 March 1973 ........................21.10
Harmony Ditch Co v Sweeney (1924) 31 Wyo 1, 222 P 577 ........................23.33
Harnedy v National Greyhound Racing Co Ltd [1940] IR 160 ........................27.04
Harris v Arnott (1889) 26 LR Ir 55 ........................44.58
Harris v James (1876) 45 LJQB 545 ........................24.75
Harrison v Armstrong (1917) 51 ILTR 38 ........................27.47
Harrison v BRB [1981] 3All ER 679 ........................20.81
Harrison v Bush (1855) 5 El & Bl 344, 119 ER 509 ........................34.165
Harrison v Carswell [1976] SCR 200 ........................23.20, 32.167
Harrison v Duke of Rutland [1893] 1 QB 142 ........................23.19
Harrison v Ennis [1967] IR 286 ........................15.34
Harrison v Michelin Tyre Co Ltd [1985] 1 All ER 918 ........................18.79, 43.33
Harrison v Shields, DPIJ: Trinity and Michaelmas Terms 1996 ........................16.22
Harrold v Watney [1898] 2 QB 320 ........................12.40
Hart v Griffith-Jones [1948] 2 All ER 729 ........................42.20
Hartery v Welltrade (Middle East) Ltd & Hurley [1978] ILRM 38 ........................34.61
........................ 34.169-34.175, 34.178, 34.199
Hartman v Fisette 66 DLR (3d) 516 ........................20.12
Harvey v Mayne (1872) IR 6 CL 417 ........................22.114
Harvey v Walters (1873) LR 8 CP 162 ........................24.99
Haseldine v Daw & Son Ltd [1941] 2 KB 343 ........................11.13
Hasselblad (GB) Ltd v Orbinson [1985] 2 WLR 1 ........................34.146
Hassett v O'Loughlin (1943) 78 ILTR 47 ........................24.17
Hassett v The Minister for Defence (SC) 7 December 1999 ........................44.95, 44.107
Hatch v Pye (1983) 59 NSR (2d) 170 ........................ 24.31-24.35
Haughey, Re [1971] IR 217 ........................1.13
Hawkes' Bay Motor Co Ltd v Russell [1972] NZLR 542 ........................9.43
Hay (or Bourhill) v Young [1943] AC 92 ........................3.05, 3.19, 3.32
Hay v Hughes [1975] 1 All ER 257, [1975] 1 QB 790 ........................42.39, 42.63
Hay v O'Grady [1992] 1 IR 210 ........................ 7.43, 10.84, 18.05-18.09, 44.61
Hay v Sheargold t/a Golden West Hotel 1996 Lexis 2732 ........................8.06
Hayden v M'Quillan [1930] IR 87 ........................15.32, 20.06
Haydon v Kent County Council [1978] QB 343 ........................21.22
Haydon v Smith (1610) 2 Browne 328 ........................4.14
Hayes v Criminal Injury Comp Tribunal [1982] ILRM 210 ........................42.40
Hayes v Finnegan [1952] IR 98 ........................2.25, 15.24
Hayes v Ireland [1987] ILRM 651 ........................ 1.16, 16.69, 32.127-32.128, 32.143, 32.175
Haynes v Harwood [1935] 1 KB 146, affg [1934] 2 KB 240 ........................2.47, 20.80, 26.34
Hazylake Fashions Ltd v Bank of Ireland [1989] IR 601 ........................ 10.107-10.115
Heald v Carey (1852) 11 CB 977, 138 ER 762 ........................30.05
Health Board v BC and the Labour Court (HC) 19 January 1994 ........................18.80, 43.15
Healy v Bray UDC [1962-1963] Ir Jur 9 ........................6.10, 7.31, 24.29, 24.85, 25.18, 25.25
Healy v Dodd [1951] Ir Jur Rep 22 ........................16.31
Healy v Ireland DPIJ: Hilary and Easter Terms 1993, p 10 ........................18.95
Healy v Minister for Defence (HC) 7 July 1994 ........................ 38.06-38.07

Healy v Nolan (1946) 80 ILTR 78 ........ 35.06, 42.02
Healy v North Western Health Board (HC) 31 January 1996 ........ 7.29, 14.30, 37.44
Heaney v Dublin Corporation, (HC) 16 May 1991 ........ 42.22
Heaney v Ireland [1997] 1 ILRM 117 ........ 32.137
Heaphy v O'Sullivan, the Commissioner of Garda Síochána, Ireland and the AG (HC) 14 July 1983 ........ 43.36
Heard v Pacitti [1933] IR 220 ........ 9.21
Heard v Woodward (1954) 12 WWR 312 ........ 25.06
Heath v Brighton (Mayor of) (1908) 98 LT 718 ........ 24.106
Heaven v Pender (1883) 11 QBD 503 ........ 11.07
Heavey v Pilotage Authority (HC) 7 May 1992 ........ 19.72
Heck v Robey (1994) 630 NE 2d 1361 ........ 20.90
Hedley Byrne & Co Ltd v Heller & Partners Ltd [1964] AC 465 ........ 1.06, 1.110
........ 6.12, 6.25, 10.02-10.09, 10.48-10.64
........ 10.73-10.78, 10.84, 10.98, 10.109-10.111
........ 10.120, 10.131, 10.138-10.141, 10.146-10.150
........ 10.153, 11.78, 11.86, 35.01, 35.10, 43.56
Heeney v Dublin Corporation (HC) 16 May 1991 ........ 7.52, 18.05, 18.09, 18.98, 26.24
Heffernan v O'Herlihy (HC) 3 April 1998 ........ 46.81
Hegan v Carolan [1916] 2 IR 27 ........ 23.43
Hegarty v O'Loughran [1990] 1 IR 148, affg [1987] ILRM 603 ........ 46.02, 46.11, 46.20
Hegarty v Shine (1878) 4 LR Ir 288 ........ 20.105, 22.18
........ 22.59, 22.65-22.66
Hegarty v Steelforms Ltd, DPIJ: Trinity and Michaelmas Terms, p 193 ........ 18.95
Heintzman & Co Ltd v Hashman Construction Ltd (1972) 32 DLR (3d) 622 ........ 25.17
Heiton and Co v McSweeney [1905] 2 IR 47 ........ 43.02
Helly v Gilhooly DPIJ: Trinity and Michaelmas Terms 1994, p 86 ........ 7.47
Henderson v Merrett Syndicates Ltd [1995] 2 AC 145 ........ 10.23, 10.141, 19.11
Henderson v Pearson Forest Products (1979) 10 CCLT 209 ........ 20.70
Henderson v Radio Corporation Pty Ltd [1960] NSWR 576 ........ 31.76
Henderson v Temple Pier Co Ltd [1998] 3 All ER 324 ........ 46.27
Henigan v Ballybunion Picture House & Baths Co [1944] Ir Jur Rep 20 ........ 30.07
Henley v Coillte Teoranta (HC) 9 March 1999 ........ 20.41
Hennerty v Bank of Ireland (HC) 5 July 1988 ........ 30.19
Hennessy (James) & Co v Keating [1908] 1 IR 43, affd [1908] 1 IR 466 ........ 31.09, 45.05
Hennessy v K-TEL Ireland Ltd (SC) 12 June 1997 ........ 34.162, 34.175, 34.199
Hennessy v Quinn and O'Donoghue [1968] IR 274 ........ 4.24
Henry (t/a Sight & Sound Film Library) v Sanderson (1972) 106 ILTR 12 ........ 2.45, 7.27
Henry, Murphy & Co v Northern Bank Ltd and McLoughlin & Harvey Ltd (HC) July 1983 ........ 24.37
Hensley v Montgomery County (1975) 25 Md App 361, 334 A 2d 542 ........ 24.29
Hercules Managements Ltd v Ernst & Young (1997) 146 DLR (4th) 577 ........ 6.31
Herd v Weardale Steel, Coal & Coke Co [1915] AC 67 ........ 22.47-22.49
Herndon v Gregory (1935) 190 Ark 702 81, SW 2d 849 ........ 9.25
Herniman v Smith [1938] AC 305 ........ 36.06

Herring v Metropolitan Board of Works 19 CBNS 510 ....................24.15
Herrington v British Rys Bd [1972] AC 877 ....................26.13
Herron v Ireland (SC) 5 December 1997 ....................38.18
Herschtal v Stewart & Ardern Ltd [1940] I KB 155 ....................11.13
Herskovits v Group Health Co-operative (1983) 99 Wn 2d 609, 664 P 2d 474 ..........2.21
Hester v MacDonald (1961) SC 370 ....................36.04
Hevican v Ruane [1991] 3 All ER 65 ....................17.33
Hewer v Bryant [1970] 1 QB 357 ....................16.12
Hewitt v Bonvin [1940] 1 KB 188 ....................43.63
Hewson v City of Red Deer (1977) 146 DLR (3d) 32 ....................8.18
Hewson v Cleeve [1904] 2 IR 536 ....................34.50
Hexagon Pty Ltd v Australian Broadcasting Commission [1976] RPC 628 ..........31.77
Hibpshman v Prudhoe Bay Supply (1987) 734 P 2d 991 ....................33.17
Hickey & Co Ltd v Roches Stores (Dublin) Ltd (HC) 14 July 1976 ....................44.18
Hickey v Electric Reduction of Canada (1970) 21 DLR (3d) 368 ....................24.05
Hickey v Sullivan (1894) 28 ILTR 150 ....................23.42
Hickman v Maisey [1900] 1 QB 752 ....................23.19, 37.05
Hicks v Faulkner (1878) 8 QBD 167,affd (1882) 46 LT 130 ....................36.06
Hicks v Stephens (1997) 40 CCLT (2d) 223 ....................34.34
Hickson v Boylan (HC) 25 February 1993 ....................23.33
Higgins v Monaghan & Reilly (1939) 74 ILTR 56 ....................34.61
Higgins v O'Reilly [1940] Ir Jur Rep 15 ....................22.28, 22.38, 43.01, 44.64
Higgins v Patterson and Gilchrist [1971] IR 253 ....................4.16, 5.02
Higgins v South of lreland Asphalt Co Ltd (1961) 101 ILTR 168 ..... 18.150, 21.52-21.55
Higgs (Billy) & Sons Ltd v Baddeley [1950] NZLR 605 ....................7.13
Hildige v O'Farrell (1880) 6 LR Ir 493 ....................21.10, 21.19
Hill v Board of School Trustees District No 35 (Langley) (2000) 2000 BCD Civ J Leix 702 ....................16.65
Hill v Chief Constable of West Yorkshire [1988] 2 All ER 238, [1989] AC 53 ....................1.33, 6.20, 6.78, 6.85, 8.25, 19.11
Hill v Finney (1865) 4 F & F 616 ....................14.176
Hill v Lundin & Associates Inc (1972) 260 La 542 256 So 2d 620 ....................2.43
Hill v Thompson (1971) 484 P 2d 513 ....................9.21
Hill v Tupper (1863) 2 H & C 121, 159 ER 51 ....................23.42
Hill v Van Earp (1997) 142 Austr LR 687 ....................6.31
Hill v Walker (1806) Peake's Nisi Prius Cas Vol 2, P 234 ....................23.29
Hills v Potter [1983] 3 All ER 716 ....................14.144
Hindle v O'Dwyer (SC) 14 February 1955 .................... 35.03,35.20-35.21, 44.58
Hinds v Direct Supply Co (Clapham Junction) Ltd, The Times, 29 January, 1966 ...16.05
Hinz v Berry [1970] 2 QB 40 ....................17.22
Hiort v Bott (1874) LR 9 Ex 86 ....................30.03
Hirst v West Riding Union Banking Co Ltd [1901] 2 KB 560 ....................35.25
Ho Kwai Loy v Leung Tin Hong [1978] HKLR 72 (CA) ....................40.26
Hoare & Co v McAlpine [1923] 1 Ch 167 ....................25.17, 25.33
Hobart v Butler (1859) 9 ICLR 157 ....................14.162

Hobbs v Bayers (1878) 2 LR Ir 496 .......... 34.175
Hodges v Webb [1920] 2 Ch 70 .......... 32.48
Hoey v Dundalk UDC (HC) 29 February 1980 .......... 24.93, 25.11
Hogan and O'Neill v Sunday World High Court 20 March, 1981 .......... 34.61
Hogan v ESB (HC) 17 December 1999 .......... 18.108, 21.50, 44.176
Hogan v McEwan (1975) 64 DLR (3d) 37 .......... 7.39, 18.03, 18.108
Hogan v Rolon Caravans Ltd (SC) 8 July 1966 .......... 21.10
Hogan v Steele & Co Ltd [2000] 1 ILRM 330 .......... 44.125, 44.129
Hogg v Keane [1956] IR 155 .......... 2.47, 6.50, 17.11, 20.20
Holderness v Goslin [1975] 2 NZLR 46 .......... 26.09
Holdings Ltd v McCormack [1992] 1 IR 151 .......... 31.62
Holgate v Lancashire Mental Hospitals Board [1937] 4 All ER 19 .......... 8.25
Holland v Dublin County Council (1979) 113 ILTR 1 .......... 24.14-24.16
Holliday v National Telephone Co [1899] 2 QB 392 .......... 24.78, 43.53
Hollington v Hewthorn [1943] KB 587 .......... 1.106, 34.125
Hollins v Fowler (1875) LR 7 HL 757 .......... 29.02, 30.04, 30.12
Hollinsworth v BCTV (1998) 44 CCLT (2d) 83 .......... 34.94
Hollywood Silver Fox Farm Ltd v Emmett [1936] 2 KB 468, [1936]1 All ER 825 .......... 24.49
Hollywood v Cork Harbour Commissioners [1992] 2 IR 457 .......... 18.108, 42.10
Holman Construction Ltd v Delta Timber Co Ltd [1972] NZLR 1081 .......... 10.149
Holmes v Ashford [1950] 2 All ER 76 .......... 11.27-11.34
Holmes v Bagge (1853) 1 E & B 782, 118 ER 629 .......... 22.114
Holmes v Heatley [1937] Ir Jur Rep 74 .......... 22.73, 22.77
Holmes v Maher (1875) LR 10 Exch 261 .......... 22.01
Holohan v Donohue [1986] IR .......... 44.66
Holohan v Minister for Defence (HC) 30 July 1998 .......... 43.08
Home Brewery plc v William Davis & Co (Loughborough) Ltd [1987] 1 All ER 637 .......... 24.52-24.55
Home Office v Dorset Yacht Co Ltd [1970] AC 1004 .......... 2.36, 6.11-6.17 .......... 6.24, 8.25, 19.08
Homer v Irwin & Son Ltd [1972] NI 202 .......... 36.19
Honan v Syntex Ireland Ltd DPIJ: Michaelmas Term 1990, p 272 .......... 44.125, 44.129
Hone v Hamilton (1875) IR 9 CL 15 .......... 23.36
Hooper v Reeve (1817) 7 Taunt 698, 129 ER 278 .......... 22.11
Hope v Leng Ltd (1907) 23 Times LR 243 .......... 34.142
Hopkins v Sadlier (1893) 28 ILTR 137 .......... 34.170
Hopp v Lepp (1980) 112 DLR (3d) 67 .......... 14.85
Horgan v Buckley [1938] IR 115, [1938] IR 675 (No 2) .......... 42.30, 42.42, 44.65-44.66
Horrocks v Lowe [1974] 1 All ER 662 .......... 34.194-34.199
Horsfall v Thomas (1862) 1 H & C 90, 158 ER 813 .......... 35.15
Horsley v MacLaren [1972] SCR 441 .......... 3.12, 7.39, 8.02, 20.81, 26.35
Horton v Jackson (CA (Civil Div)), 28 February 1996 .......... 7.28, 7.44
Horton v London Graving Dock [1951] AC 737 .......... 12.12

Hosford v John Murphy & Sons Ltd [1988] ILRM 300, [1987] IR 621 ..................... 1.06
........................................................................... 1.09, 1.22, 1.29, 1.121, 1.79
........................................................................... 17.35, 19.01, 21.69, 24.71, 33.02
........................................................................... 33.19-33.21, 37.95, 42.05
Hosford v Macken [1897] 1 IR 292 ........................................................................... 43.32
Hoskins v Woodham [1938] 1 All ER 692 ........................................................................... 13.60
Hosty v McDonagh (SC) 29 May 1973 ........................................... 16.65, 40.13, 44.66
Hotson v East Berkshire Area Health Authority [1987] AC 750 ...................... 2.21, 2.57
Hough v Irish Base Metals Ltd (SC) 8 December 1967 ................................ 18.77-18.79
........................................................................... 26.24, 43.33
House of Spring Gardens Ltd v Point Blank Ltd [1984] IR 611 ......... 30.44, 37.21-37.26
........................................................................... 37.32-37.38
Howard Electric Ltd v Mooney Ltd [1974] 2 NZLR 762 ........................................ 24.32
Howard Marine & Dredging Co Ltd v A Ogden & Sons (Excavations) Ltd
[1978] QB 574 ........................................................................... 10.147
Howard v Bergin, O'Connor & Co [1925] 2 IR 110 ................ 27.03, 27.16-27.18, 27.51
Howard v Boner (1943) 78 ILTR 3 ........................................... 22.11, 22.23, 38.01
Howard v Dublin Corporation (HC) 31 July 1996 ........................................ 6.28, 13.39
Howard v Furness, Houlder Argentine Lines Ltd [1936] 2 All ER 781 .......... 11.14, 25.19
Howard v Harris (1884) 1 Cab & E1 253 ........................................................ 30.03
Howe Scale Co v Wyckoff, Seamans & Benedict (1905) 198 US 118 ..................... 31.79
Howell v O'Regan (SC) 14 May 1970 ........................................................ 44.75
Hubbard v Pitt [1976] QB 142 ........................................... 24.97, 32.146, 37.14
Huckle v Money (1763) 2 Wils 205, 95 ER 768 ........................................ 44.09
Hudson v Ridge Manufacturing Co [1957] 2 QB 348 ................................ 18.77-18.79
Hughes v Ballynahinch Gas Co (1898) 33 ILTR 74 ................................ 7.35, 24.93
Hughes v Dundalk Harbour Commissioners [1923] 1 IR 38 ........................ 21.10, 21.19
Hughes v JJ Power Ltd (HC) 11 May 1988 ........................................ 2.27, 14.02
Hughes v Jolliffe (1957) 50 Wash 2d 554, 313 P 2d 678 ........................................ 9.21
Hughes v Lord Advocate [1963] AC 837 ........................................ 3.20, 18.124, 18.148
Hughes v Maciie (1863) 2 H & C 744, 159 ER 308 ........................................ 40.26
Hughes v Moy Contractors (HC) 29 July 1999 ........................................ 46.65
Hughes v O'Flaherty (HC) 19 January 1996 ................................ 20.41, 44.110, 44.193
Huljich v Hall [1973] 2 NZLR 279 ........................................................ 32.48
Hull v GN Ry Co of Ireland (1890) 26 LR Ir 289 ........................................ 42.42
Hulley v Silversprings Bleaching Co [1922] 2 Ch 268 ........................................ 24.100
Hulton v Jones [1910] AC 20 ........................................................ 34.111-34.114
Hume v Tennyson [1987] NILR Bull No 2, P 12 ........................................ 23.42
Humphries v Connor (1864) 17 ICLR 1 ........................................ 22.11, 22.111, 24.48
Humphrys v Pratt (1831) 4 Thigh NS 154 ........................................................ 29.05
Hunt v Severs [1994] 2 AC 350 ........................................................ 44.110
Hunter v Canary Wharf Ltd [1997] AC 655 ........................................ 22.32, 24.24, 24.43
........................................................ 24.62-24.71, 24.73, 24.112, 25.26-25.28
........................................................................... 37.02, 37.13-37.13
Hunter v Hanley 1955 SLT 213 (1st Div) ........................................................ 14.22

Hunter v Wright [1938] 2 All ER 621 ........ 9.21
Huntingburg (City of) v First (1896) 43 NE 17 ........ 7.04, 7.08
Hurley v Eddingfield (1901) 156 Ind 416, 59 NE 1058 ........ 8.01
Hurley v Imokelly Co-Operative Creamery Ltd (SC) 29 March 1973 ........ 21.42
Hussain v Lancaster City Council [1999] 2 WLR 1142 ........ 24.75
Hutchings v Nevin, 1992 LEXIS 1461 ........ 7.23
Hutchins v Maughan [1947] VLR 131 ........ 28.06
Hutchinson v Davidson 1945 SC 395 ........ 44.207
Hutchinson v York, Newcastle, and Berwick Ry Co (1950) 5 Ex 343
155 ER 150 ........ 18.02-18.02
Huth v Huth [1915] 3 KB 32 ........ 34.14
Hutton v Philippi [1982] ILRM 578 ........ 41.10
Hyett v GW Ry Co [1948] 1 KB 345 ........ 26.35
Hyland v Cleary Ltd (SC) 9 April 1964 ........ 34.175, 34.199
Hynes v Conlon [1939] Ir Jur 49 ........ 32.15
Hynes v Garvey [1978] IR 174 ........ 37.40
Hynes v Sligo Corporation, DPIJ: Trinity and Michaelmas Terms 1993 ........ 7.41
Hynes-O'Sullivan v O'Driscoll [1988] IR 436, [1989] ILRM 349 ........ 1.13, 1.121
........ 32.138, 34.08, 34.171, 34.175-34.178
........ 34.193, 34.199

## I

I v Ireland [1988] ILRM 300, (SC) 4 May 1989, affg (HC) 19 August 1988 ........ 1.29
Iarnród Éireann v Darby and O'Connor Irish Times, 23 March 1991 ........ 32.115
Iarnród Éireann/Irish Rail Ireland v Ireland [1995] 2 ILRM 161 (HC)
[1996] 2 ILRM 500 (SC) ........ 4.02-4.03, 4.20, 25.53
ICC Banl plc v Verling [1995] 1 ILRM 123 ........ 45.02
Ideal Poultry Farms Ltd v Spencer Freeman (1950) 84 ILTR 85 ........ 24.16
Ilford Urban District Council v Beal [1925] 1 KB 671 ........ 25.15
Imber v Pachtman (1975) 424 US 409 ........ 36.04
Imperial Group plc v Philip & Morris Ltd [1984] RPC 293 ........ 31.25
Imperial Tobacco v Hart 51 (1917) NSR 379, affd 51 NSR 387, 36 DLR 63 ........ 25.11
Incorporated Law Society of Ireland v Carroll (HC) 24 January 1995 ........ 31.03
Indata Equipment Supplies (t/a AutoFit) v ACL Ltd [1998] 1 BCLC 412 ........ 37.22
Independent Newspapers Ltd v Irish Press Ltd [1932] IR 615 ........ 31.41, 45.03-45.05
Indermaur v Dames (1866) LR 1 CP 274 ........ 12.03, 12.10, 12.50, 12.99, 18.81
Inland Revenue Commissioners v Hambrook [1956] 2 QB 641 ........ 32.05-32.09
Inland Revenue Commissioners v Maxse [1919] 1 KB 647 ........ 14.01
Innes v Wylie (1844) 1 C & K 257, 174 ER 800 ........ 22.14, 22.20
Insurance Commissioner v Joyce (1948) 77 Comm LR 39 ........ 6.65
Interlego AG v Croner Trading Pty Ltd (1991) 102 ALR 379 ........ 31.27
International News Service v Associated Press (1918) 248 US 215 ........ 31.77
Iowa (Leonard v State (1992) 491 NW 2d 508 ........ 37.44
Irish Equine Foundation Ltd v Robinson [1999] 2 ILRM 289 ........ 6.51, 10.09
........ 10.15, 46.20

Irish Land Commission v Murphy [1939] IR 37 ....................23.43
Irish Land Commission v Walsh (1963) 97 ILTR 91 ....................44.03
Irish Leisure Industries Ltd v Gaiety Theatre Enterprises Ltd (HC) 12 February 1975 ....................44.104
Irish National Bank v RTE [1998] 2 ILRM 196 ....................37.38
Irish Paper Sacks Ltd v John Sisk & Son (Dublin) Ltd (HC) 18 May 1972 ....................10.47
Irish People's Assurance Soc v Dublin City Assurance Co [1929] IR 25 ....................34.18
....................34.35, 34.92, 34.131, 39.03
Irish Permanent Building Society v O'Sullivan, [1990] ILRM 598 ....................43.01
Irish Shell and BP Ltd v John Costello Ltd [1981] ILRM 66 ....................23.33
Irish Shell and BP Ltd v John Costello Ltd [1984] IR 511 ....................23.22, 23.33, 45.05
Irish Shipping v Dublin Port & Docks Board (1967) 101 ILTR 182 ....................3.08
Irish Toys & Utilities Ltd v The Irish Times Ltd [1937] IR 298 ....................34.92, 34.98
.................... 35.26-35.26
Irish Transport & General Workers Union v Transport & General Workers Union [1936] IR 471 ....................35.26
Irving & Irving v Post Office [1987] IRLR 289 ....................43.35
Irwin v White Tomkins & Courage Ltd [1964] NI (HL) ....................21.10
Isaack v Clark (1615) 2 Bulst 306, 80 ER 1143 ....................29.02
Isaacs (M) & Sons Ltd v Cook [1925] 2 KB 391 ....................34.158
Island Records Ltd, ex p [1978] Ch 122 ....................21.06
Italiano v Barbero (1993) 114 ALR 21 ....................20.96
Iveagh (Earl) v Martin [1961] I QB 232 ....................23.18
Iverson v Purser (1990) 73 DLR (4th) 33 ....................26.08
Iveson v Moore (1699) 1 Ld Raym 486, 91 ER 1224 ....................44.06

## J

Jackson Soanes v Leisure Corp International Ltd (HC) 18 December 1992 ....................35.23
Jackson v Harrison (1978) 138 CLR 438 ....................20.96
Jackson v Hopperton (1864) 16 CB (ns) 829 143 ER 1352 ....................34.170
Jackson v Horizon Holidays Ltd [1975] 1 WLR 1468 ....................13.33
Jackson v LCC (1912) 28 TLR 359 ....................16.32
Jackson v Millar [1976] 1 SCR 225 ....................9.17
Jackson v Wisconsin Tel Co (1894) 88 Wis 243, 60 NW 430 ....................7.30
Jacob v O'Hara [1956] IR 89 ....................15.24
Jaensch v Coffey (1984) 54 ALR 417 .................... 17.34, 17.54-17.62
Jaffee v Redmond (1996) 518 US 1 .................... 37.56-37.57
Jaggard v Sawyer [1995] 2 All ER 189 ....................23.39
Jameson v Byrne and Maguire (1926) 60 ILTR 11 ....................43.46
Jameson v Dublin Distillers' Co [1900] 1 IR 43 ....................31.05, 31.40, 31.55, 45.05
Janiak v Ippolito [1985] 1 Can SCR 146 ....................20.30
Janvier v Sweeney [1919] 2 KB 316 ....................22.31, 37.10
Jay v Ladler (1888) 40 ChD 649 ....................31.05
JEB Fastners Ltd v Marks Bloom & Co (a firm) [1981] 3 All ER 289 ....................10.71
Jeffers v Cahill (HC) 21 May 1996 ....................44.107

Jennings v M'Carthy (1908) 42 ILTR 217 .......... 23.42
Jennings v Quinn [1968] IR 305 .......... 28.14, 45.05
Jennings v Rundall (1799) 8 TR 335, 101 ER 1419 .......... 40.32
Job Edwards Ltd v Birmingham Navigations [1924] I KB 341 .......... 26.12
Joel v Morison (1834) 6 C & P 501 .......... 43.47
John v Flynn (2000) AC WSJ Lexis 471 .......... 8.06
John v MGN Ltd [1996] 2 All ER 35 .......... 34.231
Johns v Cosgrove Chevron Queensland Ltd [1997] QSC 229 .......... 8.06
Johnson and Johnson (Ireland) Ltd v CP Security Ltd [1985] IR 362 , [1986] ILRM 559 .......... 30.42, 43.43
Johnson v Foster (1967) 202 So 2d 520 .......... 9.21
Johnson v Gresham Hotel Co (HC) 13 November 1986 .......... 18.03, 18.15, 18.81
Johnson v Larkin [1926] IR 40 .......... 4.14
Johnson v Pye (1966) 1 Sid 258, 82 ER 1091 .......... 40.31
Johnston v Dublin Corporation [1961] IR 24 .......... 7.49
Johnston v Meldon (1891) 30 LR Ir 13 .......... 19.58
Johnston v Orr-Ewing (1881) 7 AC 219 .......... 31.05
Johnstone v Bloomsbury Health Authority [1992] 1 QB 333 .......... 18.60
Johnstone v Pedlar [1921] 2 AC 262 .......... 38.14
Jones (Austin W) Co v State (1923) 122 Md 214, 119 A 577 .......... 8.25
Jones Bros (Hunstanton) Ltd v Stevens [1955] 1 QB 275 .......... 32.12
Jones v Boyce (1816) 1 Stark 493, 171 ER 540 .......... 20.18-20.20
Jones v Chappell (1869) LR 20 Eq 529 .......... 24.59
Jones v Dowle (1841) 9 M & W 19 152 ER 9 .......... 29.09
Jones v Fabbi (1973) 37 DLR (3d) 27 .......... 32.11
Jones v Festiniog Ry (1868) LR 3 QB 733 .......... 25.27, 26.25
Jones v GW Ry Co (1930) 47 TLR 39 .......... 9.06
Jones v Gwynn (1712) 10 Mod 214, 88 ER 699 .......... 36.05
Jones v Jones [1916] 2 AC 481 .......... 34.34, 34.42
Jones v Jones [1985] QB 704 .......... 33.02
Jones v Lawrence [1969] 3 All ER 267 .......... 40.26
Jones v Liverpool Health Authority (1995) 30 BMLR 1 .......... 46.50
Jones v Llaurwst UDC (No 2) [1911] 1 Ch 393 .......... 24.71
Jones v McGovern IR 1 CL 100 .......... 35.26
Jones v Northampton Borough Council (CA (CD), 15 May 1990 .......... 39.25
Jones v Pritchard [1908] 1 Ch 630 .......... 24.99
Jones v Read (1876) IR 10 CL 315 .......... 23.02
Jones v Taylor (1983) 27 CCLT 84 .......... 33.04
Joule Ltd v Poole (1924) 24 SR (NSW) 387 .......... 30.06
Joy v Newall (t/a The Copper Room) [2000] NI 91 .......... 8.11
Joyce v Motor Surveys [1948] Ch 252 .......... 35.28
Joyce v Sengupta [1993] 1 All ER 897 .......... 35.26, 35.30
JR, Re [1993] ILRM 657 .......... 42.67
Judge v Reape [1968] IR 226 .......... 20.14, 20.70
Juhlinn-Dannfelt v Crash Repairs Ply Ltd [1969] QWN 1 .......... 29.12

Junior Books Ltd v Veitchi Co Ltd [1983] 1 AC 520 ............................6.17, 6.23, 10.45
............................................ 10.75, 10.153-10.160, 11.75, 11.82-11.89, 13.55, 13.75
JUR Modes v JUR (Waterford) Ltd [1976] IR 198 ..................................................................45.05
Jury v Stoker (1882) 9 LR Ir 385 ........................................................35.03, 35.11, 35.15
Just v The Queen in Right of British Columbia [1989] 2 SCR 1228 ........................19.10

## K

K v K (1980) 114 ILTR 50 ..........................................................................................30.20
Kagan v Dept of Environment NI (HC) 6 October 1978 ..........................................21.20
Kaiser v Suburban Transportation System (1965) 65 Wash 2d 461,
398 p 2d 14 ..........................................................................................................7.15
Kamloops (City of) v Nielson (1984) 2 SCR 2, (1984) 10 DLR (4th) 641 .....19.10, 46.10
Kane v Governor of Mountjoy Prison [1988] ILRM 724 ..........................................22.37
Kane v Howth UDC [1939] Ir Jur 54 ..................................................8.04, 24.113
Kane v Kennedy, Rep of St Mary's Secondary School (HC) 26 March 1999 ............7.28
Kane v Mulvaney (1866) IR 2 CL 402 .......................................................34.142, 34.202
Kaplan v Canada Safeway Ltd (1969) 68 DLR (2d) 627 ..........................................40.10
Kars v Kars (1996) 141 ALR 37 ..........................................................................44.110
Kavanagh v Centreline Ltd [1987] ILRM 306 ..........................................27.21, 27.29
Kavanagh v Cork Corporation DPIJ: Hilary and Easter Terms 1994, p 78 .........7.42, 8.23
Kavanagh v Governor of Arbour Hill Prison (HC) 22 April 1993 .....................7.47, 8.34
Kavanagh v Hamrogue (SC) 12 March 1965 ..............................................7.39, 22.105
Kavanagh v Leader Ltd (SC) 4 March 1955 ..........................................................34.98
Kavanagh v Stokes [1942] IR 596 ................................................ 27.01-27.04, 27.29
Kaye v Robertson [1991] FSR 62 ...............................................35.26, 37.09, 37.15
KC and AC v An Bord Uchtála [1985] ILRM 302 ..................................................33.33
Kealy v Minister for Health (HC) 19 April 1999 ................. 1.171, 1.185, 44.159-44.170
Keane v Boycott (1795) 2 H Bl 511, 126 ER 676 ..................................................32.20
Keane v ESB [1981] IR 44 .................................................6.10, 12.55, 12.100, 18.15
Kearney v Clare Lime Co Ltd [1966] IR 338 ..............................................12.23, 43.32
Kearney v GS Ry Co (1886) 28 LR Ir 303 ............................................................20.20
Kearney v Ireland [1986] IR 116 ..................................34.08, 37.13, 37.20, 37.94, 43.44
Kearney v Lloyd (1890) 26 LR Ir 268 ..................................................32.58, 32.63
Kearney v Minister for Justice [1981] ILRM 266 ..................................................44.25
Kearney v Paul & Vincent Ltd (HC) 30 July 1985 ..............2.11, 2.55, 6.25, 11.11, 11.32
Kearney v The Minister for Justice, Ireland and the Attorney General
[1986] IR 116 ............................................................ 1.13-1.15, 1.39, 1.62, 44.03
Keating & Co Ltd v Jervis Shopping Centre Ltd (HC) 1 March 1996 ...........23.39, 37.06
Keating v Stephen's Green Publications Ltd and Browne, Irish Times,
15 December 1985 ..............................................................................................34.92
Keegan v Ireland (1994) 18 EHRR 342 ..................................................................33.03
Keegan v Owens [1953] IR 267 ...........................................11.15, 18.03, 18.35, 18.95
Keenan Brothers Ltd v Coras Iompair Éireann (1963) 97 ILTR 54 .....28.10, 29.02, 45.05
Keenan v Bergin [1971] IR 192 ........................................................ 18.40-18.50, 18.101
Keenan v McCreedy [1953-1954] Ir Jur 74 ..............................................................7.27

Keenan v Wallace (1916) 51 ILTR 19 .......... 34.147
Kehoe v Collen Construction Ltd DPIJ: Hilary and Easter Terms 1998, p 33 .......... 18.152
Kellagher v Walsh [1988] 2 All ER 648 .......... 44.48
Kellett v Stannard (1851) 2 Ir CLR 156 .......... 22.89, 28.06
Kelliher v Tipperary (North Riding) Board of Health and Public Assistance [1938] IR 43 .......... 9.44, 15.23, 24.17
Kelly v Boland t/a Haughey Boland & Co [1989] ILRM 373 .......... 10.71
Kelly v Crowley [1985] IR 212 .......... 14.209-14.211
Kelly v Dea (1965) 100 ILTR 1 .......... 24.25
Kelly v Donoghue DPIJ: Trinity Term 1991, p 3 .......... 44.90
Kelly v Doyle [1907] 2 IR 355 .......... 35.06
Kelly v Dublin Corporation DPIJ: Michaelmas Term 1991, p 195 .......... 18.108, 44.176
Kelly v Dublin County Council (HC) 21 February 1986 .......... 24.37, 24.93
Kelly v Fujitsu [1996] Ir L Log W 325 .......... 18.114
Kelly v Gilhooley DPIJ: Trinity and Michaelmas Terms 1994, p 86 .......... 16.17, 16.58
Kelly v Gilmore (SC) 28 July 1970 .......... 7.13-7.15, 9.44
Kelly v Gwinnell (1984) 96 NJ 538, 476 A 2d 1219 .......... 8.06
Kelly v Hennessy [1996] 1 ILRM 321, affg [1993] ILRM 530 17.02, 17.35, 17.45-17.51, 17.64- .......... 17.67, 44.176
Kelly v Ireland [1986] ILRM 318 .......... 1.106
Kelly v Jamaur DPIJ: Trinity and Michaelmas Terms 1995, p 139 .......... 18.95
Kelly v Jameson (SC) 1 March 1972 .......... 15.17, 15.27, 20.46, 20.55
Kelly v Kelly DPIJ: Michaelmas Term 1990, p 321 (HC) .......... 44.176
Kelly v Lombard Motor Co Ltd [1974] IR 142 .......... 43.63
Kelly v Mayo County Council [1964] IR 315 .......... 24.18, 24.113
Kelly v McCarron & Co Ltd (SC) 30 May 1968 .......... 18.108, 44.82
Kelly v McDonagh (CC) 15 April 1999 .......... 24.18
Kelly v McElligott (1951) 85 ILTR 4 .......... 2.19, 2.47, 3.05, 20.22, 26.06, 26.33
Kelly v Michael McNamara & Co (HC) 5 June 1996 .......... 21.10, 21.55
Kelly v Midland Gt Western Ry of Ireland Co (1872) IR 7 CL 8 .......... 36.02, 36.07
Kelly v Milliken (1840) Arm McCart & Ogle 56 .......... 23.43
Kelly v St Laurence's Hospital [1989] ILRM 437 .......... 7.04, 7.26, 7.29, 14.02, 37.44
Kelly v Sweeney [1975] 2 NSW LR 720 .......... 27.51
Kelly v Wade (1848) 12 ILR 424 .......... 27.16, 27.23
Kelly v Woolworth & Co [1922] 2 IR 5 .......... 12.08, 13.13
Kelsen v Imperial Tobacco Co Ltd [1957] 2 QB 334 .......... 23.39
Kemp v Burt (1833) 4 B & Ad 424 .......... 14.198
Kenealy v Karaka (1906) 26 NZLR 1118 .......... 16.03
Kennaway v Thompson [1980] 3 WLR 361 .......... 24.104
Kenneally v Waterford County Council (1959) 97 ILTR 97 .......... 18.12
Kennedy and Arnold v Ireland [1987] IR 587, [1988] ILRM 472 .......... 1.09, 1.16
.......... 1.39, 1.51, 1.63, 1.118, 10.26
.......... 37.13, 37.20, 37.60, 37.92
Kennedy v Allied Irish Banks Ltd [1998] 2 IR 48 .......... 10.24

Kennedy v Dublin Corporation DPIJ: Trinity & Michaelmas Terms 1992, p 134 (HC) ....................44.175
Kennedy v East Cork Foods Ltd [1973] IR 244 .................... 21.10, 21.52-21.53, 44.95
Kennedy v Fulflex Manufacturing Ltd DPIJ: Michaelmas Term 1991, p 140 ..........18.10 ....................44.176
Kennedy v Hilliard (1859) 10 ICLR 195 .................... 34.146, 34.151-34.154
Kennedy v Hughes Dairy Ltd [1989] ILRM 117 .................... 3.20, 18.16, 18.147-18.149
Kennedy v Ireland [1987] IR 587, [1988] ILRM 472 .................... 37.37, 37.86, 44.26-44.31
Kennedy v Limerick County Council (SC) 21 December 1959 ....................7.04, 18.81 ....................18.108, 44.69
Kennedy v McCabe 103 ILTR 110 ....................27.42
Kennedy v Midland Oil Co Ltd (1976) 110 ILTR 26 ....................18.150
Kennedy v Taltech Engineering Co (HC) 10 February 1989 ....................18.79, 43.12, 43.33
Kennefick v John A Wood Ltd DPIJ: Hilary and Easter Terms 1994, p 97 ..18.114, 21.30
Kennevan v Limerick Corporation DPIJ: Trinity and Michaelmas Terms 1993, p 277 ....................24.114, 44.180
Kennon and Kennon, Re (1997) 22 Fam LR 1 ....................22.27
Kenny Homes & Co Ltd v Leonard (SC) 18 June 1998 ....................23.33, 45.05
Kenny v Doran DPIJ: Hilary and Easter Terms 1993, p 214 (HC) ....................44.166
Kenny v Dublin United Tramways Co (SC) 5 March 1929 ....................7.04
Kenny v Electricity Supply Board [1932] IR 73 ....................7.44, 12.19, 12.27
Kenny v Irish Shipping Ltd (SC) 4 November 1968 ....................12.08, 18.81, 18.108
Kenny v Kelly (HC) 27 July 1988 ....................10.146
Kenny v O'Rourke [1972] IR 339 ....................2.11, 21.10, 21.22
Kent Adhesive Products Co v Ryan (HC) 5 November 1993 .................... 35.26-35.26, 45.05
Kent v Griffiths (No 3) [2000] All ER 474 , [2000] 2 WLR 1158....................26.24 6.91, 8.04
Keogh v Incorporated Dental Hospital of Ireland [1910] 2 IR 577 ......34.14, 34.61, 34.92
Keogh v Irish Forestry Board Ltd, DPIJ: Trinity Term 1991, p 18 ....................18.108
Keppel Bus Co Ltd v Ahmad [1974] 2 All ER 700 ....................43.39
Kerin v Bord na Mona (HC) 30 January 1970 ....................23.29
Kerin v Kavanagh (t/a Kavanagh Contrat Cleaners) DPIJ: Hilary and Easter Terms 1993, p 80 ....................18.84
Kerr v Belfast & Co Down Ry Co (1897) 31 ILT & Sol J 256 ....................8.14
Kerr v Kennedy [1942] 1 KB 409 ....................34.33
Kerr v Mitchell [1959] NI 21 ....................21.10
Kerr v Revelstoke Building Materials Ltd (1976) 71 DLR (3d) 134 ....................23.32
Kerr v Ulster Fireclay Works Ltd [1964] Ir Jur Rep 23 .................... 44.60-44.64
Kerry v Carter [1969] 3 All ER 723 ....................18.09
Kerwick v Minister for Defence (HC) 19 March 1999 ....................46.31
Kettle (Thomas M), Re (1906) 40 ILTR 234 ....................45.34
Keys v Belfast & Ballymena Ry Co (1858) 8 ICLR 167 ....................30.04
Khorasandjian v Bush [1993] QB 727 ....................22.32, 24.73, 37.02
Kidney v Castlemore Quarries Ltd (SC) 13 April 1973 ....................44.183
Kielthy v Ascon Ltd [1970] IR 122 ....................2.56, 18.83, 21.22, 21.42
Kiely v Carrig DPIJ: Trinity & Michaelmas Terms 1996, p 209 ....................44.90, 44.128

Kiely v McCrea & Sons Ltd [1940] Ir Jur Rep 1 .......... 43.25
Kiernan v Moneley DPIJ: Hilary and Easter Terms 1991, p 180 .......... 18.95, 18.150
Kildare County Council v Hamwood Estates Ltd (HC) 13 January 1956 .......... 24.14
Kilgarriff v Kilgarriff DPIJ: Trinity Term 1991, p 37 (HC) .......... 44.180
Kimber v Press Association [1893] 1 QB 65 .......... 34.142
Kinahan v McCullagh (1877) Ir R 11 CL 1 .......... 34.38
Kinehan v McNamara & Co (HC) 1 March 1985 .......... 13.81
King (Deeny) v Justices of County Tyrone [1909] 2 IR 400 .......... 1.105
King v Attorney General [1981] IR 233 .......... 24.03
King v Liverpool City Council [1986] 3 All ER 544 .......... 8.24
King v Phillips [1953] 1 QB 429 .......... 3.19, 17.08, 17.22
King v Walsh [1932] IR 178 .......... 29.02-29.04
King's Prerogative in Saltpetre (1606) 12 Co Rep 12, 77 ER 1294 .......... 23.51
Kingston v Kingston (1968) 102 ILTR 65 .......... 2.19, 2.47, 7.13
.......... 7.23, 20.47, 26.33, 40.04, 40.17, 40.27
Kingstown Township Commissioners v Blackrock Township Commissioners
(1876) IR 10 Eq 160 .......... 24.93-24.98, 45.05
Kinsella v Hamilton (1890) 26 LR Ir 671 .......... 43.37-43.41
Kinsella v Hammond Lane Industries Ltd (1962) 96 ILTR 1 .......... 3.05, 18.12
.......... 18.82, 18.104
Kinsella v Jefferson Smurfit & Sons Ltd (SC) 16 March 1962 .......... 18.06, 18.12
Kinsella v MIBI (SC) 2 April 1993 .......... 1.148
Kinsella v Roofing Contractors Ltd (SC) 8 February 1966 .......... 44.58
Kirby v Burke [1944] IR 207 .......... 7.03, 7.27, 9.18
.......... 11.11, 11.24
Kirby v Leather [1965] 2 QB 367 .......... 46.67
Kirby v South Eastern Health Board DPIJ: Trinity & Michaelmas Terms 1993, p 234
.......... 18.115, 44.90
Kirk v Gregory (1876) 1 Ex D 55 .......... 28.04-28.07
Kirkham v Chief Constable of Greater Manchester [1990] 2 QB 283 .......... 20.94
Kirkwood Hackett v Tierney [1952] IR 185 .......... 34.61, 34.169-34.171
.......... 34.194, 34.199
Kirwan v Bray UDC (SC) unrep,30 July 1969 .......... 7.44
Kirwan v Mackey (HC) 18 January 1995 .......... 39.15
Kirwan v National Children's Hospital (SC) 10 May 1963 .......... 18.81-18.82
Kirwin v Representative Church Body [1959] IR 215 .......... 12.13
Kitchen v RAF Association [1958] 1 WLR 563 .......... 46.82
Kleynhans v Zucker (1997) Ont CJ LEXIS 1946 .......... 22.33
Kline v Kline (1902) 64 NE 9 .......... 22.21
Kline v 1500 Massachusetts Avenue Apartment Corporation
(1970) 439 F 2d 477 .......... 8.25
Klissers Farmhouse Bakeries Ltd v Harvest Bakeries Ltd [1988] 1 NZLR 16 .......... 31.35
Knott v London Co Co [1934] 1 KB 126 .......... 27.25
Knott v Royal Exchange Assurance Company [1955] SASR 33 .......... 9.21
Knupfer v London Express Ltd [1944] AC 116 .......... 34.108

Kondis v State Transport Authority (1984) 154 CLR 672 .......................................25.49
Kooragang Invests Ply Ltd v Richardson and Wrench [1981] 3 WLR 493 ..............43.32
Krauth v Geller (1960) 31 NJ 270, 157 A 2d 129 .................................................26.35
Kreglinger and Fernau Ltd v Irish National Insurance Co Ltd [1956] IR 116 ..........35.15
Krouse v Chrysler Canada Ltd (1973) 40 DLR (3d) 15 ..........................................31.76
Krupp v Bell (1968) 67 DLR (2d) 256 .................................................................32.20
Kubach v Hollands [1937] 3 All ER 907 ..............................................................11.16
Kuddus v Chief Constable of Leicestershire [2000] 2 All ER ................................44.12
Kuhn v Banker (1938) 133 Ohio St 304, 13 NE 2d 242 ...........................................2.21
Kulyk v Board of Education for the City of Toronto (1996) 139 DLR (4th) 114 ......22.32

L

L (An Infant), Re [1968] P 119 ..........................................................................22.77
L v L [1989] ILRM 528 (HC) revd by [1992] ILRM 115, [1992] IR 77
..........................................................................................24.60, 24.71, 42.65
La Societe Anonyme de Remorquage a Helice v Bennetts [1911] 1 KB 243 .10.07, 10.46
LAC Minerals Ltd v International Corona Resources Ltd
(1989) 61 DLR (4th) 14 ..................................................................................37.38
Lacey v JD Printing Ltd (CC) 29 February 2000 ....................................................20.52
Lacroix v The Queen [1954] 4 DLR 470 ................................................................23.39
Lagan Navigation Co v Lambeg, Bleaching Dyeing and Finishing Co
[1927] AC 226 ..................................................................................................1.120
Lakatosh v Ross (1974) 48 DLR (3d) 694 ..............................................................43.39
Lake v Bushly [1869] 2 All ER 964 ....................................................................14.177
Lamb v Camden LBC [1981] QB 625 ..........................................................2.42, 2.50
Lamb v Cotongo (1987) 164 Comm LR 1 ...........................................................44.13
Lambert v Lastoplex Chemicals Ltd (1971) 25 DLR (3d) 121, [1972] SCR 569 .....11.60
Lambton v Mellish [1894] 3 Ch 163 ...................................................................24.110
Lamey v Wentworth Valley Developments Ltd (1998) 165 DLR (4th) 758 .............41.07
Lancaster v LPTB [1948] 2 All ER 796 ................................................................43.69
Landers v AC (1973) 109 ILTR 1 ..........................................................................1.13
Landon v Rutherford [1951] NZLR 975 ................................................................26.12
Lane v Biel [1971] 2 WWR 128 ..........................................................................27.51
Lange v Atkinson and Australian Consolidated Press NZ Ltd
[1998] 3 NZLR 424 ........................................................................................34.181
Langham v Wellingborough School (1932) 101 LJKB 513 .....................................16.57
Langridge v Levy (1837) 2 M & W 519, 150 ER 863 .........................11.07, 35.14, 35.20
LaPlabove v LaPlabove (1995) 125 DLR (4th 569) ...............................................16.07
Larin v Goshen (1974) 56 DLR (3d) 719 ..............................................................43.40
Larkin v Belfast Harbour Commissioners [1908] 2 IR 214 .........................23.20, 32.166
Larkin v Porter (1828) 1 Hud & BR 524..............................................................23.42
Larmour v Belfast Corporation [1945] NI 163 ......................................................18.108
Latham v Hibernian Insurance Co Ltd (HC) 4 December 1991 ...............................3.37
Latham v Johnson [1913] 1 KB 398 ....................................................................12.30
Latimer v AEC Ltd [1953] AC 643 ..............................................................7.39, 18.82

Latter v Braddell (1881) 50 LJQB 488 ........................................ 22.67
Laughan v Wellingborough School (1932) 101 LJ KB 513 ........................................ 43.68
Laurie v Ragland Building Co Ltd [1942] 1 KB 152 ........................................ 9.21
Lavelle v Brennan [1946] Ir Jur Rep 37 ........................................ 21.10, 21.20-21.22
Lavender v Diamints Ltd [1949] 1 KB 585 ........................................ 20.52
Lawler v McKenna (1905) 39 ILTR 159 ........................................ 24.18
Lawler v Sir James Mackey Ltd (1949) 83 ILTR 139 ........................................ 25.40
Lawless Dublin Port and Docks Board [1998] 1 ILRM 514 ........................................ 46.88
Lawless v Minister for Defence DPIJ: Trinity and Michaelmas Terms 1992, p 260 18.132
Lawlor v O'Connor (1929) 63 ILTR 103 ........................................ 43.36
Lawrence v Biddle [1966] I QB 504 ........................................ 33.07
Lawrence v City of New York (1981) 2 App Div 2d 485, 447 NY S 2d 506 (2d Dep't) ........................................ 18.02
Laws v Florinplace Ltd [1981] 1 All ER 659 ........................................ 24.43
Laws v Wright 2000 ACWSJ Lexis 821 (Alta QB 2000) ........................................ 27.18, 27.26
Lawson v Laferrière (1991) 78 DLR (4th) 609 ........................................ 2.22
Lawson v Wellesley Hospital (1975) 61 DLR (3d) 445, affd (1982) 76 DLR (3d) 688 ........................................ 40.41-40.43
Lawton v BOC Transhield Ltd [1987] 2 All ER 608 ........................................ 10.72
Lay v Midland Ry Co (1875) 34 LT 30 ........................................ 40.26
Lazarus v Eastern Air Lines (1961) 292 F 2d 748 ........................................ 9.25
Le Bagge v Buses Ltd. [1958] NZLR 630 ........................................ 42.17
Le Fanu v Malcolmson (1848) 1 HL Cas 637, 9 ER 910 ........................................ 34.107
Le Lievre v Gould [1893] 1 QB 491 ........................................ 6.01
League Against Cruel Sports Ltd v Scott [1986] QB 240 ........................................ 23.29-23.29
Leahy v Leader and Cork Diocesan Trustees (HC) 13 October 1999 .. 12.13, 27.34, 27.39
Leahy v Malcomson (1851) 1 Ir CLR 432 ........................................ 29.05
Leakey v National Trust [1980] 2 WLR 65 ........................................ 24.79
Leame v Bray (1803) 3 East 593, 102 ER 724 ........................................ 22.15, 23.31
Leathem v Isaac Black Ltd (1945) 80 ILTR 12 ........................................ 18.08, 18.102, 18.108
Lederev v Connecticut Co (1920) 111 Atl 785 ........................................ 20.19
Lee Cooper Ltd v CH Jenkins & Sons Ltd [1967] 2 QB 1 ........................................ 30.07
Lee v Joyce (SC) 3 December 1964 ........................................ 44.58, 44.63, 44.72, 44.145, 44.180
Leech v Reilly (HC) 26 April 1983 ........................................ 23.29, 24.31-24.31
Leech v Stokes [1937] IR 787 ........................................ 10.50
Lefroy v Burnside (No 2) (1879) 4 LR Ir 556 ........................................ 34.206
Lehane v An Comhairle Oilúna DPIJ: Hilary and Easter Terms 1992, p 12 ........................................ 21.55
Leibo v Buckman Ltd [1952] 2 All ER 1057 ........................................ 36.06
Leigh and Sullivan Ltd v Aliakmon Shipping Co Ltd [1986] AC 785 .... 6.18, 6.26, 11.85
Leigh v Gladstone (1909) 26 Times LR 139 ........................................ 22.92
Leigh v Webb (1800) Esp 165, 170 ER 574 ........................................ 36.04
Leitch & Co Ltd v Leydon [1931] AC 90 ........................................ 28.07
Lelarge v Blakney (1978) 21 NBR (2d) 100 rvsd 92 DLR (3d) 440 ........................................ 16.07
Lem v Barotto Sports Ltd (1976) 69 DLR (3d) 276 ........................................ 11.60
Lemmon v Webb [1894] 3 Ch 1, [1895] AC 1 ........................................ 1.120, 24.28, 24.99

Lemon v Simmons (1888) 57 LJ QB 260 ....................34.38
Lennard's Carrying Co v Asiatic Petroleum Co [1915] AC 705 ....................39.07
Lennon v Ganly [1981] ILRM 84 ....................22.38
Lennon v McCarthy (SC) 13 July 1966 ....................16.16, 16.26, 16.38, 16.72
Lennox-Cunningham v Louth County Council (1957) 92 ILTR 62 ....................23.29
Lertorn v Finzi [1973] RTR 161 ....................20.41
Letang v Cooper [1965] 1 QB 232 .................... 22.03-22.03
Lethbridge v Phillips (1819) 2 Stark 544, 171 ER 731. ....................30.03
Levine v Morris [1970] 1 All ER 144 ....................24.117
Leward v Basely (1695) I Ld Raym 62, 91 ER 937 ....................22.90
Lewis v City of Miami (1937) 127 Fla 426, 173 So 150 ....................21.24
Lewis v Daily Telegraph Ltd [1964] AC 234 ....................34.62
Lewis v Irish Forestry Board, DPIJ: Trinity and Michaelmas Terms 1993, p 12 ......18.82
Lewis v Olming (1983) 24 CCLT 81 ....................27.15
Lewvest Ltd v Scotia Towers Ltd (1981) 126 DLR (3d) 239 ....................23.39
Leyden v Malone (SC) 13 May 1968 .................... 3.42, 35.03, 35.15, 35.20-35.21
Liebig's Extract of Meat Co v Hanbury (1867) 17 LT 298 ....................31.29
Liesbosch Dredger v Edison SS [1933] AC 448 .................... 3.37-3.40
Lillibridge v McCann (1988) 117 Mich 84, 75 NW 288 ....................7.08
Lincoln v Daniels [l962] 1 QB 237 ....................34.155
Lind v Tipperary (North Riding) Council (HC) 9 November 1998 ....................24.84
Lindal v Lindal 129 DLR (3d) 263 ....................44.158
Lindsay v Mid-Western Health Board [1993] 2 IR 147 .................... 9.28, 9.42-9.45
....................9.53, 11.129, 43.22, 44.193
Lindsey v Maher, High Court The Irish Times, 4 February 1984 ....................34.175
Line v Taylor (1982) 3 F & F 731, 176 ER 335 ....................27.17
Linehan v Hartnett (1897) 31 ILT & Sol J 429 ....................23.42
Lingens v Austria (1986) 8 EHRR 407 ....................34.211
Lipari v Sears, Roebuck & Co (1980) 497 F Supp 185 ....................37.44
Lippiatt v South Gloucester County Council (CA) 31 March 1999 .....24.75, 24.83, 25.17
Lipschitz v Caulfields Ltd (SC) 20 December 1960 ....................15.04, 40.11
Lister v Perryman (1870) LR 4 HL 52 ....................36.07
Lister v Romford Ice and Cold Storage Co Ltd [1957] AC 555 ....................43.01
Liston v Munster & Leinster Bank [1940] IR 77 ....................14.169, 30.19
Little v Clements (1851) 1 Ir CLR 194 ....................34.199
Little v Cooper (No 1) [1937] IR 1 ....................45.05
Little v Cooper (No 2) [1937] IR 510 ....................45.05
Little v Pomeroy (1873) IR 7 CL 50 ....................34.170
Littleton v M'Namara (1875) IR 9 CL 417 .................... 23.42-23.45
Liverpool Corporation v Coghill (H) & Son Ltd [1918] 1 Ch 307 ....................24.98
Livingstone v Ministry of Defence [1984] NI 356 ....................22.07
Lloyd Corp v Tanner (1972) 407 US 551 ....................23.20
Lloyd v Grace, Smith & Co [1912] AC 716 ....................43.42
Lloyd v Osborne (1899) 20 LR (NSW) 190 ....................29.03
Local Ireland v Local Ireland-Online Ltd (HC) 2 October 2000 ....................31.64

Logan v O'Donnell [1925] 12 IR 211 .......... 20.06
London & NW Ry Co v Hughes (1889) 26 LR Ir 165 .......... 28.13, 29.05, 30.03, 30.19
London Artists v Littler [1969] 2 QB 375 .......... 34.204
London Associates for Protection of Trade v Greenlands Ltd [1916] 2 AC 15 .......... 34.175
London Borough of Southwark v Williams [1971] Ch 734 .......... 23.50
London Corporation v Appleyard [1963] 1 WLR 982 .......... 30.24
London Drugs v Kuehne & Nagle International (1992) 97 DLR (4th) 261 .......... 12.135
London Ferro-Concrete Co v Justicz (1951) 68 RPC 261 .......... 35.28
London Graving Dock v Horton [1951] AC 737 .......... 12.129
London Passenger Transport Board v Upson [1949] AC 155 .......... 15.42
Long v Dublin Corporation and ESB (CC) 13 January 1989 .......... 2.26, 2.29
Long v Gardner (1983) 144 DLR (3d) 73 .......... 16.19, 16.57
Long v O'Brien & Cronin Ltd (SC) 24 March 1972 .......... 44.82, 44.88, 44.95-44.97
Long v Saorstát & Continental Steamship Co Ltd (1959) 93 ILTR 137 .......... 12.08, 12.129
.......... 18.92, 21.34-21.35
Longdon-Griffiths v Smith [1951] 1 KB 295 .......... 39.10
Longenecker v Zimmerman (1954) 175 Kan 719, 167 P 2d 543 .......... 23.33
Longmeid v Holliday (1851) 6 Ex 761 155 ER 752 .......... 11.07
Longton v Winwick Asylum Board (1911) 75 JP 348 .......... 24.99
Lonrho Ltd v Shell Petroleum Co Ltd (No 2) [1982] AC 173 .......... 21.06, 32.58
.......... 32.74-32.79
Lonrho plc v Fayed [1992] 1 AC 448 .......... 32.58, 32.79
Loo v Harbord Administration Pty Ltd (1994) NSW LEXIS 13463, BC 9403236 .......... 41.07
Looney v Bank of Ireland (SC) 9 May 1997 .......... 36.29
Looney v Governor and Company of Bank of Ireland and Morly [1996] 1 IR 157 34.154
Lopes v Walker (SC) 28 July 1997 .......... 14.181
Lord Congregational Union Inc v Harriss & Harriss (a firm) [1988] 1 All ER 15 .......... 10.160
Loudon v Ryder (No 2) [1953] Ch 423, [1953] 2 QB 202 .......... 35.28, 37.04, 44.09
Lough v Ward [1945] 2 All ER 338 .......... 33.29-33.34
Louis v Commonwealth (1986) 87 FLR 277 .......... 22.38
Lovelace v Fossum [1972] 2 WWR 161 .......... 6.65
Lovett v Gogan [1995] 3 IR 132, [1995] 1 ILRM 12 .......... 1.39-1.46, 21.07
Lowdens v Keaveney [1903] 2 IR 82 .......... 24.18
Lowe v Collum (1877) 2 LR Ir 15 .......... 36.04
Lowery v Buchanan [1982] NI 243 .......... 12.43
Lowery v Walker [1910] 1 KB 173, [1911] AC 10 .......... 12.19
Lowns v Woods (1996) ATR 81-376 .......... 8.01, 14.40
Lucas v South Carolina Coastal Council (1992) 505 US 1003 .......... 24.01
Lumley v Gye (1853) 2 E & B 216, 118 ER 749 .......... 32.14, 32.29
Lunham v Wakefield (1863) 16 ICLR 507 .......... 36.17
Luttrell v Gouldings Fertilisers (Cork) Ltd (1969) 103 ILTR 121 .......... 18.09
Lyle-Samuel v Odhams Ltd [1920] 1 KB 135 .......... 34.203
Lynam v Gowing (1880) 6 LR Ir 259 .......... 34.143, 34.178, 34.191
Lynch v Beale (HC) 25 November 1974 .......... 3.31
Lynch v Dawson [1946] IR 504 .......... 7.28, 24.31

Lynch v Dublin Corporation DPIJ: Hilary and Easter Terms 1991, p 228 ............18.112
Lynch v Fitzgerald [1938] IR 382 ............22.91
Lynch v Hetherton [1990] ILRM 857 ............24.30, 24.85-24.87
Lynch v Knight (1861) 9 HLC 577, 11 ER 854 ............17.01, 34.42
Lynch v Lynch and Alliance v Dublin Consumers Gas Co (HC) 24 November 1976 ............4.19
Lynch v Nurdin (1841) 1 QB 29 ............16.03, 40.26
Lynch v O'Connor (HC) 28 June 1996 ............14.30
Lynch v Palgrave Murphy Ltd [1964] IR 150 ............43.10
Lynch v Rosenthal 396 SW 2d 272 ............7.24
Lynskey v Governors and Guardians of the Charitable Infirmary of Jervis Street ....14.68
Lynskey v Jervis Street Hospital (HC) 23 April 1993 ............14.30
Lynskey v Minister for Finance (SC) 8 July 1963 ............15.17
Lyon v Daily Telegraph [1963] KB 746 ............34.202

## M

M v Drury [1994] 2 IR 8 ............37.92
M v H (1991) 83 DLR (4th) 609 ............16.07
M v Ryan (1997) 143 DLR (4th) 1 ............37.57
M(K) v M(H) (1992) 96 DLR (4th) 289 ............46.99
M'Adorney v Huston (1905) 39 ILTR 148 ............44.58
M'Cormick v Ballantine (1859) 10 ICLR 305 ............28.04, 28.11
M'Cullough v Munn [1908] 2 IR 194 ............34.57
M'Daid v Milford RDC [1919] 2 IR 1 ............21.10
M'Donnell v Turf Development Board 78 ILTR 94 ............25.12
M'Greene v Hibernian Taxi Co (No 2) [1931] IR 319 ............44.66
M'Keever v M'Kain (1846) Bl Dundas & Osb 80 ............30.02
M'Kenna v Stephens and Alexander E Hull & Co Ltd [1923] 2 IR 112 ............15.32
............ 21.10-21.10, 21.25
M'Kenzie v M'Leod (1834) 10 Bing 385, 131 ER 953 ............26.08
M'Keon v Bolton (1851) 1 ICLR 377 ............ 43.49-43.50
M'Kibbin v Glasgow Corporation 1920 SC 590 ............7.13
M'Kinney v Irish NW Ry Co (1866) 11 Ir Jur (ns) 228 (QB)............18.06
M'Kinney v Irish NW Ry Co (1868) IR 2 CL 600 (Exch)............18.97
M'Lachlin v London & NW Ry Co (1907) 41 ILTR 139 ............9.23
M'Loughlin v Doey (1893) 32 LR Ir 518 ............22.15, 34.10, 34.146, 34.152
M'Manus v M'Enroe (1851) 1 ICLR 332 ............34.91
M'Morrin v Dixon (1897) 31 Ir LT & Sol J 3 ............29.05
M'Wade v Goodlake The Times, 23 June 1881 ............34.142
MacArthur v Meuser (1997) 35 CCLT (2d) 197 ............34.197
Macaulay & Co v Wyse-Power ............34.147
Macauley v Minister for Posts & Telegraphs [1966] IR 345 ............1.13, 38.03, 46.77
MacCharles v Trask (1984) 62 NSR (2d) 259 ............15.25
Macdonald v Sebastian (1987) 43 DLR (4th) 636 ............22.65
MacEnroe v Allied Irish Banks Ltd [1980] ILRM 171 ............29.02

Macintosh v Dunn [1908] AC 390 .................... 34.175
Macintyre v Coles [1966] 1 All ER 723n .................... 15.42
Macken v Munster & Leinster Bank Ltd (1959) 95 ILTR 17 .................... 10.58-10.62
Mackey v Scottish Widows Fund Life Assurance Society (1877) Ir 11 Eq 541 .................... 24.106, 45.08, 45.50
Mackie v Dumbartonshire County Council [1927] WN 247 .................... 24.29
MacKnight v Xtravision (CC) 5 July 1991 .................... 1.120, 12.140, 20.13, 22.116
MacLachlan & Mitchell Homes Ltd v Frunk's Rentals & Sales Ltd (1979) 10 CCLT 306 .................... 11.73
Maclenan v Segar [1917] 2 KB 325 .................... 20.22
Macnaghten v Baird [1903] 2 IR 731 .................... 23.33
MacNaughton v Murphy [1961] Ir Jur Rep 41 .................... 44.05, 44.144
MacSharry v McCormack and Ocline Associates Ltd Irish Times, 1 May 1985 .................... 34.59
Madden v Irish Turf Club [1997] 2 ILRM 148 .................... 1.111, 6.28-6.31, 6.48 .................... 10.09, 10.41, 10.46
Madigan v Attorney General [1986] ILRM 136 .................... 37.66
Magee v D'Arcy (1879) 4 LR Ir 312 .................... 30.04, 30.19, 45.05, 45.45
Magee v Storey [1929] NI 134 .................... 22.19
Magrath v Finn (1877) IR 11 CL 152 .................... 34.175
Maguire v Drury [1995] 1 ILRM 108 .................... 37.13
Maguire v Gaelic Athletic Association DPIJ: Trinity and Michaelmas Terms 1993 .................... 7.47
Maguire v Lagan (Contractors) Ltd [1976] NI 49 .................... 18.35, 43.11
Maher v Beirne (1959) 93 ILTR 101 .................... 45.06
Maher v Collins [1975] IR 232 .................... 1.118, 37.63, 44.18
Maher v GN Ry Co (Ir) and Warren [1942] IR 206 .................... 43.64
Mahon v Burke and Mid-Western Health Board [1991] ILRM 59, [1991] 2 IR 495 .................... 41.12, 42.14
Mahon v Celbridge Spinning Co Ltd [1967] IR I .................... 20.14
Mahon v Dublin & Lucan Electric Railway Co (1905) 39 ILTR 126 .................... 9.04
Mahon v Osborne [1939] 2 KB 14 .................... 9.28
Mahon v Trustees of the Irish Rugby Football Union [1998] 1 ILRM 284 .................... 24.10
Mahoney v Neenan (No 2) (1966) 100 ILTR 205, [1966] IR 559 .................... 23.33, 45.05
Mahony v Ford [1962] IR 146 .................... 3.05
Mahony v Lynch (1876) 10 ILT & SJ 91 .................... 22.38
Maitland v Swan (HC) 6 April 1992 .................... 9.28, 14.30, 46.31
Malcolm v Dickson [1951] SC 542 .................... 26.35
Malfroot v Noxal Ltd (1935) 51 TLR 551 .................... 11.14
Malhotra v Choudhury [1980] Ch 52 .................... 29.10
Malik v Bank of Credit and Commerce International SA [1998] AC 20 .................... 43.16
Mallett v Dunn [1949] 2 KB 180 .................... 33.16
Mallett v McMonagle [1969] NI 91 .................... 42.38
Mallon v GS & W Ry Co (1893) 27 ILTR 125 .................... 27.04
Malone v CIE (SC) 24 June 1953 .................... 15.27

Malone v Clogrennane Lime & Trading Co Ltd (HC) 14 April 1978 ........................24.31
Malone v Commissioner of Police of the Metropolis (No 2) [1979] 2 All ER 620, [1979] Ch 344 ........................37.34, 37.35, 37.38
Malone v Laskey [1907] 2 KB 144 ........................24.59
Malone v McQuaid and Registrar of Titles (HC) 28 May 1998 ........................35.28
Malone v United Kingdom (1984) 7 EHRR 4 ........................37.02
Maloney v French (1869) IR 3 CL 391 ........................22.38
Malynn v Farrell (1956) 90 ILTR 137 ........................12.37, 42.30
Malyon v Plummer [1964] 1 QB 330 ........................42.18
Malz v Rosen [1966] 1 WLR 1008 ........................36.04
Mandeville v PJ Carroll & Co Ltd DPIJ: Hilary and Easter Terms 1993, p 198 9.17, 18.95
Mangan v Atterson (1866) LR 1 Ex 239 ........................40.26
Mangan v Finglas Housing Society (1952) 86 ILTR 159 ........................12.13, 12.26
Mangan v McCarthy (1965) 99 ILTR 91 ........................45.05
Mangena v Wright [1909] 2 KB 958 ........................34.207
Mann v Saulnier (1959) 19 DLR (2d) 130 ........................23.30
Mansel v Webb (1918) 88 LJ KB 323 ........................25.19
Manton v Brocklebank (1923) 2 KB 212 ........................27.07, 27.18
Mantruck Services Ltd v Ballinlough Electrical Refrigeration Co Ltd [1992] 1 IR 351 ........................45.05
Manwanng v Billington [1952] 2 All ER 774 ........................21.49
Mapp v Gilhooley (HC) 7 November 1989 ........................16.35
Marc Rich & Co AG v British Rock Marine Co Ltd [1996] AC 211 ........................6.24
March v Stramere (E & MH) Pty (1991) 171 CLR 506 ........................2.22
Marchetti v Cantrell & Cochrane DPIJ: Hilary and Easter Terms 1991, p 112 ........................18.108, 18.152
Mare v AG for Saorstát Éireann [1930] IR 471 ........................39.10
Marinovski v Zutti [1984] 2 NSWLR 571 ........................32.09
Maritime Processing Co Ltd v Hogg (1978) 32 NSR 2d 45 ........................15.25
Markan v Galway Corporation DPIJ: Trinity and Michaelmas Terms 1995, p 57 ..18.108
Marlor v Ball (1900) 16 TLR 239 ........................27.16, 27.23
Marrinan v Vibart [1963] 1 QB 528 ........................36.29
Marris v TV3 Network Ltd, NZ (HC) 14 October 1991 ........................37.02
Marron v Cootehill (No 2) RDC [1915] 1 IR 216 ........................21.25
Marshall v Curry [1933] 3 DLR 260 ........................22.73
Marshall v Lindsey County Council [1935] 1 KB 516 ........................14.21
Martin v Dublin United Tramways Co Ltd [1909] 2 IR 13 ........................3.05, 7.09
Martin v Ford [1965] IR 42 ........................20.14
Martin v Irish Industrial Benefit Building Society [1960] Ir Jur Rep 42 ........10.50, 13.81
Martin v Miller & Co Ltd (SC) 12 May 1972 ........................2.11, 7.09, 21.10, 21.25, 21.55
Martin v Moy Contractors (SC) 9 February 1999 ........................46.65
Marx v AG [1974] 1 NZLR 164 ........................6.58, 33.02
Mason v Hill (1833) 5 B & Ad 1, 110 ER 692 ........................24.53
Masons v Levy Auto Parts of England Ltd [1967] 2 QB 530 ........................26.20

Masser (AH) Ltd v 12 Un-Named Members of AGEMOU (HC) 23 October 1979 .......... 32.162
Matheson v Dalhousie College (1983) 25 CCLT 91 .......... 22.60
Matheson v Northcote College [1975] 2 NZLR 106 .......... 25.17
Matrimonial Home Bill 1993, Re [1994] IR 305 .......... 24.71, 37.76
Matthews v Matthews [1996] Ir L Log W 168 .......... 7.28, 15.18
Matthews v The Irish Society for Autism (HC) 18 April 1997 .......... 18.119, 21.22
Maude v Murphy [1934] IR 394 .......... 24.25
Mawe v Piggott (1869) IR 4 CL 54 .......... 34.66, 34.70
Mawji v R [1957] AC 126 .......... 32.61
Maxwell v Gavin Low Ltd (SC) 11 January 1967 .......... 34.92, 34.175, 34.199
Maxwell v Gorman Cork Examiner, 12 December 1981 .......... 34.92
Maxwell v McNally [1997] Ir L Log W 13 .......... 15.32
May Ngai Gloves Factory Ltd v Nam Kam Lan [1980] HKC 175, (1980) HKC LEXIS 214 .......... 40.26
May v Burdett (1846) 9 QB 101 .......... 27.15
May v Roberts (1881) 46 Mich 160 9 NW 146 .......... 21.33
Maycock v Legg Bros Ltd (SC) 10 March 197 .......... 44.60
Maynard v West Midlands - RHA The Times, 9 May 198 .......... 14.26
Mayor v Dawsitt (1965) 240 Or 196, 400 P 2d 234 .......... 9.28
Mays v Essex County Council The Times, 4 October 1975 .......... 16.48
McAllister v Dunnes Stores Ltd High Court, 5 February 1987 .......... 22.38
McAnarney v Hanrahan [1994] 1 ILRM 210 .......... 10.09, 10.137
McArdle v McCaughey Bros Ltd [1968] IR 47 .......... 44.64, 44.74, 44.204
McArthur v R [1943] 3 DLR 225 .......... 32.05
McAuliffe v Minister for Social Welfare [1995] 1 ILRM 189 .......... 43.19
McAuliffe v Moloney [1971] IR 200 .......... 6.10, 24.77
McAuliffe v Tralee UDC DPIJ: Trinity and Michaelmas Terms 1992, p 108 .......... 19.19
McC v Town of Monaghan Co-op [1997] Ir L Log W 52 .......... 18.97
McC, Re [1985] AC 258 .......... 34.156
McCabe v Delaney [1951] Ir Jur Rep 10 .......... 3.05, 27.42-27.47
McCabe v Dolan Cosgrove & Co (HC) 14 October 1991 .......... 10.73
McCabe v Foot (1866) 11 Ir Jur (ns) 287 .......... 34.38
McCabe v Joynt [1901] 2 IR 115 .......... 34.146, 34.152
McCaffrey v Lundy (1988) ILT (ns) 245 .......... 9.26, 27.57
McCahill v New York Transportation Co (1911) 201 NY 221, 94 NE 616 .......... 2.19
McCailum v G Madill & Sons Ltd [1965] NI 187 .......... 44.209
McCallion v Dodd [1966] NZLR 710 .......... 16.09
McCann v Brinks Allied Ltd and Ulster Bank Ltd [1997] 1 ILRM 461 .......... 1.111, 6.06 .......... 6.42, 7.52, 18.84, 18.139
McCann v Edinburgh Roperie & Sailcloth Co (1889) 28 LR Ir 24 .......... 34.14, 34.91
McCann v ESB [1997] Ir L Log W 178 .......... 18.10
McCann v Mannion (1932) 66 ILTR 161 .......... 22.11, 22.23, 22.102
McCarrigle v White (1940) 74 ILTR 228 .......... 23.29
McCarry v Graham [1958] Ir Jur 9 .......... 24.18

McCartan v Belfast Harbour Commissioners [1911] 2 IR 143 .................................43.11
McCarthy v Department of Social & Health Science (1988) 759 P 2d 351 ............18.125
McCarthy v ESB DPIJ: Hilary & Easter Terms 1997, p 26 ....................................44.176
McCarthy v Garda Commission (SC) 27 Febraury 1998 ............................... 18.49-18.55
McCarthy v Maguire [1899] 2 IR 802 ....................... 34.50-34.54, 34.175, 34.199, 44.58
McCarthy v McEvoy, t/a Victoria Cross Saw Mills, (SC) 6 February 1961 ...........18.108
McCarthy v Morrissey [1939] Ir Jur Rep 82 ............................... 34.170, 34.175-34.178
McCarthy v Murphy (HC) 10 February 1998 ..........................................................3.36
McCarthy v Skibbereen UDC DPIJ: Hilary and Easter Terms 1995, p 5 ....................8.25
McCarthy v Southern Health Board DPIJ: Hilary and Easter Terms 1994, p 1 7.54, 18.83
McCarthy v Walsh [1965] IR 246 ................................................ 42.22, 44.145-44.148
McClintock v Gregg [1996] Ir L Log W 443 ........................................................18.108
McCloskey v Western Health and Social Services Board [1983] NILR Bull No 4 ...18.87
McCobb v Doyle [1938] IR 444 ....................................................32.17, 32.51, 32.108
McCombe v Read [1955] 2 QB 429 ......................................................................24.28
McComiskey v McDermott [1974] IR 75 .......................................... 6.60-6.65, 7.03-7.04
........................................................................... 15.02-15.03, 20.69, 20.77, 20.96
McConn v Laing [1939] IR 403 .............................................................................23.36
McConville v Kennelly (HC) 27 January 1984 ....................................................34.226
McCord v Electricity Supply Board [1980] ILRM 153 ................................20.14, 20.51
McCormack v Kildare County Council [1953-1954] Ir Jur 64 .....................24.18, 24.113
McCrane v Louth County Council (HC) unrep 9 December 1983 ...........................45.04
McCrystal Oil Co Ltd v Revenue Commissioners [1993] 1 IR 477 ...............29.02, 30.12
McCullagh v Lane Fox & Partners (1994) 8 EG 118,
affd (1996) 18 EG 104 .......................................................................................10.133
McCullagh v PB Gunne (Monaghan) plc (HC) 17 January 1997 .................10.09, 10.101
McCullough v Ireland, (HC) 16 March 1989 ..........................................................46.91
McCurdy (EE) Ltd v PMG [1959] NZLR 553 .........................................................29.05
McCusker v Smith [1918] 2 IR 432 ........................................................................23.20
McCutcheon v Carney [1938] Ir Jur Rep ...............................................................21.67
McDaid v Milford RDC [1919] 2 IR I .....................................................................21.25
McDaid v The Examiner Irish Times, 18 November 1999 ..........................34.03, 34.227
McDermid v Nash Dredging Reclamation Co Ltd [1987] AC 906 ..............18.33, 18.106
McDermott v Eason & Son (1913) 48 ILTR 1 .........................................................34.19
McDermott v Gargan (HC) 24 January 1997 ..........................................................44.82
McDonagh v Brian O'Connell Ltd (HC) 24 October 1996 ..........................18.23, 18.108
McDonagh v McDonagh [1992] 1 IR 119 ......................................................42.22, 42.46
McDonagh v News Group Newspapers Ltd (SC) 23 November 1993 .......................34.75
.......................................................................................................34.237, 34.252
McDonagh v O'Connell (HC) unrep 24 October 1996 ................................ 43.10-43.11
McDonagh v West of Ireland Fisheries Ltd (HC) 19 December 1986 ................ 9.17-9.19
..........................................................................................................28.05, 28.13
McDonald v CIE (1971) 105 ILTR 13 ............................................... 7.44, 15.04-15.09
McDonald v Dublin Corporation [1996] Ir L Log W 214 .........................................18.83

McDonald v Feely (HC) 30 June 1980 .................................... 21.12, 21.18, 24.84, 25.17 ................................................ 45.05-45.06, 45.37
McDonald v Galvin (HC) 23 February 1976 .................................... 22.12, 44.19
McDonald v National Coop Farm Relief Services Ltd, DPIJ: Trinity and Michaelmas Terms 1993 .................................... 18.152
McDonnell v Ireland (SC) 23 July 1997 .................................... 1.48, 1.74, 19.58 ................................................ 25.53, 32.143, 46.101
McDonnell v Preece, Irish Times, 21 November 1985 .................................... 34.59
McDonnell v Sunday Business Post Ltd (HC) 2 February 2000 .................................... 34.216
McDonnell v Sweeney DPIJ: Hilary & Easter Terms 1999 (HC) .................................... 44.176
McDonough v News Group Newspapers Ltd (SC) 23 November 1993 .................................... 34.97
McElduff v United Kingdom (1998) 27 EHRR 249 .................................... 6.84
McEleney v McCarron [1993] 1 IR 132 .................................... 15.19
McElhinney v Williams [1996] 1 ILRM 276 .................................... 38.18
McEllistrum v Etches [1956] SCR 787 .................................... 40.10, 40.26
McElroy v Aldritt (SC) 11 June 1955 .................................... 44.123
McElroy v Ireland (SC) (ex temp) 5 March 1998 .................................... 18.83
McElwaine v Hughes (HC) 30 April 1997 .................................... 4.24
McElwee v McDonald [1969] IR 437 .................................... 30.04
McEntee v Quinnsworth & Keane (SC) 7 December 1993 .................................... 34.20
McErlean v Sarel (1987) 61 OR (2d) 396, 42 DLR (4th) 577 .................................... 40.26-40.29
McEvoy v Maringe DPIJ: Trinity & Michaelmas Terms 1993, p 42 .................................... 44.90
McEvoy v Murphy Contract Management and E Smithwick & Sons Ltd DPIJ: Michaelmas Term 1991, p 154 .................................... 21.10, 21.39
McGarry v Dublin Bus [1997] Ir L Log W 278 .................................... 7.39
McGeary v Campbell [1975] NI 7 .................................... 13.11, 13.49
McGee v AG [1974] IR 284 .................................... 1.13
McGee v Cunanne (1932) 66 ILTR 147 .................................... 22.11, 22.23, 22.103
McGee v The Attorney General [1974] IR 284 .................................... 1.13, 37.60-37.69, 37.81
McGhee v National Code Board [1972] 3 All ER 1008 .................................... 2.21
McGibbon v McCorry (1909) 43 ILTR 132 .................................... 27.48
McGlynn v Clarke [1945] IR 495 .................................... 20.05
McGouran v Reynolds (HC) 27 April 1988 .................................... 20.40-20.44
McGovern v Clones UDC [1944] IR 282 .................................... 7.27, 7.49
McGowan v Harrison [1941] IR 331 .................................... 13.03
McGowan v Masterson [1953] IR 101 .................................... 8.17, 24.18, 24.85-24.89, 43.49
McGowan v Murphy (SC) 10 April 1967 .................................... 32.16, 32.70-32.77, 32.101
McGowan v Wicklow County Council (HC) 27 May 1993 .................................... 18.10, 43.11, 44.176
McGrane v Lough County Council (HC) 9 December 1983 .................................... 45.05
McGrath v Bourne (1876) IR 10 CL 160 .................................... 29.10, 44.58
McGrath v Kelly [1965] IR 497 .................................... 14.169
McGrath v Munster & Leinster Bank Ltd [1959] IR 313 .................................... 24.25, 45.05, 45.49
McGrath v Taylor [1936] NI 158 .................................... 29.10
McGregor (Robert) and Sons (Ireland) Ltd v The Mining Board (HC) 5 October 1998 .................................... 46.65

McGuigan v Iralco Ltd [1996] Ir L Log W 92 ....................18.102
McGuiggan v New England Tel & Tel Co (1986) 398 Mass 152, 496 NE 2d 141 ....................8.06
McGuinness v Fastmac Express Delivery Services Ltd, DPIJ: Michaelmas Term 1991, p 150 (HC) ....................44.176
McGuinness v O'Reilly (HC) 30 November 1992 ....................44.125
McGuinness v Vauxhall Motors Ltd (HC) 31 July 1980 ....................46.04
McGurrell v ESB (SC) 21 December 1970 ....................18.101
McHale v Watson (1964) 111 CLR 384 ....................22.03
McHale v Watson (1966) 115 CLR 199 ....................40.26
McHenry Brothers Ltd v Carey (HC) 19 November 1976 .............. 32.92, 32.102-32.105
McHugh v Commissioner of the Garda Síochána [1986] IR 228, [1987] ILRM 18 ....................1.15, 1.39, 38.10
McHugh v Minister for Defence (HC) 28 January 1999 ....................18.60
McIlveen v Charlesworth Developments [1973] NI 216 ....................11.29
McIlwrath v Harland & Wolff Ltd [1963] NI 41 ....................21.22, 21.35
McInerney v Clareman Printing & Publishing Co [1903] 2 IR 347 ....................34.70, 34.191
McIntyre v Lewis [1991] 1 IR 121 ....................22.38, 34.261, 36.03 .................... 36.06, 38.10, 43.31, 44.28-44.32, 44.35, 44.42
McKail v Hamilton [1948] Argus LR (Current Notes) 214 ....................25.13
McKay v O'Hare DPIJ: Trinity & Michaelmas Terms 1996, p 196 (HC) ....................44.55
McKee v Malcolmson [1925] NI 120 ....................24.18
McKeever v Dundalk Linen Co Ltd (SC) 15 May 1956 ....................18.155
McKeever v Dundalk Linen Co Ltd (SC) 26 May 1966 ....................18.09
McKenna v Best Travel Ltd t/a Cypriano Holidays (HC) 17 December 1996 revd by (SC) 18 November 1997 ....................6.28, 10.09, 44.140
McKenna v Commissioner of An Garda Síochána [1993] 3 IR 543 ....................29.02
McKenna v Lewis [1945] IR 66 ....................24.14, 24.18
McKenna v Longford Lifestyles DPIJ: Hilary & Easter Terms 1991, p 20 (HC) ....44.176
McKenna v McElvaney & MIBI 24 July 1998 ....................42.17, 42.28
McKenna v Meighan [1966] IR 288 ....................18.108, 18.150, 20.55 .................... 44.82-44.84
McKenna v Stephens and Alexander E Hull & Co Ltd [1923] 2 IR 112 .2.39, 3.05, 24.14
McKenzie v O'Neill and Roe Ltd (HC) 23 June 1977 ....................2.56, 26.11
McKeogh v O'Brien Moran [1927] IR 348 ....................34.55, 34.172, 34.199
McKeon v Bolton (1851) 1 ICLR 377 ....................24.18, 43.16
McKeon v Flynn (1934) 69 ILTR 61 ....................16.70
McKevitt v Ireland [1987] ILRM 541 ....................8.15, 9.29
McKew v Holland & Hannen & Cubitts (Scotland) Ltd [1969] 3 All ER 1821 ........20.26
McKinley v Minister for Defence (No 2) [1997] 2 IR 176 ....................33.14, 33.20, 44.109
McKinley v Minister for Defence [1992] 2 IR 333 .................... 33.06-33.10 .................... 33.16-33.20, 33.34
McKinley v Montgomery [1993] NI 93 ....................39.25
McKinney v Yelavich (1958) 352 Mich 687, 90 NW2d 883 ....................15.27
McIlhagger v Belfast Corporation [1944] NI 37 ....................18.108, 18.159, 21.10

McIlwrath v Harland & Wolff Ltd [1963] NI 41 ........ 21.42
McInerney v The "Clareman" Co Ltd [1903] 2 IR 375 ........ 34.100
McLoughlin v Allied Textiles Ltd (HC) 7 July 1955 ........ 18.151
McLoughlin v Antrim Electricity Supply Co [1941] NI 23 ........ 40.18
McLoughlin v Doey (1893) 32 LR Ir 518 ........ 36.04, 36.14-36.17
McLoughlin v Donegal County Council, DPIJ: Trinity and Michaelmas Terms 1994, p 114 ........ 7.39, 18.83
McLoughlin v John McGowan (Drogheda) Ltd, DPIJ: Trinity and Michaelmas Terms 1993, p 211 ........ 18.84
McLoughlin v Minister for the Public Service [1986] ILRM 28 ........ 1.135, 42.40
McLoughlin v O'Brian [1983] 1 AC 410 ........ 1.186, 17.08, 17.23-17.35
........ 17.43, 17.53-17.55, 17.66, 18.62
McLoughlin v Tuite (SC) 13 June 1989 ........ 1.105
McMahon (James) Ltd v Dunne (1965) 99 ILTR 45 ........ 32.14, 32.20-32.32
McMahon v AG [1972] IR 69 ........ 37.62
McMahon v Dunne (1965) 99 ILTR 45 ........ 32.23
McMahon v Ireland [1988] ILRM 610, [1997] 2 ILRM 148 ........ 6.26, 6.56, 10.43
........ 10.76, 19.66
McMahon v O'Sullivan [1939] IR 426 ........ 29.05, 29.10
McMahon v Wexford County Council [1996] Ir L Log W 44 ........ 24.115
McManamon v Córas Iompair Éireann [1961] IR 30 ........ 18.33, 18.108, 43.11
McManus v Bowes [1938] 1 KB 98 ........ 32.20
McManus v Cable Management, (HC) 8 July 1994 ........ 12.135
McMorrow v Knott (SC) 21 December 1959 ........ 44.58, 44.71, 44.96, 44.198
McMullan v Bradshaw (1916) 50 ILTR 205 ........ 23.23, 28.13
McMullan v Carty (HC) 13 July 1993 ........ 14.198
McMullan v Mulhall & Farrell [1929] IR 470 ........ 34.36, 34.92, 34.100, 34.175
McMullen v Clancy (HC) 3 September 1999 ........ 36.29, 37.32
McMullen v Farrell [1993] 1 IR 123, affd (SC) 9 February 1994 ........ 14.216
McNall v Farmersins Group (1979) 181 Ind Appeal 501, 392 NE 2d 520 ........ 40.29
McNally v Oldham (1863) 16 ICLR 298 ........ 34.191
McNamara (Michael) & Co Ltd v Lacken (HC) 31 May 1991 ........ 32.105
McNamara v Brown [1918] 1 IR 215 ........ 43.37, 43.41
McNamara v CIE (SC) 22 July 1972 ........ 18.108
McNamara v Duncan (1971) 26 ALR 584 ........ 22.60-22.60
McNamara v ESB [1975] IR 1 ........ 1.06, 6.01, 6.10, 6.25, 6.38
........ 6.52-6.54, 11.32, 12.01, 12.16, 12.25
........ 12.44-12.55, 12.137, 13.24, 13.63
........ 20.97, 21.38, 40.19, 42.37
McNamara v ESB [1975] IR 226 ........ 25.48, 27.14, 39.25
McNamee v Dunphy DPIJ: Hilary and Easter Terms 1993, p 192 ........ 20.17, 20.44
McNulty v J A Kilroy & Son Ltd, DPIJ: Michaelms Term 1990, p 254 ........ 18.83
McPhee v Township of Plympton (1987) 43 DLR (4th) 233 ........ 24.53
McPherson v Buick Motor Co (1916) 217 NYS 382, 111 NE 1050 ........ 11.08
McPherson v Daniels (1829) 10 B & C 263 ........ 34.123

McQuaile v Heeney and O'Connor [1959] Ir Jur 32 ....................39.10
McQuaker v Goddard [1940] 1 KB 687. ....................27.23
McShane Wholesale Fruit and Vegetables Ltd v Johnston Haulage Co Ltd
[1997] 1 ILRM 86 .................... 6.28, 6.36, 6.51, 10.09-10.10
....................10.49, 13.74, 44.111
McSharry v Waterford Post (HC) 1 May 1985 ....................34.226
McSorley v Masterson (1945) 79 ILTR 45 ....................34.107
McSorley v O'Mahony (HC) 6 November 1996 ....................4.09
McStay v Morrissey (1949) 83 ILTR 28 .................... 1.02, 27.04-27.06
McSweeney v Bourke (HC) 24 November 1980 ....................10.67
McSweeney v Cork Corporation DPIJ: Hilary & Easter Terms 1994, p 37 .....3.32, 18.09,
18.114, .................... 44.176-44.177
McSweeney v Garda Síochána Boat Club (HC) 5 June 1991 .................... 7.44-7.45
McSweeney v McCarthy (SC) 28 January 2000 .................... 18.10, 18.106-18.108, 21.55
McWilliam v Sir William Arrol & Co Ltd [1962] 1 WLR 295, [1962] 1 All ER 623
....................2.11, 18.126
Mead v Clarke Chapman & Co Ltd [1956] 1 All ER 44 ....................42.51
Mead's and Belt's Case (1823) 1 Lew 184, 168 ER 1006 ....................22.24
Meade v ITW Hi-Cone Ltd, DPIJ: Trinity and Michaelmas Terms 1998, p 55 .......18.108
Meara v Daly (1914) 48 ILTR 223 ....................24.25, 24.26
Mears v London and SW Ry Co (1862) 11 CB (ns) 850 ....................28.10, 30.20
Mee v Cruickshank (1902) 86 LT 708 ....................22.39
Meegan v Monaghan County Council, DPIJ: Hilary & Easter
Terms 1998, p 95 ....................44.96
Meehan v Reid and Murphy (HC) 5 March 1985 ....................2.11, 2.55
Melia v Meath County Council, DPIJ: Trinity and Michaelmas
Terms 1996, p 200 ....................18.108
Melling v Ó Mathgamhna [1962] IR 1 ....................1.105, 44.09
Melly v Moran and Northern Western Health Board (HC) 19 June 1997 ....................22.112
Mendez v Palazzi 68 DLR (3d) 582 ....................25.13
Menow v Jordan House Hotel [1974] SCR 239 ....................8.06
Menton v CIE (SC) 27 July 1966 ....................40.13
Mercantile Credit Co of Ireland Ltd v Cahill (1964) 98 ILTR 79 ....................29.02
Mercantile Marine Service Association v Toms [1916] 2 KB 243 ....................39.10
Meredith v Peer (1917) 35 DLR 592 ....................7.08
Merkur Island Shipping Corporation v Laughton [1983] 2 AC 570 ....................32.83
Mernagh v Bell (SC) 19 January 1956 ....................44.92
Merriman v Greenhills Foods Ltd [1997] 1 ILRM 46 ....................9.53
Merrington v Ironbridge Metalworks Ltd [1952] 1 All ER 1101 .................... 26.35-26.35
Merryweather v Nixan (1799) 8 Term Rep 186, 101 ER 1337 ....................4.19
Mersey Docks & Harbour Board v Coggins & Griffith (Liverpool) Ltd [1947] AC 1 43.11
Meskell v CIE [1973] IR 121 .................... 1.11-1.14, 1.18, 1.39-1.43
.................... 1.52, 1.65-1.66, 1.81, 8.01, 14.92
.................... 19.01, 21.19, 21.66, 32.50, 32.63-32.68
.................... 32.75, 32.129-32.140, 37.01

Metall and Rohstoff AG v Donaldson Lufkin and Jenrette [1990] 1 QB 391 32.58, 32.79
Metals & Roper Co Ltd v Tattersall [1966] 1 WLR 1500 ........................................ 29.17
Metropolitan Asylum District v Hill (1881) 6 App Cas 193 .................................... 24.07
Metropolitan Ry Co v Jackson (1877) 3 AC 193 ........................................................ 9.02
Michand v Dupuis (1977) 30 NBR (2d) 305 .............................................................. 16.07
Michelstown Co-operative Agricultural Society Ltd v Goldenvale Food
Products Ltd (HC) 12 December 1985 ................................................................ 31.35
Middleton v Humphries (1912) 47 ILTR 160 ............................................................ 24.28
Midland Bank plc v Cameron, Tong, Peterkin and Duncans 1988 SLT 611 .......... 10.132
Midland Bank Trust Co Ltd v Green (No 3) [1979] 2 All ER 193,
affd [1981] 3 All ER 744 ........................................................................................ 32.61
Midland Bank Trust Co Ltd v Hett, Scubas & Kemp [1979] Ch 384 ......... 10.153, 14.171
Midland Cold Storage Ltd v Steer [1972] Ch 630 ..................................................... 32.20
Midwood & Co Ltd v Manchester Corporation [1905] 2 KB 597 ................. 24.58, 25.19
Migliore v Gerard (1987) 42 DLR (49) 619 ............................................................... 20.34
Migotti v Colvill (1879) 4 CPD 233 ........................................................................... 22.39
Miles v Forest Rock Granite (1918) 34 Times LR 500 ................................ 25.25, 25.32
Millard v McMahon Professional Neg LR 1 ............................................................ 14.195
Miller v Jackson [1977] QB 966 .....................................7.28-7.32, 24.32, 24.98, 24.104
Miller v Kennedy (1975) 85 Wash 2d 151, 530 P 2d 334
aff'g (1974) 11 Wash App 272, 522 P 2d 852 ..................................................... 14.82
Miller v Robert Addie & Sons, Collieries [1934] SC 150 ......................................... 25.16
Millington v Coras Iompair Éireann (1974) 108 ILTR 61 ......................... 9.21, 9.38, 9.44
Mills v Baitis [1968] VR 583 ...................................................................................... 42.17
Mills v Brooker [1919] 1 KB 555 ............................................................................... 30.19
Milner v Reeves (1617) 1 Roll Abr 43 ....................................................................... 34.41
Minister for Finance & AG v O'Brien [1949] IR 91 ...........................20.06-20.12, 32.06
Ministry of Housing and Local Government v Sharp [1970] 2 QB 223 ......... 10.72, 21.19
Mint v Good [1951] 1 KB 517 .................................................................................... 24.76
Minter v Priest [1930] AC 557 .................................................................................. 34.175
Mitchell v Jenkins (1833) 5 B & Ad 558, 110 ER 908 ............................................... 36.16
Mitchelstown Co-operative Agricultural Society Ltd v Goldenvale
Food Products Ltd (HC) 12 December 1985 .............................................. 31.74, 45.05
MMDS Television Ltd v South East Community Deflector Association Ltd
(HC) 8 April 1997 ................................................................................................. 21.07
Moan v Moan [1984] NILR Bull No 3 ......................................................................... 8.22
Mobile and General Insurance Company Ltd, Re [1930] 1 KB 376 .......................... 38.17
Moddejonge v Huron County Board of Education [1972]2 OR 437 ......................... 20.80
Moffat v Kazana [1969] 2 QB 152 ............................................................................. 30.23
Molloy v Gallagher [1933] IR 1 ...................................................................... 32.62, 36.05
Molloy v Offaly County Council (1951) 85 ILTR 61 ................................. 24.18, 24.113
Moloney v Jury's Hotel plc (SC) unrep, 12 November 1999 .................................... 18.81
Moloney v Kingdom Greyhound Racing Co Ltd (1948) 82 ILTR 43 ....................... 30.19
Moloney v Stephens [1945] Ir Jur Rep 37 ................................................................. 27.48
Molson v Squamish Transfer Ltd (1969) 7 DLR (3d) 553 ........................................... 7.39

Molumby v Kearns (HC) 19 January 1999 ....................24.24, 24.31, 24.46
.................... 24.66-24.70, 37.13
Monahan v Nelson (2000) 186 DLR (4th) 193 ....................41.05
Monk v Dillon (1883) 12 LR (Ir) 321 ....................23.29
Monk v Warbey [1935] 1 KB 75 ....................21.41
Monson v Tussauds Ltd [1894] 1 QB 671 ....................34.21
Montana Hotels Pty Ltd v Fasson Pty Ltd (1986) 69 ALR 258 ....................24.86
Montex Holdings Ltd v The Controller of Patents, Designs and
Trade Marks (HC) 14 January 2000 ....................45.05
Montgomery v National C & T (1938) 186 SC 167, 195 SE 247 ....................8.03
Montgomery v Shepperton Investment Co Ltd (HC) 11 July 1995 ....................32.27
Montgomery v Thompson [1891] AC 217 ....................31.09
Mooney v Terrett [1939] Ir Jur Rep 56 ....................43.22
Moor v Foster (1696) Cro Jac 65, ER ....................34.61
Moor v Nolan (1960) 94 ILTR 153 ....................7.08
Moorcock (1889) 14 PD 64 ....................10.39
Moore v AG [1927] IR 569 ....................45.02, 45.45
Moore v AG (No 3) [1930] IR 471 ....................45.05
Moore v Atchison Topeka & Santa Fe Railway (1961) 28 Ill App 2d 340n
171 NE 2d 393 ....................9.20
Moore v Fullerton [1991] ILRM 29 ....................15.31
Moore v Hampshire County Council 80 LGR 481 ....................16.22
Moore v Nolan (1960) 94 ILTR 153 ....................15.28, 20.14
Moore v Reid (1867) 1 ILT & Sol J 229 ....................23.33
Moore v Trulock (1899) 33 ILTR 62 .................... 36.09-36.16
Moorgate Mercantile Co Ltd v Finch [1962] 1 QB 701 ....................30.06
Moorgate Tobacco Co Ltd v Philip Morris Ltd (1980) 145 CLR 457 ....................31.78
Moorhouse v City of Everett (1926) 252 P 157 ....................15.25
Moragne v States Marine Lines Inc (1970) 398 US 375 ....................42.03
Morahan v Archer [1957] NI 61 ....................44.103
Moran v Conway [1947] Ir Jur 37 ....................29.03, 29.10
Mordaunt v Gallagher (HC) 11 July 1997 ....................14.30
More v Water [1928] 2 KB 520 ....................34.157
Morgan v Fry [1968] 2 QB 710 ....................32.56
Morgan v Galway Board of Health [1943] IR 255 ....................43.22
Morgan v Lingen (1863) 6 LT 800 ....................34.67
Morgan v Maurer & Sons [1964] Ir Jur 31 ....................29.02, 30.04
Morgan v Odhams Press Ltd [1971] 1 WLR 1239 ....................34.111
Morgan v Park Developments Ltd [1983] ILRM 156 .................... 1.09, 46.09-46.13
Morgan v Smith [1953] Ir Jur 70 ....................30.04
Morley v Dubinskey (1966) 59 DLR (2d) 217 ....................24.104
Morley v Eye, Ear & Throat Hospital Incorporated [1967] IR 143 ....................12.129
Morris v Breaveglen Ltd (t/a Anzac Construction Co) [1993] ICR 766 ....................18.33
Morris v Carnarvon County Council [1910] 1 KB 159, affd [1910] 1 KB 840 ....................16.70
Morris v CW Martin & Sons Ltd [1965] 2 All ER 725 ....................43.43

Morris v Garvey [1982] ILRM 177 .......... 24.10
Morris v Luton Corporation [1946] 1 All ER 1, [1946] 1 KB 114 .......... 7.48, 15.24
Morris v West Hartlepool Navigation Co [1956] 375 AC 552 .......... 7.25
Morrison v Forsythe [1995] 6 Med LR 6 .......... 14.40
Morriss v Marsden [1952] 1 All ER 925 .......... 40.42-40.44
Morrissey v Healy [1960] IR 1 .......... 7.13, 15.02
Morrisson v Leonard, (SC) 18 April 1958 .......... 15.17
Morrow v M'Gaver (1851) 1 Ir CLR 579 .......... 34.126
Mortin v Shoppee (1828) 3 C & P 373, 172 ER 462 .......... 22.22
Morton v William Dixon Ltd [1909] SC 807 .......... 18.14, 18.19
Motherwell v Motherwell (1976) 73 DLR (3d) 62 .......... 24.60, 37.11-37.13
Motor Vehicle Assurance Fund v Dubuzane 1984 (1) SA 700 .......... 9.04
Mott v Shoolbred (1875) LR 20 EQ 22 .......... 24.97
Moulton v Ledwith (1933) 67 ILTR 233 .......... 30.19
Mount Bischoff Tin Mining Co v MB Extended Tin Co (1913) 15 CLR 549 .......... 23.45
Mount Isa Mines Ltd v Pusey (1971) 45 ALJR 88 .......... 17.22
Mountcharles v Meath County Council [1997] 1 ILRM 446 .......... 24.12
Mourneview Estate Ltd v Dundalk UDC (1967) 101 ILTR 189 .......... 45.05
Moynihan v Greensmyth [1977] IR 55 (SC), affg (HC) 1976 .. 38.12, 41.11, 46.80, 46.90
Moynihan v Gt Southern Rys Co [1936] IR 132 .......... 21.10, 21.40, 23.19
Moynihan v Moynihan [1975] IR 192 .......... 2.16, 16.15, 18.34, 33.38
.......... 43.02-43.07, 43.18, 43.68-43.69
Muckross Park Hotel Ltd v Randles [1995] IR 130 .......... 31.06
Muirhead v Industrial Tank Specialities Ltd [1986] QB 507 .......... 10.45, 11.84
Mulally v Bus Éireann [1992] ILRM 722 .......... 17.44
Mulcahy v Guardians of the Poor of Kilmacthomas Union (1886) 18 LR Ir 200 ..... 21.19
Mulcahy v Lynch and Butler (SC) 25 March 1993 .......... 15.08, 15.52
Mulcahy v Ministry of Defence [1996] 2 All ER 758 .......... 18.131
Mulcahy v R (1868) LR 3 HL 306 .......... 32.60
Mulcare v Southern Health Board [1988] ILRM 689 .......... 6.67, 7.43, 18.04-18.09
.......... 18.75, 18.86-18.90
Muldoon v Brittas Plastics Ltd, (HC) 18 March 1993 .......... 18.146
Muldoon v Ireland [1988] ILRM 367 .......... 2.42, 7.47, 8.32
Mulholland & Tedd Ltd v Baker [1939] 3 All ER 253 .......... 26.20
Mulholland v James Murphy & Co Ltd 77 ILTR 212 .......... 6.58, 33.02
Mulholland v McCrea [1961] NI 135 .......... 42.02, 42.20
Mulholland v VH McDevitt & Son Ltd NI QBD, 15 January 1998 .......... 18.33
Mullally v Bus Éireann [1992] ILRM 722 .......... 1.186, 17.35, 17.44
.......... 17.58, 17.64, 44.176
Mullan v Forrester [1921] 2 IR 412 .......... 24.18, 24.29, 24.85-24.85
.......... 25.13-25.18, 25.25, 25.40
Mullan v Omagh Meats Ltd NI (HC) 3 February 1999 .......... 18.23
Mullen v Quinnsworth Ltd t/a Crazy Prices (No 1) [1990] 1 IR 59 .......... 7.44-7.44, 9.17
.......... 9.38-9.39, 9.44, 12.08
.......... 12.53, 12.127, 25.22

Mullen v Quinnsworth Ltd t/a Crazy Prices (No 2) [1991] ILRM 439 ..............7.44, 9.38
.......................................................................................................12.08, 25.23
Mullen v Vernal Instruments Ltd (HC) 15 December 1995 ......................................18.25
Mullett v Mason (1866) LR 1 CP 559 ...................................................................35.20
Mulligan v Doherty (SC) 17 May 1966 ..................................................................16.20
Mulligan v Hewitt, DPIJ: Hilary & Easter Terms 1991, p 38 (HC) ..........................44.93
Mulligan v Holland Dredging (Ireland) Ltd (SC) 21 November 1996,
affg (HC) 23 January 1995 ...........................................................18.03, 18.33, 43.11
Mullin v Hynes (SC) 13 November 1972 ........................................... 24.31-24.34, 24.39
.........................................................................................24.56, 24.107, 45.05
Mullin v Naughton, DPIJ: Trinity & Michaelmas Terms 1996 ...............................44.90
Mullin v Richards [1998] 1 WLR 1304 ..................................................................40.26
Mulloy v Hop Sang [1935] 1 WWR 714 ...............................................................22.73
Mulrennan v Connolly (1939) 73 ILTR 94 ............................................................42.38
Mulvihill v Limerick County Council (1952) 87 ILTR 63 ............................44.58, 44.84
Municipal Tramways Trust v Ashby [1951] SASR 61 ............................................20.18
Munn & Co Ltd v Mv "Sir John Crosbie" (1965) 52 DLR (2d) 48,
affd [1967] Ex 94 ................................................................................................23.51
Munnelly v Falcon Ltd [1978] IR 387 ...................................................... 44.206-44.207
Munro v Willmott [1948] 2 All ER 983 .................................................................29.16
Murdoch v Workman & Co (1894) 28 ILTR 39 .....................................................44.03
Murgatroyd v Blackburn & Over Darwen Tramway Co 3 TLR 451 ..........................8.14
Murley v Grove (1882) 46 JP 360 .........................................................................12.19
Murnaghan v Gilhooley, DPIJ: Trinity & Michaelmas Terms 1993 .........................44.87
Murphy v Attorney General [1982] IR 241 ............................................................37.64
Murphy v Ballyclough Co-operative Creamery Ltd (HC) 27 February 1998 .....2.50, 8.11
Murphy v Brentwood District Council [1991] 1 AC 398 .........................6.03, 6.09, 6.21
.........................................................................6.29, 6.35, 6.49, 10.09, 10.45
.........................................................................10.161, 11.124, 13.56, 13.71
Murphy v Bus Éireann DPIJ: Trinity and Michaelmas Terms 1994, p 163 ..............15.47
Murphy v Casey [1997] Ir L Log W 367 .................................................................23.29
Murphy v Commissioners of Irish Lights (SC) 25 July 1973 ......................18.15, 18.108
Murphy v Cork County Council (SC) 18 November 1996 .......................................44.61
Murphy v Cronin [1966] IR 699 ................................. 15.17, 15.43, 20.55, 42.39-42.40
................................................................................................... 44.123-44.127
Murphy v De Braam (SC) 12 December 1997 .......................................................44.207
Murphy v Dow Jones Publishing Co (Europe) Inc (HC) 11 January 1995 ...34.191, 35.28
Murphy v Dublin County Council (1962) 96 ILTR 26 ...............................18.97, 18.152
.......................................................................................................21.10, 21.22
Murphy v Dublin United Tramways Co (1909) 43 ILTR 11 .......................................9.21
Murphy v ESB DPIJ: Trinity and Michaelmas Terms 1993, p 261 .....7.10, 18.83, 18.152
Murphy v Filgate (SC) 5 July 1968 ........................................................................44.58
Murphy v GN Ry Co [1897] 2 IR 301 .........................................2.39, 8.14, 8.17, 8.23
Murphy v Greene [1990] 2 IR 566 .........................................................................22.112
Murphy v Halpin (1874) IR 8 CL 127 .........................................................34.172, 34.178

Murphy v Hurley (SC) 23 March 1930 .......... 7.05
Murphy v J Donoghue Ltd [1993] 1 IR 534 .......... 4.17
Murphy v Jackson DPIJ: Trinity and Michaelmas Terms 1993, p 146 .......... 16.24
Murphy v Kirwan [1993] 3 IR 501 .......... 36.27
Murphy v McGrath [1981] ILRM 364 .......... 3.37, 20.24
Murphy v Mulcahy (1896) 30 ILT & Sol J 37 .......... 28.04
Murphy v O'Brien (1987) 6 ILT (ns) 75 .......... 6.55, 8.06-8.08, 12.53, 20.14
Murphy v PMPA Insurance [1978] ILRM 25 .......... 37.13, 37.91
Murphy v Pollock (1864) 15 ICLR 224 .......... 18.77
Murphy v Riordan (1926) 60 ILTR 113 .......... 15.27-15.32, 15.49
Murphy v Roche (HC) 15 May 1987 .......... 39.11-39.15
Murphy v Ross [1920] 2 IR 199 .......... 18.09, 18.76, 43.30
Murphy v Rucon Ltd (SC) 31 January 1969 .......... 44.75, 44.82, 44.89
Murphy v Shields, DPIJ: Hilary and Easter Terms 1994, p 89 (HC) .......... 40.11
Murphy v St Catherine's Hospital 41 DLR (2d) 697 .......... 11.34
Murphy v Stewart [1973] IR 97 .......... 1.12
Murphy v The Minister for Defence (SC) 19 July 1999 .......... 44.91, 44.99
Murphy v Wexford County Council [1921] 2 IR 230 .......... 44.207
Murray v AG [1985] IR 532 .......... 1.13
Murray v Fitzpatrick (1914) 48 ILT & Sol J 305 .......... 22.19
Murray v Gilmore (SC) 20 December 1973 .......... 7.13-7.15, 9.44
Murray v Ireland [1985] IR 532, affd [1991] ILRM 465 .......... 24.71
Murray v John Sisk & Son (Dublin) Ltd [1965] Ir Jur Rep 41 .......... 44.60, 44.202
Murray v McMurchy [1949] 2 DLR 442 .......... 22.73
Murray v Minister for Defence [1988] 1 WLR 692 .......... 22.46
Murray v Minister for Finance (HC) Irish Times, 28 May 1981;
(SC) Irish Times, 22 April 1983 .......... 38.10, 43.46
Murray v Shuter [1976] QB 972 .......... 42.40
Murray v South Carolina Railroad (1841) 26 SCL (1 McMil) 385 .......... 18.02
Murray v Times Newspapers Ltd (HC) 12 December 1995 .......... 34.49
Murray v Times Newspapers Ltd [1997] 3 IR 97 .......... 34.12
Murray v Warner Lambert [1997] Ir L Log W 267 .......... 7.32
Murtagh Properties Ltd v Cleary [1972] IR 330 .......... 1.12-1.13, 45.37
Murtagh v Board of Governors of St Emer's National School
[1991] 1 IR 482 .......... 22.104
Murtagh v Lawlor (SC) 4 December 1959 .......... 18.108
Mustad v Dosen [1963] RPC 41 .......... 37.27
Mutual Life & Citizens' Assurance Co Ltd v Evatt [1971] AC 793 .......... 10.147
Mye v Peters (1967) 68 SR (NSW) 298 .......... 15.05, 20.18, 40.26
Myerscough & Co Ltd v Kenny (HC) 18 April 1974 .......... 32.101
Myles and Gold v Ryan (CC) 19 October 1998 .......... 24.29
Myles v Supervalu [1997] Ir L Log W 159 .......... 7.44

**N**

Nader v Allegheny Airlines Inc (1980) 626 F 2D 1031 .......... 35.15

Nagle v The Tipplers Tavern DPIJ: Michaelmas Term 1991, p 161 ....................... 18.79
Nance v British Columbia Electric Ry [1951] AC 601 ....................... 20.14
Nash v Eli Lilly & Co [1993] 4 All ER 383 ....................... 46.27
Nason v Cork Corporation DPIJ: Hilary & Easter Terms 1991, p 170 (HC) ....................... 44.176
Nation Newspaper Ltd v Cheshire (1984) 2 Ken App Rep 17 ....................... 34.96
National Bank of Greece SA v Pinios Shipping Co (No 3) [1988] 2 Lloyd's Rep 126 ....................... 10.25
National Coal Board v England [1954] AC 403 ....................... 20.93
National Coal Board v Evans (JE) & Co (Cardiff) Ltd [1951] 2 KB 861 ....................... 22.01, 28.11
National Conversion Corporation v Cedar Building Corporation (1969) 23 NY 2d 621, 246 NE 2d 351, 298 NYS 2d 499 ....................... 35.09
National Engineering & Electrical Trade Union v McConnell [1983] IR 172 ....................... 23.33
National Insurance Co of New Zealand Ltd v Espagne 105 Comm LR 569 ....................... 44.114
National Irish Bank Ltd v Radio Telefís Éireann [1998] 2 ILRM 196 ....................... 45.05
National Media Ltd v Bogoshi 1998 (4) SA 1196 ....................... 34.181
National Union of General and Municipal Workers v Gillian [1946] KB 81 ....................... 39.30
Nationwide Building Society v Thimbleby & Co Ch D, 26 February 1999 ....................... 35.15
Nee v Gardiner [1949] 3 DLR 852 (BCCA), affg [1948] 4 DLR 871 ....................... 23.29
Neenan v Hosford [1920] 2 IR 258 ....................... 15.32, 20.06
Neill v Fresh Food & Ice Pty Ltd (1963) 108 Comm LR 362 ....................... 18.04
Neill v Minister for Finance [1948] IR 88 ....................... 9.21, 43.64
Nelhams v Sandells Maintenance Ltd (1995) 46 Con LR 40 ....................... 18.33
Nelles v Ontario 60 DLR (4th) 609 ....................... 36.03
Nespolon v Alford (1998) 161 DLR (4th) 646 ....................... 40.26-40.29
Ness v West Coast Airlines Inc (1965) 90 Idaho 111 410 P 2d 969 ....................... 9.25
Nestor v O'Brien, Irish Times, 21 May 1998 ....................... 34.61
Nettleship v Weston [1971] 2 QB 691 ....................... 6.65
Neumann v Shlansky (1971) 36 A 2d 540, 318 NYS 2d 925 ....................... 40.30
Neville (William) & Sons Ltd v Guardian Builders Ltd [1990] ILRM 601 ....................... 35.06
Neville v Margan Ltd (HC) 1 December 1988 ....................... 4.25, 46.87
Nevin v Johnson & Perrott Ltd DPIJ: Hilary & Easter Terms 1997, p 46 ....................... 44.176
Nevin v Roddy and Carty [1935] IR 397 ....................... 34.59, 34.175, 34.178
New Imperial & Windsor Hotel Co v Johnson [1912] 1 IR 327 ....................... 24.31, 24.37-24.39
New Ireland Assurance Co Ltd v Irish National Union of Vintners, Process & Allied Trade Assistants (HC) 1 April 1982x ....................... 23.20
New York Times v Sullivan (1964) 376 US 254 ....................... 34.180
Newbridge Industries v Bateson (HC) 7 July 1975 ....................... 32.104
News Group Newspapers Ltd v SOGAT [1986] IRLR 337 ....................... 32.161
Newstead v London Express Newspaper Ltd [1940] 1 KB 377 ....................... 34.111
Newton v Edgerley [1959] 1 WLR 1031 ....................... 16.05
Nicholls v Ely Beet Sugar Factory Ltd [1936] 1 Ch 343 ....................... 24.71
Nicholls v Ely Beet Sugar Factory Ltd [1931] 2 Ch 84 ....................... 23.45
Nichols v Marsland (1876) 2 Ex D 1 ....................... 25.39-25.42
Nielsen v Brown (1962) 232 Or 426, 374 P 2d 896 ....................... 40.29
Nobilo v Waitemata [1961] NZLR 1064 ....................... 23.29

Noble v Harrison [1926] 2 KB 332 .......... 24.29, 25.13, 25.40
Noblett v Leitrim County Council [1920] 2 IR .......... 44.09
Noel (Committee of) v Botkin [1995] 7 WWR 479, 9 BCLR (3d) 21 .......... 7.39
Nolan Transport (Oaklands) Ltd v Halligan [1998] ELR 177 (SC) revg [1995] ELR 1 .......... 32.94, 32.172-32.175, 32.184
Nolan v Fagan (HC) 8 May 1985 .......... 39.14
Nolan v Fergus DPIJ: Hilary and Easter Terms 1994, p 161 .......... 8.27
Nolan v Gilheaney (1924) 58 ILTSJ 61 .......... 38.01
Nolan v Jennings (SC) 31 January 1964 .......... 15.17
Nolan v Listowel UDC and Smyth [1966] IR 56 .......... 4.25, 24.17
Nominal Defendant v Haslbauer (1967) 117 CLR 448 .......... 9.43
Noonan v Dublin Distillery Co (1893) 32 LR (Ir) 399 .......... 18.08, 18.83 .......... 18.96, 18.108
Noonan v Hartnett (1950) 84 ILTR 41 .......... 25.17, 25.28, 27.08, 27.45
Noonan v O'Leary DPIJ: Hilary and Easter Terms 1991, p 127 .......... 44.176
Noone v Minister for Finance [1964] IR 63 .......... 20.11
Norberg v Wynrib (1992) 92 DLR (4th) 449 .......... 22.66
Norris v Attorney General [1984] IR 36, [1988] ILRM 472 ..... 37.60, 37.69, 37.93, 46.08
Norris v Ireland (1988) 13 EHRR 186 .......... 37.71, 37.80
North v Wood [1914] 1 KB 629 .......... 27.25
Northern Bank Finance Corporation Ltd v Charlton [1979] IR 149 .......... 3.42, 35.06 .......... 35.17-35.21
Northern Ireland Master Butchers' Wholesale Supply Association Ltd v Belfast Corporation [1965] NI 30 .......... 28.04, 30.05
Northern Ireland Road Transport Board v Century Ins Co Ltd [1941] NI 77 75 ILTR 44, [1942] NI 47 .......... 43.30
Northern Territory v Mengel (1995) 69 ALJR 527 .......... 19.55
Northumberland and Durham District Banking Co ex p Bigge, Re (1859) 28 LJ Ch 50 .......... 35.15
Northwestern Utilities Ltd v London Guarantee & Accident Co Ltd [1936] AC 108 .......... 24.58, 25.16, 25.28-25.31
Norton v General Accident, Fire and Life Assurance Co (1940) 74 ILTR 123 .......... 38.17
Norton v Kearon (1871) IR 6 CL 126 .......... 21.08, 21.19, 21.35
Nottingham Patent Brick and Tile Co Ltd v Butler (1866) 16 QBD 778 .......... 35.06
Nova-Mink Ltd v Trans-Canada Airlines [1951] 2 DLR 241 .......... 6.03
Nugent v DH Bushe DPIJ: Hilary and Easter Terms 1999, p 25 .......... 18.95
Nunan v Southern Rly Co [1924] 1 KB 223 .......... 42.13
Nunes Diamonds Ltd v Dominion Electric Protection [1972] SCR 769 .... 10.149, 10.153

## O

O'Beirne v Hannigan [1937] IR 237 .......... 15.01, 15.23, 24.16
O'Boyle v Attorney General [1929] IR 558 .......... 45.05
O'Brien v Armstrong (SC) 19 March 1997 .......... 15.18
O'Brien v Bergin (SC) 3 June 1965 .......... 43.36
O'Brien v Campbell Catering International Ltd (HC) 22 March 1993 .......... 10.140

O'Brien v Creaton DPIJ: Trinity and Michaelmas Terms 1996, p 92 (HC) ....................44.133, 44.166
O'Brien v Cunard SS Co (1891) 154 Mass 272, 28 NE 266 ....................22.60
O'Brien v Eason & Son (1913) 47 ILTR 266 ....................34.19, 34.108
O'Brien v Higgins (SC) 13 March 1967 .................... 42.20-42.21
O'Brien v Irish Mirror (HC) 11 November 1999, (SC) 25 October 2000 ....................34.03
O'Brien v Keogh [1972] IR 144 .................... 1.42, 46.74-46.80
O'Brien v McNamee [1953] IR 86 ....................23.38, 40.02
O'Brien v Mirror Group Newspapers Ltd (SC) 25 October 2000 ....................34.61, 34.243 ....................34.250, 34.253, 34.25634.262
O'Brien v Parker [1997] 2 ILRM 170 .................... 7.13-7.16, 7.22
O'Brien v Ulster Bank Ltd (HC) 21 December 1993 ....................4.24
O'Brien v Waterford County Council [1926] IR 1 ....................8.24, 24.113
O'Brien v Wheeler NSW 23 May 1997 ....................14.144
O'Byrne v Gloucester (SC) 3 November 1988 ....................11.35, 11.58, 11.63
O'Callaghan v Collins (HC) 1 December 1990 ....................22.103
O'Callaghan v Cross's Refrigeration Ltd (SC) 20 April 1972 ....................18.108
O'Callaghan v Meath Vocational Education Committee (HC) 20 November 1990 ....................34.20, 35.02, 35.08, 35.20, 35.26
O'Callaghan v Minister for Posts & Telegraphs (1947) 81 ILTR 162 ....................21.10
O'Conghaile v Wallace [1938] IR 526 ....................19.58, 21.10, 21.22, 22.02, 22.38
O'Connell v Bateman [1932] LJ Ir 160 ....................43.46
O'Connell v CIE (1954) 89 ILTR 95 ....................7.39
O'Connell v ESB, DPIJ: Hilary & Easter Terms 1996, p 176 (HC) ....................44.176
O'Connell v Hynes DPIJ: Hilary & Easter Terms 1991, p 257 (HC) ....................44.176
O'Connell v Kavanagh (1958) 92 ILTR 10 ....................38.01
O'Connell v Minister for Finance [1945] Ir Jur Rep 18 ....................43.64
O'Connell v Shield Insurance Co Ltd [1954] IR 286 .................... 15.01, 15.17, 15.27-15.33
O'Connor Nenagh Ltd v Powers Supermarkets Ltd (HC) 15 March 199 ....................35.08
O'Connor v Bray (1973) 56 CLR 464 ....................21.19
O'Connor v Corr (1826) Batty's Irish Reports 1825-26, 421 ....................23.50
O'Connor v First National Building Society [1991] ILRM 208 ....................14.219
O'Connor v Grand International Hotel Co [1898] 2 IR 92 ....................12.58
O'Connor v Higgisson [1946] Ir Jur 61 ....................27.06
O'Connor v Kerry County Council (1927) 61 ILTR 73 ....................21.10, 24.113
O'Connor v Martin [1949] Ir Jur Rep 9 ....................32.108
O'Connor v McDonnell (HC) 30 June 1970 ....................4.19, 20.105
O'Connor v Northeastern Health Board, DPIJ: Trinity & Michaelmas Terms 1999, p 150 ....................44.90
O'Connor v Russell (SC) 23 October 1959 ....................44.58
O'Connor v Waldron [1935] AC 76 ....................34.155
O'Connor v Wallen (1856) 6 ICLR 378 ....................34.125
O'Connor v Walsh (1907) 42 ILTR 20 ....................45.02, 45.50
O'Connor v Williams [1996] 2 ILRM 382 ....................1.39, 21.07
O'Dea v Ó Briain [1992] ILRM 364 ....................45.02

O'Doherty v Limerick Corporation, DPIJ: Michaelmas Term 1991, p 66 ............. 18.108
O'Doherty v Whelan, Prof Neg LR 440 (HC, 18 January 1993) ............................ 14.33
O'Domhnaill v Merrick [1984] IR 151 ........................................................46.54-46.62
O'Donnell (Pat ) & Co Ltd v Truck & Machinery Sales Ltd (SC) 18 February 1997
............................................................................................................ 10.26, 10.90
O'Donnell v Begley and Bord Telecom Éireann [1987] ILRM 105 ............ 18.108, 43.49
O'Donnell v Dun Laoghaire Corporation [1991] ILRM 301 ........................ 19.54, 19.67
O'Donnell v Gleeson DPIJ: Trinity and Michaelmas Terms 1996 ............................ 2.19
O'Donnell v Hannigan (SC) 19 July 1960 .................. 18.03, 18.75-18.75, 18.85, 18.108
O'Donnell v Herdmans Ltd [1987] NILR Bull 1 .................................................. 18.109
O'Donnell v Minister for Defence, DPIJ: Hilary and Easter Terms 1997, p 135 ...... 18.82
O'Donnell v Spicer (SC) 8 December 1967 ............................................................ 44.82
O'Donnell v Truck and Machinery Sales [1997] 1 ILRM 466 ............................. 10.155
O'Donoghue v Deecan & Sons Ltd (SC) 19 July 1999 ............................... 44.67, 44.83
O'Donoghue v Egan DPIJ: Trinity & Michaelmas Terms 1992, p 90 (HC) ........... 44.176
O'Donoghue v Greene [1967] IR 40 ...................................................... 12.08, 12.129
O'Donoghue v Hussey (1871) IR 5 CL 124 ........................................... 34.175, 34.178
O'Donoghue v Minister for Education (SC) 6 Febraury 1997 affg (HC) 27 May 1993
............................................................................................................................ 16.69
O'Donoghue v Nolan and Kelly (HC) 29 July 1993 .................................. 10.140, 35.03
O'Donovan v Cork County Council [1967] IR 173 .........14.05, 14.09-14.11, 14.21-14.22
.............................................................................. 14.30, 14.59, 20.18, 43.22
O'Donovan v Southern Health Board DPIJ: Michaelmas Term 1991, p 175 18.61, 44.176
O'Dowd v North Western Health Board [1983] ILRM 186 ......................... 22.112, 43.22
O'Dowd v Secretary of State [1982] NI 210 .......................................................... 17.35
O'Driscoll v Dublin Corporation [1999] 1 ILRM 106 ........................................... 46.25
O'Fiachann v Kiernan, Kiernan and Ors (HC) 11 January 1985 ............................ 43.65
O'Gara v Murray (HC) 10 November 1988 ............................................ 23.33, 45.05
O'Gorman v Crotty [1946] Ir Jur Rep 34 .......................................... 16.29, 40.13-40.18
O'Gorman v O'Gorman [1903] 2 IR 573, 36 ILTR 237 ............................ 1.02, 7.27, 7.50
.......................................................................... 11.07, 27.01-27.06, 27.23
O'Gorman v Ritz (Clonmel) Ltd [1947] Ir Jur 35 .................................. 7.32, 7.44, 12.07
O'Hanlon v ESB [1969] IR 75 .............................................. 2.26, 5.09, 18.97, 18.154
.................................................................. 18.159, 20.13, 20.64-20.67, 20.73
.................................................. 20.99-20.100, 34.18, 34.224, 38.08, 40.18, 42.12
O'Hanlon v Minister for Posts & Telegraphs [1960] Ir Jur Rep 25 ............... 24.31, 38.01
O'Haran v Divine (1964) 100 ILTR 53 .............................................. 21.72, 33.08-33.13
O'Hea v Guardians of Cork Union (1892) 32 LR Ir 629 .............................. 34.55, 34.91
O'Higgins v P Carney Ltd, DPIJ: Trinity and Michaelmas Terms 1993, p 176 ...... 18.158
O'Kane v Campbell [1985] IR 115 ........................................................... 24.31-24.37
............................................................................................................ 24.44, 24.56
O'Keefe v Ferris [1993] 3 IR 165 .......................................................................... 35.10
O'Keeffe v Cody (HC) 11 March 1994 ................................................... 14.117, 43.22
O'Keeffe v Commissioners of Public Works, (SC) 24 March 1980 .......................... 46.93
O'Keeffe v Irish Motor Inns Ltd [1978] IR 85 .................................. 7.30, 12.55, 12.100

O'Keeffe v Kilcullen, (HC) 24 June 1998 ........................................................................44.03
O'Keeffe v Ladola and Dublin Corporation (CC) 12 January 2000 ...............15.57, 26.36
O'Kelly v Harvey (1883) 14 LR Ir 105 ...........................................................................22.111
O'Leary v Bill Hanlon Offshore Supply Co Ltd DPIJ: Hilary and Easter
Terms 1994 ......................................................................................................................18.61
O'Leary v Cork Corporation (SC) 4 July 1997, affg (HC) 19 May 1993 ...............18.146
O'Leary v Dublin County Council (HC) 16 May 1988 .........................................21.15
O'Leary v Hanlon Off Shore Supply Co Ltd, DPIJ: Hilary & Easter Terms 1994, p 140
.....................................................................................................................................44.176
O'Leary v John A Wood Ltd [1964] IR 269 ...................................................7.27, 12.30
O'Leary v Lord Mayor, Aldermann and Burgesses of Cork (SC) 4 July 1997 ...........2.61
O'Leary v Melitides (1959) 20 DLR (2d) 258 ....................................................24.86
O'Leary v O'Connell [1968] IR 149 ...................................................9.02, 20.55, 44.74
O'Looney v Minister for the Public Service [1986] IR 543 .....................................1.135
O'Loughlin v Kearney [1939] Ir Jur 39 ............................................................................9.44
O'Loughlin v Teeling [1988] ILRM 617 ..................................................42.58, 44.134
O'Mahoney v Ford (Henry) & Son Ltd [1962] IR 146 ..................... 18.95-18.96, 18.109
O'Mahony v Buckley DPIJ: Trinity & Michaelmas Terms 1999, p 5 ......................44.91
..................................................................................................................44.169, 44.176
O'Mahony v District Justice Shields (HC) 22 February 1988 ................................28.15
O'Mahony v Ford [1962] IR 146 .............................................................................3.16
O'Mahony v John Sisk & Son Ltd (HC) 16 December 1994 ................................18.154
O'Mahony v O'Mahony DPIJ: Hilary and Easter Terms 1991, p 17 (HC) .............44.149
O'Mahony v Tyndale (HC) 7 April 2000 ........................................................................2.62
O'N v The Minister for Health and Children (HC) 19 October 1999 .....................44.169
O'Neill Garvan v Brennan (1988) 7 ILT (ns) 319 ..................................................12.09
O'Neill v Cork Corporation [1947] IR 103 .................................... 21.10-21.12, 21.20
O'Neill v Finn & VWD Ltd (SC) 20 May 1969 .......................................................11.14
O'Neill v Johnston [1908] IR 358 ...........................................................................30.20
O'Neill v Tipperary SR VEC [1996] Ir L Log W 369 ...............................................16.28
O'Neill v Transport & General Workers Union [1934] IR 633 ....................32.127, 45.05
O'Neill's Irish International Sports Co Ltd v O'Neill's Footwear Drying
Co Ltd (HC) 30 April 1997 ............................................31.02, 31.40, 31.54, 45.05
O'Regan v Byrne DPIJ: Hilary and Easter Terms 1993, p 238 ......................20.34, 20.41
O'Regan v Crampton Ltd (No 1) (SC) 15 June 1953 ...................................18.03, 18.108
O'Regan v Crampton Ltd (No 2) (SC) 1 June 1954 ..............................................18.108
O'Regan v Willis (1936) 71 ILT & Sol J 117 ............................................................9.17
O'Reilly v Cranville [1971] IR 90 ..........................................................................46.93
O'Reilly v Dublin Corporation, DPIJ: Hilary and Easter Terms 1991, p 194 ..........18.155
O'Reilly v Evans [1956] IR 269 .......................................................................15.02, 15.24
O'Reilly v Lavelle [1990] 2 IR 372 ............................................ 9.26, 9.39, 27.57-27.58
O'Reilly v Limerick Corporation [1989] ILRM 181 ............... 16.69, 21.13-21.18, 45.02
O'Reilly v Moroney [1992] 2 IR 145 ....................................................................22.112
O'Rourke v An Post and the Commissioner of An Garda Síochána
(CC) 27 July 2000 ...................................................................................................36.31

O'Rourke v Cavan UDC (1942) 77 ILTR 16 .......... 40.11
O'Rourke v McGuinness [1942] IR 554 .......... 9.01-9.07, 9.44
O'Rourke v Revenue Commissioners [1996] 2 IR 1 .......... 4.19
O'Rourke v Taylor (1947) 81 ILTR 69 .......... 7.28
O'Shaughnessy v Hayden (1824) 2 Fox & Smi 329, (1825) Sm & Bat 208 .......... 34.124, 34.136
O'Shaughnessy v Independent Newspapers Ltd (SC) 21 April 1955 .......... 15.39, 44.58
O'Shea v Anhold and Horse Holiday Farm Ltd (SC) 23 October 1996 .......... 9.11, 9.27 .......... 9.53, 15.18, 27.55-27.58
O'Shiel v Minister for Education [1999] 2 ILRM 241 .......... 16.69
O'Sullivan O'Connor v O'Connor (1976) 114 ILTR 63 .......... 23.42
O'Sullivan v CIE [1978] IR 407 .......... 42.19, 42.27, 42.38-42.39
O'Sullivan v Connolly DPIJ: Hilary & Easter Terms 1996, p 96 (HC) .......... 44.176
O'Sullivan v Doyle (SC) 30 July 1962 .......... 18.09
O'Sullivan v Dwyer [1971] IR 275 .......... 4.20, 7.23, 11.159, 20.46-20.50 .......... 20.55, 21.10, 21.37-21.42 .......... 21.59-21.61, 24.20, 25.34, 44.204
O'Sullivan v Iarnród Éireann (HC) 14 March 1994 .......... 18.108, 44.132
O'Sullivan v John Daly & Co Ltd (SC) unrep 31 July 1972 .......... 18.108
O'Sullivan v Mellerick (1970) 104 ILTR 8 .......... 20.55, 44.60, 44.183
O'Sullivan v Noonan (SC) 28 July 1972 .......... 11.07, 11.15, 11.25
O'Sullivan v Southern Health Board (HC) 8 December 1998 .......... 18.118
O'Sullivan v Telecom Éireann, DPIJ: Trinity & Michaelmas Terms 1998, p 265 .......... 44.91-44.93
O'Toole v Carlsbad Shell Service Station (1988) 247 Cal Rep 663 .......... 8.06
O'Toole v Dublin Corporation, (HC) 18 February 1994 .......... 12.08
O'Toole v Dublin Corporation [1997] Ir L Log W 170 .......... 24.115
O'Toole v Iarnród Éireann (HC) QBD, 19 February 199 .......... 18.109
O'Toole v Kearns (SC) 31 July 1957 .......... 44.60, 44.174
Oakes v Lynch (SC) 21 December 1954 .......... 14.169
Oblique Financial Services Ltd v The Promise Production Co [1994] 1 ILRM 74 .......... 37.21, 37.34-37.38
Office Cleaning Services Ltd v Westminster, etc Cleaners Ltd (1946) 63 RPC 39 .......... 31.40
Ogwo v Taylor [1987] 3 All ER 961, [1988] AC 431 .......... 20.80, 20.90, 26.35-26.35
Oke v Weide Transport Ltd 41 DLR (2d) 53 .......... 8.02
Oldfield v MacMillan (1998), 1998 ACWSJ LEXIS 69094 .......... 16.25
Oldham v Lawson (No 1) [1976] VR 654 .......... 24.59
OLL Ltd v Secretary of State for Transport [1997] 3 All ER 897 .......... 8.04
Organ v ESB DPIJ: Trinity and Michaelmas Terms 1992 .......... 18.10
Orme v Orme DPIJ: Trinity & Michaelmas Terms 1992, p 233 (HC) .......... 44.149
Ormrod v Crosville Motor Services Ltd [1953] 2 All ER 753 .......... 43.63
Osborn v Thomas Boulter & Sons [1930] 2 KB 266 .......... 34.161
Osborn v Veitch (1858) 1 F & F 317, 175 ER 744 .......... 22.22
Osborne v Irish Times Ltd (SC) 27 January 1954 .......... 34.216

Osman v Ferguson [1993] 4 All ER 344 ....................6.78
Osman v United Kingdom [1999] 1 FLR 193 ....................4.19, 6.68, 6.83, 8.01
....................8.25, 10.14, 14.167, 16.69, 17.64
....................18.131, 36.05, 39.25
Osterlind v Hill (1928) 263 Mass 73, 160 NE 301 ....................8.01
Otto v Bolton & Norris [1936] 2 KB 46 ....................13.03, 13.59
Overseas Tankship (UK) Ltd v Morts Dock and Engineering Co Ltd
(The Wagon Mound No 1) [1961] AC 388 .................... 3.03, 3.08-3.19
.................... 3.25-3.32, 3.42, 6.29, 18.148, 20.92
Overseas Tankship (UK) Ltd v Miller Steamship Co Ply Ltd (The Wagon Mound
No 2) [1967] AC 617 ....................3.29, 7.40, 25.19
Owens v Brimmell [1976] 3 All ER 765 ....................20.41

## P

P v P [1999] 3 FCR 547 ....................40.42
Padbury v Holliday and Greenwood Ltd (1912) 28 TLR 494 .................... 43.53-43.53
Page Motors Ltd v Epsom & Ewell BC (1982) 80 LGR 337 ....................24.83, 25.17
Page v Smith [1996] 1 AC 155 .................... 3.36, 6.50, 17.08, 17.65, 18.62-18.63, 22.30
Page v The GN Rly Co (1868) IR 2 CL 228 ....................43.30
Pai Hing Cotton Mill Ltd v Liu Chong Hing Bank Ltd [1986] AC 80 ....................18.58
Paine v Colne Valley Electrical Co [1938] 4 All ER 803 ....................18.46
Palmer v Bateman [1908] 2 IR 393 .................... 9.44-9.44, 24.85
Palmer v Byrne [1906] 1 IR 373 ....................24.28, 24.79
Palmer v Tees Health Authority (1998) 45 BMLR 88, [1999] Lloyd's Rep Med 351
....................16.69, 20.104, 37.44
Palsgraf v Long Island Railroad Co (1928) 248 NY 339, 162 NE 99 ....................3.05, 6.58
....................22.09, 32.139
Pannett v P McGuinness & Co Ltd [1972] 2 QB 599 ....................12.43
Paris v Stepney Borough Council [1951] AC 367 ....................7.37, 18.09
Park Hall School Ltd v Overend [1987] ILRM 345 ....................14.178, 14.198
Parker Knoll v Knoll International [1962] RPC 265 .................... 31.53-31.53
Parker v British Airways Board [1982] 1 All ER 834 .................... 30.24-30.27
Parker v Godin (1728) 2 Stra 813, 93 ER 866 ....................30.04, 30.38
Parker v Langley (1713) 10 Mod 145, 88 ER 667 ....................36.05
Parkes v Howard Johnson Restaurants Ltd (1970) 74 WWR 255 ....................44.21
Parkes v Minister for Finance (1979) 113 ILTR 118 ....................38.11, 43.46
Parkinson v Liverpool Corporation [1950] 1 All ER 367 ....................7.39
Parkinson v Peelo (1939) 73 ILTR 218 .................... 12.09-12.13
Parrill v Genge (1994) 52 ACWS 3d 229, (1994) ACW 5 LEXIS 9480 ....................40.29
Parry v Cleaver [1970] AC 1 ....................44.114
Parry-Jones v Law Society [1969] 1 Ch 1 ....................37.32
Parsons v BNB Laboratories Ltd [1964] 1 QB 95 ....................44.118
Parsons v Hammond Packing Co (1902) 96 Mo App 372, 70 SW 519 ....................7.08, 18.10
Parsons v Kavanagh [1990] ILRM 560 ....................21.06
Pascoe v MWTI Ltd QBD, 31 July 1990 ....................18.65

Paskiviski v Canadian Pacific Ltd [1976] 1 SCR 687 .......... 40.26
Pasley v Freeman (1789) 3 Term Rep 51, 100 ER 450 .......... 35.03
Pasternack v Poulton [1973] 2 All ER 74 .......... 20.34
Pasture Properties Ltd v Evans (HC) 5 February 1999 .......... 45.05
Patel v WH Smith (Eziot) Ltd [1987] 2 All ER 569 .......... 23.39, 45.05
Patterson v Murphy [1978] ILRM 85 .......... 4.20, 24.31, 24.32-24.37
.......... 24.45, 24.75, 45.06, 45.47
Paul & Vincent Ltd v O'Reilly 49 ILTR 89 .......... 35.15
Paul v Holt (1935) 69 ILTR 157 .......... 34.15, 34.97
Paxhaven Holdings Ltd v Attorney General [1974] 2 NZLR 185 .......... 24.112
Payne v Artane Sevice Station (t/a Castle Service Station), DPIJ: Hilary and Easter Terms 1997, p 32 .......... 18.108
Payne v Railway Executive [1952] 1 KB 26 .......... 44.114
Payne v Rogers (1974) 2 HB 1 350 .......... 24.77
Peabody Donation Fund (Governors of) v Sir Lindsay Parkinson & Co Ltd [1985] AC 210 .......... 6.17, 6.24, 6.27-6.32
.......... 6.40, 11.85, 19.39
Peacock v Amusement Equipment Co Ltd [1954] 2 QB 347 .......... 42.39, 42.51
Pearce v United Bristol Healthcare NHS Trust [1999] P 1 QR 53 .......... 14.84
Pearson & Son Ltd v Dublin Corporation [1907] AC 351 .......... 35.10-35.13, 35.15
Peek v Gurney (1873) LR 6 HL 377 .......... 35.06, 35.13
Peerless Bakery Ltd v Watt [1955] NZLR 339 .......... 34.158
Pelletier v Olson (1987) 42 CCLT 129 .......... 20.34
Pembroke v Warren [1896] 1 IR 76 .......... 24.43
Penfolds Wines Pty Ltd v Elliott (1946) 74 CLR 204 .......... 28.10, 30.20
Penny v Wimbledon UDC [1899] 2 QB 72 .......... 43.52
Penruddock's Case (1597) 5 Co Rep 100b, 77 ER 210 .......... 24.79
People (Attorney General) v Dwyer [1972] IR 416 .......... 22.89
People (Attorney General) v Edge [1943] IR 115 .......... 22.77, 24.03
People (Attorney General) v Keatley [1954] IR 12 .......... 22.90, 22.115
People (Attorney General) v O'Brien [1965] IR 142 .......... 23.03, 23.09, 28.15, 37.62
People (Director of Public Prosecutions) v Morgan (1980) 114 ILTR 60 .......... 28.07, 37.07
People (Director of Public Prosecutions) v Walsh [1980] IR 294 .......... 23.27
People v Finkel & Levine (1951) 1 Frewen 123 .......... 10.110, 35.05
People v Hayes (CCA) 9 June 1986 .......... 22.07
People v Murray [1977] IR 360 .......... 2.37
Performance Cars Ltd v Abraham [1962] 1 QB 33 .......... 2.14
Perl (P) (Exporters) Ltd v Camden LBC [1983] 3 All ER 161, [1984] QB 342
.......... 2.42, 6.57, 8.24
Perry (Howard E) & Co Ltd v British Rys Bd [1980] 1 WLR 1375 .......... 29.13
Perry v Fried (1972) 32 DLR (3d) 589 .......... 22.58
Perry v Kendrick's Transport [1956] 1 WLR 85 .......... 25.25, 25.35
Perry v Statham Ltd [1929] IR 277 .......... 12.13
Pesca Valentia v Minister for Fisheries (HC) 6 June 1989 .......... 10.146
Petch v Customs and Excise Commissioners [1993] ICR 789 .......... 18.60

Pete's Towing Services Ltd v Northern Industrial Union of Workers [1970] NZLR 32 ........ 32.43-32.46
Peter Pan Manufacturing Corporation v Corsets Silhouette Ltd [1964] 1 WLR 96 ...37.38
Peters v Prince of Wales Theatre [1943] 1 KB 73 ........ 25.11
Petersen v School District No 36, Surrey BC (1993) 104 DLR 334 ........ 16.19
Petrie v Owners of SS "Rostrevor" [1898] 2 IR 556 ........ 6.01, 6.58, 23.29
........ 23.42-23.50
PH v J Murphy & Sons Ltd [1987] IR 621 ........ 1.67
Phelan Holdings (Kilkenny) Ltd v Hogan (HC) 15 October 1996 ........ 14.226
Phelan v Coilte Teoranta [1993] 1 IR 18 ........ 43.19, 43.49
Phelan v Kilkenny County Council [1943] Ir Jur 1 ........ 8.04, 24.113
Phelps v Hillingdon London Borough Council [2000] 4 All ER 504 ........ 6.91
Phelps v White (1881) 7 LR Ir 160, affg 5 LR Ir 318 ........ 35.10, 35.15-35.20
Philips v The Medical Council [1991] 2 IR 115 ........ 20.33, 21.30
Philips v Whiteley (William), Ltd [1938] 1 All ER 566 ........ 14.73
Phillips v Britannia Hygienic Laundry Co Ltd [1923] 2 KB 832 ........ 21.11, 21.41
Phillips v Dublin Corporation DPIJ: Hilary and Easter Terms 1991, p 42 ........ 19.17
Phillips v Durgan [1991] ILRM 321 ........ 3.12, 7.39, 20.14, 20.80-20.90
........ 26.24, 26.35
Phillips v Eyre (1870) LR 6 QB 1 ........ 11.54, 31.16
Phillips v GN Ry Co Ltd (1903) 4 NIJR 154 ........ 22.37-22.42
Phillips v Soloway (1956) 6 DLR (2d) 570 ........ 40.43
Phillips v The Medical Council [1991] 2 IR 115 ........ 21.10
Picka v Porter Ont CA, 24 April 1980 ........ 8.06
Pickett v British Rail Engineering Ltd [1980] 1 AC 136, [1979] 1 All ER 774 ........ 41.07
Piel v Dublin United Tramways Co (1896) Ltd [1939] Ir Jur 88 ........ 15.48, 20.18
Pierse v Allen Professional Neg LR 486 ........ 14.211
Pigney v Pointer Transport Services Ltd [1957] 2 All ER 807 ........ 42.12
Pilford v Skog Estate (1989) 64 DLR (4th) 186 ........ 32.04
Pilmore v Hood (1838) 5 Bing NC 97, 132 ER 1042 ........ 35.14
Pine Valley Developments Ltd v Minister for the Environment [1987] ILRM 747, [1987] IR 23 ........ 1.06, 1.32, 19.53-19.60, 21.10
........ 32.84, 38.09
Pirelli General Cable Works Ltd v Oscar Faber & Partners [1983] 2 AC 1 ........ 46.10
Pitts v Hunt [1991] 1 QB 24 ........ 20.54, 20.70, 20.94-20.104
Plant v Calco Steel DPIJ : Michaelmas Term 1990, p 262 ........ 21.55
Plant v Cotterill (1860) 5 H & N 430, 157 ER 1249 ........ 30.19
Plantza v Glasgow Corporation (1910) 47 Sc LR 688 ........ 40.11
Player & Wills (Ireland) Ltd v Gallagher (Dublin) Ltd (HC) 26 September 1983 ........ 31.02, 31.74, 45.05
Playfair v Musgrove (1845) 14 M & W 239, 153 ER 465 ........ 23.24
Plummer v Webb Noy (1619) 98 74 ER 1064 ........ 27.48
Plunkett v Irish Annuals Press Ltd (1938) 72 ILTR 161 (HC) revg (1937) 71 ILTR 76 ........ 23.23, 28.11
Plunkett v St Laurence's Hospital (1952) 86 ILTR 157 ........ 7.29

Poirier v Turkewich (1964) 42 DLR (2d) 259 ........ 24.43
Polemis and Furness Withy & Co Ltd, Re [1921] 3 KB 560 ........ 3.03-3.05
........ 3.13-3.26, 3.32, 3.42, 20.92
Polsue & Alfieri Ltd v Rushmer [1907] AC 121 ........ 24.41
Polycell Products Ltd v O'Carroll and Ors t/a Dillon, O'Carroll
[1959] Ir Jur Rep 34 ........ 31.02, 31.30, 31.73, 45.05, 45.09
Pomeroy v State (1883) 94 Ind 96 ........ 22.66
Pontardawe RDC v Moore-Gwyn [1929] 1 Ch 656 ........ 25.18, 26.12
Ponting v Noakes [1894] 2 QB 281 ........ 25.13
Poole v Burns [1944] Ir Jur 20 ........ 29.05-29.05, 30.08
Poole v O'Sullivan [1993] ILRM 55 ........ 46.04
Pope v Coates (1863) 16 ICLR 156 ........ 34.21
Popular Homes Ltd v Society of African Missions Trustees [1997] Ir L Log W 367 25.11
Portelance v Board of Trustees of Roman Catholic Separate School
for School Section No 5 in Township of Grantham (1962) 32 DLR (2d) 337 ........ 16.72
Porter v Duff [1942] IR 548 ........ 22.38
Porter v Price (1960) 11 Utah 2d 80, 355 P 2d 66 ........ 7.13
Post (An) v Irish Permanent plc [1995] 1 ILRM 336 ........ 31.02, 31.21
........ 31.43, 45.05, 45.41
Potter v Carlisle & Cliftonville Golf Club Ltd [1939] NI 114 ........ 7.28, 7.44
Potterton Ltd v Northern Bank Ltd [1993] ILRM 225 ........ 10.57, 10.94
Potts v Plunkett (1859) 9 ICLR 290 ........ 18.01, 18.06
Poulton v L & SW Ry (1867) LR 2 QB 534 ........ 39.08
Powell v Boldaz [1998] Lloyd's Rep Med 116 ........ 22.30
Powell v Fall (1880) 5 QBD 597 ........ 25.19
Powell v McGlynn & Bradlaw [1902] 2 IR 154 ........ 27.03
Power v Bedford Motor Co [1959] IR 391 ........ 2.26, 2.60, 4.10
........ 11.11, 11.24, 11.74
Power v Commercial Banking Co Ltd (HC) 3 February 1975 ........ 36.05
Power v Cook (1869) IR 4 CL 247 ........ 22.12, 30.02, 30.20
Power v Crowley and Reddy Enterprises Ltd (HC) 29 October 1992 ........ 12.67, 12.129
........ 20.14, 21.10, 43.51, 44.79, 44.90
Praed v Graham (1889) 74 QBD 53 ........ 44.58
Pre-Can Exploration & Development Ltd v McTarish (1966) 57 DLR (2d) 557 ........ 37.38
Prendergast v CIE (1967) 101 ILTR 177 ........ 20.55
Prendergast v Joe Malone Self Drive Ltd (SC) 21 June 1967 ........ 44.174, 44.179, 44.181
Preston v Higgins (SC) 13 July 1962 ........ 15.49, 40.18
Preston v Mercer (1656) Hardr 60, 145 ER 380 ........ 23.32
Preston v Shannon Caravans Ltd (HC) unrep ........ 35.06
Pretty v Bickmore (1873) LR 8 CP 401 ........ 24.76
Price v Wright (1899) 35 NBR 26 ........ 27.17
Pride of Derby & Derbyshire Angling Association Ltd v British Celanese Ltd
[1953] 1 All ER 179 ........ 19.52
Priestley v Fowler (1837) 3 M &W 1, 150 ER 1030 ........ 18.02-18.02
Priestman v Colangelo [1959] SCR 615 ........ 7.39, 22.92

Primor plc v Stokes Kennedy Crowley [1996] 2 IR 459 ..................................7.01, 46.64
Pritchard v JH Cobden Ltd [1987] 1 All ER 300 ........................................................33.02
Pritchard v Ministry of Defence [1995] CLY 4726 .....................................................22.38
Private Motorists Protection Association (in liq) v Private Motorists Provident
Society (in liq) (HC) 20 February 1997 ...............................................................46.65
Private Research Ltd v Brosnan [1996] 1 ILRM 27 ..................................... 31.08-31.12
............................................................................................ 37.23-37.28, 37.38, 45.05
Prole v Allen [1950] 1 All ER 476 ........................................................................ 39.11-39.14
Prosser (A) & Son Ltd v Levy [1955] 1 WLR 1224 ..................................................25.30
Pruitt v Allied Chemical Corp (1981) 523 F Supp 975 (ED Va) ..............................24.05
Pruneyard Shopping Center v Robins (1980) 447 US 74 ............................................23.20
Public Transport Corporation v Sartori [1997] 1 VR 168 ..........................................18.66
Public Works (Commissioners of ) v Kavanagh [1962] IR 216 ..................................38.04
Purcell v Dublin County Council (SC) 28 July 1957 ....................................................8.23
Purcell v Minister for Finance [1939] IR 115 ...............................................................30.19
Purdy v Woznesensky, [1937] 2 WWR 116 .................................................................22.33
Purtill v Athlone UDC [1968] IR 205 ............................................. 6.25-6.25, 6.31, 6.38
............................................................................ 6.52-6.53, 7.25, 11.30, 11.137, 12.45
....................................................................................12.53, 12.137, 13.24, 23.14, 23.27
....................................................................................23.48, 25.48, 32.142, 39.25, 44.84
Purtle v Shelton (1971) 251 Ark 519, 474 SW 2d 123 ................................................40.30
Pyke v Hibernian Bank [1950] IR 195 ..............................................34.62, 34.67, 34.92
.............................................................................................. 34.97, 34.101, 34.175-34.177

## Q

Q v Minto Management Ltd (1985) 15 DLR (4th) 581 affd (1986) 34 DLR (4th) 767
..............................................................................................................................43.39
Quail v JJ McGovern Ltd DPIJ: Michaelmas Term 1991, p 82 ....................18.09, 18.155
Quartz Hill Gold Mining Co v Eyre (1883) 11 QBD 674 ..........................................36.19
Queegan v Bord na Mona, DPIJ: Trinity and Michaelmas Terms 1994, p 70 ...........18.10
Queen in right of Canada v Saskatchewan Wheat Pool [1983] 1 SCR 205 ....21.05, 21.08
Queen in Right of Ontario v Jennings 57 DLR (2d) 644 .........................................44.102
Queen v The Ship Sun Diamond 1983 25 CCLT 19 ......................................................24.05
Quigley v Beirne [1955] IR 62 ..........................................23.20, 32.91, 32.101, 32.150
Quigley v Byrne DPIJ: Hilary & Easter Terms 1994, p 32 (HC) ............................44.176
Quigley v Creation Ltd [1971] IR 269 ................................... 31.82, 34.10, 34.50-34.55
......................................................................34.64-34.66, 34.97-34.100, 34.229, 35.26
Quigley v Donnelly (SC) 20 December 1956 ................................................15.17, 15.39
Quigley v Ireland DPIJ: Hilary and Easter Terms 1992, p 111 ................................18.23
Quilligan v Long (1952) 87 ILTR 129 ........................................................................43.46
Quinlan v Steffens (1980) 12 CCLT 162 ....................................................................20.70
Quinlan, Re (1976) 70 NJ 10 .......................................................................................37.87
Quinn v Burch Bros (Builders) Ltd [19661 2 QB 370 ..................................................2.40
Quinn v Burrell (HC) 23 April 1993 .............................................................18.03, 21.10
Quinn v Coleman (1898) 33 ILTR 79 ..........................................................................30.24

Quinn v Hansberry, DPIJ: Trinity and Michaelmas Terms 1996, p 11 ...................... 15.05
Quinn v James Nevin Appearances DPIJ: Hilary and Easter Terms 1993, p 242 ............................................................................................................................ 8.14
Quinn v Kennedy Brothers Construction Ltd (HC) 4 March, 1994 .......................... 15.37
Quinn v Leatham [1901] AC 495 ............................................ 3.25, 32.01, 32.41, 32.48
Quinn v Ministry of Commerce [1954] NI 131 .................................................... 24.113
Quinn v Pratt [1908] 2 IR 69 ............................................................30.12, 30.19-30.20
Quinn v Quality Homes Ltd [1976-77] ILRM 314 .......................... 13.81, 20.24, 44.207
Quinn v Quinn (1905) 39 ILTR 163 ........................................................................ 27.16
Quinn v Scott [1965] 2 All ER 588 .......................................................................... 24.30
Quinn v Tedcastles & Co (1898) 32 ILTR 137 ........................................................ 11.07
Quinn v W & T Avery Ltd (1967) 103 ILTR 142 ..................................... 18.102, 44.183
Quinn, Re [1974] IR 19 .......................................................................................... 24.16
Quirke v Mid-Western Health Board, DPIJ: Trinity Term 1991, p 94 ................... 18.108

## R

R (IUDWC) v Rathmines UDC [1928] IR 260 ................................................39.26-39.28
R (Orr) v Justices of Londonderry (1891) 28 LR Ir 440 ......................................... 22.111
R (Westropp) v Clare County Council [1904] 2 IR 569 ............................................ 43.52
R Griggs Group Ltd v Dunnes Stores Ireland Co (HC) 4 October 1996 .................. 31.02 ............................................................................................................... 31.23, 45.05
R Leslie Ltd v Sheill [1914] 3 KB 607 ...................................................................... 40.31
R v Barnard (1837) 7 C & P 784, 173 ER 342 ............................................ 10.110, 35.05
R v Bournewood Community and Mental Health NHS Trust ex p L (Secretary of State for Health intervening) [1998] 3 All ER 289 ............................................ 22.46
R v Bow Street Metropolitan Stipendiary Megistrate ex p Pinochet Ugarte (No 3) [1999] 2 All ER 97 .............................................................................................. 38.19
R v Brown [1994] 1 AC 212 ...................................................................................... 22.62
R v Buchinsky 24 CCLT 266 ...................................................................................... 32.05
R v Case 1 Den CC 580 ............................................................................................. 22.65
R v Cotesworth (1704) 6 Mod 172, 87 ER 928. ....................................................... 22.11
R v Creighton [1993] 3 SCR 3 .................................................................................. 40.29
R v Cross (1892) 3 Camp 224 .................................................................................. 24.97
R v Crown Court Manchester ex p Director of Public Prosecutions [1993] 1 All ER 801 ........................................................................................................................... 38.22
R v D [1984] 2 All ER 449 ........................................................................................ 22.77
R v Dudley (1884) 14 QBD 273 ................................................................................ 22.92
R v Faulkner (1877) 13 Cox 550 .............................................................................. 22.07
R v Flattery (1877) 2 QBD 410 ................................................................................ 22.66
R v Fulling [1987] QB 426 ........................................................................................ 44.33
R v Governor of Brockhill Prison, ex p Evans (No 2) [1999] QB 1043 .................. 22.39
R v Hallett (1911) 45 ILTR 84 .................................................................................. 24.16
R v Hehir [1895] 2 IR 709 ......................................................................................... 30.12
R v Ireland [1998] AC 147 ........................................................... 22.24-22.26, 37.09
R v Jennings (1966) 57 DLR (2d) 644 .................................................................. 44.185

R v Jones [1976] 3 All ER 54 ....................23.16
R v Khan (Sultan) [1996] 3 All ER 289 ....................1.51
R v Latimer (1886) 17 QBD. 359 ....................22.07
R v Lewis (1996) 39 CRR (2d) 26 ....................37.02
R v Macquarie & Budge (1875) 13 NSWSCR 264 ....................22.38
R v Morgantaler (1988) 44 DLR (4th) 385 ....................37.81
R v O'Connor (1995) 130 DLR 4th 235 ....................37.58
R v Pagham Sussex Sewers Commissioners (1828) 8 B & C 355, 108 ER1075 .......24.55
R v Pemblition (1874) LR 2 CCR 119 ....................22.07
R v Pratt (1885) 4 E1 & BL 860, 119 ER 319 ....................23.29
R v Robinson (1746) 1 Leach 37 168 ER 121 ....................32.61
R v Secretary of State for Transport, ex parte Factortame [1997] Eu LR 475 ..1.88, 44.12
R v St George, (1840) 9 C & P 483, 173 ER 921 ....................22.22
R v Vantaudillo (1815) 4 M & S 73 ....................24.12
R v Wilson [1955] 1 All ER 744 ....................22.24
Rabbette v Mayo County Council [1984] ILRM 156 ..........3.38, 20.24, 24.31, 45.05
Radburn v Kemp [1971] 3 All ER 249 ....................15.47
Radford v Wexford Corporation (1955) 89 ILTR 184 .................... 45.03-45.05
Radio Limerick One Ltd v Treaty Radio Ltd (HC) 13 November 1997 .........31.46, 45.05
Radley v L & N W Ry (1876) 1 AC 754 ....................20.06
Rae v Strathclyde Joint Police Board [1999] SCLR 793 ....................18.125
Rafferty v Parsons (CA) of Ireland Ltd [1987] ILRM 98 ..........6.67, 18.09, 18.161
Ragget v Findlater (1873) LR 17 Eq 29 ....................31.40
Railways (NSW) (Commissioner for) v Cardy (1960) 104 CLR 274 ....................12.26
Railways (NSW) (Commissioner for) v Scott (1959) 102 CLR 392 ....................32.09
Rainham Chemical Works Ltd v Belvedere Fish Guano Co Ltd [1921] AC 465
....................25.16, 25.28
Rainville (1983) 17 U Cal Davis LR 389 ....................24.31
Rajogopal v State of TN [1994] 6 SCC 632 ....................34.181
Ralph v Henderson & Pollard Ltd [1968] NZLR 759 .................... 40.26-40.29
Rambarran v Gurrucharran [1970] 1 All ER 749 ....................43.63
Ramoo son of Erulapan v Gan Soo Swee [1971] 3 All ER 320 ....................15.48
Ramsay v Nicol [1939] VLR 330 ....................31.58
Ramsey v Northern Ireland Electricity plc, DPIJ: Hilary & Easter Terms, 1997 .......44.93
Rands v McNeil [1955] 1 QB 253 ....................18.160
Rantzen v Mirror Group Newspapers (1986) Ltd [1994] QB 670 ....................34.231
.................... 34.240-34.249, 34.255
Rappaport v Nichols (1959) 156A 2D 1 ....................8.06
Ratcliffe v Evans [1892] 2 QB 524 ....................35.26, 35.29, 44.05
Ravenscroft v Rederiaktiebolaget Transatlantic [1991] 3 All ER 73 (QB),
revg [1992] 2 All ER 470 ....................17.33
Rawlinson v Rice [1997] 2 NZLR 651 ....................19.55
Rawsthorne v Ottley [1937] 3 All ER 902 .................... 16.27-16.32
Rayson v South London Tramways Co [1893] 2 QB 304 ....................36.18
Raza v Sullivan (1970) 432 F 2d 617 ....................9.28

Read v Coker (1853) 73 CB 850, 138 ER 1437 .......... 22.20
Read v Friendly Society of Operative Stonemasons [1902] 2 KB 88 .......... 32.43-32.44
Read v GE Rly (1868) LR 3 QB 555 .......... 42.13
Read v J Lyons & Co Ltd [1947] AC 156 .......... 25.16, 25.19, 25.20, 25.25, 25.45
Reaney v Fermoy UDC DPIJ: Hilary and Easter Terms 1994 .......... 19.19
Reaney v Thomas Lydon & Son Ltd [1957] Ir Jur 1 .......... 12.08
Reavis v Clan Line Steamers Ltd [1925] SC 725 .......... 32.05
Reckitt and Colman Products Ltd v Borden Inc [1990] 1 All ER 873 .......... 31.02
Red Sea Insurance Co Ltd v Bouygues SA [1995] 1 AC 190 .......... 31.16
Redbank Oyster Co Ltd and Stassen v Fairway Fabrications Ltd and BIM [1976] IR 191 .......... 4.19
Reddaway v Banham [1896] AC 199 .......... 31.29
Reddaway v Bentham [1892] 2 QB 639 .......... 31.05
Reddlington v Thos Heiton & Co (SC) 27 February 1959 .......... 44.58
Reddy v Bates [1983] IR 141, [1984] ILRM 197 .......... 44.62, 44.76-44.79
.......... 44.90-44.91, 44.99-44.100
.......... 44.142, 44.161-44.164
Redfont Ltd v Custom House Dock Management Ltd (HC) 31 March 1998
.......... 24.01, 24.25
Redford v Courtown (Co Wexford) Golf Club Irish Times, 11 November 1983 .......... 12.52
Redmond v Equipment Company of Ireland Ltd High Court 28 July 1992 .......... 12.08
Redmond v Hayes High Court, 7 October 1974 .......... 23.48
Redmond v Kelly (1894) 28 ILT & Sol J 555 .......... 34.170
Redpath v Belfast & County Down Railway [1947] NI 167 .......... 42.39, 44.126
Reen v Bank of Ireland Finance Ltd [1983] ILRM 507 .......... 35.06
Rees v Sinclair [1974] 1 NZLR 180 .......... 14.164
Reeve v Palmer (1850) 5 CB (NS) 84, 141 ER 33 .......... 29.09
Reeves v Carthy and O'Kelly [1984] IR 348 .......... 2.27, 3.08, 3.21-3.23, 3.35
Reeves v Commissioner of Police of the Metropolis [1999] 3 All ER 897 .......... 42.12
Reeves v Metropolitan Police Commissioner [2000] 1 AC 360 .......... 20.94
Reeves v Penrose (1890) 26 LR Ir 141 .......... 23.02, 23.38
Regan v Williamson [1976] 2 All ER 244 .......... 42.64
Regina v Bishop (1975) 1 QB 274 .......... 34.78
Regina v Burko (1969) 3 DLR (3d) 330 .......... 23.20
Regina v Knuller (Publishing Printing and Promotions) Limited [1973] AC 435 .......... 34.78
Reibl v Hughes (1980) 114 DLR (3d) 1 .......... 14.79-14.85, 14.99, 14.144, 22.70
Reid v Dublin Corporation, DPIJ, Trinity Term 1991, p 86 .......... 18.83
Reid v Minister for Finance (HC) 29 July 1996 .......... 33.13
Reid v Rush & Tompkins Group plc [1990] 1 WLR 212 .......... 10.33, 18.58
Reida v Intend (1971) 18 Cal Appeal 3d 698, 96 Cal Rpt R 102 .......... 16.03
Reidy v Fry-Cadbury (Ireland) Ltd (SC) 12 May 1972 .......... 18.84
Reidy v National Maternity Hospital (HC) 31 July 1997 .......... 46.65
Reilly v Garvey [1973] IR 89 .......... 2.39, 9.07, 24.16
Reilly v Gill (1946) 85 ILTR 165 .......... 34.58, 34.165, 34.177, 34.225
Reilly v McAleer DPIJ: Hilary and Easter Terms 1992, p 204 .......... 21.22, 21.34

Reilly v Moore [1935] NI 196 .......... 21.10, 21.32-21.32
Reilly v Ryan [1991] ILRM 449 .......... 43.38
Reilly v Ryan Pettersson v Royal Oak Hotel Ltd [1948] NZLR 136 .......... 43.39
Reinhardt v Mentasi (1889) 42 ChD 685 .......... 24.31
Rendell v Associated Finance Pty Ltd [1957] VR 604. .......... 30.12
Rennick v Wexford County Council (1901) ILTR 78 .......... 24.113
Reno Engrais et Produits Chemiques SA v Irish Agricultural Wholesale Society Ltd (HC) 8 September 1976 .......... 32.14, 32.25, 45.45
Representative Church Body v Crawford (1939) 74 ILTR 49 .......... 23.29, 23.42, 23.48
Representative Church Body v Dublin Board of Assistance [1948] IR 287 ... 21.19, 21.34
Rex Pet Foods Ltd v Lamb Bros (Dublin) Ltd, (HC) 26 August 1982 .......... 45.11
Rexi Irish Mink v Dublin County Council [1972] IR 123 .......... 30.19
Reynolds v Clarke (1725) 2 LD Raym 1399, 92 ER 410 .......... 23.32
Reynolds v Molocco t/a "Patrick" [1999] 1 ILRM 289 .......... 34.75-34.77 .......... 45.05-45.05, 45.29-45.35
Reynolds v Times Newspaper Ltd [1999] 1 All ER 609 .......... 34.07, 34.82, 34.176 .......... 34.181-34.187
Rice v Chan Estate (1998) 84 ACWS .......... 40.29
Rice v Class (SC) 1954 .......... 15.29
Rich v Basterfield (1847) 4 CB 738 .......... 24.75
Rich v LCC [1953] 2 All ER 376 .......... 16.32, 16.70
Richards v Dublin Corporation (SC) 12 July 1996 .......... 23.26
Richards v Naum [1967] 1 QB 620 .......... 34.158
Richardson v Athlone Woollen Mills Co Ltd [1942] IR 581 .......... 26.03
Richardson v Atkinson (1723) 1 Stra 576, 93 ER 710 .......... 30.05
Richley v Faull (Richley, Third Party) [1965] 1 WLR 1454 .......... 9.21
Richman v McMurty (1983) 25 CC LT 152 .......... 36.04
Richmond (Mayor of City of) v Delmo Victoria SC, App Div, 13 November 1992 1992 VIL LEXIS 513 .......... 7.44
Rickards v Lothian [1913] AC 263 .......... 19.52, 25.07, 25.30-25.35
Rickes v DPP [1973] 2 AII ER 935 .......... 36.04
Riddick v Thames Board Mills Ltd [1977] QB 881 .......... 34.161
Rigby v Chief Constable of Northamptonshire [1985] 2 All ER 985 .......... 20.14, 23.29 .......... 23.37, 23.48, 25.17-25.19
Rigby v Mirror Newspapers Ltd [1964] SR (NSW) 34 .......... 34.43
Rigler v Miller (1972) 26 DLR (3d) 366 (BCSC) .......... 20.41
Ring v Power [1961] Ir Jur Rep 51 .......... 3.05, 3.28, 7.29
Riordan v Butler [1940] IR 347 .......... 32.47-32.55, 32.84
Riordan's Travel Ltd v Acres & Co Ltd (HC) 17 January 1979 .......... 20.24
Riordans Travel & Riordans Shipping Ltd v Acres & Co Ltd (No 2) [1979] ILRM 3 .......... 3.08, 3.37-3.41
Ritsas v Commonwealth of Australia (1975) 50 ALJR 104 .......... 18.04
River Valley Products Ltd v Strutt (HC) 6 February 1991 .......... 32.125
Rivers v Cutting [1982] 1 WLR 1146 .......... 43.49
Rivtow Marine Ltd v Washington Iron Works (1973) 40 DLR (3d) 530 .......... 11.60

Robb v Green [1895] 2 QB 315 .......... 37.38
Robbins v Jones (1863) 15 CB (ns) 221, 143 ER 786 .......... 13.12, 13.67
Robert J Goff & Co Ltd v Walsh [1943] Ir Jur 56 .......... 29.01
Roberts v Ramsbottom [1980] 1 WLR 823 .......... 7.20
Roberts v Ring (1919) 143 Minn 151, 173 NW 437 .......... 40.27
Roberts v Roberts (1864) 5 B & S 384, 122 ER 874 .......... 34.42
Roberts v United Kingdom (1995) 19 EHRR 112 .......... 22.104
Robertson v MacDonagh (1880) 6 LR Ir 433 .......... 14.162
Robertson v Ridley [1989] 2 All ER 474 .......... 39.14
Robinson v Balmain New Ferry Co [1910] AC 295, affg (1906) 4 CLR 379 .......... 22.55
Robinson v Chambers [1946] NI 148 .......... 34.21, 34.92
Robinson v Department of the Environment for Northern Ireland [1988] NIJB 24 .. 21.03
Robinson v ESB DPIJ: Trinity and Michaelmas Terms 1993, p 134 .......... 18.108, 18.114
Robinson v Glover [1952] NZLR 699 .......... 7.15
Robinson v Jones (1879) 4 LR Ir 391 .......... 34.178
Robinson v Jones (1979) 4 LR Ir 391 .......... 34.14
Robinson v Kilvert (1889) 41 Ch D 88 .......... 24.106
Robinson v Lindsay (1979) 92 Wash 2d 410, 598 P 2d 392 .......... 40.30
Robinson v Technico Ltd (HC) 19 February 1953, affd by (SC) 7 July 1953 .......... 6.10, 11.07, 11.14, 11.24, 11.34, 26.24
Robinson v Ward (1958) 108 L Jo 491 .......... 34.37
Robson v Marquis of Londonderry (1900) 34 ILTR 88 .......... 27.08
Roche v Kelly & Co Ltd [1969] IR 100 .......... 43.17, 44.82, 44.183
Roche v Meyler [1896] 2 IR 35 .......... 35.26
Roche v P Kelly & Co Ltd [1969] IR 100 .......... 21.10, 21.37, 43.16
Roche v Peilow [1985] IR 232, [1986] ILRM 189 .......... 10.09, 14.03 .......... 14.09-14.11, 14.130, 14.203, 14.210
Rodriguez v Shelter Canadian Properties Ltd (1997) Ont CJ LEXIS 1796 .......... 26.33
Roe v Ministry of Health [1954] 2 QB 66 .......... 9.28, 14.18, 14.27, 43.22
Roe v Wade (1973) 410 US 113 .......... 37.81
Rogers v Britton (CA (Civ Div) 4 March 1996 .......... 15.08
Rogers v Bus Atha Claith (CC) 17 January 2000 .......... 18.103
Rogers v GS Ry (1940) 74 ILTR 206 .......... 21.10, 21.12, 21.19, 24.06
Rogers v ITGWU [1978] ILRM 51 .......... 1.13
Rogers v Whitaker (1992) 175 Comm LR 479 .......... 14.79-14.85
Rogers v Wilkinson, The Times, 19 January, 1963 .......... 16.05
Rohan v Bord na Móna [1991] ILRM 123 .......... 46.69
Rohan v Minister for Finance (HC) 19 June 1992 .......... 3.35, 6.42, 7.52
Ronayne v Ronayne [1970] IR 15 .......... 44.181
Rondel v Worsley [1969] 1 AC 191 .......... 1.33, 6.20, 14.161-14.164, 14.197-14.199
Rookes v Barnard [1964] AC 1129 .......... 1.118, 32.47-32.55, 34.258-34.262 .......... 44.10-44.34, 44.41-44.52
Roomer v Atlantic Cement Co (1970) 26 NY 2d 219 .......... 24.37
Rooney v Connolly [1986] IR 57, [1987] ILRM 768 .......... 6.10, 12.13-12.14, 12.52, 27.29

Roote v Irish Box Print and Packaging Ltd DPIJ: Hilary and Easter Terms 1991, p 10 ....21.55, 44.180
Rose v Ford [1937] AC 826 ....41.05, 44.202
Rose v Plenty and Co-operative Retail Services Ltd [1976] 1 All ER 97 ....43.32
Rosenthal v Alderton & Sons Ltd [1946] KB 374 ....29.10
Ross Co Ltd v Swan [1981] ILRM 416 ....23.02, 45.05
Ross Meats v Bank of Ireland Irish Times, 10 May 1986 ....34.62
Ross v Caunters (a firm) [1980] Ch 279 ....10.72, 14.174
Ross v Curtis (HC) 3 February 1989 ....1.120, 12.55, 22.89, 22.114
Ross v Dunphy (HC) 13 February 1978 ....9.17, 23.50, 25.39, 28.12
Ross v Eason & Son Ltd [1911] 2 IR 459 ....34.19
Ross v Fedden (1872) LR 7 QB 661 ....25.11
Ross v McCarthy [1970] NZLR 449 ....27.51
Ross v McQueen [1947] NI 81 ....20.14
Ross v Rugge-Price (1876) 1 Ex D 269 ....21.19
Rosso v Ontario Jockey Club (1987) 46 DLR (4th) 359 ....23.20, 32.167
Roundabout Ltd v Beirne [1959] IR 423 .... 24.16, 32.87-32.92
Rourke v Pepper (1825) Smi & Bat 346 ....22.105
Rowdens v Keaveney [1903] 2 IR 82 ....24.16
Rowe v Bus Éireann and Wicklow County Council (HC) 3 March 1994 ....13.47, 24.116
Rowe v Richards 35 SD 201, 151 NW 1001 ....42.13
Rowling v Takaro Properties Ltd [1988] AC 473 .... 6.23, 19.10-19.11
Roy v Prior [1970] AC 470 ....36.19
Royal Aquarium and Summer and Winter Garden Society Ltd v Parkinson [1892] 1 QB 431 ....34.146
Royal Aquarium Society v Parkinson [1892] 1 QB 431 ....34.155
Royal Baking Powder Co v Wright Crossley & Co (1901) 18 RPC 95 ....35.27
Royal Dublin Society v Yates (HC) 31 July 1997 ....22.32, 23.01, 23.37 .... 24.24, 24.65-24.70, 24.73, 32.56, 37.14
Royscot Trust Ltd v Rogerson [1991] 2 QB 297 ....35.17
Ruckley v Kiernan (1857) 7 ICLR 75 ....34.38
Rudd v Rea [1921] 1 IR 223 ....23.48
Runham v Wakefield (1863) 16 ICLR 507 ....36.02
Rushton v National Coal Board [1953] 1 QB 495 ....44.07
Russell v McCabe [1962] NZLR 392 .... 26.35-26.35
Russell v Moore (1881) 8 LR (Ir) 318 ....23.33
Russell v Pope NSSCTD, 26 May 1975 ....43.14
Russell v Walsh (HC) 3 April 1995 ....14.30
Russell v Walsh and Mid-Western Health Board (HC) 3 April 1995 ....9.28
Russo v Ontario Jockey Club (1987) 43 CCLT I ....22.114
Rust v Needham 9 SASR 510 ....7.04
Ruth v Ruth 213 Tenn 82 372, SW 2d 285 ....20.81
Rutherford v Hawke's Bay Hospital Board [1949] NZLR 400 ....43.39
Ruttledge v Land [1930] IR 537 ....26.06

RWDSU Local 558 v Pepsi-Cola Canada Beverages (West) Ltd (1998) 167 DLR (4th) 220 .......... 32.145, 32.162
Ryan v Attorney General [1965] IR 294 .......... 1.13, 24.10, , 32.03-32.09, 37.86
Ryan v Clarkin [1935] IR 1 .......... 43.50
Ryan v Compensation Tribunal [1997] 1 ILRM 194 (HC) .......... 44.128
Ryan v Cooke [1938] IR 512 .......... 23.20, 32.108, 32.146 .......... 32.149-32.154, 32.166
Ryan v Dan Dooley Rent a Car Topcar Ltd and Rover (Ireland) Ltd (HC) 19 May 1994 .......... 11.16
Ryan v Fildes [1938] 3 All ER 517 .......... 22.103
Ryan v Fisher (1976) 51 Austr LJR 125 .......... 7.25
Ryan v Glover [1939] Ir Jur 65 .......... 27.42-27.47
Ryan v Hickson (1974) 7 OR (2d) 352, 55 DLR (3d) 196 .......... 40.29
Ryan v Ireland [1989] IR 177 .......... 6.06, 6.42, 6.55, 7.52 .......... 18.129-18.137, 19.01, 20.71 .......... 26.33, 32.09, 38.06-38.10
Ryan v Madden [1944] IR 154 .......... 16.17, 16.28, 40.11
Ryan v O'Callaghan (HC) 22 July 1987 .......... 23.06
Ryan v O'Connor DPIJ: Michaelmas Term, p 1 (HC) .......... 44.149
Ryan v Roscrea Bacon Factory and McNamara (SC) 20 November 1985 .......... 4.12
Ryan v Stella Picture Theatre Ltd, DPIJ: Trinity and Michaelmas Terms 1994 .......... 3.35
Ryan v Tipperary (NR) County Council [1912] 2 IR 392 .......... 24.113
Ryan v Toal DPIJ: Hilary & Easter Terms 1991, p 208 (HC) .......... 44.176
Ryeford Homes v Sevenoaks DC [1989] Con LR 75 .......... 25.27
Rylands v Fletcher (1866) LR 1 Ex 265, (1868) LR 3 HL 330 .......... 1.18, 1.50 .......... 3.42, 7.40, 9.38, 9.49, 16.15, 19.52 .......... 24.59, 24.86, 25.01-25.04, 25.09-25.18, 25.23-25.52 .......... 26.21, 26.25, 27.01, 27.08, 27.45, 38.06, 43.49

## S

S v G [1995] 3 NZLR 681 .......... 46.99
Saccardo v Hamilton [1971] 2 OR 479 .......... 25.17
Sadiq v Chief Constable of Lancashire (CA) 16 March 2000 .......... 6.91
Safeway Stores Pty Ltd v Zaluzna (1987) 162 CLR 479 .......... 25.48
Sagor v Joseph Burnett Co (1937) 122 Conn 447, 190 A 258 .......... 40.29
Said v Butt [1920] 3 KB 497 .......... 32.20
Saif Ali v Sydney Mitchell & Co (a firm) [1980] AC 198 .......... 14.161-14.164, 14.199
Salisbury v Crudale (1918) 41 R1 33, 102 A 731 .......... 16.03
Salmon v Seafarer Restaurants Ltd (British Gas Corp, third party) [1983] 3 All ER 729 .......... 26.35
Saltman Engineering Co Ltd v Campbell Engineering Co Ltd 65 RPC 203 .......... 37.23
Sammon v Dun Laoghaire County Council [1997] Ir L Log W 111 .......... 24.115
Sammon v Fleming GMbH (HC) 23 November 1993 .......... 3.35, 18.109
Sanders-Clark v Grosvenor Mansions Co [1900] 2 Ch 373 .......... 24.31
Sandys v Harrison [1926] IR 243 (SC) .......... 20.18

Sandys v Murray (1838) 1 Ir Eq Rep 29 ....................23.22, 45.05
Sargerson v McIlhagga [1963] NI 73 ....................21.22, 21.44
Saunders v Edwards [1987] 2 All ER 651 ....................20.103
Savage (JC) Ltd v Doughlas Wallace Oppermann Architects and Designers Ltd [1997] Ir L Log W 295 ....................13.81
Saville v Roberts (1698) 1 Ld Raym 374;12 Mod 208; 88 ER 1267 ....................36.17
Sayag Case 5/68 [1968] ECR 395, Case 9/69 [1969] ECR 336 ....................38.22
Sayers v Bachelor (1855) 7 IJ OS 257 ....................34.34
Sayers v Harlow UDC [1958] 1 WLR 623 .................... 2.47, 22.37-22.38
Scally v Southern Health Board [1992] 1 AC 294 ....................10.33
Scampton v Colhoun [1959] NI 106 ....................46.06
Scanlon v Abbey Service Garage (Galway) Ltd [1965] IR 700 .................... 9.01, 15.27-15.33
Scannell v O'Keefe t/a George O'Keefe & Sons DPIJ: Trinity and Michaelmas Terms 1998, p 17 (HC) ....................44.149
Schellenberg v Tunnell Holdings Pty Ltd (2000) 170 ALR 594 ....................9.43, 9.54
Schittone v George Minkensky Ltd 1997 Ont CJ LEXIS 2074 ....................32.05
Schmidt v Home Secretary of UK (SC) 24 April 1997 ....................38.18
Schmidt v Sharpe (1983) 27 CCLT 1 .................... 8.06-8.07
Scholz v Standish [1961] SASR 123 ....................7.13
Schulke & Mayr UK Ltd v Alkpharm UK Ltd Chy Dir, 31 July 1997 ....................35.26
Schuster v Whitehead [1960] OR 125, 21 DLR (2d) 609 ....................43.14
Schwarz v Hill House International Junior School (CA Civ Div) 25 May 1994 ....................33.22
Scott v Bowyer 1997 Vic LEXIS 28 ....................32.03
Scott v Brookfield Linen Co Ltd [1910] 2 IR 509 ....................21.10
Scott v Dublin & Wicklow Ry Co 11 ICLR 377 ....................20.06
Scott v Eason & Son Ltd and Batsford Ltd Irish Times, 9 August 1980 ....................34.103
.................... 45.05-45.05
Scott v Goulding Properties Ltd [1973] IR 200 ....................24.25, 44.07, 45.50
Scott v London & St Katherine Docks Co (1865) 3 H & C 596, 159 ER 665 .................... 9.15-9.17, 9.34, 9.53
Scott v McFarlane [1978] 1 NZLR 553 ....................10.147
Scott v Midland Great Western Railway Co (1853) 3 Ir CLR 573 ....................29.05, 30.07
Scott v Shepherd (1773) 2 Wm Bl 892, 96, ER 525 ....................2.47, 22.15, 22.92, 27.07
Scrimgeour v Board of Management of the Canadian District of the American Lutheran Church [1947] 1 WWR 120 ....................9.17
Scully v Marjorie Boland Ltd [1962] IR 58 ....................4.20, 6.10, 13.19, 24.85, 25.11, 25.30
Scully v Mulhall (1951) 85 ILTR 18 ....................2.25, 27.03
Seabord Air Line Ry Co v Hackney (1928) 217 Ala 382, 115 So 869 ....................7.08
Seager v Copydex (No 2) [1969] RPC 250 ....................37.22
Sealand of the Pacific Ltd v Robert C McHaffie Ltd (1975) 51 DLR (3d) 703 ....................10.149
Sea-land Services Inc v Gaudet (1974) 414 US 573 ....................42.13
Seaman v Cuppledick (1615) Owen 150, 74 ER 966 ....................22.90
Searle v Wallbank [1947] AC 341 .................... 27.50-27.54
Secretary of State for the Home Office v Robb [1995] 1 All ER 677 ....................22.92

Secretary of State for War v Studdert [1902] 1 IR 375 (HL) affg [1902] 1 IR 240 ... 1.104
Securities Trust Ltd v Hugh Moore & Alexander Ltd [1964] IR 417 ... 10.64, 10.109 ... 10.151
Security Pak Strapping v Evening Press, Cork Examiner, 20 June 1987 ... 34.67
Sedleigh-Denfield v O'Callaghan [1940] AC 880 ... 24.79-24.83, 25.40, 32.161
Seeds v Newry Traction Engine Co (1903) 37 ILTR 114 ... 24.59
Sefton v Topham's Ltd [1964] 1 WLR 1408 ... 32.30
Segal v Derrick Golf & Winter Club (1977) 76 DLR (3d) 746 ... 23.31
Semenoff v Kokan (1991) 84 DLR (4th) 76 (BC CA) ... 41.07
Senior v Ward (1859) 1 E & E 385, 120 ER 954 ... 20.58
Series 5 Software Ltd v Clarke [1996] FSR 273 ... 31.61
Serville v Constance [1954] 1 WLR 487 ... 35.28
Sevenoaks v Latimer (1919) 54 ILTR 11 ... 34.61, 34.169
Sexton v O'Keeffe [1966] IR 204 ... 42.37, 44.73, 44.95, 44.103, 44.145
SFL Engineering Ltd v Smyth Cladding Systems (HC) 9 May 1997 ... 4.24
Sforza v Green Bus Lines (1934) 150 Misc 180, 268 NYS 446 ... 7.23
Sgro v Verbeck (1980) 111 DLR (3d) 479 (Ont HC) ... 40.26
Shaddock v Parramatta City Council (1981) 36 ALR 385 ... 10.147
Sharp v Avery and Kerwood [1938] 4 All ER 85 ... 10.50
Sharp v Kaiser Foundation Health Plan of Colorado 710P 2d 1153 (solo CA 1985) ... 2.21
Shaw v Shaw [1954] 2 KB 429 ... 22.66
Shawinigan v Vokins [1961] 1 WLR 1206 ... 2.37
Sheahan v Ahearne (1875) IR 9 CL 412 ... 34.42
Shearer v Harland & Wolff Ltd [1947] NI 102 ... 21.10, 21.25, 21.54
Sheasgreen v Morgan [1952] DLR 48 ... 40.08
Sheehan v College of Dance [1996] Ir L Log W 288 ... 24.31, 45.05
Sheehan v District Justice Reilly [1992] IR 368 ... 24.12
Sheehy v Faughnan [1991] 1 IR 424 ... 29.09
Shelfer v City of London Electric Co [1895] 1 Ch 287 ... 24.37
Shelley v Shelley [1971] SASR 430 ... 20.18
Shell-Mex & BP Ltd v Belfast Corporation [1952] NI 72 ... 25.35
Shelton v Creane and Arklow UDC (HC) 17 December 1987 ... 7.27, 12.09, 19.34
Sheperd v Wakeman (1662) 1 Sid 79 82 ER 982 ... 35.26
Sheppard v Northern Ireland Housing Executive [1984] NILR Bull No 1 ... 8.24, 25.35
Sheriff v Corrigan (SC) 15 February 2000 ... 32.156
Sheriff v Dowling (SC) 26 May 1993 ... 44.62, 44.87
Sherriff v McMullen [1952] IR 236 ... 32.01, 32.14, 32.32 ... 32.110, 35.28
Sherwood v Ross/Check Stock Systems Ltd [1997] Ir L Log W 14 ... 15.17
Shield Life Insurance Co Ltd v Ulster Bank [1995] 3 IR 225 ... 30.13, 30.19
Shields v Boyle (HC) 6 November 1991 ... 15.35
Shields v Boyle DPIJ: Michaelmas Term 1991, p 88 (HC) ... 44.110, 44.176

Shields v Thomas Duffy Builders Ltd, DPIJ: Trinity and Michaelmas Terms 1996, p 129 ........ 18.152
Shiffman v Order of St John of Jerusalem [1936] 1 All ER 557 ........ 25.17, 25.25
Shimp v New Jersey Bell Telephone Co (1976) 368 A 2d 408 ........ 18.125
Shine v Irish Land Commission (1946) 81 ILTR 100 (HC) ........ 25.12
Shinwin v Quin - Con Ltd DPIJ: Trinity & Michaelmas Terms 1998, p 46 ........ 18.09
........ 18.23, 44.90
Shoshana Pty Ltd v 10th Cantanae Pty Ltd (1987) 79 Austr LR 279 ........ 31.05
Sidaway v Bethlam Royal Hospital Governors, [1985] AC 871 ........ 14.79-14.83
........ 14.95, 14.105-14.116
Siegl v Sylvester (1987) 47 DLR (49) 97 ........ 8.14
Silver Tassie Co Ltd v Cleary (1956) 90 ILTR 87, (1958) 92 ILTR 27 ........ 24.16, 32.95
Simaan General Contracting Co v Pilkington Glass Ltd (No 2) [1988] QB 758 [1988] 1 All ER 791 ........ 10.45, 10.160, 11.85
Simmonds v Dunne (1871) IR 5 CL 358 ........ 34.178
Simmons v Lilystone (1853) 8 Ex 431, 155 ER 1417 ........ 30.05
Simms v Patterson (1904) 5 NIJR 80 ........ 29.10
Simonsen v Thorin (1931) 120 Neb 684, 234 NW 628 ........ 8.03
Simple Imports Ltd v Revenue Commissioners (SC) 19 January 2000 ........ 23.07
........ 29.05, 29.10
Simpson & Co v Thompson, Burrell [1977] 3 App Cas 279 ........ 10.07
Simpson v Norwest Holst Southern Ltd [1980] 2 All ER 471 ........ 46.51
Simpson v Pollard (HC) 3 June 1963, (SC) 6 April 1967 ........ 18.12, 18.97-18.101
Simpson v Thomson (1877) 3 App Cas 279 ........ 10.46
Simpson v Weber (1925) 41 Times LR 302 ........ 23.29
Sinclair v Gogarty [1937] IR 377 ........ 34.57, 34.103, 45.05
........ 45.14, 45.30
Sindell v Abbott Laboratories (1980) 26 Cal 3d 588, 607 P 2d 924 ........ 2.60, 46.51
Siney v Dublin Corporation [1980] IR 400 ........ 6.25, 11.81, 13.05-13.11
........ 13.15-13.23, 13.31-13.36, 13.51, 19.15
........ 19.28-19.31, 19.39, 19.49, 21.10-21.12
"Singer" Machine Manufacturers v Wilson (1877) 3 AC 376 ........ 31.05
Singer Manufacturing Co v Loog (1882) 8 AC 15 ........ 31.09
Singh v Raltour (1987) The Times, 20 October ........ 43.65
Sinnott v Minister for Education (HC) 4 October 2000 ........ 16.69, 38.06, 44.51
Sinnott v Quinnsworth Ltd [1984] ILRM 523 ........ 1.171, 20.41-20.45
........ 34.243-34.245, 43.01, 44.81, 44.145-44.148
........ 44.156-44.169, 44.190
Sirros v Moore [1975] QB 118 ........ 34.148, 34.156
Sisk (John) & Son Ltd v Flinn (HC) 18 July 1984 ........ 10.71
Sisk (John) & Sons Ltd v National Silo Ltd [1963] IR 319 ........ 12.08, 18.81
Six Carpenters' Case (1610) 8 Co Rep 146a, 77 ER 695 ........ 23.23
Skeffington v Rooney [1997] 1 IR 22 ........ 37.58
Skelton v Collins (1966) 115 Comm LR 94 ........ 44.185
Skerritt v Scallan (1877) IR 11 CL 389 ........ 18.76

Skinner v Hartnett and Cork Corporation (HC) 3 February 1995 .................... 2.11, 15.37
.................................................................................................... 15.47-15.48
Skinner v LB & SC Ry (1850) 5 Ex 787, 155 ER 345 .................................. 9.13, 9.20
Slater v Swann (1730) 2 Stra 872, 93 ER 906 .................................................... 28.07
Slater v Worthington's Cash Stores [1941] 1 KB 488 ........................................ 25.40
Slattery v O'Brien, DPIJ: Hilary and Easter Terms 1993, p 98 .......................... 44.90
Slevin v Manders (1868) IR 2 CL 659 ................................................................. 22.38
Sligo Corporation v Gilbride [1929] IR 351 ........................ 28.04, 44.09, 45.02, 45.05
Slipper v Braisby [1930] NZLR 953 ................................................................... 34.172
Smeaton v Ilford Corporation [1954] Ch 450 ........................................... 19.52, 25.28
Smith Kline & French Laboratories (Australia) Ltd v Department of
Community Health Services [1990] FSR 617 ................................................. 37.35
Smith New Court Securities Ltd v Scrimgeour Vickers
(Asset Management) Ltd [1997] AC 254 ......................................................... 35.15
Smith v Austin Lifts Ltd [1959] 1 WLR 100 ........................................................ 18.10
Smith v Baker & Sons [1891] AC 325 ..................................................... 18.95, 18.159
Smith v Barking, Havering and Brentwood Health Authority [1995] 5 Med LR 285
.......................................................................................................................... 14.144
Smith v Baveystock & Co Ltd [1945] 1 All ER 531 ........................................... 21.49
Smith v Beirne (1954) 89 ILTR 24 ..................................................................... 32.108
Smith v Blackburn [1974] RTR 533 ..................................................................... 20.41
Smith v Browne (1891) 28 LR Ir 1 ........................................................................ 7.13
Smith v Carr [1937] IR 248 .................................................................................. 34.61
Smith v Chadwick (1884) 9 AC 187 .................................................................... 35.16
Smith v Coras Iompair Éireann [1991] 1 IR 314 ...................... 12.71, 12.100, 39.25
Smith v Crossley Bros Ltd (1951) 95 Sol J 655 ................................................... 18.79
Smith v Dublin Theatre Co Ltd [1936] IR 692 ..................................................... 45.50
Smith v Eric S Bush (a firm) [1990] 1 AC 831 ..................................................... 19.34
Smith v Hogg [1953-1954] Ir Jur 58 ......................................................... 23.29, 23.42
Smith v Howdens Ltd [1953] NI 131 ......................................................... 8.02, 18.127
Smith v Hugh Gormley Ltd [1997] Ir L Log W 64 ............................................... 18.95
Smith v Hughes (1871) LR 6 QB 597 .................................................................. 35.06
Smith v Ireland (HC) 16 August 1996 ................................................................ 44.111
Smith v Ireland [1983] ILRM 300 ........................................................................ 46.93
Smith v Jenkins (1970) 119 Comm LR 397 .......................................................... 22.66
Smith v Jolly (HC) 17-18 May 1984 ................................................................... 16.22
Smith v Land and House Property Corporation (1884) 28 Ch D 7 ..................... 35.08
Smith v Leavy (SC) 7 November 1960 ................................................................... 2.19
Smith v Leech Brain & Co Ltd [1962] 2 QB 405 .................................................... 3.35
Smith v Littlewoods Organisation Ltd [1987] 1 All ER 710, [1987] AC 241 ..................
6.57, .......................................................................................................... 8.24, 26.13
Smith v Lord [1962] SASR 88 ............................................................................... 7.15
Smith v Martin [1911] 2 KB 775 .......................................................................... 16.68
Smith v Mehawk Europa Ltd DPIJ: Trinity Term 1991, p 124 ............................. 18.82
Smith v Midland Ry Co (1887) 57 LT (ns) 813 ...................................................... 9.24

Smith v Mohawk Europa Ltd DPIJ: Trinity Term 1991, p 23 ................................18.151
Smith v Rae 46 OLR 518 (CA, 1919) ..........................................................................8.01
Smith v Rhone Poulenc Ireland Ltd (HC) 11 January 1995 ....................................44.91
Smith v Scott [1973] 1 Ch 314 ......................................................24.75, 25.17, 25.36
Smith v Stages [1989] 1 All ER 833 ...................................................43.25, 43.47
Smith v Stone (1647) Sty 65, 82 ER 533 ....................................................................23.38
Smith v Streatfield [1913] 3 KB 764 ....................................................................34.200
Smith v Tunbridge Wells Health Authority [1994] 5 Med LR 33 ............................14.84
Smith v Wexford County Council (1953) 87 ILTR 98 ................................................24.93
Smith v Wilson [1903] 2 IR 45 ........................................................ 22.37, 24.04-24.07
Smithies v Operative Plasterers [1909] 1 KB 210 ......................................................32.44
Smithkline Beecham plc v Antigen Pharmaceuticals Ltd [1999] 2 ILRM 190
........................................................................................ 31.02-31.05, 31.14, 31.25
.................................................................................................31.30, 31.75, 45.05
Smithwick v Hall & Upson Co (1890) 59 Conn 261 21 A 924 ................................20.15
Smyly v Glasgow & Londonderry Steampacket Co (1867) IR 2 CL 24 ...................18.06
Smyth (S) & Co Ltd v Aer Turas Teo (SC) 3 February 1997 ..................................43.21
Smyth v Dublin Theatre Co Ltd [1936] IR 692 ..........................................................24.25
Smyth v Industrial Gases (IFS) Ltd (1950) 84 ILTR 1 ...............................2.31, 24.18
Smyth v Keys (1912) 46 ILTR 68 .....................................................................12.40, 24.18
Smyth v Lynn (1950) 85 ILTR 57 ..............................................................................35.08
Smythe v Reardon [1948] QSR 74 ..............................................................................22.66
Snell v Farrell (1990) 72 DLR (4th) 289 .......................................................................2.22
Snelly v Haughton [1971] IR 305 ..............................................................................20.55
Sochacki v Sas [1947] 1 All ER 344 ..............................................................................9.21
Society for the Protection of Unborn Children (Ireland) Ltd v Grogan
(SC) 6 March 1997 ..................................................................................................22.38
Society of Motor Manufacturers v Motor Manufacturers [1925] Ch 675 .................31.05
Sodden v Image Magazine, Irish Times, 5 October 1983 ..........................................34.61
Solomons v Gertzenstein Ltd [1954] 2 QB 243 ..........................................................21.41
Soltau v De Held, (1851) 2 Sim (NS) 133, 61 ER 291 ..............................................24.07
Somers v Erskine (No 2) [1944] IR 368 ....................................................................46.04
Somers v Erskine [1943] IR 348 ............................................................1.109, 14.169
Somers v Reilly [1946] Ir Jur 44 ................................................................................15.40
Somerville v Hawkins (1851) 10 CB 583, 138 ER 231 ............................................34.170
Soronen v Olde Milford Inn Inc (1959) 46 NJ 582, 218 A 2D 630 ..............................8.06
Sorrell v Smith [1925] AC 700 ...........................................32.52, 32.58, 32.63, 32.72
Sorrell v Smith Sorrell v Smith [1925] AC 70 ..........................................................32.70
Soulah v Trinity Gate Ltd (HC) 25 November 1983 ................................................18.155
South Australian Ambulance v Wahlheim (1948) 77 Comm LR 215 ...........................7.13
South Staffordshire Waterworks Co v Sharman [1896] 2 QB 44 ...................29.09, 30.24
South Wales Miners' Federation v Glamorgan Coal Co [1905] AC 239 ..................32.41
Southcote v Stanley 1 Hurl & N 247, 156 ER 1195 ....................................................12.13
Southern Health Board v CH [1996] 2 ILRM 142 ...........................................33.03, 33.33

Southern Milling Ltd v Kantoher Food Products and Carton Brothers Ltd (HC) 26 April 1996 .......... 32.27, 32.61
Southern Portland Cement Ltd v Cooper [1974] AC 623 .......... 12.43
Southport Corporation v Esso Petroleum Co Ltd (1954) 2 QB 182, [1956] AC 218 .......... 24.03, 24.09, 24.102, 37.14
Spackman v Foster (1883) 11 QBD 99 .......... 29.02
Spaight v Dundon [1961] IR 201 .......... 21.72, 33.07-33.08, 33.14
Sparrow v St Andrews Houses Ltd QBD, 21 May 1998 .......... 18.125
Speight v Gosnay (1891) 60 LJQB 231 .......... 34.44
Spier v Barker (1974) 35 NY 2d 444 323, NE 2d 164 363, NYS 2d 916 .......... 20.44
Spiewak v 251268 Ontario Ltd 43 DLR (4th) 554 .......... 20.14
Spokane Arcades Inc v Brockett (1981) 454 US 1022, affg (1980) 631 F 2d 135 .... 24.43
Spright v Gosney (1891) 60 LJ (QB) 231 .......... 34.32
Spring v Guardian Assurance plc [1995] 2 AC 296 .......... 10.141, 10.147, 18.74, 35.28
Square D Ltd v Cook [1992] ICR 262 .......... 18.35
Square Grip Reinforcement Ltd v Macdonald (No 2) (1968) SLT 65 .......... 32.20
Squittieri v de Santis (1976) 15 OR (2d) 416, 75 DLR 3d 629 .......... 40.41-40.43
Squizzoni v McEntaggart DPIJ: Hilary and Easter Terms 1994, p 56 .......... 15.05, 15.51 .......... 40.11
SS Heranger (Owners) v SS Diamond (Owners) [1939] AC 94, [1956] IR 89 .......... 15.24
St Anne's Well Brewery Co v Roberts (1928) 140 LT 1 .......... 24.76, 25.15, 25.28
St George's Healthcare NHS Trust v S [1999] Fam 26 .......... 22.13
St Helen's Smelting Co v Tipping (1865) 11 HLC 642, 11 ER 1483 .......... 24.31-24.33 .......... 24.39
St John v Ossory (SC) 23 July 1930 .......... 24.16, 45.05
St Laurence's Hospital (Board of Governors of) v Staunton [1990] 2 IR 31 .......... 4.24
Stack v Roberts (SC) 24 July 1958 .......... 43.64
Stafford v Conti Commodity Services Ltd [1981] 1 All ER 691 .......... 10.51
Stafford v Mahony, Smith & Palmer [1980] ILRM 53 .......... 10.151
Stafford v Roadstone Ltd [1980] ILRM 1 .......... 24.10, 24.31, 24.37 .......... 45.05, 45.40
Stakelum v Bank of Ireland (HC) 27 April 1999 .......... 18.10, 18.95
Stanley v Dublin Corp (CC) 7 December 1999 .......... 13.43
Stanley v Powell [1891] 1 QB 86 .......... 22.01, 23.38
Stansbie v Troman [1948] 2 KB 48 .......... 2.43
Stanton v Ewart F Youlden Ltd [1960] 1 All ER 429 .......... 42.20
Stapleton v O'Regan (1961) 95 ILTR 1 .......... 2.19, 7.05, 15.17, 20.15
Star Village Tavern v Nield [1976] 6 WWR 80 .......... 22.37
State (Batchelor & Co (Ireland) Ltd) v District Justice O Floinn [1958] IR 155 .......... 23.06
State (DPP) v Walsh [1981] IR 412 .......... 32.61
State (Hayes) v The Criminal Injuries Compensation Tribunal [1982] ILRM 210 .......... 44.128
State (Keegan) v Stardust Victims Compensation Tribunal [1987] ILRM 202 .......... 1.16 .......... 17.35
State (M) v Attorney General [1979] IR 73 .......... 1.13, 22.38

State (Quinn) v Ryan [1965] IR 70 ........ 44.37-44.40
State (Richardson) v Govenor of Mounjoy Prison [1980] ILRM 82 ........ 37.67
State (Sheehan) v Government of Ireland [1987] IR 550 ........ 24.118, 38.12
State (Smullen) v Duffy [1980] ILRM 46 ........ 22.104
State v Brown (1986) 212 NJ Super 61, 513 A 2d 974 ........ 23.20
Staunton v Toyota (Ireland) Ltd (HC) 15 April 1988 ........ 4.19, 4.24
Staveley v Barrington (1913) 47 ILTR 296 ........ 28.06
Steadman v Erickson Gold Mining Corporation (1987) 43 DLR (4th) 712 ........ 23.32
Steel v Glasgow Iron & Steel Co [1944] SC 237 ........ 26.35
Steele v Northern Ireland Office [1988] NILR Bull 1 ........ 8.32
Stein v Gonzales (1984) 14 DLR (4th) 263 ........ 24.05, 24.43
Stelzer v Wexford North Slob Commissioners [1988] ILRM 279 ........ 21.10, 45.05
Stennett v Hancock [1939] 2 All ER 578 ........ 11.13, 11.26
Stephen v Riversdale Health Authority [1990] 1 Med LR 261 ........ 46.50
Stephens v Avery [1988] 2 All ER 477 ........ 37.21, 37.32
Stephens v Myers (1830) 4 C & P 349, 172 ER 735 ........ 22.22
Sterling Trusts Corporation v Postma [1965] SCR 324 ........ 21.10
Sterling-Winthrop Group Ltd v Farbenfabriken Bayer AG [1967] IR 97 ........ 31.05
Sterner v Lawson (1979) 11 CCLT 76 ........ 11.61
Sterwin AG v Brocades (Great Britain) Ltd [1979] RPC 481 ........ 31.15
Stevens v Stevens (1907) 24 TLR 20 ........ 45.51
Stevenson v Bagham [1922] NZLR 225 ........ 22.33
Stevenson v Lawlor (1867) IR 2 CL 77 ........ 30.19
Stewart v JJ Smith & Co (Dublin) Ltd (SC) 31 July 1957 ........ 44.58
Stewart v Killeen Paper Mills Ltd [1959] IR 436 ........ 18.152, 21.10, 21.52-21.56
Stewart v St Patrick's Hospital (1939) 73 ILTR 115 ........ 24.18
Stinnett v Buchele (1980) 598 SW 2d 469 ........ 18.10
Stockdale v Nicholls [1993] 4 Med LR 190 ........ 14.40
Stokes v Limerick Corporation DPIJ: Hilary and Easter Terms 1992, p 39 ........ 21.22
Stop & Shop Co v Fisher (1983) 387 Mass 889, 444 NE 2d 368 ........ 24.05
Storey v Challands (1837) 8 C & P 234, 173 ER 475 ........ 34.42
Storm v Jeeves [1965] Tas SR 252 ........ 17.22
Stott v Gamble [1916] 2 KB 504 ........ 32.43
Stovin v Wise [1996] AC 923 ........ 19.02, 19.10
Strand Electric Co v Brisford Entertainments [1952] 2 QB 246 ........ 29.10
Strang v Russell (1905) 24 NZLR 916 ........ 23.16
Stratford (JT) & Son Ltd v Lindley [1965] AC 269 ........ 32.23, 32.56
Stratford v Lindley [1965] AC 260 ........ 32.14, 32.32, 32.48
Strausser v Dow Chemical Co 1997 US Dist LEXIS 22136 ........ 33.21
Strehlke v Camenzind (1977) 111 DLR (3d) 319 (Alta QB) ........ 40.26
Streifel v Stroz (1957) 11 DLR (2d) 667 ........ 16.06
Strick v Treacy (HC) 10 June 1993 ........ 7.39, 15.55, 20.44, 26.36
Strong v McAuley, McRroy & Co Ltd (1929) 63 ILTR 39 ........ 43.32
Student A and Student B v Dublin Secondary School (HC) 25 November 1999 ........ 22.104

Sturdy v Dublin Corporation DPIJ: Michaelmas Term 1991, p 21 (HC) .................. 44.80
........................................................................................................44.127-44.129
Sturges v Bridgman (1879) 11 Ch D 852 ............................................24.43, 24.97-24.104
Sullivan v Creed [1904] 2 IR 317 ...................................................2.26, 7.04-7.06, 7.27
........................................................................................ 7.35, 11.07, 11.30, 16.03
Sullivan v National Bank (1939) 73 ILTR 95 ........................................................ 30.19
Sullivan v Noonan [1969] IR 253 ........................................................................ 4.16
Summers v Tice (1948) 33 Cal 2d 80, 199 P 2d 1 .................................................. 2.60
Sumner v William Henderson & Sons Ltd [1964] 1 QB 450 .................................. 18.35
Sun Life Assurance v Daryample [1965] SCR 302 ................................................ 34.200
Sunbolf v Alford (1838) 3 M & W 248,150 ER 1135 ............................................ 22.58
Sunderland v Louth County Council [1990] ILRM 658, affg [1987] IR 372 ........... 10.09
.................................................................................................. 10.43, 13.47, 19.21
.................................................................................................. 19.35, 19.47, 43.52
Sunderland v McGreavey [1987] IR 372 ......................................................... 13.68, 13.82
Superquinn Ltd v Bray UDC (HC) 18 February 1998 .......................... 3.42, 24.96, 25.02
.........................................................................................25.11, 25.41-25.42, 25.54
Superwood Holdings plc v Sun Alliance and London Assurance plc
(SC) 27 June 1995 ............................................................................................. 35.02
Sutcliffe v Pressdam Ltd [1991] 1 QB 153 ......................................................... 34.231
Sutherland Shire Council v Heyman (1985) 157 CLR 424, (1985) 60 ALR 1 ... 6.21, 6.26
......................................................................................................... 19.03, 19.10
Sutherland v Glasgow Corporation 1949 SC 563 ..................................................... 7.39
Sutherland v Stopes [1925] AC 47 ............................................................ 34.129, 34.216
Sutherland v Supervalu (CC), 11 March 1999 ........................................................ 7.46
SW Miners' Federation v Glamorgan Coal Co [1905] AC 239 ................................ 32.43
Sweeney v Cooke [1906] 1 IR 51 ................................................................ 24.51, 32.58
Sweeney v Crowley (SC) 30 May 1968 ....................................................... 44.82, 44.88
Sweeney v Duggan [1991] 2 IR 274, affd [1997] 2 ILRM 211 .............. 1.112, 6.28, 6.36
.......................................................................................10.11, 10.30-10.39, 16.25
......................................................................................................... 18.58, 18.72
Sweeney v North Western Health Board and Siemens [1996] Ir L Log W 394 ........ 26.24
Swift v Macken (1873) IR 8 CL 140 ........................................................................ 18.77
Swift v Westport UDC [1944] IR 259 ................................................................ 7.27, 12.32
Swinney v Chief Constable of the Northumbria Police [1997] QB 464 ...................... 8.25
Swords Community Council v Dunne, Ir Times, 20 March 1981 ........................... 34.170
Swords v Saint Patrick's Copper Mines Ltd [1965] Ir Jur Rep 63 .................. 7.48, 18.11
......................................................................................................... 42.02, 44.96
Sydney County Council v Dell'Ore (1964) 132 Comm LR 97 .................................. 7.36
Sykes v DPP [1962] AC 528 ................................................................................. 37.53
Sykes v Midland Bank Executor and Trustee Co [1971] 1 QB 113 ........................... 2.21
Sykes v NE Rly Co (1875) 44 LJCP 191 ............................................................... 42.18
Sylvester v GB Chapman Ltd (1935) 79 Sol J 777 ................................................. 26.35
Symonds Cider & English Wine Co Ltd v Showerings (Ireland) Ltd [1997] 1 ILRM 481
......................................................................................................... 31.64, 45.05

Symons v Toronto Dominion Bank (1997) 38 CCLT (2d) 305 ....................................34.30
Szabo v Esat Digiphone Ltd [1998] 2 ILRM 102 .........................................................45.03

## T

T (Adult: Refusal of Treatment), Re [1993] Fam 95 ...................................................22.13
T v H [1995] 3 NZLR 37 ..............................................................................................46.99
Taff Vale Railway v Amalgamated Society of Railway Servants [1901] AC 426 .....39.26
Taggart v Innes (1862) 12 UCCP 77 ............................................................... 40.38-40.44
Tai Hing Cotton Mill Ltd v Liu Chong Hing Bank Ltd [1986] AC 80 ...........10.22, 10.33
Tait v Beggs [1905] 2 IR 525 .........................................................................34.32, 34.57
Talbert v Talbert (1960) 22 Misc 2d 782, 199 NYS 2d 212 .........................................20.81
Talbot (Ireland) Ltd v ATGWU (SC) 30 April 1981 ......................................... 32.14-32.18
...................................................... 32.32-32.33, 32.41, 32.124, 32.125, 32.175
Talcott v National Exhibition Co (1911) Appeal Div 128 NYS 1059 ..........................22.44
Tallon v Ennis [1937] IR 549 .......................................................................................23.33
Tallow v Tailfeathers [1973] (1974) 6 WWR 73 ..........................................................20.96
Tarasoff v Regents of University of California (1976) 529 P 2d 553
118 Cal Rptr 129, 17 Cal 3d 425, 131 Cal Rptr 14, 551 P 2d 334 ....8.25, 37.17, 37.44
Tarleton v McGawley (1793) 1 Peake 270, 170 ER 153 ..............................................32.50
Tarrant v O'Sullivan [1949] Ir Jur 46 ...........................................3.05, 7.28, 7.44, 21.22
Tart v Chitty & Co [1933] 2 KB 453 ............................................................................15.23
Tate & Lyle Food and Distribution v Greater London Council [1983] 2 AC 509
.........................................................................................10.160, 11.84, 24.05
Tate v Minister for Social Welfare [1995] 1 ILRM 507 ..................................1.99, 46.02
Taupo Borough Council v Birnie [1978] NZLR 397 ......................................................3.37
Tauranga Electric Power Board v Karon [1939] NZLR 104 .........................................40.29
Taylor v Beere [1982] 1 NZLR 81 ...............................................................................44.13
Taylor v Director of the Serious Fraud Office [1998] 4 All ER 801 ...........................36.29
Taylor v Great Southern and Western Ry Co [1909] 2 IR 330 ..........................7.27, 9.21
Taylor v Hall (1743) 2 Stra 1189, 93 ER 1118 ............................................................34.40
Taylor v King [1993] 8 WWR 92 .................................................................................16.02
Taylor v O'Connor [1971] AC 115 ............................................................... 42.35-42.39
Taylor v Olsen (1978) 282 Or 343, 578 P 2d 779 ........................................................24.29
Taylor v Perkins (1607) Cro Jac 144, 79 ER 126 .........................................................34.41
Taylor v Rover Co Ltd [1966] 1 WLR 1491 .................................................................11.22
Taylor v Ryan [1985] IR 212 ...............................................................14.206, 14.210
Taylor v Smyth [1991] IR 142 .............................................32.27, 32.61, 32.76, 32.79
TD v Minister for Eduaction (HC) 25 February 2000 ..................................................16.69
Tear v Freebody (1858) 4 CB (ns) 28 140 ER 1071 ....................................................30.03
Teeling v Ryan (SC) 2 May 1967 ................................................................................44.58
Tefler v Wright (1978) 95 DLR (3d) 188 .......................................................................7.15
Telemak Teleproducts (Aust) Pty Ltd v Coles Myer Ltd (1988) 48 ALR 437 ..........31.35
Telnikoff v Matusevitvh [1991] 4 All ER 817 ............................................................34.220
Tenant v Goldwin (1704) 2 LD Raym 1089, 92 ER 222 ...............................................23.32
Terlin v Lisnaskea RDC [1914] 2 IR 15 .......................................................................21.10

Terrapin Ltd v Builders Supply Co (Hayes) Ltd [1967] RPC 375 .......... 37.26
Tess v Swiss Wire Ire Ltd DPIJ: Hilary and Easter Terms 1994, p 158 .......... 21.55
Tex-Jersey Oil Corporation v Beck 292 SW 2d 803 .......... 7.30
Thapar v Zezulka (1999) 994 SW 2d 635 .......... 37.44
Theaker v Richardson [1962] 1 All ER 229 .......... 34.14
Thibodeau v Cheff (1911) 24 OLR 214 .......... 16.03
Thigh v Rathangan Drainage Bd [1898] 2 IR 205 .......... 21.19
Thomas v British Rys Bd [1976] QB 912 .......... 40.10
Thomas v Leitrim County Council [1998] 2 ILRM 74 .......... 6.01, 12.08
Thomas v National Union of Ringworkers (South Wales Area) [1986] 1 Ch 20 .......... 22.22
Thomas v Quartermaine (1887) 18 QBD 685 .......... 6.13
Thomas v Thomas (1835) 2 CM & R 34 150 ER 15 .......... 24.99
Thomas v Winchester (1852) 6 NY 397 .......... 11.07
Thompson and Thompson v Gill and Macmillan et al, Irish Times, 3 November 1987 .......... 34.55
Thompson v County of Alameda (1980) 27 Cal 3d 741, 167 Cal Rep 70, 614 P 2d 728 .......... 8.25, 37.44
Thompson v Coyle Ltd [1967] IR 89 .......... 44.58
Thompson v Gibson (1841) 7 M & W 456, 151 ER 845 .......... 24.72
Thompson v Reynolds [1926] NI 131 .......... 43.64
Thompson v Ward [1953] 2 QB 153 .......... 23.46
Thompson-Schwab v Costaki [1956] 1 WLR 335 .......... 24.43
Thomson (DC) & Co Ltd v Deakin [1952] Ch 646 .......... 32.12-32.15, 32.25-32.33
Thorne v Western Australia [1964] WAR 147 .......... 8.25
Thornton v Board of School Trustees of School District No 57 (Prince George) 83 DLR (3d) 480 .......... 44.158
Thornton v Murphy Brewery (Irl) Ltd DPIJ: Hilary & Easter Terms 1993 (HC) .......... 44.79
Thorpe v Brumfitt (1873) LR 8 Ch 650 .......... 24.110
Three Rivers DC v Bank of England [1996] 3 All ER 558 .......... 22.30
Three Rivers DC v Bank of England (No 3) [2000] 2 WLR 15 .......... 19.55
Three Stripe International v Charles O'Neill & Co [1989] ILRM 124 31.61, 31.74, 45.05
Thurmond v Pepper (1938) 119 SW 2d 900 .......... 20.19
Thurogood v Van Den Berghs & Jurgens Ltd [1951] 2 KB 537 .......... 3.18, 18.12
Thwaites & Co v McEvilly [1904] IR 310 .......... 31.05
Tidy v Battman [1934] 1 KB 319 .......... 15.24
Tiernan v O'Callaghan (1944) 78 ILTR 36 .......... 12.18-12.27, 12.36, 40.18
Tillander v Gosselin (1966) 60 DLR (2d) 18, affd (1967) 61 DLR (2d) 192n .......... 40.10
Tilson Infants, Re [1951] IR 1 .......... 33.33-33.34
Timbs v Templeogue Taverns Ltd (HC) 18 December 1992 .......... 7.39
Tindale v Tindale [1950] 4 DLR 363 .......... 40.44
Tingle Jacobs & Co v Kennedy [1964] 1 All ER 888 .......... 15.48
Tinnelly & Sons Ltd v United Kingdom (1998) 27 EHRR 249 .......... 6.84
Tinsley v Mulligan [1994] 1 AC 340 .......... 20.104
Tipton v Mullinix (1973) 508 P 2d 1072 .......... 40.29
Tisdall v McArthur & Co (Steel and Metal) Ltd [1951] IR 228 .......... 24.25, 45.05

Toal v Duignan [1991] ILRM 135 ....................46.55, 46.63
Tobin v Cashell (Chairman of the Board of Management of Mayfield Community School) (HC) 21 March 2000 ....................45.02
Tock v St John's Metropolitan Area Board [1989] 2 SCR 1181 ....................19.52
Todd v Cincelli (HC) 5 March 1998 ....................44.10
Todd v Flight (1860) 9 CB (N 8) 377 ....................24.76
Todd v Hawkins (1837) 8 C & P 88, 173 ER 411 ....................34.170
Toetshinger v lhnot (1977) 312 Minn 59, 250 NW 2d 204 ....................40.08
Tolin v Terrell (1909) 117 SW 290 ....................7.08
Tolley v Fry & Sons Ltd [1931] AC 333 ....................34.94
Tolstoy Miloslavsky v United Kingdom (1995) 20 EHRR 442 ....................34.255
Tomkin Estates Ltd v O'Callaghan (HC) 16 March 1995 ....................23.33
Tomkins v Northwestern Union Truck Co of Helena (1980) 645 P 2d 402 ....................9.21
Tomlinson v Harrison [1972] 1 Ont R 670 (HC) ....................20.96
Toogood v Spyring (1834) 1 CM & R 181 ....................34.166
Toohey v Hollier (1955) 92 CLR 618 ....................33.09
Tooke v Walsh [1984] ILRM 208 ....................42.34
Tool Metal Manufacturing Co v Tungsten Electric Co [1955] 1 WLR 761 ....................10.115
Toome Eel Fishery (Northern Ireland) Ltd v Cardwell [1966] NI 1 .................... 30.19-30.20
Toppin v Feron (1909) 43 ILTR 190 ....................32.154
Topping v Warne Surgical Products Ltd [1986] NILR Bull No 9, p 14 ....................45.37
Toronto-St Catherine's Transport v Toronto [1954] 1 DLR 721 ....................21.20
Torquay Hotel Co Ltd v Cousins [1969] 2 Ch 106 ....................32.14, 32.20, 32.26
Tournier v National Provincial and Union Bank of England [1924] 1 KB 461 ....................37.32
Towell v Fallon (1912) 47 ILTR 176 ....................34.175, 35.26
Tower Homes Ltd v Brien et al (HC) 16 July 1984 ....................45.05
Towey v Ulster Bank Ltd [1987] ILRM 142 ....................1.06, 10.09, 10.25, 10.57, 10.74
Townsview Properties Ltd v Sun Construction and Equipment Co Ltd (1974) 56 DLR (3d) 330 ....................23.35
Tracey v Hagen (SC) 6 March 1973 ....................9.19, 9.44, 18.101
Transport Salaried Staffs' Association v CIE [1965] IR 180 ....................21.19
Trapp v Mackie [1979] 1 WLR 377 ....................34.155
Trauman v City of New York (1955) 143 NYS 2d 467 ....................24.18
Traynor v Fegan [1985] IR 586 ....................46.93
Treacy v McKenna (1869) IR 4 CL 374 ....................34.55, 34.97
Treacy v Robinson and Ors [1937] IR 255 ....................43.11, 43.46
Treasure Island Ltd v Zebedee Enterprises Ltd (HC) 29 May 1987 ....................29.02
Tremain v Pike [1969] 1 WLR 1556 ....................3.20
Trenberth (John) Ltd v National Westminster Bank Ltd (1980) 39 P & CR 104 ....................23.39
Tresemer v Barke (1978) 86 Cal App 3d 656, 150 Cal Rptr 384 ....................14.159
Treston v Mayo County Council (HC) 6 July 1998 ....................10.100
Trident General Insurance v McNeice (1988) 165 Comm LR 107 ....................12.135
Troute v Brassil (HC) 19 November 1999 ....................44.79, 44.169
Truck & Machinery Sales Ltd v General Accident Fire and Life Assurance Co plc (HC) 12 November 1999 ....................46.65

Trulock Ltd v District Judge McMenamin [1994] 1 ILRM 151 .............................. 24.03
Trustees of the Roman Catholic Church for the Diocese of Bathurst v Koffman 1996 NSW Lexis 3020 .............................. 16.53
Tru-Value Ltd v Switzer & Co (HC) 10 March 1972 .............................. 32.20, 32.73
Tubervell v Savage (1660) 1 Mod Rep 3, 86 ER 684 .............................. 22.18, 22.25
Tubridy v White (HC) 31 January 1974 .............................. 42.38-42.39
Tucker v News Media Ownership Ltd [1986] 2 NZLR 716 .............................. 37.02
Tucker v Tucker [1956] SASR 297 .............................. 40.29
Tughan v Craig [1918] 1 IR 245 .............................. 34.147
Tullidge v Wade (1769) 3 Wils 18, 95 ER 909 .............................. 44.09
Tully v Smith [1997] Ir L Log W 97 .............................. 23.29, 23.33-23.35
Tulsk Co-operative Livestock Mart Ltd v Ulster Bank Ltd (HC) 13 May 1993 .............................. 6.25, 10.09, 10.25, 10.74, 10.154
Tuohy v Courtney (No 2) [1994] 2 ILRM 503, [1994] 3 IR 1 .. 1.54, 32.138, 46.02, 46.20
Tuohy v March DPIJ: Trinity & Michaelmas Terms 1992, p 109 .............................. 44.176
Turner v Caldwell (1980) 36 Conn Supp 350, 421 A 2d 876 .............................. 7.23
Turner v Coates [1917] 1 KB 670 .............................. 27.18
Turner v Iarnród Éireann (HC) 14 February 1996 .............................. 3.13, 6.28, 7.39, 20.91
Turner v Metro-Goldwyn-Mayer [1950] 1 All ER 449 .............................. 34.218
Turner v Sterling (1672) 2 Vent 25, 86 ER 287 .............................. 19.55
Turton v Turton (1889) 42 ChD 128 .............................. 31.49
Tutton v Walter Ltd [1986] QB 61 .............................. 23.29
Tynan v Earls (SC) 28 March 1969 .............................. 15.17, 24.16

## U

UF (otherwise UC) v JC [1991] 2 IR 445 .............................. 34.81
UL Canada Ltd v ProCourter & Gamble Inc (1996) 65 CPR 3d 534 .............................. 35.08
Ultramares v Touche Niven & Co (1931) 255 NYS 170, 174 NE 441 .............................. 10.43, 10.50
Union Government v Ocean & Accident 1956 (1) SA 577 .............................. 32.05
Union Oil v Oppen (1974) 501 F 2d 558 .............................. 24.05
Union Transport Finance Ltd v British Car Auctions Ltd [1978] 2 All ER 385 ........ 30.12
United Bank of Kuwait v Hammond (1987) 137 NLJ 92 .............................. 43.54
United Biscuits (UK) Ltd v Burtons Biscuits Ltd [1992] FSR 14 .............................. 31.27
United Biscuits Ltd v Irish Biscuits Ltd [1971] IR 16 .............................. 31.33
United Rys & Electric Co of Baltimore v Carneal (1909) 110 Md 211, 72 A 771 .... 40.10
United States Amalgamated Food Employers Local S90 v Logan Valley Plaza Inc (1968) 391 US 308 .............................. 23.20
United States v Caltex (Philippines) Inc (1952) 344 US 149 .............................. 23.51
United States v Carroll Towing Co (1947) 159 F 2d 169 .............................. 7.25
United States v Holmes (1842) 1 Wall Jr 1 .............................. 22.92
United States v Standard Oil Co (1946) 322 US 301 .............................. 32.05
Universal City Studios Ltd v Mulligan (HC) 25 March 1998 .............................. 45.05
Universe Tankships Inc of Monrovia v International Transport Workers Federation [1980] IRLR 363 .............................. 32.127
Unsworth v Comr for Rys (1958) 101 Comm LR 73 .............................. 20.58

Uren v John Fairfax & Sons Pty Ltd (1966) 117 Comm LR 118 .................... 44.13-44.14

## V

Vaccaro v Giruzzi (1992) 93 DLR (4th) 180 .......................................................32.03
Valentine v Valentine (1892) 31 LR Ir 488 ..................................31.40, 31.73, 45.05
Van den Eynde v Ulster Ry Co (1871) IR 5 CL 328 .......................... 43.28-43.30, 43.36
Van Hoffen v Dawson (CA) 11 October 1993 ..............................................................20.70
Van Keep v Surface Dressing Contractors Ltd (HC) 11 June 1993 .............15.37, 44.139
Van Oppen v Clerk to the Bedford Charity Trustees [1989] 1 All ER 273
........................................................................................10.33, 10.147, 16.25, 16.69
Van Patter v Tillsonburg District Memorial Hospital 1997 Ont CJ LEXIS 2925
(Ont Ct (Gen Div) 16 March 1998) .............................................................................2.27
Vance v Universal Amusement Co Inc (1980) 445 US 308, affg (1978) 587 F 2d 159
.........................................................................................................................24.43
Vancouver v Burchill [1932] 4 DLR 200 .......................................................................21.48
Vandenburgh v Truax (1847) 4 Denio 464 ...................................................................23.29
Varawa v Howard Smith (1911) 13 Comm LR 35 .........................................................36.19
Varian v Kerr DPIJ: Trinity & Michaelmas Terms 1992, p 239 (HC) ....................44.176
Vaughan v Cork & Youghal Ry Co (1860) 12 ICLR 297 .............................18.02, 18.81
Vaughan v Menlove (1837) 3 Bing, NC 468, 132 ER 490 ................................ 7.05-7.05
Vaughan v Taff Vale Ry 5 (186) H & N 679 ..................................................................25.44
Venning v Chin (1974) 10 SASR 299 ................................................................................22.03
Victor Weston (Éire) Ltd v Kenny [1954] IR 191 ............................2.32, 2.39, 7.05, 7.08
.........................................................................7.29, 8.24, 13.19, 24.85, 25.07, 25.30
Victoria Park Racing & Recreation Grounds Co Ltd v Taylor (1937) 58 CLR 479
.....................................................................................................................23.19, 37.02
Victorian Railways Commissioners v Coultas (1888) 13 Appeal Cas 222 ...............17.04
.......................................................................................................... 17.08-17.17
Videan v British Transport Commission [1963] 2 QB 650 ............................12.23, 20.80
Villers v Monsley (1769) 2 Wits KB 403, 95 ER 886 .......................................................34.41
Vincent v Lake Erie Transportation Co (1910) 109 Minn 456, 124 NW 221 ............23.51
Vine Products Ltd v MacKenzie [1969] RPC 1 ..................................................................31.28
Vitalograph (Ireland) Ltd v Ennis Urban District Council and Clare County Council
(HC) 23 April 1997 .........................................................................................24.10, 24.81
Vizetelly v Mudies' Select Library Ltd [1900] 2 QB 170 ..............................................34.19
Vorvis v Insurance Corporation of British Columbia (1989) 58 DLR (4th) 193 .......44.13
Vozza v Tooth & Co Ltd (1964) 112 Comm LR 316 .........................................................18.04

## W

W v B (HC) 18 March 1999 .............................................................................................37.55
W v CIE [1967] IR 137 .........................................................................................................33.04
W v Egdell [1990] Ch 359 ....................................................................................................37.45
W v Essex County Council [2000] 2 WLR 601 ..................................................................17.66

W v Ireland (No 2) [1997] 2 IR 141 ........................................ 1.21, 1.33, 1.74, 6.28, 6.35
............................................................................ 6.87, 8.01, 14.164, 1949, 23.01, 32.136
............................................................................ 32.142, 34.06, 36.03, 36.05
W v Meah [1986] 1 All ER 935 ........................................ 22.19
W v Somers [1983] IR 122 ........................................ 23.33
W v W [1993] 2 IR 476 ........................................ 32.61, 33.34
Wade v Canadian National Ry (1977) 80 DLR (3d) 214 ........................................ 19.71, 40.26
Wade v Hegarty (SC) 13 July 1960 ........................................ 7.13
Waffen v United States 799 F 2d 911 (4th Cir 1986) ........................................ 2.21
Waggoner v Troutman Oil Company (1995) 894 SW 2d 91 ........................................ 20.90
Wagner v Fohrmann et al Case 10/63 recueil Vol X 381 ........................................ 38.22
Wagner v International Railroad Co (1921) 232 NYS 176, 133 NE 437 ........................................ 20.79
Wakefield ( CC) & Co Ltd v Purser (1928) 45 RPC 261 ........................................ 31.05
Wakelin v London & SW Ry Co (1886) 12 AC 41 ........................................ 9.05
Waldson v Junior Army & Navy Stores Ltd [1910] 2 IR 381 ........................................ 18.03
Walker (John) & Sons v Henry Ost & Co [1970] RPC 489 ........................................ 31.28
Walker v Hall (1876) 40 JP 456 ........................................ 27.25
Walker v McCormack (SC) 4 March 1968 ........................................ 3.22, 18.77-18.79
............................................................................ 18.96, 43.33
Walker v Northumberland County Council [1995] 1 All ER 737 ........................................ 18.60
Wall v Feeley (HC) 26 October 1983 ........................................ 45.05, 45.41
Wall v Hegarty [1980] ILRM 124 ........................................ 6.10, 6.25, 6.55, 10.09,
............................................................................ 10.44, 10.72-10.73, 10.153, 14.03, 14.174
Wall v Morrissey [1969] IR 10 ........................................ 3.30, 24.16, 24.18-24.19
Wallace v Fahy, DPIJ: Hilary & Easter Terms 1996, p 162 ........................................ 44.90
Wallace v McCartan [1917] 1 IR 397 ........................................ 24.31, 24.93
Walsh v BMD & Co Ltd DPIJ: Trinity and Michaelmas Terms 1994, p 104 .......... 18.108
Walsh v Bourke (HC) 25 January 1985 ........................................ 16.22
Walsh v Brown, DPIJ: Hilary & Easter Terms 1997, p 91 ........................................ 44.95
Walsh v Butler [1997] 2 ILRM 81 ........................................ 39.17
Walsh v Cronin (SC) 4 November 1935 ........................................ 9.04, 21.10
Walsh v Cullen [1997] Ir L Log W 37 ........................................ 15.17
Walsh v Dublin Corporation (HC) 23 July 1998 ........................................ 7.34, 13.42, 19.20, 24.35
Walsh v Ervin [1952] VLR 361 ........................................ 24.04, 24.07
Walsh v Family Planning Services Ltd [1992] 1 IR 496 ........................................ 1.46, 14.80, 14.85
............................................................................ 14.103-14.105, 14.115-14.128
............................................................................ 14.139-14.142, 22.12, 22.69, 22.82, 37.42
Walsh v Galway Harbour Commissioners (SC) 18 December 1972 ........................................ 15.03
Walsh v Goodman [1905] 2 IR 241 ........................................ 29.05
Walsh v Goulding (HC) 31 July 1968 ........................................ 45.50
Walsh v Ireland (SC) 30 November 1994 ........................................ 22.38, 38.10, 44.28
Walsh v Kilkenny County Council [1978] ILRM 1 ........................................ 7.28, 21.10, 21.20, 21.40
Walsh v McGauran (HC) 14 June 1979 ........................................ 23.33, 23.38
Walsh v Morgan & Sons Ltd (1938) 72 ILTR 4 ........................................ 24.06, 24.18
Walsh v Pender (1927) 62 ILTR 8 ........................................ 22.24

Walsh v Ryan (HC) 12 February 1993 ............................................................8.10, 8.28
Walsh v Securicor (Ireland) Ltd [1993] 2 IR 507 ..............................6.42, 7.52, 18.134
Walsh v St Paul & DR Co (1881) 27 Minn 367, 8 NW 145 .....................................18.10
Walsh v Tedcastle McCormack & Co Ltd (HC) 23 June 1967 ................................24.39
Walshe v Baileboro' Co-op Agricultural and Dairy Society and Gargan [1939] Ir Jur Rep 77 ..........................................................................................43.16
Walt Disney Productions v Triple Five Corp (1992) 93 DLR (4th) 739 ...................31.27
Walter D Wallet [1893] P 202 ...................................................................................36.19
Walters v Sloan (1977) 20 Cal 3d 199, 571 P 2d 609, 142 Cal Rptr 152 ..................26.35
Walters v Sloan [1988] AC 431 .................................................................................26.35
Wandsworth Board of Works v United Telephone Co (1884) 13 QB 904 ................1.120
Ward of Court, Re [1995] 2 ILRM 401 ..................................22.13, 22.73, 33.03, 37.82
Ward v Dawson (HC) 26 July 1996 .......................................................15.03, 20.18
Ward v Donegal Vocational Committee DPIJ: Hilary and Easter Terms 1993 .........16.25
Ward v Freeman (1852) 2 Ir CLR 460 .....................................................................34.146
Ward v Hertfordshire County Council [1970] 1 All ER 535, revg [1969] 2 All ER 807 ..........................................................................................16.27, 16.46, 16.72
Ward v Lewis [1955] 1 WLR 9 ............................................................32.80, 34.44
Ward v Macauley (1791) 4 Term Rep 489, 100 ER 1135 .......................................28.10
Ward v McMaster [1985] IR 29 (HC), [1989] ILRM 400, [1988] IR 337 (SC) 1.06, 1.33 ..........4.19, 6.09, 6.25-6.27, 6.33-6.40, 6.49-6.56 ..........6.87-6.88, 10.09-10.11, 10.15, 10.43, 10.77-10.84 ..........10.106, 10.141, 10.160, 11.76, 11.81, 11.89 .......... 11.100, 13.05, 13.22, 13.26-13.35, 13.45, 13.55 .......... 13.68-13.74, 13.82, 14.223, 19.21, 19.34-19.39 .......... 19.47-19.49, 20.108-21.03, 21.08, 21.18
Ward v Walsh (SC) 31 July 1991 .........................................................20.39, 44.107
Ware's Taxi Ltd v Gilliham [1949] SCR 637 ...............................................................8.20
Waring v McCaldin IR 7 CL 282 .............................................................................34.178
Warner v Riddiford (1858) 4 CB (ns) 180, 140 ER 1042 ........................................22.38
Warnink v Townsend & Sons (Hull) Ltd [1979] AC 731 .........................................31.28
Warren v King [1964] 1 WLR 1 ...............................................................................44.07
Wartman v Swindell (1892) 54 NJL 589, 25 A 356 .....................................22.29, 22.63
Wason v Walter (1868) LR 4 QB 73 .......................................................................34.192
Wasson v Chief Constable Royal Ulster Constabulary [1987] NILR Bull 34 ...........20.13
Waterford Bridge Commissioners v Waterford Corporation [1905] 1 IR 307 ...........24.16
Waterford Corporation v O'Toole (HC) 9 November 1973 ................ 29.03, 29.09-29.14
Waterford Harbour Commissioners v British Railways Board [1979] ILRM 296 .......... 21.10-21.10, 21.20, 21.35, 37.20
Waterhouse v Waterhouse (1905) 94 LT 133 ...........................................................45.51
Waters v Commissioner of Police of the Metropolis [2000] 1 WLR 1607 .......8.25, 18.80
Waters v Cruickshank [1967] IR 378 ...........................................................42.27, 42.41
Waters v O'Keefe [1937] Ir Jur Rep ........................................................................12.19
Watkins v Lee (1839) 5 M & W 270, 151 ER 115 ..................................................36.05
Watson v Davidson [1966] NZLR 853 ........................................................................9.28

Watt v Hertfordshire County Council [1954] 2 All ER 368 .......... 7.39-7.44, 15.54, 26.36
Watts Bros Ltd v Peilow High Court, 23 January 1980 .......... 23.51
Waugh v James K Allan Ltd 1974 SC 102 .......... 7.15
Waverly Borough Council v Fletcher [1996] QB 334 .......... 30.24-30.29
Weaver v Bush (1798) 8 TR 78,101 ER 1276 .......... 22.114
Weaver v Ward (1616) Hob 134, 80 ER 284 .......... 22.05, 40.38
Webb v Bloch (1928) 41 CLR 331 .......... 34.200
Webb v Ireland [1988] IR 353 (HC), [1988] ILRM 565 (SC) .......... 10.115, 10.142-10.146
.......... 23.28, 23.39, 29.02, 29.11-29.16, 30.23-30.24
.......... 30.34-30.40, 38.04
Webber v Crawford (1988) 46 CCLTI (BC SC) .......... 20.41
Webster v Paragon Bus Co [1934] IR 448 .......... 9.17
Weir v Dun Laoghaire Corporation [1983] IR 242 .......... 43.52
Weirum v RKO General Inc (1975) 15 Cal 3d 40, 539 P 2d 36, 723 Cal Rptr 468 .......... 8.18
Weitel v Moes 311 NW 2d 259 .......... 33.17
Weld-Blundell v Stephens [1920] AC 956 .......... 34.44
Weldon v Times Book (1911) 28 TLR 143 .......... 34.19
Weller & Co v Foot & Mouth Disease Research Institute [1966] 1 QB 569 .. 10.46, 25.27
Wellwood v King [1921] 2 IR 274 .......... 4.05
Wenman v Ash (1853) 13 CB 836, 148 ER 1432 .......... 34.16
Wennhak v Morgan (1888) 20 QBD 635 .......... 34.16
Wessell v Kinsmen Club of Sault Ste Marie Ontario Inc (1982) 137 DLR (3d) 96 .. 40.26
West (H) & Son Ltd v Shephard [1964] AC 326 .......... 44.07, 44.184-44.185
West London Commercial Bank Ltd v Kitson (1884) 13 QBD 360 .......... 35.09
West v Bristol Tramways Co [1908] 2 KB 14 .......... 25.06
Western Engraving Co v Film Laboratories Ltd [1936] 1 All ER 106 .......... 25.11
Westman Holidays Ltd v McCormack [1991] ILRM 833, [1992] 1 IR 151 .......... 31.64
.......... 32.93, 32.164, 32.181
Westmoreland v Schultz (1972) 2 SASR 286n .......... 40.26
Wexford County Council [1921] 2 IR 230 .......... 44.208
Whaley v Cartusiano (1990) 68 DLR (4th) 58 .......... 40.41-40.43
Whalley v Lancashire & Yorkshire Railway Co (1884) 13 QBD 131 .......... 24.55
Wheat v Lacon [1996] AC 552 .......... 12.74
Wheeler v JJ Saunders Ltd [1996] Ch 19 .......... 24.43
Wheeler v Le Merchant (1881) 17 ChD 675 .......... 37.54
Whelan v Bower (SC) 13 April 1973 .......... 44.145
Whelan v Eason & Sons [1939] Ir Jur 25, affg [1939] Ir Jur 22 .......... 8.18
Whelan v Madigan [1978] ILRM 136 .......... 23.02, 28.04, 32.56, 37.04, 44.21, 45.03
Whelan v Tipperary (SR) County Council DPIJ: Hilary and Easter Terms 1997 .......... 18.10
Whelley v Falbey DPIJ: Hilary and Easter Terms 1996 p 35 .......... 20.38, 44.180
Whipple v Grandchamp (1927) 261 Mass 40 158, NE 170 .......... 21.33
Whitby v Burt Boulton & Hayward Ltd [1947] KB 918 .......... 21.48
White v Boyle (1926) 60 ILTR 30 .......... 25.13
White v Burke DPIJ: Hilary and Easter Terms 1995, p 1 .......... 18.23

White v Chief Constable of South Yorkshire Police [1998] 3 WLR 1510, [1999] 1 All ER 1 ....................3.12, 6.22, 6.50, 17.08, 17.66, 18.61
White v Jameson (1874) LR 18 EQ 303 ....................24.78
White v Jones [1995] 2 AC 207 ....................10.141
White v Mid-Western Health Board, DPIJ: Hilary and Easter Terms 1993, p 55 ....18.118
White v Pile (1950) 68 WN (NSW) 176 ....................40.41, 40.44
White v Riley [1921] 1 Ch 1 ....................32.26
White v Stone Ltd [1939] 2 KB 827 ....................34.15
White v Store Security Ltd (CC) 21 February 1985 ....................22.12, 34.50
White v Tyrell (1856) 5 ICLR 477 ....................34.52
Whitehouse v Jordan [1981] 1 All ER 267 ....................14.19
Whiteley Ltd v Hilt [1918] 2 KB 808 ....................29.12
Whitely v Minister for Defence [1997] 2 ILRM 416 ....................46.43, 46.48
Whittaker v Sandford (1912) 110 Me 77, 85 A 399 ....................22.37, 22.47
Whittingham v Crease & Co [1978] 5 WWR 45 ....................14.174
Whooley v Dublin Corporation [1961] IR 60 ....................7.41, 8.23
Wicina v Strecker (1978) 747 P 2d 167 ....................16.25
Wicklow County Council v Hibernian Fire & General Insurance Co [1932] IR 581 21.46
Wiech v Amato (1973) 6 SASR 442 (SC) ....................40.26
Wieland v Cyril Lord Carpets Ltd [1969] 3 All ER 1006 ....................20.26
Wilchkin v Gahan (1795) Ridg Lap & Scho 591 ....................46.04
Wildgust v Bank of Ireland (HC) 28 July 1998 .....6.28, 6.34, 10.09, 10.78, 10.86, 10.106
Wiley v Synan (1937) 57 CLR 200 ....................30.38
Wilkins v Weaver [1915] 2 Ch 322 ....................32.12
Wilkinson v Ancliffe (BLT) Ltd [1986] 3 All ER 427 ....................46.50
Wilkinson v Downton [1897] 2 QB 57, 66 LJQB 493 .................... 1.83, 22.27-22.33 ....................34.85, 35.20
Willcox v Kettell [1937] 1 All ER 222 ....................23.39
William Aldred's case (1610) 9 Co Rep 576 ....................27.01
Williams (H) & Co v Dublin Corporation (1949) 84 ILTR 62 ....................23.07
Williams and Jones et al, (1736) Cast Hard 298 ....................22.18
Williams v Eady (1893) 10 TLR 41 ....................16.16, 16.68
Williams v Gilbert (1966) 239, Ark 935 SW 2d 333 ....................40.29
Williams v Holland (1833) 6 C & P 23, 172 ER 1129 ....................20.58
Williams v Mersey Docks and Harbour Board [1905] 1 KB 804 ....................42.13
Williams v Morrissey (1903) 37 ILTR 65 ....................43.30
Williams v National Life Ltd [1998] 2 All ER 577 ....................10.141
Williams v Settle [1960] 2 All ER 806 ....................44.10
Williams v Tom Duffy & Co UD 687/1986 ....................41.04
Williamson v Freer (1874) LR 9 CP 393 ....................34.178
Williamson v Honeford [1956] NI 31 ....................44.197
Williamson v Rover Cycle Co [1901] 2 IR 615 (CA) affg [1901] 2 IR 189 ....................9.19
Willis (RH) & Son v British Car Auctions Ltd [1978] 2 All ER 392 ....................30.12
Willis v Brooks [1947] 1 All ER 191 ....................39.03
Willis v Irish Press (1938) 72 ILTR 238 ....................34.170

Wills v Wisconsin-Minnesota Light & Power Co 187 Wis 626, 205 NW 556 .......... 7.32
Wilsher v Essex Area Health Authority [1988] AC 1074 .......... 2.21
Wilson Governors of Sacred Heart Roman Catholic Primary School Carlton [1998] 1 FLR 663 .......... 16.53
Wilson v Colonial Air Transport (1932) 278 Mass 420, 180 NE 212 .......... 9.25
Wilson v Finch Hatton (1877) 2 Ex Div 336 .......... 13.11
Wilson v Interlake Streel Co (1982) 32 Cal 3d 229; 185 Cal Rptr 280; 649 P 2d 922 .......... 23.32
Wilson v Lombank Ltd [1963] 1 WLR 1294 .......... 28.04, 28.13
Wilson v McGrath (HC) 17 January 1996 .......... 20.41
Wilson v Nepstad (1979) 282 NW 2d 664 .......... 26.24
Wilson v Owens (1885) 16 LR Ir 225 .......... 43.27
Wilson v Pringle [1986] 2 All ER 440, [1987] QB 237 .......... 22.03, 22.17
Wilson v Tyneside Window Cleaning Co [1958] 2 QB 110 .......... 18.84, 43.50
Wilson v Zeron [1941] OWN 353, affd [1942] OWN 195 .......... 40.41
Wilsons & Clyde Coal Co Ltd v English [1938] AC 57 .......... 18.33
Wing v London General Omnibus Co [1909] 2 KB 652 .......... 9.17
Winter v Cardiff RDC [1950] 1 All ER 819 .......... 18.106
Winterbottom v Wright (1842) 10 M & W 109, 152 ER 402 .......... 6.48, 11.04
Winters v Owens [1950] IR 225 .......... 23.42, 27.45-27.48
With v O'Flanagan [1936] Ch 575 .......... 35.06
Withers v Perry Chain Co Ltd [1961] 3 All ER 676 .......... 18.164
Wong Kwai Fun v Li Fung (1994) 1 HKC 549, (1994) HKC LEXIS 591 .......... 22.33
Wood v Leadbitter (1845) 13 M & W. 838, 153 ER 351 .......... 23.22
Wooder Investment v Wimpey Construction [1980] 1 WLR 277 .......... 13.33
Woodhouse v Newry Navigation Co [1898] 1 IR 161 .......... 23.29, 23.38, 45.02 .......... 45.05, 45.49
Woodman Matheson & Co Ltd v Brennan (1941) 75 ILTR 34 .......... 44.209
Woods v Davison [1930] NI 161 .......... 20.15
Woods v Keogh (SC) 21 December 1956 .......... 15.17
Woods v Martins Bank Ltd [1959] 1 QB 55 .......... 10.63
Woods v O'Connor [1958] Ir Jur Rep 71 .......... 26.15-26.19, 26.28
Wookey vWookey [1991] Fam 121 .......... 40.42
Woolaston v Burlington N Inc (1980) 612 P 2d 1277 .......... 40.29
Woolger v West Surrey & North East Hampshire Health Authority (1993) 16 BMLR 120 .......... 18.118
Woollerton & Wilson Ltd v Richard Costain Ltd [1970] 1 WLR 411 .......... 23.39
Workman v M'Neill (1897) 31 ILTR 144 .......... 23.29, 23.36
Wormald v Cole [1954] 1 QB 614 .......... 27.47
Worthington v Tipperary County Council [1920] 21R 233 .......... 44.09
Wren v Stokes [1902] 1 IR 167 (CA affg 1900) .......... 21.32
Wrenn v Bus Átha Cliath (SC) 31 March, 1995 .......... 7.44
Wright v Board of Managemnt of Gorey Community School (HC) 28 March 2000 .......... 22.104
Wright v McLean (1956) 7 DLR (2d) 253, Martin v Daigle (1969) 6 DLR (3d) 634 22.60

Wright v O'Neill (HC) 31 October 1991 ........................................43.65
Wright v Ramscott (1665) 1 Wms Sound 82, 85 ER 92 ........................................28.06
Wright v Tafe (1967) 208 Va 291, 156 SE 2d 562 ........................................7.24
Wright v Wilson (1699) 1 Ld Raym 739, 91 ER 1394 ........................................22.37
Wringe v Cohen [1940] 1 KB 229 ........................................24.85
Wrixon v Condran (1839) 1 Ir Eq Rep 380 ........................................ 23.38-23.39, 45.05
Wyatt v Rosherville Gardens Co (1886) 2 TLR 282 ........................................27.16, 27.23
Wymes v Tehaan [1988] IR 717 (HC) affd (SC) 9 December 1988 (ex temp) .........29.02, 30.19, ........................................45.05
Wyong Shire Council v Shirt (1980) 146 Comm LR 40 ........................................7.25

## X

X (A Minor), Re [1975] Fam 47 ........................................37.02
X v Bedfordshire County Council [1995] 2 AC 633 ........ 6.85, 16.69, 19.02, 19.11-19.14
X v Flynn (HC) 19 May 1994 ........................................37.13, 37.92
X v RTE (SC) 27 March 1990 ........................................45.15, 45.28
X v Walsh DPIJ: Hilary and Easter 1998, p 74 ........................................22.19
X v Y [1988] 2 All ER 648 ........................................37.51
XL Petroleum (NSW) Pty Ltd v Caltex Oil (Australia) Pty Ltd (1985) 155 CLR 448 ........................................44.13

## Y

Yania v Bigan (1959) 397 Pa 316, 155 A 2d 343 ........................................8.01
Yaselli v Goff (1926) 12 F 2d 396 ........................................36.04
Ybarra v Spangard (1944) 25 Cal 2d 486, 154 P 2d 687 ........................................9.28
Ybarra v Spangard (1949) 93 Cal App 2d 43, 208 P 2d 445 ........................................2.60
Yeates v Minister for Posts and Telegraphs (HC) 21 February 1978 ........................................45.46
Yepremian v Scarborough General Hospital (1980) 110 DLR (3d) 513 ........................................43.22
Young v Charles Church (Southern) Ltd 39 BMLR 146 ........................................3.36
Youssoupoff v Metro-Goldwyn Mayer Pictures Ltd (1934) 50 Times LR 581 ........34.21, 34.50, ........................................34.66
Yuen Kun Yeu v Attorney General of Hong Kong [1988] AC 175 .........6.19, 6.56, 10.76 ........................................19.66
Yun v Ford Motor Co (1994) 647 A 2d 841 ........................................11.158

## Z

Z v United Kingdom [2000] 2 FLR 245 ........................................6.85
Zarine v Owners of SS "Ramava" [1942] IR 148 ........................................38.18
Zent v Prevatte (1982) 248 Ga 832, 286 SE 2d 715 ........................................22.92
Zeppa v Coca-Cola Ltd [1955] OR 855 ........................................11.73
Zervobeakos v Zervobeakos (1969) 8 DLR (3d) 377 ........................................20.22
Zuckerberg v Munter (1950) 277 App Div 1061, 100 NYS 2d 910 ........................................16.07
Zuckerbrod v Burch (1965) 88 NJ Super 1, 210 A 2d 425 ........................................16.08
Zurla v Hydel (1997) 289 III App 3d 215, 681 NE 2d 148 ........................................7.28

# Table of Statutes

## Ireland


Accident Compensation Act 1974 .......... 1.132

Accident Rehabilitation and Compensation Insurance Act 1992 .......... 1.132

Accidental Fires Act 1943 .......... 26.15, 26.25-26.28
- s 1 (1) .......... 26.04, 26.21-26.22
  - (3) .......... 26.05

Air Navigation and Transport Act 1936
- s 7 .......... 41.08
  - (4) .......... 41.08
- 21 .......... 21.08
- 23 .......... 41.03
- 24 .......... 21.08
- 39
  - (1) .......... 23.07
- 55 .......... 21.08, 23.40, 24.93
- Pt III .......... 20.11

Air Navigation and Transport Act 1946
- s 21(1) .......... 23.40

Air Navigation and Transport Act 1959 .......... 20.11

Air Navigation and Transport Act 1973
- s 3 .......... 21.08
- 6 .......... 21.08
- 10 .......... 21.08

Air Navigation and Transport Act 1975
- s 4 (2) .......... 23.07
  - (4)(a) .......... 22.114

Air Navigation and Transport (Pre-inspection) Act 1986
- s 6 (1) .......... 21.08
  - (2) .......... 21.08

Air Navigation and Transport Act 1988
- s 18 .......... 23.07
- 33(1) .......... 23.07
- 47(1) .......... 21.08, 23.40, 24.93

Air Navigation and Trasport (Amendment) Act 1998
- s 19 .......... 23.07

Air Pollution Act 1987
- s 14 .......... 23.07
- 24(2) .......... 24.03

Air-Raid Precautions Act 1939
s 33 .......... 23.07
Administration of Justice Act 1982
s 2 .......... 33.01, 33.19
4 .......... 41.07
An Act for preventing Mischief that may happen by fire 1715 .......... 26.03
Animals Act 1985 .......... 1.121, 27.59-27.66
s 2 .......... 27.30, 27.54-27.58
3 .......... 27.27-27.29
4 .......... 27.47
5 .......... 27.47
6 .......... 27.60
Animals Remedies Act 1993
s 10(1)(c) .......... 28.16
13(1)(c) .......... 28.16
57(2)(d) .......... 28.16
Anti-Discrimination (Pay) Act 1974
s 6 (4) .......... 23.07
Adoption Act 1952 .......... 42.08, 46.71
Architectural Heritage (National Inventory) and Historic Monuments (Miscellaneous Provisions) Act 1999
s 3 (4) .......... 23.07
(5) .......... 23.06, 23.07
(8) .......... 23.06
Arterial Drainage (Amendment) Act 1995
s 10 .......... 23.07, 23.51
Abattoirs Act 1988
s 36(5) .......... 23.07
54 .......... 23.07
Attorneys' and Solicitors' Act 1870
s 7 .......... 20.66
Bill of Rights 1688
s 1 .......... 34.137
Bankruptcy Act 1988
s 27 .......... 23.04
28 .......... 23.04
Sch 1para 17(1) .......... 20.56
Broadcasting Act 1990
s 14(1) .......... 28.16
Broadcasting and Wireless Telegraphy Act 1988
s 17 .......... 23.06

Building Control Act 1990
s 8(17) ........ 23.07
Cemetries Clauses Act 1847 ........ 21.41
s 58........ 21.41
171 ........ 21.41
193 ........ 21.41
Chemical Weapons Act 1997
s 7........ 23.07, 28.16
Cheques Act 1959
s 4........ 30.14
(3) ........ 30.16
Child Care Act 1991
s 12........ 23.07
74(7) ........ 28.16
Child Trafficking and Pornography Act 1998
s 7(2)(c) ........ 28.16
Chancery Procedure Amendment Act 1858 (Lord Cairns's Act) ........ 37.39, 45.47-45.51
Civil Liability Act 1961 ........ 1.101, 1.121, 2.45-2.47, 2.52
........ 4.02, 4.07, 5.08, 11.158, 20.08, 20.13, 21.57-21.61
........ 27.28, 27.38, 33.11, 33.17, 35.15
........ 42.10, 42.21, 44.27, 44.148
s 1(b) ........ 20.67
2 ........ 4.19, 42.02
(1) ........ 20.66, 21.47, 21.58
6-10 ........ 11.120, 41.04
7(2) ........ 44.26, 44.196
8 ........ 46.89
9 ........ 41.11, 46.89
10 ........ 41.11
11 (1) ........ 4.08
(2) ........ 32.81
(a) ........ 4.09
(c) ........ 4.10, 7.40
(3) ........ 2.60, 4.10, 9.18, 27.38, 46.51
(4) ........ 34.200
(6) ........ 32.82
12 ........ 4.03, 24.112
(1) ........ 4.03, 4.09-4.12
(2) ........ 4.12
(3) ........ 4.13
14 ........ 4.03, 4.14
(1) ........ 4.14
(2) ........ 4.14
(3) ........ 4.12-4.14
(c) ........ 4.25

*Civil Liability Act 1961 (contd)*
(4) ....... 34.226, 44.18, 44.26
(5) ....... 34.226
(6) ....... 34.226
16 ....... 4.14-4.17
(1) ....... 4.17
(2) ....... 4.17
(3) ....... 4.17
(4) ....... 4.17
17 ....... 4.09
(1) ....... 4.18
(2) ....... 4.18
18 (1)(b) ....... 4.09, 4.14
19 (4) ....... 4.15
21 ....... 2.34, 4.12, 4.19-4.20, 42.16
(1) ....... 4.19, 46.87
(2) ....... 4.20
22 (1) ....... 4.20
23 ....... 4.26
(4) ....... 4.19
24 ....... 4.19
25 ....... 4.21
26 ....... 4.22
27 ....... 4.24
(1) ....... 4.21-4.24
(b) ....... 4.24
28 ....... 4.25
29 ....... 4.25
30 ....... 46.89
31 ....... 4.25, 46.87
32 ....... 4.16
(1) ....... 4.16
(2) ....... 4.16
(4) ....... 4.16
34 ....... 20.48-20.53, 20.67, 21.47, 27.26, 27.48, 34.18
(1) ....... 2.26, 4.15, 11.160, 20.10-20.13, 20.46, 20.51-20.56
....... 21.47, 21.58, 27.53, 34.224, 42.15
(b) ....... 5.09, 6.67, 11.161, 18.159, 20.63-20.73
....... 20.99, 21.50, 27.26, 34.224, 42.12
(2) ....... 20.13
(b) ....... 3.14, 20.36, 20.43-20.46, 43.69, 44.107
(c) ....... 18.158, 20.37, 20.54, 21.47
(d) ....... 30.39
(e) ....... 12.10
(f) ....... 11.28, 13.54

*Civil Liability Act 1961 (contd)*
s 35 ........ 20.58
(1) ........ 32.10
(b) ........ 42.15, 42.24
(d) ........ 42.16
(e) ........ 20.58
(f) ........ 20.59
(g) ........ 20.59
(h) ........ 20.59
(i) ........ 20.59
(j) ........ 20.59
(2) ........ 32.10, 33.16
36 (1) ........ 20.56
(3) ........ 20.56
(4) ........ 20.56
38 ........ 4.12
(1) ........ 4.19
(2) ........ 4.25
42 ........ 20.11
43 ........ 11.159, 21.50, 21.58-21.60
45 (1) ........ 20.58
(2) ........ 4.25
46 ........ 4.12
(1)(a)(ii) ........ 20.11
(2) ........ 46.88
(3) ........ 46.88
(4) ........ 46.88
47 (1) ........ 42.07
(2) ........ 42.08-42.09
47-51 ........ 11.120, 41.08, 42.01
48 ........ 1.164, 42.02
(1) ........ 42.01, 42.12-42.13
(2) ........ 42.02
(3) ........ 42.02
(4) ........ 42.02
49 ........ 42.19, 42.20
(1) (a)(i) ........ 42.19
(ii) ........ 42.19
(b) ........ 42.19
(5) ........ 42.67
49A ........ 42.11
50 ........ 42.40-42.40, 42.58, 44.118
56 ........ 2.26, 15.46, 20.12
57 (1) ........ 1.106, 4.19, 12.23, 12.114, 20.101, 21.46
(2) ........ 21.49

*Civil Liability Act 1961 (contd)*
58 ........................................................................................6.58
59 ........................................................................................38.03, 38.11
60 ........................................................................................24.118, 38.12
(1) ........................................................................................24.118
(2) ........................................................................................24.121
(3) ........................................................................................24.119
(4) ........................................................................................24.120
(5) ........................................................................................24.118
(7) ........................................................................................24.118
62 ........................................................................................20.56
Ch III ........................................................................................24.101
Pt III ........................................................................................2.60, 4.03, 11.164
Pt IV ........................................................................................1.137, 42.06, 42.13
Civil Liability (Amendment) Act 1964
s 2 ........................................................................................44.117-44.120, 44.128-44.138
(b) ........................................................................................44.127
3 ........................................................................................4.24
4 ........................................................................................32.10
5 ........................................................................................20.56
Civil Liability (Amendment) Act 1996 ........................33.10, 33.15, 42.01, 42.06, 42.19
s 1 (1) ........................................................................................42.07
(2) ........................................................................................42.10
2 ........................................................................................42.21
(1)(a) ........................................................................................42.23
(c) ........................................................................................42.67
3(2) ........................................................................................42.11
22 ........................................................................................42.40
47(1)(c) ........................................................................................33.20
Civil Liability (Assessment of Hearing Injury) Act 1998 ........................................1.191
Canals Act 1986
s 11 ........................................................................................23.07
Committee of Public Accounts of Dáil Éireann (Privilege and Procedure) Act 1970
........................................................................................34. 140
Committees of the Houses of the Oireachtas (Privilege and Procedure) Act 1976
s 2 ........................................................................................34.140
Competition Act 1991
s 21 ........................................................................................23.06
Competition (Amendment) Act 1996
s 11(2) ........................................................................................23.06
Companies Act 1963 ........................................................................................39.01
49 ........................................................................................35.10
297(1) ........................................................................................35.10

Companies Act 1990
s 39 .......... 35.10

Conditions of Employment Act 1936
s 6 .......... 38.03

Conspiracy and Protection of Property Act 1875
s 3 .......... 32.116

Consumer Credit Act 1995
s 105(1) .......... 23.07

Consumer Information Act 1978
s 6 .......... 35.01
16 (3) .......... 23.07
17 (3) .......... 1.107, 35.01, 44.137

Control of Clinical Trials Act 1987 .......... 14.150, 22.62
s 3 (1)(g) .......... 22.62
8 (4)(i) .......... 22.62
9 (7) .......... 14.29
(b) .......... 22.113
(8) .......... 22.62

Control of Clinical Trials and Drugs Act 1990 .......... 14.150, 22.62

Control of Dogs Act 1986 .......... 1.121, 27.27-27.39, 27.66
s 1 .......... 27.36
16 (1) .......... 23.07-23.07, 28.16
(2) .......... 23.07
21 .......... 27.25-27.28, 27.40, 27.66, 46.21
(1) .......... 27.30
(2) .......... 27.31
(3) .......... 22.114, 27.32-27.35
(4) .......... 27.38
23 .......... 1.120, 27.40
(1) .......... 28.06
25 .......... 27.06, 27.40
(1)(a) .......... 24.31
26 .......... 23.06
(2) .......... 23.07

Control of Dogs (Amendment) Act 1992 .......... 27.27
s 2 .......... 27.41
7 .......... 23.07, 28.16

Control of Horses Act 1996 .......... 27.61
s 17 .......... 24.03
34 .......... 23.07
35 .......... 23.06
37 .......... 28.16
(1) .......... 24.03

*Control of Horses Act 1996 (contd)*
s 40(1)(a) .......... 24.03
45 .......... 27.63
46(2) .......... 24.03
147(1) .......... 24.03

Copyright Act 1963
Pt IV .......... 21.08

Copyright and Related Rights Act 2000 .......... 31.01
s 128 .......... 30.44
131 .......... 30.44
132 .......... 23.06, 28.16
133 .......... 28.16, 30.44
(5) .......... 23.07
134(1) .......... 30.44
256 .......... 23.06, 28.16
257 .......... 28.16
(5) .......... 23.07
Ch 9 .......... 30.44

Coroners Act 1962 .......... 34.148

Court and Court Officers Act 1995 .......... 1.176

Court of Justice Act 1924
s 96 .......... 44.66

Courts (Supplemental Provisions) Act 1961
s 3 .......... 1.106
8 .......... 45.02
Sch 1 .......... 1.106

Courts Act 1971
s 6 .......... 1.164

Courts Act 1981 .......... 33.10, 42.21

Courts Act 1988 .......... 1.116, 1.164, 14.14

Courts and Legal Services Act 1990
s 8 .......... 34.255

Courts Act 1991
s 7 .......... 29.10

Courts Service Act 1998 .......... 1.177

Capital Gains Act 1975
s 24(1)(c) .......... 44.103

Credit Union Act 1966 .......... 39.10

Credit Union Act 1997
s 90(3) .......... 23.07

Criminal Damage Act 1991
s 9-11 .......... 1.108
12 (6) .......... 23.13
13 .......... 23.06

Criminal Justice Act 1951
s 11 (4) .......... 22.19

Criminal Justice Act 1964
s 4 (1) .......... 22.07
(2) .......... 22.06

Criminal Justice Act 1984
s 4-10 .......... 22.35, 22.105
6 .......... 22.113
28 .......... 22.113
274 .......... 21.08

Criminal Justice Act 1993 .......... 1.107, 1.137
s 6.......... 1.108
(1) .......... 1.108
(2) .......... 1.108
(4) .......... 1.108
(7) .......... 1.108
7 .......... 1.108
9 .......... 1.108

Criminal Justice Act 1994
s 38.......... 28.16
39 .......... 28.16
64 .......... 19.68, 28.16, 37.18

Criminal Justice (Public Order) Act 1994
s 11.......... 23.02
13 .......... 23.02
(1) .......... 23.22
(2)(b) .......... 23.22
22 .......... 28.16

Criminal Justice (Miscellaneous Provisions) Act 1997
s 10.......... 28.18
(2) .......... 28.18

Criminal Justice (Location of Victims' Remains) Act 1999
s 8.......... 23.06

Criminal Law (Amendment) Act 1885
s 11 .......... 34.81

Criminal Law Amendment Act 1935
s 1.......... 28.18
2 .......... 28.18
11 .......... 37.69

Criminal Law Act 1976
s 5 ........ 28.18
9(1) ........ 28.17
Criminal Law (Rape) (Amendment) Act 1990
s 3 ........ 28.18
4 ........ 28.18
Criminal Law (Sexual Offences) Act 1993
s 3 ........ 28.18
5 ........ 28.18
14 ........ 34.81
Criminal Law (Sexual Offences) Amendment Act 1993 ........ 37.80
Criminal Law (Suicide) Act 1993 ........ 37.83
Criminal Law Act 1997
s 2 (1) ........ 22.106
3 ........ 1.106, 37.53
(1) ........ 22.106
4 ........ 22.106-22.108
(4) ........ 22.109
6 ........ 23.12
Carriage of Dangerous Goods by Road Act 1998
s 6 ........ 23.07
7 ........ 23.06
64(4)(f) ........ 28.16
Casual Trading Act 1995
s 10 ........ 23.07
11 ........ 28.16
Custom - Free Airport Act 1947
s 7(1) ........ 23.07
Customs Consolidation Act 1876
s 267 ........ 29.05, 29.10
Customs and Excise (Miscellaneous Provisions) Act 1988
s 2 ........ 23.06
3 ........ 23.06
5 ........ 23.06
(1) ........ 23.07
Defence (Amendment) Act 1987
s 6 ........ 21.08
7 ........ 23.07
Defamation Act 1961 ........ 1.121
........ 34.09
s 2 ........ 34.142, 34.190
6 ........ 34.123

*Defamation Act 1961 (contd)*
s 14(2) ..... 34.20, 34.32
15 ..... 34.22
16 ..... 34.30
17 ..... 34.226
18 ..... 34.144-34.145
(1) ..... 34.141-34.145
(2) ..... 34.142
19 ..... 34.30-34.37
20 ..... 37.15
(1) ..... 35.30
(2) ..... 35.30
21 ..... 34.112-34.115, 34.228
22 ..... 34.127
23 ..... 34.206-34.208
24 ..... 34.144, 34.167, 34.190, 35.28
(2) ..... 34.190
(3) ..... 34.190
(4) ..... 34.192
26 ..... 34.226
Pt II ..... 34.24

Derelict Sites Act 1990
s 30..... 23.07
(3) ..... 23.06

Debtors' (Ireland) Act 1840
s 31..... 41.03

Diplomatic Relations and Immunities Act 1967 ..... 38.15

Directors' Liability Act 1890
s 2..... 35.10

Damages Act 1996
s 2..... 44.57

Dangerous Substances Act 1972 ..... 26.26

Dogs Act 1871 ..... 27.27

Dogs Act 1906 ..... 27.25, 27.36-27.39
s 1..... 27.28-27.30
7 ..... 27.36

Dogs (Protection of Livestock) Act 1960 ..... 27.27

Domestic Violence Act 1996 ..... 42.10, 45.37
s 2..... 22.27
18(1)(b) ..... 23.13

Domicile and Recognition of Foreign Divorces Act 1986
s 4..... 33.34

Data Protection Act 1988 .......... 37.98
s 7 .......... 21.08, 37.20
24 .......... 23.07

Dublin Police Act 1842
s 68 .......... 29.10, 30.19

Dublin Transport Authority Act 1986
s 18 .......... 37.20

Dumping at Sea Act 1981
s 4 (2) .......... 23.07

Dumping at Sea Act 1989
s 41 .......... 23.07

Dumping at Sea Act 1996
s 6 .......... 28.16

Electricity (Supply) Act 1927
s 98 .......... 23.07
108 .......... 23.07

Electricity Regulation Act 1999
s 11 (4) .......... 23.07
12 .......... 23.06

Electronic Commerce Act 2000
27 .......... 23.06
(2) .......... 28.16
(5) .......... 28.16

Employers Liability Act 1880 .......... 18.02

Employment Equality Act 1977 .......... 18.80

Employment Equality Act 1998
s 15 .......... 18.80
94 .......... 23.06

Energy (Miscellaneous Provisions) Act 1995
s 10 (7) .......... 23.07
s 16 .......... 23.06, 28.16
(5) .......... 23.07

Environmental Protection Agency Act 1992
s 13 .......... 23.07
(6) .......... 23.06
15 .......... 38.12
108 .......... 24.03, 24.12, 24.31

Equal Status Act 2000
s 33 .......... 23.07
(4) .......... 23.06

Education Act 1998
s 28 .......... 22.104

Education (Welfare) Act 2000
s 30 .......... 23.07
(5) .......... 23.06

Extradition Act 1965 .......... 1.34, 19.49

Finance Act 1964
s 8 .......... 44.103
9 .......... 44.103
Sch 1, para 13 .......... 44.103

Finance Act 1990
s 5 .......... 44.57, 44.103

Fire Services Act 1981 .......... 26.02, 26.15
s 9 .......... 26.31
12 (3) .......... 26.30
18 .......... 26.26
(2) .......... 26.27
(3) .......... 26.29
22
(2) .......... 23.07
27 .......... 21.08
28 .......... 23.51
(1) .......... 23.07
(2)(c) .......... 21.08
36 .......... 8.04, 21.08, 26.24, 26.32, 38.12

Firearms and Offensive Weapons Act 1990
s 15 .......... 23.06

Fisheries (Consolidation) Act 1959
s 213 .......... 23.07
215 .......... 25.44
231 .......... 23.07
233 .......... 23.07
296 .......... 23.07
298 .......... 23.07
301 .......... 23.07

Fisheries Act 1980
s 53 .......... 23.07
54 .......... 24.05
61 .......... 25.44
71 .......... 23.07

Fisheries (Amendment) (No 2) Act 1987
s 14 .......... 23.07

Fisheries (Amendment) Act 1999
s 24(4) .......... 23.07

Family Law Act 1981 .......... 33.01

Family Law (Divorce) Act 1996 .......... 33.03, 42.07
Food Safety Authority of Ireland Act 1998
s 50 .......... 23.06, 28.16
51 .......... 28.16
Forfeiture Act 1870 .......... 46.66
Friendly Societies (Amendment) Act 1953 .......... 39.10
Friendly Societies Act 1896 .......... 39.10
Fatal Accidents Act 1846 (Lord Campbell's Act) .......... 42.01
s 1 .......... 42.13
Fatal Injuries Act 1956 .......... 42.01, 44.10
s 2 .......... 42.27
3 .......... 42.27
6 .......... 41.03
Factories Act 1955 .......... 18.97, 21.35
s 3 .......... 38.03
8 .......... 21.38
21 .......... 21.36
22 .......... 21.36
23 .......... 21.10, 21.25, 21.36
34(1)(a) .......... 21.42
37 .......... 21.39
67(1) .......... 21.10
71(1) .......... 21.38
94 .......... 23.07
100 .......... 38.03
103 .......... 1.107
118 .......... 38.03
Factory and Workshop Act 1901 .......... 21.38
Gaming and Lotteries Act 1956 .......... 23.15
s 38 .......... 23.07
39 .......... 23.06
Goods and Supply of Services Act 1980
s 13 .......... 11.15
43 .......... 10.156
Garda Compensation Act 1941 .......... 42.40
Garda Síochána (Compensation) Act 1941 .......... 1.135
Garda Síochána (Compensation) Act 1945 .......... 1.135
Garda Síochána Compensation Acts 1941 .......... 33.13
Garda Síochána Compensation Acts 1945 .......... 33.13
Garda Síochána (Complaints) Act 1986
s 12 .......... 37.20

Greyhound Industry Act 1958
s 46 ........ 23.07
Grand Jury (Ireland) Act 1836 ........ 1.134
Gas Act 1976
s 26 ........ 23.07
(2) ........ 28.16
27 ........ 23.07
34 ........ 23.07
Gasworks Clauses Act 1847
s 29 ........ 24.93
Gasworks Clauses Act 1871
s 9 ........ 24.93
Guardianship of Infants Act 1964 ........ 21.62-21.69, 22.85
s 3 ........ 33.33
6 ........ 21.62
6A ........ 21.62
Health Act 1947
s 94 ........ 23.07
Health Act 1953
s 68 ........ 23.07
Health Act 1970 ........ 44.107
Health (Mental Services) Act 1981
s 36 ........ 23.07
Health (Amendment) Act 1986
s 2 ........ 44.108
Health Care Act 1947 ........ 37.50
Hepatitis C Compensation Tribunal Act 1997
s 5(15) ........ 1.184
Hire Purchase Act 1946, s 11 ........ 29.04
Holidays Employees Act 1973
s 8 (4) (c) ........ 1.107
Hotel Proprietors Act 1963 ........ 2.45, 12.143, 20.50, 21.08, 32.50
s 4 ........ 12.56-12.58
(1) ........ 12.58
(2) ........ 12.57
7 ........ 12.58
9 ........ 12.58
11 ........ 26.15
Housing Act 1966 ........ 13.11, 13.23-13.26, 13.36-13.44, 19.28, 19.39, 21.13, 21.18
s 13 ........ 21.18
39 ........ 19.23-19.31

*Housing Act 1966 (contd)*
s 40 .......... 13.40
55 .......... 21.14-21.18
66 .......... 13.11
(2) .......... 13.30
90 .......... 13.11, 13.28
111 .......... 21.12-21.17, 45.02
114 .......... 13.11
Sch 2 .......... 13.30

Housing Act 1988
s 55 .......... 21.18

Housing (Miscellaneous Provisions) Act 1992
s 12(1) .......... 23.07
18 .......... 13.11

Housing (Miscellaneous Provisions) Act 1997
s 12(2) .......... 23.07
20(4) .......... 23.07

Harbours Act 1946
s 47 .......... 21.10

Harbours Act 1996
s 14(5) .......... 23.07
49 .......... 23.07

Illegal Immigrants (Trafficking) Act 2000
s 3 .......... 28.16
7 .......... 23.06

Infants Relief Act 1874 .......... 22.85, 40.31

Interception of Postal Packets and Telcommunication Messages (Regulation) Act 1993 .......... 37.97

International Carriage of Perishable Foodstuffs Act 1987
s 8 .......... 23.07

International War Crimes Tribunals Act 1998
s 30 .......... 23.06, 28.16

Intoxicating Liquor (General) Act 1924
s 25 .......... 23.07

Intoxicating Liquor Act 1927
s 22 .......... 23.07

Intoxicating Liquor Act 1988
s 37 .......... 23.07

Industrial Relations Act 1990 .......... 32.88-32.100, 32.107-32.111, 45.05
s 8 .......... 32.92, 32.99, 32.112
9 .......... 32.115-32.115
(1) .......... 32.172

*Industrial Relations Act 1990 (contd)*
s 10 ........ 32.114-32.116, 32.172
11 ........ 23.21, 32.114-32.117, 32.145-32.147, 32.154-32.162, 32.172
(1) ........ 32.163-32.164, 32.171, 32.182
(2) ........ 32.127, 32.168-32.171
(3) ........ 32.169-32.173
(4) ........ 32.171
(5) ........ 32.171
12 ........ 32.114-32.125, 32.172
13 ........ 32.114-32.118, 32.126-32.141, 32.172, 39.32
14 ........ 32.172-32.185
16 ........ 32.172
17(1) ........ 32.117, 32.172
19 ........ 32.173, 32.180
(2) ........ 32.175-32.184
PT II ........ 32.90

Industrial and Commercial Property (Protection) Act 1927. ........ 31.01

Investment Intermediaries Act 1995
s 53 ........ 38.12
65 ........ 23.07, 28.16

Irish Aviation Authority Act 1993
s 65 ........ 23.07, 28.16

Irish Horseracing Industry Act 1958
s 51 ........ 23.07

Irish Horseracing Industry Act 1994
s 51 ........ 28.16

Joint Tortfeasor 1951 ........ 4.02
s 5 ........ 4.19

Jurisdiction of Courts and Enforcement of Judgments (European Communities) Act 1988 ........ 11.91, 34.49

Jurisdiction of Courts and Enforcement of Judgments (European Communities) Act 1993 ........ 11.91, 34.49

Licensing Act 1872
s 13 ........ 8.29
19 ........ 8.29

Licensing Act (Ireland) 1874 ........ 23.07

Licensing (Combating Drug Abuse) Act 1997
s 12 ........ 23.22
14 ........ 23.07
(3) ........ 28.16
16 ........ 28.16

Liability for Defective Products Act 1991 ........ 1.121-1.124, 11.02-11.03, 11.22
........ 11.56, 11.91-11.93, 11.129-11.131, 11.173-11.175, ,46.95

*Liability for Defective Products Act 1991 (contd)*
s 1 ........ 11.96
(1) ........ 11.99-11.103, 11.117-11.124
(2) ........ 11.94
2 ........ 11.101, 11.110
(1) ........ 11.98-11.98, 11.117-11.123, 11.135, 11.166
(2) ........ 11.102, 11.106
(b) ........ 11.103
(2)(a) ........ 11.103
(3) ........ 11.104-11.107
(c) ........ 11.104
3 (1) ........ 11.126
4 ........ 11.98, 11.115, 11.127, 11.132
5 ........ 11.108, 11.111, 11.133, 11.142
(1) ........ 11.110, 11.139
(2) ........ 11.116
6 ........ 11.136, 11.142
(b) ........ 11.138
(d) ........ 11.141
(e) ........ 11.114, 11.142, 11.144
(f) ........ 11.145
7 ........ 11.157
(1) ........ 11.148, 46.94
(2)(a) ........ 11.149
(b) ........ 11.151
(9) ........ 46.96
(3) ........ 41.11
8 ........ 11.166
9 (2) ........ 11.112, 11.158-11.160, 20.13
10 ........ 11.162, 20.66
13 ........ 11.101, 11.168

Litter Act 1982
s 11 ........ 28.16
12 ........ 28.16

Litter Pollution Act 1997 ........ 24.11
s 20 ........ 23.07, 28.16

Land Act 1927
s 37(1) ........ 23.43

Landlord and Tenant Law Amendment Act Ireland 1860 (Deasy's Act)
s 83 ........ 13.11-13.18

Landlord and Tenant Act 1931 ........ 14.217

Landlord and Tenant (Amendment) Act 1980 ........ 14.217

Local Government (Ireland) Act 1898 ........ 1.134

Local Government Act 1925 ........ 43.52
Pt III ........ 24.94

Local Government (Planning and Development) Act 1963 ........ 19.42
s 26(11) ........ 43.52
28 ........ 19.35
45(7) ........ 24.31
83 ........ 23.07

Local Government (Planning and Development) Act 1976
s 27 ........ 24.10, 24.37, 45.40
42(c) ........ 23.07

Local Government (Multi-Storey Buildings) Act 1988
s 7(1) ........ 23.07

Local Government Act 1994
s 37(2) ........ 24.03

Local Government (Planning and Development) Act 1999
s 31(3) ........ 23.07

Labour Services Act 1987
s 13 ........ 37.20

Larceny Act 1916 ........ 34.93
s 42 ........ 23.06

Law Reform (Miscellaneous Provisions) Act 1970
s 4 ........ 33.01
5 ........ 33.01

Law Reform (Miscellaneous Provisions) Act 1971 ........ 42.45

Law Reform (Personal Injuries) Act 1948 ........ 43.69

Law Reform (Personal Injuries) Act 1958 ........ 43.69

Law of Libel Amendment Act 1888
s 3 ........ 34.142
4 ........ 34.192

Medical Practitioners Act 1978 ........ 21.10

Mental Act 1945
s 260 ........ 43.22

Merchandise Marks Acts 1887-1970 ........ 44.137

Merchant Shipping Act 1894
s 206 ........ 23.07

Merchant Shipping Act 1906
s 26 ........ 23.07

Merchant Shipping (Safety Convention) Act 1952
s 37 ........ 8.02

Merchant Shipping (Salvage and Wreck) Act 1993 ........ 28.16

Merchant Shipping (Investigation of Marine Casualties) Act 2000
s 27 ........ 23.07
(3) ........ 28.16
28 ........ 23.06
Milk (Regulation of Supply) Act 1994
s 15 ........ 23.07
(1)(d) ........ 28.16
Minerals Development Act 1940 ........ 23.39
Minerals Development Act 1979 ........ 23.39
Minerals Development Act 1995 ........ 23.39
Minerals Development Act 1999 ........ 23.39
Mines and Quarries Act 1965
s 131 ........ 23 .07
137 ........ 21.08
Misuse of Drugs Act 1977
s 23 ........ 28.16
(1) ........ 23.06
Misuse of Drugs Act 1984
s 12 ........ 23.06, 28.16
Malicious Injuries (Ireland) Act 1853 ........ 1.134
Malicious Injuries Act 1981 ........ 1.107, 1.134
Malicious Injuries (Amendment) Act 1986 ........ 1.134
Married Women's Status Act 1957
s 8 (1) ........ 13.33
(ii) ........ 13.33
11 ........ 43.67
Non-Fatal Offences Against the Person Act 1997 ........ 22.32
s 2 ........ 22.11, 22.27
3 ........ 22.27
4 ........ 22.27
5 ........ 22.27
7(2) ........ 28.16
9 ........ 22.27
10 ........ 22.27, 24.73, 37.59
13 ........ 22.27
15 ........ 22.27, 22.36
23 ........ 22.74-22.85
(1) ........ 22.82
31 ........ 22.19
National Minimum Wage Act 2000
s 33 ........ 23.07
(3) ........ 23.06

National Monuments (Amendment) Act 1987
s 5 (1) .................... 23.07

National Monuments Act 1930
s 16 (1) .................... 12.86

National Monuments (Amendment) Act 1987
s 2.................... 30.25
8 (2) .................... 23.07
22 .................... 23.06

National Monuments (Amendment) Act 1994
s 8 (2) .................... 23.07
9 .................... 28.16
10 .................... 30.25

Offences Against the Person Act 1861
s 42.................... 22.19
61 .................... 34.81, 37.69
62 .................... 34.81, 37.69

Offences Against the Person Act 1939
s 29.................... 28.18

Offences Against the Person Act 1997
s 24.................... 22.104

Offences Against the State Act 1939
s 22.................... 21.08
34 .................... 1.48, 1.56

Offences Against the State (Amendment) Act 1985
s 6 .................... 21.08

Oil Pollution of the Sea Act 1956
s 21 (1) .................... 23.07

Oil Pollution of the Sea Act 1977
s 15.................... 23.07

Oil Pollution of the Sea (Amendment) Act 1977
s 2 .................... 23.51
3 .................... 23.51
4 .................... 23.51

Oil Pollution of the Sea (Civil Liability and Compensation) (Amendment) Act 1998 23.51
s 7 (2) .................... 23.51
8 .................... 23.51
32-33 .................... 23.07

Organisation of Working Time Act 1997
s 8(7) .................... 23.07

Occupiers' Liability Act 1995 ........ 1.06, 1.124, 6.01, 6.55, 12.01
........ 12.13-12.16, 12.57-12.66, 12.104, 12.143
........ 13.63, 16.70, 20.97, 23.01, 24.78, 25.36, 26.25, 27.10, 27.34, 43.44

s 1 ........ 12.131, 12.137-12.142, 13.18
(1) ........ 8.31, 12.75, 12.83, 12.96, 12.117-12.120
........ 16.73-16.77, 18.69-18.70, 24.69, 24.121, 27.09
2 (1) ........ 12.143, 16.73-16.76, 27.09-27.12, 27.33-27.34
(3) ........ 27.33
3 ........ 11.33, 12.77, 12.97, 12.130, 13.18, 16.73, 21.42
(1) ........ 12.78
(2) ........ 12.78
4 ........ 12.77, 12.82, 12.124
(1) ........ 6.38, 12.97, 12.124, 13.18, 16.76-16.79, 22.114
(2) ........ 6.38, 12.98-12.99, 12.109
(3) ........ 12.96, 12.106-12.111
(a) ........ 12.110, 22.114
(b) ........ 12.110
(4) ........ 12.115-12.120, 13.18, 16.79
5 ........ 12.82, 12.123-12.133, 16.74, 18.70-18.70
(1) ........ 12.97, 12.123
(2) ........ 12.127
(a) ........ 12.123
(b) ........ 12.123
(i) ........ 12.134, 16.74, 18.70
(c) ........ 12.123
(3) ........ 12.124
(4) ........ 12.92
(5) ........ 12.107, 12.128
6 ........ 12.132
(2) ........ 12.135
7 ........ 12.136, 12.144
8 ........ 1.120, 12.138-12.142, 16.73, 18.69, 18.81, 27.09
(a) ........ 12.113, 22.114
(b) ........ 12.141
(c) ........ 12.144
21(3) ........ 27.34

Petroleum and Other Minerals Development Act 1960
s 77 ........ 21.08
79-80 ........ 21.08

Packaged Goods (Quality Control) Act 1980
s 148(1) ........ 23.07

Package Holidays and Travel Trade Act 1995
s 21(4) ........ 23.07

Police (Property) Act 1897 ........ 28.14-28.17

Postal and Telecommunications Services Act 1983 .......... 44.90
s 37 .......... 37.20
64 .......... 32.137, 38.12
(1) .......... 21.08
(2) .......... 21.08
88 .......... 32.137, 38.12
(1) .......... 21.08
(2) .......... 21.08
105 .......... 21.08

Poynings' Law 1495 .......... 41.03

Prevention of Electoral Abuses Act 1923
s 11(5) .......... 45.34

Prevention of Forceable Entry and Occupation Act 1971 .......... 45.05

Proceeds of Crime Act 1996
s 15 .......... 28.16

Prohibition of Forcible Entry and Occupation Act 1971 .......... 22.114
s 2 .......... 23.02
6 .......... 23.02

Prohibition of Incitement to Hatred Act 1989
s 9 .......... 23.07, 28.16

Protection of Animals Kept for Farming Purposes Act 1984
s 8 .......... 23.07

Protection of Employment Act 1977
s 17 .......... 23.07

Protection of Young Persons (Employment) Act 1977
s 27 .......... 23.07

Protections for Persons Reporting Child Abuse Act 1998 .......... 34.170

Partnership Act 1890 .......... 4.19
s 10 .......... 39.09, 43.54
11 .......... 43.54
12 .......... 39.09, 43.55

Public Health Act 1878
s 107 .......... 24.03

Public Health (Ireland) Act 1878
s 17 .......... 24.96
52 .......... 23.07
55 .......... 23.07
161 .......... 21.41
181 .......... 21.08, 21.40

Public Health Act 1937 .......... 19.39

Public Health (Control of Disease) Act 1984 .......... 37.50

Punishment of Incest Act 1908 .......... 28.18

Pawnbrokers Act 1964
s 46 .......... 23.07

Quarries Act 1965 .......... 18.97

Registration of Business Names Act 1963
s 14(3) .......... 31.42

Registration of Clubs (Ireland) Act 1904 .......... 39.17

Real Property Limitation Act 1833 .......... 46.82

Rent Restrictions Act 1960 .......... 13.18
s 39 .......... 13.11

Restrictive Practices Act 1972
s 11(9) .......... 23.07
11(2) .......... 23.07

Restrictive Practices (Amendment) Act 1987
s 28 .......... 23.07

Railway Clauses Consolidation Act 1845 .......... 21.25

Railway Fires Act 1905 .......... 25.44

Railway Fires (Amendment) Act 1931 .......... 25.44

Railway Regulation Act 1871
s 7 .......... 10.13

Radiological Protection Act 1991
s 29 .......... 23.51, 28.16
33 .......... 28.16

Road Traffic Act 1933 .......... 1.141-1.145
s 78(1)(d) .......... 38.17
170 .......... 38.03
172 .......... 43.62

Road Traffic Act 1961 .......... 43.63
s 3(1) .......... 43.65
11 .......... 43.01
12 .......... 43.01
21 .......... 43.64
43 .......... 23.40
45(3) .......... 7.39, 15.53
49(8) .......... 23.10
50(10) .......... 23.10
56 .......... 1.127
(1) .......... 1.141
57 .......... 1.107
(1) .......... 1.107
(2) .......... 1.107
76(1)(d) .......... 38.17

*Road Traffic Act 1961 (contd)*
s 106 .......... 8.02
116 .......... 38.03
117 .......... 41.03
118 .......... 43.47, 43.61-43.65

Road Traffic Act 1968
s 78 .......... 1.146

Road Traffic Act 1993
s 67 .......... 15.02
70 .......... 24.31
(8) .......... 23.07
(9) .......... 23.07
(11) .......... 23.07
76(3)(b) .......... 23.07
78 .......... 23.07

Road Traffic Act 1994
s 39 .......... 23.11
(2) .......... 23.10

Road Transport Act 1999
s 15 .......... 23.06

Sea Pollution Act 1991
s 23(3) .......... 23.07
24 .......... 28.16

Sea Pollution (Amendment) Act 1999
s 4 .......... 23.07
5 .......... 23.07
14 .......... 28.16

Safety in Industry Act 1955 .......... 26.26

Safety in Industry Act 1980 .......... 21.10, 26.26
s 9(1) .......... 21.42
12(1) .......... 21.10
53 .......... 23.07

Safety, Health and Welfare (Offshore Installations) Act 1987
s 41 .......... 23.07

Safety, Health and Welfare at Work Act 1989 .......... 18.25-18.32, 18.97
s 2 .......... 21.34
6-11 .......... 18.27, 21.08
12 .......... 18.26
28 .......... 21.07-21.08
34(1) .......... 23.07
60 .......... 21.08
61 .......... 21.08, 38.12

Shannon Navigation Act 1990
s 4 ........ 23.07
Shops Act 1912
s 21(6) ........ 21.32
Sch 5 ........ 21.32
Sale of Goods Act 1893 ........ 13.03
s 14(1) ........ 11.78
22 ........ 30.07
Sale of Goods and Supply of Services Act 1980 ........ 13.03, 13.51
s 4 (1) ........ 10.157
13 ........ 11.03
(7) ........ 46.21
14 ........ 10.90
22 ........ 10.27
39 ........ 11.15, 13.51
40 ........ 20.66
43 ........ 10.146
44 ........ 10.156
45 ........ 10.90
(1) ........ 10.156
(2) ........ 10.146, 10.156
46 ........ 20.66
(1) ........ 10.157
47 ........ 30.03
Pt IV ........ 13.51
Pt V ........ 10.155
Slaughter of Animals Act 1935
s 9 ........ 23.07
Social Welfare (Occupational Injuries) Act 1966 ........ 1.121, 18.02
Social Welfare (Consolidation) Act 1993 ........ 1.121, 1.129
s 75 (1) ........ 44.131
(3) ........ 42.40
210 ........ 44.131
212(3) ........ 23.07
236 ........ 44.131-44.133
(1) ........ 42.40
237(1) ........ 44.133
281(3A) ........ 41.11
Pt II ........ 18.02
Pt VI ........ 18.02
Social Welfare Act 1996
s 41 ........ 41.11

Solicitors (Amendment) Act 1994
s 14 .... 23.07

Stock Exchange Act 1995
s 53 (1) .... 38.12

Street and House to House Collections Act 1962
s 20 .... 28.16
24 .... 23.07

Status of Children Act 1987 .... 33.03, 42.09
s 12 .... 21.62
39 (3)(a) .... 22.113
(b) .... 22.113

Statute of Frauds (Ireland) Act 1695 .... 4.19
s 2 .... 35.25

Statute of Frauds Amendment Act 1828 .... 35.24
s 6 .... 35.24

Statute of Limitations 1957 .... 1.49-1.58, 1.99, 1.110, 32.82, 32.143, 41.09, 46.02
s 2 .... 46.03
(2)(a) .... 46.04
11 (1) .... 1.56
(2) .... 1.99, 46.09
(a) .... 27.28, 46.03, 46.13-46.14
(b) .... 27.28, 46.03, 46.09-46.19
12 .... 29.10, 46.85
(1) .... 46.85
(2) .... 46.85
26 .... 46.85
48 .... 46.14
(1) .... 46.66
(2) .... 46.67
48A .... 46.100-46.102
49 (1)(a) .... 46.69
(b) .... 46.70
(c) .... 46.70
(2) .... 46.71
(a)(ii) .... 46.76
71 (1) .... 46.14, 46.81
(2) .... 46.83

Statute of Limitations (Amendment) Act 1961
s 4 .... 41.09
7 .... 41.08
8 .... 41.10
(2) .... 41.10
9 .... 41.11
10 .... 41.11

Statute of Limitations (Amendment) Act 1991 .................................. 1.58, 1.121, 11.150
........................................................ 46.02-46.07, 46.20, 46.30, 46.45, 46.95
s 2 ........................................................ 46.33, 46.47
(1) ........................................................ 46.38
(2) ........................................................ 46.45
3 (1) ........................................................ 1.59, 46.21
6 ........................................................ 46.21
(1) ........................................................ 42.02
Statute of Limitations (Amendment) Act 2000 ........................................ 46.66
s 2 ........................................................ 46.101
3 ........................................................ 46.103
Statute of Labourers 1349 ........................................................ 32.13
Supreme Court of Judicature (Ireland) Act 1877
s 28(8) ........................................................ 45.02
Telecommunications (Miscellaneous Provisions) Act 1996
s 12 ........................................................ 23.07
Trade Disputes Act 1906 ........................................ 32.88, 32.104, 32.112, 32.162
s 1 ........................................................ 32.116
2 ........................................................ 32.147, 32.160
(1) ........................................................ 23.19, 32.163-32.166
3 ........................................................ 32.43, 32.123
4 ........................................................ 1.116, 32.68, 32.129, 39.31
Trade Marks Act 1963
s 12-14 ........................................................ 21.08
Trade Marks Act 1996 ........................................................ 31.04
s 7(2) ........................................................ 31.01
10(4) ........................................................ 31.01
Trade Union Act 1871 ........................................................ 39.26
Trade Union Act 1876 ........................................................ 39.26
Trade Union Act 1941 ........................................................ 32.115
s 11 ........................................................ 32.129
12 ........................................................ 39.29
13 ........................................................ 39.29
Trade Union and Labour Relations Act 1974
s 24 ........................................................ 39.30
Traffic Act 1994
Transport Act 1950
59 ........................................................ 23.48
Transport Act 1958
s 7 (1) ........................................................ 21.08
(3) ........................................................ 21.08

Transport (Re-organisation of Coras lompair Éireann) Act 1986
s 22 .......... 37.20

Transport (Dublin Light Rail) Act 1996
s 14 .......... 23.07
19 .......... 23.48

Unfair Dismissals Act 1977 .......... 41.04

Video Recordings Act 1989
s 25 .......... 23.06, 28.16

Voluntary Health Insurance Act 1957 .......... 19.77

Wildlife Act 1976
s 68 .......... 23.07
72 .......... 28.16
73 .......... 23.07

Wireless Telegraphy Act 1926
s 8 .......... 23.06, 28.16

Women's Status Act 1957

Workmen's Compensation Act 1897 .......... 18.02

Workmen's Compensation Act 1934 .......... 18.02, 41.04
s 64(1) .......... 38.03

Waste Management Act 1996
s 7(a) .......... 23.07
14 .......... 23.07
36(2)(k) .......... 24.03
57 .......... 24.10
58 .......... 24.10
71(4) .......... 23.07


## Constitution of Ireland


Art 5 .......... 38.05
10 .......... 23.39
12.10 .......... 38.21
13.8.1° .......... 34.136
13.8.1° .......... 38.20
15.12 .......... 34.137-34.140
15.13 .......... 34.137-34.140
23 .......... 38.07
29.4.3° .......... 11.157
38.1 .......... 24.03
40 .......... 1.09, 1.29, 1.41, 23.09, 46.75, 46.91
40-44 .......... 38.05
40.1 .......... 1.09, 32.139, 37.69, 37.84, 39.25, 44.163
40.3 .......... 1.13, 1.31-1.32, 1.56, 1.71, 1.136
.......... 2.60, 24.95, 37.62, 37.69, 37.73, 37.84
.......... 46.76-46.80, 46.90

*Constitution of Ireland (contd)*
40.3.1° ........ 1.41, 34.178, 37.87, 37.94, 38.07
40.3.2° ........ 1.13, 34.05, 37.87, 38.07, 41.11, 45.23
40.3.3° ........ 37.81
40.4 ........ 1.09
40.5 ........ 1.09, 22.105, 23.03-23.05, 23.09
40.6.1°(i) ........ 1.09
40.6.1°(ii) ........ 1.09
40.6.1°(iii) ........ 1.09
40.6.1°i ........ 34.05
41 ........ 1.09, 1.23, 22.76, 22.83, 24.71, 33.03, 33.19-33.22, 37.63
41.3 ........ 37.70
41.1.1° ........ 1.26
41.1.2° ........ 1.26-1.28
42 ........ 1.09, 1.23, 22.76, 22.83
42.1 ........ 1.28
42.4 ........ 32.128
43 ........ 1.09, 46.80
44 ........ 1.09

**United Kingdom**

Accidental Fires Act (NI) 1944 ........ 26.06
Belfast Corporation Act 1845
s 142 ........ 21.44
Cheques Act 1957
s 4 ........ 30.14
Copyright Act 1956
s 17(3) ........ 44.10
22(4) ........ 44.10
Crown Proceedings Act 1947 ........ 38.03
Defamation Act 1952 ........ 34.32, 34.121
s 4 ........ 34.113
Damages (Scotland) Act 1976 ........ 42.21
Employer's Liability (Defective Equipment) Act 1969 ........ 18.101
Fatal Accidents Act 1976 ........ 42.45
Government Act 1963 ........ 19.39
Human Rights Act 1998 ........ 6.91, 34.07
Limitation Act 1963 ........ 46.15
s 1 ........ 46.08
Limitation Act 1980
s 14(2) ........ 46.45
Latent Damage Act 1986 ........ 46.01

Law Reform (Contributory Negligence) Act 1945
s 1(1) .......... 20.51

Law Reform (Miscellaneous Provisions) Act 1934
s 1(2) .......... 44.28

Misrepresentation Act 1967 .......... 10.151-10.155

Occupiers' Liability Act 1957 .......... 12.12, 12.50
s 2(40) .......... 12.136

Occupiers' Liability Act 1984
1 .......... 12.49
(1)(c) .......... 12.101

Protection from Harassment Act 1997 .......... 24.73

Quarries Act (Northern Ireland) 1927
Sch 1 .......... 21.34

Rehabilitation of Offenders Act 1974
s 8 .......... 34.123

Reserve and Auxiliary Forces (Protection of Civil Interests) Act 1951
s 13(2) .......... 44.10

Sexual Offences Act 1967
s 1 .......... 34.78

Slander of Women Act 1891 .......... 34.32

Torts (Interference with Goods) Act 1977 .......... 28.02

**European Legislation**

Commission Regulation on Imports Regulations (4024/89/EEC)
Art 1(1) .......... 1.98
4 .......... 1.98

Council Directive on Approximation of Laws relating to Insurance against Civil Liability (72/166/EEC) .......... 1.141

Council Directive on Distant Selling (97/7/EC) .......... 30.03

Council Directive on Employees Rights (77/187/EEC) .......... 32.164

Council Directive on Equal Treatment for Men and Women (79/7/EEC) .......... 1.99

Council Directive on Liability for Defective Products (85/374/EEC) .......... 1.121-1.121
.......... 11.02-11.03, 11.91-11.95, 21.61
Art 1 .......... 11.98, 11.135
2 .......... 11.99
3 .......... 11.102
(1)(d) .......... 11.103
(e) .......... 11.103
(2) .......... 11.103-11.106
(3) .......... 11.104-11.107
4 .......... 11.127-11.132
5 .......... 11.166

*Council Directive on Liability for Defective Products (85/374/EEC) (contd)*
6 ....11.108, 11.112-11.121, 11.133, 11.139
(2) ....11.116
7 ....11.136
(c) ....11.140
(d) ....11.141
(e) ....11.92, 11.144-11.144, 11.171
(f) ....11.146
8 ....11.158, 11.164
(1) ....11.98, 11.165
9 ....11.117-11.126
10 ....11.147-11.148, 11.161
11 ....11.147-11.151, 11.161, 46.06
12 ....11.161
13 ....11.91-11.93
14 ....11.126
15 ....11.144, 11.174
(3) ....11.92
16 ....11.172
17 ....11.167
19 ....11.93, 11.101, 11.167
22 ....11.92
Council Directive on Liability for Defective Products (99/34/EC) ....11.103
Council Directive on Second Motor Insurance (84/5/EEC) ....1.103, 1.141, 1.150
Art 1(4) ....1.147-1.151
Council Directive on Unfair Contract Terms (94/47/EC)
Art 1(a) ....11 .03
3(1) ....11.03
4(1) ....11.03
Council Directive on the Sale of Consumer goods and Associated Guarantees (99/44/EC) ....11.03
Council Regulation on Accident Air Carrier Liability (2027/97/EEC) ....23.40
Protocol on Privileges and Immunities of the European Communities
Art 9 ....38.22
12 ....38.22
Third Council Directive on Approximation of Laws relating to Insurance against Civil Liability (90/232/EEC) ....1.141

## International Conventions and Declarations

Brussels Convention on Jurisdiction and the Enforcement of Judgments 1968 ... 11.91, 34.48
Art 5 ... 34.12
European Convention on Human Rights and Fundamental Freedoms ... 34.04-34.08 ... 39.25
Art 3 ... 22.96-22.101
5(3) ... 34.48
6 ... 6.82-6.87
(1) ... 6.82-6.86
8 ... 24.71, 37.02, 37.80
10 ... 34.211, 34.241, 34.255-34.255, 45.30
International Covenant on Civil and Political Rights
Art 19 ... 23.20, 32.167
22 ... 23.20, 32.167
United Nations Convention on the Rights of the Child
Art 16 ... 24.71
United Nations Declaration of Human Rights
Art 12 ... 24.71
Vienna Convention on Consular Relations 1963 ... 38.15
Vienna Convention on Diplomatic Relations 1961 ... 38.15
Warsaw Convention of 1919 ... 23.40

## Statutory Instruments

Building (Safety, Health and Welfare) Regulations 1959 (SI 227/1959)
Ord 4 para 3 ... 21.22
Circuit Court Rules 1950 (SI 179/1950) ... 39.10
Control of Dogs Act 1986 (Commencement) Order 1987 (SI 16/1987) ... 27.40
Control of Dogs Act 1986 (Commencement) (No 2) Order 1987 (SI 79/1987) ... 27.06, 27.40
Control of Dogs Act 1986 (Guard Dogs) Regulations 1988 (SI 255/1988) ... 27.40
Control of Dogs (Amendment) Act 1992 (Commencement) Order 1998 (SI 443/1998) ... 27.41
European Communities (Cancellation of Contracts Negotiated Away from Business Premises) Regulations 1989 (SI 224/1989)
Reg 6 ... 30.03
European Communities (Road Traffic) (Compulsory Insurance) (Amendment) Regulations (SI 353/1995) ... 1.141
European Communities (Safeguarding of Employees, Rights on Transfer of Undertakings) Regulations 1980, (SI 306/1980) ... 32.164

European Communities (Unfair Terms in Consumer Contracts) Regulations 1995 (SI 27/1995) .......... 11.03

European Communities (Misleading Advertising) Regulations 1988 (SI 134/1988) .......... 35.08

Factories Act 1955 (Manual Labour) (Maximum Weights and Transport) Regulations 1972 (SI 283/1972)

Reg 3 .......... 18.121

6 .......... 21.27

General Bye-Laws for the Control of Traffic 1937 (SR & O 222/1937) .......... 15.40

Liability for Defective Products Act 1991 (Commencement) Order 1991 (SI 316/1991) .......... 11.93

Regulations for Burial Grounds 1888

r 1 .......... 21.08, 21.40

Road Traffic Bye-Laws 1964 (SI 294/1964) .......... 15.40

Reg 30-33 .......... 27.60

Road Traffic (Construction Equipment and Use of Vehicles) (Amendment) Regulations 1971 (SI 16/1971) .......... 20.37

Road Traffic (Construction Equipment and Use of Vehicles) (Amendment No 2) Regulations 1978 (SI 360/1978) .......... 21.48

Road Traffic General Bye-Laws 1975 (SI 281/1975) .......... 15.40

Road Traffic General Bye-Laws 1983 (SI 275/1983) .......... 15.40

Road Traffic (General Speed Limit) Regulations 1979 (SI 176/1979) .......... 7.39, 15.53

Rules of the Superior Courts 1986 (SI 15/1986)

Ord 14 .......... 39.09

15 r 4 .......... 4.06, 4.14

7 .......... 4.16

9 .......... 39.10

16 .......... 4.24

18 r 1 .......... 4.12

19 r 29 .......... 23.33

49 r 4-6 .......... 4.14

Rules of the Supreme Court (Ireland) 1905

15, r 4 .......... 4.06

Safety, Health and Welfare at Work (General Application) Regulations 1993 (SI 44/1993) .......... 18.97, 21.42

Safety, Health and Welfare at Work (Construction) Regulations 1995 (SI 138/1995) .......... 13.79

## Other Jurisdictions


Duty to Aid the Endangered Act 1973 (US)
s 519(1) ........ 8.01

Federal Tort Claims Act 1946 (US) ........ 38.04

Law Reform Amendment Act 1985, SBC 1985 (BC)
s 8........ 35.25

Law Reform (Personal Injuries) Act 1958 (NY)
s 1........ 18.02, 18.146

Ontario Negligence Act 1948
s 1........ 4.20

Chapter 1

# Overview of the Law of Torts


I. Function of the Law of Torts ........ 1
II. Recognised Interests ........ 2
III. Wrongful Interference with Constitutional Rights ........ 4
IV. European Community ........ 26
V. Definition of Tort ........ 30
VI. From Negligence to Strict Liability: from Loss Shifting to Loss Distribution ........ 37
VII. The Insurance Factor and the Problem of the Uninsured Driver ........ 44
VIII. Features of the Litigation Scene in Ireland ........ 48
IX. Recent Studies and Proposals for Reform ........ 51


## I. Function of the Law of Torts

**[1.01]** While a satisfactory definition of a tort is difficult to come by, the function of the law of torts may be more easily described. Since human beings are social animals they pursue their interests in a social context. Inevitably, this pursuit brings them into contact and into conflict with other persons pursuing their interests. This contact and conflict, of course, is not a new social phenomenon, but in the past century and a half, because of increased urbanisation, growth in population, greater and more sophisticated technology and a deeper sensitivity, interpersonal conflicts have increased in numbers and have become more complex in nature. As a result these conflicts now require more careful and more frequent resolution.

**[1.02]** One person's building may obstruct another person's view; one persons public utterances may upset another's sensitivities; one person's bees may invade another's property, one person's picket may interfere with another's business or one person's driving may interfere with another's wellbeing. In all these cases, the law has to decide whether it will tolerate or discourage the activity in question. In this way, it may be said that the law of torts is primarily concerned with adjusting conflicting interests. By and large, the plaintiff's interest is in security, whereas the defendant's interest is in freedom of action and, in attempting to solve these conflicts, the courts will have to balance the defendant's interest, in the keeping of bees for example, with the plaintiff's interest in having quiet and peaceful enjoyment of his or her property. The courts will try to give a reasonable answer to the problem before it, but in striking the balance between the parties, a third interest will be taken into account: the social interest in the activity in question. The defendant thinks that the keeping of bees is a very reasonable activity whereas the plaintiff thinks otherwise. The Court in reaching a decision may not only take the individual's interests into account but it may also have regard to the social dimensions of the problem. Is it in society's interest to permit the plaintiff in the present circumstances to keep the bees? In permitting this activity is the Court promoting the common good?[1]

> "In any society, it is inevitable that these interests come into conflict. In cases of conflict, cultures that we choose to call primitive determined who should prevail with sword and club; and there is recent melancholy evidence that the law of the jungle is not yet departed from the affairs of nations. But in a civilised community, it is the law which is called upon to act as arbiter. The administration of the law becomes a process of weighing the interests for which the plaintiff demands protection against the defendant's claim to untrammelled freedom in the furtherance of the defendant's desires, together with the importance of those desires themselves. When the interest of the public is thrown into the scales and allowed to swing the balance for or against the plaintiff, the result is a form of social engineering. A decision maker might deliberately seek to use the law as an instrument to promote the greatest happiness of the greatest number, or instead might give greater emphasis to protecting certain types of interests of individuals as fundamental entitlements central to an integrity of person that the law upholds above all else. This process of weighing the interests is by no means peculiar to the law of torts, but it has been carried to its greatest lengths and has received its most general conscious recognition in this field."[2]

**[1.03]** When the courts prohibit an activity in these circumstances we say that it is a tort or a wrong for the defendant to continue this activity. The law of torts, therefore, is no more or no less than a description of those instances of social conduct which the courts[3] consider should be prohibited and should be penalised. This book is, therefore, primarily concerned with providing a guide to these prohibited activities.

## II. Recognised Interests

**[1.04]** Without dwelling on the extent of the protection which the law will give to the plaintiff in any particular case, it might be pertinent to ask at the outset, what kinds of interest the law deems worthy of recognition and support. The answer to this question is not an easy one. One might say, for example, that people have a right to protection in the legitimate pursuit of their lawful desires and that the law should protect them by guaranteeing them the secure conditions in which they may work towards their legitimate aspirations. Thus, they may claim that physical integrity, freedom of movement, security in

---

1. In *McStay v Morrissey* (1949) 83 ILTR 28, the judge gave a direction in favour of the defendant beekeeper and refused to interfere in what he termed was a valuable industry. Compare with the successful action by the plaintiff in another bee-keeping case *O'Gorman v O'Gorman KB* [1903] 2 IR 573. It should be realised, however, that in some cases the courts, in their desire to promote justice in the case before it, may omit to take due account of the social dimension of the problem. Accordingly, the courts in their concern with the particular case may give a decision which is not in the long term interest of the community as a whole. Conversely, in stressing the general social and long term effects of a decision the courts may appear in a particular case to ignore the apparently just claims of the individuals before it. *Cf* Provine 'Balancing Pollution and Property Rights: A Comparison of the Development of English and American Nuisance Law' (1978) 7 Anglo Am LR 31.
2. PROSSER & KEETON, pp 16-17 (footnote reference omitted). See also Williams 'The Aims of the Law of Tort' (1951) 4 CLP 137; Osakwe 'An Examination of the Modern Soviet Law of Torts' (1979) 54 Tul LR 1 at 71; Vold 'The Functional Perspective for the Law of Torts' (1936) 4 Neb L Bull 217.
3. Legislative intervention has been limited in the area of tort law, although it is on the increase in recent decades.

possessions, in family life and in reputation, are all interests which the law should recognise. Indeed, the law of torts at present does recognise all of these interests when invaded in particular ways. Even if it were possible, however, to compile a complete catalogue of interests at present protected by the law it is important to note that this list would not be a definitive inventory.

**[1.05]** Society changes and so too does the catalogue of interests which deserves protection and recognition at any given time.

> "The purpose of the law of torts is to adjust these losses and to afford compensation for injuries sustained by one person as the result of the conduct of another. Such a statement of the problem indicates that the law of torts must constantly be in a state of flux, since it must be ever ready to recognise and consider new losses arising in novel ways. The introduction of printing, by facilitating the manner in which a man's reputation might be injured by the dissemination of the printed work, had a tremendous effect on the law of defamation; the radio of today presents even more serious problems, as do also the aeroplane and the modern motor car.
>
> The study of the law of torts is, therefore, a study of the extent to which the law will shift the losses sustained in modern society from the person affected to the shoulders of him who caused the loss or, more realistically in many fields, to the insurance companies who are increasingly covering the many risks involved in the conduct of business and individual activities." [4]

**[1.06]** While there are some interests, therefore, which have been recognised for a long time, other interests have had to struggle for recognition and are only recently being acknowledged. Inevitably, there are transitional problems associated with the recognition by the judiciary of new interests, and these include a degree of uncertainty and a lack of uniformity during the period when the controversy is raging as to whether the interest in question deserves recognition or not. Examples over the past few decades of new torts, or instances where the courts have shown themselves willing to allow the plaintiff recovery in circumstances where recovery was previously denied, occur in relation to injuries to trespassers,[5] economic loss caused by negligent misstatements,[6] loss caused to subsequent occupiers by the negligence of builder/vendors,[7] and wrongs done by the State.[8] It is not intended to discuss these cases here as they will be dealt with fully in more appropriate contexts in later chapters. They are mentioned merely to indicate that the law of torts is

---

4. Wright, *Cases on the Law of Torts* (4th ed, 1967). More recent examples would relate to computer technology and the internet.
5. *McNamara v ESB* [1975] IR 1. But now see Occupiers Liability Act 1995, Ch 12 below.
6. *Hedley Byrne and Co Ltd v Heller & Partners Ltd* [1964] AC 465; *Towey v Ulster Bank Ltd* [1987] ILRM 142 (HC).
7. *Ward v McMaster* [1988] IR 337, affg [1985] IR 29.
8. *Byrne v Ireland* [1972] IR 241. The tort of misfeasance of public office, characterised by STREET, p 440, in 1985, as "ill-defined and ... embryonic", has received some judicial support here: *cf Pine Valley Developments Ltd v Minister for the Environment* [1987] ILRM 747 (SC); *CW Shipping Ltd v Limerick Harbour Commissioners* [1989] ILRM 416 (HC). It is possible that the generic tort of unlawful interference with economic interests (as to which *cf Bula Ltd v Tara Mines Ltd* [1988] ILRM 157 (HC)) will be recognised by the Irish courts in the future, in view of the beneficial effects of grounding economic torts on a firmer bed of principle, but progress so far, in Ireland and in other common law jurisdictions, has been slow. See para **[32.83]** below.

particularly sensitive to social change and that new interests are continuously thrusting themselves forward as deserving of recognition.

**[1.07]** Finally, it should be noted that new risks to interests already recognised by the courts regularly present themselves from time to time. Technological developments and scientific innovations may carry unforeseen risks. For example, litigation has arisen out of personal injuries resulting from defective heart valves, breast implants and intra-uterine contraceptive devices, and in this context litigation for tobacco related illnesses should also be mentioned.

**[1.08]** Indeed, some text books dealing with the law of torts use the interests of the plaintiff as the point of departure.[9] It is true that unless the plaintiff's interest is initially recognised, he or she cannot get out of the starting blocks; and this becomes obvious in the case where new interests are being considered. In the vast majority of conflicts, however, the particular interest (eg physical integrity, property protection, etc) has long since been recognised as worthy of protection and in these cases it is natural to commence with the conduct of the defendant. Historically too, the law of torts focussed on the wrong of the defendant, rather than on the rights of the plaintiff, and the word "tort" itself refers to a wrong rather than to a right. Too much must not be made of this distinction, however. To the ordinary litigant it matters little whether the court at the end of the day says that the plaintiff has a right which is to be protected or that the defendant has committed a wrong which must be punished. For the litigant the result will be the same.

## III. Wrongful Interference with Constitutional Rights

### Introductory Observations

**[1.09]** Constitutional developments in Ireland are also relevant to the present discussion. Articles 40 to 44 of the Constitution guarantee certain fundamental rights to the citizen. Included in these provisions are guarantees in respect of the following rights: equality before the law (Article 40.1), personal liberty (Article 40.4), inviolability of the dwelling (Article 40.5), freedom of expression (Article 40.6.1°(i)), peaceful assembly (Article 40.6.1°(ii)), freedom of association (Article 40.6.1°(iii)), family rights (Article 41), educational rights (Article 42), the right to private property (Article 43), freedom of conscience and the free profession and practice of religion (Article 44). In the constitutional context these guarantees are important because they act as a check on interference by the government, and legislation which purports to interfere with these rights can be judicially reviewed and struck down if it does not respect these rights. These

8. (contd) In *Cosgrove v Ireland* [1982] ILRM 48 (HC) it was held that interference with a statutory right was actionable. In *Hosford v John Murphy and Sons Ltd* [1988] ILRM 300 (HC), however, Costello J declined to extend the action to loss of *consortium* so as to enable children to sue in relation to damage to their relationship with their father. Other new torts will inevitably be recognised over the coming years. *Cf* King 'The Tort of Unconscionability: A New Tort for New Times' (1979) 23 St Louis ULJ 97.

9. "No claim in tort can succeed, however morally reprehensible the defendants conduct, unless the court first recognises that the harm suffered by the plaintiff involves violation of an interest sufficient to confer on the plaintiff a legal right to protection of that interest. The starting point of any analysis of the law of torts must be a consideration of those rights that tort protects." STREET.

rights must be respected not only by the government and legislature, however, private citizens in the conduct of their own affairs must also respect the constitutional rights of other citizens. Wrongful interference by individuals with these rights constitutes a civil wrong which is sometimes termed a "constitutional tort". It is preferable, at the outset of our discussion, however, to speak in this context of the wrongful interference with a constitutional right.[10]

**[1.10]** An examination of these rights, and their limitations, is more properly a topic for a book on constitutional law and it is not proposed to deal with them here in detail.[11] A few examples, however, will suffice to illustrate their importance.

**[1.11]** In *Meskell v CIE*,[12] in an arrangement between the defendant company and four trade unions the defendant agreed to introduce new terms of employment for its staff whereby all employees would have to join a union. To this end it terminated all contracts with employees and offered them new contracts which contained a new and additional clause obliging the employees to join a union. The plaintiff refused to accept this new clause and was dismissed. The Supreme Court held that since the constitutional right to join a union implied a right *not* to join a union the defendants had, in attempting to coerce the plaintiff to join a union, acted unlawfully. Moreover, although the defendant company and the unions were promoting their own interests, they had used unlawful means to achieve their ends and had committed an actionable conspiracy. Damages were awarded to the plaintiff.

**[1.12]** Again in *Murtagh Properties Ltd v Cleary*,[13] the defendant who was secretary of a trade union authorised a picket on the plaintiff's property on the grounds that the plaintiff employed waitresses in his public house. The defendant contended that this was in breach of an agreement between the plaintiff and the union. In granting an interlocutory injunction Kenny J, held that the picket, although in furtherance of a trade dispute, was unlawful in that it was designed to compel the plaintiff to dismiss his female employees in breach of their personal rights under the Constitution, the right in question being the right to earn a livelihood without discrimination on the basis of sex.

**[1.13]** A further point of importance should be mentioned in this connection. In *Ryan v AG*,[14] Kenny J, suggested that the "personal rights" guaranteed in Article 40.3 of the Constitution were not exhausted by the enumeration of "life, person, good name and

10. *Cf Hosford v Murphy* [1988] ILRM 300 (HC); *Kennedy et al v Ireland and the AG* [1988] ILRM (HC); *Morgan v Park Developments Ltd* [1983] ILRM 156 (HC).
11. See generally Hogan & Morgan, *Administrative Law in Ireland* (3rd ed, 1998), p 819ff; Hogan & Whyte, *Kelly: The Irish Constitution* (3rd ed, 1994); Binchy 'Constitutional Remedies and the Law of Torts' in, *Human Rights and Constitutional Law: Essays in Honour of Brian Walsh* (O'Reilly ed 1992); p 201; QUILL, Ch 9; Cooney & Kerr 'Constitutional Aspects of Irish Tort Law' (1981) 3 DULJ (ns) 1; von Prondzynski 'The Protection of Constitutional Rights: Comparisons between Ireland and Germany' (1980) 2 Dublin ULJ 14; Butler 'Constitutional Rights in Private Litigation: A Critique and Comparative Analysis' (1993) 22 Anglo-Amer LR 1 at 17.
12. [1973] IR 121.
13. [1972] IR 330. See also *Educational Co of Ireland v Fitzpatrick (No 2)* [1961] IR 345. But *see Murphy v Stewart* [1973] IR 97 - union not obliged to accept applicant.
14. [1965] IR 294.

property rights" of the citizen in that Article. The phrase also extended to other unspecified rights "which result from the Christian and democratic nature of the State". This view has become generally accepted now and since that case the courts have been busy recognising and naming some of these unspecified rights. Among the unspecified rights now recognised by the courts are the following: the right of bodily integrity,[15] the right to work and earn a livelihood,[16] the right to litigate,[17] the right to marital privacy,[18] the right to one's good name,[19] the right of a child to live, to be fed, to be reared and educated, etc,[20] and the right to travel.[21] These rights or interests must now be protected by the law.

### Private Individuals as well as the State may be Liable for Infringement of Constitutional Rights

**[1.14]** The orthodox view in the United States is that the Constitution speaks to the government only and that it does not impose obligations on private individuals or institutions.[22] The Irish courts have not taken this option in their approach to the problem. Instead, they consider that a constitutional right in one person implies a corresponding duty in other persons to respect that right,[23] and that consequently any wrongful interference by another with the exercise of such a right amounts to a wrong for which the courts will provide a remedy.[24] In *Meskell v CIE*, Walsh J, clearly declared:

> " ... if a person has suffered damage by virtue of a breach of a constitutional right or the infringement of a constitutional right, that person is entitled to seek redress against the person or persons who have infringed that right."[25]

15. *Ryan v AG* [1965] IR 294.
16. *Murtagh Properties v Cleary* [ 1972] IR 330; *Landers v AC* (1973) 109 ILTR 1; *Rogers v ITGWU* [1978] ILRM 51 (HC).
17. *Macauley v Minister for Posts and Telegraphs* [1966] IR 345.
18. *McGee v AG* [1974] IR 284; As to the status of a more general right to privacy, see Ch 37 below.
19. Article 40.3.2° of the Constitution; See *In re Haughey* [1971] IR 217; *Hynes O'Sullivan v O'Driscoll* [1989] ILRM 349 (SC). A right to communicate has also been recognised: *AG v Paperlink Ltd* [1984] ILRM 373; *Kearney v Minister for Justice* [1986] IR 116.
20. *G v An Bord Uchtála* [1980] IR 32 (SC).
21. *The State (M) v AG* [1979] IR 73. Within the State, see *Ryan v AG* [1965] IR 294 at 313 (*per* Kenny J). As to the right to travel outside the State, see Hogan & Whyte, *Kelly: The Irish Constitution* (3rd ed, 1994), pp 67-68, 777-778, 796-810. In the context of abortion, the Supreme Court in *Attorney General v X* [1992] 1 IR 1 raised so many uncertainties that it led to the "travel" amendment to the Constitution in November 1992. Among other rights that have been recognised are the right to marry, (*Murray v AG* [1985] IR 532), the right not to have ones health put in jeopardy (*McGee v AG* [1974] IR 284) and rights to legal representation on criminal charges and to fair procedures in decision-making.
22. Individual rights under the Constitution of the USA are, for the most part, guaranteed only against governmental interference. The correlative duties are imposed not upon private citizens but upon government. See Tribe, *American Constitutional Law*, Ch 18; Cox 'The Warren Court, Constitutional Decision as an Instrument or Reform' Lecture 2.
23. *Educational Co of Ireland v Fitzpatrick (No 1)* [1961] IR 323.
24. *Byrne v Ireland* [1972] IR 241 at 279-280 (SC).
25. [1973] IR 121 at 133.

**[1.15]** In *Kearney v Minister for Justice*[26] the State was held vicariously liable for prison officers who, in breach of the prisoner's constitutional right, neglected to deliver his correspondence to him, and damages were awarded to the plaintiff. Costello J said:

> "the wrong that was committed in this case was an unjustified infringement of a constitutional right, not a tort; and it was committed by a servant of the State and, accordingly, Ireland can be sued in respect of it".

**[1.16]** Other cases illustrate the principle that the courts will award damages against the State where a constitutional interest is inadequately recognised or protected at common law. In *Kennedy et al v Ireland and the AG*[27] the plaintiff's telephone was unjustifiably tapped, and not only was the plaintiff awarded damages but substantial damages were awarded against the State because the infringement was done deliberately, consciously and without justification. Hamilton P said "the plaintiffs are in my opinion entitled to substantial damages and it is, in the circumstances of this case, irrelevant whether they be described as aggravated or as exemplary damages". (Two of the plaintiffs were awarded £20,000 each while the third was awarded £10,000.) In *Hayes v Ireland*[28] Carroll J awarded general damages of £4,000 to the plaintiffs whose constitutional right to free primary education had been infringed by the defendants. The ordinary rules of common law were adhered to in calculating the damages in this case since there was no question of aggravated or exemplary damages. In later cases[29] arising out of the same facts, pupils who suffered in their education because of the INTO's directive that other schools should not accept the pupils who were attending the school the subject of the dispute, were awarded exemplary damages.

## The Relationship between Tort Law and Infringements of Constitutional Rights

**[1.17]** One question which all this activity raises and which still remains to be definitively resolved, concerns the relationship which such constitutional torts have with the traditional nominate torts. What, for example, is the relationship between "the constitutional right to one's good name" and the tort of defamation? In this instance, can one sue, for example, on the constitutional right instead of proceeding on the traditional grounds of defamation? Instead of suing in trespass can one base one's action, in appropriate circumstances, on the inviolability of the dwelling as guaranteed in the Constitution? Does the constitutional recognition prevail over the common law or can both occupy the ground together?[30] In recent years the courts have begun to answer these questions. Some general guidelines have emerged.

---

26. [1986] IR 116. See also *McHugh v Commissioner of the Garda Síochána* [1986] IR 228; [1987] ILRM 18.
27. [1988] ILRM 472 (HC). See further para **[37.92]** below.
28. [1987] ILRM 651. It is worth noting that, in *Cosgrove v Ireland* [1982] ILRM 48, on which Carroll J relied in *Hayes*, McWilliam J considered himself entitled to award damages for mental distress for interference with a statutory right on the basis primarily of *dicta* in *Cook v Swinfen* [1967] 1 WLR 457. In the light of the later Supreme Court decision in *The State (Keegan) v Stardust Victims Compensation Tribunal* [1987] ILRM 202, this approach would have to be revised.
29. *Conway v INTO* [1991] 2 IR 305 (SC), analysed in paras **[44.36]-[44.43]** below..
30. *Cf* Heuston above, fn 20 at 222.

## The *Hanrahan* Resolution

**[1.18]** *Hanrahan v Merck Sharp and Dohme*[31] is a crucial decision. The plaintiffs complained that emissions from the defendant's factory caused damaged to their health and to their livestock and interfered with the enjoyment of their property. Although the plaintiffs pleaded trespass, negligence, nuisance and *Rylands v Fletcher*, the case was disposed of simply as a nuisance action by the trial judge, and also in the Supreme Court, in the absence of complaint by either party at such narrowing of judicial analysis. The plaintiffs' principal difficulty in the High Court was in establishing the causal link between their injuries and the defendant's conduct. One argument they put forward in support of their case on this issue was that the defendant's conduct was an interference with their constitutional rights (their property rights and their right to bodily integrity) and, since the State was obliged to vindicate and protect these rights under the Constitution, the State (through the Courts) should assist them in this by shifting the onus of proof in relation to this matter onto the defendants. In rejecting this argument the Supreme Court delivered itself of some interesting comments of a general nature. Having recognised that the tort of nuisance relied on may be said to be an implementation of the State's duties under the Constitution, the Court said it would not normally intervene to supplement the common law expression of this right except where the common law protection was clearly inadequate. Henchy J, for the Court, said:

> "So far as I am aware, the constitutional provisions relied on have never been used in the courts to shape the form of any existing tort or to change the normal onus of proof. The implementation of those constitutional rights is primarily a matter for the State and the courts are entitled to intervene only when there has been a failure to implement or, where the implementation relied on is plainly inadequate, to effectuate the constitutional guarantee in question. In many torts for example, negligence, defamation, trespass to person or property a plaintiff may give evidence of what he claims to be a breach of a constitutional right, but he may fail in the action because of what is usually a matter of onus of proof or because of some other legal or technical defence. A person may of course in the absence of a common law or statutory cause of action, sue directly for breach of a constitutional right[32] but when he founds his action on an existing tort he is normally confined to the limitations of that tort. It might be different if it could be shown that the tort in question is basically ineffective to protect his constitutional right. But that is not alleged here. What is said is that he may not succeed in having his constitutional rights vindicated if he is required to carry the normal onus of proof. However, the same may be said about many other causes of action. Lack of knowledge as to the true nature of the defendants conduct or course of conduct may cause the plaintiff difficulty but it does not change the onus of proof."[33]

**[1.19]** This passage provokes a number of comments. First, Henchy J betrays a striking reluctance to involve the courts in the role of refashioning tort law, root and branch, in the light of the Constitution. Only where the State has been guilty of a "failure to implement" or where there is a "plainly inadequate" effectuation of a constitutional guarantee will the courts intervene, since the implementation of the constitutional rights asserted by the plaintiffs in *Hanrahan's* case is "primarily a matter for the State". The import of this

31. [1988] ILRM 629 (SC).

32. Citing *Meskell v CIE* [1973] IR 121.

33. [1988] ILRM at 636.

approach would appear to be that, if the court were to consider that a particular tort was *not* "basically ineffective" in protecting the relevant constitutional right, the court should neither modify the parameters of the tort nor provide a supplementary remedy sounding in terms of infringement of the constitutional right even though the court might regard the tort as being *less than fully effective* in protecting the right in question. Henchy J's restraint, on one interpretation, appears to extend, not merely to constitutional glosses on tort law, but to the very substance of the constitutional rights themselves. On this interpretation, he is saying that the courts will also be slow to develop the jurisprudence on constitutional rights outside the specific context of tort law. This is difficult to harmonise with the development of judicial analysis of such a constitutional right as that of privacy, for example, where there has been little evidence that the courts consider themselves to be exercising a limited and subsidiary jurisdiction. Accordingly, it seems more prudent to interpret his remarks as being focused on the context of judicial modification of tort law in the light of the Constitution.

**[1.20]** It seems curious that courts should be impotent to deal with a case where the ingredients of a particular tort inadequately effectuate a constitutional guarantee and that inadequacy falls just short of "plain" inadequacy. This curiosity is enhanced when it is borne in mind that most of tort law is the creature of the common law rather than statute. The idea that this corpus of common law is surrounded by a shroud through which the light of the Constitution can penetrate in only narrow shafts is difficult to understand. The notion, implicit in Henchy J's remarks, that this corpus falls under the control of the State is also odd unless the somewhat contorted Austinian argument is made that the State's failure to amend common law principles of tort developed by the courts constitutes an implicit authorisation for their continuance as part of the State's legal system.

**[1.21]** It is worth noting that *Hanrahan's* case does not appear to prevent the courts from recognising and developing a constitutional right merely because there is already in existence a particular tort dealing with the subject-matter of that constitutional right. Nor does the existence of that tort require the court, in the articulation of the nature and limitation of that constitutional right, to be bound by the limitations and defences applying to the tort. In fact, Henchy J's observations throw no direct light on any possible inhibitions affecting the development of jurisprudence of a constitutional right as a result of the existence of a tort dealing with the general subject-matter of that constitutional right. Equally unresolved after *Hanrahan* was the converse question in respect of any particular tort, whether it was supplemented by a constitutional right or curtailed by a constitutional limitation. The whole question of the relationship between torts and infringements of constitution rights was revisited in the important High Court decision of *W v Ireland (No 2)*.[34] We will discuss the impact of *W* in detail below but first it is necessary to consider the remit of constitutional protection of certain interests.

## Limitation on Right to Damages for Infringement of Constitutional Rights

**[1.22]** There is no guarantee that the Constitution will protect every interest which is not protected by tort law. In *Hosford v John Murphy & Sons Ltd*[35] the Court held that the

34. [1997] 2 IR 141 (HC).

35. [1988] ILRM 300 (HC).

interest in question of parent-child *consortium* was not protected either by common law or by the Constitution and accordingly the plaintiffs had no remedy. The facts of the case were as follows. Mr Eugene Hosford was severely injured in 1981 in an industrial accident, he suffered irreversible brain damage and the action against his employer was settled for £420,000. In addition to this action, however, Mr Hosfords five children brought an action claiming that they were deprived of the benefits of a moral, intellectual, religious and educational nature, being the benefits which flow from the love and affection, the guidance and the example which the father of a family bestows on and gives to his children.

**[1.23]** The action was based on two separate claims. First that the defendants owed and breached a duty of care in tort to Mr Hosford's children, as well as to Mr Hosford. Second, that the defendant's careless act amounted to an infringement of the rights conferred on each of the plaintiffs by Article 41 (The Family) and Article 42 (Education) of the Constitution.[36]

**[1.24]** Having held that the plaintiffs had no right at common law because the harm which it is alleged they suffered is not of a kind for which compensation will be awarded, Costello J then addressed the constitutional arguments in the following language:

> "Their constitutional rights which the plaintiffs claim were infringed by the defendants are derived they say from Articles 41 (The Family) and Article 42 (Education). In connection with the claim for damages in respect of rights protected under both these articles, a preliminary point should be made. Whilst at Common Law a claim for an award of damages for the harm it is alleged the plaintiff sustained does not lie, this is not the case if the harm resulted from an infringement of constitutionally protected rights. If the defendant's careless act amounted to a constitutional wrong which inflicted harm on the plaintiffs then I think damages are in principle recoverable; otherwise the protective provisions of the Constitution would be vacuous and valueless. If therefore the plaintiffs can establish that the defendants were guilty of a breach of a constitutionally imposed duty which inflicted harm on the plaintiffs, then damages are recoverable even though at Common Law, an award in respect of such harm could not be made."[37]

**[1.25]** In a closely reasoned opinion which examined Article 41 and 42 of the Constitution the judge reached the conclusion, however, that the defendants had not infringed the plaintiffs' constitutional rights.

**[1.26]** In regard to Article 41, Costello J interpreted subss 1.1 and 1.2 as being closely and inexorably related to each other. Subsection 1.1 recognised rights; subs 1.2 imposed duties. Costello J considered that the claim (if sustainable) should be brought under Article 41.1.1° since it alleged a breach of constitutionally protected rights, but that:

> "the undefined rights which obtain constitutional protection by virtue of [Article 41.1.1°] must be the same as those which obtain protection under Article 41.1.2°, for it would be an unreasonable construction of the Constitution to suggest that the rights which obtain protection from the States recognition in Article 41.1.1° are either more extensive or more restricted than those which the State guarantees to protect in Article 41.1.2°."

**[1.27]** Costello J went on to examine the nature of the duties imposed on the State by Article 41.1.2° He was satisfied that, if it could be shown that the State had enacted a law

36. [1988] ILRM 300 at 301-302.
37. [1988] ILRM 300 at 303.

which in some way failed to protect the constitution or authority of the family, it would have breached its obligation; similarly, if one of its officials deliberately acted so as to attack or impair the constitution or authority of the family, unless of course the acts were justified under some other provision of the Constitution. But, in his view the States guarantee of protection did not extend to a guarantee that its officials would drive State vehicles without negligence. He cautioned that:

> "[I]t must be remembered that the Court is construing a constitutional document whose primary purpose in the field of fundamental rights is to protect [citizens] from unjust laws enacted by the legislature and from arbitrary acts committed by State officials. It would require very clear words to construe the States constitutional obligations (as distinct from its common law obligations) as including a duty to ensure that its officials would not drive carelessly."

**[1.28]** Costello J considered that if a negligent act by the State did not fall within the scope of Article 41.1.2°, it would follow that a private person's negligent act would similarly be immune, even though it fatally impaired the constitution of the family unit. He reached a similar conclusion in relation to Article 42.1.

**[1.29]** Costello J's approach was carried a stage further by Blayney J in *I v Ireland*,[38] in which, however, *Hosford*[39] was not cited by the Court. In this case the plaintiff's wife wrongfully took their infant child out of the jurisdiction in disregard of a court order. The father sought an order for mandamus directing the Minister for Foreign Affairs to withdraw his wife's passport. He claimed that since the Minister had the power to issue a passport he must likewise have power to withdraw it. He also stated that the Minister had a duty to do so as the father had been given sole custody of the child by virtue of a Circuit Court Order. Blayney J said that the crucial issue was whether, assuming that the Minister had power to withdraw the passport, he had a duty to do so and, if he had, whether that duty should be enforced by the requested order. According to Blayney J, however, there was no general obligation on the State to defend and vindicate the personal rights of the citizen. The obligation imposed on the State by Article 40.3 was to defend and vindicate by *its laws* these personal rights. There was no duty on the Minister as contended. It would appear from this that the Judge was prepared to read the Constitution literally and was not prepared to impose an obligation on the Minister to withdraw the passport. The Judge seemed also to have been influenced by the fact that the plaintiff had available to him other remedies, and could have himself prevented the situation by applying to have his wife's passport impounded prior to the removal of the child from the State.

**[1.30]** On appeal the Supreme Court affirmed Blayney J without expressing any comment on his constitutional analysis.

**[1.31]** One finds in Blayney J's interpretation of Article 40.3 a vision of the protection of personal rights being essentially a matter for State legislation rather than either State action or, more radically, action of persons having no connection with the State's relationship with its citizens. If Blayney J's view were to prevail, an infringement by one individual of another individual's constitutional rights would not be actionable and the *Meskell* principle

---

38. [1988] ILRM 300 at 305, Supreme Court, 4 May 1989, affg High Court, 19 August 1988 (Blayney J).

39. See para **[1.22]** above.

would have to be set aside unless infringements by individuals were to be actionable while those by the State were not.

**[1.32]** Of the many questions remaining to be answered in connection with constitutional infringements,[40] some have been clarified with the passage of time. For example, the Supreme Court in *Pine Valley Developments Ltd v Minister for the Environment*[41] held that, where a decision making body had acted without negligence and in a *bona fide* manner, then where it subsequently transpired that the decision was invalidly made and caused financial loss to the plaintiffs, there was no absolute right to recover damages in these circumstances. Even assuming in such circumstances that there was interference with the plaintiff's property rights, the State's obligations under Article 40.3 in this matter were not absolute. The Court held that the common good required an immunity for persons who are vested with statutory powers of decision where they act without negligence and in a *bona fide* manner. Such immunity could be justified, according to the Court, in so far as it contributes to the efficient and decisive exercise of such statutory powers and tends to avoid indecisiveness or delay.

## *W v Ireland* develops *Hanrahan* Rationale

**[1.33]** Henchy J's approach in *(HC)Hanrahan* was addressed in detail in *W v Ireland (No 2)*.[42] The case involved a claim by a victim of a convicted paedophile[43] for damages, shock and distress and consequent psychiatric problems resulting from the delay in his extradition from the Republic of Ireland to Northern Ireland. Costello P rejected the plaintiff's claim in negligence, holding that the Attorney General should not be placed under a duty of care towards potential victims of those in respect of whom the Attorney General was required to make decisions and take actions relating to their extradition.[44] Costello P then turned to consider the plaintiff's claim for damages for infringement of her constitutional rights under Article 40.3, in particular her right to bodily integrity.

40. *Cf* Forde, *Constitutional Law of Ireland* (1987), pp 788-789.

41. [1987] ILRM 747. See Hogan & Morgan, *Administrative Law in Ireland* (3rd ed, 1998), pp 823-824.

42. [1997] 2 IR 141 (HC), analysed by Gaughran 'Tort, Public Policy and the Protection of Constitutional Rights' (1998) 16 ILT (ns) 88.

43. The paedophile was a Catholic priest. The delay in his extradition led to the collapse of the coalition Government between two parties, Fianna Fáil and the Labour Party, and the formulation of a new coalition Government between Fine Gael, the Labour Party and Democratic Left.

44. Costello P applied the two-step test for determining whether a duty of care should be imposed which the Supreme Court had prescribed in *Ward v McMaster* [1988] IR 337, which largely echoed the approach of Lord Wilberforce in *Anns v London Borough of Merton* [1978] AC 728 Costello P was of the view that the Attorney General in addressing the issue of extradition was not in such a relationship of proximity with prospective victims of those whose proposed extradition was under examination as to generate a duty of care towards them. Moreover, considerations of public policy similar to those which rendered advocates (*Rondel v Worsley* [1969] 1 AC 191), Judges (*Deighan v Ireland* [1995] 2 IR 56), police investigating crime (*Hill v Chief Constable of West Yorkshire* [1989] AC 53) and the Crown Prosecuting Service (*Elguzuoli-Daf v Commissioner of Police of the Metropolis*, [1995] 1 All ER 833), immune from a duty of care in negligence applied to the Attorney General in the exercise of his statutory functions in ensuring that the State's international obligations in the field of extradition where achieved. See further paras **[6.24]** below. It is worth noting that the House of Lords in *Hall (Arthur JJ) & Co (a firm) v Simons* [2000] 3 All ER 673 repudiated *Rondel v Worsley* and abolished the traditional immunity for advocates.

**[1.34]** Costello P rejected the claim. Just as the Extradition Act 1965 (as amended) did not impose a duty of care on the Attorney General towards the plaintiff, for similar reasons it did not impose a duty on him (or on any of the other defendants) not to infringe the plaintiff's right to bodily integrity:

> "The Act created no relationship of any sort between any of the defendants and the plaintiff and no circumstances of any sort existed by which a duty to take into consideration the plaintiff's bodily integrity (and so speedily consider the extradition warrants) existed."

**[1.35]** Costello P considered that the second reason why the Attorney General at common law owed no duty of care to the plaintiff, arising from considerations of *public policy*, applied also when considering the claim based on the Constitution:

> "The rights guaranteed under the Constitution are not absolute rights (with the exception of an implied right not to be tortured which must be regarded as an absolute right which can never be abridged) and their exercise and enjoyment may be, and frequently are, limited by reason of the exigencies of the common good. I conclude, applying well established principles of the law of tort, that it would be contrary to public policy in this case to impose on the Attorney General a duty of care towards the plaintiff. The reasons why no common law duty existed also meant that no constitutional duty existed, because the exigencies of the common good (that is, in this case the need to allow the Attorney General carry out his important public functions without the threat of an action for damages for negligence at the suit of a private individual)justifies the court in depriving the plaintiff of a claim for damages for breach of duty not to infringe her right to bodily integrity. This means that none of the defendants owed under the Constitution the right asserted on the plaintiff's behalf."

**[1.36]** These two grounds were sufficient to dispose the of plaintiff's claim but Costello P thought it appropriate to express his views on the broader issue of compensation for infringement of constitutional rights. In approaching this issue he considered that constitutionally guaranteed rights might be divided into two distinct classes: first those which, independently of the Constitution, were regulated and protected by law (common law and statutory law) and secondly, those that were not so regulated and protected.

**[1.37]** In the first class were all those fundamental rights which the Constitution recognised that man had by virtue of his rational being antecedent to positive law and were rights regulated and protected by law in every State which valued human rights. In Ireland there existed a large and complex body of laws which regulated the exercise and enjoyment of these basic rights, protected them against attack and provided compensation for their wrongful infringement.

**[1.38]** Thus, for example, the right to private property was protected by laws against trespass; its enjoyment was regulated by laws against the creation of nuisance; remedies for breach of the right to private property (by way of injunctive relief and actions for damages) were available; limitation on its exercise was provided by law, allowing for its compulsory acquisition and limiting the power to dispose of it by will. The right to liberty was protected by *habeas corpus* acts and laws against wrongful imprisonment, whilst the exercise of the right was limited by provisions of the criminal code and legal powers of arrest and imprisonment. The right of freedom of expression was regulated by defamation laws and laws to protect public morality. The right of bodily integrity which was in issue in the instant case, was protected by extensive provisions in the law of tort.

**[1.39]** Costello P summarised the legal developments that had occurred in relation to the infringement of constitutional rights which were *not* regulated by law and for which *no* legal provision existed either to prohibit an anticipated infringement or to compensate for a past one. It was well established that for this class of rights the Constitution was to be construed as providing a separate cause of action for damages for breach of a constitutional right. Costello P reviewed the decisions of *Meskell v CIE*,[45] *Kearney v The Minister for Justice*,[46] *McHugh v Commissioner of Garda Síochána*[47] and *Kennedy v Ireland*,[48] all of which involved damages awards, and *Lovett v Gogan*,[49] where an injunction had been ordered.

**[1.40]** What fell for consideration in the instant case was not a guaranteed right of this second class but a right (the right of bodily integrity) in respect of which there was a large body of law (both common law and statutory), which regulated its exercise, protected it against infringment and compensated its holder should the right be breached. The question, therefore, was whether the Constitution is to be construed as conferring a discrete cause of action for damages for breach of the plaintiff's right to bodily integrity notwithstanding the existence of the law of tort and statutory provisions which conferred a right of action for damages for personal injuries sustained by the negligent act of omission of another.

> "The question can be posed this way, should the Constitution be construed so as to confer on a pedestrian injured by an army lorry a right to claim damages against the State for infringement of the right to bodily integrity in addition to, or as an alternate to, an action for damages for negligence?
>
> I am satisfied that it should not be so construed."[50]

**[1.41]** Article 40.3.1° did not require the Oireachtas to enact specific laws protecting constitutionally protected rights and the State's duty under this Article was implemented by the existence of laws (common law and statutory) which conferred a right of action for damages (or a power to grant injunctive relief) in relation to acts of omissions which might constitute an infringement of guaranteed rights. Henchy J's remarks in *Hanrahan v Merck Sharp and Dome (Ireland) Ltd*[51] supported this proposition. Thus, if the law of torts made provision for an action for damages for bodily injury caused by negligence and if the law also adequately protected the injured pedestrians guaranteed right to bodily integrity, then the State's Article 40 duties were fulfilled.

---

45. See para **[1.11]** above.
46. [1986] IR 116, discussed para **[1.62]** below.
47. [1986] IR 228.
48. [1987] IR 587, discussed para **[1.63]** below.
49. [1995] 1 ILRM 12, where the Supreme Court held that a transport company whose constitutional right to earn a livelihood was being interfered with by the defendant's breach of statute which caused a derisory penalty and did not confer a civil right on the transport company to sue for its breach was entitled to an injunction against continuing breach of the statute. *Cf O'Connor v Williams* [1996] 2 ILRM 382 (HC).
50. [1997] 2 IR 142. (HC).
51. [1988] ILRM 629 at 635-636.

**[1.42]** Costello P considered that it would be otiose for the courts to establish a new cause of action where constitutional rights were already adequately protected at common law. Taking the hypothetical example of a claim for damages for breach of the constitutional right to bodily integrity resulting from an accident involving the army lorry, Costello P observed that the court would have to consider whether there was any breach of the duty which the driver of the lorry owed to the pedestrian, since the right was not an absolute one, and, in considering the nature and scope of the duty, would decide whether the lorry driver had failed to take proper care of the plaintiff's safety, whether the pedestrian failed to take care of his own safety, apportion liability to take account of any contributory negligence on the part of the plaintiff, assess damages in accordance with established principles, and in certain circumstance consider whether the claim was statute barred - "in other words apply the law of tort to the new cause of action." Costello P acknowledged that a provision of the law to be applied might not in a given case adequately protect the guaranteed right: for example, the law might contain a limitation period which in the particular circumstance trenched unfairly on the guaranteed right and thus deprive the plaintiff of a right to compensation, as in *O'Brien v Keogh*.[52] In such a case, the law would be applied without the provision rendered invalid by the Constitution.

**[1.43]** Costello P noted that his conclusions were consistent with and followed from the views of the Supreme Court in *Hanrahan v Merck Sharp and Dohme (Ireland) Limited*.[53] They were also consistent with the views expressed in *Meskell*[54] which, by holding that a new and distinct cause of action for damages for breach of a constitutional right when the existing law failed to confer any right of damages implied that, when it did so, no new cause of action should be created.

**[1.44]** Counsel for the plaintiff had sought to argue that the crucial passage of Henchy J's judgment in *Hanrahan* was *obiter*, that the number of authorities supporting the plaintiff's contentions were more numerous and that *Hanrahan* was inconsistent with the decision of the Supreme Court in *Lovett v Gogan*.[55] Costello P did not agree. He considered that it had been clear since *Meskell* that the courts would award damages and grant injunctions for breach of constitutionally protected rights but, in each of the cases where that occurred, *Meskell* was either explicitly or implicitly applied and damages were awarded, and in the case of *Lovett v Gogan* an injunction was granted, where no remedy at law existed. None of those cases had decided that an action for damages for breach of a guaranteed right would lie in cases where the *existing* law protected the right. Costello P was satisfied that the law of tort which was applicable in the instant case was not ineffective to protect the plaintiff's constitutionally guaranteed rights:

> "It does not follow that because a plaintiff does not recover damages under the applicable law (in this case, the law of torts) ... it must be ineffective in protecting guaranteed rights. It is necessary to consider why the plaintiffs claim has failed. As already explained, the applicable principles of the law of torts established that there was neither a duty owed to the plaintiff by the defendants under the law of torts or the Constitution to process the extradition

52. [1972] IR 144.
53. See para **[9.49]**-**[9.53]** below.
54. See para **[32.64]**-**[32.68]** below.
55. [1995] 3 IR 132.

warrants speedily and so by applying the principles of the law of torts the plaintiff was not deprived of a remedy to which she was entitled under the Constitution."[56]

**[1.45]** Costello P's insistence that the court should examine why a claim in tort failed before deciding whether to grant a remedy under the Constitution is undoubtedly sensible. In cases where a court holds that the defendant was not under a duty of care in negligence relative to the plaintiff, it is doing more than merely relieving the defendant of liability: it is holding - as Costello P did in *W* - that broad consideration of social policy warrant the establishment of a zone of immunity from liability for the tort of negligence. This is a factor to which the court, in an action for damage for infringement of constitutional rights should give great weight. Plaintiffs should not have automatic "back door" access to compensation merely by reframing their cause of action.

**[1.46]** It is equally true, however, that the fact that a claim for negligence is defeated by the absence of a duty of care is not a reason why a claim for damages for an infringement of a constitutional right should also necessarily founder. This is particularly so in relation to the right of bodily integrity. No court has yet determined the scope of liability for its infringement. Undoubtedly, unjustified intentional and negligent infringements should be capable of generating liability; a plausible case can, however, be made that strict liability should attach, in at least some cases, for an unintended, non-negligent violation of bodily integrity. MacKenzie J appeared to think so in the decision of *Walsh v Family Planning Services*.[57] Whether he was right to do so is not important in the present context. The point to note is that there is nothing illogical or underhand about a claim for damages for infringement of a constitutional right in circumstances where the facts would not support the imposition of a duty of care in negligence.[58]

**[1.47]** Costello J's attempt to find a natural law basis for the constitutional rights which are regulated and protected by common law and statutory law is probably less than helpful. Of course it is true that States which value human rights will have a good record in protecting them through their positive laws, but no one would suggest that the common law of torts was perfection in this regard and the very diversity of statutory overlay on such matters as motor vehicle accident compensation, defamation and occupiers' liability makes it implausible to find an identity between the remit of natural law and positive laws in this

---

56. [1997] 2 IR 142 (HC).

57. [1992] 1 IR 496. The Supreme Court did not interpret MacKenzie J's holding in this way; but see para **[14.89]** below.

58. It is interesting to note that, in *Lovett v Grogan* [1995] 1 ILRM 12, the Supreme Court strove to grant a constitutional remedy to a plaintiff who was a person not entitled to succeed in a tort claim for breach of statutory duty. The court appeared to assume that, because the claim for damages arose in tort, it was foreclosed from granting damages as a constitutional remedy and, on that account, obliged to find another remedy, in the form of an injunction, to assist the plaintiff. The Supreme Court did not address the issue of whether the fact that a breach of statutory duty does not generate liability in tort might, of itself, be a reason for *denying* a claim for infringement of "constitutional right"; if the absence of a duty of care in the tort of negligence can (as Costello P in *W* held) have an negative effect on a claim for damages for infringement of a constitutional right, in order to maintain juridicial consistency, could it not be argued that a conscious or presumed legislative decision not to confer a civil right of action on the victim of a particular statutory breach should be respected by the courts by not permitting an award of damages for a claim framed in terms of a constitutional infrimgement.

context. Moreover, the range of constitutional rights - such as the right to bodily integrity and to privacy of communications, for example - which have been held to generate an entitlement to compensation under Costello P's second category of rights was not regulated and protected by the common law or statutory law, surely are quintessentially rights that can be based on a natural law philosophy in the broad sense.

## *McDonnell* Tames the *Meskell* Principle

**[1.48]** The most recent decision of the Supreme Court to address the issue is *McDonnell v Ireland.*[59] The plaintiff sought compensation for infringement of his constitutional right to earn a livelihood and to property by reason of having forfeited his office as a clerk with the former Department of Posts and Telegraphs in 1974 on being convicted of membership of the Irish Republican Army. This fate followed inexorably from s 34 of the Offences Against the State Act 1939, which many years later was struck down by the Supreme Court in *Cox v Ireland.*[60] The plaintiff's claim was that, having been dismissed under a constitutionally invalid statutory provision, and not having been reinstated subsequently, he had suffered considerable economic loss.

**[1.49]** The plaintiff's claim was rejected on the basis that it was defeated by the Statute of Limitations 1957. The leading judgment was delivered of Keane J, whose thorough analysis of the juridical character of the action for infringement of constitutional rights merits close attention.

**[1.50]** Keane J proceeded on the basis that the plaintiff had "some kind of action, however loosely defined and conceptually uncertain, for breach of his constitutional rights."[61] Noting the broad definition of a tort in Salmond & Heuston's text[62] as "some act done by the defendant whereby he has had without just cause or excuse caused some form of harm to the plaintiff", Keane J observed:

> "Manifestly, as this and other leading textbooks demonstrate, the law, as it has evolved, has staked out the territory within which the law of torts holds sway with more precision. For a variety of reasons, damage which at first sight may seem to have been wrongfully inflicted may not be properly remediable in tort. Even where remediable, the proceedings may still require to be brought within the constraints of a different form of action, most conspicuously in the case of actions for breach of contract, with significant consequences in areas such as the assessment of damages. But subject to these limitations, which do not require exploration in the context of the present case, it may well be said that the English law of tort has, as a matter of history, demonstrated over the centuries a flexibility and a capacity to adapt to changing social conditions, even without legislative assistance, which made it the obvious instrument of the righting of civil wrongs when the Constitution was enacted in 1937.
>
> The dynamic nature of the tort action was well understood when the 1957 Act was enacted. It had been graphically illustrated by the manner in which the action for negligence outgrew the medieval constraints of the action for trespass on the case. The law had seen new species of tortious principles such as the rule in *Rylands v Fletcher*, impose novel forms of liability on defendants. I see no reason to suppose that the Oireachtas legislated in 1957 on the basis

59. [1998] 1 IR 134 (SC affg HC).
60. [1992] 2 IR 503.
61. [1998] 1 IR 134 at 156.
62. SALMOND & HEUSTON (20th ed), p 15.

> that the law of tort was at that stage petrified for all time. It may be, however, - and to surmise on the topic would be both unjustifiable and unprofitable - that the draughtsman did not envisage the extend to which the developing constitutional jurisprudence of the High Court and the Supreme Court in later decades would powerfully reinforce the progressive development of the law of civil wrongs."[63]

**[1.51]** Keane J took by way of example the unenumerated constitutional right of privacy upheld in *Kennedy and Arnold v Ireland.*[64] While it was true that English courts had been hesitant in recognising the existence of such a tort, as was evident from *R v Khan (Sultan)*,[65] such a novel growth, even in the absence of a written constitution, might for all one knew, have flourished sturdily in Ireland. The fact that it did so in the form of an action for infringement of a constitutional right did not prevent it from being classified as a civil wrong, which was not a breach of contract but which was remediable by an action for unliquidated damages and/or an injunction.

**[1.52]** Keane J considered that the famous passage from Walsh J's judgment in *Meskell*, to the effect that constitutional rights carry within them their own entitlement to a remedy for their enforcement, was perfectly consistent with their being protected "by a new form of action in tort, provided, of course, the form of action thus fashioned sufficiently protects the constitutional right in question."[66] Nor was there anything in Henchy J's judgment in *Hanrahan* to suggest that, where a plaintiff was obliged to have recourse to an action for breach of a constitutional right, because the existing corpus of tort law afforded him no remedy, or an inadequate remedy, such an action could not in turn be described as an action in tort, albeit a tort not previously recognised by the law, within the meaning of, and for the purpose of, the Statute of Limitations 1957.

**[1.53]** Keane J acknowledged that, in considering whether other features of the general corpus of tort law apply to actions in protection of constitutional rights, questions might arise which were not relevant in these proceedings. Whatever might be the position in regard to other possible defences, no one had been able to identify in the instant case any ground for supposing that an action for breach of a constitutional right which had all the *indicia* of an action in tort should have a different limitation period from that applicable to actions in tort generally - or indeed no limitation period at all - other than its origin in the Constitution itself, which was classically a circular argument. Nor could it be seriously argued that because the action for breach of a constitutional right frequently took the form of proceedings against organs of the State, this was of itself a reason for treating a limitation statute as inapplicable. Even if it were, it had to be borne in mind that, as was made clear by *Meskell*, the defendant in such actions need not necessarily be an organ of the State.

**[1.54]** Noting the policy considerations underlying Statutes of Limitation such as the 1957 Act, which had been "succinctly and comprehensively stated" by Finlay CJ in *Tuohy v Courtney*,[67] Keane J admitted that he could:

> "see no reason why an actress sunbathing in her back garden whose privacy is intruded upon by a long-range camera should defer proceedings until her old age to provide her with a nest

63. [1998] 1 IR 134 at 157.
64. See para **[1.16]** above.
65. [1996] 3 All ER 289.
66. [1998] 1 IR 134 at 158.
67. [1994] 3 IR 1 (SC), analysed by Byrne & Binchy, *Annual Review of Irish Law 1994*.

> egg, while a young man or woman rendered a paraplegic by a drunken motorist must be cut off from suing after three years. The policy considerations identified by the [Finlay CJ] in [*Tuohy v Courtney*] are applicable to actions such as the present as much as to actions founded on tort in the conventional sense."[68]

**[1.55]** Keane J's judgment on the limitations issue received the overt support of O'Flaherty J, who expressed his "total agreement"[69] with it. Hamilton CJ also concurred. Barrington J did not think it necessary to decide for the purposes of the case, whether all breaches of constitutional rights are torts within the meaning of the Statute of Limitations. His analysis as to the character and scope of the action for breach of constitutional rights appears to follow closely that of Henchy J in *Hanrahan* and, indeed, to adopt a narrow view of the circumstances in which such an action will be available.

**[1.56]** It may be useful to quote *in extenso* what Barrington J had to say on this question:

> "The general problem of resolving how constitutional rights are to be balanced against each other and reconciled with the exigencies of the common good is, in the first instance, a matter for the legislature. It is only when the legislature has failed in its constitutional duty to defend or vindicate a particular constitutional right pursuant to the provisions of Article 40, s 3 of the Constitution that this Court, as the Court of last resort will feel obliged to fashion its own remedy. If, however, a practical method of defending or vindicating the right already exists, at common law or by statute, there will be no need for this Court to interfere ...
>
> There is no doubt that constitutional rights do not need recognition by the legislature or by common law to be effective. If necessary the courts will define them and fashion a remedy for their breach. There may also be cases where the fact that a tort is also a breach of a constitutional right may be a reason for awarding exemplary or punitive damages.
>
> But, at the same time, constitutional rights should not be regarded as wild cards which can be played at any time to defeat all existing rules. If the general law provides an adequate cause of action to vindicate a constitutional right it appears to me that the injured party cannot ask the Court to devise a new and different cause of action. Thus the Constitution guarantees the citizens right to his or her good name but the cause of action to defend his or her good name is the action for defamation. The injured party, it appears to me, has to accept the action for defamation with all its incidents including the time limit within which the action must be commenced. Likewise the victim of careless driving has the action for negligence by means of which to vindicate his rights. But he must, generally, commence his action within three years. He cannot wait longer and then bring an action for breach of his constitutional right to bodily integrity."[70]

---

68. [1998] 1 IR 134 at 160.
69. [1998] 1 IR 134 at 144.
70. [1998] 1 IR 134 at 147-148. Barron J took a different approach. In his view the plaintiff's case was not grounded on breaches of constitutional rights because s 34 of the 1939 Act, being null and void on account of its constitutional invalidity, had never applied to the plaintiff and therefore could not have infringed his constitutional rights. His position had never been forfeited. The refusal to reinstate him was a breach of the terms of his contract. This was the true basis of his claim, which was clearly barred by s 11(1) of the Statute of Limitations 1957, which applies to actions for breach of contract. Any claim the plaintiff had in relation to any right guaranteed by the Constitution would be co-extensive with his right of action for breach of contract; once the 1957 Act applied to the latter it equally applied to any co-extensive right in relation to the Constitution. Noting that the instant case was not one where the cause of action stemmed solely from the provisions of the Constitution itself, Barron J reserved for another time the question whether such cause of action would be barred under the Statute of Limitations.

**[1.57]** The judgments of Keane, Barrington and Barron JJ raise interesting questions. There is much to be said for Keane J's view that an action for damages or an injunction for breach of a constitutional right is capable of juridical classification as a tort but this is so only because of the breadth and virtual vacuity of so many traditional definitions of a tort. It would seem quite mistaken to proceed from the fact that the action for breach of constitutional right is capable of being juridically characterised as a tort to the automatic conclusion that a judicial and statutory corpus of law which has developed over centuries under the rubric of the law of torts should be applied, without further deep reflection, to this newly-named tort.

**[1.58]** There are undoubtedly good policy reasons for having a limitation period or periods for actions for breaches of constitutional rights, but this does not mean that the reasons are identical with those applying to (other) torts. The Statute of Limitations 1957 does not treat all torts identically: it prescribes different periods for certain different torts. Moreover, the Statute of Limitations (Amendment) Act 1991 prescribes a new, and potentially much longer, period for particular actions involving personal injuries or death. There is no basis for assuming that a single period of limitation will do justice to the complexity of circumstances that can arise in respect of breaches of constitutional rights.

**[1.59]** At a formal technical level of statutory interpretation, it is hard to see how an infringement of a constitutional right which results in personal injury can be regarded as "negligence, nuisance or breach of duty ...", as s 3(1) of the Statute of Limitations (Amendment) Act 1991 provides. Of course, a court disposed to squeeze claims for damages into the proscrustean tort model could always hold that there is a duty resting on citizens and the State not to infringe constitutional rights and that to do so is a "breach of duty", but this is surely to argue backwards.

## Some Difficult Questions

**[1.60]** The present state of Irish law is less than ideal. The courts, having established the principle that the infringement of constitutional rights, by the State or by private individuals, warrants a remedy in the form of damages or an injunction, have baulked at the prospect of replacing the pre-existing statutory and common law remedies by a new constitutional remedial regime but they have not repudiated the principle. Instead they have sought to mitigate its practical effects by looking to the pre-existing law as the medium through which the constitutional remedy should be channelled in most cases. The result is that all the conceptual difficulties relating to the principle are left unanswered (though their range of application has been reduced), whilst new difficulties arise on such issues as when a particular tort "is basically ineffective to protect [the plaintiff's] constitutional right."

## Are Constitutional Infringements Actionable *Sine Damno*?

**[1.61]** Let us first consider the difficulties relating to the *Meskell* principle. Perhaps the most significant concerns the very concept of infringement of a constitutional right. Should a constitutional right be regarded as infringed only on proof of actual damage, such as physical or mental injury, physical damage or economic loss, or is it possible for a constitutional right to be infringed without any such damage? Does the answer depend on which particular constitutional right is in question? It will be recalled that, in the law of torts, precisely such a distinction is made: for some torts, most obviously the tort of negligence, the plaintiff must establish proof of damage; for other torts, notably the torts of trespass to the person and to land, no such proof of damage is required. For these latter torts, it is a case of *injuria sine damno*.

**[1.62]** It would seem that, in *Kearney v The Minister for Justice, Ireland and the Attorney General*[71] where the plaintiff, a prisoner, suffered an unjustified infringement of his constitutional right to communicate as a result of the failure of the prison authorities to deliver certain letters to him promptly, Costello J regarded the infringement of this particular right as actionable *per se*. He noted that, "[f]ortunately, the plaintiff suffered no pecuniary or other loss as a result of the delay in delivering him the letters ...".[72] He considered that exemplary damages should not be awarded as there was not sufficient evidence to show that the wrongful conduct was so oppressive or vindictive as to justify such an award. He awarded the plaintiff nominal damages of £25.

**[1.63]** One should not conclude from *Kearney* that all infringements of constitutional rights are actionable *per se*. Of necessity, some constitutional rights simply cannot be infringed without damage: the rights not to be tortured or have ones health impaired, for example. Other infringements of constitutional rights are more controversial. Take the right to privacy in communications, for example. In *Kennedy and Arnold v Ireland and Attorney General*,[73] Hamilton P awarded £20,000 damages to two of the plaintiffs and £10,000 to the third plaintiff where their telephones were unlawfully tapped. He noted that damages, may be "compensatory, aggravated, exemplary or punitive."[74] He considered that the plaintiffs were entitled to substantial damages and that it was, in the circumstances of the case, irrelevant whether they were described as aggravated or exemplary. He was satisfied that the plaintiffs had "not suffered any loss"[75] though they had "significant"[76] distress as a result of the injury done to their of privacy.

**[1.64]** Hamilton P's observations make it difficult to state with confidence that his holding was to the effect that all infringements of the right to privacy of communications are actionable *per se*. It is perhaps significant that his list of the categories of damages did not include nominal damages, which would be appropriate in some cases where the plaintiff's right was infringed without damage occurring.[77]

**[1.65]** A strong argument can be made that infringement of the constitutional right to privacy of communication should be actionable *per se*. Protection of privacy interests is at the heart of the trespassory torts, which are actionable without proof of damage. The point of wider importance, however, is that *Meskell* offers no guidance on the general question whether some, or all, infringements of constitutional rights are actionable *per se*. Simply characterising the claim for damages for an infringement of a constitutional right as a tort, as *McDonnell* does, does not advance the analysis of the issue as to actionability *per se*.

71. [1986] IR 116 (HC).
72. [1986] IR 116.
73. [1987] IR 587 (HC).
74. [1987] IR 587 at 594.
75. [1987] IR 587 at 595.
76. [1987] IR 587.
77. *Cf Constantine v Imperial Hotels Ltd* [1944] KB 693.

## When does Infringement occur?

**[1.66]** *Meskell* and its progeny are also unhelpful on the manner in which a constitutional right may be infringed. Three principal approaches may be considered. The first would proceed on the basis that the definition of the scope of a right should prescribe the circumstances in which the right may be exercised rather than focus on the question of the intention or carelessness to generate liability under *Meskell*, regardless of the defendant's due care or lack of intent to infringe the right in question. In favour of this approach, it may be argued that it best harmonises with the underlying concept of a right, which envisages a range of activities or a particular state or condition deserving of protection from external attack or compromise. As against this, the truth of the matter is that there is no way of avoiding the legitimacy and relevance of the question whether, in a specific case, it is just to impose what is, in effect strict liability for an infringement of a particular constitutional right. For a court to argue that, because the right has been infringed, liability ensues automatically, would be to resort to definitional resolution rather than to confront the issue. The prior question is whether the concept of infringement should inevitably be shorn of reference to the intent or carelessness of the alleged infringer.

**[1.67]** The second approach would seek to establish a general criterion for infringement by reference to the intent or negligence of the alleged infringer. Costello J appeared to favour this line of attack in *PH v J Murphy & Sons Ltd.*[78] The difficulty with this second approach is that it fits somewhat uncomfortably into a rights-based *schema*. It may well be that, in specific instances, the issues of the alleged infringer's negligence or intent may be crucial but there are dangers in establishing a universal or general requirement that liability for infringement be premised on intention or negligence.

**[1.68]** The third approach would eschew the first approach's definitional disposition of troublesome questions and the second approach's generic criteria. Instead, it would favour a more contextualised process of enquiry, whereby issues of intention and negligence would be addressed in precise and detailed factual contexts. This would require the courts to engage in a great deal of fine-tuning of the concept of infringement and of the circumstances in which compensation for infringement would be appropriate. This may seem to involve much toil but there is no way of avoiding the labour involved in translating general rights into specific application. It may be argued that it is better that the courts should equip themselves with precision instruments for conceptual analysis rather than claw hammers.

**[1.69]** It is in this context that Henchy J's approach in *Hanrahan* can perhaps best be understood. The system of tort law was perceived as offering a ready-made, pre-packaged, detailed *schema* for translating general constitutional rights into specific detail. Subject to the minimalist qualification that the courts should refashion this *schema* only when the tort in question was "basically ineffective" to protect a constitutional right and to the entitlement of a person to sue directly for infringement of a constitutional right, in the absence of a common law or statutory cause of action, tort law should be left to do the work of prescribing the scope of compensation under the *Meskell* principle.

---

78. [1987] IR 621.

**[1.70]** The difficulties with this solution have already been adumbrated. The core problem is that tort law simply was not designed to do this task. The medieval English judges who fashioned the contours of trespass to the person, chattels and land exercised no prophetic role in seeking to anticipate the Irish Constitution's protection of citizen's rights to life, bodily integrity, health and property. Of course, the substance of many of these constitutional rights is in no sense novel: there must be a continuous respect in the law for basic human values if a legal system is to have any real claim to respect and continuity. The difficulty with looking to the corpus of tort law to discharge the lion's share of the burden of conferring specificity onto the range of compensation for infringement of constitutional rights is not that tort law is poorly equipped for the task, but rather that it is not the most appropriate model, in that it concentrates on the question of the defendant's conduct rather than the plaintiff's rights.

**[1.71]** Even if courts proceed on the basis that most tort principles are likely to be in accordance with constitutional requirements, they should not accept the quite different premise that these principles represent a presumptive incarnation of the *Meskell* mandate. No court would, or should, accept the proposition that the limits of tort law[79] represent the limits of the range of compensation for constitutional infringements. Plainly, it is open to the courts to declare previously undiscovered personal rights under Article 40.3. There is no reason to presume that the judges who developed the corpus of tort law necessarily anticipated future decisions which as yet remain a matter of speculation among legal commentators.

## The Concept of "Basic Ineffectiveness" of a Tort

**[1.72]** It may be useful to examine the question of when a tort is "basically ineffective" to protect a persons constitutional rights and to consider how the court should respond to such finding.

**[1.73]** From a conceptual standpoint, it seems that ineffectiveness may be regarded as generic or contextual. The court could stigmatise a particular tort as so "basically ineffective" to protect the constitutional rights of citizens that it should be subjected to remodelling in the light of general constitutional requirements. Thus, for example, the present definition to the tort of assault might be regarded as basically ineffective to protect the rights of bodily integrity and health, in that the tort fails to impose liability for a *non-imminent* threat to injure another.[80] The court would be faced with a choice in such circumstances, either to modify the definition of the tort or to leave it as it is but to permit a victim of a non-imminent threat to sue for damages for infringement of his or her constitutional rights.

**[1.74]** Does it matter which approach the court takes? The answer depends on whether the courts will continue the process of "taming" the action for damages for infringement of constitutional rights. In *McDonnell*, as we have seen the majority characterised this action as a tort, subject to the same hesitation periods as other torts; and, in *W*, Costello P appeared to think that the defence of contributory negligence and the assessment of damages were the same for this action as for an action for negligence.

---

79. Subject to proviso in *Hanrahan* regarding "basically ineffective" protection of constitutional rights.

80. *Cf Barton v Armstrong* [1969] 2 NSWR 451 and see para **[0.00]** below.

**[1.75]** Yet in *Conway v Irish National Teachers Organisation*, the Supreme Court appeared to regard the issue of when exemplary damages should be awarded for infringements of constitutional rights as one requiring resolution in terms of an overtly constitutional analysis rather than leaving the matter to be determined by principles applicable to torts.

**[1.76]** As regards limitation periods for actions for infringement of constitutional rights they must be addressed in the context of these actions: the notion that there should be no such periods in any circumstances is clearly unsustainable. But treating these actions separately from the mainstream of tort actions does not lead inexorably to such an imprudent solution. Instead it imposes on the judiciary the troublesome task of fashioning distinctive limitation periods for these actions, to take account of the values that they protect. Undoubtedly the courts would be wise to have regard to the statutory limitation periods applying to specific torts; but they should not let these periods foreclose their own analysis of what the appropriate periods for these actions should be. It is not self-evident, for example, that certain violations of bodily integrity, such as torture by servants of the State, should automatically be governed by the limitation periods applying to the tort of battery.

## Interpersonal Infringements of Constitutional Rights

**[1.77]** The Irish courts proceeded too quickly and perhaps too eagerly to construct a theoretical model of constitutional rights in which the public and private realms were fused. The State as a juristic person was reduced to the same status as a private individual and constitutional guarantees were treated as conferring or recognising rights inhering in individuals and enforceable *contra mundum*. Two strands of philosophy may be identified as fuelling this process. The first was related to the fact that the Irish Constitution is based to a significant extent[81] on a natural law philosophy. In natural law theory, rights inhere in people by virtue of their very humanity.[82] They are not the gifts of a positive legal system which are conferred from above by the State on its subjects. These rights, on this approach, predated the promulgation of the Constitution, which recognised rather than created them. The State, in this theory, is regarded as the creation of the People rather than the People's master. There was an understandable tendency for the judges, therefore, to regard constitutional rights as enforceable against all who infringe them.

**[1.78]** The second philosophical strand which encouraged this outcome was the strong assertion of judicial independence from the executive and the legislature which characterised the Supreme Court, especially in the formative years under the leadership of Ó Dálaigh CJ and more particular Walsh J. A stream of judicial decisions made it clear that the executive, in the eyes of the Court, was largely answerable to the judiciary in the conduct of its affairs. This perception of a diminished executive power made it less likely for the courts to limit the actions for infringement of constitutional rights to cases where the State, as opposed to private individuals, was guilty of an infringement.

**[1.79]** Completely undeveloped in Irish judicial analysis of the action for infringement of constitutional rights is the investigation of whether *all* constitutionally protected rights are

81. Other philosophical streams also make a contribution. There is clear evidence of the influence of British constitutional theory relating to the separation of powers and the protection of individual liberties.

82. *Cf* Finnis, *Natural Law and Natural rights* (1980); Greenawalt 'How Persuasive is Natural Law Theory?' (2000) 75 Notre Dame LR 1647.

enforceable against the State and against individuals without discrimination. Indeed in *H v Murphy*,[83] Costello P proceeded on the basis that the court could determine whether an individual was liable for an infringement by asking whether the State would be liable in the circumstances and then simply applying the answer to that question to the matter of an individual's liability. Inevitably some constitutional rights relate exclusively to the relationship between the right-holder and the State. Some of these, by their very definition, clearly apply only in this context, for example, the right to trial by jury for non-minor offences. Other rights are not so unambiguous but they nonetheless can best be understood as excluding the possibility of interpersonal interference. The courts will surely be called on in the future to engage in analysis on these lines and abandon the assumption that all constitutional rights embrace the possibility of interpersonal infringement.

## Concluding Observations

**[1.80]** There is much to be said in favour of a private law system of compensation which is fully sensitive to constitutional rights. Undoubtedly the system of torts is largely in harmony with constitutional considerations but it was neither created nor developed with those considerations in view. The Irish courts therefore have the task of reviewing the torts system to ensure that it does indeed give full effect to constitutional rights.

**[1.81]** *Meskell* seemed like a simple way of achieving this but it frankly has been less than successful. The judiciary could either have developed a radically new system of actions for damages for infringement of constitutional rights, with all the headache that this involves in terms of working out new rules for the remoteness and measure of vicarious liability and so on. To do this the judiciary would in effect have had to legislate an entire corpus of law. Instead, the judiciary, intimidated by the prospect, has largely tamed the beast that *Meskell* released by shackling it to the pre-existing tort law.

**[1.82]** No judge has gone so far as to declare that the *Meskell* experiment is over. Yet the product of over twenty five years of judicial development of *Meskell* has been surprisingly modest.

## Innominate Torts

**[1.83]** One further point should be mentioned in this connection. While there are many torts which have names and can be readily identified (eg negligence, nuisance, defamation, etc) there are also other instances where the defendant will certainly be liable for his or her actions, but which, perhaps, because of the infrequency of their occurrence, are not given any specific names. So, for example, the person who for a practical joke gives another person false information, on which he intends that other to act, is liable for damage caused to that other.[84] That we have no specific name for this last incidence of liability does not mean that it is any the less of a tort, and this book being concerned with liability will deal, of course, with both nominate and innominate torts.[85]

---

83. [1987] IR 621 (HC).

84. *Wilkinson v Downton* [1897] 2 QB 57.

85. See Smith 'Torts Without Particular Names' (1921) 69 U Pa LR 91; Winfield 'The Foundations of Liability in Tort' (1927) 27 Col LR 1. It should also be mentioned that some torts overlap with each other and there is no reason why the same set of facts should not render the defendant liable in two separate torts. Double recovery will not, however, be allowed.

## IV. European Community

**[1.84]** Since Ireland joined the EEC in 1973, Community legislation has full effect within the State.[86] The issue whether damages for "Euro-torts" should be awarded and, if so, in what circumstances, has come to be of crucial practical importance over the years. [87]

**[1.85]** In *Francovich and Bonifaci v Italy*[88] the Court of Justice held that a Member State is obliged to pay compensation for harm caused to individuals by breaches of Community law for which it can be held responsible. In *Francovich*, the complaint was that the member state failed to implement properly a Community directive so that the plaintiff suffered a loss.

**[1.86]** The Court prescribed three conditions which had to be met before there would be a right to compensation:

> "The first of those conditions is that the result prescribed by the directive should entail the grant of rights to individuals. The second condition is that it should be possible to identify the content of those rights on the basis of the provisions of the directive. Finally, the third condition is the existence of a causal link between the breach of the States obligation and the harm suffered by the injured parties."[89]

**[1.87]** The Court went on to make it clear that it was in accordance with the rules of national law on liability that the State must make reparation for the harm. In the absence of any Community legislation, it was a matter for the internal legal order of each member state to determine the competent courts and lay down the detailed procedural rules for legal proceedings to safeguard the rights that individuals derived from Community law. The substantive and procedural conditions laid down by the national law of the various member states on compensation for harm might not be less favourable than those relating to similar internal claims and might not be "so framed as to make, it virtually impossible or excessively difficult to obtain compensation."[90]

---

86. Temple Lang, 1 J Ir Soc for Eur Law 20; Temple Lang, *The Common Market and The Common Law*, pp 482; La reparation des consequences dommageables d'une violation des Articles 85 et 86 du traits instituant la CEC, CEE Etudes, (1966) Serie Concurrence No 1.

87. For detailed analysis of this complex area of the law, see *Remedies for Breach of EC Law* Lonbay & Biondi eds (1997); *The Action for Damages in Community Law* Heukels & McDonnell eds (1997); Craig & De Búrca, *EU Law: Text Cases and Materials* (2nd ed, 1998), Ch 5; Craufurd Smith, *Remedies for Breaches of EU Law in National Courts: Legal Variation and Selection* Ch 8 of *The Evolution of EU Law* Craig & De Búrca eds (1998); Flynn 'State Liability in Damages for Failure to Observe EC Law' (1996) 14 ILT (ns) 170; O'Neill 'Reliance on EC Directives in the National Court: The Direct Effect of EC Directives – The Current Position' (1995) 2 CLP 36; Flynn '*Francovich* in the National Courts' (1995) 13 ILT (ns) 16; O'Neill 'Member State Liability for Damages for Breach of Community Law Obligations' (1996) 14 ILT (ns) 146; Spink 'Contravening EC Law: The Liability of the Member State' (1997) 48 NILQ 111.

88. [1991] ECR I–5357, [1993] 2 CMLR 66. The holding in *Francovich* had been anticipated by Temple Lang 'The Development of European Community Constitutional Law' (1991) 13 DULJ (ns) 36 at 44. For analysis of *Francovich*, see Craig, '*Francovich*, Remedies and the Scope of Damages Liability' (1993) 109 LQR 595; Ross 'Beyond *Francovich*' (1993) 56 MLR 55; Steiner 'From Direct Effects to *Francovich*' (1993) 18 European LR 3; Editorial 'Following *Francovich*' (1993) 2 Ir J of European L 3.

89. [1993] 2 CMLR 66 .

90. [1991] ECR I-5357.

**[1.88]** The Court of Justice took matters further in *Brasserie du Pêcheur SA v Germany* and *R v Secretary of State for Transport, ex parte Faetortame Ltd.*[91] The Court rejected the argument (favoured, incidentally by the Irish Government)[92] that member states were required to make good loss or damage caused to individuals only where the provisions breached were not directly effective. It went on to hold that member states' obligation of reparation was applicable where the national legislation was responsible for the breach in question.

**[1.89]** Turning to the conditions under which the State might incur liability for acts and omissions of the national legislation contrary to Community law, the Court acknowledged the wide margin of discretion available to the institutions in implementing Community policies. In the instant case, the German and British legislature had been faced with situations involving choices comparable to those made by the Community institutions when adopting legislative measures pursuant to a Community policy:

> "In such circumstances Community law confers a right to reparation where three conditions are met: the rule of law infringed must be intended to confer rights on individuals; the breach must be sufficiently serious; and there must be a direct causal link between the breach of the obligation resting on the State and the damage sustained by the injured parties."[93]

**[1.90]** As to the second of these three conditions, the Court gave the following guidance. The competent court might take into consideration such factors as the clarity and precision of the rule breached, the measure of discretion left by that rule to the national or Community authorities, "whether the infringement and the damage caused was intentional or involuntary",[94] whether any error of law was excusable or inexcusable, the fact that the position taken by a Community institution might have contributed towards the omission, and the adoption or retention of national measures or practices contrary to Community law.[95]

**[1.91]** These factors clearly require the court to address in these specific contexts issues that can show the national (or Community) authorities acted badly. The Court of Justice accepted that "certain objective and subjective factors connected with the concept of fault under a national legal system"[96] might well be relevant for the purpose of determining whether or not a given breach of Community law was serious. The Court went on to state, however, that the obligation for loss or damage caused to individuals could not depend upon a condition based on any concept of fault going beyond that of a sufficiently serious breach of Community law:

> "Imposition of such a supplementary condition would be tantamount to calling in question the right to reparation founded on the legal order."[97]

**[1.92]** On the actual extent of the reparation due by a member state responsible for a breach affecting individuals, the Court counselled that reparation had to be

---

91. [1991] ECR I-5357.
92. [1991] ECR I-5357.
93. [1991] ECR I-5357.
94. [1991] ECR I-5357.
95. [1991] ECR I-5357.
96. [1991] ECR I-5357.
97. [1991] ECR I-5357.

"commensurate with the loss or damage sustained so as to ensure the effective protection of their rights".[98]

**[1.93]** It was for each member state to set the criteria for determining the extent of reparation but (echoing what it had said in *Francovich*) the Court of Justice insisted that there criteria must not be less favourable then those applying to similar claims based on domestic law, nor such as in practice to make it impossible or excessively difficult to obtain reparation. In particular, in order to determine the loss or damage for which reparation might be granted, the national court might inquire whether the injured person showed reasonable diligence in order to avoid the loss of damage or limit its extent – contributory negligence, in the parlance of a domestic tort action in Ireland – and whether, in particular, the injured person availed himself or herself in time of all the legal remedies available to him.[99]

**[1.94]** Regarding the possibility of the national court restricting the scope of damages recoverable, the Court of Justice laid down that the total exclusion of loss of profit as a head of damages for which reparation might be recovered in the case of a breach of Community law could not be accepted:

> "Especially in the context of economic or commercial litigation, such a total exclusion of loss of profit would be such as to make reparation of damage practically impossible."[100]

**[1.95]** As regards the award of exemplary damages, the Court of Justice noted that the basis of the claim for such an award in the British case (*Factortame*) was that the public authorities had acted oppressively arbitrarily or unconstitutionally. It stated:

> "In so far as such conduct may constitute or aggravate a breach of Community law, an award of exemplary damages pursuant to a claim or an action founded on Community law cannot be ruled out if such damages could be awarded pursuant to a similar claim or action founded on domestic law."[101]

**[1.96]** Finally the Court made it clear that the damage for which reparation might be awarded extends to harm before a judgment is delivered by the Court finding that an infringement has been committed.

**[1.97]** The repercussions of these crucial decisions of the Court of Justice are gradually being worked out.[102] The Court has held in *Dillenkofer v Federal Republic of Germany*,[103] that the failure to implement a directive (on package holidays) on time constituted a sufficiently serious breach to generate liability. The language used by the Court suggests clearly that a failure of this kind, regardless of the content or purpose of the particular directive, will have this consequence, provided, of course, that the plaintiff's claims fulfils all the other conditions specified in *Francovich* and *Brasserie du Pêcheur/Factortame*.

**[1.98]** In the Supreme Court decision of *Emerald Meats Ltd v The Minister for Agriculture*,[104] the state was in breach of a duty in failing to include the plaintiff company

98. [1991] ECR I-5357.
99. [1991] ECR I-5357.
100. [1991] ECR I-5357.
101. [1991] ECR I-5357.
102. See Craig & De Búrca, *EU Law: Text Cases and Materials* (2nd ed, 1998), Ch 5
103. [1991] ECR I-5357, [1993] 2 CMLR 66.
104. No 2 [1977] 1 ILRM 275.

as a qualified applicant in making its returns to the Commission. Commission Regulations 4024/89/EEC required that 90% of the GATT meat quota should be apportioned among importers who had imported GATT meat within the previous three years. In forwarding the list of qualified applicants, the Minister for Agriculture had omitted the plaintiff's name with the result that the plaintiff lost its quota and suffered loss through disruption of its business and its trade relationships. The Supreme Court, upholding Costello P held there was a breach of duty, which was in effect a breach of statutory duty, awarded both special and general damages to the plaintiff.[105] In this case the Minister was in breach of the duty to the plaintiff which arose under Articles 1(1) and 4 of Regulation 4024/89, a Community measure which, by definition, does not require to be transposed into Irish law.

**[1.99]** In *Tate v Minister for Social Welfare*[106] Carroll J characterised the Government's failure to implement Directive 79/7/EEC as a tort, and held that the limitation period applicable to torts under the Statute of Limitations Act 1957, applied to such an action also. She observed:

> "There is nothing strange in describing the States failure to fulfil its obligations under the Treaty as a tort. Therefore I am satisfied that s 11(2) of the Statute of Limitations does apply to a breach of obligation to observe a community law."[107]

**[1.100]** Carroll J's approach to the classification problem was addressed in her judgment in the following way:

> "In my opinion, the wrong committed by the State in continuing the discrimination by failing to implement the directive is a wrong arising from community law which has domestic effect. It is not a breach of constitutional rights; it is not a breach of statutory duty[108] and it is not a breach of the duty of care. It is a breach of a duty to implement the directive and its approximates to a breach of a constitutional duty. Every type of action which would be available in the national domestic law to ensure the observance of national law is available to ensure observance of the directive once it took on the mantle of direct effect."[109]

**[1.101]** Carroll J's approach was further endorsed by Geoghegan J in *Coppinger v Waterford County Council.*[110] In that case the plaintiff was injured when he drove his car into the stationary tipper truck owned by the defendants. The plaintiffs injuries were greatly exacerbated because the defendant's truck was not fitted with an under-run protection barrier. EC directives required Member States to make such barriers compulsory. The Irish legislation, however, in implementing the directives wrongly exempted tipper-trucks such as the County Council's vehicle in the present case: the exemptions contemplated in the directive did not cover tipper-trucks and the State was wrong in making exceptions in this case. Geoghegan J agreed with Carroll J's characterisation of the State's failure in this regard as a tort, which is a "wrong" within the

---

105. Costello Ps refusal to award general damages, although willing to award special damages, was overturned by the Supreme Court. See Byrne & Binchy, *Annual Review of Irish Law 1995*, pp 785-787.

106. [1995] 1 ILRM 507.

107. [1995] 1 ILRM 507 at 525.

108. See Byrne and Binchy, *Annual Review of Irish Law 1995*, pp 541-543; and see Ch 21 below on Breach of Statutory Duty.

109. [1995] ILRM 507 at 522.

110. [1996] 2 ILRM 427.

meaning of the Civil Liability Act 1961. On the evidence the judge went on to hold that this breach had caused "the serious aspect of the plaintiff's injuries". He also held that the defendant Council was an "emanation of the State" and as such was liable for the State's breach of duty in failing to properly implement the community measure. In awarding damages to the plaintiff the judge, however, reduced the plaintiff's award by 75% for contributory negligence. The Court also held that the defendant was not liable in common law negligence since it was entitled to assume that the State had properly implemented the directive. In these circumstances, if the defendant was a private person, presumably the plaintiff would have failed in his action and would have had to issue separate proceedings against the State.

**[1.102]** In *Dublin Bus v MIBI*[111] the respondent/plaintiff sued the appellant/defendant in respect of property damage caused to its buses by hit and run drivers. The cars had been taken without the consent of the owners and the drivers, after crashing into the buses, ran away and were never indentified or apprehended. The MIBI Agreement of 1988, which was designed to compensate victims in these type of cases, created an exception where the MIBI did not have to pay for property damage if the damage was caused by a vehicle "the owner or user of which remains unidentified or untraced". The MIBI relied on this provision in resisting the plaintiff's claim.

**[1.103]** The 1988 Agreement was drafted to give effect to EEC Directive 84/5 which permitted Member States to make such an exception only where the *vehicle* was untraced. Had the Directive been properly transposed into Irish law Dublin Bus would have been entitled to recover for its property damage. McMahon J held that the Directive intended to confer rights on individuals, and that the breach by the MIBI, who were aware of the flawed transposition and had made public commitments that it would not rely on the national measure but had not lived up to its promise in the present case, was a serious one. Further the MIBI had not taken any reasonable steps to amend the Agreement in the interim. Finding that there was a causal nexus between the failure to properly implement the Directive and the plaintiff's damages, McMahon J, held that it was entitled to compensation. In McMahon J's opinion the MIBI was a clear emanation of the State in this matter. It was a party with the Minister for the Environment to the agreement and it managed the scheme on behalf of the State:

> "The State's yoke of responsibility for transforming community respensibility in this regard lies equally on the shoulders of the Bureau as well as on the shoulders of the Minister. Indeed, in so far as the Bureau knew of the State's failure ... for several years and failed to remedy the matter it cannot avoid responsibility".[112]

## I. Definition of Tort

**[1.104]** A tort may be defined as a civil wrong (other than a breach of contract or a breach of trust) for which the normal remedy is an action for unliquidated damages.[113] It must be noted that this is a purely formal or procedural definition which might help lawyers to distinguish the law of torts from other branches of law, but it does little to indicate to lay

111. Circuit Court, 29 October 1999 (McMahon J).

112. Page 14 of judgment. McMahon J did not use the word "tort" in imposing liability.

113. *Cf Secretary of State for War v Studdert* [1902] 1 IR 375 (HL) affg [1902] 1 IR 240 (CA).

persons the acts or omissions for which the law will hold them liable. It does not provide them with a list of the instances where the law allows an injured person the right to recover for his/her injuries.

## Tort v Crime

**[1.105]** The law of torts is primarily concerned with private disputes between individuals, whereas criminal law has a greater public dimension.[114] Tort is principally concerned with the provision of compensation whereas criminal law is concerned with the regulation of conduct and the maintenance of social order and, to this end, with the imposition of penalties. Nevertheless, there can be an overlap between the two areas and the same set of facts may at the same time constitute both a tort and a crime. For example, a drunken driver who kills a pedestrian may be prosecuted for manslaughter or dangerous driving causing death and sued for negligence. Similarly, a thief may be prosecuted for larceny and sued for conversion. Since the overlap is partial only, there are, of course, some crimes which are not torts and some torts which are not crimes. The drunken driver who mercifully causes no damage commits no tort because he or she injures no one, yet he has committed a criminal offence. Similarly, perjury is an offence but does not generate civil liability. Conversely, a defamatory statement, while it might render the author liable in tort, does not normally involve the author in criminal liability.

**[1.106]** Since a crime is essentially an offence against society, enforcement is normally left in the hands of public officials such as the Director of Public Prosecutions or a member of the Garda Síochána. Individuals, it is true, have certain rights to bring a prosecution[115] but, even when they exercise them, they are acting in the public interest. In tort the injured party sues for compensation for the injuries he or she has suffered and the public interest in the act is less central. When the same set of facts gives rise to criminal and civil liability parallel proceedings may be instituted. There is no reason why one set of proceedings should precede the other.[116] There is a technical advantage in the normal road traffic case for the injured person to delay the suit until criminal proceedings have terminated. As well as getting a preview of the evidence that is likely to be produced in the civil action, if the criminal action is successfully prosecuted, the plaintiff's negotiating position in seeking to secure an insurance settlement in the civil context will be greatly strengthened, although the criminal conviction in itself creates no presumption of negligence.[117]

---

114. *Cf The King (Deeny) v Justices of County Tyrone* [1909] 2 IR 400 at 404 (KBD) See also *Melling v Ó Mathghamhna* [1962] IR 1; *McLoughlin v Tuite* Supreme Court, 13 June 1989.

115. See Ryan & Magee *The Irish Criminal Process* (1983), pp 74-75.

116. There was an old common law rule which provided that, where a wrong was also a felony, the wrongdoer should first be prosecuted before civil proceedings could be instituted. The Criminal Law Act 1997, s 3, abolished all distinctions between felony and misdemeanour. See also the Criminal Justice Act 1951, s 26, repealed by the Courts (Supplemental Provisions) Act 1961, s 3, Sch 1.

117. *Hollington v Hewthorn* [1943] KB 587. See Glanville, 'Litigation and Evidence: The Rule of *Hollington v Hewthorn & Co Ltd*' (1996) 14 ILT (ns) 25. *Cf Kelly v Ireland* [1986] ILRM 318 (HC). In *Dockery v O'Brien* (1975) 109 ILTR 127 at 128 (CC) McWilliam J said: "In so far as there was a breach of the Highway Code, I accept that this creates no presumption of liability, but it is a circumstance which I am entitled to consider in deciding whether there was negligence or not." - The defendant had left the car key in the ignition. The car was taken by an intoxicated person and he damaged the plaintiff's car. The defendant was held liable. See also the Civil Liability Act 1961, s 57(1). The relationship between breach of a criminal statute and civil liability is analysed in detail in Ch 15.

**[1.107]** In a couple of cases schemes have been established where the State, in discharge of its welfare functions, provides compensation to the injured person for criminal injuries done to his or her property or person. Included in these are the malicious injury code covering malicious injury to property,[118] compensation for Gardaí injured in the course of their duties and compensation for injuries inflicted by crimes of violence.[119] The State is moved to act in these schemes because of the absence, in most cases, of an identifiable or insured defendant. Similar recent examples of the conscious departure from traditional roles attributed to crime (punishment) and tort (compensation) occur in the Factories Act 1955 (s 103), the Road Traffic Act 1961 (s 57), the Holidays Employees Act 1973 (s 8(4)(c)) and the Consumer Information Act 1978 (s 17(3)) where an offender may be ordered to compensate the injured party,[120] and more generally the provision of compensation orders in the Criminal Justice Act 1993.

**[1.108]** The 1993 Act should be regarded as a watershed as it reflects a wider cultural shift, discernible in the past decade or so, to blur the sharp boundaries between the criminal and the civil law. Section 6 enables the court, on conviction of any person for an offence, instead of or in addition to dealing with that person in any other way and "unless it sees reason to the contrary",[121] to make a "compensation order", requiring the convicted person to pay compensation in respect of any personal injury or loss resulting to another from the offence. The sum ordered must not exceed the amount of the damages that, in the courts opinion, the injured party would be entitled to recover in a civil action.[122] The court must also take into account the convicted persons means.[123] Where a compensation order has been made and damages in respect of the injury or loss fall to be assessed in civil proceedings, the court must, in effect, subtract the amount ordered under the compensation order from its award.[124] If the amount ordered under the compensation order was greater than what the court in civil proceedings wishes to award as damages the convicted person is entitled to a rebate.[125]

## Tort v Breach of Contract

**[1.109]** The same set of facts may give rise to both contractual and tortious liability. Liability in both is civil as opposed to criminal and both simple contracts and torts have

118. Malicious Injuries Act 1981.

119. See fn 166 to 171 below and accompanying text.

120. Section 57(1) and (2) of the Road Traffic Act 1961 was held to be unconstitutional in *Cullen v AG* [1979] IR 394. For criticism, see Casey (1976) 11 Ir Jur (ns) 326.

121. Section 6(1) of the 1993 Act. For analysis of the legislation see Bird 'Annotation to the Criminal Justice Act 1993' [1993] ICLSA; Byrne & Binchy, *Annual Review of Irish Law 1993*, pp 216-217. The 1993 Acts provisions repeal and enlarge upon the more limited provision contained in the Criminal Damage Act 1991, ss 9 to 11.

122. Section 6(2). As regards road accidents, the court's power to make a compensation order is limited to cases where the convicted person was not insured or the vehicle was taken out of the owners possession and damaged while out of his or her possession (as, for example, where a "joyrider" crashes the car): s 6(4).

123. Section 6(5). Payments under a compensation order are made to the District Court clerk for transmission to the injured party: s 7.

124. Section 9.

125. Section 9.

common origins in the writ of assumpsit. The dentist, the doctor or the solicitor who does his job badly may at one and the same time be liable for negligence and for breach of contract. The common law was not consistent in its handling of the concurrence problem here, declaring in the case of carriers, bailees and innkeepers that concurrent liability in both contract and tort existed, whereas in the case of solicitors, architects, and others there was a tendency until recently to say that there was liability only in contract.[126]

**[1.110]** *Donoghue v Stevenson*,[127] of course exploded the fallacy that since there was no contract between the plaintiff and the defendant there could be no liability in tort between the parties. In that case the ultimate consumer was held to have a good tort action against the manufacturer even though there was no contract between them. Conversely, Irish courts have also affirmed, in general terms, that the existence of a contract between the parties does not mean that there can be no liability in tort. In *Finlay v Murtagh*[128] in an action against a solicitor for not prosecuting a claim within the period allowed by the Statute of Limitations the question was raised as to whether the action was based in contract or in tort. If it was based in tort the plaintiff would have been entitled to a jury trial. In the course of his judgment Henchy J (with whom O'Higgins CJ and Parke J agreed) made the following statement of the law:

> "It has to be conceded that for over a hundred years there has been a divergence of judicial opinion as to whether a client who has engaged a solicitor to act for him, and who claims that the solicitor failed to show due professional care and skill, may sue in tort, or whether he is confined to an action in contract ...
>
> ... It is undeniable that the client is entitled to sue in contract for breach of that implied term. But it does not follow that, because there is privity of contract between them, and because the client may sue the solicitor for breach of the contract, he is debarred from suing also for the tort of negligence. Since the decision of the House of Lords in *Hedley Byrne & Co Ltd v Heller & Partners Ltd* [1964] AC 465 and the cases following in its wake, it is clear that, whether a contractual relationship exists or not, once the circumstances are such that the defendant undertakes to show professional care and skill towards a person who may be expected to rely on such care and skill, and in fact does so rely, then that person may sue the defendant in the tort of negligence for failure to show such care and skill, if he has been damnified by such default. For the purpose of such an action, the existence of a contract is merely an incident of the relationship. If, on the one side, there is a proximity of relationship creating a general duty and, on the other, a reliance on that duty, it matters not whether the parties are bound together in contract ... The coincidence that the solicitor's conduct amounts to a breach of contract cannot affect either the duty of care or the common law liability for its breach, for it is the general relationship, and not any particular manifestation such as a contract, that gives rise to the tortious liability in such a case: see per Lord Devlin in the *Hedley Byrne* case ..."

---

126. *Cf Somers v Erskine* [1943] IR 348. See also Reynolds 'Tort Actions in Contractual Situations' (1985) 11 NZLR 215; Jaffey 'Contract in Torts Clothing' (1985) 5 Legal Studies 77; Mason 'Contract and Tort: Looking Across the Boundary from the Side of Contract' (1987) 61 Austr LJ 228.

127. [1932] AC 562.

128. [1979] IR 249. See also *Chariot Inns Ltd v Assicurazioni Generali SPA et al* [1981] IR 199 - Liability of insurance broker.

**[1.111]** The Irish courts have not fully worked out in all cases the basis of liability when both contract and tort occupy the same legal space. In spite of *Donoghue v Stevenson* there is still a tendency for the courts, in some cases, to refer to the contract in seeking to determine whether the duty of care exists in the first instance or to determine the content of the duty or the measure of care required in the second instance. Three recent Supreme Court cases can be cited as illustrating the different circumstances which can give rise to these difficulties. In *Madden v Irish Turf Clubs*[129] the plaintiff bet on a horse that had come second at Punchestown Races. When the "winner all right" announcement was made, the totalisator with whom the plaintiff had placed his bet, paid out in accordance with its rules. It was subsequently discovered that the horse first past the post was ineligible for the race and should not have been allowed run. The second horse was then elevated to first place. The plaintiff did not sue the totalisator which had already paid out according to its rules which provided that a subsequent disqualification would not affect the payout; instead he sued the Turf Club and the Irish National Hunt Steeple Chase Committee which administered and regulated flat and steeple chasing in Ireland. He claimed that in carelessly permitting an ineligible horse to run they had breached their duty of care to him. He claimed in excess of £18,000 which was what he would have won had his horse been first past the post. The plaintiff lost his case on the basis that there was not sufficient proximity between the defendants and the plaintiff. In the course of his judgement O'Flaherty J stated that the plaintiff's contract was with the tote management and that "that erected a barrier so as to prevent such close and direct relations to occur as is necessary to give rise to a duty of care between the plaintiff and the defendants".[130] O'Flaherty J adopted the same approach in *McCann v Brinks Allied Ltd and Ulster Bank*[131] in a more serious case where bodily integrity was the invaded interest. When sued by the employees of a security firm who were injured while transporting the bank's moneys, the Supreme Court held that the bank could escape liability by inserting an immunity provision in its contract with the security firm. These two cases raise the question as to when a contractual term with a third party might affect the existence of a duty of care in the first instance to a person who is not a party to the contract.

**[1.112]** In *Sweeney v Duggan*[132] the Supreme court dismissed the plaintiffs claim where he tried to escape "out" of contract into the domain of tort.[133] The plaintiff was a labourer who was injured during the course of his work and successfully sued the company which employed him for negligence and breach of statutory duty. Because the company went into liquidation and had no employer's liability insurance, the plaintiff could not recover his award fully. He then decided to sue the defendant who was the managing director and who also owned all but one of the shares in the company. The plaintiff argued, *inter alia* that the defendant had a duty to ensure that the company obtained such insurance or, if not, to warn him that it had not done so. The particular duty to insure against liability, it was argued by

129. [1997] ILRM 148.

130. O'Flaherty J adopted the same approach in *McCann v Brinks Ltd and Ulster Bank* [1997] 1 ILRM 461.

131. [1997] 1 ILRM 461.

132. [1997] 1 ILRM 211.

133. See MARKESINIS AND DEAKIN, pp 7-17 where these issues are discussed at length. The English authorities are also confused and inconsistent.

the plaintiff, was an implied term of the employment contract. The Supreme Court held that such a term could not be implied and since there was no duty on the company, there could be no duty on the defendant in tort.

**[1.113]** It is probably now becoming clear that the problems created by the contract/tort overlap are not easily resolved. Perhaps this is because the courts are still trying to deal with the overlap problem as if all situations were the same and admitted of a single analysis. The truth may be that the courts need to be more refined in their approach, distinguishing between different relationships and different kinds of damage. It would seem to be well established, for example, that in the cases of an employer's obligations to his or her employee and a professional's (doctor, lawyer etc) duties to his client, the courts will not restrict the injured employee or client to either a tortious or contractual remedy. Both will be available. In the case of a bank's dispute with its customer or a holiday makers dispute with his travel agent (where consumer protection measures may be available) should more weight be given to the terms of the contract? The final answer to this question may be no but one may be justified in showing more hesitation before pronouncing definitively on the matter.

**[1.114]** The contract/tort problems adverted to here will be dealt with more fully in Chapter 10.

**[1.115]** On the troubled question of "non-dangerous" defects in products, Irish courts have shown greater consistency than their British counterparts in holding that liability in tort as well as contract may arise.[134]

**[1.116]** The distinction between contract and tort, nevertheless, remains and continues to have some importance. For instance, different limitation periods apply to contract and tort actions. Remoteness is not determined in the same way in both branches of the law and the object of damages in tort is to compensate the plaintiff by restoring him to the position which he would have held if the tort was not committed, whereas in contract loss of expectations and the loss of profit may also be allowed. Again in a contract case the plaintiff must show consideration whereas this is not necessary in tort. Moreover, it is said that the obligation imposed in contract is imposed by the parties, whereas in tort the obligation is imposed by law.[135] In tort, liability is normally imposed because of misfeasance,[136] whereas in contract, liability is common both for misfeasance and for nonfeasance. In tort there is also difficulty about awarding damages for pure economic loss.[137] Until recently the distinction was also of immense practical importance in Ireland

---

134. See para **[11.72]** below.

135. This may be more apparent than real, as is the distinction that a tort duty is to persons in general while contractual duties are to specific persons.

136. Liability for nonfeasance in tort requires a duty (usually based on some existing relationship) between the parties. See Shapo, *The Duty to Act* (1977); *cf* Logic, [1988] Camb LJ 115.

137. *Cf* Ch 10 below. Exemplary damages, are allowed in tort but not the traditional view was that they were not available for breach of contract. See, however, *Garvey v Ireland* [1981] ILRM 266 (HC) and the analysis of the Law Reform Commission in its *Report on Aggravated, Exemplary and Restitutionary Damages* (LRC 60-2000), paras 1.48-1.49.

where tort (but not contract) actions were heard by juries.[138] The right to trial by jury for personal injury actions was abolished in Ireland as from 1 August 1988 (The Courts Act 1988).

## Restitution and Breach of Trust

**[1.117]** The law of restitution imposes an obligation, on a person who receives an unintended benefit, to repay the sum by which he or she has been "unjustly enriched". The action here, however, is for a fixed ascertained sum and so can be distinguished from the typical tort action which is for unliquidated damages. The law of restitution, however, typically applies to cases where the person who received the benefit may have done no wrong, and this too distinguishes it from tort. Finally, restitution is not concerned with compensation for losses, but rather with the return of unjust enrichments.[139] The same characteristic of the tort action also helps to distinguish tort liability from liability for breach of trust, an area of liability which should be fenced off from the tort area because it is more properly considered to relate to the law of property.[140]

## Unliquidated Damages

**[1.118]** One of the principal ways of distinguishing liability in tort from other forms of liability is that in tort the action by the plaintiff is for an unfixed sum. The plaintiff in his claim may, of course, put a figure on his loss but this in practice indicates no more than the upper limit beyond which the court will not usually go. The principal object of the law of torts is to restore the plaintiff to the position which he or she occupied before the wrong was committed, and the principal means it has of attempting to do this is through compensation in monetary form. In some cases, notably involving damage to property, the law may more or less achieve its objective; in other cases, however, most obviously those involving personal injuries, and pain and suffering, the conversion of the injuries into monetary sums can never really pretend to be anything more than notional compensation. Exceptionally, the courts depart from their compensatory role and award exemplary damages to the plaintiff, but the limited circumstances in which the courts will indulge in this punitive role indicate how unusual these awards are.[141]

**[1.119]** There are areas, however, where the courts, while admitting an injury, will hesitate to award any damages to the plaintiff, for example, in the case of pure economic loss and emotional distress. The courts caution here, however, is caused, it would seem, by "floodgate fears" rather than by the inability to convert and quantify such losses into monetary terms.

**[1.120]** Finally, it would be wrong to think that, while an award of damages is the principal remedy available to the plaintiff in a tort action, it is the only remedy available. As well as

138. It should also be noted that trade unions are immune from tortious but not from contractual liability. See Trade Disputes Act 1906, s 4. Furthermore, the privileged position of minors in contract cannot be circumvented by suing in tort.

139. See Birks *Introduction to the Law of Restitution* (1985); Eoin O'Dell 'Restitution' in Byrne and Binchy *Annual Review of Irish Law 1997*, pp 607-665.

140. *Cf* WINFIELD & JOLOWICZ, pp 14-15.

141. *Rookes v Barnard* [1964] AC 1129. See also *Maher v Collins* [1975] IR 232. *Cf Kennedy and Arnold v Ireland* [1988] ILRM 472 (HC); *Conway v Ireland* High Court, 2 November 1988 (Barron J).

seeking an injunction from the courts the law also permits the plaintiff to resort to self-help in appropriate circumstances. Accordingly, a person may enter another person's property to recover his or her goods[142] or shoot a dog worrying his or her livestock;[143] a reasonable amount of force may be used to expel a trespasser,[144] and a nuisance may be removed or abated by the affected individual.[145] Great caution must be taken in the exercise of such remedies, however, as the courts tend to discourage unlimited measures of self-help.[146]

## VI. From Negligence to Strict Liability: from Loss Shifting to Loss Distribution[147]

**[1.121]** In the areas of tort law that seem to need most urgent reform nowadays there have been many advocates for a solution based on strict liability. Strict liability already exists in respect of occupational injuries[148] and there have been many suggestions for a similar system in respect of road traffic accidents. The most comprehensive proposal in these islands is to be found in the Pearson Commission's Report,[149] published in Britain in 1978. The EEC's Directive on Products' Liability also favours a no-fault approach in respect of defective products. In view of the tendency of reformers in these areas to advocate strict (no-fault) liability it seems worthwhile to note this move away from the fault concept. This development also illustrates two other important characteristics of the law of torts: first, the sensitivity of tort rules to social, economic and industrial pressures, especially when tort rules are viewed in an evolving way and in a continuing time-frame; and second, the important role which the judiciary has played in the development of these rules. With regard to the latter point it has already been noted that much of the law of torts is judicially developed law, and that legislation has played a relatively subordinate role until recently in the development of the principles of liability. There have been notable exceptions of course the Civil Liability Act 1961, the Defamation Act 1961, to mention but two in Ireland - and one might expect greater statutory reform in the future because of the harmonisation impetus from the EU (eg the directive on products liability) which will necessarily have to

---

142. *Anthony v Haney* (1832) 8 Bing 186, 131 ER 372. See also *Cope v Sharpe (No 2)* [1910] KB 168; on appeal [1912] 1 KB 496.
143. Control of Dogs Act 1986, s 23.
144. See *Ross v Curtis*, High Court, 3 February 1989 (Barr J); Occupiers' Liability Act 1995, s 8..
145. *Lemmon v Webb* [1895] AC 1; *Wandsworth Board of Works v United Telephone Co* (1884) 13 QB 904.
146. See *Lagan Navigation Co v Lambeg, Bleaching Dyeing and Finishing Co* [1927] AC 226 at 244; *McKnight b Xtravision* Circuit Court, 5 July 1991 (Judge Carroll).
147. *Cf* McMahon (1968) 3 Ir Jur (ns) 18-32 and 284-298. See also Sheldon 'Return to Anonymous: The Dying Concept of Fault' (1976) 25 Emory LJ 163; Leflar 'Negligence in Name Only' (1952) 27 NYU LR 564.
148. The Social Welfare (Occupational Injuries) Act 1966, replacing earlier Workmans Compensation legislation from the late 19th century. See now the Social Welfare (Consolidation) Act 1993.
149. *Report of the Royal Commission on Civil Liability and Compensation for Personal Injury*, 1978, Cmnd 7054, Vol I, (*Pearson Report*), para 1086 and Annex 8. See also 'Accident Compensation after Pearson' (1979); Allen, Bourn & Holyoak (eds), Veitch 'The Pearson Report: Guidelines for Canada?' (1979) 28 UN Brunswick LJ 19; Fleming, (1979) 42 MLR 249; Marsh (1979) 95 LQR 513; Weir, [1978] Camb LJ 222.

be implemented in Irish law by Act of the Oireachtas or by Statutory Instrument. The EEC's (now the EU's) Directive on products' liability, for example, was implemented in Ireland by the Liability for Defective Products Act 1991. Moreover, recommendations of the Law Reform Commission on various tort matters will, if adopted by the Government, obviously find ultimate expression in legislative form.[150] Nevertheless, the role of the judge as law maker in the tort area is, and will for some time remain, considerable and deserves attention.

**[1.122]** In early society when an accident occurred and an injury was incurred the natural thing was to leave the loss lie where it fell. Certainly one who wished to shift it had the onus of providing a good reason as to why it should be moved. Causation of itself was hardly a sufficient reason for moving the loss on to the person who caused the loss. When causation combined with culpability, however, one then had a justification for shifting the loss on to the causal agent who was to blame. Fault became the lever which moved the loss, and without fault the loss lay where it fell. The rule became no fault, no liability. Without fault the law could not justify shifting the loss from one individual to another individual. Shifting the loss, of itself, did not reduce the cost of the accident to society. If someone was at fault, however, it seemed fair that he should bear the loss rather than the innocent victim. The fault concept dominated the law of torts from the nineteenth century and is still a major factor when we are considering the modern tort of negligence.

**[1.123]** This view of tort law suggests that the function of the law is to address these problems in an interpersonal way, shifting the loss from one person to another when justification for doing so exists.

**[1.124]** In more recent times, however, when individualist philosophies gave way to notions of collectivism, it was felt, especially in the context of welfare programmes, that such losses should not lie with the individual, but should perhaps be shared among the community. This approach was favoured especially when the act which attracted liability in the first instance, was not fault in the true sense of wrongdoing, but merely a lapse of concentration or an error of judgment. Where the activity in question inevitably brought with it a risk, then it seemed more equitable to look away from the immediate action and seek a method of imposing liability on the person who created the risky product or

---

150. See Animals Act 1985, the Control of Dogs Act 1986 and the Statute of Limitations (Amendment) Act 1991. Other reports dealing with tort law published by the Commission some time ago but not yet implemented include those dealing with the liability of builders, vendors and lessors of premises and the liability of minors and of the mentally disabled. The Commission's proposals in relation to torts affecting family relations, contained in its *First Report on Family Law*, published in 1981, were in part rejected by the Oireachtas in the Family Law Act 1981. The Oireachtas has yet to respond to the Commission's proposals in that report dealing with the actions for loss of consortium and for seduction, enticement and loss of services of a child. So far, at least, as the latter torts are concerned, it seems most unlikely that the Commission's proposals will see the light of day. The need for energetic law reform on these matters is apparent from the reluctance of the judiciary to engage in active development of areas of the law where the Commission has reported (*cf Hosford v J Murphy & Sons Ltd* [1988] ILRM 300 (HC)) or even where there is only a prospect of the Commission's engaging in a study of the area in question (*cf Hynes O'Sullivan v O'Driscoll* [1989] ILRM 349 at 361 (SC). The Occupiers' Libility Act 1995 is another legislative reforming measure which is dealt with full in Ch 12. In the past decade the Commission has produced Consultation Papers and Reports on defamation, personal injuries, aggravated, exemplary and restitutionay damges, privacy and the aspects of the Statutes of Limitation, most of which stand a good chance of implementation.

intiiated the risky activity in the first place - the manufacturer, for example. Further justification for this approach could be found when it was appreciated that the manufacturer could handle the loss better by passing it on to the consumer by way of price increase. This meant that the loss was now being spread among a group of people who took part in this risky activity. Spreading of the loss was further facilitated when liability insurance became generally available to the manufacturer.[151] This development manifests itself in the emergence of judicial tendencies which favoured injured plaintiffs at the expense of deep-pocketed defendants in a more or less incremental and clandestine fashion which characterises judicial law making in the common law tradition. Examples of this can be found in the development of *res ipsa loquitur* and the curtailment of the doctrine of common employment. In recent decades the acceptance of the collectivist approach has reflected itself in statutory form[152] or by more direct methods of government intervention to cater for special cases where large scale disasters have occurred.[153]

**[1.125]** Economists who began to examine critically the traditional tort system were also able to justify the development from loss shifting to loss distribution as being a development which "internalised" the costs of accidents, and by making the group who availed of the beneficial activity, carry the costs of such inevitable accidents, the deterrent effect was also maintained.[154]

## Insurance and Other Schemes of Compensation

**[1.126]** One must not think that tort liability operates in a vacuum. Injuries suffered by a person may be the object of compensation from sources other than a successful action against a tortfeasor. In particular, the injured person may receive compensatory payments from insurance sources or from the State in the form of welfare payments of one sort or another. Perhaps it is just as well that the injured plaintiff does not have to rely entirely on the hope of compensation from a tort action, especially where the success of his or her action depends on the ability to prove fault. The defects of the fault system are easily listed: it is expensive; it is slow; it is uncertain in outcome and in the amount of the award; the unpredictability of the jury in cases where it still operates places undue pressure on both plaintiff and defendant to make unwise settlements; and, compensation in a "once and for all" lump sum[155] takes inadequate account of future developments.[156] Where the

---

151. This development can also be explained in philosophical terms as a move from corrective justice to distributive justice

152. Eg the Liability for Defective Products Act 1991 which imposes strict liability on the producer. The earliest example occurred in the case of workers injured at work. The Workers Compensation Acts established a system of payments to such workers which applied irrespective of fault. It has now been taken a step further in the Occupational Injury Code. The Occupiers' Liability Act 1995, in reducing the occupiers' liability to recreational users and trespassers, may be seen as going counter to this general trend.

153. Eg the establishment of Special Tribunals to pay compensation to the victims of defective blood products – discussed at para **[1.188]**.

154. On the Economic analysis of tort law see MARKESINIS AND DEAKIN, pp 23-36.

155. The Law Reform Commission, in its *Report on Personal Injuries Periodic Payments and Structural Settlements* (LRC 54–1996) has proposed modifications to the "once-off" award approach. See Byrne and Binchy, *Annual Review of Irish Law 1996*.

156. The arguments for the fault system are that it reflects a deep-seated concept of justice ("he who is to blame should pay"), that it acts as a deterrent and that it educates the public as to what is socially acceptable behaviour. See generally Fleming, *An Introduction to the Law of Torts* (2nd ed, 1985), Ch 1.

plaintiff's hope of compensation is dependent on fault it is probably just as well in these circumstances that there may be other sources to which he can look more confidently. Although it is not the object of this book to outline the insurance and welfare aspects of a persons injuries, a brief description of their operation and relevance to tort liability cannot be avoided.

**[1.127]** A person who suffers injuries may benefit from private insurance coverage in two ways. First, he may have an insurance policy of his own for which he pays a regular premium and which covers him for such injuries. Such a policy is known as a personal accident or first party policy, and is normally taken out by the insured for accidental injuries which might happen to himself. The second party to such a policy is the insurance company. Second, the person who injures him may have a liability policy which covers the risk that he, the insured, will become liable in law to the injured person. The injured person in such circumstances will sue the insured and, in the event of liability being established, the insurance company will indemnify the insured for the amount of his liability.[157] Such a liability policy is sometimes referred to as a "third party policy", the third party being the injured person.[158] Under the Road Traffic Act 1961, s 56, owners of motor vehicles are obliged by law to carry such third party policies. Many cautious drivers, however, take out "comprehensive cover" which is in reality no more than a combined "liability" and "personal accident" policy in respect of car driving. Because third party insurance cover is compulsory in respect of car driving, the real contest in the legal sequel to a car crash, therefore, is between the plaintiff and the defendant's insurance company. More often than not, where two cars are involved and there is a dispute as to who was at fault the real contest is then between the two insurance companies carrying the cover. In such circumstances and to save administrative costs the insurance companies operate what is known as a "knock-for-knock" agreement. Under this arrangement the companies agree in advance that should an accident occur between persons having third party cover with the companies, then each company will compensate its own policy holder rather than engage in a legal dispute in which each company tries to establish that the other companys policy holder is liable. Under this arrangement a company may loose out in an individual case, but in the long run both companies stand to gain since both avoid legal expenses and both save on administrative costs.

**[1.128]** Although some large organisations may employ sufficiently large numbers which enable them to carry their own insurance (self-insurers), most organisations, and most individuals, transfer the risk together with an insurance premium to private insurance companies. State insurance, that is, where the State collects the premiums and pays out the losses, as a general approach to the problem is an option adopted in some countries (eg New Zealand[159]) but is not favoured in Ireland. Such an option involves a political/philosophical preference for a socialist approach to the problem which some western

157. Intentional torts generally cannot be insured against.

158. The first party is the insured; the second party is the insurance company.

159. See the Pearson Commission Report, para 219 *et seq* for description of New Zealand Comprehensive approach. See also Palmer, *Compensation for Incapacity* (1979); Palmer, (1977) 25 Am J Comp L 1; Dahl, (1976) 53 J Urban L 925; Harris, (1974) 37 MLR 361; Szakats, (1973) 8 UBC LR 1; Garkins, (1980) 18 OHLJ 238; Anderson, (1969) 1 Aukland ULR No 2, 1. See also Atiyah 'No Fault Compensation: A Question that Will Not Go Away' (1980) 54 Tul LR 271.

countries are reluctant to embrace. Particular state run insurance schemes, however, do exist in respect of particular kinds of risks and these must be noted.

**[1.129]** Generally speaking, under the Social Welfare (Consolidation) Act 1993, almost all employees over 16 years must be covered by pay-related social insurance regardless of their earnings. Contributions[160] are levied from employers and employees, and on the occurrence of certain events (including injuries at work or occupational diseases) the State makes payments to the affected employee. A variety of benefits[161] are available.[162] For our purposes the occupational injuries benefit is the most important. In many of the other cases there is normally no question of tort liability at all whereas in the case of occupational injuries the possibility of a tort action against the employer is strong.y[163] Such common law remedies the injured person may have are not abolished by the scheme of State insurance payments and are frequently preferred by injured persons since damages at common law are more generous than payments under the statutory scheme. Under the present system:

> benefits are payable under the occupational injuries insurance scheme to insured persons who are injured in the course of their employment or who contract prescribed occupational diseases. When an insured person dies as a result of such an injury or disease, provision is made, under the scheme, for the payment of benefits to the dependents of the deceased. The benefits payable under the scheme are: (1) injury benefit; (2) disablement benefit; (3) medical care; (4) death benefits.[164]

**[1.130]** The scheme is characterised by the facts that to recover the injured person need not prove fault and payments to the injured person are fixed and provide partial compensation only.

**[1.131]** No-fault compensation schemes for road injuries have found favour in some North American jurisdictions. The American systems have been usefully summarised in the Pearson Commission in the following language:

> "The two-tier systems operating in North America include no-fault first party insurance and third party liability insurance. The policy in respect of a motor vehicle provides first party insurance for the owner of the vehicle, any authorised driver of it, any passenger in it and any person struck by it (unless he is driven or a passenger in another vehicle and so covered by insurance in respect of that vehicle). If any person for whom such first party insurance is provided suffers an injury while travelling in or embarking in or disembarking from the

---

160. Employees are classified into different categories and contributions vary from category to category.

161. The schemes are administered by the Department of Social Welfare. For fuller description of these benefits see most recent edition of the Department's own publication entitled *Summary of Social Insurance and Social Assistance Services*. See generally Casey 'The Occupational Injuries Act: Some Reflections' (1969) 4 Ir Jur (ns) 234. See also the *Report of the Commission of Inquiry on Safety, Health and Welfare at Work*, paras 21.121.25 (PI 1868, 1983) (the *Barrington Report*).

162. Other welfare benefits are also available from the State but are not related to the State's insurance schemes and need not concern us here.

163. The Social Welfare (Occupational Injuries) Act 1966 replaced earlier Workman's Compensation legislation dating from the end of the last century. See Egner, (1980) 18 UW Ont LR 269. The provisions of the 1966 Act became part of the consolidating measure on social welfare enacted in 1981 and again in 1993.

164. *Summary of Social Insurance and Social Assistance Services*, fn 161 above, p 43.

vehicle or is struck by the vehicle, he has a direct claim under the policy against the insurer for pecuniary loss. If his claim is disputed, he has a right of action in his own name against the insurer. The same policy also provides third party insurance for the owner and any authorised driver of the vehicle against any liability which he may incur for injury caused by his negligence in the driving or control of the vehicle."[165]

**[1.132]** New Zealand has gone one step further and has introduced a comprehensive no-fault compensation scheme for *any* accidental injury however it is incurred. Where the scheme is applicable the right to sue in tort is abolished.[166] Pressures on the economic viability of the scheme led to a singificant retrenchment within the past decade.

**[1.133]** Before ending this chapter two other compensation schemes which exist in Ireland should also be mentioned.[167] Both codes were introduced to assist injured persons whose property was maliciously damaged on the one hand, or who suffered criminal injuries to their person on the other. In many of these cases tortious compensation for the injuries suffered was seen as a remote possibility either because the criminal was not likely to be apprehended or, if apprehended, the criminal did not represent "a good mark" for tortious proceedings.

**[1.134]** Compensation for malicious[168] injury to property could be claimed, since 1836,[169] from the ratepayers of the area where the injury occurred, and the instances where such recovery was permitted were extended by the Local Government (Ireland) Act 1898. Moreover, injuries to property caused by unlawful assemblies, riots, etc could also be the subject for compensation by virtue of the Malicious Injuries (Ireland) Act 1853.

165. *Pearson Report*, para 192. The common law tort action for motor vehicle accidents has not been abolished in states which have adopted these no-fault schemes, but indications are that this position may not last indefinitely, para 193. For an excellent survey of these and other schemes see WINFIELD & JOLOWICZ, Ch 1. See also O'Connell & Henderson, *Tort Law, No-fault and Beyond* (1975); Browne 'Deterrence and Accident Compensation Schemes' (1979) 17 UW Ont LR 111. For comprehensive survey of Irish position see Osborough, 'Regime of Protection for Road Victims' (1970) 5 Ir Jur (ns) 217. See also Clarke 'Absolute Liability in Motor Accident Cases: Loss insurance versus Common Law' (1967) 2 Ir Jur (ns) 78.

166. Accident Compensation Act 1974 substantially amended by the Accident Rehabilitation and Compensation Insurance Act 1992. See the New Zealand Law Commission's Report No 3, *The Accident Compensation Scheme Interim Report on Aspects of Funding* (NZLC R3, 1987) and its Report No 4, *Personal Injury: Prevention and Recovery: Report on the Accident Compensation Scheme* (NZLC R4, 1988). The *Barrington Report* fn, 87, paras 21.31-21.33, referred briefly to the advantages and drawbacks of a no-fault system for occupational injuries, although it made no recommendations on the matter.

167. See generally, Kennedy & McWilliam, *The Law on Compensation for Criminal Injuries in the Republic Of Ireland* (1978); Miers 'Compensation and Rights in Property' (1973) 24 NILQ 539; Kelly 'The Malicious Injuries Code and the Constitution' (1969) 4 Ir Jur (ns) 221. For Northern Ireland see, Greer & Mitchell, *Compensation for Criminal Injuries to Persons in Northern Ireland*; Greer 'Criminal Injuries Compensation for Nervous Shock: Freezing the Law in a Rigid Posture?' (1992) 43 NILQ 396.

168. "Malice in the legal sense and for the purpose of the Code means a wrongful act done intentionally without just cause or excuse, whether associated with ill-will or spite or not, or done recklessly without caring whether injury resulted or not." Kennedy & McWilliam, *The Law on Compensation for Criminal Injuries In The Republic Of Ireland* (1978), p 27, (footnotes omitted). The onus on the claimant is a heavy one.

169. Grand Jury (Ireland) Act 1836.

Compensation awarded under these Acts was levied on the ratepayers in the area where the injury occurred rather than from central funds, and the normal defendants in such proceedings were either the county council or the corporation within whose jurisdiction the injury occurred. The Malicious Injuries Act 1981 brought the law on this matter up to date but the whole scheme was greatly restricted by the Malicious Injuries (Amendment) Act 1986. The 1986 Act, in an effort to reduce public expenditure, introduced a new and more limited scheme under which compensation is paid from public funds for damage to property. Compensation is no longer paid for all damage caused "maliciously" but only for damage caused by riot or by persons acting on behalf of or in connection with unlawful or certain other organisations.[170]

**[1.135]** Compensation for *personal* injuries criminally inflicted was also possible under the 1836 legislation[171] but only to a very limited extent. A more comprehensive right to compensation for personal injuries (from central funds) was made available to the Garda Síochána (police) under the Garda Síochána (Compensation) Acts 1941 and 1945.[172] More generally, since 1974, *ex gratia* payments to any person injured by a crime of violence can be made by virtue of a scheme laid before the Oireachtas (Parliament) in that year. The increase in undetected political acts of violence in the early 1970s seems to have been the immediate spur to the introduction of this scheme.

**[1.136]** Since April 1986, however, the award of general damages has been severely restricted under the scheme,[173] and since such awards do not now compensate for pain and suffering, they are perceived as being inadequate. In recognition of the victim's rights, the National Crime Forum was impressed by suggestions that payments for pain and suffering

---

170. See the Annotation to the 1986 Act by Professor Greer, *ICLSA Irish Current Law Statutes Annotated 1986*, No 27. The position in Northern Ireland is analysed in Greer's *Compensation for Criminal Injury in Northern Ireland* (1990); the position in britain, following the coming into force of the Criminal Injuries Compensation Scheme in 1990, analysed by Greer in *Criminal Injuries Compensation* (1991)..

171. See Greer 'Criminal Injuries Compensation for Nervous Shock: Freezing the Law in a Rigid Posture?' (1992) 43 NILQ 396.

172. See Walsh, *The Irish Police* (1998), paras 2-36-2-39; *O'Looney v Minister for the Public Service* [1986] IR 543 (SC); *McLoughlin v Minister for the Public Service* [1986] ILRM 28 (SC).

173. For details of this scheme see Kennedy & McWilliam, *The Law on Compensation for Criminal Injuries In The Republic Of Ireland* (1978), Appendix M, p 69 *et seq*. The scheme is administered by the Criminal Injury Compensation Tribunal the members of which are appointed by the Minister for Justice. From the annual reports of the tribunal it can be seen that substantial claims were being awarded by the Tribunal until 1986. See the detailed analysis by Osborough, (1978) 13 Ir Jur (ns) 320. In *AG v Ireland* [1994] 1 IR 369, analysed by Byrne & Binchy, *Annual Review of Irish Law 1992*, pp 137-139, Carroll J held that the changes brought about in 1986 to the scheme did not conflict with the right to bodily integrity under Article 40.3 of the Constitution. For comparative studies of compensation systems in other countries, see Edelhertz & Geiss, *Public Compensation to Victims of Crime* (1974) Chs 9-10; Childers 'Compensation for Criminally Inflicted Personal Injury' (1965) 50 Minn LR 271; 'Symposium: Governmental Compensation for Victims of Violence' (1970) 43 S Calif LR 1, including articles on Australia (by Chappell, p 69), California (by Shank, p 85) and New Zealand (by Weeks, p 107); Cheeseman 'Victim Compensation: Law and Economic Analysis' (1981) 4 Hamline LR 451; Murphy 'Comment: Compensation for Victims of Crime: Trends and Outlooks' (1984) 8 Dalhousie LR 530. A historical analysis is made by Wolfgang 'Victims Compensation in Crimes of Personal Violence' (1965) 50 Minn LR 223.

should be re-introduced and estimated that the costs of such a change would be at least £40 million a year as opposed to the present cost of £3.5 million.[174]

**[1.137]** In connection with criminal acts it should further be noted that since the Criminal Justice Act 1993, the court hearing the criminal case can also make compensation orders, requiring the criminal to pay compensation for personal injury or loss caused by him. The advantage for the victim who seeks such an order, of course, is that he does not have to go through the trauma of a second court case to get compensation. Such orders may cover pain and suffering and they are available not only to the primary victims, but also to the victims' family in respect of a fatal injuries action ("wrongful death") under Part IV of the Civil Liability Act 1961, where the primary victim has died as a result of his injuries. Such orders are only available, however, when the perpetrator is apprehended, charged and convicted, and is of little value where the criminal has no means or, because of a prison sentence, is in no position to make any reparation payments. On a more practical level this option may be less attractive to victims or their families when it is appreciated that if the sentencing judge agrees to make such a compensation order he is entitled to take this into account in sentencing the perpetrator. The likelihood that such an order will result in a reduced sentence may make the victim reluctant to seek the order in the criminal context preferring to exercise his civil remedies at a later date in the civil courts. This may be the reason for the poor take-up by victims of this option. [175]

## VII. The Insurance Factor and the Problem of the Uninsured Driver

**[1.138]** Loss handling in the tort system is, in the first instance, based on the idea of shifting loss from the injured party to the party liable, or at fault, for that injury. It remains the case, however, that while the right to seek compensation exists under the system, it may be of little benefit to a party who has the misfortune to be injured by an impecunious defendant. Even when the defendant is not totally impecunious, however, it remains the case that few individuals possess sufficient private funds to compensate persons to whom they cause serious injury.

**[1.139]** The tort system has as a result become reliant on liability insurance to support it and to ensure that funds are available out of which compensation awarded by the courts can be paid. Indeed, it has been suggested that without the support of liability insurance the tort system would long since have collapsed.[176]

**[1.140]** Within the general tort system motor accident compensation produces particular difficulties. The number of persons exposed to liability is great and most motorists could not meet the cost of damage caused by them. Furthermore, the imposition of such costs on the average motorist could be ruinous to him and might not be in the social interest.

---

174. See National Crime Forum, Report, 1998. By the Public Institute of Public Administration Dublin.

175. There are no procedural rules drafted in respect of the victims application for such compensatory order.

176. See also more generally for the position in the USA see Priest 'The Current Insurance Crisis and Modern Tort Law' (1988) 96 Yale LJ 1521; McMahon 'Tort Reform in USA and Lessons for Ireland' (1968) 82 Incorp L Soc of Ireland Gaz 33.

**[1.141]** To solve this problem compulsory insurance against liability for motor accidents was first introduced in Ireland in 1933[177] and the present legislative rule[178] provides that every motorist must insure without limit against liability for personal injury incurred by him. There is also an obligation to insure against liability for property damage up to £90,000[179] since 1 January 1996.

**[1.142]** The Irish motorist is thus required to take out third-party insurance, that is insurance cover against claims by third parties (which includes passengers in the vehicles) in respect of the careless management of his motor vehicle. The driver himself is not covered, however, and he is not required under legislation to insure himself against any injuries he may sustain. He may, if he wishes, take out first party insurance to cover himself but this is not obligatory.[180]

**[1.143]** Despite its merits, however, first party insurance remains relatively uncommon. The prime reason for this is that a large number of motorists view insurance simply as a prerequisite to driving (similar to having the vehicle correctly taxed), and therefore try to keep their liability insurance premium to a minimum. The legal minimum, especially in recessionary periods, has a tendency to become the maximum and motorists tend to avoid supplementary insurance save for the type of cover which indemnifies against damage to the vehicle itself (such as "Fire and Theft" policies).

## The Operation of Insurance

**[1.144]** The State has a fundamental interest in the efficient operation of insurance in the country as it provides the basic support to the whole motor compensation system as it stands. The insurance industry is regulated by the Minister for Enterprise, Trade and Employment. Each insurer must be licensed and is subject to rigorous examination at the outset to ensure its expertise, and once licensed it is subject to continuous scrutiny to ensure its solvency. The efficacy of "the watchdog system" must now be in doubt, however, as the well documented difficulties of both ICI and PMPA occurred while subject to government scrutiny. Insurance premiums are subject to price control under the Prices Acts and here the Minister tries to strike a balance between low premiums for the benefit of the individual motorist and commercially viable premiums in the interest of the insurer.

**[1.145]** The State further intervenes to compel the insurance industry to fill the gaps in the compensation system. This is done primarily through two organisations to which each insurer has to be affiliated:

(i) The Declined Cases Committee: If a motorist is refused motor insurance cover by five or more insurers, he may apply to this committee which will compel one of its members to provide a quotation for the motorist. Without this facility, a bad risk driver might not be able to drive legally in the State. Similar

177. Road Traffic Act 1933.

178. The Road Traffic Act 1961, s 56(1). A challenge to regulations issued under this section failed in *Greaney v Scully* [1981 1 ILRM 340. (SC).

179. See SI 353/1995 implementing EEC Council Directives 72/166/EEC, 84/5/EEC and 90/232/EEC.

180. *Committee of Enquiry into the Insurance Industry Interim Report on Motor Insurance 1972* (prl 2843) (the *O'Connor Report*) at paragraph 8.2.1(x) recommended that the value of first party insurance be brought home to motorists and that it be included as an optional extra in all motor insurance policies.

provision is made in most other jurisdictions with compulsory insurance requirements. The Committee may, in exceptional cases, refuse to compel a member to provide cover.

(ii) The Motor Insurers Bureau of Ireland: Since the coming into force of the Road Traffic Act 1933, which required compulsory insurance in respect of the driving of motor vehicles, there was public concern for innocent third parties who received personal injuries as a result of being struck by a motor vehicle for which there was no valid insurance at the time of the accident. To fill this gap in the compensation scheme the Minister for Local Government entered into a voluntary agreement with the insurance industry. This became effective in 1955 and was amended in 1962 and again in 1964 to accommodate problems relating to passengers in uninsured vehicles. Changes necessitated by the EEC caused a new agreement to come into effect as and from 1 January 1988.[181]

**[1.146]** The effect of the principal agreement signed in 1955 is to provide for the establishment of the Motor Insurers Bureau of Ireland which undertakes to pay the amount of an unsatisfied judgment against a motorist who is not effectively insured in so far as such judgment relates to personal injury coming within the scope of the Road Traffic Act. Section 78 of that Act provides that all insurers licensed in the motor insurance field in this country must belong to the MIBI. These insurers then fund the Bureau in proportion to their individual share of the motor insurance market. Ultimately the cost of doing so is passed on to the consumer by way of higher insurance premiums. Thus, an increasing incidence of uninsured motor accidents has the direct effect of increasing the premiums of those drivers who are insured.

**[1.147]** The old agreement relates solely to compensation for personal injuries and thus claims for damage to property are not entertained. The Second EEC Motor Insurance Directive (84/5/EEC), Article 1(4), however, provides that innocent victims of uninsured drivers or drivers of stolen cars should be able to claim for property damage as well as for personal injuries. As a result the 1988 agreement provides that the MIBI will compensate for such damage but only as and from 31 December 1992.

**[1.148]** Furthermore, only personal injuries to third parties contemplated in the insurance requirements of the provisions of the Road Traffic Act are covered in the scheme. Accordingly, since there is no obligation under the Road Traffic Act to insure against liability to passengers in vehicles, not generally designed or constructed to carry passengers (eg agricultural tractors/trailers) or to passengers in the rear of goods vehicles, neither of these can claim as beneficiaries from the Motor Insurance Bureau. Another limitation in the scheme occurs where a passenger is being driven in a car which at the time of the accident, he knows or ought reasonably know, is being used without the owners consent.[182] In addition, the new scheme does not apply where the person injured either

181. Agreement signed on 21 December 1988 between Minister for the Environment and MIBI. See generally Buckley, *Insurance Law in Ireland* (1997), p 242. It is understood that this agreement is being revised at the moment and an amended Agreement will issue in the near future. See para **[1.102]** above.

182. The onus is on the defence in such a case to prove that the claimant knew or should reasonably have known that the car was uninsured. Moreover, the question as to the claimant's knowledge is to be determined objectively. See *Kinsella v MIBI* Supreme Court 2 April 1993; *Curran v Gallagher and MIBI* Supreme Court, 17 May 1997.

stole the car or was in collusion with the parties who did. Neither does it apply where both parties in a collision are uninsured.

**[1.149]** As the liability of the Bureau before 1 January 1989 was to pay unsatisfied judgments only, a person sustaining injuries from an untraced motorist in a hit and run type accident could not up to that date apply for compensation in the usual manner. Once more, however, under the old agreement the Bureau in such circumstances made ex *gratia* payments on two conditions:

(i) The injured party must have suffered serious and permanent disablement or died as a result of the injuries.

(ii) The liability of the driver would not have been in doubt if traced.

**[1.150]** The Second EEC Directive on Motor Insurance (84/5/EE) affected this area also, and in order to comply with the standards of the Directive as implemented in the new agreement the MIBI now covers all personal injuries incurred in hit and run accidents from 31 December 1988. The victim of the "hit and run" driver is now entitled to compensation as of right and not on an *ex gratia* basis from 1 January 1989.

**[1.151]** Attention should be drawn to Clause 7(2) of the 1988 Agreement which provides: "The Liability of the MIBI for damage to property shall not extend to damage caused by a vehicle the owner or user of which remains unidentified or untraced". This clause attempted to transpose into Irish law Article 1.4, para 4, of EC Directive 30/12/1983 (84/5/EEC) but did so incorrectly. The relevant provision of the Directive reads as follows: "Member States may limit or exclude the payment of compensation by that body [the MIBI] in the event of damage to property by an unidentified vehicle". An examination of Clause 7(2) shows that the MIBI's exclusion is not justified by the directive in so far as it attempts to exclude payment when the owner, etc, is untraced even though the vehicle is located, and in doing so, the exclusion is contrary to EU obligations. If the vehicle which caused the property damage is traced, then the directive obliges the MIBI to pay for such damage, even if the owner or user remains untraced.[183]

**[1.152]** Under the old agreement, the uninsured driver was usually asked to sign a mandate authorising the Bureau to deal with the claim and effect a settlement on his behalf. The mandate also incorporated an indemnity to reimburse the Bureau for damages paid. If the driver failed to sign, the Bureau simply paid off the unsatisfied judgment and then proceeded in any event against the uninsured driver on indemnity principles. As an incentive to sign, if he completed the mandate the Bureau offered to pay the costs of the uninsured person's defence and did not subsequently seek repayment of these. Now, under the new agreement, a victim of an accident involving uninsured motor vehicles will be able to apply directly to the MIBI for compensation. He will not have to secure first a judgment against the uninsured driver, as a precondition to compensation. Moreover, he will have a right of redress to the Courts if he is refused compensation by the MIBI or if he is not satisfied with the amount of compensation offered by the MIBI.

---

183. This view was adopted by McMahon J in *Dublin Bus v MIBI* Circuit Court, 29 October 1999. See para **[1.102]** above for note of this case.

### Uninsured Drivers

**[1.153]** It is estimated that somewhere between 15 to 20% of all Irish motorists drive without insurance, and this causes a serious problem for the whole system. For example, the Motor Insurers Bureau of Ireland has to pay very large amounts of compensation each year to the victims of these insurance dodgers. This has the knock-on effect of further increasing the insurance premiums of insured drivers. This in turn causes a greater incidence of evasion.[184]

**[1.154]** The problem of the uninsured driver has been of concern to both politicians and insurance companies in recent years. Attempts to improve the situation have focused on three courses of action:

(i) Improved and more enthusiastic enforcement of remedies

(ii) Increased advertising to heighten social awareness;

(iii) Greater attempts to reduce insurance premiums.

These measures would appear, however, to have had limited affect in reducing the overall numbers of uninsured drivers.

## VIII. Features of the Litigation Scene in Ireland

**[1.155]** The experience of accident victims seeking compensation in the tort system has been likened to that of runners in an uncertain and ever changing obstacle race:

> "The victims, without their consent, are placed at the starting line, and told that if they complete the whole course, the umpire at the finishing line will compel the race-promoters to give them a prize; the amount of the prize, however, must remain uncertain until the last moment because the umpire has discretion to fix it individually for each finisher. None of the runners is told the distance he must cover to complete the course, nor the time it is likely to take. Some of the obstacles in the race are fixed hurdles (rules of law), while others can, without warning, be thrown into the path of a runner by the race-promoters, who obviously have every incentive to restrict the number of runners who can complete the course. As the runners physical fitness, and their physchological preparedness for the race, varies greatly, the relative difficulty of the obstacles also varies from runner to runner. In view of all the uncertainties, and particularly the difficulties which could be presented by the unknown future obstacles many runners drop out of the race at each obstacle; others press on, but are progressively weakened by their exertions. At any stage of the race, the promoters alongside the racetrack are permitted to induce a runner to retire from the race in return for an immediate payment, which they fix at a figure less than the prize which they expect to be awarded by the umpire upon completion of the course. After waiting to see how many runners drop out at the early obstacles without any inducement, the promoters begin to tempt the remaining runners with offers of money to retire; the amounts of the offers tend to increase the longer the runner stays in the race. In view of the uncertainties about the remaining obstacles, their ability to finish the course, and the time it might take, most

184. The *McLiam Report* studied the problem of uninsured driving in fourteen other European countries and found that Ireland has probably one of the worst rates of uninsured driving among them. There is no evidence to suggest that the problem has diminished in the years since the report was published and indeed the likelihood is that it has increased because of the recession. A Garda Survey in 1987 indicated that 68% of vehicles were not properly insured. Since a properly insured vehicle may be driven without consent one would expect the figure for uninsured motorists to be considerably higher.

runners accept an offer and retire. The few hardy ones who actually finish may still be disappointed with the prize-money."[185]

**[1.156]** Plaintiffs rarely have more than one major negligence action in a lifetime. Insurance companies fight thousands of such cases every year. It is their business. As such it may be said that plaintiffs are risk-averse. Insurance companies are not. The odds favour the insurer. It does not matter whether a particular case costs more to settle than the insurance company would actually have expected, as long as the insurance company gets its annual sums right on balance. As long as premium income exceeds liability payments and running expenses then the insurers make a profit. Variations in individual transactions have little significance for insurance companies.

**[1.157]** The injured person, on the other hand, is only concerned with the outcome of his or her particular case. If his injuries are sufficiently serious, then the forensic lottery becomes a particularly hazardous game. He or she must obtain as much money in compensation as possible, so that he or she will have a reasonable income to sustain him or her during the period of continuing disability. To avoid the risk of losing his or her case the injured person may have to settle for less than the injury is worth.

**[1.158]** Insurance companies have vast expertise and experience at their disposal when it comes to handling claims. Injured persons generally have little experience of the legal process. They select their solicitor frequently for reasons other than for his or her litigating or negotiating expertise. Insurance companies know the strengths and weaknesses of the small group of counsel who specialise in the motor accident field. They know whom to settle with or whom to fight with in court. Plaintiffs, for the most part, select their solicitor because of a personal and continuing relationship. Frequently, they do not know which lawyers specialise in the area. Moreover, they have no way of gauging the advice their lawyers give them.

**[1.159]** The plaintiff generally has a pressing need for money. He or she has bills to pay now and the prospect of a large sum of money after he or she eventually gets to court may be of little help in settling accounts owed today. The insurance company can afford to hold off. Interest on awards, if payable at all, runs only from the judgment and not from the date of the accident. Although insurance companies may try to effect an early settlement to save administrative and legal costs, there is no interest penalty to encourage them to do so.

**[1.160]** Related to the "fault system" there are other pressures on the plaintiff to settle. The plaintiff must prove (i) that the defendant was negligent, and (ii) that the defendants conduct caused the plaintiff's injury. Moreover, the plaintiff may have his award reduced because (iii) he contributed to his own injury. All of these problems may involve substantial evidentiary difficulties for the plaintiff thereby inducing reasonable fears and apprehensions.

**[1.161]** Further problems can arise in relation to the damages awarded the plaintiff at the end of the day. The plaintiff may have (iv) difficulty in proving the full extent of his or her injuries. Conflict between medical experts may confuse the issue. Moreover, (v) uncertainties in medical prognoses may mean that the full extent of the injuries cannot be fully appreciated until years after the accident and the trial. The lump sum, once and for all

185. Harris, *et al*, *Compensation and Support for Illness and Injury* (1984), pp 132-133.

system of compensation obliges a single assessment and prevents periodic revision. The injured party must risk all on one throw. Again, (vi) it is difficult to calculate, in the bargaining process, the value to be placed on subjective damages for such things as pain and suffering. Also, (vii) uncertainty may exist as to whether the law will allow recovery for certain kinds of injury (eg nervous shock) and, if so, how damages are to be calculated in these cases. Finally, (viii) there may be the pressures associated with immediate financial need (groceries, school-bills, medical bills, etc.) and the apprehension with regard to ultimate legal bills in the event of losing the case. There is also the undoubted psychological strain associated with a prolonged unresolved dispute of great personal concern.[186] In the light of these forces many plaintiffs may be tempted to "get shut" of the case for a greatly discounted sum.

**[1.162]** Many of the shortcomings associated with personal injury litigation in Ireland were formerly attributed to the jury form of trial and a move to abolish the jury trial, spearheaded by the insurance industry, got under way some years ago.

**[1.163]** The principal arguments that could be levelled against the jury form of trial were that: juries were inconsistent and unpredictable; the jury trial was slower and more expensive; juries were too generous in their awards; the jury system was inconvenient and involved a heavy time commitment from the jurors and was wasteful; the jury award could not be reviewed; and the assessment of damages had become too sophisticated in recent years for lay juries. Against this it was argued that: the jury form of trial was a traditional institution of proven value; the jury system involved the citizen in the administration of justice; juries were more likely to give more realistic awards than a judge sitting alone; there was a relative finality in jury awards; and if the legal system shows Constitutional confidence in juries for serious criminal cases why should it lose faith in it for civil cases?[187]

**[1.164]** In the event the debate on the jury issue was settled by the Courts Act 1988 which as and from 1 August 1988 abolished the right to a jury in High Court proceedings in respect of personal injuries or wrongful death actions (ie fatal injuries actions under s 48 of the Civil Liability Act 1961). The right to a jury trial in lower courts for such injuries had been previously abolished by s 6 of the Courts Act 1971. The right to a jury still remains, however, in High Court actions for false imprisonment, intentional trespass to the person and defamation.[188]

**[1.165]** Moreover, curious as it may seem, it would appear that the right to a jury trial still exists in respect of negligently or intentionally inflicted damage to property alone in excess of Circuit Court jurisdiction. If, therefore, the defendant through his negligence destroys my BMW motor car, which is valued at £35,000, while inflicting no personal injuries, then I am still entitled to a jury trial in such an action.

186. Tharsh & Roystan 'A Follow-up Study of Accident Neurosis' (1985) 146 Br J of Psychiat 18.
187. The merits of these arguments were fully examined in McMahon 'Judge or Jury? Trial for Personal Injury Cases in Ireland' (1985) Cork University Press.
188. See further Byrne & Binchy, *Annual Review of Irish Law 1988.*

## IX. Recent Studies and Proposals for Reform

**[1.166]** In recent decades the high cost of insurance for businesses in Ireland has been the subject of much debate. The insurance industry blamed the high level of court awards and the high frequency of claims for the high premiums.

**[1.167]** It also targeted the jury trial as a factor which contributed to the high awards. When the abolition of the jury trial for personal injury claims failed to yield the reduction in awards as anticipated by the insurance industry, further proposals were advanced to introduce legislation to provide for a maximum level of judicial awards ("a cap") for general damages in personal injuries cases. The basic argument for such a "capping" measure was that insurance costs were making Irish businesses uncompetitive in the international market and in particular uncompetitive vis-à-vis businesses in the UK.[189] In 1995 the Minister for Commerce, Science and Technology commissioned a firm of management consultants, Deloitte and Touche, to report on the economic evaluation of insurance costs and its report was published in 1996.

**[1.168]** Some of the reports findings relate to the litigation process and are worth considering.

1. The average estimated claims costs for Employer's Liability and for Public Liability, during the period 1986 to 1994 rose by 50% and 100% approximately;
2. There was a rise also in the average cost of combined liability claims (which include motor claims) during the same period and this was due to (i) increases in medical costs; (ii) the relationship between special damages and general damages (ie as special damages increase so too do general damages and overall costs, and where special damages are low, lower courts tend to over-compensate in their awards for general damages);[190] (iii) the high level of legal costs, which tend to increase the longer the claims remain outstanding [191]
3. Insurance premiums for combined liability cover for Employer's Liability and Public Liability, were three times more expensive in Ireland than in UK[192] (Irish motor premiums are probably as expensive in a similar ratio).
4. Personal Injury settlement costs in Ireland in 1994 amounted to £410m of which Motor Claims accounted for 74%, Employers Liability for 14% and Public Liability for 12%. In the area of personal injuries, therefore, it should be constantly borne in mind that 88% of all such claims relate to Employer's Liability and Motor Accidents. It is probable that the dominance of these

---

189. Studies have shown that in Employer Liability and Public Liability, Irish premium quotations can be up to three times similar quotations in UK. See *Deloitte & Touche report* published by Department of Enterprise and Employment, October 1996, Appendix 1 – Table 1, hereinafter referred to as Deloitte & Touche report. For analysis of the Deloitte Touche Report, see O'Regan Cazabon 'Cutting Insurance Costs in Ireland' 1 Ir Ins LR 8.

190. *Deloitte & Touche report*, p 7.

191. *Deloitte & Touche report*, p 5.

192. *Deloitte & Touche report*, p 6.

claims in the insurance books is also reflected in the kinds of cases heard by the courts.

**[1.169]** With regard to the level of awards the report examined a sample of High Court cases and found, contrary to the general perception that the majority of High Court awards of general damages, in the most serious cases, "clustered around an average level of approximately twice the level of average industrial earnings" and very high awards (in excess of IR£60,000) were exceptional.[193]

**[1.170]** The sample survey found that in the cases which related to leg, back and neck injuries, the bulk of the awards clustered around £10K to £35K in the case of leg and back injuries, and around £20K to £26K in the case of neck injuries. Higher awards tended to be exceptional and the results suggest, again contrary to preconceptions, a strong element of consistency among the High Court judiciary. Moreover, the survey found that 85% of the Irish awards fell within the UK 'Guidelines for the Assessment of Damages for Personal Injuries'.[194] It is suspected that, at the lower level, Irish Courts are more generous than their UK counterparts and one claims manager with experience in both jurisdictions indicated to the consultants that a whiplash in the UK costs about £3,000 compared to £8,000 to £12,000 in Ireland. This would accord with the authors' experience also. Given the frequency of, and the increased legal costs associated with these claims, these smaller claims may account in part for the higher costs of insurance in Ireland.

**[1.171]** Because of these reassuring findings the Deloitte & Touche report does not recommend the introduction of any measure which would place a ceiling or "cap" on damages. According to the report there would be no guarantee that the introduction of any such capping regime would result in the reduction of insurance premiums. In any event, the introduction of any such capping legislation would be likely to face a constitutional challenge in Ireland. The enthusiasm for such a measure has waned further as policy makers come to appreciate that the introduction of such capping measures in the US was partly influenced by the spiralling punitive damage awards there (a factor that does not operate in Ireland) and by the unusual features of medical malpractice suits peculiar to that country. Finally, it should also be noted that a judicial "cap" of £150,000 on general damages was introduced by the Supreme Court in *Sinnott v Quinnsworth, CIE and Durrings*[195] and this has been recently raised by Morris P to £250,000.[196]

**[1.172]** Although it was not specifically adverted to in the Deloitte and Touche report, it is also probable that there has been an increase in the amount of claims being made in Ireland in recent years. All legal practitioners will testify to the increase in litigation in relation to professional malpractice; doctors, accountants and lawyers are targeted with increasing frequency nowadays. Employers are almost unanimous in voicing their view that there is an increase in claims. Public authorities also are continuously complaining of the

193. *Deloitte & Touche report*, p 7.

194. The report is justifiably cautious on these comparisons because of the differences in the sources of information and the impossibility of finding identical factual situations to compare in both jurisdictions. Accordingly, the reports suggests the results must only be viewed "indicatively" (*Deloitte & Touche report*, p 5-6).

195. [1984] ILRM 523.

196. *Kealy v The Minister for Health*, High Court, unrep,19 April 1999.

increasing cost of claims that are forcing them to reconsider the provision of playgrounds and other recreational facilities, which are the source of many accidents. These laments are frequently accompanied by allegations of fraudulent and exaggerated claims and suggestions that the legal profession is encouraging what has become known as "the compo culture". This last accusation has been asserted in recent years, because with the change of rule which now allows solicitors to advertise, there is a suggestion that an element of "ambulance chasing" has crept into legal practice. Further, since solicitors are also allowed now to advertise the "no foal, no fee" charging practice, it is suggested that this too has fuelled litigation fires. The worst aspect of these practices has been addressed by the Law Society of Ireland which controls the solicitors profession and which it should be noted was, from the outset, against the move which allowed solicitors to advertise, but which had the advertising culture thrust upon it on the grounds that the alternative restrictions would be anti-competitive. Accordingly, solicitors who advertise the "no foal, no fee" approach, must now also draw to the attention of their clients the rule which may oblige a losing plaintiff to pay the defendant's legal costs if he loses his action.

**[1.173]** The Deloitte and Touche report recommends as a solution to the high costs in personal injury litigation (i) that the Irish judiciary should draw up a guideline for general damages to ensure consistency and to eliminate overgenerous awards and (ii) that a Personal Injuries Tribunal should be established.

**[1.174]** A subsequent working group was set up in December 1996 to further examine the nature such a Personal Injury Tribunal might take and its first report was published in May 1997. Its examination was confined to personal injuries sustained at work. Two of the three members favoured a Tribunal within the Courts structure, whereas the other member preferred a "Greenfield" option that would operate outside the courts structure. Both suggestions, however, have a good deal in common in that both would recommend the availability of a mediation process to encourage willing litigants to participate on a voluntary basis in a non-adversarial procedure in an initial effort to settle the employee's claim. If such a process failed the parties would then be free to take the alternative routes to arbitration or litigation through the courts. It is proposed that the Tribunal would only entertain cases up to a value of £50,000 in which there is no substantial dispute on liability between the parties. It is also recommended that there be a 12 months limitation period for cases going before the Tribunal. While it is proposed that the parties be entitled to legal representation it should be an important characteristic of the mediation process that the employer and the employee should be able to participate fully in the process. An enforcement process should be available to ensure that the mediators or the arbitrators awards are implemented effectively.

**[1.175]** No action has been taken on this proposal to date, and it would seem unlikely to be adopted in the near future.[197] First, there is a clear danger that such a facility would be used as a "first step or dual claim facility"[198] thereby adding to the costs and delays associated

197. "The proposal is confined to occupational injuries and would require further study if it were extended to road traffic accidents, where liability is frequently at issue". For consideration of the first report, see O'Regan Cazabon 'First Report of the Special Working Group on Personal Injuries Tribuanl' (1997) 1 Ir Ins LR 19; (1998) 2 Ir Ins LR 22.

198. Page 28 of 1997 Report.

with claims settlements. Secondly, the vested interests within the legal process itself have clearly signalled their reservations. At p 12 of the Report of the Special Working Group these reservations are recorded and would appear to sound the death knell for the proposal:

> *Law Society*
>
> Issues of liability were the prerogative of the Courts to determine. In serious injury cases it would be difficult to separate assessment of liability from assessment of the extent of the injury;
>
> The role of a tribunal could only be as a mediation process where both parties submitted to arbitration by agreement. In such cases, mediation could be used to reduce the burden on the judiciary;
>
> In the case of serious injury, medical prognosis may take considerable time and, in such case, the processing of the claim would have been progressed to an advanced stage before the tribunal would come into play;
>
> *Bar Council views*
>
> While there was no legal objection to assessment of compensation by a tribunal, with the consent of the parties, a Greenfield tribunal would be likely to cut across the proposals of the Working Group on a Courts Commission (the Denham Reports) for reforming the Courts system;
>
> A personal injuries tribunal could only be a step in the legal process;
>
> Barristers already engage in mediation as a matter of course. The Bar Council could make people available as mediators/commissioners, if required.
>
> *Mrs Justice Denham*
>
> The concept of a tribunal as envisaged in the Deloitte & Touche report had been overtaken to a large extent by the reform of the courts and further radical reforms had been proposed for the courts by the Working Group on a Courts Commission;
>
> Personal injury cases were being heard more quickly in the courts and the concept of case conferencing or mediation, if utilised by the parties, would help to remove the adversarial element of personal injury assessments;
>
> The structures already exist within the courts for mediation of personal injury claims.

## County Registrars

**[1.176]** Following the establishment of the Working Group, representatives of the Association of County Registrars had approached the Minister for Commerce, Science and Technology and submitted that their enhanced powers under the Court and Court Officers Act 1995 enabled them to undertake, inter alia, assessments of personal injury compensation, with the consent of the parties or under the direction of the Courts. In effect, therefore, they were now in a position to undertake the type of assessment envisaged for a personal injuries tribunal.

**[1.177]** In relation to the administration and the management of the courts a great deal has been done recently by the Denham Working Group on a Courts Commission. Established in October 1995, it published six reports and two working papers by November 1998. As well as focusing on problems within the court's system, the working group proposed that there should be established an independent and permanent body to manage a unified court system, to be known as the Courts Service. This was accepted and passed into law by the Courts Service Act 1998. Functions relating to the courts previously performed by the

Department of Justice, were transferred to the Courts Service. In addition the working group focused attention not only on institutional reform but also on the concept of judicial case management which involves active oversight by the court on the progress of court proceedings. This represents a fundamental change of approach and signals a significant transfer of the responsibility for the management of civil litigation from the litigants and their legal advisers to the courts and will, hopefully, reduce delays. This is a continuing process which will undoubtedly improve the administration of justice in the area of civil litigation, and the concept of case conferencing or mediation, if availed of by the parties, would, additionally minimise the adversarial element of personal injuries assessments.

**[1.178]** Delays in civil litigation are now at an acceptable level. The most recent statistics show that the backlog in the Supreme Court has decreased in a period of two years from 219 cases to 43. By July, 1998, in the High Court the number of cases being disposed of exceeded the number of cases being set down for hearing, while in the Circuit Court by December 1997, the maximum delay in all but one Circuit was six months.[199] This indicates a notable improvement in efforts to reduce delays in recent years, with the consequent reduction in the costs of litigation.

**[1.179]** These changes, and the general emphasis, within the Courts Service, on modern management techniques, partnership and team-work based on a new management ethos, should continue to improve the quality of service provided to the public in the future in the area of civil litigation.

**[1.180]** Because delays in hearing cases have now been reduced to acceptable levels, and because the Deloitte and Touche report itself found that there was a lot of clustering in the awards given by the High Court judges in Ireland (which suggests consistency), the rationale advanced by the management consultants for the establishment of a Tribunal in Employer Liability cases is greatly weakened. In the teeth of opposition from practising lawyers and from Mrs Justice Denham's Working Group, it is unlikely to find the necessary support for its adoption.

## Tribunals

**[1.181]** There have been instances in recent decades where the State has felt that the tort system may not have offered an appropriate mechanism for handling the losses in question and where it has sought to manage the losses by establishing Tribunals. The first arose out of a fire in a discotheque on St Valentine's night 1981: forty eight young people died and many were severely burned in the tragedy. There was huge public shock and sympathy for the victims and their families, and the government interpreted public sympathy as authorising it to take action to alleviate the situation. It decided that the victims should not have to suffer additionally, the uncertainties and delays of the tort system and that compensation should be paid, irrespective of the victims ability to prove fault and this was to be done by establishing a tribunal to administer the compensation scheme. Compensation awarded under the scheme was to be comparable to that available in the civil courts, but no exemplary or punitive damages were allowed. The Tribunal was composed of three members and the Chairman was a judge. Procedures were informal and

---

199. In the Cork Circuit the delay was 9 months. (See Working Group on A Courts Commission, 6th report, Nov 1998, p 116).

the rules of evidence were relaxed. The applicants were not obliged to accept the Tribunal's award but could opt for a hearing in the civil courts where ordinary liability rules would apply. In the event 953 applications were dealt with and a total of £10.5 million was paid out to 823 applicants. The vast majority (759) of these awards were below £30,000.[200]

**[1.182]** The same Tribunal technique, as an alternative to the regular civil courts dealing with the problem, was favoured in 1995 when nearly 1,600 people became infected with Hepatitis C from blood products (principally Human Immunoglobulin – Anti D) or from a transfusion of blood, supplied by the Blood Transfusion Service Board (BTSB). The BTSB was a state-sponsored body for which the State was responsible. Subsequent reports clearly suggested negligence on the part of the BTSB and some of its employees. The Government, once more, decided to address the apparently legitimate complaints of those infected by establishing a Tribunal to, in effect, assess damages. Initially, the Tribunal was non-statutory, but in the wake of a celebrated civil action taken by one Mrs McCole, the Tribunal was given a statutory basis.[201] Mrs McCole had commenced her proceedings in the High Court and because of the seriousness of her illness, had sought to have her case brought forward for early hearing. Shortly before the trial was due to commence the plaintiff settled on satisfactory terms. In the ensuing publicity, in which the litigation strategy adopted by the State was widely criticised, the Government decided to set up a Tribunal of Inquiry into the Blood Transfusion Board under the chairmanship of the former Chief Justice Finlay and when the Finlay Report was published the Government felt obliged because of the adverse findings to put the Compensation Tribunal on a statutory basis.

**[1.183]** In the Hepatitis C Tribunal (like the Stardust Tribunal) the claimants for compensation did not have to prove fault, the proceedings were informal to a large extent and, the proceedings were in private. Damages were to be awarded on the same basis as that which prevailed in an ordinary tort action before the High Court but awards could, in the blood cases, include sums for aggravated or exemplary damages. Interestingly, the Hepatitis Tribunal may also make a provisional award that may be increased at a later date in appropriate circumstances.

**[1.184]** Claimants had a choice of rejecting or accepting the Tribunal's award. If they accepted the Tribunal's award they could not proceed in the civil courts in tort; if they rejected the award, they could have their day in court where the ordinary liability rules would apply or they could appeal the award under sub-s 15 of s 5 of the Act. In its early non-statutory form the Tribunal could not entertain applications for exemplary or aggravated damages, but because of the findings in the Finlay report, the Tribunal's powers in this respect were extended. If a claimant is awarded a sum for general and special damages, then if he or she wishes to renounce a claim for aggravated or exemplary damages the claimant will be entitled under the Act to an additional 20% of the award for this renunciation.[202]

---

200. See *Report of the Stardust Tribunal Victims Compensation Tribunal*, PL 7831, p 10 25 Sept 1985.

201. Hepatitis C Compensation Tribunal Act 1997. For detailed analysis of the Act, see Blánaid Clarke's *Annotation* ICLSA.

202. Section 11.

**[1.185]** The Tribunal has five members and the chairman (Egan J) is a retired judge. It sits in chambers of three. At the time of writing the Tribunal has disposed of approximately 1,300 cases, and there have been appeals in about 200 cases. Many of these have been filed by cautious lawyers in the wake of Morris P's decision in *Kealy v The Minister for Health*[203] where he held that the ceiling for general damages should nowadays be raised from £150,000 to £250,000. Of the 200 cases where appeals have been filed only those cases where the maximum of £150,000 in respect of general damages was awarded, are likely to be affected by the new ceiling announced by Morris P, and it is not anticipated that many adjustments will have to be made in the majority of these cases.

**[1.186]** Both the Stardust and Hepatitis Tribunals are interesting in that they illustrate cases where the State, for political and legal reasons, finds it more satisfactory to take the losses out of the tort system and manage them in a different way. In the Stardust case public sympathy was enormous and there was a clear signal from the public that something should be done to alleviate, insofar as money could, the pain and the distress of the injured and their families. The entitlement at common law of the families of the deceased, who were for the most part, young single people, was modest as the dependency was in many cases non-existent. Moreover, when the Compensation Tribunal was announced the spectre of large sums being paid for nervous shock was not a serious inhibiting factor.[204] Finally, the numbers involved were limited and the financial dimensions of the assistance required were not open-ended. Nevertheless, the scheme was not put on a statutory basis and all payments were *ex gratia*, both factors indicating a certain amount of caution on the part of the State. As noted above, in later Hepatitis C Tribunal, was eventually, put on a statutory basis.

**[1.187]** An earlier model, it is worth noting was set up in November 1977 in respect of persons who it was claimed were damaged by whooping cough vaccination. According to Morgan and Hogan:

> "Of the 93 cases which presented themselves to the Group, the Group found that there was a reasonable possibility that the vaccine was responsible for damage in 16 of the cases. An offer of an *ex gratia* payment of £10,000 was made in each case where the Expert Medical Group had found in favour of the children on the understanding that it did not involve the acceptance of any liability on the part of the State or any public authority in respect of the child's disability. Thirteen families accepted the offer of the *ex gratia* payments". [205]

**[1.188]** Again, it can be noted that in this instance, the number of potential victims was small and the sums offered by way of *ex gratia* payments were modest and the State was not willing to accept any liability. It was a cautious recognition of the State's responsibility but it was a gesture that was more an acknowledgement of the State's Welfare role than an acceptance of legal liability.

**[1.189]** The more recent Blood Tribunal involves a shift towards a more open acknowledgement of the State's legal responsibility. This is understandable in the light of

---

203. High Court, 19 April 1999.

204. *McLoughlin v OBrian* [1983] AC 410; [1982] 21 All ER 298 had not been decided in England, and its Irish counterpart *Mullally v CIE* [1992] ILRM 722 was some eleven years off. See Ch 17 on Nervous Shock.

205. Hogan and Morgan, *Administrative Law in Ireland* (3rd ed, 1998), p 291, fn 221.

the findings of the Finlay report. Further, the close connection between the BTSB and the State and the likelihood that the ordinary civil courts would have found against the State and, because of the facts of the case, might very well have been tempted to award aggravated or punitive damages, encouraged the State to take a pro-active approach in managing the loss. The size of the problem and the clear public sympathy together with sustained political pressure eventually determined the shape and the nature of the Tribunal.

**[1.190]** The more recent flood of "army deafness" cases once more presented the State with serious problems of compensation and naturally suggested that the best way for the State to handle the problem was to try to "tribunalise" the claims. These cases arose out of claims by soldiers in the Irish Army that the State did not take reasonable care for their safety, by failing to provide ear protection for members of the forces engaged in weapons training, when the State long knew the dangers involved in such exercises when soldiers were not wearing ear muffs.

**[1.191]** Prospective claimants in such cases faced the usual problems in mounting their actions: they had to prove fault on the part of the State, damage to their hearing and also they had to make the causal connection between the State's omission and the hearing loss. Further there was the additional problem of claims being barred by the limitation period. Initially, the State toughened it out, but once the first award was made in the courts the floodgates were opened. The sheer scale of the claims was daunting: the total number of claims in early 1999 was estimated to stand at 14,000 with about 2,500 already dealt with by the courts or by out-of-court settlement. The final cost to the State is estimated conservatively to be somewhere in the region of £360 million. It is little wonder, therefore, in these circumstances that the Minister for Defence should propose a tribunal for handling these cases. It has been suggested that managing the claims in this way will speed up the hearings, reduce the overall costs of the claims, reduce legal costs and standardise the awards. At present, before the Courts, different judges have different approaches to the claims and awards vary greatly. One problem that has arisen is how to measure the hearing loss involved and this has led to some disparity in the judicial determinations. In an effort to bring some moderation and predictability to the court verdicts in these hearing injury cases, the Civil Liability (Assessment of Hearing Injury) Act 1998[206] was introduced. This Act obliges the courts to take judicial notice of the report of an Expert Hearing Group and, in determining the extent of the injuries, to have regard to the classification method contained therein. This in effect imposes on the courts a method of measuring the hearing loss, known as the "Green Book" method. In turn, this it was hoped, would restrain judicial awards.

**[1.192]** Those hopes were ultimately vindicated when the Supreme Court, in *Hanley v Minister for Defence*[207] gave an authoritative ruling which had the effect of keeping damages within fairly narrow controls. The "army deafness crisis" has now eased and projections for future payments have been radically reduced.

---

206. For a detailed analysis, see Pamela Boutin *Annotation* ICLSA; Humphries and Craven, Defence Forces Chapter in Byrne and Binchy, *Annual Review of Irish Law 1998*, pp 237-238. For a wider picture, see Humphries and Craven, *Military Law in Ireland*, (1997), pp 226-227.

207. [2000] 2 ILRM 276 (SC).

# Chapter 2

# Causation[1]


I. Introduction ........ 59
II. Factual and Legal Causation ........ 60
III. Novus Actus Interveniens ........ 67
IV. Proof ........ 78
V. Causation and medical Negligence ........ 82


## I. INTRODUCTION

**[2.01]** Normally speaking when the plaintiff sues for damages in tort three separate questions arise under the heading of damages: causation; remoteness; and quantum or measure. To succeed the plaintiff must first show that the defendant *caused* the damage. Second, for the plaintiff to recover, the damage must not be too remote. Third, if recovery is allowed, the Court must decide how much money the plaintiff is entitled to in respect of his injuries.

**[2.02]** Although these three questions can sometimes intermingle, it greatly facilitates initial appreciation and analysis if for the most part they are considered as if they were separate and independent problems. It is true that this approach may lead to an over-simplification of the problems involved, but this is a risk well worth running when one considers the confusion, the complexity and the chaos that is traditionally associated with these problems. Separate consideration is essential if one is to pick one's way safely through the chaotic thicket that surrounds the whole area.

**[2.03]** It may be helpful at this juncture to identify in a summary fashion what the problems are before going on to examine the issues in greater detail. First there is the problem of causation. It is said that the defendant cannot be liable to the plaintiff unless he has caused the damage in question. This means at the outset that the act of the defendant must be linked in a factual or scientific way to the injury of the plaintiff if the defendant is to be considered as being potentially liable. This involves a factual investigation. If there is no connection between the defendant's conduct and the plaintiff's injury then the defendant cannot be liable to the plaintiff. But just because the defendant caused in a *factual sense* the plaintiff's injury does not necessarily mean that he will be *liable in law* to the plaintiff. Before the courts will hold the defendant liable in law they must also be

1. For a detailed treatment of this subject see Hart & Honoré, *Causation in the Law* (2nd ed, 1985). See also White, *Civil Liability for Industrial Accidents* (1993), Ch 2; Kennedy & Grubb, *Medical Law* (3rd ed, 2000), pp 465-507; James & Perry, 'Legal Cause', (1951) 60 Yale LJ 761; Wright 'Causation in Tort Laws' (1985) 73 Calif LR 1735; Pincus 'Progress on the Causal Chain Gang: Some Approaches to Causation in Tort Law and Steps Toward a Linguistic Analysis' (1986) 24 Os HLJ 961; Pardy 'Fault and Cause: Rethinking the Role of Merchant Conduct' (1995) 3 Tort LR 143; Mullany 'Common Sense Causation - An Australian View' (1992) OJLS 431; Fleming 'Probabilistic Causation in Tort Law' (1989) 68 Can B R 661; Fleming 'Probabilistic Causation in Tort Law - A Postscript' (1991) 70 Can BR 137.

satisfied, on policy grounds, that the defendant *legally caused* the damage to the plaintiff. When the courts have established to their satisfaction both factual and legal cause then the second problem of remoteness arises.

**[2.04]** The remoteness problem is concerned with the consequences of the defendant's actions. Even though the defendant may be liable for injuring the plaintiff he may not be liable for *all* the consequences of his actions. There is no legal system which is so strict that it saddles the person liable for *all* the consequences of his actions. The courts must introduce a limit, a cut-off point beyond which the defendant will not be liable. The standard or criterion which the courts use in locating the cut-off point has changed over the years and it is with this criterion that one is primarily concerned when one is dealing with remoteness.

**[2.05]** An examination of the third question, the quantum or measure of damages issue, can be postponed. Logically and analytically, it does not arise until after the other two questions have been dealt with, but even at this early juncture it can be pointed out, that in many cases, and in all cases concerning personal injuries, the task of reducing the plaintiff's injuries to monetary terms, is in one sense impossible. At best, all one can hope for is some consistency and some predictability in the awards.

## II. Factual and Legal Causation

**[2.06]** The question of causation is fraught with difficulty. As Fleming says, the topic:

> "has plagued courts and scholars more than any other ... in the law of torts. Some of the perplexity that has been experienced is due to the undifferentiated use of the word 'cause' accompanied by such adjectives as 'legal', 'proximate' or 'remote', in dealing with two rather distinct inquiries."[2]

### Factual Causation[3]

**[2.07]** In the law of torts a person cannot be liable unless he caused the injury to the plaintiff. There must be some causal connection between the defendant's actions or omissions and the plaintiff's injury. If P is run over by D he may have an action against D because D caused the injury in a factual or scientific sense. Conversely, of course, P cannot sue an innocent bystander who in no way contributed to the accident or a person who, having no connection with the accident, was miles away in another city. These latter persons cannot be held liable simply because they were in no way causally connected to the event which is the basis of the plaintiff's complaint. In many ways it is the negative formulation of the causation rule that is most helpful to the lawyer at this point. We may

2. FLEMING, p 218.

> "There is perhaps nothing in the entire field of law which has called forth more disagreement, or upon which the opinions are in such a welter of confusion. Nor, despite the manifold attempts which have been made to clarify the subject, is there yet any general agreement as to the proper approach. Much of this confusion is due to the fact that no one problem is involved, but a number of different problems, which are not distinguished clearly and that language appropriate to a discussion of one is carried over to cast a shadow upon the others".

PROSSER & KEETON, pp 264-265 (footnotes omitted).

3. See Becht & Miller, *The Test of Factual Causation* (1961); Malone 'Ruminations on Cause-in-fact' (1956) 9 Stan LR 60; Boon, Note: 'Causation and the Increase of Risk' (1988) 51 MLR 508.

say that if there is no factual causal link between the defendant's conduct and the plaintiff's injury, then the defendant *cannot* be liable.[4]

**[2.08]** On the other hand, if the defendant did cause the plaintiff's injury in a factual sense, then all we may say at this point, is that the defendant *may* be liable for the plaintiff's injuries. Whether he will or will not be held liable depends on questions of legal policy which are debated sometimes under the heading "legal cause" or alternatively, under the heading of "remoteness".

**[2.09]** The question of causation, therefore, is primarily a question of fact,[5] in the scientific or physical sense of cause and effect, and secondly a question of legal policy, whereas the remoteness question is in essence a question of law. In studying these problems our main concern is to discover the criteria used by the courts in determining whether the matter is a factual cause or a legal cause or whether the particular head of damage is too remote. It is appropriate therefore to address ourselves first to the question as to how the courts decide whether the defendant has in fact caused the plaintiff's injury.

**[2.10]** In a sense, of course, when one is speaking about causation, one might say as a philosopher might, that events have an infinite number of causes and that all events were caused initially by Adam and Eve's alleged misdemeanour in the Garden of Eden.[6] Practical considerations in the administration of the law, however, mean that the courts cannot afford such philosophical indulgences and must take a more pragmatic approach to the problem. The rule they most commonly favour in distinguishing the relevant causes from the irrelevant causes is what has come to be known as the "but for" rule. An act is a cause of an event if the event would not have occurred without ("but for") the act in question. If the event or effect would have occurred without the act in question then the act cannot be deemed to be a cause.

**[2.11]** The "but for" test is helpful in attempting to understand most of the cases and it can be usefully illustrated from the courts' jurisprudence. Some straightforward examples can be dealt with first. In *Kenny v O'Rourke*[7] the plaintiff, who was a painter employed by sub-contractors, was injured when he fell off a ladder which was provided by the general contractors on the building site. Although the ladder was defective, the general contractors were held not to be liable on this account as the plaintiff testified that he fell because he lent over too far. His fall was in no way caused by the defect in the ladder.[8] In *Meehan v Reid and Murphy*[9] the plaintiff claimed damages for structural damage to his house which he said was due to the defendants' quarry operations and in particular to vibrations caused

4. On the unusual rule where a person will be liable vicariously even though he or she has not personally caused the injury. See Ch 43 below.
5. Although some policy element is also inevitably present here too: *cf* Malone 'Ruminations on Cause-in-Fact' (1956) 9 Stan LR 60 at 72-79 and see Cohen 'Field Theory and Judicial Logic' (1950) 59 Yale LJ 238 at 252-253
6. *Atlantic Coastline R Co v Daniels* (1911) 70 SE 203 (CA).
7. [1972] IR 339 (SC); *McWilliams v Errol (Sir William) & Co Ltd* 1962 SC 70, [1962] 1 All ER 623, noted by Henderson, (1962) 25 MLR 599. See also *Martin v Miller & Co Ltd* Supreme Court, 12 May 1972.
8. Contrast *Cuckian v Cully* Supreme Court, 9 March 1972 (Ó Dálaigh CJ).
9. High Court, 5 March 1985 (Murphy J).

by the discharge of explosives at the defendants' quarry. Having heard all the scientific evidence, however, the High Court was able to conclude "with virtual certainty, that no structural damage was caused to the plaintiff's premises by the defendants ..."[10] In *Kearney v Paul and Vincent Ltd*[11] the plaintiff, who claimed that his calves died as a result of feeding them an actified milk replacer marketed by the defendant company, lost his case when he failed to provide sufficient scientific evidence to convince the Court that the death of the calves was caused by the defendants' product. This was also the problem which the plaintiffs faced in *Berkery v Flynn*[12] and in the celebrated *Hanrahan* case.[13] In *Berkery* the plaintiff had to introduce a great deal of technical evidence from geologists and others before he finally convinced the Court that the contamination to his well was in fact caused by the defendant's slurry pit. In *Hanrahan* it was only at the Supreme Court level that the plaintiffs finally secured a judicial determination to the effect that the technical and other evidence produced at the High Court warranted a finding that the damage to the plaintiffs' health and to the farm stock was caused by the toxic emissions from the defendant's chemical factory.[14]

**[2.12]** Where the plaintiff claims that his injuries were caused by the defendant's failure to act, then the causal link (in the factual sense) must also be proved if the defendant is to be liable. In *Barnett v Chelsea and Kensington Hospital Management Committee*[15] the plaintiff's husband and two other night watchmen were negligently turned away from the defendant's hospital without proper examination by a doctor. They had complained of vomiting after drinking tea and the plaintiff's husband subsequently died of arsenic poisoning. The widow's action against the hospital failed because it was held that, even if an examination had been made, the probability was that the deceased would have died anyway. The defendants' negligence did not cause the death. Damage to the deceased's system was so advanced that death would have occurred no matter what the defendant did.

**[2.13]** In *Collier v Earl of Mountcharles and Others*[16] another example of the usefulness of the "but for" test occurs. In that case the plaintiff, a fee-paying visitor, was injured when a stone stairway collapsed in the defendant's castle. The Court held that there was no liability on the defendants as they had no reason to suspect any defect in the structure which had stood firmly for 180 years. The plaintiff argued that the defendant should have engaged an architect to examine the stairs and the defendants successfully replied that in the circumstances there was no duty on them to do this. The defendants also produced

---

10. At p18 of unreported judgment.
11. High Court, 30 July 1985 (Barron J). This is frequently a problem for plaintiffs who sue for food poisoning.
12. High Court, 10 June 1982 (Costello J).
13. *Hanrahan v Merck, Sharp and Dohme (Irl) Ltd* [1989] ILRM 629 (SC).
14. See Ch 24 below. In *Skinner v Hartnett and Cork Corp* High Court, 3 February 1995, the plaintiff cyclist was injured when he collided with the defendant's vehicle. It was accepted that the traffic lights were set to give a cyclist starting from a stationary position insufficient time to cross the junction. The second defendant, however, was not liable on this account in the instant case, since it was found that the plaintiff broke the red light rather than wait for green. The timing of the lights did not causally contribute to the accident.
15. [1969] 1 QB 428. See also *The Empire Jamaica* [1957] AC 386; *Conley v Strain* [1988] IR 628, (HC).
16. Supreme Court, 19 December 1969.

professional evidence, however, that even if they had engaged an architect he would not have warned them that the stairway was dangerous. The collapse would thus have occurred anyway, so the omission was not a factual cause of the accident. Again, in *CIE v Carroll and Wexford County Council*[17] it was alleged that the failure by the Council to post notices and warnings contributed to the damage which Carroll caused to the plaintiff's bridge when he drove under it with too high a load. The Supreme Court, reversing the High Court, held, having regard to the fact that Carroll lived only four miles away from the bridge and regularly drove high vehicles under it, that on the occasion in question he assumed (wrongly) that his load was no higher than usual, and that he did not know its height, that the absence of signs did not contribute to the accident happening.

**[2.14]** The "but for" test as illustrated here is especially useful where one can fairly say that the event in question had only one cause. It is less helpful, and must be modified in its application, where multiple causes operate to bring about the same event or damage.[18] If, for example, two independent fires converge simultaneously on the plaintiff's property, each of which on its own is sufficient to destroy the plaintiff's property, the strict application of the "but for" test in these circumstances would mean that neither person responsible for the fires would be liable. Neither common sense[19] nor the law accepts this proposition, and both parties would be liable to the plaintiff nowadays.[20] Again, if the plaintiff suffers injury because of the successive wrongs of more than one defendant, the "but for" test is not very helpful. If Dl crashes into my car and damages my right wing (in the amount of £40) and shortly thereafter while driving to the garage to have repairs carried out D2 crashes into the same wing, totally destroying it (and the replacement value is £100) the question arises whether Dl is liable for the full £100? On a strict application of the "but for" test the answer would be yes. The law, however, again trusting more to pragmatic common sense makes Dl liable only for the damage he caused, ie £40, and D2 liable for the balance of £60.[21]

**[2.15]** It is because of these difficulties with the "but for" test that *Prosser & Keeton* favour another test in determining whether a thing was a cause of an event or not.

> "The defendant's conduct is a cause of the event if it was a material element and a substantial factor in bringing it about."[22]

17. [1986] ILRM 312.
18. See McGregor 'Successive Causes of Personal Injury' (1970) 30 MLR 378 and Strachan 'The Scope and Application of the "But for" Causal Test', Journal (1970) 30 MLR 386; Malone 'Ruminations on Cause-in-fact' (1956) 9 Stan LR 60 at 88-97.
19. "We demand that we be allowed to judge as we observe. Drama has triumphed over the syllogism": Malone 'Ruminations on Cause-in-fact' (1956) 9 Stan LR 60 at 89.
20. *Cf* PROSSER & KEETON, pp 266-268, *Anderson v Minneapolis St Paul & Sault Ste Marie Ry Co* 1920 146 Minn LR 430, 179 NW 45 (SC). The plaintiff, however, cannot recover more than his total loss. With regard to contribution, see Ch 4 below.
21. See *Baker v Willoughby* [1970] AC 467; *Performance Cars Ltd v Abraham* [1962] 1 QB 33. *Cf Fitzgerald v Lane* [1987] 2 All ER 455 (CA), noted by Gearty [1988] Camb LJ 8, affd by HL, [1988] 2 All ER 961.
22. PROSSER & KEETON, p 267. See further White, *Civil Liability for Industrial Accidents* (1993), para 2.2.18.

If the defendant's conduct was not "a material element and a substantial factor" then he should not be liable since he will not have caused the plaintiff's injury in a factual sense. The formulation is attractive and appealing in that it properly emphasises the importance of the circumstances of each particular case in determining the causal question. Its weakness, of course, is its lack of philosophical depth or definitional certainty.

**[2.16]** A final illustration is to be found in *Duffy v Rooney and Dunnes Stores (Dundalk) Ltd*[23] the infant plaintiff was burned when her coat caught fire while standing too close to the sitting room fire in her grandparent's home. The grandfather, who was about to take the three year old for a walk, went to the hall to get his overcoat and while he was so engaged, the infant's coat came in contact with an unguarded fire. The plaintiff sued both her grandfather and Dunnes Stores, who sold the coat. Laffoy J found that the grandfather was liable as the person to whom the safety of the infant was entrusted and also as occupier of the premises where the accident happened (but not vicariously liable for another member of the household who removed the fireguard).[24] With regrad to the second-named defendant, who sold the garment, the judge found that the retailer was negligent in not affixing a notice warning that the garment should have been kept away from fire. The learned judge, however, held that this failure was not a legal cause of the injury, being of the view that the grandmother who purchased the garment would not have considered the garment inappropriate had such a warning notice been affixed at the time of the purchase. Further, even if such a warning notice had been affixed its circumstances would not have been any different in the house on the day of the accident, it being noted that the plaintiff's other garments, did have such warning notices attached on the day in question and these did not alter the grandparents arrangements to prevent the accident. The accident was entirely attributable to the first-named defendant's negligence in not supervising the child; the second named defendant's omission in no way contributed to the accident. The Supreme Court upheld the trial judge's judgment.[25]

## Legal Causation

**[2.17]** From the above, therefore, it should be clear that the search for factual causes is a preliminary one. The purpose of the "but for" test is:

> "to act as a preliminary filter and to eliminate the irrelevant rather than to allocate legal responsibility."[26]

**[2.18]** When the field is narrowed by the elimination of the factually irrelevant causes the inquiry must continue among those causes considered to be factually relevant, to establish whether they are legally relevant to the court's inquiry.[27]

**[2.19]** It is clear that an event may be brought about by more than one cause. And this is openly acknowledged nowadays.[28] P may crash his car because the road was wet at the

---

23. Supreme Court, 23 April 1998 (Hamilton CJ).
24. *Cf Moynihan v Moynihan* [1975] IR 192. See Ch 43 below.
25. Supreme Court, 23 April 1998 (Hamilton CJ).
26. WINFIELD & JOLOWICZ (12th ed), p 121. See now the 15th ed, p 197.
27. FLEMING, pp 218-232.
28. It is true that there may have been a tendency when contributory negligence was a complete defence, for the courts in their efforts to assist the plaintiff, to avoid a finding that the plaintiff's acts partly caused the accident.

time of the accident, because he was driving too quickly, because the corner of the road was too sharp and because his brakes were defective. One could say here that the accident was caused by the wet road, the excessive speed, the bad corner and by the defective brakes. The courts approach the matter by distinguishing between mere conditions, on the one hand, and causes on the other. Mere conditions, which are not sufficient to amount to "the cause" of the event, tend to be inanimate or normal; a cause, on the other hand, is more likely to be a voluntary human act or an abnormal contingency.[29] "There is no precise legal rule, but common sense and law unite in looking for the abnormal or the deliberate human act, and regarding that as 'the cause'."[30] In the example just given the courts would be more likely to find as the cause of the accident the driver's negligence rather than the wet road.[31] If, however, the weather conditions were so abnormal that they amounted to a hurricane, the courts might be satisfied to declare this to be the cause of the event.[32] In *Smith v Leavy*,[33] in a fatal injuries case, Kingsmill Moore J had this to say on an appeal against a High Court decision to withdraw the case from the jury:

---

28. (contd) To do so would have been to deny the plaintiff any recovery. In such circumstances, between the plaintiff and defendant in any event, the tendency may have been to declare that there was only one cause: the defendant's conduct. Certainly the doctrine of the "last clear chance" (*cf* paras **[20.04]**-**[20.07]** below) reflected this policy. Nowadays, with apportionment available, no such pressure operates on the courts. If the defendant alleges contributory negligence he too, of course, must make the causal link between the plaintiff's conduct and the accident. *Stapleton v O'Regan* (1961) 95 ILTR 1 (SC) "If the plaintiff, using all caution reasonably required of him would nevertheless have been unable to avoid the accident then his failure to use such caution is not an effective contributory cause of the accident and the accident must be attributed solely to the negligence of the defendant. The plaintiff's negligence is '*nihil ad rem*'" *per* Kingsmill Moore J at 5. But see also *Kingston v Kingston* (1968) 102 ILTR 65 (SC); *Kelly v McElligott* (1951) 85 ILTR 4 (SC). The technical problems associated with joint tortfeasors at common law may also have encouraged the Courts to hesitate in attributing loss to multiple defendants. See Ch 4 below.

29. See SALMOND, & HEUSTON, p 508-510.

30. STREET (8th ed), p 224. See now 10th ed, pp 264-265. See *Burke v John Paul and Co Ltd* [1967] IR 277; *Connolly v South of Ireland Asphalt Co* [1977] IR 99.

31. In *Dunne v Clarke Oil Products Ltd* Irish Times Law Report, 25 November 1996, where there was a conflict as to whether the collision was caused by worn tyres or by the negligence of the driver, the Supreme Court affirmed the High Court's finding that the more probable cause was that the plaintiff/driver was driving too fast.

32. The use of qualifying epithets adds little by way of clarification in this area. Thus, to say that the condition is the "proximate", the "dominant", the "real", the "effective", the "immediate" or the "precipitating" cause does not help. Either the condition is to be considered relevant or not; if it is then we may simply call it a cause, as opposed to a mere condition and move on to examine the question of remoteness. Whether a cause is to be regarded as a legal or proximate cause:

> "is always to be determined on the facts of each case upon mixed considerations of logic, common sense, justice, policy and precedent ... The best use that can be made of the authorities on proximate cause is merely to furnish illustrations of situations which judicious men upon careful consideration have adjudged to be on one side of the line or the other".

Street, *Foundations of Legal Liability* (1906), p 110.

33. Supreme Court, 7 November 1960. See also *O'Donnell v Gleeson* DPIJ: Trinity and Michaelmas Terms 1996, p 39 (HC). The plaintiff, an elderly man, injured in an accident caused by the negligence of one of the defendants, suffered a stroke nearly two and a half years later. The accident was held not to be the cause of the stroke.

> "There was evidence from which a jury might reasonably conclude that the accident had brought on a very rapid development of the aortic stenosis rendering an operation necessary at a much earlier period in the patient's life than would have been the case if there had been no accident. If this is so the risk of death by a proper and necessary operation had to be incurred earlier in life. The risk turned out adversely. The man's life was cut short at an earlier period than if there had been no accident and an operation, performed at a later date, had turned out equally fately. The accident was truly the cause of this operation being performed at an earlier date than would otherwise have been necessary, and in consequence accelerated the death. It *was* the cause of his death occurring *at that time.* This is sufficient to satisfy the wording of the relevant section. Death at some time comes to all, but in the eyes of the law to accelerate that time is equivalent to causing death at that time so as to attach liability for the pecuniary loss to the dependents arising from such acceleration of death."

It is submitted that the same reasoning would apply if the question was causing death at common law.[34]

**[2.20]** This brings us to an important issue which our courts have yet to address. Let us take the case of a person with a serious medical condition, whose prospects of survival with a timely diagnosis would be 40%. The defendant doctor, through negligence, fails to make the diagnosis and the person dies.

**[2.21]** In an action against the doctor for wrongful death should it be a good defence for the doctor that the patient's prospects of survival had at best been less than 50%? Or should compensation be provided? If compensation is to be permitted, what should be its quantum? The traditional answer would be that no compensation would be due.[35] More recently, commentators[36] and courts[37] in the United States have shown increasing willingness to permit compensation, with damages reflecting the limited prospect of survival which the plaintiff had before the defendant's act. From the standpoint of fairness this seems the better solution, though the process of compensation of the loss may in some

---

33. (contd)

> "It may hypothetically be a possible argument that the hypertension may have been contributed to by the complications arising from the fall, but it seemed to be worth noting [a medical witness]'s detailed evidence that the plaintiff in fact had made a very commendable and good recovery over the period of two years and somewhat more prior to his stroke. [O]n ordinary principles of causation and probability it would be unsafe and unwarranted to attribute the very significant further losses accruing to [the plaintiff] to [the original accident]".

34. See also *McCahill v New York Transportation Co* (1911) 201 NY 221, 94 NE 616.

35. *Cf* eg *Kuhn v Banker* (1938) 133 Ohio St 304, 13 NE 2d 242. See also *Sykes v Midland Bank Executor and Trustee Co* [1971] 1 QB 113 (CA), critically analysed by Schaefer, 'Uncertainty and the Law of Damages' (1978) 19 W & MLR 719 at 763-765.

36. King 'Causation, Valuation and Chance in Personal Injury Torts Involving Pre-existing Conditions and Future Consequences' (1981) 90 Yale LJ 1353; Robinson 'Probabilistic Causation and Compensation for Tortious Risk' (1985) 14 J Leg Stud 779; PROSSER & KEETON, p 272; Anon 'Note: Damages Contingent Upon Chance' (1964) 18 Rutgers LR 875 at 893-896; Wright 'Causation in Tort Laws' (1985) 73 Calif LR 1735 at 1814-1816.

37. *Cf Falcon v Memorial Hosiptal* (1990) 436 Mich 443, 462 NW 2d 44; *Borowski v Sacheti* (1996) 43 Conn App 294, 682 A 2d 1095; *Herskovits v Group Health Co-operative* (1983) 99 Wn 2d 609, 664 P 2d 474 (concurring opinion of Pearson J); *Sharp v Kaiser Foundation Health Plan of Colorado* 710 P 2d 1153 (Colo CA 1985); *Waffen v United States* 799 F 2d 911 (4th Cir 1986).

cases be somewhat complex. In England, the House of Lords did not in its express holding exclude the possibility of developing the law on these lines, in *Hotson v East Berkshire Area Health Authority*,[38] though a number of the speeches evinced hostility to it.

**[2.22]** In the light of its subsequent decision in *Wilsher v Essex Area Health Authority*,[39] however, it would seem that a plaintiff would have very great difficulty in succeeding in such a case.

### Legal Cause and Remoteness of Damage

**[2.23]** The above presentation looks at the problem from the event backwards to the causes of the event. It is an approach which essentially looks at the problem from the plaintiff's point of view back to potential defendants, and it is an approach which favours the view that causation is primarily concerned with locating defendants. Sometimes, however, the courts will look at the problem from the defendant's point of view and ask whether the damage of which the plaintiff complains was "too remote", that is, a consequence of the defendant's conduct for which he ought not in law to be liable. We will examine this approach in greater detail in Chapter 3. Briefly, it may be mentioned here that, as a general rule, a plaintiff may be compensated only to the extent that the loss or injury of which he complains was reasonably foreseeable by the defendant.

## III. Novus Actus Interveniens

**[2.24]** Conventional terminology in connection with the question of legal causation frequently describes the occasions where the courts are unwilling to impose liability on the defendant in the language of *novus actus interveniens*. It is proposed to adhere to this terminology for the time being and to examine the rules on this matter before moving on to discuss the concept of remoteness. It should be mentioned, however, that while the language used may differ, the underlying problem in both cases may be the same in some instances at least.

**[2.25]** Sometimes the causal link between the defendant's act and the plaintiff's injury is said to be broken by an intervening act which is of such a kind that it must be deemed to be

38. [1987] AC 750. Lord Mackay's analysis of the House of Lords decision in *McGhee v National Code Board* [1972] 3 All ER 1008 must be read in the light of Lord Bridge's interpretation of that case in *Wilsher v Essex Area Health Authority* [1988] AC 1074.

39. [1988] AC 1074, analysed by Boon 'Note: Causation and the Increase of Risk' (1988) 51 MLR 508 and Grubb [1988] Camb LJ 350. In *Wilsher*, Lord Bridge, delivering the only speech, interpreted *McGhee* in such a way as to deprive it of virtually any force. It had involved merely a "robust and pragmatic conclusion based on the undisputed primary facts of the case", and had "laid down no new principle of law whatever". He expressly repudiated Lord Wilberforce's statement in *McGhee* that one who, by breach of duty of care, creates a risk, the injury occurring within the area of that risk should bear the loss unless he shows that it had some other cause. Lord Bridge noted that such a reversal in the onus of proof would run counter to the "unanimous and emphatic" opinions expressed in the earlier decision of the House of Lords in *Bonnington Castings Ltd v Wardlaw* [1956] AC 613. See further MARKESINIS & DEAKIN, pp 178-181. *Cf Snell v Farrell* (1990) 72 DLR (4th) 289 (SCC); *Lawson v Laferrière* (1991) 78 DLR (4th) 609 (SCC). It is worth noting that Lord Wilberforce's approach found support in *March v Stramere (E & MH) Pty* (1991) 171 CLR 506 at 514 and in *Chappel v Hart* (1998) 72 ALJR 1344 Kirby J admitted to finding it "compelling". See Waddams 'Causation, Physicians and Disclosure of Risks' (1999) 7 Tort LR 5.

the sole or new cause of the plaintiff's injuries. Thus, the defendant may do something for the consequences of which he could fairly be said to be responsible, but because of the supervening and subsequent act of another he may be relieved of this responsibility. In those cases the intervening act may be said to hi-jack the causal investigation, and the courts will not go behind the intervening act in their search for the legal cause. The intervening act may be that of a third party, that of the plaintiff himself or an independent physical event.[40]

**[2.26]** Where the act of a third party combines with the act of the defendant to cause the harm of which the plaintiff complains, the third party and the defendant are concurrent wrongdoers and both are liable to the plaintiff for the full amount of the damage suffered. The defendant may allege, however, that the supervening act of the third party is of such a nature as to relieve him totally from responsibility for the plaintiff's damage, ie, is such as to negate the defendant's causal contribution.[41] Similarly, where the act of the plaintiff supervenes on the wrongful act of the defendant and the acts of both defendant and plaintiff contribute to cause the harm of which the plaintiff complains, *prima facie* the case is one of contributory negligence on the part of the plaintiff leading to an apportionment if the plaintiff is found not to have been exercising reasonable care for his own protection. In this latter case, the defendant may allege that the supervening act of the plaintiff was of such a nature as to relieve him entirely from responsibility for the plaintiff's damage.[42] Finally, where a physical event supervenes on the act of the defendant, the latter may allege

---

40. *Cf Ashworth v General Accident Fire and Life Assurance Corporation Ltd* [1955] IR 268 (SC revg HC 1950); *Hayes v Finnegan* [1952] IR 98, at (SC); *Carslogie Steamship Co Ltd v Royal Norwegian Government* [1952] AC 292 (HL). See also *Scully v Mulhall* (1951) 85 ILTR 18 (CC) (The owner of a bullock, with a quiet reputation, which was driven down the main street of Portlaoise, was held not liable when it suddenly broke into a gallop and fell on top of the plaintiff's bicycle. There was no evidence that the owner was negligent but Gleeson J observed that, even if he had been it was not the cause of the accident, "because the animal fell on the street which was an unforeseeable occurrence in the nature of a *novus actus*. The chain of causation was definitively broken at that point".

41. See *Power v Bedford Motors* [1959] IR 391 (SC).

42. It should be noted that under the doctrine of contributory negligence as prescribed by the Civil Liability Act 1961, s 34(1), to which the courts faithfully subscribe, "fault" is to be equated with blameworthiness rather than the causative factors moving from each side. Section 56 of the Act abolishes the last opportunity rule. It should be noted that this is connected exclusively with the *careless failure to avoid the consequences of the act of another*. It is not concerned with a case where the defendant alleges that a *new careless act* attributable to the plaintiff has *broken* the causal chain. On the reluctance of Irish Courts to find that plaintiff's contribution was the sole cause, see *O'Hanlon v ESB* [1969] IR 75; *Doran v Dublin Plant Hire Ltd* [1990] 1 IR 488 (HC 1989, Barron J). In *Long v Dublin Corporation and ESB* Circuit Court, 13 January 1989, Irish Times, 14 January 1989, p 12, the plaintiff sued for injuries he received when trying to rescue his pet dog who came in contact with a "live" lamp-post on a wet night. In his rescue effort the plaintiff was bitten and received shocks. The defendant corporation argued unsuccessfully that the plaintiff was author of his own misfortune in attempting to rescue his dog. The plaintiff was awarded £3,150. Contrast *O'Hanlon's* case with *Ginty v Belmont Building Supplies Ltd* [1959] 1 All ER 414. In *Coyle v An Post* [1993] ILRM 508, O'Flaherty J (diss) said of the defendant's arguments:

> "It represents a serious confusion between the concept of *novus actus interveniens* and what should more properly be dealt with as possible contributory negligence. It is of the essence of *novus actus interveniens* that the damage ... should have resulted from the act of another person who is independent of the plaintiff and defendant".

At 526.

that such event is of a type which wholly negates his causal connection with the resultant harm. If an intervening act can have the effect of breaking the chain between the defendant's conduct and the plaintiff then the decisive question relates to the character of the supervening act or event which will cause it to have the effect of constituting a *novus actus interveniens* relieving the original wrongdoer from responsibility for the harm to the plaintiff.[43]

**[2.27]** Before going on to examine the quality of the intervening act required to sunder the chain between the original wrongdoer and the plaintiff, one should perhaps mention that the conduct of the third party need not necessarily be a positive act: indeed it can be a negligent *omission*. In *Crowley v AIB and O'Flynn*[44] the plaintiff was seriously injured when he fell from the flat roof of premises owned by the AIB. The second named defendants were the architects who had designed the roof without specifying the need for a railing around the roof. In the High Court the architect was ordered to pay 30% of the damages for its faulty design. The Supreme Court reversed this and held that there was no nexus between the negligence of the architect and the plaintiff's injury. The link between the plaintiff's injury and the architect's negligence was broken by the fact that the bank knew that boys regularly played on this unguarded roof and did not attempt to prohibit or prevent this conduct. The inactivity of the Bank in this instance constituted a *novus actus interveniens* which relieved the architects.[45]

## Reasonable Foresight of Intervening Act and Recklessness on the Part of the Intervener

**[2.28]** In examining the circumstances when the inervening act will have the effect of relieving the original perpetrator, two factors feature in the judge's approach: first, whether, and to what extent the intervening act was foreseeable by the original actor, and

---

43. *Cf Sullivan v Creed* [1904] 2 IR 317, at 339 (CA, affg KB Div):

> "All third party cases are difficult, because in tracing the chain of cause and effect, circumstances often make it almost impossible to distinguish between a flow and a break, or to say whether the intervention of the third party has not so far predominated the bringing about of the injury as to make it right to say that the act of the original party was not an effective cause of the ultimate result."

44. [1988] ILRM 225.

45. See further Byrne & Binchy, *Annual Review of Irish Law 1987*, pp 328-329; *Emeh v Kensington and Chelsea* [1985] 2 WLR 233. Contrast *Hughes v JJ Power Ltd* High Court, 11 May 1988, where unsuccessful repair work designed to undo damage done by negligent defendant was held not to constitute a *novus actus interveniens*. See also *Reeves v Carthy and O'Kelly* [1984] IR 348 (SC), where the Supreme Court held that the trial judge should not have withdrawn from the jury the plaintiff's claim for negligence against two doctors who had treated him, some time before he had a stroke. O'Higgins CJ (Hederman J concurring) rejected the notion that the doctor who provided the earlier treatment should be relieved of causal responsibility by reason of the intervention of the second doctors. "I appreciate that the administration of largacty by [the second doctor] was, so far as [the first doctor] is concerned, a complicating factor. However, in my view, a jury could well take the view on the evidence that the administration of that drug was merely an accelerating factor in the circulatory collapse which was meritable so long as the plaintiff's condition was not properly diagnosed and treated in hospital, and that for this both defendants could be held responsible". *Cf Conley v Strain* [1988] IR 628 (HC) (defence of *novus actus interveniens* not successful). See also *Van Patter v Tillsonburg District Memorial Hospital* 1997 Ont CJ LEXIS 2925 (Ont Ct (Gen Div) 16 March 1998); *Elofson v Davis* (1997) 144 DLR (4th) 143 (Alta QB); *Ferguson v National Life Assurance Co of Canada*, 1996 Ont CJ LEXIS 1663 (Ont Ct of Justice (Gen Div) 18 April 1996, Bell J).

second, what was the mental attitude of the subequent intervenor - was he careless, neligent, grossly negligent, reckless or did he intend to do damage.

**[2.29]** Clearly, if the original wrongdoer could not foresee any subsequent intervening act he will not be liable. but if he has not the comfort of this degree of unforeseeability he may be liable for subsequent intervening acts, in appropriate cases. Liability will certainly continue to attach to him where the *novus actus* was predictable and inevitable. Accordingly, if I throw a baby into a river it is predictable that the babysitter will attempt a rescue,[46] and likewise if I drive my car in a reckless manner it is predictable that a policeman will attempt to intervene. Neither of these interventions will relieve me of any causative role in the ensuing drama.

**[2.30]** But the degree of foreseeability on the part of the original perpetrator may be less clear.

**[2.31]** In *Smyth v Industrial Gases (IFS) Ltd*,[47] the plaintiff, a six year old boy, returning home from school, was seriously injured when a fellow pupil threw lime putty in his eyes. The lime putty had leaked onto the road from a cart driven by the defendants' servant. In an action for negligence and public nuisance,[48] the trial judge had withdrawn the case from the jury on the ground, *inter alia*, that the plaintiff's injury had been caused by the intervention of a third party. The Supreme Court held that he should not have done so.

**[2.32]** Maguire CJ, delivering the judgment of the Court, considered that, if the jury accepted the evidence that lime putty when scattered on the road looked like snow, it would be reasonable for it to hold that it "had the attribute of attractiveness for children ..., while its injurious effect upon the human eye would constitute its concealed peril."[49] As regards the submission that the defendants were not liable because the act of the boy who threw the lime putty should be treated as a *novus actus interveniens*, the Chief Justice expressed the view that:

> "the question as to whether an intervention of a third party should be regarded as breaking the chain of causation depends on whether, in the circumstances of the case, the defendants ought reasonably to have foreseen that such an intervention might take place. In view of the natural propensity of children to throw such things as snow at each other, the jury might reasonably take the view that in this case the intervention of the boy who threw the lime putty at the plaintiff was something which a reasonably prudent person ought to anticipate. Putting it another way, the person guilty of the original negligence cannot escape liability by showing that there was intervention by a third person, if it be shown that he ought reasonably to have foreseen that there might be such intervention, and to have foreseen, if such interventions occurred, that injury would result."[50]

---

46. See *Long v Dublin Corporation and ESB* Circuit Court, 13 January 1989, Irish Times, 14 January 1989 - plaintiff rescuing his dog.
47. (1950) 84 ILTR 1 (SC).
48. The report speaks simply of "nuisance" but in view of the fact that the case involved a danger to the public on the highway and that the plaintiff had no connection with any neighbouring property it seems clear that the action must have been for public nuisance.
49. (1950) 84 ILTR 1 at 6.
50. See also *Victor Weston (Éire) Ltd v Kenny* [1954] IR 191 (HC); *Hall v John McKone (1968) Ltd* [1975] IR 292 (HC).

**[2.33]** It should be noted that, in cases where a person acts in a deliberate way which results in an injury to himself or another, this will not break the chain of causation if the deliberate act is affected, and rendered dangerous, by the prior negligence of the defendant. Thus in *Doran v Dublin Plant Hire Ltd*,[51] a supervisor fitter who used a crowbar to loosen the flange of a roller after it had collapsed when he was moving it, was held guilty of contributory negligence but was not characterised as the *causa causans* of the accident that followed from the use of the crowbar. Unknown to the plaintiff the roller was of a new design. The earlier failure by his employer to have directed him to consult the service manual contributed to his decision to use the crowbar, even when he was put on notice by the collapse that the roller might be of a different design to that with which he was familiar.

**[2.34]** If foreseeability alone is rejected as the test for determining the effect of the *novus actus interveniens* (as it is submitted it must be), we are left then with the traditional doctrine that only the voluntary (ie, reckless or intentional) act of the plaintiff or third party is sufficient to negative causal connection. This question as to whether the voluntary act of the plaintiff or third party negatives causal connection has been considered in those cases where one wrongdoer, having been held responsible to an injured person, claims contribution from another person whose act, *prima facie*, contributed with that of the claimant in causing the injured person's damage. The Supreme Court has correctly stated that the words "or would if sued at the time of the wrong have been liable in respect of the same damage", used in s 21 of the Civil Liability Act 1961, establish that:

> "a defendant is entitled to recover contribution from a person who is not sued in the original action only if the plaintiff in the action could have succeeded in proceedings against the person from whom the contribution is claimed".[52]

This requirement brought into question the issue of *novus actus* in *Conole v Redbank Oyster Co*[53] and *Connolly v South of Ireland Asphalt Co Ltd*.[54]

**[2.35]** In *Conole v Redbank Oyster Co* the defendants knew that the boat built for them by Fairway Fabrics Ltd was unseaworthy and unsafe. Defects in the construction had shown up when, at a local ceremony to launch the boat, trial runs were being made. In spite of these defects and in contravention of an order to tie up the boat, the captain, while refreshments were being served in the local community hall, took some fifty children out in the boat. The boat capsized with the overload and the plaintiff's daughter (together with nine others) was drowned. Damages were awarded against the defendants who in the present action sought to recover contribution from Fairway Fabrics Ltd. The Supreme Court refused to award contribution declaring that the sole cause of the accident was the defendants' negligence, through the reckless act of their captain. The manufacturer's negligence did not cause the accident. Henchy J, delivering judgment said that putting to sea in a boat which the defendants knew to be unsafe:

---

51. [1990] 1 IR 488 (HC).
52. *Connolly v South of Ireland Asphalt Co Ltd* [1977] IR 99 at 107.
53. [1976] IR 191 (SC).
54. [1977] IR 99.

> "meant that the defendants were consciously undertaking the primary responsibility if an accident happened, and that Fairway were being relegated to an area of remoteness within which responsibility in negligence does not operate. Of course, the defendants are entitled to say that there would have been no accident if Fairway had not been in default in supplying an unseaworthy boat ... However, as far as the negligence that resulted in the drownings is concerned, any such default by Fairway would have been merely a *causa sine qua non* and not a *causa causans*.
>
> In terms of legal causation, there was only one act of negligence in this case: it was the defendants' act of putting to sea in a boat which they knew to be unseaworthy and which was overloaded with unsupervised young people ...
>
> The direct and proximate cause of this accident was the decision of the defendants ... to put to sea with passengers when they had a clear warning that the boat was unfit for the task. The defendants were the sole initiators of the causative negligence ..."[55]

**[2.36]** The Court was clearly dealing with an issue of legal causation. On the *Wagon Mound* doctrine approaching it from the remoteness perspective, the problem should and could easily have been resolved in terms of "reasonable foresight". Could Fairway have reasonably anticipated the conduct of the defendant company in putting to sea in the manner in which it did? Nowhere in the judgment, however, is reference made to foresight. The Court contented itself with saying that the sole cause of the accident was the negligence of the defendants. What we have here, it is submitted, is the development previously discussed in relation to *McKew's* case and *Home Office v Dorset Yacht Co*: the reversion back to causal terminology unencumbered by reference to foreseeability to determine the issue of *novus actus interveniens*. This approach was endorsed in the Supreme Court more recently in *Crowley v AIB and O'Flynn*.[56] The more outrageous and reckless the conduct of the intervenor, the more likely is it to break the chan of causation.

## Recklessness

**[2.37]** It is now necessary to describe the precise quality of the defendant's act in *Conole's* case. If reasonable foreseeability by the original wrongdoer is not the standard, but the act in question must be reckless to amount to a *novus actus*, we must ask what is meant by recklessness in this context? In the context of the criminal law, the prevalent view is that recklessness involves a conscious acceptance of the risk of doing harm. The doer of a reckless act need not desire harm to follow: he may hope and expect that harm will not follow; but he realises that harm is not unlikely to follow and he deliberately takes the risk that it will follow.[57] Another view is that recklessness is no more than gross carelessness and that a person may be reckless if he or she does an act involving an unjustifiable risk whether he or she appreciates the risk or not. The meaning of recklessness in the law of tort was considered by Kingsmill Moore J, in *Donovan v Landys Ltd*[58] where he preferred

---

55. [1976] IR 191 at 196-197.
56. [1988] ILRM 225.
57. *Russell on Crime* (12th ed, 1964) pp 41-43; Williams 'Criminal Law: The General Part' (2nd ed, 1961) 53ff; the Law Reform Commission's Report on Receiving Stolen Property, paras 114-115(LRC 23-1987); McAleese 'Just What is Recklessness'? [1981] DULJ 29; *People v Murray* [1977] IR 360 at 403 (SC).
58. [1963] IR 441 at 461-462.

the second "objective" meaning of the word, adopting the definition of recklessness "as gross carelessness" given by Megaw J, in *Shawinigan v Vokins*.[59]

**[2.38]** Clearly, in *Conole's* case it would not be inaccurate to describe the act of the defendants as being subjectively reckless, as "flying in the face of an apprehended risk, indifferent as to its outcome". The question remains open as to whether gross negligence, objective recklessness, by its intervenor is sufficient to negative causal connection with the original wrongdoer.

**[2.39]** In *Connolly (Defendant) v South of Ireland Asphalt Co Ltd (Thirdparty)*,[60] a Mr Wade had been killed when struck by the defendant's Connolly's motor car. The circumstances of the accident were that the third party had a premises bordering on a public roadways and their heavy lorries when travelling to and from their premises created several unconnected pot holes in a line along the margin of the road nearest the gates, part of each hole extending into the public road. From time to time the holes filled with water which was splashed on to the undamaged surface of the road by the wheels of vehicles passing along the road on that side. On the date of the accidents there had been a heavy fall of rain followed by a frost which caused patches of ice in the immediate vicinity of the holes. Mr Wade, driving a motor-cycle lost his balance on the icy surface and fell off his machine. While picking his machine up he was struck and killed by the defendant's car. Mr Wade's widow brought an action against the defendant alleging negligence and she was awarded damages under a settlement of the action. The defendant claimed from the third party a contribution towards the damages payable by the defendant to the plaintiff on the ground that the third party had been negligent and had created a public nuisance. Murnaghan J in the High Court dismissed the claimant's action. He held that the defendant was grossly negligent in failing to see Mr Wade and in not putting on his brakes and this finding was not disputed by the judges of the Supreme Court. The Courts, however, unanimously allowed the appeal on both grounds. O'Higgins CJ, gave a reasoned argument only in relation to the issue of nuisance. Kenny J, confined himself substantially to the claim in negligence. The effect of both judgments, however, is that the gross negligence of the claimant, Connolly, did not constitute a *novus actus* rendering the negligence of the company in failing to maintain the road which they had damaged inoperative. O'Higgins CJ, was of the opinion that "what happened was clearly foreseeable". Kenny J considered that while the third party through its employees should have foreseen the sequence of events up to the point that riders of motorcycles could be thrown onto the road and struck by following vehicles, they could not be expected to have anticipated in addition "that a driver of a car travelling behind a motor-cyclist who was crossing this icy patch and who had fallen would drive with gross negligence and so kill or injure the motor-cyclist". He held, however, that the third party would nonetheless be liable to Mr Wade's dependents as the type of harm which in fact occurred was a foreseeable consequence of the third party's

59. [1961] 1 WLR 1206 at 1214. See McMahon 'Occupier's Liability in Ireland' (1975) at 41 (Prl 4403). and Ch 12 below.

60. [1977] IR 99. See also *Murphy v GN Ry* [1897] 2 IR 301 (CA affg QBD); *McKenna v Stephens and Alexander E Hull & Co Ltd* [1923] 2 IR 112 (CA (IFS)); *Victor Weston (Éire) Ltd v Kenny* [1954] IR 191 (HC); *Reilly v Garvey* [1973] IR 89 (SC, 1972). *Cf Hall v McKone (1968) Ltd* [1975] IR 292 (HC), where *novus actus interveniens* was not pleaded.

original negligence and it was irrelevant that the precise manner in which the harm eventuated was unforeseeable. Implicit in his judgment is the view that foresight of the supervening act is not the determining factor in deciding whether that act constitutes a *novus actus*. Implicit in the unanimous decision of the Court is the view that the gross negligence (ie objective recklessness) of the intervening actor is insufficient to break the chain of causation.

**[2.40]** It is submitted that the conclusion to be drawn from the Irish and English decisions on this matter is that foreseeability of the intervening act is not the criterion for determining whether an act amounts to a *novus actus* to relieve the original wrongdoer. As Salmon LJ has said:

> "Although the foreseeability test is a handmaiden of the law, it is by no means a maid-of-all-work. To my mind it cannot serve as the true criterion when the question is, how was the damage caused?"[61]

**[2.41]** The true criterion, it is submitted, is that the voluntary act of a human being will negative causal connection when and only when such act is intentional or reckless. And "recklessness" in this context must, in the light of *Connolly's* case, mean subjective recklessness and not merely gross negligence.

**[2.42]** In *Lamb v Camden LBC*[62] the defendant through its negligence caused the plaintiff's premises to be flooded. The plaintiff, who resided abroad, caused the premises to be vacated and removed the furniture. Squatters moved in and caused considerable further damage to the premises. The Court held the squatters' action was not foreseeable and so the defendants were not liable for this further damage. Watkins LJ also held that although reasonable foreseeability was the usual test in the case of human intervening acts, the test must give way if the intervenor's act is "anti-social" and "criminal". In such a case the chain of causation will be broken by the intervening act. Similarly, in *Perl (Exporters) Ltd v Camden LBC*[63] the defendant council owned an unoccupied basement flat which they had been warned was not secure. Other flats in the block had been burgled and vagrants had been seen in the area. In spite of complaints the defendant council did nothing. Thieves entered the vacant flat and from there broke through a wall into the plaintiffs' premises from which they stole several hundred garments. The Court of Appeal in England held that the defendants owed no duty of care to the plaintiffs in the absence of a special relationship between the occupiers and the burglars. According to Walker LJ a very high degree of foreseeability is required if liability is to be imposed on a person for the acts of an independent third party. In other words, the criminal act of the third party broke the nexus between the defendant's act and the plaintiff's injury. In *Muldoon v Ireland and AG*[64] no liability was imposed on the prison authorities for injuries inflicted with a blade by one prisoner on another. Here, even though there was a relationship between the defendant (the prison authorities) and both prisioners, Hamilton P held that there had been no breach of duty by the prison authorities.

---

61. *Quinn v Burch Bros (Builders) Ltd* [19661 2 QB 370 at 394.
62. [1981] QB 625.
63. [1983] 3 All ER 161.
64. [1988] ILRM 367.

**[2.43]** An apparent exception to the rule that the voluntary act of a third party negatives causal connection is to be found in cases such as *Cunningham v McGrath Bros*[65] and *Stansbie v Troman.*[66] In the first of these cases the defendants were engaged to do some work on a shop front in Grafton Street, Dublin. Unattended ladders which were being used for the job were causing a nuisance and were removed by an unknown third party to a less obtrusive and less obstructive place where they fell and injured the plaintiff. In rejecting the defendants' argument that they did not cause the accident Kingsmill Moore J said:

> "I am of the opinion that the test to be applied is whether the person responsible for creating the nuisance should anticipate as a reasonable and probable consequence that some person in pursuance of his rights would attempt to abate the nuisance and in so doing would create the danger."

**[2.44]** In truth, no question of proximate cause or *novus actus* entered into the Court's decision inasmuch as the risk of a third party acting in the manner in which he did was the very thing which the defendants were under a duty to take precautions to avoid. The case merely demonstrates that in certain circumstances the defendant may be under an obligation *as part of his original duty* to take precautions to protect the plaintiff from the negligent or, indeed, in some cases, even the intentional acts of third parties.

**[2.45]** In *Stansbie v Troman*,[67] a householder was obliged to leave a painter working alone in his house. The painter also left the house for about two hours and (although warned by the householder to shut the door when he left the house) failed to lock the door. The painter was held liable for the loss of jewellery stolen by a third party who entered the house in his absence. Theft by another was, in the circumstances, the very thing which the painter was under a duty to take precautions against. The question in such cases. as *Prosser & Keeton* correctly state, "is essentially one of the defendant's original obligation, and far removed from causation".[68]

**[2.46]** It should be noted that, in cases where a person acts in a deliberate way which results in an injury to himself or another, this will not break the chain of causation if the deliberate act is affected, and rendered dangerous, by the prior negligence of the defendant. Thus in *Dublin Plant Hire Ltd*,[69] a supervisor fitter who used a crowbar to loosen the

65. [1964] IR 209. *Cf Hill v Lundin & Associates Inc* (1972) 260 La 542 256 So 2d 620.

66. [1948] 2 KB 48.

67. [1948] 2 KB 48.

68. PROSSER & KEETON, p 305. In the Circuit Court decision of *Dockery v O'Brien* (1975) 109 ILTR 127. A person who in contravention of a bye-law left his car unlocked in a public place with the key in the ignition switch was held liable when the car was taken by an unauthorised person and caused damage to another person's parked motor vehicle. This case may be contrasted with *Douglas Iron Works & Colquhoun v Owen* [1951] IR 93 and *Henry (t/a Sight & Sound Film Library) v Sanderson* (1972) 106 ILTR 12 (HC). In the former the plaintiff left his car in a hotel garage with the key in the ignition. The porter took the car and damaged it. In an action against the hotel owner the plaintiff failed because of his contributory negligence. (The action pre-dated the apportionment provisions of the Civil Liability Act 1961 and the Hotel Proprietors Act 1963). In the latter case the defendant left his car open and property belonging to the plaintiff was stolen from the car. The Court held that the defendant was in breach of his duty as bailee.

69. [1990] 1 IR 488 (HC). See also liability of carers and Garda Síochána for persons in their care paras **[8.14]-[8.44]** below.

flange of a roller after it had collapsed when he was moving it, was held guilty of contributory negligence but was not characterised as the *causa causans* of the accident that followed from the use of the crowbar. Unknown to the plaintiff the roller was of a new design. The earlier failure by his employer to have directed him to consult the service manual contributed to his decision to use the crowbar, even when he was put on notice by the collapse that the roller might be of a different design to that with which he was familiar.

**[2.47]** Finally, it should be remembered that the intervening actor's conduct will not be regarded as "voluntary" (ie reckless or intentional) so as to relieve the original wrongdoer, if it is a reflex action on the part of the third party,[70] or if it is performed in pursuance of a moral or legal duty (as where one rescues another or a servant in pursuance of his contract of service takes steps to protect his master's property),[71] or, where the original wrong of the defendant has forced the intervening actor into taking the course that he did, as where P fearing injury, if she remains a passenger in the defendant's runaway car jumps out hoping to escape greater injury.[72] The real question to be asked in these "alternative danger" cases is whether a reasonable person in the position of the plaintiff would have acted as she did. In putting this question the Court will adopt the objective test of what a reasonable person would do and will ignore personal infirmities peculiar to the plaintiff at the time of the accident.[73] This objective view was confirmed in *Kingston v Kingston*[74] where the defendant was taking his family on an outing to the seaside and while driving down a steep incline exclaimed "My brakes have gone". The plaintiff, the defendant's wife, who was sitting in the passenger seat jumped from the car and suffered injuries. The defendant succeeded in "nosing" the car to a halt and none of the children travelling in the car at the time suffered any injury. There was evidence that the plaintiff was of nervous disposition, a condition that had been heightened by a miscarriage some time previously. The Supreme Court refused to disturb the jury's finding that the plaintiff was guilty of contributory negligence (which was a total defence at the time) and Walsh J, delivering the Court's judgment said:

> "The test does not, and to my view properly so, permit to be taken into account the pre-accident nervous or anxious condition of the plaintiff which was peculiar to her only."[75]

70. *Scott v Shephard* (1773) 2 W Bl 892, 96 ER 525 - the "squib" case; *Brandon v Osborne Garrett & Co Ltd* [1924] 1 KB 548.
71. *Haynes v Harwood* [1935] 1 KB 146, *Baker v TE Hopkins & Sons Ltd* [1959] 1 WLR 966. But the principle does not sanction unreasonable or foolhardy heroism.
72. *Hogg v Keane* [1956] IR 155 at 158: "It is not contested that if the plaintiff can connect her injuries to the accident by showing that her fright was reasonable, she is entitled to recover damages against the defendant". See also *Kelly v McElligott* (1951) 85 ILTR 4 (SC). This case preceded the Civil Liability Act 1961 and contributory negligence was a total defence. Where the plaintiff's own act is the supervening act then it is a question of degree whether it is of such a kind that it relieves the wrongdoer completely or merely amounts to contributory negligence which allows apportionment. See *Sayers v Harlow UDC* [1958] 1 WLR 623 - plaintiff injured while climbing out of lavatory with defective lock (a harsh decision on the facts).
73. *Kingston v Kingston* (1968) 102 ILTR 65 at 68 (SC). But the question of the standard required of a plaintiff who is either physically or mentally infirm is still open.
74. (1968) 102 ILTR 65 (SC).
75. *Hogg v Keane* [1956] IR 155 at 158; *Kelly v McElligott* (1951) 85 ILTR 4 followed. Nowadays, a finding of contributory negligence would only result in an apportionment of damages.

**[2.48]** *Carslogie Steamship Co Ltd v Royal Norwegian Government*[76] provides an example of a case where an intervening natural event constituted a *novus actus*. In this case a ship was damaged through the negligence of the defendants. Temporary repairs were effected and the plaintiffs then undertook a voyage which they would not have undertaken but for the collision. During this voyage the ship suffered additional damage because of heavy weather. It was held that this extra damage was not a consequence of the collision "and must be treated as a supervening event occurring in the course of a normal voyage".[77]

**[2.49]** Likewise normal weather conditions will not relieve the wrongdoer even if they intervene, but a frost beyond all prior experience may well amount to a *novus actus*.[78]

## Summary: Novus Actus Interveniens

**[2.50]** In view of the above discussion it is useful to attempt a summary of the law relating to the vexed question of *novus actus interveniens*. Sometimes another act or event is interposed between the original act of the defendant and the damage to the plaintiff. The question then arises as to whether the defendant is liable for the damage caused by this new intervening act. Whether the intervening act is such that it is still to be considered as having been caused by the defendant or amounts to an independent cause which relieves the defendant (ie it breaks the chain of causation between the defendant's act and the plaintiff's damage) is a question that has troubled the courts for some time. All the cases cannot be reconciled on this matter but it is clear that two factors become important when the courts consider this matter. First, the courts are concerned with whether the intervening act was foreseeable by the defendant, and second, if it was foreseeable and a human act, the courts also concern themselves with the nature, the character and, in particular, the mental element of the intervening actor. From the case law we may state the following propositions with some degree of confidence:

(1) If the third party's act is *wholly unforeseeable* then the original defendant will not be liable.

(2) If the third party's act is intended by the original wrongdoer, or is as good as programmed by him, or if it is an inevitable response to defendant's act or is *very likely*, then the original defendant is still considered to be the operative cause in law. The third party's intervention in these circumstances is not a *novus actus* which will break the chain of causation between the plaintiff's damage and the defendant's conduct. This is even more obviously true where the intervening event is not a voluntary act at all: where A pushes B against C.

(3) If the third party's action is foreseeable (though not probable or likely) then the courts will look especially closely at the nature of the intervenor's act in addressing this problem. If the intervenor's act is criminal or reckless in the subjective sense, then it is likely to be considered as a *novus actus*. Similarly if the third party's act is intentional. In *Lamb*[79] Watkins LJ described the squatters' acts as "unreasonable conduct of an outrageous kind" when he held

76. [1952] AC 292; [1952] 1 All ER 20.

77. [1952] 1 All ER 22. This passage does not appear in the official report.

78. *Blyth v Birmingham Waterworks Co* (1856) 11 Ex 781, 156 Eng Rep 1047.

79. [1981] QB 625.

that the defendant wrongdoer could not be responsible for it. In *Perl*[80] the act of thieves, interposed between the defendant's conduct and the plaintiff's injury, meant that the defendants were not liable.[81] If the intervenor's act, however, is merely careless, negligent, or perhaps even grossly negligent, it may not be considered sufficiently strong to break the chain of causation between the original defendant and the plaintiff's injury,[82] although much will depend on the facts of the case. In *Crowley v AIB and O'Flynn and Others*[83] we have seen that a *negligent omission* by the third party was deemed sufficient to break the chain and relieve the defendant.

**[2.51]** Sometimes the courts arrive at these determinations by one of two routes of rationalisation: (1) the approach of the ordinary person (who would the ordinary person say caused the accident?); (2) who should be liable on policy grounds? The *novus actus* may be the act of the plaintiff himself. In this case the analysis is usually done under the rubric of contributory negligence. In extreme cases such consideration may cause the court to impose full liability on the plaintiff, but in most cases the court will nowadays apportion liability between the plaintiff and the defendants on the basis of their respective degrees of fault.

**[2.52]** This suggests another important development in recent times. The courts are no longer obsessed with seeking a single cause for accidents or injuries. They are willing to admit that there may be two or more causes sufficient to attract liability. In this event the courts are likely to settle for a multiple cause finding and apportion losses between the parties on this basis. Where the *novus actus* in question is the plaintiff's act they do this under the rubric of contributory negligence, being required by the Civil Liability Act 1961 to address the issue, overtly at least, in terms of comparative blameworthiness rather than of the potency of the causal factors moving from each side. Where the act of a third party is involved they will make their finding as between concurrent wrongdoers when they allow the statutory provisions relating to contribution to come into play.

**[2.53]** All this means is that the courts are less likely to find that a *novus actus* is the sole cause of the plaintiff's injury nowadays. It is only in very extreme cases that the nature of the third party's act will break the chain completely between the defendant's original conduct and the plaintiff's damage.

## IV. Proof

**[2.54]** It is frequently said that it is for the plaintiff to prove the causal connection between the defendant's conduct and the plaintiff's injury, and as a general principle this is undoubtedly true.[84] In *Guilfoyle v Linders*[85] for example, the plaintiff purchased from the

80. [1983] 3 WLR 769.

81. See TRINDADE & CANE, pp 504-505 on the relationship between causation and remoteness.

82. See also *Murphy v Ballyclough Co-operative Creamery Ltd* High Court, 27 February 1998 (Morris P) where the plaintiff sued several defendants who had served him drink on the day of the accident. Morris P was of the view that only the seventh named defendant, who served the last drink to the plaintiff and who drove him to his car, should be liable, if the appropriate evidence was forthcoming. See **[8.11]-[8.13]** below.

83. [1988] ILRM 225.

84. *Hanrahan v Merck, Sharp and Dohme (Irl) Ltd* [1988] ILRM 629 (SC).

defendants a second-hand car, part of the deal being that the defendant would replace a worn tyre on the off-side rear. Although the car already had three Michelin ZX radial tyres the defendant fitted a Dunlop SP radial to the car and when the plaintiff crashed some time later he claimed that the mixing of the tyres caused the accident. A High Court award of £4,988 in favour of the plaintiff was reversed by the Supreme Court which held that the plaintiff had not discharged the onus of proof that the mixing of the tyres caused the accident. Henchy J, in delivering the unanimous judgment of the Court, said the skid might have been caused by the plaintiff's braking as he rounded the bend on the wet day on which the accident occurred. The technical evidence relating to the dangers of mixing different radial tyres (as opposed to mixing radials with non-radial tyres) was inconclusive.

**[2.55]** We have seen above[86] that the plaintiff's difficulty in the matter of proof may be most acute when he is trying to establish factual causation. In *Meehan v Reid and Murphy* and in *Kearney v Paul and Vincent Ltd* we saw that the plaintiff failed to satisfy the Court, and even where the plaintiff succeeded in *Berkery v Flynn* and in the *Hanrahan* case, the scientific proof and the technical evidence required were daunting.

**[2.56]** In many cases, however, the plaintiff's task will not be a difficult one, and in the typical car accident, for example, the causal link will be easily shown. Moreover, the plaintiff must show the existence of the link only as a matter of probability. And even where proof is more difficult because of the plaintiff's inability to testify or because of the absence of independent witnesses, the Courts may not be too unsympathetic to the plaintiff's predicament, by accepting circumstantial evidence as sufficient to establish the causal link. In *McKenzie v O'Neill and Roe Ltd*[87] an extensive area of gorse and heather on the plaintiff's property was destroyed by fire. Evidence was given that earlier in the day in question the defendant's men had started a rubbish fire on the defendant's premises. The men in charge of the fire, however, testified that the fire was continuously watched until it was out and that there was at least an hour's interval between the exhaustion of the rubbish fire and the moment when the fire on the plaintiff's property was noticed. No other evidence of a specific nature was offered, although the Court did take notice that the fire occurred during a lengthy period of dry weather. Nevertheless, the trial judge was, in the circumstances, prepared to find that the defendant's fire caused the fire on the plaintiff's property. Again in *Kielthy v Ascon Ltd*[88] a workman was found dead at the bottom of a wall on a building site. Evidence was produced that a recognised route to the defendant's office at the building site was along the narrow nine-inch wide wall in question, although this was not the only, or the safest, route. There was no direct evidence as to how the deceased fell, but the Supreme Court held that there was sufficient evidence for the lower Court to find that the deceased's fall was caused by the defendant's failure to provide a safe system of access and that there was no evidence of contributory negligence on the part of the deceased.

85. Supreme Court, 23 November 1979; Irish Times, 24 November 1979, p 8.

86. Above, text accompanying fns 9-14. *Meehan v Reid and Murphy* High Court, 5 March 1985; *Kearney v Paul and Vincent Ltd* High Court, 30 July 1985; *Berkery v Flynn* High Court, 10 June 1982; *Hanrahan v Merck, Sharp and Dohme (Irl) Ltd* [1988] ILRM 629.

87. High Court, 23 June 1977.

88. [1970] IR 122 (SC).

**[2.57]** Finally, in *Clark v MacLennan*,[89] in a medical negligence case, it was held that where the defendant departs from established practice and the plaintiff suffers injury, then it is for the defendant to show that his act did not cause the accident.

**[2.58]** The most recent pronouncement on these matters occurs in *Hanrahan v Merck Sharp and Dohme*.[90] In that case the plaintiffs, in proceedings for nuisance (*inter alia*), claimed that emissions from the defendants' factory interfered with the enjoyment of their land and caused damage to the health of the plaintiffs and to their farm stock. Henchy J, in delivering the judgment of the Supreme Court, said on this issue:

> "The ordinary rule is that a person who alleges a particular tort must, in order to succeed, prove (save where there are admissions) all the necessary ingredients of that tort and it is not for the defendant to disprove anything."

**[2.59]** Having referred to the rule of *res ipsa loquitur* which, when a particular element of the tort of negligence lies pre-eminently within the defendants' knowledge, operates to allow the act relied on to be evidence of negligence and (according to most Irish decisions) has the effect of shifting the onus of proof onto the defendant, he continued:

> "That is not the case here. What the plaintiffs have to prove in support of their claim in nuisance is that they suffered some or all of the mischief complained of and that it was caused by emissions from the defendants' factory. To hold that it is for the defendants to disprove either or both of those matters would be contrary to authority and not be demanded by the requirements of justice. There are of course difficulties facing the plaintiffs in regard to proof of those matters, particularly as to the question of causation, but mere difficulty of proof does not call for a shifting of the onus of proof. Many claims in tort fail because the plaintiff has not access to full information as to the true nature of the defendant's conduct. The onus of disproof rests on the defendant only when the act or default complained of is such that it would be fundamentally unjust to require the plaintiff to prove a positive averment when the particular circumstances show that fairness and justice call for disproof by the defendant. The argument put forward in this case for putting a duty of disproof on the defendants would be more sustainable if the plaintiffs had to prove that the emissions complained of were caused by the defendants' negligence. Such is not the case. In my view having regard to the replies given by the defendants to interrogatories and notices for particulars and to the full discovery of documents made by them, it is not open to the plaintiffs to complain that for want of knowledge on their part it would be unjust or unfair to require them to bear the ordinary onus of proof."[91]

**[2.60]** The plaintiffs in *Hanrahan* also tried to pray in the Constitution to help them in the matter of proof. In essence their argument was that the Constitution guaranteed (Article 40.3) to protect their personal right to bodily integrity and the property right to their land and livestock. They claimed that the tort of nuisance may be said to be an implementation

---

89. [1983] 1 All ER 416. Whether this decision can still stand in the light of *Hotson v East Berkshire Area Health Authority* [1988] AC 750 (HL), may be debated.

90. [1988] ILRM 629 (SC).

91. At 635. This passage gives rise to difficulty in that it suggests that the same causal issue could involve different onuses of proof depending on whether the proceedings sounded in nuisance or negligence. This is particularly a matter of concern when it is recalled that negligence can play a significant role in determining liability in nuisance. For critical analysis of Henchy's remarks in relation to *res ipsa loquitur*, see paras **[9.49]**-**[9.53]** below.

of the State's duties, but that the State was not vindicating the citizens' rights adequately if it obliged the plaintiff (once damage was shown) to prove that it was the defendant's conduct that caused it. The plaintiffs claimed that in such circumstances a proper recognition of the plaintiff's constitutional rights should put the onus on the defendants to show that they did not cause the damage. The Court roundly rejected this argument. Henchy J said:

> "So far as I am aware, the constitutional provisions relied on have never been used in the courts to shape the form of any existing tort or to change the normal onus of proof. The implementation of those constitutional rights is primarily a matter for the State and the courts are entitled to intervene only when there has been a failure to implement or, where the implementation relied on is plainly inadequate, to effectuate the constitutional guarantee in question. In many torts - for example, negligence, defamation, trespass to person or property - a plaintiff may give evidence of what he claims to be a breach of constitutional right, but he may fail in the action because of what is usually a matter of onus of proof or because of some other legal or technical defence. A person may of course in the absence of a common law or statutory cause of action, sue directly for breach of a constitutional right but when he founds his action on an existing tort he is normally confined to the limitations of that tort. It might be different if it could be shown that the tort in question is basically ineffective to protect his constitutional right. But that is not alleged here. What is said is that he may not succeed in having his constitutional rights vindicated if he is required to carry the normal onus of proof. However, the same may be said about many other causes of action. Lack of knowledge as to the true nature of the defendants' conduct or course of conduct may cause the plaintiff difficulty, but it does not change the onus of proof''.[92]

It is worth noting in this context that s 11(3) of the Civil Liability Act 1961 provides that, where two or more persons are at fault and one or more of them is or are responsible for damage while the other is or are free from causal responsibility, but it is not possible to establish which is the case, such two or more persons are deemed concurrent wrongdoers in respect of the damage. This provision catches the obvious case of where two persons (not acting in concert) negligently fire their guns in the direction of the plaintiff and a bullet from one of the guns strikes him or her but it is not possible to say from which gun it emerged.[93] Of perhaps greater potential interest is the possibility of using s 11(3) in relation to multiple polluters where causation difficulties present themselves, as well as in relation to cases where an entire industry engages in the negligent production of a dangerous item (such as a drug) and the plaintiff is unable to prove which particular producer manufactured the product that caused him or her injury.[94]

---

92. [1988] ILRM 636. In cases where there is a "conspiracy of silence" among those who are aware of what caused the plaintiff's injury, especially where the plaintiff had placed himself or herself in a relationship of trust or dependency on whose who remain silent, a shift in the burden of proof on constitutional grounds might be considered desirable: *cf Ybarra v Spangard* (1949) 93 Cal App 2d 43, 208 P 2d 445.

93. *Cf Cook v Lewis* [1952] 1 DLR 1 (SC of Canada); *Summers v Tice* (1948) 33 Cal 2d 80, 199 P 2d 1. The latter decision did not greatly impress Kingsmill Moore J, dissenting, in *Power v Bedford Motor Co Ltd* [1959] IR 391 (SC).

94. *Cf Sindell v Abbott Laboratories* (1980) 26 Cal 3d 588, 607 P 2d 924, adopting a "share-of-market" test of liability. Note that s 11(3) would allow the plaintiff total recovery against any of the defendants in such a case, leaving it to the producers to work out liability *inter se* in accordance with the rules as to contribution contained in Part III of the Civil Liability Act 1961. See Handsten 'Market Share Liability and the Nature of Causation in Tort' (1993) 1 Torts LJ 24.

## V. Causation and Medical Negligence

**[2.61]** As we have seen in our general discussion of the subject, causation is frequently put in issue in medical negligence cases, partly, no doubt because in many cases medical knowledge is limited and the relevant medical research has not been undertaken or has not produced definitive answers. In such cases witnesses citing different authorities can be enlisted by the parties and the ensuing battle of the experts invites the court to pronounce on matters which, in truth, are still very much open to debate. Given that the onus is on the plaintiff to prove the factual connection, it is in the defendant's interest to argue that the causal link between the plaintiff's injury and the defendant's negligence is far from accepted in existing medical literature. A recent example of such a dispute made its appearance before the Irish courts when the defendant argued that there was no objective proof from existing research to support a claim by the plaintiff that he suffered multiple scleriosis because of negligently inflicted trauma.[95] Similar causal problems arise for plaintiffs who try to link illnesses with the "three in one" injection administered to children with the support and encouragement of the State.

**[2.62]** One example will suffice to illustrate the point. In *O'Mahony v Tyndale*[96] the paintiff claimed that the cerebral palsy, the severe mental and physical handicap and the epilepsy he suffered from was caused by the negligence of the defendants at the time of his birth. The trial judge found that the hospital system and procedures were found wanting in two respects: a delay in the delivery by about 7-12 minutes longer than the hospital's system comtemplated; and the inadequate system in use at the time for recording the medication prescribed for and given to mothers in the "24 hour nursery" where the plaintiff was kept for 19 hours after his birth. Neither of these factors, however, was shown by the plaintiff to have caused or contributed to his disability. The experts were not able to convince the Court as to what caused the plaintiff's injury and the plaintiff in particular had not discharged the onus of proving on the balance of probabilities that his disability was caused because he developed hypoglycaemia (low blood sugar levels) due to inadequate nursing care during the period immediately after his birth.

**[2.63]** No doubt the question of causation will continue to be pressed as a defence in medical negligence cases in future.[97]

---

95. *O'Leary v Lord Mayior, Aldermann and Burgesses of Cork* Supreme Court, 4 July 1997. The possibility of such connection was accepted, but the plaintiff failed to prove that his MS was caused by the accident which befell hom in July 1985 and for which the defendants accepted liability.

96. High Court, 7 April 2000 (Quirke J).

97. See para **[2.20]-[2.21]** below. In *Bolitho v Hackney Health Authority* [1998] AC 232, the House of Lords held that the casual connection between a defendant's negligent omission and a plaintiff's injury is not broken by showing that the damage would have occurred in any event because he or she would have committed some other breach of duty had he or she not been guilty of the negligent omission.

## Chapter 3

# Remoteness[1]


I. Introduction .......... 83
II. Direct Consequences .......... 84
III. Reasonable Foreseeability .......... 85
IV. Types of Damage .......... 90
V. Conclusion .......... 98


## I. Introduction

**[3.01]** In this chapter we examine the criteria which the courts use in fixing the cut-off point in the line of consequences, beyond which the defendant will not accountable.[2]

**[3.02]** When proceeding to examine the remoteness standard it may be helpful if one bears in mind a concrete fact situation which might be used as a reference point to prevent one from becoming over-abstract about the problem. Suppose the defendant in negligently driving her car knocks down and injures the plaintiff. In the accident, the plaintiff's leg is broken. The plaintiff is operated on but is left with a permanent and noticeable limp in his right leg. As a result he suffers a personality change, he loses his job and takes to the drink. His health deteriorates, his wife leaves him, and his children are alienated. Moreover, in an unsuccessful attempt to commit suicide the plaintiff inflicts serious injuries on himself. One could continue, but there is probably sufficient in this example to serve our purposes and to meaningfully ask in a concrete fashion for which of these consequences should the defendant be liable in law?

**[3.03]** At common law two approaches are discernible: the direct consequence rule and the reasonable foreseeability rule. The direct consequence rule is usually associated with the 1921 case, *Re Polemis and Furness Withy & Co Ltd*[3] and this approach held sway until the

---

1. The literature on this topic is extensive. It includes White *Civil Liability for Industrial Accidents* (1993) Vol 1, paras 7.601-7.612; Williams 'The Risk Principle' (1961) 77 LQR 179; Goodhart 'Liability and Compensation' (1960) 76 LQR 567; Goodhart 'The Unforeseeable Consequences of a Negligent Act' (1930) 39 Yale LJ 449. Seavey 'Mr Justice Cardozo and the Law of Torts' (1939) 52 Harv LR 372; Dias 'Remoteness of Liability and Legal Police' [1962] Camb LJ 178; Fleming 'The Passing of Polemis' (1961) 39 Can BR 439; Dworkin 'Risk and Remoteness - Confusion Worst Confounded' (1964) 27 MLR 344; McLaren 'Negligence and Remoteness - The Aftermath of the Wagon Mound' (1967) 32 Sask LR 45; Fuerst 'Foreseeability in American and English Law' (1965) 14 Clev-Mar LR 552; Foster, Grant and Green 'Note: The Risk Theory and Proximate Cause - A Comparative Survey' (1953) 32 Neb LR 72; Cooke 'Remoteness of Damages and Judicial Discretion' [1978] Camb LJ 288; Coval, Smith & Rush 'Out of the Maze, Towards a Clear Understanding of the Test for Remoteness of Damages in Negligence' (1983) 61 Can BR 559.
2. The Statutes of Limitations are another way in which the law attempts to introduce another cut-off point: a temporal one.
3. [1921] 3 KB 560 (CA).

reasonable foreseeability rule established itself with a vengence in 1961 in *Overseas Tankship (UK) Ltd v Morts Dock and Engineering Co Ltd (The Wagon Mound (No 1)*.[4] Put succinctly, *Re Polemis* stated that the defendant was liable for all the *direct consequences* of his or her negligence, whereas in the *Wagon Mound (No 1)* the Privy Council held that the defendant was liable only for those consequences which flowed from his or her negligence which were *reasonably foreseeable.*

**[3.04]** Before examining these two rules, two preliminary points must be made. First, as we shall see, a person is always liable for the consequences he or she *intends* to cause, even if these are unforeseeable. If I throw a stone at a person some 70 metres away from me intending to hit him, then I will be liable if I do hit him even though the chances of my succeeding are extremely slim. Second, in unintentional torts the question of remoteness does not arise unless liability is first established, and there can be no liability unless the defendant could foresee damage of *some sort* resulting from his or her act. If the defendant could not foresee any damage whatsoever from his or her actions, then the defendant cannot be liable and the question of remoteness will not arise. It is only when the threshold question of liability is first established that one can address the next question: liable for *what?* Both of these points are more fully developed later in this chapter.

## II. DIRECT CONSEQUENCES

### *Re Polemis*[5]

**[3.05]** The facts in *Re Polemis* were as follows: An agent of the charterers of a ship, while unloading the vessel in Casablanca, negligently knocked a plank into the hold of the ship. The impact of the plank in the hold caused a spark which ignited petrol vapour which had accumulated in the hold. The ensuing explosion caused a fire which destroyed the ship. In the action by the owners of the ship against the charterers, the latter alleged that the damage was too remote. The Court held that, if the charterers could reasonably foresee some damage, liability in negligence was established; and in such circumstances the charterers should be liable for all the *direct* consequences of their acts. Scrutton LJ put the matter this way:

> "To determine whether an act is negligent, it is relevant to determine whether any reasonable person would foresee that the act would cause damage; if he would not, the act is not negligent. But if the act would or might probably cause damage, the fact that the damage it in fact causes is not the exact kind of damage one would expect is immaterial, so long as the damage is in fact directly traceable to the negligent act ...".[6]

In the present case it was clear that negligence in knocking down the plank might cause some injury to other workmen, to the cargo or to the ship and in such event, liability being

---

4. [1961] AC 388 (PC).

5. See Goodhart 'The Brief Life Story of the Direct Consequences Rule in English Tort Law' (1967) 53 Va LR 857; Tilley 'The English Rule as to Liability for Unintentional Consequences' (1935) 33 Mich LR 829; White *Civil Liability for Industrial Accidents* (1993) Vol 1, para 7.605.

6. [1921] 3 KB at 577.

established,[7] the charterers were liable for all the direct consequences including the burning of the ship. This approach clearly distinguishes between the initial issue of liability, where *foreseeability* is the test, and the issue of the extent of the liability (liable for which consequences?) where *directness* is the criterion.[8]

## III. Reasonable Foreseeability

### *The Wagon Mound (No 1)*[9]

**[3.06]** The facts in *Wagon Mound* were as follows: the appellants chartered the SS Wagon Mound and while the ship was taking on bunkering oil in Sydney harbour their employees carelessly allowed some of the oil to spill into the bay. The oil spread over the bay and accumulated in large quantities near the respondents' wharf. The employees of the respondents on noticing the oil suspended work which involved the use of electric and oxy-acetylene welding equipment. On making further enquiries about the risk of the oil catching fire the respondents' works manager considered that work could safely be resumed, but ordered that extra precautions should be taken to prevent inflammable material getting into the oil from the wharf. Two days later some molten matter fell into the oil, ignited a piece of debris and set the oil on fire. The respondents' wharf was damaged by the fire. They sued, and were awarded damages. This award was confirmed by the Full Court of the Supreme Court of New South Wales and an appeal was taken to the Judicial Committee of the Privy Council. The appeal was allowed.

**[3.07]** The Judicial Committee decided that in resolving the remoteness issue it was illogical and unjust to use two different standards. One could not use the reasonable foreseeability test to determine liability (or culpability) and direct (or natural) consequences to determine the extent of the liability or the remoteness of consequences

7. The decision is less than entirely clear, in regard to the requirement (recognised in *Palsgraf v Long Island Railroad Co* (1928) 248 NY 339, 162 NE 99 and *Hay (or Bourhill) v Young* [1943] AC 92) that the defendant should have been negligent *towards the plaintiff*. Indeed Scrutton LJ's judgment might, in part, be interpreted as not insisting on this requirement. It is interesting to note that in *Palsgraf*, Cardozo CJ had no rooted objection to the *Polemis* test, provided the threshold issue of the defendant's negligence in *risking some foreseeable injury* to the plaintiff (though not necessarily the injury that the plaintiff actually suffered) was resolved in the plaintiff's favour.

8. See generally Dias 'Remoteness of Liability and Legal Police' [1962] Camb LJ 178. In *Ring v Power* [1961] Ir Jur 51 it was pointed out that although *Re Polemis* had been acted on on several occasions in the Supreme Court the case was never specifically approved in Ireland. See also *Kinsella v Hammond Lane Industries Ltd* (1962) 96 ILTR 1 at 2 (SC), were *Polemis* had "been the subject of much controversy", that it had not yet been considered in the House of Lords nor the Supreme Court, and that, in *Ring v Power*, Lavery J, in citing some passages from the judgments in *Polemis* had observed that if the statements in these passages were to be treated as general propositions, they raised questions fundamental to the law of negligence. But what appears to be unambiguous support for *Polemis* is evident in *McKenna v Stephens and Alexander E Hall & Co Ltd* [1923] 2 IR 112 (CA(IFS)). See also *O'Mahony v Ford* [1962] IR 146 at 153. *Cf Kelly v McElligott* (1951) 85 ILTR 4 at 13. *McCabe v Delany* [1951] Ir Jur 10 at 13-14 (HC). *Tarrant v Sullivan* [1949] Ir Jur 46 (CC) would also appear consistent with the *Polemis* approach. A confusion of approaches is apparent in the earlier decision of *Martin v Dublin United Tramways Co Ltd* [1909] 2 IR 13 (KB).

9. See Goodhart, 'The Brief Life Story of the Direct Consequences Rule in English Tort Law', (1967) 53 Va LR 857.

issue. In its view reasonable foreseeability was the sole standard to be applied at both stages - or in truth, was to be applied only once since there was really only one question to be determined, namely, was the defendant liable for this damage?

> "It is, no doubt, proper when considering tortious liability for negligence to analyse its elements and to say that the plaintiff must prove a duty owed to him by the defendant, a breach of that duty by the defendant, and consequent damage. But there can be no liability until the damage has been done. It is not the act but the consequences on which tortious liability is founded. Just as (as it has been said) there is no such thing as negligence in the air, so there is no such thing as liability in the air. Suppose an action brought by A for damage caused by the carelessness (a neutral word) of B, for example a fire caused by the careless spillage of oil. It may, of course, become relevant to know what duty B owed to A, but the only liability that is in question is the liability for damage by fire. It is vain to isolate the liability from its context and to say that B is or is not liable, and then to ask for what damage he is liable. For his liability is in respect of that damage and no other. If, as admittedly it is, B's liability (culpability) depends on the reasonable foreseeability of the consequent damage, how is that to be determined except by the foreseeability of the damage which in fact happened - the damage in suit? And, if that damage is unforeseeable so as to displace liability at large, how can the liability be restored so as to make compensation payable?"[10]

**[3.08]** The decision is not without conceptual difficulties and has been the subject of some criticism. It nevertheless represents the majority opinion as to the current state of the law on the issue.[11]

**[3.09]** An interesting application of the reasonable foreseeability test can be seen clearly in the case of *Condon v CIE et al*[12] The background to this case was a tragic railway accident in Buttevant, Co Cork, when the Dublin to Cork passenger train was derailed, causing the death of 18 people and injuries to 75 more. The plaintiff was a railway employee who was suspected of being responsible for the accident. The Minister for Transport and Tourism set up a statutory inquiry and the plaintiff in the present action sought to recover damages from CIE (who did not deny negligence), including the costs of being legally represented at the inquiry. In adopting the reasonable foreseeability test and citing *Burke v John Paul & Co Ltd* and *Wagon Mound (No 1)*, Barrington J said:

> "I accept that in determining liability for the consequences of a tortious act of negligence the test to be applied is whether the damage is of such a kind as a reasonable man should have foreseen. I also accept that if the damage is of such a kind as a reasonable man should have foreseen it is quite irrelevant that no one foresaw the actual extent of the damage."

**[3.10]** Barrington J then went on to hold that although the Minister had a discretion with regard to holding such an inquiry, this was not an arbitrary discretion. Indeed, it was not only foreseeable that the Minister would establish an inquiry in such circumstances, but it was almost unthinkable that he would not:

---

10. [1961] AC 425.

11. *Wagon Mound (No 1)* has been approved in Ireland in several decisions including *Riordans Travel & Riordans Shipping Ltd v Acres & Co Ltd (No 2)* [1979] ILRM 3 (HC); *Irish Shipping v Dublin Port & Docks Board* (1967) 101 ILTR 182 (SC); *Dockery v O'Brien* (1975) 109 ILTR 127 (CC); *Reeves v Carthy* [1984] IR 348 (SC); *Egan & Sons Ltd v John Sisk & Sons Ltd* [1986] ILRM 283 (HC); *Burke v John Paul & Co Ltd* [1967] IR 277 (SC), and *Condon v CIE et al*, High Court, 16 November 1984.

12. High Court, 16 November 1984.

"This being so it appears to me to be also reasonably foreseeable that the Plaintiff as a person immediately involved in the events leading up to the disaster and whose actions must require minute examination from the Court of Inquiry, should, in his own interest, seek representation before the inquiry and be granted such representation."[13]

**[3.11]** Since the plaintiff was placed in this position because of the negligence of CIE, and since the plaintiff acted reasonably, he was entitled to his legal costs in the circumstances as these were a reasonably foreseeable consequence of the defendants' negligence.

**[3.12]** Where a defendant's negligence has occasioned a reasonably foreseeable rescue attempt in which the rescuer receives reasonably foreseeable injuries, liability will be imposed.[14] The courts no longer heed the argument that the rescuer's conscious exposure of himself or herself to danger represents a *novus actus interveniens* or a voluntary assumption of risk. It should be noted that if the rescue attempt was not reasonably foreseeable, however heroic it may have been, the defendant will not be liable for the rescuer's injuries. Thus, in the famous case of *Horsley v MacLaren*,[15] the majority of the Supreme Court of Canada held that a passenger who jumped from a boat to rescue his friend who had already fallen over board, was acting in an unforeseeable manner because it should have been obvious to him that the water of Lake Ontario in the early spring were so cold that no one could survive for more than the briefest exposure to it.

**[3.13]** It is also worth emphasising that the foreseeability for the rescue does not depend on there being anyone (or any property) in actual danger. The negligence consists simply of carelessly and foreseeably inducing the rescue attempt by creating a situation of apparent peril. Thus, in *Turner v Iarnród Éireann/Irish Rail*,[16] where a mother fell on the railway track when searching agitatedly for her six year old daughter whom she mistakenly believed to have gone through an opening in the fence beside the track, Flood J imposed liability on the railway company and the local authority for negligently creating the situation of apparent danger. Although on that point Flood J mentioned that the plaintiff's injuries were "a direct consequence"[17] of the railway company's breach of duty of care in failing to provide adequate fencing, the tenor of his judgment as a whole appears clearly to harmonise with the requirement of *Wagon Mound (No 1)* rather than *Re Polemis*.

**[3.14]** In *Egan v Sisk*[18] the plaintiff's warehouse was flooded due to the negligence of the first named defendant. The flood destroyed brochures which were stored there and which the plaintiffs planned to use in connection with their mail order business. Fliers had already been sent out to the American market and 9,000 applications for brochures at $2

13. At p 24.
14. See para **[3.07]** below. A clear instance in *Phillips v Durgan* [1991] ILRM 321 (SC). In England, the question of compensating professional rescuers for psychiatric damage has been hotly debated in the wake of the House of Lords decision in *White v Chief Constable of the South Yorkshire Police* [1999] 1 All ER 1. See Lomax & Treece 'Liability to the Professional Rescuer: Who Pays' (1999) 15 Prof Neg 139.
15. [1972] SCR 441 (SC, Can).
16. High Court, 14 February 1996, analysed by Byrne & Binchy, *Annual Review of Irish Law 1996*, pp 592-595.
17. At p 9 of Flood J's judgment.
18. [1986] ILRM 283.

each had been received. The plaintiffs could calculate from this response for brochures how many orders for advertised goods could be expected for the Christmas market. Because the plaintiffs lost the brochures, and because they could not have them reprinted in time for the Christmas demand, they incurred substantial losses, including loss of profits on anticipated sales amounting to £140,307. Carroll J, in awarding total damages of £196,000, made the following statement on the remoteness issue.

> "If a defendant through its negligence injures property in a warehouse, it must take the responsibility for damaging whatever goods are there. There might be expensive furs, old masters, priceless antiques, first editions, etc. It is also foreseeable that because a warehouse is part of the world of commerce, there will be economic loss and possible loss of profits. If the goods can be replaced at cost, so much the better for the defendant; if the goods cannot be replaced, then the economic loss, including loss of profits, is foreseeable.
> In my opinion the economic consequences of the loss of the brochures was immediately predictable at the time of the damage. What was unforeseen in this case was that the plaintiff could not get a reprint of the brochures in time. But this is a separate issue and concerns the duty of the plaintiff to mitigate. Different considerations apply. The plaintiffs' duty is to take all reasonable steps to mitigate. If the Court is satisfied that this was done, then the fact that the inability of the plaintiff to mitigate was unforeseeable, is not relevant."[19]

**[3.15]** In this case the plaintiffs were able to quantify their claim in a convincing fashion because of previous annual figures available to them.

**[3.16]** It is interesting to note that disenchantment with *Re Polemis* was evident in Ireland as early as 1960 in *O'Mahony v Ford*,[20] a decision of the Supreme Court given a year before *Wagon Mound (No 1)*. In this case the plaintiff was employed as a riveter by the defendant company which manufactured and assembled motor vehicles. The rivet gun and the electric drill which the plaintiff used in his employment was operated by resting it against his chest. During its use the rivet gun and the drill vibrated constantly against the plaintiff's chest and in 1956 he noticed a small swelling which was diagnosed as scirrhus carcinoma of the left breast. He sued his employers. At the end of the plaintiff's case the defendant's company sought a direction. The trial judge refused and left one question to the jury: "Were the defendants negligent?" The jury failed to agree and the defendants appealed to the Supreme Court asking that the plaintiff's case should be dismissed and seeking an order which would set aside the trial judge's refusal to withdraw the case from the jury. The Supreme Court allowed the appeal and entered judgment for the defendants. Lavery J delivering the majority opinion declared the question for the Court to be as follows:

> "Whether an act or omission which might have caused but, in fact, did not cause injury or damage which the reasonable man might be held to have foreseen and had, therefore, a duty not to commit or to omit, is actionable negligence because injury or damage of a different

---

19. At pp 284-285. The latter paragraph can perhaps best be understood as going no further than to assert that a foreseeable type of injury may be compensated even where the particular circumstances in which it unfolds may not reasonably have been foreseen. The mere fact that the plaintiff is not guilty of negligent failure to mitigate his or her damages, in terms of contributory negligence under Civil Liability Act 1961, s 34(2)(b) does not, of itself, render a defendant liable to compensate a plaintiff for unforeseeable loss resulting from this inability to mitigate damages.
20. [1962] IR 146.

kind not foreseeable and one, therefore, in respect of which there was no duty, has been suffered?"[21]

**[3.17]** In other words, Lavery J felt that although the defendants could foresee physical injury (bruising, etc) no such injury had in fact occurred, and he posed the question whether in such circumstances the defendants could be liable for a different kind of injury (cancer) which could not be reasonably foreseen. In the event he refused to impose liability in such circumstances because in respect of the former injury no damage had in fact occurred and in respect of the latter there was no negligence or duty.

> "The breach of duty which might be established did not cause any injury and an award of damages in respect of an injury which the defendants could not foresee and had no duty to guard against would lack the necessary support that the injury was caused by their negligence and breach of duty".[22]

**[3.18]** In the same judgment and in the context of remoteness of damage he put the matter this way:

> "In neither [*Re Polemis* nor *Thurogood v Van Den Berghs & Jurgens Ltd*[23]] was the question considered whether any damage of the nature reasonably foreseeable had in fact been caused. This consideration was treated as irrelevant.
>
> Though not considered, it was the position that in the *Polemis* Case the foreseeable damage which might be caused by the fall of the plank was not suffered and the damage actually caused, but not foreseeable, was certainly not of the same 'exact kind'."[24]

**[3.19]** In denying the plaintiff a right to recover in these circumstances Lavery J was greatly modifying *Polemis* and was anticipating the approach favoured in *Wagon Mound (No 1)*. He was insisting that for the defendant to be liable the foreseeable damage must be of the same "kind" as the damage which actually occurred. Not only must the defendant foresee some damage but he must foresee *the type* of damage which occurred before he should be liable for it. One year later in *Wagon Mound (No 1)*, although damage to the plaintiffs' wharf was foreseeable and damage to the plaintiffs' wharf occurred, the Privy Council would not allow recovery because the damage which was foreseeable was fouling by oil, whereas the damage which occurred was damage by fire:

> "We have come back to the plain common sense stated by Lord Russell of Killowen in *Hay (or Bourhill) v Young*.[25] As Denning LJ said in *King v Phillips*: 'there can be no doubt since *Hay (or Bourhill) v Young* that the test of *liability for shock is* foreseeability of *injury by shock*'.[26] Their Lordships substitute the word 'fire' for 'shock' and endorse this statement of the law."[27]

---

21. At 155.
22. At 158.
23. [1951] 2 KB 537.
24. [1962] IR 155.
25. [1943] AC 92.
26. [19531 1 QB 429 at 441.
27. |1961] AC 426.

## IV. Types of Damage

**[3.20]** The crucial question then becomes how does one distinguish one type of damage from another?[28] What do we mean by different kinds of damage? In addressing the liability issue, even before *Re Polemis*, the Courts used three broad categories of damages as being separate and distinct from each other: physical, psychological and economic. In the area of remoteness, however, the courts are much more detailed in their efforts to distinguish the various types of damage from each other. This analysis is not in any sense reducible to a scientific categorisation. Underlying the judicial approach is the desire to ensure that too precise an application of the test of reasonable foreseeability would relieve admittedly negligent defendants of liability.[29] Unfortunately, once the courts invoked the somewhat robust notion of "types" of damage, they were inevitably called on to give some conceptual force to this notion. By and large they have sensibly declined to define it too precisely, and have preferred to adopt a pragmatic, intuitive resolution of the problem,[30] without any philosophical pretensions.

**[3.21]** In *Reeves v Carthy and O'Kelly*[31] an attempt was made by the defendant doctors to defend themselves by saying that, even if they were negligent in their diagnosis and prescription, they were not liable for the fact that the plaintiff suffered a stroke because, unknown to them at the time, the patient also had Crohn's Disease. The defendants, it was argued, might have foreseen an abdominal perforation, but they could not have foreseen the occurrence of a stroke as such which was not the consequence of the perforation but of a perforation with Crohn's Disease. The Supreme Court refused to accept this argument:

> "In this case, the damage which occurred was of a type that was foreseeable (ie circulatory damage and shock), so that, even if the stroke was not foreseeable by the defendants, if either

28. See *Tremain v Pike* [1969] 1 WLR 1556, where the plaintiff contracted a rare disease (Weils disease) because the farm where he worked was allowed to be overrun with rats. In his action he failed because the damage suffered was both unforeseeable and "entirely different in kind" from that which might have been foreseeable such as injury from a rat bite or from eating food contaminated by the rats.

29. This probably explains the decision of *Hughes v Lord Advocate* [1963] AC 837 (HL). See also *Connolly v South of Ireland Asphalt Co Ltd* [1977] IR 99 (SC). *Cf Kennedy v Hughes Dairy Ltd* [1989] ILRM 117 (SC) considered para **[18.147]-[18.149]** below; *Fitzsimons v Bord Telecom Éireann* [1991] ILRM 276 (HC), analysed by Byrne & Binchy *Annual Review of Irish Law 1990*, pp 488-493.

30. *Cf* eg *Doughty v Turner Manufacturing Co Ltd* [1964] 1 QB 518 (CA); *Kennedy v Hughes Dairy Ltd* [1989] ILRM 117 (SC) analysed by Byrne & Binchy *Annual Review of Irish Law 1988*, pp 414-415. TRINDADE & CANE, pp 377-378 make the pertinent observation that where the injury occurs in two distinct stages it is easier to apply the "type of damage" analysis than where the loss is indivisible and the question is how to describe it. This is particularly apparent in cases where the plaintiff suffers some serious emotional disturbance as a result of the defendant's negligence and the court is required to characterise the condition as "nervous shock", "grief" or "guilt neurosis".

31. [1984] IR 348 (SC). See also *O'Donovan v Cork County Council* [1967] IR 173 (SC) - risk of ether convulsions a foreseeable risk in administration of anaesthetic even though it occurs only rarely; *per* Walsh J (at 202):

> "The fact that it may manifest itself gradually in some instances and come on with unheralded severity and suddeness in other cases does not make the latter circumstances a different risk. It is but a variant of the foreseeable risk, namely the risk of either convulsions occuring."

of them was held to have been negligent then he would be answerable for the stroke because that was the extent of the damage suffered."[32]

**[3.22]** In *Burke v John Paul & Co Ltd*[33] the plaintiff suffered a hernia because he was obliged to use a blunt cutter in the course of his employment and thereby exert greater pressure than if the blades had been properly maintained. The defendants argued that they could not reasonably anticipate that the plaintiff would suffer a hernia because of his exertions. They might have anticipated a tearing or straining of muscles but not the hernia which was due to a congenital predisposition of the plaintiff. The Court once more refused to accept this argument. The injuries were of the same type and the egg-shell principle applied:

> "... the test is not whether the defendants could reasonably have foreseen that a straining or tearing of the muscles would cause a hernia in this particular man, but the question is rather whether they could have reasonably foreseen the type of injury that he did suffer, namely, the tearing or straining of the muscles which resulted in the hernia ... [I]t is immaterial that the defendants could not anticipate the full extent of the damage."[34]

**[3.23]** In this case a hernia was held to be of the same type as the straining or tearing of muscles, while in *Reeves v Carthy and O'Kelly* a stroke was held to be of the same type as circulatory damage and shock. It could be suggested therefore that Irish Courts are not too willing to engage in refined rule-manipulation to the detriment of plaintiffs, although it is clear that, should they wish to do so, the freedom which they possess in relation to distinguishing between different types of damage in the remoteness area provides them with an easy means of doing so.

**[3.24]** Against the above background, and although uncertainty still pervades the area, it might be helpful if the more or less fixed rules of remoteness were set out in a somewhat simplified manner.

## Intentional Damage

**[3.25]** A person is always liable for the damage he *intends* to cause. *Re Polemis* and *Wagon Mound (No 1)* are principally concerned with unintentional damage. If a person intends to cause damage to another person and does an act to effect the same, then he cannot in a subsequent action for such damage be heard to say: "I may have intended the damage but it

32. At 367. Griffin J noted that, in *Salmond on the Law of Torts* (16th ed), para 202 at p 564, Professor Heuston, "with his customary clarity" had conveniently summarised this branch of the law as follows:

> "... It has been made plain that the precise details of the accident or the exact concatenation of circumstances need not be foreseen. It is sufficient if the type, kind, degree category or order of harm could have been foreseen in a general way. The question is, was the accident a variant of the perils originally brought about by the defendant's negligence? The law of negligence has not been fragmented into a number of distinct torts."

See now the 21st ed, p 519.

33. [1967] IR 277 (SC).

34. [1967] IR 277 at 285 (*per* Budd J, Ó Dálaigh CJ and Haugh J concurring). See also *Garry v John Sisk & Son (Dublin) Ltd* Supreme Court, 29 January 1973; *Walker v McCormack* Supreme Court, 4 March 1968.

was not foreseeable or likely to happen." The defendant's intention is paramount here and displaces other criteria such as foreseeability and direct consequences.[35]

## Unintentional and Unforeseeable Damage

**[3.26]** Even in unintentional torts there is no liability where the defendant could not foresee any damage resulting from his acts. For the defendant to be liable he must be able to foresee damage in some shape or form. If no damage whatsoever is foreseeable then there will be no liability. And this rule holds whether the *Re Polemis* approach or the *Wagon Mound (No 1)* approach is followed. For even in *Re Polemis* it was an important element that the defendant could have foreseen that carelessness in dropping the plank could cause some damage by injuring someone in the hold or breaking cargo or denting the hold, etc.

**[3.27]** *Carey v The Cork Consumers Gas Company*[36] illustrates the point. In this case the plaintiff was employed by the defendant company and his duties were such that for short periods of the year he was exposed to a process which involved the inhalation of a lot of silica dust. He claimed that as a result he contracted silicosis. The trial judge withdrew the case from the jury and the plaintiff appealed. The appeal was dismissed on the grounds that the defendants did not know, nor could they reasonably have known, that the plaintiff's employment was dangerous. The evidence in the defendants' favour was substantial. Although silicosis had first been discovered in 1924 it was not very common in Ireland. The plaintiff was exposed to the dust process for only short periods of the year and there was no evidence of any previous complaints. No breach of statutory regulation was suggested and the routine complained of had been carried on without incident over a great number of years. Nor was there any evidence that any other case had occurred in Cork or elsewhere in the country. Maguire J delivering the judgment of the Supreme Court, said:

> "In my opinion the evidence for the plaintiff, while concerned with establishing that the plaintiff was now suffering from silicosis, was not directed to establishing that the defendants at any relevant time should have known that there was any danger to the plaintiff in carrying out his duties."

**[3.28]** The Supreme Court also took the same line in *Ring v Power*,[37] where the plaintiff who was a passenger in the defendant's van was thrown against the door as the van was taking a right-hand turn and fell from the van, sustaining injuries. The High Court's verdict in favour of the defendant was appealed on the grounds that the trial judge had misdirected the jury. The Supreme Court dismissed the appeal, holding that the defendant could not have foreseen that the door would open and, since there was no evidence that she might have suffered any other injury as a result of the defendant's driving (eg, by being bruised or crushed against the door), the defendant could not be liable.

---

35. Intention "disposes of any question of remoteness of damage". *Quinn v Leatham* [1901] AC 495 at 537 (*per* Lord Lindley) "Intended consequences are never too remote" WINFIELD & JOLOWICZ p 219. See also *Bettel v Yim* 20 OR (2d) 617, 88 DLR (3d) 543 Ont Ct 1973). *Allan v New Mount Sinai Hospital* (1980) 109 DLR (3d) 634 (Ont HC).
36. Supreme Court, 5 March 1958.
37. [1961] Ir Jur Rep 51.

## Foreseeability and the Remoteness of Damage

**[3.29]** In negligence and nuisance nowadays foreseeability is the test to be applied in determining remoteness of damage. In *Wagon Mound (No 2), Overseas Tankship (UK) Ltd v Miller Steamship Co Ply Ltd*[38] the plaintiff was different from the plaintiff in *Wagon Mound (No 1)* and the action was principally pursued in nuisance. Moreover, different evidence was produced in *Wagon Mound (No 2)* which tended to show that furnace oil might after all ignite on water. In those circumstances the Court was willing to impose liability on the defendants. To the argument that nuisance could in some circumstances be a strict tort and that it would be more appropriate to apply the "direct consequences" rule, it was pointed out that even in those cases of nuisance which involved strict liability the reasonable foreseeability rule was preferable to ensure uniformity for all types of nuisance.

**[3.30]** *Wagon Mound (No 2)* has been approved in Ireland in *Wall v Morrissey.*[39] In the latter case Walsh J, delivering the majority judgment, made the following statement:

> "I am content to adopt the reasoning of Lord Reid in *Wagon Mound (No 2)* and to accept the conclusion which he arrives at, namely, that while negligence is not an essential ingredient of nuisance in an action in public nuisance, foreseeability is an essential ingredient. In the present case the defendant created a danger on the highway which did amount to a public nuisance, but before the plaintiff can establish his right to damages he must satisfy the jury that the injury which he suffered was a reasonably foreseeable event on the part of the defendant."[40]

**[3.31]** Furthermore, as has been mentioned above, not only must the defendant foresee some damage, but certainly since *Wagon Mound (No 1)* the defendant must also foresee the *type* of damage for which the plaintiff seeks to make him or her liable.[41] The defendant is not liable if he or she could not foresee any damage; neither is the defendant liable for a particular type of damage if he or she could not have foreseen this type of damage.

## The Egg-Shell Skull and the Impecunious Plaintiff

**[3.32]** The "egg-shell skull" rule[42] has survived the reasonable foreseeability rule introduced by *Wagon Mound (No 1)*. According to this rule if the defendant could foresee a particular type of physical or psychological injury to the plaintiff then he or she will be

---

38. [1967] AC 617 (PC). For analysis of the decision see Goodhart 'The Brief Life Story of the Direct Consequences Rule in English Tort Law' (1967) 53 Va LR 857. Green 'The Wagon Mound No 2 - Foreseeability Revisited' [1967] Utah LR.
39. [1969] IR 10 (SC).
40. [1969] IR 10 at 15.
41. *Cf Lynch v Beale* High Court, 25 November 1974 Hamilton J:

    > "Having regard to the decision of the Supreme Court in *Burke v John Paul & Co Ltd* [1967] IR 277 in the course of which the *Wagon Mound (No 1)* was referred to, the current test appears to be not whether the extent of the damage could have been foreseen but whether the type of injury could have been foreseen".

    The court went on to hold that if inadequate beams are used in construction it should be reasonably foreseeable that a collapse will follow.
42. See Linden 'Down with Foreseeability! Of Thin Skulls and Rescuers' (1969) 47 Can BR 545, at 548 557; Comment 'Taking the Plaintiff as You Find Him' (1967) 16 Drake LR 49; Rowe 'The Demise of the Thin Skull Rule' (1977) 40 MLR 377; Bahr & Graham 'The Thin Skull Plaintiff Concept: Evasive or Pervasive?' (1982) 15 Loyola LR 409.

liable for all the physical or psychological injury that follows on account of the plaintiff's particularly vulnerable pre-accident condition, even if it turns out that the injuries to the plaintiff were far more than might reasonably have been expected in normal circumstances. This rule was well established at common law[43] and its survival reduced the practical differences between the *Re Polemis*[44] and the *Wagon Mound (No 1)*[45] approaches. Whether the rule is a fair one is a matter of debate. In *McSweeney Cork Corporation*[46] Murphy J said that he thought it to be "very harsh in its application ...".

**[3.33]** *Burke v John Paul & Co Ltd*[47] provides a good example of the operation of the rule. In this case, the plaintiff, an employee of the defendant was injured while cutting steel bars by means of a hand-operated cutting machine. The blades of the cutter were blunt and caused the plaintiff to exert a greater physical effort during his work than would have been necessary had the blades been maintained properly. The plaintiff complained about the inadequate sharpness but nothing was done. On the day of the accident the plaintiff felt a snap while he was operating the cutter and later he developed a hernia.

**[3.34]** At the end of the plaintiff's case the defendant asked for a direction on the grounds that the defendant could not reasonably be expected to anticipate and foresee that the plaintiff might develop a hernia from having to exert such extra pressure as might be involved in the use of a blunt instrument. The judge withdrew the case and the plaintiff appealed.

**[3.35]** On the remoteness issue the defendant suggested that the medical evidence showed that before a person can develop a hernia there must be some congenital weakness and since this could not be discovered by an ordinary examination it was impossible for the defendant to know of the predisposition, and consequently the defendant could not reasonably foresee that the plaintiff in using the extra pressure would develop a hernia. The Court dealt with the problem in the following language:

> "It was clearly implicit in the medical evidence that unwonted bodily exertion may cause straining or tearing of the muscles. It cannot. I think, be suggested that it is necessary to have the statement of a medical expert that an employer should know that if one of his employees is forced to use great exertion in the course of his work that may cause a straining, or even a tearing, of muscles, as that is a matter of common knowledge; but the point taken is that it could not be reasonably anticipated that a hernia would result without knowledge that the plaintiff had a predisposition to hernia. The answer to this, I think, is what is generally referred to as 'the egg-shell skull rule' and I do not think that the rule has been impugned in any way by the *Wagon Mound (No 1)* decision."[48]

In other words the tortfeasor takes his victim as he finds him.[49]

---

43. See *Dillieu v White* [1901] 2 QB 669 at 697; *Hay (or Bourhill) v Young* [1943] AC 92 at 109.
44. [1921] 3 KB 560.
45. [1961] AC 388.
46. DPIJ: Hilary and Easter Terms (1994), p 37 at 42 (HC, 15 April, 1994).
47. [1967] IR 277.
48. [1967] IR 277 at 283.
49. The Court followed *Smith v Leech Brain & Co Ltd* [1962] 2 QB 405. For a critical analysis of the rule see Rowe 'The Demise of the Thin Skull Rule?' (1977) 40 MLR 377. See also *Reeves v Carthy and O'Kelly* [1984] IR 348 (SC 1982), especially at 361 (*per* O'Higgins CJ).

**[3.36]** In *McCarthy v Murphy*[50] in 1998, McCracken J applied *Burke v John Paul & Co Ltd* where the plaintiff, who suffered foreseeable soft-tissue injury in a minor traffic accident caused by the defendant's negligence developed a depressive reaction which was attributable in part to an underlying depressive condition. McCracken J observed:

> "Of course the defendant could not have anticipated that [the plaintiff] was a person with a pre-disposition to depression, but he could have reasonably foreseen a soft tissue injury and, that being so, he is liable for damage which flows from that injury, as he has to take the plaintiff as he finds her."[51]

**[3.37]** In an English decision over half a century ago, where the defendant could foresee damage of a pecuniary nature to the plaintiff, but where this damage was exacerbated because of the plaintiff's impecuniosity the House of Lords refused to award damages in respect of the additional element caused by the plaintiff's poverty.[52] In principle it is difficult to see why the "egg-shell skull" principle should not also extend to the plaintiff's impecuniosity and in any event it now seems that if the plaintiff is obliged to borrow and pay interest to mitigate his loss he will be allowed to recover for the interest so incurred.[53] In *Riordan's Travel Ltd v Acres and Co Ltd*[54] the defendants, in demolishing a building, damaged the plaintiffs' business premises. The plaintiffs claimed damages for damage to property, rent for alternative accommodation, loss of profits, and interest on money they had to borrow for rent for alternative premises. McWilliam J had little difficulty with the first two headings of damage and he also awarded a sum for loss of profits, although, because of the many imponderables and the uncertainty of the projections made to the Court, the sum awarded was less than that claimed by the plaintiffs. There was a little more difficulty with regard to the interest incurred by the plaintiffs by virtue of the fact that they had to borrow to pay for the rented alternative accommodation. *The Edison* suggested that this was irrecoverable as this was due to the plaintiffs' impecuniosity. Although

---

49. (contd) For consideration of the medical dimensions of the type of problem raised in *Smith v Leech Brain & Co Ltd*, see Halpern 'Legal Relation of Trauma to Cancer' (1963) 12 Clev-Mar LR; Ladanyi 'Impact Trauma as "Legal Cause" of Cancer?' (1971) 20 Clev St LR 409; Small 'Gaffing at a Thing Called Cause: Medico-Legal Conflicts in the Concept of Causation' (1953) 31 Texas LR 630 at 634ff; Computation of damages in the "egg-shell" cases may raise some difficulties: see Perlmutter & Kafka, 'Comment: Measure of Damages - Aggravation of Previous Injury, Disease, Disability or Latent Weakness' (1947) 22 St John's LR 135; *Ryan v Stella Picture Theatre Ltd*, DPIJ: Trinity and Michaelmas Terms 1994, High Court, 14 June 1994, p 45; *cf Rohan v Minister for Finance* High Court, 19 June 1992 (O'Hanlon J), analysed by Byrne & Binchy *Annual Review of Irish Law 1992*, pp 570-571; *Sammon v Fleming GMbH* High Court, 23 November 1993 (Barron J), analysed by Bryne & Binchy *Annual Review of Irish Law 1993*, pp 539-541.
50. High Court, 10 February 1998.
51. Page 4 of McCracken J's judgment. *Cf Page v Smith* [1996] 1 AC 155 (HL, 1995), *Young v Charles Church (Southern) Ltd* 39 BMLR 146 (CA (Civil Div), 1997).
52. *Liesbosch Dredger v Edison SS* [1933] AC 448, distinguished by the Privy Council in *Alcoa Minerals of Jamaica Ltd v Broderick* [2000] 3 WLR 23.
53. *Riordans Travel Ltd v Acres & Co Ltd (No 2)* [1979] ILRM 3. See also *Taupo Borough Council v Birnie* [1978] NZLR 397; *AG v Geothermal Produce (NZ) Ltd* [1987] 2 NZLR 348.
54. Analysed by Kerr, 'The End of the "Edison"?' 74 (1980) ILSGI 51. See also *Latham v Hibernian Insurance Co Ltd* High Court, 4 December 1991 (Blayney J), analysed by Byrne & Binchy *Annual Review of Irish Law 1991*, pp 410-411; Jones 'The Impecunious Claimant' (2000) 16 Prof Neg 165.

McWilliam J was prepared to say that in circumstances such as the present any reasonable man in business circles must appreciate at the present time that the plaintiffs would "not have money in a stocking or under a mattress or even in a current account for that purpose, but will either have to apply money which is bearing interest and so to lose such interest or will have to borrow money and pay interest on the money borrowed", he nevertheless was more inclined to approach the problem as one where the plaintiff had to mitigate his loss. In McWilliam J's view the plaintiffs' obligation, once the tort was committed, was to act reasonably to mitigate their loss, and if this involved borrowing and paying interest this was a loss which they were entitled to recover from the defendants.[55]

**[3.38]** A more interesting and puzzling case arose in *Rabbette v Mayo County Council.*[56] In that case the plaintiff obtained an injunction to prevent the defendant council from carrying out blasting operations near the plaintiff's property. Although no blasting was in fact carried out because of these proceedings, the plaintiff nevertheless suffered damage because of the defendants' threat to start blasting. In particular, the plaintiff, a speculative builder, claimed that the threatened blasting operations had the following effects on his business: he had to cancel the sale of two houses and pay one prospective purchaser £750; he had to redecorate the houses which remained vacant because of the dispute with the County Council; moreover, he was out of pocket until he eventually sold the houses and he claimed interest for this out-of-pocket loss. He eventually sold the houses at a profit and this factor was also allowed for by the Court. More interestingly, however, the plaintiff claimed that he had been offered options on other building sites which he would have taken up had the original sales gone through. Because they did not he was obliged to pay a higher price at a later date. According to O'Hanlon J:

> "this represented a loss to him of about £3,000/4,000, but it is quite clear that it would not have arisen but for the impecuniosity of the plaintiff, so it was attributable in part to the activity of the defendants and in part to an outside circumstance of which they had not obvious knowledge or means of knowledge."[57]

**[3.39]** Having referred to *The Edison* and to the inroad made by *Riordan's Travel Ltd v Acres and Co Ltd*, he allowed £3,500 in respect of this claim. He then went on to say:

> "I would also hold that it should have been within the contemplation of the defendants that the interference with his cash flow which was the inevitable consequence of the litigation about threatened nuisance would produce a temporary curtailment of credit and I propose to allow the claim for bank interest of £2,573.56 and £2,100 for loss of discount on materials

---

55. See also *Murphy v McGrath* [1981] ILRM 364 (HC), where compensation was awarded for interest accruing on money borrowed from the bank by the plaintiff for repairs to his car which had been negligently damaged by the defendant. The Chief Justice stated (at 365):

> "The plaintiff had to be put to the necessary task of borrowing finance and accordingly, I see no break in the chain of causation from the original tort. This I believe to be the common sense view and I say this without studying the authorities that if a man has to go to a bank to borrow the necessary finance to effect repairs to his motor car which was damaged as a result of the defendant's negligence then … the claim for interest is not too remote or extreme".

In fact *Riordan's Travel* had been cited in argument; *cf* at 364 of CJ's judgment.

56. [1984] ILRM 156 (HC).

57. [1984] ILRM 156 at 159.

purchased at a time when his credit with suppliers had dried up and he was obliged to pay cash for any materials he needed to continue in business."[58]

**[3.40]** O'Hanlon J, however, considering the continuing relevance of *The Edison*, refused to compensate the plaintiff for a claim in respect of all the options the plaintiff might have taken up if an ordinary building programme had not been disrupted by the defendant's conduct or for the loss which the plaintiff claimed he suffered because he had eventually to go out of business completely. These claims were too remote.

**[3.41]** In *Doran & Doran v Delaney & Others*[59] Geoghegan J endorsed McWilliam J's approach in *Riordan's Travel.* This was a case where solicitors and the vendors of a site for a dwelling house were sued by disappointed purchasers, for breach of contract and misrepresentation. Noting that the *Edison* has been greatly modified by subsequent decisions in England Geoghegan J held that the loss would not be too remote if it could have been reasonably within the contemplation of the parties at the time the misrepresentation was made. He found in the case before him that the plaintiffs "acted perfectly reasonably after the debacle had occured and that losses flowing from their having to salvage the situation as best they could due to their inability to raise alternative funds to put them back in the position which they would have been in but for breaches of duty and misrepresentation are all reasonably forseeable losses."[60]

## Strict Torts

**[3.42]** Although not totally free from doubt the better opinion suggests that the direct consequences of *Re Polemis* may still survive in the strict torts. In *Wagon Mound (No 1)* itself it is suggested that the reasonable foreseeable test might not apply to *Rylands v Fletcher.*[61] And the Supreme Court in Ireland and the Court of Appeal in England have ruled that the direct consequences rule of *Polemis* applies to deceit.[62] Moreover it has been suggested that the *Polemis* approach is the proper one for breach of absolute statutory duty.[63] At all events it seems clear that liability in trespass[64] continues to be determined by the directness test, which owes nothing to *Polemis,* having antedated it by several centuries.

---

58. At 159-160.
59. High Court, 25 November 1998, Geoghegan J.
60. At 16.
61. [1961] AC 388 at 426-427. See, however, the modifications adopted by the House of Lords in *Cambridge Water Co Ltd v Eastern Counites Leather plc* [1994] 2 AC 264; *cf Superquinn Ltd v Bray Urban District Council* High Court, 18 February 1998 (Laffoy J).
62. *Leyden v Malone* Supreme Court, 13 May 1968; *Northern Bank Finance Corporation Ltd v Charlton* [1979] IR 149 (SC). See paras **[35.17]-[35.20]** below. See also *Doyle v Olby (Ironmongers) Ltd* [1969] 2 QB 158. Decisions in other common law jurisdictions are in accord; *cf* WINFIELD & JOLOWICZ, p 289.
63. As in *Galashiels Gas Co Ltd v O'Donnell* [1949] AC 275.
64. See para **[23.30]-[23.32]** above.

## V. CONCLUSION

**[3.43]** By way of summary it might be concluded that the extended meaning given to "reasonably foreseeable", the liability for "big bangs" when "little bangs" only were foreseeable, and the survival of the "egg-shell skull" rule, have all meant that the difference in practice between the *Polemis* approach of direct consequences and the *Wagon Mound (No 1)* approach of reasonable foreseeability may not be as great as was initially thought.

Chapter 4

# Concurrent Wrongdoers: Joint and Several Tortfeasors


I. Introduction .......... 99
II. Concurrent Wrongdoers .......... 102


## I. Introduction

**[4.01]** In tort, as in other branches of law, responsibility for the plaintiff's injuries may rest on more than one person. The plaintiff may be entitled to sue multiple defendants in respect of the injuries he or she has suffered. If the injury complained of is tortious then the defendants may be spoken of as concurrent tortfeasors; if the injury is contractual or a breach of trust the more general term, concurrent wrongdoers, is now more appropriate in Ireland. Traditionally, concurrent tortfeasors were classified into two categories: joint tortfeasors and several tortfeasors. Generally speaking, the law considered persons to be joint tortfeasors whenever it felt that in addition to being liable individually they should also be liable to the plaintiff as a group. When no group activity was involved, however, (eg where there was no conspiracy or concerted action) liability to the plaintiff was said to be several only, ie each defendant might be liable to the plaintiff individually, but there was no liability as a group.

**[4.02]** Until 1961 the law relating to joint tortfeasors and several concurrent tortfeasors in Ireland was contained in common law principles as amended and supplemented by the Joint Tortfeasors Act 1951. The Civil Liability Act 1961 now contains the principal rules on this subject.[1] Part III of the 1961 Act, however, is not confined to joint tortfeasors or several concurrent tortfeasors, it also purports to cover wrongdoers other than tortfeasors,

1. See the comprehensive analysis in Kerr, *The Civil Liability Acts* (1999), pp 11-39. See also Williams, *Joint Torts and Contributory Negligence* (1951). Williams's work is particularly important since the substance of Professor Williams's recommendations found legislative expression in the 1961 Act. The historical background is well analysed by O'Flaherty J in *Iarnród Éireann/Irish Rail Ireland v Ireland* [1996] 2 ILRM 500 at 506 (SC). See also Keane J's judgment in the same case [1995] 2 ILRM 161 (HC) and by Prosser 'Joint Torts and Several Liability' (1937) 25 Calif LR 413. A detailed comparative bibliography is contained in Kutner 'Bibliography: Contribution Among Tortfeasors' (1983) 3 Rev of Litigation 297. Other discussions of the subject include Dugdale 'Proposals to Reform the Law of Civil Contribution' (1984) 2 Canterbury LR 171; Mallon 'Civil Contribution Where a Party Has Settled: Proposals for Reform' (1987) 6 Otago LR 499; 'Reforms to the Law of Joint and Several Liability - Introduction of Proportionate Liability' (1997) TLJ Vol 5; Green & Graves 'Allocation of Fault: Joint Tortfeasos in Court and the ones who Should Be' (1994) 63 Miss L J 647; Vanall 'A Cirtique of the Restatement (Third), Apportionment, As It Affects Joint and Several Liability' (2000) 49 Emory LJ 565.

such as persons in breach of contract or in breach of trust. Consequently, Part III of the 1961 Act deals with the liability of concurrent wrongdoers, which term, it may be noted for our purposes, embraces joint tortfeasors and several concurrent tortfeasors. Subsequent references in this chapter to "the Act" refer to the Civil Liability Act 1961 unless otherwise stated.

**[4.03]** Three principles underlie Part III of the Civil Liability Act 1961:

(i) Subject to the rule that the plaintiff cannot recover more than the total amount of the damages he has suffered, the injured plaintiff must be allowed full opportunity to recover the full compensation for his injuries from as many sources as possible;

(ii) Concurrent wrongdoers should be entitled to recover fair contributions from each other in respect of damages paid to the plaintiff;

(iii) All matters relating to the plaintiff's injuries should as far as possible be litigated in one action.[2]

**[4.04]** In general, it may be said that any common law rule which impedes these principles is repealed by the 1961 Act. In particular the Act also aims at abolishing unnecessary refinements which had developed at common law between joint concurrent wrongdoers and several concurrent wrongdoers.

**[4.05]** Before examining the statutory provisions relating to these matters, three possible factual situations relating to the plaintiff's injuries must be distinguished. First, the injury to the plaintiff may be caused by the joint or concerted action of two or more persons: for example, where two persons decide to assault or rob the plaintiff, or where a principal orders his agent to commit a tort on the plaintiff. These are true cases of joint liability. Second, although not acting in concert, the acts of two or more persons may concur to produce the same damage to the plaintiff. This might be the case, for example, where the plaintiff, a passenger in a motor car is injured by the negligence of the driver of the car in which he is a passenger and by the negligence of the driver of another car, or where the

---

2. An unsuccessful assault on the constitutional validity of ss 12 and 14 of the 1961 Act was made in *Iarnród Éireann/Irish Rail v Ireland* [1996] 2 ILRM 500 (SC) on the grounds that these provisions violated the railway company's property rights and rights to basic fairness of procedure. A train had been derailed after a collision with a herd of cattle owned by a farmer. In proceedings by a passenger, the railway company and the farmer were held to have been concurrent wrongdoers. Liability was apportioned 30% - 70% between them. Under s 12(1) each was liable for all of the damages. The farmer did not have sufficient funds to pay his portion. The railway company argued that to require it to pay in excess of the 30% of the total sum was unconstitutional.

Rejecting this argument O'Flaherty J (for the Court) stated:

> "[T]he legislation marked an amelioration and rationalisation of the liability of concurrent wrongdoers *inter se* from what had been there before. The possibility that one of a number of defendants may be insolvent and unable to meet his or her liability is an unfortunate aspect of litigation; that the risk should fall on the other solvent defendants who are concurrent wrongdoers whether because they are independent or otherwise rather than upon the plaintiff seems to the court to be a solution that is in harmony with the core principles underlying civil liability."

See also Keane J's judgment in High Court [1995] 2 ILRM 161.

negligence of the architect combined with the negligence of the builder causes the plaintiff's house to subside. At common law, liability here was said to be several only. The wrongdoers were not jointly liable, although each was liable individually for the full amount of damages to the plaintiff.[3] Third, the plaintiff may be injured by the independent wrongs of two or more persons, where, for instance, the plaintiff has been injured by the negligent driving of D1 and while on the roadway awaiting assistance, D2 negligently injures him further. In this case the plaintiff has suffered different injuries at the hands of different and independent tortfeasors. The plaintiff has two distinct actions against D1 and D2. The torts are separate and the tortfeasors have acted independently of each other. Moreover, the defendants have caused different damage to the plaintiff and in general are liable only for the damage which they have caused. D1 and D2 are in no sense joint tortfeasors or several concurrent wrongdoers. The injured person has two distinct actions against two separate tortfeasors in respect of different damage or injuries.[4] The confusion that surrounds this branch of the law might be dispelled if the following terminology, "joint concurrent tortfeasors", "several concurrent tortfeasors" and "several independent tortfeasors", were adopted to describe the above three categories. Traditional usage, which favours "joint tortfeasors", "several tortfeasors" and "independent tortfeasors", lacks precision.

**[4.06]** In the first situation just mentioned the defendants have committed the same *iniuria* (wrong) and have caused the same *damnum* (damage); in the second case the defendants have committed different *iniuriae* but have caused the same *damnum*; in the third case the defendants have committed different *iniuriae* and have caused different *damna*. Defendants in the first factual situation are considered to be joint tortfeasors and even before 1961 such persons were said to be both jointly and severally liable for all the damage suffered by the plaintiff. In the second factual situation - where the acts of the defendants concurred to produce the same damage - the defendants were considered to be severally liable only. From the plaintiff's point of view this meant that in the first case (ie the case of joint tortfeasors) the plaintiff could sue any one of the tortfeasors for all of the damage he suffered or he could sue all the tortfeasors together. In the second case, (ie the case of several liability) although each tortfeasor could be sued for the whole damage there was no possibility at common law of bringing a joint action against all the tortfeasors.[5] The distinction between joint and several liability on the one hand, and several liability only on

3. "The general principle of our law is that if a man is injured in his person or in his property by the *combined* negligence of others he can sue and recover damages from those who caused his injuries and his action may at his option. be taken against them jointly or against any one or more of them." *Wellwood v King* [1921] 2 IR 274 at 307 (emphasis added). One must distinguish between joint liability and the possibility of being sued jointly in one action. The former concept expresses a substantive rule whereas the latter expresses a procedural facility.

4. See eg *Dillingham Constructions v Steel Mains Ply* (1975) 6 ALR 177.

5. The rule as to non-joinder in relation to several concurrent tortfeasors disappeared with the introduction of the provision in RSC (Ir) 1905, O 15, r 4 which is now re-enacted in Rules of the Superior Courts 1986, O 15 r 4:

> "All persons may be joined as defendants against whom the right to any relief is alleged to exist whether jointly severally or in the alternative. Judgment may be given against such one or more of such defendants as may be found liable according to their respective liabilities without any amendment."

the other, was important at common law principally for two reasons: where persons were jointly and severally liable (joint concurrent wrongdoers), a judgment against one tortfeasor discharged the other tortfeasors; and second, release of, or accord with, one, discharged all. The rationale of these rules was that there was only one cause of action linking the plaintiff to the defendants and when this was extinguished, either by judgment against one or by the release of one, the cause of action was destroyed and there remained nothing on which to sue. Neither of these rules applied in the case of persons severally liable only.

**[4.07]** The distinction between joint liability and several liability in tort law (and in contract and breach of trust also) has to a large extent now been abolished in Ireland by the Civil Liability Act 1961 which treats joint tortfeasors and several concurrent tortfeasors in a similar fashion under the generic name of concurrent wrongdoers.

## II. Concurrent Wrongdoers

**[4.08]** Section 11(1) of the Civil Liability Act 1961 declares persons to be concurrent wrongdoers when:

> two or more persons ... are wrongdoers and are responsible to a third person ... for the same damage, whether or not judgment has been recovered against some or all of them.

**[4.09]** This definition includes both the first and second factual situations adverted to above. The 1961 Act itself specifically declares that, without prejudice to the generality of s 11(1), persons may become concurrent wrongdoers as a result of (i) the vicarious liability of one for another, (ii) the breach of a joint duty, (iii) conspiracy or concerted action to a common end.[6] Moreover, persons are also considered to be concurrent wrongdoers if their independent acts cause the same damage.[7] The 1961 Act, therefore, treats both the first and second factual situations above in the same way: persons in both situations are considered to be concurrent wrongdoers and are liable to the extent provided for in s 12(1), discussed below. The principal differences at common law between joint and several liability, namely, that a release of one joint tortfeasor released all, and that judgment against one joint tortfeasor discharged the others, are specifically abolished in ss 17 and 18 of the Act. Section 17 of the 1961 Act now provides that release of, or accord with, one wrongdoer discharges the other wrongdoers only if such a release or accord indicates an intention that the other wrongdoers are to be discharged. If the release or accord does not indicate this, then the plaintiff will be identified with the wrongdoer released, in any action against the other wrongdoers. Section 18 provides that an action against one wrongdoer will not be a bar against other concurrent wrongdoers, subject to the rule that the plaintiff cannot recover more damages than he or she has suffered.[8] The plaintiff may, however, be penalised in costs by the court if the taking of successive actions by him or her was unreasonable.[9]

---

6. Civil Liability Act 1961, s 11(2)(a). These are the situations contemplated in the first factual situation above.
7. Civil Liability Act 1961, s 11(2)(a). That is the second factual situation above.
8. *Cf* Kerr, *The Civil Liability Acts* (1999), p 21; *McSorley v O'Mahony* High Court, 6 November 1996, Costello P.
9. Civil Liability Act 1961, s 18(1)(b).

**[4.10]** Two other points should be mentioned before examining the regime of liability which the 1961 Act imposes on concurrent wrongdoers. The Act specifically recognises that concurrent wrongs do not have to be contemporaneous: they may be successive. So, where a manufacturer negligently manufactures a machine which is installed in a factory, and later the plaintiff, an employee, is injured because of the defect in the machine and because of the negligence of a fellow employee, both fellow employee and manufacturer may be concurrent wrongdoers.[10] Secondly:

> "where two or more persons are at fault and one or more is or are responsible for damage while the other or others is or are free from causal responsibility, but it is not possible to establish which is the case, such two or more persons shall be deemed to be concurrent wrongdoers in respect of the damage".[11]

**[4.11]** Such a situation might arise, for example, where two people hunting a deer negligently discharge their guns but it is impossible to determine which bullet first lodged in the plaintiff's brain.

**[4.12]** Section 12(1) of the 1961 Act declares that concurrent wrongdoers as defined in the Act are each liable for the whole of the damage in respect of which they are concurrent wrongdoers.[12] The Act also declares that where persons cause independent items of damage of the same kind, (the third factual situation described earlier) the court may apportion liability between such persons in such a manner as may be justified by the probabilities of the case. The relevant provision on this, s 12(2), reads as follows:

> "Where the acts of two or more persons who are not concurrent wrongdoers cause independent items of damage of the same kind to a third person or to one of their number, the court may apportion liability between such persons in such manner as may be justified by the probabilities of the case, or where the plaintiff is at fault may similarly reduce his damages; and if the proper proportions cannot be determined the damages may be apportioned or divided equally."[13]

---

10. Civil Liability Act 1961, s 11(2)(c).
11. Civil Liability Act 1961, s 11(3). See further on this subsection Kerr, *The Civil Liability Acts* (1999), pp 12-13; White 'Selected Aspects of the Civil Liability Acts 1961 and 1964' unpublished LLB thesis University College Cork 1978; Murnaghan J 'Lecture 36 of Society of Young Solicitors'. *Bowes v O'Connor* High Court, 21 February 1964 (Murnaghan J). *Cf Power v Bedford Motor Co* [1959] IR 391 at 420 (SC). See also Thomson 'Remarks on Causation and Liability' (1984) 13 Philosophy and Public Affairs 101; Miller 'Cases of Uncertain and Unknown Causation and Negligence: Relationship Analysis as a Real Alternative to Present Inadequate Concept' (1968) 16 U Kansas LR 209. See further paras **[9.18]** and **[27.38]** below.
12. Subject (i) to s 38 where a reduction is allowed where the plaintiff has been guilty of contributory negligence, (ii) to s 46 relating to maritime cases, and (iii) to s 14(3). There is no obligation in an action against concurrent wrongdoers, where all are liable, for the judge in the main action to apportion liability between the defendants. Such apportionment will properly be made in the contribution action taken under s 21 of Civil Liability Act 1961.
13. The procedural problems that can arise in such a case were illustrated in *Byrne v Triumph Engineering Ltd* [1982] IR 220 (SC). In that case the plaintiff was injured when he was struck on the head while working for D1, due to the alleged negligence of D1 and D2. Some four months later while working for D3 he was struck on the wrist and suffered personal injuries.

**[4.13]** This section is also meant to apply specifically to persons whose acts combine to cause a nuisance to the plaintiff, but neither of whom, if taken alone, would be liable in an action for nuisance as their activities would not on their own be unreasonable.[14]

**[4.14]** The action against concurrent wrongdoers may be brought against all of them, or against any one or more of them,[15] and the judgment in an action against concurrent wrongdoers who are sued together will take effect as if it were given against them separately.[16] In such a case, however, the plaintiff may agree to accept an apportionment of his damages among the defendants, and in this event: (a) the satisfaction of one judgment will not operate as satisfaction of another; (b) the defendants will not have any right of contribution among themselves; and (c) if one judgment is unsatisfied the plaintiff may apply to have the deficiency distributed by way of secondary judgment among the other defendants.[17]

**[4.15]** If the plaintiff sues concurrent wrongdoers successively and judgment is given for one defendant, the plaintiff will be bound in any subsequent actions against other concurrent wrongdoers by the findings of fact in favour of such defendant in the first action. Moreover, where an action is brought against concurrent wrongdoers and judgment is given against one without a reduction of damages because of the plaintiff's contributory negligence, but against another subject to a reduction under s 34(1), because of the plaintiff's contributory negligence, then the damages under the first mentioned judgment will be assessed subject to the same proportionate reduction.[18]

**[4.16]** In an action against concurrent wrongdoers, each defendant has the right to present evidence against the other or others.[19] Decisions of the Supreme Court, however, emphasise that neither s 32 nor the provision in Order 15, rule 7 of the Rules of the Superior Courts 1986 alters the incidence of burden of proof cast on the plaintiff in civil actions.[20] Moreover, a concurrent wrongdoer may appeal against a judgment in favour of

---

13. (contd). The plaintiff brought both claims in the same proceedings, suing D1 and D2 for the first injury and D3 for the second. Rules of Superior Courts 1986, O 18 r 1 allows for this. The Rules provide, however, that if the cases cannot be conveniently heard together they should be tried separately. The Supreme Court held that in the circumstances the defendants had not discharged the onus of establishing that a joint trial could not conveniently take place. See also *Ryan v Roscrea Bacon Factory and McNamara* Supreme Court, 20 November 1985.

14. Civil Liability Act 1961, s 12(3).

15. The High Court can make an order to have several actions consolidated: Rules of the Superior Courts 1986, O 49 r 4-6. Indeed several independent tortfeasors may be joined as co-defendants under O 15, r 4.

16. Section 14(1) and (2). The earlier rule to the contrary had been approved in *Damon v Mc Clelland* [1899] 2 IR 486 (following *Haydon v Smith* (1610) 2 Browne 328). *Dawson's* case was followed and approved in *Johnson v Larkin* [1926] IR 40 (SC).

17. Civil Liability Act 1961, s 14(3). An apportionment of the plaintiff's costs is not sanctioned by s 14, so that the defendants remain liable *in solidum* in respect of these, but with rights of contribution *inter se*. That the plaintiff should not recover more damages than he or she has suffered is explicitly recognised in s 16 of the Act. See also s 18(1)(b).

18. Civil Liability Act 1961, s 19(4).

19. Civil Liability Act 1961, s 2(1).

20. See *Sullivan v Noonan* [1969] IR 253; *Higgins v Patterson and Gilchrist* [1971] IR 253.

the injured person even where the judgment has been satisfied by another concurrent wrongdoer, and may also contest as respondent an appeal by another concurrent wrongdoer.[21] Where the injured person has succeeded against one defendant and fails against another, the unsuccessful defendant may appeal against the judgment in favour of the successful defendant.[22]

## Satisfaction, Release and Accord

**[4.17]** Satisfaction, for the purpose of the Civil Liability Act 1961, means "payment of damages, whether after judgment or by way of accord and satisfaction, or the rendering of any agreed substitution thereof".[23] Release is satisfaction under seal. Section 16(1) provides that satisfaction by one concurrent wrongdoer (ie payment of the full damages adjudged or agreed[24]) discharges all other concurrent wrongdoers. Partial payment, however, will operate only as partial satisfaction. To prevent the plaintiff from making a profit in such circumstances the plaintiff who has accepted satisfaction from one wrongdoer will be estopped from denying that the person who made satisfaction was liable to him or her, in a subsequent proceeding against another wrongdoer for the same damage.[25] Thus if P accepts £1,000 as satisfaction from C1 and subsequently sues C2 for the same damage, he cannot deny C1's liability to him in the action against C2, although he is permitted to litigate any other questions of fact or law relative to C2's liability.[26]

**[4.18]** Section 17(1) provides that the release of, or accord with, one concurrent wrongdoer discharges the others if it indicates an intention that the others are to be discharged. If no such intention can be gleaned from the release or accord and the injured party sues other concurrent wrongdoers, then the injured person will be identified with the person with whom the release or accord is made. So if P who has suffered damages in the amount of £1,000 releases C1 for the sum of £600 and subsequently sues C2 and C3 for damages, the fact that P has already received £600 must be taken into account.[27] This subsection enshrines two ideas: (i) the principle that partial satisfaction by one concurrent wrongdoer will operate in favour of all, and (ii) the desirability of facilitating settlements out of court.[28] This rule abolishes unnecessary refinements that existed between a release and a covenant not to sue, and between accord and satisfaction, at common law.

---

21. Civil Liability Act 1961, s 32(2).
22. Civil Liability Act 1961, s 32(4).
23. Civil Liability Act 1961, s 16(2).
24. Civil Liability Act 1961, s 16(3). In *Murphy v J Donoghue Ltd* [1993] 1 IR 534 at 555 (SC) McCarthy J observed that s 16 "is probably declaratory of the common law ...". See further Kerr, *The Civil Liability Acts* (1999), p 19.
25. Civil Liability Act 1961, s 16(4).
26. Civil Liability Act 1961, s 16(4).
27. Civil Liability Act 1961, s 17(2) *Cf Bula v Flynn, Taxing Master of the High Court* High Court, 7 March 2000 (McGuiness J); *ACC Bank plc v Malocco* High Court, 7 Febraury 2000 (Laffoy J); Twomey, *Partnership Law* (2000), para 11.95.
28. See Explanatory Memorandum to Civil Liability Bill 1960, p 7.

## Contribution Between Concurrent Wrongdoers[29]

**[4.19]** Section 21(1) provides for contribution[30] between concurrent wrongdoers and generally follows s 5 of the Joint Tortfeasors Act 1951.[31] Contribution is allowed where concurrent wrongdoers are "liable in respect of the same damage"[32] and it should be noted that because of the definition given in s 2 of the 1961 Act to the word "liable", contribution may exist even if the liability of a concurrent wrongdoer to the plaintiff is not enforceable. Thus, although an injured person's right against one concurrent wrongdoer may be unenforceable (eg by virtue of diplomatic immunity, or where a party can show that a contract does not comply with the Statute of Frauds),[33] such a wrongdoer may yet be liable in a contribution action by another concurrent wrongdoer. If, however, the claimant

29. See eg *Redbank Oyster Co Ltd and Stassen v Fairway Fabrications Ltd and BIM* [1976] IR 191 (SC) There is no contribution if the defendants are not concurrent wrongdoers.

30. A judgment for contribution in respect of costs as opposed to damages may also be given under s 24. See Kerr, *The Civil Liability Acts* (1999), pp 11-39; *Gillespie v Fitzpatrick* [1970] IR 102 (SC).

31. The old common law rule prohibiting such contribution was expressed in *Merryweather v Nixan* (1799) 8 Term Rep 186; 101 ER 1337; See Reath (1898) 12 Harv LR 176. For a full analysis of s 21 see Kerr, *The Civil Liability Acts* (2nd ed, 1999), pp 22-24. The right of contribution is a restitutionary right which survives for the benefit of the claimant's estate and against the contributor's personal representatives: s 30.

32. Civil Liability Act 1961, s 21. See *Staunton v Toyota (Ireland) Ltd* High Court, 15 April 1988 (Costello J). Contribution may be recovered from another wrongdoer who "is or would if sued at the time of the wrong have been liable in respect of the same damage." A party who has been sued but not to judgment may fall outside this definition. See *James Hardie & Coy Pty Ltd v Seltsam Pty Ltd* analysed by Kerr, *The Civil Liability Acts* (1999), pp 23-24. A trial court's apportionment of contribution based on an incorrect ascription to one of the parties of the status of concurrent wrongdoer will, of course, be overturned on appeal: *Doran v Cosgrove* Supreme Court, 12 November 1992.

33. The concept of "legal liability [that is] not enforceable by action" presents difficulty in the context of the duty of care in negligence. See Kerr, *The Civil Liability Acts* (1999), pp 23; Kutner (1985) 63 Can BR 1 at 7; Williams, *Joint Torts and Contributory Negligence* (1951), pp 99-110. Clearly a party to whom no duty of care is owed by reason of failing the *Wagon Mound (No1)* or *Palsgraf* test will not be able to claim that this is a case of legal liability which is not enforceable by action: there is simply no legal liability relative to that person who is outside the circle of reasonable foresight and thus of a duty of care. Where, however, the party is within that circle but nonetheless not owed a duty of care under the two-step test favoured by the Supreme Court in *Ward v McMaster* [1989] ILRM 400 the position is somewhat less clear. A straightforward interpretation of s 2 is that a party to whom no duty of care is owed for whatever reason - whether lack of foreseeability, lack of proximity under the first step in *Ward* or for reasons of policy under the second step - is simply one in respect of whom no legal liability arises. The decision of the European Court of Human Rights in *Osman v United Kingdom* [1999] 1 FLR 193, however, casts a shadow of doubt on this analysis. The Court there appeared to accept that some form of at least putative liability actually arises where a plaintiff passes the first but falters on the second step. If that view were to be accepted by an Irish court the argument that there is a form of unenforceable legal liability in such a case is perhaps plausible. For critical analysis of *Osman* see paras **[6.68]-[6.90]**.

pays a sum to the injured party, even though the injured person's claim is barred by the Statute of Limitations, the claimant will not be entitled to enforce a contribution claim against other concurrent wrongdoers unless at the time the payment was made the injured person's cause of action against the contributor was not barred.[34] No contribution will be allowed to a concurrent wrongdoer from a person who is entitled to be indemnified by him. Consequently, a master or a principal will not be entitled to claim contribution from a servant or agent who would in the circumstances be entitled to be indemnified by the master or principal.[35]

**[4.20]** The amount of the contribution will be what the court considers "to be just and equitable having regard to the degree of the contributor's fault", and includes a power to exempt completely any person, or direct that the contribution shall amount to a complete indemnity.[36] The Supreme Court in *Connolly v South of Ireland Asphalt Co*[37] expressly refrained from deciding the principles upon which the amount of contribution should be assessed, and the meaning of fault within s 21(2), but it is now clear that the test to be adopted in apportioning the plaintiff's damages among the wrongdoers under s 21 should be that of the comparative blameworthiness of the defendants.[38] Moreover, a tortfeasor

34. Civil Liability Act 1961, s 23(4). On the problem associated with the maxim *ex turpi causa non oritur actio*, see s 57(1) of 1961 Act, Kerr, *The Civil Liability Acts* (1999), pp 67-68. *Cf O'Connor v McDonnell* High Court, 30 June 1970, Murnaghan J, noted by O'Reilly 7 Ir Jur (ns) 98; criticised by White 'Selected Aspects of the Civil Liability Acts 1961 and 1964', pp 38-39. On practice relating to apportionment of fault between concurrent wrongdoers where plaintiff may also be guilty of contributory negligence see the Civil Liability Act 1961, s 38(1) as interpreted in *Lynch v Lynch and Alliance v Dublin Consumers Gas Co* High Court, 24 November 1976 (Murnaghan J). See also Fleming 'Note: Contributory Negligence and Multiple Tortfeasors' (1988) 104 LQR 6 at 9.

35. Indemnity may be available under contract, under statute (eg Partnership Act 1890), or under the rules relating to vicarious liability etc. Indemnity is usually only available, however, to "innocent" persons, as for example where an innocent auctioneer liable in conversion can sue the thief for indemnity: *Adamson v Jarvis* (1827) 4 Bing 66; 130 ER 693. Money paid by a concurrent wrongdoer on the basis of a High Court apportionment between concurrent wrongdoers, and which is reversed on appeal by the Supreme Court, must be repaid by way of contribution to the concurrent wrongdoer who overpaid. Interest on same, however, is not allowable: *East Cork Foods v O'Dwyer Steel* [1978] IR 103 (SC). A subsequently developing viewss of interest in restitution cases, in decisions such as *O'Rourke v Revenue Commissioners* [1996] 2 IR 1 (HC), might call into question the denial of interest on the facts in *East Cork Foods*; though *cf Goodman v Minister for Finance* [1999] 3 IR 356 (HC).

36. Section 21(2). See *Collen Bros (Dublin) Ltd v Scaffolding Ltd* [1959] IR 245; *Scully v Marjorie Boland Ltd* [1962] IR 58; *Patterson v Murphy* [1978] ILRM 85; *Connolly v Dundalk UDC* [1990] 2 IR 1. Section 43 of the Act expresses the rule which is implicit in s 21(2), namely that where the wrong of one of the concurrent wrongdoers consists of a breach of strict statutory or common law duty without fault, the Court has a discretion to grant such wrongdoer an indemnity. See *O'Sullivan v Dwyer* [1971] IR 275 (SC); *Daly v Avonmore Creameries Ltd* [1984] IR 131 (SC) and paras **[11.159]**.

37. [1977] IR 99.

38. *Cf Patterson v Murphy* [1978] ILRM 85; *Connolly v Dundalk UDC* High Court, 7 February 1990. See now *Iarnród Éireann v Ireland* [1996] 2 ILRM 500 (SC). In the High Court Keane J, after examining the matter in some detail, concluded:

who makes a reasonable settlement with the injured person so as to bar an action against other concurrent wrongdoers can also claim a contribution from the other wrongdoers. If the amount of the settlement was excessive the court can fix the amount at a reasonable figure and allow a contribution in respect of such a reasonable sum.[39] Even if the settlement does not bar an action against other concurrent wrongdoers, contribution may still be allowed provided, however, that in such circumstances justice is done in the final allocation between the concurrent wrongdoers.

> "Suppose that P (the injured person) settles with a wrongdoer D1, (the claimant) for £600, and D1 obtains £300 from another wrongdoer D2, (the contributor) in a claim for contribution, both being held equally to blame. Then, in a subsequent action by P (who is identified with D1) against D2, if P recovers £400 out of a total assessed damages of £1,000, D2 would pay in all £700; but he will be entitled to recover from D1 part or whole of the contribution he has already paid. In the example, he should recover £200, which makes his final liability £500; and D1's final liability will also be £500."[40]

**[4.21]** Provision is made in s 25 for the case where one wrongdoer is omitted from the claim for contribution. For example, three wrongdoers, C1, C2 and C3, may be equally responsible to the injured person P. P sues C1 who joins only C2; then if damages are awarded in the amount of £900, C1 will get a contribution of £450 from C2. C1 may (at the discretion of the court under s 27(1)) claim further contribution from C3. So also may C2. C1's and C2's judgments will be executable only if C1 and C2 have paid the sum levied against them and C2's judgment against C3 can never exceed an amount greater than the sum that, when added to the amount still due to P. will equal C3's just proportion (£300) of the damages. In other words, C3 will be subject to C1's executable judgment only to the extent that C3 is safe from a further claim by P. If P's damages have been fully paid, then C3 becomes liable for £300. If, however, P is still owed £200, then the extent of C's executable judgment is only £100 (ie £300 less £200).

**[4.22]** A claim for contribution will also lie (eg against a thief) where a person (for example, a person who innocently handles stolen goods) restores the property to the owner. The innocent party may have an action against the thief for contribution even though he or she is not a tortfeasor, if, for example, he or she has committed no conversion.[41]

**[4.23]** The rules relating to the procedure for claiming contribution are designed to ensure that, where possible, claims for contribution will be made and determined in the injured person's action. They are set out in s 27 of the Act, sub-s (1) of which contains the principal rules and reads as follows:

---

38. (contd)

> "I am, accordingly, satisfied that the view exposed by the Supreme Court, that the criterion to be adopted in determining the reduation in a plaintiff's damages because of his or her contributory negligence is that of blameworthiness and not causation, is also applicable to the apportionment of liability between concurrent wrongdoers" ([1995] 2 ILRM 161 at 197).

39. Civil Liability Act 1961, s 22(1). Based on Ontario Negligence Act 1948, s 1.

40. Explanatory Memorandum to Civil Liability Bill 1960, pp 9-10. For further provisions as to payment by a settling wrongdoer see ss 27(4) and 29(7).

41. Civil Liability Act 1961, s 26. *A fortiori* if he or she is a tortfeasor.

A concurrent wrongdoer who is sued for damages or for contribution and who wishes to make a claim for contribution under this Part -

(a) shall not, if the person from whom he proposes to claim contribution is already a party to the action, be entitled to claim contribution except by a claim made in the said action, whether before or after judgment in the action;

and

(b) shall, if the said person is not already a party to the action, serve a third party notice upon such person as soon as reasonably possible and, having served such notice, he shall not be entitled to claim contribution except under the third party procedure. If such third party procedure is not served as aforesaid, the Court may in its discretion refuse to make an order for contribution against the person from whom contribution is claimed.[42]

**[4.24]** Regarding s 27(1)(b),[43] it has been determined that if the defendant in the main action does not serve the third party notice as soon as reasonably possible he loses his right to contribution.[44] This does not mean, however, that he cannot claim damages in negligence or breach of contract.[45] The right to contribution is a statutory remedy and does not replace other common law rights of action. Loss of the right of contribution although it may have procedural disadvantages, eg the claimant's having to prove his case *de novo*, does not mean the loss of other common law remedies. Section 3 of the Civil Liability (Amendment) Act 1964 amends s 27 of the 1961 Act by expressly providing that a person may serve a notice pursuant to s 27(1) without conceding that he was a wrongdoer.[46] The procedure by way of third party notice is governed by Order 16 of the Rules of the Superior Courts 1986.[47]

**[4.25]** Provision is also made for the distribution of loss caused by the failure to obtain satisfaction from one of three or more concurrent wrongdoers[48] and for the circumstances

42. For the advantages which third party notice offers over an independent action for contribution, see Williams, *Joint Torts and Contributory Negligence* (1951), p 181. Where an action is brought by two injured persons against a wrongdoer, and that wrongdoer claims that, as regards the action by one of the injured persons, the other plaintiff is a concurrent wrongdoer with him, and claims contribution against the plaintiff, the proper mode of enforcing his claim is by counterclaim against the plaintiff with whom he alleges he is a concurrent wrongdoer: *Cullen v Clein* [1970] IR 146.

43. Considered in *Gilmore v Windle* [1967] IR 323.

44. See Kerr, *The Civil Liability Acts* (1999), pp 29-34 for a comprehensive analysis and review of the decisions, which include *Board of Governors of St Laurence's Hospital v Staunton* [1990] 2 IR 31 (SC); *O'Brien v Ulster Bank Ltd* High Court, 21 December 1993; *Dillon v MacGabhann* High Court, 24 July 1995; *SFL Engineering Ltd v Smyth Cladding Systems* High Court, 9 May 1997 (Barron J); *McElwaine v Hughes* High Court, 30 April 1997, (Barron J); *Dowling v Armour Pharmaceutical Co Inc* [1996] 2 ILRM 417 (HC); *Connolly v Casey* Supreme Court, 17 November 1999.

45. *Cf A & P (Ireland) Ltd v Golden Vale Products Ltd* High Court, 7 December 1998.

46. See discussions of this problem in *Gilmore v Windle* [1967] IR 323; *cf Staunton v Toyota (Ireland) Ltd* High Court, 15 April 1988; Kerr, *The Civil Liability Acts* (1999), p 32.

47. On third party costs see *Hennessy v Quinn and O'Donoghue* [1968] IR 274.

48. Civil Liability Act 1961, s 28; compare with ss 14(3)(c), 38(2) and 45(2).

in which estoppel may apply in a contribution action.[49] The period of limitation for contribution actions is the same period allowed to the injured person to bring his or her action against the contributor, or two years after the claimant's liability is ascertained or the injured person's damages are paid, whichever is the greater.[50]

**[4.26]** The 1961 Act, of necessity, draws a distinction between the right to obtain a judgment for contribution and the right to execute and actually recover damages under that judgment. A right to contribution having been established and judgment in respect thereof having been obtained, it does not follow that such judgment is immediately executable. Suppose P to have sued D1 and D2 in respect of their concurrent negligence causing him harm and it is held that both D1 and D2 are concurrent wrongdoers so that a several judgment for the full amount of P's damage is given against both D1 and D2. D1 and D2 will seek contribution against each other in respect of their liability to pay more than their fair share of P's damages and, if both defendants are held equally at fault, a judgment for 50% of P's damages will be given to each defendant as against the other. To allow each to execute immediately and before payment by either of any portion of the injured person's damages would negative the purpose of the proceedings. Accordingly, s 23 distinguishes between the right to obtain a judgment for contribution and the right to levy execution thereunder: the claimant will not be allowed to execute his judgment for contribution until after satisfaction in whole or in part by him of the damages for which the claimant is liable at the time when satisfaction is made to the injured person or his representatives or lawful assignees and then he may execute only "in respect of the amount by which the sum paid by him exceeds his just proportion of that particular amount" as determined by the court in the action for contribution.

49. Civil Liability Act 1961, s 29. The general law of estoppel has not been restricted by s 29: *Nolan v Listowel UDC and Smyth* [1966] IR 56; (HC); White 'Selected Aspects of the Civil Liability Acts 1961 and 1964', p 56 *et seq*. See further Kerr, *The Civil Liability Acts* (1999), p 36.

50. Civil Liability Act 1961, s 31. *Buckley v Lynch* [1978] IR 6 (HC); *Neville v Margan Ltd* High Court, 1 December 1988 (Blayney J); Kerr, *The Civil Liability Acts* (1999), pp 37-38.

# Chapter 5

# Negligence

I. Introduction .................................................... 111
II. Elements of the Tort .................................................... 111

## I. Introduction

**[5.01]** Until the earlier part of the last century, negligence was not regarded as a separate tort.[1] The word was used in a number of senses, generally suggesting inadvertence or inattention on the part of the defendant. In the nineteenth century negligence began to emerge as a separate basis of liability, but it was not until the twentieth century that the conceptual elements of the tort were fully developed.

## II. Elements of the Tort

**[5.02]** There are four elements in the tort of negligence. These are:

1. A duty of care, that is, the existence of a legally recognised obligation requiring the defendant to conform to a certain standard of behaviour for the protection of others against unreasonable risks.[2]
2. A failure to conform to the required standard.
3. Actual loss or damage to recognised interests of the plaintiff.
4. A sufficiently close causal connection between the conduct and resulting injury to the plaintiff.[3]

**[5.03]** The first element of this formula - the duty question - raises complex issues of law and policy, considered in detail below.[4] The courts have been called on to determine whether liability should attach to certain forms of conduct regarding particular relationships or types of injury. Thus, such questions can arise as whether there is a duty to rescue those in peril,[5] whether a bystander, as well as a parent or spouse of the victim, may sue for psychic disturbance ("nervous shock") resulting from witnessing an accident,[6] and

---

1. See Winfield 'The History of Negligence in the Law of Torts' (1926) 42 LQR 184; Wigmore 'Responsibility for Tortious Acts: Its History' (1894) 7 Harv LR 315, 441, 453; Baker, *An Introduction to Legal History* (2nd ed, 1979), Ch 19.
2. In *Gilmour v Belfast Harbour Commrs* [1933] NI 114, at 148 (CA), Megaw J considered it "elementary law that an action for negligence is based on the breach of a duty to exercise reasonable care in the circumstances of a particular case. Duty and negligence are co-related."
3. *Cf Higgins v Patterson* Supreme Court, 2 April 1971, at p 1 *per* FitzGerald J. Leading textbooks on the subject include Buckley, *The Modern Law of Negligence* (3rd ed, 1999) and *Charlesworth & Percy On Negligence* (9th ed, 1996) by Percy & Walton.
4. See Ch 6.
5. See Ch 8.
6. See Ch 17.

whether there should be liability for causing pure economic loss, unaccompanied by any physical injury or damage.[7]

**[5.04]** With regard to the standard of care demanded once the duty is acknowledged, the courts have tended to ask whether the defendant acted as "the reasonable person" would have done. As we will see, this test is prescriptive rather than descriptive: it will not avail a defendant to show that most people jaywalk or throw litter on the pavement if the court is satisfied that "the reasonable person" would not engage in such conduct. The factors to which the courts give weight in assessing whether conduct is negligent include the probability of an accident, the gravity of the threatened injury, the social utility of the defendant's conduct and the cost of eliminating the risk. Of course, itemising these factors can give no indication of their weight in any particular case; determining this question involves a complex value-judgment, rather than merely some mathematical process.

**[5.05]** The third element of the negligence formula requires actual loss or damage to the interests of the plaintiff. The tort of negligence, unlike trespass,[8] for example, is not actionable *per se*. Much judicial energy in recent years has been expended on determining the range of loss and damage for which compensation in negligence should be available. Of particular difficulty has been the question of recovery for defective, but non-dangerous, products.[9]

**[5.06]** The general principle of "remoteness" of damage is that the loss should have been reasonably foreseeable.[10] This broad formula is sufficiently flexible to expand or contract as the courts desire. Thus it is not necessary that the precise circumstances in which the injury occurred should be foreseeable if the injury is of a type that ought to have been foreseen.[11] Moreover, of further assistance to the plaintiff is the rule that, once the defendant's negligence risked reasonably foreseeable injury to the plaintiff, he or she may claim compensation for injuries that are more serious than could have been foreseen on account of some physical or psychological weakness on his or her part. The key to the understanding of this principle, known widely as the "egg-shell skull" rule,[12] is that it can apply only to cases where the defendant risked reasonably foreseeable injury of some degree to the plaintiff. Thus, if a person lets a book fall on a library floor and a reader forty yards away has a heart attack from the shock, liability should not be imposed on the careless custodian of the book.

**[5.07]** The final element of the tort of negligence requires a sufficiently close causal connection between the conduct and resulting injury to the plaintiff. This aspect of the subject is dealt with in Chapter 2.

**[5.08]** A few words about defences to a negligence action may be in order. The defence of contributory negligence arises where, although the defendant is guilty of negligence, the plaintiff has also been at fault in failing to take due care of himself or herself or his or her

7. See Ch 10.
8. See para **[23.33]** below.
9. See para **[11.77]-[11.77]** below.
10. See para **[3.29]-[3.31]** above.
11. See para **[3.29]-[3.31]** above.
12. See para **[3.32]-[3.41]** above.

property. In these circumstances the plaintiff's compensation will be reduced in proportion to the respective degrees of fault of the plaintiff and the defendant. Prior to the Civil Liability Act 1961, contributory negligence afforded a complete defence, save in cases where, in spite of the plaintiff's contributory negligence, the defendant had the last opportunity to avoid the accident - in which case the defendant had to compensate the plaintiff without any deduction. This arbitrary distinction had few attractions and its demise was widely welcomed.

**[5.09]** The traditional defence of voluntary assumption of risk was also modified by the Civil Liability Act 1961. The position since then has been that, if the defendant can show that the plaintiff before the act complained of agreed to waive his or her legal rights in respect of it, the plaintiff's action must be dismissed.[13] The notion of agreement here involves "some intercourse or communication"[14] between the plaintiff and the defendant from which it may reasonably be inferred that the plaintiff assured the defendant that he or she waived any right of action he or she might have in respect of the defendant's negligence. A "one-sided secret determination" on the part of the plaintiff to give up his or her right of action does not afford the defendant a complete defence but may be treated as contributory negligence in appropriate cases.[15]

13. Civil Liability Act 1961, s 34(1)(b). See Kerr, *The Civil Liability Acts* (1999), pp 43-44 and see paras **[20.72]-[20.77]** below.

14. *O'Hanlon v ESB* [1969] IR 75 at 92 (SC).

15. *O'Hanlon v ESB* [1969] IR 75.

Chapter 6

# The Duty of Care


I. Introduction ........ 115
II. Concepts and Policy ........ 116
III. The Judicial Development of the Duty of Care ........ 118
IV. The Duty of Care in Particular Contexts ........ 128
V. Proximity: Levels of Generality ........ 132
VI. Some Troublesome Duty Issues ........ 133
VII. The European Dimension ........ 138


## I. Introduction

**[6.01]** It has been observed that a person "is entitled to be as negligent as he pleases towards the whole world if he owes no duty to them".[1] The concept of duty[2] is a control device whereby the courts may, as a matter of law, limit the range of liability within what they consider to be reasonable bounds. Important areas of the law where the courts were reluctant to recognise a duty of care include those relating to recovery for pure economic loss, emotional suffering, injury resulting from failure to act, and injuries suffered by entrants on property. Over the years most of those areas of exemption from responsibility have gradually been set aside in favour of extending the range of "duty" to allow recovery for a considerable range (though still far from all) of damage that was reasonably foreseeable to the regular actor. Failure to act and pure economic loss are the principal remaining areas where the courts are still hesitant to impose a wide-ranging duty of care.[3]

**[6.02]** It is worth noting at the outset that although the duty concept in Negligence is obviously concerned with the range of persons to whom the defendant may be obligated, the duty issue is also concerned with the kind of damage which the defendant may cause. It is understandable and perhaps inevitable, because of the dominance of Lord Atkin's

1. *Le Lievre v Gould* [1893] 1 QB 491 at 497 (CA), quoted with approval by Fitzgibbon LJ in *Petrie v Owners of SS "Rostrevor"* [1898] 2 LR 556 at 575 (CA).
2. See generally, Fleming 'Remoteness and Duty: The Control in Liability for Negligence' (1953) 31 Can BR 471; Green 'The Duty Problem in Negligence Cases' (1928) 28 Col LR 1014; Morison 'A Re-examination of the Duty of Care' (1948) 12 MLR 9; Dias 'The Duty Problem in Negligence' [1955] Camb LJ 198; Heuston '*Donoghue v Stevenson* in Retrospect' (1957) 20 MLR 1; Symmons 'The Duty of Care in Negligence: Recently Expressed Policy Elements' (1971) 34 MLR 394; Heuston '*Donoghue v Stevenson*: A Fresh Appraisal' [1971] CLP 37; Lawson 'Duty of Care in Negligence' (1947) 22 Tulane LR 111; Williams 'The Risk Principle' (1961) 77 LQR 179; 'Smith & Burns, *Donoghue v Stevenson*-The Not So Golden Anniversary' (1983) 46 MLR 147.
3. This judicial extension of the duty of care on the part of occupiers to trespassers - *McNamara v ESB* [1975] IR 1 and (more tentatively) to other entrants - *Foley v Musgrave Cash and Carry Ltd* Supreme Court, 20 December 1985; *Thomas v Leitrim County Council* [1998] 2 ILRM 74 (HC); *cf Rooney v Connolly* [1987] ILRM 768 - was thrawted by a lobby-driven legislative response: Occupiers' Liability Act 1995, analysed, see para **[12.59]** below.

"neighbour principle" (articulated in *Donoghue v Stevenson*[4]), in the development of the concept of duty of care, that the focus should be on the range of persons who are owed the duty. In addressing the question whether a manufacturer owed a duty of care to the consumer, Lord Atkin declared that everyone owed such a duty to his "neighbour". He then went on to define who are our neighbours. Some forty-six years later, the House of Lords, in *Anns v Merton Urban District Council*,[5] per Lord Wilberforce, when updating the duty problem, also emphasised that in society persons normally owe a duty of care to persons who are "proximate" or who pass the "neighbourhood" criterion. So both of these influential precedents, the emphasis was on the *range of persons* to whom the defendant ought to have regard when doing his business. But it is worth emphasising that the duty issue is not only concerned with answering the question "To whom is the defendant liable?" but equally is it concerned with answering the question "for what kind of damage is the defendant liable?". It may be that the plaintiff is within the range of persons for whom the defendant ought to have regard when considering his actions, but the courts may still not recognise a duty in the circumstances because of the nature of the damage suffered, where for example, the damage is "pure economic loss" or "nervous shock". The negligent motorist may cause physical damage to a pedestrian, may cause another motorist economic loss because of the delay caused by the accident, and may cause a spectator "nervous shock". While all three injured parties might be classified as "neighbours", only the pedestrian is sure of recovery. Traditionally, the courts denied the others recovery on the ground that the defendant owed them no duty in respect of their damage. For the beginner, therefore, it is well to remember that the courts discuss under the heading of duty, not only "To whom?", but also "For what?".

## II. Concepts and Policy

**[6.03]** At the threshold of our analysis of the duty of care, it is desirable to examine why the courts in any particular case hold that the defendant was, or was not, under a duty of care. Many commentators regard the concept of the duty of care as empty of any meaning- "a shorthand statement of a conclusion, rather than an aid to analysis in itself".[6] When, therefore, a court says that the defendant should not be liable because he or she was not under a duty of care towards the plaintiff, this really means nothing more than that, having regard to broad considerations of social policy, the court is of the opinion that it would not be wise to require the defendant, and others similarly acting, to compensate persons injured by that conduct. The court thus fashions the duty of care and specifies its scope with the simple aim of accomplishing social goals. The value system of which the duty of care is part is one of limited economic and utilitarian horizons rather than of nobler ethical pedigree.[7] This reductionist interpretation of the duty of care explains how the courts have

---

4. [1932] AC 562.
5. [1978] AC 728.
6. PROSSER & KEETON, p 358. See also *Nova-Mink Ltd v Trans-Canada Airlines* [1951] 2 DLR 241 at 255; *Earp v Nobmann* (1981) 175 Cal Rptr 767 at 778 (CA); *Caparo Industries plc v Dickman* [1990] 2 AC 605 (HL); *Murphy v Brentwood DC* [1991] 1 AC 398 (HL).
7. *Cf* Lord Atkin's express acknowledgement that the "neighbour" to whom a duty of care in negligence is owed is a more restricted category than the Christian neighbour: *Donoghue v Stevenson* [1932] AC 562 at 580 (HL(Sc)) *Cf* para **[6.10]** below.

found many forms of immoral and anti-social conduct not to involve a breach of duty of care in negligence. It is noteworthy that, over the past decade or so, the British courts have gone to some lengths to make it plain that they have not been bewitched by the conceptual framework of traditional duty of care analysis into believing that the crucial concepts have tangible reality. Thus, in *Caparo Industries plc v Dickman*,[8] Lord Bridge observed that the concepts of proximity and fairness, which had been emphasised in earlier decisions:

> "are not susceptible to any such precise definition as would be necessary to give them utility as practical tests, but amount in effect to little more than labels to attach to the features of different specific situations which, on a detailed examination of all the circumstances, the law recognises pragmatically as giving rise to a duty of care of a given scope."[9]

**[6.04]** Lord Oliver was equally frank in puncturing the metaphysical bubble:

> "'Proximity' is, no doubt, a convenient expression so long as it is realised that it is no more that a label which embraces not a definable concept but merely a description of circumstances from which, pragmatically, the courts conclude that a duty of care exists."[10]

**[6.05]** As we shall see, there are problems associated with trying to develop a coherent law of negligence where the courts have eschewed broad principle in favour of an incremental pragmatism. No one would deny that Lord Atkin's "neighbour" principle in *Donoghue v Stevenson*[11] or that Lord Wilberforce's "two-step" test in *Anns v Merton London Borough Council*[12] can lead an unreflective court to imposing too expansive a range of liability, but they have the definite virtue of encouraging courts to raise their eyes beyond immediate pragmatic considerations and develop liability principles which are sensitive to such basic values as the protection of human life, bodily integrity and economic interests from careless or otherwise socially unwarranted violations.

**[6.06]** The Irish courts have generally preferred to adhere to the conceptual language of proximity and neighbourhood and have not resorted to incremental pragmatism. Of course they are also conscious of the social and economic implications of an overbroad definition of the duty of care and are perfectly able to tailor the scope of the duty in the light of these considerations but their starting point is one of broad principle. With very few exceptions[13] they have translated the concepts of proximity and neighbourhood, mediated by policy considerations, into an impressive body of jurisprudence.

---

8. [1990] 2 AC 605 (HL).

9. [1990] 2 AC 605. See Lord Roshill's observations in the same case:

> "Phrases such as 'foreseeability', 'proximity', 'neighbourhood', 'just and reasonable', 'fairness', 'voluntary acceptance of risk' or 'voluntary assumption of responsibility' will be found used from time to time in the different cases. But ... such phrases are not precise definitions. At best they are but labels or phrases descriptive of the very different factual situations which can exist in particular cases and which must be carefully examined in each case before it can be pragmatically determined whether a duty of care exists and, if so, what is the scope and extent of that duty."

10. [1990] 2 AC 605.

11. [1932] AC 562 at 580 (HL).

12. [1978] AC 728 at 751-752 (HL).

13. It may be argued that *McCann v Brinks Allied Ltd and Ulster Bank Ltd* [1997] 1 ILRM 461 (SC) did not extend the duty of care far enough - *cf* Byrne & Binchy, *Annual Review of Irish Law 1996*, pp 577-579 and that *Ryan v Ireland* [1989] IR 177 extended it somewhat too far - *cf* Byrne & Binchy, *Annual Review of Irish Law 1989*.

## III. The Judicial Development of the Duty of Care

**[6.07]** The process of judicial development of the duty of care has been complicated and uncertain. Two distinct matters must be identified. The first concerns the conceptual scaffolding supporting the duty of care; the second relates to the scope of this duty in particular contexts. These two matters have become intertwined: judicial debate has concentrated on the extent to which the conceptual scaffolding should seek to define the actual scope of the duty of care. Briefly, it may be said that the Irish courts, taking their lead from a decision[14] of the House of Lords in 1977, are considerably more willing than the House of Lords now is to let the conceptual scaffolding go some way towards defining the actual scope of the duty of care in particular cases.

**[6.08]** What do we mean here by "conceptual scaffolding"? Essentially that the duty of care in negligence has been defined in conceptual terms: rather than merely deciding at an intuitive level whether there was or was not a duty of care in a particular case, the courts address this question by reference to key concepts which enlarge on the meaning of the duty of care.

**[6.09]** It seems desirable to examine first the development of British thinking on this matter, before going on to examine Irish judicial analysis. In contrast to the creative and subtle development of its constitutional jurisprudence, the Supreme Court has yet to make a distinctive contribution to the jurisprudence on the duty of care in negligence. Save for the strikingly forthright incorporation of negligence principles into the law relating to occupiers' liability to trespassers,[15] Irish decisions on the conceptual aspects of negligence law have tended to accept somewhat uncritically a conceptual agenda set by British decisions. There is perhaps some evidence over the past decade or so that the Irish courts have decided to build on these importations. What we now find is that the foundation stone[16] for this new Irish edifice[17] is one that has since been emphatically rejected by those who laid it.[18]

### British Developments 1932-2000

**[6.10]** In *Donoghue v Stevenson*,[19] in a passage which has been cited with approval many times in our courts,[20] Lord Atkin outlined "a general conception of relations giving rise to

14. *Anns v Merton London Borough Council* [1978] AC 728 (HL).
15. *Cf* para **[12.16]** below.
16. *Anns v Merton London Borough Council* [1978] AC 728.
17. *Cf Ward v McMaster* [1988] IR 337.
18. *Cf Murphy v Brentwood DC* [1991] 1 AC 398.
19. [1932] AC 562 (HL).
20. As, for example, by O'Higgins CJ, in *Keane v ESB* [1981] IR 44 at 50 (SC). See also *Healy v Bray UDC* [1962-63] Ir Jur Rep 9 at 15 (SC); *Donaldson v Irish Motor Racing Club* Supreme Court, 1 February 1957 (Kingsmill Moore J), pp 7, 8 of judgment; *Finlay v Murtagh* [1979] IR 249 at 264 (SC); *Wall v Hegarty* [1980] ILRM 124 at 127 (HC); *McAuliffe v Moloney* [1971] IR 200 at 202 (SC); *Scully v Marjorie Boland Ltd* [1962] IR 58 at 64-65 (HC); *Robinson v Technico Ltd* High Court, 19 February 1953 (Davitt P) at pp 10-11 (affd SC); *McNamara v ESB* [1975] IR 1 at 16 (SC); *Rooney v Connolly* [1987] ILRM 768 at 778 (SC). See also *Ward v McMaster* [1988] IR 337, affg [1985] IR 29 (HC).

a duty of care, of which the particular cases found in the books are but instances".[21] He stated:

> "The rule that you are to love your neighbour becomes in law you must not injure your neighbour; and the lawyer's question, who is my neighbour? receives a restricted reply. You must take reasonable care to avoid acts or omissions which you can reasonably foresee would be liable to injure your neighbour. Who, then, in law, is my neighbour? The answer seems to be - persons who are so closely and directly affected by my act that I ought reasonably to have them in contemplation as being so affected when I am directing my mind to the acts or omissions which are called in question."[22]

**[6.11]** The "neighbour principle" has operated as a "general road sign"[23] rather than a binding rule. In the House of Lords decision of *Home Office v Dorset Yacht Co Ltd*[24] in 1969, Lord Reid stated that the principle "ought to apply unless there is some justification or valid explanation for its exclusion".

**[6.12]** In *Anns v Merton London Borough Council*,[25] Lord Wilberforce sought to provide a new conceptual formulation of the duty of care, to take account of judicial developments over the years. He said:

> "Through the trilogy of cases in this House, *Donoghue v Stevenson*,[26] *Hedley Byrne & Co Ltd v Heller & Partners Ltd*[27] and *Home Office v Dorset Yacht Co Ltd*[28] the position has now been reached that in order to establish that a duty of care arises in a particular situation, it is not necessary to bring the facts of that situation within those of previous situations in which a duty of care has been held to exist. Rather the question has to be approached in two stages. First, one has to ask whether, as between the alleged wrongdoer and the person who has suffered damage, there is a sufficient relationship of proximity or neighbourhood such that, in the reasonable contemplation of the former, carelessness on his part may be likely to cause damage to the latter, in which case a prima facie duty of care arises. Secondly, if the first question is answered affirmatively, it is necessary to consider whether there are any considerations which ought to negative, or to reduce or limit the scope of, the duty or the class of person to whom it is owed or the damages to which a breach of it may rise ..."

**[6.13]** The first of these two steps sounds very similar to Lord Atkin's language in *Donoghue v Stevenson*. As we shall see, the word "proximity" has played an important role in the Irish cases. The concept of proximity[29] may perhaps be criticised as involving a mercurial metaphor. It suggests a closeness between the parties, but on analysis it turns out that the legal notion of proximity does not require closeness in either space or time. Liability in negligence may attach to conduct that results in injury or damage thousands of miles away and decades later[30] to a plaintiff not born at the time when the conduct was

21. [1932] AC 580.
22. [1932] AC 580.
23. FLEMING, p 136 (5th ed, 1977).
24. [1970] AC 1004 at 1027.
25. [1978] AC 728 at 751.
26. [1932] AC 562.
27. [1964] AC 465.
28. [1970] AC 1004.
29. The word has a long pedigree: *cf Thomas v Quartermaine* (1887) 18 QBD 685 at 688.
30. Note that the limitations issue in negligence cases relating to discoverability for injury, for example, (as to which *cf* Ch 46), is premised on there being a duty of care in such a case.

completed. It is true that distance in space and time are factors to which due weight is to be given when deciding the question of legal proximity, but these factors are far from the only ones.

**[6.14]** The second step of Lord Wilberforce's formula comes into play only where a *prima facie* duty of care arises on the basis of the first step. It envisages that there may be considerations which ought to negative or reduce or limit the scope of the duty of care, or the class of person to whom it is owed, or the damages which its breach may occasion. It may be argued, on one view, that, if the second step is to avoid redundancy, these negativing considerations should not come into play at the stage when the court is taking the first step. If this is so, then although the first step mentions "a sufficient relationship of proximity or neighbourhood ...", these terms cannot be co-extensive with Lord Atkin's "neighbour" formula, since plainly the court could hold that there was (or was not) a sufficient relationship of neighbourhood under Lord Atkin's formula only after addressing the negativing considerations and weighing them against the considerations supporting a finding of a sufficient degree of neighbourhood to impose a duty of care.

**[6.15]** Lord Wilberforce's two-step formula can be interpreted as merely expressing Lord Atkin's "neighbour" formula in more expansive language, without any implication of its embracing a *wider scope* of duty. On another view, Lord Wilberforce's fromula hints at precisely this extension of scope of duty. The reference to "a *prima facie* duty of care" may suggest to some judges that the first step is one that should not give them cause to hesitate too long. Although the formula does not expressly state this, its overall effect may be to encourage the imposition of a duty of care in all situations, however novel, or, conversely, however strongly repudiated in earlier judicial precedents, unless there is some most unusual reason, based on public policy, not to do so or to do so only partially.

**[6.16]** A still more radical (and heterodox) interpretation of Lord Wilberforce's test is that the first step actually equates the duty of care with reasonable foreseeability of injury. This would drain the expressions "proximity" and "neighbourhood" of all their traditional meaning, since the distinguishing feature of these concepts is that they demand something more than reasonable foreseeability.

**[6.17]** Lord Wilberforce's formula initially received fairly widespread support.[31] In time, however, the tide turned, at least in England. In *Governors of the Peabody Donation Fund v Sir Lindsay Parkinson & Co Ltd*[32] in 1984, Lord Keith noted that there had been a tendency in recent cases to treat this formula and Lord Reid's observations in *Dorset Yacht Co* as being themselves of a definitive character. He added:

> "This is a temptation which should be resisted ... [I]n determining whether or not a duty of care of particular scope was incumbent on a defendant it is material to take into consideration whether it is just and reasonable that it should be so."[33]

**[6.18]** This "note of criticism"[34] was reinforced in later decisions. In *Leigh and Sullivan Ltd v Aliakmon Shipping Co Ltd*[35] in 1986, Lord Brandon[36] observed that the key passage

31. *Cf*, eg *Junior Books Ltd v Veitchi Co Ltd* [1983] 1 AC 520 (HL).
32. [1985] AC 210 (HL).
33. [1985] AC 210 at 240.
34. *Curran v Northern Ireland Housing Co-ownership Association Ltd* [1987] AC 718 at 724 (HL).
35. [1986] AC 785 at 815 (HL).
36. The other members of the Court concurring.

from Lord Wilberforce's judgment in *Anns* did not provide, and could not have been intended to provide, "a universally applicable test of the existence and scope of a duty of care in the law of negligence". Lord Wilberforce had been dealing with the approach to the questions of the existence and scope of a duty of care in a novel type of factual situation which was not analogous to any factual situations in which the existence of a duty of care in a factual situation in which such a duty had already been held to exist. He "was not ... suggesting that the same approach should be adopted to the existence of a duty of care in a factual situation in which such a duty had repeatedly been held not to exist."[37] In *Curran v Northern Ireland Housing Co-ownership Association Ltd*[38] Lord Bridge[39] observed that *Anns*:

> "may be said to represent the high-water mark of a trend in the development of the law of negligence by [the] House [of Lords] towards the elevation of the 'neighbourhood principle' ... into one of general application from which a duty of care may always be derived unless there are clear countervaluing considerations to exclude it".

He noted that this trend has been "cogently criticised"[40] by academic commentators,[41] "particularly in its tendency to obscure the important distinction between misfeasance and non-feasance".[42]

**[6.19]** In the Privy Council decision of *Yuen Kun-yeu v AG of Hong Kong*[43] the destruction of Lord Wilberforce's formula was carried a good deal further. The Judicial Committee was of the view that the two-step test had "been elevated to a degree of importance greater than it merits, and greater perhaps than its author intended".[44] The first step carried a risk of misinterpretation. It might be considered either to equate "proximity" with reasonable foreseeability or to make the expression "proximity or neighbourhood" import "the whole concept of necessary relationship between plaintiff and defendant discussed by Lord Atkin in *Donoghue v Stevenson*".[45] In the view of the Judicial Committee, the first interpretation was clearly wrong:

> "Foreseeability of harm is a necessary ingredient of such a relationship, but it is not the only one. Otherwise there would be liability in negligence on the part of one who sees another about to walk over a cliff with his head in the air, and forbears to shout a warning."[46]

**[6.20]** The Judicial Committee favoured the second interpretation. On this basis, a serious doubt would arise as to how the second step could have any efficacy, since the Atkinian neighbourhood formula required the court to address negativing factors before

---

37. [1986] AC 785 at 815.
38. [1987] AC 724.
39. The other members of the Court concurring.
40. [1987] AC 724.
41. Smith & Burns '*Donoghue v Stevenson* - The Not So Golden Anniversary' (1983) 46 MLR 147.
42. [1987] AC at 724.
43. [1987] 2 All ER 705 (PC).
44. [1987] 2 All ER 705 at 710.
45. [1932] AC 562.
46. [1987] 2 All ER 705. The example is not perhaps the happiest that might have been chosen.

determining whether or not a sufficient degree of neighbourhood existed to warrant the information of a duty of care. The Privy Council resolved this difficulty by interpreting the second stage as involving only the most exceptional instances where, "notwithstanding that a case of negligence is made out on the proximity basis, *public policy* requires that there should be no liability".[47] Lord Keith mentioned as examples the immunity from suit in negligence of barristers[48] in respect of their conduct of proceedings in court and the immunity of the police in relation to the investigation of crime.[49] In view of the direction in which the law had been developing since *Anns*, the Judicial Committee considered that for the future "it should be recognised that the two-stage test ... is not to be regarded as in all circumstances a suitable guide to the existence of a duty of care".[50]

**[6.21]** The end for Lord Wilberforce's formula came with *Caparo Industries plc v Dickman*[51] and *Murphy v Brentwood District Council*.[52] In these two decisions, the House of Lords made it clear that it would no longer proceed by broad strides, based on the concepts of proximity, neighbourhood and duty, instead it would inch forward incrementally, sceptical of general principles and loose concepts, venturing cautiously by way of close analogy with what had gone before. Lord Bridge's observations in *Caparo*[53] encapsulate this *volte face*:

> "Whilst recognising, of course, the importance of the undeveloping general principles common to the whole field of negligence, I think the law has now moved in the direction of attaching greater significance to the more traditional categorisation of distinct and recognisable solutions as guides to the existence the scope and the limits of the varied duties of care which the law imposes. We must now, I think, recognise the wisdom of the words of Brennan J, in the High Court of Australia in *Sutherland Shire, Council v Heyman*,[54] where he said:
>
>> 'It is preferable in my view that the law should develop novel categories of negligence incrementally and by analogy with established categories, rather than by a massive extension of a *prima facie* duty of care restrained only by undefinable 'considerations which ought to negative, or to reduce or limit the scope of the duty of the class of person to whom it should be owed.'

**[6.22]** The incremental approach now in vogue in Britain is closely associated with a predilection to break the duty of care into three categories by reference to the consequences of negligent conduct. These are, firs, cases of physical injury or damage, the infliction of which "universally requires to be justified"[55]; second, cases of pure economic loss, which should largely go uncompensated[56]; and third, cases of psychiatric injury, in

47. [1987] 2 All ER 705 at 712 (emphasis added).
48. *Rondel v Worsley* [1969] 1 AC 191 (HL).
49. *Hill v Chief Constable of West Yorkshire* [1988] 2 All ER 238 (HL).
50. [1987] 2 All ER 705 at 712. See also *D & F Estates Ltd v Church Commissioners for England* [1988] 2 WLR 368 (HL) where the ratio in *Anns* was placed under a shadow of uncertainty.
51. [1990] 2 AC 605.
52. [1991] 1 AC 398.
53. [1990] 2 AC 605.
54. (1985) 60 ALR 1 at 43-44 (HC, Austr).
55. [1990] 2 AC 605.
56. *Cf Murphy v Brentwood DC* [1991] 1 AC 398.

respect of which an elaborate (and unhelpful) distinction is now drawn between primary and secondary victims.[57]

**[6.23]** Why should there have been such a disenchantment in Britain with the two-step test? Several reasons may be suggested. First, the decision in *Junior Books*, which was almost immediately regarded as having gone too far, was seen as having involved too facile an application of the two-step test. If this could happen at the level of the House of Lords, how much more likely was it to do so at the level of the trial judge, who might resort to the test as a substitute for clear thought on the policy issues raised in the case before the court. Secondly, the test itself was perceived as having been expressed too widely. Unless narrowly and unconvincingly interpreted, it would call into question all previous decisions on the duty issue. Thirdly, it would be wrong to ignore the long tradition of pragmatism among the British judiciary.[58] Finally, uncertainty as to the breadth of the duty of care led to difficulties for business in forward planning and in assessing how much insurance cover they should seek for their enterprises.

**[6.24]** The two-step test stated the law in terms of principle which had a sharper bite than the Atkinian formula. A modification was called for, and the gloss that the duty of care be recognised only when it is "just and reasonable that it should be so"[59] provided an attractive blurring of principle.

## Irish Developments

**[6.25]** In Ireland, the courts have long endorsed the Atkinian test. In the important decisions of *Purtill v Athlone UDC*[60] and *McNamara v ESB*[61] - both decided before *Anns* - there was a strong emphasis on proximity as the lynchpin of the duty of care. This trend has continued unabated.[62] In *Tulsk Co-op v Ulster Bank Ltd*,[63] for example, Gannon J said:

> "In every case in which a claim for damages is founded in negligence it is essential to examine the circumstances which bring the parties into relation with each other and in which the risks of reasonably foreseeable harm can be identified, and the extent to which each or

57. *White v Chief Constable of South Yorkshire Police* [1999] 1 All ER 1.
58. In *Rowling v Takaro Properties Ltd* [1988] AC 473 at 501 (PC), Lord Keith described the question of imposing a duty of care in negligence as being "of an intensely pragmatic character, well suited for gradual development but requiring most careful analysis". See also *Caparo Industries plc v Dickman* [1989] 1 All ER 798 (CA).
59. *Governors of the Peabody Donation Fund v Sir Lindsay Parkinson & Co Ltd* [1985] AC 10 at 241. It is worth noting the source of the "just and reasonable" formula endorsed in *Peabody*. In *Home Office v Dorset Yacht Co Ltd* [1970] AC 1004 at 1038-1039, Lord Morris had observed that "[p]olicy need not be invoked where reason and good sense will at once point the way". This suggests an emphasis more on intuition than on extended rational deliberation. Moreover, in no sense is it limited only to holdings against the recognition of a duty of care. Yet, since *Peabody*, the "just and reasonable" formula has tended to be regarded in that light. See further *Marc Rich & Co AG v British Rock Marine Co Ltd* [1996] AC 211 (HL).
60. [1968] IR 205 (SC).
61. [1975] IR 1 (SC).
62. *Cf*, eg, *Siney v Dublin Corporation* [1980] IR 400 (SC); *Wall v Hegarty* [1980] ILRM 124 (HC); *Ward v McMaster* [1988] IR 337 (SC).
63. High Court, 13 May 1983 (Gannon J).

either has control of the circumstances, with a view to determining what duty of care, if any, may exist, the nature and extent of the duty, and whether and to what extent there may have been a breach of duty of care to which the damage complained of can properly be attributed. There are many types of relationships created by circumstances which lend themselves to easy classification with identifiable duties as in cases where the parties have entered into contracts or formal agreements, or where informal or fiducial; relations exist, or there may be circumstances of social encounter such as invitor and invitee, or casual encounter or physical proximity such as road traffic conditions. But it is demonstrable from consideration of the judgments of Walsh J, in *Purtill v Athlone UDC*[64] and of the opinions expressed in the House of Lords in *Hedley Byrne v Heller & Co Ltd*[65] that liability in negligence for damages is not derived solely from identifiable classification of relationships, however variable, the existing circumstances may import with the duty of care they demand."[66]

**[6.26]** Some High Court judges[67] were attracted by the early somewhat moderate, retrenchment from *Anns* that was apparent in English decisions in the 1980s. The Supreme Court, however, has taken a different view. In the crucial decision of that Court of *Ward v McMaster*[68] McCarthy J preferred "not ... to dilute the words of Lord Wilberforce". He considered the duty of care "arose" from the proximity of the parties, the foreseeability of the damage, and the absence of any compelling exemption based upon public policy.[69] He was of the view that such an exemption would have to be "a very powerful one" if it was to be used to deny an injured party his "right to redress".[70] McCarthy J showed no enthusiasm[71] for Brennan J's preference in *Sutherland Shire Council v Heyman*[72] that "the law should develop novel categories of negligence incrementally and by analogy with established categories ..." In McCarthy J's opinion, this "verbally attractive proposition of incremental growth ... suffers from a temporal defect - that rights should be determined by the accident of birth". On one interpretation, this suggests that McCarthy J perceived specific judicial declarations of "new" situations importing a duty of care as doing no more than articulating duties and rights already included in the established general principle of proximity. On another interpretation, he was repudiating Lord Brandon's attempt in *Leigh & Sullivan* to limit the two-step test to the questions of the existence and scope of a duty of care in a novel type of factual situation rather than in cases where the existence of such a duty had repeatedly been held not to exist.[73]

---

64. [1968] IR 205.
65. [1964] AC 465.
66. Pages 37-38 of Gannon J's judgment. See also *Kearney v Paul & Vincent Ltd* High Court, 30 July 1985 (Barron J), at p 20.
67. *Cf Ward v McMaster* [1985] IR 29 (HC), noted by Murray [1986] Dublin ULJ 109; *McMahon v Ireland* [1988] ILRM 610 (HC).
68. [1988] IR 337 (SC). See Kerr, [1988] Dublin ULJ 182.
69. [1988] IR 337 .
70. [1988] IR 337 .
71. [1988] IR 337 .
72. (1985) 60 ALR 1 at 43 (HC, Austr).
73. It is worth noting that McCarthy J considered that, in view of the finding on the facts of *Ward v McMaster* that there was a *prima facie* duty of care, against which no negativing or limiting consideration had been argued, it "follow[ed]" that the plaintiff should succeed, "without entering into the question of whether or not it is 'just and reasonable' to impose the duty". For full discussion of *Ward v McMaster* and its implications for the development of duty of care analysis in Ireland, see Byrne & Binchy, *Annual Review of Irish Law 1988*.

**[6.27]** McCarthy J considered that, in view of the finding on the facts of the case in *Ward v McMaster* that there was a *prima facie* duty of care, against which no negativing or limiting considerations had been argued, it "follow[ed]" that the plaintiff should succeed "without entering into the question of whether of not it is 'just and reasonable'[74] to impose the duty."[75]

**[6.28]** McCarthy J's expression of how the court should approach the duty of care issue has proved to be the definitive one.[76] It contains two strong and simple conceptual requirements: the proximity of the parties and the foreseeability of the damage. Against this it balances "the absence of any compelling exemption based upon public policy", which in order to "trump" the factors of proximity and foreseeability, "must be a very powerful one if it is to be used to deny an injured party his right to redress at the expense of the person or body that injured him."

**[6.29]** This formula differs from the British approach, prior to the *Caparo*[77]-*Murphy*[78] retrenchment, in a number of ways. First, the emphasis on foreseeability of the damage as a distinct element in the formulation of the duty of care is somewhat surprising in that the need to establish such foreseeability was already accepted as a pre-condition of liability about which there could be no controversy. Certainly, since *Wagon Mound*,[79] there were no voices claiming recovery for one who suffered unforeseeable injury in his or her action against a negligent defendant.

**[6.30]** One clear benefit of McCarthy J's isolation of the issue of foreseeability as a distinct matter for the court to address, separate from the proximity issue, is that it makes his test imperious to the criticism widely levelled against Lord Wilberforce's "two-step" test in *Anns*, that the proximity question dispenses with foreseeability. A plaintiff under McCarthy J's test must clear the two separate hurdles of foreseeability and proximity and must not be brought down by the public policy provisio if he or she is to succeed.

**[6.31]** McCarthy J's invocation of proximity of relationship between the parties is scarcely surprising. The phrase has been part of the lexicon of the duty of care for generations.

---

74. *Cf Peabody Fund v Sir Lindsay Parkinson Ltd* [1985] AC 210.
75. [1989] ILRM 400.
76. See, eg *Sweeney v Duggan*, [1991] 2 IR 274 (HC), affd [1997] 2 ILRM 211 (SC); *Doherty Timber Ltd v Drogheda Harbour Commissioners* [1993] ILRM 401 (HC); *McShane Wholesale Fruit and Vegetables Ltd v Johnston Haulage Co Ltd* [1997] 1 ILRM 86 (HC); *Turner v Iarnród Éireann/Irish Rail* High Court, 14 February 1996 (Flood J); *Howard v Dublin Corporation* High Court, 31 July 1996 (Lavan J) (revd by SC); *McKenna v Best Travel Ltd t/a Cypriana Holidays* High Court, 17 December 1996 (Lavan J); *Madden v Irish Turf Club* [1997] 2 ILRM 148 (SC) (*nem diss*); *W v Ireland (No 2)* [1997] 2 IR 141 (HC) - involving a complex analysis of the duty of care issue, considered at para **[32.137]** below; *Forshall and Fine Arts and Collections Ltd v Walsh*, High Court, 18 June 1997 (Shanley J), affd by Supreme Court, 31 July 1998 - where *Ward* and *Caparo* were cited as though they adopted an identical approach to the duty of care issue; *Hanahoe v Judge Hussey* High Court, 14 November 1997 (Kinlen J); *Wildgust v Bank of Ireland* High Court, 28 July 1998 (Morris P) - where Lord Bridge's speech in *Caparo* was quoted.
77. *Caparo Industries plc v Dickman* [1990] 2 AC 605 (HL).
78. *Murphy v Brentwood DC* [1991] 1 AC 398 (HL).
79. *Overseas Tankship (UK) Ltd v Morts Dock & Engineering Co Ltd (The Wagon Mound) (No 1)* [1961] AC 388 (PC).

Although judges internationally seem in recent years to delight in deflating its metaphysical pretensions,[80] with the enthusiasm of children who have just discovered the facts of life about Santa Claus, proximity remains a potent metaphor, going to the core of human empathy and moral decision making. Lord Atkin was surely wise to point to the fact that the law sets a somewhat lower standard that the parable of the Good Samaritan: traditionally it has not required us, under legal sanction, to go to the aid of others, especially strangers.[81] It would seem mistaken, however, to dismiss out of hand the capacity of the proximity metaphor to guide judicial decisonmaking, albeit at a somewhat primitive level. The word seems to capture the true basis in *Purtill v Athlone UDC*,[82] for finding a duty of care on the part of the custodians of detonators to a young boy tempted by these obvious, unguarded attractions and conversely, for not identifying a duty of care on the part of the racing authorities to a disappointed wagerer in *Madden v Irish Turf Club*.[83]

**[6.32]** McCarthy J's emphasis on public policy as being capable of negating or limiting the duty of care and his rejection of the *Peabody*[84] "just and reasonable" proviso contrasts strongly with the contemporary British preference[85] for stressing the latter and downplaying the former consideration.

---

80. *Cf* the passages from the speeches of Lords Bridge, Roskill and Oliver, in *Caparo Industries plc v Dickman* [1990] 2 AC 605, quoted at para **[6.03]-[6.04]** above. In *Hill v Van Earp* (1997) 142 Austr LR 687 at 700 (HC, Austr), Dawson J considered that "proximity" served a purpose, indicating that "something more is required" than simple proof of foreseeability in order to create a duty of care; that term signified that "the process of reasoning must be undertaken". Dawson J added:

> "Proximity, in that sense, expresses the result of a process of reasoning rather than the process itself, but it remains a useful term because it signifies that a process of reasoning must be undertaken. But to hope that proximity can describe a common element underlying all those categories of case in which a duty of care is recognised is to expect more of the term than it can provide."

A similar scepticism is apparent in La Forest J's judgment in *Hercules Managements Ltd v Ernst & Young* (1997) 146 DLR (4th) 577 (SC, Can), echoing what he, Stevenson and McLaughlin JJ had said in *Canadian National Railway Co v Norsk Pacific SS Co* (1992) 91 DLR (4th) 289 (SC Can):

> "[T]he term 'proximity' itself is nothing more than a label expressing a result, judgment or conclusion; it does not, in and of itself, provide a principled basis on which to make a legal determination."

81. It has, however, recognised that family members, employers and others in position of authority or trust may owe an affirmative duty of care towards those in situation of danger of dependency. The metaphor of proximity here seems to have vitality in assisting judicial determination of how widely to cast the net of duty.

82. [1968] IR 205 (SC).

83. [1997] 2 ILRM 148 (SC).

84. [1985] AC 210.

85. Thus in *Caparo Industries plc v Dickman* [1990] 2 AC 605 at 617, Lord Bridge stated:

> "What emerges is that, in addition to the foreseeability of damage, necessary ingredients in any situation giving rise to a duty of care are that, there should exist between the party owing the duty and the party to whom it is owed a relationship characterised by the law as one of 'proximity' or 'neighbourhood', and that the situation should be one in which the court considers it fair Just and reasonable that the law should impose a duty of a given scope on the one party for the benefit of the other."

In the light of this frequently-cited statement of the guiding principles to determining the existence (or otherwise) of a duty of care, WINFIELD & JOLOWICZ, p 108 consider that "it is difficult to see how there can be a 'public policy' interest which cannot be handled in the court's analysis of what is 'fair, just and reasonable'."

**[6.33]** Over the years since *Ward v McMaster*, McCarthy J's three-step approach of proximity and public policy has received strong support. Most courts are content to cite or summarise it without comment and then to proceed to apply it to the facts of the case before them. In only a couple of decisions has anything been said that raises even the most tangential doubt about the continuing efficacy of the approach.

**[6.34]** In the Supreme Court decision of *Forshall and Fine Arts Collection Ltd v Walsh*,[86] Barrington J had "no doubt" that the plaintiff "fell within the 'proximity' or 'neighbourhood' principle as described in the cases of *Ward v McMaster* and *Caparo Industries plc v Dickman*." It is somewhat curious that *Ward* and *Caparo* should be cited as bedfellows when they are far from identical in their respective approaches to the duty of care. These differences were, however, largely irrelevant to the determination of the duty of care issue in *Forshall* since it seemed that Barrington J considered that, on either approach, the duty of care to the plaintiff was established.

**[6.35]** In *W v Ireland (No 2)*,[87] the parties were agreed that Costello P should approach the case by applying McCarthy J's test, and Costello P proceeded on that basis. He did, however, make the following, somewhat puzzling, observation:

> "I am, of course aware that subsequent to the decision of *Ward v McMaster* criticisms were made of it and the test suggested by Lord Wilberforce in the English courts to which reference was made in the judgment of McCarthy J. These were carried a step further by the House of Lords in *Murphy v Brentwood* in which the *Anns* decision was decided that the House of Lords should depart from *Anns* 'insofar as it affirmed a private law duty of care to avoid damage to property which causes present or imminent danger to the health and safety of owners or occupiers resting upon local authorities in relation to their function of supervising complicane with building by-laws or regulations ...'[88] Irish law has therefore parted company with English law but I am no means certain that the departure is a major one. The view of the Irish courts has been that *Anns* was a 'confirmation' of the long established principles of the law of tort contained in *Donoghue v Stevenson* and was not (as some commentators in England seem to consider) a major innovation in the law of tort."[89]

The argument here is not entirely plain. It may be to the effect that *Anns*, having merely "confirmed" the earlier law, did not represent any significant development of legal principle so that its overruling in *Murphy* did not create any major difference between the Irish courts (which continues to follow *Anns*) and the British courts (which do not). This would be a somewhat difficult argument to sustain. Certainly the rejection of Lord Wilberforce's "two-step" test in *Anns*, to which Costello P did not explicitly refer, has created a philosophic gulf between Irish and British law on the question of the definition and scope of the duty of care.

---

86. Supreme Court, 31 July 1998. Lynch and Barron JJ concurred. See also *Wildgust v Bank of Ireland*, quoted from Lord Bridge's speech in *Caparo*, quoted at para **[6.21]** above, while stating that he accepted as "a correct statement of law" what had been said on the issue in *Ward v McMaster*.
87. [1997] 2 IR 141 (HC).
88. [1991] AC 398 at 457.
89. [1997] 2 IR 141 at 148.

## IV. THE DUTY OF CARE IN PARTICULAR CONTEXTS

**[6.36]** Let us now examine how the courts have addressed the issue of the duty of care in particular contexts. What is striking about the Irish decisions is that they have shown little of the willingness apparent in English cases to pigeon hole duty issues into the broad categories of physical injury, psychiatric damage and pure economic loss. Indeed, in *McShane Wholesale Fruit and Vegetables Ltd v Johnston Haulage Co Ltd*,[90] Flood J appeared to consider that no such categories should be recognised. He treated the question posed as a preliminary issue - "whether economic loss consequential on a negligent act is recoverable as damages, within this jurisdiction" - as though it were entirely unproblematic. Having quoted McCarthy J's test in *Ward v McMaster*, Flood J stated:

> "The quality of the damage does not arise. It can be damage to property, to the person, financial or economic ...[91] The question as to whether the damage (of whatever type) is recoverable is dependent on proximity and foreseeability subject to the caveat of compelling exemption of public policy.
>
> In short, the proximity of the parties giving rise to the duty of care must be such, as a matter of probability to be causal of the damage. If it is not, the damage is too remote and the action will fail. It will fail not because the damage is of a particular type but because the relationship between the wrongdoer and the person who suffers the damage does not have the essential, of sufficient relationship of proximity of neighbourhood.
>
> It therefore follows that the fact that the damage is economic is not in itself a bar to recovery where the other elements above stated are present.
>
> Whether the damage in this instance is or is not too remote is a question of fact to be determined on evidence."[92]

In spite of Flood J's preference for a holistic approach, it is nonetheless convenient to channel our consideration of the cases into the categories of physical injury or damage, psychiatric injury and pure economic loss. This is the "Liable for what?" apsect of the duty issue referred to earlier.

### Physical injury or damage

**[6.37]** If one person carelessly, physically injures another or damages that other person's property, the courts generally will hold that the careless person was under a duty of care to avoid the injury or damage. In road accident litigation it is hard to find a judicial reference to the duty of care because all parties take it for granted that a road user has a duty of care not to injure other roadusers.[93]

**[6.38]** There are, however, situations where the careless infliction of physical injury or damage takes place in circumstances where the careless person owes no duty of care to the person suffering the injury or damage. The traditional position in relation to occupiers' liability to trespassers was that the occupier owed the trespasser no duty of care and was liable only for injuries intentionally or recklessly inflicted.[94] Even after the liberalising

---

90. [1997] 1 ILRM 86 (HC), analysed by Byrne & Binchy, *Annual Review of Irish Law 1996*, pp 573-574.

91. Citing *Sweeney v Duggan* [1991] IR 274.

92. [1997] 1 ILRM 86.

93. *Cf Gorey v Gorey* High Court, 10 June 1993 (Flood J), analysed by Byrne & Binchy, *Annual Review of Irish Law 1993*, pp 533-534 - plaintiff injured when trying to start tipper truck, which had broken down on the highway.

94. *Cf* para **[12.17]** below.

decisions of *Purtill*[95] and *MacNamara*,[96] the courts fell short of imposing a duty of care on occupiers to all trespassers. As a result of the enactment of the Occupiers' Liability Act 1995,[97] the occupier returns to the position of owing no duty of care to any trespasser in respect of damages due to the state of the premises. The occupier must not injure the trespasser intentionally or recklessly[98] and, if the trespasser is a criminal entrant, there is no requirement to avoid injuring him or her recklessly, save in cases where justice requires otherwise.[99]

**[6.39]** There are other circumstances in which a person is not under a duty of care to avoid causing physical injury or damage to another. One such case is *John C Doherty Timber Ltd v Drogheda Harbour Commissioners*.[100] The plaintiffs, who were timber importers, received a consignment of timber at Drogheda harbour. Having paid the appropriate tonnage dues and cargo dues levied by the defendant harbour authority, the plaintiffs left the consignment on the quayside with the permission of the defendant. It could have lain there for at least a fortnight without incurring any charge or rental. The defendant provided no security of any type in relation to the timber. The day after it was placed on the quayside, it was set on fire by children and destroyed.

**[6.40]** On the question of negligence, Flood J approached the matter from the standpoint of Lord Wilberforce's "two-step" test in *Anns*,[101] as modified by Lord Keith's "just and reasonable" addendum, expressed in *Peabody*.[102] Flood J also noted that, in *Ward v McMaster*,[103] McCarthy J had considered that the duty of care arose from the proximity of the parties, the foreseeability of the damage and the absence of any compelling exemption based on public policy.

**[6.41]** Applying these conditions to the facts of the instant case, Flood J considered that the foreseeability of damage must have been just as apparent to the plaintiff as to the defendant:

> "It seems to me that the reality of the relationship was a bare permission which carried no further obligations of care on the part of the defendant for the very simple reason that it would be virtually impossible to effectively implement. In my opinion the inference to be drawn from the relationship of the parties is that each party knew that the goods were placed and retained on the quayside at the consignee's risk. Further, the consignee being the person primarily involved, it was for him to evaluate and assess the damage of his goods. If damage flowed from his failure to take steps to eliminate or mitigate such risk the proximate cause of the damage would be his failure to act rationally, and reasonably, and in my opinion, in the circumstances, would negative and override any duty of care on the part of the defendant alleged to arise from any proximity or neighbourhood of the parties. It follows that I am of

95. *Purtill v Athlone UDC* [1968] IR 205 (SC).
96. *McNamara v ESB* [1975] IR 1 (SC).
97. *Cf* para **[12.59]** below.
98. Occupiers' Liability Act 1995, s 4(1).
99. Occupiers' Liability Act 1995, s 4(2).
100. [1993] 1 IR 315 (HC).
101. [1978] AC 728.
102. [1985] AC 10.
103. [1989] ILRM 400 (SC).

> opinion that in this instance there was no common law duty of care imposed on the defendant..."[104]

This holding seems eminently sensible. The idea that the Harbour Commissioners should be required to take care of the plaintiff's property, under pain of civil liability, seems quite misplaced.

**[6.42]** Issues relating to the scope of the duty of care in employers' liability have raised the question as to the limits of that duty in particular situations. Obviously employers generally owe a duty of care to their employees to protect them from personal injury when they are carrying out their duties, but does the duty extend to all kinds of work environments? In *Ryan v Ireland*,[105] the Supreme Court held that the army owes a duty of care to its soldiers to take reasonable care to protect them from the risk of injury or death in situations of armed conflict. Security firms similarly owe a duty to protect their employees from careless exposure to the risk of violence.[106] However, what duty of care does a third party owe to employees of a security firm who are exposed to danger as a result of a particular contractual provision which the third party negotiates with the security firm in the knowledge of the danger that this causes the employees? None, said the Supreme Court in *McCann v Brinks Allied Ltd and Ulster Bank Ltd*.[107]

**[6.43]** In this case Morris J imposed liability in negligence on a security firm which exposed its employees to danger in making deliveries to a bank by requiring them to park their vehicle on the roadside, some distance from the bank. The plaintiffs had been violently attacked when attempting to make a delivery to the bank. The bank had refused to let the vehicle drive closer to the premises over a slabbed forecourt, saying that the slabs were not intended to support the weight of vehicles such as the van the employees were using. In the previous three years, two attempted robberies had taken place outside this bank. The security firm had requested the bank to provide a better access to its premises and a Garda Síochána inspector had given the bank similar advice. This could have been done by strengthening the forecourt or by providing a chute at the side of the bank.

**[6.44]** Morris J, while holding the security firm liable, held that the bank was not guilty of negligence in unreasonably exposing the plaintiffs to the danger of criminal assault. The security firm appealed to the Supreme Court, arguing that the bank should be held a concurrent wrongdoer. The Supreme Court, controversially, dismissed the appeal.

**[6.45]** The only judgment delivered in the Court was by O'Flaherty J, which whom Blayney and Murphy JJ concurred. O'Flaherty J reasoned as follows. If it could be held that the bank owed a duty of care to the plaintiffs, then it was "clear that there was enough

---

104. [1993] 1 IR 315.

105. [1989] IR 177 (SC), analysed by Byrne & Binchy, *Annual Review of Irish Law 1989*, pp 410-418. *A fortiori* where the injury is sustained during athletics training: *Rohan v Minister for Finance* High Court, 19 June 1992 (O'Hanlon J); *Dowdall v Minister for Defence* High Court, 23 July 1992 (Denham J).

106. *Walsh v Securicor (Ireland) Ltd,* [1993] 2 IR 507 (SC, affg HC), analysed by Byrne & Binchy, *Annual Review of Irish Law 1993*, pp 541-543; *McCann v Brinks Allied Ltd and Ulster Bank,* [1997] 1 ILRM 461 (SC, affg HC).

107. [1997] 1 ILRM 461. For analysis of *McCann*, see Byrne & Binchy, *Annual Review of Irish Law 1996*, pp 577-579.

to have alerted the bank to take steps to minimise, at least, the risk of injury to [them]".[108] In his view, no such duty was owed:

> "The legal solution to the problem posed is to say that the parties reached an agreement that the risk would lie with Brinks to make sure that the cash was delivered safely; that was the extent of the bank's interest; possibly the bank could have done more in the way of co-operating with Brinks as regards the proposal made about easier access to the bank premises and so forth but the fact that it did not do more does not give rise to any liability in law. In this case the contract was a circumstance which prevented any duty of care arising on the part of the bank *vis-à-vis* Brinks' employees. It is, therefore, a preventative factor, rather than an intervening one, which negatives the existence of a duty of care here."[109]

**[6.46]** The contractual provision which had the effect of thus immunising the bank from liability in negligence to the plaintiffs was to the following effect:

> "The company [Brinks] reserves to itself absolute discretion as to the means, route and procedure to be followed in the storage, guarding and transportation of any goods to which this contract relates. Further, if in the opinion of the company it is at any stage necessary or desirable in the customer's interests to depart from any instructions given by the customer as to such matters the company shall be at liberty to do so."

**[6.47]** This clause, as O'Flaherty J conceded, did not amount to an agreement by Brinks to assume the risk of any damage or injury to its employees. Quite clearly, on the facts of the case, the parties had acted on the basis that the bank's demands had secured the acquiescence of Brinks. Far from running the operation as it wanted, in pursuance of its contractual entitlement, Brinks had deferred to a policy adopted by the bank which, to the bank's own knowledge, exposed the plaintiffs to a danger which both Brinks and the garda inspector understood to be unacceptable. It seems frankly astounding that the bank should be considered not to have owed, and breached, a duty of care to the plaintiffs, whose lives and physical safety were placed at risk.

**[6.48]** The judgment contains no analysis of the reason why the contractual provision should have had the effect of extinguishing a duty of care that would otherwise have arisen. It seems as if O'Flaherty J regarded the very existence of a contract as being, of itself, the explanation why the putative duty expired. He took a somewhat similar view in *Madden v Irish Turf Club*[110] a gambler on the tote sought compensation for his failure to win a bet because an ineligible horse had carelessly been permitted to enter the race. O'Flaherty J stated that the fact that the plaintiff's contractual relationship was with the tote management "erected a barrier so as to prevent such close and direct relations to occur as is necessary to give rise to a duty of care between the plaintiff and the defendants". In the nineteenth century, courts in England[111] and Ireland[112] used to favour such an approach but what became known as the "privity of contract fallacy" was repudiated over six decades

---

108. [1997] 1 ILRM 461 at 464.
109. [1997] 1 ILRM 461 at 465.
110. [1997] 2 ILRM 148 at 146 (SC). See further para **[6.31]** below.
111. *Winterbottom v Wright* (1842) 10 M & W 109, 152 ER 402.
112. *Corry v Lucas* (1868) IR 3 CL 208.

ago in *Donoghue v Stevenson*.[113] Even within the law of contract itself, the privity doctrine is under increasing attack.[114]

**[6.49]** In most cases of negligent damage to property the liability issue is entirely non-problematic. If I negligently drop your Ming vase causing it to smash into pieces, I will have to compensate you for your loss. If I carelessly manufacture a toaster which burns down your kitchen, I will have to pay for the damage. Some other cases are more controversial, however. In Irish law,[115] but no longer in British law[116] a manufacturer (or builder) may be liable in negligence if the product (or building) turns out to be dangerously defective and the purchaser suffers economic loss in taking remedial action. Again in Irish,[117] but not British,[118] law, a producer (or builder) may be liable for a qualitative non-dangerous defect in a product (or building).

### Psychiatric Damage

**[6.50]** In the area of psychiatric disturbance - "nervous shock" - our courts, going back to the last century,[119] have generally adopted a progressive attitude which regards psychiatric and physical injuries as unitary rather than involving a Cartesian divergence.[120] One should, however, acknowledge that, so far, the cases that have required resolution have not been particularly problematic: we have yet to find out how an Irish court would regard factual situations such as arose in *Alcock*[121] or *White*.[122] When the Supreme Court had an opportunity to structure its analysis to the general subject, the result was disappointing.[123]

### Pure Economic Loss

**[6.51]** We have seen that, in *McShane Wholesale Fruit and Vegetables Ltd v Johnston Haulage Co*,[124] Flood J did not regard cases of negligently caused pure economic loss as raising a distinct problem for the courts in terms of setting the contours of liability. This is in stark contrast with contemporary judicial attitudes in Britain. In Chapter 10 we examine in detail the policy issues that arise in this context.

## V. Proximity: Levels of Generality

**[6.52]** It may be useful to examine how the single concept of "proximity" can have differing effects, depending on the degree of generality which is ascribed to it. The cases of *Purtill v Athlone UDC*[125] and *McNamara v ESB*[126] make this process clear.

---

113. [1932] AC 562 (HL).
114. See Friel 'The Failed Experiment with Privity' (1996) 14 Ir L Times (ns) 86.
115. *Ward v McMaster* [1988] IR 337.
116. *Murphy v Brentwood DC* [1991] 1 AC 398 (HL); STREET, pp 213-214.
117. *Ward v McMaster* [1988] IR 337.
118. *Murphy v Brentwood DC* [1991] 1 AC 398; STREET, p 213.
119. *Byrne v Southern and Western Ry Co* Court of Appeal February 1884; *Bell v GN Ry Co* (1890) 26 LR (Ir) 428.
120. *Contrast Hogg v Keane* [1956] IR 155 (SC) with *Page v Smith* [1996] AC 155 (HL).
121. *Alcock v Chief Constable of South Yorkshire* [1992] 1 AC 310 (HL).
122. *White v Chief Constable of South Yorkshire Police* [1999] 1 All ER 1 (HL).
123. *Kelly v Hennessy* [1996] ILRM 321 (SC). See Ch 17 below.
124. [1997] 1 ILRM 86 (HC). See also *Irish Equine Foundation Ltd v Robinson* [1999] 2 ILRM 289 (HC); *Hanahoe v Hussey* High Court, 14 November 1994.
125. [1968] IR 205 (SC).
126. [1975] IR 1 (SC).

**[6.53]** In *Purtill*, Walsh J's judgment hinges on "proximity", but that proximity appeared to many readers of the decision to be of the specific kind that linked the custodians of dangerous chattels with children likely to be injured by those chattels if given access to them. On the basis of this specific relationship, liability might be imposed in spite of the fact that the plaintiff was a former trespasser. *Purtill* looked like an unusual exception to the general, well-established[127] principle that an occupier owed no duty of care in negligence to a trespasser. Yet the language used was elastic, capable of a broad or a narrow interpretation.

**[6.54]** By the time *McNamara* was decided seven years later, Walsh J could interpret *Purtill* as having laid down the unambiguously broad principle:

> "that the occupier of premises could not claim exemption from liability on the grounds that the person injured by the occupier's acts or omissions was a trespasser ...".[128]

While he noted that in *Purtill*, "the duty was stated in relation to a situation where the proximity was known",[129] it seems clear from the facts of *McNamara* that in no sense was the duty of care therein articulated conditional on the defendant's knowing the identity of the plaintiff as a foreseeable entrant or on the existence of a prior relationship between the parties. We thus find from these two cases that a single concept - "proximity" - can support an initially narrow exceptional principle which itself can then be made a stepping stone for a wide-ranging replacement of a former rule to which the concept as originally stated was a mere exception.

## VI. Some Troublesome Duty Issues

**[6.55]** The whole spectrum of human relationships in society raises questions of social policy as to whether regulation of these relationships, backed by the sanction of damages, is appropriate in particular cases. The answer can be expressed in terms of a judicial finding - or rejection - of a "duty of care'' in negligence. Thus, for example, it has been accepted by our courts that the occupier of premises owes a duty of care to trespassers,[130] that a builder of a house owes a duty of care to the purchaser in relation to its safety,[131] that a solicitor owes a duty of care to his or her client,[132] that the State is not immune from a duty of care[133] either generally[134] or specifically in relation to soldiers involved in armed

---

127. *Donovan v Landy's Ltd* [1963] IR 441. See para **[12.31]** below.

128. [1975] IR 1 at 13.

129. [1975] IR 1 at 14.

130. *Purtill v Athlone UDC* [1968] IR 205 (SC); *McNamara v ESB* [1975] IR 1 (SC). The Oireachtas has, however, restored the draconian immunity from a duty of care to trespassers (throwing in "recreational users" for good measure) with the passage of the Occupiers' Liability Act 1995. See para **[12.97]** below.

131. *Ward v McMaster* [1988] IR 337. The duty can extend more widely to non-dangerous defects.

132. *Finlay v Murtagh* [1979] IR 249 (SC).

133. *Wall v Hegarty* [1980] ILRM 124 (HC).

134. *Byrne v Ireland* [1972] IR 241 (SC).

conflict or hostilities,[135] and that a publican owes a duty of care to intoxicated persons on[136] the premises.[137]

**[6.56]** In *McMahon v Ireland*[138] Blayney J held that the Registrar of Friendly Societies did not owe a prospective depositer in a friendly society a duty of care, so that his failure to use his statutory powers in the manner advocated as reasonable by the plaintiff in the proceedings could not involve him in any liability. Blayney J followed the principles of law stated by the Privy Council in *Yuen Kun-yeu v AG of Hong Kong*.[139] In view of the fact that the Supreme Court in *Ward v McMaster*[140] showed a preference for Lord Wilberforce's two-step definition of the duty of care, which *Yuen Kun-yeu* thought should be treated "with some reservation",[141] it seems that *McMahon* has uncertain status as a precedent.

**[6.57]** In England, the courts[142] have evinced no enthusiasm for imposing a duty of care on owners of property to secure it so that it does not become a danger, through human intervention, to their neighbours - by vandals, burglars or arsonists, for example. While these courts have not completely foreclosed the possibility of a duty of care arising in exceptional circumstances, their general attitude is one of fairly unremitting hostility to claims of this type. It seems that the fear of imposing too onerous a duty in this context has led the courts to decline to impose a duty, even in cases where it might be considered just and equitable to do so. Irish courts may prove less reluctant when the issue presents itself to them. They may have a good deal less sympathy for property owners who leave their premises vulnerable to incursion with foreseeable risks to their neighbours.

## The Defendant must have been in Breach of his or her Duty to the Plaintiff

**[6.58]** After some uncertainty, the view has prevailed throughout the common law world that the plaintiff must show that the defendant was in breach of his or her duty to the

135. *Ryan v Ireland* [1989] IR 177.

136. Irish courts have yet to produce a considered analysis of the question of the duty of care of publicans to persons injured off the premises by patrons who were served drink beyond the point of intoxication.

137. *Murphy v O'Brien* (1987) 6 ILT (ns) 75 (CC), where, it should be noted, the report does not state that the plaintiff, who had had "plenty to drink" elsewhere, was served any drink on the defendant's premises.

138. [1988] ILRM 610 (HC), analysed by Byrne & Binchy, *Annual Review of Irish Law 1987*, pp 322-324. See also *Glencar Exploration plc v Mayo County Council* High Court, 20 August (Kelly J) - no duty of care owed by the defendants to pliantiffs, when imposing mining ban:

> "It would be neither fair nor reasonable nor would the proximity of the parties suggest that there was any duty of care extant between the [defendant] and the [plaintiffs] when the mining ban was imposed. The [plaintiffs] were even then applicants for a planning permission and indeed there was no guarantee that they would ever become so. The most that can be said for then [is] that they were prospectors who had a hope, nay even an expectation of bieng applicants for planning permission at some stage in the future."

139. [1987] 2 All ER 705 (PC).

140. [1989] ILRM 400 (SC).

141. [1987] 2 All ER at 710.

142. *Cf Perl (P) (Exporters) Ltd v Camden LBC* [1984] QB 342 (CA); *Smith v Littlewoods Organisation Ltd* [1987] 1 All ER 710 (HL). See STREET, pp 170-171.

plaintiff and "not as the vicarious beneficiary of a breach of duty to another".[143] In other words, a plaintiff will not win his or her case even where the defendant was guilty of the grossest negligence to others, unless the plaintiff can show that the defendant breached a duty of care owed to him or her.[144]

**[6.59]** In the United States of America, the leading decision on this question is *Palsgraf v Long Island Railroad Co.*[145] There, when railway staff of the defendant company were negligently assisting two passengers onto a moving train in a station, one of the passengers dropped a parcel containing explosives. There was an explosion which resulted in a weighing scales, some considerable distance down the platform, falling on the plaintiff and injuring her. The jury found that she was an unforeseeable plaintiff, and the question for the New York Court of Appeals was whether this finding disentitled her to recover. The majority of the Court held that it did. Cardozo J (for the majority) said:

> "What the plaintiff must show is 'a wrong' to herself, ie, a violation of her own right, and not merely a wrong to someone else, nor conduct, 'wrongful' because unsocial, but not 'a wrong' to any one ... The risk reasonably to be perceived defines the duty to be obeyed and risk imports relation; it is risk to another or to others within the range of apprehension.[146]

The conduct of the railway staff:

---

143. *Palsgraf v Long Island Railroad Co* (1928) 162 NE 99. See Prosser 'Palsgraf Revisited' (1952) 52 Mich LR; Green 'The Palsgraf Case' (1930) 3 Col LR 789; Cowan 'The Riddle of the Palsgraf Case' (1938) 23 Minn LR 46; Ehrenzweig 'Loss-Shifting and Quasi-Negligence: A New Interpretation of the Palsgraf Case' (1941) 8 U Chi LR 729. See also *Bourhill v Young* [1943] AC 92 at 108 (HL). *Cf Petrie v Owners of SS "Rostrevor"* [1898] 2 IR 556 at 575-576 (CA). Sometimes the courts use broad language to describe the duty owed: eg *Connolly v South of Ireland Asphalt Co Ltd* [1977] IR 99 at 107 (SC): "[Negligence] is a breach of duty owed generally"; but it seems clear that the concept of negligence as a breach of duty to specific individuals is firmly established in our jurisprudence.

144. A decision that probably went too far is *Mulholland v James Murphy & Co Ltd* 77 ILTR 212 (CC), where an infant forced onto bottle feeding as a result of injury to his mother was denied a right of action for consequent lack of development (although, strangely, the Court would have allowed the mother to claim for this loss). The question the court should have asked was whether such injury to the child was reasonably foreseeable. *Cf* Binchy 'Note: Duty and Foresight in Negligence: The "Control Devices" Out of Control' (1975) 38 MLR 468. Presumably the court was reluctant to countenance an action by a child for loss resulting from injury to a parent akin to the spouse's action for loss of consortium. But the facts in *Mulholland*'s case were probably strong enough to allow for recovery of damages without conceding an unnecessarily broad principle. See also *Marx v AG* [1974] 1 NZLR 164 (CA). It should be noted that one may owe a direct, rather than derivative duty of care to one yet to be borm, as where a manufacturer puts a drug on the market for use by pregnant women. Section 59 of the Civil Liability Act 1961 provides for recovery of damages for prenatal injuries provided the child is subsequently born alive. Kerr, *The Civil Liability Acts* (1990), p 70. The courts have not addressed in the context of a *Meskell*-based analysis. For consideration of related issues, see Donnelly 'The Injury of Parenthood: The Tort of Wrongful Conception' (1997) 48 NILQ 10.

145. (1928) 248 NY 339, 162 NE 99.

146. Contrast the potent dissent by Andrews J, to the effect that negligence should be regarded as anti-social conduct, wherein the defendant breaches his duty to the world at large, rather than merely to those in respect of whom harm might reasonably be expected to result. The extent of a defendant's liability should not be determined by a conceptual formula based on individuated relationships but rather by "practical polities", with emphasis on broad questions of public policy and common sense. "It is all a question of expediency. There are no fixed rules to govern our judgment."

> "if wrong in its relation to the holder of the package, was not a wrong in its relation to the plaintiff, standing far away. Relative to her it was not negligence at all. Nothing in the situation gave notice that the falling package had in it the potency of peril to persons thus removed. Negligence is not actionable unless it involves the invasion of a legally protected interest, the violation of a right. 'Proof of negligence in the air, so to speak, will not do'.[147] "[148]

## To What Extent is the Duty Concept determined by Objective Criteria?

**[6.60]** It has been said that the law of negligence "lays down that the standard of care is that which is to be expected from a reasonably careful man in the circumstances."[149]

**[6.61]** The issue was debated by the Supreme Court in *McComiskey v McDermott*,[150] in 1973. The plaintiff, acting as a navigator in a motor-car rally, was injured when the defendant, the driver of the car, overturned the car by driving it into a ditch by the public road, in order to avoid an obstacle. The driver was at the time of the accident attempting to maintain an average speed of 35 mph through winding mountain roads in Co Wicklow. The jury found that the defendant was not guilty of negligence.

**[6.62]** The plaintiff appealed against this finding[151] contending that it was not reasonably open to the jury on the evidence to have made such a finding. By a majority[152] the Supreme Court rejected the plaintiff's contention.

**[6.63]** Henchy J, for the majority, considered it important to bear in mind that:

> "While the general duty owed by a motorist to other users of the road is the objective one of showing due and reasonable care, the duty becomes particularised and personalised by the circumstances of the case. For example, it might be negligence to drive at 50 mph past a group of boisterous children coming from school, and yet it may not be negligence to drive at that speed past a group of adults. Therefore, it is necessary in each case to consider who is the person claiming to be owed the duty of care, who is the person it is claimed against, and what are the circumstances."[153]

**[6.64]** In his view the duty of care owed by the defendant to the plaintiff was to drive as carefully as a reasonably careful competitive rally-driver would be expected to drive in the prevailing circumstances.[154]

---

147. Pollock, *Torts*, (11th ed, 1923), p 455.
148. See further Prosser 'Palsgraf Revisited' (1953) 52 Mich LR 1.
149. *McComiskey v McDermott* [1974] IR 75 at 89 (SC).
150. *McComiskey v McDermott* [1974] IR 75. The decision is analysed by Symmons, (1974) 9 Ir Jur (ns) 79 and Symmons 'The Impact of Third Party Insurance Legislation on the Development of the Common Law' (1975) 4 Anglo-Am LR 426 at 436-437. A decision applying the former "directness" test of Polemis is *Donaldson v Irish Motor Racing Club* Supreme Court, 1 February 1957. Lavery J's dissent is worthy of note in the present context.
151. The issue of voluntary assumption of risk is considered see para **[20.61]** below.
152. Henchy and Griffin JJ; Walsh J dissenting.
153. *McComiskey v McDermott* [1974] IR 75 at 88.
154. *McComiskey v McDermott* [1974] IR 75 at 89. See also *McComiskey v McDermott* [1974] IR 75 at 95 (*per* Griffin J).

**[6.65]** Henchy J distinguished the facts of the case from decisions in England[155] and Australia[156] which had differed on whether to apply the "objective" standard of duty owed to all road-users to "learner" drivers driving with passengers who were aware of their inexperience.[157] In Henchy J's view, such cases were:

> "not to the point in the present case where the passenger, far from committing himself to the care of a driver whom he knew to be incompetent, allied himself to the driver as navigator in the hope that by the assiduous application of their respective skills they would win a prize in the competition."[158]

**[6.66]** In the view of Walsh J, dissenting, the governing circumstance in the case was that the car was being driven on the public highway at a time when the highway was being used as such:

> "The duty which the defendant owed to all persons using that highway, including the passenger in his own car, was the same. To hold otherwise would lead to rather absurd results. For example, if during the course of the rally the defendant had picked up a passenger who knew that he was in a participating motor car (but who was not himself in any sense a participant) and if the car had been involved in an accident, due to the negligent driving of the defendant, which injured not merely the navigator but also the casual passenger and a pedestrian who happened to be walking along the road at the same time, it could not be seriously contemplated that the liability of the driver of the motor car to each of the injured parties would be governed by different standards of duty."[159]

In Walsh J's view, the concept of contributory negligence rather than that of duty should differentiate between the various claimants in such a case.

**[6.67]** The decision raises important issues of policy. The defence of voluntary assumption of risk, as we shall see,[160] has been emasculated by legislation in 1961.[161] If, therefore, the duty concept is to be understood in objective terms (as Walsh J would prefer) the effect will be to make the scope of compensation broader than if the concept is to be determined by reference to more individuating circumstances (as the majority favour). It would be unfortunate if defendants should be able too easily to convince the courts of the existence of a constricted "special" duty of care, especially in such contexts as employers' liability,[162] where social policy over recent years has sought to protect employees from too harsh an operation of the concepts of contributory negligence and voluntary assumption of risk.

---

155. *Nettleship v Weston* [1971] 2 QB 691 (CA), noted by Goodhart, (1971) 87 LQR 444.
156. *Insurance Commissioner v Joyce* (1948) 77 Comm LR 39.
157. The Court did not cite the British Columbia decision of *Lovelace v Fossum* [1972] 2 WWR 161, which favoured the *Nettleship v Weston* analysis.
158. *McComiskey v McDermott* [1974] IR 75 at 89. See also Griffin J at 95. *Cf* Walsh J at 81.
159. *McComiskey v McDermott* [1974] IR 75 at 82. See also *Downey v Limerick Motor Club Ltd* High Court, 28 April 1989 (Lynch J).
160. See para **[20.63]** below.
161. Civil Liability Act 1961, s 34(1)(b). In this context, *cf* the helpful analysis by Fleming 'Comparative Negligence at Last- By Judicial Choice' (1976) 64 Calif LR 239 at 264-265.
162. *Cf* the discussion in Ch 18 of the decisions of *Rafferty v CA Parsons of Ireland Ltd* [1987] 1 ILRM 98 (SC) and *Mulcare v Southern Health Board* [1988] ILRM 689 (HC).

## VII. The European Dimension

**[6.68]** We now must consider the European dimension. The decision of the European Court of Human rights in *Osman v United Kingdom*[163] has potentially vast implications for the development of the concept of the duty of care in negligence.

**[6.69]** It is necessary to give the facts of the case in some detail. A male teacher formed an attachment with Ahmet Osman, a male pupil who was aged sixteen. Efforts were made by the school authorities to deal with the situation. The police came to be involved. The boy was transferred to another school for a time but, owing to curriculum difficulties, had to return to the original school. The teacher changed his name to that of the boy. Files involving personal details about the boy went missing and graffiti appeared in the school which involved obscene allegations about him.

**[6.70]** A brick was thrown through a window of the Osman family's house and on two occasions the tyres of their car were deliberately burst. The police investigated the brick incident to the extent of preparing a crime report. Although the acts of vandalism on the car were both reported, no police records relating to these offences could be found.

**[6.71]** The teacher left the school, originally on sick leave. He was later suspended from teaching duties pending an ILEA investigation for "unprofessional behaviour" towards Ahmet Osman. The outcome was an official reprimand and a severe warning but his suspension was lifted on the basis that he was not to return to the school which he had left. He took up work as a supply teacher at two other local schools.

**[6.72]** Shortly thereafter the Osman family was subjected to serious acts of vandalism: engine oil and paraffin were poured on the area outside their home; their car windscreen and windows were smashed; their front door lock was jammed with superglue; dog excrement was smeared on their doorstep and on their car, and the bulb was repeatedly taken from the light in the outside porch. All of these incidents were reported to the police, who interviewed the teacher but kept no records of what he said.

**[6.73]** The teacher was involved in an incident in which he allegedly rammed a van which had, as a passenger, a friend of Ahmet Osman. The teacher was jealous of this young man's relationship with Ahmet Osman. In a statement to the police, the driver recalled that, after the accident, the teacher had said: "I'm not worried because in a few months I'll be doing life".

**[6.74]** After this incident the police interviewed the Osman family and the family of the friend who was a passenger. The friend told the police of threats that the teacher had allegedly made to "get him" whether it took "30 days or 30 years".

**[6.75]** The teacher was interviewed by ILEA officers at his own request. He said that he was in a totally self-destructive mood and "that it was all a symphony and the last chord had to be played." He blamed the headmaster for all his troubles; he said that he "would

163. [1999] 1 FLR 193 (ECHR, 1998). See Vranten 'Duty of Care, Public Policy and the European Convention on Human Rights: *Osman v United Kingdom*' (1999) 7 Torts LJ 40; Walter, *Policing in a Changing Constitutional Order* (2000), pp 132-138; Mullender 'Negligence, the Policy/Operational Distinction and the European Convention on Human Rights' (1999) 7 Tort LR 98; Weir 'Down Hill - All the Way?' [1994] CLJ 4; Hoffman 'Human Rights and the House of Lords' (1999) 62 MLR 159.

not do a 'Hungerford' in a school but would see him at his home". A detailed report explaining the ILEA's concerns was left with the receptionist of the detective sergent who had been investigating the case. The detective sergent went to the school where he allegedly gave the assurance that the police would undertake the measures necessary to protect the Osman family and school personnel.

**[6.76]** The police sought to arrest the teacher on suspicion of criminal damage but could not find him. Over subsequent months he was sighted in the vicinity of the Osman family home. The police were notified of this though the report did not properly get communicated to the detective sergent. One night the teacher came to the Osman home, armed with a stolen shotgun. He shot and killed Mr Osman and seriously wounded Ahmet. He then drove to the headmaster's home where he shot and wounded him and killed his son. He pleaded guilty to manslaughter on grounds of diminished responsibility and was sentenced to detention in a mental hospital without limit of time.

**[6.77]** The Osman family commenced proceedings for negligence against the Commissioner of Police of the Metropolis. They argued that although the police had been aware of the teachers' activities for ten months, they had failed to apprehend or interview him, search his home or charge him with an offence before the fateful night.

**[6.78]** An application by the Metropolitan Police Commissioner to have the statement of claim struck out on the ground that it disclosed no reasonable cause of action was dismissed by the High Court judge but succeeded in the Court of Appeal.[164] McCowan LJ (Simon Brown LJ concurring) was of the opinion that the plaintiffs had an arguable case, that they passed the first step of the Wiberforce two-step test in *Anns*,[165] on the basis of the existence of "a very close degree of proximity amounting to a special relationship."[166] In contrast to the victims of the Yorkshire Ripper,[167] the Osman family members were as individuals, identifiably at risk of being injured or killed by the person whose apprehension had not been accomplished by the police. However, McCowan LJ was satisfied that the plaintiffs had no prospect of surmounting the second step, of public policy. Lord Keith's and Lord Templeman's action of this factor in *Hill*[168] applied with equal force to the instant case. The fact that the culprit had been identified was not a satisfactory ground for distinguishing the case from Hill:

> "It is one thing for the police to say 'We believe that a particular man has committed or has threatened to commit a crime' but it is another matter for them to bring it home to him. Here the police were still in the process of gathering evidence against [the teacher] which would include evidence of what he said when found and interviewed. Searching for him was all part of the investigation.
>
> When one looks at the particulars of negligence one sees, among other things, failure to interview him, failure to search his home, failure to trace him through cars he hired and failure to link the theft of the shotgun with him. These all appear to me to be properly described as failures in investigation."[169]

164. *Osman v Ferguson* [1993] 4 All ER 344.
165. *Anns v Merton London Borough* [1978] AC 728 at (HL).
166. [1993] 4 All ER 344.
167. *Hill v Chief Constable of West Yorkshire* [1988] 2 All ER 238.
168. [1988] 2 All ER 238.
169. [1993] 4 All ER 344.

**[6.79]** Neither was McGowan LJ impressed with the argument that the ratio of *Hill* was that policy decisions were protected by public policy immunity but operational decisions were not, and that the failures alleged in the instant case, being of an operational nature, should involve the imposition of a duty of care. He considered such a dividing line to be "artificial and impossible to draw in the present case".[170]

**[6.80]** Finally, McCowan LJ rejected the plaintiffs' submission that, if the class of victim was sufficiently proximate and sufficiently small, the public policy argument might not apply. He noted that, in *Hill*, Lord Keith had "plainly treat[ed] public policy as a separate point which is not reached at all unless there is a duty of care".[171] If counsel for the plaintiff were right on this point:

> "public policy would not be a separate argument at all because, if a plaintiff were proved to be sufficiently proximate and a member of a sufficiently small class, public policy would not arise."[172]

In McCowan LJ's view, the House of Lords decision on public policy "doom[ed] the action to failure ..."[173]

**[6.81]** Beldam LJ, agreed that the plaintiff's claim was not maintainable on public policy grounds. He preferred to express no opinion on the proximity issue. The Court of Appeal refused leave to appeal to the House of Lords and the House of Lords refused a similar application.

**[6.82]** The Osman family took the case to Europe, arguing that their rights under Article 6 of the European Convention on Human Rights had been infringed. Article 6(1) provides (in part) that, "[i]n one determination of his civil rights and obligations ..., everyone is entitled to a ... hearing by [a] tribunal ..."

**[6.83]** The European Court of Human Rights held in favour of the Osman family. It considered that the applicants:

> "... must be taken to have had a right, derived from the law of negligence, to seek an adjudication on the admissibility and merits of an arguable claim that they were in a relationship of proximity to the police, that the harm caused was foreseeable and that in the circumstances it was fair, just and reasonable not to apply the exclusionary rule outlined in the *Hill* case. In the view of the Court the assertion of that right by the applicants is in itself sufficient to ensure the applicability of Article 6(1) of the Convention."[174]

**[6.84]** The question to be determined was whether the restriction that was imposed on the exercise of the applicants' right under Article 6(1) was lawful. In this respect, the contracting State enjoyed a "certain margin of appreciation",[175] though the Court had to be satisfied that the limitations applied did "not restrict or reduce the access left to the individual in such a way or to such an extent that the very essence of the right is impaired".[176] Moreover, a limitation would not be compatible with Article 6(1) if it did not

---

170. [1993] 4 All ER 344.
171. [1993] 4 All ER 344.
172. [1993] 4 All ER 344.
173. [1993] 4 All ER 344.
174. *Osman v United Kingdom* [1999] 1 FLR 193 at 229.
175. [1999] 1 FLR 193 at 231.
176. [1999] 1 FLR 193 at 231

pursue a legitimate aim and if there was not a reasonable relationship of proportionality between the reasons employed and the aim sought to be achieved.[177]

**[6.85]** Referring to the *Hill*[178] decision, the Court stated:

> "Although the aim of such a rule may be accepted as legitimate in terms of the Convention, as being directed to the maintenance of the effectiveness of the police service and hence to the prevention of disorder or crime, the Court must nevertheless, in turning to the issue of proportionality, have particular regard to its scope and especially its application in the case at issue. While the [British] Government have contended that the exclusionary rule of liability is not of an absolute nature and that its application may yield to other public policy considerations, it would appear to the Court that in the instant case the Court of Appeal proceeded on the basis that the rule provided a watertight defence to the police and that it was impossible to prise open an immunity which the police enjoy from civil suit in respect of their acts and omissions in the investigation and suppression of crime.
>
> The Court would observe that the application of the rule in this manner without further inquiry into the existence of competing public interest considerations, only serves to confer a blanket immunity on the police for their acts and omissions deriving from the investigation and suppression of crime, and amounts to an unjustifiable restriction on the applicants' right to have a determination on the merits of his or her claim against the police in deserving cases.
>
> In its view, it must be open to a domestic court to have regard to the presence of other public interest considerations which pull in the opposite direction to the application of *Hill*. Failing this, there will be no distinction made between the degrees of negligence or of harm suffered, or any consideration of the justice of a particular case. It is to be noted that in the instant case McCowan LJ appeared to be satisfied that the applicants, unlike the plaintiff in *Hill*, had complied with the proximity test, a threshold requirement which is, in itself, sufficiently rigid to narrow considerably the number of negligence cases against the police which can proceed to trial. Furthermore, the applicants' case involved the alleged failure to protect the life of a child and their view that that failure was the result of a catalogue of acts and omissions which amounted to grave negligence as opposed to minor acts of incompetence. The applicants also claimed that the police had assumed responsibility for their safety. Finally, the harm sustained was of the most serious nature.
>
> For the Court, there are considerations which must be examined on the merits and not automatically excluded by the application of a rule which amounts to the grant of an immunity to the police. In the instant case, the Court is not persuaded by the Government's argument that the rule as interpreted by the domestic court did not provide an automatic immunity to the police."[179]

**[6.86]** The Court accordingly concluded that the application of the exclusionary rules in the instant case constituted a disproportionate restriction on the applicants' right of access to a court and that there had been a violation of Article 6(1) of the Convention.

**[6.87]** The *Osman* decision clearly has potentially huge implications for the Irish law of negligence. The Courts' holding calls in question, at a minimum, the practice of dismissing cases on the basis that the plaintiff has no reasonable prospect of success, where the plaintiff has passed the first stage of McCarthy J's three-step test in *Ward v*

177. In this context the Court cited *Tinnelly & Sons Ltd v United Kingdom* (1998) 27 EHRR 249 and *McElduff v United Kingdom* (1998) 27 EHRR 249.

178. [1988] 2 All ER 238.

179. [1999] 1 FLR 193 at 231-232. See also the decision of the European Commission of Human Rights in *Z v United Kingdom* [2000] 2 FLR 245, which involved a successful invocation of Article 6 of the Convention by the unsuccessful plaintiffs in *X v Bedford County Council* [1995] 2 AC 633 (HL).

*McMaster*,[180] which is largely similar to that of Lord Wilberforce in *Anns*.[181] More radically, it must raise an issue as to the consistency with Article 6 of blanket immunities, such as that of the advocate in court[182] or the prosecuting authorities.[183]

**[6.88]** A common lawyer reading the Court's analysis might conclude that the Court did not fully understand how the duty of care concept really operates. It was surely mistaken in imagining that paving the first step, of proximity of relationship, conferred on a plaintiff any substantive legal right.[184] All common law courts which have adopted the *Anns*[185] test, or some modification such as in *Ward v McMaster*,[186] have proceeded on the basis that a duty of care crystalises only where a plaintiff has surmounted both hurdles. The public policy enquiry does not take away from a plaintiff a pre-existing legal right; no such right attaches until this enquiry has been completed successfully from the plaintiff's standpoint.

**[6.89]** A second major difficulty with the Court's approach is that it appears to insist on an individuated judicial enquiry into the public policy issue in every case, whereas the whole purpose of the concept of duty of care is to exclude such an enquiry across a wide range of cases.[187] The judicial decision that no duty of care should be imposed on the police in the detection of crime is a decision designed to make it clear to future potential litigants that it is futile to sue members of police forces for this kind of default. The very rationale of this holding that there is no such duty is to prevent such litigation, which would encourage defensive police practices and divert the time, energy and resources of the police.

**[6.90]** Having said that the courts, in holding that in particular contexts there is no duty of care, are intending to foreclose future individuated investigation of conduct falling within the zone of immunity, it must also be acknowledged that there is in fact always the possibility for further re-assessment. A plaintiff in a subsequent case can seek to convince the court that it should refine, modify or even abandon an earlier judicial holding that there is no duty of care across a broad sweep of human conduct. This is what the plaintiffs in *Osman* sought to do in the English Court of Appeal. They argued that the *Hill* ratio

---

180. [1989] ILRM 400.

181. [1978] AC 728.

182. *Cf* para **[6.12]** below.

183. *Cf W v Ireland (No 2)* [1997] 2 IR 141 (HC).

184. *Cf Barrett v London Borough of Enfield* [1999] 3 All ER 193 (HL).

185. *Barrett v London Borough of Enfield* [1999] 3 All ER 193; Weir 'Down Hill - All the Way' [1999] CLJ 4 at 5-6.

186. *Barrett v London Borough of Enfield* [1999] 3 All ER 193.

187. *Cf Barrett v London Borough of Enfield* [1999] 3 All ER 193 (*per* Lord Browne-Wilkinson):

> "In English law the decision as to whether it is fair, just and reasonable to impose liability in negligence on a particular class of would be defendants depends on weighing in the balance the total detriment to the public interest in all cases from holding such class liable in negligence as against the toll loss to all would be plaintiffs if they are not to have a cause of action in respect of the loss they have individually suffered.
>
> In English law questions of public policy and the question whether it is fair and reasonable to impose liability in negligence, are decided as questions of law. Once the decision is taken that, say, company auditors though liable to shareholders for negligent auditing are not liable to those proposing to invest in the company ..., that decision will apply in all future cases of the same kind. The decision does not depend on weighing the balance between the extent of the damage to the plaintiff and the damage to the public in each particular case."

regarding public policy did not apply to a case where the plaintiffs passed the proximity test and were personally identifiable as being at risk or where the culprit's identity was actually known to the police. The Court of Appeal, after due reflection, rejected all of these arguments. The point to note is that the Court did not unthinkingly apply a blanket immunity but rather was open to reconsideration of the application of the immunity to the particular circumstances that the instant case involved. It moved from one level of generality to a more specific level of generality; it did not do as the European Court of Human Rights would apparently have preferred, which was to dispense with the idea that an immunity can exist on the basis that the particular facts fall within a defined category of relationship.

**[6.91]** It is interesting to witness how the British appellate courts, in anticipation of a new jurisprudence under the Human Rights Act 1998, have shown a discernible willingness to take a considerably softer approach than formerly toward blanket immunities from a duty of care.[188] One may expect that the Irish courts, which never embraced these immunities so wholeheartedly will also be sensitive to *Osman's* emphasis on a proportionate and individuated approach to the duty of care.

---

188. See, eg, *Kent v Griffiths* [2000] 2 WLR 1158 (CA); *Sadiq v Chief Constable of Lancashire* English Court of Appeal, 16 March 2000, Lexis transcript; *Hall (Arthur JJ) & Co (a firm) v Simons* [2000] 3 All ER 673 (HL); *Phelps v Hillingdon London Borough Council* [2000] 4 All ER 504 (HL); *Darker v Chief Constable of the West Midlands Polcie* [2000] 2 WLR 747 (HL).

Chapter 7

# The Standard of Care


I. Introduction ........ 145
II. The Reasonable Person ........ 145
III. Physical Capacities ........ 149
IV. Mentally Disordered Persons ........ 153
V. Specific Factors Assessing Whether Conduct is Negligent ........ 154


## I. INTRODUCTION

**[7.01]** As we have seen in Chapters 5 and 6, the tort of negligence involves the failure by the defendant to conform with the required standard of behaviour. This notion is relatively easy to understand; indeed it may seem so bland as to have no clearly defined cutting edge. Thus it is scarcely enlightening to learn that:

> "Negligence is the omission to do something which a reasonable person, guided upon those considerations which ordinarily regulate the conduct of human affairs, would do or doing something which a prudent and reasonable person would not do."[1]

**[7.02]** As may readily be seen, this simple formula suffers from lack of particularised standards against which to judge a person's behaviour. However vague the concept may be, there is little doubt that the one standard which has gained general support in this context is that of the "reasonable person". We must therefore examine the concept more closely.

## II. THE REASONABLE PERSON[2]

**[7.03]** In *Kirby v Burke*[3] Gavan Duffy J stated:

---

1. *Blyth v Birmingham Waterworks Co* (1856) 11 Ex Ch 781 at 784, 156 ER 1047 at 1049. See also *Cunningham v Frontier SS Co* [1906] 2 IR 12 at 36 (KB affd by CA); *Duffy v Rooney and Dunnes Stores (Dundalk) Ltd* High Court, 23 June 1997 at p 14 of Laffoy J's judgment; *Primor plc v Stokes Kennedy Crowley* [1996] 2 IR 459 at 501 (SC) .
2. See generally Terry 'Negligence', (1915) 29 Harv LR 40; Green 'The Negligence Issue', (1928) 37 Yale LJ 1029; Parsons 'Negligence, Contributory Negligence and the Man Who Does Not Ride the Bus to Clapham' (1958) 1 Mel ULR 163; Seavey 'Negligence - Subjective or Objective?' (1927) 41 Harv LR 1; James 'The Qualities of the Reasonable Person in Negligence Cases' (1951) 16 Missouri LR 1; Bannerman 'Negligence - The Reasonable person and the Application of the Objective Test in Anglo-American Jurisprudence' (1969) 6 UGLJ 69; Reynolds 'The Reasonable person of Negligence Law: A Health Report on the "Odious Creative"' (1970) 23 Oklahoma LR 410.
3. [1944] IR 207 at 214 (HC). See also *McComiskey v McDermott* [1974] IR 75 at 89 (SC):

   > "The law of negligence lays down that the standard of care is that which is to be expected from a reasonably careful man in the circumstances."

   In *Tarrant v O'Sullivan* [1949] Ir Jur 46 at 48 (CC) O'Connor J stated that negligence "is the doing of a thing which a reasonable person would not do, or failing to do what a reasonable person would do, having regard to the circumstances."

> "... the foundation of liability at common law for tort is blameworthiness as determined by the existing average[4] standards of the community; a man fails at his peril to conform to these standards. Therefore, while loss from accident generally lies where it falls, a defendant cannot plead accident if, treated as a man of ordinary intelligence and foresight, he ought to have foreseen the danger which caused injury to his plaintiff."

**[7.04]** Thus, the standard is expressed in terms of a hypothetical person[5]- "the reasonable man"[6] or, more neutrally, "the reasonable person".[7] A host of questions may be asked of that "reasonable person". What, for example, is the reasonable person expected to know or to feel? When does he or she act, react or fail to act? May he or she take risks?[8] How brave must the reasonable person be? How forgetful or selfish may he or she be allowed to be? Whilst the standard purports to be objective, "eliminat[ing] the personal equation",[9] the law of negligence in practice, as we shall see,[10] has made allowance in at least some cases for the particular capacities of the actor whose conduct is under scrutiny.

## Standard of the Reasonable Person

**[7.05]** Several descriptions of the standard of the reasonable person have been provided by the courts over the years, but, since they are little more than synonyms, they do not cast any light on the inner nature of the concept. In a search for the essence of the reasonable person, one is not greatly assisted to be told that he is the "careful man"[11] or the man of "ordinary prudence".[12] In spite of this difficulty, a number of points are clear. It is not

---

4. This word is misleading: *cf* para **[7.06]** below.

5. *Cf Sullivan v Creed* [1904] 2 IR 317 at 330 (KB affd by CA).

6. *Kenny v Dublin United Tramways Co* Supreme Court, 5 March 1929, *per* FitzGibbon J at 2. The expression is also used by Ó Dálaigh J in *Kennedy v Limerick Co* Supreme Court, 21 December 1959 at p 7 and by the same judge (dissenting) in *Byrne v Sheedy* [1955] IR 1 at 12 (SC). *Cf McComiskey v McDermott* [1974] IR 75 at 89 (SC), "a reasonably careful man in the circumstances"; *Callaghan v Killarney Race Co Ltd* [1958] IR 366 at 375 (SC), "a reasonable and prudent man".

7. *Kelly v St Laurence's Hospital,* [1989] ILRM 437 (SC). In *Connolly v South of Ireland Asphalt Co Ltd* [1977] IR 99 at 109 (SC), Kenny J spoke of "a reasonable human being". Feminist analysis is divided on the question whether, instead of applying a genderless "reasonable person" test, the courts should apply a differential test of the "reasonable man" or "reasonable woman", depending on the sex of the defendant (or, perhaps, victim) or should instead refashion the "reasonable man" test so as to place a greater emphasis on the experience and values of women: see, eg, Parker "The Reasonable Person" A Gendered Concept?', (1993) 23 Victoria U Wellington LR No 2, 105; Forell 'Reasonable Woman Standard of Care' (1992) 11 U of Tasmania LR 1; Martyn 'A Feminist View of the Reasonable Man: An Alternative Approach to Liability in Negligence for Personal Injury' (1994) 23 Anglo-American LR 334.

8. *Cf City of Huntingburg v First* 43 NE 17 at 18 (Ind CA) speaking of contributory negligence: "The most prudent persons take some risks, but in taking the risk they must exercise ordinary care to avoid being injured".

9. *Glasgow Corporation v Muir* [1943] AC 448 at 457 (HL *per* Lord Macmillan). Thus a person should not be judged by a higher standard of care simply because he or she habitually adopts more care than is required of a reasonable person:

   > "... the common law has never recognised this subjective standard. If a man's conduct complies with the standard of care of the reasonable person it does not matter that it falls short of some higher standard of care habitually adopted by himself"

   *Rust v Needham* 9 SASR 510 at 523 (*per* Bray CJ, 1974).

10. See para **[7.12]-[7.14]** below.

11. *Murphy v Hurley* Supreme Court, 23 March 1930, *per* FitzGibbon J at p 25.

12. *Vaughan v Menlove* (1837) 3 Bing, NC 468 at 475, 132 ER 490 at 493; *Cunningham v Blake* [1937] Ir Jur 20 at 21 (HC); *Curry v Foster* [1960] Ir Jur 33 at 34 (HC, NI) "the reasonable and prudent man". See also *Victor Weston (Éire) Ltd v Kenny* [1954] IR 191 at 200 (HC).

sufficient for a person to do his or her best if that best is not up to the standard of the reasonable person.[13] Conversely, the standard of perfection is not required, since even "the most excessively careful person will sometimes have an accident".[14]

**[7.06]** The question is a normative one: the judge or jury members should ask, not "How would I have acted?" or "How would the average person have acted?" but rather "How ought the defendant, as a reasonable person, have acted?". Clearly, of course, the way people normally behave will affect the determination of this question,[15] if the standard is to be effective, there must be a close correspondence between "is" and "ought". In this context, one may regret the abolition of juries in personal injury litigation. The different experience of each of the jurors can be a useful - if not a necessary - ingredient in determining precisely the level at which the standard of reasonableness should be pitched.[16]

## Knowledge

**[7.07]** In *Byrne v McDonald*,[17] Kingsmill Moore J, speaking of contributory negligence, observed:

> "The act or omission must be judged in the light of the knowledge, actual or imputed, which the plaintiff has, for if there is, or should be, no knowledge that the act or omission involves danger then the plaintiff cannot be convicted of failing to take reasonable care. To every adult is imputed the knowledge of risks which the normal reasonable person may be assumed to have ..."

**[7.08]** Thus a reasonable person will be expected to know facts of common experience, such as the basic laws of nature,[18] and physics,[19] the normal incidents of the weather, the

---

13. *Cf Vaughan v Menlove* (1837) 3 Bing, NC 468 at 475, 132 ER 490 at 493. The exceptions to this rule are considered para **[7.12]-[7.24]** below.
14. *Carrat v Matthews* (1921) 59 DLR 505 (Alta, CA). See also *Stapleton v O'Regan* Supreme Court, 21 December 1956 (at p 10 of his judgment): "A driver is not required to possess more than normal reactions and normal skill."
15. *Cf* FLEMING, p 118. See also Morris 'Custom and Negligence' (1942) 42 Col LR 1147 at 1154, negligence is not determined "by invoking unworldly values". In *Coyle v An Post* [1993] ILRM 508 (SC) Hederman J observed that:

    > "[w]hile negligence is not determined by reference simply to how people in fact act, nevertheless the courts are entitled to have regard to common experience when determining the scope of negligent conduct."
16. *Cf Sullivan v Creed* [1904] 2 IR 317 at 330:

    > "[A]s the experience of one man usually differs from that of another, our law wisely says that what is reasonable is to be determined by the jury- that is, it is to be the result of the to a certain extent varying, opinions of twelve different persons."

    This passage was quoted with approval by Circuit Judge Clark in the US decision of *Pease v Sinclair Refining Co* (1939) 104 F 2d 183 at 187 (2 Cir).
17. Supreme Court, 7 February 1957 at p 10 of Kingsmill Moore J's judgment. See also *Sullivan v Creed* [1904] 2 IR 317 at 331 (KB, 1903, *per* Palles CB; affd by CA 1903).
18. As, for example, the general laws of gravity: *Meredith v Peer* (1917) 35 DLR 592 (Ont SC); *Seabord Air Line Ry Co v Hackney* (1928) 217 Ala 382, 115 So 869; *Brown v Swift & Co* (1912) 91 Neb 532, 136 NW 726, although not every practical application of these laws, *cf Parsons v Hammond Packing Co* (1902) 70 SW 519 at 522 (Mo CA). A reasonable person may be held to know about the combustible qualities of certain materials: *Vaughan v Menlove* (1837) 3 Bing, NC 468 at 475, 132 ER 490 at 493; *Lillibridge v McCann* (1988) 117 Mich 84, 75 NW 288.
19. *Cooke v Midland GW Ry of Ireland* [1909] AC 229 at 237 (HL (Ir)).

inquisitiveness and "frequently mischievous disposition"[20] of young children, the habits of ordinary animals[21] and the basic properties of ordinary machinery.[22] Moreover, in certain cases, even where more complex matters are in question, a reasonable person will frequently be expected to appreciate his or her ignorance of possible dangers and act accordingly. Thus, a person who enters a factory should not interfere with the machinery, and if he does so, and thereby injures another, he cannot excuse his conduct by pleading lack of knowledge of how the machinery worked. Similarly, a person from Switzerland who is unfamiliar with Irish traffic regulations will not be excused if his ignorance leads to an accident.[23]

**[7.09]** The Courts do not insist that every person should remember everything that he or she has been told, forgetfulness, especially when brought about by pressures of employment, may in some cases be excused.[24] Thus, in *Martin v Dublin United Tramways Co Ltd*,[25] a tram conductor was held not to have been negligent for failing to remember that a passenger had mentioned that he wished to alight at a specific destination about three miles from where he had boarded the tram. At the time the tram passed the destination point the conductor was on the roof collecting fares. In the view of Boyd J, the court:

> "ought not impose on the defendants, or their servants, the responsibility of remembering orders that a passenger may give them, unless that order be given within a reasonable time before the passenger may desire to leave the car".[26]

**[7.10]** And Andrews J was:

> "not ... inclined to hold that the forgetfulness of the conductor, in such circumstances, considering his numerous duties on a journey, was so unreasonable as to amount to such negligence as would make the Company responsible".[27]

---

20. *Cf City of Huntingburg v First* (1896) 43 NE 17 at 18 (Inc CA).

21. *Cf Tolin v Terrell* (1909) 117 SW 290 at 291 (Ky SC):

> "In spite of the fact that there was testimony to show that this mule was of so gentle a disposition that children could play at its heels, it is a matter of common experience that there is no telling when or under what circumstances a mule will or will not kick. The only way to escape danger from the feet of a mule is not to go within the radius of its heels."

See also *Fulton v Randall, Gee & Mitchell Ltd* [1918] 3 WWR 331 (BC) - "common knowledge" that grain is allurement to animals which may induce them to overeat so as to injure or kill themselves.

22. Liability may not be imposed of course, where machinery, apparently harmless contains a latent danger not capable of being appreciated by a reasonable person: *Byrne v McDonald* Supreme Court, 7 February 1957. In *Victor Weston (Éire) Ltd v Kenny* [1954] IR 191 at 198 (HC), Davitt P observed that "[e]very house owner must ... be presumed to know that cisterns may go out of order."

23. See *Moor v Nolan* (1960) 94 ILTR 153 (SC). *Cf* Seavey 'Negligence - Subjective or Objective?' (1927) 41 Harv LR 1 at 19. See also *The Lady Gwendolene*: *Guinness (Arthur) Son & Co (Dublin) Ltd v The Freshfield (Owners)* [1965] P 294 (CA) - brewers who transported stout from Dublin to Liverpool in a ship required to conform to general standard of care appropriate to shipowners; *per* Winn LJ at 350:

> "The law must apply a standard which is not relaxed to cater for their factual ignorance of all activities outside brewing: having become owners of ships, they must behave as reasonable ship-owners."

24. *Cf Martin v Miller & Co Ltd* Supreme Court, 12 May 1972.

25. [1909] 2 IR 13 (KB).

26. [1909] 2 IR 13 at 22.

27. [1909] 2 IR 13 at 21. It may be negligent for a person in some circumstances to fail to anticipate, and mitigate the danger of potential injury resulting from, the forgetfulness of others: see *Murphy v Electricity Supply Board* DPIJ: Trinity Terms 1993, 261 (HC).

**[7.11]** It would be wrong, of course, to conclude from this case that a conductor would necessarily be exempt from being held negligent merely because the destination point was some distance away when the request was made. If a passenger made it plain that he or she was placing exclusive reliance on the conductor and that the implications of failure to be informed properly would involve the passenger in loss, it is possible that a court today would take a serious view of the conductor's forgetfulness. Much would depend on the particular circumstances of the case.

## III. Physical Capacities[28]

**[7.12]** A certain standard of physical dexterity is required of persons in their dealings with others. As Oliver Wendell Holmes put it:

> "If, for instance, a man is born hasty and awkward, is always hurting himself or his neighbours, no doubt his congenital defects will be allowed for in the courts of Heaven, but his slips are no less troublesome to his neighbours than if they sprang from guilty neglect. His neighbours accordingly require him, at his peril, to come up to their standard, and the courts which they establish decline to take his personal equation into account."[29]

**[7.13]** Clearly, if the courts were to "eliminate the personal equation" completely and to apply relentlessly the objective standard of the reasonable person in all cases, this could result in considerable injustice and hardship for persons who are physically disabled.[30] Accordingly, it seems[31] that the law will modify its objective approach somewhat in relation to these persons. The test it applies in these circumstances is the standard of a reasonable person afflicted with the particular physical disability in question. Thus, a blind, person will not be required to see,[32] nor a deaf person required to hear,[33] nor will a

---

28. See generally Vance 'Note: Negligence: Physical Defects as Affecting the Standard of Care in Civil and Criminal Laws' (1942) 30 Ky LJ 220 at 220-222; Weisiger 'Negligence and the Physically Infirm' (1946) 24 N Carolina LR 187; More 'Note', (1955) 34 N Carolina LR 142.
29. Holmes, *The Common Law* (1881) 108. See also Seavey 'Negligence - Subjective or Objective?' (1927) 41 Harv LR 1.
30. The dividing line between physical disability and mere incompetence is, of course, difficult, if not impossible, to draw: *cf* James & Dickinson 'Accident Proneness and Accident Law' (1950) 63 Harv LR 769. See, however, Schwartz 'Contributory and Comparative Negligence: A Reappraisal' (1978) 87 Yale LJ 697 at 715.
31. The position is surprisingly unclear. In *Kingston v Kingston* (1968) 102 ILTR 65 at 67 (SC). Walsh J stated:

    > "In the case of plaintiffs suffering from physical or mental defects the matter does not appear to have been finally determined, although in the case of plaintiffs suffering from physical defects the standard could vary with their actual physical abilities while still remaining an objective test."

    It should be noted that in the same case Walsh J stated that in actual practice "greater indulgences have been granted to plaintiffs which have not been granted to defendants".
32. FLEMING, p 125; Lowry 'The Blind and the Law of Tort: The Position of a Blind Person as Plaintiff in Negligence' (1972) 20 Chitty's LJ 253; *M'Kibbin v Glasgow Corporation* 1920 SC 590. See, however, *Duffy v Fahy* [1960] Ir Jur 69 at 75 (SC).
33. *South Australian Ambulance v Wahlheim* (1948) 77 Comm LR 215. *Cf Smith v Browne* (1891) 28 LR Ir 1 (QB); *Gaffney v Dublin United Tramways Co* [1916] 2 IR 472 (CA); *Wade v Hegarty* Supreme Court, 13 July 1960. For a critical analysis, see ten Broek 'The Right to Live in the World: The Disabled in the Law of Torts' (1966) 54 Calif LR 841 at 898-899.

lame person be required to be agile,[34] nor will the victim of a heart attack[35] an epileptic seizure,[36] insulin reaction,[37] or other sudden medical[38] or physical[39] emergency be required to behave as though all was well. The law does not ask of such a person that he achieve "the impossible by conforming to physical standards which he cannot meet".[40]

**[7.14]** This does not mean, however, that physically disabled persons may act as they please. As has been mentioned, they will be judged by the standard of a reasonable person suffering from their particular disability. Thus, for example, although a blind person is not required to see, he may have to take particular precautions on account of his disability which sighted persons need not.[41] To take an extreme example: if a blind person drives a car and crashes it into the back of another, he will not be permitted to plead his lack of sight as an excuse. He may, however, venture into the street unaided, even at the risk of

---

34. *Goodman v Norwalk Jewish Center* (1958) 139 A 2d 812. See further ten Broek 'The Right to Live in the World: The Disabled in the Law of Torts' (1966) 54 Calif LR 841 at 899-900. In this regard, some judicial deference to age is apparent. In *Condon v Cork Corporation and An Bord Telecom* High Court, 1 February 1991, where the sixty-six year old plaintiff fell on a cracked concrete pavement, Barr J acquitted her of contributory negligence in failing to see the danger. Pedestrians were not obliged to look out for and avoid every minor defect:

 > "If the law so required, then, bearing in mind the state of numerous footpaths in the older parts of our cities and towns, pedestrians not infrequently would find themselves involved in something broadly akin to hop-scotch which, for elderly people, in particular, might well be more dangerous than the minor hazards sought to be avoided."

35. See Kraig 'Heart Attack as a Defense in Negligence Actions' (1963) 12 Clev-Mar LR 59.
36. See Perr 'Epilepsy and the Law' (1958) 7 Clev-Mar LR 280 at 292-296; Smith 'Medico - Legal Facets of Epilepsy' (1953) 31 Tex LR 765 at 773-776; Littlejohn 'Note' (1949) 1 Baylor LR 499. *Cf O'Brien v Parker* [1997] 2 ILRM 170 (HC) discussed paras **[7.16]-[7.22]** below.
37. *Porter v Price* (1960) 11 Utah 2d 80, 355 P 2d 66.
38. *Kelly v Gilmore* Supreme Court, 28 July 1970. *Murray v Gilmore* Supreme Court, 20 December 1973. *Cf Government v Marine & Trade Insurance Co Ltd* 1973 (3) SA 797 - the onus of proof was on the defendant driver to show that the accident had resulted from a blackout following a coughing fit; this onus was not discharged. Voluntary intoxication does not count. Some of the issues concerning the relationship between intoxication and negligence are more complex than might at first appear: see McCoid, 'Intoxication and its Effect Upon Civil Responsibility', (1956) 42 Iowa LR 38. It has been held that a person running into a fellow-worshipper when in a state of religious fervour could be "compared to voluntary intoxication": *Barr v Aetna Insurance Co* (1979) 370 So 2d 511 at 513 (La SC). As to the possible relevance of pre-menstrual tension in this context, see Stewart 'Pre-menstrual Tension in Automobile Accidents' (1957) 6 Clev-Mar LR 17 at 25-30; Perr 'Pre-menstrual Tension, Medicine and Law' (1958) 7 Clev-Mar LR 52 at 63-64. Whether this development would be generally welcomed by women has been debated: see Laws 'The Sexual Politics of Pre-Menstrual Tension' (1983) 6 Women's Studies Int Forum 19.
39. *Cf Donoghue v Burke* [1960] IR 314 (SC) - the driver was dazzled by headlights of approaching car; *Morrissey v Healy* [1960] IR I (SC) - plaintiff driver was "mesmerised" by the defendant's negligent driving and therefore should be excused of negligence; *Scholz v Standish* [1961] SASR 123 - bee sting. See also *Billy Higgs & Sons Ltd v Baddeley* [1950] NZLR 605 (CA).
40. PROSSER & KEETON, p 176. Where the affliction rendered the action involuntary this may constitute a defence to the effect that there was no act. Of course this would not necessarily relieve the defendant of liability for prior negligence in failing to take adequate advance precautions.
41. *Cf* Young 'Note: The Limits of Objectivity in Negligence' (1940) 28 Ky LJ 242 at 244-245.

occasionally impeding traffic.[42] Where precisely the line is to be drawn is a difficult task for the courts, since the question raises issues regarding the manner in which freedom of movement and indeed of life fulfilment for disabled persons should be reconciled with the security or convenience of other persons.[43]

**[7.15]** In *Kelly v Gilmore*,[44] the Supreme Court by a 3-2 majority held that the case should have been withdrawn from the jury. The defendant's car mounted the pavement and struck the plaintiff after the defendant had been the victim of a sudden onset of unconsciousness. The defendant, although a 60 year-old man with a condition of high blood pressure, had not previously suffered any fainting attacks or fits of dizziness. In the subsequent proceedings of *Murray v Gilmore*,[45] taken by a different plaintiff arising from the same accident, the Supreme Court, again by a 3-2 majority, held that the case should not have been withdrawn from the jury. One important difference between the two actions was that the defendant had given evidence in the first but had died before the second; his evidence established that he had not had sufficient time after the onset of the attack to take any steps to avoid the accident. Without this direct evidence, the evidence of the bystanders on this issue "was not so coercive that the case should not have been allowed to go to the jury".[46]

**[7.16]** In *O'Brien v Parker*,[47] the defendant had been involved in a traffic accident in which his car had crashed into the plaintiff's vehicle. There was no dispute that, if no particular individuating circumstances were taken into account, the defendant's driving would be considered negligent. The defence lodged by the defendant, however, asserted that he had "suffered an attack of epilepsy without prior indication or warning" and that "[i]n the circumstances the defendant was not negligent." It appeared from the evidence that the defendant had never previously been treated for epilepsy; that on the fateful day, he had

---

42. FLEMING, p 125. A blind pedestrian may rely on the guidance of others in crossing a street; *cf Chan Shin-nin v Tang Kam-ho* [1974] HKLR 1 (Cons J) however, the negligence of a sighted woman who carelessly led her blind husband across the road into the path of a car was attributed to her husband. Although the husband "relied quite properly" upon his wife, the court considered that "in this particular marriage, the husband was in fact the dominant personality ... actively involved in control of their progress in every respect except that he relie[d] on his wife to warn him of dangers that he would not himself notice by reason of his blindness" (at 7). As to the position of deaf pedestrians *cf* the decisions cited in fn 33 above.

43. *Cf* ten Broek 'The Right to Live in the World. The Disabled in the Law of Torts' (1966) 54 Calif LR 841 at 886 ff.

44. Supreme Court, 28 July 1970.

45. Supreme Court, 20 December 1973. See also *Tefler v Wright* (1978) 95 DLR (3d) 188 (Ont CA,).

46. See also *Waugh v James K Allan Ltd* 1974 SC 102 (HL); *Smith v Lord* [1962] SASR 88; *Robinson v Glover* [1952] NZLR 699. As to the question of the possible liability of a doctor for failing to diagnose a condition in his or her patient which makes the patient a potential hazard to other road users, or for failing to advise the patient properly as to his or her condition or the effects on driving of taking prescribed medication, see Hirsh 'Physicians' Liability to Non-patients - A Panoramic View' (1977) 1 L Med Q 211. *Cf Dennehy v Kildare Co Board of Health* [1936] IR 384 (HC), where Hanna J baulked at the (hypothetical) prospect of liability attaching to the defendant for a fever epidemic resulting from the premature release from hospital of a patient suffering from scarlatina. See also Streitwieser 'Note' (1974) Creighton LR 724; *Freese v Lemmon* (1973) 210 NW 2d 576 (Iowa, SC); *Kaiser v Suburban Transportation System* (1965) 65 Wash 2d 461, 398 p 2d 14, amended 65 Wash 2d 461, 401 p 2d 350.

47. [1997] 2 ILRM 170 (HC), analysed by Byrne & Binchy, *Annual Review of Irish Law 1997*, pp 716-723.

had "certain experiences at home" before driving; that when he was driving, he had a minimal sense of smell and had intense images of light; and that he did not recollect the final hundred yards of his journey before collision.

**[7.17]** What the defendant had suffered was a condition of temporal lobe epilepsy which had manifested itself "out of the blue". The consultant neurologist was of the opinion that the defendant had experienced a complex partial seizure. They would "allow for some consciousness on an objective basis [and] would allow a person suffering from this condition to make a decision. There was a degree of awareness ...".

**[7.18]** Counsel for the defendant argued that, where a defendant proved that his or her actions were the result of a sudden illness, the defence of inevitable accident was made out. He conceded that the illness in the case had to result in autonomism or a state of unconsciousness in which the defendant had been left without control of his actions.

**[7.19]** Lavan J after a review of some British authorities on the defence of automatism in criminal prosecutions, noted that these decisions had prescribed strict limits to its scope. It was necessary for the defendant to establish "a total destruction of voluntary control on [his or her] part". Impaired, reduced or partial control would not suffice. In the instant case, the defendant had not succeeded in establishing such a total destruction of voluntary control. He had made the decision to drive even though he had experienced "some difficulties" at home. He had when driving been conscious of experiencing some symptoms before the accident had occurred.

**[7.20]** Lavan J's conclusions are understandable in the light of the parameters of the defence put forward in the case, but the question can be raised as to whether the scope of any defence in a civil action should be determined by reference to judicial authorities dealing with criminal responsibility. In England, in *Roberts v Ramsbottom*,[48] Neill J thought it appropriate to make such a transposition but the Court of Appeal, in *Mansfield v Weetabix Ltd*, soundly criticised this approach.

**[7.21]** It is necessary to unravel two quite separate issues here that are in danger of becoming improperly enmeshed. The first is whether it can truly be said that a defendant in a negligence action engaged in any legally cognisable conduct at all, for which he or she should be called to answer. If the defendants has not in fact engaged in any voluntary conduct - because of a heart attack, stroke, or epileptic episode, then no liability should be imposed. The second issue can only arise where the first issue has been answered in the affirmative. Assuming the defendants conduct was not involuntary, was it negligent? There are many situations in which a person engaging in voluntary conduct will be confronted by a sudden emergency, which calls for a reasonable response, making due allocations of the "agony of the moment". The emergency may come from within - an epileptic attack, for example - or without - as in the case of the bee sting that has already been mentioned. In determining whether the defendant has acted reasonably in this context the court will not simply restrict itself to the precise seconds in which the accident occurred but will examine the background circumstances which led to the defendant being in a dangerous position.

---

48. [1980] 1 WLR 823.

**[7.22]** In *O'Brien v Parker*, only the first of these issues was addressed *expressis verbis*. Nonetheless, it is clear from Lavan J's judgment that, in imposing liability on the defendant, he was strongly affected by the defendant's failure to respond to the forewarning of the epileptic seizure.

## IV. Mentally Disordered Persons

**[7.23]** The position of a mentally ill person regarding negligence or contributory negligence is not at all clear.[49] There is no recorded Irish decision in which the issue was thoroughly analysed,[50] and the decisions in other common law jurisdictions are divided on the issue.[51] An objective test which ignores the mental condition of the actor cannot be reconciled with the policy of excusing a temporary loss of consciousness by persons who are not affected by mental illness. It has been defended[52] on the basis that it encourages accident compensation, but it must be admitted that it does so at the expense of consistency[53] and (arguably) justice to the innocent defendant.

---

49. See the Law Reform Commission's Report on the *Liability in Tort of Mentally Disabled Persons*, Ch 1 and pp 62-71 (LRC-1985); Hornblower 'Insanity and the Law of Negligence' (1905) 5 Col LR 278; Cook 'Mental Deficiency in Relation to Tort' (1921) 21 Col LR 333; Casto 'Comment: The Tort Liability of Insane Persons for Negligence: A Critique' (1972) 30 Tenn LR 705; Splane 'Note: Tort Liability of the Mentally Ill in Negligence Actions' (1983) 93 Yale LJ 153; Goldstein 'Asking the Impossible: The Negligence Liability of the Mentally Ill' (1995) 12 J Contemporary Health Law & Policy 67; Korrell 'The Liability of Mentally Disabled Tort Defendants' (1995) 19 L & Psychol LR 1; Shuman 'Therapeutic Jurisprudence and Tort Law: A Limited Subjective Standard of Care' (1992) 46 SMU LR 409.

50. *Cf Kingston v Kingston* (1968) 102 ILTR 65 at 67 (SC): "It is sufficient to say that the question of the standard of care required of a plaintiff who is ... mentally infirm is still open ...". See also *Duffy v Fahy* [1960] Ir Jur 69 at 75 (SC); *O'Sullivan v Dwyer* [1971] IR 275 at 286 (SC); *Carroll v Clare Co* [1975] IR 221 at 226-227 (SC). In *Armstrong v Eastern Health Board*, High Court, 5 October 1990, where a mentally disturbed patient who fell from a building after having received inadequate medical care, Egan J held that she was not guilty of contributory negligence because she was "not really in control of her thoughts" at the time. Egan J did not cite any of the precedents on the issue of mental disability and the holding can perhaps be understood as involving a perception of the plaintiff as a distraught, socially deprived person in a state of serious anxiety about where she would find accommodation. See further Byrne & Binchy, *Annual Review of Irish Law 1990*, pp 523-526, 532-533.

51. The Australian decision of *Adamson v Motor Vehicle Trust* (1957) 58 WALR 56 makes no allowance for mental illness; in favour of recognising mental illness as a factor precluding the defendant from appreciating the duty to take care is the Canadian decision of *Buckley v Smith Transport* [1946] 4 DLR 721, followed, with some apparent reluctance, in *Hutchings v Nevin*, 1992 LEXIS 1461 (Ont CJ, 5 August 1992), where Haines J observed that "[i]t may be that this issue should be re-examined in light of legislative and social developments that have occurred since *Buckley* was decided in 1946". In *Attorney General of Canada v Connolly* (1989) 64 DLR (4th) 84 (BC SC), Paris J reserved on the question whether *Buckley* had been rightly decided. One line of authority in the United States relieves a defendant in cases of sudden onset of insanity: the leading decision in *Breunig v American Family Insurance Co* (1970) 45 Wis 2d 536, 173 NW 2d 619. Other decisions (notably *Sforza v Green Bus Lines* (1934) 150 Misc 180, 268 NYS 446 and *Turner v Caldwell* (1980) 36 Conn Supp 350, 421 A 2d 876), as well as the Restatement (Second) of Torts, s 283, require conformity with an objective standard.

52. FLEMING, p 127.

53. If the physically disabled are to be allowed their own standard, so also should the mentally disabled. Conversely, if the mentally disabled may not invoke their condition in their defence, why should the physically disabled be permitted to do so?

**[7.24]** The position regarding adult defendants with limited intellectual capacity[54] defendants is not entirely clear. Eliminating the personal equation[55] would suggest that an objective test should prevail, but the injustice of such a rule, especially in cases of serious retardation, surely calls for some modification to take account of the defendant's particular qualities. There appears to be a dearth of decisions on this question.[56] Only in the United States do we find a body of jurisprudence, mainly dealing with contributory negligence, where, it must be pointed out, the policy issues are radically different from those relating to negligence. Various strategies have been adopted; these range from making no allowance for the plaintiff's condition,[57] through an intermediate position where allowance will be made for the plaintiff's condition if it prevented him or her from understanding the danger in question[58], to the more generous solution of making allowance for the plaintiff's mere inability to exercise the judgment of a reasonable person.[59] It is to be hoped that our Courts would apply a subjective test, at all events in cases of serious retardation. It will be noted that the Law Reform Commission in its 1985 report made wide-ranging proposals for reform of the liability in tort of mentally disabled persons.[60] Their recommendations extended to those who are mentally retarded as well as those who are mentally ill.[61] The effect of the Commission's proposals[62] in relation to negligence would be that serious mental retardation would relieve a person of liability save in respect of road accidents, where the objective test would largely[63] apply.

## V. Specific Factors in Assessing Whether Conduct is Negligent

**[7.25]** Whilst the standard of the reasonable person gives some substance to the concept of negligence, a number of more specific indicators have been identified[64] in an effort to elaborate more particularly what is or is not reasonable in particular circumstances. Four

---

54. The subjective test applicable to children has regard to their particular mental development. Thus, due allowance will be made for the limited intellectual capacity of children.
55. *Cf Glasgow Corporation v Muir* [1943] AC 448 at 457.
56. See Flynn 'Note: Contributory Negligence of Incompetents' 3 Washburn LJ 215 (1964).
57. *Cf* the Restatement (Second) of Torts, s 464, Comment g; *Wright v Tafe* (1967) 208 Va 291, 156 SE 2d 562.
58. See Flynn 'Note: Contributory Negligence of Incompetence' (1964) 3 Washburn LJ 215.
59. See also *Lynch v Rosenthal* 396 SW 2d 272 (Mo CA, 1965).
60. LRC 18-1985.
61. *Cf* LRC 18-1985, p 1.
62. *Cf* Ch 4 of the Report.
63. Save in cases where the defendant's conduct was involuntary.
64. *Cf Purtill v Athlone* UDC [1968] IR 205 at 212-213 (SC 1967 *per* Walsh J):

> "What amounts to sufficient care must vary remarkably with the circumstances, the nature of the danger, and the age and knowledge of the person likely to be injured."

See also *Donaldson v Irish Motor Racing Club*. Supreme Court, 1 February 1957 *per* Kingsmill Moore J (p 9 of judgment):

> "What is reasonable care depends on all the circumstances, including the probability of an occurrence causing danger, the probability of injury ensuing if such an occurrence takes place, the practicability of precautions, the legal categories involved, and other matters too diverse and numerous to be catalogued."

factors in particular have been discussed in the decisions[65] and among the commentaries on negligence. These are:

(a) the probability of an accident;

(b) the gravity of the threatened injury;

(c) the social utility of the defendant's conduct; and

(d) the cost of eliminating the risk.

**[7.26]** Before examining these factors in detail, it is as well to point out that none of them contains any particular predetermined "weight" relative to any of the others. At the end of the day, the determination of what constitutes unreasonable conduct involves a value-judgment. These four factors highlight the factual considerations on which that value judgment is to be based but they do not of themselves contain the resolution of the negligence issue. It should also be noted that at times the courts in their judgments concentrate on one of the factors, to the apparent neglect of the others. The first of these factors - the probability of an accident - tends to receive the most disproportionate attention, perhaps because the requirement[66] that the plaintiff's injuries be "reasonably foreseeable" suggests a test of mere predictability without regard to the three other factors. As recently as 1988, the Supreme Court had to re-emphasise that "a test for liability in a case of alleged negligence, based on mere foreseeability or on some degree of possibility or probability, is not correct".[67]

## The probability of an Accident

**[7.27]** The greater the likelihood of harm to the plaintiff, the more probable it is that the court will regard it as unreasonable for the defendant to engage in the risky conduct or to

---

64. (contd) And see *Callaghan v Killarney Race Co* [1958] IR 366 at 375 (SC *per* Kingsmill Moore):

> "In judging what a reasonable and prudent man would think necessary more than one element has to be considered. The rarity of the occurrence must be balanced against the gravity of the injury which is likely to ensure if the occurrence comes about, and some consideration must be paid to the practicability of precautions suggested."

65. *Cf Christie v Odeon Ltd* (1957) 91 ILTR 25 at 29 (SC) - mentioning factors (a), (b) and (d). See also *Morris v West Hartlepool Navigation Co* [1956] 375 AC 552 at 574; *Ryan v Fisher* (1976) 51 Austr LJR 125 at 126 (HC); *United States v Carroll Towing Co* (1947) 159 F 2d 169 at 172 (US, CC App, 2nd Circuit); *Conway v O'Brien* (1940) 111 F 2d 611 at 612 (US, CC App, 2nd Circuit), motion denied 61 S Ct 610, reversed 312 US 492, 61 S Ct 634; *Wyong Shire Council v Shirt* (1980) 146 Comm LR 40 at 47-48 (HC of Austr); TRINDADE & CANE, pp 438, 442-443.

66. *Cf* Ch 3.

67. *Kelly v St Lawrence's Hospital* [1989] ILRM 437 at 448 (SC *per* Henchy J). See also Finlay CJ at 441. Also Walsh J (with whose observations on this matter McCarthy J agreed) stated at 444:

> "In my view, once there is a foreseeable possibility [of injury] then the persons involved are put on notice. Undoubtedly the standard of care which might reasonably be expected may be sufficient if it is commensurate with the degree of possibility, but that is different from saying that no standard of care is expected until the possibility reaches such a high degree as to be classified as a probability."

*Cf Fitzsimons v Bord Telecom Éireann* [1991] ILRM 276 (HC), analysed by Byrne & Binchy, *Annual Review of Irish Law 1990*, pp 489-493.

fail to take steps to avert the threatened injury.[68] The presence of children in dangerous situations frequently involves a high risk of injury,[69] as does their propensity to meddle with articles of danger.[70] The risk of contamination from flies in the manufacture of jam is a real one since flies are "as notoriously ubiquitous as they are notoriously dirty".[71] Flax is "a particularly combustible substance", which imposes on a mill owner a heavy obligation to prevent a fire - not discharged where the employees are permitted to smoke.[72]

**[7.28]** The possibility of injury from a golf shot that is badly directed or taken before the players ahead are out of range[73] should not be discounted (as many golfers and their

---

68. *Cf* Stephenson 'Note' (1942) 30 Ky LJ 321. But of course the other considerations, mentioned in headings (b) to (d), must be balanced against this consideration. *Cf* Green 'The Duty Problem in Negligence Cases' (1928) I, 28 Col LR 1014 at 1032, fn 43: "Danger has never stopped a useful invention". See also *Beatty v Central Iowa Ry Co* 12 NW 332 at 334 (Iowa SC): "The price of progress cannot be withheld".

69. *Cf Breslin v Brennan* [1937] IR 350 (SC) - the driver negligent in restarting his car without checking whether children, who had been on the running-board a few minutes previously, had safely departed; *Davoren v FitzPatrick* [1935] Ir Jur 23 (CC) - similar facts; *Glanfield v CIE* (1946) 80 ILTR 72 (CC): ticket-checker on train slammed door on child's fingers; *cf Taylor v GS & W Ry* [1909] 2 IR 330 (CA): no liability in similar circumstances); *Fleming v Kerry Co* [1955-1956] Ir Jur 71 (SC): steam roller and tar boiler likely to injure children who "swarmed around". *Cf O'Leary v John A Wood Ltd* [1964] IR 269 (SC): no liability where boy injured when stealing ride on "low-loader"; *per* Kingsmill Moore J (at 278):

> "For myself, I cannot consider the low-loader to have been either an allurement or a concealed danger to this unfortunate boy. If the case be looked at from the *Donoghue v Stevenson* point of view I cannot see that the driving of this low-loader through the streets of Cork without a man seated on it could be regarded as an act which the defendants would 'reasonably foresee as likely to injure their neighbours'. I think the learned Judge was correct in withdrawing the case from the jury.".

70. *Sullivan v Creed* [1904] 2 IR 317 (CA affg KB) - defendant was negligent in leaving a loaded gun where his son was likely to find it and use it without due care; *Cunningham v Blake* [1937] Ir Jur 20 (HC) - no liability where son used gun in anger; *Swift v Westport UDC* [1944] IR 259 (SC; on referral, HC) - a gully-trap in the street was "a manifest danger to little children with no playgrounds"; *McGovern v Clones UDC* [1944] IR 282 (HC) - similar facts but no liability found; *Shelton v Creane* High Court, 17 December 1987 - a metal cover over an armstrong junction on the path to a local authority rented house was removed, resulting in plaintiff's fall; neither the tenant nor the local authority was liable as this removal "was something altogether exceptional which had never occurred before". The meddling propensity of adults is easy to foresee in some cases. In *Cahill v Kenneally* [1955-1956] Ir Jur 15 (CC), a bus driver was held to have been negligent in leaving his bus unattended with keys in the ignition and allowing men into bus to rest; it was "clearly dangerous to do so." See also *Henry (t/a Sight & Sound Film Library) v Sanderson* (1972) 106 ILTR 12 (HC).

71. *Kirby v Burke* [1944] IR 207 at 215 (HC). See also *O'Gorman v O'Gorman* [1903] 2 IR 573 (KB) - liability was imposed on defendant for smoking hives where bees swarmed from the hives and stung a horse which the plaintiff was riding, causing the horse to throw the plaintiff.

72. *Keenan v McCreedy* [1953-1954] Ir Jur 74 at 75 (CC).

73. *O'Rourke v Taylor* (1947) 81 ILTR 69 (CC). *Cf Horton v Jackson,* English CA (Civil), 28 February 1996 (LEXIS transcript); *Zurla v Hydel* (1997) 289 Ill App 3d 215, 681 NE 2d 148. The possibility of suing the golf club for negligence in its organisation of how the game is to be played should not be discounted: *cf Carey v Albany Golf Club* 4 SR (WA) 168 (DC) and contrast *Potter v Carlisle & Cliftonville Golf Club Ltd* [1939] NI 114. Schools organising the game of rounders in a sports hall must take account of its size and adapt the rules as necessary for the safety of the players: *Kane v Kennedy, Rep of St Mary's Secondary School* High Court, 26 March 1999. More generally see *Donaldson v Irish Motor Racing Club* Supreme Court, 1 February 1957; *Callaghan v Killarney Race Co Ltd* [1958] IR 366 (SC).

victims will attest). Factory work may be so managed as to make the risk of injury a real one for employees.[74] A tree overhanging the highway may become increasingly dangerous not because it changes but because the volume of traffic on the highway does.[75] Similarly, constant use of the highway by heavy lorries going to and from an adjoining property may create potholes so that it "should have been obvious that a serious road hazard was being created".[76] On the other hand, where a farmer places poison on his own land, the risk of its being transported to the lands of another by birds and other animals may be so small as to prevent his conduct from constituting negligence.[77]

**[7.29]** Whereas it may not be foreseeable that a quiet patient, suspected of spinal injury and "hardly able to move", would fall off an X-ray couch,[78] the likelihood of an obviously intoxicated railway passenger causing injury to another passenger in an altercation with railway staff may be far greater.[79] It has been held that it would be "entirely fanciful"[80] to

---

74. *Crowe v Brennan* [1967] IR 5 (SC) - the risk of an inadvertently dangerous and careless greasing of a machine by an employee when the machine is in motion is an "ever-present" one.
75. *Lynch v Dawson* [1946] IR 504 (HC). See also *Miller v Jackson* [1977] QB 966 (CA). *Cf Alliance & Dublin Consumers Gas Co v Dublin County Council* [1901] 1 IR 492 (CA, affg with modification, Porter MR, 1900).
76. *Connolly v South of Ireland Asphalt Co Ltd* [ 1977] IR 99 at 104 (SC).
77. *Tarrant v O'Sullivan* [1949] Ir Jur 46 (CC) See also *Matthews v Matthews* [1996] Ir L Log W 168 (CC) - driver on very narrow road "should have had within his contemplation the possibility that there m[ight] have been cattle on the road"; *Walsh v Kilkenny County Council* [1978] ILRM I (HC) - it was not foreseeable that the plaintiff's cows would break through a weakened wall onto the defendant's property and be poisoned by eating yew, since the plaintiff, although aware of the wall's condition, had not informed the defendant of this fact.
78. *Plunkett v St Laurence's Hospital* (1952) 86 ILTR 157 (HC). Contrast *Kelly v St Laurence's Hospital* [1989] ILRM 437 (SC) - liability was imposed where an in-patient admitted to hospital for observation when being taken off all drug therapy for epilepsy, was permitted to go to first-floor toilet, unattended, resulting in his falling from a window. In *Armstrong v Eastern Health Board* High Court, 5 October 1990, Egan J imposed liability in negligence for a patient's apparent attempted suicide on the ground that the medical assessment of her condition had been based on insufficient information when more information was available: see Byrne & Binchy, *Annual Review of Irish Law 1990*, pp 523-526. In *Healy v North Western Health Board*, High Court, 31 January 1996, Flood J held it to have been negligent to discharge a patient from a mental hospital without an assessment, immediately beforehand, of his medical condition to confirm that he had reached the status of firm remission from depression. The patient, shortly after discharge, had committed suicide. In *C v North Western Health Board* [1997] Ir L Log W 133 (CC), where a recently admitted mental patient left the hospital without permission and injured the plaintiff, no liability was imposed as the letter of referral had not mentioned the patient's propensity for violence. See also *Hanser v Chicago, Rhode Island & Pacific Ry* (1928) 205 Iowa 946, 219 NW 60 - it was not foreseeable that a passenger using the lavatory on a train would faint and fall in such a way that her head would come in contact with very hot steam pipes under the lavatory; *cf Victor Weston (Éire) Ltd v Kenny* [1954] IR 191 (HC) - landlord was liable for flooding damage resulting from an over-flow of water from a basin with a choked waste-pipe where an unknown person left the tap running:

   > "Human nature being what it is, any person of ordinary prudence, if he gave the matter any thought, must have considered that it was not impossible that some individual using the basin might fail to turn off the tap".

79. *Cf Adderley v GN Ry Co* [1905] 2 IR 378 (CA).
80. *Ring v Power* [1961] Ir Jur 51 at 52 (SC).

require a driver to foresee that turning a corner at speed in a van might cause a passenger bruising or other physical injury from impact with the door, (perhaps not everyone would agree with this view).

**[7.30]** The risk of a premises being struck by lightning is, of course, generally very low, but one that may have to be taken into account, at least in cases[81] where the building is particularly vulnerable by reason of height or isolation. In the area of occupier's liability, the contention that hotel staff should have expected a non-resident patron to be running in darkness at 4 am outside the rear kitchen quarters was regarded by O'Higgins CJ, in *O'Keeffe v Irish Motor Inns Ltd*,[82] as "bordering on the absurd".[83] As Kenny J observed: "No prudent person could have anticipated this."[84]

**[7.31]** So also, in *Healy v Bray UDC*,[85] where the plaintiff was injured by a loose rock which was dislodged and rolled down Bray Head and through a gap in a surrounding wall before hitting her, the defendant Council was relieved of liability in negligence. As Kingsmill Moore J stated:

> "The combination of all these unlikely events seem to me to reduce the risk to such minute proportions that the Council cannot be held negligent."[86]

**[7.32]** As these last two decisions demonstrate, the less the risk of injury, the less the likelihood is that the defendant will be guilty of negligence.[87] Thus, in *O'Gorman v Ritz (Clonmel) Ltd*,[88] the plaintiff, a patron at the defendant's cinema, stretched her legs under the seat in front of her, which was occupied by another person. When that person stood up to let another patron pass, his seat tilted backwards and caught the plaintiff's legs, cutting her left shin. The injury became septic and she required medical treatment for two months.

**[7.33]** The evidence disclosed that, in the previous seven years, approximately one million people had used the parterre seats in the defendant's cinema and no complaint had been received by the management regarding them. The plaintiff's action was dismissed. Geoghegan J stated:

> "The defendants are not insurers and it seems to me that the plaintiff seeks a degree of diligence, foresight, and precaution to which an ordinary threatre-goer is not entitled. I am satisfied on the particular facts, that to guard against a remote contingency such as that

81. *Cf* the United States decisions of *Jackson v Wisconsin Tel Co* (1894) 88 Wis 243, 60 NW 430 and *Tex-Jersey Oil Corporation v Beck* 292 SW 2d 803 (Text Civ App 1956). Although the likelihood of lightning in Ireland is less than in the United States, the general statement of principle would appear valid for this country.

82. [1978] IR 85 (SC).

83. [1978] IR 85 at 95.

84. [1978] IR 85 at 102.

85. [1962-1963] Ir Jur 9 (SC, 1961).

86. [1962-1963] Ir Jur 9 at 18.

87. *Cf Bolton v Stone* [1951] AC 850 (HL); *Fardon v Harcourt-Rivington*, 146 LT 391 at 392 (1932, *per* Lord Dunedin); Contrast *Miller v Jackson* [1977] QB 966 (CA); *Wills v Wisconsin-Minnesota Light & Power Co* 187 Wis 626, 205 NW 556 (SC 1925).

88. [1947] Ir Jur Rep 35 (HC, Geoghegan J). See also *Murray v Warner Lambert* [1997] Ir L Log W 267 (CC) - defendant manufacturer, who had received only three complaints out of a million sales of its product, a home perming kit, none of which had been substantiated, was found not liable in negligence for failure to warn of risk of allergic reaction where the plaintiff suffered such a reaction having used the product for many years.

which led to the injuries here would need precautions of a well-nigh fantastic nature, which could not reasonably be expected in the construction or management of a theatre."[89]

**[7.34]** In *Walsh v Dublin Corporation*,[90] in 1998, Smith J invoked the *Ritz* decision when dismissing the claim of a visitor to a flat, of which the defendant was the landlord, where a door from the hallway to the kitchen slammed shut, injuring her thumb. There was a "wind tunnel effect" when this door and the doors at the front and back of the flat were open at the same time. The plaintiff argued that a restraining mechanism should have been attached to the door. Smith J disagreed. The apartment in question was "small and compact" and space was "at a premium". The accident, while unfortunate, "was one that could befall any of us at any time, whether in our own homes or elsewhere".

## The gravity of the Threatened Injury

**[7.35]** Where the potential injury is great, the creation of even a slight risk may constitute negligence. An obvious case would be where highly poisonous materials are being transported in a public place.[91] In *Hughes v Ballynahinch Gas Co*,[92] liability was imposed on a gas company for injuries sustained in a gas explosion. Palles CB noted that:

> "These escapes of gas are matters most dangerous to human life, and, therefore, the highest degree of reasonable care is that which is due by this company that makes its living by supplying gas to the public."[93]

**[7.36]** The question of risk must be determined according to the information reasonably available to the defendant. Thus, secret information to which the defendant ought not reasonably have had access, which establishes a high degree of risk, must be ignored in determining whether the act was negligent.[94] In times of rapid technological development, this may result in problems for persons injured by defects in products which take some time to reveal themselves.[95]

**[7.37]** The gravity of the threatened injury is a relative matter: although the risk of an accident's happening may be exactly the same for two people, the results may be more serious for one than the other, and accordingly greater care may be owed to the former. An

---

89. [1947] Ir Jur Rep 35 at 36.
90. High Court, 23 July 1998 (Smith J). See also *Cassells v Marks & Spencer plc* High Court, 25 March 1999, where the fact that apparently hundreds of thousands of children's dresses made of the same fabric as caused injury, in this case its inflammability had previously been manufactured without a similar claim for fire injury was an element weighing against the imposition of liability for retailing the product without subjecting it to fire retardant chemicals.
91. *Cf Sullivan v Creed* [1904] 2 IR 317 at 325-326 (*per* Gibson J). See also *Collen Bros (Dublin) Ltd v Scaffolding Ltd* [1959] IR 245 at 247 (HC 1957, Davitt P):
"The necessity for the scaffolding to be safe, and the risk of life and limb if it were not, is obvious and must have been foreseeable by the defendants."
In accord is *Swinton v The China Mutual Steam Navigation Co* (1951) 83 Comm LR 553 at 566-567.
92. (1898) 33 ILTR 74 (Palles CB).
93. At 74.
94. *Cf Sydney County Council v Dell'Ore* (1964) 132 Comm LR 97.
95. *Cf* Bazelon, 'Science and Uncertainty: A Jurist's View' (1981) 5 Harv Environmental LR 209 at p 211.

obvious example is where an employee with sight in only one eye is required to do work that involves the risk of his losing the sight in his other eye.[96]

## The Social Utility of the Defendant's Conduct

**[7.38]** Regard must be had to the object of the defendant's conduct. Where it has a high social utility it will be regarded with more indulgence than where it has little or none.

**[7.39]** A person attempting to save the life of another may drive with less care than a Sunday driver.[97] Similarly, a person attempting to make an arrest of a suspect may be given some leeway relative to the risk of injuring others, although, of course, the likelihood of injury and the gravity or otherwise of the offence will be taken into consideration.[98] Moreover, businesses cannot be always carried on without some risk, as

---

96. *Cf Paris v Stepney Borough Council* [1951] AC 367. Whether imposition of liability in such circumstances assists accident prevention has been debated. There is evidence in England that the result of the *Paris* decision was a reduction in employment prospects for disabled persons rather than a decrease in industrial accidents: Wrigglesworth 'Legislation and Injury Control' (1978) 18 Med Sci & L 191 at 193.

97. *Cf O'Connell v CIE* (1954) 89 ILTR 95 (HC) - a bus driver braking and swerving to avoid a child who ran in his path was not guilty of negligence; *McGarry v Dublin Bus* [1997] Ir L Log W 278 (CC) - a bus driver braking to avoid car which had crossed without warning into the bus lane was not guilty of negligence; *Frawley v CIE* (1950) 84 ILTR 189 (HC) - a busdriver braking to avoid a dog was not guilty of negligence; *Parkinson v Liverpool Corporation* [1950] 1 All ER 367. See, however, *Molson v Squamish Transfer Ltd* (1969) 7 DLR (3d) 553 at 557 (BC), *Sutherland v Glasgow Corporation* 1949 SC 563. The size of the animal is important: obviously, the bigger the animal, the more reasonable it is for the driver to try to avoid hitting it - out of concern for the safety of his passengers and himself, if not for the life of the animal: *Hogan v McEwan* (1975) 64 DLR (3d) 37 (Ont HC). Emergency vehicles are exempted from ordinary speed limits: Road Traffic Act 1961, s 45(3), Road Traffic (General Speed Limit) Regulations 1979 (SI 176/1979) (*cf* Pierse, para 3.1.4); this does not, of course, relieve their drivers from liability for negligence where, in the circumstances, they drive without care; but, in determining whether due care was taken, the social object of the journey should be given due weight: *cf Phillips v Durgan* [1991] ILRM 321 (SC); *Turner v Iarnród Éireann* High Court, 14 February 1996; *Watt v Hertfordshire County Council* [1954] 2 All ER 368 (CA); *McLoughlin v Donegal County Council* DPIJ: Trinity and Michaelmas Terms 1994, p 114 (HC); *Coderre v Ethier* (1978) 85 DLR (3d) 621 (Ont HC). In *Strick v Treacy*, High Court, 10 June 1993, the driver of a Garda car and the driver of a fire tender on their way to a fire at a school were held guilty of negligence towards other road-users: see Byrne & Binchy, *Annual Review of Irish Law 1993*, pp 537-538. In determining whether a rescuer was guilty of contributory negligence, the court will also have regard to the fact that he or she is involved in a socially beneficial act, in which caution may legitimately be set on one side. *Cf Corothers v Slobodian* (1975) 51 DLR (3d) 1 (SC Can), Binchy, (1974) 52 Can Bar Rev 292). But even a rescuer cannot recover compensation if totally foolhardy: *cf Horsley v MacLaren* [1972] SCR 441, Binchy, 'The Good Samaritan at the Crossroads: A Canadian Signpost', (1974) 25 NILQ 147.

98. *Priestman v Colangelo* [1959] SCR 615; *Noel (Committee of) v Botkin* [1995] 7 WWR 479, 9 BCLR (3d) 21 (SC); *Blaz v Dickinson*, 23 MVR (3d) 70, 1996 Ont CJ LEXIS 3410 (1996); *Doern v Phillips (Estate)* 43 BCLR (3d) 53 (CA). *Cf Kavanagh v Hamrogue,* Supreme Court, 12 March 1965 - risk of injury to suspect himself at issue: see especially Kingsmill Moore J's judgment at pp 4-5. Contrast *Beim v Goyer* (1966) 57 DLR (2d) 253 (SC Can). In *Akers v P* (1986) 42 SASR 30 (SC), police officers intervening in a domestic dispute were held liable in negligence where they directed a man involved in the dispute, who was obviously intoxicated, to leave on his motorcycle, the man crashing shortly afterwards.

Kingsmill Moore J noted in *Christie v Odeon (Ireland) Ltd*:[99] "to make accidents impossible would often be to make work impossible".

**[7.40]** Conversely, where certain conduct has little or no social utility[100] it may be regarded as unreasonable even where the risk of injury is relatively small. As Professor Fleming has observed, "there is a world of difference between throwing a burning object into the street below just for the fun of it or in order to save a house on fire."[101]

**[7.41]** Thus, in *Whooley v Dublin Corporation*,[102] the defendant was relieved of liability where the plaintiff sustained injuries through putting her foot into an open fire hydrant box when she was walking along the footpath of a street in Dublin. It appeared that the lid of the box had been removed by a mischievous person. The box was designed so as to be easily accessible to the fire brigade in case of fire, and therefore the lid was capable of being removed without very great difficulty. In denying the plaintiff's claim, McLoughlin J. expressed the opinion that "no other type of hydrant which could be devised, consistent with its necessary purpose, would be safe from ... malicious interference".[103]

**[7.42]** In *Kavanagh v Cork Corporation*,[104] a case involving similar facts, Keane J observed that:

> "a fire hydrant, of its nature, has to be readily and quickly accessible to the fire brigade, or anyone else who has to make use of it rapidly in order to deal with an emergency. That is the whole point of it and, consequently, to have them locked in any way would obviously be more

---

99. (1957) 91 ILTR 25 at 29 (SC). See also *Latimer v AEC Ltd* [1953] AC 643 (HL); *Timbs v Templeogue Taverns Ltd* High Court, 18 December 1992 analysed by Byrne & Binchy, *Annual Review of Irish Law* (1992), pp 586-588; *Boyle v Marathon Petroleum Ireland Ltd* High Court, 1 November 1995 analysed by Byrne & Binchy, *Annual Review of Irish Law 1995*, pp 483-485, affd by Supreme Court, 12 January 1999 - there was no way offshore oil rig could have been constructed without inherent danger of low ceilings and obstructions.

100. As, for example, the illegal release of oil into a bay (*The Wagon Mound (No 2)* [1967] 1 AC 617 (PC)). Several commentators sympathetic to common law actions as a means of environmental protection consider that proceedings based in negligence may provide a useful adjunct to actions for public and private nuisance, trespass, and under the rule in *Rylands v Fletcher*; problems of proof of causation and reasonable foreseeability of the injury may, however, weaken the effectiveness of negligence proceedings: see generally Juergensmeyer 'Control of Air Pollution Through the Assertion of Private Rights' [1967] Duke LJ 1126 at 1142-1148; Reitze 'Private Remedies for Environmental Wrongs' (1971) 5 Suffolk ULR 779 at 808-810; Lohrmann 'Comment: The Environmental Lawsuit: Traditional Theories to Control Pollution' (1970) 16 Wayne LR 1085 at 1121-1123. Section 11(2)(c) of the Civil Liability Act 1961 could be of particular use in this context to mitigate some of the causation problems. The doctrine of *res ipsa loquitur* may also be called in aid by the plaintiff in some of these cases. In *Hanrahan v Merck, Sharp & Dohme (Ireland) Ltd* [1988] ILRM at 634-35 (SC), Henchy J expressed this doctrine so widely as to fail to accord with the conventional understanding of its scope.

101. FLEMING, p 130. See also *Watt v Hertfordshire County Council* [1954] 2 All ER 368 at 371 (CA); *The Wagon Mound (No 2)* [1967] 1 AC 617 at 642; *Daborn v Bath Tramways Motor Co Ltd* [1946] 2 All ER 333 (CA).

102. [1961] IR 60 (HC).

103. [1961] IR 60 at 64. See also *Carroll v Kildare County Council* [1950] IR 258 (SC, 1946) *per* Maguire CJ at 262: "... it would be absurd to argue that the use of steamrollers in the work of road construction is not normal and proper", but care must be taken in operating them. And see *Bradley v CIE* [1976] IR 217 at 223 (SC). *Hynes v Sligo Corporation* DPIJ: Trinity and Michaelmas Terms 1993, p 36 (HC).

104. DPIJ: Hilary and Easter Terms 1994, p 78 at p 80 (HC).

dangerous than the dangers caused by the sort of vandalism apparently common in parts of the city ...."

**[7.43]** The courts have found particular difficulty in resolving the extent to which desirable social policies should be achieved by requiring employees to carry the risk of injury without compensation. No doubt, the elderly derive great support from the home-help service, but should home-helps have to subsidise the service by being denied a remedy when, for example, they fall in a dilapidated house? And should the policy of integrating the mentally disabled into the community mean that a house-parent should have no recourse when a mentally handicapped patient who had previously had engaged in mischievous and slightly dangerous behaviour, assaults her? In *Mulcare v Southern Health Board*,[105] a home help's claim was dismissed on the basis that the house was not all that dilapidated and in *Hay v O'Grady*[106] a houseparent lost her action, the trial judge, Lynch J, emphasising the "most laudable" state policy that "those fit for community living should not, as far as possible, be locked away in large institutions for the rest of their lives".[107]

## The Cost of Eliminating the Risk

**[7.44]** Regard may be had to the cost of eliminating the risk of injury: "A slight risk may be run if the cost of remedying it is unreasonably high".[108] Thus, as we have seen, a cinema need not be constructed in such a manner as to prevent all risk of injury to patrons from seats in front of where they are sitting.[109] Clearly, it would be possible to design such a cinema but it would be too much to ask of cinema proprietors. Similarly, the proprietors of a fruit and vegetable market are not required to keep floors absolutely clear of vegetable

105. [1988] ILRM 689, analysed by Byrne & Binchy, *Annual Review of Irish Law 1988*, pp 422-424.

106. [1992] 1 IR 210 (SC, affg HC)

107. [1992] 1 IR 210 at 215. On appeal to the Supreme Court, McCarthy J noted that "there was no evidence whatever from any expert source to the effect that the management of [the patient] fell short of any reasonable standard of care". At 218.

108. *Kirwan v Bray* UDC Supreme Court, unrep,30 July 1969 *per* Ó Dálaigh CJ at pp 5-6. See also *Watt v Hertfordshire County Council* [1954] 2 All ER 368 at 371 (*per* Denning LJ); *Fortune v Jacob* Supreme Court, 22 June 1977 *per* O'Higgins CJ at pp 4-5. Much interest has been recently displayed by torts scholars in the United States in a cost-benefit analysis of negligence: *cf*, eg, Lanser & Posner *The Economic Structure of Tort Law* (1987); Posner, *Economic Analysis of Law* (3rd ed, 1992); Brown 'Toward an Economic Theory of Liability' (1973) 2 J Leg Studies 323. But whether this approach gives an accurate picture has been doubted. "The reasonable person is by no means a caricature cold-blooded, calculating Economic Man": FLEMING, p 132. See further Cane, *Tort Law and Economic Interests* (2nd ed, 1996), Ch 10; Shavell *Economic Analysis of Accident Law* (1987).

109 *O'Gorman v Ritz (Clonmel) Ltd* [1947] Ir Jur 35 (HC). See also *Potter v Carlisle & the Cliftonville Golf Club Ltd* [1939] NI 114 (CA): golfcourse need not be constructed so that green and tees are not close to one another for safety reasons - "such rule would impose serious limitations on the places where [golf] can be played" *per* Babington LJ at 137, *Potter* was approved in *Ellison v Rogers* (1967) DLR (2d) 21 (Ont HC). *Cf Mayor of City of Richmond v Delmo* Victoria SC, App Div, 13 November 1992, 1992 VC LEXIS 513; *Horton v Jackson* English CA (Civil Div), 28 February 1996. See also *Callaghan v Killarney Race Co Ltd* [1958] IR 366 (SC) - race-course proprietors were not negligent in failing to provide a fence at a hurdle which a horse could not crash through; *per* Kingsmill Moore J at 375: "If there was an obligation to double fence the whole perimeter, or to surround it with an unbreakable fence, the expense might well put an end to many of the smaller race-courses, or involve a higher price for admission"); *Butterly v Mayor of Drogheda* [1907] 2 IR 134 (KB) - corporation was held not to have been negligent for failing to place any protection around a pile of stones its employees had placed on the road: *per* Lord O'Brien LCJ (at 143):

leaves and other matter, where to do so "would require an army of cleaners".[110] Whilst the traditional obligation of shop proprietors in relation to spillages was expressed in terms of a duty to provide a reasonable system for monitoring and removing the danger to customers, the courts in recent years have imposed a very high standard especially on large

109. (contd)

> "Under the circumstances, there was no obligation, in my opinion, on the part of the Corporation to have, in broad daylight, any protection around the heap that was to be immediately spread. Why? If there was to be a protection put round heaps of this character that were to be immediately spread, the task of spreading would take at least four times as long as it otherwise would, and it would be attended with great expense. The erection and removal of the protection would cause great delay and great expense. In fact, the protection should be put up to be immediately pulled down; and why all this? To dispense a way-farer from the obligation of using his eyes."

*Kenny v Dublin United Tramways Co* Supreme Court, 5 March 1929 - it was too much to expect that a tram company should so construct a starting bell on tram that only conductor could reach it with a walking stick, as counsel for injured passenger had submitted! See also *Kingsport Utilities v Brown* (1950) 201 Tenn 393, 299 SW 2d 656. In *Nooney v Royal Canal Co* Batty's Irish Reports 1825-26, 357 (KB), a canal company was held not to have been negligent in failing to prevent damage to the plaintiff's boat which struck a large stone at the bottom of the canal. Unlike carriers, who owed a higher duty, the canal company was answerable merely "for the consequences of such accidents as ... reasonable care could have provided against". *Cf Butler v M'Alpine* 11904] 2 IR 445 (CA affg KB). See also *Martin v Dublin United Tramways Co* [1909] 2 IR 13 (KB).

110. *Ahern v Cork Corporation* (1950) 85 ILTR 97 at 98 (HC). *A fortiori* where the duty to keep the floor clear of slippy material rests on the plaintiff: *Courtney v Minister for Defence*; [1996] Ir L Log W 157 (CC, Lynch J). The courts generally are ill-disposed to tolerate spillages in shops, especially supermarkets: see, eg, *Mullen v Quinsworth t/a crazy Prices (No 1)* [1990] 1 IR 59 (SC) and *Mullen v Quinnsworth t/a Crazy Prices (No 2)* [1991] ILRM 439 (SC), but on occasion the odd shop escapes liability: see, eg *Myles v Supervalu* [1997] Ir L Log W 159 (CC). A spillage on a disco dance floor did not result in liability in *McSweeney v Garda Síochána Boat Club*, High Court, 5 June 1991; O'Flaherty J considered that, since the spillage had occurred only a very short time previously, it would be "a counsel of perfection" to expect it to be cleared up immediately. See also *Curry v Foster* [1960] Ir Jur 33 at 34 (HC, NI, QB) - "it would be a counsel of perfection to suggest that a farmer was bound to remove completely every trace of clay dropped on the highway by washing or some other method". In *Tarrant v O'Sullivan* [1949] Ir Jur 46 (CC), when holding the defendant not liable in negligence for poisoning the plaintiff's pigs, O'Connor J said (at 48):

> "If an occupier of land hides the poison in the ground it is of no value; if he places it in a drain or sewer it may be of value only in killing rats. Where then is he to put it?"

And see *McDonald v CIE* (1971) 105 ILTR 13 at 19 (SC), where Budd J rejected the proposition that a driver has an obligation to avoid hitting a child no matter how unexpected and speedy his movements may be, on the ground, inter alia, that it would "make the movement of traffic impossible ...". *Cf Davoren v FitzPatrick* [1935] Ir Jur 23 (CC) - children started defendant's car and caused injury; "It was urged in the course of the arguments that this car was constructed without any key or any other effective means of preventing what happened, but that does not relieve the defendant from taking all proper precautions". See also *Cannon v Midland GW Ry (Ireland) Co* (1879) 6 LR Ir 199 (CA) - railway company was not obliged to provide extra platform staff to control an unruly group of harvest-men taking special excursion train at a cheap rate; *Devine v Iarnród Éireann* [1996] Ir L Log W 419 (CC): plaintiff was attacked when on the train; defendant had no case to answer, Smith J considering that "would amount to 'virtual security men'". *Cf Wrenn v Bus Átha Cliath/Dublin Bus,* Supreme Court, 31 March, 1995: conductor liable for ineffective response to violence on a late-night bus. See also *Kenny v ESB* [1932] IR 73 at 93 (SC): "... a jury is not entitled to lay down that all considerations of every kind are to be subordinated to the object of preventing boys from climbing".

supermarkets, which frankly borders on strict liability. McCarthy, J. actually went so far as to countenance the possibility of giving formal endorsement to a test of "absolute liability", in *Mullen v Quinnsworth t/a Crazy Prices (No 1)*,[111] though his enthusiasm for this opportunity appeared to wane when the case came back on a second appeal to the Supreme Court.[112]

**[7.45]** Spillages on disco dance floors have proved more problematic. In *McSweeney v Garda Síochána Boat Club*,[113] O'Flaherty J acquitted the defendants of negligence, in spite of the fact that patrons had been permitted to bring glasses of drink into the area where dancing took place, with the inevitable result that drinks were spilled from time to time. Impressed by the defendants' evidence as to their system for mopping up these spillages, O'Flaherty J concluded that the spillage which caused the plaintiff injury could have been there only for a very short length of time and that "it would be a counsel of perfection to expect [it] to be cleaned up immediately". In *Duffy v Carnabane Holdings Ltd t/a The Glencarn Hotel*,[114] the Supreme Court accepted that any analogy with the duty of factory owners to their employees would set an inappropriately high standard of care for dance hall proprietors in relation to spillages.

**[7.46]** In *Sutherland v Supervalu*,[115] where a six-year-old girl's arm became trapped in a conveyor belt when she was helping her mother place goods on the check-out conveyor, the shopkeeper was held not to have been negligent[116], Smithwick P noting that:

> "it would be imposing an unreasonable duty of care on shopkeepers to ask them to continuously police children helping their mothers putting goods on conveyor belts at check-outs."

**[7.47]** In *Donaldson v Irish Motor Racing Club*,[117] the Supreme Court relieved of liability in negligence the organisers of a motor race through the Curragh, where one of the cars veered off the road and ploughed into the spectators. Kingsmill Moore J noted that sports and games "usually involve violence in the form of high speed or vigorous muscular exertion or both, and it is impossible to confine the results of such violence entirely to the arena in which the performance is taking place".[118] He considered that:

> "To remove spectators to such a distance, or to guard them with such protective screens as would ensure complete safety, would in most cases so diminish the view as to render watching unattractive and put an end to the entertainment. Where the arena of the sport extends linearly over a great distance, as in horse or motor racing, the provision of an

---

111. [1990] 1 IR 59 (SC). *Cf* Byrne & Binchy, *Annual Review of Irish Law 1990*, pp 518-521.

112. *Mullen v Quinnsworth t/a Crazy Prices (No 2)* [1991] ILRM 439. *Cf* Byrne & Binchy, *Annual Review of Irish Law 1991*, pp 393-395. See also *Myles v Supervalu,* [1997] Ir L Log W 159 (CC): no liability was imposed. In *Foley v Quinnsworth*, High Court, 10 April 1992, Carroll J evinced no approval of the concept of imposing "absolute liability" in this context, though her remarks can perhaps best be understood as referring specifically to the application of the doctrine of *res ipsa loquitur*: see Byrne & Binchy, *Annual Review of Irish Law 1992*, pp 598-600.

113. High Court, 5 June 1991 (CCA); *cf* Byrne & Binchy, *Annual Review of Irish Law 1991*, pp 395-396.

114. [1996] 2 ILRM 86; *cf* Byrne & Binchy, *Annual Review of Irish Law 1996*.

115. Circuit Court, 11 March 1999, Irish Times, 12 March 1999.

116. The supplier of the check-unit was held liable in negligence in its design.

117. Supreme Court, 1 February, 1959.

118. Page 11 of Kingsmill Moore's judgment.

unbreakable barrier alongside the whole course would be impracticable on the ground of expense. Yet it is in the public interest, alike from the point of view of players, competitors, and spectators that games and sports should be carried on."[119]

**[7.48]** The cost factor tends to lose most of its force, however, where the risk of injury becomes substantial.[120] Moreover, the fact that the cost of removing the risk is small will be a factor that may suggest that the failure to make that expenditure was negligent.[121]

**[7.49]** In *McGovern v Clones UDC*[122] the plaintiff was injured when struck by a gully-tap installed by the defendant on a public street in Clones. About three hundred children under the age of twelve lived on the street and were accustomed to assembling there and playing on it. Some of them had meddled with the gully-trap and had placed it in a dangerous condition.

**[7.50]** The plaintiff's action in negligence was dismissed because the court considered that the defendant ought not reasonably to have anticipated that the children would meddle with the gully-trap. Black J added, however, that his decision was:

> "in no way influenced by any view that it would be impracticable to render these street gratings incapable of being opened by a child like the plaintiff. No doubt to do so would be troublesome, and if even confined to localities like [the street where the plaintiff resided], might involve an unwelcome increase in expense. If the defendants had had to convince me that such precautions would have been impracticable the evidence put forward with that object would not have satisfied me."[123]

---

119. Pages 11-12 See also *Burke v Good,* [1997] Ir L Log W 336 (CC). In *Maguire v Gaelic Athletic Association* DPIJ: Trinity and Michaelmas Terms 1993, 95 (HC) where the plaintiff spectator had fallen from the roof of a toilet on which barbed wire had been placed, but there was a gap in the barbed wire which had not been refilled, Lynch J held that the organisers of the sports event were not guilty of negligence. He rejected the argument that the roof should have been rendered totally inaccessible; the barriers that it had erected "made it perfectly clear that patrons should not attempt to go on to the roof in question" and, insofar as there was a gap in the barrier, the roof was very difficult to climb upon because of its smooth surface and the absence of a proper hand-holds. In *Helly v Gilhooly* DPIJ: Trinity and Michaelmas Terms 1994, 86 (HC), where a pupil was knocked down by two dogs while walking down a path in the school premises, the school was relieved of liability in failing to keep the dogs out. If such a duty existed, "it would mean putting a teacher or other employee on every gate. This seems much too high a standard of care in the circumstances." *Cf Muldoon v Ireland* [1988] ILRM 367 (HC): prison authorities in Arbour Hill were not required to search every prisoner every time they were moved from one area of the prison to another to ensure that no prisoner had an offensive weapon with which he might injure another prisoner; more frequent searches than those in operation would be regarded by the prisoners as excessive and arguably would amount to harassment of them. In accord are *Kavanagh v Governor of Arbour Hill Prison* High Court, 22 April 1993; *(Arbour Hill)* and *Boyd v Ireland,* High Court, 13 May 1993; *Bates v Ireland* High Court, 18 May 1995; *Bolger v Governor of Mountjoy Prison* Supreme Court, 1998. See further McDermott, *Prison Law* (2000), pp 232-249.

120. *Cf Morris v Luton Corporation* [1946] 1 All ER 1 at 4; *Edwards v National Coal Board* [1949] 1 KB 704 at 710.

121. *Cf Swords v St Patrick's Copper Mines Ltd* [1965] Ir Jur 63 (SC).

122. [1944] IR 282 (HC, Black J). See also *Johnston v Dublin Corporation* [1961] IR 24 (HC, McLoughlin J, on appeal from Circuit Ct, 1960): an inadequate system of inspection of a water mains valve box on a footpath of a Dublin Street.

**[7.51]** Particular difficulties arise in the context of employment. Some jobs cannot be done without risk.[124] The problem for the courts is to determine the scope of the employers' duty to mitigate or remove danger. In *Bradley v Coras Iompair Éireann*,[125] Henchy J observed that:

> "even where a certain precaution is obviously wanted in the interests of the safety of the workman, there may be countervailing factors which would justify the employer in not taking that precaution".

**[7.52]** One suspects that no judge today would use quite the same language. Indeed, the courts have shown themselves solicitous to protect the lives and bodily security of those with such manifestly dangerous avocations as soldiers,[126] firefighters,[127] and security guards.[128] In *Ryan v Ireland*,[129] Finlay CJ went so far as to express the view that "[t]here could ... be no objective in a master and servant relationship which would justify exposing the servant to a risk of serious injury or death other than the saving of life itself."

**[7.53]** The courts have, however, kept some sense of proportion. In *Barclay v An Post*,[130] the defendant was relieved of liability in negligence for requiring employees to deliver post to premises with letter boxes at the base of the door.[131] The defendant had sought (unsuccessfully) to encourage the Department of the Environment to introduce regulations to remedy the matter. It had also provided a training course in manual handling for its employees. Whilst there was "no practical satisfactory answer to this problem other than to eliminate low letter boxes",[132] the defendant had done all that was reasonable, within its power to protect its employees.

---

123. At 294. See also *Collen Bros (Dublin) Ltd v Scaffolding Ltd* [1959] IR 249 (HC); *Burell v Tuohy* [1898] 2 IR 271; *O'Gorman v O'Gorman* [1903] 2 IR 573 (KB) where the defendant was held to have been negligent in keeping an unreasonable number of bees at an unreasonable place, close to his neighbour's property; the defence that "bee-keeping is an ancient and useful industry" (at 586) did not relieve him of the obligation to take care not to injure his neighbour.

124. Those working in bomb-disposal or acting as test pilots, for example, confront the risk of death or injury as a real aspect of their employment. In *Depuis v Haulbowline Industries Ltd* Supreme Court, 14 February 1962, Lavery J observed that shipbreaking was employment "of a sort that admittedly has a certain degree of risk."

125. [1976] IR 217 at 223 (SC).

126. *Ryan v Ireland* [1989] IR 177 (SC); *Dowdall v Minister for Defence* High Court, 23 July 1992; *Rohan v Minister for Finance*, High Court, 19 June 1992.

127. *Heeney v Dublin Corporation,* High Court, 16 May 1991 analysed by Byrne & Binchy, *Annual Review of Irish Law 1991*, pp 398-399.

128. *Walsh v Securicor (Ireland) Ltd* [1993] 2 IR 507 (SC), analysed by Byrne & Binchy, *Annual Review of Irish Law 1993*, 541-543; *McCann v Brinks Allied Ltd and Ulster Bank Ltd,* High Court, 12 May 1995; Morris J analysed by Byrne & Binchy, *Annual Review of Irish Law 1995*, pp 487-490, affd by Supreme Court [1997] 1 ILRM 461 analysed by Byrne & Binchy, *Annual Review of Irish Law 1996*, pp 577-579 and by O'Dell, pp 215-217 (Contract Chapter of the Review).

129. [1989] IR 177 at 183.

130. [1998] 2 ILRM 385 (HC)

131. In the particular circumstances of the case, the defendant was held liable to the plaintiff employee in failing to ensure that, in the short term after a back injury, he was not exposed to work involving "undue and extraordinary strain" on his back: [1998] 2 ILRM 385 at 399.

132. [1998] 2 ILRM 385 at 398.

**[7.54]** In *Coyle v An Post*,[133] the Supreme Court (by a four to one majority[134]) baulked at the proposition that an employer was guilty of negligence by reason of the fact that its employee, a sub-postmaster, found it necessary to take his car out in icy weather conditions, to obtain money to replenish funds which had run low because of a surprising level of demand on the day, resulting in an accident. Hederman J observed:

> "The law of negligence is not a system whose primary purpose is to ensure that injured persons will receive monetary compensation. It is a system premised on the establishment of fault on the part of the defendant. The present case has no precedent; certainly none was cited to us in argument. If the court were to impose liability in relation to the circumstances that arose in this case, it is hard to see why it would not follow that every employer, whose employees journey in frosty weather, a journey which could be avoided by the employer taking other steps, is under a duty of care, under pain of being found liable in negligence, to arrange to have the journey called off. This is a bold proposition which goes well beyond what the law of negligence should demand. In my view the court cannot slip into a strict liability regime."[135]

---

133. [1993] ILRM 508 (SC), analysed by Byrne & Binchy, *Annual Review of Irish Law 1992*, pp 573-576.

134. Finlay CJ, Hederman, Egan and Blayney JJ, O'Flaherty J dissenting, reversing High Court, 15 February 1991 (Johnson J).

135. [1993] ILRM 520. See also *McCarthy v Southern Health Board* DPIJ: Hilary and Easter Terms 1994, p 1 (HC, 11 January 1994): an employee slipped on an icy patch on a path outside his place of work; a non-suit was granted; *per* Keane J at p 2:

> "It really does come to an imposition of absolute liability because the most careful occupier of property imaginable could never ensure that there could not be an occasional accumulation of water save by constant supervision, constant attention to the surface. Th[is] standar[d] .... could not be possibly imposed on any person."

It is suggested that this statement should be read in the context of the facts of the particular case in question. It cannot be understood as holding that the occupier can never be liable in such situations: see *Connolly v South of Ireland Asphalt Co* [1977] IR 99 at para **[2.39]** above.

Chapter 8

# Affirmative Duties


I. Introduction .......... 169
II. Duty to Protect Incapacitated Persons (and their Potential Victims) from Injury .......... 171
III. Duty to Control Others .......... 176


## I. Introduction

**[8.01]** Unlike civil law jurisdictions,[1] the common law has historically taken a harshly individualistic position on the question of affirmative duties. The courts have recognised "a basic difference between doing something and merely letting something happen".[2] There is no general duty to go to the assistance of another person who is in peril,[3] even where to do so would involve no danger or real inconvenience to the would-be-rescuer.[4] Thus, a doctor may pass a road accident with impunity even though he or she could give

1. *Cf* Dawson 'Negotiorum Gestio: The Altruistic Intermeddler' (1961) 74 Harv LR 1073. Anon 'Failure to Rescue: A Comparative Study' (1952) 52 Colum LR 631, Ratcliffe ed, *The Good Samaritan and The Law* (1966), p 63; von Bar, *The Common Law of Torts* (2000), Vol 2, pp 208-232. One effect of the decision of the European Court of Human Rights in *Osman v United Kingdom* [1999] 1 FLR 193 may be to extend to common law jurisdiction the spirit of the civil law systems in this context: see McBride 'Protecting Life: A Positive Obligation to Help' [1999] Eur LR, 24 Supp HRS 43-54. A matter that has yet to be considered by the Irish courts is the extent to which the entitlement to compensation for infringement of constitutional rights, recognised in *Meskell v CIE* [1973] IR 121, extends to infringement through culpable neglect. Costello P's analysis in *W v Ireland* [1997] 2 IR 141 might suggest that the limitations on the duty of care in negligence should in this context be respected by the courts when assessing the question of eligibility to damages under the *Meskell* principle. No doubt that is so, but one suspects that a modern judicial reassessment of the traditional immunity for liability for omissions could lead to its rejection or, at least, substantial modification.
2. Smith & Burns, '*Donoghue v Stevenson* - The Not So Golden Anniversary', (1983) 46 MLR 147, at 154.
3. See generally Bohlen 'The Moral Duty to Aid Others as a Basis of Tort Liability' (1908) 56 U Pa LR 217, 316; Linden 'Rescuers and Good Samaritans' (1971) 34 MLR 241; Binchy 'The Good Samaritan at the Crossroads: A Canadian Signpost' (1974) 25 NILQ 147; Wright 'Negligent Acts or Omissions' (1941) 19 CBR 465; Snyder 'Liability for Negative Conduct' (1949) 35 Va LR 446; McNeice & Thornton 'Affirmative Duties in Tort' (1949) 58 Yale LJ 1272; Scheid 'Affirmative Duty to Act in Emergency Situations - The Return of the Good Samaritan' (1969) 3 John Marshall J of Practice and Procedure 1; Logie 'Affirmative Action in the Law of Tort: the Case of the Duty to Warn' [1989] Camb LJ 115; Brady 'Note: The Duty to Rescue in Tort Law: Implications of Research on Altruism' (1980) 55 Ind LJ 551; Weinrib 'The Case for a Duty to Rescue' (1980) 90 Yale LJ 247; Gordon 'Moral Challenge to the Legal Doctrine of Rescue' (1965) 14 Clev-Mar LR 334; Rudolph 'The Duty to Act: A Proposed Rule' (1965) 44 Neb LR 499.
4. Some particularly horrible decisions are cited by PROSSER & KEETON, p 373.

valuable assistance to the injured,[5] and an adult may let a toddler drown in shallow water without lifting a finger to help the infant.[6]

**[8.02]** Whilst there is no general duty to act, specific relationships may give rise to a particular affirmative duty. The relationship of occupier and entrant is one such case.[7] Statute, moreover, may impose such an obligation.[8] The employment relationship may impose an affirmative duty in certain cases,[9] and a Canadian decision[10] imposes a similar obligation on the captain of a boat respecting his passengers.

**[8.03]** Cases[11] in other jurisdictions have imposed an obligation on persons who having, without negligence, created a situation of danger, fail to take reasonable steps to protect others from being injured. Thus, for example, on the relatively rare occasion when two cars crash without either driver being negligent, an obligation may fall on both drivers to take positive steps to protect other road users from the risk of injury from the obstruction on the road.

**[8.04]** Whilst failure to perform an act - or nonfeasance, as it is sometimes called - will not normally involve a person in liability, nevertheless, if that person elects to perform the act and does it negligently, so as to cause harm to another, he or she will be liable for

---

5. *Cf Smith v Rae* 46 OLR 518 (CA, 1919); *Hurley v Eddingfield* (1901) 156 Ind 416, 59 NE 1058; Gray & Sharpe 'Doctors, Samaritans and the Accident Victim' (1973) 11 Os HLJ. In the United States, with a view to encouraging altruism, "Good Samaritan" legislation in every jurisdiction has conferred immunity from liability in negligence on persons rendering emergency care to accident victims. The statutes differ widely in their scope: see Brandt 'Comment: Good Samaritan Laws - The Legal Placebo: A Current Analysis' (1983) 17 Akron LR 303. Vermont has taken a more positive approach. Under s 519(1) of the Duty to Aid the Endangered Act (Vt Stat Ann title 12, 1973):

   > "a person who knows that another is exposed to grave physical harm shall, to the extent that the same can be rendered without danger or peril to himself or without interference with important duties to others, give reasonable assistance to the exposed person unless that assistance or care is being provided by others."

   A statutory obligation on these lines was proposed as long ago as 1908 by Ames 'Law and Morals' 22 Harv LR 97 at 113. See further Stewart 'How Making the Failure to Assist Illegal Fails to Assist: An Observation on Expanding Criminal Omission Liability' (1998) 25 Am J Crim 385 at 390-391.

   As to the duty of a hospital to treat persons seeking medical attention, *cf Barnett v Chelsea & Kensington Hospital Management Committee* [1969] 1 QB 428. *Cf* Anon 'Hospital's Duty of Emergency Care: A Functional Approach' (1970) 6 Col J of L & Soc Problems 454 at 460ff. See further *Collins v Mid-Western Health Board* Supreme Court, 12 November 1999. In *Lowns v Woods* (1996) Aust Torts Reps 81-376, the New South Wales Court of Appeal imposed a duty on a general practioner to go to the assistance of a person who was not his patient. This holding has been criticised by Haberfield '*Lowns v Woods* and the Duty to Rescue' (1998) 6 Tort LR 56, but approved of by FLEMING, p 65

6. *Cf Osterlind v Hill* (1928) 263 Mass 73, 160 NE 301; *Yania v Bigan* (1959) 397 Pa 316, 155 A 2d 343. Where the adult is related or (semble) *in loco parentis* to the infant, a duty to give assistance arises.

7. *Cf* Ch 12.

8. Eg Road Traffic Act 1961, s 106, Merchant Shipping (Safety Convention) Act 1952, s 37. *Cf Oke v Weide Transport Ltd* 41 DLR (2d) 53 (Man CA, 1963).

9. *Smith v Howdens Ltd* [1953] NI 131 (CA). *Cf* para **[18.127]** below.

10. *Horsley v MacLaren* [1972] SCR 441, analysed by Binchy in (1974) 25 NILQ 147.

11. *Cf Montgomery v National C & T* (1938) 186 SC 167, 195 SE 247; *Simonsen v Thorin* (1931) 120 Neb 684, 234 NW 628; *Hardy v Brooks* (1961) 103 Ga App 124, 118 SE 2d 492; see also the dissenting judgment of Freedman JA, in *Oke v Weide Transport Ltd* 41 DLR (2d) 53 (Man CA, 1963).

misfeasance. Thus, if a road authority, which is not under an obligation to keep the roads in good repair, elects to repair a road but leaves it in a dangerous condition, liability may be imposed.[12] So also if those responsible for the running of an ambulance service respond to an emergency call by undertaking to send an ambulance, they may fall under a duty of care to deliver on that promise.[13]

**[8.05]** Failure to act, and in particular failure to warn, can give rise to liability in several other contexts, treated elsewhere in this work. These include such matters as fraudulent and negligent non-disclosure and failure to warn of dangers in relation to products.

## II. Duty to Protect Incapacitated Persons (and their Potential Victims) from Injury

**[8.06]** A duty to control incapacitated persons so that they do not cause injury to others or to themselves[14] may also arise in certain cases. Although it seems clear that one may with legal impunity pass an intoxicated person on the street even though he or she is a menace to traffic and in danger of being injured, the position is a good deal less clear where a dispenser of alcohol serves drink to a person beyond the point of intoxication, and as a result the intoxicated person injures himself or herself or an entirely innocent third party. Decisions in Canada[15] and the United States of America[16] impose liability on commercial purveyors, such as the owners

---

12. *Cf Phelan v Kilkenny County Council* [1943] Ir Jur 1 (SC); *Kane v Howth DC* [1939] Ir Jur 54 (CC, 1938, Shannon J). In England, in *Capital & Counties plc v Hampshire County Council* [1997] QB 1004, the Court of Appeal held that fire authorities could be held liable in negligence if their actions worsened the position but not if their default consisted of an omission. In Ireland s 36 of the Fire Services Act 1981 probably excludes liability for both acts and omissions. See *Cullinane v Waterford County Council* [1997] Ir L Log W 309 (CC). *Kent v Griffiths* [2000] 2 WLR 1158. Police responding to a burglar alarm: *Alexandrou v Oxford* [1993] 4 All ER 328 (Ct App (Cir Div)) or the coastguard responding to an emergency at sea: *OLL Ltd v Secretary of State for Transport,* [1997] 3 All ER 897 (QB Div, May J).
13. *Kent v Griffiths* [2000] 2 WLR 1158 (CA).
14. *Cf Dunbar v Guardians of Ardee Union* [1897] 2 IR 76 (CA, 1896).
15. *Cf Menow v Jordan House Hotel* [1974] SCR 239, analysed by Binchy 'Drink Now-Sue Later' (1975) 53 Can BR 344; Silberberg 'The Intoxicated Patron: A Re-Appraisal of the Duty of Care' (1974) 20 McGill LJ 491; *Schmidt v Sharpe* (1983) 27 CCLT 1 (Ont HC); *Picka v Porter* Ont CA, 24 April 1980, considered by Kligman 'Innkeeper's Liability: of the Alcoholic Excuses of Patrons' (1984) 22 CCLT 49 at 56. See also *Crocker v Sundance, Northwest Resorts Ltd* [1988] 1 SCR 1186, where the Supreme Court of Canada, as in *Menow,* rejected the defence of voluntary assumption of risk. In *Stewart v Pettie* [1995] 1 SCR 131, however, the Court appeared to have drawn in its horns. It stressed that liability does not flow from the mere fact that the publican has over-served the patron. There must be some foreseeable risk of harm to the patron or a third party. For critical analysis of *Stewart*, see Kostal (1996) 75 Can BR 169. As to employers' liability for traffic accidents sustained by employees who drank during hours of work see *John v Flynn* 2000 AC WSJ LEXIS 471 (Ont, SC).
16. See, eg, *Rappaport v Nichols* (1959) 156A 2D 1 (NJ SC); *Soronen v Olde Milford Inn Inc* (1959) 46 NJ 582, 218 A 2D 630 (SC). See Moore Walsh 'The Roundabout Tavern Settlement: A Reflection of American Publican Liability' (2000) 18 Ir LT (ns) 205. The issue has yet to be addressed directly by courts in Australia: see Solomon & Payne 'Alcohol Liability in Canada and Australia: Sell, Serve and Be Sued' (1996) 5 Tort LR 198 at 220.

of bars and hotels.[17] Some decisions in the United States[18] have gone so far as to impose liability on social hosts who give their intoxicated guests "one for the road".[19]

**[8.07]** It seems difficult to deny a remedy to third parties who are injured or killed in either such case.[20] It is clearly foreseeable that, if a drunken driver is released onto the highway, he or she may be involved in an accident. The only way that the supplier of the drink could be absolved from legal liability would be to argue that, even today, a fundamental premise of tort law is that I am not my brother's keeper, and that the intoxicated person should be regarded as a *novus actus interveniens*. Whatever about the claim of an intoxicated person who is injured, it would seem that the injured third party's claim to entitlement to sue is a very strong one. If I am liable for carelessly leaving the keys in my car when others, without my knowledge, meddle with it and cause injury,[21] how can I be absolved from responsibility when (possibly for motives of commercial profit and in breach of the criminal law),[22] I participate in transforming a safe driver into a lethal one and then release him onto the highway?

---

16. (contd) In *Hay v Sheargold t/a Golden West Hotel* 1996 LEXIS 2732 (NSW SC CL Div), on obligation was considered to fall on the hotel staff to ensure that a drunken guest was conducted safely to his room and in *Johns v Cosgrove Chevron Queensland Ltd* [1997] QSC 229 (cited and discussed by Dunne 'Publicans' Liability for Injuries Off the Premises' (1999) 5 BR 152 at 155) a publican who served drink to a patron beyond the point of intoxication was held liable for his injury where he staggered out in from of a moving car. In England the general issue of liability for serving alcohol to an intoxicated person came before the Court of Appeal in *Barrett v Ministry for Defence* [1995] 3 All ER 87, in the context of employers, rather than publicans. While the Court imposed liability for failure to have protected an employee, a naval airman, who had collapsed from the quantum of drink served to him in the mess, the Court made it clear that it did not consider the defendant legally culpable for having facilitated the employee in becoming intoxicated. "To dilute self-responsibility and to blame one adult for another's lack of self-control is neither just nor reasonable and in the development of the law of negligence an increment too far" (*per* Bedlam LJ). In *Griffiths v Brown* [1999] P 1 QR 131 (HC, QB Div) Jones J declined to impose an affirmative duty of care on a taxi-driver carrying an intoxicated passenger.

17. In *O'Toole v Carlsbad Shell Service Station* (1988) 247 Cal Rep 663 (CA), noted in (1988) 102 Harv LR 544, liability was imposed on a petrol station which furnished petrol to a visibly intoxicated driver who later injured a third party.

18. Eg, *Kelly v Gwinnell* (1984) 96 NJ 538, 476 A 2d 1219; *Clark v Mincks* (1985) 364 NW 2d 226 (Iowa SC); *McGuiggan v New England Tel & Tel Co* (1986) 398 Mass 152 at 161, 496 NE 2d 141 at 146; *Gariup Construction Co v Foster* (1988) 519 NE 2d 1224 at 1227-1229 (Ind SC). The large majority of Courts that have addressed this question have, however, declined to impose liability on social hosts: see Anon 'Note' (1988) 102 Harv LR 549; *D'Amico v Christie* (1987) 71 NY 2d 76, 518 NE 2d 890; Ashmea (1989) 55 Brooklyn LR 995. Moreover legislation in California, Iowa and Oregon has overturned court decisions in favour of liability: Anon 'Note' (1988) 102 Harv LR 549 at 555.

19. This passage, in the first edition at p 165, was quoted by Judge Sheridan in *Murphy v O'Brien* (1987) 6 ILT (ns) 75 at 76 (CC).

20. See Binchy 'Suing Publicans: The Weak Links in Management that Can be Strengthened' paper delivered at a conference on publicans' liability at Trinity College Dublin on 21 November 1998.

21. *Cf Cahill v Kenneally* [1955-1956] Ir Jur 15 (CC); *Davoren v Fitzpatrick* [1935] Ir Jur 23 (CC). See also *Dockery v O'Brien* (1975) 109 ILTR 127 (CC), in which the meddling party was intoxicated.

22. The breach of statute has been strongly relied upon in many of the decisions in Canada and the United States, *cf* Binchy 'Comment: Drink Now - Sue Later' (1975) 53 Can BR 344; *Schmidt v Sharpe* (1983) 27 CCLT 1 (Ont HC); Nelson 'Note' (1972) 6 Creighton LR 110; Meagher 'Note' (1979) 1 Miss College LR 303.

**[8.08]** So far we have no definitive determination of the issue in this jurisdiction, but there are harbingers of imposing liability in these circumstances. In the Circuit Court decision of *Murphy v O'Brien*[23] the question arose as to the duty of a publican to protect an intoxicated patron against the risk of injury. The plaintiff, who had "had plenty to drink"[24] elsewhere, was assisted by friends into the defendant's public house. The defendant permitted the party to come in, and did not prevent three drinks being served to them. It is important to note that the report does not state that the plaintiff was served or drank anything on the premises.

**[8.09]** The plaintiff went downstairs to go to the toilet. She slipped and fell because the handrail did not run all the way down the stairs. Expert evidence led Judge Sheridan to conclude that the handrail would have been perfectly adequate for a sober person but not for one who was somewhat intoxicated. The plaintiff's action against the proprietor of the public house was successful, though her damages were reduced by two-thirds on account of her contributory negligence. Judge Sheridan's analysis is of considerable interest. Having held that the case should be determined on ordinary principles of negligence rather than occupiers' liability, he quoted Lord Atkin's "neighbour" test in *Donoghue v Stevenson*[25] and went on to say:

> "Lord Atkin, in that passage, was dealing with liability of manufacturers ... It cannot, in my opinion, be overlooked that this case involved a public house which was there to receive persons for the purpose of the purchase and consumption of intoxicating liquor. It, of course, should be in the contemplation of the defendant that persons in varying states of intoxication might attempt to use the stairs, and she certainly knew ... that the plaintiff was in a state of considerable intoxication. She therefore must be taken to have foreseen that the plaintiff might well attempt to negotiate the stairs in her evidence, and, this being so, she might well have difficulty in negotiating the last step ... without the benefit of the hand rail. It seems to me that once the defendant declined to refuse admission to the plaintiff, and to permit the serving of further drink, she had to take the consequences of any foreseeable risk to the plaintiff in her then state, and this, in my opinion, she failed to do. In my opinion, therefore, the defendant was guilty of fault."[26]

**[8.10]** Liability was thus imposed on the basis that the proprietor of the public house had willingly entered into a relationship of prospective, if not actual, economic dimensions with the plaintiff. If the plaintiff had merely called at the door of the premises and requested to use the toilet, making it clear that she was not going to look for any alcoholic drink, it seems probable that Sheridan J would not have imposed liability on the basis of *Donoghue v Stevenson*, but rather - if at all - by applying the relevant principles relating to the duty owed by an occupier to a licensee.[27]

---

23. (1987) 6 ILT (ns) 75 (CC).
24. At 75.
25. [1932] AC 562 at 580.
26. At 76.
27. See also *Walsh v Ryan* High Court, 12 February 1993 (Lavan J); *cf Hall v Kennedy* High Court, 20 December 1993 (Morris P).

**[8.11]** *Murphy v Ballyclough Co-operative Creamery Ltd*,[28] is worth noting in the present context. The plaintiff had received hospitality at a free bar provided by the first-named defendant, after which he had gone to a number of other licensed premises. He was driven by the seventh-named defendant (the owner of the last public house where he was drinking) to the place where he had left his car. When he drove the car he was involved in an accident and suffered catastrophic injuries. The plaintiff's case against the defendants was that they were negligent in serving him with alcoholic drink at a time when they knew or ought to have known that he was already intoxicated and as a result were wholly or partly to blame for the accident.

**[8.12]** In granting an order for dismissal of the proceedings against the first and second defendants (on the basis of estoppel), Morris P said that he was:

> "satisfied that from a practical point of view the claim which [the plaintiff] now seeks to make against the first and second-named defendants is of minimal value. In paragraphs 3 to 8 of the amended Statement of Claim it is apparent that, whilst the plaintiff may have attended at the premises of the first or second-named defendant at the outset, he visited another licensed premises thereafter and in fact was driven back to his car by the sixth and seventh-named defendants [who were] the owners of [a named public house] so as to enable him to collect his car at a time when, it is alleged, he was 'obviously intoxicated'. It may well be that any negligence there was on the part of the first and second-named defendants in providing alcohol to the plaintiff would have been overwhelmed by the alleged negligence of the remaining defendants, if established."

**[8.13]** It would, perhaps, be unwise to place too much emphasis on Morris P's observations, which were made on a motion, without having heard the evidence. It is noteworthy, nonetheless, that Morris P appeared not to be too disturbed about the general proposition that a publican can be liable in negligence for serving too much drink to a patron who later crashes his or her car. Morris P limited himself to the question of causation. In this context it should be noted that it would not be necessary for the later drinks to have been supplied negligently; the supply would be capable of breaking the causal connection (depending, of course, on the evidence) even where those supplying the drinks did so in ignorance of how much the plaintiff had already consumed.[29]

**[8.14]** Some of these considerations are reflected in the approach of the law towards the responsibility of carriers for injury caused by intoxicated persons whom they permit to use their transport. In *Adderley v GN Ry Co*,[30] the plaintiff was injured when a drunken

---

28. High Court, 27 February 1998 (Morris P). See Moore Walsh 'The Roundabout Tavern Settlement: A Reflection of American Publican Liability' (2000) 13 Ir LT (ns) 205. See also *Joy v Newall (t/a The Copper Room)* [2000] NI 91, where the Court of Appeal of Northern Ireland, in a considered judgment, with full reference to commonwealth authorities, declined to impose liability on a publican for injuries sustained by an intoxicated customer who fell off a bar stool. The Court's analysis was hostile to recognising any duty of care for injuries accruing to intoxicated patrons who drive dangerously.

29. The plaintiff's claim against two other defendants was settled on 14 October 1998: see Cleary, 'Insurers put pressure to settle case, says publican', Irish Times, 15 October 1998.

30 [1905] 2 IR 378 (CA). *Cf Kerr v Belfast & Co Down Ry Co* (1897) 31 ILT & Sol J 256 (QBD) - no liability where disturbance arose on train, there was no question of drink being involved. See also *Cannon v Midland GW Ry (Ireland) Co* (1879) 6 LR Ir 199 (CA) - unruly crowd of harvest-men waiting in a station for a special train at a reduced fare rushed forward, causing other passengers to be killed by the train; railway company not liable for not providing extra staff to control the crowd.

passenger, in an altercation with the defendant company's porter, broke a window of a train in which the plaintiff was being transported. FitzGibbon LJ stated that:

> "when the Company chooses to accept a drunken passenger, the measure of responsibility is to be governed by the same principle which regulates the responsibility of carriers of dangerous things. A carrier who accepts a dog, or a carboy of vitriol, does not become absolutely answerable for everything that may happen, but he accepts a responsibility, and he undertakes a duty, regulated by the nature and circumstances of the case. It was the duty of the man who checked the ticket to use reasonable care to admit no one who was dangerous, and if he did allow a man to come in who was ... 'obviously drunk', it became the duty of the Company to take due and reasonable care, having regard to his condition, to prevent any inconvenient or injurious consequences to other passengers arising from his condition."[31]

**[8.15]** In *McKevitt v Ireland*[32] the members of the Supreme Court were agreed that gardaí owed a duty to an intoxicated plaintiff in their custody in a cell at a garda station to take all reasonable steps to ensure that he would not injure himself accidentally or deliberately. Thus, they were obliged to carry out a proper search to ensure that he was not carrying any boxes of matches and to respond to any intimation that he would start a fire in his cell.[33]

**[8.16]** In *Byrne v Ireland*,[34] a Circuit Court decision a year before *McKevitt*, Martin J had dealt with the same duty issue, in regard to somewhat different facts. A 39-year-old woman, Mrs Phillips, was arrested by the Gardaí for being drunk and disorderly and placed in a cell in a Garda station. That evening she died when a fire broke out in her cell. The Gardaí had checked Mrs Phillips in her cell at regular intervals. The last time was at 7.15 pm, when the sergeant said she was shouting and muttering; fifteen minutes later, he noticed smoke coming from the door of the cell block. He and other Gardaí tried unsuccessfully to rescue Mrs Phillips.[35] A matchbox was later found in the cell and, Martin J held, Mrs Phillips probably also had had cigarettes. Martin J found the Gardaí negligent in having failed adequately to search Mrs Phillips before placing her in a cell. He attributed this failure to "reasons of delicacy". Garda regulations made it clear that women were to be searched by a female searcher. Martin J observed that, if a telephone call had

30. (contd) Contrast *Murphy v GN Ry* [1897] 2 IR 301 (CA affg QBD), where lack of supervision was not pleaded. See also *Devlin v GN Ry Co (Ireland)* [1936] Ir Jur 55 (NI HC, KB). *Cf* Rose (1977) 40 MLR 420, at 431; *Siegl v Sylvester* (1987) 47 DLR (49) 97 (BC SC). In *Quinn v James Nevin Appearances* DPIJ: Hilary and Easter Terms 1993, p 242 (High Court, 24 February 1993, Geoghegan J), liability was imposed on the organisers of a bingo session where the person in charge caused an unruly exodus from the hall, in which the plaintiff was injured, by stating that there was a risk of an explosion from a hissing sound (which was later traced harmlessly, to the amplification system rather than the gas heaters). The lack of an effective stewarding system to deal with an emergency exacerbated the negligence. *Cf* the harsh decision of the Supreme Court of Canada in *Bradford v Kanellos* (1973) 40 DLR (3d) 578.

31. [1905] 2 IR at 405-406. See also *Murgatroyd v Blackburn & Over Darwen Tramway Co* 3 TLR 451 (CA, 1887).

32. [1987] ILRM 541 (SC, 1986). For a comprehensive analysis of the civil liability of members of the Garda Síochána see Walsh *The Irish Police: A Legal and Constitutional Perspective*, (1998), Ch 10.

33. The Court ordered a re-trial of the issue of liability because the trial judge had left the negligence issue to the jury as one question rather than two. The case is scarcely a strong precedent on the duty issue in view of the fact that there was "no dispute" between the parties as to the duty owed by the Gardaí to persons in their custody: at 548.

34. Circuit Court, 28 January 1985 (Judge Martin); Irish Times, 29 January 1985, p 8, col 4.

35. Judge Martin commended the bravery of the gardaí concerned.

been made to a station nearby for a ban-gharda to search Mrs Phillips, "the regrettable fatality would not have occurred".

## III. Duty to Control Others

**[8.17]** Formerly the Courts were not disposed to impose liability for failure to provide against the misconduct (whether intentional or negligent) of other persons. As late as 1897, O'Brien J, in *Murphy v GN Ry Co* asserted that "there is no rule of law that obliges persons to provide against the possible misconduct of others".[36] However, even in 1897 it is probable that this statement went too far, and nowadays it is accepted that it may be negligent to facilitate the commission of a dangerous act by others, either by lack of control or the provision of inadequate protection,[37] lack of warning,[38] failure to remove a source of danger created by a person falling within one's "area of influence",[39] or by the creation of a source of temptation.[40]

**[8.18]** Thus, in *Cahill v Kenneally*,[41] the driver of a bus left it unattended, with two passengers in it and with the ignition capable of being switched on merely by turning a knob. One of the passengers succeeded in starting the bus and drove it against the plaintiff's car. Liability was imposed on the bus owner for the negligence of the driver in facilitating the act which caused the damage.[42] On the other hand, in *Whelan v Eason & Sons*,[43] a motorist visiting a hotel, who placed his car in the porter's charge with

---

36. [1897] 2 IR 301 at 308-309 (QBD).

37. In the United States, victims of criminal injury have sued their employers, landlords, carriers and hotel proprietors for negligent failure to protect them against foreseeable attacks: see PROSSER & KEETON, p 383; Ballou 'Recourse for Rape Victims: Third Party Liability' (1981) 4 Harv Women's LJ 105; Carrington 'Victims' Rights Litigation: A Wave of the Future?' (1977) 11 U Richmond LR 447 at 459; Hanson & Thomas 'Third Party Tort Remedies for Crime Victims - Searching for the "Deep Pocket" and a Risk Free Society' (1988) 18 Stetson LR 1.

38. *Cf Crowe v Brennan* [1967] IR 5 (SC).

39. *Cf* Murnaghan J's judgment in *McGowan v Masterson* [1953] IR 101 at 106 (SC), discussed at paras **[24.89]-[24.92]** below.

40. See generally Harper & Kime 'The Duty to Control the Conduct of Another' (1934) 43 Yale LJ 886; Eldredge 'Culpable Intervention as Superseding Liability for Negligence' (1940) 24 Minn LR 635; Weinrib 'The Dorset Yacht Case: Causation, Care and Criminals' (1971) 4 Ottawa LR 389; Hanson 'Escaping Borstal Boys and the Immunity of Police' [1969] Camb LJ 273.

41. [1955-1956] Ir Jur 15 (CC). See also *Davoren v Fitzpatrick* [1935] Ir Jur 23 (CC) – was a car started by children. See, however *Byrne v Dun Laoghaire Corporation* [1940] Ir Jur 40 (HC) - children made a see-saw out of roadworks materials, a child was injured, defendant was held not liable for letting materials be appropriated by the children; *Hewson v City of Red Deer* 146 DLR (3d) 32 (Alta SC, App Div, 1977 – keys were left in the ignition in a tractor during a coffee break late at night; interference was held not to be reasonably foreseeable. See generally Von Wald 'Comment: Failure to Remove Ignition Key - The Key to Liability' (1969) 14 S Dakota LR 115; Young, 'Negligent Parking of Automobiles' (1965) 14 Clev - Mar LR 356 at 362-364; Peck, 'An Exercise Based Upon Empirical Data: Liability for Harm Caused by Stolen Automobiles', [1969] Wis LR 909.

42. See also *Weirum v RKO General Inc* (1975) 15 Cal 3d 40, 539 P 2d 36, 723 Cal Rptr 468 - radio station was held liable for the death of a road user killed by a car driven recklessly by teenagers rushing to a location named on the radio where a peripatetic disc jockey was giving away money to first comers.

43. [1939] Ir Jur 25 (HC), affg [1939] Ir Jur 22 (CC).

instructions to place it in the hotel garage, was held not to have been bound to anticipate that the porter would instead take the car for a joy ride and injure the plaintiff.

**[8.19]** For liability to attach, the persons who cause the damage need not necessarily themselves be guilty of actionable negligence. They may, for instance, be children acting as children are wont to do.

**[8.20]** In *Curley v Mannion*,[44] the plaintiff cyclist was injured when the defendant's thirteen-year-old daughter suddenly opened the door of the defendant's car in which she was a passenger. The trial judge withdrew the case from the jury, but the Supreme Court held that there was evidence of negligence which should have gone to the jury. Ó Dálaigh CJ stated simply that, in his judgment:

> "a person in charge of a motor car must take reasonable precautions for the safety of others, and this will include the duty to take reasonable care to prevent conduct on the part of passengers which is negligent. In the present case that duty is, it seems to me, reinforced by the relationship of parent and child; and a parent, while not liable for the torts of his child, may be liable if negligent in failing to exercise his control to prevent his child injuring others."[45]

**[8.21]** More expansively, but in very clear terms, Walsh J stated:

> "In my view the defendant, as the owner and driver of the motor car in question, owed a duty to other persons using the highway not merely not to use or drive the car negligently but to take reasonable precautions to ensure that the car, while under his control and supervision, was not used in a negligent fashion. It would indeed be a startling proposition that a person in charge of a motor vehicle on the public highway should not owe any duty to third parties save in respect of his own negligent act in the use of the vehicle, or in respect of omissions relating to his own use of the vehicle, and that he should not be liable in negligence for failing to take reasonable steps to prevent the negligent use of a motor car by a passenger therein while it is under his control and supervision when such negligent use is actually known to or ought to be foreseen by him."[46]

**[8.22]** Regarding the specific negligent conduct alleged against the defendant, Walsh J stated:

> "In the streets of a town the opening and closing of doors on the traffic side of a stationary motor car is so notoriously fraught with danger that a person in control of a motor car who permits this to be done in his motor car without first ascertaining that it is safe to do so or without taking reasonable steps to ensure that it is done without danger, is in my view failing in the duty which he, as the person in control and supervision of the motor car, owes to the other users of the highways."[47]

**[8.23]** The Courts are not, however, disposed to impose too heavy a burden on a defendant to guard against the intentional wrongdoing of adults. Thus, in *Purcell v Dublin County Council*,[48] the Supreme Court held that the plaintiff's case had been correctly withdrawn from the jury where he claimed that the defendant county council had been negligent in

44. [1965] IR 543 (SC); *Cf Ware's Taxi Ltd v Gilliham* [1949] SCR 637.
45. At 546.
46. At 549.
47. *Cf Moan v Moan* [1984] NILR Bull No 3 (CA).
48. Supreme Court, 28 July 1957.

failing to keep a night watchman on duty or arranging for some form of periodic inspection where it had created an obstruction on the road. The defendant had placed storm lamps around the obstruction but these had been deliberately extinguished "by some evilly disposed person or persons".[49]

**[8.24]** Maguire CJ stated:

> "It is said on behalf of the County Council that it had fulfilled its duty to give warning of danger by placing the lighted lamps in position, that they had no reason to anticipate that the lamps would not remain burning during the hours of darkness and that there was no evidence which entitled the Jury to say that the County Council should have anticipated that the lamps would deliberately be put out by evilly disposed persons as happened on this occasion. The court accepts this contention."[50]

**[8.25]** Nevertheless, certain relationships impose an obligation on one party to protect others from injury resulting from the intentional conduct of the other party.[51] Thus, a psychiatrist or a mental hospital may be liable for injury caused by a patient who is negligently released from, or not committed to, appropriate medical care, or by a patient who is allowed to escape[52] or otherwise cause injury.[53] Similarly, a prison or other custodial institution may be legally responsible for damage or injury caused by an inmate who

---

49. Page 1 of Maguire CJ's judgment. *Cf Murphy v GN Ry Co* [1897] 2 IR 301 at 308-309 (QB, affd by CA). See also *Whooley v Dublin Corporation,* [1961] IR 60 (HC); *Kavanagh v Cork Corporation* DPIJ: Hilary and Easter Terms 1994, p 78 (HC, 24 January 1994, Keane J).

50. Page 4 of Maguire CJ's judgment. See also *Victor Weston (Éire) Ltd v Kenny* [1954] IR 191 (HC) - landlord was held liable for flooding caused by the failure of a person using a basin on premises to turn off the tap, which, on account of a choked waste-pipe, led to flooding of the premises. *Cf O'Brien v Waterford County Council* [1926] IR 1 (SC); *Sheppard v Northern Ireland Housing Executive* [1984] NILR Bull No 1 (HC). In Britain, the courts have made plain their considerable reluctance to impose liability on proprietors of premises subject to acts of vandalism by trespassers save when they are aware of a real risk of injury to neighbours: see *Smith v Littlewoods Organisation Ltd* [1987] AC 241; *Perl (P) (Exporters) Ltd v Camden London BC* [1984] QB 342; *King v Liverpool City Council* [1986] 3 All ER 544.

51. *Cf Tarasoff v Regents of University of California* (1976) 529 P 2d 553, 118 Cal Rptr 129 (1974), and 17 Cal 3d 425, 131 Cal Rptr 14, 551 P 2d 334, critically analysed by Stone 'The *Tarasoff* Decisions: Suing Psychotherapists to Safeguard Society' (1976) 90 Harv LR 358; see also *Bradley Center Inc v Wessner* (1982) 250 Ga 199, 296 SE 2d 693, analysed by Kyle 'Comment: From *Tarasoff* to *Bradley*: Courts Struggle to Apply the Duty to Control Mental Patients' (1984) 14 Camb LR 165; and see *Austin W Jones Co v State* (1923) 122 Md 214, 119 A 577. *Cf Thorne v Western Australia* [1964] WAR 147; Hirsh 'Physicians' Liability to Nonpatients - a Panoramic View' 1 L Med Q 211 at 211-212 (1977). See generally Cohen 'Note: *Tarasoff v Regents of University of California*: The Duty to Warn: Common Law and Statutory Problems for California Psychotherapists' (1978) 14 Cal WLR 153, Griffith & Griffith 'Duty to Third Parties, Dangerousness and the Right to Refuse Treatment; Problematic Concepts for Psychiatrist and Lawyer' (1978) 14 Cal WLR 241; Slovenko 'Psychotherapy and Confidentiality' (1975) 24 Clev St LR 375.

52. *Cf Holgate v Lancashire Mental Hospitals Board* [1937] 4 All ER 19. Contrast *C v North Western Health Board* [1997] Ir L Log W 133 (CC).

53. *Cf* Brandt 'Liability of Custodial Institutions for Torts of Patient-Inmates' (1977) 1 Legal Med Q 193.

should not have been let out[54] or should otherwise have been kept under control.[55] So also landlords,[56] employers,[57] hoteliers,[58] carriers,[59] and disco proprietors,[60] as well as school proprietors[61] and parents[62] may be liable where they fail to take reasonable steps to ensure that those in their charge do not injure others.

---

54. *Home Office v Dorset Yacht Co* [1970] AC 1004, analysed in Weinrib 'The Dorset Yacht Case: Causation, Care and Criminals' (1971) 4 Ottawa LR 389; Hanson 'Escaping Borstal Boys and the Immunity of Police' [1969] Camb LJ 273; *Grimm v Arizona Bd of Pardons & Paroles* (1977) 115 Ariz 260, 564 P 2d 1227; *Estate of Armstrong v Pennsylvania Bd of Probation and Parole* (1979) 46 Pa Commw 33, 405 A 2d 1099; see, however, *Thompson v County of Alameda* (1980) 27 Cal 3d 741, 167 Cal Rep 70, 614 P 2d 728 (with strong dissent by Tobriner J), Carrington 'Victim's Rights Litigation: A Wave of the Future?' (1977) 11 U Richmond LR 447 at 460-465. In *Hill v Chief Constable of West Yorkshire* [1989] AC 53, the House of Lords held that police officers should be immune from a duty of care to potential victims of criminals in regard to their detection and apprehension. To impose such a duty, in its view, would lead to "defensive" policing and a diversion of scarce resources. The police have been held immune from a duty of care to respond to burglar alarms (*Alexandrou v Oxford* [1993] 4 All ER 328) or to protect roadusers from hazards such as a road or which diesel fuel has spilled (*Ancell v McDermott* [1993] 4 All ER 355) or a road junction where the traffic lights are out of order (*Clough v Bussan* [1990] 1 All ER 431). A duty of care can, however, result from the assumption of responsibility, as where an informant is assured of confidentiality (*Swinney v Chief Constable of the Northumbria Police* [1997] QB 464), or where a police officer assumes the responsibility to act on his or her "police duty" to go to the assistance of a fellow officer in danger. The English Court of Appeal so held in *Costello v Chief Constable of the Northumbria Police* [1999] 1 All ER 550, though it failed to clarify the precise scope of this "police duty" or to explain how the notion of assumption of responsibility in this case was other than a cloak for the ascription of responsibility. The European Court of Human Rights, in its decision in *Osman v UK*, [1999] 1 FLR 193, has cast doubt on the principles underlying *Hill*. There are early signs that *Osman* has already had an impact: see *Waters v Commissioner of Police of the Metropolis* [2000] 1 WLR 1607 (HL); *Gibson v Chief Constable of Strathclyde Police* 1999 SC 420 (Outer House of the Court of Session, Lord Hamilton).
55. *Cf* Levin Flight 'Flee, Submit, Sue: Alternatives for Sexually Assaulted Prisoners' (1985) 18 Col J of L & Soc Problems 505 at 522-523.
56. *Cf Kline v 1500 Massachusetts Avenue Apartment Corporation* (1970) 439 F 2d 477 (DC Cir); *Braitman v Overlook Terrace Corporation* (1975) 68 NJ 368, 346 A d 76; *Butler v Acme Markets, Inc* (1982) 89 NJ 270 445 A 2d 114. From a somewhat different standpoint, *cf Brooke v Bool* [1928] 2 KB 578. See generally Lesar 'Tort Liability of Illinois Landlords for Crimes of Third Persons' [1983] S Illinois ULJ 415; Maynard 'Landlord's Liability for Criminal Acts Committed Against His Tenants' (1970) 7 Calif WLR 197. Haines 'Landlords or Tenants: Who Bears the Cost of Crime' (1981) 2 Cardozo LR 299.
57. *Cf* Ch 18 below. See also Kime & Harper 'The Duty to Control the Conduct of Another' (1934) 9 Indiana LJ 498 at 515-516.
58. *Cf* FLEMING, pp 139, 435; *Garzilli v Howard Johnson's Motor Lodges Inc* (1976) 419 F Supp 1210 (EDNY).
59. *Cf* FLEMING p 168; Kime & Harper 'The Duty to Control the Conduct of Another' (1934) 9 Indiana LJ 498 at 515-516.
60. *Cf Clohessey v Tara Club Ltd* Circuit Court, Evening Press p 5, 25 March 1985 (Judge Smith) - a disco was not liable where a plate was thrown by an unknown person, without provocation or prior warning and injured the plaintiff. In *McCarthy v Skibbereen UDC* Doyle's Personal Injury Judgements: Hilary and Easter Terms 1995, p 5 (High Court, 25 January 1995, O'Hanlon J), liability was imposed on the organisers of a disco for failing to prevent, or, alternatively, to stop rowdy behaviour resulting in injury to the plaintiff.
61. *Cf* para **[16.16]** below.
62. *Cf* para **[16.02]** below.

**[8.26]** Bar-room assaults have frequently resulted in litigation by the injured person against the proprietors of the bar. In *Hall v Kennedy*,[63] Morris J held that proprietors of a public house had not been guilty of negligence in failing to prevent an assault on the plaintiff, a customer, by another customer. The violent customer had shown "none of the signs or manifestations of drink such as should have alerted a reasonable publican or his staff to the prospect that he might assault another customer"[64]. The assailant's "hot-headed, spontaneous"[65] response to what he had regarded as an insult by the plaintiff could not have been foreseen by the publican.

**[8.27]** Morris J set out with commendable succinctness the relevant principles of law:

> "The obligation of the [publican] at law is to take all reasonable care for the safety of the [customer] while on the premises. This would include in this case ensuring that [another] customer in the premises did not assault him. The necessary steps would include, in an appropriate case, removing such a customer from the premises, refusing to serve him drink [and] staffing the bar with sufficient barmen or security staff so as to ensure the safety of the [customer]".[66]

**[8.28]** *Hall v Kennedy* may be contrasted with *Walsh v Ryan*,[67] where Lavan J imposed liability on a publican when a female customer was seriously assaulted on the premises by another customer who had arrived at the premises in a drunken condition and caused a row. He had been served drink while in the premises. The publican had evicted the plaintiff and the assailant from the premises and declined to call an ambulance for the plaintiff. The defendant knew the assailant and had been aware of his violent or unruly propensity for a considerable time previously. The defendant had had to intervene twice in the row which the assailant had caused and which culminated in the assault.

**[8.29]** Lavan J rejected the plaintiff's argument that, by virtue of ss 13 and 19 of the Licensing Act 1872, the defendant was negligent in that he had permitted drunkenness on his premises and had failed to exclude a drunkard from his premises. Lavan J observed that

> "[t]hese two sections of the Act ... create two statutory offences[;] they do not, in my view, constitute evidence of negligence."[68]

**[8.30]** The plaintiff also contended, successfully, that the defendant was liable as an occupier of the premises. Lavan, J characterised the plaintiff as a contractual invitee, in regard to whom the defendant owed a duty to take reasonable care to ensure that his premises were conducted without risk. In view of the defendant's knowledge of the assailant's drunkenness and propensity towards violence and his two interventions in the row, that duty had been violated.

**[8.31]** It is interesting to speculate as to the effect of the enactment of the Occupiers Liability Act 1995 in this context. That legislation limits itself to dangers "due to the state

---

63. High Court, 20 December 1993 (Morris J).
64. Page 5 of Morris J's judgment.
65. Page 5 of Morris J's judgment.
66. Page 5 of Morris, J's judgment. See also *Nolan v Fergus* Doyle's Personal Injury Judgements: Hilary and Easter Terms 1994, p 161 (High Court, 18 January 1994, Kinlen J) - no liability was held as sudden violent assault by another person could not have been foreseen.
67. High Court, 12 February 1993 (Lavan J).
68. Page 7 of Lavan, J's judgment.

of the premises".[69] It is open to a customer who has been assaulted by another, violent, customer to contend that the publican's duty of care is based on a proximity of relationship that depends on the commercial context rather than the publican's status as occupier. If a court were to insist on treating the case as one falling within the scope of the legislation, the injured customer, as a "visitor", would surely have as strong a claim since the duty of an occupier to a visitor is in essence one of negligence. The question whether the legislation covers cases such as this is not, however, merely an academic one. In certain circumstances it can have a crucial significance. In a case where the injured customer had himself or herself played an active role in a brawl, then if the legislation governed the case, he or she would be characterised as a criminal entrant to whom the publican would owe only the duty not to intentionally injure him or her.[70] Accordingly, the belligerent plaintiff could not succeed. Under common law principles of negligence, the court might, of course, find that in the circumstances the plaintiff was guilty of contributory negligence and reduce his or her damages; it might even apply the *ex turpi causa* principle in a particularly egregious case. However, there is no rule at common law which in all such cases defeats the plaintiff's claim *in limine*.

**[8.32]** The prison authorities may be liable for failure to take due care to protect prisoners in their charge from being injured by other prisoners. In *Muldoon v Ireland*,[71] the plaintiff, who was serving a prison sentence in Arbour Hill, was suddenly attacked from behind by another prisoner during a recreation period in the prison recreation yard. The other prisoner later admitted to having used a blade, though this had not been recovered by the authorities at the scene of the assault. At the time the incident occurred there were around forty or fifty prisoners in the yard, with several supervisors - ten or twelve, according to the plaintiff; seventeen, according to the evidence of the Chief Officer. No search of any prisoner had apparently taken place before the recreation period that day. It appeared that prisoners were searched initially when committed into custody and that searches, of their person and their cells, were made on a very regular basis. Moreover, before and after they went to the workshops, an inventory was made of all implements, supplemented by a rub down search of all prisoners when they were leaving the workshop.

**[8.33]** The plaintiff sued Ireland and the Attorney General, claiming that the prison authorities had been guilty of negligence. Hamilton P withdrew the case from the jury. He considered that no case had been made out based on the lack of staff on duty in the yard to exercise proper supervision. In view of the sudden, unprovoked nature of the attack, the incident could not have been prevented even if there were fifty officers in the yard. Nor could it be said that the prison authorities had been wanting in care in permitting a prisoner to reach the recreation yard with a sharp instrument such as a blade. Reasonable care did not dictate that every prisoner should be searched every time he moved from one area of

---

69. Section 1(1) of the of the Occupiers Liability Act 1995.

70. Section 4(3). The most the plaintiff could hope for would be that the court would hold that justice required it in the circumstances to impose a duty on the publican not to be reckless in regard to the plaintiff.

71. [1988] ILRM 367 (HC). See also *Ellis v Home Office* [1953] 2 All ER 149 (CA); *Steele v Northern Ireland Office* [1988] NILR Bull 1 (QBD). For a comprehensive analysis of civil liability of prison authorities for injuries caused by fellow prisoners, see McDermott, *Prison Law* (2000), pp 232-249.

the prison to another. In spite of the regime of searches prevailing in the prison, an incident such as arose in the present care could always happen. More frequent searches would without doubt be regarded by the prisoners as excessive, and arguably would amount to harassment of them.

**[8.34]** In *Kavanagh v Governor of Arbour Hill Prison*,[72] on somewhat similar facts, Morris P reached the same conclusion, acquitting the prison authorities of negligence.

**[8.35]** *Boyd v Ireland*,[73] concerned an attack on the prisoner by co-prisoners in the exercise yard of Portlaoise prison. The deputy governor of the prison testified that it was not the practice to search prisoners from the block where these prisoners were housed as they were going into the exercise yard as by and large they were well behaved. In the past fifteen years, there had been no incidents in the yard.

**[8.36]** As to supervision of the yard, Budd J noted that the deputy governor had explained that, "after an incident on 30 December 1974", prison officers and Garda "had been in the exercise yard but that this had caused constant confrontation between the staff, the prisoners and the garda". Eventually the staff had been placed outside a chain-link fence surrounding the yard. There was no need for prison officers to be in the yard and it was also understandable for security reasons. Budd J dismissed the plaintiff's case. In his view, there had been no failure to provide adequate searches of the prisoners or to supervise them adequately.

**[8.37]** In the Supreme Court decision of *Bates v Minister for Justice*,[74] the plaintiff, a prisoner in Limerick prison was the victim of a horrific attack by another prisoner, who threw a jug of hot water containing sugar in his face, as well as striking him with a heavy object and cutting him with a knife or blade. The basis of the plaintiff's case in negligence was that hot water should not have been made available to prisoners in the way that the prison authorities had permitted. Johnson J rejected the claim and the Supreme Court affirmed.

**[8.38]** The area where the incident took place housed seven or eight high security prisoners in separate cells. It was supervised by five prison officers. The system in place was that breakfast food was brought to a room in the area; the prisoners were released from their cells, collected the food and returned to their cells where they ate it. To that extent, as Murphy J[75] noted, breakfast was a form of self-service. The prisoners made their own tea. Since 1987, there as an electrically operated boiler in the area, which maintained the water at a permanent temperature during the breakfast period. The prisoners filled teapots or jugs from the boiler. They then usually took the water to their own cell or, at their choice, to a fellow inmate's cell. In the instant case, the assailant was seen by the prison officers to go to the plaintiff's cell with his hot water. This was not regarded as unusual or undesirable by the prison authorities or by the prisoners who gave evidence.

**[8.39]** The essence of the plaintiff's case was that, in contrast to the cases where unsuccessful actions for negligence against the prison authorities involved the use of

72. High Court, 22 April 1993 (Morris P).
73. High Court, 13 May 1993 (Budd J).
74. Supreme Court, 4 March 1998.
75. Lynch and Barron JJ concurring.

weapons unlawfully taken into the prison, in the instant case the weapon - the jug of hot water - had actually been provided by the prison authorities. The plaintiff's criticism was not that the general level of supervision was inadequate, but that, having regard to the known propensity of some of the inmates to violence and the obvious danger to prisoners and wardens from the throwing of hot water or tea, the availability of these missiles should have been more carefully supervised. The authorities, his counsel contended, should not have permitted one prisoner to enter the cell of another carrying a container full of hot water.

**[8.40]** Murphy J rejected this argument on the basis that its logic was that one prisoner could not be permitted to have such a container anywhere in the presence of another inmate or indeed a prison officer as it would be impossible to prevent an assault with the hot liquid although it might be possible to prevent the incident from escalating. Moreover, there would be little difficulty in identifying the culprit and imposing sanctions.

**[8.41]** Murphy J rejected other systems for providing tea which had been canvassed. Transporting large urns of tea that had already been brewed in the kitchen - an option that had been tried before 1987 and which was resurrected after the assault - "involved some dangers and difficulties in the transportation of the tea but more particularly the addition of milk to the urns was resented by some prisoners who preferred to have their tea without milk." Requiring the inmates to drink their tea in a single room together would merely transfer the problem from the cells to that room. Service of the hot water to each inmate in his cell "might afford a solution but would involve a major change in the management of the prison and perhaps a risk to security." Furthermore, if the tea or hot water was to be served by other prisoners, these prisoners would have the potential for causing injury.

**[8.42]** There was, in Murphy J's view, no obvious way for serving tea of a reasonable quality and temperature to prisoners whereby their safety could be ensured without causing an excessive hardship on the prisoners or an excessive burden on the prison authorities:

> "No doubt prison management is a constant battle between the need to preserve security and safety on the one hand and on the other hand, the obligation to recognise the constitutional rights of the prisoners and their dignity as human beings. Procedures for the provision of food and hot drink and the means by and the location in which it will be provided will require to be reviewed from time to time but it would seem unfortunate if the requirements of safety precluded access to tea or necessitated further restrictions on communal eating and social intercourse between the inmates. It is a difficult balance to achieve but it is in that context that the duty of care owed by the defendants to the plaintiff must be tested."

**[8.43]** Ultimately cases of this nature had to depend on what should have been anticipated by the prison authorities. The wardens had been unaware of any antagonism by his assailant to the plaintiff. Neither ought they have known of any objection by the plaintiff or other prisoners to any other inmate visiting them in their cells. There was obviously a danger that boiling water could be thrown but "there was no evidence to suggest that there was any particular risk to inmates from such conduct; only to wardens."

**[8.44]** As one views these decisions, from *Muldoon* to *Bates*, one has to ask whether the courts have adopted a tacit policy decision to dismiss actions by prisoners against prison authorities for negligent supervision save in egregious cases. Prisons are potentially violent, dangerous places, filled with risk for prisoners. If, as in *Boyd*, a strategic withdrawal two decades previously by prison officers from the exercise yard can be regarded as tolerable protection of the prisoners within (to avoid "constant confrontation" with the prisoners) and if, as in *Bates*, the preference by some prisoners to have their tea without milk was a factor in leading the authorities to adopt a system with inherent and obvious dangers to other prisoners, then it will have to be a case of supreme neglect or systematic incompetence of the highest order before compensation will be awarded to prisoners who are the victims of assault by other prisoners.

Chapter 9

# Proof of Negligence


I. Introduction ........................................ 185
II. Res Ipsa Loquitur ........................................ 187
III. The *Hanrahan* Restatement of the *Res Ipsa Loquitur* Doctrine ........................................ 199


## I. Introduction

**[9.01]** As a general rule a plaintiff in an action for negligence must plead and prove negligence[1] on the part of the defendant in order to succeed. The plaintiff must convince the judge, on the balance of probabilities, that the defendant was negligent. Anything less will not be sufficient.

**[9.02]** Where there was a judge and a jury in a negligence action, each served important different functions. The position was well expressed by Lord Cairns in an English decision in 1877:

> "The judge has to say whether any facts have been established by evidence from which negligence may reasonably be inferred; the jurors have to say whether, from these facts ... negligence ought to be inferred. It is ... of the greatest importance in the administration of justice that these separate functions should be maintained, and should be maintained distinct. It would be a serious inroad on the province of the jury if, in a case where there are facts from which negligence may reasonably be inferred, the judge were to withdraw the case from the jury upon the ground that, in his opinion, negligence ought not to be inferred and it would, on the other hand, place in the hands of the jurors a power which might be exercised in the most arbitrary manner, if they were at liberty to hold that negligence might be inferred from any state of facts whatever."[2]

This statement has received the approval of the Supreme Court.[3]

**[9.03]** In 1988, as we have seen, juries were abolished generally in relation to personal injuries litigation. This had been the position in Circuit Court proceedings for many years prior to that. Similarly, the District Judge acts without a jury in such cases. The distinction between establishing that negligence may reasonably be inferred and establishing that, on the balance of probabilities, it ought to be reasonably inferred is accordingly given less attention nowadays in proceedings in courts where the fact finder is a judge. This has had the effect of muddying the waters in relation to the doctrine of *res ipsa loquitur*.[4]

**[9.04]** As has been mentioned, the plaintiff must show on the balance of probabilities that the defendant was guilty of negligent conduct which caused the accident. Mere surmise

1. *Cf O'Rourke v McGuinness* [1942] IR 554 at 557 (SC). So also with proving the plaintiff's contributory negligence: *cf Scanlon v Abbey Service (Galway) Ltd* [1965] IR 700 (SC).
2. [1965] IR 700 (SC). *Metropolitan Ry Co v Jackson* (1877) 3 AC 193 at 207.
3. *Cf Gallagher v ESB* [1933] IR 558 (SC). In *O'Leary v O'Connell* [1968] IR 149 at 152-153 (SC).
4. *Cf* para **[9.11]** *et seq* below.

will not be sufficient. In *Mahon v Dublin & Lucan Electric Railway Co*,[5] the body of the plaintiff's husband was found by a policeman on a railway line in front of an engine, which had been derailed. These facts clearly indicated that the man had died as a result of a collision with the train, but the evidence went very little further, other than to indicate that the deceased had been sober shortly before the collision. In upholding a directed verdict for the defendant, Lord O'Brien LCJ stated briefly that the Court was "of opinion that there is no evidence of actionable negligence".[6]

**[9.05]** The facts in *Mahon's* case are similar to those in the English decision of *Wakelin v London & SW Ry Co*,[7] where the House of Lords adopted the same approach as the Irish King's Bench Division.

**[9.06]** This does not mean, however, that the plaintiff "has got to have a story"[8] which explains how the accident occurred:

> "All that is required for a plaintiff to succeed is to establish facts from which an inference of negligence on the part of the defendant may reasonably be inferred . . . 'It is a mistake to think that because an event is unseen its cause cannot be reasonably inferred.'[9]"[10]

**[9.07]** Thus, in *O'Rourke v McGuinness*,[11] the Supreme Court held that an inference of negligence could be drawn where, after a collision between the plaintiff's car and the defendant's lorry, the lorry was lying on the plaintiff's side of the road and impact marks were also found on that side of the road. In holding that the trial Judge should not have withdrawn the case from the jury, Sullivan CJ stated:

> "From that evidence the jury could in my opinion legitimately have drawn the inference that at the time of the collision the lorry was entirely on its wrong side of the road without any apparent reason, that this caused the collision and that the lorry driver was negligent. I do not say the lorry driver was negligent. I do not say that the jury would have been bound to draw that inference in the absence of any evidence by the defendant, but I am satisfied that they would have been entitled to do so if they thought fit"[12]

**[9.08]** Similarly, in *Denniston v McNamara, Maxwell & Co*,[13] where the plaintiff swallowed a tack when eating a slice of bread baked by the defendant, Judge Gleeson, of the Circuit Court, considered it "a reasonable inference of fact that [the tack] was in the loaf before it left the defendant's premises" and imposed liability on the defendants.

---

5. (1905) 39 ILTR 126 (KB).
6. (1905) 39 ILTR 126 at 127. See also *Walsh v Cronin* Supreme Court, 4 November 1935 where Ua Cinnéidigh CJ considered that "a jury steeling their hearts to considerations of sympathy" for the plaintiff widow could not on the evidence find that a case of negligence had been made out. *Cf Motor Vehicle Assurance Fund v Dubuzane* 1984 (1) SA 700 (App Div).
7. (1886) 12 AC 41.
8. *Gahan v Engineering Products Ltd* [1971] IR 30 at 32 (SC).
9. *Jones v GW Ry Co* (1930) 47 TLR 39 at 41.
10. *Gahan v Engineering Products Ltd* [1971] IR 30 at 32-33.
11. [1942] IR 554 (SC). See also *Reilly v Garvey* [1973] IR 89 (SC).
12. At 557. See also *Finlay v Price* [1932] NI 81 (CA) - disagreement in CA as to whether there was sufficient evidence of negligence on the part of motorist to go to jury. *Alexander v Anderson* [1933] NI 158 (CA), facts similar to *O'Rourke v McGuinness*; dissent of Moore LCJ worthy of note.
13. (1950) 84 ILTR 168 at 169 (CC). *Cf Fleming v Henry Denny & Sons* Supreme Court, 29 July 1955.

**[9.09]** In the Supreme Court decision of *Clancy v Dublin Corporation*,[14] McCarthy J (for the Court) warned that it was not sufficient:

> "to prove facts upon which a jury or, as would now be the case, a judge might properly hold that a conclusion of negligence could be inferred; ... the facts must be such that the jury or judge may on the balance of probabilities reasonably make such an inference - whether negligence ought to be inferred".

**[9.10]** The Supreme Court held that the trial judge had wrongly withdrawn the case from the jury, where the plaintiff, who had spent a number of hours drinking at his brother's home, fell down the stairs, after having descended a few steps. At about this point the handrail was defective in such a manner that a person who caught his fingers in it would be turned around. The plaintiff had been found on his back facing in the direction from which he had fallen. These facts established a prima facie case from which a jury might properly have concluded that the admittedly unsafe nature of the handrail caused or contributed to the accident.

## II. Res Ipsa Loquitur[15]

**[9.11]** The doctrine of *res ipsa loquitur* has been variously described as "one of the great mysteries of tort law",[16] and as being "curiously complex".[17] The meaning and scope of the doctrine have given rise to much discussion and no lack of confusion. It is impossible to reconcile all the decisions on the subject. The matter has been complicated still more by Henchy J's controversial restatement of the doctrine in the Supreme Court decision of *Hanrahan v Merck Sharp & Dohme (Ireland) Ltd.*[18]

### Origins of the Doctrine

**[9.12]** The doctrine of *res ipsa loquitur* traces its origins to "an off-hand remark to counsel by Chief Baron Pollock during the course of argument"[19] in *Byrne v Boadle*.[20] The plaintiff had been injured by a barrel of flour which fell from a window above the defendant's shop. The defendant did not explain how the accident occurred. The assessor granted a non-suit. On appeal to the Court of Exchequer, counsel for the defendant contended that the plaintiff

---

14. Supreme Court, 22 November 1988, at p 5.
15. See generally Lewis 'A Ramble with *Res Ipsa Loquitur*' 11 Camb LJ 74; *Paton 'Res Ipsa Loquitur'* [1954] Camb LJ 118; Atiyah '*Res Ipsa Loquitur* in England and Australia' (1972) 35 MLR 337; Schiff 'A *Res Ipsa Loquitur* Nutshell' (1976) 26 U Toronto LJ 451; Prosser '*Res Ipsa Loquitur* in California' (1949) 37 Calif LR 193; Miller 'Cases of Uncertain or Unknown Causation and Negligence: Relationship Analysis as a Real Alternative to Present Inadequate Concept' (1968) 16 U Kansas LR 209; Malone '*Res Ipsa Loquitur* and Proof by Inference - A Discussion of the Louisiana Cases' (1941) 4 La LR 70; Khan '*Res Ipsa Loquitur*: An Update' (1984) 128 Sol J 232; Anon '*Res Ipsa Loquitur*' (1950) 84 ILT & Sol J 165.
16. LINDEN, p 214.
17. SALMOND & HEUSTON, p 244.
18. [1988] ILRM 629 (SC). Finlay CJ and Hederman J concurred with Henchy J's judgment. See further para **[9.49]-[9.53]** below. In *O'Shea v Tilman Anhold and Horse Farm Ltd* Supreme Court, 23 October 1996, Keane J noted that Henchy J's judgment had been criticised and might "need to be reconsidered at some stage." Hamilton CJ reserved his position regarding this suggestion.
19. LINDEN, p 215.
20. (1863) 2 H & C 722, 159 ER 299.

"was bound to give affirmative proof of negligence. But there was not a scintilla of evidence, unless the occurrence is of itself evidence of negligence".[21] Pollock CB responded that "there are certain cases of which it may be said *res ipsa loquitur* and this seems one of them ..."[22] In his judgment Pollock CB stated that:

> "The learned counsel was quite right in saying that there are many accidents from which no presumption of negligence can arise, but I think it would be wrong to lay down as a rule that in no case can presumption of negligence arise from the fact of an accident."[23]

**[9.13]** It is fairly clear that Pollock CB "was totally unaware that he was creating a new doctrine"[24] in *Byrne v Boadle.*[25] He was speaking at a time when litigation regarding railway accidents was beginning to fashion a rule of law that a presumption of negligence should arise in certain cases - as, for example, where there was a collision between trains run by the same company.[26] Whilst there was nothing amiss in Pollock CB's making the Latin remark in *Byrne v Boadle*,[27] it was very shortly afterwards elevated to the status of a principle,[28] in respect of which some courts have been guilty of very loose language and lack of conceptual clarity.

**[9.14]** Two fundamental questions arise in relation to the principle: when will it apply and what is its procedural effect?

## When Will the Principle Apply?

**[9.15]** In *Scott v London & St Katherine Docks Co*,[29] Erle CJ, in a passage that has been very influential in subsequent decisions,[30] stated:

> "There must be reasonable evidence of negligence. But where the thing is shown to be under the management of the defendant or his servants, and the accident is such as in the ordinary circumstances does not happen if those who have the management use proper care, it affords reasonable evidence, in the absence of explanation by the defendants, that the accident arose from want of care."

**[9.16]** These elements require specific elucidation, bearing in mind the shadow of uncertainty cast by the recent decision of *Hanrahan v Merck Sharp & Dohme (Ireland) Ltd*,[31] whose implications we will examine[32] after we have set out the traditional understanding of the principle.

---

21. (1863) 2 H & C 722, 159 ER 299 at 725-726 and 300 respectively.
22. (1863) 2 H & C 722, 159 ER 299 at 726 and 300 respectively.
23. (1863) 2 H & C 722, 159 ER 299 at 727 and 301 respectively.
24. LINDEN, p 216.
25. See para **[9.12]**.
26. *Cf Skinner v LB & SC Ry* (1850) 5 Ex 787, 155 ER 345; *Ayles v SE Ry Co* (1868) LR 3 Ex 146.
27. As to its classical antecedents see Carmody '*Res Ipsa Loquitur* in an Ancient Roman Trial' (1974) 2 J of Legal Med No 6 p 41.
28. *Cf Ballard v NB Ry* 1923 SC 43 at 56 (*per* Lord Shaw): "If it had not been in Latin nobody would have called it a principle". See also Prosser '*Res Ipsa Loquitur* in California' (1949) 37 Calif LR 183 at 215.
29. (1865) 3 H & C 596 at 601, 159 ER 665 at 667.
30. In *Flannery v W & L Ry Co* (1877) IR 11 CL 30 at 38 (Exch), Palles CB described *Scott* as being "distinguished from the chaos of authorities depending on particular facts by an attempt at the application of something in the nature of principle to cases of this class". He "entirely subscribe[d]" (at 39) to the doctrine laid down in the decision.
31. [1988] ILRM 629 (SC).
32. See paras **[9.49]-[9.53]** below.

### *(a) Management of the defendant*

**[9.17]** According to the principle of *res ipsa loquitur* as widely understood in the cases and as mentioned by Erle CJ, "the thing" must be "under the management of the defendant or his servants". Almost every aspect of this requirement has elements of uncertainty. A clear case of management of the thing being under the control of the defendant arises where a barrel rolls out of premises to which only the defendant and his servants have access.[33] Another clear case may arise in relation to the operation of a motor vehicle,[34] although much will depend on the circumstances.[35] Airplanes are also normally capable of being regarded as being under the management of their proprietors.[36] So also guns may be regarded as under the management of those who use them.[37] Conversely, an electric lamp in a student dormitory was held not to have been under the control of the school at the time of the accident.[38]

**[9.18]** Courts have been uncertain as to whether they should limit the application of *res ipsa loquitur* to cases in which the "thing" was under the actual management of the defendant or his servants. Some have done so[39] (and have been criticised for their pains).[40] Others have taken the view - surely a reasonable one - that the concept of management or control should be broadly understood, so as to extend beyond physical custody or possession to include cases of former possession[41] - most importantly in relation to products liability[42] - or the right to control.[43]

---

33. *Cf Byrne v Boadle* (1863) 2 H & C 722, 159 ER 299; *Scott v London & St Katherine Docks Co* 3 H & C 596 at 60, 159 ER 665 at 667. In *Mullen v Quinnsworth Ltd t/a Crazy Prices* [1990] IR 59 (SC) a supermarket floor on which colourless cooking oil had been spilled, causing the plaintiff a 74-year-old customer to slip and fall, was held to be under the management of the proprietors.
34. *Cf Corcoran v West* [1933] IR 210 (HC); *Halliwell v Venables* (1930) 99 LJKB 353; *Doxtator v Burch* (1973) 41 DLR (3d) 768; *Jackson v Millar* [1976] 1 SCR 225.
35. *Cf Wing v London General Omnibus Co* [1909] 2 KB 652 (CA); *Webster v Paragon Bus Co* [1934] IR 448 at 455 (SC).
36. *Cf Fosbroke-Hobbes v Airwork Ltd* [1937] 1 All ER 108. As regards boats, see *Ross v Dunphy* High Court, 13 February 1978 as explained in *McDonagh v West of Ireland Fisheries Ltd* High Court, 19 December 1986, Blayney J.
37. *Cf O'Regan v Willis* (1936) 71 ILT & Sol J 117 at 118 (HC).
38. *Scrimgeour v Board of Management of the Canadian District of the American Lutheran Church* [1947] 1 WWR 120 (Sask, CA). In *Mandeville v PJ Carroll & Co Ltd* DPIJ: Hilary and Easter Terms 1993, p 198 (HC), where a chair in the mechanics room of the defendant's premises broke when the plaintiff employee sat on it, the doctrine of *res ipsa loquitur* was held to apply.
39. *Cf Bloom v Creed & Consumers' Gas Co* [1937] OR 626 (CA).
40. *Cf* LINDEN, pp 231.
41. *Cf Collen Bros v Scaffolding Ltd* [1959] IR 245 (HC).
42. *Cf* FLEMING, p 539-541; *Kirby v Burke and Holloway* [1944] IR 207 (HC); *Fleming v Henry Denny & Sons* Supreme Court, 29 July 1955; *cf Denniston v McNamara Maxwell & Co* (1950) 84 ILTR 168 (CC). See also para **[9.08]** below.
43. *Cf Mandeville v PJ Carroll & Co Ltd* DPIJ: Hilary and Easter Terms 1993 p 198 (HC, 13 May 1993) where a chair broke under an employee; *per* O'Hanlon J at 200: "[C]hairs provided for the use of the workers should not normally collaps[e] when used in the orthodox and ordinary manner unless [they have] been allowed to get into a dangerous condition ...".

**[9.19]** It is clear, however, that a former right to control the "thing" that causes the damage will not be sufficient to give rise to the application of the *res ipsa loquitur* concept where the "thing" is no longer in the condition in which it was when the control was exercised. In *Tracey v Hagen*,[44] the Supreme Court held that the case had correctly been withdrawn from the jury where the plaintiff had been injured when he was servicing a machine used to make plastic bottles. The machine had been manufactured by the defendant and supplied to the plaintiff six months previously, the servicing of the machine being carried out by the plaintiff. Walsh J considered that *res ipsa loquitur* was not applicable:

> "on the ground that the machine, not being under the control or management of the defendant, had not been proved to have been in the condition in which he provided it".[45]

***(b) Accident is such as in ordinary circumstances does not happen with the use of care by those in control of the thing***

**[9.20]** This is really the key ingredient in the operation of the maxim: if the plaintiff can establish it, he or she is well on the way to winning the case. Certain accidents suggest that those who were in control of the thing that did the injury were not exercising due care. Trains run by the same company do not normally[46] collide without negligence on the part of someone in the company's employment;[47] a barrel of flour does not usually drop from a warehouse[48] or a bale from a lorry,[49] nor does scaffolding normally collapse[50] without carelessness on the part of those in control. Of course there may be a perfectly innocent explanation for the accident, but too heavy an onus should not be placed on the plaintiff to disprove such a possibility.

**[9.21]** On the other hand, experience tells us that a fire may spread from an ordinary domestic grate without negligence on anybody's part.[51] Whether a skid by a motor vehicle suggests negligence on the part of the driver is a question that has given some difficulty. After some hesitation,[52] it appears that the courts are now prepared to accept that it may.[53]

---

44. Supreme Court, 6 March 1973. See also *Williamson v Rover Cycle Co* [1901] 2 IR 615 (CA) affg [1901] 2 IR 189 (QB).

45. Page 4 of Walsh J's judgment. See *McDonagh v West of Ireland Fisheries Ltd* High Court, 19 December 1986.

46. The test is not whether or not the event happens rarely but rather whether, if the event happens, it rarely happens without negligence on the part of someone in control: *Cf Brannon v Wood* (1968) 251 & 349, 444 P 2d 558.

47. *Skinner v LB & SC Ry* (1850) 5 Exch 787. See also *Moore v Atchison Topeka & Santa Fe Railway* (1961) 28 Ill App 2d 340n, 171 NE 2d 393.

48. *Byrne v Boadle* (1863) 2 H & C 722, 159 ER 299; *Hake v George Wiedemann Brewing Co* (1970) 23 Ohio St 65, 262 NE 2d 703 (SC).

49. *Bellizia v Meares* [1971] VR 641.

50. *Collen Bros (Dublin) Ltd v Scaffolding Ltd* [1959] IR 245 (HC).

51. *Sochacki v Sas* [1947] 1 All ER 344. Other types of fires may give rise to an inference of negligence: *cf Farrell v Alliance & Dublin Consumers' Gas Co* [1939] Ir Jur 41 (CC). For United States cases see, Anon 'Note: *Res Ipsa Loquitur* in Actions Against Owner or Occupant of Premises for Personal Injury Death or Property Damage Caused by Fire' (1966) 8 ALR (3d) 974.

52. *Cf Laurie v Ragland Building Co Ltd* [1942] 1 KB 152; *Hunter v Wright* [1938] 2 All ER 621.

53. *Cf Corcoran v West* [1933] IR 210 (HC); *Richley v Faull (Richley, Third Party)* [1965] 1 WLR 1454; *Knott v Royal Exchange Assurance Company* [1955] SASR 33.

This is consistent with the general trend of the law, which is to be more willing than formerly to draw an inference of negligence on the part of the defendant. Where a vehicle which has been parked starts into motion shortly afterwards, courts have applied the *res ipsa loquitur* principle;[54] but where several hours have elapsed the principle will normally be less easy to apply.[55] In *Neill v Minister for Finance*,[56] the plaintiff, aged two and a half years, injured his hand in the door of a postal delivery van. He might have sustained the injury when the postman shut the door but the evidence was not clear. All that was clear was that the postman had been delivering a parcel to the child's home and that the child had followed him to the van. Maguire CJ could:

> "not see how the [*res ipsa loquitur*] principle can be applied in the present case. The gap which exists between the evidence as to the movements of the driver and the injury to the child could reasonably be filled in a number of ways. Granted that it is reasonable to conclude that the child's fingers were caught in some way in the door of the van when it was being closed, the actions of the child may have been such as could not reasonably have been anticipated by the driver."[57]

**[9.22]** Similarly Black J considered that:

> "... there was not sufficient evidence as to how the accident was caused to eliminate all reasonable possibility that the driver was not to blame, or to justify a verdict for the [plaintiff]."[58]

**[9.23]** So also in *M'Lachlin v London & NW Ry Co*[59] it was held that no inference of negligence was permissible where a horse, transported by train and boat operated by the defendant from Crewe to Belfast, left in sound condition but arrived with a punctured hock. The defendant company gave evidence "of an exhaustive character" to show that the animal had been properly boxed and looked after during the journey.

**[9.24]** In dismissing the claim, Wright J referred to the English decision of *Smith v Midland Ry Co*,[60] which, in his view, decided:

---

53. (contd) Where a vehicle merely jerks, an inference of negligence may not be drawn: *Heard v Pacitti* [1933] IR 220; *Breslin v Dublin United Tramways Co* (1911) 45 ILTR 220 (CA); *Murphy v Dublin United Tramways Co* (1909) 43 ILTR 11 (CA); nor does a swerve on to the wrong side of the road, without more give rise to an inference of negligence: *Gilmore v Irish Omnibus Co* (1930) 64 ILTR 48 (HC) (*semble*). See, however, *Tomkins v Northwestern Union Truck Co of Helena* (1980) 645 P 2d 402 (Mont SC): and *cf Badela v Karpowich* (1965) 152 Conn 360, 260 A, 2d 838 (SC of Errors); *Johnson v Foster* (1967) 202 So 2d 520 (Miss SC). In *Millington v Coras Iompair Éireann* (1974) 108 ILTR 61 (SC) the sudden braking of a bus was held to give rise to the application of the *res ipsa loquitur* doctrine. For consideration of the authorities in the United States on accidents involving only one car, see Young 'Note' (1987) 18 Tex Tech LR 1331 at 1336-1346.
54. *Cf Glaser v Schroeder* (1929) 269 Mass 337, 168 NE 809 (SC); *Borg & Powers Furniture Co v Clark* (1935) 194 Minn 305 260, NW 316 (SC).
55. *Cf Hughes v Jolliffe* (1957) 50 Wash 2d 554, 313 P 2d 678 (SC). See, however, *Hill v Thompson* (1971) 484 P 2d 513 (Okla SC).
56. [1948] IR 88 (SC). *Cf Taylor v Great Southern and Western Ry Co* [1909] 2 IR 330 (CA)
57. [1948] IR 88 at 92.
58. [1948] IR 88 at 93. See Also *Dully v North Eastern Health Board* High Court, 3 November 1988 (Hamilton P).
59. (1907) 41 ILTR 139 (Civil Bill Appeal).
60. (1887) 57 LT (ns) 813 (QB). The facts of this case were different in an important respect from those in *M'Lachlin's* case: they involved the transportation together of eight cows which on a reasonable inference might through restlessness have injured each other as well as themselves.

"that the mere fact of an injury having occurred, there being no express evidence of negligence, does not discharge the onus of proof which is on the plaintiff. Applying that principle to the present case, I find that though this horse sustained the injury while under the care of the railway company, there is no evidence going to show want of care. I must therefore, decide against the plaintiff's claim. To hold otherwise would impose on railway companies too onerous a burden. A plaintiff must at least give some evidence to show how it was probable the animal sustained, or might have sustained, the injury."[61]

**[9.25]** Changes in technology may lead to an inference of negligence being drawn today which would not have been drawn in former times.[62] Thus, courts are now more disposed to infer negligence from the occurrence of an airplane crash than they were when aviation was a novelty.[63]

**[9.26]** So also contemporary social and economic realities can influence the court's decision whether or not to apply the *res ipsa loquitur* doctrine. Farmers today have generally sufficient resources to fence their lands properly so as to prevent their livestock straying on the highway. In *O'Reilly v Lavelle*,[64] Johnson J observed that:

"[c]attle properly managed should not wander on the road and therefore the burden of proof ... shifts to the defendant to show that he took reasonable care of his animals."

**[9.27]** The Supreme Court took the same view in *O'Shea v Tilman Anhold and Horse Holiday Farm Ltd*,[65] where Keane J considered it:

"self-evident that a horse will not normally escape from land on to the public road if adequate fencing is provided and any gates are kept in a closed position."

---

61. (1907) 41 ILTR 140.

62. *Cf* eg *Wilson v Colonial Air Transport* (1932) 278 Mass 420, 180 NE 212 (SC); *Herndon v Gregory* (1935) 190 Ark 702 81, SW 2d 849 (SC).

63. *Cf* McLarty '*Res Ipsa Loquitur* in Airline Passenger Litigation' (1951) 37 Va LR 55; Shawcross & Beaumont, *Air Law* (4th ed, 1977) Vol 1, pp 79-82; Goldin 'The Doctrine of *Res Ipsa Loquitur* in Aircraft Law' (1946) 18 So Cal LR 15124; Anon '*Res Ipsa Loquitur* in Aviation Accidents' (1949) 6 ALR 2d 528; Horton 'Note: Torts - *Res Ipsa Loquitur* - Mid-Air Explosion of Aircraft' (1955) 33 N Car LR 670; *Cox v Northwest Airlines Inc* (1967) 379 F 2d 893 (USCA, 7th Crt) cert denied 389 US 1044. Of course even in modern times *res ipsa loquitur* may not necessarily apply to accidents in the air: a sudden lurch of a plane which throws a passenger from a seat (*Cudney v Mid-Continent Airlines* (1953) 363 Mo 922, 254 SW 2d 662 (SC)) or which causes hot tea to be spilled over a passenger (*Lazarus v Eastern Air Lines* (1961) 292 F 2d 748 (KC Ct)) will not give rise to the application of *res ipsa loquitur* (although the airline may be under a legal duty to avoid or minimise precisely such dangers by a judicious use of the "fasten seat belts" sign - *Ness v West Coast Airlines Inc* (1965) 90 Idaho 111 410 P 2d 969 (SC) and warning its stewards to take particular care during periods of predicted turbulence or more radically, by avoiding foreseeable turbulence where this can reasonably be done: see Cimino 'Comment: Air Turbulence Liability' (1999) 64 J Air L & Com 1163)). *Cf Fosbroke-Hobbes v Airwork Ltd* [1937] 1 All ER 108, a relatively early decision where an inference of negligence was drawn. For consideration of the possibility of invoking *res ipsa loquitur* in respect of computer malfunction see Hanson 'Comment' (1983) 69 Iowa LR 241.

64. High Court, 2 April 1990 of Johnson J's judgment. *Cf McCaffrey v Lundy* (1988) ILT (ns) 245 (DC) where Brennan DJ relied on the "peculiar knowledge" principle, rather than on an inference deriving from the unusualness of an occurrence such as happened without negligence in the past of the person in charge.

65. Supreme Court, 23 October 1996 of Keane J's judgment.

**[9.28]** The courts formerly evinced some reluctance to go beyond the experience of ordinary persons[66] in determining whether the happening suggested negligence on the part of those in control of the object that caused the damage.[67] This is no longer the position. A plaintiff may introduce expert evidence to show that the inference of negligence should be drawn. Thus, in relation to medical negligence, for example, where the judge's knowledge of the intricacies of medical practice is necessarily limited, the plaintiff can invoke the assistance of medical witnesses to show that the injury of which he or she complains does not normally result from the treatment given in the absence of negligence on the part of the doctor treating the patient.[68]

**[9.29]** In *McKevitt v Ireland*,[69] an interesting issue of *res ipsa loquitur* arose at trial but was not taken up on appeal. The plaintiff, arrested for being drunk and incapable, was taken to a garda station and placed in a cell, having been searched for matches and other items of potential danger. Two hours later his cell (in which he was the sole occupant) was found to be on fire. He received extensive burns.

**[9.30]** The plaintiff's case centred[70] on the search carried out by the gardaí. He claimed that it was inadequate, since it had allowed him to retain two boxes of matches. The garda vigorously contested this assertion and during the trial the plaintiff conceded that they had made a thorough search.

**[9.31]** At the trial, counsel for the plaintiff unsuccessfully submitted that the doctrine of *res ipsa loquitur* applied. On appeal, Griffin J endorsed the trial judge's rejection of this argument. In his view:

---

66. As to what an ordinary member of the jury may be expected to know see *Coughlan v Marks* [1918] 2 IR 306 at 324-325 (*per* Sir Ignatius J O'Brien C) and at 342-343 (*per* Ronan LJ), (CA affg KB).

67. *Cf Mahon v Osborne* [1939] 2 KB 14 (CA Scott LJ's judgment; Goddard LJ dissenting on this question).

68. *Cassidy v Ministry of Health* [1951] 2 KB 343; *Roe v Ministry of Health* [1954] 2 QB 66; *Watson v Davidson* [1966] NZLR 853; *Raza v Sullivan* (1970) 432 F 2d 617 - tooth extraction resulting in fracture of jaw; *Mayor v Dawsitt* (1965) 240 Or 196, 400 P 2d 234 (SC) - paralysis after use of anaesthetic during child-birth. *Cf Daniels v Heskin* [1954] IR 73 (SC) discussed para **[9.34]** below; see also *Lindsay v Mid-Western Health Board* [1993] 2 IR 147 (SC 1992 reversing HC 1991) analysed by Symmons 'Medical Negligence and the Doctrine of *Res Ipsa Loquitur* in Ireland' (1992) 9 Prof Neg 17; *Maitland v Swan and Sligo County Council* High Court, 6 April 1992; *Barrett v Southern Health Board* High Court, 5 December 1988; *Dully v North Eastern Health Board* High Court, 3 November 1988; *Russell v Walsh and Mid-Western Health Board* High Court, 3 April 1995. In a number of these cases the court held that the doctrine of *res ipsa loquitur* did not on the evidence apply or that the defendant had discharged the burden of proof. See generally Renswick '*Res Ipsa Loquitur* Hospital and Malpractice Cases' (1960) 9 Clev-Mar LR 179; Rossen 'Defense Against Res Ipsa in Medical Malpractice' 13 Clev-Mar LR 128 (1964); Louisell & Williams '*Res Ipsa Loquitur*- Its Future in Medical Malpractice Cases' (1960) 48 Calif LR 252; Fricke 'The Use of Expert Evidence in *Res Ipsa Loquitur* Cases' (1959) 5 Vill LR 59; BIB 'Note: The Use of Expert Evidence in *Res Ipsa Loquitur* Cases' (1958)106 U Pa LR 731. *Cf Ybarra v Spangard* (1944) 25 Cal 2d 486, 154 P 2d 687.

69. [1987] ILRM 541 (SC).

70. Another important issue not of present relevance related to whether the plaintiff had warned the Gardaí of his intention to set fire to his cell.

> "on no version of how the fire started could the doctrine apply. Only the plaintiff could say (if even he could) how this fire started, so the onus of rebutting negligence could not pass to the defendants."[71]

**[9.32]** Perhaps this understates the force of the argument. It may be the case that a properly administered search could conceivably have failed to find matches; if so, *res ipsa loquitur* might indeed be difficult to establish. However, it may be useful to consider a somewhat different set of facts in order to test the relevance of *res ipsa loquitur* to situations involving the care of intoxicated persons. Let us imagine a case where a search fails to find a large knife on an intoxicated person, who later injures himself with it in the cell. Assuming that the knife should have been found in the search, would it be an effective rebuttal of *res ipsa loquitur* to contend that only the plaintiff could say how he had sustained his injury? In such a case the answer would surely be that the plaintiff sustained his injury - however precisely this happened does not matter- by reason of the authorities' negligently having enabled him to have access to something with which he might hurt himself. If the plaintiff is characterised as the "instrumentality" which caused the accident, could it not be said that in such a case the accident is such as in the ordinary course of things, does not happen with the use of care by those in control of intoxicated, arrested persons?

**[9.33]** It is interesting to contrast McCarthy J's observation that, if the jury, properly directed, were to conclude that they could not rely on the evidence of the plaintiff himself, and merely had the evidence of the fire's having occurred, "they could properly conclude that, the burden being on them, the defendants had failed to prove that they had not been negligent".[72] Although McCarthy J did not expressly invoke the *res ipsa loquitur* principle, this is surely the reason why the onus of proof would have thus shifted to the defendants. That the principle was not far from McCarthy J's thoughts is suggested by his statement that:

> "there was no evidence that could take away from the very fact that there was a fire and that it could only have been caused by the plaintiff, lacking any Promethean qualities, by the use of matches".[73]

**[9.34]** The courts have been less than forthcoming about how they determine whether the particular accident is "such as in the ordinary circumstances does not happen if those who have the management [of the thing causing the injury] use proper care ...".[74] They generally eschew on overt statistical calculus. In *Daniels v Heskin*,[75] however, Lavery J went some way towards doing so. The case involved a home birth, which took place in 1951. The defendant doctor and a midwife were in attendance. While the defendant was stitching the mother after the birth, a needle broke. One of the issues in the case was whether this breakage constituted negligence on the defendant's part.

**[9.35]** Counsel for the mother (and her husband) conceded that the case was one where the *res ipsa loquitur* principle did not apply and that the needle might have broken through a

---

71. [1987] ILRM 541 at 553.
72. [1987] ILRM 541 at 554.
73. [1987] ILRM 541.
74. *Scott v London & St Katherine Docks Co* (1865) 3 H & C 596 at 60, 159 ER 665 at 667 (*per* Erle CJ).
75. [1954] IR 73 (SC)

flaw in itself not discoverable by the defendant or otherwise without negligence on his part. Three doctors gave evidence to this effect. The trial judge directed a verdict in favour of the defendant and the Supreme Court, by a four-to-one majority,[76] held that he had been right to do so.

**[9.36]** Counsel for the appellants submitted that, as there was evidence that the breaking of needles in the course of a surgical operation was more often due to an imperfection of technique on the part of the operator than to a defect in the instrument, it would have been open to the jury on the balance of probabilities to find that it had been caused by negligence. Lavery J considered that this amounted to a claim to apply the *res ipsa loquitur* principle in another form:

> "It is certainly not open to a jury, in my opinion, in th[e] state of facts [established in the instant case], to hold that the breaking was caused by imperfection of technique, on the ground that say in 60 per cent of cases of broken needles it is so caused, and the same is true of any other statistical record of such happenings until the point is reached where the preponderance is such as to make it a case of *res ipsa loquitur* shifting the burden of proof to the defendant to give an explanation and to establish that the mishap was not due to his negligence."[77]

**[9.37]** The suggestion here appears to be that the doctrine is to be applied only where the preponderance of statistical unlikelihood of the accident without occurring negligence on the part of the person in charge of the harmful agency is well over 60%.

**[9.38]** If this is so, it might be considered curious that later judgements have not generally[78] reflected a similar approach. Perhaps the courts are reluctant to commit themselves to any particular statistical threshold in order to preserve their flexibility in the application of the *res ipsa loquitur* principle, as well as to disguise the fact that there can be formidable methodological difficulties in defining the parameters of the category of accident in respect of which the statistical analysis should be effected. To take a simple example: if the driver of a motor vehicle brakes suddenly, so that a passenger is slightly injured, how narrowly or broadly should the category of accident be formulated for the purposes of the, *res ipsa loquitur* principle?[79] Does it depend on the size or function of the vehicle? The speed at which it was travelling? The character of the location - urban, suburban or rural? The time of day at which the braking took place? The truth of the matter is that the court retains considerable elasticity in its characterisation.[80] In most instances, it relies not on sharply measured statistical empirical data, but on a common-sense robust assessment of

76. Murnaghan, O'Byrne, Lavery and Kingsmill Moore JJ; Maguire CJ dissenting.

77. [1954] IR 73 at 79.

78. *Cf Barrett v Southern Health Board* High Court, 5 December 1988 where Blayney J, in a case alleging negligence in an operation on fractures on the plaintiff's arm in which a nerve was damaged observed:

> "Th[e] doctrine [of *res ipsa loquitur*] has no application in the context of an operation which necessarily involved risk and where the evidence is that in more than 7% of the cases some nerve damage is sustained. Where such damage could occur without any negligence on the part of the surgeon the mere fact that there was damage is not evidence of negligence."

The displacement of the potential application of the doctrine at such a low percentage point is not replicated *expressis verbis* in other decisions.

79. *Cf Millington v CIE* (1974) 108 ILTR 61 (SC).

80. In *Mullen v Quinnsworth Ltd t/a Crazy Prices (No 1)* [1990] 1 IR 59 (SC) where an elderly customer of a supermarket slipped on some colourless cooking oil that had been knocked onto the floor of the aisle, the Supreme Court held that the *res ipsa loquitur* principle applied.

"how things are" in the real world. No doubt such common-sense lies at the heart of adjudication in negligence litigation but one can question whether it should be the linchpin for the application or non application of a technical doctrine with potentially massive implications for the parties, so far as it determines which party is to have to discharge the burden of proof.

***(c) Res ipsa loquitur need not be expertly pleaded***

**[9.39]** In the Supreme Court decision of *Mullen v Quinnsworth Ltd t/a Crazy Prices (No 1)*,[81] Griffin J (Finlay CJ concurring) expressed the view that the *res ipsa loquitur* doctrine does not have to be pleaded before a plaintiff may rely on it. "If the facts pleaded and the facts proved show that the doctrine is applicable to the case, that is sufficient ..." In *O'Reilly v Lavelle*,[82] Johnson J followed Griffin J's lead on this question.

***(d) Where an explanation is found, res ipsa loquitur does not apply***

**[9.40]** The *res ipsa loquitur* principle applies only where an explanation of what actually occurred is not forthcoming. Once such an explanation is adduced and accepted, the situation is no longer one calling for the application of the principle. Of course the explanation may be one which either excuses the defendant or confirms his or her liability.

## The Procedural Effect of *Res Ipsa Loquitur*[83]

**[9.41]** One of the most difficult and unsatisfactory aspects of the operation of the *res ipsa loquitur* principle arises in relation to its procedural effect. If the plaintiff has established that *res ipsa loquitur* applies, this could have one of a number of consequences. First, it could mean no more than that he has established a case sufficient to go to the jury. The jury would be free to find for either plaintiff or defendant, but the plaintiff would have the assurance that he would at least get the case to the jury for this consideration. In some (albeit rare) cases, the evidence which merits the application of the *res ipsa loquitur*

---

80. (contd) Griffin J (Finlay CJ concurring) observed that "the floor was under the management of the defendant ... and the accident was such as in the ordinary course of things would not happen if floors were kept free from spillages of this nature." This is a curious way of applying the test unless supermarket proprietors are under a strict obligation to keep the floors free of spillages rather than (as traditionally understood) an obligation to take reasonable care to keep the floors free of them. Since it was acknowledged that supermarkets have an inevitable risk of items breaking and spilling, Griffin J's test and surrounding analysis tilt towards the conclusion that supermarkets can only rarely escape liability for falls by customers. McCarthy J (Finlay CJ concurring) actually toyed with the idea of imposing what he termed "absolute liability", using the rule in *Rylands v Fletcher* as an inspiration. When the case returned to the Supreme Court (*Mullen v Quinnsworth Ltd t/a Crazy Prices (No 2)* [1991] ILRM 439) McCarthy J's enthusiasm for this approach had abated. Not every slip in a supermarket will give rise to the application of the *res ipsa loquitur* doctrine, however. *Cf Foley v Quinnsworth Ltd* High Court, 10 April 1992 where the plaintiff slipped on a floor on which no spillages could be found immediately afterwards.

81. [1990] 1 IR 59 at 63 (SC). McCarthy J took no definitive position on the issue though his laconic reference perhaps suggests a contrary view. Griffin J quoted the English decision of *Bennett v Chemical Construction (GB) Ltd* [1971] 3 All ER 822 in support.

82. [1990] 2 IR 372 (HC), (CCA).

83. See Prosser 'The Procedural Effect of *Res Ipsa Loquitur*' (1936) 20 Minn LR 241; Kauffman 'Comment: *Res Ipsa Loquitur* - An Analysis of Its Application and Procedural Effects in Nebraska' (1962) 41 Neb LR 747; Harlow '*Res Ipsa Loquitur* - A Progress Report' (1972) 3 Kingston LR 1.

principle might be sufficiently strong to entitle the plaintiff to a directed verdict in his favour.[84] Secondly, it could mean that the defendant is obliged to establish either that he was not negligent or to provide a reasonable explanation, equally consistent with negligence and no negligence on his part. On this interpretation (in contrast to the first), if the defendant elects not to give evidence, the plaintiff must (not may) win his case. Thirdly, it could shift the onus onto the defendant to establish affirmatively that the accident was not caused by his negligence.

**[9.42]** The courts have been somewhat remiss in the language they have used to describe the law on this question. One even finds decisions[85] in which inconsistencies are apparent within the same judgment.

**[9.43]** There is much to be said in favour of the first interpretation,[86] which has won favour in courts in the United States,[87] Canada,[88] Australia,[89] and, it seems, New Zealand.[90] Why should one species of circumstantial evidence (which is referred to as *res ipsa loquitur*) have greater evidential weight than direct evidence? To regard *res ipsa loquitur* as merely having the effect of ensuring that the plaintiff gets the case before the jury means, however, that it ceases to be a distinctive doctrine and such concepts as "control" of the object that causes the danger lose their crucial significance.

**[9.44]** The tendency in the Irish courts is not to favour the first interpretation (although a few decisions[91] seem to give some support to it).

---

84. With the abolition of the jury in personal injuries litigation the judge takes on the responsibility of trier of fact. Experience in other common law jurisdictions is that this first interpretation of the procedural effect of *res ipsa loquitur* tends to give way to the second or third once the judge assumes this responsibility. There is no logical necessity for this change, however. *Cf* WINFIELD & JOLOWICZ, p 191.

85. Including the decision of *Byrne v Boadle* (1863) 2 H & C 722 which started the whole problem! See also *Lindsay v Mid-Western Health Board* [1993] 2 IR 147 (SC revg HC) where O'Flaherty J appeared to adopt the third interpretation whilst expressly approving of a quotation from FLEMING (7th ed), p 291 which advocated acceptance of the first interpretation. *Cf* Byrne & Binchy, *Annual Review of Irish Law 1992*, pp 594-595. FLEMING (9th ed), pp 360-364 maintains advocacy for the first interpretation.

86. *Cf* STREET, p 262-263.

87. *Cf* PROSSER & KEETON, pp 257-258.

88. *Cf* FLEMING, p 361; TRINDADE & CANE, pp 466-467; *Nominal Defendant v Haslbauer* (1967) 117 CLR 448; *Government Insurance Office of New South Wales v Fredrichberg* (1968) 118 CLR 403; *Schellenberg v Turnell Holdings Pty Ltd* (2000) 170 ALR 594.

89. *Hawkes' Bay Motor Co Ltd v Russell* [1972] NZLR 542.

90. The Supreme Court of Canada, in *Fontaine v British Columbia (Official Administrator)* [1998] 1 SCR 424, frustrated by the confusion surrounding the *res ipsa loquitur* concept, held (at 435) that "the law would be better served if the maxim was treated as expired and no longer used in negligence actions. After all, it was nothing more than an attempt to deal with circumstantial evidence." See McInnes 'The Death of *Res Ipsa Loquitur* in Canada' (1998) 114 LQR 547.

91. *Cf O'Rourke v McGuinness* [1942] IR 554 (SC); *Palmer v Bateman* [1908] 2 IR 393 at 399 (KB); *Coughlan v Marks* [1918] 2 IR 306 at 319 (CA 1917 affg KB 1917) *Tracey v Hagen* Supreme Court, 6 March 1973, (Walsh J); *Millington v CIE* (1974) 108 ILTR 61 at 67 (SC).

The second,[92] and, more particularly, the third[93] interpretations are generally adopted.[94]

**[9.45]** If it is accepted that the Irish courts have committed themselves to the view that an onus rests on the defendant, once the *res ipsa loquitur* principle applies, the question arises as to what precisely the defendant must do to avoid liability. The Supreme Court addressed the issue in *Lindsay v Mid-Western Health Board*.[95] The case concerned a girl who, nine years before the trial, when she was aged eight, had been admitted to the defendant's hospital with suspected appendicitis. An alternative diagnosis of mesenteric adonitis was also considered by the medical staff. The plaintiff was operated on. She appeared initially to be recovering consciousness after the operation but had a sudden epileptic-form attacks and lapsed into a deep coma from which she had not regained consciousness at the time of the litigation.

**[9.46]** The plaintiff's action for negligence against the hospital involved the invocation of the *res ipsa loquitur* doctrine. The expert witness on her behalf, a highly qualified and experienced anaesthetist, identified three possible causes for the plaintiff's condition: sub-arachnoid haemorrhage, hypoxic insult and "miscellaneous possibilities". Morris J held in favour of the plaintiff on the basis that the defendant's hypothesis of a viral explanation was speculative, but the Supreme Court reversed.

---

92. *Cf Farrell v Alliance & Dublin Consumers' Gas Co* [1939] Ir Jur 41 (CC). *Fleming v Henry Denny & Son Ltd* Supreme Court, 29 July 1955 (*semble*); *O'Loughlin v Kearney* [1939] Ir Jur 39 (CC) (*semble*).

93. *Cf Coughlan v Marks* [1918] 2 IR 306; *Flannery v Waterford & Limerick Ry Co* (1877) IR 11 CL 30; *Corcoran v West* [1933] IR 210; *Collen Bros (Dublin) Ltd v Scaffolding Ltd* [1959] IR 245; *Palmer v Bateman* [1908] 2 IR 393; In *Millington v CIE* (1974) 108 ILTR 61 (SC) (Fitzgerald J's judgment); *Mullen v Quinnsworth Ltd t/a Crazy Prices* [1990] IR 59 (SC) (Griffin J's judgment, Finlay CJ concurring). In *Kelliher v Tipperary (North Riding) Board of Health and Public Assistance* [1938] IR 43 (SC) FitzGibbon J, (with whom Sullivan CJ concurred), favoured the third view. He said (at 62):

> "In actions founded upon negligence the principle embodied in the maxim *res ipsa loquitur* is called in aid to shift the onus of proof, and to relieve the party who relies upon the maxim, from the necessity of producing any evidence other than the bare occurrence of an accident. Where the maxim is applied, the mere occurrence of an accident of a particular kind is treated as casting upon the defendant without any further evidence on behalf of the plaintiff, the onus of showing that the accident was not caused by his negligence."

Meredith J dissenting favoured the second approach. He said (at 67-68):

> "[W]here th[e] *res ipsa loquitur* principle is the sole foundation of the allegation of negligence, an explanation merely consistent with the evidence, though not affirmatively substantiated as the actual explanation, and consistent also with the absence of negligence may be relied upon to show that the principle does not apply."

In *Daniels v Heskin* [1954] IR 73 at 79 (SC) Lavery J proffered a hybrid test, which can perhaps best be interpreted as tilting more towards the third than the second approach. See also *Moore v Fox (R) & Sons* [1956] 1 QB 596; *Henderson v Jenkins (Henry) & Sons* [1970] AC 282. For recent examples of judicial support for the third interpretation see eg *Lindsay v Mid-Western Health Board* [1993] 2 IR 147 (SC revg HC); *O'Reilly v Lavelle* High Court, 2 April 1990 (Johnson J); *Merriman v Greenhills Foods Ltd* [1997] 1 ILRM 46 (SC); *O'Shea v Tilman Anhold and Horse Holiday Farm Ltd* Supreme Court, 23 October 1996.

94. *Collen Bros (Dublin) Ltd v Scaffolding Ltd* [1959] IR 245 (HC); *Kelly v Gilmore* Supreme Court, 28 July 1970; *Murray v Gilmore* Supreme Court, 20 December 1973.

95. [1993] 2 IR 147 (SC revg HC) analysed by Byrne & Binchy, *Annual Review of Irish Law 1992*, pp 593-597.

**[9.47]** O'Flaherty J (Finlay CJ and Egan J concurring) was of the view that, in the instant case, the most that the defendant should be required to do was to show that it had exercised all reasonable care; it should not be required to take the further step of proving, on the balance of probabilities, what had caused the plaintiff's brain damage.

**[9.48]** The effect of this holding is that a defendant can escape liability in a case where *res ipsa loquitur* applies even where a mystery remains as to the cause of the accident. Once the defendant has established that, whatever the actual cause, it can not be attributed to his or her negligence, then the defendant has done enough. Of course, if the defendant can establish the actual cause of the plaintiff's injury, he or she will also escape liability, in spite of having been guilty of negligence, if that negligence was not the cause of the injury.

## III. The *Hanrahan* Restatement of the *Res Ipsa Loquitur* Doctrine

**[9.49]** We now must consider the implications of the restatement of the *res ipsa loquitur* doctrine in the Supreme Court decision of *Hanrahan v Merck Sharp & Dohme (Ireland) Ltd.*[96] The plaintiffs had claimed damages for negligence and nuisance and under the rule in *Rylands v Fletcher*. They contended that the injuries which they had suffered - in regard to their health, their farm animals and plant life - had been caused by noxious emissions which they alleged had been discharged from the defendants' factory, where pharmaceutical products were processed. The central issue was one of causation, though the question of the quantum of the injuries was also a matter of dispute.

**[9.50]** Keane J dealt with the claim as essentially one of nuisance. Since no appeal had been taken alleging that this was erroneous, the Supreme Court was content to treat the claim similarly. This did not, however, prevent Henchy J (for the Court) from preferring an important observation on the *res ipsa loquitur* doctrine:

> "The ordinary rule is that a person who alleges a particular tort must, in order to succeed, prove (save where there are admissions) all the necessary ingredients of that tort and it is not for the defendant to disprove anything. Such exceptions as have been allowed to that general rule seem to be confined to cases where a particular element of the tort lies, or is deemed to lie, pre-eminently within the defendant's knowledge, in which case the onus of proof as to that matter passes to the defendant. Thus, in the tort of negligence, where damage has been caused to the plaintiff in circumstances in which such damage would not usually be caused without negligence on the part of the defendant, the rule of *res ipsa loquitur* will allow the act relied on to be evidence of negligence in the absence of proof by the defendant that it occurred without want of due care on his part. The rationale behind the shifting of the onus of proof to the defendant in such cases would appear to lie in the fact that it would be palpably unfair to require a plaintiff to prove something which is beyond his reach and which is peculiarly within the range of the defendant's capacity of proof."[97]

**[9.51]** Central to this analysis is the notion of the defendant's superior knowledge of how the tort was caused: it would be "palpably unfair" to require the plaintiff to prove that which is "peculiarly within the range of the defendant's capacity of proof". This approach gives rise to difficulty.[98] It is not the case that *res ipsa loquitur* may be invoked only where the evidence is more accessible to the defendant. Of course, proof of the elements of a case based on *res ipsa loquitur* frequently shows superior or exclusive knowledge on the part of

---

96. [1988] ILRM 629 (SC).
97. [1988] ILRM 629 at 634-635.

the defendant as to how the accident occurred: of the nature of things, those in control of the instrumentality causing the injury are generally more likely to have such knowledge than their victims. However the *res ipsa loquitur* doctrine is neither reducible to, nor dependent on, this element.

**[9.52]** Henchy J's statement that *res ipsa loquitur* applies "where damage has been caused to the plaintiff in circumstances in which such damage would not usually be caused without negligence on the part of the defendant" involves an unfortunate elision of the separate elements of the doctrine. In fact the plaintiff does not have to discharge such an onus. The whole point of the doctrine is to permit the making of an inferential conclusion that the defendant's negligent conduct caused the plaintiff's injury from the fact that (a) the thing causing the injury was under the defendant's control, and (b) accidents such as the one befalling the plaintiff do not ordinarily happen if those in control exercise due care. Under Henchy J's approach, the inferential conclusion has become, in effect, a premise. In *Hanrahan*, the issue at the core of the case was whether in fact the "thing" that was under the control of the defendants was the "thing" which caused injury to the plaintiffs. Unless it could be proven on the balance of probabilities that it was, the plaintiffs could not succeed. The *res ispa loquitur* doctrine would not assist in providing this proof.

**[9.53]** The *Hanrahan* restatement has not become deeply rooted in Irish law. The Supreme Court made no reference to it in *Lindsay v Mid-Western Health Board*[99] or *Merriman v Greenhills Foods Ltd*[100] and in *O'Shea v Tilman Anhold and Horse Holiday Farm Ltd*,[101] Keane J noted that "the recent restatement of the doctrine by this court in *Hanrahan* ... has been criticised[102] and may need to be reconsidered at some stage." He preferred to use the "classic formulation"[103] of *res ipsa loquitur*, contained in the famous passage of Erle CJ's judgment in *Scott v London & St Katherine Docks Co*,[104] O'Flaherty J merely referred to his own earlier judgment in *Lindsay*, which had derived no apparent inspiration from *Hanrahan*. Hamilton CJ expressly reserved his position with regard to Keane J's suggestion that the *Hanrahan* restatement be reconsidered. Eleven years after *Hanrahan*, the restatement seems to have little vitality.

---

98. *Cf* PROSSER & KEETON, pp 254-255:

> "If the circumstances are such as to create a reasonable inference of the defendant's negligence it cannot be supposed that the inference would ever be defeated by a showing that the defendant knew nothing about what had happened, and if the facts give rise to no such inference, a plaintiff who has the burden of proof in the first instance could scarcely make out a case merely by proving that the plaintiff knew less about the matter than the defendant."

99. [1993] 2 IR 147 (SC 1992 revg HC 1991)

100. [1997] 1 ILRM 46 (SC). It is true that a central paragraph in Blayney J's judgment (with which O'Flaherty J concurred) appears to place much weight on the plaintiff's lack of knowledge of the cause of the accident, and on the extent to which the defendant may have exercised due care. He was "satisfied that to enable justice to be done, the [*res ipsa loquitur*] doctrine should be applied to throw the onus on the [defendant] to prove that it was not negligent." There are perhaps resonances here of the *Hanrahan* restatement. As against this Blayney J made no reference to it and instead relied on the *locus classicus* of *Scott v London & St Katherine Docks Co* (1865) 3 H & C 596 at 601; 159 ER 665 at 667.

101. Supreme Court, 23 October 1996, p 5 of Keane's judgement.

102. Citing the second edition of this work (1990), pp 142-144.

103. Page 5 of Keane J's judgment.

104. See para **[9.15]** above.

**[9.54]** It remains to be seen whether the Irish courts will take the entirely different course, favoured by the Supreme Court of Canada[105] and finding certain sympathy in the High Court of Australia,[106] of announcing the demise of the *res ipsa loquitur* doctrine, leaving negligence litigation involving circumstantial evidence to be resolved simply on the weight of that evidence. Such a development could only contribute to clarity in our law.

105. *Fontaine v British Columbia (Official Administrator)* [1998] 1 SCR 424.
106. *Schellenberg v Tunnell Holdings Pty Ltd* (2000) 170 ALR 594.

## Chapter 10

# Negligence and Economic Loss[1]


I. Introduction .......... 203
II. The Contemporary Irish Approach to Pure Economic Loss .......... 206
III. The Contractual Dimension .......... 208
IV. The Hedley Byrne Principle .......... 216
V. Pure Economic Loss in Products Liability .......... 246


## I. Introduction

**[10.01]** Attention was drawn earlier, when discussing the duty of care in negligence, to the fact that the duty issue is not only concerned with the range and class of people to whom the duty is owed, but also to the kind of damage that is recognised by the law as deserving compensation. The duty issue, we said, is concerned with answering two questions: duty to whom? and duty for what?

**[10.02]** Pure economic loss, that is economic or financial loss, unaccompanied by physical injury or damage to property, was one kind of injury for which the courts at common law were loathe to compensate. Undoubtedly, this was because pure economic loss, historically and in the general order of natural priorities, was regarded as less important than physical injury or damage to property. Secondly, like "nervous shock", the judiciary was apprehensive about recognising such kind of damage because of floodgate fears. Finally, it was felt that pure economic loss was more properly a matter exclusively related to breach of contract, and should not for that reason be compensated in tort claims. The general feeling was that the streams of contract and tort should not be allowed to mingle. Each of these objections has diminished in recent years, and the rigid division between contractual and tortious liability has weakened considerably as an inhibiting factor in this area. It is now possible for plaintiffs to sue professional advisers in both contract and tort for economic loss at the same time, and product liability cases frequently involve both contract and tort issues. It is not surprising, therefore, that the recent debate as to whether the plaintiff can recover for pure economic loss in tort, has tended to rage around the overlap between contract and tort and in this case it frequently arises where professional advisers such as solicitors, architects, auctioneers, bankers and stockbrokers and the like,

1. See generally MacGrath 'The Recovery of Pure Economic Loss in Negligence - An Emerging Dichotomy' (1985) 5 Oxford J of Legal Stud 350; Atiyah 'Negligence and Economic Loss' (1967) 83 LQR 248; Harvey 'Economic Losses and Negligence: The Search for a Just Solution' (1972) 50 Can BR 580; Fleming James 'Limitations on Liability for Economic Loss Caused by Negligence: A Pragmatic Appraisal' (1972-1973) 12 JSPTL 105; Craig 'Negligent Misstatements, Negligent Acts and Economic Loss' (1976) 92 LQR 213; Todd 'Negligence, Economic Loss and the Ambit of the Duty of Care' (1980) 1 Canterbury LR 29; Hayes 'The Duty of Care and Liability for Purely Economic Loss' (1979) 12 Melb ULR 79.

are offering advice. This in turn raises the question of liability for contractual (or pre-contractual) representations and liability under the *Hedley v Byrne* principle.

**[10.03]** It should also be mentioned at this stage that what we are speaking of here is the defendant's liability for *negligently* inflicted economic loss. The common law was not so hesitant in awarding damages for intentionally inflicted economic loss, and this it did in the tort of deceit. Absent the intention to injure, however, the courts were less resolute and showed more reserve.

**[10.04]** As a general comment on the courts' willingness in this area, it might be fair to say that where there was a contractual relationship between the plaintiff and the defendant (or something "equivalent to contract") the courts were more inclined to award such damages in tort, presumably because the presence of the additional contractual element justified it. The "near contractual" context further ensured the tortious requirement of proximity. In addition, if the plaintiff relied on the defendant's assurances, to the knowledge of the defendant, the courts were likely to be more favourably disposed to the plaintiff's claim for pure economic loss.

**[10.05]** Finally, it is interesting to note also, that many of the cases where the issue of pure economic loss arises occur in relation to negligent mis-statements, and this complicates analysis somewhat. The law had traditionally distinguished between negligent acts and negligent statements in considering whether a duty of care arises, being somewhat hesitant again in relation to the latter. Pure economic loss is the typical kind of damage which flows from negligent advice, and so a plaintiff who suffered as a result of such negligent counsel, frequently faced a double disadvantage at common law; judicial hesitancy in relation to negligent statements and a similar reluctance in relation to the pure economic loss generated by bad advice or negligent representations.

**[10.06]** In reading the cases, therefore, it may be helpful to remember that the courts will award damages for economic loss if it is intentionally inflicted or if it is accompanied by personal injuries. In other tort claims the following distinctions run through the tangled analysis: the distinction between contract and tort; between pure economic loss and personal injury; between acts and statements; between pre-contractual and contractual representations; and between intentional statements and negligent statements. Which feature predominates in any given judgment seems to be determined by the particular facts of the case, rather than by a settled, coherent approach dictated by principle. Furthermore, there would not appear to be any inevitability about the courts' approach in this area. In the absence of coherent judicial analysis, a great deal of discretion appears to be available to the judge as to what judicial route he or she chooses to follow when confronted with a plaintiff who has suffered pure economic loss.

**[10.07]** "Few areas in modern tort law are darker and more uncertain"[2] than that concerned with liability in negligence for economic loss unaccompanied by injury to the person or property of the plaintiff. The comforting conceptual symmetry of breach of duty, reasonable foresight, and remoteness of damage does not always give clear guidance as to what is the best solution in particular cases. Historically, the courts rejected the right to

---

2. Harvey 'Economic Losses and Negligence: The Search for a Just Solution' (1972) 50 Can BR 580.

recover for pure economic loss[3] which "has long been a pariah in tort".[4] After *Donoghue v Stevenson*,[5] the position became somewhat uncertain, since the precise scope of the "neighbour" principle had to be worked out in the courts.

**[10.08]** There was little judicial analysis of the issue for some time, but in recent years the matter has been exhaustively analysed by the courts in most common law jurisdictions.

**[10.09]** The picture that emerges, using broad brush strokes, is as follows. It is now universally accepted, throughout all common law jurisdictions, that there is no rule of law excluding liability in negligence for pure economic loss in all circumstances. The British courts for more than a decade have taken a narrow approach. The *Anns*[6] formula has been effectively displaced as a test to determine the issue in new contexts.[7] Instead the British courts have had to resort to an inflated and less than fully convincing rendition of the *Hedley Byrne*[8] principle, based on an "assumption of responsibility" for the plaintiff's economic welfare. In Ireland, the courts have evinced less tension on the issue. They have been content to invoke the language of "neighbourhood" and "proximity of relationship", meditated by public policy considerations,[9] when addressing the scope of liability in negligence for pure economic loss.[10] It is interesting to note, however, that the Irish courts have also interpreted the *Hedley Byrne* principle widely,[11] even to the point of merging its doctrinal basis with the broader concept of the duty of care, deriving from *Donoghue v Stevenson*.[12] Another striking feature of Irish jurisprudence is the judicial propensity to have resort to the *Hedley Byrne* principle in the context of professional practice.[13] This

3. *Cattle v Stockton Waterworks Co* (1875) LR 10 QB 453; *Simpson & Co v Thompson, Burrell* [1977] 3 App Cas 279 (HL, SC); *La Societe Anonyme de Remorquage à Helice v Bennetts* [1911] 1 KB 243. *Cf Dublin Port & Docks Board v Bank of Ireland* [1976] IR 118 at 141 (SC): "[C]ommercial life would become impossible if foreseeability that one's action or inaction would cause economic loss to another were to create liability …".
4. James *The Fallacies of Simpson v Thomson* (1971) 33 MLR 149 at 160.
5. [1932] AC 562 (HL, SC). *See* Heuston '*Donoghue v Stevenson* in Retrospect' (1957) 20 MLR 1 at 18-19; Heuston '*Donoghue v Stevenson*: A Fresh Appraisal' (1971) 24 CLP 37 at 45-49.
6. *Anns v Merton London Borough Council* [1978] AC 728 at 751-752 (HL, Eng).
7. *Caparo Industries plc v Dickman* [1990] 2 AC 650 (HL, Eng); *Murphy v Brentwood District Council* [1991] 1 AC 398 (HL, Eng).
8. *Hedley Byrne & Co Ltd v Heller and Partners* [1964] AC 465 (HL, Eng).
9. *Ward v McMaster* [1989] ILRM 40 (SC) is the *locus classicus*.
10. *Cf*, eg *John C Doherty Timber Ltd v Drogheda Harbour Commissioners* [1993] 1 IR 315 (HC); *Sunderland v Louth County Council* [1990] ILRM 658 (SC); *McShane Wholesale Fruit and Vegtables Ltd v Johnston Haulage Co Ltd* [1997] 1 ILRM 86 (HC); *Madden v Irish Turf Club* [1997] 2 ILRM 148 (SC); *Irish Equine Foundation Ltd v Robinson* [1999] 2 ILRM 289 (HC).
11. *Cf*, eg, *Wall v Hegarty* [1980] ILRM 124 (HC); *Tulsk v Ulster Bank Ltd* High Court, 13 May 1983 (Gannon J); *Towey v Ulster Bank Ltd* [1987] ILRM 142 (HC); *Cotter v Minister for Agriculture* Supreme Court, 1 April 1993; *Forshall v Walsh* Supreme Court, 31 July 1998; *Wildgust v Bank of Ireland* High Court, 28 July 1998 (Morris P); *Doolan v Murray* High Court, 21 December 1993 (Keane J); *McKenna v Best Travel t/a Cypriano Holidays* High Court, 17 December 1996 (Lavan J) revd by Supreme Court, 18 November 1997.
12. [1932] AC 562 (HL, SC).
13. *Cf Wall v Hegarty* [1980] ILRM 124; *Doran v Delaney* [1998] 2 ILRM 1 (SC); *Forshall v Walsh* Supreme Court, 31 July 1998; *McAnarney v Hanrahan* [1994] 1 ILRM 210 (HC); *McCullagh v PB Gunne (Monaghan) plc* High Court, 17 January 1997 (Carroll J).

means that the professional person whose conduct has been impugned is unable to shelter behind the deferential criterion[14] that applies to professional negligence in general.

## II. The Contemporary Irish Approach to Pure Economic Loss

**[10.10]** The most appropriate starting-point for our analysis of the contemporary Irish approach to liability for negligently caused pure economic loss is *McShane Wholesale Fruit and Vegetables Ltd v Johnston Haulage Co Ltd.*[15] The plaintiffs' factory had been brought to a halt by the loss of electrical power caused by a fire in the defendants' adjoining premises. The plaintiffs sued for damages for the economic loss[16] that they sustained. Their central point was, a claim in negligence.

**[10.11]** Flood J was called on to try a preliminary issue as to "whether economic loss consequent on a negligent act is recoverable as damages, within this jurisdiction". He disposed of the issue in twelve sentences:

> "In Ireland since the Supreme Court decision in *Ward v McMaster*[17] the test for actionable negligence is:
>
> (a) A sufficient relationship of proximity between the alleged wrongdoer and the person who has suffered damage.
>
> (b) Such relationship that in the reasonable contemplation of the former carelessness on his part may be likely to cause damage to the latter - in which case a *prima facie* duty of care arises.
>
> (c) Subject always to any compelling exemption based on public policy.
>
> McCarthy J[18] stated the position as follows:
>
>> 'I prefer to express the duty as arising from the proximity of the parties, the foreseeability of the damage and the absence of any compelling exemption based on public policy. I do not in any fashion seek to exclude the latter consideration although I confess that such a consideration must be a very powerful one if it is to be used to deny any injured party his right to redress at the expense of the person or body that injured him.'
>
> The quality of the damage does not arise. It can be damage to property, to the person, financial or economic.[19] The question as to whether the damage (of whatever type) is recoverable is dependent on proximity and foreseeability subject to the caveat of compelling exemption on public policy.

14. *Cf Roche v Peilow* [1985] IR 232 (SC); *Dunne v National Maternity Hospital* [1989] IR 91.
15. [1997] 1 ILRM 86 (HC).
16. Flood J in his judgment did not describe the loss suffered by the plaintiff as being of purely economic character and he quoted the plaintiff's "Particulars of Negligence", which included a claim that the defendant had failed to take adequate precautions to ensure that the fire "would not spread to and *cause damage to the plaintiff and its said premises*" (emphasis added). Nonetheless the only loss identified by the plaintiff was "a loss of electrical power in consequence of which is suffered loss and damage in carrying out its ... business." Moreover, the tenor of Flood J's judgment is that he was addressing the issue of the duty to avoid causing pure economic loss rather than merely economic loss consequent on physical injury sustained by the plaintiff.
17. [1989] ILRM 400 (SC).
18. [1989] ILRM 400 at 409
19. Citing *Sweeney v Duggan* [1991] IR 274.

In short, the proximity of the parties giving rise to the duty of care must be such, as a matter of probability to be causal of the damage. If it is not, the damage is too remote and the action will fail. It will fail not because the damage is of a particular type but because the relationship between the wrongdoer and the person who suffers the damage does not have the essential, of sufficient relationship of proximity or neighbourhood.

It therefore follows that the fact that the damage is economic is not in itself a bar to recovery where the other elements above stated are present.

Whether the damage in this instance is or is not too remote is a question of fact to be determined on evidence."[20]

**[10.12]** The analysis provokes a number of observations. The first, and most obvious, is that Flood J appears to regard claims based on pure economic loss as essentially non-controversial and non-distinctive: the fact that the damage is economic "is not in itself a bar to recovery where the other elements above stated are present."

**[10.13]** A closer inspection of what he had to say, however, suggests a more nuanced interpretation. Flood J was, after all, answering a preliminary issue, expressed in the broadest terms: "whether economic loss consequent on a negligent act is recoverable as damages, within this jurisdiction." His reply goes no further than to confirm that such loss *is not inevitably irrecoverable*; the precise extent of recoverability will depend on proximity, foreseeability[21] and the absence of any "compelling exemption o[f] public policy" but clearly the court retains control over the scope of the actionable duty of care in this context.

**[10.14]** As we shall see below, courts have had a tendency to exclude a duty of care for certain types of pure economic loss, as, for example, where a plaintiff suffers such loss consequent on damage to property in which he or she has no proprietary interest.[22] It remains to be seen whether Flood J's observations will be interpreted as inconsistent with

---

20. [1997] 1 ILRM 86 at 88-89.

21. It is perhaps unfortunate that foreseeability should be mentioned in this precise context, since the requirement of reasonable foreseeability as a condition of liability is endemic to all actions for negligence: *cf* Ch 3 above. Of course it is true that the issue whether a pure economic loss sustained by the plaintiff was reasonably foreseeable may on occasion require to be determined, but this will be addressed from the standpoint of remoteness of damage rather than the duty of care. *Condon v Coras Iompair Éireann* High Court, 4 November 1984 (Barrington J) is instructive. In this case, the plaintiff, a railway employee, obtained compensation for the legal and other costs and expenses of being represented at an inquiry ordered by the Minister for Transport and Tourism, under the Railway Regulation Act 1871, s 7, arising out of a serious railway accident for which CIE was responsible. Barrington J considered it "almost unthinkable" that the Minister would not have ordered an inquiry. This being so, it was reasonably foreseeable that the plaintiff, as a person immediately involved in the events leading up to the disaster, should, in his own interest seek to be represented before the inquiry. The issue as fought before Barrington J was one of remoteness of damage rather than of the duty of care. It may be noted that the plaintiff had sustained personal injuries in the accident; this aspect of his case was, however, dealt with in separate proceedings. Nothing in Barrington J's judgment suggests that the plaintiff would not have succeeded in his claim for pure economic loss if he had emerged physically unscathed from the accident.

22. This appears to be the approach favoured by the Supreme Court of Canada in *Bow Husky (Bermuda) Ltd v St John Shipbuilding Co Ltd* (1997) 153 DLR (4th) 385. See Rafferty, 'Pure Economic Loss in the Supreme Court of Canada – the Final Word?' (1999) 15 Professional Neg 13.

the development of such focused sub-categories of immunity from liability. Perhaps the shadow of the judgment of the European Court of Human Rights in *Osman v United Kingdom*[23] will discourage the Irish courts from doing so, and instead address the issues of proximity and public policy on an individual case-by-case basis.

**[10.15]** The most recent judicial utterance on the subject is that of Geoghegan J in *Irish Equine Foundation Ltd.*[24] Having described the British retrenchment over the past decade, he observed, *obiter*, that "... the law relating to the recovery of pure economic loss in a negligence action would appear to be different in Ireland having regard to *Ward v McMaster*".[25]

## III. The Contractual Dimension

**[10.16]** The interrelationship between the law of contract and the law of tort is crucial to the determination of the scope of liability in negligence for pure economic loss.[26] Of course the law of contract can involve potential liability for physical injury, as will be the case with employment contracts and contracts for the provision of certain professional services, such as those of medicine. Most contracts nonetheless are concerned with pure economic gain (or, in the case of their breach, loss). The law of contract mainly protects economic rather than physical security.

**[10.17]** The courts have addressed the question whether the law of contract should exclusively govern the potential liability of the parties or whether concurrent liability, in both contract and tort, is permissible. They have concluded that concurrent liability is indeed permissible but it must be acknowledged that not everything they have said on this issue is entirely clear or consistent.

**[10.18]** A number of propositions can, however, be made with confidence. First, where the plaintiff, who is in a contractual relationship with the defendants, sues the defendant in negligence, arguing that the defendant has breached his or her duty of care to the plaintiff and the plaintiff does not seek to rely on any specific term of the contract, express or implied, but rather on some other source of the duty, the claim in negligence is not excluded by reason of the existence of the contract. Thus, in *Finlay v Murtagh*,[27] where the Supreme Court recognised for the first time that the client of a solicitor may sue the solicitor in tort for negligence as well as in contract for breach of contract, Henchy J stated:

> "The coincidence that the [solicitor]'s conduct amounts to a breach of contract cannot affect either the duty of care or the common-law liability for its breach, for it is the general relationship, and not any particular manifestation such as contract, that gives rise to the tortious liability in such a case ..."[28]

23. [1999] 1 FLR 193.
24. [1999] 2 ILRM 289 (HC).
25. [1999] 2 ILRM 289 at 295.
26. See STREET, pp 196-198; FLEMING, pp 203-207.
27. [1979] IR 249 (SC). See further para **[14.171]-[14.174]** below.
28. [1979] IR 257

**[10.19]** Equally, it is accepted that the *Hedley Byrne* principle, relating to tortious negligent misrepresentation, can apply where the parties are in a contractual relationship with each other.[29]

**[10.20]** In these cases, whether the court in addressing the "general duty of care" of a professional or the assumption of responsibility in the context of *Hedley Byrne* liability, it should be noted, however, that the existence of a contractual relationship between the parties is not a complete irrelevancy. On the contrary, it may be of considerable relevance in determining whether the defendant owed, and breached, a duty of care to the plaintiff; but in factoring in the contractual dimension of the parties' relationship, the court will not simply engage in a process of characterising a contractual term as a tortious obligation. In *Finlay v Murtagh*, Henchy J sought to make this distinction clear when he explained that no tortious liability attaches where the solicitor is in breach, not of his or her general duty of care arising form the professional relationship with the client, but of "a particular and special term of the contract in respect of which the solicitor would not be liable if the contract had not contained such a term".[30]

**[10.21]** Let us now turn to the situation where the plaintiff points to a contract between himself or herself and the defendant and argues that, *by virtue of the contractual relationship*, the defendant owed the plaintiff a duty of care to avoid causing the plaintiff physical or economic injury. Of course many contracts will contain a term (usually implied rather than express) that the defendant will take due care to avoid causing such injury, but the question has arisen as to whether the plaintiff is limited in such cases to the terms of the contract or may instead make a separate claim in negligence.

**[10.22]** In Britain, *Tai Hing Cotton Mill Ltd v Liu Chong Hing Bank Ltd*[31] represents the high water mark of the policy of excluding the claim in negligence. Lord Scarman stated:

> "Though it is possible as a matter of legal semantics to conduct an analysis of the rights and duties inherent in some contractual relationships either as a matter of contract law when the question will be what, if any, terms are to be implied or as a matter of tort law when the task will be to identify a duty arising from the proximity and character of the relationship between the parties, their Lordships believe it to be correct on principle and necessary for the avoidance of confusion in the law to adhere to the contractual analysis, on principle because it is a relationship in which the parties have, subject to a few exceptions, the right to determine their obligations to each other, and for avoidance of confusion because different consequences do follow according to whether liability arises from contract or tort, eg in the limitation of action."[32]

**[10.23]** In the later decision of the House of Lords in *Henderson v Merrett Syndicates Ltd*,[33] this approach was rejected.[34] Lord Goff expressed the belief that, in the context of the facts of the case before the House:

---

29. See para **[10.80]** below.
30. [1979] IR 257.
31. [1986] AC 80 (HL, Eng).
32. [1986] AC 80 at 107.
33. [1995] 2 AC 145 (HL, Eng).
34. *Cf* STREET, p 197, observing that, after *Henderson v Merrett Syndicates Ltd*, "[t]he old restrictive rules Lord Scarman sought to resurrect in *Tai Hing* remain dead and buried."

> "the common law is not antipathetic to concurrent liability, and that there is no sound basis for a rule which automatically restricts the claimant to either a tortious or a contractual remedy. The result may be untidy; but given that the tortious duty is imposed by the general law, and the contractual duty is attributable to the will of the parties, I do not find it objectionable that the claimant may be entitled to take advantage of the remedy which is most advantageous to him, subject only to ascertaining whether the tortious duty is so inconsistent with the applicable contract that, in accordance with ordinary principle the parties must be taken to have agreed that the tortious remedy is to be limited or excluded."[35]

**[10.24]** In the Supreme Court decision of *Kennedy v Allied Irish Banks Ltd*,[36] Hamilton CJ accepted that this passage from Lord Goff's speech contained "the correct statement of the law".

**[10.25]** One should be cautious about the Chief Justice's endorsement of Lord Goff's approach in *Henderson* since he went on immediately thereafter to quote a quite inconsistent proposition from an earlier English Court of Appeal decision[37] before observing that:

> "[t]he case clearly establishes that, when parties are in a contractual relationship, their mutual obligations arise from their contract and are to be found expressly or by necessary implication in the terms thereof and that obligations in tort which may arise from such contractual relationship can not be greater than those to be found expressly or by necessary implication in their contract."[38]

With respect, that is exactly what Lord Goff denied in *Henderson*.[39]

---

35. [1995] 2 AC 193-194.
36. [1998] 2 IR 48 at 56 (O'Flaherty and Denham JJ concurring).
37. *National Bank of Greece SA v Pinios Shipping Co (No 3)* [1988] 2 Lloyd's Rep 126 where Lloyd LJ stated:

    > "[S]o far as I know it has never been the law that a plaintiff who has the choice of suing in contract or tort can fail in contract yet nevertheless succeed in tort."

38. *Kennedy v Allied Irish Banks Ltd* [1998] 2 IR 48 at 56.
39. Hamilton CJ went on to affirm the dismissal of the plaintiffs' case by the trial judge on the basis, first that, on the facts the bank was not liable to the plaintiffs, its customers, under the *Hedley Byrne* principle and, secondly, that the bank had not been in breach of a duty of care owed to the plaintiffs in considering its own interests to their detriment when deciding whether to grant them a loan facility that the plaintiffs considered was necessary to ensure the viability of a property development in which it was engaged having received the previous support of the bank. It is one thing to deny liability on these grounds; it is quite another to contend that no more extensive obligations were *capable* of arising in tort than under the contract. Of course, there may be good policy reasons for a court's concluding that, with regard to particular relationships, such as that of banker and customer, the limits of the contractual terms should represent the limits of the duty of care in negligence, so far as pure economic loss is concerned (subject to the *Hedley Byrne* principle, which is not founded on a contractual base). If that is the true rationale of *Kennedy*, then its holding may perhaps be defended but it remains the case that Hamilton CJ's judgment include statements of law inconsistent with such an approach and inconsistent with the observations of Lord Goff with which the Chief Justice expresses agreement. It seems clear, in any event, from the decision of *Tulsk Co-operative Livestock Mart Ltd v Ulster Bank Ltd* High Court, 13 May 1993 (Gannon J), *Brennan v Bank of Ireland* High Court, 23 May 1985 (Murphy J) and *Towey v Ulster Bank Ltd* [1987] ILRM 142 that a bank's duty of care to its customer is not necessarily co-incidental with the terms of its contract with the customers. See further Donnelly, *The Law of Banks and Credit Institutions* (2000), Ch 7; Breslin, *Banking Law in the Republic of Ireland* (1998), Ch 11.

**[10.26]** The issue was revisited by the Supreme Court in *Pat O'Donnell & Co Ltd v Truck & Machinery Sales Ltd.*[40] There O'Flaherty J invoked the passage from Hamilton CJ's judgment in *Kennedy* that endorsed Lord Goff's approach in support for the following proposition:

> "[T]he general duty of care in tort cannot be manipulated so as to override the contractual allocation of responsibility between the parties. Thus if, for instance, a contract provides – whether expressly or by necessary implication – that the defendant is not liable for a particular risk, then the law of tort should not be allowed to contradict it."[41]

**[10.27]** The idea of a corpus of responsibility which is broken down between the parties to a contract is curious. A contract does not normally involve such a distribution but rather the assumption of *separate* responsibilities by the parties. If I buy a bar of chocolate from you, my responsibility is to pay you the price; yours is to give me the chocolate. Our respective responsibilities are quite different from each other. If you wish to reduce your responsibility in respect of the bar of chocolate by a contractual waiver, you can do so (if I agree) subject to the restrictions laid down by pro-consumer legislation.[42] In reducing your contractual responsibility you are not imposing any extra responsibility on me (though you may be adding to my practical worries).

**[10.28]** There are, however, some cases where a particular activity or process may involve a true contractual allocation of responsibilities as between the parties. For example, two people who are jointly involved in designing a lamp may ascribe particular responsibilities to each other in the context of testing the materials from a safety standpoint. If the prototype of the lamp burns down the premises of one of the parties because of an unsafe ingredient and that party sues the other in negligence, the other is perfectly entitled to invoke the terms of the contract, with their allocation of respective responsibilities, in aid of the argument that he or she is not liable in tort.

**[10.29]** One may doubt whether O'Flaherty J envisaged such a scenario. It seems far more likely that what he had in mind was an allocation of *risk* between the parties, as mentioned in his example. Such an allocation of risk may of course be made by the express or implied terms of the contract, *for the purposes of the contract itself.* But this will not necessarily exclude a claim based on the tort of negligence. A court should conclude that it has this effect only where it so construes the contract or where it considers that, in the light of the totality of the relationship between the parties, including their contractual relationship, it would not be appropriate to impose a duty of care.

**[10.30]** Another recent decision of the Supreme Court has analysed the relationship between breach of contract and the duty of care in negligence not to cause economic loss. In *Sweeney v Duggan*,[43] the plaintiff, a labourer was injured when working for a company of which the defendant was managing director and owner of all but one of its shares. The plaintiff initially sued the company for damages for negligence and breach of statutory duty but was able to enforce only part of the judgment against the company as it had no

---

40. Supreme Court, 18 February 1997.
41. Supreme Court, 18 February 1997.
42. *Cf* the Sale of Goods and Supply of Services Act 1980, s 22.
43. [1997] 2 ILRM 211 (SC).

employers' liability insurance and at the time of liquidation was unable to pay all its creditors in full.

**[10.31]** The plaintiff, then sued the defendant personally and in his action for negligence and breach of contract against the defendant, argued that the company ought to have procured employers' liability insurance or, failing that, to have warned him that no such policy was in existence. The plaintiff also claimed that the defendant had a duty to ensure that the company obtained such insurance or, if not, he had a duty to warn him that it had not done so.

**[10.32]** It was contended on behalf of the plaintiff that the obligations, so far as they fell on the company, derived primarily, and perhaps exclusively, from the contractual relationship between the employer and employee. The particular duty to insure against liability was, it was argued, an implied term of the contract.

**[10.33]** Murphy J (Hamilton CJ and Barrington JJ concurring) gave a detailed analysis of the latter issue, concluding that such a term could not be implied, in spite of the great danger to employees working in quarries where the accident rate was about eight times worse than on building sites generally. Murphy J placed considerable emphasis on British decisions,[44] in support of his view that "the obligation[s] as between the employer and employee in a case such as the present are to be found in contract and not in tort."[45]

**[10.34]** If the company had no liability in contract to the plaintiff, then neither had the defendant. It was true that the defendant had a variety of duties to the plaintiff as "a fellow workman" and in his capacity as quarry manager, the breach of which would involve him in tortious liability, but in the instant case the plaintiff had not alleged that any of these duties had been neglected nor would the breach of any of them provide the remedy which the plaintiff sought to assert.

**[10.35]** Murphy J found it:

> "difficult to accept that a director or shareholder as such has the necessary relationship with an employee of his company to give rise to any duty on the part of the director/shareholder for the economic welfare of the employee. I find it inconceivable that any such duty on the part of a corporator, if it did exist, could be more extensive than that of the corporation itself."[46]

Accordingly, the Supreme Court dismissed the plaintiff's appeal.

**[10.36]** *Sweeney v Duggan* throws little light on the juridical relationship between contractual and delictual claims. It appears to hold that the limits of liability in negligence on the part of an employer are broadly co-extensive with those of contractual liability. It is true that Murphy J does not go quite so far, since he restricts his remarks to "a case such as the present". His judgment gives no clear guidance on what particular distinguishing

44. *Reid v Rush & Tompkins Group plc* [1990] 1 WLR 212; *Van Oppen v Bedford Charity Trustees* [1990] 1 WLR 235; *Scally v Southern Health Board* [1992] 1 AC 294 (HL, Eng). Murphy J noted that, in *Reid* and in *Scally*, the passage from Lord Scarman's speech in *Tai Hing Cotton Mill Ltd v Liu Chong Hing Bank Ltd* [1986] AC 80 at 107 set out in para **[10.22]** above had been quoted with approval.

45. [1997] 2 ILRM 211 at 222.

46. [1997] 2 ILRM 211 at 222.

features of the instant case made it appropriate to restrict the employer's liability to the contractual aspects of its relationship with its employee.

**[10.37]** It is, of course, true that very many of the breaches by an employer of its duty of care in negligence to an employee will also generate contractual liability. This does not mean, however, that the starting and finishing point for judicial analysis should be in the field of implied contractual terms. Where the plaintiff's case centres on two matters in particular, it seems that the courts should give the right of way to the negligence action.

**[10.38]** The first of these matters is whether the employer has acted as a reasonable employer ought to have acted in relation to the employee. It is better for the courts to deal with this question by reference to the standard criteria appropriate to actions for negligence rather than to ask whether it is possible to fashion an implied contractual term. It is not the case that every employment contract contains an implied term that the employer will comply with the requirements of the standard of care in every aspect of the employment relationship.

**[10.39]** The second matter is one that was raised in *Sweeney v Duggan* which concerns the duty of care in negligence. A characteristic of the law of negligence is that it allows a plaintiff to assert that the defendant owed a duty of care in totally novel circumstances where no court previously held there to be such a duty. The court may, of course, reject the claim but equally a court may hold that, in spite of the novelty of the claim, a duty of care did indeed arise. There is simply no way in which the same outcome could be reached by the route of an implied contractual term. It would be implausible to suggest that a novel duty of care could pass the *Moorcock* test,[47] nor could it often be convincingly claimed that an implied term to this effect derives from the nature of the contract itself.

**[10.40]** We now must consider whether being party to a contract can kill off a claim for economic loss taken either by a party to the contract against a third party or *vice versa*.

**[10.41]** In *Madden v Irish Turf Club*,[48] this issue fell for consideration. The plaintiff had bet on a horse on the totalisator in a race where that horse came second to an ineligible horse which was later disqualified on account of its failure to fulfil the necessary qualification to compete in the race. The rules of the totalisator were that payment was made after the "All right" had been announced and that no subsequent disqualification would change the position. The plaintiff, who would have won £18,000 if his horse had come first, sued the Irish Turf Club, which administers flat racing in Ireland, and the Irish National Hunt Steeple Chase Committee, which has a similar function in relation to steeple chasing, both of these defendants sharing facilities and employees. He argued that, in carelessly permitting the ineligible horse to run, they had breached their duty of care in negligence to him.

**[10.42]** The Supreme Court, reversing Morris J, dismissed the claim. O'Flaherty J (Blayney and Murphy JJ concurring) reasoned as follows. The betting aspect of race meetings was separate from the defendants' "essential function", which was to regulate and control horse races at various courses around the country. The Rules of Racing and the

47. (1889) 14 PD 64.
48. [1997] 2 ILRM 148 (SC).

Irish National Hunt Steeple Chase Rules expressly provided that stewards were to take no cognisance of any disputes or claims with respect to bets. Further:

> "the plaintiff's contractual relationship was with the tote management and that erected a barrier so as to prevent such close and direct relations to occur as is necessary to give rise to any duty of care between the plaintiff and the defendants."[49]

**[10.43]** If the suggestion here is that the existence of a contractual relationship between A and B automatically erects a barrier to the establishment of a relationship of proximity between A and C, involving a duty of care on C's part to A, this would clearly be insupportable. What O'Flaherty J surely meant was that, in the particular circumstances of the case, the plaintiff's contractual relationship with the tote management represented the limits of the plaintiff's justifiable expectations and the limits of how others, who were not parties to it, might reasonably be called on to act. What was involved was a bet, those who wager about an uncertain outcome cannot reasonably call on others to act in a way that makes their assessment of that outcome more reliable.[50] The possibility that others may act carelessly is simply part of the risk.

**[10.44]** If we take the converse case, where C is seeking to establish a duty of care towards him or her on the part of A, who is in a contractual relationship with B, it is now clear that there can be no objection in principle to such a claim, even where the duty relates to the avoidance of pure economic loss. The existence of the contract, far from automatically exempting A from a duty of care to C, may well be the very reason why a duty of care should be imposed. Thus, for example, in *Wall v Hegarty*,[51] a disappointed beneficiary was held entitled to sue a solicitor whose negligent breach of contract with the testator resulted in loss to the intended beneficiary.

**[10.45]** *Junior Books Ltd v Veitchi Co Ltd*[52] is perhaps the clearest, if most controversial, instance of a contractual obligation with one party generating a duty of care not to cause pure economic loss to another person, who is not a party to contract. *Junior Books* has effectively been sidelined in subsequent British decisions[53] but still holds sway in Ireland. We examine this aspect of the subject in greater detail below.[54]

---

49. [1997] 2 ILRM 148 at 155.

50. This appears to have been the thrust of the argument by counsel for the plaintiffs, who went on to contend, on the basis of *Ward v McMaster* [1988] IR 337, *Sunderland v Louth County Council* [1990] ILRM 658 and *McMahon v Ireland* [1988] ILRM 610, that, in claims for economic loss, whatever about claims for personal injury or physical damage, "a duty of care must be established through the *relationship* of the parties" [1997] 2 ILRM 148 at 152 (*per* O'Flaherty J) summarising, with apparent approval, the asignment of counsel for the defendants. O'Flaherty J was clearly concerned about the public policy implications of imposing liability on the defendants for carelessness in permitting an ineligible horse to run in a race. He invoked Cardozo CJ's famous warning in *Ultramares Corporation & Touche* (1931) 255 NY 170 at 179 against "liability in an indeterminate amount for an indeterminate time to an indeterminate class". Since the public policy argument had not been debated in the High Court and was not necessary for the decision, O'Flaherty J left over consideration of it to another day.

51. [1980] ILRM 124 (HC).

52. [1983] 1 AC 520 (HL, SC).

53. *Cf Muirhead v Industrial Tank Specialties* [1986] QB 507 (CA); *Simaan General Contracting Co v Pilkington Glass Ltd (No 2)* [1988] QB 758 (CA); *Murphy v Brentwood District Council* [1991] 1 AC 398 (HL, Eng).

54. See para **[11.75]** below.

**[10.46]** Let us now consider how the courts deal with cases where the economic loss sustained by the plaintiff consists of damage to his or her contractual expectancies, either by making it more difficult for the plaintiff to discharge his or her contractual obligations or by reducing the profits that the plaintiff might have expected from the contract. The judicial attitude towards claims of this character has been hostile.[55] Thus, for example, an insurance company that pays out on a policy because the insured has been injured or killed or the insured's property has been damaged through the negligence of another will not be permitted to recoup its loss by suing the negligent person.[56] As Fleming observes:

> "it is doubtful if the insurer can be said to have recovered injury in any real sense. For how can realisation of the risk insured against constitute a loss when that very risk was calculated into the premium? For that matter, how can the fact that one is called upon to perform a contractual obligation ever constitute an injury, let alone a tortious injury?"[57]

Perhaps *Madden v Irish Turf Club*[58] can best be understood as an example of a case where negligent damage to a contractual expectancy was held not to generate liability.

**[10.47]** It is well established in English law that:

> "[a] plaintiff who suffers economic loss consequent on physical damage to another person, or to property in which at the time damage is suffered he has no proprietary interest, cannot recover that loss in tort."[59]

In Ireland, support for this approach can be found in the High Court decision of *Irish Paper Sacks Ltd v John Sisk & Son (Dublin) Ltd.*[60] There, the defendant's employees, when excavating a trench on the highway, severed a cable that supplied electricity to the plaintiff's factory. This resulted in a power failure lasting two days, during which time the plaintiff had to cease production at the factory. The company suffered economic losses in relation to labour, overheads and loss of profits. It suffered no damage, however, since the severed cable was not on its property.

**[10.48]** Recovery was denied. After referring to the English decisions of *Electrochrome Ltd v Welsh Plastics Ltd,*[61] *Elliott v Sir Robert McAlpine & Sun Ltd*[62] and *Hedley Byrne & Co Ltd v Heller & Partners Ltd,*[63] O'Keefe P stated:

> "The principle to be derived from these cases is that a plaintiff suing for damages suffered as a result of an act or omission of the defendant cannot recover if the act or omission did not directly injure the plaintiff's person or property, but merely caused consequential loss. After a full consideration of the matter I think that I must apply the principle to the[se] cases."[64]

---

55. *Cf Cattle v Stockton Waterworks* (1875) *Co* LR 10 QB 453; *La Societé de Remorquage à Hélice v Bennetts* [1911] 1 KB 243; *Weller & Co v Foot and Mouth Disease Research Institute* [1966] 1 QB 569.
56. *Simpson v Thomson* (1877) 3 App Cas 279.
57. FLEMING, pp 196-197.
58. [1997] 2 ILRM 148 (SC).
59. STREET, p 227 (footnote references omitted)
60. High Court, 18 May 1972 (O'Keefe P).
61. [1968] 2 All ER 205.
62. [1966] 2 Lloyds LR 482.
63. [1964] AC 465 (HL, Eng).
64. Page 4 of O'Keefe P's judgment.

**[10.49]** It seems that Flood J in *McShane Wholesale Fruit and Vegetables Ltd v Johnston Haulage Co Ltd*[65] has taken a more liberal approach and has expressly rejected the idea that the court should, *a priori*, exclude liability for negligently caused pure economic loss, without first investigating whether, on the facts the particular case, there is sufficient proximity of relationship between the parties to impose a duty of care, subject to the caveat of a "compelling exemption on public policy".[66]

## IV. The *Hedley Byrne* Principle[67]

### The Old Approach

**[10.50]** Tort law was slow to give a remedy for pure economic[68] loss resulting from negligent misstatements unless there was a contractual or fiduciary relationship between the parties[69] or unless the defendant was guilty of fraud. The Courts were fearful of imposing "liability in an indeterminate amount for an indeterminate time to an indeterminate class".[70] People notoriously are less careful about what they say than about what they do. Moreover, "words are more volatile than deeds, they travel fast and far afield, they are used without being expended".[71]

**[10.51]** For many years after the decision of *Donoghue v Stevenson*[72] negligent[73] misstatements continued[74] to be regarded as immune from the application of the "neighbour" principle of negligence. In time, however, the old law gave way.

---

65. [1997] 1 ILRM 86. See further paras **[10.10]-[10.15]** above.

66. For further consideration of the various attempts by the courts throughout the common law world to produce meaningful criteria for restricting the scope of liability for negligently caused pure economic loss, see the second edition of this work, pp 162-168. More recent developments in Australia are comprehensively analysed by TRINDADE & CANE, pp 369-399.

67. See Donnelly *Recent Developments in the Tort of Negligent Misstatement* (1996) 14 ILT (ns) 123; Stevens '*Hedley Byrne & Co Ltd v Heller & Partners Ltd:* Judicial Creativity and Doctrinal Possibility' (1964) 27 MLR 121; Honore *Hedley Byrne & Co Ltd v Heller & Partners Ltd* (1965) 8 JSPTL 284; Weir *Liability for Syntax* [1963] CLJ 216; Symmons *The Problem of Applicability of Tort Liability to Negligent Misstatements in Contractual Situations* (1975) 21 McGill LJ 79; Goodhart *Liability for Innocent but Negligent Misrepresentations* (1964) 74 Yale LJ 286; *James & Gray Misrepresentation* (1978) 37 Maryland LR 286 at 488; Gordon *Hedley Byrne v Heller in the House of Lords* (1965) 2 UBC LR 113.

68. In contrast to physical injury or damage: *cf Forsythe v GN Ry Co (Ireland)* [1937] Ir Jur Rep 18 (HC); *Brogan v Bennett* [1955] IR 119 (SC); *Sharp v Avery and Kerwood* [1938] 4 All ER 85 (CA).

69. *Leech v Stokes* [1937] IR 787 (SC affg HC). *Cf Martin v Irish Industrial Benefit Building Society* [1960] Ir Jur Rep 42 (CC).

70. *Ultramares v Touche Niven & Co* (1931) 255 NYS 170 at 179, 174 NE 441 at 444. For criticism of this approach see Godwin 'Negligent Interference with Economic Expectancy: The Case for Recovery' (1964) 16 Stan LR 664.

71. *Hedley Byrne & Co Ltd v Heller & Partners Ltd* [1964] AC 465 at 534 (HL, Eng).

72. [1932] AC 562.

73. Of course advice may be *wrong* without necessarily being negligent: *Stafford v Conti Commodity Services Ltd* [1981] 1 All ER 691 (QBD).

74. *Cf Candler v Crane, Christmas & Co* [1951] 2 KB 164, analysed by Seavey (1951) 67 LQR 466; Wilson (1952) 15 MLR 160.

## The *Hedley Byrne* Breakthrough

**[10.52]** The decision which established definitely in England that liability could arise from negligent misstatement is *Hedley, Byrne & Co Ltd v Heller & Partners Ltd.*[75] The case concerned a reference as to the creditworthiness of its customer given by one bank to another where in giving the reference the bank knew or ought to know that this information would be passed on to the plaintiff company, which was about to do business with the customer.

**[10.53]** The reference was negligent and as a result the plaintiff company suffered loss. The reference contained a disclaimer which the House of Lords held was sufficient to relieve the defendant bank of responsibility, but the case is important on account of the fact that the speeches delivered in the House of Lords, despite differences of emphasis, were to the effect that there can be liability for negligent misstatement in cases where a party seeking information from the defendant relies on his special skill and trusts him to exercise due care.

**[10.54]** The several speeches in *Hedley Byrne* contain different statements of the circumstances in which this duty of care will arise. On the one hand, Lord Morris considered that:

> "it should now be regarded as settled that if someone possessed of a special skill undertakes, quite irrespective of contract, to apply that skill for the assistance of another person who relies upon that skill, a duty of care will arise ... Furthermore, if, in a sphere in which a person is so placed that others could reasonably rely upon his judgment or his skill or upon his ability to make careful inquiry, a person takes it upon himself to give information or advice to, or allows his information or advice to be passed on to, another person who, as he knows or should know, will place reliance upon it, then a duty of care will arise."[76]

**[10.55]** In contrast, Lord Devlin contented himself with the proposition that:

> "Wherever there is a relationship equivalent to contract, there is a duty of care. Such a relationship may be either general or particular. Examples of a general relationship are those of solicitor and client and of banker and customer ... There may well be others yet to be established."[77]

**[10.56]** As we shall see, the law has ultimately developed more on the lines proposed by Lord Morris than on those favoured by Lord Devlin.

**[10.57]** It is worth noting that the duty envisaged by the judges of the House of Lords was not considered to be one imposed on people against their free will. Lord Reid, for example, observed that:

> "A reasonable man, knowing that he was being trusted or that his skill and judgment were being relied on, would, I think, have three courses open to him. He could keep silent or decline to give the information or advice sought: or he could give an answer with a clear qualification that he accepted no responsibility for it or that it was given without the reflection or inquiry which a careful answer would require: or he could simply answer without any such qualification. If he chooses to adopt the last course he must, I think, be held

75. [1964] AC 465 (HL, Eng).
76. [1964] AC 465 at 502-503.
77. [1964] AC 465 at 530.

> to have accepted some responsibility for his answer being given carefully, or to have accepted a relationship with the inquirer which requires him to exercise such care as the circumstances require."[78]

## An Irish Harbinger of *Hedley Byrne*?

**[10.58]** Four years before the House of Lords decided *Hedley Byrne*, an Irish Circuit Court case, *Macken v Munster & Leinster Bank Ltd*,[79] had addressed the issue of negligent misrepresentation. The manager of a branch of the defendant bank assured the plaintiff, a grocer, who was not a customer of the bank, that if he signed a promissory note for a third party there would not be the slightest risk of the third party's default. In fact the third party was a fraudulent person who had engaged in a series of lies and who later defaulted. The plaintiff in the meantime had lent him money and given him credit in his shop, which the third party failed to repay.

**[10.59]** The plaintiff sued for damages in respect of his potential liability under the promissory note, as well as for the credit he had advanced. His counsel based the case on the principle that:

> "a person carrying on a business or profession who takes upon himself to give advice on a matter on which he professes skill or knowledge, in such circumstances that the person advised relies upon his special skill and knowledge, is under a duty to that person in advising him."[80]

**[10.60]** So far as the claim in relation to the promissory note was concerned Deale J narrowed his holding by stating that the judicial and academic authorities on the question of the liability of a banker volunteering advice as to the financial standing of a person about whom he was in a position to answer appeared:

> "not to be in point for this reason, that here [the manager and the bank] were in a special position vis-à-vis [the plaintiff], namely that they were either inviting or inducing him to enter into the contract to sign the promissory note and [the manager] knew that [the plaintiff] was to some extent relying on the information he was furnishing concerning [the third party]. So the parties were about to contract with each other and one of them was in possession of material information upon which the other was, to his knowledge, relying. [Counsel for the plaintiff] suggests that, this fact places the transaction in the category of a contract *uberrima[e] fidei*. I am not deciding that this was such a contract, though there is a resemblance, but I am of opinion that a banker in such a situation is bound to take reasonable care in the statements he makes to a person about to sign a promissory note as a guarantor."[81]

On the evidence, the judge concluded that the bank manager had not taken that care.

---

78. In *Towey v Ulster Bank Ltd* [1987] ILRM 142 at 149 (HC), O'Hanlon J, having quoted this passage, sounded a warning note. In the case of a banker asked by his own customer to advise him on a matter concerning the customer's business relations with another party, and in circumstances where the banker might be expected to be in a position to give worthwhile advice, the banker was "not quite as free to wash his hands of the hypothetical reasonable man in Lord Reid's example, and his duty of care may be somewhat more clearly defined than that of the banker who is merely doing an obligement for a fellow-banker". See also *Potterton Ltd v Northern Bank Ltd* [1993] ILRM 225 (HC), discussed at paras **[10.97]-[10.99]** below.
79. (1959) 95 ILTR 17 (CC).
80. (1959) 95 ILTR 17 at 18.
81. (1959) 95 ILTR 17 at 22-23.

**[10.61]** Deale J rejected the plaintiff's claim for damages in relation to the money he had afforded the fraudulent third party. Although the bank manager had over a period of months on several occasions reassured the plaintiff that the money was safe, this was, in the judge's view, merely a repetition of the manager's original belief already stated to the plaintiff and not a decisive factor in his decision to lend money to the third party. In "no way"[82] did these assurances set up any legal liability on the part of the Bank. Nor could the plaintiff's claim in relation to the supply of credit succeed. Although the manager's assurances "no doubt, had their influence"[83] on the plaintiff, no connection in law had been established between them and the giving of credit some time later, the plaintiff having desired to retain the goodwill of the household into which the third party had married and where he was staying at the time.

**[10.62]** Does *Macken v Munster & Leinster Bank Ltd* amount to a judicial recognition of a duty of care in negligence on the part of bankers volunteering advice as to financial standing? In favour of this view, it may be argued that this is precisely the basis on which counsel for the plaintiff presented the case; moreover Deale J rejected two of the three heads of the plaintiff's case, not apparently because there *could* be no legal liability attaching to the bank but because, on the particular facts, there *was* not. As against this, a formidable argument to the contrary may be made. First Deale J expressly dismissed the plaintiff's authorities on the broad issue of negligence as appearing "not to be in point"[84] because the case could be decided on the far narrower ground of the liability attaching to one who induces another to enter into a contract to sign a promissory note as a guarantor. The particular context would justify the imposition of due care under classic principles of contract and fiduciary relationships without necessarily venturing into the mainstream of tort law. Moreover Deale J's holding that, when he later received further information from abroad about the fraudulent third party, the bank manager owed "no duty in law to the plaintiff, the promissory note having been signed",[85] suggests that the judge considered that due care was required of the manager only in respect of the period prior to the signing of the note. It is, however, not easy to explain why the judge did not reject the other two headings of the plaintiff's claim out of hand. One possible, and scarcely convincing, reason may have been that he preferred to deal with the causation issue first, and that this disposed of these two headings without requiring him to address the difficult legal issue in the broader context of bankers' advice as to creditworthiness in general.

**[10.63]** Finally, it is perhaps worth noting that the authorities cited by the plaintiff were virtually[86] all prior to *Candler* (which was not cited to the Court by either side, so far as

---

82. (1959) 95 ILTR 17 at 22.
83. (1959) 95 ILTR 17 at 23.
84. (1959) 95 ILTR 17 at 22.
85. (1959) 95 ILTR 17 at 23.
86. The only exception was *Woods v Martins Bank Ltd* [1959] 1 QB 55, where Salmon J was willing to impose a duty of care as regards investment advice on a bank advising a potential customer. In *Hedley Byrne* [1964] AC 465 at 510-511, Lord Hodson observed that, although Salmon J had based liability on the existence of a fiduciary relationship, thus bringing the case within the scope of *Candler's* case, by which he was bound, the decision could nonetheless be properly sustained as an example of a "special relationship'' recognised in *Hedley Byrne* as importing a duty of care.

may be gleaned from the report of the case). The plaintiff cited the third edition of Paget's *Law of Banking*, published in 1947, four years before *Candler's* case.

### *Hedley Byrne* Reaches Ireland

**[10.64]** In the High Court decision of *Securities Trust Ltd v Hugh Moore & Alexander Ltd* in 1964,[87] *Hedley Byrne* made its way into Irish law. Counsel for the defendant in the *Securities Trust* case did not attempt to dispute the proposition in *Hedley Byrne* (as summarised by Davitt P) that:

> "circumstances may create a relationship between two parties in which, if one seeks information from the other and is given it, that other is under a duty to take reasonable care to ensure that the information is correct".[88]

The *Securities Trust* case arose out of a printing error in the Articles of Association of the defendant company. The Articles were sent by the company to a shareholder (pursuant to statutory obligation) in response to his request. The shareholder was the managing director of the plaintiff company, which, on foot of the inaccuracies in the Articles, invested money in the defendant company, eventually suffering financial loss as a result. The plaintiff company's action for negligent misstatement failed since the Articles had been supplied to the shareholder in his personal capacity. Davitt P considered that it could:

> "hardly be seriously contended that the defendant company owed a duty to the world at large to take care to avoid mistakes and printing errors in the reprint of their Articles".[89]

**[10.65]** Two years after *Securities Trust*, *Hedley Byrne* was again considered by the High Court in *Bank of Ireland v Smith*.[90] The defendant auctioneer published an advertisement for the sale of lands in which it was stated incorrectly that part of the lands had been undersown with permanent pasture. The plaintiff purchased the land on foot of this statement. On the assumption that the auctioneer had been negligent (which, on the evidence, the Court did not consider to have been the case[91]), it was contended by the plaintiff that the case fell within the scope of the *Hedley Byrne* principle on the basis that an auctioneer acting for a vendor should anticipate that any statement made by him about the property would be relied on by the purchaser.

**[10.66]** Kenny J rejected this argument, holding that liability could be imposed only where there was a relationship between the parties "equivalent to contract", namely, where there was an assumption of responsibility in circumstances in which, but for the absence of consideration, there would be a contract.

**[10.67]** *McSweeney v Bourke*[92] is a decision involving facts almost the converse of the *Securities Trust* case. A group of companies, in financial difficulties, engaged the defendant as a financial consultant to advise the group in respect of a possible takeover bid. The bid fell through, but the defendant subsequently set out a series of alternative courses open to the group, one of which involved the injection of capital into the group by

87. [1964] IR 417 (HC).
88. [1964] IR 417 at 421.
89. [1964] IR 417 at 422. *Cf Caparo Industries plc v Dickman* [1989] 1 All ER 798 (CA).
90. [1966] IR 646 (HC).
91. *Cf* [1966] IR 646 at 660.
92. High Court, 24 November 1980 (Carroll J).

the two plaintiffs, who were majority shareholders in the group and who had been in close consultation with the defendant during the formulation of his proposal. The plaintiffs made further investment into the group in line with the defendant's proposal. As events transpired over the following months, this investment proved costly.

**[10.68]** The plaintiffs' action against the defendant for negligent misstatement was dismissed. Carroll J held that, since the defendant was advising the group of companies rather than the plaintiffs personally, then, if he discharged his duty of care to the group, he could not in the circumstances of the case be liable to the plaintiffs. Carroll J stated that:

> "irrespective of contract, the adviser has a primary duty of care to the client and there may or may not be a duty to third parties. If the advice given is not given negligently *vis-à-vis* the client in the first instance but is given with all due care, there is no breach of duty to the client. If an adviser is not negligent vis-à-vis the client and does not purport to advise any person other than the client, I do not see how a third party who knows of the advice given to the client and who carries out steps outlined in that advice (ultimately to his own detriment) can claim that the advice was negligent in relation to him."[93]

**[10.69]** Turning to the facts of the case, Carroll J adopted a syllogistic approach: if, on the one hand the respective interests of the group and the shareholders were identical, then, once the advice to the group was given with due care, there was no breach of duty to the shareholders; on the other hand, if the respective interests were not identical, then:

> "the only reliance the two shareholders, as such, could place on the advice was that it was good advice for the group as a whole. They were intended to act on the advice but in the context that the advice was given with the interest of the group in mind. Once [the defendant] did not hold himself out as advising the shareholders as well as the group there was no additional duty imposed on [him] to add any words of warning in relation to the risks attached to further capital investment in the group. There is no evidence that [the defendant] undertook an additional and separate duty of advising shareholders, as such, with a conflicting interest."[94]

**[10.70]** After a review of the evidence, which showed that the defendant had not been negligent "in any way"[95] in the formulation of proposals on behalf of the group, Carroll J reiterated her finding that there was no evidence that the defendant had held himself out as advising any shareholder as such. If either of the plaintiffs assumed that he was advising them as shareholders, this "was not a reasonable assumption". If they placed reliance on the advice, they could do so only in the context that it was advice for the benefit of the group.

**[10.71]** The approach adopted by Carroll J might be considered to be somewhat indulgent to those who give negligent advice in contexts where they are aware that the advice will reasonably be relied upon by third parties even though those giving the advice "d[o] not purport to advise"[96] such parties. Auditors can owe a duty, under the *Hedley Byrne* principle, not only to the shareholders of the audited company but also to prospective investors. So far as the latter are concerned the foreseeability of such investors must be

---

93. High Court, 24 November 1980 at p 17 of judgment.
94. High Court, 24 November 1980 at p 18.
95. High Court, 24 November 1980 at p 22.
96. High Court, 24 November 1980.

very real and immediate before the courts will be disposed to impose a duty of care on the auditors in regard to them.[97]

## Judicial Development of the *Hedley Byrne* Principle

**[10.72]** Some of the decisions that have been discussed might suggest that it is well-nigh impossible to impose a duty of care outside relationships "equivalent to contract", but this is not the case. In many decisions a broader view is taken.[98] Thus, for example, it is now accepted that the plaintiff need not actually have solicited the information from the defendant, provided the defendant ought to have foreseen that it would be relied upon by the plaintiff.[99]

**[10.73]** This was the position in *Wall v Hegarty*[100] where, by reason of the negligence of the defendant solicitors in the execution of a will, the will was condemned. The plaintiff, an executor and disappointed legatee, was held entitled to recover damages, not only for the legacy that he lost, but also for the expense to which he was put in attempting to have the will admitted to probate. Barrington J, following the lead of the Supreme Court in *Finlay v Murtagh*[101] and, impressed by the "unanswerable"[102] reasoning of Sir Robert Megarry in the English decision of *Ross v Caunters (a firm)*,[103] imposed liability for the lost legacy on the basis of the broad "neighbour" principle first recognised in *Donoghue v Stevenson.*[104] He accepted that the same principle would also justify recovery for the expense involved in attempting to have the will admitted to probate. But Barrington J noted that this latter item of loss could also be recovered on *Hedley Byrne* principles even if the plaintiff's loss had

---

97. *Cf Caparo Industries plc v Dickman* [1989] 1 All ER 789 (CA), in which Bingham LJ (at 813) interpreted Woolf J's judgment in *JEB Fastners Ltd v Marks Bloom & Co (a firm)* [1981] 3 All ER 289 narrowly. In *Kelly v Boland t/a Haughey Boland & Co* [1989] ILRM 373 (HC), Lardner J had quoted with approval from Woolf J's judgment. No liability was found, on the facts, in *Kelly v Boland.* See also *Sisk (John) & Son Ltd v Flinn* High Court, 18 July 1984 (Finlay P), where the *Hedley Byrne* principle was held to apply but no liability was found on the facts. Accountants investigating the affairs of a company on behalf of the plaintiffs who were considering whether to engage in a rescue operation to keep the company in business were held negligent in *Golden Vale Co-Operative Creameries Ltd v Barrett* High Court, 16 March 1987 (O'Hanlon J). Although the defendants had done "an extremely good job ... within a remarkably short space of time", they had nevertheless failed in certain limited respects to protect the plaintiffs from falling into error. Although their Report had contained "all kinds of reservations", the overall impression created by certain extracts was "much more encouraging than was warranted" by the company as known to the defendants.

98. *Cf,* eg *Curley v Mulcahy* High Court, 21 December 1977 (McMahon J) at p 3 - architects who advised two companies with whom they were not in a contractual relationship owed them a duty of care since advice was given in circumstances in which reasonable men would know that their professional skill and judgment was being relied upon. See also *Ministry of Housing and Local Government v Sharp* [1970] 2 QB 223 (CA) - especially Salmon LJ's judgment; *Ross v Caunters (a firm)* [1980] Ch 279; *Lawton v BOC Transhield Ltd* [1987] 2 All ER 608 (QBD); *Wall v Hegarty* [1980] ILRM 124 (HC); *Finlay v Murtagh* [1979] IR 249 (SC).

99. *Cf Curley v Mulcahy* High Court, 21 December 1977; *Wall v Hegarty* [1980] ILRM 124.

100. [1980] ILRM 124.

101. See paras **[14.171]-[14.174]** above.

102. [1980] ILRM 124 at 129.

103. [1980] Ch 279.

104. [1932] AC 562.

not flown directly from the defendants' original carelessness in drafting the will. This was because the defendants had sent the plaintiff a copy of the will:

> "without drawing to his attention a fact (which someone in the firm must have known) that while the testator's signature appeared on the face of the will to have been properly attested it had not in fact been properly attested".[105]

One thus finds in *Wall v Hegarty* a willingness to use general negligence principles in imposing liability for pure economic loss in respect of relationships whose proximity is sealed by elements similar to, and overlapping with, those founding liability under *Hedley Byrne*, namely, trust, reliance, reasonable expectations, and an identified and finite group of persons whose expectations are thwarted.

**[10.74]** The same approach is apparent in *Tulsk v Ulster Bank Ltd.*[106] There, Gannon J considered that *Hedley Byrne* was one of the decisions which demonstrated that:

> "liability in negligence for damages is not derived solely from identifiable classifications of relationships but may derive from whatever relationships, however variable, the existing circumstances may import with the duty of care they demand."

**[10.75]** If this trend were to continue, the *Hedley Byrne* principle could in time become obsolete, having served its purpose in encouraging the courts to confront the difficult issue of compensation for pure economic loss. Nevertheless, it would seem premature to

---

105. [1980] ILRM 124 at 130. *Cf McCabe v Dolan Cosgrove & Co* High Court, 14 October 1991 (Lynch J) analysed by Byrne & Binchy *Annual Review of Irish Law 1991*, pp 388-390.

106. High Court, 13 May 1983 (Gannon J) at p 38. In *Tulsk* liability in negligence was imposed on the defendants, who gave comforting advice to the plaintiffs, who were their customers, about the creditworthiness of another customer, a cattle dealer, who did a very big business with the plaintiffs. and whose practice was to pay them large sums of money by cheques payable through an English bank but in Irish currency, which took some weeks to clear. The defendants failed to disclose a substantial body of disturbing information which became available to them as to their customer's financial standing. Gannon J considered that:

> "there was a relationship between the parties in which special information and advice of a confidential nature concerning the financial position of a mutual customer was required by the Mart from the Bank. The nature of the information required by the Mart was known to the Bank and the reason why it was required by the Mart was known to the Bank, and the fact that the Mart was dependent upon having the information truly and timely conveyed to them was known by the Bank. The means of acquiring the information which the Mart needed was within the control of the Bank who would have been more skilled than the Mart in assessing correctly the quality of the information, and who would have been more skilled than the Mart in recognising the nature and extent of the financial risks involved ... [T]he circumstances were such that the Bank was under a duty to the Mart to investigate actively and fully so far as Bank resources made possible the financial standing of [the other customer], to make an honest an financially skilful assessment of the business risks, if any, for the Mart involved in any trading with [the other customer], and to make honest but discreet disclosure of the information obtained to the Mart sufficient to enable the Mart to make their own business decision." (pp 44-45 of judgment).

Though Gannon J apparently preferred not to base liability specifically on the *Hedley Byrne* principle, it surely applied to the facts of the case, even if the Bank's functions as collecting bank and advising bank tended to merge.

In *Towey v Ulster Bank Ltd* [1987] ILRM 142 (HC), in litigation by a different plaintiff based on similar facts, O'Hanlon J also found the defendants liable in negligence. It seems that *Hedley Byrne* constituted at least one pillar in the foundations of such liability: *cf Towey v Ulster Bank Ltd* [1987] ILRM 142 at 148-149.

announce its eclipse by the notions of proximity and neighbourhood. Experience in Britain over the past few years shows how *Hedley Byrne* can act as a haven for courts intimidated by the experience of open discussion of these notions.[107]

**[10.76]** It is worth considering one aspect of the relationship between the *Hedley Byrne* principle and the wider duty of care in negligence. Even if *Hedley Byrne* is no longer to constitute a specific basis of liability, the questions it seeks to resolve will continue to call for resolution, albeit under the mantle of the general duty of care. We thus find in *Yuen Kun-yeu v AG of Hong Kong* the Privy Council holding that the Hong Kong Commissioner of deposit-taking companies owed no duty of care in negligence to future depositors in one such company since "no *special relationship* existed between [him] and the *unascertained members of the public* who might in future become exposed to the risk of financial loss through depositing money with the company". [108] This approach was endorsed by Blayney J in *McMahon v Ireland, the AG and the Registrar of Friendly Societies.*[109]

**[10.77]** In Britain over the past decade the courts have resiled from the *Anns*[110] "two-step" formula for determining whether a duty of care arises in any particular fact situation, preferring a more pragmatic, incremental approach, as is evidenced in *Caparo Industries v Dickman.*[111] In Ireland, the general policy has been to continue to favour McCarthy J's formula in *Ward v McMaster*,[112] which was largely influenced by *Anns* but was even more liberal in its enunciation, since it placed less emphasis on the policy factors inhibiting recognition of a duty of care. No Irish judge has repudiated McCarthy J's approach.

**[10.78]** In the context of *Hedley Byrne*, however, there has been a recent judicial tendency to merge the *Hedley Byrne* philosophy with what was said in *Ward v McMaster* and *Caparo*. Since there is no doctrinal symmetry between the two latter decisions, this raises new uncertainties. The two recent Irish decisions are *Forshall v Walsh*[113] and *Wildgust v Bank of Ireland.*[114]

**[10.79]** In *Forshall v Walsh*,[115] Shanley J held that one Michael McSweeney, a bank manager, who failed to exercise due care to the plaintiff in making representations that the company of which his brother Timothy was director was a concessionaire of Lamborghini Motor Cars, was liable for negligent misrepresentation and negligent misstatement to her when she gave moneys to the company, which she would not otherwise have done, to her detriment. Shanley J made it clear that he did not believe that the bank manager was guilty of telling conscious untruths to the plaintiff.

---

107. Thus, the bold decision of the House of Lords in *Junior Books Ltd v Veitchi Co Ltd* [1983] 1 AC 520 (HL (Sc), 1982) was followed by such profound retrenchment that the majority holding came to be interpreted (unconvincingly) in *D & F Estates v Acrecrest Ltd* [1988] 2 All ER (HC (Eng)) as merely an application of the *Hedley Byrne* principle.
108. [1987] 2 All ER 705 (PC) (emphasis added).
109. [1988] ILRM 610. See Byrne & Binchy *Annual Review of Irish Law 1988*, pp 321-323.
110. [1978] AC 728.
111. [1990] 2 AC 605.
112. [1989] ILRM 400.
113. Supreme Court, 31 July 1998, affg High Court, 18 June 1997 (Shanley J).
114. High Court, 28 July 1998 (Morris P).
115. See para **[6.34]** above.

**[10.80]** Shanley J proceeded on the basis that a party seeking damages for negligent misrepresentation had to establish that the representor had failed to exercise due care in making the representation, as a result of which the representee "was induced to enter into the particular agreement and suffered damage in consequence of the inaccurate representation."[116] Closely aligned to the claim of negligent misrepresentation was the wider tort of negligent misstatement. In relation to this latter tort, the plaintiff had to establish that the defendant owed him or her a duty of care. In this context, Shanley J noted that, in *Ward v McMaster*[117] McCarthy J had considered that the duty of care arose from the proximity of the parties, the forseeability of the damage and the absence of any compelling exemption based on public policy. In *Caparo Industries plc v Dickman*,[118] Lord Bridge had stated:

> "What emerges is that, in addition to the foreseeability of damage, necessary ingredients in any situation giving rise to a duty of care are that there should exist between the party owing the duty and the party to whom it is owed a relationship characterised by the law as one of 'proximity' or 'neighbourhood' and that the situation should be one in which the Court considers it fair, just and reasonable that the law should impose a duty of a given scope on the one party for the benefit of the other."

**[10.81]** Lord Bridge had observed, in relation to decided cases in which a duty of care in respect of negligent misstatement had been held to exist, that the limit on the liability of a wrongdoer towards those who had suffered economic damage:

> "… rested on the necessity to prove, in this category of the tort of negligence, as an essential ingredient of the 'proximity' between the plaintiff and the defendant, that the defendant knew that his statement would be communicated to the plaintiff, either as an individual or as a member of an identifiable class, specifically in connection with a particular transaction or transactions of a particular kind (eg in a prospectus inviting investment) and that the plaintiff would be very likely to rely on it for the purpose of deciding whether or not to enter on that transaction or upon a transaction of that kind."[119]

**[10.82]** Shanley J considered that in the instant case there had been "clearly a most exceptional relationship"[120] between Michael McSweeney and the plaintiff:

> "It started with the fact that he was doing business with a customer of the bank. It was compounded by the fact that the Managing Director of the customer of the bank was a brother of Michael McSweeney. That the relationship was exceptional is illustrated, first by the number of unsolicited phone calls made by Michael McSweeney to [the plaintiff] and that, when in trouble, [the plaintiff] phoned Michael McSweeney, not just as his office, but at his home, using a number which he himself had given her."[121]

**[10.83]** Whether one adopted McCarthy J's test in *Ward v McMaster* or Lord Bridge's test in *Caparo*, all the necessary ingredients which might give rise to a duty of care existed in relation to the bank and the plaintiff:

---

116. High Court, 18 June 1997.
117. [1989] ILRM 400.
118. [1990] 2 AC 605 at 647-648.
119. [1990] 2 AC 605.
120. High Court, 18 June 1997.
121. High Court, 18 June 1997.

> "[T]here was a relationship which can undoubtedly be characterised as one of the 'proximity' or 'neighbourhood', a relationship of such a nature that the bank, in the person of Michael McSweeney, was aware that statements he might make would most likely be relied upon by [the plaintiff] and that carelessness in making such statements might cause her damage. There can be no doubt in my mind that in such circumstances it is fair, just and reasonable that the law should impose a duty of care on the bank in relation to the representations it made to [the plaintiff]."[122]

**[10.84]** The Supreme Court affirmed Shanley J's judgment. Barrington J (Lynch and Barron JJ concurring) stayed close to the haven of *Hay v O'Grady*.[123] There is thus only limited substantive legal analysis. It is notable, however, that Barrington J was willing to endorse Shanley J's location of the discussion on negligent misrepresentation and negligent misstatement in the context of the *general* duty of care rather than the narrow focus in *Hedley Byrne*. He considered that there was "no doubt … that [the plaintiff] fell within the 'proximity' or 'neighbourhood' principle as described in the cases of *Ward v McMaster* and *Caparo Industries plc v Dickman*."[124]

**[10.85]** There is little indication here that *Ward v McMaster* and *Caparo* represent opposing views as to the nature and scope of duty of care in negligence. The facts in *Forshall* were sufficiently strong to ensure that the defendant was within the range of proximity to the plaintiff judged by the more demanding test of *Caparo*.

**[10.86]** In *Wildgust v Bank of Ireland and Norwich Union Life Assurance Society*,[125] decided three days before the Supreme Court judgment in *Forshall*, Morris P applied the principles on negligent misstatement set out by Shanley J at trial in *Forshall*. The plaintiff had borrowed money from Hill Samuel Merchant Bankers to finance a property purchase. Part of the security of the loan was that he and his wife should assign to Hill Samuel a policy of insurance taken out on their lives from the second defendant. As a result of a breakdown in the system of payment of the premium by bankers' order, the policy lapsed. The plaintiff's wife died subsequently and the second defendant declined to pay out on the policy.

**[10.87]** The plaintiff sued his bank for the non-payment of the premium. These proceedings were settled. He also sued the second defendant. Part of his claim was that an employee of the second defendant had assured a manager of Hill Samuel, who had telephoned because the direct debit had been returned unpaid, that the cheque had in fact been received and that everything was in order. On this basis, it was alleged, the manager took no action; had he been told that the premium remained unpaid, he would have arranged for Hill Samuel to pay it so as to keep the policy alive.

**[10.88]** At the close of the plaintiff's case, counsel for the second defendant applied unsuccessfully for a non-suit. Morris P considered that nothing that Shanley J had said in *Forshall* on the issue of negligent misrepresentation differed from what had been established in *Ward v McMaster*.[126] The plaintiff had presented the court with evidence

---

122. [1990] 2 AC 605.
123. [1992] 1 IR 210.
124. Supreme Court, 31 July 1998.
125. High Court, 28 July 1998 (Morris P).
126. [1989] ILRM 400.

which, if accepted, would establish that there had been a negligent misstatement of fact by the second defendant's employee to Hill Samuel and "by reason of the relationship between Hill Samuel and the plaintiff (ie that of mortgagor and mortgagee) there was a proximity between the [second defendant] and the plaintif[f]".[127] Evidence had also been tendered which showed that damage as a result of the alleged misstatement was foreseeable:

> "The fact that [the plaintiff] personally knew that the premium had not been paid is in dispute as he has given evidence, which the court could accept, that he believed he was in credit with his premium payment. The fact that he did not rely on the representations made by the [second defendant] is in my view of no relevance; once [the manager] of Hill Samuel did rely on these representations and damage resulted to the plaintif[f] who [w]as in proximity to [the second defendant] the cause of action is established."[128]

Morris P was further satisfied that the plaintiff had adduced evidence which, if accepted, could lead the court to conclude that Hill Samuel's manager's enquiry of the second defendant had been made by Hill Samuel in its capacity as agent for the plaintiff and his company and that "the making of a negligent misstatement to Hill Samuel equated in all respects to the making of the statement to the plaintif[f]".[129]

## The Scope of the Representation

**[10.89]** In order to be actionable the defendant must have negligently made an incorrect representation whose incorrectness led the plaintiff to detriment. The scope of the representation thus needs to be scrutinised by the court.

**[10.90]** In *Pat O'Donnell & Co Ltd v Truck & Machinery Sales Ltd*[130] the plaintiff supplied mechanical shovels to the defendant, who sold and rented out the machinery. In a counter-claim taken by the defendant against an action for the price of the goods sold, Moriarty J held that the plaintiff was liable for negligent misrepresentation at common law and under s 45 of the Sale of Goods and Supply of Services Act 1980, but not for breach of implied terms of merchantability and fitness for purpose under s 14 of that Act.[131] The Supreme Court reversed. The defendant had claimed that the plaintiff had represented that the mechanical shovel was comparable to a category of machines previously supplied when in fact, by reason of a different wheel construction, the adjustment necessary to render them

---

127. Page 10 of Morris P's judgment.

128. Page 10 of Morris P's judgment.

129. Page 11 of Morris P's judgment. Morris J went on to hold that the plaintiff's pleadings had not asserted with sufficient clarity that a case based on the *Hedley Byrne v Heller* principle was being alleged. Had the defendant been aware that this was the case it was being called on to meet, it would have adopted a different strategy. Morris J permitted the plaintiff to amend his statement of claim, penalising him in costs, and granted leave to amend its pleadings accordingly. The Supreme Court, on 13 April 2000, held that it would be preferable in the light of this amendment, that the proceedings not be sent for a new trial but rather that they should continue to be heard by Morris P. McGuinness J (Denham and Murphy JJ concurring) noted that counsel for the defendant had been somewhat critical of what he regarded as an undue broadening by Morris P of the tort of requisite misstatement in the light of *Forshall*. McGuinness J observed: "Perhaps the President inclined to a generous interpretation of the tort but that is not an issue for this Court".

130. Supreme Court, 18 February 1997.

131. [1997] 1 ILRM 466 (HC), analysed by Byrne & Binchy *Annual Review of Irish Law 1996*, pp 199-201.

suitable for work in quarries and gravel pits made them more sluggish than their predecessors.

**[10.91]** Only two judges in the Supreme Court, Lynch and O'Flaherty JJ, dealt with the issue of misrepresentation. Lynch J emphasised the vagueness of the representation as to comparability:

> "The [new model] might be inferior to the [old one] in some respects, much the same in many respects but superior in some others and this would satisfy the representation that it was comparable to the [older model]."[132]

**[10.92]** In the absence of a plea that there was a representation by the plaintiff that the new model would be comparable specifically for heavy quarrying and gravel pit work, Lynch J found it difficult to see how Moriarty J could find no breach of s 14 consistent with his finding of common law and statutory misrepresentation. Perhaps the answer lies in the fact that the implied terms of merchantability and reasonable fitness for purpose do not exhaust the reasons why a party might be induced to enter into a contract. If that party has acted on the basis of a misrepresentation and as a result of entering the contract has suffered loss, remedies at both common law and under section 45 should be available, and then will not be defeated by the mere fact that no breach of an implied term under s 14 has occurred.

**[10.93]** In O'Flaherty J's view, Moriarty J had appeared:

> "to have imported into the case a finding that Mr O'Donnell was negligent, aside from being guilty for any misrepresentation, by omitting to give a warning as regards the unsuitability of the larger tyres and wheels."[133]

With respect, it is difficult to locate such a finding in Moriarty J's judgment, which imposed liability, not on some failure or disclosure, but rather on the inconsistency of the goods supplied with the representations made about them.

**[10.94]** In *Potterton Ltd v Northern Bank Ltd*,[134] the plaintiff, whose business was in auctioneering and livestock sales, had sold cattle at its mart to a farmer for many years. The purchases were paid by means of cheques drawn on the farmer's company account with the defendant bank. At one sale the farmer bought cattle to the value of just under £40,000 and paid with a post-dated cheque. When the cheque was sent on for clearance, the defendant bank returned it with the words marked on it "refer to drawer present again alteration req's drawer's conf" – shorthand for "alteration requires drawer's confirmation". It was re-presented for clearance without alteration and without seeking the drawer's confirmation of any part of the writing on the cheque; the defendant once more returned it with the same message, save that the words "present again" were struck out. In the meantime the farmer had bought more cattle with a separate post-dated cheque for over £13,000 which when presented was returned marked "refer to drawer". The plaintiff never received payment on either cheque as the farmer's company went into liquidation.

**[10.95]** It transpired that the query raised by the defendant regarding the "alteration" on the cheque had been merely a device invented to extricate the defendant bank from an

132. Supreme Court, 18 February 1997.

133. Supreme Court, 18 February 1997.

134. [1993] ILRM 225 (HC).

awkward situation where more cheques were coming in for payment than the account could meet, in circumstances where the bank was unwilling to dishonour the farmer's cheques because of its belief, based on previous experience, that it was likely to be put in funds if more time was given. O'Hanlon J was satisfied that there had been no justification for returning the cheque uncashed on the basis that the word "nine" had been written in block letters and the other words in ordinary script. It had all the appearance of having been written at the same time, and with the same writing instrument, and by the same hand as all the rest of the writing on the cheque; moreover, the bank had previously cleared without question cheques similarly written by the farmer.

**[10.96]** In O'Hanlon J's opinion:

> "the words written in when returning the cheque unpaid were calculated to, and did, lull the payee into a false sense of security and led the plaintiff to believe that payment was only being withheld for some technical reason having to do with the manner in which the cheque had been written. If this were, in fact, a cause of concern to the bank, they could have cleared it up immediately by means of a simple one minute telephone call to their own customer."[135]

**[10.97]** O'Hanlon J considered that, while a bank generally does not owe any duty to one who is not its customer when a cheque is presented for payment, this rule:

> "must be subject to qualification if the bank deliberately embarks on a course of conduct for its own purposes which is calculated to deceive the payee of the cheque in a manner which may result in financial loss to such payee, and where there is no lawful justification for such action on the part of the bank".[136]

In contrast to the facts of *Dublin Port & Docks Board v Bank of Ireland*,[137] which concerned the obligation of a bank on which a cheque was drawn to make payment on foot of it, the issue in the instant case related to the *message communicated by the defendant bank* to the plaintiff's bank, and thus to the plaintiff also, when declining to make payment on foot of the cheque. The plaintiff's case was that this message giving the alleged reason for dishonouring the cheque amounted to a negligent misrepresentation of the true situation which induced the plaintiff to act to its detriment or to forbear from taking steps for its own protection which it would have taken had the true position been made known.

**[10.98]** O'Hanlon J noted that, in the instant case, the defendant was under the ordinary banker's obligation either to pay the cheque forthwith if there were sufficient funds or otherwise to refuse payment at once. Had it done so in an unqualified manner, no liability could have attached to it and the plaintiff would have been alerted to take whatever steps were then open to it to secure payment or otherwise protect its interests. But, said O'Hanlon J:

> "[t]he defendant elected to go further … and took it upon itself to communicate to the plaintiff its reason for refusing to honour the cheque at that point in time. In doing this I consider that it assumed an obligation to act honestly and carefully and not to deceive the plaintiff by putting forward a reason which was not the true reason, but was a spurious reason (as alleged in the statement of claim in this case, and as supported by the evidence adduced on behalf of the plaintiff)."[138]

---

135. [1993] ILRM 225 at 229.
136. [1993] ILRM 225 at 229.
137. [1976] IR 118.
138. [1993] ILRM 225 at 233.

This brought the case, "assuming that it is still necessary to do so",[139] within the scope of the situation envisaged by Lord Reid in *Hedley Byrne*, where a reasonable man knows that he is being trusted or that his skill and judgment are being relied on.[140]

**[10.99]** In the instant case, the defendant had taken the course of answering without qualification as to its potential liability for doing so and had breached its obligation to reply in a careful and honest manner once it indicated its reason for refusing payment on foot of the cheque. This had caused the plaintiff economic loss and damages were awarded against the defendant.

**[10.100]** In *Treston v Mayo County Council*,[141] the defendant council was found liable for negligent misrepresentation in influencing the plaintiff's decision to buy a house in its housing estate (though no longer owned by it) by the statement that it intended to upgrade and sell off houses in the estate, wherever possible, to tenants already in occupation; after the plaintiff had proceeded with the purchase, the defendant gave possession of a neighbouring house to a family who were known to be troublemakers. The difficulties caused to the plaintiff by this family were immense. Moriarty J left to another day resolution of the question whether a local housing authority was under *general* duty of care to an incoming purchaser in one of its estates "in the context of housing inordinately disruptive or unruly tenants in close proximity".[142] He inclined to the view that:

> "such a duty, given the core functions and duties of such authorities, would be inordinately far-reaching and oppressive, or at most should be found only in the most coercive and flagrant instances".[143]

**[10.101]** In some cases, the plaintiff's claim will not concentrate on a specific misrepresentation but will be based on a more diffused and protracted process of communication. In *McCullagh v PB Gunne (Monaghan) plc*[144] Carroll J gave important guidance on the legal position of auctioneers. Briefly, the case concerned the purchase of licensed premises by a naive married couple with no business experience, where the price of £125,000 was just beyond their means. The business venture was a disaster. When the property was put up for resale, in spite of the earlier representation by the defendant auctioneer's employee at the time of purchase that he could get the plaintiffs a profit of £10,000 to £20,000 if they resold, the highest offer received was only £85,000. There were problems with the licence, because there was no money to stamp the deed of conveyance, it could not be produced at the annual licensing sessions.

**[10.102]** The facts thus stated, while unfortunate, would not necessarily involve any question of liability on the part of the auctioneer. In the particular circumstances of the case, however, it appeared that the employee of the defendant auctioneer had taken a proactive role. The plaintiffs had told him that they had never previously bought property and they asked him to keep them straight. He had told them not to worry and that he could

139. [1993] ILRM 225 at 233.
140. See paras **[10.72]-[10.78]** above.
141. High Court, 6 July 1998 (Moriarty J)
142. High Court, 6 July 1998.
143. High Court, 6 July 1998.
144. High Court, 17 January 1997 (Carroll J).

arrange finance. He sold their farm for £35,000 sterling. He kept the deposit of (IR£11,657) in the clients' account. He arranged to open an account with a building society for the balance of the purchase money of the farm in the name of the plaintiffs c/o Gunnes. This employee later told the plaintiffs that the licensed premises which they subsequently bought was ideal for them. He said he was not going to advertise because, if he did, the phone would never stop ringing and they would not get a chance to buy. In fact the owner of the premises had asked him to put the property on the market but to keep it very quiet. The plaintiffs inspected the premises and decided they were happy with it. They asked him to buy it at the best price, as cheaply as possible. Having bought the premises for £125,000, he kept telling the plaintiffs not to worry about money and that he could get a loan of 60% to 65% from a financial institution.

**[10.103]** The plaintiffs claimed that Gunnes had held itself out to find them premises at a price they could afford and that it would arrange finance. Mr. McCullagh acknowledged that he was aware that Gunne's employee had been acting as an auctioneer and had been paid a commission by the vendor but he said that the employee had never told him that he could not also act for the McCullaghs or advise them. Mr McCullagh "did not understand figures, [nor] what turnover meant"[145] and the plaintiffs had put their trust in the auctioneer's employee.

**[10.104]** Carroll J imposed liability for negligent misrepresentation on the defendant auctioneer. She noted that the defendant's employee had told the plaintiffs that he was not advertising the property and that, if he did, the phone would not stop ringing:

> "This gave the impression that he was on the McCullaghs' side and that they were on some kind of inside track compared to other prospective purchasers. This may be a ploy of auctioneers but, if it is, it is wholly unjustified. An auctioneer is employed by a vendor to get the best price and should always make it clear that the vendor is his only client, not the purchaser as well. Auctioneers cannot be all things to all men."[146]

**[10.105]** Carroll J concluded that, in the circumstances of the instant case, the auctioneer's employee had taken over the burden of assisting the McCullaghs to arrange adequate finance in their quest for a suitable business. He had sold the farm for them and opened an account for them in the building society; he had not demurred when they said they wanted him "to keep them straight" nor when they asked him to buy the licensed premised at the best price. He had supplied the turnover and projections to the building society. He had found the plaintiffs not one but two solicitors. He had encouraged them by telephone to believe they would get as much money as they needed for the purchase. He had got them to sign the loan approval form without solicitor's advice.

**[10.106]** It must have been obvious to him that the plaintiffs were depending on him and his expertise to get them adequate finance. He had done nothing to disabuse them of the reliance which they had obviously placed in him. Even after he got them a second solicitor, he had not sent them off to him for advice on the loan application which showed the purchase price inaccurately at £130,000 and the promoters' input at £65,000. As late as at

145. High Court, 17 January 1997.

146. High Court, 17 January 1997.

the stage of post contract/preclosing, he had promised them as much as they needed. Even at that point they probably could have refused to close. Carroll J observed in conclusion:

> "The plaintiffs are naive but they impressed me as very straight honest people. They did not deserve the treatment they had [received from the defendant's employee] and this was certainly a case where it is fair, just, equitable and reasonable that a duty of care be recognised by the Court."[147]

**[10.107]** In *Hazylake Fashions Ltd v Bank of Ireland*[148] the bank had over a period of months discounted several bills of exchange that had not been accepted. This was done by the plaintiff company inconsistently with its own constitutional undertaking to the plaintiff, which had been limited to bills that had been accepted. When the bank discovered its mistake it informed the plaintiff that for the future, only accepted bills would be discounted. This placed a strain on the plaintiff's cash flow, resulting in the plaintiffs' being forced to cease production some time later.

**[10.108]** The plaintiff claimed damages on a number of grounds. One of these was that, having regard to the particular relationship between the parties, the bank would have been liable to the plaintiff for any statement made negligently which resulted in economic damage to the plaintiff; in that context, it claimed, the actions of the bank in discounting unaccepted bills within a few days of their receipt amounted to an implied statement.

**[10.109]** Murphy J rejected the claim. He stated:

> "It seems to me that it would be impossible to extend the decision in *Hedley Byrne and Co Ltd v Heller and Partners Ltd*[149] or indeed the subsequent Irish decision in *Securities Trust Ltd v Hugh Moore and Alexander Ltd*[150] to the facts of the present case.
>
> Where *Hedley Byrne v Heller* extended the concept of negligent actions causing economic loss to negligent misstatements having the same result, this case would involve the further extension of the law to include implied statements. But even if that extension is justifiable it is difficult to extract from the actions of the parties the statement which is said to have been made negligently and caused economic loss. It could not be contended that the bank negligently or otherwise led the company to believe that the bills were accepted before they were discounted. Manifestly this was impossible having regard to the dates on which the various transactions took place. If it is suggested that the premature discounting of the bills was a representation that his procedure would continue then effectively the company is contending that the original contract had been amended and there is no evidence (or indeed argument) to support that conclusion. The reality of the matter is that the bank acted negligently in the sense that they failed to take appropriate steps to safeguard their own interests. They did not await notification of acceptance before discounting and they may

147. Carroll J's reference to the fairness, justice and reasonableness of recognising a duty of care reflects the formula adopted by Lord Bridge in *Caparo Industries plc v Dickman* [1990] 2 AC 605, which was endorsed by Shanley J in *Forshall v Walsh* High Court, 18 June 1997 and by Morris P in *Wildgust v Bank of Ireland* High Court, 28 July 1998. It represents an expansion on the test of fairness and reasonableness, favoured by Costello J in *Ward v McMaster* [1985] IR 400, which was somewhat eclipsed by McCarthy J's approach on appeal to the Supreme Court: [1989] IR 400.

148. [1989] IR 601 (HC).

149. [1964] AC 465.

150. [1964] IR 417.

> have lost the protection of the insurance cover as a result. In my view they were making no 'statement' express or implied to the company. The company was simply the beneficiary of an unfortunate administrative error made within the banking system. I accept that the correction of this error on very short notice to the company must have added to the serious financial problems which it was then undergoing but I cannot see that the bank acted in breach of its duty by making a mistake in relation to the conduct of its own business or correcting the error when it was identified. In the circumstances it seems to me that this argument ... must fail."[151]

**[10.110]** Several comments on the issues raised in this case seem in order. First, the notion of an implied statement is scarcely different in principle from that of an express statement. Courts have for a long time dealt with implied statements in both civil and criminal contexts of fraudulent misrepresentation. In *R v Barnard*[152] it was accepted that a man in Oxford who wore a student's cap and gown was representing that he was a student. Similarly in *Gill v McDowell*,[153] the notion of a "tacit" or "implied" representation was accepted by the Court.

**[10.111]** Is there any reason in principle why, if a *fraudulent* representation may be implied rather than expressed, the tort of *negligent* misrepresentation should exclude implied statements? The answer appears to be that there is not. The *Hedley Byrne* principle, in its original exposition, required representation and reliance as central elements. Provided these requirements are adhered to, it seems that an implied representation should be capable of generating liability under the *Hedley Byrne* principle.

**[10.112]** This is not to suggest that a court should be over-eager to find implied representations inhering in conduct which is either unsupported by any linguistic representations, or indeed, contrary to them. Equally, courts should closely scrutinise claims by plaintiffs that they relied on representations of this type. But this caution extends merely to the application of principle to fact rather than to the acceptability of the principle itself.

**[10.113]** Next, it is worth considering whether the plaintiff's argument in *Hazylake*, that there had been an implied representation that the procedure of discounting unaccepted bills would continue, *necessarily* amounted to a contention that the original contract had been amended. The circumstances in which a contract may be amended do not exactly coincide with those in which a representation inconsistent with that contract may occasion liability in tort.

**[10.114]** A person may sue for negligent misrepresentation in the context of the performance of contractual obligations without having to base his or her case on the breach of those obligations or on the misrepresentations having had the effect of varying any contractual term. To take a more straightforward case than *Hazylake*, if a bank has contractually agreed to discount only accepted bills, and the manager calls in the client and says: "I know we're not contractually bound to do this, and I'm not wishing to change our

---

151. [1989] IR 601.

152. (1837) 7 C & P 784; 173 ER 342. See also *The People v Finkel & Levine* (1951) 1 Frewen 123; *Brogan v Bennett* [1955] IR 119. In the law of evidence, the concept of implied statements is an important (and troubling) feature of the rule against hearsay.

153. [1903] 2 IR 463.

contractual position, but I want you to know that we'll discount unaccepted bills for the next year", it is clear that the client can sue for negligent misrepresentation if the client relies on this assurance, without being forced to show that the contract had (contrary to the manager's express statement) been varied by the manager's representation.

**[10.115]** A striking feature of *Hazylake* is the absence of discussion in the judgment of the principle of estoppel. *High Trees*[154] was, after all a case involving the forbearance of one party to stand on his contractual rights, and in *Tool Metal Manufacturing Co v Tungsten Electric Co*[155] the issue concerned the period of grace which must be given when a person decides to reassert contractual rights having not done so for some time. All of this touches on the question whether a bank, having been guilty of an error in providing a service beyond that which it had contractually undertaken, can turn round, on discovering the error, and leave the client to work out the cash flow problems resulting from a withdrawal of the extra service (save to the extent to ensuring that the client's overdraft in the bank is cleared).

## Assumption of Responsibility

**[10.116]** Not every careless statement will engender liability in tort. Loose talk at a party about the prospects of "dot.com" shares on the stock market will not render the speaker liable to one who invests with an unhappy outcome even if the speaker is a stockbroker. If I am in a railway station and I am asked the time by an agitated passenger who says that he or she is rushing to an important interview, I will not be exposed to a *Hedley Byrne* claim if my watch is slow and the passenger misses the interview and damages the prospects of new, better-paid employment. There has to be some assumption of responsibility on my part that what I say can be relied on by the person seeking my help.

**[10.117]** As we shall see, there has been a debate in recent years as to whether the notion of assumption of responsibility should be understood as an empirical or juridical phenomenon. Is it a question of assuming responsibility for *the task* or assuming responsibility *in law* for what one says? Does liability depend on a conscious assumption of this responsibility or can the court ascribe legal responsibility to a party who is seeking earnestly to avoid it?

**[10.118]** Let us examine the cases in which the courts have addressed these issues. In *Gayson v Allied Irish Banks plc*,[156] the plaintiff, a customer of the defendant bank with a bogus foreign account, claimed that the bank had negligently advised him not to avail himself of tax amnesty in 1988. In answer to his question "Is there anything in this amnesty for us?", a senior official at the branch where he was a customer allegedly replied: "Not really". She also was alleged to have stated: "Why would you; it could still cost you a good bit of money; I would leave it alone if I were you."

**[10.119]** Geoghegan J accepted that "some sort of conversation of a kind in very broad terms similar to what is alleged did take place, though the precise nature of it must be quite

154. *Central London Property Trust Ltd v High Trees House Ltd* [1947] KB 130.

155. [1955] 1 WLR 761. Murphy J did not refer to the Supreme Court judgment in *Webb v Ireland* [1988] ILRM 565.

156. High Court, 28 January 2000 (Geoghegan J).

uncertain ...".[157] Geoghegan J was satisfied that what the plaintiff was effectively saying to the bank official was: "What should I do about this amnesty? Would I be safer to own up and avail of it or continue hiding the money in the hope that I might get away with it?" The evidence of his allegation against the bank official was that she had advised him to continue hiding the money because, although he would not have to pay penalties and interest, he would still have to pay a great deal of money to the Revenue.

**[10.120]** Geoghegan J was satisfied that "any such conversation which the plaintiff had with [the bank official] was of an 'off the cuff' nature and that it would never have reasonably occurred to either of them that any answer given by her could have given rise to an action against the bank".[158] On this ground (among others) Geoghegan J dismissed the action based on *Hedley Byrne* principles.

**[10.121]** Another good example of the approach adopted is *Doolan v Murray*[159] where Keane J awarded damages against the owner of a site on which premises had been built and subsequently sold to the plaintiff. The owner of the site had retained a right of way in relation to part of the site. She had successfully applied for outline planning permission for the construction of the premises. The person who built the premises deviated from the plans, so that is was necessary to obtain permission for its retention; in giving the necessary permission, the planning authority required an access capable of admitting cars and also three car spaces. The plaintiff, when she bought the premises, was unaware of this requirement. She and the owner of the site drew up a deed relating to the right of way. The manner in which the owner of the site negotiated and executed the deed implicity represented that the right of way as originally reserved, had been intended to be for pedestrian use only and was capable of being locked, whereas, in view of the planning permission requirement, vehicular access was necessary. When the plaintiff subsequently sought to erect a barrier on the path, with the provision of keys for those with a right of way, she discovered the existence of the planning authority's requirements for the first time.

**[10.122]** Keane J provided a wide-ranging analysis of the principles of negligence law. He considered that Lord Atkin's statement of the "neighbour" principle in *Donoghue v Stevenson*[160] was relevant, in conjunction with the speeches of Lords Reid and Devlin in *Hedley Byrne & Co v Helller & Partners*.[161] He noted that, while Lord Atkin's statement had expressly extended to omissions, the authorities in England and other common law jurisdictions had reflected a reluctance to extend liability to "pure omissions". He quoted from Slade LJ's judgment in *Banque Financière v Westgate Insurance Co*:[162]

> "The same reluctance on the part of the courts to give a remedy in tort for pure omission applies, perhaps even more so, when the omission is a failure to prevent economic harm ...

157. High Court, 28 January 2000.
158. High Court, 28 January 2000.
159. High Court, 21 December 1993 (Keane J).
160. [1932] AC 562 at 580.
161. [1964] AC 465.
162. [1989] 2 All ER 952 at 1009.

> [A] corresponding distinction is drawn by the law of contract which in general imposes no liability by virtue of a failure to speak as opposed to a misrepresentation."

**[10.123]** Keane J commented that, as the citation suggested:

> "the general principle of *caveat emptor*, based as it is on the recognition by the law that parties should be left free to determine their obligations to each other, is not to be eroded by the inappropriate invocation of tortious liability."[163]

**[10.124]** Where, however, a person elected to make a representation on a matter which was capable of being misleading because of its partial nature, there seemed no reason why liability in tort for negligent misstatement should not arise, provided there was a duty to take care in relation to the making of the representation. Whether such a duty of care arose in the circumstances of the instant case had to be determined having regard to the legal principles laid down in *Hedley Byrne* and subsequently adopted by the Irish courts.

**[10.125]** The owner of the site had made a misrepresentation as to private rights; such a misrepresentation was capable of being actionable, in contrast to misrepresentation as to the law in general.

**[10.126]** Whilst the *Hedley Byrne* doctrine had its most obvious application in cases where persons holding themselves out as having professional or other skills made statements on which others foreseeably relied, it was not necessarily confined to that category:

> "The authorities demonstrate that what the court must do in each case is to examine the facts and determine whether the circumstances of the case were such that the maker of the statement should have had within his or her contemplation at the time when it was made a person or persons who might reasonably rely on it to their possible detriment. There must be, as the cases make clear, an assumption of responsibility in circumstances where the maker of the statement ought to have foreseen that it would be relied on and it was in fact relied on by the plaintiff."[164]

**[10.127]** The owner of the site clearly must have known of the plaintiff's concern in relation to the right of way. In her negotiations prior to the execution of the deed, it must have been obvious to her that her silence as to the true nature of the right of way left the plaintiff under a false impression which could well result in adverse financial consequences to her. She should have been aware that the plaintiff would rely on her silence as indicating that there were no problems of which she knew in regard to the right of way. Accordingly Keane J imposed liability on the owner of the site for negligent misstatement.

**[10.128]** An important statement of law by Keane J in respect of two other defendants should be noted. He stated that the fact that they had entered into a contract with the plaintiff did not mean that their duties to the plaintiff were necessarily to be ascertained from the terms of the contract alone. A vendor of property might well be under an additional duty of care *quoad* the purchaser in accordance with the principles of *Heldey Byrne*.

**[10.129]** The Supreme Court addressed the issue of the scope of the assumption of responsibility under *Hedley Byrne* in the important decision of *Doran v Delaney*.[165] The

---

163. High Court, 21 December 1993.

164. High Court, 21 December 1993.

165. [1998] 2 ILRM 1 (SC), revg [1996] 1 ILRM 490 (HC).

case concerned the sale of land to the plaintiffs. The fourth and fifth named defendants acted as solicitors for the vendors. One of the requisitions raised by the plaintiff's solicitor enquired whether any litigation was pending or threatened in relation to any part of the property and whether any adverse claim thereto had been made by any person. The reply given by the fifth named defendant was "vendor says none". In fact the fourth and fifth named defendants were aware that there had been a boundary dispute as they had been told by one of the vendors that it "had been settled and sorted out and that there was no queries." They had not, however, ascertained from the vendors the terms on which the dispute had allegedly been resolved. The dispute had not finally gone away; when the plaintiffs bought the property the dispute re-emerged, causing them significant financial loss. They sued their own solicitor, the vendors and the vendors' solicitors for negligence.

**[10.130]** Hamilton P held the plaintiffs' solicitor and the vendors liable but not the vendors' solicitors. He considered it:

> "clear from the nature of the replies to the requisitions that the fourth and fifth named defendants were transmitting their clients' instructions and were not assuming responsibility for or the role of principal in relation to that information so far as the plaintiffs or their solicitor was (*sic*) concerned."[166]

**[10.131]** The plaintiffs appealed successfully to the Supreme Court. Keane J (Barrington J concurring) invoked Lord Devlin's speech in *Hedley Byrne & Co v Heller and Partners*,[167] for the general propositions that:

> "[w]hile there was no contractual relationship between the vendor's solicitors and the purchasers, that would not of itself negate the existence of a duty of care. Moreover, in determining whether such a duty of care arose in the particular circumstances, it is a material factor that such replies to requisitions are made by a solicitor acting as such and not in some casual social context. Again, while the primary duty of the solicitor acting for the vendor in circumstances such as arose here is under common law and by virtue of contract, to protect his own client, that obligation is perfectly consistent with the existence of a duty of care in certain circumstances to the purchaser."

**[10.132]** In *Midland Bank plc v Cameron, Tong, Peterkin and Duncans*,[168] Lord Jauncey had identified four factors as relevant to a determination of the question whether in a particular case a solicitor, while acting for a client, also owed a duty of care to a third party:

(1) The solicitor must assume responsibility for advice or information furnished to the third party.

(2) The solicitor must let it be known to the third party expressly or impliedly that he claims, by reason of his calling, to have the requisite skills or knowledge to give the advice or furnish the information.

(3) The third party must have relied on that information as a matter for which the solicitor has assumed personal responsibility.

(4) The solicitor must have been aware that the third party was likely so to rely.

166. [1996] 1 ILRM 490.
167. [1964] AC 465 at 528.
168. 1988 SLT 611.

**[10.133]** Keane J considered it clear, at least in cases where these four factors were present, that a solicitor might be held liable to a third party "under the more general principle laid down in *Hedley Byrne* ...".[169] The fact that the vendors had been found liable for misrepresentation made directly by themselves to the plaintiffs or in the form of statements transmitted in good faith by their solicitors was not a relevant consideration in determining whether the solicitors themselves were in breach of a duty of care which they owed the plaintiffs.[170]

**[10.134]** Keane J accepted that in many cases the solicitor for the vendor replying to requisitions should not be considered to be assuming any responsibility for the information transmitted to the purchaser. If, for example, the solicitor was expressing a professional opinion on matters of title or was giving a reply where the purchaser's solicitor from his or her own experience would be well aware that the reply had to have been on the client's instruction, the vendor's solicitor would not be regarded as assuming responsibility for the accuracy of the response. From this, it is clear, that there are circumstances in which the vendor's solicitor would assume at least some degree of responsibility for the information being furnished to the purchaser's solicitors:

> "Specifically, in a case such as the present, where the vendor's solicitor is asked whether there is any litigation pending or whether any adverse claim has been made to the property and is aware of his or her own knowledge of threats or litigation and adverse claims having been made, he or she assumes at least some responsibility for the information given in reply and cannot be exonerated from responsibility solely on the ground that he or she is simply transmitting the vendor's instructions. Whether he or she can be regarded as so relieved from responsibility must depend upon the circumstances of the particular case and whether it was reasonable, in those circumstances, for the vendor's solicitor simply to transmit what he or she was told without further enquiry.
>
> It is also clear that, in such a situation, the vendor's solicitor in assessing the instructions he or she is given, determining whether further enquiries should be made and deciding on the information to which the vendors' solicitors are entitled, is acting in a professional capacity and must be assumed to be applying the skill and knowledge to be expected of a solicitor in such circumstances."[171]

In the circumstances of the case the fourth and fifth defendants must have known that, whether or not their reply accurately reflected the vendor's instructions to them, it would unquestionably be relied on by the plaintiffs.

**[10.135]** Keane J therefore concluded that the fourth and fifth defendants had owed, and breached, a duty of care to the plaintiffs when they replied to the requisition:

> "There are many instances in which a solicitor acting in a transaction such as this would be perfectly entitled to convey without comment the information furnished to him by his client, but this was not one of them ... In failing to ascertain the terms on which the dispute had been settled and conveying that information to the plaintiffs, the [fourth and fifth defendants]

---

169. [1998] 2 ILRM 1 at 15.

170. Keane J preferred the approach on this matter that Coleman J had taken in *McCullagh v Lane Fox & Partners* (1994) 8 EG 118, affd (1996) 18 EG 104 to that adopted in *Gran Gelato v Richcliff (Group) Ltd* [1992] Ch 560: the fact that there would be a duplication of remedy should not negate the existence of liability.

171. [1998] 2 ILRM 1 at 17.

> were in breach of their duty of care to them. On one view – that urged on behalf of the plaintiffs – they had, in any event, not accurately transmitted the vendor's instructions, since those merely indicated that the dispute had been settled: they did not indicate, as the reply to the requisition on one reading did, that no claim to the triangular portion was at the date of the reply being made by [the other disputant]. At the very least, however, the reply, because of the manner in which it was framed, did not convey all the information to which the plaintiffs were entitled and ... a partial statement in such circumstances may be equivalent to a misstatement or misrepresentation."[172]

Keane J emphasised that there had been no suggestion in the case that the fourth and fifth defendants had *deliberately* intended to mislead the plaintiffs or their solicitors.

**[10.136]** Barron J, concurring, made the following forthright observations:

> "In my view a solicitor's responsibility, if any, for replies to requisitions should not depend upon the wording used. Answers such as 'vendor says no', or 'not to vendor's knowledge', all mean the same thing: 'it is believed that there is no information of relevance'.
>
> The solicitor is not a conduit pipe. Once he is acting professionally he warrants that so far as his own acts are concerned he has taken the care and applied skill and knowledge expected of a member of his profession. He cannot therefore accept his client's instructions without question when it is reasonable to query them. That is the difference between innocent and negligent misstatement. It is not enough that the solicitor was acting *bona fide*. For that reason, the submission made by the defendants' counsel sought to apply the wrong test. Of course, as against his own client, if the solicitor acted on the client's express instructions, this is generally a good defence to a claim by his own client."[173]

**[10.137]** In *McAnarney v Hanrahan*[174] is another important decision in this context. The plaintiffs had bought the leasehold interest in a public house for £45,000 on the basis of assurances by the defendant auctioneer that a bid for £54,000 had been received at auction and that previous negotiations with the ground landlords justified the assessment of the purchase price for the freehold at a maximum of £3,000. Neither of these assurances was correct. Some time after buying the property, the plaintiffs sought to acquire the freehold. The ground landlord's price was £40,000 (ultimately reduced to £30,000). They sued the auctioneer and his principal for negligent misstatement.

**[10.138]** Costello J held that the case fell within the principles laid down by the House of Lords in *Hedley Byrne v Heller & Partners Ltd.*[175] He quoted with approval the passage from Lord Morris's speech which has been set out above.[176]

**[10.139]** In the instant case the auctioneer had taken upon himself responsibility for giving his opinion about the purchase of the freehold. He should have known that the plaintiffs would place reliance on what he told them, particularly as he expressly stated that negotiations had already taken place with the ground landlords. A special relationship had thus arisen between the parties, which imposed on the auctioneer the duty of care in giving

---

172. [1998] 2 ILRM 1 at 18-19.
173. [1998] 2 ILRM 1 at 19.
174. [1994] 1 ILRM 210.
175. [1964] AC 465.
176. See para **[10.54]** above.

the information. He had breached that duty in that, before making the statement, he had taken no care to see what price the landlords would require for their interest.

**[10.140]** The case was different from *Bank of Ireland v Smith*[177] where Kenny J had held that no duty of care towards prospective purchasers was imposed on an auctioneer placing an advertisement that contained misleading information. In the instant case the responsibility that the auctioneer had taken upon himself and the particular circumstances of the negotiations created a special relationship which was absent in the circumstances that Kenny J had been considering.[178]

**[10.141]** In Britain, in recent years, the courts have adopted[179] a broad interpretation of assumption of responsibility under the *Hedley Byrne* principle as a way of permitting recovery for negligently caused pure economic loss which can in British eyes no longer be justified on the basis of *Donoghue v Stevenson*.[180] In Ireland the courts find no great doctrinal problem with using the lexicon of "proximity of relationship" and neighbourhood. It is interesting to note that *Ward v McMaster*[181] could well have been based on *Hedley Byrne* rather than proximity of relationship, having regard to the assumption of responsibility for obtaining an effective survey which Louth County Council was found to have undertaken. In *Cotter v Minister for Agriculture*,[182] the Supreme Court was content to invoke *Ward v McMaster*, distinguishing it on its facts, in rejecting a claim that the Minister had not been negligent to farmers or the plaintiff, a contractor who tendered for a drainage operation, in failing to have a full survey of the river carried out or to give them warnings about the possibility of extra cost. O'Flaherty J found it:

> "impossible to formulate such a duty of care in the situation that prevailed which was, to recapitulate: the farmers were left in no doubt that they would have to arrange for a contractor to carry out the work; they took twelve months preparing themselves, raising funds and engaging a contractor and while the Minister agreed that he would provide a grant, that was clearly going to be the height of his involvement. Indeed, some of the conditions set out in the documentation that accompanied the letter providing for the grant would suggest that the Minister was distancing himself as far as possible from having any responsibility for anything that might go wrong. This was akin to a form of exemption clause."

## Promissory Estoppel

**[10.142]** We must now consider the potential impact on the *Hedley Byrne* principle of the doctrine of promissory estoppel, articulated in very broad terms by the Supreme Court in *Webb v Ireland*[183] in 1987. There the plaintiffs, a father and son, while trespassing on the

---

177. [1966] IR 646. See para **[10.65]** above.

178. See also *O'Brien v Campbell Catering International Ltd* High Court, 22 March 1993 (Morris J) and *O'Donoghue v LV Nolan* High Court, 29 July 1993 (Carroll J). These decisions are noted in Byrne & Binchy, *Annual Review of Irish Law 1993*, pp 548-549.

179. *Henderson v Merrett Syndicates Ltd* [1995] 2 AC 145 (HL, Eng); *White v Jones* [1995] 2 AC 207 (HL, Eng); *Williams v National Life Ltd* [1998] 2 All ER 577 (HL, Eng); *Spring v Guardian Assurance plc* [1995] 2 AC 296 (HL, Eng). See further STREET, 220-224.

180. [1932] AC 562 (HL, SC).

181. [1988] IR 337.

182. Supreme Court, 2 April 1993.

183. [1988] ILRM 565 (SC). See O'Connor, *Legitimate Expectation* (1988) 6 ILT (ns) 147.

property of two farmers found the "Derrynaflan Hoard", a number of very valuable antique religious objects which had been buried by their owner over a thousand years ago. They delivered it to the National Museum; the father was told by its Director that he would be honourably treated. On the basis of this assurance the plaintiffs were each held entitled to £25,000 from the State.

**[10.143]** Finlay CJ stated that:

> "Applying the law as there stated, which seems to me to accord with fundamental equitable principles, I am satisfied that the unqualified assurance given to the first-named plaintiff by the Director ... that he ... would be honourably treated was an integral part of the transaction under which the Hoard was deposited in the Museum and accepted on behalf of the State, and that the State cannot now go back on the assurance. It must be given effect to in the form of a monetary award of an amount which is reasonable in all the circumstances."

**[10.144]** Walsh J, in his concurring judgment, dealt with the issue in two vital sentences. Having expressed his conclusion that the owners of the land, who had been compensated by the State, were not entitled to assert a claim for ownership to the Hoard, and that it was their good fortune that the State had seen fit to pay them, he added:

> "On the basis of ordinary justice it appears to me that the plaintiffs should be equally entitled, if not more entitled, legitimately to expect to be rewarded on a no less generous scale. I agree with the opinion of the Chief Justice on this topic already expressed in his judgment."

**[10.145]** McCarthy J stated that, while it might be contended that the plaintiffs were "merely complying with law" when they brought the Hoard to the attention of the National Museum, in his view, for the reasons stated in the Chief Justice's judgment, they "were entitled to rely on a legitimate expectation that the State would make to them a substantial reward", and they were entitled to enforce this in the Courts. In this area he believed that public policy played a significant role.

**[10.146]** The implications of *Webb* for the development of the doctrine of promissory estoppel appeared, initially at least, to be wide-ranging.[184] But the implications for the law relating to negligent misstatement are equally significant. Nothing in the judgments of the Supreme Court expressly requires that the representation be fraudulent or negligent; thus, the possibility of obtaining damages (however described[185]) for an innocent misrepresentation[186] cannot be excluded. Equally, the judgments do not in express terms require proof that the plaintiffs had acted to their detriment, nor even, indeed, that they had altered their position as a result of the representation.[187] The range of those who may claim to have been affected by a representation and seek compensation on the basis of promissory estoppel is also unclear. The son was held entitled to succeed on the basis of an

---

184. See Byrne & Binchy, *Annual Review of Irish Law 1987*, pp 162-164. Subsequent judicial developments belie this expectation, however: see Delany, *Equity and the Law of Trusts in Ireland* (2nd ed, 1999), 606-609.

185. See Byrne & Binchy, *Annual Review of Irish Law 1987*, p 164.

186. As to the present position, see Clark, *Contract Law in Ireland* (4th, ed 1998), pp 250-251. Under s 45(2) of the Sale of Goods and Supply of Services Act 1980, damages may be awarded in lieu of rescission in respect of contracts defined by s 43.

187. See Byrne & Binchy, *Annual Review of Irish Law 1987*, p 164.

assurance given to his father, presumably because the judges were of the view that the assurance had been intended to extend to the son, and (perhaps) that the father had been acting as his son's agent. In the immediate aftermath of *Webb* it seemed scarcely fanciful to suggest that precedents dealing with the range of reliance under the *Hedley Byrne* principle might yet find their way into the jurisprudence on promissory estoppel. As against this, the invocation of the legitimate expectation/promissory estoppel doctrine had the aura of an *ad hoc* solution to a troublesome "political" issue[188] rather than developing the doctrine on a systematic basis.[189] Thus far, save for *Webb*, its role has been confined to administrative law contexts and judges at the High Court level have yet to evince any enthusiasm for developing the doctrine in private law.

## Areas of Competence

**[10.147]** If a person on whom a business reliance is already placed in one context (insurance for example) gives advice in another (investment, for example), should he or she be excused merely because he or she did not have expertise in the latter area? A Privy Council decision[190] has taken the view that no liability should be imposed in such circumstances. Other courts are less willing to take such an indulgent view.[191]

**[10.148]** In *Gaysan v Allied Irish Banks plc*,[192] Geoghegan J held that the defendant bank could not be held liable for advice allegedly given by one of its senior officials to the

---

188. The Court had a difficulty: it surely wanted to hold (as it did) that the State had a constitutional claim to old artefacts of cultural significance; it also must have wished to discourage the plundering of historical sites, especially by finders. But the plaintiffs, though trespassers, had acted with frankness and responsibility in delivering the Hoard to the National Museum. That they should have been left with nothing might well have seemed harsh and might encourage future finders to be less public spirited.

189. The *Webb* version of promissory estoppel was fully applied in *Kenny v Kelly* High Court, 27 July 1988 (Barron J) in a case which appears from the judgment to have been well capable of disposition on *Hedley Byrne* principles. It was also applied in *Duggan v An Taoiseach* High Court, 11 April 1988 (Hamilton P), where Hamilton P described the doctrine as "being in accord with equitable principles ...". The "equity of the other's case" demanded that the plaintiffs be compensated in damages for the frustration or breach of their legitimate expectations. See also *Egan v Minister for Defence* High Court, 24 November 1988 (Barr J), distinguishing the *Webb* principle. *Webb* was also distinguished (on the basis of lack of reliance) in *Devitt v Minister for Education* High Court, 13 May 1988 (Lardner J). In *Garda Representative Association v Ireland* [1989] ILRM 1, Murphy J interpreted Finlay CJ's judgment in *Webb* as betraying a reluctance to recognise legitimate expectation as a new or separate concept in our legal system. The tenor of Keane J's judgment in *Pesca Valentia v Minister for Fisheries* High Court, 6 June 1989 seems sceptical as to the merits of the *Webb* doctrine.

190. *Mutual Life & Citizens' Assurance Co Ltd v Evatt* [1971] AC 793 (PC, Austr) analysed by Griffith, (1971) 45 Law Institute J 298; Stevens, (1972) 5 NZU LR 39; Lindgren, (1972) 46 Austr LJ 176; Farmer [1972] Camb LJ 189. See, however, *Esso Petroleum Co Ltd v Mardon* [1976] QB 801 (CA); *Howard Marine & Dredging Co Ltd v A Ogden & Sons (Excavations) Ltd* [1978] QB 574; *Van Oppen v Clerk to the Bedford Charity Trustees* [1989] 1 All ER 273 at 287-288 (QBD); *Spring v Guardian Assurance plc* [1995] 2 AC 296 at 320.

191. See also *Scott v McFarlane* [1978] 1 NZLR 553; *Shaddock v Parramatta City Council* (1981) 36 ALR 385; MacCormick 'What is Wrong with Deceit?' (1983) 10 Sydney LR 5 at 14-16.

192. High Court, 28 January 2000 (Geoghegan J).

plaintiff, its customer, that he should not avail himself of a tax amnesty. Geoghegan J observed that:

> "the kind of illegal advice given by the bank in connection with setting up particular types of deposit accounts is ultimately connected with the banking business and is of a totally different order from direct advice given to the plaintiff as to whether he should avail of the amnesty or not. The bank is in no sense in the business of advising customers as to whether they should avail of a tax amnesty or not. If, therefore, [the bank official] gave such advice in circumstances that went beyond a mere casual conversation ..., she was, to use the traditional terminology, 'on a frolic of her own'. The bank could not be vicariously liable for the advice."[193]

Perhaps this states the scope of a bank's potential liability under the *Hedley Byrne* principle in somewhat narrow terms.[194]

## Statements in a Contractual Setting

**[10.149]** A problem arises concerning negligent statements made in a contractual setting.[195] Some courts[196] and commentators[197] have perceived dangers in permitting the tort of negligence to encroach too far into the area of contract; the law of contract seeks to promote values based on individual autonomy,[198] in contrast negligence seeks to impose on individuals a standard of behaviour determined by objective societal norms.

**[10.150]** In *Esso Petroleum Co Ltd v Mardon*,[199] the English Court of Appeal applied *Hedley Byrne* to a pre-contractual misrepresentation culminating in a contract to the detriment of one of the contracting parties. Lord Denning MR stated:

> "It seems to me that *Hedley Byrne*, properly understood, covers this particular proposition: if a man, who has or professes to have special knowledge or skill, makes a representation by

193. High Court, 28 January 2000.

194. The illegality allegedly underlying the relationship between the parties was undoubtedly a factor in the outcome. Geoghegan J held that it was such as to prevent the establishment of a duty of care in negligence.

195. *Cf* the comprehensive analysis by Symmons 'The Problems of the Applicability of Tort Liability to Negligent Misstatements in Contractual Settings' (1975) 21 McGill LJ 79. More generally, see Phillips 'The Concurrence of Remedies in Contract and Tort' (1977) 12 Ir Jur (ns) 234; Poulton 'Tort or Contract?', (1966) 82 LQR 346; French 'The Contract/Tort Dilemma' (1982) 5 Otago LR 236; Fridman The Interaction of Tort and Contract (1977) 93 LQR 422; Rafferty 'Liability for Pre-Contractual Misstatements' (1984) 14 Manitoba LJ 63; Schwartz 'Hedley Byrne and Pre-Contractual Misrepresentations: Tort Law to the Aid of Contract?' (1978) 10 Ottawa LR 581; Considine 'Some Implications from Recent Cases on the Differences Between Contract and Tort' (1978) 12 U Br Col LR 85; Irvine 'Contract and Tort: Troubles Along the Border' (1979) 10 Can Cas L Torts 281; Morgan 'The Negligent Contract - Breaker' (1980) 58 Can BR 299; Sutton & Mulgan 'Contract and Tort' [1980] NZLJ 366; Reiter 'Contracts, Torts, Relations and Reliance' in B Reiter & J Swan, eds, *Studies in Contract Law*, (1980) p 235, Cane 'Contract, Tort and Economic Loss', in Furmston, ed, *The Law of Tort* (1986).

196. Notably in Canada: *cf J Nunes Diamonds Ltd v Dominion Electric Protection* [1972] SCR 769; *Sealand of the Pacific Ltd v Robert C McHaffie Ltd* (1975) 51 DLR (3d) 703 (BCA). See also the New Zealand decision of *Holman Construction Ltd v Delta Timber Co Ltd* [1972] NZLR 1081.

197. *Cf* Sealy [1975] CLJ, 194; Sealy [1978] CLJ 229; Fleming [1978] CLJ 226; Jolowicz [1979] CLJ 54

198. Note the distinction drawn by Henchy J, in *Finlay v Murtagh* [1979] IR 249 at 256 (SC).

199. [1976] QB 801.

virtue thereof to another - be it advice, information or opinion - with the intention of inducing him to enter into a contract with him, he is under a duty to use reasonable care to see that the representation is correct, and that the advice, information or opinion is reliable. If he negligently gives unsound advice or misleading information or expresses an erroneous opinion, and thereby induces the other side into a contract with him, he is liable in damages."[200]

**[10.151]** This passage from *Mardon* was quoted in the Irish decision of *Stafford v Mahony, Smith & Palmer.*[201] The references[202] by Doyle J to the approach adopted by the English Court of Appeal might appear to suggest some reluctance to endorse its holding, but a close reading of *Stafford's* case reveals that Doyle J, on the authority of *Securities Trust Ltd v Hugh Moore & Alexander Ltd,*[203] accepted that pre-contractual misrepresentation could give rise to liability for negligent misstatement.[204]

**[10.152]** In *Greyhill Property Co Ltd v Whitechap Inn Ltd (in receivership),*[205] Barr J also applied the principles stated in *Esso Petroleum Co Ltd v Mardon*, that a person who was managing the receivership of a company was guilty of negligent misrepresentation (*inter alia*) in indicating to the solicitor of purchasers of the premises owned by the company that there were no unusual or onerous requirements by the fire officer still outstanding which might affect licences relating to the premises. Barr J was:

> "of opinion that there is a 'special relationship' between a receiver and a prospective purchaser of property belonging to the company in receivership within the ... *Hedley Byrne* [principle] which gives rise to a duty to take such care as is reasonable in all the circumstances. This includes a duty not to give misleading information and to take reasonable care that such information is reliable. A receiver negotiating the sale of such property owned by a company in receivership has by reason of his office a particular interest in the proposed contract which in my view creates a special relationship between him and the proposed purchaser which gives rise to a duty of care to the latter ... In terms of the present case the receiver was not under a duty to volunteer information to the prospective purchasers as to the fire officer's requirements relating to the premises for sale[206] but, having been asked about them, the duty of care ... thereupon arose."[207]

---

200. [1976] QB 801 at 820.

201. [1980] ILRM 53 (HC).

202. Eg, the following passages:

> "in [*Mardon*] the Court of Appeal purported to find their judgment upon ... *Hedley Byrne*. It would, I think, be generally considered that the Court of Appeal in *Mardon* considerably extended the application of the principle which had been laid down in *Hedley Byrne* ... [I]t is difficult to avoid the suspicion that the views of [the judges in *Mardon*] were to some extent coloured by the provisions of the English Misrepresentation Act of 1967 which was already law for some years at the date of the judgment but which had not been effective in 1963 at the date of the matters complained of by Mr Mardon the appellant":

[1980] ILRM at 62.

203. [1964] IR 417.

204. See also *Campbell v T & J Barrington Ltd* High Court, 3 October 1977 (Gannon J) - negligent advice given (through its consultant) to poultry farmer by supplier of feeding stuffs concerning nature and quality of feeding required; *Donnellan v Dungoyne Ltd* [1995] 1 ILRM 388 (HC); *Central & Eastern Trust Co v Rafuse* (1986) 31 Dec 31 DLR (4th) 481 (SC, Can).

205. High Court, 5 October 1993.

206. Citing *Re Flynn and Narman's Contract* [1948] IR 104 (HC).

207. Pages 22-23 of Barr J's judgment.

**[10.153]** Where the negligent misstatement occurs at some time after the contract has been made, the judicial authorities[208] are less clear. On principle, it seems that the defendant should not be exempt by reason only of the fact that the parties are in a contractual relationship.[209] He is always free, by way of a contractual provision or otherwise, to disclaim or modify his potential liability under the *Hedley Byrne* principle. It is to be hoped that our courts will resist the temptation to follow recent English decisions which seek to prevent the extension of tort into areas where traditionally contract had reigned supreme.

**[10.154]** Certainly the Irish decision of *Tulsk Co-operative Livestock Mart Ltd v Ulster Bank Ltd*[210] gives reason for hope that our Courts will not deviate down this path. Gannon J was satisfied that the fact that there was a contractual relationship between the plaintiffs and the defendants did not limit the duty owed by the defendants to the plaintiffs since there were in the general relationship between the parties many other factors from which the law would impute a duty of care to avoid harm under the "neighbour principle.[211]

## Statutory Misrepresentation

**[10.155]** Statute has supplemented the protection available to victims of misrepresentation in a contractual context. Part V of the Sale of Goods and Supply of Services Act 1980[212] introduces provisions broadly similar to those of the English Misrepresentation Act 1967.[213] An important limitation, however, is that only a narrow range of contracts falls within its scope; other contracts, notably contracts for the sale of land, continue to be subject to the common law.

---

208. Contrast *J Nunes Diamonds Ltd v Dominion Electric Protection* [1972] SCR 769 with *Midland Bank v Hett Stubbs & Kemp* [1979] Ch 384. *Cf Wall v Hegarty* [1980] ILRM 124 (HC), which, though not based on any finding of a contractual relationship between the executor and the solicitors, involved facts from which it would scarcely be difficult to infer such a relationship. As has already been mentioned *Junior Books Ltd v Veitchi Co Ltd* [1983] 1 AC 520 (HL, SC) was unconvincingly interpreted as involving an application of the *Hedley Byrne* principle, in *D & F Estates v Church Commissioners* [1988] 2 All ER 992 (HL, Eng).

209. See also *Finlay v Murtagh* [1979] IR 249 (SC), where Henchy J invoked *Hedley Byrne* as authority for the proposition that, whether a contractual relationship exists or not, once the circumstances are such that a defendant undertakes to show professional care and skill towards a person who may be expected to rely on such care and skill and who does so rely, the failure to show such care and skill is actionable:

> "The coincidence that the defendant's conduct amounts to breach of contract cannot affect either the duty of care or the common-law liability for its breach, for it is the general relationship. and not any particular manifestation such as a contract, that gives rise to the tortious liability in such a case."

*Finlay v Murtagh* was concerned with the general duty of care of a solicitor, rather than a duty based on the *Hedley Byrne* principle, but Henchy J's reliance on *Hedley Byrne* strongly suggests support for recognising a *Hedley-Byrne*-based action in respect of conduct also constituting a breach of contract.

210. High Court, 13 May 1983 (Gannon J).

211. *Donoghue v Stevenson* [1932] 562 at 580 (HL, SC), *per* Lord Atkin. See further para **[0.00]** above.

212. See Clark, *Contract Law in Ireland* (4th ed, 1998), pp 252-255; *O'Donnell v Truck and Machinery Sales* [1997] 1 ILRM 466 (HC).

213. Leading commentaries on this Act include Atiyah & Trietel (1967) 30 MLR 369 and Fairest [1967] Camb LJ 239.

**[10.156]** Three principal changes have been brought about by the legislation. First, s 44 of the Act removes the bars to rescission of a contract[214] for innocent misrepresentation imposed by the common law where the misrepresentation has become a term of the contract or the contract has been performed. Secondly, s 45(1) provides that:

> Where a person has entered into a contract after a misrepresentation has been made to him by another party thereto and as a result thereof he has suffered loss, then, if the person making the misrepresentation would be liable to damages in respect thereof had the misrepresentation been made fraudulently, that person shall be so liable notwithstanding that the misrepresentation was not made fraudulently, unless he proves that he had reasonable ground to believe and did believe up to the time the contract was made that the facts represented were true.

The third change brought about by the Act is to enable the court to award damages in lieu of rescission:

> if of opinion that it would be equitable to do so, having regard to the nature of the misrepresentation and the loss that would be caused by it if the contract were upheld, as well as the loss that rescission would cause to the other party .[215]

This power may be exercised only where the person to whom the representation has been made "would be entitled, by reason of the misrepresentation, to rescind the contract".[216] It would seem therefore that the remedy of rescission must still be available to him at the time of the action.

**[10.157]** Provisions excluding liability for misrepresentation are not enforceable unless shown to be "fair and reasonable".[217] In determining what is "fair and reasonable", regard is to be had to such factors as the strength of the bargaining position of the parties relative to each other and whether the contractor received an inducement to agree to the term.

## V. Pure Economic Loss in Products Liability

**[10.158]** Later[218] we examine in detail the question of recovery of damages for pure economic loss in products liability cases. The matter can arise in two principal ways. First, a plaintiff may sue the manufacturer of a chattel, claiming that, on account of his negligence, the chattel is defective in a way that involves neither injury nor the risk of injury to the person or property.[219] Secondly, a plaintiff may sue for compensation for the expenditure of money in the repair of a dangerous chattel.

**[10.159]** As regards the first of these cases, the House of Lords decision of *Junior Books Ltd v Veitchi Co Ltd*[220] appeared to open the door to recovery for non-dangerous defects, at

214. "Contract" in Part V of the Act means a contract of sale of goods, a hire-purchase agreement, an agreement for the letting of goods or a contract for the supply of a service: s 43.

215. Section 45(2). Damages may be awarded against a person under this provision whether or not he is liable to damages under s 45(1); but where he is so liable any award under s 45(2) is to be taken into account in assessing his liability under s 45(1).

216. Section 45(2).

217. Section 46(1). Unlike the other provisions in the Act (*cf* s 4(1)), this provision is retrospective.

218. See Ch 11 below.

219. Cases involving such injury fall readily within the scope of the *Donoghue v Stevenson* principle: *cf* Ch 11 below.

220. [1983] 1 AC 520 (HL, SC). See para **[10.45]** below.

all events when there was a high degree of proximity between the parties. In *Junior Books* itself, the interrelationship of expertise and reliance was particularly clear. It is interesting to note how the judges in the majority could not agree among themselves as to how to categorise the facts of the case. Lords Fraser, Russell and Roskill regarded the case as one involving liability for a defective chattel, while Lord Keith characterised it as one involving liability for causing foreseeable economic loss. In his view to introduce a general liability for manufacturing a defective product would be disruptive of commercial practice.[221]

**[10.160]** In *Ward v McMaster*,[222] Costello J warmly endorsed *Junior Books*. The fact that the British decisions subsequent to *Junior Books* have effectively disowned it[223] is worth noting in the Irish context. It may well be that Irish courts will prove more steadfast to the extension of liability it involves than their British counterparts.

**[10.161]** As regards compensation for the costs of repair of a product that is dangerous to the person or property on account of the defendant's negligence, we again have the spectacle of rapid British retreat from a position formerly endorsed. In *D & F Estates v Church Commissioners*,[224] the House of Lords held that such costs involved "pure economic loss" and were thus irrecoverable in tort. This conclusion is of questionable merit and is unlikely to appeal to the Irish courts. Indeed, so clear is the entitlement in justice of a party who is put to such expenditure that the courts here would surely have to examine the constitutionality of a common law rule denying compensation.

---

221. [1983] 1 AC 520 at 537

222. [1985] IR 29 (HC). The Supreme Court appeal on 10 May 1988 did not involve a consideration of the issue of non-dangerous defects as the defendant against whom judgment was given on this matter did not appeal.

223. See para. **[10.11]** and **[10.45]** below. Rarely has the eclipse of a House of Lords precedent been so undignified. Rather than abandon it in express terms, subsequent decisions have treated it as having been decided on its special facts, have vaunted the dissenting speech of Lord Brandon, (*cf D & F Estates Ltd v Church Commissioners* [1988] 2 All ER 992 (HL, Eng), and characterised it as a case involving damage to property (*Tate & Lyle Ltd v Greater London Council* [1983] 2 AC 509 at 530 (HL (Eng) *per Lord* Templeman)); *Lord Congregational Union Inc v Harriss & Harriss (a firm)* [1988] 1 All ER 15 at 25 (CA *per* Ralph Gibson LJ); see also *Simaun General Contracting Co v Pilkington Glass Ltd (No 2)* [1988] 1 All ER 791 at 803 (CA).

224. [1989] AC 177. See further *Murphy v Brentwood DC* [1991] 1 AC 398 (HC).

Chapter 11

# Manufacturers' and Producers' Liability for Defective Products[1]


I. Introduction ............ 249
II. By Whom is the Duty Owed? ............ 253
III. To Whom is the Duty Owed? ............ 257
IV. Non-Dangerous Defects ............ 268
V. Strict Liability: The European Regime ............ 274


## I. Introduction

**[11.01]** In previous editions of this work we gave to this chapter the heading *Products Liability*. We have changed the heading in this edition because we feel that *Manufacturers' and Producers' Liability for Defective Products* better describes the problems dealt with in the text, and follows closer the terminology preferred in the European Union, and now derivitively in the Irish legislation also.

**[11.02]** At common law a person injured by a defective product was confined by contract to suing those with whom he or she had privity. In 1932 the House of Lords in *Donoghue v Stevenson*[2] allowed a consumer to sue the manufacturer when she found a snail in her bottle of soda. The Law Lords recognised her right to sue the manufacturer even though the parties were not in a contractual relationship with each other. From 1932 to date, the English courts, and all those common law jurisdictions which followed *Donoghue v Stevenson*, have been concerned with expanding, refining and developing the principle established in that seminal decision. These judicial developments will be traced in the first

1. See *Product Liability*, Schuster ed, Irish Centre for European Law, 1989; *The New Product Liability Regime*, Schuster ed, Irish Centre for European Law, 1992; Stapleton, *Product Liability* (1994); Waddams, *Products Liability* (3rd ed, 1993); Frumer & Friedman, *Products Liability* (1998); Clark, *Product Liability* (1989); Miller, *Product Liability & Safety Encyclopedia*; Kelly & Attree eds, *European Product Liabilities* (2nd ed, 1997), especially Ch IX (on Irish law) by Hugh Garvey; Hodges ed, *Product Liability: European Laws and Practice* (1993), especially Ch 13 (on Irish law) by Clarke & Kennedy; Howells & Weatherill, *Consumer Protection Law* (1995), Ch 6; Heuston 'Donoghue v Stevenson in Retrospect' (1957) 20 MLR 1; Heuston 'Donoghue v Stevenson: A Fresh Appraisal' [1971] CLP 37; Gibson 'Products Liability in the United States and England: The Difference and Why' (1974) 3 Anglo Am LR 493; Carbonneau & Garvey 'Judicial Experimentation with a Strict Products Liability Rule: A Comparison of the Law in the United Kingdom, Louisiana and the United States' Common Law Jurisdictions' (1982) 5 Loyola of LA Int & Comp LJ I; Owen 'Products Liability: Principles of Justice' (1991) 20 Anglo-Amer LR 238; Goldring 'Consumer Protection Globalization and Democracy' (1998) 6 Cardozo J of Int'l & Comp L 1; Delany 'Note: Dangerous Chattels in the Irish Courts' (1954) 70 LQR 170; McMahon 'Liability for Defective Products: the Draft European Convention' (1973) 8 Ir Jur (ns) 227and short articles in (1923) 57 ILT & SJ; (1939) 55 73 ILT & SJ 201; (1970) 94 ILT & SJ 261, 267; (1940) 74 ILT & SJ 339; (1960) 94 ILT & SJ 139, 139.

2. [1932] AC 562 (HL).

five sections of this chapter. In spite of these developments, however, largely to the advantage of the plaintiff, it should be appreciated that liability under *Donoghue v Stevenson* was a fault-based liability: the manufacturer was liable to the consumer pnly when the manufacturer was at fault or was negligent, and in most cases the consumer had to discharge the onus of proof in that regard. In more recent times, and for different reasons, there has been a trend within the European Union to make the manufacturer strictly liable (ie liable without fault), whenever its product causes damage to the consumer. Recent Irish legislation, the Liability for Defective Products Act 1991, implementing the European Community's Directive in this matter, will be dealt with in Section VI of this chapter.

**[11.03]** Bearing the above general comments in mind, we can fairly say that nowadays liability in negligence for defective products is in the course of a radical restatement. Originally, the courts evinced little desire to hold manufacturers of products responsible for injuries suffered by consumers: to do so would, according to the thinking of former times, contradict the basic privity rule of contract law, whereby a person who is not a party to a contract[3] may not derive rights of action under it. In recent years the position has been transformed. The changes in marketing of products, the increase in consumerism, and the internationalisation of commerce have all led to a changed approach. The concept of

---

3. The law of contract offers increasingly wide-ranging remedies for consumers injured or merely disappointed by products. The Sale of Goods and Supply of Services Act 1980 implies warranties of merchantability and fitness for purpose of goods sold, from which the vendor may not attempt to resile contractually where the buyer deals as a consumer. Exemption clauses in other contracts to which the Act relates are enforceable only if "fair and reasonable". See Clark, *Contract Law in Ireland* (4th ed, 1998), Ch 8 for a comprehensive analysis. Section 13 of the 1980 Act which implies a condition in the sale of a motor vehicle that it is free from any defect that would render it a danger to the public, is considered see para **[11.13]** fn 33 below. The European Communities (Unfair Terms in Consumer Contracts) Regulations 1995 (SI 27/1995) give effect to the Unfair Contract Terms Directive 94/47/EC [1994]; OJ 1982 L280 which is "undoubtedly the most important piece of consumer protection legislation to emanate from the European Community": Clark, *Contract Law in Ireland* (4th ed, 1998), p 194. The Directive provides in Article 3(1) that:

> "[a] contractual term which has not been individually negotiated shall be regarded as unfair if, contrary to the requirement of good faith, it causes a significant imbalance in the parties' rights and obligations arising under the contract to the detriment of the consumer."

Article 4(1) provides in part that:

> "... the unfairness of a contractual term shall be assessed, taking into account the nature of the goods or services for which the contract was concluded, and by referring at the time of the conclusion of the contract to all the circumstances attending the conclusion of the contract and to all the other terms of the contract or of another contract on which it is dependent."

The Annex to the Directive contains an indicative and non-exhaustive list of the terms which may be regarded as unfair. One of the more important of these is contained in s 1(a) of the Annex which refers to terms that have the object or effect of excluding or limiting the legal liability of a seller or supplier in the event of the death of a consumer or personal injury to the consumer, resulting from an act or omission of the seller or supplier. A further development has come over the horizon. The Sale of Consumer Goods and Associated Guarantees Directive (99/44/EC, OJ 1999 L171/12), which must be transposed into Irish law by 1 January 2000, stipulates that consumer goods must be in conformity with the contract of sale. See Zollers, Hurd and Shears 'Consumer Protection in the European Union: An Analysis of the Directive on the Sale of Consumer Goods and Associated Guarantees' (1999) 20 Pa J of Int'l Econ L 97.

negligence has been applied and expanded. Ireland has crossed the threshold of strict liability[4] with the passage of the Liability for Defective Products Act 1991,[5] which (belatedly) gives effect to the EEC Directive on Products Liability of 1985.

## The Historical Background

**[11.04]** In the nineteenth century, as has been mentioned, courts in this country and elsewhere showed considerable reluctance in recognising the right of persons injured by products to recover damages in negligence against those with whom there was no privity of contract. In one of the leading decisions, *Winterbottom v Wright*,[6] in 1842, the plaintiff, a coachdriver of the mail from Hertford to Holyhead, was seriously injured when the coach which he was driving broke down on account of a latent defect. The plaintiff's employer was contractually bound to supply coachmen to the Postmaster-General to convey the mail. The defendant had contracted with the Postmaster-General to keep the coach in a proper state of repair. The plaintiff's action was dismissed on a demurrer.

**[11.05]** The judges of the English Court of Exchequer were of the view that to allow an action would impose too severe an obligation on the defendant. Lord Abinger CB considered that:

> "[u]nless we confine the operation of such contracts as this to the parties who entered into them, the most absurd and outrageous consequences to which I can see no limit, would ensue ... By permitting this action, we should be working this injustice, that after the defendant had done everything to the satisfaction of his employer, and after all matters between them had been adjusted, and all accounts settled on the footing of their contract, we should subject them to be ripped open by this action of tort being brought against him."[7]

Alderson B contended that:

> "The only safe rule is to confine the right to recover to those who enter into the contract; if we go one step beyond that, there is no reason why we should not go fifty"[8]

**[11.06]** So also in *Corry v Lucas*,[9] the Irish Court of Common Pleas sustained a demurrer where a worker was killed by an allegedly defective boiler supplied by the defendant to his employer. The court was unable to distinguish the facts from those in *Winterbottom v Wright*. In fairness to the court, however, if it was guilty of "privily of contract fallacy", it was perhaps encouraged by the plaintiff's pleadings which laid great stress on the defendant's contractual undertakings to the employer rather than attempting to base liability in negligence on broader principles.

---

4. Strict liability in various forms has been the preferred test in the United States for more than a quarter of a century. See Leigh-Jones 'Products Liability: Consumer Protection in America' (1969) 27 Camb LJ 54; Pasley 'The Protection of the Purchaser and Consumer under the Law of the USA' (1969) 32 MLR 241; Prosser 'The Assault Upon the Citadel' (1960) 69 Yale LJ 1099; Prosser 'The Fall of the Citadel' (1966) 50 Minn LR 791.
5. See Byrne & Binchy *Annual Review of Irish Law 1991*, pp 420-434.
6. (1842) 10 M & W 109, 152 ER 402; *Cf* Atiyah, *The Rise and Fall of Freedom of Contract* (1979), pp 501-504.
7. 10 M & W at 114-115; 152 ER at 405.
8. 10 M & W at 115; 152 ER at 405.
9. (1868) IR 3 CL 208 (Com Pleas).

**[11.07]** Gradually the courts became less reluctant to extend liability beyond the privity nexus of contract law. A false representation of safety in the knowledge that a product was dangerous had been recognised, even before *Corry v Lucas*[10] as a basis for recovery.[11] Liability was also recognised in the case of failure to give a warning when there was an awareness of a defect.[12] Moreover, liability in respect of "inherently dangerous things" was recognised.[13]

## Abolition of the Privity Requirement

**[11.08]** Eventually in all Common Law jurisdictions, the privity limitation was set aside in favour of a more general principle of liability in relation to the negligent manufacture and supply of defective products. In the United States, the seminal decision was *McPherson v Buick Motor Co*,[14] where the New York Court of Appeals in 1916 held that the category of "inherently dangerous things" should include "anything which would be dangerous if negligently made".[15] In Canada general liability for negligent manufacture was imposed eight years later in *Buckley v Mott*;[16] in Britain, the decision taking this step was *Donoghue v Stevenson*,[17] in 1932. The pursuer averred that she had gone to a cafe in Paisley, Scotland, with a friend who had bought some refreshments for both of them. The refreshments consisted of ice-cream in a tumbler with ginger-beer poured over it. The ginger-beer had been manufactured by the defendant and sold by him to the cafe proprietor. It was contained in a stoppered bottle of dark opaque glass. When the ginger-beer was being poured on the pursuer's ice-cream, the remains of a decomposed snail emerged. As a result of seeing this, the pursuer alleged, she suffered from shock and severe gastro-enteritis.

**[11.09]** By a majority of three to two, the House of Lords held that the pursuer had stated a good cause of action. Lord Atkin, having set forth the broad "neighbour" formula of negligence that has been mentioned above,[18] expressed the obligation owed by a manufacturer of chattels to the consumer, which in the circumstances specified in its formulation "has never been questioned [and] has been adopted and expanded in over one

10. (1868) IR 3 CL 208 (Com Pleas).

11. *Langridge v Levy* (1837) 2 M & W 519; 150 ER 863.

12. *Cf Heaven v Pender* (1883) 11 QBD 503 at 517. See also *Quinn v Tedcastles & Co* (1898) 32 ILTR 137 (QB).

13. *Longmeid v Holliday* (1851) 6 Ex 761 155 ER 752. *Thomas v Winchester* (1852) 6 NY 397. *Cf O'Gorman v O'Gorman* [1903] 2 IR 573 at 584-595 (KB). An interesting echo of this approach is apparent in *O'Sullivan v Noonan* Supreme Court, 28 July 1972 in Walsh J's judgment. It is also noteworthy that as late as 1953 in *Robinson v Technico Ltd* High Court, 19 February 1953; affd by Supreme Court, 7 July 1953, Davitt P adopted the same approach the most recent Irish decision cited in his judgment being *Sullivan v Creed* [1904] 2 IR 317. *Cf* Delany (1954) 70 LQR 170.

14. (1916) 217 NYS 382; 111 NE 1050.

15. (1916) 217 NYS 382; 111 NE 1050.

16. (1920) 50 DLR 408 (NS SC).

17. [1932] AC 562 (HL). See Heuston 'Donoghue v Stevenson in Retrospect' (1957) 20 MLR 1; Heuston 'Donoghue v Stevenson: A Fresh Appraisal' [1971] CLP 37.

18. [1932] AC 562, para **[6.09]** above.

hundred reported cases throughout the common law world".[19] The obligation, as expressed by Lord Atkin, was to the effect that:

> "... a manufacturer of products, which he sells in such a form as to show that he intends them to reach the ultimate consumer in the form in which they left him, with no reasonable possibility of intermediate examination, and with the knowledge that the absence of reasonable care in the preparation or putting up of the products will result in an injury to the consumer's life or property, owes a duty to the consumer to take that reasonable care."[20]

**[11.10]** The extent to which this statement represents the law of this country today will require further consideration.

## II. By Whom is the Duty Owed?

**[11.11]** In the Supreme Court decision of *Power v Bedford Motor Co*,[21] Lavery J stated that the *Donoghue v Stevenson*[22] principle "must now be taken as settled".[23] He continued:

> "It is clear in principle that the obligation is not confined to manufacturers of goods but extends to persons undertaking repairs to articles which will be dangerous to users who should be in contemplation if there is a want of reasonable care in the work. It must also apply to persons doing work on an article which they foresee would be used by others without examination."[24]

These categories require further consideration.

### Manufacturers

**[11.12]** It is clear from *Donoghue v Stevenson* and *Power v Bedford Motor Co*, that the manufacturer of a product owes a duty of care towards those who may foreseeably be injured or damaged by the product.

### Repairers

**[11.13]** It is equally clear from the passage quoted above that a repairer of goods may be liable under the *Donoghue v Stevenson*[25] principle. Accordingly, in the *Power*[26] case liability was imposed on the defendant garage for the negligent repair of a car, which left the steering mechanism in a dangerous state after the repairs had been completed.[27]

---

19. SALMOND & HEUSTON, p 297 (footnote reference omitted).
20. [1932] AC 562 at 599.
21. [1959] IR 391 (SC). The earlier High Court decision of *Kirby v Burke and Holloway* [1944] IR 207 in which Gavan Duffy J imposed liability on a manufacturer using a straightforward standard of reasonable care unencumbered by further conceptual refinements, had little influence in the further development of the law.
22. [1932] AC 562 (HL). See also *Kearney v Paul & Vincent Ltd* High Court, 30 July 1985 (Barron J), p 20.
23. [1959] IR 391 at 408.
24. [1959] IR 391 at 408.
25. [1932] AC 562 (HL).
26. [1959] IR 391 (SC).
27. See also *Gilna v Maguire and 3M Ireland Ltd* High Court, 19 May 1999 (Johnson J) - manufacturer and servicer; *Stennett v Hancock* [1939] 2 All ER 578 (KBD); *Herschtal v Stewart & Ardern Ltd* [1940] I KB 155; *Haseldine v Daw & Son Ltd* [1941] 2 KB 343 (CA).

### Installers and Assemblers

**[11.14]** Installers and assemblers have been held liable in a number of reported decisions.[28] An unusual application of the principle was made in *Brown v Cotterill*[29] (decided only two years after *Donoghue v Stevenson*[30]), where liability was imposed on a monumental mason when a tombstone that he had erected fell on a little girl who was placing flowers on her grandmother's grave. The court rightly held that the mason could not shift responsibility away from himself onto the person who had contracted with him for the erection of the tombstone, since:

> "persons who employ monumental masons to erect tombstones rely on the mason's skill and not on their own examination, and there is therefore, nothing in their acceptance of the mason's work to exempt him from liability for the defective work which he has erected in a place to which the public have access."[31]

### Suppliers

**[11.15]** It is clear that the supplier of a chattel for reward is under a duty of care in respect of the safety of those to whom the chattel is supplied or indeed in respect of the safety of any person who is likely to use it when so supplied. In *Keegan v Owens*,[32] the Supreme Court held that the supplier for reward of swing-boats for a charity carnival owed a duty to protect a worker employed by the carnival committee from injury in operating the swing-boats.[33]

### Retailers

**[11.16]** As well as being under wide-ranging contractual obligations to purchasers,[34] retailers fall under a duty of care in tort to those who may foreseeably be injured by the products they sell.[35] There is, however, a difference in the scope of duty owed by

28. Eg *Brown v Cotterill* (1934) 51 TLR 21 (KBD); *Malfroot v Noxal Ltd* (1935) 51 TLR 551 (KBD); *Howard v Furness Houlder Argentine Lines Ltd* [1936] 2 All ER 781 (KBD). *Cf O'Neill v Finn & v WD Ltd* Supreme Court, 20 May 1969; *Robinson v Technico Ltd* High Court, 19 February 1953.
29. See fn 28.
30. [1932] AC 562 (HL Sc).
31. See fn 28 at 22.
32. [1953] IR 267 (SC). The Sale of Goods and Supply of Services Act 1980, s 39 implies in every contract for the supply of a service by a supplier acting in the course of a business a term that materials used will be sound and reasonably fit for the purpose for which they are required.
33. Liability has also been extended to the suppliers of second-hand goods. See *O'Sullivan v Noonan* Supreme Court, 28 July 1972. See also *O'Neill v Finn & VWD Ltd* Supreme Court, 20 May 1969. Under s 13 of the Sale of Goods and Supply of Services Act 1980 there is an implied condition in the sale of a motor vehicle (including a secondhand car) that it is free from any defect which would render it a danger to the public. Persons using the vehicle with the consent of the buyer, may maintain an action for breach of this condition as if they were the buyers. *Cf Glorney v O'Brien* High Court, 14 November 1988 (Lynch J).
34. See para **[2.16]** above.
35. *Andrews v Hopkinson* [1957] 1 QB 229; *Fisher v Harrods* [1966] 1 Lloyd's Rep 500; *Kubach v Hollands* [1937] 3 All ER 907; *Duffy v Rooney and Dunne's Stores (Dundalk) Ltd* High Court, 23 June 1997 (Laffoy J), affd by Supreme Court, 23 April 1998; *Browne v Primark t/a Penneys* DPIJ:: Michaelmas Term 1990 p 182 (HC); *Cassells v Marks & Spencer plc* High Court, unrep 25 March 1999 (Barr J).

manufacturers and retailers; respectively.[36] A manufacturer of chocolate bars, for example, must have a system for checking the quality of the bars that are put onto the market. A retailer, of course, has a duty of care in relation to the chocolate bars sold in the shop but it is limited to taking reasonable steps to ensure that the stock is not out of date. Customers would not thank the retailer for opening the wrapping to inspect the contents.

**[11.17]** In *Duffy v Rooney and Dunnes Stores (Dundalk) Ltd*,[37] Laffoy J took an expansive view of the scope of the duty of care of retailers. A very young child was burnt when she went too close to the fire, wearing an inflammable raincoat bought in the second defendant's retail premises. Laffoy J held that the second defendant had been guilty of negligence in failing to attach a warning[38] label to the raincoat but she relieved the second defendant of liability as this negligence had not caused the child's injury, since the evidence indicated that, had the appropriate warning been given, the child would probably still have been wearing the raincoat.

**[11.18]** In *Duffy*, the second defendant did not dispute that, as retailer of the coat, it owed a duty of care to the plaintiff, as the ultimate user of the coat. The only question was whether it had "observed the standard of care in retailing that product which the law required of it". Nowhere in her judgment did Laffoy J address the proposition that the scope of a retailer's duty might be narrower than, or at all events different in scope from, that of a manufacturer. Instead, one finds an elision between the two. Thus, for example, Laffoy J was not satisfied on the evidence that in 1991:

> "a reasonable or prudent *manufacturer or retailer,* if he had addressed the issue, would have considered it necessary to substitute a low flammability fabric ... in order to protect the plaintiff'.[39]

**[11.19]** A similar elision may be noted in Laffoy J's observation that:

> "a reasonably prudent *manufacturer or retailer*, had he properly addressed the issue would have, and the second defendant ought to have, affixed a label to [the plaintiff]'s coat warning that it should be kept away from fire".[40]

On Laffoy J's approach there is, in effect, an identical duty resting on the manufacturer and the retailer to ensure that a product is made of safe ingredients and to ensure that the consumer is adequately warned as to any dangers inhering in the product. There may well be justification for expanding the duty of the retailer to meet that of the manufacturer in a case where the retailer is a large commercial organisation with adequate resources to engage in close scrutiny of products that it actually commissions, but nothing in Laffoy J's

---

36. *Ryan v Dan Dooley Rent a Car Topcar Ltd and Rover (Ireland) Ltd* High Court, 19 May 1994 (Kinlen J) (Circuit Appeal) is an example of how the duties of manufacturer, wholesaler and retailer may differ. The plaintiff bought a car which had a propensity to cut out too often. The retailer was held liable in contract. The manufacturer was held liable in negligence and the wholesaler was also found to have been negligent in failing to have absorbed properly the information which the manufacturer had sent to it in bulletins alerting it of the problem with cars of the type that the plaintiff had bought. As between manufacturer and wholesaler, liability was divided on a two thirds/one third basis.
37. High Court, 23 June 1997 (Laffoy J), affd by Supreme Court, 3 November 1998.
38. See further para **[11.41]-[11.53]** below.
39. Emphasis added.
40. Emphasis added.

judgment expressly confirms that this is why she articulated the respective duties of manufacturer and retailer in identical terms.

**[11.20]** It is worth noting that the manufacturer in this case was a large and reputable one. The evidence was to the effect that the Irish standards as to warnings followed rather than led those in England. Yet there is no suggestion in Laffoy J's judgment that the second defendant, as retailer, might be entitled to assume that the manufacturer had addressed the requirements as to warning. As against this, it may be responded that the case was not comparable to one where a retailer sells contaminated tinned food. Here the second defendant had full information as to the constituent fabrics in the coat. The question of formulating an appropriate warning was not more difficult, and no less urgent, for the second defendant to address than it was for the manufacturer.

## Liability of Manufacturer for Negligence of Supplier of Component Part

**[11.21]** A further question of some importance arises here and requires our attention. Where a product is disseminated by a manufacturer containing a component part supplied by an outside contractor, is the manufacturer liable for damage caused by the product which is attributable to the outside contractors' lack of due care? In *Fleming v Henry Denny & Sons Ltd*,[41] Kingsmill Moore J stated:

> "It is, I think, impossible to lay down a universal rule. The nature of the material purchased, the reputation of the dealer from whom it is purchased, the obligations imposed by law on a vendor, the processes through which the materials have already passed in the hands of the manufacturer or dealer, the past experience of the purchaser and the general experience of mankind, all these have their bearing upon the remoteness or otherwise of the contingency. The manufacturer is not bound to take precautions against any contingency however remote, and the nature of the precautions which he is obliged to take must bear a relation to the probability or improbability of the risk. A manufacturer of cakes may well be bound to take great care that stones are not incorporated in the currants which he uses, for the occasional presence of such stones is notorious, but it does not follow that, if he purchases flour from millers of unblemished reputation he is bound to test it for the presence of ergot, and still less would he be bound to examine the sugar which he purchases from reliable sources to see that it is not contaminated with strychnine or other poisonous crystals ..."

**[11.22]** In *Fleming's* case, the Supreme Court held that the manufacturers of black pudding were entitled to rely on the firms that supplied them with oatmeal, rusk meal and spices (which formed part of the ingredients of the black pudding) to take care that what they supplied to them was free from hidden dangers, such as a piece of steel. Kingsmill Moore J stated that it seemed to him that:

> "a manufacturer whose duty is to take reasonable care not to send out food containing any harmful substance may, insofar as the ingredients of that food are concerned, discharge his duty by obtaining the ingredients from firms of high repute who have a like responsibility to see that the ingredients are free from any harmful substance. It may not be so in every case. The defect may be so obvious that it is a failure of reasonable care not to observe it. There may be special facts which require special precautions."[42]

41. Supreme Court, 29 July 1955, pp 7-8.

42. See also *Taylor v Rover Co Ltd* [1966] 1 WLR 1491. It is worth noting that, under the Liability for Defective Products Act 1991 the manufacturer of a product is not able to avoid liability in respect of a component part or raw material by showing that the supplier was reputable: *Cf* para **[11.98]** below.

## III. To Whom is the Duty Owed?

**[11.23]** In *Donoghue v Stevenson*[43] Lord Atkin described the duty as being owed to "the ultimate consumer". The courts have taken a broad view of this element in the duty, and have extended its scope significantly.

**[11.24]** Clearly, of course, the "consumer" in the narrow sense of the word, namely, the user of a retail product, will come within the scope of the definition.[44] However, a wider view has been taken. In *Power v Bedford Motor Co*,[45] where the purchaser of a car from another person was killed as a result of negligent repair work done by the defendants for the former owner, liability was imposed on the repairer. Lavery J, in the Supreme Court, stated in his conclusion that:

> "the deceased did belong to the class of persons whom [the defendants] should have contemplated as being exposed to the danger if the work were done wrongly. That class of persons included any person who might drive or be a passenger in the car and perhaps others who might be injured if the car went out of control - though it is unnecessary to consider them."[46]

**[11.25]** The Supreme Court has since recognised that the supplier of a car with a defect that renders it dangerous may be liable for resulting damage, not only to passengers in the car but also to "other users of the highway or other parties who would foreseeably come into proximity with the motor vehicle."[47]

**[11.26]** In many other decisions, the "ultimate consumer" test has also been broadened. Thus, in *Barnett v H & J Packer & Co Ltd*,[48] a confectioner who was injured by a sweet which he was placing in a display tray[49] was permitted to sue, though quite clearly the goods in question had never reached the "ultimate consumer". Similarly, in *Brown v Cotterill*,[50] as we have seen, the child in the churchyard was entitled to recover when hit by the tombstone, Lawrence J considering that the mason was under a duty:

> "to every member of the public who might lawfully enter the churchyard and be injured by the fall of the tombstone."[51]

---

43. [1932] AC 562 at 599 (HL (SC)).
44. See eg *Donoghue v Stevenson* [1932] AC 562; *Kirby v Burke and Holloway* [1944] IR 207 (HC); *Denniston v McNamara Maxwell & Co* (1950) 84 ILTR 168 (CC); *Grant v Australian Knitting Mills Ltd* [1936] AC 85 (PC); *Fleming v Henry Denny & Son Ltd* Supreme Court, 29 July 1955; *Conole v Redbank Oyster Co Ltd* [1976] IR 191 at 196 (SC); in *Robinson v Technico Ltd* High Court, 19 February 1953.
45. [1959] IR 391 (SC).
46. [1959] IR 391 at 411.
47. *O'Sullivan v Noonan* Supreme Court, 28 July 1972 at p 14 of his judgment.
48. [1940] 3 All ER 575 (KBD).
49. The sweet contained a piece of wire or steel which pricked the plaintiff's hand and gave him serious blood-poisoning.
50. (1934) 51 TLR 21 (KBD).
51. (1934) 51 TLR 21 at 22. See also *Stennett v Hancock* [1939] 2 All ER 578 (KBD) - pedestrian injured by lorrywheel.

## Intermediate Examination

**[11.27]** The principle on which liability was based in *Donoghue v Stevenson*[52] was limited by the restriction that there should be "no reasonable possibility of intermediate examination". Thus it was held that the defendant was not liable where the plaintiff was actually aware of the danger and disregarded it[53] or where an examination was so carelessly carried out as not to reveal the defect.[54]

**[11.28]** The courts, however, in keeping with the general trend to favour the injured plaintiff, gradually relaxed their attitude regarding intermediate inspection. Section 34(2)(f) of the Civil Liability Act 1961, went no further than what the courts had already decided in providing that, where an action is brought for negligence in respect of a "thing" that has caused damage, the fact that there was a reasonable possibility or probability of examination after the thing had left the hands of the defendant does not, by itself, exclude the defendant's duty, but may be taken as evidence that he was not in the circumstances negligent in parting with the thing in its dangerous state.

**[11.29]** Thus a technical approach to the issue has been set aside in favour of an approach that makes the issue a question of fact, formerly for the jury, to be determined according to common sense, albeit with the likelihood of sympathy for the plaintiff. In *Colgan v Connolly Construction Company (Ireland) Ltd*,[55] McMahon J went so far as to express the view that s 34(2)(f) of the 1961 Act has "shifted the onus of proof to the defendants in products liability cases".

## Dangerous Substances

**[11.30]** In *Bolands Ltd v Trouw Ireland Ltd*[56] Finlay P accepted the proposition that:

> "a person in control of a dangerous substance, whether as a supplier, manufacturer or vendor, has a duty to take reasonable care that any person acquiring it from him, whether by sale or otherwise, does not suffer injury or loss".

This duty will override any limitations in the duty of the occupier to those entering the premises in which the chattel is kept.[57] Thus, in *Purtill v Athlone UDC*,[58] the fact that an eleven-year-old boy was a trespasser in the defendant's abattoir did not on that account relieve the defendants of a duty to protect him from being injured by a detonator kept on the premises within easy access of the boy.

---

52. [1932] AC 562 at 599 (HL).
53. *Farr v Butters Bros & Co* [1932] 2 KB 606 (CA). See also *Conole v Redbank Oyster Co Ltd* [1976] IR 191 at 196 (SC).
54. *Buckner v Ashby & Horner Ltd* [1941] 1 KB 321; *Holmes v Ashford* [1950] 2 All ER 76. *Cf Dowsett Engineering Construction Ltd v Sloan* [1955-1956] Ir Jur 31 (HC, NI). *Cf Conole v Redbank Oyster Co Ltd* [1976] IR 191 at 196 discussed at para **[2.35]** above.
55. [1980] ILRM 33. See also *McIlveen v Charlesworth Developments* [1973] NI 216 (CA).
56. High Court, 1 May 1978 at pp 19-20. *Cf Purtill v Athlone UDC* [1968] IR 205 (SC) - especially at 211 *per* Walsh J; *Sullivan v Creed* [1904] 2 IR 317; *Cahill v Kenneally* [1955-1956] Ir Jur 15. See also *Campbell v O'Donnell* [1967] IR 226 at 231 (SC); *Byrne v McDonald* Supreme Court, 7 February 1957; *Breslin v Brennan* [1937] IR 350 at 362 (SC).
57. *Cf Purtill v Athlone UDC* [1968] IR 205; *Byrne v McDonald* Supreme Court, 7 February 1957.
58. [1968] IR 205.

## Duty to Warn

**[11.31]** In *Bolands v Trouw Ireland Ltd*,[59] Finlay P rejected the contention that the vendor of an ingredient of a poultry foodmix owed a duty to explain to the purchaser who compounded the foodmix, the manner in which the ingredient could be used safely with other ingredients. The President considered that the ingredient was:

> "a dangerous substance only in the sense that a great majority of chemical drugs are dangerous substances, namely, the application of them to humans or animals in excessive doses may be injurious or even fatal."[60]

**[11.32]** This decision may be contrasted with *Kearney v Paul & Vincent Ltd*,[61] where Barron J preferred the following conceptual analysis:

> "A manufacturer of a product which is not dangerous in itself is not absolved from all duty of care to the users of his product. This duty arises upon the basis of the neighbour principle established in *Donoghue v Stevenson*[62] and approved by the Supreme Court in *McNamara v ESB*[63] ... The extent of the duty of a manufacturer whose product is alleged to have caused damage is not to be determined therefore with regard to the damage alleged to have been sustained, but with regard to what he knew or ought to have known when he released the product on the market. In *McNamara v ESB* the court was dealing with the duty of care towards a trespasser. In the present case, it seems to me that the duty of care should be analogous to that of the duty owed by an invitor to an invitee as in both cases the relationship between the parties arises in the interests of the party owing the duty.
>
> There must be many matters which come or should come to the notice of a manufacturer placing a new product on the market which, if he gave or had given proper consideration to such matters, he should have realised were such that the user of the product required to be told about them because otherwise in ignorance of them he might use the product in such a way as to sustain damage as a result. It is his duty to ensure that such matters are brought to the attention of the users of the product."

**[11.33]** Whether the analogy with the duty owed by an invitor to an invitee is the happiest one may be debated. That duty, after all, was historically a circumscribed one, falling short of the duty of care in negligence. It would, moreover, be unjust if the duty to warn invariably extended no further than to purchasers. It is surely better that the duty to warn should embrace the flexibility of the duty of care in negligence than that it should endorse a categorical approach or analogy with one now that has recently been dismantled in relation to occupier's liability.[64]

**[11.34]** Cases in other common law jurisdictions are to the effect that, while the supplier of a dangerous product to a professional or business buyer may (within limits) assume that the buyer will be aware of the danger,[65] different considerations apply to the supply of

---

59. High Court, 1 May 1978.
60. At p 20.
61. High Court, 30 July 1985 (Barron J) at pp 20-21.
62. [1932] AC 562 at 580.
63. [1975] IR 1.
64. *Cf* Ch 12; Occupiers' Liability Act 1995, s 3.
65. *Holmes v Ashford* [1950] 2 All ER 76 (CA); *Murphy v St Catherine's Hospital* 41 DLR (2d) 697 at 711-712.

dangerous products to an unsophisticated general public: here, clear warnings regarding dangers in use (or even foreseeable abuse) of the product may be required.[66]

**[11.35]** In *O'Byrne v Gloucester*,[67] in 1988, the Supreme Court upheld Johnson J's finding of negligence against the makers of a brushed cotton skirt for failure to attach to it a warning that the skirt was highly flammable. The plaintiff, aged fifteen, had been severely burned after the hem of her skirt had touched a butane gas heater in her living room. Finlay CJ[68] said:

> "Having regard to the nature of the risk involved in this particular dangerous aspect of this material, namely, major physical injury to the wearer, which was a danger foreseeable by the defendants, and having regard to the simplicity of the precaution which it is alleged the defendants should have taken, namely, the attaching to the garment of a simple warning that it was dangerous if exposed to a naked flame and would burn rapidly, ... this was a precaution which a reasonably careful manufacturer and vendor of this type of clothing should have taken."[69]

**[11.36]** The defendants argued that, even if a warning had been placed on the garment, it was improbable that the plaintiff would have adverted to it or, if she had, would have acted any differently from how she had in fact acted. No questions had been asked of the plaintiff or her mother by counsel on either side. Finlay CJ was satisfied that there was sufficient evidence before the trial judge to raise an inference that, if a warning had been attached in the proper way, the plaintiff would probably have taken precautions, or her parents (who had given the skirt to her as a present) would probably have urged her to take such precautions in the use and wearing of the skirt, or possibly have chosen instead a less dangerous material.

**[11.37]** McCarthy J went further. He considered that, once the trial judge had concluded that the absence of an appropriate warning constituted negligence on the part of the defendants:

> "it was for the defendants to establish, by cross-examination or otherwise, that the warning would not have affected the purchase or the conduct of the wearer of the garment".[70]

**[11.38]** *O'Byrne* may be contrasted with *Browne v Primark t/a Penneys*,[71] where again the plaintiff was a young person whose clothing went on fire. There were, however, significant differences between the two cases. In *Browne* the plaintiff was a boy aged "five or six years".[72] When he was playing with matches, his cotton flannelette pyjamas caught fire and he was badly burned. He sued the manufacturer and the retailer in negligence. The

---

66. *Lambert v Lastoplex Chemicals Ltd* [1972] SCR 569. See *Robinson v Technico Ltd* High Court, 19 February 1953. The question whether there is a duty at common law to warn of dangers that may result from cigarette-smoking has been discussed in Courts in the United States: see Garner, (1980) 53 S Cal LR 1423; McCarthy, (1989) 23 U Richmond LR 257.
67. Supreme Court, 3 November 1988.
68. With whose judgment Walsh J concurred.
69. Pages 9-10 of Finlay CJ's judgment.
70. Page 1 of McCarthy J's concurring judgment. As to the circumstances in which warning labels may be efficacious in actual practice, see Lebto & Miller in J of Products Liability (1988), p 225.
71. DPIJ: Michaelmas Term 1990, p 182 (High Court, 10 December 1990, (Lardner J)).
72. DPIJ: Michaelmas Term 1990, p 182.

pyjamas contained a warning label with the words "Keep away from fire", as the standards prevailing in Ireland and England at the time required. The essence of the plaintiff's case was that the standards were wrong to make a distinction between nightdresses and pyjamas by requiring for only the former that they should comply with prescribed flammability criteria.

**[11.39]** In granting a non-suit, Lardner J said:

> "It has been very forcefully urged that I should find the defendants have been guilty of want of reasonable care in marketing these pyjamas. I find I am not persuaded that a reasonably careful retailer, or maker of the garments of this kind, should, in 1986, in this country, have used only flame-resistant fabrics in children's pyjamas. Public standards, which are declared by the Institute which is set up by statute and which are under the control of the Department of State do not require it and there is no evidence that such standards were commonly applied here and I am not satisfied that a reasonably carefully trader should, as a matter of legal duty at common law, have observed the higher standard of safety claimed on behalf of the plaintiff. It may well be that such a higher standard should be required by law, but if that is the case, it's a matter for the legislature."[73]

**[11.40]** *Browne* was really a case in which the issue was whether or not the article should have been placed on the market in its existing condition. The questions of the nature and scope of the duty to warn were secondary though it seems clear that, had there been no warning, a non-suit would not have been granted.

**[11.41]** In *Duffy v Rooney and Dunnes Stores (Dundalk) Ltd*,[74] Laffoy J gave the most comprehensive analysis thus far in Ireland of the issue of duty to warn of dangers inhering in products.

**[11.42]** The plaintiff, a girl aged two years and ten months, was seriously burned when a coat she was wearing on a visit to her grandparent's home came in contact with an open fire in the sitting room. The coat had been purchased in the second defendant's store.

**[11.43]** The accident took place in 1992. The coat, which had been manufactured in 1991, was designed and sold as a hooded raincoat. The outer fabric was a full flared skirt, which was designed to stand out from the body in a bell shape. The coat contained no warning that the fabrics were flammable or that it should be kept away from fire.

**[11.44]** The coat was one of a range of over five thousand sold by companies in the Dunnes Stores Group which were manufactured for the Group by an English Company. This company was a large reputable manufacturer specialising in children's outer wear for many of the leading multiple chain stores in Britain and Ireland as well as North America and other countries. Its annual turnover was three million pounds and it manufactured 120,000 garments a year. The fabrics for the raincoat that the plaintiff wore had been sourced by the manufacturer from a large reputable British supplier. The coats were of a standard design and style popular in the market at the time of manufacture. In 1991 there were no standards or regulation in force in Britain in relation to the manufacture or assembly of outer garments for children. The manufacturer did not carry out flammability testing on the fabrics. No warning label was attached to the coats and there was no

73. DPIJ: Michaelmas Term 1990, p 189.

74. High Court, 23 June 1997 (Laffoy J) affd by Supreme Court, 23 April 1998.

standard or regulation in Britain requiring warning labels to be affixed. From 1992 onwards the Dunnes Stores Group put warning labels on all children's garments.

**[11.45]** In 1991, the only Irish standard in force in relation to the children's apparel was IS 148:1988, under which the National Standards Authority of Ireland (EOLAS) prescribed the flammability and labelling requirements of fabrics and fabric assemblies used in children's nightwear. Children's night-dresses, dressing gowns and pyjamas fell within the scope of these requirements but there was no dispute that the plaintiff's coat did not come within their remit. Had it done so, the fabrics of which it was made up would not have been used; and the words "Keep away from fire" would have been necessary if the fabrics had been permitted to be used as nightware.

**[11.46]** In the instant case, Laffoy J noted that IS 148:1988 was not directly relevant, since the coat was worn by the plaintiff was not a garment to which the standard applied. Nevertheless, this standard was relevant insofar as it evidenced:

> "an official awareness of the risk inherent in using fabric other than fabric of low flammability for lightweight, long, loose garments such as night-dresses, pyjamas, and dressing gowns intended primarily for indoor wear and an official determination that, insofar as it is not necessary to proscribe the use of fabrics other than fabrics of low flammability in the manufacture of such garments, a warning, by means of labelling, of that risk is necessary to protect the public, as evidenced by the requirement of a warning label on pyjamas and terry-towelling bathrobes. It is also of relevance in that official awareness was communicated to the public, and, in particular, to manufacturers and retailers through publication of IS 148:1988 and, indeed, through publication of the standards and the enactment of the regulations which preceded it."

**[11.47]** Applying these principles to the facts of the case, Laffoy J was not satisfied that the plaintiff's coat was so inherently dangerous that it should not have been put in circulation. The court was required to have regard to "demands of the market place and the popularity of this type of garment", which was "entirely understandable in the light of its attractiveness and utility", and to weigh these factors against the risks the coat presented and the manner in which those risks might adequately be addressed.

**[11.48]** Moreover, Laffoy J was not satisfied on the evidence that in 1991 a reasonable and prudent manufacturer or retailer, if it had addressed the issue, would have considered it necessary to substitute a low flammability fabric, such as nylon, for the cotton/polyester outer layer of the plaintiff's coat. The resulting garment would have been of a different type from the one that found favour with customers. To have treated the outer fabric with flame retardant would have detracted from the attractiveness and comfort of the coat because it would have rendered the fabric stiffer and less comfortable where it met the body.

**[11.49]** Laffoy J was, however, of the view that a reasonably prudent manufacturer or retailer, if it had properly addressed the issue, would have affixed a label on the coat warning that it should be kept away from the fire, taking into account the following seven factors:

(a) that the trend in recent times had been to use lighter weight and more flammable fabrics for garments intended for wear by children out of doors than had formerly been the case;

(b) that in design terms there were many similarities between a coat of the type worn by the plaintiff and a night-dress or dressing gown, particularly in terms of length and looseness and the fact that frequently with garments such as raincoats and wintercoats the child wore a size bigger than was appropriate to the child's age (as was the situation in the instant case);

(c) that very young children had to be dressed by a parent or other adult and that even a garment primarily designed for outdoor wear was normally put on the child in the house and might be worn around the house for some time before the child went out;

(d) that open fires and gas heaters were a common feature of domestic life in Ireland;

(e) that young children were unpredictable and lacked a sense of danger;

(f) the gravity of the consequences of fire accidents; and

(g) the relatively low cost of labelling garments.

**[11.50]** It was not enough, however, for the plaintiff to establish that the second defendant had been guilty of negligence in failing to affix a warning label to the coat; it was essential for her to show that this negligence had resulted in her injuries. This, in Laffoy J's judgment, the plaintiff had failed to do. The plaintiff's grandmother, who had bought the coat in 1991 and given it to her as a Christmas present, gave evidence, that if there had been a warning label, she would have adverted to it and been hesitant to buy something which would have been dangerous, particular for her granddaughter. While Laffoy J had no doubt that the grandmother honestly believed this, she considered that the belief was "informed by more than a modicum of hindsight" and was not satisfied that the grandmother would not in fact have bought the coat if the warning had been attached. Similarly, Laffoy J rejected the plaintiff's mother's belief that she would not have dressed her daughter in the coat if it contained a warning. On the fateful day, the plaintiff was wearing trousers and a sweatshirt to which warning labels were attached.

**[11.51]** Neither did Laffoy consider that, if the warning label had been affixed, affairs in the household on the day in question would have been conducted in such a way that the plaintiff's coat would not have come in contact with the fire. Accordingly the plaintiff's action against the second defendant was dismissed.

**[11.52]** The first defendant appealed unsuccessfully to the Supreme Court, his appeal concentrating on the issue of causation. The Supreme Court rejected the argument that the onus on the causation question should rest on the second defendant.

**[11.53]** Laffoy J's approach in *Duffy* is markedly different from that of Lardner J in *Browne*. Both judges professed to derive guidance from the standards in operation at the time of the accident. Whereas Lardner J was strongly influenced by the limits of the regulatory code in determining the scope of the duty of care in negligence, Laffoy J perceived in the relatively limited standards a wider concern for the safety of children on which she built a common law duty of care.

**[11.54]** The fourth and final case that needs to be considered in this context is *Cassells v Marks & Spencer plc*.[75] Here a five-year-old girl was burnt when her cotton day dress went

75. High Court, 25 March 1999 (Barr J). For further analysis of both *Duffy* and *Cassells* see Schuster 'Proofs in Product Liability Cases: Some Aspects of Practice and Procedure in Burn Injuries Claims' (1999) 1 P & P 60.

too near the fire. The dress had been bought in the defendant's retail store in Brixton.[76] It contained a tag with the words "Keep away from fire" in red capital letters. There had two cardboard tags "in significant size" hanging below the hem which were intended to be removed after purchase. One of them contained a warning, again in large red capital letters: "In the interest of safety it is advisable to keep your child away from fire". The same warning, in smaller writing, appeared on the reverse side of this tag.

**[11.55]** Irish and English standards were identical in requiring inflammability tests and the provision of warnings for children's nightwear and in having no similar requirements for children's day wear. Marks & Spencers had their own flammability standard for children's day wear. This fell "substantially short" of the flammability standard required by the English and Irish children's night-gown regulations and it did not cover the use of fire retardant chemicals. The fire warning labels for day wear garments were also part of Marks & Spencers' self-imposed safety standards.

**[11.56]** The case was concerned only with the position at common law; an alternative claim on the breach of the Liability for Defective Products Act 1991 was not argued before the Court.

**[11.57]** Barr J dismissed the case. He did not think that children's dresses and night-dresses required identical treatment. Night-dresses were generally loose, ankle length garments intended for indoor use primarily in the evening or night when, at least in winter, the wearers were likely to spend significant time at home near domestic fires. Day dresses were almost invariably worn with underclothes, which gave the child some degree of greater protection. Dresses were, moreover, intended for outdoor as well as indoor use, which probably lessened the risk of association with fire. Moreover, the use of chemical fire retardants caused significant practical problems, including skin irritation, loss of fabric strength, a less comfortable feel and unreliability in efficacy. This militated "against the merchantability of children's dresses". The defendant was entitled to take into account universal trade practice "in conjunction with other relevant factors", including the public demand for quality wearable cotton garments. Finally, and perhaps most importantly, the defendant was entitled to take into account that the official independent bodies in Britain and Ireland which regulated the maker had not deemed it necessary in the interest of public safety to impose any flammability test or fire warning for children's day dresses.

**[11.58]** Barr J accepted that cotton material presented "a major fire hazard" for the wearer if not subjected to an appropriate retardant process. It had been established in *O'Byrne* and *Duffy* that, in these circumstances, "an effective fire warning must be appended to each garment by way of alternative precaution." The plaintiff had contended that, in the light of Finlay, CJ's observation in *O'Byrne*[77] as to the explicit nature of the fire warning that is required, the warnings on her dress were inadequate. Barr J conceded that, on its face, this

---

76. The conflicts of law aspects of the case were not addressed by the Court. Clearly there could be no problem with the jurisdiction of the Irish Courts: *Cf Grehan v Medical Incorporated* [1986] ILRM 627. It would seem that the rule in *Phillips v Eyre* (1870) LR 6 QB 1 was also complied with, assuming that this has any vitality after the assault on it in *Grehan*. If the new regime for choice of law in tort advocated in *Grehan* were to apply, the Court would have to determine whether Irish or English law should apply to each of the issues that fell for adjudication.

77. Quoted at para **[11.35]** above.

was "a formidable argument" but nonetheless rejected it because the Chief Justice's remarks had been *obiter* to the judgment of the Supreme Court, which was that the defendants had been negligent in not giving *any* fire warning with the plaintiff's skirt. The precise nature of the warning which ought to have been given had not been an issue in *O'Byrne*.

**[11.59]** Barr J dismissed the action, holding that the defendant had discharged its duty of care by adopting the form of words specified by the regulatory authorities in both jurisdictions for children's nightwear. It had gone "significantly beyond the requirement" by appending the second more prominent and more specific warning on the tag hanging from the hem of the dress.

**[11.60]** Apart from inflammable clothing, it is worth noting that with the expansion of do-it-yourself activities around the home, what was formerly an adequate warning (because only skilled users of the product might be foreseen) may no longer be sufficient.[78] Furthermore, where a manufacturer, after the product has been supplied to customers, learns of a danger in the product, it must take reasonable steps to acquaint the customers of this fact.[79]

## Transfer by way of gift

**[11.61]** The extent of the duty of care owed by a donor of a present or by a person who gratuitously lends a product to another is uncertain.[80] Traditionally, the law has required the donor, at all events, to give a warning of any danger known to him or her.[81] Moreover dangerous products may involve particular care when being let into the hands of the young or the incompetent.[82] Beyond that, the present law is unclear. The onward march of negligence in relation to licensors and to those who give advice gratuitously suggests that the mere absence of consideration should no longer exempt a donor or gratuitous lender from a duty of care. Of course, in assessing the scope and content of that duty the courts would have regard to all the circumstances of the case, including such factors as the likelihood of reliance by the donee or borrower on the donor's or lender's having taken care in relation to the item transferred.

## Causation

**[11.62]** It is not sufficient for the plaintiff to establish that the defendant manufacturer, retailer, assembler or supplier was negligent in respect of the dissemination of the product.

---

78. *Cf Lem v Barotto Sports Ltd* (1976) 69 DLR (3d) 276 (Alta CA); *Lambert v Lastoplex Chemicals Ltd* (1971) 25 DLR (3d) 121 (SC, Can); *Buchan v Ortho Pharmaceuticals (Canada) Ltd* (1986) 25 DLR (4th) 658 (Ont, CA)..

79. *Rivtow Marine Ltd v Washington Iron Works* (1973) 40 DLR (3d) 530 (SC, Can). See Binchy, (1974) 90 LQR 181; Harvey, (1974) 37 MLR 320.

80. See generally Marsh 'The Liability of the Gratuitous Transferor: A Comparative Survey' (1950) 66 LQR 39.

81. *Cf Campbell v O'Donnell* [1967] IR 226 at 229 (SC).

    "There is now ample authority for the proposition that, independently of any contractual relationship between the parties, the donor owes at least the duty to give warnings of any dangers actually known to him."

82. *Cf Campbell v O'Donnell* [1967] IR 226 at 231. A decision going very far is *Sterner v Lawson* (1979) 11 CCLT 76 (BCCA) - loan of powerful motorcycle by teenager to teenage friend.

The plaintiff must also show that that negligence caused injury to the plaintiff or damage to the plaintiffs' property.

**[11.63]** The issue of causation arose in the important case of *Best v Wellcome Foundation Ltd*,[83] where Hamilton P held that the defendant manufacturer had been negligent in releasing a particular batch of whooping cough vaccine but that this had not caused the plaintiff's injuries. The Supreme Court reversed Hamilton P's finding on the causation issue.

**[11.64]** The proceedings raised an important issue of general public importance: whether the pertussis (whooping cough) component of the DTP (diphtheria, tetanus and pertussis) vaccine could cause encephalopathy. The plaintiff had developed this condition shortly after having received the vaccine. There was evidence that the particular batch from which the plaintiff had been injected had not complied with the accepted standards with regard to potency and toxicity but that the defendant manufacturer had nevertheless released the batch for commercial distribution.

**[11.65]** Much of the case was concerned with what was a crucial question of evidence relating to the time when the plaintiff first manifested the condition of encephalopathy. If this was not shortly after the time he was vaccinated there was little possibility that the vaccination was the cause; if it was shortly afterwards, then the issue of the vaccine's possible causal role would have to be investigated and determined.

**[11.66]** Hamilton P held that the condition first manifested itself so long after the vaccination as to exclude its possible causal role. He did, however, hold that the defendant manufacturer had been negligent in releasing the batch in view of its failure to comply with the accepted standards. On the general scientific question whether encephalopathy could result (albeit in rare cases) from the vaccine when it *complied* with the accepted standards, Hamilton P received a great deal of conflicting evidence. He expressed the conclusion that "there was a possibility that the pertussis component in the vaccine could in some rare cases cause encephalopathy". It is not clear whether he envisaged that these "rare cases" were limited to cases where the accepted standards had not been complied with. The point is of great significance, since important and difficult questions concerning the possibilities of negligence liability would arise if *properly tested* whooping cough vaccine is capable of causing encephalopathy.

**[11.67]** The Supreme Court reversed Hamilton P on the evidential question relating to the time of the occurrence of the plaintiff's first convulsion. It upheld his holding on the link between the vaccine distributed by the defendant manufacturer and the onset of the plaintiff's condition. Accordingly, it held that the plaintiff was entitled to succeed against the defendant manufacturer.

**[11.68]** In an important passage in his judgment, Finlay CJ said that he was:

83. [1992] ILRM 609 (SC revsg HC). See Byrne & Binchy, *Annual Review of Irish Law 1991*, p 434; Byrne & Binchy, *Annual Review of Irish Law 1992*, pp 610-611. Other Product liability cases in which the issue of causation was raised include *O'Byrne v Gloucester* Supreme Court, 3 November 1988, analysed in paras **[11.35]-[11.37]** above and *Duffy v Rooney and Dunnes Stores (Dundalk) Ltd* Supreme Court, 23 April 1998 affg High Court, 23 June 1997 (Laffoy J), analysed in paras **[11.41]-[11.52]** above.

> "satisfied that it is not possible either for a judge of trial or for an appellate court to take upon itself the role of a determining, scientific authority resolving disputes between distinguished scientists in any particular line of technical expertise. The function which a court can and must perform in the trial of a case, in order to acquire a just result, is to apply common sense and a careful understanding of the logic and likelihood of events to conflicting opinions and conflicting theories concerning a matter of this kind."

**[11.69]** With respect, the task of the judiciary on some occasions cannot be sidestepped so easily. This case raised the clear question as to whether or not the vaccine, when complying with accepted standards, could cause encephalopathy. No doubt the court would not wish to have to decide such a controversial question especially when an affirmative answer would have such important downstream effects, but this does not mean that the court can avoid responsibility on the unconvincing basis that it is not its function to determine a scientific issue on which the scientific community is divided. The court does this every day in medical malpractice litigation. What was distinctive about the *Best* case was not that the court had to determine a scientific controversy but rather that the particular scientific controversy had such a significant political dimension, with major consequences for public health policy.

**[11.70]** In his concurring judgment, O'Flaherty J interpreted Hamilton P's judgment as involving a finding that post-pertussis vaccine encephalopathy existed. O'Flaherty J's observations give no clear indication that he considered this finding to be limited to cases where the accepted standards had not been complied with, but the tenor of his remarks does not appear to provide clear support for that limitation.

## *Res Ipsa Loquitur* in Products Liability

**[11.71]** Although *Donoghue v Stevenson*[84] might have appeared to suggest to the contrary, it is clear that the doctrine of *res ipsa loquitur* may apply in products liability cases.[85] In the Supreme Court decision of *Fleming v Henry Denny & Sons Ltd*,[86] Kingsmill Moore J (speaking for the court) stated:

> "It appears to me that the maxim is applicable. But its application only shifts the onus of proof. The defendant can give evidence to negative negligence on his part by demonstrating that his system of production is one which is reasonably safe (or, as I would prefer to phrase it, that he has taken all reasonable care to provide a safe system) and that there has been no negligence on the part of his servants in the operation of the system provided."

**[11.72]** In *Fleming's* case, the Supreme Court went so far as to hold that, in the light of the evidence tendered on behalf of the defendant, a jury would be unreasonable if it held that the defendant had not rebutted the presumption arising from the doctrine..

**[11.73]** It has been noted that in other jurisdictions where the general doctrine of *res ipsa loquitur* has only the effect of raising an inference of negligence rather than involving an onus shift, *res ipsa loquitur* has been applied with particular effect in products liability cases so as to shift the onus of proof onto the producer, manufacturer or supplier, as the

84. [1932] AC 562 at 622.
85. See Garvey, 'Ireland' Ch IX of *European Product Liabilities*, Kelly & Attree eds (2nd ed, 1997), pp 245-246.
86. Supreme Court, 29 July 1955. See also *Grant v Australian Knitting Mills* [1936] AC 85 (PC).

case may be, to show that it was not negligent.[87] It has been suggested by some commentators[88] that this development constitutes a tacit move in the direction of strict products liability though the courts have denied this.[89]

## IV. Non-Dangerous Defects

**[11.74]** We now must consider the difficult issue of whether liability should attach for the negligent manufacture, sale or repair of a product with a nondangerous defect. In *Donoghue v Stevenson*,[90] as we have seen, Lord Atkin spoke of "injury to the consumer's life or property"; and in *Power v Bedford Motor Co*,[91] Lavery J referred to articles being "dangerous to users" in the absence of reasonable care. Gradually the Courts began to articulate a distinction between "dangerous" and "non-dangerous" defects. The former involved physical damage to the person or to property, as, for example, where a product was in such a state that it went on fire, burning the plaintiff or his house or goods. The latter involved no such danger; they included, for example, a watch that would not work or a suit that did not fit. Many of the cases spelling out the distinction between "dangerous" and "non-dangerous" defects were concerned with the issue whether the old immunities for builders, venders and lessors of real property should be retained. *Colgan v Connolly Construction Co (Ireland) Ltd*,[92] was one such case. There, McMahon J held that contract rather than tort was the proper avenue of compensation for "non-dangerous" defects. Referring to the duty of care recognised by the principle of *Donoghue v Stevenson*[93] he said:

> "I think that it is a duty to take care to avoid defects in the product which may cause personal injury or damage to property, but the product itself has not been regarded as falling within the scope of the duty. The obligation of the builder or manufacturer in regard to the quality of his product is, in my view, something which ought to rest in contract only. It is not the same nature as his common law duty under the principle of *Donoghue v Stevenson* because that duty is founded upon the concern of the law to see that the product is not a cause of injury or damage to persons or property subsequently affected by it. Where a defect is such that no question of such injury or damage arises I see no good reason for expanding the principle of *Donoghue v Stevenson* to defects in the quality of the product itself."[94]

**[11.75]** Two years later, in Britain, the House of Lords, on an appeal from Scotland, supported more wide-ranging principles of liability. In *Junior Books Ltd v Veitchi*,[95] the owners of a factory sued specialist flooring contractors who had been engaged as subcontractors to lay a floor in the factory which turned out to be defective. The owners of the factory had the floor relaid - a process which put them to considerable expense, not

87. *Cf* eg *Zeppa v Coca-Cola Ltd* [1955] OR 855 (CA). See further LINDEN, pp 505-508.
88. *Cf* FLEMING, p 540.
89. *MacLachlan & Mitchell Homes Ltd v Frunk's Rentals & Sales Ltd* (1979) 10 CCLT 306 at 330 (Alta SC).
90. [1932] AC 562 at 599 (HL (SC)).
91. [1959] IR 391 at 408 (SC).
92. [1980] ILRM 33 (HC) analysed by Kerr [1981] Dublin ULJ 118.
93. [1932] AC 562.
94. [1980] ILRM 33 at 37.
95. [1983] 520 (HL).

only in having the job done but also in removing machinery (with consequent loss of profits) while the floor was being relaid. The pursuers did not allege that the floor was likely to cause any personal injury or injury to property. The House of Lords held that none the less they had stated a good cause of action. Three separate speeches were delivered for the majority.

**[11.76]** Lord Roskill delivered what Costello J in *Ward v McMaster*[96] described as "the leading" speech for the majority. He was guided by Lord Wilberforce's two-step approach towards the duty issue in *Anns v Merton London Borough Council*.[97] The first step was to ask whether there was a sufficient degree of proximity between the plaintiff and the defendants to give rise to a duty of care on the part of the defendants.[98] Lord Roskill regarded *eight* facts as being "of crucial importance in requiring an affirmative answer to that question".[99] These were:

(1) the defendants were nominated sub-contractors;

(2) they were specialists in flooring;

(3) they knew what products were needed and they specialised in the production of these products;

(4) they alone were responsible for constructing the floor;

(5) the plaintiffs relied on their skill and experience;

(6) the defendants as nominated subcontractors must have known that the plaintiffs relied on their skill and experience;

(7) the relationship between the parties was as close as it could be short of actual privity of contract;

(8) the defendants must be taken to have known that, if they did the work negligently, the resulting defects would at some time require remedying, with the plaintiffs spending money on the remedial measures, as a consequence of which the plaintiffs would suffer economic loss.

**[11.77]** The second step of Lord Wilberforce's formula was to decide whether there were any considerations which ought to negative or reduce or limit the scope of duty, or the class or persons to whom it was owed, or the damages to which a breach of it might give rise. Lord Roskill said that "on the facts I have just stated, I see nothing whatever to restrict the duty of care arising from the proximity of which I have spoken."

**[11.78]** It is worth looking closely at the eight facts mentioned by Lord Roskill. A number of them - especially facts (2), (3), (4), (5), (6), (7) and (8) - have a strong flavour of the *Hedley Byrne* principle. Indeed, fact (5) reflects almost *verbatim* the (rather narrow) approach favoured by Lord Devlin in *Hedley Byrne*[100] which influenced Kenny J in *Bank of*

---

96. [1985] IR 29 at 43 (HC).

97. [1978] AC 728 at 751. *Cf* see para **[6.11]** above.

98. *Cf* SALMOND & HEUSTON (19th ed), pp 229-320 where it is pointed out that in fact in *Junior Books* no question arose as to the first step because counsel had conceded that there was a breach of duty. Equally, no question properly arose as to the second step since on the facts no issue involving restriction or negation of a new duty was raised.

99. [1983] 1 AC 520 at 546.

100. *Hedley Byrne & Co Ltd v Heller & Partners Ltd* [1964] AC 465 at 530 (HL). *Cf* see para **[10.44]** above.

*Ireland v Smith*.[101] The point to note is that Lord Roskill did not take the view that reliance of the type falling within the scope of the *Hedley Byrne* principle was in every case a precondition of liability for negligently producing defective goods (as opposed to defective advice). But Lord Roskill did express the view that "the concept of proximity must always involve, at least in most cases, some degree of reliance". He went on to say:

> "I have already mentioned the words 'skill' and 'judgment' in the speech of Lord Morris in *Hedley Byrne*. These words seem to me to be an echo, be it conscious or unconscious, of the language of s 14(1) of the Sale of Goods Act 1893. My Lords, though the analogy is not exact, I do not find it unhelpful for I think the concept of proximity of which I have spoken and the reasoning of Lord Devlin in the *Hedley Byrne* case involve factual considerations not unlike those involved in a claim under s 14(1); and as between an ultimate purchaser and a manufacturer would not easily be found to exist in the ordinary everyday transaction of purchasing chattels when it is obvious that in truth the real reliance was on the immediate vendor and not on the manufacturer."[102]

**[11.79]** Lord Roskill was probably trying to put a rein on the potential scope of the decision by highlighting the significance of reliance, but two points can none the less be stressed. First, he does not say, nor does the case hold, that reliance is in every case a precondition of liability. Of course, it will normally be an important, often a vital, ingredient in deciding whether there is sufficient proximity between the parties, but that is not the same as a precondition of liability. Secondly, one could disagree with Lord Roskill's opinion that, in the ordinary everyday transaction of purchasing chattels, the purchaser's "real reliance" is on the immediate vendor and not the manufacturer. Often, because of the vast sums spent by manufacturers in promoting their products, it is not.

**[11.80]** Lord Brandon's dissent should here be noted briefly in view of its subsequent elevation. He considered that there were two important considerations which ought to limit the scope of the duty of care. First, to dispense with the requirement of danger, or the threat of danger, of physical damage to persons or their property (excluding the very piece of property whose defective condition gave rise to the danger) would involve a radical departure from long-established authority. Secondly, to impose a duty of care to avoid producing defective, non-dangerous products would, in substance:

> "create, as between two persons ... not in any contractual relationship with each other, obligations ... which are only really appropriate as between persons who do have such a relationship between them".[103]

Imposing warranties of good design and merchantability on manufacturing and distribution of goods was "contrary to any sound policy requirement".[104] Moreover, it was difficult to see how the notion of defectiveness had any real meaning in the absence of a contractually prescribed criterion.

101. [1966] IR 646.
102. [1983] 1 AC 520 at 546-547.
103. [1983] 1 AC 546 at 551.
104. [1983] 1 AC 546 at 551.

**[11.81]** *Junior Books* first came in for close scrutiny in Ireland in *Ward v McMaster.*[105] In *Ward*'s case the first defendant built a bungalow with both dangerous and non-dangerous defects. Later he sold it to the plaintiffs. Costello J referred to Lord Roskill's speech in *Junior Books* in some detail, without criticism. In a central passage of his judgment, Costello J said:

> "There is no doubt that this case has extended the liability of a builder for loss sustained by defective workmanship. I find this reasoning persuasive and I have no difficulty in applying it. It follows from it that the concept of reasonable foresight is one to be employed not only in deciding in a given case whether a duty of care *exists,* but also can be employed in determining its *scope.* Applying this concept to the present case it seems to me that the duty of care which the defendant owed to a purchaser of the bungalow which he built was one relating to hidden defects not discoverable by the kind of examination which he could reasonably expect his purchaser to make before occupying the house. But the duty was not limited to avoiding foreseeable harm to persons or property other than the bungalow itself (that is a duty to avoid dangerous hidden defects in the bungalow) but extended to a duty to avoid causing the purchaser consequential financial loss arising from hidden defects in the bungalow itself (that is a duty to avoid defects in the quality of the work). It also seems to me that the defendant should have foreseen that if he caused the bungalow to be so badly constructed as to force the plaintiff and his wife to leave it ... this would cause them both inconvenience and discomfort, and so he owed a duty both to the plaintiff and his wife not to cause hidden defects which would result in such inconvenience. This conclusion is consistent with the decision of the Supreme Court in *Siney*[106] in which the Court upheld an award for damages in negligence to the plaintiff and his family for the inconvenience they each suffered."[107]

**[11.82]** This passage is interesting for several reasons. First, it represents a clear and enthusiastic endorsement of *Junior Books.* Secondly, and in contrast to *Junior Books,* it appears to regard the question raised in *Junior Books* as being one related to the scope rather than the existence of a duty of care. In *Ward's* case, it was easy for the Court to adopt a two-step process: (1) Does an owner-builder owe a duty of care to a purchaser? and (2) If so, what is the scope of that duty? This was because, on the facts of *Ward,* it was clear that there were both dangerous and non-dangerous defects. But *Junior Books* had not involved such a factual situation and it seems plain that the case was concerned with whether a duty of care existed, rather than the scope of an admitted or apparent duty of care. Thus, there was a concentration in Lord Roskill's speech (as we have seen) on the several specific factual elements which, in combination, justified the imposition of a duty of care on the defender. In *Ward's* case there is no explicit examination of these, or equivalent, factors because Costello J approached this aspect of the case as involving only an issue as to the scope, rather than the existence, of the duty. It may be of interest to compare the factual circumstances of *Ward* with the eight factors mentioned by Lord Roskill as being "of crucial importants". First, the owner-builder's identity was, of course, known to the purchaser. (This is not too far from factor (1) in *Junior Books.*) Second, the owner-builder was far from being a specialist in building (in contrast to factor (2) in *Junior Books*). Nor,

105. [1985] IR 29 (affd on grounds of present relevance) [1988] IR 37. For consideration of the issue of an owner-builder's immunity in this case see para **[13.68]** below.

106. *Siney v Dublin Corporation* [1980] IR 400 (SC). *Cf* para **[13.23]** below.

107. [1985] IR 29 at 44.

thirdly, could it easily be said of the owner-builder (in contrast to factor (3) that he "knew what products were needed and ... specialised in the production of these products"). Fourthly, the owner-builder was alone responsible for the construction of the building (similar to factor (4)). Fifthly, the purchaser relied on his skill and experience (as in factor (5)). Sixthly, the owner-builder must have known of this reliance (as in factor (6)). Seventhly (and in contrast to factor (7)), there was actual privity of contract between the parties. Finally (as in factor (8)), the defendant owner-occupier must have known that if the house had been negligently built, the purchaser and his wife would suffer economic loss.

**[11.83]** This somewhat tedious comparison of factors as between the two cases makes it plain that in *Ward's* case there were many similar elements in the relationship between the parties which would support the imposition of liability on the owner-builder.

## The Eclipse of *Junior Books* in Britain

**[11.84]** In Britain *Junior Books* has been treated with such unmitigated hostility that it can now be regarded as "only a momentary interruption to the slow pragmatic development of the law".[108] In *Tate and Lyle Ltd v Greater London Council*,[109] Lord Templeman referred to *Junior Books* as a case in which the plaintiff had suffered "damage to his property".[110] In *Muirhead v Industrial Tank Specialities Ltd*,[111] Goff LJ treated *Junior Books* as a case in which, on its particular facts, there had been considered to be such a very close relationship between the parties that a statable case of negligence had been averred.

**[11.85]** The same process was apparent in the House of Lords decision of *Peabody Donation Fund (Governors) v Sir Lindsay Parkinson & Co Ltd*,[112] and *Leigh & Sullivan Ltd v Aliakmon Shipping Co Ltd*[113] In *D & F Estates Ltd v Church Commissioners for England*,[114] in 1988, Lord Bridge delivered the *coup de grace*:

> "The consensus of judicial opinion, with which I concur, seems to be that the decision of the majority [in *Junior Books*] is so far dependent upon the unique, albeit non-contractual, relationship between the pursuer and the defender in that case and the unique scope of the duty of care owned by the defender to the pursuer arising from that relationship that the decision cannot be regarded as laying down any principle of general application in the law of tort or delict."

**[11.86]** He pointedly praised Lord Brandon's dissenting speech in *Junior Books* for its "cogency and clarity". Similarly, Lord Oliver did not consider *Junior Books* to be "of any

108. SALMOND & HEUSTON (19th ed), p 230. See also the 21st ed, pp 206-207
109. [1983] 2 AC 509.
110. [1983] 2 AC 509 at 530.
111. [1986] QB 507.
112. [1985] AC 210.
113. [1986] AC 785.
114. [1988] 2 All ER 992 at 1003 (HL). See Binchy 'Defective Building Work: Who Should Pay?'(1989) 83 Incorp L Soc of Ireland Gaz 41. See also *Simaan General Contracting Co v Pilkington Glass Ltd (No 2)* [1988] 1 All ER 791 at 805 (CA) where Dillon LJ expressed the view that *Junior Books* had been:

> "subject to so much analysis and discussion with differing explanations of the basis of the case that the case cannot now be regarded as a useful pointer to any development of the law whatever Lord Roskill may have had in mind when he delivered his speech. Indeed I find it difficult to see that future citation from *Junior Books* can ever serve any useful purpose".

help in the present context". He agreed with Lord Bridge that it depended on so close and unique a relationship with the plaintiff that it was "really no use as an authority of the general duty of care", adding that "it rests, in any event, upon the *Hedley Byrne* doctrine of reliance". So far as the general limits of the general duty of care in negligence were concerned, he adopted what had been said in Lord Brandon's dissenting speech.

**[11.87]** There is something quite unsatisfactory about this manner of dealing with *Junior Books*. It betrays a timidity and unprincipled subtlety unworthy of an ultimate appellate court. It is not true (as asserted by Lord Oliver) that *Junior Books* rested on the *Hedley Byrne* doctrine of reliance. *Junior Books* is not a species of the *Hedley Byrne* genus. Of course, the reliance element played a most important role in establishing a sufficient degree of proximity, on the particular facts, between the pursuer and the defender; but nothing in *Junior Books* incorporated the *Hedley Byrne* "doctrine of reliance" as an essential ingredient of liability in every case involving a defective, non-dangerous product. It is, moreover, disingenuous to interpret the majority speeches as involving the application of no general principles relating to the duty of care in negligence, while enthusiastically endorsing Lord Brandon's dissenting analysis. In fact the majority speeches are replete with a consideration of general principles; moreover, Lord Roskill's speech took issue with Lord Brandon's dissenting analysis and went some way to answering his concerns; yet neither Lord Bridge nor Lord Oliver mentioned this attempted rebuttal.

**[11.88]** It is, of course, futile to argue that the British courts have misunderstood their own decision since they plainly are now resolute that, as a general principle, liability under the *Donoghue v Stevenson* formula should not arise in respect of qualitative defects in products.[115] But the question is very much a live one in Ireland so let us return to consider how the law is likely to develop here.

## Future Developments

**[11.89]** The Irish courts have not so far sought to isolate the *Junior Books ratio* in the way the British courts have done. It is perhaps significant that in *Ward v McMaster*[116] Costello J endorsed the principle enthusiastically, in spite of the fact that even by then a degree of judicial disenchantment with *Junior Books* had already become plain. If the experience[117] with the *Anns*[118] principle is any guide, it may well be that the Irish courts will adhere to the *Junior Books* principle in spite of the *volte face* in Britain. The *volte face,* in relation to both *Anns* and *Junior Books* represents a desire to return to a process of incremental development of the duty of care rather than one based on deeper principle. The Irish courts have shown a preference for a principled approach, unadorned by too many refinements. On this basis the *Junior Books* principle may well thrive here.

**[11.90]** This is not, of course, to suggest that the Irish courts will promiscuously impose liability on manufacturers in negligence for qualitative defects. Proximity must always be

---

115. See also *Murphy v Brentwood DC* [1991] 1 AC 398 (HL); WINFIELD & JOLOWICZ, pp 315-320, 335-338; STREET, p 344-345.

116. [1985] IR 29.

117. *Cf* para **[6.25]** above.

118. [1978] AC 728 at 751-752 (HL).

established and, in most cases, as the majority in *Junior Books* recognised, it will not be possible for the plaintiff to do this.

## V. STRICT LIABILITY: THE EUROPEAN REGIME

**[11.91]** We must now consider the regime of strict liability prescribed by the EC Directive on Products Liability and implemented belatedly in Ireland by the Liability for Defective Products Act 1991.[119] This Act supplements, rather than replaces, the existing remedies in tort and contract.[120] In conjunction with the Jurisdiction of Courts and Enforcement of Judgments (European Communities) Act 1988,[121] and the Jurisdiction of Courts and Enforcement of Judgments (European Communities) Act 1993,[122] implementing, respectively, the Brussels and Lugano Conventions,[123] which have now been the subject of consolidating legislation - the Jurisdiction of Courts and Enforcement of Judgments Act

119. See *Product Liability*, Schuster ed, Irish Centre for European Law, 1989; *The New Product Liability Regime*, Schuster ed, Irish Centre for European Law (1992); Weatherill, *EC Consumer Law And Policy* (1997), Ch 5; Bird 'Annotation to the Liability for Defective Products Act 1991' *Irish Current Law Statutes Annotated 1991*; Schuster 'The New Product Liability Regime' (1995) 39 St Louis LJ 917; Albanese & Del Duca 'Note Defining the Limits of Liability: Developments in European Product Liability' (1987) 5 Dickinson J of Intl L 193'; Shapo 'Comparing Products Liability: Concepts in European and American Law' (1993) 26 Cornell Intl J 279; Binchy 'The EEC Directive on Products Liability'(1986) 80 Incorp L Soc of Ireland Gazette 37, 73; Coe 'Products Liability in the European Community -An Introduction to the 1985 Council Directive' (1987) 10 J of Products Ly 197; Dielmann The European Economic Community's Council Directive on Product Liability (1987) 20 Intl Law 1391; Stapleton 'Products Liability Reform - Real or Illusory?' (1986) 6 Oxford J of Legal Stud 392; Shettler 'Products Liability: A Comparison of US and EEC Approaches' (1986) 13 Syr J of Int L & Com 155; Leibman 'Note The European Community's Products Liability Directive: Is the US Experience Applicable?' (1986) 18 L & Poly in Intl Bus 795; Nilles 'Note: Defining the Limits of Liability: A Legal and Political Analysis of the European Community Products Liability Directive' (1985) 25 Va J of Intl L 729; Borrie 'Product Liability in the EEC' (1987) 9 Dublin ULJ 82; Vranken 'The First Decennium of the European Product Liability Directive: A Cause for Celebration?' (1996) 4 Torts LJ 225; Malden 'Strict Liability for Defective Products: A Changing Basis?' (1982) 33 NILQ 229; Bourke 'Product Liability and Product Safety: EC Directives and Implementation in Ireland' in Heusel ed, *Community Law in Practice: Including Facets of Consumer Protection Law* (1996), p 161; Spacone 'Strict Liability in the European Union - Not a United States Analog' (2000) 5 Roger Williams ULR 341; Taschner 'Harmonization of Product Liability in the European Community' (1999) 34 Tex Int'l 321.

120. Article 13 of the Directive.

121. See Binchy 'Annotation' [1988] ICLSA; O'Reilly & Hogan, *Guide to Changes in the Rules of the Superior Courts 1986 as a Consequence of the Coming into Operation of the Jurisdiction of Courts and Enforcement of Judgments (European Communities) Act 1988* (1989). For a consideration of the Judgments Convention and related Conventions to which the Act gives effect see Binchy *Irish Conflicts of Law* (1988), pp 181-191, 612-616; Kaye, *Civil Jurisdiction and Enforcement of Foreign Judgments* (1987); Gill, (1980) 4 J of Irish Soc for Eur L 3; Terry, (1980) 4 J of Irish Soc for Eur L 26; Moloney & Kremlis, (1985) 79 Incorp L Soc of Ireland Gaz, pp 329, (1986) 80 Incorp L Soc of Ireland Gazette 5. See also the Irish Centre for European Law's Conference *A Practical Guide to the New Superior Court Rules Relating to the Judgments Convention* 11 February 1989.

122. See Byrne & Binchy *Annual Review of Irish Law 1993*.

123. See Hardy 'Conventions on Jurisdiction and Governing Law', Ch 4, *Product Liability: European Laws and Practice*, Hodges ed, 1993.

1998 - in our domestic law, the directive has the effect of broadening the options available to injured parties, so far as the type of liability, the range of potential defendants, the choice of jurisdiction, and the modes of enforcement of judgments are concerned.

## The Preparation of the Directive

**[11.92]** The Commission of the European Economic Communities presented its draft Directive on Product Liability to the Council in September 1976.[124] Negotiations between the EEC countries then followed simultaneously resulting in final implementation on 25 July 1985.[125] The Directive extends to all Member States.[126]

**[11.93]** Article 19 of the Directive required Member States to bring into force, not later than three years from the date of notification of the Directive - 30 July 1985 - the laws, regulations and administrative provisions necessary to comply with the Directive. In fact Ireland did not meet the Directive's deadline, and implemented the Directive only in 1991. The Liability for Defective Products Act 1991 came into operation on 16 December 1991,[127] thus raising questions as to the principle of direct effect[128] and the possibility that a plaintiff denied a remedy under the terms of the Directive during the period 1988-1991,[129] might seek to impose *Francovich*[130] liability on the State.

## The Main Features of the 1991 Act and the Community Directive

**[11.94]** The nature of a directive in Community law is that is obliges Member States to achieve certain targets set out in the directive but leaves to the Member States the discretion as to how these community objectives are to be achieved in the national legal system. It is for each Member State to assess its own laws and see what national changes are required and then to select the appropriate means necessary to comply with the communtity requirements. Much of the directive will be mandatory, but some provisions may be optional and in such cases the Member States will be free to ignore such optional recommendations. The mandatory provisions must be implemented into national law, however, although how this is achieved is a matter for the Member State itself. Ireland chose to comply with the directive in this instance, by enacting the Liability for Defective Products Act 1991. In reading the Act it is therefore important to appreciate the historical

---

124. See Dashwood [1977] J of Bus L 202.

125. 85/374/EEC published in OJ No L210/29.

126. Article 22. Article 15(3) required the Commission to report on the operation of the "development risks" defence contained in Article 7(e). The Commission did so in 1995 (Com (95) 617) in "a profoundly uninspiring document": Weatherill, *EC Consumer Law and Policy* (1997), p 100. For an analysis of the wider picture see 'The Consumer Protection Programme of the EC in the 1990's', Ch 2, *Enhancing the Legal Position of the European Consumer*, Lonbay ed, 1996; Askham & Stoneham *EC Consumer Safety* (1994).

127. SI 316/1991.

128. *Cf* Garvey 'Ireland' Ch IX, *European Product Liabilities*, Kelly & Attree eds, (2nd ed, 1997), p 249.

129. Since the Directive makes it plain in Article 13 that the strict liability regime it establishes is not to affect any rights an injured person has under the national law, the plaintiff in a *Francovich*-based action would have to show that he or she had no claim under common law negligence principles or in contract.

130. *Francovich v Italy* [1991] ECR 1 537. *Cf* Hyland 'State Liability for Non-Implementation of Directives - Further and Better Particulars' (1997) 3 BR 40; Schuster 'Review of Case-law under Directive 85/374/EEC on Liability for Defective Products' (1998) 6 Consumer LJ 195 at 208-209.

background to the Act and to realise that although the 1991 Act may (and in some cases does) go beyond what is injuncted by the directive, it cannot disregard any mandatory provision of the directive. This is clearly recognised by the Act itself which reproduces in its schedule the entire directive, and provides specifically in s 1 that words and expressions used in both the Act and the directive shall have the meaning it has in the directive (sub-s (2)) and further that a court in contruing a provision of the Act will give effect to the directive (sub-s (3)). It is clear from this that the 1991 Act may be challenged by any litigant on the ground that it does not properly or faithfully implement the directive or that it fails to give effect to the directive. In those circumstances it is not suprising that the Irish draftsmen responsible for the 1991 legislation, carefully transposed the directive and in many cases adopted the provision in the directive *verbatim* so that no conflict is likely. For these reaons we propose to outline the provisions of the 1991 Act as representing the law in Ireland, and where there are differences between the 1991 Act and the Directive we will draw attention to such differences as they arise. If the 1991 Act does not properly transpose the Directive into Irish law, a litigant may, of course, in appropriate cases appeal to the superior force of the directive to assert its rights.

**[11.95]** Let us now consider the main features of the legislation of 1991 and of the Directive. In doing so, it is easiest to refer to the relevant sections of the 1991 Act, adding appropriate references to the specific Articles of the Directive. In any case where the drafting of the section is such as to call for special comment, we discuss the questions that arise.

**[11.96]** The essence of liability under the Act is contained in s 2(1), which is drafted with commendable simplicity:

> The producer shall be liable in damages in tort for damage caused wholly or partly by a defect in his product.

The rest of the Act is largely concerned with defining the terms used in this basic principle of liability.

**[11.97]** There are, of course, some important qualifications to this statement of general principle, but the main notion is clear: liability is based, not on *wrongful conduct* by the producer, which (in theory at least) is the hallmark of negligence, but merely on proof of *a fact*, that a defect in the product caused the plaintiff damage. Inevitably normative considerations enter into the picture when deciding what constitutes "defectiveness" in this context. As we shall see, however, the range of liability under the Act and under the Directive is not radically different from that under common law principles.

**[11.98]** Section 2(1) of the 1991 Act gives effect to Article 1 of the Directive which is even more succint. Article 1 provides that:

> [t]he producer shall be liable for damage caused by a defect in his product.

The words "in tort", which do not appear in Article 1, are important. They achieve two goals. First, it makes it clear beyond argument that the nature of liability envisaged by the Directive is delictual; secondly it ensures that the whole apparatus of domestic tort law is applied to the new right of action. Thus, the 1991 Act integrates this right of action with the pre-existing legal structure of tort litigation on such matters as contributory negligence, concurrent wrongs, fatal accidents and damages. The addition of the words "or partly" should also be noted. They harmonise, to some degree with Article 8(1) of the Directive, which provides that:

> ... the liability of the producer shall not be reduced when the damage is caused both by a defect in the product and by the act or omission of a third party.

If it is accepted that a causal ascription may be made to an occurrence that does not involve a human act or omission - a meterological phenomenon such as a flood, rain or lightning, for example, or the fall of an ancient building - it may be appreciated that cases can arise where a person's injury may be caused partly by a defect in a product and partly by such an occurrence. Section 2(1) ascribes responsibility to the producer in such a case, going beyond Article 8(1) of the Directive, which is limited to partial causation attributable to human act or omission.[131]

***The meaning of "product"***

**[11.99]** A "product" is defined in s 1(1) of the Act as including all movables *except* "primary agricultural products", even where the movables are incorporated into other movables or into immovables. (Section 1(1) of the 1991 Act is substantially in accord with Article 2 of the Directive). "Primary agricultural products" are defined by the same section as meaning "the products of the soil, of stock-farming and of fisheries and game, excluding products which have undergone initial processing", and goes on to define "initial processing" as "any processing of an industrial nature of those products which could cause a defect therein". Since no processing (of any kind) is immune from the possibility of causing a defect,[132] it seems that the key words of the definition are "of an industrial nature". Once the processing can be so characterised, the exception ceases. Because of recent concerns related to variant CJD and other diseases transmitted from animal meat, agricultural products are no longer an exception. They are treated to the same strict regime as other products now, and all Member States are obliged to make the necessary legal adjustments in this regard from 4 December 2000.[133] The exception applies in Irish law, however, for primary agricultural products before that date. Electricity is deemed a "product" for the purpose of the Directive. Section 1(1) of the Act brings electricity within the scope of the definition of "product" where "damage is caused as a result of a failure in the process of generation of electricity".

**[11.100]** The general exclusion of immovables should be noted. In the law of negligence, as we shall see,[134] immovables (or, in ordinary tort parlance, land)[135] tended to remain

---

131. Section 4 of the Act does not affect the position. It places an onus on the injured person to prove the damage and the defect, and the causal relationship between the defect and the damage. This is merely an adjectival, evidential provision and does not affect the substantive aspects of causal attribution.

132. An alternative interpretation is that the court should treat the issue as raising an empirical question, requiring it to assess the process in order to decide whether it was one that was capable of causing a defect. This seems a mistaken approach since, even if the process was entirely satisfactory, the court could not discount the possibility that nonetheless, a defect might at some time be caused by it. The purpose of the definition is to establish a threshold not to police industrial processes in order to find deficiencies.

133. Directive 1999/34/EEC, OJ L141, 4.6.1999, p 20.

134. See Ch 13 below.

135. The notions of immovables and of land are not identical: see Binchy *Irish Conflicts of Law* (1988), Ch 19.

outside the scope of a full duty of care. It is only in recent years that the exemptions from liability for owners and builders have gradually been swept away.[136] The Directive does not apply, for example, to a defective house which collapses, save to the extent that any movable "incorporated into" the house is defective. Thus, if a girder installed in a home is defective and this brings about the collapse, the Act may apply. Since most immovables are composed of movables which are "incorporated into" the whole, this potential range of application should not be ignored. In such cases, however, it would be necessary to show that the particular movable (or movables) was itself (or were themselves) defective; in other words, a *defective incorporation* into an immovable of movables which themselves are not defective would not appear to fall within the scope of the Act or the Directive.

**[11.101]** Finally, it should be noted that s 13 provides that the Act is not to apply to products (as defined by s 2) put into circulation before the commencement of the Act.[137]

***Who is a "producer"?***

**[11.102]** The definition of "producer" in the 1991 Act is substantially in accord with Article 3 of the Directive, but one or two refinements may be noted. Section 2(2) provides as follows:

> In this Act 'producer' means -
>
> (a) the manufacturer or producer of a finished product or
>
> (b) the manufacturer or producer of any raw material or the manufacturer or producer of a component part of a product or
>
> (c) in the case of the products of the soil of stock-farming and fisheries and game which have undergone initial processing the person who carried out such processing or
>
> (d) any person who by putting his name trade mark or other distinguishing feature on the product or using his name or any such mark or feature in relation to the product has held himself out to be the producer of the product or
>
> (e) any person who has imported the product into a Member State from a place outside the European Communities in order in the course of any business of his to supply it to another or
>
> (f) any person who is liable as producer of the product pursuant to subsection (3) of this section.

**[11.103]** In contrast to Article 3 of the Directive, s 2(2)(a) and (b) refer to the "manufacturer *or producer*" of a finished product (emphasis added). It is not clear who this non-manufacturer producer is. Section 1(1) requires us to find the answer exclusively by reference to s 2 and s 2 throws no further light on the question. As regards paragraph (c) the reference to "the person who carried out such processing" could refer to the employed operative or operatives who actually did the work, or to the proprietor of the enterprise. One would have thought that the proprietor should be the party personally responsible. Undoubtedly the ordinary principles of vicarious liability would in almost all cases result

---

136. See *Ward v McMaster* [1985] IR 29 (HC). In the United States some courts have imposed strict liability: see Frizzell 'Note: Strict Liability in Tort for Builder -Vendors of Homes' (1988) 24 Tulsa LJ 117 at 128-131.

137. By virtue of Article 19, as has already been mentioned, Member States were required to do this before 30 July 1988.

in such an ascription, but the language of the subsection appears more easily to characterise the employee rather than the employer as the "producer". Once primary agricultural products cease to be an exception, this will have no relevance beyond 4 December 2000.[138] Paragraph (d) goes further than Article 3, para 1 by including those who *without* putting their name trademark or other distinguishing feature on a product, have *used* it in such a way as to hold themselves out to be the producer. While it may be argued that this extension captures the spirit of the principle recognised in Article 3, para 1, there may be a concern that it nonetheless goes too far. In the amorphous world of marketing where representations as to authorship of products fade into endorsements or associations, the tangible requirement in Article 3, para 1 that to be characterised as a producer one should actually have engaged in the verifiable tangible process of putting one's name, trademark or other distinguishing features on the product, is a limitation in the Directive which Member States' legislation should respect. Since, however, as the Directive is the minimum required of Member States. Member States may go further if they so wish, and the 1991 Act clearly chooses to do so in this instance. Under para (e) a person who imports into the Community a product for sale, hire, leasing or any form of distribution in the course of his business is deemed to be a producer within the meaning of the Act and is accordingly responsible as a producer.[139]

**[11.104]** Finally, under s 2(3) of the Act where the producer of the product cannot by taking reasonable steps be identified, each supplier of the product is treated as its producer unless he informs the injured person "within a reasonable time" of the identity of the producer, or of the person who supplied him with the product. Section 2(3)(c) treats the requirement as to "reasonable time" as applying not merely to the supplier after he or she has received the request for information, but also to the injured person in making the request. The request must be made "within a reasonable time after the damage occurs and at a time when it is not reasonably practicable for the injured person to identify" the producer. One may question whether it is possible for the implementing legislation to extinguish a right of action against the supplier by the addition of this requirement.The same rule applies in the cases of an imported product, if this product does not indicate the identity of the importer, even if the name of the producer is indicated.[140]

**[11.105]** It is scarcely surprising that manufacturers of finished products, producers of raw materials and manufacturers of component parts should be treated as "producers" for the purposes of the Act and Directive. Nor, on reflection, should it be a matter of serious debate that those who present themselves as producers by putting their name, trade mark or other distinguishing feature on a product should also be treated as "producers". This practice is "particularly common amongst large retail organisations"[141] and has been part of Irish mercantile life for several years. It would be curious if, having presented products as their own to the public, retail organisations should later be allowed to disclaim strict liability on the basis that the articles were not really "their" products.

138. Directive 99/34/EC, OJ L141, 4.6.1999, p 20.

139. See Article 3, para 2 of the Directive.

140. Article 3, para 3.

141. Eng Law Com No 82 & Scot Law Com No 45, para 99.

**[11.106]** So far as imported products are concerned, it should be noted that only the person who imports the product into the European Community, in order, in the course of his or her business, to supply it to another will be characterised as producer.[142] Thus, for example, there is no question that the legislation will affect the non-commercial importation of food or gadgets purchased abroad by holidaymakers, a fear that troubled the English and Scottish Law Commissions.[143] The argument in favour of imposing strict liability on the commercial importer is that his or her business involves exposing consumers within the Community to the risk of being injured by the imported products. Realistically, the consumers will be grateful for being presented with a relatively easy target within the Community rather than having to face the prospect of expensive and uncertain litigation in some foreign jurisdictions outside the Community.[144]

**[11.107]** Where the producer cannot be identified, there is much to be said for effectively treating the supplier as the producer,[145] unless he or she discloses the identity of the actual producer. As the English and Scottish Law Commissions[146] observed:

> "First, it assists the injured person in tracing the 'anonymous' producer in circumstances where assistance is needed; second, it encourages retailers and other suppliers to keep records from which it may be possible to establish the identity of the supplier (or producer) of the product in question; third, by making it harder for the producer to remain anonymous it encourages him to reveal his identity by labelling his products where practicable."[147]

***When is a product defective?***

**[11.108]** Section 5 of the 1991 Act is concerned with the circumstances in which a product is defective. Section 5 implements the provisions of Article 6 *verbatim*. Section 5 provides as follows:

> (1) For the purposes of this Act a product is defective if it fails to provide the safety which a person is entitled to expect, taking all circumstances into account, including -
>
> (a) the presentation of the product,
>
> (b) the use to which it could reasonably be expected that the product would be put, and
>
> (c) the time when the product was put into circulation.
>
> (2) A product shall not be considered defective for the sole reason that a better product is subsequently put into circulation.

**[11.109]** Under Irish law, as we have seen, a person may, in some circumstances, be liable in negligence for producing a defective, non-dangerous product. Under s 5, however, "defectiveness" does not have this wider meaning. Products that are safe but shoddy do not fall within its scope.

**[11.110]** The key word in this section is *safety:* a product is defective when it *does not provide the safety which a person is entitled to expect*, taking all the circumstances into

---

142. Article 3, para 2 and s 2(2).

143. Eng Law Com No 82 & Scot Law Com No 45, para 103.

144. *Cf* the Pearson Report *op cit* Vol 1, para 1250.

145. Article 3, para 3 and s 2(3).

146. In respect of an equivalent provision in the Council of Europe's Convention on Products Liability.

147. Para 101. *Cf* Schuster 'Review of Case-law under Directive 85/374/EEC on Liability for Defective Products' (1998) 6 Consumer LJ 195 at 197 - reviewing German decisions on this provision.

account.[148] Section 5(1) mentions three specific circumstances, giving them no particular weight relative to each other or relative to other unspecified circumstances. What weight each should have must depend on the facts of the particular case. The first of these circumstances is "the presentation of the product". If, for example, a product is represented in the advertising literature or in the detailed descriptive literature accompanying its sale as being of a particular quality, then a consumer who is injured or suffers damage as a result of the product's dangerousness in lacking this quality may have a right to action.[149] So, where a hot water bottle is represented as being capable of taking boiling water, and it is not, an injured user who relies on this representation may well succeed, on this account, in showing that the hot water bottle did not provide the safety which he was entitled to expect. It would appear that the "presentation" of the product includes an *omission* to provide information which ought to have been given, to protect the user from harm.[150] Thus, the failure by a producer to refer to an allergic reaction which was known to the producer to affect the product could in some instances be relied on by an injured consumer.

**[11.111]** The developing Irish jurisprudence[151] on "the duty to warn" will be of relevance here. Although the cases have so far been dealing with common law negligence rather than liability under the 1991 Act, the question as to whether a warning was adequate will usually in practice be answered in the same way under both tests. It is striking that these placed significant emphasis on consumer preferences for purchasing inflammable clothes. It would be difficult for the same courts to hold that a person to whom they had ascribed

---

148. The influence of the American Law Institute's *Restatement (Second) of Torts*, is notable. Comment to Section 402A stated that a product is defective if it is "dangerous to an extent beyond that which would be contemplated by the ordinary consumer who purchases it with the ordinary knowledge, common to the community, as to its characteristics." *Cf* Little 'The Place of Consumer Expectations in Product Strict Liability Actions for Defectively Designed Products' (1994) 61 Tenn LR 1189; Korzec 'Dashing Consumer Hopes: Strict Products Liability and the Demise of the Consumer Expectations Test' (1997) 20 Boston College Int L & Comp LR 227. The American Law Institute's *Restatement (Third) of Torts: Products Liability*, s 2 adopts a less consumerist approach. Three categories of defectiveness each with a distinct test for liability are prescribed. A *manufacturing* defect exists "when the product departs from its intended design even though all possible care was exercised in the preparation and marketing of the product": section 2(a). A *design* defect exists when the foreseeable risks of harm posed by the product could have been reduced or avoided by the adoption of a reasonable alternative design and renders the product not reasonably safe: s 2(b). A defect because of *inadequate instructions or warnings* occurs when the foreseeable risks of harm posed by the product could have been reduced or avoided by the provision of reasonable instructions or warnings and the omission renders the product not reasonably safe: section 2(c). This transformation which in some respects leaves European Community law more pro-consumer than that of the United States of America has provoked much discussion at times acrimonious. See the *Symposia* in (1994) 61 Tenn LR 1043-1454; (1993) 10 Touro LR 1-237; (1998) 6 Consumer LJ 135-194; also Vargo 'The Emperor's New Clothes: The American Law Institute Adorns a "New Cloth" for Section 402A; Products Liability Design Defects - A Survey of the States Reveals a Different Weave' (1996) 26 U Memphis LR 493.

149. See Shapo 'A Representational Theory of Consumer Protection: Doctrine Function and Legal Liability for Product Disappointment' (1974) 60 Va LR 1109.

150. *Cf* Coe 'Products Liability in the European Community -An Introduction to the 1985 Council Directive' (1987) 10 J of Products Ly 197 at 208. See generally Madden, (1988) 11 J of Products Ly 103. See also Kidner 'Toxic Waste and Strict Liability for Products' (1988) 138 NLJ 379 at 379.

151. See para **[11.41]** above.

such propensity, could nonetheless be "entitled to expect", under s 5 a level of safety which he or she had consciously rejected

**[11.112]** The second circumstance specified in s 5 (and Article 6) is "the use to which it could reasonably be expected that the product would be put". Clearly there are limits to what reasonably may be expected: it is unreasonable, for example, to expect that a hammer should be capable of being used successfully as a car jack. Moreover, a competent adult who deviates widely from the specified instructions as to the use of a product may have no right to complain about injuries resulting from his or her failure to comply with the directions. It seems that mere proof of misuse by a plaintiff of the product will not suffice to exempt the producer from liability. Culpable misuse can of course, constitute contributory negligence, which is dealt with specifically by s 9(2).[152] The misuse may be so unforeseeable as to be outside the range of what "could reasonably be expected." If so, that is a telling, though not necessarily conclusive, factor against characterising the product as defective. The point to note here is that it is the unlikelihood of the use rather than the culpability of the user that is in question.

**[11.113]** The third circumstance specified by s 5 (and Article 6) is "the time when the product was put into circulation". This factor may operate in one of two ways. First, the passage of time may be relevant as throwing light on what a person is "entitled to expect". To take an obvious case, one would not be entitled to expect that a chocolate cake would be edible after a year. Indeed, one should surely expect that any consumer product, after sufficient wear and tear, will eventually become likely to be unsafe. That is one of the reasons why we change our cars and electrical appliances periodically.

**[11.114]** The second way the time factor specified by s 5 (and Article 6) operates is somewhat different. It relates to the fact that safety standards may change over a period of time. This change may be as a result of a development in the state of scientific and technical knowledge: such a case is also covered by s 6, clause (e) and will be considered below. Safety standards may also change without direct reference to such scientific and technical developments. What may have been an acceptable risk from a product twenty years ago may simply cease to be acceptable to the community over this period. For example, there is a greater sensitivity to questions of hygiene and road safety today than there was some time ago. The thrust of s 5 (and Article 6) is to seek to ensure that producers will not suffer unduly from these changes in attitude. The Article does not give the producer an absolute defence to show that the product complied with the standards of the time when the product was put into circulation; but this will be a factor to be considered as one of a number of circumstances, in determining whether the product was defective.

**[11.115]** The passage of time since the product was put onto the market may also be relevant to the question of proof, which is addressed by s 4.[153] As *Prosser & Keeton,* note:

---

152. *Cf* para **[11.158]** below. In a recent decision in the Circuit Court, Judge McMahon held that liability could arise when the plaintiff stood on a kitchen table to reach a shelf. The table collapsed due to a defect in the way it was constructed. Liability imposed such usage of the kitchen table in a modest modern house was foreseeable. Judge McMahon made a deduction for contributory negligence.

153. Implemented by s 4 of the 1991 Act. See para **[11.127]** below.

"[t]he older the product, the less likely it is that evidence of malfunctioning will suffice as an inference of a construction flaw, although some Courts would permit [the] plaintiff to negative misuse and overuse in such a case."[154]

**[11.116]** Finally in this context it should be noted that s 5(2) of the Act and Article 6, para 2 of the Directive states that a product is not to be considered defective "for the sole reason that a better product is subsequently put into circulation". This recognises the fact that production processes are inevitably subject to constant technological change: to stigmatise a product as "defective" merely because a better one has later been produced would be unfair and impractical. In some cases, however, the later circulation of a better product may be potent evidence that greater safety could earlier have been achieved. Section 5(2) does not prevent this inference from being made.

***The scope of "damage"***

**[11.117]** "Damage", for the purposes of s 2(1), is defined in s 1(1) as meaning:

(a) death or personal injury;

(b) loss of, damage to, or destruction of, any item of property other than the defective product itself; provided that the item of property:

  (i) is of a type ordinarily intended for private use or consumption, and

  (ii) was used by the injured person mainly for his own private use or consumption.

Article 9 of the Directive which is substantially in the same terms, is specified as being without prejudice to national provisions relating to non-material damage.[155]

**[11.118]** In the original draft Directive, presented by the Commission to the Council in September 1976, "damage" had been defined somewhat differently. The relevant Article (then Article 6) had defined damage as meaning:

(a) death or personal injuries;

(b) damage to or destruction of any item of property other than the defective article itself where the item of property

  (i) is of a type ordinarily acquired for private use or consumption; and

  (ii) was not acquired or used by the claimant for the purpose of his trade, business or profession.

---

154. PROSSER & KEETON, p 696.

155. *Cf* Crossick 'The Future of Liability for Defective Products in the European Community' at p 13 (Paper delivered at the ESC Conference. The New EEC Product Liability Directive Implementation and Implications 16 October 1986, at pp 8-9):

"In this area any attempt to provide a Community solution would have been extremely difficult because the Member States are themselves not capable of reaching agreement on a definition of such damage. Moreover, it was not politically acceptable to exclude such damages in all the Member States by reason only of the fact that they did not have their place in their system of strict liability as in German Law. Such an exclusion could not moreover be justified, 'Dommage moral', 'Pain and suffering' and 'Schmerzengeld' are concepts appropriate to each national legislation. They represent only a small part of the total system of compensation. There is no need to fear that provisions under this title constitute an excessive burden on the producer."

Not everyone will agree with this sanguine view. The difference in national laws encourages some degree of "forum-shopping".

**[11.119]** The Explanatory Memorandum to the draft Directive made it clear that, so far as the death of the user of the defective article was concerned, the Article was:

> "intended to cover both rights to compensation arising for the benefit of th[at] person in the period between the event giving rise to injury and his death, and rights to compensation arising for the benefit of persons who had rights against the deceased. These will be primarily rights to maintenance of the spouse or close relatives."

**[11.120]** In terms of Irish law, the claim would cover both survival of actions and the fatal injuries provisions in ss 6-10 and 47-51, respectively, of the Civil Liability Act 1961 (as amended). So far as personal injuries were concerned the Explanatory Memorandum to the draft Directive stated[156] that:

> "[t]he term 'personal injuries' comprises the cost of treatment and of all expenditure incurred in restoring the injured person to health and any impairment of earning capacity as a result of the personal injury".[157]

The Explanatory Memorandum noted that the draft Directive did:

> "not include payment of compensation for pain and suffering or for damage not regarded as damage to property (non-material damage). It is therefore possible to award such damages to the extent that national laws recognise such claims, *based on other legal grounds*." [emphasis added]

**[11.121]** The Directive, as it finally emerged in Article 9, involved some drafting changes from what originally appeared as Article 6, but on the questions of death and personal injuries the substantial position has not been altered.

**[11.122]** It is perhaps significant that the ninth recital to the Directive, having referred to the fact that the protection of the consumer requires compensation for death and personal injury as well as damage to property, goes on to state that the Directive:

> "should not prejudice compensation for pain and suffering and other non-material damages payable, where appropriate, under the law applicable to the case".[158]

**[11.123]** It seems beyond argument that the manner in which the 1991 Act has implemented the Directive permits the award of damages for pain and suffering in proceedings under the Act. Section 2(1) of the Act proclaims simply that the producer "shall be liable to damages in tort" for damage caused by a defect in a product. A hallmark of damages in tort is the award for pain and suffering. Section 1(1) defines "personal injury" as including "any disease and any impairment of a person's physical or mental condition". The same subsection provides that "damage" means (*inter alia*) "death or personal injury". Alex Schuster's analysis of the position is surely correct:

> "Given that the 1991 Act implemented the Directive through the creation of a statutory tort, it is suggested that the Irish courts will have little difficulty in shaping this new tort to

156. Crossick 'The Future of Liability for Defective Products in the European Community'. para 17.

157. Crossick 'The Future of Liability for Defective Products in the European Community' at p 13.

158. See the second edition of this work, p 194, for discussion of this provision. See also the interesting exchange of views between Alex Schuster and Michael McGrath in *Product Liability*, Schuster ed, Irish Centre for European Law 1989, at pp 10-12, 22. See also Coe 'Products Liability in the European Community -An Introduction to the 1985 Council Directive' (1987) 10 J of Products Ly 197 at 210-211.

encompass pain and suffering as a recoverable head of loss. In any event, might it not be argued that the broad definition of 'personal injury' enshrined in the 1991 Act - which includes 'any disease and any impairment of a person's physical or mental condition' - should be interpreted to include recovery for pain and suffering. Indeed it is arguable that pain and suffering constitutes an amalgam of both physical and mental injury. If the Irish legislature had intended to exclude such losses from the ambit of the new regime, this exercise in subtraction would have been clearly enunciated in the 1991 Act".[159]

**[11.124]** So far as property damage is concerned, s 1(1), as may be seen, requires, first, that the damage be to any item of property *other than the defective product itself*. Thus, if an electric kettle self-destructs and burns to a cinder, but causes no damage to other property, no liability accrues under the Act or the Directive.[160]

**[11.125]** Section 1(1) requires, secondly, that the item of property damaged by the defective product be of a type "ordinarily intended for private use or consumption" and that it had been "used by the injured person mainly for his own private use or consumption". Clearly what the Act is seeking to exclude is damage to property used in the course of a trade, business or profession and the draft Directive makes this a clear objective also.

**[11.126]** On the issue of the 500 ECU threshold, the 1991 Act has taken a controversial stance. The Directive was clearly concerned that the regime of strict liability might release a rush of small trivial claims and to prevent this it defined damage as extending out to property damage, other than the defective product itself, "with a lower threshold of 500 ECU" (Article 9). This could mean that claims below this threshold may not be maintained but that claims which reach or exceed it will be compensated in full or, less convincingly, it could be interpreted as requiring the court to deduct 500 ECU from every property claim that passes the threshold, so that, for example, a plaintiff whose property compensation is valued at ten thousand ECUs should be entitled only to nine thousand, five hundred ECUs. Such a bizarre outcome, as well as the language of the text, suggests that the former interpretation is far preferable but s 3(1) of the 1991 Act has adopted the latter, requiring a deduction of £350 in every case, for which it might be open to challenge.[161]

### *Questions of proof and causation*

**[11.127]** Section 4 provides tersely that:

> The onus shall be on the injured person concerned to prove the damage, the defect and the causal relationship between the defect and damage.

---

159. Schuster 'The New Product Liability Regime' in *The New Product Liability Regime* at 13-14, Schuster ed, (1992).

160. *Cf* the *Explanatory Memorandum to the Draft Directive* para 20. It is interesting to note how in *D & F Estates Ltd v Acrecrest* [1989] AC 177 the House of Lords adopted a similar approach on this matter. The issue was revisited in *Murphy v Brentwood DC* [1991] 1 AC 398. *Cf* WINFIELD & JOLOWICZ, pp 335-336. *Cf* paras **[11.84]-[11.88]** above.

161. It should be noted that by virtue of Article 14 the Directive does not apply to injury or damage "arising from nuclear accidents and covered by international conventions ratified by the Member States". Article 16 enables a Member State to limit a producer's total liability for damage resulting from death or personal injury subject to that limit being not less than 70 million ECU (about IR £53 million). Ireland did not avail itself of this option when implementing the Directive in 1991. See further para **[11.172]** below.

Section 4, which implements Article 4, places *expressis verbis*, the onus of proving these three elements on the injured person. What must be proved is, of course, less conceptually encumbered than what is necessary to establish in a negligence action. There is no need to establish any breach of a duty of care on the part of the defendant: all that need be shown is that the product was defective, that the plaintiff suffered damage. and that "the causal relationship between the defect and damage" existed.

**[11.128]** One or two questions arise about this approach. To what extent, if at all, may some analogue of the *res ipsa loquitur* doctrine be applied? This is a formidable issue since, under present law, as we have seen,[162] it is less than fully clear what precisely the doctrine means and what are its effects on the onus of proof.

**[11.129]** It is beyond argument that the *res ipsa loquitur* doctrine, in its pure form, can have no application since it is concerned with the issue of the defendant's negligence. A defendant who can establish that his or her negligence was not the cause of the plaintiff's injury will escape liability even if a fog of uncertainty as to the actual cause remains unresolved.[163] The 1991 Act, however, is concerned, not with the defendant's negligence, but the product's defectiveness. Many cases which would formerly have involved an application of the *res ipsa loquitur* doctrine, usually resulting in the imposition of liability on the defendant,[164] can now proceed, with greater honesty, on the basis of a strict liability test, with the same outcome in practice. Yet there will be cases where the plaintiff is injured by a product in circumstances where it could plausibly be said that injuries such as happened do not usually occur without the product's having some defect. This is about as close an analogy as one can find to the classic "trigger" for the application of the *res ipsa loquitur* doctrine. Should the courts invent a new *res ipsa loquitur* principle for proceedings under the 1991 Act and, if so, what should its procedural effect be?

**[11.130]** The answer is not obvious. It could be argued that the courts should indeed go down this road, for two reasons. First, because it would be a curious anomaly if a plaintiff suing both in negligence and under the 1991 Act should receive the benefit of an onus shift in the former action where the *res ipsa loquitur* doctrine applied but not in the latter action, where the doctrine should plausibly be applied by analogy. Secondly, the rationale for *res ipsa loquitur* in negligence litigation which Henchy J propounded in *Hanrahan v Merck Sharp & Dohme (Ireland) Ltd*,[165] that:

> "it would be palpably unfair to require a plaintiff to prove something which is beyond his reach and which is peculiarly within the defendant's capacity of proof,"

could be considered to apply with equal force to litigation under the 1991 Act.

**[11.131]** To attack these arguments, it is necessary to call into question, in the first case, the wisdom of the shifting of the onus of proof which the *res ipsa loquitur* doctrine involves in negligence actions and, in the second case, to cast doubt on the plausibility of Henchy J's rationale for the doctrine. In Chapter 9, we have done both of these things.[166] If

---

162. See para **[9.11]** above.
163. *Lindsay v Mid Western Health Board* [1993] 2 IR 147 (SC) analysed by Byrne & Binchy, *Annual Review of Irish Law 1992*, pp 592-598.
164. *Cf* paras **[9.41]** and **[9.44]** above.
165. [1988] ILRM 629 (SC).
166. *Cf* para **[9.43]** and **[9.52]** above.

these criticisms have validity they should have at least equal force in the context of actions under the 1991 Act, and this would argue against adopting a *res ipsa loquitur* analogue in the context of the 1991 Act.

**[11.132]** A second question arises about the causation issue to which Article 4 of the Directive and s 4 of the 1991 Act refer: what exactly is meant by "the causal relationship between the defect and damage"? Obviously, if there is *no* causal relationship, the plaintiff cannot succeed, but the converse is not necessarily the case, as the doctrine of "proximate cause" or remoteness of damage in tort actions makes clear. As we have seen,[167] in tort law not every case involving a causal relationship will be sufficient to impose liability on the defendant, and this limitation applies even in cases of strict liability. Thus, in negligence cases, "factual" causes will not attract liability; it is only if the cause is the "proximate" or "legal" cause that liability will attach. Moreover, on the remoteness of damage issue, in negligence actions reasonable foreseeability of the damage is the outer limit of liability ("egg shell skull" cases aside) and, in trespass, directness is the limit. Article 4 specifies no similar limitations and s 4 of the 1991 Act does nothing to clarify the opacity of the Article. Should Article 4 be interpreted as implicitly imposing liability, however indirect and distant the causal relationship may be?

**[11.133]** We suggest the answer is no because the true limit to liability is contained in the concept of defectiveness itself. It will be recalled that the Article provides, simply, that the producer "shall be liable for damage caused by a defect in his product". It does not say that the producer is liable for damage caused by a defective product. The defect must be the cause of the damage. Section 5 (echoing Article 6) as we have seen, provides that a product is defective "if it fails to provide the safety which a person is entitled to expect, taking all the circumstances into account ..." Whilst not defining "defect" specifically, s 5 makes it reasonable for a court to identify as a defect the condition of a product which results from the failure to provide the requisite safety.

**[11.134]** Integral to defectiveness (and thus "defect") is the disappointed expectation of the hypothetical person. Thus, foreseeability (albeit reversed into a failure to perform as might reasonably have been expected), is at the heart of liability. So the car whose axle breaks and kills the driver can be stigmatised as having a defect that causes damage because the circumstances of the damage's occurrence manifest a defect in the product.

**[11.135]** It is easy to conjure up unusual instances of the occurrence of the accident - for example, the car may have been "driven" by a five-year-old child who stole the keys for it. It seems impossible, however, to envisage cases where the product could convincingly be characterised as defective in circumstances where the product did not carry with it a foresight (actual or constructive) of a safety standard that was defeated by the character of the product itself. In other words, to be liable under s 2(1) and Article 1 the product must in some foreseeable respect (albeit retrospectively reconstructed) have been defective since to be defective is to violate reasonable expectations. The range of reasonable expectations of any products' safety is finite and its principle capable of being stated in advance. It is only this predictable range of expectations that generates liability for injury caused by breach of these expectations.

---

167. See Ch 3 above.

### *Defences*

**[11.136]** Section 6 of the 1991 Act, which gives effect *verbatim* to Article 7, provides six defences to the strict liability principle. A producer will not be liable if he proves:

(a) that he did not put the product into circulation; or

(b) that, having regard to the circumstances, it is probable that the defect which caused the damage did not exist at the time when the product was put into circulation by him or that this defect came into being afterwards; or

(c) that the product was neither manufactured by him for sale or any form of distribution for economic purpose, nor manufactured or distributed by him in the course of his business; or

(d) that the defect is due to compliance of the product with mandatory regulations issued by the public authorities; or

(e) that the state of scientific and technical knowledge at the time when he put the product into circulation was not such as to enable the existence of the defect to be discovered; or

(f) in the case of a manufacturer of a component, that the defect is attributable to the design of the product in which the component has been fitted or to the instructions given by the manufacturer of the product.

**[11.137]** Regarding the first defence, that the producer did not "put the product into circulation", the Commission was of the view that it was not necessary to define this term further since it was "self-explanatory in the ordinary meaning of the words".[168] The Commission considered that "[n]ormally, an article has been put into circulation when it has been started off on the chain of distribution".[169] Thus, if a product is released onto the market as a result of theft, the producer would not be strictly liable. Of course, if the theft was foreseeable, the producer could in some circumstances be liable in negligence for reasonably foreseeable injuries resulting from this.[170] It would appear, however, that strict liability would not attach to the producer in such circumstances, unless (which seems unlikely) a very broad, and strained, interpretation were given to the words "put ... into circulation".

**[11.138]** The defence contained in ground (b) in s 6 is designed to protect the producer from liability for defects coming into being some time after the product was put into circulation by him. As the Commission noted:

> "[o]ne of the conditions for the liability of the producer is that the defect in the article should arise in the producer's production process ... Liability is therefore excluded where the defect arose only after th[e] time [it was put into circulation] ..."[171]

Although the difference may be easy enough to state in the abstract, it does raise some troublesome conceptual - indeed philosophical - issues. If a defect appears in a product

---

168. *Explanatory Memorandum to the Draft Directive*, para 15.

169. *Explanatory Memorandum to the Draft Directive.* It appears that an element of intention is necessary. Thus as Alex Schuster points out: "If a factory emits toxic waste into the atmosphere the 'producer' will not be regarded as having put it into circulation". 'Annotated Text of the Liability for Defective Products Act 1991' in *The New Product Liability Regime*, Schuster ed, Irish Centre for European Law 1992, p 83.

170. *Cf* Ch 3. *Purtill v Athlone Urban District Council* [1968] IR 205 (SC).

171. *Explanatory Memorandum to the Draft Directive*, para 14.

two years after the product was put into circulation, by what criteria can it be judged to have "come into being" at any particular time? And when should that time be? Are we not here attempting to resolve the problem of "actualisation of potential", which has troubled philosophers since the time of Aristotle? If a car develops a weakness in its brakes after two years, and the technical evidence is to the effect that if a car is so manufactured that the brakes generally start weakening dangerously at this time, is that a defect "coming into being" at the time of manufacture or two years later? Would the answer be the same if the relevant period were two weeks? Or twenty years?

**[11.139]** The truth of the matter is that the concept of a defect under the 1991 Act is in the normative rather than empirical order. A product is defective when it "does not provide the safety which a person is entitled to expect taking all the circumstances into account ..."[172] The gradual weakening and decay of any product is a process that is integrally related to such expectation. When the process is in accord with reasonable expectations, then the product may be characterised as not suffering from a defect. When the process is premature, then the product will be held to be defective and normally the weakness in the product will be regarded as a defect inhering in it from the time it was put into circulation.

**[11.140]** The defence contained in ground (c) of Article 7 protects the non-commercial producer, such as the home-brew enthusiast who poisons his family or the grandparent who makes a doll's house for a favourite grandchild with sharp nails sticking out of the roof. "Free samples" in supermarkets, however, will not normally fall within this defence.[173]

**[11.141]** Ground (d) ensures that a commercial producer will not be faced with the dilemma of having to comply with mandatory regulations issued by the public authorities and at the same time run the risk of being liable under the strict regime established by the Act and by the Directive: if such a potential clash arises, the producer will have a good defence under the Act if it complies with the mandatory regulations.[174]

**[11.142]** Ground (e) of s 6 contains an important modification to the strict liability principle, generally known as the "development risks" defence. A producer will be relieved of liability that would otherwise attach if he can prove that the state of scientific and technical knowledge at the time when he put the product into circulation was not such as to enable the existence of the defect to be discovered. In other words, if the product was as safe as the "state of the art" would allow at the time of production, subsequent improvements in safety in the production process with respect to this product may not be

172. Article 6 of the Directive; s 5(1) of the 1991 Act.

173. As to the expression "course of business" see *Davies v Sumner* [1984] 1 WLR 1301 cited by Schuster 'Note to Section 6, Annotated Text of the Liability for Defective Products Act 1991' in *The New Product Liability Regime*, Schuster ed, Irish Centre for European Law 1992, p 83.

174. *Cf* Schuster (p 83):

> "It is unclear whether the phase 'any enactment' refers exclusively to Irish law. Suppose for example that an Irish producer adapts his product to comply with mandatory German legislation. If it subsequently injures a German consumer the Irish manufacturer will be able to rely on the mandatory compliance defence before the German courts. If, however, the victim of the defective product is a forum shopper the Irish producer may well find himself defending his action before the Irish courts. It would seem unfair to deny him a defence which he would automatically enjoy under the German product liability regime".

relied on by an injured plaintiff as setting the standard of safety. To some degree this specific defence is contained, in general terms, in s 5: for why should a person be "entitled to expect" a standard of safety which, *ex hypothesi,* was *impossible* to attain at the time the product was put into circulation? Moreover, s 5, as we have seen, specifies "the time when the product was put into circulation" as a circumstance to be taken into account in determining whether a product is defective. This would appear to give some scope to the development risks defence to operate, even without the express ground to this effect contained in s 6.[175]

**[11.143]** It is perhaps worth raising the question whether the development risks defence contained in s 6 of the Act would be more effective in exempting a producer from strict liability under the Act than from liability in negligence at common law. Mere proof that the state of scientific and technical knowledge at the time the product was put into circulation "was not such as to enable the existence of the defect to be discovered" will relieve the producer of strict liability; but in a negligence action the matter would not be so easily decided in its favour. A separate question could arise in some cases as to whether, in view of the limited level of scientific knowledge and relatively undeveloped "state of the art", it was negligent to have put the product into circulation at all. The risk to the consumer could well outweigh the benefits, especially where the desire to make profits encouraged a premature release of a product onto the market.

**[11.144]** It should be noted that any Member State may, by way of derogation from Article 7(e), provide that the producer is to be liable even where it proves that the state of scientific knowledge at the time when it put the product into circulation was not such as to enable the existence of a defect to be discovered.[176] Ireland did not avail itself of this

---

175. In the United States, conformity with the state of the art will generally result in the producer's escaping liability either as an affirmative defence, or on the basis that the product should not be regarded as being defective, in such a way as to be *unreasonably dangerous* - the core concept in products liability law there. PROSSER & KEETON, p 700 observe that:

> "[i]f inability to discover a risk or hazard related to product design is regarded as a defence, then it is true that the only practical difference between strict liability for design hazards using a danger-utility test and negligence is a change in the burden of proof".

176. Article 15. *Cf* para **[11.171]** below. Britain's seemingly overbroad translation of the development risks defence survived the scrutiny of the Court of Justice in Case C-300/95 *EC Commission v United Kingdom* [1997] 3 CMLR 923 which adopted a benevolent teleological interpretation. Alex Schuster warns that:

> "... it is by no means certain that the finding by the Court of Justice to the effect that section 4(1)(e) of the [Consumer Protection] Act ... 1987 .... does not introduce an element of subjectivity into the 'development risks' defence will be mirrored in future decisions by the UK courts (even though they are obliged to interpret the 1987 Act in line with the wording and purpose of the Product Liability Directive)":

'Review of Case-law under Directive 85/374/EEC on Liability for Defective Products' (1998) 6 Consumer LJ 195 at 212. See generally Newdick 'The Development Risk Defence of the Consumer Protection Act 1987' (1988) 47 Camb LJ 455; Newdick 'Risk Uncertainty and Knowledge in the Development Risks Defence' (1991) 20 Anglo-Amer-LR 309; Howells & Mildred 'Is European Products Liability More Protective than the Restatement (Third) of Torts: Products Liability? (1998) 65 Tenn Lr 985; Stapleton 'Products Liability in the United Kingdom: The Myths of Reform' (1999) 34 Tex Int'l LJ 45 at 59-61; Owen 'American Products Liability Law Restated' (1998) 6 Consumer LJ 161.

option. Section 6(e) of the 1991 Act contains the development risks defence in language that is identical to that used in Article 7(e) of the Directive.

**[11.145]** Ground (f) of s 6 allows the manufacturer of a component part to escape liability under the Directive where, in effect, the responsibility lies with the manufacturer of the product in which the component is fitted, ie the "host" product. That responsibility can arise where the defect is attributable (i) to the design of the product in which the component is fitted, or (ii) to the instructions given by the manufacturer of the "host" product. It is possible to imagine cases where the defect is attributable to a combination of causes, including the act of the manufacturer of the component and the instructions given by the manufacturer of the "host" product. In such instances joint and several liability, rather than liability imposed solely on the manufacturer of the product, would appear appropriate. In other words it seems that, "attributable" in ground (f) should be interpreted as meaning "attributable exclusively" to the matters specified in the ground.

**[11.146]** Accordingly, s 6(f), which implements Article 7(f) uses the expression "attributable entirely to the design of the product ..." to give effect to this view. In doing so it runs the risk, remote it is submitted, of not complying with the Directive, which does not use the word "entirely" in its corresponding provision. It also places the producer of a raw material (who is not mentioned in Article 7(f)) in the same position as the manufacturer of a component so far as its integration into a product is concerned.[177]

***Limitation period and extinction of liability***

**[11.147]** The idea of a limitation period[178] is based on two policies: first, that a defendant should be protected from stale, possibly fraudulent, claims, where accessibility to evidence has been diminished; and, secondly, that a plaintiff who sleeps on his rights is not entitled to an indefinite period within which to take the action. As one commentator has pointed out:

> "The conflict generated by these two often contradictory currents of thought is responsible for much of the discord in this area. One school of thought emphasises the security to the defendant, while the other emphasises the lack of diligence on the part of the plaintiff."[179]

The thrust of the Directive seems, on balance, to favour the first school of thought. Though Article 10 is framed in terms generous to plaintiffs, the benefit of this is largely, if somewhat arbitrarily, subverted by Article 11.

---

177. In the United States a somewhat similar defence has been recognised. PROSSER & KEETON, p 706, explain that if an assembled product was unreasonably dangerous because the component part was unfit for the particular use that the assembler was making of it, "then arguably the defect is in the design of the assembled product rather than in the design of the component part". This does not mean, however that the manufacturer of the component part will always be able to escape liability:

> "If the maker of the component part ... knows or has reason to know that the part will be used in a way that will make the assembled product unreasonably dangerous, then such a seller may well be subjected to liability on a warranty of fitness theory if the purchaser was relying on the seller, or a negligent entrustment theory, or perhaps strict liability in tort without regard to reliance."

178. The subject is dealt with in greater detail in Ch 46.

179. Kahan 'Statutes of Limitations Problems in Cases of Insidious Diseases: The Development of the Discovery Rule' (1978) 2 J of Products Ly 127 at 134.

**[11.148]** Section 7(1) of the 1991 Act provides, in accordance with Article 10 of the Directive, that a limitation period of three years is to apply to proceedings for the recovery of damages as provided for in the Directive. The limitation period begins to run from the date on which the action accrued or the date (if later) on which the plaintiff became aware, or should reasonably have become aware, of the damage, the defect and the identity of the producer. However, the laws of Member States regulating suspension or interruption of the limitation period are not affected by the Directive.

**[11.149]** Section 7(2)(a) provides, in the "long stop" provision that the rights conferred on the injured person pursuant to the Act are to be extinguished on the expiry of a period of ten years from the date on which the producer put into circulation the actual product which caused the damage, unless the injured person has in the meantime instituted proceedings against the producer.

**[11.150]** Some points about these implementing provisions should be noted. First, as mentioned in relation to s 7(1), as an alternative to the accrual of the action, time begins to run from the time the plaintiff was, or ought to have become, aware of the damage, the defect and the identity of the producer. Under Irish law, outside the present context, a distinction is made in the legislation between claims for damages for personal injury or death, which are based on a "discoverability" test[180] broadly similar to that provided in s 7(1) and Article 10, and other claims - for property damage or economic loss - where the clock starts ticking even before the plaintiff could reasonably have become aware that he or she was the victim of a tort.[181] Section 7(1), uniquely in Irish law, applies a "discoverability" test to claims for personal injury or death *and* property damage.[182]

**[11.151]** It should also be noted that the effect of s 7(2)(a) in extinguishing the injured person's rights after the expiry of ten years from the date the producer put the product into circulation, is to render inoperative the law of Member States regulating suspension or interruption of the limitation period - on the basis of minority or mental incapacity, for example. True, Article 10 provides that these laws "shall not be affected by this Directive"; but Article 11 is concerned, not with a limitation period within which an action must be taken, but the extinction of rights. Section 7(2)(b) of the 1991 Act gives a clear priority to Article 11 over Article 10.

**[11.152]** The merits and disadvantages of the "long stop" provision in s 7(2)(a) and Article 11 have been widely debated. In favour of the absolute cut-off point, the English Law Commission has observed that:

> "[i]t is in the producer's interests that he should be able to close his books on a product after it has been in circulation for a fixed period. It assists him in assessing the risk and it facilitates insurance and amortisation, thus keeping the insurance premium down. There is thus some saving, albeit marginal, which redounds to the general benefit of the public. More important, perhaps, it sets a date after which the producer no longer has the burden of

---

180. Statute of Limitations (Amendment) Act 1991. See further Ch 46 below.

181. *Cf* Brady & Kerr, *The Limitation of Actions in the Republic of Ireland* (2nd ed, 1994), pp 79-85.

182. See Brady & Kerr, *The Limitation of Actions in the Republic of Ireland* (2nd ed, 1994), pp 85-86; Schuster 'Note to section 7 Annotated Text of the Liability for Defective Products Act 1991' in *The New Product Liability Regime*, Schuster ed, Irish Centre for European Law 1992, p 85.

> proving that a product which has caused an accident was not defective when he put it into circulation. This burden is increasingly difficult for him to discharge as the years pass and it seems only fair that there should come a point when it is entirely removed."[183]

**[11.153]** As against this, several objections may be made to the ten-year cut-off point. First, it is crude and arbitrary. Some products - various types of machinery or aircraft, for example - may well be expected to last for more than ten years, so that it could properly be said of them, say, twelve years after they were put into circulation, that, in spite of their age, they were "defective". For other products - a loaf of bread, for example - ten years is an entirely inappropriate figure. The Council of Europe, which favoured the same approach as was ultimately adopted by the EEC Directive, was conscious of the problem but none the less considered ten years "an acceptable period in view of the need to fix some limit (ten years being a fair average) and the desirability of affording producers some security".[184]

**[11.154]** Similarly, the framers of the draft Directive considered that ten years "appeared appropriate as an average period".[185] This notion of an "average period" may be challenged; the vast range of products, each with their appropriate life-span of use, makes it quite inapt to select *any* particular period as a general cut-off point, since that period will be quite unsuitable for many of these products.[186]

**[11.155]** The ten-year cut-off period has not been met with universal support by producers, some of whom:

> "argue that the period is too long, that for them to maintain records to establish that goods were not defective when originally sold will be an expensive exercise, and the longer the period for which records must be kept the greater the expense. As the consumer must bear this cost in the price of the goods is it to his advantage to pay for record keeping which can be of benefit on only the most rare occasion?"[187]

**[11.156]** One of the grounds on which the Scottish Law Commission objected to the ten-year cut-off point was that it would be unfair to an injured person, who normally would not know on what date the product had been put into circulation. Different cut-off periods would apply in respect of each component:

> "an injured person wishing to sue a component maker would have at the very least a complicated task in ascertaining whether his action was likely to be time-barred, and evidence to this effect might not emerge until after the injured person had incurred considerable expense in pursuing his claim."[188]

The effect of the cut-off point, moreover, is in some cases to deprive a person of a right of action before he or she sustains an injury.

---

183. Eng Law Com No 82, para 152.
184. *Explanatory Report to the Strasbourg Convention on Products Liability in Regard to Personal Injury and Death*, para 68. See generally on Council of Europe Convention McMahon 'Liability for Defective Products: the Draft European Convention' (1973) 8 Ir Jur (ns) 227.
185. *Explanatory Memorandum to the draft Directive*, para 28
186. *Cf* the views of the Scottish Law Commission expressed in Eng Law Com No 82 & Scot Law Com No 45, para 156.
187. Marriott 'Products Liability in Europe - What of the Future?' (1979) 3 J of Products Ly 15 at 16.
188. Scottish Law Commission expressed in Eng Law Com No 82 & Scot Law Com No 45, para. 158.

**[11.157]** The constitutional aspects of such a rule are considered below.[189] Of course, the provisions of the Directive as implemented by s 7 may not be challenged on constitutional grounds.[190]

***(h) Contributory negligence***

**[11.158]** Contributory negligence comes into play in the Act and under the Directive.[191] Section 9(2) provides that:

> (2) Where any damage is caused partly by a defect in a product and partly by the fault of the injured person or of any person for whom the injured person is responsible, the provisions of the Civil Liability Act, 1961, concerning contributory negligence, shall have effect as if the defect were due to the fault of every person liable by virtue of this Act for the damage caused by the defect.

Thus, contributory negligence is permitted to have much the same role as it does at present in a negligence action. Even the notion of imputed contributory negligence[192] is allowed to operate.

**[11.159]** Relevant to s 9(2) is the present judicial debate in Irish law as to how a case should be resolved where the plaintiff is guilty of contributory negligence and the defendant is strictly liable (for breach of statutory duty, for example) without any "fault", as that notion is understood under the Civil Liability Act 1961. As we have seen,[193] in the Supreme Court decision of *O'Sullivan v Dwyer*,[194] Walsh J literally interpreted s 43 of the 1961 Act as disentitling the plaintiff to any compensation in such circumstances. However, in *Daly v Avonmore Creameries*,[195] McCarthy J raised a question as to whether s 43 was mandatory or discretionary. It is perhaps worth noting that in several jurisdictions in the

---

189. See ch 46 below.

190. *Cf* Article 29.4.3° of the Constitution.

191. As well as to express treatment of the issue in Article 8, the Directive implicitly has regard to careless conduct by the plaintiff. The definition of defectiveness in Article 6 requires the court to take account of "the use to which it could reasonably be expected that the product would be put". Thus, an unreasonable use of the product *may* mean that the plaintiff will be unable to establish that the product was defective. This is not to say that all unreasonable uses of products have such an effect. If a misuse may reasonably be expected then the product may well be held to be defective (though all the other circumstances must also be taken into account under Article 6). It should also be noted that Article 6 does not in express terms provide that a use to which it could *not* reasonably be expected that the product would be put automatically defeats a claim. Since the court is required to take all the circumstances into account in determining whether the product was defective, it is theoretically possible that it could conclude that in spite of the unforeseeable use to which it was put, the product was still defective. Under the Directive the defect must have caused the plaintiff's injury. Thus it is possible that the plaintiff's misuse in particular cases may be characterised as the sole cause of his or her injury: *Cf Yun v Ford Motor Co* (1994) 647 A 2d 841 (NJ App Div). In the Circuit Court, Judge McMahon held that liability could arise when the plaintiff stood on a kitchen table to reach a shelf. The table collapsed due to a defect in the way it was constructed. Liability was imposed on the basis that such usage of the kitchen table in a modest modern house was foreseeable. Judge McMahon made a deduction for contributory negligence.

192. *Cf* para **[20.57]** below.

193. See para **[21.59]** above.

194. [1971] I R 275.

195. [1984] IR 131 (SC).

United States[196] it is possible to operate contributory negligence rules of apportionment (referred to there as "comparative" negligence) in products liability cases where the defendant is strictly liable and the plaintiff is guilty of contributory negligence.

**[11.160]** Section 9(2) is clearly in accord with this approach. Unlike s 34(1) of the 1961 Act, it does not require the Court to compare the respective degrees of fault of the plaintiff and defendant. On the contrary, it envisages reduction or disallowance of the claim by virtue of a consideration of "all the circumstances" where the damage is caused by a defect in the product and the fault of the plaintiff or his proxy.

***Prohibition on "contracting out"***

**[11.161]** Article 12 of the Directive prohibits "contracting out". It provides that the liability of the producer arising from the Directive may not, in relation to the injured person, be limited or excluded by a provision limiting his liability or exempting him from liability. In its original draft, the relevant provision (then Article 10) had specified that liability might not be excluded or limited, without reference to any "provision" to this effect. The original draft, therefore, overrode not merely contractual exclusions of liability but also any assertion by the producer that the consumer, by using the product, had voluntarily assumed the risks that might arise from the defectiveness of the product. The inclusion in the final text of the reference to a "provision" limiting the injured person's liability appears to restrict the scope of the Article. The precise extent of the change is a matter for debate: there may, of course, be a "provision" in a contract, but it would also seem possible for there to be a "provision" in a non-contractual agreement, or even (perhaps) in a unilateral notice, involving some degree of communication between the parties. The parallel with the constriction of the *volenti* defence as a result of s 34(1)(b) of the Civil Liability Act 1961 is worth considering.[197]

**[11.162]** Section 10 of the 1991 Act, implementing Article 12, has taken a broad view of its scope. It provides as follows:

> "The liability of a producer arising by virtue of this Act to an injured person shall not be limited by any term of contract by any notice or by any other provision."

**[11.163]** It may be argued that this provision should be interpreted as being limited to the protection of the injured person from the dilution or extinction of his or her rights against the producer under the Directive and the Act. It should not be interpreted as restricting the entitlement of those in the chain of distribution between (and including) the producer and the retailer to regulate their contractual relationships *inter se*. Thus it would not be a legitimate contention that an exemption clause or indemnity provision in a contract between the producer and the wholesaler whereby the producer offloaded its potential liability to consumers under the 1991 Act onto the wholesaler was prohibited by Article 12 or s 10.[198]

196. For a stimulating critical analysis see Roszkowski & Prentice 'Reconciling Comparative Negligence and Strict Liability: A Public Policy Analysis'(1988) 33 St Louis ULJ 19.

197. *Cf* para **[20.61]**. If the notion of a "provision" in Article 12 is limited to documents and excludes oral communications it is more restrictive than s 34(1)(b).

198. See Schuster 'Note to section 10 Annotated Text of the Liability for Defective Products Act 1991' in *The New Product Liability Regime*, Schuster ed, Irish Centre for European Law 1992, pp 86-87.

### *Concurrent wrongdoers*

**[11.164]** The net of liability among several defendants is cast widely by the Directive. In view of the broad range of liability under Part III of our Civil Liability Act 1961 and our liberal third-party procedure, this approach is generally in harmony with the present law. Article 8 provides that:

> [w]here, as a result of the provisions of this Directive, two or more persons are liable for the same damage, they shall be liable jointly and severally without prejudice to the provisions of national law concerning the rights of contribution or recourse.

**[11.165]** And Article 8, para 1, provides that:

> [w]ithout prejudice to the provisions of national law concerning the right of contribution or recourse, the liability of the producer shall not be reduced when the damage is caused both by a defect in [the] product and by the act or omission of a third party.

**[11.166]** Section 8 of the 1991 Act gives effect, *verbatim*, to Article 5. Section 2(1), as we have seen, goes further than Article 8, para 1 in providing that the producer "shall be liable in tort for damage caused wholly or partly by a defect in his product."

### *Retrospection*

**[11.167]** The Directive is not retrospective in its operation. Article 17 provides that the Directive "shall not apply to products put into circulation before the date on which the provisions referred to in Article 19 enter into force". Article 19 provides that Member States shall bring into force, not later than three years from the date of notification of the Directive, the laws, regulations and administrative provisions necessary to comply with the Directive. As has been mentioned, the Directive was notified to the Member States on 30 July 1985.

**[11.168]** As we have mentioned, Ireland's implementing legislation, the Liability for Defective Products Act 1991, did not come into force until 16 December 1991, raising the spectre of *Francovich* liability. Section 13 of the Act provides that the legislation "shall not apply to any product put into circulation within the territory of any Member State before the commencement of this Act".

**[11.169]** There is some degree of uncertainty as to when precisely a product is "put into circulation". Clearly, commercial distribution will suffice. It may well be that a product is "put into circulation" earlier than this when it leaves the factory, even before title has passed to any intermediate party. It seems clear that, while it is in the course of manufacture at the manufacturer's premises, the product has not been "put into circulation".[199]

### *Opt-ins and opt-outs*

**[11.170]** The Directive gave Member States certain choices, either to "opt in" or "opt out" of particular provisions, on three issues:

(i) the development risks defence,

(ii) a cap on damages, and

(iii) primary agricultural products.

---

199. *Cf* Guarino 'Product Liability Directive: Who is Liable and When?', pp 8-9 (Paper delivered at ESC Conference The New EEC Product Liability Directive: Implementation and Implications 16 October 1986).

*(i) Development risks defence*

**[11.171]** As regards the development risks defence,[200] Ireland has chosen to retain it, being anxious to encourage pharmaceutical companies to retain and expand their connections in Ireland.

*(ii) Cap on damages*

**[11.172]** Article 16 of the Directive permits Member States to provide a limit for a producer's total liability for damage resulting from death or personal injury and caused by identical items with the same defect, but requires that this limit be not less than 70 million ECU (about £IR53 million). This Article provoked a great deal of debate during the formation of the Directive. Most Member States regarded a ceiling on damages as unjust in giving an unwarranted preference to early claimants and in inducing inflated claims.[201] As against this, a few Member States favoured the limit, either because it was in harmony with their own national laws or because they considered that it would help industry in its planning and in acquiring insurance.

**[11.173]** A Discussion Document issued by the Department of Industry and Commerce on 17 August 1987, noted that the view of the majority, including Ireland, was that 70 million ECU was such a high amount that there would be no material difference from an unlimited liability system:

> "There would, therefore, be no significant difference in the level of insurance premiums and consequently little, if any, difference in the competitive position in industry. Accordingly, while there could be disadvantages, there was no discernible benefit for anyone, including industry, in setting a limit."[202]

70 million ECU looks a good deal smaller today but nonetheless the 1991 Act did not contain this cap on damages.

*(iii)Primary agricultural products*

**[11.174]** Article 15, as we have seen, enables Member States to include primary agricultural products and game within the scope of the definition of "products" in their legislation. The main argument in favour of taking this step is that, from the consumer's standpoint, the fact that a product is a "primary agricultural" one is irrelevant: whether a person chokes on a piece of broken glass or a broken chicken bone is not important as far as he or she is concerned. As against this it has been argued that primary agricultural products are particularly prone to hidden defects caused by environmental factors beyond the control of the producer.[203] Moreover, it has been said that the thrust of the Directive is

---

200. Article 7(e).

201. This is also the provisional view of the Law Reform Commission of Australia: Working Paper No 34, *Product Liability*, para 108 (1988). The Directive has been criticised by Leibman 'Note: The European Community's Products Liability Directive: Is the US Experience Applicable?' (1986) 18 L & Poly in Intl Bus 795 at 807 for not defining "identical items" and "same damage".

202. At p 19.

203. *Cf* At p 20. The revelations about practices in relation to feeding animals over the past decade and the growing concerns about BSE and related detrimental consequences of these practices have weakened the attraction of this argument.

to cover industrially manufactured or processed products. In any event, the consumer is already protected under the laws of negligence and contract.

**[11.175]** Again, as a matter of practical politics there was much to be said for derogation by Ireland, in view of the relative importance in our economy of agriculture. It came as no great surprise, therefore, that the 1991 Act excluded primary agricultural products and game from liability. It is, however, worth noting the argument that in the long run our international stature as food producers would have been more enhanced by including primary agricultural products within the scope of our legislation. This debate is only of historical interest now, since, as already noted,[204] Member States are no longer entitled to derogate in respect of agricultural products and are obliged as from 4 December 2000, to ensure that the products' liability regime of the European Community also extends to agricultural products.[205]

204. See fn 133 and accompanying text.

205. Directive 1999/34/EEC OJ L141, 4.6.1999, p 20.

Chapter 12

# Occupiers' Liability[1]


I. Introduction .......... 299
II. The Common Law .......... 299
III. Trespassers .......... 303
IV. The Hotel Proprietors Act 1963 .......... 314
V. The Occupiers' Liability Act 1995 .......... 315


## I. Introduction

**[12.01]** The law on occupiers' liability to entrants on land or buildings was radically overhauled by the Occupiers' Liability Act 1995. The 1995 Act clarified the law in certain areas, improved the legal entitlements of some entrants and significantly reduced the entitlements of others.

**[12.02]** It is impossible to understand fully the impact of the 1995 legislation without reference to the legal developments that led to its enactment. By way of introduction, therefore, a brief review of the common law on the subject will be given.

## II. The Common Law

**[12.03]** The law relating to occupiers' liability for injuries to entrants on their premises represented one piece of dry land which was not swamped when Lord Atkin, in *Donoghue v Stevenson*,[2] opened the floodgates of the modern law of negligence. In theory, the problems of occupiers' liability and manufacturers' liability were, in essence, similar enough to be governed by the same legal principles and a different approach to both problems was hard to justify, in logic or in law. Only historical accident could explain the differing attitudes that the common law took to these problems. This difference in attitudes was undoubtedly due, to a large extent, to the historical fact that the crucial decision of *Indermaur v Dames*[3] predated *Donoghue v Stevenson* by more than 60 years. Although it was of narrow application and, in theory, could have been easily engulfed by the principles of modern negligence, the principle enunciated in *Indermaur v Dames* had become too firmly entrenched by 1932 (promoted and perpetuated as it was by the doctrine of judicial precedent) to be swamped by another judicial cross-current.[4]

**[12.04]** When the rules governing occupiers' liability were being formulated in 1867, social, economic and industrial conditions favoured the interest of the land occupier rather

1. The analysis of the law prior to *McNamara v ESB* [1975] IR 1 (SC) is largely based on McMahon 'Occupiers' Liability in Ireland' in *Reform of Law of Occupiers' Liability in Ireland* (1975) Prl 4403.
2. [1932] AC 562 (HL (SC)).
3. (1866) LR 1 CP 274.
4. See McDermott CJ in *Gallagher v N McDowell Ltd* [1961] NI 26 at 32.

than that of the entrant. It was a period when the economic theory of laissez-faire was rife; it was considered first, that people should be left to look after themselves and, secondly, that economic resources should not be inhibited. Consequently, rules of law were developed which generally favoured the landowners. Entrants were categorised according to the benefit they endowed on the occupier: the greater the benefit the entrant conferred on the occupier, the greater the duty of the latter. Contractual entrants, invitees, licensees and trespassers all found their places in the stratification. At the top of this scale a comparatively high duty of care was demanded of the occupier; at the bottom, little or no duty was required. In choosing this approach, it must be noted that the judiciary were opting for a solution that was based on legal criteria rather than one that proceeded on a case by case basis, where emphasis would be placed on the facts of each case. By developing a legal stratification the judges were ensuring that they would keep the development of the law to themselves, and out of the hands of jurors, who they feared might be more favourably disposed to plaintiffs rather than to landowners.[5]

**[12.05]** In this context modern pressures, which, by and large, favoured the plaintiff-entrant, were obliged to operate and make their presence felt within an inimical framework determined by the 19th century outdated principles. Judicial goodwill was cramped within an anachronistic structure, which was propelled and perpetuated by *stare decisis*, with the result that the justice of the entrant's claim was not making its proper impact in the law.

## Categories of Entrant[6]

**[12.06]** The courts developed four categories of entrant, to each of which a distinctive duty was owed by the occupier. These were (1) contractual entrants; (2) invitees; (3) licensees; and (4) trespassers.

### *(a) Contractual entrants*

**[12.07]** A contractual entrant was a person who entered premises in pursuance of a contract between himself or herself and (normally) the occupier. Cinema patrons[7] or spectators at a sporting event[8] were classic examples of this category. The duty owed to the contractual entrant was determined by the terms of the contract. Thus, express terms could range from rendering the occupier's warranting the safety of the contractual entrant to the complete abnegation of any potential liability by the occupier. In the absence of express terms dealing with the matter, the courts implied a term on the part of the occupier that he or she had taken reasonable care to make the premises safe for the contemplated purposes.

### *(b) Invitees*

**[12.08]** An invitee was an entrant who went onto the property with the consent of the occupier in circumstances where the occupier had a material advantage in the visit. The

---

5. Marsh 'The History and Comparative Law of Invitees, Licensees and Trespassers', (1953) 69 LQR 182 at 185; Law Reform Commission of New South Wales 'Working Paper on Occupiers' Liability' pp 38-40.

6. For a detailed consideration, see the first edition of this work, pages 230-262.

7. *O'Gorman v Ritz (Clonmel) Ltd* [1947] Ir Jur 35 (HC).

8. *Coleman v Kelly* (1951) 85 ILTR 48 (SC); *Callaghan v Killarney Race Co Ltd* [1958] IR 366 (SC); *Donaldson v Irish Motor Racing Club* Supreme Court, 1 February 1957, extracted in McMahon & Binchy, *A Casebook on the Irish Law of Torts* (1st ed, 1983).

idea here was that, if the occupier was deriving a financial benefit from the visit, the entrant should receive a high level of care. Thus, a customer in a shop was the quintessential invitee.[9]

**[12.09]** We need no longer concern ourselves with attempting to identify the parameters of this category, which did not survive the 1995 legislation. We may merely note that the concept of a material advantage was somewhat broader than requiring a financial dimension, though it was generally accepted that social guests were not invitees.[10] The courts also took the long view on what constituted a material advantage. Thus the occupier, who clearly had a material interest in receiving deliveries of milk, bread or food to his or her home,[11] was considered to have a similar interest when the milkman or other delivery person came to the premises later, looking for payment. So also a customer going back to a shop with a complaint about a product was still regarded as an invitee. In *Thomas v Leitrim County Council*,[12] McCracken J was willing to accept that attracting tourists into an area was a sufficent material interest to render a visitor to Glencar Waterfall, which was open to the public, an invitee.

---

9. *Foley v Musgrave Cash and Carry Ltd* Supreme Court, 20 December 1985, extracted in McMahon & Binchy, *A Casebook on the Irish Law of Torts* (2nd ed, 1991); *Mullen v Quinnsworth t/a Crazy Prices* [1990] 1 IR 59 (SC); *Mullen v Quinnsworth t/a Crazy Prices* (No 2) [1991] ILRM 439 (SC) analysed, respectively, by Byrne & Binchy, *Annual Reveiw of Irish Law 1990*, pp 518-520 and Byrne & Binchy, *Annual Review of Irish Law 1991*, pp 393-395. *Cf Duffy v Carnabane Holidays Ltd* [1996] 2 ILRM 86, analysed by Byrne & Binchy, *Annual Review of Irish Law 1996*, pp 587-589. Other examples of invitees were: a person who paid a fee for a conducted tour of a castle (*Collier v Earl of Mountcharles* Supreme Court, 19 December 1969), a visitor to a tourist amenity (*Thomas v Leitrim County Council* [1998] 2 ILRM 74 (HC)), a paying patron at a dance (*Kelly v Woolworth* [1922] 2 IR 5 (CA)), people on a premises for refreshments, while using toilet facilities (*Reaney v Thomas Lydon & Son Ltd* [1957] Ir Jur 1; *O'Donoghue v Greene* [1967] IR 40), a stevedore on deck superintending the unloading of a cargo from a berthed ship (*Long v Saorstát & Continental Steamship Co Ltd*, (1959) 93 ILTR 137), employees (*Christie v Odeon (Ireland) Ltd* (1957) 91 ILTR 25 (SC), *Kenny v Irish Shipping Ltd* Supreme Court, 4 November 1968; *Sisk (John) & Sons Ltd v National Silo Ltd*, [1963] IR 319 (SC affg HC); *Redmond v Equipment Company of Ireland Ltd* High Court 28 July 1992 (Budd J) - employee working on defendant's premises as a security guard, a boy living with his family, who were tenants in the defendant's flat complex (*O'Toole v Dublin Corporation*, High Court, 18 February 1994 (Lynch J)), and the wife of a tenant while on the property to which all the tenants had resort, but which was retained by the landlord in the lease (*Geraghty v Montgomery* [1953] IR 89).

10. The fact that the entrant was a friend or relation, however, did not prevent him or her from being elevated to the status of invitee if the entrant performed acts of clear economic benefit, such as child minding: *cf Shelton v Creane and Arklow UDC* High Court, 17 December 1987 (Lardner J), analysed by Byrne & Binchy, *Annual Review of Irish Law 1987*, pp 324-325, 331-332. See also *O'Neill Garvan v Brennan* (1988) 7 ILT (ns) 319 (CC), analysed by Byrne & Binchy, *Annual Review of Irish Law 1988*, pp 428-429. In *Doyle v Magill* [1999] 2 ILRM 66 (HC), a social guest was treated, without debate, as an invitee.

11. *Cf Parkinson v Peelo* (1939) 73 ILTR; *Cooney v Dockrell* [1965] Ir Jur 31; *Daly v Greybridge Co-op Creamery Ltd* [1964] IR 497.

12. [1998] 2 ILRM 74 (HC) analysed by Byrne & Binchy, *Annual Review of Irish Law 1997*, pp 740-744.

**[12.10]** The duty owed to an invitee was stated by Willes J in the leading case of *Indermaur v Dames*:

> "[W]ith respect to such a visitor, at least, we consider it settled law, that he, using reasonable care on his own part for his own safety, is entitled to expect that the occupier shall on his part use reasonable care to prevent damage from unusual danger which he knows or ought to know, and that where there is evidence of neglect, the question whether such reasonable care has been taken by notice, lighting, guarding, or otherwise, and whether there was contributory negligence in the sufferer, must be determined by a jury as a matter of fact ..."[13]

**[12.11]** Much judicial energy was expended on the question of when a danger should be regarded as "unusual".[14] Summarising a complex and not always consistent body of case law, it may be said that the answer depended, not on the statistical infrequency of the danger as an empirical occurrence, but rather on the normative issue of whether the danger was one that the invitee might reasonably have expected to encounter.

**[12.12]** The Irish courts treated invitees in one important respect more favourably than did their English counterparts.[15] Recognising that Willes J had imposed a duty to use reasonable care to prevent damage from unusual dangers, they held that a warning of unusual danger would not discharge that duty unless it left the invitee in the position, in the light of receiving it, that he or she could safely proceed to do what he or she had come onto the premises to accomplish.[16]

***(c) Licensees***

**[12.13]** Licensees were entrants who came onto the property with the occupier's permission (express or implied) but who conferred no material benefit on the occupier. They could range from social guests[17] to children whose presence on the premises for their own purposes was tolerated without objection by the occupier.[18]

**[12.14]** The occupier's duty was limited to warning the licensee of concealed dangers[19] of which the occupier was actually aware. Thus, there was no duty to warn of dangers that

---

13. (1866) LR 1 CP 274 at 287. Section 34(2)(e) of the Civil Liability Act 1961, ensured that the contributory negligence of the invitee should lead to apportionment of damages rather than constituting an obstacle to the establishment of a duty on the part of the occupier. See further WILLIAMS, para 77. For a detailed analysis of the duty owed to invitees under Willes J's test, see the first edition of this work, pp 238-243 (1981).

14. See the first edition of this work, pp 239-40. See also *Doyle v Magill* [1999] 2 ILRM 66 (HC), analysed by Byrne & Binchy, *Annual Review of Irish Law 1999* (Torts Chapter).

15. *Horton v London Graving Dock* [1951] AC 737 (HL). This decision was one of the reasons why legislative reform, culminating in the Occupiers' Liability Act 1957, was deemed an urgent necessity in England.

16. See the first edition of this work, pp 240-42.

17. *Southcote v Stanley* 1 Hurl & N 247, 156 ER 1195 (Ex). See, however, *Doyle v Magill* [1999] 2 ILRM 66 (HC).

18. *Cf Boughton v Bray UDC* [1964] Ir Jur 57; *Cooke v Midland GW Ry Co of Ireland* [1909] AC 229 (HL). Other examples include: the owner of a car admitted, by a mechanic after hours, to the garage where the car was kept (*Perry v Statham Ltd* [1929] IR 277); a delivery man on the tenant's business while crossing, of necessity, property retained by the landlord (*Ahearne v Rudd* [1945] Ir Jur 45; *cf Parkinson v Peelo* (1939) 73 ILTR 218); worshippers visiting a church (*Kirwin v Representative Church Body* [1959] IR 215);

were patent to the particular licensee, nor was there any duty to go beyond a warning even where the warning would not, in itself, effectively protect the licensee from the danger. An occupier who was not aware of a hidden danger, but which he or she ought to have known was not liable to the licensee for this omission. If, however, the occupier was in fact aware of all the facts that constituted the hidden danger but for some reason failed to appreciate the danger, liability would be imposed.[20]

***(d) Trespassers***

**[12.15]** At common law, a trespasser was, and under the recent legislation still is, as a person who enters (or remains) on property without the express or implied consent of the occupier. Clearly a burglar is a trespasser but many other less unpleasant people must also be so characterised. A neighbouring child who persists in coming onto the property to collect his ball after a clear prohibition may be considered a trespasser as may a tipsy guest who refuses to go home when the party is over.

## III. Trespassers

### Trespassers Defined

**[12.16]** This branch of the law was drastically overhauled twenty five years ago in Ireland. After *McNamara v ESB* was handed down by the Supreme Court in 1975, the duty owed to trespassers in Ireland was the duty to take reasonable care. The Occupiers' Liability Act 1995, however, has reversed this and has restored the old pre-*McNamara* common law standard, that is, that the duty owed to trespassers is not to injure them intentionally and not to act with reckless disregard their person or property. All the common law case law on this branch of the law, which had become largely redundant during the period 1975 to 1995, is once more very relevant in determining what recklessness means in this context. Furthermore, the judicial techniques which were developed to mitigate this harsh common law rule must all be revisited as they represent real options for a judiciary wishing to avoid a draconian rule in particular situations.

---

18. (contd) *Rooney v Connolly* [1987] ILRM 768); people resorting to public parks and playgrounds (*Ellis v Fullam Borough Council* [1938] 1 KB 359 (CA)); a pupil at school (*Bohane v Driscoll* [1929] IR 428; and a person who had with others frequently used, without objection, a short cut through a development lot (*Mangan v Finglas Housing Society* (1952) 86 ILTR 159). In *Leahy v Leader and Cork Diocesan Trustees* High Court, 13 October 1999, McCracken J held that no liability attached to the defendant Parish Priest when a person taking a shortcut through Church grounds which were open to the public, was bitten by a dog owned by other persons who were drinking cider on the Church grounds. The judge held that the dog ("Lassie type collie") was no a concealed danger. The incident occurred in 1994 and the Occupiers' Liability Act 1995 did not apply. The case is also considered in Ch 27.

19. The courts emphasised that the quality of being concealed lay, not in the danger itself, but in the perception of the licensee. Thus the same phenomenon - a burning candle for example - might be a patent danger for an adult but a concealed danger for a child: *Rooney v Connolly* [1987] ILRM 768 (SC); *Boughton v Bray UDC* [1964] Ir Jur 57; *Bohane v Driscoll* [1929] IR 428. In *Rooney*, Hederman J put the matter well: "Clearly the danger may be obvious to the child's eyes, but equally clearly it may be concealed from her understanding or appreciation."

20. *Cf Rooney v Connolly* [1987] ILRM 768.

**[12.17]** It was commonly said at common law that the occupier owed no duty to a person coming on to the premises as a trespasser. The trespasser as a wrongdoer was entitled to little or no consideration and it used to be said that he or she was certainly not entitled to that degree of care reserved for contractual entrants, invitees and licensees.[21]

**[12.18]** A qualification, however, was hastily added: the occupier (even when the law was most indulgent to his or her interests) might do no act that was intended to injure or was so reckless as to be likely to injure the trespasser, whose presence was known or ought to have been known. In this connection, however, it was well said that:

> "The exact limits of the act otherwise lawful, which he is under an obligation to a trespasser to refrain from doing, are more difficult to define; but I am prepared to hold that neither upon principle nor authority can they extend beyond acts done with the wilful intention of doing harm, and acts the direct and immediate effect of which would be to do harm to a trespasser".[22]

**[12.19]** Accordingly, a trespasser could not complain if he or she fell down a defective stairway, but would of course have a good action against the occupier if the latter shot him or her simply because he or she was trespassing. Similarly, and for the same reason, the occupier could not set spring-guns and the like which were really designed to injure trespassers who came on to the premises.[23] A nice distinction, which still survives, was made here by the courts; they declared that the occupier was entitled to keep potential trespassers off his or her property and to this end to erect a barbed wire fence or a spiked-wall; once on the premises, however, the trespasser might not be recklessly or intentionally injured. Preventive or deterrent measures were thus permitted; retributive measures were not. Accordingly, a trespasser who fell into a dangerous excavation in a private road,[24] or who was injured by a savage horse,[25] or who was injured by falling through a window the sash of which had been removed[26] could not recover.[27]

**[12.20]** With regard to the acts of the occupiers as opposed to the condition of the premises the following passage from *Salmond* was quoted with approval by Kingsmill Moore J in *Landy*'s case.[28]

> "... the occupier is liable even to a trespasser for positive acts of negligence misfeasance done by himself with knowledge of the trespasser's presence. The occupier's exemption from any duty of care to a trespasser applies only to the dangerous state of the premises, not to acts done on the premises with knowledge of the trespasser's presence. He who shoots upon his land owes a duty of care not only to persons lawfully there, but also to trespassers whom he

---

21. *Donovan v Landy's Ltd* [1963] IR 441 at 459, where all the important cases, English and Irish, are reviewed.
22. *Coffey v McEvoy* [1912] 2 IR 95 at 111, (*per* Palles CB); (affd [1912] 2 IR 290; see also *Tiernan v O'Callaghan* (1944) 78 ILTR 3.
23. *Bird v Holbrook* 4 Bing (1828) 628, 130 ER 911.
24. *Murley v Grove* (1882) 46 JP 360.
25. *Lowery v Walker* [1910] 1 KB 173, revd on other grounds [1911] AC 10.
26. *Coffey v McEvoy* [1912] 2 IR 290.
27. See also *Kenny v ESB* [1932] IR 73; *Waters v O'Keefe* [1937] Ir Jur Rep 1.
28. *Donovan v Landy's Ltd* [1963] IR 441 at 450.

knows (or perhaps reasonably ought to have known) to be there. He must not act with reckless disregard of such persons."

**[12.21]** Kingsmill Moore J then continued:

> "I consider this to be a correct statement of the effect of the authorities for us, except that, in Ireland at least, the word 'perhaps' should be omitted."[29]

**[12.22]** Three arguments in particular seem to have been responsible for the "hard line" adopted by the judiciary *vis-à-vis* the trespasser at common law:

(i) the trespasser was a wrongdoer and as such was entitled to no protection from the law;

(ii) the trespasser was usually not anticipated and so could not reasonably be provided for;

(iii) the occupier's position as a land occupier ought not, according to the laissez-faire theory, be unduly clogged and cluttered by duties imposed for the benefit of persons not lawfully on the land.

**[12.23]** These arguments, however, are not as cogent nowadays as they appeared in the 19th century when they were first formulated. In the first place, it is generally recognised nowadays that the mere fact that a person is a wrongdoer does not *ipso facto* deprive him or her of all rights in law. This was clearly shown by the legislation[30] in which it was established that contributory negligence was no longer an absolute bar to recovery in negligence.[31] Similarly, "... a man does not forfeit his rights by becoming a trespasser and is not *caput lupinum* to be treated as the occupier pleases."[32] In *Kearney v Clare Lime Co Ltd*,[33] the plaintiff was injured while standing on the tow-bar of the defendant's spreading machine. The trial judge, holding the plaintiff was a trespasser, said there was, therefore, no case to go the jury. On appeal to the Supreme Court it was held that, even if the jury found that the plaintiff was a trespasser, whether the defendant company was in breach of the duty to such a trespasser was a further question to be answered by the jury. A new trial was accordingly ordered. From this it can be seen that a trespasser even at common law was entitled to some measure of care, however small that measure was. The modern viewpoint was put even more cogently by Pearson LJ, in an English case[34] in 1963, when he stated:

---

29. See para **[12.34]** below for meaning of recklessness. This is also the proper way in which cases like *Breslin v Brennan* [1937] IR 350, and *Griffin v Daniels* (1952) 86 ILTR 38 should be interpreted. In both of these cases children, who had been playing around stationary vehicles and who had been warned off by the driver, had remounted again unknown to the driver, and were injured when the vehicle was put in motion. In both cases the plaintiff child recovered.

30. Section 57(1) of the Civil Liability Act 1961 provides that it is not a defence in an action of tort merely to show that the plaintiff is in breach of the civil or criminal law. *Cf* see para **[12.114]** below.

31. *Cf* s 34. See further para **[20.48]-[20.33]** below.

32. *Tiernan v O'Callaghan* (1944) 78 ILTR 36 at 38 (CC).

33. [1966] IR 338 See now *Brennan v Savage Smyth & Co Ltd* [1982] ILRM 223 a "scutting" case which was dealt with on pure negligence principles.

34. *Videan v British Transport Commission* [1963] 2 QB 650 at 678.

> "It is true that the trespasser commits his wrong against the occupier, but the occupier is not entitled to have his revenge by being less mindful of the trespasser's safety than some other person ought to be in the same situation."

**[12.24]** Moreover, as already mentioned, it is no longer fair to picture the trespasser as a wrongdoer in all cases; in modern conditions the most innocent people can become trespassers. Nor is it reasonable to say that the trespasser by his wrongdoing has consented the injury. Secondly, it is frequently untrue nowadays to say that the trespasser is not anticipated. Many of the cases show that the trespasser was not only anticipated but had been warned by the occupier on previous occasions. If the occupier is not to be held liable in these cases it must be on the grounds other than he did not anticipate the trespasser's presence. In some cases it is closer to the truth to say he knew or ought to have known of his presence. Thirdly, the political and social system which perpetuated the privileged position of the landed classes has collapsed. The laissez-faire theory has been supplanted by somewhat more communitarian values, and the availability of liability insurance has meant that the owners and occupiers of property can, for what is still generally a relatively modest premium, insure themselves against these potential losses.

**[12.25]** For these reasons, a leavening process had become evident in the judicial attitude towards the trespasser even before the Supreme Court took the bold stop of applying ordinary negligence principles to the trespasser in *McNamara v ESB*[35] in 1975. Before that the judiciary moved more discreetly, unable in common law decency to overthrow completely the old rules with regard to the trespasser's position. These were too firmly ensconced by the doctrine of precedent to be lightly set aside, and so any liberalizing approach had, of necessity, to be worked out within the framework of the already existing rules. This humane judicial effort was especially evident in the following developments:

***(a) Frequent trespassers***

**[12.26]** Frequent trespasses which were known by the occupier to occur and which were not prevented by him were increasingly construed by the courts as licences simply because of their frequency and because of the inactivity of the occupier. This tendency is even more evident where the entrants also happened to be children.[36]

***(b) Child trespassers***

**[12.27]** It is clear from the case law that infancy *per se* did not create a duty of care. If a duty of care existed, infancy might increase the amount of care required of the occupier, but infancy alone could not create a duty if none would exist to an adult in the same circumstances.[37] As Lord Dunedin said in the *Addie* case:

> "The truth is that in cases of trespass there can be no difference in the case of children and adults, because if there is no duty to take care that cannot vary according to who is the

---

35. [1975] IR 1.

36. *Cooke v Midland GW Ry Co of Ireland* [1909] AC 229; *Mangan & Another v Finglas Housing Society* (1952) 86 ILTR 159. See also *Commissioner for Railways (NSW) v Cardy* (1960) 104 CLR 274.

37. *Kenny v Electricity Supply Board* [1932] IR 73, esp at 91; *Addie & Sons v Dumbreck* [1929] AC 358; *Tiernan v O'Callaghan* (1944) 78 ILTR 36.

trespasser. It is quite otherwise in the case of licensees, because there you are brought into contact with what is known as a trap ..."[38]

**[12.28]** This reasoning is not easy to follow, and the whole argument collapses once the premise (that there is no duty to trespassers) is questioned. The truth is that the occupier has always owed some duty to trespassers, albeit a limited one: he never could intentionally or recklessly cause them injury and, in deciding whether the defendant was reckless or not, that the trespasser was a child was a relevant factor.[39]

**[12.29]** The courts, however, chose a different method of assisting the child who came on to premises as a trespasser. They showed an increasing tendency to hold that a child-trespasser could have his status raised from that of a trespasser to that of a licensee if it could be shown that he was at an age when he would "follow a bait as mechanically as a fish" and that the occupier's premises contained "an allurement". Once the infant was categorised as a licensee it is not difficult to prove that the danger was a concealed danger *vis-à-vis* a child of such tender years.[40] This allurement theory has operated greatly for the benefit of children.

**[12.30]** Once this concession was made, however, there was a natural and inevitable attempt by the judiciary to delimit the area of its own interference. It should cause no wonder, therefore, that in defining what was an "allurement" in law, the courts offered a fairly restricted definition. To be an "allurement" in law, it was declared that the object had to be both "fascinating and fatal".[41] In *O'Leary v John A Wood Ltd*,[42] Kingsmill Moore J, declared that:

> "... an object should not be considered an allurement unless the temptation which it presents is such that no normal child could be expected to restrain himself from intermeddling even if he knows that to intermeddle is wrong."

**[12.31]** On the facts of that case he held that a low-loader on tow through Cork city did not possess these hypnotic or fascinating qualities, and did not, in that particular instance, amount to an allurement. The same judge said in *Donovan v Landy's Ltd*[43] that a bread-van on which children were stealing rides, by inserting their fingers through perforated holes in the rear of the van while the vehicle was in motion, was not an allurement:

> "I am of opinion that though, together with every other vehicle on which a child can find a place to perch, it afforded an attractive opportunity for trespass, yet it did not possess that combination of compulsive temptation and concealed danger which may involve liability to an infant intermeddler, by converting his status from that of a trespasser to a licensee."[44]

**[12.32]** This restrictive definition of allurement, however, must be understood as simply being an attempt by the judiciary to impose reasonable limits on the creature they

38. [1929] AC 358 at 376.
39. *Donovan v Landy's Ltd* [1963] IR 441 at 463.
40. See *Bohane v Driscoll* [1929] IR 428; *Boughton v Bray UDC* [1964] Ir Jur 57.
41. *Latham v Johnson* [1913] 1 KB 398.
42. [1964] IR 269 at 277.
43. [1963] IR 441. For more recent approach to this problem see *Brennan v Savage & Smyth* [1982] ILRM 223.
44. [1963] IR 441 at 446.

themselves had created, and as such was merely the last step in the natural process of judicial law-making. To give but two examples, a turn-table for train engines on railway property[45] and a gullytrap on a public road[46] have both been held by Irish courts to possess the qualities of fascination and fatality that would make them allurements in law.

**[12.33]** The foregoing examples of judicial goodwill in favour of the trespasser attempted to assist the latter by upgrading him into the licensee category, thereby qualifying him for a higher standard of care. It is interesting that these judicial devices will be possible options for the judiciary now that trespassers and recreational users are distinguished from other visitors under the 1995 legislation. But judicial ingenuity was also evident in the interpretation of the word "recklessness", the word which was, and once more is, the limit of the occupier's duty to the trespasser. In an effort to spread the net of liability, and catch the occupier within the haul, the judiciary at common law, interpreted this word very liberally.

***(c) Recklessness***

**[12.34]** Two questions in particular need to be asked at this point: first what is the difference between reckless conduct and unreasonable conduct?; secondly, is the occupier to be liable only for injuries caused to trespassers of whose presence he actually knows or is he also to be liable to trespassers whose presence he should reasonably expect?

**[12.35]** In dealing with the above two problems, the Irish courts have not given separate answers but have preferred to treat the second question as one aspect of the first. They have defined recklessness from an objective rather than from the subjective point of view of the occupier and in doing so the second question melts into, and is really only one aspect of, the first question. The higher the probability of trespassers being present, the greater the likelihood that the conduct of the occupier would be reckless.[47]

**[12.36]** The adoption of the objective standard of recklessness, as opposed to the subjective attitude of the occupier, may be seen as the development of a rule favouring the trespasser and this may especially be true when one looks at some of the cases where the defendant's conduct was construed as having been reckless.[48]

**[12.37]** A realisation that "objective recklessness" is the criterion that has been used by the courts in this area, helps to clear away much of the confusion that surrounds the case-law here, for, in applying the criterion of "recklessness" all the considerations relevant to ordinary negligence became relevant except that the impact of their cumulative effect had to be greater if the trespasser (as opposed to the "legal neighbour") was to recover. Both the neighbour and the trespasser had the same hurdle to clear if they were to recover, but in the case of the trespasser the cross-bar was raised a little higher. And so considerations like the gravity of the risk, the likelihood of the injury, whether the trespasser was a child, the probability of his presence on the property, the cost of prevention, etc, were all relevant in

45. *Cooke v Midland Great Western Railway Co of Ireland* [1909] AC 299.

46. *Swift v Westport UDC* [1944] IR 259.

47. *Donovan v Landy's Ltd* [1963] IR 441, especially at 462. See also *Griffin v Daniels* (1952) 86 ILTR 38; *Breslin v Brennan* [1937] IR 350.

48. See eg *Breslin v Brennan* [1937] IR 350; *Fleming v Kerry Co Council* [1955] Ir Jur Rep 71; *Griffin v Daniels* (1952) 86 ILTR 38; *Tiernan v O'Callaghan* (1944) 78 ILTR 36.

the case of the trespasser as well as in the case of the "neighbour", and this factor may explain why so many of the cases in this area at common law seem to have been decided on straight negligence principles rather than by the criterion of recklessness. The truth of the matter seems to be that the courts in these cases were not looking for negligence, despite some misleading language, but were in reality searching for "objective recklessness".[49]

**[12.38]** Nevertheless, in some of the cases, especially those which involve trespass on motor vehicles, one sometimes had the distinct feeling that what the court was talking about was negligence rather than recklessness. This is not so surprising when one remembers that the area in which the negligence criterion is more frequently used in tort law concerns motor collisions; perhaps the courts sometimes forgot that where a trespasser was injured by falling off a motor vehicle the principles that governed the situation were those concerned with occupiers' liability, rather than straight negligence principles. Furthermore, it seems fair to say that in the case where the injury resulted from an activity (a misfeasance as opposed to a nonfeasance) the courts were more likely to apply ordinary negligence principles, or a least a more generous interpretation of recklessness, and in most of the trespass-on-vehicles cases the damage is, in fact caused when the vehicle is put in motion.

***(d) Nuisance near highway***

**[12.39]** Another area where one might expect judicial activity in favour of trespassing plaintiffs is where the occupier maintains a dangerous condition close to the highway. To be injured, it is true the road-user must leave the road and become a trespasser, but the trespass is only a "little one" and frequently the injury can be serious.

**[12.40]** The traditional cause for recovery here has been under the tort of nuisance:

> "A rotten fence close to a highway is an obvious nuisance. If I were on the highway and wanted to tie my boot, or got tired and leaned against the fence, should I not have been lawfully using the highway?[50]
>
> [T]he defendant, in having made the excavation, was guilty of a public nuisance, even though the danger consisted in the risk of accidentally deviating from the road."[51]

The law reports are full of such statements.[52]

**[12.41]** Contrary to what one might expect from the few cases that have come before the Irish courts there has not been great enthusiasm on the part of the judiciary to extend the occupiers' liability in this situation under the rubric of nuisance. Indeed, there seems to have been a reluctance on the part of the plaintiffs to proceed in public nuisance, at all, and this is probably due to the fact that "if there was no liability in public nuisance, it was fatally easy to argue that there could be no liability at all."[53]

---

49. See cases cited in last note. Also *Malynn v Farrell* (1956) 90 ILTR 137.

50. *Harrold v Watney* [1898] 2 QB 320 at 322

51. *Barnes v Ward* (1850) 9 CB 392 at 420, 137 ER 945 at 956.

52. If the plaintiff deliberately left the highway he or she may not be able to recover. Contrast *Smyth v Keys* (1912) 46 ILTR 68 with *Fitzgerald v Brangan* (1905) 39 ILTR 116.

53. Marsh 'The History and Comparative Law of Invitees, Licencees and Trespassers' (1953) 69 LQR 182 at 187.

## A New Approach to Trespassers (and Other Entrants?) 1974-1995

**[12.42]** The English or Northern Ireland law on trespassers was not changed by the Occupiers' Liability legislation introduced in those jurisdictions in the late fifties so that the hard line approach to trespassers that characterised the common law in this matter continued in these jurisdictions for some time afterwards. Some improvement, however, was brought about by the House of Lords' decision in *British Railways Board v Herrington*[54] in 1972.

**[12.43]** At the risk of oversimplifying, the Court decided in that case, that if the occupier knows or as good as knows of the presence of a trespasser and that there is a likelihood of serious danger then a duty of care arises. When the duty arises the content of the duty requires the occupier to act in a "humane manner". Although there may be some uncertainty as to what humaneness meant in the present context it seems clear that while it falls short of requiring the occupier to act with reasonable care, it certainly requires something more of the occupier than that he should avoid reckless conduct.[55]

**[12.44]** The Supreme Court in Ireland was given an opportunity to restate the law on this matter two years later in *McNamara v Electricity Supply Board*.[56] The facts of the case were as follows: The plaintiff , an eleven-year-old boy, having climbed over a wire fence which surrounded an electricity transformer station, was injured when, in an effort to catch the drain-pipe and slide down from a flat-roofed addition to the station, his hand came in contact with a high tension cable some 13 inches distant from the drain-pipe. Since the original station was first built, in 1929, and since the flat-roofed addition was built in 1956, the area around the station had become considerably built-up and the danger which the station offered to children was well appreciated by the authorities. At the time of the accident the wire fencing surrounding the station was being repaired and, so far from acting as a barrier, actually facilitated access to the flat-roofed addition to the station. In the High Court the jury found that the defendant was negligent and that the plaintiff had not been guilty of contributory negligence; it awarded damages in the amount of £74,772. The defendant appealed to the Supreme Court against the whole judgment. All the judges in the Supreme Court held that the damages were excessive and three of the five judges found that the jury below was wrong in finding that the plaintiff was not guilty of contributory negligence. A retrial on all issues was ordered. For our purposes, however, the interesting portions of the Supreme Court's judgment relate to the long discussion on the legal basis of the defendant's liability to injured trespassers. Only three judgments were issued in the case,[57] as Fitzgerald CJ concurred with Griffin J and Budd J concurred with Walsh J; the other judgment was issued by Henchy J.

---

54. [1972] AC 877. For analysis, see Weaver 'The Occupiers' Liability to Trespassers - Still a Problem Child?' (1973) 3 Kingston LR 72.

55. See McMahon 'Occupiers' Liability in Ireland' in *Reform of Law of Occupiers' Liability in Ireland* (1975) Prl 4403. See also *Pannett v P McGuinness & Co Ltd* [1972] 2 QB 599 and *Southern Portland Cement Ltd v Cooper* [1974] AC 623; *cf* Symmonds, (1974) 37 MLR 468. For an application of *Herrington* in Northern Ireland see *Lowery v Buchanan* [1982] NI 243 (CA).

56. [1975] IR 1.

57. Fitzgerald CJ did deliver a judgment in Court but died before he was able to certify it. It seems that his view of the law, on the present issue, favoured a retention of the *Addle* formulation and he recommended a retrial on all issues.

**[12.45]** Briefly, the three judgments were in basic harmony, not only that *Addie* (and *Donovan v Landy's Ltd*,[58] its Irish equivalent) should be abandoned, but also that the rule relating to the occupier's duty towards trespassers should be restated in a form that would better reflect modern concepts of justice on the matter. *Herrington's* case was cited with approval but a more valuable line was taken from the earlier Irish case of *Purtill v Athlone UDC*.[59] In that case a boy who had been on the premises of an abattoir and who had stolen some detonators from the premises was injured when he was exploding them at his home. Walsh J delivering the judgment of the Court stated the duty of the occupier in such circumstances in the following terms:

> "When the danger is reasonably foreseeable, the duty to take care to avoid injury to those who are proximate, when their proximity is known, is not abrogated because the other party is a trespasser. The duty of those in proximity is not based on any implied term of an invitation or a licence, or upon any warranty for safety which might be thought to be inherent in any such invitation or licence. Rather it is based upon the duty that one man has, to those in proximity to him, to take reasonable care that they are not injured by his acts. What amounts to sufficient care must vary necessarily with the circumstances, the nature of the danger, and the age and knowledge of the person likely to be injured."[60]

**[12.46]** In short, it seems that the Court in *McNamara* decided that the occupier owed a duty to trespassers whom he could reasonably foresee and that the duty in such case was to take such reasonable care as the circumstances demand.

**[12.47]** A few quotations will undoubtedly illustrate the Court's attitude. Walsh J having examined the common law on the matter and having examined *Purtill*'s case, posed the following question:

> "Was it reasonably foreseeable to the defendants that the children might enter their premises unless reasonable steps were taken to keep them out? On the evidence placed before the jury, I think they were quite entitled to answer that question in the affirmative. The question must then arise of whether the steps taken by the defendants to keep out children were, in all the circumstances, reasonable. Again, on the evidence before the jury, I think the jury was quite entitled to answer that question in the negative."[61]

**[12.48]** Later in his judgment he made the following statement:

---

57. (contd) Information supplied by the late Niall McCarthy, SC, one of the plaintiff's counsel in the case, who later became a Judge of the Supreme Court. Judgments supplied by the Supreme Court office merely state that Fitzgerald CJ concurred with Griffin J but do not give the Chief Justice's judgment as delivered in Court. A judgment culled from reporter's notes is given in the Irish Reports. See [1975] IR 1 at 4.
58. [1964] IR 441.
59. [1968] IR 205. Although *Purtill* might be seen as a dangerous products case it was clearly dealt with as an occupiers' liability case by the context.
60. [1968] IR 205 at 212. It is extraordinary that a Supreme Court decision, on almost identical facts, and given 11 years previously was not referred to by counsel or by the Court itself. In *Byrne v McDonald* High Court, 7 February 1957, the Supreme Court, in giving a decision in favour of the plaintiff, ordered a retrial. The unsatisfactory state of law reporting then prevailing in Ireland must be blamed for this oversight.
61. [1975] IR 14.

> "The known physical facts were the condition of the fence, its proximity to the building, the habit of the local children to play around the immediate area of the fence. In those circumstances it was the duty of the defendants to take reasonable steps to ensure that the children, or any of them, would not be able to enter the danger area. In a case such as the present, that means taking reasonable steps to prevent the children trespassing."[62]

**[12.49]** In attempting to assess the full implications of *McNamara* a few general remarks may be appropriate. First, in so far as the Supreme Court in *McNamara* opted for the reasonable care standard it was opting for a standard with which the Court was comfortably familiar. True, in its application to specific cases, the reasonable care standard could prove as elastic as *Herrington's* "humane" test, but the Supreme Court was not as apprehensive about its own preferred standard as it might have been for the novel criterion suggested in *Herrington*. Secondly, the Irish solution seemed to avoid the problems that arose in England in the wake of *Herrington*, namely, whether trespassers must be "extremely likely", whether a higher duty is owed when the occupier has "created" the danger and whether non-occupying contractors owe a higher duty than the occupier. Thirdly, the subjective element in *Herrington* - that the trespasser must take the occupier as he finds him and that more might be expected of an occupier with great resources - does not seem to have found express favour in *McNamara*: Nevertheless, since the relationship of occupier and trespasser is one thrust upon the occupier against his wishes, the courts must inevitably have regard to the occupier's resources in determining what is reasonable.[63]

**[12.50]** The greatest problem with *McNamara*, for Irish lawyers, however, related not to trespassers at all but to invitees and licensees. What was the effect of *McNamara* on *Indermaur v Dames* and on *Fairman v Perpetual Investment Building Society*?[64] In England when the House of Lords was addressing itself to the problem of the trespasser in *Herrington* it had a clear pitch in which it could do so. The problems relating to invitees and licensees had already been dealt with by the legislature in the Occupiers' Liability Act 1957. In Ireland, however, the common law rules relating to invitees and licensees had never expressly been overruled. Could it be argued that they had been impliedly overruled in 1974 by *McNamara*? The argument for such a proposition was as cogent as it was simple: surely the trespasser was not entitled to a higher standard of care than the lawful entrant? If the trespasser was elevated, surely the invitee and the licensee must likewise be

---

62. See also Griffin J's judgment with whose judgment Fitzgerald CJ, concurred, to the same effect. Henchy J, also favoured a straight negligence approach (*cf* [1975] IR 25). But other parts of his judgment may not be without difficulty (*cf* At 24). Henchy J's tendency there to divide the issue of due care into several elements, each of which must be established separately by the trespasser, would make it harder for the trespasser to succeed in his action. This propensity was also apparent in *Keane v ESB* [1981] IR 44. where Henchy J placed emphasis on the foreseeability of the trespasser's entry as a threshold issue to be determined in isolation; only where that issue was resolved in the trespasser's favour should the court address the question whether the occupier had failed to take reasonable steps to prevent the entry and the consequent injury.

63. It is interesting to note that, in England, s 1 of the Occupiers' Liability Act 1984 favours the *McNamara* approach in replacing the subjective test applied in *Herrington* regarding the occupier's resources by an objective test: see SALMOND & HEUSTON, p 281.

64. [1923] AC 74.

raised? It would certainly be anomalous if the invitee and the licensee had still to concern themselves with "unusual dangers" and "concealed dangers".[65]

**[12.51]** Nowhere in the *McNamara* decision did the court address itself to this problem, however, and the spotlight of uncertainty that focussed for so long on the trespasser shifted after *McNamara* to the invitee and licensee.

**[12.52]** *McNamara* did not usher in the general negligence principles to the area of invitees and licensees without question. The tenacity of the old classifications meant that a new regime would not be born without a difficult labour. In 1983, in *Redford v Courtown (Co Wexford) Golf Club*,[66] a visiting golfer, who was injured when he mistook a glass panel for the door itself, was awarded substantial damages. The trial judge instructed the jury in the traditional terminology of invitees, "usual dangers" and "ought to know". Similarly, in 1984, the Supreme Court, in an action taken by the widow of the deceased contractor who had fallen through a perspex skylight, dismissed her case on the grounds, *inter alia*, that the deceased was not an invitee and the danger was not an unusual one.[67] *Rooney v Connolly*[68] also saw the Supreme Court, albeit for curious procedural reasons, still willing to trade in the old "licensee-concealed danger" coinage.

**[12.53]** The *Rooney* case went to trial in the High Court before the decision in *Foley v Musgrave Cash and Carry Ltd*.[69] In this latter case the Supreme Court was prepared to extend the *McNamara* approach to the area of invitees. It appeared after *Foley* that the stratification of entrants with their distinctive rights had been swept away. In *Foley* an invitee tripped over a shopping trolley in a wholesaler's cash and carry shop. The defendants appealed to the Supreme Court and an award of damages was made in favour of the plaintiff. McCarthy J in reply to the defendant's argument that there was no unusual danger, held that we should no longer be talking about "unusual dangers" in this type of case, and that the general negligence approach was to be preferred.[70] Griffin J, while

---

65. However, see *Coughlan v The Mayor, Aldermen and Burgesses of Limerick* (1977) 111 ILTR 141, a Circuit Court decision where the old approach seems to have been applied. Also *Rooney v Connolly* [1987] ILRM 768.

66. Irish Times, 11 November 1983, p 13.

67. *Daly v Avonmore Creameries Ltd* [1984] IR 131. Some passages of Henchy J are more ambiguous and could be interpreted as favouring the new approach.

68. [1987] ILRM 768.

69. Supreme Court, 20 December 1985. See also *Murphy v O'Brien* (1987) 6 ILT (ns) (CC) where Sheridan J preferred to apply on straight negligence in relation to an intoxicated plaintiff who fell in a pub. See Byrne & Binchy, *Annual Review of Irish Law 1987*, pp 324-325, 332, and pp 123-124. In *Mullen v Quinnsworth Ltd (No 1)* [1990] 1 IR 59 and *Duffy v Carnabane Holdings Ltd* [1996] 2 ILRM 86, the Supreme Court adopted an unencumbered standard of reasonable care in relation to invitees, with no indication that this represented a change in the law. In *Clancy v Commissioners of Public Works in Ireland* [1992] 2 IR 460 and *Duggan v Armstrong* [1992] 2 IR 161, McCarthy J maintained his campaign against differentiating the duties owed to invitees and licensees respectively.

70. Earlier in *Daly v Avonmore Creameries Ltd* [1984] IR 131 at 138, McCarthy J, in a dissenting judgment, had signalled his views:

> "I am by no means satisfied that the Court should look any longer to the artificial concepts derived from a Common Law founded upon property to determine issues of legal liability more properly related to the proximity between individuals -be they private individuals or corporate ones."

admitting that the plaintiff was an invitee, stated that nowadays the duty of the defendant was to take reasonable care in all the circumstances to see that the premises were reasonably safe for the invitee. And in this, it mattered not to Griffin J whether one used this test or Walsh J's test in *Purtill*,[71] or Lord Atkin's test in *Donoghue v Stevenson*.[72] Finlay CJ, the third member of the court, agreed with both judgments but did not deliver a separate judgment of his own.

**[12.54]** *Rooney*, delivered in 1986, caused greater negligence uncertainty in this area. Clearly, general principles did not yet rule in respect of licensees, and it could be said that *Rooney* also cast doubt as to whether the general negligence principles applied to invitees in spite of *Foley*.

**[12.55]** *McNamara* represented a brave judicial attempt to remedy the trespasser's position. Unfortunately, it also indicated the problems that arise when sweeping reform is attempted by way of judicial decision. The general principle that legislation was the most efficient means of effecting substantial reform in our system was still valid. In the particular sphere of occupiers' liability, *McNamara's* case hardly reduced the arguments for statutory reform.[73]

## IV. THE HOTEL PROPRIETORS ACT 1963[74]

**[12.56]** An interesting statutory provision should also be noted at this stage. According to s 4 of the Hotel Proprietors Act 1963:

> where a person is received as a guest at a hotel, whether or not under special contract, the proprietor of the hotel is under a duty to take reasonable care of the person of the guest and to ensure that, for the purpose of personal use by the guest, the premises are as safe as reasonable care and skill can make them.

**[12.57]** From this it would seem that a guest's statutory right against a hotel proprietor is wider than an invitee's right against an invitor at common law and a visitor's claim under the Occupiers' Liability Act 1995. For, as it is phrased in the statute, it would seem that the hotel proprietor is also liable for the acts of his independent contractors. That this section is intended to extend the hotel proprietor's liability, rather than to consolidate the common

71. *Purtill v Athlone UDC* [1968] IR 205.

72. [1932] AC 562.

73. The statement of the law in *McNamara* was endorsed in *O'Keeffe v Irish Motor Inns Ltd* [1978] IR 85. See also *Keane v ESB* [1981] IR 44. It is interesting to note that in both of these cases the liberalisation of the law by the *McNamara* decision did not enable the trespassers to recover. Fears that *McNamara* would open the floodgates appear to have been unfounded. In *Ross v Curtis* High Court, 3 February 1989 (Barr J) an action by an intruder against the defendant (a supermarket owner) who, it was alleged, negligently discharged a .22 calibre rifle and injured him, failed. The court accepted that the defendant believed he was being attacked and intended to fire a warning shot only. Unfortunately, the defendant had failed to aim the gun sufficiently high. Barr J was satisfied that the defendant had acted reasonably in all the circumstances and had not been reckless.

74. See Anon, (1963) 28-29 Ir Jur 19, McDonald 'Reform of the Hotel Proprietors Act 1963' [1999] Internat Travel J 156.

law position, seems to be affirmed by sub-s (2) of s 4 which declares that the "... duty is independent of any liability of the proprietor as occupier of the premises."

**[12.58]** Section 4 has provoked a paucity of litigation in spite of the hig level of casre which it demands of hotel proprietors.[75] Nor should s 7 of the Act[76] (a section which imposes a financial limit of £100 on the proprietor's liability) discourage a s 4 action since this limitation applies only to damage to the guest's property and does not apply to an action under s 4 for personal injuries. This omission by plaintiffs' lawyers is all the more extraordinary when it is realised that the hotel proprietor is prohibited from contracting out of his or her liability by s 9 of the 1963 Act. Such an action, however, is of course confined to hotel "guests" and does not extend to other lawful visitors. The 1963 Act does not define "guests", but it appears to cover persons on the premises for food and drink: apparently one does not have to contract for sleeping accommodation to be a guest. Decisions on the earlier legislation were clearly to this effect.

## V. The Occupiers' Liability Act 1995

**[12.59]** Let us now turn to consider the radical changes brought about by the Occupiers' Liability Act 1995.[77]

**[12.60]** The 1995 Act marginally improves the position of some entrants, essentially by stating in legislative terms what was generally presumed to be the existing law but without a definitive judicial authority putting the matter beyond doubt. The more distinctive feature of the legislation, however, is that it reduces the extent of occupier's obligations to trespassers and to "recreational users" (a new concept) of the premises. The 1995 Act was the product of a strong lobby by farming organisations, supported by organisations, such as hunting and fishing groups, who were concerned with the recreational use of agricultural property. The voice of the trespasser, notably the adventurous urban child, was

---

75. See *Duggan v Armstrong*, [1993] ILRM 222 (SC), analysed by Byrne & Binchy, *Annual Review of Irish Law 1992*, pp 588-591. McCarthy J's judgment may be criticised for addressing the liability issue under common law without refering to the relevant decisions on the duty owed to invitees and for dismissing the argument that s 4 of the 1963 Act imposes an additional duty on the hotel proprietor with the laconic observation that he found it "difficult to discern the nature of this case". Section 4(2) could not be clearer that the duty imposed by s 4(1) is *independent* of the hotel proprietor's liability as occupier. McCarthy J's approach may be contrasted with that of Blayney J in *Coleman v Kilternan Hotel and Golf Club Ltd* Supreme Court, 19 July 1996, where he described the test laid down by s 4 as being "if anything ... the more stringent test" than that at common law.

76. A decision on a similar statutory provision of limitation of liability - the Innkeepers Act 1863, s 3 - was construed in *O'Connor v Grand International Hotel Co* [1898] 2 IR 92 (QB).

77. For analysis of the 1995 Act, see Hall 'The Occupiers' Liability Act 1995: Codification of Occupiers' Duty to Entrants' (1989) 89 Incorp L Soc of Ireland Gaz 189; MacNamee 'The Occupiers' Liability Act 1995: A Farewell to *McNamara v ESB*' (1997) 1 Ir Ins L Rev 3; Shannon 'Public Liability' (1998) 2 Ir Ins L Rev 47, 72; Doherty, Annotation to the Act, ICLSA; Walsh, *Agriculture and the Law* (1996), Ch 9 and Byrne & Binchy, *Annual Review of Irish Law 1995*, pp 493-518. For a perceptive examination of the policy issues, see O'Dell, 'Reform of Occupiers' Liability?' Part 2 (1992) 86 Incorp L Soc of Ireland Gaz 359 at 361-363. The Act came into effect on 17 July 1995, one month after the date of its passing: s 9(2).

not heard. Where politicians are responding to a lobby from one side of an argument, there is always the danger of lopsided legislation. Undoubtedly there are important social and economic reasons for taking steps to ensure that agricultural land will remain open to hikers and other recreational users; tourism would not be well served by farmers turning their holdings into fortresses. One may nonetheless wonder whether a coherent case, from the standpoint of justice, was made out in favour of releasing occupiers from the duty of care to trespassers, especially in crowded urban environments where the trespasser is a child. The concerns of the members of the Law Reform Commission on this matter[78] suggest that the legislation may have gone too far in aid of the occupier.

## The Lobby is Marshalled

**[12.61]** Around a decade ago, a fear arose in the agricultural community when it became plain that no lawyer could give an assurance that a claim brought by a trespasser or recreational user of a farmer's lands, arising from injuries sustained on the lands, would inevitably fail. The right legal advice was surely that, in the light of *Purtill* and *McNamara*, a farmer is in principle capable of falling under a duty of care to either of these entrants but that the requirements of proximity and foreseeability would ensure that an undue burden of care would not be placed on the farmer - unless the court was affected by sympathy for the injured plaintiff or the insurance company decided, on cost considerations, to settle. Two further points could be made to ease the farmer's anxiety. First, there was no volume of cases in which courts had shown themselves hostile to farmers in relation to negligence claims; indeed, for a country where agriculture has such an important role, there was a surprising dearth of reported litigation on the subject. Secondly, the cost of insurance in this area was very small indeed, so small that the issue for farmers was apparently one of principle rather than of practical economics.

**[12.62]** Nevertheless, the fear, once planted, grew to awesome dimensions and became the basis of a strong political lobby. The farmers' organisations were less than happy with the Law Reform Commission's recommendations on the subject. They kept up the pressure and the legislation that ultimately went onto the statute book represents a victory for those interests.

## The Main Features of the Act

**[12.63]** Under the 1995 Act, persons who come onto another persons premises are divided into three categories: (i) visitors; (ii) trespassers and (iii) recreational users. By and large, a visitor means an entrant who is lawfully on the premises of the occupier, and is there either at the invitation or with the permission of the occupier or at the invitation or with the permission of a member of the occupiers family. It would also include persons who are present on the premises by virtue of an express or implied term in the contract, or persons who are on the premises as of right. The category of visitor, broadly speaking, encompasses entrants who formerly would have been categorised as contractual entrants, invitees and licensees, but with one important exception. A new concept of recreational user is introduced. This is an entrant who, with or without the occupier's permission, enters premises without a charge, to engage in a recreational activity, such as hiking or hunting or

78. In its Consultation Paper on *Occupiers' Liability* (1993) and its *Report on Occupiers' Liability* (LRC-1994).

exploring caves or visiting buildings of historical or scientific interest. Clearly, under the former law, a recreational user would normally be categorised as a licensee; courts were disposed to take a broad view of what amounted to implied permission to be on the occupier's lands.

**[12.64]** Briefly speaking, the occupier owes a duty of care ("its common duty of ease") to a visitor, and this duty is defined in the act as a duty "to take such care as is reasonable in all the circumstances ... to ensure that a visitor to the premises does not suffer injury or damage by reason of any danger existing thereon." This duty of care is akin to the standard of care in ordinary negligence, and like the ordinary duty in Negligence it may be affected by the plaintiff's own contributory negligence. More interestingly, the occupier's "common duty of care" may be reduced when the injured person is on the premises in the company of another person who may be expected to supervise the visitor, such as would be the case where a child visitor is accompanied by its, parent, its supervisor, or its minder.

**[12.65]** Trespassers and "recreational users", however, are not treated so generously under the act. Under the new dispensation, the occupier does not owe any duty of care in negligence to recreational users or trespassers with regard to dangers due to the state of the premises. All that the occupier must do is ensure that he or she does not injure the recreational user or trespasser intentionally or act with reckless disregard for the recreational user or trespasser. This change represents the overturning of *Purtill* and *McNamara*, not just in the agricultural context but in respect of all premises, urban and rural. The trespassing child in a large city, just as in an open field, is no longer owed a duty of care by the occupier *qua* occupier.

**[12.66]** Other important features of the legislation include the restriction of duty owed to criminal entrants - in regard to whom occupiers are now free to act recklessly; the introduction of an entitlement on the part of the occupier to restrict the scope of his or her duty to visitors under the legislation, by express agreement or by reasonable notice; and the preservation by the 1995 Act of special defences (such as self-defence and defence of property) and special duties (notably the duty of an employer to his or her employees). Let us now turn to examine the provisions of the legislation in detail.

***(a) The scope of liability***

**[12.67]** A crucial limitation in the legislation is that it relates only to dangers due to the state of the premises.[79] Thus, what are known as "activity" duties remain unaffected by the Act. If, for example, an occupier fells a tree or knocks down a wall on his or her land or drives a vehicle there, the activity will be judged by the negligence standard, regardless of the status of the entrant.[80]

---

79. Section 1(1).

80. *Cf* FLEMING, pp 506-507. It is worth bearing in mind that an occupier may be liable for negligent misrepresentation in respect of a danger on the premises, whether resulting from the state of the premises or an activity taken place there. Here the only "activity" is the representation itself. In *Power v Crowley and Reddy Enterprises* High Court, 29 October 1992, Blayney J imposed liability on an occupier for what, in essence, was regarded as a negligent misrepresentation about the condition of a wall. The holding in the case seems somewhat harsh on the facts: see Byrne & Binchy, *Annual Review of Irish Law 1992*, pp 591-592.

**[12.68]** The problem here is that, for the past two decades and more, Irish courts have not been required to make the conceptual distinction between "activity" and "occupancy" duties because frankly the outcome of the case would not be affected by it. A trespasser who was owed the duty of care could invoke the negligence standard however the facts were characterised.

**[12.69]** Now that the legislation draws this crucial distinction between "activity" and occupancy duties, courts will be obliged to address the issue. Clearly it will be in the interests of a trespasser or recreational user to rest the case on an "activity" rationale since then the occupier can be held to a standard of negligence, assuming, of course, that the plaintiff is considered by the court to have sufficient proximity and foreseeability to generate a duty of care on the part of the "active" occupier.

**[12.70]** Who is to say when the facts of the case should be characterised one way or the other? Very often the plaintiff's story will include elements of passive "occupancy" default coupled with an activity on the part of the defendant. Neither element of the whole picture can easily be identified as predominant.

**[12.71]** *Smith v Coras Iompair Éireann*,[81] is a good example of this characterisation dilemma. The plaintiff, who came onto the defendant's railway line by means of a wall that had not been kept fully repaired, could point to either the train (active) or the wall (passive occupancy) as the basis of liability. In truth, his case depended on a complex intermingling of both elements. The plaintiff's case was defeated by insufficient proximity and lack of foreseeability.[82]

**[12.72]** It is worth noting in this context that, in respect of a danger existing on premises, s 4(1)(b) imposes on the occupier the obligation "not to act with reckless disregard" for the person or property of the recreational user or trespasser. Of course it is quite possible to envisage acts by an occupier that are distinctively centered upon dangers due to the state of the premises. For example, an occupier might excavate ground near a building rendering it unsafe. There are, however, other cases where the act of the occupier has some connection with the state of the premises but that connection does not feature centrally in the manner in which the recreational user or trespasser is injured. For example, a farmer spraying a crop with material that is injurious to inhale might carelessly turn the hose in the direction of the recreational user or trespasser. The activity of spraying seems undoubtedly one that creates a danger "due to the state of the premises", but could not the injured recreational user or trespasser claim that the injury from the misdirected hose had such an immediate and intimate nexus with the careless activity that, in spite of the fact that the activity generated a danger in respect of the premises, it should nonetheless be capable of being characterised as negligent activity rendering the farmer liable in a straightforward negligence action taken by the recreational user or trespasser?

**[12.73]** Would the position be different if, ten minutes after the farmer had stopped spraying the crop, another recreational user or trespasser entered the field, inhaled the spray and was injured? The notion of a danger "due to the state of the premises" connotes some element of continuity over time. But for how long?

---

81. [1991] 1 IR 314.

82. *Cf* Byrne & Binchy, *Annual Review of Irish Law 1990*, pp 508-513.

### *(b) Who are occupiers?*

**[12.74]** Formerly, "occupation", for the purposes of occupiers' liability, was identified with the right to exclude. Gradually the element of control became crucial. Courts came to accept that the concept of control is a relative rather than absolute one and that it is possible for more than one person to be an occupier in this sense.[83]

**[12.75]** Section 1(1) of the 1995 Act provides that an "occupier", in relation to any premises, means:

> a person exercising such control over the state of the premises that it is reasonable to impose upon that person a duty towards an entrant in respect of a particular danger thereon and, where there is more than one occupier of the same premises, the extent of the duty of each occupier towards an entrant depends on the degree of control each of them has over the state of the premises and the particular danger thereon and whether, as respects each of them, the entrant concerned is a visitor, recreational user or trespasser.

**[12.76]** This amalgam of questions of responsibility and control is a source of potential confusion, since the court, in determining whether or not a particular defendant is an "occupier" - a threshold characterisation issue - is in some sense engaging, even inchoately, in an assessment of the liability issue.[84]

### *(c) The concept of "premises"*

**[12.77]** Under the 1995 Act "premises" include not only land, water and any fixed or moveable structures on land or water but also vessels, vehicles, trains, aircraft and other means of transport:[85] This breadth of definition reflects the former common law. When it is recalled that one may sue only in relation to a danger "due to the state of the premises"[86] it becomes clear that there is no prospect of running-down cases succeeding under the Act. A passenger who was burned by defective electrical fittings in a vehicle would, however, have a right of action under s 3, if a visitor, or s 4 otherwise. "Activity" duties are still dealt with under the common law principles.

### *(d) Who are visitors?*

**[12.78]** A "visitor" for the purposes of the Act, is:

(1) an entrant as of right (such as a member of the Garda Síochána or a fire fighter, for example);

(2) an entrant, other than a recreational user (of which more anon), who is present on premises by virtue of an express or implied term in a contract (such as a patron of the local cinema, for example);

(3) an entrant (other than a recreational user) who is present on premises at the invitation, or with the permission, of the occupier (such as a shop customer or a social guest, for example, or a person permitted to be on the premises for his or her own purposes); and

(4) an entrant present on premises on which "recreational activities" are capable of taking place, without a charge being imposed for the purpose of engaging in a recreational activity, where the entrant is:

83. *Cf Wheat v Lacon* [1996] AC 552.
84. *Cf* HOWARTH, p 371.
85. Section 1(1).
86. Section 1(1).

(a) a member of the occupier's family who is ordinarily resident on the premises;

(b) an entrant who is present at the express invitation of the occupier (or family member of the occupier);

or

(c) an entrant who is present with the permission of the occupier (or member of his or her family) for social reasons connected with the occupier (or family member).[87]

**[12.79]** Broadly speaking, therefore, visitors are those entrants who would formerly have been categorised as contractual entrants, as of right, invitees and licensees, save for those licensees who fall within the definition of "recreational user". One is a visitor while he or she is present on the premises for the purpose for which he or she is invited or permitted to be there, for the purpose of the performance of the contract or for the purpose of the exercise of the right. So if a person invited onto premises engages in conduct inconsistent with that purpose he or she loses the status of visitor and becomes a trespasser. The legislation has removed any uncertainty that might formerly have attached to the status of a shoplifter, for example.

***(e) The occupier's duty to visitors***

**[12.80]** An occupier owes what is called "the common duty of care" towards a visitor.[88] This is a duty to take such care as is reasonable in all the circumstances to ensure that a visitor does not suffer injury or damage by reason of any danger existing on the property.[89] In essence the test is that of reasonable care; in other words, the same as the negligence criterion of common law.

**[12.81]** Some points about this duty may be noted. First, in determining what care is reasonable in the circumstances, the court must have regard to the care which a visitor may reasonably be expected to take for his or her own safety and, if the visitor is on the premises in the company of another person, the extent of the supervision and control the latter person may reasonably be expected to exercise over the visitor's activities.[90] Thus, an occupier is entitled to take into account that an adult normally can look after his or her own welfare; but this general expectation may, of course, have to be modified where the occupier is or ought to be aware that an adult visitor is more vulnerable, on account of mental incapacity, for example. Similarly, when a child comes onto the premises in the company of an adult, the occupier may normally place some reliance on the likelihood that the adult will take reasonable care of the child, but again circumstances may alter the strength of this reliance and in no case may an occupier contend that, merely because the adult was in charge of the child, the occupier was relieved of any duty of care towards the child.

**[12.82]** Secondly, the common duty of care towards visitors applies in all cases save where it is extended, restricted, modified or excluded in accordance with s 5. We shall see, when considering s 5, that the occupier is not permitted to reduce the level of his or her duty

87. The term "visitor" is defined in s 1(1).

88. Section 3(1).

89. Section 3(2).

90. Section 3(2).

below that owed to recreational users and trespassers, which requires the occupier not to injure these entrants intentionally or act with reckless disregard for them.[91]

### *(f) What are recreational activities?*

**[12.83]** The legislation defines "recreational activity" as meaning:

> any recreational activity conducted, whether alone or with others, in the open air (including any sporting activity), scientific research and nature study so conducted, exploring caves and visiting sites and buildings of historical, architectural, traditional, artistic, archeological or scientific importance.[92]

**[12.84]** Thus, most obviously, such activities as hunting, shooting, fishing, hiking and picnicking will come within the earlier part of the definition. A few points should be noted. First, the reference to scientific research is limited to cases where it takes place in the open air, but visiting a building of scientific importance also comes within the scope of the definition. Secondly, the only indoor activities envisaged by the definition, apart from exploring caves, consist of "visiting sites and buildings of historical, architectural, traditional, artistic, archeological or scientific importance". Obviously a visit to an ancient tower or castle to examine it from an historical, architectural, traditional, artistic, archeological or scientific standpoint will fall within the scope of the definition, but what about the case where a person enters a building of this kind with no such lofty purpose? Take, for example, a person who goes to a three-hundred-year old house to canvass for a political party. Is he or she engaging in a "recreational activity", for the purposes of the Act, because, as a matter of definition, the house is admittedly of scientific importance? The "right" answer, from the standpoint of the policy of the 1995 Act, is of course in the negative; but the drafting is not as clear as one might have wished. As we shall see presently, the legislation excludes three categories of entrant from the definition of "recreational user", but the political canvasser does not fall within any of these categories.

**[12.85]** Perhaps the courts would interpret the expression "visiting" in a narrow way as being limited to cases where the motivation for entry springs from a concern for the historical (or other definitionally-relevant) aspect of the building.

### *(g) Who are recreational users?*

**[12.86]** The legislation defines a "recreational user" as:

> an entrant who, with or without the occupier's permission or at the occupier's implied invitation, is present on premises without a charge (other than a reasonable charge in respect of the cost of providing vehicle parking facilities) being imposed for the purpose of engaging in a recreational activity, including an entrant admitted without charge to a national monument pursuant to section 16(1) of the National Monuments Act 1930, but not including an entrant who is present and is -
>
> (a) a member of the occupier's family who is ordinarily resident on the premises,
>
> (b) an entrant who is present at the express invitation of the occupier or such a member, or
>
> (c) an entrant who is present with the permission of the occupier or such a member for social reasons connected with the occupier or such member.[93]

---

91. *Cf* s 4.
92. Section 1(1).
93. Section 1(1).

**[12.87]** Several points about this definition are worth noting. First, as is plain, to be a recreational user, one must not have paid for the privilege of entry (other than for parking one's car). Thus, owners of ancestral homes who charge members of the public to see around the building are required to discharge the "common duty of care" to the entrants, who are visitors rather than recreational users.

**[12.88]** Secondly, the three exclusions are obviously necessary to ensure that those who are not in truth recreational users should retain their entitlement to hold the occupier to the common duty of care. We have suggested already that the political canvasser (or other entrant who has no interest in the recreational potential of the premises) should also be entitled to the common duty of care. It is unfortunate that so much has to depend on the scope of the term "visiting" in the definition of "recreational activity".

**[12.89]** Thirdly, it is worth reflecting on the implications of the exclusion from the definition of "recreational user" of an entrant who is present at the express invitation of the occupier or a member of the occupier's family. If the occupier (or family member) meets a would-be recreational user and welcomes him or her onto the land, there is a danger that this will raise the entrant's status to that of visitor. At what point does casual civility give way to an "express invitation"? If there is a doubt on the matter, should solicitors be advising occupiers of agricultural land or of historical sites to shun conversations with would-be recreational users lest they be transformed into visitors?

**[12.90]** It appears clear that, to fall within the definition of "recreational user", the entrant must be present on the premises for the purpose of engaging in a recreational activity. It might be thought that the reference to such a purpose should be read as part of the phrase "without a charge ... being imposed for the purpose of engaging in a recreational activity", and that therefore, if no such charge is imposed, the entrant's purpose is of no further relevance to the definition. Such an interpretation cannot be right, since it would mean that all entrants on the premises would have to be characterised as recreational users if present at the occupier's implied invitation or with or without the occupier's permission, unless either a charge was imposed for engaging in a recreational activity or they fell within one of the three exceptions specified in paragraphs (a), (b) and (c) of the definition. Manifestly that was not the intent of the Oireachtas. The more plausible interpretation, therefore, is that, to be a recreational user, the entrant must be present for the purpose of engaging in a recreational activity. Note that the definition does not require that the recreational user should have entered the premises with this purpose: all that is necessary is that he or she be "present" there with this purpose. It would seem, therefore, that a person who came onto the premises without this purpose, either as a visitor or as a trespasser, could in certain circumstances change his or her status by forming the purpose of engaging in a recreational activity. It is not necessary that the occupier be aware of the purpose. Thus, an entrant's status can depend on a state of mind that may or may not be known, or knowable, to the occupier.

**[12.91]** Further uncertainties are attached to the definition of "recreational user".[94] Section 1(1) defines a recreational user as an entrant who, "with or without the occupier's

94. We are grateful to Dr Clive Symmons, Research Associate of the Law School of Trinity College, for identifying these uncertainties.

permission or at the occupier's implied invitation", is present on the premises, in the circumstances prescribed by the subsection. The absence of the occupier's permission, prior to the legislation, rendered an entrant a trespasser. The effect of the definition is thus to remove from certain trespassers this stigmatic character and to place them into a different, new, category.

**[12.92]** Since the 1995 Act imposes on the occupier the same duty in relation to both trespassers and recreational users in all circumstances save those falling within the scope of s 5(4), this transformation of status for unpermitted entrants may seem to be a matter of no importance, but it does raise a question about the occupier's entitlement to prevent such entrants from coming on to the premises or to exclude them once they have entered the premises, as well as the implications for the traditional rules of law in this context. An occupier is under common law entitled to use reasonable force to prevent a trespasser from coming onto the property or to expel the trespasser. Section 8 of the legislation provides that nothing in the 1995 Act is to be construed as affecting any enactment or rule of the law relating, inter alia, to "the defence of property". If the traditional rule of law relating to the entitlement to exclude trespassers is unaffected by the legislation, does this mean that the occupier is not permitted to prevent entry by, or to expel, a recreational user who wishes to be, or is, on the premises without the occupier's permission? The answer must surely be that an occupier is still entitled to prevent entry or to expel any entrant on the premises without the occupier's consent. The fact that some entrants without consent are not characterised as trespassers under the 1995 Act does not change the fundamental basis of the entitlement to exclude, which is the absence of consent to be on the premises rather than the particular label attached by particular legislation to particular entrants. The idea that an occupier would be obliged to tolerate without redress the unpermitted presence of entrants on his or her property seems quite unconvincing.

**[12.93]** In this context it is useful to consider the position of children. The definitions of "recreational activity" and "recreational user" are capable of embracing children. Certainly children are not excluded from them, thought it is fair to say that the definition of "recreational activity" connotes a degree of purposeful maturity that is not easy to ascribe to the carefree activities of childhood. If some children go into a neighbour's garden and play tig there, this can no doubt be designated a "recreational activity ... in the open air," but the children may be oblivious of the location of the game and certainly pay no attention to whether it is indoors or in the open air. They fall within the definition accidentally, as it were.

**[12.94]** The point is of crucial importance because of the distinction in duties owed to a visitor and a recreational user. Under the legislation, an entrant who is present with the permission of the occupier will be a visitor, and will be owed a high level of care, even though he or she confers no economic benefit on the occupier, unless the entrant is a recreational user. There thus are many entrants who would formerly have been characterised as licensees who are now designated visitors. They will be reduced to the lower category of recreational user only if they are present for the purpose of engaging in a recreational activity. When children come onto a neighbour's premises, they may intend to have a game of tig; often, they will have no particular game plan. Mooching is part of the condition of being young; it is a collaborative exercise. Yet the legislation makes a crucial distinction in relation to their status, and the level of care owed to them, on the basis of whether or not they formed a sufficiently focused intention to characterise their purpose as being to engage in a recreational activity.

**[12.95]** So alien is this line of enquiry from the reality of childhood experience that one is forced to look again at the definition of "recreational activity". It is at least worth arguing that the courts should construe the concept narrowly, so as to embrace only activities that are of greater focus and organisation than mooching, even if the moochers kick a stone or a ball (a "sporting activity") as they progress somewhat aimlessly through their neighbour's property. This is not to suggest that the concept requires any particular formality: an ad hoc game of football, with three a side, is surely a sporting activity for the purpose of the definition. It may well turn out that the courts will disdain any attempt to distinguish between activities on the basis suggested above and will characterise as recreational users all children engaging in open-air activities who do not fall within the exceptions specified in the definition.[95]

***(h) Who are trespassers?***

**[12.96]** A trespasser, for the purposes of the legislation, is an entrant other than a recreational user or visitor.[96] Thus, one can be a "good" or "bad" trespasser, a mischievous child or a burglar. Later in the 1995 Act, distinctions are made between different types of trespasser. The purpose of committing (or attempting to commit) an offence or the commission of an offence on the premises radically reduces the scope of the duty owed to the entrant.[97]

***(i) Duty owed to recreational users and trespassers***

**[12.97]** An occupier, in respect of a danger existing on premises, owes recreational users and trespassers on the premises only the limited duty not to injure them or damage their property intentionally and not to act with reckless disregard for them or their property.[98] The occupier is not required to discharge the standard of reasonable care (the "common duty of care"), which visitors can insist upon by virtue of s 3. The owner is, of course, free to extend this duty, by express agreement or notice in accordance with s 5(1).

**[12.98]** In determining whether or not an occupier has acted with reckless disregard for a recreational user or trespasser (or his or her property), the court must have regard to all the circumstances of the case, including nine factors specified in s 4(2). It may be useful to identify these nine factors and say a few words about some of them.

*Whether the occupier knew or had reasonable grounds for believing that a danger existed on the premises*

**[12.99]** We have seen that, at comon law, prior to the legislation, an occupier would be held liable to an invitee for failure to protect an invitee from an unusual danger of which the occupier was, or ought to have been aware.[99] We have also noted that the duty to a licensee

95. For consideration of the legal status of children engaging in recreational activities on school premises outside school hours, see para **[16.46]-[16.64]** below.

96. Section 1(1).

97. Section 4(3).

98. Section 4(1).

99. *Indermaur v Dames* (1866) LR 1 CP 274.

was far more restricted: it arose only where the danger was a hidden one, of which the occupier was actually aware. Thus a failure - even if culpable - to be aware of a danger immunised the occupier against liability to a licensee. This factor might at first sight seem to apply to recreational users and trespassers the level of duty formerly appropriate to invitees but this is not so. The court is required to have regard to this factor among nine specified factors, which in turn are but elements of the entirety of the circumstances of the case. Sections 4(2) does not give any indication or guidance as to what should be the implications of a finding that the occupier had knowledge of the danger or that he or she had reasonable grounds for believing that it existed. Nothing crucial attaches to their finding; it is but part of the tapestry of facts in relation to which the court is to form a view as to the issue of reckless disregard.

*Whether the occupier knew or had reasonable grounds for believing that the person and, in the case of damage, the property of the person, was or was likely to be on the premises and whether the occupier knew or had reasonable grounds for believing that the person or property of the person was in, or was likely to be in, the vicinity of the place where the danger existed.*

**[12.100]** We can consider these two factors together. Even under the progressive principles of *Purtill* and *McNamara*, the courts required a high degree of foreseeability of a trespasser's presence on the property in the danger area. This is evident from such Supreme Court decisions as *Keane v ESB*,[100] *O'Keeffe v Irish Motor Inns Ltd*,[101] and *Smith v Coras Iompair Éireann*,[102] for example. Again there is no express requirement under s 4(2) to dismiss a case taken by a trespasser (or recreational user) whose presence was not highly foreseeable. This factor is part of the picture; the court must have regard to it; but it is not in itself a reason for dismissing a case where other factors, in the totality of circumstances, weigh in favour of the plaintiff.

*Whether the danger was one against which, in all the circumstances, the occupier might reasonably be expected to provide protection for the person and property of the person*

**[12.101]** This provision echoes s 1(1)(c) of England's Occupiers' Liability Act 1984, which was the legislature's response to the House of Lords decision in *British Railways Board v Herrington*.[103] It is singularly devoid of factual specificity and frankly, in view of the inclusion of the eight other factors, adds almost nothing to the quality of the judicial assessment of the recklessness issue.

*The burden on the occupier of eliminating the danger or of protecting the person and property of the person from the danger, taking into account the difficulty expense or impracticability, having regard to the character of the premises and the degree of the danger of doing so*

**[12.102]** This factor is inherent in all assessments of whether or not the defendant in a negligence action should be held to have breached the duty of care. For example, in *Callaghan v Killarney Race Co*,[104] Kingsmill Moore J stated:

---

100. [1981] IR 44 (SC).
101. [1978] IR 85 (SC).
102. [1991] 1 IR 314 (SC) analysed by Byrne & Binchy, *Annual Review of Irish Law 1990*, 508-515.
103. [1972] AC 877 (HL).
104. [1958] IR 366 at 375 (SC).

> "In judging what a reasonable and prudent man would think necessary, more than one element has to be considered. The rarity of the occurrence must be balanced against the gravity of the injury which is likely to ensue if the occurrence comes about, and some consideration must be paid to the practicality of precautions suggested."

**[12.103]** In that case, the defendants, who were race-course proprietors, were held not to have been negligent in failing to provide a double fence at a hurdle sufficiently durable to prevent a horse from crashing through it. Kingsmill Moore J observed that, if there was to be an obligation to double fence the whole perimeter or to surround it with an unbreakable fence, "the expense might well put an end to many of the smaller race-courses or involve a higher price for admission".

**[12.104]** In the context of the 1995 Act, this calculation of the balance of advantage will take place at the level of recklessness rather than of negligence but the calculus is similar.

*The character of the premises including, in relation to premises of such a character as to be likely to be used for recreational activity, the desirability of maintaining the tradition of open access to premises of such a character for such an activity*

**[12.105]** This factor reminds the court of the policy considerations that inspired the enactment of the legislation. If the law lays too heavy a burden on occupiers, they will withdraw the permission they gave to recreational users to come on their lands.

*The conduct of the person, and the care which he or she may reasonably be expected to take for his or her own safety, while on the premises, having regard to the extent of his or her knowledge thereof*

**[12.106]** The inclusion of conduct as a factor to be considered by the court ensures that a distinction may be made between "innocent" trespassers, such as young children, for example, and "guilty" trespassers, such as burglars, thieves and entrants who will not leave when asked. We shall see presently, that there is a specific additional provision[105] dealing expressly with entrants who commit an offence or enter the premises for that purpose.

*The nature of any warning given by the occupier or another person of the danger*

**[12.107]** This factor, in contrast to s 5(5), relating to warnings to visitors, makes the nature of every warning given to the recreational user or trespasser an element to be assessed in conjunction with all the other circumstances of the case. There is no rule of law requiring an occupier to give the recreational user or trespasser a warning in every, or any specific, case. It may be, of course, that in a particular case the court will conclude that the failure to have given a warning renders the occupier liable, having regard to all the circumstances or that a particular warning was so deficient that the occupier should be held to have been reckless.

*Whether or not the person was on the premises in the company of another person and, if so, the extent of the supervision and control the latter person might reasonably be expected to exercise over the other's activities.*

**[12.108]** An occupier might reasonably expect that an adult in charge of children will take proper care of them when on the occupier's premises. This is not an inflexible rule, however. There will be some cases where it is clear the adult is not exercising proper care:

---

105. Section 4(3).

many people have had the experience of wondering whether to intervene in situations of danger to children where their parents seem blithely unaware of the risk. Of course it is possible for an injured child to sue parents for negligence.[106] This does not happen in practice for several reasons, not least the fact that parents are rarely insured for this type of liability. A theoretical right of joinder of the parents is of little comfort to the occupier.

### *(j) The nature of "recklessness" under the Act*

**[12.109]** It is clear from consideration of the several factors prescribed in the legislation that recklessness connotes objective default rather than necessarily requiring any subjective advertence on the part of the occupier to the risk of injury. An occupier who culpably failed to discover, or who forgot about, a particular danger will not on that account be relieved of liability. In favouring the objective test of recklessness, the legislation is merely echoing the approach formerly adopted by the Irish courts, in relation to the occupier's duty to trespassers, before the *Purtill/McNamara* reform.[107] One can only speculate about the extent to which the courts are in practice going to set the standard at a lower level than the (equally objective) standard of reasonable care. The 1995 Act gives no guidance as to how much lower the level should be. The nine factors specified in s 4(2) contain no such yardstick; indeed, they might constitute a trap to an unwary judge who could easily seek to apply them without adverting to the fact that, although they are similar to criteria applicable for determining the issue of negligence, they have to be pitched at a level more indulgent to the defendant.

### *(k) Criminal entrants*

**[12.110]** The spectre of liability to a burglar or other law-breaker haunted the Oireachtas Debates. Non-lawyers have great difficulty in contemplating that an occupier could ever owe such unpleasant entrants any duty of care. The solution adopted by s 4(3)(a) of the legislation is that the occupier should be relieved of the obligation not to act with reckless disregard of a person who enters onto premises for the purpose of committing an offence or a person who, while present on premises, commits an offence there. An "offence", either intended or actually committed, embraces an attempted offence.[108]

**[12.111]** A few points about s 4(3) should be noted. First, the immunity is not absolute: it does not apply in a case where a court determines otherwise "in the interests of justice". It is impossible to predict with any degree of certainty how the court will exercise this function. One may anticipate that it would be disposed to hold occupiers to the recklessness standard where the offender was very young or the offence was trivial - such as picking a flower.

**[12.112]** Secondly, it is not necessary that the person should have entered the premises where the injury occurs for the purpose of committing an offence there. A would-be thief who enters one premises as a means of access to another, where he intends to steal, falls within the section. Conversely, a person who goes into a café to pass the time before a bank robbery has not entered the cafe "for the purpose of" committing an offence, but merely

106. *Cf* para **[16.02]-[16.15]** below.

107. *Cf* para **[12.34]** above.

108. Section 4(3)(b).

with the intention of doing so afterwards, there being no connection between the café and the bank.

**[12.113]** Thirdly, the occupier is relieved only of the duty not to act with reckless disregard for the entrant; he or she is still under the duty not to injure the entrant (or damage the entrant's property) intentionally. In some cases, of course, that obligation will in turn be "trumped" by the occupier's entitlement to use proportionate force for his or her self-defence, the defence of others or the defence of property.[109]

**[12.114]** Finally, one should not ignore the entitlement of the court, without prejudice to s 4(3), to discuss proceedings taken by a plaintiff on the basis of the *ex turpi causa* principle. The scope of this principle in Irish law is not entirely clear. What is beyond argument is that the mere fact that the plaintiff is in breach of the law is not, of itself, a defence in an action in tort.[110]

### *(l) Structures on premises*

**[12.115]** An occupier owes a duty to take reasonable care to recreational users in one situation: this is where a structure on premises is provided for use primarily by recreational users. The occupier must take reasonable care to maintain it is a safe condition.[111] A few comments about this requirement are warranted.

**[12.116]** First, the kinds of structure here envisaged include such equipment as playground slides, benches in public parks and viewing points in scenic areas.

**[12.117]** Secondly, it is not necessary that the occupier should have provided the structure; a duty of reasonable care with respect to its maintenance attaches to the occupier even where someone else provided it. As a result, "if the Office of Public Works has built a stairway or gate to allow access to a national monument on private land, it is the landowner who is responsible if it becomes dangerous".[112] Certainly, the landowner has a duty of care, by virtue of s 4(4). The subsection does not purport to exclude the duty of care resting on the Office of Public Works. Whether such a duty of care arises and, if so, has been discharged will of course depend on the particular circumstances of the case. It is possible that, in the particular circumstances, the Office of Public Works could have retained sufficient control over the stairway or gate or fall within the definition of 'occupier' in s 1(1).

**[12.118]** Thirdly, s 4(4) contains a proviso to the effect that:

> where a stile, gate, footbridge or other similar structure on premises is or has been provided not for use primarily by recreational users, the occupier's duty towards a recreational user thereof in respect of such structure shall not be extended by virtue of this subsection.

**[12.119]** This provison appears to be otiose, since the duty of reasonable care arises in the first place only where the structure "is or has been provided for use primarily by recreational users".

---

109. *Cf* s 8(a).
110. Civil Liability Act 1961, s 57(1).
111. Occupiers' Liability Act 1995, s 4(4).
112. Doherty 'Annotation to the Act' ICLSA, General Note to section 4.

**[12.120]** Fourthly, it is worth considering the position of a recreational user who is present on the premises without the occupier's permission. As we have seen, s 1(1) characterises this entrant as a recreational user inspite of the absence of permission. Can it be that s 4(4) imposes a duty of reasonable care on the occupier to maintain the structure in a safe condition for such an unpermitted entrant? The point is one of some practical significance. It is easy to envisage premises that are subject to frequent unpermitted incursion by people who fall within the definition of recreational user. Can it be that s 4(4) imposes on the occupier a full duty of care in relation to them ?

**[12.121]** Against this condition, the following argument may be considered. Section 4(4) states that where a structure is or has been provided "for use primarily by recreational users", the occupier owes a duty of care "towards such users". Manifestly the occupier has not provided the structure for use by unpermitted recreational users; the only objects of the occupier's beneficence are recreational users permitted by the occupier to come onto the premises. This being so, the reference to "such users" should be interpreted as being limited to permitted recreational users. This argument can no doubt be attacked on the basis that the reference to "use primarily by recreational users" embraces the entire class of recreational users, permitted and unpermitted.

**[12.122]** We can assume that the occupier, when providing the structure primarily for the use of recreational visitors, did not thereby intend to provide it for the use of unpermitted recreational users, but as long as it can correctly be said that the occupier provided the structure "for use primarily by recreational users", the language of s 4(4), and in particular its reference to "such users", requires the conclusion that all members of the class of recreational users were intended by the Oireachtas to receive the benefit of the duty of care imposed on the occupier by s 4(4). This interpretation is probably strengthened by the fact that the subsection, as we have seen, is not concerned with who actually provided the structure for this purpose. Since the occupier is not necessarily the person who did so, the particular attitude of the occupier towards certain recreational users should scarcely be decisive in determining the duty of care owed to them under the subsection.

***(m)Modification of occupiers' duty to entrants***

**[12.123]** Section 5 of the 1995 Act deals with modification of the occupier's duty towards entrants. It enables an occupier, by express agreement or notice, to extend his or her duty towards any category of entrant.[113] This of course does not happen often in practice. It also enables an occupier, again by express agreement or notice, to restrict, modify or exclude his or her duty towards visitors,[114] subject to certain qualifications. The visitor will not be bound unless the restriction, modification or exclusion is reasonable in all the circumstances.[115] Moreover, where the occupier seeks to accomplish his or her goal by notice rather than by obtaining the visitor's express agreement, the occupier must take reasonable steps to bring the notice to the attention of the visitor.[116] The occupier will be

113. Section 5(1).

114. Section 5(2)(a).

115. Section 5(2)(b)(ii).

116. Section 5(2)(b)(ii).

presumed unless the contrary is shown, to have taken such reasonable steps if the notice is prominently displayed at the normal means of access to the premises.[117]

**[12.124]** There is a minimum level of obligation to visitors below which the occupier is not permitted to venture: the occupier may not exclude liability to injure a visitor or damage the visitor's property intentionally or to act with reckless disregard for a visitor or the property of a visitor.[118] So the minimum level that the occupier can engineer by agreement or notice is identical to the duty an occupier owes under the legislation to recreational users and trespassers.[119] The 1995 Act does not permit the occupier to reduce that level of obligation to recreational users by agreement or notice. This seems clear from the drafting of s 5, which does not expressly permit such a reduction, and more particularly by the drafting of s 4, which prescribes the duty to recreational users and trespassers and goes on to provide that this duty is owed "except in so far as the occupier extends the duty in accordance with s 5". That exception, thus expressly limited, does not allow the occupier to restrict or exclude his or her duty to these entrants.

**[12.125]** It may be useful to consider how the court would respond to a situation where an occupier puts up a notice at "the normal means of access to the premises", which states:

> "No liability shall attach to the occupiers of these lands in respect of any injury sustained on these lands by any visitor, recreational user or trespasser, howsoever caused."

**[12.126]** Recreational users and trespassers are unaffected by it, because, being restrictive of the occupier's duty, it has potential application only to visitors. Should the notice be interpreted, in relation to them, as having no legal validity because it professes to exclude liability which the occupier is not permitted to exclude by virtue of s 5(3)? We consider that the answer is no, and that instead the notice should be interpreted as restricting the occupier's liability as far as s 5(3) permits, but no further. Section 5(3) provides that a restriction, modification or exclusion "shall not be taken as allowing" an occupier to injure the visitor intentionally or to act in reckless disregard for the visitor. That expression strongly suggests that the court, in interpreting the scope of the notice, should artificially restrict it to the permitted level of reduction of obligation. Nevertheless, courts do not like rewriting contractual terms and it may be that, although the notice is not such a term, the court would adopt the traditional "blue pencil" rule. The moral is clear. Notices should not overreach; they should be drafted in terms that go no further than the law permits. Otherwise confusion will result.

**[12.127]** It may be worth considering briefly the question of when a restriction, modification or exclusion is "reasonable in all the circumstances". This is extremely hard to predict since the relationship between the occupier and visitor is by no means always contractual. Why should it ever be unreasonable for an occupier to restrict his or her liability? Clearly s 5(2) is premised on the acceptance of the judgment that there are cases where a restriction of liability is unreasonable. Perhaps the courts will have regard to social factors, such as the necessity of people to go on certain premises, such as social welfare offices or hospitals. One suspects that the courts would not look with favour on a notice

---

117. Section 5(2)(c).

118. Section 5(3).

119. *Cf* s 4(1).

purporting to restrict liability to "entrants as of right", such as the gardaí, bailiffs or fire fighters for example. The courts may even engage in an "enterprise theory" approach, echoing that with which McCarthy J briefly flirted,[120] to the effect that supermarkets, which generate large profits through a system that exposes customers to an inevitable risk of slip-and-fall injuries, should not be entitled to restrict their liability under this subsection.

### *(n) The adequacy of a warning to a visitor*

**[12.128]** Let us turn to another, related but separate matter covered by s 5. Where injury or damage is caused to a visitor (or the visitor's property) by a danger of which the visitor had been warned by the occupier or another person, the warning is not to be treated as absolving the occupier from liability unless, in all the circumstances, it was enough to enable the visitor, by having regard to the warning, to avoid the injury or damage so caused.[121]

**[12.129]** This extends the scope of liability from what had formerly been the position. In England, as has been mentioned, the House of Lords had taken the view that a warning to an invitee would disentitle the invitee to sue for injury resulting from the risk that had thus been brought to his or her attention.[122] The Irish courts took a more nuanced approach: only if the warning was such as to "enable[e] the careful invitee to perform his task without danger" would it render the occupier immune from liability.[123] The present legislation extends potential liability in this context to all visitors, not just invitees. There are many entrants who are characterised as visitors who were not invitees. Social guests are one group; also those permitted by the occupier to use the premises as a short-cut or even, for example, the neighbouring boy who comes over the wall to retrieve his ball.

**[12.130]** Under the former approach, the rationale was that, if a person is coming onto your property to confer an economic benefit upon you, it is only fair that your warning should have the effect of making it possible for him or her to confer that benefit upon you in safety. Where there is no such benefit flowing to the occupier, it is more debatable whether an occupier should be required, by the warning, to render the premises safe for the visitor. If, for example, the ball that has been kicked over the wall lands in an area where weedkiller has been placed, and the neighbour who wants it back is a twelve year old boy, a warning will not suffice unless it is enough to enable the youth to avoid injury from the weedkiller. Merely apprising him of the danger is not necessarily enough. Contrast this with a situation where the danger is of the same level but the occupier is out when the boy comes over the wall and thus no question of a warning arises. Here there is no rule of law which imposes liability on the occupier unless a certain specified level of care is delivered by the occupier; the case is reduced to the opaque standard of "the common duty of care"

---

120. In *Mullen v Quinnsworth t/a Crazy Prices (No 1)* [1990] 1 IR 59 (SC). *Cf* para **[25.22]** below.
121. Section 5(5).
122. *London Graving Dock v Horton* [1951] AC 737.
123. *O'Donoghue v Greene* [1967] IR 40 at 46. See also *Long v Saorstát and Continental Steamship Co Ltd* (1953) 93 ILTR 137 (SC); *Morley v Eye, Ear & Throat Hospital Incorporated* [1967] IR 143 and *Power v Crowley and Reddy Enterprises Ltd* High Court, 29 October 1992 (Blayney J). *Cf* Byrne & Binchy, *Annual Review of Irish Law 1992*, 591-592.

to visitors under s 3. The result may in some cases be the same but it will not necessarily be so.

### *(o) Duty of occupiers to strangers to contracts*

**[12.131]** There are many situations where an occupier who is in a contractual relationship with one person - a builder or repairer, for example - permits other persons - the employees of the builder or repairer, or independent contractors engaged by the builder or repairer - to come on the premises. The occupier will not normally be in a contractual relationship with these other persons though the contract between the occupier and builder or repairer may envisage, and sometimes specifically prescribe, that they are to come onto the property. What should the occupier's position be relative to these persons? They are undoubtedly visitors. Under s 1, the term "visitor" includes an entrant present with the occupier's permission or one present "by virtue of an express or implied term in a contract". (Note that the contract need not necessarily be with the occupier.) The "stranger to the contract" comes within both of these criteria. Should the occupier be permitted, by a term in the contract between him or her and the builder or repairer, to exclude or modify the liability that would otherwise arise under s 3 to these visitors?

**[12.132]** Section 6 of the Act makes it plain that the answer is no. Under subs (1), the duty that an occupier owes an entrant under the 1995 Act is not capable of being modified or excluded by a contract to which the entrant is a stranger, whether or not the occupier is bound by the contract to permit the entrant to enter or use the premises. Section 6(2) provides that an entrant is deemed a stranger to a contract if he or she is not for the time being entitled to the benefit of the contract as a party to it or as the successor, by assignment or otherwise, of a party to it; accordingly, a party to the contract who has ceased to be so entitled is deemed a stranger to the contract.

**[12.133]** Two points may here be noted. First, s 6 merely prevents the occupier from using a contract with one person (for example, the builder or repairer) to reduce or remove his or her liability to other persons (the builder's or repairer's employees or independent contractors). It does not prevent the occupier from using s 5 of the 1995 Act to achieve the same purpose. This could be done by express agreement with the employees or independent contractors or by the notice procedure prescribed by the subs (2).

**[12.134]** A question of policy arises as to whether s 5(2)(b)(i) has the inevitable effect of defeating this strategy. That clause renders ineffective any express agreement or notice seeking to restrict, modify or exclude the occupier's liability towards visitors unless it is "reasonable in all the circumstances". No doubt the employees and independent contractors would argue that, in the light of s 6, an employer should not be permitted to achieve directly what he or she is not permitted to achieve indirectly by means of a provision in the contract with the employer or engage of these visitors. As against this, it can credibly be replied that the policy underlying s 6 is to ensure that entrants do not lose their statutory protection by virtue of a provision in a contract to which they are not parties and from which they derive no benefit. It is not intended to go further than this and prevent an occupier from entering into a contract with these entrants which contains such a restriction, modification or exclusion of liability.

**[12.135]** This brings us to the second point, which relates to the present law relating to privity of contract and consideration. The traditional view was that only parties to a contract who provided consideration should be able to enforce the contract. Specific exceptions were conceded, notably that of the contractual trust. The accepted wisdom for many years was that the privity doctrine had sufficient vitality to resist third party beneficiary claims and that the contractual trust doctrine was in decline. Recently, courts throughout the common law world, notably in Canada[124] and Australia,[125] have been willing to countenance an assault on the privity doctrine. Irish courts have yet to confront the issue squarely.[126] If they follow the example of other common law jurisdictions, they may well extend the scope of entitlement to enforce a term of a contract to which one is not privy. For practical purposes, this change would have little effect under s 6. Section 6(2) defines a "stranger to a contract" in such a way that, even if the entrant who is not a party to the contract is entitled to the benefit of the contract, and to enforce that entitlement, he or she remains a stranger because he or she is not so entitled as a party to the contract. If the law develops in the future in such a way that parties to the contract who do not provide consideration have the right to sue to enforce the benefit prescribed to them under the contract, they will clearly not be "strangers". One cannot be definitive about parties to a contract which contains a term conferring benefit on them where they do not provide consideration. Are they "entitled to the benefit as a party to it" because (let us assume) some other party, who has provided consideration, could enforce the term for their benefit? Or does "entitlement" necessarily encompass a personal right of action on the part of the person so entitled? It may be predicted (tentatively) that the latter approach is the one the court would favour.

***(p) Liability of occupiers for the negligence of independent contractors***

**[12.136]** Under s 7 of the legislation, an occupier is not liable to an entrant for injury or damage caused to the entrant (or his or her property) by reason of a danger existing on the premises due to the negligence of an independent contractor employed by the occupier if the occupier has taken all reasonable care in the circumstances, unless the occupier has or ought to have had knowledge of "the fact that the work was not properly done". Taking reasonable care in this context includes taking such steps as the occupier ought reasonably have taken to satisfy himself or herself that the independent contractor was competent to do the work concerned.[127]

---

124. *London Drugs v Kuehne & Nagle International* (1992) 97 DLR (4th) 261 (SC, Can).

125. *Trident General Insurance v McNeice* (1988) 165 Comm LR 107 (HC, Austr).

126. *Cf Bula Ltd v Tara Mines Ltd* [1988] ILRM 157 and *McManus v Cable Management*, High Court, 8 July 1994 (Morris J).

127. Section 7 avoids the uncertainties created by a similarly drafted provision in English law (Occupiers' Liability Act 1957, s 2(40)) which limited the occupier's immunity to cases where the damage was caused by a danger "due to the faulty execution of any work of construction, maintenance or repair" by the independent contractor. This forced the English courts to provide "a broad and purposeful interpretation" of this limitation (*Ferguson v Welsh* [1987] 1 WLR 1553 at 1556 (HL)), so as to include demolition or a builder's failure to take adequate precautions against flooding, for example. *Cf AMF International v Magnet Bowling Ltd* [1988] 1 WLR 1028 at 1043. The Law Reform Commission rightly recommended that the provision should be drafted in a manner that was free of these unnecessary confusions.

**[12.137]** One commentator has pointed out[128] that an independent contractor can sometimes be an occupier, as, for example, where a builder takes over a site long enough to fall within the definition of "occupier" under s 1 of the 1995 Act. Of course, the injured person will always have a right of action against the independent contractor for negligence, regardless of whether the independent contractor falls, within that definition. The 1995 Act has nothing to say on the nature and extent of the duty of care of a general contractor to trespassers (or other entrants). The philosophical basis of *Purtill* and *McNamara* suggests that the courts should be slow to deny a foreseeable trespasser a right of action against the independent contractor by reason of the fact that he or she is a low-prestige entrant. The passage of the Occupiers' Liability Act 1995 should not have altered this position. There may (or may not) be good reasons for reducing the duty owned by occupiers to recreational users or trespassers. These reasons relate to the encouragement of tourism and of access to rural areas and the removal of a potentially oppressive level of liability from occupiers. They do not impact to any similar extent in relation to independent contractors who choose to do work for occupiers and have no long-term stake in the property.

**[12.138]** An important point to note here, which we shall consider in more detail in a moment, when we consider s 8, is that paragraph (c) makes it plain that nothing in the 1995 Act is to be construed as affecting any enactment or rule of law relating to (*inter alia*) the liability imposed on an occupier for a tort committed by another person in circumstances where the duty imposed on the occupier is of such a nature that its performance may not be delegated to another person. It is well established under common law that the occupier has a non-delegable duty with regard to "ultra-hazardous activities".[129] In *Crowe v Merrion Shopping Centre Ltd*,[130] Spain J held that an occupier may not avoid liability by delegating to an independent contractor menial tasks that are within the occupier's competence to perform. This notion is extending deeply into the realm of employers' liability.[131] In practice, the concept of a non-delegable duty means that the court will hold the occupier liable for the negligence of an independent contractor on the basis of what amounts to vicarious liability.

***(q) Preservation of higher duties***

**[12.139]** Section 8 of the Act makes it plain that nothing in the 1995 Act is to be construed as affecting any enactment or rule of law relating to three specific areas.

*(i) Self defence, defence of others and defence of property*

**[12.140]** This is an area where the law allows a fairly robust response by the occupier. It is fair to say that the courts have not injected many legal refinements into what ultimately is a somewhat primitive value judgment about the limits of protection of the values of life, bodily integrity and property, all of which are endowed with constitutional status. The litigated cases tend to be decided "on the facts", with little precedental worth for later

128. Doherty, 'Annotation to the Act', ICLSA, General Note to section 7.

129. *Cf* para **[12.144]** below.

130. (1995) 15 ILT (ns) 302 (CC), analysed by Byrne & Binchy, *Annual Review of Irish Law 1995*, pp 518-519.

131. See *Connolly v Dundalk Urban District Council*, [1990] 2 IR 1 (SC), and para **[18.41]-[18.48]**.

cases. The law requires reasonable proportionality between the threat to these values and to the response by the occupier. Where the line is to be drawn depends on "all the circumstances", but one or two principles at least are clear. In the defence of my property I am not permitted to subject a trespasser to the imposition of retributive force. Thus for two centuries the use of spring guns[132] or other engines of retribution have rendered the occupier liable to the unwelcome entrant. Moreover, there is recent authority that commercial enterprises should seek injunction proceedings rather than have recourse to "private violence" in protection of their property interests.[133]

*(ii) Liability imposed on an occupier as a member of a particular class of persons*

**[12.141]** The second situation which is unaffected by the Occupiers' Liability Act 1995 is that relating to any liability imposed on an occupier as a member of a particular class of persons. Section 8(b) of the 1995 Act states three examples in a non-exclusive list:

(a) persons by virtue of a contract for the hire of, or for the carriage for reward of persons or property in, any vessel, vehicle, train, aircraft or other means of transport;

(b) persons by virtue of a contract of bailment; and

(c) employers in respect of their duties towards their employees.

**[12.142]** A few words about these three classes may be of assistance. Carriers and bailees have for centuries been subjected to onerous duties, in excess of that of the common law duty of care, in certain circumstances. This is because those who place themselves or their goods in their charge are sometimes in a vulnerable situation. Five hundred years ago, it was always possible for carriers to conspire with highway men and for bailees to facilitate the theft of goods in their care. Human nature has not changed markedly over the years. Carriers are mentioned by s 8 because of the broad definition of "premises" in s 1, which embraces vessels, vehicles, trains, aircraft and other means of transport.

**[12.143]** Hotel proprietors are not mentioned in s 8. As we have seen, the Hotel Proprietors Act 1963 prescribes the duties owed by hotel proprietors to guests. For either of two reasons, this legislation is unaffected by the 1995 Act. Section 2(1) appears not to extend to it because it is limited to replacing the duties "heretofore" attached by the common law. If the 1963 Act nonetheless is putatively affected by the 1995 Act, s 8 makes it plain that nothing in the 1995 legislation is to be construed as affecting "any enactment or rule of law" relating to any liability imposed on an occupier "as a member of a particular class of persons ..."[134]

*(iii)Non-delegable duties*

**[12.144]** We have already mentioned the tendency of the courts in recent years to expand the scope of employers' liability under the characterisation of the non-delegable duties. Section 8(c) of the 1995 Act removes from its scope non-delegable duties. Thus, a non-delegable duty, whether relating to an employers' liability to an employee or otherwise will

132. *Cf Bird v Holbrook* (1828) 4 Bing 628, 130 ER 911.

133. *MacKnight v Xtravision* Circuit Court, 5 July 1991 (Carroll J) extracted in McMahon & Binchy, *Casebook on the Irish Law of Torts* (2nd ed, 1991), p 407.

134. Section 8(b). For consideration of the possible effect of the 1995 Act or s 21(3) of the Control of Dogs Act 1986, under which negligence is the exclusive test for determining liability for damage caused by a dog to a trespasser, see para **[27.28]** below.

be capable of rendering the person on whom that duty is imposed liable for the tortious acts or omissions of an independent contractor. In our discusstion of s 7, we have referred to Judge Spain's holding in *Crowe v Merrion Shopping Centre Ltd*,[135] which characterises an occupier's menial duties relating to the safety of the premises as non-delegable.

135. (1995) 15 ILT (ns) 302 (CC).

## Chapter 13

# Liability of Vendors, Lessors and Builders for Quality and Fitness of Premises[1]


| | | |
|---|---|---|
| I. | Introduction | 337 |
| II. | Liability of Vendor and Lessor | 337 |
| III. | Liability of the Builder | 350 |
| IV. | Liability of Builder/Vendor and Builder/Lessor | 353 |


## I. Introduction

**[13.01]** We are primarily concerned in this chapter with an examination of the rules of liability that apply to vendors, lessors and builders for defective premises. Consideration of this branch of the law brings us inevitably into contact with both tortious and contractual concepts and in this connection "defective premises" may have two different meanings.

> "From the point of view of tort liability premises are defective only if they constitute a source of danger to the person or property of those who are likely to come on to them or to find themselves in their vicinity. In the contractual sense they are defective if their condition falls short of the standard of quality which the purchaser or lessee was entitled to expect in the circumstances. We refer to these different kinds of defects as dangerous defects and defects of quality respectively ...". [2]

**[13.02]** Although the distinction is a valuable one and should be borne in mind constantly in this chapter, it should be pointed out that the distinction has been subjected to criticism in Ireland in recent years. Further attention will be given to this later in the chapter.

## II. Liability of Vendor and Lessor

### Defects of Quality: Contract

**[13.03]** Generally speaking, neither the vendor nor the lessor of real property is under any obligation to ensure that the premises are free from any defects in quality. *Caveat emptor* or *caveat lessee* are the contractual rules that govern the situation. Unless there are express warranties the purchaser must look out for himself or herself. The law will not normally imply into such contracts any warranties and there are, subject to what is said hereafter, no implied conditions or warranties relating to fitness for purpose, etc, analogous to those contained in the Sale of Goods Act 1893 and the Sale of Goods and Supply of Services Act

---

1. See generally LRC Working Paper No 1 1977, *The Law Relating to the Liability of Builders, Vendors and Lessors for the Quality and Fitness of Premises* and the Commission's *Report on Defective Premises* (LRC-3 1982); see also Smillie 'Liability of Builders, Manufacturers and Vendors for Negligence' 8 NZULR 1(19 (1)78); Wylie *Irish Conveyancing Law* (1978), p 156 *et seq*; Rowntree 'Negligence, *Caveat Emptor* and Defective Premises' 54 Law Institute J 29 (1980).
2. *Civil Liability of Vendors and Lessors for Defective Premises* (1970) English Law Com, No 40, para 2.

1980 in respect of the sale of goods. In accepting land or buildings the purchaser or lessee is expected to have examined the property and to have taken it with knowledge of all its defects. One judicial quotation from an English court will suffice to illustrate the strength of this rule:

> "It is settled law that the vendor of a house, even if also the builder of it, gives no implied warranty as to its safety. A purchaser can make any examination he likes, either by himself or by somebody better qualified to do so. He can take it or leave it, but if he takes it, he takes it as he finds it. It is, perhaps, the strongest example of the application of the maxim 'caveat emptor'."[3]

**[13.04]** This view was affirmed in the High Court, in *Curling v Walsh*,[4] where Hamilton P dismissed an action by the plaintiff for breach of contract, fraudulent or negligent misrepresentation, and unjust enrichment in respect of a house purchased by the plaintiff which was badly infected by dry and wet rot. The plaintiff claimed he had been reassured by the defendant that it would be a waste of money to engage the services of a surveyor as there was nothing wrong with the house. As Hamilton P found on the evidence that no such warranty or representation had been made, *caveat emptor* applied and the plaintiff failed.

**[13.05]** The plaintiff might have fared better had he framed his action in negligence simpliciter, rather than in negligent misrepresentation. Irish decisions in *Siney v Dublin Corporation*[5] and *Ward v McMaster*,[6] both discussed below,[7] would suggest that this would have been a better route to travel for the plaintiff.

**[13.06]** It is difficult for the court to imply terms into such agreements because of the "four corners rule" which prohibits, in normal circumstances, parol evidence to supplement the written terms of the contract. In any event, contractual terms when they do exist cannot, because of the privity rule, benefit third parties.

**[13.07]** In exceptional cases, however, circumstances may be such that the courts will imply warranties in relation to the building, but they will not do so automatically. In *Brown v Norton*,[8] Davitt P said:

> "I am strongly inclined to the opinion that the only general proposition which can be safely derived from the earlier authorities is that there is no rule of law which provides that, on the mere sale or letting of an unfurnished but completely built house, there shall be implied a warranty that it is reasonably fit for habitation. To say that in no case of such a sale or letting, no matter how compelling the circumstances, can a Court hold that such a warranty is implied seems to me to be a wholly different and very much wider proposition. The Legislature may be competent to lay down such a sweeping provision but I take leave to doubt whether it is within the competence of a Court to do so."[9]

---

3. *Otto v Bolton & Norris* [1936] 2 KB 46 at 52 cited with approval in *McGowan v Harrison* [1941] IR 331 at 337. Although accurate in respect of vendors, the quotation has to be qualified now where the vendor is also the builder. See para **[13.57]** below.
4. High Court, 23 October 1987. See Byrne & Binchy *Annual Review of Irish Law 1957* (1988), p 333; Clarke, *Contract Law in Ireland* (4th ed, 1998), p 127.
5. [1980] IR 400.
6. [1988] IR 337.
7. See paras **[13.23]**, **[13.35]** and **[13.51]**.
8. [1954] IR 34.
9. [1954] IR 34 at 55-56.

**[13.08]** He concluded that the authorities on the matter might suggest that implied warranties are not normally implied by the vendor, but he was unwilling to accept that the authorities precluded the courts from ever implying such warranties in appropriate circumstances.

**[13.09]** What is true of the vendor is also true of the lessor, who, in making a lease, does not normally give any undertakings other than those expressly provided for in the lease. In particular the lessor does not warrant that the premises are suitable for habitation.[10]

**[13.10]** It is not surprising, however, that the scope of these nineteenth century *laissez faire* type rules should have been reduced somewhat both by judicial and by legislative action in the course of the twentieth century. The majority of these derogations, however, benefit the lessee or tenant rather than the purchaser of real property, as, the weak, unequal and vulnerable position of the tenant evokes more sympathy than that of the purchaser. In regard to the vendor/purchaser relationship, the presumption still generally remains that the parties are more or less on equal footing, however untrue this may be in fact nowadays.

**[13.11]** The main exceptions to the rule that no warranties are implied by the vendor or lessor of real property are as follows:

(i) Where the vendor sells, or the lessor sells by way of lease, a house in the course of construction, certain terms relating to the completion of the house, the materials used and the quality of the workmanship will be implied by the courts.[11]

(ii) The lessor impliedly covenants in a lease for furnished premises to be used for residential occupation that the premises are fit for such occupation at the commencement of the tenancy.[12]

(iii) In *Siney v Dublin Corporation*[13] the Supreme Court held, in the case of an unfurnished letting under the Housing Act 1966, that there is an implied warranty that the premises are reasonably fit for human habitation. The Corporation was clearly under a statutory obligation here to end substandard housing and it may be that the decision does not extend to ordinary lettings. However, this has yet to be decided. Further, the principle is the same whether the plaintiff takes a lease or a tenancy.[14]

---

10. *Chambers v Lord Mayor et al of Cork* (1958) 93 ILTR 45; *Brown v Norton* [1954] IR 34 at 45; Wylie, *Landlord and Tenant Law* (2nd ed, 1998), para 15.04; Deale *The Law of Landlord and Tenant in the Republic of Ireland* (1968), p 214.
11. *Brown v Norton* [1954] IR 34; *cf Brohan v Crossplan Developments* [1985] ILRM 702; *McGeary v Campbell* [1975] NI 7.
12. *Collins v Hopkins* [1923] 2 KB 617; *Wilson v Finch Hatton* (1877) 2 Ex Div 336; Wylie, *Landlord and Tenant Law* (2nd ed, 1998), para 15.04; Deale *The Law of Landlord and Tenant in the Republic of Ireland* (1968), pp 214-215. *Cf* an unfurnished house, *Murray v Lace* (1872) IR 8 CL 396; *Beaver v McFarlane* [1932] LJ Ir 128.
13. [1980] IR 400. Followed in *Coleman v Dundalk UDC* Supreme Court, 17 July 1988. An argument seeking to base a distinction on the fact that *Coleman* involved a long lease whereas in *Siney*, a weekly tenancy was in question, was rejected in *Coleman*. See Clarke, *Contract Law in Ireland* (4th ed, 1998), p 126
14. *Coleman v Dundalk UDC* Supreme Court, 17 July 1988.

(iv) Several statutory provisions also impose repairing obligations on the lessor of property, but these need only be noted at this point.[15]

## Dangerous Defects: Tort

**[13.12]** With regard to the tortious liability of vendors and lessors the position at common law was equally unfavourable for the purchaser or lessee. The general rule of negligence, that a person has a duty to take care that his or her actions do not injure his or her neighbour, appeared, until recently at least, to have no application in the case of the vendor or lessor of real property. According to *Salmond & Heuston,* this immunity "escaped the flood tide of liability released by *Donoghue v Stevenson*".[16] Earlier *dicta* in relation to the landlord's tortious immunity in this matter occurred in *Robbins v Jones*[17] and in *Cavalier v Pope.*[18] In *Robbins v Jones,* Erle CJ stated the rule as follows:

> "A landlord who lets a house in a dangerous state is not liable to the tenants, customers or guests for accidents happening during the term; for, fraud apart, there is no law against letting a tumbledown house; and the tenant's remedy is upon his contract, if any."[19]

**[13.13]** And in *Cavalier v Pope,* Lord Atkinson used the following language:

> "... it is well established that no duty is, at law, cast upon a landlord not to let a house in a dangerous or dilapidated condition and further, that if he does let it while in such a condition, he is not thereby rendered liable in damages for injuries which may be sustained by the tenant, his (the tenant's) servants, guests, customers, or others invited by him to enter the premises by reason of this defective condition."[20]

**[13.14]** *Chambers v Lord Mayor of Cork*[21] provides a good illustration of the vigour of this rule in operation. The plaintiff was injured when her foot caught in the iron grating covering a gully trap in the yard of a house leased by the defendant Corporation to her tenant husband. The tenant had previously complained of the trap and a housing official from the Corporation had inspected the trap and agreed that it was dangerous. Nothing, however, was done to remedy the matter. In rejecting the plaintiff's claim Dixon J said:

> "As to the issue of negligence, it is well settled law that in circumstances such as those present here a landlord owes no duty to the wife of a tenant. Even if it were found that the gully trap was defective, the law is that a tenant takes a house as he finds it with all its defects. And, except by special agreement, the landlord is not liable to the tenant for defects in the house rendering it dangerous and unfit for occupation, even if he has brought about the defects himself or is aware of their existence. That, of course, is all the more so where, as here, the defects are obvious to the tenant, and if the landlord owes no duty to the tenant in

---

15. See eg Housing (Miscellaneous Provisions)Act 1992, s 18 and the Housing Act 1966, s 114; Rent Restrictions Act 1960, s 39; Housing Act 1966, s 66 and s 90; The Landlord and Tenant Law Amendment Act Ireland 1860 (Deasy's Act), s 83. See further Wylie, *Landlord and Tenant Law* (2nd ed, 1998), para 15.05-15.11.
16. SALMOND & HEUSTON, p 287.
17. 15 CB (ns) 221, (1863)143 ER 768.
18. [1906] AC 428.
19. 15 CB (ns) 221 at 240, (1863) 143 ER 768 at 776.
20. [1906] AC 428 at 432, citations omitted. *Cf Kelly v Woolworth & Co* [1922] 2 IR 5 at 9 where Ronan LJ appeared to proceed on the basis of this principle.
21. (1958) 93 ILTR 45.

this respect then the wife of the tenant could be in no better position and could have no greater claim."[22]

**[13.15]** Because of the Supreme Court's decision in *Siney v Dublin Corporation*[23] this may no longer represent the law on this matter. The Court's decision on this will be dealt with below, but it should first of all be noted that although the vendor or the lessor is not liable in tort *qua* vendor or *qua* lessor, this does not mean that he or she may not be liable under some other heading in tort. This is particularly important in the case of the lessor, of course, because he or she may still figure in relation to the property after the lease has been granted, whereas the vendor is usually removed from the picture once the sale is completed. In particular, the lessor may be liable in tort for dangerous defects on the premises under any of the following headings: (1) defects created after the demise (activity duty or liability for current operations), (2) liability as occupier of buildings, and (3) liability in nuisance. In addition we must now look at (4) liability in negligence in the wake of the *Siney* decision.

**[13.16]** It is not intended to develop these at any great length at this stage, but a brief word about each may not be out of place.

### *(a) Defects created after demise (activity duty or liability for current operations)*

**[13.17]** If the landlord by a positive act of misfeasance alters the condition of the premises after the lease is made the lessor may render himself or herself liable for damage caused by the changed conditions. In those circumstances ordinary *Donoghue v Stevenson* principles apply.[24] Needless to say, if the vendor reenters the sold property and commits a negligent act which causes injury to the purchaser or any of the purchaser's family or indeed anyone who could reasonably be foreseen, the vendor too will be liable on ordinary negligence principles. The lessor or vendor in those circumstances is in no better position than a stranger would be in the same circumstances. Because of the lessor's continuing interest in the property, however, the contemplated circumstances are more likely to arise in his case than in the case of the vendor who has presumably left the premises.

### *(b) Lessor's liability as occupier of the premises*

**[13.18]** The lessor's liability may also arise because he or she continues to be the occupier of the premises let or retains control over common stairways, etc. Liability here depends, not on his or her position as lessor, but on his or her position as occupier. Apart from liability which the lessor may incur because of express provisions in the contract or provisions implied by the law (eg under Deasy's Act or Rent Restrictions Acts), the lessor's liability usually arises here when the injury occurs on passages or staircases, etc, retained by the lessor. The effect of the Occupiers' Liability Act 1995[25] is to place the lessor under a "common duty of care"[26] – in other words, the obligation to use due care, as it would be assessed in a negligence claim – towards "visitors"[27] in relation to these areas. Visitors

22. (1958) 93 ILTR 45 at 48.
23. [1980] IR 400.
24. See McMahon, *Reform of Law of Occupier's Liability in Ireland* (Prl 4403), pp 10-11. With regard to a local authority's liability for nonfeasance see *Anns v Merton London Borough Council* [1978] AC 728.
25. See Ch 12 above.
26. Section 3 of the Act.

embrace contractual entrants, entrants as of right (such as the police or fire fighters) and other entrants who are present with the occupier's consent, regardless of whether or not they confer an economic benefit on the occupier. Where the entrants are "recreational users"[28] – a category of entrant created by the 1995 Act epitomised by the hiker across farmland, but more broadly defined - they are not owed a duty of care by the occupier[29] and can make a legal complaint only when intentionally or recklessly injured[30] by the occupier.

**[13.19]** It would seem that a straight negligence approach is also favoured in Ireland nowadays in determining whether a lessor is liable for injuries caused on the demised premises because of a defect in the condition of the premises retained by the lessor. In *Scully v Marjorie Boland Ltd*[31] and *Victor Weston (Éire) Ltd v Kenny*,[32] Davitt P, clearly favoured the straight negligence approach. In the *Weston* case he held that the owner of premises is:

> "under a legal obligation to take reasonable care to prevent any part of the premises which he retain[s] from becoming a source of danger or damage to the adjoining occupiers, his tenants, and so to prevent water from escaping from his top lavatory and doing damage [to tenants lower down]".[33]

***(c) Lessor's and vendor's liability in nuisance***

**[13.20]** The lessor may also be liable if he or she creates a nuisance on the property or authorises a usage of the property which necessarily involves wrongful interference with another person's enjoyment of his property. Moreover, if the lessor interferes with a public right, then a member of the public who suffers special damage over and above the public injury will have an action in public nuisance also.

**[13.21]** Liability for nuisance may also attach to the vendor of property. Of course, instances of this would be rarer, but could arise, for example, where the vendor created the nuisance in the first place. Liability would follow the vendor in this case even though he or she may no longer be in a position to abate the nuisance.[34]

***(d) Liability of lessor or vendor in negligence when the lessor is a public authority under statutory duties***

**[13.22]** As already noted above, the common law immunity which inured for the benefit of the lessor or the vendor in tort must now be in doubt because of recent decisions in England and Ireland.[35]

27. *Cf* s 3.

28. *Cf* s 1.

29. Save in respect of structures (placed on the premises) by the occupier for the benefit of recreational users: s 4(4).

30. Section 4(1).

31. [1962] IR 58.

32. [1954] IR 191.

33. [1954] IR 191 at 198

34. Ch 24.

35 *Dutton v Bognor Regis UDC* [1972] 1 QB 373; [1972] 1 All ER 462; *Anns v Merton London Borough* [1978] AC 728; *Siney v Dublin Corp* [1980] IR 400; *Ward v McMaster* [1988] IR 337 (SC), affg [1985] IR 29 (HC).

**[13.23]** In *Siney v Dublin Corporation*[36] the defendant corporation had a statutory duty under the Housing Act 1966 to provide housing for poorer sections of the community. In discharging its functions it employed the National Building Agency to build houses on its behalf. The plaintiff, tenant of the premises, claimed he suffered damages as a result of defects (dampness) in the building. The Court held in favour of the plaintiff on the basis that there was in the circumstances an implied warranty that the premises should be fit for habitation. There were strong *obiter dicta*, however, by both O'Higgins CJ and Henchy J (with Kenny J agreeing), that if the issue of the negligence of the corporation as a landlord were to arise, the principle of *Donoghue v Stevenson* should apply. In this case the defendant was a municipal corporation and was under a statutory obligation to exercise certain functions. Whether the court would adopt a similar rule in the absence of these two special considerations (ie in the case of an ordinary landlord), is, it might be claimed, still an open question.

**[13.24]** On the issue of whether vendors and lessors continued to inherit the common law immunities in tort in relation to negligence, both O'Higgins CJ and Henchy J strongly voiced opinions that the immunities were now gone. Kenny J agreed with both. O'Higgins CJ is particularly strong in his judgment:

> "On behalf of the defendants it was submitted that, as the lessors of the flat, they could be under no liability at common law in respect of injury or damage caused by a defect existing in the premises at the time of the letting. If correct, this submission means that what is known as the principle in *Donoghue v Stevenson* has no application in the circumstances of this case and that, as landlords, the defendants cannot be made liable in negligence in respect of defects existing in the premises which they have let. This submission is supported by an impressive series of decisions . . . It is not easy to see the basis in logic for the existence of such an immunity, particularly where the defect which causes the damage was known or could have been known to the lessor, were it not for his carelessness, and was not known and could not have been known to the tenant or to those whom he brought into the building or the house pursuant to the letting."

Adverting to Lord McDermott's judgment in *Gallagher v N McDowell Ltd* the Chief Justice continued:

> "In that last passage from his judgment Lord McDermott seems to assume a continuing immunity for landowners, as such, from the rule in *Donoghue v Stevenson* in respect of defects or dangers on their land. Such a view of the law is not consistent with the decisions of this Court in *Purtill v Athlone UDC* and *McNamara v ESB*."[37]

**[13.25]** More explicitly later in his judgment, O'Higgins CJ, noting that the defendants carried out an inspection of the premises, declared:

35. See also Wallace 'Tort Demolishes Contract in New Construction' (1978) 92 LQR 60; Wylie *Irish Conveyancing Law* (1978), pp 162-64; Gravells 'Defective Premises: Negligence Liability of Builder' [1979] Conv 97; Seddon 'The Negligence Liability of Statutory Bodies: Dutton Reinterpreted' (1978) 9 Fed LR 326; Cane 'The Liability of Builders and Surveyors for Negligence: *Dutton v Bognor Regis Urban District Council'* (1974) 7 Sydney LR 284.

36. [1980] IR 400. See Kerr & Clark 'Council Housing, Implied Terms and Negligence A Critique of *Siney v Dublin Corporation*' (1980) 15 Ir Jur (ns) 32.

37. [1980] IR 412 at 414. Footnotes omitted.

> "The inspection should have been carried out on the basis that the flat was to be handed over for occupation as a dwelling to a family entitled to expect that it would be one which was fit for human habitation. Because the inspection was defective, the flat was handed over in a condition in which it was not so fit. The result was that damage and injury was caused to the incoming family. In my view, on the facts found by the Circuit Court judge the defendant ought to be held liable in negligence."[38]

**[13.26]** Henchy J was of a similar view. Referring to the inadequate inspection he declared:

> "The plaintiff was entitled, apart from any contractual obligation, to rely on the defendants to ensure that the flat would be habitable. The duty placed on the defendants by the Act of 1966 justified the plaintiff in so thinking. It is the defendants' failure, vis-à-vis the plaintiff as tenant under the Act, to observe that duty that was the particular source of negligence."[39]

**[13.27]** In *Burke v Dublin Corporation*,[40] three plaintiffs sued the defendant Corporation for damage caused by heaters installed into a house provided by the defendant under powers and obligations imposed again in the Housing Act 1966. The original oil-based heating system was replaced in 1978-79 by the defendant who, after extensive investigations and trials, opted for a new solid fuel-fired heating system, called "Conserva". It was alleged that the new heaters were defective in that they emitted smoke and fumes, and that they rendered the houses unfit for human habitation. The plaintiffs alleged breach of "implied warranty", negligence and breach of duty including breach of statutory duty.

**[13.28]** Of the three plaintiffs who pursued claims, the third plaintiff was a tenant who claimed that she had contracted asthma and had to redecorate her house more frequently. The second plaintiff was a tenant-purchaser who purchased her house from the defendant under s 90 of the 1966 Act. She contracted bronchitis from the fumes and she claimed that she was entitled as a purchaser to the same implied warranty of fitness for human habitation as the tenant was. The first plaintiff was a minor who was not even born when his parents first became tenants. This plaintiff, the defendant argued, had no privity with the defendant and could not benefit from any warranties that might exist between the contracting parties.

**[13.29]** The Supreme Court, upholding the trial judge (Blaney J) in regard to the second and third plaintiffs, held, *inter alia*, that the implied warranty as to fitness for habitation under the legislation applied to purchasers entitled to be housed under the Act and those plaintiffs were to benefit from its holding. No view was expressed on whether any warranties applied when the housing authority let or sold to persons who were not in need of assisted housing. It would appear also that the Court's decision does not apply to ordinary vendors and landlords.

---

38. [1980] IR 412 at 415.
39. [1980] IR 412 at 421-422. This view of the law is supported by Costello J in *Ward v McMaster* [1985] IR 29 (HC) affd by Supreme Court, [1988] IR 337 and by Kerr & Clark 'Council Housing, Implied Terms and Negligence A Critique of *Siney v Dublin Corporation*' (1980) 15 Ir Jur (ns) 32 at 44-45. Henchy J's earlier qualification that such a holding would he beyond "the true scope of the essential circumstances of the case" scarcely weakens his strong statement just quoted in the text. See especially his statement of the principle at 421.
40. [1991] 1 IR 341 (SC).

**[13.30]** The Court's willingness to assist the second and third plaintiffs in this case can also be seen from its reluctance to confine its interpretation of what was unfit for habitation to the twelve matters set out in the Second Schedule of the 1966 Act. The defendant argued that a proper construction of s 66(2) of the Act should be confined to those matters, but the Supreme Court refused to be constrained in this way. It was for the court and not the housing authority to determine what was fit for habitation and, while the second schedule might assist the court, it ought not to confine it.

**[13.31]** That the Court in *Burke*, and earlier in *Siney*, should have opted for the contractual solution to assist the plaintiff, as opposed to the more orthodox possibility of relying on a breach of statutory duty, is surprising. It may be suggested that a straightforward application of the conventional principles of liability in tort for a breach of statutory duty would have been the more satisfactory course for it to have adopted. To regard those duties as being for the benefit of the public rather than for those who need housing seems to involve an unconventional interpretation of the legislation.[41]

**[13.32]** It should be borne in mind that, in finding for the plaintiffs in contract, for breach of implied warranty, the Supreme Court was imposing contractual strictness instead of the reasonableness standard which is more characteristic of tortious liability. In other words, the liability, when it arose, was strict and the obligation placed on the defendant did not admit of remission or mitigation merely because the defendant had acted with due care or because the defect might be obvious to a tenant. Presumably, however, the Court could still entertain the concepts of contributory negligence and causation in coming to its final conclusion.

**[13.33]** The position of the first plaintiff in *Burke*, however, was different. He was not even born when his parents took the premises from the defendant, he was not privy to the contract and was not entitled to claim a breach of the tenancy agreement. In the Supreme Court the infant plaintiff advanced two further arguments to overcome the privity obstacle: (i) that he had an interest in the contract by virtue of the provisions of the Married Women's Status Act 1957, s 8(1) and (ii) more generally, that the tenancy agreement was a contract made for his benefit by analogy with holiday contracts and the like.[42]

**[13.34]** The Supreme Court rejected both arguments, holding that any derogation to the privity rule must be looked as an exception and accordingly confined in its application.[43]

**[13.35]** On the question of negligence, Blayney J held that there was no breach of duty by the defendant corporation in the circumstances of the case. Adopting the *Ward v McMaster* formulation, he held that, although there might have been proximity between the parties, there was no negligence since the defendant had carried out thorough investigations and tests and could not foresee any damage when the heaters were installed. The Supreme Court, however, declared that although this was not in breach of its duty under the contract,

41. *Cf* Byrne & Binchy, *Annual Review of Irish Law 1989*, p 119.

42. *Cf Jackson v Horizon Holidays Ltd* [1975] 1 WLR 1468; *Wooder Investment v Wimpey Construction* [1980] 1 WLR 277. See Clark, *Contract Law in Ireland* (3rd ed, 1998), p 406

43. It might be asked what contract could be more fundamental to the needs of a child than one providing home and shelter?

its obligation in relation to "fitness for human habitation" was a *continuing* one which ran throughout the duration of the tenancy.

**[13.36]** Finlay CJ observed:

> "The question obviously arises in this case as to whether in the case of a dwelling having been provided for a tenant under the Act of 1966 without negligence, which is in fact unfit for habitation, there is a continuing obligation on the housing authority if the fact of unfitness is established to it or ought to have discovered it, to render if fit.
>
> In my view, there is. The judgments in *Siney v Corporation of Dublin*[44] are entirely dependent on the broad scope of the objectives identified by and the obligations imposed by the Housing Act 1966, in regard to unfit or uninhabitable housing accommodation. The housing authorities are, under the broad terms of that Act, obliged to eradicate such housing in their areas and to substitute for it habitable housing. I am satisfied that that is a duty they owe to the inhabitants of a house who are lawfully in occupation under a letting agreement from them. It is not a single or once-off duty imposed upon the authority at the commencement of a letting, but is one which, in my view, must as a matter of law be taken to continue during the course of the letting."[45]

**[13.37]** Since the question of a continuing obligation and the issue as to whether there had been a breach of it was not dealt with by the trial judge, the Supreme Court ordered a re-trial on that issue.

**[13.38]** From *Burke*, therefore, it is clear that only the parties to the tenancy can benefit from the implied warranty as to "fitness for human habitation". Third parties, to succeed in these type of situations, must recover in negligence by proving proximity, foreseeability of damage, and breach of duty.

**[13.39]** The nature of the corporation's "continuing duties" in these type of cases can be seen from *Howard v Dublin Corporation*[46] and from very similar fact situations which arose in *Dyer v Dublin Corporation*[47] and *Felloni v Dublin Corporation*.[48]

**[13.40]** In *Howard*, the plaintiffs had been tenant purchasers since approximately 1976. Three years later, they obtained a loan from the Corporation (under Housing Act 1966, s 40) to install a new heating system. The system proved defective and the plaintiffs sued the Corporation. The nature of the "continuing duty" was considered. Lavan J held that there was no breach of a continuing duty in the case where the borrower was a tenant purchaser and was merely provided with a loan to improve the heating. Lavan J observed:

> "The duty in the instant case is tenuous: a duty to take care with respect to such representation as to approval of the heating system as may be implicit in the making of a s 40 loan. It has not been established that the defendants were negligent in this regard. Nor is the plaintiffs' claim stateable on other grounds: I find the implied warranty identified in *Burke*[49] to be inapplicable to the facts of this case: here, the first and second named plaintiffs themselves installed the heating system after the transfer. The making of a loan is at a clear

---

44. [1980] IR 400.
45. [1991] 1 IR 341 at 355-356.
46. High Court, 31 July 1996 (Lavan J).
47. High Court, 10 June 1993 (Morris J).
48. [1998] 1 ILRM 133.
49. [1991] 1 IR 341 (SC).

> remove from the transfer of a house with the defective system already installed. A plaintiff's status as tenant-purchaser must shift the balance of relationship between him and the housing authority and the duties of the latter are relaxed accordingly. Such warranty as to fitness for human habitation as existed at the time of the transfer must be regarded as spent by the time of the installation. In the absence of negligence on the housing authority's part, no breach of duty is established. Nor is there a continuing duty (as in the case of a letting agreement), breach of which can give rise to liability in negligence, because of the status of the plaintiffs as tenant-purchaser."[50]

**[13.41]** *Dyer*[51] and *Felloni*[52] had very similar facts and both were decided by Morris J. In *Dyer* the plaintiff had moved into the premises in August 1984. The previous tenant had altered the position of the front door and had removed the door furniture. To close the door, the plaintiff had as a result, to put his hand around the door's edge and pull sharply. To execute this manoeuvre safely it was necessary to make sure one's hand was clear when the door slammed. In February 1985, the plaintiff lost part of his finger when he failed to clear the door in time. The plaintiff succeeded in his action against the corporation. The learned judge held that the absence of the door furniture rendered the house unfit for habitation. Further, the defendants were made aware of the danger and although one of its employees undertook to repair the door, there was an unreasonable delay in attending to it. There was negligence on part of the defendant arising out of the letting agreement and also out of the undertaking to repair. The plaintiff, however, had his damages reduced by 50% for contributing to the injury.

**[13.42]** In *Felloni*, decided some five years later, the same judge came to a different conclusion on similar, but distinguishable, facts. The plaintiff aged fifteen, resided with her aunt who was the tenant of the premises. Door furniture had originally been provided by the defendant corporation, but over the years, the knocker became defective and for the tenant and her invitees to close the door, they had to pull the door using the key as a pulling mechanism or by putting their fingers around the door and pulling the door out. The plaintiff lost the tip of her finger in carrying out this manoeuvre. In this case, Morris J dismissed the claim as he found the Corporation had never been made aware of the defect. The tenant had never complained as she did not see it as a problem. There was, therefore, no liability on the Corporation: the flat as originally delivered was fit for habitation, and there was no evidence that the defendant failed to respond to the legitimate complaint. Morris J went further:

> "[E]ven if I were to find that there was negligence ... and a failure to comply with [the Corporation's] obligations under the Housing Act 1966, ... I believe that negligence on the part of [the tenant] and on the part of the plaintiff in this case in allowing the state of affairs to continue whereby presumably a number of times a day they would voluntarily expose themselves to what must have been a risk of injury in the slamming of the door when the remedy was available to them at little or no expense to remedy the problem by fixing some sort of handle onto the door at minimal expense."[53]

---

50. Pages 6-7 of Lavan J's judgment.
51. High Court, 10 June 1993 (Morris J).
52. [1998] 1 ILRM 133.
53. [1998] 1 ILRM 133 at 135-136, citing *Crowley v Allied Irish Banks* [1987] IR 287 and *Conole v Redbank Oyster Co* [1976] IR 191. See further para **[0.00]** above. See also *Walsh v Dublin Coproation* para **[19.20]** below.

**[13.43]** It might be questioned in this regard whether the plaintiff's carelessness should have been permitted to immunise the Corporation from liability on causal grounds. The negligence of the tenant in failing to remedy or report the problem with the door might be equated to the bank's omissions in *Crowley*,[54] but the failure by the plaintiff surely savoured, at worst, of contributory negligence rather than constituting a *novus actus interveniens*. She had no duty to report the problem to the Corporation or, indeed, to repair the door. In *Stanley v Dublin Corp*,[55] Judge McMahon in the Circuit Court in purporting to follow the above High Court authorities held in favour of the plaintiff. In that case the plaintiff had complained to the Corporation about an internal door that was jamming and was not properly aligned. To open it the plaintiff had to push hard against it or kick it at the base. In trying to open the door one night the plaintiff pushed her hand through the glass panel and cut herself. In its defence the defendant claimed that, when its workmen visited the apartment, they offered to replace the door with a fireproof door. The plaintiff refused. Judge McMahon, however, did not think this was determinative. The plaintiff had four children living in the apartment and the glass door enabled her to remain connected with the children in the small area. Just because the plaintiff refused a fire door, did not justify the Corporation's leaving the existing door in a state of disrepair where there were children as well as adults on the premises, who would, because of the jamming of the door, inevitably have to push and kick it open sometime. When the plaintiff refused the fire door, the Corporation, in keeping with its "continuing duty", should have repaired the existing door. After the plaintiff refused the offer of a "fire door", the corporation was not entitled to wash its hands of the matter.

**[13.44]** In the light of those decisions, one may summarise the law on this matter in the following propositions:

(1) In a private vending or letting situation:

a There normally is no implied warranty as to fitness for habitation. *Caveat emptor* or *caveat lessee* applies except in the case of a house in the course of construction[56] or in the case of a lease of furnished premises. Where there is in these exceptional cases an implied warranty, only the parties to the agreement can avail of it. It is possible that there may be other circumstances where a court might also imply a warranty in exceptional circumstances.

b The purchaser and the tenants can also sue the vendor and lessor in negligence if they can show proximity, reasonable foreseeability of damage and breach of duty. The existence of a contractual relationship does not exclude a tortious obligation as well.

(2) In a Public Authority Housing situation under the Housing Act 1966:

a There is an implied warranty that the housing is fit for habitation. This warranty is implied in lettings or leases or where there is a tenant-purchase and where the letting, lease or sale relates to assisted housing. Whether it also applies to sales to persons who are not beneficiaries under the Housing Acts

54. [1987] IR 287.

55. Circuit Court Dublin, 7 December 1999.

56. *Brown v Norton* [1954] IR 34.

is not decided, but must be doubtful. When the warranty is implied it benefits only the parties to the contract.

b In addition the tenant can sue in negligence if he or she can show proximity, reasonable foreseeability of damage and breach of duty. The existence of a contractual relationship does not exclude an action in negligence.

c Other parties claiming to be injured on the premises by the housing authorities can recover only under the negligence heading. Again, assuming there are no policy reasons excluding liability, the plaintiff must show proximity, reasonable foreseeability of damage and breach of duty. As well as an original duty on the defendant in respect of the provision of the housing, there may also be a "continuing duty" on the authority. The authority may have fulfilled its obligation in the original provision of the housing, but may become liable later if dangers develop and go unattended. In this case, whether the housing authority is liable will depend on whether it has or ought to have notice of the danger, and what response it has made, where it has notice.

**[13.45]** It is important when considering the public authority's liability in negligence to remember that in determining the existence, and the nature and scope of the duty of care, the contract between the authority and the leasee or purchaser does not solely control the situation. When the plaintiff is also the tenant or the tenant-purchaser he or she may, in addition, be entitled to benefit as a "neighbour", to use *Donoghue v Stevenson* terminology. The plaintiff's rights are independent of each other and, although there may be a tendency to conflate the grounds of the authority's obligations, this tendency should be resisted. The authority has a contractual obligation to tenants and tenant-purchasers (represented by the implied warranty for fitness for habitation) and it also has tortious obligations to those who are in a proximate relationship with it in the terms of *Ward v McMaster*. When addressing the issue of tortious liability there is a real danger that the court, when considering the extent and the content of the duty of care, will resort to the "implied warranty" concept. In tort the duty is to those who are sufficently proximate, whereas in contract the obligation is to the parties (the tenant or the purchaser); in tort the duty is to take reasonable care, whereas in contract the obligation (under the Housing Acts at least) is derived from the implied warranty that the property is fit for habitation.

**[13.46]** In determining, therefore, the content and the extent of the duty of care of the authority the truth of the matter is that, while the warranty should not be ignored in the determination of the authority's duty of care, both at the commencement and during the currency of the tenancy, the nature and scope of the duty of care should be fashioned in the light of the authority's statutory functions untrammeled by any limitation (or, indeed, extension) of liability which the warranty might involve.[57]

**[13.47]** Finally, it might be suggested that some, at least, of the confusion that surrounds this area might have been avoided if the liability of the housing authorities under the Housing Acts had been approached using the traditional terminology of breach of statutory

57. *Cf* Byrne & Binchy, *Annual Review of Irish Law 1989*, p 125.

duty and identifying those "proximate" as being the class for whose benefit the legislation was passed.[58]

## III. LIABILITY OF THE BUILDER

**[13.48]** Under this heading we are contemplating the position of a builder as such: that is, the builder who is not also a vendor or lessor of property. In other words, we are not concerned with the "spec builder" here. A "spec" (ie speculative) builder is one who builds a house (or houses) without having a definite buyer in mind. Such a builder takes a chance that a buyer will emerge for the completed product. A "contract builder" on the other hand, is a builder who undertakes to build a house on specified instructions and to fixed specifications. The distinction is important because liability for defects used to be different in both cases.

### Defects of Quality: "Contract Builders"

**[13.49]** In relation to the "contract builder" the courts have recognised that in the absence of express words to the contrary there was to be implied

> "a threefold undertaking by the builder: (i) that the builder will do the work in a good and workmanlike manner; (ii) that he or she will supply good and proper materials; and (iii) that the house, built or to be built, will be reasonably fit for human habitation".[59]

### Dangerous Defects: "Contract Builders"

**[13.50]** In tort nowadays, the contract builder is liable for negligence in the same way as the manufacturer is liable for defective products which cause injury to the ultimate consumer. In other words *Donoghue v Stevenson* principles apply.

**[13.51]** With regard to contractual liability two further points can be made in the present context. First, the owner of the premises may benefit from the Sale of Goods and Supply of Services Act 1980, which as its name suggests applies to services provided, as well as to the sale of goods now. The 1980 Act may well imply into the contract between the builder and the owner of the premises terms in relation to the quality of the work and materials

---

58. See more generally Ch 21 below. See Byrne & Binchy, *Annual Review of Irish Law 1989*, pp 124-125. In relation to public authorities' liability under statute other than as housing authorities, the Courts have been more reluctant to find the necessary proximity to bring negligence into play. See *Sunderland v Louth County Council* [1990] ILRM 658 - planning authority; *Convery v Dublin County Council* [1996] 3 IR 153 (SC rev HC) - planning and road authority, especially Keane J at 23 judgment; *Rowe v Bus Éireann and Wicklow County Council* High Court, 3 March 1994 (Carroll J) - Road Authority, see also Ch 24 below. In *Convery*, the plaintiff sued the defendant in its capacity as a planning and road authority. Keane J in his judgment dismissing the plaintiff's claim, said (at 174):

> "As to the claim founded in negligence, it is clear that the plaintiff has failed to establish that there was a relationship between her and the County Council which created a duty to take reasonable care arising from their public duty under statute. The powers and duties of the County Council as planning authority and roads authority are vested in them in order to ensure the proper planning and development of their area and the provision and maintenance of an appropriate network in that area. While their exercise of those powers and duties can be regulated by the High Court by means of judicial review process so as to ensure that they are exercised only in accordance with law, the plaintiff does not belong to any category of persons to whom the Council, in the exercise of those powers, owed a duty of care at common law."

59. SALMOND & HEUSTON (19th ed), p 329, citing *Billyack v Leyland Construction Co Ltd* [1968] 1 WLR 471 and *McGeary v Campbell* [1975] NI 7.

which would not have been implied at common law.[60] Secondly, the existence of a contract between the builder and the owner does not mean that the owner's rights are confined to contract: the owner may also in appropriate cases sue in tort. In facing in this argument in *Siney v Dublin Corporation*, Henchy J dismissed the argument in a rather brusque fashion:

> "I do not think that the existence of a contract of tenancy, or of liability under that contract, excludes liability in negligence. Liability under both heads may exist simultaneously: this Court so held in *Finlay v Murtagh.*"[61]

**[13.52]** It is clear, therefore, that the builder does not, as such, inherit any of the immunities that may have applied at one time to the vendor or lessor. The restrictive interpretation of the common law immunity to vendors and lessors of real property only, had been adopted in the Northern Ireland case of *Gallagher v N McDowell Ltd.*[62] In this case a dwelling house was erected by the defendants, a firm of building contractors, for the Northern Ireland Housing Trust. It was inspected by the Housing Trust's architect, and the plaintiff's husband was the first tenant. The plaintiff was injured shortly afterwards when the heel of her shoe went through a floor board. The floor board, when being laid, had a defect which was improperly repaired by the insertion of a plug of wood which gave way under the plaintiff's heel. The Court of Appeal, reversing the trial judge, held that the defendants were under a duty to the plaintiff, as a lawful user of the house they had constructed, to take reasonable care in the repair of the hole in the defective floor board. Lord McDermott LCJ, having examined all the authorities, held that, while the immunities of vendors and lessors were well established they must be confined to vendors and lessors: others could be liable for defects in realty. And the suggestion that *Donoghue v Stevenson* never applied to realty was a proposition with which he could not agree.

> "In my opinion, the cases since *Donoghue v Stevenson* show that the landowner's immunities, which I have described as settled before that decision, have not been disturbed by it. But the fact that these immunities arise in relation to defects and dangers on land does not mean that the law imposes no neighbourly duty of reasonable care as respects defects and dangers of that kind. The immunities attach to landowners as such, and I do not think one is at liberty to jump from that to saying that the law of negligence in relation to what is dangerous draws a clear distinction between what are chattels and what, by attachment or otherwise, form part of the realty. Why should it? Such a distinction does not justify itself, and it is not required by the immunities I have mentioned when one is not dealing with landowners as such."[63]

**[13.53]** In *Colgan v Connolly Construction Company (Ireland) Ltd*[64] the plaintiff who was the second owner and occupier of a dwelling house sued the defendant building company for damages in respect of defects in the dwelling house. The High Court had no difficulty in applying *Donoghue v Stevenson* to the case (citing *Gallagher v N McDowell Ltd*). McMahon J stated:

---

60. See Part IV of the Act especially s 39. See further Clark, *Contract Law in Ireland* (4th ed, 1998), pp 180-181.
61. [1980] IR 422.
62. [1961] NI 26.
63. [1961] NI 26 at 38. Whether the immunity still applies even to vendors and lessors is now very much doubted. *Cf* fns 33, 34 and 35 above and accompanying text.
64. [1980] ILRM 33 (HC).

> "I am satisfied ... that the principle of *Donoghue v Stevenson* applies to the relationship between the builder of a house and a subsequent occupier so as to entitle the occupier to recover damages against the builder for personal injuries caused by defects in the house which are attributable to the negligence of the builder and which are not discoverable by the kind of examination which the builder could reasonably expect the occupier to make before occupying the house."

**[13.54]** Apart from applying negligence principles the decision clearly indicates that the builder is not automatically excused in this type of case by the fact that the plaintiff might have discovered the defects if he or she had taken the opportunity of having the property professionally surveyed. With regard to the possibility and effect of an intermediate examination, McMahon J said:

> "Section 34(2)(f) of the Civil Liability Act 1961 seems to me to have shifted the onus of proof to the defendants in product liability cases. That section provides that the fact that there has been a reasonable possibility or probability of examination after the thing had left the hands of the defendants shall not, by itself, exclude the defendants' duty but may be taken as evidence that he was not in the circumstances negligent in parting with the thing in its dangerous state."

**[13.55]** The damages which the plaintiff would be entitled to in such an action would, of course, include damages for personal injuries caused by defects in the building (this did not arise in the *Colgan* case) and damages in respect of expense incurred in removing "defects in the dwelling which threaten the health or safety of the occupier". With regard to defects of quality, however, which did not pose a threat to the health or safety of the occupier, the Court held that the liability of the builder rested in contract only. Accordingly, the plaintiff in the *Colgan* case was not able to recover damages for defects in the internal plaster or for defects in the porch roof. Defects in the main roof of the dwelling, however, were recoverable in so far as they could easily result in personal injury. In *Ward v McMaster*,[65] however, Costello J, in a decision which was not challenged in the Supreme Court, held, in effect, that the Court in *Colgan* was wrong in refusing to award damages for defects in the quality of workmanship which did not threaten health or safety. Costello J "explained" *Colgan*[66] on the basis that it had been handed down before *Junior Books Ltd v Veitchi*[67] which changed the law on this matter and which was approved by Costello J. Having examined the holding in *Junior Books*, Costello J concluded:

> "There is no doubt that this case has extended the liability of a builder for loss sustained by defective workmanship. I find its reasoning persuasive and I have no difficulty in applying it. It follows from it that the concept of reasonable foresight is one to be employed not only in deciding in a given case whether a duty of care *exists*, but also can be employed in determining its *scope*. Applying this concept to the present case it seems to me that the duty of care which the defendant owed to a purchaser of the bungalow which he built was one relating to hidden defects not discoverable by the kind of examination which he could reasonably expect his purchaser to make before occupying the house. But the duty was not limited to avoiding foreseeable harm to persons or property other than the bungalow itself (that is a duty to avoid dangerous hidden defects in the bungalow) but extended to a duty to avoid causing the purchaser consequential financial loss arising from hidden defects in the

65. [1985] IR 29 (HC), affd by Supreme Court, 10 May 1988. See further para **[10.09]-[10.11]** below.
66. [1980] ILRM 33 (HC).
67. [1983] 1 AC 520.

> bungalow itself, (that is a duty to avoid defects in the quality of the work). It also seems to me that the defendant should have foreseen that if he caused the bungalow to be so badly constructed as to force the plaintiff and his wife to leave it that this would cause them both inconvenience and discomfort, and so he owed a duty both to the plaintiff and his wife not to cause hidden defects which would result in such inconvenience. The conclusion is consistent with the decision of the Supreme Court in *Siney* in which the Court upheld an award of damages in negligence to the plaintiff and his family for the inconvenience that each suffered."[68]

**[13.56]** The House of Lords in *D & F Estates Ltd v Church Commissioners*[69] took a very different view on this matter, and later decisions[70] of that tribunal have sounded a further retreat from imposing liability on builders for negligently performed work. The possible impact of these decisions on Irish law will be assessed below.[71]

## IV. Liability of Builder/Vendor and Builder/Lessor

**[13.57]** We have seen from the above discussion that the common law conferred immunities on vendors and lessors of real property, but that the builder as such was fully liable for his or her negligent acts. At common law the more interesting question of the builder/vendor and the builder/lessor had then to be addressed. How was such a person to be dealt with? Was he or she to be classified as a builder, in which case he or she would be liable for negligence, or was he or she to be classified with vendors and lessors, in which event he or she would be entitled to common law immunities? In other words, is the bat to be classified as a mouse or a bird? If, as is suggested above, the vendors' and lessors' immunities are gone now in this jurisdiction, then the classification problem is not important because the vendors are treated in the same way as builders. This cannot be stated with such certainty at the moment, however, to render a discussion of the builder/vendor's problem superfluous.

**[13.58]** The importance of the problem can be fully appreciated when one recalls that the "spec builder" who accounts for so much of the housing needs of our society is indeed the typical builder/vendor. The "spec" builder builds on his or her own ground and sells the completed house to a member of the public. Can the disappointed purchaser whose spouse or child is injured when the roof collapses sue the builder/vendor and claim that as a builder he or she is liable in negligence?

**[13.59]** Earlier cases classified the builder/vendor as a vendor and so gave him or her the protection that the law conferred on this class. The force of precedent ensured that this position continued even after *Donoghue v Stevenson* was decided. Atkinson J in *Otto v Bolton and Norris*[72] stated that he could:

---

68. [1980] ILRM 33 at 44.
69. [1988] 3 WLR 368.
70. *Murphy v Brentwood DC* [1991] AC 398; *Department of the Environment v Thomas Bates & Son* [1991] 1 AC 499.
71. See para **[13.71]-[13.76]** below.
72. [1936] 2 KB 46.

"find in no case any suggestion that a builder selling a house after completion is, in his capacity of builder, under any obligation to take care towards a future purchaser, let alone other persons who may come to live in it."[73]

**[13.60]** In *Hoskins v Woodham*[74] Macnaghten J expressed the rule in the following language:

"It is quite certain that, in the sale of a completed house, where a sale is duly executed, and possession taken of the house after conveyance, there is no implied warranty that the house is reasonably fit for habitation."[75]

**[13.61]** The decision by the courts to emphasise the vending aspect of the builder/vendor's activities as opposed to his building role was of immense importance to speculative builders. A "spec builder" could, by selling or leasing the premises, immunise himself from negligence actions.

**[13.62]** Conditions change, however, and conditions that once argued for the builder/vendor's immunity gave way to different pressures:

"When the rules relating to this branch of law were being formulated in the nineteenth century the purchaser or tenant was primarily concerned with the land. Accordingly, his interest in the house or buildings that might have been on the property were incidental to the main concern of the transaction. Moreover, the purchaser or tenant, in the agricultural context of the time, had sufficient skill to execute the relatively simply maintenance needs of his house. He was also less mobile, and when he was a tenant this continuity of residence provided him with the incentive to repair. The modern purchaser/tenant, however, is more properly characterised as a highly mobile unit living in an urban environment, who posseses 'a single specialized skill unrelated to maintenance work', lives in a complex building unit, lacks the finance to make more than minor repairs, and whose primary concern is not addressed to the land as such, but to securing for himself and his family a place to live. Rules which were developed and articulated in the former factual situation must now be reassessed in the light of these new social facts."[76]

**[13.63]** The immunity conferred on builder/vendors gradually came to be perceived as an unacceptable anomaly in the law of torts. After *Donoghue v Stevenson* had established the general principle that a person should be liable for foreseeable damage caused by his or her negligent acts, the position of several privileged persons was eroded. In particular, the person who makes negligent statements,[77] the occupier of premises[78] and probably the gratuitous bailor of goods[79] have all seen their privileged positions overtaken by

73. [1936] 2 KB 46 at 52. *Cf* Heuston, '*Donoghue v Stevenson* in Retrospect' (1957) 20 MLR 1 at 1921.
74. [1938] 1 All ER 692.
75. [1938] 1 All ER 692 at 695.
76. LRC Working Paper No 1 1977, *The Law Relating to the Liability of Builders, Vendors and Lessors for the Quality and Fitness of Premises* and the Commission's *Report on Defective Premises* (LRC-3 1982) at 36-37.
77. *Hedley Byrne & Co Ltd v Heller and Partners Ltd* [1964] AC 465. *Cf Bank of Ireland v Smith* [1966] IR 646.
78. *McNamara v ESB* [1975] IR 1. The Occupiers' Liability Act 1995, in response to strong lobbying from farming organisations, has largely restored the *status quo ante* in respect of claims by trespassers and has reduced the level of duty owed to "recreational users": see Ch 12 above.
79. *Campbell v O'Donnell* [1967] IR 226.

negligence principles. Why, it may well be asked, should not the builder/vendor be also subjected to the same standard nowadays? Why should the act of selling or leasing protect the housebuilder from liability?

**[13.64]** The case law on this topic over the past thirty years has recognised the force of these arguments and from it one may perceive an inexorable trend towards depriving the builder/vendor and the builder/lessor of the immunities heretofore granted by the law. *Dutton v Bognor Regis UDC*[80] was the first important recent English decision on this matter.

**[13.65]** In that case a builder applied for and received planning permission to erect a detached house on a piece of leasehold owned by him. During the course of construction the foundations were inspected by an officer of the Urban District Council who negligently certified that the foundations complied with local bylaws. The house was completed and was sold by the builder/owner to a Mr Clarke in January 1960. In December 1960 Mr Clarke sold the house to the plaintiff Mrs Dutton. Some months later the house began to subside because of the defects on the foundations. Mrs Dutton brought an action against the builder and against the Council for negligence. The action against the builder was settled for £625 in spite of the fact that legal authorities on the matter at the time suggested that builder/vendors were immune from liability. There both Lord Denning MR, and Sachs LJ were prepared to say that the immunity conferred on the builder/vendor of a house no longer existed.

**[13.66]** The correctness of the majority in *Dutton* was confirmed by the House of Lords in *Anns v Merton London Borough Council.*[81] In the *Anns* case the owners of some property built seven maisonettes which they let in 1962 on long leases. In 1970 structural defects manifested themselves in the buildings and the plaintiffs sued the builder/owners. They also sued the Borough Council for negligence in approving the foundations on which the block was erected and in failing to inspect the said foundations. Some of the plaintiffs were the original lessees while others held an assignment from original lessees.

**[13.67]** The House of Lords, in respect of the supposed immunity enjoyed by the builder/ vendor or lessor at common law, agreed with the Court of Appeal in *Dutton's* case.

> "That immunity, as I understand it, rests partly on a distinction being made between chattels and real property, partly upon the principle of '*caveat emptor*' or, in the case where the owner leases the property, on the proposition 'for fraud apart there is no law against letting a tumbledown house'. But leaving aside such cases as arise between contracting parties, when the terms of the contract have to be considered ..., I am unable to understand why this principle or proposition should prevent recovery in a suitable case by a person, who has subsequently acquired the house, on the principle of *Donoghue v Stevenson*: the same rules should apply to all careless acts of a builder: whether he happens also to own the land or not. I agree generally with the conclusions of Lord Denning MR on this point (*Dutton's* case). In the alternative, since it is the duty of the builder (owner or not) to comply with the byelaws, I would be of opinion that an action could be brought against him, in effect, for breach of

---

80. [1972] 1 QB 373, analysed by Goldberg 'The Tortious Duties of Care: Reflections on *Dutton v Bognor Regis UDC*' (1972) 1 Anglo-American LR 509.

81. [1978] AC 728. See Stanton (1977) 93 LQR 488; Buxton (1978) 41 MLR 85; Banahas [1977] Camb LJ 245; Oliver [1980] CLP 269.

> statutory duty by any person for whose benefit or protection the byelaw was made. So I do not think that there is any basis here for arguing from a supposed immunity of the builder to immunity of the council."[82]

**[13.68]** Some of the statements of O'Higgins CJ and Henchy J in *Siney*[83] could be interpreted as resolving the issue,[84] but a clearer holding that the builder/vendor was to be classified in accordance with his building activity and therefore liable for negligence to the occupier is to be found in *Ward v McMaster*.[85] The facts of this case were as follows. The plaintiffs, a married couple, purchased a house from McMaster and moved into possession in 1981. Shortly thereafter they discovered that the house was grossly substandard, was structurally unsound, a source of danger, and a risk to health. They vacated the house and sued the vendor/builder, the local authority (for breach of statutory duties), and the auctioneer who valued the property for the local authority. No negligence was found against the auctioneer and the verdict against the local authority was appealed to the Supreme Court (see below). It is with Costello J's judgment against the vendor/ builder that we are concerned here. It should be noted that the vendor was not in any sense a trained builder: he bought the site and built the house with the help of his father ("a handyman") and his brother. He lived in the house for four years before selling it to the first named plaintiff, Mr Ward. Having examined the existing authorities Costello J concluded as follows:

> "These developments justify me in holding that in this country, as in England, the immunity in tort of a builder who owns the land on which the house is built and who subsequently sells it to a purchaser (or who lets it to a lessee) no longer exists. And I am satisfied both in principle and on authority that in this case the first named defendant when building the bungalow owed a duty of care to the person to whom he might subsequently sell it, based on the neighbour principle established in *Donoghue v Stevenson*. There are no facts here arising under contract or otherwise that require that that duty should be restricted or limited in any way; ..."[86]

**[13.69]** In particular it made no difference that the defendant lived in the house for some years before selling it to the plaintiff.

**[13.70]** With regard to the scope of the duty, Costello J held, as already noted, that the plaintiff could recover for quality defects and for inconvenience as well as for dangerous defects.[87]

---

82. [1978] AC 728 at 759 - internal citation to *Robbins v Jones* (1863) 15 CB (ns) 221 at 240, 143 ER 786 at 776.

83. [1980] IR 400.

84. See para **[13.24]** and Costello J in *Ward v McMaster* Supreme Court, 10 May, 1988, affg [1985] IR 29 (HC).

85. [1985] IR 29, affd by Supreme Court on other grounds, 10 May 1988.

86. [1985] IR 29 at 42. See also *Sunderland v McGreavey* [1987] IR 372 (HC). Liability imposed on builder/vendor when site on which house was built was liable to flooding. Measure of damages was difference between house as it was and house as it would have been if not susceptible to flooding. Consequential loss of £3,000 also awarded. No liability on architect or on planning authority which authorised retention of house built without authority.

87 See *Bowen v Paramount (Builders) Hamilton Ltd* [1977] 1 NZLR 394; *Batty v Metropolitan Property Realizations Ltd* [1978] QB 554.

## Qualitative Defects and Dangerous Defects Discovered before Injury or Damage is Caused

**[13.71]** It is necessary to look a little closer at two questions. First we must ask whether there is a good basis for imposing liability on a builder for qualitative, non-dangerous defects attributable to the builder's negligence in the construction of the premises. Secondly, we must examine the policy arguments surrounding the issue of compensating a purchaser of a premises who discovers that the premises contain a dangerous defect that risks causing injury and who is out of pocket as a result of removing the risk (by repair, for example, or by selling at a loss). In *Ward v McMaster*, Costello J had no difficulty in imposing liability in both cases. Yet in Britain, subsequent to *Ward v McMaster*, the House of Lords has taken a different view.[88] Is there anything in its later analysis that would encourage a similar *volte face* in Ireland?

**[13.72]** So far as qualitative defects are concerned, the arguments are finely balanced. Against imposing liability for negligently caused qualitative defects in buildings it may be suggested that contract law deals adequately and sensitively with this kind of loss, that the very concept of a qualitative defect is one that has to be sourced from contractually driven expectations and that pure economic loss resulting from qualitative defects is of too broad and uncertain character to generate liability in tort. In favour of imposing liability, it may be replied that there can be no objection in principle to awarding compensation in appropriate cases. It all depends on the degree of proximity between the parties and the foreseeability of the loss. In the case of builders and purchasers (even subsequent purchasers), the degree of proximity and foreseeability can be very high. When one adds a heavy degree of reliance, which often exists in this relationship, the argument for liability is still stronger.

**[13.73]** The position relating to dangerous defects that are discovered before they cause injury is quite different. The British courts have rejected liability for such defects on the formalistic and unconvincing basis that the loss sustained by the plaintiff in removing the danger is purely economic.[89] Of course it is – Lord Denning MR was guilty of a barefaced mischaracterisation when he claimed it was "physical damage"[90] – but that is no good reason for denying compensation. The economic loss was suffered for the purpose of preventing physical injury. What more deserving reason could there be for suffering it?[91] Moreover, the class of claimants for this kind of loss will be very narrow and identifiable. The likelihood is that in most cases the degrees of proximity and foreseeability will be

---

87. (contd) In the appeal to the Supreme Court in *Ward v McMaster* this part of Costello J's holding was not contested and McCarthy J apparently approved Costello J's statement of the law relating to builder/vendors when he said: "The vendor/builder had no answer was decreed and has not appealed ..."

88. *D & F Estates Ltd v Church Commissioners* [1989] AC 177; *Murphy v Brentwood DC* [1991] AC 398; *Department of the Environment v Bates* [1991] AC 449. See further FLEMING, pp 525-529.

89. *D & F Estates Ltd v Church Commissioners* [1989] AC 177; *Murphy v Brentwood DC* [1991] AC 398; *Department of the Environment v Bates* [1991] AC 499.

90. *Dutton v Bognor Regis United Building Co* [1972] 1 QB 373 at 396 (CA). *Cf Murphy v Brentwood DC* [1991] 1 AC 470 (*per* Lord Keith).

91. For discussion of the issues raised see Cooke 'An Impossible Distinction?' (1991) 107 LQR 46; O'Dair 'A House Built on Firm Foundations?' (1991) 54 MLR 561.

high. If, in one odd case, it emerges that they are not, the court is under no obligation to award damages. Finally, there are compelling reasons of policy to impose liability for this kind of loss where the requisite proximity and foreseeability are established. To leave plaintiffs uncompensated would discourage them from taking the necessary steps, with due expedition, to make the premises safe. Where the premises are of a public character – such as a cinema or football stadium, for example – the law should strive to encourage a sense of urgency rather than lethargy in the person who learns of the danger. Even in relation to private residences the case in favour of imposing liability is very strong. The law of contract will not always be available against the negligent builder: certainly it will not be available where a subsequent purchaser discovers the danger.[92]

**[13.74]** Will the Irish courts go down the same road as their British counterparts on these two issues? There has not been a case since *Ward v McMaster* squarely raising either of them. Nothing that the courts have said on the general matter of the duty of care or the more specific question of liability for pure economic loss suggests a judicial propensity to depart from *Ward v McMaster*. Indeed, *McShane v Wholesale Fruit & Vegtables Ltd v Johnston Haulage Company Ltd*[93] would indicate the complete absence of judicial anxiety about liability for pure economic loss.

**[13.75]** Having said this, it should be acknowledged frankly that the arguments relating to liability for qualitative defects are finely balanced and that those against imposing liability have yet to be put to an Irish court in a case where the qualitative defects were not accompanied by other, dangerous, defects. If an Irish court in the future were to contemplate rejecting *Junior Books* and Costello J's judgment in *Ward v McMaster*, it would have to contemplate embarking on a difficult philosophical journey to distinguish between those defects that are qualitative and those that are incipiently dangerous and between damage to the premises itself and damage to other property. The British courts have been driven to develop a "complex structure" theory to deal with the anomalies flowing from the latter distinction, with the inevitable result of creating new anomalies.[94]

**[13.76]** We reiterate our firm view that the Irish courts will not, and ought not, deny compensation to plaintiffs who suffer economic loss as a result of neutralising a danger to health and safety in premises that was caused by the negligence of the defendant. The arguments in favour of continuing to adhere to the approach adopted in *Colgan* and *Ward v McMaster* are compelling from the standpoints of justice and of social policy.

## Voluntary Schemes

**[13.77]** For many years the construction industry in many countries has seen the desirability of improving building standards in a selfregulatory manner. In some countries this desire sprang from a genuine concern with poor standards within the industry itself and with the plight of the purchaser in particular. In other countries this concern displayed itself so late that its altruism must be suspected. It would not be unfair to suggest that, in

92. *Cf* the convincing analysis by Mason CJ, Deane and Gaudron JJ in *Bryan v Maloney* (1985) 182 CLR 609 (HC, Austr 1995).

93. [1997] 1 ILRM 86.

94. *Cf* MARKESINIS & DEAKIN, pp 106-107.

Ireland, it was in part the fear that threatened legislation would impose strict standards which drove the industry to suggest some forms of self-regulation.

**[13.78]** Such self-regulatory measures usually take the form of a registration scheme for builders which attempts to ensure the quality and the financial stability of builders registered therein.

**[13.79]** The Construction Industry Federation with the support of the Department of the Environment and the building societies now runs a limited guarantee scheme in respect of new houses in Ireland.[95]

## Proposals for Reform

**[13.80]** The Law Reform Commission, in Working Paper No 1 (1977), *The Law Relating to the Liability of Builders, Vendors and Lessors for the Quality and Fitness of Premises, and in its Report on Defective Premises,*[96] published in 1982, has proposed a more radical solution. Very briefly, the approach favoured by the Commission would impose a duty on persons undertaking any building work to carry out the work in a proper manner with suitable materials, so that the premises, if they consist of a dwelling, will be reasonably fit for occupation and habitation. This duty would be owed, not only to the person who commissioned the work, but also to every other person who acquired an interest in the premises. Persons selling or leasing premises would owe a duty to all persons who might unreasonably be affected by defects in the condition of the premises to take reasonable care that they are left reasonably secure from personal injuries or from damage to their property caused by the defects, provided that the vendor or lessor ought to have known of the defects at the time of the sale or lease.

## Architects, Engineers, Surveyors, etc

**[13.81]** It is worth noting finally that architects, engineers, surveyors and auctioneers may also be negligent in the building context and, accordingly, may be considered as suitable defendants in appropriate circumstances. Liability here may arise in contract and in tort. The same principles of law that apply to any professional doctor, solicitor, accountant apply also to architects, engineers, surveyors and auctioneers. If I engage any such person to design, supervise or report for me I may sue him or her in contract if he or she fails to discharge his contractual obligations. In addition, I may sue him or her in tort also.[97] Even if no contract exists I may still sue such a person in the appropriate case where he or she

95. For criticism for the Scheme as introduced see (LRC 1-1977), pp 80-81. The Safety, Health and Welfare at Work (Construction) Regulations 1995 (SI 138/1995) extend the scope of duties and the range of those falling under a duty in regard to construction work. See MacNamee 'The 1995 Construction Regulations - The Widening Legal Net' (1998) 2 Ir Ins LR 43.

96. (LRC 3-1982).

97. *Finlay v Murtagh* [1979] IR 249. Cases involving litigation (sometimes unsuccessful) against architects, engineers and surveyors include *Curley and Dowley v Mulcahy* High Court, 21 December 1977 (McMahon J); *Quinn v Quality Homes Ltd* [1976-77] ILRM 314 (HC); *Flanagan v Griffith* (1985) Prof Neg LR 95 (HC); *Kinehan v McNamara & Co* High Court, 1 March 1985; *Savage (JC) Ltd v Wallace Oppermann Architects and Designers Ltd* [1997] Ir L Log W 295 (CC); *Martin v Irish Industrial Benefit Society* [1960] Ir Jur Rep 42.

owed me a duty of care (ie where proximity exists) and where he or she failed to take reasonable care thereby causing me foreseeable damage.[98]

**[13.82]** Whether the defendant will be liable for not taking reasonable care, however, will vary depending on the circumstances of each case. In *Sunderland v McGreavey*,[99] for instance, an architect who was asked to do a visual inspection (as opposed to a complete survey) in a hurry, was held not liable when it transpired that the property was liable to flooding. In *Crowley v Allied Irish Banks*,[100] the assumption was clearly accepted that architects would be liable for injuries caused by defective design, although in that case the court held that there was a *novus actus interveniens* which sundered the *nexus* between the architect's negligence and the plaintiff's injuries and that, for this reason the architects could not be liable. Furthermore, a professional engaged to carry out a task will not be expected to possess qualifications which he does not profess or hold himself out as possessing. In *Ward v McMaster*[101] the local authority employed an auctioneer to value a house and when the house turned out to be structurally unsound an attempt by the purchaser to sue the auctioneer failed because the auctioneer had no professional expertise to assess the structure etc of the building. His function was merely to value the property on what he saw and on the assumption that there was no latent defect.

---

98. See generally Jackson & Powell *Professional Negligence* (4th ed, 1997), Ch 2; Yule 'Architects and Engineers' Ch 3 (1999) *Professional Liability: Law and Insurance* (Hodgin ed) Fernyhough & Franklin *The Liability of the Architect in Contract and Tort*, Ch 2 (1994) *The Legal Obligations of the Architect* (Burns ed); Leong & Chan 'Architects' Design Duties: A Shift from *Bolam* to the Objective Test' (1999) 15 Prof Neg 3; *Irish Building and Engineering Case Law* (1989) Lyden ed; Keane *Building and the Law* (3rd ed, 1998), Ch 9; Ross & Gwillim 'Architects, Engineers and Quality Surveyors', Ch 5 *Professional Negligence Cases* (1998) (Pittway & Hammerton ed).

99. *Sunderland v McGreavey* [1987] IR 372 (HC). *Cf Bedford v Lane* (1991) Prof Neg LR 355 (HC).

100. [1988] ILRM 225.

101. [1985] IR 29.

# Chapter 14

# Professional Negligence

## I. INTRODUCTION

**[14.01]** The law relating to professional negligence contains some distinctive principles which merit particular attention.[1] The unenviable task of defining a "profession" in this context has yet to be addressed comprehensively by our courts.[2] The traditional view has been that professions are characterised by the specialised intellectual work involved, the underlying moral duties to the client and the community, and the high social status attaching to their members.[3] All of these characteristics can, of course, be challenged and debated: the notion of attributing prestige to a limited number of occupations has been criticised as elitist, arbitrary and undemocratic.

**[14.02]** So far as medicine is concerned, the Supreme Court, in *Kelly v St Laurence's Hospital*,[4] was satisfied that nursing care is not to be subjected to these distinctive principles. In contrast, in *Hughes v JJ Power Ltd*,[5] Blayney J considered that these principles should be applied to mechanics, as persons "exercising and professing to have [a] special skill".[6]

---

1. See generally Jackson & Powell, *Professional Negligence* (4th ed, 1997); Dugdale & Stanton, *Professional Negligence* (3rd ed, 1998); Hodgin ed, *Professional Liability: Law and Insurance* (2nd ed, 1999).
2. In England, in the Court of Appeal decision of *Commissioners of Inland Revenue v Maxse* [1919] 1 KB 647 at 657 (where the issue related to taxation rather than negligence), Scrutton LJ dealt with the definitional question as follows:

   > "The next question is what is a profession? I am very reluctant finally to propound a comprehensive definition. A set of facts not present to the mind of the judicial propounder, and not raised in the case before him, may immediately arise to confound his proposition. But it seems to me as at present advised that a 'profession' in the present use of language involves the idea of an occupation requiring either purely intellectual skill, or of manual skill controlled, as in painting and sculpture, or surgery, by the intellectual skill, of the operator, as distinguished from an occupation which is substantially the production or sale or arrangements for the production or sale of commodities. The line of demarcation may vary from time to time. The word 'profession' used to be confined to the three learned professions, the Church, Medicine and Law. It has now, I think, a wider meaning."

3. *Cf* Jackson & Powell, *Professional Negligence* (4th ed, 1997), para 1.01. Our courts have generally applied distinctive principles to "traditional" professions, such as medicine and law.
4. [1989] ILRM 437 (SC).
5. High Court, 11 May 1988 (Blayney J).
6. Page 6 of judgment. In favouring this approach, Blayney J may have brought the notion of professional negligence back to its historical origins: *Cf* Kaye 'The Liability of Solicitors in Tort' (1984) 100 LQR 680 at 687.

**[14.03]** Of course, professional persons owe contractual duties to their clients.[7] For a time, these contractual duties were regarded[8] as excluding liability in tort for negligence, but today the two headings of potential liability are regarded as concurrent.[9]

**[14.04]** A central distinctive principle of professional negligence relates to the deference which courts give to customary practice. By virtue of their traditions, their rules of self-regulation, and the high intellectual calibre of their members, professionals are regarded by the courts as being substantially competent to determine, and require, a satisfactory standard of competence in the performance of professional duties. Thus, if a member of a profession can show that he or she adhered to the customary practice of his or her profession, this should normally be sufficient to relieve him or her of the accusation of negligence. However, the courts reserve to themselves the power to have the last word on the question, though it is a power they will exercise sparingly, in only the clearest of cases.

**[14.05]** In *O'Donovan v Cork County Council*[10] Walsh J expressed the position as follows:

> "A medical practitioner cannot be held negligent if he honours general and approved practice in the situation with which he is faced ...[11] That proposition is not, however, without qualification. If there is a common practice which has inherent defects, which ought to be obvious to any person giving the matter due consideration, the fact that it is shown to have been widely and generally adopted over a period of time does not make the practice any the less negligent. Neglect of duty does not cease by repetition of neglect of duty. Furthermore, if there be a dispute of fact as to whether or not a particular practice is a general and approved practice, it is for a jury to determine whether or not the impugned treatment is general and approved practice. In such circumstances a jury would be told that if they find that there is such a general and approved practice they must acquit the practitioner where there is not the qualification which I have referred to above. If some witnesses say that a particular practice is a general and approved one and other medical witnesses deny that, then it is an issue of fact to be determined as any other issue of fact. This particular issue cannot be withdrawn from a jury merely because the practice finds support among some medical witnesses if there be others who deny the fact that it is general and approved practice."[12]

**[14.06]** In *Roche v Peilow*,[13] the Supreme Court reasserted this approach. Henchy J observed that the reason for the exception or qualification mentioned by Walsh J in *O'Donovan* was that:

> "the duty imposed by the law rests on the standard to be expected from a reasonably careful member of the profession, and a person cannot be said to be acting reasonably if he automatically and mindlessly follows the practice of others when by taking thought he would have realised that the practice in question was fraught with peril for his client and was readily avoidable or remediable. The professional man is, of course, not to be judged with the benefit of hindsight, but if it can be said that, if at the time, on giving the matter due

---

7. *Cf* Jackson & Powell, *Professional Negligence* (4th ed, 1997), paras 1.08-1.12.
8. *Cf* para **[14.169]** below.
9. *Finlay v Murtagh* [1979] IR 249 (SC); *Wall v Hegarty* [1980] ILRM 124 (HC); *Roche v Peilow* [1986] ILRM 189 at 195 (SC).
10. [1967] IR 173 (SC).
11. Citing *Daniels v Heskin* [1954] IR 73.
12. [1967] IR 173 at 193-194.
13. [1986] ILRM 189 (SC).

consideration, he would have realised that the impugned practice was in the circumstances incompatible with his client's interest, and if an alternative and safe course of conduct was reasonably open to him, he will be held to have been negligent."[14]

**[14.07]** And McCarthy J was of the view that:

> "it cannot be a legal principle that a professional is, so to speak, entitled to 'one free bite' - to wait until damage has occurred before taking an obvious means of avoiding such damage."[15]

## II. Medical Negligence[16]

**[14.08]** While some have argued[17] that a strict liability regime could with benefit be applied to medical mishaps, the present law is not so stringent. A doctor is not considered to have failed in his or her duty towards a patient on mere proof that the patient's condition has not improved or has, in fact, deteriorated. The essential test is whether the doctor has behaved reasonably. Thus, conduct falling short of perfection does not inevitably amount to negligence.[18]

**[14.09]** The standard of care required of medical practitioners has been analysed in a number of decisions over the past fifty years.[19] The *locus classicus* is *Dunne v National*

---

14. [1986] ILRM 189 at 197 (Hederman J concurring).
15. [1986] ILRM 189 at 204. See also Walsh J at 194-195, and Griffin J at 199.
16. See generally White, *Medical Negligence Actions* (1996); Power & Harris eds, *Clinical Negligence* (3rd ed, 2000); Phillips, *Medical Negligence Law: Seeking a Balance* (1997); Tomkin & Hanafin, *Irish Medical Law* (1995), Ch 5; *Suing Doctors, Hospitals and Health Board*, a conference held at the Law School of Trinity College, Dublin on 14 October 2000; Delany 'The Civil Responsibility of Medical Practitioners' (1952) 9 NILQ 206; Anon 'Hospitals, Doctors, Nurses and Negligence' (1943) 77 ILT & Sol J 83, 89; Nathan, *Medical Negligence* (1952); Fleming 'Developments in the English Law of Medical Liability' (1959) 12 Vand LR 633; Sherman 'The Standard of Care in Malpractice Cases' (1966) 4 OHLJ 222; Quest 'Recent Developments in Medical Negligence' (1980) 1 Med & L 483; Linden 'The Negligent Doctor' (1973) 11 Osgoode Hall LJ 31; Rozovsky 'Medical Malpractice in Canada' (1977) I Legal Med Q 2; Johnson 'Note: An Evaluation of Changes in the Medical Standard of Care' (1970) 23 Vand LR 729; Oppenheim 'Standard of Care of Medical General Practitioners' (1960) 9 Clev-Mar LR 227; Bryce-Smith 'Malpractice in the United Kingdom' (1961) 10 Clev-Mar LR 10; McCoid 'The Care Required of Medical Practitioners' (1959) 12 Vand LR 549; Keeton 'Compensation for Medical Accidents' (1973) 121 U Pa LR 591; Fricke 'Medical Negligence' (1982) 56 Austr LJ 61; Deutsch 'Medical Negligence Reviewed' (1983) 57 Austr LJ 674; Gamble, *Professional Liability*, Ch 7 or McLean ed, Legal *Issues in Medicine* (1981).
17. Eg Ehrenzweig, 'Compulsory "Hospital-Accident" Insurance: A Needed First Step Towards Displacement of Liability for "Medical Malpractice"' (1964) 31 U Chicago LR 279; O'Connell 'Expanding No-Fault Beyond Auto Insurance: Some Proposals' (1973) 59 Va LR 749; but see Keeton 'Compensation for Medical Accidents' (1973) 121 U Pa LR 590. In Britain, in response to a rapid rise in insurance premiums, the BMA has recently proposed a no-fault compensation scheme, with a cap on damages, as an alternative (though not a mutually exclusive one) to tort litigation: see Bolt 'Compensating for Medical Mishaps - A Model "No Fault" Scheme' (1989) 139 New LJ 109; Mildred 'Reforming the Tort System', p 124.
18. *Daniels v Heskin* [1954] IR 73 at 84.
19. In *Daniels v Heskin* [1954] IR 73 at 75 (SC) Maguire CJ stated:

    > "A medical practitioner is liable for injury caused to another person to whom he owes a duty to take care if he fails to possess that amount of skill which is usual in his profession or if he neglects to use the skill which he possesses or the necessary degree of care demanded or professed."

*Maternity Hospital.*[20] Finlay CJ's judgment contains the modern authoritative statement of principle:

> "The courts have consistently recognised certain features in the general law of negligence which have particular reference to allegations of negligence made against professional persons in the carrying out of their professional duties. These particular features applicable to allegations of medical negligence have been fully set out by this Court in *O'Donovan v Cork County Council*...[21] The reasoning of *O'Donovan v Cork County Council* was ... approved and applied to a case of professional negligence by a solicitor in *Roche v Peilow*.[22] There was no argument submitted to us on the hearing of this appeal which constituted any form of challenge to the correctness of the statements of principle thus laid down, although there was controversy concerning their application to the facts of this case. The principles thus laid down related to issues raised in this case can in this manner be summarised:
>
> 1. The true test for establishing negligence in diagnosis or treatment on the part of a medical practitioner is whether he has been proved to be guilty of such failure as no medical practitioner of equal specialist or general status and skill would be guilty of if acting with ordinary care.
> 2. If the allegation of negligence against a medical practitioner is based on proof that he deviated from a general and approved practice, that will not establish negligence unless it is also proved that the course he did take was one which no medical practitioner of like specialisation and skill would have followed had he been taking the ordinary care required from a person of his qualification
> 3. If a medical practitioner charged with negligence defends his conduct by establishing that he followed a practice which was general, and which was approved of by his colleagues of similar specialisation and skill, he cannot escape liability if in reply the plaintiff establishes that such practice has inherent defects which ought to be obvious to any person giving the matter due consideration.
> 4. An honest difference of opinion between doctors as to which is the better of two ways of treating a patient does not provide any ground for leaving a question to the jury as to whether a person who has followed one course rather than the other has been negligent.
> 5. It is not for a jury (or for a judge) to decide which of two alternative courses of treatment is in their (or his) opinion preferable, but their (or his) function is merely to decide whether the course of treatment followed, on the evidence, complied with the careful conduct of a medical practitioner of like specialisation and skill to that professed by the defendant.

---

19. (contd) In the same case, (at 86) Kingsmill Moore J expanded somewhat on the duties owed by the doctor to his patient:

> "He must possess such knowledge and skill as conforms to the recognised contemporary standards of his profession and, if he is a specialist, such further and particularised skill and knowledge as he holds himself out to possess. He must use such skill and knowledge to form an honest and considered judgment as to what course, what action, what treatment, is in the best interests of his patient. He must display proper care and attention in treating, or in arranging suitable treatment for, his patient."

See also *Boyle v Martin* (1932) 66 ILTR 187 (CC); *O'Donovan v Cork County Council* [1967] IR 173 at 183-184 (SC).

20. [1989] IR 91 (SC).
21. [1967] IR 173.
22. [1985] IR 232.

6. If there is an issue of fact, the determination of which is necessary for the decision as to whether a particular medical practice is or is not general and approved within the meaning of these principles, that issue must in a trial held with a jury be left to the determination of the jury.

In order to make these general principles readily applicable to the facts of this case, with which I will later be dealing, it is necessary to state further conclusions not expressly referred to in the cases above mentioned. These are:

'General and approved practice' need not be universal but must be approved of and adhered to by a substantial number of reputable practitioners holding the relevant specialist or general qualifications.

Though treatment only is referred to in some of these statements of principle, they must apply in identical fashion to questions of diagnosis.

In an action against a hospital, where allegations are made of negligence against the medical administrators on the basis of a claim that practices and procedures laid down by them for the carrying out of treatment, or diagnosis by medical or nursing staff were defective, their conduct is to be tested in accordance with the legal principles which would apply if they had personally carried out such treatment or diagnosis in accordance with such practice or procedure."[23]

**[14.10]** The Chief Justice went on to observe:

"In order fully to understand these principles and their application to any particular set of facts, it is, I believe, helpful to set out certain broad parameters which would appear to underline their establishment. The development of medical science and the supreme importance of that development to humanity makes it particularly undesirable and inconsistent with the common good that doctors should be obliged to carry out their professional duties under frequent threat of unsustainable legal claims. The complete dependence of patients on the skill and care of their medical attendants and the gravity from their point of view of a failure in such care, makes it undesirable and unjustifiable to accept as a matter of law a lax or permissive standard of care for the purpose of assessing what is and is not medical negligence. In developing the legal principles outlined and in applying them to the facts of each individual case, the courts must constantly seek to give equal regard to both of these considerations."[24]

**[14.11]** A few points about the principles spelt out by the Chief Justice are in order. First, proposition 3 is in harmony with *O'Donovan* and *Roche v Peilow*. It represents a compromise between absolute deference to customary professional practice and what might be considered to be undue intrusion by the courts. By virtue of their traditions, their rules or of self-regulation, and the high intellectual calibre demanded of their members, professions are regarded by the courts as being substantially competent to determine and require a satisfactory standard of care in the performance of professional duties. But if customary practice has inherent defects which ought to be obvious to any person giving the matter due consideration, then the courts consider they can no longer stand idly by.

**[14.12]** A second point worth noting about the Chief Justice's proposition of law in *Dunne* is the reference, in propositions (1) and (2), to "*no* medical practitioner"[25] of equal

23. [1989] IR 91 at 108-110.
24. [1989] IR 91 at 110.
25. Emphasis added.

specialisation and skill. This might suggest that, if a defendant could dig up a *single* medical practitioner who acted as he or she had done, liability could not be imposed (subject to the "inherent defects" long-stop). In fact, this is not so, because even that single practitioner, to be of use to the defendant, would have to pass the test of ordinary care. The reference to "no medical practitioner ..." has a long and distinguished pedigree and, provided it is understood in context, need not confuse.

**[14.13]** Thirdly, the reference in proposition (4) to an "honest" difference of opinion between doctors as to which is the better of two ways of treating a patient should not be understood as providing an exemption from liability on the basis of an honest though unreasonable belief as to the desirability of a particular mode of treatment.

**[14.14]** Fourthly, the fact that the Courts Act 1988 abolished juries for personal injuries litigation renders the fourth ground largely otiose; it can still have relevance to the extent that the trial judge may dismiss a case at the conclusion of the plaintiff's evidence.

**[14.15]** In *Dunne*, the jury had awarded the plaintiff over a million pounds in a claim in which he had alleged negligence in the management of his mother's labour and of his birth, resulting in his sustaining brain damage. The Supreme Court held that the trial judge had erred in his direction to the jury in failing to make it clear that *deviation* from general and approved practice would constitute negligence only if no other hospital medical administrator or consultant obstetrician would have so deviated if he were taking the appropriate ordinary care, and that *adherence* to such practice would not involve negligence unless it was one which had inherent defects which should have been obvious on due consideration to a hospital administrator or consultant obstetrician.

**[14.16]** The court accordingly ordered a retrial, which later took place before Carroll J sitting without a jury as a result of the 1988 Act. The case was settled for £400,000 plus costs, payable by the hospital. The action against the consultant was dismissed without admission of liability.[26]

## Courts Should Guard Against Being Wise After the Event

**[14.17]** The courts have frequently stressed the dangers of being wise after the event and of failing to make allowances for the complicated task facing the doctor, the wide range of possible solutions, the element of emergency that may be present, and the less than ideal surroundings in which decisions may sometimes have to be made. As Kingsmill Moore J said in a Supreme Court decision in 1952:

> "Any attempt to substitute a rule of law, or even a rule of thumb practice, for the individual judgment of a qualified doctor, doing what he considers best for the particular patient, would be disastrous. There may be cases where the judgment of the physician is proved by subsequent events to have been wrong, but if it is honest and considered and if, in the circumstances known to him at the time, it can fairly be justified, he is not guilty of negligence. There may indeed be cases where the nature of the judgment formed or the advice given is such as to afford positive evidence that the physician has fallen short of the required standard of knowledge and skill, or that his judgment could not have been honest and considered, but it lies on the plaintiff to adduce evidence from which such a failure of duty can reasonably be inferred."[27]

---

26. See Irish Times, 9 December 1989.

27. *Daniels v Heskin* [1954] IR 73 at 86-87 (SC).

**[14.18]** Denning LJ echoed somewhat similar sentiments in the English case of *Roe v Ministry of Health*:[28]

> "... it is so easy to be wise after the event and to condemn as negligence that which was only misadventure. We ought always to be on our guard against it, especially in cases against hospitals and doctors. Medical science has conferred great benefits on mankind, but these benefits are attended by unavoidable risks. Every surgical operation is attended by risks. Every advance in techniques is also attended by risks. Doctors, like the rest of us, have to learn by experience. Experience often teaches in a hard way ...."

## Error of Judgment[29]

**[14.19]** A doctor will not be liable where he or she makes an error of judgment, provided that the error was not an unreasonable one. At first sight, this might appear to be an unduly lenient approach for the law to take, but when regard is had to the complicated task facing the doctor, as discussed above, the approach may be seen to have much to recommend it. That it does not constitute a licence to malpractice is apparent from the balanced statement on the subject by Kingsmill Moore J in *Daniels v Heskin*. [30]

**[14.20]** In England an attempt by Lord Denning MR to maintain that an error of judgment by a professional man "is not negligent"[31] was politely but forcibly criticised by the House of Lords on appeal. Lord Fraser said:

> "[I]n my respectful opinion, the statement as it stands is not an accurate statement of the law. Merely to describe something as an error of judgment tells us nothing about whether it is negligent or not. The true position is that an error of judgment may, or may not, be negligent; it depends on the nature of the error. If it is one that would not have been made by a reasonably competent professional man professing to have the standard and type of skill that the defendant held himself out as having, and acting with ordinary care, then it is negligent. If, on the other hand, it is an error of a man, acting with ordinary care, might have made then it is not negligence."[32]

## Different Schools of Thought

**[14.21]** In relation to many medical conditions, doctors may disagree among themselves as to the best treatment. Where more than one school of thought has a respectable place in the medical profession, a doctor will not be forced at his or her peril to choose between them. In *Daniels v Heskin*[33] and again in *O'Donovan v Cork County Council*,[34] Lavery J quoted with approval Maugham LJ's statement in *Marshall v Lindsey County Council*[35] that:

> "... in this matter, as in so many others, the doctors differ, and in the presence of this undoubted honest difference of opinion it is not open in my opinion to a jury to hold that it is negligent to accept one view rather than the other."

28. [1954] 2 QB 66.
29. Weber 'Misdiagnosis or Error of Judgment?' (1974) 2(4) J of Legal Med 18.
30. See para **[14.17]** above. See also *Whitehouse v Jordan* [1981] 1 All ER 267 (HL, 1980).
31. *Whitehouse v Jordan* [1981] 1 All ER 267 at 658.
32. [1981] 1 All ER 267 at 281 (HL, 1980).
33. [1954] IR 73 at 79-80.
34. [1967] IR 173 at 183 (SC).
35. [1935] 1 KB 516 at 551.

**[14.22]** Adopting a similar view, Kingsmill Moore J stated in *Daniels v Heskin:*[36]

> "I should like to say with emphasis that an honest difference of opinion between eminent doctors, as to which is the better of two ways of treating a patient, does not provide any ground for leaving a question to the jury as to whether a person who has followed one course rather than the other has been guilty of negligence. It would be different if a doctor had expressed the opinion that the course adopted was definitely erroneous."

**[14.23]** It seems clear that, after *Dunne v National Maternity Hospital*,[37] these principles continue to apply, subject to the proviso that protection will not be given to a school of thought that suffers from an inherent defect which ought to be obvious to any person giving the matter due consideration.

## Keeping up-to-date

**[14.24]** Particular problems may arise where the doctor adheres to a school of thought that is going out of fashion. As was said in the Scottish decision of *Hunter v Hanley*[38] in 1955:

> "... the practitioner must not obstinately and pigheadedly carry on with the same old technique if it has been proved to the contrary to what is really substantially the whole of informed medical opinion ..."

**[14.25]** Thus, as one commentator has observed: "it would be indefensible [for a doctor] to say, 'That is what I was taught at university and I shall go on doing it".[39]

**[14.26]** To what extent in practice must doctors keep up with changing medical thinking?[40] Are they obliged to spend the weekends reading the literature on their particular area of expertise? Are they bound to heed what is reported in the journals or is readily available on the Internet and change their behaviour accordingly? Of course, each case depends very much on the circumstances, but from reported decisions it seems that there *is* a duty to keep reasonably abreast with the literature in what might be called the mainstream journals although the courts in no sense impose an oppressive burden on medical practitioners in this regard. As Lord Denning observed in an English decision in 1953:

> "... it would, I think, be putting too high a burden on a medical man to say that he has to read every article appearing in the current medical press; and it would be quite wrong to suggest that a medical man is negligent because he does not at once put into operation the suggestions which some contributor or other might make in a medical journal. The time may come in a particular case when a new recommendation may be so well proved and so well known and so well accepted that it should be adopted, but that was not so in this case."[41]

---

36. [1954] IR 73 at 85. See also [1954] IR 73 at 76 *(per* Maguire CJ ) and *O'Donovan v Cork County Council* [1967] IR 173 at 184 (*per* Lavery J) approving *Hunter v Hanley* 1955 SC 200 at 204, 206 (*per* Lord President Clyde).

37. [1989] IR 91 (SC).

38. 1955 SLT 213 (1st Div).

39. Whincup 'The Legal Obligations of Doctors and Health Authorities', Ch 1 of *Legal Proceedings Against Doctors and Health Authorities* (1983) Freeman ed, p 3.

40. *Cf* Oleck 'New Medical Standards of Skill and Care' (1962) 11 Clev-Mar LR 443.

41. *Crawford v Board of Governors of Charing Cross Hospital*, The Times, 8 December 1953 (CA), cited by Mason & McCall Smith, *Law and Medical Ethics* (1983), p 132. See also *Maynard v West Midlands - RHA* The Times, 9 May 1983 noted in *Negligence: Further Guidance from the Courts*, 286 Br Med J 2069 (25 June 1983).

**[14.27]** Thus, to fail to read one particular article may be excusable, while to disregard a series of warnings in the medical press could well amount to negligence.[42] The courts have yet to address the impact of the Internet in this area. Highly, sophisticated, completely up-to-date, information is now available to doctors (and their patients, to the dismay of some doctors) on the Internet. It seems reasonable to predict that a court will in due course recognise the reality and impose on doctors a duty to take reasonable steps to keep informed of latest developments through this medium. The scope of this duty will, of course, depend on the particular specialism of the doctor in question.

## Innovative Treatment

**[14.28]** Having looked briefly at the problem of old-fashioned and discredited medical theories and techniques, we must now consider the other side of the coin: the question of ultra modern, innovative treatment. The law has a real problem here. If it comes down too heavily on this type of treatment, it will damage the prospects of medical progress, on which the interests of patients and the community depend in the long run. On the other hand, it cannot allow doctors to experiment without restraint. It is true that, with informed consent properly obtained, the doctors may legitimately perform a fairly wide range of innovative treatment without the risk of being sued. But there remains a range of experimental treatment for which, in the nature of things, it may be impossible to obtain the patient's informed consent: the patient may, for example, be unconscious or mentally ill.[43] In such circumstances by what criterion is this innovative treatment to be judged?

**[14.29]** When one examines what the courts and commentators have to say on this question, one finds a disappointing lack of conceptually clear guiding principle. Instead there is a tendency to dispose of the issue with somewhat bland generalities about not straying too far from the accepted ways. That this should be so is perhaps not surprising. The general approach in relation to medical negligence has been to depend on judges (and juries prior to their abolition in this context) to use their common sense and discretion in specific cases rather than to attempt to resolve the question in conceptual terms.[44]

---

42. In England in *Roe v Ministry of Health* [1954] 2 QB 66, the defendant anaesthetist was held not to have been negligent where paralysis followed a spinal injection administered by him. The injury was caused because ampoules contained nupercaine percolated through miniscule flaws in the glass jars in which the nupercaine was stored and contaminated the anaesthetic. In the year before the accident, two American medical publications had drawn attention to this danger. It was held that these publications were outside the range of the ordinary anaesthetist in England at the time so the defendant could not be expected to have been aware of the need to take the precautions which would have prevented the injury. See further Frenkel 'Anaesthesiologists and the Law' (1981) 5 Legal Med Q 74; Wasmuth 'Standards of Care in Anaesthesiology' (1958) 7 Clev-Mar LR 403; Harland 'Anaesthetic Malpractice in Canada' (1961) 10 Clev-Mar LR 19; Auerbach 'How to Handle An Anesthesia Injury Case' (1966) 15 Clev-Mar LR 399.

43. *Cf* Macklin 'Some Problems in Gaining Informed Consent from Psychiatric Patients' (1982) 31 Emory LJ 345.

44. *Cf* the Control of Clinical Trials Act 1987, s 9(7).

## Specialists

**[14.30]** In *O'Donovan v Cork County Council*,[45] Walsh J concisely stated the position regarding specialists:

> "A medical practitioner who holds himself out as being a specialist in a particular field is required to attain to the ordinary level of skill amongst those who specialise in the same field. He is not required to attain to the higher degree of skill and competence in that particular field."

## General Practitioners[46]

**[14.31]** General practitioners are not in the front line of litigation for negligence. Several reasons explain this.[47] By and large, patients with serious ailments will be referred on by their general practitioner, to specialists or to hospital. The expertise of the general practitioner is to distinguish between these serious cases and others which he or she can resolve himself or herself. Thus diagnosis is a most important part of the general practitioners art. The law requires that he or she make a reasonable diagnosis, not necessarily a correct one, and in cases where the general practitioner is uncertain or where the symptoms clearly call for specialist investigation, that the general practitioner make the necessary referral of the patient.

**[14.32]** An important element in the general practitioner's daily (or nightly) work concerns the decision to make a house-call in response to a communication from a patient or a

---

45. *O'Donovan v Cork County Council* [1967] IR 173 at 190. See also Linden 'The Negligent Doctor' (1973) 11 OHLJ 31 at 35-36; Bryce-Smith 'Malpractice in the United Kingdom' (1961) 10 Clev-Mar LR 10 at 13-16; Keohne & Young 'Special Law for Medical Specialists' (1972) 16 St Louis ULJ 497. For an account of the standard applicable to psychiatrists, see Casey & Craven, *Psychiatry and the Law* (1999); Craven 'Litigation Against Psychiatrists 1997-1999' (1999) 5 Medico-Legal J of IR 70; *Healy v North Western Health Board* High Court, 31 January 1996; *Armstrong v Eastern Health Board* High Court, 5 October 1990; *C v North Western Health Board* [1997] Ir L Log W 133 (CC). These and other decision are analysed by Craven in 'Medical Negligence: Litigation against Paediatricians, Psychiatrists and Surgeons', a paper delivered at a Conference, *Suing Doctors, Hospitals and Health Boards*, held at Trinity College, Dubin on 14 October 2000. As to negligence claims against paediatricians, Dr. Craven analyses *Goonan v Dooley* High Court, 23 March, 1994; *Buckley v National Maternity Hospital* High Court 21 December 1998 and *Lynch v O'Connor* High Court, 28 June 1996 (Kinlen J). In his review of litigation against surgeons, Dr Craven analyses *Maitland v Swan* High Court, 6 April 1992; *Dunleavy v Devitt* Supreme Court, 19 February 1992; *Fitzpatrick v Midland Health Board* High Court, 1 May 1997; *Conley v Strain* [1988] IR 629 (HC); *Duffy v North Eastern Health Board* Professional Negligence Reports 199 (HC, 1988); *Edwards v Southern Health Board* Supreme Court, 26 July 1994; *Russell v Walsh* High Court, 3 April 1995; *Ewing v North Western Health Board* High Court, 2 December 1998; *Lynskey v Jervis Street Hospital* High Court, 23 April 1993; *Mordaunt v Gallagher* High Court, 11 July 1997; *Barrett v Southern Health Board* Professional Negligence Reports 211 (HC 1988); *Caffrey v North Eastern Health Board* High Court, 10 February 1995 and *Collins v Mid-Western Health Board* Supreme Court, 12 November 1999. Most of these decisions are also discussed by Byrne and Binchy in the relevant *Annual Review of Irish Law*.

46. See Kennedy & Grubb (eds) *Principles of Medical Law*, paras 5.25-5.36; Craven 'Medical Negligence: Litigation Against Surgeons, Psychiatrists, Paediatricians and General Practitioners', paper delivered at a symposium on medical negligence litigation held at Trinity College Dublin Law School in June 1998.

47. One reason is the personal dimension. Most patients know their general practitioners well and have a good personal relationship with them. It is far easier to sue an anonymous hospital or health board.

member of the patient's family. In what circumstances will a decision not to visit be stigmatised as negligent?

**[14.33]** This question arose in *O'Doherty v Whelan*.[48] The plaintiff, a "very highly strung and at times hysterical" person, became ill at a time when she was in the eleventh week of pregnancy. She had previously suffered two miscarriages in the first trimester. She attended the defendant's surgery on Friday afternoon. The defendant, who was aware of her medical history and of her excitable disposition, diagnosed a "flu like" illness, probably viral, with a probable urinary tract infection. She did not, however, ask the plaintiff to provide her with a urinary sample, on account of time constraints. The surgery time was drawing to a close; laboratory facilities were not readily available at the weekend; it was approaching closing time for the chemists and there was a prescription for antibiotics to be filled.

**[14.34]** The plaintiff's condition worsened overnight and the following morning. She vomited up the tablets she had been prescribed. Her husband telephoned the defendant at least twice over the weekend and asked her to come to visit the plaintiff and on each occasion she was unwilling to do so. On the first call, she recommended to the husband that he bring his wife to the hospital forthwith. The exchanges between them were acrimonious, the defendant complaining that the husband slammed down the phone on her in mid-sentence on both occasions. On the second occasion, the defendant was very angry and upset that her earlier advice had been disregarded. She repeated that advice to the husband. When eventually, on the following Tuesday, the plaintiff was brought to the hospital, her condition continued to deteriorate but, over time, it improved and she was in due course discharged. No definitive diagnosis was ever made. Although the medical staff at the hospital administered antibiotics, they could not determine whether the treatment helped or hindered the plaintiff's recovery.

**[14.35]** O'Hanlon J, applying the *Dunne* criteria, imposed liability on the defendant. The crucial question of liability related to the telephone calls and the defendant's failure to visit the plaintiff in her home. O'Hanlon J noted that, although the plaintiff was a very highly-strung person, she was undoubtedly vomiting and unable to retain food or medicine; this was "calculated to cause in her feelings of alarm and concern for the well-being both of herself and of her baby, at the early stage of her pregnancy".[49]

**[14.36]** O'Hanlon J concluded that the defendant should be regarded as having failed to respond adequately to the situation that arose after the Friday consultation. In an important passage, he observed:

> "That is not to say that an obligation can arise in every case where a request is made to a general practitioner to visit the patient at home, to comply with such request. That would be wholly unreasonable. Every case must be judged on its own particular circumstances."[50]

**[14.37]** O'Hanlon J had regard to a number of factors. The plaintiff was a young mother, with one child of two years who had to be looked after. She had suffered two miscarriages, both in the first trimester of the pregnancy, and she was now expecting another baby and

48. Prof Neg LR 440 (HC, 18 January 1993).
49. Prof Neg LR 440.
50. Prof Neg LR 440.

was in or about the eleventh week of the pregnancy. She was undoubtedly ill when she had attended the defendant's surgery and sufficiently ill in the defendant's opinion to be put on a course of antibiotics. She was known to the defendant to be of a nervous and highly-strung and excitable disposition.

**[14.38]** It was a situation where the plaintiff and her husband needed reassurance and where the plaintiff's condition needed to be monitored closely. The defendant felt that she had responded appropriately by telling the husband to have the plaintiff brought to the hospital, but on the defendant's own account of the telephone calls there was little to indicate that this discretion or suggestion was being well received at the other end or that it was going to be complied with. O'Hanlon J thought it was unfortunate to respond angrily to a young couple who had good reason to be worried about the situation, and a message such as, "Get her into the hospital and stop telephoning me", was not, in his opinion, an appropriate way to obtain co-operation in having the plaintiff's fears set at rest and in having her illness attended to properly.

**[14.39]** On the defendant's account of the two telephone calls O'Hanlon J did not think she was entitled, after either of them, to feel confident that the plaintiff was on her way to hospital and that the defendant need have no further cause for concern.

**[14.40]** It appeared to O'Hanlon J that the response given by the defendant to the telephone calls was in all probability affected by the difficulties with which the defendant herself had to contend at the time:

> "It was a week-end; she was suffering from a painful and troublesome back injury; her father was seriously ill; she had a young child of her own to look after, and her husband was dead. She knew from a previous experience that the plaintiff was highly-strung and liable to dramatise her complaints.
>
> These are all ameliorating factors which should not be minimised, but they are not sufficient to provide an answer to the claim that the response of the defendant to the patient's pleas for help was neither adequate nor appropriate."

The damages awarded in the case were the small sum of £1,000 for the pain and distress caused to the plaintiff between the first telephone call and the time she was admitted to the hospital on the following Tuesday. This was because the illness from which she suffered was of unknown origin and it proceeded apparently unaffected by the medical care she received in the hospital. O'Hanlon J considered it would be entirely speculative to contend that the effects of the plaintiff's illness would have been any less severe if she had been seen at home by the defendant.[51]

**[14.41]** In *Collins v Mid Western Health Board*,[52] the Supreme Court prescribed a heavy duty on general practitioners to factor into their examination of patients who consult them any other relevant information received from other credible sources on which reliance should be placed. The deceased was a man who did not make a practice of going to

---

51. See also *Lowns v Woods* (1996) ATR 81-376 (NSW CA); *Cavan v Wilcox* (1973) 44 DLR (3d) 42 (NBCA); *Stockdale v Nicholls* [1993] 4 Med LR 190; *Durrant v Burke* [1993] 4 Med 248; *Morrison v Forsythe* [1995] 6 Med LR 6 (Court of Senior; Outer House, Lord Clyde); Kennedy & Grubb (eds) *Principles of Medical Law*, paras 6.48-6.49.

52. Supreme Court, 12 November 1999, analysed by Sheikh & Cusack (2000) 6 Medico-Legal J of Ir 4.

doctors. He was suddenly affected by a very bad headache, which forced him to stop work. His wife, when telephoning the general practitioner, expressed her serious concern about his condition, mentioning that he "must be very bad", in view of his usual policy of avoiding doctors. When he presented to the general practitioner and on a subsequent visit by the general practitioners to his home, the deceased did not lay any strong emphasis on the headache. The general practitioner's initial diagnosis was that of upper respiratory tract infection. It later transpired that he had a subarachoid haemorrhage. His condition worsened and some weeks later he died. The Supreme Court, reversing Johnson J, held that the general practitioner was negligent in failing to have adopted a more pro-active inquisitorial strategy in the light of information he had received from the deceased's wife. It has to be said that this stringent requirement is not echoed in the decisions of other common law jurisdictions and may possibly encourage defensive referrals to scarce hospital beds.

## Other Medical Personnel and Hospital Administration

**[14.42]** Other medical personnel may be held guilty of negligence if they fail to act in accordance with the standards of reasonable members of their various areas of work. Thus, for example, nurses may be liable for negligence. Sometimes the real complaint is not that any particular person in the medical team had been negligent but rather that there is a systematic weakness in the delivery of health services which is really of an administrative rather than medical character. So, for example, if the admissions procedure for prospective patients into a hospital is not properly thought through this may constitute negligence. In *Collins v Mid-Western Health Board*,[53] the Supreme Court considered that a system that rested total authority in a senior house officer to determine who should be admitted into the hospital was one that, in Keane J's words, "clearly suffered from an inherent defect which should have been obvious to any person giving it due consideration".

## Diagnosis

**[14.43]** Let us now turn to the question of diagnosis. The law does not require doctors to make a correct diagnosis in every case. All that it asks it that the diagnosis be a reasonable one in the circumstances. These circumstances will, of course, include the category of practice in question. Thus, a specialist will be expected to have the diagnostic skill of a reasonable specialist in the particular discipline. A general practitioner will not be judged by the same test. This does not mean that general practitioners are free to make incorrect diagnosises without fear of sanction: the law requires them to be conscious of the need to refer a patient for specialist attention where the symptoms are puzzling, ambiguous and complex.

**[14.44]** In *Goonan v Dooley*,[54] the plaintiff, who was born in 1977, was found in 1979 to have a seriously dislocated left hip. She sued the hospital where she was born, arguing that those who treated her at that time should have discovered the condition. Had they done so,

53. Supreme Court, 12 November 1999. See also *Fitzpatrick v Midland Health Board* High Court, 1 May 1997 (Johnson J) - defective system for delivery of report on culture of swab led to late administration of appropriate antibiotic treatment, resulting in partial amputation of finger. See Byrne and Binchy, *Annual Review of Irish Law 1997*, pp 734-735.

54. High Court, 23 March 1994 (Lynch J).

she claimed, the condition could have been amerliorated to a significant degree. The essential issue was whether in fact there had been a congenital condition capable of being identified at the time of the birth.

**[14.45]** Lynch J concluded on the evidence that there had not. The plaintiff had been given the Ortolani Barlo examination, a standard test as to whether there was abnormality in her hips at the time of her birth, by two junior house doctors and a public health nurse. The public health nurse had given the examination again some weeks afterwards.

**[14.46]** Lynch J observed that one could readily accept as a reasonable probability that a medical examiner might slip up and culpably fail to diagnose a present and ascertainable dislocation of the hip but this did "not so readily follow as a probability" when three separate medical persons had examined the plaintiff on four occasions within two months of her birth and concluded that there was no abnormality. The evidence of one of the medical experts in the case was to the effect that the Ortolani Barlo examination was not a very sensitive test and would not show up abnormalities in 20%-30% of cases that emerged later. Two experts were of the view that the condition might not be congenital but might develop later.

**[14.47]** Lynch J acquitted the defendants of negligence in failing to detect the abnormality in the plaintiff's hip. He was, moreover, of the view that the abnormality was probably not present in the first few months following birth and had developed later. The crucial holding, thus, was one of the absence of negligence on the defendants' part.

**[14.48]** What is the position where the doctor in nonplussed and simply *cannot* make a diagnosis. This was the position in *Coughlan v Whelton*.[55]

**[14.49]** The plaintiff consulted the defendant consultant, complaining of severe pain in his chest and right arm after consuming small amounts of alcohol. The defendant subjected him to a battery of tests, involving radiography, but this revealed nothing useful. He contacted the plaintiff's general practitioner explaining that he had not been able to make a conclusive diagnosis.

**[14.50]** The plaintiff had Hodgkin's disease. Lavan J accepted evidence that "only two persons in the Irish population of 3.5 million would present with symptoms of Hodgkin's disease including a symptom of alcohol induced pain" and that there had been no recorded case where a patient presented with only the single system of alcohol induced pain.

**[14.51]** Applying the principles enunciated in *Dunne*, Lavan J acquitted the defendant of negligence. He could:

> "not see how a doctor can be guilty of negligence if he carried out all appropriate tests and all of those tests prove normal as a result of which he cannot come to a conclusion and conveys that clear view to the patient's general practitioner."

**[14.52]** A difficulty can arise when attempting to make a correct diagnosis of a patient who is less than fully frank about the provenance and nature of his or her symptoms. In *Caffrey v North Eastern Health Board*,[56] the plaintiff had received injuries to his throat in a traffic accident. He was admitted to the casualty department of the defendant's hospital in

---

55. High Court, 22 January 1993.
56. High Court, 10 February 1995.

a country town at 7.50 am on a Saturday. He initially said that he could not remember anything. He complained of suffering from asthma and maintained that position until the following Monday. His symptoms included difficulty in swallowing, stridor, breathlessness, pain in the area of the neck and inability to speak.

**[14.53]** There was no ear, nose and throat surgeon on duty in the hospital that weekend. The following Monday, the plaintiff told the hospital staff that he has suffered an injury to the larynx. He explained that he had said that he could remember nothing because he thought he was in trouble as the car which crashed was not his own. A correct diagnosis was then made and the plaintiff was moved to a Dublin hospital where he was operated upon. This left him with a permanent flap in his throat for the purpose of assisting him in breathing, as well as some other disabilities not identified in Johnson J's judgment.

**[14.54]** The plaintiff sued the surgeon into whose care he had been placed in the first hospital. He claimed that the doctor ought to have diagnosed his condition earlier than the Monday. With "a great deal of doubt",[57] Johnson J held that the defendant could be criticised for having failed to examine the exterior or the interior of the throat before Monday, having regard to the symptoms that were present. He balanced this finding with a very severe criticism of the plaintiff for his lack of candour.

**[14.55]** On the issue of causation, Johnson J was bemused at the failure of either party to have called as a witness the surgeon who had operated on the plaintiff in the Dublin hospital. Johnson J recorded in his judgment that it had been left to him "to force the parties"[58] to call this witness; he observed that, if they had failed to do so, he would have been obliged to do so himself, in view of the surgeon's crucial role. The evidence of this surgeon was to the effect that the delay in diagnosis had no effect on the outcome. Accordingly, Johnson J held that the defendants were not liable to the plaintiff for his injury.

## Treatment[59]

**[14.56]** The law does not require doctors to treat all patients successfully; what is necessary is that doctors act reasonably in the provision of treatment. If they do this, they will not be liable, even where the treatment proves unsuccessful. It will be recalled that, in *Dunne*,[60] Finlay CJ said that the principles relating to treatment were identical to those relating to diagnosis.

**[14.57]** In regard to many medical conditions, doctors may disagree among themselves as to the best treatment. As we have seen, where more than one school of thought has a respectable place in the medical profession, a doctor will not be forced at his or her peril to choose between them, provided that neither can be stigmatised as constituting a practice which "has inherent defects which ought to be obvious to any person giving the matter due consideration".[61]

57. High Court, 10 February 1995.

58. High Court, 10 February 1995.See also *Collins v Mid-Western Health Board* Supreme Court, 12 November 1999, discussed in para **[14.41]** above.

59. See Kennedy & Grubb (eds) *Principles of Medical Law*, paras 5.25-5.36.

60. *Dunne v National Maternity Hospital* [1989] IR 91 (SC).

61. *Dunne v National Maternity Hospital* [1989] IR 91.

**[14.58]** In *Edwards v Southern Health Board*,[62] the Supreme Court affirmed O'Hanlon J's dismissal[63] of proceedings for negligence based on the claim that the defendants had failed to provide the correct treatment for a post-operative infection. The essence of the plaintiff's case was that, with proper treatment, the infection would have been cured earlier.

**[14.59]** O'Hanlon J, applying the principles laid down by Walsh J in *O'Donovan v Cork County Council*,[64] had held that the conservative treatment adopted by the defendants, in providing antibiotics and draining the wound by wicks had the support of a substantial body of medical practitioners and did not have inherent defects which ought to have been obvious to any medical practitioner caring for the plaintiff at the time. Accordingly he had dismissed the proceedings.

**[14.60]** The Supreme Court affirmed. Finlay CJ[65] rejected specific legal inferences which the plaintiff proposed should be drawn from the evidence.

**[14.61]** In *Fitzpatrick v The Midland Health Board*,[66] Johnson J addressed two issues: the adequacy of the treatment regime adopted by a surgeon employed by the hospital where the plaintiff went with a pain and swollen finger and the manner in which a report of a medical test should have been communicated to the surgeon so that he could act upon it expeditiously. On the first visit to the hospital, the plaintiff was placed on antibiotics; his finger was operated on by the surgeon; a culture was taken and sent for analysis. It was found to be sterile and the plaintiff was discharged, his finger now in a satisfactory condition. He was seen again two days later and told to return after a week. When he did so, it was found that he was suffering from a severe pulp space infection of the right index finger.

**[14.62]** The surgeon operated on the plaintiff for a debridement of the finger; he removed the tissue from the distal phalanx, took a swab and sent it for culturing. He decided at this stage not to give the plaintiff any antibiotics.

**[14.63]** The result of the culturing did not return until three days later. It was not seen by the surgeon for a further two days. He then prescribed antibiotics, which were not given to the plaintiff until yet another day had passed. The condition of the finger deteriorated. The tip of the index finger proved to be necrotic. The surgeon removed two millimetres of bone. The care of the patient was transferred to another surgeon, because the first surgeon was going on vacation. The second surgeon, responding to the fact that osteomyelitis had set in, amputated the distal phalanx of the right index finger.

**[14.64]** The essence of the plaintiff's case was that the first surgeon ought to have prescribed antibiotics earlier. There was a conflict of opinion as to whether it would have been appropriate to have treated the plaintiff with broad spectrum antibiotics before the swab was taken and cultured or whether it would have been preferable to wait until the swab had been cultured and the specific antibiotic which ought to be used identified.

62. Supreme Court, 26 July 1994.

63. High Court, 20 January 1989.

64. [1967] IR 173 (SC).

65. Egan and Denham JJ concurring.

66. High Court, 1 May 1997.

There was no disagreement among the medical witnesses, however, that the delay in starting the antibiotics after the culture had been taken was unreasonable.

**[14.65]** Johnson J, in the light of the division of professional opinion of the first issue, held that one could "not say that the failure to apply the broad spectrum antibiotics immediately was negligent".[67] But he was satisfied that the delay in starting the treatment after the culture had been taken was negligent and that this had exacerbated the plaintiff's injuries, meriting an award of £20,000 general damages.

**[14.66]** Johnson J reiterated the fact that:

> "it is essential where a course is adopted by the [treating doctor] not to apply broad spectrum antibiotics … that (a) a report be delivered regarding the culture of the swab as soon as it is practicable to the treating doctor, (b) that it is brought to his attention and (c) that he is therefore enabled to act upon it as soon as is possible."[68]

**[14.67]** The question of internal communications between doctors, technicians, scientists, nurses and administrators in a hospital setting is sometimes perceived as a matter to be resolved by the *Dunne* test. In the instant case, this was not problematical as there was no dispute among the professional witnesses. In truth, practical strategic questions as to what and when medical services are delivered to the patient should not be determined by the *Dunne* test but rather on the basis of straightforward negligence principles.

**[14.68]** In *Lynskey v Governors and Guardians of the Charitable Infirmary of Jervis Street*,[69] the plaintiff, a married man aged sixty-one, with three children, had an operation conducted by the defendant's medical team, for the removal of bilateral epididymal cysts. During the course of the operation, the testicular artery, with the diameter of a thread, was severed. The person carrying out the operation, who was Registrar in Urology, considering that the best course was orchidectomy, removed the testis on the basis that it had been deprived of its blood supply.

**[14.69]** The plaintiff's action for negligence rested on three grounds. First he contended that the operation was of such complexity that it should have been carried out by a person with greater experience. This Costello J rejected on the evidence. The Registrar in Urology had ten years' experience of general surgery and, six months after the operation, had acted as locum for the Consultant Urologist who expressed himself "quite happy to let him operate on any member of my family".[70]

**[14.70]** The second ground was that the Registrar in Urology had been negligent in severing the artery. Costello J rejected this contention on the basis that, having regard to the nature, size and position of the cysts, there had been a risk of severance even with the exercise of reasonable skill and care.

**[14.71]** Finally, the plaintiff argued that the testis should not have been removed. An expert witness supported this view. As against this, an expert witness on behalf of the defence contended that the Registrar in Urology had acted correctly in making a balanced decision. Whereas the course suggested by the plaintiff's expert witness would be applicable to a

67. High Court, 1 May 1997.
68. High Court, 1 May 1997.
69. High Court, 23 April 1993 (Costello J).
70. High Court, 23 April 1993.

young boy whose testicular inability might be perilous, one had to set against this the risk of the development of an acutely gangrenous condition, or infection or extrusion. The expert witness concluded that, "[f]aced in th[ese] circumstances by a 61 year old man, one would be tempted not to replace the testis".

**[14.72]** Costello J agreed with this witness. He was satisfied that the Registrar in Urology, in having to make a balanced decision, had "expressed reasonable care in the making of that decision for good reasons..."[71]

## Medical Treatment by Unqualified Persons

**[14.73]** The Courts have taken a common-sense approach in determining the standard of care appropriate to unqualified persons performing medical treatment. In the English decision of *Philips v Whiteley (William), Ltd.*[72] in 1938, Goddard J dismissed an action for negligence brought against a jeweller where it was alleged that he had not taken sufficient precautions to sterilise an instrument used for piercing the plaintiff's ears. Goddard said, bluntly:

> "If a person wants to ensure that the operation of piercing her ears is going to be carried out with that proportion of skill and so forth that a Fellow of the Royal College of Surgeons would use, she must go to a surgeon. If she goes to a jeweller, she must expect that he will carry it out".[73]

This would include taking some means of disinfecting the instrument, as a lay person would, but Goddard J did:

> "not think that a jeweller holds himself out as a surgeon or professes that he is going to conduct the operation of piercing a lady's ears by means of aseptic surgery, about which it is not to be supposed that he knows anything".[74]

**[14.74]** This reference to "holding out" is important. Clearly, if I hold myself out to be a qualified medical practitioner, then, apart from any question of fraud, I may be held to the standard of care appropriate to qualified medical practitioners. Equally, as the ear-piercing case makes plain, if I make no claim to medical skill or qualifications, the standard appropriate to qualified medical practitioners will not be relevant. There is, however, an intermediate position, where I make no claims to medical *qualifications,* but I make definite claims to medical *skill.* In such circumstances, the law requires that I should have the competence which I claim. In truth, this is primarily a case of imposing liability for negligent misstatement, based on the plaintiff's reliance.

**[14.75]** Thus, in *Brogan v Bennett*,[75] in 1952, the Supreme Court held that:

> "if a person is induced to become a patient of an unqualified person on the recommendation that that person is skilled, the latter owed a duty to use care in using the skill and administering the treatment which he has offered. He is not expected to employ the degree of skill which would be expected from a qualified man. He is only liable for failure to employ such skill as he said he had".

---

71. High Court, 23 April 1993.
72. [1938] 1 All ER 566 (KBD).
73. [1938] 1 All ER 566 at 569.
74. [1938] 1 All ER 566.
75. [1955] IR 119 at 126 (*per* Maguire CJ). See also, to similar effect at 128-129 (*per* O'Byrne J).

In this case the defendant, in the words of O'Byrne J, professed "not only to have particular skill in the treatment of tuberculosis, but to have effected cures which were scarcely short of miracles".[76] He said he could guarantee to effect a cure within three months of a tuberculosis patient who consulted him. Instead, the trial judge held, the defendant's treatment resulted in the death of the patient. The Supreme Court held, on a case stated, that on these findings the trial judge could hold the defendant liable to the deceased patient's dependents under the fatal accidents legislation.

## Informed Consent[77]

**[14.76]** The extent to which a medical practitioner is obliged to inform his or her patient of the nature of proposed treatment - of its risks and the chances of success - is a question that has given rise to much analysis in the past couple of decades. Important philosophical and social questions are involved: at the base is a clash between the values of autonomy and paternalism. Let us examine some of the more important aspects of the subject in turn.

### *(a) Is treatment without informed consent battery or negligence?*[78]

**[14.77]** The first question concerns the nature of the tort committed where a doctor performs treatment on a patient without having properly explained to him or her the nature of the treatment. Is it a battery or is it negligence?[79]

**[14.78]** In favour of the former, it can be argued that unauthorised physical contact constitutes a battery, and where a patient consents to the contact in ignorance of the true position, his or her consent is defective. In favour of the latter, it can be argued that the question of what should be told to patients is essentially one of professional discretion and competence, and accordingly that failure to comply with this standard constitutes professional malpractice.

---

76. [1954] IR 119 at 127.

77. Amongst the vast literature on the subject see bibliography at the end of this chapter.

78. See Healy, *Medical Negligence: Common Law Perspectives* (1999), Ch 6; Tomkin & Hanafin, Irish Medical Law (1995), Ch 3; Kennedy & Grubb (eds), *Principles of Medical Law* (1998), paras 3.101-3.142; Shuck 'Rethinking Informed Consent' (1994) 103 Yale LJ 899; Keown 'The Ashes of AIDS and the Phoenix of Informed Consent' (1989) 52 Mod LR 790; McCoid 'A Reappraisal of Liability for Unauthorized Medical Treatment' (1957) 41 Minn LR 381; Walz & Scheuneman 'Informed Consent to Therapy' (1970) 64 Nw UL Rev 628; Skegg '"Informed Consent" to Medical Procedures' (1975) 15 Med Sci & L 124; Robertson 'Informed Consent to Medical Treatment' (1981) 97 LQR 102; Brazier 'Informed Consent to Surgery' (1979) 19 Med Sci & L 49; Glass 'Note: Restructuring Informed Consent: Legal Therapy for the Doctor-Patient Relationship' (1970) 79 Yale LJ 1533; Kirby 'Informed Consent: What Does It Mean?' (1983) LJ of Med Ethics 69; Tancredi 'Competency for Informed Consent: Conceptual Limits of Empirical Data' (1982) 5 Int J of L & Psychiat 51; McNorrie 'Medical Malpractice. The Scope of Informed Consent in Negligence' (1983) 32 Int & Comp LQ 229; Meisel & Roth 'Toward an Informed Discussion of Informed Consent: A Review and Critique of the Empirical Studies' (1983) 25 Ariz LR 265; Feng 'Failure of Medical Advice: Trespasser Negligence?' (1987) 7 Legal Studies 149.

79. Battery was favoured in earlier decision in the United States, (*Cf* Smith 'Battery in Medical Torts' (1967) 16 Clev-Mar LR 22 at 32-37) but the trend is now towards negligence: Hale & Podell 'Medical Malpractice in New York' (1976) 27 Syracuse LR 657 at 732.

**[14.79]** Decisions in Canada,[80] Australia[81] and England[82] prefer to characterise as negligence rather than battery medical treatment carried out on a patient whose informed consent has not been obtained, provided the patient has been advised in broad terms of the procedure to be preferred.

**[14.80]** In *Walsh v Family Planning Services Ltd*[83] the members of the Supreme Court were agreed that negligence was the appropriate pigeon-hole.[84] (The issue was strictly *obiter*, since the majority found that the warning had in fact been adequate.) O'Flaherty J, expressed the view that:

> "If there had been such a failure to give a warning as to possible future risks that would not involve the artificial concept of an assault, but, rather, a possible breach of a duty of care giving rise to a claim in negligence. A claim of assault should be confined to cases where there is no consent to the particular procedure and where it is feasible to look for a consent."[85]

**[14.81]** O'Flaherty J placed much reliance on Laskin CJ's analysis of the issue in *Reibl v Hughes*[86] where the Chief Justice of Canada stated:

> "I can appreciate the temptation to say that the genuineness of consent to medical treatment depends on proper disclosure of the risks which it entails, but in my view, unless there had been misrepresentation or fraud to secure consent to the treatment, a failure to disclose the attendant risks, however serious, should go to negligence rather than to battery. Although such a failure relates to an informed choice of submitting to or refusing recommended and appropriate treatment, it arises as the breach of an anterior duty of care, comparable in legal obligation to the duty of due care in carrying out the particular treatment to which the patient has consented. It is not a test for the validity of the consent."

***(b) The duty of disclosure***

**[14.82]** If the duty of disclosure raises the issue of negligence rather than battery, what is the proper test for deciding whether the doctor has given sufficient information to the patient? Three principal solutions have been proposed. The first resolves the question by reference to the generally accepted practice in the medical profession. This approach, which is an application of the *Bolam*[87] test, stresses the fact that the decision of what to tell the patient has traditionally been regarded as primarily a matter of medical judgment and discretion. The second solution,[88] at the other end of the spectrum, concentrates on the patient's right of self determination in regard to what is to be done to his body. It requires

80. *Reibl v Hughes* (1980) 114 DLR (3d) (SC).
81. *Rogers v Whitaker* (1992) 175 Comm LR 479. See TRINDADE & CANE, p 285
82. *Cf Chatterton v Gerson* [1981] 1 QB 432 (QBD); *Sidaway v Bethlam Royal Hospital Governors*, [1985] AC 871 (HL); *Freeman v Home Office (No 2)* [1984] 1 All ER 1036 (CA).
83. [1992] 1 IR 496 (SC).
84. The issue was strictly *obiter*, since the majority found that the warning as to the risks inherent in the proposed treatment had in fact been adequate.
85. [1992] 1 IR 496.
86. (1980) 114 DLR (3d) 1 at 10.
87. *Bolam v Friern Hospital Management Committee* [1957] 2 All ER 118.
88. *See* Seidelson 'Medical Malpractice: Informed Consent Cases in 'Full Disclosure" Jurisdictions' (1976) 14 Duquesne LR 309.

full disclosure of all material risks incident to the proposed treatment, so that the patient, rather than the doctor, makes the real choice as to whether treatment is to be carried out:

> "The patient has the right to chart his own destiny, and the doctor must supply the patient with the material facts the patient will need in order to intelligently chart that destiny with dignity."[89]

**[14.83]** The third approach lies between these two extremes. While tilting somewhat towards the first, it applies the *Bolam* test save where disclosure of a particular risk "was so obviously necessary to an informed choice on the part of the patient that no reasonably prudent medical man would fail to make it".[90]

**[14.84]** Courts in other jurisdictions have shown no unanimity on this matter. In England, in *Sidaway v Governors of the Bethlem Royal Hospital*,[91] different members of the House of Lords favoured each of these positions: Lord Diplock the first, Lord Scarman the second, and Lords Bridge and Keith the third.[92] The initial response in the courts in England below the level of the House of Lords to the competing views expressed in *Sidaway* was to favour Lord Diplock's approach.[93] The *Bolam* test, on which Lord Diplock's approach was based, had since been rejected by the House of Lords in *Bolitho v City and Hackney Health Authority*,[94] in which their Lordships were careful to avoid becoming embroiled in a debate on informed consent. It might have been expected that the Bridge-Keith approach would move into the ascendancy since it is most easy to harmonise with the *Bolitho* philosophy on medical treatment. There are indications, however, that Lord Scarman's test, based on disclosure of material risks, may ultimately triumph in England.[95]

**[14.85]** This liberal approach has been favoured by the Supreme Court of Canada[96] and the High Court of Australia.[97] In Ireland the subject was first addressed substantively[98] by the

---

89. *Miller v Kennedy* (1975) 85 Wash 2d 151, 530 P 2d 334 affg (1974) 11 Wash App 272, 522 P 2d 852.
90. *Sidaway v Governors of the Bethlem Royal Hospital* [1985] AC 871 at 900.
91. See fn 91 above. See Teff 'Consent to Medical Procedures: Paternalism, self-determination or Therapeutic Alliance' (1985) 101 LQR 432; Grubb 'Comment' [1985] Camb LJ 199.
92. Lord Templeman's approach was *sui generis:* the duty of the doctor, subject to his overriding obligation to have regard to the best interests of the patient, is "to provide the patient with information which will enable the patient to make a balanced judgment if the patient chooses to make a balanced judgment." MARKESINIS & DEAKIN, p 270, describe Lord Templeman's speech as, "to say the least, idiosyncratic" and his analysis as being "as 'clear as mud'."
93. *Gold v Haringey Health Authority* [1987] 2 All ER 888 (CA), analysed by Grubb [1988] Camb LJ 12; *Blyth v Bloomsbury Health Authority* [1993] 4 Med LR 151 (CA), analysed by Grubb, (1993) 1 Med LR 115; see, however, *Smith v Tunbridge Wells Health Authority* [1994] 5 Med LR 334 (Moreland J); Markesinis & Deakin, p 271
94. [1998] AC 232 (HL, Eng). *Cf* Grubb (1998) 6 Med LR 378.
95. *Cf Pearce v United Bristol Healthcare NHS Trust* [1999] P 1 QR 53 (CA), analysed by Grubb, (1999) 7 Med LR 61. See further MARKESINIS & DEAKIN, p 272; See Kennedy & Grubb (eds) *Principles of Medical Law*, paras 3.136-3.138.
96. *Hopp v Lepp* (1980) 112 DLR (3d) 67 (SC, Can); *Reibl v Hughes* (1980) 114 DLR (3d) 1 (SC, Can).
97. *Rogers v Whitaker* (1992) 175 Comm LR 479.
98. The Supreme Court had addressed a related question nearly four decades previously in *Daniels v Heskin* [1954] IR 73 (SC). There the issue involved, not disclosure of the risks of *proposed* treatment, but rather a doctor's duty to disclose to a patient the fact that treatment *already carried out* had resulted in an untoward danger to the patient.

Supreme Court in 1992, in *Walsh v Family Planning Services*.[99] It cannot be said that *Walsh* left the law in a clear or satisfactory state.

**[14.86]** The plaintiff, aged forty-four, married with five children, sought to have a vasectomy performed at the first defendant's clinic. He and his wife had an interview with one of the doctors associated with his clinic, in which aspects of the proposed operation were discussed. On the day scheduled for the operation, the plaintiff met another doctor who enquired whether he had changed his mind; he said that he had not. At that point a third doctor came into the room. The operation was conducted by the third doctor. The plaintiff claimed that the third doctor had to be given instructions by the second doctor as to the correct procedure.

**[14.87]** The operation turned out very unfortunately for the plaintiff who developed a condition of orchialgia, involving impotence and constant nagging pain, which required surgical treatment.

**[14.88]** The plaintiff's action was for trespass to the person and battery. He argued that he had never consented to the third doctor's participation in the operation; that it had been carried out without due care; and that he had not been given a sufficient warning of the risks attached to an operation of this kind.

**[14.89]** MacKenzie J held in his favour. He considered that there had been "a technical assault and battery"[100] in that the plaintiff had never consented to the third doctor's participation:

> "He was confronted with a situation which, having regard to the nature of the position, made him powerless to do anything but submit to [this doctor]'s assistance."[101]

**[14.90]** MacKenzie J went on to hold that the plaintiff had not proved his case in negligence. All the evidence was that the operation had been performed properly. The first doctor had given sufficient warning. MacKenzie J added:

> "The plaintiff must have known this to be a consequence of the operation, otherwise he would have followed the direction in the circular to report immediately if anything unusual should have happened to him. Why he did not do this is a mystery, but in my view his constitutional right, that is an unspecified constitutional right to bodily integrity, has been violated. It is to be noted that it is conceded by some of the witnesses for the defence... that all the plaintiff's troubles stem from the operation ..."[102]

**[14.91]** MacKenzie J awarded the plaintiff £30,000 damages for violation of his constitutional rights as well as special damages.

**[14.92]** A mystery of MacKenzie J's judgment is the precise basis of the award for interference with the plaintiff's constitutional right to bodily integrity. The judges in the Supreme Court, notably McCarthy and O'Flaherty JJ, considered that the unconstitutional

99. [1992] 1 IR 496, (SC revg HC). The Supreme Court judgment is analysed by Healy, *Medical Negligence: Common Law Perspectives* (1999), Ch 5; Tomkin & Hanafin, *Irish Medical Law* (1995), Ch 3; Symmons, (1994) 10 Professional Neg 134; Donnelly, (1997) 2 Medico-Legal J of Ireland 3.

100. [1992] 1 IR 486.

101. [1992] 1 IR 486.

102. [1992] 1 IR 486.

violation consisted of the "technical assault and battery" resulting from the third doctor's participation.[103]

**[14.93]** The defendants appealed successfully to the Supreme Court against MacKenzie J's judgment and the Supreme Court dismissed the plaintiff's cross-appeal. The court divided three to two: Finlay CJ, Hederman and O'Flaherty JJ for the majority with McCarthy and Egan JJ dissenting. A number of issues arose, on which there was a wide variety of judicial views.

**[14.94]** Four of the judges[104] held that MacKenzie J had been mistaken in holding that there had been a technical assault and battery on account of the participation by the third doctor. One of those in the majority, O'Flaherty J, observed that it seemed to him that "what the plaintiff was agreeing to was that the operation should be carried out by a person or persons with the requisite skill and that it should be competently done".[105]

**[14.95]** As to the appropriate test for determining the duty of disclosure, the members of the Court were divided as to which approach should be adopted. Finlay CJ considered that the same standard of care should govern medical treatment, advice and the giving of a warning of the consequences of proposed surgical treatment and that this standard was that which the Supreme Court (in his own judgment) had spelt out in *Dunne v National Maternity Hospital*.[106] That test as we have seen,[107] protects conduct that adheres to a general and approved practice, save where the particular practice has inherent defects which ought to be obvious to any person giving the matter due consideration. The *Dunne* test, when applied to the context of informed consent, is essentially the same as that favoured by Lords Bridge and Keith in *Sidaway*.[108] Interestingly, Finlay CJ's desire to have a unified test for the several aspects of medical practice echoes that of Lord Diplock in *Sidaway*; the Chief Justice differed from Lord Diplock in the *Dunne* test, in contrast to that of *Bolam* and makes it clear that the court is not required to give its benediction to practices with inherent defects, even if they have general or universal endorsement from the medical profession.

**[14.96]** Whilst declaring an unambiguous preference for the application of the *Dunne* test to the informed consent context, Finlay CJ made the following observations, which merit extensive quotation:

> "I am satisfied that there is, of course, where it is possible to do so, a clear obligation on a medical practitioner carrying out or arranging for the carrying out of an operation, to inform the patient of any possible harmful consequence arising from the operation, so as to permit the patient to give an informed consent to subjecting himself to the operation concerned. I am also satisfied that the extent of this obligation must, as a matter of common sense, vary

103. Another possible interpretation is that MacKenzie J considered that there should be strict liability for infringing the plaintiff's constitutional right to bodily integrity under the principles set out by the Supreme Court in *Meskell v Coras Iompair Éireann* [1973] IR 121. See Byrne & Binchy, *Annual Review of Irish Law 1992*, pp 559-560.

104. Finlay CJ, Hederman, O'Flaherty and Egan JJ, McCarthy JJ, discenting.

105. [1992] 1 IR 496. *Cf* Byrne & Binchy, *Annual Review of Irish Law 1992*, p 560.

106. [1989] IR 91.

107. See paras **[14.11]** above.

108. See paras **[14.84]** above.

with what might be described as the elective nature of the surgery concerned. Quite obviously, and apart even from cases of emergency surgery which has to be carried out to persons who are unconscious or incapable of giving or refusing consent, or young children, there may be instances where a matter of medical knowledge, notwithstanding substantial risks of harmful consequence, the carrying out of a particular surgical procedure is so necessary to maintain the life or health of the patient and the consequences of failing to carry it out are so clearly disadvantageous that limited discussion or warning concerning possible harmful side-effects may be appropriate and proper. On the other hand, the obligation to give warning of the possible harmful consequences of a surgical procedure which could be said to be at the other end of the scale to the extent to which it is elective, such as would undoubtedly by the operation of vasectomy, may be more stringent and more onerous."[109]

**[14.97]** Finlay CJ made it clear that these observations were subject to the *Dunne* test. He went on to express the view that, in response to a defence of general practice:

> "it may be, certainly in relation to very clearly elective surgery, that the court might more readily reach a conclusion that the extent of warning given or omitted contained inherent defects which ought to have been obvious to any person giving the matter due consideration than it could do in a case of complicated medical or surgical procedures, and an allegation that, although generally adopted, they were inherently unsafe."[110]

**[14.98]** These passages from Finlay CJ's judgment are of particular interest since they reveal a willingness on the part of the Chief Justice to articulate broad principles as to the requirement of disclosure in particular contexts which are hard to reconcile with the "long-stop" strategy of *Dunne*. Under the *Dunne* test, a court should look first to generally approved practices and only if a particular practice can be stigmatised as obviously containing inherent defects should the court depart from it. *Dunne* thus does not involve the court in the process of lying down general rules as to what constitutes negligence, yet this is what Finlay CJ does in the first of the two passages quoted above. The second passage formally subjects the first to the language of *Dunne* but nonetheless the tenor of the Chief Justice's analysis is to favour a significant dimension of judicial control over the principles of what must be disclosed. This indicates a sensitivity to the fact that disclosure of risk to patients involves issues ranging beyond matters of medical judgment.[111]

**[14.99]** O'Flaherty J stated unambiguously that he did not accept that *Dunne* governed the question of disclosure. Rather he thought that it was:

> "a matter for the trial judge, in the first instance, to find whether there has been a breach of the duty of care owed by the defendants to a person such as the plaintiff. That is to be resolved on the established principles of negligence. This was the approach of the Supreme Court of Canada in *Reibl v Hughes*.[112]"[113]

This amounts to an acceptance of the position endorsed by Lord Scarman in *Sidaway*.

**[14.100]** O'Flaherty J went on to express "no hesitation" in subscribing to the view that, in cases of *elective* surgery:

---

109. [1992] 1 IR 496.
110. [1992] 1 IR 496.
111. *Cf Geoghegan v Harris* High Court, 21 June 2000 (Kearns J) at p 28 of Kearns J's judgment.
112. See paras **[14.79]** above.
113. [1992] 1 IR 496.

> "if there is a risk – however exceptional or remote – of grave consequences involving severe pain stretching for an appreciable time into the future and involving the possibility of further operative procedures, the exercise of the duty of care owed by the defendants requires that such possible consequences should be explained in the clearest language to the plaintiff."[114]

Hederman J concurred with O'Flaherty J's judgment.

**[14.101]** It is necessary to examine the respective approaches of McCarthy and Egan JJ since their dissents related essentially to the application of the relevant legal principles to the facts of the particular case. Their position on whether the *Dunne* test applied to disclosure was not entirely clear.

**[14.102]** McCarthy J quoted a passage from the second edition of this work which refers to the differing approaches of Lords Bridge and Scarman in *Sidaway*. He considered that these two solutions "in a case such as the present" were:

> "essentially the same. In determining whether or not to have an operation in which sexual capacity is concerned, it seems to me that to supply the patient with the material facts is so obviously necessary to an informed choice on the part of the patient that no reasonably prudent medical doctor would fail to make it. What then is material? Apart from the success ratio of the operation, what could be more material than sexual capacity after the operation and its immediate sequelae?"[115]

**[14.103]** While the Bridge/Keith and Scarman formulae may sometimes yield the same outcome to legal proceedings, they are not of course "essentially the same" in their definition. Is it possible to discern how McCarthy J would approach a case which was not "such as the present"? We suggest that the most reasonable answer is that McCarthy J was essentially a proponent of the Bridge/Keith test, which is consistent with that favoured in *Dunne*. McCarthy J quoted with approval the *Dunne* criteria, including the passage from Finlay CJ's judgment to the effect that a doctor who adheres to a customary practice will be held negligent if the practice has inherent defects which ought to be obvious to any person giving the matter due consideration. McCarthy J considered that his task was to consider "the application of th[is] principle, adapted, as needs be, to the special circumstances of what is called elective surgery."[116] These special circumstances made it clear to him that failure to disclose material risks would render the doctor liable on account of his or her adherence to a practice with inherent defects. Thus, McCarthy J joined Finlay CJ in *Walsh* in adopting *Dunne* as the appropriate test for informed consent issues.

**[14.104]** With O'Flaherty and Hederman JJ rejecting *Dunne's* application in favour of a straightforward negligence test involving the requirement to disclose material risks, Egan J's judgment assumed a decisive role. It is difficult to discern precisely where Egan J stood on this issue. He referred to the opposing judgments of McCarthy and O'Flaherty JJ and noted that they were agreed in the view that:

> "if there is a risk, however exceptional or remote, of grave consequences involving severe pain stretching for an appreciable time into the future and involving further operative procedures, the exercise of the duty of care owed by the defendants requires that such

114. [1992] 1 IR 496.

115. [1992] 1 IR 496.

116. [1992] 1 IR 496.

> possible consequences should be explained in the clearest language to the prospective patient".[117]

This passage does not give any inkling as to Egan J's opinion on whether the formulation of such a duty depends of *Dunne* or an unemcumbered negligence criterion. Perhaps it is best to read Egan J's judgment as affording no real support for *Dunne*, since he made no reference to the *Dunne* test and did not refer to all Finlay CJ's judgment, which had given *Dunne* a clear endorsement.

**[14.105]** *Walsh* left the law on informed consent in an unsatisfactory and confused state. There was no clear consensus on the scope of the duty of disclosure. Summarising the decision as a whole it may be observed that the Diplock approach in *Sidaway* found no support in *Walsh*. The Bridge/Keith approach was supported by Finlay CJ and (less certainly) by McCarthy J. The Scarman approach was endorsed by O'Flaherty J, with whom Hederman J concurred. So far as elective treatment is concerned, Finlay CJ, while formally remaining within parameters of the Bridge/Keith approach, postulated a degree of judicial policing of the disclosure requirement that brings it, in substance if not form, far closer to the materiality test favoured by Lord Scarman in *Sidaway* and O'Flaherty and Hederman JJ in *Walsh*. Similarly McCarthy J tilted towards a materiality test in relation to elective treatment.

**[14.106]** It is not perhaps surprising that the High Court judges found difficulty in locating a clear *ratio* in *Walsh*. Their strategies have been to make no reference to *Walsh*[118] to endorse one approach favoured in *Walsh*, without referring to any other,[119] or to choose between the compelling approaches.[120]

**[14.107]** In *Farrell v Varian*[121] O'Hanlon J addressed the issue. The plaintiff had consulted the defendant, a specialist in hand surgery, in relation to a condition of bilateral Dupuytren's contracture affecting both hands. It was agreed to operate first on the right hand. The operation was not successful. A rare progressive and incapacitating condition developed known as reflex sympathetic dystrophy syndrome; this affected, not only the plaintiff's hand, but also his arm and shoulder. His hand was contracted, discoloured and covered with scaly skin; he was in constant serious pain and, he said in evidence, he had lost his employment as a result of the condition.

**[14.108]** O'Hanlon J rejected, after an extensive review of the evidence, the plaintiff's claim for professional negligence in the defendant's post-operative treatment of the plaintiff. He was satisfied that, on crucial issues of fact, the defendant's evidence was more reliable.

**[14.109]** The plaintiff's other claim was that the defendant had failed to give him sufficient information as to the risks involved in the operation to enable him to make an informed decision whether he wished to undergo it. O'Hanlon J rejected this also. He accepted the

117. [1992] 1 IR 496.

118. *Farrell v Varian* High Court, 19 September 1994 (O'Hanlon J).

119. *Bolton v Blackrock Clinic Ltd* High Court, 20 December 1994 (Geoghegan J) affd by Supreme Court, 23 January 1997.

120. *Geoghegan v Harris* High Court, 21 June 2000 (Kearns J).

121. *Farrell v Varian* High Court, 19 September 1994.

defendant's evidence that he had an invariable practice to explain briefly to the patient the nature of Dupuytren's contracture, to convey the information that the appropriate treatment to alleviate the condition was by surgery, to explain that the cause of the condition was unknown and that the condition tended to recur in a significant number of cases after surgery and to stress that no guarantee could be given of full correction of the contracture, particularly where the proximal interphalangeal joint was involved.

**[14.110]** In O'Hanlon J's opinion, this represented an adequate warning of what the operation involved so as to enable the plaintiff to make an informed decision on the matter. The plaintiff said in evidence that, had he known of the risks involved, he would not have undergone the operation, but O'Hanlon J believed he was making this assertion with hindsight, influenced by the terrible misfortune that had befallen him in the aftermath of the operative treatment. In view of his earlier medical history, before he had consulted the defendant, he already had first-hand knowledge that it was not possible to guarantee the lasting success of the treatment by operation and that the condition was liable to recur.

**[14.111]** As regards the nature and extent of the warning which should be given to a patient contemplating an operation, O'Hanlon J was of opinion that:

> "the doctor's obligation does not extend to enumerating all the possible risks, however remote, which are involved. Such a procedure could only subject many patients to unnecessary fears and worries, and possibly have the effect of deterring many patients from submitting to treatment which it was obviously in their best interests to undergo."[122]

**[14.112]** If there was some significant danger of serious consequence the patient would have an entitlement to be warned of it. O'Hanlon J noted that in *Sidaway v Bethlem Royal Hospital* it had been suggested, by way of example that, if there was an operation involving a substantial risk of grave adverse consequences, such as 10% risk of a stroke, a judge would be entitled to conclude that, in the absence of some cogent clinical reason why the patient should not be informed, a doctor could hardly fail to appreciate the necessity for an appropriate warning.

**[14.113]** All the expert evidence in the present case was to the effect that the onset of reflex sympathetic dystrophy was a rare phenomenon. The plaintiff's case had been described by all the doctors as the worst they had ever seen; the general incidence of the condition in a severe form had been put at lower than 1% of cases arising from operative treatment. O'Hanlon J observed that:

> "in view of the extremely small number of actual cases seen by these medical gentlemen of great experience in their field, their evidence would suggest a much smaller incidence than 1%."[123]

There appeared also to be an incidence "of a much less serious character", which cleared up within a relatively short period, even without remedial treatment, in a significantly larger number of cases.

**[14.114]** In a crucial passage, O'Hanlon J said that he agreed with:

> "the view expressed by the House of Lords in the *Sidaway* case that 'the decision what degree of disclosure of risks is best calculated to assist a particular patient to make a rational

122. High Court, 19 September 1994.
123. High Court, 19 September 1994.

> choice as to whether or not to undergo a particular treatment must primarily be a matter of clinical judgment', although, as also observed by their Lordships, a case might arise where a judge could conclude that disclosure of a particular risk was so obviously necessary to an informed choice on the part of the patient that no reasonably prudent medical man would fail to make it."[124]

O'Hanlon J was satisfied that the warning given by the defendant in the instant case had been "adequate in all the circumstances to meet his obligation in this respect."[125]

**[14.115]** O'Hanlon J's approach merits two observations. First, the failure to mention the Supreme Court judgment in *Walsh v Family Planning Services* is striking. The list of authorities included as an appendix to the judgment makes it clear that the case was cited by counsel. Why should it not have been considered worthy of discussion, especially since the High Court is bound by the Supreme Court precedent? Perhaps the answer is that O'Hanlon J regarded the divisions among the Judges in *Walsh* as so great as to neutralise the decision's precedential influence.

**[14.116]** Secondly, O'Hanlon J's discussion of *Sidaway* gives little impression of the internal divisions in that case. It seems that O'Hanlon J preferred the approach favoured by Lords Bridge and Keith but he has no word of criticism for the competing approaches of Lords Diplock, Scarman and Templeman.

**[14.117]** *O'Keeffe v Cody*,[126] also raised the issue of consent. In this case Lynch J dismissed the plaintiff's action for negligence in relation to the administration of an epidural injection when she was giving birth. The plaintiff claimed this had damaged her spinal cord, causing her an incomplete paralysis. Lynch J, on the evidence, concluded that the plaintiff was in fact suffering from multiple sclerosis, even before the time of this injection. He also addressed the issue of informed consent, which was clearly moot, in view of his holding as to the nature of the plaintiff's medical condition. He held that the consultant anaesthetist, before administering the injection, had warned the plaintiff of its possible side effects. That warning "was the customary [one] given by anaesthetists and was adequate and proper in the absence of any inquiry as to the possibility of other adverse effects".[127] The anaesthetist had not mentioned the rare possibility of paralysis but, having regard to the plaintiff's anxiety to have an epidural injection when giving birth previously and her similar, "if not greater", anxiety to have an epidural injection on the instant occasion, Lynch J was satisfied that she would have opted to have the injection even if she had received this warning.

**[14.118]** Lynch J's failure to discuss *Walsh* or even *Sidaway* makes it difficult to assess with confidence his precise view on the best approach to the issue of informed consent. What he had to say on the subject suggests a position somewhere between Lord Diplock and Lords Bridge and Keith. This is not at all unlike the approach adopted by the Supreme Court in the old case of *Daniels v Heskin*.[128]

---

124. High Court, 19 September 1994.
125. High Court, 19 September 1994.
126. High Court, 11 March 1994 (Lynch J)
127. High Court, 11 March 1994.
128. [1954] IR 73, discussed paras **[14.153]** below.

**[14.119]** In *Bolton v Blackrock Clinic Ltd*,[129] the plaintiff, who had undergone bronchial and lung surgery on two occasions, with permanent distressing and incapacitating sequelae, sought to impugn the treatment she had been given by her cardiac physician and her cardio-thoracic surgeon. Part of her case was that the cardio-thoracic surgeon had failed to obtain her informed consent to a sleeve resection of her left main bronchus.

**[14.120]** Geoghegan J dismissed the plaintiff's claim against both specialists. On the specific issue of the consent to the sleeve resection, he accepted that the surgeon had "told [the plaintiff] that there would be a 1% risk of death but that in reality chances of survival were better than 99%.

**[14.121]** He had explained to her where the narrowing of the bronchus was and warned her that if no surgery was carried out it could get slowly worse, affecting the function of her left lung and her whole lung could become destroyed ultimately. He had advised that sleeve resection was the most appropriate procedure, particularly having regard to her cardiac condition. He had told the plaintiff he would remove the cylinder of the left main bronchus. He had further told her that the success rate was 95% but that there was a 5% risk of restenosis. The plaintiff had apparently been somewhat alarmed by this and wondered why he would not do a full pneumonectomy. With the help of diagrams the surgeon had explained to her that sleeve resection was more appropriate. He had advised her of wound pain.

**[14.122]** Geoghegan J stated that he had "noted the view"[130] of O'Flaherty J in *Walsh v Family Planning Services Ltd*[131] with which Hederman J had concurred. He applied this test to the facts of the case and concluded that the information imparted had been "adequate" and that it had represented a reasonable exercise of care on the part of the surgeon. He also held that the consultant thoracic physician had not been in any way negligent in this communication with the plaintiff who had "quite clearly" given an informed consent to both operations.

**[14.123]** Geoghegan J made no reference to the other approaches in *Walsh*, which were quite opposed to that favoured by O'Flaherty and Hederman JJ, nor did he discuss O'Hanlon J's judgment in *Farrell v Varian*.[132] It seems clear that the plaintiff would have fared no better if the other approaches in *Walsh* had been applied to the facts of the case.

**[14.124]** The plaintiff appealed unsuccessfully to the Supreme Court.[133] Hamilton CJ (Barrington an Murphy JJ concurring) held that Geoghegan J's finding that the plaintiff had given "a fully informed consent" was supported by the evidence. He quoted from Finlay CJ's judgment in *Walsh*, which includes the passage where Finlay CJ stated that the question of disclosure of risk should be determined by the test laid down by the Supreme Court in *Dunne v National Maternity Hospital*.[134]

---

129. High Court, 20 December 1994 (Geoghegan J) affd by Supreme Court, 23 January 1997.
130. High Court, 20 December 1994.
131. [1992] 1 IR 496.
132. High Court, 20 December 1994.
133. Supreme Court, 23 January 1997.
134. [1989] IR 91.

**[14.125]** Hamilton CJ made no reference to that fact that Geoghegan J had applied the more stringent test preferred by O'Flaherty and Hederman JJ. It seems clear from Hamilton CJ's judgment, which is largely composed of extracts from the transcript of the evidence given at trial, that the Chief Justice supported the test set down by Finlay CJ in *Walsh*. It is unfortunate that the radical division of judicial opinion apparent in *Walsh* has not been resolved, one way or the other, by a thorough analysis of the competing approaches. After *Bolton*, it was still open to a litigant to argue that O'Flaherty and Hederman JJ's approach retained vitality since Hamilton CJ made no critical references to it or to the fact that Geoghegan J had adopted it, and the Chief Justice did not expressly state his preference for the approach favoured by Finlay CJ and (it would seem) McCarthy J in *Walsh*. Hamilton CJ ignored, not only O'Flaherty J's judgment (with which Hederman J concurred) but also the judgments of McCarthy and Egan JJ.

**[14.126]** The O'Flaherty/Hederman flag was raised in the most recent High Court analysis of the duty of disclosure in *Geoghegan v Harris*.[135] This decision represents the most sophisticated and closely-reasoned discussion of the subject of an Irish court.

**[14.127]** The plaintiff complained that a dental implant procedure, involving a bone graft taken from his chin, had been carried out negligently by the defendant, leaving him with chronic neurapathic pain in his chin. He also claimed that the defendant had failed to disclose to him the risk that pain of this character might result from the procedure. Kearns J, with the consent of the parties, delivered a judgment on the latter issue first, leaving to a later date the issue of negligence.

**[14.128]** Kearns J subjected *Walsh v Family Planning Services Ltd* to serious critical scrutiny. He expressed his opposition to the approach favoured by Finlay CJ since he did not consider that the *Dunne* test for medical treatment is general, which in essence the Chief Justice applied in *Walsh*, could convincingly be so extended.

**[14.129]** Kearns J observed:

> "where the medical professional standard is adopted, subject to a caveat or saver, then, to me at least, it make no great sense to oust from any meaningful role the views of the self-same medical practitioners as to the materiality of a risk or the need for a warning. Their views are received and relied upon in ordinary medical negligence cases. Who else can supply evidence of inherent defects? To substitute its own view, effectively in opposition to the experts on whose views, at least in the first instance, it purports to rely, the Court sets at nought the professional standard test and the result in the instant case is that the defendant must be found to be in breach of duty when not a single expert from either side believes a warning to be necessary."[136]

**[14.130]** Kearns J quoted from passages from the judgments in *Roche v Peilow*[137] which dealt with the court's power to override an established professional customary practice. Henchy J had expressed the view that a person could not be considered to be acting reasonably if he mindlessly followed the practice of others when by taking thought he would have realised that the practice in question was "fraught with peril" for his client and was readily avoidable or remediable. McCarthy J had considered it was the solicitors' duty

---

135. High Court, 21 June 2000 (Kearns J).

136. Page 28 of Kearns J's judgment.

137. [1985] IR 232 (SC).

to warn against "a clear and present danger" of financial loss for the client. Kearns J placed emphasis on the quoted phrases. In a crucial passage, he stated:

> "*Roche v Peilow* strongly suggests that the exception should only operate where a high onus is met and the defect, ignored or tolerated by the approved practice of a profession, relates to an obvious risk or danger, which is in very marked contrast to the instant case. The exception is there to address an obvious lacuna in professional practice usually arising from a residual adherence to out-of-date ideas. It seems an inappropriate mechanism to find fault with medical practitioners for failing to warn of very remote risks which for that very quality cannot be regarded an obvious or 'clear and present danger' even on due consideration. It is yet another reason to think that the third principle in *Dunne*, though suitable for medical treatment, is perhaps inappropriate in the distinctly different context of disclosure. One must surely conclude that the more remote the risk, the harder it is to judge any practice of not disclosing it to be 'blind, lax or inherently negligent'. The converse approach adopted in *Walsh* was justified by reference to the elective nature of the surgery, but that consideration … is more appropriate to the issue of causation than any duty of disclosure, where the seriousness of the consequences and the frequency of the risk are the real concern."[138]

**[14.131]** Perhaps this analysis can be debated. There is nothing illogical or implausible in a court's conclusion that in particular circumstances, it is obviously necessary for a doctor to disclose to a patient a very small risk relating to the proposed treatment. It is not the risk that must be obvious; what is essential is that the situation be one in which disclosure is obviously necessary. Whether disclosure of a small risk is obviously necessary involves a value-judgment on the part of the court. If a small risk of very serious injury is an element of a particular treatment, where the patient has other options, on could envisage a court's concluding that disclosure was "obviously necessary" thus keeping requirements as to disclosure in broad harmony with the approach favoured in *Dunne*.

**[14.132]** What is interesting about the passage just quoted from Kearns J's judgment is that Kearns J did not regard the elective nature of the proposed treatment as a distinctive reason for expanding the range of disclosure of risks. He proceeded to give a warning to the patient of any material risk that is a "known complication" of an operative procedure carefully carried out, even if the risk of its occurrence is very small. The only proviso or clarification that Kearns J considered necessary was that:

> "clearly the duty must be confined to such consequences or consequence which may be described as foreseeable or predictable consequences arising from such complications. Mere coincidental and unrelated risks, for example, could not properly fall within the compass of any duty, any more than consequences which might flow from the practitioner's negligence."[139]

**[14.133]** In the instant case, Kearns J held that nerve damage had to be characterised as a "known complication" of the procedure, "be it implants *per se*, or bone grafts, in the chin area".[140] The particular symptom of neuropathic pain was " a subdivision, not in a different species of risk or unrelated risk".[141] It was "foreseeable as a consequence of damaging

138. Page 31 of Kearns J's judgment

139. Page 20 of Kearns J's judgment.

140. Page 24 of Kearns J's judgment.

141. Page 24 of Kearns J's judgment.

nerves and certainly those nerves with which this case is concerned".[142] Once that was established, the fact that the particular manifestation of the nerve damage was very remote and unusual – "one in multiple thousands"[143] – was legally immaterial, since it was within the range of what was known or should be known by the medical practitioner.

**[14.134]** What is not entirely clear from Kearns J's judgment is whether the materiality test should require disclosure of "known complications" in every case. In favour of the view that it does, it can be argued that, if a risk of "one in multiple thousands" had to be disclosed in the instant case by reason of its being a known complication (in the sense of being a complication capable of being identified in advance), there would seem no obvious reason in principle for setting the bar higher in another case. As against this, Kearns J did make it clear that the disclosure standard he prescribed was to apply in the instant case, and his judgment contained an important passage in which he appeared to accept that what must be disclosed is less than every possible known risk and will depend on the particular circumstances of each case:

> "The application of the reasonable patient test seems more logical (than that of *Dunne*) in respect of disclosure. This would establish the proposition that, as a general principle, the patient has the right to know and the practitioner a duty to advise of all material risks associated with a proposed form of treatment. The Court must ultimately decide what is material. 'Materiality' includes consideration of both (a) the severity of the consequences and (b) statistical frequency of the risk. That both are critical is obvious because a risk may have serious consequences and yet historically or predictably be so rare as not to be regarded as significant by many people. For example, a tourist might be deterred from visiting a country where there had been an earthquake causing loss of life, but if told the event happened fifty years ago without repetition since, he might well wonder why his travel agent caused him unnecessary worry by mentioning it at all.
>
> The reasonable man, entitled as he may be to full information of material risks, does not have impossible expectations nor does he seek to impose impossible standards. He does not invoke only the wisdom of hindsight if things go wrong. He must be taken as needing medical practitioners to deliver on their medical expertise without executive restraint or gross limitation on their ability to do so.
>
> The decision in *Walsh* effectively confines the test of materiality to severity of consequences only …
>
> However, [there is a] possibility that at times a risk may become so remote, in relation at any rate to the less than most serious consequences, that a reasonable man may not regard it as material or significant. While such cases may be few in number, they do suggest that an absolute requirement of disclosure in every case is unduly onerous, and perhaps in the end counter productive if it needlessly deters patients from undergoing operations which are in their best interests to have.[144]

142. Page 24 of Kearns J's judgment.

143. Page 24 of Kearns J's judgment.

144. This sentence, savouring of Lord Diplock's approach in *Sidaway*, is curiously paternalistic in its assumptions and somewhat out of harmony with the general thrust of Kearns J's analysis, which is based on the value to be ascribed to patient autonomy.

As pointed out by Mr Healy: 'materiality is not a static concept'.[145] If the assessment of materiality is to 'abide a rule of reason',[146] any absolute requirement which ignores frequency seems much at variance with any such rule.

Every case it seems to me should be considered in the light of its own particular facts, evidence and circumstances to see if the reasonable patient in the plaintiff's position would have required a warning of the particular risk."[147]

**[14.135]** Looking at Kearns J's analysis of the issue of duty of disclosure in its entirety, it seems clear that he favours the "material disclosure" test and that he envisages that this involves a very wide range of disclosure of risk, at all events where what is at stake is the risk of serious injury or death. Precisely how this translates into practice in specific cases other than the instant case awaits further judicial analysis. It is fair to say that no other Irish judge has examined the issue of informed consent to treatment in as thorough and philosophical manner as Kearns J did in *Geoghegan v Harris*.

## The "Therapeutic Privilege"

**[14.136]** Brief mention may be made of the doctor's "therapeutic privilege", whereby no liability will attach to a doctor's failure to mention to the patient a risk inhering in a proposed treatment because to mention it would cause the patient some serious, disproportionate injury – a heart attack or nervous breakdown, for example. There is reasonably general (though not unanimous) judicial acceptance that such a privilege should be recognised.[148] Courts should, however, be on their guard lest paternalistic values are enabled to reassert themselves too strongly in this context.

## Causation and Non-Disclosure

**[14.137]** A patient who complains that the doctor failed to make proper disclosure of a risk in proposed treatment and who convinces the court that such a culpable failure has occurred will not have done enough to win the case. In any negligence proceedings it is not sufficient to show that the defendant has been guilty of negligence: one must go further

---

145. Healy, *Medical Negligence: Common Law Perspectives* (1999), p 99.

146. *Canterbury v Spence* (1972) 464F 2d 772 at 788 (US Court Apps DC Circ). It may be useful to quote the passage surrounding the phrase (at 787-788):

> "The topics importantly demanding a communication of information are the inherent and potential hazards of the proposed treatment, the alternatives to that treatment, if any, and the results likely if the patient remains untreated. The factors contributing significance to the dangerousness of a medical technique are, of course, the incidence of injury and the degree of harm threatened. A very small chance of death or serious disablement may well be significant, a potential disability which dramatically outweighs the potential benefit of the therapy or the detriments of the existing malady may summons discussion with the patient.
>
> There is no bright line separating the significant from the insignificant; the answer in any case must abide a rule of reason. Some dangers – infection, for example – are inherent in any operation; there is no obligation to communicate those of which persons of average sophistication are aware. Even more clearly, the physician bears no responsibility for discussion of hazards the patient has already discovered, or those having no apparent materiality to patients' decision on therapy. The disclosure doctrine, like others marking lines between permissible and impermissible behaviour in medical practice, is in essence a requirement of conduct prudent under the circumstances. Whenever non disclosure of particular risk information is open to debate by reasonable-minded men, the issue is for the finder of fact."

147. Pages 31-33 of Kearns J's judgment.

148. *Cf* Healy, *Medical Negligence: Common Law Perspectives* (1999), p 118-122.

and establish that the negligence foreseeably caused injury to the plaintiff. Many a negligence claim involving clear proof of culpability on the part of the defendant has failed for lack of proof of causation.

**[14.138]** In the context of a doctor's failure to make the appropriate level of disclosure of risks inhering in proposed treatment, two principal approaches have found favour in the decisions. The first permits recovery where the patient establishes that he or she would not in fact have undergone the proposed treatment if the doctor had made the appropriate disclosure. This approach is entirely consistent with the general principles of causation but has been criticised by some judges as being unrealistic in practice since almost every patient will be so affected by hindsight as to deny that he or she would have undergone the treatment if proper disclosure had been made.

**[14.139]** The second approach, conscious of the frailties of human recollection and hindsight, applies what is known at the "prudent patient" test, whereby liability will be imposed if a prudent patient, in the position of the plaintiff, would not have undergone the treatment if the proper degree of disclosure had been made. This approach can perhaps be criticised on the basis that it suspends the general requirements of proof of causation on the basis of a concern that may have no application in particular cases. It raises an interesting question as to whether, in conjunction with the *Scarman* test, which requires disclosure of material risks, it completely dispenses with a causal enquiry. The answer to this question depends on whether there are some risks which ought to be disclosed under the Scarman test but which nevertheless are not such that a reasonable patient, on learning of them, would inevitably decline to go through with the proposed treatment. There surely are risks of this category. In *Walsh*,[149] there was general agreement among the judges in the Supreme Court that, with elective treatment, the doctor is required to disclose risks that are remote and not necessarily serious. In *Geoghegan v Harris*,[150] there was a duty to disclose a risk of "one in multiple thousands". Even though a patient is entitled to be told of all these risks, it can hardly be considered that such disclosure would necessarily have resulted in his or her declining to go through with the proposed treatment in *every case*.

**[14.140]** In *Walsh* the judges gave no clear guidance on what test should be applied to the casual question. The only judge to address the general issue unambiguously was Egan J, who did not consider it necessary that the plaintiff should have to prove that, had a proper warning been given to him, he would not have submitted to the original operation:

> "If he never, in fact, received a proper warning, his answer to a question asking how it would have affected his attitude would necessarily be hypothetical and, unless it was by any unlikely chance in the negative, the court would be entitled to come to the conclusion that the failure to give the advice was negligent and actionable."[151]

**[14.141]** McCarthy J appeared to consider that the fact that the plaintiff had testified that, if he had known the risk, he would not have undergone the procedure, determined the causation issue in his favour.

---

149. [1992] 1 IR 496.
150. High Court, 21 June 2000 (Kearns J).
151. [1992] 1 IR 496.

**[14.142]** The complicating factor in *Walsh* was that the plaintiff had alleged that he received no warning from the first doctor whereas MacKenzie J held that he had received some warning from his doctor. O'Flaherty J derived no assistance from the plaintiff's assertion that, if he had received the correct warning from this doctor, he would not have undergone the operation:

> "This is because he must now be taken to speak with the wisdom of hindsight and, naturally, no rational human being who has undergone what the plaintiff has, undoubtedly, undergone would say that he would go through it all again for the sake of what was to be achieved by the operation. The plaintiff is bound by the primary finding of fact made by [MacKenzie J] in his regard, *viz* that the warning was given to the plaintiff and, in those circumstances, it seems to me that I am precluded from engaging in any examination of whether if a more powerful warning was given the plaintiff would have acted on it in the light of his flat contradiction that any warning at all was given."[152]

**[14.143]** This passage merges two quite separate issues. The first is that of causation; the second that of some species of estoppel, whereby a plaintiff who alleges that no warning was given is denied the entitlement to argue, as a matter of law, that the scope of the warning which the trial judge found was given was inadequate. Egan J was surely correct to reject the proposition that the court was in these circumstances precluded from engaging in an examination of whether the warning was adequate. It should be noted that the hypothetical quality of the answer to the question whether the plaintiff would have undergone the treatment if a proper disclosure had been given is exactly the same regardless of whether no disclosure or partial disclosure had occurred. This does not appear to have been fully appreciated by O'Flaherty J. Nor, it seems, by the Chief Justice.[153]

**[14.144]** In *Geoghegan v Harris*,[154] Kearns J expressed the view that Egan J's approach on the causation issue appeared to be "at variance with established principles on causation..."[155] and that it was "not perhaps as simple an issue as McCarthy J suggested".[156] He discussed decisions from the United States[157] and Canada[158] which favoured the objective "prudent patient" test, as well as decisions from Australia[159] favouring the subjective plaintiff-centered test. Noting that English decisions[160] also favoured the subjective test, he eventually adopted a hybrid test.

152. [1992] 1 IR 496.
153. *Cf* [1992] 1 IR 496 at 512.
154. High Court, 21 June 2000 (Kearns J).
155. Page 35 of Kearns J's judgment.
156. Page 35 of Kearns J's judgment.
157. *Canterbury v Spence* (1972) 464F 2d 772 at 788.
158. *Reibl v Hughes* (1980) 114 DLR (3d) 1. See also *Arndt v Smith* (1997) 148 DLR (4th) 48 (SCC).
159. *Ellis v Wallsend District Hospital* (1989) 17 NSWLR 553; *Bustos v Hair Transplant pty* NSWCA, 15 April 1997; *O'Brien v Wheeler* NSW 23 May 1997.
160. *Chatterton v Gerson*, [1981] 1 QB 432; *Hills v Potter* [1983] 3 All ER 716. Kearns J also discussed *Smith v Barking, Havering and Brentwood Health Authority* [1995] 5 Med LR 285, where Hutchison J adopted a hybrid approach to causation. See further Kennedy & Grubb (eds) *Principles of Medical Law*, paras 3.139–3.142, *O'Keefe v Harvey-Kemble* (1998) 45 BMLR 74 (CA), adopting subjective test.

**[14.145]** In the first instance, the court should consider the problem from an objective point of view by asking itself what a reasonable person, in the plaintiff's position would have done if properly informed. Taking account of the plaintiff's position would involve having regard to the plaintiff's age, pre-existing health, and family and financial circumstances, as well as the nature of the surgery: "in short, anything that can be objectively assessed, though personal to the plaintiff".[161] The objective test would sometimes have to yield to a subjective test, "but only when credible evidence, and not necessarily that of the plaintiff, in the particular case so demands".[162]

**[14.146]** Kearns J, having considered that, wherever possible, the Court should look beyond the testimony of the parties for credible confirmation, went on to observe:

> "If this dual and combined approach smacks of pragmatism, so be it. It is in my view well justified if it achieves a better result in terms of deciding what probably would have occurred. At the end of the day it seems to me that the different approaches are more about methodology than any legal principle. It is an exercise in 'fact construction'. In any such hypothetical though necessary exercise, there are dangers in dogmatically adopting one approach to the exclusion of the other, and certain aids to analysis would be forsaken by doing so."[163]

**[14.147]** This passage makes it plain that Kearns J was applying causal criteria that are faithful to the general approach in negligence litigation which is to enquire into what would have been the position if the negligent act had not taken place. In the context of the issue of informed consent, that question can be answered by reference to the particular plaintiff: what would this plaintiff have done had he or she been told of the risks involved in the proposed treatment. Kearns J was surely correct to place emphasis on the objective facts, external to the parties' testimony, in determining the answer to the question but, in doing so, he was conscious that this was not transforming the test into that of a hypothetical "prudent patient". At the end of the day, the judicial definition is about how the plaintiff in the proceedings would have acted if properly informed.

**[14.148]** Kearns J, expressing his agreement with Dr White's analysis[164] of the issue of the relevance of the elective character of the treatment to the duty of disclosure and causation, respectively, went on to re-emphasise that he considered that the significance of the elective dimension lay in causation rather than the duty to inform. It was obvious common sense to hold that a person might forego surgery when he had a real choice in the matter but, even in making a decision as to whether or not to undergo elective surgery, the reasonable man would be very greatly influenced by the statistical likelihood of the particular adverse consequence ever taking place:

> "If the risk is virtually off the spectrum, then I believe a reasonable man might accept or disregard such a risk where it is not in the more serious category and when he has regard to the perceived benefits attaching to the proposed procedure."[165]

161. Page 45 of Kearns J's judgment.
162. Page 46 of Kearns J's judgment.
163. Page 46 of Kearns J's judgment.
164. White, *Medical Negligence Actions* (1996), p 190.
165. Page 47 of Kearns J's judgment.

**[14.149]** In the instant case, Kearns J, placing more emphasis on the objective than the subjective factors, in view of their greater reliability, concluded that, had there been proper disclosure, the plaintiff would still have undergone the treatment. He had been keen to have it and his conduct clearly suggested that he was not going to be put off by some very remote risk when balanced with the perceived benefits of the procedure. Accordingly Kearns J held against the plaintiff on the causation issue, with the result that no liability attached to the defendant in respect of the claim based on lack of disclosure of risk.

## Consent in Relation to Medical Research[166]

**[14.150]** Where the consent of a person to undergo treatment for the purposes of medical research is being sought, a very high standard of disclosure and explanation is required. This was well put in a Canadian decision:

> "There can be no exceptions to the ordinary requirements of disclosure in the case of research as there may well be in ordinary medical practice. The researcher does not have to balance the probable effect of lack of treatment against the risk involved in the treatment itself. The example of risks being properly hidden from a patient where it is important that he should not worry can have no application in the field of research.
>
> The subject of medical experimentation is entitled to a full and frank disclosure of all the facts, probabilities and opinions which a reasonable man might be expected to consider before giving his consent."[167]

**[14.151]** A "professional disclosure" standard, whereby the profession has the last word on what should be told the patient, would seem clearly inappropriate in relation to research,

---

166. See Dickens 'Contractual Aspects of Human Medical Experimentation' (1975) 25 U Toronto LJ 406; Mulford 'Note: Experimentation on Human Beings' (1967) 20 Stanford LR 99; Samuels 'Medical Research: Law and Ethics' (1981) 21 Med Sci & L 295; Bowker 'Experimentation on Humans and Gifts of Tissue: Articles 2-23 of the Civil Code' (1973) 19 McGill LJ 161 a more comparative study then title suggests; Waddams 'Medical Experiments on Human Subjects' (1967) 25 U Toronto Faculty LR 25; Boyce 'Comment: Organ Transportation Crisis: Should the Deficit Be Eliminated Through Inter Vivos Sales?' (1983) 17 Akron LR 283 at 299-301; Treat 'Proposed Changes for Obtaining Consent from Experimental Subject[s,]' (1977) L & Human Behavior 403; Perlman 'Human Experimentation' (1974) 2(1) J of Legal Med 40; Morse 'Legal Implications of Clinical Investigation' (1967) 20 Vand LR 747; McClellan 'Informed Consent to Medical Therapy and Experimentation The Case for Invoking Punitive Damages to Deter Infringement of Individual Autonomy' (1982) 3 J of Legal Med 81; Cahill 'Compensation of Subjects Injured in Experimental Medicine Programs: The Ethical and Legal Considerations (1980) I J of Legal Med 110; Frenkel 'Human Experimentation: Codes of Ethics' (1977) 1 Legal Med Q 7; Rozovsky 'Informed Consent and Investigational Drugs' (1977) 1 Legal Med Q 162; Rozovsky 'Informed Consent and Investigational Drugs' (1977) 1 Legal Med Q 162.

167 *Halushka v University of Saskatchewan* 53 DLR (2d) 436 at 442-443 (Sask CA, 1965). Medical experimental research has given rise to particular difficulties in relation to children, since it is not clear whether they (or their parents on their behalf) can give an informed consent to treatment that is not directly for their benefit: *Cf* Somerville *Consent to Medical Care* 75ff. (Study Paper in the Protection of Life Series published by the Law Reform Commission of Canada 1979); Perlman 'Human Experimentation' (1974) 2(1) J of Legal Med 40 at 46; Morse 'Legal Implications of Clinical Investigation' (1967) 20 Vand LR 747; Cahill 'Compensation of Subjects Injured in Experimental Medicine Programs: The Ethical and Legal Considerations (1980) 1 J of Legal Med 110 at 121. For ethical guidelines drawn up by the British Paediatric Association, see 55 Archives of Disease in Childhood (1980) 75.

since those carrying out medical research have such significant incentives, not primarily of concern to the volunteer, such as the desire to produce medical information beneficial to future patients.[168] To require of them that they set their own legally binding standards would place them in an invidious position.

## Disclosure of Problems Arising in Medical Treatment

**[14.152]** Sometimes, in the course of treatment, an unexpected problem arises. In such a case, is the doctor required to tell the patient and, if so, subject to what qualifications?

**[14.153]** This problem arose in *Daniels v Heskin.*[169] The defendant, a dispensary doctor, was called to the plaintiff's house by a midwife to attend the female plaintiff, who, when giving birth at home to a baby, suffered a tear of the perineum. While the defendant was stitching the tear, the needle broke without his negligence, and portion of it remained embedded in the patient's flesh. The defendant did not inform the patient or her husband[170] of this fact fearing that to do so would damage the plaintiff's health. Instead, he instructed the midwife to watch for anything unusual occurring to the patient and to inform him if it did, telling her if the needle was not found within a period of six weeks the patient was to be x-rayed.

**[14.154]** The patient and her husband learned of the position some time later and another doctor successfully removed the broken portion of the needle. They sued the defendant in negligence.

**[14.155]** Lavery J considered that the failure by the defendant to inform the plaintiff for fear of causing her unnecessary mental anxiety was a reasonable one. In the circumstances "no purpose" could have been served by informing either the patient or her husband. It was not necessary to hold that the decision had been the right one:

> "In order to establish negligence or breach of duty the plaintiff would have to show that it was a decision incompatible with the proper exercise of the defendant's functions as a doctor."[171]

**[14.156]** On the question of damages, assuming there had been a duty to inform, the plaintiff would have to prove that her injuries had been caused by the failure to disclose. But since the needle had been successfully removed by another doctor at the appointed time there was no evidence that the non-disclosure had caused any damage to the plaintiff.

**[14.157]** Kingsmill Moore J stated:

> "I cannot admit of any abstract duty to tell patients what is the matter with them or, in particular, to say that a needle has been left in their tissues. All depends on the circumstances

167. (contd) The Control of Clinical Trials Act 1987 and Control of Clinical Trials and Drugs Act 1990 contain important procedural limitations. The Acts are analysed by Pearce 'Annotation' [1987] ICLSA and by Byrne & Binchy, *Annual Review of Irish Law 1987*; Byrne & Binchy, *Annual Review of Irish Law 1990* and Casey & Craven, *Psychiatry and the Law* (1999), pp 527-534.

168. *Cf* Schneyer 'Informed Consent and the Danger of Bias in the Formation of' Medical Disclosure Practices' [1976] Wisc LR 124 at 160-161. See also Treat 'Proposed Changes for Obtaining Consent from Experimental Subject[s,]' (1977) L & Human Behavior 403.

169. [1954] IR 73 (SC).

170. The husband was also a plaintiff in the proceedings, claiming damages for loss of *consortium*.

171. [1954] IR 73 at 81.

- the character of the patient, her health, her social position, her intelligence, the nature of the tissue in which the needle is imbedded, the possibility of subsequent infection, the arrangements made for future observation and care and innumerable other considerations."[172]

**[14.158]** He considered that there was no evidence indicating that the defendant had failed in his duty towards his patient in not informing her of the position.

> "In the present case the patient was passing through a *post-partum* period in which the possibility of nervous or mental disturbance is notorious; the needle was not situate in a place where any immediate damage was to be anticipated; husband and wife were of a class and standard of education which would incline them to exaggerate the seriousness of the occurrence and to suffer needless alarm and arrangements were made to keep the patient under observation during the period when sepsis might occur and to have the patient x-rayed at a period when the bruising caused by the birth should have subsided."[173]

**[14.159]** In the United States, a broad duty to warn patients about newly discovered dangers in previously administered treatment has been recognised.[174] In principle such a duty is easy to understand: the real difficulties attach to the scope of the duty - the nature and extent of the steps the doctor must take to warn the patient, the degree of danger which is necessary to create the obligation to inform, and the time that may have elapsed since the patient was last actively treated by the doctor.

**[14.160]** Our courts have yet to decide whether, for example, merely writing a letter to all former patients would be sufficient when it may be foreseen that the letter will inevitably not reach some of them because they will have moved without leaving a forwarding address. Naturally the answer will depend on the degree of risk which has been discovered about the former treatment; but where the former patient is continuing to act on the advice given, it seems clear that there should be a stringent duty to go to considerable lengths to communicate urgently with the former patient.

## Barristers

**[14.161]** The question whether a barrister should be liable in negligence[175] raises particularly difficult issues of policy. A number of arguments have been voiced in favour of conferring immunity on a barrister, at all events insofar as his or her work relates to litigation (actual or contemplated). It has been said that the administration of justice requires that a barrister should be allowed to perform his or her duty independently and

---

172. [1954] IR 73 at 81.

173. [1954] IR 73 at 81.

174. *Tresemer v Barke* (1978) 86 Cal App 3d 656, 150 Cal Rptr 384, analysed by Calfee 'Note: What you Don't Know Will Hurt You: 'Physicians' Duty to Warn Patients About Newly Discovered Dangers in Previously Administered Treatment' (1982) 31 Clev St LR 649.

175. See Dunlop 'Lawyer's Negligence' (1971) 65 Gaz of Incorp L Soc of Ireland 71; Roxburgh 'Rondel v Worsley: Immunity of the Bar' (1968) 84 LQR 513; Zander 'Note' (1979) 42 MLR 319; Keane 'Note: Negligence of Barristers' (1967) 2 Ir Jur (ns) 102; Smith 'Liability for the Negligent Conduct of Litigation: The Legacy of Rondel v Worsley' (1983) 47 Sask LR 211. The subject is analysed by the Committee on Court Practice and Procedure in its Fourteenth Interim Report, *Liability of Barristers and Solicitors for Professional Negligence* (Prl 2348, 1971).

discharge fully his or her higher duty to the Court.[176] Moreover, actions against barristers for negligence in the performance of courtroom work would prolong litigation, against the public interest.[177]

**[14.162]** A barrister is perhaps unique among professionals in being obliged (subject only to limited exceptions) to accept any client.[178] It has been argued that a barrister must be permitted, in the interests of the efficient administration of justice, to prepare his or her case and make decisions as to what is relevant and what is not: if the barrister were constantly looking over his or her shoulder at a prospective action for negligence by the client he or she would burden the Court with much unnecessary evidence and argument as an insurance against having his or her discretionary judgment questioned subsequently.[179] Another possible rationale for the immunity is that all participants in judicial proceedings- judges, lawyers, the parties to the litigation, and the witnesses- are rightly relieved of the stress and tension of a possible lawsuit.[180] Finally, a collateral attack on a judgment of the Court could bring the administration of justice into disrepute.[181]

**[14.163]** The thrust of these policy considerations would extend immunity to all those acting in the capacity of Court advocate - whether solicitor or barrister.[182] Where Court work ends and other legal work begins is "a grey area"[183] which may be difficult to determine in many cases.

**[14.164]** There appears to be no decision in this country in which the matter was comprehensively addressed as an issue in the proceedings.[184] In *W v Ireland (No 2)*,[185]

---

176. *Rondel v Worsley* [1969] 1 AC 191 at 231-232 (HL Eng), *per* Lord Reid); Fourteenth Interim Report, para 22; Miller 'The Advocate's Duty to Justice: Where Does it Belong?' (1981) 97 LQR 127. *Cf Saif Ali v Sydney Mitchell (a firm)* [1980] AC 198 at 220 (*per* Lord Diplock, doubting the strength of this argument).

177. [1969] 1 AC at 249 (*per* Lord Morris of Borth-y-Gest). *Cf* the Fourteenth Interim Report, para 21.

178. [1969] 1 AC at 281 (*per* Lord Upjohn). In Ireland, the constitutional right of access to the courts may strengthen this policy consideration: *Cf* Keane 'Note: Negligence of Barristers' (1967) 2 Ir Jur (ns) 102 at 103. Moreover, a barrister may not sue for his fees: *Hobart v Butler* (1859) 9 ICLR 157 (Exch). *Cf Robertson v MacDonagh* (1880) 6 LR Ir 433 (QBD). Lord Diplock was not impressed with this argument either: [1980] AC at 221.

179. [1969] 1 AC at 273 (*per* Lord Pearce). Fourteenth Interim Report, paras 21-24.

180. *Saif Ali v Sydney Mitchell & Co (a firm)* [1980] AC 198 at 222 (*per* Lord Diplock).

181. *Saif Ali v Sydney Mitchell & Co (a firm)* [1980] AC 198 at 222-223 (*per* Lord Diplock).

182. Divergent views on this question were expressed in *Rondel v Worsley* [1969] 1 AC 191. The Committee on Court Practice and Procedure in its Fourteenth Interim Report, para 6, expresses the view that, "in respect of advocacy in court, the solicitor is probably immune from an action for negligence". See also para 33. In England, a solicitor has been held to come within the scope of the immunity.

183. WINFIELD, 11th ed, p 73. The view is there expressed that it will be very much more difficult to bring within the immunity advice not to take proceedings than, for example, decisions not to call a witness or put in a particular piece of evidence. See now the 15th ed, pp 157-158.

184. *Cf Robertson v MacDonagh* (1880) 6 LR IR 433 (QBD) where a client, suing in contract for the non-performance by a barrister of his duties as an advocate, "admitted that in an ordinary case arising between client and counsel ... a client [could not] sue his counsel for the non-performance of his duties as advocate, or for negligence in the performance of such duties": at 436-437 (*per* May CJ).

185. [1997] 2 IR 141 (HC). See para **[1.33]** above.

Costello P appeared completely satisfied as to the merits of not imposing a duty of care in relation to the discharge of advocacy functions. In England the House of Lords, in *Rondel v Worsley*,[186] unanimously held that a barrister acting as advocate was immune from a duty of care to his or her client. In that case the negligence alleged against the defendant related to his conducting of the case in Court, in regard to the calling of witnesses and the putting of certain questions to them. The Court did not therefore have to address the difficult question of where the lines around the immunity should be drawn. That issue arose in *Saif Ali v Sydney Mitchell & Co (a firm)*.[187] There the alleged negligence was the failure within the limitation period to advise whether to sue certain defendants in a running-down case. The majority held that, on the facts pleaded, the immunity would not run so far. They approved of the formula contained in a decision of the New Zealand Court of Appeal, to the effect that, while the immunity extended to some pre-trial work, each piece of such pre-trial work:

> "should ... be tested against the one rule: that the protection exists only where the particular work is so intimately connected with the conduct of the cause in court that it can fairly be said to be a preliminary decision affecting the way that cause is to be conducted when it comes to a hearing. That protection should not be given any wider application than is absolutely necessary in the interests of the administration of justice ..."[188]

The majority in *Saif Ali* did not give any clear indication on how this somewhat opaque formula should be transplanted into the specifics of a barrister's practice. All that Lord Diplock could offer was that, where the barrister advises on evidence at some stage before the trial, "his protection from liability in the conduct of the case at trial is not to be circumvented by charging him with negligence in having previously advised the course of conduct at the hearing that was subsequently carried out".[189] Lord Salmon was of the view that drafting pleadings or advising on evidence might, but not necessarily would, come within the scope of the immunity.

**[14.165]** Recently, under the shadow of the European Convention on Human Rights, the House of Lords, in *Hall (Arthur JJ) & Co v Simons*[190] has abolished the advocates' immunity for both civil and criminal cases (with some dissenting voices on the latter aspect). Their Lordships no longer were impressed by the arguments against imposing a duty of care which had convinced their predecessors. Advocates, like other professions, could confront the risk of being sued without undue apprehension or compromising their standards. Whilst the problem of character attack on earlier verdicts, especially in criminal proceedings, had to be acknowledged, it was not sufficiently serious to justify the immunity.

---

186. See paras **[14.161]** above..

187. [1980] AC 198 (HL Eng), 1979), analysed by Zander (1979) 42 MLR 319.

188. *Rees v Sinclair* [1974] I NZLR 180 at 187 (CA).

189. [1980] AC 198 at 224.

190. [2000] 3 All ER 673 (HL). For a most perceptive analysis of the implication of this decision, see Williams '"May There Be No Moaning of the Bar"' (2000) 16 Prof Neg 225.

**[14.166]** The position in Canada[191] is not indulgent to advocates. In the United States[192] no immunity has been recognised.

**[14.167]** How an Irish Court would approach the question if it required resolution is not absolutely clear. Constitutional issues might be relevant.[193] Moreover, as the fact, if not the analysis, of the House of Lords' decision in *Hall* indicates, there are significant doubts as to whether the non-imposition of a duty of care in this context complies with Article 6 of the European Convention on Human Rights.[194] We suggest that the best solution would be for the court to grasp the nettle and abolish the immunity. The arguments in its favour are not strong and would surely not withstand an *Osman* standard of scrutiny. The court should prescribe a duty in negligence which, consistent with general principles, would be tempered by the fact that an advocate (whether barrister or solicitor) owes not only a duty to his client in the performance of his or her work in Court, but also a broader duty to assist the administration of justice.[195] As an historical footnote, we must record that, in 1971, the matter was the subject of a report by the Committee on Court Practice and Procedure,[196] under the chairmanship of Walsh J. It stated that:

> "The present legal position as to the liability of a barrister for professional negligence seems to be that he is immune from actions for negligence in advocacy in court. With regard to advising and preliminary work in connection with litigation the position is doubtful but the better opinion seems to be that he cannot be made liable. In non-litigious work the position is also doubtful but since the decision in *Rondel v Worsley* the better opinion seems to be that he is liable."[197]

**[14.168]** The Committee considered that, since the existing law had given rise to no public disquiet and since few claims for professional negligence had been brought against solicitors, it would not be advisable to recommend legislative change.[198] It approved[199] of what it considered to be the existing position that, in regard to advocacy work, both solicitors and barristers were immune from suit in negligence. With regard to the preparatory work in litigation, where the legal position was in doubt, the Committee considered[200] that it would be best to let the position be clarified by judicial decisions in appropriate cases. Finally, the Committee considered[201] that it would not be desirable to alter what they believed to be the present situation in regard to non-litigious work, namely that both solicitors and barristers are liable for professional negligence.

---

191. Jackson & Powell, *Professional Negligence* (4th ed, 1997), para 5.12.
192. *Cf* PROSSER & KEETON, pp 185-186.
193. *Cf* Keane 'Note: Negligence of Barristers' (1967) 2 Ir Jur (ns) 102 at 103.
194. *Cf Osman v United Kingdom* [1999] 1 FLR 193.
195. *Cf* Sgayias 'Liability of a Lawyer for Negligence in the Conduct of Litigation' (1978) 8 Manitoba LJ 661 at 668.
196. Fourteenth Interim Report, *Liability of Barristers and Solicitors for Professional Negligence* (Prl 2348 1971).
197. Fourteenth Interim Report, para 5. This statement of the law appears to extend the immunity somewhat wider than in *Saif Ali*.
198. Fourteenth Interim Report, paras 32-35.
199. Fourteenth Interim Report, para 33.
200. Fourteenth Interim Report, para 34
201. Fourteenth Interim Report, para 35.

## Solicitors

**[14.169]** Formerly, the duty of a solicitor to his or her client was regarded as resting exclusively on contract,[202] and no right of action in tort for negligence was recognised.[203] With the development and extension of the "neighbour" principle, this limitation came to be questioned but was slow to be abandoned.[204]

**[14.170]** Thus, in *Deignan v Greene*,[205] the Supreme Court evinced little enthusiasm to recognise a tortious right of action in negligence. Ó Dálaigh J stated:

> "It may indeed be that the categories of negligence are never closed; but it does not necessarily follow that all the rejected claims of other branches of the law can there find a sanctuary ... I much doubt if refuge can be found for claims which must flee the inconvenience of the doctrine of consideration."

**[14.171]** A different approach was taken in the Supreme Court decision of *Finlay v Murtagh*[206] in 1978. Henchy J stated:

> "The coincidence that the [solicitor]'s conduct amounts to a breach of contract cannot affect either the duty of care or the common-law liability for its breach, for it is the general relationship, and not any particular manifestation such as a contract, that gives rise to the tortious liability in such a case ..."[207]

**[14.172]** No liability, however, would attach in tort where the solicitor was in breach, not of his general duty of care arising from his or her professional relationship, but of "a particular and special term of the contract in respect of which the solicitor would not be liable if the contract had not contained such a term".[208] In this regard, Henchy J instanced cases where the solicitor was to issue proceedings within a specified time or to close a sale

202. For a comprehensive analysis of the present law, see O'Callaghan, *The Law on Solicitors in Ireland* (2000), Ch 11. See also Kaye 'The Liability of Solicitors in Tort' (1984) 100 LQR 680; Crowley 'Professional Negligence: The Liability of Solicitor in Negligence' (1987) 5 ILT (ns) 94; Stanton 'Note' (1979) 43 MLR 207; Dias 'Comment' [1980] Camb LJ 45; Dugdale & Stanton 'Solicitors and Professional Negligence' (1980) 130 New LJ 384; Dwyer 'Solicitor's Negligence - Tort or Contract?' (1982) 56 Austr LJ 524. For accounts of the position in the United States, see the Symposium in (1978) 14 Willamette LR 355; Haughey 'Lawyers Malpractice: A Comparative Appraisal' (1973) 48 Notre Dame L 888.

203. An excellent statement of what this duty may be in specific cases is made in a memorandum submitted by the Incorporated Law Society of Ireland to the Committee of Court Practice and Procedure during the preparation of its Fourteenth Interim Report, *Liability of Barristers and Solicitors for Professional Negligence* (Prl 2348, 1971) summarised in paras 13 to 16.

204. *Cf Liston v Munster & Leinster Bank* [1940] IR 77; *Somers v Erskine* [1943] IR 348 (HC). *Deignan v Greene* Supreme Court, 21 October 1954. The right of a client to sue his solicitor for conspiracy to defraud and fraud was recognised in *Oakes v Lynch* Supreme Court, 21 December 1954. *Cf McGrath v Kelly* [1965] IR 497 (HC), where it was "argued that the liability sought to be imposed on [the] defendant [solicitor] is a liability *ex contractu*" (at 510).

205. Supreme Court, 21 October 1954.

206. [1979] IR 249 (SC).

207. [1979] IR 249 at 257. See also *Midland Bank Trust Co Ltd v Hett, Scubas & Kemp* [1979] Ch 384 (Oliver J), noted by Stanton (1979) 42 MLR 207. As to Canada. see *Central & Eastern Trust Co v Refuse* (1986) 37 CCLT 117 at 165 (SC Can, *per* Le Dain J delivering the judgment of the Court). *Finlay v Murtagh* was quoted (160-161).

208. [1979] IR 249.

by a particular date - stressing that the particular obligation must not fall within the general duty of care owed by the solicitor. (Thus, a specific undertaking to take proceedings within the relevant period of limitation would fall within the general duty of care rather than be regarded as a special term.)

**[14.173]** The solicitor's liability in tort under the general duty of care extended, stated Henchy J, not only to a client for reward but also:

> "to any person for whom [he] undertakes to act professionally without reward, and ... to those (such as beneficiaries under a will, persons entitled under an intestacy, or those entitled to benefits in circumstances such as a claim in respect of a fatal injury), with whom he has made no arrangement to act but who, as he knows or ought to know, will be relying on his professional care and skill."[209]

**[14.174]** In the High Court decision of *Wall v Hegarty*,[210] where, on account of a solicitor's admitted carelessness, an intended legatee was not legally entitled to a legacy, Barrington J held that the legatee was entitled to recover. He accepted the reasoning of Sir Robert Megarry VC, in *Ross v Caunters*[211] that in such circumstances there was a close degree of proximity between the parties, and stated[212] that he was satisfied that on the basis of *Finlay v Murtagh*,[213] the solicitor owed a legatee a duty of care:

> "to ensure that the wishes of the legator are not frustrated and the expectancy of the legatee defeated ..."

## The Standard of Care for Solicitors

**[14.175]** The standard of care for solicitors covers such aspects of a solicitor's practice as the giving of advice, selection of counsel, acting on the advice of counsel, and conducting conveyances and other transactions with due care. Let us look briefly at some of the cases in point.

### *(a) Giving advice*

**[14.176]** A solicitor who gives incorrect advice on "a point of common occurrence, where the law is clear",[214] will be liable in negligence.[215] Where, however, the law is difficult, advice may be reasonable even though it later turns out to be incorrect.[216]

### *(b) Failing to give advice*

**[14.177]** A solicitor may sometimes fail to give advice either initially or as the transaction for which he has been engaged progresses through its several stages. Depending on the relevance and urgency of that neglected advice, the solicitor may be guilty of negligence. Thus, for example, if a solicitor engaged to act for a person who has contracted to purchase

209. [1979] IR 249.

210. [1980] ILRM 124 (HC). See generally Eisenberg 'Note Attorney's Negligence and Third Parties' (1982) 57 NYULR 126.

211. [1980] Ch 297. See also *Whittingham v Crease & Co* [1978] 5 WWR 45 (BC SC).

212. [1980] Ch 297.

213. [1980] Ch 297. *Cf Clarke v Bruce Lane & Co (a firm)* [1988] 1 WLR 881 and see the comments in [1988] All ER Ann Rev 271-272, 295, 329.

214. Jackson & Powell, *Professional Negligence* (2nd ed, 1987), para 4.67.

215. *Cf* eg *Hill v Finney* (1865) 4 F & F 616.

216. *Cf Bell v Strathairn & Blair* (1954) 104 LJ 618.

a property discovers from a search that it lacks proper (or any) planning permission, he should let his client know.[217]

**[14.178]** In *Park Hall School Ltd v Overend*,[218] the plaintiff offered lands for sale. After negotiations with a prospective purchaser had gone some distance, a contract was drawn up but not signed by that party within the specified time. The plaintiff withdrew the offer, and later advertised the lands for sale. Before any tenders had been accepted, the disappointed party, who had until then appeared to accept his fate without protest, issued a plenary summons claiming specific performance of an oral agreement to sell him the lands. In the belief that this claim had no prospect of success, the plaintiff proceeded with the sale by tender to another party. To the plaintiff's surprise and financial detriment, the disappointed party was successful in his action. The plaintiff sued the solicitors, whom it had engaged to act in respect of the sale, alleging that they had been negligent.

**[14.179]** O'Hanlon J dismissed the action at the conclusion of the plaintiff's case. He reviewed the difficult state of the law as to offer and acceptance at the time of the transaction and came to the conclusion that when the relevant details about the negotiations became available to the defendants, the right course for them was to proceed on the assumption that no binding contract had yet been concluded, while recognising at the same time that a doubtful situation existed. This the defendants had done. After the intending purchaser had been told that the offer had been withdrawn, any later enquiry to him as to his intentions would only have disclosed an uncertainty as to the plaintiff's legal position. Once the intending purchaser had sued, the proper course, again adopted by the defendants, was to brief counsel. Thereafter, it would have been extremely rash and unwise for them to challenge the expert opinion on the legal situation which was made available to them by distinguished members of the Bar.[219] As the plaintiff's representatives had been present at a series of meetings with counsel after the litigation had commenced, the plaintiff had been duly apprised of counsel's views, including the reservations ultimately expressed as to the probable outcome of the case.

### *(c) Negligence in litigation*

**[14.180]** A solicitor may be guilty of actionable negligence in regard to litigation in a number of ways. These relate to the following areas (1) the choice of which court to proceed in (2) the manner in which a solicitor liaises with counsel on behalf of the client (3) the solicitor's performance of advocacy duties and (4) delay in initiating or processing litigation.

#### *(i) Choice of court*

**[14.181]** In *Lopes v Walker*,[220] the issue of solicitor's duties in relation to strategy as to court jurisdiction fell for consideration. The Court, by a majority[221] overturned a verdict against the plaintiff by Morris J in the High Court.

217. *Cf Lake v Bushly* [1869] 2 All ER 964.
218. [1987] ILRM 345 (HC).
219. [1987] ILRM 345 at 356.
220. Supreme Court, 28 July 1997.
221. Lynch and Barron JJ; Murphy J dissenting.

**[14.182]** The plaintiff, was involved in a traffic accident in 1988. He had worked previously in the merchant navy, but at the time of the accident was owner of a newsagent's business. The accident was attributable to the negligence of an intoxicated driver. Within three weeks, and before medical reports were received, the plaintiff's original solicitor had issued a civil bill in the Circuit Court. The plaintiff wished to have the case transferred to the High Court. Counsel advised against this. The plaintiff changed from his original solicitor to the defendant solicitor on 1 March 1991. The defendant had for many months been aware of the plaintiff's dissatisfaction with the proceedings continuing in the Circuit Court. The case was heard on 14 May 1991, the plaintiff was awarded £10,000 general damages and just over £2,000 special damages. The Circuit Court judge awarded nothing for loss of earnings.

**[14.183]** The threshold for the High Court jurisdiction at the time of the litigation was £15,000.

**[14.184]** The plaintiff sued the defendant for negligence, contending that he should not have let the case proceed to judgment in the Circuit Court without further adjournment. The essence of his claim was that the defendant ought to have sought another expert medical opinion when the neurologist who examined the plaintiff regarded the arachnoid cyst on the left side of his brain as being congenital rather than as being attributable to the accident. The plaintiff also contended that greater attention should have been paid to his claims for loss of earnings. He argued that his injuries were such as to prevent him returning to his career as a merchant seaman, which yielded an income of £18,000 per annum.

**[14.185]** Morris J dismissed the claim but, as has been mentioned, the Supreme Court, by a majority upheld the plaintiff's appeal.

**[14.186]** Barron J, one of the two judges upholding the appeal, considered that the defendant ought to have arranged through the neurologist for a second opinion. Moreover, although the evidence of the neurologist, an orthopedic surgeon and a psychiatrist had been fairly presented, the reports of the neurologist and psychiatrist had contained provisos, to which no attention appeared to have been paid. These might have been asked about them but they never had been. Furthermore, a certificate by a doctor approved by the Minister for Communications to the effect that he had examined the plaintiff and found him unfit for seafaring, had not been followed up. It was true that counsel's opinion as to the value of the case was in favour of remaining in the Circuit Court, but his assessment was clearly affected by his view of the medical evidence and it was hard to see how he had taken such a strong view of it. Contrary to his assertion that there was no positive evidence of physical injury, there was in fact such evidence "albeit soft tissue injury and not bony injury".[222] In addition, counsel's view as to loss of earnings seemed to be based on the proposition that, since the plaintiff had not been earning a seaman's wages at the date of his accident, he could not then claim such a loss:

> "Undoubtedly, counsel's opinion was supported by the assessment of damages by the trial judge. But that is not really the true test of what the plaintiff could or should have recovered

[222] Supreme Court, 28 July 1997.

as of that date. It is merely an assessment of what was the proper sum to award to the plaintiff on the basis of the manner in which his case was presented to the Court."[223]

**[14.187]** Even if the plaintiff had never expressed any intention before the accident of returning to sea and even if his newsagent's business would have failed anyway, the fact still remained that, had he still been in full health he would have been in a position to return to sea.

**[14.188]** The plaintiff had been happy to proceed in the Circuit Court provided he could subsequently sue the neurologist. It must, however, have been obvious to the defendant that a hypothetical action against a doctor, which was highly unlikely to be successful, was no remedy for proceeding in a court and under a jurisdiction when the plaintiff did not want. The defendant's failure to tell him so meant that the plaintiff could not make an informed decision to let the case proceed in the Circuit Court.

**[14.189]** Lynch J, the other judge in the majority, expressed the defendant's failure somewhat more narrowly in terms of not having sought an adjournment of the case as soon as he received the file on 1 March 1991 to give him "breathing space to sort the matter out properly one way or the other".[224]

**[14.190]** Murphy J, dissenting, pointed to a number of potent factors weighing against liability. In relation to the reports of the neurologist and the orthopedic surgeon, the defendant had expressly advised his client in writing that he was entitled to obtain a second expert medical opinion if he wished. During the pre-trial consultation at the courthouse, counsel had made the position clear to the plaintiff. A memorandum kept by the defendants' assistant recorded counsel advising the plaintiff as follows:

> "In his estimation the valuation based on [his] knowledge of the Judge and on the knowledge of what the doctors would say was about £10,000. He reiterated that Mr Lopes must be absolutely satisfied that he was happy to go into Court today for a maximum of £15,000. He did not have to follow the opinion of his legal advisors. If he was not happy he must bring the case in another Court and this decision must be made today. If he felt that the compensation was not adequate then he should tell us today and go to another Court. Mr Lopes said that it would be silly of him to go to the High Court if no more damages [be] awarded in that Court."

**[14.191]** On the issue of loss of earnings, the memorandum recorded that counsel had pointed out that there was

> "no proof of loss of earnings. The court would compensate Mr Lopes on the basis of what he was actually working at the time. The test was one of probabilities and not possibilities and the probability was that he would not be working at sea."

**[14.192]** In the plaintiff's later case against the defendant, counsel gave evidence before Morris J to similar effect. The medical reports did not paint a picture of a person who would have been incapable of carrying on the business of a shopkeeper; moreover, since the plaintiff had not been engaged as a ship's officer for some years before the accident and had no immediate plans of taking up that occupation before the accident, it could not be used as the basis for calculating his loss. Such a claim was in fact made before the Circuit

---

223. Supreme Court, 28 July 1997.

224. Supreme Court, 28 July 1997.

Court Judge who had expressly rejected it. Morris J had not merely upheld counsel's advice as a tenable, competent, professional opinion but had confirmed that it represented his own assessment of the interpretation of the medical evidence available to the legal advisor on the date of the hearing of the personal injury action.

**[14.193]** As regards the medical evidence, there had been no suggestion that the plaintiff had relied upon any guidance from the defendant as to what doctors he should consult. While the plaintiff had wished for the neurologist to be called as a witness in order to be cross-examined by the plaintiff's counsel as to the provenance of the cerebral cyst, such a course would have been extremely imprudent, in Murphy J's view.

**[14.194]** Murphy J concluded by noting that the proceedings had been issued, particulars delivered and all of the medical examinations conducted before the defendant came on record as the plaintiff's solicitor. Furthermore, and even more importantly, the fundamental responsibility as to the witness to be called and as to the advice to be given to the client in relation to the valuation of the claim was a matter for counsel. The defendant had, therefore, a more limited role in the proceedings and Morris J had been entirely correct in concluding that there was no evidence that he had failed to discharge those duties.

*(ii) Liaising with counsel*

**[14.195]** In *Millard v McMahon*,[225] Henchy J observed that it was:

> "well settled that where a solicitor lays his client's claim fully before competent counsel and acts on counsel's advice, he is not liable for negligence".

**[14.196]** In *Fallon v Gannon*,[226] in an action for negligence against a solicitor, the plaintiff alleged that the counsel representing the plaintiff in the action against the plaintiffs by the purchasers of the plaintiff's premises failed adequately or properly to cross-examine witnesses, resulting in the decision going against the plaintiff. This allegation was rejected by the Supreme Court. Finlay CJ (for the Court) said:

> "The duty of a solicitor with regard to the conduct of a case in court where he has briefed counsel is firstly to brief appropriate and competent counsel and secondly to instruct them properly with regard to the facts of the case which he has obtained from his client; and to make provision for the attendance of appropriate witnesses and other proofs. A solicitor has not got any vicarious responsibility for the individual conduct of counsel."[227]

**[14.197]** It should be borne in mind that the traditional view had been that counsel engaging in advocacy functions may not be sued for negligence.[228] Thus, there would be no question of vicarious liability attaching to a solicitor, even where a barrister conducts a case carelessly, unless a court were (surprisingly) to hold that the immunity should not confer protection on the solicitor so far as his or her vicarious liability is concerned. Of course, it would be possible, as the Supreme Court apparently recognises, that a solicitor

---

225. Professional Neg LR 1 at 11 (HC, 1968).

226. [1988] ILRM 193 (SC).

227. [1988] ILRM 193 at 197.

228. *Rondel v Worsley* [1969] 1 AC 191, overruled by the House of Lords in *Hall (Arthur JJ & Co) v Simons* [2000] 3 All ER 673. See para **[14.165]** above for discussion of the case and para **[14.167]** for consideration of how the Irish courts may in future decide this issue.

might be sued for the negligent selection of counsel. Here, if liability attached, it would be in the solicitor's personal capacity rather than vicariously.

**[14.198]** Courts traditionally have held that a solicitor who acts on the advice of properly instructed counsel is not negligent.[229] It seems that this rule should not be stated without any qualification.[230] If the solicitor in question is a specialist, and holds himself or herself out to the client as such, it may well be that blind adherence to the advice of a barrister may (albeit rarely) fail the requirements of due care.

*(iii) Immunity when acting as advocate*

**[14.199]** It appears to be beyond debate that, to the extent that a barrister may have an immunity from being sued in respect of his work as advocate,[231] a solicitor doing the same work will have a similar immunity.[232] In *Rondel v Worsley*,[233] Lords Pearce, Reid and Upjohn accepted that the barristers immunity extended to a solicitor acting as advocate, and in *Saif Ali v Sydney Mitchell & Co. (a firm)*,[234] Lords Diplock, Salmon and Wilberforce took the same view. In neither case did the specific question arise of whether the parameters of that immunity were identical as between barristers and solicitors; it is, however, very difficult to see why they should differ in any way.

***(d) Buying and selling property***

**[14.200]** Buying and selling property for clients are markedly dangerous activities for solicitors to engage in, from the standpoint of negligence litigation. Solicitors can be sued for what they did or failed to do, said or failed to say, or the manner in which they did or said it.

*(i) Requisitions*

**[14.201]** In *Hanafin v Gaynor*,[235] the plaintiff unsuccessfully sued the defendant solicitor for professional negligence. The plaintiff had purchased premises on an industrial estate for over half a million pounds. As a result of planning defects, he had to sell it at a very substantial loss. The plaintiff claimed that the defendant had negligently recommended to the plaintiff that he should buy the premises, which could be worth over a million pounds. Egan J rejected this on the evidence, as he did the plaintiff's claim that the defendant had warranted, represented or advised that the property had full planning permission and bye-law approval for light industrial and office use.

**[14.202]** At contract stage, certain documents had been furnished to the defendant, including planning permission in 1970 for a proposed industrial building on the site of the

---

229. *Cf*, eg *Kemp v Burt* (1833) 4 B & Ad 424. In *Park Hall School Ltd v Overend* [1987] ILRM 345 at 356 (HC), O'Hanlon J noted that it would have been "extremely rash and unwise" for the defendant solicitors to have sought to challenge the expert opinion of a distinguished members of the Bar". See also *McMullan v Carty* High Court, 13 July 1993 (Carroll J).

230. *Cf* Jackson & Powell, *Professional Negligence* (2d ed, 1987), paras 4.48-4.49.

231. *Cf* para **[14.167]** above.

232. *Cf* Jackson & Powell, *Professional Negligence* (2d ed, 1987), para 4.45.

233. [1969] 1 AC 191 (HL, Eng).

234. [1980] AC 198 (HL, Eng).

235. Professional Neg LR 278 (HC, 1990). See also the important decision of *Doran v Delaney* [1998] 2 ILRM 1 (SC) discussed in paras **[10.129]-[10.136]** above.

premises. Proper requisitions of title by the defendant ensued; Egan J was satisfied that "one would certainly assume from reading the replies that this 1970 permission was the only permission in existence which affected the property". Nothing was disclosed about a permission in 1972. Searches handed over revealed that there had been a permission in 1973. The defendant had made a query about this and was told in reply that it did not affect the site being sold. In Egan J's opinion, the defendant had had no reason to query the accuracy of this reply, nor to believe that a 1972 permission was in existence.

**[14.203]** Applying the test for professional negligence spelt out by the Supreme Court in *Roche v Peilow*[236] and in *Dunne v National Maternity Hospital*,[237] Egan J held that the defendant was not guilty of professional negligence. He had been perfectly entitled to accept the reply to his query regarding the 1973 permission. The existence of the 1972 permission had never been disclosed even though professional law searchers had carried out searches "so how was the defendant to know about it?"[238] Egan J rejected the plaintiff's argument that the defendant should have carried out a further search before closing: the plaintiff or his tenants "were actually in possession during this period."[239] (Whether lawyers should thus be able to transfer the burden onto non-lawyers may be debated.)

**[14.204]** Egan J stressed that the title had been accepted by the solicitor of the plaintiff's financiers as by the vendor's solicitor, who was actually buying the property for his own clients while at the same time selling it to the plaintiff.

**[14.205]** Egan J concluded that it could not be said that the defendant was guilty of such failure as no other solicitor of equal status and skill would be guilty of if acting with ordinary care. He did not address in express terms the question whether the evidence had revealed any professional practice which had inherent defects which ought to have been obvious to any person giving the matter due consideration. Presumably he considered this proviso irrelevant to the evidence in the case.

*(ii) Liquor licences*

**[14.206]** The examination of liquor licences calls for particular care.[240] In *Taylor v Ryan*,[241] the defendant solicitor was found to have been negligent in the following circumstances. The plaintiff agreed by contract to buy a seven-day publican's ordinary licence and premises in a rural area. He then engaged the defendant to carry out the legal work concerning the purchase. The defendant's requisitions on title asked the vendor's solicitors to specify the exact type of licence and to give full particulars of all exemptions or other privileges attached to it. The vendor's solicitors replied by stating "copy licence furnished ordinary licence". Previous to the delivery of the requisition, the vendor's solicitor had furnished the defendant with a photostat copy of the current licence, which was stated to be a publican's ordinary licence in the name of the vendor. This copy was of the face of the licence only. On the back of this, and on all licence papers applicable to ordinary

236. [1985] IR 232.
237. [1989] IR 91.
238. Professional Neg LR 278
239. Professional Neg LR 278.
240. Practitioners should heed the advice set out in Cassidy, *The Licensing Acts 1833-1995*, Ch 29.
241. [1985] IR 212.

publicans' licences, was a note stating that this form of licence was used for both public houses and certain hotels and that hotel licences were subject to certain restrictions which did not apply to public houses. Although the copy did not contain this note, the defendant stated in evidence that he was aware of the existence of such a note on all such licence papers.

**[14.207]** The plaintiff later put the defendant on notice "in a persistent fashion"[242] of his doubt about the validity of a licence. The defendant relied on his knowledge of the fact that the premises had for twenty years traded with all the outward appearances of an ordinary seven-day public house, that they had never been a hotel during that period and that the licence had been annually renewed without opposition in the courts. Some time after the sale it transpired that the licence was not an ordinary seven-day publican's licence but was a hotel licence only. Since the premises were incapable of being reconstructed into a hotel and there was a seven-day ordinary publican's licensed premises within a mile, it was not possible under the licensing code to have them licensed even by the extinction of existing licences. The plaintiff thus sustained considerable loss.

**[14.208]** Finlay P imposed liability. He noted that "a simple, direct enquiry"[243] to the District Court Office of the appropriate town would have revealed the true position. In his view:

> "in the particular circumstances of this case and on the express warnings given, such an enquiry was a necessary reasonable standard of professional skill and care on the part of this defendant."[244]

**[14.209]** In *Kelly v Crowley*,[245] Murphy J imposed liability in negligence on a solicitor who failed to pursue further his requisition as to the "exact type of licence attached to the property", when the reply from the vendor's solicitors merely had referred him to the licence which was attached but had made no statement as to the nature of the licence or the privileges attached to it. Even earlier than this, however, the defendant ought to have sought clarification of the position regarding the licence. Although he had been instructed only two days before the auction of the premises, this did not afford him a defence. Murphy J observed that:

> "[i]n many cases it will happen that a professional man is entrusted with a task of such complexity that it cannot be competently performed in the time available. Where that problem arises it seems to me that the professional man would have to advise the client as to that state of affairs and warn him of the risks which might be involved in dispensing with appropriate enquiries or of otherwise dealing with a complex matter on the basis of inadequate information."[246]

**[14.210]** Murphy J, considered that the defendant should have enquired from the vendor's solicitor before the auction, or the auctioneer at the auction itself, as to whether the licence advertised in the brochure was one granted in respect of a hotel or some other type of premises. A reassurance thus acquired "might well"[247] have been an adequate discharge of

242. High Court, 10 March 1983, p 9
243. High Court, 10 March 1983, p 10.
244. High Court, 10 March 1983.
245. [1985] IR 212 (HC).
246. [1985] IR 212 at 228.
247. [1985] IR 212.

his duty. Murphy J was of the view that, particularly in view of *Taylor v Ryan*[248] it might be the case that a solicitor acting on behalf of a purchaser of licensed premises is not required to inspect the Register of Licences before the sale unless there are "some circumstances giving rise to suspicion".[249]

**[14.211]** In *Pierse v Allen*,[250] Murphy J had an opportunity to review and explain the *ratio* of his earlier decision on legal malpractice in *Kelly v Crowley*.[251] In *Kelly*, as we have seen, he had imposed liability in negligence on a solicitor who had bought a licensed premises for the plaintiff, knowing that the plaintiff wanted to acquire what is normally called a publican's licence, without enquiring from the vendor's solicitors whether the licence was publican's or an hotel licence. In *Pierse v Allen*, the solicitor had acted in 1983 for clients who bought premises on the representation of the vendor that it was an hotel. It turned out that it had lost its status an hotel some time previously. The clients invoked *Kelly v Crowley* but Murphy J distinguished the earlier decision:

> "[T]he error of the solicitor in that case was a failure to establish the nature of the property or interest offered for sale. It was not a failure to establish the right or title of the vendor to that property. That is a consideration which in general must be postponed. For detailed investigation subsequent to the contract and prior to completion and on the footing that if, for any reason, the vendor is unable to make title to the property which he has contracted to sell, that at the very least the purchaser will recover the deposit paid and be discharged of any liability in respect of the balance of the purchase price."[252]

**[14.212]** In the instant case there was no doubt whatever about the nature of the property offered for sale. Insofar as it had enjoyed a particular value or status, it had clearly been represented to be an "hotel". Murphy J was accordingly of the view that the solicitor had not been guilty of negligence in relation to any specific pre-contract enquiry; expert evidence had been given to the effect that there was not at the time of trial, or more particularly in 1983 had not been, any general practice with regard to making pre-contract enquiries or requisitions. Of course the absence of any such general practice would not inevitably be fatal to the plaintiffs' claim.[253] Murphy J must have been of the view that there was no question that the practice should be stigmatised as one obviously lacking in due care.

**[14.213]** In *Fallon v Gannon*[254] the Supreme Court addressed a number of allegations of negligence against a solicitor and upheld the High Court's order withdrawing the plaintiff's case from the jury at the conclusion of his case. Briefly, the case arose out of an abortive

248. [1985] IR 212.

249. [1985] IR 212 at 228. Other cases dealing with the question of solicitors' duty of care include *Roche v Peilow* [1985] IR 232, in which the defendant was held to have been negligent in adhering to a universal practice of his profession in failing to execute a search against a building company (which had agreed to build a house for the plaintiffs, the defendant's clients) until after the completion of the building and the payment of some instalments of the purchase price. See also *Desmond v Brophy* [1985] IR 449 (HC).

250. Professional Neg LR 486 (HC, 1993).

251. [1985] IR 212.

252. Professional Neg LR 486 (HC, 1993).

253. *Cf Roche v Peilow*, [1985] IR 232 (SC) and paras **[14.04]-[14.07]** above.

254. [1988] ILRM 193 (SC).

sale by auction of the plaintiff's public house, in which (earlier proceedings had so held) the plaintiff had falsely warranted that the annual turnover was £60,000 to £65,000 whereas in fact it was considerably less.[255] The plaintiff had been ordered to return the purchaser's deposit and auction fees. He later sued his solicitor, arguing that the solicitor had been negligent in relation to this abortive sale. He appeared to believe that his solicitor either had been in collusion with the purchaser's solicitor or had sought to protect his professional colleague.

**[14.214]** The first ground of alleged negligence was that his solicitor had been negligent in sending a town agent to attend the auction in his stead. He argued that, if the solicitor had been present, he would have prevented the plaintiff from making a false representation or that he would have been subsequently available as a witness to deny the making of any representation by the plaintiff.

**[14.215]** The Supreme Court had no difficulty in rejecting this argument. There were "no conceivable grounds" whereby the solicitor could have anticipated the making of any representation by the plaintiff at the auction, nor were there any grounds for him to anticipate any issue or dispute about the making of any representation at the auction.

*(iii) Other premises*

**[14.216]** In *McMullen v Farrell*[256] the plaintiff sued three firms of solicitors for negligence. His action succeeded at trial against the second and third firms but failed against the first firm; the Supreme Court affirmed.

**[14.217]** The essence of the plaintiff's case was that, having leased a castle just outside the town of Tullamore in 1972 (and thus unable to benefit from the Landlord and Tenant Act 1931), he had not been fully informed by the second and third firms of the effect of the Landlord and Tenant (Amendment) Act 1980. He had been informed that it provided that a landlord's consent to an assignment of the premises could not be unreasonably withheld; but he had not been advised that a similar provision applied to change of user of the premises. This was of some importance as the plaintiff, who was required to use the premises as a private residence, realised that the prospects of selling his interest would be enhanced if the castle could be used as a hotel or put to some other commercial use.

**[14.218]** Barron J set out in some detail what he considered a solicitor's duty to be, in a manner that Finlay CJ, on appeal, considered to be entirely correct. It is worth recording what Barron J had to say, in view of its general application:

> "A solicitor cannot in my view fulfil his obligations to his client merely by carrying out what he is instructed to do. This is to ignore the essential element of any contract involving professional care or advice. The professional person is consulted by the client for the very reason that he has specialist or professional skill and knowledge. He cannot abrogate his duty to use that skill or knowledge. To follow instructions blindly is to turn himself into a machine. In my view a solicitor when consulted by a client has an obligation to consider not only what the client wishes him to do but also the legal implications of the facts which the client brings to his attention. If necessary, he must follow up these facts to ensure that he appreciates the real problem with which he is being asked to deal. When he is sure that he is

255. Griffin J's judgment deals in detail with this aspect of the case

256. [1993] 1 IR 123 (HC), affirmed in part by Supreme Court, 9 February 1994).

clear as to the way forward, then he advises his client accordingly. In most cases, perhaps, this will involve doing what his client wants. Where a client has been involved in a road traffic accident, he wants to know whether he can recover damages. It is sufficient for a solicitor, having been given the facts and being satisfied that it is an appropriate case to sue, to indicate to his client that he will issue proceedings. Even in such a case, where the cause of action is weak, for example, and the client is a person of means, he cannot just issue proceedings. His client is entitled to advice as to the wisdom of so proceeding.

In more complicating cases, the duties of the solicitor are also more complex. If his opinion corresponds with what he is asked to do, then there is no problem. When it does not, he must advise his client of his views and all reasonable approaches to the problem. The solicitor then acts on the basis of the instructions which he receives in the light of these advices. It is probably better that the solicitor's advice should be in writing, but that is a matter for him. In other words, as part of his duty to his client, a solicitor is obliged to exercise his professional skill and judgment in the interests of his client. The extent of this particular obligation is dependant on the nature of the case presented to him."[257]

**[14.219]** In *O'Connor v First National Building Society*,[258] a bus driver who had retired permanently on the ground of ill-health and was living on a social welfare pension was, with his wife, anxious to buy a somewhat larger house that the one in which they were at present living, which had been bought with a mortgage from the defendant building society. After consulting with the building society, he was informed of its approval of a loan of £15,000 provided the house to be purchased would be adequate security for that amount.

**[14.220]** The plaintiffs found a house that interested them. They looked over it and noted that it was in a very bad state of decorative repair though it seemed otherwise to be sound. They agreed to buy it for £21,5000 and paid the auctioneer a booking fee of £1,000. They then obtained a loan application from the building society, which they returned having filled in most of it. They completed the form on the society's premises with the assistance of the representative of the society. During their discussion with the representative they enquired whether or not they should obtain an independent inspection of the house. The representative indicated that such an inspection might cost £100 or £200 or even as much as £700 but that a vendor would never allow an inspection of such detail as to cost £700; he also pointed out that the society would be having it own valuation or survey or inspection of the premises and, if it showed up anything structurally serious or any rot of a serious nature, the society could not advance a loan on the security of that house. The plaintiffs paid the society £29.80 in respect of the cost to be incurred by the society in having the premises valued or surveyed or inspected. The loan application form which they completed specifically provided in clause 8 that '[n]o responsibility can be accepted by the society for the condition of the property.' This paragraph occurred immediately above the plaintiffs' signatures. Lynch J was satisfied that the plaintiffs were aware 'in a general way' of this clause.

**[14.221]** A few days later, the plaintiffs went to see a member of the staff of their solicitors. They brought him up to date as to how matters had progressed. While the

257. [1993] 1 IR 123.

258. [1991] ILRM 208.

solicitor was obtaining particulars for Mr O'Connor, Mrs O'Connor, by way of interjection, sought to enquire whether they should arrange for their own survey of the premises; the solicitor brushed this enquiry aside as he was concentrating on what Mr O'Connor had to say. The solicitor advised Mr O'Connor to jump on certain floors and to test walls to see if the plaster was sound. The solicitor was under the impression that Mr O'Connor was in the building trade; because of this, because Mr O'Connor had said the premises were in very poor condition and because the purchase price seemed relatively cheap, the solicitor did not think it necessary to advise that the plaintiffs should have any independent inspection or survey by a suitably qualified person. Equally he did not seek to dissuade them from doing so. Had he known of Mr O'Connor's actual qualifications he would have advised that an independent survey be obtained.

**[14.222]** The plaintiffs, having purchased the house, found that it contained a number of defects in the chimney and flues. They sued their building society and solicitors in negligence.

**[14.223]** Lynch J dismissed their claim against the building society. They had to be fixed with notice of the provisions and meaning of clause 8. The society's representative had told them nothing but the truth as regards the cost of independent inspections and of the implications of the society's inspection revealing serious structural faults. His remarks about the cost of independent inspections was 'undoubtedly off-putting' so far as the plaintiff's thought about obtaining an independent investigation. Insofar as the representative might have referred to the valuation which the society might obtain as a 'survey', Lynch J did not consider that the plaintiffs would have been in any way misled as to the nature of what was being obtained, having regard to the contrast between the price they had to pay for this valuation and the figures for an independent inspection mentioned by the representative:

> "It must have been clear to the plaintiff that whatever valuation or survey might be obtained by the [society] for the £29.80 fee could hardly be anything other than a walk around and visual inspection."[259]

**[14.224]** Lynch J imposed liability on the firm of solicitors. He accepted that there could be no absolute rule of law that a solicitor must always advise a purchaser that he ought o have an independent inspection of the property by a suitably qualified person, but, having regard to the evidence of Mr John Buckley from the Law Society Conveyancing Committee about established practice, he thought that:

> "such a duty *prima facie* arises and it is for a solicitor who contends that no such duty arose in any particular case to show circumstances such as [where the purchaser is an architect who has himself carefully examined the property] if he is to negative the existence of the duty."[260]

**[14.225]** Since Mr O'Connor was no more than a do-it-yourself enthusiast, rather than the person with experience in the building trade who the solicitor believed him to be, a duty

259. [1993] 1 ILRM 208. *Cf Ward v McMaster* [1988] IR 337, discussed at paras **[13.68]** *et seq* above, where the plaintiffs' reasonable inferences regarding the payment of a small fee for what they believed was a valuation were construed somewhat differently; but the facts of that decision were in many respects different from those in *O'Connor*.

260. [1991] ILRM 208.

arose to advise an independent inspection. Had it been carried out, it would have revealed the defects and the plaintiff would have withdrawn from the purchase.

*(iv) Conflict of interest*

**[14.226]** In *Phelan Holdings (Kilkenny) Ltd v Hogan*,[261] Barron J imposed liability in negligence on the defendant solicitor who allowed a conflict of interest to develop between himself and the plaintiff, his client. The plaintiff, a building contractor, sought to develop property by purchasing land and building houses on it. Part of the project involved buying a right of way over a strip of land from a company of which the defendant was beneficial owner. The defendant also acted for him as his solicitor. The development ran into local opposition, planning problems and financial difficulties, which resulted in the plaintiff having to abort his plans, at a financial loss.

**[14.227]** Barron J considered that, when the defendant agreed to grant to the plaintiff the right of way over the green strip, he should have advised him to be represented by a different solicitor:

> "It was not just a case of a solicitor acting for both parties; one of the parties was in reality the solicitor himself. Once this transaction had been completed there would have been no ban per se to his acting in relation to the purchase of the site or in relation to any other legal matter."[262]

**[14.228]** As the development strategy proceeded, the conflict of interest should have become apparent to the defendant. By the time that local residents were threatening proceedings, the defendant "had no alternative but to advise the plaintiff that he could no longer act for him. The likelihood of prejudice to the plaintiff if he continued to do so was all too clear."[263]

**[14.229]** Barron J noted that "[u]nfortunately the facts .... in the proceedings by [the residents] were such that the conflict was no technical breach of a technical rule."[264] The defendant was in a position where he was quite incapable of dealing objectively with the situation which presented itself. When he sought advice from senior counsel, he had professed to do so on behalf of the plaintiff. The problem was in reality his own, since his company would have been liable in damages to the plaintiff if he could not have used the right of way which had been agreed, through the defendant, to be granted to him. If senior counsel had known the defendant's real involvement, he would have pointed out the conflict and required separate representation for each defendant.

**[14.230]** It had been submitted on behalf of the defendant that the conflict of interest was potential only. Barron J could not accept that this was so. The defendant had been "in clear breach of the duty as a solicitor towards his client."[265] He had deprived him of the opportunity to obtain proper independent advice in relation to all his various problems.[266]

---

261. High Court, 15 October 1996 (Barron J).

262. High Court, 15 October 1996.

263. High Court, 15 October 1996.

264. High Court, 15 October 1996.

265. High Court, 15 October 1996.

266. For consideration of the issue of compensation of damages in the case, see Byrne & Binchy, *Annual Review of Irish Law 1996*.

**[14.231]** It is interesting to note by way of conclusion that the Irish courts when discussing liability for solicitors' negligence, appear to focus much more on the facts of the case, whereas in relation to medical negligence judicial discussion seems to take place at a much higher level of abstraction where principles and policy are more openly acknowledged. One might reasonably ask why this should be so.

Chapter 15

# Negligence on the Roads


I. Introduction .......... 419
II. The Duty of the Driver .......... 420
III. General Rules of Behaviour on the Highway .......... 424


## I. Introduction

**[15.01]** Road accidents[1] have given rise to a huge volume of litigation in this country. The cases are sometimes difficult to reconcile.[2] Not a great deal of law of general application can normally be learnt from these cases since, as Lavery J stated in *O'Connell v Shield Insurance Co Ltd*:

> "The circumstances to be considered where two moving parties come into collision are infinitely various. The time, the weather, the place, the possibility of view, the light - daylight or artificial - the vehicle or vehicles involved and many other matters will all affect the question of whether there has been a breach of duty."[3]

**[15.02]** On this account the Supreme Court "has frequently expressed its view ... that little or no help is to be derived from comparison of cases in relation to matters of fact".[4] As Maguire CJ noted in *Morrissey v Healy*:

> "Judges have frequently deprecated the citation of cases which are relied upon because the facts are said to be similar to those in the case which is being considered. It need hardly be stated that no case is binding on this Court save in so far as it lays down some principle of law."[5]

This should be borne in mind when considering the possible precedential force of the decisions that will be cited in this chapter.

---

1. See generally Duffy, *A Chapter of Accidents* (1942). *Bingham's Motor Claim Cases* (8th ed, 1980). Criminal and administrative aspects of the subject are comprehensively dealt with by Pierse, *Road Traffic Law* (2nd ed, 1995) and by O'Keeffe & Hill, *Dangerous Driving Cases* (1999).
2. *Cf O'Beirne v Hannigan* [1937] IR 237 at 244 (SC *per* FitzGibbon J):
   > "No cases with which this Court has had to deal have caused more difficulty, or given rise to a greater divergence of judicial opinion, than those which arise out of actions for negligence, and especially negligence upon the roads."
3. [1954] IR 286 at 290 (SC). Many of the cases turn on determinations of fact.
4. *Dillon v Ryan* Supreme Court, 7 April 1960, at p 3 (Maguire CJ). See also *McComiskey v McDermott* [1974] IR 75 at 89 (SC). See further STREET, pp 235-236, FLEMING, p 348.
5. [1960] IR 1 at 3 (SC). See also, to similar effect, *Colgan v Shannon* Supreme Court, 23 October 1958, at pp 5-6 (Lavery J); *O'Reilly v Evans* [1956] IR 269 at 272 (SC). Road Traffic Act 1993, s 67 requires users of public roads to take reasonable care for their own safety and that of other road-users and to take "all reasonable measures" to avoid injury or damage to property.

## II. The Duty of the Driver

**[15.03]** The Courts have frequently stressed the somewhat obvious fact that the duty of a driver varies according to the particular circumstances of the case. Thus, for example, greater care is required of a driver of a car in a dock area than on a public highway away from water.[6] Nor should one require of a rally driver the same duty of care to his or her navigator as to the other road users.[7] In *Coleman v O'Hara*,[8] FitzGerald J stated:

> "I do not accept that the concentration of attention required of a driver in a city street amidst other morning traffic, or on a suburban road with children on the footpath, or on emerging from a side-road on to a main road, is the same as that to be expected when driving on a clear straight road in the country without any warning that something may emerge from a concealed position and block the road."

### The Presence of Children

**[15.04]** Children present particular difficulties, not only for drivers and for those who have the duty to keep them under their care, but also for courts. Vigilance is particularly necessary "at a time of day when school children may be 'creeping like snails unwillingly to school'...".[9] The courts have made it plain that a driver is not obliged to avoid hitting a child, in every circumstance, and no liability will attach when the child's movement is wholly unexpected and reasonably unpredictable.[10] To impose such an obligation would:

> "make the movement of traffic impossible once it was shown that there were children on a footpath in front of the driver of a vehicle."[11]

**[15.05]** When juries were used in personal injury litigation, the trial judges preferred to adopt a broader, less closely-defined approach, giving general pointers to the jury but essentially relying upon their common sense and "road ethics" to determine the question. The proper charge to the jury, according to Budd J (speaking for the Court) in the Supreme Court decision of *McDonald v CIE*, would be on the following lines:

---

6. *Walsh v Galway Harbour Commissioners* Supreme Court, 18 December 1972.
7. *McComiskey v McDermott* [1974] IR 75 (SC), discussed at para **[6.60]-[6.63]** above.
8. Supreme Court, 16 March 1977 at p 1. See also *Coleman v Clarke* [1991] ILRM 841 (SC), analysed by Byrne & Binchy, *Annual Review of Irish Law 1991*, pp 404-406, where the majority of the Supreme Court, reversing MacKenzie J, acquitted a driver of negligence where he braked severely and sounded his horn when confronted by the plaintiff's vehicle which had drifted into his direct path but he had not veered onto the pavement to avoid the plaintiff's vehicle. In *Ward v Dawson* High Court, 26 July 1996 (Flood J), the plaintiff driver, who had responded to "a confusion of cars" ahead of him, where a collision had just occurred, was held not to have been guilty of contributory negligence in braking and slowing down to ten miles per hour. See also *Browne v Barry's Tea Ltd* [1996] Ir L Log W 142 (CC). In *Corcoran v Core Electrical* [1996] Ir L Log W 228 (CC), the defendant driver was acquitted of negligence in responding to a sudden change of the plaintiff's mind and of the consequent change of position of the car in front of him, by braking and sounding his horn. As to the situation where the emergency comes from within - from a heart attack or epileptic attack, for example, see paras **[7.13]-[7.22]** above.
9. *Byrne v CPI Ltd* High Court, 3 February 1993 (Budd J) at p 3 of judgment.
10. See, eg, *Lipschitz v Caulfields Ltd* Supreme Court, 20 December 1960; *Gallagher v Concarr* DPIJ: Hilary and Easter Terms 1993, p 139 (High Court, 4 May 1993 (Keane J)).
11. *McDonald v CIE* (1971) 105 ILTR 13 at 19 (SC).

"The jury should be told that the presence or expected presence of children on or near the travelling surface of a highway casts a heavy responsibility on the driver of a vehicle approaching such children. He must alert himself to their presence and be mindful that they may act in the heedless fashion that children do. He must then place himself in such a position and be in readiness to take all such precautions as he reasonably can to avoid causing injury to any one of them who acts in a heedless fashion. This will involve, inter alia, such matters as keeping a careful watch on the children, possibly giving warning of his presence, keeping a reasonable distance from them and having his vehicle under such control and travelling at such speed and otherwise acting in such fashion as will enable him to take all such steps as are reasonably possible to avoid their heedless movements and actions. The details of what is said must of course vary with the circumstances of the case. The time, place, presence of other traffic and other relevant matters must influence what is said. It is also necessary to avoid conveying the impression to the jury that it is the duty of a driver in the presence of young children to ensure their safety in all circumstances. What is required is that he should take all such steps as can reasonably be expected of him as a prudent man bearing in mind the heavy responsibility resting on him in the presence of young children. A direction on these lines having been given with such variations on the facts as the case calls for, it is then for the jury to decide whether, having regard to the heavy responsibility cast on him and the surrounding circumstances, the driver had taken all reasonable precautions."[12]

**[15.06]** This model charge is based largely on the judgments of Lavery J in *Duffy v Fahy*,[13] and *Donovan v Landys Ltd.*[14] Reference should also be made to *Hackett v Horan*,[15] which is discussed in *McDonald v CIE*.

**[15.07]** Budd J's judgment gives us an insight into how, in effect, the Court "passed the buck" to the jury, giving them little more than vague generalities to guide them, with little cutting edge. It would seem that the Courts were reluctant to define the duty of drivers in relation to children too specifically lest to do so would impose an unrealistic burden on road users, yet they were equally reluctant to call attention to their lenience in this regard. There is some evidence that the abolition of the jury in personal injury litigation has had the effect of encouraging trial judges to define the duty in somewhat fuller and franker terms.

### School Buses

**[15.08]** In *Mulcahy v Lynch and Butler*,[16] an eight-year-old boy who ran out from behind a school bus, from which he had alighted, into the path of an oncoming car which was

12. *McDonald v CIE* (1971) 105 ILTR 13 at 20. See also *Mye v Peters*, 68 SR (NSW) 298 (CA); *Griffiths v Doolan* [1959] Qd R 304 (SC); *Quinn v Hansberry* DPIJ: Trinity and Michaelmas Terms 1996, p 11 (High Court, 23 October 1996 (Smyth J)). In *Squizzoni v McEntaggart* DPIJ: Hilary and Easter Terms 1994, p 56 at p 64 (High Court, 11 May 1994), Budd J observed that:

   "when you drive a mechanically propelled vehicle, which is a lethal weapon, through a residential housing estate on a summer evening, you have to be on your guard for children coming at you from every angle. They are going to be chasing footballs on the pathways, they are likely to come out of the trees at you and you have to be on your guard."

13. [1960] Ir Jur 69.
14. [1963] IR 441.
15. Supreme Court, 14 May 1953.
16. Supreme Court, 25 March 1993. See also *Rogers v Britton*, English Court Appeal (Civ Div) 4 March 1996.

travelling at between five and ten miles per hour in second gear succeeded in an action for negligence against the driver of the car. In the High Court, Lynch J dismissed the claim, but the Supreme Court reversed.

**[15.09]** Blayney J (Finlay CJ and Egan J concurring) held that the driver's failure to sound the horn constituted negligence. Invoking Budd J's observations in *McDonald v CIE*,[17] Blayney J went on to say:

> "Where a driver is approaching a school bus which has stopped to let children out, one of the obvious things that must be anticipated is that one of the children will want to cross the road and may do so by running out suddenly from behind the bus. The approaching driver should be aware that the approach of his car is obscured from view by the presence of the bus so that the only way that he can give warning of his approach is by blowing the horn. In such circumstances it seems to me that the heavy responsibility referred to by Budd J can only be satisfied by not only driving slowly and keeping a careful look out but also by blowing the horn. This is a case in which giving warning of her presence by doing this was of major importance."[18]

**[15.10]** The plaintiff had also sued the driver of the school bus alleging that he had been negligent in not having insisted that children who intended to cross the road after leaving the bus should always wait until the bus had gone. He contended that the driver should have established a safety code containing such a prescription. The Supreme Court affirmed Lynch J's dismissal of this claim. The driver's duty, said Blayney J, was confined to transporting the children safely from the place where he picked them up to the place where he left them off:

> "His function was to drive the bus. So his primary duty was to drive the bus carefully with a view to ensuring that it was not involved in any accident. In addition, he had to keep order amongst the children while they were on the bus. And finally, in picking up the children, or letting them off, he had to choose a place where this could be done safely without exposing the children to any risk. These were of themselves duties requiring considerable attention and concentration, and it seems to me that it would be unreasonable to impose any additional duty on [the driver] once the children had left his bus and no more, I consider that he ceased to have any duty of care in regard to them."[19]

**[15.11]** The Supreme Court was surely right in the particular circumstances of the case not to impose liability on the driver but it is another proposition entirely to assert that all drivers of school buses should have no duty of care to the children under their charge once they have left the vehicle. It is easy to envisage some cases where a duty might indeed arise, as, for example, where a very young child had to be left off at a place that the driver knows is completely new to the child, and where the child will be obliged to cross a busy highway to reach his or her destination.

**[15.12]** In *Doherty v McKelvey*,[20] Johnson J had to consider a situation where the plaintiff, aged five, had been injured when, after alighting from a school bus, he had run across the road into the path of an oncoming car. He sued the owners of the school bus for negligence

17. (1971) 105 ILTR 13.
18. Supreme Court, 25 March 1993, at p 6.
19. Supreme Court, 25 March 1993, at pp 8-9.
20. DPIJ: Trinity and Michaelmas Terms 1994, p 91 (High Court, 1994 (Johnson J)).

on the basis that the bus contained no insignia to designate its character and had no flashing lights. Imposing liability, Johnson J expressed the view that:

> "anyone who gets the contract for driving a school bus has an enormous duty imposed on them to make absolutely clear that whoever passes it on the road or coming in contact with it will see quite clearly that it is a school bus ... I am not saying that it is necessary that a flashing red light should be put on top of a school bus but I certainly consider that, if the Minister for the Environment wished to avoid accidents like this, then it would be good to do ...
>
> Now, it is absolutely necessary that if you go around with a container containing children, as the school bus is, ... you alert all passers by in a manner which is absolutely unmistakable to the fact that you are releasing onto the public highway persons that may behave in an irrational and undisciplined fashion, irrespective of what age they are."[21]

**[15.13]** In *Connolly v Bus Éireann*,[22] the question of the duties surrounding the transport of school-children again fell for consideration. The plaintiff, a fourteen year-old girl, was seriously injured when crossing the road at 5 pm on a summer's evening, having just alighted from a bus. The bus was on a scheduled run from Ballyshannon to Sligo. Whereas primary school children in the area were transported by school buses dedicated to that function, with distinct identification as such, secondary school children were transported in the ordinary scheduled bus service. The bus which carried the plaintiff served two secondary schools in Bundoran; that afternoon it had collected about thirty pupils and twelve adult passengers.

**[15.14]** The driver of the vehicle which struck her was found to have been guilty of negligence; but a question arose as to whether the bus should have had attached to it some suitable sign or writing to indicate that it was in fact school transport and therefore was likely to contain a substantial number of children returning from school. Barr J rejected such a basis of liability, stating:

> "That might be a counsel of perfection but in my view it was not a duty in negligence which Bus Éireann owed to other road users. The distinction between the standard type of school bus and a bus operating on a scheduled service is that the former is concerned with conveying primary school children to and from schools. Such children, who may be as young as four years of age, have a potential for causing traffic hazards on leaving the bus. There is no doubt that such vehicles should be clearly identified. A scheduled service bus which incidentally carries secondary school children at certain times of day is in a quite different situation. First, the children are substantially older, being from twelve to eighteen years of age, and their presence on the bus is for a comparatively short part of the total bus journey, ie in the ordinary course, in circumstances such as those under review, all of the children will have dismounted long before the bus reaches its destination. In short, for the greater part of its route the bus leads a normal existence and cannot be regarded as a partial school bus. I am not satisfied that Bus Éreann had any obligation to warn other road users that for part of its scheduled journey it carried a large number of secondary school children."[23]

---

21. At p 92.
22. High Court, 29 January 1996 (Barr J).
23. High Court, 29 January 1996, at p 12 of judgment.

**[15.15]** From the decisions it is clear that carriers transporting primary school children have an obligation to clearly mark the bus, but probably not in the case of secondary school children at least where the bus is a non-dedicated bus.

## III. General Rules of Behaviour on the Highway

**[15.16]** In relation to behaviour on the highway, certain general rules for drivers have been established through the years. Most of these rules involve the application of no more than obvious common sense and thus scarcely rise above the commonplace. Bearing this in mind, it may not be inappropriate to advert briefly to some of these rules.

### Failure to Keep a Proper Look Out

**[15.17]** The failure of either a driver or a pedestrian to keep a proper look out[24] may be negligence (or contributory negligence as the case may be). This issue is usually one for the fact-finder to resolve. As Walsh J stated in the Supreme Court decision of *Nolan v Jennings*:[25]

> "It cannot be held as a matter of law that a person must be found guilty of negligence if he fails to observe the whole of an area which it is possible to observe. The test is whether the area he did in fact observe was in the circumstances reasonably sufficient and consistent with his obligation to himself to anticipate the emergence of traffic from [another] street."

**[15.18]** A road user may not proceed on the assumption that other road users will not act negligently without at the same time keeping a reasonable look-out to see if they are so acting.[26] As Kingsmill Moore J observed in *O'Connell v Shield Insurance Co Ltd*:[27]

> "When coming to a blind corner I may be entitled initially to assume that a person driving in the opposite direction will not be driving on his wrong side of the road, but I must keep a good look-out so that if he appears on the wrong side of the road I can do my part in avoiding an accident."[28]

---

24. *Stapleton v O'Regan*, Supreme Court, 21 December 1956; *Quigley v Donnelly*, Supreme Court, 20 December 1956; *Woods v Keogh*, Supreme Court, 21 December 1956; *Morrisson v Leonard*, Supreme Court, 18 April 1958; *Colgan v Shannon*, Supreme Court, 23 October 1958; *Farrell v Prendergast* Supreme Court, 22 May 1958; *Lynskey v Minister for Finance* Supreme Court, 8 July 1963; *Fowler v O'Mahoney* Supreme Court, 6 February 1973; *Kelly v Jameson* Supreme Court, 1 March 1972; *Tynan v Earls* Supreme Court, 28 March 1969; *Candy v Minch Norton & Co Ltd* [1953] IR 192 (SC); *Green v Pickering* [1952] IR 274 (SC); *O'Connell v Shield Insurance Co, Ltd* [1954] IR 286 (SC), *Byrne v Sheedy* [1955] IR 1 (SC, 1954); *Murphy v Cronin* [1966] IR 699 (SC, 1964); *Butterly v Mayor of Drogheda* [1907] 2 IR 134 (KB Div 1906); *Braund v Henning*, 62 ALJR 433 (H Austr, 1988), *Walsh v Cullen* [1997] Ir L Log W 37 (CC); *Sherwood v Ross/Check Stock Systems Ltd* [1997] Ir L Log W 14 (CCJ) - "a classic centre-of-the-road collision".
25. Supreme Court, 31 January 1964, p 3.
26. *O'Connell v Shield Insurance Co Ltd* [1954] IR 286 at 294 (SC, 1964).
27. [1954] IR 286.
28. See also: *O'Brien v Armstrong* Supreme Court, 19 March 1997 (ex temp) – a driver of cattle truck rounding a corner on a narrow country road was not negligent in failing to anticipate that another vehicle would attempt to pass him out; *O'Shea v Tilman Anhold and Horse Holiday Farm Ltd* Supreme Court, 23 October 1996 – a driver at night was not guilty of contributory negligence when, out of the blue, a horse, "resembl[ing] Pegasus", leapt from a field and crashed into the roof of the car;

**[15.19]** In *McEleney v McCarron*,[29] the plaintiff, when returning home from a disco by bus in a comatose state of drunkenness, was helped off the bus and propped against a wall. Two young women who knew him tried to get him home but he kept falling, eventually lying with his feet on the path and his torso and head on the road. The women pulled him further in from the road but had not completed this operation when the defendant's car approached. One of the young women signalled to the defendant, who interpreted this as an attempt to thumb a lift, which he was not willing to provide. He then caught a half glimpse of what looked like a shadow adjacent to the young women. This was the plaintiff; the defendant's car came in contact with his head almost immediately and injured him severely.

**[15.20]** Carney J imposed liability in negligence. He stated:

> "The case comes down to whether the ... defendant kept a proper look-out. On the defendant's own evidence he did not, for presumably by reason of concentration on the girls he never saw the plaintiff's torso and head on the road until after he had run over it. Accordingly I find the ... defendant guilty of negligence ..."[30]

**[15.21]** The Supreme Court reversed this finding. Finlay CJ (Hederman and O'Flaherty JJ concurring) stated:

> "It seems to me that the manner in which the conclusion of the learned trial judge is stated would appear to assume that the mere fact that the defendant failed to see, in the very short space which was available and in the short space of time which was available, the torso of the plaintiff lying on the road, of itself, must establish a negligent failure to keep a proper look out.
>
> I do not think that this is so, and I am satisfied that it would be placing upon the defendant an absolute duty and not what is required by law, namely a duty to take reasonable care."[31]

**[15.22]** The Chief Justice considered that the defendant's "major obligation" was to keep an eye on the two women whom he understood to be trying to thumb a lift. The road was 19 feet wide; the defendant's car was over 5 feet wide. There was probably only about 2 feet between the side of the car and the footpath. The defendant owed a duty by keeping them under his observation, to ensure that neither of the young women stepped forward to further their apparent intention of trying to get a lift. The defendant's concentration on them "was the proper reasonable care which he should have exercised on that occasion". Once the trial judge concluded that this was the explanation for the defendant's failure to see the part of the plaintiff's body on the road, "it would be a wholly artificial standard of care to hold him guilty of negligence ..."[32]

---

28. (contd) *Basmajian v Haire* High Court, 2 April 1993 (Barr J) - one driver was negligent in attempting to pass car as she approached the apex of a hill; the other driver was negligent in driving so fast as to be prevented from reacting adequately to the plaintiff's vehicle; *Matthews v Matthews* [1996] Ir L Log W 168 (CC) - driver should have moderated speed to take account of possibility of cattle on the road; *Bradshaw v Grimes* [1997] Ir L Log W 332 (CC) - plaintiff driver was guilty of 20% contributory negligence in failing to keep a proper look out when coming on "a puff of smoke in the middle of the road" resulting from an earlier collision.
29. [1993] 1 IR 132 (SC revg HC).
30. [1993] 1 IR 132 at 135.
31. [1993] 1 IR 132 at 136.
32. [1993] 1 IR 132 at 136.

## Negligence Per Se - and Driving When Blinded

**[15.23]** Formerly it was considered that it was negligence *per se* to drive so as to be unable to stop within the limits of one's vision. In *O'Beirne v Hannigan*,[33] where the plaintiff had been dazzled by the defendant's lights, so that he could see only "a black shadow" in front of him, he was held to have been guilty of contributory negligence as a matter of law in continuing to drive at a speed of 15 to 20 mph, Fitzgibbon J stated:

> "In my opinion, it was a negligent act, per se, in the words of the Chief Baron,[34] on the part of the plaintiff to plunge at 15 to 20 miles an hour into a 'black shadow', which, for all he knew, might enshroud a car or a foot passenger whose presence his own headlights, which are designed to illuminate the road before him, would not enable him to detect. Surely it would be a negligent act for a driver to proceed at 15 to 20 miles per hour along a road with his eyes shut. Is it any less negligent to do so with eyes blinded, as the plaintiff says his were, by the lights of a stationary car, and deprived of the assistance of his own headlights?"

**[15.24]** This approach no longer commands support. The question has been reduced to one depending on all the circumstances of the case rather than involving an absolute rule of law.[35]

**[15.25]** As Kingsmill Moore J stated in *O'Reilly v Evans*:

> "There may be circumstances of an embarrassing nature, or such as are not reasonably to be anticipated, which are sufficient to account for a collision without necessarily involving negligence on the part of the [driver]. I may instance deceptive lighting, a sudden drift of fog, interference or confusion caused by other road users, the small size and partial concealment of the obstacle, and so on."[36]

---

33. [1937] IR 237 at 246 (SC). See also *Baker v Longhurst & Sons Ltd* [1933] 2 KB 461 at 468 (*per* Scrutton LJ); *Tart v Chitty & Co* [1933] 2 KB 453; *cf Kelliher v Tipperary (North Riding) Board of Health and Public Assistance* [1938] IR 43 (SC).

34. *Coyle v GN Ry* (1887) 20 LR Ir 409 at 418.

35. *Kelliher v Tipperary County Council* [1938] IR 43 (SC); *Hayes v Finnegan* [1952] IR 98 (SC); *O'Reilly v Evans* [1956] IR 269 (SC); *Carroll v Clare County Council* [1975] IR 221 (SC); *Tidy v Battman* [1934] 1 KB 319; *Morris v Luton Corporation* [1946] 1 KB 114; *SS Heranger (Owners) v SS Diamond (Owners)* [1939] AC 94. *Cf Jacob v O'Hara* [1956] IR 89 (SC). In *Carroll v Clare County Council* [1975] IR 221 (SC) at 228-229, the Supreme Court rejected the argument that a person placing an unlighted danger on the highway must, as a principle of law, be regarded as more blameworthy than the person who collides into it.

36. [1956] IR 269 at 273-274 (SC). The position was well put by Wheeler J, in *Emerson v Bailey* 156 A 2d 762 at 764 (NH SC, 1959):

> "We are not of the view ... that without prior warning or reason to anticipate dangers ahead due care requires that every driver must bring his motor vehicle to a stop upon the approach of headlights to await the diminution of the blind spot which every driver knows occurs when approaching a vehicle coming in the opposite direction in the night time. If such was the required standard of care under normal circumstances, the flow of traffic would be intermittently interrupted creating a chaotic traffic situation which would undoubtedly cause more accidents than it prevented"

Similarly, in *Moorhouse v City of Everett* (1926) 252 P 157 at 160 (Wash Sup Court), Bridges J said that to impose an obligation to stop when blinded by a sudden fog "must do infinitely more harm than good". See, however, *MacCharles v Trask* (1984) 62 NSR (2d) 259 at 261 (SC, Tr Div). Where the fog is not sudden, a duty to stop may arise: *Maritime Processing Co Ltd v Hogg* (1978) 32 NSR 2d 451 at 506-507 (Tr Div).

**[15.26]** Of course, the truth of the matter is that the courts decline to impose an absolute obligation to avoid driving when dazzled or otherwise blinded, not because these occasions are so rare and unpredictable as to be unforeseeable but because the price of total safety is considered too expensive. Our society distinguishes between a person driving with his eyes shut and one driving when blinded by external conditions. Accidents at night could presumably be reduced by a maximum speed limit of thirty miles per hour, but the social and economic cost is considered to outweigh the benefit.

## Pedestrians

**[15.27]** The Courts have striven to balance the interests of pedestrians with those of other road users. They start from the principle that it "is not of course necessarily negligent for a pedestrian to walk out on the highway when a vehicle is approaching".[37] Nor is a person required to use a pedestrian crossing, if one is available.[38] Moreover, a pedestrian "has a right to expect some co-operation from other traffic.[39] Whether a pedestrian used due care is "pre-eminently a question for the jury",[40] or, since the abolition of juries in personal injury litigation in 1988, trial judge. But this does not mean that there can never be coercive evidence that the pedestrian is guilty of negligence or contributory negligence, as the case may be. As Kennedy CJ stated in *Murphy v Riordan*:

> "Having regard to modern conditions and modern life, it may be said that people cannot step off a footpath on to a busy road without looking around without being guilty of negligence."[41]

**[15.28]** In *O'Connell v Shield Insurance Co Ltd*, Maguire CJ observed:

> "A pedestrian who looks in the direction from which traffic is to be expected[42] and sees none may proceed without again looking if at the time he last looked before crossing there was no reasonable possibility that a vehicle driven at a normal pace would reach him on his way across."[43]

**[15.29]** But in *Rice v Class*,[44] the same judge sought to "amplify"[45] this statement by making it clear that when the pedestrian gets to the middle line of the highway "he must realise that there is a change in direction of the traffic from which the risk may come".[46]

---

37. *Malone v CIE* Supreme Court, 24 June 1953 (Lavery J) at p 9.
38. *Cf Kelly v Jameson* Supreme Court, 1 March 1972 (Fitzgerald J) at p 2 - dissenting, but dissent not affecting this point.
39. *Scanlon v Abbey Service Garage (Galway) Ltd* [1965] IR 700 at 705 (SC).
40. *O'Connelly v Shield Insurance Co Ltd* [1954] IR 286 at 288 (SC). See also *McKinney v Yelavich* (1958) 352 Mich 687, 90 NW2d 883 (SC).
41. (1926) 60 ILTR 113 at 114 (SC).
42. According to Kingsmill Moore J in *Moore v Nolan* 94 ILTR 153 at 161 (SC, 1956), the pedestrian may expect an elephant but not a helicopter making a forced descent onto the highway! With the decline in circuses and increase in the use of helicopters perhaps the contemporary expectations should be reversed.
43. [1954] IR 286 at 288.
44. Supreme Court, 1954.
45. At p 1.
46. At p 2.

**[15.30]** A driver is under the obligation to take reasonable care not to strike a pedestrian. Naturally this duty is affected by the circumstances. A person driving down a remote country road need not normally anticipate that a pedestrian will run out into his or her path but a person driving past a primary school will have to take particular care that a young child will not do so.

**[15.31]** In *Moore v Fullerton*,[47] the Supreme Court, by a majority,[48] upheld Costello J's finding that the defendant, who was driving his large, laden lorry through a village at about 12 to 14 miles per hour had not been guilty in striking the plaintiff, a nine year-old boy, who had run out into his path from behind a lorry, which was straightening itself having crossed the road. Finlay CJ was satisfied that to hold the driver liable in these circumstances would be to impose on him an artificially high and unreasonable standard of care.

**[15.32]** It is clearly negligent to walk onto the road from behind a stationary vehicle without looking to see what traffic may be passing.[49] Similarly, a pedestrian is guilty of contributory negligence if he walks across a busy city street and fails to see an approaching car until it is upon him.[50] Moreover, standing on the road - even a country road - in the evening may amount to negligence or contributory negligence.[51] In *M'Kenna v Stephens and Alexander E Hull & Co*,[52] in 1923, Ronan LJ said:

> "On an infrequented country road a person may without much danger walk along the road, but in a street where there is traffic the person who takes to the roadway incurs a definite intelligible risk which he does not incur on the footpath. The use of the roadway of a street in a crowded place is really to cross from one side to the other. In a crowded thoroughfare like Grafton Street or Cheapside to walk up or down the roadway would be evidence of negligence for you to run the chance of a vehicle overtaking you. That is not so in crossing the street, for you can see both sides as you cross over."

**[15.33]** The Courts are, however, reluctant to stigmatise pedestrians' carelessness as contributory negligence as a matter of law. Thus, in *Connolly v Murphy*,[53] the Supreme

47. [1991] ILRM 29 (SC 1990, affg HC (Costello J)). For analysis, see Byrne & Binchy, *Annual Review of Irish Law 1990*, pp 526-528.

48. Finlay CJ and Hederman J, O'Flaherty J dissenting.

49. *Cf Hayden v M'Quillan* [1930] IR 87 (SC 1929). See also *Murphy v Riordan* (1926) 60 ILTR 113 (SC); *Maxwell v McNally* [1997] Ir L Log W 13 (CC); *Duffy v Brodigan* (1998) 17 ILT (ns) 28 (CC).

50. *Green v Pickering* [1952] IR 274 (SC). See also *Crosbie v Boland National Car Ltd t/a Euro Dollar Rent-A-Car* High Court, 7 July 1995 Morris J - a plaintiff pedestrian who was crossing a dual carriageway slip road near Dublin Airport at noon when a car was approaching fast was held guilty of 50% contributory negligence.

51. *Morrisroe v Leonard* Supreme Court, 18 April 1958. See also *Neenan v Hosford* [1920] IR 258 (CA).

52. [1923] 2 IR 112 at 127 (CA(IFS)). *Cf* [1923] 2 IR 112 at 134 (*per* O'Connor LJ). In view of the fact that Grafton Street has been pedestrianised, perhaps Nassau Street would be a more useful contemporary example.

53. Supreme Court, 11 October 1971, especially *per* Walsh J at p 5. See also *Guerin v O'Driscoll* Supreme Court, 7 February 1966; *O'Connell v Shield Insurance Co Ltd* [1954] IR 286; *Scanlon v Abbey Service Garage (Galway) Ltd* [1965] IR 700 (SC).

Court held that it was a matter for the jury to decide whether the plaintiff had been guilty of contributory negligence where he had been walking on the line between the road and hard shoulder in the same direction as the car that struck him, on a wet and windy night.

**[15.34]** When it comes to apportioning responsibility between a pedestrian and the driver of a motor vehicle which injured the pedestrian, there may be an understandable tendency to be unduly lenient to the pedestrian. This tendency offends against legal principle. In *Harrison v Ennis*,[54] Walsh J said:

> "While I would agree ... that the position in the case of a collision between a motor car and a pedestrian is not the same as for two motor vehicles, it does not follow that in every collision between a pedestrian and a motor vehicle, in which both parties are negligent, a greater degree of fault must always be apportioned to the driver of the motor car. All the circumstances attendant upon the accident must be taken into account including [such questions as whether] the accident occurred at night and in circumstances in which the [pedestrian] had a better opportunity of seeing the [driver] than the [driver] had of seeing the [pedestrian]."

**[15.35]** In *Shields v Boyle*,[55] O'Hanlon J addressed the question of the contributory negligence of a pedestrian injured when crossing a street in a country town after dark. There was two hundred yards clear visibility up the street and the lighting in the area was good. The road was about thirty two feet wide. The plaintiff, emerging from between parked cars, had formed the view that the vehicle that struck her was sufficiently far away to make it safe for her to cross in its path. O'Hanlon J held that the driver of that vehicle had been negligent in driving at an unsafe speed and in failing to keep a careful look out. He held that the plaintiff was guilty of contributory negligence in clearly having failed to ensure that it was safe for her to cross and in having failed to keep the car in view as she crossed the road. O'Hanlon J reduced the plaintiff's damages by 33$^{1}/_{3}$% when apportioning fault between the parties. If it had been a simple matter of apportioning causation, he would have tended towards a division in equal shares but, since fault was the test, at a 33$^{1}/_{3}$% reduction was more correct on the basis that the negligent driving of the defendant's car was a source of real danger to all other users of the road in that vicinity, whereas the plaintiff's negligence was merely a careless failure to take care for her own safety.

**[15.36]** Normally, of course, the pedestrian will be the plaintiff in legal proceedings, the only issue regarding his conduct being whether it amounted to contributory negligence.[56] It is, however, clear that pedestrians owe a duty of care to other road users, and if they fail to

54. [1967] IR 286 at 294 (SC).
55. High Court, 6 November 1991.
56. In *Harding v Barrett*, DPIJ: Trinity and Michaelmas Terms 1993, p 246 (High Court, 7 October 1993), Geoghegan J rejected the argument of counsel for the plaintiff that the defendant driver's negligence had been so gross that he should not even consider the issue of the plaintiff pedestrian's contributory negligence. Such an argument "might have some validity if the defendant had driven out of the hospital at 100 miles an hour, blind drunk ...". Nothing like that arose in the case, where Geoghegan J reduced the plaintiff's damages by 20% for failing to keep a proper look out as she crossed in front of the exit lanes from the hospital.

discharge this duty they may be liable for injury or damage that results.[57] Unlike motorists, pedestrians are not obliged to insure themselves against such liability: this has meant that many pedestrians will not be good financial marks, at all events in the case of serious injury. Nevertheless, it is interesting to note how few reported cases there have been throughout the common law world involving defendant pedestrians. It seems not to have occurred to some motorists (or their legal advisers) to take proceedings in many of these cases.

## Cyclists

**[15.37]** The courts have naturally been called on to prescribe a *via media* for cyclists and car drivers on the highway. In *Buckley v Maloney*,[58] the Supreme Court affirmed Johnson J's finding of negligence against the defendant driver where he had collided with the plaintiff cyclist who had come onto the road from the hard shoulder to avoid some potholes. O'Flaherty J stated:

> "The law on this matter I would lay down as follows: that when vehicles are travelling in the same direction and when one is a lorry travelling at some speed, at about 30 miles an hour ... and there is a cyclist on the hard shoulder, and then it is clear that the cyclist must move out from the hard shoulder to the main carraigeway - it was his entitlement to be on the main highway in the first instance - then a duty devolves on the lorry driver to give him a goodly clearance. [The defendant driver] felt that he had done this but I am clear in my mind that he did not do so. Further, he could have checked further in advance that there was not traffic behind; in addition, he could have slowed down sufficiently to give a cyclist a chance to come outside the potholes and could indeed, have stayed behind him for some distance. It is clear that he had many options open to him in the circumstances because there was no traffic behind, nor was there any traffic approaching. None of these options were effectively exercised, I am satisfied."[59]

## Road junctions

**[15.38]** Accidents at road junctions have given rise to much litigation, if only because of the conflict of evidence that frequently arises in such cases.

**[15.39]** An intersection of roads of equal status "impose[s] a very high degree of caution on the users of both roads".[60] In the Supreme Court decision of *O'Shaughnessy v Independent Newspapers Ltd*,[61] Maguire CJ stated:

> "Somervell LJ, in *France v Parkinson*[62] puts the position very neatly when he says that in case of a collision at a cross-roads where both roads are equally important in the absence of

57. *Cf Barry v MacDonald* (1966) 110 Sol J 56; *Green v Hills* The Times, 22 April 1969.

58. Supreme Court, 2 July 1996 (ex temp).

59. See also *Van Keep v Surface Dressing Contractors Ltd* High Court, 11 June 1993 (Budd J); *Skinner v Hartnett and Cork Corporation* High Court, 3 February 1995 (O'Hanlon J); *Quinn v Kennedy Brothers Construction Ltd* High Court, 4 March, 1994 (Barron J). The position relating to cyclists coming from side roads onto main roads is considered, para **[15.43]-[15.44]** below.

60. *Quigley v Donnelly* Supreme Court, 20 December 1956 (Kingsmill Moore J), p 4 of judgment.

61. Supreme Court, 21 April 1955, p 3.

62. [1954] 1 All ER 739 at 740. *Cf* Goodhart (1954) 70 LQR 302 at 302: "This may be described as an almost double *res ipsa loquitur* case."

special circumstances the balance of probability is in favour of both drivers having been negligent. He prefaces this by saying that each case turns on its own facts."

**[15.40]** In *Somers v Reilly*,[63] it was held that a driver "might reasonably anticipate that [another] driver would comply with the requirement of the rule[64] to yield the road to the vehicle approaching from the right",[65] and that accordingly the other driver, who did not yield, was "the main and effective cause"[66] of the collision. The Courts have, however, shown a sense of considerable realism in handling this rule. In *Byrne v Sheedy*,[67] the former Supreme Court rejected the argument that the person approaching from the right may, without qualification, assume that no precautions are necessary against a breach of the law by a driver on the other road. Kingsmill Moore J said:

> "To make those bye-laws operate reasonably they must be read with some qualifications. If a person is bound always to give way to all traffic coming from the right, irrespective of its distance or its visibility, he could never get across a junction. It is not necessary to define the exact scope of the bye-law, but it seems to me that it is intended to regulate the actions of two drivers who have come into view of each other at such speeds and at such a distance that if one did not yield to the other there would be a danger of a collision."

**[15.41]** Every driver must approach a junction with such reasonable caution as the circumstances require and should have his car in such control that he is able to yield the right of way to a car which approaches the junction from his right and is being driven in such a manner as may reasonably be expected. But if the car coming from his right emerges suddenly at an excessive speed, or is otherwise driven in a negligent manner, he cannot be required to do more than to take all reasonable and proper steps to avoid a contingency which he is not bound to anticipate.

**[15.42]** Similarly the bye-law which requires a driver to yield the right of way to a vehicle actually crossing cannot become mandatory till the vehicle is in sight, though again it imposes a duty of caution on all drivers so to approach a junction as to be able to give way to a vehicle emerging in a manner or [at a] speed reasonably to be expected.

> "Even if the [driver coming from the right] were entitled to drive on the assumption that other drivers would obey the letter of the law and would not be guilty of negligence (a proposition which requires some qualification ...),[68] yet he is under an obligation to keep a good look-out to see if other drivers are so acting and, if they are not so doing, to take all proper steps to avoid the consequences of their breach or negligence."[69]

---

63. [1946] Ir Jur 44 (HC).
64. General Bye-Laws for the Control of Traffic 1937 (SR & O No 222 of 1937). See now the Road Traffic General Bye-Laws 1964 (SI 294/1964, as amended by SI 281/1975 and SI 275/1983). See further Pierse, *Road Traffic Law* (2nd ed, 1995), para 7.4.5, especially at p 455.
65. *Somers v Reilly* [1946] Ir Jur 44 at 45.
66. The case was decided before the apportionment legislation but it may be presumed that the same approach would be followed today. See also *Eaton v Dineen* Supreme Court, 26 July 1971.
67. [1955] IR 1 (SC). See also *Blay v Daly* [1997] Ir L Log W 99 (CC).
68. Citing *London Passenger Transport Board v Upson* [1949] AC 155 at 173, 175, 176 and 181.
69. [1955] IR at 8-9. See also *Macintyre v Coles* [1966] 1 All ER 723n (CA). See also *Creed v Cunningham*, [1996] Ir L Log W 404 (CC) – it is not responsible to expect a driver to weave in and out on the roadway approaching a T-junction on the right where cars were parked on the left side of road; *Burke v McDonald* (1989) 17 ILT (ns) 64 (CC).

**[15.43]** The courts are, moreover, reluctant to give the impression that the driver on a major road is free to ignore a possible source of danger from a person emerging from a minor road. In the Supreme Court decision of *Murphy v Cronin*,[70] Kingsmill Moore J (speaking for the majority) stated that a driver on a main road:

> "was entitled to make the *prima facie* assumption that a cyclist would not come out of a side road and cross his path when he was so near that there was an imminent risk of a collision. His primary duty was to watch the road straight ahead of him. But he was not absolved from paying a measure of attention to the side road in the event of a careless cyclist emerging and continuing his course and, despite the bad and misleading street lighting, he should have been able to pick up the light of the bicycle lamp coming in from his right. He cannot in my view be absolved from some fault and some responsibility for the collision."

**[15.44]** Cyclists coming from a minor road onto a major road will be guilty of contributory negligence if they fail to ensure that they do not cycle into the path of an oncoming vehicle.[71]

**[15.45]** In *Grace v Fitzsimon and O'Halloran*,[72] the Supreme Court affirmed a finding by Barr J that the first defendant was 40% to blame and the second defendant 60% to blame for an accident causing injury to the plaintiff. The first defendant, wishing to turn left into a street in the direction that the plaintiff was approaching, nudged out into a yellow "box" on the street and stopped there for perhaps a minute, waiting for a clearance. The second defendant came "at some speed" in the opposite direction. He collided with the plaintiff. He argued later that he had been forced onto the wrong side of the road because of the obstruction created by the first defendant.

**[15.46]** The first defendant unsuccessfully sought to convince the Supreme Court that, although he should not have needlessly been in the yellow hatched area, nevertheless, since he had been there for so long, the second defendant ought to have seen him, so that the first defendant's wrong should not be regarded as having contributed to the accident at all. In essence this was an invocation of the doctrine of *novus actus interveniens* or at least an attempt to apply the doctrine of the "last clear opportunity", abolished by s 56 of the Civil Liability Act 1961.[73] O'Flaherty J observed that the first defendant:

> "was in a place where he should not legally have been. There is no doubt that if [the second defendant] was going somewhat slower he would have been able to stop and not have had to swerve onto the wrong side of the road. But that is where [the second defendant] was at fault."

---

70. [1966] IR 699 at 707 (SC).

71. *Hanley v Morrissey* Supreme Court, 20 December 1974 – the plaintiff cyclist was held guilty of contributory negligence of more than 50%; a retrial was ordered. See also *Coleman v O'Hara* Supreme Court, 16 March 1977 (FitzGerald J) at p 1; *Murphy v Cronin* [1966] IR 699 (SC); *Fagan v Cochrane* DPIJ: Trinity and Michaelmas Terms 1993, p 112 (High Court, 13 December 1993, Flood J), *Brennan v O'Meara* DPIJ: Trinity and Michaelmas Terms 1996, p 45 (High Court, 1 July 1996, Moriarty J); *Conlon v Kenney* [1996] Ir L Log W 177 (CC) – a cyclist weaving through stationary traffic in the middle of the road junction was held to be 60% contributorily negligent.

72. Supreme Court, 14 June 1996 (ex temp).

73. See para **[2.26]** above.

## Junctions Controlled by Traffic Lights

**[15.47]** Where a junction is controlled by traffic lights, clearly it will normally be negligent for a driver to defy a red light, or to attempt to cross the junction when the light has gone green without keeping a look-out, especially for stragglers.[74] Even where the light is already at green before the driver comes near it, this does not relieve him or her of the duty to keep a proper look-out, though the care expected will naturally be less than at an uncontrolled crossing.[75] Budd J provided a good statement of the law, in *Doyle v HF Murray Ltd*,[76] in 1967:

> "I would venture to make these observations on the duty of a motorist to take care, especially as regards look-out, when entering a crossing when the green light is in his favour. The duty to keep a look-out is not so heavy as at an uncontrolled crossing. The driver does not have to take such a comprehensive and extended look to his right and to his left as he should at an uncontrolled crossing, because he is entitled to have regard to the fact that traffic on either side of him is restricted from crossing. But there is still a duty on such a driver to keep a reasonable look-out commensurate with the circumstances existing at the time. Such a driver is obviously not entitled, for example, to start forward immediately to come across his intended course. It would seem to me that likewise he ought not to proceed without regard to similar traffic which he would be bound to observe if he took the precaution of looking in the direction in which he intended to proceed and the immediate vicinity thereof, in which vicinity there might be traffic just about to cross his path. Such traffic might be in that position perfectly legitimately at the moment the light changes to green for one reason or another, such as its being impeded in its progress. Even if it is not there legitimately the motorist is not entitled to proceed to the danger of other persons or vehicles that he ought to have seen had [h]e observed the restricted look-out which I have envisaged as reasonably called for on proceeding when the lights turn green in a motorist's favour. This comes to no more than saying that the reasonable degree of care demanded in law of a motorist entering a junction with the traffic lights in his favour requires him to keep a look-out for, and to exercise due care with regard to, traffic or persons in the positions I have mentioned.
>
> To this should be added that what is a reasonable look-out, how far it should extend, and the degree of care required will, of course, vary with the nature of the crossing and the prevailing circumstances. For example, greater care and a wider extension of the area to be looked at will be called for in a crowded city area at a busy time of the day for traffic than on a wide open suburban crossing carrying little traffic. The variety of circumstances that may arise are infinite. No hard and fast rules can be stated, only a general guidance can be given and what I have said should be read as being no more than what one is called upon to state for the purposes of this case."

---

74. *Cf Radburn v Kemp* [1971] 3 All ER 249 at 252 (CA):

> "[T]he driver had no business, despite the light being in his favour, to enter the junction at all unless he was satisfied that it was safe for him to do so, and, once he had entered it, no right to proceed further across the junction without taking the utmost care to save harmless people who rightly were already on the junction before he entered it."

75. In *Murphy v Bus Éireann* DPIJ: Trinity and Michaelmas Terms 1994, p 163 at 169 (HC), Murphy J observed that, to require a driver to blow the horn after receiving the green light in his favour when travelling on a temporary single lane as a result of roadworks, would set "an excessive degree of care, paranoia care".

76. [1967] IR 390 at 403-404 (SC). See also *Skinner v Hartnett and Cork Corporation* High Court, 3 February 1995 (O'Hanlon J).

**[15.48]** On occasions, traffic lights cease to operate at all, or operate improperly.[77] This fact will not necessarily exempt the road user from liability: indeed, in certain instances it may impose a higher degree of caution. If the road user has no reason to apprehend that the lights are out of order, then he or she will be judged by the standard applicable to road users where the lights are working.[78] There is no reported Irish case dealing with the position where the road user ought to be aware of the fact that the lights are not working. The general standard of "what is reasonable in the circumstances" should afford the test, though it may be doubted whether this soft-centred formula is particularly helpful in determining how these cases should be resolved.

## Sounding Horn

**[15.49]** Failure to sound one's horn may be negligent.[79] Moreover, it is not good enough to sound one's horn outside the range of ordinary hearing:

> "There is no use in sounding a horn which is not heard; common sense as well as the Act of Parliament requires that there shall be 'audible and sufficient warning'."[80]
>
> Of course it must be shown that if the horn had been sounded the accident would not have taken place.[81]

**[15.50]** In *Darcy v Torpey*,[82] Lynch J observed that:

> " ... of course, one does not have to blow one's horn every time one passes a motorcar on a good wide straight road but, where ... the driver intending to overtake is aware that there is a right turn ahead of the car which he is going to overtake and that that car is going slow enough that it might be going to take that turn and that the car appears to be moving out a bit towards the centre, then it seems to me that those circumstances clearly call for a warning by the intending overtaking driver, whether by flashing his lights or blowing his horn ... [O]ne is not entitled to drive on the assumption that all other drivers on the road will behave perfectly and one must be alert for errors by other drivers, one of the commonest of which, certainly in this country, is the giving of a signal far too late."

**[15.51]** Commonsense also dictates when a driver should sound the horn in the presence of children. In *Squizzoni v McEntaggart*[83] Budd J said that he had:

---

77. In *Tingle Jacobs & Co v Kennedy* [1964] 1 All ER 888 at 889 (CA) Lord Denning MR considered that "the presumption should be that [the lights are] in proper working order unless there is evidence to the contrary ...". See also *Frank v Cox* (1956) 54 LGR 142 (Div Court).

78. *Cf Doyle v HF Murray Ltd* [1967] IR 390, where the parties were held not to have been remiss in failing to anticipate that the amber light would only last for 1.3 seconds, but were nonetheless in breach of their duty of care in failing in all the circumstances to keep a proper lookout. See also *Ramoo son of Erulapan v Gan Soo Swee* [1971] 3 All ER 320 (PC); *Piel v Dublin United Tramways Co (1896) Ltd* [1939] Ir Jur 88 (CC). The authorities responsible for installing and maintaining the traffic light system must take reasonable care that the green light is of sufficient duration to allow traffic to cross the junction: *Skinner v Hartnett and Cork Corporation* High Court, 3 February 1995.

79. *Cf Connolly v O'Brien* Supreme Court, 28 October 1955; *Preston v Higgins* Supreme Court, 13 July 1962 (semble). See also para **[15.08]** above.

80. *Casey v Martin* (1920) 54 ILTR 185 at 187 (CA).

81. *Murphy v Riordan* (1926) 60 ILTR 113 (SC).

82. DPIJ: Hilary and Easter Terms 1993, p 208 at p 209 (High Court, 2 March 1993, Lynch J).

83. DPIJ: Hilary and Easter Terms 1994, p 56 at pp 63-64 (High Court, 11 May 1994).

> "to sympathise with th[e] point of view that when you are going through a residential estate of a sunny evening you watch out for children but you don't go blasting your horn every time you see a child. [Y]ou might toot your horn if you notice a child that you think is going to kick a ball out or chase it or something of that sort but I don't think that the residents would be too happy if every time a child was seen in the distance in a residential estate that people start to blast their horns at them."

**[15.52]** We have already noted[84] that in *Mulcahy v Lynch and Butler*,[85] the Supreme Court held that a driver approaching a schoolbus that has stopped to let children out must blow the horn, under pain of being found guilty of negligence.

## Emergency Vehicles

**[15.53]** How should the courts assess the negligence of drivers of ambulances, fire brigades or other emergency vehicles on their way to a situation of danger? They are exempted from ordinary speed limits[86] but this is a matter directly affecting their criminal rather than civil liability. Undoubtedly, the social utility of saving life or property or of approaching criminal suspects should be a factor meriting some weight in applying the test of "the reasonable person", which underlies the standard of care in negligence.[87]

**[15.54]** It is, however, clear that drivers of emergency vehicles have nothing like a blanket immunity. As Denning LJ observed in *Watt v Hertfordshire County Council*:[88]

> "I quite agree that fire engines, ambulances and doctors' cars should not shoot past the traffic lights when they show a red light. That is because the risk is too great to warrant the incurring of the danger. It is always a question of balancing the risk against the end."

**[15.55]** In *Strick v Treacy*,[89] the plaintiff, driving her car on the Tallaght By-Pass highway, approaching a junction controlled by traffic lights that were in her favour, found that first a garda car with flashing lights emerged from the road to her left, against the traffic lights, and halted close to the centre of the highway and then a yellow Civil Defence fire tender, travelling "some considerable distance" behind the garda car, also emerged from the same road, with its own flashing lights, still against the traffic lights. She collided with the fire tender and was injured. Some of the cars in the outside lane of the highway had come to a halt in response to the garda car's activity, but traffic in the slow lane had continued to flow.

**[15.56]** It transpired that the garda car was escorting the fire tender which was in action because of a strike in the ordinary fire services. The two vehicles were on their way to attend a fire that had broken out in a local school. O'Hanlon J held that all three drivers were at fault. He reduced the plaintiff's damages by 50% on account of her contributory negligence. The driver of the fire tender had been negligent because he had had a clear

---

84. See para **[15.08]** above.
85. Supreme Court, 25 March 1993.
86. Road Traffic Act 1961, s 45(3), Road (Traffic General Speed Limit) Regulations 1979 (SI 176/1979).
87. *Cf* para **[7.03]-[7.11]** above. See also *Daborn v Bath Tramways Motor Co Ltd* [1946] 2 All ER 333.
88. [1954] 2 All ER 368 at 371 (CA).
89. High Court, 10 June 1993 (O'Hanlon J). See Quill, pp 82-83.

unobstructed view for a long distance to his right when he neared the junction. He ought to have ensured that the plaintiff had seen what was happening and was yielding to him the right of way before he drove into her path at a time when the lights were in her favour. The garda car driver had been unreasonable in proceeding on the basis that it could clear a path for itself through all the traffic on the way to the fire, leaving the fire tender "to solve its own problems ...", he should have done more to halt the traffic, particularly having regard to the large gap that had opened up between him and the fire tender. The plaintiff should have been alerted by the presence of the garda car on the highway and the halting of the traffic to her right, notwithstanding that it had the lights in its favour. She should have been "doubly cautious" when she saw the large yellow fire tender approaching from her left with its lights flashing. Moreover her failure to wear a seat belt had "contributed significantly to the seriousness of her injuries".

**[15.57]** In *O'Keeffe v Ladola and Dublin Corporation*[90] the plaintiff was a passenger in a bus which collided with an ambulance flashing its emergency light. The bus driver was approaching a main road intersection intending to turn right. He slowed down looking first to his right and then to his left. A motorist coming from the bus driver's left on the main road, flashed his lights to the bus driver indicating that the bus could emerge across the motorist's path. The bus driver did not look to his right again, but moved into the junction. An ambulance driving fast in an emergency struck the bus from the right. The bus driver, if he looked to his right, had a clear view for 300 yards on the main road. The ambulance driver was travelling at between 40 and 41 mph in a 30 mile an hour speed zone, and had his strobe lights and siren operating. The ambulance had come through a red light some distance back from the scene of the crash and from some 70 yards back had a full view of the bus emerging. Girls travelling in the bus saw the ambulance approaching as the bus drove into the junction. Judge McMahon held the bus driver liable for 80% and the ambulance driver 20%.

90. Circuit Court Dublin, 12 January 2000 (McMahon J).

Chapter 16

# Negligent Care of Children


I. Introduction .......... 437
II. Parental Negligence .......... 437
III. The Negligence of Schools .......... 441


## I. Introduction

**[16.01]** In this chapter we examine the ways in which liability can arise for the negligent care of children. We divide the analysis into two categories: parental negligence and the negligence of schools.

## II. Parental Negligence

**[16.02]** There is no general rule that parents are liable for the torts of their children by virtue of their status of parents *per se*.[1] A parent may, however, be negligent in affording his child an opportunity to injure another.[2] The negligence may consist of a wide range of behaviour, which may relate to:

(a) dangerous things;

(b) the child's dangerous propensities; and

(c) failure to control the child properly.

### Dangerous Things

**[16.03]** It may be negligent for a person to leave dangerous things within reach of a child in circumstances where injury to the child or another is foreseeable. A clear case is where a person leaves a loaded gun within reach of a young child. Liability will not depend simply on the relationship between parent and child that may exist in such a case but rather on the foreseeability of harm[3] and the reasonableness of attributing blame to the defendant for his lack of care. This was well illustrated in the leading Irish decision on the subject,

1. *Taylor v King* [1993] 8 WWR 92 (BCCA). Indeed, a parent who pays compensation to the victim of her or her child's wrongdoing in the mistaken belief of the existence of a principle of automatic parental liability may have a restitution claim to recover the money paid, see *B v Arkin* (1996) 138 DLR 4th 309 (Man QB).
2. See generally Waller 'Visiting the Sins of the Children. The Liability of Parents for Injuries Caused by their Children' (1963) 4 Mel ULR 17 at 24-29; Fridman 'Children and Negligence' (1967) 117 New LJ 35 at 36; Binchy, (1980) 74 Inc L Soc Gaz of Ir 35; Kime & Harper 'The Duty to Control the Conduct of Another' (1934) 9 Ind LJ at 498 at 506-509; Freer 'Parental Liability for Torts of Children' (1965) 53 Ky LJ 254; Hefey 'Dennis the Menace and the Wonder/and of Children's Torts, Children's Torts and Parental Responsibility' (1984) 58 Law Institute J 661, Prescott & Kundin, 'Toward a Model Parental Liability Act' (1984) 20 Cal WLR 187.
3. See *Dixon v Bell M & S* (1816) 198, 105 ER 1023; *Lynch v Nurdin* (1841) 1 QB 29 at 35, 113 ER 1041 at 1043; *cf Good-Wear Treaders Ltd v D & B Holdings Ltd* (1979) 8 CCLT 87 at 101-102 (NS SC). See also *Dickinson v Dickinson* (1986) 3 SR (NSW) 233 (DC).

*Sullivan v Creed*.[4] There, the defendant, a farmer who had been shooting rabbits on his property, left his gun loaded and at full cock standing inside a fence on his lands. His fifteen-year-old son, not realising that the gun was loaded, pointed it in play at the plaintiff and accidentally shot him. A verdict for the plaintiff was upheld by the Court of Appeal.

**[16.04]** FitzGibbon LJ stated:

> "The scope of the duty is the scope of the danger, and it extends to every person into whose hands a prudent man might reasonably expect the gun to come, having regard to the place where he left it. The ground of liability here is not that the boy was the defendant's son, but the fact that the gun was left without warning, in a dangerous condition, within reach of persons using the pathway, and the boy was one of the very class of persons whom the defendant knew to be not only likely but certain to pass by, *viz* his own household."[5]

**[16.05]** It has been held that a parent (or another person) may also be liable where he or she negligently entrusts a dangerous thing to a child in circumstances where injury to the child or another is foreseeable. Instances of liability under this heading are not confined to parents of course, but because examples may frequently occur in the domestic context, it is worth emphasising that parenthood provides no immuntiy when third parties suffer. Whether or not the entrustment was negligent "... must depend upon the exact facts of every case".[6]

## Child's Dangerous Propensities

**[16.06]** A parent may be liable in negligence where he or she knows or ought to know[7] of a particular dangerous propensity of his or her child and fails to protect others against injury likely to result from it.

**[16.07]** Thus, for example, if the parent is aware that his or her child has attacked other persons previously,[8] or has displayed a tendency to steal,[9] or to set fire to property,[10] or to

4. [1904] 2 IR 317 (CA 1903). The decision has been widely cited and discussed in many common law jurisdictions: see eg, *Reida v Intend* (1971) 18 Cal Appeal 3d 698, 96 Cal Rpt R 102 (CA 2nd Dist); *Dickens v Barnham* (1920) 69 Colo 349, 194 P 356 (SC); *Salisbury v Crudale* (1918) 41 R1 33, 102 A 731 (SC) (describing the decision as being "of great weight"); *Thibodeau v Cheff* (1911) 24 OLR 214 (Div Court); *Kenealy v Karaka* (1906) 26 NZLR 1118 (CA).

5. *Sullivan* v Creed [1904] 2 IR 317 at 340. *Cf Cunningham v Blake* [1937] Ir Jur 20 (HC).

6. *Newton v Edgerley* [1959] 1 WLR 1031 at 1032. See also *Donaldson v McNiven* [1952] 2 All ER 691 (CA); *Bebee v Sales* (1916) 32 TLR 413; *Court v Wyatt* The Times, 24 June, 1960, p 12, Col 2 (QBD), *Rogers v Wilkinson*, The Times, 19 January, 1963, p 4, Cols 3-4 (QBD); *Hinds v Direct Supply Co (Clapham Junction) Ltd*, The Times, 29 January, 1966, p 15, cols 6-7 (QBD).

7. On principle, it would appear that a parent who culpably fails to learn of his child's particular dangerous propensities should not be able to shelter behind his ignorance. Nevertheless, some decisions appear to require something akin to *scienter* on the part of the parent: see eg *Streifel v Stroz* (19571) 1 DLR (2d) 667 (BC SC).

8. *Cf Gorely v Codd* [1966] 3 All ER 891 at 896; *Court v Wyatt*, The Times, 24 June, 1960, p 12, Col 2 (QBD); *Michand v Dupuis* (1977) 30 NBR (2d) 305 (SC, QBD) - father knew of eleven year-old son's propensity to throw stones and did nothing to control it. *Zuckerberg v Munter* (1950) 277 App Div 1061, 100 NYS 2d 910 (2nd Dept) – eight-year-old son attacked domestic servant with baseball bat.

9. *Streifel v Stroz* (1957) 11 DLR (2d) 667 (BC, SC).

10. *Thibodeau v Cheff* (1911) 24 OLR 214 (Div Court). *Agnesini v Olsen* 277 App Div 1006,100 NYS 2d 338 (2nd Dept, 1950); *cf M v H* (1991) 82 DLR (4th) 609 (BCCA) – arson was not foreseeable in the circumstances.

drive dangerously,[11] he or she may be liable for failing to take the steps necessary to protect others from harm likely to result from a repetition of such conduct.

**[16.08]** The steps that the parent will be required to take will depend on the circumstances of the case. The proper approach may be to discipline the child, encourage him to mend his ways, remove him from likely sources of temptation or warn his potential victims. Clearly the age of the child and the nature of the danger will greatly affect how the parent should behave. It is settled, however, that the parent is not an insurer: he/she will not be liable where his/her reasonable best was not sufficient to prevent the injury.[12]

## Failure to Control Child Properly

**[16.09]** Where parents fail to control a child properly, they may be liable for injuries resulting to others (or, indeed, to the child itself).[13]

**[16.10]** In *Curley v Mannion*,[14] the Supreme Court held that it might be negligence for the owner and driver of a car to permit his passenger to open a door without ensuring that other road users would not thereby be endangered. The case involved the thirteen year-old daughter of the driver opening a door in the path of a cyclist. Ó Dálaigh CJ stated that, in his judgment:

> "a person in charge of a motor car must take reasonable precautions for the safety of others, and this will include the duty to take reasonable care to prevent conduct on the part of passengers which is negligent. In the present case that duty is, it seems to me, reinforced by the relationship of parent and child; and a parent, while not liable for the torts of his child, may be liable if negligent in failing to exercise his control to prevent his child injuring others."[15]

**[16.11]** Walsh J observed that the steps which the person in charge of a car should take to protect others from injury must be determined in the light of the exact circumstances of each case:

> "In this case the defendant by reason of the fact that he was the parent of the tortious child could be held to have had an authority over the child. By reason of his proximity to the child he could be held to have been in a position to exercise that authority."[16]

---

11. *Cf Lelarge v Blakney* (1978) 21 NBR (2d) 100 rvsd 92 DLR (3d) 440 - son's propensity to drive dangerously was known to his parent; *LaPlabove v LaPlabove* (1995) 125 DLR (4th 569) (BCCA) - father should not have allowed his 16-year-old son to drive, in view of son's diminished mental capacity and impairment of leg and arm movement in consequence of medical accident 14 years previously. *Golembe v Blumberg* (1941) 262 AD 759, 27 NY 2d 692 - jury issue as to whether father's awareness of son's epileptic condition rendered it negligent to entrust son with car. Contrast *Estes v Gibson* (1953) 257 SW 2d 604 (Ky CA), where the gift of a car by a mother to her son, whom she knew to be "an inebriate and drug addict" gave rise to no liability on her part when he injured the plaintiff. The strong dissent of Duncan J is worthy of note.
12. *Cf Zuckerbrod v Burch* (1965) 88 NJ Super 1, 210 A 2d 425 (App Div,).
13. *Cf Gambino v Dileo* (1970) 17 DLR (3d) 167 (Ont HC); *Arnold v Teno* (1978) 83 DLR (3d) 609 (SC Can); *McCallion v Dodd* [1966] NZLR 710 (CA).
14. [1965] IR 543 (SC). What degree of control is desirable for children when they are at play raises some difficult questions as to the psychological nature of play. It may be that the values of children conflict directly with the "adult" values of negligence law here: *cf* Bahr 'Tort Law and the Games Kids Play' (1978) 23 S Dakota LR 275.
15. [1965] IR 546.
16. [1965] IR 546 at 549-550. See also *Carmarthenshire County Council v Lewis* [1955] AC 549 at 566 (HL). *Cf Galaskey v Stauffer* (1994) 112 DLR (4th) 109 (SC, Can) - driver of a car, being "in a position of control" has responsibility to see that seatbelts are worn by younger passengers, even where children are accompanied by their parents; *per* Cory J at 120:

A number of specific aspects of parental liability based on negligence require a further brief comment.

### *(a) The age of the child*

**[16.12]** Clearly, where the child is very young, the parents' responsibilities are high and they will not be permitted to excuse themselves by having relied on their child to behave carefully when the child's immaturity and lack of experience would not warrant that trust. It has been well observed, however, that:

> "[a]s they approach maturity, and as an aid in their attaining it, adolescents require more freedom, and hence less supervision, than ... young children. As a child grows older there are fewer situations in which his parents have the ability to control him. Concomitantly, as he grows older there should be fewer situations in which they have a legal obligation to do so."[17]

### *(b) Which parent is liable?*

**[16.13]** Somewhat surprisingly the decisions on parental liability do not contain a detailed analysis of this question. Usually the father alone is sued; sometimes both parents are defendants; most rarely, the mother alone is sued. Clearly, the question of which parent is the proper one to sue will depend greatly on the facts of the case. If a mother lets her child escape onto the roadway while she is shopping, it will not usually occur to a driver who is injured while swerving to avoid the child to sue the father who is at the time busy at work many miles away. If the roles are reversed, there is no objection in principle, and no difficulty in practice, in suing the father. The facts of each case will make it clear who should be sued.

**[16.14]** If the marriage has broken down and there is a new partner involved in the rearing of the children again there would seem to be no problem in principle in determining who should be sued. The answer depends on where the courts consider that the duty of supervision lay in the context of the facts giving rise to the injury to the child. Of course there will be some cases where the new partner's level of integration into the domestic life of the family may be a matter of debate. Clearly the scope of his or her duty of supervision will depend on the resolution of this issue. The courts, no doubt, will in the future be called on to give practical translation of contemporary social morals and expectations in this context. If the boyfriend of a mother of a two-year old child is left in the home with the child in his company, he will not be permitted to shuffle off his resonsibility for letting the child play with matches by saying that he did not want to take on the role of step-father.

### *(c) The Law Reform Commission's Seventeenth Report*

**[16.15]** The Law Reform Commission addressed the subject of the liability of parents for damage caused by minors, in their Seventeenth Report,[18] published in 1985. The Commission considered and ultimately rejected, three options for reform: vicarious

---

16. (contd)

> "The presence of a parent in a car may mean that the responsibility is shared, but it cannot negate the duties owed by the driver to the passenger under the age of sixteen."

17. Alexander, *Tort Liability of Children and their Parents*, Ch 14, *Studies in Canadian Family Law* Mendes Da Costa ed, (1972), p 867.*Cf Hewer v Bryant* [1970] 1 QB 357 at 369 (CA).

18. *Report on the Liability in Tort of Minors and the Liability of Parents for Damage Caused by Minors*, Ch 3 (LRC 17-1987).

liability, strict liability and a presumption of parental negligence where a person is injured by a minor child. As regards vicarious liability, it considered that the analogy between parents and employers was not entirely helpful. The family is "not primarily directed towards impersonal goals".[19] The Commission was unwilling to extend the range of vicarious liability that can occur under existing law.[20] The Commission considered strict liability too drastic a solution. Analogies with wild animals[21] and the rule in *Rylands v Fletcher*[22] were not appropriate, since parenthood fulfils "a vitally important social and moral function".[23] The Commission was drawn to the option of establishing a presumption of negligence, which is the approach favoured in many civil law jurisdictions.[24] Ultimately it rejected it on the basis that (inter alia) it could work hardship in some cases on parents and that it would be difficult to draw the line fairly in relation to such matters as whether it should apply to absent parents, to persons *in loco parentis*, to minors of all ages, to all kinds of damage, to cases where the minor had acted wilfully or negligently or to all cases of damage, even where the minor had done no wrong. Thus, the Commission recommended no change in the existing law relating to parental liability. This approach is to be welcomed, as being in harmony with the constitutional protection of the family; strict liability or even a presumption of negligence would be likely to cause the greatest hardship for parents with the least economic resources.

## III. The Negligence of Schools[25]

**[16.16]** Clearly teachers and those involved in the management of schools have a duty of care in relation to pupils who attend the school. The elements of proximity of relationship and foreseeability of potential injury could scarcely be more pronounced. A very general guiding principle was expressed by Lord Esher in *Williams v Eady*, that:

---

19. LRC Report at p 67.
20. *Cf Moynihan v Moynihan* [1975] IR 192 (SC).
21. *Cf* Alexander, *Tort Liability of Children and their Parents*, Ch 14, *Studies in Canadian Family Law*, Mendes Da Costa (ed), (1972), Vol 2 at p 846.
22. *Cf AG v Corke* [1933] Ch 89.
23. LRC Report at p 69.
24. *Cf Travaux du Premier Colloque International de Droit Compare* (1963 Ottawa), Vol 2, p 43. As to the United States, see Prescott & Kundin 'Toward a Model Parental Liability Act' (1984) 20 Cal WLR 187.
25. The subject has been most recently analysed in Glendenning *Education and the Law* (1999), Ch 9; see also Mahon, *Negligence and The Teacher* (1995) (Ennis Teacher's Centre); Farry *Vocational Teachers and the Law* (1998), pp 20-33; Glendenning 'Schools and the Law of Negligence' (1997) 2 BR 241; Linehan 'The School Teacher and the Law of Negligence' (1965) 31 Ir Jur 38; Anon 'School Teachers and School Managers - Their Liability for Negligence' (1954) 88 ILT & Sol J 1, 11; Anon 'Liability for Accidents Happening in Schoolrooms' (1890) 24 ILT & Sol J 629; Delany 'Injuries to School Children: The Principles of Liability' 28, 29 Ir Jur 15 (1962-1963); Brown 'Injuries to School' (1970) 114 Sol J 216; Lowe 'The Liability of Teachers and School Authorities for Injuries Suffered by Students' (1983) 13 U Queensland LJ 28; Heffey 'The Duty of Schools and Teachers to Protect Pupils from Injury' (1985) 11 Monash ULR 1; Dugan 'Teachers' Tort Liability' (1962) 11 Clev MRL 512 at 513-517; Seitz 'Tort Liability of Teachers and Administrators for Negligent Conduct Towards Pupils' (1971) 20 Clev St LR 551; Anon 'Safety in School and the Danger Without' (1969) 119 New LJ 939; Binchy 'Schools' Liability in Negligence' (1984) 78 Incorp L Soc of Ireland Gaz 153, 185.

> "the schoolmaster [is] bound to take such care of his boys as a careful father would take of his boys ..."[26]

**[16.17]** Although this statement has been quoted widely with approval in several decisions in this country and abroad, it has been criticised for being "unrealistic, if not unhelpful"[27] especially where the number of pupils in the school is high. The problems of care and control in a school bear some resemblance to those confronting a parent in the home but they are far from identical. It is possible that in a future decision an Irish court will drop the reference to the "careful parent" and stress the fact that it is the standard of the reasonable school teacher or manager which should prevail.[28] The degree of care required of the teacher, naturally, will vary with the circumstances and especially the age of the child.[29] As Costello J observed in *Kelly v Gilhooley*:

> "the duty of care which school authorities owe to children differs from moment to moment and from place to place and the duty is different in different times of the day and in different places in the school."[30]

**[16.18]** The types of negligence of which a school teacher or school management may be guilty cover a wide range of activities. These may be conveniently summarised under six headings:

(a) negligence in instruction;
(b) supervision in school playgrounds;
(c) supervision outside hours;
(d) injuries sustained off the premises;
(e) other acts of negligence;
(f) structural dangers.

## Negligence in Instruction

**[16.19]** An allegation of negligence may arise where accidents take place during the course of instruction by teachers. Most of the cases have been concerned with injuries suffered during gymnastic and sports training, where the allegations centre around dangerous exercises, inadequate equipment and lack of supervision. As one judge pointed out:

> "The potential for danger in these cases can be easily imagined. Young students are apt to try different and more daring manoeuvres than a more mature person would permit."[31]

**[16.20]** In the Supreme Court decision of *Mulligan v Doherty*[32] in 1966, the plaintiff was a seventeen-year-old girl who was injured when preparing a new gymnastic exercise. The

---

26. (1893) 10 TLR 41 at 429 (CA), cited with approval in *Lennon v McCarthy* Supreme Court, 13 July 1966 (Ó Dalaigh CJ), p 2.

27. *Beaumont v Surrey County Council* (1968) 112 Sol J 704.

28. *Cf* Ramsay 'Teachers' Liability: The Standard of Care' (1992) 8 Prof Neg.

29. *Cf Ryan v Madden* [1944] IR 154 at 156-157 (HC); *Faranda v Minister for Education* [1981] 1 SR (WA) 312 (DC).

30. DPIJ: Trinity and Michaelmas Terms 1994 p 86 at p 88 (High Court, 1 November 1994).

31. *Long v Gardner* (1983) 144 DLR (3d) 73 at 81 (Ont HC). See generally Drowatsky 'On the Firing Line. Negligence in Physical Education' (1977) 6 J & L & Educ 481. In *Petersen v School District No 36, Surrey BC* (1993) 104 DLR 334 (BCCA), a physical education teacher was held negligent in positioning the plaintiff too close to the batter in a baseball game.

32. Supreme Court, 17 May 1966.

exercise had been demonstrated by the physical training teacher, who had also supervised one girl in repeating the exercise. The teacher then went to another part of the gymnasium to instruct another class. In her absence other girls in the class repeated the exercise without mishap but the plaintiff toppled from the bars and injured her back. The gymnastic exercise involved a somewhat elaborate descent down the wall bars, with the hands changing bars alternately in descending order. The plaintiff did not exactly remember what the teacher had done in the demonstration and released both hands simultaneously, resulting in her fall.

**[16.21]** The plaintiff's case in negligence was based on allegations that there had been inadequate instruction and that the teacher had failed to remain with the class until each of the pupils knew the correct sequence of movements for the safe performance of the exercise.

**[16.22]** Henchy J directed the jury to hold that the defendants were not liable and the Supreme Court affirmed. The Supreme Court regarded the exercise as a "routine" one which a 17 year-old girl of ordinary intelligence "could not have failed to apprehend".[33] Ó Dalaigh CJ considered that no one could reasonably have foreseen that such a girl would fail to understand the safe way of carrying out the exercise, and would substitute her own patently risky mode of descent so as to require that the teacher remain at hand to supervise further:

> "Something might be said for such a view in the case of young children; but a woman over 17 years of age is a person whose conduct in performing a simple gymnastic exercise might reasonably be expected to be intelligent and sensible ..."[34]

**[16.23]** In *Delaney v O'Dowd*,[35] a teacher supervising children practising defensive manoeuvres from Olympic Handball was held not to have been negligent where two pupils aged about 11 or 12 collided. The children had been placed in pairs two to three metres apart and were instructed to run parallel to one another. Judge Carroll considered that this was a perfectly safe distance for the exercise. He rejected any criticism that the teacher had

---

33. Supreme Court, 17 May 1966.

34. Supreme Court, 17 May 1966 at 3-4. See also *Smith v Jolly* High Court, 17-18 May 1984 (O'Hanlon J); *Walsh v Bourke* High Court, 25 January 1985 (Hamilton J), in neither of which the plaintiff succeeded. In *Harrison v Shields*, DPIJ, Trinity and Michaelmas Terms 1996, p 235 (High Court, 15 November 1996), Laffoy J dismissed the plaintiff's action where she fell when participating in a high jump competition in her school. On the evidence, Laffoy J concluded that the accident should be attributed to the plaintiff's inability to control her landing, on account of her relative inexperience, rather than to her falling on ground outside the area protected by two mats. Laffoy J stated that, if the plaintiff had fallen on such unprotected ground, she would have imposed liability on the basis of the inadequacy of the matting, "irrespective of the expert views", which were divided on the question whether the rules of the International Amateur Athletic Association relating to matting should be considered an appropriate standard for school sports events. See also *Gilroy v Ní Cheallaigh* [1996] Ir L Log W 310 (CC); *Cf Gard v Board of School Trustees of Duncan* [1946] 2 DLR 441 (BCCA) - not negligent to permit pupils play hockey unsupervised; the plaintiff injured as a result of breach of rules of the game; *Moore v Hampshire County Council* 80 LGR 481 (CA (Civil Div)), 4 November 1981 – the school authorities were negligent in permitting twelve-year-old pupil with two dislocated hips to do handstands; plaintiff, desperately anxious to join the gymnastics class had "told a whopper" to the teacher that her doctor had given her permission to participate; teacher should have sought confirmation.

35. [1997] Ir L Log W 157 (CC).

not kept his eyes focused on the children at all times. Such an obligation could not reasonably be expected in the circumstances and no prudent parent would have objected to the way the class had been supervised.

**[16.24]** In *Murphy v Jackson*,[36] where a six-year-old pupil was injured in a "perfectly supervis[ed]" piggy-back race, Costello J held that the school had not been guilty of negligence in allowing boys of this age to engage in such an activity.

**[16.25]** In *Ward v Donegal Vocational Committee*,[37] Keane, J considered it "an impossible proposition to sustain" that a school should be "ipso facto, automatically negligent" for organising a Gaelic football competition where boys of significantly different weights and physiques played in the same match. In the instant case, the plaintiff had been injured when he and another boy had gone for possession of the ball at the same time. Keane J observed that:

> "it would be paternalistic for a court to be saying that teams must be chosen by the teachers on such a basis and that effectively people won't get hurt. Of course people will get hurt and people [who] were of stronger physique than this young man was at the time he met with his injury can get hurt because it is in the nature of these games ... w[h]ere bodies collide sometimes quite violently ... people will get injuries at greater or less severity. That is a hazard of the game."

## Supervision in School Playgrounds

**[16.26]** It is beyond argument that some degree of supervision is necessary where children are playing in school playgrounds but the courts have been anxious to make it plain that too high a standard of care will not be demanded. As O'Dalaigh, CJ said in *Lennon v McCarthy*:

> "When normally healthy children are in the playground it is not necessary that they should be under constant supervision."[38]

---

36. DPIJ: Trinity and Michaelmas Terms 1993, p 146 (High Court, 1993, Costello J). See also *Flynn v O'Reilly*, DPIJ: Trinity and Michaelmas Terms 1996, p 55 (High Court, 31 October 1996, Smyth J).

37. DPIJ: Hilary and Easter Terms 1993, p 116 (HC). In *Van Oppen v Bedford Charity Trustees* [1990] 1 WLR 235, the English Court of Appeal held that a school was not liable in negligence for failing to have insurance cover for injuries sustained by pupils playing rugby and for failing to inform their parents of the absence of such cover. Courts in the United States of America have come to the same conclusion: *Friederich v Board of Education* (1978) 375 NE 2d 141 (Ill App Ct); *Wicina v Strecker* (1978) 747 P 2d 167 (Kan Sup Ct); see, however, *Oldfield v MacMillan* (1998), 1998 ACWSJ LEXIS 69094 (NBQB). If the Irish courts were to adopt the same approach as that which the Supreme Court favoured in *Sweeney v Duggan* [1997] 2 ILRM 211 (in which *Van Oppen* was cited and distingusihed in Murphy J's judgment), liability in negligence would not be likely to be imposed.

38. Supreme Court, 13 July 1966 at p 2 of his judgment. See also *Courtney v Masterson* [1949] Ir Jur 6 at 7 (HC): "... I should have thought it unheard of that teachers should have to watch all the children at every instant when under their care." In accord are *Flesk v King* DPIJ, Trinity and Michaelmas Terms 1996, p 87 at p 90 (High Court, 29 October 1996, Laffoy J) discussed in paras **[16.33]-16.34]** below; *Clark v Monmouthshire County Council* (1954) 2 LGR 246 at 247-248 (CA) at 250 (*per* Morris LJ) and at 251 (*per* Evershed MR); *Board of Education for City of Toronto & Hunt v Hiffs* (1959) 22 DLR (2d) 49 at 55 (SC Can). See also *Commonwealth of Australia v Stokes* 1996 Aust ACTSC LEXIS 65; BC 96054-75 (SC).

**[16.27]** Similarly, in the English decision of *Rawsthorne v Ottley*,[39] Hilbery J expressed the view that:

> "it is not the law, and never has been the law, that a schoolmaster should keep boys under supervision during every moment of their school lives."

**[16.28]** The Irish cases present interesting examples of the range of cases that can arise under the general heading of supervision. In *Ryan v Madden*,[40] the failure of a national school teacher to supervise young pupils, including the plaintiff, aged five, when they were leaving the building at the end of school hours was held to be negligence where the child slid down the banisters from the upper floor (where the class-room was).

**[16.29]** In *O'Gorman v Crotty*,[41] a ten-year-old pupil, when being chased during play in the school playground, fell over one of several wooden blocks which were lying in the playground. The blocks were sometimes used to support boards for use as seats, but appear to have served no positive function as play objects. In holding the school manager and principal teacher liable, O'Byrne J stated:

> "In circumstances such as those in this case careful supervision is essential, and the persons having charge of the school are bound to see that there is supervision of the playground during play intervals. It was the duty of the principal teacher to see that the playground was clear and not a source of danger to boys playing there, who could not be expected to keep their eyes fixed."[42]

**[16.30]** The plaintiff was held not to have been guilty of contributory negligence on the basis that "boys naturally run in a playground",[43] and that the accident took place during a period of recreation, in a place specially set aside for play which the boy "was entitled to assume ... was reasonably safe for this purpose".[44]

**[16.31]** In *Healy v Dodd*,[45] an 11-year-old pupil was injured when he fell while using handcuffs in a game known as "still" - where "police" arrested "poteen makers". The use of handcuffs had been forbidden two years earlier and a pair of handcuffs had been confiscated. In order to keep up the deception of the game imaginary handcuffs were put on by the boys after the real handcuffs were taken by the master.[46] Two days before the

---

39. [1937] 3 All ER 902 at 905 (KBD). In *Ward v Hertfordshire County Council* [1970] 1 All ER 535 at 538 (CA) Lord Denning MR stated: "Before the school began the staff were indoors preparing for the day's work. They can't be expected to be in the playground, too"
This seems a poor argument. The problem of staff being in two places at once can be resolved for the simple device of a roster system, or the employment of extra personnel.
40. [1944] IR 154 (HC). Contrast *O'Neill v Tipperary SR VEC* [1996] Ir L Log W 369 (CC), where a 12 year-old student was injured by another student of similar age who was sliding down the banisters. The student who injured her was guilty of one other sliding episode. No liability was imposed on the school. See also *Greene v Mundow* Circuit Court, 20 January 2000, Irish Times 21 January 2000 (Judge McMahon).
41. [1946] Ir Jur Rep 34 (HC).
42. [1946] Ir Jur Rep 34 at 36.
43. [1946] Ir Jur Rep 34 at 36.
44. [1946] Ir Jur Rep 34.
45. [1951] Ir Jur Rep 22 (HC).
46. [1951] Ir Jur Rep 22 at 23.

accident the handcuffs made their way back to the school - being brought there by the son of the principal teacher, unknown to him.[47]

**[16.32]** O'Byrne J in the High Court dismissed the action. The teacher had been supervising play at the time of the accident and there was "nothing to arouse his suspicion" that the real handcuffs had returned.[48]

**[16.33]** In *Flesk v King*,[49] the plaintiff, a seven-year-old pupil, was injured by a toy boomerang which another pupil threw at him, in the school playground. The boomerang had been taken to school by a pupil in his schoolbag and released by him into the playground unknown to the teacher. It was thrown from person to person, as if it were a ball, for five or six minutes before the accident occurred. The school principal who was in charge of playground supervision had to patrol three separate areas where different groups of children played.

**[16.34]** Laffoy J dismissed the case. A proper system of supervision was in place "in that in general the small children were segregated from the older pupils and [they] played on the safer grassy area". The principal had been "constantly ... patrolling the entire play area on foot so as to supervise all eighty five pupils and he was not merely relying on observation from school windows".

**[16.35]** A case which runs against this tread of other Irish decisions is *Mapp v Gilhooley*.[50] There Barr J imposed liability on a school manager where the plaintiff, aged five, was injured in the school playground. At the time there were over two hundred boys in the playground. The accident occurred when one "train", made up of about ten boys, holding each other by the waist, collided with another train, similarly composed. Two teachers were supervising the recreation period, supported by six eight-year-olds who acted as prefects. The headmaster was also in the yard at the time, though not in the vicinity where the accident happened.

**[16.36]** The plaintiff, also aged eight at the time of trial, gave the unsworn evidence, because he had not yet learned the meaning of the oath. He impressed Barr J who considered him a "remarkably bright and intelligent boy". He attested that the "trains" game was a well-established practice, with up to five trains operating at the same time. On the fateful day, the game had been in progress for some time before the accident took place. The teachers who were on duty gave evidence that they had no indication that the "trains" game was in progress before the plaintiff received his injury.

**[16.37]** Barr J imposed liability. He stated:

> "In measuring the duty of care owed by a school authority to a pupil or pupils in given circumstances, the court must take into account all the relevant factors, including the ages of the children in question, the activities in which they are or may be engaged, the degree of supervision (if any) required having regard to the prevailing circumstances and the

47. [1951] Ir Jur Rep 22 at 23.
48. See also the English decisions of *Rawsthorne v Ottley* [1937] 3 All ER 902 (KBD), *Jackson v LCC* (1912) 28 TLR 359 (CA), and *Rich v LCC* [1953] 2 All ER 376 (CA), analysed in detail by Binchy, (1984) 78 Incorp L Soc of Ireland Gaz at 156-157.
49. DPIJ: Trinity and Michaelmas Terms 1996, p 87 (High Court, 29 October 1996 Laffoy J).
50. High Court, 7 November 1989 (Barr J).

opportunity (if any) which those in charge of the child had to prevent or minimize the mischief complained of. It goes without saying that the duty ought to be measured realistically and should take into account also that children, particularly small boys, are high spirited by nature and some are inclined to be mischievous. In the absence of a regime of draconian servitude, it is impossible to keep very young children under complete control when at play. Disciplinary and supervisory measures required of a school authority should be construed within the reasonable bounds."

**[16.38]** Barr J considered that the statement in *Lennon v McCarthy*,[51] that the duty of a schoolmaster is to take such care of its pupils as a careful father would of his children, was not at variance with his own approach. The proposition approved in *Lennon v McCarthy* that, where normally healthy children are in the playground it is not necessary for them to be under constant supervision, however, "clearly relate[d] to the circumstances of that particular case and [was] not intended to have general application." It was "not any authority that two hundred and twenty four boys from four to eight years of age do not require some continuous supervision when playing in a small schoolyard".

**[16.39]** In the instant case, over a hundred and sixty small boys from four to six years had been running around in half the yard in an area measuring thirty paces by fifteen paces. In these circumstances it was not surprising that the supervisors had failed to notice the "trains" forming and running about before the collision.

**[16.40]** On what Barr J characterised the "crucial aspect" of the case, as to whether the game had been in progress long enough to have given the supervisors the opportunity to stop it before the accident occurred, Barr J concluded that it had: the boys in the junior section had been playing the game "for [a] significant period which was sufficiently long prior to the accident to allow one or other or both supervision teachers to see what was happening and to end it before the accident occurred if they had been keeping a reasonable watch". It followed that they had been negligent in not supervising the children adequately.

**[16.41]** The conclusion is not easy to reconcile with Barr J's earlier explanation of the teachers' failure to see the "trains", not in terms of their neglect, but rather because of the large number of boys in such a small area. If that was the reason then the school might well still be held liable, either for having too many pupils in the yard at the time or too few supervisors, but the teachers themselves should not have to bear the opprobrium of having failed in their duty of supervision.

51. Supreme Court, 13 July 1966 (Barr J). The Supreme Court allowed an appeal on a separate matter (the plaintiff's capacity to give unsworn evidence). On the retrial, the Circuit Court in Sligo held in favour of the school on the liability issue. An appeal to the High Court by the plaintiff was unsuccessful: see Glendenning, *Education and the Law* (1999), p 290, fn 69. See also *Coffee v St Pins National School* Circuit Court Dublin, 18 October 1999, where Judge Smyth imposed liability on a school for lack of a sufficient number of supervisors in a yard, slightly larger than that in *Mapp v Gilhooley*, in which there were 144 pupils and only one supervisor. The plaintiff had been punched by another pupil, who broke his wrist. Judge Smyth appeared to make some consession to the particular resources available to schools since he noted that in the instant case it had "not been suggested that there could not have been an extra teacher supervising".

**[16.42]** *Clarke v O'Gorman*[52] seems a somewhat stringent application of the legal principles. In that case a ten year old boy was injured when he was carried by some older boys across the playground, kicking and screaming, during playtime and deposited with no great ceremony, fracturing his forearm. The trial judge characterised this behavour as "a dangerous kind of horseplay". There was no conflict of evidence and the trial judge found that "it [was] an extremely well run school and that it operate[d] a system of supervision which [could] not seriously be criticised"[53] With regard to the system he said:

> "... one's own common sense will tell ... to have one teacher looking after 35 lively and volatile children and the headmaster moving between the four playgrounds and keeping an eye on each of them is really as much as one could expect and probably more than one would found in a great many schools. I have no doubt that [it] represented a perfectly adequate and proper system."[54]

**[16.43]** The trial judge also accepted the evidence of the teacher who was supervising the yard at the time. She gave evidence that at the time she was correcting another pupil who was in breach of school rules in running onto the grassy bank next to the yard. The teacher was reprimanding "the recalcitrant boy" and was in fact entering his name in her notebook at the time the plaintiff was being carried away.

**[16.44]** The trial judge took the view that the teacher had a momentary lapse of attention to where her attention should have been, even though she was not conscious of what was happening to the plaintiff; the system was fine but it broke down on this occasion and for this he held the school liable. In an interesting passage the learned judge gave his reason in the following language:

> "I accept fully her [the teacher's] evidence that she was not conscious and was not aware of this happening until the boy had actually fallen on the ground. That I am satisfied was so because her attention was distracted by the significantly less serious matter of disciplining the young man who was breaking the rule of going on to the grass. This was the sort of momentary loss of concentration that people in responsible positions and in the ordinary course of life is bound to happen on occasions ... It was unfortunate that on this occasion her attention was distracted more than it should have been by the incident she was dealing with."[55]

**[16.45]** On appeal the Supreme Court upheld the trial judge's approach. A couple of comments are called for. First, the trial judge held that the system of supervision which allocated one teacher to 35 lively students in the playground was faultless. This necessarily involved some risk as being acceptable. It meant, of necessity, that if one student got into difficulty, 34 students could lawfully be ignored for an appropriate amount of time. In normal circumstances in such a case the teacher would not be liable say, if while one student was being attended for a stab wound, another pupil was hit by a third student out of the teacher's sight. That is what acceptance of a 35:1 student-teacher ratio means. It would of course be different if an injury occurs while the teacher is not paying attention, if, for example, he or she was listening to a walkman or doing the crossword. But this is not what

52. Supreme Court affg High Court, 13 February 1996 (Keane J).
53. High Court, 13 February 1996, p 2.
54. High Court, 13 February 1996, p 3.
55. High Court, 13 February 1996, p 5

happened here. In this case the teacher was carefully supervising the playground and attending to an infraction of the rules. There was no lapse of attention. She was carrying out her duties faithfully in the circumstances in a system that the judge found to be faultless. Surely, the injury to the plaintiff was due to the system (35:1 ratio) and not to the carelessness of the teacher. She was, in fact, held liable for not comparing the infringement she was attending to with the infringement that occurred to the plaintiff, even though she was not aware of it, and then for not concluding that the plaintiff's incident was more serious even though she did not know of it. It seems strange to impose liability in such circumstances when her unawareness was solely due to paying proper attention to her supervisory function. It would seem that liability should be imposed only in those circumstances if she was aware of both incidents and did not attend to the more serious or threatening event, or if she was unaware of the second incident because she was not carrying out her supervisory role in a proper fashion. Would any leeway be given to such a teacher if in assessing two simultaneous incidents she does not pick the more serious incident at the time. Perhaps the Supreme Court's holding can be based on a specific perception that the infraction that diverted the reader's attention was so trivial that she should simply have ignored it, having regard to the more pressing demands of supervising potentially more pressing situations of danger and dealt with the infringement at some later time when her attention was not diluted. The difficulty with this rationale is that the Court did not give any clear indication that this was the basis of its decision.

### Supervision Outside Hours

**[16.46]** Clearly it would be wrong to impose on day schools a duty to supervise children day and night: there must be temporal limits to the scope of this duty. Equally clearly, it would seem legalistic and unjust to restrict the duty to the exact limits of school hours. The courts have therefore tried to strike a reasonable balance. In *Ward v Hertfordshire County Council*,[56] an eight-year-old child was injured when she fell against a wall while racing unsupervised in the playground a few minutes before school classes began at 8.55 am. Imposing liability, Hinchcliffe J said:

> "If it is thought necessary to supervise children at 10.45 am, midday and 2.30 pm, surely it is just as necessary to supervise them between 8.30 am and 8.45 am and 8.55 am ... In my judgment reasonable supervision was required, not only during the working day, but also when the children were collected together in the playground before the school starts. I do not suggest that there should necessarily be a continuous supervision from 8.15 am onwards, but there should have been supervision from time to time controlling any risky activity of the children having regard to the proximity of this dangerous wall; and really it is not too much to ask that there should be supervision between 8.30 am or 8.45 am and 8.55 am when the supervision might well have been continuous."

**[16.47]** The judges of the Court of Appeal, reversing Hinchcliffe J, were more anxious to stress the causal irrelevance of lack of supervision at the time of the accident, on the facts of the case, than to address the issue of when a duty to supervise commenced. Salmon LJ appeared to concede tentatively that a duty to supervise existed before the beginning of school hours, but Lord Denning MR seemed unsympathetic to this argument. Cross LJ did not address the issue.

---

56. [1970] 1 All ER 535 (CA).

**[16.48]** In *Mays v Essex County Council*,[57] an eight-year-old pupil was very seriously injured when sliding on ice in the playground a few minutes before school was scheduled to being at 9 am. His action for negligence failed. The Court considered that "unless the school voluntarily adopted responsibility for early arrivals, it was under no legal duty to provide supervision in the playground". The school Head had sent a circular letter to parents requesting them not to bring their children to school too early in the morning and he had quite reasonably thought that most children in November, would have wanted to go straight indoors.[58]

**[16.49]** The High Court of Australia considered the question in far greater detail in *Geyer v Downs*[59] in 1977. The case also was concerned with injuries sustained in a playground before school opened but at a time when a significant number of children had already assembled. The evidence disclosed that the headmaster had some time earlier given instructions that the children were not to run about or play games before school opened but were to sit down and read or talk quietly.

**[16.50]** The High Court held that in these circumstances, the school was under a duty of care for the period before school hours - a duty which the jury had already held had been breached. Stephen J said that:

> "The duty which a schoolmaster owes to his pupil arises from the relationship between them and its temporal ambit will be determined by the circumstances of the relationship on the particular occasion in question."[60]

**[16.51]** In an important passage, he stated that:

> "It is for the schoolmasters and for those who employ them .... to provide facilities whereby the schoolmasterly duty can adequately be discharged during the period for which it is assumed. A schoolmaster's ability or inability to discharge it will determine neither the existence of the duty nor its temporal ambit but only whether or not the duty has been adequately performed. The temporal ambit of the duty will, therefore, depend not at all upon the schoolmaster's ability, however derived, effectively to perform the duty but, rather, upon whether the particular circumstances of the occasion in question reveal that the relationship of schoolmaster and pupil was or was not then in existence. If it was, the duty will apply. It will be for the schoolmaster and those standing behind him to cut their coats according to the cloth, not assuming the relationship when unable to perform the duty which goes with it."[61]

**[16.52]** The concept of "assuming the relationship" suggests a new application of the Hedley Byrne principle. To those who say that they simply cannot discharge the obligation the riposte of the court is that they should have thought of that before undertaking it in the first place. Applied to the question of playground supervision before school hours, the

57. The Times, 4 October 1975.

58. Commenting on this decision, Bloy and Harrison, in *Essential Law for Teachers*, (1980), p 94, state: "The 'early arrivals' mentioned in *Mays v Essex County Council* could be taken to refer only to those children arriving on the premises at such an early hour that it would be unreasonable to expect staff to supervise them. It would be reasonable to expect a teacher to be on duty to supervise children arriving fifteen to twenty minutes before school starts. It would certainly be reasonable for a headteacher to expect members of staff to comply with a request that they should do so."

59. (1977) 138 CLR 91.

60. (1977) 138 CLR 91 at 93.

61. (1977) 138 CLR 91 at 94.

lesson of *Geyer v Downs* is clear: if a school opens its gates to children before school hours it must supervise them adequately. If it cannot provide the necessary supervision then it must close its gates to the children or risk the consequences. Whether this decision encourages or discourages the prevention of accidents has been questioned.

**[16.53]** In *The Trustees of the Roman Catholic Church for the Diocese of Bathurst v Koffman*[62] a twelve year-old pupil at a primary school was injured when he got into an altercation with older pupils of a neighbouring high school while waiting for the school bus outside the high school, which was about three hundred yards from the primary school. The bus did not provide a pick-up service for the primary school. The incident occurred about twenty minutes after the primary school's activities for the day had ended. The primary school provided no supervision for pupils going home by this route.

**[16.54]** The Court of Appeal of New South Wales, by majority, upheld the imposition by the trial court of liability in negligence on the primary school. Counsel for the school sought to derive support from Stephen J's observations in *Geyer v Downs* for the proposition that the school's duty of care was "circumscribed by time": it had a beginning point and an ending point, depending on the period that the school allowed the pupils onto the school premises and "during such further times as the school held itself out as able or willing to supervise the pupils".

**[16.55]** Sheller JA, for the majority of the Court, responded:

> "... I do not think the relationship of teacher and pupil begins each day when the pupil enters the school ground and terminates when the pupil leaves the school ground ... In my opinion the extent and nature of the duty of the teacher to the pupil is dictated by the particular circumstances. I do not think its extent is necessarily measured or limited by the circumstances that the final bell for the day has rung and the pupil has walked out the school gate. The circumstances of a small country high school located beside a quiet street and a primary school located on a busy highway in a big city may be contrasted. In the first case older children leave the environs of the school in comparative safety. In the second small children emerge from the school into a situation of immediate danger. School buses and parents may arrive late. Major streets have to be crossed and so on. Moreover, as happened at Bathurst High School, high spirited children congregate outside the school waiting to be taken home ....
>
> Counsel for the school, legitimately asked rhetorically, whether the duty extended to the journey on the bus or in the case of other pupils during the time they spent walking from the school to their homes. The answer must be that this depends upon the circumstances. Ordinarily I would not expect the duty to be so extended. But if the school were aware that a particular bus driver, who transported its children, was a dangerous driver or that on a particular journey older children habitually and violently bullied younger children, the duty may well extend so far as to require the school to take preventative steps or to warn parents. This duty would be founded in the relationship of teacher and pupil."

**[16.56]** It is also worth nothing that in the Canadian decision of *Bourgeault v Board of Education, St Paul's Roman Catholic School District No 20*,[63] a school was held not liable for injuries sustained by a 14 year-old pupil who fell off a ladder when hanging

---

62. 1996 NSW LEXIS 3020; BC 9603487 (NSW SC). *Cf Wilson Governors of Sacred Heart Roman Catholic Primary School Carlton* [1998] 1 FLR 663.

63. (1977) 82 DLR (3d) 701 (Sask QB).

decorations in the gymnasium for the Christmas concert. The girl had remained on in the school after classes had been completed and after she had been told to go home. Hughes J said that he had considered:

> "whether a duty rested with the defendant to have a member of the teaching staff responsible for touring the school premises after dismissal of classes, to be sure that all students left the building before he or she leaves as the last person, other than the caretaker, to depart the premises ... while the age and grade of children might prompt different responses as to whether such a duty can be said to exist, I do not believe it can be said any such duty was owed to a student of 14 years of age .... and who had received, when possessed with ability to comprehend, instructions to depart for home."

**[16.57]** These decisions in other common law jurisdictions serve as a useful backdrop to another significant Irish decision of five years ago. In several other cases,[64] where a sudden danger arose during playtime which resulted in injury to a child but which was of its nature difficult for the school authorities to foresee or provide against, the Courts have not imposed liability.

**[16.58]** In *Kelly v Gilhooley*,[65] Costello J held that the school authorities were not liable in negligence where a pupil was knocked down by two racing dogs as he was walking down a path on the school premises on his way to class. The school gates were open at the time. Costello J rejected the plaintiff's contention that the gates should have been kept closed:

> "[T]here is very large traffic going into schools such as this in the morning tim[e] and it would be impossible to keep the gates closed even if such a duty was to be cast upon [the authorities], and in order to ensure that if that duty did exist ... if it was fulfilled it would mean putting a teacher or other employee on every gate. This seems too high a standard of care in the circumstances."

**[16.59]** Costello J did not consider that an analogy could be drawn from the position where children were hurt by other children in the playground. There was simply no duty on school authorities to keep stray dogs from getting onto the school premises.

**[16.60]** In *Greene v Mundow*[66] the plaintiff recovered on similar, but perhaps distinguishable, facts. The plaintiff was bitten by a stray dog while playing with other children on the school premises shortly before school commenced. School class began at 9.00 am, but the main gate was opened to admit teachers who drove to school early to avoid the traffic rush. At approximately 8.45, the gates for vehicular traffic were then

---

64. Eg *Clark v Monmouthshire County Council* 52 LGR 246 (CA) – an unintended knife injury during scuffle; *Langham v Wellingborough School* (1932) 101 LJKB 513 (CA) - golf shot in playground; *Gow v Glasgow Education Authority* 1922 SC 260 – a boy unexpectedly jumped on the back of another boy at a school for blind children; *Chilvers v LCC* (1916) 32 TLR 363 (KBD) - child injured eye when he fell on movable lance of a toy soldier. See also *Long v Gardner* (1983) 144 DLR (3d) 73 (Ont HC) - summer camp was not liable for knife injury sustained by a boy at camp during an argument with another boy; event held not foreseeable; *Durham v Public School Bd of Township School area of North Oxford* (1960) 23 DLR (2d) 711 (Ont CA) - wire spring flew into a boy's eye in playground: school was not liable; *H v Pennell* (1987) 46 SASR 158 (SC (In Banco)) - school was not liable where piece of car radio aerial broke away on being violently flicked by pupil over his shoulder; aerial had been returned to pupil after confiscation; irresponsible use not foreseeable.

65. DPIJ: Trinity and Michaelmas Terms 1994, p 86 (High Court, 1 November 1994, Costello J).

66. Circuit Court, 20 January 2000 (Judge McMahon).

closed and the pedestrian gates admitting pupils were opened at approximately 8.50. The children played in the yard until the whistle blew for class to commence, usually about 9.05. The plaintiff arrived at about 8.55 and went around the building to play with her friends. There was between fifty and sixty children in this area when a dog started to chase them. The dog first knocked the plaintiff's elder sister and then chased other children before biting the plaintiff. Judge McMahon had no difficulty in holding that once on the property there was an obligation to supervise the children. The headmaster, in evidence, said that even though most of the teachers were on the premises since 8.30 he did not think it right that he should ask them to supervise before the official class began. (There was a suggestion that there might be a union problem). It was acknowledged that the school had a problem with straying dogs and used to ask individuals walking dogs not to come on the premises; the caretaker used to put the dogs out when he noticed them; and finally, the dog warden was called if a dog persisted or if there was more than one dog on the grounds. Since the gates were open to dogs from 8.00, the possibility of dogs being on the grounds before the children arrived was real. Judge McMahon held that the duty to supervise commenced once the children were allowed onto the premises even if this was before official class time. In the present case this certainly commneced when the pedestrian gates were opened. By then, there were several teachers on the premises, and if there was a union problem with them, the school should make alternative arrangements for that short period. He commented that the school had a caretaker and an assistant caretaker and the period in question, 10-15 minutes, was very short. He had no difficulty in concluding that, were the children supervised, the plaintiff would not have been bitten, since the dog was worrying the other children for some minutes before biting the plaintiff. The duty to supervise was not, according to Judge McMahon, confined to the "official" day, but spilled over to a short period before school when pupils were arriving and to a short period after school when pupils were dispersing. The length of those "spill-over" periods would depend on the facts of each case.

**[16.61]** In *Dolan v Keohane*,[67] a nine-year-old pupil at the defendant's primary school was injured when swinging on the entrance gate of the defendant's secondary school which was across the road from the primary school at a distance of thirty yards. The accident happened at about 3 pm when the primary school pupils were coming home. Children who lived near the school walked or cycled home. Those who lived at a further distance either were collected by car or went home by bus under a private arrangement between their parents and the bus operator. The bus drivers had formerly collected the pupils at a pre-arranged spot at the entrance to the primary school but, after consultation with the Gardaí, had recently moved to a point close to the entrance to the secondary school.

**[16.62]** Keane J at trial and the Supreme Court on appeal rejected the plaintiff's case for negligence. So far as it rested on the allegation of lack of supervision it was accepted that the duty in some cases to supervise did not end at the school gate but, where it did the degree of supervision required varied with the circumstances including the age of the child. In the case of very young children, the duty might include the obligation to ensure that they did not escape from the school where there was any significant traffic, but no

67. Supreme Court, 8 February 1994, affg High Court, 14 February 1992 Keane J. See Byrne & Binchy, *Annual Review of Irish Law 1992*, pp 579-581.

such considerations arose in the instant case. It would be unreasonable to treat the teachers in the primary school as being under any obligation to supervise the plaintiff when he had crossed to the other side of the road and walked an appreciable distance to the gates of the secondary school. Equally, the teachers in the secondary school had not been under any duty to supervise the plaintiff at that point, their duty being confined to their own pupils.

**[16.63]** What is the best approach, therefore, for primary school management to take in relation to supervision before and after school hours? It is plain from the decisions, that there is no specific moment at which the duty of care starts or ends. It all depends on the circumstances of each case. The Department of Education's view[68] that supervision should be provided for a period of at least twenty minutes before school begins is likely to be reflected in court decisions, not because there is any magic in twenty, as opposed to nineteen, minutes but because clearly the duty starts before the bell rings and twenty minutes is a reasonable enough estimate of the minimum period when a sound system of supervision may be expected.

**[16.64]** It is equally clear that there may be cases where the duty to supervise goes well beyond twenty minutes. To a significant extent the existence and scope of this duty can be controlled by effective communication between school management and the parents, involving written notes of acceptance by the parents that pupils are not to arrive before a certain time. Such notes would not however constitute them as magic exemptions from prospective liability. They could be overtaken by events. If all parents signed notes accepting that their children should not arrive before 9 am yet the school playground is full every day at 8.45 am, the court might well hold that a duty to supervise arose because the management had acquiesced in a practice that contradicted the assurances given in the notes.

## Injuries Sustained Off the Premises

**[16.65]** An allegation of negligence may be made against the school where a child is injured off the premises, on account of lack of supervision or because of an inadequate safety system. In *Hosty v McDonagh*[69] in 1973, a ten-year-old child was injured by a car when she came through the school gate at lunch time and ran onto the road. Liability was imposed on the school manager for not having a suitable exit from the school, not having it supervised and allowing the plaintiff onto the road unattended.[70] The judgment of FitzGerald CJ (for the Court) does not expressly state why the child went onto the road or what she should have been doing at the time.

**[16.66]** The liability of a school in this context may extend to injuries sustained by third parties. In *Carmarthenshire County Council v Lewis*[71] a four-year-old pupil at a nursery school got out of the classroom when he was not being supervised and ran through an

---

68. Expressed in a communication to school principals.

69. Supreme Court, 29 May 1973.

70. *Cf* pp 4-5 of FitzGerald CJ's judgment. Liability was also imposed on the teacher in charge, but the basis of liability was not spelt out. *Cf Barnes v Hampshire County Council* [1969] 3 All ER 746 (HL), revsg (1968) 67 LGR 53 (CA); *Hill v Board of School Trustees District No 35 (Langley)* (2000) 2000 BCD Civ J LEXIS 702 (BC, SC).

71. [1955] AC 549 (HL (Eng)).

unlocked gate down a lane into a busy highway. He caused a driver of a lorry to make it swerve so that it struck a telegraph pole, as a result of which the driver was killed.

**[16.67]** Liability was imposed on the school authorities by the English Court of Appeal, on the basis that the lack of supervision by the teacher had been negligent. The House of Lords held that the teacher had not been negligent but still imposed liability on the school authorities because they ought to have anticipated the danger of a child "escaping" in the absence of supervision, whatever the cause of that absence.

## Other Acts of Negligence

**[16.68]** Other acts of negligence may occur in the course of a school day. Two examples will suffice: a teacher or other school employee may leave dangerous things, such as phosphorus,[72] within access of the pupils, or a pupil may be sent on a risky task that is beyond his or her abilities.[73]

**[16.69]** The extent to which schools owe a duty of care towards pupils (and their parents) outside the context of physical injury has yet to be litigated by our Courts. It is possible that they will have to consider whether a badly educated child would have a right of action in negligence against the school on the basis of the school's poor teaching performance.[74]

---

72. *Williams v Eady* (1893) 10 TLR 41 (CA).

73. *Smith v Martin* [1911] 2 KB 775.

74 See, Glendenning, *Education and the Law* (1999), pp 313-317; McGlade-Cooney 'Educational Malpractice - Another American Import?' (1991) 1 Student LR 4; Foster 'Educational Malpractice - Tort for the Untaught?' (1985) V Br Col LR 161; Elson 'A Common Law Remedy for the Educational Harms Caused by Incompetent or Careless Teaching' (1978) 73 Nw ULR 641; Parker 'Educational Malpractice: A Tort is Born' (1991) 39 Clev St LR 301; Rapp 'Note: Reconsidering Educational Liability: Property-Owners as Litigants, Constructive Trust as Remedy' (2000) 18 Yale L & Pol'y R 463. Courts in the United States of America, where this argument has been pressed most strongly, have generally proved unreceptive to it. In England, there is a growing judicial interest in contemplating liability in certain instances: see *X v Bedfordshire County Council* [1995] 2 AC 633 (HL); *Palmer v Tees Health Authority* [1999] Lloyd's Rep Med 351 (CA); *Gallagher v Barrow Wood School Ltd* English CA, 7 October 1999 (LEXIS transcript). In Ireland, litigants have preferred to proceed down the constitutional path. It is clear that a conscious infringement of the right to education under Article 42 can generate liability to pay damages: *Crowley v Ireland* [1980] IR 102 (SC); *Hayes v Irish National Teachers Organisations* [1987] ILRM 651 (HC); *Conway v Irish National Teachers Organisation* [1991] ILRM 497 (SC). The explosion of litigation designed to compel the State to give practical effect to the constitutional guarantee, especially in regard to children (or, indeed, adults: *Sinnott v Ireland* High Court, 4 October 2000 (Barr J)) with special needs (eg *O'Donoghue v Minister for Education* Supreme Court, 6 February 1997 affg with modifications High Court, 27 May 1993 (O'Hanlon J); *FN v Minister for Education* [1995] 1 IR 409 (HC); *Comerford v Minister for Education* [1997] 2 ILRM 134 (HC); *O'Shiel v Minister for Education* [1999] 2 ILRM 241 (HC); *DG v Eastern Health Board* [1998] 1 ILRM 241 (SC); *DB v Minister for Education* [1999] 1 IR 29; *TD v Minister for Education* High Court, 25 February 2000; *cf* Ruane 'The Separation of Powers and Grant of Mandatory Orders to Enforce Constitutional Rights' (2000) 5 BR 416) would suggest that a claim for infringement of the constitutional right to education represents an attractive route for children who have received a deficient education at school. (This appears to be the interpretation given the *Sinnott* judgment by the Minister for Education who has appealed the decision to the Supreme Court: see Oliver 'Anxious Parents, State Await Sinnott Appeal' Irish Times, 1 November 2000).

## Structural Dangers

**[16.70]** A school manager or principal may be liable as occupier of the premises where there is a structural danger.[75] Prior to the enactment of the Occupiers' Liability Act 1995, the pupils were sometimes regarded as invitees[76] but the language used on this question was sometimes not exact and criteria more appropriate to a licensor-licensee relationship were on occasion invoked.[77] There was an added complication. In cases involving schools the injured plaintiff would frequently be alleging a twofold breach of duty, arguing that there was a structural danger and that the school authorities did not adequately supervise the children, having regard to this danger. In such circumstances the school authorities' duty as occupiers tended to be clouded with their broader duty in negligence.[78]

**[16.71]** The language of the occupiers' cases was used in *Courtney v Masterson*,[79] where it was held that a barbed wire fence did not constitute a "concealed trap" to a ten-year-old boy. The fence was, however, in a field adjoining the school playground, which was out-of-bounds for the pupils. The case is really one involving an issue of supervision rather than occupation duties.

**[16.72]** So also in *Lennon v McCarthy*,[80] the Supreme Court held that the case had rightly been withdrawn from the jury where a nine-year-old pupil playing "tig" in a field adjoining his school playground was struck in the eye by a rebounding hawthorn bush

---

74. (contd) One obvious advantage of framing a claim in constitutional terms is that it avoids the threshold difficulty of establishing a duty of care in negligence (though clearly the European Court of Human Rights' decision in *Osman v United Kingdom* [1999] 1 FLR 193 is having the effect of mitigating that problem). It would be rash, however, to suggest that such a constitutional claim would have a great prospect of success. At some point, political decisions as to the provision of resources and personnel to schools become non-justiciable. *O'Reilly v Limerick Corporation* [1989] ILRM 81. For an insightful analysis, see Whyte 'The Right to Education of Children with Special Needs' paper delivered at a Conference on the Law Affecting Primary Schools, held at Trinity College Dublin Law School on 9 October 1999.

75. See also North, *Occupiers' Liability* (1971), pp 68-70.

76. *Cf McKeon v Flynn* (1934) 69 ILTR 61 (CC); *Fryer v Salford Corporation* [1937] 1 All ER 617 (CA) (especially at 622, *per* Scott LJ). See also *Morris v Carnarvon County Council* [1910] 1 KB 159 (KBD), affd [1910] 1 KB 840 (CA). In the King's Bench Division, especially *per* Phillimore J at 167. There was strong emphasis on the fact that the defendants had "invited" the plaintiff to be on the school premises. The Court of Appeal applied a broader general concept of negligence, with less emphasis on the "occupation" element in determining liability. In Canada it has been held that the duty of care owed in the school to a pupil is "higher than that ordinarily owing by an invitor to an invitee": *Cropp v Potashville School Unit No 25* (1977) 81 DLR (3d) 115 at 118 (Sask QB) - reversing previous authorities).

77. *Cf Bohane v Driscoll* [1929] IR 428 (SC); *Courtney v Masterson* [1949] Ir Jur 6 (HC); *Boryszko v Bd of Education of City of Toronto and Bennett-Pratt Ltd* (1962) 33 DLR (2d) 257 (Ont HC), where a child returned from home to play in the school playground after having had his evening meal, he was held to be a licensee: *cf* At 262-263. In *Dolan v Keohane* Supreme Court, 8 February 1994, affg High Court, 14 February 1992 Keane J; counsel for the proprietors of primary and secondary schools, whilst alleging that primary pupil swinging on the gate of secondary school was a trespasser, acknowledged that negligence test should be applied.

78. See, eg *Rich v LCC* [1953] 2 All ER 376 (CA).

79. [1949] Ir Jur 6 at 51.

80. Supreme Court, 13 July 1966.

when chasing another pupil. Ó Dálaigh CJ rejected the argument that a careful father, looking at the field, would have considered it unsuitable to play in. He stated:

> "I am wholly unable to accept this view. It is unreal. Its effect would be to proscribe the playing of ordinary simple games like 'tig' in the ordinary surroundings of rural Ireland. What happened here was an accident such as is inseparable from life ..."[81]

**[16.73]** The Occupiers' Liability Act 1995 has had the following effect in relation to schools. Pupils are clearly "visitors", for the purposes of s 1(1).[82] The school authorities owe "the common duty of care" towards pupils under s 3. In essence this is the same duty as is imposed by the common law in negligence cases. It should be remembered that the Act replaces the former law in relation to occupiers' liability only in respect of dangers existing on the premises.[83] Thus, in those hybrid cases where the claim involves an alleged structural danger combined with an alleged lack of supervision, the court will be called on either to characterise the claim as falling exclusively under, or outside, the legislation, as the case may be or to sever the claims, giving the plaintiff pupils two bites at the cherry: one, under the Act, relating to the structural danger, and the other, under common law negligence principles, for lack of supervision.

**[16.74]** In truth, the difference between the two categories of claim will in most cases be entirely academic, since the essence of both is negligence. One can, however, envisage three principal contexts where the difference may have practical implications. The first concerns the impact of s 5, which enables the occupier by express agreement or notice to restrict his or her duty arising under s 3 to visitors. This entitlement is subject to the requirement (*inter alia*) that the modification be "reasonable in all the circumstances".[84] It may well be that a court would hold any such attempt by the school to limit its duty of care towards its pupils as entirely unreasonable. Most pupils are compelled by law to attend school. They have no option, having read such a notice, to turn on their heel.

---

81. Page 3 of Ó Dálaigh CJ's judgment. See also *Portelance v Board of Trustees of Roman Catholic Separate School for School Section No 5 in Township of Grantham* (1962) 32 DLR (2d) 337 (Ont CCA) a Canadian decision very similar in its facts and legal holding to *Lennon v McCarthy*. *Cf Ward v Hertfordshire County Council* [1970] 1 All ER 535 (CA 1969), revsg [1969] 2 All ER 807 (QBD). See also *Flynn v O'Reilly* DPIJ Trinity and Michaelmas Terms 1996, p 55 (High Court, 31 October 1996, Smith J) affd by Supreme Court, [1999] 1 ILRM 458 - school was not liable where eleven year-old pupil, in a race running backwards, fell on the ground "which may have had slight tufting or indentation" but was not "holed or rutted or so rough or uneven as to be ... hazardous or dangerous ...".
82. A blinkered literal parsing of the definition of "recreational activity" and "recreational user" in s 1(1) could yield an argument that in some instances a pupil attending school falls within the scope of these definitions. A pupil competing in a race on the school's sports day is engaging in a "sporting activity" which is one of the activities specifically identified as a recreational activity. It is to be hoped that the court would adopt a broader purposive interpretation.
83. Section 2(1). Section 8 provides that nothing in the Act is to be construed as affecting any rule of law relating to "any liability imposed on an occupier as a member of a particular class of persons ... including carriers, bailees and employers". It could possibly be argued that school authorities constitute "a particular class of persons", since children have a specific constitutional entitlement of access to education (albeit not inevitably to be provided by schools). It is submitted that this argument should be rejected. The pre-legislation law imposed no distinct principles of liability on school authorities, in contrast to the three categories specifically mentioned in para (6) of s 8.
84. Section 5(2)(b)(i).

**[16.75]** No similar limitation attaches to an agreement between the school authorities and pupils whereby the school authorities purport to restrict the scope of their potential liability in negligence under common law, in respect of their duty to supervise the pupils.[85]

**[16.76]** The second context in which the difference may be important is where a pupil is a trespasser on the school premises. Under the legislation, the occupier owes only a limited duty of care, in respect of dangers existing on the premises,[86] to trespassers. The occupier is merely obliged not to injure the trespasser intentionally nor act with reckless disregard for the trespasser.[87] If we take a fairly common scenario: pupils are strictly instructed not to come to school until fifteen minutes before the classes start. They and their parents are told in clear terms that the school playground is out of bounds before then. A particular pupil turns up twenty minutes before the start of the school day. If he is injured in the playground within a couple of minutes of his arrival, he may be characterised as a trespasser and thus unable to assert a duty of care on the part of the school so far as structural dangers are concerned but he will nonetheless be able to press a claim for negligent lack of supervision at common law.[88] The court would, of course, be entitled to hold that, in the circumstances there was no duty to supervise but it can not reach this conclusion automatically by reason of the mere fact that the pupil had the status of trespasser. The common law is no longer so crude an instrument as to require it to do so.

**[16.77]** Finally it is worth considering the implications for school and for pupils of the establishment of the new category of "recreational users" which the 1995 Act introduced. Section 1(1) of the Act defines "recreational activity" as:

> "any recreational activity conducted, whether alone or with others, in the open air (including any sporting activity), scientific research and nature study so conducted, exploring caves and visiting sites and buildings of historical, architectural, traditional, artistic, archaeological or scientific importance."

**[16.78]** A "recreational user" is defined by s 1(1) as:

> "an entrant who, with or without the occupier's permission or at the occupier's implied invitation, is present on premises without a charge ... being imposed for the purpose of engaging in a recreational activity, but not including an entrant who is present and is -
>
> (a) a member of the occupier's family who is ordinarily resident on the premises,
>
> (b) an entrant who is present at the express invitation of the occupier or such member, or
>
> (c) an entrant who is present with the permission of the occupier or such a member for social reasons connected with the occupier or such member."

**[16.79]** Recreational users are in a very disadvantaged position under the 1995 Act. The occupier of the premises does not owe them any duty of care in negligence in respect of

85. It might be thought unlikely that the court would, under common law, give effect to an agreement between the school and the pupil which it regarded as unreasonable. Yet the common law imposes no function on the courts to police agreements for their reasonableness. The hallmark of contract theory is that the parties, and not the courts, carve out their respective entitlements. The whole question of the validity and enforcement of contracts with minors is, of course, relevant in this context.

86. Section 2(1).

87. Section 4(1).

88. *Green v Mundow* Circuit Court Dublin, 20 January 2000 (McMahon J), Irish Times, 21 January 2000.

dangers existing on the premises. All that the occupier is required to do is not injure them intentionally and not act with reckless disregard for them.[89] The only instance where a higher duty is imposed is where a structure on the premises is provided for use primarily by recreational users. The occupier, in such a case, must take reasonable care to maintain it in a safe condition.[90] Recreational users, thus, are in virtually as bad a position as trespassers under the 1995 legislation.

**[16.80]** Could it be argued that a pupil playing football during break at school is a "recreational user" who is not owed a duty of care in negligence by the school authorities in respect of dangers existing on the premises? The answer is no. The pupil is on the premises, not "for the purpose of engaging in a recreational activity", but because the law requires him or her to be there, because his or her parents so ordain and because, so far as the pupil's own motivation determines the issue, school is where one receives an education. Even if one envisages the case of a student, with no academic interests, who devotes himself or herself tentatively to the sports side of the curriculum it seems inconceivable that a court would hold that his or her presence on the premises on a normal school day during school hours was "for the purpose of engaging in a recreational activity". It might conceivably be otherwise, where pupils, after school hours, or at weekends, resort to the school football or hurling pitch, as they do regularly in many rural areas and perhaps now urban areas also.

**[16.81]** It may be useful to refer to the Idaho case of *Bauer v Minidoka School District No 331*,[91] where a pupil tripped over sprinkler pipes while he was playing football in the school grounds a few minutes before classes commenced. The school obtained summary judgment in its favour by invoking a legislative provision regarding recreational users similar to the1995 Act. The Supreme Court reversed.

**[16.82]** Johnson J, for the Court said:

> "Here, [the plaintiff] was a public school student participating in a game being played at school as the school day was getting under way. [He] was not merely a recreational user of the school premises; he was there as a student entitled to the protection of the district. This relationship is crucial to our decision in holding that the recreational use statute does not apply to this case ...
>
> This special relationship that a student has to a school district would be substantially impaired if the recreational use statute were applied to injuries children suffered while on school premises as students. Students would then bear the risk of defects in school premises.
>
> [The plaintiff] was not the type of recreational user contemplated in the recreational user statute. He was a public school student who came to the school early before classes began to play football with his classmates. If he had come to the school grounds to play a game of football that was not organised or sanctioned by the school on a day when school was not in session, we would have no trouble in applying the statute to limit the liability of the district. Nor would we have any difficulty in applying the statute, if he had come to the school grounds on a school day to play a game of football that was not organised or sanctioned by

89. Section 4(1).

90. Section 4(4).

91. (1989) 116 Idaho 586, 778 P 2d 336.

> the school before the faculty and other students who were not involved in the game began arriving.
>
> The problem we have in applying the recreational use statute to these facts is that [the plaintiff] arrived to play football at the very time that the school was beginning its operations for the day, although no classes had begun. He was not just a member of 'the public' referred to in the recreational use statute. He was there as a student to begin the school day with a game of football. Some students may come early to talk to their teachers, some to visit with their classmates, some to study and others to participate in informal activities such as football. All of these are legitimate activities within the scope of a student's special relationship with the school.
>
> It would be entirely artificial to apply the recreational use statute to activities of students up to the moment the first bell rings and classes begin. No purpose would be served by drawing this line for application of the recreational use statute. When the principal is present some faculty members are on duty and students have arrived, the school day has begun and the recreational use statute has no application to a student who is injured on the school grounds."[92]

**[16.83]** This analysis is helpful but of course one should bear in mind the social, educational and legal differences between Idaho and Ireland. It seems certain that in Ireland, a pupil playing football on school grounds a few minutes before classes commence will be characterised as a visitor and not a recreational user. It is doubtful whether the Irish courts will take the same view as was adopted in the *Bauer* case on the question whether there are some situations where the recreational user characterisation should be attached to pupils on school premises. It is likely that an Irish court would consider a pupil who arrives with a football at the school very early in the morning, before the time that supervision is scheduled to begin, as a visitor rather than a recreational user. He or she is still attending school as a pupil, for predominantly academic purposes. Of course, if the school managers had prohibited attendance before a particular time, the pupil would be a trespasser.

**[16.84]** Where the pupil comes onto school premises with the football on a day when no academic activities are taking place, the pupil should be characterised as a visitor if the sporting activity is, in the broad sense, part of the school programme. So a child who comes on a Saturday to play an organised match against a team from another school will certainly be a visitor. If, however, the school had no organisational input into the game, which was entirely informal, and if the game took place on a day where absolutely no school activities were scheduled, it has to be acknowledged that the case for holding the child to be a recreational user is very much stronger. Again, in the event of an actual prohibition, the pupil should be characterised as a trespasser.

---

92. 778 P 2d 336 at 338-339.

# Chapter 17

# Negligently Inflicted Psychiatric Damage


I. Introduction .......... 461
II. Recent Developments in Irish Law on Nervous Shock .......... 470


## I. INTRODUCTION

**[17.01]** In this chapter we examine the circumstances in which compensation may be due for negligently inflicted psychiatric damage.[1] In 1861, in an Irish appeal to the House of Lords, Lord Wensleydale asserted that:

> "mental pain or anxiety the law cannot value, and does not pretend to redress, when the unlawful act complained of causes that alone."[2]

**[17.02]** We have come a long way since then in our understanding of mental injury and in the willingness of the courts to compensate those who suffer such harm. Nonetheless, as we shall see, there is still a certain judicial hesitation to mental injury as simply an aspect of a broader category of what might be called psycho-physical injury and instead of pigeon-hole mental injury, or even particular sub-species of mental injury, separately from physical injury. This propensity has led the English courts in recent years to refuse compensation to deserving plaintiffs, as a result of blindly following a categorical approach which frankly makes no medical sense. Up to now, the Irish courts have avoided

---

1. See generally Casey & Craven, *Psychiatry and the Law* (1999), Ch 8; Mullany & Handford, *Tort Liability for Psychiatric Damage: the Law of Nervous Shock* (1993); Trindade 'The Principles Covering the Recovery of Damages for Negligently Caused Nervous Shock' [1986] Camb LJ 476; Greer 'A Statutory Remedy for Nervous Shock?' (1986) 21 Ir Jur (ns) 57; Handsley 'Mental Injury Occasioned by Harm to Another: A Feminist Critique' (1996) 14 L & Inequality J 391; Bailey 'The Relevance of Defences to Accident Liability in Nervous Shock Cases' (1983) 3 Legal Stud 43; Goodhart 'Shock Cases and the Area of Risk' (1953) 16 MLR 14; Rendall 'Nervous Shock and Tortious Liability' (1962) 20 OHLJ 291; Goodhart 'Emotional Shock and the Unimaginative Taxicab Driver' (1953) 69 LQR 347; Taff 'The Requirement of "Sudden Shock" in Liability for Negligently Inflicted Psychiatric Damage' (1996) 4 Tort LR 44; Burrows 'Liability for Psychiatric Illness: Whre Sould the Line be Drawn?' (1995) 3 Tort LR 220; Butler 'Identifying the Compensable Damage in "Nervous Shock" Cases' (1997) 5 Torts LJ 67; Green 'Injuries from Fright without Contact' (1966) 15 Clev-Mar LR 331; Merring 'Note: Administering the Tort of Mental Infliction of Mental Distress: A Synthesis' (1973) 4 Cardozo LR 487; Anon 'Damages for Shock Caused by Fear of Immediate Personal Injury to Another Person' (1924) 58 ILT & Sol J 30; Obst 'Nervous Shock - The English Position' (1982) 56 Law Institute J 746; Lambert 'Tort Liability for Psychic Injuries: Overview and Update' (1978) 37 ATLA LJ 1 at 4ff; Anon 'Fright and Its Consequences' (1901) 35 ITL & Sol J 495; Anon 'Negligence Causing Damage by Terror' (1888) 22 ILT & Sol J 347; Burdick 'Tort Liability for Mental Disturbance and Nervous Shock' (1905) 5 Col LR 179.
2. *Lynch v Knight* (1861) 9 HLC 577 at 598, 11 ER 854 at 863 (HL).

going down the same path, but the Supreme Court decision of *Kelly v Hennessy*,[3] gives cause for concern.

**[17.03]** Let us first summarise how the courts approach the subject. There is no problem with a broken leg or a facial scar: these are simply and immediately characterised as physical injuries. However, a plaintiff's loss may be more complex. The scar may cause distress or anxiety and may lead to the development of a psycho-somatic condition. The immobility and loss of employment may result in depression, leading to a suicide attempt. A person may suffer mental injury without any accompanying physical injury such as a broken leg or a scar. The sudden death of a loved one, caused by the defendant's negligence, will foreseeability lead to mental distress, which in turn may lead to depression. The circumstances in which this death comes to the attention of the relative or close friend may themselves be traumatic and may lead to post-traumatic stress disorder (or, as the courts over many years have described it, "nervous shock").

**[17.04]** How should the courts approach the question of compensating mental injury to these various types? Before one can attempt to answer this question, it is surely necessary to address the empirical question of the relationship between "physical" and "mental" injury. Formerly there was a widespread acceptance of the view that some scientifically meaningful distinction could be drawn between the two: physical injuries were real; mental injuries were imagined. They had, no doubt, a reality to the sufferer, but they were considered subjective and variable, incapable of scientific measurement, exposing courts to the risk of self-deceiving or even fraudulent claims.[4] A further reason for segregating mental injury in Victorian times was the social stigma surrounding it and the sense that people of strong moral character should not succumb to their emotions. At a philosophical level, the mental self was regarded as a morally free agent, located in the body but, in some fundamental way, severable from it.

**[17.05]** All of these factors encouraged the courts to remove mental injury from the category of physical injury and to treat it separately, dividing it into discrete sub-groups, where mental distress and post-traumatic stress disorder are considered to generate entirely different legal claims.

**[17.06]** It is most unfortunate that outdated medical thinking should continue to have such an influence on the judicial approach. The modern approach in medicine regards the person as a psycho-physical unit, in which no sharp distinction can be drawn between mental and physical injury. Of course certain injuries can usefully be characterised as mental or physical, but there is a large corpus of conditions where the physical and mental blend or at least affect each other. No medical person today feels comfortable with pigeon-holing conditions into "mental distress", "nervous shock" and so on.

**[17.07]** It would be naive to ignore the wider cultural context. Contemporary psychiatric theory is largely (though by no means exclusively) deterministic. The notion of the morally free mental self "residing in" the body, as it were, has been largely replaced by a

3. [1996] 1 ILRM 321 (SC).

4. *Cf Victorian Railways Commissioners v Coultas* (1888) 13 Appeal Cas 222 (PC). See further Sprince 'Negligently Inflicted Psychiatric Damage: A Medical Diagnosis and Prognosis' 18 Legal Studies 55 (1998).

perception of human emotions and decision-making as the objective product of material scientifically measureable causes.

**[17.08]** Let us now consider the legal dimension. The law of negligence permits compensation where the defendant's negligent conduct has breached a duty of care towards the plaintiff, causing injury of a kind that was reasonably foreseeable by the defendant.[5] In approaching the question of liability for negligently caused mental injury, the courts have addressed primarily the issues of duty, foreseeability and the "egg-shell skull" rule. The solutions they have reached at various times are very much influenced by their empirical starting-point in terms of their understanding of mental injury. Thus, a century ago, the dominant view in common law jurisdictions[6] - though, interestingly, not in Ireland[7] - was that there was no duty to avoid causing "nervous shock" to another. Gradually the judicial opposition crumbled, but came to be replaced by an approach which contained the potential for further injustice and anomalies. This approach was to make the foreseeability of "nervous shock" a necessary (although not always a sufficient) condition of liability.[8] The House of Lords balked at such a conclusion in a case where a plaintiff who was at risk of a foreseeable physical injury, in the traditional sense of that term, in fact suffered an unforeseeable psychiatric response (ME). To resolve the problem, their Lordships rashly launched[9] a new distinction: primary victims, that is, those who were at risk from a foreseeable physical injury in the traditional sense, could recover compensation if instead they suffered an unforeseeable psychiatric response; secondary victims, that is, those who were not at risk from foreseeable physical injury in the traditional sense, could not recover for an unforeseeable psychiatric response. Once the concepts of primary and secondary victims had been adopted as part of the judicial lexicon, they quickly became enmeshed in the complex issue of the duty of care. The House of Lords in *White v Chief Constable of South Yorkshire*[10] held that, whereas the duty of care owed to primary victims was non-problematic, secondary victims had to surmount a series of hurdles, inspired by policy considerations, which had been erected in *McLoughlin v O'Brian*[11] and refined in *Alcock v Chief Constable of South Yorkshire Police*.[12]

**[17.09]** Let us examine briefly the historical development of the law on the subject, before attempting to synthesise the main issues.

**[17.10]** With regard to allowing recovery in respect of what came to be referred to as "nervous shock", the courts hesitated, being fearful of exposing persons to a multiplicity of claims by plaintiffs taking "unrighteous or groundless"[13] actions. Moreover, as we have mentioned there was a feeling, consistent with the philosophy of the times, that mere fright was a somewhat ignoble emotion.

---

5. *Cf* Ch 2.
6. *Cf Victorian Railways Commissars v Coultas* (1888) 13 Appeal Cas 222.
7. *Cf* paras **[17.12]-[17.21]** below.
8. "[T]he test of liability for shock in foreseeability of injury by shock": *King v Phillips* [1953] 1 QB 429 at 441 (CA).
9. *Page v Smith* [1996] AC 155 (HL).
10. [1999] 1 All ER 1 (HL).
11. [1983] AC 410 (HL). See para **[17.26]** below.
12. [1992] 1 AC 310 (HL(Eng) 1991). See para **[17.30]**.
13. *Dulieu v White & Sons* [1901] 2 KB 669 at 681 (CA).

**[17.11]** Over the past century, however, the courts have become increasingly willing to afford such injuries compensation. In this respect, Irish law has been ahead of most other common law jurisdictions. It is only fair to point out that the two leading Irish cases, which were decided in the nineteenth century,[14] concerned plaintiffs who had actually been in the zone of physical danger. The ease with which the courts in both instances were willing to impose liability may thus be deceptive. It is far from clear that the courts would necessarily have been equally receptive to a plaintiff's claim if he or she had suffered nervous shock from merely witnessing an accident involving another person or from being told about it afterwards.

**[17.12]** In *Byrne v Southern and Western Ry Co*,[15] decided in 1882 and affirmed two years later by the Court of Appeal, the plaintiff was superintendent of the telegraph office at the Limerick Junction station of the defendant's railway. His office consisted of a small building at the end of one of the railway sidings, between it and the office a buffer was strongly fixed. One day, on account of the railway points having been negligently left open, a train entered the siding and broke down the buffer and the wall of the telegraph office. On hearing the noise and seeing the wall falling he "sustained a nervous shock which resulted in certain injuries to his health".[16]

**[17.13]** The plaintiff gave somewhat graphic evidence to the effect that:

> "[a] hair of my head was not touched; I swear I received no physical injury; I got a great fright and shock: I do not mean a physical shake; it was the crash and falling in of the office, and shouts of the clerks saying they were killed; I saw part of the office falling in; I believed it was all falling in."

**[17.14]** The plaintiff obtained a verdict of £325 - a substantial figure at that time. A motion to set aside the verdict on the ground that there had been no evidence of injury sufficient to sustain the action was refused by the Common Pleas Division, and this refusal was affirmed by the Court of Appeal.

**[17.15]** This straightforward approach contrasts strongly with that of the Privy Council four years later in *Victoria Ry Commrs v Coultas*.[17] There the plaintiff suffered a severe nervous shock crossing the defendant's railway line when, on account of the defendant's

---

14. A somewhat unclear, more recent decision on the subject is *Hogg v Keane* [1956] IR 155 (SC). It also involved a plaintiff in the zone of physical danger. The plaintiff alleged that she was seated in a stationary car in the town of Carrick-on-Shannon, when the defendant reversed his car into the car in which she was seated. She claimed that she had become so frightened that she attempted to escape from the car and in doing so she struck her head on the interior of the car. She alleged that she had suffered shock and traumatic neurosis which prevented her from attending to her household and family duties. The trial judge withdrew the case from the jury, holding that on the evidence the jury could not reasonably find for her. The Supreme Court ordered a new trial.
There was considerable uncertainty as to whether the plaintiff's injuries resulted from the fright she had sustained or the knock on the head. The Court appears to have favoured the view that in either case she was entitled to claim damages. Maguire J stated that:

> "It was open to her to make the case that her present state was due either to the knock or the fright which she received at that time. Those alternative cases were, in my view open to her."

15. Court of Appeal, February 1884; discussed in *Bell v GN Ry Co* (1890) 26 LR (Ir) 428 at 441-442.
16. 26 LR (Ir) at 442 (*per* Palles CB, referring to plaintiff's case in *Byrne*).
17. (1888) 13 AC 222. Black J, of the former Supreme Court, (extra-judicially) described *Coultas* as a "particularly bad decision"; Black, 'The Doctrine of Precedent in Modern Irish Law', public lecture delivered at Trinity College, Dublin on 5 March 1952).

negligence, a train nearly hit her. A verdict in her favour was reversed on appeal to the Privy Council. Sir Richard Couch stressed the fear that to grant a remedy in such cases would greatly increase the difficulty in determining whether the injury was caused by the defendant's negligence and that "a wide field [would be] opened for imaginary claims".[18]

**[17.16]** In 1890, the issue arose again in Ireland, in *Bell v GN Ry Co.*[19] There the plaintiff, a forty-nine-year-old woman, was a passenger in the defendant's train when part of the train was unhooked and reversed with great speed down a hill. This caused great panic among the passengers. At a curve the train stopped suddenly, and the plaintiff, who was then standing up, was thrown down. The plaintiff suffered severe shock. Her mental health was affected and the medical evidence disclosed that her condition might result in subsequent paralysis. The plaintiff was awarded £50 at trial.

**[17.17]** On appeal, the Exchequer Division was faced with an interesting problem. Its own Court of Appeal in *Byrne's*[20] case had only six years previously held that a case would lie on such facts, yet the Privy Council in *Coultas*[21] scarcely two years before *Bell*[22] had taken the opposite view.

**[17.18]** The Court unanimously took the view that *Byrne*[23] was the preferable decision. Palles CB, with a perception of the relationship between mind and body which was well ahead of his time,[24] criticised *Coultas* for:

> "assum[ing], as a matter of law, that nervous shock is something which affects merely the mental functions, and is not in itself a peculiar physical state of the body. This error pervades the entire judgment."[25]

**[17.19]** Concluding his judgment Palles CB, expressed the view that:

> "as the relation between fright and injury to the nerve and brain structures of the body is a matter which depends entirely upon scientific and medical testimony, it is impossible for any Court to lay down, as a matter of law, that if negligence causes fright, and such fright, in its turn, so affects such structures as to cause injury to health, such injury cannot be 'a consequence which, in the ordinary course of things would flow from the' negligence unless such injury 'accompany such negligence in point of time'."[26]

---

18. (1888) 13 AC 222 at 226. *Cf* Wasmuth 'Medical Evaluation Mental Pain and Suffering' (1957) 6 Clev Mar LR 7 at 7-10.
19. (1890) 26 LR (Ir) 428 (Ex Div).
20. Court of Appeal, February 1884.
21. (1888) 13 AC 222.
22. (1890) 26 LR (Ir) 428.
23. Court of Appeal, February 1884.
24. *Cf* Ryle *The Concept of Mind* (1949).
25. (1890) 26 LR (Ir) 428 at 441. For support of Palles CB's approach in modern medical thinking on nervous shock, *cf* Havard 'Reasonable Foresight of Nervous Shock' (1956) 19 MLR; Smith 'Relation of Emotions to Injury and Disease: Legal Liability for Psychic Stimuli' (1944) 30 Va LR 193; Anon (1971) 59 Geo LJ 1237 at 1248-1253; Crean 'Injuries from Fright Without Contact' (1966) 15 Clev-Mar LR 331 at 340-342.
26. (1890) 26 LR (Ir) 428 at 442.

**[17.20]** Adopting the same approach, Murphy J stated that it appeared to him:

> "immaterial whether the injuries may be called nervous shock, brain disturbance, mental shock or injury. The only questions to be considered, in my opinion, are: was the health or capacity of the plaintiff for the discharge of her duties and enjoyment of life affected by what occurred to her whilst in the carriage? Next, was this caused by the negligence of the defendants?"[27]

**[17.21]** The law in Ireland following *Byrne* and *Bell* appeared reasonably easy to state. The general principle had been accepted that a person who suffered a nervous shock leading to some physical or psychiatric injury might recover damages from the one whose negligence caused this shock. It was not necessary that the nervous shock be accompanied contemporaneously with physical injury: to reject the plaintiff's case where the injury resulted from the shock would be as foolish, in Palles CB's view, as saying that:

> "a death caused by poison is not to be attributed to the person who administered it because the mortal effect is not produced contemporaneously with its administration."[28]

**[17.22]** In both *Byrne*[29] *and Bell*,[30] the foreseeability of the plaintiff's injury was not seriously in doubt. Other cases are, however, less easy to determine.[31] Should a person who witnesses an accident involving a relative and thereupon suffers nervous shock be entitled to recover damages?[32] Does it make any difference that the witness is not related to the victim?[33] What of the case where the "victim" emerges unscathed? May a person who is merely informed[34] of a tragedy or sees its immediate after-effects[35] rather than personally witnessing it recover damages?

**[17.23]** The courts have here faced a dilemma. A straightforward application of the foreseeability test could cast the net of liability very far, since we can easily understand how a person might suffer serious shock from learning of an accident to another, even where there had been no particularly strong bonds of affection between them beforehand. To prevent liability from ranging so widely, courts, in embracing this test, may tend either to come to the unconvincing conclusion that the shock was not foreseeable,[36] or else seek to introduce what are in fact policy limitations under the guise of "factors" to which "due

27. (1890) 26 LR (Ir) 428 at 443.
28. (1890) 26 LR (Ir) at 439.
29. Court of Appeal, February 1884.
30. (1890) 26 LR (Ir) 428.
31. *Cf* Mullany & Handford *Tort Liability for Psychiatric Damage: the Law of Nervous Shock* (1993).
32. *Cf Hambrook v Stokes Bros* [1925] I KB 141 (CA); *Hinz v Berry* [1970] 2 QB 40 (CA).
33. *Cf Chadwick v British Transport Commn* [1967] 2 All ER 845 - rescuer, analysed by Glasbeek 'Nervous Shock and the Rescuer' (1968) 46 Can BR 299; *Mount Isa Mines Ltd v Pusey* (1971) 45 ALJR 88; *Bourhill v Young* [1943] AC 92.
34. *Cf King v Phillips* [1953] 1 QB 429, analysed by Goodhart 'Emotional Shock and the Unimaginative Taxicab Driver' (1953) 69 LQR 347.
35. *Cf Chester v Waverley Corporation* (1939) 62 Comm LR 1; *Storm v Jeeves* [1965] Tas SR 252; *Benson v Lee* [1972] VR 879.
36. *Cf* eg, *King v Phillips* [1953] 1 QB 429 (CA), critically analysed by Goodhart 'Emotional Shock and the Unimaginative Taxicab Driver' (1953) 69 LQR 347; *Brown v Hubar* (1974) 3 OR (2d) 448, criticised by Binchy, (1977) 9 Ottawa LR at 350-352.

regard" must be paid when determining whether the particular plaintiff's shock was foreseeable.[37]

**[17.24]** Some judges have been willing to dispense with such covert limitations, and to declare openly that shock that is without question foreseeable should nonetheless not occasion liability on policy grounds. This approach exposes these judges to the easy criticism that the net has been cast arbitrarily and too narrowly.

**[17.25]** Internationally the balance tilts slightly in favour of the latter approach, but there are some sharp differences of judicial opinion in the highest courts of England and Australia.

**[17.26]** In England, the issue came to the fore in *McLoughlin v O'Brian*.[38] The plaintiff's husband and three children had been involved in a traffic accident caused by the defendant's negligence. One of the children died almost immediately; the husband and the two other children were injured. The plaintiff, who was at home two miles away, was later told of the accident by a motorist who had come on the immediate aftermath of the accident.[39] The motorist drove her to the hospital, where she came upon the surviving members of her family who were in a state of great distress and disarray. The plaintiff suffered severe shock, organic depression and a change of personality.

**[17.27]** The House of Lords[40] held that the plaintiff was entitled to succeed, but there was a clear division of opinion as to why this should be so. Lords Russell, Scarman and Bridge favoured the straightforward application of the reasonable foreseeability test. Lord Bridge accepted the importance of the factors of space, time and relationship "as bearing on the degree of foreseeability of the plaintiff's illness"[41] but opposed the drawing of hard and fast lines of policy. Thus, whether the plaintiff was close to the accident, whether the shock resulted from witnessing the accident rather than hearing about it, and whether the plaintiff and the accident victim were closely related were all matters impinging on the issue of foreseeability rather than constituting criteria by which "a largely arbitrary limit of liability"[42] should be determined.

**[17.28]** Lords Wilberforce and Edmund-Davies did not agree with this approach. Lord Wilberforce considered that, because nervous shock was capable of affecting so wide a range of people, there was "a real need for the law to place some limitation on the extent of admissible claims".[43] He considered that this limitation should affect the class of persons whose claims were to be recognised, the proximity of these persons to the accident and the

37. *Cf* Lord Bridge's speech in *McLoughlin v O'Brian* [1983] AC 410, relying of the lead of Tobriner J, in the California Supreme Court decision of *Dillon v Legg* (1968) 68 Cal 2d 728 at 740 741.

38. [1983] 1 AC 410, analysed by Teff, (1983) 99 LQR 100; Owen, [1983] Camb LJ 41; Hutchinson & Morgan, (1982) 45 MLR 694; Street, (1983) 34 NILQ 53.

39. Another child of the plaintiff was a passenger in this motorist's car. He was not injured.

40. Reversing Boreham J (who held the plaintiff's nervous shock was not reasonably foreseeable) and the Court of Appeal (who considered that the nervous shock was reasonably foreseeable but that either on grounds of policy (*per* Stephenson LJ) or lack of duty of care (*per* Griffiths LJ) no action lay: [1981] QB 599).

41. [1983] 1 AC 410 at 442.

42. [1983] 1 AC 410 at 442.

43. [1983] 1 AC 410 at 442.

means by which the shock was caused. Thus, only those with a very close relationship to the person injured in the accident could sue. This class would certainly include parents, children, husbands and wives, but beyond this he was not willing to commit himself, save to note that "[t]he closer the tie (not merely in relationship, but in care) the greater the claim for consideration".

**[17.29]** As regards proximity to the accident, Lord Wilberforce regarded it as "obvious that this must be close in both time and space". A strict test of proximity by sight or hearing should be applied, save for those who came on the scene very soon after the accident or those "of whom it could be said that one could expect nothing else than that [they] would come immediately to the scene - normally a parent or spouse.[44] As regards communication, Lord Wilberforce ruled out cases where a person suffers nervous shock on being informed of a calamity affecting a loved one: the shock would have to come through either sight or hearing of the event or its immediate aftermath, or possibly through some equivalent of sight and hearing, such as simultaneous television.[45]

**[17.30]** *McLoughlin v O'Brian* was reconsidered by the House of Lords nine years later in *Alcock v Chief Constable of South Yorkshire Police*.[46] The case resulted from the tragedy at Hillsborough where nearly a hundred people died and many hundreds were injured in a crush at a football stadium; the overcrowding had been caused by negligent management on the part of the police. Several relatives and close friends of those who had died or been injured sought compensation for the psychiatric injuries they sustained from the trauma.

**[17.31]** Broadly speaking, Lord Wilberforce's approach triumphed in *Alcock*. As regards his first policy requirement, of close relationship between the plaintiff and the person who was injured or killed their Lordships were willing to express it in terms of reasonable forseeability. Spouses, parents and children would normally come within the scope of reasonable foreseeability without any great difficulty; others were not excluded *a priori* and in some cases could have a demonstrably strong claim, as, for example, where the plaintiff has lived with the primary victim "for forty years, both being under the belief that they were lawfully married".[47] *Sillinap* would not pass the test so easily – their claims failed in *Alcock* – but a plaintiff who was engaged to the primary victim would be likely to claim a higher degree of foreseeability of suffering nervous shock. While bystanders would generally not be able to assert that their psychiatric injuries were foreseeable, there should be no inflexible rule of exclusion. Lord Ackner gave the example of a petrol tanker running out of control into a school in session and busting into flames.[48]

**[17.32]** Lord Wilberforce's second and third requirements, of proximity of time and space and of the means of communication, were applied in *Alcock* without modification. So far as time was concerned, many of the plaintiffs' claims failed because of the fact that several hours had elapsed before they came upon their deceased loved ones in the morgue.

44. [1983] 1 AC 410 at 442.

45. [1983] 1 AC 410 at 441 and 423. In the United States, proceedings for shock resulting from what was seen on television have fared badly for plaintiffs, even where the shock was based on concern for relatives whose injury or death was portrayed on the screen: see Andrews (1987) 17 Sw ULR 65.

46. [1992] 1 AC 310 (HL).

47. [1992] 1 AC 310 at 416 (*per* Lord Oliver).

48. [1992] 1 AC 310 at 403.

Witnessing a horrifying event on television or radio would not generally suffice though no absolute barrier to a claim based on such an experience was adopted. Lord Achner adopted[49] the example proffered by Nolan LJ in the Court of Appeal[50] of the transmission by television of a special event of children travelling in a balloon, in which there was media interest, particularly among the parents, where the balloon suddenly burst into flames.

**[17.33]** Their Lordships in *Alcock* did not flinch at the rule that psychiatric injury resulting from being informed of a horrifying event, rather than witnessing it or its aftermath directly, should not be compensated. On that basis, Lord Ackner considered it:

> "open to serious doubt whether *Hevican v Ruane*[51] and *Ravenscroft v Rederiaktiebolaget Transatlantic*[52] were correctly decided, since the psychiatric illness would appear to have been the fact of a son's death and the news of it."[53]

**[17.34]** In *Jaensch v Coffey*,[54] the High Court of Australia addressed the issue, on facts similar to those in *McLoughlin v O'Brian*. The plaintiff's husband had been injured in a traffic accident. She suffered severe anxiety and depression after having gone to the hospital and witnessed his condition. The High Court unanimously upheld the trial Court's verdict in favour of the plaintiff, but the judges were divided as to the basis of liability. Brennan J echoed Lords Bridge and Scarman in requiring only reasonable foreseeability of the plaintiff's injury. Gibbs CJ, Deane and Murphy JJ echoed Lords Wilberforce and Edmund-Davies in requiring the plaintiff to surmount an additional barrier of policy.[55] However, they were not willing to draw the lines of liability as narrowly as Lord Wilberforce had done. Thus, Deane J was willing to allow recovery in a case where the plaintiff was so devastated by being told of the accident involving members of his or her family that he or she was unable to attend at the scene. In rejecting a rationale based on considerations of physical proximity, in the sense of space and time, between the accident and its immediate aftermath, and the injury, Deane J posited an alternative criterion of reference to "considerations of causal proximity".[56] This admixture of causation and duty issues[57] is not likely to assist clarity of judicial thought on the subject.

---

49. [1992] 1 AC 310 at 405.
50. [1992] 1 AC 310 at 386-387.
51. [1991] 3 All ER 65 (QB).
52. [1991] 3 All ER 73 (QB), revg [1992] 2 All ER 470n (CA).
53. [1992] 1 AC 310 at 398.
54. (1984) 54 ALR 417 (HC, Austr), analysed by Trindade, (1975) 5 Oxford J of Legal Stud 305; O'Connell & Evans, (1985) 15 Melbourne ULR 164 and Partlett, (1985) 59 Aust LJ 44.
55. Dawson J also preferred to limit the foreseeability test by policy considerations but was not disposed to spell them out.
56. 54 ALR at 462.
57. In *Beecham v Hughes* (1988) 45 CCLT 1 (BCCA), Lambert JA saw merit in this approach, going so far as to propose (at 54) "a composite answer, based on foreseeability, proximity, causation and remoteness ...".

## II. Recent Developments in Irish Law on Nervous Shock

**[17.35]** The Irish courts have addressed the issue in detail[58] in two recent decisions: *Mullally v Bus Éireann*[59] and *Kelly v Hennessy*.[60] In *Mullally v Bus Éireann*, the plaintiff's husband and children were involved in a serious bus accident caused by the negligence of the defendants' employee. The plaintiff learned of the accident when on a visit to another town with her brother and mother. Her brother received a telephone message from his sister-in-law as well as a visit from the Gardaí. The plaintiff, aware that something was wrong, telephoned one hospital and was told that one of her sons, Francis, was "very bad"; she telephoned another hospital and was told that her husband was dying and that a second son, Tom, was also there. She could not at this time establish where her third son, Paul, had been taken.

**[17.36]** The plaintiff was first driven to her home, when she was told that Paul was in the same hospital as Francis. She went to that hospital where she discovered a scene familiar to a field hospital. Denham J stated that "[t]here were bodies" everywhere, people moaning and groaning and many distressed relatives around. Her son, Paul, presented a most distressing sight, with blood oozing from his wounds and with tubes attached to his arms and nose and in his mouth. The plaintiff became very aggressive and angry with the medical personnel. She later came upon Francis, who was "beyond recognition", with serious injuries to his face, nose, teeth and head.

**[17.37]** The plaintiff then went to the other hospital. The scene there was not as bad because the passage of time since the accident had enabled matters to be more under control. Her husband nonetheless presented a very distressing sight. He was obviously very ill and fighting for his life. The plaintiff then went to see Tom, who was having his ear stitched. He was crying and upset but in a much better condition than his father. At this time the plaintiff was walking and talking mechanically but when she went home she became hysterical and rejected attempts by others to comfort her.

58. In two earlier decisions, Irish courts have addressed the issue of nervous shock, but in neither did the question of the range of entitlement to sue require resolution. *State (Keegan) v The Stardust Victims Compensation Tribunal* [1987] ILRM 202 involved proceedings for judicial review of the failure to make an *ex gratia* award of compensation for nervous shock by the Tribunal set up after the Stardust fire tragedy. The Tribunal had adjudicated the claim in the light of the concession of the Attorney General, that the proper test to apply was that set out by Lord Wilberforce in *McLoughlin v O'Brian*. Finlay CJ and Henchy and Griffin JJ went to some lengths to reserve their position as to the correctness of this test. The only matter of substance which can be gleaned from the decision so far as the parameters of liability are concerned is that grief will not give rise to liability for damages (save, of course, under the specific statutory provisions relating to mental distress). The same point was reiterated by Costello J in *Hosford v Murphy* [1988] ILRM 300. See further Greer 'A Statutory Remedy for Nervous Shock?' (1986) 21 Ir Jur (ns) 57. Another Irish decision in which *McLoughlin v O'Brian* played a less than central role was *O'Dowd v Secretary of State* [1982] NI 210 (CA), considered by Greer 'A Statutory Remedy for Nervous Shock?' (1986) 21 Ir Jur (ns) 57, and by Street, (1983) 34 NILQ 53.

59. [1992] ILRM 722 (HC).

60. [1996] 1 ILRM 321.

**[17.38]** In the months afterwards, the condition of plaintiff's husband and of Francis and Tom gradually improved. The outcome for Paul was tragic. After nine months' of disability, accompanied at times by great suffering, and after several operations, he died.

**[17.39]** The plaintiff's psychological state had changed radically from what it had been before the accident. Denham J noted that:

> "[s]he put down the shutters. She became very reserved. A new person emerged. She put all emotion aside ... Her personality changed. She appeared frozen ..."[61]

**[17.40]** Denham J found that the plaintiff had the symptoms consistent with post-traumatic stress disorder. She accepted the DSM III-R criteria for this condition, as set out in Brian McGuire's article in the Irish Journal of Psychology 1990, at p 4. These are:

1. Exposure to a recognisable stress or trauma outside the range of usual human experience, which would evoke significant symptoms of distress in almost anyone.
2. Re-experiencing the trauma through intrusive memories, nightmares or flashbacks or intensification of symptoms through exposure to situations resembling or symbolising the event.
3. Avoidance of stimuli related to the trauma or numbing of general responsiveness indicated by avoidance of thoughts or feelings, or of situations associated with the trauma, amnesia for important aspects of the trauma, diminished interest in activities, feelings of estrangement from others, constricted affect, sense of foreshortened future.
4. Increased arousal indicated by sleep disturbance, anger outbursts, difficulty concentrating, higher vigilance, exaggerated startle response, psychologically reactivity to situations resembling or symbolising the trauma.
5. Duration of disturbance at least one month.

**[17.41]** Denham J for the purpose of the judgment, found that post-traumatic stress disorder "is a psychiatric disease".[62] The plaintiff's condition had been caused by the accident and its aftermath, not her grief. Applying "the ordinary criteria of reasonable foreseeability"[63] to the facts, and in view of the "ever-advancing awareness of medical knowledge of mental illness",[64] Denham J considered that it was readily foreseeable that a mother exposed to the experience that the plaintiff had gone through would break down and suffer illness. She considered that there was:

> "no policy in Irish law opposed to a finding of nervous shock, an old term covering post-traumatic stress disorder. Indeed the Irish courts were one of the first to find that such an illness existed and was compensatable ..."[65]

**[17.42]** Denham J here quoted passages from *Byrne v Southern & Western Rly Co* and *Bell v GN Rly Co*. In a crucial passage, she stated:

> "Thus the law is that a person who suffers nervous shock which results in psychiatric illness

61. [1992] ILRM 722 at 727.
62. [1992] ILRM 722 at 728. See further Casey & Craven, *Psychiatry and the Law* (1999), Ch 6 and 7.
63. [1992] ILRM 722 at 730.
64. [1992] ILRM 722 at 730.
65. [1992] ILRM 722 at 730.

may succeed against the person who caused the nervous shock. The question then is whether the causation nexus exists between the defendants' negligence and the plaintiff's illness as the plaintiff was not at the scene of the accident.

It appears to me that the causal link is there; that the illness was reasonably foreseeable. The facts of this case clearly establish an horrific situation for the plaintiff from the time of learning of the accident, through her journey to the hospital, to the appalling sights at the hospital, the terrifying sights of her sons Paul and Francis, and the fact of her apparently dying husband. All these events were caused by the accident caused by the defendants. It would be unjust, and contrary to the fundamental doctrine of negligence, not to find that there is a legal nexus between the actions of the defendants causing the accident, and the resultant aftermath in the scenes in the hospital ... and the injuries of the plaintiff's three sons and husband. There was no ... cause of the scenes in the hospital or the injuries to the children and the husband other than the defendant's negligence. The shock of the plaintiff was foreseeable. The duty of care of the defendants extends as to injuries which are reasonably foreseeable. Thus the defendants had a duty of care to the plaintiff. I consider that there is no bar in law, or under the Constitution, to this determination. If it causes commercial concern then that is a matter for another place, where a policy can be established in the law. It appears to me to come under the fundamental principles of the law of negligence to hold the defendants liable for reasonably foreseeable psychiatric illness caused by [their] negligence."[66]

**[17.43]** Denham J went on to observe that she had been assisted by the House of Lords decision in *McLoughlin v O'Brian*.[67] She added that, while the instant case appeared to fall within the parameters set by Lord Wilberforce, she was "guided more by Lord Bridge".[68]

**[17.44]** It should be noted that at the time when Denham J delivered her judgment in *Mullally*, the House of Lords had not yet handed down the judgment in *Alcock*.[69] There is a striking contrast between Denham J's approach and that favoured by the Lord Wilberforce in *McLoughlin* which was substantially endorsed in *Alcock*. For Denham J the policy question as to compensation for nervous shock was a threshold one, which should be resolved in favour of permitting compensation for this category of injury. Denham J evinced no interest in prescribing the three limitations favoured by Lord Wilberforce. Does this mean, therefore, that *Mullally* is a clear precedent for a victory for plaintiffs in a factual situation similar to *Alcock*? Specifically, should brothers and brothers-in-law be entitled to recover, and should the fact that they witness the shocking event on television be no barrier to their claims? The general tenor of Denham J's judgment would suggest that these plaintiffs would succeed, but it is wise to sound two notes of caution. First, she expressed no dissent from Lord Wilberforce's approach and went so far as to note that the facts of *Mullally* appeared to fall within the parameters that Lord Wilberforce had set. Secondly, Lord Bridge's favoured approach of foreseeability, as we have seen, contains a strong element of underlying policy. This suggests that, even applying a foreseeability test, an Irish court could well hold against some plaintiffs who suffer nervous shock. There are precedents in other jurisdictions that show that such an outcome could well occur.

66. [1992] ILRM 722 at 731.
67. [1983] 1 AC 410.
68. [1992] ILRM 722 at 731.
69. *Alcock v Chief Constable of South Yorkshire Police* [1992] 1 AC 310 (HC).

**[17.45]** In *Kelly v Hennessy*,[70] the Supreme Court addressed the issue. Again the facts were tragic. The plaintiff was a married woman, the mother of two daughters and a son. One evening, her husband and daughters left the family home in County Meath to travel to Dublin Airport to collect the plaintiff's niece, who was arriving on a flight from abroad. Some time after 9.30 pm the niece telephoned the plaintiff and informed her that her husband and daughters had been seriously injured in a road accident. The plaintiff "immediately went into shock, became upset and commenced vomiting". Her neighbours took her to Jervis Street Hospital to see her family. She was ill during the journey. When she arrived at the hospital she saw her husband and daughters "each of whom w[as] in an appalling condition and one of whom she .... described as looking like mince meat".[71]

**[17.46]** Thereafter, the plaintiff "lead a traumatised existence".[72] Her husband remained in hospital for over three months. He suffered permanent brain damage, needing to be bathed and cared for by the plaintiff. One of the plaintiff's daughters, who was hospitalised for over a year, was also brain damaged "and a serious problem to her mother at home".[73] The other daughter, who was in hospital for nine months, made a full recovery from her injuries.

**[17.47]** At trial, Lavan J accepted that the plaintiff was "a genuine, gentle and caring human being".[74] He added "No greater love for one's family have I ever witnessed."[75] The medical evidence established that the plaintiff had suffered immediate shock resulting in vomiting on receiving the telephone call and that this condition had been "gravely aggravated by scenes she immediately thereafter witnessed in Jervis Street Hospital".[76] The post-traumatic stress disorder had continued until 1992, at the earliest; the plaintiff continued to suffer a serious depression and Lavan J doubted whether she would ever fully recover from what he perceived to be a clear psychiatric illness. He rejected the defendant's argument that the plaintiff's failure to acknowledge her pain, grief and depression constituted in law a failure to mitigate her damages. This conclusion would seem eminently sustainable. The doctrine of failure to mitigate damages is not intended to capture complex internal psychological strategies for coping with personal tragedy. The "egg shell skull" rule ensures that a plaintiff will receive compensation in such circumstances.

**[17.48]** In his legal discussion of the substantive issue of the scope of liability for negligently caused nervous shock, Lavan J noted that *Mullally* was not binding on him but that it was "of strong persuasive authority, being a judgment of the High Court".[77] Having considered all of the leading judicial authorities in Ireland and England, he adopted the view of Denham J in *Mullally* and held that the plaintiff was entitled to recover as against the defendant for nervous shock. He awarded the plaintiff £75,000.

---

70. [1996] 1 ILRM 321. See Bredin 'Nervous Shock and the Secondary Victim' (1997) 3 BR 133.
71. [1993] ILRM 530 at 532 (HC).
72. [1993] ILRM 530 at 532 (HC).
73. [1993] ILRM 530 at 533 (HC).
74. [1993] ILRM 530 at 533 (HC).
75. [1993] ILRM 530 at 533 (HC).
76. [1993] ILRM 530 at 533 (HC).
77. [1993] ILRM 530 at 534 (HC).

**[17.49]** The Supreme Court affirmed Lavan J. Two judgments were delivered: by Hamilton CJ (Egan J concurring) and Denham J. Since nuanced differences as to the basis and scope of liability can be detected in the judgments, it may be useful to subject them to close analysis.

**[17.50]** Hamilton CJ identified five requirements of a successful claim for nervous shock:

1. The plaintiff must establish that he or she suffered a recognisable psychiatric illness.
2. This illness must have been "'shock induced'".[78]
3. The nervous shock must have been caused by the defendant's act or omission.
4. The nervous shock must have been "by reason of actual or apprehended physical injury to the plaintiff or a person other than the plaintiff".[79]
5. The plaintiff must show that "the defendant owed him or her a duty of care not to cause him [or her] a reasonably foreseeable injury in the form of nervous shock".[80]

**[17.51]** From the standpoint of the general development of the law in this area, only the fifth of these requirements is a matter of debate (though, in the particular context of *Kelly v Hennessy*, the second requirement was strongly contested by the defendant).

**[17.52]** As regards the fifth requirement, Hamilton CJ noted that the question of who came within the scope of those to whom a defendant owed a duty of care had arisen in many cases and was the subject of continuing debate. The fact that the plaintiff came within the scope of the defendant's duty of care was not, however, an issue in the instant case.

**[17.53]** The Chief Justice nonetheless enlarged on the duty question in a way that makes it difficult to state with confidence how he wished to resolve the issues that had divided courts of ultimate resort in other jurisdictions. It appears that he broadly favoured the notion that a rein should be applied to the scope of duty of care and that there was merit in Lord Wilbeforce's approach in *McLoughlin v O'Brian* but there is also evidence in his analysis suggesting that he did not favour resorting (*expressis verbis*, at all events) to policy considerations and that the parameters of liability be preferred were framed more broadly that those of Lord Wilberforce or of the House of Lords in *Alcock*.

**[17.54]** Hamilton CJ observed that:

> "the law permits of the recovery of damages for nervous shock and psychiatric illness induced thereby where a plaintiff comes on the immediate aftermath of the accident." [81]

This appears to echo Lord Wilberforce's second policy requirement, though it is to be noted that the Chief Justice did not expressly limit liability at this point. His approving references to *McLoughlin v O'Brian* and *Jaensch v Coffey* on the aftermath issue suggest strongly that he was willing to draw the line at the same point as was done in these cases.

**[17.55]** The Chief Justice went on to state that "[t]he relationship between the plaintiff and the person injured must be close".[82] He specifically endorsed Lord Wilberforce's comment

78. [1996] 1 ILRM 321 at 325 (SC).
79. [1996] 1 ILRM 321 at 326 (SC)
80. [1996] 1 ILRM 321 at 326 (SC)
81. [1996] 1 ILRM 321 at 385 (SC)
82. [1996] 1 ILRM 321 at 328 (SC).

in *McLoughlin v O'Brian* that "[t]he closer the tie (not merely in relationship, but in care) the greater the claim for consideration."[83]

**[17.56]** Hamilton CJ commented that the plaintiff's ties to her husband and daughter "could not be closer...".[84] He said nothing more on this issue so it is a matter of wasteful speculation as to whether his cut-off point for closeness of relationship coincided with *McLoughlin v O'Brian* or *Alcock* or was somewhat more expansive than either of them.

**[17.57]** Hamilton CJ went on to consider, and reject, the defendant's argument that the plaintiff's injury could in substantial part be attributed to the extra strain placed on her from having to care on an ongoing basis for her seriously injured husband and daughter.

**[17.58]** Denham J's judgment is of particular interest because she moved perceptibly from the position she had adopted in *Mullally*, where she had expressed a clear preference for a simple foreseeability test of liability. She now laid a far greater emphasis on the matter of proximity:

> "This case turns on the issue of proximity. These may include: (a) proximity of relationship between persons; (b) proximity in a spatial context; and (c) proximity in a temporal sense."[85]

**[17.59]** Denham J considered that "[t]he proximity of relationship between the primary victim and the secondary victim" was "a critical factor".[86] In the instant case there was "a close relationship"[87] between the plaintiff and those who were injured in the accident. This concept was thus not an issue.

**[17.60]** As regards spatial proximity, Denham J noted that, while the plaintiff had not been at the scene of the accident, she had been told of the event on the telephone shortly thereafter and had gone immediately to the hospital where she had "viewed her loved ones who were in a very serious condition".[88] As far as Denham J was concerned this meant that the plaintiff had "perceived the aftermath of the road traffic accident in the hospital".[89] Therefore this element was not in contention.

**[17.61]** Denham J observed that it was on the issue of proximity in time that the case turned. She noted that the defendant's contention had been that the plaintiff's post-traumatic stress disorder had arisen later in time than the accident, as a result of the events in the weeks and months after the accident. She considered that Lavan J's holding to the contrary was based on credible evidence and that it should be upheld.

**[17.62]** Denham J then proceeded to review the law on the duty issue as it had been stated by Lords Bridge and Wilberforce in *McLoughlin v O'Brian* and the judges of the High Court of Australia in *Jaensch v Coffey*. She referred to the verdict at which she had arrived in *Mullally v Bus Éireann*, without making any reference to its basis in principle.

83. [1983] 1 AC 401 at 422 (HC).
84. [1996] 1 ILRM 321 at 329 (SC).
85. [1996] 1 ILRM 321 at 335 (SC).
86. [1996] 1 ILRM 321 at 336 (SC).
87. [1996] 1 ILRM 321 at 336 (SC).
88. [1996] 1 ILRM 321 at 336 (SC).
89. [1996] 1 ILRM 321 at 336 (SC).

**[17.63]** Denham J's conclusions must be quoted in full:

> "I have considered the above cases and the 'neighbour' principle in *Donoghue v Stevenson*. It is not necessary in this case to choose between either the general or the more restricted approach in common law. I have used the cases to isolate factors which are relevant in law and applied these factors to the facts in this case. The relationship of the [plaintiff] to the victims who were participants in the accident could not be closer, the victims were her daughter and husband who with her formed a close loving family. The [plaintiff] was drawn into the trauma by a telephone call. She went to the hospital as soon as practicable. She saw the seriously injured victims in the immediate aftermath of the accident when they were in so serious a state of injury as to be disturbing to the normal person. She was told of the serious nature of the injuries of her husband, but especially the serious injuries of her daughter ...
>
> I am satisfied that a person with a close proximate relationship to an injured person, such as the [plaintiff], who, while not a participant in an accident hears of it very soon after and who visits the injured person as soon as practicable, and who is exposed to serious injuries of the primary victims in such a way as to cause a psychiatric illness, then she becomes a secondary victim to the accident."[90]

**[17.64]** In the wake of *Kelly v Hennessy*, it is not easy to state with any certainty the principles of law that govern the question of liability for negligently caused "nervous shock". It seems that the straightforward foreseeability test favoured by Denham J in *Mullally* has not sufficient judicial support to claim for it the orthodox position: Hamilton CJ did not embrace it and Denham J herself did not do so unequivocally in *Kelly*. Clearly, the issue will be determined by reference to the metaphor of proximity of relationship. While there are some phrases in the judgments of Hamilton CJ and Denham that lend support to the view that the Irish courts will look with sympathy on the strict policy limitations as to time and means of communication which found favour in *Alcock*, it seems more likely that instead the Irish courts will prefer to decide future cases, raising more troublesome borderline issues of liability than either *Mullaly* or *Kelly*, by reference to the proximity mantra rather than by invoking *a priori* policy-based rules of exclusion. Doubtless the decision of the European Court of Human Rights in *Osman v United Kingdom*[91] cases it shadow over this area of the law.

## III. Primary and Secondary Victims

**[17.65]** Finally, we must refer briefly to a distinction between "primary" and "secondary" victims which has gained currency in the British courts in recent years. Those who are primary victims benefit from the characterisations in two ways: they may obtain compensation for unforeseeable psychiatric injury[92] and they are not subject to the policy limitations prescribed by the House of Lords in *Alcock*. It is thus a matter of some practical significance whether a plaintiff is characterised as a primary or secondary victim. The essence of the distinction appears to be based on whether or not one was a foreseeable participant in the accident which generated the psychiatric injury: if one was, and

90. [1996] 1 ILRM 321 at 340 (SC).

91. [1999] 1 FLR 193.

92. *Page v Smyth* [1996] AC 155. *Cf* the Australian decisions analysed by Butler 'A "Kind of Damage": Removing the "Shock" from "Nervous Shock" (1997) 5 Torts LJ 255.

sustained physical injury or psychiatric injury, compensation for the psychiatric injury will be forthcoming.

**[17.66]** Much criticism has been made of this distinction. Two may be mentioned. It extends the scope of liability too far in one respect, by requiring a defendant to compensate a plaintiff for entirely unforeseeable psychiatric injury merely because the defendant risked causing, but did not in fact cause, physical injury to the plaintiff. If a distinction is to be made between physical and psychiatric injuries for the purposes of remoteness of damage, this outcome cannot easily be supported unless one has resort to the "egg shell skull" rule. Secondly, and of greater relevance in the present context, the judicial acceptance of a distinction between primary and secondary victims is likely to have the effect of writing in stone the policy limitations prescribed in *Alcock*, removing the possibility, in the short term at least, of the courts' moving to embrace a more flexible proximity criterion or, more radically, the reasonable foreseeability test favoured by Lord Bridge in *McLoughlin v O'Brian*. Moreover, as the British case-law[93] shows, judicial consideration of the scope of duty owed to such claimants as police and fire fighters who suffer "nervous shock" in the course of their employment can get side-lined into a semantic debate about whether they can aspire to the rosette of a "primary victim" characterisation.

**[17.67]** In *Curran v Cadbury Ireland Ltd*,[94] Judge McMahon noted the criticisms that the English Law Commission had made[95] of the distinction between primary and secondary victims. He observed:

> "For my own part, I am not convinced that the separation of victims into these two categories does any thing to assist the development of legal principles that should guide the courts in this complex area of the law. Hamilton CJ (with whom Egan J agreed) did not refer to the distinction in *Kelly v Hennessy*, the leading Irish case on the matter, and while Denham J in the same case used the term 'secondary victim' to describe the aftermath relatives who were plaintiffs in that case, her primary focus was naturally on the plaintiffs before her rather than on persons who were more directly involved in the accident."[96]

**[17.68]** In the instant case, Judge McMahon awarded compensation to the plaintiff, who sustained psychiatric injury when, on turning on a machine where she worked, she believed with good reason that she had killed or seriously injured a fellow employee who was working inside the machine without her knowledge. It was clear that, on Denham J's definition of a primary victim, the plaintiff came within its scope. The plaintiff had unwittingly become an essential link in the causative chain that resulted in injury to her colleague. Her injury was foreseeable in the circumstances.

---

93. *White v Chief Constable of South Yorkshire Police* [1999] 2 AC 455, analysed by Williams & Segal 'Psychiatric Injury, Policy and the House of Lords' [1999] JPIL 102; Rogers 'Psychiatric Trauma: "Thus Far and No Further" - In Fact Not Quite So Far As Hitherto' (1999) 7 Torts LJ 23; Kelly 'Post-Traumatic Stress Disorder: Military and Police: The Legality of Hillsborough' (1999) 14 Ir LT (ns) 217, 235; *Cullin v London Fire and Civil Defence Authority* [1999] P 1 QR 314 (CA); *Greatorex v Greatorex* [2000] 1 WLR 1970 (QBD); *W v Essex County Council* [2000] 2 WLR 601 (HL).
94. [2000] 2 ILRM 343 (CC). *Cf Campbell v North Lanarkshire Council* 2000 SCLR 373 (Outer House). For analysis of *Curran*, see Dunne 'Secondary Victims and Nervous Shock' (2000) 5 BR 383.
95. English Law Commission's Report *Liability for Psychiatric Illness* (Law Com 249, 1998), para 5.50.
96. [2000] 2 ILRM 343 at 347 (CC).

**[17.69]** Judge McMahon, in a useful summary,[97] which deserves extended quotation contrasts the position in England with the Irish position, and highlights the remaining issues which have to be unequivocally addressed by future Irish courts:

> *Summary of English and Irish law now*
>
> After *White* the English position is as follows; persons who suffer negligently inflicted psychiatric illness are divided into two groups: primary victims and secondary victims. Primary victims are variously defined as those who were also exposed to physical injury *or* who were in the area of risk of physical injury *or* who were participants *or* directly involved in the accident. Secondary victims include mere bystanders and spectators. There appear to be no other categories, so that all claimants are either primary or secondary victims. The law views secondary victims as being less deserving and consequently, it demands that those victims must, for policy reasons, satisfy the courts in addition to the ordinary negligence requirements, that there was a 'close' relationship between the claimant and the victim, that they were spatially and temporally near the accident and that they perceived the events through their own senses. *White*, in effect, held that rescuers and employee claimants who up to then had been considered to be entitled to recover without having to concern themselves with 'the control mechanisms', are now treated as secondary victims also. To succeed, therefore, a rescuer must now show that he has a 'close' relationship with the injured person(s) and that he complies also with the other policy requirements. *White* also decided that there is no general duty of care owed by the employer to his employees in respect of psychiatric illness, and employees, like other secondary victims, must now also surmount the policy control mechanisms if they wish to recover. Finally, the English courts have held *in Page v Smith, supra*, that if the defendant could foresee personal injury (ie physical or psychiatric illness) he will be liable if the claimant only suffers psychiatric illness.
>
> In contrast, to recover for this type of injury in the Irish courts, the claimant must comply with the five conditions laid down by Hamilton CJ (with whom Egan J agreed) in *Kelly v Hennessy*. Nowhere in the Chief Justice's judgment is there any reference to primary or secondary categories. Denham J in the same case seemed to accept the distinction, and indicated that to be a primary victim one had to be a 'participant' in the events. As opposed to the English position, Hamilton CJ also held that to recover in Ireland for nervous shock, the defendant had to foresee nervous shock and not merely personal injury in general. When addressing these issues in *Kelly*, the Irish courts relied heavily on the Australian approach as expressed in *Jaensch v Coffey, supra*, an approach which has been rejected by the English Courts.
>
> Two things become clear from this: first, the law on this topic is far from settled in either jurisdiction; second, a divergence of approach between the two jurisdictions is becoming increasingly obvious and perhaps inevitable. Several questions have yet to be confronted by the Irish courts: should the law in this jurisdiction accept the primary/secondary classification?; are there to be other classes - tertiary victims for example?; if not, are there to be exceptions to the primary/secondary categories - eg rescuers and/or employees?; is 'participation' to be the criterion in determining primary victims?; is it necessary for a defendant to foresee nervous shock or is it sufficient if he foresees 'personal injury' of some kind?; are the occupational stress cases like *Walker v Northumberland County Council* [1995] 1 All ER 737 where the plaintiff is clearly a primary victim, but where the injury is not shock induced, affected by these developments?; and perhaps, most fundamental of all: is the distinction between physical and psychiatric injury medically or legally defensible nowadays? (See Lord Lloyd of Berwick in *Page v Smith* [1996] 1 AC 155, at p 188.)

97. [2000] 2 ILRM 343 at 359-360.

Chapter 18

# Employers' Liability


I. Introduction .......... 479
II. An Employer's Duty of Care to an Employee .......... 480
III. Assessment of Employers' Liability .......... 500
IV. Voluntary Assumption of Risk .......... 529


## I. INTRODUCTION[1]

**[18.01]** The law was slow to impose liability in negligence on employers in relation to injuries sustained by their employees. The *laissez-faire* philosophy, which prevailed during the earlier part of the nineteenth century, was reflected in judicial attitudes to work-related injuries: industry was admittedly dangerous but was clearly regarded as being socially beneficial in the long run; employees could look after their own interests, and if they chose to accept dangerous employment for an appropriate payment, they should not impose on their employer the obligation to compensate them when things went wrong.[2]

**[18.02]** This philosophy was given effect through the legal concepts of implied contractual terms, absence of a legal duty of care,[3] contributory negligence, voluntary assumption of risk and the doctrine of "common employment". This latter doctrine, the "most common nefarious judicial ploy for reducing the charges on industry",[4] relieved employers from

1. See White, *Civil Liability for Industrial Accidents* (1993); Munkman, *Employers' Liability at Common Law* (12th ed, 1995); Forde, *Employment Law* (1992), Ch 5; Coleman, *An Employer's Duties at Common Law in Ireland* (1961); Delany, 'An Employer's Duty of Care to his Workmen: What is a Safe System?' (1959) 25 Ir Jur 29; Anon 'The Duty of a Master to Provide a Safe System of Working' (1949) 83 ILT & Sol J 237; Fleming, 'Tort Liability for Work Injury', Vol 15 of the *International Encyclopedia of Comparative Law* (1975); Anon, 'Vicarious Liability and the Standard of Care' (1957) 2 Victoria U of Wellington LR No 3, 199; Kornhauser 'An Economic Analysis of the Choice Between Enterprise and Personal Liability for Accidents' (1982) 70 Calif LR 1345; Schwartz, 'Tort Law and the Economy in Nineteenth Century America: A Reinterpretation' (1981) 90 Yale LJ 1717 at 1768-1771; Posner 'A Theory of Negligence' (1972) 1 J of Legal Stud 29 at 44-46; Epstein 'The Historical Origins and Economic Structure of Workers' Compensation Law' (1982) 16 Ga LR 775.

2. *Cf Potts v Plunkett* (1859) 9 ICLR 290 at 297-298 (QB); *cf* Rabin 'The Historical Development of the Fault Principle: A Reinterpretation' (1981) 15 Ga LR 925 at 940-941:

   "[T]he history of workmen's compensation reform is singularly free of any reference to laborers protesting against the legislation on the grounds that a compulsory safety premium was likely to have a depressing effect on wages. Where were the risk-preferring workers when their wage premiums were under siege? If the historical record is to be believed, they were unappreciatively on the side of unseating their judicial protectors."

3. *Cf* eg, *Potts v Plunkett* (1859) 9 ICLR 290 (QB); *Vaughan v Cork & Youghal Ry Co* 12 (1860) ICLR 297 (Exch).

4. FLEMING, p 570. See Friedman & Ladinsky 'Social Change and the Law of Industrial Accidents' (1967) 67 Col LR 50 at 63, quoting the remarks of the Secretary for Ireland in the House of Commons in 1897: "Lord Abinger planted it [in *Priestley v Fowler* (1837) 3 M &W 1, 150 ER 1030], Baron Alderson watered it [in *Hutchinson v York, Newcastle, and Berwick Ry Co* (1950) 5 Ex 343, 155 ER 150], and the devil gave it increase". See further Tucker, 'The Law of Employers' Liability in Ontario 1861-1900: The Search for a Theory' (1984) 22 Os Hall LJ 213 at 218ff.

vicarious liability for injuries caused to employees by the negligence of their fellow employees.[5] In the latter part of the nineteenth century, this philosophy was tempered somewhat,[6] and over the past century the progress in dismantling this judicial mechanism has been rapid and radical. Thus we find that the concepts of duty, contributory negligence and voluntary assumption of risk have been transformed, the doctrine of "common employment" has been abrogated by statute[7] and a state system of compensation for work-related injuries established, in 1897,[8] originally under judicial control[9] but now administered as part of the mainstream of the social welfare regime.[10]

## II. An Employer's Duty of Care to an Employee

**[18.03]** It is settled law that:

> "[t]he duty of an employer[11] towards a servant is to take reasonable care for the servant's safety in all circumstances of the case."[12]

The courts have constantly stressed, however, that the employer's duty is not an unlimited one and that "the employer is not an insurer".[13] In *Bradley v CIE*, Henchy J stated that:

5. The English decisions in which the doctrine was first recognised, *Priestley v Fowler* (1837) 3 M & W 1 and *Hutchinson v York, Newcastle, and Berwick Ry Co* (1950) 5 Ex 343, 155 ER 150 were enthusiastically applied in this country. A similar pattern developed in the United States: *Murray v South Carolina Railroad* (1841) 26 SCL (1 McMil) 385; *Farwell v Boston & Worcester Railroad* (1842) 45 Mass (4 Met) 49.

6. *Cf* Woodard 'Reality and Social Reform: Transition from Laissez-Faire to Welfare State' (1962) 72 Yale LJ 286.

7. Law Reform (Personal Injuries) Act 1958 (No 38), s 1. The doctrine was abolished by judicial decision in New York in *Lawrence v City of New York* (1981) 2 App Div 2d 485, 447 NY S 2d 506 (2d Dep't), where the Court considered that it was not founded on "natural justice but on an absurd and disingenuous public policy": at 503 and 517, respectively. See Koester 'Note' (1982) 56 St John's LR 388.

8. Workmen's Compensation Act 1897.

9. *Cf* Workmen's Compensation Act 1897 and the Workmen's Compensation Act 1934; see (1945) 11 Ir Jur 58. The legislation preserved the employee's rights of action in tort against the employer, and contained provisions controlling the power to contract out: see further Epstein 'The Historical Origins and Economic Structure of Workers' Compensation Law' (1982) 16 Ga LR 775 at 797-799. There is evidence that in some high risk employments, notably railways and mines, there were already voluntary workers' compensation schemes in operation, whose efficacy the courts had sought to ensure in their interpretation of the Employers Liability Act 1880: *cf* at 793-794, *Clements v London & Northwestern Ry* [1894] 2 QB 482 (CA).

10. *Cf* the Social Welfare (Occupational Injuries) Act 1966 (No 16), analysed by Casey 'The Occupational Injuries Act: Some Reflections' (1969) 4 Ir Jur (ns) 234; Kaim-Caudle 'Compensation for Occupational Injures' (1966) 14 Administration 24. See now the Social Welfare (Consolidation) Act 1993, Pts II and VI.

11. As to who is an employer, see *Keegan v Owens* [1953] IR 267 (SC); *Waldson v Junior Army & Navy Stores Ltd* [1910] 2 IR 381 (CA *affg* KB); *Quinn v Burrell* High Court, 23 April 1993 (Hamilton P); *Mulligan v Holland Dredging (Ireland) Ltd* High Court, 23 January 1995 (O'Hanlon J).

12. *Dalton v Frendo* Supreme Court, 15 December 1977, p 4 of O'Higgins CJ's judgment; *cf* p 5 of Griffin J's judgment. See also *O'Donnell v Hannigan* Supreme Court, 19 July 1960 (Maguire CJ) at p 3; *Burke v John Paul & Co Ltd* [1967] IR 277 at 281 (SC).

13. *Dalton v Frendo* Supreme Court, 15 December 1977, p 4 of O'Higgins CJ's judgment. See also *Fennell v E Stone & Sons Ltd* [1967] IR 204 at 207 (SC); *Christie v Odeon (Ireland) Ltd* (1957) 91 ILTR 25 at 29 (SC); *O'Regan v Crampton Ltd (No 1)* Supreme Court, 15 June 1953 *per* O'Byrne J at p 1; *Johnson v Gresham Hotel Co* High Court, 13 November 1986 at p 2 (Lynch J).

"The law does not require an employer to ensure in all circumstances the safety of his workmen. He will have discharged his duty of care if he does what a reasonable and prudent employer would have done in the circumstances."[14]

**[18.04]** Henchy J went so far as to state that:

"even where a certain precaution is obviously wanted in the interests of the safety of the workman, there may be contervailing factors which would justify the employer in not taking that precaution."[15]

**[18.05]** In *Daly v Avonmore Creameries Ltd*,[16] McCarthy J took the edge off this statement. Having referred to this passage from Henchy J's judgment, he observed that he was:

"not to be taken as supporting a view that, where lives are at stake, considerations of expense are any more than vaguely material. Where a danger is very rare, such considerations may be irrelevant."[17]

**[18.06]** It is not sufficient for the injured employee to seek compensation on a bare allegation of negligence: he or she must make sure to state how and why the employer was in breach of its duty of care.[18] In this regard, the words of caution by Kingsmill Moore J, in *Christie v Odeon (Ireland) Ltd*,[19] may be noted:

"It is of little avail to show, after an accident has happened, that such and such a precaution might in the circumstances have avoided a particular accident. The matter must be considered as it would have appeared to a reasonable and prudent man before the accident."

---

14. [1976] IR 217 at 223; see also *Hogan v McEwan* (1975) 64 DLR (3d) 37 at 62 (Ont HC).
15. [1976] IR 217 at 223. See also *Mulcare v Southern Health Board* [1988] ILRM 689 (HC); *Vozza v Tooth & Co Ltd* (1964) 112 Comm LR 316; *Neill v Fresh Food & Ice Pty. Ltd* (1963) 108 Comm LR 362; *Ritsas v Commonwealth of Australia* (1975) 50 ALJR 104 at 106.
16. [1984] IR131 (SC).
17. [1984] IR131 at 147. (McCarthy J was dissenting but this did not affect the present issue.) The several Irish decisions (discussed at para **[18.127]** below) relating to the duty owed to members of the Defence Forces and employees of security firms are centrally relevant to this issue. Persons employed in the emergency services may find themselves exposed to risks greater than in most other jobs without liability on their employer's part. In *Folan v Galway County Council* DPIJ: Trinity and Michaelmas Terms 1998, p 99 (HC), a fire-fighter who was struck by boulders or planks that fell out of a building, in a "somewhat freakish" accident, after he had been instructed to enter the building by his superior officer, who "could not … have assumed that nobody inside … could have been alive", lost his action. Geoghegan J commented that:

    "[n]o doubt, in the immediate vicinity of a fire different superior officers might apply different conclusions or make different decisions. It does not necessarily mean that one is right and the other is wrong".

    The failure to provide effective breathing apparatus or to ensure that fire-fighters are medically fit the for job constitutes negligence: *Heeney v Dublin Corporation* High Court, 16 May 1991 (Barron J). See further fn 28 below. As to other employees working in positions of high social utility but involving personal risk, see *Mulcare v Southern Health Board* [1988] ILRM 689 (HC); *Hay v O'Grady* [1992] 1 IR 210 (SC).
18. *Cf Smyly v Glasgow & Londonderry Steampacket Co* (1867) IR 2 CL 24 (Exch); *Potts v Plunkett* (1859) 9 ICLR 290 (QB); *M'Kinney v Irish NW Ry Co* (1866) 11 Ir Jur (ns) 228 (QB). Apart from the proposition for which they are cited, these old decisions should be read with great caution, as many of the principles which they support have long since been repudiated.
19. (1957) 91 ILTR 25 at 29 (SC). See also *Kinsella v Jefferson Smurfit & Sons Ltd* Supreme Court, 16 March 1962.

**[18.07]** In *Brady v Beckmann Instruments (Galway) Inc*,[20] in 1985, the Supreme Court held that the employer was not liable in negligence where the employee contracted folliculitis, a form of dermatitis by inhaling chemical fumes at his workplace. The uncontradicted evidence was that the safety precautions were superior to those to be found in a like plant anywhere in Ireland or Britain and that the tests made in the factory indicated a level of exposure of only about 5% of the recommended statutory level in Ireland, Britain and the United States of America. This evidence would not have determined the issue of negligence had it been reasonable to anticipate what happened to the plaintiff. However, there was also evidence that none of the literature available indicated any case of folliculitis or any essentially similar condition ever having resulted from the degree of exposure to which the plaintiff had been subjected.[21] His injury was thus "so unique and improbable as not to be one which could be said to have been reasonably foreseeable by his employers".[22]

## The Duty Varies According to the Employee's Circumstances

**[18.08]** The courts have not laid down one single duty of care, to be applied without regard to employees' individual circumstances. In *Dalton v Frendo*,[23] Griffin J stated that:

> "Actions of negligence are concerned with the duty of care as between a particular employer and a particular workman ... That duty may vary with the workman's age, knowledge and experience."

**[18.09]** Thus, an employee's lack of work experience[24] or expertise,[25] his or her youth[26] or mental[27]

20. [1986] ILRM 361 (SC).
21. *Cf* [1986] ILRM 361 at 363.
22. [1986] ILRM 361.
23. *Dalton v Frendo* Supreme Court, 15 December 1977, p 5 of Griffin J's judgment. See also p 4 of O'Higgins CJ's judgment. *cf Leathem v Isaac Black Ltd* 80 ILTR 12 at 13 (KBD NI 131, 139-140 (CA)); *Noonan v Dublin Distillery Co* (1893) 32 LR (Ir) 399 at 405 (Ex Div).
24. *Cf Luttrell v Gouldings Fertilisers (Cork) Ltd* (1969) 103 ILTR 121 (SC); *Byrne v Jefferson Smurfit & Son Ltd* [1962-1963] Ir Jur 49 (SC); *Barrett v Anglo Irish Beef Producers Ltd* High Court, 6 March 1989 (Barr J); *Quail v JJ McGovern Ltd* DPIJ: Michaelmas Term 1991, p 82 (HC); *Shinkwin v Quinn Con Ltd and Quinlan* DPIJ: Trinity and Michalemas Terms 1998, p 46 (HC); *Egan v Crown Equipment Ltd* DPIJ: Trinity and Michaelmas Terms 1995, p 29 (HC).
25. *Cf Campbell v Cox* Supreme Court, 15 May 1956.
26. *Cf Murphy v Ross* [1920] 2 IR 199 (CA); *McKeever v Dundalk Linen Co Ltd* Supreme Court, 26 May 1966; *Kerry v Carter* [1969] 3 All ER 723 (CA), where Lord Denning MR considered that the fact that the plaintiff was still an apprentice whom the defendant had agreed to instruct put on the defendant "a higher duty, if anything", than that owed to a boy employed at the agricultural wage. In *Gies v Gunwall* (1982) 143 DLR (3d) 126 at 129 (BC SC), Berger J expressed the view that the master-apprentice relationship entailed a wider, rather than higher, duty than the ordinary duty of care in that the master "is obliged ... to instruct the apprentice in the use of the tools with which he must do his job". In fact, an employer may in some cases have such a duty; the better approach seems to be to prescribe no distinctions, *a priori*, as between the duties owed to employees and apprentices respectively.
27. In *McSweeney v Cork Corporation* DPIJ: Hilary and Easter Terms, 1994, p 37 (HC) the plaintiff, an adult who had experienced "fairly serious difficulties" with education, was injured when working on a work scheme organised to reduce unemployment. While Murphy J awarded compensation, he sounded a note of caution as to the wisdom of imposing too onerous a test for liability.

or physical disability[28] may all be taken into consideration in determining the duty of care owed. Conversely, of course, an employee's particularly extensive experience or abilities[29] or the risks inherent in the particular work[30] may also be taken into consideration.

## General Guidelines

**[18.10]** In spite of the importance of particular circumstances, the courts have laid down general guidelines regarding the duty owed to employees. There is generally no obligation to warn of obvious risks: the relationship between the parties should not be regarded as equivalent to that between a nurse and a child.[31] Thus, an experienced building contractor

---

27. (contd) Noting that unemployment was "most particularly … a disaster for those who are handicapped in any way, be it physical, mental or learning", he expressed the view that it was:

> "great credit to the Corporation that they provide these schemes to give people an opportunity of earning money and, above all, achieving personal dignity by so doing and one would like that people would not be deterred from providing schemes such as this by visiting them with damages when very minor accidents occur unless the law so requires". at p 38.

This is but one of several instances of the difficulty facing the court in employers' liability claims where the defendants conduct has a high social utility. *Cf Mulcare v Southern Health Board* [1988] ILRM 689 (HC); *Hay v O'Grady* [1992] 1 IR 210 (SC); Byrne & Binchy *Annual Review of Irish Law 1992*, pp 576-579.

28. *Paris v Stepney Borough Council* [1951] AC 367 (HL); *Cf Rafferty v Parsons (CA) of Ireland Ltd* [1987] ILRM 98 (SC). In *Heeney v Dublin Corporation* High Court, 16 May 1991 (Barron J), where a station officer with a fire brigade died when fighting a fire, Barron J held the fire authority liable in negligence for not having earlier carried out a medical examination on him and other colleagues who had reached the age of fifty five. A Labour Court recommendation in favour of annual medical examinations had been resisted by the union pending resolution of what was to be the fate of those who failed the test. Barron J considered that this had not prevented the employer from taking action. *cf Bryson v Gardner Merchant Ltd* NI CA (Civil Div), 11 October 1996, Lexis transcript NICA 2196, where the claim that an employer should have had a pre-employment medical examination for employees at risk of dermatitis from using detergents was rejected on causal grounds by the Court of Appeal. Campbell J at trial stating that he did "not believe that the courts have yet reached the stage where they are entitled to expect employers to reach the levels of ideal rather than reasonable care".

29. *Dalton v Frendo* Supreme Court, 15 December 1977; *cf Hanratty v Drogheda Web Offset Printers Ltd* Supreme Court, (*ex temp*) 2 June 1994 where Finlay CJ adopted a passage from Lord Oaksey's speech in *General Cleaning Contractors v Christmas* [1953] AC 180 at 689, to the effect that:

> "[e]mployers are not exempted from th[e] duty [of reasonable care] by the fact that their men are experienced and might, if they were in the position of an employer, be able to lay down a reasonably safe system of work themselves. Workmen are not in the position of employers. Their duties are not performed in the calm atmosphere of a board room with the advice of experts. They have to make their decisions on narrow window sills and other places of danger and in circumstances in which the dangers are obscured by repetition."

30. *Cf Depuis v Haulbowline Industries Ltd* Supreme Court, 14 February 1962 - ship-breaker injured when propeller fell on him; *per* Lavery J at pp 5-6:

> "In this case the employment is of a sort that admittedly has a certain degree of risk. There is risk in the breaking up of ships ... for scrap. Particularly the use of an oxy-acetyline burner has risks of an infinite variety. It seems to me that the jury must accept the evidence that no one is better able to appreciate and deal with the risks than the plaintiff himself."

See also *O'Sullivan v Doyle* Supreme Court, 30 July 1962, especially *per* Kingsmill Moore J (dissenting) at p.4.

31. *Dalton v Frendo* Supreme Court, 15 December 1977, p 6 (*per* Griffin J), quoting *Smith v Austin Lifts Ltd* [1959] 1 WLR 100 at 105. See also *Kennedy v Fulflex Manufacturing Ltd* DPIJ: Michaelmas Term 1991, p 140 (HC).

need not be warned of the danger of placing one set of legs of a step-ladder in a flowerbed with the other set on a lawn.[32] Similarly, a building labourer need not be warned of the possibility that a long scaffolding pole he is carrying may come into contact with a lamp suspended from the ceiling in the room.[33] Nor need an employer instruct employees as to the location of a particular light switch on the premises where it is at a height and in the general area that might be expected, though not in the most convenient position.[34]

**[18.11]** Where, however, an employer fails to take the necessary steps to remove an unnecessary risk created by him, and contents himself with giving a detailed warning to the employee of the dangerous condition thus resulting, he may be liable if the employee is injured. In the Supreme Court decision of *Swords v St Patrick's Copper Mines Ltd*,[35]

---

32. *Dalton v Frendo* Supreme Court, 15 December 1977. See also *Stakelum v Bank of Ireland* High Court, 27 April 1999, critically analysed by Byrne and Binchy *Annual Review of Irish Lawi 1999* (Torts chapter). In *McSweeney v McCarthy* Supreme Court, 28 January 2000, the failure to give an experienced painter clear instructions as to what she should do when she confronted a potential danger when working unaccompanied on a ladder was held to constitute an unsafe system of work. Employees may be presumed to know how the general laws of gravity work "and govern themselves accordingly": *Brown v Swift & Co* (1912) 91 Neb 532, 136 NW 726 at 728. See also *Walsh v St Paul & DR Co* (1881) 27 Minn 367, 8 NW 145); but this presumed knowledge may not extend to more complex applications of these laws in the course of work: *Parsons v Hammond Packing Co* (1902) 96 Mo App 372, 70 SW 519 at 522.

33. *Fennell v E Stone & Sons Ltd* [1967] IR 204, especially at 209. See also *Stinnett v Buchele* (1980) 598 SW 2d 469 (Ky SC). In *Whelan v Tipperary (SR) County Council* DPIJ: Hilary and Easter Terms 1997 (HC), where an employee involved in the construction of a wall fell when a stone forming part of a heap moved as he was carrying another large stone, Carney J held that the employer was not guilty of negligence, stating it would amount to a "total molly-cuddling" to expect that the employee be supervised in relation to the path he was travelling at the time as he was the person whose job it was to disturb the stones from the heaps and carry them to where the wall was being constructed. *Cf Queegan v Bord na Mona*, DPIJ: Trinity and Michaelmas Terms 1994, p 70 (HC) where an employee who was injured when two pieces of metal went into his eye lost his action against his employer. Two kinds of goggles were available on the premises but he had not used them, though he had personally attended a safety course in which the dangers of working without goggles had been emphasised. Noting that it was "hard to think what else the [the employer] could do", Carroll J rejected the idea that the foreman's duty had extended to going up on the roof on the fateful day to see if the plaintiff was wearing goggles while at work there. See also *McCann v ESB* [1997] Ir L Log W 178 (CC) - employee who was removing electricity pole from premises fell into the hole left in the ground. Employer not liable for failing to cover the hole. "This was just one of those areas where the law must leave the plaintiff to take care of himself".

34. *Organ v ESB* DPIJ: Trinity and Michaelmas Terms 1992, p 41 (HC). Murphy J observed:

> "There are some matters which employers are entitled to assume that the employees will take the obvious steps which are necessary and appropriate for them in any given circumstances. In my view an employer is entitled to assume that an adult employee will locate a switch which is in the vicinity of a staircase which the adult employee is going to mount in conditions of some degree of darkness ... This is not a matter of ... contributory negligence by an employee. It seems to me simply to be the case that an employer has no duty and his intervention would, I believe, be resented if he w[ere] to explain or point out to an adult employee the whereabouts of a switch which was some three or four feet off the ground in the general area on which anyone would expect to find it."

See also *McGowan v Wicklow County Council* High Court, 27 May 1993 (Morris J) - no obligation to give superfluous warnings to highly skilled labourers as to dangers arising from working too close to JCB diggers.

35. Supreme Court, 30 July 1963, p 3. See also *Daly v Ballyclough Co-Operative* DPIJ: Trinity Term 1991, p 92 (HC).

Walsh J (speaking for the Court) went so far as to say of an employer who had adopted this course in relation to a machine operated by an employee that:

> "The instruction ... might well have reduced to minimal the probability of injury but did not alter the mechanical condition which rendered the machine a dangerous one and it therefore continued to be a dangerous thing. Instruction and warning, however explicit, cannot be equated to the presence of a physical guard."

**[18.12]** Nevertheless, reasonable care is all that is required of the employer, who is not required to foresee every risk that may possibly cause injury. In *Kenneally v Waterford County Council*,[36] for example, the Supreme Court held that the case had been correctly withdrawn from the jury where the driver of a traxcavator had been injured by a fall of soil from a bank he was removing. The soil was dislodged as a result of frost; it would not have injured the driver had he not been at the rear of his vehicle attempting to restart it after it had stalled. This double contingency was regarded as beyond the bounds of reasonable foresight. Where, however, an employer has created or permitted a dangerous condition to arise, he should foresee and provide against the possibility of injury arising from it:

> "even though it so results through the intermediation of an act of inadvertence by the employee and even though that act of inadvertence be of a character which cannot be precisely forecast and remains in the event 'unexplained'".[37]

The same considerations apply to acts of similar inadvertence or lack of skill on the part of fellow employees.[38]

## Omissions

**[18.13]** It is very easy to be wise after the event and to assert that an employer ought to have done something which he failed to do in order to have avoided the accident.[39] Courts will scrutinise closely an argument that the defendant was guilty of negligence by omission.

**[18.14]** Formerly, the employer charged with negligence by omission could be found to have been negligent only where his negligence fell within one or two compartments; where what was omitted by way of protection:

> "either was a thing commonly done by other employers[40] in like circumstances, or was so obviously required that it would be folly for an employer to neglect to provide it; in other words, that no reasonable and prudent employer would have omitted it."[41]

---

36. (1959) 97 ILTR 97 (SC). See also *Dalton v Frendo* Supreme Court, 15 December 1977; *Kinsella v Hammond Lane Industries Ltd* (1962) 96 ILTR 1 (SC); *Simpson v Pollard* Supreme Court, 6 April 1967; *Kinsella v Jefferson Smurfit & Sons Ltd* Supreme Court, 16 March 1962.
37. *Connor v Malachy Burke (Contractors) Ltd* Supreme Court, 31 March 1955 *per* Kingsmill Moore J, p 7 quoting from *Thurogood v Vanden Berghs & Jurgens Ltd* [1951] 2 KB 537 at 554.
38. *Connor v Malachy Burke (Contractors) Ltd* Supreme Court, 31 March 1955 *per* Kingsmill Moore J, p 7.
39. *Cf Christie v Odeon (Ireland) Ltd* (1957) 91 ILTR 25 at 29 (SC).
40. *Cf Kenneally v Waterford County Council* (1959) 97 ILTR 97 at 99 (SC); *Depuis v Haulbowline Industries Ltd* Supreme Court, 14 February 1962.
41. *Caulfield v George Bell & Co Ltd* [1958] IR 326 at 334 (HC), echoing Lord Dunedin's test in *Morton v William Dixon Ltd* [1909] SC 807 at 809 (1st Div).

**[18.15]** Today, the courts are somewhat less concerned with whether the omission can be stigmatised as "folly":[42] the ordinary criterion of reasonableness has been applied,[43] so as to reduce the force of the more restrictive approach. In the Supreme Court decision of *Bradley v CIE*[44] in 1976, Henchy J said that the old formulation, as glossed by qualifications in subsequent cases:

> "does no more than provide a mode of testing whether in the class of cases to which it refers the employer has taken reasonable care for the safety of his employee or, as it is sometimes put, whether he has subjected him to unnecessary risk."

**[18.16]** In *Kennedy v Hughes Dairy Ltd*,[45] in 1988, the Supreme Court examined the issue somewhat more closely. Differences of emphasis as to the effect of Henchy J's statement in *Bradley* are apparent in the judgment of McCarthy J and the dissenting judgment of Finlay CJ.

**[18.17]** McCarthy J appeared satisfied with the restatement of the test as being one of reasonable care. He said:

> "In my view *Bradley's* case is not to be construed as laying down for all time two unchanging compartments into one or both of which every plaintiff's claim must be brought if it is to succeed. Indeed, the judgment of Henchy J in *Bradley* itself demonstrates the manner in which in different jurisdictions the wording used has been qualified or added to by gloss or otherwise. The essential question in all actions of negligence is whether or not the party charged has failed to take reasonable care whether by act or omission. That prime question may be broken down to subsidiary questions appropriate to the circumstances of different cases."[46]

**[18.18]** McCarthy J went on to say that in actions resulting from injuries sustained "in what may be termed static conditions - those prevailing in a particular employment or a particular premises or the like",[47] expert evidence might properly point, as a primary matter, to the foreseeable risk of injury and the consequent requirement of special care. The practice of the trade or of occupiers of similar premises might be "powerful rebutting evidence but, ... in a changing world, it should seldom, if ever, be conclusive".[48] Consequently, the failure to comply with a trade practice would be powerful evidence in support of expert testimony as to the breach of duty.

---

42. *Cf Anon* 'Folly' (1961) 95 ILT & Sol J 83.
43. *Cf Cavanagh v Ulster Weaving Co* [1959] NI 109 (HL (NI)), analysed by Delany 'An Employer's Duty of Care to His Workmen: What is a "Safe System"?' (1959) 25 Ir Jur 29; Fricke 'General Practice in Industry' (1960) 23 MLR 653; Anon 'Note' (1960) 76 LQR 6; *Christie v Odeon (Ireland) Ltd* (1957) 91 ILTR 25 (SC); *cf Callaghan v Killarney Race Co Ltd* [1958] IR 366 at 374-375.
44. [1976] IR 217 at 221 (SC). See also *Murphy v Commissioners of Irish Lights* Supreme Court, 25 July 1973 *per* Henchy J at p 3 of his judgment. *Cf Keane v ESB* [1981] IR 44 (SC); *Callaghan v Killarney Race Co Ltd* [1958] IR 366 at 374-375 (SC); *Hamilton v Nurouf (WA) Pty* (1956) 96 Comm LR 18 at 26; *Johnson v Gresham Hotel Co* High Court, 13 November 1986 at p 8 (Lynch J).
45. [1989] ILRM 117 (SC).
46. [1989] ILRM 117 at 123.
47. [1989] ILRM 117 at 123.
48. [1989] ILRM 117 at 123.

**[18.19]** McCarthy J added that, if *Bradley's* case were to be construed as excluding any approach other than that specified in *Morton v William Dixon Ltd*,[49] he "would want a conclusion to that effect expressed by a full court".[50]

**[18.20]** In contrast to this approach, Finlay CJ addressed the issue of the employer's negligence exclusively in terms of the two compartments set out by Lord Dunedin in *Morton v William Dixon Ltd*. Although he quoted Henchy J's restatement of the principle in terms of a reasonable care formula, he appeared to see no reason to address the issue of negligence outside the framework of the two compartments. It is perhaps fair to point out that Henchy J, having articulated the reasonable care formula, had similarly disposed of the issue in compartmental terms.

**[18.21]** Hederman J's judgment appears to lean more in the direction of McCarthy J's approach. Although he referred with apparent approval to the compartmental approach, he added immediately afterwards:

> "In other words, a question should have been left to the jury ... 'Had the employer taken reasonable care for the safety of his employee or had he subjected him to unnecessary risks?'"[51]

This broad question contains none of the narrowness of the compartmental approach.

**[18.22]** It thus remains to be seen whether the Supreme Court will in the future give actual substance to Henchy J's restatement of the duty in terms of reasonable care.

## The Relationship Between Employers' Liability and Claims for Breach of Statutory Duty

**[18.23]** There is a clear conceptual distinction as regards the basis of liability, between a common action in negligence for employers' liability and an action for breach of statutory duty by an employee against an employer. The negligence action is not fixated with technical definitions as to what constitutes being an "employer" since *Donoghue v Stevenson* principles are capable of embracing relationships similar to that of employment.[52] Moreover, it requires proof that the employer acted unreasonably.[53] The

---

49. [1909] SC 807.

50. [1989] ILRM 117 at 123.

51. [1989] ILRM 117 at 123. See also *English v Anglo-lrish Meat Products Ltd* High Court, 2 December 1988 (O'Hanlon J).

52. *Cf White v Burke* DPIJ: Hilary and Easter Terms 1995, p 1 (HC) - elderly woman who engaged a nineteen-year-old to clean the front windows of her house, which was on a street with a severe incline, without checking how the operation was being carried out or having some assurance of his skill, held to have owed and breached a duty to him, not as his employer, but on *Donoghue v Stevenson* principles. Contrast *Deegan v Wholey t/a Stoneridge Plant Hire* DPIJ: Hilary and Easter Terms 1997, p 121 (HC), where a self-employed handy man "prepared to do 'nixers'" was held not to be owed a duty of care. *Cf McDonagh v Brian O'Connell Ltd* High Court, 24 October 1996 (Barr J) - liability imposed on "*de facto* employer"; *Allen v Ó Súilleabháin* High Court, 28 July 1995 (Kinlen J) - obstetrician, though not employer of student midwife attending the birth, "certainly owed a duty" to her "under the principles of 'the good neighbour' [in *Donoghue v Stevenson*]"; *Shinkwin v Quin-Con Ltd and Quinlan* DPIJ: Trinity and Michaelmas Terms 1998, p 46 (HC)) - manager of factory premises, whom plaintiff "regarded ... as his boss", held to owe a duty of care to plaintiff under *Donoghue v Stevenson* principle; *Quigley v Ireland* DPIJ: Hilary and Easter Terms 1992, p 111 (HC) - inmate of Loughan House told to paint ceiling; started task by climbing onto table; no step ladder provided. State liable but damages reduced by 50% as plaintiff should have asked for ladder.

53. See Ch 7 above.

action for breach of statutory duty depends on the precise terms of the particular statutory provision to determine who is an "employer" and what is the character of the duty prescribed by the particular statutory provision. Sometimes it demands no more than reasonable care on the part of the employer but many statutory provisions impose a more stringent test,[54] ranging as far as strict liability. Moreover, the scope of the defences of contributory negligence[55] and voluntary assumption of risk,[56] are considerably more restricted in claims for breach of statutory duty than for employers' liability claims at common law.

**[18.24]** An employee is, of course, free to sue for either or both of these causes of action. Each must be considered separately by the court. While this is formally the position, courts in employers' liability claims have inevitably been affected by the whole code of legislation imposing specific statutory duties on employers to protect the safety, health and security of their employees. That statutory code sends three messages to guide the court in employers' liability litigation. First, it emphasises the social support that exists for paternalistic protective values underlying the employer-employee relationship. Secondly, the specificity of its provisions gives guidance as to what an employer might be expected to do for his or her employees in concrete situations.[57] Finally, the procedures prescribed by statutes may easily translate into useful models for what constitutes a "safe system of work" for the purposes of employers' liability litigation at common law.

**[18.25]** The Safety, Health and Welfare at Work Act 1989 has had a particular influence on employers' liability claims in this context, as Barron J's decision in *Mullen v Vernal Instruments Ltd*,[58] demonstrates. The plaintiff was employed as a manageress of the drapery and household section of the defendant's retail premises in Carlow. Once every month she went to Dublin to buy goods for sale in her section of the store. She used to buy from five wholesalers in the city centre and carry or, if needs be, drag what she had bought, in plastic sacks, to a car-park nearby. On the occasion in question, she injured her back when using the staircase in the car-park while half carrying, half dragging four sacks containing the purchases for the day, which were too heavy for her.

**[18.26]** The plaintiff claimed that the defendant had failed to take any steps to prevent the danger to her because of the weight of the purchases. She relied on the statutory duties imposed on employers by Part II of the Safety, Health and Welfare at Work Act 1989, with special emphasis upon the provisions of s 12, which requires the preparation of a safety statement to deal with the identification of the hazards and an assessment of the risks of

---

54. *Cf Boyle v Marathon Petroleum (Ireland) Ltd* Supreme Court, 12 January 1999; *Mullan v Omagh Meats Ltd* NI High Court (QBD), 3 February 1999 (McCollum LJ).

55. See para **[21.52]** below.

56. See para **[20.61]** below.

57. This can work both ways. In *Dunne v Dublin Cargo Handling Ltd (in liquidation)* Supreme Court, 30 August 1997, a communication system in relation to unloading ships was held to be negligent, Barron J seeing "significan[ce] in the fact that there had been "no contest but that the [statutory] regime [regulating the work] was being followed". *Cf* Byrne & Binchy *Annual Review of Irish Law 1997*, pp 739-740.

58. High Court, 15 December 1995 (Barron J), analysed by Byrne & Binchy *Annual Review of Irish Law 1995*, pp 490-492.

safety and health at the place of work to which the statement relates. Evidence was adduced on her behalf that the weight of the sacks – twenty one kilograms – exceeded the weight which should reasonably have been required of a female employee.

**[18.27]** The defendant sought unsuccessfully to resist liability on the basis that the accident that befell the plaintiff was one that was likely to occur in a non-work environment. Barron J stated:

> "The whole tenor of ... the 1989 Act is to ensure that thought is given to work situations so that dangers from carelessness or from failure to give any thought to a particular danger may be eliminated. Even though the provisions contained in ss 6 to 11 of Part II of the Act do not by virtue of s 60 confer any right of action in civil proceedings an employer cannot escape liability for failure to consider possible dangers merely because the employee can meet the same problems or dangers in her ordinary life where she must deal with them herself."[59]

**[18.28]** Barron J went on to express the view that, although there had been no safety statement, none had been required by the section in the circumstances of the case. Such a statement would relate to the place of work, not to places where an employee might be in the course of his or her work. Thus, s 12 would not require safety statements for employees who travelled throughout the State or abroad on the business of their employers. This did not, however, absolve employers from a *common law* duty to give consideration to the health and safety of employees who in the course of their employment had to leave their main place of work to carry out their duties elsewhere.

**[18.29]** In the instant case, the employer had not given any consideration to what problems might arise during a buying trip, regarding the plaintiff's safety or health. The question to be answered was whether, if he had done so, he would have anticipated the need to give the plaintiff any advice or to formulate a particular system of work which would have avoided the injury. He was aware that, following these buying trips, the plaintiff arrived into work bringing with her goods carried in black plastic sacks, but there was no evidence to suggest that he was aware that the plaintiff carried the sacks with her in the course of her trip, regardless of how many there were, or that to do so caused her any physical problems.

**[18.30]** The system whereby the manager of the drapery section had made a monthly visit to Dublin for the purpose of buying had existed for many years. During the entirety of this period and during the several months during which this work had been carried out by the plaintiff, there had never been any question of any problems involved in it other than one remark made by the plaintiff in relation to whether or not a helper might be provided. That remark had "not [been] made in the context of any particular problem."[60]

**[18.31]** Barron J concluded:

> "Where [the plaintiff] bought the goods and how she got them back to the shop was a matter for [her]. She alone knew what was involved. There was nothing in those facts which should have led the defendant to anticipate the need to give any particular advice to the plaintiff nor to formulate any particular system of work. In the circumstances, the plaintiff's claim fails."[61]

---

59. Page 3 of Barron J's judgment.
60. Page 4.
61. Page 5.

**[18.32]** Barron J's emphasis on the obligation of employers to give *consideration* to the health and safety of their employees reflects the approach favoured by the 1989 Act, which encourages employers to adopt procedures in which these concerns are addressed in a structured manner. This philosophy gives substance to the notion of a safe *system* of work.[62]

## Employer's Duty to Employees is "Non-Delegable"

**[18.33]** Since *Wilsons & Clyde Coal Co Ltd v English*,[63] it has been recognised that an employer's duty of care to his or her employees is "non-delegable" in the sense that it cannot be shaken off by delegating it to some other person to discharge.[64] Of course, if the person to whom the duty is discharged is an employee of the employer, ordinary principles of vicarious liability would lead to this result, but the law in this context ranges more widely. Even if the person is an independent contractor, the employer will be liable where the employer's duty has thus been delegated.

**[18.34]** In truth, the liability based on an non-delegable duty is a form of vicarious liability,[65] even though the judicial rhetoric characterises it as "personal" to the employer. Clearly it is not dependent on establishing proof of control[66] – or even the right to control – on the part of the employer.

**[18.35]** Many of the cases involve situations where an employee is allocated by his or her general employer to work for a temporary employer. Here the courts tend to have little difficulty in finding that the general employer remains under a non-delegable duty to the employee.[67] Similarly, they have made it clear that an employer is not automatically immunised from liability to his or her employees by engaging the services of a person who

62. See *Allen v Ó Súilleabháin* High Court, 28 July 1995. *Cf Conway v Cniotail Gaeltarra* DPIJ: Michaelmas Term 1990, p 285 (HC), where the failure by employees' representatives to make complaints at safety committee meetings as to the safety of seating was interpreted as indicating that the employees had no problem with it.

63. [1938] AC 57.

64. See *McDermid v Nash Dredging and Reclamation Ltd* [1987] AC 906 (HL); *Morris v Breaveglen Ltd (t/a Anzac Construction Co)* [1993] ICR 766 (CA (Civil Div)); *Nelhams v Sandells Maintenance Ltd* (1995) 46 Con LR 40 (CA (Civil Div)); *Mulholland v VH McDevitt & Son Ltd* NI QBD, 15 January 1998; *Mulligan v Holland Dredging (Ireland) Ltd* Supreme Court, 21 November 1996, aff'g High Court, 23 January 1995 (O'Hanlon J)), analysed by Byrne & Binchy *Annual Review of Irish Law 1995*, pp 483, 485-487; *McManamon v Córas Iompair Éireann* [1961] IR 30 (SC); *cf Crowe v Brennan*, [1967] IR 5 (SC).

65. *Cf* para **[43.50]** below.

66. *Cf Moynihan v Moynihan* [1975] IR 192. Control by the permanent employer may in some cases be established on the evidence: see *McDermid v Nash Dredging and Reclamation Ltd* [1987] AC 906; *cf McManamon v CIE* [1961] IR 30 (SC).

67 See, eg *McDermid v Nash Dredging and Reclamation Ltd* [1987] AC 906; *Morris v Breaveglen Ltd (t/a Anzac Construction Co)* [1993] ICR 766; *Nelhams v Sandells Maintenance Ltd* (1995) 46 Con LR 40; *Mulholland v VH McDevitt & Son Ltd* NI QBD, 15 January 1998. See also *Mulligan v Holland Dredging (Ireland) Ltd* Supreme Court, 21 November 1996, where, in the High Court, O'Hanlon J distinguished *McDermid* on the basis that, in the instant case, the plaintiff had not been in the employment of the defendant company at the time of the accident and therefore was not owed any duty of care by it in respect of the safety of his place of work in Israel where he was employed by a Dutch subsidiary company of a parent company of which the defendant company was also a subsidiary.

is characterised as an independent contractor rather than an employee. However, as Lord Tucker observed in *Davie v New Merton Board Mills Ltd*:

> "this does not mean that every person with whom the employer may have entered into some contractual relationship connected with the manufacture or supply of some machinery, appliance or tool which is ultimately used in his business automatically becomes a person entrusted by the employer with the performance of his common law duty. Still less can the negligence of some person with whom the employer has never been in contact contractually or otherwise, or of whom perhaps he has never been heard, be imputed to him."[68]

**[18.36]** So how should the line be drawn? The courts have been slow to give guidance as to the principles on which this question is to be resolved. In *Davie* Viscount Simonds made it clear that the concept of delegation by the employer was not metaphorical: some genuine process of delegation was required. On this basis it could not be said that a manufacturer of equipment which happened to be used by an employer had been delegated to produce it:

> "[B]y what use or misuse of language can the manufacturer be said to be a person to whom the employer delegated a duty which it was for him to perform? How can it be said that it was as the delegate or agent of the employer that the manufacturer failed to exhibit due skill and care? It is, to my mind, clear that he cannot."[69]

**[18.37]** Lord Morton noted that the non-delegability doctrine had "never been extended … to a case where the [employer] has ordered a standard tool from a reputable supplier …".[70]

**[18.38]** Lord Reid saw "no difficulty in principle in extending vicarious liability beyond liability for those who are, strictly speaking, servants",[71] but he thought that it would:

> "be going far beyond anything reasonable to extend it to cover a case where there was no relationship whatever between the master and the negligent person or his employer at the time when the negligence occurred".[72]

**[18.39]** Lord Reid went on to ask:

> "Where, then, is the line to be drawn? On the one hand it appears that an employer is liable for the negligence of all independent contractors whom he has engaged to carry out one of what have been described as her personal duties on his own premises and whose work might normally be done by the employer's own servant – at least if the negligent workmanship is discoverable by reasonable inspection. On the other hand, … I am of opinion that he is not liable for the negligence of the manufacturer of an article which he has bought, provided that

67. (contd) This was so even though there was an inter-company arrangement whereby the defendant company initially paid the plaintiff his wages. The Supreme Court affirmed without discussing this issue in any detail. *Cf Square D Ltd v Cook* [1992] ICR 262 (CA); See also *Keegan v Owens* [1953] IR 267 (SC), where the fact that the plaintiff's general employers had no control over the work for which he was engaged by the temporary employer was considered to remove the status of employers from the general employers and thus defeat his action against them resulting from injury sustained while working with the temporary employer. This conclusion runs contrary to the modern approach, exemplified by a number of the decisions cited earlier in this footnote.

68. [1959] AC 604 at 647 (HL (Eng)). See also *Sumner v William Henderson & Sons Ltd* [1964] 1 QB 450, *Maguire v PJ Lagan (Contractors) Ltd* [1976] 1 NIJB (CA (Civil Div)).

69. [1959] AC 604 at 625.

70. [1959] AC 604 at 629.

71. [1959] AC 604 at 642.

72. [1959] AC 604 at 642.

> he has been careful to deal with a seller of repute and has made any inspection which a reasonable employer would make. That leaves a wide sphere regarding which it is unnecessary … to express any opinion here. Various criteria have been suggested and it must be left for the further development of the law to determine which is correct."[73]

**[18.40]** Progress thus far has been slow. In the Supreme Court decision of *Crowe v Brennan*,[74] Walsh J took a neutral position on whether *Davie* has been correctly decided. In *Keenan v Bergin*,[75] however, he referred to "the type of case where an employer discharges his duty by buying from a reputable supplier a standard tool whose latent defect he had no means of discovering and which causes injury." Walsh J added: "In such a case an employer may be held to have discharged his duty by taking care to buy a standard tool from a reputable supplier."[76]

**[18.41]** In *Connolly v Dundalk Urban District Council and Mahon & McPhillips*,[77] the plaintiff, an assistant caretaker at the Council's waterworks, was severely injured when he inhaled a dense cloud of chlorine gas which had escaped when a plastic pipe carrying chlorine mixed with water became disconnected from a rigid plastic pipe. The point of connection, O'Hanlon J held, had been inadequately secured. The type of joint used was:

> "quite unsuitable for its purpose and was likely to fail at some stage, and the failure of the joint, which should have been foreseeable to the plaintiff's employers, was the primary cause of the accident …"[78]

**[18.42]** Accordingly, O'Hanlon J held that the Council had failed in its duty as employer to the plaintiff to take all reasonable steps to ensure that his place of employment was safe and free from danger of a type which should have been foreseen by it.

**[18.43]** The second defendant had erected the waterworks for the Council in 1968. Having completed the design and construction of the waterworks, the contractors at a later stage agreed to service the installation by providing three services visits *per annum*.

**[18.44]** Expert evidence adduced in the case was to the effect that, while alarm systems and ventilation systems were not at the time part and parcel of the conventional installation where chlorine gas was used for water treatment, these additional protective features had since become commonplace, being widely used for many years prior to 1986, when the plaintiff met with his accident. The Council was at the time of the accident in the process of arranging for their introduction. O'Hanlon J stated that, while the Council had obviously been activated at all times by the desire to keep the waterworks up to the best

---

73. [1959] AC 604 at 646.
74. [1967] IR 5.
75. [1971] IR 192 at 199.
76. [1971] IR 192 at 199. See also *Connolly v Thorn EMI (Irl) Ltd* DPIJ: Trinity and Michaelmas Terms 1992, p 193 (HC), where an employee who suffered strain when lifting a shutter failed in her action for negligence against her employer. Keane J considered that the shutter had been functioning perfectly well; even if it had not, he observed (at p 194) that it was:

    > "hard to see what an employer is expected to do, who orders a shutter in a perfectly ordinary way from a reputable source and puts it in and find none of his employees experience any difficulty with it …. [I]t's hard to see how the employer can stand indicted of negligence, as it were, in that situation."
77. [1990] 2 IR 1 (HC affd SC, 18 November 1992).
78. [1990] 2 IR 1 at 6.

standards of safety, he was forced to conclude that it again must be held liable, for failing to acquaint itself in time with the development of safety procedures which had come to be regarded as standard for some significant time before the accident and to give effect to them in the plaintiff's place of employment.

**[18.45]** The Council had sought unsuccessfully to avoid liability on the basis that the responsibility for any failure of the pipework or any failure to implement safety measures should be laid at the door of the second defendant who was responsible for the original design and installation and for all aspects of service and maintenance of the system. O'Hanlon J considered it:

> "well-established … that an employer owes a duty to his employee to provide a safe place of work, and cannot escape liability for breach of such duty by employing an independent contractor – no matter how expert – to perform the duty for him."[79]

**[18.46]** He invoked two English authorities in support, one judicial, the other academic. In *Paine v Colne Valley Electrical Co*,[80] Goddard LJ said: "This is a duty which cannot be avoided by delegation. It is no answer to say … 'We employed competent contractors to provide a safe place or plant'". *Charlesworth on Negligence* stated:

> "The employer is liable if the failure to exercise reasonable care and skill is that of an independent contractor, and is only excused from liability if the danger is due to a latent defect not discoverable by reasonable care and skill on the part of anyone."[81]

**[18.47]** The Supreme Court on 18 November 1992, affirmed O'Hanlon J's imposition of liability on the Council. Of particular interest is O'Flaherty J's statement of the principles relating to an employer's liability for the negligence of an independent contractor:

> "The common law duties to take reasonable steps to provide safe plant and a safe place of work – I speak of the place of work as being part of the employer's property … are such they cannot be delegated to independent contractors so as to avoid the primary liability that devolves on employers to make sure that these duties are carried out. These are responsibilities which cannot be put to one side; they must remain with the employer. They are owed to each individual employee. That is not to say, of course, but that the employer on occasion is entitled to and very often should get the best expert help that he can from an independent contractor to perform those duties. If he does so and the contractor is negligent causing injury to an employee, the employer retains a primary liability for the damage suffered though if he is not himself negligent he may obtain from the contractor a contribution to the damages and costs which he has to pay which will amount to full indemnity."[82]

**[18.48]** This statement goes further than what was said in the High Court, where O'Hanlon J's observations were entirely consistent with the Supreme Court's holding in *Keenan v Bergin*.[83] O'Flaherty J speaks in unqualified terms of the employer's non-delegable duty's embracing the negligence of the independent contractor to whom the duty has been cast. Nevertheless it would seem prudent to read these remarks in the context of the facts of

79. [1990] 2 IR 1 at 7.
80. [1938] 4 All ER 803 at 807.
81. 4th ed, para 845.
82. Pages 2-3 of O'Flaherty J's judgment.
83. [1971] IR 192.

*Connolly*, where the independent contractor had been specifically engaged in work on the employer's premises and retained an ongoing contractual relationship with the employer. This case is far removed from the situation where an employer engages in a once-off transaction with the independent contractor such as the purchase of equipment from a supplier where there is no question of the purchase involving any precise specifications by the employer in relation to the employer's particular needs in regard to the equipment.

**[18.49]** The Supreme Court's broad statement on the concept of the employer's non-delegable duty in *Connolly* may be contrasted with its failure to address the issue at all in *McCarthy v Garda Commissioner*,[84] where a member of the Garda Siochána was injured when he sought to draw his truncheon from his trouser pocket only to discover that the pocket was too narrow to enable him to do so effectively. His action in negligence against his employers for failing to take reasonable care in relation to his uniform was unsuccessful in the High Court and on appeal to the Supreme Court. In an *ex tempore* judgment, Murphy J noted that the Garda authorities had given the correct specifications as to pocket size to the tailors with whom they had contracted for the supply of uniforms. Having done this, they were not under an obligation to inspect the many thousands of pockets on the uniforms that were supplied.

**[18.50]** Nowhere in the judgments is there any reference to the possibility that the employers might have been under a non-delegable duty in relation to the supply of uniforms. The case is closer to the facts of *Connolly* that of *Keenan v Bergin* in that the tailors had been specifically recruited for a task with customised requirements. Certainly O'Flaherty J's language would seem broad enough to involve the imposition of liability on the employers, leaving them with an action against the tailors, if the tailors failed to comply with instructions.

**[18.51]** Finally we may note Morris P's judgment in *Armstrong v William J Dwan & Sons Ltd*,[85] in 1999. The plaintiff, a lorry driver employed by the first defendant was injured when the side crash bars on the vehicle he was driving collapsed under him as he was dismounting from it. The second defendant, Westpark Motor Company, had carried out repairs on the vehicle in a negligent manner.

**[18.52]** Morris P held that the employer had not been guilty of any negligence. He was:

> "satisfied that [Westpark Motor Company] being main Ford truck dealers are a reputable company upon whom the first named defendants were entitled to rely. I do not consider that it would be reasonable to expect the first named defendants to inspect the work prior to putting the truck back into service. I believe that they were entitled to assume that the job was satisfactorily carried out given the straightforward nature of the work to be done, the fact that Westpark Motor Company were main Ford dealers and the fact that they had

84. Supreme Court, 1998.

85. High Court, 8 February 1999 (Morris P). See also *Gilna v Maguire and 3M Ireland* High Court, 19 May 1999 where Johnson J improsed liability in negligence on an employer for "failing to provide the plaintiff with safe equipment in the course of her employment as her employer". The equipment in question was a laser imaging processor, which gave off electro static shocks because its manufacturer had not fitted correctly an electro static brush. It is hard to see how the employer failed to use due care since it had the machine regularly serviced by the manufacturer. Perhaps this is an instance of the application, *sub silentio*, of the non delegability principle.

satisfactorily carried out repairs to the [first defendants]'s fleet of trucks for some time in the past. They were not in breach of obligation towards the plaintiff by failing to inspect the work done on the side crash bar."[86]

**[18.53]** Morris P made it clear that there was no question of addressing the issue of contribution or indemnity as between the first and second defendants since he had found "no liability whatever"[87] on the part of the first defendant to compensate the plaintiff.

**[18.54]** Morris P made no reference to O'Flaherty J's observations in *Connolly* to the effect that an employer who had engaged a reputable independent contractor should be entitled to an indemnity on the basis that the employer retains a non-delegable duty towards the employee.

**[18.55]** It seems clear from the pattern of these decisions that the employer's non-delegable duty of care cannot be shaken off by employing independent contractors who come onto the premises to do a job that impacts on the employer's duty of care to the employees, whether in respect of "safe plant", a "safe place of work" or (though not specifically mentioned in *Connolly*) a safe system of work. It seems equally clear, as we have already indicated, that the employer's non-delegable duty does not extend to the purchase of equipment from a supplier on a once-off basis with no customised specifications. However, *McCarthy v Garda Commission*[88] and *Armstrong v William J Dwan & Sons Ltd*,[89] suggest that the non-delegable duty does not even reach a case where the supplier of equipment, or one who services or repairs equipment, used by employees is in an ongoing commercial relationship with the employer. Perhaps it would be unwise to read too much into these two decisions as in neither of them was the issue of the employer's non-delegable duty specifically addressed.

## Does an Employer's Duty of Care Extend Beyond Physical Injury?

**[18.56]** The employer's duty of care to employees is generally addressed in the context of *physical* injury but there is no reason in principle why this should represent the limit of that duty. Provided the classic ingredients of the duty of care[90] – proximity and reasonable foresight – can be established, an employee who suffers psychiatric injury, property damage or even pure economic loss as a result of the employer's negligence *qua* employer should be entitled to compensation.

**[18.57]** There is, of course, an element of circularity in this reasoning. Of course a claim will be conceded where the necessary ingredients of the duty of care can be established but the prior question relates to when these ingredients should be considered to have been established. The answer lies in the realms of values and social policy. Is the employment relationship to be regarded as a neutral bargain between autonomous individuals (as the courts did controversially, in the nineteenth century[91]) or should the social function of

86. High Court, 8 February 1999, pp 7-8 of Morris P's judgment.

87. High Court, 8 February 1999, p 17.

88. Supreme Court, 27 Febraury 1998.

89. High Court, 8 February 1999.

90. *Cf* Ch 6 above.

91. It was on this basis that the doctrines of voluntary assumption of risk and common employment could flourish. It is interesting to note that, even today, uncertainty prevails as to the possibly continuing vitality of the defence of common employment in relation to property damage or loss caused by the negligence of a fellow employee: see para **[43.69]** below.

being an employer carry with it duties of concern for the welfare of one's employees, which translate into enforceable legal obligations going beyond the arid assessment of the implied terms of the employment contract? Should all employers be treated on falling under an identical set of duties or should paternalistic duties be premised on the size and complexity of the employment enterprise?

**[18.58]** The courts have yet to provide a coherent answer to these questions. The general thrust of judicial decisions on employers' liability is paternalistic, requiring the employer to go to considerable lengths to protect the physical welfare of employees. Indeed, common law principles of employers' liability blend comfortably with the social policies underlying statutory duties on employers which are clearly paternalistic in their purpose and which could not easily be interpreted on the basis of an implied contractual terms model. There is, however, a strand of judicial authority[92] favouring the implied terms approach. In Ireland[93] this has been limited to the context where the claim is one for economic loss (albeit linked to physical injury) rather than for physical injury *per se*. It would have been better for the matter to have been addressed and resolved by reference to considerations of proximity and policy rather than by resort to the contract paradigm.

**[18.59]** Let us consider how the courts have dealt with claims by employees that range beyond physical injury.

### *(a) Psychiatric injury*[94]

**[18.60]** Psychiatric injury in the workplace has given rise to litigation in recent years. It is now clear that an employer who is or ought to be aware that an employee is working under such pressures that his or her mental health is likely to break down owes a duty to take reasonable steps to deal with the problem.[95] Equally, the careless failure by an employer to recognise and treat the obvious symptoms of post-traumatic stress disorder in an employee may generate liability. Budd J so held in *McHugh v Minister for Defence*,[96] where a solider on a tour of duty in the Lebanon developed such a condition after he had been exposed to a life-threatening incident involving an unexpected and negligent discharge of a gun by a sergeant who was standing beside him and, a couple of months later, was involved in a number of distressing incidents where he witnessed the dead bodies of other soldiers. Although he displayed clear symptoms of post-traumatic shock disorder, his employers were slow to recognise the condition and to deal with it effectively. Budd J stated:

---

92. *Pai Hing Cotton Mill Ltd v Liu Chong Hing Bank Ltd* [1986] AC 80; *Reid v Rush & Tompkins Group plc* [1990] 1 WLR 212; *Sweeney v Duggan* [1997] 2 ILRM 211 (SC).

93. *Sweeney v Duggan* [1997] 2 ILRM 211.

94. See Handford 'Psychiatric Injury in the Workplace' (1999) 7 Tort LR 126; Dolding & Mullender 'Law, Labour and Mental Harm' (1996) 59 MLR 296; McNamee 'Mental and Emotional Stress in the Workplace (1998) 2 Ir Ins LR 4.

95. The leading English authority is *Walker v Northumberland County Council* [1995] 1 All ER 737. *Cf Johnstone v Bloomsbury Health Authority* [1992] 1 QB 333 (CA); *Petch v Customs and Excise Commissioners* [1993] ICR 789 (CA); *Beard v Jevans Furnishings Co Ltd* CA (Civil Div), 6 October 1999. The leading Australian authority in *Gillespie v Commonwealth* (1991) 104 ACTR 1, appeal dismissed (1993) Aust Torts Reports 81-217. See generally McKenna 'Stress Injuries at Work' (1994) 144 New L J 1652, Wilson 'Stress at Work' (1999) 149 New L J 1036; Kelly 'Post Traumatic Stress Disorder: Military and Police: The Legacy of Hillsborough' (1979) 14 Ir LJ (ns) 217, 235.

96. High Court, 28 January 1999 (Budd J).

"The plaintiff was employed by the defendants as a member of the defence forces and as such the [Minister for Defence] owed to the plaintiff a duty to take reasonable care for the health and safety of the plaintiff. In my view there was a negligent failure to take appropriate care for the health of the plaintiff in that once he became subject to stress, which was likely to happen and was reasonably foreseeable in the dangerous and macabre situations in the Lebanon, the defendants failed to spot the obvious manifestations of post traumatic stress or else negligently failed to recognise the significance of the symptoms and also failed to obtain remedial therapy for the plaintiff."[97]

**[18.61]** What should be the situation where an employee suffers psychiatric injury – "nervous shock", in the traditional lexicon of the lawyers[98] – as a result of carelessness on the part of the employer? In Britain the House of Lords[99] has rejected the idea that an employee who is a "secondary" rather than a "primary" victim should be owed a distinct duty of care, however careless the employer may have been and regardless of the fact that the psychiatric injury may be highly foreseeable. Unless the employee can succeed in surmounting the several policy restrictions attaching to the claims of secondary victims generally – and in most cases he or she will not be able to do so – the claim will fail.

**[18.62]** This harsh consequence follows from a succession of developments in Britain in relation to claims for nervous shock. The policy limitations prescribed in *McLoughlin v O'Brian*,[100] and refined in *Alcock*,[101] coupled with the controversial distinction between primary and secondary victims developed in *Page v Smith*,[102] led the House of Lords, by a majority, in *White v Chief Constable of South Yorkshire*,[103] to impose the policy limitations on all secondary victims and to deny that employees were owed any distinct duty of care to be protected from "nervous shock". Of course the odd employee will be able to come

97. Page 42 of Budd J's judgment.

98. *Cf* Ch 17 above. *Cf Berry v Brandon Hotel* Circuit Court, 7 May 1999 (Judge Lynch), where the plaintiff, a chambermaid cleaning a hotel room, injured her hand with a syringe needle that had been discarded in an ashtray. She suffered extreme stress following the incident and feared contracting AIDS or hepatitis, despite blood tests having proved negative. The hotel was held liable "in the matter of instruction" to her, damages being reduced by 75% to take account of her contributory negligence. See also *Dunne v Lawter Products Ltd*, DPIJ: Hilary and Easter Terms 1997, p 66 (HC) - plaintiff suffered anxiety state and phobia after being injured in explosion on factory premises; *O'Leary v Bill Hanlon Offshore Supply Co Ltd* DPIJ: Hilary and Easter Terms 1994 (HC) - employee trapped under containers on oil rig suffered from depression after the traumatic event; *Gilna v Maguire* High Court, 19 May 1999 (Johnson J) - radiographer suffered from chronic pain syndrome and post traumatic stress disorder following trauma of electro magnetic shock when using laser imager processor; *Clancy v Micro Bio (Irl) Ltd* DPIJ: Hilary and Easter Terms 1996, p 67 (HC) - plaintiff suffered severe physiological injury from three incidents involving, exposure to chlorine gas and the release of a blast of chlorine into his face; liability not contested; *O'Donovan v Southern Health Board* DPIJ: Michaelmas Term 1991, p 175 (HC) - nurse who was struck by linen bag, thrown from top of stairs, suffered serious depression, leading to suicide attempt. It should be noted that in all of these cases, the plaintiff had suffered some physical injury.

99. In *White v Chief Constable of South Yorkshire Police* [1998] 3 WLR 1510. See Handford, *Psychiatric Injury in the Workplace* (1999) 7 Tort LR 126 at 153-154.

100. [1983] 1 AC 410.

101. *Alcock v Chief Constable of South Yorkshire Police* [1992] 1 AC 310.

102. [1996] 1 AC 155.

103. [1999] 2 AC 455.

within the narrow confines of the category as rescuer or will be able to show that he or she was a primary victim[104] but in all other cases the employee will have no claim.

**[18.63]** It is to be hoped that the Irish courts will not follow down this harsh and ultimately indefensible line of thought. They have not yet committed themselves unambiguously to *Alcock's* policy limitations; nor have they yet been called on to take a position on the issue raised in *Page v Smith*.[105] They thus are free to reflect on the question unencumbered by compromising precedent.

**[18.64]** Why should an employer, who owes a duty of care to an employee not to cause him or her physical injury, not also owe a duty of care to avoid causing the employee psychiatric injury resulting from nervous shock? The only justification proferred for the absence of such a duty is one that applies to claims for "nervous shock" in general, namely that the potential range of claimants could be very wide. While this concern has some validity in cases where bystanders (or, *a fortiori*, television viewers) suffer nervous shock, it has far less in the context of the workplace, where the potential number of claimants will be small (often a single person). Moreover, the moral claim of the employee is surely a strong one. Horrific accidents take place in work environments. The employee who witnesses a colleague suffering dreadful injuries or actually dying from them will inevitably be greatly affected by what he or she has seen. Why should the employer who is responsible for the accident not be responsible to the employee for the psychiatric injury that he or she suffers? Few negligence actions have more compelling elements of proximity and foreseeability.

***(b) Property damage***

**[18.65]** There is a marked judicial reluctance to extend the employer's duty of care as far as the employee's property.[106] Of course, if an employee suffers physical injury as a result of the employer's breach of his or her duty of care in respect of the employee's safety and in the accident the employee's watch (for example) is broken, the employer will have to compensate the employee for the value of the watch.[107] This will be so even where by good fortune the employee completely escapes physical injury. In such circumstances however, the employee's liability springs from a breach of duty of care to avoid physical injury: the damage to the watch falls within the foreseeable consequences of that breach. Where, however, the property is damaged or otherwise lost – by theft, for example – in circumstances where the employer has not risked causing physical injury to the employee, the position is different. It is one thing to say that an employer must take care of the employee's physical safety; it is another to say that a similar obligation arises in relation to the employee's property. The policy arguments in favour of imposing such a burden are clearly less pressing, though they still have some force.

---

104. *Curran v Cadbury (Ireland) Ltd* [2000] 2 ILRM 343 (CC), where the plaintiff was, by the employer's negligence, given cause to believe that she had seriously injured a fellow employee, was awarded damages in respect of psychiatric injury. See Judge McMahon's comments on this at pp 356-359 [2000] 2 ILRM *and* analysis of Deane Jane, 'Pressure Points' 95 Law Soc Gazette 14-17.

105. [1996] 1 AC 155.

106. For a thorough analysis, see White, *Civil Liability for Industrial Accidents* (1993), paras 7.3.08-7.3.10.

107. Equally, so if the watch was stolen from the employee's wrist when he was incapicitated from the accident: *cf Pascoe v MWTI Ltd* QBD, 31 July 1990 (Tyrell QC).

**[18.66]** The English cases that have addressed the issue have done so in the narrow context of the theft by a third party of the employee's property form the workplace.[108] Perhaps not too surprisingly they have rejected the employee's attempt to impose liability on the employer. In *Deyong v Shenburn*[109] Du Parcq LJ observed:

> "There has never been a decision that a master must, merely because of the relationship which exists between a master and servant, take reasonable care for the safety of his servants' belongings in the sense that he must take steps to insure, so far as he can, that no wicked person shall have an opportunity of stealing the servants' goods. That is the duty which is contended for here, and there is not a line of authority which suggests that any such duty exists or ever has existed."

**[18.67]** These words were uttered over half a century ago and in the meantime the scope of the general duty of protection from intentional wrong-doing by third parties has widened to some degree. It is nonetheless true that theft claims by employees are a species of claim for negligently caused pure economic loss, where courts continue to evince reluctance about imposing a duty of care. This combination of an affirmative duty of protection and a duty to prevent pure economic loss (caused directly by another) makes the claim by employees in this context a particularly difficult one to sustain.

**[18.68]** There are, however, other kinds of cases involving damage to an employee's property where the argument for imposing a duty of care on the employer, and liability for its breach, seems unanswerable. In the nature of things, most employees bring few of their possessions with them to work: their clothes, a case or bag and the tools of their trade will often be all that is involved. They may leave their car or bicycle somewhere on the premises. The potential scope of liability on the part of the employer is therefore relatively limited; but who can deny that an employer should have to compensate an employee for the discolouration of the clothes he or she is wearing as a result of some default on the employer's part – such as the failure to put a "wet paint" sign on a recently painted office wall? Where physical damage rather than pure economic loss relating to property is involved, there seems no principled objection to imposing a duty of care on the employer.

**[18.69]** Cars and bicycles raise a somewhat different issue. If the employer provides space for employees' vehicles on the premises, undoubtedly a duty of care arises but it may be argued that that duty should be characterised as one resting on bailment or occupancy rather than *qua* employer. The point is far from academic. The Occupiers' Liability Act 1995, which relates to the occupier's duty to protect the person *and property*[110] of the entrant, contains a proviso in s 8 that nothing in the Act is to be construed as affecting any enactment or rule of law relating to (*inter alios*) "employers in respect of their duties towards their employees".

**[18.70]** If the employer's duty of care extends to protecting employees' vehicles parked on the premises as part of the employment contract, then the 1995 Act does not affect this duty. If that is so, a notice in the area where the cars are parked professing to comply with s 5 of the Act and reducing the scope of the employer's duty, as occupier, in respect of

108. *Deyong v Shenburn* [1946] KB 227; *Edwards v West Herts Group Hospital Management Committee* [1957] 1 WLR 415; *cf Public Transport Corporation v Sartori* [1997] 1 VR 168 (SC Austr CA).

109. [1946] KB 227 at 233.

110. Section 1(1) of the Act defines "damage" as including loss of property.

visitors'[111] vehicles to avoid damaging the vehicles intentionally or reluctantly, would not defeat a claim by an employee whose vehicle is damaged negligently by the employer.[112]

***(c) Pure economic loss***

**[18.71]** As our discussion of the cases dealing with the theft of employees' property has indicated, courts are notoriously reluctant to impose a duty of care on employers to protect their employees from pure economic loss.[113] This is so even where the economic loss is integrally related to the sustaining of physical injury by an employee in the workplace.

**[18.72]** In *Sweeney v Duggan*[114] the plaintiff who had been employed by a quarrying company, had been injured when working there. He sued his employer and was awarded damages against the company. At the time of the award the company had gone into voluntary liquidation. He then sued the defendant who was the managing director and effectively the only shareholder of the company, arguing that the defendant had had a duty to ensure that the company either had employers' liability insurance to meet claims such as his or, alternatively, to ensure that the company apprised its employees of the absence of such insurance cover.

**[18.73]** The Supreme Court, affirming Barron J, rejected the claim. Such a term could not, it considered, be implied into the employment contract either on the "officious bystander" test or on the basis that it derived "from the nature of the contract itself". Nor could tort law assist the plaintiff since the court should look to the contract to determine the scope of the obligations undertaken by the employer in relation to the employee.

**[18.74]** It is, perhaps, not surprising that the Court should have hesitated about imposing liability in *Sweeney v Duggan*, since the practical implications would be wide-ranging. It is also understandable that the implied terms model should have an appeal when responding to employees' claims in negligence for pure economic loss.[115]

## III. Assessment of Employer's Liability

**[18.75]** Whilst the scope of the duty of care is a matter for individual determination in each case, the Courts have tended to analyse the duty under four general headings:[116]

(1) the provision of competent staff;

(2) the provision of a safe place of work;

---

111. The Act defines "visitor" in s 1(1). See further para **[12.78]** above.

112. If the court were to hold that, at least so far as employees' vehicles are concerned, the employer should be treated as an occupier falling under the terms of the 1995 Act, then it would have to consider whether in any circumstances (and, if so, in which) a purported restriction of liability under s 5 is "reasonable in all the circumstances": s 5(2)(b)(i). See further para **[12.123]** above.

113. See generally Hibbs 'Employee Accidents and Economic Loss – Any Duty of Care?' (1990) 87 Incorp L Soc Gaz of Ireland No 11, p 16

114. [1997] 2 ILRM 211 (SC), analysed by Byrne & Binchy *Annual Review of Irish Law 1997*, pp 704-706 and by Eoin O'Dell in the Contract Law Chapter of that volume, pp 212-220.

115. *Cf Spring v Guardian Assurance plc*, [1995] 2 AC 296 (HL, 1994) - former employers liable in negligence for carelessly prepared reference, arising (*per* Lords Goff, Slynn and Woolf) from an implied term of the employment contract. See further STREET, pp 223-224.

116. *Cf O'Donnell v Hannigan* Supreme Court, 19 July 1960 *per* Maguire CJ at p 3; *Dowling v CIE* Supreme Court, 1 March 1956 *per* Kingsmill Moore J at p 6.

(3) the provision of proper equipment; and

(4) the provision of a safe system of work.

Each of these requires separate consideration, although it should be noted that in certain factual situations, these headings tend to be difficult to separate, and in some cases it may not be clear under which heading it is most appropriate for the plaintiff to proceed. This difficulty should not, of course, defeat his case.[117]

## The Provision of Competent Staff

**[18.76]** "The duty which a master owes to his servant is to use due care to select proper and competent fellow servants".[118] This duty, which inheres in the employer, may be contrasted with vicarious liability whereby the employer will be responsible for the torts of the fellow employees of the plaintiff committed in the course of their employment. This distinction was formerly of considerable importance, where the doctrine of "common employment" relieved the employer of vicarious liability in such circumstances. Since its abolition, the plaintiff generally has had less need to rely on the employer's failure to provide competent staff, although it is still possible to imagine circumstances where it would be wise to do so. Where an employer requires an employee to perform a new operation which the employee quite reasonably fails to appreciate is beyond his or her capacities and the employee injures another employee as a result, the employer, although perhaps not vicariously liable - since the employee carrying the injury might not be guilty of negligence - will be liable to the injured employee under this personal heading of responsibility.

**[18.77]** Before an employer will be liable for having failed to provide competent staff it must be shown that the employer had reason to be aware of their incompetence.[119] This may be proved by specific evidence of knowledge of their incapacity; but it can also be established by proof of a negligent system of "no questions asked". Moreover, where an employer discovers that an employee is incompetent some time after engaging the employee, and then continues to employ the employee on work which the employer now appreciates is beyond the employee's capacity, the employer does so at his or her peril.[120]

---

117. *Cf O'Donnell v Hannigan* Supreme Court, 19 July 1960 *per* Maguire CJ at p 3. See also *Mulcare v Southern Health Board* [1988] ILRM 689 at 692 (HC).

118. *Skerritt v Scallan* (1877) IR 11 CL 389 at 401 (Exch). See also *Murphy v Ross* [1920] 2 IR 199 at 209 (CA). *Cf* Loftus 'Employer's Duty to Know Deficiencies of Employees' (1967) 16 Clev-Marshall LR 143; Kime & Harper 'The Duty to Control the Conduct of Another' (1934) 9 Indiana LJ 498 at 515-516; Armstrong 'Comment, Negligent Hiring and Negligent Entrustment: The Case Against Exclusion' (1973) 52 Ore LR 296; Walker 'Comment, Negligent Hiring: Employer's Liability for Acts of an Employee' (1984) 7 Am J of Trial Ad 603; Haerle 'Comment, Employer Liability for the Criminal Acts of Employees Under Negligent Hiring Theory' (1984) 68 Minn LR 1303; Anon, 'Comment, Recognition of Negligent Hiring Expands Employer Liability' (1983) 10 Wm Mitch LR 361.

119. *Cf Murphy v Pollock* (1864) 15 ICLR 224 (Exch); *Skerritt v Scallan* (1877) IR 11 CL 389 (Exch); *Swift v Macken* (1873) IR 8 CL 140 (Exch); *Hough v Irish Base Metals Ltd* Supreme Court, 8 December 1967 - plaintiff's case based on lack of adequate supervision of employees as constituting unsafe system; *Walker v McCormack* Supreme Court, 4 March 1968; *Barrett v Anglo Irish Beef Producers Ltd* High Court, 6 March 1989 (Barr J) but see *Murphy v Ross* [1920] 2 IR 199 (CA).

120. *Hudson v Ridge Manufacturing Co* [1957] 2 QB 348; *Antoniak v Commonwealth* (1962) 4 FLR 454.

The same applies to cases where the employee has behaved in such a way that the employer ought to have become aware of his or her incompetence but failed to do so.

**[18.78]** In some cases, failure to provide competent staff may more conveniently be regarded as falling under the heading of failure to provide a safe system of work through inadequate supervision of the employees.

**[18.79]** In *Hough v Irish Base Metals Ltd*,[121] the Supreme Court held that no case of negligence had been made out where an employee was injured when jumping away from a gas fire which had been placed near him for "a bit of devilment" by another employee. This was a "lark" that was often practised in the repair shop where they worked. The Supreme Court held that since no evidence had been proferred concerning the supervision in this repair shop or the degree of supervision that would ordinarily be required in a repair shop, the employer could not be held to have been negligent. Ó Dálaigh CJ (which whom Walsh and Haugh JJ concurred) stated that the larking was regarded by all as "a bit of fun", that it would be over in an instant, that the practice had not been reported to anyone in authority by either the plaintiff or any of his fellow employees, and was not easily detectable by the employer. It could not reasonably be said, therefore, that an employer who did not detect it had failed in his duty to provide a safe system of supervision "as the larking in question was of such recent origin and was not of such frequency as must necessarily have been detected in any system of reasonable supervision".[122]

**[18.80]** An employer may be personally liable for sexual harassment or bullying of an employee, either on the basis that the employer ought to have been aware of the offending employee's propensity to act in this way or on the basis of an unreasonable failure to provide a safe system of work.[123] In *Eustace v The Ashtown Tin Box Co Ltd*, Hamilton P dismissed such a claim against an employer. He was not satisfied that there had been a lack of supervision on its part. Moreover, while there had been evidence that the offending

121. Supreme Court, 8 December 1967.

122. Page 4 of judgment. See also *Walker v McCormack* Supreme Court, 4 March 1968; *Smith v Crossley Bros Ltd* (1951) 95 Sol J 655; *cf Hudson v Ridge Manufacturing Co* [1957] 2 QB 348. Of course, the employer may be liable *vicariously* for damage caused to one employee by a practical joke played on him by another employee: *see Harrison v Michelin Tyre Co Ltd* [1985] All ER 918 (QBD), noted by Hodgkinson 'Vicarious Liability for the Practical Joker' (1985) 135 New LJ 1252; *Kennedy v Taltech Engineering Co Ltd* High Court, 10 February 1989 (Barr J). *Cf Nagle v The Tipplers Tavern* DPIJ: Michaelmas Term 1991, p 161 (HC), where two teenage colleagues of the fifteen-year-old plaintiff, working at a licensed premises, as a prank offered him a glass of corrosive detergent which looked like water. The employer was held not to be vicariously liable but was held liable in negligence for failing to instruct the employees as to the corrosive character of the detergent, of which the pranksters were completely unaware.

123. Of course an employer may also be liable vicariously for conduct of this kind where it can be regarded as having occurred in the course of the offending employee's employment. Such a claim failed in the High Court decision of *The Health Board v BC and the Labour Court* High Court, 19 January 1994 in the context of the Employment Equality Act 1977. The Employment Equality Act 1998, s 15, has remedied the position. See generally Meenan, *Working within the Law* (2nd ed, 1999), pp 218-224; Twomey, 'Sexual Harassment' (1999) BR 64; Harvey & Twomey *Sexual Harassment in the Workplace* (1995), Ch 3; Flynn 'The Limits of Sexual Harassment Liability' (1994) ILT 215; *Waters v Commissioner of Police of the Metropolis* [2000] 1 WLR 1607 (HL). For discussion of recent developments in the USA, see Baldrate, (1999) 31 Connecticut LR 1149; Gill, (1999) 32 Creighton LR 1651; Brama 'The Changing Burden of Employer Liability for Workplace Discrimination' (1999) 83 Minn LR 1481.

employee had engaged in offensive conduct against a number of female employees, there was no evidence that they had made any complaint to their employer.[124]

## The Provision of a Safe Place of Work

**[18.81]** The employer must ensure that a reasonably safe place of work is provided and maintained for the benefit of the employee.[125] It is no longer[126] sufficient for the employer to show that the employee was aware of the danger on the premises. Prior to the enactment of the Occupiers Liability Act 1995, the courts had sometimes addressed the question of the employer's liability to the employee in respect of the condition of the premises in terms of *occupiers'* rather than employers' liability. They tended to characterise the employee as an invitee.[127] The problem with this approach is that it emmeshed the courts in the inappropriate task of assessing whether dangers on the employer's premises were "unusual" ones.[128] Other courts realised that employers' liability – even in respect of premises – should not be diverted down the path of occupiers' liability and that the better approach would be to apply the straightforward negligence test to dangers resulting from the condition of the employer's premises, unencumbered by the distinctive rules traditionally attaching to the different categories of entrant.[129] Section 8 of the Occupiers' Liability Act 1995 provides that nothing in the Act is to be construed as affecting any enactment or any rule of law relating (*inter alios*) to "employers in respect of their duties towards their employees". It seems clear that the effect of this provision is to re-enforce the strong strand of judicial authority prior to the Act favouring a straightforward negligence test.[130]

---

124. DPIJ: Hilary and Easter Terms 1991, p 31 (HC). One might reasonably ask in the light of the *Hough* case (see para **[18.79]**) to what extent is there a positive obligation on the employer to be pro-active in the context of bullying and harrassment. Should he or she make regular enquiries, hold meetings or distribute literature on the subject, even if he or she has no specific reason to suspect it is prevalent in the work place? The trend of social policy, envinced clearly by legislation, is to require employers to be vigilant and concerned for the welfare of thier staff even in the absence of specific incidents.
125. See *Gallagher v Mogul of Ireland Ltd* [1975] IR 204 (SC); *Kirwan v National Children's Hospital* Supreme Court, 10 May 1963, especially Walsh J's judgment at p 3, expressing the duty (in terms similar to that owed to a contractual entrant) as being "to make the premises as safe as reasonable care and skill could make them".
126. *Cf Vaughan v Cork & Youghal Ry Co* (1860) 12 ICLR 297 (Exch), articulating the former approach.
127. *Cf Christie v Odeon (Ireland) Ltd* (1957) 91 ILTR 25 (SC); *Kenny v Irish Shipping Ltd* Supreme Court, 4 November 1968; *Sisk (John) & Sons Ltd v National Silo Ltd* [1963] IR 319 (SC aff'g HC). *Ewart v Polytechnic Touring Association Ltd* [1933] IR 230 (SC), in its formulation of the duty sought to be imposed on the employer, appears to fall between the duties owed to an invitee and a licensee, respectively.
128. *Cf Indermaur v Dames* (1866) LR ICP 274 at 288 (Willes J).
129. See *Carriere v Board of Gravelbourg School District No 2244 of Saskatchewan* (1977) 79 DLR (3d) 662 (Sask CA). Alternatively, plaintiffs have based their case on failure to provide a safe system: *cf Kennedy v Limerick County Council* Supreme Court, 21 December 1959; *Kenny v Irish Shipping Ltd* Supreme Court, 4 November 1968 - hybrid test of occupier/safe system applied. In *Johnson v Gresham Hotel Co* High Court, 3 November 1986 (Lynch J); the plaintiff failed under both headings. *Cf Moloney v Jury's Hotel plc* Supreme Court, 12 November 1999.
130. One can surely discount the prospect that a court today would place any reliance on earlier decisions expressing the employer's duty in terms of that appropriate to an invitee (or, *a fortiori*, licensee). Those decisions were clearly guided by the common law principles relating to occupiers' liability, which have been displaced by the 1995 Act.

**[18.82]** Courts applying the straightforward negligence test are entitled to take account of the fact that the employee is on the premises to do a job of work. As Kingsmill Moore J noted in *Christie v Odeon (Ireland) Ltd*,[131] "to make accidents impossible would often be to make work impossible."

**[18.83]** Nevertheless, an employer is not entitled to expect that the employees will always act with regard for their own safety in response to dangers on the premises. In *Kielthy v Ascon Ltd*,[132] Ó Dálaigh CJ stated:

> "In my opinion if an employer offers without distinction a number of modes of access to the company's office, all of which, except one, are safe, he cannot be relieved of his liability because a workman happens to choose to use the one which turns out to be unsafe. His duty is, not to see that *some* modes of access which he offers are safe, but that all of them are safe."

---

131. (1957) 91 ILTR 25 at 29 (SC). See also *Latimer v AEC Ltd* [1953] AC 643 (HL); *Depuis v Haulbowline Industries Ltd* Supreme Court, 14 February 1962; *Kinsella v Hammond Lane Industries Ltd* (1962) 96 ILTR 1 (SC); *Kirwan v National Children's Hospital* Supreme Court, 10 May 1963, pp 2-4 *per* Lavery J (dissenting); *Bradley v CLE* [1976] IR 217 at 223 (SC). *Cf Smith v Mehawk Europa Ltd*, DPIJ: Trinity Term 1991, p 124 (HC). In *O'Donnell v Minister for Defence*, DPIJ: Hilary and Easter Terms 1997, p 135 (HC), a solider injured when he stumbled in a competition involving running failed in his complaint about the roughness of the terrain (in Finner Camp). *Per* Costello P at p 138:

> "Of course the ground wasn't that of a bowling green, of course there was unevenness ... There may well have been rabbit holes … but to require a battalion to hold its competition in this particular terrain did not in itself, in my opinion, amount to an act of negligence …"

See also *Lewis v Irish Forestry Board*, DPIJ: Trinity and Michaelmas Terms 1993, p 12 (HC).

132. [1970] IR 122 at 129 (SC); *cf Noonan v Dublin Distillery Co* (1893) 32 LR (Ir) 399 (Ex Div), predicated on a degree of passivity on the part of the employer which would scarcely command support today. See also *Murphy v ESB* DPIJ: Trinity and Michaelmas Terms 1993, p 261 (HC) - employer ought to have anticipated that employees driving tip-up trucks to and from an ash pit would sometimes drive off leaving the body of the truck in a tipped-up position and should therefore have installed a "goal post" to alert them; *Reid v Dublin Corporation*, DPIJ, Trinity Term 1991, p 86 (HC) - unsafe means of access to pit because grease and dirt were on steps; *Bedford v Minister for Defence*, DPIJ: Hilary and Easter 1998, p 1 (HC) - system for removing mud from gymnasium steps after return of football team failed on the day; *McNulty v J A Kilroy & Son Ltd*, DPIJ: Michaelms Term 1990, p 254 (HC) - employer liable for providing access to premises by an "extremely dangerous" ladder; *McDonald v Dublin Corporation* [1996] Ir L Log W 214 (CC) - co-employee fell on plaintiff because of absence of ladder. *Cf McElroy v Ireland*, Supreme Court, (*ex tempore*) 5 March 1998 - defect in metal strip across doorway; *Dowling v ESB*, DPIJ: Hilary and Easter Terms 1997, p 40 (HC) - employee with three years' experience of barrier on employer's premises which was down during certain periods of the day failed in action; Carney J was "not concerned with a roving inquiry in relation to what is desirable in the construction and design of gates of this type"; *McLoughlin v Donegal County Council*, DPIJ: Trinity and Michaelmas Terms 1994, p 114 (HC) - employer of fire fighter not obliged to have a system for grating frosty pathways to facilitate safe access by employees to fire station; such a requirement would be unrealistic; *McCarthy v Southern Health Board*, DPIJ: Hilary and Easter Terms 1994, p 1 (HC) - employee who slipped on icy patch on footpath on hospital premises failed in her action; *per* Keane J at p 2 "… [T]he most careful occupier of property could never ensure that there could not be an occasional accumulation of water save by … constant attention to the surface". In *Gallagher v Premier Dairies*, DPIJ: Michaelmas Term 1990, p 316 (HC), liability was imposed where an employee slipped on a path where there was ice under light snow. The employer's failure on the fateful day to have adhered to its system for making the path safe in adverse weather conditions may have told against it.

**[18.84]** The extent to which an employer must protect an employee from injury on premises not under the employer's control is somewhat less certain. Whilst the fact that the premises are not under his control does not constitute an automatic ground for exemption from responsibility, clearly it is an important factor to which the Court will have regard.[133] There are obvious limits to the employer's duty in this regard:

> "if a master sends his plumber to mend a leak in a respectable private house, no one could hold him negligent for not visiting the house himself to see if the carpet in the hall creates a trap"[134]

**[18.85]** Although some decisions[135] have approached this issue under the fourth heading, of failure to provide a safe system of work, whatever approach is favoured, it seems that no hard-and-fast rules have been articulated on this question, and that the Courts have generally been content to hide behind the rationale that it is no more than a "question of fact".[136]

**[18.86]** In *Mulcare v Southern Health Board*[137] a home help employed by the defendant injured her ankle on an uneven floor in a dilapidated house of an elderly woman whom she had visited for several years. She alleged that the defendant was negligent in failing to have surveyed the house. Murphy J, having quoted with approval the previous paragraph (which appeared in the first edition of this text), said:

> "I have no wish to hide behind the paragraph I have quoted, but it seems to me that what was involved in this case is a question of degree. A distinction must be drawn between an employee on his employer's property, and an employee on the property of others. There can be multiple variations, for example a skilled craftsman who is sent out on a domestic emergency to a premises where no danger is likely, and where the premises would be safe. This must differ from the case of an apprentice who is sent out to the demolition of a premises. It is a matter of degree and fact in every case. I think it unhelpful to consider the problem under the four general headings of workmen or competent staff, safe place of business, safe tools, safe premises, or safe system. I think that all that can be done is to simply state that the employer is bound to exercise reasonable care. The employer fixes the condition in which an employee works."[138]

---

133. The occupier of the premises may also, of course, be sued in appropriate cases: *cf* eg *Reidy v Fry-Cadbury (Ireland) Ltd* Supreme Court, 12 May 1972 - occupier, but not employer, sued; *McLoughlin v John McGowan (Drogheda) Ltd*, DPIJ: Trinity and Michaelmas Terms 1993, p 211 (HC) - employer and occupier equally liable; *Daly v Securicor (Ireland) Ltd* DPIJ: Hilary and Easter Terms 1991, p 142 (HC) - employer, but not occupier, liable to security guard; *McCann v Brinks (Ireland) Ltd and Ulster Bank Ltd* [1996] 1 ILRM 461 (SC), analysed by Byrne & Binchy *Annual Review of Irish Law 1996*, pp 577-579 - similar holding; *Kerin v Kavanagh*, DPIJ: Hilary and Easter Terms 1993 - employers 20% liable, occupier 80% liable.

134. *Wilson v Tyneside Window Cleaning Co* [1958] 2 QB 110 at 121 (CA).

135. Eg *General Cleaning Contractors v Christmas* [1953] AC 180 (HL). *Cf O'Donnell v Hannigan* Supreme Court, 19 July 1960 - employer directed employee to travel in dangerous van owned and driven by third party; Maguire CJ (for the Court) acknowledged difficulty of categorising liability under any of the four conventional heads, but held that case should not have been withdrawn from jury.

136. *Wilson v Tyneside Window Cleaning Co* [1958] 2 QB 110 at 122 (CA). See also *Kerin v Kavanagh (t/a Kavanagh Contrat Cleaners)* DPIJ: Hilary and Easter Terms 1993, p 80 at p 92 (HC).

137. [1988] ILRM 689.

138. [1988] ILRM 689 at 692.

**[18.87]** Murphy J noted that if the defendant had carried out a survey, the condition of the house, might have been only slightly better than when the accident occurred. He went on:

> "What would the duty have been then? Are those[139] conditions where the employer must say to an employee 'You cannot work there'? Is one to say that a reasonable employer must say to the owner of the premises, 'My man will not go in there until certain works are done', [be it in writing, or, in this case, remedying defects to a floor?] At what stage is one to say the home help can only go to a moderately dilapidated premises?
>
> I take the view that a Health Board is not bound by a duty, where an employee provides this type of service, to require the premises in which the employee is to provide those services to be improved to modern standards."[140]

**[18.88]** Murphy J considered that the floor, though short of the ideal, was not unsafe. He noted that the plaintiff had not fallen there in the previous seven years and concluded that the premises were not so unsafe as to require the defendant to oblige the elderly woman to carry out improvements or lose the services of the home help.

**[18.89]** The case raises a most interesting policy question to which the empty formula of due care can provide no helpful answer. Murphy J reveals a commendable concern for the implications of requiring elderly and infirm members of our community to spend high sums of money on house repairs as the price for necessary medical and social care. However, if the answer is not to deprive the people of care that they may urgently need, why should the employees of the Health Board have to run the risk of injury without compensation?

**[18.90]** The house in *Mulcare v Southern Health Board* was not really unsafe; but where the dilapidation is worse and a house is unquestionably unsafe, are home helps in future to venture therein at their physical and legal peril?

**[18.91]** The Supreme Court also considered the question of the employer's liability in relation to a third party's premises in *Cooney v Thomas Dockrell Sons & Co Ltd.*[141] There, the plaintiff, a carter, was employed to deliver plywood to a customer's timber-yard, which he knew from previous experience contained heaps of debris over which his horse-drawn vehicle had to pass. In negotiating a large heap, the plaintiff fell off the vehicle and was injured. He had frequently spoken to his employer of the delay and inconvenience caused by these heaps of debris, but had not specifically referred to the danger. There was evidence, however, that another employee had mentioned the danger to the employer.

**[18.92]** The plaintiff's action against the customer as occupier failed on the basis that the heap was not an unusual danger and that, even if it was, his knowledge of it in the circumstances relieved the customer of liability.[142] The majority of the Supreme Court also held that there was no case to go to the jury in respect of the liability of his employer. In the view of Haugh J (with whom Lavery J concurred):

---

139. Perhaps the word should be: "there".

140. [1988] ILRM 689 at 692. *Cf McCloskey v Western Health and Social Services Board* [1983] NILR Bull No 4 (CA).

141. [1965] Ir Jur Rep 31 (SC).

142. Applying *Long v Saorstat & Continental SS Co Ltd* (1953) 93 ILTR 137 (SC).

"it follows logically that if there was no case made out against [the customer], equally and for substantially the same reasons there was no case to go in respect of [the employer]."[143]

**[18.93]** Whilst it may be that in most cases the absence of liability on the part of the occupier/customer will coincide with the absence of liability of the employer, there is no *logically* necessary correlation, as Haugh J suggests. It is quite possible that the occupier might not in the circumstances be liable to the employee - as, for instance, where he is not aware of the employee's particular condition, such as deafness or poor sight - where the employer, who is aware of the employee's condition, would nonetheless be liable.

**[18.94]** Finally, in this context we may note the important decision of *Barclay v An Post*,[144] where McGuinness J held that An Post and its statutory predecessor, the Department of Posts and Telegraphs, had not been guilty of negligence in exposing postal workers to the risk of back injury when delivering mail to estates where many of the front doors of the houses had their letter boxes at foot height. The Department of Environment and other statutory bodies had attempted to introduce regulations regarding the positioning of letter boxes, but with no success. Its employees had received training in safe manual handling. McGuinness J, with some reluctance, held that these initiatives had discharged the employer's duty of care.[145]

## The Provision of Proper Equipment

**[18.95]** The employer has the duty to take "reasonable care to provide proper appliances, and to maintain them in a proper condition, and so to carry on his operations as not to subject those employed by him to unnecessary risk".[146] Thus, for example, in *Deegan v Langan*,[147] liability was imposed on an employer who supplied his employee, a carpenter, with nails of a type that the employer knew was apt to disintegrate when struck by a hammer.

143. [1965] Ir Jur Rep 31 at 40. *Cf* Kingsmill Moore J's dissent on this question at 34.

144. [1998] 2 ILRM 385 (HC) analysed by Byrne & Binchy *Annual Review of Irish Law 1998*, pp 624-627.

145. The plaintiff did, however, succeed in his action for injuries sustained when he had been prematurely re-assigned to delivery to low-positioned doors after he had earlier hurt his back when engaged in this kind of work.

146. *Burke & John Paul & Co Ltd* [1967] IR 277 at 281 (SC), quoting from *Smith v Baker & Sons* [1891] AC 325 at 362 (HL). See also *Keegan v Owens* [1953] IR 267 at 274 (SC); *O'Mahoney v Ford (Henry) & Son Ltd* [1962] IR 146 at 150-151 (SC).

147 [1966] IR 373 (SC). See also *Furmeaux v Willis Oil Tools Ireland Ltd*, DPIJ: Trinity and Michaelmas Terms 1993, p 53 (HC) - employer negligent in providing saw with rotating blade to carpenter where a job required a vertical band saw to be done safely; *Hegarty v Steelforms Ltd*, DPIJ: Trinity and Michaelmas Terms, p 193 (HC) - insufficient supply of safety equipment for workforce; *Kiernan v Moneley*, DPIJ: Hilary and Easter Terms 1991, p 180 (HC) - builder's labourer injured when chisel fell on toe; employer negligent in failing to ensure that he was wearing boots; *Smith v Hugh Gormley Ltd* [1997] Ir L Log W 64 (CC) - similar facts; *Brennan v Teagasc* Circuit Court, 30 October 1998 (O'Leary J) - farm advisory development officer whose job required him to walk over hilly ground failed in action against employer alleging that it had not provided him with proper footwear; *Goring v ESB*, DPIJ: Trinity and Michaelmas Terms 1993, p 169 (HC) - employee fell from top of electricity pole as climbing irons had not been kept in "absolute[ly] pristine condition", as safety required; liability imposed; *Mandeville v PJ Carroll & Co Ltd*, DPIJ: Hilary and Easter Terms 1993, p 198 (HC) - unsafe chair, *res ipsa loquitur* principle applied; *Healy v Ireland*, DPIJ: Hilary and Easter Terms 1993, p 10 (HC) - top-heavy filing cabinet;

**[18.96]** Similarly, in *Garry v John Sisk & Son (Dublin) Ltd*[148] liability was imposed on an employer who ignored his employee's complaints about the erratic operation of a cement mixer, when the employee was subsequently injured by the machine. A less direct form of injury arose in *Burke v John Paul & Co Ltd*,[149] where liability was imposed on an employer who supplied a "guillotine" machine for cutting steel bars which, though quite safe for its purpose, had blunt blades, thereby involving its operator in increased physical pressure, with consequent damage to his health.

**[18.97]** As well as being liable for the supply of dangerous equipment, an employer may be liable for the failure to provide equipment essential to the safety of the employee[150] or the failure to maintain equipment in a safe condition.[151] The Factories Act 1955, the Mines and Quarries Act 1965, Safety, Health and Welfare at Work Act 1989 and the Safety, Health and Welfare at Work (General Application) Regulations 1993 of course, afford much statutory protection[152] to employees in this regard by specifying safety requirements which have been reinforced by civil action, but the liability also exists, in more general terms, at common law.

---

147. (contd) *Egan v Crown Equipment Ltd*, DPIJ: Trinity and Michaelmas Terms 1995, p 29 (HC) - loose clothing provided resulting in entanglement of plaintiff's sleeve in machine; *Kelly v Jamaur*, DPIJ: Trinity and Michaelmas Terms 1995, p 139 (HC) - earmuffs kept on plant hire company's premises in a cage as part of the stock of the business for sale to customers rather than for use by employees; *Nugent v DH Bushe* DPIJ: Hilary and Easter Terms 1999, p 25 (HC) - defective ladder; *Stakelum v Bank of Ireland* High Court, 27 April 1999 (O'Donovan J) - employer ought to have ensured that the employee read warning on ladder as to how it should be used.

148. Supreme Court, 29 January 1973; *Cf Noonan v Dublin Distillerv Co* (1893) 32 LR Ir 399 at 406 (Ex Div).

149. [1967] IR 277 (SC); *cf O'Mahony v Ford (Henry) & Son Ltd* [1962] IR 146 (SC) - unforeseeable illness resulted from use of riveting machine and driller. See also *Carlisle v O'Sheas (Dublin) Ltd* Supreme Court, 15 March 1968 - car with defective tyres supplied to employee by employer. *Cf Walker v McCormack* Supreme Court, 4 March 1968 - air compressor used by one employee as a "lark" in such a manner as to injure another employee; *per* Walsh J (p 1):

> "Even if the instrument in question can be regarded as being a dangerous instrument, and I do not think the evidence does more than suggest that it is potentially dangerous, the particular misuse of it in this case is not one of the dangers which could be reasonably foreseen."

150. *Cf O'Hanlon v ESB* [1969] IR 75 (SC); *Gahan v Engineering Products Ltd*, [1971] IR 30 (SC); *M'Kinney v Irish NW Ry Co* (1868) IR 2 CL 600 (Exch Ch); but see *Murphy v Dublin County Council* (1961) 96 ILTR 26 (SC).

151. *Cf Simpson v Pollard* Supreme Court, 6 April 1967; *McC v Town of Monaghan Co-op* [1997] Ir L Log W 52 (CC). In *Daly v Securicor (Ireland) Ltd*, DPIJ: Hilary and Easter Terms 1991, p 142 (HC), a security guard who fell when on a tour of duty around a factory premises because he had not the use of a torch supplied by his employer, as it was defective, succeeded in his action for negligence against the employer. Damages were reduced by 50% to take account of his contributory negligence in failing to have reported to his employer the fact that the torch was not working.

152. See White, *Civil Liability for industrial Accidents* [1993] Part 3; Byrne, *A Guide to Safety, Health and Welfare at Work Regulations* (1995); Garavan, *The Irish Helath and Safety Handbook* (1997), Chs 3-4; Byrne and Binchy, *Annual Review of Irish Law 1993*, pp 379-393; Byrne and Binchy 'The Extension of the Scope of Breach of Statutory Duty for Accidnts at Work' (1995) 13 Ir LT (ns) 4, 28; McNamee 'Employers' Liability: Recent Legislative and Common Law Developments' (1997) 1 Ir Ins LR No 1, p 15, No 2, p 3.

**[18.98]** In *Heeney v Dublin Corporation*,[153] a fatal injuries action, the deceased had been employed as station officer with a fire brigade. He died after inhaling gases while fighting a fire in a building without breathing apparatus. His death took place in October 1985. The evidence established that the fire authority in 1977 had started to provide their crews with breathing apparatus and to organise courses for the training of firemen. By 1984, all the permanent fire brigades in the country had been issued with breathing apparatus, but certain retained brigades, including the one employing the deceased, had not yet received any training nor had been issued with the apparatus.

**[18.99]** The deceased had enquired when these matters would be remedied and had been informed that breathing apparatus training would be provided for retained firemen when the training programme had been finalised. An order for the purchase of breathing apparatus for the deceased's appliance had been made in 1983 but is was not issued until 1988 because personnel were not trained in its use until then.

**[18.100]** In imposing liability, Barron J had no doubt that the fire authority ought to have provided breathing apparatus for its retained crews before it had done and that the brigade where the deceased was employed should not have been allowed to go into buildings without breathing apparatus in cases where the station officer would have authorised the use of breathing apparatus, had it been available. The absence of any instruction to the station officer or his men not to enter the building without breathing apparatus had been wrong. Barron J rejected the argument that the deceased should have waited at the fire for the arrival of the brigade with breathing apparatus before going into the building. The deceased "was in control of the fire and had to act as he saw fit when he arrived at the fire...".

**[18.101]** It should be pointed out that an employer is not an insurer of the safety of the equipment supplied to his employees. As Kingsmill Moore J stated in the Supreme Court decision of *Dowling v CIE*,[154] "this duty is not a warranty but only a duty to exercise all reasonable care". Thus, where an employer buys from a supplier a standard tool whose latent defect the employer has no means of discovering,[155] the employer may be relieved of liability in negligence in the event of injury to an employee.[156] Much will depend on the circumstances as to whether an employer has taken sufficient care regarding equipment

---

153. High Court, 16 May 1991 (Barron J).

154. Supreme Court, 1 March 1956, at p 11.

155. *Cf Simpson v Pollard* High Court, 3 June 1963 - bacon-slicing machine in shop put in motion by employee's hip brushing against it; Supreme Court held that case should have gone to jury; *per* Ó Dálaigh CJ (pp 3-4):

> "We are here concerned not with the intricacies of machine design or with latent defect but with a condition which a jury might consider was reasonably discoverable to be quite unsafe and, particularly so, for the bustle and jostling associated with work behind a shop counter."

See also *Hanrahan v Ardnamult Steamship Co* (1887) 22 LR Ir 55 (Ex Div); *Cf Burrell v Tuohy* [1898] 2 IR 271 (QBD affg 1897).

156. *Keenan v Bergin* [1971] IR 192 at 199 (SC). See further paras **[18.33]** *et seq* above in relation to the possible application of the concept of a "non-delegable duty" in this context. See also *Bissett v Heiton & Co* [1930] IR 17 (SC); *Bissett v Heiton & Co (No 2)* [1933] IR 242 (SC); *Flynn v Irish Sugar Manufacturing Co* [1928] IR 525 at 532 (SC).

used by an employee.[157] The duty is not limited to equipment owned by the employer. Thus, a high degree of care may be required of an employer who authorises the manhandling of heavy equipment owned by a third party that is on the employer's premises: prior inspection of the equipment may be called for to ensure that the employee will not be injured.[158] Where the equipment is on the premises of a third party, the employer's duty of care may be easier to discharge.[159]

**[18.102]** In many cases the difference between supplying defective equipment and failing to provide a safe system of work ceases to be conceptually clear, as where an employer is aware that a machine is being used quite unnecessarily in a dangerous manner by an employee, but fails to explain to the employee how the danger may be avoided,[160] or where an employee is required to work on a machine that is too low, resulting in the employee's knees coming in contact with metal pegs protruding from underneath the work table[161] or where work that involves the risk of appliances becoming dangerous through no-one's fault is not supported by an adequate system of inspection and reporting which would mitigate the consequent dangers to employees.[162]

**[18.103]** In *Rogers v Bus Atha Claith*[163] the question of safe equipment/safe system arose in the context of a bus driver being assaulted on two separate occasions in February and November 1995. There had been a dramatic increase in the number of serious assaults on bus drivers in the Dublin area in the period 1991-95. As far back as 1985, the vulnerability of bus drivers had been recognised by the employers who met with the drivers, the Unions and gardaí to discuss the problem. Various solutions were proposed as to how the driver in one-man buses might be protected. Some of these were installed but were vetoed by the drivers who in one case, said the modified structure was too claustrophobic and in another, that the perspex surround caused a glare. A horizontally sliding screen was then tried, but after trials in November 1993 it was found to have two faults; first, the driver did not use it frequently, and second, it was not totally secure in so far as a determined assailant could

---

156. (contd) In accord is the English decision of *Davie v New Merton Board Mills Ltd* [1959] AC 604 (HL (Eng)), discussed at paras **[18.35]** above and analysed by Osborough 'Employer's Liability and Defective Tools' (1969) 4 Ir Jur (ns) 119; Webber 'Safety of Tools and Employer's Liability' (1959) 12 CLP 56 and Hamson 'Note' [1959] Camb LJ 157. Scottish decisions have held to the contrary: *cf Crowe v Brennan* [1967] IR 5 at 8 (SC). For critical analysis of the Employer's Liability (Defective Equipment) Act 1969, enacted in England in response to *Davie's* case, see Lang 'The Employer's Liability (Defective Equipment) Act - Lion or Mouse?' (1984) 47 MLR 48; Lemon & James 'The Employer's Liability (Defective Equipment) Act, 1969' (1970) 2 Kingston LR 57.

157. In some cases, of course, it may not be clear whether the employer or the supplier of the defective chattel is liable. The difference may be vital where the employee himself or herself is charged with the task of ensuring the chattel is safe: *Tracey v Hayes* Supreme Court, 6 March 1973. In other cases, both the employer and the supplier may both be separately liable: see, eg, *Gilna v Maguire* High Court, 19 May 1999 (Johnson J).

158. *Keenan v Bergin* [1971] IR 192 (SC).

159. *Cf McGurrell v ESB* Supreme Court, 21 December 1970; *Campbell v Cox* Supreme Court, 15 May 1956.

160. *Cf Crowe v Brennan* [1967] IR 5 (SC), see also *Burns v Irish Fibres Ltd* (1967) 101 ILTR 172 (SC); *Leathem v Isaac Black Ltd* (1945) 80 ILTR 12 (KBD NI); *Quinn v W & T Avery Ltd* (1967) 103 ILTR 142 (SC).

161. *McGuigan v Iralco Ltd* [1996] Ir L Log W 92 (CC).

162. *Cf Dowling v CIE* Supreme Court, 1 March 1956 - plaintiff unsuccessful on facts.

163. Circuit Court, January 2000 (Judge McMahon).

get around it. Eventually by the middle of 1995 an agreed structure was adopted and all new buses were fitted with this structure, and all existing stock was scheduled for modification. The plaintiff's bus had not been fitted with the structure when he was attacked in February or in November 1995. Judge McMahon, held that the employers had acted reasonably in all the circumstances: they recognised the problem, they addressed it seriously, they spent considerable amounts of money in trying to design an acceptable frame, they continuously discussed the proposed solutions with the workers and the Unions and when finally, an acceptable solution was devised they bean to implement the solution in a reasonable fashion. The plaintiff further argued that, given the bad record of assaults on the plaintiff's particular route, the employers should have prioritised the conversion of his bus. Judge McMahon did not accept this argument, and in any event, he held that even had the conversion been done, this would not have deterred the assailant since, the new agreed screens were not assault-proof and the assailant in the November assault, wearing a balaclava and armed with a butcher's knife, would have as easily rounded the proposed screen, as he did the existing one.

## The Provision of a Safe System of Work[164]

### *Introduction*

**[18.104]** In *Kinsella v Hammond Lane Industries Ltd*,[165] McLoughlin J stated:

> "If an accident causes injury to a workman and the accident results from a risk of an unsafe system of work, against which the employer should have [taken], but did not take, reasonable precautions to guard, then the employer is liable for damages."

**[18.105]** Since the demise of the doctrine of "common employment", this heading of liability (like the first heading) has lost some of its importance, as vicarious liability will normally provide a suitable alternative avenue for compensation, but there will be cases where a claim could succeed under this heading although not on the basis of vicarious liability - as where negligence on the part of the employee who injured the plaintiff cannot be established or where no other employee was responsible for the injuries.

### *What is a "system" of work?*

**[18.106]** In *Caulfield v George Bell & Co Ltd*,[166] Murnaghan J noted that the expression "a safe system of work" had never previously, to his knowledge, been defined. Stating that "the obligation presupposes a *system*"[167] he added that:

---

164. See Anon 'The Duty of a Master to Provide a Safe System of Working' (1949) 83 ILT & SJ 237; Delany 'An Employer's Duty of Care to his Workmen: What is a "Safe System"?' (1959) 25 Ir Jur 29; Anon 'Master and Servant- Common Law Duty to Provide a Safe System of Working - Cases Where the Doctrine of Common Employment Does not Apply' (1939) 73 ILT & SJ 165; Anon 'Master and Servant, Duty to Provide a Safe System of Working' (1948) 82 ILT & SJ 143 at 153.

165. (1962) 96 ILTR 1 at 4 (SC).

166. [1958] IR 326 (HC).

167. [1958] IR 326 at 333. The obligation may, however, arise in respect of a single transaction: *Winter v Cardiff RDC* [1950] 1 All ER 819. The test is not simply whether the employer has *devised* a safe system but also whether the employer is *operating* one: *McDermid v Nash Dredging Reclamation Co Ltd* [1987] AC 906 (HL), noted by Holgate, (1988) 9 Bus LR 51; *Gallagher v Premier Dairies*, DPIJ: Michaelmas Term 1990, p 316 (HC). Simply leaving matters to an employee to decide, even where the employee is experienced, may be stignatised as constituting an unsafe system of work: *McSweeney v McCarthy* Supreme Court, 28 January 2000.

> "The expression has to be considered in every case, to which it is appropriate, in relation to the particular circumstances of the job in hand. In the expression the word, 'safe', means no more than 'as safe as is reasonably possible in the circumstances'. The degree of safety would depend on the particular job and would vary between wide limits."[168]

***Some specific instances of an unsafe system***

**[18.107]** Bearing these considerations in mind, it is easy to appreciate why the Court found there to have been an unsafe system where, in a bakery, a baker was prohibited from using a piece of wood to push dough from the sides of a dangerous machine on to the ground because there was "a danger that a piece of wood might be cut by the cutter and ... get into the dough which would be baked into loaves", but the baker was allowed to use his finger for the task.[169]

**[18.108]** Other examples of failure to provide a safe system of work include: the provision of unstable scaffolding;[170] the failure to fence a tank of sewage around which an employee has to walk in darkness during a gale ;[171] requiring employees to use ladders when carrying lengthy and heavy rods;[172] providing an unseaworthy raft to convey employees across a river in the course of their work;[173] requiring a seaman, working under pressure of an emergency, to pass close to an unfenced revolving stub axle;[174] improperly loading a van which is to be driven by an employee,[175] or arranging for the unloading of a vehicle in a

168. [1958] IR 326 at 333.

169. *Guckian v Cully* Supreme Court, 9 March 1972.

170. *Leathem v Isaac Black Ltd* (1945) 80 ILTR 12 (KBD NI). See also the other decisions cited in fn 159 above. And see *O'Regan v Crampton Ltd (No 1)* Supreme Court, 15 June 1953; *O'Regan v Crampton Ltd (No 2)* Supreme Court, 1 June 1954 - plank held not to have broken but alleged to have been too narrow to walk on with safety.

171. *McIlhagger v Belfast Corporation* [1944] NI 37 (KBD).

172. *Larmour v Belfast Corporation* [1945] NI 163 (CA). See also *McKenna v Meighan* [1966] IR 288 (SC) - employee required to mount trailer in a dangerous manner; *Devers v Bourke Builders Ltd*, DPIJ: Trinity and Michaelmas Terms 1991, p 3 (HC) - failure to provide ongoing help in holding ladder for painter working on a very shiny and slippery floor was negligent; *McSweeney v McCarthy* Supreme Court, 28 January 2000 - foreman should have made it clear to the painter using ladder alone what to do if he encountered a potential danger; the fact that the painter was an experienced one did not remove this obligation. See also *Walsh v BMD & Co Ltd*, DPIJ: Trinity and Michaelmas Terms 1994, p 104 (HC).

173. *Flynn v Irish Sugar Manufacturing Co* [1928] IR 525 (SC).

174. *Murphy v Commissioners of Irish Lights* Supreme Court, 25 July 1973. *Cf McCarthy v McEvoy, t/a Victoria Cross Saw Mills*, Supreme Court, 6 February 1961; *O'Doherty v Limerick Corporation*, DPIJ: Michaelmas Term 1991, p 66 (HC).

175. *O'Callaghan v Cross's Refrigeration Ltd* Supreme Court, 20 April 1972 - plaintiff unsuccessful on the facts. *Cf Daly v Ballyclough Co-operative*, DPIJ: Trinity Term 1991 (HC) - plaintiff successful. See also *O'Donnell v Hannigan* Supreme Court, 19 July 1960 - employer alleged to have been negligent in letting plaintiff drive in motor truck unsafe and unsuitable for transportation of bulls; truck overturned and plaintiff injured; case should not have been withdrawn from jury. *Cf Hogan v McEwan* (1975) 64 DLR (3rd) 37 (Ont HC) - not negligence to transport eight employees in van not intended for passengers and having no seats. *Per* Henry J at 62: "The evidence indicates that it was not feasible to modify the vans by adding seats. The alternative would be to carry the men in a second (passenger) vehicle but that clearly poses economic problems"; *Burke v Minister for Defence*, DPIJ: Hilary and Easter Terms 1991, p 234 (HC) - loading blocks onto truck by passing them between the loaders at too fast a pace was an unsafe system.

dangerous manner;[176] permitting operators of a bottle-cleaning machine to lift bottles by putting their fingers in the top, with consequent risk of injury;[177] providing hand-washing facilities for employees in a barrel containing water contaminated by cement;[178] requiring an employee to carry quarters of beef through a narrow opening in a yard, thus risking a fall;[179] requiring a fitter to carry out electrical work on a plug without adequate instruction;[180] arranging transportation for employees to be provided by a driver (another employee) who is suffering from fatigue resulting from hard work over many hours;[181] requiring two employees to travel on a tractor where there was safe seating for one;[182] transporting an employee in a car with no windscreen;[183] requiring nurses in a hospital cafeteria to clean away food they might spill on the floor and failing to provide any other protection to patrons against slipping;[184] requiring a carpenter to demolish a shed without a

---

176. *McManamon v CIE* [1961] IR 30 (SC revg 1957); *Kelly v Dublin Corporation*, DPIJ: Michaelmas Term 1991, p 195 (HC). *Cf Cazabon v Westinghouse Electric Irl Ltd t/a Thermoking (Europe) Ltd*, DPIJ: Hilary and Easter Terms 1994, p 104 (HC) - unloading heavy boxes from shelves into trolley; *Marchetti v Cantrell & Cochrane* DPIJ: Hilary and Easter Terms 1991, p 112 (HC) - door of delivery van jammed, requiring employee to exit in a risky manner.

177. *O'Sullivan v John Daly & Co Ltd* Supreme Court, unrep 31 July 1972 - practice not established on the evidence. *Cf Barrett v Anglo Irish Beef Producers Ltd* High Court, 6 March 1989 (Barr J).

178. *Boyne v Commissioner for Public Works in Ireland*, DPIJ: Hilary and Easter Terms 1992, p 58 (HC).

179. *Brady v McCarren & Co Ltd* Supreme Court, 6 June 1957. See also *Robinson v Electricity Supply Board*, DPIJ: Trinity and Michaelmas Terms 1993, p 134 (HC) - employee dragged out a cast iron lintel from under ledge for inspection rather than used forklift truck; employer liable but employee held 15% contributory negligence; *Markan v Galway Corporation*, DPIJ: Trinity and Michaelmas Terms 1995, p 57 (HC); *McClintock v Gregg* [1996] Ir L Log W 443 (CC) - system involving farm hand carrying newborn calf across uneven farmyard, resulting in fall, held unsafe; *O'Sullivan v Iarnród Éireann – Irish Rail* High Court, 14 March 1994, Morris J) - plate-layer fell when carrying heavy sleeper in station yard full of scrap metal and wire that had been left lying on the ground.

180. *Campbell v Cox* Supreme Court, 15 May 1956. See also *Hogan v ESB* Supreme Court, 17 December 1999 - failure to warn employee to remain clear of live transformers.

181. *Murtagh v Lawlor* Supreme Court, 4 December 1959.

182. *Keogh v Irish Forestry Board Ltd*, DPIJ: Trinity Term 1991, p 18 (HC).

183. *Canning v Cahill*, DPIJ: Hilary and Easter Terms 1995, p 42 (HC).

184. *Kennedy v Limerick County Council* Supreme Court, 21 December 1959; *cf Kenny v Irish Shipping Ltd* Supreme Court, 4 November 1968 - adequate precautions taken to prevent donkeyman-greaser from slipping on greasy deck in ship's engine room. *Donahue v Irish Shipping Ltd* Supreme Court, 28 November, 1958 - similar facts); *Flanagan v Robert Usher & Co Ltd*, DPIJ: Michaelmas Term 1991, p 84 (HC) - plaintiff slipped on bobbin that had escaped onto a factory floor from a machine, causing his hand to fly into the machine; liability imposed; *Payne v Artane Sevice Station (t/a Castle Service Station)*, DPIJ: Hilary and Easter Terms 1997, p 32 (HC) - no system to cope with spillages, leading to accumulation of diesel and water at service station. Contrast *Quirke v Mid-Western Health Board*, DPIJ: Trinity Term 1991, p 94 (HC) where a domestic worker, whose duties included keeping tidy the floor of a ward in a hospital where geriatric patients and patients with mental disability were being tended, slipped on food that a patient had let spill onto the floor. Relieving the employer of liability Johnson J observed that:

> "Every job has an inherent risk. Some risks vary to a greater or lesser extent and the …. obligation of an employer is to minimise the risk within reason. Here we have [a] situation which causes great difficulty in the management of elderly and geriatric and psychiatric patients. Part of the risk involved in this is going to be the spillage of food. No method has yet been devised to prevent this happening and someone has got to clean it up and part of the risks of any cleaning staff in any establishment [is] to actually go on to the floor when it is not clean for the purposes of cleaning it. All that can be done is to warn [the employee] …"

helper;[185] requiring an employee to work on top of a container on the deck of a vessel when a crane was moving suspended loads over his head;[186] arranging work in a trench so as to make the labourers run the risk of being struck by stones dislodged by their fellow-employees;[187] and organising work on a railway in such a manner that an employee is struck by a reversing engine.[188]

**[18.109]** On the other hand, in *Carey v Cork Consumers Gas Co*[189] a general labourer was held not to have established an unsafe system where he had contracted silicosis over a period of twenty-four years, by inhaling silica dust when periodically demolishing silica bricks. The former Supreme Court considered that there was no evidence that his employers ought to have known of the health danger. Whether the same view would be taken today is very doubtful in the light of greater knowledge of such risks and increased sensitivity to work-related health dangers.[190]

**[18.110]** In *Coyle v An Post*,[191] the Supreme Court, by a majority, rejected the contention that an employer should be held negligent for having an employee make a journey by road on a winter's morning when conditions were icy, resulting in his crashing his car. The plaintiff, the sub-postmaster of Raphone, had been driving to Lifford to collect cash. The Supreme Court did not consider that the employer's failure to have an available source of funds at a Lifford bank, thus exposing the plaintiff to the risks of the journey, constituted negligence.

---

184. (contd) See also *Buckley v Southern Health Board*, DPIJ: Hilary and Easter Terms 1994, p 115 (HC); *Meade v ITW Hi-Cone Ltd*, DPIJ: Trinity and Michaelmas Terms 1998, p 55 (HC); *Cassidy v Wellman International Ltd*, DPIJ: Trinity and Michaelmas Terms 1998, p 171 (HC). *Cf Evans v Doranbrook Services Ltd (t/a The Baggot Inn)*, [1997] Ir L Log W 389 (CC) - differentiating system of cleaning required on a small premises from that in a large supermarket or hotel. Not a safe system to require staff in public house to clean up their own spillages at busy Christmas period.

185. *Kelly v McCarron & Co Ltd*, Supreme Court, 30 May 1968 (22-1967 - a jury question, on which expert evidence was divided, the defence witness regarding it as "crackers" to require a helper in such a case.

186. *Hollywood v Cork Harbour Commissioners* [1992] 2 IR 457 (HC).

187. *Connor v Malachy Burke (Contractors) Ltd* Supreme Court, 31 March 1955. See also *O'Donnell v Begley* [1987] ILRM 105 (HC) - jury question whether removal of joint box cover, weighing 3 cwts, by one employee with one key amounted to an unsafe system of work (affd SC); *Coughlan v Birr UDC* Supreme Court, 22 July 1996 - stone mason required to work on uneven surface when building a wall, by reason of decision to create temporary narrow channel between wall and kerb of footpath; *Melia v Meath County Council*, DPIJ: Trinity and Michaelmas Terms 1996, p 200 (HC) - employer liable for collapse of trench which had been routed close to water main rendering soil less stable; *McDonagh v Brian O'Connell Ltd* High Court, 24 October 1996 (Barr J) - trench collapse.

188. *McNamara v CIE* Supreme Court, 22 July 1972. Contrast *Noonan v Dublin Distillery Co* (1893) 32 LR (Ir) 399 (Ex Div).

189. Supreme Court, 5 March 1958; *Cf O'Mahoney v Ford (Henry) & Son Ltd* [1962] IR 146 (SC). See also *Brady v Beckmann Instruments (Galway) Inc* [1986] ILRM 361 (SC). *O'Donnell v Herdmans Ltd* [1987] NILR Bull 1 (QBD); *Sammon v Fleming GmbH* High Court 23 November 1993 (Barron J) analysed by Byrne & Binchy *Annual Review of Irish Law 1993*, pp 539-54.

190. *Cf O'Toole v Iarnród Éireann* English High Court, QBD, 19 February 1999 (Hayward J), where liability was imposed on an employer for the death of an employee as a result of exposure to asbestos dust thirty years previously.

191. [1993] ILRM 508 (SC), analysed by Byrne & Binchy *Annual Review of Irish Law 1992*, pp 573-576.

### *Lifting weights*

**[18.111]** If an employee is required to lift excessive weights in the course of his or her work, the system of work can be stigmatised as an unsafe one. The whole subject of lifting excessive weights has for many years been dealt with by statutory provisions and the regulations made pursuant to statute.[192] The statutory code is more favourable to the plaintiff than the common law action for negligence, which requires only that the employer take reasonable care to protect employees from injury. Often the success of the plaintiff is an action for breach of statutory duty renders his or her common law claim in negligence otiose.

**[18.112]** Parallel to the employer's obligation to protect the employees from injury by lifting weights that are excessive is the obligation to train them in the proper way to lift weights that they are likely to encounter in their employment. An employee who fails in the claim that a weight was excessive can still succeed in establishing that although the weight was within acceptable limits, he or she had not received the appropriate training in how to lift it safely. In *Lynch v Dublin Corporation*,[193] the plaintiff, a labourer, was injured when, with another employee, he attempted to lift a wheelbarrow containing tools onto a low-loader, at a height of over three feet. The fellow employee let the wheelbarrow fall in the middle of the manoeuvre.

**[18.113]** Morris J rejected the plaintiff's contention that it was negligent for his employer to have required him and his co-employee to engage in this manoeuvre, observing that he was:

> "not prepared to accept that for two men to be required to lift a load which would be calculated at somewhere between 90 and 100 lbs between them onto a low-loader [of] a height of three feet is something that is basically dangerous and that it is improper to require a workman to do it. I feel that if one were to make a finding that such a process was dangerous and improper, then it would mean that virtually all manual work would have to stop and I would not be prepared to accept that the load in this case was such as to make a loading of it onto a three-foot high low-loader a dangerous or improper manoeuvre to require a workman to perform".[194]

**[18.114]** Morris J went on, however, to impose liability on the employer, both vicariously for the co-employee's default and in the employer's own right for failing to provide proper training to its employees in lifting techniques.[195]

---

192. See generally White, *Civil Liability for Industrial Accidents* (1993), Ch 16. *Cf Dunleavy v Glen Abbey Ltd* [1992] ILRM 1 (HC), analysed by Byrne & Binchy *Annual Review of Irish Law 1991*, pp 406-409.

193. DPIJ: Hilary and Easter Terms 1991, p 228 (HC).

194. DPIJ: Hilary and Easter Terms 1991, p 228 (HC), pp 230-231.

195 See also *Kennefick v John A Wood Ltd*, DPIJ: Hilary and Easter Terms 1994, p 97 (HC) - storeman injured back when lifting toolbox that was obstructing access to store room; employer liable in negligence and breach of statutory duty for having failed to instruct him on how to lift weights properly, damages reduced by 15% for employee's contributory negligence; *Robinson v ESB*, DPIJ: Trinity and Michaelmas Terms 1993, p 134 (HC) - employee injured when dragging heavy mantelpiece; liability imposed on employer subject to 15% reduction for contributory negligence as plaintiff could have used forklift truck;

**[18.115]** Nurses have frequently been subjected to undue demands, in the course of the employment, in regard to lifting patients or otherwise bearing their weight. In *Kirby v South Eastern Health Board*,[196] Morris J stigmatised as negligent a turning procedure by nurses which required them to clasp their hands under a patient's lower back and thigh, to lift a patient at a given signal and to turn the patient thereafter on her side. This involved the plaintiff in stretching forward across the bed to move the patient over to the far side of the bed. The plaintiff hurt her back in the process.

**[18.116]** This method of turning a patient had been recognised by the nursing profession in the late 1970 and the early 1980's as being dangerous. In a number of publications before the date of the accident – in January 1988 – attention had been drawn to this danger. The Southern Health Board had published instructions for the training of the nurses which condemned the practice for exposing the nurse who was moving the patient away from her to the danger of injuring her back.

**[18.117]** Morris J also accepted expert evidence from an engineer that, apart altogether form the nursing and medical profession, it had been well recognised for many years in industry that the general safety of employees required that a lift must not be performed in this way and that to incorporate such a lift in a system of work was potentially dangerous to employees.

**[18.118]** Morris J rejected the allegation of contributory negligence. The plaintiff "could not reasonably have been aware of the danger present in using this method of lifting without instruction from the defendants."[197]

---

195. (contd) *Byrne v Newman Sheeting Centre* [1996] Ir L Log W 229 (CC) - shortage of available staff to help plaintiff; *McSweeney v Cork Corporation* DPIJ: Hilary and Easter Terms 1994, p 37 (HC) - slow learner inadequately trained in lifting techniques. *Dennehy v Counter Equipment Ltd* DPIJ: Hilary and Easter Terms 1992, p 193 (HC) - excessive weights and lack of instruction in lifting techniques, liability for breach of statutory duty and negligence; *Bowdren v Southern Health Board*, DPIJ: Trinity and Michaelmas Terms 1993, p 65 (HC) - not foreseeable that plaintiff, carrying "a very minor load" of x-ray photographs weighing 28 pounds would sustain a back injury even though the shelf from which he was taking them was crowded and he was working from a ladder; *Kelly v Fujitsu*, [1996] Ir L Log W 325 (CC) - employer negligent in failing to put warning label on box indicating it was heavy, "especially where the majority of the boxes were quite light"; employee 50% contributorily negligent in failing to have checked the weight himself.

196. DPIJ: Trinity and Michaelmas Terms 1993, p 234 (HC).

197. DPIJ: Trinity and Michaelmas Terms 1993, p 234 (HC). See also *Allen v O'Suilleabhain and the Mid-Western Health Board* High Court, 28 July 1995 (Kinlen J), analysed by Byrne & Binchy *Annual Review of Irish Law 1995*, pp 479-482 - nurse required to support a woman's leg on her shoulder as woman was giving birth; *White v Mid-Western Health Board*, DPIJ: Hilary and Easter Terms 1993, p 55 (HC) - nurse injured when lifting fourteen stone, non-cooperative patient with assistance of only one other colleague; liability imposed for lack of sufficient trained personnel; *Firth v South Eastern Health Board* High Court, 27 July 1994 (Barr J) - ward attendant injured when turning a patient in bed; health board liable for failing to have the nursing staff retrained and kept up to date in lifting techniques prior to the accident; *O'Sullivan v Southern Health Board* High Court, 8 December 1998 (Smyth J) - nurse required to lift patients with assistance of untrained domestic staff member; damages reduced by 1/3% for contributory negligence as she could have insisted that a qualified nurse help her and ensured that the domestic staff member was aware of need to lift in unison. *Cf Woolger v West Surrey & North East Hampshire Health Authority* (1993) 16 BMLR 120; *Dewing v St Luke's (Anglican Church in Australia) Association* 1999 TAS LEXIS 9; BC 9901351 (Tas SC).

**[18.119]** Issues of causation and foreseeability can complicate litigation involving claims against employers relating to excessive weights. In *Matthews v The Irish Society for Autism and the National Autistic Association*,[198] the plaintiff was the office manager of the defendant corporations, of which she and her husband were founding members, her husband being their executive director. On a wet afternoon, when she was carrying fifty information packs in her arms and a large briefcase over her shoulder, she rushed across the footpath at O'Connell Street, Dublin, towards her husband's car. As she did so, an unidentified woman who was coming along the footpath to her left slipped and fell. In falling, she grabbed the plaintiff who in turn, lost her balance and fell heavily on her arm and shoulder, fracturing her neck.

**[18.120]** The plaintiff claimed (*inter alia*) that the defendants were negligent in failing to provide a safe system of working for her and in failing to provide appropriate equipment for the task she was required to do.

**[18.121]** The essence of the plaintiff's claim was that, under the system in place at the time, she was required to handle manually an excessive load or weight of material and that the environment through which she had to carry it exposed her to risk. The weight she was carrying – forty three pounds – exceeded the limit prescribed for female employees under Article 3 of the Factories Act 1955 (Manual Labour) (Maximum Weights and Transport) Regulations 1972. These regulations had no application to the instant case but the plaintiff nonetheless contended that the load was too heavy for one female. Her counsel argued that requiring her to cradle loose information packs in her arm when crossing a busy urban footpath on a wet afternoon, when pedestrians tended to rush, was not a safe way to transport the material, even if the weight was acceptable.

**[18.122]** Laffoy J dismissed the plaintiff's case. The accident was "entirely attributable" to the fact that the unidentified female pedestrian had collided with the plaintiff. The fact that the plaintiff was carrying a heavy and an awkward load had not contributed to her fall. There was "a high degree of probability" that the accident would have happened in the same way, with the same consequences, if the plaintiff had not been encumbered by the information packs or the briefcase and if she had not been rushing. It was probable that the same result would have ensued if she had been going with the flow of pedestrian traffic in front of the woman who collided with her. The hazard which the accident had highlighted was not of a type that would reasonably be anticipated by the defendants' employee who had responsibility for preparing a safety statement and not something which would have been required to have been identified and addressed in the formulation of such a safety statement, had there been one.

**[18.123]** Laffoy J's characterisation of the kind of accident that occurred was of crucial relevance to the outcome of the proceedings. The essence of the event was that the plaintiff had been knocked down by another person whose fall would have brought about the plaintiff's accident regardless of what she was carrying. The heavy load that she was carrying had not, in Laffoy J's view, increased the prospects of an accident occurring. Laffoy J, although describing in detail the plaintiff's argument that the defendants had been

198. High Court, 18 April 1997 (Laffoy J), analysed by Byrne & Binchy *Annual Review of Irish Law 1997*, pp 736-738.

negligent in failing to provide a safe system of work, or proper equipment, never specifically held that the defendants had in fact been guilty of negligence. The general tenor of her discussion of this argument, however, suggests that she did not demur from the proposition that they had been negligent.

**[18.124]** The reason why the plaintiff lost her case was, thus, not (necessarily) that the defendants were not negligent, but that any such negligence could not have been the cause of the plaintiff's injuries. It is true that in *Hughes v Lord Advocate*,[199] the House of Lords held that a negligent defendant will be liable, even where the precise circumstances of an accident are unforeseeable, if the injury is of a *kind* that was foreseeable. This case could not assist the plaintiff, however, since Laffoy J did not hold that the accident was not of a different kind from that which was foreseeable: on her analysis the cause of the injury was the unidentified woman's fall, so the defendants simply had not caused the plaintiff' s injury, whether foreseeable or otherwise.

***Passive smoking***

**[18.125]** Our courts have yet to address the question whether an employer is under a duty of care to have a system of work that protects employees from risks to their health as a result of passive smoking.[200] In the recent Scottish case, *Rae v Strathclyde Joint Police Board*,[201] Lord Bonomy declining to dismiss such a claim *in limine*, observed that:

> "... smoking is a non-industrial activity indeed, a social activity indulged in by workers and tolerated by employers which has got absolutely nothing to do with the industrial process. If to the knowledge of an employer smoking in the workplace gives rise to the risk that an employee will contract illness through working regularly in close proximity to smokers, then it may well, depending on the circumstances, be very easy to regard the employer as under a duty to stamp out smoking, or at the very least mitigate the effects of smoking since there may well in the circumstances be no difficult issues of practicability or expenses to be weighed against the risk. No question arises of modifying the method of production."[202]

***Non-use of safety equipment***

**[18.126]** While, as has been mentioned,[203] there is no obligation on an employer to treat the employees as children and warn them of obvious dangers, the task of accident prevention should not be regarded as the employees' sole preserve. A "system" that is perfectly safe in its conception but not carried out in practice may not be sufficient to save the employer. Where, however, the employer can show that it is probable that the employee would not

---

199. [1963] AC 837. See further para **[3.20]** above.

200. See genearlly, Becean 'No Smoking at the Workplace' (1998) 148 New LJ 10; Nolan 'Passive Smoking Litigation in Australia and America: How an Employee's Health Hazard May Become an Employer's Wealth Hazard' (1993) 9 J of Contemp Health L & Poly 563; Fox 'An Assessment of the Current Legal Climate Concerning Smoking in the Workplace' (1994) 13 St Louis U Pub LR 591; Ezra, '"Get Off Your Butts": The Employers' Right to Regulate Employee Smoking' (1993) 60 Tenn LR 905, Vallone 'Note: Employer Liability for Workplace Environmental Tobacco Smoke: Get Out of the Fog' (1996) 30 Valparaiso ULR 811.

201. [1999] SCLR 793 (Court of Session).

202. [1999] SCLR 793 at 799. *Cf Sparrow v St Andrews Houses Ltd* QBD, 21 May 1998 (Manchester District Registry, Holland J); *Shimp v New Jersey Bell Telephone Co* (1976) 368 A 2d 408 (NJ SC ChD); *McCarthy v Department of Social & Health Science* (1988) 759 P 2d 351 (Wash).

203. See para **[18.03]** above.

have used the safety equipment if it had been provided, or would not have obeyed instructions to use it, the employer may escape liability on the grounds of lack of causation.[204]

### *Affirmative obligations of employer*

**[18.127]** It appears that the duty of an employer to take care for the safety of an employee may extend beyond merely preventing an accident in at least some cases. In *Smith v Howdens Ltd*,[205] the Northern Ireland Court of Appeal[206] held that the trial judge had been wrong in holding that the failure of shipowners to provide adequate first-aid equipment for their employees who sustained injuries on the ship through no fault of the shipowners could not constitute negligence. Lord MacDermott LCJ was unable to accept the proposition that:

> "irrespective of circumstances, an employer's duty at common law to take reasonable care for the safety of his workmen never involves an obligation to provide for the treatment of those injured at work. Much may, of course, depend on such matters as the nature of the injury, the efficacy of immediate treatment, and the alternative facilities available ... Why should the precautions which an employer ought at common law to take for the safety of those who work for him cease with the injury and disregard all effective first-aid measures to reduce the gravity of its consequences which might reasonably be taken? I can think of no answer to this question which does not give safety an artificial and sardonic meaning."[207]

### *Dangerous work environments*

**[18.128]** The Irish courts have in several cases addressed the problem of fashioning principles of employers' liability in relation to employees whose job requires them to confront enhanced danger of physical attack. Two categories of care are worthy of distinct notice: (1) the Defence Forces and (2) Employees of security firms.

#### *(i) The defence forces*

**[18.129]** Members of the Defence Forces are sometimes in the course of their employment placed in situations where there is an unavoidable risk of death or serious injury. In the Supreme Court decision of *Ryan v Ireland*,[208] Finlay CJ observed:

> "In such situations considerations of standards of care drawn from the experience of the workplace may be of little assistance. There could, I think, be no objective in a master and servant relationship which would justify exposing the servant to risk serious injury or death other than the saving of life itself. In the execution of military service, exposing a solider to

---

204. *McWilliam v Sir William Arrol & Co Ltd* [1962] 1 WLR 295 see also (more generally) *Caulfield v Bell & Co Ltd* [1958] IR 326 at 334 (HC). *Cf Fraser v Harland & Wolff Ltd* [1978] NIJB (Part 2) (CA).

205. [1953] NI 131 (CA). See Osborough, (1971) 6 Ir J (ns) 205 at 210.

206. MacDermott LCJ and Porter LJ; Black LJ, *dubitante.* Black LJ considered that if such a duty existed is was "very remarkable" (at 147) that it had never previously been laid down in any reported decision or in any text book.

207. See fn 113 above at 139. See also *Barrett v Ministry of Defence* [1995] 3 All ER 87 (CA) - liability imposed on employer who having "assumed responsibility" for an intoxicated employee who was "in a collapsed state "thereafter took inadequate steps to care for him, resulting in his death; the holding in the case does not extend to recognising that, in the absence of such assumption of responsibility, an affirmative obligation would have attached to the employer.

208. [1989] IR 177 at 183-184 (SC). See Byrne & Binchy *Annual Review of Irish Law 1989*, pp 410-418.

> such risk may often be justified by the nature of the task committed to the forces concerned. Furthermore, there can in relation to armed conflict be many situations where those in authority must make swift decisions in effect in the agony of the moment. Mere proof of error in such decisions would not in itself establish negligence. Importance may be attached, I am satisfied, in regard to alleged negligence in a military situation to the question as to whether the role of solider at the time of the alleged negligence is one of attack or defence, or, to put the matter in another way, whether he is engaged actively in armed operation or is only passively engaged in them."

**[18.130]** In *Ryan*, the plaintiff, an army private, was a member of the defence forces serving as a volunteer with the United Nations International Force in the Lebanon. He was placed on guard duty in a guard post which was a likely target for mortal attack by the Chetuhian militia. When such an attack took place, he was injured. He sued the State for negligence, claiming that the guard tent should have been more elaborately sandbagged to protect him from the effects of the attack. The Supreme Court rejected the defence of immunity from liability and ordered a retrial following a withdrawal of the case from the jury in earlier High Court proceedings. The retrial[209] resulted in a verdict in the plaintiff's favour.

**[18.131]** It is clear from Finlay CJ's judgment that he rejected the argument that the State had no duty of care to soldiers even in times of war or armed conflict.[210] As the passage quoted above makes plain, however, the Chief Justice recognised that the particular circumstances of each case would be crucial in determining how the duty of care would be discharged. Naturally situations calling for immediate decisions should be assessed in a way that recognises their emergency character.[211] Equally, where soldiers are engaged passively in armed operations, such as being on guard duty, there will often be a greater opportunity to address the requirements of their safety in a calmer and more systematic way. There is, however, no magic in the distinction between active and passive engagement in armed operations: one can envisage situations where an active engagement may involve plenty of opportunity for deliberate and considered decision-making and other situations of passive engagement which require split-second assessments.

---

209. High Court, Barr J.

210. English courts do not impose a duty of care in these circumstances, thus raising the question whether this approach complies with the European Convention on Human Rights, as interpreted in *Osman v United Kingdom* [1999] 1 FLR 193: case: see *Mulcahy v Ministry of Defence* [1996] 2 All ER 758 (CA).

211. Thus, in *Carey v Ireland*, DPIJ: Michaelmas Term 1990, p 293 (HC), Lardner J dismissed proceedings arising from an incident at a check-point in the Lebanon in which the plaintiff, who was acting as sentry, was accidentally shot by a colleague who was attempting to immobilise a vehicle which was seeking to break through the check-point. Lardner J observed that, if the colleague's conduct was open to criticism, it was nonetheless:

> "entitled to be regarded in the light of the fact that he made [his] decisions quickly, when an emergency arose and they do not seem to me to be .... so unreasonable, so outlandish, so extravagant and uncontrolled as to warrant a finding of negligence against him. They seem to me to be quite reasonable in all the circumstances": at 306.

**[18.132]** In *Lawless v Minister for Defence*,[212] another case emerging from the Lebanon, Keane J imposed liability on the State where the absence of a protection on the perimeter of premises in which the plaintiff, a private was billeted facilitated its penetration and destruction by two people who detonated explosive changes in it, injuring the plaintiff. Keane J characterised the case as one of "passive" engagement to which the "agony of the moment" principle did not apply. The plaintiff's officer:

> "had, ... to quote the words of the Chief Justice [in *Ryan*], 'time and opportunity' to consider the position of the plaintiff and the other persons under their control at the relevant time. Indeed, … the circumstances in the *Ryan* case approximated more closely to conditions of actual warfare than the circumstances which obtained in this case."[213]

*(ii) Employees of security firms*

**[18.133]** Echoing the strong emphasis in *Ryan v Ireland*[214] on the obligation of an employer to take stringent precaution to protect employees from the risk of serious injury and death, the Irish courts have insisted that security firms must adopt wide-ranging, well-thought-out, measures to ensure that their staff are not casually exposed to undue danger from criminals.

**[18.134]** In *Walsh v Securicor (Ireland) Ltd*,[215] the plaintiff, an employee of the defendant security company, collected a large amount of money from a bank in Cork city and drove a van in the direction of Cobh, where he intended to deliver the money to smaller banks and a post office. There was another employee driving with him in the van, which had a Garda escort. They encountered an ambush, in which the van's path was blocked by a tractor and bullets were fired at the windscreen which began to shatter. The plaintiff was eventually forced to open the door of the van and was hit on the head with what he believed to be the butt-end of a rifle. The robbers made off with most of the money.

**[18.135]** The plaintiff sued the defendant for negligence. Barrington J held in his favour and the Supreme Court affirmed.

**[18.136]** The essence of the plaintiff's case was that the time of delivery had been the same every week for a period of seven years and that, in view of the fact that the journey was by a high-risk route, the time should have been varied periodically. This argument appealed to Egan J, with whose judgment Finlay CJ and Hederman J concurred. The defendant's contention that it was contractually tied to the delivery time was swept aside with the observation that there had been "no evidence at all of any discussions at the appropriate levels about the desirability of reviewing or changing the times of delivery from time to time".[216] Moreover, the evidence supported Barrington J's finding that the Garda authorities were quite flexible as to even short notice of alteration in time. "In any event", said Egan J "this was a high risk operation and the defendant was bound to avail of every safety precaution, not just the provision of a Garda escort".[217]

---

212. DPIJ: Trinity and Michaelmas Terms 1992, p 260 (HC).

213. DPIJ: Trinity and Michaelmas Terms 1992, p 260 (HC).

214. [1989] IR 177.

215. [1993] 2 IR 507 (SC affg HC). See Byrne & Binchy *Annual Review of Irish Law 1989*, pp 425-427; Byrne & Binchy *Annual Review of Irish Law 1993*, pp 541-543.

216. [1993] 2 IR 507 at 509-510.

217. [1993] 2 IR 507 at 510.

**[18.137]** Egan J went on to quote Finlay CJ's statement in *Ryan v Ireland*[218] that, in his opinion:

> "[t]here could ... be no objective in a master and servant relationship which would justify exposing the servant to a risk of serious injury or death other than the saving of life itself."

**[18.138]** Egan J noted that Barrington J had not dealt specifically with the defendant's argument that the attack had been unforeseeable in view of the seven years' experience of safe passage. He rejected this argument because the provision of a Garda escort had minimised, but not eliminated, the risk:

> "Every device or precaution must be taken in a high risk operation such as this and there was expert evidence to the effect that it was unwise to retain a clockwork precision in relation to the time factor."[219]

**[18.139]** In *McCann and Cummins v Brinks Allied Ltd and Ulster Bank Ltd*,[220] a more complicated situation arose. The plaintiffs were security men who were employed by Brinks Allied Ltd. They were injured when delivering a cash payment of £1,000,000 to the Rochestown Avenue branch of the Ulster Bank, in south County Dublin in 1990. They were assaulted by bank raiders who shot the first plaintiff in the leg.

**[18.140]** The branch in question was a relatively modern purpose-built bank set back from the public road with a paved or slabbed forecourt and a service road running up beside the bank and around the rear of the building. Because bollards had been erected on the road side of the slabbed forecourt and because the bank objected to the van driving over the slabs, which it said were not intended to support the weight of the van, it was necessary to park the van on the service road. This meant that the closest the van could get to the hall door was forty-seven feet. While the plaintiffs were traversing the forty-seven feet to the door of the bank they were set upon by two armed and masked men and they were kicked and beaten and ultimately the first plaintiff was shot in the leg.

**[18.141]** The plaintiffs argued that their *employer*[221] had been negligent. They contended that the location of the branch of the bank made it a peculiarly attractive target for bank raiders because is was situated close to a shopping centre car park, from which the raiders could survey the scene and lie in wait and also because it was adjacent to a roundabout which provided a satisfactory escape route. The branch had been raided on three previous occasions; two of the raids involved the theft, or attempted theft, of money from security officers in the process of making deliveries to the bank. It was fundamental to the safe delivery of cash to a bank that provision should be made for the van to drive as close as possible to the bank. To require the security personnel to traverse forty-seven feet exposed them to such a high risk that Brinks were, they said, negligent in requiring them to work in these circumstances. Brinks should have ensured that arrangements were put in place to enable the delivery van to be brought close to the bank door or alternatively provide for a

218. [1989] IR 177 at 182.

219. [1993] 2 IR 507 at 510.

220. High Court, 12 May 1995 (Morris J), affd by Supreme Court, 4 November 1996.

221. They also argued, unsuccessfully that the Bank had breached its duty of care to them. For critical analysis of the rejection of this aspect of their claim by both Morris J and the Supreme Court, see Byrne & Binchy *Annual Review of Irish Law 1995*, pp 577-579 and Eoin O'Dell's analysis in the Contract Chapter of Byrne and Binchy *Annual Review of Irish Law 1996*, pp 215-217.

chute or "bank-link" facility which would enable the funds to be transferred from the van to the bank without exposing the men to risk.

**[18.142]** Morris J fortified by expert evidence from a former Detective Chief Superintendent, accepted the plaintiffs' argument about the foreseeability of a raid. He believed that it was "a self-evident fact that the shorter the distance that the money is exposed to potential raiders then the safer the delivery would be."[222]

**[18.143]** He also accepted the evidence of the expert witness that cash-link units had been on the market for some years prior to the date of the incident and could, without undue expense, have been fitted to the side wall of the bank. This would have negated the necessity to expose the security men to the dangers associated with the walk to the front door of the bank. While Morris J was prepared to hold that it had not been the practice in banking circles at the relevant time to use the cash-link units, he was of the view that, given the fact that the branch had already been singled out for two previous raids on the delivery security men and given that the cost of erecting these units and making them compatible with a corresponding unit on the side of the van was small, this work should have been carried out by Brinks if they chose to take on the contract of delivering money to this bank.

**[18.144]** It was impossible to prove as a mathematical certainty that, had the appropriate steps been taken, the bank would not have been raided on the fateful day. The plaintiff had, however, established on the balance of probabilities that, if the relevant steps had been taken to shorten the walk or install a cash-link unit, the injuries of which they complained would not have occurred.

**[18.145]** Therefore Brinks, as the employers of the plaintiffs, were liable in negligence for their failure to provide the plaintiffs with a safe system of work and to take all proper and reasonable precautions for their safety.

## Employer's Negligence Must Have Caused the Injury Complained Of

**[18.146]** As in all cases of negligence, it is not sufficient for the plaintiff to establish that the defendant has been negligent: it is also necessary for the employee to show that the negligence *caused* the injury of which he or she complains.[223] In an older decision, it was suggested that mere proof of a breach by an employer of his duty to provide a safe system of work coupled with proof of an accident of the kind which a safe system would be designed to guard against "discharged the onus of connecting the accident with the breach of duty",[224] in the absence of any other explanation of the accident. This approach was unquestionably affected by the shadow of the doctrine of common employment, which by

222. Pages 4-5 of Morris J's judgment.

223. In *O'Leary v Cork Corporation* Supreme Court, 4 July 1997, affg High Court, 19 May 1993 (Murphy J), the plaintiff sought unsuccessfully to establish that he had developed multiple sclerosis as a result of a work related accident involving negligence on the part of his employer. See Byrne & Binchy *Annual Review of Irish Law 1993*, pp 543-545; Byrne & Binchy *Annual Review of Irish Law 1997*, p 740. See also *Muldoon v Brittas Plastics Ltd*, High Court, 18 March 1993 (Morris J) - lack of training in how to operate fork-lift truck had not caused driver's injury when its mast struck an overhead door beam as he was fully aware of the need to keep the mast lower than the door (lintel).

224. *Connor v Malachy Burke (Contractors) Ltd* Supreme Court, 31 March 1955 *per* Ó Dálaigh J, p 6.

then had become discredited (being abolished by legislation[225] only three years later). It would seem advisable, therefore, not to regard this statement as qualifying the normal rules of proof of causation in the context of employers' negligence. Of course the evidence may be such as to support, or indeed compel, a verdict in favour of an employee where the inferential options are narrow and point in the direction of liability but it would be most unfortunate if the courts were to develop, without serious advance reflection, a doctrine that shifts the onus of proof on the causation issue onto the defendant. Employers should compensate employees not simply because the employer had an unsafe system of work but because that unsafe system actually caused injury to the employees.[226] Criminal sanctions and official safety monitoring processes should penalise employers for unsafe system that happily do not result in injury to the employees.

## Necessary Precautions and Coincidental Injuries

**[18.147]** We must now consider whether an employer should be liable to an employee who sustains injury which might have been avoided or lessened if he had been provided with some protective clothing or equipment, which itself was required not to prevent the injury actually sustained but to prevent another type of injury. In *Kennedy v Hughes Dairy Ltd*,[227] McCarthy J gave the example of workers on a building site who are required by law to be supplied with helmets in order to lessen the risk of injury sustained from falling objects. He asked (but in the circumstances of the case considered it not necessary to answer) the question:

> "Where such an employee has not been provided with a helmet but is injured, not by a falling object, but by, for instance, contact with some equipment being carried, may the employer be liable when the injury sustained is not that against which the precaution [should have been] taken?"[228]

**[18.148]** The answer, according to classic principles of negligence law, is that the employer should not be liable if the injury which the employee happens to sustain is not the reasonably foreseeable result of the employer's negligent conduct. The whole purpose of *Wagon Mound (No 1)*[229] was to assert the principle that defendants should not have to compensate plaintiffs outside the range of the reasonably foreseeable results of their conduct.[230]

**[18.149]** Having said this, it is as well to point to the realities of the workplace. Although a particular precaution may well be considered advisable to deal with a specific risk, this

225. Law Reform (Personal Injuries) Act 1958, s 1.

226. See para **[18.103]** and **[18.121]** above.

227. [1989] ILRM 117 (SC).

228. [1989] ILRM 117 at 124.

229. [1961] AC 388. The modification prescribed by *Hughes v Lord Advocate* [1963] AC 837 and *Burke v John Paul & Co* [1967] IR 277 (SC) would, of course, mitigate the full force of the *Wagon Mound* doctrine in this context.

230. Finlay CJ, dissenting in *Kennedy*, was surely right in principle in saying (at 119) that:

> "[t]he mere fact that a precaution which could be considered necessary to prevent a different type of accident would by coincidence have also ameliorated or prevented injury from this type of accident, is not ... a good ground for reaching a conclusion that it was a precaution which a reasonable and prudent man would consider obviously necessary to provide against the happening of this accident and injury."

does not exclude the possibility that the same precaution may also afford necessary protection against other, less prominent but no less real, risks. Our Courts would be most unwise to concentrate on seeking to identify particular risks to the exclusion of all others. Such an approach, apart from its doubtful social consequences could introduce a dangerous artificiality. *Kennedy v Hughes Dairy Ltd*[231] is itself an example of how the risk may be perceived narrowly or broadly. The majority in the Supreme Court were satisfied that the plaintiff's case should not have been withdrawn from the jury where he had adduced some evidence of negligence on the part of his employers in failing to have afforded him a gauntlet leather glove when tidying away crates of milk bottles, a number of which were broken. The plaintiff had slipped (on a broken milk bottle) and knocked down a crate of bottles, which broke and injured his arm. The majority was of the view that the issue of the defendant's alleged negligence should be defined in broad terms: whether the plaintiff "should have been provided with adequate protective gloves for the work in which he was engaged".[232] However, Finlay CJ, dissenting, concluded from the description of the accident that the injury which the plaintiff had sustained to his arm "might just as easily have been inflicted on his side, his shoulder or his chest."[233] It would:

> "clearly not be reasonable or practicable for an employer to seek to protect his workm[a]n as to the whole of his body or the upper part of his body from cutting by broken glass in the carrying out of the type of work which the plaintiff was doing on this occasion".[234]

## Contributory Negligence of Employee

**[18.150]** The question whether the employee was guilty of contributory negligence in an action based on the employer's breach of duty at common law will be determined according to a somewhat less lenient standard than applies in relation to actions for breach of statutory duty.[235] The courts are, however, aware that the employer sets the standards of care and that the employee may, in his own economic interests, be obliged to accept a less-than adequate level of safety.[236] As Walsh J observed in the Supreme Court decision of *McKenna v Meighan*:[237]

> "It is well established that the workman's knowledge of the danger is not in itself contributory negligence as knowledge is only an ingredient in negligence."

---

231. See para **[3.20]** above.
232. [1989] ILRM 117 at 122 (*per* Hederman J). See also at 124 (*per* McCarthy J).
233. [1989] ILRM 117 at 119. The question may be asked as to whether the failure to provide the glove caused the injury in this case, would the plaintiff have been injured in any event, even if he had been wearing a glove provided by his employer.
234. [1989] ILRM 117.
235. *Higgins v South of Ireland Asphalt Co Ltd* (1961) 101 ILTR 168 (SC). It should be noted that, where the defendant is not in possession of evidence to support a plea of contributory negligence and can thus give no particulars of contributory negligence, the plea will be struck out: *Kennedy v Midland Oil Co Ltd* (1976) 110 ILTR 26 (HC).
236. *Cf Kiernan v Moneley*, DPIJ: Hilary and Easter Terms 1991, p 18 (HC); *Canning v Cahill*, DPIJ: Hilary and Easter Terms 1995, p 42 (HC).
237. [1966] IR 288 at 290 (SC).

**[18.151]** Thus, in *Deegan v Langan*,[238] where a carpenter was injured by a nail supplied by his employer of a type that both he and his employee knew to be dangerous, the Supreme Court held that he could not be found guilty of contributory negligence in using nails of this type in such circumstances. Walsh J stated that the employee's instructions had been:

> "clear and unambiguous and bearing in mind their respective positions it is my view that it would be unreasonable to hold that there still remained an obligation upon the servant to make further representations about the matter to his master. In reality the alternatives open to him were either to do the job as he had been instructed to do it or to refuse to do it. He could not be held guilty of [contributory] negligence because he chose to do the job he was directed to do."[239]

**[18.152]** From this point of view, the desire of an employee to get on with the job may be regarded as praiseworthy rather than automatically amounting to contributory negligence on his or her part.[240] Thus, where an employer could without difficulty have supplied a safety device to a machine operated by his employee, the employee was regarded as being guilty of only slight contributory negligence where he failed to stop the machine every time an adjustment was necessary and injured himself in consequence of the absence of the safety device.[241] So also, in *Stewart v Killeen Paper Mills Ltd*,[242] an employer customarily failed to keep in its correct place a protective guard on a dangerous machine in

---

238. [1966] IR 373 (SC). *Cf Garry v John Sisk & Son (Dublin) Ltd* Supreme Court, 29 January 1973. See also the discussion of *McLoughlin v Allied Textiles Ltd* High Court, 7 July 1955 (Teevan J), in Coleman, *An Employer's Duties at Common Law in Ireland*, (1961) 22.

239. [1966] IR 373 at 376. *Cf Smith v Mohawk Europa Ltd*, DPIJ: Trinity Term 1991, p 23 (HC).

240. *Cf Murphy v Dublin County Council* (1962) 96 ILTR 26 (SC). See also *Shields v Thomas Duffy Builders Ltd*, DPIJ: Trinity and Michaelmas Terms 1996, p 129 (HC) - "counsel of perfection and well beyond the reasonable standard of care which any workman must take for his own safety" to expect employee to inspect bricks close to which scaffolding is placed for possible looseness. In *Furmeaux v Willis Oil Tool Ireland Ltd*, DPIJ: Trinity and Michaelmas Terms 1993, p 53 (HC), a carpenter was held not to have been guilty of contributory negligence for "an instant of inattention" when using a saw at a time when he was hurrying on an urgent order. In *Goring v ESB*, DPIJ: Trinity and Michaelmas Terms 1993, p 169 (HC) O'Hanlon J reduced the employee's damages by 25% where he slipped from the top of an electricity pole because his climbing irons were not in proper condition; the fall was attributable in part to "some relaxation by the plaintiff of the pressure applied [by] him on the irons immediately before the fall, through inadvertence on his part". This appears a somewhat high reduction in view of the dangerous character of the work and the employer's default. *Cf Farmview Dairies Ltd* NI HC (QBD), 18 December 1998 (Coghlin J) - employee who fell from ladder held 60% contributorily negligent in failing to wear wellington boots supplied by employer; *Feeney v John Sisk & Sons Ltd*, DPIJ: Hilary and Easter Terms 1993, p 254 (HC) - employee found 60% contributory negligent in setting ladder on tiles which he knew were wet and slippery; this was "the height of folly". In *Kehoe v Collen Construction Ltd*, DPIJ: Hilary and Easter Terms 1998, p 33 (HC), an employee who fell over an obstruction on the only path onto a building site when he was running back to work, having absented himself without permission was found to have been guilty of contributory negligence to the extent of 75%. Barr J found it "difficult to envisage a greater disregard for personal safety than running on a large industrial building site".

241. *Burns v Irish Fibres Ltd* (1967) 101 ILTR 172 (SC). See also *Barrett v Anglo Irish Beef Producers Ltd* High Court, 6 March 1989 (Barr J).

242 [1959] IR 436 (SC). See also *Murphy v ESB*, DPIJ: Trinity and Michaelmas Terms 1993, p 261 (HC) - employer should have anticipated that employees driving tip-up trucks to and from ash pits would sometimes drive off leaving the body of the truck in a tipped-up position. Employer liable where employee's truck later struck a bridge. *Per* Lynch J (at pp. 261-262):

a paper mill and thereby caused the employee operating the machine to take a chance in grabbing at paper and injuring himself. He was acquitted of contributory negligence. Kingsmill Moore J, in the Supreme Court, stated:

> "Where it can be shown that a regular practice exists unchecked it is difficult to convict of contributory negligence a workman who follows such practice."[243]

**[18.153]** Nonetheless, the role of employees in keeping the workplace safe should not be ignored. In *Aherne v Showerlux (Cork) Ltd*,[244] the plaintiff fell over a pallet that had been prematurely placed by a colleague in the area where he was working, in breach of the employer's safety regulations, Murphy J reduced the plaintiff's damages by 50% on account of his contributory negligence. It was the responsibility of the plaintiff and his colleagues to see that this area was properly maintained and every worker was "bound to have some regard for his own safety". Murphy J observed that:

> "this always must be read in the context that a person who is working, perhaps at a delicate ... or a dangerous task, is keeping his eye on one piece of equipment and ... cannot be expected to have his eye on some dirt ... or grease on the floor ... But here the fact is that the obstruction was the same, in kind, as the material with which [the plaintiff] was constantly concerned ..."[245]

**[18.154]** Of course, where the risk of injury is very great and the employee is injured while disobeying a clear prohibition, he may be regarded as the author of his own misfortune, and damages may be reduced to zero.[246]

**[18.155]** The youthfulness or lack of experience[247] of an employee will be taken into consideration in determining whether he was guilty of contributory negligence. Thus, in

---

242. (contd)

> "It was ... the duty of the defendant to take all reasonable steps to avoid accidents. Employers can not guarantee the safety of careless workers at all times but, if there is a foreseeable danger [which] can be guarded against relatively easily and economically, then the employer should take such steps to guard against it. In this case, the likelihood of a slip up by some driver was, in my view, foreseeable and was capable of being guarded against both easily and economically by the goal-post system ..."

Employee's damages reduced by 50% to take account of his contributory negligence.

243. [1959] IR at 450. See also *Guckian v Cully*, Supreme Court, 9 March 1972; *Marchetti v Cantrell & Cochrane*, DPIJ: Hilary and Easter Terms 1991, p 112 (HC). *Cf McDonald v National Coop Farm Relief Services Ltd*, DPIJ: Trinity and Michaelmas Terms 1993 (HC) - employee guilty of 10% contributory negligence where, on an impulse to get a machine started after it had given trouble, he climbed onto it with a claw hammer which slipped and injured his hand when he sought to lever wire into pulley.

244. DPIJ: Hilary and Easter Terms 1992, p 73 (HC).

245. DPIJ: Hilary and Easter Terms 1992, p 73 at p 78.

246. *Cf O'Hanlon v ESB* [1969] IR 75 (SC). See also *Garry v John Sisk & Son (Dublin) Ltd* Supreme Court, 29 January 1973 - finding of 38% contributory negligence too generous to careless employee who "threw elementary caution aside and went out of his way to bring injury on himself" (*per* Henchy J at pp 5-6); *O'Mahony v John Sisk & Son Ltd* High Court, 16 December 1994 (Barron J) - employer could not reasonably anticipate that labourer would not use available scaffold.

247. *Cf Soulah v Trinity Gate Ltd* High Court, 25 November 1983 (D'Arcy J) - plaintiff, a vegetable porter employed at defendant's restaurant, told to use food-mixing machine to make spaghetti.

> "He asked the chef how he would do it and he replied that he would show him later and left. While [the plaintiff was] breaking an egg the shell fell in the mixture and in a reflex action his hand went in after it. He tried to pull it out but could not":

Irish Times, 25 November 1983, p 13.

*McKeever v Dundalk Linen Co Ltd*,[248] the Supreme Court held that the issue of the plaintiff's contributory negligence should not have been left to the jury where a fifteen-year-old, on the first day that he was taken to clean rust off a particular machine in his employers' factory, was injured by slowly revolving steel rollers on the machine. He had not been warned of the danger of approaching the machine while it was in motion. O'Keeffe J accepted that an adult might reasonably be expected to appreciate the danger but considered that, since the negligence found against the employers was their failure to have warned him of the danger:

> "it would be setting too high a standard for this young plaintiff to expect him to appreciate it without any warning."[249]

**[18.156]** The junior status of an employee may discourage him or her from protesting about working conditions. In *Allen v Ó Súilleabháin*,[250] a twenty-five-year old student midwife sustained a serious back injury when holding the leg of a woman who was giving birth by caesarean section for more than fifteen minutes. This system of work was held to have been an unsafe one by Kinlen J, who acquitted the plaintiff of any contributory negligence. Although she was "a highly intelligent, well-schooled trained nurse", Kinlen J thought, as one witness had stated, that:

> "it would be extremely cheeky for a student midwife to interrupt the obstetrician or the other fully trained midwives. She stood grimacing, doing the best she could, and she is not to be faulted for doing that."

**[18.157]** It has to be said that a system of work that forces a worker into silence when undergoing pain severe enough to render her unemployable for the rest of her life is one that would benefit from review.

**[18.158]** When considering the question of employees' contributory negligence it is worth bearing in mind the general rule[251] that a plaintiff's failure to exercise reasonable care for his or her own protection will not amount to contributory negligence in respect of damage unless the damage results from the particular risk to which the plaintiff's conduct has exposed himself or herself. Thus, if an employee fails to wear goggles to protect him from sparks and he loses his sight because of the negligent discharge of fumes into the factory, his carelessness will not count against him as the risk to which he exposed himself was not the one that actually transpired.

---

247. (contd) Defendant did not deny liability but alleged contributory negligence. Jury found that plaintiff had not been contributorily negligent. See also *Quail v JJ McGovern Ltd*, DPIJ: Michaelmas Term 1991, p 82 (HC). Conversely, of course, the fact that an employee is experienced will be a factor capable of weighing against him or her when determining the issue of contributory negligence: see, eg, *O'Reilly v Dublin Corporation*, DPIJ: Hilary and Easter Terms 1991, p 194 (HC).

248. Supreme Court, 15 May 1956; *Buckley v Avonmore Creamery* Circuit Court, 7 May 1985 (Roe J).

249. Page 4 of O'Keeffe J.'s judgment.

250. High Court, 28 July 1995 (Kinlen J).

251. Civil Liability Act 1961, s 34(2)(c). See para **[20.15]** above. *Cf O'Higgins v P Carney Ltd*, DPIJ: Trinity and Michaelmas Terms 1993, p 176 (HC).

## IV. VOLUNTARY ASSUMPTION OF RISK

**[18.159]** Formerly the defence of voluntary assumption of risk was fairly readily accepted in cases dealing with employer's liability.[252] "In recent years", however, the defence, "has virtually disappeared in [such] cases which turn on common-law negligence".[253] The Courts, even before the statutory reform of 1961,[254] had shown an increasing sympathy for the dilemma of an employee who was aware of a dangerous work practice for which his employer was responsible. If he said nothing, he might be held to have accepted the risk; if he protested, he might have lost his livelihood.[255] Today, only a communicated waiver of a right of action will constitute a voluntary assumption of the risk: an uncommunicated determination will not suffice.[256] The employee may, however, still be defeated by a holding that, having regard to the risks inherent in a particular business, the employer was not in breach of his duty of care to the employee.

**[18.160]** This was the fate of an acetylene burner, employed by shipbreakers and scrapmerchants, who was injured by a falling propeller, in *Depuis v Haulbowline Industries Ltd*.[257] In the Supreme Court, Lavery J, for the majority,[258] noted that shipbreaking was employment "of a sort that admittedly has a certain degree of risk".[259] In his view, the jury was obliged to accept the evidence that "no one is better able to appreciate and deal with the risks than the plaintiff himself".[260] If the same case were to come before the courts today, it is likely that a less indulgent view would be taken of the employer's obligations.

**[18.161]** In *Rafferty v Parsons (CA) of Ireland Ltd*,[261] in 1986, a most interesting issue on the question of voluntary assumption of risk was presented to the Supreme Court, but, in the event, was not resolved. The plaintiff employee had been employed as a storeman by the defendants. He developed a recurrent condition of pain in his back. His doctors advised him to do only light work, and one gave him a note for his foreman, suggesting[262] or requesting[263] that he be given light work. The foreman told him that the employers had no light work for him and that if he was not able to do the full work there would be no work for him.

---

252. *Cf Flynn v Irish Sugar Manufacturing Co* [1928] IR 525 (SC).
253. *O'Hanlon v ESB* [1969] IR 75 at 90 (SC).
254. Civil Liability Act 1961, s 34(1)(b).
255. *Cf Smith v Baker* [1891] AC 325 (HL(Eng)); *Bowater v Rowley Regis Corporation* [1944] KB 176 (CA); *McIlhagger v Belfast Corporation* [1944] NI 37 (KBD); Anon 'Negligence as Between Master and Servant' (1921) 55 ILT & SJ 115.
256. *Cf O'Hanlon v ESB* [1969] IR 75 at 92 (SC).
257. Supreme Court, 14 February 1962.
258. Lavery and Haugh JJ; Kingsmill Moore J dissenting.
259. Page 5 of Lavery J's judgment.
260. Page 6 of Lavery J's judgment. See also *Rands v McNeil* [1955] 1 QB 253 (CA).
261. [1987] ILRM 98 (SC), analysed by Binchy '"Light Work": A Dilemma for Employers' (1988) 82 Incorp L Soc of Ireland Gazette, p 47.
262. *Cf* [1987] ILRM 98 at 99 and 100.
263. *Cf* [1987] ILRM 98 at 103, McCarthy J at 104, spoke of "certificates or letters".

**[18.162]** The plaintiff gave evidence that the need to support his family forced him to resume work, which, he said, caused him further pain in his back over the following few years. The trial judge withdrew the case from the jury; the Supreme Court, by a majority,[264] affirmed. Unfortunately the disposition of the case was clouded by several factors: the plaintiff, in his particulars for negligence, had not clearly made out the argument, pressed at the end of the hearing in reply to the defendant's application to have the case withdrawn from the jury, to the effect that the defendants had been negligent in allowing him to attempt to do his normal work when they knew him to be fit only for light work; there was, moreover, no transcript of the trial; nor did either party put forward in evidence the note from the plaintiff's doctor. These various elements affected the outcome of the appeal and necessarily diverted the Court's attention to some extent away from the issue of voluntary assumption of risk.

**[18.163]** For the majority, Finlay CJ considered that it would be "a wholly artificial and unreal standard of care"[265] to impose on the employers to hold them liable in negligence for having reacted to a single application for light work, "even if supported by a medical certificate suggesting that he was fit for light work",[266] by simply informing him that they had not got any, and then taking no further action when he "voluntarily"[267] resumed his ordinary work and kept at it for significant periods for some years afterwards. There was no *prima facie* evidence of negligence, in his view. On the other hand, Henchy J, also for the majority, expressly declined to decide whether it could be negligence for an employer to allow an employee to attempt to do his normal work when he was known to be fit only for light work. If such an argument were to be made, it would have to be pleaded so that the defendants "could meet that case in evidence and properly raise a plea of contributory negligence and for a plea of *volenti non fit injuria*".[268] He considered, however, that this argument was not open on the evidence because all that the evidence showed was that the plaintiff's doctor had *requested* of his employees that he be given light work - not that he had supplied a medical certificate proving that he was fit for light work only.

**[18.164]** McCarthy J's dissent is of particular interest. So far as the doctor's note to the employers was concerned he did not accept the proposition:

> "that it would not be open to a jury to conclude that certificates or letters of this kind would not be adequate notice to the defendant that the plaintiff should not do other than light work; if that were not so, such a certificate would scarcely be necessary at all".[269]

McCarthy J considered that the case should have been allowed to go to the jury with, on the defendants' request, an ancillary issue as to voluntary assumption of risk.

**[18.165]** It is unfortunate that the Court did not have to confront the central issues of policy raised by the employment of a person known by the employer to be at risk of

---

264. Finlay CJ and Henchy J.; McCarthy J dissenting.
265. [1987] ILRM 98 at 100.
266. [1987] ILRM 98 at 100.
267. [1987] ILRM 98 at 100.
268. [1987] ILRM 98 at 102.
269. [1987] ILRM 98 at 104. *Cf Withers v Perry Chain Co Ltd* [1961] 3 All ER 676, where the English Court of Appeal's analysis skimmed the surface of the issues of principle and policy.

damage to his health on account of the work to which he is to be put. If we accept that the *volenti* defence will not generally protect an employer who adopts substandard work practices, the question must arise as to whether the same position applies in a case where the only negligence alleged against the employer consists of employing the plaintiff in the knowledge of his inability to do a job, safe for employees generally, without risk of particular injury to him. Ultimately this question can be answered only by resort to the court's social philosophy; whether paternalistic or *laissez faire* principles are applied, the solution may comfortably be articulated in the legal language of duty, contributory negligence and *volenti non fit injuria*.[270]

270. *Cf Bolger v Queally Pig Slaughtering Ltd*, High Court, 8 March 1996 (Barron J), analysed by Byrne & Binchy *Annual Review of Irish Law 1996*, pp 586-587, where an employer who ignored a complaint from an employee who had developed a swelling around his left elbow was held to have been negligent in letting the condition worsen. Barron J rejected the defendant's argument that, if it had responded to the complaint, it would have been obliged to discharge the employee. Barron J was satisfied that "some arrangement would have been made to enable the plaintiff to work but at the same time ... to work without injuring himself." Not all cases will be capable of such easily resolution on the causation issue. See also *Doyle v Atlantic Mills Ltd*, DPIJ: Trinity and Michaelmas Terms 1995, p 124 (HC) where an employee who returned to work after being out with a back injury subsequently hurt his back when emptying waste material from a trolley. Budd J held that the employer had a duty to take into account the plaintiff's vulnerable back when allotting him his range of tasks. He considered, however, that the particular task was a light one and that the employer could not have foreseen that it would expose the plaintiff to injury.

# Chapter 19

# Public Authorities


I. Introduction .......... 533
II. Negligence .......... 535
III. Nuisance .......... 547
IV. Breach of Statutory Duty .......... 547
V. *Rylands v Fletcher* .......... 547
VI. Misfeasance of Public Office .......... 547


## I. Introduction

**[19.01]** Public authorities present the courts with distinctive issues in relation to tortious liability.[1] It is easy to see why this should be so. Tort law has tended historically to regard conduct by private individuals as the paradigm;[2] its central principles were developed at a time when public authorities played a far less significant part in most people's lives;[3]

1. For a comprehensive analysis, see Hogan & Morgan *Administrative Law* (3rd ed 1998), Ch 15. See also Harlow 'Fault Liability in Public Law' (1976) 39 MLR 516; Cohen & Smith 'Entitlement and the Body Politic: Rethinking Negligence in Public Law' (1986) 64 CBR 1; Harlow '"Public" and "Private" Law: Definition Without Distinction' (1980) 43 MLR 241; Samuel 'Public and Private Law: A Private Lawyer's Response' (1983) 46 MLR 558, Smith & Burns '*Donoghue v Stevenson* - The Not So Golden Anniversary' (1983) 46 MLR 147; Bowman & Bailey 'Negligence in the Realm of Public Law - A Positive Obligation to Rescue?' [1984] Pub L 277; Craig 'Negligence in the Exercise of a Statutory Power' (1978) 94 LQR 429; Smillie 'Liability of Public Authorities for Negligence' (1985) 23 W Ont LR 213; Rubinstein 'The Liability of Bodies Possessing Statutory Powers for Negligent Failure to Avoid Harm' (1987) 13 Monash ULR 75; Phegan 'Public Authorities, Nonfeasance and Breach of Statutory Duty' (1977) 11 U Br Col LR 187; Phegan 'Public Authority Liability in Negligence' (1977) 22 McGill LJ; Baker 'Maladministration and the Law of Torts' (1985) 10 Adelaide LR 207; Todd 'The Negligence Liability of Public Authorities: Divergence in the Common Law' (1986) 102 LQR 370; Bailey & Bowman 'The Policy/Operational Dichotomy - A Cuckoo in the Nest' [1986] Camb LJ 430; Klar 'The Supreme Court of Canada: Extending the Tort Liability of Public Authorities' (1990) 28 Alta LR 648; Reynolds & Hicks 'New Directions for the Civil Liability of Public Authorities: Drawing the Line' (1993) 1 Tort LR 123; Lowry & Oughton 'A Saga of Neglect by England's Town Halls' (1996) 4 Tort LR 12; Mullender 'Negligence, The Policy/Operational Distinction and the European Convention on Human Rights' (1999) 7 Tort LR 98; Murray [1986] Dublin ULJ 109; Kerr [1985] Dublin ULJ 139; Kerr [1988] Dublin ULJ 182.
2. It is a striking feature of Irish constitutional analysis that judicial thinking on the nature of constitutional rights and their enforcement has largely neutralised the distinction between private individuals and public authorities, national or local. Thus, there is no sovereign immunity from suit by the citizen (*Byrne v Ireland* [1972] IR 241 (SC)), citizens may sue each other, as well as the State, for infringement of their constitutional rights (*Meskell v Coras Iompair Éireann* [1973] IR 121 (SC)), the conduct of State servants is used on a model for determining liability in respect of the conduct of private individuals (*H v Murphy* [1987] IR 621 (HC)) and the Defence Forces' obligations as employer are subject to no immunity (*Ryan v Ireland* [1989] IR 177 (SC)).
3. This explains the old rule (yet to be finally abrogated) that highway authorities should not be held liable for injuries resulting from non-feasance as opposed to misfeasance.

moreover, public law remedies went some way towards ensuring that public authorities played by the rules.[4] A more fundamental reason why the courts have hesitated about applying with full rigour the principles of tort law is that public authorities engage in decision-making of a political nature: policies as to the allocation of scarce resources, and as to priorities among selected options, may be considered matters beyond the proper remit of the judiciary.[5]

**[19.02]** There are other reasons for judicial caution. To impose liability on public authorities for the failure to exercise a statutory power (or, in some cases, statutory duty) can involve the court in recognising an affirmative duty to act, which is something that the common law has been reluctant to do,[6] unless the particular relationship is one that calls out for altruism.[7] It is one thing to hold that parents or employers, for example, owe paternalistic obligations of an affirmative nature towards children or employees. It is quite another for the court to interpret local authorities' statutory powers as involving an affirmative legal obligation in respect of this exercise. The extent to which paternalism should be a feature of the relationship between a local authority and the several groups or wider public that it serves might well be considered a political question to be determined by the Oireachtas when enacting legislation prescribing these powers.

**[19.03]** As against this, there are certain statutory functions - whether characterised as duties or powers - which appear so essential to maintaining the social scaffolding that it is reasonable for society, through the courts, to insist that they be discharged properly, under sanction of a damages award. This type of case had been characterised by Australian courts as involving a "general reliance" on the part of those at risk of injury or damage if the statutory function is neglectfully discharged.[8]

**[19.04]** It may perhaps be better if our own courts reach the same conclusion as to liability by the more conventional route of *Donoghue v Stevenson.* There are dangers in postulating a reliance which is largely metaphorical and incapable of validation or refutation in any particular case. In contrast to the language of proximity and neighbourhood, which does not pretend to refer to the empirical order, the concept of reliance is a curious one to adopt where no useful evidence can be adduced that particular people actually relied on any specific representation or assurance emanating from the defendant. The law can well do without such a judicial fiction. There is a subtle distinction between the empirical proposition that "people generally expect" and the normative proposition that "people are entitled to expect" that a particular function will be exercised with due care.

---

4. See Hogan & Morgan *Administrative Law* (3rd ed, 1998).
5. See STREET, pp 182-188.
6. See Ch 8 above; also *Stovin v Wise* [1996] AC 923 (HL); *X (Minors) v Bedfordshire County Council* [1995] 2 AC 633 (HL); *Capital and Counties plc v Hampshire County Council* [1997] QB 1004 (CA). *Cf Cullinane v Waterford County Council* [1997] Ir L Log W 309 (CC).
7. *Cf* FLEMING, p 211, fn. 485:

   "Arguably the sacrifice of individual liberty, implicit in affirmative duties on private individuals, has no counterpart in the case of public authorities specifically entrusted with powers and resources for the sake of public health and safety ...."
8. *Cf Sutherland Shire v Heyman* (1985) 157 Comm LR 424.

## II. Negligence

**[19.05]** Discussion for the past forty years or so has concentrated on the question of the liability in negligence of public authorities. The position regarding their liability for breach of statutory duty,[9] or, conversely, their immunity from liability for torts resulting from conduct authorised by statute,[10] was relatively clear. With the general extension of the duty of care in negligence, especially in relation to the supervision and control of third parties,[11] the question inevitably began to arise in the courts as to the extent to which public authorities could be held liable in negligence for their policy decisions and the day-to-day implementation of those decisions, usually (though not invariably) against the background of some statutory power rather than a duty to act in the particular context.

**[19.06]** The courts might easily enough have determined the question of the negligence of public authorities in accordance with classic principles of negligence which are of general application. Thus, for example, in determining the standard of care, courts are obliged to have regard, *inter alia,* to the *social utility* of the defendant's conduct[12] and the *cost of preventing the injury.*[13] These elements are perfectly sensitive to the position in which public authorities may find themselves. If this is not sufficient, the concept of the duty of care[14] should ensure that no public authority would have to bear a burden that the courts considered too heavy.

**[19.07]** What actually happened in Britain however, was that the House of Lords added yet more complex layers of conceptualisation, to no great advantage as far as the clarity or fairness of the law is concerned.

**[19.08]** Three stages in this process may be identified. The first involved identifying the remit of discretion afforded by the particular statutory power and immunising from liability all conduct on the part of the public authority that fell within that remit. Only if the discretion had been exercised so unreasonably that there had been "no real exercise of the discretion which Parliament ha[d] conferred"[15] could liability in negligence be imposed. In *Anns v Merton London Borough Council,*[16] Lord Wilberforce sought to draw a distinction between policy and operational matters:

> "Most, indeed probably all, statutes relating to public authorities ... contain in them a large area of policy. The courts call this 'discretion', meaning that the decision is one for the authority or body to make, and not for the courts. Many statutes also prescribe or at least presuppose the practical execution of policy decisions: a convenient description of this is to say that, in addition to the area of policy or discretion, there is an operational area. Although this distinction between the policy area and the operational area is convenient, and illuminating, it is probably a distinction of degree; many 'operational' powers or duties have in them some element of 'discretion'. It can safely be said that the more 'operational' a power or duty may be, the easier it is to superimpose on it a common law duty of care."

---

9. See para **[19.02]-[19.03]** above and Ch 21 below; see also Hogan & Morgan *Administrative Law* (3rd ed 1998), Ch 15
10. See para **[19.02]-[19.03]** above; see also Hogan & Morgan *Administrative Law* (3rd ed 1998), Ch 15.
11. See Ch 8 above.
12. See para **[7.38]-[7.43]** above.
13. See para **[7.44]-[7.54]** above.
14. See Ch 6 above.
15. *Home Office v Dorset Yacht Co Ltd* [1970] AC 1004 at 1031 (HL (Eng)).
16. [1978] AC 728 at 754 (HL (Eng)).

**[19.09]** Lord Wilberforce noted than an operational duty might contain a discretionary element in its exercise, "discretionary as to the time and manner of inspection, and the techniques to be used".[17] A plaintiff complaining of negligence would have to prove that the action taken was "not within the limits of a discretion *bona fide* exercised"[18] before he or she could begin to rely on a common law duty of care.

**[19.10]** The policy/operational distinction was subjected to academic criticism over the years,[19] in which the British courts[20] joined. Their concerns concentrated on the impossibility of making a clear division between the two elements since policy considerations can be reflected even in micro operational choices. There was also a view that the distinction offers courts the opportunity to hide behind an apparently rigorous legal criterion when in truth it represents no more than a conclusory formula adopted by courts when they decide, on undisclosed policy grounds, that the public authority's conduct that is under scrutiny should not be justiciable.[21]

**[19.11]** One might have thought that this judicial frankness would have led to the simplification of analysis in Britain in relation to the scope of liability of public authorities. Instead, the House of Lords in *X v Bedfordshire County Council*,[22] adopted an elaborate *schema*, expressed by Lord Browne-Wilkinson as follows:

> "Where Parliament has conferred a statutory discretion on a public authority, it is for that authority, not for the courts, to exercise the discretion. Nothing which the authority does within the ambit of the discretion can be actionable at common law.

---

17. [1978] AC 728 at 755.

18. [1978] AC 728 at 755.

19. See Cohen & Smith 'Entitlement and the Body Politic: Rethinking Negligence in Public Law' (1986) 64 Can BR 1; Smillie 'Liability of Public Authorities for Negligence' (1985) UW Ont LR 213; Woodall 'Private Law Liability of Public Authorities for Negligent Inspection and Regulation' (1992) 37 McGill L J 83; Bailey & Bowman 'The Policy/Operational Dichotomy – A Cuckoo in the Nest' [1986] Camb LJ 430; Sopinka 'The Liability of Public Authorities: Drawing the Line' (1993) 1 Tort LR 123 (Justice of the Supreme Court of Canada, writing extra-judicially)

20. *Rowling v Takaro Properties Ltd* [1988] AC 473 at 501 (PC); *Stovin v Wise* [1996] AC 923 at 951 (HL (Eng)). The High Court of Australia was more measured in its caution in *Sutherland Shire Council v Heyman* (1985) 157 CLR 424 and the Supreme Court of Canada has been positively enthusiastic about the policy/operational distinction: *City of Kamloops v Nielson* [1984] 2 SCR 2; *Just v The Queen in Right of British Columbia* [1989] 2 SCR 1228; *Brown v The Queen in Right of British Columbia* [1994] 1 SCR 420.

21. Thus in *Rowling v Takaro Properties Ltd* [1988] AC 473 at 501, Lord Keith said that the Judicial Committee inclined to the opinion that:

    > "this distinction does not provide a touchstone of liability, but rather is expensive of the need to exclude altogether those cases in which the decision under attack is of such a kind that a question whether it has been made negligently is unsuitable for judicial resolution, of which notable examples are discretionary decisions on the allocation of scarce resources or the distribution of risks .... If this is right, classification of the relevant decision as a policy or planning decision in this sense may exclude liability but a conclusion that it does not fall within that category does not, in their Lordships' opinion, mean that a duty of care will necessarily exist."

    FLEMING, p 215, considers that "[the English courts'] new mantra, justiciability, is no more precise" than what it replaced.

22. [1995] 2 AC 633 (HL (Eng)), analysed by STREET, pp 185-187, Brodie 'Public Authorities - Negligence Actions – Control Devices' (1998) 18 Legal Studies 1; Lowry & Oughton 'A Saga of Neglect by England's Town Halls' (1996) 4 Tort LR 12.

> Where the decision complained of falls outside the statutory discretion, it can give rise to common law liability but where the factors relevant to the exercise of the discretion include matters of policy, the court cannot adjudicate on such policy matters and therefore cannot reach the conclusion that the decision was outside the ambit of the statutory discretion.
>
> Therefore, a common law duty of care in relation to the taking of decisions involving policy matters cannot exist.[23]"[24]

**[19.12]** The more recent decision of the House of Lords in *Barrett v London Borough of Enfield*[25] suggests some softening of the judicial hostility to imposing a duty of care on public authorities in the exercise of their statutory powers.

**[19.13]** Lord Slynn rejected the suggestion that, if an element of discretion is involved in an act that is done subject to an overriding statutory power, common law negligence is necessarily ruled out:

> "Acts may be done pursuant and subsequent to the exercise of a discretion where a duty of care may exist - as has often been said, even knocking a nail into a piece of wood involves the exercise of some choice or discretion and yet there may be a duty of care in the way it is done. Whether there is an element of discretion to do the act is thus not a complete test leading to the result that, if there is, a claim against an authority for what it actually does or fails to do must necessarily be ruled out."[26]

**[19.14]** Later in his speech, Lord Slynn went some way towards rationalising and reducing the complexity of the elaborate structure of analysis that had been constructed in *X v Bedfordshire County Council.*[27] He stated:

> "Where a statutory power is given to a local authority and damage is caused by what it does pursuant to that power, the ultimate question is whether the court should accept that it has no role to play. The two tests (discretion and policy/operational) ... are guides in deciding that question. The greater the element of policy involved, the wider the area of discretion accorded, the more likely it is that the matter is not justiciable so that no action in negligence can be brought ... A claim in negligence in the taking of a decision to exercise a statutory discretion is likely to be barred, unless it is wholly unreasonable so as not to be a real exercise of the discretion, or if, it involves the making of a policy decisions involving the balancing of different public interests; acts done pursuant to the lawful exercise of the discretion can, however, in my view be subject to a duty of care, even if some element of discretion is involved."[28]

---

23. *Cf Rowling v Takaro Properties Ltd* [1988] AC 473; *Hill v Chief Constable of West Yorkshire* [1989] AC 53 (HL (Eng)); *Caparo Industries plc v Dickman* [1990] 2 AC 605 (HL (Eng)) and *Henderson v Merrett Syndicates Ltd* [1995] 2 AC 145 (HL (Eng)), discussed in Lord Browne-Wilkinson's speech.
24. [1995] 2 AC 633 at 738-739
25. [1999] 3 WLR 79 (HL (Eng)).
26. [1999] 3 WLR 79 (HL (Eng)) at 96.
27. See para **[19.11]** above.
28. [1999] 3 WLR 79 at 96-97. See also 108 (*per* Lord Hutton):

    > "[I am of] the provisional view that the fact that the decision which is challenged was made within the ambit of a statutory discretion and is capable of being described as a policy decision is not in itself a reason why it should be held that no claim for negligence can be bought in respect of it ... It is only where the decision involves the weighing of competing public interests and is dictated by considerations which the courts are not fitted to assess that the courts will hold that the issue is non-justiciable on the ground that the decision was made in the exercise of a statutory discretion."

**[19.15]** The Irish decisions have largely avoided an over-elaborate conceptual approach to the question, although the Irish courts are clearly conscious of the social and political dimensions of the exercise of public authorities statutory functions. Thus in *Siney v Dublin Corporation*,[29] for example, the Supreme Court's analysis placed no emphasis on the range of delegated discretion afforded to those carrying out the inspection on behalf of the defendant.

**[19.16]** The Irish courts have adopted two main strategies in assessing the negligence of public authorities. They may be summarised as (i) the standard of care test and (ii) the proximity/policy test.

## The Standard of Care Test

**[19.17]** There are countless cases in which the Irish courts have approached the issue of the negligence of public authorities as one that raises merely a question of the standard of care, with none of the complex preliminary problems of discretion, policy-operational distinctions, justifiability or the duty of care. Thus, for example, in *Phillips v Dublin Corporation*,[30] where the twelve-year-old plaintiff fell down a lift shaft in one of the Ballymun tower blocks when the lift door opened into a void, Barron J acquitted the defendant corporation of negligence. It had taken considerable steps to combat the problems of vandalism and of young teenagers joy-riding on the roof of the lift. Barron J stated:

> "The defendant was, in my view, under an obligation to take reasonable steps to prevent unauthorised entry to the lift shaft or unauthorised interference with the lift mechanism ... In considering whether [the defendant act[ed] reasonabl[y], it must be remembered that an occupier is not an insurer [a]nd the defendant must expect [that] perhaps parental supervision would be lacking for a variety of reasons, but it is not justice to require an occupier, even in the position of a local authority, to have to bear the ultimate responsibility for other than its own actions, and failure to have someone in constant attendance, as has been suggested is unreasonable."[31]

**[19.18]** There is no evidence here of judicial agonising over threshold issues relating to the duty of care. Instead there is a simple, thoughtful application of the principles relating to the standard of care.

**[19.19]** So also in *McAuliffe v Tralee UDC*,[32] where a 23-year-old fell from a see-saw in a public park, Lynch J dismissed the claim without an elaborate preliminary analysis of resource allocations by public bodies. The see-saw was an old one, it and two others:

> "had been there for some fifty years and no doubt hundreds and thousands of children and probably many an adult had used them in the intervening time, and there is no evidence of any claim against the Urban District Council during that fifty years on the basis of any alleged accident with the see-saws. The see-saw was not the most modern but it was in good

29. [1980] IR 400. See para **[13.23]** above.
30. DPIJ: Hilary and Easter Terms 1991, p 42 (HC).
31. DPIJ: Hilary and Easter Terms 1991 at p 46. See also paras **[13.27]-[13.44]** above.
32. DPIJ: Trinity and Michaelmas Terms 1992, p 107 (HC).

repair and safe for normal and proper use.[33] The defendants were not bound to discard the older model as soon as a newer model came on the market ..."[34]

**[19.20]** Similarly in *Walsh v Dublin Corporation*,[35] Smith J applied the conventional standard of care criteria in rejecting a claim that the Corporation had been negligent in failing to put a stopper on a door in a flat which blew closed on the plaintiff's hand when a wind tunnel was created by the opening of the front and back doors. It is interesting to note that Smith J was happy to apply to public authorities the same standard as is applicable to private individuals. Commenting that the phenomenon of doors banging in draughts created by other doors opening "arises in most homes throughout the country and [is] one with which we are all familiar",[36] Smith J drew inspiration from a decision[37] involving the design of seating in a cinema in private ownership. He observed in conclusion that "[t]he accident ... was one that could befall any of us at any time whether in our own homes or elsewhere."[38]

## The Proximity/Policy Approach

**[19.21]** The Irish courts have addressed the more complex issues of negligence relating to public authorities in terms of the proximity of the relationship between the pubic authority and the plaintiff and the possible public policy grounds for denying, or restricting the scope of the duty of care.[39] Three Supreme Court decisions over the past twelve years are of particular importance and require specific consideration. These are *Ward v McMaster*,[40] *Sunderland v Louth County Council*[41] and *Convery v Dublin County Council*.[42]

### *(a) Ward v McMaster*

**[19.22]** *Ward v McMaster*[43] is a decision of some greatness in this context. As we have seen,[44] much of its importance lies in Costello J's rejection of the last vestiges of the immunity from negligence of vendors and builders and his enthusiastic endorsement of the principle of recovery of damages for non-dangerous defects.

**[19.23]** These matters did not arise directly on appeal but the Supreme Court's decision is nonetheless of considerable interest. It will be recalled that Mr Ward bought a house from

33. Lynch J found that the accident was attributable to the failure of the plaintiff's husband to hold onto "the perfectly adequate handle provided for his use and safety", as a result of which he was suddenly thrown off the see-saw, causing the plaintiff to be dislodged.

34. *McAuliffe v Tralee UDC* DPIJ: Trinity and Michaelmas Terms 1992, p 108 (HC). See also *Reaney v Fermoy UDC* DPIJ: Hilary and Easter Terms 1994 (HC).

35. High Court, 23 July 1999 (Smith J).

36. At p 2.

37. *O'Gorman v Ritz (Clonmel) Ltd* [1947] Ir Jur Rep 35 (HC) (CCA). See para **[7.32]** above.

38. Page 4 of Smith J's judgment.

39. The further hurdle that British courts require a plaintiff to surmount – that it be "just and reasonable" to impose a duty of care – was treated by McCarthy J in *Ward v McMaster* [1988] IR 337 at 352, as a redundancy once the plaintiff had passed the first two hurdles.

40. [1988] IR 337.

41. [1990] ILRM 658.

42. Supreme Court, 12 November 1996.

43. [1988] IR 337 (SC) affg [1985] IR 29 (HC).

44. See para**[13.55]** above.

the first named defendant with the assistance of a loan granted by Louth County Council under regulations made by virtue of s 39 of the Housing Act 1966. The house turned out to be riddled with both dangerous and non-dangerous defects, which made it uninhabitable.

**[19.24]** Mr Ward had no difficulty in bringing a successful claim against the builder-vendor,[45] which was not appealed. He also sued the County Council in negligence. The essence of his claim was that the County Council, by requiring him to pay a fee with his loan application, led him to believe that the fee was for a valuation of the house which would be carried out carefully. In fact the fee was designed to discourage frivolous applications, though Mr Ward was not told this.

**[19.25]** The Council employed the services, not of a surveyor but of an auctioneer, who was unable to discover the hidden defects in the bungalow. The auctioneer was acquitted of negligence in the High Court since he had done all that might be asked of one of his profession. The failure by the County Council to carry out the valuation with due care resulted, the plaintiff argued, in reasonably foreseeable loss to him.

**[19.26]** Costello J imposed liability on the County Council on the basis that:

> "there was a sufficient relationship of proximity or neighbourhood between the plaintiff and the Council such that in the reasonable contemplation of the Council carelessness on their part in the carrying out of the valuation of the bungalow ... might be likely to cause him damage".[46]

The Council ought to have been aware, in view of Mr Ward's very limited means and his knowledge that it was going to value the premises, that he would not employ a professional valuer. Echoing Lord Wilberforce's two-step test for the duty of care in *Anns*,[47] Costello J held that there was nothing in the dealings between the parties which should restrict or limit the *prima facie* duty of care that arose. In particular no warning against reliance on the proposed valuation had been given.

**[19.27]** On appeal by the County Council, the Supreme Court unanimously affirmed Costello J's finding of liability. Two judgments were delivered.

**[19.28]** After a wide-ranging review of cases in Ireland and other common law jurisdictions dealing with the duty of care in negligence, McCarthy J concluded that the County Council was under a duty of care to Mr Ward. He said:

> "The proximity of the parties is clear: they were intended mortgagor and mortgagees. This proximity had its origin in the Housing Act 1966 and the consequent loan scheme. This Act imposed a statutory duty upon the County Council and it was in the carrying out of that statutory duty that the alleged negligence took place. It is a simple application of the principle in *Donoghue,* confirmed in *Anns* and implicit in *Siney,* that the relationship between [Mr Ward] and the County Council created a duty to take reasonable care arising from the public duty of the County Council under the Statute. The statute did not create a private duty but such arose from the relationship between the parties."

**[19.29]** This passage is of some significance since it makes it clear that the breach by a public body of a statutory duty to which the Oireachtas did not intend to attach the

---

45. See para **[13.57]** above.

46. [1985] IR at 52.

47. [1978] AC 728 at 751.

sanction of civil liability can nonetheless constitute the tort of negligence when it embraces sufficient circumstances of proximity between the parties. In one sense, of course, this is not remarkable since proximity can arise in *any* context, whether or not a statute plays any part in the generation of that proximity in any particular case. However, it would surely be sensible to interpret McCarthy J's holding as having more significance. The description of the duty of care arising under the statute suggests that he considered that the duty of care owed to Mr Ward was not limited to the unique circumstances of the case but rather would apply to any applicant for a loan under the scheme. In other words, the Council owed a general duty of care to all applicants arising from its public duties under the statute. If this interpretation is correct, then McCarthy J may be considered to have confirmed what was apparent in *Siney*, in effect if not in express terms, that the law of negligence can be used to subvert the well-established principle that where a statutory provision is enacted for the benefit of the public rather than private individuals it does not generate civil liability for its breach. Many lawyers over the years have questioned why statutes of clear social purpose should be impotent when it comes to civil sanctions.

**[19.30]** Henchy J's judgment in favour of Mr Ward is of narrower scope than McCarthy J's. That much is tolerably clear. What is somewhat less clear is the precise basis of the imposition of liability. Henchy J disdained to embark on a broad analysis of the duty of care since he considered that the salient features of the case were "sufficiently clear and distinctive to enable the point at issue to be decided on well-established principles".

**[19.31]** Henchy J went on to state that the breach by the Council of its public duty under the Regulations made under s 39 of the 1996 Act "would not in itself give a cause of action in negligence to the plaintiff".[48] It was necessary for the plaintiff to show that the relationship between him and the Council was one of proximity or neighbourhood which cast a duty on the Council to ensure that, regardless of anything left undone by him, he would not end up as the mortgagor of a house which was not a good security for the amount of the loan. A paternalistic or protective duty of that kind would not normally be imposed on a mortgagee in favour of a mortgagor, but the plaintiff was in a special position. To qualify for a Council loan, the plaintiff had to show first, that he was unable to obtain one from a commercial agency and, secondly that his circumstances were such that he would otherwise need to be re-housed by the council. A borrower of that degree of indigency could not have been reasonably expected to incur the further expense of obtaining a structural survey of the house. The plaintiff, like the Council, had relied on the auctioneer's opinion. He considered that the Council would have the house approved by a surveyor and that it would be superfluous for him to engage a surveyor. That was an understandable attitude and one that ought to have been foreseen by the Council, particularly when one of the preconditions of the loan required the plaintiff to insure the home against fire for at least its full value. The council "must be taken to have impliedly assured the plaintiff that the house would be a good security for the loan".

**[19.32]** Henchy J considered that "[i]n the light of the special relations between the plaintiff and the Council ..., apart from their public duty in the matter", the Council owed a duty to the plaintiff to ensure by a proper valuation that the house would be a good security for the loan. "In the light of the statutory rights and duties of the Council", it owed a duty to the plaintiff to observe due care in the valuation of the house; it had failed to carry out

48. Citing *Siney v Dublin Corporation* [1980] IR 400.

that duty. If the Council had wished to avoid the incidence of that duty, it could have so provided in one of the preconditions of the loan.

**[19.33]** Henchy J's judgment is clearly narrower in its holding than McCarthy J's. Its emphasis on the special circumstances of the case contrasts with McCarthy J's broad statement of the Council's duty. Moreover, Henchy J's judgment falls well short of an equation, or near-equation, of the Council's statutory duties with the duty of care in negligence. In his view, these duties are not irrelevant to the establishment of proximity of relationship between the Council and loan applicants but equally do not automatically generate that proximity. Having said this, it is difficult to see how, in the light of Henchy J's analysis, he could deny that a duty of care would be owing to *all* loan applicants, since the factors creating the duty towards Mr Ward - his need to be rehoused and his inability to obtain a loan from a commercial agency - would be shared by *all* loan applicants.

**[19.34]** As regards the question of the discharge of the Council of its duty of care or, at all events, its immunisation from liability, it is to be noted that Henchy J was satisfied that some unspecific insertion as a "pre-condition of the loan" would suffice. Whether that pre-condition should be that the applicant should conduct his or her own survey or merely that the Council was accepting no legal responsibility for the accuracy of its own survey is not clear. The question may, perhaps, arise as to whether such a pre-condition would *always* suffice. It is possible to envisage loan applicants with a degree of indigency so pressing that even the payment of a surveyor's fee would involve serious financial hardship. The robust reply may be that such people, if anxious to become property-owners, should be expected to pay such a small sum; but the whole tenor of the judgments in *Ward v McMaster* is that conventional economic assumptions have to be modified to have regard to social realities.[49]

### *(b) Sunderland v Louth County Council*

**[19.35]** In *Sunderland v Louth County Council*,[50] the defendant county council, pursuant to its powers under the Local Government (Planning and Development) Act 1963,[51] granted one McGreavey permission to build a house on a particular location. McGreavey, who had no previous building experience went ahead without checking on the suitability of the site. He later discovered that planning permission did not apply to the site on which he had built the house and, pursuant to s 28 of the Act, obtained permission for its retention. The

---

49. *Cf Smith v Eric S Bush (a firm)* [1990] 1 AC 831 (HL(Eng)). Costello J's analysis of proximity arising out of a statutory function was applied by Lardner J in *Shelton v Creane and Arklow UDC* High Court, 17 December 1987, which was decided some months before the Supreme Court decision in *Ward v McMaster*. The plaintiff, a visitor to a house rented from a local authority, fell over a drain whose unlocked metal cover had been removed in unknown circumstances. She sued the tenant as occupier and the local authority for negligence. As regards the latter claim Lardner J, having quoted from Costello J's judgment in *Ward v McMaster*, held that the plaintiff "simply as an invitee or visitor" was not within "the class of persons which the statute was designed to assist". It is interesting to speculate on whether Lardner J would have come to a different view in the light of the Supreme Court judgment in *Ward v McMaster*. This seems unlikely. It would, of course, have been open to the court to impose liability on the general principle of neighbourhood articulated in *Donoghue v Stevenson*. Lardner J specifically addressed this issue, even though no argument had been directed to the question. He noted that the evidence fell far short of satisfying him that the local authority ought reasonably to have foreseen that the cover might be removed.

50. [1990] ILRM 658 (SC), affg [1987] IR 372 (HC).

51. See Scannell, *Environmental Planning Law* (1995), Ch 6.

plaintiffs' bought the house from McGreavey, following an inspection but without carrying out a survey. The county council confirmed to the plaintiffs' solicitors "that in general the conditions of the planning permission granted have been complied with".

**[19.36]** The plaintiffs, in buying the house, "also bought disaster"[52] Because of the unsuitability of the site and the way the septic tank had been built, the house and garden were constantly in a state of dampness, with periodic flooding. The house was thus uninhabitable.

**[19.37]** The plaintiff's obtained judgment against McGreavey who was no mark. Their action against the county council failed before Lardner J and on appeal to the Supreme Court. The essence of the plaintiffs' case against the county council, was that the council breached a duty of care to them, as foreseeable and proximate persons liable to be detrimentally affected by the council's failure properly to exercise its functions in the granting of planning permission. To grant planning permission, the plaintiffs argued, implied that the development plan would at least not be at variance with the county development plan and not be an environmental or health hazard. The council ought to have refused planning permission on the ground that there was no effective drainage.

**[19.38]** On the evidence the council might well have been held in breach of its duty of care to the plaintiffs if such a duty existed. They had carried out no inspection of the constructed house before granting planning permission; there had been no investigation of the site; all that had occurred was an inspection carried out by a planning assistant, who was a geographer or economist. It was conceded by the plaintiffs that the council owed no duty of care to McGreavey. The essence of their case was that the council owed a duty to them *as occupiers*, over and above such duty as it owed to the public as a whole, pursuant to the statutory obligations imposed by the Planning Act.

**[19.39]** In rejecting the plaintiffs' argument that the council owed them a duty of care, McCarthy J, delivering the judgment of the Court, developed his analysis as follows:

> "In *Siney v Dublin Corporation*[53] a legal relationship of landlord and tenant existed between the parties; in *Ward v McMaster*[54] a mortgagor-mortgagee relationship existed. True it is that the damage that was caused to the plaintiffs could be foreseen; but it would require that the council could reasonably foresee that a prospective occupier would not carry out an investigation to learn whether or not the site was suitable for drainage by means of a septic tank; that, equally, future purchasers would not carry out such an inspection. Both *Siney* and *Ward* were cases where the statutory duty of the local authority arose under the Housing Act 1966, an Act which is demonstrably and unequivocally designed towards the protection and improvement of the housing conditions of persons who are not able by their own resources to provide it for themselves. So also a number of the English cases cited ... were cases under the Public Health Act 1937, an Act directed towards the protection of the public health and welfare or, in *Peabody*,[55] under the London Government Act 1963 which prohibited the erection of buildings unless drains were constructed to the satisfaction of the council."[56]

---

52. [1990] ILRM 658 at 659 (*per* McCarthy, J).
53. See para **[13.23]** above.
54. See para **[19.22]** above.
55. *Governors of Peabody Donation Fund v Sir Lindsay Parkinson & Co Ltd* [1985] AC 210 (HL (Eng)).
56. [1990] ILRM 658 at 662.

**[19.40]** McCarthy J went on to state:

> "The fundamental difference between what may be called planning legislation and housing legislation is that the first is regulatory or licensing according to the requirements of the proper planning and development of the area but the second is a provision in a social context for those who are unable to provide for themselves; if they are unable to provide for themselves then the duty on the provider reaches the role that would be taken by professional advisers engaged on behalf of the beneficiary. This is in marked contrast to the watchdog role that is created under the Planning Act, a watchdog role that is for the benefit of the public at large. This is emphasised by the existence of the appeals procedure, formerly to the relevant minister of the government, assigned by him to a junior minister, and since 1976 carried out by the planning appeals board (An Bord Pleanála). This latter body has national jurisdiction but must still deal with any planning appeal by the test of local standards - the proper planning and development of the area. It would follow from the plaintiffs' argument that there would be imposed upon the planning appeals board, in the case of an application for retention of a dwelling house constructed without permission, a duty to carry out an examination of the drainage system including the suitability of the soil, presumably irrespective of whether or not the applicant for such permission had done so. Such a duty would lie upon the board as much in the case of a large scale housing development, and, presumably, separately in respect of each house, as it would for a single development such as here. The liability, whether it be of the planning authority or of the planning appeals board, would remain indefinitely towards any occupier.
>
> I point to these consequences, not *in terrorem* but, rather, to seek to identify on a reasonable approach the intention of the legislature in enacting the relevant parts of the Planning Act. That Act was to make provision, in the interest of the common good, for the proper planning and development of the cities, towns and other areas, whether urban or rural; the Act permits the making of building regulations, which, if they had existed, might well enure to the benefit of the plaintiffs. There are no such regulations relevant to County Louth."[57]

**[19.41]** On the basis of this analysis, McCarthy J concluded that, in conferring statutory powers on planning authorities, the Oireachtas:

> "did not include a purpose of protecting persons who occupy buildings erected in the functional area of planning authorities from the sort of damage which the plaintiffs ... suffered."[58]

This being so, the council, in the exercise of those powers, owed no duty of care at common law to the plaintiffs.

**[19.42]** The holding in *Sunderland* was widely welcomed. To have engrafted onto the 1963 Act such as onerous duty of care as the plaintiffs asserted would surely have laid too heavy a burden on local authorities and on An Bord Pleanála.

### *(c) Convery v Dublin County Council*

**[19.43]** In *Convery v Dublin County Council*,[59] the plaintiff a resident in a suburban estate, sought a mandatory injunction directing the defendant to abate a nuisance caused by the vehicular traffic using the roads in her area as an access route to an urban centre. She

57. [1990] ILRM 658 at 663.
58. [1990] ILRM 658 at 663.
59. [1996] 3 IR 153 (SC revg (HC). See Byrne & Binchy *Annual Review of Irish Law 1996*, pp 611-612.

argued that the defendant had not taken sufficient steps to deal with the traffic "rat run" through the area.

**[19.44]** The estate had not been designed for through traffic. The urban centre - Tallaght Town Square - had been developed a decade after the estate had been completed. The County Manager had advertised his intention temporarily to close access to the junction of the roads near to where the plaintiff lived. Well over two thousand objections to this proposal were lodged. The County Manager decided not to proceed with the intended closure. Earlier a proposal by elected members of the Council to install bollards in the area has been met by about 2,000 objections and had not been pursued further. Carroll J proceeded on the basis that the defendant could be liable for public nuisance if the nuisance arose from its negligence in the exercise of its statutory duties. She considered that the evidence established that the defendant had been negligent in this regard. The Council as planning authority had "imposed a particular type of development on the builder with the result that the three roads affected are unsuitable for the traffic which now uses them in breach of the original scheme or design."[60] The planning department had permitted extensive development of the urban centre without ensuring that the road infrastructure was adequate. It had not required substantial contributions from developers to ensure that a particular road could be constructed which would have eased the problem.

**[19.45]** Carroll J went on to observe, robustly:

> "The Council has been aware for many years of the appalling conditions which the residents [in the area] have to endure. But the members of the Council bowed to the number of objections (representing votes) who have become used to inflicting themselves on the residents ... They have placed the unjustified convenience of a large number of voters over the legitimate complaints of a comparatively small number of householders. Tyranny of numbers is not democracy. The Council is elected to make decisions in the interest of the common good which does not always coincide with popular approval.
>
> The Council is responsible to ensure proper roads are constructed so that there is proper traffic management. In my opinion the failure of the Council to take any concrete steps to alternate the problem amounted to negligence.
>
> While the immediate nuisance is created by the volume of traffic, the real cause lies in the Council permitting the type of road required at the time of the initial development to be used far beyond its capacity as a distributor road long after the estate was completed.
>
> The Council cannot hide behind the efforts which it did make and blame the local opposition for their inaction. All it has done so far is to talk, commission a report, and talk some more. This is not good enough."[61]

**[19.46]** Accordingly, Carroll J made it clear that she was disposed to grant the injunction requiring the Council to abate the nuisance, and, after a period of time, made the order.

**[19.47]** The Supreme Court reversed. Keane J (O'Flaherty and Barrington JJ concurring) considered it "clear"[62] from the judgments in *Ward v McMaster*[63] that the fact that the plaintiff belonged to a particular category of persons for whose benefit the powers and duties of the housing authority under the Act were to be exercised was "of critical

60. [1996] 3 IR 153 at 160.
61. [1996] 3 IR 153 at 160-161.
62. [1996] 3 IR 153 at 170.
63. [1988] IR 337 (SC) affg [1985] IR 29 (HC). See para **[19.22]** above.

importance"[64] in determining whether the Council owed him a duty of care in the exercise of those powers and duties. This was "in sharp contrast"[65] to the decision in *Sunderland v Louth County Council*,[66] Keane J quoted *in extenso* from McCarthy J's judgment in that case, without further comment.

**[19.48]** In the instant case, Keane J rejected the claim based on public nuisance as the traffic had not originated in any premises owned or occupied by the Council nor generated as a result of any activities carried on by the Council on land in the area. He succinctly disposed of the claim founded on negligence as follows:

> "[I]t is clear that the plaintiff has failed to establish that there was a relationship between her and the County Council which created a duty to take reasonable care arising from its public duty under any statute. The powers and duties of the County Council as planning authority and local authority are vested in it in order to ensure the proper planning and development of its area and the provision and maintenance of an appropriate road network in that area. While its exercise of those powers and duties can be regulated by the High Court by means of the judicial review process so as to ensure that they are exercised only in accordance with law, the plaintiff does not belong to any category of persons to whom the Council, in the exercise of those powers, owed a duty of care at common law."[67]

**[19.49]** The Court's conclusion is clear in its rejection of the plaintiff's claim, its precise basis is a matter of debate. The reference to the possibility of judicial review to regulate the exercise of the statutory functions of planning authorities and road authorities might suggest that this is the exclusive route of complaint. This cannot be so, however, and a close reading of Keane J's judgment makes this more apparent. It is perfectly possible for a claim in negligence to succeed against a planning authority or road authority.

From these cases, therefore, we can see that the Supreme Court was unwilling to concede that individuals have civil rights under the Planning Acts, which are regulatory acts passed for orderly developments and for the benefit of the common good in general, and this is so even were the affected group and small and indentified as in *Convery*. Beneficiaries under the Housing Acts, however, were a more indentifiable and deserving group to whom the Supreme Court was willing to recognise a duty of care in *Ward* and *Siney*. The nature and the purpose of the particular legislation seems to have been the determining factor in the Supreme Court's conclusions.[68]

---

64. [1996] 3 IR 153 at 170.
65. [1996] 3 IR 153 at 170
66. [1990] ILRM 658 (SC) affg [1987] IR 372 (HC). See para **[19.35]** above.
67. [1996] 3 IR 153 at 174.
68. In *HMW(nee F) v Ireland, the AG and the Government of Ireland (No 2)* [1997] 2 IR 141 (HC), Costello J examined these cases where the plaintiff, a victim of sexual assault, claimed that the Attorney General caused her damage by not *speedily* processing an extradition application in respect of the priest who allegedly committed the assaults. Costello J, whose decision is dealt with more fully in Ch 1 (see also para **[6.34]**), followed the *Ward v McMaster* line of analysis, in holding that under the relevant legislation (The Extradition Act 1965) the Attorney General owed no common law duty of care to the plaintiff. Costello J was also prepared to hold that, even if there was proximity, public policy reasons existed why it should not be recognised in this case by the Court: *Ward v McMaster* makes it clear, when the court is required to consider whether a duty of care at common law arises in the exercise of statutory duties, powers or functions the issue is largely determined by the scope and nature of the relevant statutory provisions." (at 153).

## III. Nuisance

**[19.50]** Elsewhere[69] we consider the present exemption of road authorities from liability for nonfeasance. We also consider[70] the question of legislative authorisation to commit a nuisance - an important matter where public authorities are concerned. The Supreme Court's analysis of the possible liability of the defendant in *Convery v Dublin County Council*[71] for the tort of public nuisance is discussed below.[72]

## IV. Breach of Statutory Duty

**[19.51]** In a later Chapter[73] we set out the main features of the action for breach of statutory duty. Of importance in the present context is the matter there touched on, of legislative exemptions and immunities for certain governmental and administrative authorities. The constitutionality of these provisions is a matter of some uncertainty and debate.[74]

## V. Rylands v Fletcher

**[19.52]** Public authorities may of course be liable under the rule in *Rylands v Fletcher.*[75] The concept of "non-natural" use of property is not however, completely hostile to activities in which a public authority may engage since it excludes "such a use is proper for the general benefit of the community."[76]

## VI. Misfeasance of Public Office[77]

**[19.53]** The courts have had to consider the extent to which *ultra vires* or otherwise wrongful acts by public officials should be actionable in damages. Thus far, Irish law has generally protected decisions made in good faith, provided, of course, they are not

---

69. See para **[24.19]-[24.23]** and **[24.113]-[24.121]** below.
70. See para **[24.93]-[24.96]** below.
71. [1996] 3 IR 153.
72. See para **[19.21]** below.
73. Ch 21.
74. See Hogan & Morgan *Administrative Law* (3rd ed 1998), pp 365-366.
75. See Ch 25 below.
76. *Rickards v Lothian* [1913] AC 263 at 280 (PC). Williams 'Non-natural Use of Land' (1973) 32 Camb LJ 310 at 319, invoked with approval by La Forest J (with Dickson CJ) in *Tock v St John's Metropolitan Area Board* [1989] 2 SCR 1181 at 1189. See, however, *Smeaton v Ilford Corporation* [1954] Ch 450 (Ch Div), rejecting Denning LJ's attempt to provide a still broader exemption for local authorities in *Pride of Derby & Derbyshire Angling Association Ltd v British Celanese Ltd* [1953] 1 All ER 179 at 202 (CA). FLEMING, p 380 envinces strong opposition to judicial deference to public authorities in this context.
77. See Hogan & Morgan *Administrative Law* (3rd ed 1998), pp 802-808. Kneebone 'Misfeasance in a Public Office After Mengel's Case: A "Special" Tort No More?' (1999) 7 Tort LR 111; McBride 'Damages as a Remedy for Unlawful Administrative Compensation in Public Law Action' [1979] Camb LJ 323; Craig 'Compensation in Public Law' (1980) 96 LQR 413, Dench 'The Tort of Misfeasance in a Public Office' (1981) 4 Auckland U L Rev 182; Sadler 'Liability for Misfeasance in a Public Office' (1992) 14 Sydney LR 131; Baker 'Maladministration and the Law of Torts' (1985) 10 Adelaide LR 207 at 242-251.

actionable under the rubric of some well-recognised tort such as false imprisonment or trespass. In the Supreme Court decision of *Pine Valley Developments Ltd v Minister for the Environment*[78] Finlay CJ referred to the "weighty considerations of the public interest" supporting these limitations. If the law were to range more broadly, "there would be an inevitable paralysis of the capacity for decisive action in the administration of public affairs".[79]

**[19.54]** The Chief Justice adopted with approval Wade's "clear summary"[80] of the law:

> "The present position seems to be that administrative action which is *ultra vires* but not actionable merely as a breach of duty will found an action for damages in any of the following situations:
>
> 1. If it involves the commission of a recognised tort, such as trespass, false imprisonment or negligence.
> 2. If it is actuated by malice, eg personal spite or a desire to injure for improper reasons.
> 3. If the authority knows that it does not possess the power which it purports to exercise."[81]

**[19.55]** The tort of misfeasance of public office embraces the latter two situations.[82] It has a long history yet even today its precise contours are a matter of debate.[83] Perhaps the best way of analysing its role in Irish law is, first, to discuss the Irish cases in which the tort has been litigated and then to attempt to address issues that have yet to be fully debated before the Irish courts.

## The Irish Cases

**[19.56]** In *Pine Valley* the defendant Minister, acting on the advice of his officials, had granted outline planning permission in relation to property later acquired by the plaintiffs. It transpired that this permission was *ultra vires* as the development materially contravened the plan. This resulted in financial loss for the plaintiffs. The plaintiffs sought damages from the Minister for misfeasance of public office, negligence and negligent misrepresentation. They were unsuccessful in all these claims, at trial before McMahon J and on appeal to the Supreme Court.

**[19.57]** The plaintiffs made no allegation of *mala fides* against the Minister. The Minister was acquitted of negligence and negligent misrepresentation because he had acted on the advice of the senior legal adviser of his Department.[84] It was "obvious"[85] that he had believed the planning permission to be valid.

---

78. [1987] ILRM 747 at 758 (SC).
79. [1987] ILRM 747 at 758.
80. [1987] ILRM 747 at 757.
81. Wade *Administrative Law* (5th ed, 1982), p 673. This passage was also quoted by Costello J, in *O'Donnell v Dun Laoghaire Corporation* [1991] ILRM 301 at 320 (HC).
82. The earliest case appears to be *Turner v Sterling* (1672) 2 Vent 25, 86 ER 287, followed by the famous decision of *Ashby v White* (1703) 2 Ld Raym 938, 92 ER 126.
83. *Cf Northern Territory v Mengel* (1995) 69 ALJR 527 (HC, Austr); *Garrett v Attorney General* [1997] 2 NZLR 332 (CA); *Three Rivers DC v Bank of England (No 3)* [2000] 2 WLR 15 (CA); *Rawlinson v Rice* [1997] 2 NZLR 651 (CA).
84. This advice echoed that given to other Ministers by successive senior legal advisers to the Department.
85. [1987] ILRM 762 (*per* Henchy J).

**[19.58]** So also in *McDonnell v Ireland*,[86] where the plaintiff's employment had been terminated on the basis of a statutory provision which many years later was found to be constitutionally invalid, Keane J, in the Supreme Court, observed that, since the tort of misfeasance of public office was committed only where the act in question was performed either maliciously or with actual knowledge that it was committed without jurisdiction and with the known consequence that it would injure the plaintiff, the tort would be of no avail to the plaintiff in the present circumstances.

**[19.59]** In *CW Shipping Co Ltd v Limerick Harbour Commissioners*[87] the plaintiff's application for a tug operating licence was refused by the defendants. In proceedings for judicial review and damages, O'Hanlon J came to the conclusion that the plaintiff's craft was one for which no licence was necessary.

**[19.60]** As regards the plaintiff's claim for damages, O'Hanlon J was satisfied that the correct approach was that adopted by the Privy Council in *Dunlop v Woollahra Municipal Council*[88] to the effect that one could recover damages in an action on the case for loss suffered as an inevitable consequence of the unlawful, intentional and positive act of another only where the act was illegal or forbidden by law and not where it was merely null and void and incapable of affecting rights. As in *Pine Valley* (which was not recorded as having been among the authorities cited to O'Hanlon J) the defendant council in *Woollahra* was not guilty of negligence as it has acted on legal advice.

**[19.61]** In *Woollahra*, the Privy Council held that the failure by a public authority to give a person an adequate hearing before exercising a statutory power which affects him or his property was not of itself a breach of a duty of care giving rise to damages, since the effect of that failure was merely to render the exercise of the power void, which fact the person affected was just as able to deduce as the offending public authority. In the light of this realisation the affected party would be entitled to ignore the void exercise of the power since it was incapable of affecting his legal rights.

**[19.62]** In *Woollahra*, the Privy Council had gone on to hold that misfeasance was a necessary element in the tort of abuse of public office, and, in the absence of malice, the passing by a public authority of a resolution which was devoid of legal effect when the authority had no prior knowledge of the invalidity was not conduct capable of amounting to misfeasance.

**[19.63]** In *CW Shipping*, O'Hanlon J held that the defendants should not be condemned in damages merely for having construed the provisions of s 53 incorrectly. They had acted in a *bona fide* manner in what they conceived to be the best way of organising the provision of towing services in their area. There was no evidence suggesting that they had acted maliciously or in pursuance of a conspiracy to inflict damage on the applicants or that there had been any abuse of public office on their part.

---

86. Supreme Court, 23 July 1997. See also *Johnston v Meldon* (1891) 30 LR Ir 13; *Ó Conghaile v Wallace* [1938] IR 526 (SC); *Farrell v Minister for Agriculture and Food* High Court, 11 October 1995 Carroll J, all discussed by Hogan & Morgan *Administrative Law* (3rd ed 1998), pp 812-815, where liability was not imposed in the absence of *mala fides*.

87. [1989] ILRM 416 (HC).

88. [1981] 1 All ER 1212.

**[19.64]** The only reservation O'Hanlon J expressed as to the "very helpful statement of principle" in *Woollahra* concerned the ability of a person whose interests are sought to be affected by an invalid resolution of an administrative tribunal to ignore the resolution and proceed as if it had never been passed. O'Hanlon J considered it "somewhat unrealistic" to expect people in such cases to proceed to spend money in the belief that the courts will later uphold their view of the law. Moreover, even if in the present case the applicants had been willing to so act, the local shipping agents would have been unhappy about engaging the services of their tugs once it became known that the Research Harbour Commissioners had contended that this was in breach of s 53.

**[19.65]** O'Hanlon J's reservation is eminently sensible. It will be in only rare cases that the void quality of an administrative authority's act will be so patent that it will warrant being ignored in the manner envisaged in *Woollahra*.

**[19.66]** It remains also to be seen whether legal advisers to governmental and administrative authorities can be subjected to a duty of care in negligence to all persons likely to be detrimentally affected by negligent advice.[89] It may be that our courts, on policy grounds, will be disposed to spell out significant limitations on that duty in view of the quasi-political context in which the advice is given, the competing claims and interests, and the inevitable uncertainty involved in predicting judicial interpretations of constitutional and statutory provisions.

**[19.67]** Next, we must examine a couple of more recent cases in which the tort of misfeasance of public office was considered. In *O'Donnell v Dun Laoghaire Corporation*,[90] the plaintiffs, a married couple, claimed (*inter alia*) damages for this tort where the defendant corporation, acting *ultra vires* but in good faith, had disconnected their water supply. Costello J dismissed their action. The Corporation had not been activated by malice but rather was:

> "carrying out its different responsibility in an impartial and unbiased manner, satisfied that it possessed the statutory power to cut off defaulting householders, like the plaintiff[s], who failed to pay the charges which it believed had been validly imposed."[91]

**[19.68]** In *Hanahoe v Judge Hussey*,[92] Kinlen J addressed the question of the scope of liability for misfeasance of public office. The plaintiff, who was a solicitor had been subjected to a "media circus" by the leaking of information by a member of the Garda Síochána that a search of his office was to take place on a warrant under s 64 of the Criminal Justice Act 1994. Kinlen J awarded £100,000 damages for negligence against An Garda Síochána.[93] Counsel for the plaintiff argued that the deliberate leaking of this information amounted to the tort of misfeasance of public office. Kinlen J disposed of the argument as follows:

---

89. *Cf* Kneebone 'Misfeasance in a Public Office After Mengel's Case: A "Special" Tort No More?' (1996) 4 Tort LR 111 at 134-135; *McMahon v Ireland* [1988] ILRM 610 (HC); *Yuen Kun Yeu v Attorney General of Hong Kong* [1988] AC 175 (PC); *Davis v Radcliffe* [1990] 1 WLR 821 (PC).
90. [1991] ILRM 301 (HC), analysed Byrne & Binchy *Annual Review of Irish Law 1990*, pp 549-551.
91. [1991] ILRM 301 at 320.
92. High Court, 14 November 1997, Kinlen, J.
93. See para **[37.18]** above.

"For the tort of misfeasance of public office to be made out there must be either a malicious act or a knowing and conscious abuse of power. It was submitted [by counsel for the Garda Síochána] that in the absence of a finding that there was a deliberate and conscious leak on the part of senior Garda management ... there could be no finding of the tort of misfeasance of public office. If the Court found that an individual Garda or other officer of the State had either maliciously or in conscious breach of his public duty deliberately leaked the relevant information, the actions of such officer would be wholly outside the scope of his employment and [An Garda Síochána] could not be liable. The clear evidence of all the [Garda] witnesses was to the effect that secrecy and discretion were fully impressed upon them as part of their obligations."[94]

**[19.69]** Kinlen J did not return to the question thereafter in his judgment. His remarks can perhaps be regarded as disposing of the issue, in favour of An Garda Síochána and it is clear that the plaintiff did not succeed on this ground. He did, however, succeed on another ground and there is no reason to regard Kinlen J's remark as going further than summarising the argument of counsel for An Garda Síochána rather than necessarily fully endorsing it.

**[19.70]** It can hardly be the case that the tort of misfeasance of public office may be committed only by "senior Garda management". Clearly, a Garda of any rank is capable of doing so. Nor can the fact that a Garda had acted "maliciously or in conscious breach of his public duty" necessarily insulate his employers from vicarious liability on the basis that the act was "wholly outside the scope of his employment". Defiance of orders does not, of itself, defeat the remit of vicarious liability. If the Garda who leaked the information had done so with the view of improving the hand of the Gardaí in their attempt to bring about the conviction of the plaintiff's client, his act might well be characterised as coming within the scope of his employment.

**[19.71]** Thus far we have been dealing with cases where the plaintiff alleged that the defendant had purported to exercise a power which the defendant knew it did not possess. What is the situation, however, where the claim is that the defendant exercised a power which it *did* possess but exercised it (to quote *Wade* again) in circumstances where it was "actuated by malice, eg personal spite or a desire to injure for improper reasons"?[95]

**[19.72]** This question was addressed by Blayney J in *Heavey v Pilotage Authority*.[96] The plaintiff, a licensed pilot employed by the Dublin Port and Docks Board, which is the Pilotage Authority of the Dublin Pilotage District, applied to be made a Pilot Class I. The relevant bye-law provided that "[t]he Authority may, on the recommendation of the Pilot Superintendent, accede to the application".[97] The Pilot Superintendent did not make such a recommendation as he was awaiting a proper report from the plaintiff in respect of a collision between two vessels which had occurred twenty minutes after the plaintiff had left one of the vessels. Accordingly the plaintiff's application was not successful.

**[19.73]** The plaintiff sued both the Pilotage Committee of the Authority and the Pilotage Superintendent for misfeasance of public office.[98] His counsel accepted that the claim

94. Page 49 of Kinlen, J's judgment.

95. Wade *Administrative Law* (5th ed, 1982), p 673. See also the 7th ed, 1992, p 795.

96. High Court, 7 May 1992, Blayney J.

97. Pilotage Bye-Laws 1987, Art 8.

98. The plaintiff also applied unsuccessfully for an order for *certiorari*.

could succeed only if malice was proved. Blayney J was satisfied on the evidence that there had been no malice on the part of either defendant. Insofar as the Committee was concerned, Blayney J could see "no grounds whatsoever"[99] for the suggestion that its members had purported to exercise a power they knew they did not have. The plaintiff's claim in regard to the Pilotage Superintendent was that he had made his mind up that the plaintiff should not be endorsed as a Pilot Class I and that his actions had been motivated by a desire to have the application refused. Blayney J held that there was no evidence to support this submission. The "sole reason"[100] that he had not given the necessary application was that the plaintiff had not complied with the bye-laws regime regarding the making of a report.

**[19.74]** The basis of Blayney J's rejection of the plaintiff's claim was clearly that the Pilotage Superintendent had done nothing wrong: his conduct was simply beyond reproach. The case therefore throws little, if any, light on what constitutes malice for the purposes of the tort of misfeasance of public office.

**[19.75]** The Supreme Court decision of *Callinan v Voluntary Health Insurance Board*[101] threw light on this issue. The case arose out of the way in which the defendant had sought to come to terms with a difficult financial period by attempting to negotiate new contractual arrangements with hospitals. When it failed to reach agreement with the plaintiffs, who owned a private hospital, it excluded the hospital from full participation in the VHI scheme, which meant that hospital cover was not provided to VHI subscribers admitted to the hospital.

**[19.76]** The plaintiffs sued the defendants, claiming, *inter alia*, damages and an injunction for breach of statutory duty. Keane J granted an injunction but declined to award damages.[102] The Supreme Court held that damages should be awarded.

**[19.77]** In holding that the defendant had been in breach of its statutory duty under the Voluntary Health Insurance Act 1957, Keane J reasoned as follows:

> "The VHI is not a private commercial organisation: it is a public body established by the Oireachtas with statutorily defined objects and powers. While the enabling Act undoubtedly confers on the VHI a wide discretion, under the ultimate control of the Minister, as to how it carries out those objectives and the manner in which it uses its powers, in common with other bodies of this nature it must use the powers entrusted to it fairly and reasonably. That obligation which must, if necessary, be enforced by the courts, exists not merely in the case of its subscribers and potential subscribers, but also in the case of the providers of health care, such as the plaintiffs, with whom the VHI may have reason to deal and who, for their part, have no practicable alternative to dealing with the VHI … The actions of the VHI … might have been unexceptional in legal terms in the case of a private commercial firm vigorously protecting its own interests. They were not, however, a fair and reasonable use of the powers entrusted expressly and by implication to the VHI by the Oireachtas for the common good and I am, accordingly, satisfied that the plaintiffs are entitled to appropriate relief in respect of those actions."[103]

---

99. Page 14 of Blayney J's judgment.
100. Page 15 of Blayney J's judgment.
101. Supreme Court, 28 July 1994.
102. High Court, Keane J.
103. Pages 97-102 of Keane J's judgment

**[19.78]** The analysis might be considered to fall easily enough within the traditional framework of the action in tort for breach of statutory duty.[104] Keane J adopted the words "The breach of statutory duty issue" as a heading under which he presented his analysis. He identified the nature and scope of the statutory duty in question and found that the plaintiffs were persons of a category to whom the duty was owed.

**[19.79]** Nonetheless, on appeal to the Supreme Court, a different view of Keane J's judgment found favour. Blayney J (O'Flaherty and Denham JJ concurring) interpreted Keane J's holding as being based on the fact that "the VHI had *abused their statutory powers*" - not that the VHI had breached a statutory duty. Blayney J went on to observe that Keane J:

> "did not categorise the tort constituted by the VHI's exercising their powers unreasonably and unfairly but, if he had done so, the probability is that, having regard to its ingredients, he would have classified it as misfeasance in public office ..."[105]

**[19.80]** If the case is to be understood as one of misfeasance of public office, one must scrutinise the basis of liability. A statutory power may be exercised unreasonably and unfairly without involving any subjective animus malice or ulterior motive. Unreasonableness and unfairness are objective concepts which do not require the court to attempt to get into the mind of the defendant. If an unreasonable exercise of a statutory power is to generate civil liability, one might have thought that the tort of negligence should be the appropriate avenue. If unfairness in conjunction with unreasonableness transforms the tort into that of misfeasance of public office, it would be helpful to have some judicial guidance as to how unfairness differs from unreasonableness.

**[19.81]** The decisions in other common law jurisdictions do not set the boundaries of liability for misfeasance of public office so widely.[106] They require that the defendant was knowingly[107] recklessly *outside* the scope of his or her legal powers or, if professedly acting *within* them, was doing so "maliciously" in the sense of being activated by an ulterior predominant purpose, such as to hurt the plaintiff for conduct unconnected with the exercise of the power.

---

104. See Ch 21 below.
105. Supreme Court, 28 July 1994, p 29.
106. See Kneebone 'Misfeasance in a Public Office After Mengel's Case: A "Special" Tort No More?' (1999) 7 Tort LR 111 at 126-138.
107. *Cf Bourgoin SA v Ministry of Agriculture* [1986] QB 716 (cited by Blayney J in *Callinan*).

## Chapter 20

# Defences


I. Introduction .......... 555
II. Contributory Negligence .......... 555
III. Volenti Non Fit Injuria .......... 577
IV. Illegality .......... 584


## I. Introduction

**[20.01]** In this chapter we examine three of the principal defences to an action for negligence: contributory negligence, voluntary assumption of risk and illegality (or *ex turpi causa*). All of these defences may be relevant in other proceedings; where actions for trespass to the person, goods or land are concerned, the defence of voluntary assumption of risk tends to be treated as one of consent.

## II. Contributory Negligence[1]

**[20.02]** Under present law, the general rule in an action for tort is that, where the plaintiff is partly at fault, damages will be reduced in proportion to his fault. This was not always the position. From the early part of the nineteenth century, a stricter doctrine prevailed: once the defendant could establish any fault on the part of the plaintiff which contributed to his injury, the plaintiff would be denied compensation. One of the earliest decisions was *Butterfield v Forrester*.[2] It involved proceedings for public nuisance arising from the obstruction of a street by the defendant by placing a pole across it. The plaintiff, riding his horse "violently", had failed to see the pole and had collided with it. The jury's verdict for the defendant was upheld on appeal, Lord Ellenborough stating that:

> "One person being in fault will not dispense with another's using ordinary care for himself. Two things must concur to support this action, an obstruction in the road by the fault of the defendant, and no want of ordinary care to avoid it on the part of the plaintiff."[3]

---

1. See Williams, *Joint Torts and Contributory Negligence* (1951) (hereafter in this chapter cited as Williams); Gregory, *Legislative Loss Distribution in Negligence Actions* (1936); Schwartz, *Comparative Negligence* (3rd ed, 1994); Kerr, *The Civil Liability Acts* (1999); James 'Contributory Negligence' (1953) 62 Yale LJ 691; Bohlen 'Contributory Negligence' (1946) 21 Harv LR 151; Lowndes 'Contributory Negligence' (1934) 22 Geo LJ 674; Malone 'Some Ruminations on Contributory Negligence' [1981] Utah LR 91; Johnson 'Comparative Negligence and the Duty/Risk Analysis' (1980) 40 La LR 319.
2. (1809) 11 East 60, 103 ER 926; SALMOND & HEUSTON, p 486, fn 75, note that although this decision is commonly cited as the source of the doctrine of contributory negligence that term is not used in it and the concept can be traced further back.
3. (1809) 11 East 60, 103 ER 926 respectively. See also *Butterly v Mayor of Drogheda* [1907] 2 IR 134 at 141-142 (KB).

**[20.03]** Why should such a doctrine have been formulated? Perhaps the tendency then prevalent in the common law to look for the cause of an accident rather than to regard an event as being capable of having more than one cause, may have had some influence in relation to contributory negligence.[4] A more likely factor was the individualistic philosophy of the day, which stressed personal autonomy and regarded people as being able to look after themselves. From this standpoint, to deny a careless plaintiff any damages might be regarded as encouraging accident prevention: certainly, the policy of compensating those who acted carelessly would have been considered an unjust and socially destructive one. The denial of damages in cases of contributory negligence has been perceived by some commentators as being the product of the same economic outlook as the doctrines of voluntary assumption of risk[5] and common employment, which:

> "subsidised the growth of industrial and business enterprise by lightening the burden of compensation losses for accidents inevitably associated with a rapidly expanding economy and the faster and greater volume of transport."[6]

## Erosion of the Doctrine

**[20.04]** The full rigour of the doctrine of contributory negligence did not hold sway for very long. By the middle of the last century, a mitigating doctrine had developed known as "last clear chance" or "ultimate negligence".[7] The decision on which this doctrine was constructed is *Davies v Mann*[8] in 1842. The facts were similar to those in *Butterfield v Forrester*,[9] but in reverse. The plaintiff had left his donkey on the highway, with its feet fettered. The defendant's horses and wagon, coming "at a smartish pace", collided with the donkey and killed it. Liability was imposed on the defendant. Parke J stated that:

> "although the ass may have been wrongfully there, still the defendant was bound to go along the road at such a pace as would be likely to prevent mischief. Were this not so, a man might justify the driving over goods left on a public highway, or even over a man lying asleep there, or the purposely running against a carriage going on the wrong side of the road."[10]

**[20.05]** From this decision the doctrine of the last clear chance was constructed,[11] whereby a plaintiff, despite his contributory negligence, would be entitled to full recovery if the defendant had the last opportunity to avoid the accident and by his negligence failed to do so.[12]

---

4. *Cf* FLEMING, p 303.
5. See para **[20.61]**.
6. FLEMING, p 304 citing Malone 'The Formative Era of Contributory Negligence' (1946) 41 Ill LR 151.
7. See Munday 'The Last Clear Chance Doctrine' (1942) 21 Neb LR 347. See on this and more generally McMahon 'Reactions of Tortious Liability to the Industrial Revolution: Part II' 3 Ir Jur (ns) 284.
8. (1842) 10 M & W 547, 152 ER 588 (Exch).
9. (1809) 11 East 60, 103 ER 926. See Schofield '*Davies v Mann*: Theory of Contributory Negligence (1890) 3 Harv LR 263; *cf* Hayden '*Butterfield* Rides Again: Plaintiff's Negligence As Superseding or Sole Proximate Cause in Systems of Pure Comparative Responsibility' (2000) 33 Loyola LALR 887.
10. (1842) 10 M & W 547, 152 ER 588 at 549 and 589 respectively.
11. Salmond's role in this development was critical: *cf* SALMOND & HUESTON, pp 486-487. See also VTH D[elany] 'Contributory Negligence: "The Third Question"' (1958) 24 Ir Jur 4 and articles in (1939) 73 ILT & Sol J 185 and (1957) 91 ILT & Sol J 175 181.
12. See eg *McGlynn v Clarke* [1945] IR 495 (SC). *Cf Butterly v Mayor of Drogheda* [1907] 2 IR 134 (KB).

**[20.06]** The doctrine became refined further so as to allow the plaintiff to recover where the defendant, on account of inattention, failed to appreciate that an opportunity to avoid the accident existed[13] or where the defendant would have had the last opportunity had it not been for his prior negligence.[14]

**[20.07]** Clearly, the doctrine of the last clear chance was a crude device,[15] which went both too far and not far enough: too far because full compensation would in many cases be inappropriate and unjust; not far enough because in many other cases a deserving plaintiff guilty of relatively trivial contributory negligence would still be awarded nothing simply because no last opportunity arose.[16]

## The Civil Liability Act 1961

**[20.08]** The law was set on a modern footing with the enactment of the Civil Liability Act 1961.[17] The Act contains detailed provisions regarding contributory negligence. They are based very largely on draft legislation prepared by Professor Glanville Williams in his influential treatise *Joint Torts and Contributory Negligence*.[18] The legislation, therefore, has all the advantages of a thorough and incisive analysis by a legal expert of world renown who took full account of the strengths and weaknesses of statutory reforms in other jurisdictions.

**[20.09]** Under the 1961 Act, contributory negligence ceases to be an absolute defence: instead a system of apportionment of damages is employed, whereby the plaintiff's damages are reduced having regard to the respective degrees of fault of plaintiff and defendant.[19] This approach has for a long time been part of the law in civil law jurisdictions and has been part of our admiralty law in dealing with collisions at sea.

---

13. *Radley v L & N W Ry* (1876) 1 AC 754.
14. Maclntyre 'The Rationale of Last Clear Chance' (1940) 18 Can BR 669. The question whether this doctrine was part of Irish law was resolved finally only in 1948 by a 3/2 majority of the Supreme Court in *Minister for Finance & AG v O'Brien* [1949] IR 91 (SC), previous decisions had been divided: *cf Neenan v Hosford* [1920] 2 IR 258 (CA). *Logan v O'Donnell* [1925] 12 IR 211 (SC); *Hayden v M'Quillan* [1930] IR 87 (SC). The older decision of *Scott v Dublin & Wicklow Ry Co* 11 ICLR 377 (Exch), which made its way to the Supreme Court in *O'Brien's* case through the devious route of Ontario (*Brenner v Toronto Railway Co* 13 Ont LR 423) and the Privy Council (in the famous decision of *BC Electric Ry v Loach* [1916] 1 AC 719) scarcely resolves the question in definitive terms.
15. *Cf* Anon 'Contributory Negligence and the Comparison of Fault' (1957) 91 ILT & Sol J 175 at 175.
16. In *Daly v Lawless* [1952] Ir Jur 20 (SC) the Supreme Court declined an invitation to abandon the last opportunity doctrine in the light of English legislative changes in regard to contributory negligence enacted in 1945.
17. No 41. For a comprehensive analysis of the legislation and the later amendments to it see Kerr, *The Civil Liability Acts* (1999). See also McCartney 'Contributory Negligence and the Civil Liability Act 1961' (1961) 27 Ir Jur 25. A detailed explanatory memorandum to the legislation was published by the Department of Justice at the time it was enacted. Just how revolutionary were some of the changes in the Act may be gleaned from a comparative study published fifteen years later: Fleming 'Comparative Negligence at Last - By Judicial Choice' (1976) 64 Calif LR 239.
18. (1951) reviewed by Lord Wright (1951) 67 LQR 528 and Hall (1952) 15 MLR 258.
19. *Cf* WILLIAMS, pp 256-257. Ontario was the first common law jurisdiction to enact apportionment legislation (in 1924); the fact that it borders on the civil law province of Quebec may be significant: WILLIAMS, pp 257-258

**[20.10]** Section 34(1) of the 1961 Act provides that:

> Where, in any action brought by one person in respect of a wrong committed by any other person, it is proved that the damage suffered by the plaintiff was caused partly by the negligence or want of care of the plaintiff or of one for whose acts he is responsible (in this Part called contributory negligence) and partly by the wrong of the defendant, the damages recoverable in respect of the said wrong shall be reduced by such amount as the court thinks just and equitable having regard to the degrees of fault of the plaintiff and defendant ..."

**[20.11]** This provision is subject to three qualifications:

(i) If, having regard to all the circumstances of the case, it is not possible to establish different degrees of fault, liability is to be apportioned equally;

(ii) The provision will not defeat any defence that the plaintiff before the act complained of agreed to waive his legal rights in respect of it;[20]

(iii) Where any contract or enactment[21] providing for the limitation of liability is applicable to the claim, the amount of damages awarded to the plaintiff by virtue of s 34(1) is not to exceed the maximum level so applicable.[22]

**[20.12]** Section 56 of the 1961 Act specifically abolishes the last opportunity rule. The fact that any person:

> (a) had an opportunity of avoiding the consequences of the act of any other person but negligently or carelessly failed to do so, or
>
> (b) might have avoided those consequences by the exercise of care, or
>
> (c) might have avoided those consequences but for previous negligence or want of care on his part;[23]
>
> is not, by itself, to be a ground for holding that the damage was not caused by the act of that other[24] person.[25]

**[20.13]** The scope of the statutory reform is wider than might at first appear. Formerly, the defence of contributory negligence did not apply to cases of intentional wrongdoing, such

---

20. This is considered in detail, see para **[20.61]** below.

21. Eg Part III of the Air Navigation and Transport Act 1936 as amended by the Air Navigation and Transport Act 1959. See also s 46(1)(a)(ii) of the Civil Liability Act 1961.

22. As a general principle where damages are awarded on claim and counterclaim subject in each case to a reduction for contributory negligence under s 34(1) costs should be awarded in the same proportion as damages but a judicial discretion still remains: see s 42 of the Civil Liability Act 1961 and *Noone v Minister for Finance* [1964] IR 63 (HC).

23. *Cf Minister for Finance & AG v O'Brien* [1949] IR 91 (SC).

24. Note that the legislation is so drafted as to deny the possibility of any last opportunity rule applying in the future to the conduct of either party although at common law it appears never to have been invoked specifically against the plaintiff since such a plaintiff would in any event be destined to lose by virtue of his or her contributory negligence: FLEMING, p 312.

25. The failure by many other legislatures to abolish the last opportunity rule when introducing apportionment legislation has led to some confusion: FLEMING, pp 312-313. *Cf Gillespie v Fitzpatrick* [1970] IR 102 (SC); *Hartman v Fisette* 66 DLR (3d) 516 (SC Can); *Brown v George* 294 SE 2d (SC) noted by Folline (1983) 35 SC LR 177. For a discussion of the relationship between s 56 and causal detrimators, see byrne and Binchy *annual Review of Irish Law 1999* (Torts Chapter).

as battery[26] or false imprisonment, where the defendant meant to punch or confine the plaintiff, rather than where he did so by negligence. Section 34(1) refers to "a wrong", a term embracing all delictual liability[27] as well as breach of contract.[28]

## The Nature of Contributory Negligence

**[20.14]** Contributory negligence essentially involves a lack of reasonable care for one's own safety[29] or the safety of one's property[30] in contrast to negligence which involves a

26. See Hudson 'Contributory Negligence as a Defence of Battery' (1984) 4 Legal Stud 332 at 338-342. This article provides a useful analysis of the relationship between the defences of provocation and contributory negligence. For a policy analysis of applying the defence of contributory negligence to torts involving wrongful intentional conduct see Crocker 'Apportionment of Liability and Intentional Torts: The Time is Right for Change' (1982) 7 Dalhousie LJ 172. See also *Wasson v Chief Constable Royal Ulster Constabulary* [1987] NILR Bull 34 (QBD). In *MacKnight v Xtravision* Circuit Court, 5 July 1991, extracted in McMahon & Binchy, *Casebook on the Irish Law of Torts* (2nd ed, 1991), pp 407-410, Judge Carroll reduced the plaintiff's damages in an action for trespass to the person by 50% to take account of his contributory negligence. For analysis of the decision see Byrne & Binchy, *Annual Review of Irish Law 1991*, pp 417-419, 443.

27. Delictual liability, arising under legislative measures implementing directives under European Community law, is sometimes specifically characterised as a tort to which the provisions of the Civil Liability Act 1961 relating to the contributory negligence, apply. See eg the Liability for Defective Products Act 1991, s 9(2). Even in the absence of such specificity these provision may be considered to operate by analogy: *cf Coppinger v Waterford County Council* [1996] 2 ILRM 427 (HC) analysed by Byrne & Binchy, *Annual Review of Irish Law 1996*, pp 601-603.

28. *Cf* Civil Liability Act 1961, s 34(2). See also *O'Hanlon v ESB* [1969] IR 75. The law in other jurisdictions has given rise to difficulties in the absence of clear statutory guidance: see Andrews 'Note: No Apportionment for Contributory Negligence in Contract' [1986] Camb LJ 8; Taylor 'Note: Contributory Negligence - A Defence to Breach of Contract?' (1986) 49 MLR 102; Anderson 'Contributory Negligence in Contract - Again' [1987] Lloyds Mar & Com LQ 10; Burrows 'Note Contributory Negligence: A Defence to Breach of Contract?' (1985) 101 LQR 161; McPherson 'Note' (1986) 35 U New Brunswick LJ 197; Swanton 'Contributory Negligence as a Defence to Actions for Breach of Contract' (1981) 55 Austr LJ 278 - a most perceptive analysis.

29. *Cf Judge v Reape* [1968] IR 226 (SC) - a passenger travelling with intoxicated driver; *Murphy v O'Brien* 6 ILT (ns) 75 (CC) - an intoxicated patron of a public house fell on steps with an inadequate hand rail; *Dyer v Dublin Corporation* High Court, 10 June 1993 - a tenant injured his hand when attempting to close a damaged door by putting his hand around the edge and pulling it sharply towards him; the damages were reduced by 50% as the plaintiff, a clerical assistant with An Post and "an articulate and intelligent man", ought to have taken some remedial measures such as fitting a temporary handle to the door rather than persist in what his own counsel had stigmatised, as the "Russian Roulette" method of closing the door. *Cf Allen v Ó Súilleabháin and the Mid-Western Health Board* High Court, 28 July 1995 (Kinlen J) - 25-year-old student midwife was held not guilty of contributory negligence in failing to communicate verbally to the obstetrician and midwives, that she was in great pain resulting from holding the leg of a patient during childbirth; to have interrupted them "would be extremely cheeky for a student midwife". In *Power, Crowley and Reddy Enterprises Ltd* High Court, 29 October 1992 - a 50% reduction for contributory negligence was made where the plaintiff, a carpenter with no experience of demolishing walls, permitted a labourer working under his charge to knock a line of bricks three feet from the ground out of a ten-foot-high wall. See Byrne & Binchy, *Annual Review of Irish Law 1992*, pp 601-603, 604-605.

30 *Cf Cody v Player & Wills (Ir) Ltd* (1975) 109 ILTR 32 (CC) - a plaintiff who let a horse stray on a highway, where it was struck by defendant's car held guilty of contributory negligence; damages reduced accordingly by 20%;

breach of duty towards others.[31] An act may of course constitute both contributory negligence and negligence at the same time - a foolhardy lack of caution for one's own safety, such as climbing a mountain without the proper equipment, may induce a rescue attempt, resulting in injury to the rescuer.[32]

## Contributory Negligence and Particular Risk

**[20.15]** A plaintiff's failure to exercise reasonable care for his or her own protection will not amount to contributory negligence in respect of damage unless that damage results from the particular risk to which the plaintiff's conduct has exposed the plaintiff. In other words,[33] the fact that the plaintiff has been careless for his or her safety in one respect will not assist the defendant unless that carelessness gave rise to a risk of injury that in fact transpired. This question arises frequently in road accident cases where a defendant alleges that the plaintiff has been guilty of contributory negligence. He or she may indeed have been, but unless the defendant can show that it related to a danger which in fact transpired, proof of even the grossest lack of care will not avail the defendant. Thus the fact that a plaintiff pedestrian was extremely intoxicated will not be relevant if he would still have been struck if sober.[34] Similarly, to accept a lift on a motorbike whose lights to your knowledge are defective may well constitute contributory negligence, but this may not be invoked by the driver of the bike if she runs into a plainly visible vehicle coming towards her.[35]

**[20.16]** The sound sense of the rule was stressed by Kingsmill Moore J, in *Moore v Nolan*,[36] when he said that if it were otherwise:

> "the way of a transgressor with an ingenious imagination would be made easy, for he could call in his aid a series of possible and potential dangers which in theory a careful man should

---

30. (contd) *Rigby v Chief Constable of Northamptonshire* [1985] 2 All ER 985 (QB) - defence rejected on the facts; *Spiewak v 251268 Ontario Ltd* 43 DLR (4th) 554 (Ont HC) - real estate agent liable under *Hedley Byrne* principle for giving the plaintiff prospective purchaser of an apartment building a misleading estimate of likely rental income; the plaintiff, who was "no babe in the woods", was held guilty of contributory negligence for failing to have retained a lawyer.

31. *Cf Moore v Nolan* (1960) 94 ILTR 153 (SC); *Ross v McQueen* [1947] NI 81 at 84 (KB); *Nance v British Columbia Electric Ry* [1951] AC 601 at 611 (PC). In *McCord v Electricity Supply Board* [1980] ILRM 153 (SC), O'Higgins CJ considered that unreasonable conduct "without regard to the comfort and convenience of [one's] family" could "fairly be regarded as contributory negligence or want of care within the meaning of the section". This would seem hard to justify unless the lack of concern for others reveals a want of care for one's own welfare. Some of the complexities of the conceptual difference between negligence and contributory negligence were left unaddressed by the Supreme Court in *Phillips v Durgan* [1991] ILRM 321; *cf* Byrne & Binchy, *Annual Review of Irish Law 1990*, pp 493-500.

32. See further para **[20.78]** below. But see *Moore v Nolan* (1960) 94 ILTR 153 at 160. As to what particulars of contributory negligence must be pleaded by the defendant see *Mahon v Celbridge Spinning Co Ltd* [1967] IR I (SC) overruling *Martin v Ford* [1965] IR 42 (HC).

33. Section 34(2)(c) reaffirming previous law. See *Moore v Nolan* (1960) 94 ILTR 153 at 159 (SC); *Stapleton v O'Regan* (1961) 95 ILTR 1 at 5 (SC). *Cf Guckian v Cully* Supreme Court, 9 March 1972, (Ó Dalaigh CJ's judgment p 1).

34. *Woods v Davison* [1930] NI 161 (HL).

35. *Gent-Diver v Neville* [1953] QSRI. See also *Smithwick v Hall & Upson Co* (1890) 59 Conn 261 21 A 924.

36. (1960) 94 ILTR 153 at 160 (SC).

anticipate and take steps to guard against. As against his own proved and effective negligence he could set a hypothetical negligence of the injured man."

**[20.17]** However, the courts will not adopt an unduly specific investigation in determining the risk to which the plaintiff's conduct exposed him: "it is sufficient if it is a danger of a particular class whose occurrence he should anticipate and take reasonable precautions to guard against."[37]

## The "Agony of the Moment"

**[20.18]** When proof of contributory negligence afforded an absolute defence, the courts developed a doctrine, known as that of the "agony of the moment", whereby a plaintiff acting reasonably in an attempt to extricate himself from a sudden emergency for which he or she was not responsible,[38] or had no reason to anticipate,[39] was held not guilty of contributory negligence if he or she unintentionally aggravated the situation.[40] In truth there was no need for any distinctive rule: application of the ordinary principles of negligence and contributory negligence should clearly be able to distinguish between the standard required of one making a decision in calm and unhurried circumstances and one being forced to decide quickly in an emergency.[41] The rule may have been applied with somewhat undue leniency towards plaintiffs before apportionment was allowed.[42] Under present law, undue leniency is clearly not permissible. The rule does not, of course, affect merely the plaintiff, it applies equally to situations of emergency for the defendant brought about by the plaintiff's conduct.[43] Moreover, it can arise in respect of a situation of peril for either party that has been created by a third party or by no party at all (as in the case of

---

37. (1960) 94 ILTR 153 at 161. *Cf Judge v Reape* [1968] IR 226 at 230 (SC). See also *McNamee v Dunphy* DPIJ: Hilary and Easter Terms 1993 p 192 (HC) - injuries sustained by motor cyclist attributable in part to failure to wear crash helmet.

38. See eg *Ward v Dawson* High Court, 26 July 1996, plaintiff driver not guilty of contributory negligence in behaving "as any ordinary motorist would behave in the circumstances unfolding before him", by braking sharply when "a confusion of cars ahead of him" was involved in a collision. *Cf Municipal Tramways Trust v Ashby* [1951] SASR 61; *Gallant v Oickle* (1982) 53 NSR (2d) 331 (SC) - tailgating. In cases where the plaintiff himself brought about the emergency it is:

> "not the conduct in the emergency that the law does not excuse. There is no culpability in such conduct. It is the negligent conduct which brought about the emergency that the law does not excuse. The act done in the emergency, immediately causing the injury, is a mere link in the causal chain connecting the negligent act which brought about the emergency with the injury. It is this negligent act and not the non-negligent act done in the emergency, that liability springs from":

*Windsor v McKee* (1928) 22 SW 2d 65 at 67 (Mo Appeal). See also *Lunzer v Pittsburgh & L ER Co* (1929) 296 Pa 303 at 145, Atl 907 at 908

39. *Cf Mye v Peters* (1967) SR (NSW) 298 at 300-301 (CA).

40. See WILLIAMS, pp 360-364; *The Bywell Castle* (1879) 4 PD 219 (CA); *Jones v Boyce* (1816) 1 Stark 493, 171 ER 540; Reynolds 'Put Yourself in an Emergency - How Will You Be Judged?' (1974) 62 Ky LJ 366; 'Note The Sudden Emergency Doctrine' (1965) 36 Miss LJ 392'; Thode 'Imminent Peril and Emergency in Texas' (1962) 40 Texas LR 441; Brown 'Note: Act of God, Unavoidable Accident, Sudden Emergency' (1966) 19 Okla LR 308; Evans 'The Standard of Care in Emergencies' (1943) 31 Ky LJ 207; Hollingsworth 'Note: The Sudden Emergency Doctrine in Florida' (1969) 21 U Fla LR 667. See *Ward v Dawson* High Court, 26 July 1996.

41. WILLIAMS, p 361.

42. WILLIAMS, p 361. But see the Irish decisions discussed para **[20.23]**.

43. *Cf Sandys v Harrison* [1926] IR 243 (SC); *Delany v Dublin United Tramways Co* 30 LR Ir 725 (CA). In some cases less indulgence has been shown to defendants than to plaintiffs: see eg *Shelley v Shelley* [1971] SASR 430.

some natural disaster, such as a landslide, or a medical emergency[44] or the more mundane happening of traffic lights changing as one attempts to get clear of a crossing).[45]

**[20.19]** We have already seen how drivers of vehicles who are obliged to stop suddenly in an unforeseen emergency to avoid colliding with a person or even an animal may be excused if they injure a passenger or other road user in the process.[46] The court will not be guided by hindsight, instead the difficult circumstances of the emergency during which a quick decision was required will be given due weight. This does not mean, however, that persons are given a *carte blanche* to act as they wish in situations of apparent emergency, they may be liable if they unreasonably imagine that an emergency exists when it does not[47] or if, in a condition of actual emergency, their response was an unreasonable one.[48] The difficult question of the entitlement of a person in an emergency to place his own interests over those of people around him has not yet come before an Irish court. Courts in other jurisdictions have been sympathetic to defendants in such circumstances,[49] one judge taking the view that "self-preservation is the first law of nature".[50] Clearly, however, there must be limits to what is reasonable in this context; there is no unqualified privilege to ignore the rights of others even in situations of emergency. Where the action in aid of oneself is instinctive and unthinking, the Courts will have less difficulty in excusing it than in cases where the actor, after deliberation, chooses in an emergency to sacrifice the interests of another to his or her own benefit.

**[20.20]** In some of the Irish cases the Courts have evinced a surprising lack of sympathy for plaintiffs faced with an emergency. In *Kearney v GS Ry Co*,[51] the plaintiff was a passenger on a train when the connecting-rod broke, which led to her carriage being filled with steam. At the same time, some pebbles struck the window. A man in the same carriage looked out of the window and cried out that the train was on fire. The plaintiff, believing that the steam was smoke, jumped out of the carriage and was injured.

**[20.21]** The plaintiff's action was dismissed by direction of the trial judge and her appeal was unsuccessful. The Queen's Bench Division regarded her action as rash and unwarranted, in jumping out "without inquiry"[52] as to whether the cry of "fire" was correct. Had the carriage been over-turned by the defect in the machinery, the position would have been different.

---

44. *Cf O'Donovan v Cork Co Co* [1967] IR 173 at 200 (SC).
45. *Piel v Dublin United Tramways Co* (1896) Ltd [1939] Ir Jur 88 (CC).
46. See para **[20.18]**.
47. *Cf Lederev v Connecticut Co* (1920) 111 Atl 785 at 788 (Cone CA).
48. *Cf* PROSSER & KEETON, p 197.
49. *Cf* eg *Gordan v Peerless Transportation Co* (1941) 27 NYS 2d 198 (City Court of NY).
50. *Thurmond v Pepper* (1938) 119 SW 2d 900 at 903 (Texas Cir App). It should be noted that in this case the defendant did make some attempt albeit limited and futile to prevent injury to the other person.
51. (1886) 28 LR Ir 303 (QB) (distinguishing *Jones v Boyce*). *Cf Hogg v Keane* [1956] IR 155 (SC).
52. (1886) 28 LR Ir 303 at 308. Another harsh decision is *Bradford v Kanellos* (1973) 40 DLR (3d) 578 (SC, Can) - a patron was injured when he was trampelled upon by other panic-stricken patrons rushing from a restaurant to avoid fire; the fire had been extinguished, but the extinguisher had made a popping sound which another patron, (described by the judge as "an idiotic person"), mistook for gas, shouting that there might be an explosion; liability denied on basis of *novus actus interveniens*.

**[20.22]** This approach seems unduly harsh, and would be unlikely to be followed today. The fact that the engine-driver and stoker had been injured (the former breaking his leg) was surely some corroboration of the plaintiff's assessment of the seriousness of the situation. Moreover, it is scarcely satisfactory to say (as Johnson J did)[53] that the defendants were not responsible for the cry of fire, on the basis that "it was unfounded, in fact". To be too willing to apply hindsight in such cases may yield an unjust result.

## The Dilemma Principle

**[20.23]** The "agony of the moment" principle has been extended into a broader principle, known as the "dilemma principle". This relates to cases where the defendant's negligence places the plaintiff in a position where, to avoid a greater inconvenience (not necessarily one involving risk of personal injury) he, with due deliberation, chooses to run a slight risk of injury or damage.[54] Whereas courts were formerly somewhat indulgent to plaintiffs in this regard, they are, since apportionment has been introduced, freer to stigmatise such conduct as contributory negligence, albeit of a relatively small proportion.[55]

## Failure to Mitigate Damage

**[20.24]** A negligent or careless failure to mitigate damage is deemed[56] contributory negligence in respect of the amount by which such damage exceeds the damage that would otherwise have occurred.

**[20.25]** Under previous law, contributory negligence might be contrasted with failure to mitigate damage in that contributory negligence applied before the wrong had been committed, whereas failure to mitigate could only arise afterwards. Where the plaintiff, as a result of carelessness after sustaining the injury, worsened his condition or delayed his

53. (1886) 28 LR Ir 303 at 310. See also *Kelly v McElligott* (1951) 85 ILTR 4 (SC) where scant sympathy was shown to an hotel guest injured when escaping from a fire. *Cf Maclenan v Segar* [1917] 2 KB 325; *Zervobeakos v Zervobeakos* (1969) 8 DLR (3d) 377 (NS SC). In *Armstrong v Eastern Health Board* High Court, 5 October 1990 a patient with a history of physchiatric illness who, having been inadequately assessed, jumped from a balcony was held not to have been guilty of any contributory negligence as "she was not really in control of her thoughts" at the time.

54. *Cf Clayards v Dethick* (1848) 12 QB 439, 116 ER 932. See also *Billings (AC) & Sons Ltd v Riden* [1958] AC 240 (HL); WILLIAMS, pp 362-363.

55. *Cf Sayers v Harlow UDC* [1958] 2 All ER 342 (CA) - a woman locked in public lavatory was injured when trying to escape: damages reduced by 25% as she adopted an unduly hazardous manner of escape. Contrast *Caterson v Commissioner for Rys* (1973) 128 Comm LR 99 (HC, Austr) - a jury was not bound to find a plaintiff guilty of contributory negligence for jumping off a moving train; the train had left the station without warning while he was seeing a passenger off; the next station was 80 miles away; and the plaintiff's 14-year old son had been left alone on the platform 40 miles from home. *Cf Martin v Dublin United Tramways Co Ltd* [1909] 2 IR 13 (KB). See also *Galvin v Griffin* DPIJ: Trinity and Michaelmas Terms 1994, p 58 (HC) - customer who went into shop after noticing wet muddy tracks or footprints on the floor and then slipped held not guilty of contributory negligence: "[I]t was not her function to put the shop into quarantine by not entering it."

56. Section 34(2)(b). Impecuniosity on the part of the plaintiff is regarded with some indulgence by the courts in determining whether there has been a failure to mitigate damages: *cf Quinn v Quality Homes Ltd* High Court, 21 November 1977; *Riordan's Travel Ltd v Acres & Co Ltd* High Court, 17 January 1979; *Murphy v McGrath* [1981] ILRM 364 (HC). See *Kerr* (1980) 74 Gaz ILSI 51. See also *Rabbette v Mayo County Council* [1984] ILRM 156 (HC) and para **[3.38]**.

recovery, an issue of causation arose; if his conduct could be regarded as a *novus actus interveniens* he would not be permitted to recover any damages for injuries that could be traceable to his conduct.

**[20.26]** Thus, where a person whose leg had been weakened in an accident for which the defendant was responsible, placed himself in a situation of danger by climbing unassisted a steep stair with no handrail, he was regarded as responsible for his subsequent fall and for the damage flowing from it, since, even though it was foreseeable, he had acted unreasonably, in the circumstances.[57] Had the plaintiff not acted unreasonably, of course, the defendant would have been liable for the subsequent injury.[58]

**[20.27]** Such a rule was clearly "lacking in sophistication".[59] As Professor Williams argued:

> "It is not satisfactory that in cases like these the plaintiff should recover the whole of his damages or nothing according as his conduct is put at the reasonable or unreasonable end of what is in fact a continuous gradation. Justice can best be served by considering the conduct of both parties and then, if necessary, apportioning the loss between them. Slight negligence on the part of the plaintiff can be allowed for by a slight reduction in his damages, and the court no longer has to make the painful choice between denying the plaintiff's slight lapse and refusing the plaintiff any remedy."[60]

**[20.28]** Does this mean that, under existing law, apportionment of damages will be the proper solution in every case of negligent or careless failure to mitigate damage?[61] Surely not. There are some failures to mitigate which clearly do not even raise a question of apportionment. If a plaintiff with an injured thumb chooses to recuperate in the Bahamas, no question of splitting that bill should arise. The reform brought about by the statutory provision was designed to ensure that the apportionment philosophy was not thwarted by too mechanical an application of a causal rule in respect of what Professor Williams calls "slight negligence" on the part of the plaintiff after sustaining the injury. It was scarcely its purpose to impose on the defendant liability for damage brought by the plaintiff freely upon himself for his own selfish indulgence. Probably the court would reject such a claim on the basis that it was not a "negligent or careless" failure to mitigate damages, but rather that the plainitff's deliberate act represented a *novus actus interveniens*.[62]

---

57. *McKew v Holland & Hannen & Cubitts (Scotland) Ltd* [1969] 3 All ER 1821 (HL).
58. *Cf Wieland v Cyril Lord Carpets Ltd* [1969] 3 All ER 1006 (QB); LINDEN, p 345.
59. LINDEN, p 345.
60. WILLIAMS, pp 292-293.
61. *Cf Campbell v T & J Barrington Ltd* High Court, 3 October 1977, which appears to reject this proposition.
62. In *Baldwin v Foy and Forest Way Riding Holidays Ltd* High Court, 1 July 1997, Laffoy J held that the plaintiff who had been injured in a horse-riding accident caused by the defendants' negligence had failed to mitigate her damages and was accordingly guilty of contributory negligence in deciding not to continue to pursue a career in catering but instead to take training courses in skills related to "the advertising business - copywriting and graphics and such like". The evidence in the case was to the effect that three years after the accident the plaintiff would have been able to obtain employment in the catering business. Her losses thereafter, in Laffoy J's view, were attributable to her decision to engage in a career change.

**[20.29]** Similarly, if a plaintiff who has been injured declines to undergo necessary medical treatment in circumstances where that refusal is unreasonable having regard to the nature of the treatment, damages will be computed on the basis that the treatment was carried out.

**[20.30]** In *Bohan v Finn*,[63] Murphy J so held, where the plaintiff, suffering from a psychosomatic illness, declined to undergo treatment in a psychiatric hospital which carried an 85% to 90% probability of a cure. Murphy J observed that:

> "... the refusal to accept that treatment to my mind is unreasonable. Nobody is bound to undergo experimental or unusual remedies for the illness or disability imposed upon them by a wrongdoer, but they are bound to undertake reasonable steps to procure their recovery. I appreciate [the plaintiff]'s concern about the stigma of attending a psychiatrist hospital, or indeed attending a psychiatrist. It is part, or perhaps a feature of our tradition and culture, that people dislike going to such hospitals or attending such specialists, whereas in other countries it is, I think, more notorious that distinguished and wealthy people, film stars amongst them, wouldn't dream of doing anything without attending frequently their retained psychiatrist, and that there is no disgrace involved in that, but it does seem to me, whoever it is done by, ... that [the plaintiff] really must, in her own interests and in fairness to the defendants, and should before now have, undergone a treatment which doesn't seem to involve any particular degree of pain, in the sense of what an operative or surgical treatment might well involve.
>
> I don't think it is open to the plaintiff to say: 'I am disabled. I will continue to go about on crutches unable to walk, and unable to work, and unable to enjoy the amenities of life, even though there is a treatment available to me which would take a year and has a success rate of over 85%.' I don't think that is acting reasonably."[64]

**[20.31]** Accordingly, Murphy J calculated the plaintiff's damages on the basis that her disability would have been completely cured by the time of trial.

**[20.32]** So also, if a plaintiff declines to take up an offer of employment that is within his or her capacity to undertake, the reduction of compensation to take account of that failure to mitigate damages should be based on a calculation of the full financial loss thereby unnecessarily sustained by this deliberate decision.[65]

**[20.33]** An instance of a reasonable failure to mitigate damages occurred in *Philips v The Medical Council*,[66] where the plaintiff lost three years' earnings of around £20,000 per annum while the Medical Council unreasonably delayed the registration on the General Register of Medical Practitioners. The plaintiff had not claimed a social welfare benefit of £30 per week as he had not considered it worth his while applying for it. Costello J regarded this attitude as "a reasonable one"[67] and made no deduction on its account.

63. DPIJ: Trinity and Michaelmas Terms 1994, p 61 (HC).

64. DPIJ: Trinity and Michaelmas Terms 1994, pp 65-66. *Cf Cazabon v Westinghouse Electrical Irl Ltd t/a ThermoKing (Europe) Ltd* DPIJ: Hilary and Easter Terms 1994, p 104 (HC) - the plaintiff was "not unreasonable in being slow to undergo" further surgery "attended with some risks". Where the refusal to undergo treatment is attributable to a pre-existing psychological infirmity no deduction in damages should be made: *Janiak v Ippolito* [1985] 1 Can SCR 146.

65. *Cf* Kinlen J's discussion of the issue in *Ecock v MF Kent & Co* DPIJ: Hilary and Easter Terms 1994, p 178 (HC).

66. High Court, 11 December 1990.

67. High Court, 11 December 1990.

## The Seat Belt Defence[68]

**[20.34]** After some earlier uncertainty, it is now generally accepted that the use of seat belts helps to reduce the level of injuries resulting from traffic accidents.[69] Where a driver or passenger fails to use an available seat belt, ought the damages be reduced if, on account of that failure, he or she suffers injuries that would not have occurred had he or she been wearing the seat belt? The answer given with increasing uniformity by courts in common law jurisdictions[70] is that they should be reduced.

---

68. See Kerr 'Seatbelts Crash, Helmets and Contributory Negligence' (1979) 73 Incorp L Soc of Ireland 122; Slattery 'Seat Belts and Contnbutory Negligence' (1977) 4 Dalhousie LJ 86; Kirk *The Seat-Belt Defence*, Ch 6 of Law Reform Reconnaissance Pt 3 (Legal Research Institute of the University of Manitoba 1974); Kliest 'The Seat Belt Defense - An Exercise in Sophistry' (1967) 18 Hastings LJ 613; Wilton & Campbell 'Recognizing the Value of Seat Belts in Motor Vehicle Products Liability Cases' (1988) 11 J of Prod Ly 1; Ackerman 'The Seat Belt Defense Reconsidered: A Return to Accountability in Tort Law?' (1986) 16 New Mex LR 221; Goe 'Comment Buckling Up: How the Mandatory Seatbelt Law Affects the Seatbelt Defense' (1988) 17 SW LJ 597; Wayand 'Seat Belts - A Comparative Study of the Law and Practice' (1981) 30 Int & Comp LQ 165; Linden 'Seat Belts and Contributory Negligence' (1971) 49 Can BR 475; Reynolds & Kirschman 'The Ten Myths of Product Liability' (2000) 27 Wm Mitchell LR 551 at 578-581; Nielsen 'Note: The New Case for the "Seat Belt Defence"' (2000) 30 NM LR 403; Hicks 'Seat Belts and Crash Helmets' (1974) 37 MLR 308; Williams 'Comment' (1975) 53 Can BR 113.

69. *Cf* O'Flynn 'Safety Belts' 17 An Foras Forbatha, October 1969, RS 56:

> "Researchers seem to be unanimous in their agreement that safety belts of all types are effective in reduction of injury severity and ejection control."

More recent research findings are substantially in accord: see eg Berard-Anderson 'Use and Effects of Seat Belts in 21 Countries' (1978), pp 13-18.

70. This is clearly so in England: *Froom v Butcher* [1976] QB 286 (CA). Courts in Australia and the USA were slower to recognise the defence. In Canada most decisions now favour the view that failure to use a seatbelt constitutes contributory negligence. It should be noted that the question may arise as to whether the driver of a car (or other person) has a duty to advise a passenger to use a seat belt. In *Pasternack v Poulton* [1973] 2 All ER 74 (QB), Kenneth Jones J QC, imposed liability on this ground (as well as on the ground of the defendant's reckless driving), although he reduced the damages on account of the plaintiff's contributory negligence. The relative infrequency with which seat belts were then installed in cars must be compared with the position today where they are mandatory and almost universal. The issue of the driver's negligence would now be limited to cases where some special reason (such as the passenger's youth or lack of mental capacity) would call for action by the driver. In *Migliore v Gerard* (1987) 42 DLR (49) 619 (Ont HC) parents were relieved of liability for what was "at most a momentary lapse in judgment" in failing to ensure that their children aged 7 and 3 wore seat belts. It should be noted that the accident occurred in 1981 when only four of the Canadian provinces (admittedly comprising 75% of the population) were covered by mandatory seat belt legislation. Further O'Brien J noted (at 626) that in 1981 "there was a question in the minds of many people about the safety of small children in seat-belts". See also *Beaver v Crowe* (1974) 49 DLR (3d) 116 (NS SC) repudiating the *Pasternack v Poulton* rationale; and see *Pelletier v Olson* (1987) 42 CCLT 129 (Sask QB). In *O'Regan v Byrne* DPIJ: Hilary and Easter Terms 1993, p 238 at 241 (HC) Murphy J mooted in general terms the possibility that:

> "a driver of a motorcar particularly the driver of a certain vehicle would have [the] duty to remind the passenger to look after his own welfare."

**[20.35]** The issue did not arise at appellate level in this country until 1977. In *Hamill v Oliver*[71] the Supreme Court held that:

> "any person who travels in the front seat of a motor car, be he passenger or driver, without wearing an available seat belt must normally be held guilty of contributory negligence if the injuries in respect of which he sues were caused wholly or in part as a result of his failure to wear a seat belt."

**[20.36]** The Court seemed not to regard as relevant the statutory rule[72] that failure to mitigate damages should be regarded as contributory negligence.

**[20.37]** It is interesting to note that reliance was placed by the Court on the fact that the legislature had made it compulsory[73] to fit seat belts to cars: in doing so "it must have been intended that they should be worn although the wearing of seat belts was not made compulsory".[74] Today it is compulsory to wear a seat belt (save in exceptional cases). It might therefore be contended that a plaintiff's failure to wear a seat belt now even more clearly constitutes contributory negligence than formerly, since it is surely a breach of statutory duty resulting in "damage that the statute was designed to prevent".[75]

***(a) Excuses for not wearing a seat belt***

**[20.38]** In *Hamill v Oliver*,[76] Griffin J stated that there might be excusing circumstances for failure to wear a seat belt, "such as obesity, pregnancy,[77] post-operative convalescence, and the like, where the wearing of a seat belt might be thought to do more harm than good", but he stressed[78] that it is for the person who has not worn the seat belt to raise and prove such excusing circumstances.

**[20.39]** In *Ward v Walsh*[79] the Supreme Court saw no reason to excuse a plaintiff whose failure to wear a seat belt was attributable to a fear of being trapped in a car. Upholding a reduction of 20% for his contributory negligence, the Supreme Court gave no consideration to whether his fear derived from an inadequate assessment of the respective risks of wearing or not wearing a seat belt or from some phobia.

**[20.40]** In *McGouran v Reynolds*,[80] the plaintiff, a helper in a van, argued that it would have been impracticable to use a seat belt, having regard to the number of stops and starts

---

71. [1977] IR 73 at 76 (SC J). The decision is perceptively analysed by Kerr 'Seatbelts, Crash Helmets and Contributory Negligence' (1979) 73 Incorp L Soc of Ireland Gaz 122. Too much must not be read into the phrase that the duty is confined to front seat passengers. In 1977, back seat belts were rare in this jurisdiction.
72. Section 34(2)(b) of the Civil Liability Act 1961.
73. Road Traffic (Construction Equipment and Use of Vehicles) (Amendment) Regulations 1971 (SI 16/1971). In the United States the first mandatory seat belt law was as late as 1984 (in New York).
74. *Hamill v Oliver* [1977] IR 73 at 76 (SC).
75. Section 34(2)(c) of the Civil Liability Act 1961.
76. [1977] IR 73 at 76. *Cf McKay v Borthwick* 1981 SLT 265.
77. In *Whelley v Falbey* DPIJ: Hilary and Easter Terms 1996 p 35 (HC), the defence of contributory negligence failed by reason of the plaintiff's pregnant condition.
78. [1977] IR at 76.
79. Supreme Court, 31 July 1991 analysed by Byrne & Binchy, *Annual Review of Irish Law 1991*, pp 441-443.
80. High Court, 27 April 1988. See also *Conley v Strain* [1988] IR 628 (HC).

involved in his work. O'Hanlon J rejected this contention, not, it seems, because an argument on these lines was inherently defective, but because the driver had estimated that the journey was "a good half mile" between their previous stop and the one to which they were proceeding.

### *(b) Proof of causation*

**[20.41]** That the plaintiff's failure to wear a seat belt contributed to injury, must be established on the evidence.[81] In *Hamill v Oliver*, it was held that "in most cases"[82] no special evidence was required to prove that the wearing of the seat belt would have prevented or reduced the injuries. This contrasts with the approach of the courts in many other jurisdictions,[83] where clear proof of a causal connection is required. In some Irish cases, the courts have referred to the issue of causation in a manner indicating that they appreciated its relevance but that, consistent with the Supreme Court's guidance, proof need not be unduly specific. Thus, for example, in *McGouran v Reynolds*,[84] O'Hanlon J reduced the plaintiff passenger's damages by 15% where he had been "thrown violently against the side of a van, in a manner which would probably have been minimised to a significant extent were he wearing a seat belt at the time."[85] On other occasions, the Courts have accepted evidence of causation expressed in terms of enhancement of the risk of injury. In *Sinnott v Quinnsworth*,[86] the Supreme Court considered that the plaintiff's contributory negligence was in the order of 15% where a neuro-surgeon testified[87] that had the plaintiff been wearing a seat belt the chances of his sustaining the very severe injury which he suffered would have been reduced by about 25%. Thus, the plaintiff's damages were reduced, even though the evidence was not to the effect that failure to wear a seat belt, on balance, caused a sufficient enhancement of his injury.

**[20.42]** *Sinnott v Quinnsworth* may be contrasted with *Conley v Strain*,[88] where the plaintiff's damages were reduced by 14% on the basis of evidence by his surgeon that a person thrown out of a motor vehicle is thirty times more likely to suffer serious injuries in an accident than one who remains in the crashed vehicle. Taking this evidence together with the evidence that the plaintiff was lying under his car after the accident, Lynch J came

---

81. *Wilson v McGrath* High Court, 17 January 1996; *Hughes v O'Flaherty* High Court, 19 January 1996; *Coppinger v Waterford County Council* [1996] 2 ILRM 427; *Conley v Strain* [1988] IR 628 (HC).

82. [1977] IR 73 at 76. See also *Froom v Butcher* [1976] QB 286.

83. *Cf* McCann 'The Seat Belt Defence in Canada' (1977) 42 Sask LR 75 at 103 who states that in Canada: "the failure rate of the [seat belt] defence is high because of a lack of proper proof of causation ...". See also Feince 'Comment' (1970) 10 Santa Clara L 370 at 380-381; Slattery 'Seat Belts and Contributory Negligence' (1977) 4 Dalhousie LJ 96 at 108. The position is similar in the United States: see Fischer 'Comment: The Medical and Legal Problems Arising from the Failure to Wear Seat Belts' (1972) 27 U Miami LR 130 at 146 ff. See also *Webber v Crawford* (1988) 46 CCLTI (BC SC); *Rigler v Miller* (1972) 26 DLR (3d) 366 (BCSC); *Smith v Blackburn* [1974] RTR 533; *Lertorn v Finzi* [1973] RTR 161; *Owens v Brimmell* [1976] 3 All ER 765 (QB).

84. High Court, 27 April 1988.

85. Page 4 of O'Hanlon J's judgment. See also *Conley v Strain* [1988] IR 628 at p 4; *O'Regan v Byrne* DPIJ: Hilary and Easter Terms 1993, p 238 (HC); *Cronin v Mulligan* Supreme Court, 14 May 1999; *Henley v Coillte Teoranta* High Court, 9 March 1999.

86. [1984] ILRM 523.

87. McCarthy J would have preferred to rely on the expertise of a motor engineer "or perhaps ... any individual driver or passenger" on the question of causation: [1984] ILRM 523 at 534.

88. [1988] IR 628.

to "the inevitable conclusion"[89] that the plaintiff's failure to wear the seat belt has contributed to the gravity of his injuries.

***(c) Apportionment of damages***

**[20.43]** In determining apportionment of damages an important question arises as to whether failure to wear an available seat belt should be regarded as contributory negligence simpliciter or as failure to mitigate damages - in which case it is also contributory negligence, but with an important difference, namely, that it is contributory negligence "in respect of the amount by which such damage *exceeds the damage that would otherwise have occurred*".[90] An example will perhaps make this clearer. P, a passenger, is injured as a result of D's negligence. The evidence shows that, if he had worn his seat belt, the damages would have been £20,000. In fact, as a result of not wearing it, P breaks his neck and the damages are £60,000. If P is guilty of contributory negligence *simpliciter*, the apportionment is carried out on the full sum of £60,000, but if P is guilty of contributory negligence by reason of failure to mitigate damages, then apportionment can be carried out only on £40,000 - the amount by which his damage "exceeds the damage that would otherwise have occurred". In some cases, no practical difference will result from applying the different criteria, but in others, especially where the enhanced injuries are small but the degree of fault on the part of the injured person is great, the difference could be of considerable importance.

**[20.44]** In *Hamill v Oliver*,[91] the Supreme Court appears to have favoured the view that failure to use a seat belt constitutes contributory negligence *simpliciter* (though the issue does not seem to have been argued). Subsequent decisions[92] are generally[93] in accord. It is

---

89. [1988] IR 628.
90. Section 34(2)(b) of the Civil Liability Act 1961 (emphasis added). In some cases of course, the failure to wear a seat belt may result in injury, when wearing a seat belt would have resulted in no injury at all. This is not a case of failure to mitigate damages and can best be regarded as "simple" contributory negligence: *cf Curry v Moser* (1982) 89 Appeal Div 2d 1 454 NYS 2d 311 (2d Dept). Noted by Tonma (1983) 57 St John's LR 430.
91. [1977] IR 73 (SC).
92. *Cf* eg *McGouran v Reynolds* High Court, 27 April 1988; *Conley v Strain* [1988] IR 628; *Sinnott v Quinnsworth Ltd* [1984] ILRM 523 (SC). In *Strick v Treacy* High Court, 10 June 1993 O'Hanlon J reduced the plaintiff's damages by 50% where her failure to wear a seat belt "contributed significantly to the seriousness of her injuries". These included injuries to her head, neck, arm, shoulder and knee. It should be noted that the plaintiff's contributory negligence extended to failure to keep a proper look out when driving her car. O'Hanlon J did not allocate specific proportions of the 50% reduction to the two headings of contributory negligence.
93. It is interesting to note that in *McNamee v Dunphy* DPIJ: Hilary and Easter Terms 1993, p 192 (HC), where the plaintiff motorcyclist sustained among other injuries a fracture of the skull and a serious injury to his left ear as a probable result of his failure to wear a crash-helmet, O'Hanlon J observed (at p 195):

> "I thought at one stage I could meet the situation by merely eliminating from consideration altogether those injuries, which in my opinion he would not have sustained had he worn the crash-helmet, and simply given him the full amount for all his other injuries, but I think on reflection that this is not a correct approach and accordingly I proceed on the orthodox basis to apportion fault as between the parties. I consider that the proportion of injuries, both in amount and seriousness, attributable to his contributory negligence, is of a relatively small variety by comparison with the remainder of his injuries and I propose therefore to apportion fault between the parties as to 95% against the defendant and 5% against the plaintiff."

submitted, however, that there is much to be said for the view that a failure to mitigate damages is involved.[94]

**[20.45]** As regards the extent of the reduction in damages to take account of the plaintiff's contributory negligence, most findings are in the range of 10% to 20%. In *Sinnott v Quinnsworth Ltd*[95] the Supreme Court raised to 15% a jury finding of 2% contributory negligence, O'Higgins CJ noting that the Court had "frequently stated that in no case can such a small percentage as 2% be warranted".[96]

## Degrees of Fault

**[20.46]** Section 34(1), as we have seen, requires an apportionment of damages to be made "... having regard to the degrees of fault of the plaintiff and defendant". The Supreme Court has made it clear on more than one occasion that fault "is equated to blameworthiness and not to the potency of the causative factors moving from each side".[97]

**[20.47]** What does "blameworthiness" mean? In *O'Sullivan v Dwyer*,[98] Walsh J (with whose judgment Ó Dálaigh CJ and Fitzgerald J agreed) stated that:

---

93. (contd) In *Cassidy v Clarke* DPIJ: Trinity and Michaelmas 1999, p 183 (HC), Finnegan J gave what is perhaps the most sophisticated judicial analysis of the assessment of contributory negligence. The plaintiff had sustained injuries to her head, neck, wrist, thumb and back in a traffic accident where she had failed to wear a seat-belt. Her head injuries were caused by her striking her head off the mirror. Finnegan J reduced the compensation *for that particular injury* by 15%, since it was attributable to her failure to wear the seat belt, but made no other reduction.

94. *Cf Guldenschuh* (1980) 56 Notre Dame L 272 at 275-277; *Spier v Barker* (1974) 35 NY 2d 444 323; NE 2d 164 363, NYS 2d 916.

95. [1984] ILRM 523 (SC).

96. [1984] ILRM 523 at 528.

97. *Kelly v Jameson* Supreme Court, 1 March 1972 *per* Walsh J at p 4. See also *O'Sullivan v Dwyer* [1971] IR 275 (SC); *Carroll v Clare Co Co* [1975] IR 221 (SC). See also *Conley v Strain* [1988] IR 628 at p 5:

> "Usually a person is either negligent or not negligent, and the addition of adjectives does not alter the legal position. When one comes to apportion fault under section 34 ... however, it seems to me that one must fall back on adjectives."

The distinction between causation and culpability is not always easy to draw: *cf Ashworth v General Accident Fire & Life Assurance Corporation* [1955] IR 268 at 296-297 (SC *per* Black J, dissenting). In *Shields v Boyle* High Court, 6 November 1991, O'Hanlon J reduced the plaintiff pedestrian's damages of 33¹/3% on the basis of a comparison of the parties' respective degrees of blameworthiness while indicating that if it had been a simple matter of apportioning causation he would have tended towards a division in equal shares. In truth, the court will often be required to address the parties' respective causal roles (if not "contributions" - a term that may suggest an inevitable ascription of partial causal responsibility). It is possible, for example, that the plaintiff may have been uniquely causally responsible for the injury. The fact that the plaintiff's negligent failure to mitigate damage is contributory negligence, in respect of the amount by which the damage that exceeds the damage that would otherwise have occurred (s 34(2)(b) of the 1961 Act) complicates the issue. A further complication, at a more fundamental philosophical level, is that to make a causal ascription in respect of human conduct is inevitably to involve oneself in a normative evaluation in which blameworthiness is a tacit ingredient.

98. [1971] IR 275 at 286 (SC). See also *Snell v Haughton* [1971] IR 305 at 309 (SC) - with whose judgment Ó Dálaigh CJ, Budd, Fitzgerald and McLoughlin JJ concurred.

"... a judge in directing a jury, must direct their minds to the distinction between causation and fault and that they should be instructed that degrees of fault between the parties are not to be apportioned on the basis of the relative causative potency of their respective causative contributions to the damage, but rather on the basis of the moral blameworthiness of their respective causative contributions. However, there are limits to this since fault is not to be measured by purely subjective standards but by objective standards. The degree of incapacity or ignorance peculiar to a particular person is not to be the basis of measuring the blameworthiness of that person. Blameworthiness is to be measured against the degree of capacity or knowledge which such a person ought to have had if he were an ordinary reasonable person ...[99] Fault or blame is to be measured against the standard of conduct required of the ordinary reasonable man in the class or category to which the party whose fault is to be measured belongs ...."

**[20.48]** This passage was quoted by Kenny J in the Supreme Court decision of *Carroll v Clare County Council*,[100] where some concern was evinced about the effect that reference to "moral" blameworthiness might have on juries. Kenny J stated:

"I think that 'fault' in s 34 ... means a departure from a norm by a person who, as a result of such departure, has been found to have been negligent and that 'degrees of fault' expresses the extent of his departure from the standard of behaviour to be expected from a reasonable man or woman in the circumstances. The extent of that departure is not to be measured by moral considerations, for to do so would introduce a subjective element while the true view is that the test is objective only.[101] It is the blameworthiness, by reference to what a reasonable man or woman would have done in the circumstances, of the contributions of the plaintiff and defendant to the happening of the accident which is to be the basis of the apportionment. I think that the use of the word 'moral', when addressing a jury in connection with blameworthiness, is likely to mislead them."[102]

**[20.49]** The language used by Walsh J and Kenny J appears unsuitable for cases where the defendant is guilty of intentional rather than negligent wrongdoing. This is scarcely surprising since neither judge was addressing such a case. It seems reasonable to anticipate that measuring intentional "fault" will present no particular difficulty in practice, though it may not be that easy to express in convincing conceptual terms. One approach would be for the Court to refer without embarrassment to the moral quality of the defendant's conduct, since this is the only real basis on which intentional wrongdoing may be measured.

**[20.50]** We examine elsewhere[103] the position where the defendant's wrong consists only in a breach of strict statutory or common-law duty without fault, and the specific question as to whether in such a case the court must[104] or may[105] hold that it is not just and equitable to cast any part of the liability upon him, if the plaintiff is guilty of contributory negligence. For the present it is worth noting that the phrase "a breach of strict statutory or common-

99. Citing *Kingston v Kingston* (1968) 102 ILTR 65.
100. [1975] IR 221 at 226-227 (SC).
101. *Cf Conroy v AC* [1965] IR 411 at 435 (SC).
102. [1975] IR at 227. *Cf* Fleming (1976) 64 Calif LR 239 at 249.
103. See para **[21.52]**.
104. *Cf O'Sullivan v Dwyer* [1971] IR 275 at 275 (SC).
105. *Cf Daly v Avonmore Creameries* [1984] IR 131 (SC).

law duty" seems appropriate to describe a breach of tortious liability, at common law and under statute, supplemented by the liability of those in "public callings", such as inn (now "hotel")[106] keepers and carriers.

**[20.51]** Limited to this issue is the question on whether a court, where both parties have been guilty of some fault but the overwhelming preponderance is on one side, may as the case may be, make no deduction from the amount to be awarded, when that preponderance is on the defendant's side and award nothing, declaring the plaintiff to be 100% contributory negligent, where the preponderance of fault lies on his or her side. In *McCord v Electricity Supply Board*,[107] the Supreme Court was divided on the possibility of a 100% reduction. O'Higgins CJ, disenting, considered that s 34 "authorises the reduction, not the negativing or annulment of [the] damages".[108] The majority took a different view but did not speak with one voice on the issue. Griffin J's analysis was the most extensive. He quoted from Williams's discussion of the matter in *Joint Torts and Contributory Negligence*,[109] where Williams had referred to the words "shall be reduced" which appear in both s 34(1) (based on Williams's own model Act) and in the equivalent English legislation:

> "If these words are read alone they may be taken to imply that where contributory negligence is found there must be some differences between the total loss recorded and the damages awarded. On the other hand the words just quoted are followed by 'to such extent as the court thinks just and equitable,' and it may be that if the fault of one person is minute justice and equity would not be thought to demand apportionment."[110]

**[20.52]** Griffin J noted that Denning J had taken the same view in *Lavender v Diamints Ltd*[111] Griffin J observed:

> "In an appropriate case, therefore, where the fault of the plaintiff is slight as against the fault of the defendant being gross, the plaintiff may be given full damages, whereas conversely, where the defendant's fault is slight and the plaintiff's fault is gross, the reduction in damages may be total and the plaintiff will be denied any damages."[112]

In the instant case, the fault of the plaintiff had so outweighed that of the defendant that, in Griffin J's opinion, "justice and equity require[d] that the entire of the damage should lie upon the plaintiff".[113]

---

106. *Cf* the Hotel Proprietors Act 1963 and para **[12.56]** above.
107. [1980] ILRM 153 (SC).
108. [1980] ILRM 153 (SC).
109. Williams, *Joint Torts and contributory Negligence*, p 392.
110. Law Reform (Contributory Negligence) Act 1945, s 1(1) (Eng).
111. [1949] 1 KB 585.
112. [1980] ILRM 153 (SC). See also *Lacey v JD Printing Ltd* Circuit Court, 29 February 2000, Judge McMahon where a very senior printer with long experience put his hand in to unblock paper, and in his own evidence said it was "stupid in hindsight", when he could have easily switched off the machine which did not on restarting have any warm up period. Judge McMahon found that the plaintiff was the sole cause of the accident in what he said were "extreme and unusual circumstances".
113. [1980] ILRM 153 (SC).

**[20.53]** Henchy J's analysis was somewhat different. He considered that "the real source of the plaintiff's damages"[114] was to be found in his failure to take all reasonable steps to mitigate his damage:

> "whether the matter be judged in terms of contributory negligence or failure to mitigate the damage, the plaintiff's conduct must be deemed the real and ultimate cause of [the damage he suffered]."[115]

The essence of Henchy J's analysis is that the defendant should be relieved of liability on account of the fact that the plaintiff's damage was not caused by its wrong. Of course a defendant should not have to pay for damage that it did not cause but the issue whether the court is permitted to make a 100% reduction (or, indeed, a 0% reduction) where both parties are guilty of causally relevant fault was the one that Griffin J sought to address. Whilst Henchy J expressed agreement with Griffin J's analysis and while Parke and Kenny JJ expressed agreement with the judgments of Henchy and Griffin JJ, *McCord* remains an unsatisfactory judgment because of its contamination, with causal considerations involving, it seems, some judicial confusion as to the effects of s 34 on the former law relating to the failure to mitigate damages.[116]

**[20.54]** As to the competing views of O'Higgins CJ and Griffin J on the entitlement of a court to reduce the plaintiff's damages by 100%, we suggest that O'Higgins CJ has the better of the argument. This is not simply because of the language of s 34(1) but also because of the nature of the operation in which a court is engaged when investigating the nature, relevance and blameworthiness of the plaintiff's negligence in any case. A plaintiff who was not guilty of any contributory negligence or one who was guilty of contributory negligence where the damage does not result from the particular risk to which his or her conduct has exposed the plaintiff,[117] will be entitled to 100% of the damages without the court's entering into a consideration of the respective blameworthiness of the parties. Commonly, where the defendant has not been guilty of negligence that resulted in the plaintiff's injury, the defendant should not have to pay, again with no consideration of respective blameworthiness.[118] However, where both parties are guilty of causally relevant fault, it seems wrong that, even in cases where the overwhelming proportion of fault lies

---

114. [1980] ILRM 153 (SC).

115. [1980] ILRM 153 (SC). See also *Felloni v Dublin Corporation* [1998] 1 ILRM 133 (HC) - the plaintiff's case was defeated on the ground that the defendant's negligence had been "overwhelmed and overtaken" by the negligence of a third party, and the contributory negligence of the plaintiff.

116. *Cf* see para **[20.24]-[20.33]**.

117. *Cf* s 34(2)(c) of the 1961 Act and see para **[20.15]**.

118. In determining the causal issue, cases will sometimes arise where the plaintiff's blameworthy conduct intervenes between the defendant's negligent act and the plaintiff's injury. If the court characterises that intervention as a *novus actus interveniens* then the defendant will be free from liability but not because the defendant was 100% at fault for the purposes of s 34(1). The subsection applies only where the damage was caused partly by the plaintiff's contributory negligence and "partly by the wrong of the defendant". If the case is one of *novus actus interveniens* the wrong has not been caused partly by the defendant.

on one side, the court should discount the small, or even tiny, fault resulting on the other.[119] As Beldam LJ observed in *Pitts v Hunt*,[120] such an approach is "logically insupportable".

## Appeal Regarding Apportionment of Fault

**[20.55]** The appellate court will interfere with an apportionment of fault only where, in its opinion, gross error on the part of the jury (or trial judge) has been shown to have existed.[121] The principle to be applied is the same as that which arises when it is alleged that damages awarded are wholly inadequate or grossly excessive.[122] Thus, the Court will overturn the verdict of the jury (or trial judge) only where the percentages or degrees of fault fixed by it were so grossly disproportionate that no reasonable factfinder could make such a determination.

## Set-Off of Claims

**[20.56]** The general rule is that where a judgment is given for the plaintiff on a claim and for the defendant on a counterclaim under sub-s (1) of s 34 (dealing with contributory negligence), the one judgment is to be set off against the other and only the balance owing is to be recoverable.[123] This rule, however, operates only in relation to the satisfaction of debts,[124] and where the parties are insured, they will be able to recover from their respective insurance companies the balances outstanding.[125] An example[126] will perhaps clarify the position. Let us take the case where A and B are involved in an accident, A's damages being assessed at £10,000 and B's at £8,000, fault being apportioned at 50% each. A will get judgment for £5,000 and B will get judgment for £4,000, thus making A entitled to £1,000 after set-off of B's claim. The sum of £1,000 will be paid to A by B's insurance company, but B will be entitled to recover from his insurance company the sum of £4,000 deducted by the company in settling A's claim; similarly A has a right to recover

119. It would seem invidious to place emphasis on the words "shall be reduced" so as to interpret s 34(1) as preventing the court from holding a blameworthy plaintiff 100% at fault, while enabling it to hold a blameworthy defendant 100% at fault where the plaintiff was guilty of some causally relevant fault.

120. [1991] 1 QB 24 (CA). See also *Greene v London Borough of Hadiney* Court Appeal (Civil Div) 18 February 1992.

121. See *Snelly v Haughton* [1971] IR 305 (SC); *O'Leary v O'Connell* [1968] IR 149 (SC); *Kelly v Jameson* Supreme Court, 1 March 1972; *Murphy v Cronin* [1966] IR 699 (SC); *Prendergast v CIE* (1967) 101 ILTR 177 (SC); *O'Sullivan v Mellerick* (1970) 104 ILTR 8 (SC); *O'Sullivan v Dwyer* [1971] IR 275 (SC); *Carroll v Clare Co Co* [1975] IR 221 (SC); *McKenna v Meighan* [1966] IR 288 (SC). *Cf Donoghue v Burke* [1960] IR 314 (SC). See also *Gillespie v Fitzpatrick* [1970] IR 102 at 107 (SC).

122. *O'Leary v O'Connell* [1968] IR 149 at 152 (SC).

123. Section 36(1) of the Civil Liability Act 1961.

124. Section 36(3).

125. Section 36(4) of the Civil Liability Act 1961, see s 5 of the Civil Liability (Amendment) Act 1964.

126. The example is taken from the speech of the Minister for Justice, Mr Haughey on the Second Reading of the Civil Liability Bill 1964: Dail Debates Vol 211, Col 568. The position of set offs in the context of bankrupt parties is dealt with in s 36(3) of the Civil Liability Act 1961, as amended by the Bankruptcy Act 1988 inserting reference to para 17(1) of the First Schedule to that Act and s 5 of the 1964 Act; (*cf* also s 62 of the 1961 Act). The general effect of these provisions is to ensure that insurance companies do not enrich themselves at the expense of injured parties: *cf* Dail Debates Vol 211 Col 568 and para 40 of the Explanatory Memorandum to the Civil Liability Bill 1961 (as passed by both Houses). See further Kerr *The Civil Liability Acts* (1999), pp 46-47.

from his own insurance company in respect of B's claim for £4,000. Thus, between them, the two insurance companies will meet their aggregate liability for £9,000 in full.

### Imputed Contributory Negligence[127]

**[20.57]** In some circumstances the plaintiff in an action for tort will have the negligence of another person imputed to him, by virtue of some special relationship between them. This doctrine, known as the doctrine of identification, arises primarily in cases of a consequential or derivative nature, where the plaintiff has not been directly injured by the wrongdoer, but bases his claim on the wrong done to another.[128]

**[20.58]** The identification provisions are contained in s 35 of the Civil Liability Act 1961.[129] This section lays down the following rules.

(i) Sub-section (1) of s 35 provides that a plaintiff is to be responsible for the acts of a person for whom he is, in the particular circumstances, vicariously liable.[130] The effect thus is that identification for the purposes of contributory negligence is co-extensive with vicarious liability,[131] whether by virtue of the common law or statute. Suppose, for example, M's servant S crashes into a motor vehicle driven by D. If S was 20% at fault and M sues D for damage to the van driven by S, then M will be identified with his servant's contributory negligence, and accordingly will have his damage reduced by 20%. Why should the principle of identification apply in such a case? Certainly it seems to involve a "misguided sense of symmetry".[132] Vicarious liability is designed to ensure fully effective redress for injury or damage; such a policy is scarcely consistent with protecting a tortfeasor against the claim of an employer.[133] In the face of this analysis, the "both ways" principle, which prevailed in the United States, is now under attack there.[134] As against this, Williams has argued that there is a general policy behind both forms of imputed negligence, namely that a person who employs another to do an act instead of doing it himself should be as

127. See WILLIAMS, paras 115-120.

128. *Cf* Cheifetz, *Apportionment of Fault in Tort*, (1981) p 213.

129. See also s 45(1) of the Civil Liability Act 1961, which provides that where the defendant, owing to ignorance of the facts, omits to claim the benefit of the identification provisions, he will have a right to repayment by the plaintiff of such sum as, by reason of these provisions the plaintiff should not have recovered. This right arises notwithstanding that judgment has been given in the plaintiff's favour.

130. Section 35(1)(a). See also *Chaplin v Hawes* (1828) 3 C & P 554, 172 ER 543; *Williams v Holland* (1833) 6 C & P 23, 172 ER 1129; *The Bernina* (1888) 13 AC 1; *Unsworth v Comr for Rys* (1958) 101 Comm LR 73; Gregory 'Vicarious Responsibility and Contributory Negligence' (1932) 41 Yale LJ 831.

131. For a detailed analysis of vicarious liability see Ch 43. There is no need for the section to refer to the relationship of principal and agent because, if an agent does a negligent act under instructions, the principal will be personally rather than vicariously liable: WILLIAMS, pp 432-433.

132. FLEMING, p 323.

133. *Cf* FLEMING, p 323. See also MacIntyre 'The Rationale of Imputed Negligence' (1944) 5 U Toronto LJ 368 at 373; Gregory 'Vicarious Responsibility and Contributory Negligence' (1932) 41 Yale LJ 831.

134. *Cf* 'Annotation' (1973) 53 ALR 3d 664 and (1974) 57 ALR 3d 1226.

responsible for that act and for the way in which it is done as though it were his own.[135]

(ii) The subsection provides[136] that a plaintiff in an action brought for the benefit of the dependents of a deceased person under Part IV of the Act - the Fatal Injuries Part - (whether the plaintiff is the personal representative or a dependent of the deceased) is deemed responsible for the acts of the deceased.[137]

(iii) The subsection provides[138] that a person suing as personal representative of the person suffering the damage is deemed responsible for his acts.

(iv) The subsection deals[139] with cases of negligence on the part of persons on whose behalf the action is being taken. A simple example would be where a fatal accident case is taken on behalf of certain dependents of the deceased, one of whom acted in a negligent manner, partly contributing to the death of the deceased. Here, the person suing on behalf of the dependents will be deemed responsible for the acts of that negligent dependent.

(v) The subsection provides[140] that a plaintiff suing as assignee of another, whether by operation of law[141] or otherwise, is to be deemed to be responsible for the acts of the other. It would clearly be improper that the assignee, an insurance company, for example, should have a better claim than the assignor.

**[20.59]** The subsection goes on to specify a number of instances of identification all of which involve identifying the plaintiff with one of two or more wrongdoers. These instances are:

(a) where the plaintiff has by contract made before the occurrence of the damage excluded that wrongdoer's liability;[142]

(b) where he has not excluded such liability but by contract again made before the occurrence of the damage, limited that wrongdoer's liability to a sum less than that wrongdoer's just share;[143]

(c) where he has settled with that wrongdoer by release or accord;[144]

(d) where his claim against that wrongoder has become statute-barred;[145] and

(e) where, in an action by him against the wrongdoer, judgment is given in favour of the wrongdoer.[146]

---

135. WILLIAMS, p 433.

136. In clause (b).

137. This is consistent with the former law: *Senior v Ward* (1859) 1 E & E 385, 120 ER 954.

138. In clause (c).

139. In clause (d).

140. Section 35(1)(e).

141. As in the case of bankruptcy.

142. Section 35(1 )(f).

143. Section 35(1)(g).

144. Section 35(1)(h).

145. Section 35(1)(i).

146. Section 35(1)(j). Here it is necessary for another concurrent wrongdoer, when sued, to prove that he and the successful defendant were in fact concurrent wrongdoers.

**[20.60]** These provisions harmonise with the provisions relating to contribution, to ensure fair treatment, not only between plaintiffs and defendants, but among the defendants themselves.

## III. *VOLENTI NON FIT INJURIA*

**[20.61]** The doctrine of voluntary assumption of risk has changed radically over the years. In its earliest development it was little different from the concept of contributory negligence, having the same fatal effect on the plaintiff's case. As we shall see regarding the defence of consent to trespass,[147] where a person consents to the harm that is directly inflicted upon him by way of trespass, he will have no right of action. The same applies to negligence: where a person consents to the negligent act, he may not complain when it occurs.

**[20.62]** The question as to when a person will be regarded as having consented in this manner is a matter on which the courts have changed their policy over the years. Formerly, some decisions held that if a person, knowing of the likelihood of some injury resulting from the negligence of another, nevertheless subjected himself to the physical risk, he could not succeed in an action for negligence if injury resulted. Over the years, the defence -which had worked much hardship in cases relating to employees injured in work accidents - mellowed significantly.

**[20.63]** Statute has now intervened. Section 34(1)(b) of the Civil Liability Act 1961 provides that:

> this subsection [which deals with contributory negligence] shall not operate to defeat any defence arising under a contract or the defence that the plaintiff before the act complained of agreed to waive his legal rights in respect of it, whether or not for value; but, subject as aforesaid, the provisions of this subsection [which deals with contributory negligence] shall apply notwithstanding that the defendant might, apart from this subsection, have the defence of voluntary assumption of risk.

**[20.64]** Since this provision was enacted:

> "what used to be called the defence of *volenti non fit injuria* ... can now properly be described in the words of that ... Act ... as 'the defence that the plaintiff before the act complained of agreed to waive his legal rights in respect of it'."[148]

**[20.65]** The present position therefore may be summarised as follows. The defence of *volenti* is gone, but a defendant can escape any liability in two cases: (a) where he shows that by contract he is not liable; or (b) where he shows that the plaintiff before the act agreed to waive his legal rights in respect of it. In either case the burden of establishing the defence falls on the defendant.[149]

### Contract

**[20.66]** Contract[150] may exempt the defendant but the Courts will not regard such a defence with any great enthusiasm. In *O'Hanlon v ESB*[151] Walsh J noted that:

---

147. See para **[22.59]-[22.85]** below.

148. *O'Hanlon v ESB* [1969] IR 75 at 90 (SC).

149. *O'Hanlon v ESB* [1969] IR 75 at 90 (*per* Walsh J).

150. "Contract" is defined as meaning a contract under seal or by parol: s 2(1).

151. [1969] IR 75 at 91 (SC)

"It is already settled that such contracts are construed strictly against the party claiming the benefit of the exception and there are instances[152] where such contracts are actually prohibited by statute."

## Agreement

**[20.67]** It is now clear that the "agreement" contemplated by s 34(1)(b):

> "necessarily contemplates some sort of intercourse or communication between the plaintiff and the defendants from which it could be reasonably inferred that the plaintiff had assured the defendants that he waived any right of action he might have in respect of the negligence of the defendants. A one-sided secret determination on the part of the plaintiff to give up his right of action for negligence would not amount to an agreement to do so. Such a determination or consent may be regarded as 'voluntary assumption of risk' in the terms of the Act but, by virtue of the provisions of the Act and for the purposes of the Act, this would be contributory negligence and not the absolute defence mentioned in the first part of sub-s 1(b) of section 34"[153]

**[20.68]** There are very considerable difficulties in determining whether there was:

> "some sort of intercourse or communication between the plaintiff and the [defendant] from which it could reasonably be inferred that the plaintiff had assured the [defendant] that he waived any right of action he might have ..."

Where the communication is expressed by means of language used by both parties, no particular problem arises, the Court's task being merely one of interpretation, but where it is non-verbal, or where only one party speaks, the position is less clear.

**[20.69]** If I say to a passenger to whom I am giving a lift: "I am a bad driver, and you may travel with me only if you do not sue me for any injury I cause you by my negligent driving" and he says nothing but gets into the front seat, it would seem that there has been sufficient evidence of "communication" for the purposes of the statutory defence. What is the position, however, if there is merely a notice in the front window stating: "All passengers travel at their own risk", which the passenger reads?[154] In *McComiskey v McDermott*,[155] the Supreme Court held that such a notice did not bind the passenger, as it was (to the plaintiff's knowledge) already in the car when the defendant bought it, and as the defendant had not shown that he had adopted it "as coming from him" or that he intended it to bind the plaintiff or that the plaintiff so accepted it. Griffin J cautioned, however, that:

> "in an appropriate case the affixing of a notice to the dashboard might lead to the inference that there was agreement between the passenger and the owner sufficient to set up the statutory defence ..."[156]

---

152. *Cf* Attorneys' and Solicitors' Act 1870, s 7. See also the Sale of Goods and Supply of Services Act 1980, ss 40 and 46 and the Liaibility for Defective Products Act 1991, s 10. See para **[11.162]** above.
153. *O'Hanlon v ESB* [1969] IR 75 at 92.
154. *Cf* Tan Keng Feng 'Dashboard Notices - Motor Insurer's Saviour' [1983] 1 Malaya LJ clxxix.
155. [1974] IR 75 (SC).
156. [1974] IR 75 at 94. *Cf Bennett v Tugwell* [1971] 2 QB 267. *Birch v Thomas* [1972] 1 All ER 705 (CA). *Geier v Kujawa, Weston & Warner Bros (Transport) Ltd* [1970] 1 Lloyds LR 364. See also Symmons (1974) 9 Ir Jur (ns) 79; 'Note' (1969) 32 MLR 88.

**[20.70]** The problem of passengers taking lifts from drunken drivers[157] is one that has caused much discussion. Williams has argued that the defence of voluntary assumption of risk is not appropriate, because "the passenger's knowledge of the driver's state [is] not equivalent to consent to negligent driving".[158] Yet this seems to be too bald a statement. There are surely some cases where an agreement to waive the right of action may be inferred. The courts should be reluctant to make such a finding, but to exclude such a possibility *a priori* seems to be improper.

**[20.71]** In *Ryan v Ireland*,[159] in 1989, the Supreme Court rejected the *volenti* defence in relation to a soldier injured in the Lebanon, where he had enlisted for United Nations service. No express contract waiving his right to sue if injured by the negligence of his superior officers had been suggested. He had "accepted the risks inherent in the possibility of being involved in armed conflict",[160] but it could not be implied that he had accepted the risk of being unnecessarily exposed to injury by negligence. The Court did not refer to the possibility that the plaintiff had waived his right to sue by agreement other than of a contractual nature - presumably because no evidence to this effect had been tendered by the defendant.

**[20.72]** In *Baldwin v Foy and Forrest Way Riding Holidays Ltd*[161] s 34(1)(b) fell for consideration. The plaintiff, a novice horse-rider, succeeded in her action for negligence against the horse-riding establishment for exposing her to danger by letting her ride on a cross-country course adjacent to boggy land, resulting in her being thrown from her horse during a sudden hailstorm.

157. See Gordon 'Drunken Drivers and Willing Passengers' (1966) 82 LQR 62; Stefani 'Comment: Assumption of Risk and the Automobile Guest: Time to Re-evaluate Their Relationship' (1959) 13 Creighton LR 251; Spector 'Contributory Negligence of Automobile Passengers' (1963) 12 Clev-Mar LR 447 at 450. In *Judge v Reape* [1968] IR 226 (SC) the jury negatived the defence and no appeal was taken against this funding.

158. WILLIAMS, p 305. In substantial accord in *Dann v Hamilton* [1939] 1 KB 509; but in Canada the *volenti* defence "is still available ... under special circumstances": *Cherrey v Steinke* 13 CCLT 50 at 63 (Man CA). Not infrequently passengers who willingly travel with drunken drivers have been held *volens* as, for example, in *Cherrey v Steinke* itself, *Henderson v Pearson Forest Products* (1979) 10 CCLT 209 (Ont HC); *Quinlan v Steffens* (1980) 12 CCLT 162 (Ont HC) and the other decisions cited by Irvine 'Annotation' (1980) 13 CCLT 51 at 55. The decision of the Supreme Court of Canada in *Dubé v Labar* (1986) 27 DLR (4th) 653 has, however, emphasised the requirement of bargaining away rights rather than mere foolhardiness. Estey J observed (at 658-659) that the acceptance of risk:

> "may be express or may arise by necessary implication from the conduct of the parties but it will arise ... only where there can truly be said to be an understanding on the part of both parties that the defendant assumed no responsibility to take due care for the safety of the plaintiff and that the plaintiff did not expect him to".

In England, where statute has intervened to block the *volenti* defence for road traffic accidents, the courts have had resort to the defence of illegality in serious cases (*Pitts v Hunt* [1991] 1 QB 24 (CA) but prefer to characterise the plaintiff's default as one of contributory negligence in less serious cases (*Van Hoffen v Dawson* Court of Appeal, 11 October 1993, Lexis transcript).

159. [1989] IR 177.

160. Page 13 of Finlay CJ's judgment (for the Court).

161. High Court, 1 July 1997 (Laffoy J).

**[20.73]** The defendants unsuccessfully invoked s 34(1)(b). Laffoy J expressed the view, laconically, that it was:

> "not possible to draw an inference from the evidence that the plaintiff agreed to waive any right of action she might have in respect of negligence on the part of the defendants."

Laffoy J made no reference to *O'Hanlon v ESB*,[162] although of course that decision, of the Supreme Court, bound her.

**[20.74]** The defendants also sought to avoid liability on the basis of disclaimer notices displayed at their premises. Both were headed "AIRE Association of Irish Riding Establishments". The first read as follows:

> "The Association of Riding Establishments Schemes for the registration of riding establishments is a voluntary non-statutory scheme under which the Association has set up and maintains a register of riding establishments which have been inspected by the Association and the owners of which have been advised of AIRE's minimum requirements in relation to the provision of facilities, equipment, supervision, safety requirements, insurance, etc. Non-compliance by a riding establishment with these standards would automatically result in cancellation of the registration of that riding establishment. The AIRE wishes to make it clear that it cannot accept legal liability in respect of any accident, however caused, arising out of the operation of any riding establishment."

**[20.75]** The second notice was in the following terms:

> "Riding is a risk sport. Your choice to ride is voluntary. We take care to provide suitable and safe horses and ponies for our customers, but all animals can be unpredictable. We strongly advise you to take out full personal accident cover."

**[20.76]** In Laffoy J's view, neither of these notices was open to the construction that the defendants, as distinct from AIRE, were disclaiming liability for negligence and breach of duty.

**[20.77]** One of the difficulties with the manner in which s 34(1)(b) has been drafted is that a free choice to undertake a particular risk caused by the defendant's negligence must be ignored, and the plaintiff permitted to recover in full, if that choice does not implicate the plaintiff with contributory negligence[163] and there is, in the circumstances of the case, no "intercourse or communciation" between plaintiff and defendant on the issue.[164] The requirement of an agreement between the parties denies efficacy to free, but uncommunicated, choice. Of course, the courts may respond to the problem in specific cases by adopting a constricted "individuated" duty of care to take account of the willingness of the plaintiff to undergo the risk,[165] but there is no guarantee that they will do so in every case.

---

162. [1969] IR 75.

163. *Cf* Simons 'Assumption of Risk and Consent in the Law of Torts: A Theory of Full Preference' (1987) 67 Boston ULR 213 at 234.

164. *Cf* Simons 'Assumption of Risk and Consent in the Law of Torts: A Theory of Full Preference' (1987) 67 Boston ULR 213 at 226 fn 45.

165. *Cf McComiskey v McDermott* [1974] IR 75 (SC). See also *Condon v Basi* [1985] 1 WLR 866 (CA) analysed by Opie (1986) 15 Melb ULR 756.

## Rescuers[166]

**[20.78]** The legal position of the rescuer has changed radically in recent years. "Once the Cinderella of the law, he has since become its darling."[167] Formerly the courts rejected[168] claims in respect of injuries sustained during rescue operations resulting from the negligence of others: the rescuer was regarded as having voluntarily assumed the risk or as having broken the causal link between the negligence and his injuries.

**[20.79]** Today, the approach is different. As Cardozo J said in the famous United States decision of *Wagner v International Railroad Co*:[169]

> "Danger invites rescue. The cry of distress is the summons to relief. The law does not ignore these reactions of the mind in tracing conduct to its consequences. It recognizes them as normal. It places their effects within the range of the natural and probable. The wrong that imperils life is a wrong to the imperiled victim; it is a wrong also to his rescuer. The risk of rescue, if only it be not wanton, is born of the occasion. The emergency begets the man. The wrongdoer may not have foreseen the coming of a deliverer. He is accountable as if he had."

**[20.80]** It is easy to see why persons whose employment carries with it a legal or moral obligation to go to the assistance of others should be held entitled to sue; thus, the courts have had little difficulty in recognising the claim of policemen,[170] doctors[171] or even stationmasters,[172] for example. But it is now clear that altruism umprompted by professional duty will suffice. Thus, a person who helps in rescue operations after a train wreck,[173] car crash[174] or fire[175] or who goes to the assistance of a friend in danger of drowning,[176] may recover damages if injured in the attempt. Some specific aspects of the rescuer's claim may be noted.

---

166. See VTH; D[elany] 'The Duty of Care to a Rescuer' (1959) 25 Ir Jur 7; Tiley 'The Rescue Principle' (1967) 30 MLR 25; Linden 'Rescuers and Good Samaritans' (1971) 34 MLR 241; Linden 'Down with Foreseeability: Of Thin Skulls and Rescuers' (1969) 47 Can BR 545 at 558-570; Goodhart 'Rescue and Voluntary Assumption of Risk' (1934) 5 Camb LJ 192; Binchy 'The Good Samaritan at the Cross-roads: A Canadian Signpost?' (1974) 25 NILQ 147; Blake 'The Plight of the Rescuer' (1978) 128 New LJ 476; Anon 'A Rescuer's Rights' (1941) 75 ILT & Sol J 113. More generally see Rose 'Restitution for the Rescuer' (1989) 9 Oxford J of Legal Stud 167.

167. FLEMING, p 186.

168. *Cutler v United Dairies (London) Ltd* [1933] 2 KB 297 (CA) criticised by WILLIAMS, p 306. See also *Grainger v Cullen* (1909) 43 ILTR 132 (CC) where the plaintiff injured himself pulling a cart off his pony, which had fallen into a ditch when frightened by an obstruction negligently placed on the highway by the defendant; it was held that, although the injury to pony and damage to cart were recoverable the injury to the plaintiff was not, being "too remote".

169. (1921) 232 NYS 176, 133 NE 437.

170. *Haynes v Harwood* [1935] 1 KB 146 (CA), affg [1934] 2 KB 240. Also firemen: see *Ogwo v Taylor* [1987] 3 All ER 961 (HL); *Cunningham v O'Brien* [1982] NI 75.

171. *Baker v Hopkins* [1959] 3 All ER 225 (CA), affg [1958] 3 All ER 147 (QB); *Chapman v Hearse* (1961) 106 CLR 112, affg [1961] SASR 51.

172. *Videan v British Transport Commission* [1963] 2 QB 650 (CA), see also *Canadian National Railway v Bakty* (1977) 18 OR (2d) 481 (Co Court) - conductor on train.

173. *Chadwick v British Transport Commission* [1967] 2 All ER 845 (KBD).

174. *Corothers v Slobodian* (1974) 2 SCR 633.

175. *Phillips v Durgan* [1991] ILRM 321 (SC).

176. *Moddejonge v Huron County Board of Education* [1972]2 OR 437 (HC).

### *The conduct of the defendant*

**[20.81]** Liability will attach to a defendant only where he has been guilty of negligence in creating the situation of actual or apparent peril. Clearly if my negligence results in peril to another which induces a rescue attempt by a third party, I will also be liable to the rescuer.[177] It is now equally clear[178] that, if by my own carelessness I place myself in a position of peril of a kind that invites rescue, I will be liable for injuries sustained by my rescuer. Thus, foolhardy mountaineers, potholers or even, in some cases, swimmers risk not only their own lives but also a lawsuit if they are rescued. It should be noted that we are not dealing with contributory negligence here: I may well be regarded as being guilty of contributory negligence if I attempt to swim across Galway Bay, with no previous training, but if a person is injured in rescuing me, I am liable to him for the breach of my duty of care to him.

**[20.82]** Conversely, it has been held[179] that even a rescuer owes a duty to another potential rescuer to carry out the rescue attempt with reasonable care. Of course the fact that the situation is an emergency will be taken into account in determining this question.[180]

**[20.83]** Since the rescuer's right of action is an independent one, not deriving from any breach of duty by the defendant to another,[181] it is clear that the rescuer may recover damages even where there has in fact been no such breach of duty to another, provided that the defendant by his or her negligence brought about a situation of apparent danger.[182]

### *The conduct of the rescuer*

**[20.84]** On principle, the outer limit of recovery should not extend beyond reasonable foreseeability. The Courts have generally confined liability within this range, but have tended to use terminology which arguably could go somewhat beyond this: a rescue that is neither "rash", "wanton" nor "reckless" could nonetheless be quite unforeseeable.

---

177. *Phillips v Durgan* [1991] ILRM 321. The rescue may consist of an act of complete altruism, as where a person sacrifices himself or herself rather than injure a potential victim of another's negligence; *cf Carmarthenshire Co Co v Lewis* [1955] AC 549 (HL).

178. *Baker v Hopkins* [1959] 3 All ER 225 (CA), affg [1958] 3 All ER 147 (QBD); *Chapman v Hearse* (1961) 106 CLR 112, affg [1961] SASR 51; *Horsley v MacLaren* [1972] SCR 441; *Canadian National Ry v Bakty* (1977) 18 OR (2d) 481 (Co Court); *Harrison v BRB* [1981] 3All ER 679 analysed by McConnell 'The Duty Owed to Rescuers' (1981) 131 New LJ 225; *Ruth v Ruth* 213 Tenn 82 372, SW 2d 285 (SC); *Carney v Buyea* (1944) 271, Appeal Div 338, 65 NYS 2d 902; *Brugh v Bigelow* 310 Mich 74, 16 NW 2d 668, 158 ALR 184 (SC) noted by Groefoema (1945) 43 Mich LR 980. In *Talbert v Talbert* (1960) 22 Misc 2d 782, 199 NYS 2d 212, a father who attempted to commit suicide in a locked garage was held liable for injuries sustained by his son, who was injured in the successful attempt to save his life.

179. *Horsley v MacLaren* [1972] SCR 441; see Binchy 'The Good Samaritan at the Crossroads; A Canadian Signpost?' (1974) 25 NILQ 147.

180. *Cf Corothers v Slobodian* (1974) 2 SCR 633 revg 36 DLR (3d) 597 (Sask CA). (The Court of Appeal's decision is criticised by Binchy in (1974) 52 Can BR 292.)

181. *Cf* WILLIAMS, p 365.

182. So, for example, if students during a "rag week" stage a bogus kidnap scenario in a public place and attract an intervention by a public-minded citizen, they will have to compensate the citizen for any injuries he or she sustains in the rescue attempt in spite of the fact that nobody was in fact in peril.

**[20.85]** Where the rescuer is guilty of contributory negligence his damages should, of course, be reduced and, in the case of a totally foolhardly rescue, it might be proper to deny him any damages at all.

**[20.86]** In *Phillips v Durgan*,[183] the Supreme Court addressed for the first time, the position in tort law of a rescuer. The defendant owned and lived in a house in which his late mother had also lived prior to her death in 1975. The house was not in a good state of upkeep: the kitchen was in a condition of extreme dirt and filth, most of which consisted of many years' accumulation of grease from constant frying on a gas cooker. The floor was greasy and its linoleum covering was broken. The cooker and wall beside it were heavily coated with grease.

**[20.87]** In 1981 the defendant engaged the first plaintiff, his sister, to paint and decorate the house for a price of £100. The second plaintiff, her husband, drove her to the house. The first plaintiff placed a kettle of water to boil on the only jet on the cooker that worked. She started to scrape away grease from the cooker and the wall, but stumbled, probably because of the greasy condition of the floor. The cloth in her hand came into contact with the flame under the kettle. It immediately took light because of the grease that had accumulated on it. She dropped it on the floor and tried to extinguish the flame by stamping on it but in an extraordinarily short time the whole area around the cooker, as well as the cooker itself, went on fire. The first plaintiff was extensively burned. The second plaintiff dragged her from the room. He was injured in doing so as well as in his attempts to put out the fire.

**[20.88]** The Supreme Court affirmed a verdict in favour of both plaintiffs, basing liability to the first plaintiff on negligent failure to warn of the risks involved in the work and of "the sort of preparations which might be necessary and the sort of equipment which it might be necessary to bring in order to carry out the work with safety",[184] and liability to the second plaintiff on his status as a person whose rescue efforts were foreseeably prompted by the defendant's negligence to the first plaintiff.[185]

**[20.89]** The Supreme Court reduced the first plaintiff's damages by 15% to take account of her contributory negligence in failing to take some special precautions about where she was working until such time as the kettle had boiled and the flame had been turned off. The second plaintiff was not found guilty of any contributory negligence: what he had done after the fire started "was the natural and obvious thing to do, and could not be an act of contributory negligence, namely, an attempt to put out the fire to save his wife".[186]

183. [1991] ILRM 321 (SC) analysed by Byrne & Binchy, *Annual Review of Irish Law 1990*, pp 493-500.

184. [1991] ILRM 321 (SC).

185. Finlay CJ (Griffin and Hedermann JJ concurring) expressed clear support for the requirement that the rescue be foreseeable, and appeared to go so far as to characterise all rescue attempts in case of fire as foreseeable: see Byrne & Binchy, *Annual Review of Irish Law 1991*, pp 497-498. Griffin J used language consistent with permitting recovery of damages for unforeseeable rescue attempts, provided only they are "not wanton", but not to question the requirement of foreseeability.

186. [1991] ILRM 321 (SC). The question of the first plaintiff's possible liability in negligence to the second defendant for carelessly contributing to her plight was not addressed by the Court. Whilst there is no necessary translation from contributory negligence to negligence in this context the facts of the case would appear to support such liability: *cf* Byrne & Binchy, *Annual Review of Irish Law 1991*, p 498.

**[20.90]** In *Philips v Durgan*, the judgments in the Supreme Court gave clear support to the English decision of *Ogwo v Taylor*,[187] where the House of Lords rejected the "fire fighter's rule", which still commands widespread support in the United States of America. Under this rule, a professional fire fighter injured in the course of fighting a fire will not be entitled to sue the person whose negligence caused the fire, save in exceptional cases, such as where the injury is attributable to a hidden danger on the premises about which the occupier failed to provide an adequate warning.[188]

**[20.91]** In *Turner v Iarnród Éireann/Irish Rail*,[189] liability was imposed on the operators of the Tralee Mallow railway line and on a local authority where a mother sustained injuries when seeking to protect her child from the risk of being struck by a train. The child, aged six, had been permitted by her mother to play in front of her house in a local authority housing estate in Tralee on a summer's afternoon. She wandered away down the road, went through an opening in a post-and-wire fence and proceeded onto the railway line. The mother went looking for her, naturally became agitated, ran along the track and tripped on some signal wires, injuring her knee. The child emerged unscathed. The mother's case in negligence centred on the case with which her child could penetrate the fence and her own status as a rescuer.

**[20.92]** Flood J held that the plaintiff's injuries were "a direct consequence" of the failure to provide adequate fencing. It would seem unwise to interpret this as an attempt to resurrect the directness test for remoteness of damage favoured in *Re Polemis*[190] and later displaced by a foreseeability test in *The Wagon Mound (No 1)*.[191] It is clear from the facts, and Flood J's view of them, that the plaintiff's agitation and consequent stumble were entirely foreseeable.

## IV. Illegality

**[20.93]** Courts throughout the common law world have found great difficulty in developing a coherent philosophy on the subject of the disentitlement of a plaintiff to succeed in an action for negligence or other tort because the claim is morally or legally

187. [1988] AC 431 (HL).

188. See eg *Butler v Union Pacific RR Co* (1995) 68 F 2D 378 (USC Appeal 10th CIR); *Heck v Robey* (1994) 630 NE 2d 1361 (Ind Appeal); *Fox v Hawkins* (1992) 594 NE 2d 493 (Ind Appeal); *Gray v Russell* (1993) 853 SW 2d 928 (Mo). *Cf Edwards v Honeywell Incorporated* (1995) 50 F 3d 484 (USC Appeal 7th CIR). The rule has even been extended to voluntary fire fighters: *Waggoner v Troutman Oil Company* (1995) 894 SW 2d 913; (Ark) noted by Wood (1997) 50 Ark LR 363. For analysis of the operation of the rule see Russell (1994) 59 Mo LR 479; Wright (1990) 58 UMKC LR 329; Franzlaw (1994) 23; Steson LR 843; Berger (1998) 44 Wash & Lee LR 1555; Dreiman (1998) 8 Ind Int'l & Comp LR 381. Some decisions have adopted a similarly restrictive rule in relation to police officers: see eg *Newton v New Hanover County Board of Education* (1996) 342 NC 554 467 SE 2d 58; *Kreski v Modern Wholesale Electric Supply Co* (1987) 415 NW 2d 178 (Mich).

189. High Court, 14 February 1996 (Flood J) analysed by Byrne & Binchy, *Annual Review of Irish Law 1996*, pp 592-595.

190. [1921] 3 KB 560.

191. *Overseas Tankship (UK) Ltd v Morts Dock and Engineering Co Ltd (The Wagon Mound) (No 1)* [1961] AC 388 (PC). See Ch 3 above.

tainted in some way.[192] It is easy enough in clear cases to apply or reject the defence. If one burglar sues another for negligence in his use of explosives to crack a safe, he is destined to lose the case;[193] equally clearly the driver of an untaxed car will not lose his action against a negligent roaduser on account of the driver's failure to have had the car taxed. An adulterer *in flagrante delicto* on whom the roof falls will still be able to sue the architect and a professional burgular who travels by bus on the way to a "job" is almost certainly entitled to compensation if the busdriver is so drunk that the bus crashes, injuring the burglar.[194]

**[20.94]** The problems, however arise in the cases in-between. How should they be decided? If two teenage drivers crash while drunkenly racing each other down a highway in the wrong lane, should the action by one against the other be dismissed on the ground of illegality, or because the action springs from a wrongful source (*ex turpi causa non oritur actio*)?[195] Would it make any legally significant difference to show that, having wrongfully taken the cars, they were joyriders? Why should their illegal and wrongful conduct relative to the owners of the cars an hour previously affect the claim between them? Would it make a difference if the accident took place a few days after the cars were taken? Should a person, injured in an accident caused by another's negligence, be entitled to compensation if he unsuccessfully attempts to commit suicide and thereby worsens his physical injuries?[196] And how should the court regard the claim of a person with a history of mental illness who kills another after an alleged deficiency in treatment of his psychiatric condition and finishes up in prison after being convicted for manslaughter?[197]

**[20.95]** As these hypothetical examples make plain, the illegality or wrongful conduct which is part of the account of the circumstances giving rise to the plaintiff's claim may be serious or trivial, central or peripheral, necessarily integrated in the claim or contingent to it, limited to the dealings between the plaintiff and defendant or directed towards some third party.

---

192. See Kerr *The Civil Liability Acts* (1999), pp 66-70; Symmons 'Ex Turpi Causa in English Tort Law' (1981 44 MLR 585; Prentice 'Of Tort Reform and Millionaire Muggers: Should an Obscure Equitable Doctrine be Revived to Dent the Litigation Crisis?' (1995) 32 San Diego LR 53; Debattista 'Ex Turpi Causa Returns to the English Law of Torts: Taking Advantage of a Wrong Way Out' (1984) 13 Anglo-American LR 15; Crago 'The Defence of Illegality In Negligence Actions (1964) 4 Melb ULR 534 Fridman 'The Wrongdoing Plaintiff' (1972) 18 McGill LJ 275; Gibson 'Illegality of Plaintiff's Conduct as a Defence' (1969) 47 Can BR 89; Swanton 'Plaintiff a Wrongdoer: Joint Complicity in an Illegal Enterprise as a Defence to Negligence' (1981) 9 Syd LR 304; Ford 'Tort and Illegality: The *Ex Turpi* Defence in Negligence Law' (1978) Melb ULR 32 164.

193. *Cf National Coal Board v England* [1954] AC 403 at 429 (HL).

194. Though the burglar will not be entitled to compensation for loss of "earnings" that evening: *cf Burns v Edman* [1970] 2 QB 541. On the dependants' claim in a fatal injuries action, where the deceased's income had been under-returned to the Revenue, see para **[42.29]** below.

195. Cases involving the issue of grossly irresponsible conduct on the highway include *Pitts v Hunt* [1991] 1 QB 24 (CA) - drunken pillion passenger on motor cycle "egging on" drunken driver to drive recklessly.

196. *Cf Reeves v Metropolitan Police Commissioner* [2000] 1 AC 360 (HL); (CA); *Kirkham v Chief Constable of Greater Manchester* [1990] 2 QB 283 (CA).

197. *Cf Clunis v Camden and Islington Health Authority* [1998] 3 All ER 180 (CA).

**[20.96]** If the courts had never developed an *ex turpi causa* defence, they could still have dismissed the plaintiff's case in many instances. Applying an individuated definition of the duty of care, which found favour with the majority in the Supreme Court decision of *McComiskey v McDermott*,[198] courts could hold that, having regard to the particular relationship between the parties, either no duty, or a severely attenuated duty, of care arose. If a rally driver owes a distinctive duty of care to the navigator, as in *McComiskey v McDermott*, which is narrower in its scope than the duty of care owed by the driver to other road users, one can understand why a court might hold that joyriders racing each other or burglars departing at speed from the scene of the crime should not be regarded as owing each other any duty of care. At a formal level the court's definition of the existence (or absence) or scope of the duty of care having regard to the nature of the particular relationship is merely a function of its general task in every negligence action. The substance of the matter, however, is that a court that concludes that no duty of care arises in such cases is engaging, not in a "no fault" analysis, but in closet value judgments about the moral merits of the claim.[199]

**[20.97]** Of course, even if the courts were to eschew the sophistication of the theory of a particularised duty of care, fashioned by the nature of the individual relationship of the parties, and were to treat the case as falling within more general categories of relationship - occupier - trespasser, driver - passenger, for example - the outcome for a plaintiff whose conduct was tainted by wrongdoing would often be equally fatal. The burglar who slips on marbles in the children's playroom has no case, not because a duty was breached and liability avoided by application of the illegality defence but rather because there simply was no duty of care in the first place. Even before the passage of the Occupiers' Liability Act 1995, the burglar would have failed to pass the *McNamara*[200] test.

**[20.98]** A further defence, which would formerly have defeated many a claim by plaintiffs tainted with illegality, was that of voluntary assumption of risk (*volenti non fit injuria*). On a broad view, a plaintiff who willingly exposed himself or herself to the risk of being injured by the defendant's negligent conduct could have no complaint if the injury occurred. So, for example, a person who chose to be a passenger with a driver known to be intoxicated would be held to have been *volens* relative to the accident. Much risky behaviour has a criminal dimension. The degree of voluntary assumption of risk would kill off the claim before the issue of illegality, in its own right, fell for consideration.

**[20.99]** The effect of s 34(1)(b) of the Civil Liability Act 1961 was to require, not merely a unilateral willing exposure to risk but a bilateral agreement between the parties, whereby the plaintiff waived his or her right of action.[201] Such agreement, the Supreme Court held, was dependent on some "intercourse or communication" between the parties from which a waiver could be informed.[202]

---

198. [1974] IR 75 (SC). See para **[6.60]-[6.63]**.

199. *Cf Gala v Preston* (1991) CLR 243 (HC, Austr); *Italiano v Barbero* (1993) 114 ALR 21 (HC, Austr); *Jackson v Harrison* 138 CLR 438 (HC, Austr 1978); *Pitts v Hunt* [1991] 1 QB 24 (CA); WINFIELD & JOLOWICZ, p 869; *Tomlinson v Harrison* [1972] 1 Ont R 670 (HC); *Tallow v Tailfeathers* [1973] (1974) 6 WWR 732 (Alta CA).

200. *McNamara v ESB* [1975] IR 1 (SC). See para **[12.44]** above.

201. See para **[20.65]** above.

202. *O'Hanlon v ESB* [1969] IR 75 (SC).

**[20.100]** No doubt some cases of illegality will fall at the *volenti* hurdle, even under the statutory restriction, but others will not, in the absence of proof of the requisite connection between the parties. Possibly the fact that the parties have engaged in a joint criminal or immoral enterprise may make it easier for a court to infer such communication on the basis that the parties, in engaging in the enterprise together, must be expected to have communicated about what was to take place and who was to do what. *O'Hanlon v ESB*[203] does not require that the communication itself address, *expressis verbis*, the legal implications for the plaintiff; all that is necessary is that the communication justify the inference that "the plaintiff had assured the defendan[t] that he waived any right of action he might have in respect of the negligence of the defendan[t]".

**[20.101]** Let us now attempt to review the different approaches that the legislature and courts in common law jurisdictions have favoured at different times. Our starting point has to be s 57(1) of the Civil Liability Act 1961, which provides that:

> "[i]t shall not be a defence in an action merely to show that the plaintiff is in breach of the civil or criminal law."

**[20.102]** The crucial word here is "merely". Section 57(1) does not abolish the defence of illegality and says nothing whatsoever about morally wrongful conduct on the plaintiff's part. All that it achieves is to ensure that the mere fact that the defendant can show that the plaintiff is in breach of the law will not, of itself, be a defence. Frankly this achievement is scarcely a measurable one since no court in any common law jurisdiction has ever maintained the draconian policy of dismissing a claim automatically on proof of some illegality on the plaintiff's part. The crucial question concerns the circumstances that are necessary to trigger the defence. Section 57(1) gives no guidance whatsoever as to how that question should be answered.

**[20.103]** Among the various approaches that have found judicial favour at some time is the "public conscience" test. The idea here is that the court should not give a remedy to a plaintiff if, in doing so, "the court would thereby appear to assist or encourage the plaintiff in his illegal conduct or to encourage others in similar acts".[204] Thus, not every illegality would defeat the claim: unless there was a significant public dimension, the illegality might be forgiven. The case would be dismissed only *pour décourager les autres*.[205]

**[20.104]** The "public conscience" test has much to be said for it. It retains flexibility, is sensitive to changing mores and has regard to the societal dimension to human conduct. It has, however, been criticised for its deviation from the traditional, more uncompromising, approach,[206] its lack of predictability or, indeed, consistency in application in particular cases and for the fact that it places a somewhat overgraphic emphasis on society's response to individual wrongdoing. It is worth noting that "public conscience" works both ways. It can be a reason for imposing a duty of care in some cases.[207]

---

203. See para **[20.64]-[20.66]** above.

204. *Euro-Diam Ltd v Bathurst* [1990] 1 QB 1 at 35 (CA). *Cf Saunders v Edwards* [1987] 2 All ER 651 (CA).

205. *Cf* Howarth, *Textbook on Tort* (1995), p 667 who is sceptical about the efficiency of deterrence in this context.

206. *Tinsley v Mulligan* [1994] 1 AC 340 (HL); *Clunis v Camden and Islington Health Authority* [1998] QB 978 (CA); *Pitts v Hunt* [1991] 1 QB 24 (CA).

207. *Cf Palmer v Tees Health Authority* (1998) 45 BMLR 88 (QB) - where, though the phrase was used, no duty of care was held to arise.

**[20.105]** The approach that finds favour with the English courts at present is that a plaintiff who bases his or her claim on a criminal or immoral act that he or she has done should be defeated by the *ex turpi* defence. Thus, in *Clunis v Camden and Islington Health Authority*,[208] a claim by a man who had pleaded guilty to the manslaughter of another person, on the grounds of diminished responsibility by reason of his mental illness, had his action for negligence against the health authority, alleging that its treatment had failed to prevent him from committing the offence, dismissed on the ground of illegality. Even though the plaintiff's mental disorder had led to the causation of the offence of manslaughter, it had not justified a verdict of not guilty by reason of insanity. Consequently, though his responsibility for the killing was diminished, he had to be taken to have known what he was doing and that it was wrong. Public policy would preclude the court from entertaining the plaintiff's claim unless he lacked such knowledge.

**[20.106]** The merit of this approach is that it ensures that the *ex turpi* defence will defeat a claim only where the illegality or immorality is the rock on which the plaintiff's claim is built.

**[20.107]** The weakness of this approach, however, is that it lacks subtlety. It does not enable the court to distinguish between serious offences (against law or morality) and the more trivial transgressions or to take into account mitigating factors based on the personal circumstances of the plaintiff.

**[20.108]** When faced with the *ex turpi causa* defence, rather than cleaving to any particular restrictive criterion, it might well be better for Irish courts to take a broader approach (as they do when determining the scope of the duty of care in negligence, where public policy also plays a role).[209] The courts should require that if the *ex turpi* defence is to apply, the illegality or immorality should play a central rather than peripheral role in the plaintiff's claim, that it be serious and that there be no countervailing considerations, based on the particular circumstances of the parties which would render application of the defence oppressive or unjust. The fact that the parties were engaging in a joint criminal enterprise should encourage, though not inevitably require, the court to apply the defence and dismiss the claim. All courts, regardless of the particular theory of *ex turpi causa* that they are applying, find it well-nigh impossible to reward the plaintiff in these cases.[210] Even here, however, the court should be sensitive to the nature of the crime and the circumstances of the participants. There is a difference between a gang of robbers "doing a job", and a couple of immature youths who drink too much and drive with gross irresponsibility while intoxicated. The criminal law should deal with all criminal offenders with the appropriate degree of severity.[211] Courts should hesitate before "recreat[ing] the class of outlaws"[212] too broadly, merely to accommodate "the moral populism of the outraged public conscience".[213]

---

208. [1998] 3 All ER 180 (CA). See also *Hegarty v Shine* (1878) 4 LR Ir 288 (CA); *O'Connor v McDonnell* High Court, 30 June 1970 (Murnaghan J).

209. *Cf Ward v McMaster* [1988] IR 337 (SC).

210. *Cf* Howarth, *Textbook on Tort* (1995), pp 667-668.

211. It is worth taking into account that the goals of sentencing are not merely retributive but include such other purposes as deterrence rehabilitation and containment. *Cf* the divided views on the philosophy of sentencing in the Law Reform Commission's Report on Sentencing (LRC 53-1996), analysed by Byrne & Binchy, *Annual Review of Irish Law 1996*.

212. Howarth, *Textbook on Tort* (1995), p 666.

213. Howarth, *Textbook on Tort* (1995), p 667.

# Chapter 21

# Statutory Duties and Rights


I. Introduction .......... 589
II. Breach of Statutory Duty .......... 589
III. Interference with Statutory Rights .......... 612


## I. Introduction

**[21.01]** The relationship between rights, duties, powers and immunities has given rise to much discussion by legal scholars. The issues go to the heart of jurisprudential analysis: are rights always the creation of the law, or can they ever be antecedent to it? What relationship is there between a right and a duty? Is the answer reducible to semantics, or is something more at stake?

**[21.02]** In tort litigation, the courts have tended to regard their function as one of compensating the victims of breach of duties by others. Thus at common law, such torts as negligence, deceit and malicious prosecution are seen as involving wrongdoing by the defendant rather than primarily an interference with the plaintiff's rights. Of course, it can be said that a person has *a right* not to be injured by a negligently driven car, for example, but it seems more natural to say that the driver ought not to breach his *duty* to drive with due care. In other torts this emphasis on duties rather than rights may seem misplaced. For example, it may be considered that an action for defamation seeks primarily to protect people's *right* to a deserved reputation. Other common law torts seem to fall midway between these two notions: the action for nuisance, for example, involves primarily a *balancing process* between *competing rights*.

**[21.03]** Statutes reflect the common law emphasis on duties; they tend to be drafted in terms imposing liabilities rather than conferring rights.[1]

**[21.04]** In this chapter we will examine first the conventional principles relating to liability in tort for breach of statutory duty. We will then go on to consider the less certain principles relating to the recovery of damages for interference with a statutory right.

## II. Breach of Statutory Duty[2]

**[21.05]** The question whether a breach of statute gives rise to civil liability is a difficult one in tort law. In general, the orthodox approach at common law suggests that whether a

1. It is, of course, a feature of many statutes that they impose *powers* rather than duties. As we have seen (pp 247ff) the trend of negligence law has been to extend the duty of care to embrace many of these powers requiring due care in their discharge: *cf* eg *Ward v McMaster and Louth County Council* [1989] ILRM 400 (SC), affg [1985] IR 29 (HC); *Robinson v Department of the Environment for Northern Ireland* [1988] NIJB 24 (QBD).

2. See Stanton, *Breach of Statutory Duty in Tort* (1986); Horgan & Morgan, *Administrative Law* (3rd ed, 1998), pp 816-818; Buckley 'Liability in Tort for Breach of Statutory Duty' (1984) 100 LQR 204; Fricke 'The Juridical Nature of the Action Upon the Statute' (1960) 76 LQR 240; Williams 'The Effect of Penal Legislation in the Law of Tort' (1960) 23 MLR 233 and short articles in (1937) 71 ILT& SJ 335; (1947) 81 ILT & SJ 293-299; (1887) 21 ILT & SJ 549-563; (1940) 74 ILT & SJ 239; (1965) 99 ILT & SJ 248; (1949) 83 ILT & SJ 261.

statute gives a remedy to an injured person is essentially a matter of interpretation in each case. The courts in this country have been quick to express "principles of interpretation" but slower to attempt to articulate the policy on which this interpretation should be based. This formalism contrasts with the position in North America[3] (but not in other jurisdictions[4]), where much discussion of policy is apparent.

**[21.06]** In England the House of Lords in *Lonrho Ltd v Shell Petroleum*,[5] rejected the principle, endorsed by Lord Denning MR in *Ex parte Island Records Ltd*,[6] that a civil right of action should in all cases accrue to the proprietor of a lawful business who suffers damage in consequence of a contravention by another individual of *any* statutory prohibition. In the Irish decision of *Parsons v Kavanagh*,[7] O'Hanlon J appeared to favour *Lonrho,* so far as the position at common law was concerned. However, he considered:

> "the constitutional right to earn one's livelihood by any lawful means carries with it the entitlement to be protected against any unlawful activity on the part of another person or persons which materially impairs or infringes that right."[8]

**[21.07]** Accordingly, he granted an injunction in favour of the plaintiff, a private bus operator, whose livelihood had been threatened and actually interfered with by operations conducted outside the law by the defendants.[9]

---

3. *Cf* Morris 'The Role of Criminal Statutes in Negligence Actions' (1949) 49 Col LR 21; Morris 'The Relation of Criminal Statutes to Tort Liability' (1933) 27 Harv LR 453; Lowndes 'Civil Liability Created by Criminal Legislation' (1932) 16 Minn LR 361; James 'Statutory Standards and Negligence in Accident Cases' (1950) 11 La LR 95; Thayer 'Public Wrong and Private Action' (1914) 27 Harv LR 317; Alexander 'Legislation and the Standard of Care in Negligence' (1964) 42 Can BR 243; Linden 'Tort Liability for Criminal Nonfeasance' (1966) 44 Can BR 25; *The Queen in right of Canada v Saskatchewan Wheat Pool* [1983] 1 SCR 205.
4. *Cf* FLEMING, pp 114-115.
5. [1982] AC 173 (HL).
6. [1978] Ch 122 (CA).
7. [1990] ILRM 560 (HC).
8. [1990] ILRM 560.
9. O'Hanlon J was inclined to the view that even if the plaintiff's claim for an injunction could not be maintained for breach of a constitutional right, it would still be enforceable on the basis of the principle expressed by Costello J in *AG v Paperlink* [1984] ILRM 373, that "whenever Parliament has enacted a law and given a particular remedy for the breach of it, such remedy being in an inferior court, nevertheless the High Court always has a reserve power to enforce the law so enacted by way of an injunction or other suitable remedy. The High Court has jurisdiction to require obedience to the law whenever it is just and convenient to do so". O'Hanlon J considered that the plaintiff's claim was enforceable "having regard to the present day inadequacy of the penalties provided by the Road Transport Acts 1932 and 1933, for such breaches of the provisions of the Acts. These monetary penalties have remained unchanged for some fifty-five years and with the fall in the value of money in the meantime, they appear to me at the present time to be somewhat derisory as a deterrent against possible breaches of the Act". In *Lovett and O'Neill (t/a Lovett Transport)* [1995] 1 ILRM 12 (SC), Finlay CJ (Egan and Denham JJ concurring) said that he was "satisfied that the decision reached by O'Hanlon J in the case of *Parsons v Kavanagh*, was a decision which was correct in law on the findings of fact made by him in that case". The Chief Justice went on to observe that, in *Parsons v Kavanagh*, O'Hanlon J had concluded that the 1932 Act could not be construed so as to protect other licensed providers of road passenger services; this was "a correct conclusion" in the Chief Justice's view. In the instant case which concerned the same legislation, the plaintiff would be entitled to an injunction as he could establish that it was the only way of protecting him from the threatened invasion of his constitutional rights.

**[21.08]** In certain cases no problem arises. A statutory provision sometimes provides explicitly that a civil action may[10] or may not[11] be taken in relation to breach of certain of its provisions. A clear example is s 7 of the Data Protection Act 1988, which imposes a statutory duty of care on data controllers and data processors, to the extent that tort law does not already provide, as regards the collection of personal data and their dealing with the data; the duty is owed to "the data subject concerned". Where, however, the statute is

---

9. (contd) Having regard to the small amount of the price that could be imposed on a person running a road passenger service without a licence, Finlay CJ had no doubt that if the plaintiff was entitled to an injunction it was the only remedy that could protect him. Though the defendants had given evidence that the plaintiff had been guilty of individual breaches of individual conditions in his licence this "fell far short indeed" of establishing that he was a person earning his livelihood by illegal means. Accordingly the Supreme Court affirmed the injunction awarded in his favour by Costello J. Where the criminal penalties are substantial and prosecutions are being mounted the court may conclude that the criminal law is sufficiently strong to prevent the damage in respect of which an injunction is being sought and accordingly decline to grant the injunction: *O'Connor v Williams* [1996] 2 ILRM 382 (HC). *Cf MMDS Television Ltd v South East Community Deflector Association Ltd* High Court, 8 April 1997 (Carroll J).

10. *Cf* Air Navigation and Transport Act 1936, s 21. See further Edwards 'The Liability of Air Carriers for Death and Personal injury to Passengers' (1982) 56 Austr LJ. Other examples of specific statutory imposition of liability arise in relation to infringement of copyright (*cf* Part IV of the Copyright Act 1963, see also *Green v Irish Independent Co Ltd* [1899] 1 IR 386 (CA) reg [1899] 1 IR and the infringement of the right to use a trade mark. *Cf* Trade Marks Act 1963, ss 12-14); see also Rule 1 of the Regulations for Burial Grounds, 6 July 1888 made pursuant to s 181 of the Public Health (Ireland) Act 1878; the Hotel Proprietors Act 1963 and the Petroleum and Other Minerals Development Act 1960, ss 77, 79-80. *Cf Collins v Gypsum Industries Ltd* [1975] IR 331 (SC).

11. *Cf* eg the Transport Act 1958, s 7(3) - duty of CIE (under s (1)) to provide "reasonable, efficient and economical transport services ..." not to impose "any form of duty or liability enforceable by proceedings before any court" to which CIE would not otherwise be subject; Postal and Telecommunications Services Act 1983, s 64(1) - An Post immune for all liability for loss or damage suffered by a person, in the use of a postal service by reason of (a) failure or delay in providing operating or maintaining a postal service, (b) failure interruption suspension or restriction of postal service, s 64(2) - members of staff of An Post similarly immune save at the suit of the company; s 88(1) and (2) - similar exemptions for Bord Telecom Éireann and its staff for loss or damage resulting from (a) failure or delay in providing operating or maintaining a telecommunications service, (b) failure interruption suspension or restriction of a telecommunications service, (c) any error or omission in telephone directory or in any telegram or telex messages transmitted by it; and s 105 - An Post immune from all liability for loss arising out of any payment made, or action taken in accordance with Post Office Savings Bank legislation or the 1983 Act itself; staff similarly immune save at the suit of An Post; Criminal Justice Act 1984, s 274 - failure to comply with Ministerial regulations for the recording by electronic means of the questioning of persons by gardaí not by itself to render a person liable to civil proceedings; Offences Against the State (Amendment) Act 1985, s 6 - no action or prosecution "of any kind" to lie against bank in respect of acts done by the bank in compliance with a Ministerial document requiring forfeiture of moneys held by the bank, or the non-payment by the bank of the moneys to the person who, but for s 22 of the Offences Against the State Act 1939, would be owner; Air Navigation & Transport (Pre-inspection) Act 1986, *s* 6(1) - a citizen of the United States who is a permanent employee of the United States government and is assigned to carry out duties at a pre-inspection facility, is not amenable to the jurisdiction of the State in respect of acts (itemised in s 6(2)) performed by him in the exercise of his duties; this immunity may be waived by the United States government: s 6(2); Air Navigation and Transport Act 1973, *s* 10 - no liability in damages in any civil action in the State attaches to commander of an aircraft, member of its crew, passenger, owner or operator, or any person on whose behalf a flight was performed for any action taken against any person pursuant to a provision of the Act, eg restraint (s 3) or disembarkation (s 6);

silent as regards any civil remedy, the courts may be called on to determine whether it was the intent of the legislature that such a remedy should exist. In truth, the legislature probably had no "intent", one way or the other, on the matter; indeed, its failure to provide explicitly for a remedy might reasonably be considered to imply that it did not intend that any remedy should be available to persons injured by breach of any of the statute's provisions.[12] Nevertheless, there are good reasons why the courts should exercise themselves in the task of pursuing this "will o' the wisp of a non-existing legislative intention".[13] To recognise a civil right of action in controlled circumstances arising from a breach of statute may be seen as strengthening the criminal sanction,[14] as well as assisting the judiciary in controlling the jury.[15] To describe the Court's deliberation as strictly that of legislative interpretation would be naive: a considerable element of judicial creativity is also involved.[16]

**[21.09]** A number of guidelines have been developed by the courts in determining the legislative "intent" of such statutory provisions. These will be considered in turn.

## Benefit of the Public or a Class of Persons

**[21.10]** The courts have frequently held that where a legislative provision was enacted for the benefit of a particular class of persons rather than for the benefit of the general public,

---

11. (contd) Defence (Amendment) Act 1987, s 6 - similar provision with regard to service aircraft. See also s 36 of the Fire Services Act 1981 (considered para **[26.31]-[26.32]** below), which provides that no action lies against the Minister for the Environment, or against a fire authority, or sanitary authority in respect of injury to persons or property alleged to have been caused or contributed to by the failure to comply with any functions conferred by the Act. Section 28(2)(c) exempts from liability fire authorities, persons in control at a fire (*cf* s 27) and persons acting under their control under sub-s (2). The effect of the provision appears to be that no civil liability attaches in respect of the use and control of water on property, including the directing of water against property not on fire, where the person in control considers this necessary for its protection. See also s 61 of the Safety Health and Welfare at Work Act 1989. Whether all, or any of these exemptions from liability can withstand constitutional scrutiny is uncertain. In *Byrne v Ireland* [1972] IR 241 (SC), Walsh J expressly declined to state an opinion on whether legislation could exempt the State from liability. *Cf* Mines and Quarries Act 1965, s 137 which provides a defence in respect of proceedings under certain provisions of the Act to a defendant who can prove that "it was impracticable to avoid or prevent the contravention". See also Air Navigation and Transport Act 1936 (No 40), s 24 - limitation of liability, and s 55 as amended by the Air Navigation and Transport Act 1988, s 47(1) - exclusion of liability. The Safety Health and Welfare at Work Act 1989, s 60 provides that nothing in the Act is to be construed as conferring a right of action in any civil proceedings, in respect of any failure to comply with any duty imposed by ss 6 to 11. However, breach of a duty imposed by regulations made under s 28 is to be actionable, so far as it causes damage, except in so far as regulations provide otherwise.
12. *Cf* FLEMING, p 114. See also *Norton v Kearon* (1871) IR 6 CL 126 (Exch). See, however, Evershed 'The Judicial Process in Twentieth Century England' (1961) 61 Col LR 761 at 783-784.
13. Harper & James, p 995, n 5. See also *The Queen in Right of Canada v Saskatchewan Wheat Pool* [1983] 1 SCR 205 at 215-216.
14. *Cf* Fricke 'The Juridical Nature of the Action Upon the Statute' (1960) 76 LQR 240 at 225. Williams 'Aims of the Law of Tort' (1951) 4 CLP 137 at 150. The abolition of juries in personal injuries litigation is unlikely to alter the practice of statutory interpretation significantly, though it may encourage the judges to greater frankness in articulating the underlying policy factors. This trend is already apparent in actions for negligence in the exercise of statutory functions: *cf Ward v McMaster and Louth County Council* [1989] ILRM 400 (SC) affg [1985] IR 29 (HC).
15. *Cf* LINDEN, pp 167-168. *Bissett v Thomas Heiton & Co Ltd* [1930] IR 17 (SC).
16. See Lowndes 'Civil Liability Created by Criminal Legislation' (1932) 16 Minn LR 361. *Cf* Fuller 'Positivism and Fidelity to Law - A Reply to Professor Hart' (1958) 71 Harv LR 68.

members of that class ought to be able to obtain damages for breach of the provision.[17] A right of action has been recognised in relation to such persons as workers in factories[18] (or similar industrial premises), building workers[19] in mines or quarries,[20] or on railways,[21] agricultural labourers,[22] barmen,[23]

17. *Cf M'Kenna v Stephens and Alexander E Hull & Co Ltd* [1923] 2 IR 112 at 128-129 (CA) - The fact that in addition to benefiting a particular class of person the statutory provision is *also* designed to protect the public will not deprive the member of the class of an entitlement to sue: *Waterford Harbour Commissioners v British Railways Board* [1979] ILRM 296 at 339 (SC). The statutory code relating to planning is generally regarded by the courts as being directed at the public good rather than affording a civil remedy to private parties for breach of its positions: see *Pine Valley Developments Ltd v Minister for the Environment* [1987] IR 23 (SC); *Glencar Exploration plc v Mayo County Council* High Court, 20 August 1998 (Kelly J).

18. *Cf Stewart v Killeen Paper Mills Ltd* [1959] IR 436 (SC); *Doherty v Bowaters Irish Wallboard Mills Ltd* [1968] IR 277 (SC); *Hogan v Rolon Caravans Ltd* Supreme Court, 8 July 1966; *Daly v Greybridge Co-operative Creamery Ltd* [1964] IR 497 (SC); *Shearer v Harland & Wolff* [1947] NI. 102 (KB); *Campbell v John A Best & Co Ltd* [1969] NI 123 (CA); *Irwin v White Tomkins & Courage Ltd* [1964] NI (HL); *Kennedy v East Cork Foods Ltd* [1973] IR 244 (SC); *Barry v Nitrigin Éireann Teo* [1994] 2 ILRM 522 (HC) - breach of noise regulations; *Byrne v Jefferson Smurfit & Son Ltd* [1962-1963] Ir Jur Rep 49 (SC); *Bissett v Thomas Heiton & Co Ltd* [1930] IR 17 (SC); *Harley v Imokelly Co-Operative Creamery Ltd* Supreme Court, 29 March 1973 - breach of Factories Act 1955, s 67(1) - lifting too heavy load; *Scott v Brookfield Linen Co Ltd* [1910] 2 IR 509 (KB) - machinery not securely fenced; *Martin v Millar Co Ltd* Supreme Court, 12 May 1972 - inadequate fencing under the Factories Act 1955, *s* 23 alleged but not found; *Lavelle v Brennan* [1946] Ir Jur Rep 37 (HC) - threshing machine not a "factory" under 1901 Act; *Kerr v Mitchell* [1959] NI 21 (CA) - farm premises, save in exceptional circumstances are incapable of constituting a factory under Northern Ireland's 1938 Act; *Murphy v Dublin County Council* 96 ILTR 26 (SC affg HC) - manhole, not a "factory" under 1955 Act; *Mcllhagger v Belfast Corporation* [1944] NI 37 (KB) - sewage pumping station not a "factory" under Northern Ireland's 1938 Act. *Dunne v Honeywell Control Systems Ltd and Virginia Milk Products* [1991] ILRM 595 (HC) - analysed by Byrne & Binchy, *Annual Review of Irish Law 1990*, pp 500-505 - electrical technician who had gone to the second defendants' premises pursuant to his employee's service contract to carry out repair work on a machine was held entitled to invoke the protection of Factories Act 1955, s 37(1) as amended by the Safety in Industry Act 1980, s 12(1). *Cf McEvoy v Murphy Contract Management and E Smithwick & Sons Ltd* DPIJ: Michaelmas Term 1991, p 154 (HC) - employee of first defendant doing work on premises of second defendant entitled to invoke the Factories Act 1955, s 23. See also the articles on the duty to fence machinery in factories, in (1951) 85 ILT& SJ 215; (1962) 96 ILT& SJ 27. For general analysis of the 1955 Act, see Shillman, *The Factory Legislation of Ireland* (1956). The Safety in Industry Act 1980 (No 9) extends the definition of "factory" under the Factories Act 1955, as well as enlarging the duties owed by employers in respect of the safety of their employees. For a general analysis see Cashell 'Safety in Industry Act 1980' (1981) 75 Gaz ILSI 9. See also the Construction Industry Federation & Incorporated Law Society of Ireland's *Joint Seminar on Accidents in the Construction Industry* (Dublin, 4 February 1985). *Cf Quinn v Burrell* High Court, 23 April 1993 (Hamilton P) analysed by Byrne & Binchy *Annual Review of Irish Law 1993*, pp 562-563.

19. *Roche v P Kelly & Co Ltd* [1969] IR 100 (SC); *Kenny v O'Rourke* [1972] IR 339 (SC); *O'Sullivan v Dwyer* [1971] IR 275 (SC); *Delaney v Mather & Platt Ltd* High Court, 1 December 1976 (Murnaghan J); *cf Murphy v Dublin County Council* (1962) 96 ILTR 26 (SC); *Power v Crowley and Reddy Enterprises Ltd* High Court, 29 October 1992 (Blayney J) analysed by Byrne & Binchy *Annual Review of Irish Law 1992*, pp 601-603; *Kelly v Michael McNamara & Co* High Court, 5 June 1996 (Budd J).

20. *Hamilton v Niblock* [1956] NI 109 (CA); *Gallagher v Mogul of Ireland Ltd* [1975] IR 204 (SC).

21. *Cf* article in (1948) 82 ILT & SJ 277. See, however, *Rogers v GS Ry* 74 ILTR 206 (CC).

22. *Cf Terlin v Lisnaskea RDC* [1914] 2 IR 15 (KB) overruled by *M'Daid v Milford RDC* [1919] 2 IR 1 (CA).

23. See *Reilly v Moore* [1935] NI 196 discussed in greater detail para **[21.32]** below.

roadusers[24] tenants[25] landowners,[26] port pilots,[27] schoolchildren,[28] harbour commissioners,[29] sailors,[30] prisoners,[31] medical practitioners[32] and even shareholders.[33]

---

24. *O'Callaghan v Minister for Posts & Telegraphs* (1947) 81 ILTR 162 (CC); *O'Connor v Kerry County Council* (1927) 61 ILTR 73 at 74 (HC); *CIE v Carroll* [1986] ILRM 312 (SC) - breach of statutory obligation to keep minimum clearance between railway bridge and road was not actionable as plaintiff had not relied on compliance with obligation. *Cf Cullen v Williams & Co Ltd* [1931] LJ Ir 50 (CC) - breach of statutory regulation requiring rear light to be in order was held not to be a ground for damages in a court action. See also *Walsh v Cronin* Supreme Court, 4 November 1935 *per* Ua Cinnéidigh CJ at p 4. A different conclusion has been reached in Canada: *Sterling Trusts Corporation v Postma* [1965] SCR 324 discussed by Alexander in (1968) 2 Ottawa LR 44 and Linden in (1967) 45 Can BR 121. As to the impact of insurance on statutory interpretation of road traffic regulations, see Symmons 'The Impact of Third Party Insurance Regulation on the Development of the Common Law' (1975) 4 Anglo-Amer LR 426. See also *M'Kenna v Stephens and Alexander E Hull & Co* [1923] 2 IR 112 (CA) - obstruction on footpath; defendant failed to comply with condition of statutory licence; pedestrian injured by lorry when she stepped into street; liability in negligence imposed.
25. *Siney v Dublin Corporation* [1980] IR 400 (SC); *cf O'Neill v Cork Corporation* [1947] IR 103 (SC); *Hildige v O'Farrell* 6 LR Ir 493 (CA).
26. *Bohan v Clements* [1920] 2 IR 117 (CA); *Bonfield v Tipperary (North Riding) County Council* [1941] Ir Jur 76 (HC); *cf Walsh v Kilkenny County Council* [1978] ILRM 1 (HC); *Greer v Belfast & Co Down Ry* [1926] NI 68 (CA); *Moynihan v Gt Southern Rys Co* [1936] IR 132 (HC); *Stelzer v Wexford North Slob Commissioners* [1988] ILRM 279 (HC).
27. *Hughes v Dundalk Harbour Commissioners* [1923] 1 IR 38.
28. *Ching v Surrey County Council* [1910] 1 KB 736 (CA).
29. *Waterford Harbour Commissioners v British Ry Bd* [1979] ILRM 296 (SC affg with variations HC). Conversely, the statutory duty of a harbour authority under s 47 of the Harbours Act 1946, to take all proper measures for the management, control and operation of the harbour, and to provide reasonable facilities and accommodation therein for vessels, goods and passengers does not give the owners of a consignment of timber, which they were permitted by the harbour authority to leave on the quayside, an action for breach of statutory duty where it was destroyed by fire caused by young children: *Doherty Timber Ltd v Drogheda Harbour Commissioners* [1993] 1 IR 315 (HC).
30. *Boucher v Clyde Shipping Co* [1904] 2 IR 129 (KB); *Cunningham v Frontier SS Co* [1906] 2 IR 12 (CA affg KB).
31. *O'Conghaile v Wallace* [1938] IR 526 (SC) - plaintiff's case held not to have been made out on the evidence; Meredith J's strong dissenting judgment is worthy of note.
32. In *Phillips v The Medical Council* [1991] 2 IR 115 (HC), Costello J awarded over £40,000 damages to the plaintiff for breach by the Medical Council of its statutory duty under the Medical Practitioners Act 1978, to determine his application for full registration on the General Register of Medical Practitioners within a reasonable time. Costello J did not refer to the questions of whether the 1978 Act had been enacted for the benefit of the public or a specific category of persons, or if so whether the plaintiff fell within that favoured category. He did, however, note that the Medical Council:

   > "is not a body established to manage the affairs of the medical profession or to protect its interests; it is a statutory body entrusted with important statutory functions to be performed in the public interest. In particular, the register of medical practitioners which it is required to maintain has been established to ensure that those who practice medicine in the State are properly qualified to do so".

   While this passage emphasises the public policy grounding of the legislation, it in no sense excludes the possibility of interpreting the legislation as also being designed to protect the legitimate interests of medical practitioners including applicants for full registration on the General Register. See also *Bakht v The Medical Council* [1990] 1 IR 515, where the Supreme Court awarded damages in judicial review proceedings arising from similar facts. See further Horgan & Morgan, *Administrative Law* (3rd ed 1998), pp 816-817.
33. *Coey v Belfast & Co Down Ry Co* (1866) IR 2 CL 112 (Com Pleas).

**[21.11]** At first blush it might appear anomalous that an Act which is passed for the protection of a limited class should be reinforced by a civil remedy whereas a statute passed for the benefit of the public at large should not be so reinforced.[34] It is to be hoped that our courts will critically re-examine this rule at some time.[35]

**[21.12]** A controversial instance of a finding of public duty arose in *Siney v Dublin Corporation*.[36] The plaintiff, a tenant of a flat let to him by the defendant, claimed damages for breach of statutory duty *(inter alia)*, on the basis that the flat was not fit for habitation as, he alleged, the Housing Act 1966 required. This claim was unsuccessful. O'Higgins CJ in the Supreme Court held that:

> "the statutory duties imposed by the Housing Act 1966 are so imposed for the benefits of the public. Under the Act they are enforceable under s 111 by the Minister. In these circumstances no right of action is given to a private citizen if the complaint is merely that the duties so imposed or any one of them have or has not been carried out. The mere fact that a housing authority has failed to discharge a duty imposed upon it does not give to a complaining or aggrieved citizen a right of action for damages."[37]

**[21.13]** *Siney* may be contrasted with the later decision of the Supreme Court in *McDonald v Feely*[38] and Costello J's decision in *Reilly v Limerick Corporation*.[39] Both of these cases dealt with housing authorities' statutory duties in relation to travellers. In *McDonald v Feely*, O'Higgins J (for the Court) referred to Dublin County Council's duty under s 60 of the Housing Act 1966, to make a scheme determining priorities among those to be housed. He considered that this duty:

> "would seem to involve a corresponding duty to operate such and in so doing to have regard to the housing needs of those living in unsuitable or overcrowded conditions and those in need of housing and unable to provide for themselves".[40]

He raised the question (though, on the facts of the case, did not feel obliged to determine) whether a Housing Authority could lawfully evict trespassing traveller families from its property, having regard to its statutory duty to look to the housing needs of those unable to provide for themselves.

**[21.14]** In *Reilly v Limerick Corporation*, Costello J held that a Housing Authority had a duty under s 55 of the Housing Act 1966 to have regard to the provision of suitable housing accommodation for persons who were in need of it and were unable to provide it from their own resources. If, therefore, it was established that there was a group of persons whose need was for housing accommodation in caravans situated on serviced sites because their needs could not be met by the provision of ordinary dwelling houses, then, said Costello J:

---

34. *Phillips v Britannia Hygienic Laundry Co Ltd* [1923] 2 KB 832 at 841.

35. *Cf* WINFIELD & JOLOWICZ, p 165

36. [1980] IR 400 (SC). *Cf O'Neill v Cork Corporation* [1947] IR 103 (SC); *Rogers v GS Ry* 74 ILTR 206 (CC). See also *McDonald v Feely* Supreme Court, 23 July 1980. The *Siney* decision is analysed in another context, see Ch 13. *Cf Brannon v Guthrie* [1988] 5 NIJB 54 (CA).

37. [1980] IR at 412.

38. Supreme Court, 23 July 1980.

39. [1989] ILRM 181 (HC) analysed by Whyte [1988] DULJ 189.

40. P 7 of O'Higgins CJ's judgment (*nem dis*).

> "the housing authority must have regard to the needs of those persons. This does not mean that having considered them they may then ignore them."[41]

**[21.15]** Costello J went on to spell out the four conditions which had to exist before the Housing Authority fell under a duty to include proposals to meet these needs in its building programme:

(i) financial resources would permit the work involved in the proposals to be carried out;

(ii) sites were either in the Housing Authority's possession or capable of being acquired by it;

(iii) these rules were suitable:

> "bearing in mind the reasonable needs of the travellers and the reasonable needs of the members of the settled community, as well as the responsibilities and duties of the Corporation as planning authority in the area";[42] and

(iv) the provision of serviced sites would not conflict with the achievement of other statutory objectives laid down in the Act or other statutory duties of the Corporation which in their opinion should reasonably take precedence.

**[21.16]** Costello J held that the Housing Authority had a duty to review an existing building programme if it was established that there were housing needs in the functional area in respect of which no proposals had been made in the programme; unless those needs were being met informally and by some other means, the Authority was under a duty to review the programme and vary it by the insertion of proposals to remedy these newly ascertained needs, once the four conditions already mentioned could be shown to exist.

**[21.17]** After a review of the evidence, Costello J went on to hold that, whilst the plaintiffs were not entitled to an order requiring the Housing Authority to provide them with serviced sites, they were entitled to a declaration that the Housing Authority was obliged to review its building programme, which it had adopted three years previously, and to vary it so as "to include proposals relating to the work [it] proposes] to undertake to provide serviced sites for the members of the travelling community in its functional area".[43] He did not consider it appropriate to make a mandatory injunction as he could not assume that the Housing Authority would neglect to perform the statutory duty thus shown to exist or that, if it should be guilty of such neglect, the Minister would not exercise his powers under s 111 in the light of the Court's order.

**[21.18]** Although neither *McDonald v Feely* nor *Reilly v Limerick Corporation* involved a claim for damages for breach of statutory duty,[44] it may be argued that the decisions call

41. [1989] ILRM 190.

42. *Cf O'Leary v Dublin County Council* High Court, 16 May 1988 (O'Hanlon J).

43. [1989] ILRM at 191.

44. In *Reilly* the plaintiffs sought damages for interference with their *constitutional rights;* in *McDonald* the plaintiffs sought an injunction to prevent their eviction from property on which they were trespassing. *Cf* Whyte [1988] Dublin ULJ 189 at 193-197. See also *Ward v McMaster and Louth County Council* [1989] ILRM 400 (SC) affg [1985] IR 29 (HC). The Housing Act 1988, s 55 repeals the Housing Act 1966, s 55; s 13 expressly extends the power of housing authorities to provide manage and control sites for travellers.

seriously into question the view that none of the provisions of the Housing Act 1966 is capable of sustaining an action for breach of statutory duty.

## Nature of Penalty or Remedy Provided by the Statutory Provision

**[21.19]** In attempting to define whether a civil remedy ought to be made available under a statute the courts also look to the penalty provisions of the Act in question for inspiration in their deliberations. Here, however, the courts have attempted the impossible in trying to draw a conclusion, one way or the other, from the nature of the penalty or remedy provided by the statutory provision. If the penalty is low, or if no penalty at all or some other remedy not involving a specific right to damages is provided, does this mean that the legislature regarded it as improper for there also to be a civil action (as some courts have concluded),[45] or does it indicate, on the contrary, that the legislature must have intended that the criminal sanction should be supplemented and reinforced by a civil remedy (as other courts have said)?[46] Conversely, if the penalty is high, does this suggest that the legislature regarded it as sufficient punishment, or can one conclude that a breach which the legislature so clearly considered to be serious must be supplemented by a civil remedy?[47] Even a cursory glance at the authorities shows that the courts have not been consistent in their approach to this general question.

## Other Techniques of Statutory Interpretation

**[21.20]** The courts also use other techniques of statutory interpretation. They may, for example, examine the preamble,[48] or other sections[49] of the statute in order to determine whether an intention to create civil liability for breaches of specific sections may be inferred. The previous statutory[50] or common law[51] background to the Act under

45. *Cf Atkinson v Newcastle and Gateshead Waterworks Co* (1877) 2 Ex D 441, explained by Palles CB in *Thigh v Rathangan Drainage Bd* [1898] 2 IR 205 at 224-225 (QB); *Glynn v Smith* (1921) 55 ILTR 67 (HC); *Norton v Kearon* (1871) IR 6 CL 126 (Exch) - a decision which goes very far in foreclosing the right to take civil proceedings for breach of bye-law. See also *Mulcahy v Guardians of the Poor of Kilmacthomas Union* (1886) 18 LR Ir 200 (QB); *Handley v Moffat* (1872) IR 6 CL 104 (Com Pleas); *Hildige v O'Farrell* (1880) 6 LR Ir 493 (CA); *Representative Church Body v Dublin Board of Assistance* [1948] IR 287 at 303-304 (SC).

46. *Cf Bohan v Clements* [1920] 2 IR 117 at 124 (CA); *Transport Salaried Staffs' Association v CIE* [1965] IR 180 (SC 1963 affg 1962). See also *Meskell v CIE* [1973] IR 121 at 138 (SC); *Rogers v GS Ry* (1940) 74 ILTR 206 at 208 (CC); *Groves v Wimbourne* [1898] 2 QB 402 (CA); *Dormont v Furney Ry* (1883) 11 QBD 496; *Ross v Rugge-Price* (1876) 1 Ex D 269; *Cutler v Wandsworth Stadium Ltd* [1949] AC 398; *Ministry of Housing and Local Government v Sharp* [1970] 2 QB 223; *O'Connor v Bray* (1973) 56 CLR 464 at 486.

47. *Cf Hughes v Dundalk Harbour Commissioners* [1923] IR 38 (Ch Div).

48. LINDEN, p 160-161.

49. *Walsh v Kilkenny County Council* [1978] ILRM 1 (HC); *Bohan v Clements* [1920] 2 IR 117 at 124 (CA); *Adderley v Great Northern Ry Co* [1905] 2 IR 378 (CA). *Cf Waterford Harbour Commissioners v British Railways Board* [1979] ILRM 296; *Doherty v Bowaters Irish Wallboard Mills Ltd* [1968] IR 277 (SC); *Cunningham v Frontier SS Co* [1906] 2 IR 12 (CA affg KB 1904).

50. *Cf Lavelle v Brennan* [1946] Ir Jur 37 at 38 (HC); *Gallagher v Mogul of Ireland Ltd* [1975] IR 204 (SC); *Kagan v Dept of Environment* NI High Court, 6 October 1978 (Gibson LJ). See also *Walsh v Kilkenny County Council* [1978] ILRM 1 (HC).

51. *Harbinson v Armagh County Council* [1902] 2 IR 538 (KB).

consideration or the contrast between the language of the Act under consideration and that of other Acts[52] may also throw light on its interpretation. The Courts may also apply the principle of construction, *expressio unius est exclusio alterius*, so as to deny a civil remedy where civil liability is expressly stated in certain sections of the Act but not in the particular section under consideration.[53]

## Limitations on Recovery

**[21.21]** Even where the courts hold that a statutory provision gives rise to civil liability, this does not necessarily mean that the plaintiff will be entitled to recover damages. Certain other limitations, considered now, have also been recognised.

### *(a) Breach of statute required*

**[21.22]** Where the plaintiff fails to show that the defendant was in breach of a statutory provision, as alleged, the defendant will be excused of liability[54] on that account (although he may still on the facts be liable for common law negligence[55] or for some other wrong[56]). This may seem to be a truism, but in certain cases the issue may be one that gives rise to

52. *Cf O'Neill v Cork Corporation* [1947] IR 103 at 116 (SC).

53. *Commerford v Halifax School Commissioners* [1950] 2 DLR 207 (ns); *Toronto-St Catherine's Transport v Toronto* [1954] 1 DLR 721, 732-737.

54. See *Bill v Short Brothers & Harland Ltd* [1963] NI 1 (HL (NI)); *McIlwrath v Harland & Wolff Ltd* [1963] NI 41 (CA); *Lavelle v Brennan* [1946] Ir Jur Rep 37 (HC). *Cf Murphy v Dublin County Council* (1962) 96 ILTR 26 (SC); *O'Conghaile v Wallace* [1938] IR 526 (SC).

55. *Cf Byrne v Sheedy* [1955] IR I (SC); *Tarrant v O'Sullivan* [1949] Ir Jur Rep 46 (CC) - action for negligence unsuccessful on the facts. *Sargerson v McIlhagga* [1963] NI 73. A statutory provision, though not breached by the defendant (or plaintiff), may be relevant in determining the issue of negligence (or contributory negligence). Thus, although until relatively recently statutory regulations required merely the installation but not the wearing of seat belts in cars, the existence of this regulation might be taken into account in determining whether a passenger was guilty of contributory negligence in not wearing an available seat belt. *Cf Hamill v Oliver* [1977] IR 73 at 75-76 (SC). See also *Duffy v Rooney and Dunnes Stores (Dundalk) Ltd* High Court, 23 June 1997 (Laffoy J) (affd by Supreme Court 23 April 1998) - safety standards, requiring warnings of inflammability to be attached to nightclothes worn by children were held to be evidence of an official awareness of a risk attaching to a wider range of clothes including coats worn by children, thus supporting the imposition of a duty on manufacturers and retailers to place warnings on these coats. *Cf Matthews v The Irish Society for Autism* High Court, 18 April 1997 (Laffoy J) analysed by Byrne & Binchy *Annual Review of Irish Law 1997*, pp 736-738. Also *Stokes v Limerick Corporation* DPIJ: Hilary and Easter Terms 1992, p 39 (High Court, 7 February 1992, O'Hanlon J) *Reilly v McAleer* DPIJ: Hilary and Easter Terms 1992, p 204 (High Court, 19 March 1992, Morris J). Sometimes the regulatory code may be regarded by the court as setting the outer limits of liability for a common law action sounding in negligence: see eg *Dunne v Dublin Cargo Handling Ltd (in liquidation)* Supreme Court, 30 August 1997 (*ex temp*), critically analysed by Byrne & Binchy, *Annual Review of Irish Law 1997*, pp 738-740. In England, the Court of Appeal has evinced reluctance to impose liability in negligence on a public authority, in respect of its discretionary functions, where breach of statutory duty has been catered for by the statute under scrutiny: *Haydon v Kent County Council* [1978] QB 343 (CA) analysed by Oliver '*Anns v London Borough of Merton* Reconsidered' [1980] CLP 269 at 276-278. It should also be added that where a court interprets a statutory provision as not conferring a right of civil action on the injured party it may nonetheless have regard to the provision in measuring whether the defendant is guilty of common law negligence: *cf Adderley v GN Ry Co* [1905] 2 IR 378 (CA).

56 *Cf Governors of Barrington's Hospital v Minister for Health* High Court, 14 March 1988 (Costello J), where the plaintiffs unsuccessfully sought an injunction against the Minister for Health's decision to terminate funding for their hospital.

considerable debate. In *Kenny v O'Rourke*,[57] the defendant, who had failed to provide scaffolding for his employee who was painting a window at first-storey level, was held not to have been in breach of a building regulation[58] which required scaffolding to be provided "for all building operations that cannot safely be carried out without it". The Supreme Court held that the trial judge was correct in ruling that there was no evidence which would warrant a finding on this provision. Whilst scaffolding would clearly have been a safer system than a ladder, the evidence on behalf of the plaintiff fell well short of showing that the job could not safely be carried out without scaffolding.[59]

**[21.23]** In two situations, however, this may not be so obviously a correct policy. First, where the defendant's conduct falls *just outside* the scope of a statutory obligation, it might be considered proper that the plaintiff should be able to give evidence of that obligation as a standard of care that might guide the court in negligence proceedings. The English Court of Appeal has rejected this approach, fearing that:

> "undue complications will be brought into these cases if, whenever the courts were considering common law obligations, they had to consider all the statutory regulations which nearly apply but which do not in fact apply."[60]

**[21.24]** Secondly, where a statutory provision was not violated because of some technicality (as where road traffic regulations were defectively enacted), it might be argued that civil liability should not be defeated on that account. If the legislature intended to enact legislation that would have the effect of conferring a right of action of parties injured by the type of conduct that it meant to prohibit, why should that intention be frustrated by what, from the parties' standpoint, was an irrelevant technical hitch? This view has been favoured in the United States of America,[61] but the issue has not yet arisen in our courts. Having regard to the narrow constructionist approach favoured in this country, it is far from certain that the American approach would be followed here.

---

56. (contd) The plaintiffs conceded that the Minister had no mandatory duty to fund the hospital and that only the Oireachtas could relieve them of this duty; the Minister's decision, they said, was an unlawful arrogation of the legislature's powers. Costello J rejected this argument. he said (at p 6): ...

> "Once [the Minister] was under no legal requirement to provide the governors with funds to run their hospital his knowledge of the consequences of his decisions cannot in itself invalidate it."

Costello J provided no further discussion on the question of unlawful abrogation of the legislature's powers.

57. [1972] IR 339 (SC). See also *Kielthy v Ascon Ltd* [1970] IR 122 (SC).
58. Building (Safety, Health and Welfare) Regulations 1959, Reg 4 para 3 (SI 227/1959)
59. As to the respective functions of judge and jury in determining whether there has been a breach of the statutory provision see *Bissett v Thomas Heiton & Co Ltd* [1930] IR 17 (SC).
60. *Chipchase v British Titan Products Co* [1956] 1 QB 545 (CA). The existence of statutory controls, which do not prohibit the conduct that gave rise to the damage but which throw light on the legislature's attitude to that conduct, may be relevant, however, in determining whether the conduct constitutes negligence or contributory negligence: *cf* fn 54 above.
61. *Clinkscales v Carver* (1943) 22 Cal 2d, 72 136 p 2d 777; *Lewis v City of Miami* (1937) 127 Fla 426, 173 So 150. See further, James 'Statutory Standards and Negligence in Accident Cases' (1950) 11 La LR 95 at 109-110.

### *(b) Offending conduct must cause loss*

**[21.25]** The plaintiff must establish on the balance of probabilities that, but for the defendant's conduct which constituted a breach of the statutory provision, he would not have suffered the loss or injury complained of.[62] Thus, in *Martin v Millar & Co Ltd*,[63] the Supreme Court held that, even if the fencing on the machine could be regarded as inadequate[64] when the machine was in operation, the plaintiff could not rely on this fact since he had been injured when the machine was not working, the fencing in such circumstances being regarded as adequate. Moreover, the "chain of causation" between breach of statute and injury must not have been broken, as for example by a *novus actus interveniens*.[65]

**[21.26]** The thrust of recent decisions is to regard defence claims of lack of causal connection with less than full enthusiasm. In *Dunleavy v Glen Abbey Ltd*[66] the plaintiff, whose duties included moving heavy loads, was injured when carrying a very heavy package. The background to the accident was that he would have used a fork lift truck but this was inoperative because its battery was dead; so he had asked another person to assist him. The employee had let go of the package when it was near to the ground. The result was that the plaintiff was jerked by the weight of the load and suffered an injury to his back.

**[21.27]** The crucial issue related to the Factories Act 1955 (Manual Labour) (Maximum Weights and Transport) Regulations 1972, regulation 6 provided as follows:

> (1) Every person shall, prior to being assigned to - (a) a process to which these regulations relate ..., receive adequate training or instruction in working techniques relating to the process for the purposes of safe-guarding health and preventing accidents.
>
> (2) The training or instruction mentioned in paragraph (1) of this regulation shall include methods of lifting, carrying, putting down, unloading and stacking different types of loads, and shall be given by a suitably qualified person.
>
> (3) Whenever a person receives training or instruction required by this regulation, such training or instruction shall, whenever practicable, be followed by adequate supervision to ensure that the correct methods are used by the person while engaged in the process to which the training or instruction relates.

---

62. *Cf McDaid v Milford RDC* [1919] 2 IR I (CA); *Condon v Mitchelstown RDC* [1914] 1 IR 113 (CA); *Marron v Cootehill (No 2) RDC* [1915] 1 IR 216 (HL(Ir)). In some cases the plaintiff's injury may have been only *partially* caused by the breach of the statutory provision. Here the court will attempt to sever and award appropriate compensation for the quantum of injury that is attributable to this breach. See eg *Barry v Nitrigin Éireann Teo* [1994] 2 ILRM 522 (HC) - plaintiff employee's loss of hearing not exclusively attributable to breach of noise regulations at work, but the contribution of other factors was relatively slight requiring a reduction in the damages from £60,000 to £50,000).
63. Supreme Court, 12 May 1972. See also *CIE v Carroll* [1986] ILRM 312 (SC) - reduction of clearance under a bridge below the limit prescribed by the Railway Clauses Consolidation Act 1845 was not material as there was no evidence that the driver, who ran an excavator into the bridge aware of this limit and relied on it in approaching the bridge with a high load.
64. *Cf* Factories Act 1955, s 23.
65. *Cf Shearer v Harland & Wolff Ltd* [1947] NI 102 (KB) - defence was rejected on the facts. See also *M'Kenna v Stephens and Alexander E Hull & Co Ltd* [1923] 2 IR 112 (CA (IFS)).
66. [1992] ILRM 1 (HC).

(4) In case a person is required by this regulation to receive training or instruction it shall be the duty of the person by whom such person is employed to provide or arrange for the provision of such training or instruction.

**[21.28]** Also of relevance was regulation 7, which provided that:

> [i]n order to avoid the necessity for the manual transport of loads, suitable mechanical devices shall be used, so far as is reasonably practicable, in ... every factory or premises mentioned in regulation 3(1)...

**[21.29]** The regulation applied to the plaintiff, who had received no training such as the regulations envisaged. There was no dispute on the evidence that the plaintiff was aware that the fork lift truck was inoperative from time to time and that he had complained about this. In these circumstances, Barron J concluded that the defendant was in breach of its statutory duties both as to training and as to the provision of suitable mechanical devices.

**[21.30]** The defendant urged that the causal link between its breach of the statutory provision and the plaintiff's injury was missing. Even if the plaintiff had been properly trained in accordance with the regulations, he would still have carried out his work in the way that he had done. The plaintiff had used the proper posture for lifting and putting down loads. Barron J rejected this argument, on the basis that, if the employer had carried out its statutory obligations, the plaintiff would have learned more than the correct posture:

> "He would have learned that in some circumstances it is safer to take the whole weight himself rather than to share it with another. He would have learned that in appropriate circumstances of which this was one it is advisable to break up the load. Had he been given such advice, it is clear that he would not have set about his particular task in the way he did. It is reasonable to suppose that because of this he would not have met with the accident."[67]

**[21.31]** As regards the fork-lift truck, Barron J was satisfied that, if the truck had been available, the plaintiff would have used it and thus not met with the accident. He did not accept that regulation 7 applied only to *repetitive* actions. In his view the failure to have the fork-lift truck adequately maintained when the employer was aware that it was breaking down from time to time was itself a breach of the regulations.

**[21.32]** *Reilly v Moore*[68] raised an interesting question regarding proof of loss. The plaintiff, a barman, sought damages for breach by his employer of the statutory duty[69] to give him a fortnight's holiday with full pay every year. The defendant contended that the plaintiff had suffered no injury as a result of the breach, but Best LJ rejected the argument, stating:

---

67. [1992] ILRM 1 at 5. See also *Dennehy v Counter Equipment Ltd* DPIJ: Hilary and Easter Terms 1992 p 193 (HC); *Kennefick v John A Wood Ltd* DPIJ: Hilary and Easter Terms 1994 p 97 (HC). In *Philips v The Medical Council* [1991] 2 IR 115 (HC) Costello J awarded over £40000 to an applicant for full registration on the General Register of Medical Practitioners whose application had not been determined by the Medical Council within a reasonable time. As well as making this award, Costello J declared that the Medical Council should consider and determine an issue on which Costello J had held that the plaintiff would have succeeded, had the Council made that determination earlier.

68. [1935] NI 196 (KB). See also *Wren v Stokes* [1902] 1 IR 167 (CA affg 1900); *Gill v Wilson* 3 ICLR 544 (QB). *Cf Boucher v Clyde Shipping Co* [1904] 2 IR 129 (KB).

69. Shops Act 1912, *s* 21(6) and Fifth Schedule (2 Geo 5 c 3).

"It is true that no evidence was given on the subject of injury and it is not suggested that any apparent physical damage, such as may result to a person involved in an accident, affects the plaintiff, but if the Legislature deemed it necessary for the well-being of the class to which the plaintiff belongs that holidays should be provided for members of that class it is not an unwarranted inference that plaintiff's health must have been impaired to some extent by his having been deprived of the holidays provided for in ... the Act."[70]

**[21.33]** Where a defendant has been in breach of a licensing requirement, and as a result of his or her conduct injures another person, may that person base an action on the breach of this requirement? For example, may an unlicensed driver or medical practitioner be sued if injuries result from his or her driving or medical treatment where no case for negligence can be made out at common law? Courts in other jurisdictions have generally said no,[71] either on the basis that the purpose of the statutory licensing requirement was fiscal or administrative rather than designed to protect potential victims,[72] or on the ground that the plaintiff has not shown that the defendant's failure to obtain the license was the *cause* of the plaintiff's injury.[73] A leading American commentator has offered another explanation: the real reason is that the licensing statute of itself "establishes no standard of conduct - it does not stipulate any particular human act ..."[74]

### *(c) Accident must be of a type the statute sought to prevent*

**[21.34]** A plaintiff may not recover damages for the defendant's breach of statutory duty admittedly causing him injury unless the injury falls within the scope of the risk contemplated by the statutory provision. *Gorris v Scott*[75] provides a good observation of this rule. The defendants, who were shipowners, in breach of statute, failed to provide pens for the transportation of the plaintiff's sheep; as a result the sheep were swept overboard and lost. Liability was denied since "the damage was of such a nature as was not contemplated at all by the statute".[76] The statute was directed towards preventing the spread of disease rather than protecting the animals from the perils of the sea.[77]

---

70. [1935] NI 206. *Cf* generally Malone 'Ruminations on Cause-In-Fact' (1956) 60 Stan LR 6 at 73-75. *Reilly v Moore* [1935] NI 196 (KB) goes close to making the tort of breach of statutory duty actionable *per se*. It can perhaps better be understood as enforcing an implicit statutory entitlement rather than penalising a statutory breach. *Cf Cosgrove v Ireland* [1982] ILRM 48 (HC) discussed below para **[21.63]**.

71. Eg *Brown v Shyne* (1926) 242 NY 176, 151 NE 197 (CA) criticised by Linowitz 'Note' (1937) 22 Cornell LQ 276. *Cf Whipple v Grandchamp* (1927) 261 Mass 40 158, NE 170.

72. *Cf Annot* (1931) 73 ALR 156; PROSSER WADE & SCHWARTZ, p 234.

73. *Cf* LFO 'Note: Highways - Unlicensed Automobile- Effect on Rights of Parties' (1929) 7 Neb L Bulletin 203 at 204-205.

74. Gregory 'Breaches of Criminal Licensing Statutes in Civil Litigation' (1951) 36 Cornell LQ 622 at 631. The possibility of other actions notably of negligent misstatement, deceit and even battery (*cf De May v Roberts* (1881) 46 Mich 160 9 NW 146 (SC) should not be discounted however.

75. (1874) LR 9 Exch 125.

76. (1874) LR 9 Exch 125 at 128. See James 'Statutory Standards and Negligence in Accident Cases' (1950) 11 La LR 95 at 112-113. In *Curran v Cadbury Ireland Ltd* [2000] 2 ILRM 343 (CC) Judge McMahon raised the question whether the definition of "personal injury" under s 2 of the Safety, Health and Welfare at Work Act 1989 might include unforeseeable mental impairment where foreseeable physical injury to the plaintiff had been risked but not actually sustained.

77 See also *Long v Saorstát & Continental Steamship Co* (1953) 93 ILTR 137 (SC); *Representative Church Body v Dublin Board of Assistance* [1948] IR 287 (SC); *Egan v Dublin Health Authority* Supreme Court, 30 July 1965;

### (d) Plaintiff must be a person whom the statute sought to protect

**[21.35]** A person who is in breach of a statutory duty will only be liable to those whom the statutory provision seeks to protect.[78] In *Long v Saorstát & Continental Steamship Co*,[79] the plaintiff, a stevedore, was injured when a gangway fell on him while he was on a ship in port. He called in aid a statutory regulation requiring that there be "safe means of access for the use of persons employed" on ships when lying at a wharf or quay for the purpose of unloading, as those persons "ha[d] to pass from the ship to the shore or from the shore to the ship". The Supreme Court held that, assuming there had been a breach of the regulation, the plaintiff could not base his action upon it since, it appears, the Court did not regard him as a person for whose protection the regulation was designed.[80] Similarly, in *Daly v Greybridge Co-operative Creamery*,[81] the Supreme Court held that certain provisions of the Factories Act 1955 could not be invoked by a child who was injured while in the boiler-house of the defendant's creamery. The child was fetching milk from the creamery and was sheltering in the boiler house when his hand got caught in a pumping machine. The boiler-house constituted a "factory" for the purposes of the Act and the plaintiff contended that the Act[82] required that it be fenced.

**[21.36]** Walsh J stated:

> "In the present case the plaintiff was quite clearly not 'employed or working on the premises' within the meaning of ss 21, 22, or 23 of the Act of 1955 and, indeed, I doubt if he could be held to have been employed or working in any sense of those terms on the occasion of the accident. He was lawfully on the premises but I cannot subscribe to the view ... that the fact is in itself sufficient to give him the benefit of the statute as I think it is abundantly clear that

---

77. (contd) *Hamilton v Niblock* [1956] NI 109 at 117-118 (CA) - query as to whether a plaintiff worker injured when lifting stone onto a truck in a quarry, could recover where statute expressed to be in "prevention of dangerous accidents in a quarry": Quarries Act (Northern Ireland) 1927, First Schedule (17 & 18 Geo 5 C 19);

> "Was this a dangerous accident? Was it an accident? Was it an accident of a type or kind peculiar to a quarry which occurred not merely while but because the plaintiff was working in a quarry or was it an accident dangerous or otherwise which with a like truck and a like heavy and unwieldy load could have happened just as readily in a warehouse or on a farm? I confess to difficulty in answering my own query in favour of the plaintiff."

See also *Reilly v McAleer* DPIJ: Hilary and Easter Terms 1992 p 204 (HC) (Morris J) - building regulations placing limitations for the length of stride for stairways were held to relate to the safety rather than merely the comfort of those using the stairways, accordingly they were capable of generating civil liability for a fall attributable to violation of regulations; in this case where the steps were outside the premises, Morris J did not take a final view on the question whether the regulations governed only internal steps since he considered that "if it is necessary to comply with a given standard in the interest of safety for internal steps, it is no less valid that these structures should conform to that standard if they are built out of doors". Liability was thus imposed on the basis of negligence at common law rather than for breach of statutory duty.

78. *Cf Norton v Kearon* (1871) IR 6 CL 126 at 128. See also *Waterford Harbour Commissioners v British Railways Board* [1979] ILRM 296 at 341 (SC).
79. (1953) 93 ILTR 137 (SC). *Cf McIlwrath v Harland & Wolff Ltd* [1963] NI 41 (CA).
80. *Long v Saorstát & Continental Steamship Co* (1953) 93 ILTR 137 at 146. A somewhat different analysis is presented by Maguire CJ at 139.
81. [1964] IR 497 (SC).
82. Sections 21-23.

> the object of the Act is to protect only those persons who, broadly speaking, are employed in the factory premises at the work in which the factory is engaged or at work incidental to it."[83]

**[21.37]** In *Roche v P Kelly & Co*,[84] however, this passage was repeated by Walsh J, who stated that the expression

> "quite clearly did not exclude independent contractors as such and an independent contractor is 'a person employed' or 'person working in' a factory when he is there working for the purpose of the factory or when his work there is incidental to the purpose of the factory."

**[21.38]** In *McNamara v ESB*,[85] the Supreme Court held that no statutory duty towards a person trespassing on a sub-station was imposed on the Electricity Supply Board by Article 30 of the Electricity Regulations 1932. That article required that every sub-station should be substantially constructed and so arranged that no unauthorised persons could obtain access to the sub-station otherwise than by the proper entrance. The 1932 Regulations were made under the Factory and Workshop Act 1901 and were carried over by s 8 of the Factories Act 1955. Accordingly, they fell within the scope of s 71(1) of the 1955 Act which enabled the Minister for Industry and Commerce to make special regulations for safety where any such appliance was "of such nature as to cause risk of bodily injury to the persons employed, or any class of those persons". Henchy J stated that he read s 71(1):

> "as limiting the power of the Minister to make regulations for the benefit of 'persons employed' in the sense in which that expression is used in the Factories Act in relation to a factory. The regulations, being normally made under s 71, subs 1, do not apply, and could not have been made so as to apply, to the plaintiff who was a mere trespasser and in no sense a person employed. Therefore, he is not entitled to assert a breach by the defendants of a duty owed to him under article 30 of the Regulations of 1932. No such duty was owed to the plaintiff because he does not come within the category of persons to whom a duty could be owed under that article."[86]

**[21.39]** Griffin J considered that:

> "[t]he fact that the regulations do not innure for the benefit of a trespasser and that a person relying on the safeguards provided by the Factories Acts must show that he was 'employed' on the premises is so well settled that it is unnecessary to consider the matter further.[87]

---

83. See para **[21.35]** above.

84. [1969] IR 100 at 110 (SC). See also *O'Sullivan v Dwyer* [1971] IR 275 (SC). *Cf Delaney v Mather & Platt Ltd* High Court, December 1976 (Murnaghan J).

85. [1975] IR 1 (SC).

86. [1975] IR 1 at 30.

87. [1975] IR 1 at 38. See also *Daly v Avonmore Creameries Ltd* [1984] IR 131 (SC) - a sub-contractor who gratuitously undertook work on part of factory roof outside the range of services he had been engaged to carry out, died when he fell through a skylight; Factories Act 1955, s 37 which requires protective measures to be taken in relation to any person who "has to" or "is to" work in certain places, held irrelevant as the deceased was neither required nor expected to work where he did on the roof. See further *Dunne v Honeywell Control Systems Ltd and Virginia Milk Products* [1991] ILRM 595 (HC); *McEvoy v Murphy Contract Management and E Smithwick & Sons Ltd* DPIJ: Michaelmas Term 1991 p 154 (HC) (Lynch J).

**[21.40]** In *Walsh v Kilkenny County Council*,[88] the plaintiff's cattle were poisoned by eating yew trees when trespassing in a graveyard for whose upkeep the defendant was responsible. A boundary wall had fallen into disrepair some time previously, but the plaintiff had not informed the defendant of this fact. The plaintiff claimed damages for breach of statutory duty (*inter alia*), relying on a statutory regulation[89] which required that burial grounds be "sufficiently fenced". The regulation provided no penalty for failure to perform the duty, and the plaintiff argued that this absence meant that "the remedy in damages lies for any person damnified by the breach of statutory duty".[90]

**[21.41]** Gannon J quoted Maugham LJ's statement in *Monk v Warbey*,[91] that the Court has to make up its mind whether the harm "ought to be remedied by the statute is one of the kind the statute intended to prevent. He analysed a number of the sections of the Act and concluded without hesitation that:

> "[t]aking the provisions of this Act as a whole ... this is an enactment for the benefit only of the public at large, and that the duties and obligations therein are imposed for the benefit only of the public at large, and not for the benefit of any class of persons nor of any individuals ... Having regard to ss 161 to 181 ... it would appear that the declared and primary purposes of the duties imposed on the defendants are the protection of public health, the maintenance of public decency, and the prevention of the violation of the respect due to the remains of deceased persons. The provisions of s 171 and of s 58 of the Cemetries Clauses Act 1847, incorporated by s 193, which confer powers on the defendants to punish trespassers are inconsistent with the imposition of any duty on the defendants to trespassers. The duty to fence imposed by the Regulations of the 6th July 1888 made pursuant to s 181 seems to be a duty to protect the property vested in the Burial Board from desecration or other interference by trespassers. The plaintiff, who is admittedly a trespasser, cannot claim that he is a person for whose benefit this duty is laid upon the defendants"[92]

## Nature of Obligation Imposed by Statute

**[21.42]** It is a matter of statutory construction to determine the nature of the obligation imposed by the statute on the defendant. Generally it will not be sufficient for the defendant to show that he or she behaved with all due care.[93] Frequently the courts hold the defendant "absolutely" or "strictly" liable for the breach. Thus, in *Doherty v Bowaters*

---

88. [1978] ILRM I (HC). *Cf Moynihan v Gt. Southern Rys Co* [1936] IR 132 (HC).
89. Regulations for Burial Grounds, r 1, dated 6 July 1888 made pursuant to the Public Health (Ireland) Act 1878, s 181.
90. [1978] ILRM 1 at 4.
91. [1935] 1 KB 75 at 85. Gannon J also quoted extracts from *Phillips v Britannic Hygienic Laundry Co* [1923] 2 KB 832 at 840 (CA) and *Solomons v Gertzenstein Ltd* [1954] 2 QB 243 at 266 (CA).
92. [1978] ILRM 5.
93. *Cf O'Sullivan v Dwyer* [1971] IR 275 at 285 (SC) and see *Cunningham v Frontier SS Co* [1906] 2 IR 12 at 49 (KBD affd CA). *Cf Mcllwrath v Harland & Wolff Ltd* [1963] NI 41 (CA); *Hurley v Imokelly Co-Operative Creamery Ltd* Supreme Court, 29 March 1973 *per* Walsh J (p 4 of judgment). Almost without exception, the Safety, Health and Welfare at Work (General Application) Regulations 1993 provide for strict and even absolute duties. On occasion the statute may, of course, specifically prescribe an obligation to act with due care, or its equivalent: *cf eg* Safety in Industry Act 1980, s 9(1); Occupiers' Liability Act 1995, s 3. *Cf Conway v Cniotáil Gaeltarra* DPIJ: Michaelmas Term 1990, p 285 (HC) (Barron J) - interpreting the Factories Act 1955, s 55. As to what the phrase "so far as practicable" connotes, see *Boyle v Marathon Petroleum Ireland Ltd* Supreme Court, 12 January 1999.

*Irish Wallboard Mills Ltd*,[94] the Supreme Court held that s 34(1)(a) of the Factories Act 1955 imposed distinct and absolute duties on the defendant in requiring *inter alia* that:

> "a chain, rope or lifting tackle shall not be used unless it is of good construction, sound material, adequate strength and free from patent defect."

**[21.43]** The approach favoured by the Court is made clear in the following passage of the judgment of Walsh J, who considered that:

> "One must ... look at s 34 itself to see whether there is anything in the section which qualifies or weakens the absolute nature of the terms of the duty imposed. It is quite clear from a perusal of the different paragraphs of the section, and indeed of other sections of the Act, that the legislature made a distinction between taking something into use in a factory for the first time and the user described in the phrase 'shall not be used'. In my view the distinction emphasises the continuing nature of the duty imposed by s 34, sub-s 1(a), and far from weakening its primary meaning, rather strengthens it by contrast. The phrase 'free from patent defect' is, in my view, an additional duty and not a qualification of the duty that the lifting tackle should be of good construction, sound material, and adequate strength. The freedom from patent defect is itself an absolute obligation and such a defect is not one which is captured under the headings of good construction, sound material or adequate strength."[95]

**[21.44]** Conversely where a statute requires (or authorises) the performance of some obligation, it may not be sufficient for the persons under that obligation to show that they have complied with the express terms of the statutory obligation if they nevertheless fail to take reasonable care not to injure others when doing so as required by common law. Thus, in *Sargerson v McIlhagga*,[96] the defendants were held to have been in breach of their common law duty of care to a pedestrian who tripped over an iron drain gutter that the defendants had set in the footpath to carry away rain water from their premises, as required by statute.[97] The top of the gutter had become raised from the level of the pavement and this condition had existed for some time before the accident.

---

93. (contd) It is interesting to note Murnaghan J's view, expressed extra judicially, that proof of the breach of a statutory duty is no more than "*prima facie* evidence of negligence on the basis that a reasonable man would perform any duty laid by statute or statutory regulation": Society of Young Solicitors, Lecture No 36 'The Civil Liability Acts 1961 and 1964' (3 November 1968) at p 2. This approach is favoured in North America. As we have seen our courts have become increasingly disposed to invoke statutory functions as an element in a claim for common law negligence *distinct from a claim for breach of statutory duty.*

94. [1968] IR 277 (SC). See also *Hamilton v Niblock* [1956] NI 109 (CA); *Campbell v John A Best & Co Ltd* [1969] NI 123 at 133 (CA); *Kielthy v Ascon Ltd* [1970] IR 122 at 136 (SC). *Gallagher v Mogul of Ireland Ltd* [1975] IR 205 (SC) may be contrasted in its approach with certain English decisions which have been criticised for their somewhat surprising construction of statutory provisions relating to safety in mines and quarries as being *less* onerous than those enacted at around the turn of the century: see Friedman 'Security in Mines' (1969) 32 MLR 174; Hamson 'Note' [1962] Camb LJ 26. So also with factory legislation: see Howells 'Note: New Wave of interpretations of the Factories Acts' (1962) 25 MLR 98; Evans 'Note' (1966) 29 MLR 94; *cf* Reid 'Note' (1967) 30 MLR 455.

95. [1968] IR at 282-283. See also *Byrne v Jefferson Smurfit & Sons Ltd* [1962-1963] Ir Jur Rep 49 (SC).

96. [1963] NI 73.

97. Belfast Corporation Act 1845, s 142 (8 & 9 Vict c 142).

**[21.45]** In imposing liability, Black LJ stated:

> "It is well settled that persons exercising a statutory power or a statutory duty such as we find [here] are under a legal obligation at common law to take care not to injure other members of the community when exercising the power or duty, unless indeed there is something expressed in the statute or to be inferred from its wording exempting them from such an obligation ... No such exemption from this obligation to take care not to injure other members of the public could possibly be inferred from the Act ... for owners or occupiers exercising the duties imposed under [the] section [in question]".[98]

## Breach of Statutory Duty by Plaintiff not of itself a Bar in Tort Action

**[21.46]** It is not a defence in an action of tort merely to show that the plaintiff is in breach of the civil or criminal law.[99] Thus, a defendant in an action for tort will not escape liability merely by establishing that the plaintiff was in breach of a statutory duty. That much is clear. What is less clear are the circumstances in which the breach of statutory duty by the plaintiff may be taken into account in determining whether the defendant is liable.

**[21.47]** Breach of statutory duty by the plaintiff should be regarded as "negligence",[100] for the purposes of apportionment of liability under s 34 of the Civil Liability Act 1961.[101] The section comes into operation where the damage suffered by the plaintiff was caused "partly by the *negligence* or want of care of the plaintiff ..."[102] Therefore, whilst it is not a defence in an action for tort merely to show that the plaintiff was in breach of the law, that fact may, in conjunction with other facts, relieve the defendant of liability in some cases, and may be capable of constituting contributory negligence subject to the limitation that it will not do so "unless the damage of which [the plaintiff] complains is damage that the statute was designed to prevent."[103]

**[21.48]** Determining whether the damage suffered was "damage that the statute was designed to prevent" involves the court in analysing the underlying policy of the statute. Thus, for example, where the plaintiff driver breaches a statutory provision designed to raise revenue for the State rather than to encourage the safety of road users,[104] this breach will not defeat his claim. Conversely, where a plaintiff breaches a statutory provision specifically designed to prevent him from injuring himself, apportionment may be allowed. The regulations[105] requiring the use of seat belts and crash helmets would appear to be clear examples.

**[21.49]** It has always been accepted that as a general rule a person subjected to a statutory duty will not be relieved of liability by delegating the duty or its performance to another person.[106] Where the duty has been delegated to the plaintiff, however, this is not so

98. [1961] NI 73.
99. Civil Liability Act 1961, s 57(1) (No 41). *Cf Wicklow County Council v Hibernian Fire & General Insurance Co* [1932] IR 581 (SC).
100. *Cf* Civil Liability Act 1961, s 2(1).
101. (No 41).
102. Section 34(1) (emphasis added).
103. Section 34(2)(c) of the Civil Liability Act 1961 (No 41).
104. *Cf Vancouver v Burchill* [1932] 4 DLR 200; FLEMING, p 278.
105. Road Traffic (Construction Equipment and Use of Vehicles) (Amendment No 2) Regulations 1978 (SI 360/1978). See Pierse, *Road Traffic Law*, para 1.5.5.4 and Ch 20.
106. *Gray v Pullen* (1864) 5 B & s 970 122, ER 1091; *Whitby v Burt Boulton & Hayward Ltd* [1947] KB 918.

obviously a sound a policy, and Courts have taken the view that the plaintiff in such a case should not be entitled to recover where the only reason a breach of statute occurred was because he acted as he did. There was a tendency to articulate the rejection of the plaintiff's case in such circumstances in terms of the theory of *delegation* of the duty by the employer.[107] This approach was already losing support[108] when s 57(2) of the Civil Liability Act 1961 provided that:

> "It shall not be a defence in an action for breach of statutory duty merely to show that the defendant delegated the performing of the duty to the plaintiff."

**[21.50]** This does not, of course, mean that the defendant will be liable (in full or in part) in every case where he delegated the performance of the duty to the plaintiff. The principles of contributory negligence and causation will apply, and it may very often be the case that the plaintiff will be regarded as fully responsible for his injuries;[109] alternatively, the plaintiff may be held to have agreed to waive his legal rights in respect of the breach of statutory duty.[110]

**[21.51]** Moreover, where the statutory duty involves a standard of care which is more akin to negligence than to strict liability, it would appear that the circumstances of the delegation may be taken into account in determining whether a breach of statutory duty has occurred.

## Contributory Negligence

**[21.52]** The courts have consistently held that the term "contributory negligence" has "a different meaning"[111] in an action for breach of statutory duty from that in an action for common law negligence. In *Stewart v Killeen Paper Mills Ltd*,[112] Maguire CJ stated that there is:

> "an essential difference in the nature and quality of the acts of the plaintiff which would amount to contributory negligence in the one case and in the other. The distinction is very fine. It is nevertheless well established."

**[21.53]** The care required of a plaintiff in an action for breach of statutory duty is *less* extensive than in actions for common law negligence. The Court must take into account:

---

107. *Cf Beale v Gomme Ltd* (1949) 65 TLR 543; *Manwanng v Billington* [1952] 2 All ER 774; *Smith v Baveystock & Co Ltd* [1945] 1 All ER 531; *Gallagher v Dorman Long & Co Ltd* [1947] 2 All ER 38; *Barcock v Brighton Corp* [1949] 1 KB 339.

108. It has since "fallen into disrepute" in England: WINFIELD & JOLOWICZ, p 173.

109. *Cf* Explanatory Memorandum of the Bill as passed by both Houses of the Oireachtas p 27 (Lunasa 1961). See also s 43 of the 1961 Act discussed below, pp 393-395. See *Hogan v ESB* High Court, 17 December 1999 (O'Higgins J) - no liability for breach of statutory duty as breach "was caused by the act or default of the plaintiff himself" whose job it was to do the specific task which, if completed would have saved him from the risk of injury.

110. Civil Liability Act 1961, s 34(1)(b).

111. *Kennedy v East Cork Foods Ltd* [1973] IR 244 at 249 (SC). See also *Byrne v Jefferson Smurfit & Son Ltd* [1962-1963] Ir Jur Rep 49 (SC); *Higgins v South of Ireland Asphalt Co Ltd* (1961) 101 ILTR 168 (SC).

112. [1959] IR 436 at 441 (SC).

"all the circumstances of work in a factory and ... it is not for every risky thing which a workman in a factory may do in his familiarity with the machinery that a plaintiff ought to be held guilty of contributory negligence."[113]

**[21.54]** It has been stated that:

> "The policy of the statutory protection would be nullified if a workman were held debarred from recovering because he was guilty of some carelessness or inattention to his own safety, which though trivial in itself threw him into the danger consequent on the breach by his employer of the statutory duty. It is the breach of a statute, not the act of inadvertence or carelessness, which is then the dominant or effective cause of the injury."[114]

**[21.55]** The essential difference between breach of statutory duty and common law negligence therefore seems to be that, in respect of breach of statutory duty:

> "[a]n error of judgment, heedlessness or inadvertence on the part of a workman does not amount to contributory negligence."[115]

Whereas, in respect of common law negligence:

> "[a]n act of inadvertence, even although momentary if it is an act which a reasonably careful workman would not do, will in a common law action amount to contributory negligence."[116]

---

113. *Flower v Ebbw Vale Steel Iron & Coal Co* [1934] 2 KB 132 at 140 which "is accepted here as a correct statement of the law"; *Stewart v Killeen Paper Mills Ltd* [1959] IR 436 at 442 (SC). *Cf* at 450 (*per* Kingsmill Moore J). See also *Higgins v South of Ireland Asphalt Co Ltd* (1961) 101 ILTR 168 (SC); *Kennedy v East Cork Foods Ltd* [1973] IR 244 at 249.

114. *Caswell v Powell Duffryn Associated Collieries Ltd* [1940] AC 152 at 178-180. *Caswell* is a decision "which has been followed many times" in the Supreme Court: *Kennedy v East Cork Foods Ltd* [1973] IR 244 at 250. See also *Higgins v South of Ireland Asphalt Co Ltd* (1967) 101 ILTR 168; *Stewart v Killeen Paper Mills Ltd* [1959] IR 436 at 442; *Shearer v Harland & Wolff Ltd* [1947] NI 102 at 106 (KBD). Both *Flower* and *Caswell* are discussed in Anon 'Liability for Dangerous Machinery Defence of Contributory Negligence' (1949) 83 ILT & SJ 127 at 133.

115. *Stewart v Killeen Paper Mills Ltd* [1959] IR 436 at 442 (*per* Maguire CJ). A distinction has sometimes been drawn between inattentiveness (which is not considered contributory negligence) and some positive act of carelessness (which is). In *Kennedy v East Cork Foods Ltd* [1973] IR 244 (SC) the Supreme Court approved of a direction to the jury by the trial judge which was to the following effect:

> "When a factory owner is bound to have a machine fenced or guarded and the operative manages to get his hand caught in the machine, the operative is not guilty of contributory negligence merely because he was careless, or inattentive, or forgetful, or inadvertent. It must be shown that he did something rather more than that. He must enter into the realm of downright carelessness because the Factory (*sic*) Act was passed for the express purpose of saving factory workers from their own carelessness and their inattention. The plaintiff would not be guilty of contributory negligence unless you were satisfied that what he did was not simply inadvertence, normal forgetfulness or normal inattention but was in fact negligent and careless in a more positive and definite way."

The distinction was applied by Barron J in *Dunne v Honeywell Control Systems and Virginia Milk Products Ltd* [1991] ILRM 595 (HC), where the plaintiff's claim for breach of statutory duty was not reduced as his failure to take sufficient care for his own safety was attributable to inadvertence rather than any positive act. In *Kelly v Michael McNamara & Co* High Court, 5 June 1996 (Budd J), the distinction was again applied with the plaintiff employee's damages being reduced by 10% to take account of his "minimal" incapability in walking on the top of battens. See also *Brown v Robert Wilkes Ltd* DPIJ: Michaelmas Term 1990 p 159 (High Court, 11 December 1990, Lavan J); *Plant v Calco Steel* DPIJ: Michaelmas Term 1990, p 262 (High Court, 23 November 1990, Lardner J); *Lehane v An Comhairle Oilúna* DPIJ: Hilary and Easter Terms 1992, p 12 (HC).

**[21.56]** In *Stewart v Killeen Paper Mills Ltd*,[117] Kingsmill Moore J stated:

> "Where the injury could not have occurred but for the breach of statutory duty on the part of the master, a jury, in considering whether the conduct of the workman in all the circumstances amounted to contributory negligence, are entitled to take into account that the action was taken by the workman in furtherance of the interest of his master and that zeal may have dulled the edge of caution: that the action was one undertaken to meet a situation where if anything effective was to be done it had to be done rapidly and without deliberation: and that, if the act was one which was customarily performed, the master ought to have been aware of the practice and its danger and ought to have taken steps to forbid it. Where it can be shown that a regular practice exists unchecked it is difficult to convict of contributory negligence a workman who follows such a practice."

**[21.57]** In drawing a distinction between common law negligence and breach of statutory duty, so far as the contributory negligence of an employee is concerned, the courts have been engaging in the formulation of robust policy-making for which there is no express warrant in the Civil Liability Act 1961. Echoing the approach of some American courts,[118] our judges have taken the view that social policy requires that legislation prescribing safety standards in industry should not too easily be diluted by the doctrine of contributory negligence.

**[21.58]** Where a defendant is in breach of statutory duty but is not guilty of any fault,[119] it is clear, as has been stated, that he will nonetheless be liable for the damage caused. There is an important exception to this general rule. In cases where either contribution or reduction of damages under s 34(1) of the Civil Liability Act 1961 is in issue, the Court:

> may take account of the fact that the negligence[120] or wrong of one person consisted only in a breach of strict statutory or common-law duty without fault, and may accordingly hold that it is not just and equitable to cast any part of the damage upon such person.[121]

**[21.59]** In the Supreme Court decision of *O'Sullivan v Dwyer*,[122] Walsh J referred to this provision and stated:

---

115. (contd) In *Tess v Swiss Wire Ire Ltd* DPIJ: Hilary and Easter Terms 1994, p 158 (High Court, 2 February 1994, Flood J) the employee's contributory negligence was 50%. A similar reduction was made in *Roote v Irish Box Print and Packaging Ltd* DPIJ: Hilary and Easter Terms 1991, p 10 (High Court, 1 February 1991, Johnson J). In *McSweeney v McCarthy* Supreme Court, 28 January 2000, a 40% deduction was made. *Per* Murray J:

> "In this case ... the conduct of the plaintiff amounted to more than mere inadvertence referred to in the authorities. It consisted of a deliberate act on his part when he knew of the risk involved."

116. *Higgins v South of Ireland Asphalt Co Ltd* (1961) 101 ILTR 168 at 171, who conceded that "[t]here may of course be acts of momentary inadvertence which a jury will properly excuse as being acts which a reasonably careful workman should do." See also *Martin v Miller & Co* Supreme Court, 12 May 1972 at p 4.
117. [1959] IR 436 at 450 (SC).
118. See *Bexiga v Havir Manufacturing Co* (1972) 60 NJ 402, 290; A 2d 281.
119. As to the meaning of "fault" see above pp 362-364.
120. It will be recalled that Civil Liability Act 1961, s 2(1) defines "negligence" as including breach of statutory duty.
121. Civil Liability Act 1961, s 43.
122. [1971] IR 275 (SC).

> "The result ... appears to be somewhat anomalous. Under the terms of the Act of 1961 a person who has caused damage by the commission of a wrong which amounts to a breach of strict duty is liable in damages to the person injured thereby, even though the wrongdoer was not guilty of any fault,[123] provided that the person injured was not guilty of contributory negligence. The position appears to be that, once he has been found guilty of contributory negligence, the person injured will fail to recover anything if the defendant wrongdoer cannot be shown to have been at fault."[124]

**[21.60]** In *Daly v Avonmore Creameries Ltd*,[125] McCarthy J expressed "difficulty in understanding this interpretation"; in his view, s 43 permitted, but did not compel, absolution from fault in such a case.

**[21.61]** This difference of opinion is one of considerable practical importance. The underlying policy issue is whether strict liability safety standards should *automatically* be inoperative where the employer is not negligent and the employee is careless. The trend of the law is against an automatic disentitlement. Neither strict liability for injury caused by dogs nor strict liability under the EEC Products Liability Directive involves such a fate for a careless plaintiff. It is of course true that the Civil Liability Act 1961 seeks to assess the extent of reduction of damages for contributory negligence by comparing the *respective degrees of fault* of the plaintiff and the defendant. If the defendant is guilty of no fault then, it seems, the scales should fall completely to the side of the contributory negligent plaintiff. As against this, judges and juries in many common law jurisdictions have experienced no difficulty in simply reducing damages in such a case. The plaintiff's fault, even though it cannot be compared with any fault of the defendant, can be analysed and assessed in terms of the seriousness of its degree of deviation from how a reasonable person would have behaved. In the employment context, there may seem good reason to distinguish between an employee who takes a "short cut" on safety procedures and one who seeks to operate a dangerous machine when blind drunk. To deny both a remedy merely because both are guilty of contributory negligence is arguably too crude an approach.[126]

---

123. Walsh J considered (at 285) that "where a defendant's causative contribution to damage has been his breach of ... strict [statutory] duty, there must also be negligence on his part before any apportionment of the fault can be attributed to him."

124. Walsh J added (at 286) that, in a case of breach of strict duty only, "a plaintiff could scarcely be found guilty of contributory negligence unless he had knowledge of the breach of strict duty found against the defendant."

125. [1984] IR 131 at 148 (SC).

126. Walsh J's approach in *O'Sullivan v Dwyer* is not easy to reconcile completely with the approach he adopted in *Gallagher v Mogul of Ireland Ltd* [1975] IR 204 (SC), where he stated that:

    > "[t]he Civil Liability Act 1961, permits the appointment of fault between the parties in a case where there was an absolute duty on one side and a less than absolute duty on the other ...; it is the latter's failure of duty to himself to take care for his own safety, that may carry a degree of moral culpability."

    The host of decisions in which an employee's contributory negligence was held to reduce his or her damages in actions for breach of absolute statutory duty rather than completely defeat his or her claim, are further *indicia* of lack of judicial acceptance for the approach taken in *O'Sullivan v Dwyer*.

## III. Interference with Statutory Rights

**[21.62]** We now must consider the rare cases in which a statute, instead of imposing a duty, confers a right. One such instance is the Guardianship of Infants Act 1964, which provides that, if married to each other[127] the mother and father of an "infant" (a child who has not reached the age of majority) are to be joint guardians of the infant's person and estate, and are to be entitled to apply to the Court for its direction on any question affecting the welfare of the infant.

**[21.63]** In *Cosgrove v Ireland*,[128] the plaintiff, an Irish national and resident, was married to a Netherlands national. They lived for some years in Ireland, but the marriage relationship seriously deteriorated. When the wife indicated that she wanted to take the children on holidays to the Netherlands, the plaintiff refused to consent to the children's obtaining passports and contacted the Department of Foreign Affairs making his objection plain. Nonetheless passports were issued, with the result that the wife took the children to the Netherlands, never to return.

**[21.64]** In an action brought by the plaintiff against the Minister for Foreign Affairs, for interference with his constitutional and statutory rights, McWilliam J held that the plaintiff's rights as joint guardian under the 1964 Act had been infringed. On the Judge's view of the Act, neither parent might deprive the other of his or her children without an order of the Court. The Department had been wrong to issue the passports without an application to the Courts for such an order; moreover, the Department was aware that the plaintiff had failed to sign forms requiring his signature and that he had actually telephoned the Department his objection. Since he held in the plaintiff's favour in his statutory claim, McWilliam J did not address his claim based on the violation of the constitutional rights.

**[21.65]** McWilliam J awarded the plaintiff damages for the expense to which he had been put as a result of the issue of the passports, as well as damages for mental distress. The total amount thus awarded was, however, small - £1,250 - since the judge was of the opinion that, in view of the history of the spouses' relationship, and in particular the plaintiff's behaviour, it was "quite inconceivable that he would have been given custody of the children when the parties separated".[129]

**[21.66]** McWilliam J was content to rely primarily on Holt CJ's bold assertion in *Ashby v White*[130] that if the plaintiff has a right "he must of necessity have the means to vindicate it and a remedy if he is injured in the enjoyment or exercise of it". He also derived inspiration from the holding in *Meskell v CIE*[131] that infringement of a constitutional right

---

127. The Act has been amended by the Status of Children Act 1987, s 12 which inserts a new s 6A into the Guardianship of Infants Act 1964, providing that, where the mother and father have not married each other the court may appoint the father of the child to be a guardian. This is a discretionary power subject to constitutional considerations and s 6 of the 1964 Act; see further Byrne & Binchy *Annual Review of Irish Law 1987*, pp 179-182 and Woulfe 'Annotation' [1987] ICLSA, General Note to this section of the Act.

128. [1982] ILRM 48 (HC).

129. [1982] ILRM 48 at 55.

130. (1703) 2 Ld Raym 938 at 953. Holt CJ was dissenting but the House of Lords upheld his judgment.

131. [1973] IR 121.

entitled the victim to sue for damages. These are scarcely clear authorities for the proposition that every infringement of a statutory right similarly entitles the victim to sue for damages.

**[21.67]** At common law, in spite of Holt CJ's statement, it is far from the case that the principle, *ubi jus, ibi remedium,* prevails. On the contrary, the position historically was that the forms of action largely determined the scope of particular remedies; so strong was this limitation that the principle might more appropriately have been *ubi remedium, ibi jus.* There was an innominate class of actions for disturbances of franchise rights attaching to markets[132] or ferries, and offices of profit, for example.[133] The development of this class "reached its furthest point"[134] in *Ashby v White*, which concerned the disturbance of the right to vote. That case was decided in 1703. Although it concerned a statutory entitlement, it did not result in any fundamental restatement of the law relating to liability for interference with statutory or common law rights.

**[21.68]** McWilliam J did not concern himself with much doctrinal analysis of the right of action he had identified. It is necessary, therefore, to raise some questions as to its possible scope.

**[21.69]** The first of these questions relate to *the type of conduct* which amounts to a breach of statutory entitlements. The possible range of conduct extends from wilful, intentional conduct, through negligence, to acting with complete propriety and, perhaps, with no way of knowing the possible impact of one's conduct on the plaintiff's statutory right. In *Cosgrove,* the defendant Department had been "put on notice that the plaintiff was exercising his rights as joint guardian under the Guardianship of Infants Act".[135] It may be presumed that liability would also attach in relation to a deliberate action (such as the issuing of a passport) in circumstances where a defendant ought to have been aware of the probable consequences of interference with the plaintiff's statutory rights. But what is a good deal less clear is whether action lacking such deliberation would involve liability, even though it was reasonably foreseeable that the occurrence of such undeliberate and unintended action would probably result in interference with a person's statutory rights. Does McWilliam J's decision mean, for example, that a person whose negligent driving permanently injures a child could be sued for wrongful interference with that child's parents' statutory guardianship rights?[136]

**[21.70]** The uncertainty as regards this issue may be contrasted with the position in relation to breach of statutory *duties.* Where a breach of statutory duty is involved, the language of the statutory provision will define the range of conduct falling within the scope of that duty. This language will make clear, for example, whether liability is to be strict, to be limited to cases involving negligence, or to involve some intermediate standard.[137] Where statutory *rights* are concerned, however, the statutory provision will only very rarely refer to the question of the range of conduct by others against which the

132. *Cf McCutcheon v Carney* [1938] Ir Jur Rep (HC).
133. See Baker, *An Introduction to English Legal History* (2nd ed, 1979), p 359.
134. Baker, *An Introduction to English Legal History* (2nd ed, 1979), p 359.
135. [1982] ILRM at 52.
136. *Cf Hosford v John Murphy & Sons* [1988] ILRM 300 (HC).
137. *Cf Hosford v John Murphy & Sons* [1988] ILRM 300 at 388-390.

particular holder of a statutory right is entitled to be protected. Thus, the courts will have to do their best in each case in articulating what this range of conduct is to be. Apart from cases of intentional interference, the Courts will largely have to work on a common sense basis, seeking to keep the range of conduct within manageable bounds.

**[21.71]** On one aspect of the outer ranges of such conduct, *Cosgrove* affords us some guidance. McWilliam J was:

> "not satisfied that there is any duty imposed on the State or the Department by the Constitution or otherwise to take any particular steps to protect rights which they have no reason to suppose are being infringed".[138]

Whether the State or the Department would be liable for infringement of rights, where they culpably failed to learn of the risk of their being infringed, is not certain, but seems implicit in McWilliam J's statement.

**[21.72]** This brings us to consideration of the nature of the right that is being infringed. In *Cosgrove* the plaintiff's loss involved a total rupture of his relationship with his children, which completely damaged his statutory rights. Guardianship embraces the totality of parental functions, including such matters as care and control of the child, decisions as to his or her education, as well as moral and religious formation; it also extends to the ordinary, day-to-day communication between parent and child. The question arises as to whether *all* interferences with the entitlement to guardianship warrant compensation, on the *Cosgrove* principle, or whether it is only in cases of total destruction of the statutory entitlement that the action should be upheld. Subject to the *de minimis* principle, it is difficult to see why an arbitrary threshold of total destruction should apply.[139]

**[21.73]** The next question raises an important issue of principle: if the Department of Foreign Affairs may be liable for interference with the statutory right of guardianship, may an individual - specifically, the other parent - also be liable? Courts in other common law jurisdictions are divided on the question whether tort law should have any place in inter-parental disputes. Some have taken the view that it exacerbates disharmony and may be damaging to the child's interests; others consider that the flagrant rupturing of the parent-child relationship is sufficiently serious to warrant the support of tort law.[140]

**[21.74]** Finally, the question of defences must be considered briefly. On principle, it would seem that justice requires that a plaintiff's damages should be capable of being reduced in cases of contributory negligence. Thus, for example, if one parent's misbehaviour had encouraged the other to leave the home, this could be relevant in assessing damages for interference with the statutory right of guardianship. Again, on principle there seems no reason why the voluntary waiver of the right to sue for interference with a statutory right should not afford a defence.

---

138. [1982] ILRM at 52. *Cf Minister for Foreign Affairs* High Court, 19 August 1988, affd by Supreme Court, 4 May 1989 (Blayney J) considered in Ch 1 and by Byrne & Binchy *Annual Review of Irish Law 1988*, Constitutional Law and Torts Chapters (1989) - where the unsuccessful claim was based on infringement of constitutional rather than statutory rights.

139. *Cf* the requirement in actions for damages for loss of *consortium* that there be a total loss of *consortium* even for a limited period or periods: *Spaight v Dundon* [1961] IR 201 (SC) as modified in *O'Haran v Divine* (1964) 100 ILTR 53 (SC) and Ch 33 below.

140. See Allen 'Note: Interference with Visitation As an Independent Tort' (1986) 24 Fam L 481.

# Chapter 22

# Trespass to the Person


I. Intoduction ........ 615
II. Trespass Against the Person ........ 617
III. Defences to Trespass to the Person ........ 633


## I. INTODUCTION

### Trespass and Negligence[1]

**[22.01]** The essence of trespass is that wrongful conduct should cause a direct injury to the plaintiff. The Courts in earlier times were primarily concerned with the directness of the injury to the plaintiff and were not interested in investigating questions of intention or negligence on the part of the defendant. With the development of the tort of negligence in the nineteenth century, however, they were obliged to look closer at the problem of unintended trespass. The view arrived at (although with questionable historical support[2]) was that, to amount to trespass, the defendant's conduct had to be either intentional or negligent: other unintended injuries directly caused could not be regarded as trespass.[3]

**[22.02]** This shift in favour of the defendant was, however, modified somewhat by the establishment of the rule that, once the plaintiff proved direct injury, the onus shifted to the defendant to show that he had acted neither intentionally nor negligently.[4] (Trespasses on or near the highway were regarded as exceptional: here intention or negligence had to be proved by the plaintiff.)

**[22.03]** In England, the Court of Appeal in *Wilson v Pringle*[5] in 1986 considered that the action for trespass for battery should rest on "deliberate" contact, in contrast to negligence, where the contact "is normally though by no means always unintended". The same approach has for long been followed in the United States[6] and New Zealand[7] but other

1. Bates 'Accidents, Trespass and Burden of Proff: A Comparative Study' (1976) 11 Ir Jur (ns) 88; Blay 'Onus of Proof of Consent in an Action for Trespass to the Person' (1987) 61 Austr LJ 25; Fridman Trespass or Negligence (1971) 9 Alta LR 250; Goodhart & Winfield 'Trespass and Negligence' (1933) 49 LQR 358; Hertz 'A Teacup Tempest: Onus to Prove Consent in Trespass to the Person' (1979) 17 Alta LR 318; Millner 'The Retreat of Trespass' 18 CLP 20; Picard 'Onus of Proving Consent in Trespass to the Person: On Whom Does It Rest?' p 322; Trindade 'Some Curiosities of Negligent Trespass' (1971) 20 ICLQ 706.
2. *Cf* POLLOCK, pp 128-134 (Editor's Excursus B).
3. *Cf Holmes v Maher* (1875) LR 10 Exch 261; *Stanley v Powell* [1891] 1 QB 86; *National Coal Board v Evans (JE) & Co (Cardiff) Ltd* [1951] 2 KB 861.
4. *Cf O'Conghaile v Wallace* [1938] IR 526 at 569 (SC) (semble).
5. [1986] 2 All ER 440 (CA). See also the earlier case, *Fowler v Lanning* [1959] 1 QB 426, approved, obiter, in *Letang v Cooper* [1965] 1 QB 232.
6. *Cf* PROSSER & KEETON, pp 30-31; Gregory 'Trespass to Negligence to Absolute Liability' (1951) 37 Va LR 359; Roberts 'Negligence: Blackstone to Shaw to?' (1965) 50 Cor LQ 191.
7. *Beals v Hayward* [1960] NZLR 131.

countries[8] have been slow to adopt it. In this country, this step has not yet been taken, so it remains the case that on proof of direct injury, the onus shifts to the defendant to show that he acted neither intentionally nor negligently.

**[22.04]** In practice, most plaintiffs will sue for negligence rather than trespass, even though the injury may have been directly caused, as proof that the injury was directly caused does not arise in negligence, but the advantages of suing in trespass should not be discounted. Apart from the clear benefit of shifting the onus onto the defendant to show that he acted neither intentionally or negligently,[9] there may be other advantages in trespass regarding the question of remoteness (directness rather than foreseeability) and proof of damage (since trespass is actionable *per se*).

## Voluntariness, Intention and Motive

**[22.05]** For a defendant to be liable in trespass his action must be voluntary, in the sense that the action must be under conscious control. Thus, "if a man by force takes my hand and strikes you"[10] I am not guilty of a trespass.

**[22.06]** Clearly, if I do an act with a desire of bringing about a physical result which constitutes trespass I will (in the absence of excusing circumstances[11]) be liable for it. Where I do not desire to bring about the physical result, but I believe that the result is "substantially certain",[12] it seems that I will still be regarded as having acted intentionally. If I do not have this belief, I should not be held to have acted intentionally (although of course I may be found to have acted negligently) even in cases where the result was reasonably foreseeable.

**[22.07]** As the conceptual development of the law on these questions is somewhat primitive (in contrast to criminal law, where much judicial and academic analysis has been made of intention and related concepts), it can not be said with confidence when the notion

---

8. For Canada, see Hertz 'A Teacup Tempest: Onus to Prove Consent in Trespass to the Person' (1979) 17 Alta LR 318, Picard 'Onus of Proving Consent in Trespass to the Person: On Whom Does It Rest?' p 322; *Cook v Lewis* [1951] SCR 830. In Australia, the onus still remains on the defendant to show that he was guilty of neither an intentional nor negligent contact: *McHale v Watson* (1964) 111 CLR 384 (HC, Austr); *Venning v Chin* (1974) 10 SASR 299 (SC (In Banco)). In *Hackshaw v Shaw* (1984) 155 CLR 614 at 619 (HC Austr), however, Gibbs CJ expressed a tentative preliminary preference, *obiter*, for the approach favoured in *Fowler v Lanning* [1959] 1 QB 426 and *Letang v Cooper* [1965] 1 QB 232. He noted that, "perhaps unfortunately", the court had not been called on to resolve this difference of opinion. See Blay 'Onus of Proof of Consent in an Action for Trespass to the Person' (1987) 61 Austr LJ 25; TRINDADE & CANE, pp 328-339.

9. This could be of particular importance where the defendant is a child of tender years.

10. *Weaver v Ward* (1616) Hob 134 at 134, 80 ER 284. *Cf Gibbons v Pepper* (1695) 1 Ld Raym 38 at 38-39, 91 ER 922.

11. Eg, necessity, self-defence.

12. STREET, p 26. This analysis has been followed in the United States: PROSSER & KEETON, p 35; *Garratt v Dailey* (1955) 46 Wash 2d 197, 279 p 2d 109, second appeal, (1956) 49 Wash 2d 499, 304 P 2d 681. Tort law, in relation to intention, requires proof of a subjective element, whether of desire to bring about the result or of a belief that the result is substantially certain. In criminal law, s 4(2) of the Criminal Justice Act 1964 introduces a rebuttable presumption, in murder prosecutions only, that the accused person is to be presumed to have intended the natural and probable consequences of his conduct.

of "substantial certainty" gives way to mere "foreseeability". The whole area has yet to be articulated clearly by our courts. To attempt, therefore, in these circumstances to discuss the question of "transferred intent" might be regarded as unduly optimistic. At criminal law, if I throw a stone or a bomb at A intending to injure him and it hits B, I will be liable for the injury to B.[13] Does the same rule apply in tort? Technically, the question resolves itself to whether "intention" should be interpreted narrowly as meaning "intention to injure the plaintiff" or more broadly as meaning "intention to injure anyone".[14] Since the decided cases do not address this question, it may perhaps be desirable to look to the policy dimensions of the problem.

**[22.08]** The notion of "transferred intent" can be justified in criminal law, which is "understandably preoccupied with moral guilt"[15] and with the stigmatisation of wrongful conduct as criminal in the sense that it is a wrong against society in general. The position in tort is somewhat different. Tort law does not involve the same social pursuit against wrongdoing. If I am guilty of the grossest negligence towards A and unforeseeable injure to B, I am not liable to B in negligence.[16] Why, therefore, should I be liable to him in trespass? It can, of course, be said that intentional conduct is morally worse than (or at all events of a different order to) negligent conduct, but it is easy to conceive of cases where the intentional wrongdoing is trivial - mischievously pulling away a chair from under a person as he is about to sit down, for example[17] - in contrast to negligent conduct - as where one drives when almost insensible from drink.

**[22.09]** The question is an open one,[18] and it is submitted, with some hesitation, that the better view is that the doctrine of "transferred intent" should not be regarded as part of the law of tort. This means that in some cases the victim of the injury may not be able to have redress under any heading of tort,[19] but this should not in itself be a reason for doubting the desirability of this approach. For why should my ineffective malevolence towards one person be a reason for making me liable in trespass to a person to whom I am neither guilty of intentional nor negligent[20] wrongdoing?

## II. Trespass Against the Person

> "Security for the person is among the first conditions of civilized life. The law, therefore, protects us, not only against actual hurt and violence, but against every kind of bodily

13. *R v Latimer* (1886) 17 QBD. 359, *R v Pemblition* (1874) LR 2 CCR 119; *R v Faulkner* (1877) 13 Cox 550 (Ir Court for Cr Cas Res); *People v Hayes* Court of Criminal Appeal, 9 June 1986: *cf* the LRC's *Report on Malicious Damage*, para 26 (1988 LRC 26). See also the Criminal Justice Act 1964, s 4(1).
14. *Cf* STREET, pp 31-32; *Livingstone v Ministry of Defence*, [1984] NI 356 (CA).
15. PROSSER & KEETON, pp 37-38.
16. See PROSSER & KEETON, Ch 3.
17. *Cf Garratt v Dailey* (1955) 46 Wash 2d 197, 279 p 2d 109.
18. The doctrine of transferred intent is part of American law: Prosser, 'Transferred Intent' (1967) 45 Tex LR 650. Winfield accepted that it was also part of English law: (1935) 83 U Pa LR 416, n 15, but the modern English commentators are not so strongly of this view: *cf* STREET, p 31 - "point is undecided".
19. Negligence would not normally be available where the injury to the third party was unforeseeable; it is possible to envisage certain other torts - of strict liability - being relevant.
20. *Cf Palsgraf v Long Island Railroad Co* (1928) 162 NE 99 (NY CA).

interference and restraint not justified or excused by allowed cause, and against the present (immediate) apprehension of any of these things."[21]

**[22.10]** The law has developed along specific avenues, each of which will be explored in turn. Our analysis will involve considering the torts of battery, assault, intentional or reckless infliction of emotional suffering and false imprisonment. Whether these torts will continue to be the principal avenues of recovery for such types of interference remains to be seen. As several commentators have noted, there is a real possibility that they will be supplemented by a jurisprudence of constitutional infringements. Although the Supreme Court has recently evinced reluctance to rewrite the ingredients of torts in the light of constitutional guarantees, this does not prevent the Court from supplementing particular torts with a parallel remedy for infringement of a constitutional right. Thus, for example, although traditionally the tort of assault does not allow compensation for threats of non-imminent violence, there surely is a remedy for this type of misconduct under the rubric of infringement of the constitutional rights to health and bodily integrity. Having recorded this proviso, let us examine the various torts in turn.

## Battery

### *(a) Nature of the tort*

**[22.11]** The direct application of physical contact upon the person of another without his or her consent, express or implied, may constitute a battery. An attack is an obvious example,[22] but the tort may be committed by spitting in a person's face,[23] overturning a chair on which he or she is sitting,[24] or striking a horse so that it throws the rider to the ground.[25] In *Humphries v Connor*,[26] the Court of Queen's Bench was agreed that the removal by a policeman of an orange lily from the clothes of a woman could constitute a battery.

**[22.12]** It seems that neither force nor physical injury[27] is an ingredient of the tort. The tort of battery protects the person against physical contact to which he or she does not expressly or impliedly consent. Thus, whilst I will not commit a tort if I kiss my child when he or she is asleep, I will be guilty of battery if I lean forward in a railway carriage

---

21. *Dullaghan v Hillen* [1957] Ir Jur Rep 10 at 13 (CC). See generally Trindade 'Intentional Torts: Some Thoughts on Assault and Battery' (1982) 2 Oxford J of Legal Studies 211.

22. See, eg *Dullaghan v Hillen* [1957] Ir Jur Rep 10; *Donohue v Coyle* [1953-54] Ir Jur Rep 30 (CC); *Howard v Boner* (1943) 78 ILTR 3 (CC); *McGee v Cunanne* (1932) 66 ILTR 147 (CC); *McCann v Mannion* (1932) 66 ILTR 161 (CC); *Grealy v Casey* (1901) 1 NIJR 121 (CA). In criminal law, the offence of assault embraces conduct that in civil law would be characterised as either a battery or an assault, eg the Non-Fatal Offences Against the Person Act 1997, s 2. See further Bacik 'Striking a Blow for Reform? A Note on the Non-Fatal Offences Against the Person Act 1997 and Its Effect on the Law of Assault' (1997) 7 Ir Crim LJ 48.

23. *R v Cotesworth* (1704) 6 Mod 172, 87 ER 928.

24. *Hooper v Reeve* (1817) 7 Taunt 698 at 699, 129 ER 278.

25. *Dodwell v Burford* (1670) 1 Mod 24, 86 ER 703.

26. (1864) 17 Ir CLR 1 (QB). See also *Corcoran v W & R Jacob & Co* [1945] IR 446 (SC) - action for 'assault', but probably battery envisaged.

27. *Cf McDonald v Galvin* High Court, 23 February 1976 (McWilliam J). See also *Power v Cook* (1869) IR 4 CL 247 (Comm. Pleas) - only a push; *White v Store Security Ltd* Circuit Court, 21 February 1985 (Judge Martin) - plaintiff shopper suffered a 'technical assault' when grabbed by security man.

and kiss a stranger who is sleeping in the seat opposite me.[28] Although courts generally have preferred to base the concept of informed consent to medical treatment on negligence principles,[29] it is at least arguable that the tort of battery also protects persons against such contacts to which they have not fully consented.[30]

**[22.13]** It seems plain from the Supreme Court decision of *Re a Ward of Court*[31] that an autonomous person has the legal right to refuse physical contact, however benevolent the motives of the other party and however necessary that contact may be for the health or even life of the person who refuses it.

**[22.14]** Mere passive obstruction does not constitute a battery.[32] The line between passive obstruction and the active application of force may be difficult to draw in some cases and may be in need of some further refinement. If I see my enemy being dragged towards me (by a car or a wave, for example) and I stand my ground so that we come into contact, surely I should be regarded as having been guilty of battery? True, I would not be guilty in negligence for having failed to go to his aid,[33] but where my failure results (and is intended by me so to result) in injury to him, when he has in no way willingly brought the injury upon himself, I should, it is submitted, be liable for battery.

***(b) The contact must have directly resulted from defendant's act***

**[22.15]** In order to constitute a battery, the contact must have directly resulted from the defendant's act.[34] This is because battery is a species of trespass, which stresses the need for direct relationship between the defendant's act and the injury suffered. Where the defendant's conduct results in indirect injury, the plaintiff may not be bereft of any recompense: a separate action on the case may be available to him,[35] although the scope of such action has not yet been clearly articulated by the courts.

---

28. *Cf* STREET (8th ed, 1988), p 24, fn 7: "Is kissing a sleeping lady in the presence of her friends a battery? It is suggested that it is." *Cf* (10th ed, 1999), p 34, fn 8: "Today presumably, a lady reversing the roles is equally liable?" Compare the problem of 'unconscious' confinement, discussed para **[22.45]** below, in respect of the tort of false imprisonment.

29. *Cf* para **[14.76]** above.

30. *Cf Walsh v Family Planning Services Ltd* [1992] 1 IR 496 (SC revg HC). In the United States, battery has been restricted to harmful or offensive contact: see PROSSER & KEETON, pp 39, 41-42. Since offensiveness is a broad concept, the scope of the tort is not significantly narrower than in Irish law, but some rather complex problems can arise as regards the requisite intent of the defendant.

31. [1995] 2 ILRM 401 (SC). *Cf* Byrne & Binchy, *Annual Review of Irish Law 1995*. See also *Re T (Adult: Refusal of Treatment)* [1993] Fam 95; *F v West Berkshire Health Authority* [1990] 2 AC 1 (HL); *Airedale NHS Trust v Bland* [1993] AC 789 (HL); *St George's Healthcare NHS Trust v S* [1999] Fam 26 (CA); Kennedy & Grubb *Medical Law* (2000), Ch 16.

32. *Innes v Wylie* 1 C & K 257, at 263, 174 ER 800 at 803. But see *Bruce v Dyer* (1966) 58 DLR (2d) 211 at 216-217 (Ont HC), (affd (1970) 8 DLR (3d) 592n (CA)); *Fagan v Metropolitan Commissioner* [1969] 1 QB 439, and PROSSER & KEETON, p 34, fn 6.

33. *Cf* PROSSER & KEETON, ch 8.

34. *Cf Leame v Bray* (1803) 3 East 593, at 603; *Scott v Shephard* (1773) 2 Wm B 892 at 899, 96 ER 525 at 528. See also *M'Loughlin v Doey* (1893) 32 LR Ir 518 at 529 (Ex Div).

35. *Cf* STREET, p 33.

### *(c) Disposition of the defendant*

**[22.16]** Whilst "the least touching of another in anger is a battery",[36] a hostile intention is not a necessary ingredient in the tort: "excessive zeal"[37] in the discharge of one's obligations may suffice. We must now consider a question which has led courts to differing conceptual solutions, though the practical results are less significant than might at first appear. There must surely be some contacts which do not need express approval.

**[22.17]** But how is this range of permissible contacts to be rationalised? One approach is that of implied consent. This is the easiest, but conceptually unconvincing, solution, since it offers a label to a conclusion reached by the court on another, possibly intuitive, basis, rather than constituting a truly enlightening test. Another approach, favoured in England in *Wilson v Pringle*,[38] is to exempt from liability all contacts that are not "proved to be ... hostile ..." Hostility is here given an artificial meaning. Far from being equated with ill-will or malevolence, it appears to extend to "unlawful" conduct in the sense that the conduct may interfere with one or more person's legal rights. This approach would mean that a friendly push would be called "hostile" when it went beyond what the court considered permissible. The "hostility" solution suffers from the same weakness as that of implied consent, compounded only by the artificiality of the meaning ascribed to the term. The third approach, favoured in the United States,[39] restricts liability for battery to harmful or offensive contact. Contact is offensive "if it offends a reasonable sense of personal dignity".[40] It must be such as would offend the ordinary person, and must therefore be unwarranted by the social usages prevalent at the time and place at which it is inflicted.[41]

**[22.18]** Whichever of these approaches is to be adopted by our courts, it is clear that a certain leeway should be given to persons in the ordinary day-to-day contacts of contemporary life: thus, no liability will normally attach for bumping into other pedestrians on a crowed footpath[42] or touching them during an amicable conversation,[43] or when playing a sport.[44]

---

36. *Cole v Turner* (1704) 6 Mod 149 at 149, 87 ER 907 at 907.
37. *Corcoran v W & R Jacob & Co* [1945] IR 446 at 454 (SC).
38. [1987] QB 237 (CA).
39. *Restatement of the Law of Torts, Second*, ss 13, 18.
40. *Restatement of the Law of Torts, Second*, s 19.
41. *Restatement of the Law of Torts, Second*. See PROSSER & KEETON, p 42. In *Collins v Wilcock* [1984] 3 All ER 374 at 378 (QB), Goff LJ (as he then was) sought to rationalise the lawfulness of everyday physical contacts, such as jostling and handshakes, in terms of a general exception embracing all physical contact which is generally acceptable in the ordinary conduct of everyday life. This criterion was eclipsed by the (dubious) "hostility" test put forward in *Wilson v Pringle*. In *F v West Berkshire Health Authority* [1990] 2 AC 1 (HL), however, Lord Goff (as he had since become) reaffirmed his earlier opinion.
42. *Cole v Turner* (1704) 6 Mod 149 at 149, 87 ER 907 at 907, respectively.
43. *Tubervell v Savage* (1660) 1 Mod Rep 3 at 3, 86 ER 684 at 684. *Williams and Jones et al*, (1736) Cast Hard 298 at 301, 95 ER 193 at 196.
44. *Hegarty v Shine* (1878) 4 LR Ir 288 at 291 (CA).

**[22.19]** Before 1951, the adjudication in criminal proceedings of a complaint for common assault or battery was a bar to civil proceedings.[45] Section 11(4) of the Criminal Justice Act 1951[46] removed this bar. It provided as follows:

> "The adjudication of a complaint as to common assault or battery shall not affect any civil remedy that the complainant may have against the defendant in respect of the subject matter of the complaint."

## Assault[47]

**[22.20]** An assault consists of an act that places another person in reasonable apprehension of an immediate battery being committed upon him.[48] Accordingly, if I brandish a stick or point a gun in such a manner that I induce a reasonable apprehension in another of imminent physical contact, I commit the tort of assault. Mere passive obstruction, however does not constitute an assault,[49] although taking active steps to block or obstruct another may do so.[50]

**[22.21]** Where a person has no apprehension of a battery before it takes place - as where he is asleep or where he is stabbed in the back - he may not sue for assault, for the tort consists of "a touching of the mind, not the body".[51] Moreover, apprehension, not fear, is the test.

**[22.22]** The apprehension must be of an immediate battery, a limitation that the courts have interpreted narrowly.[52]

---

45. Offences Against the Person Act 1861, s 42 (24 & 25 Vict, c 100). See North 'Civil and Criminal Proceedings for Assault' (1966) 29 MLR 16; Anon 'The Effect of a Conviction for Assault' (1877) 11 ILT & Sol J 201; *Murray v Fitzpatrick* (1914) 48 ILT & Sol J 305; *Donnelly v Ingram* (1877) 31 ILTR 139 (CC); *Magee v Storey* [1929] NI 134 (CA).
46. Repealed by the Non-Fatal Offences Against the Person Act 1997, s 31 in the light of the replacement of an array of common law offences by a new statutory code. The possibility of an action for battery against a violent criminal should not be discounted. See *W v Meah* [1986] 1 All ER 935. *Cf X v Walsh* DPIJ: Hilary and Easter 1998, p 74 (HC) - exemplary damages awarded for "vicious and degrading assaults" by person exercising authority over him. For consideration of this theme, see Schutz 'The Violated: A Proposal to Compensate Victims of Violent Crime' (1965) 10 St Louis ULJ 238; Carrington 'Victims' Rights Litigation: A Wave of the Future?' (1977) 11 U Richmond LR 447; Lowder 'Comment: The Civil Action for Rape: A Viable Alternative for the Rape Victim?' [1978] S Illinois ULJ 399. For a thorough analysis of the competing issues in attempting to find a just harmony between the civil and criminal law, see Stapleton 'Civil Prosecutions - Part 1: Double Jeopardy and Abuse of Process' (1999) 7 Torts LJ 244; Stapleton 'Civil Prosecutions - Part 2: Civil Claims for Killing or Rape' (2000) 8 Torts LJ 15.
47. See generally Handford 'Tort Liability for Threatening or Insulting Words' (1976) 54 Can BR 563, Crickson 'What Constitutes an Assault?' 16 Clev Marshall LR 14 (1967).
48. *Cf Dullaghan v Hillen* [1957] Ir Jur Rep 10 at 12 (CC); *Read v Coker* (1853) 73 CB 850 at 860, 138 ER 1437 at 1441.
49. *Innes v Wylie* (1844) 1 C & K 257, 174 ER 800.
50. *Bruce v Dyer* [1970] 1 OR 482 (CA).
51. *Kline v Kline* (1902) 64 NE 9, at 10 (Ind SC).
52. *Cf Stephens v Myers* (1830) 4 C & P 349, 172 ER 735; *Mortin v Shoppee* (1828) 3 C & P 373, 172 ER 462. *Cf Osborn v Veitch* (1858) 1 F & F 317, 175 ER 744 at 318 and 744, respectively:

> "Pointing a loaded gun at a person is in law an assault. It is immaterial that it is at half-cock; cocking it is an instantaneous act, and there is a 'present ability' to execute the threat".

Where the apprehension is mistaken, but reasonably held - as where an empty gun is pointed at the plaintiff - the tort is still committed.[53]

**[22.23]** Whether words of themselves may constitute an assault has given rise to some discussion. In *Dullaghan v Hillen*,[54] where a customs officer responded to "a filthy and insulting remark" by breaking the nose of its author, the Court held that the remark could not be regarded as an assault. Fawsitt J noted that the defendant had failed to recollect:

> "the commonplace but trite couplet which runs: 'Sticks and stones may break your bones but words will never hurt you', and in which there is a definition of the law of assault, namely that mere words, no matter how harsh, lying, insulting and provocative they may be, can never amount in law to assault."[55]

**[22.24]** Whilst the statement is consistent with older authority[56] and is clearly correct so far as it relates to provocative and insulting words, it might be misleading in suggesting[57] that words can never constitute an assault: when spoken in particular contexts suggesting the imminent use of force, words may well do so.[58] Since words are always spoken in some context rather than in a void, the real question is whether the words in the particular context in which they were spoken were sufficient to induce a reasonable apprehension of physical contact.[59]

---

52. (contd) *Thomas v National Union of Ringworkers (South Wales Area)* [1986] 1 Ch 20, (which WINFIELD & JOLOWICZ, p 67, fn 60, regard as "a rather 'tough-minded' decision in this respect"). For critical consideration of the requirement of imminence in the tort of assault, see Seitz 'Insults - Practical Jokes - Threats of Future Harm - How New As Torts?' (1940) 28 Ky LJ 411 at 422-423. It may be that the courts will in the future take the view that the requirement of imminence is designed to ensure that the apprehension of future contact is credible and that accordingly, if credibility can be established by the evidence as a whole, the plaintiff should not be required to establish proof of nuisance as well: see *Barton v Armstrong* [1969] 2 NSWR 451. The idea that an entirely credible threat to blow a person's head off in one hour's time should not be actionable seems offensive to justice. If the tort of assault does not provide the remedy, some other tort (such as the intentional inflection of emotional suffering) should serve the task. If there is a lacuna in the protection afforded by the tort system, this is surely one that should be filled by an action for damages for infringement of constitutional rights, under the (timid) formula set out by Henchy J (for the Court) in *Hanrahan v Merck Sharp & Dohme (Ireland) Ltd* [1988] ILRM 629 (SC). *Cf* para **[1.18]** above.

53. *R v St George*, (1840) 9 C & P 483 at 490, 493, 173 ER 921, 926. *Cf* Turner 'Assault at Common Law' (1939) 7 Camb LJ 56.

54. *Dullaghan v Hillen* [1957] Ir Jur Rep 10; *Donohue v Coyle* [1953-54] Ir Jur Rep 30 (CC); *Howard v Boner* (1943) 78 ILTR 3 (CC); *McGee v Cunanne* (1932) 66 ILTR 147 (CC); *McCann v Mannion* (1932) 66 ILTR 161 (CC); *Grealy v Casey* (1901) 1 NIJR 121 (CA).

55. *Dullaghan v Hillen* [1957] Ir Jur Rep 10 at 14.

56. *Mead's and Belt's Case* (1823) 1 Lew 184, 168 ER 1006. Whilst it is true that Holroyd J did say that "no words or singing are equivalent to an assault" (at 185 and 1006, respectively), his subsequent remarks clearly indicated that he regarded the context in which the words were spoken as being relevant in determining whether an assault had been committed.

57. As the judgment does, more strongly, at 12: "Words cannot of themselves amount to an assault, under any circumstances".

58. *Cf* FLEMING, p 32; Handford, Tort Liability for Threatening or Insulting Words (1976) 54 Can BR 563 at 566-571; *R v Wilson* [1955] 1 All ER 744 at 745 (CCA); *Fairclough v Whipp* [1951] 2 All ER 834. See also *Grealy v Casey* (1901) 1 NIJR 121 at 122 (CA); *Walsh v Pender* (1927) 62 ILTR 8 (HC).

59 *Cf R v Ireland* [1998] AC 147 at (HL), Lord Steyn observed:

> "The proposition that a gesture may amount to an assault, but that words can never suffice, is unrealistic and indefeasible. A thing said is also a thing done.

**[22.25]** Conversely, however, words may have the effect of rendering harmless conduct that would otherwise constitute an assault. Thus, no liability attached to a man who laid his hand menacingly on his sword but remarked: "If it were not assize-time, I would not take such language from you."[60]

**[22.26]** Silence may in particular contexts be the basis of liability for assault. In *R v Ireland*,[61] Lord Steyn stated:

> "Take .... the case of the silent [telephone] caller. He intends by his silence to cause fear and he is so understood. The victim is assailed by uncertainty about his intentions. Fear may dominate her emotions, and it may be the fear that the caller's arrival at her door may be imminent. She may fear the possibility of immediate personal violence."

Of course, in the large majority of cases, such silent communications, however intimidating, will not amount to assaults[62] because the victim does not apprehend any imminent physical contact.

**[22.27]** Finally, it is worth noting that assaults can take place in a wider context of abuse such as domestic violence. There is no reason why the statutory system of protection[63] that has grown up over recent years should not, in appropriate cases be supplemented by a tort action for assault.[64]

---

59. (contd)
There is no reason why something said should be incapable of causing an apprehension of immediate personal violence, eg a man accosting a woman in a dark alley saying, 'Come with me or I will slap you'. I would therefore, reject the proposition that an assault can never by committed by words."

60. *Tubervell v Savage* (1669) 1 Mod 3, 86 ER 684.

61. [1998] AC 147.

62. Though they may constitute another tort, such as the intentional infliction of emotional suffering or a violation of the victim's constitutional right to health, bodily integrity, privacy and liberty.

63. *Cf* the Domestic Violence Act 1996, analysed by Shatter, *Family Law* (4th ed, 1997), Ch 16; Byrne & Binchy, *Annual Review of Irish Law 1996*. A safety order under s 2 of the 1996 Act is, in effect, an injunction against (*inter alia*) an assault. See also the Non-Fatal Offences Against the Person Act 1997, s 2 assault, s 3 assault causing harm, s 4 causing serious harm, s 5 threats to kill or cause serious harm, s 9 coercion, s 10 harassment, s 13 endangerment, s 15 false imprisonment. What amounts to a power of injunction against harassment, even where a prosecution for the offence of harassment fails on the evidence, is nothing of particular note in s 10. Victims of violence can, of course sue for the tort of battery. The possibility of suing for damages under the *Wilkinson v Downton* principle (examined para **[22.28]** below) should also be considered in cases falling short of physical violence. The desirability of such actions in a family law system where the remedies have largely moved away from allegations of wrongful conduct is a matter of some controversy. See Orsinger 'Asserting Claims for Intentionally or Recklessly Causing Severe Emotional Distress in Connection with Divorce' (1994) 25 St Mary's LJ 1254; Bradley 'Note, Turning Marital Misery into Financial Fortune: Assertion of Intentional Infliction of Emotional Distress Claims by Divorcing Spouses' (1974) 33 U Louisville J Fam L 101; Karp & Karp 'Beyond the Normal Ebb and Flow ... Infliction of Emotional Distress in Domestic Violence Cases' (1994) 28 Fam LQ 390. The judicial decisions and policy arguments are clearly analysed by Taylor 'Comment, Infliction of Emotional Distress During Marriage' (1997) 32 Wake Forest LR 1261.

64. *Cf* In *Re Kennon and Kennon* (1997) 22 Fam LR 1.

## Infliction of Emotional Suffering[65]

**[22.28]** Where a person intentionally or recklessly inflicts emotional suffering on another he may be guilty of a tort.[66] The precise scope of the tort is somewhat uncertain.

**[22.29]** The leading decision is *Wilkinson v Downton*.[67] The defendant, as a practical joke, told the plaintiff that her husband had been injured in a road accident, that he was lying on the ground with both legs broken and that she was to go at once to fetch him. The entire tale was false. It gave the plaintiff a violent shock resulting in severe injuries. The action did not fit easily into any established categories, but as the Court "obviously had no love for the defendant; and as in many another hard case, the enormity of the outrage overthrew the settled rule of law".[68] Liability was imposed on the basis that the defendant had:

> "wilfully done an act calculated to cause physical harm to the plaintiff, that is to say, to infringe her legal right to personal safety, and has in fact thereby caused physical harm to her. That proposition without more appears to me to state a good cause of action, there being no justification alleged for the act. The wilful *injuria* is in law malicious, although no malicious purpose to cause the harm which was caused nor any motive of spite is imputed to the defendant."[69]

**[22.30]** Wright J's use of the word "calculated" needs some explanation for the modern reader: it connotes an objective likelihood of a high degree rather than requiring a specific subjective intent. Once willfulness of conduct (as opposed to negligent inadvertence) combines with this element of likelihood of harm, liability can flow under the *Wilkinson v Downton* principle.[70]

---

65. See Prosser, 'Insult and Outrage' (1956) 44 Calif LR 40; Prosser 'International Infliction of Mental Suffering: A New Tort' (1939) 37 Mich LR 874; Glasbeek, 'Outraged Dignity: Do We Need a New Tort?' (1968) 6 Alta LR 77, Magruder 'Mental and Emotional Disturbance in the Law of Torts' (1936) 49 Harv LR 1033, Handford 'Intentional Infliction of Mental Distress: Analysis of the Growth of a Tort' (1979) 8 Anglo-Am. LR 1; Burdick 'Tort Liability for Mental Disturbance and Nervous Shock' (1905) 5 Col LR 179 at 187-189; Vold 'Tort Recovery for Intentional Infliction of Emotional Distress' (1939) 18 Neb LR 22; Vinson 'Torts' (1984) 72 Ky LJ 457 at 458-464; Givelber 'The Right to Minimum Social Decency and the Limit of Evenhandedness: Intentional Infliction of Emotional Distress by Outrageous Conduct' (1982) 82 Col LR 42.

66. Of course, if emotional suffering is inflicted in the course of the commission of a particular tort, such as malicious prosecution or false imprisonment, for example, damages may be awarded to compensate the plaintiff for this injury: *cf Higgins v O'Reilly* [1940] Ir Jur Rep 15 (HC).

67. [1897] 2 QB 57 (Wright J); 66 LJQB 493 is a fuller report.

68. PROSSER & KEETON, p 60.

69. [1897] 2 QB 57 at 58-59. In some circumstances a practical joker may claim that the defence of implied consent should apply, as, for example, where a pair of friends have a habit of playing tricks on each other which involve some degree of emotional suffering: *cf Wartman v Swindell* (1892) 54 NJL 589, 25 A 356.

70 In *Powell v Boldaz* [1998] Lloyd's Rep Med 116 at 125 (CA), Stuart-Smith LJ (Morritt and Schieman LJJ concurring) considered that *Wilkinson v Downton* was authority for the following two propositions:

> "First, that the making a statement known to be false with the intention that it should be believed and with the intention of causing injury, which in fact results, is actionable;

**[22.31]** In *Janvier v Sweeney*[71] a threat by a private detective, representing himself to be a policeman, to charge the plaintiff with espionage unless she handed over private letters in her possession was held to be actionable, where the plaintiff became ill from shock.

**[22.32]** In recent years courts in England have debated the utility of the *Wilkinson v Downton* principle in developing a substantive tort of harassment.[72] The process was overtaken by the creation there of a statutory tort of harassment under section of the Non-Fatal Offences Against the Person Act 1997. The court in criminal proceedings under the section was able to grant what amounts to an injunction, even where the prosecution fails for lack of evidence. This gives somewhat clumsy protection to the victims of harassment.

**[22.33]** Litigation under the *Wilkinson v Downton* principle has developed, slowly, in Canada,[73] Australia,[74] New Zealand,[75] and Hong Kong.[76] In the United States an avalanche

70. (contd)

> and, secondly, that where the defendant's act is plainly calculated to produce some effect of the kind which was produced, an intention to produce it ought to be imputed to the defendant, regard being had to the fact that the effect was produced on a person on an ordinary state of health and mind. Another way of putting the second proposition is to say that a man who foresees the consequences of his act is to be taken to intend the consequences, even when he does not desire them."

See also *Page v Smith* [1996] 1 AC 155 (HL) *per* Lord Jauncey, dissenting, dissent not affecting this issue, 1995):

> "I take from the[e quoted] passage from *Wilkinson v Downton* that the judge thought it appropriate to apply the foreseeability test in the context of a person of normal susceptibility to such an act."

*Cf Three Rivers District Council v Bank of England* [1996] 3 All ER 558 (QB), where Clarke J interpreted "calculated" as incorporating a mental element. It may be suggested instead that the requirement of a subjective mental element is contained in the word "wilfully". See further WINFIELD & JOLOWICZ, pp 86-87 for a helpful discussion.

The reference to "a person of normal susceptibility" ought not be understood to mean that those of particular physical, mental or emotional susceptibility should be deprived of the entitlement of suing under the *Wilkinson v Downton* principle. On the contrary, the law should make special efforts to protect them from such harm. All that is in question in the present context is that the injury of which the plaintiff claims should have been foreseeable. In most cases the defendant will not be able to have foreseen that his or her conduct would harm those of particular susceptibility; but of course in some instances (as where the defendant knows the victim well) there will be a high degree of foreseeability of injury and liability should follow.

71. [1919] 2 KB 316 (CA).

72. See *Burnett v George* [1992] 1 FLR 525 (CA); *Khorasandjian v Bush* [1993] QB 727 (CA). The Court of Appeal's attempt in *Khorasandjian* to characterise such conduct as a private nuisance was repudiated subsequently by the House of Lords in *Hunter v Canary Wharf Ltd* [1997] AC 655. *Cf Royal Dublin Society v Yates* High Court, 31 July 1997 (Shanley J). See also *Kulyk v Board of Education for the City of Toronto* (1996) 139 DLR (4th) 114 (Ont Court (Gen Div)); *Bateman v Newcourt Credit Group Inc* (1995) Ont CJ LEXIS 614 (Ont Court (Gen Div)).

73. *Cf* eg *Bielitski v Obadiak* (1922) 15 Sask LR 153 (CA); *Purdy v Woznesensky,* [1937] 2 WWR 116 (Sask CA); *Kleynhans v Zucker* (1997) Ont CJ LEXIS 1946 (Ont Court of Justice).

74. *Bunyan v Jordan* (1937) 57 Comm LR 1 (HC, Austr); *Gimson v Victorian Work Authority* [1995] 1 VR 209 (SC); *Church of Scientology In v Transmedia Productions Pty Ltd* (1997) NSW LEXIS 7075, BC 8701 359 (NSW SC).

75. *Bradley v Wingnut Films Ltd* [1993] 1 NZLR 415 (HC); *Stevenson v Bagham* [1922] NZLR 225.

76. *Wong Kwai Fun v Li Fung* (1994) 1 HKC 549, (1994) HKC LEXIS 591 (HC).

of cases has given some shape to the tort.[77] There the tort is committed where the defendant by extreme and outrageous conduct intentionally or recklessly causes severe emotional distress to another.[78] There is a certain lack of conceptual attraction to this definition since it is a matter more of emotion than of intellect to determine when conduct becomes "extreme and outrageous". Nevertheless, this approach is surely preferable to the complete lack of definitional precision in other common law jurisdictions.

> "Whilst the precise nature of the defendant's state of mind necessary to engender liability for this tort is a matter of debate, in the absence of any clear predent in this country it is worth bearing in mind the fact that, for some plaintiffs who fail in proceedings based on the *Wilkinson v Downton* principle, the tort of negligent infliction of emotional suffering[79] may well still be available."

**[22.34]** Although the reported cases deal only with the imposition of shock, fear or other psychological harm, is there any reason in principle why liability should not extend to all intentionally caused physical harm which the plaintiff suffers other than that falling within the scope of actions for trespass to the person? Is there to be no remedy for indirectly caused intentional injury, such as putting poison[80] in another's tea or digging a pit into which he is intended to fall? Winfield & Jolowicz[81] and Street[82] consider that the principle in *Wilkinson v Downton* is sufficiently broad to cover these types of cases, and there is much to be said for this conclusion from the standpoint of both principle and policy.[83] It seems beyond question that, if no tort remedy is capable of being fashioned to deal with this misconduct, the plaintiff should have recourse to the protection afforded by the Constitution against infringement of the rights to health and bodily integrity.

## False Imprisonment[84]

**[22.35]** In *Dullaghan v Hillen*,[85] Fawsitt J stated:

---

77. See PROSSER & KEETON, pp 54-66; Prosser (1939) 37 Mich LR 874; Borda, (1939) 28 Geo LJ 55; Givelber 'The Right to Minimum Social Decency and the Limit of Evenhandedness: Intentional Infliction of Emotional Distress by Outrageous Conduct' (1982) 82 Col LR 42; McCubbin, (1980) 20 Washburn, LJ 106; Hayden, (1993) 34 Wm St Mary LR 580. Courts in the United States have imposed liability for such disparate types of outrageous behaviour as sexual solicitation (*cf* (1962) 1 Washburn LJ 621), racial slurs (*cf* (1978) 17 Washburn LJ 706), and harassment of tenants (*cf* PROSSER & KEETON, p 62; Harrington, 12 Cumberland LR 527 at 540, fn 94). Serious neglect of tenants' interests may also come within the scope of the tort: *cf Birkenhead v Coombs* (1983) 143 Vt 167, 465 A. 2d 244; similarly intimidatory debt-collection practices: *cf* (1973) 37 Alb LR 497 Harrington, 12 Cumberland LR 527 at 540, fn 92; Honsburger 'Harassment of Borrowers by Licensed Lenders' (1965) 1 Col J of L & Soc Problems 39 at 53-59; Nelson 'Note: Mental Distress from Collection Activities' (1965) 17 Hastings LJ 369; Riselli 'Note' (1971) 6 Suffolk ULR 140. Mistreatment of employees can also give rise to liability: see the critical analysis of the jurisprudence by Duffy, (1994) 74 Boston ULR 387.

78. *Restatement, Second, On Torts* (1965), p 846.

79. *Cf* Green, 'Fright' Cases (1933) 27 Ill LR 761, 873 at 881.

80. *Cf Bell v GN Ry Co of Ireland* (1890) 26 LR (Ir) 428 at 439 (Ex Div).

81. WINFIELD & JOLOWICZ, p 85

82. STREET, p 33.

83. *Cf Bird v Holbrook* (1828) 4 Bing 628, 130 ER 911.

84. See generally NHN 'False Imprisonment' [1931] LJIFS 141; Heffey 'Negligent Infliction of Imprisonment: Actionable 'Per Se' or 'Cum Damno"'? (1983) 14 Melbourne ULR 53; Vold 'The Legal Allocation of Risk in Assault, Battery, and Imprisonment - The Prima Facie Case' (1938) 17 Neb L Bull 149 at 178-193, Halliday 'How Much Detention Constitutes False Imprisonment?' (1966) 15 Clev-Mar LR 75.

85. [1957] Ir Jur 10 at 15 (CC).

"False imprisonment is the unlawful[86] and total restraint of the personal liberty of another whether by constraining him or compelling him to go to a particular place or confining him in a prison or police station or private place or by detaining him against his will in a public place. The essential element of the offence is the unlawful detention of the person, or the unlawful restraint on his liberty. The fact that a person is not actually aware that he is being imprisoned does not amount to evidence that he is not imprisoned, it being possible for a person to be imprisoned in law, without his being conscious of the fact and appreciating the position in which he is placed, laying hands upon the person of the party imprisoned not being essential. There may be an effectual imprisonment without walls of any kind. The detainer must be such as to limit the party's freedom of motion in all directions. In effect, imprisonment is a total restraint of the liberty of the person. The offence is committed by mere detention without violence."

**[22.36]** This is an admirably succinct statement of the principal features of the tort.[87] Each of the main ingredients will now be considered in turn.

***Confinement within fixed bounds***

**[22.37]** As the passage quoted above makes clear, the tort of false imprisonment will be committed only where a person is confined within fixed bounds. Where one's way is merely blocked so that one has to return whence one came or make a diversion, this does not constitute false imprisonment[88] (although it may give rise to liability for other torts, such as public nuisance[89] or negligence[90]). However, a person is not required to risk injuring himself or herself[91] or undergo some major humiliation (such as walking naked in the street[92]) to avoid an obstacle created by the defendant's action. In such circumstances the law will not permit the defendant to avoid liability by saying that the confinement was not total. The Supreme Court has held that overt surveillance does not amount to detention, provided the person under surveillance is permitted to go where he or she wants.[93]

---

86. As to lawful detention of arrested persons, *cf* para **[22.105]** below and the Criminal Justice Act 1984, ss 4 to 10.

87. False imprisonment is also a criminal offence under the Non-Fatal Offences Against the Person Act 1997, s 15.

88. *Bird v Jones* (1845) 7 QB 742, 115 ER 668; *Phillips v GN Ry Co Ltd* (1903) 4 NIJR 154 (KBD).

89. *Cf Boyd v GNR* [1895] 2 IR 555; *Smith v Wilson* [1903] 2 IR 45.

90. *Cf Star Village Tavern v Nield* [1976] 6 WWR 80 (Man QB); see also *Cullen v Dickenson* (1913) 33 SD 27, 144 NW 656 - action on the case recognised. *Cf* Halpern 'International Torts and the Restatement: A Petition for Rehearing' (1957) 7 Buffalo LR 7 at 16-17.

91. *Sayers v Harlow UDC* [1958] 1 WLR 623 (CA). *Cf Wright v Wilson* (1699) 1 Ld Raym 739, 91 ER 1394; *Whittaker v Sandford* (1912) 110 Me 77, 85 A 399 (SC).

92. *Cf* SALMOND & HEUSTON, p 125, fn 79.

93. *Kane v Governor of Mountjoy Prison* [1988] ILRM 724 (SC) (especially at 735, *per* Finlay CJ). Whether overt surveillance is otherwise unlawful as, for example, amounting to an unconstitutional (or possibly, tortious) interference with privacy, depends on the particular purpose of the surveillance and all the circumstances of the case.

**[22.38]** The extent of the confinement may vary: it can include confinement not only in a prison[94] or barracks,[95] but also in a house,[96] shop,[97] or hotel,[98] a car,[99] a polling booth,[100] a station,[101] a boat[102] or a lavatory,[103] for example. At some point, the area of the confinement becomes so large[104] that the tort of false imprisonment gives way to remedies under the Constitution protecting a citizen's right to travel within the State and internationally.[105]

***Continuance of imprisonment***

**[22.39]** A person who helps to continue a wrongful detention commits the tort of false imprisonment, although he or she may not have been responsible for the original detention.[106] So where one in lawful custody becomes entitled to be discharged, if the person who has him or her in charge fails to set that person free, the gaoler will be guilty of falsely imprisonment.[107]

***Physical and psychological imprisonment***

**[22.40]** Imprisonment may be physical, in the sense that the victim will be unable physically to escape - as where he or she is locked in a room with barred windows.

---

94. *Gildea v Hipwell* [1942] IR 489 (SC); *Slevin v Manders* (1868) IR 2 CL 659 (Exch); *Mahony v Lynch* (1876) 10 ILT & SJ 91; *Maloney v French* (1869) IR 3 CL 391 (QB). *Cf Ó'Conghaile v Wallace* [1938] IR 526 (SC).
95. *Dunne v Clinton* Supreme Court, 12 December 1931, affg [1930] IR 366 (HC). See also *Curley v Ireland* Circuit Court, 2 July 1984 (Sheridan J); *Walsh v Ireland*, Supreme Court, 30 November 1994, noted by Hogan & Morgan, pp 811-812 and Byrne & Binchy, *Annual Review of Irish Law 1994*, pp 461-462; *McIntyre v Lewis* [1991] 1 IR 121 (SC).
96. *Warner v Riddiford* (1858) 4 CB (ns) 180, 140 ER 1042; *Dillon v Dunnes' Stores Ltd* Supreme Court, 20 December 1968 - room.
97. *McAllister v Dunnes Stores Ltd* High Court, 5 February 1987 (Barron J).
98. *Cf Porter v Duff* [1942] IR 548 (HC).
99. *Burton v Davies* [1953] QSR 26, *Cieplinski v Severn* (1929) 269 Mass 261, 168 ER 722.
100. *Higgins v O'Reilly* [1940] Ir Jur Rep 15 (HC).
101. *Farry v Marshall*; *Farry v GN Ry Co* [1898] 2 IR 352 (QB); *Phillips v GN Ry C Ltd* (1903) 4 NIJR 154 (KBD).
102. *R v Macquarie & Budge* (1875) 13 NSWSCR 264.
103. *Sayers v Harlow UDC* [1958] 1 WLR 623 (CA).
104. *Cf* WINFIELD & JOLOWICZ, pp 71-72:

 > "What will amount to a complete restraint must be a question of degree. A person would plainly be imprisoned if locked inside a large building, even though he had full freedom to roam around inside it, and it has been suggested [in *Pritchard v Ministry of Defence* [1995] CLY 4726] that unlawful conscription is theoretically capable of being false imprisonment. But it seems unlikely that an action for false imprisonment would lie if, for example, the plaintiff was wrongfully prevented from leaving this country [Citing *Louis v Commonwealth* (1986) 87 FLR 277]."

105. See Hogan and Whyte, *Kelly: The Irish Constitution* (3rd ed, 1994), pp 777-778, 798-810; *The State (M) v Attorney General* [1979] IR 73 (HC); *Lennon v Ganly* [1981] ILRM 84 (HC). The issue gave rise to much controversy in the context of travel abroad for the purposes of abortion. See *Attorney General v X* [1992] 1 IR 1 (SC); *Re Article 26 of the Constitution and the Regulation of Information (Services outside the State for the Termination of Pregnancies) Bill 1995* [1995] 1 IR 1 (SC); *Society for the Protection of Unborn Children (Ireland) Ltd v Grogan*, Supreme Court, 6 March 1997; *A and B v Eastern Health Board* [1998] 1 ILRM 460 (HC).
106. *Griffin v Coleman* (1859) 4 H & N 265, 157 ER 533. See also *R v Governor of Brockhill Prison; ex parte Evans (No 2)* [1999] QB 1043 (CA), analysed by Fordham 'False Imprisonment in Good Faith' (2000) 8 Tort LR 53.
107. *Migotti v Colvill* (1879) 4 CPD 233; *Mee v Cruickshank* (1902) 86 LT 708.

**[22.41]** It may also be psychological,[108] in the sense that the victim goes along with the wishes of the other party, fearing that force will be used to confine him or her if he or she does not. Thus, there may be an imprisonment without walls of any kind.[109] The classic case of this type of imprisonment is where a person is arrested without actually being touched by the other party.

**[22.42]** In *Phillips v GN Ry Co Ltd*,[110] a person of "unimpeachable" integrity was suspected by railway personnel of attempting to defraud the railway by travelling on a train without the proper ticket. On the arrival of the train in Dublin, while ordering a cab, she was told by the ticket collector not to move. She asked the cabman whom he was to obey - the ticket collector or herself. The cabman replied: "You; but we dare not move". The ticket collector went away and brought the stationmaster to the plaintiff. After some further conversation, the plaintiff got into the cab and drove off, the stationmaster shouting: "We have the number of that cab."

**[22.43]** The plaintiff's action for false imprisonment succeeded before a jury (who awarded her £5.00 damages), but the King's Bench Division held that there was no evidence to go to the jury and set the verdict aside. Lord O'Brien LCJ considered that, whilst the plaintiff had been subjected to some delay, there was no evidence that she had been:

> "so dominated by the action of the ticket-collector that, succumbing to that domination, she lost her liberty. Her intended means of egress were interfered with but she plainly could have left the station, and . . . there was not 'a total restraint of the liberty of the person'.[111]" [112]

**[22.44]** Another case of psychological imprisonment may be considered briefly. This arises where the defendant brings about an apparent total confinement of the plaintiff. If in fact there is a way out available, but one which neither is or ought reasonably to be apparent to the plaintiff, then on principle the defendant ought to be liable.[113]

### *Consciousness of confinement*[114]

**[22.45]** As the passage quoted above from *Dullaghan v Hillen*[115] indicates, one can be falsely imprisoned even when not aware of this fact - as where a sleeping person or a child or a mentally handicapped individual is confined without his knowledge. This appears to be the better view.[116]

---

108. *Cf Chaytor v London, New York & Paris Assoc of Fashion Ltd* (1961) 30 DLR (2d) 527 (Nfld SC), where the term is used.
109. *Dullaghan v Hillen* [1957] Ir Jur Rep 10 at 15 (CC).
110. (1903) 4 NIJR 154 (KBD).
111. *Bird v Jones* (1845) 7 QB 742, 115 ER 668.
112. *Phillips v GN Ry Co Ltd* (1903) 4 NIJR 154 at 155.
113. *Cf Talcott v National Exhibition Co* (1911) Appeal Div 128 NYS 1059.
114. See Prosser 'False Imprisonment: Consciousness of Confinement' (1955) 55 Col LR 847.
115. [1957] Ir Jur Rep 10 at 15 (CC).
116 The academic commentators generally favour imposing liability . The leading analysis is by Prosser 'False Imprisonment: Consciousness of Confinement' (1955) 55 Col LR 847; see also 'Note, Is Knowledge of the Fact of imprisonment by the Plaintiff a Necessary Element in False Imprisonment?' (1944) 32 Ky LJ 212;

**[22.46]** In *Murray v Minister for Defence*,[117] the House of Lords (on appeal from the Northern Ireland Court of Appeal) held that neither consciousness of confinement nor proof of special damage was a necessary ingredient in the tort. The "supreme importance"[118] which the law attached to the liberty of the individual made it necessary to define the tort so broadly, said Lord Griffiths, though he pointed out that "[i]f a person is unaware that he has been falsely imprisoned and has suffered harm, he can normally expect to recover no more than nominal damages".[119]

***Failure to release***

**[22.47]** As a general principle, it will not be false imprisonment for a person to fail to release another who has become imprisoned on his property, as where he falls down his well, for example. Where, however, the defendant has induced the other person to get into that position, with an assurance - express or implied - that he will release him, liability for false imprisonment[120] will attach if he does not do so.[121] Furthermore, where a person agrees with another to have restrictions placed on his movement, the normal rule is that he may call on that other to release him only in accordance with the terms of the agreement.[122] Thus, in *Burns v Johnston*,[123] liability was denied in the following circumstances. The defendant factory owner extended by half an hour the period for work in his factory so that employees would have to work a 12½ hour day ending at 6.30 pm, as was the former rule. He was legally entitled to do this as most of his employees failed to give notice within the time agreed upon between the parties of their intention to leave the employment. The factory was run in a fashion which involved the yard gate's being closed during work hours. This was, "in accordance with familiar factory discipline, to control the works, avoid irregularity of work, and prevent absence without knowledge of the employer".[124] A

---

116. (contd) Cohen 'False Imprisonment: A Re-examination of the Necessity for Awareness of Confinement' (1975) 43 Tenn LR 109; Prosser 'False Imprisonment: Consciousness of Confinement' 55 Col LR 847 (1955); Halpern 'Intentional Torts and the Restatement: A Petition for Rehearing' (1957) 7 Buffalo LR 7 at 23-29; Reed 'Note: Is Knowledge of the Fact of Imprisonment by the Plaintiff a Necessary Element in False Imprisonment?' (1944) 32 Ky LJ 212; The *Restatement, Second, of Torts* (1965), s 35 takes a compromise position, imposing liability for imprisoning a person not conscious of the fact of confinement only in cases where he suffers harm; but *cf* Goodhart (1935) 83 U Pa LR 411 at 418.

117. [1988] 1 WLR 692.

118. [1988] 1 WLR 692 at 703.

119. [1988] 1 WLR 692 at 703. Lord Griffiths resisted the temptation to redefine the tort in the terms of s 35 of the *Restatement, Second, of Torts*. See also *R v Bournewood Community and Mental Health NHS Trust ex p L (Secretary of State for Health intervening)* [1998] 3 All ER 289 (HL).

120. The possibility of the courts' also recognising an affirmative duty in negligence should not be discounted.

121. *Restatement, Second, of Torts*, p 845. See also *Whittaker v Sandford* (1912) 110 Me 77, 85 A 399 (SC).

122. *Cf Herd v Weardale Steel Co* [1915] AC 67. See also *Balmain New Ferry Co v Robinson* [1910] AC 295 (PC), affg (1906) 4 Comm LR 379. See generally Amos 'A Note on Contractual Restraint of Liberty' (1928) 44 LQR 464; Keng Feng Tan 'A Misconceived Issue in the Tort of False Imprisonment' (1981) 44 MLR 166; Vold, 'The Legal Allocation of Risk in Assault, Battery, and Imprisonment- The Prima Facie Case' (1938) 17 Neb L Bull 149 at 188 190; GGL 'Note' (1933) 7 So Calif LR 102.

123. [1917] 2 IR 137, affg [1916] 2 IR 444.

124. [1916] 2 IR 444 at 453 (KB).

pass could, however, be obtained from the gate-keeper for adequate personal reasons. On the first day that the extended working hours came into operation, the plaintiff with 129 other employees demanded to be let out at 6 p.m. The defendant refused to accommodate them and they were detained until 6.30 pm. The plaintiff sued for false imprisonment.

**[22.48]** The trial judge stated a case to the King's Bench Division,[125] which held that no action lay. The Court of Appeal affirmed.[126]

**[22.49]** Cherry LCJ considered that the case came within the principles laid down by the House of Lords in *Herd v Weardale Steel, Coal & Coke Co*,[127] in the previous year, where a coal mine proprietor had been held not liable for false imprisonment in failing to release a miner from a mine when he insisted on being brought to the surface in breach of his contract before the shift had been completed and at a time earlier than the lift would normally be available. Lord Haldane had stated that the plaintiff:

> "chose to go to the bottom of the mine under these conditions - conditions which he had accepted. He had no right to call upon the employers to make use of special machinery put there at their cost, and involving cost in its working, to bring him to the surface just when he pleased."[128]

**[22.50]** In the *Burns* case, Cherry LCJ stated:

> "It was part of the conditions of his employment that the plaintiff should remain at work until 6.30 pm; and although the defendant might not be entitled to interfere actively to prevent his leaving before that time, he was not bound to afford facilities to him for doing so. Had the plaintiff applied for and been refused a pass out, different considerations might arise, but this he did not do."[129]

**[22.51]** Moreover, even if the defendant's inaction had been designed to punish the plaintiff for having broken his contract this would not assist him.[130]

**[22.52]** In similar vein, Gibson J stated that

> "The plaintiff by wrongfully refusing to work cannot get rid of the employer's right to maintain the existing physical condition of the factory premises, or impose on him a duty of doing an act which he never undertook to do, and which would be contrary to the terms of his bargain with the plaintiff."[131]

**[22.53]** He stressed the fact that the plaintiff could not impose a positive obligation on the defendant, which might involve him in difficulty or inconvenience, stating that:

> "Whether the means of egress is by a cage from a mine, or by laying a gangway, or by using a key in a lock, though the cost may be different, all agree in this, that assistance is required from an affirmative act. Suppose a cook in the middle of the night - the outer door being locked, and her employer in bed - wished on a sudden nocturnal caprice to get away, could she sue for false imprisonment if her master declined to get up and open the door to enable her to carry out her breach of contract? The opening of a locked door involves voluntary

125. [1916] 2 IR 444 (KB).
126. [1917] 2 IR 137 (CA).
127. [1915] AC 67.
128. *Herd v Weardale Steel Co* [1915] AC 67 at 73.
129. [1916] 2 IR 444 at 450.
130. [1916] 2 IR 444 at 451. See also, to similar effect, *Herd v Weardale Steel Co* [1915] AC 67 at 72.
131. [1916] 2 IR 444 at 455.

action which may cause trouble and delay, especially if the staff controlling the key was away at any distance, or where (as here) a number were going and many remaining. If all the dissatisfied workers did not go at the same time, was the gate-keeper to keep unlocking and locking the gate for the thirty minutes."[132]

**[22.54]** On appeal, the Court of Appeal summarily[133] affirmed the judgment of the King's Bench Division.

**[22.55]** Reading *Herd* and *Burns* today, it is hard not to be diverted by the harshness of the social and economic circumstances that led to the proceedings in both cases and by the assumption as to the broad scope of employees' obligations and the still broader scope of their employees' entitlements. Nonetheless questions of principle remain. Should a crucial distinction be made between act and omission in this context? Is there a difference between requiring one's imprisioner to go to some degree of bother to effect one's release (such as opening and closing the gate repeatedly, as in *Burns*) or requiring of the imprisioner that he or she simply press a button once? If *Herd* and *Burns* were to rest on the unreasonableness of the demand, in terms of undue bother, then their legal holding (though not necessarily their application of that holding to the facts) could be supported. The distinction between a reasonable and unreasonable demand was the criterion adopted by the Privacy Council in *Robinson v Balmain New Ferry Co.*[134] It offers a more convincing rationale than an elaborate working back from a conclusion to a constructed ascription of an implied term.

**[22.56]** If this test is applied to situations where a person (even one in breach of contract) wishes to leave a place of confinement and calls on another to take some positive step, however unburdensome, to effect the release, the implication is that liability should be imposed on the other person for failing to take this unburdensome step. Does this commit the courts to the proposition that there is a general duty resting on all members of society to take positive unburdensome steps to release strangers who are imprisoned? The answer is simply no, just as, at present, there is no general affirmative duty in the law of negligence to go to the assistance of others.[135] In negligence proceedings, if court is satisfied that, in the particular circumstances of the case, a duty of care arose, then it can impose liability on the party under that duty for failure to act or for acting carelessly.

**[22.57]** One does not wish to complicate the law relating to false imprisonment by overelaborate conceptualisation and the courts may well prefer to avoid incorporating the language of duty, proximity and neighbourhood into their analyses in this context. If they limit themselves to addressing whether, in the circumstances - which, of course, will include the particular relationship between the parties - the defendant was reasonable in failing to release the plaintiff, that should ensure that the important value of liberty is appropriately protected.

## Confinement as a Sanction

**[22.58]** One may not confine a person to enforce a civil debt.[136] Resort to the civil proceedings in the courts is the proper solution for dissatisfied creditors.

132. [1916] 2 IR 444 at 454.
133. [1916] 2 IR 444.
134. [1910] AC 295.
135. *Cf* see para **[8.01]** above
136. *Cf Sunbolf v Alford* (1838) 3 M & W 248,150 ER 1135; *Perry v Fried* (1972) 32 DLR (3d) 589 (NS).

## III. Defences to Trespass to the Person

### Consent

**[22.59]** Where an individual consents to physical contact that would otherwise constitute a trespass to his person this will render the contact lawful.[137]

**[22.60]** Consent may be expressed or implied. If I stick out my arm when a doctor wishes to innoculate me, I can scarcely claim later that my silence indicated a refusal to consent.[138] What the law regards is external acts manifesting a consent, so far as the reasonable perceptions of the other party are concerned. Thus, even in a case where the victim did not subjectively consent, the defendant will be relieved of liability if the victim's external conduct indicated consent. Whether it is wise to base the exemption from liability on "implied" consent may perhaps be debated, since in truth it is the reasonableness and social acceptability of the defendant's conduct which is the proper basis for the absence of liability. Courts in Ireland and elsewhere have yet to consider the reverse case, where a person gives no external manifestation of consent but in fact does subjectively consent. So far as the defendant is concerned, of course, he has the requisite intent on which to base liability, but none the less it would seem wrong to do so because, in spite of this, his act was done with the consent of his intended victim.[139] Consent may be implied in respect of a wide range of human activities. We will put up with minor buffetings when walking down a busy street, for example. Similarly, in the playing of sports, consent to contact which frequently involves actual injury is implied. The limits of consent in sporting activities[140] have not been litigated upon in this country or in England to anything like the same extent as in the United States,[141] Australia[142] and

---

137. *Cf Hegarty v Shine* (1878) 4 LR Ir 288 at 296 (CA, *per* Palles CB,):
"It is indisputable that an act cannot be an assault unless it be against the will of the person assaulted."

138. *Cf O'Brien v Cunard SS Co* (1891) 154 Mass 272, 28 NE 266. *Cf* Tobias, (1988) 18 Golden Gate LR 495 at 520-521. See also *Beatty v Illingworth* Br Med J 21 Nov 1896, p 1525; *Dicenzo v Berg* (1940) 340 Pa 305, 16A, 2d 15; *cf Barfield v South Highland Infirmary* (1915) 191 Ala 553, 68 So 30.

139. *Cf* PROSSER & KEETON, p 113.

140. *Cf* Luntz 'Compensation for Injuries Due to Sport' (1980) 54 Austr LJ 588.

141. *Cf* Schubert, Smith & Trentadue, *Sports Law* (1986), Ch 7; Tucker, [1980] Duke LJ 742; Gulotta, (1980) 48 Fordham LR 764; Hink, (1980) 55 NYUL Rev 971; Carroll, (1982) 16 Akron LR 537; Turro, (1980) 44 Albany LR 696; Amador, (1980) 17 Cal WLR 149; Schuett, (1978) 57 Neb LR 1128; Di Nicola & Mendeloff 'Controlling Violence in Professional Sports: Rule Reform and the Federal Professional Sports Violence Commission' (1983) 21 Duquesne LR 843 at 865-877; Lambert 'Tort Law and Participant Sports: The Line Between Vigor and Violence' (1978) 4 J Contemp L 211; Champion & Swygert 'Non-professional Sport-Related Injuries and Assumption of Risk in Pennsylvania: Is There Life After *Rutter*?' (1983) 54 Pa Bar Assoc Q 34; 'Note, Violence in Professional Sports' [1975] Wis LR 771; 'Comment: Controlling Violence in Professional Sports' (1978) 2 Glendale LR 323; Carroll, (1982) 16 Akron LR 537; *Hackbart v Cincinnati Bengals Inc* (1977) 435 F Supp 352 (D Colo), revd (1979) 601 F 2d 516 (10th CIr), cert den 444 US 931; Nabel 'Comment: On Finding Civil Liability Between Professional Football Players: *Hackbart v Cincinnati Bengals Inc*' (1980) 15 New England LR 741; Lambert 'Tort Law and Participant Sports' (1978) 4 J of Contemp L 211.

142. *Cf McNamara v Duncan* (1971) 26 ALR 584 (ACT SC); *Ginmelli v Johnston* (1991) Aust Torts Reps 81-085. See further the excellent analysis by Kelly, *Sport and the Law: An Australian Perspective* (1987), Ch 9, which discusses the position in several common law jurisdictions and Yeo 'Determining Consent in Body Contact Sports' (1998) 6 Tort LR 199.

Canada,[143] so some of even the basic questions cannot be answered with certainty. It seems clear, however, that a flagrant intentional breach of the rules of the game involving physical injury to the victim consitutes a battery;[144] it is possible that dangerous play in breach of the rules of the game is also a battery,[145] and it could even be contended that dangerous play within the rules would in at least some cases constitute a battery.

**[22.61]** Whilst consent must be freely given, it may be "bought": employees may, for example, consent to physical contact by others as part of the terms of their employment.[146]

**[22.62]** So also, there appears to be no legal rule that renders unlawful in all circumstances the purchase of a person's consent to become the subject of non-therapeutic medical or scientific research.[147] Of course this is an area bristling with ethical issues and the courts are likely to recognise that social, economic or personal pressures may render such a "bought" consent unfree and therefore unlawful. Even where the consent is freely made, there may be limits on the legality of its scope, inspired by consideration of public policy.[148]

**[22.63]** Consent to a particular contact may in some cases be inferred from previous tolerated similar contact. If, for example, two friends have a practice of playing practical jokes on one another, involving contact with the body, then it may be that consent will be implied to a later surprise contact, such as squirting a water pistol in the face.[149] The courts would be likely, however, to look on such a defence with some caution.

### *Excess of consent*

**[22.64]** Clearly, when consent is pleaded by the defendant, it must be shown that the terms of the consent were not exceeded. In *Corcoran v W & R Jacob & Co*,[150] where employees

---

143. *Cf Agar v Canning* (1965) 54 WWR 302 (Man QB) (affd 55 WWR 384 (Man CA)); *Wright v McLean* (1956) 7 DLR (2d) 253; *Martin v Daigle* (1969) 6 DLR (3d) 634 (NBCA); *Champagne v Cummings* 1999 Ont Sup CJ LEXIS 12.

144. *Cf McNamara v Duncan* (1971) 26 ALR 584. Recent newspaper reports in this jurisdiction indicate an increase in this type of litigation nowadays.

145. *Cf* STREET, p 83; Luntz 'Compensation for Injuries Due to Sport' (1980) 34 Austr LJ 588 at 589; *McNamara v Duncan* (1971) 26 ALR 584. See, however, *Agar v Canning* (1965) 54 WWR 302 (Bastin J); *Matheson v Dalhousie College* (1983) 25 CCLT 91 (NS SC). In *Condon v Basi* [1985] 1 WLR (CA), analysis of the matter was limited to a consideration of the duty of care in negligence as the plaintiff had based his action exclusively on the ground.

146. *Corcoran v W & R Jacob & Co* [1945] IR 446 (SC). Since the abolition of the doctrine of "common employment", an employee is not deemed to have consented to negligent contacts by fellow-employees. See further Ch 18 above.

147. Neither the Control of Clinical Trials Act 1987 nor the Control of Clinical Trials and Drugs Act 1990 expressly prohibits the payment of money to research subjects. Indeed the 1987 Act appears to be premised on acceptance of the principle that there can be no *a priori* objection to such payment. Those proposing to undertake a clinical trial must supply to the Minister "details of any proposed inducements or rewards, whether monetary or otherwise, to be made for becoming or being a participant": s 3(1), clause (g). The ethics committee, when considering the justification for the trial, must have regard to this factor: s 8(4), clause (i). See also s 9(8). See further Casey & Craven, *Psychiatry and the Law* (1998), p 527-534.

148. *Cf R v Brown* [1994] 1 AC 212 (HL).

149. *Cf Wartman v Swindell* (1892) 54 NJL 589 at 25 A 356 - taking away reins from plaintiff's horse as a joke.

150. *Wartman v Swindell* (1892) 54 NJL 589.

as part of the terms of their employment agreed to be liable to be searched by security personnel, this was held by the former Supreme Court not to justify a security officer making a "power dive" at an employee when attempting to search him.

***Consent vitiated by fraud or duress or illegality***

**[22.65]** As in other areas of the law where consent is in issue, it must of course be shown to be genuine consent. So, if fraud, duress or illegality is present, the consent may be vitiated. The approach which the courts have[151] adopted regarding fraud has caused controversy. Following the lead of the criminal law, they have held that consent obtained by fraud going to the quality of the conduct will be invalid but that fraud which is merely collateral will not vitiate the consent. The decision which has given rise to most controversy is *Hegarty v Shine*.[152] There, the Court of Appeal dismissed an action for battery by a woman who had been infected by her paramour with a venereal disease, the existence of which he had concealed. The Court dismissed the action of the basis that it arose *ex turpi* but also on the basis that the woman's consent was real and had not been vitiated by fraud. Ball LC stated:

> "We are not dealing with deceit as to the nature of the act to be done, such as occurred in the instance[153] ... of the innocent girl who was induced to believe that a surgical operation was being performed. There was here a lengthened cohabitation; deliberate consent to the act or acts out of which the cause of action has arisen. If deceit by one of the parties to such a cohabitation as to the condition of his health suffices to alter the whole relation between them, so as to transform their intercourse into an assault on his part, why should not any other deceit have the same effect? Suppose a woman to live with her paramour, under and with a distinct and reiterated promise of marriage, not fulfilled nor, it may be, ever intended to be fulfilled - is every separate act of sexual intercourse an assault? Let the same happen in conjunction with a violated engagement to provide for her maintenance and protection against poverty - does a similar consequence here also follow? No one, I think, would be prepared to answer these questions in the affirmative."[154]

The Court was clearly affected by the fact that the relationship was between unmarried persons. It regarded it as impossible to contend that, out of this "meretricious relationship", it should find a legal duty of disclosure whose object would be "the aiding of its continuance".[155]

---

151. But *cf Macdonald v Sebastian* (1987) 43 DLR (4th) 636 (NSSCTD), where Burchell J saw merit in the suggestion that the defendant's conduct amounted to a battery when the defendant, a landlord, failed to disclose to his tenants that the water supply at the rented premises was contaminated by arsenic.

152. (1878) 4 LR Ir 288 (CA).

153. *R v Case* 1 Den CC 580.

154. 4 LR Ir 288 at 294.

155. (1878) 4 LR Ir 288, (*per* Ball LC). Decisions in the United States do not take this approach: regardless of whether the parties are married to one another, liability may attach in respect of sexually transmitted diseases: see Kaganas, 'Compensation for AIDS victims' (1987) 16 Anglo-Amer LR 117 at 133; Baruch 'AIDS in the Court: Tort Liability for the Sexual Transmission of Acquired Immunity Deficiency Syndrome' (1987) 22 Tort Ins. LJ 165 at 181-186; Murray & Winslett 'The Constitutional Right to Privacy and Emerging Tort Liability for Deceit in Interpersonal Relationships' [1986] U Ill LR 779. Corliss 'Comment, Aids-Liability for Negligent Sexual Transmission' (1988) 18 Cumb LR 691 at 702-709, 717-719. See generally Gostin & Hodge 'Piercing the Veil of Secrecy in HIV/AIDS and other Sexually Transmitted Diseases: Theories of Privacy and Disclosure in Partner Notification' (1998) 5 Duke J of Gender L & Policy 9.

**[22.66]** The decision was met with little enthusiasm by foreign courts[156] and most commentators.[157] Their criticisms have some force, so far as they condemn the actual holding in the case, but there remains in this context a difficulty in defining the line between central and collateral fraud.[158] If a man convinces an inexperienced girl that sexual intercourse is a medical operation which will cure her asthma,[159] is that not a different case, legally speaking, from where a man convinces a less inexperienced girl that sexual intercourse will improve her looks or her humour? It is submitted that what is wrong with *Hegarty v Shine* is not that it failed to address these issues (which it did, somewhat cumbersomely) but that it let moralistic considerations cloud its resolution of the question. Why the decision is unconvincing is that the defendant's fraud was surely central rather than collateral. He induced the plaintiff to engage in conduct which, to his knowledge but not hers, was very likely to injure her. The conduct itself was injurious. This was not a case bearing any close parallel with one of breach of promise of marriage,[160] contrary to Ball LC's suggestion.

**[22.67]** Consent may be vitiated by duress. The case-law on the subject is scanty; so far as it has established clear principles, it appears that mere economic duress will not suffice.[161] Whether this approach would be favoured by the courts today is, however, far from clear. The change in judicial attitude towards economic duress in the context of the defence of voluntary assumption of risk would certainly suggest that the older decisions on this question would carry little weight today.[162]

***Consent to medical procedures***[163]

**[22.68]** Medical procedures raise particular problems relating to consent. Clearly, where the medical practitioner fully explains to the patient the nature of the proposed treatment

156. In *Smith v Jenkins* (1970) 119 Comm LR 397 at 413 (HC Austr), Windeyer J described *Hegarty v Shine* as a "miserable" case. In *Hall v Hebert* (1993) 101 DLR (4th) 129 (SC, Can), Cory J observed that the case was "perhaps a notorious example of the unfairness which results from transferring the doctrine from contract to tort law." In *Norberg v Wynrib* (1992) 92 DLR (4th) 449 (SC, Can), Sopinka, J had "no doubt that such a case would be viewed quite differently today."

157. *Cf* WINFIELD & JOLOWICZ, p 849; SALMOND & HEUSTON, p 477-478; STREET, p 84; Prentice 'Of Tort Reform and Millionaire Muggers: Should An Observe Equitable Doctrine Be Revived To Dent The Litigation Crisis?' (1995) 32 San Diego LR 53 at 109 - "infamous and often condemned decision".

158. WINFIELD & JOLOWICZ, p 849.

159. *Cf R v Flattery* (1877) 2 QBD 410; Williams [1923] 1 KB 340; *Pomeroy v State* (1883) 94 Ind 96; see also *Hegarty v Shine* 4 LR Ir 297. More generally, see the LRC's Consultation Paper, *Rape*, (1987) para 17 and its Report, *Rape and Allied Offences* (LRC 24-1988), paras 16-17.

160. Even in such cases, a remedy may be forthcoming, in deceit (*Graham v Saville* [1945] OR 301 (CA); *Smythe v Reardon* [1948] QSR 74) or, where still available, for breach of promise of marriage (*Shaw v Shaw* [1954] 2 KB 429).

161. *Cf Latter v Braddell* (1881) 50 LJQB 488 (CA), noted in (1881) 15 ILT & SoLJ 126. *Cf Freeman v Home Office (No 2)* [1984] QB 524 affd [1984] 1 All ER 1036 (CA); STREET, p 84, fn 11.

162. *Cf* Bankier 'The Avoidance of Contracts for Economic Duress Threats to Employment: American Developments and Anglo-Canadian Prospects' (1974) 22 Chitty's LJ 73; Reard, (1979) 17 Alberta LR 322.

163 See Skegg 'A Justification for Medical Procedures Performed Without Consent' (1974) 90 LQR 512; Skegg 'Consent to Medical Procedures on Minors' (1973) 36 MLR 370; Skegg 'Capacity of Minors to Consent to Medical Treatment' [1969] Recent L 295;

and the patient consents, there is no problem: the difficulties arise where no such explanation is given or no attempt is made to obtain the patient's consent at all, whether on account of the patient's unconscious condition or his or her young age.

**[22.69]** The question of "informed consent" has already been considered.[164] On this matter the Supreme Court has made it plain that it does not regard actions for failure to obtain an informed consent to a proposed course of medical treatment as ordinarily entitling the plaintiff to an action for battery (or "assault" as it was described colloquially in the judgments). In *Walsh v Family Planning Services Ltd*,[165] O'Flaherty J expressed the belief that:

> "if there had been ... a failure to give a warning as to possible future risks that would not involve the artificial concept of an assault, but, rather, a possible breach of a duty of care giving rise to a claim in negligence. A claim of assault should be confined to cases where there is no consent to the particular procedure and where it is feasible to look for a consent."

**[22.70]** O'Flaherty J approved of the Supreme Court of Canada's decision in *Reibl v Hughes*,[166] where Laskin CJ had restricted the operation of the tort of battery in this context to cases where there has been "misrepresentation or fraud to sever consent to medical treatment." Finlay CJ agreed with O'Flaherty J's approach.

**[22.71]** Let us now turn to consider cases of failure to obtain any consent for the treatment carried out.

**[22.72]** It is quite possible, of course, that consent may be implied in the circumstances of the case. The patient may well have authorised the practitioner to behave in the way he or she did by a general permission, such as telling the practitioner to "do what you consider best", or some similar injunction. The failure by the patient to prohibit ordinary and foreseeable modes of treatment, the possible effects of which are known to the patient, may also be considered to amount to implied consent in certain cases.

**[22.73]** Where, however, something out of the ordinary is done by the practitioner, it is less easy to establish implied consent. Decisions[167] in several common law jurisdictions have held that it will not be sufficient for the practitioner to show that what he or she did was for the benefit of the patient: the practitioner must show that it was urgently necessary for him or her to do so without letting the patient first decide on whether the patient wishes the

---

163. (contd) Rozovsky 'Consent to Treatment' (1973) 11 OHLJ 103; Bates 'Consenting to the Necessary' (1972) 46 ALJ 73, Institute of Law Research & Reform, Alberta, Background Paper No 9, *Consent of Minors to Medical Treatment* (1975); McCoid 'A Reappraisal of Liability for Unauthorised Medical Treatment'(1957) 41 Minn LR 381; Smith 'Antecedent Grounds of Liability in the Practice of Surgery' (1942) 14 Rocky Mt LR 233, Kelly 'The Physician, the Patient, and the Consent' (1960) 8 U Kansas LR 405; Foley 'Note: Consent as a Prerequisite to a Surgical Operation' (1940) 14 U Cincinnati LR 161; LTW 'Note: Surgical Operations Without Consent' (1946) 19 Tennessee LR 374; Smith 'Battery in Medical Torts' (1967) 16 Clev LR 22.

164. See Ch 14 above.

165. [1992] 1 IR 496.

166. [1980] 114 DLR (3d) 1.

167. *Marshall v Curry* [1933] 3 DLR 260 (Nova Scotia SC); *Murray v McMurchy* [1949] 2 DLR 442 (BC SC); *Mulloy v Hop Sang* [1935] 1 WWR 714 (CA); *Allan v New Mount Sinai Hospital* (1980) 109 DLR (3d) 634 (Ont HC); *Brushett v Cowan* (1987) 40 DLR (4th) 488 (Nfld SCTD); *Holmes v Heatley* [1937] Ir Jur Rep 74 (HC) is not inconsistent with these decisions.

treatment to be carried out. Whether the entitlement of the doctor to act in cases of emergency should properly be regarded as being based on the implied consent of the patient or on the broader concept of necessity has been debated in the decisions. In England, there has been a trend towards adopting a broad welfare test for interventions such as sterilisation, where the person is mentally incompetent, either temporarily or on a long-term basis.[168] Irish courts should hesitate before adopting this approach too readily. Principles of bodily integrity and autonomy should be given due weight; paternalism, outside the context of judicial exercise of its *parens patriae* jurisdiction, should not be let run rampant, merely because the object of the benevolent intervention lacks the capacity to refuse it.[169]

### *Minors*

**[22.74]** The capacity of minors to consent to medical treatment - and, more broadly, any types of physical contact - is a matter of debate.[170] The position has recently been changed, and clarified to some extent, by s 23 of the Non-Fatal Offences Against the Person Act 1997 but some important questions remain unsolved.

**[22.75]** Let us first consider the common law position prior to the statutory change. The better view appeared to be that:

> "[i]t all depends on whether the minor can understand what is involved in the procedure in question. At least in theory, this is a factual test, the application of which cannot be determined in the abstract."[171]

**[22.76]** One should not overlook the constitutional dimensions of the question (which of course have not been altered by the recent statutory change). Where, for example, the responsibilities of parents as guardians of their children and the rights of children to be protected from precocious sexual activity are interfered with or imperilled, the courts will protect the members of the family against infringement of their constitutional rights. It would seem prudent to treat with some reserve any suggestion that pronouncements in Britain[172] in relation to minors and procreation would receive the unthinking imprimatur of an Irish court.[173]

---

168. *Cf Re F; F v West Berkshire Health Authority* [1990] 2 AC 1 (HL).

169. *Cf* In *Re a Ward of Court (No 2)* [1996] 2 IR 100 (SC).

170. See the references cited in fn 164 above, and Tomkins 'Health Care for Minors: The Right to Consent' (1974) 40 Sask LR 41; Wadlington 'Minors and Health Care: The Age of Consent' (1973) 11 Os Hall LJ 115; Foley 'Note: Consent as a Prerequisite to a Surgical Operation' (1940) 14 U Cincinnati LR 161 at 172-177; Engum 'Expanding the Minor's Right to Consent to Non-Emergency Health Care: A Psycho-Legal Rationale', (1982) 3 J of Legal Med 557; Frankel 'Consent of Incompetents (Minors and the Mentally Ill) to Medical Treatment' (1977) 1 Legal Med Q 187; Picard 'Recent Developments in Medical Law' (1977) 1 L Med Q 206 at 204-205.

171. Skegg, 'Consent to Medical Procedures on Minors' (1973) 36 MLR 370 at 375.

172. Eg *Gillick v West Norfolk and Wisbech Area Health Authority* [1986] AC 112. See Parkinson 'The Gillick Case - Just What Did It Decide?' (1986) 16 Fam L 11.

173 The constitutional issues are complex and their resolution is made more difficult to predict because, over the past decade, the Supreme Court's philosophy on general themes impacting on the subject has been in a state of flux. There has been an increasing emphasis on individualistic values - autonomy, privacy and bodily integrity - as well as a greater stress on the rights of children.

**[22.77]** Where a minor is incapable of providing consent, and, indeed, even in some cases where he or she is, the practice in this country and abroad has been for medical practitioners to obtain the consent of the parents or guardian for the proposed treatment. How such consent, given by a third party, can logically provide a defence is difficult to understand[174] but it clearly has had the support of decisions in this country[175] and in other jurisdictions.[176] It may perhaps be justified on the ground of necessity, implied consent, agency or the welfare of the minor.

**[22.78]** In the only reported decision regarding medical treatment of minor in this country, *Holmes v Heatley*,[177] Maguire J, of the High Court, absolved the medical practitioner from liability. The parents of a sixteen-year-old boy gave their consent for an operation on his toxic exopthalmic goitre. They had been informed that only a local anaesthetic would be required. During the operation, when it was time to stitch up the wound, the boy became excitable so a general anaesthetic was administered. The boy died as a result through no negligence in the administration of the anaesthetic.

**[22.79]** Maguire J dismissed the plaintiffs' action under the fatal accidents legislation at the close of their case. He stated:

> "There is no evidence here which would entitle a jury to hold that there was an assault. I am not deciding the question as to whether there is any necessity for the consent of the parents for an operation or whether the consent of the boy of the age of the deceased is sufficient. In my view the surgeon was bound to act as he did in the emergency with which he was faced. On the uncontradicted evidence in this case the giving of the general anaesthetic was the only course open to him."[178]

**[22.80]** Let us now consider the change brought about by s 23 of the Non-Fatal Offences Against the Person Act 1997. It provides as follows:

> (1) The consent of a minor who has obtained the age of 16 years to any surgical, medical or dental treatment which, in the absence of consent, would constitute a trespass to his or her person, shall be as effective as it would be if he or she were of full age; and where a minor has by virtue of this section given an effective consent to any treatment it shall not be necessary to obtain any consent for it from his or her parent or guardian.

---

173. (contd) Parental rights have been less emphasised, especially where those rights conflict with the rights of children. There has also been a development of what might be characterised as "neo-family privacy", which regards the family has having some degree of entitlement, at a constitutional level, to make decisions affecting the continuation, or otherwise, of the lives of the unborn or those with a very limited cognitive capacity. If the Irish courts address the issue that arose in *Gillick* - the provision of contraceptives to minors under sixteen without the prior knowledge or approval of their parents - these competing values will require resolution. In highlighting the recent changes, it would be unwise to ignore the fact that the express language of Articles 41 and 42 of the Constitution represents a potent statement of protection for the trustee role of parents in relation to the rearing and nurture of their children.

174. WILLIAMS, p 315. More generally, see *The People (AG) v Edge* [1943] IR 115 (SC); *cf R v D* [1984] 2 All ER 449 (HL); Williams 'Can Babies Be Kidnapped?' [1989] Crim LR 473.

175. *Holmes v Heatley* [1937] Ir Jur Rep 74 (HC) (semble).

176. *Cf* In *Re L (An Infant)* [1968] P 119 (CA); *B(BR) v B(J)* [1968] p 466 (CA). See further Skegg, 'Consent to Medical Procedures on Minors' (1973) 36 MLR 370 at 375

177. [1937] Ir Jur Rep 74 (HC).

178. [1937] Ir Jur Rep 74 at 76.

(2) In this section 'surgical, medical or dental treatment' includes any procedure undertaken for the purposes of diagnosis, and this section applies to any procedure (including, in particular, the administration of an anesthetic) which is ancillary to any treatment as it applies to that treatment.

(3) Nothing in this section shall be construed as making ineffective any consent which would have been effective if this section had not been enacted.

**[22.81]** A few points about this section may be noted. First, it says nothing expressly about the position relating to the consent of a minor under the age of sixteen years. If sub-s (1) were viewed in isolation, the *inclusio unius est exclusio alterius* rule of construction might possibly indicate a legislative intent that sixteen should be the minimum age for a lawful consent by a minor. When one takes account of sub-s (4), however, it seems that the Oireachtas has decided to leave open the question whether a minor under sixteen has the capacity in any circumstances to consent, without reference to the minor's parents or guardians. Section 23, therefore, only partially clarifies the law.

**[22.82]** The second point concerns the nature of a consent by a minor who has obtained the age of sixteen. The section throws no light on what is necessary to constitute such a consent. The reference in sub-s (1) to "an effective consent" does not refer to the quality of the consent; it merely relates back to the earlier part of the sentence where legal effectiveness is conferred on the consent by reason of the fact of its being provided by the minor. The courts may be disposed to treat the question of the minor's consent as "one of fact", dependent on the circumstances of the case, including the particular minor's age and maturity (or lack of it) as well as the nature of the medical treatment. It can be predicted that the courts will closely scrutinise elective interventions of a cosmetic nature.[179]

**[22.83]** This leads to the third point, which concerns the implications of the section for parents or guardians. There has been no recent judicial pronouncement directly on the issue, but it is plain that Articles 41 and 42 recognise the trusteeship role of parents in the upbringing and protection of their children. Legislation cannot subtract from this constitutional remit though it can attempt to clarify it in specific contexts.

**[22.84]** Even if s 23 had never been enacted, it is generally accepted that the trusteeship role of parents in relation to the details of the lives of their children is to recognise and respect the burgeoning capacities of their teenage offspring to make autonomous decisions regarding their values, beliefs and choices as to life plans, associations, friendships and loves.[180] While fully acknowledging the difficult task of parenting, it seems certain that a court would not hold to be unlawful the decision of a sixteen-year-old minor to undergo a small medical intervention - such as an operation on his or her broken finger - without the consent of the minor's parents. But if the case involves a serious medical intervention with significant risks, and if there is a strong argument that the intervention is not truly for the minor's welfare, the legal position becomes less clear. Presumably the parents could take wardship proceedings, in which the welfare of the minor would be the paramount

179. On elective treatment in general, see *Walsh v Family Planning Services Ltd* [1992] 1 IR 496 (SC) and compare Kearns J's approach in *Geoghegan v Harris* High Court, 21 June 2000.

180. The trend of international conventions and covenants is to regard autonomy interests as inhering in children even of a very young age. See Jackson 'Note: The War Over Children's Rights: And Justice for All? Equalizing the Rights of Children (1999) 5 Buff Hum Rts LR 223.

consideration. In the absence of wardship proceedings, a doctor, before the enactment of s 23, might have apprehended that to go ahead with the intervention without the consent of the parents could expose the doctor to the risk of litigation, either by means of a claim for damages[181] or an injunction.[182]

**[22.85]** The enactment of s 23 must have eased these anxieties, though it cannot have removed them completely. The provision that a minor's consent is legally effective and that "it shall not be necessary to obtain any consent for [the treatment] from his or her parent or guardian" could be interpreted in one of two ways. On one view, it means that the parents or guardians are thereby disentitled in any case to take any legal steps in respect of the treatment, so far as it impacts on the welfare of the minor, their trusteeship role under the Constitution or otherwise. On the other view, what s 23 does is to render the consent lawful to the extent that it can not be regarded as unlawful by reason merely of the failure to obtain the consent of the parents or guardians. On this latter view, the trusteeship function is not disturbed and parents or guardians remain entitled (to the uncertain extent that they have such an entitlement) to take proceedings with respect to the treatment in the same way as they can with respect to any other lawful activity - an employment contract, for example - in which their minor child engages.[183]

### Self Defence

**[22.86]** In *Dullaghan v Hillen*,[184] Fawsitt J, of the Circuit Court set out clearly the law relating to self-defence:

> "When one is wrongfully assaulted it is lawful to repel force by force, provided that no unnecessary violence is used. How much force and of what kind it is reasonable and proper to use, in the circumstances, is a question of fact. Resistance must 'not exceed the bounds of mere defence and prevention' or ... the force used in defence must be not more than commensurate with that which provoked it."

**[22.87]** In *Gregan v Sullivan*[185] O'Byrne J sounded a note of caution:

> "I am inclined to agree that we ought not to weigh a method of self-defence on too fine a scales, but steam hammers ought not to be used to crush flies."

**[22.88]** In this case the High Court held perverse a Circuit Court jury finding of self-defence where the defendant, a man aged under forty, had used a pitchfork to inflict thirteen punctured wounds on the arms of the 65-year-old plaintiff, as well as breaking one of his arms, in response to being struck on the lip by the plaintiff.

**[22.89]** It is none the less true that a person threatened with assault is "not bound to wait until the other has given a blow, for perhaps it will come too late afterwards".[186]

---

181. *Cf Cosgrove v Ireland* [1982] ILRM 48 (HC).

182. *Cf A & B v Eastern Health Board* [1998] ILRM 460 (HC).

183. One should note here the potential dissonance between tort law and contract law and the difficulty of reconciling the antiquated statutory rules relating to contractual capacity, contained in the Infants Relief Act 1874 with contemporary constitutional values. The thinking underlying contracts for "necessaries" and analogous contracts for the benefit of a minor contains the germ of the welfare principle underlying the Guardianship of Infants Act 1964 and related legislation, but this welfare principle is only crudely and anomalously effectuated by the 1874 legislation.

184. [1957] Ir Jur Rep, 10 at 13 (CC). See also *Cockcroft v Smith* (1705) 11 Mod 43, 88 ER 872.

185. [1937] Ir Jur Rep 64 at 65 (HC).

186. *Chaplin of Gray's Inn's Case*, YB 2 Hen IV, fo 8, pi 40. See also *Kellett v Stannard* (1851) 2 Ir CLR 156 at 158 (Exch); Ross v Curtis High Court, 3 February 1989 (Barr J). For the criminal law standard see *The People (AG) v Dwyer* [1972] IR 416 (SC).

## Defence of Third Persons

**[22.90]** Historically, the law recognised the right of a master to defend his servant against attack;[187] it recognised the same privilege for servants regarding their masters,[188] husbands regarding their wives[189] and wives regarding their husbands.[190] Beyond this it did not go, although logically "there seems to be no good reasons why the relationship of brothers should not be included".[191] In modern times this essentially proprietary[192] approach has fallen into disfavour. Salmond & Heuston[193] expressed the view that:

> "[it] may be safely assumed. . . that at the present day all such distinctions are obsolete, and that everyone has the right of defending any person by reasonable force against unlawful force, even if he has made a genuine mistake about the perilous position of that other".

In the criminal law decision of *People (AG) v Keatley*,[194] Maguire CJ, of the Court of Criminal Appeal, stated that "[t]he true position seems to the Court to be correctly stated" in a virtually identical passage, from an earlier edition of that work.[195]

**[22.91]** The limits of the defence appear to be the same as that of self-defence.[196] Mistake, if reasonable, will excuse the defendant.[197]

## Necessity

**[22.92]** The scope of the defence of necessity in respect of trespass to the person[198] is uncertain. The authorities are either very old,[199] controversial[200] or not directly in point.[201]

---

187. *Seaman v Cuppledick* (1615) Owen 150, 74 ER 966.
188. *Barfott v Reynolds*, (1733) 2 Str 953, 93 ER 963.
189. *Anon*, YB 19 Hen VI, 31 pl 59 (1440).
190. *Leward v Basely* (1695) I Ld Raym 62, 91 ER 937.
191. *People (AG) v Keatley* [1954] IR 12 at 17 (CA).
192. *Cf Seaman v Cuppledick* (1615) Owen 150, 74 ER 966 at 150-151, and 967, respectively.
193. SALMOND & HEUSTON, p 128.
194. *People (AG) v Keatley* [1954] IR 12 at 17.
195. SALMOND, (10th ed, 1945), p 334.
196. *Cf Lynch v Fitzgerald* [1938] IR 382 (SC, affg HC).
197. *Cf Gambriell v Caparelli* (1975) 7 OR (2d) 205 (CA,), analysed by Binchy, (1977) 9 Ottawa LR, at 362-364. *Cf* Wilson 'The Defence of Others - Criminal Law and the Good Samaritan' (1988) 33 McGill LJ 756.
198. See Williams, 'Defence of Necessity'(1953) 6 CLP 216 at 234-235.
199. *Cf Scott v Shepherd* (1773) 2 WBI 892, 96, ER 525; *Greeson v Gilbert* (1783) 3 Dougl 232, 99 ER 629 - action on a policy of insurance, to recover value of slaves thrown overboard ship for want of water.
200. *Cf Leigh v Gladstone* (1909) 26 Times LR 139; Zellick 'The Forcible Feeding of Prisoners: An Examination of the Legality of Enforced Therapy' [1976] Public L 153; *Leigh v Gladsone* was not followed in *Secretary of State for the Home Office v Robb* [1995] 1 All ER 677 (Fam Div). The constitutional dimension to that issue is discussed by Walsh J, extrajudicially, in 'The Judicial Power and the protection of the Right of Privacy' [1977] Dublin ULJ 3 at 9. For the US approach, see Aushbacher, 'Note: Forcefeeding Hunger-Striking Pressmen: A framework for Analysis' (1983) 35 U Fla LR 99; Greenberg 'Note: Hunger Striking Prisoners: The Constitutionality of Force-Feeding' (1983) 51 Fordham LR 747; *cf Zent v Prevatte* (1982) 248 Ga 832, 286 SE 2d 715 - holding hunger-strikes unconstitutional -contrary to general trend of US decisions. More generally, see Costello 'The Terminally Ill The Law's Concerns' (1986) 21 Ir Jur (ns) 35.
201. *Cf Priestman v Colangelo* [1959] SCR 615.

It appears that it is open to a defendant to justify a trespass against the person on the ground of necessity but that the Courts will be very reluctant to recognise the defence. Whilst minor trespasses may be tolerated,[202] serious interferences will scarcely be excused. Whether necessity could ever justify killing another is debatable: the criminal authorities[203] are against the defence in such a case, but it has been contended by one commentator that drawing lots to decide who is to die, where all participants are agreed on the course of action might be "acceptable" in civil law "in the direst of emergencies in the absence of any possible alternative".[204]

### Discipline

**[22.93]** Traditionally, parents had a broad discretion in the manner in which they maintained discipline among their children.[205] The use of physical force or confinement remains permissible, provided it is not excessive. No cases appear to have been reported in which a child has sued his or her parents for battery or false imprisonment. Of course, there is no reason in principle why such an action should not be taken. The victim of physical or sexual abuse may sue the perpetrator, regardless of the question of familial relationship.

**[22.94]** Contemporary attitudes are increasingly uncomfortable with the infliction of physical force on children. The Law Reform Commission, in its Report on Non-Fatal Offences Against the Person[206] made it clear that it would have wished to recommend making it an offence for parents to use force in discipling their children but it considered that such a legislative change would, in the short term at least, be counterproductive:

> "[I]t is important that change be made in stages. The sudden introduction of criminal liability for any assault into the home without more education and information would be inimical to good reform and the interests of children. Foundations have to be laid with prudence. Without proper guidance in effective, enlightened, non-violent powering, parents will feel lost, resentful and resistant to change."[207]

**[22.95]** The Commission considered that, while it would be premature to abolish the common law chastisement exception immediately, "the re-education of parents should proceed without delay and the exception should be abolished at the right time."[208]

---

202. As, for example, where a member of the Garda Síochána pushes through a crowd of shoppers in Grafton Street when pursuing a suspected shoplifter.
203. *R v Dudley* (1884) 14 QBD 273; *US v Holmes* (1842) 1 Wall Jr 1.
204. Linden, *Tort Law*, p 72, referring to Fuller 'The Case of Speluncean Explorers' (1949) 62 Harv LR 616.
205. *Cf* Eekelaar 'What Are Parental Rights?' (1973) 89 LQR 210 at 223-224. More generally, see Herman 'A Statutory Proposal to Prohibit the Infliction of Violence upon Children' (1985) 19 Fam LQ 1; Edwards 'Corporal Punishment and the Legal System' (1996) 36 Santa Clara LR 983; Davidson 'Note: When is Parental Discipline Child Abuse? The vagueness of Child Abuse Law' (1996) 34 U Louisville J of Fam L 403 and the truly comprehensive analysis by Bitensky 'Spare the Rod, Embrace Our Humanity: Toward a New Legal Regime Prohibiting Corporal Punishment of Children' (1998) 31 U Mich J L Reform 353 which discusses statutory reforms in Europe and Minnesota, the decision of the Italian Supreme Court of Cassation abolishing the parental immunity and the impact of international instruments including the European Convention on Human Rights and Fundamental Freedom.
206. LRC 45-1994.
207. LRC 45-1994, para 9.211.
208. LRC 45-1994, para 9.214.

**[22.96]** That time may be closer than the Commission envisaged. A decision of the European Court of Human Rights in 1998 - *A v United Kingdom*[209] - found English law to be in violation of Article 3 of the European Convention, which prohibits torture or inhuman or degrading treatment or punishment. The stepfather of a nine-year-old child had struck him on a number of occasions, with a garden cane, causing bruising on several parts of his body. He was charged with causing him actual bodily harm but acquitted by a majority jury verdict, his defence being that the boy was a difficult child who had not responded to parental or school discipline. The child argued that English law had failed to protect him from ill-treatment by his step-father.

**[22.97]** In holding that Article 3 had been violated, the European Court of Human Rights noted that the British government accepted that there had been such a violation. Relying on an earlier decision, also involving the United Kingdom,[210] the Court observed that ill-treatment must attain a minimum level of severity if it is to fall within the scope of Article 3:

> "The assessment of this minimum is relative: it depends on all the circumstances of the case, such as the nature and context of the treatment, its duration, its physical and mental effects and, in some instances, the sex, age and state of health of the victim."[211]

**[22.98]** The Court considered that the beating of a nine-year-old child with a garden cane using considerable force, on more than one occasion, reached the level of severity prohibited by Article 3.

**[22.99]** Holding the British government liable, the Court stated that:

> "[c]hildren and other vulnerable individuals, in particular, are entitled to state protection, in the form of effective deterrence, against such serious breaches of personal integrity ..."[212]

Noting that, under English law, it is a defence to a charge of assault on a child that the treatment in question amounted to "reasonable chastisement", that the burden is on the prosecution to prove beyond reasonable doubt that the assault went beyond the limits of lawful punishment and that the jury had acquitted the step-father in spite of the fact that the child had been subjected to treatment of sufficient severity to fall within the scope of Article 3, the Court concluded that English law had not provided adequate protection to the applicant against treatment or punishment contrary to Article 3.

**[22.100]** The Court clearly did not regard the position as being mitigated by the fact that, under English (as under Irish) civil law, the victim was entitled to sue for battery was on the balance of probabilities and where the issue of justification rested on the defendant.

**[22.101]** The case indicates an impatience at the European level with the possibility that physical chastisement of a severe degree might go unpunished. The Court's antipathy appears to cast a shadow on the common law system of criminal justice since the possibility that a jury will acquit an accused - for whatever reason - even where the offence charged is very serious - murder or rape, for example - is an integral part of a system that requires proof beyond reasonable doubt. To stay in harmony with the Court's critique,

---

209. [1998] 2 FLR 959 (ECHR).
210. *Costello-Roberts v United Kingdom* (1993) 19 EHRR 112.
211. [1998] 2 FLR 959.
212. [1998] 2 FLR 959.

English and Irish legislators could take the radical step of abandoning the general requirement of proof beyond reasonable doubt in criminal proceedings, shifting the burden of proof onto the defendant, once violence of an objective level sufficient to violate Article 3 has been established or abolishing parental immunity from criminal liability for reasonable "chastisement of children". Whether that strategy would be consistent with the constitutional guarantee of due process may be a matter of debate.

**[22.102]** Schoolteachers[213] formerly had a similarly broad discretion to inflict violence on their charges. In *McCann v Mannion*,[214] Judge Moonan of the Circuit Court, stated that:

> "Teachers must be protected against any unjust attacks upon them concerning what they do in maintaining discipline. A teacher is justified in inflicting proper corporal punishment when it is necessary. The person most competent to estimate the conduct which deserves such punishment is the teacher himself, and it would require proof of malice or of something approaching to malice to induce me to interfere with his discretion."

**[22.103]** The mode and extent of the punishment were matters that excited greater judicial concern: whilst the court might not "compute the number of strokes to be given in punishment"[215] and whilst "[a] stubborn, mutinous child might require abnormal treatment"[216] - that is, more corporal punishment than the norm- modes of punishment involving particular risk of injury such as striking a child on the legs or on the cheek, were almost certain to amount at least to a technical assault.[217]

**[22.104]** The matter is now dealt with by legislation. Section 24 of the Offences Against the Person Act 1997 provides that "[t]he rule of law under which teachers are immune from criminal liability in respect of physical chastisement of pupils is hereby abolished."[218]

---

213. For a comprehensive analysis, see Glendenning, *Education and the Law* (1999), Ch 10. See also Anon 'Schoolmaster's Right to Punish Children' (1941) 75 ILT & SJ 41; Wallington 'Corporal Punishment in Schools' [1972] Jurid R 124; Bates 'Corporal Punishment in Legal, Historical and Social Context' (1983) 12 Manitoba LJ 337; Tripp Acting 'In *Loco Parentis* as a Defense to Assault and Battery' (1967) 16 Clev-Mar LR 39. Bridlinger 'Discipline by Teachers in Loco Parentis' (1957) 6 Clev-Mar LR 313; Dugan, Teachers' Tort Liability (1962) 11 Clev-Mar LR 512 at 517-520; Baeckle 'Corporal Punishment in Schools; An Infringement on Constitutional Freedoms' (1971) 20 Clev St LR 560.

214. (1932) 66 ILTR 161 (CC).

215. *McGee v Cunanne* (1932) 66 ILTR 147 at 148 (CC).

216. *McGee v Cunanne* (1932) 66 ILTR 147.

217. In *McGee v Cunanne* (1932) 66 ILTR 147, damages of £1 were awarded in 1932 for 'a technical assault', where there had been 'an attempt to victimise the teacher'; in *McCann v Mannion* (1932) 66 ILTR 161, the same judge in the same year awarded £2, again, for 'a technical assault' where there had been no similar attempted victimisation of the teacher. See also *Ryan v Fildes* [1938] 3 All ER 517; *Fitzgerald v Northcote* (1865) 4 F & F 656, ER. A teacher successfully defended an action in *O'Callaghan v Collins* High Court, 1 December 1990.

218 Section 18 gives a general defence in respect of the use of force, concerning such matters as self-defence, defence of others and defence of property. See further Glendenning, *Education and the Law* (1999), paras 10.06-10.16, 10.56-10.50. The Law Reform Commission had so recommended in its *Report on Non-Fatal Offences Against the Person*, (1994) LRC 45, para 9.205. Corporal punishment in national schools had already been "abolished" by Circular 9/82 issued by the Department of Education. For consideration of the legal effectiveness of this circular, see Hogan & Morgan, *Administrative Law in Ireland* (3rd ed, 1998), p 51.

While s 24 refers only to criminal liability, it is plain that the immunity at civil law must also have expired. This development is in line with changing mores throughout Europe.[219]

## Lawful Authority

**[22.105]** The law permits conduct that would otherwise constitute a trespass to the person where its purpose is to prevent, control or respond to antisocial behaviour, most notably of a criminal nature. Thus, members of the Garda Síochána[220] have broad powers of arrest under warrant[221] or, in certain cases, without a warrant.[222] Civilians too have powers of arrest but they always were more narrowly defined and have been further curtailed by

---

218. (contd) The first prosecution of a teacher after the legislative change took place on 13 January 1999; 'Principal Fined for Assault on 12-Year-Old Pupil', Irish Times, 14 January 1999. The legislative abolition of the immunity in relation to physical chastisement still leaves teachers with a formidable range of legal protection in relation to disciplinary matters. The Irish courts have given schools considerable latitude in formulating and administering disciplinary procedures: see The *State (Smullen) v Duffy* [1980] ILRM 46 (HC); *Murtagh v Board of Governors of St Emer's National School* [1991] 1 IR 482 (SC); Byrne & Binchy, *Annual Review of Irish Law 1991*. See also *Student A and Student B v Dublin Secondary School* High Court, 25 November 1999 (Kearns J); *Wright v Board of Managemnt of Gorey Community School* High Court, 28 March 2000 (O'Sullivan J). Formal procedures, with rights of appeal, have been introduced by ss 28 and 29 of the Education Act 1998: see Glendenning, *Education and the Law* (1999), Ch 10; Glendenning 'School Discipline: The Impact of Section 29 of the Education Act 1998 in Primary Schools' a paper delivered at a Conference at Trinity College Dublin Law School, Irish courts have yet to examine the lawfulness of disciplinary powers not affected by s 24 of the 1997 Act, such as those relating to confiscation of pupils' property or detention of pupils. STREET, p 96 (footnote reference omitted) expresses the view that:

> "[a] pretty serious breach of discipline would have to be shown to justify detaining or, in particular, locking up a child. Disciplinary powers may afford a defence to trespass to goods as where a teacher removed from a boy a pocket book which, he thought, would identify the ringleaders in a school conspiracy to disturb order".

In Ireland, no court has yet sought to reconcile in express terms the competing interests of school discipline and the constitutional rights of pupils to liberty, free expression and property. The urgency of the case in *Smullen* and the apparent triviality of the case in *St Emer's* led the judges to make sweeping statements which do not give sufficient indication of the strength of pupils' constitutional claims in other school disciplinary contexts.

219. For analysis of the problem from the perspective of the United States Constitution, see Baechle, *Corporal Punishment in Schools; An Infingement on Constitutional Freedoms* (1971) 20 Clev St LR 560. This issue has also been considered by the European Court of Human Rights: *cf Campbell & Cosans v UK* (1982) 4 EHRR 293, noted by Lonbay, (1983) 46 MLR 345; *Costello - Roberts v United Kingdom* (1995) 19 EHRR 112.

220. See generally Walsh, *The Irish Police, A Legal and Constitutional Perspective* (1998), paras. 6-12ff. The arresting officer must make it clear to the arrested person that he or she is under arrest: *DPP v McCormack* High Court, 8 July 1999 (McGuinness J).

221. It should be noted that at common law there was no notion of detention falling short of arrest: see *Dunne v Clinton* [1930] IR 366 (HC affd SC); *AG v Cox* CCA 9 April 1929; *cf Doherty v Liddane* [1940] Ir Jur Rep 58 (HC). Sections 4 to 10 of the Criminal Justice Act 1984 contain provisions relating to the detention of arrested persons in Garda Síochána's custody. As to constitutional inhibitions, in regard to the inviolability of the dwelling under Article 40.5, see Byrne & Binchy, *Annual Review of Irish Law 1987*, pp 85-88.

222. See Williams 'Arrest for Felony at Common Law' [1954] Crim LR 408; Sandes, *Criminal Law and Procedure in the Republic of Ireland* (3rd ed, 1951), pp 42-45.

recent legislation. Briefly, at common law, an arrest by a member of the Garda Síochána was lawful where he or she reasonably believed that a felony has been committed and that the arrested party was guilty of that offence[223] A civilian was not quite so privileged. He or she was entitled to use force to prevent the commission of a felony or to arrest a person reasonably suspected of having committed a felony but, if it transpired that no felony had in fact been committed, he or she was liable in false imprisonment (and in some cases battery) to the arrested party.[224]

**[22.106]** The position has been changed by recent legislation. The Criminal Law Act 1997 abolished the traditional distinctions between felony and misdemeanor.[225] In place of felony, it introduced the concept of an "arrestable offence" which is one carrying punishment of at least five years imprisonment.[226] Section 4 contains the crucial provision on arrest without warrant. These broadly reflect the former law but differ in an important respect. The section may be quoted in full:

> (1) Subject to subsections (4) and (5), any person may arrest without warrant anyone who is or whom he or she, with reasonable cause, suspects to be in the act of committing an arrestable offence.
>
> (2) Subject to subsections (4) and (5), where an arrestable offence has been committed, any person may arrest without warrant anyone who is or whom he or she, with reasonable cause, suspects to be guilty of the offence.
>
> (3) Where a member of the Garda Síochána, with reasonable cause, suspects that an arrestable offence has been committed, he or she may arrest without warrant anyone whom the member with reasonable cause, suspects to be guilty of the offence.
>
> (4) An arrest other than by a member of the Garda Síochána may only be effected by a person under subsection (1) or (2) where he or she, with reasonable cause, suspects that the person to be arrested by him or her would otherwise attempt to avoid, or is avoiding, arrest by a member of the Garda Siochána.
>
> (5) A person who is arrested pursuant to this section by a person other than a member of the Garda Síochána shall be transferred into the custody of the Garda Síochána as soon as practicable.

**[22.107]** A few points about s 4 may be noted. First, it retains the requirements in respect of an arrest without warrant by a person other than a member of the Garda Síochána, not only that the person have reasonable cause to believe that the arrested party was guilty of

223. *Cf Kavanagh v Hamrogue* Supreme Court, 12 March 1965 - sergeant attempted to arrest cyclist in belief that bicycle had been stolen; High Court ruling that reasonable grounds existed for suspecting that cyclist was guilty of felony was not challenged on appeal but, in Lavery J's view, in Supreme Court, the ruling was "extremely lenient".

224. Sandes, *Criminal Law and Procedure in the Republic of Ireland* (3rd ed, 1951), p 43; *Cf Rourke v Pepper* (1825) Smi & Bat 346. In *Dillon v Dunnes' Stores Ltd* Supreme Court, 20 December 1968 a shop proprietor who employed members of the Garda Síochána in their spare time as store detectives was relieved of liability for false imprisonment where they were alleged to have been over-zealous in attempting to abstract confessions from shop assistants suspected of pilfering, since the proprietor's conduct fell "short of authorising or agreeing to falsely imprison" *per* Ó Dálaigh CJ at p 8).

225. Criminal Law Act 1997, s 3(1).

226. Criminal Law Act 1997, s 2(1).

an offence, but also that the offence should in fact have been committed.[227] Thus, for example, if a store detective reasonably believes that a customer committed a shop-lifting offence and it turns out that no such offence occurred (or, as will sometimes be the case, that it cannot be shown that the suspect was guilty of the offence), then the arrest will be unlawful and the store detective[228] is open to civil liability for false imprisonment, battery, assault and perhaps defamation.

**[22.108]** Secondly, subs (4) renders unlawful an arrest without warrant by a person other than a member of the Garda Síochána, even though it complies fully with the requirements of subss (1) or (2), if the person carrying out the arrest does not, with reasonable cause, suspect that the person to be arrested by him or her "would otherwise attempt to avoid, or is avoiding arrest by a member of the Garda Síochána". The practical impact of sub-s (4) on the power of arrest by civilians, especially retailers or the security staff engaged by them, is potentially significant. When would a retailer (or member of the security staff) be likely to have such reasonable suspicion? It can be argued that the circumstances are rarely likely to occur. Of course, if the retailer actually witnesses a suspected shoplifter running away from an arresting guard, the retailer will comply with the requirements of sub-s (4) if he or she apprehends the fleeing figure. But this is not a normal occurrence. What the retailer will have to deal with is a person walking out of the shop who has apparently stolen some goods. The retailer will hardly ever have any reasonable cause for suspecting that, if he or she does not arrest the customer, the customer "would otherwise attempt to avoid" arrest by a member of the Garda Síochána. The person is seeking to consummate a successful shoplifting experience. No doubt, in walking away from the store, the prospects of his or her being arrested, by a member of the Garda Síochána or anyone else, are increasing with each stride. But, since no member of the Garda Síochána will normally be actually present or even aware of the fact of the theft, there is something unconvincing about attributing to the departing thief the attempt to avoid an arrest by a particular person or category of persons where no persons of that category have at this moment the slightest intent to carry out an arrest of the thief or even any knowledge of the offence.

**[22.109]** It is true that s 4(4) speaks of "avoiding" rather than "resisting" arrest. No doubt the former expression includes, but is not limited to, the latter. The use of "avoiding" does extend to a furtive course of action. But, at the end of the day, it is hard to translate the action of a thief in leaving a premises into an actual attempt to avoid arrest by a member of the Garda Síochána, where no such member has any knowledge of the facts that would justify the arrest and consequently no arrest is being contemplated.

**[22.110]** The motivation underlying the introduction of subs (4) appears to have been to discourage vigilantism but it is a crude instrument.

**[22.111]** Members of the Garda Síochána may also do acts that would constitute a trespass where they are designed to prevent a breach of the peace[229] that they reasonably believe is

---

227. Subsection (2). The only instance where a person other than a member of the Garda Síochána is protected where an arrestable offence has not in fact been committed and where he or she makes the arrest warranted, is where the arresting party reasonably suspects that the party arrested is in the act of committing the offence: subs (1).

228. As to the question of vicarious liability of the store, see *Dillon v Dunnes Stores Ltd* Supreme Court, 20 December 1968.

229. See Williams 'Arrest for Breach of the Peace' [1954] Crim. LR 578.

otherwise likely to take place. The person whose liberty or whose person is affected need not have been the one likely to breach the peace.[230] Thus in *Humphries v Connor*[231] in 1864, where a constable removed an orange lily from a woman who was walking through the street of the town of Swanlinbar, it was held to be a good defence that the act was done to preserve the public peace, in that the woman, although being followed by a threatening crowd, refused to remove the lily. A similar approach was followed in *O'Kelly v Harvey*[232] in 1883, where a public meeting organised by the Land League at Brookeborough was forcibly dispersed by a magistrate after an inflammatory poster had been published by certain persons of opposing political views, calling on opponents of the Land League to assemble in large numbers "and give Parnell and his associates a warm reception".

**[22.112]** The courts have, however, made it clear that compulsory "protective custody" is not to be permitted. Thus in *Connors v Pearson*[233] the arrest and incarceration of a child witness could not be justified on the basis that his life was in jeopardy. As O'Connor LJ put it:

> "You cannot incarcerate a man or a boy merely because his going abroad or his doing something that he is minded to do exposes him to some danger. If that were so, the adventurous spirits that sought the North Pole or the interior of Africa, or that conquered the Atlantic in flight, might have been locked up for their own good. Nor does the fact that the supposed danger arises from the designs of wicked men warrant interference with the wish of him who wishes to brave it. If it were otherwise, every informer in Irish history could have been locked up for life"[234]

**[22.113]** The extent to which other compulsory bodily contacts may be lawfully justified is a matter of uncertainty. The constitutional right to bodily integrity must set some limits to these interventions. Statutory provisions permitting bodily contacts without consent can probably withstand constitutional scrutiny on the basis of the social policy they seek to serve: the need for the effective detection of crime may be considered sufficient to warrant compulsory fingerprinting of suspects[235] (though it would not justify torture or inhuman treatment), the process of proxy consent for the taking of a blood test from an immature

230. *Cf Humphries v Connor* (1864) 17 ICLR 1 (QB); *O'Kelly v Harvey* (1883) 14 LR Ir 105 (CA); *Coyne v Tweedy* [1898] 2 IR 167 (CA, affg QBD); *Beatty v Gillbanks* (1882) 9 QBD. 308; *Duncan v Jones* [1936] 1 KB 218.

231. (1864) 17 ICLR 1 (QB).

232. (1883) 14 LR Ir 105 (CA). See also, to similar effect, *Coyne v Tweedy* [1898] 1 IR 167 (CA, affg QBD). *Cf R (Orr) v Justices of Londonderry* (1891) 28 LR Ir 440 (QB), favouring an approach that is difficult to reconcile with these decisions: Kelly, *Fundamental Rights in the Irish Law and Constitution* (2nd ed, 1967), p 147; Hogan and Whyte, *Kelly: The Irish Constituion* (3rd ed, 1998), pp 966-967.

233. [1921] 2 IR 51 (CA).

234. [1921] 2 IR 51 at 91. As to the powers of compulsory confinement of persons considered to be mentally ill, under the Mental Treatment Act 1945, Pt XIV (as amended), see eg *O'Dowd v North Western Health Board* [1983] ILRM 186 (SC), *In re Clarke* [1950] IR 235 (SC); *Murphy v Greene* [1990] 2 IR 566; *O'Reilly v Moroney* [1992] 2 IR 145; *Bailey v Gallagher* [1996] 2 ILRM 433; *Croke v Smith* Supreme Court, 31 July 1996; *Melly v Moran and Northern Western health Board* High Court, 19 June 1997; *Blehein v Murphy* Supreme Court, 17 January 2000. The meeting is comprehensively analysed in Casey and Craven, *Psychiatry and the Law* (1999), Ch 18. A new Bill brings Irish law into line with the requirements of the European Community on Human Rights.

235. *Cf* ss 6 and 28 of the Criminal Justice Act 1984. Where the suspect refuses to give his or her consent to be fingerprinted he or she will be guilty of an offence (ss 6(5) and 28(4)), but it is not clear whether the suspect can be physically forced to undergo this process.

minor[236] or a mentally ill adult[237] in cases where paternity is in question may be adjudged necessary to fill in what would otherwise be a lacuna which would work against the interests of the minor or adult in question.[238] Corporal punishment in prisons and places of detention, which had not been a feature of the Irish penological systems for many years, was formally abolished 1997.

## Defence of Property

**[22.114]** Where a person enters another's land or premises, with force and violence, that other may thereupon evict the intruder,[239] using no more force than is reasonably necessary to do so.[240] Where, however, the entry is without force or violence, it is necessary to request that the trespasser leave before resorting to physical measures.[241] Similar principles apply to trespass to goods.[242] In order to exercise this privilege one must have such possession of the land (or goods) as to ground an action in trespass.[243]

---

236. *Cf* the Status of Children Act 1987, s 39(3)(a), analysed by Woulfe 'Annotation to the Act' [1987] ICLSA, General Note to s 39; Byrne & Binchy, *Annual Review Of Irish Law 1987*, pp 187-189. In England, at common law, it was held that the court had no power to compel an adult to take a blood test: *W v W (No 4)* [1974] p 67; *H v H* [1966] 3 All ER 560.

237. *Cf* s 39(3)(b) of the 1987 Act and the Irish references cited above.

238. *Cf* s 9(7)(b) of the Control of Clinical Trials Act 1987 providing for proxy consent in relation to clinical trial on an ill person who is incapable of comprehending nature, significance and scope of the requisite consent.

239. *Cf Russo v Ontario Jockey Club* (1987) 43 CCLT I (Ont HC). As to the position at criminal law, see the Prohibition of Forcible Entry and Occupation Act 1971. For the historical background, see Anon 'Forcible Entry' (1881) 15 ILT & Sol J 653. See also the Air Navigation and Transport Act 1975, s 4(4)(a) - authorising removal from aircraft of persons committing or about to commit offence.

240. *Green v Goddard* (1798) 2 Salk 641, 91 ER 540.

241. *Green v Goddard* (1798) 2 Salk 641, 91 ER 540; *Weaver v Bush* (1798) 8 TR 78,101 ER 1276. See also *Ross v Curtis* High Court, 3 February 1989 (Barr J), analysed by Byrne & Binchy, *Annual Review of Irish Law 1989*, pp 438-441, where Barr J had to deal with the twin defences of self-defence and defence of property. There is of course, no conceptual identity between them. A burly landowner who evicts two six-year-old boys from his orchard will be concerned to protect his property without even addressing the question of his own physical welfare. Barr J's test, so far as the defence of property was concerned, appeared to incorporate recklessness. It will be recalled that the Occupiers' Liability Act 1995 limits the duty owed by occupiers towards trespassers to that of not injuring them intentionally and not acting with reckless disregard for them: s 4(1). The duty owed to a person who enters the premises for the purpose of committing an offence or who, while present there, commits an offence is even more restrictive: the occupier is not required to avoid acting with reckless disregard for this entrant "unless a court determines otherwise in the interests of justice": s 4(3)(a). Section 8(a) provides that nothing in the Act affects any enactment or rule of law relating to "self defence, the defence of others or the defence of property". Thus, the changes brought about by the Act in respect of the duty owed to trespassers generally have no effect on the previous law so far as these defences are concerned. It appears that s 21(3) of the Control of Dogs Act 1986, which prescribes negligence as the exclusive test to determine liability for an attack by a dog on a trespasser, has survived the Occupiers' Liability Act 1995 unscathed, although there is a respectable argument to be contrary: see para **[27.33]** below.

242. *Blades v Higgs* 10 CB (ns) 713, 142 ER 634 (1861) affd on other grounds, (1865) 11 HL Cas 621, 11 ER 1474. Whilst that case 'shows that the owner of goods, which are wrongfully in the possession of another, may justify an assault involving no unnecessary violence, in order to re-possess himself of his property, ... there is nothing in [it] to justify the extension of the principle ... to an imprisonment and detention for an indefinite time', *Harvey v Mayne* (1872) IR 6 CL 417 at 419 (Com Pleas).

243. *Holmes v Bagge* (1853) 1 E & B 782, 118 ER 629.

**[22.115]** It seems that the privilege extends to the protection of the property of other members of one's household.[244] Whether such a broader right of protection of their property would be recognised has not been tested in the courts, and it is true that historically the law has discouraged interventions on behalf of others, which were regarded as a form of intermeddling.[245] This philosophy is scarcely consistent with modern thinking and is diametrically opposed to the approach favoured in *People (AG) v Keatley*,[246] which recognised the right to protect the safety of others, irrespective of whether they are members of one's household. Whilst it could perhaps be argued that protection of the person raises somewhat different considerations from that of protection of property, the better view seems to be that the privilege would today be recognised (within reasonable limits) as extending to the protection of property as well as of the person.[247]

**[22.116]** A thoughtful analysis of the limits of the defence was provided by Carroll J in the Circuit Court decision of *MacKnight v Xtravision*.[248] The defendants were tenants of a lockup shop in a shopping centre in Palmerston, County Dublin. In the course of a dispute with their landlord, the owner of the centre, the defendants withheld payment of service charges to the landlord. One morning the defendants' staff arrived to find that they were unable to enter the shop because a chain and lock had been placed on the door by the landlord. The plaintiff "a security man about the place", was aware of the fact that a landlord had done this because of the defendants' non-payment of the service charges. In taking this step, the landlord was, in Carroll J's view, a trespasser.

**[22.117]** Some time later the defendants' marketing manager and the head of their security department arrived, as did the gardaí. The plaintiff was in the vicinity of the shop, allegedly telling passers-by that the rent was unpaid. He told the gardaí that this was a civil matter and that they had no jurisdiction. The gardaí, "perhaps wisely", accepted what the plaintiff said and departed.

**[22.118]** The defendants consulted their solicitor at some stage and were advised that they might use force to remove the lock and chain. The exact terms of this advice were not given clearly in evidence. The Xtravision party went to Donnybrook where they purchased bolt clippers and collected "another very hefty member" of the security department; asked, when giving evidence, whether he was a heavyweight boxer, he explained he was a light-middle weight. On their return the Xtravision party found that the plaintiff had anchored himself to the handles of the double doors of the shop, facing the doors, an arm through each handle. In acting this way he was a trespasser, in the judge's view.

**[22.119]** An altercation then ensued in which, it appears, the plaintiff's arms were restrained and he was punched by the marketing manager and the boxer. His arm and upper chest were bruised and his back and abdomen were very painful.

---

244. *Cf* STREET, p 92, citing Blackstone, Book III, 3, adding that no modern cases have been traced.
245. *Cf* Dawson '*Negotiorum Gestio*: The Altruistic Intermeddler' (1961) 74 Harv LR 1073.
246. [1954] IR 12 (SC).
247. For critical analysis of the historical development of aspects of moral thinking on the general subject, see Sullivan, *Killing in Defense of Private Property: Development of a Roman Catholic Moral Teaching, Thirteenth to Eighteenth Centuries* (1976).
248. Circuit Court, 5 July 1991, extracted in McMahon & Binchy, *Casebook on the Law of Torts* (2nd ed, 1991), pp 407-410

**[22.120]** Carroll J was satisfied that the "roughing up" administered to the plaintiff would certainly support a charge of assault causing actual bodily harm against the defendants. The question was whether it could be justified on the ground that it was the consequence of using no more force than was reasonably necessary to remove from the shop doors a man who was undoubtedly a trespasser.

**[22.121]** Carroll J's forceful, yet highly thoughtful, discussion of the issue may be quoted in extenso.

> "What is reasonable force? Is it merely the amount of energy which is required to move a man out of a room [or] a house or, as here, to loosen his grip on a door and move him away from it, no matter what may be the other consequences? I think not. It is necessary to take into account the occasion upon which the force is used. It is here essential to point out that the present case bears only ... remote resemblance to that of a householder who is disturbed by an intruder who invades his or her house or flat, the shopkeeper or tradesman who finds a person forcing his way into his shop or premises where business is being carried out so as to threaten or discommode his customers or staff or one who refuses to go when asked; even less does it resemble the case of any such person who has to deal with a criminal who forces or tries to force an entry with threat to life or limb or property.
>
> The danger of causing confusion in the minds of such persons is one of the features of the case which has troubled me. The degree of force used here would be perfectly justifiable in such types of case and much more if necessary to defend a man's home. Nothing which I am about to say should in any way render such citizens hesitant or fearful about defending their persons or property.
>
> In this case, up to the arrival of [the Xtravision party], no one had been in any way threatened or put in fear: it was a simple case of the defendants, being prevented from entering a lock-up shop and, no doubt, some threat to commercial interests.
>
> The Xtravision party were undoubtedly entitled to lay hands lightly on the plaintiff to move him aside. But when that failed, in the circumstances of the case, they should have desisted. They were not upon such cause entitled to assault him so as to inflict the type of injuries [he sustained].
>
> On their way to Donnybrook to buy the bolt clippers and pick up the light-middle weight ... they must have passed the open doors of these courts where, their solicitors might have advised them, they could have had an injunction against [the plaintiff] and his employers for the asking. It may be objected that this would have involved a delay which would have been damaging to their commercial interests. But it is of the essence of a civilised state regulated by law that its citizens in very many - indeed in all but a very small minority of - cases, forego the right to redress their grievances by private violence and instead look to the courts for their remedy. If parties were to resort to private violence in cases such as this, there would be an end to all law or order."

**[22.122]** While imposing liability, Carroll J reduced the plaintiff's damages by a half on account of his contributory negligence.

# Chapter 23

# Trespass to Land


I. Introduction ........ 653
II. Trespass by Entering on Land ........ 653
III. Trespass by Remaining on Land ........ 662
IV. Trespass by Placing Things on Land ........ 664
V. The Defendant's State of Mind ........ 668
VI. Interference with Possession ........ 670
VII. Defences ........ 672


## I. Introduction

**[23.01]** The tort of trespass to land consists of intentionally or negligently entering or remaining on, or directly causing anything to come into contact with, land in the possession of another without lawful justification.[1] The tort may be regarded as protecting the right to private property[2] or, more abstractly and less effectively, the right to privacy.[3]

## II. Trespass by Entering on Land

**[23.02]** The slightest crossing of the boundary onto the plaintiff's land will constitute a trespass. Thus, even putting a finger through the plaintiff's door will suffice. Indeed it is not necessary to cross the boundary: physical contact with it may constitute trespass.[4]

---

1. *Cf* STREET, p 73, SALMOND & HEUSTON, pp 40; Magnet 'International Interference with Land', Ch 10 of *Studies in Canadian Tort Law*, Klar ed, (1977); Keeton 'Trespass, Nuisance and Strict Liability' (1959) 59 Col LR 457. In *Royal Dublin Society v Yates* High Court, 31 July 1997, Shanley J stated:

   "Trespass to land consists in any unjustifiable intrusion by one person upon land in the possession of another. The intrusion may be intentional or it may be negligent: in either case, it is actionable in the absence of lawful justification."

2. In *W v Ireland (No 2)* [1997] 2 IR 141 at 164-165 (HC), Costello P stated: "The right to private property is protected by laws against trespass ..:". The duty of occupiers to trespassers is now governed by the Occupiers' Liability Act 1995. See Ch 12.

3. *Cf* Ch 37 below.

4. *Cf* SALMOND & HEUSTON, p 40; *Gregory v Piper* (1829) 9 B & C 591, 109 ER 220. *Whelan v Madigan* [1978] ILRM 136 (HC) - striking door with intention of breaking it. A complete ouster of the plaintiff from the property will, of course, constitute a trespass: *Clarke v Cooper* (1859) 5 Ir Jur (ns) 38 (Exch). Where there has been a forcible entry, the criminal penalty may take account of whether compensation has been made to the owner: Prohibition of Forcible Entry and Occupation Act 1971, s 6. Section 2 of the Act exempts from criminal liability the owner or one entering the land forcibly in pursuance of a *bona fide* claim of right. The court may prefer not to imprison a trespasser who is in contempt of an injunction, leaving the matter to the Gardaí to enforce under the provisions of the 1971 Act: see *Ross Co Ltd v Swan* [1981] ILRM 416 (HC).

## Constitutional, Common Law and Statutory Rights of Entry

**[23.03]** Article 40.5 of the Constitution provides that "[t]he dwelling of every citizen is inviolable and shall not be forcibly entered save in accordance with law". In the Supreme Court decision of *The People (Attorney General) v O'Brien*,[5] Walsh J, having quoted the provision, said:

> "That does not mean that the guarantee is against forcible entry only. In my view, the reference to forcible entry is an intimation that forcible entry may be permitted by law but that in any event the dwelling of every citizen is inviolable save where entry is permitted by law and that, if necessary, such law may permit forcible entry."

**[23.04]** *O'Brien's* case was concerned with the question of the admissibility of evidence obtained during a search of a person's home[6] rather than of trespass. Walsh J considered that evidence should not be admitted if:

> "obtained or procured by the State or its servants or agents as a result of a deliberate and conscious violation of the constitutional rights of the accused person where no extraordinary excusing circumstances exist, such as the imminent destruction of vital evidence or the need to rescue a victim in peril. A suspect has no constitutional right to destroy or dispose of evidence or to imperil the victim. I would also place in the excusable category evidence obtained by a search incidental to and contemporaneous with a lawful arrest although made without a valid search warrant."[7]

---

4. (contd) See also *Beattie v Mair* (1882) 10 LR (Ir) 208 (Ex Div). The Criminal Justice (Public Order) Act 1994, s 13 makes it an offence to trespass on a building or its curtilage, without reasonable excuse in such a manner as causes fear or is likely to cause fear in another person. Section 11 of the Act makes it an offence to enter a building with the intent to commit an offence. *Cf Reeves v Penrose* (1890) 26 LR Ir 141 (Ex Div). Where construction work on an adjoining property leads to the collapse of the building possessed by the plaintiff, an action in trespass will lie: *cf Etchingham v Acres & Co Ltd* High Court, 24 July 1975 (Butler J). In *Jones v Read* (1876) IR 10 CL 315 (Exch), the defendant knocked down a "ruinous" wall of which he and the plaintiffs were tenants in common, which had stood between their separate properties. In the absence of an intention by the defendant to rebuild the wall, this was held to constitute a trespass. As to damage from blasting, see Smith 'Liability for Substantial Physical Damage to Land by Blasting - The Rule of the Future' (1970) 33 Harv LR 542, 667. See also *Boylan v Northern Bank Ltd* High Court, 21 July 1977 (Costello J). *Daly v Cullen* (1957) 92 ILTR 127 (CC); *Clancy v Whelan* (1957) 92 ILTR 39 (HC).

5. [1965] IR 142 at 169 (SC). Walsh J added:

> "In a case where members of a family live together in the family home, the house as a whole is for the purpose of the Constitution the dwelling of each member of the family. If a member of a family occupies a clearly defined proportion of the house apart from the other members of the family, then it may well be that the part not so occupied is no longer his dwelling and that the part he separately occupies is his dwelling as would be the case where a person not a member of the family occupied or was in possession of a clearly defined portion of the house".

See also *Director of Public Prosecutions v Gaffney* [1988] ILRM 39 (SC), analysed by Byrne & Binchy, *Annual Review of Irish Law 1987*, pp 85-8.

6. On this question see Hogan and Whyte, *Kelly: The Irish Constitution* (3rd ed, 1994), pp 613-614; Casey, *Constitutional Law in Ireland*, (3rd ed, 2000), pp 530-535; Forde, *Constitutional Law of Ireland* (1987), pp 369-373; Ryan & Magee, *The Irish Criminal Process* (1983), pp 156-176; O'Connor, The Admissibility of Unconstitutionally Obtained Evidence in Irish Law', (1982) 17 Ir Jur (ns) 257.

7. [1965] IR at 170. See further Hogan & Whyte, *Kelly: The Irish Constitution* (3rd ed, 1994), pp 914-920.

**[23.05]** It seems reasonably clear that if these or other "extraordinary circumstances" exist, an entry would not be contrary to Article 40.5. Whether it would destroy the occupant's right of action for trespass to land (or to goods) is not certain, but in some cases at least - the rescue of a victim in peril, for example - it may be argued with some confidence that it does have this effect. As we shall see public necessity has traditionally afforded a broad defence to the tort of trespass to land. It would be curious if an entry that is immune from challenge under Article 40.5 were nonetheless to fall outside the parameters of this defence.

**[23.06]** At common law, a search warrant may be issued by a District Justice or Peace Commissioner, on information being sworn before him or her alleging a suspicion that goods have been stolen and are in the house sought to be searched.[8] This common law power has been supplemented by statute.[9]

**[23.07]** Statutes have also conferred on certain persons in certain circumstances the right of entry onto private property for other purposes.[10] Thus, for example, inspectors have broadly drafted powers of entry and inspection of any place they have reasonable cause to

---

7. (contd) *Cf* the Bankruptcy Act 1988, ss 27 and 28, reflecting the constitutional concerns of the Bankruptcy Law Committee Report, para 8.6.1 (Prl 2714), not shared by the Law Reform Commission in their *Report on Debt Collection: (I) The Law Relating to Sheriffs*, para 81 (LRC 27-1988). The Commission's analysis should be read in the light of judicial developments noted by Byrne & Binchy, *Annual Review of Irish Law 1987*, pp 85-86.

8. *Cf* Hogan & Whyte *Kelly: The Irish Constitution* (3rd ed, 1994), p 560; *The Garda Síochána Guide* (1981), p 1202.

9. Sandes, *Criminal Law and Procedure in the Republic of Ireland* (3rd ed, 1951), pp 50 51. Examples include the Misuse of Drugs Act 1977, s 23(1), as amended by Misuse of Drugs Act 1984, s 12, see O'Connor, 'Annotation to the Act' [1984] 1 CLSA - General Note to section 12, *Byrne v Grey,* High Court, 9 October 1987, Hamilton P and Charleton, *Controlled Drugs and the Criminal Law* (1986), pp 34-40; the Gaming and Lotteries Act 1956, s 39; *DPP v McMahon* [1987] ILRM 87; the Customs and Excise (Miscellaneous Provisions) Act 1988, ss 2, 3, 5; the Wireless Telegraphy Act 1926, *s* 8; as amended by the Broadcasting and Wireless Telegraphy Act 1988, *s* 17; the Video Recordings Act 1989, s 25; the Criminal Damage Act 1991, s 13; the International War Crimes Tribunals Act 1998, s 30; the Firearms and Offensive Weapons Act 1990, s 15; the Food Safety Authority of Ireland Act 1998, s 50; the Employment Equality Act 1998, s 94; the Energy (Miscellaneous Provisions) Act 1995, s 16; the Environmental Protection Agency Act 1992, s 13(6); the Derelict Sites Act 1990, s 30(3); the Carriage of Dangerous Goods by Road Act 1998, s 7; the Competition Act 1991, s 21, as amended by the Competition (Amendment) Act 1996, s 11(2); the Control of Dogs Act 1986, s 26; the Control of Horses Act 1996, s 35; the Road Transport Act 1999, s 15; the Criminal Justice (Location of Victims' Remains) Act 1999, s 8; the Architectural Heritage (National Inventory) and Historic Monuments (Miscellaneous Provisions) Act 1999, s 3(5)-(8) (see Lyall, Annotation to the Act, ICLSA, General Note to s 3); the Electricity Regulation Act 1999, s 12; the National Minimum Wage Act 2000, s 33(3); the Equal Status Act 2000, s 33(4); the Merchant Shipping (Investigation of Marine Casualties) Act 2000, s 28; the Copyright and Related Rights Act 2000, ss 132, 256; the Electronic Commerce Act 200, s 27; the Education (Welfare) Act 2000, s 30(5); and the Illegal Immigrants (Trafficking) Act 2000, s 7; and the National Monuments (Amendment) Act 1987, *s* 22. Note also, the Larceny Act 1916, *s* 42 (*cf Ryan v O'Callaghan,* High Court, 22 July 1987 (Barr J); *Farrell v Farrelly,* High Court, 5 February 1988 (Hanlon J)) and the Merchandise Marks Act 1887, *s* 12(1); *cf The State (Batchelor & Co (Ireland) Ltd) v District Justice Ó Floinn* [1958] IR 155 (SC rev HC).

10. See Ryan & Magee, *The Irish Criminal Process* (1983), p 143.

believe is being used as a place of work,[11] as have authorised persons in relation to air transport[12] and persons ensuring the humane slaughter of animals.[13] Similarly, the gardaí

11. Safety, Health and Welfare at Work Act 1989, s 34(1). This provision was reflected in earlier legislation. *Cf* the Factories Act 1955, *s* 94; see also the Safety in Industry Act 1980, s 53; the Safety, Health and Welfare (Offshore Installations) Act 1987, s 41; and the Mines and Quarries Act 1965, s 131; the Merchant Shipping Act 1894, s 206; Merchant Shipping Act 1906, s 26; the Abattoirs Act 1988, ss 36(5), 54; Health Act 1953, s 68, the Health Act 1947, s 94. See, however, *Brannigan v Dublin Corporation* [1927] IR 513 (SC); - Public Health (Ireland) Act 1878, ss 52 and 55 did not authorise defendant to dump rubbish on plaintiff's land. Other examples include the International Carriage of Perishable Foodstuffs Act 1987, s 8; the Abattoirs Act 1988, s 54; the Building Control Act 1990, s 8(17); the Housing (Miscellaneous Provisions) Act 1992, s 12(1); the Housing (Miscellaneous Provisions) Act 1997, ss 12(2), 20(4); the Wildlife Act 1976, s 73; the Prohibition of Incitement to Hatred Act 1989, s 9; the Organisation of Working Time Act 1997, s 8(7) and the National Monumnets (Amendment) Act 1994, s 8(2).

12. Air Navigation and Transport Act 1936, s 39(1); Custom - Free Airport Act 1947, s 7(1); Air Navigation and Transport Act 1988, ss 18, 33(1); Air-Raid Precautions Act 1939, s 33; Air Navigation and Transport Act 1975, s 4(2); Gas Act 1976, ss 26-27, 34, Electricity (Supply) Act 1927, s 98 - given a constitutional *imprimatur* in *Electricity Supply Board v Gormley* [1985] IR 129 (SC), and s 108; Defence (Amendment) Act 1987, s 7.

13 Slaughter of Animals Act 1935, s 9. Other examples of a statutory right of entry include the Oil Pollution of the Sea Act 1956, s 21(1), as amended by the Oil Pollution of the Sea Act 1977, s 15; the Oil Pollution of the Sea (Civil Liability and Compensation) Act 1988, ss 32-33; Air Pollution Act 1987, s 14; (see Scannell, *Annotation* [1987] ICLSA - General Note to the section); the Restrictive Practices Act 1972, s 11(2), (9); the Packaged Goods (Quality Control) Act 1980, s 148(1); the Protection of Animals Kept for Farming Purposes Act 1984, s 8 (as to common law, see *H Williams & Co v Dublin Corporation* (1949) 84 ILTR 62 (CC): see further Clark, *Annotation* [1984] ICLSA, General Note to section 8); the National Monuments (Amendment) Act 1987 s 8(2) 5(1); the Canals Act 1986, s 11; the Control of Dogs Act 1986, ss 16(1) & (2) and 26(2); the Pawnbrokers Act 1964, s 46; the Data Protection Act 1988, s 24; the Local Government (Multi-Storey Buildings) Act 1988, s 7(1); the Dumping at Sea Act 1981, s 4(2); the Roads Act 1993, s 70(8), (9), (11), 76(3)(b); the Waste Management Act 1996, ss 7(a), 14 and 71(4); the Energy (Miscellaneous Provisions) Act 1995, s 10(7), 16 (5); the Harbours Act 1996, s 14(5) and s 49; the Consumer Credit Act 1995, s 105(1); the National Monuments (Amendment) Act 1994, s 8(2); the Credit Union Act 1997, s 90(3); the Sea Pollution Act 1991, s 23(3); the Health (Mental Services) Act 1981, s 36; the Restrictive Practices (Amendment) Act 1987, s 28; the Consumer Information Act 1978, s 16(3); the Shannon Navigation Act 1990, s 4; the Solicitors (Amendment) Act 1994, s 14; the Street and House to House Collections Act 1962, s 24; the Telecommunications (Miscellaneous Provisions) Act 1996, s 12; the Package Holidays and Travel Trade Act 1995, s 21(4); the Milk (Regulation of Supply) Act 1994, s 15; the Local Government (Planning and Development) Act 1963, s 83, as amended by the Local Government (Planning and Development) Act 1976, s 42(c) and the Local Government (Planning and Development) Act 1999, s 31(3); the Wildlife Act 1976, s 68; the Licensing (Combating Drug Abuse) Act 1997, s 14; the Litter Pollution Act 1997, s 20; the Investment Intermediaries Act 1995, s 65; the Irish Aviation Authority Act 1993, s 65; the Irish Horseracing Industry Act 1958, s 51; the Gas Act 1976, s 26; the Greyhound Industry Act 1958, s 46; the Employment Equality Act 1998, s 94; the Energy (Miscellaneous Provisions) Act 1995, s 16; the Environmental Protection Agency Act 1992, s 13; the Derelict Sites Act 1990, s 30; the Dumping at Sea Act 1989, s 41; the Carriage of Dangerous Goods by Road Act 1998, s 6; the Casual Trading Act 1995, s 10; the Chemical Weapons Act 1997, s 7; the Child Care Act 1991, s 12; the Control of Dogs Act 1986, s 16(1) ; as amended by the Control of Dogs (Amendment) Act 1992, s 7; the Control of Horses Act 1996, s 34; the Sea Pollution (Amendment) Act 1999, ss 4 and 5 (see Symmons, Annotation to the Act, ICLSA, General Notes to ss 4 and 5);

may enter licensed premises to prevent or detect a violation of the licensing laws;[14] they may also search club premises on suspicion that any unregistered excisable liquor is being sold there[15] and they may enter the premises being used for public dancing in order to prevent or detect drug trafficing offences. Powers of entry in relation to gaming and lotteries range widely: a member of the Garda Síochána may at all reasonable times enter any amusement hall, funfair, circus, travelling show, carnival, bazaar, sports meeting, local festival, exhibition, "or other like event" in which gaming or a lottery is or is likely to be carried on.[16] Moreover, inspectors have wide powers of entry under the Social Welfare (Consolidation) Act 1993.[17] Similar powers are given to authorised officers under employment legislation.[18] So also persons authorised by a fire authority have a right of entry to premises "at all reasonable times" for the purposes of the Fire Services Act 1981;[19] the same Act, in s 28(1), permits persons in control of a fire or other emergency to enter any building, to cause it to be vacated by its occupants, and to pull the building down. Powers of entry may be given to undertakings that confer general social or economic benefit on the community. thus, for example, statutory powers of entry are prescribed by the Transport (Dublin Light Rail) Act 1996, s 14, the Roads Act 1993, s 78, the Air Navigation and Trasport (Amendment) Act 1998, s 19 and the Arterial Drainage (Amendment) Act 1995, s 10. Finally it is worth noting the very wide powers of entry, search and seizure conferred on authorised persons by the fisheries legislation.[20]

**[23.08]** In the Supreme Court decision of *DPP v Forbes*,[21] O'Flaherty J considered that:

> "[i]t must be regarded as axiomatic that any householder gives an implied authority to a member of the garda to come onto the forecourt of his premises to see to the enforcement of the law or prevent a breach thereof."[22]

**[23.09]** O'Flaherty J made it clear that in the instant case no question of entering the dwelling house arose and that, therefore, there was not "any question of any form of

---

13. (contd) the Architectural Heritage (National Inventory) and Historic Monuments (Miscellaneous Provisions) Act 1999, s 3(4) and (5); the Electricity Regulation Act 1999, s 11(4); the Fisheries (Amendment) Act 1999, s 24(4); the National Minimum Wage Act 2000, s 33; the Equal Status Act 2000, s 33; the Merchant Shipping (Investigation of the Marine Casualties) Act 2000, s 27; the Copyright and Related Rights Act 2000, ss 133(5), 257(5); the Education (Welfare) Act 2000, s 30 and the Customs and Excise (Miscellaneous Provisions) Act 1988, s 5(1) - *cf Simple Imports Ltd v Revenue Commissioners* Supreme Court, 19 January 2000. For further examples, see McMahon, *Report on Irish Economic Law*, p 130 (Commission of European Communities, Vol 7 in Competition - Approximation of Legislation Series, 1976), Hogan & Whyte, *Kelly: The Irish Constitution* (3rd ed, 1994), pp 918-919.
14. Licensing Act (Ireland) 1874, as amended by the Intoxicating Liquor Act 1927, *s* 22. See *DPP v McMahon* [1987] ILRM 87 (SC). See also the Intoxicating Liquor Act 1988, s 37.
15. Intoxicating Liquor (General) Act 1924, s 25.
16. Gaming and Lotteries Act 1956, s 38. See *DPP v McMahon* [1987] ILRM 87.
17. Social Welfare (Consolidation) Act 1993, s 212(3).
18. Anti-Discrimination (Pay) Act 1974, s 6(4); Protection of Employment Act 1977, s 17; Protection of Young Persons (Employment) Act 1977, *s* 27.
19. Fire Services Act 1981, s 22(2).
20. *Cf*, eg, the Fisheries (Consolidation) Act 1959, ss 213, 231, 233-236, 296, 298, 301; Fisheries Act 1980, ss 53, 71; Fisheries (Amendment) (No 2) Act 1987, s 14.
21. [1994] 2 IR 542 (SC).
22. [1994] 2 IR 542 (SC) at 548.

implied waiver of any constitutional right".[23] Furthermore, O'Flaherty J sought to make it plain that "like any implied authority it is an implication which the evidence may, on occasion, rebut".[24]

**[23.10]** Subsequent to *DPP v Forbes*, the Oireachtas enacted the Road Traffic Act 1994, s 39(2) of which provides that:

> "[a] member of the Garda Síochána may for the purpose of arresting a person under section 49(8) or 50(10) of the [Road Traffic Act 1961], enter without warrant (if need be by use of reasonable force) any place (including the curtilage of a dwelling but not including a dwelling) where a person is or where the member, with reasonable cause, suspect him to be."

**[23.11]** In *DPP (Dooley) v Lynch*,[25] Costello P rejected the argument that the totality of the power of entry for the purpose of effecting an offence was contained in s 39 of the Traffic Act 1994 and that accordingly the principles established in *DPP v Forbes* no longer applied. It seemed to Costello P that:

> "the section made lawful what might otherwise not be lawful. However, the section does not make unlawful acts which are, according to *Forbes*, perfectly lawful. When Gardaí enter on private property .... there is an implied consent to enter the property to allow the Gardaí to carry out their duties."[26]

**[23.12]** Section 6 of the Criminal Law Act 1997 now deals comprehensively with the power of members of the Garda Síochána to enter (and search) premises to effect an arrest. It provides as follows:

> (1) For the purpose of arresting a person on foot of a warrant of arrest or an order of committal, a member of the Garda Síochána may enter (if need be, by use of reasonable force) and search any premises (including a dwelling) where the person is or where the member, with reasonable cause, suspects that person to be, and such warrant or order may be executed in accordance with section 5.[27]
>
> (2) For the purpose of arresting a person without a warrant for an arrestable offence a member of the Garda Síochána may enter (if need be, by use of reasonable force) and search any premises (including a dwelling) where that person is or where the member, with reasonable cause, suspects that person to be, and where the premises is a dwelling the member shall not, even acting with the consent of an occupier of the dwelling or other person who appears to the member to be in charge of the dwelling, enter that dwelling unless -
>
> (a) he or she or another such member has observed the person within or entering the dwelling, or

---

23. [1994] 2 IR 542 (SC) at 548. In *DPP v Corrigan* [1986] IR 290 at 296 (HC), Blayney J interpreted Walsh J's remarks in *The People (Attorney General) v O'Brien* [1965] IR 142 at 169, as:

    "saying ... that 'dwelling' in [Article 40], section [5] means a house, or part of a house, and that this is what is made inviolable by the Constitution. The protection would not extend accordingly to a garden surrounding the dwelling, or leading to it, and so would not in my opinion extend to the driveway of the defendant's house where he was arrested".

24. [1994] 2 IR 542 (SC) at 548.
25. [1998] 4 IR 437 (HC).
26. [1998] 4 IR 437 at 440-441.
27. Section 5 gives power to a member of the Garda Síochána to execute a warrant for the arrest of a person or an order of committal notwithstanding that it is not in the member's possession at the time but it requires that the warrant or order to be shown to that person "as soon as practicable".

(b) he or she, with reasonable cause, suspects that before a warrant for arrest could be obtained the person will either abscond for the purpose of avoiding justice or will obstruct the course of justice, or

(c) he or she, with reasonable cause, suspects that before a warrant of arrest could be obtained the person would commit an arrestable offence, or

(d) the person ordinarily resides at that dwelling.

(3) Without prejudice to any express amendment or repeal made by this Act, this section shall not affect the operation of any enactment or rule of law relating to powers of search or powers of arrest.

**[23.13]** Two other statutory provisions of some particular social significance should also be noted. Section 12(6) of the Criminal Damage Act 1991 gives members of the Garda Síochána power to enter any place where a person is or, where they reasonably believe the person to be, for the purposes of arresting that person without a warrant in respect of an offence under the Act. A similar power is conferred on members of the Garda Síochána in respect of arrest without warrant, under s 18(1)(b) of the Domestic Violence Act 1996.

## Abuse of Right of Entry

**[23.14]** Where a person enters land on the basis of an invitation (express or implied) or other ostensible lawful justification, should that person's entry be regarded as none the less constituting a trespass if in fact he or she enters for some other purpose?[28] In the Supreme Court decision of *Purtill v Athlone UDC*,[29] Walsh J left this question open, although his remarks appear to evince sympathy for the view that a trespass is committed.

**[23.15]** In *DPP v McMahon*,[30] which dealt with the admissibility of illegally obtained evidence, Finlay CJ (Walsh, Henchy and Hederman JJ concurring) held that gardaí, who entered a licensed premises without a search warrant in the course of investigating suspected offences under the Gaming and Lotteries Act 1956, were "in law trespassers"[31] as they had no statutory authority to do so and "were outside, by reason of their intention in so doing, the implied invitation of the owner of the licensed premises".[32] The Director of Public Prosecutions, on the basis of the trial judge's findings had "correctly"[33] conceded that the general invitation implied by law in the case of a person running a licensed premises was not applicable to the gardaí in the case. It was "clear that the owner of a licensed premises issues by implication an invitation to members of the public to have resort to his premises for the purposes of buying drink or consuming drink or food therein and for ancillary and consequential purposes".[34] It was also clear, however, that the gardaí did not have that purpose and they "proper[ly] and commendabl[y]"[35] had made no attempt to colour their activity by pretending to be interested in food or drink. *McMahon* thus

28. The position resulting from abuse or excess of authority *after* entry on the land is considered at para **[23.23]** below, in the discussion of trespass *ab initio*.
29. [1968] IR 205 at 210 (SC).
30. [1987] ILRM 87 (SC).
31. [1987] ILRM 87 at 91.
32. [1987] ILRM 87.
33. [1987] ILRM 87 at 89.
34. [1987] ILRM 87.
35. [1987] ILRM 87.

stands unequivocally for the proposition that entry for a sole purpose extraneous to the terms of the invitation (express or implied) renders the entrant a trespasser.

**[23.16]** Courts in other jurisdictions are divided on this question.[36] In the High Court of Australian High Court decision of *Barker v The Queen*[37] in 1983, Brennan and Deane JJ considered that, "[u]nless the consent to enter is limited by reference to purpose, an entry which is otherwise lawful does not become trespassory because it is effected for a purpose of which the person giving the consent is ignorant and of which he would not have approved".[38] Of course in one sense, consent to entry is always "limited by reference to purpose";[39] unless the *Barker* formula were to be read subject to the gloss that the purpose be communicated expressly to the entrant, it might well work out in practice closer to *McMahon* than might at first appear.

**[23.17]** The issue arises frequently in relation to use of the highway. The public have a right to use a highway for the purposes of passing and repassing "and for such other reasonable purposes as it is usual to use the highway".[40] If the highway is used by a person for some extraneous purpose he or she will be a trespasser against the owner of the subsoil.[41]

**[23.18]** The position was well expressed in an English decision:

> "On a highway I may stand still for a reasonably short time, but I must not put my bed upon the highway and permanently occupy a portion of it. I may stoop to tie up my shoelace, but I may not occupy a pitch and invite people to come upon it and have their hair cut. I may let my van stand still long enough to deliver and load goods but I must not turn my van into a permanent stall."[42]

**[23.19]** Thus, using the highway to interfere with the enjoyment of the owner of the subsoil in the shooting of game on a grouse moor adjoining the highway,[43] or to spy on racehorse trials[44] will constitute a trespass. Using the highway for the purposes of picketing was possibly a trespass[45] before the Trade Disputes Act 1906,[46] s 2(1) which rendered lawful attendance "at or near" a house or place where a person resides or works or carries on

---

36. *Cf Strang v Russell* (1905) 24 NZLR 916 (SC); *Byrne v Kinematograph Renters Society Ltd* [1958] 2 All ER 579 (Ch Div); *Reg v Jones* [1976] 3 All ER 54 (CA, CR Div), *Barker v The Queen* (1983) 153 Comm LR 338 (HC, Austr).

37. (1983) 153 Comm LR 338 at 359.

38. (1983) 153 Comm LR 338 at 359.

39. One is reminded here of Scrutton LJ's now well-worn observation in *The Carlgarth* [1927] P 93 at 110 that "[w]hen you invite a person into your house to use the staircase you do not invite him to slide down the bannisters".

40. Clerk & Lindsell, *The Law of Torts* (17th ed, 1995), para 1342.

41. Normally the owner of the adjoining land, though this presumption can be rebutted: *cf* Kerr & Whyte, *Irish Trade Union Law* (1985), p 288.

42. *Iveagh (Earl) v Martin* [1961] I QB 232 at 273.

43. *Harrison v Duke of Rutland* [1893] 1 QB 142.

44. *Hickman v Maisey* [1900] 1 QB 752. See also *AG v Mayo County Council* [1902] 1 IR 13 at 19-20. *Cf Moynihan v GS Ry Co* [1936] IR 132 (HC). *Cf Victoria Park Racing & Recreation Grounds Co Ltd v Taylor* (1937) 58 Comm LR 479 (HC, Austr).

45. *Cf Harrison v Duke of Rutland* [1893] 1 QB 142 at 146.

46. 6 Edw 7, c 47.

business, if those attending there are acting in contemplation or furtherance of a trade dispute and are there merely for the purpose of peacefully obtaining or communicating information, or of peacefully persuading any person to work or abstain from working. It is clear that in the absence of such statutory authority, a tresspass would be committed. Pickets, therefore, which are not protected by industrial relations legislation may be trespasses.

**[23.20]** In *Ferguson v O'Gorman*,[47] the Supreme Court held that picketing on the highway (as opposed to on the premises of another[48]) was rendered lawful by this provision. Sullivan CJ stated:

> "When the legislature declared it lawful for persons to attend at or near a house or place where a person resides, or works, or carries on business, it cannot reasonably have contemplated that such a house or place would be situated in a waste or no man's land. The usual approach to a residence or place of business is by a public highway and unless the right to attend at or near a residence or place of business is a right to attend on a public highway I do not see how such a right can be exercised at all, consistently with the decisions in *Larkin's Case*[49] and *McCusker's Case*[50] that private property may not be invaded."[51]

**[23.21]** The matter is now dealt with by s 11 of the Industrial Relations Act 1990, which permits attendance "at, or, where that is not practicable, at the approaches to, a place" where the picketers' employer[52] (or, in certain instances, another employer, who is not a party to the trade dispute[53]) works or carries on business. It may safely be assumed that a

47. [1937] IR 620 (SC). See also *Ryan v Cooke* [1938] IR 512 (HC); *Quigley v Beirne* [1955] IR 62 (SC revs HC).

48. *Cf Larkin v Belfast Harbour Commissioners* [1908] 2 IR 214; *McCusker v Smith* [1918] 2 IR 432. There is a possibility that the constitutional right of free speech (eg in picketing) could be regarded as circumscribing the right of property - another constitutional right - in certain cases, especially where the private area trespassed upon has a "public" dimension, as in the case of a shopping centre. *Cf* the developments in the United States *Amalgamated Food Employers Local S90 v Logan Valley Plaza Inc* (1968) 391 US 308; *Lloyd Corp v Tanner* (1972) 407 US 551; *Pruneyard Shopping Center v Robins* (1980) 447 US 74 and the dissenting judgment of Laskin CJ in *Harrison v Carswell* [1976] SCR 200, analysed by Ulmer 'Picketing in Shopping Centres' (1975) 13 Os HLJ 879. See also *Regina v Burko* (1969) 3 DLR (3d) 330 (Ont Kitchener Mag Court); *Rosso v Ontario Jockey Club* (1987) 46 DLR (4th) 359 at 363 (Ont HC); *Attorney General of Ontario v Dieleman* (1994) 117 DLR (4th) 449 (Ont Court (Gen Div)). As to the scope of a "public" dimension in this context, see *State v Brown* (1986) 212 NJ Super 61, 513 A 2d 974 (Appeal Div), critically analysed by Sama, (1987) 17 Seton Hall LR 486. The issue was touched on by Barrington J in *New Ireland Assurance Co Ltd v Irish National Union of Vintners, Process & Allied Trade Assistants* High Court, 1 April 1982, analysed in 1J of the Irish Soc for Labour L 21-22 (1982) and Kerr & Whyte, *Irish Trade Union Law* (1985), pp 304, 305. There an injunction was granted against the picketing of a shopping centre with 27 units, on the basis that the owners of the shopping centre would permit reasonable picketing of one unit by the defendant. In Australia the claim by trespassing trade unionists to immunity by virtue of Articles 19 and 22 of the International Covenant on Civil and Political Rights was given short shrift by Morling J, in *Concrete Constructions (NSW) Pty Ltd v Australian Building Construction Employees' and Builders Labourers' Federation* (1988) 83 ALR 385 (Fed Court of Austr).

49. *Larkin v Belfast Harbour Commissioners* [1908] 2 IR 214.

50. *McCusker v Smith* [1918] 2 IR 432.

51. [1937] IR 620 at 648.

52. Subsection (1) of s 11.

court would reject the argument that the replacement of the phrase "or near" by "or, where that is not practicable, at the approaches to" has had the effect of overturning *Ferguson v O'Gorman*. Indeed, it is worth noting that Sullivan CJ used language very close to s 11 when he referred to the fact that "t]he usual approach to a residence or place of business is by public highway ...."

## III. Trespass by Remaining on Land

**[23.22]** Where persons have lawfully entered land in the possession of another, they will commit a trespass if they remain there after their right to stay has ended.[54] Thus, the refusal or failure to leave after being requested to do so will constitute a trespass. The occupier, after a lapse of reasonable time to enable the visitor to do so, may use reasonable force to eject the entrant, whose status is now that of trespasser.[55]

**[23.23]** The doctrine of trespass *ab initio*[56] must now be considered. From early times it has been held that, where a person enters land[57] under authority of law rather than by private invitation,[58] and subsequently abuses or exceeds that authority, he or she is deemed to become a trespasser *ab initio,* that is, from the time of entry onto the premises.[59] Hotel guests or police officers executing a search warrant are examples of persons falling within the scope of the doctrine.

**[23.24]** A person becomes a trespasser *ab initio* only by an act of positive misfeasance: mere non-feasance, such as failing to pay for goods or services at an inn,[60] does not constitute trespass *ab initio.* However, remaining on the land longer than is necessary for the purpose of entry constitutes misfeasance.[61]

**[23.25]** Where an abuse takes place after entry, the entry does not become a trespass *ab initio* if there remains an independent ground or reason for the entry which is unaffected by the abuse.[62]

---

53. Subsection (2) of s 11.

54. *Wood v Leadbitter* (1845) 13 M & W. 838, 153 ER 351; *Duffield v Police* [1971] NSLR 381. *Cf Sandys v Murray* (1838) 1 Ir Eq Rep 29 (Eq Exch); *Carson v Jeffers* [1961] IR 44 (HC); *Irish Shell and BP Ltd v John Costello Ltd* [1984] IR 511 (SC). See also *Dehn v Attorney-General* [1988] I NZLR 564 (HC).

55. It is an offence to trespass on any building or its curtilage "in such a manner as causes or is likely to cause fear in another person": Criminal Justice (Public Order) Act 1994, s 13(1). The failure to leave immediately the vicinity of the place concerned in a peaceable and orderly manner, after being directed to do so by a member of the Garda Síochána who reasonably suspects that such an offence is being, or has been committed is itself an offence: s 13(2)(b). See also the Licensing (Combating Drug Abuse) Act 1997, s 12.

56. See Williams 'A Strange Offspring of Trespass *ab initio*' (1936) 52 LQR 106.

57. The principle also applies to trespass to goods or to the person.

58. *Cf Delta Hotels Ltd v Magrum,* (1975) 59 DLR (3d) 126 (BC SC).

59. *The Six Carpenters' Case* (1610) 8 Co Rep 146a, 77 ER 695. See also *McMullan v Bradshaw* (1916) 50 ILTR 205 (CA); *cf Plunkett v Irish Annuals Press Ltd* (1938) 72 ILTR 161 (HC), revg (1937) 71 ILTR 76 (CC); *Byrne v Duckett* (1882) 10 LR (Ir) 24 (Ex Div).

60. As was the situation in *The Six Carpenters' Case* (1610) 8 Co Rep 146a, 77 ER 695.

61. *Playfair v Musgrove* (1845) 14 M & W 239, 153 ER 465; *Aitkenhead v Blades* (1813) 5 Taunt 199, 128 ER 663.

**[23.26]** The doctrine of trespass *ab initio* met with some criticism in the English Court of Appeal in 1968,[63] but the general view of commentators is that, although the doctrine is very old, it serves a useful function in modern times where there has been a great increase in the powers of entry by public officials, including police.[64]

**[23.27]** In the Supreme Court decision of *Purtill v Athlone UDC*,[65] Walsh J raised, but did not consider it necessary to resolve, a number of questions regarding the doctrine. He enquired whether the plaintiff, if on the premises in the category of either invitee or licensee,

> "and, having entered without any intention of stealing, ... then formed the intent to steal, ... he become[s] a trespasser as from the moment he forms the intent on the grounds that once he exceeds the terms of his invitation or his licence he becomes a trespasser *ab initio*? If the answer to that question is in the affirmative then *a fortiori* he is a trespasser if he forms the intention before he enters at all."[66]

**[23.28]** It is difficult to see how a person who abuses a private entitlement to enter premises should be, or becomes, a trespasser *ab initio*, as opposed to a simple trespasser, by virtue of a secret intention to steal or act otherwise contrary to the terms of the invitation or licence. As we have seen, the doctrine historically has been limited to cases of entry by authority of law rather than private invitation or licence. We find, however, in *Webb v Ireland*,[67] a willingness on the part of Finlay CJ to characterise as trespassers *ab initio* persons who came onto private property with the implied licence of the owners to visit an ancient church and tomb, but who dug into a pit to remove valuable chalices (the Derrynaflan Hoard). It would perhaps be possible to regard access to historical monuments as involving a public rather than a private entitlement, but nothing said by the Chief Justice suggests any such distinction.

---

62. *Elias v Pasmore* [1934] 2 KB 164 - police officers who had lawfully entered property to arrest a man wrongfully seized documents; it was held that they were trespassers only as to the goods and not trespassers *ab initio*. As to the position of persons entering premises pursuant to an improperly obtained court order, see *McMullan v Bradshaw* (1916) 50 ILTR 205 (CA); *Plunkett v Irish Annuals Press Ltd* (1938) 72 ILTR 161 (HC).

63. *Chic Fashions (West Wales) Ltd v Jones* [1968] 2 QB 299 (CA). Lord Denning had previously taken a different view extra-judicially, in *Freedom Under The Law* (1949), p 109. Subsequently, in *Cinnamond v British Airports Authority* [1980] 1 WLR 582 at 588 (CA), Lord Denning invoked the doctrine as a justification for a byelaw enabling the management of Heathrow Airport to exclude from the Airport "mini cab" drivers with convictions for touting and alleged overcharging.

64. See Clerk & Lindsell, *The Law of Torts* 17th ed, 1995, paras 22-29. *Cf* FLEMING, p 48. The rule received the benediction of a Supreme Court judge as recently as in 1996: *Richards v Dublin Corporation* Supreme Court, 12 July 1996 (Keane J) (*ex tempore*) at p 1 of his judgment.

65. [1968] IR 205 (SC).

66. [1968] IR 205 at 210. It should be noted that in *The People (DPP) v Walsh* [1980] IR 294 at 304 (SC), O'Higgins CJ, speaking in a different context, stated that he

> "would regard it as illogical and contrary to reason to contend that something done by a person in accordance with the law could be rendered unlawful merely because that person subsequently acted contrary to his obligation under the law".

67. [1988] ILRM 565 at 589 (SC).

## IV. Trespass by Placing Things on Land

**[23.29]** It is a trespass for a person to place any chattel[68] on the land of another[69] or to

---

68. Including animals: Williams, *Liability For Animals*, (1971), p 171; LRC, Working Paper 3-1977, *Civil Liability for Animals*, paras 30-38; *Hill v Walker* (1806) Peake's Nisi Prius Cas Vol 2, P 234; *R v Pratt* (1885) 4 E1 & BL 860, 119 ER 319; *Beckwith v Shordyke* (1797) 4 Burr 1092, 98 ER 91; *Buckle v Holmes* (1925) 42 TLR 147 at 148 (KBD) (affd [1926] 2 KB 125 (CA)). In *League Against Cruel Sports Lid v Scott* [1986] QB 240, Park J held that, where the master of a hunt takes out a pack of hounds and deliberately sets them in pursuit of a stag or hind, knowing that there is a real risk that in the pursuit hounds may enter or cross prohibited land, the master will be liable for trespass if he intended to cause hounds to enter such land, or if by his failure to exercise proper control over them he caused them to enter such land. Contrast *Crean v Nolan* (1963) 97 ILTR 12 (CC) where no liability was imposed on the organisers of a drag hunt where some of the beagles, a considerable time after the hunt had been completed, went onto the plaintiff's property and killed sheep, *per* Judge Ó Briain: "*prima facie* there is no liability for trespass of cats and dogs in the absence of proof of *scienter*, or the incitement by the owner of the dogs to trespass and commit damage". - In view of the fact that the tort of trespass to land is actionable *per se*, the requirement of incitement to commit damage would seem mistaken. (On this general theme, Edward Parkyns Levinge, *Game Laws of Ireland* (1857), Ch 6 is still of some interest.) It seems clear that a person may be liable in trespass where he directs bees in his possession to invade his neighbour's property. This principle is in no way inconsistent with Henry QC's reluctance in *Tutton v Walter Ltd* [1986] QB 61 (QB), to apply the anthropomorphic label of "trespassers" to bees which (with no such direction by their owners) were attracted to neighbouring property.

69. See *Dwyer Nolan Developments Ltd v Dublin County Council* [1986] IR 130 (HC) - deposit of rubble; *Gibbings v Hungerford* [1904] 1 IR 211 (CA) - discharge of sewerage onto plaintiff's lands; *Brannigan v Dublin Corporation* [1927] IR 513 (SC) - rubbish dumped on plaintiff's land; *Flynn v Ross* High Court, 19 February 1974 (Pringle J); *Woodhouse v Newry Navigation Co* [1898] 1 IR 161 (CA) - stones, ballast and rubbish placed within the ambit of oyster beds in Lough; *Buckley v Healy* [1965] IR 618 (HC) - stones from blasting operations; *cf Petrie v Owners of SS "Rostrevor"* [1898] 2 IR 556 (CA); *Workman v M'Neill* (1897) 31 ILTR 144 (CC) - gate placed at entrance to defendant's bog; *Murphy v Casey* [1997] Ir L Log W 367 (CC) - fencing of a section of plaintiff's lands; *Tully v Smith* [1997] Ir L Log W 97 (CC) - gravel surface of over 1000 feet placed on land; *Representative Body of the Church of Ireland v Warnock* [1898] 2 IR 532; - erection of headstone; *Lennox-Cunningham v Louth County Council* (1957) 92 ILTR 62 (CC) - in malicious damage proceedings, the placing of explosives and firearms in an outhouse held to be a trespass; *Kerin v Bord na Mona* High Court, 30 January 1970 (Kenny J) - deposit of silt and other bog waste on plaintiff's land. For consideration of the action for trespass as a remedy against pollution, see Moloney 'Judicial Protection of the Environment - A New Role for Common-Law Remedies' (1972) 25 Vand LR 145 at 149-150; Juergensmeyer 'Control of Air Pollution Through the Assertion of Private Rights' [1967] Duke LJ 1126 at 1138-1142; Reitze 'Private Remedies for Environmental Wrongs' (1971) 5 Suffolk ULR 779 at 807-808; Lohrmann, 'Comment: The Environmental Lawsuit: Traditional Doctrines and Evolving Theories to Control Pollution' (1970) 16 Wayne LR 1085 at 115-1117; Benham 'Comment: Acid Rain - The Limitations of Private Remedies' [1983] s Illinois ULJ 515 at 535-536; Woodruff 'Pollution Control, Present and Potential: A Jurisprudential Evaluation of Cost Allocation as an Alternative' (1972) 61 Ky LJ 22 at 35; Prince 'Compensation for Victims of Hazardous Substance Exposure' (1985) 11 Wm Mtchell LR 657 at 712-713. Disputes about graves have inspired a considerable amount of litigation. As Moonan J noted in *Representative Church Body v Crawford* (1939) 74 ILTR 49 at 50 (CC), "the right of interment is one which is fondly cherished and jealously guarded". In *Crawford's* case, there is a review of previous decisions, many of which involve actions sounding in trespass. See also *McCarrigle v White* (1940) 74 ILTR 228 (CC); and *Smith v Hogg* [1953-1954] Ir Jur 58 (CC). *Cf* Stopford, *A Handbook of Ecclesiastical Law and Duty for the Use of Irish Clergy* (1861), pp 287-291.

cause any object or substance directly[70] to cross the boundary of another's land,[71] or even to reach the boundary. Thus, to grow a creeper on another's wall[72] or lean a ladder against it will constitute a trespass. There seems no reason why one should not be liable in trespass for inducing an incursion by a person as well as a thing, as, for example, where one brings[73] or chases[74] a person onto the plaintiff's property. But this notion should not be extended unduly: it would be wrong to impose liability in trespass (as opposed to negligence) for conduct that merely increased the likelihood of such an incursion.[75]

## Nature of Interference

**[23.30]** To constitute an actionable trespass, the injury must be direct rather than consequential. *Salmond & Heuston's* definition of these concepts is authoritative, having been adopted in a leading Canadian decision[76] on the subject:

> "An injury is said to be direct when it follows so immediately upon the act of the defendant that it may be termed part of that act; it is consequential, on the other hand, when, by reason of some obvious and visible intervening cause, it is regarded, not as part of the defendant's act, but merely as a consequence of it."[77]

**[23.31]** The classic example of the distinction was given in the English decision of *Leame v Bray*[78] where Le Blanc J referred to a man throwing a log onto the highway:

> "If at the time of its being thrown it hit any person, it is trespass; but if after it be thrown, any person going along the road receives an injury by falling over it as it lies there, it is case."

---

70. See *Leech v Reilly*, High Court, 26 April 1983 (O'Hanlon J), where water pouring from a gutter on a structure on the defendant's property caused flooding on the plaintiff's premises; this was held to constitute *nuisance. Cf Nobilo v Waitemata* [1961] NZLR 1064.

71. *Cf Rigby v Chief Constable of Northamptonshire* [1985] 2 All ER 985 (QB) - police discharging CS gas canister onto plaintiff's premises, resulting in fire.

72. *Simpson v Weber* (1925) 41 Times LR 302.

73. *Cf Nee v Gardiner* [1949] 3 DLR 852 (BCCA), affg [1948] 4 DLR 871.

74. See *Vandenburgh v Truax* (1847) 4 Denio 464 (NY SC); *cf Monk v Dillon* (1883) 12 LR (Ir) 321 (CA). So also with animals: *cf League Against Cruel Sports Ltd v Scott* [1986] QB 240.

75. *Cf Guille v Swan* (1823) 19 Johns 381, 10 AM Dec 234 (NY SC), the famous case of a descending balloonist, dangling from the basket "in a very precarious situation", whose 200 rescuers broke into the plaintiff's garden and trampled on his flowers and vegetables. Liability was imposed on the balloonist for the damage caused by the crowd. The decision has subsequently been narrowly interpreted: *cf* Ross 'Comment: Caligula Wasn't So Wrong: Tort Liability for Damages Caused by the Attraction of Crowds' (1984) 54 Miss LJ 513 at 523-528.

76. *Mann v Saulnier* (1959) 19 DLR (2d) 130 (NB CA).

77. SALMOND & HEUSTON, pp 5-6. See also *Hamilton v Donegall (Marquis of)* (1795) 3 Ridg PC 267 at 316-317. At common law a plaintiff had to fit his claim into one of two writs: the writ of trespass (for direct damage) and the writ of case (for non direct damage) which later covered negligence and breach of contract).

78. (1803) 3 East 593 at 602, 102 ER 724 at 727. In *Segal v Derrick Golf & Winter Club* (1977) 76 DLR (3d) 746 (Alta SC), the "invasion" of the plaintiff's property by golf balls overshooting a green on a course nearby was held to be "unquestionably a trespass" (as well as a nuisance).

**[23.32]** Helpful as the definitions are, however, the difference between direct and consequential injury may be difficult to determine in some cases.[79] Thus, whether water[80] or sewage[81] has been sent directly onto the plaintiff's property or merely allowed by the defendant to accumulate on his own property and then flow onto the plaintiff's land may be a matter of argument. The courts have regarded the spread of tree branches and roots as consequential rather than direct, even where an occupier stands idly by for years, knowing that ultimately the inevitable result will be damage to his neighbour's property. Intrusions of a less tangible, though no less real, nature, such as noise or smell, are generally treated as nuisances[82] rather than trespasses, though the line may be difficult to draw in some cases.[83]

## Trespass Actionable *Per Se*

**[23.33]** Trespass to land is actionable *per se.* This means that the plaintiff needs show no damage[84] to succeed, although, if he wishes to obtain substantial damages, he will normally have to prove appreciable loss.[85] The fact that trespass is actionable *per se* has encouraged persons to invoke the tort to settle disputed rights over land.[86]

---

79. For a rigorous analysis of the underlying policy considerations, see Merrill 'Trespass, Nuisance, and the Costs of Determining Property Rights' (1985) 14 J Legal Stud 13.

80. *Cf Preston v Mercer* (1656) Hardr 60, 145 ER 380; *Reynolds v Clarke* (1725) 2 LD Raym 1399, 92 ER 410. In *Steadman v Erickson Gold Mining Corporation* (1987) 43 DLR (4th) 712 (BC SC), the discharge of silt into water was held not to constitute a trespass.

81. *Cf Tenant v Goldwin* (1704) 2 Ld Raym 1089, 92 ER 222.

82. *Cf* Ch 24 below. See also *Bridges Bros Ltd v Forest Protection Ltd* (1976) 72 DLR (3d) 335 (NB SC); *Wilson v Interlake Streel Co* (1982) 32 Cal 3d 229, 185 Cal Rptr 280, 649 P 2d 922. But *cf Kerr v Revelstoke Building Materials Ltd* (1976) 71 DLR (3d) 134 (Alta SC).

83. See Rainville, 'Remedies for Intangible Intrusions: The Distinction Between Trespass and Nuisance Actions Against Lawfully Zoned Business in California' (1983) 17 U Cal Davis LR 389 at 389-396.

84. *Cf Russell v Moore* (1881) 8 LR (Ir) 318 (CA). Indeed the action may succeed even though the defendant's trespass actually resulted in physical or financial benefits for the plaintiff: *Harmony Ditch Co v Sweeney* (1924) 31 Wyo 1, 222 P 577 - trespass by sheep; *Longenecker v Zimmerman* (1954) 175 Kan 719, 167 P 2d 543 - topping trees.

85. *Cf Tallon v Ennis* [1937] IR 549 at 552-553 (HC, Gavan Duffy J).

86 STREET, p 73. See also *Church Representative Body v M'Loughlin* (1896) 31 ILTR 43 (CC); *Representative Body of the Church of Ireland v Warnock* [1898] 2 IR 532 (QB); *Macnaghten v Baird* [1903] 2 IR 731 (CA revg KBD); *Moore v Reid* (1867) 1 ILT & Sol J 229 (CC); *W v Somers* [1983] IR 122 (SC); *Irish Shell & BP Ltd v John Costello Ltd* [1981] ILRM 66 (SC, revg HC); *Walsh v McGauran* High Court, 14 June 1979 (Hamilton J). *Cf Tomkin Estates Ltd v O'Callaghan* High Court, 16 March 1995 (McCracken J); *Hickson v Boylan* High Court, 25 February 1993 (Carroll J); *Daly v Cullen* (1957) 92 ILTR 127 (CC); *Clancy v Whelan* (1957) 92 ILTR 39 (HC); *Browne v Dowie* (1959) 93 ILTR 179 (Recorder's Court, Belfast); *Mahoney v Neenan* [1966] IR 559 (HC); *Carroll v Sheridan* [1984] ILRM 451 (HC) - declaration of entitlement to right of way granted; *Flanagan v Mulhall* [1985] ILRM 134 (HC); *Irish Shell and BP Ltd v John Costello Ltd* [1984] IR 511 (SC); *Tully v Smith* [1997] Ir L Log W 97 (CC); *Collins v Stack* [1996] Ir L Log W 427 (CC); *Kenny Homes & Co Ltd v Leonard* Supreme Court, 18 June 1998. The tort of trespass to land has even been invoked as an indirect means of testing the legal validity of an expulsion of a union official: *cf National Engineering & Electrical Trade Union v McConnell* [1983] IR 172 (SC); *O'Gara v Murray* High Court on Circuit, 10 November 1988, (McCarthy J).

## Continuing Trespass

**[23.34]** Whilst a person who places an object on the land of another will be guilty of a continuing trespass if he fails to remove it, he will not be guilty of a continuing trespass where, as a result of his wrong, the plaintiff's land is otherwise damaged. A man who cuts down and removes his neighbour's tree or digs a hole in his lawn will have to pay damages, of course, for his wrong, but, unlike the case where he builds a wall in his neighbour's yard, he will not be liable on a continuing basis until the tree is brought back or the hole is filled. Why should this be so?

**[23.35]** Some interesting light was cast on the problem by Holmes J, in *Clarke v MGW Ry Co*:[87]

> "Continuous torts are simple enough in theory, but it is not always easy to distinguish them for practical purposes. A man builds a wall on another's land. This is a continuing trespass, and a judgment against the wrongdoer will not be a bar to a second action, if the wall is permitted to remain. On the other hand, a man digs a hole or cuts down a tree on another's land, and only one action can be brought ... What is the principle that underlies [this distinction]? It cannot depend upon the nature of the injury sustained or upon the fact that such injury is of a continuing character. The right to enjoy one's land free from the encumbrance of a wall does not differ in kind from the right to enjoy it free from the inconvenience of a hole. The element of continuity must, I think, be looked for not in the right interrupted but in the acts that cause the interruption. Where a man commits a trespass by placing something on another's land, it is reasonable to regard him as responsible for its continuance until he takes away what is in its nature removeable, or until the owner of the lands by refusing him permission to remove it adopts what has been done. But a tree cut down is gone forever. Compensation can be made for it, but it cannot be brought back. So, too, in the case of an excavation; it may no doubt be filled up, but not so as to make the excavated place what it was before. An equivalent can be given, but restoration, strictly speaking, is impossible. The distinction I have suggested will be found to accord with ordinary thought and language. We naturally think and speak of the man who has built a wall as keeping the wall where he placed it. He has taken possession of certain land by building on it, and he retains possession of it as long as the building is allowed to stand. No such idea attaches to the person who makes an excavation or cuts down a tree. He may retain for his own use, or otherwise dispose of the matter excavated, or the timber, but his trespass on the land ceases when the act is done."[88]

**[23.36]** In this case, liability on a continuing basis was held to attach to the defendants, who had interfered with the water supply of the plaintiff some time previously and who

---

86. For consideration of the policy basis of the *sine damno* rule, see Keeton 'Trespass, Nuisance and Strict Liability' (1959) 59 Col LR 457 at 468 469. Declaratory judgments may also serve a role in this context: see Order 19, rule 29 of the Rules of the Superior Courts 1986; Ó Floinn, *Practice and Procedure in the Superior Courts* (1996), p 177, *Acton Corporation v Morris* [1953] 2 All ER 932 (CA).

87. [1895] 2 IR 294 at 304-305 (QB).

88 Holmes J's statement regarding excavations is in accord with English authority: *Clegg v Dearden*, (1848) 12 QB 576 at 601, 116 ER 986 at 995. However, in the Canadian case of *Townsview Properties Ltd v Sun Construction and Equipment Co Ltd* (1974) 56 DLR (3d) 330 (Ont CA), the Ontario Court of Appeal upheld the trial court's finding, that an excavation constituted a continuing trespass, since "[t]he soil had been disturbed and it continued in that disturbed state and still continues ...": at 357.

had paid damages in respect of this interference already. To remedy the injury they would have had to enter the land of the plaintiff. This, of course, did not excuse them, but it appears that their liability would cease if the plaintiff on request refused them entry.[89]

## V. The Defendant's State of Mind

**[23.37]** Trespass to land is subject to the general rules applicable to all forms of trespass, so far as the defendant's state of mind is concerned. Thus, it would appear that where the plaintiff establishes an act which physically constitutes a trespass, the onus is upon the defendant to show that he was neither negligent nor intentional.[90]

**[23.38]** If the defendant did not act voluntarily, of course, no liability will be incurred, as properly speaking, he has no act to be reponsible for. Thus, if I am carried against my will[91] or sleepwalk onto my neighbour's property I do not commit a trespass. Where I merely mistake his house for mine, however, I will be guilty of trespass[92] (unless the mistake was brought about by my neighbour's conduct).[93]

### Trespass Above and Below the Surface of the Land

**[23.39]** It has been stated: *Cujus est solum, ejus est usque ad coelum et usque ad inferos*.[94] From the standpoint of the law of trespass, however, the proposition requires some qualification. It is true that any entry beneath the surface of land, however deep, is

---

88. In *Townsview*, the defendants had a continuing licence to be on the plaintiffs' property, and this factor, rather than the qualities and location of the soil, may best explain the holding in *Tully v Smith* [1997] Ir L Log W 97, where the plaintiff had trespassed on the defendant's property by putting down a gravel surface over a thousand feet of it Judge Smith awarded the defendant (in a counterclaim) £2,000 damages for the trespass but said that "he would not direct [the plaintiff] to undo what he had already done."

89. To the same effect is *Workman v M'Neill* (1897) 31 ILTR 144 at 144 (CC). *Cf Cullen v Cullen* [1962] IR 268 at 283 (HC). See also *McConn v Laing* [1939] IR 403 (SC, revg HC); *cf Hone v Hamilton* (1875) IR 9 CL 15 (Com Pleas); *Carroll v Kildare County Council* [1950] IR 258 (SC).

90. *Cf* STREET, p 69. See also *ESB v Hastings & Co Ltd* [1965] Ir Jur 51 (HC) - trespass to goods; *Rigby v Chief Constable of Northamptonshire* [1985] 2 All ER 985 (QB); *Royal Dublin Society v Yates* High Court, 31 July 1997 (Shanley J).

91. *Cf Smith v Stone* (1647) Sty 65, 82 ER 533; *O'Brien v McNamee* [1953] IR 86 (HC). Davitt P's assertion that, where the defendant's act was voluntary, liability will be imposed even in the absence of "intention or malice" overlooks the possibility that a defendant can escape liability for trespass to land where he or she was not negligent. Davitt P misinterpreted *Stanley v Powell* [1891] 1 QB 86 as negativing negligence "on the ground of the act being involuntary".

92. *Basely v Clarkson* (1682) 3 Lev 37 83 ER 565. *Cf Walsh v McGauran* High Court, 14 June 1979. As to the effect of mistake on the decision to grant an injunction, see *Woodhouse v Newry Navigation Co* [1898] 1 IR 161 at 169 (CA). More broadly, a mistaken claim of right will not afford a defence: see *Wrixon v Condran* (1839) 1 Ir Eq Rep 380; *Reeves v Penrose* (1890) 26 LR (Ir) 141 (Ex Div); *O'Brien v McNamee* [1953] IR 86 at 88.

93. Magnet 'International Interference with Land' Ch 10 of *Studies in Canadian Tort Law* Klar, ed (1977), p 299. In this case my act is voluntary, though executed while I was labouring under an error.

94. Co Litt 4a. The maxim is cited (in translation) by Sir WM James VC, in *Corbet v Hill* (1870) IR 9 Eq 671 at 673. See Wylie, *Irish Land Law* (2nd ed, 1986), para 4.002; Thurston, 'Trespass to Air Space' in *Harvard Legal Essays*, p 501 (1934), (reprinted 1967); Becker 'Common Law Sun Rights: An Obstacle to Solar Heating and Cooling' (1976) 3 J of Contemp L 19 at 22-23.

actionable as a trespass.[95] It is also true that a direct infringement over the air-space of a person's land may constitute a trespass,[96] at all events up to "such height as is necessary for the ordinary use and enjoyment of his land and the structures upon it".[97] Where the line is to be drawn may vary: I may well be guilty of trespass if I fly my kite near a building or radio mast that is five hundred feet high; I may not be guilty of a trespass if my kite flies at a far lower height over my neighbour's back garden.[98]

**[23.40]** By statutory provision,[99] no action lies in respect of trespass or nuisance by reason only of the flight of aircraft over any property at a height above the ground, which, having regard to wind, weather and all the circumstances of the case is reasonable; nor will

---

95. *Willcox v Kettell* [1937] 1 All ER 222. *Cf Wrixon v Condran* (1839) 1 Ir Eq Rep 380. The State has the right to most minerals, by virtue of Article 10 of the Constitution and statutory enactment: *cf* Wylie, *Irish Land Law* (3rd ed, 1997), para 4.022; Hogan & Whyte, *Kelly: The Irish Constitution* (3rd ed, 1994); Donelan, *Energy and Mineral Resources in Law in Ireland*, (1985), Ch 3; McMahon, *Report on Irish Economic Law*, p 130 (Commission of European Communities, Vol 7 in *Competition - Approximation of Legislation Series*, 1976). See further the Minerals Development Act 1940; the Minerals Development Act 1979; the Minerals Development Act 1995 and the Minerals Development Act 1999, analysed by Clarke 'Annotation to the Act' ICLSA). *Cf Webb v Ireland* [1988] ILRM 565 (SC). Whether in all circumstances the rule should apply *ad inferos* at common law has been doubted: *cf Edwards v Sims* (1929) 232 Ky 791 at 24 SW 2d 619 at 622 (*per* Logan J, dissenting). For consideration of some of the broader issues, see Blomquist 'Geophysical Trespass: The Guessing Game Created by the Awkward Combination of Outmoded Laws and Soaring Technology' (1996) 48 Baylor LR 21.

96. *Kelsen v Imperial Tobacco Co Ltd* [1957] 2 QB 334.

97. *Bernstein of Leigh (Baron) v Skyviews & General Ltd* [1978] QB 479 at 488 (QBD). See also *Gello v Brownstone Condominium Association* (1980) 82 III Appeal 3d 334, 37 Ill Dec 805, 402 NE 2d 807 - no liability where intrusion of scaffolding into plaintiff's airspace was not "such as to subtract from the owner's use of the property" (*per* McNamara J); *Lacroix v The Queen* [1954] 4 DLR 470, but *cf Lewvest Ltd v Scotia Towers Ltd* (1981) 126 DLR (3d) 239 (Nfld SC). The question whether to grant an injunction against the incursion into the plaintiff's air-space by cranes or scaffolding in connection with necessary building work has provoked a wide range of solutions: see, eg, *Woollerton & Wilson Ltd v Richard Costain Ltd* [1970] 1 WLR 411; *Trenberth (John) Ltd v National Westminster Bank Ltd* (1980) 39 P & CR 104; *Patel v WH Smith (Eziot) Ltd* [1987] 2 All ER 569 (CA); *Anchor Brewhouse Developments Ltd v Berkley House (Docklands Developments) Ltd* [1987] 2 EGLR 173; *Jaggard v Sawyer* [1995] 2 All ER 189 (CA). *Wollerton*, which sought to apply the principle of poetic justice, has been harshly treated in subsequent English decisions, but it received the support of Keane J in *Keating & Co Ltd v Jervis Shopping Centre Ltd*, High Court, 1 March 1996, analysed by Byrne & Binchy, *Annual Review of Irish Law 1996*. See further Wilkinson, *Trespass to Air Space*, (1988) 138 NLJ 385.

98. See further SALMOND & HEUSTON, pp 45-46. As to the possible interference with a constitutionally-protected right of privacy in this context, see O'Connor J's concurring opinion in *Florida v Riley* (1989) 102 LED 2d 835.

99. Air Navigation and Transport Act 1936, s 55, as amended by the Air Navigation and Transport Act 1988, s 47(1). For a brief historical account of the liability for aircraft, see Coblentz 'Limitation of Liability for Aircraft' (1950) 23 S Cal LR 473. Contemporary texts on aviation tort law include Shawcross & Beaumont, *Air Law* (Vol I, Ch 4 and 5B); Speiser & Krause, *Aviation Tort Law* (3 Vols, 1978-1980); and Kreindler, *Aviation Accident Law* (2 Vols loose leaf). See also Krause, (Chairman), *Aviation Accident Litigation* (1980, Law Journal Seminars- Press Inc NY); Loggans, 'Personal Injury Damages in International Aviation Litigation: The Plaintiff's Perspective' (1980) 13 J MLR 541. As to incursion by space objects, see Schwartz & Berlin 'After the Fall: An Analysis of Canadian Legal Claims for Damage Caused by Cosmos 954' (1982) 27 McGill LJ 676 at 678-691, 713-714.

liability attach for the "ordinary incidents of the flight", provided that the provisions of any order made under Part II of the Air Navigation and Transport Act 1946, to give effect to, or to supplement, the Chicago Convention[100] have been duly complied with.[101]

## VI. Interference with Possession

**[23.41]** Since trespass is essentially an interference with possession, the tort generally may not be availed of by persons out of possession at the time of the intrusion. Thus (subject to what is stated below), a purchaser cannot sue for a trespass occurring before title passes to him, and a landlord may not sue during the subsistence of a lease.[102]

**[23.42]** Similarly, mere use of land without exclusive possession[103] will not be sufficient to support an action for trespass,[104] But the grantee of a legal or equitable interest in land in the nature of an easement or *profit à prendre*[105] may sue for direct interference with that interest. A licensee,[106] even one in perpetuity, has not sufficient interest to support an

99. (contd) It should be noted that, so far as Community air carriers are concerned, the financial limits on liability for death or personal injury of passengers in the course of carriage by air, prescribed by the Warsaw Convention of 1919 (as amended) have been removed by Council Regulation (EC) 2027/97 on air carrier liability in the event of accidents. See further Grief 'Challenging the EC Regulation on Air Carrier Liability' [2000] J of Business L 92.

100. The text of the Convention is set out in Shawcross & Beaumont, Appendix A, p 91.

101. Liability without proof of negligence is, however, imposed by s 21(1) where "material damage or loss is caused to any person or property on land or water by, or by the person in, or any article or person falling from, an aircraft while in flight, taking off or landing", save in the case of contributory negligence. It would seem that the better view is that, although it does not refer to this provision specifically, the Civil Liability Act 1961 would allow for apportionment in such a case: *cf* Shawcross & Beaumont, *Air Law*, (4th ed, 1977) Vol 1, p 512 (revised reference, updated to 1982 legislation: Ch 20, para 144). Where, however, the defendant's breach was "without fault", s 43 of the 1961 Act would come into operation: *cf* WILLIAMS, paras 45, 79.

102. *Cf Cooney v Cooney* (1920) 54 ILTR 60 (CC).

103. Exclusive possession in a pew in a church was upheld in *Bret v Mullarkey* (1873) IR 7 CL 120 (Com Pleas); but see *Linehan* v *Hartnett* (1897) 31 ILT & Sol J 429. It is otherwise with respect to graves: *Hickey v Sullivan* (1894) 28 ILTR 150 (CC); *Jennings v M'Carthy* (1908) 42 ILTR 217; *Connor v Moran* (1894) 29 ILTR 32 (Co Court); *Representative Church Body v Crawford* (1939) 74 ILTR 49 (CC); *cf Coyne v Tweedy* [1898] 2 IR 167 (CA affg QB). *Brennan v O'Donnell,* [1996] Ir L Log W 129 (CC). See also *Carson v Jeffers* [1961] IR 44 (HC) - reviewing earlier Irish authorities on agistment and conacre lettings. In *O'Sullivan O'Connor v O'Connor* (1976) 114 ILTR 63 (CC), Judge Wellward held that where the parties were entitled to grazing rights in common, the appropriate action for overgrazing was that of overstint rather than trespass. As counsel for the plaintiff explained, a stint is the right to common pasturage according to a fixed rate measured in collops alloted to each grazier "One collop represents the grass of a full-grown horse or cow for a year .... The grass of six sheep or eighteen geese also represents a collop". See further Bland, *The Law of Easements and Profits a Prendre* (1997), p 314. *Cf Winters v Owens* [1950] IR 225 (HC) - conacre tenant with licence to till the land and a right to entry on, and the use of, the land for that purpose entitled to maintain action of trespass for damage to his crop by "wild Leitrim sheep" from lands grazed so extensively that they were "roaring with hunger".

104. *Hill v Tupper* (1863) 2 H & C 121, 159 ER 51. *Cf Bellaney v Reilly* [1945] IR 542 at 602 (HC); *Hume v Tennyson* [1987] NILR Bull No 2, P 12 (HC).

105. *Cf Cronin v Connor* [1913] 2 IR 119 (KB Div). See, however, *Coffey v Burriss* (1845) 7 ILR 509 (Exch).

action for trespass,[107] but he has rights of abatement similar to those of the victim of trespass.[108] A guest in a hotel may not sue for trespass if ousted from his bedroom, as he does not have exclusive possession.[109]

**[23.43]** What amounts to actual possession in a particular case may be difficult to determine. In *Hegan v Carolan*,[110] the Court held that cutting down trees, breaking a lock on the gate of the field in question and placing cattle in it were sufficient acts of possession by the owner to entitle him to maintain an action for trespass. Pim J stated:

> "It cannot be necessary for one who is asserting his rights to walk over every inch of a field. That would be absurd. All that is necessary is that he should do some act from which it may reasonably be inferred that he claimed the whole, and intended to assert his right to the whole."[111]

**[23.44]** Two important qualifications to these principles should be noted. First, a landlord may sue for trespass where the wrongful act of the defendant has caused permanent damage to the land, leading to a reduction in the value of his reversion.[112] Secondly, where a person entitled to possession actually enters on the land and so acquires possession, he is deemed to have been in possession from the moment that his right to it accrued. This fiction is known as "trespass by relation". Its effect is that the person may sue for any act of trespass committed while he was out of possession whilst having the immediate right to possession. It provides the foundation for the claim for "mesne profits", or compensation for having been kept out of possession of one's land.

### *Jus Tertii* No Defence

**[23.45]** It will not normally be a good defence for a person sued for trespass to allege that the plaintiff has no right to possession of the lands in question because the right (*jus*) rests in a third party (*tertii*).[113] Where, however, the defendant has entered the premises with the authority of the person with the true right to possession he will have a good defence.[114]

---

106. See, however, *Littleton v M'Namara* (1875) IR 9 CL 417 (Com Pleas).

107. *A fortiori* a person who has sought, but has been refused, a licence: *cf Petrie v Owners of SS "Rostrevor"* [1898] 2 IR 556 (CA).

108. *Smith v Hogg* [1953-1954] Ir Jur 58 (CC).

109. *Larkin v Porter* (1828) 1 Hud & BR 524, [1916] 2 IR 27 (KB Div).

110. [1916] 2 IR 27.

111. [1916] 2 IR 27 at 29-30. See also *Colbert v Smithwick* (1986) 30 ILT & Sol J 436 (CC) - planting trees sufficient; *Kelly v Milliken,* (1840) Arm McCart & Ogle 56 - carrying out repairs sufficient; *Irish Land Commission v Murphy* [1939] IR 37 (SC affg HC) - in delivery of possession of a holding by Sheriff, under the Land Act 1927, s 37(1), it was not necessary to place the furniture out on the road; thus the persons evicted had no right to sue for trespass to land. See also *Coyne v Tweedy* [1898] 2 IR 167 (CA affg KBD); *Daly v Murray* (1885) 17 LR (Ir) 185 (CA); *Hamilton v Attorney-General* (1881) 9 LR (Ir) 271 (CA); *Bristow v Cormican* (1874) IR 10 CL 398 (Exch).

112. *Cf Cosgrave v National Telephone Co* [1901] 2 IR 611 (KBD).

113. *Graham v Peat* 1 East 244, (1801); *Nicholls v Ely Beet Sugar Factory* [1931] 2 Ch 84; *Mount Bischoff Tin Mining Co v MB Extended Tin Co* (1913) 15 CLR 549. See also *Hagan v Pasley* (1878) 2 LR (Ir) 573 (QB) - trespass to goods and conversion. *Gannon v Walsh* High Court, 20 June 1996 (Keane J).

114. *Cf Daly v Murray* (1885) 17 LR (Ir) 185 where this defence was not successful on the facts. See also *Littleton v M'Namara* (1875) IR 9 CL 417 (Com Pleas).

**[23.46]** The defence of *jus tertii* will not even mitigate damages,[115] although the wrongful possessor may have to account to the person with the right of possession for the damages recovered in the action against the defendant.[116]

## VII. Defences

**[23.47]** A number of defences to the action for trespass to land may be available:

### Consent

**[23.48]** Clearly, where the plaintiff has invited or permitted the defendant to come onto the property the defendant will not be a trespasser,[117] unless he abuses the terms of the invitation,[118] or where he has some secret purpose for being there which negates his consent.[119] The invitation or permission may be expressed or implied, and may be for consideration[120] or gratuitous.

### Lawful authority

**[23.49]** A person who enters property with lawful authority will not be guilty of the tort of trespass (unless, of course, he or she abuses that entitlement, in which case he or she becomes a trespasser *ab initio*).[121] Earlier in the chapter,[122] we have given several instances of where a statutory provision confers a right of entry on specified person in particular circumstances.

### Necessity[123]

**[23.50]** It seems that necessity will afford a good defence where there was an emergency (not caused by the prior negligent conduct of the defendant himself)[124] of such a nature as

115. *Cf Eastern Construction Co v National Trust Co* [1914] AC 197; *Glenwood Lumber Co v Phillips* [1904] AC 405; *Thompson v Ward* [1953] 2 QB 153.

116. *Eastern Construction Co v National Trust Co* [1914] AC 197 at 210.

117. *Cf Representative Church Body v Crawford* (1939) 74 ILTR 49 (CC) - defence of consent successful; *Redmond v Hayes* High Court, 7 October 1974 (Kenny J) - defence successful; *Brannigan v Dublin Corporation* [1927] IR 513 (SC) - defence rejected; *Flynn v Ross* High Court, 19 February 1974 - defence rejected. See also *Rigby v Chief Constable of Northamptonshire* [1985] 2 All ER 985 (QB), where the consent given by a shopkeeper to the police to discharge a gas canister into the premises to remove a thief was held to extend to what was necessary for this purpose but no more. The *offence* of trespass on the railways requires proof of the existence of a notice at the level of crossing nearest the spot where the trespass is alleged to have been committed, warning against trespass on the railways: Transport Act 1950, s 59. See also a similar provision in the Transport (Dublin Light Rail) Act 1996, s 19.

118. *Cf Rudd v Rea* [1921] 1 IR 223.

119. *Cf Purtill v Athlone UDC* [1968] IR 205 at 210 (SC) - raising, but not deciding the question.

120. *Cf Rudd v Rea* [1921] 1 IR 223.

121. *Cf* para **[23.23]** above.

122. See para **[23.07]** above.

123. See Williams, *The Defence of Necessity* (1953) 6 CLP 216.

124 *Esso Petroleum v Southport Corporation* [1956] AC 218; *Rigby v Chief Constable of Northamptonshire* [1985] 2 All ER 985. *Cf Ross v Dunphy*, High Court, 13 February 1978 (Finlay P) - chattel. See also *Petrie v Owners of SS "Rostrevor"* [1898] 2 IR 556 (CA).

would justify a person reasonably to take the action that the defendant took, even where, in the light of hindsight, the action was not necessary.[125]

**[23.51]** Whether a defendant who successfully pleads necessity is obliged to compensate the person on whose land he trespassed on the basis of a restitutionary obligation is a matter of controversy.[126] Old authority[127] suggests that no compensation is due where the action was done for the benefit of the public (as, for example, to prevent a fire from spreading to a neighbouring village), but it has been doubted[128] whether this represents the law today. Where the action was done merely to protect the interests of the defendant, the plaintiff's moral claim is much stronger: it is recognised in the law in the United States[129] but has been rejected in Canada.[130] *Fleming* favours the former approach, arguing that "it is obviously more appealing to one's sense of fairness that he, whose interests have been advanced by the act, should bear that expense rather than someone who derived no benefit from it at all".[131]

---

124. For criticism of Lord Denning MR's restrictive approach to the issue in *London Borough of Southwark v Williams* [1971] Ch 734 (CA), see Weaver 'Common Sense and the Homeless: A Study in the Limits of Judicial Discretion' (1978) 8 Kingston LR 167 at 179-183.

125. *Cope v Sharpe (No 2)* [1912] 1 KB 496. *Cf Hargreaves v Meade* (1859) 10 ICLR 117; *O'Connor v Corr* (1826) Batty's Irish Reports 1825-26, 421 (KB).

126. See Bohlen 'Incomplete Privilege to inflict Intentional Invasion of Property and Personality' (1926) 39 Harv LR 307; Sussman 'The Defence of Private Necessity and the Problem of Compensation' (1967) 2 Ottawa LR 184. The defence of necessity will not be construed broadly: see *Hargreaves v Meade* (1858) 10 ICLR 117 (Com Pleas) and *cf Watts Bros Ltd v Peilow* High Court, 23 January 1980 (McWilliam J).

127. *The King's Prerogative in Saltpetre* (1606) 12 Co Rep 12, 77 ER 1294.

128. *Burmah Oil Co v Lord Advocate* [1965] AC 75; but see *United States v Caltex (Philippines) Inc* (1952) 344 US 149. *Cf* the Fire Services Act 1981, s 28, authorising demolition of buildings when necessary or expedient to extinguish fire or rescue persons or property, the resulting damage being deemed for all purposes to have been caused by the fire. Of course the fact that the resultant damage is deemed to have been caused by the fire does not, of itself, entitle a plaintiff to recovery for that damage against the author of the fire. The deeming provision may certainly be considered to remove the defence of *novas actus interveniens* but, in a case where the particular intervention raises an issue of reasonable foreseeability, this provision does not automatically resolve that issue against the defendant. See also the Arterial Drainage (Amendment) Act 1995, s 10 - power of entry on land to prevent flooding); the Radiological Protection Act 1991, s 29 - broad powers of entry, seizure and exclusion given to inspectors. As to the position of a person directed by the Minister for Industry and Commerce to prevent or reduce oil pollution, see the Oil Pollution of the Sea (Amendment) Act 1977, ss 2-3. The Minister's right of action against those causing a "maritime casualty" by negligence or default is preserved by s 4 of the Act. Where pollution damage in the State is caused by a ship carrying oil in bulk as cargo, the owner is generally liable for the damage (Oil Pollution of the Sea (Civil Liability and Compensation) Act 1988, s 7(2)); one case in which he will not be liable, however, is where he proved that the discharge of the oil resulted from '... a natural phenomenon of an exceptional, inevitable and irresistible character' (s 8). It may be argued that a discharge following a deliberate decision to do so in the light of such a natural phenomenon could fall within the scope of this exemption; but a narrow interpretation of "inevitable" could defeat this argument. (The restrictions on liability under the 1988 Act introducted by ss 34-6 of the Oil Pollution of the Sea (Civil Liability and Compensation) (Amendment) Act 1998 should be noted).

129. *Vincent v Lake Erie Transportation Co* (1910) 109 Minn 456, 124 NW 221.

130. *Munn & Co Ltd v Mv "Sir John Crosbie"* (1965) 52 DLR (2d) 48, aff'd [1967] Ex 94.

131. FLEMING, p 95 (5th ed, 1981). To similar effect, 9th ed, 1998, p 106.

Chapter 24

# Nuisance


| | | |
|---|---|---|
| I. | Introduction | 675 |
| II. | Public Nuisance | 676 |
| III. | Private Nuisance | 685 |
| IV. | Defences | 709 |
| V. | Ineffectual Defences | 711 |
| VI. | Highway Authorities | 714 |


## I. Introduction

**[24.01]** Nuisance in tort law consists essentially of the unreasonable interference with another person in the exercise of his or her rights generally associated with the occupation of property.[1] The action traces its origins to mediaeval times,[2] yet it displays a continuing vitality, being capable of adjustment to contemporary notions of ecological balance and the control of pollution.[3]

---

1. In *Redfont Ltd v Custom House Dock Management Ltd* High Court, 31 March 1998, Shanley J stated: "Any interference with a person's use and enjoyment of his land is actionable in nuisance ..." See generally Gearty 'The Place of Private Nuisance in the Modern Law of Torts' [1989] Camb LJ 214; Winfield 'Nuisance as a Tort' (1931) 4 Camb LJ 189; Newark 'The Boundaries of Nuisance' (1949) 65 LQR 480; Eekelaar 'Nuisance and Strict Liability' (1973) 8 Ir Jur (ns); Keeton 'Trespass, Nuisance and Strict Liability' (1959) 59 Col LR 457; Vennell 'The Essentials of Nuisance: A Discussion of Recent New Zealand Developments in the Tort of Nuisance' (1977) 4 Otago LR 56; Prosser 'Nuisance without Fault' (1942) 20 Texas LR 399 at 410; Oleck 'Nuisance in a Nutshell' (1956) 5 Clev-MLR 148, and anonymous articles in (1938) 72 ILT & Sol J 213, (1955) 89 ILT & Sol J 113 and (1961) 95 ILT & Sol J 95. The lack of a clear underlying framework of principle has been widely criticised in *Lucas v South Carolina Coastal Council* (1992) 505 US 1003 at 1005, Blackmun J, dissenting, observed that "one searches in vain ... for anything resembling a principle in the common law of nuisance". See further Halper 'Untangling the Nuisance Knot' (1998) 28 BC Envtl Aff LR 89; McLaren 'Nuisance Law and the Industrial Revolution Some Lessons from History' (1983) 3 Oxford J of Legal Studies 155; Brenner, 'Nuisance Law and the Industrial Revolution' (1974) 3 J of Legal Studies 403.
2. *Cf* Winfield 'Nuisance as a Tort' (1931) 4 Camb LJ 189 at 190-191; Newark 'The Boundaries of Nuisance' (1949) 65 LQR 480 at 481-482; Leongard 'The Assize of Nuisance Origins of an Action at Common Law', (1978) 37 Camb LJ 144.
3. For general consideration of the utility of nuisance actions in the environmental context, see Scannell, *Environmental and Planning Law in Ireland* (1995) 42-46; Juergensmeyer 'Common Law Remedies and Protection of the Environment' (1971) 6 UBC LR 215 at 216-220; Wade 'Environmental Protection, the Common Law of Nuisance and the Restatement of Torts' (1972) 8 Forum 165; Maloney, 'Judicial Protection of the Environment - A New Role for Common Law Remedies', (1972) 25 Vand LR 145 at 146-149, 153ff; Reitze 'Private Remedies for Environmental Wrongs' (1971) 5 Suffolk ULR 779 at 799-805; Warren 'Nuisance Law as an Environmental Tool' (1971) 7 Wake Forest LR 211; Lohrmann 'Comment: The Environmental Lawsuit: Traditional Doctrines and Evolving Theories to Control Pollution' (1970) 16 Wayne LR 1085 at 1106-1114;

**[24.02]** In *Connolly v South of Ireland Asphalt Co*,[4] O'Higgins CJ stated:

> "It has been said that actionable nuisance is incapable of exact definition. The term nuisance contemplates an act or omission which amounts to an unreasonable interference with, disturbance of, or annoyance to another person in the exercise of his rights. If the rights so interfered with belong to the person as a member of the public, the act or omission is a public nuisance. If these rights relate to the ownership or occupation of land, or of some easement, profit, or other right enjoyed in connection with land, then the acts or omissions amount to a private nuisance."

Public nuisance and private nuisance will be considered in turn.

## II. PUBLIC NUISANCE[5]

**[24.03]** A public nuisance is a crime.[6] Its scope is somewhat difficult to define with exactitude, since it "covers a multitude of sins, great and small".[7] It includes such disparate forms of conduct as keeping a common gaming-house and creating an obstruction on the

---

3. (contd) Sokolow 'Comment: Hazardous Waste Liability and Compensation: Old Solutions, New Solutions, No Solutions' (1982) 14 Conn LR 307 at 320-321; Juergensmeyer 'Control of Air Pollution Through the Assertion of Private Rights' [1967] Duke LJ 1126 at 1130-1137; Benham 'Comment: Acid Rain - The Limitations of Private Remedies' [1983] S Illinois ULJ 515 at 536-537; Delogu, 'Legal Aspects of Air Pollution Control and Proposed State Legislation for Such Control' [1969] Wis LR 884 at 887-889; Woodruff 'Pollution Control, Present and Potential: A Jurisprudential Evaluation of Cost Allocation as an Alternative' (1972) 61 Ky LJ 22 at 31-33; Prince 'Compensation for Victims of Hazardous Substance Exposure' (1985) 11 Wm Mitchell LR 657 at 713-715. *Locus standi* may present a problem; *cf* Scannell 'Aspects of Pollution Control in Ireland' (1977) 2 Dublin ULJ 18 at 20. See also Rheingold 'Comment: A Primer on Environmental Litigation' (1971) 38 Brooklyn LR 113 at 115-119. As to the possibility of suing under European Community Environmental Directives, see Fitzsimons 'Cause of Action Where Damage Has Been Suffered as a Result of the Improper Treatment and Disposal of Sewage' (2000) 6 IR Planning & Envir LJ 11.
4. [1977] IR 99 at 103 (SC).
5. *Cf* Prosser 'Private Action for Public Nuisance' (1966) 52 Va LR 997; Spencer 'Public Nuisance - Critical Examination' [1989] Camb LJ 55; Loengard 'The Assize of Nuisance: Origins of an Action at Common Law' [1978] Camb LJ 144.
6. See Quinn, *Criminal Law in Ireland* (3rd ed, 1998), p 321; Gabbett, *A Treatise on the Criminal Law*, (1835) Ch 39. The lack of specificity in the definition of this crime raises doubts as to its consistency with due process requirements under Article 38.1 of the Constitution (*cf The People (AG) v Edge* [1943] IR 115 (SC); *King v Attorney General* [1981] IR 233 (SC); Hogan & Whyte, *Kelly: The Irish Constitution* (3rd ed, 1994), pp 573-577). The growth of legislative measures in the Nineteenth and Twentieth centuries dealing with special aspects of environmental law reduced the practical significance of the offence of public nuisance to a large degree. See, eg, the provisions relating to nuisance contained in Public Health Act 1878, s 107 as amended (*cf* Maguire, O'Reilly & Roche, *Irish Environmental Legislation*, (1999) 431ff); the Air Pollution Act 1987, s 24(2); the Environmental Protection Act 1992, s 108; the Local Government Act 1994, s 37(2); the Control of Horses Act 1996, ss 17, 37(1), 40 (1)(a), 46(2), 47(1); the Waste Management Act 1996, s 36(2)(k). One possible strategy would be for the courts to sever the tort of public nuisance from the crime of that name and to redefine the tort in terms of anti-social conduct without any formal insistence that this conduct necessarily come within the offence of public nuisance. *Cf Attorney General v Dieleman* (1994) 117 DLR (4th) 449 (Ont Court (Gen Div)).
7. *Southport Corporation v Esso Petroleum Co Ltd* (1954) 2 QB 182 at 195 (CA). See further Spencer 'Public Nuisance- Critical Examination' [1989] Camb LJ 55 at 55-66, 76-80.

highway. The essence of the crime is injury to the reasonable comfort and convenience of the public or a section of the public.[8]

**[24.04]** Where the public or some section of it is injured by the public nuisance, only the Attorney-General may take civil proceedings.[9] The reason for this rule appears to be that it prevents a multiplicity of actions, and protects the wrongdoer against the risk of being punished a hundred times for the same cause.[10] Only where a person has suffered "particular" or 'special' damage over and above that suffered by other members of the public may he or she take civil proceedings.[11] This rationale is somewhat dubious as it does not apply in respect of the tort of private nuisance; moreover, it runs contrary to the mainstream of contemporary tort law, in particular negligence, which is to afford a remedy for injuries that are suffered as a result of wrongful conduct, even though the number of claimants may be very large.

## What is "Particular" or "Special" Damage?[12]

**[24.05]** There is some uncertainty as to what constitutes "particular" or "special" damage. Some courts have held that the plaintiff's injury must be different in kind rather than degree from that suffered by the general public.[13] The more popular view, which appears to be favoured by our courts, is that recovery may be allowed where the plaintiff's injury is

8. *Cf Re Article 26 and the Employment Equality Bill 1996* [1997] 2 IR at 321 (SC): "[P]ublic nuisance ... is an act which obstructs, or causes inconvenience or damage to, the public in the exercise of rights common to all citizens". In *Trulock Ltd v District Judge McMenamin* [1994] 1 ILRM 151 (HC), O'Hanlon J observed that the offence of public nuisance:

> "is committed by every person who (a) does an act not warranted by law, or (b) omits to discharge a legal duty, if the effect of the act or omission is to endanger the life, health, property, morals or comfort of the public, or to obstruct the public in the exercise or enjoyment of rights common to all subjects. It is immaterial whether the annoyance arises from noise, stench, unwholesomeness or interference with public health or convenience" [Citations omitted].

9. *Cf Smith v Wilson* [1903] 2 IR 45 at 65 (KBD); *AG v Mayo County Council* [1902] 2 IR 13 at 20; *Walsh v Ervin* [1952] VLR 361 at 368.

10. *Anon* (1535) YB 27 H VIII, fn 27, Mich, pl 10 cited by FLEMING, p 461, who is not convinced by Baldwin CJ's argument.

11. *Cf Coppinger v Sheehan* [1906] 1 IR 519 at 522-523. It should be noted that, unlike in cases of private nuisance (discussed below), the person suffering the injury does not have to have an interest in land in order to succeed in his action.

12. See Fridman 'Definition of Particular Damage in Nuisance' (1953) 2 WA Annual LR 490; Kodilinye 'Public Nuisance and Particular Damage in the Modern Law' (1986) 6 Legal Stud 182; Jones 'Public Rights, Private Rights and Particular Damage' (1983) 34 NILQ 341.

13 Eg *Hickey v Electric Reduction of Canada*, (1970) 21 DLR (3d) 368 - commercial fishermen could not complain about pollution of public waters as their interests were not different in kind from those who fished for recreation. This decision has been criticised by Kodilyne in 'Public Nuisance and Particular in Damage in Modern Law' (1986) 6 Legal Stud 182 at 189-191; Estey 'Public Nuisance and Standing to Sue' (1972) 10 Os HLJ 563; McLaren 'The Common Law Nuisance Action and the Environment Battle -Well-Tempered Swords or Broken Reeds?' (1972) 10 Os HLJ 505. It has not been adopted in the United States: *Union Oil v Oppen* (1974) 501 F 2d 558 (CA) - a leading decision on the subject of recovery for pure economic loss; see also Mulhern 'Marine Pollution, Fishers and the Pillars of the Land: A Tort Recovery Standard for Pure Economic Loss' (1990) 18 BC Envtl Aff L Rev 85; *Pruitt v Allied Chemical Corp* (1981) 523 F Supp 975 (ED Va), analysed by Benham 'Comment: Acid Rain - The Limitations of Private Remedies [1983] S Illinois ULJ 515 at 536-537;

appreciably more serious than that suffered by the general public, to such degree that it may be regarded as particular to him or her.

**[24.06]** Special or particular damage may consist of injury to the plaintiff's pecuniary interests, as where, most obviously, his or her person[14] or property[15] is damaged or where, less directly, he or she is deprived of the opportunity to earn a livelihood. Thus, in *Boyd v Great Northern Ry*,[16] the plaintiff, a doctor, who was delayed for twenty minutes at a level crossing by reason of the default of the defendant's servants, recovered ten shillings damages. The plaintiff, who was "in very large practice" and "whose time was of pecuniary value", was held to have suffered "some appreciable damage peculiar to himself beyond that suffered by other members of the public ordinarily using the highway".[17]

**[24.07]** In *Smith v Wilson*,[18] the plaintiff, an elderly small farmer, used frequently to walk to market in Ballymena on a public road, until the defendant obstructed the road by removing a bridge and erecting a fence. As a result, the plaintiff was obliged to take a longer and more circuitous route, and sometimes had to pay for a car in doing so. The majority of the King's Bench Division held that he was entitled to damages. Gibson J stated:

> "I think there is some evidence on which a jury might find that the plaintiff had sustained peculiar, direct and substantial damage in farm business, and expenses. No doubt the case is not as strong as if a carriage road had been stopped; but still there is some distinctive injury. It may be said that if the plaintiff can sue, every other farmer in the neighbourhood who used the path may be able to do the same. This may be so; but every nuisance which affects large sections of the community, eg, nuisance from chemical works or a small-pox hospital,[19] or

---

13. (contd) *Stop & Shop Co v Fisher* (1983) 387 Mass 889, 444 NE 2d 368, noted by Gladstone, (1984) 18 Suffolk ULR 114; *Burgess v M/V Tamanfo* (1973) 370 Supp 247 (5D Maine); *The Queen v The Ship Sun Diamond* 1983 25 CCLT 19 (Fed Court of Can) and *Dagi v Broken Hill Pty Co Ltd* 1995 Vic Lexis 1182; BC9502519 (Vic SC). *Hickey* may also be contrasted with the approach favoured by the House of Lords in *Tate & Lyle Food and Distribution v Greater London Council* [1983] 2 AC 509, critically analysed by Jones 'Public Rights, Private Rights and Particular Damage' (1983) 34 NILQ 341 at 346-347. While the *Hickey* rationale still commands some respect: *cf Stein v Gonzales* (1984) 14 DLR (4th) 263 at 267 (BC SC), Low J in *Gagnier v Canadian Forest Products Ltd* (1990) 1990 ACW SJ LEXIS 19321 (BC SC), citing old decisions from Ontario, expresses doubts about the narrow breadth of the holding in *Hickey*. Legislation in Ontario has since expanded the entitlement to sue for public nuisance: see the Environmental Bill of Rights SO Ch 28 (1993); Castrill 'Environmental Rights Statutes in the United States and Canada: Comparing the Michigan and Ontario Experiences' (1998) 9 VIII Entvl LJ 349. Preventive action may also be possible, whether by injunction or under statutory entitlement (eg the Fisheries Act 1980, s 54: see *Courtney v Minister for the Marine* High Court, 21 December 1988 (O'Hanlon J).
14. See *AG v Mayo County Council* [1902] 2 IR 13 at 20.
15. Eg *Halsey v Esso Petroleum Co Ltd* [1961] 1 WLR 683; *Walsh v Morgan & Sons Ltd* (1938) 73 ILTR 4 (CC) - damage to car; *Dougan v Allen* (1912) 46 ILTR 221 (CC) - plaintiff's greyhounds poisoned.
16. [1895] 2 IR 555 (Ex Div).
17. [1895] 2 IR 555 at 557. See also *Rogers v GS Ry* (1940) 74 ILTR 206 (CC). See further Smith 'Private Action for Obstruction to Public Right of Passage' (1915) 15 Col LR 1, 142 at 149, fn 84, and Kodilinye's criticism of *Boyd*, at 187.
18. [1903] 2 IR 45 (KBD). *Cf Dunne v Rattigan* [1981] ILRM 365 (CC).
19. Citing *Metropolitan Asylum District v Hill* (1881) 6 App Cas 193. See also *AG (Boswell) v Rathmines & Pembroke Joint Hospital Board* [1904] 1 IR 161 (CA). *Cf Dennehy v Kildare Co Board of Health* [1936] IR 384 (HC).

from a collection of explosives,[20] is open to the same remark. Everyone who individually sustains particular injury can apply for damages or an injunction[21]."[22]

**[24.08]** It seems, moreover, that where other persons are inconvenienced by the public nuisance and as a result the plaintiff suffers loss, he or she may be entitled to sue.[23] If, for example, members of the public are obstructed or otherwise prevented from gaining access to the plaintiff's shop by the nuisance, the plaintiff may recover.[24]

**[24.09]** A person who suffers particular or special damage in the form of personal injury will also have a right of action.[25] This is of considerable importance because an injured person who may experience some difficulties in pursuing an action based on negligence would be well advised to contemplate also suing in public nuisance. The concept of unreasonableness is not necessarily of the same dimensions in the two torts. Moreover, once public nuisance is proved and the defendant is shown to have caused it, the onus is shifted on to the defendant to exculpate himself or herself.[26]

**[24.10]** The fact that special injury must be shown in this context serves, however, to blunt the edge of public nuisance as a weapon used by environmentalists to counter pollution.[27] The problem here is that if a factory pollutes a stream or the air, all persons in the area suffer from it. As will be seen below, an action for private nuisance or for interference with riparian rights may be more effective in such cases. The possibility of judicial recognition of the class action[28] or of successful constitutional litigation to protect the citizen's right to bodily integrity[29] should also not be discounted. Finally it should be noted that, by virtue of s 27 of the Local Government (Planning & Development) Act 1976, if an activity

20. Citing *Cowper Essex v Local Board of Acton* (1889) 14 AC 153.

21. Citing *Soltau v De Held*, (1851) 2 Sim (NS) 133, 61 ER 291.

22. [1903] 2 IR 45 at 75. *Cf Walsh v Ervin* [1952] VLR 361 at 368 where Scholl J praised this statement for its "common sense and good law". But see Kodilinye 'Public Nuisance and Particular Damage in the Modern Law' (1986) 6 Legal Stud 182 at 188.

23. *Cf Amalgamated Theatres Ltd v Lumley Ltd* [1962] NZLR 226 at 229. See further SALMOND & HEUSTON, p 88.

24. *Cf Clifford v Drug Treatment Centre Board* High Court, 7 November 1997 (McCracken J).

25. *Castle v St Augustine's Links* (1922) 38 Times LR 615. See also the many decisions involving personal injury cited, para **[24.14]** below, in respect of public nuisances on the highway. In *Connolly v South of Ireland Asphalt Co Ltd* [1977] IR 99 (SC), the death of a road-user was held to constitute "particular damage" so far as his widow was concerned.

26. *Southport Corporation v Esso Petroleum Co Ltd* [1954] 2 QB 182 at 197.

27. *Cf* the articles by Estey 'Public Nuisance and Standing to Sue' (1972) 10 Os HLJ 563 and McLaren 'The Common Law Nuisance Action and the Environment Battle -Well-Tempered Swords or Broken Reeds?' (1972) 10 Os HLJ 505.

28. *Cf* Rothstein 'Private Action for Public Nuisance: The Standing Problems' (1974) 76 W Va LR 453; Jaffe 'Standing Again' (1971) 84 HLR 633, Davis 'The Liberalized Law of Standing' (1970) 37 U Chi LR 450.

29. *Cf AG v Ryan* [1965] IR 294 (SC); Walsh J 'Existence and Meaning of Fundamental Rights in Ireland' (1980) 1 Human Rights LJ 171 at 178-179. But see *Hanrahan v Merck Sharp & Dohme (Ireland) Ltd* [1988] ILRM 629 (SC) and the discussion of the case in Ch 1. For consideration of constitutional issues from the standpoint of the United States, see Reitze 'Private Remedies for Environmental Wrongs' (1971) 5 Suffolk ULR 779 at 816-819; Lohrmann 'Comment: The Environmental Lawsuit: Traditional Doctrines and Evolving Theories to Control Pollution' (1970) 16 Wayne LR 1085 at 1131-1134.

constitutes a breach of the planning law, it may be prohibited by the High Court at the suit of any person.[30] (*Quia timet* injunctions may not, however, be granted under s 27[31]). Moreover, any person may seek an injunction or other remedy against one who in holding, recovering or disposing of waste, causes, or may cause, environmental pollution.[32]

**[24.11]** In contrast, the Litter Pollution Act 1997 does not give a specific statutory right of redress to the individual citizen - "a serious oversight", in the view of one commentator.[33]

## Types of Public Nuisance

**[24.12]** As has been indicated,[34] the types of public nuisance are infinitely various. They include such diverse wrongs as exposing in the public streets a person suffering from an infectious disease[35] and holding a pop festival which generates an excessive degree of noise and traffic congestion.[36]

---

30. In *Morris v Garvey* [1982] ILRM 177 at 180 (SC), Henchy J said:

> "When s 27(2) is invoked, the court becomes the guardian and supervisor of the carrying out of the permitted development according to its limitations, and in carrying out that function it must balance the duty and benefit of the developer under the permission as granted against the environmental and ecological rights and amenities of the public, present and future, particularly those closely or immediately affected by the contravention of the permission. It would require exceptional circumstances (such as genuine mistake, acquiescence over a long period, the triviality or mere technicality of the infraction, gross or disproportionate hardship, or such like extenuating or excusing factors) before the court should refrain from making whatever order (including an order of attachment for contempt in default of compliance) as is 'necessary to ensure that the development is carried out in conformity with the permission'."

See also *Stafford v Roadstone Ltd* [1980] ILRM 1 (HC). More generally see Walsh, *Planning and Development Law* (2nd ed, 1984) paras 12.39-12.42; McGrath 'Planning Injunctions under Section 27' (1996) 18 DULJ 1. In *Vitalograph (Ireland) Ltd v Ennis Urban District Council* High Court, 23 April 1997, Kelly J declined to make an order under s 27 where he had already granted an interlocutory injunction against the continuance of a private nuisance. The effect of granting a statutory injunction under s 27 "would be the same" as that of the interlocutory injunction and there was "little point in having two injunctions which bring about the same result".

31. *Mahon v Trustees of the Irish Rugby Football Union* [1998] 1 ILRM 284 (SC), critically analysed by Flynn 'Pop Concerts and Planning' (1997) 4 Irish Planning & EnvironmentalLJ 127.

32. Waste Management Act 1996, ss 57, 58. ("waste" is defined in s 4). See Meehan 'The Waste Management Act 1996: The Last Green Bottle' (1996) 3 Irish Planning & Environmental LJ 59, esp at 66-67.

33. Flynn 'The Litter Pollution Act 1997' (1997) 4 Ir Planning & Environmental LJ 47 at 52.

34. See para **[24.08]** above.

35. *R v Vantaudillo* (1815) 4 M & S 73. See Mulholland 'Public Nuisance - A New Use for an Old Tool' (1995) 11 Prof Neg 70.

36. *AG for Ontario v Orange Productions Ltd* (1971) 21 DLR (3d) 257. On the general subject of urban noise as a public nuisance, see Anon 'Urban Noise Control' (1968) 4 Col J of L & Soc Problems 105 at 107-108. The planning legislation offers an alternative route: *Mountcharles v Meath County Council* [1997] 1 ILRM 446 (HC); *Mahon v The Trustees of the Irish Rugby Football Union* [1998] 1 ILRM 284; *cf Sheehan v District Justice Reilly* [1992] IR 368 (HC). Another option for an aggrieved person (whether resident or otherwise) is to make a complaint under s 108 of the Environmental Protection Agency Act 1992 in the District Court, where the noise is

> "so loud, so continuous, so repeated, of such duration or pitch, or occurring at such times as to give reasonable cause for annoyance to a person in any premises in the neighbourhood or to a person lawfully using any public place ...".

See Mulloy 'Noise Regulations 1994' (1996) 1 Ir Planning & Environmental LJ 103 at 105 ff.

**[24.13]** Public nuisances on the highway have probably given rise to most litigation, so these will be considered in some detail.

## Public Nuisance on the Highway

### *(a) Obstructions*

**[24.14]** In *Cunningham v McGrath Bros*,[37] Kingsmill Moore J stated that speaking generally, any obstruction of the public[38] highway is a public nuisance. But this is not a universal rule: As Molony CJ said in *McKenna v Stephens and Alexander E Hull & Co*:

> "It is quite clear that every obstruction of the roadway does not create a cause of action in a person injured or inconvenienced thereby."[39]

**[24.15]** Molony CJ cited with approval the observation of Byles J in *Herring v Metropolitan Board of Works*,[40] that a wide range of everyday activities do not constitute a public nuisance:

> "Carts and wagons stop at the doors of shops and warehouses for the purpose of loading and unloading goods. Coal-shoots are opened in the public footway for the purpose of letting in necessary supplies of fuel. So for the purpose of building, rebuilding, or repairing houses abutting on the public way in populous places hoardings are frequently erected enclosing a part of the way. Houses must be built and rebuilt - and hoarding is necessary in such cases to shield persons passing from danger from falling substances."

**[24.16]** Examples of obstructions that may constitute a public nuisance are: leaving a ladder for an unreasonable period on a public footpath;[41] digging a trench in the highway;[42] leaving a vehicle on the highway for an unreasonable time;[43] leaving railway gates closed

---

37. [1964] IR 209 at 213 (SC). See also *Holland v Dublin County Council* (1979) 113 ILTR 1 (HC); *Kildare County Council v Hamwood Estates Ltd* High Court, 13 January 1956 (Dixon J) at pp 7-8; *McKenna v Lewis* [1945] IR 66 at 74 (SC). See generally Smith 'Private Action for Obstruction to Public Right of Passage' (1915) 15 Col LR 1, 142.

38. Where the public highway has been closed by order of the Minister for the Environment acting under statutory authority, it seems that an action for public nuisance may not lie: *cf Donaldson v Irish Motor Racing Club* Supreme Court, 1 February 1957 - allegation of nuisance not pursued in Supreme Court, rightly, according to Kingsmill Moore J.

39. [1923] 2 IR 112 at 122 (CA).

40. 19 CBNS 510 at 525.

41. *Cunningham v McGrath Bros* [1964] IR 209.

42. In *Wall v Morrissey* [1969] IR 10 at 21 (SC), Fitzgerald J stated:

> "The unauthorised opening of a trench on a public road is a public nuisance. The failure to refill a trench lawfully opened and to restore the surface of the highway to make it fit for traffic may also amount to a public nuisance."

43. *Cf* at 20 (*per* Fitzgerald J): "A stationary, or even an unlighted, vehicle on a highway may not amount to a nuisance unless the owner permits it to remain for longer than a reasonable time." See also *Dymond v Pearce* [1972] 1 QB 496 (CA); *Chesterfield Corporation v Arthur Robinson (Transport) Ltd* (1955) 106 LJ (News) 61; *St John v Ossory* Supreme Court, 23 July 1930 - dumping and loading timber in front of plaintiff's entrance to byroad. *Cf Tynan v Earls* Supreme Court, 28 March 1969 - tar boiler parked overnight on highway; proceedings sounding in negligence; *Reilly v Garvey* [1973] IR 89 (SC) - proceedings sounding in negligence. *O'Beirne v Hannigan* [1937] IR 237 (SC, 1937, rev HC, 1936) - proceedings sounding in negligence; no liability on facts. *Ideal Poultry Farms Ltd v Spencer Freeman* (1950) 84 ILTR 85 (HC).

longer than is reasonably necessary;[44] allowing picketers[45] or queues[46] to form so as to obstruct the passage of road users or pedestrians or the access of customers to shops or other premises; building a structure which obstructs a road[47] or navigable river;[48] and allowing a mass of animals to obstruct the highway.[49]

***(b) Dangers***

**[24.17]** In *Hassett v O'Loughlin*,[50] Briain J stated:

> "A nuisance is not confined to an obstruction on the highway; it may consist of anything which makes the use of the highway unsafe or dangerous to the public."

Liability was there imposed on the defendant for putting a tiny heap of stones on the highway.[51]

**[24.18]** Other examples of dangers to the highway include leaving an unauthorised no parking notice on the footpath;[52] failing to remove a disused gas pipe projecting from the

---

44. *Boyd v GN Ry Co* [1895] 2 IR 555 (Ex Div).

45. *Cf EI Co Ltd v Kennedy* [1968] IR 69 at 91 (SC). In several cases, injunctions have been sought against picketing on the ground (inter alios) of nuisance, the pleadings generally not specifying public or private nuisance. See, eg, *Beckton, Dickinson & Co Ltd v Lee* [1973] IR 1 (SC); *Ardmore Studios (Ireland) Ltd v Lynch* [1965] IR 1 (HC); *Crowley v Cleary* [1968] IR 261 (HC); *Roundabout Ltd v Beirne* [1959] IR 423 (HC); *Silver Tassie Co Ltd v Cleary* 90 ILTR 87 (HC). *Cf Educational Co of Ireland Ltd v Craig* [1961] IR 345, Kingsmill Moore J observed:

> "That picketing as ordinarily conducted interferes very seriously with the user and enjoyment of the premises picketed and amounts to a common law nuisance can hardly, I think, be contested".

See further Vorspan 'The Political Power of Nuisance Law: Labor Picketing and the Courts in Modern England 1871-Present' (1998) 46 Buffalo LR 593.

46. *Cf Barber v Penley* [1893] 2 Ch 447. See also Anon 'Cinema Queues and Nuisance', (1947) 81 ILT & Sol J 139 at 410, referring to an unreported Circuit Court decision of Judge Ó Briain in Limerick which held that a queue of people at a cinema constituted a nuisance, although Judge Ó Briain stated in very clear words that his decision was not to be taken as a decision that a queue must constitute a nuisance in every case. See also Sylvester 'Shopping Centre Parking Lot Liability' (1965) 14 Clev-Mar LR 570 at 577. *Cf Re Quinn* [1974] IR 19 (SC). As to processions moving through streets *cf Rowdens v Keaveney* [1903] 2 IR 82 (KBD).

47. *AG v Mayo County Council* [1902[ 1 IR 13. *Cf Holland v Dublin County Council* 113 ILTR 1 (HC).

48. *Rex v Hallett* (1911) 45 ILTR 84 (HC). See also *Waterford Bridge Commissioners v Waterford Corporation* [1905] 1 IR 307 (CA 1905, affg 1904). *Cf Coppinger v Sheehan* [1906] 1 IR 519 - heaps of stones placed on foreshore obstructed right of access to lands bounded by the sea, for the purposes of navigation. Injunction granted on the basis apparently, of private rather than public nuisance: *cf* [1906] 1 IR at 522-523, 525-526). See also *AG v Northern Petroleum Tank Co Ltd* [1936] IR 450 (HC).

49. *Cunningham v Whelan* (1918) 52 ILTR 67 (CC); *Hall v Wightman* [1926] NI 92 at 102-103 (CA *per* Andrews LJ); *cf* at 106 (*per* Best LJ); See also *Gillick v O'Reilly* [1984] ILRM 402 (HC).

50. (1943) 78 ILTR 47 at 48 (CC).

51. See also *Clements v Tyrone County Council* [1905] 2 IR 415 (KBD) and *Butterly v Mayor of Drogheda* [1907] 2 IR 134 (KB Div, affd, CA), where the actions sounded in negligence for placing heaps of stones and debris on the highway. In *Kelliher v Board of Health & Public Assistance for Co Tipperary (North Riding)* [1938] IR 43 (SC), there was some uncertainty as to whether the proceedings should be regarded as being based on negligence or public nuisance, but nothing hinged on this issue. The facts concerned the danger to road users created by pipes and excavated materials during sewerage work on the highway. *Cf Nolan v Listowel UDC* [1966] IR 56 (HC).

52. *Walsh v Morgan & Sons Ltd* (1938) 72 ILTR 4 (CC). *Cf McCarry v Graham* [1958] Ir Jur 9 (NI).

soil on property close to the footpath;[53] damaging the road surface[54] or rendering it hazardous[55] or damaging property under it,[56] placing dangerous materials on[57] or near[58] the highway; holding unauthorised motor-bicycle speed trials on an unsuitable road;[59] camping on the roadside at an unserviced site, thereby causing rat infestation, litter and a traffic hazard,[60] maintaining a golf club in a manner designed so that players are likely to slice the ball onto the highway;[61] projecting a stone step and metal scraper into the highway,[62] letting a wall adjoining a highway fall onto it,[63] reconstructing the side portion of a highway in a dangerous manner,[64] or causing the road[65] or footpath[66] to subside.

---

53. *Stewart v St Patrick's Hospital* (1939) 73 ILTR 115 (CC). See also *Fitzgerald v Brangan* (1904) 39 ILTR 116. *Cf Smyth v Keys* (1912) 46 ILTR 68.
54. *Molloy v Offaly County Council* (1951) 85 ILTR 61 (CC); *McCormack v Kildare County Council* [1953-1954] Ir Jur 64 (CC); *Kelly v Mayo County Council* [1964] IR 315 (SC); *Wall v Morrissey* [1969] IR 10 (SC); *Connolly v South of Ireland Asphalt Co* [1977] IR 99 (SC).
55. *Smyth v Industrial Gases (IFS) Ltd* (1950) 84 ILTR 1 (SC) - lime putty leaked onto highway; children playing with it injured plaintiff's eye; trial judge ought to have left the question of negligence "and possibly of nuisance" to the jury.
56. *Armagh Union (Guardians of) v Bell* [1900] 2 IR 371 (QBD) - sewer pipes under street damaged by steam traction-engine; see also *Alliance & Dublin Consumers Gas Co v Dublin County Council* [1901] 1 IR 492 (CA).
57. *Cf McGowan v Masterson* [1953] IR 101 (SC) - oil spilt on footpath; *Curry v Foster* [1960] Ir Jur 33 (HC NI, QBD) - clay on road; *Grainger v Cullen* (1909) 43 ILTR 132 - large mortar board left on road frightened horse; case sounding in negligence; *Byrne v British & Irish Steampacket Co Ltd* Supreme Court, 27 July 1966 - barrow placed at edge of footpath whilst person pushing it waited to cross road in safety held not to constitute a public nuisance; *Cregan v ESB* (1936) 71 ILTR 62 (SC) - shock from electricity pole; no liability as negligence not established; *McKeon v Bolton* (1851) 1 ICLR 377 (QB) - rubbish on highway led to overturning of plaintiff's vehicle.
58. *Dougan v Allen* (1912) 46 ILTR 221 (CC) - plaintiff's greyhounds attracted to poisoned meat on defendants land close to highway. See also *Lawler v McKenna* (1905) 39 ILTR 159; *Emery v Knox* (1896) 30 ILTR 106 (CC). The decisions are discussed in Anon 'Placing Poison or Poisonous Matter on Lands, Rights and Liabilities' (1949) 83 ILT & Sol J 69.
59. *McKee v Malcolmson* [1925] NI 120 (CA). See, however, *Donaldson v Irish Motor Racing Club and Thompson* Supreme Court, 1 February 1957. In *Conroy v Attorney General* [1965] IR 411, Kenny J referred to Gibson J's observations in *Lowdens v Keaveney* [1903] 2 IR 82 at 89 that use of the highway, which is excessive or unreasonable and excessive is a nuisance and commented:

    > "Driving a motor car on a public highway when the driver is incapable of exercising effective control over it is, in my opinion, an unreasonable use of the highway".
60. *Kelly v McDonagh* Circuit Court, 15 April 1999 (Buttimer J).
61. *Castle v St Augustine's Links* (1922) 38 Times LR 615. *Cf Campion v Chicago Landscape Co* (1938) 295 Ill Appeal 225, 14 NE 2d 879; *Trauman v City of New York* (1955) 143 NYS 2d 467 (SC); Mandel 'Negligent Design of Sports Facilities' (1967) 16 Clev-Mar LR 275 at 275-276; *Bolton v Stone* [1951] AC 850 (HL). See also Keeton 'Trespass, Nuisance and Strict Liability' (1959) 59 Colum LR 457 at 474. More generally, see O'Kane, Lynch & Schaller 'Injuries from Errant Golf Balls: Liability Theory and Defenses' (1987) 37 Fedn Ins & Corp Couns Q 247 at 248-251; DeVoto 'Injury on the Golf Course: Regardless of Your Handicap, Escaping Liability Is Par for the Course' (1993) 24 U Toledo LR 859 at 874-876.
62. *Early v Flood* [1953-1954] Ir Jur 65 (HC) - defendant not liable as land dedicated to public subject to existing state of danger.
63. *Mullan v Forrester* [1921] 2 IR 412 (KBD).
64. *McKenna v Lewis* [1945] IR 66 (SC).
65. *Hall v McKone Ltd* [1975] IR 292 (HC).
66. *Baker v Alliance & Dublin Consumers' Gas Co* [1946] Ir Jur 48 (CC). *Cf Ahearne v Rudd* [1945] Ir Jur 45 (HC).

## Extent of Liability for Public Nuisance

**[24.19]** It appears that the principle of a non-delegable duty arises in relation to public nuisance. Certainly it does in respect of excavation on the public highway. In *Wall v Morrissey*,[67] Walsh J stated:

> "A person who makes an excavation on the highway has imposed upon him a duty of care which cannot be discharged by the employment of an independent contractor, nor can such person delegate to a contractor the work of taking the precautions necessary to prevent the mischievous consequences of the excavation on the highway. The person who procures the excavation is primarily liable for the actionable consequences which may flow therefrom; he is not simply liable vicariously for the acts of the independent contractor."

**[24.20]** The reference to the duty of care may mislead. It cannot refer to the Atkinian duty of care in negligence,[68] since *Wall v Morrissey* makes plain that negligence is not an essential ingredient of the tort of public nuisance. Liability will be imposed, however, only where the injury suffered by the plaintiff was "a reasonably foreseeable event on the part of the defendant".[69]

**[24.21]** *Convery v Dublin County Council*[70] establishes that liability in public nuisance is contingent on the defendant's ownership or occupation of premises in the area or the fact that the defendant has caused some activity on land in the area. The Supreme Court, reversing Carroll J,[71] held that the defendant council was not liable for public nuisance in permitting extensive development without ensuring that the general road infrastructure was adequate. The plaintiff complained about the large volumes of traffic using the road in front of her house as a rat run. The Supreme Court considered that this problem was the result of a combination of several factors:

> "[T]he development of large scale residential and commercial projects by private interests, the decisions of thousands of individual drivers to use this particular route, and the failure of central government to allocate funds for the provision of the necessary roads infrastructure, to mention the most obvious."[72]

**[24.22]** The decisions of the council to which objection had been taken represented only one of a number of factors which had resulted in the position of which the plaintiff complained. To treat the council, in these circumstances, as being the legal author of a public nuisance would be entirely contrary to principle and wholly unsupported by authority.[73]

---

67. [1969] IR 10 at 14 (SC). *Cf Connolly v South of Ireland Asphalt Co Ltd* [1977] IR 99 (SC).
68. *Donoghue v Stevenson* [1932] AC 562 at 580 (HC).
69. [1969] IR 10 at 15. It is interesting to note that, in *O'Sullivan v Dwyer* [1971] IR 275, Walsh J, stated that he regarded those liable for public nuisance as guilty of fault, on the basis of the foreseeability of the injury. This conclusion is hard to reconcile with *Wall v Morrissey* [1969] IR 10, where Walsh J made it plain that negligence is not a necessary ingredient in the tort of public nuisance. Foreseeability in this context is merely a precondition of the imposition of liability. It does not of itself necessarily connote any fault, moral or legal, on the part of the defendant.
70. [1996] 3 IR 153 (SC revg HC), analysed by Byrne & Binchy, *Annual Review of Irish Law 1996*, pp 611-617.
71. [1996] 3 IR 153.
72. [1996] 3 IR 153 at 173 *per* Keane J, (O'Flaherty and Barron JJ concurring).
73. [1996] 3 IR 153 at 174

**[24.23]** The decision is non-problematic so far as it rests on the lack of causal potency of the council's actions in the particular circumstances of the case. It would be wrong, however, to believe that a defendant in an action for public nuisance who neither owns nor occupies premises and who does not himself or herself engage in activities on land in the area will inevitably escape liability. If, for example, a county council exercised its functions in such a way as to encourage vermin-infested vehicles to throng the highway, carrying diseases to neighbouring houses, there is no reason in principle why it should not be held in public nuisance.

## III. PRIVATE NUISANCE[74]

**[24.24]** Private nuisance is "really a field of tortious liability rather than a single type of tortious conduct: the feature which gives it unity is the interest invaded - that of the use and enjoyment of land".[75] In *Royal Dublin Society v Yates*,[76] Shanley J went so far as to observe that the tort of private nuisance consists of any interference without lawful justification with a person's use and enjoyment of his property. The dimensions of the tort have changed somewhat over the years, the trend being to expand the scope of liability in terms of who may sue and who may be sued,[77] but contracting its scope so far as the standard of liability is concerned - here the movement is towards aligning nuisance with negligence, by judging the question of the reasonableness of the defendant's conduct through the eyes of the neighbouring plaintiff rather than of the defendant himself. Thus we find Henchy J, delivering the judgment of the Supreme Court in *Hanrahan v Merck, Sharp & Dohme (Ireland) Ltd*,[78] in 1988, stating that it was:

> "clear from the authorities on the law of nuisance that what an occupier of land is entitled to as against his neighbour, is the comfortable and healthy enjoyment of the land to the degree that would be expected by an ordinary person whose requirements are objectively reasonable in all the particular circumstances."

**[24.25]** A private nuisance is not generally actionable *per se*,[79] and actual damage must be proved. The damage may consist of (a) physical injury to land, (b) a substantial interference with the enjoyment of land, or (c) an interference with servitudes, where the

---

74. See the articles cited in fn 1, above. See also Gearty 'The Place of Private Nuisance in a Modern Law of Torts' [1989] Camb LJ 214. Dr Gearty presents a strong case for restricting the tort of private nuisance to the protection of property from non-physical damage and letting the tort of negligence handle indirectly caused damage to land.

75. SALMOND & HEUSTON, p 53.

76. High Court, 31 July 1997 (Shanley J).

77. This issue is one that had provoked much judicial concern in recent years. In *Hunter v Canary Wharf Ltd* [1997] AC 655, the House of Lords sought to restrict the scope of claimants. Later Irish decisions have not gone so far: see *Royal Dublin Society v Yates* High Court, 31 July 1997; *Molumby v Kearns* High Court, 19 January 1999 (O'Sullivan J). See further paras **[24.59]** and **[24.72]** below.

78. [1988] ILRM 629 at 634 (SC). In *Molumby v Kearns* High Court, 19 January 1999 at p 45 of his judgment, O'Sullivan J expressed the view that this passage "... captures the essence of the tort in Irish law ...".

79. Three exceptions have been recognised: (i) the court may infer damage where none is proved if to require such evidence would be superfluous: *Fay v Prentice* (1845) 1 CB 828, 135 ER 769; *cf Meara v Daly* (1914) 48 ILTR 223 (CC); (ii) no damage need be proven by a plaintiff seeking damages for interference with an easement or profit *à prendre*; (iii) an injunction may be granted in a *quia timet* action where harm is reasonably feared to be imminent, but has not yet occurred.

disturbance constitutes a substantial interference with the plaintiff's rights.[80] The last of these categories overlaps with the mainstream of property law and will not be discussed in this work.[81]

## Physical injury to Land

**[24.26]** Certain nuisances of this kind are closely akin to trespass.[82] Indeed, sometimes it is difficult to see why the injury is not regarded as having been directly caused. Encroachment by trees raises particular difficulties in this regard.

### *(a) Roots*

**[24.27]** It has been observed that:

> "It is somewhat remarkable that in a country so largely agricultural as Ireland, there has been such a marked scarcity of decisions touching upon the rights and liabilities of occupiers of land resulting from the spreading of the roots or trees beyond the boundary of their owner's property."[83]

---

80. Bland, *The Law Of Easements and Profits à Prendre*, (1997), para 18-02, citing *Fitzgerald v Firbank* [1897] 2 Ch 96 at 104. *Cf*, eg, *Redfont Ltd v Custom House Dock Management Ltd* High Court, 31 March 1998 (Shanley J); *Tisdall v McArthur & Co (Steel and Metal) Ltd* [1951] IR 228 (SC); *McGrath v Munster & Leinster Bank Ltd* [1959] IR 313 (HC); *Kelly v Dea* (1965) 100 ILTR 1 (HC). *Scott v Goulding Properties Ltd* [1973] IR 200 (SC); *Gannon v Hughes* [1937] IR 284 (HC); *Smyth v Dublin Theatre Co Ltd* [1936] IR 692 (HC); *cf Daly v Cullen* (1957) 92 ILTR 127 (CC); *Black v Scottish Temperance Life Assurance* [1908] 1 IR 541 (HL rev CA, restoring order of Barton J, 1906), *Maude v Murphy* [1934] IR 394 (HC). It is of interest to note that in the United States, where courts long ago rejected the right of action for interference with ancient lights there is a growing willingness to reconsider that policy in the context of protection of the right of access to sunlight for residential solar energy systems: *cf* Isban 'Note: Tort Law - Private Nuisance - Access to Sunlight - Residential Solar Energy Systems' (1983) 21 Duquesne LR 1159; Hollis 'Comment: A Private Nuisance Remedy for Obstructions to Solar Access' (1983) 48 Missourri LR 769. See also Kraemer, *Solar Law* (1978), Chs 7-8; Zillman 'Common-Law Doctrines and Solar Energy' Ch 2, *Legal Aspects of Solar Energy* (Minan & Lawrence eds 1981). Blenkhorn 'Note: Access to Sunlight in Ohio: The Dismal Outlook' (1984) 32 Clev St LR 497 at 499 505; Lyden, 'Note: An Integrated Approach to Solar Access' (1984) 34 Case WLR 367; Gevartz 'Obstruction of Sunlight as a Private Nuisance' (1977) 65 Cal LR 94; Mostowitz 'Legal Access to Light: The Solar Energy Imperative' 9 Nat Resources Law (1976) 177 at 204-206; Miller 'Legal Obstacles to Decentralized Solar Energy Technologies -1' (1980) 1 Solar L Reporter 595 at 602-603; Becker 'Common Law Sun Rights: An Obstacle to Solar Heating and Cooling' (1976) 3 J of Contemp. L 19 at 26-31. Other common law jurisdictions have also taken note of the question: *cf* Bradbrook 'The Tortious Liability of the User of a Solar Energy System' (1983) 14 MULR 151; Bradbrook 'Nuisance and the Right of Solar Access' (1983) 15 UW Austr LR 148.

81. For detailed discussion see Bland, *The Law of Easements and Profits à Prendre* (1997) (especially Ch 18); Wylie, *Irish Land Law* (3rd ed, 1997), Ch 6; Coughlan *Property Law* (2nd ed, 1998), Ch 3; Lyall *Land Law in Ireland* (2nd ed, 2000), Ch 22.

82. The difference between nuisance and trespass is important: in nuisance damage must be proved, but trespass is actionable *per* se. *Cf Meara v Daly* (1954) 48 ILTR 223 (CC) - the holding in the case, that economic loss sustained by an occupier in protecting horses from barbed wire was not "damage," is questionable. In *Hanrahan v Merck, Sharp & Dohme (Ireland) Ltd* [1988] ILRM 629 (SC), the issue of causation was at the centre of the case. For consideration of the Supreme Court's analysis, see para **[9.49]** above.

83. Anon 'Roots of Trees: Liability for Injury caused to Neighbour's Premises' (1940) 6 Ir Jur 39 at 39. *Cf* Anon, 'Trees', (1940) 74 ILT & Sol J 289 at 290-291.

**[24.28]** The principles of law are, however, reasonably clear. Where the encroachment of tree roots onto the property of a neighbouring occupier causes damage,[84] this constitutes a nuisance, which entitles the injured party in an appropriate case to seek damages[85] or an injunction,[86] or to abate the nuisance himself or herself.[87] Moreover, he or she need not wait until damage is done: he may take protective action by cutting the roots as soon as they project into his property[88] or may seek a *quia timet* injunction[89] (provided that the stringent requirements of that remedy have been fulfilled).

***(b) Branches***

**[24.29]** Branches occasion largely the same liability as roots,[90] but some differences may be noted. Where a branch encroaches onto another's property and causes damage, the occupier of that property will have the same remedies as in the case of encroaching roots.[91] Where, however, a tree overhangs the highway, and a branch falls as a result of a latent defect not discoverable by any reasonable inspection, liability will not be imposed.[92]

---

84. *Middleton v Humphries* (1912) 47 ILTR 160 (Ch Div), approved and applied in *Butler v Standard Telephones & Cables Ltd* [1940] 1 KB 299. See Anon 'Trees' (1940) 74 ILT & Sol J 289 at 290-291, and D[elany] 'Injuries Caused by Growing Trees' (1959) 25 Ir Jur 20, analysing *Davey v Harrow Corporation* [1958] 1 QB 60 (CA).

85. *Middleton v Humphries* 47 ILTR 160; *Davey v Harrow Corporation* [1958] 1 QB 60 (CA).

86. In *McCombe v Read* [1955] 2 QB 429, Harman J, after referring to the approach to this question favoured in *Middleton v Humphries* stated (at 436): "In my opinion this must be right". See also *Black v Zager* (1982) 22 CCLT 231; *Cf Palmer v Byrne* [1906] 1 IR 373.

87. *Butler v Standard Telephones & Cables Ltd* [1940] 1 KB 299 at 403; *Lemmon v Webb* [1894] 3 Ch 1 at 24, [1895] AC 1. Some cases in the United States have permitted self-help as the only remedy: *cf* Mollit 'Note: Remedies for Intruding Branches and Roots' (1982) 40 Ky LJ 211.

88. *Lemmon v Webb* [1894] 3 Ch 1 at 24, [1895] AC 1; *Davey v Harrow Corporation* [1958] 1 QB 60 at 70.

89. See Ch 45 below.

90. See Anon 'Injuries Arising from Overhanging Branches' (1904) 38 ILT & Sol J 325; Anon 'Actions for Damage Caused by Overhanging Trees' (1919) 53 ILT & Sol J 123, Anon 'Some Recent Decisions on the Liability of Occupiers for Defective Trees Bordering the Highway' (1950) 84 ILT & Sol J 159; Anon 'Trees' (1940) 74 ILT & Sol J 289; Anon 'Some Cases on the Liability to Users of the Highway for Injuries Caused by Defective Premises, Fences, Trees, etc' (1937) 71 ILT & Sol J 197 at 199-201; Neel 'Nuisance from Land In Its Natural Condition' (1943) 56 HLR 772 at 786-791.

91. *Lemmon v Webb* [1894] 3 Ch 1 at 24, [1895] AC 1. *Cf Myles and Gold v Ryan* Circuit Court, 19 October 1998, - defendant guilty of trespass in cutting down far more than was his entitlement in responding to branches overhanging his property; plaintiffs had agreed to have the overhanging branches cut back but the defendant's workmen had "engaged in the wholesale destruction of a twenty-foot elderberry planting" in the plaintiff's garden; three trees, twenty feet high, had been reduced to three foot stumps.

92. *Gillen v Fair* (1956) 90 ILTR 119 (HC); *Noble v Harrison* [1926] 2 KB 332. See also *Mullan v Forrester* [1921] 2 IR 412 at 433 (KBD). *Cf Mackie v Dumbartonshire County Council* [1927] WN 247 (HL) - patent defect alleged. Other relevant decisions are discussed in (1950) 74 ILT & (1919) Sol J 159, and 53 ILT & Sol J 123. See also *Healy v Bray UDC* [1962-1963] Ir Jur 9 at 16 (SC). In *Gillen v Fair* 90 ILTR 119 at 120, Lavery J, is reported as having stated that the standard of care required of a farmer in County Mayo having trees growing on his land adjoining a highway might not be as high as that required of an owner of a tree growing beside a highway in a thickly populated built-up area. This remark was made in the context of the tort of negligence, but the same would necessarily appear to apply in nuisance. A similar trend is discernible in the United States. See, eg, *Taylor v Olsen* (1978) 282 Or 343, 578 P 2d 779; *Hensley v Montgomery County* (1975) 25 Md App 361, 334 A 2d 542.

**[24.30]** It seems that the court should take into account the location of the premises, so as to require more of the occupiers of urban premises whose trees overhang the highway than of those living in the heart of the country.[93] In *Lynch v Hetherton*,[94] where an ash tree fell on the plaintiff's car which was driving along a country road in County Westmeath, O'Hanlon J held that the defendant occupier was not liable in nuisance or negligence. The tree was rotten inside but this fact was not known by the defendant. The tree was located on an out-farm, which the defendant passed five days a week. He had tightened a row of wire on a ditch, which was connected to the tree, with stakes ten days before the accident at a point two feet above ground level, which was very sound and firm. The defendant had inspected all his trees, though he had not employed an expert to look at them, and had cut down several before the accident. O'Hanlon J was satisfied that the defendant was not under an obligation to employ an expert; even if he had done so, it was probable that the decay would not have been detected.

**[24.31]** In *Lynch v Dawson*,[95] liability was imposed on the owner of land adjoining a highway where a branch of a tree which projected onto the highway became entangled in the top part of a turf lorry, resulting in the plaintiff's being injured. The Court considered that the defendant ought to have been aware of the danger, and stressed that changing times could change the level of vigilance required of the defendant. Murnaghan J. stated:

> "This tree, about sixteen feet in length and, growing as it was, would not obstruct much of the present users of the highway and certainly would not have obstructed the user at all forty years ago. Of recent years, however, motor lorries carrying creels have come into common use. Although the principles of the common law remain the same, the application of these principles must move with the times."[96]

In other instances trees are not, of course, the only offenders. Physical injury constituting a nuisance may result from blasting;[97] vibrations;[98]

---

93. *Caminer v Northern & London Investment Trust Ltd* [1951] AC 88 (Lords Radcliff and Reid's speeches); *Quinn v Scott* [1965] 2 All ER 588 (QB).

94. [1990] ILRM 857 (CCA), analysed by Byrne & Binchy, *Annual Review of Irish Law 1990*, pp 539-542.

95. [1946] IR 504 (HC).

96. [1946] IR 504 at 507-508. *Cf O'Hanlon v Minister for Posts & Telegraphs* [1960] Ir Jur 25 (SC). For consideration of the statutory powers of abatement of a nuisance in this context, under the Local Government (Planning and Development) Act 1963, s 45(7) and s 70 of the Roads Act 1993, see Galligan, *Irish Planning Law and Procedure*, (1997), p 42.

97. *Malone v Clogrennane Lime & Trading Co Ltd* High Court, 14 April 1978 (McWilliam J); *Buckley v Healy* [1965] IR 618 (HC); *Halpin v Tara Mines Ltd* High Court, 16 February 1976 (Gannon J). *Patterson v Murphy* [1978] ILRM 85 (HC); *Stafford v Roadstone Ltd* [1980] ILRM 1 (HC). See also *Rabbette v Mayo County Council* [1984] ILRM 156 (HC). *Cf* Green 'Fright Cases' (1933) 27 Illinois LR 761, 873 at 879-881.

98. *Goldfarb v Williams & Co* [1945] IR 433 (HC); *Bellew v Cement Ltd* [1948] IR 61 (SC); *Halpin v Tara Mines Ltd* High Court, 16 February 1976; *Patterson v Murphy* [1978] ILRM 85. See also *Rainville* (1983) 17 U Cal Davis LR 389.

noise;[99] dust;[100] water;[101] the emission of toxic substances;[102] fumes;[103] smoke[104] or sewage[105] causing excessive heat to pass into adjoining premises[106] or, conversely, obstructing heat so as to reduce the adjoining premises to arctic conditions.[107]

**[24.32]** Courts tended in the past to limit the scope of compensation for personal injuries in proceedings for private nuisance since the tort historically was based on interference with the use of land or premises. It was not invoked where personal injuries were sustained except in cases where the injuries were the incidental consequence of some clear interference with the use of the property - as with illness caused by noxious gases from an

99. *Dewar v The City and Suburban Racecourse Company* [1899] 1 IR 345; *O'Kane v Campbell* [1985] IR 115 (HC); *Mullin v Hynes* Supreme Court, 13 November 1972; *Stafford v Roadstone Ltd* [1980] ILRM 1; *New Imperial & Windsor Hotel Co v Johnson* [1912] 1 IR 327; *Sheehan v College of Dance* [1996] Ir L Log W 288 (CC); *Molumby v Kearns* High Court, 19 January 1999 (O'Sullivan J). *Cf Attorney General (ex rel McGarry) v Sligo County Council* [1991] 1 IR 99 (HC); *Cagney v Murphy* Circuit Court, 13 February 1999 (Judge Lindsay), Irish Times, 12 February 1999 - injunction ordered under s 25(1)(a) of the Control of Dogs Act 1986 to abate nuisance from non-stop "yelping and whinning" of dogs in boarding kennel. See also Anon 'Nuisance by Noise' (1930) 64 ILT & Sol J 163, Anon 'Urban Noise Control' (1968) 4 Col J of L & Soc Problems 105 at 108; Bennett 'Airport Noise Litigation: Case Law Review' (1982) 47 J of Air L & Commerce 449; Testro 'Noise-A Strategy for Attack' (1983) 57 Law Institute J 431 at 432-433; *Patterson v Murphy* [1978] ILRM 85; *Leech v Reilly* High Court, 26 April 1983 (O'Hanlon J). In *Halpin v Tara Mines Ltd* High Court, 16 February 1976 at p 21 of his judgment, when dealing with explosions in relation to mining activities which occurred at irregular intervals, Gannon J observed:

> "Intermittent noises of their nature unusual to a locality which come at irregular or unpredictable intervals are likely to be more disagreeable than such noises which form part of the norm for the locality, such as passing traffic. When these unusual noises are of such nature that they instil apprehension and anxiety into the mind of the listener the sensitivity of the ear is likely to be more acutely perceptive of such noises, despite the amplitude of other more familiar and more acceptable noises simultaneously heard but instinctively disregarded."

In *Baxter v Camden Borough Council* [1999] 1 All ER 237 at 242 (CA), Tuckey, LJ observed:

> "[I]n the case of noise nuisance ... the court will obviously have to consider the locality, age and physical characteristics of the premises in question. Occupiers of low cost, high density housing must be expected to tolerate higher levels of noise from their neighbours than others in more substantial and spacious premises".

In *Hampson v Roddy* Dublin District Court, 2 March 2000, Irish Times 3 March 2000, Judge MacBride, acting under s 108 of the Environmental Protection Agency Act 1992, ordered the defendant to have no more than three parties a year, ending no later than 2 am. His neighbour had complained that there had been two all-night parties in the previous four months, one of which ended at 11 am. See generally Adams & McManus, *Noise and Noise Law: A Practical Approach* (1994).

100. *Malone v Clogrennane Lime & Trading Co Ltd* High Court, 14 April 1978 (McWilliam J); *Leech v Reilly* High Court, 26 April 1983.

101. *Grace v Dwyer Nolan Developments* Circuit Court, 9 November 1998 (Judge Groarke) Irish Times, 10 November 1998.

102. *Hanrahan v Merck, Sharpe & Dohme (Ireland) Ltd* [1988] ILRM 629 (SC).

103. *St Helens Smelting Co, v Tipping* (1865) 11 HLC 642, 11 ER 1483.

104. *Hatch v Pye* (1983) 59 NSR (2d) 170.

105. *Gibbings v Hungerford* [1904] 1 IR 211 (CA); *Wallace v M'Cartan* [1917] 1 IR 397; *Casey v Daughters of Charity of St Vincent de Paul* [1996] Ir L Log W 68 (CC).

106. *Reinhardt v Mentasi* (1889) 42 ChD 685; *Sanders-Clark v Grosvenor Mansions Co* [1900] 2 Ch 373.

107. *Dublin (South) City Market Co v McCabes Ltd* [1953] IR 283 at 311 (HC).

adjoining factory, for example.[108] On principle, compensation should be due for personal injuries to the same extent as for other injuries.[109]

## Substantial interference in the Enjoyment of Land

**[24.33]** A nuisance under this heading results in:

> "personal inconvenience and interference with one's enjoyment, one's quiet, one's personal freedom, anything that discomposes or injuriously affects the senses or the nerves."[110]

**[24.34]** Clearly, this is a very broad criterion: much will depend on a common sense approach towards what is reasonable to expect between neighbours. The courts will thus apply the principle of "give and take, live and let live",[111] since they are required "to act as arbiter between the competing interests of the respective property users".[112]

**[24.35]** One finds in nuisance a conceptual approach towards what is reasonable that is remarkably similar to some of the questions asked in respect of the tort of negligence:[113] thus the court must examine:

(i) the utility of the defendant's conduct, and
(ii) the gravity of the harm resulting or likely to result from it.

**[24.36]** In resolving these questions, a different approach is taken in nuisance actions than that adopted in negligence actions. In negligence, only the conduct of the defendant is under central examination (although of course the wider social context is not ignored): in nuisance, the court is more conscious of being involved in a balancing process between the interests of the plaintiff and the defendant, with (in at least some instances) an undisguised sympathy for the plaintiff.[114] Let us therefore examine in turn each of these elements as understood in a nuisance action.

### *(a) The utility of the defendant's conduct*

**[24.37]** It is clear that "the law, in judging what constitutes a nuisance, does take into consideration ... the object ... of that which is said to constitute a nuisance".[115] Thus, some allowance may be made for the social and economic contexts in which the interfering

---

108. See *Patterson v Murphy* [1978] ILRM 85; *Gibbings v Hungerford* [1904] 1 IR 211; *Hanrahan v Merck, Sharp & Dohme (Ireland) Ltd* [1988] ILRM 629.

109. *Cf Howard Electric Ltd v Mooney Ltd* [1974] 2 NZLR 762; *Miller v Jackson* [1977] QB 966 (CA). See generally Rabin 'Nuisance Laws: Rethinking Fundamental Assumptions' (1977) 63 Va LR 1299.

110. *St Helens Smelting Co v Tipping* (1865) 11 HLC 642 at 650, 11 ER 1483 at 1486.

111. *Bamford v Turnley* 3 B & S 66 at 84, 122 ER 27 at 33. See also Smith 'Reasonable Use of One's Own Property as a Justification for Damage to a Neighbour' (1917) 17 Col LR 383.

112. *Mullin v Hynes* Supreme Court, 13 November 1972 (Henchy J) at p 6. See also *O'Kane v Campbell* [1985] IR 115 at 118 (HC).

113. *Cf* para **[7.25]** above. See also *Hatch v Pye* (1983) 59 NSR (2d) 170; *cf* Shelton 'Anyone for Tennis?' (1984) 58 Law Institute J 639. On occasion, in cases where the plaintiff has pleaded nuisance and negligence, the court directs its attention solely to the latter actions: see, eg, *Walsh v Dublin Corporation* High Court, 23 July 1998 (Smith J).

114. *Cf*, eg, *Bellew v Cement Ltd* [1948] IR 61 (SC), and see Henchy J's language in *Hanrahan v Merck, Sharp & Dohme (Ireland) Ltd* [1988] ILRM 629 at 633, 634 (SC).

115. *Cf Mullin v Hynes* Supreme Court, 13 November 1972 (Henchy J) at p 8. See also *Kelly v Dublin County Council* High Court, 21 February 1986 (O'Hanlon J), at p 7.

conduct takes place. The courts appreciate that the construction of buildings in a city[116] or the running of hotels[117] or shops,[118] for example, must necessarily involve more likelihood of some degree of personal discomfort for neighbouring property owners than if these premises were put to exclusively domestic purposes. This does not mean that the benefit the defendant's conduct confers on the public will be given decisive weight. Indeed, the courts have gone so far as to deny that this should be a factor in determining whether the defendant's conduct was a nuisance. Thus, in the leading decision, *Bellew v Cement Ltd*,[119] Maguire CJ stated:

> "... I am of opinion that the Court is not entitled to take the public convenience into consideration when dealing with the rights of private parties."

And Murnaghan J said:

> "I do not think that we are entitled to deprive [the plaintiff] of his legal rights on some idea of public convenience."[120]

**[24.38]** It is difficult to reconcile these statements with the holdings in some of the decisions.[121] It seems that the courts will be reluctant to listen to the plea of public benefit where the injury to the plaintiff is out of the ordinary rather than part and parcel of urban life, the courts being conscious of the fact that what is ordinary (and thus, they hold, acceptable) in one part of a city may be unusual (and thus unacceptable) in another.[122]

---

116. *Cf Andrae v Selfridge* [1938] Ch 1. See, however, *Henry, Murphy & Co v Northern Bank Ltd and McLoughlin & Harvey Ltd* High Court, July 1983 (Barrington J), where the Court awarded £10,000 damages for nuisance for excessive noise during the reconstruction of the old Hibernian Bank for the Northern Bank at the corner of College Green, Dublin. The builders were required to pay 80% of the damages; the Bank 20%. The Judge said he was satisfied from the evidence that there was considerable interference from the adjacent development work with the enjoyment of the plaintiffs property.

117. *Cf New Imperial Hotel Co v Johnson* [1912] 1 IR 327.

118. *Cf O'Kane v Campbell* [1985] IR 115 at 118 (HC).

119. [1948] IR 61 at 64 (SC). See also *Shelfer v City of London Electric Co* [1895] 1 Ch 287 at 316; *Halpin v Tara Mines Ltd* High Court, 16 February 1976 (Gannon J), at p 5. *Aliter* with respect to proceedings under the Local Government (Planning and Development) Act 1976, s 27: *Stafford v Roadstone Ltd* [1980] ILRM 1 at 19-20 (HC).

120. [1948] IR 61 at 65. See, however, *AG (Boswell) v Rathmines & Pembroke Joint Hospital Board* [1904] 1 IR 161 at 185 (CA): "... The public advantage should not be forbidden unless the danger and injury to the individual are clearly proved". See also *Patterson v Murphy* [1978] ILRM 85 at 100 (HC). *Cf Roomer v Atlantic Cement Co* (1970) 26 NY 2d 219 and Hashim 'Note; Private Nuisance Law: Protection of the Individual's Environmental Rights' (1974) 8 Suffolk ULR 1162 at 1175.

121. In *Clifford v Drug Treatment Centre Board* High Court, 7 November 1997, McCracken J declined to grant an interlocutory injunction reducing the numbers of drug addicts eligible to attend the defendant's drug treatment centre, where the plaintiffs, the proprietors of businesses in the area, claimed that the addicts were damaging the businesses by antisocial activities. The immediate result of granting such an injunction "would be that less drug addicts would be treated, which is clearly against the public interest, besides depriving possibly hundreds of individuals of badly needed treatment." He did, however, enjoin the expansion of numbers, noting that "[a]n injunction restraining such expansion will not affect existing patients".

122. *Cf Adams v Ursell* [1913] 1 Ch 269 at 271-272: "It by no means follows that because a fried fish shop is a nuisance in one place it is a nuisance in another."

**[24.39]** The Courts have accordingly articulated a rule that has regard to the character of the neighbourhood in which the conduct occurs.[123] Thus, in *New Imperial & Windsor Hotel Co v Johnson*,[124] Barton J stated:

> "One of the necessary incidents of the social life of an industrial city is a certain amount of recreation and innocent amusement, taking the form of social gatherings of the respectable young men and women who do a large proportion of the daily work of the city."

**[24.40]** In that case only a limited injunction[125] was given against the proprietor of tea-rooms and a restaurant, who used the premises opposite the plaintiff's hotel in Belfast for dancing and other entertainment at night.

**[24.41]** This does not, of course, mean that industrial and recreational proprietors are given a *carte blanche* to make as much noise (or other disturbances) as they wish in some sections of town,[126] and smoke from factory chimneys may constitute a nuisance even in an industrial town.[127]

**[24.42]** In *Dewar v City & Suburban Racecourse Co*,[128] the defendants organised race-meetings on Sundays on property in Drumcondra, a residential area in Dublin. The residents of the area complained of noise and other disturbances, including interruption of religious services. The area at the time - the 1890s - was described by the Court as follows:

> "Though nearly adjoining the thickly inhabited portions of the city, it was till recent years not closely built on and it retained somewhat of the nature of a country district. The very field converted into the racecourse was, until the year 1894, a market garden ... The houses were few and scattered; but since then it has been closely built on, and consists almost entirely of dwelling-houses erected in streets or terraces, which became a favourite locality for persons in employments in the city during the day, and who enjoyed the quiet and better air of the place in their hours at home. It was essentially a residentiary district for the middle classes."[129]

The Court granted an injunction against the defendants, prohibiting the holding of race-meetings on Sundays.

---

123. See Penner 'Nuisance and the Character of the Neighbourhood' (1993) 5 J of Environmental L 1. The rule has no operation where the plaintiff suffers "material injury" - that is, actual physical damage - to his or her property: *cf St Helen's Smelting Co v Tipping* (1865) 11 HLC 642 at 650, 11 ER 1483 at 1486 (HL). See also *Halsey v Esso Petroleum Co Ltd* [1961] 1 WLR 683 noted in (1961) 77 LQR 306; *Halpin v Tara Mines* High Court, 16 February 1976 (Gannon J); *Hanrahan v Merck, Sharp & Dohme (Ireland) Ltd* [1988] ILRM 629 (SC).

124. [1912] 1 IR 327 at 332. A large dancehall in a residential area of a country town (Templemore, Co Tipperary) was regarded as an entirely different proposition in *Mullin v Hynes* Supreme Court, 13 November 1972. *Cf Walsh v Tedcastle McCormack & Co Ltd* High Court, 23 June 1967 (Kenny J).

125. The injunction was limited in effect to keeping the windows of the premises shut after midnight and to preventing patrons leaving and entering the premises from making undue noise.

126. See *Polsue & Alfieri Ltd v Rushmer* [1907] AC 121 (HL). *Cf Dublin Corporation v Moore* [1984] ILRM 339 at 346 (SC).

127. *Crump v Lambert* (1867) LR 3 Eq 409.

128. [1899] 1 IR 345.

129. [1899] 1 IR 345 at 351-352.

**[24.43]** The decision provides a good example of judicial zoning,[130] whereby the courts perform the function of "rightly giving more weight to the demands of a stable, as distinct from a changing, society".[131] Where the character of a neighbourhood is fixed it is a relatively easy task for the court to determine the appropriate standard,[132] but where the locality is in a state of transition (whether from rural or urban or, within a city, from residential to industrial or vice versa), the task facing the court is more difficult.[133]

**[24.44]** *O'Kane v Campbell*[134] involved an interesting question of how the locality should be characterised. A shop was positioned on the corner of North Circular Road and Glengarriff Parade in Dublin. North Circular Road is "a wide busy street both by day and

---

130. In the United States "judicial zoning" has been used to reinforce legislative zoning of neighbourhoods: *cf* Benscher & Morrison 'Judicial Zoning Through Recent Nuisance Cases' [1955] Wisc LR 440; 'Comment: Nuisance as a Modern Mode of Land Use Control', (1970) 46 Wash LR 47. This process has extended into some contentious social and moral contexts, such as the operation of pornshops, massage parlours and abortion clinics. See O'Connor, (1977) 46 Fordham LR 57. Control of obscenity through civil nuisance statutes, being subject to stringent constitutional safeguards, has proved a less than fully effective remedy: *cf* Gorman 'The Demise of Civil Nuisance Actions in Obscenity Control' (1982) 14 Loyola U of Chicago LJ, Catlett 'Note' (1984) 84 Col LR 1616; *Vance v Universal Amusement Co Inc* (1980) 445 US 308, affg (1978) 587 F 2d 159; *Spokane Arcades Inc v Brockett* (1981) 454 US 1022, affg (1980) 631 F 2d 135. See also Rendleman 'Civilizing Pornography: The Case for an Exclusive Obscenity Nuisance Statute' (1977) 44 U Chi LR 509; Gorman 'The Demise of Evil Nuisance Actions in Obscenity Control' (1983) 14 Loy U Chi LJ 31, Trachtman 'Note' (1983) 58 NYU LR 1478. In England, the tort of public nuisance has been invoked to enjoin the use of a private residence for the purposes of prostitution: *Thompson-Schwab v Costaki* [1956] 1 WLR 335; see also the Canadian decision of *AG for British Columbia v Couillard* (1984) 11 DLR (4th) 567 (BC SC); but *cf Stein v Gonzales* (1984) 14 DLR (4th) 263 (BC SC); *AG for Nova Scotia v Beaver* (1985) 67 NSR (2d) 281 (NSCA), affg (1985) 66 NSR (2d) 419 (NS SC); private nuisance was successfully pleaded in the Canadian decision of *Poirier v Turkewich* (1964) 42 DLR (2d) 259, but failed in *Stein v Gonzales* 14 DLR (4th) 263. See also *Laws v Florinplace Ltd* [1981] 1 All ER 659. More generally, see Canch 'Prostitution and Public Nuisance: Desperate Measures and the Limits of Civil Adjudication' (1985) 63 Can BR 764.

131. FLEMING, p 470. See also Oleck 'Nuisance in a Nutshell' (1956) S Clev-Mar. LR 148 at 160-161; VVC 'Note: The Modern Tendency Toward the Protection of the Aesthetic' (1937) 44 W Va LQ 58.

132. *Cf Sturges v Bridgman* (1879) 11 Ch D 852 at 865 (CA); *Pembroke v Warren* [1896] 1 IR 76 at 140.

133. *Cf* Friedmann 'Modern Trends in the Law of Torts' (1937) 1 MLR 39 at 46-47:

> "The first factory in a farming district, the running or by-products of which attract noxious animals which injure crops in the neighbourhood, causes obviously a nuisance ... A second factory may already be in a better position. The standard of comfort may no longer be so clearly that of a farming community, and eventually a solitary farmer may possibly be held to cause a nuisance to the workers of a factory nearby through the noise of cattle or the smell of farm-yard manure. A parallel problem occurs when a quiet residential quarter is invaded by business and industry."

See also Grossman and Fischer 'Protecting the Right to Farm: Statutory Limits on Nuisance Actions Against the Farmer' [1983] Wis LR 9S, Levitin 'Change in Neighbourhood in Nuisance Cases' (1964) 13 Clev-Mar LR 340, Anon 'Note: Home Owners' Rights versus Industrial Expediency' (1944) 19 Indiana LJ 167. In England, a judicial willingness to regard a grant of planning permission as being capable of constituting a change in the character of a neighbourhood, apparant in *Gillingham BC v Medway (Chatham) Dock Co Ltd* [1993] QB 343, has been radically tempered and refined in subsequent decisions: *Wheeler v JJ Saunders Ltd* [1996] Ch 19; *Hunter v Canary Wharf Ltd* [1996] 1 All ER 482 (CA; issue now arising on appeal to HL).

134. [1985] IR 115 (HC).

by night"; Glengarriff Parade is "an old established residential street ... just removed from the bustle of other more busy places in the area".[135] The shop began to trade on a 24-hour basis. This involved a degree of noise throughout the night, which disturbed the plaintiff, who lived opposite the shop, in Glengarriff Parade. The noise was the normal and inevitable result of "ordinary law abiding people"[136] going to and from the shop, revving the engines of their cars or motor-bikes, banging car-doors,[137] and playing car radios. There was no question of disorderly behaviour or breaches of the peace.

**[24.45]** Lynch J was satisfied that, had the shop been on Glengarriff Parade itself it would have constituted a clear nuisance on account of traffic congestion and noise; conversely, if it had been completely on North Circular Road and a little distance away from Glengarriff Parade, there would be "hardly any doubt that there was no actionable nuisance".[138] In view of the position of the shop at the junction of the two streets, the case was less clearcut, but Lynch J was satisfied on the evidence that the trading carried on through the night had "drastically altered the amenity of Glengarriff Parade as a residential street".[139] Accordingly he enjoined the defendant from carrying on business between midnight and 6 am.[140]

**[24.46]** In *Molumby v Kearns*,[141] O'Sullivan J was called on to adjudicate competing interests in relation to a somewhat complex location. The plaintiff lived on Foster Avenue, Mount Merrion, a prestige residential address in Dublin 4. They complained of noise and fumes associated with traffic movements on an adjoining industrial estate. In ordering that the working hours on the industrial estate should be restricted to daytime from Monday to Friday and to Saturday morning, that no commercial vehicles should be permitted access to the estate when the gates were closed and that fork-lift and pallet trucks should be electric or battery operated units with rubber wheels, O'Sullivan J observed:

> "I treat the locality not as an exclusively residential area but as a residential area, so zoned, adjoining a busy road in front and with an industrial estate, authorised by appropriate planning, in its midst.
>
> I do not think that the fact that the residences immediately adjoin the industrial estate means that the estate must close down. I do not think this would be reasonable. Equally, I do not think that the noise, fumes and general activity and traffic movements on the estate should be such as to cause an undue impact on the amenities of the nearby residences."[142]

**[24.47]** Where there is no good purpose in the defendant's conduct, it will constitute a nuisance. Thus, whilst the concept of abuse of rights, familiar in Civil Law

---

135. [1985] IR 115 at 118.
136. [1985] IR 115 at 117.
137. *Per* Lynch J ([1985] IR 115 at 117): "[a]nd they have to be banged to some extent to close them at all."
138. [1985] IR 115 at 118.
139. [1985] IR 115.
140. See also *Patterson v Murphy* [1978] ILRM 85, where the Court had to decide whether the locality should be characterised as agricultural or one of quarrying.
141. High Court, 19 January 1999 (O'Sullivan J).
142. Page 46 of O'Sullivan J's judgment.

jurisidictions,[143] has not yet been developed in Irish law, it is clear that malice plays an important part in actions for nuisance.[144]

**[24.48]** Where the defendant, with the intention of causing annoyance to a neighbour, uses his or her property in an unneighbourly manner, the court will have regard to this intention in determining whether the use of the property was reasonable. Thus, in *Christie v Davey*,[145] the defendant, exasperated by the noise from the music lessons given up to a late hour by the plaintiff, his neighbour, attempted by a clumsily-written letter to have the noise discontinued. When this failed, he resorted to playing instruments, blowing whistles, knocking on trays and making other noise in mock concerts designed to annoy the plaintiff. The defendant was held to have committed a nuisance,[146] North J stating:

> "If what has taken place had occurred between two sets of persons both perfectly innocent, I should have taken an entirely different view of the case. But I am persuaded that what was done by the defendant was done only for the purpose of annoyance, and in my opinion it was not a legitimate use of the defendant's house to use it for the purpose of vexing and annoying his neighbours."[147]

---

143. *Cf* Gutteridge 'Abuse of Rights' (1933) 5 Camb LJ 22; Leake 'Abuse of Rights in Louisiana' (1933) 7 Tul LR 426. Crabb 'The French Concept of Abuse of Rights' (1964) 6 Inter-Amer LR 1.

144. *Cf* Fridman 'Motive in the English Law of Nuisance' (1954) 40 Va LR 583; Williams 'The Foundation of Tortious Liability' (1939) 7 Camb LJ 111 at 125 ff; Anon 'Some Recent Cases on Nuisance' (1938) 72 ILT & Sol J 213 at 214-215.

145. [1893] 1 Ch 316. *Cf* Ames 'How Far an Act May Be a Tort Because of the Wrongful Motive of the Actor' (1905) 18 Harv LR 411 at 421.

146. An injunction was granted, damages not having been claimed. The Court advised the plaintiff's son when practising the violincello, not to begin any fresh piece after 11 pm (although North J did "not believe that his playing has been open to any objection ..:" at 328).

147 [1893] 1 Ch 316 at 326-327. *Cf Humphries v Connor* (1864) 17 Ir CLR 1 at 7-8. In *Boyle v Holcroft* [1905] 1 IR 245, the Court granted an injunction against the defendant, the judicial tenant of the plaintiff, restraining him from trespassing upon the plaintiff's fishery and from erecting or maintaining any wire paling or other obstruction so as to obstruct the plaintiff in the exercise of his exclusive right of fishing. Barton J said (at 250-251):

> "I take it that, as a general rule, so long as the tenant is *bona fide* and reasonably managing and using the lands, the owner of the fishing rights might be content to exercise his right upon the lands in the condition in which they may happen to be from time to time. On the other hand, the tenant must not, under cover of farm user or management, unreasonably or *mala fide* cause or maintain an obstruction to the exercise of the right of fishing, and may be restricted by injunction from doing so ..."

The defendant having adopted a kind of paling which prevents the exercise of a legal right, questions of motive and reasonableness become legitimate subjects of inquiry. In the present case, he said (at 251):

> "[t]here was evidence pointing to a personal *animus* against the plaintiff, and an attitude of hostility to his exclusive right of fishing, which cannot be left out of consideration upon the question of *bona fides*."

The paling had not been erected until after the defendant had been imprisoned for fishing at the place in question. His brother had been fined for a similar offence, and "[a]n atmosphere of opposition to fishing rights in general, and in particular to plaintiff's fishing right, permeated the evidence upon defendant's side. The element of personal *animus* has significance when taken in connection with the absence of any adequate explanation of the use of barbed wire at this place" (at 251). Barton J did not consider it necessary, in view of the clear evidence, to decide whether the burden of proof on the issues of *bona fides* and reasonableness rested on the plaintiff or defendant.

**[24.49]** In *Hollywood Silver Fox Farm Ltd v Emmett*[148] the defendant's farm bordered the plaintiff's fox farm. The defendant objected to a notice-board on the plaintiff's property, since he thought that it was detrimental to a scheme of his to sell some of his land as plots for bungalows. When the plaintiff's proprietor refused to take down the signs, the defendant threatened to shoot on his own property as near as he could to the breeding pens, saying: "You will not raise a single cub". In time the defendant carried out his threat. The effect of noise was that vixens were put off mating and induced to kill and devour their young.

**[24.50]** The defendant tried to excuse his conduct by stating that he was attempting to keep down rabbits, but the Court regarded this explanation as manifestly untrue.[149] Liability was imposed by MacNaghten J, who considered that the matter had been "put beyond all doubt"[150] by *Christie v Davey.*[151]

**[24.51]** Some difficulty has been caused by the decision of *Mayor of Bradford v Pickles*,[152] where the defendant deliberately dammed percolating water that flowed through his land so as to diminish the supply of water reaching the plaintiffs land. His purpose was to coerce the plaintiffs into buying the land. It had previously been established[153] that no interest in percolating water exists until it is appropriated. The House of Lords held that the defendant had not behaved unlawfully. Lord Halsbury LC stated:

> "This is not a case in which the state of mind of the person doing the act can affect the right to do it. If it was a lawful act, however ill the motive might be, he had a right to do it. If it was an unlawful act, however good his motive might be he would have no right to do it. Motives and intentions in such a question as is now before your Lordships seem to me to be absolutely irrelevant."[154]

---

147. (contd) The injunction was claimed in terms which did not extend to actions by the defendant which were the necessary result of the *bona fide* and reasonable exercise by [him] of his right, as the tenant of the "... lands, in the proper cultivation and management thereof" (at 252). *Cf Caldwell v Kilkelly* [1905] 1 IR 434; *Fetherstonhaugh v Hagarty* (1878) 3 LR Ir 150. See also *Palmer v Byrne* [1906] 1 IR 373 - tenant was required to permit landlord, in the exercise of his fishery rights, to cut sallies and bushes which had become overgrown, but under "no active obligation ... to take upon himself the responsibility and expense of cutting and logging trees for the [landlord]'s benefit - injunction accordingly refused". *Per* Barton J at 377:

> "If the [tenant], after the date of the restriction of the fishing right, had planted these sallies and bushes so as to be or become an obstruction to the fishing right, different considerations might arise. I express no opinion upon a state of facts which is not before the Court".

148. [1936] 2 KB 468 - facts and judgment set out in greater detail in [1936]1 All ER 825. For analysis of the decision see Goodhart 'Note' (1936) 52 LQR 460 and Rejoinder, (1937) 53 LQR 3, Holdsworth 'Note' (1937) 53 LQR 1, Cronkite, (1937) 2 Sask BR 36. *Cf Annaly Hotel Ltd v Bergin* (1967) 104 ILTR 65 (HC) - defendant blocked windows of neighbouring hotel with sheets of galvanised iron which gave off an "unearthly" sound when wind blew; liability in nuisance imposed. See also *Atlantic Aviation v Nova Scotia Light & Power Co* (19655) 5 DLR (2d) 554 (NS SC).

149. [1936] 1 All ER 827.

150. [1936] 1 All ER 827 at 829 (*Cf* [1936] 2 KB 468 at 475, where this passage is omitted).

151. [1893] 1 Ch 316.

152. [1865] AC 587 (HL). See also *Sweeney v Cooke* [1906] 1 IR 51 at 100.

153. *Broadbent v Ramsbotham* (1856) 11 Ex 602, 156 ER 971, *Chasemore v Richards* (1859) 7 HL Cas 349, 11 ER 140 (HL).

154. At 594. See also *Sweeney v Cooke* [1906] 1 IR 51 at 100 (CA). For criticism of Lord Halsbury's statement as constituting no more than a tautology, see Williams 'The Foundation of Tortious Liability' (1939) 7 Camb LJ 111 at 127.

**[24.52]** It is now agreed that there is no inconsistency between these three decisions. *Pickles*[155] stands for no more than the proposition that the abstraction of water flowing in undefined channels is an absolute privilege and it is not contingent on reasonable use.[156] Thus, motive will not enter into the question. Where, however, the court is examining the question whether a neighbour's conduct was reasonable - and this will ordinarily be the case in actions for nuisance - the motive of the defendant will be an ingredient in determining this question.[157]

**[24.53]** The cases dealing with the passage of water from one property to another reveal an underlying principle of reasonableness as the basic test of rights and duties. Thus, the occupier of land through which water flows in defined channels, whether on the surface or underground, is not entitled to deprive the downstream occupier of its flow, but equally may insist that the water be received by him or her.[158] Where the water flows in undefined channels, as we have seen, the occupier may appropriate it, even maliciously.[159] If this water is allowed to flow to the lower occupier's land, the lower occupier is "under no obligation"[160] to receive it, but "if the user of his land by him is unreasonable and is resulting in damage to a higher occupier, ... then a nuisance is created".[161]

**[24.54]** The commercial exploitation of land may well be considered a "reasonable" user of property in this context,[162] but the courts will seek to ensure that the higher occupier should be protected as far as is reasonably practicable. Thus, in *Fitzpatrick v O'Connor*,[163] Costello J held that a lower occupier was liable in nuisance in putting up an earth mound which had the effect of interfering with the natural drainage of the plaintiff's lands. The mound had been designed to facilitate landscaping of the defendant's property, with a view to complying with planning requirements but did not in fact achieve this purpose. Costello J concluded that the defendant:

> "acted unreasonably in putting up the earth mound, particularly when he was not required to do so and particularly when alternative methods of screening were available to him."[164]

**[24.55]** In the more urgent case of flooding, from sea or river, an occupier:

> "is entitled to protect his land against floodwater, ... by erecting an embankment on his land, and, if the erection of such an embankment causes floodwater to flow onto his neighbour's land in greater quantities or with greater violence than it would otherwise have done, he is

155. [1895] AC 587 (HL).

156. FLEMING, p 471-473. See also *Home Brewery plc v William Davis & Co (Loughborough) Ltd* [1987] 1 All ER 637 (QB).

157. See Cronkite, (1937) 2 Sask LR 36 at 38.

158. *Mason v Hill* (1833) 5 B & Ad 1, 110 ER 692. See the helpful summary of the relevant legal principles by Wilkinson 'The Natural Drainage of Land' (1987) 137 New LJ 867 at 868.

159. *Mayor of Bradford v Pickles* [1865] AC 587 (HL). *Cf* SALMOND & HEUSTON, p 23.

160. *Fitzpatrick v O'Connor* High Court, 11 March 1988 (Costello J) at p 7.

161. In accord are the Australian decisions of *Gartner v Kidman* (1962) 108 CLR 12 and the English decision (cited by Costello J) *Home Brewery plc v William Davis & Co (Loughborough) Ltd* [1987] 1 All ER 637. Canadian decisions appear to be more indulgent to the owner occupier: see *McPhee v Township of Plympton* (1987) 43 DLR (4th) 233 (Ont DC) and the decisions cited therein.

162. *Home Brewery plc v William Davis & Co (Loughborough) Ltd* [1987] 1 All ER 637; see also Spencer 'Comment: Flooding, Fault and Private Nuisance' [1987] Camb LJ 205 at 207.

163. High Court, 11 March 1988 (Costello J).

164. At p 7. *Cf Grace v Dwyer Nolan Developments Ltd* Circuit Court, 9 November 1998 (Groarke J).

under no liability to his neighbour. If the neighbour wishes to protect his land it is for him to erect his own embankment."[165]

Once the floodwater has actually come onto his or her land, however, an occupier may not later discharge it onto a neighbour's land.[166]

### *(b) Gravity of harm*

**[24.56]** The courts have frequently stressed that some allowance should be made for the ordinary incidents of neighbourly relations, and that the injury must be of "a substantial character, not fleeting or evanescent".[167] Thus, in *Mullin v Hynes*,[168] Henchy J, referred to "the unwillingness of the courts to grant relief where the damage claimed is in respect of trivial, fanciful or exaggerated inconvenience". On this basis, a specially sensitive plaintiff will not be permitted to compel a neighbour to accommodate his or her particular needs.[169] This does not mean that the court should ignore certain characteristics of the plaintiff. As Lynch J, observed in *O'Kane v Campbell*,[170] when enjoining a shop at the corner of a residential street from trading throughout the night: "Elderly people perhaps sleep more lightly [than young people] but they are not abnormal for that and they are entitled to their night sleep".

**[24.57]** Once the injury is of a material nature which causes damage to the property, as we have seen, the courts will not have regard to competing considerations, such as public benefit or the character of the neighbourhood. In this regard, nuisance differs from negligence, where proof of material injury does not so effectively foreclose consideration of other factors.

## Nuisance as a State of Affairs

**[24.58]** It seems proper to regard nuisance as a continuing wrong, in the sense of a wrongful state of affairs for which the defendant is responsible.[171] Thus, where an interference is of a fleeting nature, which is unlikely to recur, the Courts are reluctant to stigmatise it as a nuisance. This does not mean, however, that the tort of nuisance cannot be committed where damage results from a single act[172]

165. *Home Brewery plc v William Davis & Co (Loughborough) Ltd* [1987] 1 All ER 637 at 642. See *R v Pagham Sussex Sewers Commissioners* (1828) 8 B & C 355, 108 ER1075, *Gerrard v Crowe* [1921] 1 AC 395.

166. *Whalley v Lancashire & Yorkshire Railway Co* (1884) 13 QBD 131.

167. *Benjamin v Storr* (1874) LR 9 CP 400 at 407. See also *Halpin v Tara Mines Ltd* High Court, 16 February 1976 (Gannon J) at p 5, and *Hanrahan v Merck, Sharp & Dohme (Ireland) Ltd* [1988] ILRM 629 at 634 (SC).

168. Supreme Court, 13 November 1972 at p 7.149 *Cf* para **[24.107]** below.

169. *Cf* para **[24.106]-[24.108]** below.

170. [1985] IR 115 at 118 (HC).

171. *Cf Halpin v Tara Mines Ltd* High Court, 16 February 1976 (Gannon J), at p 4 of judgment.

172. *Cf* FLEMING, p 468-469. It is true that, in *Hanrahan v Merck, Sharp & Dohme (Ireland) Ltd* [1988] ILRM 629 at 633 (SC), Henchy J noted that the plaintiffs had to show that their use and enjoyment of their farm had been interfered with "over a substantial period of time, and that no remedy in nuisance would lie where the damage complained of was not so repeated or continuous as to be what in ordinary parlance could be described as nuisance." The Court in *Hanrahan* was not dealing with an allegation of damages having been sustained by a single calamitous occurrence for which the defendants were responsible. It would therefore perhaps be unwise to treat the case as definitively rejecting liability in nuisance in such circumstances, in spite of Henchy J's broad language. The failure to refer to significant authorities to the contrary on this question supports a cautious interpretation.

such as the escape of gas[173] for example. The gist of the claim is not the isolated act but the continuuous or permanent organisation by the defendant of his or her affairs on his or her own property in such a way as to result in the injury.[174]

## Who may Sue for Private Nuisance?

**[24.59]** The question of who may sue for the tort of private nuisance is one that has recently been subjected to close analysis by the Irish and English courts. Traditionally it was accepted that the occupier of land may sue in respect of an interference with it and that a tenant in possession may sue, even where there is only a weekly tenancy[175] or a tenancy at will.[176] Conversely, the traditional view was that a person who used the land without either possession of it or any other proprietary interest in it has no right of action.[177] Thus it was held that a member of the family[178] of the occupier or a lodger or guest might not sue.

**[24.60]** In recent years, there was evidence internationally of an increasing judicial willingness to go beyond the traditional restrictions and to permit actions by plaintiffs who had no legal proprietary interest. Thus wives[179] and children[180] of the person with the proprietary interest were able to sue; sometimes the claims of other family members were also acknowledged.[181]

**[24.61]** This process was not always overtly acknowledged by the courts as involving any development in the law. Thus, for example, in *Hanrahan v Merck, Sharp and Dohme (Ireland) Ltd*,[182] the High Court and Supreme Court accepted without discussion that the son and daughter-in-law of the registered owner of the premises were as entitled as she was to claim damages for nuisance.

---

173. *Midwood & Co Ltd v Manchester Corporation* [1905] 2 KB 597; *Northwestern Utilities Ltd v London Guarantee & Accident Co Ltd* [1936] AC 108. *Cf Flynn v Ross* High Court, 19 February 1974 (Pringle J) - inflammable material deposited on plaintiff's property by defendant went on fire; plaintiff entitled to damages for trespass or nuisance. See also *Carroll v Kildare County Council* [1950] IR 258 (SC).

174. *Cf* SALMOND & HEUSTON, pp 55-56.

175. *Jones v Chappell* (1869) LR 20 Eq 529 at 544.

176. *Burgess v City of Woodstock* [1955] 4 DLR 615 (Ont HC).

177. *Cf Seeds v Newry Traction Engine Co* (1903) 37 ILTR 114. Henchy J expressed the lack of entitlement to sue in broad terms in *Hanrahan v Merck, Sharp & Dohme (Ireland) Ltd* [1988] ILRM 629 at 633 (SC). Contrasting the respective circumstances in which proceedings may be brought for nuisance and under the rule in *Rylands v Fletcher,* he said that in some cases liability requires to be determined under *Rylands v Fletcher* only, such as where the plaintiff is not an occupier of land.

178. *Malone v Laskey* [1907] 2 KB 144 (CA); *Canard v Antifyre Ltd* [1933] 1 KB 551; *Oldham v Lawson (No 1)* [1976] VR 654. *Chambers v Cork Corporation* (1958) 93 ILTR 45 (HC).

179. *Cf L v L* High Court, October 1988 (Barr J). In *Motherwell v Motherwell* (1976) 73 DLR (3d) 62 (Alta SC), it was held that a wife who had a right to live in the family home could sue for nuisance.

180. In *Devon Lumber Co Ltd v MacNeill* (1987) 45 DLR (4th) 300 (NBCA); the New Brunswick Court of Appeal (Rice JA dissenting) extended the entitlement to children of the family who, while "lack[ing] any legal title to the property" had a right of occupation in the house. *Cf Attorney General of Ontario v Dieleman* (1994) 117 DLR (4th) 449 (Ont Ct); *Motherwell v Motherwell* (1976) 73 DLR (3d) 62 (Alta SC); *Devon Lumber Co Ltd v MacNeill* (1987) 45 DLR (4th) 300 (NBCA).

181. *Motherwell v Motherwell* (1976) 73 DLR (3d) 62.

182. [1988] ILRM 629.

**[24.62]** In England, in *Hunter v Canary Wharf Ltd*,[183] the House of Lords sought to reverse this trend and to restrict the claim, in the ordinary event, to those "who ha[ve] a right to the land affected",[184] such as freeholders, tenants in possession or licensees with exclusive possession. The majority emphasised the fact that the action for private nuisance is one based on interference with land. To the extent that personal injuries or discomfort might generate compensation under this tort, the award should be justified on the basis of the diminution of the amenity value of the property. For those members of the family (or others without the requisite "right to the land affected") who suffered personal injury from incursions onto the land, a remedy in negligence would normally be available.

**[24.63]** The majority opposed the extension of the action, not only on the ground that it was inconsistent with the true character of the tort of private nuisance but also out of fear of descending from the "slippery slope". Once family members were permitted to sue, the question would arise as to whether the category of claimants was:

> "also to include the lodger upstairs, or the au pair girl or resident nurse caring for an invalid who makes her home in the house while she works there? If the latter, it seems strange that the category should not extend to include places where people work as well as places where they live, where nuisances such as noise can be just as unpleasant or distracting."[185]

**[24.64]** Lord Cooke, dissenting, robustly responded:

> "Occupation of the property as a house is, to me, an acceptable criterion, consistent with the traditional concern for the sanctity of family life and the English man's home - which need not in this context include his workplace."[186]

**[24.65]** Two Irish cases have addressed this issue after *Hunter*. In *Royal Dublin Society v Yates*[187] Shanley J having referred to the *Hunter* restrictions, observed that, in *Hanrahan v Merck Sharp & Dohme (Ireland)*,[188] "a different and more flexible approach appears to have been taken on the issue of who has the right to sue". In the instant case, the plaintiff was not just the occupier of the lands but also their owner and was entitled to their exclusive possession. Since on any view it had the right to sue for private nuisance, Shanley J found in unnecessary to consider the difference of approach that appeared to have emerged between the Supreme Court and the House of Lords.

**[24.66]** In *Molumby v Kearns*,[189] in proceedings for an interlocutory injunction, the defendants argued that certain of the plaintiffs lacked *loci standi* to sue in private nuisance because there was not sufficient affidavit evidence to establish that they had a legal interest in the properties in question. O'Sullivan J rejected this argument, stating that he accepted that *locus standi* was "established by a plaintiff who sues in nuisance if he or she is the occupier of the land. I do not think it is necessary that the plaintiff establish a legal interest over and above this".[190]

---

183. [1997] AC 655.

184. [1997] AC 655 at 724 (*per* Lord Hope).

185. [1997] AC 655 at 693 (*per* Lord Goff).

186. [1997] AC 655 at 718.

187. High Court, 31 July 1997 (Shanley J), at p 38 of his judgment.

188. [1988] ILRM 629.

189. High Court, 19 January 1999 (O'Sullivan J), analysed by Dunleavy 'Not in my Back Yard: *Molumby & Others v Kearns & Others*' (2000) 6 Ir Planning & Envir LJ 8.

190. At p 44 of O'Sullivan J's judgment.

**[24.67]** He stated in passing from this topic that, it was interesting to note that Lord Hoffman had observed in *Hunter* that:

> "[t]he courts today will readily assume that a wife has required a beneficial interest in the matrimonial home. If so, she will be entitled to sue for damage to that interest."[191]

**[24.68]** O'Sullivan J understood this observation to indicate that the court would "readily infer such an interest from relatively slight evidence".[192] On this basis, he concluded that, even if it had been necessary for the plaintiffs to establish as a matter of probability, they had discharged the onus, even where, in one instance, the legal title to the home showed that the husband had the sole interest and, in another instance, the wife had in her affidavit and supplemental affidavit, referred to the property as "my house" and the husband had made no reference to having any interest in the property.

**[24.69]** O'Sullivan J's preference for a test based on the plaintiff's being the "occupier of the land", with no necessity to establish a legal interest over and above this, clearly intended this to be broader that the *Hunter* approach; precisely how much broader is not entirely clear. The concept of occupier is a somewhat elastic one, dependant on the particular context. Sometimes it is encompasses a legal interest;[193] in other cases it is determined by more empirical factors, such as the nature and extent of the control actually exercised by the putative occupier.[194] The general tenor of O'Sullivan J's observations suggests the latter tendency.

**[24.70]** It would be wrong to imagine that the Irish position has yet been definitively determined. In *Royal Dublin Society v Yates*,[195] the plaintiff satisfied even the narrowest of tests of eligibility to sue and in *Molumby v Kearns*,[196] all the plaintiffs were regarded as having, or being presumed to have, a sufficient legal interest to sue, even under the *Hunter* approach. Neither case established that he or she had no legal interest; nor did either case raise the issue of the entitlement of the children of the person with the legal interest to sue for private nuisance.

**[24.71]** There is force in the argument that the members of the family of the occupier should be permitted to sue. The emphasis in Article 41 of the Constitution on the rights of the family[197] and the developing international human rights protection on family and

---

191. [1997] AC 655 at 708.
192. At p 44.
193. *Cf* eg, Wylie, *Landlord and Tenant Law* (2nd ed, 1998), para 3.13.
194. Section 1(1) of the Occupiers' Liability Act 1995 defines "occupier", in relation to any premises, as "a person exercising such control over the state of the premises that it is reasonable to impose upon that person a duty towards an entrant in respect of a particular danger thereon ...". This test ultimately involves a judgment of value rather than of fact but in making that judgment the court is required to have regard to the particular factual quantum of control exercised by the person in question.
195. High Court, 31 July 1997 (Shanley J).
196. High Court, 19 January 1999 (O'Sullivan J).
197 One should not seek to make too much of this argument, since Article 41 has been interpreted in a way that makes it hard to translate the protection it professedly affords into actual enforceable legal entitlements for family members. See, eg, *Greene v Minister for Agriculture* [1990] 2 IR 17 (HC); *H v J Murphy & Sons Ltd* [1987] IR 621, *Murray v Ireland* [1985] IR 532 (HC); affd [1991] ILRM 465 (SC). Perhaps the most striking aspect of this judicial failure is in relation to the position of wives who have no paper title to the family home.

private life,[198] and the right of children to be protected in their homes,[199] add support to the view that it would be invidious to deny certain members of the family a right of action for private nuisance for personal injury or discomfort by reason of their lack of a legal interest in the family home. A reversioner has a right of action where there is a likelihood that permanent injury will be caused to the reversion. A permanent injury is one which will continue indefinitely if something is not done to remove it.[200] The distinction between permanent and merely temporary injuries may be difficult to apply in some cases. The owner of an incorporeal hereditament may sue for the disturbance of his or her right.[201]

## Who may be Sued?[202]

### *(a) Creator of the nuisance*

**[24.72]** The person who created the nuisance will be liable, whether or not he or she is in occupation of the land. Normally the creator of the nuisance will at some stage have been in control or occupation of the land, but this does not appear to be essential. Thus, for example, one who constructs a building that constitutes a nuisance will be liable, and will continue to be liable, for the nuisance even where he or she has no power to abate it.[203]

---

197. (contd) The courts denied any recognition to their work within the home. "It is not ... disputed that work undertaken by a wife in the home as a carer and rearer of the family does not result in a beneficial interest being acquired": Shatter's *Family Law* (4th ed, 1997), p 778. In *L v L* [1992] IR 77, the Supreme Court overturned Barr J's valiant attempt ([1989] ILRM 528]) to find a constitutional basis in Article 41 for recognising a property entitlement in the family home for such wives. The Supreme Court indicated that the Oireachtas was the appropriate forum to generate this entitlement. When the Oireachtas got round to doing so with a mildly reforming measure, the Supreme Court declared it invalid on the ground that it interfered with

> "the right of a married couple to make a joint decision as to ownership of a matrimonial home [which] is one of the rights possessed by the family which is recognised by the State in Article 41, s 1, sub-s 1 of the Constitution as antecedent and superior to all positive law ...":

In *Re the Matrimonial Homes Bill* [1994] 1 IR 305 at 325, the idea that legislation establishing a regime of joint ownership, from which the spouses were free to resile (s 5) and which could be overridden by court order where justice so required (s 6) is contrary to natural law is hard to accept. In *Hunter v Canary Wharf Ltd* [1997] AC 655 at 708, Lord Hoffman observed that "[t]he courts today will readily assume that a wife has acquired a beneficial interest in the matrimonial home. If so, she will be entitled to sue for damage to that interest". Although O'Sullivan J saw merit in this approach in *Molumby*, it may be argued that, in the context of actions for private nuisance, the Irish courts might hesitate before travelling down this path. The assumption that Lord Hoffman envisages is, sadly, not one that is consistent with the present legal position in Ireland and is frankly a device to achieve a goal - the entitlement of wives to sue for nuisance - which should be done by facing the issue of principle squarely.

198. European Convention for the Protection of Human Rights and Fundamental Freedom, Article 8. See also the United Nations Declaration of Human Rights, Article 12.

199. United Nations Convention on the Rights of the Child, Article 16. See the speech of Lord Cooke in *Hunter* above at 713-714.

200. *Cf Jones v Llaurwst UDC (No 2)* [1911] 1 Ch 393.

201. *Cf Nicholls v Ely Beet Sugar Factory Ltd* [1936] I Ch 343.

202. See Friedmann 'The Incidence of Liability in Nuisance' (1943) 59 LQR 63.

203. *Thompson v Gibson* (1841) 7 M & W 456, 151 ER 845.

**[24.73]** In *Royal Dublin Society v Yates*[204] Shanley J held that the defendant's presence on the plaintiff's premises was capable of constituting a private nuisance. This is surely mistaken. The tort consists of a wrongful incursion *ab extra*[205] rather than behaviour occurring exclusively on the plaintiff's premises.[206]

***(b) The landlord***

**[24.74]** In general a landlord will not be liable for a nuisance on the demised premises[207] as he or she is not the occupier: in such a case the tenant will normally be liable. The landlord may, however, be liable in the following cases:

*(i) Where the landlord has authorised the creation or continuation of a nuisance*

**[24.75]** Authorisation may be express or implied. An example of implied authorisation occurs in *Goldfarb v Williams & Co*,[208] where liability was imposed on the lessors of premises let to an employees' social and athletic club, when the club operated dances and other social activities so as to cause a nuisance by noise to the plaintiffs. The premises were constructed in a fashion which transmitted the noise with exceptional clearness and loudness[209] to the floors above and below. Overend J stated:

> "As between the club and their lessors I am of opinion that, in as much as dancing was one of the purposes specifically mentioned during the negotiations, the club was entitled to use the premises for that purpose in a reasonable manner, notwithstanding the restrictive provision against causing nuisance or annoyance. I therefore think the lessors are responsible as having authorised such nuisance, which was inevitable if the premises were used as intended ...[210]

---

204. High Court, 31 July 1997 (Shanley J).

205. Though not necessarily from private premises elsewhere: "[a] nuisance can emanate from a public place": *Attorney General of Ontario v Dieleman* (1994) 117 DLR (4th) 449 at 688 (Ont Ct).

206. It is true that Shanley J observed that the defendant's presence must be considered in the context of the acrimonious and offensive correspondence he was having with a female employee of the plaintiff, together with the threatening correspondence he was having with other parties. If Shanley J was seeking to derive any support from the English Court of Appeal decision of *Khorasandjian v Bush* [1993] QB 727, which he had earlier mentioned in his judgment, this, we suggest, would not be a sound foundation. The majority in *Hunter v Canary Wharf Ltd* [1997] AC 655 was surely correct in the view that the tort of private nuisance should not be used as an indirect means of creating a tort of harassment. Section 10 of the Non-Fatal Offences Against the Person Act 1997 creates an offence of harassment, backed by an injunctive power: sub-s (3). It does not, however, create a tort of harassment, as was done in England by of the Protection from Harassment Act 1997. Conceivably, an action in tort for breach of statutory duty under s 10 could be maintained successfully. Alternatively, a claim (or damages) for infringement of the constitutional right to bodily integrity or to health could be available. See also Birks 'Harassment and Hubris: The Right to an Equality of Respect' (1997) 32 Ir Jur (ns) 1.

207. It is, of course, a question of fact as to whether the area in which the injury was caused was part of the demised premises: see *Ahearne v Rudd* [1945] Ir Jur 45 (HC). In *Byrne v Martina Investments Ltd* High Court, 30 January 1984 (O'Hanlon J) (CA) - a landlord was held liable for the incursion of water onto the demised premises from premises under the landlord's control.

208. [1945] IR 433 (HC).

209. At 444. See further Wylie, *Landlord And Tenant Law* (2nd ed, 1998), para 14.11

210. Citing *Harris v James* (1876) 45 LJQB 545. *Cf Rich v Basterfield* (1847) 4 CB 738; *Smith v Scott* [1973] 1 Ch 314; *Hussain v Lancaster City Council* [1999] 2 WLR 1142, as explained in *Lippiatt v South Gloucester County Council* CA 31 March 1999. See also *Patterson v Murphy* [1978] ILRM 85; *De Jager v Payneham & Magill Lodges Hall Inc* (1984) 36 SASR 498 (SC).

The lessors must be deemed to know the construction and properties of their own building."[211]

*(ii) Where the landlord has let the premises with a nuisance on them*

**[24.76]** A landlord will be liable where a nuisance of which he was aware or ought to have been aware existed at the commencement of the tenancy.[212] There is old authority[213] for the view that he may exempt himself from liability in such a case by extracting a covenant to repair from the tenant. Whether the courts today would take the same view, however, is doubtful.[214]

*(iii) Where the landlord has covenanted to repair*

**[24.77]** Where the landlord has covenanted to keep the demised premises in a state of repair, he may be sued in nuisance if injury results from the breach of this covenant.[215] If the tenant has covenanted to keep the interior of the premises in good repair and the lease is silent as to the question of exterior repairs, the landlord does not thereby become responsible for external repairs.[216] Moreover, where the landlord has carried out repairs whilst expressly disclaiming his liability to do so, he will not be liable.[217]

***(c) The occupier***

**[24.78]** Where an occupier creates a nuisance he or she will, of course be liable for it. Moreover, where the occupier authorises its commission, he or she will also be liable where his or her servants or, in certain circumstances, his or her independent contractors[218] or even invitees or licensees are guilty of the nuisance.[219]

**[24.79]** In other cases, the occupier is no longer held responsible unless, in effect, he or she was aware or ought to have been aware of the nuisance and failed to remove it, or worse still, positively endorsed or "adopted" it. Thus, where the nuisance is created by a trespasser or stranger or results from natural causes, the occupier will be liable if, within a reasonable time after acquiring knowledge or presumed knowledge of its existence he or she fails to take reasonable steps to bring it to an end.[220] The same applies to cases where the occupier acquires property with a nuisance already existing on it.[221] So also where the nuisance results from the escape of things naturally on the land: the occupier will be liable where he has failed to take reasonable care, due allowances being made for the fact that the

---

211. At 445. *Dublin (South) City Market Co v McCabes Ltd* [1953] IR 283 (HC).

212. *St Anne's Well Brewery Co v Roberts* (1928) 140 LT 1 at 7-8 (CA); *Todd v Flight* (1860) 9 CB (N 8) 377; *Gwinnell v Eamer* (1875) LR 10 CP 658.

213. *Pretty v Bickmore* (1873) LR 8 CP 401.

214. *Cf Mint v Good* [1951] 1 KB 517 (CA); *Brew Bros Ltd v Snox (Ross) Ltd* [1970] 1 QB 612 (CA).

215. *Payne v Rogers* (1974) 2 HB 1 350. *Cf McAuliffe v Moloney* [1971] IR 200 (SC).

216. *Gray v Siev* (1949) 83 ILTR 67 (CC).

217. *Farrell v Burke* (1953) 87 ILTR 70 (CC).

218. *Cf Bower v Peate* (1876) 1 QBD 321; *Dalton v Angus* (1881) 6 AC 740; *Holliday v National Telephone Co* [1899] 2 QB 392. Australian authorities adopt a somewhat more restrictive approach: *cf* FLEMING, p 436.

219. *White v Jameson* (1874) LR 18 EQ 303. *Cf Connell v Porter* High Court, 21 December 1967 (Teevan J). Presumably, after the changes brought about by the Occupiers' Liability Act 1995, the occupier's lliability will extend to a nuisance created by his or her visitors or recreational users.

220. *Sedleigh-Denfield v O'Callaghan* [1940] AC 880. See, however, *Palmer v Byrne* [1906] 1 IR 373.

221. *Penruddock's Case* (1597) 5 Co Rep 100b, 77 ER 210; *St Anne's Well Brewery Co v Roberts* (1928) 140 LT 1.

hazard has been "thrust upon him through no seeking or fault of his own".[222] The courts will have regard to the fact that the occupier's resources may be of a very modest character either in relation to the magnitude of the hazard or as compared to those of his or her threatened neighbour.[223] The standard required of the occupier is thus no more than what is reasonable to expect of him or her in his or her individual circumstances.[224]

**[24.80]** The position of local authorities in relation to Travellers has been analysed by the courts in this particular context. The subject, of course, raises far broader social issues. Over the past thirty years, Travellers have been driven from many of their traditional camping sites; there has been a move towards urbanisation; their traditional trades have been displaced and some of their newer economic activities, such as trading in scrap metal, involve accumulations displeasing to the settled community.[225] Attempts (sometimes fitful and hesitant) by local authorities to discharge their statutory duty to provide accommodation, including halting sites for Travellers, have met with much resistance from certain sections of the settled community. Yet, where the local authorities are driven by this opposition to neglecting their statutory obligations, they then find themselves sued for failing to remove the nuisance caused by Travellers remaining on unofficial sites.

**[24.81]** In *Vitalograph (Ireland) Ltd v Ennis Urban District Council and Clare County Council*,[226] Kelly J granted an interlocutory injunction in favour of companies carrying on business at an industrial estate in Ennis against Clare County Council, the owner of a strip of land at the entrance to the estate which was occupied by Travellers, requiring it to restrain acts of nuisance by them. It appeared that a number of caravans had forced their way onto the land, which was a former car park. Further caravans had arrived later. The plaintiffs complained of the existence of large amounts of scrap metal, the steady accumulation of litter, the presence of horses and dogs and the total lack of any sanitary facilities on the site.

**[24.82]** The County Council sought to deny responsibility on the basis that those on the land had entered and remained their without any authorisation. The only step it had taken to remove them, however, was to write a letter, after the proceedings had begun, asking them to leave.

**[24.83]** Kelly J was satisfied that the County Council had in these circumstances adopted the nuisance[227] in failing to take appropriate steps within a reasonable period to bring it to an end. He did not accept that the plaintiffs should be refused an injunction because they

222. *Goldman v Hargrave* [1967] 1 AC 645 at 664; see also *Leakey v National Trust* [1980] 2 WLR 65.

223. *Cf Goldman v Hargrave* [1967] 1 AC 645 at 664.

224. This passage was quoted by Buckley J in *Daly v McMullan* [1997] 2 ILRM 232 (CC). The boundaries between nuisance and negligence are crumbling at this point: see Markesinis 'Negligence, Nuisance and Affirmative Duties of Action' (1989) 105 LQR 104 at 118-119, Gearty 'The Place of Private Nuisance in the Modern Law of Torts' [1989] Camb LJ 214 at 233ff.

225. See *Irish Travellers: Culture And Ethnicity*, McCann, Ó Síocháin and Ruane eds, (1994).

226. High Court, 23 April 1997.

227. Kelly J cited with approval Lord Wright's speech in *Sedleigh-Denfield v O'Callaghan* [1940] AC 880, and the English Court of Appeal decision in *Page Motors Ltd v Epson and Ewell Borough County* (1982) 80 LGR 337. See also *Lippiatt v South Gloucestershire County Council* Court Appeal, 3 March 1999.

had a remedy against the Travellers. They were entitled to choose the remedy they considered to be the more suitable one for their requirements. Whilst they might obtain an injunction against the occupiers restraining nuisance, they could not obtain an order for possession of the site as they had no entitlement to it. An injunction against the County Council might, in the circumstances, be the only practical and effective way of terminating the nuisance. The policing and enforcement of an injunction prohibiting nuisance alone "would probably be difficult".

**[24.84]** It appears from Kelly J's judgment that the County Council had made attempts over the years to provide appropriate accommodation for Travellers. In October 1995 it had been restrained from using lands at Drumcliffe, Ennis, as a halting site. It later obtained another site in the Ennis area, with a view to providing a temporary halting site on it. Once this became known, immediate objections were raised by a number of local residents. Kelly J noted that there were allegations of intimidation and threats being made towards the servants or agents of the County Council and its contractors concerning the site. The County Council had identified a third site as a possible permanent halting site, but:

> "[s]uch was the level of protest concerning tests to be carried out on that site that the Council itself had to apply to the High Court [for] .... injunctions restraining trespass on the lands".[228]

## Premises Adjoining the Highway

**[24.85]** There is some doubt as to whether the occupier owes a more extensive duty in respect of dangers in or on premises adjoining the highway. The decisions are difficult to reconcile. There is respectable authority[229] for the view that no extra duty arises in such a

---

228. See also *Lind v Tipperary (North Riding) Council* High Court, 9 November 1998 (Carroll J), noted by Byrne & Binchy, *Annual Review of Irish Law* (1997), pp 762-763, where an injunction was granted against a local authority for intensifying a nuisance that already existed by providing an inadequately supervised halting site. Other decisions sounding in nuisance include *McDonald v Feely* High Court, 30 June 1980 (Barrington J) and *Ellis v Dun Laoghaire Corporation* Circuit Court 29 January 1982 (Ryan J). See also *Casey v Tralee UDC* DPIJ: Hilary and Easter Terms 1995, p 49 - injury to child from horse placed by (unidentified) members of the Travelling community on open grass area near housing estate; the Council was liable for not having addressed the problem of regular grazing of horses in the area more effectively.

> "[A]t the very least, there should have been vigorous and energetic monitoring and identifying of the owners of the horses and ... pursu[it of] those owners by way of threatened or actual injunction proceedings"

At p 50. The controversial extension of the rule in *Rylands v Fletcher* in this context in *AG v Corke* [1933] Ch 89, has been universally condemned in later decisions. In *Kelly v McDonagh* Circuit Court, 15 April 1999, Judge Buttimer, an injunction was granted against a widowed Traveller living in a caravan on the side of the road near New Ross for the previous eight years. The site was illegal and unserviced, it contributed to rat infestation and litter and was a traffic hazard. Judge Buttimer was told that the local authority had no available housing or halting site for the defendant. She directed that a house be allocated to the defendant temporarily, and that she should retain her position on the housing list. See 'Traveller Allocated House After Injunction Hearing', Irish Times, 16 April 1999. See further Elder 'An Overview of the Statutory Duty to Provide Halting Sites' (1998) 16 Ir LT (ns) 232.

229. *Cf Palmer v Bateman* [1908] 2 IR 393; *Mullan v Forrester* [1921] 2 IR 412; *Scully v Marjorie Boland Ltd* [1962] IR 58 at 69 (HC); *Gillen v Fair* (1956) 90 ILTR 119 (HC); *Victor Weston (Éire) Ltd v Kenny* [1954] IR 191 at 197 (HC). See also *Healy v Bray UDC* [1962-63] Ir Jur 9 at 16 (SC) and *Lynch v Hetherton* [1990] ILRM 857 (CCA), discussed at para **[24.30]** above.

case, but there is an equally strong line of cases[230] going the other way, imposing what is, in effect, strict liability on the occupier, save in cases where the nuisance was caused by a trespasser or by a secret and unobservable operation of nature.[231]

**[24.86]** The imposition of strict liability in such a case has been defended on the basis that:

> "the interests of highway users require special protection from such dangers, and that a standard of ordinary diligence is not enough to achieve a sufficient degree of protection."[232]

The trend of analysis has however, been critical[233] (although it should be noted that much of it appeared before the emergence of a strong pro-plaintiff bias among academic commentators).[234] It has been argued that the distinction between premises and natural objects (such as trees, which may have been planted at the same time as the house was built) is an unconvincing one[235] and that a stringent liability akin to *Rylands v Fletcher* should not be extended to what is no more than a normal user of land.[236]

**[24.87]** In *Lynch v Hetherton*,[237] the scope of landowners' obligations in relation to trees adjoining rural highways was considered. The plaintiff's car had been damaged when an ash tree fell on it as he was driving down a country road in Westmeath. The Circuit Court judge found in favour of the plaintiff, who sued for nuisance and negligence, but O'Hanlon J reversed on appeal. The parties were agreed on the general principle that a landowner was bound to take reasonable care to prevent damage from falling trees. The plaintiff did not contend that a stricter test should be imposed.

**[24.88]** Echoing Lavery J's observation, in *Gillen v Fair*,[238] that he did not think that every farmer in the country should employ an expert to examine every tree growing on their lands beside a highway, and that the standard of care would have regard to whether the trees were in a rural or an urban area, O'Hanlon J was satisfied that what the plaintiff had done was sufficient to discharge his legal obligation. Although the tree was rotten inside, the evidence fell short of establishing that this rotten state had been perceptible externally before the accident. The tree was on an out-farm, which the defendant passed five days a week. The defendant had tightened a row of wire on a ditch, which was connected to the tree, with staples ten days before the accident at a point two feet above ground level. He had inspected all his trees, though he had not employed an expert to look at them, and had cut down several before the accident.

---

230. *Mullan v Forrester* [1921] 2 IR 412; *Wringe v Cohen* [1940] 1 KB 229 (CA); *Bruton's Ltd v Milletts' Stores Ltd* (1951) 85 ILTR 42 (CC). *Cf Farrell v Burke* (1953) 87 ILTR 70 (CC); *McGowan v Masterson* [1953] IR 101 at 106 (SC); *Fitzgerald v Brangan* (1904) 39 ILTR 116.

231. See FLEMING, pp 398-399.

232. CLERK & LINDSELL, para 1430.

233. *Cf* Friedmann in (1940) 3 MLR 305, and in (1943) 59 LQR 63, Winfield in (1940) 56 LQR 1; Landon in (1940) 56 LQR 140. For judicial criticism in Canada see *O'Leary v Melitides* (1959) 20 DLR (2d) 258.

234. *Cf* Heuston '*Donoghue v Stevenson*: A Fresh Appraisal' [1971] CLP 37 at 49.

235. FLEMING, p 479.

236. See also *Montana Hotels Pty Ltd v Fasson Pty Ltd* (1986) 69 ALR 258 at 263-264 (PC).

237. [1990] ILRM 857 (HC), analysed by Byrne & Binchy, *Annual Review of Irish Law 1990*, pp 539-542.

238. (1956) 90 ILTR 119 at 120 (HC).

**[24.89]** In *McGowan v Masterson*,[239] in 1952, the Supreme Court held that no action in nuisance lay against the occupier of premises or his wife for injuries sustained by the plaintiff who slipped on a pool of liquid paraffin on the footpath outside the premises. The paraffin had been in a bottle in the basket of a bicycle which a visitor to the premises had left at the kerb of the premises during her visit. The bicycle had fallen and the bottle had broken. The occupier's wife had removed the broken bottle (by throwing it across a nearby fence) but had not removed the paraffin. The occupier, returning to the premises, also saw the paraffin but did nothing about it either. The trial judge found that neither the occupier nor his wife had known that the paraffin was dangerous; but there was no finding as to whether they ought to have known this rather elementary fact. The visitor/cyclist's role in the events was somewhat shadowy. It is clear that she saw the broken bottle and the paraffin on the footpath,[240] but she appears to have done nothing to remedy the situation.

**[24.90]** Though the Supreme Court was of one mind that neither the occupier nor his wife should be liable in nuisance, there was a difference of approach among the members of the Court. Maguire CJ took the view that

> "by dedicating property to the public the occupier of premises adjoining the highway loses control of that property to the extent at least that he ceases to be liable for nuisance proceeding from it. The liability which rests upon an occupier of premises adjoining the highway does not extend to nuisance on the highway."[241]

**[24.91]** And Lavery J said:

> "The ownership of the soil [under the highway to the middle line], actual or presumed, has in no authority to which we have been referred, established the obligation to keep the highway clear or safe. The owner is in no sense in occupation of the adjoining highway. In principle it is the fact of occupation and the right and obligation to control which imposes liability ... It was not suggested that the defendant created the nuisance by bringing the oil to the path, and if he had not any duty to clean the pavement his omission to do so cannot make him liable for the damage. I have already expressed the view that no such duty arose from the defendant's ownership or occupation ... It seems to me sufficient to say that the visitor while on the highway was there as a member of the public and her acts or omissions while thereon, cannot be attributed to the invitation, if there was one, of the defendant to visit his house. It is unnecessary to deal with obligations arising from the acts or omissions of servants, agents, contractors or other persons for whose acts or omissions the defendant may be responsible."[242]

**[24.92]** Murnaghan J took a different view of the law. In his opinion the case was one of a class in which the owner or occupier of premises *could* be liable for nuisance committed by a stranger, but "in order to impose liability ... the owner or occupier should not only know of the existence of the object, but the object must also be such than an ordinary man would know it to be a danger".[243] In Murnaghan J's opinion, the trial judge's finding that "the defendant did not know or appreciate that the ... oil was dangerous made it impossible

239. [1953] IR 101 (SC).

240. [1953] IR 101 at 105.

241. [1953] IR 101 at 106.

242. [1953] IR 101 at 107-108.

243. [1953] IR 101 at 106.

for the plaintiff to succeed in this action".[244] It could, however, be argued that the trial judge's finding addressed only the factual question of whether the defendant was aware of the danger from the oil, not the normative issue of whether he ought to have been so aware. Perhaps it is legitimate, in the absence of a finding that the defendant ought to have known of the danger, to infer that the trial judge was not of this view; but it scarcely follows inexorably from this express, limited finding of fact. Negligence was apparently not pleaded in the case: it is interesting to speculate on the outcome had the action included that plea.

## IV. Defences

### Legislative Authority

**[24.93]** Legislation may in express terms[245] authorise the commission of what would be a nuisance at common law or it may by necessary implication do so.[246] Conversely, legislation may specifically preserve the right of action in nuisance, despite legislative authority for the commission of certain undertakings.[247] In other cases, where legislation authorises conduct which may constitute a nuisance, the person or authority so acting must not behave in a negligent fashion.[248]

**[24.94]** In *Kelly v Dublin County Council*,[249] the defendants carried out extensive road-works in South County Dublin, under statutory authority[250] which permitted it to cause a nuisance in the discharge of its functions. It used a site as a storage depot for vehicles and materials, close to the plaintiffs home. The plaintiffs complained of noise, dust and diesel fumes caused by the vehicles and machinery leaving the premises every working day, and returning in the evening.

**[24.95]** O'Hanlon J found the defendant guilty of actionable nuisance. The statutory authorisation to commit a nuisance extended only to its functions of maintenance and construction of roads; in setting up the depot, the council had been engaging in an ancillary activity which was not protected by the statute. If he was wrong on the matter -

244. [1953] IR 101.

245. *Cf* eg, Air Navigation and Transport Act 1936, s 55, as amended by the Air Navigation and Transport Act 1988, s 47(1).

246. *Allen v Gulf Oil Refining Co* [1981] 1 All ER 353; *cf Kingstown Township Commissioners v Blackrock Township Commissioners* (1876) IR 10 Eq 160; *Clifford v Drug Treatment Centre Board* High Court, 7 November 1997 (McCracken J).

247. *Cf* Gasworks Clauses Act 1847, s 29 (10 & 11 Vict, c 15); Gasworks Clauses Act 1871, s 9 (34 & 35 Vict, call); *Baker v Alliance & Dublin Consumers' Gas Co* [1946] Ir Jur 48 (CC).

248. *Cf Cregan v ESB* (1936) 71 ILTR 62 (SC); *Wallace v McCartan* [1917] 1 IR 397; *Smith v Wexford County Council* (1953) 87 ILTR 98 (HC), noted in (1953) 87 ILT & Sol J 106; *Burniston v Corporation of Bangor* [1932] NI 178 (CA); *Geddis v Proprietors of Bann Reservoir* (1878) 3 AC 430 at 455-456; *Hughes v Ballynahinch Gas Co* (1898) 33 ILTR 74; *Hoey v Dundalk UDC* High Court, 29 February 1980 (McWilliam J); *Kelly v Dublin County Council* High Court, 21 February 1986 (O'Hanlon J). See also the very brief report of *Crowley v Town Commissioners of Youghal* (1986) 30 ILT & Sol J 151.

249. High Court, 21 February 1986 (O'Hanlon J). Distinguished in *Convery v Dublin County Council* [1996] 3 IR 153 (SC).

250. Local Government Act 1925, Pt III (as amended).

and his respectful reference to authorities to the contrary[251] indicated some doubts - he held that liability should nonetheless be imposed; in view of the location of the depot and the lack of any evidence that the council had had no alternative or no reasonable alternative, the council had not shown that it had acted without negligence.

**[24.96]** In *Superquinn Ltd v Bray Urban District Council*,[252] where the plaintiff's premises were flooded when a river burst its banks during 'Hurricane Charlie' in 1987, the defendant council was acquitted of liability in respect of the manner in which it had carried out its drainage construction works in the area where the river flowed. As the local authority it was under a statutory duty, by virtue of the Public Health (Ireland) Act 1878, s 17 to drain the area. Laffoy J accepted as correct the proposition that, "[t]hat being the case, .... the Council is immune from an action based on negligence and is free from liability unless it was negligent in the exercise of its statutory duty and power".[253] On the evidence, and having regard to "the social utility of the conduct of th[e Council]" and the object of the works - to improve drainage in the Bray area,[254] Laffoy J held that the council had not been negligent and that therefore was free of liability.

## Prescription

**[24.97]** Prescription affords no defence for public nuisance.[255] With regard to certain private nuisances, however, twenty years continuance will, by prescription, legalise the activity which constitutes the nuisance, converting it into an easement appurtenant to the land on which it exists, as though the right had been authorised at the commencement of the nuisance by a grant from the owner of the servient land.[256]

**[24.98]** For prescription to apply, the defendant must throughout the period have been acting, openly and with the knowledge of the owner of the servient tenement.[257] Moreover, the period runs from the time the nuisance was created: this may be some time after the activity which constitutes a nuisance commenced. Thus, in *Sturges v Bridgman*,[258] where a physician built a consulting room at the end of his garden, the defendant, who had used heavy machinery nearby, which by its noise constituted a nuisance to the consulting room, could not argue that he had a prescriptive right to do so since, although the machinery had

---

251. *Dunne v North Western Gas Board* [1964] 2 QB 806. See also *Allen v Gulf Oil Refining Ltd* [1981] AC 1001. It may be that the constitutional protection of individual personal rights under Article 40.3 in Ireland should encourage a narrow interpretation of legislative authorisation: see Hogan & Morgan, *Administrative Law* (3rd ed), pp 809-810.

252. High Court 18 February 1998 (Laffoy J).

253. High Court 18 February 1998, p 62 of Laffoy J's judgment.

254. High Court 18 February 1998, at p 65 of Laffoy J's judgment. This judicial reference, *expressis verbis*, to social utility is rare.

255. *R v Cross* (1892) 3 Camp 224; *Mott v Shoolbred* (1875) LR 20 EQ 22; *Hubbard v Pitt* [1976] QB 142. This is one reason why public nuisance may in some cases be a more attractive option for environmentalists in pollution suits: *cf* Maloney 'Judicial Protection of the Environment - A New Role for Common Law Remedies' (1972) 25 Vand LR 145 at 162.

256. *Sturges v Bridgman* (1879) 11 ChD 852 at 863.

257. *Liverpool Corporation v Coghill (H) & Son Ltd* [1918] 1 Ch 307.

258. (1879) 11 ChD 852. *Cf Miller v Jackson* [1977] QB 966 (CA), discussed at fn 270. See also *Kingstown Township Commissioners v Blackrock Township Commissioners* (1876) IR 10 Eq 160.

been in operation for more than twenty years, it had not constituted a nuisance to the plaintiff until he had built his consulting room.

**[24.99]** Whether there is a prescriptive right to commit all types of nuisance is doubtful. It is clear that a person may acquire a right to discharge rain-water from his eaves on to a neighbour's land,[259] to send smoke through flues in a party wall,[260] or to discharge surface water onto adjoining land.[261] On the other hand, one cannot acquire a prescriptive right to let the branches or roots of a tree intrude onto one's neighbour's property.[262]

**[24.100]** No reported decision has held squarely that one may otherwise acquire by prescription the right to annoy a neighbour by smoke, smells, noise or vibrations.[263] It has been argued[264] that such a right would be impossible to acquire since the quantity of interference would be variable, thus lacking the degree of certainty and uniformity required of rights capable of acquisition by prescription.

### Contributory Negligence

**[24.101]** The contributory negligence of the plaintiff will afford a defence in an action for nuisance, under the provisions of Chapter III of the Civil Liability Act 1961.[265] Apportionment principles apply.

### Inevitable Accident

**[24.102]** It seems that inevitable accident will be a good defence where liability in nuisance depends on negligence.[266]

## V. Ineffectual Defences

**[24.103]** A number of defences which will not avail a defendant in nuisance actions may be mentioned briefly.

### Coming to the Nuisance

**[24.104]** It is no defence to assert that the plaintiff "came to the nuisance", as where a person buys property which he or she is aware is being subjected to a nuisance from the neighbouring land.[267] In *Bliss v Hall*[268] the Court held that where the defendant's tallow

---

259. *Thomas v Thomas* (1835) 2 CM & R 34 150 ER 15; *Fay v Prentice* (1845) 1 CB 828, 135 ER 769; *Harvey v Walters* (1873) LR 8 CP 162.

260. *Jones v Pritchard* [1908] 1 Ch 630.

261. *AG v Copeland* [1902] 1 KB 690; *Longton v Winwick Asylum Board* (1911) 75 JP 348; Appeal compromised, 76 JP 113.

262. *Lemmon v Webb* [1895] AC 1.

263. *Cf* WINFIELD & JOLOWICZ, p 525, fn 59.

264. *Cf Hulley v Silversprings Bleaching Co* [1922] 2 Ch 268 at 281. See also *Lemmon v Webb* [1895] AC 1, affg [1894] 3 Ch 1.*Cf* the broad statement of Bird CCJ, reported in *Cronin v O'Shea* (1896) 30 ILT & Sol J 436.

265. For a good discussion of the policy aspects of the defence, see FLEMING, pp 491-492.

266. *Southport Corporation v Esso Petroleum Co Ltd* [1956] AC 218 at 286.

267. *Bliss v Hall* (1838) 4 Bing NC 183, 132 ER 758, *Morley v Dubinskey* (1966) 59 DLR (2d) 217; *Sturges v Bridgman* (1879) 11 Ch D 852; *Elliotson v Feetham* (1865) 2 Bing NC 134 132 ER 53. See also *Armagh Union (Guardians of) v Bell* [1900] 2 IR 371 at 378-379 (QB).

268. (1838) 4 Bing NC 183, 132 ER 758.

chandlery had been emitting offensive smells and vapours onto the plaintiff's property for three years before the plaintiff arrived, this afforded him no defence since the plaintiff had come to the "house with all rights which the common law affords, and one of them is a right to wholesome air".[269]

**[24.105]** An enterprising defendant might allege that the plaintiff's conduct in coming to a nuisance amounted in the circumstances to contributory negligence. The better view, however, seems to be that:

> "it is not reasonable to expect a person to refrain from buying land in a neighbourhood merely because a nuisance already exists there: and conduct cannot amount to contributory negligence unless it is unreasonable."[270]

**[24.106]** It is, however, clear that, since the tort is based on reasonable give-and-take between neighbours, a person who carries on a trade or profession or hobby that is "specially sensitive", may not demand of a neighbour an unduly high standard of conduct.[271] As Henchy J said in *Hanrahan v Merck, Sharp & Dohme (Ireland) Ltd*,[272] the plaintiff "is not entitled to insist that his personal nicety of taste or fastidiousness of requirements should be treated as inviolable".

**[24.107]** The Supreme Court decision of *Mullin v Hynes*[273] might seem to suggest that the defendant may not escape liability by asserting that the plaintiff was unduly sensitive. Henchy J after a partial review of dicta in the relevant decisions[274] did express the view that they were:

> "but examples of the unwillingness of the courts to grant relief where the damage is in respect of trivial, fanciful or exaggerated inconvenience. They do not enshrine any wider principle and, in particular, they are no warrant for the proposition that the dominant test is the tolerance of an average or reasonable or ordinary person of the inconvenience complained of."[275]

---

269. In *Miller v Jackson* [1977] QB 966 (CA), the English Court of Appeal expressed some dissatisfaction with the application of this general rule without some qualification, especially where a long-established and innocent pastime - in this case cricket - becomes a nuisance by reason of housing moving into rural areas. See, however, *Kennaway v Thompson* [1980] 3 WLR 361 (CA), noted with approval in (1981) 97 LQR 3.

270. WILLIAMS, para 56.

271. *Cf Gaunt v Fynney* (1872) LR 8 Ch; *Eastern & South African Telephone Co v Cape Town Tramways* [1902] AC 381; *Robinson v Kilvert* (1889) 41 Ch D 88; *Bridlington Relay Ltd v Yorkshire Electricity Board* [1965] Ch 436; *Heath v Brighton (Mayor of)* (1908) 98 LT 718; *Bloodworth v Cormack* [1949] NZLR 1058; *Mackey v Scottish Widows Fund Life Assurance Society* (1877) Ir 11 Eq 541. See also *Connell v Porter* High Court, 21 December, 1967 (Teevan J); *Devon Lumber Co Ltd v McNeill* (1987) 45 DLR (4th) 300 (NBCA).

272. [1988] ILRM 629 at 640 (SC).

273. Supreme Court, 13 November 1972.

274. Only two decisions were discussed. No reference was made to *Bloodworth v Cormack* [1949] NZLR 1058, although it was of particular relevance, since it dealt with invalids, the plaintiff in *Mullin v Hynes* who suffered the injury now complained of also being an invalid.

275. Pages 7-8 of unreported judgment.

**[24.108]** Nevertheless, a close reading of the decision makes it clear that Henchy J did not seek to deny that "the over-fastidious or over-sensitive plaintiff"[276] cannot impose a higher obligation on a neighbour.

**[24.109]** The decision is important in its holding that where a nuisance caused by a defendant brings about a hypersensitive condition in a formerly healthy person, the defendant may be enjoined thereafter from so conducting his or her operations that they constitute an intolerable interference with that person's beneficial user of his or her premises although they do not constitute such an interference for persons not so affected.

## Acts of Others Combining with Defendant's Act to Make Nuisance

**[24.110]** It is no defence that the nuisance of which the plaintiff complains was made by the combination of acts of the defendant and of others where, viewed in isolation, none of these acts in itself constitutes a nuisance. This may be regarded as somewhat rough justice but can be defended on the basis that to allow the defence would cause greater hardship. In the English decision of *Lambton v Mellish*,[277] where two rival merry-go-round proprietors carried on their business, with fair ground organs, close to the plaintiff's house, an injunction was granted against both of them, Chitty J stating:

> "If the acts of two persons, each being aware of what the other is doing, amount in the aggregate to a cause of complaint."[278]

**[24.111]** Professor Glanville Williams has commented that at first sight the decision seems to be rather hard on the proprietor of the merry-go-round, held to be not in itself a nuisance, which arrived first, arguing that:

> "The solution may be that whereas both are liable to the innocent plaintiff, the one that arrived second is additionally liable to the one that arrived first."[279]

**[24.112]** However, this solution no longer appears to be open to an Irish court. The question of apportionment of damages in these cases is now the subject of specific statutory provision. Sub-sections (3) of s 12 of the Civil Liability Act 1961 applies to "two or more persons whose acts taken together constitute a nuisance, even though the act of any one of them taken alone would not constitute a nuisance, not being unreasonable in degree" and sub-s (2) allow the court to apportion liability between such persons "in such manner as may be justified by the probabilities of the case ... and if the proper proportions cannot be determined the damages may be apportioned or divided equally".[280] A plaintiff in *de facto* exclusive possession of the affected property will not be defeated by a plea of *jus tertii*.[281]

276. Page 10.
277. [1894] 3 Ch 163. See also *Thorpe v Brumfitt* (1873) LR 8 Ch 650.
278. [1894] 3 Ch at 166.
279. WILLIAMS, para 7, fn 12.
280. Section 12(2). The implications in respect of pollution caused by an accumulation of discharges not in themselves harmful have yet to be considered On powers of abatement, see the first edition of this work, pp 495-497.
281. *Foster v Warblington UDC* [1906] 1 KB 648 (CA); *Paxhaven Holdings Ltd v AG* [1974] 2 NZLR 185 (SC); *Hunter v Canary Wharf Ltd* [1997] AC 655 (HL).

## VI. Highway Authorities[282]

**[24.113]** It is well established[283] that, whereas a highway authority may be liable for misfeasance, that is, acts of positively negligent character regarding the maintenance or repair of the highway, it will not be liable for non-feasance, that is, the failure to maintain the highway, however negligent that failure may have been.[284]

**[24.114]** It has been noted by Kingsmill Moore J that "[t]his may be an unsatisfactory state of the law, but law it is,"[285] and in a Supreme Court decision of 1925, the rule was described as "anomalous".[286]

**[24.115]** Judges continue to examine the rule. In *Condon v Cork Corporation*,[287] in 1996, Moriarty J observed that:

> "the present state of our substantive law with regard to misfeasance and non-feasance is artificial and outmoded. And indeed it can sometimes provide an incentive to a road authority to lack diligence and to allow hazards to accumulate with wear and tear but nonetheless it remains the law of the land."

---

282. See Hogan & Morgan *Administrative Law in Ireland* (3rd ed, 1998), pp 684-686, 802-804; Anon 'Liability for the Non-Repair of Roads' (1954) 88 ILT & Sol J 99, 105, 111; Harrison Moore 'Misfeasance and Non-feasance in the Liability of Public Authorities' (1914) 30 LQR 276, 415. Denning 'Note' (1939) 55 LQR 343, Sawer 'Non-feasance Revisited' (1955) 18 MLR 541 at 545-550; Bland 'The Strange Death of the Nonfeasance Defence' (1998) 16 Ir LT (ns) 172.

283. See *AG v Mayo County Council* [1902] IR 13; *Clements v Tyrone County Council* [1905] 2 IR 415; *Harbinson v Armagh County Council* [1902] 2 IR 538; *Rennick v Wexford County Council* (1901) ILTR 78 (CC); *McCormack v Kildare County Council* [1953-1954] Ir Jur 64 (CC); *Molloy v Offaly County Council* (1951) 85 ILTR 61 (CC); *Kelly v Mayo County Council* [1964] IR 315 (SC); *Gallagher v Leitrim County Council* (1955) 89 ILTR 151 (HC); *Quinn v Ministry of Commerce* [1954] NI 131; *Ryan v Tipperary (NR) County Council* [1912] 2 IR 392; *O'Brien v Waterford County Council* [1926] IR 1 (SC); *Breen v Tyrone County Council* [1905] 2 IR 542 (CA); *Kane v Howth UDC* [1939] Ir Jur 54 (CC); *Phelan v Kilkenny County Council* [1943] Ir Jur 1 (SC); *O'Connor v Kerry County Council* 61 ILTR 73 (HC).

284. *Cf Kelly v Mayo County Council* [1964] IR 315 at 318-319:

> "[Highway authorities] are liable in damages for injuries suffered by a road user if they have been negligent in doing repairs or in interfering with the road. They are not liable for injuries suffered or caused by the want of repair of a road. This is the familiar distinction - they are liable for misfeasance but not for non-feasance".

285. [1964] IR 318 at 324.

286. *O'Brien v Waterford County Council* [1926] IR 1. In *Kennevan v Limerick Corporation* DPIJ: Trinity and Michaelmas Terms 1993, p 277 at p 278 (HC, 18 June 1993), Geoghegan J observed that the rule was anomalous and that it could work injustice. He raised the question that "maybe sometime it will be challenged".

287. DPIJ: Trinity and Michaelmas Terms 1996, p 214 (HC, 16 October 1996 (Moriarty J)). The same Judge had earlier voiced similar criticism, in *McMahon v Wexford County Council* [1996] Ir L Log W 44 at 44 (CC). Other Judges of the Circuit Court have joined the refrain: see, eg, *Fitzhenry v Geraghty* [1997] Ir L Log W 146 at 147 (CC). Cases applying the rule include *Sammon v Dun Laoghaire County Council* [1997] Ir L Log W 111 (CC) - misfeasance; *O'Toole v Dublin Corporation* [1997] Ir L Log W 170 (CC) - misfeasance.

**[24.116]** Where there is misfeasance, however, The Supreme Court has recognised that a highway authority may be liable even to incompetent drivers. In *Danaher v Roscommon County Council*,[288] Fitzgerald CJ stated that local authorities were:

> "not entitled to erect on or near a roadway, an obstruction or some unusual feature which may create an undue risk for a person lawfully using the roadway. They should anticipate not only that people will use the roadway normally, but that, through unforeseen circumstances, or something in the nature of fog, or something of a character not to be expected by the motorist ... that (sic) cars may, when driven incompetently, leave the travelling surface."[289]

**[24.117]** Henchy J, speaking in the more limited context of the duty owed to motorists by the local authorities prior to the completion of the road works stated:

> "Clearly they are bound to make it in such a way that it will be safe for its normal use by motorists who are not negligent. But the duty does not end there. They are also bound to see that the uncompleted road is not a hazard to persons using it negligently if the negligence is of a kind which experience shows drivers to be prone to, and if the particular hazard causing the accident could have been reasonably obviated or guarded against."[290]

**[24.118]** The present position will be changed when - or if - s 60 of the Civil Liability Act 1961[291] comes into operation. The section in-waiting provides[292] that a road authority[293] is to be liable for damage caused as a result of their failure to maintain adequately a public road.[294]

**[24.119]** In determining whether a road was adequately maintained, particular regard is to be had to three matters:

---

288. Supreme Court, 21 December 1973. *Cf Breivo v City of Aberdeen* (1976) 15 Wn Appeal 520, 550 P 2d 1164, noted by Anon, in (1977) 12 Gonzaga LR 728. More generally, see Erlsten 'Defectively Designed Highways' (1967) 16 Clev-Mar LR 264.

289. Page 7 of Fitzgerald CJ's judgment. See also *Rowe v Bus Éireann and Wicklow County Council* High Court, 3 March 1994 (Carroll J); *Copaz v Louth County Council* [1997] Ir L Log W 402 (CC).

290. Pages 4-5 of Henchy J's judgment. See also *Levine v Morris* [1970] 1 All ER 144; *CIE v Carroll* [1986] ILRM 312 (SC).

291. Section 60(7) provides that the section is to come into operation on such day, not earlier than 1 April 1967, as may be fixed therefore by order made by the Government. No such order has yet been made. In *The State (Sheehan) v Government of Ireland* [1987] IR 550, the Supreme Court, by a majority, held that s 60(7) was merely an enabling provision, vesting a complete discretion in the Government. Henchy J considered that the language of the subsection:

> "would seem to point to the parliamentary recognition of the fact that the important law reform to be effected by the section was not to take effect unless and until the Government became satisfied that, in the light of factors such as the necessary deployment of financial and other resources, the particular reform could be brought into effect".

See further Hogan 'Judicial Review of Executive Discretion' (1987) 9 DULJ 91; Hogan & Morgan *Administrative Law in Ireland* (3rd ed, 1998), pp 684-686; Byrne & Binchy, *Annual Review of Irish Law 1987*, pp 17-21, 313-314, 329.

292. By subs (1).

293. The term "road authority" means a county council or country or other borough corporation or urban district council: s 60(5).

294. The term public road is widely defined, extending not only to roads the responsibility for whose maintenance lies on a road authority, but also any bridges, pipes, arches, pulleys, footways, pavements, fences, railing or walls which form such roads and which it is the responsibility of a road authority to maintain.

(a) the construction of the road and the standard of maintenance appropriate to a road of such construction;
(b) the traffic using the road;
(c) the condition in which a reasonable person would have expected to find the road.[295]

**[24.120]** In determining whether a road authority had a reasonable opportunity to give warning that a road was a danger to traffic or had taken reasonable precautions to secure that a road was not such a danger, regard is to be had to the standard of supervision reasonable for a road of such character.[296]

**[24.121]** Subsection (2) provides that in proceedings under s 60, it will be a defence for the road authority to prove that:

(a) they had given sufficient warning that the road was a danger to traffic; or
(b) they had taken reasonable precautions to secure that the road was not a danger to traffic; or
(c) they had not a reasonable opportunity to give such warning or take such precautions; or
(d) the damage resulted from a wrong committed by any person other than the road authority.

As already mentioned no Government order bringing the section into operation has issued as yet.[297]

295. Section 60(3).

296. Section 60(4).

297. An Impressive argument is made by Bland 'The Strange Death of the Nonfeasance Defence' (1998) 16 Ir LT (ns) 172 that the enactment of the Occupiers' Liability Act 1995 has had the effect of abolishing this defence, since it prescribes a "common duty of care", with regard to both acts and omissions, in relation to "visitors", who are defined in s 1(1) as including entrants "as of right". The latter term is not defined in the legislation. Mr Bland argues that it embraces persons lawfully exercising a public right of way over a road. Whether this argument will succeed is, however, unclear. The Oireachtas debates do not support this interpretation of a legislative intent to abrogate the old defence. Moreover, the entrants "as of right" which the legislation envisages are probably person, such as Members of the Garda Síochána and firefighters, whose status under common law was somewhat uncertain. Mr Bland's thesis is nonetheless, well researched and powerfully argued and is sure to cause difficulties to those called on to oppose it.

# Chapter 25

# The Rule in *Rylands v Fletcher*


I. Introduction .......... 717
II. Scope of the Rule .......... 719
III. Defences .......... 727
IV. The Future of the Rule in Irish Law .......... 731


## I. INTRODUCTION

**[25.01]** The rule in *Rylands v Fletcher*[1] is a source of much controversy.[2]

> "There are few cases upon which such magnificent edifices of theory have been erected, and few which in the process have been so sadly misunderstood."[3]

**[25.02]** Blackburn J's judgment has been described as "one of the masterpieces of the Law Reports," the rule stated therein has, on the other hand, been stigmatised as "largely bereft of current authority or validity ... all but obliterated by subsequent judicial explanations and qualifications".[4] It has recently been rejected by the High Court of Australia and subsumed within the tort of negligence.[5] The House of Lords has preferred a more modest restatement of the rule.[6] At the end of this chapter we shall attempt to assess the probable trend of Irish law in the light of these international developments.

**[25.03]** The rule has given rise to very little reported litigation in Ireland.[7] It is difficult to see why this should be: the volume of reported cases in regard to the related tort of nuisance, for example, is high. Moreover, the clash of rural and industrial values which the

---

1. (1868) LR 3 HL 330, affg (1866) LR 1 Ex 265.
2. See Shields '*Rylands v Fletcher* Revitalised' (1999) 2 Trinity College LR 124; Carroll, 'The Rule in *Rylands v Fletcher*: A Re-Assessment' (1973) 8 Ir Jur (ns) 208; Bohlen, 'The Rule in *Rylands v Fletcher*' (1911) 59 U Pa LR 298; Pollock, 'Duties of Insuring Safety: The Rule in *Rylands v Fletcher*' (1886) 2 LQR 52; Prosser 'The Principle of *Rylands v Fletcher*', Ch 3 in *Selected Topics in the Law of Torts* (1954); Malloy '*Fletcher v Rylands*: A Re-examination of Judicial Origins' (1942) 9 U Chi LR 266; Morris 'Hazardous Enterprises and Risk Bearing Capacity' (1952) 61 Yale LJ 1172; Newark 'Non-Natural User and *Rylands v Fletcher*' (1961) 24 MLR 557; West 'Nuisance and *Rylands v Fletcher*' (1966) 30 Conv (ns) 95; Anon *Rylands v Fletcher* [1933] LJ Ir 105; Eekelaar 'Nuisance and Strict Liability' (1973) 8 Ir Jur (ns) 191; Stallybrass 'Dangerous Things and the Non-Natural User of Land' (1929) 3 Camb LJ 376; Wharaw 'Opening the Floodgates' (1974) 3 Anglo-Am LR 65; Green, 'Tort Law Public Law in Disguise' (1959) 38 Tex LR 1 at 4-6.
3. 'The Principle of *Rylands v Fletcher*', Ch 3 of Prosser, *Selected Topics in the Law of Torts* (1954), p 135.
4. SALMOND & HEUSTON, p 314.
5. *Burnie Port Authority v General Jones Pty Ltd* (1994) 179 CLR 520 (HC, Austr). *Cambridge Water Company v Eastern Counties Leather plc* [1994] 2 AC 264 (HL).
6. *Cf Superquinn Ltd v Bray Urban District Council* High Court, 18 February 1998 (Laffoy J).
7. *Cf* Anon 'The Rule in *Rylands v Fletcher*' [1933] LJ Ir 105 at 105.

rule seeks in part to superintend, is surely one that has been of continuing importance in this country.[8]

**[25.04]** The facts in *Rylands v Fletcher*, briefly, were that the plaintiff was mining coal with the permission of the land-owner. The defendant was mining coal on premises adjoining the defendant. The defendant built a reservoir to supply water to their mill on his land. This work was done by independent contractors. The contractors negligently failed to discover that there was a disused shaft of a mine under the reservoir which communicated with the plaintiff's mine. In due course water from the reservoir broke into the shaft and flooded the plaintiff's mine.

**[25.05]** The plaintiff in launching his action faced some formidable difficulties. The defendants had not been negligent (the arbitrator found), no trespass had been committed since the damage by flooding had not been a direct consequence of the defendants' activity, the defendants were not guilty of nuisance, since there had been a single escape only[9] nor (at that time)[10] would they be considered liable for any negligence created by an independent contractor. Liability was nonetheless imposed on the defendants. Blackburn J in the Court of Exchequer Chamber stated:

> "We think that the true rule of law is that the person who for his own purposes brings on his lands and collects and keeps there anything likely to do mischief if it escapes, must keep it in at his peril, and, if he does not do so, *is prima facie* answerable for all the damage which is the natural consequence of its escape."[11]

The House of Lords affirmed. Lord Cairns included in his speech a passage that has caused some confusion in subsequent decisions:

> "If the defendants, not stopping at the natural use of their close, had desired to use it for any purpose which I may term a non-natural use for the purpose of introducing into the close that which in its natural condition was not in or upon it, for the purpose of introducing water either above or below ground in quantities and in a manner not the result of any work or operation on or under the land; and if in consequence of their doing so, or in consequence of any imperfection in the mode of their doing so, the water came to escape and pass off into the close of the plaintiff, then it appears to me that that which the defendants were doing they were doing at their own peril; and if in the course of their doing it the evil arose to which I have referred - the evil, namely, of the escape of the water and its passing away to the close of the plaintiff and injuring the plaintiff, then for the consequence of that, in my opinion, the defendants would be liable ..."[12]

---

8. The relevance of the rule in *Rylands v Fletcher* to environmental pollution has been much discussed in North America: see, eg Lohrmann 'Comment: The Environmental Lawsuit: Traditional Doctrines and Evolving Theories to Control Pollution' (1970) 16 Wayne LR 1085 at 1117-1121; Juergensmeyer 'Control of Air Pollution through the Assertion of Private Rights [1967] Duke LJ 1126 at 1148-1152; Maloney 'Judicial Protection of the Environment A New Role for Common-Law Remedies' (1972) 25 Vand LR 145 at 150 151; Sokolon 'Comment: Hazardous Waste Liability and Compensation Old Solutions, New Solutions, No Solutions' (1982) 14 Conn LR 307 at 318-319; Prince 'Compensation for Victims of Hazardous Substance Exposure' (1985) 11 Wm Mitchell LR 657 at 715-719.
9. *Cf* PROSSER & KEETON p 545.
10. *Cf Bower v Peate* (1876) 1 QBD 321.
11. *Fletcher v Rylands* (1866) LR 1 Ex 265 at 278.
12. *Rylands v Fletcher* (1868) LR 3 HL 330 at 338.

**[25.06]** In the Supreme Court decision of *Hanrahan v Merck Sharp & Dohme (Ireland) Ltd*[13] Henchy J quoted from Blackburn J's judgment but made no reference to the modification proposed by Lord Cairns. Henchy J defined the rule by reference to "a thing which is likely to do mischief if it escapes,"[14] rather than mentioning any requirement of "non-natural" use. It would appear unwise, however, to infer from Henchy J's failure to address the adequacy or otherwise of the requirement of "non-natural" use that he was rejecting the body of case-law that has been built up around this concept. It is significant that in *Hanrahan's* case, the defendant's activity engaging in the processing of "dangerous chemical substances,"[15] would almost certainly have been considered a "non-natural" use of their land. In any event, Henchy J's remarks are *obiter,* since the Supreme Court proceeded[16] on the basis that only the plaintiff's claim in nuisance should be considered on appeal.

## II. Scope of the Rule

### "Non-Natural" Use[17]

**[25.07]** The concept of liability contingent on "non-natural" use is ambiguous. It could mean merely that land, in its natural state, should not be the subject of liability or it could, on the other hand, relieve the defendant from responsibility in respect of an artificial but nonetheless ordinary (and in that sense "natural") accumulation onto his land. After some confusion, the latter interpretation gained supremacy: "non-natural" is to be understood in the sense of:

> "some special use bringing with it an increased danger to others, and must not merely be the ordinary use of land or such a use as is proper for the general benefit of the community".[18]

**[25.08]** "Non-natural use" therefore, does not oblige the owner to leave his land to nature. Rather does it mean something close to "excessive" or "extra-ordinary use". If, for example, I pipe onto my land, sufficient water for my domestic requirements, I would not be making a "non natural use" of my property. If, however, I build a reservoir to store unusually large quantities of water, that might well constitute a "non natural" user. In this

13. [1988] ILRM 629 at 633 (SC).
14. [1988] ILRM 629 at 633.
15. *Cf West v Bristol Tramways Co* [1908] 2 KB 14; *Heard v Woodward* (1954) 12 WWR 312, *Cairns v Canada Refining Co* (1914) 6 OWN 562.
16. *Cf Hanrahan v Merck, Sharp and Dohme* [1988] ILRM 629 at 634.
17. See Newark, 'Non-natural User and *Rylands v Fletcher*' (1961) 24 MLR 557; Carroll J 'The Rule in *Rylands v Fletcher*: A Re-Assessment' (1973) 8 Ir Jur (ns) 208 at 218-219.
18. *Rickards v Lothian* [1913] AC 263 at 280 (PC). For criticism of the developments leading to this interpretation, see Newark 'Non-natural User and *Rylands v Fletcher*' (1961) 24 MLR 557. In *Ellison v Ministry of Defence* (1996) 81 Build LR 101 (QB) bulk fuel installations for the storage of aviation fuel at the United States Army Air Force airfield at Greenham Common were held not to constitute a non-natural use of the property. "Taking the community as the national community as a whole, there is no doubt that the works were for the benefit of the community." As to the requirement that the "thing" brought onto the property should itself be dangerous, see Stallybrass 'Dangerous Things and the Non-Natural User of Land' (1929) 3 Camb LJ 376. In *Victor Weston (Éire) Ltd v Kenny* [1954] IR 191 at 197, Davitt P stated that, under the rule in *Rylands v Fletcher*, there was "an absolute obligation to prevent dangerous matter from escaping."

sense, the defendant is liable because he engaged in conduct which he knew or ought to have known was unduly risky. But what is this if it is not *negligence*? Surely, it may be said, the essence of negligence is taking an improper risk, whether the risk may result in immediate damage or damage at some unknown time in the future?

**[25.09]** This seems to be a valid analysis,[19] but for reasons of history this rationalisation has not taken place. Strict liability of the kind ultimately articulated in *Rylands v Fletcher* predated the recognition of negligence as a distinctive tort; the principle of *res ipsa loquitur* had not been developed; and the concepts of fault and of "social engineering" inherent in a modern torts system were still at a fairly primitive stage.

**[25.10]** As a practical matter, the characterisation of the particular use as "non-natural" is of crucial significance in litigation: if the plaintiff can pass this hurdle, then the case will be decided on a strict liability principle. As we shall see, the judicial precedents on the issue are confusing and inconsistent. The problems can be traced to its source: a definition of "non-natural user" which pulls in several conflicting directions, with no clear underlying principle.[20]

### *(a) Examples of non-natural use*

#### *(i) Water*[21]

**[25.11]** The decision of *Rylands v Fletcher*[22] is of course itself an authority for holding that the accumulation of water may constitute a non-natural use of land.[23] That case involved

---

19. *Cf* Prosser 'The Principle of *Rylands v Fletcher*', Ch 3 in *Selected Topics in the Law of Torts* (1954), p 181. See also Carroll 'The Rule in *Rylands v Fletcher*: A Re-Assessment' (1973) 8 Ir Jur (ns) 208 at 210-214, Millner, *Negligence in Modern Law* (1967) pp 190-199. The High Court of Australia agreed, in *Burnie Port Authority v General Jones Pty Ltd* (1994) 179 Comm LR 520. In their joint judgment, Mason CJ Deane, Dawson, Toohey and Gaudron JJ noted at pp 538-539 that the definition in *Rickards v Lothian* seemed to focus on the nature of the use but that:

    "other cases have made clear that, in determining whether a use satisfies the 'non-natural', 'special' or 'not ordinary' description, regard may be had to the manner as well as the nature of the use. Increasingly, *Rylands v Fletcher* liability has come to depend on all the circumstances surrounding the introduction, production, retention or accumulation of the relevant substance. That being so, the presence of reasonable care or the absence of negligence in the manner of dealing with a substance or carrying out an activity may intrude as a relevant factor in determining whether the use of land is a 'special' and 'not ordinary' one".

20. In *Burnie Port Authority v General Jones Pty Ltd* (1994) 179 Comm LR 520 at 544, Mason CJ, Deane, Dawson, Toohey and Gaudron JJ stated of the test of "non-natural" use:

    "Far from representing a unifying principle and a general conceptual explanation and determinant of different categories of care, it has ... become a source of disunity and disparity within the individual category. Thus the introduction to or retention on land of trees, water, gas, electricity, fire and high explosives, amongst other things, have all been seen, as a result of the application of the test to the particular circumstances, as both attracting and not attracting the operation of the rule. Indeed, the test of 'non-natural use' has probably done more than anything else to vindicate Sir Frederick Pollock's identification, almost a century ago, of *Rylands v Fletcher* as one of those authorities that are followed only in the letter, and become slowly but surely choked and crippled by [judicially imposed] exceptions'..."

21. See Kadirgamar 'The Escape of Water from Domestic Premises' (1973) 37 Conv (ns) 179.
22. Kadirgamar 'The Escape of Water from Domestic Premises' (1973) 37 Conv (ns) 179.
23. See also *Superquinn Ltd v Bray Urban District Council* High Court, 18 February 1998 (Laffoy J). *Cf Popular Homes Ltd v Society of African Missions Trustees* [1997] Ir L Log W 367 (CC); *Dockery v Manor Park Homebuilders Ltd* High Court, 10 April 1995 (O'Hanlon J).

the construction of a reservoir: it has also been held[24] that carrying water in large quantities in mains under the street constitutes a non-natural use. On the other hand, domestic uses of water, such as for heating,[25] and plumbing[26] do not constitute non-natural use.[27] Moreover, some other uses of water, such as a sprinkler system,[28] for example, do not fall within the scope of the rule.

**[25.12]** The drainage of bogs is, of course, a matter of considerable importance in this country.[29] The position appears to be that a farmer's opening drains on his bog[30] probably does not fall within the scope of the rule in *Rylands v Fletcher* but that the commercial exploitation of bogs with heavy machinery may do so, on the basis that this is not an ordinary and "natural" user of land. At all events there was a High Court decision[31] in 1944 to this effect, but its correctness today has been doubted[32] on the basis that the public interest is better served by the use of such machinery.

*(ii) Trees*

**[25.13]** Trees are not normally regarded[33] as falling under the rule in *Rylands v Fletcher*.[34] Where, however, the trees are poisonous,[35] liability may be imposed under the rule, provided the branches of the tree have "escaped" (by encroachment[36] or otherwise) onto the neighbouring property[37] or the highway.

---

24. *Charing Cross Electricity Supply Co v Hydraulic Power Co* [1914] 3 KB 722 (CA); *Hoey v Dundalk UDC* High Court, 29 February 1980 (McWilliam J). See also *Western Engraving Co v Film Laboratories Ltd* [1936] 1 All ER 106 (CA).
25. *Imperial Tobacco v Hart* 51 (1917) NSR 379, affd 51 NSR 387, 36 DLR 63 (CA).
26. *Carstairs v Taylor* (1871) LR 6 Ex 217; *Ross v Fedden* (1872) LR 7 QB 661; *Blake v Woolf* [1898] 2 QB 426. See also *Scully v Marjorie Boland Ltd* [1962] IR 58 (HC) - sounding in negligence.
27. *Cf Fitzpatrick v O'Connor* High Court, 11 March 1988 (Costello J) - sounding in nuisance.
28. *Peters v Prince of Wales Theatre* [1943] 1 KB 73 (CA). It has been contended by an Australian commentator that swimming pools in private residences probably do not come under the rule in *Rylands v Fletcher*. Shelton 'Anyone for Tennis?' (1984) 58 Law Institute J 639 at 640. Whether the social realities of Irish life on this matter are similar to those in Australia is a matter for debate.
29. *Cf Connolly v Congested Districts Board for Ireland* 52 ILT & Sol J 52 at 59.
30. See *M'Donnell v Turf Development Board* (1944) 78 ILTR 94 at 95 (HC); see also *Connolly v Congested Districts Board for Ireland* 52 ILT & Sol J 52; *Shine v Irish Land Commission* (1946) 81 ILTR 100 (HC). *Cf Doona v O'Donoghue* [1957] Ir Jur 85 (CC).
31. *M'Donnell v Turf Development Board* 78 ILTR 94.
32. Carroll (1973) 8 Ir Jur (ns) at 219.
33. *Noble v Harrison* [1926] 2 KB 332. Wright J stated (at 342) that a beech tree:

    "is a usual and normal incident of the English country; it develops by slow natural growth, its branches are not likely to cause danger, even if permitted to expand outwards over the highway. Such a tree cannot be compared to a tiger, a spreading fire, or a reservoir in which a huge weight of water is artificially accumulated to be kept in by dams, or noxious fumes or sewage."

    See also *Mullan v Forrester* [1921] 2 IR 412 at 433 (KB). But *cf McKail v Hamilton* [1948] Argus LR (Current Notes) 214 (Melbourne Co Court, Gamble J).
34. (1868) LR 3 HL 330.
35. *Crowhurst v Amersham Burial Board* (1878) 4 Ex Div 5.
36. In *Mendez v Palazzi* 68 DLR (3d) 582 (Ont Co Court 1976), it was held that encroachment of roots did not constitute an "escape", *sed quare*.
37. *Ponting v Noakes* [1894] 2 QB 281. *Cf White v Boyle* (1926) 60 ILTR 30 (HC) - liability based on contract.

**[25.14]** Despite *dicta* seemingly to the contrary,[38] it seems consistent with the basic principles of the rule in *Rylands v Fletcher*[39] that liability should not attach to the occupier in respect of a tree not artificially grown by him unless he was aware or ought to have been aware of a danger arising in respect of it.

*(iii) Walls*

**[25.15]** In *Mullan v Forrester*,[40] Pim J appeared to support the view that the collapse of a wall onto the highway might fall within the scope of the rule of *Rylands v Fletcher*. Whether building an ordinary wall[41] should be regarded as a "non-natural user" is, however, extremely doubtful.[42]

*(iv)Electricity, gas and explosives*

**[25.16]** As in the case of water and fire,[43] domestic use of electricity[44] or gas[45] will not fall within the scope of the rule, but non-domestic uses[46] of these substances or of explosives[47] or other highly inflammable materials[48] may give rise to strict liability.

***(b) Other "accumulations"***

**[25.17]** A wide range of other "accumulations" has fallen within the rule. Thus, a flagpole,[49] a fairground chair-o-plane,[50] vibrations,[51] building materials and debris allowed to fall on neighbouring buildings and block drains, while a new building was being constructed,[52] Christmas street decorations[53] and even a group of gypsy caravaners on the

38. *Cf Davey v Harrow Corporation* [1958] 1 QB 60. See also, Pettit 'Note: Trespass or Case' (1957) 20 MLR 499 at 500.
39. Pettit 'Note: Trespass or Case' (1957) 20 MLR 499.
40. [1921] 2 IR 412 at 421, 425 (KB), *cf* at 433 (*per* Moore J dissenting).
41. The wall was, admittedly, part of a business enterprise - a dyeworks, but this fact does not appear to have been regarded as crucial.
42. English authorities are to the contrary: *cf Ilford Urban District Council v Beal* [1925] 1 KB 671 at 675; *St Anne's Well Brewerey Co v Roberts* (1928) 140 LT 1 at 3 (CA) discussed by Anon 'The Doctrine of *Rylands v Fletcher* and Afterwards' (1929) 63 ILT & Sol J 7. *Cf Daly v McMullan* [1997] 2 ILRM 232 (CC) (rule in *Rylands v Fletcher* had no application to embankment as there was "no question of any unnatural user of land").
43. Anon 'The Doctrine of *Rylands v Fletcher* and Afterwards' (1929) 63 ILT & Sol J 7.
44. *Collingwood v Home & Colonial Stores Ltd* [1936] 1 All ER 74, affd [1936] 3 All ER 200 (CA).
45. *Miller v Robert Addie & Sons, Collieries* [1934] SC 150.
46. Eg *Northwestern Utilities Ltd v London Guarantee and Accident Co* [1936] AC 108 (PC); *Hanson v Wearmouth Coal Ltd* [1939] 3 All ER 47 (CA); *Eastern & South African Telephone Co v Cape Town Tramways Co* [1902] AC 381 at 392 (PC); *Fullarton v North Melbourne Electric Tramway & Lighting Co* (1916) 21 CLR 181 (HC Austr).
47. *Rainham Chemical Works Ltd v Belvedere Fish Guano Co* [1921] 2 AC 465; *cf Read v Lyons & Co Ltd* [1947] AC 156. For an account of the position in the United States, see Max 'Blasting - An Abnormally Dangerous Activity in Need of a Strict Liability Standard' (1980) 11 Cumberland LR 23 at 24 26.
48. *AG of Canada v Diamond Weatherproofing Ltd* (1974) 48 DLR (3d) 353 (Ont CA).
49. *Shiffman v Order of St John of Jerusalem* [1936] 1 All ER 557 (KB).
50. *Hale v Jennings Brothers* [1938] 1 All ER 579 (CA).
51. *Hoare & Co v McAlpine* [1923] 1 Ch 167.
52. *Heintzman & Co Ltd v Hashman Construction Ltd* (1972) 32 DLR (3d) 622 (Alta SC). The Court emphasised that the failure to place the material in receptacles was an ingredient in the defendant's liability.
53. *Saccardo v Hamilton* [1971] 2 OR 479 at 492.

defendant's campsite[54] have given rise to strict liability. In *Rigby v Chief Constable of Northamptonshire*,[55] in 1985, it was accepted without argument that the police action in discharging a CS gas canister was "non-natural" for the purposes of the rule in *Rylands v Fletcher.*

## Defendant Must Have Brought Source of Danger onto Property

**[25.18]** The rule in *Rylands v Fletcher*[56] applies only where the defendant "brings on his lands and keeps there" the source of the danger. Thus, in *Healy v Bray UDC*,[57] liability was not imposed under the rule where the plaintiff was injured by a rock which was dislodged from the defendant's land and rolled down a hill towards her. Kingsmill Moore J stated:

> "The defendants did not bring the rocks or outcrop on to [their] land for their own purpose (or at all). They are there as the result of natural forces operating in geological time, as indeed is the land. They are, in short, the land itself and not things brought onto it."[58]

## Escape

**[25.19]** Liability under *Rylands v Fletcher*[59] will not be imposed unless there has been an "escape"[60] from a place where the defendant has occupation of or control over land[61] to a

54. *AG v Corke* [1933] Ch 89, criticised in (1933) 49 LQR 158 by Kennedy, (1933) 11 Can BR 693, also in *Matheson v Northcote College* [1975] 2 NZLR 106 at 117-118. *Cf Smith v Scott* [1973] Ch 314 and the interesting discussion by Weinrib 'The Dorset Yacht Case: Causation, Care and Criminals' (1971) 4 Ottawa LR 389 at 401-402. See also *McDonald v Feely* High Court, 30 June 1980 (Barrington J) at p 8 - nuisance; *Ellis v Dun Laoghaire Corporation* Circuit Court, 29 January 1982 (Ryan J), Irish Times 30 January 1982; *Boharmor Ltd v Belfast City Council* [1987] NILR Bull 1 (CA); *cf Page Motors Ltd v Epsom & Ewell BC* (1982) 80 LGR 337 (CA), noted by Cane [1983] Pub L 202; *Lippiatt v South Gloucestershire County Council* Court Appeal (Civ Div), 31 March 1999. In *Gibb v Comerford* [1942] IR 295 at 304 (HC), Maguire P stated: "I can understand that the rule in *Rylands v Fletcher* may apply in the case of wild animals, but it appears to me to have no application to a domestic animal." In *Brady v Warren* [1900] 2 IR 632 at 652, however, Johnson J cited *Rylands v Fletcher* as authority for the proposition that "a person who keeps a fox keeps him at his peril if he escapes". From his discussion of *The Anonymous Case* 1 Vent 295, it appears that Johnson J envisaged a tame fox which reverted to its wild state after the escape. Whether cattle trespass should be regarded as falling under the rule in *Rylands v Fletcher* has led to some confusion: *cf Noonan v Hartnett* (1950) 84 ILTR 41 (CC). See also para **[27.45]** below.
55. [1985] 2 All ER 985. See also *Hanrahan v Merck Sharp & Dohme (Ireland) Ltd* [1988] ILRM 629 at 633 (SC *per* Henchy J, for the Court) "dangerous chemical substances" brought into factory for processing considered to be "things which were likely to do mischief if they escaped"; issue of "non-natural" use not addressed.
56. (1868) LR 3 HL 330, affg (1866) LR 1 Ex 265.
57. [1962-1963] Ir Jur 9 (SC).
58. [1962-1963] Ir Jur 9 at 15. See also *Pontardawe RDC v Moore-Gwyn* [1929] 1 Ch 656 (Eve J) and *cf* Noel 'Nuisances from Land in its Natural Condition' (1943) 56 HLR 772. *Cf Mullan v Forrester* [1921] 2 IR 412 at 433 (KB).
59. (1868) LR 3 HL 330, affg (1866) LR 1 Ex 265.
60. Whether an intentional release comes within the notion of "escape" for the purpose of the rule has yet to be decided. In *Rigby v Chief Constable of Northamptonshire* [1985] 2 All ER 985 at 996, Taylor J was "inclined to the view" that liability in such a case should rest, if at all, on trespass rather than on *Rylands v Fletcher.*
61. Thus there is authority for the proposition that an escape from a ship will not fall within the rule: *The Wagon Mound (No 2)* [1963] 1 Lloyd's R 402 at 426 - point was not raised on appeal. See, however, *Howard v Furness, Houlder Argentine Lines Ltd* [1936] 2 All ER 781.

place which is outside his occupation or control ...".[62] But it is clear that the defendant need not have any proprietary interest in the land.[63] Public utilities and others who, under licence, introduce a dangerous substance (such as gas or electricity) into mains on or under the highway, will be liable if it escapes from there onto the neighbouring premises.[64] Moreover, where a person brings a source of danger onto the highway, such as a locomotive which emits sparks onto the neighbouring property,[65] strict liability may be imposed.

**[25.20]** The requirement of escape has been criticised. There is something curious about a law which entitles a person, ordered by Ministerial direction to work in a munitions factory,[66] to bring an action based on strict liability in respect of an explosion which injures him as he is approaching the factory but denies him this right where the explosion occurs when he is actually in the factory, where the danger of injury would be that much greater.[67] The justification[68] for the rule must be that what is involved here is *strict* liability and that, whilst it is not unfair to impose strict liability in the event of escape, it would be unfair to impose such liability where an occupier is behaving without negligence on his own property: persons who enter his property should demand of him no more than that he conduct his operations with reasonable care towards them.

**[25.21]** Whether an Irish Court would look with sympathy on the American refinement of the rule, so as to impose strict liability for ultra-hazardous activities[69] irrespective of any question of escape, is difficult to predict.[70] It would have the advantage of rationalising the policy basis of the rule, but would possibly involve too radical a departure from established principles to encourage the Court here to take this step.[71]

---

62. *Read v Lyons* [1947] AC 156 at 168. For a more narrow expression of the test see Lord Macmillan, at 173.
63. *Benning v Wong* (1969) 122 CLR 249 at 294. In *Rigby v Chief Constable of Northamptonshire* [1985] 2 All ER 985 at 996, Taylor J could see "no difference in principle between allowing a man-eating tiger to escape from your land into that of another and allowing it to escape from the back of your wagon parked on the highway".
64. *Midwood & Co Ltd v Manchester Corporation* [1905] 2 KB 597; *Charing Cross Electricity Supply Co v Hydraulic Power Co* [1914] 3 KB 772 (CA). For an attempt to explain these decisions in orthodox terms, see *Read v J Lyons & Co Ltd* [1947] AC 156 at 177 (*per* Lord Porter), 168 (*per* Viscount Simon) and 183 (*per* Lord Simonds).
65. *Powell v Fall* (1880) 5 QBD 597; *Mansel v Webb* (1918) 88 LJ KB 323.
66. These were the facts in *Read v J Lyons & Co Ltd* [1947] AC 156.
67. *Cf* the judgment of Cassels J in the lower court proceedings in *Read v J Lyons & Co* (1944) 60 Times LR 363. See also Linden 'Whatever Happened to *Rylands v Fletcher*?', Ch 11, *Studies in Canadian Tort Law,* Klar ed, (1977), pp 334 335.
68. *Cf* Stallybrass 'Note' (1944) 60 LQR 207 at 208.
69. *Cf* King 'A Goals - Oriented Approach to Strict Tort Liability for Abnormally Dangerous Activities' (1996) 48 Baylor LR 341.
70. The English courts have not evinced a willingness to take this step; *cf Read v J Lyons & Co Ltd* [1945] QB 216 (CA), and (briefly) on appeal [1947] AC 156.
71. For some of the conceptual and practical difficulties, see English Law Com No. 32, *Civil Liability for Dangerous Things and Chattels* (1970) paras 14-16. *Cf* Shields 'Liability without fault: *Rylands v Fletcher* Revitalised' (1999) 2 Trinity College LR 124 at 132-133.

**[25.22]** In *Mullen v Quinnsworth Ltd t/a Crazy Prices*,[72] McCarthy J (Finlay, CJ concurring) quoted the previous paragraph from the second edition of this work[73] and observed:

> "It remains for another day to consider whether or not, by way of application of the rule in *Rylands v Fletcher* or otherwise, balancing the rights of people and the rights of property, a principle of absolute liability may be appropriate to claims arising out of certain forms of accidents occurring in large supermarkets."[74]

That McCarthy, J was willing to give this proposal serious consideration is evident from the following analysis:

> "The supermarket is a modern phenomenon derived from a combination of events such as cash and cash only purchasing, efficient and attractive packaging, competition itself, convenience of customers, the increase in the number of gainfully employed housewives, the growth of family shopping and the availability of 'fast foods', the purchasing power of store chains or other groups of traders, the efficiency and speed of transport, both traders and private customers, and, no doubt, a variety of other circumstances. The supermarket has supplanted the family grocer in whose shop the risk of an accident such as befell the plaintiff was virtually non-existent. If a customer on taking a package from the grocer were to let it fall she would know it; it would not arise that another customer would come so near as to be endangered. The customer in the supermarket has sacrificed the personal touch of the family grocer for the sake of lower prices and possibly other advantages but she has taken on a very much greater risk of personal injury."[75]

**[25.23]** When the case returned to the Supreme Court after a retrial, McCarthy J noted that, although the notice of appeal had contained "a detailed contention as to absolute duty and, therefore, to absolute liability,"[76] on the hearing of the appeal, at the court's invitation, the argument had been confined to the issue of whether the defendant had exercised reasonable care. He added: "The question must therefore remain for another day".[77] Although *Mullen (No 1)* and *Mullen (No 2)* have been discussed or cited in later decisions, no judge has taken up the invitation to discuss the question of the extension of the rule in *Rylands v Fletcher* to slip-and-fall accidents in supermarkets.

**[25.24]** Let us give some brief consideration to McCarthy J's ruminations. Why should large supermarkets be subject to a system of strict liability[78] for these accidents? The underlying tone of McCarthy J's remark about the social phenomenon that supermarkets represent is one of distaste for these new cathedrals of commerce and a concern for the risks to customers which the placing of thousands of items on open shelves entails. Even the most attentive system of sweepers will inevitably be less than fully successful in avoiding slip-and-fall accidents. Perhaps there is something in the argument that this systematic deficiency should generate liability. Whether it should be characterised as strict

72. [1990] 1 IR 59 (SC).
73. (2nd ed, 1990), p 505.
74. [1990] 1 IR 59 at 69.
75. [1990] IR 59 at 68-69.
76. [1991] ILRM 439 at 448.
77. [1991] ILRM 439 at 448.
78. Although McCarthy J spoke of his "absolute" liability his supporting reference to the rule in *Rylands v Fletcher* indicates that he envisaged strict liability.

liability rather than as an application of the negligence principle, akin to the concept of an unsafe system of work in employers' liability[79] may be debated. Against imposing liability *a priori*, as it were, without regard to the efficacy of the particular sweeper system, two points may be made. First, customers clearly are attracted to supermarkets and happy to shop there. Every activity or process has some risk. If the customer purchasing preferences can mould and narrow the scope of a retailer's duty to warn about the dangerous potential of particular products,[80] why should these preferences not also be taken into account in the slip-and-fall context? Secondly, the practical implications of imposing strict liability on supermarkets are not clear. Certainly such a change would reduce the incentive to management to have a good sweeper system, proof of which can defeat a negligence claim.

## Entitlement to Sue

**[25.25]** Although the rule in *Rylands v Fletcher* is based on unneighbourliness in occupation of property, it appears that entitlement to sue is not limited to adjoining occupiers but extends to any person who sustains material or personal injuries as a result of the escape.[81] In *Read v Lyons*[82] Lord Macmillan appeared to question whether the action could ever support a claim for personal injuries, but this approach has not been supported by decisions in England[83] or elsewhere in common law jurisdictions.[84]

**[25.26]** The position in England appears to be that the adjoining occupier may sue for personal injuries but that the right of a non-occupier to sue for such injuries is a matter of debate. The question is whether the House of Lords would follow the analogy of nuisance[85] so as to keep the rule in *Rylands v Fletcher* within as narrow a compass as possible or will instead treat *Rylands v Fletcher* liability either as *sui generis* or close to negligence liability.[86] As we have seen, that broader question is an open one in the Irish context. On the specific issue of the entitlement of a non-occupier to sue for personal injuries, the authorities here would appear to support such a right of action.[87]

---

79. *Cf* para **[18.104]** above.

80. *Cf Duffy v Rooney and Dunnes Stores (Dundalk) Ltd* Supreme Court, 23 April 1998, affg High Court, 23 July 1997 (Laffoy J); *Cassells v Marks & Spencer plc* High Court, 25 March 1999 (Barr J).

81. *Cf*, eg, *Mullan v Forrester* [1921] 2 IR 412; *Healy v Bray UDC* [1962-1963] Ir Jur 9 (SC); *Shiffmann v Order of St John of Jerusalem* [1936] 1 All ER 557; *Charing Cross Electricity Co v Hydraulic Power Co* [1914] 3 KB 772 (CA); *British Celanese Ltd v Hunt (AH) (Capacitors) Ltd* [1969] 1 WLR 959 at 964 (QB). See also *Hanrahan v Merck Sharp & Dohme (Ireland) Ltd* [1988] ILRM 629 at 633 (SC).

82. [1947] AC 156 at 173. However, see SALMOND & HEUSTON, p 312.

83. *Miles v Forest Rock Granite* (1918) 34 Times LR 500 (CA); *Shiffman v Order of St John* [1936] 1 All ER 557; *Hale v Jennings Bros* [1938] 1 All ER 579; *Perry v Kendrick's Transport* [1956] 1 WLR 85 at 92. See, however, *Dunne v North Western Gas Board* [1964] 2 QB 806 at 838, indicating that the question may still be open.

84. Eg *Benning v Wong* (1969) 122 CLR 249 (HC Austr); *Aldridge v Van Patter* [1952] 4 DLR 93. *Cf Burnie Port Authority v General Jones Pty Ltd* 179 CLR 520 at 546 (HC Austr):

> "In this country, ... damages ... extend to personal injury or damage to property sustained outside the relevant premises by persons having no relationship to neighbouring land apart from being on it."

85. *Hunter v Canary Wharf Ltd* [1997] AC 655.

86. STREET, p 401-402 presents a very clear and convincing analysis of this issue.

87. *Cf Healy v Bray UDC* [1962-1963] Ir Jur 9 (SC).

**[25.27]** As regards injury to goods, it seems that the occupier may sue[88] but again the claim of the non-occupier is doubtful. It has been held that mere financial loss suffered by a non-occupier is not actionable.[89] Whether the occupier may sue for such loss has not been decided.[90] The commentators internationally are divided on the issue.[91] Perhaps the relaxed approach of the Irish courts to claims for pure economic loss, which is in stark contrast to that of their British counterparts, will lead to recognition of such a claim.

### Status of Defendant

**[25.28]** Clearly, of course, an occupier[92] may be liable under the rule in *Rylands v Fletcher.* It seems clear also that liability may attach to those on the land by statutory authority[93] or by private permission;[94] and it has been said that persons "cannot escape ... liability ... merely because they have no tenancy or independent occupation of the land but use it thus by permission of the tenants or occupiers".[95] There is divided authority on the question whether an owner not in occupation of the land at the time when the thing escapes is liable where he has authorised the accumulation.[96] In this specific context one can witness yet again the tension between characterising the rule in *Rylands v Fletcher* as as aspect of the tort of private nuisance[97] and treating it either as *sui generis* or akin to the tort of negligence.

## III. Defences

**[25.29]** Although a wide range of defences to the rule in *Rylands v Fletcher*[98] has been recognised, the process has fallen short of admitting absence of negligence as a good defence. A further word about permissible defences is now called for.

### Consent of the Plaintiff

**[25.30]** The rule does not apply to the escape of things brought by the defendant onto his premises with the consent of the plaintiff. In such a case the plaintiff will be limited to an

88. *Jones v Festiniog Ry* (1868) LR 3 QB 733; *British Celanese Ltd v AH Hunt (Capacitors) Ltd* [1969] 1 WLR 959 (QB).
89. *Cattle v Stockton Waterworks Co* (1875) LR 10 QB 453; *Weller & Co v Foot & Mouth Disease Research Institute* [1966] 1 QB 569. See, however, *Ryeford Homes v Sevenoaks DC* [1989] Con LR 75. See Carroll 'The Rule in *Rylands v Fletcher*: A Re-Assessment' (1973) 8 Ir Jur (ns) 208 at 223-224.
90. STREET, p 353.
91. *Cf* LUNNEY & OLIPHANT, pp 573-574; STREET, p 402; FLEMING, pp 384-385.
92. Whether or not with a valid title, provided he exercises control: *cf Benning v Wong* (1969) 122 CLR 249 (HC, Aust).
93. *Smeaton v Ilford Corporation* [1954] Ch 450.
94. *Northwestern Utilities Ltd v London Guarantee Ltd* [1936] AC 108.
95. *Rainham Chemical Works Ltd v Belvedere Fish Guano Co Ltd* [1921] AC 465 at 479 (HL). *Cf* English Law Com No 32, *Civil Liability for Dangerous Things and Chattels*, Appendix 1, para 5. Whether *Noonan v Hartnett* (1950) 84 ILTR 41 (CC) throws any light on this question is doubtful: *cf* Carroll 'The *Rule in Rylands v Fletcher*: A Re-Assessment' (1973) 8 Ir Jur (ns) 208 at 215-216.
96. Dicta in the *Rainham Chemical Works Ltd v Belvedere Fish Guano Co Ltd* [1921] AC 465 at 479, support the imposition of liability: against holding the occupier liable is *St Anne's Well Brewery Co v Roberts* (1928) 140 LT 1.
97. *Cf Hunter v Canary Wharf Ltd* [1997] AC 655.
98. See fn 2.

action in negligence.[99] Consent may be express or implied. The most common application of the latter involves the escape of water from an upper storey premises in the occupation of several tenants.[100] The courts have considered that it would be unfair on the tenant of the upper floor to carry the risk of strict liability for an accidental non-negligent escape where the tenant of the lower floor would be free of the risk.[101]

**[25.31]** The defence of consent extends to certain other cases of "common benefit" (sometimes regarded as a separate ground of defence to the application of the rule in *Rylands v Fletcher*). Where rain water is collected on a roof of premises for the benefit of the several occupants[102] for example, strict liability will not be imposed. The courts have, however, been reluctant to apply this approach to the relationship between consumers and suppliers of public utilities, such as gas and water.[103]

## Default or Special Sensitivity of the Plaintiff

**[25.32]** In *Rylands v Fletcher*,[104] Blackburn J recognised the plaintiff's own default as a ground for excluding the application of the rule. Thus, in *Dunn v Birmingham Canal*,[105] a mine-owner who worked his mine under the defendant's canal in the knowledge of the danger and brought the water from the canal down upon himself was denied a remedy.

**[25.33]** The defence has been extended, on analogy with nuisance, to cases of special sensitivity on the part of the plaintiff in his use of his property. Thus, in *Eastern and South African Telegraph Co v Cape Town Tramways*,[106] the plaintiffs failed in their action for disturbance of their telegraph cable by electricity escaping from the defendant's tramway system since their operation of the cable constituted a special use of their property. In contrast, the fact that a building may be structurally unsound so as to be affected by vibrations coming from the defendant's property will not afford a good defence to the defendant, since the property has not been put to any special use.[107]

---

99. *AG v Cory Bros & Co* [1921] 1 AC 521 at 539; *Victor Weston (Éire) Ltd v Kenny* [1954] IR 191 at 197 (HC); WILLIAMS, p 314.

100. *Victor Weston (Éire) Ltd v Kenny* [1954] IR 191 at 197; *Rickards v Lothian* [1913] AC 263; *Prosser (A) & Son Ltd v Levy* [1955] 1 WLR 1224. See Kadirgamar 'The Escape of Water from Domestic Premises' (1973) 37 Conv (ns) 179.

101. The fact that water used for domestic purposes is generally regarded as not constituting non-natural use of property would also defeat the plaintiff's claim: *cf* see para **[25.08]** above; *Scully v Marjorie Boland Ltd* [1962] IR 58 (HC). See also Buckley, *The Law of Nuisance* (1981) pp 51-52.

102. *Carstairs v Taylor* (1871) LR 6 Exch 217.

103. *Northwestern Utilities Ltd v London Guarantee & Accident Co Ltd* [1936] AC 108 at 120 (PC); *Gilson v Kerrier RDC* [1976] 1 WLR 904.

104. LR 1 Ex 265 at 279.

105. (1872) LR 7 QB 244, affd (1872) LR 8 QB 42. *Cf Miles v Forest Rock Granite* (1918) 34 Times LR 500, doubted by SALMOND & HEUSTON, p 316, fn 80. See also *Fitzpatrick v O'Connor* High Court, 11 March 1988 (Costello J) - counterclaim sounding in nuisance.

106. [1902] AC 381.

107. *Hoare v McAlpine* [1923] 1 Ch 167.

**[25.34]** Where the plaintiff's fault is not the sole cause of the escape, it would seem that the defence should be assimilated with that of contributory negligence, so as to reduce the damages awarded.[108]

## Act of a Stranger

**[25.35]** The defendant will not be liable if the escape was due to the deliberate act of a stranger which could not reasonably have been anticipated by the defendant. The scope of the defence is somewhat uncertain. It has been clearly established that, where a trespasser intentionally creates a danger on a person's property which results in an escape onto the plaintiff's property which causes damage to the plaintiff, that person will not be liable unless, with knowledge or presumed knowledge of the danger, he or she fails to take reasonable steps to remove it.[109] The same rule applies where the creator of the danger, without actually entering the land of the defendant, brings about the injurious escape.[110]

**[25.36]** The occupier will, however, be responsible under the rule not only for the wrongful act of an employee acting in the course of his or her employment but also for that of an independent contractor engaged to do work on his behalf.[111] Moreover, it appears that the occupier may also be responsible for the acts of invitees,[112] (or visitors, under the Occupiers' Liability Act 1995), licensees,[113] and probably the members of his family also,[114] unless "in all the circumstances the occupier had no control over the activities of the person in question".[115] Where, however, the defendant is not in occupation or control, he will not be liable: thus, a landlord will not incur responsibility under *Rylands v Fletcher*[116] for the misconduct of his tenants.[117]

**[25.37]** The defence of "act of a stranger" is difficult to harmonise with a strict liability approach.[118] It is noteworthy that it does not seem to apply in respect of liability for dangerous animals,[119] for example.

---

108. *Cf* FLEMING, p 387; Carroll 'The Rule in *Rylands v Fletcher*: A Re-Assessment' (1973) 8 Ir Jur (ns) 208 at 221. If the rule in *Rylands v Fletcher* truly involves strict liability it is possible to envisage cases where a defendant liable under the rule is devoid of any fault. Under Walsh J's reasoning in *O'Sullivan v Dwyer* [1971] IR 275 at 285, the plaintiff guilty of contributory negligence should receive no compensation in these circumstances. One strongly suspects that this logic would not appeal to a court today. *Cf* FLEMING, pp 386-387.
109. *Goldman v Hargrave* [1967] 1 AC 645; *Rickards v Lothian* [1913] AC 263; *Perry v Kendrick's Transport* [1956] 1 WLR 85 at 92; *Shell-Mex BP Ltd v Belfast Corporation* [1952] NI 72 (CA).
110. *Cf Box v Jubb* (1879) 4 Ex D 76; *Shell-Mex & BP Ltd v Belfast Corporation* [1952] NI 72 (CA). See also *Sheppard v Northern Ireland Housing Executive* [1984] NILR Bull No 1 (HC).
111. *Rylands v Fletcher* (1868) LR 3 HL 330.
112. *Hale v Jennings Bros* [1938] 1 All ER 579 (CA).
113. SALMOND & HEUSTON, p 387, Contrast FLEMING, p 389; and see *Fenn v Peterborough* (1979) 104 DLR (3d) 174 (Ont CA).
114. *Cf* SALMOND & HEUSTON, p 318, WINFIELD & JOLOWICZ, p 441.
115. SALMON & HEUSTON, p 318.
116. SALMON & HEUSTON (19th ed, 1985), p 372.
117. *Smith v Scott* [1973] Ch 314. So also where occupier is required by law to tolerate without objection the bringing of a thing onto his property by a person with statutory authority, he may not be liable: see *Burchett v Commissioner for Rys* [1958] SR (NSW) 366.
118. *Cf* eg *Shell-Mex & BP Ltd v Belfast Corporation* [1952] NI 72 (CA); STREET, pp 408-409.
119. *Cf* FLEMING, p 406.

## Act of God

**[25.38]** In *Rylands v Fletcher*,[120] Blackburn J stated that a defendant could "excuse himself by showing that the escape was the consequence of *vis major*, or the act of God."

**[25.39]** In only one reported British decision, *Nichols v Marsland*,[121] has the defence been successful. There the defendant had formed some artificial ornamental lakes on his property by damming up a stream. Owing to an extraordinarily violent storm, described by some witnesses as the heaviest in living memory, the embankments broke down and the rush of escaping floodwater carried away some of the plaintiff's bridges. Liability was not imposed on the defendant, the jury finding that the defendant could not reasonably have anticipated the events that occurred.

**[25.40]** It would appear that only the most extreme of natural phenomena will afford a good defence. Thus, gales in this country,[122] heavy rainfalls in Wales[123] and Scotland[124] and heavy snowfalls in England[125] have been held on the evidence not to have been "Acts of God". There is, however, some *obiter* support[126] for the view that a latent defect in a tree branch would fall within the concept of *vis major*.

**[25.41]** The issue has been analysed in two recent Irish decisions. In *Dockery v Manor Park Homebuilders Ltd*,[127] in 1995, O'Hanlon J held that the defence of "Act of God" had not been made out where rainfall of a kind that would occur once every twenty years led to flooding. In *Superquinn Ltd v Bray UDC*[128] in 1998, Laffoy J applied the defence apparently for the first time in an Irish court. The meteorological phenomenon involved in that case - Hurricane Charlie, in 1987 - was a far rarer occurrence. Laffoy J Gave a very thorough analysis of the law, in which she examined the conflicting lines of authority deriving from *Nichols v Marsland*[129] and *Greenock Corporation v Caledonian Railway*,[130] respectively. She preferred the former, which, she considered:

> "was more in line with the current concept of tortious liability under the rule in *Rylands v Fletcher*, as exemplified by the decision of the House of Lords in *Cambridge Water Co v Eastern Counties Leather plc* [131]..."[132]

---

120. (1866) LR 1 Ex 265 at 278.
121. (1876) 2 Ex D 1, criticised by Goodhart 'The Third Man' [1951] CLP 177 at 178-182. *Cf Greenock Corporation v Caledonian Ry* [1917] AC 556; see also *Ross v Dunphy* High Court, 13 February 1978 (Finlay P).
122. *Lawler v Sir James Mackey Ltd* (1949) 83 ILTR 139 (CC). See also *Mullan v Forrester* [1921] 2 IR 412; *Ross v Dunphy* High Court, 13 February 1978.
123. *AG v Cory Bros* (1919) 35 Times LR 570 at 574. *Cf* [1921] 1 AC 521 at 536; *Sedleigh Denfield v O'Callaghan* [1940] AC 880 at 889.
124. *Greenock Corporation v Caledonian Ry* [1917] AC 556.
125. *Fenwick v Schmaltz* (1868) LR 3 CP 313 at 316; *Slater v Worthington's Cash Stores* [1941] 1 KB 488 at 492.
126. *Noble v Harrison* [1926] 2 KB 332 at 343.
127. High Court, 10 April 1995 (O'Hanlon J).
128. High Court, 18 February 1998 (Laffoy J).
129. (1876) 2 Ex D 1.
130. [1917] AC 556.
131. [1994] 2 AC 264 (HL).
132. Page 76 of Laffoy J's judgment.

**[25.42]** In its formal enunciation, the rule stated in the *Cambridge Water Co* case would not assist a defendant in an almost all cases where the defence of "Act of God" is advanced, since what is usually in issue is not the foreseeability of the kind of damage that occurred but rather the foreseeability of the occurrence of an escape which caused the damage. In *Superquinn* there could, clearly be no debate about the fact that, if the water escaped, it would cause flood damage. What was in issue was the foreseeability of such an escape occurring. Nevertheless, *Cambridge Water Co* was a decision taking the edge off the strictness of the liability that the rule in *Rylands v Fletcher* had represented. In that regard, it was not too surprising that Laffoy J might be disposed to follow the precedent of *Nichols v Marsland* rather than the very strict approach favoured in *Greenock Corporation*. If the High Court of Australia's decision in *Burnie Port Authority v General Jones Pty Ltd*[133] were to find favour in Ireland, "Act of God" would no longer be a distinct defence but would be subsumed within the issue of whether the defendant had been negligent. The unlikelihood of the escape would be a factor, but not a distinctive one on which liability would depend.

### Statutory Authority

**[25.43]** A statute may authorise the defendant to act in a manner that would otherwise involve liability under *Rylands v Fletcher*.[134] More frequently, a statute will authorise or require the performance of an activity that is likely to cause danger to others but be silent as to the application of the rule in *Rylands v Fletcher*.[135]

**[25.44]** In such cases, it appears that where the harm is a necessary incident of the activity authorised by the statute, liability under the rule will not attach (although the defendant may, of course, still be liable in negligence, unless the statutory provision goes so far as to exclude liability in negligence). Thus where a railway is authorised to run steam locomotives, it will not be liable if operating the trains causes sparks or vibrations.[136] Similar protection has been extended to public utilities which supply water, gas and electricity.[137]

## IV. The Future of the Rule in Irish Law

**[25.45]** As we mentioned at the beginning of our analysis of the subject, the rule in *Rylands* came under sudden judicial assault over the past decade. It did not withstand the scrutiny of the High Court of Australia, in *Burnie Port Authority v General Jones Pty Ltd*.[138] In their joint judgment, Mason CJ, Deane, Dawson, Toohey and Gaudron JJ

133. (1994) 179 CLR 520 (HC Austr).

134. (1868) LR 3 HL 330, affg (1866) LR 1 Ex 265.

135. (1868) LR 3 HL 330, affg (1866) LR 1 Ex 265.

136. *CPR v Roy* [1902] AC 220; *Vaughan v Taff Vale Ry* 5 (186) H & N 679; *Hammersmith Ry v Brand* (1869) LR 4 HL 171; *Cf* the Railway Fires Act 1905, as amended by the Railway Fires (Amendment) Act 1931.

137. *Benning v Wong* (1969) 122 CLR 249; *Dunne v NW Gas Board* [1964] 2 QB 806. See also the Fisheries (Consolidation) Act 1959, s 215, and the Fisheries Act 1980, s 61.

138. (1994) 179 CLR 520, analysed by Heuston & Buckley 'The Return of *Rylands v Fletcher*' (1994) 110 LQR 506; Fisher 'The Demise of the Rule in *Rylands v Fletcher*: Occams Razor and the Unifield Law of Negligence' (1994) 68 Austr LJ 462; Dziobon & Mullender 'Formalism Forever Thwarted: *Rylands v Fletcher* in Australia' [1995] Camb LJ 23.

analysed the core concepts on which the rule was founded. Noting that, in *Read v Lyons & Co Ltd*,[139] Lord Porter had referred to a possible future need to lay down principles for determining whether the requirements of danger and non-natural use had been satisfied, they found themselves:

> "unable to extract any such principles from the decided cases. Indeed, if the rule in *Rylands v Fletcher* is regarded as constituting a discrete area of the law of torts, it seems to us that the effect of past cases is that no such principles exist. In the absence of such principles, those twin requirements compound the other difficulties about the content of the 'rule' to such an extent that there is quite unacceptable uncertainty about the circumstances which give rise to its so-called 'strict liability'. The result is that the practical application of the rule in a case involving damage caused by the escape of a substance is likely to degenerate into an essentially unprincipled and *ad hoc* subjective determination of whether the particular facts of the case fall within undefined notions of what is 'special' or 'not ordinary'."[140]

**[25.46]** If the problems of the rule in *Rylands v Fletcher* were confined to the uncertainties of its content an application, it would be necessary for the courts to continue their "so far spectacularly unsatisfactory efforts" to resolve them. This was not, however, the position. Over the century and a quarter since its formulation, the rule had been progressively weakened and confined from within and the area of its operation had been progressively diminished by increasing assault from without, whence negligence had "progressively assumed dominion".[141]

**[25.47]** The intrusion of negligence principles into the rule could be identified in several aspects. Blackburn J's qualification, "which he [the owner/defendant] knows to be mischievous", had been refined into an objective test which was, at the least, a close equivalent of foreseeability of damage of the relevant kind. Negligence was a factor in determining whether the use of land was "not-natural". Moreover the defences of consent and "default of plaintiff" closely corresponded with the negligence defences of voluntary assumption of risk and contributory negligence. Taken in conjunction with the other defences to the rule, there was not much left of the strict liability principle on which it was ostensibly founded.

**[25.48]** The gradual dismantling of the original restriction on damages recoverable under the rule also reduces the difference between it and the negligence principle. In contrast to occupiers' liability towards entrants,[142] the rule in *Rylands v Fletcher* had never been seen as *exclusively* governing the liability of an occupier of land in respect of injury caused by the escape of a dangerous substance. This had allowed "ordinary" negligence principles to encompass and overlay the territory in which the rule in *Rylands v Fletcher* operated.

**[25.49]** The time had come for the rule to be restated in terms of negligence rather than strict liability. The principle of "non-delegable duty" was capable of embracing the kind of

139. [1947] AC 176.

140. (1994) 179 CLR 520 at 540.

141. (1994) 179 CLR 520 at 541.

142. *Commissioner for Railways v Quinlan* [1964] AC 1054 (PC). Of course, in Ireland, the Supreme Court decisions in *Purtill v Athlone UDC* [1968] IR 205and *McNamara v ESB* [1975] IR 226 destroyed this principle of exclusivity in relation to occupiers' liability. The equivalent breakthrough in Australia occurred in *Safeway Stores Pty Ltd v Zaluzna* (1987) 162 CLR 479.

case that arose under the rule in *Rylands v Fletcher*. The principal categories of care in which this principle should be applied were:

(i) adjoining owners of land in relation to work threatening support or common walls;

(ii) employers' duty to provided a safe system of work for their employees;

(iii) hospitals relative to patients;

(iv) school authorities relative to pupils, and (arguably)

(v) occupiers relative to invitees.

In most, if not all of these categories of case, the common element in the relationship, which generated the special responsibility to see that care was taken, was that:

> "the person on whom [the duty] is imposed has undertaken the care, supervision or control of the person or property of another or is so placed in relation to that person or his property as to assume a particular responsibility for his or her safety, in circumstances where the person affected might reasonably expect that due care will be exercised."[143]

Viewed from the perspective of the person to whom the non-delegable duty was owed, the cases were marked by "special dependence or vulnerability"[144] on his or her part.

**[25.50]** These elements were present in relationships where *Rylands v Fletcher* - liability was imposed:

> "One party to that relationship is a person who is in control of premises and who has taken advantage of that control to introduce thereon or to retain therein a dangerous substance or to undertake thereon a dangerous activity or to allow another person to do one of those things. The other party to that relationship is a person, outside the premises and without control over what occurs therein, whose person or property is thereby exposed to a foreseeable risk of danger 'which he knows to be mischievous if it gets on his neighbour's [property]'.[145] In such a case the person outside the premises is obviously in a position of special vulnerability and dependence. He or she is specially vulnerable to danger if reasonable precautions are not taken in relation to what is done on the premises. He or she is specially dependent upon the person in control of the premises to ensure that such reasonable precautions are in fact taken. Commonly, he or she will have neither the right nor the opportunity to exercise control over, or even to have foreknowledge of, what is done or allowed by the other party within the premises. Conversely, the person who introduces (or allows another to introduce) the dangerous substance or undertakes (or allows another to undertake) the dangerous activity on premises which he or she controls is 'so placed in relation to [the other] person or his property as to assume a particular responsibility for his or its safety'."[146]

**[25.51]** While in most cases, the rule in *Rylands v Fletcher* should be subsumed under the principle of a non-delegable duty in negligence, there might remain cases where it was "preferrable to see a defendant's liability in a *Rylands v Fletcher* situation as lying in nuisance (or even trespass) and not in negligence".[147] The joint judgment did not expand

---

143. *Kondis v State Transport Authority* (1984) 154 CLR 672 at 687 (HC, Austr).

144. *Burnie Port Authority v General Jones Pty Ltd* (1994) 179 CLR 520 at 551.

145. *Fletcher v Rylands* (1866) LR 1 Ex 265 at 280.

146. (1994) 179 CLR 520 at 551-552 (latter internal citation to Thayer 'Liability without Fault' (1916) 29 HLR 801 at 809.

147. (1994) 179 CLR 520 at 556.

on the circumstances in which this latter approach should be favoured. It did, however, include a laconic supporting footnote, in a reference to the English decision of *Cambridge Water Co v Eastern Counties Leather plc*.[148] To that case we now turn.

**[25.52]** In *Cambridge Water Co*, the House of Lords, guided by the law of nuisance,[149] which was considered to represent the natural home of the rule in *Rylands v Fletcher*, held that liability under the rule should be imposed only where the damage suffered by the plaintiff was of a kind that was reasonably foreseeable by the defendant. Their Lordships considered that the general tenor of Blackburn J's statement of principle of liability was that knowledge, or at least foreseability, of the risk was a prerequisite of the recovery of damages under the principle but that the principle was still one of strict liability in the sense that the defendant might be held liable notwithstanding that he had exercised al due care to prevent the escape from occurring. In *Cambridge Water Co* itself, the House of Lords held that no liability should be imposed because it was not foreseeable that chlorinated solvent used for industrial purposes seeping into the ground would find its way into a borehole more than a mile away.

**[25.53]** How are the Irish courts likely to respond to these developments? It is hard to make a confident prediction. Keane J, in *en passant* observations subsequent to *Burnie* and *Cambridge Water Co*, has indicated that he perceives the rule in *Rylands v Fletcher* as a "novel for[m] of liability"[150] (contrary to the understanding of the House of Lords in *Cambridge Water Co*) and involving a form of liability "where it could not be said that the injury or damage has been the result of any blameworthy conduct"[151] (contrary to the understanding of the High Court of Australia in *Burnie*). In adopting this traditional interpretation of the rule, Keane J was not attempting to review the present status of the rule in other common law jurisdictions. Clearly, in neither case were the decisions of *Burnie* or *Cambridge Water Co* cited to the Court because they were of no relevance to the issues before it.

**[25.54]** The *Cambridge Water Co* decision was, however, applied by Laffoy J in *Superquinn Ltd v Bray UDC*.[152] She observed that "[t]he nature of the liability of a defendant been clarified recently"[153] by *Cambridge Water Co*. She made no reference to *Burnie*. If *Burnie* had been applied to that facts of the case (which involved a flood in the wake of Hurricane Charlie) there would scarcely have been a doubt about the inevitability of a favourable outcome for Coillte.

**[25.55]** A strong argument can be made that the Irish courts should adopt *Burnie's* approach. Its devastating critique of the crucial concepts in the rule of *Rylands v Fletcher* is hard to refute. The time has surely come to abandon them in favour of the negligence principle.

---

148. [1994] 2 AC 264 (HL) analysed by Wilkinson '*Cambridge Water Company v Eastern Counties Leather plc*: Diluting Liability for Continuing Escapes' (1994) 57 MLR 799; Heuston & Buckley 'The Return of *Rylands v Fletcher*' (1994) 110 LQR 185; Weir '*Rylands v Fletcher* Reconsidered' [1994] Camb LJ 216. More generally, see Cross 'Does Only the Careless Polluter Pay? A Fresh Examination of the Nature of Private Nuisance' (1995) 111 LQR 445.

149. *Overseas Tankship (UK) Ltd v Miller Steamship Co Ltd* [1967] 1 AC 617 (PC).

150. *McDonnell v Ireland* Supreme Court, 23 July 1997 (Keane J).

151. *Iarnrod Éireann v Ireland* [1995] 2 ILRM 161 at 203 (HC).

152. High Court, 18 February 1998.

153. Page 70 of Laffoy J's judgment.

## Chapter 26

# Liability for Fire[1]


I. Introduction ........ 735
II. Occupiers' Liability for Fire ........ 736
III. Liability of Persons Other than the Occupier ........ 741


## I. Introduction

**[26.01]** The law of torts has had some difficulty in establishing a coherent set of principles of liability for injury or damage caused by fire. The very nature of fire raises problems in attempting to set out an orderly and fair balance between competing human interests. Fire is capable of inflicting enormous damage, with no regard for legal boundaries, yet it is a basic necessity in personal and economic life. It can be started easily, by accident or design, by adult or child, by the sane or the insane, by occupier or trespasser, or indeed by forces of nature without any human intervention. The concepts that tort law normally adopts - such as negligence, trespass, occupation duties, strict liability, and vicarious liability - are not very satisfactory in relation to fire, since the contexts in which it may result in injury or damage are so various and complex. Since fire of its nature, can bring benefit or disaster, potential destroyer, the law has necessarily been obliged to adopt a somewhat ambiguous response when addressing its liability isue for damage caused by fire.

**[26.02]** Historically, liability for fire was perceived principally as arising in the context of the spread of fire from one person's property to the property of another. Accordingly the law has tended to be discussed even today in the context of liability arising from occupation or ownership of land. In truth, of course, liability for injury resulting from fire may arise in many other contexts. An arsonist is liable in tort, for example, just as is a driver of a car whose negligence causes injury by fire to another road user. More controversially, it may be claimed that governmental or local authorities should be held liable for the negligent discharge of their supervisory functions in relation to fire safety. In this chapter, we examine first the matter of occupiers' liability for fire. We then turn to the question of liability arising in other contexts, including the position under the Fire Services Act 1981. Finally, we consider the legal position of those affected by the threat of fire, and of those who are injured in attempting to extinguish or control a fire.

1. The leading analysis is Osborough 'Liability in Tort for Unintended Fire Damage' (1971) 6 Ir Jur (ns) 205. See also Anon 'The Accidental Fires Act, 1943' (1943) 9 Ir Jur 5; Newark 'The Accidental Fires Act (Northern Ireland) 1944' (1945) 6 NILQ 134; Foote 'Liability for Fire Before 1800' (1969) 20 NILQ 141; Ogus 'Vagaries in Liability for the Escape of Fire' [1969] Camb LJ 104; PROSSER & KEETON, pp 543-545.

## II. Occupiers' Liability for Fire

**[26.03]** At common law, strict liability was imposed on occupiers for the spread of fires.[2] By an Act in 1715,[3] however, it was provided that no action should be taken against any person in whose "house or chamber" a fire accidentally began. In *Richardson v Athlone Woollen Mills Co Ltd*,[4] in 1942, the Supreme Court held that a factory could not be regarded as a "house or chamber". O'Byrne J referred to legislation in England which had extended the scope of protection to other buildings and commented:

> "It may well be that the time has arrived when similar provision should be made in this country; but, in the meantime, the Courts must administer the law as they find it."[5]

**[26.04]** The following year legislation was enacted on these lines.[6] Section 1(1) of the Accidental Fires Act 1943[7] (the 1943 Act) provides that:

> "Where any person (in this section referred to as the injured person) has suffered damage by reason of fire accidentally occurring ... in or on the building or land of another person, then, notwithstanding any rule of law ... no legal proceedings shall be instituted in any court by the injured person or any person claiming through or under him or as his insurer against such other person on account of such damage."

**[26.05]** "Building" is defined as including "any structure of whatsoever material or for whatever purpose used".[8] The expression "building or land of another person" might suggest that that person must be the owner of the premises in question. The precise limits of the term have not been laid down by the courts but it seems safe to state that it extends also to persons who are in occupation of the premises.

**[26.06]** It seems that "accidentally" means "without negligence". This is the effect of the decisions[9] but, as Professor Osborough notes,[10] legislation[11] enacted in Northern Ireland the following year might suggest that the term could extend to all non-intentional fires.

---

2. Newark 'The Accidental Fires Act (Northern Ireland) 1944' (1945) 6 NILQ 134; Wigmore 'Responsibility for Tortious Acts: Its History' (1894) III, 7 Harv LR 441 at 448 449; *cf* Winfield 'The Myth of Absolute Liability' (1926) 42 LQR 37 at 46 50.
3. An Act for preventing Mischief that may happen by fire (2 Geo 1 c 5).
4. [1942] IR 581 (SC).
5. [1942] IR 581 (SC).
6. The legislation was clearly in response to the *Athlone Woollen Mills* decision. The Minister for Industry and Commerce, Mr Lemass, explained that this was the case, adding that the legislation "simply proposes to make it clear that the legal position will henceforth be what until the recent Supreme Court decision, it was always commonly assumed to be": 89 Dail Debates Col 1405 (24 March 1943).
7. Accidental Fires Act 1943 (No 8).
8. Section 1(3).
9. *Cf Ruttledge v Land* [1930] IR 537; *Gaynor v McGinn* [1933] LJ Ir 70 (CC), (noted by Anon, *Rylands v Fletcher* [1933] LJ Ir 105); *Kelly v McElligott* (1951) 85 ILTR 4. See Osborough 'Liability in Tort for Unintended Fire Damage' (1971) 6 Ir Jur (ns) 205 at 206-207. Where injury or damage is intentionally caused by fire - arson, for example - the transgressor will be liable for trespass (to the person, chattels or land). In the unlikely event of trespass not applying on account of a difficulty in showing that the injury or damage was directly sustained, it seems reasonable to assume that an innominate basis of liability would be recognised by the court.
10. Osborough 'Liability in Tort for Unintended Fire Damage' (1971) 6 Ir Jur (ns) 205 at 207.
11. Accidental Fires Act (NI) 1944, analysed by Newark in (1945) 6 NILQ 134.

**[26.07]** Let us first examine the range of persons for whose negligence the occupier may be vicariously liable.

**[26.08]** A somewhat imprecise dividing line recognised in the decisions is that an occupier is liable for the spread of fire caused upon his or her land by anyone but a stranger,[12] but who is a "stranger" for this purpose? It seems clear that members of the occupier's family are not strangers,[13] nor are their guests[14] or employees,[15] at least where they are acting within the course of their employment.[16]

**[26.09]** It also seems that an occupier will be liable for fires caused by persons on the property with his or her licence.[17] It has been observed that imposing liability in such a case:

> "is more consistent with justice than in its absence. The occupier, knowing the nature of the licence he grants, and the characteristics and tendencies of the persons to whom he grants it, can, by the exercise of proper care, safeguard his property and his neighbours from the danger of fire. The neighbour is not in the same advantageous position."[18]

**[26.10]** In truth, of course, the occupier often will have no opportunity to exert any control over the licensees in respect of many activities involving the risk of fire. The occupier will not be standing by their side when they throw away a lighted match, for example. The law here in many cases is really selecting between two innocent persons as to who should bear the loss. This is also the case in respect of damage caused by fires created on the occupier's land by his or her independent contractors: again liability may be imposed on the occupier for the acts of such persons.[19]

**[26.11]** The next question we must examine concerns the nature of conduct that is denominated "negligent". Negligence may arise either in respect of the creation of the fire or in failure to control it adequately. Clearly it would be negligent for a person to start a fire by carelessly dropping a lighted match on inflammable material. An interesting example of the failure to control a fire adequately arose in the High Court decision of *McKenzie v O'Neill & Roe Ltd*[20] On a summer's day after a dry spell, a director of the defendant company burned papers that had accumulated on the company's premises on the slopes of the Dublin mountains. The day in question was windy and, although after a time the fire seemed to the director's satisfaction to have been extinguished, it later spread to a

---

12. *Boulcott Golf Club Inc v Engelbrecht* [1945] NZLR 556 at 558 (SC); *Balfour v Barty-King* [1957] I QB 496 at 504 (CA).
13. *Cf* WINFIELD & JOLOWICZ, p 560 (referring to the wife of the occupier).
14. *Crogate v Morris* (1617) 1 Brown & Gold 197, 123 ER 751; *Iverson v Purser* (1990) 73 DLR (4th) 33.
15. WINFIELD & JOLOWICZ, p 560.
16. *Cf M'Kenzie v M'Leod* (1834) 10 Bing 385, 131 ER 953.
17. *Cf Holderness v Goslin* [1975] 2 NZLR 46.
18. *Boulcott Golf Club Inc v Engelbrecht* [1945] NZLR 556 at 559.
19. *Balfour v Barty-King* [1957] I QB 496. *Cf Eriksen v Clifton* [1963] NZLR 705; *H & N Emanuel Ltd v Greater London Council* [1971] 2 All ER 835 (CA). See further WINFIELD & JOLOWICZ, p 560; FLEMING, p 394.
20. High Court, 23 June 1977 (Hamilton J). The case is discussed at para **[2.56]** above, in relation to the issue of proof of causation.

neighbouring property where it burned gorse, heather and other shrubs planted by the plaintiff. In imposing liability, Hamilton J stated that he was:

> "satisfied that having regard to the conditions prevailing at the time, the nature of the wind and the dryness of the conditions and the nature of the growth in the area it was negligent on the part of [the director] to light a fire on the defendant company's premises without taking adequate precautions to ensure that it was extinguished or that no portion of the material being burned or sparks would be blown by the wind on to the adjoining premises."[21]

**[26.12]** Although (as has been mentioned) an occupier will not as such be vicariously liable in negligence for the acts of a stranger, such as a trespasser, the occupier may be personally liable, as where he or she fails to extinguish a fire caused by such a stranger, or, indeed, a fire arising from natural causes, such as lightning.[22] In the Privy Council decision of *Goldman v Hargrave*,[23] the Judicial Committee accepted that this was so, but stressed that the individual circumstances of the occupier would have to be taken into account in determining whether the occupier had acted reasonably:

> "Thus, less must be expected of the infirm than of the able-bodied: the owner of a small property where a hazard arises which threatens a neighbour with substantial interests should not have to do so much as one with larger interests of his own at stake and greater resources to protect them: if the small owner does what he can and promptly calls on his neighbour to provide additional resources, he may be held to have done his duty: he should not be liable unless it is clearly proved that he could, and reasonably in his individual circumstance should, have done more."[24]

**[26.13]** It seems reasonable to assume that our courts would adopt a broadly similar approach. Indeed, it is possible that they would lay somewhat less stress than did the Judicial Committee on the individual circumstances of the occupier as a basis for exempting the occupier from responsibility.[25] A decision of the House of Lords in 1987 addressed the question of when an occupier should be liable in negligence for damage to neighbouring property resulting from a fire lit by an intruder on the occupier's property. In *Smith v Littlewoods Organization Ltd*,[26] the owners of an empty and unattended cinema,

---

21. Page 6 of Hamilton J's judgment. See also the decisions cited in fn 9 above.

22. *Cf Goldman v Hargrave* [1967] 1 AC 645 (PC). See also *Boatswain v Crawford* [1943] NZLR 109 (SC); *Landon v Rutherford* [1951] NZLR 975 (SC) - fires of unknown origin.

23. [1967] 1 AC 645, analysed by Roberts, (1967) 30 MLR 445; Harris, [1967] Camb LR 25 and Anderson, (1968) 3 UBC LR 211.

24. [1967] 1 AC at 663. In adopting this subjective standard, the Judicial Committee were influenced by cases drawn from the law of nuisance: *Job Edwards Ltd v Birmingham Navigations* [1924] I KB 341; *Pontardawe RDC v Moore-Gwyn* [1929] 1 Ch 656. *Cf* Roberts, (1967) 30 MLR 445 at 450.

25. The English decision of *Herrington v British Rys Bd* [1972] AC 877 (HL) stressed the individual circumstances of the occupier as a factor in determining the scope of his duty to trespassers; the philosophy of *Goldman v Hargrave* appears to have had some influence: see, especially, [1972] AC at 920-921. *Cf* Matthews, [1927] Camb LJ 214. at 216, (1972) 35 MLR 409 at 413.

26. [1987] 1 All ER 710 (HL), noted by Fleming, [1987] Camb LJ 208. In *Doherty Timber Ltd v Drogheda Harbour Commissioners* [1993] ILRM 401 (HC), Flood J held that the defendants were not liable in negligence for the destruction by fire of the plaintiff's timber. The fire had been caused by children. The plaintiff, to whom the timber had been consigned, had been permitted to leave it for a period on the quayside at its own risk. Flood J considered that in the circumstances "there was no common law duty of care imposed on the harbour commissioners".

which they intended in due course to demolish, were held not liable to a neighbouring owner for damage caused by a fire lit by children trespassing in the cinema. There was some degree of disagreement as to the scope of an occupier's duty in such circumstances. This matter has been dealt with earlier.[27]

**[26.14]** On the general question of negligence, it should be noted, finally, that, the occupier may, of course, be liable in negligence in some capacity other than that of occupier. Thus, for example, where an employee is injured by fire on the employer's premises as a result of the employer's negligence or breach of statutory duty as employer, the employee may recover damages.

**[26.15]** It seems clear[28] that the 1943 Act confers immunity (in the absence of negligence on the part of the defendant) even where there has been no spread of fire from the defendant's premises to those of the victim. Thus, if a fire on the defendant's premises injures or damages the person or property of another on the premises at the time - in a public building,[29] such as a library or hospital, for example - the 1943 Act will apply. (As we shall see presently, the Fire Services Act 1981 alters the position in relation to such buildings. )

## Fire and Causation of Damage

**[26.16]** Where a person is injured or killed because of the failure of an occupier to provide a safe means of escape,[30] will the Accidental Fires Act 1943 exempt the occupier from responsibility? This question arose in *Woods v O'Connor*,[31] where an hotel guest was injured in a fire because the windows in his room could not be opened. Deale J held that the hotel keeper was not liable.

**[26.17]** He stated:

> "It is of course true that the means of exit used by the plaintiff was not safe, and that there was no other means open to him when the fire cut him off from the stairs. But, he was only using this exit because of the fire; if there had been no fire, and he had wished to leave his room, he would have used the door, landing and stairs. It is clear therefore that the fire was the cause of the injuries, and there is no evidence to show what started the fire. This means that the plaintiff has failed to show that the fire was not accidental, and so has failed to take the case out of the protection afforded by the . . . Act ',[32]

**[26.18]** This approach has rightly been criticised[33] because it wrongly identifies the fire as the only cause of the plaintiff's injuries. To regard the defendant's negligence in failing to provide a safe means of escape as devoid of causal potency is surely unconvincing.

---

27. *Cf* paras **[26.08]-[26.10]** above.
28. *Cf* Osborough 'Liability in Tort for Unintended Fire Damage' (1971) 6 Ir Jur (ns) 205 at 209-210; Anon 'The Accidental Fires Act 1943' (1943) 9 Ir Jur 51 at 52.
29. Hotels are now dealt with under specific legislation: *cf* Hotel Proprietors Act 1963 (No 7), especially s 11. The section was designed to overrule *Woods v O'Connor* [1958] Ir Jur Rep 71 (CC), which had conferred immunity under the 1943 Act on hotel proprietors. *Cf Hanley v Bethell Hotels Ltd* (1917) 52 ILTR 10 (CC), holding the opposite in respect of the 1715 Act.
30. *Cf* Malone 'Ruminations on Cause-In-Fact' (1956) 9 Stan LR 60 at 77-81.
31. [1958] Ir Jur 71 (CC).
32. [1958] Ir Jur 71 at 72.
33. By Osborough 'Liability in Tort for Unintended Fire Damage' (1971) 6 Ir Jur (ns) 205 at 210.

## Does "Damage" Include Personal injures?

**[26.19]** It has been held[34] that immunity under the Act extends beyond mere property damage to personal injuries. This interpretation has been questioned[35] by Professor Osborough who argues that the value placed on human life might be one reason, in terms of social policy, why immunity should be restricted to property damage.

## The Burden of Proof Under the Act

**[26.20]** There is divided authority[36] on the question of the burden of proof under the Act. The better view appears to be that the plaintiff must show that the fire was caused otherwise than by accident.

## Remedies Not Defeated by the Act

**[26.21]** The Act, as we have seen, provides that in the case of damage suffered by reason of fire accidentally occurring on another's premises "then, notwithstanding any rule of law",[37] no legal proceedings may be instituted against him. This appears to close the door[38] to the possibility of taking proceedings against him under the rule in *Rylands v Fletcher*.[39] The view has been canvassed[40] that there might be a way around this difficulty by identifying the anterior risk as the effective cause of the damage; whether the Courts would be willing to subscribe to this analysis is, however, far from certain.

**[26.22]** At all events the remedy in negligence remains,[41] though, as we have seen,[42] its precise scope may give rise to difficulty. Moreover an occupier who intentionally burns down his neighbour's property through the medium of a fire started and allowed to spread

---

34. *Woods v O'Connor*, [1958] Ir Jur Rep 71 (CC).

35. Osborough 'Liability in Tort for Unintended Fire Damage' (1971) 6 Ir Jur (ns) 205 at 211.

36. *Gaynor v McGinn* [1933] LJ Ir 70 (CC) - onus was on the defendant to show that he had not been negligent: *Woods v O'Connor* [1958] Ir Jur 71 (CC) - onus was on the plaintiff to show the fire had been caused otherwise than by accident. English authority favours the latter approach: *Masons v Levy Auto Parts of England Ltd* [1967] 2 QB 530; *Collingwood v Home & Colonial Stores Ltd* [1936] 3 All ER 200 (CA). *Mulholland & Tedd Ltd v Baker* [1939] 3 All ER 253 (KB). Canadian authority is in accord: *Franks v Sanderson* (1988) 25 BCLR (2d) 248 (CA).

37. Section 1(1) of the Act.

38. *Cf* Osborough 'Liability in Tort for Unintended Fire Damage' (1971) 6 Ir Jur (ns) 205 at 214 215, Carroll '*The Rule in Rylands v Fletcher*: A Re-Assessment' (1973) 8 Ir Jur (ns) 208 at 222. Where the fire occurs off the defendant's premises, then the language of s 1(1) of the 1943 Act would not appear to exclude liability under the rule in *Rylands v Fletcher*, since the exemption from responsibility which it affords arises only where the fire "accidentally occur[s] in or on the building or land" of the defendant.

39. See Ch 25 above.

40. *Cf* Osborough 'Liability in Tort for Unintended Fire Damage' (1971) 6 Ir Jur (ns) 205 at 214-215. Some support for this approach towards analysing the true policy basis of the rule in *Rylands v Fletcher* maybe gleaned in Goodhart 'The Third Man or Novus Actus Interveniens' (1951) 4 CLP 177. *Cf* Hart & Honoré, *Causation in the Law* (1959), p 265ff.

41. *Cf* Osborough 'Liability in Tort for Unintended Fire Damage' (1971) 6 Ir Jur (ns) 205 at 215-216. An action for breach of statutory duty might also be available: *cf* at 216; and see *Gaynor v McGinn* [1933] LJ Ir 70.

42. See para **[26.16]** above, discussing *Woods v O'Connor* [1958] Ir Jur Rep 71.

from the occupier's own property will not be allowed to invoke s 1(1) of the 1943 Act as the fire has not "accidentally occurred".

## III. Liability of Persons Other than the Occupier

**[26.23]** As has been already mentioned, liability for fire may attach to persons other than an occupier of a building or land. An arsonist will, of course, be liable in tort - almost certainly for trespass (to land, chattels or the person) - but in the unlikely event of the damage being regarded as indirect and thus outside the scope of trespass, it seems inconceivable that the Court would deny a remedy in case.

**[26.24]** The case of the negligent road user, which has already been mentioned, is another obvious case where liability may be imposed. So also, the manufacturer of a dangerous product which goes on fire when in the possession of a consumer may be liable for the damage caused.[43] An employer may be liable in negligence for exposing an employee to unreasonable risk in relation to fire. This could happen where the employer ought to be aware of another employee's propensity to injure the plaintiff employee by fire[44] or where the employer carelessly supplies equipment which involves the risk of fire,[45] fails to provide the equipment necessary to prevent or reduce injury from fire[46] or fails to take reasonable care in relation to the premises where the employee is working.[47] Other less direct types of negligence may also arise; with the recent extension of liability on the part of governmental or local authorities for negligent discharge of their supervisory functions, it is possible that the negligent discharge of these functions in relation to fire safety legislation and regulations could give rise to liability in negligence.[48] So far as the Fire

---

43. *Robinson v Technico Ltd* Supreme Court, 1954, affg High Court, 1953. *Cf Sweeney v North Western Health Board and Siemens* [1996] Ir L Log W 394 (CC) - manufacturer of physiotherapy hydrotherm machine not liable for misuse of equipment by physiotherapist, resulting in fire that injured patient.

44. *Hough v Irish Base Metals Ltd* Supreme Court, 8 December 1967.

45. *Cf Phillips v Durgan* [1991] ILRM 321 (SC) - independent contractor.

46. *Heeney v Dublin Corporation* High Court, 16 May 1991 (Barron J).

47. *Cf Dillon v Irish Industrial Explosives Ltd* High Court, 27 October 1998 (Johnson J). It is worth noting that *Cullinane v Waterford County Council* [1997] Ir L Log W 309 (CC), Judge Sheridan, while rejecting the argument that a negligence claim by a farmer against a fire authority for sending a brigade with an allegedly faulty gauge fell outside the immunity conferred on the defendant by s 36 of the Fire Services Act 1981, is reported (at 310) as having:

 > "expressed the view that it would be going too far suggests that s 36 would allow a fire authority to ignore the essential duties it had under statute and common law to provide a safe place of work in a safe system of work and proper and safe plant and appliances."

 See further Hogan and Morgan, *Administrative Law in Ireland* (3rd ed, 1998), pp 809-810.

48. The English Court of Appeal so held in *Capital & Counties plc v Hampshire County Council* [1997] QB 1004 but only to the extent that the fire authority's actions *made matters worse* (by switching off a sprinkler system). For critical analysis of this restrictive approach, see Bartlett & Waite 'Searching for Duties of Care: The Fire Brigade Cases' [1997] JPIL 147; 'Negligence in the Public Sphere: Is Clarity Possible?' (2000) 51 NILQ 25; 'The Emergency Services, "999" Calls and the Duty of Care' (2000) 16 Prof Neg 171; '"*Caparo under Fire*": A Study into the Effects upon the Fire Services of Liability in Negligence' (2000) 63 MLR 502. *Capital & Counties* was distinguished (unconvincingly) in *Kent v Griffiths (No 3)* [2000] All ER 474 (CA), on the basis that an ambulance service protects individual patients rather than the general public, which the fire service was considered to protect.

Services Act 1981 is concerned, s 36 appears to have the effect of rendering the authorities exempt from such a claim, though the scope of that section is less than fully clear. We examine it below.

**[26.25]** Persons who are not owners or occupiers of a building or land may also, of course, be liable for other torts where damage results from fire. Whilst, as has been mentioned, the better view is that the Accidental Fires Act 1943 excludes liability on the part of occupier or owner under the rule in *Rylands v Fletcher*, this protection will not extend to other persons - such as licensees under common law. The merging of licensees and invitees into the category of visitors, effected by the Occupiers Liability Act 1995, raises an issue as to how the courts should now draw the line. In view of the breadth of definition of visitors, it may be argued that the 1943 Act does not extend to them. Moreover, fires causing damage to agricultural land or crops "arising from sparks or cinders emitted from any locomotive engine used on a railway,"[49] now controlled by statute,[50] have been recognised[51] as falling under the rule in *Rylands v Fletcher*.

**[26.26]** The Fire Services Act 1981 (the 1981 Act) was enacted in the wake of the "Stardust" tragedy in March of that year. The Act makes provision for the establishment of fire authorities and the organisation of fire services and for fire safety, fire fighting, and the protection and rescue of persons and property. It lays down wide-ranging duties, backed by criminal sanctions. Of particular relevance is s 18, which prescribes general obligations with regard to fire safety in relation to a defined list[52] of premises used for

---

48. (contd) In *Cullinane v Waterford County Council* [1997] Ir L Log W 309 (CC), Judge Sheridan discussed the High Court judgment in *Capital & Counties*. He conceded that the fire authority, as employer, might be liable for a negligent omission relative to its employees, but so far as its duty to property owners was concerned, he appeared to favour the distinction between a positive act that made matters worse (which could involve liability, subject possibly to the immunity conferred by s 36 of the Fire Services Act 1981) and an omission, such as arriving to fight a fire with a faulty gauge. Judge Sheridan is reported as having stated (at 311) that:

> "he did not believe it would be a sound proposition that modern, effective and working equipment should be a *sine qua non* for a fire brigade hastening to the scene of a conflagration pursuant to its duties under the Act of 1981".

49. *Cf* Harper & Harper 'Establishing Railroad Liability for Fires' (1929) 77 U Pa LR 629.

50. Railway Fires Act 1905, as amended by the Railway Fires (Amendment) Act 1931 (£200 maximum award).

51. *Jones v Festiniog Ry* (1868) LR 3 QB 733.

52. Subsection (1) provides that the section applies to premises or any part of them put to any of the following uses:
    - (a) use as, or for any purpose involving the provision of, sleeping accommodation, excluding premises consisting of a dwelling house occupied as a single dwelling;
    - (b) use as, or as part of, an institution providing treatment or care;
    - (c) use for purposes of entertainment, recreation or instruction or for the purpose of any club, society or association;
    - (d) use for purposes of teaching, training or research;
    - (e) use for any purpose involving access to the premises by members of the public, whether on payment or otherwise; and
    - (f) use for any other prescribed purpose, but excluding -
      - (i) premises used as a factory within the meaning of the Safety in Industry Acts, 1955 and 1980;
      - (ii) premises used as a store and subject to licensing under regulations made under the Dangerous Substances Act, 1972.

prescribed purposes, such as hostels, hospitals, places of entertainment, schools and colleges, but not premises used as a factory within the meaning of the Safety in Industry legislation.

**[26.27]** Section 18(2) imposes a duty on every person having control over any of these premises:

> "to take all reasonable measures to guard against the outbreak of fire on such premises and to ensure as far as is reasonably practicable the safety of persons on the premises in the event of an outbreak of fire."

**[26.28]** A strong case may be made for interpreting this provision as generating civil liability in the event of its breach, at least in regard to the failure to protect the safety of people on the premises. This is scarcely a great expansion of liability, however, since the subsection appears to go little further than the position at common law. However, it surely guarantees that an unjust decision such as *Woods v O'Connor*[53] will not recur; in an assault on an over-broad interpretation of the immunity afforded by the 1943 Act, there may well be a strategic advantage to the plaintiff in clothing what is in essence a negligence claim in the language of a provision of the 1981 Act.

**[26.29]** Section 18(3) provides that it is the duty of every person on one of these premises:

> "to conduct himself in such a way as to ensure that as far as is reasonably practicable every person on the premises is not exposed to danger from fire as a consequence of any act or omission of his".

This is a broad provision, with uncertain implications in relation to civil liability. Even more strongly than for s 18(2), it may be argued that s 18(3) clearly identifies the persons whom it seeks to protect and the type of damage (personal injury to them) which it seeks to prevent. However, the very generality of the language in the subsection may tell against it when the question whether it generates civil liability arises. It is to be hoped that our courts interpret it as having this function. Again, it is expressed in language very similar to that of common law negligence.

**[26.30]** The reference to an "omission" might suggest that failure to rescue a person could come within the scope of s 12(3). If so, this would mean that the subsection had introduced a statutory duty to rescue, limited to the control of fires, quite similar to that already existing in some other jurisdictions. Such an interpretation could however, be challenged. For liability to arise the omission must result in a person's being "exposed to danger from fire"; if he is already exposed to fire and thus in need of rescue, it would seem more natural to say that a failure to rescue enhanced the existing danger or at the least failed to mitigate it, rather than it "exposed" the person in peril to some new danger. As against this, if the criticisms[54] of Judge Deale's narrow interpretation of causation in *Woods v O'Connor*[55] is sound, there may be an argument for taking an expansive approach to the interpretation of exposing a person to danger.

**[26.31]** A most important provision is contained in s 36, to the effect that:

> [n]o action or other proceeding shall lie or be maintainable against the Minister [for the Environment], or against a fire authority[56] or a sanitary authority or any officer or servant of,

53. See paras **[26.16]-[26.17]** above.

54. See paras **[26.18]** above.

55. [1958] Ir Jur 71 (CC).

or person engaged by, any such authority for the recovery of damages in respect of injury to persons or property alleged to have been caused or contributed to by the failure to comply with any functions conferred by this Act.

**[26.32]** Clearly the intention here is to exempt governmental and local authorities (and their employees) from civil liability as a result of their failure to comply with any functions conferred on them by the Act.[57] An action for breach of statutory duty under the Act against these authorities would therefore fail. However, what of an action for negligence where the gravamen of the claim is one of negligent exercise of powers or other functions prescribed by the Act? One interpretation is that s 36 excludes this action as well, on the basis that, to succeed in the action, the plaintiff is obliged to allege that his injury has been "caused" - or at all events, "contributed to" - by "the failure to comply with" a function conferred by the Act. Another, opposite, interpretation is that the claim for negligence is concerned, not so much with the failure to comply with a statutory function, as with common law negligence in the performance of that statutory function. That is, apart altogether from s 36, such a claim in negligence would not be defeated by proof merely of an authority's compliance with its statutory functions. The failure of compliance is not always integral to the plaintiff's claim: an authority which had without question complied with its functions, in the sense of satisfying the requirements of the Act, could equally without question have done so in a manner that involves it in liability in negligence at common law. This being so, it seems that s 36 should not kill an action against an authority for negligence in the discharge of its functions under the Act. However, where an action either for breach of statutory duty or in negligence is based on the failure to comply with these functions, it would fall under the exclusion prescribed by s 36.

## Contributory Negligence

**[26.33]** As a general principle, an attempt to escape from a fire affords a classic example of conduct in "the agony of the moment"[58] in respect of which a somewhat indulgent standard should be applied when determining whether the person so attempting to escape

56. *Cf* Fire Services Act 1981, s 9.

57. Whether this attempt to confer immunity from suit is constitutional is a separate question. *Cf* Forde, *Constitutional Law of Ireland* (1987), pp 286-287; Casey, *Constitutional Law in Ireland* (1987), p 47; Hogan & Whyte, *Kelly: The Irish Constitution* (3rd ed, 1994), p 1152.

58. It is interesting to note that in the Circuit Court decision of *Cullinane v Waterford County Council* [1997] Ir L Log W 309, Judge Sheridan did not completely exclude the possibility that an appropriate claim for negligence against a fire authority might fall outside the immunity afforded by section 36. He acknowledged that s 36 did not defeat a claim by employees of an authority, for its failure to provide a safe place of work, a safe system of work or proper sale plant and appliances. He did not consider, however, that the fact that a fire brigade had arrived at the scene of a fire on the plaintiff's farm to fight the fire with a faulty gauge "was ... sufficient to take it out of the scope of section 36". What Judge Sheridan appeared to envisage here was the distinction between omissions and acts positively worsening the situation, which has found favour with the English courts in relation to local authorities. Judge Sheridan's particular solicitude for the rights of employees echoes that of the Supreme Court in *Ryan v Ireland* [1989] IR 177. In this context, Hogan & Morgan, *Administrative Law in Ireland* (3rd ed, 1998), pp 809-810 observe that:

> "... surely a shadow must hang over the validity of s 36 of the Fire Services Act 1981, at least in so far as it precludes a fireman from suing a fire authority in respect of the negligent discharge of their statutory duties. It is difficult to see how such an immunity could survive if an analogous common law immunity enjoyed by the Defence Forces has been condemned as unconstitutional."

was guilty of contributory negligence. In *Kelly v McElligott*,[59] however, the one reported decision in which the question was analysed, a somewhat strict approach appears to have been adopted by the majority of the former Supreme Court. The plaintiff, a hotel guest, was injured when making her escape from her bedroom when fire had broken out in the hotel. She chose to leave via a flat roof because the staircase was full of smoke. In crossing the roof, she fell through a skylight which was clearly visible to her and sustained the injuries for which she sought compensation. A jury finding that she had not been guilty of contributory negligence was overturned by a majority[60] of the Supreme Court, who gave judgment for the defendant. O'Byrne J for the majority, stressed the fact that the skylight was plainly visible, and stated[61] that the trial judge should have ruled inadmissible evidence that the plaintiff was terrified on account of a previous experience of having seen a hospital fire in England during a wartime air raid. The majority holding, which appears very harsh to the modern reader, can probably best be understood as a product of the unsatisfactory "all-or-nothing" approach which then prevailed in respect of contributory negligence, no question of the "last opportunity" arising on the facts of the case.

## Rescuers[62]

**[26.34]** It is now clear that persons who are injured while rescuing others trapped by a fire may claim damages on the ordinary principles of negligence. In *D'Urso v Samson*,[63] in 1939, a night-watchman, after coming out of his employer's factory to give warning of a fire, returned and was burnt to death. The defences of voluntary assumption of risk and *novus actus interveniens* were rejected (although at that time rescuers as a general class had only recently come to be looked on with favour by the courts).[64] Simonds J stressed that the deceased had been employed to protect the premises from fire and that his actions should be regarded:

> "as merely part of the single transaction which consisted of discovering the fire, taking some steps (it may be) to put it out, going out of the premises and calling for aid, and returning to do what more he could to save these premises".[65]

**[26.35]** It gradually came to be recognised that a fire fighter[66] should not normally be defeated by the claim of voluntary assumption of risk. In *Ogwo v Taylor*[67] in 1987, Lord

59. (1951) 85 ILTR 4 (SC). *Cf Rodriguez v Shelter Canadian Properties Ltd* (1997) Ont CJ LEXIS 1796. See para **[26.18]** above.

60. Murnaghan, Geoghegan and O'Byrne JJ; Maguire CJ and Black J dissenting.

61. 85 ILTR at 7. O'Byrne J's stress on the fact that contributory negligence is "to be determined by objective, and not subjective standards" finds support in *Kingston v Kingston* (1968) 102 ILTR 65 (SC).

62. This topic is considered in more detail in the general context of negligence actions, see paras **[20.78]**-**[20.92]** above.

63. [1939] 4 All ER 26 (KBD).

64. Contrast *Cutler v United Dairies (London) Ltd* [1933] 2 KB 297 with *Haynes v Harwood* [1935] 1 KB 146. The change in thinking in English law owed a great deal to the influence of United States decisions, brought to the attention of the profession by Professor Goodhart, (1935) 5 Camb LJ 192.

65. [1939] 4 All ER at 30.

66. *Merrington v Ironbridge Metalworks Ltd* [1952] 1 All ER 1101; *Russell v McCabe* [1962] NZLR 392 (CA); *Salmon v Seafarer Restaurants Ltd (British Gas Corp, third party)* [1983] 3 All ER 729; *Ogwo v Taylor* [1988] AC 431.

67. It should be noted that counsel for the defendant had expressly disclaimed any intention to rely on the defence of *volenti*.

Bridge in the House of Lords expressed the view that applying the *volenti* defence to professional fireman would be "utterly repugnant to our contemporary notions of justice". The Supreme Court in *Phillips v Durgan*[68] in 1990 approved of the reasoning in *Ogwo v Taylor* when it held that a husband who went to the assistance of his wife when she was involved in a fire was entitled to be compensated by the defendant whose negligence had occasioned the fire. The preference today in many common law jurisdictions[69] is that any person who fights a fire, whether from professional duty or out of disinterested benevolence, should not be excluded from entitlement to sue, provided of course that he or she can show that his or her conduct was the reasonably foreseeable result of the defendant's negligence and that it was not totally foolhardy.[70] Contributory negligence rather than voluntary assumption of risk or *novus actus interveniens* is likely to be the worst that will face most overenthusiastic fire rescuers today, especially where life, rather than property,[71] is in peril.[72]

**[26.36]** A person who is engaging in a rescue attempt in response to a fire is not immune from liability in negligence in all circumstances. While it is well established that, in assessing the question of negligence of emergency vehicles, the court should take account of the great social utility of rescue,[73] fire fighters must still exercise due care.[74] This is

---

68. [1991] ILRM 321 (SC), analysed by Byrne & Binchy, *Annual Review of Irish Law 1990*, pp 493-500.

69. *Cf Ogwo v Taylor* [1988] AC 431; *Russell v McCabe* [1962] NZLR 392; Linden 'Rescuers and Good Samaritans' (1971) 34 MLR 241 at 256. In almost all jurisdictions in the United States, however, the "fire fighter's rule" denies recovery in negligence by professional fire fighters injured in the course of their work, from hazards caused by the fire on the basis that policy considerations demand either that no duty of care be imposed on occupiers of premises or that fire fighters be held to have consented to the risk. See *Krauth v Geller* (1960) 31 NJ 270, 157 A 2d 129; *Walters v Sloan* (1977) 20 Cal 3d 199, 571 P 2d 609, 142 Cal Rptr 152. In *Ogwo v Taylor*, Lord Bridge evinced no enthusiasm for the American doctrine. Having read the majority judgment delivered by Clark J, in *Walters v Sloan*, as well as Tobriner AC J's dissent, he was "left in no doubt whatever" that the doctrine had no place in English Law [1988] AC 431. Unfortunately Lord Bridge shed no light on why he preferred Tobriner ACJ's dissent. Two basic policy questions not addressed in *Ogwo v Taylor* are, first, whether imposition of liability may discourage property owners from calling the fire brigade, with unfortunate possible consequences for their neighbours as well as themselves, and second, whether the pay of firefighters should reflect the risks inherent in their employment and, if so, whether it should be supplemented by a right of action in negligence.

70. *Cf Sylvester v GB Chapman Ltd* (1935) 79 Sol J 777 (CA) - an attempt to rescue a leopard.

71. The Courts have accepted that liability may be imposed in respect of injuries sustained by a person in an attempt to save property from a fire, whether his employer's (*Merrington v Ironbridge Metalworks Ltd* [1952] 1 All ER 1101; *Hyett v GW Ry Co* [1948] 1 KB 345 (CA); *Steel v Glasgow Iron & Steel Co* [1944] SC 237), or his own - (*Russell v McCabe* [1962] NZLR 392 at 403), provided, of course, that the injury is reasonably foreseeable: *Malcolm v Dickson* [1951] SC 542.

72. It is possible to conceive of cases where a fire would be so intense that a rescue attempt would be manifestly futile: *cf Horsley v McLaren* [1972] SCR 441 - water in Canadian lake in early spring so cold as to make rescue attempt unforeseeable. Even in cases where the fire is of such intensity the courts are likely to be very slow to hold the rescue attempt unforeseeable.

73. See *Daborn v Bath Tramways Motor Co Ltd* [1946] 2 All ER 333; *Watt v Hertfordshire County Council* [1954] 2 All ER 368 (CA).

74. In *Watt v Hertfordshire County Council* [1954] 2 All ER 368 at Denning, LJ observed:

> "I quite agree that fire engines, ambulances and doctors' cars should not shoot past the traffic lights when they show a red light. That is because the risk is too great to warrant the incurring of the danger. It is always a question of balancing the risk against the end."

clear from *Strick v Treacy*,[75] where liability in negligence was imposed on the driver of a fire tender (among others) on his way to fight a fire in a school, which was involved in a collision with the plaintiff's vehicle at a road junction. O'Hanlon J considered that the driver of the tender, who had a clear view to his right as he neared the junction, should have made sure that the plaintiff had seen and responded to him before driving into her path when the lights were in her favour.

75. High Court, 10 June 1993 (O'Hanlon J). See also *O'Keeffe v Ladola and Dublin Corporation* Circuit Court Dublin, unrep 12 January 2000 (Judge McMahon) and para **[15.53]** above.

# Chapter 27

# Liability for Injuries caused by Animals


I. Introduction ... 749
II. Liability under the General Principles of Tort ... 750
III. Liability under Special Rules ... 754
IV. Law Reform Commission Proposals ... 768


## I. INTRODUCTION

**[27.01]** The rules relating to the liability for injury or damage caused by animals[1] are both special and general. Special rules, usually imposing strict liability, have been developed by the common law and imposed by statute in some cases. These rules of special liability, however, do not exclude the possibility of liability under the general rules of tort. This point needs to be emphasised, for frequently it is assumed that if the plaintiff cannot recover under the special rules, then he or she cannot recover at all. Because the special rules frequently impose strict liability on the owner of the animal it is understandable that the plaintiff should first of all seek to fit the case into the special rules. Failure to do so, however, may not be fatal: if the plaintiff can prove negligence, or can show that the act amounted to a nuisance or a trespass, or fall within the rule in *Rylands v Fletcher*, he or she will be able to recover under the general principles of the law of tort.[2]

---

1. See generally North *The Modern Law Of Animals* (1972); Williams *Liability For Animals* (1939); LRC WP No 3-1977; Walsh ed, *Agriculture and the Law* (1993), Ch 11; 'Civil Liability for Animals', analysed by Osborough (1978) 13 Ir Jur (ns) 182 and *Report on Civil Liability for Animals* (LRC2-1982). Animals have played such a central role in the social and economic life of communities that it is scarcely surprising to find that ancient legal systems had very sophisticated rules of civil and criminal liability in relation to their ownership and control. The Code of Hamurabi contains fine distinctions familiar to lawyers today who are called on to apply the principles of the *scienter* action: see Driver & Miles, *The Babylonian Laws* (1952), Vol I, pp 441-444. In *Dunphy v Bryan* (1963) 97 ILTR 4 at 6 (DC), Coghlan DJ expressed the hope that the Brehon Laws on the subject would be "carefully studied when we embark upon law reform".

2. *Cf* LRC WP No 3, p 5:

> "If for example a person brings a dog onto the highway he may be liable in negligence if he does not exercise a reasonable care in controlling the dog (*Gomberg v Smith* [1963] 1 QB 25, [1962] 1 All ER 725). Again, if a person keeps animals in such numbers that they unreasonably interfere with his neighbour's enjoyment of his property then the owner of the animals may be liable in nuisance (*O'Gorman v O'Gorman* [1903] 2 IR 573 36 ILTR 237). Similarly, will the owner be liable if the noise or stench which such animals emit unreasonably interferes with the quiet enjoyment of adjoining property (*William Aldred's* case (1610) 9 Co Rep 576)? In trespass too the owner who commands a dog to attack a person or who drives a beast onto another's land may be liable: *Cronin v Connor* [1913] 2 IR 119. The occupier of premises may be liable if, for example, injury is caused to a lawful entrant by the occupier's dog (*Kavanagh v Stokes* [1942] IR 596). Finally, within the principle expressed in *Rylands v Fletcher* (1868) LR 3 HL 330, if animals are collected on property in such a way as to amount to a non-natural use of the land, and if they are likely to do damage if they escape the owner may then be liable for all injuries caused by such an escape."

**[27.02]** This chapter is primarily concerned with examining the special rules relating to animals and in particular, with the *scienter* action, liability for dogs, cattle trespass, and the liability for animals on the highway. Before examining these rules, however, it is worth taking a closer look at some of the leading cases where liability has been imposed for damage caused by animals under the general principles of tort law.

## II. LIABILITY UNDER THE GENERAL PRINCIPLES OF TORT

### Negligence

**[27.03]** In *Howard v Bergin, O'Connor & Co*[3] cattle which were being unloaded at Kingsbridge (Heuston) Railway station were negligently allowed to escape onto the road, where, after various escapades, they knocked down and injured the plaintiff. The court allowed recovery in negligence, the unreasonable conduct consisting of not using the platform provided for unloading cattle, leaving a gate onto the public road open during the unloading operation and leaving the cattle unattended while one of the drovers went in search of assistance. Moreover, the court held that this was not a case of quiet animals being allowed onto the road, but rather a case where the animals "got wild" in the unloading, and were negligently allowed to get onto the roadway where they "dashed blindly along colliding with or overturning human impediments to [their] wild progress".[4] In *Powell v McGlynn & Bradlaw*[5] the negligence consisted of leaving a pony and trap unattended while the defendant, McGlynn, said goodnight to a woman friend.[6] Liability will not be imposed in negligence, however, if an animal known to be quiet is brought onto the highway and, through no negligence on the part of the handler, the animal suddenly runs off and injures another.[7]

**[27.04]** In *Kavanagh v Stokes*[8] liability was imposed in negligence for injuries done by the defendant's dog to the plaintiff, a paying guest, who was returning from a dance, and in *Mallon v GS & W Ry Co*[9] liability was imposed when the defendant's servant, a railway porter, in negligently handling a dog, caused injury to the plaintiff, a transit passenger on a crowded platform. Both *O'Gorman v O'Gorman*[10] and *McStay v Morrissey*[11] clearly establish that negligence in the keeping and management of bees will render the beekeeper liable.

### Nuisance

**[27.05]** The defendant will also be liable in nuisance if in the keeping or managing of animals he or she wrongfully interferes with a public right or with another landowner's

3. [1925] 2 IR 110 (SC).
4. [1925] 2 IR 110 at 125. *Cf Grace Provision Co v Dortch* (1961) 350 SW 2d 409 (Tenn Appeal).
5. [1902] 2 IR 154 (CA).
6. See also *Furlong v Curran* [1959] Ir Jur 30 (HC).
7. *Scully v Mulhall* (1951) 85 ILTR 18.
8. [1942] IR 596.
9. (1893) 27 ILTR 125 (CA). See also *Harnedy v National Greyhound Racing Co Ltd* [1940] IR 160 (HC).
10. [1903] 2 IR 573.
11. (1949) 83 ILTR 28 (CC).

reasonable use or enjoyment of his or her property.[12] In *Cunningham v Whelan*[13] liability was imposed where the plaintiff's horse and cart were overturned when some 24 bullocks belonging to the defendant, which were unattended on the roadway, pressed against the cart. Although there was normally no liability at that time for damage caused by animals straying on the highway, the court held that it was different when one was dealing with a "combined mass" of animals causing an obstruction on the highway. Although the language of the court seems to suggest that liability was imposed in negligence, there was no evidence of negligence on the part of the defendant and a statement by the judge that it was immaterial how the animals got on the highway suggests that liability was in nuisance.[14]

**[27.06]** If animals are kept in unreasonable numbers so that by noise,[15] or smell or otherwise they interfere with the lawful user or enjoyment of private property the owner of the animals may clearly be liable in private nuisance. In *O'Gorman v O'Gorman*[16] the defendant, who kept about twenty beehives near the plaintiff's haggard was held liable when the bees swarmed, while the defendant was taking honey from them, and attacked the plaintiff's horse:

> "The defendants were entitled to the natural and reasonable use of their own land, and the jury had to consider whether this keeping of bees in the manner and place which they did, went beyond the lawful use of their own land in relation to their neighbour. It was a jury question, and there was, in my opinion, evidence upon which they could properly act. They found in effect that the defendant had set up what was an actionable nuisance, and that it resulted in injury to his neighbour. I do not think that that finding can be quarrelled with ..."[17]

## Trespass

**[27.07]** The defendant may be liable in trespass if he or she throws or drives an animal onto another's land in the same way as if he or she threw or drove some inanimate object onto the property.[18] Liability here, however, must be distinguished from liability under the

12. See generally. Simmons 'Comment: The Nuances of Nuisance: Forty Cats are Too Many; Four Just Enough' (1960) 5 Dakota LR 86.
13. (1918) 52 ILTR 67 (CC). See also *Furlong v Curran* [1959] Ir Jur 30; *Gillick v O'Reilly* [1984] ILRM 402.
14. This interpretation seems to be supported by *Hall v Wightman* [1926] NI 92.
15. *Cf O'Connor v Higgisson* [1946] Ir Jur 61 (HC).
16. [1903] 2 IR 573.
17. [1903] 2 IR 573 at 582-583 (*per* Kenny J). Wright J also based his decision on nuisance although Barton J preferred to give the plaintiff the verdict on negligence principles. In *McStay v Morrissey* (1949) 83 ILTR 28 the court refused the plaintiff an injunction on the grounds that bees were not kept in unreasonable numbers or in an unreasonable place. See also *Grainger v Finlay* (1858) 7 ICLR 417. And *cf Brady v Warren* [1900] 2 IR 632 variously interpreted by Goodhart 'Liability for Things Naturally on the Land' (1930) 4 Camb LJ 13 at 20-21 and Noel 'Nuisances from Land in its Natural Condition' (1943) 56 Harv LR 772 at 781-782. With regard to remedies available in the District Court for nuisance by barking dogs see Control of Dogs Act 1986, s 25 and, for prescribed form of notice to be served, see the Control of Dogs (No 2) Regulations 1987 (SI 59/1987).
18. *Scott v Shepherd* (1773) Wils KB 403 at 408 95; ER 1124 at 1127. See also *Manton v Brocklebank* [1923] 2 KB 212 at 219.

special rule of cattle trespass. If I drive my cattle on to your land I am committing a trespass through the animals; if, however, my cattle stray on to the property of their own volition, this is cattle trespass properly so-called, and the special rules of liability described hereafter apply. The distinction is important for three reasons:

> "First, liability in cattle trespass is strict whereas liability in some kinds of trespass at least requires intention or negligence on the part of the defendant; second, cattle trespass is confined to 'cattle', and does not extend to other animals such as cats and dogs; third, the defences in both torts are not the same."[19]

## Rylands v Fletcher[20]

**[27.08]** In theory there seems to be no reason why in appropriate circumstances the owner of some kinds of animals at least would not be liable if these animals escaped and did mischief.[21] As a practical matter, however, the application of the *Rylands v Fletcher* rule to normal animal cases must be rare, because the more recent versions of the rule confine it to "dangerous things".[22] Moreover, the plaintiff to succeed must show first that there was an escape, and second, that there was a "non-natural" use of land. The keeping of cattle and domestic dogs and cats, for example, could hardly be considered non-natural in normal circumstances.[23] If animals, however, are kept in unreasonable numbers the user may easily become non-natural.[24]

## Occupier's Liability

**[27.09]** The position under the Occupiers' Liability Act 1995 (the 1995 Act),[25] of a person who owns or is in charge of an animal is less than entirely clear. Section 2(1) of the Act provides that, subject to s 8, the duties, liabilities and rights provided for by the Act are to have effect:

> "in place of the duties, liabilities and rights which heretofore attached by the common-law to occupiers of premises as such in respect of dangers existing on their premises to entrants thereon."

Section 1(1) provides that "danger", in relation to any premises, means danger due to the state of the premises. Section 8 provides that nothing in the Act is to be construed as

---

19. LRC WP No 3 p 18, (footnotes omitted). The distinction is not always observed by the courts however: see *Cronin v Connor* [1913] 2 IR 119.
20. (1866) LR 1 Exch 265 affd (1868) LR 3 HL 330.
21. It is sometimes suggested that cattle trespass is but one example of *Rylands v Fletcher* liability - see eg Blackburn J in *Rylands v Fletcher* (1866) LR 1 Exch 265 at 280 *et seq*. and Judge Ó Briain in *Noonan v Hartnett* (1950) 84 ILTR 41 at 43. See also *Dalton v O'Sullivan* [1947] Ir Jur 25 (CC). Better opinion nowadays however suggests that these are separate heads of liability and should be viewed independently: North, *The Modern Law of Animals*, p 275; Williams *Liability for Animals*, pp 197-199. See also LRC WP No 3, pp 23 24.
22. SALMOND & HEUSTON, p 315 considers that "[n]owadays the most satisfactory approach is to treat the whole concept of 'dangerousness' as but another way of saying that harm must have been in some sense foreseeable.
23. See LRC WP No 3 - 1917 p 24.
24. *Brady v Warren* [1900] 2 IR 632; See also *Robson v Marquis of Londonderry* (1900) 34 ILTR 88: number of pheasants bred not unreasonable having regard to the acreage of the demesne.
25. See para **[12.59]** above.

affecting any enactment or rule of law relating to, *inter alia*, "any liability imposed on an occupier as a member of a particular class of persons ...", including carriers, bailees and employers, as well as any liability imposed on an occupier for a tort committed by another person "in circumstances where the duty imposed on the occupier is of such a nature that its performance may not be delegated to another person".

**[27.10]** The 1995 Act prescribes three categories of entrant: the visitor,[26] the recreational user[27] and the trespasser.[28] In Chapter 12, we examine the law in this context in some detail. Here, it may be noted, by way of broad summary, that the occupier owes visitors "the common duty of care" - in effect, the standard that applies in actions for common law negligence. To recreational users and non-criminal trespassers, the occupier is merely required not to injure them intentionally nor to act with reckless disregard for them. To criminal trespassers, the occupier generally is not even under an obligation to avoid acting with reckless disregard for them.

**[27.11]** Let us take the case where a ferocious bull gores an entrant or a frisky pony knocks an entrant down. (We leave till later in the chapter consideration of the more troublesome questions surrounding dogs.) The crucial question is whether the 1995 Act replaces the common law, both in respect to its general grounds of liability, such as negligence, and in respect of specific grounds such as the *scienter* rule, considered later in this chapter.

**[27.12]** There is a strong argument that it does not have this effect. Three reasons may be proffered for this conclusion. First, the 1995 Act expresses itself in s 2(1) to be limited to the replacement of the duties, liabilities and rights which formerly "attached by the common law to occupiers of premises as such". Certainly the special grounds of liability, notably the *scienter* rule, have an independent existence which cannot be reduced to occupiers' liability "as such". Secondly, to the extent that the 1995 Act replaces earlier common law occupiers' liability, it does so only in respect of dangers existing on the premises which are "due to the state of the premises". The tenor of this language suggests a continuous condition. It is hard to see a rampaging bull in this way, though perhaps the retention of an animal for a period of time might be considered by the court to amount to sufficient continuity to transform the situation into one capable of being described as involving "the state of the premises".

**[27.13]** At the heart of this dilemma is the distinction between "activity duties" and "occupancy duties", which has been recognised by the courts and which we discuss in greater detail in Chapter 12. It is only if the court takes the view that the presence of the animal on the premises can, either generally or in the particular circumstances of the case, be characterised as "a danger due to the state of the premises" that the 1995 Act can have potential application in relation to animals.

**[27.14]** In the event that the court were so to characterise the animal's presence, this would not inevitably mean that the new duties, liabilities and rights should replace those arising under the common law. Section 8 clearly preserves non-delegable duties. As we have seen,[29] there is a narrow band of authority suggesting that an occupier has a non-delegable

26. See para **[12.78]** above.
27. See para **[12.86]** above.
28. See para **[12.96]** above.
29. See para **[12.144]** above.

duty in certain instances. If an animal were to feature within the parameters of this (somewhat speculative) band of authority, then the case would have to be dealt with under the common law rules. More plausably, a plaintiff suing for injury caused by an animal on the defendant's premises could argue that the proceedings are against the defendant, not in respect of his or her status as occupier but, as s 8 envisages, by reason of his or her "member[ship] of a particular class of persons" - the class being that of owner or controller of an animal.[30]

## III. LIABILITY UNDER SPECIAL RULES

### The *Scienter* Principle

#### *(a) The rule*

**[27.15]** One of the special rules relating to animals depends on a distinction drawn in law between wild animals and domestic animals.[31] The owner of a wild animal keeps it at his peril and if such an animal causes damage the owner is strictly liable.[32] The owner of a tame animal, however, is liable only if he knows that the animal has a "mischievous propensity" to do the damage of the kind complained. As Professor Williams explains:

> "Such knowledge had originally to be proved in all cases, but in modern law it is presumed if the animal in question is one of a dangerous class. The principle is known as the *scienter* principle (from the words *scienter retinuit* in the old form of the writ), and proof of knowledge is called, somewhat ungrammatically, proof of *scienter*."[33]

**[27.16]** This statement of principle finds ample support in the Irish authorities.[34] In *Quinn v Quinn*[35] the defendant's sow attacked and killed the plaintiff's cow. Proof that the sow had previously attacked and killed fowl to the defendant's knowledge was held to be sufficient to make the defendant liable. In contrast, where injury is caused by a wild animal (a zebra,[36] a bear[37] or elephant,[38] for example) recovery is not dependent on alleging or proving a vicious propensity in the animal in question.

**[27.17]** The "mischievous propensity" must be a "vicious, mischievous or fierce" tendency.[39] The propensity must be one which indicates "bad blood". The plaintiff who

30. Ch12 and *McNamara v ESB* [1975] IR 226.
31. The traditional Latin phrases were animals *ferae naturae* and *mansuetue naturae*.
32. *May v Burdett* (1846) 9 QB 101; *Behrens v Bertram Mills Circus Ltd* [1957] 2 QB 1. See also Levin and Spak 'Lions and Lionesses, Tigers and Tigresses, Bears and ... Other Animals: Sellers' Liability for Dangerous Animals' (1983) 58 Notre Dame LR 537 at 544-545. In Canada, in *Lewis v Olming* (1983) 24 CCLT 81 (Alta QB), liability was premised on "*escape* from the custody and control of the owner" (emphasis added). For criticism of this extra requirement: see Irvine 'Annotation' (1983) 24 CCLT 82.
33. Williams, *Liability For Animals* (1939), p 273.
34. *Kelly v Wade* (1848) 12 ILR 424; *Quinn v Quinn* 39 ILTR 163; *Howard v Bergin O'Connor & Co* [1925] 12 IR 110.
35. 39 ILTR 163.
36. *Marlor v Ball* (1900) 16 TLR 239.
37. *Wyatt v Rosherville Gardens Co* (1886) 2 TLR 282.
38. *Filburn v Peoples Palace and Aquarium Co Ltd* (1890) 25 QBD 258.
39. *Fitzgerald v ED & AD Cooke Bourne (Farms) Ltd* [1964] 1 QB 249 at 270.

shows that a foal has a tendency to frolic around people or that a dog was in the habit of bounding enthusiastically on strangers[40] has not demonstrated a mischievous propensity. However, it is sufficient for the plaintiff to show that a dog "was always growling" and that it used to run at a child and climb up on children.[41] In *Duggan v Armstrong*,[42] McCarthy J (Hederman and Costello JJ concurring) observed:

> "One does not have to wait for the growling and frightening dog to bite someone in order to know that it may do so; the requirement of *scienter* is not that the dog will bite somebody but that, having displayed a vicious propensity, it may do so."

**[27.18]** The malicious tendency need not be a chronic or permanent element of the animal's nature. Kennedy CJ, in *Howard v Bergin, O'Connor & Co*,[43] put it in the following language:

> "In my opinion, however, what is called a 'mischievous propensity' may be as well a passing or temporary phase of character or temper of the particular animal as a chronic or permanent element of its nature.
> ... I understand by the expression 'a mischievous propensity', a propensity to do mischief, a tendency to do harm or cause injury, whether, in one case, by some single characteristic action such as kicking or goring or biting or, in another case, generally when mischief may be done in any of a variety of ways."[44]

**[27.19]** These *dicta* are not without difficulty, however, because they indicate that knowledge of a passing phase may amount to *scienter* even though the defendant may have no knowledge of any previous disposition to such activity, and they have been criticised by Williams.[45]

**[27.20]** The knowledge which the defendant must have is actual knowledge, although it does not matter whether it is acquired from personal observation, from hearsay, or through an employee.[46] Nor does it matter whether the knowledge was acquired recently or a long time before the injury. In *Bennett v Walsh*,[47] the knowledge of a nine year old girl of a mischievous propensity rendered her father liable in *scienter*.

**[27.21]** An illustration of the rule occurred in *Forster v Donovan, Ireland and the AG*[48] A postman was bitten by an Alsation watch dog. The plaintiff was a share-postman and it was the second day he delivered post to Donovan's home. Shortly before this Mr Donovan had

---

40. *Line v Taylor* (1982) 3 F & F 731; 176 ER 335. Contrast *Price v Wright* (1899) 35 NBR 26.
41. *Duggan v Armstrong* [1992] 2 IR 161 (SC).
42. *Duggan v Armstrong* [1992] 2 IR 161.
43. [1925] 2 IR 110 at 124 125.
44. Citing in support of this proposition *Turner v Coates* [1917] 1 KB 670; *Manton v Brocklebank* (1923) 2 KB 212. In *Laws v Wright* 2000 ACWSJ Lexis 821 (Alta QB 2000) McBain J held that knowledge of a horse's tendency to nip constituted *scienter* in regard to a subsequent bite, since "a nip is but a gentle bite".
45. Williams *Liability For Animals* (1939), pp 291-292; See also LRC WP No 3, p 37.
46. Williams *Liability For Animals* (1939), p 305.
47. (1936) 70 ILTR 252 (CC). *Cf* McCarthy J's curious ruminations on constitutional aspects of the *scienter* rule in this context in *Duggan v Armstrong* [1993] ILRM 222. See further Byrne & Binchy *Annual Review of Irish Law 1992*, pp 588-590.
48. (1980) 114 ILTR 104 (HC).

placed a letter-box near the entrance to his property, some 100 yards from the house, and had also erected a warning sign which read "Beware of Alsatian". On the first day the postman delivered to the front door of the house, but on that occasion the dog was inside. On that afternoon Mr Donovan's wife telephoned the post office to instruct the postman not to deliver to the door of the house in future but to use the letter box at the entrance to the property. The warning was not relayed to the postman and as he was delivering at the hall door the second day he was bitten by the Alsatian. The plaintiff sued Mr Donovan and the State (representing the Post Office). With regard to the dog owner's liability Costello J said:

> "I have sympathy for the first named defendant but when he keeps a dog, like the one referred to in the evidence, he runs the risk of some person being injured. This defendant had knowledge of the propensity of the dog and, accordingly, the plaintiff must succeed against him and there must be a decree against him."[49]

**[27.22]** The judge went on to find that the Post Office was also negligent in not conveying the warning to the postman and that in the circumstances the plaintiff did not contribute to his own injury. The judge, however, gave effect to his sympathy for Mr Donovan's position by ordering the Post Office to provide a full indemnity to Mr Donovan in considering the issue of contribution *inter se*.

### *(b) Wild and domestic animals*

**[27.23]** The criterion used to classify animals into the wild or tame categories seems to be whether the animal belongs to a species which is a danger to mankind in general, although in determining this issue it seems that regard may be had to other countries' experience with the animal.[50] Precedents now exist which treat the following as domestic animals: cats,[51] dogs,[52] cattle, "horses, pheasants and partridge"[53] and bees[54] and the following as wild animals: elephants,[55] bears,[56] and zebras.[57] In *McQuaker v Goddard*[58] an English court, taking into account the realities of life in the countries where the animal was indigenous, treated a camel as a domestic animal.

### *(c) Incidence of liability*

**[27.24]** Although there are not many Irish authorities on the point, liability in *scienter* seems to be attracted by possession or control rather than by ownership.[59]

---

49. (1980) 114 ILTR 104 at 105-106. See also *Kavanagh v Centreline Ltd* [1987] ILRM 306.
50. LRC WP No 3, p 32.
51. *Buckle v Holmes* [1926] 2 KB 125.
52. *Kelly v Wade* (1848) 12 ILR 424.
53. *Filburn v People's Palace and Aquarium Co Ltd* (1890) 59 LJQB 471-472. *Cf Curley v Gregan* [1895] 2 IR 320 (CA).
54. *O'Gorman v O'Gorman* [1903] 2 IR 573.
55. *Filburn v People's Palace and Aquarium Co Ltd* (1890) 59 LJQB 471-472; *Behrens v Bertram Mills Circus Ltd* [1957] 2 QB 1.
56. *Wyatt v Rosherville Gardens Co* (1886) 2 TLR 282.
57. *Marlor v Ball* (1900) 16 TLR 239.
58. [1940] 1 KB 687.
59. LRC WP No 3, p 39.

**[27.25]** In *Walker v Hall*[60] the trainer of a horse was made liable; and, although the owner as such may not be liable,[61] if he obliges a servant to keep an animal as part of his employment he will attract liability in *scienter* or at any rate in negligence.[62] In *Crean v Nolan*,[63] where the plaintiff's sheep were killed by beagles, it was suggested that the organising committee of the drag hunt, although not the owners of the dogs, might have been liable in *scienter* had the sheep been killed during the hunt. In the event, however, no liability was imposed on the Committee because the killing had been done long after the hunt was over.

***(e) Defences in the* scienter *action***

**[27.26]** The contributory negligence of the plaintiff will reduce the liability of the defendant in the *scienter* action.[64] Before 1961, the contributory negligence of the plaintiff was a total defence[65] but since the Civil Liability Act 1961 (s 34) the plaintiff's negligence will only have the effect of apportioning liability. Moreover, if the plaintiff's action was the sole cause of the damage the plaintiff will fail on the issue of causation. The act of a third party and an act of God ought also to be considered as defences in the appropriate circumstances in the *scienter* action.[66]

## Dogs

**[27.27]** Special statutory provisions relating to damage caused by dogs were consolidated by the Control of Dogs Act 1986 (the 1986 Act). This Act repealed earlier legislation[67] and introduced some modest reforms. The Control of Dogs Act 1992 has carried the process somewhat further.

---

60. (1876) 40 JP 456.
61. Williams *Liability For Animals* (1939), pp 325-326.
62. But not seemingly if he kept it as a pet: *Knott v London Co Co* [1934] 1 KB 126; *cf North v Wood* [1914] 1 KB 629.
63. (1963) 97 ILTR 125 (CC). This case affords a good illustration of the difficulties which may face a plaintiff in framing an action in such circumstances. He cannot sue the owners of the dogs because he has no way of knowing which dogs killed the sheep. But see *Arneil v Paterson* [1931] AC 560. He cannot sue in cattle trespass since (as we shall see) dogs are not "cattle" for the purposes of the rule. Nor could the plaintiff in *Crean v Nolan* make the organizing committee liable under the Dogs Act 1906, which imposed strict liability in the case of dogs worrying cattle because liability under that Act attached only to the owners of the dogs, and the organizing committee was not the owner of the dogs. The same is true nowadays under Control of Dogs Act 1986, s 21. In *Lyons v Kelly et al* a motor cyclist who was knocked off his bike when a hunt dog ran into his path recovered in the Cork Circuit Court in an action for negligence against the members of the club: Cork Examiner, 10 December 1983 p 10.
64. Civil Liability Act 1961 s 34. *Cf Campbell v Wilkinson* (1909) 43 ILTR 237. As to question of apportionment principle when the defendant is only in breach of strict statutory obligation see *Daly v Avonmore Creameries Ltd* [1984] IR 131.
65. *Carroll v Kehoe* (1927) 61 ILTR 192 (HC).
66. See LRC WP No 3, p 43. Voluntary assumption of risk also constitutes a defence: *Laws v Wright* 2000 ACWSJ Lexis 821 (Alta QB 2000). In view of the constricted scope of this defence under s 34(1)(b) of the Civil Liability Act 1961, a court disposed to dismiss a claim by a foolhardy plaintiff meddling with a dangerous animal might seek to characterise the plaintiff as the author of his or her own misfortune, thus resolving the issue in exclusively causal terms.
67. The Dogs Act 1871; Dogs Act 1906; Dogs (Protection of Livestock) Act 1960 and Animals Act 1985, s 3.

**[27.28]** The principal rule relating to the civil liability for damage caused by dogs is now contained in s 21 of the 1986 Act, and this addresses the anomaly that existed before 1986 whereby, because of earlier statutory provisions,[68] the owner of a dog was strictly liable for injury which a dog did to "cattle", but for injury done to human beings the injured person was still obliged to prove negligence. In such situations the law protected property interests more assiduously than it protected interests to the person. Section 21 of the 1986 Act attempts to correct this anomaly by imposing strict liability for injuries caused by dogs to livestock and for damage caused when a dog attacks a person. The section reads in full as follows:

> (1) The owner of a dog shall be liable in damages for damage caused in an attack on any person by the dog and for injury done by it to any livestock; and it shall not be necessary for the person seeking such damages to show a previous mischievous propensity in the dog, or the owner's knowledge of such previous propensity, or to show that such injury or damage was attributable to neglect on the part of the owner.
>
> (2) Where livestock are injured by a dog on land on to which they had strayed, and either the dog belonged to the occupier of the land or its presence on the land was authorised by the occupier, a person shall not be liable under this section in respect of injury done to the livestock, unless the person caused the dog to attack the livestock.
>
> (3) A person is liable in damages for any damage caused by a dog kept on any premises or structure to a person trespassing thereon only in accordance with the rules of law relating to liability for negligence.
>
> (4)(a) Any damage or injury for which a person is made liable under this section shall be deemed to be attributable to a wrong within the meaning of the Civil Liability Act, 1961, and the provisions of that Act shall apply accordingly.
>
> (b) Sections 11(2)(a) and 11 (2)(b) of the Statute of Limitations 1957 shall apply to such damage."

**[27.29]** This provision calls for a number of comments. First, the 1986 Act does not abolish the *scienter* action (as was proposed by the Law Reform Commission), so that a person injured by a dog may still proceed under that rule where he or she can show that the dog had a mischievous propensity and the keeper knew of this.[69] Accordingly, the keeper of a guard dog will be held to be strictly liable for injuries caused by a dog trained to attack and hold, when the dog is out of his or her control and where the injury results from such propensity. Furthermore, the injured person may also have remedies under the general rules of negligence and trespass.[70]

---

68. The Dogs Act 1906, s 1.

69. *Kavanagh v Centreline Ltd* [1987] ILRM 306. See also *Forster v Donovan, Ireland and the AG* (1980) 114 ILTR 10. It should be noted that sub-s (3) is drafted in such a manner as to exclude a *scienter* action by a trespasser, whose only claim can be one based on negligence. In *Rooney v Connolly* [1986] IR 572 at 595 (SC), McCarthy J observed that "[t]he doctrine of *scienter* ... has been abolished by statute [Animals Act 1985, s 3]." Section 3 was replaced by s 21 of the 1986 Act. The language of s 3(1) (which is identical to that of s 21 (1)) appears to contradict McCarthy J's interpretation since it is permissive rather than mandatory in relation to dispensing with the *scienter* action.

70. *Kavanagh v Centreline Ltd* [1987] ILRM 306, where liability was also imposed under *Rylands v Fletcher* principles; *Kavanagh v Stokes* [1942] IR 596. See also *Green v Mundow* Circuit Court, 20 January 2000, Irish Times (McMahon J) where liability was imposed on school authorities for failure to supervise pupils in the school yard. The plaintiff was bitten by a stray dog when there was a recognised problem of dogs coming on to the premises.

**[27.30]** Second, the new section imposes strict liability for injuries to the person only when there is "an attack" on a person by the dog. In contrast, with regard to dogs and livestock, the section does not require an attack but imposes strict liability "for injury done by it to any livestock". Although "an attack" probably does not require physical contact and strict liability would certainly attach for injuries received in trying to avoid a lunging dog, it seems clear from the manner in which sub-s (1) is drafted that strict liability under it does not arise where the dog attacks the motor cycle or the motor car thereby causing the driver to swerve and injure himself or herself. Similarly, there would be no strict liability for personal injuries inflicted by a prancing Irish Wolfhound which caused injuries to the person because of its size or its awkwardness rather than because of an intent to do injury. In such cases the injured person would still have to rely on *scienter* or negligence. Because of the wording of the 1986 Act the owner of livestock is better protected for similar injuries to his or her animals, because in this case an attack is not required and strict liability is imposed for any injury done to the livestock.[71] The phrase "injury done by it"[72] (ie the dog) was held not to cover injuries which two foals suffered when they were travelling on a public road and when the defendant's dog rushed out and barked at them. The foals broke away and were not recovered until the next day. They later died from the injuries received in the flight.

**[27.31]** Section 21(2) creates an exception to the strict liability rule in the case of a dog causing injury to livestock which have strayed on to the dog owner's land (or on to land where the dog is authorised). In such a case liability will be imposed on the defendant only when he or she caused the dog to attack the livestock.

**[27.32]** When a trespasser is injured by a dog, s 21(3) of the 1986 Act provides that the ordinary rules of negligence apply instead of strict liability rules. Apparently the rationale is that a trespasser is entitled to less consideration than a lawful entrant and an owner of property is entitled to take reasonable steps to protect his or her property.[73] A literal interpretation of sub-s (3) excludes *scienter* liability towards trespassers.

**[27.33]** Some uncertainty surrounds the effect of the passing of the Occupiers' Liability Act 1995 on sub-s (3). On one view, the 1995 Act leaves sub-s (3) entirely unchanged. Section 2(1) of the 1995 Act provides for the replacement (by new duties) of the duties, liabilities and rights:

> which heretofore attached by the common law to occupiers of premises as such in respect of dangers existing on their premises to entrants thereon.

The duty attached by sub-s (3), being part of a statute, is not a common law one and, the argument goes, is therefore unaffected by s 2(1) of the 1995 Act. A further reason why s 2(1) might be considered not to affect sub-s (3) is that s 2(1) affects duties, liabilities and rights attached by the common law to occupiers of premises as such. The 1986 Act establishes liabilities on owners of dogs, not occupiers of premises.

---

71. *Campbell v Wilkinson* (1909) 43 ILTR 237. It should be noted that, where a dog is negligently let go onto the highway, where it injures a road-user, liability may be improved: Animal Act 1985, s 2. *Cf Aleksoske v State Rail Authority of New South Wales* [2000] NSW CA.

72. The Dogs Act 1906, s 1 repeated in s 21(1) of the 1986 Act.

73. See Ch 12.

**[27.34]** As against this, it can be argued (albeit somewhat tentatively) that the duty that is imposed by s 21(3) is, in essence a common law duty of negligence rather than a statutory duty. The subsection has, as it were, returned liability in this context to the common law: common law principles will determine the outcome of proceedings taken by trespassers against owners. To adopt a concept familiar in conflicts of law: a *renvoi* to common law has occurred. That being so, s 2(1) of the 1995 Act would be capable of replacing it with a radically more restricted basis of liability. A trespasser can succeed under the 1995 Act only where the occupier has intentionally injured him or her, or has acted with reckless disregard for the trespasser. A criminal trespasser, as we have seen, is generally not even permitted to sue for recklessly caused injury. It would be a curious dissonance of social policy if the criminal trespasser could be able to sue in negligence for being attacked by a dog but not for any other negligent exposure by the occupier to the risk of injury. As to the contention that the 1995 Act relates only to duties, liabilities and rights attached formerly by the common law to occupiers of premises as such, it may be pointed out that the 1986 Act contains a definition of "owner" of a dog which includes the occupier of premises where the dog is kept, subject to proof to the contrary.[74]

**[27.35]** On balance, the argument that s 21(3) has been left undisturbed by the 1995 Act appears stronger. The more formalistic rules of statutory interpretation tilt in this direction and the course of the Oireachtas Debates does not support a contrary view. Undoubtedly, the result is anomalous, but the 1995 Act is the source of far more wide-ranging anomalies than merely this particular one.

**[27.36]** Having raised these questions about the present status of s 21(3) let us return to some further points about the section as a whole. Section 1 of the 1986 Act defines livestock to include "cattle, sheep, swine, horses and all other equine animals, poultry, goats and deer not in a wild state". The old Dogs Act 1906 imposed strict liability only for the protection of "cattle", which was not as widely defined as livestock under the 1986 Act.[75]

**[27.37]** It should also be noted that s 21(1) imposes strict liability in respect of "damage" to the person and in respect of "injury" to livestock. "Damage" is the wider of the two words and is defined in the 1986 Act to include:

> death or injury to any person (including any disease caused to a person or any impairment of his physical or mental condition) and includes injury to, or total or partial destruction of, property.

**[27.38]** Finally, s 21(4) provides that the Civil Liability Act 1961 applies to damage or injuries caused by dogs under the section, and so the provisions relating to contributory negligence, concurrent wrongdoers and fatal injuries all apply to those type of injuries. In a case where two dogs attacked livestock in concert, and it was not possible to attribute

---

74. In *Leahy v Leader and Cork Diocesan Trustees* High Court, 13 October 1999, the plaintiff while lawfully on the defendant's church property was bitten by a dog belonging to some cider drinkers also on the property. The 1986 Act provides that an owner of a dog included the occupier where the dog was kept or permittted to live or remain at any particular time. McCraken J refused to impose liability since in his view "permitted" implied consent and knowledge. The plaintiff had not proved any knowledge on the part of the Parish Priest, and the Parish Priest had given evidence that he had no such knowledge.

75. The Dogs Act 1906, s 7.

what particular damage was caused by which dog, the House of Lords has held[76] that the owner of each dog may be liable for the whole damage. This would appear to be a sensible rule and one which would be followed in Ireland.[77] Subsection (4) also provides that the ordinary periods of limitation - three years for personal injuries and six years for injury to property - apply to s 21 actions.

**[27.39]** The presumption to the effect that the occupier of premises where a dog was kept or "permitted to live or remain ...." was the owner of the dog, and which was contained in the Dogs Act 1906 has been retained in the Dogs Act 1986.[78]

**[27.40]** On the regulatory and criminal side, the Control of Dogs Act 1986 also made provision for the control and licensing of dogs, including greyhounds, for the control and seizure of stray dogs, for the duties of local authorities and the power of dog wardens, and for the regulation of premises and dogs. The Act created offences and provides penalties in respect of these matters. In the case of nuisance by barking dogs provision was made for recourse to the District Court for appropriate remedies.[79] Regulations controlling the use of guard dogs came into force on 1 February 1989. These Regulations required that guard dogs used at business premises must be accompanied by a handler or secured so that they could not go freely about the premises or escape. A warning notice had to be displayed at all entrances to the premises. Guard dogs had to have identification collars and were also required to have an electronic device implanted under the skin containing a permanent identification code allotted by the Irish Society for the Prevention of Cruelty to Animals.[80] Breach of these criminal rules, it is submitted, would not give rise to a civil action for breach of statutory duties in light of s 21 which specifically makes provisions for civil remedies in certain cases. The specific provision of civil remedies under s 21 would weaken the inference of civil remedies under other sections of the 1986 Act. It might be also noted that the Act provides the defendant with a defence in an action for damages for shooting a dog which was worrying or about to worry livestock, or where there was a threat to such livestock from a stray dog.[81] The Act was brought into effect on 1 February 1987 and 1 April 1987 by the Control of Dogs Act 1986 (Commencement) Order 1987[82] and the Control of Dogs Act 1986 (Commencement) (No 2) Order 1987.[83]

76. *Arneil v Paterson* [1931] AC 560.

77. Compare with Civil Liability Act 1961, s 11(3) regarding concurrent wrongdoers. Even in cases where only one dog has been involved problems of proof of identity can arise: *cf Flinter v Ryan* DPIJ: Hilary and Easter Terms 1993 p 262 (HC, 11 February 1995).

78. See the definition of "owner" in s 1. In *Leahy v Leader* DPIJ: Trinity & Michaelmas Terms 1999, p 126 (HC), McCracken J held that the occupier's permission was contingent on his awareness of the dog's presence on the property; permission to individuals to be on the premises would not involve the occupier in liability for an attack by a dog they brought with them unless the occupier knowingly consented to the dog's coming onto the property.

79. Section 25.

80. Control of Dogs Act 1986 (Guard Dogs) Regulations 1988 (SI 255/88).

81. Section 23.

82. SI 16/1987.

83. SI 79/1987.

**[27.41]** Further changes were made by the Control of Dogs (Amendment) Act 1992,[84] designed to strengthen the measures available to deal with dangerous dogs. Section 2 of the 1992 Act amended section of the 1986 Act by introducing a new definition of "general dog licence" to ensure that a licence relates to a location, thus preventing an organisation from obtaining a simple licence for an unlimited number of dogs. It strengthened the hand of the Minister for Environment in the whole area of licensing. The powers of local authorities and of dog wardens were also enhanced.

## Cattle Trespass

### *(a) The rule*

**[27.42]** Cattle which stray from their owner's land onto another person's property will render their owner liable irrespective of negligence.[85] This is a special rule and, at the outset, it must be repeated that this liability arises only where the cattle stray of their own volition. If the cattle are driven onto the property then liability will be in trespass not in cattle trespass. The rule applies where the cattle break from one field into an adjoining field and also where cattle stray from their own field onto the highway and thence onto another person's property.[86] It does not apply, however, where cattle which are being lawfully driven on the highway break onto property adjoining the road. Liability in such circumstances depends on the plaintiff being able to prove negligence on the part of the owner of the animals and in this connection it must be noted that landowners adjacent to the highway accept the inevitable risk of damage done by animals lawfully using the highway, provided there has been no negligence.[87]

### *(b) "Cattle" defined*

**[27.43]** This rule of strict liability applies only to "cattle", which as a term, although it does not include cats and dogs or wild animals on one's property, comprises more than the bovine species. For the purpose of the rule it also includes horses, sheep, goats, pigs, asses,[88] domestic fowl[89] and apparently domesticated deer.[90]

**[27.44]** In *Brady v Warren*[91] it was held that the defendant could not be liable for damage caused by rabbits which trespassed onto the plaintiff's property even though it was shown that the defendant who trapped and exported the rabbits had encouraged the propagation of the species by importing a foreign strain. The rabbits were wild and did not belong to the defendant and therefore he could not be liable for damage caused by them. In the same case, however, the court imposed liability on the defendant for damage caused by deer which strayed from his land deeming them to be "cattle" for the purose of the rule. In respect of these, however, it was shown that the defendant used to feed the deer in the

84. See Byrne & Binchy *Annual Review of Irish Law 1992*, pp 439-440, the Control of Dogs (Amendment) Act 1992 (Commencement) Order 1998 (SI 443/1998).

85. *Ryan v Glover* [1939] Ir Jur 65; *McCabe v Delaney* [1951] Ir Jur 10; *Brady v Warren* [1900] 2 IR 632. See also *Carroll v Parkes* (1912) 47 ILTR 88 (CC).

86. *Kennedy v McCabe* 103 ILTR 110; Williams, *Liability for Animals* (1939) at 373.

87. See LRC WP No 3, pp 51-53. On the necessity to prove negligence in such circumstances see *Buckley v Fitzgerald* (1881) 15 ILT Jo 118.

88. LRC WP No, 3 p 49

89. Williams *Liability For Animals* (1939), pp 27 and 136.

90. *Brady v Warren* [1900] 2 IR 632.

91. *Brady v Warren* [1900] 2 IR 632.

winter, and the court was willing to hold that the deer were tame and under the defendant's control.[92]

***(c) Incidence of liability***

**[27.45]** A question which frequently arises in relation to cattle trespass is whether it is the owner of the cattle or the owner of the land who is the proper defendant in such an action. The question becomes crucial when the cattle do not belong to the owner of the land from which they stray. The question has been discussed in three Irish cases which concerned agistment agreements. Under such an agreement the owner of the animals takes lands on a grazing letting but as part of the agreement the lessor undertakes to herd the cattle.[93] In *Dalton v O'Sullivan*[94] the action against the owner of the cattle failed because the defendant, who lived nearly 100 miles from the land, neither had possession of the cattle nor occupation or the land. Ownership of the animals alone was not sufficient to make him liable. In *Winters v Owens*,[95] however, the defendant (the owner of the animals) was held liable in a similar arrangement because, in spite of the agreement, he fed and tended the animals himself. In fact, he retained possession and control of the animals. In the third case, *Noonan v Hartnett*,[96] which had facts almost identical to *Winters v Owens*, the plaintiff brought the action against the owner of the land from which the cattle strayed. The defendant was held liable but probably not as landowner only, as it seems that he was also in possession of the cattle in question. The case is suspect insofar as it states that liability for cattle trespass is based on *Rylands v Fletcher* principles.

**[27.46]** From these cases it would seem that the crucial factor is possession and control of the animals rather than ownership of either the animals or the land.

***(d) Extent of liability***

**[27.47]** As cattle trespass is primarily considered to be a wrong against land it is quite clear that a complainant under this action can recover for damage to his land and crops.[97] Recovery can also be had for injury done by the trespassing cattle to the plaintiff's animals.[98] Although the older authorities doubted whether the defendant would be liable for personal injuries inflicted by the trespassing cattle,[99] *Wormald v Cole*[100] has allowed recovery for physical injuries suffered by the owner-occupier of land onto which the cattle had come. Similarly, it has been suggested that recovery should be allowed if the landowner's servant is injured while putting trespassing cattle off the property.[101] Indeed, if

---

92. See also *Foley v Berthoud* (1903) 37 ILTR 123 (County Court) - rabbits and pheasants; *Farrar v Nelson* (1885) 15 QB 258 where the defendant was held liable in nuisance. *Cf Diversified Holdings Ltd v The Queen in Right of British Columbia* (1982) 23 CCLT 156 (BC CA).

93. As to the nature of such lettings see Wylie, *Irish Land Law*, Ch 20, paras 25-27.

94. [1947] Ir Jur 25.

95. [1950] IR 225.

96. (1950) 84 ILTR 41 (CC).

97. *Cf Cronin v Connor* [1913] 2 IR 119.

98. *McCabe v Delaney* [1951] Ir Jur Rep 10 and *Ryan v Glover* [1939] Ir Jur 65.

99. See generally North *The Modern Law Of Animals* (1972), p 94; Williams *Liability For Animals* (1939), pp 163-173.

100. [1954] 1 QB 614.

101. *Harrison v Armstrong* (1917) 51 ILTR 38 (CC) which, however, may be based more on negligence. See also *Winters v Owens* [1950] IR 225-231; Williams *Liability For Animals* (1939), p 163; *Cox v Burbridge* (1863) 13 CB (ns); 430 143 ER 171.

this is so, the defendant should be liable for any personal injuries inflicted on any person lawfully on the property, provided the damage is not too remote.[102]

### *(e) Defences*

**[27.48]** The defences[103] which are available to the defendant in an action for cattle trespass are Act of God,[104] the plaintiff's own fault,[105] contributory negligence[106] and, probably, inevitable accident.[107] After some initial doubt it seems to be clear now that the wrongful act of a third party is also a defence. In *Moloney v Stephens*[108] where a third person left the defendant's gate open so that his cattle strayed onto the plaintiff's property, it was held following an earlier Irish case of *McGibbon v McCorry*,[109] that the defendant was not liable.

## Animals on the Highway

**[27.49]** Animals brought onto the highway are subject to the normal rules of negligence and nuisance and the liability in this context has been described earlier in the chapter.

**[27.50]** A curious immunity, however, existed until very recently in respect of damage which is caused by animals that have strayed onto the highway. In such cases the owner of the animal was not liable at common law. This rule was established in *Searle v Wallbank*[110] and had been followed in several Irish cases.[111]

**[27.51]** The justification for the rule seemed to be first, that a rule which would oblige the owner of cattle to keep them from straying onto the highway was too onerous a burden for landowners,[112] and second, that road users must take the ordinary risks inherent in road travel including the presence of straying animals. This immunity was strangely anachronistic in recent times. It had been frequently criticised and its abolition had been recommended by the Law Reform Commission[113] in 1977. The limits of the rule as it operated in Ireland should be noted. Firstly, it appeared that it did not apply where the animals were straying on the road in sufficiently large numbers to cause an obstruction.[114] Secondly, an animal might have been known to have such characteristics as to impose upon its owner a duty to take steps to prevent it from endangering the public by getting on to the highway and there exhibiting its characteristics to the danger of users of the highway.[115]

---

102. For powers of gardaí to impound wandering animals now see Animals Act 1985 ss 4 and 5.
103. See generally LRC WP No 3, pp 60-62.
104. See Delany 10 NILQ 135; Williams *Liability For Animals* (1939), pp 184-185.
105. *Plummer v Webb Noy* (1619) 98 74 ER 1064.
106. Civil Liability Act 1961, s 34.
107. YBP 21 E4 28b pl 23 continued in YBP 22 E4 8a pl 24 (Bro Custom 51 Trespas 351). Cited in Williams, *Liability For Animals* (1939), p 191. See generally Williams *Liability For Animals* (1939), p 185-194; *cf Winters v Owens* [1950] IR 225-231 at 232.
108. [1945] Ir Jur Rep 37.
109. (1909) 43 ILTR 132.
110. [1947] AC 341.
111. *Gibb v Comerford* [1942] IR 295; *Dunphy v Bryan* (1963) 97 ILTR 4 (DC); *Cunningham v Whelan* (1918) 52 ILTR 67 and *Hall v Wightman* [1926] N1 92.
112. *Cf* Delany 10 NILQ 140.
113. See LRC WP No 3 pp 70 *et seq.*
114. *Cunningham v Whelan* (1918) 52 ILTR 67.
115. *Brock v Richards* [1951] I KB 529 at 535 (CA); *Howard v Bergin O'Connor & Co* [1925] 12 IR 110.

Thus, if a person knew that his or her dog had a mischievous propensity to chase passing motor-cyclists, the owner would be liable in *scienter* if he or she allowed the dog to stray onto the highway. Thirdly, the rule did not apply where animals were brought onto the highway.[116] Fourthly, in *Howard v Bergin O'Connor & Co*,[117] O'Connor J was inclined to limit the application of the rule to rural conditions, being of the view that city dwellers should be under an obligation to fence. This line of argument received general support among academic commentators,[118] and decisions in other jurisdictions[119] also tended in this direction. Indeed, in *Gillick v O'Reilly*[120] McWilliam J cast strong doubt on the justice of the rule in modern times:

> "It seems to me that, in each age, circumstances arise, different from those of previous ages, which entail that acting or failing to act in the way in which a reasonable man might be expected to act constitutes a breach of duty to others. In determining negligence the circumstances must be considered in each case so that there cannot be any hard and fast rule governing all cases. I am of opinion that this applies equally to consideration of the liability for negligence with regard to animals wandering the public road. An unfenced road running through rough mountain pasture gives rise to different considerations from those arising on a modern main motor road running through fenced farm land and I cannot see any logical reason for a principle which ignores the entirely different circumstances of each when considering the duty owed to users of the road."[121]

**[27.52]** Lastly, where there were special circumstances such as peculiar topography or where the animal was engaged in an activity that could properly be carried on only under a high degree of human control, it had been suggested[122] that liability might also arise.

**[27.53]** It should also be noted that where a person crashed a car into an animal straying on the highway the driver might not only find himself or herself remediless under the old law, but might even be sued by the owner of the animal for damage to the animal. In such a case, however, there was no reason why the defendant could not successfully plead contributory negligence on the part of the plaintiff. No duty of care needs to be established for contributory negligence. All that was required was "want of care" on the part of the plaintiff.[123]

**[27.54]** The pressures for reform of the rule in *Searle v Wallbank* continued to mount, however, until in 1985 they became irresistible. Legislative intervention finally removed the immunity and exposed landowners adjoining the highway to the ordinary law of negligence. Section 2 of the Animals Act 1985 now provides as follows:

---

116. *Gomberg v Smith* [1963] 1 QB 25.

117. [1925] 2 IR 110 at 133-134.

118. Eg Delany (1954) 10 NILQ 135 at 141.

119. *Cf Fleming v Atkinson* [1959] SCR 513; *Gash v Wood* (1960) 22 DLR (2d) 625; *Kelly v Sweeney* [1975] 2 NSW LR 720; *Gardiner v Miller* 1967 SLT 29; but see *Lane v Biel* [1971] 2 WWR 128 (Sask); *Ross v McCarthy* [1970] NZLR 449 (CA).

120. [1984] ILRM 402.

121. [1984] ILRM 402 at 405

122. *Ellis v Johnstone* [1963] 2 QB 8; *Bativala v West* [1970] 1 QB 716; North, *The Modern Law Of Animals* (1972), pp 150-151.

123. Civil Liability Act 1961, s 34(1). See *Coady v Player & Wills (IR) Ltd* (1979) 114 ILTR 32 (CC) where the plaintiff's damages were reduced by 20%.

(1) So much of the rules of the common law relating to liability for negligence as excludes or restricts the duty which a person might owe to others to take such care as is reasonable to see that damage is not caused by an animal straying on to a public road is hereby abolished.

(2)(a) Where damage is caused by an animal straying from unfenced land on to a public road, a person who placed the animal on the land shall not be regarded as having committed a breach of the duty to take care by reason only of placing it there if -

(i) the land is situated in an area where fencing is not customary, and

(ii) he had a right to place the animal on that land,

(b) In this subsection 'fencing' includes the construction of any obstacle designed to prevent animals from straying, and 'unfenced' shall be construed accordingly.

**[27.55]** Although the landowner's immunity is now gone, the section does not make the adjoining landowner strictly liable in these circumstances. All that is required of him or her is to take reasonable care in respect of the fencing and provided the landowner does this, liability will not be imposed. This is clear from the Supreme Court in *O'Shea v Anhold and Horse Holiday Farm Ltd*.[124] In O'Shea's case, a horse collided with a motor vehicle on a public road. The trial judge found that the defendant was negligent, but the Supreme Court reversed. Keane J stated that:

> "Section 2 of the Animals Act 1985 has abolished the somewhat anomalous immunity from the ordinary law of negligence which the owners of land for which animals strayed on to the highway previously enjoyed. It has not, however, imposed any form of absolute liability on such persons."[125]

**[27.56]** At the trial the defendant, through experts, had given evidence that the fencing of the field was adequate and the defendant had also given evidence that he closed the gate after leaving the field. This evidence was not challenged by the plaintiff and in these circumstances the plaintiff could not succeed.

**[27.57]** The question whether the plaintiff may rely on the *res ipsa loquitur* doctrine had arisen in *O'Reilly v Lavelle*,[126] where the plaintiff while driving his car collided with a freisan calf at approximately 10 pm on a summer evening. Johnson J held that the *res ipsa loquitur* applied and on the facts before him imposed liability on the defendant cattle owner. He stated:

> "Cattle properly managed should not wander on the road and therefore the burden of proof in this case shifts to the defendant to show that he took reasonable care of his animals. I believe that there is no matter more appropriate for the application of the doctrine of *res ipsa loquitur* than cattle wandering on the highway."[127]

---

124. Supreme Court, 23 October 1996.

125. Keane J's judgment, p 7.

126. [1990] 2 IR 372 (HC), (CCA).

127. [1990] 2 IR 372. Johnson J considered that Brennan DJ had been "absolutely correct in his view of the law" in *McCaffrey v Lundy* (1988) ILT (ns) 245 (DC). See further Needham 'Straying Animals: The Burden of Proof' (1988) 82 Gaz Incorp L Soc of Ireland Gaz 171. *Cf* Byrne & Binchy, *Annual Review of Irish Law 1990*, p 554. Developments in the United States of America are analysed by Wall 'Note: *Res Ipsa Loquitur* and the Great Cattle Caper: Inferred Negligence in Escaped Livestock - Automobile Collisions after Roberts v Weber & Sons Co (1995) 248 Neb 243, 533 MW 2d 664', (1996) 75 Neb LR 308.

**[27.58]** The Supreme Court in *O'Shea v Anhold and Horse Holiday Farm Ltd*,[128] without citing *O'Reilly*, adopted the same approach. Although O'Flaherty J seemed to suggest that s 2 of the Animals Act 1985 itself imposed an onus on the defendants to show that they had taken reasonable care, Keane J, stated that "[t]his would seem to be a case in which the *res ipsa loquitur* principle clearly appears".[129] The horse in this case was under the management and control of the defendants and Keane J considered it:

> "self evident that a horse will not normally escape from lands on to the public road if adequate fencing is provided and any gates are kept in a closed position."[130]

Like O'Flaherty J, however, Keane J found that the defendants had discharged the onus of proof in this case.

**[27.59]** Two other matters may be noted. First, the 1985 Act itself provides that it is no breach of duty for a person to place animals on unfenced lands adjoining the highway where the owner of the animals has a right to place them on the land and the area is one where fencing is not customary.[131]

**[27.60]** Secondly, where animals wander from an undeveloped or uncompleted housing estate which has been designated by the local authority as "a designated area", the occupier of such a site (the builder/developer) is liable for damage caused by such straying animals unless the occupier has notified the authorities in advance that the animals are not there with his or her permission (s 6). This section addresses the problem of animals straying from unfinished building sites and makes the occupier liable as if he were the owner.[132]

## The Control of Horses Act 1996

**[27.61]** The Control of Horses Act 1996 is a legislative response to the growing phenomenon of horse ownership in urban areas. It is largely a regulatory law and as such not of great significance to the law of torts. Principally it aims to protect people and their property from the dangers of wandering horses and to improve the welfare of horses. At the time of its enactment, there were around three thousand stray horses in the State of which at least a thousand were in the Dublin area.

**[27.62]** Under the provision of the 1996 Act, all horses in designated areas have to be licensed. Officials are given wide powers to deal with uncontrolled horses and their owners.

**[27.63]** Section 45 is of particular relevance. Headed "Criminal liability for injury or damage caused by horses", it provides as follows:

---

128. Supreme Court, 23 October 1996.
129. Keane J's judgment, p 4.
130. Keane J's judgment, p 5.
131. See Bland *The Law of Easements and Profits a Prendre* (1997), pp 167-168 discussing the unreported decision of *Bryant v Snell* Circuit Court, 18 June 1997 (Judge Lynch).
132. Regulations regarding the control of animals when on the highway are contained in the Road Traffic Bye-Laws 1964 (SI 294/1964), Articles 30-33: see Walsh ed, *Agriculture and the Law* (1993), p 165.

> (1) The owner, keeper or person in charge or control of a horse who willfully or recklessly permits the horse to pose a danger to a person or a property or to cause injury to a person or damage to any property shall be guilty of an offence.
>
> (2) A person who willfully or recklessly causes a horse to pose a danger to a person or property or to injure a person or damage any property shall be guilty of an offence.

**[27.64]** The question arises as to whether this section gives an injured individual a civil right of action. The use of the phrase "criminal liability" in the heading may not be determinative. When the legislation was being enacted, the Minister for Justice, Mr Deenihan, noted that originally it had been intended to provide for civil liability in this context but that this policy had been abandoned.

**[27.65]** A strong case can be made that s 45 does indeed confer a civil right of action. It clearly seeks to protect an identified, relatively narrow, class of potential victims rather than the public as a whole. The section is noteworthy in making it plain that it is not some general measure concerned with the environment or even the broad goal of road safety, but rather the risk of injury to particular persons or their property. Having said this, it should be acknowledged that the heading is less than fully supportive of this argument and that the Oireachtas Debates are similarly unhelpful. In practice, the issue may not be very important since it is hard to conceive of a case where a common law action for negligence would fail in circumstances under civil liability, and nonetheless be imposed under s 45.

## IV. Law Reform Commission Proposals

**[27.66]** The Animals Act 1985 and Control of Dogs Act 1986 go only a small distance towards implementing the radical proposals on the subject made by the Law Reform Commission in its *Report on Civil Liability for Animals*[133] published in 1982. The Commission had recommended that the owner of any animal which causes damage should be made liable on the principles of strict liability irrespective of fault. Act of God and contributory negligence would be recognised as defences in such a regime of strict liability. As an exception to this, however, it was suggested that where the plaintiff was a trespasser on the defendant's property when injured by the defendant's animal ordinary negligence principles should apply. Section 21 of the Control of Dogs Act 1986 reflects the spirit of these proposals, but only in respect of dogs, and even here, as we have seen, certain types of damage-causing acts do not fall within its scope.

---

133. LRC 2-1982. For analysis of the Commission's proposals on similar lines made in its Working Paper on the subject (LRC WP No 3, p 90) see Osborough (1978) 13 Ir Jur (ns) 182. For criticism of the narrow scope of the Animals Act 1985 see 'Editorial: A Tame Piece of Law Reform' (1985) 3 ILT (ns) 157.

# Chapter 28

# Trespass to Goods

I. Introduction .................... 769
II. Elements of the Tort of Trespass to Goods .................... 769

## I. Introduction

**[28.01]** The law relating to wrongful interference with chattels lacks clarity and consistency.[1] There is force in Sir John Salmond's observation that it is:

> "a region still darkened with the mists of legal formalism, through which no man will find his way by the light of nature or with any other guide save the old learning of writs and forms of action and the mysteries of pleading".[2]

**[28.02]** The present law represents an interim stage in the historical process[3] whereby the old actions for trespass *de bonis asportasis*, detinue and replevin were supplemented by the action for trover, which in turn was modified into the present tort of conversion. The judiciary seem unwilling to pursue the task of rationalisation very much further, so perhaps it is best to look instead to the legislature as a more likely source of restatement and reform.[4]

## II. Elements of the Tort of Trespass to Goods

**[28.03]** In *Farrell v Minister for Agriculture and Food*,[5] Carroll J observed that this tort "consists of wrongfully and directly interfering with the possession of chattels". A number of aspects of the tort are uncertain in the absence of clear Irish authorities in point.

### Nature of the Interference

**[28.04]** The interference may take many forms. It may consist, for example, of taking the chattel out of the possession of another,[6] moving it from one place

1. *Farrell v Minister for Agriculture and Food* High Court, 11 October 1995 (Carroll J) at 19 approving the statement to this effect in the second edition of this work p 522.
2. Salmond 'Observations on Trover and Conversion' (1905) 21 LQR 43 at 43.
3. See Ames 'The History of Trover' (1898) 11 HLR 277 at 374. Baker, *An Introduction to English Legal History* (2nd ed, 1979), Ch 18.
4. Moderate reforms were enacted in England by the Torts (Interference with Goods) Act 1977 (c 12) based on the (more radical) 18th Report of the Law Reform Committee (Cmnd 4774 1971) analysed by Bentley (1972) 35 MLR 171. Proposals for reform been made by the Law Reform Committee of South Australia in its Ninety-Fifth Report Law of Detinue Conversion and Trespass to Goods (1987) have yet to receive a legislative response.
5. High Court, 11 October 1995 at p 19 of the judgment.
6. Eg *Brewer v Dew* (1843) 11 M & W 625 152 ER 955 - wrongful seizure of goods; *Gahan v Maingay* Ridg Lap & Scho (1793) 62; *Conway v Archdall* (1826) 1 Bat 182; *Wilson v Lombank Ltd* [1963] 1 WLR 1294 - removal of car from garage where plaintiff had left it for repairs;

to another,[7] or doing damage to it with one's person[8] or property.[9] Therefore, in *Farrell v Minister for Agriculture and Food*,[10] Carroll J held that there had been a direct interference with the plaintiff's right to possession of his cattle where the Minister, "with the mantle of statutory regulations assumed to be valid around him", but which were in fact *ultra vires*, constrained the plaintiff to have his herd taken for slaughter:

> "The Minister did it knowingly and intended the consequences, though he did not act [with] *mala fides* because he did not know the regulations were *ultra vires*. To my mind that is a direct interference with the plaintiff's right to possession of his animals and therefore the tort of trespass to chattels was committed ..."

**[28.05]** The requirement that the interference be direct was emphasised in *McDonagh v West of Ireland Fisheries Ltd*,[11] where Blayney J held[12] the defendant not liable in trespass where a boat, which the defendant had temporarily removed from the moorings in a harbour, was later damaged in uncertain circumstances. Blayney J said:

> "The injury to the [boat] was clearly not direct; in so far as it is possible to ascertain how it was caused, it was probably due to her settling on some obstruction on the sea-bed. Such an injury, not being direct, would not have constituted a trespass."[13]

**[28.06]** Where precisely the line is to be drawn between direct and indirect interference is, of course, not easy to say.[14] It is clearly a trespass to shoot at racing pigeons[15] or beat a dog,[16]

---

6. (contd) *GWK Ltd v Dunlop Rubber Co Ltd* (1926) 42 Times LR 593 (CA) - removal of tyres from cars; *Sligo Corporation v Gilbride* [1929] IR 351 (SC) - removal of stones from wall; *Northern Ireland Master Butcher Wholesale Supply Association Ltd v Belfast Corporation* [1965] NI 30 - seizure by sanitary authority officers of unsound meat with a view to disposing of it in manner contrary to statute held a trespass; *Whelan v Madigan* [1978] ILRM 136 (HC) - removal of chairs by landlord; *Murphy v Mulcahy* (1896) 30 ILT & Sol J 37 - wrongful removal of sand and gravel from public road on plaintiff's land; *Cooney v Cooney* (1920) 54 ILTR 60 - defendant was liable for taking possession of crops planted by plaintiff while licensee of defendant and depriving the plaintiff of them.
7. *Kirk v Gregory* (1876) 1 Ex D 55.
8. *Cf Fouldes v Willoughby* (1841) 8 M & W 540 at 549; 151 ER 1153 at 1157. See also *Deering v Mahon* (1851) 2 Ir CLR 25 (Comm Pleas) - where sheriff had lawfully seized furniture he could nonetheless be sued for trespass for damage "unnecessarily done" when furniture was in his custody.
9. *M'Cormick v Ballantine* (1859) 10 ICLR 305 (QB).
10. *Farrell v Minister for Agriculture and Food* High Court, 11 October 1995.
11. High Court, unrep 19 December 1986 (Blayney J).
12. The plaintiff did not press the trespass issue Blayney J considering him right not to have done so: p 5 of judgement.
13. *McDonagh v West of Ireland* High Court, 19 December 1986 (Blayney J).
14. *Farrell v Minister for Agriculture and Food* High Court, 11 October 1995 at p 19 of Carroll J's judgment approving the statement to this effect in the second edition of this work p 523.
15. *Hamps v Darby* [1948] 2 KB 311 (CA).
16. *Wright v Ramscott* (1665) 1 Wms Sound 82 85 ER 92. See also *Kellett v Stannard* (1851) 2 Ir CLR 156 - shooting of a dog; *Staveley v Barrington* (1913) 47 ILTR 296 - shooting trespassing dog was justified as reasonably necessary to protect sheep; *cf Brown v Belfast Water Commissioners* (1912) 47 ILTR 153 (Craig KC); The Dogs Act 1986 s 23(1) provides a defence in an action for shooting a dog, that the dog was worrying livestock (or was about to do so) and there was no other means of preventing it from doing so or that it was a stray dog in the vicinity of a place where livestock had been injured or killed and the defendant (being the person in charge of the livestock) reasonably believed the dog had been involved in the injury or killing, the gardaí being notified within 48 hours.

but is it trespass[17] to lay poison for an animal?[18] And what about chasing an animal? Is there a difference between chasing it over a cliff and chasing it until it dies of exhaustion? The courts have not yet given clear answers to these questions.

## Is Trespass to Goods Actionable *Per Se*?

**[28.07]** The commentators[19] are generally of the view that trespass to goods is actionable *per se*, but the judicial authorities[20] are less than compelling on this question. On principle, it would seem that such trespass should be actionable *per se*, and there seems to be no reason to introduce such refinements as the requirement of asportation or dispossession, as some of the commentators have suggested.[21]

**[28.08]** The policy basis that has been articulated for making trespass to goods actionable *per se* is scarcely convincing. It has been said that otherwise "persons could touch museum exhibits with impunity";[22] it has even been contended that making the tort actionable *per se* protects "the perhaps not oversensitive person who declined to use his toothbrush any more after another had used it without his consent".[23] The problem of unauthorised post-mortem examination of bodies is also considered relevant in this context (although there is uncertainty as to whether any action would be available to the executors in such a case).[24] It would seem that these attempted rationalisations of the rule ignore the fact that the courts in such cases would surely find that damage had been sustained.

---

17. It may of course be another tort such as negligence for example.
18. *Cf* STREET, p 68; TRINDADE & CANE, p 134; *Hutchins v Maughan* [1947] VLR 131; see also WINFIELD & JOLOWICZ, p 585.
19. Eg SALMOND & HEUSTON, p 95; POLLOCK (15th ed) pp 264-265; STREET, p 69.
20. *Leitch & Co Ltd v Leydon* [1931] AC 90 at 106 (*per* Lord Blanesburgh); *cf Slater v Swann* (1730) 2 Stra 872, 93 ER 906; *Kirk v Gregory* (1876) 1 Ex D 55. See also *Demers v Desrosier* [1929] 3 DLR 401 (Alta SC); TRINDADE & CANE p 135-136. The New Zealand decision of *Everitt v Martin* [1953] NZLR 298 (SC) is a clear authority denying that the tort is actionable *per se*. In Ireland a dictum in a criminal case appears to support the view that trespass to chattels is actionable *per se*. In *The People (DPP) v Morgan* (1980) 114 ILTR 60 at 62 (CC) Judge Sheridan observed that:

    ".... an examination of the private effects of another person is clearly an act of trespass. In the case of a ladies' handbag which is very often a recepticle for the most private documents and effects apart from money, I cannot think of many better examples of gross trespass ...".

    In *Flannery v Dean* [1995] 2 ILRM 393 (HC) Costello P awarded no damages to the plaintiff as she had not established any loss. It is not clear from Costello P's judgment what exactly was the nature of the plaintiff's claim which may perhaps have been one sounding exclusively in contract or bailment rather than tort: *cf* the headnote to the report at p 393.
21. Clearly, however, if the tort is not to be actionable *per se* a strong case can be made for holding that proof of asportation or dispossession would be sufficient proof of damage; this is the position in the United States: PROSSER & KEETON, p 87
22. STREET, p 69. This example is used widely by the commentators.
23. STREET (8th ed), p 60.
24. In the United States the Courts have recognised the true basis of such wrongdoing which is not interference with a property right but instead involves wrongful intrusion into the privacy of the personal feelings of the bereaved: *cf* PROSSER & KEETON, p 63; Restatement Second on Torts section 218; Comment e, *Clidden v Szybiak* (1949) 95 NH 318 63 A 2d 233; Anon 'Note' (1934) 18 Minn LR 204.

**[28.09]** The policy issue is, therefore, a more stark one: should I have a right of action where my property is wrongfully interfered with, even though absolutely no damage whether of a financial nature (as in the museum example) or of a psychological nature (as in the toothbrush case) has been sustained? The answer will surely depend to some extent on one's evaluation of the degree of importance that attaches to the use and possession of private property, but it will also depend on values that are perhaps more in harmony with more contemporary themes - the protection of privacy being the clearest of these values. It has been suggested that trespass to land historically carried "a connotation of an affront to honour",[25] which was lacking in trespass to goods. Whether that distinction would appeal to a court today may be doubted.

## The Title of the Plaintiff

**[28.10]** As in the case with trespass to land the tort of trespass to goods is "founded on possession"[26] and not ownership.[27] Thus, in *Keenan Bros Ltd v CIE*,[28] in 1962, where the plaintiffs' goods had been delayed in *transitu* as a result of a labour dispute, Budd J declined to grant an interlocutory mandatory injunction compelling the carriers to deliver the goods or to permit the plaintiffs' employees to remove the goods from the railway wagons in which they were languishing. He said:

> "Prima facie it is the right and function of the defendant company to open its own wagons and remove goods out of them. It would seem a clear act of trespass at common law for any person to open the defendants' wagons and remove goods from them unless by virtue of the defendants' permission or by virtue of some legal right. The fact that the goods may be the plaintiffs' does not alter the position and entitle them to commit an act of trespass to recover them. The only right that they could rely on to do what they claim they are entitled to do is one that can properly be spelled out in the contract [between the parties]."[29]

## Defendant's State of Mind

**[28.11]** In order to be actionable a trespass must be either wilful or negligent.[30] This was held by O'Keeffe J, in *ESB v Hastings & Co Ltd*[31] where, after referring to the English decisions of *National Coal Board v Evans (JE) & Co (Cardiff) Ltd*,[32] and *Fowler v*

---

25. Todd Burrows Chambers, Mulgan & Mcgregor, VENNELL, p 486.
26. *Ward v Macauley* (1791) 4 Term Rep 489 at 490; 100 ER 1135 at 1135.
27. SALMOND & HEUSTON, p 97; HARPER JAMES & GRAY, pp 134-135.
28. (1963) 97 ILTR 54 (HC).
29. (1963) 97 ILTR 54 at 59. It should be noted that courts in a number of common law jurisdictions have recognised that an owner out of possession whose goods are permanently damaged or destroyed may have a right of action in case - *Mears v London & SW Ry* (1862) 11 CB (ns) 850: *Penfolds Wines Pty Ltd v Elliott* (1946) 74 CLR 204 at 230; *Dee Trading Co Pty Ltd v Baldwin* [1938] VLR 175 (SC). For discussion as to what constitutes permanent damage in this context see KLAR, p 83; TRINDADE & CANE, pp 170-171; Tattenborn 'Reversionary Damage to Chattels' [1994] CLJ 326.
30. See *M'Cormick v Ballantine* (1859) 10 ICLR 305 (QB); but *cf Plunkett v Irish Annuals Press Ltd* (1938) 72 ILTR 161 (HC) revg (1937) 71 ILTR 76 (CC). Involuntary contact such as breaking a vase while sleepwalking should not on principle constitute trespass to goods: *Beals v Haywood* [1960] NZLR 131 at 137.
31. [1965] Ir Jur 51 (HC). *Cf* Combs 'Note: Torts - Accidental Trespass' (1945) 33 Ky LJ 203.
32. [1951] 2 KB 861 (CA).

*Lanning*,[33] the judge stated that "[t]hese cases appear to support th[is] proposition sufficiently for me to accept it as being correct".[34]

**[28.12]** On the facts of the case, liability was imposed on account of the negligent conduct of the defendants. The defendants, in resurfacing a road, opened a trench and allowed their mechanical shovel to damage a high tension cable in the possession of the plaintiffs. The defendants had been made aware by the plaintiffs of the presence of the cable in the general vicinity of their operations and the Court held that this put the defendants "on notice sufficiently to render them liable for the trespass".[35] O'Keeffe J did not discuss the question of which party bore the onus of proof. It is therefore submitted that the decision should not be interpreted as altering the previously accepted principle that the onus rests on the defendant to show that he was guilty of neither an intentional or negligent wrong.[36]

## Character of Defendant's Conduct

**[28.13]** The defendant will be liable even where the defendant did not appreciate that the interference was wrongful.[37] Thus, the deliberate use of a chattel in the mistaken belief that it is one's own will constitute a trespass.[38] However where the defendant uses a chattel without having obtained the permission of the owner, he or she may be excused where the situation was one of some urgency (albeit created by the defendant himself or herself) if the intervention is in protection of the owner's interests and it is not possible to obtain the consent of the owner beforehand.[39]

## Lawful Authority

**[28.14]** In some circumstances, an action that would otherwise constitute a trespass to goods may not be tortious because the actor has lawful authority to do the action. In the Supreme Court decision of *Jennings v Quinn*,[40] in 1966, O'Keeffe J summarised the position in relation to the seizure of goods by the Gardaí when effecting a valid arrest. He said:

> "In my opinion the public interest requires that the police, when effecting a lawful arrest, may seize, without a search warrant, property in the possession or custody of the person

---

33. [1959] 1 QB 426 (Diplock J).
34. [1965] Ir Jur 51 at 54.
35. [1965] Ir Jur 51 at 54 at 55.
36. *Cf Ross v Dunphy* High Court, 13 February 1978 (Finlay P) which may perhaps be interpreted as lending support to this proposition. See also *Bell Canada v Bannermount Ltd* 35 DLR (3d) 267 (Ont CA 1973).
37. *Farrell v Minister for Agriculture and Food* High Court, 11 October 1995, Carroll J; *Cf McMullan v Bradshaw* (1916) 50 ILTR 205 (CA).
38. *Cf Wilson v Lombank Ltd* [1963] 1 WLR 1294; *Dexter v Cole* (1858) 6 Wis 319 70 Am Dec 465.
39. *Cf Ross v Dunphy* High Court, 13 February 1978. Note that although Finlay P stated that the defendant's conduct did not constitute "a wrongful act" the onus rested on the defendant to show that damage sustained to the chattel during the period it was under his control without the permission of the owner had occurred without his negligence. See also *London & NW Ry Co v Hughes* (1889) 26 LR Ir 165 (QB). In *McDonagh v West of Ireland Fisheries Ltd* High Court, 19 December 1986 Blayney J interpreted Finlay P's remarks as involving the application of the *res ipsa loquitur* principle.
40. [1968] IR 305 (SC). See Casey *Constitutional Law in Ireland* (3rd ed, 2000), pp 531-532.

arrested when they believe it necessary to do so to avoid the abstraction or destruction of that property and when that property is:

(a) evidence in support of the criminal charge upon which the arrest is made, or

(b) evidence in support of any other criminal charge against that person then in contemplation, or

(c) reasonably believed to be stolen property or to be property unlawfully in the possession of that person;

and that they may retain such property for use at the trial of the person arrested, or of any other person or persons, on any criminal charge in which the property is to be used as evidence in support of the charge or charges; and that thereafter they should return the property to the person from whom it was seized, unless the disposal of the property otherwise has been directed by a court of competent jurisdiction.[41]"[42]

**[28.15]** O'Keeffe J considered that the public interest also requires that property, which the police might lawfully retain for use as material evidence in a charge against a person arrested if that charge were brought against him within the jurisdiction, may also be lawfully retained by them for the purpose of sending it into another jurisdiction where a charge on which that property is material evidence has been laid against the person arrested, "at least in cases where the lawful arrest of the person within the jurisdiction was made in aid of the jurisdiction of the country in which the charge is laid".[43]

**[28.16]** The statute books since Independence are replete with provisions entitling members of the Garda Síochána and others to seize goods in certain circumstances. Thus, for example, under s 13(1)(c) of the Animals Remedies Act 1993, members of the Garda Síochána or officers of Customs and Excise are entitled to seize anything found in the course of a search under the section.[44] Similar powers, are conferred on members of the

---

41. *Cf* the Police (Property) Act 1897 (60 & 61 Vict c 30).

42. [1968] IR 305 at 309. See further Walsh, *The Irish Police: A Legal and Constitutional Perspective* (1998), pp 153-154.

43. [1968] IR 305 at 310. See also *Dillon v O'Brien* (1887) 20 LR Ir 300. In *Chic Fashions (West Wales) Ltd v Jones* [1968] 2 QB 299 at 313 (CA) Lord Denning MR expressed the opinion that a policeman entering a house by virtue of a search warrant for stolen goods may seize:

> "not only the goods which he reasonably believes to be covered by the warrant but also may seize other goods which he believes on reasonable grounds to have been stolen and to be material evidence on a charge of stealing or receiving against the person in possession of them *or anyone associated with him*". (Emphasis added.)

One should not ignore the constitutional dimensions: *cf The People (Attorney-General) v O'Brien* [1965] IR 142 at 170 (SC). See also *O'Mahony v District Judge Shields* High Court, 22 February 1988 (Lardner J).

45 See also the Animals Remedies Act 1993, s 26. *Cf* the Criminal Justice Act 1994, especially ss 38, 39 and 64; the Criminal Justice (Public Order) Act 1994, s 22 - surrender of liquor to member of Garda Síochána at public event; the Sea Pollution Act 1991, s 24 - seizure of ship that has caused or may cause pollution; the Street and House to House Collections Act 1962, s 20 - seizure of money and collection boxes; the Video Recordings Act 1989, s 25 - seizure of evidence for prosecution under the Act; the Wildlife Act 1976, s 72 - seizure of evidence; the Radiological Protection Act 1991, s 29 - wide-ranging seizure power and s 33 - powers of slaughter of animals, destruction of crops and disposal of eggs, fish, etc; the Wireless Telegraphy Act 1926, s 8 - considered in *O'Mahony v District Justice Shields* High Court, 22 February 1988 (Lardner J); the Irish Aviation Authority Act 1993, s 65 - detention of aircraft involved in accident or other incident;

Garda Síochána and receivers of wrecks under ss 10(1)(c) and 57(2)(d), respectively, of the Merchant Shipping (Salvage and Wreck) Act 1993 and on members of the Garda Síochána under s 14 (1) of the Broadcasting Act 1990.

**[28.17]** Section 9(1) of the Criminal Law Act 1976 Act confers a very broad power of retention. It provides as follows:

> "where in the course of exercising any powers under this Act or in the course of a search carried out under any other power, a member of the Garda Síochána, a prison officer or a member of the Defence Forces finds, or comes into possession of, anything which he believes to be evidence of any offence, it may be seized and retained for use as evidence in any criminal proceedings in relation to a breach of prison discipline, for such period from the date of seizure as is reasonable or, if proceedings are commenced in which the things so seized is required for use as evidence, until the conclusion of the proceedings, and thereafter the Police (Property) Act 1897 shall apply to the thing so seized in the same manner as that Act applies to property which has come into the possession of the Garda Síochána in the circumstances mentioned in that Act."[45]

44. (contd) the Irish Horseracing Industry Act 1994, s 51 - removal of books or accounts of bookmaker; the Gas Act 1976, s 26(2) - removal of soil for tests; the Food Safety Authority of Ireland Act 1998, s 50 - removal of records and s 51 - taking of samples; the Energy (Miscellaneous Provisions) Act 1995, s 16 - seizure of evidence; the Dumping at Sea Act 1996, s 6 - detention of vessel or offshore installation; the Carriage of Dangerous Goods by Road Act 1998, s 64(4)(f) - power to take samples of goods from premises, place or transport equipment on suspicion of its having been, or intended to be, used for a purpose connected with the carriage of dangerous goods; the Casual Trading Act 1995, s 11 - seizure of goods by member of Garda Síochána; the Chemical Weapons Act 1997, s 7 - wide-ranging powers of removal; the Child Trafficking and Pornography Act 1998, s 7(2)(c) - seizure of evidence; the Control of Dogs Act 1986, s 16(1), as amended by the Control of Dogs (Amendment) Act 1992, s 7 - dog warden's power to seize and detain dogs; the Control of Horses Act 1996, s 37 - seizure and detention of horses; the Sea Pollution (Amendment) Act 1999, s 14 - see Symmons 'Annotation to the Act' ICLSA, General Note to s 14; the International War Crimes Tribunals Act 1998, s 30 - seizure of evidence; the Investment Intermediaries Act 1995, s 65 - power of authorised officer, subject to warrant of District Court Judge, to remove books, records and documents for examination; the Non-Fatal Offences Against the Person Act 1997, s 7(2) - seizure of syringe by member of Garda Síochána; the Milk (Regulation of Supply) Act 1994, s 15(1)(d) - inspector entitled to take sample of milk from tankard; the Proceeds of Crime Act 1996, s 15 - seizure of property to prevent its removal from the State; the Prohibition of Incitement to Hatred Act 1989, s 9 - seizure of recordings, materials or scripts; the National Monuments (Amendment) Act 1994, s 9 - power of Director of the National Museum of Ireland to take possession of archaeological object; the Child Care Act 1991, s 74(7) - seizure of solvents; the Misuse of Drugs Act 1977, s 23, as amended by the Misuse of Drugs Act 1984, s 12 - seizure and detention of evidence; the Licensing (Combating Drug Abuse) Act 1997, ss 14(3) and 16 - seizure and retention of sound equipment; the Litter Act 1982, ss 11 and 12 - removal of abandoned or environmentally damaging vehicles from land; the Litter Pollution Act 1997, s 20 - removal of environmentally damaging articles or advertisements from structures; the Merchant Shipping (Investigation of Marine Casualties) Act 2000, s 27(3) - removal of object believed relevant to conduct of investigation; the Copyright and Related Rights Act 2000, ss 132 and 133 - seizure of infringing copies, articles or devices, ss 256 and 257 - seizure of illicit recordings; the Electronic Commerce Act 2000, ss 27(2) and 27(5) - seizure and retention of evidence; the Illegal Immigrants (Trafficking) Act 2000, s 3 - Garda power to detain vehicles and s 7 - Garda power to seize evidence.

45. Seizure of documents made solely for obtaining or communicating legal advice are exempt: s 9(2).

**[28.18]** Draconian powers of search and seizure of documents under s 29 of the Offences Against the Person Act 1939, as amended by s 5 of the Criminal Law Act 1976, should also be noted. So also s 10 of the Criminal Justice (Miscellaneous Provisions) Act 1997 provides[46] for the issuing of search warrants by judges of the District Court for prescribed serious offences,[47] and for the seizure[48] by members of the Garda Síochána of anything found which they reasonably believe to be evidence of or relating to a prescribed offence.

46. In sub-s (1).

47. These are: (a) an indicatable offence involving the death of or serious bodily injury to any person; (b) false imprisonment; (c) rape; (d) an offence under the Punishment of Incest Act 1908; Criminal Law Amendment Act 1935, ss 1 or 2; Criminal Law (Rape) (Amendment) Act 1990, ss 3 or 4 or Criminal Law (Sexual Offences) Act 1993, ss 3 or 5.

48. Section 10(2).

# Chapter 29

# Detinue


I. Introduction .......... 777
II. Adverse Possession .......... 777
III. Bailment and Finding Contrasted .......... 780
IV. Remedies .......... 780


## I. Introduction

**[29.01]** The essence of the tort of detinue[1] is the wrongful refusal by the defendant to deliver up to the plaintiff a chattel after demand has been made by the plaintiff to do so. Frequently, the same facts will give rise to actions for detinue and for breach of contract; in this regard, detinue may prove a particularly useful remedy where the contractual claim is thwarted[2] (as in the case of infancy, for example). A number of aspects of the action may be noted.

## II. Adverse Possession

**[29.02]** A detention is not wrongful unless the defendant's possession is adverse to or in defiance of the plaintiff's right.[3] A bailee who merely holds onto a chattel after the termination of the contract of bailment may be liable for breach of contract but not in detinue. The finder of a chattel who is not aware of the true owner of it may keep it in safe custody without being guilty of detinue.[4] The action may lie even where the chattel is no longer in the defendant's possession.[5]

**[29.03]** Normally, adverse possession will be proved by establishing a demand for the return of the chattel and a refusal by the defendant to do so.[6] Thus, in *Cullen, Allen & Co v*

1. See Ames 'The History of Trover' (1898) 11 Harv LR 277, 374 at 375 ff.
2. *Cf Ballett v Mingay* [1943] KB 281. Detinue will not, however, be permitted to run roughshod over the principles of contract law: *cf Robert J Goff & Co Ltd v Walsh* [1943] Ir Jur 56 (CC affd HC).
3. *Spackman v Foster* (1883) 11 QBD 99; *King v Walsh* [1932] IR 178 (SC); *Treasure Island Ltd v Zebedee Enterprises Ltd* High Court, 29 May 1987. See also *Webb v Ireland* [1988] ILRM 565 (SC revg HC); *McKenna v Commissioner of An Garda Síochána* [1993] 3 IR 543 (SC); *McCrystal Oil Co Ltd v Revenue Commissioners* [1993] 1 IR 477 (HC); *Wymes v Tehaan* [1988] IR 717 (HC) affd by Supreme Court 9 December 1988 (ex temp); *MacEnroe v Allied Irish Banks Ltd* [1980] ILRM 171 (SC); *Mercantile Credit Co of Ireland Ltd v Cahill* (1964) 98 ILTR 79 (CC); *Keenan Brothers Ltd v Coras Iompair Éireann* (1963) 97 ILTR 54 (HC).
4. *Isaack v Clark* (1615) 2 Bulst 306 at 312 80 ER 1143 at 1148; *Hollins v Fowler* (1875) LR 7 HL 757 at 766.
5. *Cf Morgan v Maurer & Sons* [1964] Ir Jur 31 (CC).
6. *Cf France v Gaudet* (1871) LR 6 QB 199; *Moran v Conway* [1947] Ir Jur 37 (CC); *King v Walsh* [1932] IR 178 (SC); *Waterford Corporation v O'Toole* High Court, 9 November 1973. See also *British Wagon Co Ltd v Shortt* [1961] IR 164 (HC); *Lloyd v Osborne* (1899) 20 LR (NSW) 190 (SC); *Treasure Island Ltd v Zebedee Enterprises Ltd* High Court, 29 May 1987, noted by Byrne & Binchy, *Annual Survey of Irish Law 1987*, p 340.

*Barclay*,[7] the defendant, a potato salesman, was held not liable in detinue where in breach of contract he failed to return certain sacks which the plaintiffs, who were potato merchants, had supplied him to be filled with potatoes. The Court of Appeal considered that the correspondence between the parties could not be read as involving a demand for the return of the sacks. FitzGibbon LJ stated that:

> "... though a plaintiff could bring his action for breach of contract without any demand, he could not bring an action of detinue until, by a demand of, and a refusal or neglect to return, the goods, the breach of contract was turned into a wrongful detainer."[8]

**[29.04]** For a demand for the return of the chattel to be effective, it must as a general rule be "brought to the knowledge of the person of whom it is made".[9] Therefore, in *King v Walsh*,[10] a claim for detinue failed where a demand contained in a letter delivered to the defendant's house in Dublin was followed by a writ, before the defendant, who was then in the south-west of the country, had returned home. The fact that the defendant had not been keeping out of the way to avoid service of notice of the demand was stressed by the Supreme Court.

**[29.05]** Where the refusal to return a chattel is reasonable - as, for instance, where the defendant wishes to investigate the legality of the plaintiff's claim[11] - adverse possession

7. (1881) 10 LR Ir 224. See also *King v Walsh* [1932] IR 178 (SC).
8. At 233.
9. *King v Walsh* [1932] IR 178 at 189 (SC).
10. [1932] IR 178 (SC). It is worth noting the Hire Purchase Act 1946, s 11 which provides as follows:

> Where in an action by an order of goods which have been under a hire-purchase agreement to enforce a right to recover possession of the goods from the hirer the owner proves that before the commencement of the action and after the right to recover possession of the goods accrued the owner made a request in writing to the hirer to surrender the goods the hirer's possession of the goods shall for the purpose of the owner's claim to recover possession thereof be deemed to be adverse to the owner. Nothing in this section shall affect a claim for damages for conversion.

11 *Clayton v Le Roy* [1911] 2 KB 1031; *EE McCurdy Ltd v PMG* [1959] NZLR 553 (SC); *Poole v Burns* [1944] Ir Jur 20 (CC); *Leahy v Malcomson* (1851) 1 Ir CLR 432 (QB); *cf Scott v Midland Great Western Railway Co* (1853) 3 Ir CLR 573 (Exch Ch). See also *London & NW Ry Co v Hughes* (1889) 26 LR Ir 165 (QB) - carriers entitled to detain cattle where consignor refused to pay amount due under contract of carriage. So also it may be lawful for a member of the Garda Síochána when lawfully arresting a person to detain chattels for the purpose of producing them as evidence in the prosecution of that person in respect of the offence for which he is arrested: *cf Dillon v O'Brien* (1887) 20 LR Ir 300 (Ex Div). But where goods are lawfully seized (by the customs authorities for example) care must be taken during their detention: *cf McMahon v O'Sullivan* [1939] IR 426 (SC affg HC) upholding an award for damages for trespass conversion and detinue for damage to a lorry while lawfully seized; Customs Consolidation Act 1876, s 267 limiting damages to two pence in cases where there was reasonable or probable cause for the seizure, was held inapplicable since (*per* Sullivan CJ at 435).

> "[t]he uncontradicted evidence established that during that time it was lying uncovered in an open yard beside the sea exposed to the weather and covered with the salt that had been used in the treatment of the sheep skins and that as a result it was covered with rust the chassis and the steel parts were destroyed the engine was seized and the four new tyres were perished. That damage was not such as would result from the mere detention of the lorry it resulted from the reckless neglect to take any care of the lorry while it was in the appellant's custody."

See also *Simple Imports Ltd Revenue Commissioners* Supreme Court, 19 January 2000 *per* Keane CJ, at p 24 of his judgment.

will not be established. In *Poole v Burns*,[12] the defendant auctioneer retained the plaintiff's horse in her possession for five weeks, refusing to return it to the plaintiff because she had been informed by another person that the horse had been stolen from her. A day after the defendant had this information, a Garda officer called to her premises, "took statements from the defendant's manager and the plaintiff, and told the defendant's manager to retain the horse while the investigations were going on".[13] Correspondence between the parties ensued and, five weeks afterwards, the defendant's solicitor[14] telephoned the gardaí. A day later the plaintiff served a civil bill on the defendant in response to which the defendant returned the horse.

**[29.06]** Liability in detinue was imposed on the defendant. Davitt J accepted the proposition that "a bailee of property, who is in bona fide doubt as to the ownership thereof, is legally entitled to detain that property for a reasonable time in order to have enquiries made as to who is the proper owner".[15] That principle did not, however, apply in the present case. He stated that he had:

> "great sympathy with auctioneers and pawnbrokers and other people of that sort who are frequently placed in such a difficult position. But I have come to the conclusion that in this case the defendant detained the animal for more than a reasonable time. If she had made an effort she would probably have speeded up the police investigation, and it was the duty of her and not the plaintiff to do everything possible to secure the release of the animal. Instead of that she did nothing [for five weeks]."[16]

**[29.07]** With respect, this approach may be questioned. To hold that there is a duty on the innocent bailee to "speed up" police investigations is surely too harsh.

**[29.08]** Finally, on the question of adverse possession, it should be noted that the necessity of a demand and refusal may be dispensed with where it is clear that the demand would have been futile.[17]

---

11. (contd) As to seizures by sheriffs and related matters see *Challiner v Burgess* (1856) 3 Saunders Co Court Cas 147 (QB); *M'Morrin v Dixon* (1897) 31 Ir LT & Sol J 3 (CA); *Walsh v Goodman* [1905] 2 IR 241 (KB Div 1904). The Courts are conscious of the fact that a sheriff may be "placed between two fires" (*per* Lord Tenterden as reported in *Humphrys v Pratt* (1831) 4 Bligh NS 154 at 164); thus where a sheriff on the representation of a plaintiff in a suit seizes goods under a *fieri facias* as belonging to the defendant in that suit and later a third person claiming the goods obtains damages against the sheriff the sheriff may sue that plaintiff for deceit. See generally Dixon & Gilland, *The Law Relating to Sheriffs in Ireland*, (1888) pp 109-131, 222-223. The Law Reform Commission in its *Report on Debt Collection: (1) The Law Relating to Sheriffs* (LRC 27-1988), para 96 recommended that a sheriff should not be liable to a third party if he seized goods in the joint or sole possession of the judgment debtor unless he had notice (factual or constructive) of any right of that third party infringed by the seizure. The person to whom the seized goods belonged if they proved not to be the property of the debtor should be entitled to recover their value and any other damage he had sustained from the debtor.
12. [1944] Ir Jur 20 (CC).
13. [1944] Ir Jur 20.
14. Davitt J states this at 21. The statement of facts refers merely to "the defendant". Nothing hinges on the point however.
15. [1944] Ir Jur 20 at 21.
16. [1944] Ir Jur 20. Nominal damages of one shilling were awarded since only "a technical wrong" had been committed by the defendant
17. *Baud Corporation NV v Brook* (1974) 40 DLR (3d) 418 analysed by Palmer (1975) 53 Can BR 121.

## III. Bailment and Finding Contrasted

**[29.09]** An important distinction is made between cases where the chattel was originally bailed to the defendant and where it was found by him. In the former case, even if the bailee wrongfully[18] loses possession of the chattel, he will still be liable for detinue when he fails to return it at the end of the contracted period of bailment.[19] In the latter case, the finder of a chattel will not be liable in detenue if he loses possession of the chattel,[20] but in a case where he wrongfully disposes of it he will be liable to the plaintiff for conversion.

## IV. Remedies

**[29.10]** One of the advantages of the action for detinue over that of conversion lies in the breadth of remedies[21] available to the plaintiff.[22] Three possible forms of judgment exist:

18. Ie intentionally or negligently.

19. *Reeve v Palmer* (1850) 5 CB (NS) 84 at 93; 141 ER 33 at 36; *Jones v Dowle* (1841) 9 M & W 19 152 ER 9; *Ballett v Mingay* [1943] KB 281; *Waterford Corporation v O Toole* High Court, 9 November 1973 (Finlay J); *Sheehy v Faughnan* [1991] 1 IR 424 (HC).

20. *Cf South Staffordshire Waterworks Co v Sharman* [1896] 2 QB 44; *Coldman v Hill* [1919] 1 KB 443 at 449.

21. See *General & Finance Facilities Ltd v Cooks Cars (Romford) Ltd* [1963] 1 WLR 644 at 650-651 (CA). Statutes may limit the amount recoverable in certain cases (eg Customs Consolidation Act 1876, s 267) but they will be construed narrowly: *cf McMahon v O'Sullivan* [1939] IR 426 (SC); see also *McGrath v Taylor* [1936] NI 158 (CA); *Simple Imports Ltd Revenue Commissioners* Supreme Court, 19 January 2000 per Keane CJ, at p 24 of his judgment. Special provisions concerning limitation of actions for detinue and conversion are contained in the Statute of Limitations 1957, s 12 discussed at para **[46.86]**. Summary proceedings in detinue brought under the Dublin Police Act 1842, s 68 must be commenced within six months of the time the case of complaint first arose: *Moran v Conway* [1947] IR Jur Rep 37 (CC). The jurisdiction of the District Court in cases of detinue was raised to £5000 by s 7 of the Courts Act 1991. As to the degree of precision required in pleadings for detinue see *Friedel v Castlereagh* (1877) IR 11 CL 93 (Com Pleas). On damages see *M'Grath v Bourne* (1876) IR 10 CL 160 (ExCh). On costs *cf Birmingham v Billing* (1875) IR 9 CL 287; *Bradley v Archibald* [1899] 2 IR 108 (QB); *Donnelly v Donnelly* [1899] 2 IR 111 (QB); *Donnelly v Coyne* [1901] 2 IR 7 (CA); *Simms v Patterson* (1904) 5 NIJR 80 (KB).

22. In *Hanley v ICC Finance Ltd* [1996] 1 ILRM 463 (HC) Kinlen J was impressed by Denning LJ's ruminations in *Strand Electric Co v Brisford Entertainments* [1952] 2 QB 246 at 255 to the effect that the action for conversion resembles one for restitution rather than tort because the defendant has had the benefit of the goods. Kinlen J interpreted Denning LJ's remarks as "subsuming th[e] two distinctive torts [of detinue and conversion] into a claim for restitution". Kinlen J found such a proposition "very attractive". He considered that "the trial judge should look at all aspects of the case and decide the relevant periods and nature of damage having regard to all the particular circumstances of each individual case". Kinlen J was of the view that "[t]he matter should be clarified by statute." Eoin O'Dell, [1997] *Restitution LR* 139 suggests (surely correctly) that Kinlen J's dictum:

> "should be read only as endorsing the availability of a claim for restitution measure ... for the tort of conversion but should not be seen as precluding a claim for damages in the compensation measure ... for the tort of conversion where that is appropriate".

On the basis of Kinlen J's elision of the torts of detinue and conversion the same reasoning may perhaps be applied to the tort of detinue. For a comprehensive analysis of the subject see Eoin O'Dell's 'Submission to the Law Reform Commission on Damages in the Restitution Measure for Tort and Breach of Contract' (1999) and O'Dell in Byrne and Binchy *Annual Review of Irish Law 1998*.

(i) for the value of the chattel as assessed[23] and damages for its detention,

(ii) for the return of the chattel or its value as assessed and damages,

(iii) for return of the chattel and damages for its detention.

## Order for the Value of the Chattel as assessed and Damages for its Detention

**[29.11]** This is appropriate where the chattel is an ordinary article of commerce, or where the plaintiff does not want the goods back or where it is not possible for them to be returned.[24]

## Order for the Return of the Chattel or its Value as assessed[25] and Damages

**[29.12]** The power vested in the court to order the return of a chattel is discretionary, and:

> "ought not to be exercised when the chattel is an ordinary article of commerce and of no special value or interest, and not alleged to be of any special value to the plaintiff, and where damages would fully compensate".[26]

**[29.13]** So far as the exercise of discretion is concerned, the court should be very slow to heed an argument by a defendant to the effect that he is afraid to return the chattel for fear of what may happen to him as a result of a threat made by a third party; save in exceptional cases "it is the unlawful that must yield to the lawful, and not vice versa".[27]

**[29.14]** *Waterford Corporation v O'Toole*[28] involved an interesting use of judicial discretion. Corporation officials had given into the defendant's possession two stone plaques, which had sixty years previously been designed to commemorate the composer William Vincent Wallace. The idea was that the defendant would erect the plaques on his house, which was "in a prominent and suitable public place"; however, the bailment was subject to permission of the Corporation at a meeting to be held shortly afterwards. It was envisaged that this permission would be a mere formality. Before the meeting the defendant had the plaques erected on the wall of his home embedded "in a massive area of concrete with iron bars". In fact the Corporation refused its permission and demanded the return of the plaques. To do this would have been possible only by the "massive operation" of removing a very considerable section of the corner of the house, having supported the balance, and taking a large part of the structure of the house away with the plaques.

**[29.15]** Finlay J exercised his discretion against ordering the specific return of the plaques, which would have involved "an altogether unwarranted expense and damage to the

23. "[A]t the date of judgment and not at the date of breach": *Malhotra v Choudhury* [1980] Ch 52 at 79 (CA). See also *Rosenthal v Alderton & Sons Ltd* [1946] KB 374; *Hanley v ICC Finance Ltd* [1996] 1 ILRM 463 (HC).

24. *General & Finance Facilities Ltd v Cooks Cars (Romford)* [1963] 1 WLR 644 at 650, quoted with approval by Blayney J in *Webb v Ireland* [1988] IR 353 reversed on other grounds [1988] ILRM 565 (SC).

25. The reason for assessing its value is to provide for cases where the sheriff is unable to find the chattel: *General & Finance Facilities Ltd v Cooks Cars (Romford) Ltd* [1963] 1 WLR 644 at 651; *Juhlinn-Dannfelt v Crash Repairs Ply Ltd* [1969] QWN 1.

26. *Whiteley Ltd v Hilt* [1918] 2 KB 808 at 819 (CA).

27. *Perry (Howard E) & Co Ltd v British Rys Bd* [1980] 1 WLR 1375 at 1385.

28. High Court, 9 November 1979, Finlay J.

defendant's property". Instead he awarded nominal damages, since the plaques had finished up in a place where they were preserved for the benefit of the citizens of Waterford, thus giving effect to the proper interest of the Corporation in the matter.

**[29.16]** Where a court orders the return of a chattel in circumstances where the defendant has added to its value by his or her own work, creativity or expenditure, the court should make an allowance to the defendant for this increase in value.[29] In *Webb v Ireland*[30] Blayney J, in the High Court, held that the State was entitled to such an allowance in respect of expenditures made on the Derrynaflan Hoard after it had been given by the plaintiff into its custody but only to the point when the plaintiffs made a demand for its return.

**[29.17]** It should be noted finally that, in a case where the court makes an order for the return of a chattel, the defendant may not "merely wait and remain inert in all respects".[31] He or she must take some steps at least to make it clear to the plaintiff that he or she regards the chattel as being entirely at the plaintiff's disposal.[32]

## Order for the Return of the Chattel and Damages for its Detention

**[29.18]** This remedy is much the same as the second, but lacks the element of assessment of the value of the chattel. Since the only pecuniary redress that may be given under this head is damages for detention, it is essential from the plaintiff's point of view that there be no risk of the chattel's not being capable of being returned on foot of the decree.

**[29.19]** In *Webb v Ireland*,[33] where the plaintiffs, finders of the "Derrynaflan Hoard", sought its return and damages for detinue from the State, Blayney J held in their favour but the Supreme Court reversed. The case is considered in greater detail elsewhere.[34] For present purposes, it is worth noting that Blayney J was of the view that, on the special facts of the case, he should make an order for the return of the Hoard, or recovery of its value assessed (£5,536,000), and nominal damages, subject to the reduction of £25,800 to which the State was entitled for remedial work done by the staff of the National Museum on the Hoard in the bona fide belief that the State was its owner, but not for work done after they had received notice of the plaintiffs' claim for its return. Since the Supreme Court held that the State was not liable in detinue, the issue of remedies for this tort did not there arise.

29. *Greenwood v Bennett* [1973] QB 195 (CA); *Munro v Willmott* [1948] 2 All ER 983 (HC); *Webb v Ireland* [1988] IR 353 (HC); revd by the Supreme Court on other grounds 1987.

30. [1988] IR 353.

31. *Metals & Roper Co Ltd v Tattersall* [1966] 1 WLR 1500 at 1503-1504 (CA).

32. *Metals & Roper Co Ltd v Tattersall* [1966] 1 WLR 1500 at 1504.

33. [1988] IR 353 reversed on other grounds [1988] ILRM 565 (SC).

34. See paras **[30.25]-[30.35]** above.

# Chapter 30

# Conversion[1]


I. Introduction ........ 783
II. Taking Possession ........ 783
III. Abusing Possession ........ 784
IV. Denying Title ........ 786
V. Scope of the Tort of Conversion ........ 788


## I. INTRODUCTION

**[30.01]** Conversion consists of any act relating to the goods of another that constitutes an unjustifiable denial of his or her title to them, or, as is sometimes said, the wrongful assertion of dominion over them. This is not an easy or certain concept to understand or apply with any precision.[2] The borderlines of liability have been drawn more by judicial instinct than by the clear application of principles with a cutting edge. Conversion may be committed by the wrongful taking possession of the goods, abusing possession already acquired, or otherwise denying the title of the other person to them, whether or not possession has been acquired.

## II. TAKING POSSESSION

**[30.02]** Taking possession of another's property may constitute conversion[3] but not always: it is only where the defendant deals with the goods in a manner inconsistent with the right of the true owner that conversion (as opposed to trespass) will be committed.[4] Thus, in *Fouldes v Willoughby*,[5] where, after a dispute about fares with a passenger, a ferry-boat operator turned two horses that he was transporting loose on the landing-place, he was held not to have been guilty of conversion of the animals. Lord Abinger CB stated:

---

1. See Simpson 'The Introduction of the Action on the Case for Conversion' (1959) 75 LQR 364. Anon 'Detinue and Conversion' (1964) 98 ILT & Sol J 305; Ames 'The History of Trover' (1898) 11 Harv LR 277 374; Clark 'The Test of Conversion' (1908) 21 Harv LR 408; Warren 'Qualifying as Plaintiff in an Action for a Conversion' (1936) 49 Harv LR 1084; Rubin et al 'Comment: Conversion of Choses in Action' (1941) 10 Fordham LR 415; Prosser 'The Nature of Conversion' (1957) 42 Cornell LQ 168. Gordon 'Anomalies in the Law of Conversion' (1955) 71 LQR 346; Tettenborn 'Conversion, Tort and Restitution' Ch 32 of *Interests in Goods* (2nd ed, 1998) (Palmer and McKendrick eds).
2. *Cf* Clark 'The Test of Conversion' (1908) 21 Harv LR 408 at 412-414. Even the Restatement Second on Torts, s 222A contains a disappointedly circular definition of the tort.
3. *M'Keever v M'Kain* (1846) Bl Dundas & Osb 80; *Power v Cook* (1869) IR 4 CL 247 (Com Pleas). *Cf Hanley v ICC Finance Ltd* [1996] 1 ILRM 463 (HC) analysed by O'Dell [1997] Restitution LR 139 and by Byrne & Binchy *Annual Review of Irish Law 1995* pp 535-536.
4. *Cf* FLEMING, pp 70-71.
5. (1841) 8 M&W 540, 151 ER 1153. See further Bell, *Modern Law of Personal Property in England and Ireland and Ireland* (1989), pp 469-470.

> "It has never yet been held, that the simple act of removal of a chattel, independent of any claim over it, either in favour of the party himself or anyone else, amounts to a conversion of a chattel. In the present case, therefore, the simple removal of these horses by the defendant, for a purpose wholly unconnected with any the least denial of the right of the plaintiff to the possession and enjoyment of them, is no conversion ...."[6]

**[30.03]** It should be noted that dealing with goods in a manner inconsistent with the right of the true owner need not involve any intention on the part of the defendant permanently to deprive the owner of the goods: taking a car for a joy ride[7] can be as much of a conversion as stealing it. In general, the voluntary reception[8] of another's goods without his authority constitutes conversion. An involuntary reception does not, however, constitute conversion. A person upon whom goods are thrust - by an aggressive tradesman, for example - is not regarded as a bailee in the strict sense.[9] He or she may not be charged with negligence in respect of the safe custody of the goods.[10] Whilst it appears that the recipient may not always wilfully damage or destroy them,[11] the law will look with sympathy on any action he takes regarding them where they have become a nuisance to him or her.[12] He must act reasonably in attempting to return the goods to their owner.[13]

## III. Abusing Possession

**[30.04]** Where possession has been lawfully acquired, subsequent abuse of it may constitute conversion. Pawning another's goods[14] or sale and delivery of them[15] are examples of such abuse. The delivery of the goods to some other third party may not constitute conversion in certain cases. In *Morgan v Maurer & Sons*,[16] a watch repairer in Ennis sent a watch given in for repair to Dublin, without having been authorised to do so

---

6. (1841) 89 M&W 540 at 547, 151 ER 1153 at 1156. *Cf Hagan v Pasley* (1878) 2 LR Ir 573 at 578 (QB). *Aitken Agencies Ltd v Richardson* [1967] NZLR 65 (SC).
7. See also *Tear v Freebody* (1858) 4 CB (ns) 28, 140 ER 1071.
8. See Burnett 'Conversion by an Involuntary Bailee' (1960) 76 LQR 364.
9. *Cf Lethbridge v Phillips* (1819) 2 Stark 544 171 ER 731.
10. *Howard v Harris* (1884) 1 Cab & El 253.
11. *Cf Hiort v Bott* (1874) LR 9 Ex 86 at 90 (*per* Bramwell *obiter*).
12. *Cf* CLERK & LINDSELL (16th ed), p 676.
13. *Cf Elvin & Powelle Ltd v Plummer Roddis* (1933) 50 TLR 158; *Hiort v Bott* (1874) LR 9 Ex 86 criticised by Burnett 'Conversion by an Involuntary Bailee' (1960) 76 LQR 364. See also *London & NW Ry Co v Hughes* (1889) 26 LR Ir 165 (QB). See now The Sale of Goods and Supply of Services Act 1980, s 47. See also the European Communities (Cancellation of Contracts Negotiated Away from Business Premises) Regulations 1989 (SI 224/1989), Reg 6 and the Distant Selling Directive 1997 (97/7/EC), analysed by McMahon 'Contracts Negotiated Away from Business Premises and the 1997 Distance Selling Directive' (1999) 19 ILT (ns) 139.
14. *Parker v Godin* (1728) 2 Stra 813, 93 ER 866.
15. *Hollins v Fowler* (1875) LR 7 HL 757; *Hagan v Pasley* (1878) 2 LR Ir 573 (QB); *Magee v D'Arcy* (1879) 4 LR Ir 312 (Ex Div) - an interlocutory injunction against the sale of ponies refused as damages would be an adequate remedy. *Cf London & NW Ry Co v Hughes* (1889) 26 LR Ir 165 - sale was justified by circumstances of necessity.
16. [1964] Ir Jur 31 (CC). *Cf Morgan v Smith* [1953] Ir Jur 70 (HC). *Keys v Belfast & Ballymena Ry Co* (1858) 8 ICLR 167 (Com Pleas); *McElwee v McDonald* [1969] IR 437 (HC).

by the owner. The watch was lost in the post on the way back. Judge O'Briain, of the Circuit Court, held that the defendant was not guilty of conversion (although he was liable for breach of the terms of the contract of bailment).

**[30.05]** A clear case of abuse of possession is where the chattel is wilfully destroyed[17] - as, for example when it is burnt or broken up so that its identity is destroyed. If the chattel retains its identity in spite of being damaged, the defendant will not be guilty of conversion, though he or she will be liable in trespass.[18] The question whether there has been a destruction of identity rather than mere damage is difficult to resolve in some cases. Clearly, however, a change of identity may result from even a slight act, as where I draw some wine out of a cask and fill up the deficiency with water.[19]

**[30.06]** An abuse of possession may result in the loss of the chattel without involving its destruction. An interesting example of this type of case arose in *Moorgate Mercantile Co Ltd v Finch.*[20] A car that had been borrowed for the smuggling of goods into England was seized and confiscated by the Customs authorities. The borrower was held liable for conversion because he had used the car in a manner that was likely to result in the owners being deprived of it for ever. Even though he had not intended this to happen, "he must be taken to [have] intend[ed] the consequences which were likely to happen from the conduct of which he was guilty, and which did in fact result in the loss of the car to plaintiffs".[21]

**[30.07]** Where possession is not transferred, the act will not normally constitute conversion. The law provides otherwise, however, in the case of market overt.[22] Mere failure to prevent another from interfering with the goods does not amount to conversion,[23] although it may, of course, amount to negligence.[24]

**[30.08]** The refusal to return goods to their owner in response to a demand to do so is normally conclusive evidence of conversion, unless the refusal is reasonable (as, for

17. *Cf Heald v Carey* (1852) 11 CB 977, 138 ER 762.

18. *Cf Simmons v Lilystone* (1853) 8 Ex 431, 155 ER 1417.

19. *Richardson v Atkinson* (1723) 1 Stra 576, 93 ER 710. Ironically the failure to destroy the article taken was the basis of liability in *Northern Ireland Master Butchers' Wholesale Supply Association Ltd v Belfast Corporation* [1965] NI 30 (Ch D) where the reprocessing and sale of carcasses taken by a sanitary authority acting under statutory powers which required them to destroy the meat was held to constitute a conversion the carcasses having been surrendered for a purpose entirely different from that to which they were put.

20. [1962] 1 QB 701 (CA).

21. [1962] 1 QB 701 at 706. This case may be contrasted with the situation where a person lawfully in temporary possession of the plaintiff's goods simply loses them: *Joule Ltd v Poole* (1924) 24 SR (NSW) 387 at 390.

22. *Cf* Sale of Goods Act 1893, s 22. See *Delaney v Wallis & Son* (1884) 15 Cox CC 525; *Ganly v Ledwidge* (1876) IR 10 CL 33 (QB); Davenport & Ross 'Market Overt' Ch 14 *Interests in Goods* (2nd ed, 1998) (Palmer & McKendrick eds).

23. *Ashby v Tolhurst* [1937] 2 KB 242.

24. *Lee Cooper Ltd v CH Jenkins & Sons Ltd* [1967] 2 QB 1; *cf Henigan v Ballybunion Picture House & Baths Co* [1944] Ir Jur Rep 20 (CC); *Scott v Midland Great Western Railway Co* (1853) 3 Ir CLR 573 (Exch Ch); *Joule Ltd v Poole* (1924) 24 SR (NSW) 387.

example, where a person wishes to authenticate the claims of the other that he is the owner).[25]

**[30.09]** In *British Wagon Company Ltd v Shortt*,[26] bulldozing machinery which was the subject-matter of a hire purchase agreement was purportedly sold to the defendant, who was ignorant of the existence of the previous agreement. The owner sought the return of the machinery but the defendant refused to do this unless he received compensation for repairs that he had carried out on it - a condition to which the plaintiff would not submit. The plaintiff's action proceeded on the basis of detinue and, in the alternative, conversion, but at the trial the plaintiff abandoned the claim for detinue and limited the claim to damages for conversion.

**[30.10]** Davitt P, in the High Court, considered that the plaintiff was entitled to succeed on either claim. When the defendant had refused to hand back the machinery unconditionally he had "converted it to his own use".[27]

## IV. Denying Title

**[30.11]** Where the defendant has never been in possession (actual or constructive) of the goods of another, the defendant may nonetheless be guilty of conversion if he or she deals with them in such a way as to amount to an absolute denial of that other's title to them.

### Bona Fides of Defendant

**[30.12]** An honest but mistaken belief of the defendant that he or she has the right to deal with the goods generally does not constitute a good defence to a claim for conversion. The leading decision is *Hollins v Fowler*.[28] There, the defendant, a cotton broker, quite innocently bought cotton from a person who had acquired it fradulently from the plaintiff. The defendant resold the cotton to another person, receiving only broker's commission. He was held liable for conversion. Blackburn J stated that "[w]hen a loss has happened through the roguery of an insolvent, it must always fall on some innocent party; and that must be a hardship ...".[29]

**[30.13]** The issue of negligence fell for consideration in *Shield Life Insurance Company Ltd v Ulster Bank Ltd,*[30] Costello P held the defendant bank liable for having converted a cheque for £30,000 of which the plaintiffs were payees, which an insurance broker who was a fraudster had lodged in a branch of the bank for collection, having either endorsed the cheque himself or having had it endorsed on his direction, in an ambiguous fashion

---

25. *Cf Poole v Burns* [1944] Ir Jur 20 (CC).

26. [1961] IR 164 (HC).

27. [1961] IR 164 at 168

28. (1875) LR 7, HL 757. See also *Union Transport Finance Ltd v British Car Auctions Ltd* [1978] 2 All ER 385 (CA); *RH Willis & Son v British Car Auctions Ltd* [1978] 2 All ER 392 (CA); *Rendell v Associated Finance Pty Ltd* [1957] VR 604.

29. *Hollins v Fowler* (1875) LR 7 HL 757 at 764. *Cf Hagan v Pasley* (1878) 2 LR Ir 573 (QB). The same approach was adopted in *Ganly v Ledwidge* (1876) IR 10 CL 33 (QB) and *Delaney v Wallis & Son* (1884) 15 Cox CC 525 (CA affg Ex Div) in respect of the sale of cattle and sheep in market overt. The salesmaster could not invoke the protection afforded to the purchaser in respect of such a sale. *Cf Reg v Hehir* [1895] 2 IR 709 at 749. See also *Quinn v Pratt* [1908] 2 IR 69 at 82-83 (KB); *McCrystal Oil Co Ltd v Revenue Commissioners* [1993] 1 IR 477 (HC).

30. [1995] 3 IR 225 (HC).

which could have been an endorsement executed by him, as broker, on behalf of the payee or an endorsement by him, as broker, claiming to be its holder in favour of the bank. The broker asked the bank to pay the proceeds of the cheque into his client's account and to transfer £5000 to his office account. His office account had been continuously overdrawn for the previous fifteen months and the bank had refused to honour a number of cheques.

**[30.14]** Section 4 of the Cheques Act 1959 gives a substantial element of protection to collecting banks, provided they have acted "in good faith and without negligence".[31]

**[30.15]** In the instant case, Costello P stated that the plaintiffs were entitled to damages for conversion unless the defendants could establish that they had taken reasonable care that their customer's title to the cheque was not defective. What facts were sufficient to cause a bank reasonably to suspect that its customer was not the true owner of the cheque depended on current banking practice. All the circumstances surrounding the transaction might be relevant.

**[30.16]** Section 4(3) of the 1959 Act made it clear that a banker was not to be treated as having been negligent by reason only of his failure to concern himself with an irregularity in the indorsement of a cheque but, if there were other circumstances either antecedent to the transaction in suit or part of that transaction which, taken in conjunction with the irregularity of the indorsement and the failure of the banker to concern himself with the irregularity, these might be considered by the court in considering whether the banker had been guilty of breach of duty to the cheque's true owner.

**[30.17]** Costello P observed:

> "Each case must ultimately depend on its own facts. But there may be special circumstances in a case which affect the banker's duty of care to which the banker should pay particular regard. Those special circumstances may include, as in this case, a situation in which a customer maintains two accounts, an office account and a clients' account, and in which it is clear that the customer is holding money in an account as a trustee. Previous movements in and out of that account by the customer which may suggest that it is not being operated in a manner consistent with the customer's duty as a trustee may be relevant in considering the bank's duty in relation to the payment into a client's account of a cheque which has been irregularly indorsed."[32]

**[30.18]** In the instant case the endorsement was ambiguous. The bank could have inferred from the fact that the broker asked the bank to pay the proceeds of the cheque into his client's account that the proceeds did not belong to him. The broker's instruction to the bank to transfer £5,000 to his office account amounted to an instruction to pay to himself a substantial sum out of the proceeds of a cheque which the payee had not endorsed. Bearing in mind the inference as to the possible impropriety of the transfers from the customer to the client's account, the nature of the irregularity of the endorsement and the circumstances

31. In *Harfani & Co Ltd v Midland Bank Ltd* [1968] 2 All ER 573 at 579, Diplock LJ observed in respect of s 4 of England's Cheques Act 1957 (which was the model for the Irish provision) that:

> "[t]he only respect in which this substituted statutory duty differs from a common law cause of action in negligence is that since it takes the form of a qualified immunity from a strict liability at common law the onus of showing that he did take such reasonable care lies on the defendant banker".

32. [1995] 2 IR 225 at 238-239. See Breslin *Banking Law in the Republic of Ireland*, pp 193-194;Donnelly 'The Law of Banks and Credit Institutions (2000), pp 307-308; Johnston *Banking and Security Law in Ireland* (1998), pp 129-134.

surrounding its lodgement, Costello P came to the conclusion that a prudent banker would have made enquiries about the cheque before accepting it for collection. The bank had been negligent in the manner it discharged its duty to the plaintiffs and the plaintiffs' claim for damages for conversion had to succeed.

## V. Scope of the Tort of Conversion

### Subject Matter of Conversion

**[30.19]** One may be guilty of conversion of any corporeal personal property,[33] including papers and title deeds. Money may be converted[34] as may negotiable instruments,[35] title deeds[36] and realty when severed.[37] Animals and birds may also be converted: domestic animals[38] in all cases and animals *ferae naturae* when they have been reduced into possession.[39]

---

33. TRINDADE & CANE, pp 137-138; *Allen v Sharp* (1848) 2 Exch 352, 154 ER 529. The wrongful interference with a dead body or its parts may possibly be actionable in conversion in spite of old statements to the effect that there is no property in a human body: see *Jervis on Coroners* (11th ed, 1993), Ch 7; Farrell *Coroners, Practice and Procedure* (2000), paras 4.05-4.06; Magnusson 'Proprietary Rights in Human Tissue' Ch 2 *Interests in Goods* (2nd ed, 1998) (Palmer & McKendrick eds).

34. See CLERK & LINDSELL, pp 684-685; *Dillon v O'Brien* (1887) 20 LR Ir 300 (Ex Div) - bank notes *inter alia*; *Fitzpatrick v Dunphy* (1851) 1 Ir CLR 366 (Exch); *Shield Life Insurance Co Ltd v Ulster Bank* High Court, 5 December 1995. But see *Sullivan v National Bank* (1939) 73 ILTR 95 (HC) holding that no action lies in detinue for retention of money. *Cf Hennerty v Bank of Ireland* High Court, 5 July 1988 (O'Hanlon J).

35. *Alsager v Close* (1842) 10 M&W 576, 152 ER 600; *Bradley v Archibald* [1899] 2 IR 108 (QB) - promissory notes, action in detinue; *Liston v Munster Leinster Bank Ltd* [1940] IR 77 (HC) - cheques and pay orders. See also Rubin et al 'Comment: Conversion of Choses in Action' (1941) 10 Fordham LR 415 at 416-419. *Cf* SALMOND & HEUSTON, p 102:

> "This principle .... may .... be extended to cover the tokens which are such a feature of contemporary life - eg cheque cards, credit cards, both tokens and gaiming chips."

36. *Plant v Cotterill* (1860) 5 H & N 430, 157 ER 1249; *Birmingham v Billing* (1875) IR 9 CL 287 (Exch Ch) - title deeds; action in detinue; *Byrne v M'Evoy* (1871) IR 5 CL 568 (Com Pleas) - mortgage deed; detinue and trover; *Donnelly v Donnelly* [1899] 2 IR 111 (QB) - title deeds, detinue; *Curry v Rea* [1937] NI 1 (CA) - title deeds; *Donnelly v Coyne* [1901] 2 IR 7 (CA) - receipts, action in detinue; *cf Moulton v Ledwith* (1933) 67 ILTR 233 (CC) - insurance agent's collection book not a deed or muniment of title so as to be excluded from the provisions of Dublin Police Act 1842, s 68.

37. *Mills v Brooker* [1919] 1 KB 555; *Quinn v Pratt* [1908] 2 IR 69 (KB). *Cf Stevenson v Lawlor* (1867) IR 2 CL 77 (Exch).

38. *Cf London & NW Ry Co v Hughes* 26 LR Ir 165 (QB); *Ganly v Ledwidge* (1876) IR 10 CL 33 (QB); *Delaney v Wallis & Son* (1884) 15 Cox CC 525 (CA affg Ex Div); *Devine v London & NW Ry Co* (1864) 17 ICLR 174; *Magee v D'Arcy* (1879) 4 LR Ir 312 (Ex Div); *Clooney v Watson* (1851) 2 Ir CLR 129 (Exch); *Moloney v Kingdom Greyhound Racing Co Ltd* (1948) 82 ILTR 43 (SC); *Wymes v Tehan* [1988] IR 717 (HC).

39. TRINDADE & CANE, p 138. *Cf Toome Eel Fishery (Northern Ireland) Ltd v Cardwell* [1966] NI 1 at 29 (CA):

> "... I do not think one can distinguish in this connection between game which is reduced into possession by killing and taking and eels which are reduced into possession by packing them alive in boxes which then are taken to market".

See also *Rexi Irish Mink v Dublin County Council* [1972] IR 123 (SC) - criminal injury; *Purcell v Minister for Finance* [1939] IR 115 (SC) - malicious injury.

## Title of Plaintiff[40]

**[30.20]** A plaintiff may maintain an action if, at the time of the defendant's act, he had either (a) ownership and possession of the goods[41]; or (b) possession of them; or (c) merely an immediate right to possess them, unless the defendant can prove that the title to the goods is in some other party. As between co-owners[42] there is unity of possession so one co-owner cannot be guilty of conversion as against the other merely by using the goods in a particular fashion, unless he or she goes so far as to destroy them, sell them in market overt or completely exclude the other from possession of them.

**[30.21]** As stated above, it will be sufficient for the plaintiff to establish ownership and possession or possession of the goods at the time of their conversion. In either case the plea of *jus tertii* is not available.[43]

**[30.22]** Where the plaintiff establishes merely an immediate right to possess the goods, *jus tertii* may be pleaded. An exception relates to bailment: a bailee, if sued by the bailor for conversion, is estopped from denying the bailor's title, unless the baliee has been evicted from the goods by another who has a title paramount to that of the bailor or unless the bailee is defending the action on behalf, and by the authority, of a third person. Where the bailee is subjected to competing claims by the bailor and a third party, he or she may have the issue resolved by interpleader proceedings.

## Finders[44]

**[30.23]** The law relating to finders of chattels is in a confused state. Certain aspects are, however, clear. The true owner of the chattel has a better title to it than either its finder or the occupier of the land or premises where it is found.[45]

**[30.24]** The finder is regarded as a sub-bailee, who owes the owner a duty to take reasonable care of the chattel and to return it to the owner if this is possible.[46] Where the true owner cannot be found the finder has a title as against all others save, in certain

---

40. See *Quinn v Pratt* [1908] 2 IR 69. *Cf Cantrell & Cochrane Ltd v Neeson* [1926] NI 107 (CA). *Toome Eel Fishery (Northern Ireland) Ltd v Cardwell* [1966] NI 1; *Fitzpatrick v Dunphy* (1851) 1 Ir CLR 366 (Exch); *Bristow v Cormican* (1878) 3 AC 641 (HL); *O'Neill v Johnston* [1908] IR 358.

41. An owner not in possession may have an action on the case for injury to his or her reversionary interest: *Mears v London and SW Ry Co* (1862) 11 CB (NS) 850; *Penfold Wines Pty Ltd v Elliot* (1946) 74 CLR 204. See further TRINDADE & CANE, pp 170-171; FLEMING, p 72.

42. See Derham, 'Conversion by Wrongful Disposal as Between Co-Owners' (1952) 68 LQR 507. *Cf Power v Cook* (1869) IR 4 CL 247 - separated spouses. Protection against the unreasonable or vindictive disposal of household chattels by a spouse is afforded by the Family Home Protection Act 1976, s 9. See also *K v K* (1980) 114 ILTR 50 (HC).

43. *Armory v Delamirie* (1721) 1 Stra 505, 93 ER 644. *Cf Haggan v Pasley* (1878) 2 LR Ir 573 (QB); *Quinn v Pratt* [1908] 2 IR 69; *Fitzpatrick v Dunphy* (1851) 1 Ir CLR 366.

44. See Marshall, 'The Problem of Finding' (1950) 2 CLP 68; Harris, *Oxford Essays in Jurisprudence*, Ch 4; *Report of the English Law Reform Committee Annex I* (1971 Cmnd), p 4774; Goodhart, 'Three Cases of Possession' 3 Camb LJ 195; Anon 'The Civil and Criminal Liability of the Finder of Lost Articles' (1948) 82 ILT & Sol J 235-241; Anon 'Are Findings Keepings?' (1964) 98 ILT & Sol J 205.

45. *Webb v Ireland* [1988] ILRM 565 (SC 1987 revg HC 1986); *Moffat v Kazana* [1969] 2 QB 152.

46. *Gilchrist Watt and Sanderson Pty Ltd v York Products Pty Ltd* [1970] 1 WLR 1262.

instances mentioned below, the occupier of the land or premises where the chattel is found. Thus, in *Quinn v Coleman*,[47] where a young girl found a purse which was subsequently taken from her by false pretences, it was held that the constabulary authorities who took possession of the purse when apprehending the criminal were obliged to hand it back to the girl after a reasonable time for establishing the true ownership had elapsed. An exception has been made where the chattel is found when either attached to or lying under the surface of the land: here, according to English decisions, the occupier of the land has rights superior to those of the finder.[48] Where, however, the chattel is on or in, but not attached to, a building,[49] the occupier will have rights superior to those of the finder "if, but only if, before the chattel is found, he has manifested an intention to exercise control over the building and the things which may be in or on it".[50]

**[30.25]** In *Webb v Ireland,*[51] in 1987, the Supreme Court analysed the question. The plaintiffs, who were trespassing on property of two farmers, found the "Derrynaflan Hoard", a number of very valuable antique religious objects which had been buried by their owner over a thousand years ago. One of the questions addressed by the Court was whether the plaintiffs, as finders, or the farmers, as occupiers, had a better claim to the Hoard. The occupiers had conveyed their interest, such as it might be, to the State for a financial consideration.

**[30.26]** The Court was divided on the issue. Finlay CJ (with whom Griffin and Henchy JJ concurred) was:

> "satisfied that the true legal position is that there might be distinguished, with regard to the question of control, things which are on land and things which are attached to or under it."[52]

**[30.27]** In his view, in cases where objects are attached to or under the land, the extent to which an absence of control may deprive the owner of a claim against a finder is probably limited to cases such as *Hannah v Peel*,[53] "where the owner of a house had never entered into possession of it though the title had devolved him".[54] The Chief Justice regarded the

---

47. (1898) 33 ILTR 79; *cf Armory v Delamirie* (1721) 1 Stra 505, 93 ER 644; also *Bridges v Hawkesworth* (1851) 21 LJQB 75; *Hannah v Peel* [1945] KB 509.

48. *Elwes v Brigg Gas Co* (1866) 33 Ch D; *South Staffordshire Waterworks Co v Sharman* [1896] 2 QB 44; *London Corporation v Appleyard* [1963] 1 WLR 982; *Parker v British Airways Board* [1982] 1 All ER 834 at 843 (CA). For analysis of *Parker*, see Roberts (1982) 45 MLR 683; *Tettenborn* [1982] Camb LJ 242.

49. Or, *semble* on the land.

50. *Parker v British Airways Board* [1982] 1 All ER 834 at 843. See also *Webb v Ireland* [1988] ILRM 565; *Waverly Borough Council v Fletcher* [1996] QB 334 (CA).

51. [1988] ILRM 565 (SC rev HC), analysed by Kelly 'Hidden Treasure and the Constitution' (1988) 10 DULJ 15; Hogan and Whyte *Kelly: The Irish Constitution* (3rd ed, 1994), pp 1132-1137; Lenihan 'Royal Prerogatives and the Constitution' (1989), pp 45-46. The Oireachtas responded to *Webb* with the National Monuments (Amendment) Act 1987, 2 restricting the use of detection devices at the sites of monuments or in archeological areas, and the National Monuments (Amendment) Act 1994, providing a comprehensive code for the ownership and possession of archeological objects, with possession (s 10) for payment to finders. See further Casey *Constitution Lawa in Ireland* (3rd ed, 2000), pp 51-53.

52. [1988] ILRM 565 at 588.

53. [1945] KB 509.

54. [1988] ILRM 565 at 588.

general propositions of law set out by Donaldson LJ, in *Parker v British Airways Board*,[55] though obiter, as "a careful and ... correct assertion of the relevant principles applicable".[56] Two of these propositions were relevant to *Webb*. The first was that "[a]n occupier of land has rights superior to those of a finder over chattels in or attached to that land ...". The second was that "[t]he finder of a chattel acquires very limited rights over it if he takes it into his care and control ... in the course of trespassing".

**[30.28]** On the basis of these propositions, Finlay CJ concluded that the occupiers had a right to possession of the chattels, superior to the plaintiffs, and that by virtue of the conveyance to the State of their interests by the occupiers, their rights had become vested in the State.

**[30.29]** Although it was not necessary for the purposes of the decision, Finlay CJ went on to consider whether a finder's rights should be diminished on account of the fact that he had entered the property as a trespasser. In the view of the Chief Justice, public policy required that a person should not, because of the trespass, "acquire any rights of ownership to the land or things found in it",[57] save in cases of prescription. The principle was based on the requirement of the common good that the ownership and right to possession of land is to be protected from unlawful invasion. Rejecting the argument that this principle should be qualified where the trespass was minimal and the trespassing finder behaved responsibly in relation to what he found, Finlay CJ said that there did not appear to him to be:

> "any grounds in logic or justice for a rule of law that a person who by trespass of little extent obtained possession of a very valuable chattel would be exempt from this provision of the law, whereas a person committing a larger or more extensive trespass, and possibly deriving a much smaller profit would be penalised by it."[58]

**[30.30]** Walsh J favoured a somewhat different approach. Limiting himself to the case where the chattels were left for safe keeping, as opposed to having been lost or abandoned, and declining to address the question whether some distinction should be drawn between chattels found on the land and those found in or under the land, he took the view that the owner of the land has bare possession, as distinct from ownership, of chattels on his lands, against any claimant who unearths the chattels. He said:

> "Notwithstanding the number and the weight of the authorities cited it is my opinion that the owner of the land upon which mislaid or unremembered chattels are intentionally placed for safe keeping, whether in or under the surface, cannot claim to be the owner of the chattels simply by reason of his being the owner of the land. To so hold would fail to vindicate the rights of property of the true owners of the chattels so placed and would permit the type of injustice which Article 40 section 3 of the Constitution is designed to prevent. The owner of such land is to be deemed to be in bare possession of the chattels even if he does not know of their existence on his lands. He can assert a good claim to possession, as distinct from

55. [1982] 1 All ER 834 at 843.
56. [1988] ILRM 565 at 589.
57. [1988] ILRM 565 at 589.
58. [1988] ILRM 565 at 590. Finlay CJ's analysis received strong support in *Waverly Borough Council v Fletcher* [1996] QB 334 (CA).

ownership, against any claimant whether it be trespasser, or otherwise, whose claim is based on simply unearthing and removing the chattels in question. Even the former royal prerogative of treasure trove acknowledged that in so far as treasure trove was concerned the true owner, or his successors in title, could always claim ownership and possession of the treasure if he could establish title."[59]

**[30.31]** In the present case the owners of the land had never sought to recover possession in the land. The "right of title" that they sold to the State was nil, in Walsh J's view, since they could not assign a right to bare possession divorced from ownership when they had already lost possession.

**[30.32]** McCarthy J was even less enthusiastic about the claim of an owner of land. He was:

> "far from satisfied that ownership of land necessarily carries with it either ownership or a right to possession or other right in respect of chattels found in or over the land as against the claim of a finder. By definition, the owner, until the find, is unaware of the presence of the chattels; if the owner is a purchaser, he has bought and the vendor has sold for a price that takes no account of the chattels; these circumstances are quite apart from the problems that arise from the possible existence of a series of superior or inferior titles to the land, which term must, for this purpose, include real property of any kind."[60]

**[30.33]** McCarthy J was unimpressed by Donaldson LJ's invocation of public policy, in aid of an occupier against a trespassing finder, to prevent the "free-for-all situation" which would arise if anyone could take the article from a trespassing finder with no rights. McCarthy J expressed no concluded view on the question but he commented tartly:

> "Public policy is an unruly horse; it is a form of judicial policy making, in this instance to be used to establish a right in someone who was unaware of the subject matter of that right until it was brought to his attention by the person who is to be denied that right."[61]

**[30.34]** *Webb* thus leaves the law relating to finders still in an uncertain state. So far as any general trend may be discerned, it seems that the occupier of the land has at least a right to bare possession against a non-trespassing finder. Where, however, the finder is a trespasser, the majority of the Court would deny the finder any claim, whilst Walsh J would apparently concede his claim subject only to any right of bare possession on the part of the occupier. McCarthy J seemed willing to recognise the claim of the finder in such a case unencumbered by any claim by the occupier.

**[30.35]** It remains to be seen whether any distinctions will be made as between articles lost, mislaid and hidden, and as between articles found in, on or under the land. Since these distinctions did not arise in *Webb*, it is most difficult to make even tentative assessments on such issues.

**[30.36]** The position changes where the finder is under a duty - statutory or contractual - to hand over property found to another. In *Crinion v Minister for Justice*,[62] a member of the

59. [1988] ILRM 565 at 600-60.

60. [1988] ILRM 565 at 607.

61. [1988] ILRM 565 at 607.

62. [1959] Ir Jur 15 (CC).

Garda Síochána found £184 on the public footpath. He handed the money to his station sergeant for safe custody pending enquiries as to ownership, which proved fruitless. After a year and a day, the guard sought the return of the money, and claimed damages for conversion.

**[30.37]** The Minister pleaded that the plaintiff had been under a duty at the time of the finding to hand the money to the sergeant.

**[30.38]** The plaintiff's action was dismissed. Judge Conroy, in a short judgment, stated that the general principle of law was that a servant or agent acts for his principal. The plaintiff was in the service of the State and on duty at the time when he found the money. He "never took full possession of the money so as to establish his own claim to it".[63]

## Conversion and Contributory Negligence

**[30.39]** Section 34(2)(d) of the Civil Liability Act 1961 provides that the plaintiff's failure to exercise reasonable care in the protection of his own property will, except to the extent that the defendant has been unjustly enriched, be deemed to have committed contributory negligence in an action for conversion of the property. Formerly it seems that contributory negligence was not a defence though there was some doubt on the matter.[64]

## Damages

**[30.40]** The measure of damages for conversion is generally the value of the article converted at the date of the conversion.[65] This contrasts with the action for detinue, where "the cause of action ... is a continuing one up to the date of judgment and the value of the chattel is assessed as at that date."[66]

**[30.41]** In calculating the value of the article at the date of conversion, the court should not ignore the effects of inflation or deflation; otherwise the plaintiff would not be restored to the same position as if the tort had not been committed.[67]

**[30.42]** Assessment of the value of the article is made on common-sense commercial principles. Thus, in *Johnson and Johnson (Ireland) Ltd v CP Security Ltd,*[68] where ten van loads of pharmaceutical products were stolen from the premises of the plaintiff, which manufactured and retailed these products, Egan J awarded damages on the basis of

63. [1959] Ir Jur 15 at 17. See also *Grafstein v Holme* (1958) 12 DLR (2d) 727 - employer entitled to money found in a box in his basement by an employee; *Wiley v Synan* (1937) 57 CLR 200 at 216-7. See also *Parker v Godin* (1728) 2 Stra 813, 93 ER 866 at 843.

64. WILLIAMS, pp 210-212, 328; Goldring 'The Negligence of the Plaintiff in Conversion (1977) 11 MULR 91; Burnett 'Conversion by an Involuntary Bailee' (1960) 76 LQR 364; Anon 'Contributory Negligence in Action for Conversion I' (1955) Victorian U of Wellington LR No 234.

65. *Allibert SA v O'Connor* [1982] ILRM 40 at 43 (HC).

66. *Webb v Ireland* [1988] IR 353 at 371 (HC) reversed on other grounds by Supreme Court [1988] ILRM 565.

67. *Cf* FLEMING, p 76.

68. [1985] IR 362 (HC).

replacement cost. He "entirely reject[ed]"[69] the argument that the goods should be valued at the prices at which the plaintiff could have sold them for profit:

> "It had vast quantities of goods in its possession to meet existing orders and those which were stolen could have been replaced at cost without any difficulty."[70]

**[30.43]** Where the converted article would have been put to profitable use - such as being hired out - losses for this use may also be recovered.[71]

**[30.44]** Chapter 9 of the Copyright and Related Rights Act 2000 contains provisions prescribing remedies for infringement of copyright which are of present relevance. These include actions for damages[72] and for orders for delivery up.[73] The copyright owner also has the right to seize infringing copies, articles or devices.[74] Section 134(1) specifically confers on the owner of a copyright the entitlements to:

> all such rights and remedies, in respect of conversion or detention by any person -
>
> (a) infringing copies of a worth,
>
> (b) articles that have been or are to be used to make infringing copies, or
>
> (c) protection - defeating devices
>
> as he or she would be entitled to if he or she were the owner of every such copy, article or device and had been the owner thereof since the time when it was made.

69. [1985] IR 362 at 366.
70. [1985] IR 362 at 366.
71. FLEMING, pp 77-78.
72. Copyright and Related Rights Act 2000, s 128.
73. Copyright and Related Rights Act 2000, s 131.
74. Copyright and Related Rights Act 2000, s 133. For discussion of the former law, which is likely to influence judicial interpretation of the new remedies, see Clark & Smyth *Intellectual Property Law in Ireland* (1997), para 18.18. *Cf Allibert SA v O'Connor* [1982] ILRM 40 (HC); *House of Spring Gardens Ltd v Point Blank Ltd* [1984] IR 611 (SC affg HC).

# Chapter 31

# Passing Off[1]



| | | |
|---|---|---|
| I. | Introduction | 795 |
| II. | Scope of the Tort of Passing Off | 797 |
| III. | Interlocutory Injunction Proceedings for Passing Off | 811 |



## I. INTRODUCTION

**[31.01]** Much of the law relating to intellectual property is now the subject of statutory control. The law relating to trade marks,[2] copyright,[3] and industrial design,[4] for example, has been regulated by statute in relatively recent times. There remains, however, an area of common law protection falling within the scope of the tort of passing off.

**[31.02]** The tort appears to have its origins[5] in the concept of deceit, but the requirement of fraudulent intent has long since been abandoned. The essence of the tort is that one trader represents its goods or services as those of another, so as to be likely to mislead the public and involve an appreciable risk of detriment to the plaintiff. In *Polycell Products Ltd v O'Carroll and Ors t/a Dillon, O'Carroll*,[6] Budd J stated:

---

1. See generally Clark & Smyth *Intellectual Property Law In Ireland* (1997), Ch 24; Hunt 'The Law of Passing Off in Ireland' (M Litt Thesis, Trinity College Dublin, 1998), Wadlow *The Law of Passing Off* (2nd ed, 1995); Cornish *Intellectual Property*, (3rd ed, 1996), Ch 16; Drysdale & Silverleaf *Passing Off Law and Practice* (2nd ed, 1992); Tierney *Irish Trade Marks Law and Practice* (1987), Ch 2; Healy 'The Tort of Passing Off' (1997) 15 ILT (ns) 196, 218; Rose 'Passing Off, Unfair Competition and Community Law' [1990] EIPR 123; Schricker 'European Harmonisation of Unfair Competition Law - A Futile Venture?' (1991) 22 IIC 788; Lewis 'Passing Off and Unfair Competition' [1981] LMCLQ 341; Meyer-Rochow 'Passing Off - Past, Present and Future' (1994) 84 Trademark Rep 38; Morcom 'Developments in the Law of Passing Off' [1991] EIPR 380; Knight 'Unfair Competition: A Comparative Study of its Role in Common Law and Civil Law Systems' (1978) 53 Tulane LR 164.
2. Trade Marks Act 1996, s 7(2) of the Act provides that "... nothing in this Act shall affect the law relating to passing off." A ground for refusing to register a trade mark is that its use in the State is liable to be preindicated "by virtue of any rule of law (in particular the law of passing off) protecting an unregistered trade mark or other sign used in the course of trade": s 10(4).
3. Copyright and Related Rights Act 2000. As to the remedies for the copyright owner, see Chapter 9 of the Act. Criminal offences are specified in Chapter 13. The remedies for infringement of performers' rights are contained in Chapters 14 and 15 of the Act.
4. Industrial and Commercial Property (Protection) Act 1927.
5. Historical aspects of the tort are comprehensively analysed by Clark & Smyth *Intellectual Property Law In Ireland* (1997), Ch 24; Wadlow *The Law of Passing Off* (2nd ed, 1995); Cornish *Intellectual Property*, (3rd ed, 1996).
6. [1959] Ir Jur Rep 34 at 36 (HC). *In Player & Wills (Ireland) Ltd v Gallagher (Dublin) Ltd* High Court, 26 September 1983 at pp 1-2, Barron J offered a useful summary:

   "The essence of passing off is the adoption by the defendant of some element in the manner in which the plaintiff's goods are marketed in a manner calculated to deceive persons intending to buy the plaintiff's product into thinking that they have bought it when in fact they have bought the defendant's product.

> "The legal principles affecting an action for 'passing off' are well established. To establish merchandise in such a manner as to mislead the public into believing that it is the merchandise or product of another is actionable. It injures the complaining party's right of property in his business and injures the goodwill of his business. A person who passes off the goods of another acquires to some extent the benefit of the business reputation of the rival trader and gets the advantage of his advertising."

More recently, in *O'Neills Irish International Sports Co Ltd v O'Neills Footwear Dryer Co Ltd*,[7] Barron J observed:

> "The nature of the tort is to be found in its name. The wrong is that of passing-off one's goods as those of another. This can be done by similarity of name, appearance, get-up or any other similarity which achieves the same purpose. How it is done is immaterial so long as the

---

6. (contd)

> The element so adopted must be one for which the plaintiff can establish a reputation in the sense that those purchasing goods involving such element do so because of their awareness of the connection between that element and the plaintiff. The element may inter alia be the name, the particular mark or design attached to the goods or its get up. In each case, it indicates a badge of origin."

7. High Court, 30 April 1997 (Barron J) at p 4 of his judgment. Two definitions of the tort in English decisions have had influence in Ireland. In *Reckitt and Colman Products Ltd v Borden Inc* [1990] 1 All ER 873 at 880 (HL), Lord Oliver expressed the view that the plaintiff had to establish these elements in order to succeed:

> "'First, he must establish a goodwill or reputation attached to the goods or services which he supplies in the mind of the purchasing public by association with the identifying 'get-up' (whether it consists simply of a brand name or a trade description, or the individual features of labelling or packaging) under which his particular goods or services are offered to the public, such that the get-up is recognised by the public as distinctive specifically of the plaintiff's goods or services. Second, he must demonstrate a misrepresentation by the defendant to the public (whether or not intentional) leading or likely to lead the public to believe that goods or services offered by him are the goods or services of the plaintiff. Whether the public is aware of the plaintiff's identity as the manufacturer or supplier of the goods or services is immaterial, as long as they are identified with a particular source which is in fact the plaintiff. For example, if the public is accustomed to relying on a particular brand name in purchasing goods of a particular description, it matters not at all that there is little or no public awareness of the identity of the proprietor of the brand name. Third, he must demonstrate that he suffers or, in a *quia timet* action, that he is likely to suffer damage by reason of the erroneous belief engendered by the defendants' misrepresentation that the source of the defendants' goods or services is the same as the source of those offered by the plaintiff."

In *DSG Retail Ltd v PC World Ltd* High Court, 13 January 1998, Laffoy J adopted this test, which also has the support of the Supreme Court of Canada see *(Ciba-Geigy Canada Ltd v Apotex Inc* [1992] 95 DLR 385. In *Erven Warnick BV v J Townsend & Sons (Hull) Ltd* [1979] AC 731 at 742 (HL), Lord Diplock had identified the characteristics of passing off as:

> "(1) a misrepresentation (2) made by a trader in the course of trade (3) to prospective customers of his or ultimate consumers of goods or services supported by him, (4) which is calculated to injure the business or goodwill of another trader (in the sense that this is a reasonably foreseeable consequence) and (5) which causes actual damage to a business or goodwill of the trader by whom the action is brought or (in a *quia timet* action) will probably do so."

Lord Diplock's test was applied by Murhpy J in *Falcon Travel Ltd v Owners Abroad Group plc t/a Falcon Leisure Group* [1991] 1 IR 175 at (HC); by Kinlen J in *An Post v Irish Permanent plc* [1995] 1 ILRM 336 (HC) and by McCracken J in *B & S Ltd v Irish Auto Trader Ltd* [1995] 2 ILRM 152 (HC); *R Griggs Group Ltd v Dunnes Stores Ireland Co* High Court, 4 October 1996 and *Smithkline Beecham plc v Antigen Pharmaceuticals Ltd* [1999] 2 ILRM 190 (HC) and by Barron J in *O'Neills Irish International Sports Company Ltd v O'Neills Footwear Dryer Co Ltd* High Court, 30 April 1997.

similarity is calculated to deceive those who might buy or otherwise deal in the goods. Deliberate intention is not necessary."

**[31.03]** The tort is therefore essentially designed to protect the plaintiff's proprietary interest in his goodwill rather than to protect the interests of the consumer or the wider public, thus it is no defence to show that the defendant's goods or services are better or cheaper than those of the plaintiff or that the resultant competition is good for the consuming public.[8]

**[31.04]** Since most of the decisions dealt with in this chapter are concerned with passing off in relation to products it is perhaps desirable to stress at this point the fact that passing off of services is also actionable. In this regard, Clarke has commented:

> "Until the passing of the Trade Marks Act 1996, an action for passing off was the only method by which service mark holders could defend their goodwill in such marks. With the advent of service mark registration and with the wider test for trade mark infringement, it remains to be seen whether the tort will retain the importance it haas had up to now."[9]

## II. Scope of the Tort of Passing Off

### Intention to Deceive Not Essential

**[31.05]** It is clear that neither actual deception[10] nor even an intention to deceive[11] is necessary,[12] but proof of such intention[13] or that a member of the consuming public has been deceived will clearly assist the plaintiff's case. As McWilliam J stated in *Grange Marketing Ltd v M & Q Plastic Products Ltd*:[14]

> "if an intention to deceive is established, it is more probable that the goods were marketed in a way calculated to deceive."

---

8. *Incorporated Law Society of Ireland v Carroll* High Court, 24 January 1995. See also *Michael B Costelloe Ltd v Simek Ltd* High Court, 26 February 1981 (Costello J).
9. Clarke, *Intellectual Property*, para 12.04 in O'Connor & Ussher *Doing Business in Ireland* (Rel 11-8/99).
10. *Jay v Ladler* (1888) 40 ChD 649 at 656; *Reddaway v Bentham* [1892] 2 QB 639; *Jameson v Dublin Distillers' Co* [1900] 1 IR 43 at 55 (Chatterton VC). *Cf Askjorn Horgard AlS v GibbslMortac Industries Ltd* (1987) 38 DLR (4th) 544 (Fed CA).
11. *"Singer" Machine Manufacturers v Wilson* (1877) 3 AC 376 at 391; *Johnston v Orr-Ewing* (1881) 7 AC 219; *Shoshana Pty Ltd v 10th Cantanae Pty Ltd* (1987) 79 Austr LR 279 (Fed CA); *Guinness Ireland Group v Kilkenny Brewing Co Ltd* [1999] 1 ILRM 531 (HC); *Smithkline Beecham plc v Antigen Pharmaceuticals Ltd* [1999] 2 ILRM 190 (HC). *Cf Thwaites & Co v McEvilly* [1904] IR 310 at 326.
12. *Grange Marketing Ltd v M & Q Plastic Products Ltd* High Court, unrep 17 June 1976 (McWilliam J) at p 6. See also *Sterling-Winthrop Group Ltd v Farbenfabriken Bayer AG* [1967] IR 97 at 104 (HC) quoting with approval from SALMOND (14th ed, 1965 by Heuston, p 573). See now SALMOND & HEUSTON (21st ed, 1996), p 385.
13. *Society of Motor Manufacturers v Motor Manufacturers* [1925] Ch 675 at 686. Thus, Kenny J said *Sterling-Winthrop Group Ltd v Farbenfabriken Bayer AG* [1967] IR 97 was in error in holding that, because an intention to deceive was not essential to establish liability, intention was "not relevant on the issue of passing off". As to proof by "trap orders", *see Dickson v Dickson* [1909] IR 185; *CC Wakefield & Co Ltd v Purser* (1928) 45 RPC 261.
14. High Court, 17 June 1976 (McWilliam J) at p 6. See also *Cantrell & Cochrane (Dublin) Ltd v Savage Smythe & Co Ltd* High Court, 1 August 1976 (Kenny J).

**[31.06]** So also, in the Supreme Court decision of *C & A Modes v C & A (Waterford) Ltd*,[15] Henchy J stated that, while intention to deceive is not the essence of the action, it "shows that the conduct complained of was in fact likely to deceive -which goes to the gist of the action for passing off".

**[31.07]** Where there was no intention to deceive, it appears that nominal damages will generally be in order.[16] Moreover this factor may have some effect on the decision whether or not to grant an interlocutory injunction.[17]

## Risk of Confusion

**[31.08]** The courts have made it clear that there must be a likelihood of confusion: "isolated incidents of confusion will not in themselves amount to passing off ...".[18] They have not gone much further than this, however, in spelling out the requisite level of probability or potential scope of confusion.[19]

**[31.09]** The test for determining whether confusion is probable is the likely impression on the casual and unwary customer[20] who is typical of those who seek the goods in question. It is not a defence to contend that an observant person making a careful examination of the goods would not have been misled.[21]

**[31.10]** In an action for passing off it is not necessary for the plaintiff to establish that the public associated the goods with any particular firm. "It is sufficient to establish that the goods are known by a particular name ... or even by a particular get-up."[22] Likelihood of confusion may be established even where the defendant intends to engage in a different type of business than that of the plaintiff's. So in *Guinness Ireland Group v Kilkenny Brewing Co Ltd*,[23] Laffoy J granted an injunction against the use of the name Kilkenny Brewing Company by a company whose purpose was merely to hold land (a micro brewery premises) rather than to be a trading company for the business carried on, or the products produced, in the micro brewery. Evidence from three persons "very experienced in the licensed trade"[24] was to the effect that consumers would be likely to get the

15. [1976] IR 198 at 211. See also *Muckross Park Hotel Ltd v Randles* [1995] IR 130 at 135 (HC).
16. *Draper v Trist* [1939] 3 All ER 513 at 525 (*per* Clauson LJ) and 528 (*per* Goddard LJ), *cf* at 519 (*per* Greene LJ).
17. *Cf B & S Ltd v Irish Auto Trader Ltd* [1995] 2 ILRM 152 (HC).
18. *Private Research Ltd v Brosnan* [1996] 1 ILRM 27 at 31 (HC).
19. See Cornish, *Intellectual Property* (3rd ed, 1996), p 548.
20. *Singer Manufacturing Co v Loog* (1882) 8 AC 15 at 18. See also *An Bord Trachtála v Waterford Foods plc* [1994] FSR 316 (HC).
21. *Cf Montgomery v Thompson* [1891] AC 217 at 225 (*per* Lord MacNaughten): "Thirsty folk want beer, not explanations". Brandy-drinkers may be more discriminating: *cf Hennessy (James) & Co v Keating* [1908] 1 IR 43 at 100-101 (affd [1908] 1 IR 466 (HL)). *Cf* Naresh 'Passing off; Goodwill and False Advertising: New Wine in Old Bottles' [1986] Camb LJ 97, criticising the breadth of a number of English decisions, notably *Erven Warnick BV v J Townsend & Sons (Hull) Ltd* [1979] AC 731.
22. *Cantrell & Cochrane (Dublin) Ltd v Savage Smythe & Co Ltd* High Court, 1 August 1976 at p 10 of Kenny J's judgment, referring to *Kerly on Trade Marks* (8th ed), p 342.
23. [1999] 1 ILRM 531 (HC).
24. [1999] 1 ILRM 531 (HC) at 538.

impression that the defendant brewed Kilkenny Irish Beer (the plaintiffs' product) or that it was posed by one of the plaintiffs.

**[31.11]** It should be noted that, in the absence of proof of likely confusion as between the plaintiff's and the defendant's products, the plaintiff's claim must fail, even though the commercial success of the plaintiff's product has inspired the defendant to adopt the same style or design. In the Supreme Court decision of *Adidas Sportsschuhfabricken Adi Dassler KG v Charles O'Neill & Co Ltd*,[25] O'Higgins CJ said that the plaintiff had no right to complain:

> "if a trader, attracted by the design [of the plaintiff's product] or susceptible to the fashion which its prominence creates, decides to copy or imitate. The mere copying of a design or the anticipation of a fashion or the taking advantage of a market or demand created by another's advertising is not of itself sufficient to support an action for passing off if the trader against whom the complaint is made has sufficiently distinguished his goods so that confusion is not created."

**[31.12]** And Henchy J stressed that:

> "a person who has initiated or exploited a trend or fashion in clothes or other goods does not thereby acquire a right, by means of a passing-off action, to warn off competitors who might wish to trade in such articles or goods. In such circumstances, competitive trading remains open to all until, by the use of a name, a mark, a get-up or other novel or distinctive feature, a particular trader acquires a goodwill as a result of such use. Even then, that trader does not get a right of action against a rival trader for passing off until that rival puts forth goods for sale bearing that distinctive indication or a colourable imitation thereof, thereby misrepresenting his goods as those of the person who has acquired the goodwill or proprietary repute created by the distinctive feature and, by such unfair trading, causing a degree of financial loss, actually incurred or likely to be incurred by the person who has acquired the goodwill or 'the intangible property right' created by the idiosyncratic mark, design or get-up."[26]

**[31.13]** In *Gabicci v Dunnes Stores Ltd*,[27] Carroll J distinguished the *Adidas* holding where the designer of men's co-ordinated casual clothing sought an interlocutory injunction against the sale of sweaters by the defendants which were very similar in design to those of the plaintiff's though they were sold under the defendants' "St Bernard" label. Carroll J commented:

> "This is not a case of Dunnes following a fashion trend and giving good value. It concerns the sale of sweaters which to all intents and purposes are 'the plaintiff's sweaters' and which it is alleged has created confusion to the public with resultant damage to the plaintiff's goodwill."[28]

**[31.14]** When assessing the risk of confusion, the courts must address the question of who is likely to be confused. In *Smithkline Beecham plc v Antigen Pharmaceuticals Ltd*,[29] the

25. [19831 ILRM 112 at 117 (SC) (Hederman J, concurring).
26. [1983] ILRM 112 at 124. (Henchy J dissented in this case but the dissent did not affect this statement of the law.) *Cf Private Research Ltd v Brosnan* [1996] 1 ILRM 27 (HC) noted by Byrne & Binchy, *Annual Review of Irish Law 1995*, pp 270, 540.
27. High Court, 31 July 1991 (Carroll J).
28. High Court, 31 July 1991 at p 3 of Carroll J's judgment.
29. [1999] 2 ILRM 190 (HC).

defendants marketed an analgesic named Solfen which, the plaintiffs claimed, was likely to be confused in customers' minds with its product named Solpadene. Neither product could be sold on open shelves, they had to be sold over the counter, "when asked for by name by the purchaser and under the supervision of a qualified pharmacist".[30] The plaintiffs were concerned that "a customer with an uncertain recollection"[31] (which McCracken J acknowledged was "the correct test"[32]) might ask a pharmacist for a pain killer with a phrase such as "sol something" and that confusion would occur. McCracken J considered that "[t]hat confusion would be the confusion of the pharmacist, or the carelessness of the pharmacist in not asking further questions, rather than the confusion of the customer purchasing the product".[33]

**[31.15]** McCracken J, with some reluctance, held that there was a serious issue to be tried in relation to the risk of confusion, though he considered that the plaintiffs' case was "very much weakened" by the fact that the products were not on open access on a supermarket shelf but were "dispensed by a person trained to take care".[34]

**[31.16]** In *An Bord Tráchtála v Waterford Foods plc*,[35] Keane J addressed the issue of the risk of confusion in an international context[36] where the plaintiff was not a conventional business. An Bord Tráchtála, was charged with the task of developing and promoting the export of Irish produce throughout the world. It designed a logo to assist its marketing of Irish agri-food products abroad, by the creation of a single identity representative of all Irish food-related products. The logo consisted of a symbol representing the sun rising over a valley of green hills leading down to the sea; it was accompanied by the legend "Food Ireland". It prominently displayed the logo on all its exhibition stands at international trade fairs, and in supermarkets displays abroad, as well as in advertising at home and abroad.

**[31.17]** The defendant, a company with a range of milk and cheese products sold extensively abroad, developed a logo consisting of a yellow sun above a blue and green valley, with the accompanying legend "Waterford Foods". The plaintiff sought an interlocutory injunction against the use of the defendant's logo, on the basis that it constituted passing off. Keane J declined to grant the injunction.

---

30. [1999] 2 ILRM 190 at 195.
31. [1999] 2 ILRM 190 at 195.
32. [1999] 2 ILRM 190 at 195.
33. [1999] 2 ILRM 190 at 195.
34. [1999] 2 ILRM 190 at 195. *Cf Sterwin AG v Brocades (Great Britain) Ltd* [1979] RPC 481.
35. [1994] FSR 316 (HC) analysed by Byrne & Binchy *Annual Review of Irish Law 1993*, pp 580-582.
36. The choice-of-law issues in this case were of interest. Keane J declined to follow the lead of the Supreme Court in *Grehan v Medical Incorporated Inc* [1986] IR 528, where Walsh J (Finlay CJ and Griffin J concurring) had lambasted the rule in *Phillips v Eyre* (1870) LR 6 QB 1. Keane J treated this criticism as *obiter*, since *Grehan* was concerned with the issue of jurisdiction, and followed the rule, which has subsequently been modified in important respects by *Red Sea Insurance Co Ltd v Bouygues SA* [1995] 1 AC 190 (PC). For a comprehensive analysis of the subject, see Fawcett & Torremans *Intellectual Property and Private International Law* (1998), especially pp 652-668. See also Binchy *Irish Conflicts of Law* (1988), Ch 32.

**[31.18]** Keane J held that the plaintiff had not adduced any evidence that the logo on which it relied was well known, or known at all, in Ireland or any other country in connection with it or any business in which it might be regarded as engaged, principally the promotion of Irish exports abroad. Nor was there the slightest reason why it should be so known:

> "[F]rom the point of view of the plaintiff, provided the logo achieves, or helps to achieve, its object of identifying Irish food products abroad with a pure and pollution-free environment, it is hardly a major consideration that the name and reputation of the sponsoring body is not known to the prospective customers in Birmingham or Glasgow. It is 'Food Ireland' that the logo seeks to promote, not 'An Bord Tráchtála'." [37]

## Survey Evidence

**[31.19]** Market research surveys have come to play an important role internationally in passing off litigation.[38] They can serve a number of functions,[39] the most important of which, in practice, relates to the issue of actual or likely confusion between the plaintiff's and the defendants' business in the mind of the prospective customers.

**[31.20]** This evidential status has provoked controversy. Should they be regarded as a record of the opinion of the public or a class of the public and thus not violative of the rule against hearsay on the basis that they may be characterised as original evidence of the fact that this group held such opinions?[40] The problem with this approach is that there is no guarantee that the interviewees communicated truthfully their opinion to the researchers carrying out the survey.[41] Moreover, the researchers will normally have made written records of the interviews, which will then be pooled and processed to yield results about which an expert representative of the enterprise carrying out the survey may give evidence in court. That expert's evidence depends on what the researchers asserted in their records and originally is hearsay evidence on that account.[42] In *Hanafin v Minister for the Environment*,[43] opinion poll evidence was accepted.

**[31.21]** In *An Post v Irish Permanent plc*,[44] in an application for an interlocutory injunction for passing off, Kinlen J accepted survey evidence apparently without question. He observed that, allowing for the statistical evidence that applies to sample surveys, he believed that the two surveys of which affidavit evidence had been addressed on behalf of the plaintiff had established several specific facts. He referred to criticisms made of these findings by an expert who carried out a survey for the defendant. Kinlen J referred to the

37. [1994] FSR at 316.
38. See Clark & Smyth *Intellectual Property Law in Ireland* 1997, paras 31.31-31.35; Wadlow, *The Law of Passing Off* (2nd ed, 1995), paras 8.45-8.50; Pattinson 'Market Research Surveys - Money Well Spent? The Use of Survey Evidence in Passing Off Proceedings in the UK' [1990] 3 EIPP 99; Stephenson-Burton 'UK: Survey Evidence in Trade Mark and Passing Off Proceedings'(1996) 9 Trademark World 28; Fellner 'Survey Evidence in Passing Off Cases' (1985) 5 J of Media L & Practice 273; Farmen 'The Admissibility of Survey Evidence in Intellectual Property Cases' [1984] UNSW LJ 57.
39. See Pattinson 'Market Research Surveys - Money Well Spent? The Use of Survey Evidence in Passing Off Proceedings in the UK' [1990] 3 EIPP 99.
40. See McGrath 'Evidence' in Byrne & Binchy, *Annual Review of Irish Law 1997*, p 416.
41. See McGrath 'Evidence' in Byrne & Binchy, *Annual Review of Irish Law 1997*, p 416.
42. *Cf* Wardlow, *The Law of Passing Off* (2nd ed, 1995), para 8.46.
43. High Court, 24 January 1996.
44. [1995] 1 ILRM 336 (HC).

findings from this survey highlighted in this expert's affidavit (without giving his express endorsement to them). Kinlen J went on to observe that counsel for both plaintiff and defendant had used the surveys "to great effect"[45] and that they each had "quarried suitable portions to support their respective cases".[46]

**[31.22]** All of this suggests that Kinlen J saw no difficulty in principle with survey evidence. It may, however, be significant that, in finding that there was a serious question to be tried, Kinlen J observed that it was "undoubtedly clear from the affidavits (leaving aside the aforementioned surveys) that there ha[d] been some confusion."[47] The fact that the survey evidence had been subjected to considerable criticism by the defendant may have encouraged Kinlen J to take this course.[48]

**[31.23]** In *R Griggs Group Ltd v Dunnes Stores Ireland Co*,[49] where the plaintiffs sought an interlocutory injunction against alleged passing off its "Doc Martens" boots, McCracken J evinced considerable dissatisfaction with the "very informal" survey conducted by the plaintiffs' solicitors, which had consisted of stopping people in the street, showing them a pair of boots and asking them "What brand of shoes are these?".

**[31.24]** McCracken J observed:

> "The courts have always been sceptical of survey evidence, particularly when it is taken in such an informal way, and certainly this survey is open to much criticism. For example, parts of the survey were carried out on the street after dark, and we are not told whether the persons questioned were given an opportunity to examine the boots in the same way as would be possible in a shop." [50]

**[31.25]** In *Smithkline Beecham plc v Antigen Pharmaceuticals Ltd*,[51] McCracken J considered that, with regard to the survey evidence, he could "do no more that quote" from the judgment of Whitford J in *Imperial Group plc v Philip & Morris Ltd*,[52] to the effect that:

> "[h]owever satisfactory market research surveys may be in assisting commercial organisations as to how they can best conduct their business, they are by and large, as experience in other cases has indicated, an unsatisfactory way of trying to establish questions of fact which are likely to be matters of dispute."

**[31.26]** McCracken J was of the view that survey evidence was:

> "of little or no value in interlocutory applications, where that evidence is not tested by cross-examination, and indeed all the background facts relating to that evidence, such as the actual questionnaires and answers are not put in evidence."[53]

---

45. [1995] 1 ILRM 336 at 342.
46. [1995] 1 ILRM 336 at 342.
47. [1995] 1 ILRM 336 at 343.
48. *Cf* Clark & Smyth, *Intellectual Property Law in Ireland* (1997), para 24.41.
49. High Court, 4 October 1996 (McCracken J).
50. High Court, 4 October 1996 (McCracken J).
51. [1999] 2 ILRM 190 at 196 (HC).
52. [1984] RPC 293 at 302.
53. [1999] 2 ILRM 190 at 197.

**[31.27]** It should be noted that Whitford J did not exclude survey evidence completely but instead laid down stringent conditions for its acceptance by a court in passing-off litigation:

> "Of course, if a survey is to have any validity at all, the way in which the interviewees are selected must be established as being done by a method such that a relevant cross-section of the public is interviewed ... Any survey must of course be of a size which is sufficient to produce some relevant result viewed on a statistical basis. It must be conducted fairly ...
> If survey evidence is to be of any weight at all it can only be of weight if in any case where ... a number of surveys have been carried out the plaintiffs give - and they must give this to the defendants before ever the action comes on - the fullest possible disclosure of exactly how many surveys they have carried out, exactly how those surveys were conducted and the totality of the number of persons involved ...
> It is also important that the totality of all answers given to all surveys should be disclosed and made available to the defendants ...
> Great importance inevitably attaches to the way in which the questions are cast ... It must necessarily be the case that the exact answers given and not some sort of abbreviation or digest of the exact answer should be recorded. For the purpose of an analysis coding is in general carried out ... and it is of vital importance that [it] be accurately carried out. Of course one has to know exactly what instructions were given to persons carrying out the interview upon which answer to questionnaires are secured ..." [54]

## Shared Goodwill[55]

**[31.28]** It is not clear that parties who share goodwill may, individually or collectively, protect it by a passing off action against those who damage it. Thus successful actions have been taken by the producers of champagne,[56] sherry,[57] scotch, whisky,[58] and advocaat[59] in protection of their shared goodwill. In *Warnink v Townsend & Sons (Hull) Ltd*,[60] Lord Diplock considered:

> "the principle must be the same whether the class of which each member is severally entitled to the goodwill which attaches to a particular term as descriptive of his goods is large or

54. [1984] RCP 293. See also *United Biscuits (UK) Ltd v Burtons Biscuits Ltd* [1992] FSR 14; *Walt Disney Productions v Triple Five Corp* (1992) 93 DLR (4th) 739). In *Interlego AG v Croner Trading Pty Ltd* (1991) 102 ALR 379 (Fed Ct, Austr), Sheppard J, having quoted with approval the passage form Whitford J's judgment in *Imperial Group* quoted above and from the *Manual for the Conduct of Complex Litigation*, (2nd ed, 1985), para 21.484, published by the Federal Judicial Center of the United States of America, commented that:

> "one can[not] lay down rules which come necessarily to govern each case. The facts and circumstances of one case will differ so much from those of another that it would be unwise to lay down, whether in a judgment or a practice note, guidelines which are to rigid. Nevertheless, ... I think it wise that surveys should be conducted on notice to the opposing side, that attempts be made to conduct surveys jointly and that the court, in appropriate cases, exercise some supervision in relation to the formation of the questions and the manner in which the survey is to be administered."

55. See Cornish *Intellectual Property* (3rd ed, 1996), pp 540-541; Clark & Smyth *Intellectual Property Law In Ireland* (1997), p 451.
56. *Bollinger v Costa Brava Wine Co* [1960] RPC 16, [1961] RPC 116.
57. *Vine Products Ltd v MacKenzie* [1969] RPC 1.
58. *Walker (John) & Sons v Henry Ost & Co* [1970] RPC 489, analysed by Hobbs [1979] EIPR 141.
59. [1979] AC 731.
60. [1979] AC 731 at 744.

small. The larger it is the broader must be the range and quality of products to which the descriptive term used by the members of the class has been applied, and the more difficult it must be to show that the term has acquired a public reputation and goodwill as decorating a product endowed with recognisable qualities which distinguish it from others of inferior reputation that complete with it in the same market. The larger the class, the more difficult it must also be for an individual member of it to show that the goodwill of his own business has sustained more than minimal damage as a result of deceptive use by another trader of the widely shared descriptive term."

## Description of Goods

**[31.29]** Where the plaintiff's case is based on the contention that the defendant has used a name similar or identical to that of his own goods, the question arises as to whether the name used actually connotes goods manufactured or sold by him or is merely descriptive of those goods. Clearly, descriptive words may by usage become distinctively attached to a product: "camel-hair" clothing,[61] for example. In such a case it will constitute passing off to misappropriate the name. What is distinctive today, however, may through business usage become descriptive tomorrow: everyone may now sell "gramophones", for example, because the word has long since ceased to suggest that those products are manufactured by the original producers who used the name.[62]

## Packaged Products

**[31.30]** In deciding whether a defendant alleged to have packaged his goods in a manner similar to those of the plaintiff is guilty of passing off, the court must consider:

> "the general 'get up' of the packages; their size and shape; the material used; combination of colours; the decoration and lettering; the arrangement of labels; the spacing of words; and finally, the overall picture presented from the entire combination."[63]

**[31.31]** In *Polycell Products Ltd v O'Carroll and Ors t/a Dillon, O'Carroll*,[64] an interlocutory injunction was granted against the sale of a cellulose adhesive by the defendant in packages very similar in colour and design to those of the plaintiff's product. The fact that the name was reasonably dissimilar- "Clingcell" in comparison to "Polycell" - was not sufficient to prevent the risk of confusion in the mind of the consumer.

**[31.32]** In *Grange Marketing Ltd v M & Q Plastic Products Ltd*,[65] the defendant company was found liable for passing off where its product -"body shaping" rope equipment - was packaged in a box very similar in size and illustration to that of the plaintiff's, and where the slogan written on the defendant's box- "one five minute exercise twice daily slims, trims and shapes you" - was identical to the one on the plaintiff's.

**[31.33]** In *United Biscuits Ltd v Irish Biscuits Ltd*,[66] the plaintiff company, who manufactured biscuits called "Cottage Creams", claimed that the defendant company, who

---

61. *Reddaway v Banham* [1896] AC 199.
62. *Gramophone Co's Application* [1910] 2 Ch 423. See also *Liebig's Extract of Meat Co v Hanbury* (1867) 17 LT 298. In this context one might also consider the descriptive term "hoover".
63. *Polycell Products Ltd v O'Carroll and Ors t/a Dillon, O'Carroll* [1959] Ir Jur Rep 34 at 38 (HC). See also *Smithkline Beecham plc v Antigen Pharmaceuticals* High Court, 25 March 1999 (HC).
64. [1959] Ir Jur Rep 34 at 38 (HC).
65. High Court, 17 June 1976 (McWilliam J).
66. [1971] IR 16 (HC).

manufactured biscuits called "College Creams", were guilty of passing off. The packages in which the biscuits were sold to the public were entirely different in design and colour. The biscuits were, however, similar to each other.

**[31.34]** Counsel for the plaintiff contended that a person who had eaten and enjoyed Cottage Cream biscuits might, on being told their name, subsequently buy College Creams in the belief that he was getting the biscuit that had pleased him. Kenny J rejected this argument on the basis that, since both brands were sold in packages, the appearance, size and texture of the biscuits were irrelevant. He went so far as to state that: "Similarities in the biscuit which is sold in packages can never be a passing off".[67]

**[31.35]** In *Michelstown Co-operative Agricultural Society Ltd v Goldenvale Food Products Ltd*,[68] in 1985, Costello J granted an interlocutory injunction against the use by the defendants of a form of packaging and wording for their new butter substitute, which the plaintiffs claimed was misleadingly close to their own product. The products were packaged in tubs of identical dimensions. The trademarks under which the two products were sold were separately registered and not confusingly similar. The plaintiffs did not make any claim to a monopoly in the use of a tub for marketing a dairy spread; but they strongly objected "to another product['s being] sold in a tub whose general colour scheme, strength, shape, dimensions and overall-printing correspond[ed] to theirs and which moreover [also] use[d] the symbol of a yellow flower".[69]

## Clothes

**[31.36]** Some particular difficulties arise in relation to passing off actions regarding designs or fashions in clothes. In *Adidas Sportsschuhfabriken Adi Dassler KA v Charles O'Neill & Co Ltd*,[70] the well-known German sports company, Adidas, sought an injunction and damages against the defendant, a family concern which had been making sports garments for a number of years.

**[31.37]** The gravamen of the plaintiff's case was that the use, by the defendant, of three stripes on sports clothes amounted to passing off, since the plaintiff's products had become well-known for using this design.

**[31.38]** McWilliam J dismissed the action, and the Supreme Court, by a majority, affirmed. O'Higgins CJ (Hederman J concurring) stressed the fact that the defendant was a well-established firm, whose products were delivered to retail outlets in boxes clearly marked with its name. The Chief Justice endorsed McWilliam J's view that the defendant had done no more than to adopt a fashion in the trade. There had been no suggestion of any attempt to deceive customers, who might in any event be expected to look fairly at the

---

67. [1971] IR 16 at 20. See also *Cantrell & Cochrane (Dublin) Ltd v Savage Smythe & Co Ltd* High Court, 1 August 1976; *Beecham Group Ltd v Eiraf Pharmaceuticals Ltd* High Court, 27 March 1985 (Barron J) - interlocutory injunction against sale or distribution of antibiotic in capsules confusingly similar to the distinctive black and red-coloured capsule of plaintiff company.

68. High Court, 12 December 1985 (Costello J).

69. High Court, 12 December 1985, p 4. *Cf Klissers Farmhouse Bakeries Ltd v Harvest Bakeries Ltd* [1988] 1 NZLR 16 (CA); *Telemak Teleproducts (Aust.) Pty Ltd v Coles Myer Ltd* (1988) 48 ALR 437 (Fed Ct Austr); *Dalepak Foods plc v Frezmet Daily Pack Ltd* [1987] NILR p 1.

70. [1983] ILRM 112 (SC), affg High Court, 20 May 1980 (McWilliam J).

goods on display. By the time the plaintiff posed a real challenge to the defendant for the Irish market in sporting gear, the defendant's products with a three-stripe design had become "well-established and well-known". They were, moreover, clearly marked as the defendant's products.

**[31.39]** Henchy J, dissenting, placed emphasis on the fact that no witness had attested that he had associated the get-up relied on by the plaintiff with any manufacturer other than the plaintiff. That get-up, in Henchy J's view, had become part of the plaintiff's goodwill, even if this was "an unwelcome conclusion to those who resent the power over ... personal taste and preference exercised by lavish advertising, free handouts and such like influences on purchasing habits that are a feature of the media-dominated society in which we live".[71]

## Descriptive Expressions

**[31.40]** The plaintiff who alleges that an expression *prima facie* descriptive should be regarded as sufficiently associated with his product as to have acquired a distinctive meaning associated with his goods has a hard task. The burden of proof upon him is high and the Court will tend to accept small differences between the plaintiff's and the defendant's descriptions of their respective products as adequate to justify the defendant's conduct.[72] Nevertheless, the differences must be real ones.[73] An example of the approach favoured by the Courts arose in *Ragget v Findlater*,[74] where it was held that a brewer accustomed to putting on the label of his bottles and words "nourishing stout" had no monopoly to this expression.

**[31.41]** The assignee of a trade name is not debarred from seeking compensation for passing off in respect of that name even though the assignee has not in fact used the name subsequent to the assignment. It is always possible that the goodwill attaching to the name will have retained sufficient potency to be damaged even after a period of non-use. However, the fact, or probability, of this damage must be established before an injunction will be ordered. Thus, in *"Independent" Newspapers Ltd v "Irish Press" Ltd*,[75] in 1932, Meredith J refused to grant a *quia timet* injunction against the defendant company, who had declared their intention of publishing the "Evening Press" under the title of the "Evening Telegraph". The plaintiff company had been assigned that title seven years previously from the "Freeman's Journal" which had published an "Evening Telegraph" for

---

71. [1983] ILRM 112 at 123.

72. *Office Cleaning Services Ltd v Westminster, etc Cleaners Ltd* (1946) 63 RPC 39 at 42 (*per* Lord Simonds,). See also *Cellular Clothing v Maxton* [1899] AC 326 at 343.

73. *Effluent Disposal Ltd v Midlands Effluent Disposal Ltd* [1970] RPC 238.

74. (1873) LR 17 Eq 29. *Cf Grand Hotel Co of Caledonia Springs v Wilson* [1904] AC 103; *Fels v Hedley* (1903) 20 TLR 69. *Cf Griffin v Kelly's Strand Hotel* High Court, 24 January 1980 (McWilliams J) - interlocutory injunction granted in respect of use of hotel name. Where a surname is adopted so as to cause confusion liability will generally follow: *cf Dockrell & Co v Dockrell & Co* (1941) 75 ILTR 226 (HC) where Black J conceded (at 227) that if the defendants had actually possessed the same surname, the position might be considerably more difficult, because it might be said that they were entitled to the use of their own name, even though the result should be to confuse. See also *Valentine v Valentine*, (1892) 3 ILR (Ir) 488*; Jameson v Dublin Distillers' Company* [1900] I IR 43; *Dickson (Alex) & Sons Ltd v Dickson (Alexander) & Sons* [1909] 1 IR 185 (CA); *O'Neill's Irish International Sports Co Ltd v O'Neill's Footwear Drying Co Ltd* High Court, 30 April 1997 (Barron J).

75. [1932] IR 615 (HC).

several years, the paper enjoying a large and steady circulation. The plaintiff company had never used the name for any of their publications.

**[31.42]** Meredith J, in dismissing the plaintiffs' application, said:

> "Property in the name of a business does not exist in the name *per se* but only *per accidens*. Hence if a firm discards a name that has no attractive force save as a good name, another has as much right to adopt it as to take vacated business premises for the purpose of carrying on a similar business therein. Many firms use names included to suggest the specific virtues of their goods and many such names have become household words. The rights acquired in respect of such names are, however, acquired by virtue of use and as indicating that the goods are the goods of the firm, and do not attach to the name as an appropriate and suggestive name. So the name, 'Evening Telegraph', may suggest the latest political news or sporting intelligence, but if it is only calculated to draw away custom from [the plaintiff's paper] the 'Evening Herald' by attractiveness of that kind the plaintiffs can have no grievance by reason of the defendants adopting the name ... The exclusive right of the plaintiffs to the name 'Evening Telegraph' cannot survive the extinction of the goodwill of the old 'Evening Telegraph' as a practical reality. The conveyance of 1925 did not immortalise that goodwill. To my mind the onus is on the plaintiffs to show that the goodwill of the old 'Evening Telegraph' is still an attractive force that would come into active operation if the defendants call their evening paper the 'Evening Telegraph'. I do not think they have discharged that onus."[76]

In this context it is perhaps worth stressing that compliance with the Registration of Business Names Act 1963 gives a person no propriety rights in the name thus registered. Moreover, s 14(3) makes it plain that registration of a name under the Act does not authorise the use of the name if apart from that registration its use could be prohibited.

**[31.43]** In *An Post v The Irish Permanent plc*,[77] Kinlen J granted an interlocutory injunction against the use by the defendant to the phrase "Savings Certificates" to describe its system of investment bonds. The essential question was whether the plaintiff could establish that it had such a strong association in the public mind with the phrase used to describe its investment bond system, that the adoption of the same phrase, albeit precedent by the distinguishing phrase "Irish Permanent", would be likely to confuse some would-be purchasers into believing that the defendant's system was the plaintiff's.

**[31.44]** Recognising that the plaintiff had only to establish a prima facie case, Kinlen J was of the view that it had done this. He referred to several English dictionaries in which the phrase was said to connote a governmental dimension.

**[31.45]** Perhaps it can be argued that, while it is undoubtedly the case that the public, in Britain and in Ireland, should make an association between the phrase "saving certificates" and the government for as long as the government remained the sole provider of savings certificates, that association would not necessarily continue if some other agency became a provider. The crucial question was not how the public understood the phrase during the period of governmental monopoly but rather how it understood, and was likely in the future to understand, that phrase once that monopoly was broken. In this context, the use by the defendant of the identification "Irish Permanent" in conjunction with the phrase

76. [1932] IR 615 at 628.
77. [1995] 1 ILRM 336 (HC).

"savings certificates" may, or may not have been sufficient to remove the inevitable initial potential confusion resulting from the inevitable association with the government (and An Post as its successor) during the period of monopoly.

**[31.46]** In *Radio Limerick One Ltd v Treaty Radio Ltd*,[78] Costello P declined to grant an interlocutory injunction restraining an alleged passing off. The plaintiff's contract with the Independent Radio and Television Commission to broadcast on FM channel and on the 95 wave-length in the Limerick area had been terminated by the Commission for serious and persistent breaches of the contract. The plaintiff took unsuccessful legal proceedings challenging the termination as far as the Supreme Court.[79] The plaintiff also had a license to broadcast on the Astra satellite granted by the BBC. There were around 7,000 satellite dishes in the Limerick area capable of receiving what the plaintiff transmitted. The plaintiff also sold advertising space on its broadcast service. It used different call signs on its radio broadcast and is promotional literature: these were "Limerick 95 FM", "Limerick 95" and "Radio Limerick".

**[31.47]** The plaintiff claimed that the defendant was not entitled to use the word "Limerick" in its style or in its call signal, or the figure and letters "95 FM" in its call or promotional literature.

**[31.48]** In the instant case the defendant had merely represented that it was broadcasting on a certain wavelength on a certain waveband in a certain area. It was not representing that it was carrying on the plaintiff's business but rather that it was now broadcasting on the wavelength on which the plaintiff had formerly broadcast and in the same area. There was no misrepresentation involved in what the defendant was doing and in Costello P's opinion no tort had been established.[80]

## The Use of One's Actual Name

**[31.49]** The courts have had difficulty in setting out clear legal principles to apply to cases where confusion results from the use by the defendant of his or her actual name.[81] In the nineteenth century judicial sympathy tended towards the defendant. Thus, for example, in *Turton v Turton*,[82] Lord Esher felt that he could dispatch the case for imposing liability for passing off against such a defendant in strong and simple terms:

---

78. High Court, 13 November 1997 (Costello J).

79. [1997] 2 IR 291 (SC).

80. Costello P considered that there was a further reason why injunctive relief should be refused. The plaintiff had lost its licence to broadcast in the Limerick area because it had been in serious breach of the conditions of its licence. It would now be illegal for the plaintiff to broadcast in the Limerick area. In these circumstances the plaintiff had no longer any goodwill in the business of sound broadcasting on the FM wavelength which the Court could protect. Although the plaintiff had apparently applied to the Minister for a licence to re-transmit the signal from the Astra satellite this licence had not yet been obtained. The Court could not exercise its discretion on the basis of a possibility that a licence might be granted by the Minister.

81. See Kodilinye 'Passing Off and the Use of Personal Names' (1975) 26 NILQ 177; Coleman 'The Unauthorised Commercial Exploitation of the Names and Likenesses of Real Persons' (1982) 7 EIPR 189; Clark & Smyth, *Intellectual Property Law in Ireland* (1997), paras 24.29-24.31; Wadlow, *The Law of Passing Off* (2nd ed, 1995), paras 7.10-7.14; Cornish, *Intellectual Property* (3rd ed, 1996), para 16.13.

82. (1889) 42 Ch D 128 at 136 (CA).

> "[T[he proposition goes to this length that if one man is in business, and has so carried on business that his name has become a value in the market, another man must not use his own name. If that other man comes in and carries on business, he must discard his own name and take a false one. The proposition seems to me so monstrous that the statement of it carries its own reflection."

**[31.50]** At that time the courts were only beginning to accept that liability could be imposed in those kinds of actions where there was no actual intention to deceive. Once the test became whether the misrepresentation was "calculated to" mislead in the sense of it being foreseeable that it would do so, the legal dilemma about the use of personal names became more acute, since clearly there will be cases where identical names are likely to cause confusion. Indeed, if the parties have a common activity, the likelihood of confusion may be inevitable.

**[31.51]** Many courts accordingly have tended to concentrate on the defendant's *mens rea*. They have insisted that he or she act "honestly" or "*bona fide*". Bad faith may be found where the defendant has cheated by decorating the name with an addition which is factually untrue and which is designed to mislead customers. So, in *Dickson & Sons v Dickson & Sons*,[83] the Irish Court of Appeal enjoined the defendant from using "& Sons" in its title as the defendant's sons were not partners. Fitzgibbon LJ observed:

> "The elder son [had] asked to be made a partner and he was positively refused. The younger son, who had only just come home from school, was employed by his father about the place... But he had no qualifications as a partner, and the 'Sons' can have been introduced only for the purpose of creating confusion".[84]

**[31.52]** This case is really no authority against the use by a person of his or her own name: it was the untruthful addition that alone was impugned. So what does dishonesty consist of in relation to the use of one's actual name? Cornish considers that "[s]eeking out an individual with an appropriate name in order to lend colour to the imitation of a rival's name is not likely to be false honest".[85] No doubt the person doing the seeking out would be held to have acted dishonestly but it would be necessary for the plaintiff to establish that the person with the appropriate name was also a knowing party to the scheme before he or she could be held liable. Often the facts will be such that this knowledge can fairly easily be inferred.

**[31.53]** If a name has assumed a secondary meaning so that it "denotes or has come to mean goods made by a particular person and not goods made by another person even though such other person may have the same name",[86] then an action for passing off will be against a person with the same name, "whatever may be his intention, [who] is so

---

83. [1909] 1 IR 185 (CA).
84. [1909] 1 IR 185 at 199. Holmes LJ (at 202) observed that, if the defendant had not included the reference in the title to the sons, "it is probable that this action would not have been brought, and, if it had, I have no doubt as to how it ought to have ended."
85. Cornish, *Intellectual Property* (3rd ed, 1996),para. 16.13. Cornish goes on to observe:

    > "Likewise where the name of a person genuinely associated with an enterprise its nevertheless used as part of a scheme to suggest an association with the plaintiff which does not exist".
86. *Parker Knoll v Knoll International* [1962] RPC 265 (HL, *per* Lord Morris of Borth-y-Gest).

describing his goods that there is a likelihood that a substantive section of the purchasing public will be misled into behaving that his goods are the goods of the plaintiff."[87]

**[31.54]** A recent Irish decision in which the use of names was considered is *O'Neill's Irish International Sports Co Ltd v O'Neill's Footwear Drying Co Ltd*,[88] where the defendant company, formed by one John O'Neill, sold an electronically operated shoe dryer in boxes with the label "O'Neill's Footwear Dryer" in sports outlets. Barron J granted an interlocutory injunction in favour of the plaintiffs, who manufactured and sold sports goods under the name of O'Neills. Barron J observed:

> "[T[he plaintiffs maintain that they have acquired a reputation in the name O'Neill and that the defendant is deliberately trading on their reputation in that name. From the evidence which I have heard I am satisfied that the words O'Neill's is associated with the plaintiffs in relation to sports goods and that they have built up a considerable reputation in the name. I am equally satisfied that the manner in which the defendants' product is being marketed is calculated to lead persons seeing that product ... to believe that the product is the product of the plaintiffs ... In my view, it is no accident that the defendant is marketing the product in the way in which it does so. It was clearly expected that more sales would be obtained by using the word O'Neills and by doing so the defendant is deliberately trading on the reputation of the plaintiffs.... No doubt John O'Neill believed that since his name was O'Neill he could form a company with O'Neill in its name and market his product under that name. In that belief he was wrong. While a person may use his own name in the course of trade and cannot be faulted on that ground alone, that does not entitle him to use his own name in such a way as is calculated to lead others to believe his goods are those of another. That is the case here."[89]

**[31.55]** A few points about Barron J's judgment may be noted. First, it is reasonable to assume that he was using the word "calculated" in the sense of "likely" rather than "intended".[90] This is the conventional practice in passing-off litigation. Secondly, the tenor of Barron J's observations is that the defendant was seeking to deliberately trade on the plaintiff's reputation. Thus it was not simply a case of a person with a particular name using it in business in the knowledge that it was likely to be confused with the business of another person with the same name. This distinction is important. Thirdly, the judicial indulgence to the use of personal names is somewhat diluted where company names are concerned.[91]

**[31.56]** Whilst Barron J made no specific reference to this factor, it may nonetheless have come into the equation.

## Businesses Not Trading in the State

**[31.57]** The fact that a plaintiff's business does not trade in the State will not be a reason for denying it a remedy for passing off with regard to the use of its name, where it has acquired a goodwill in the State. In *C & A Modes v C & A (Waterford) Ltd*,[92] the Supreme

87. *Parker Knoll v Knoll International* [1962] RPC 265 (*per* Lord Morris of Borth-y-Gest).
88. High Court, 30 April 1997 (Barron J).
89. High Court, 30 April 1997 at pp 3-4 of Barron J's judgment.
90. *Cf Jameson v Dublin Distillers' Co* [1900] 1 IR 43 at 52 (ChD).
91. *Cf* Cornish, *Intellectual Property* (3rd ed, 1996), para 16.13; Wardlow, *The Law of Passing Off* (2nd ed, 1995), para 7.14. It should be noted that the courts evince no desire to protect defendants' use of first names or nicknames: *cf Biba Group Ltd v Biba Boutique* [1980] RPC 413.
92. [1976] IR 198 (SC affg HC).

Court strongly endorsed this proposition. The plaintiff company carried on a retail clothing business in a chain of 65 shops throughout Britain and Northern Ireland. The Belfast shop attracted many customers from the Republic, and the company advertised extensively on television and in newspapers which reached many people in the Republic. It did not, however, actually carry on business in the Republic.

**[31.58]** In permitting an action for passing off, Henchy J stated:

> "Goodwill does not necessarily stop at a frontier ... What has to be established for the success of the plaintiff's claim ... is that by his business activities - be they by direct selling within the State or otherwise -he has generated within the State a property right in a goodwill which will be violated by the passing-off." [93]

**[31.59]** Kenny J drew a distinction between passing off by the use of a name and passing off by the use of a given mark or get up. In the former case, a plaintiff could sue even though none of its products were on sale in the State; in the latter case it would be necessary to show that the disputed mark or get up had become by user in the State distinctive of the plaintiff's goods, so that the use of that mark or get up in relation to any goods of the kind dealt in by the plaintiff would be understood by the trade and the public here as meaning that the goods were the plaintiff's.[94]

**[31.60]** In the later decision of the Supreme Court, in *Adidas Sportsschuhfabriken Adi Dassler KA v Charles O'Neill & Co Ltd*,[95] the majority endorsed this approach. The plaintiff, who manufactured sportswear with a distinctive triple stripe, claimed that the use by the defendant of a triple stripe design constituted passing off. The trial judge was not satisfied that the plaintiff had established in the State an exclusive association of this design with its garments; he found that no confusion had been caused. The majority of the Supreme Court came to the same conclusion. O'Higgins CJ noted that, if the complaint had been that the name "Adidas" (or a name similar to it or an imitation of it) had been used in association with the defendant's goods, although no Adidas products were on sale in this country, he had no doubt that a goodwill existed and a potential confusion in relation to customers would have been established and protection given:

> "We are dealing, however, not with a well known name but with a particular design and its exclusive association with the goods of Adidas in Ireland must be established if the claim made is to succeed."[96]

## III. Interlocutory Injunction Proceedings for Passing Off

**[31.61]** We must now consider the issue of the proper test for determining applications of interlocutory injunctions in relation to passing off. The judicial resolution of this question has changed over time. Some decisions of Costello J - *Three Stripe International v Charles O'Neill*[97] and *Benchkiser GmbH v Fibrisol Service Ltd*[98] - favoured the view that, if the

93. [1976] IR 198 at 212. See also *Ramsay v Nicol* [1939] VLR 330; *Dominion Rent A Car Ltd v Budget Rent A Car Systems (1970) Ltd* [1987] 2 NZLR 395 (CA) and Gummow 'Carrying On Passing Off' (1974) 7 Sydney LR 224 at 230-232.

94. [1976] IR 198 at 215-216.

95. [1983] ILRM 112 (SC, O'Higgins CJ and Hederman J, Henchy J dissenting).

96. [1983] ILRM 112 at 117. See also *DSG Retail Ltd v PC World Ltd* High Court, 13 January 1998 (Laffoy J).

97. [1989] ILRM 124.

98. High Court, 13 May 1988 (Costello J); see Byrne & Binchy *Annual Review of Irish Law 1988*, pp 199-203.

interlocutory injunction is likely to represent the end of the road for the parties, with no prospect of proceedings going on to a plenary hearing, the court should seek to determine the merits of the substantive legal issue rather than proceed immediately to address the questions of irreparable damage and the balance of convenience once satisfied that there is a serious question to be tried. Support for this general approach is also apparent in Laddie J's judgment in *Series 5 Software Ltd v Clarke*.[99]

**[31.62]** It will be recalled that the Supreme Court decision of *Holdings Ltd v McCormack*,[100] Finlay CJ expressed the view that, having regard to the Court's earlier decision in *Campus Oil Ltd v Minister for Industry and Energy (No 2)*[101] and in particular O'Higgins CJ's judgment in that case, the position was that, once the plaintiff had raised a fair question to be tried, the court should not express any view on the strength of the contending submissions, but should proceed to consider the issues of irreparable damage and balance of convenience.

**[31.63]** In *B & S Ltd v Irish Auto Trader Ltd*,[102] a case dealing with an application for an injunction for passing off, McCracken J, echoing the approach favoured by the House of Lords in *American Cyanamid Co v Ethicom*,[103] acknowledged that consideration of the respective strengths of the competing arguments should be allowed, after the court had established that there was a fair issue to be tried. As one of five matters the court should there address, McCracken J stated that:

> "where the arguments are finely balanced, the court may consider the relative strength of each party's case as revealed by the affidavit evidence adduced at the interlocutory stage where the strength of one party's case is disproportionate to that of the other."

**[31.64]** In *Symonds Cider & English Wine Co Ltd v Showerings (Ireland) Ltd*,[104] Laffoy J quoted McCracken J's five point test in *B & S Ltd v Irish Auto Trader Ltd* with apparent approval. She went on, however, to say that she was satisfied that, having regard to the *Westman Holidays* decision of the Supreme Court, it was not open to the High Court, where the plaintiff had established a fair and *bona fide* question to be tried, to express any view on the strength of the contending submissions on this issue. Even if this were permissible, it would be impossible to do so in the instant case, which was "bristling with difficult issues of fact arising from conflicting affidavit evidence and difficult issues of law."[105]

---

99. [1996] FSR 273.
100. [1992] 1 IR 151 at 157-158 (SC).
101. [1983] IR 88 (SC).
102. [1995] 2 IR 142 at 145 (HC).
103. [1975] AC 396 (HL).
104. [1997] 1 ILRM 481 (HC).
105. [1997] 1 ILRM 481 at 491. See Byrne & Binchy *Annual Review of Irish Law 1997*, pp 773-775. In *Local Ireland v Local Ireland-Online Ltd* High Court, 2 October 2000, where the plaintiff sought an interlocutory injunction of passing off in regard to its Internet address and domain name, Herbert J considered himself, on the authority of *Campus Oil Ltd v The Minister for Industry and Energy (No 2)* [1983] IR 88 "not entitled at this juncture to inquire into the merits of the case or consider the probabilities of success of any party at the trial of the action"

**[31.65]** Briefly, the facts were as follows. The plaintiff was an English company, part of the HP Bulmer group, the world's largest cider maker. Since the early 1980's, it had been selling cider in England under the trade mark "Scrumpy Jack". This had come onto the Irish market in 1991, reaching 17% of the canned cider market in 1995. It was widely advertised in Ireland.

**[31.66]** Originally, the product was marketed and sold in Ireland in a gold coloured can with the name "Scrumpy Jack" in large brown script and a logo whose dominant feature was a display of red apples on either side of an old-fashioned cider press, with the words "strong cider" below. A newly designed can was put on the Irish market in the late summer of 1996. The gold colour was darker and more matt in appearance; the cider press logo appeared without the display of apples; the product was described as "traditional" rather than "strong" cider.

**[31.67]** The defendant sold a number of brands of cider. One of these bands was called "Annerville Golden Scrumpy" and appeared on the market in June 1996. This cider was sold in a gold coloured can with a gold cap, and the name "Golden Scrumpy" appeared in large brown script with a logo consisting of two barrels surrounded by red apples and green leaves above it.

**[31.68]** The plaintiff sought, *inter alia*, an interlocutory injunction against passing off. The proceedings were instituted about a month before the new product was launched on the Irish market. The new product quickly replaced the old product in Irish retail outlets.

**[31.69]** Although the thrust of the plaintiff's case was that the defendant had imitated its old can, the plaintiff contended that it had, and would continue to have, a residual and persistent reputation in the get-up of the old can and in the name of "Scrumpy Jack" which was sufficient to found an action for passing off.

**[31.70]** The defendant argued that the word "scrumpy" was part of the common-age of the English language, being a descriptive term denoting rough dry cider. It could not be monopolised by any trader. The plaintiff contested the accuracy of this assertion in respect of Ireland, contending that the word "scrumpy" was only of dialectal significance in certain parts of England and that, before the Irish launch of "Scrumpy Jack", it had no particular significance in Ireland.

**[31.71]** Laffoy J had no difficulty in holding that there was a fair question to be tried. Nor was there any doubt that damage would not adequately compensate either party if an interlocutory injunction were, or were not, granted at the case might be. The respective detriments to the parties were "evenly balanced in terms of nature and degree" but for one factor. This was that the plaintiff's new cans were by now on the Irish market. The plaintiff's case had focused on its old can and Laffoy J was not satisfied that the plaintiff had shown on the affidavit evidence before the court that there was a fair issue to be tried as to the likelihood of confusion between the plaintiff's new can and the defendant's can or that there had been actual confusion.

---

105. (contd) once the plaintiff had established that there was a *bona fide* question to be tried. He regretted his inability to determine the case on its merits, since most, if not all, of the relevant facts were before the court on affidavit and counsel for both parties appeared to accept that the outcome of the application for interlocutory relief was likely to determine the dispute.

**[31.72]** Accordingly Laffoy J declined to grant an interlocutory injunction.

**[31.73]** In proceedings for an interlocutory injunction for passing off, the plaintiff must show that he would suffer irreparable damage if the injunction was not granted. This requirement, however, does not appear to be too stringently applied. In *Polycell Products Ltd v O'Carroll and Others t/a Dillon, O'Carroll*,[106] Budd J stated:

> "The expression ... means that the injury which is to be expected, if an injunction is not granted, would be material and one which could not be adequately remedied by damages. No one can tell what damage will result from a successful passing off of goods. It is impossible to prove what customers are lost. Further, the person 'passing off' goods may build up his trade on the reputation and advertising of his rival. Injury of that nature is almost impossible to assess in damages."[107]

**[31.74]** In *Mitchelstown Co-operative Agricultural Society Ltd v Goldenvale Food Products Ltd*,[108] where, as has been mentioned,[109] Costello J granted an interlocutory injunction against the use of a form of packaging and wording on a new dairy spread, the judge observed that it was "axiomatic"[110] that in most passing off actions damages would be an inadequate remedy for a successful plaintiff. An "additional factor of considerable importance"[111] in this context was that the plaintiffs had been responsible for introducing a better substitute on to the Irish market. They had informed the public that it was made from fresh cream and vegetable oil. The defendants' product was made from butter and vegetable oil, though they had said it was the same as the plaintiffs'. It was "quite impossible"[112] to calculate what damage this might do to the reputation of the plaintiff's product. An interlocutory injunction would not exclude the defendants from the market until the full trial of the action, since they could obtain an alternative form of packing within eight to ten weeks.

**[31.75]** The weakness of the plaintiff's case on the issue of confusion may tell against the granting of an interlocutory injunction, even though the plaintiff has established that there is a serious issue to be tried. In *Smithkline Beecham plc v Antigen Pharmaceuticals Ltd*,[113] where the plaintiffs complained about the defendants' marketing of an analgesic named Solfen, which the plaintiffs claimed engendered confusion with their product named Solpadeine, McCracken J declined to grant an interlocutory injunction since he was not greatly impressed by the evidence on the issue of confusion. He placed little weight on hearsay evidence concerning pharmacists' averrals that they had been confused and still less on survey evidence. Noting that the defendant's product had come on the market five months previously, McCracken J expressed astonishment that in all that time the plaintiffs

---

106. [1959] Ir Jur Rep 34 at 39 (HC).

107. This approach encourages the court to grant an interlocutory injunction where the plaintiff's conduct is beyond reproach. See *Valentine v Valentine* (1892) 31 LR (Ir) 488. *Cf Aksjeselskapet Jotul v Waterford Iron Founders Ltd* High Court, 8 November 1977 (McWilliam J).

108. High Court, 12 December 1985 (Costello J).

109. See para **[31.35]** above.

110. High Court, 12 December 1985, p 7 of Costello J's judgment.

111. High Court, 12 December 1985, p 7.

112. High Court, 12 December 1985, p 7. See *also Player & Wills (Ireland) Ltd v Gallagher (Dublin) Ltd* High Court, 26 September 1983 (Barron J); *Three Stripe International v Charles O'Neill* [1989] ILRM 124 (HC); *Benckiser GmbH v Fibrisol Service Ltd* High Court, 13 May 1988 (Costello J); *Dalepak Foods plc v Frezmet Daily Pack Ltd* [1987] NILR, p 1.

113. High Court, 25 March 1999 (HC).

had been unable to find anybody to give evidence that they had been confused. He went on to observe:

> "Of course, this is not a prerequisite for success in the action itself, but it is in my view a highly relevant matter in relation to the balance of convenience. If there is no evidence that anybody was confused in the last five months, then I think there is only a weak case for saying that anybody will be confused, or the plaintiffs will suffer loss, in the next three or four months pending the full hearing of this action."[114]

## Future Developments

**[31.76]** It is possible that the action for passing off may yet develop into a broader tort of misappropriation of business reputation.[115] The present limitations may be considered in some respects arbitrary. Why should the tort not cover all cases of the wrongful invasion, for economic gain, of another's name or personality?[116] Should not there be compensation for invasions of dignitary and privacy interests?[117]

**[31.77]** Courts in the United States[118] have extended tort law into these areas, under the rubric of unfair competition[119] rather than passing off. An Australian decision[120] also favours this approach. In *Cadbury-Schweppes Pty Ltd v Public Squash Co Pty Ltd*[121] a claim on these lines was not pursued before the Privy Council. Nevertheless, the tenor of the Judicial Committee's judgment was not supportive of recognition of a right of action for unfair competition outside the conventional parameters of misappropriation of the plaintiff's goodwill.

**[31.78]** After *Public Squash* was decided, the High Court of Australia in *Moorgate Tobacco Co Ltd v Philip Morris Ltd*[122] decisively rejected a general action for unfair competition.

**[31.79]** Nevertheless it is in Australia that the most ambitious development of the law relating to "character merchandising" has taken place in recent years.[123] This reflects the

---

114. High Court, 25 March 1999 (HC) at p 7.
115. *Cf Henderson v Radio Corporation Pty Ltd* [1960] NSWR 576.
116. *Cf* Frazer 'Appropriation of Personality - A New Tort' (1983) 99 LQR 281 - a comprehensive analysis. See also Vaver 'What's Mine is not Yours: Commercial Appropriation of Personality under the Privacy Acts of British Columbia, Manitoba and Saskatchawan' (1981) 15 U Br Cot LR 241; Treece 'Commercial Exploitation of Names, Likenesses, and Personal Histories' (1973) 51 Tex LR 637; Gordon 'Right of Property in Name, Likeness, Personality and History' (1960) 55 NWULR 553; *Krouse v Chrysler Canada Ltd* (1973) 40 DLR (3d) 15 (Ont CA); *Athans v Canadian Adventure Camps Ltd* (1977) 80 DLR (3d) 583 (Ont HC); *cf Canada Safeway Ltd v Manitoba Food & Commercial Workers Local* 832 (1983) 25 CCLTI (Man CA) - appropriation of symbol.
117. *Cf* Bloustein 'Privacy as an Aspect of Human Dignity: An Answer to Dean Prosser' (1964) 39 NYULR 962.
118. *Cf* PROSSER & KEETON, pp 1013-1023, Chafee 'Unfair Competition' (1940) 53 Harv LR 1289; Handler 'False and Misleading Advertising' (1929) 39 Yale LJ 22.
119. *International News Service v Associated Press* (1918) 248 US 215.
120. *Hexagon Pty Ltd v Australian Broadcasting Commission* [1976] RPC 628.
121. [1981] 1 All ER 213 (PC).
122. (1980) 145 CLR 457.
123. See Terry 'Unfair Competition and the Misappropriation of a Competitor's Trade Values' (1988) 51 MLR 296 at 306-319.

huge international growth in the exploitation of the fame of actual or fictional personalities in contexts very different from the one in which the fame has been acquired.[124] Of course the traditional remedies for the protection of copyright may always be invoked[125] but sometimes they will not be sufficiently wideranging. As Cornish points out:

> "[T]here is no copyright in a fictional character or a performer's art outside the confines of the particular texts or scenarios in which the character or act is developed. Copyright does not extend to Biggles, or the character repeatedly played by Charles Chaplin, whatever they are made to do or say."

**[31.80]** The practice of famous people or the creators of famous fictional characters licensing the commercial exploitation of that fame has become widespread. A plausible, though not necessarily convincing, argument can be made that those who seek to exploit the fame without obtaining the necessary license are causing damage to the source of the fame since they are falsely conveying that their product has been licensed and that it has been subjected to the requisite quality control of the licensor.

**[31.81]** Australian courts have been willing to accept an argument on these lines. British courts were generally hostile to it but opposition has been crumbling over the past decade. So far the matter has not been litigated in Ireland. Clark & Smyth observe that:

> "[i]n Ireland, the constitutional protections in relation to property and a good name would arguably assist any Irish litigant whose name has been used prejudically [in] obtaining vindication in the courts ..."[126]

**[31.82]** Certainly the law of defamation has been stretched to provide a remedy to one whose name has been wrongfully exploited without any clear impugnment of reputation.[127] It could, perhaps, be argued that the traditional limitations on the scope of the tort of passing off represent not a judicial failure to protect fully the constitutional right to property but rather a judicial assessment that at some point it is necessary to give way to free competition. It might be hard for a plaintiff to convince a court that the tort of passing off is "basically ineffective"[128] in protecting his or her constitutional right to property where there are strong social and economic arguments in favour of keeping the tort within fairly narrowly drawn contours.

---

124. See *Mirage Studios v Counter-Feat Clothing Co Ltd* [1991] FSR 145 (ChD) (the Teenage Mutant Hero Turtles case). *Elvis Presley Trade Marks* [1999] RPC 567 (CA) where Robert Walker LJ expressed *obiter* support for Brown-Wilkinson VC's approach.

125. Clark & Smyth *Intellectual Property Law in Ireland* (1997).

126. Clark & Smyth *Intellectual Property Law in Ireland* (1997)

127. *Cf Quigley v Creation.*

128. *Hanrahan v Merck Sharp & Dohme (Ireland) Ltd* [1988] ILRM 629 (SC). See further para **[9.49]-[9.53]** above.

# Chapter 32

# Torts Affecting Business Relations


| | | |
|---|---|---|
| I. | Introduction | 817 |
| II. | The Action Per Quod Servitium Amisit | 817 |
| III. | Action for Enticement or Harbouring of a Servant | 820 |
| IV. | Interference with Contractual Relations | 821 |
| V. | Intimidation | 830 |
| VI. | Conspiracy | 834 |
| VII. | Intentional Interference with Economic Interests | 841 |
| VIII. | Trade Disputes | 842 |


## I. INTRODUCTION

**[32.01]** Just as the law of negligence is built on the philosophy of a broad principle of liability encompassed by the "neighbour" formula expounded by Lord Atkin in *Donoghue v Stevenson*,[1] so the law regarding intentional interference with contractual relations is based on:

> "the well-established principle that 'a violation of legal right committed knowingly is a cause of action ... it is a violation of legal right to interfere with contractual relations recognised by law if there be no sufficient justification for the interference'."[2]

**[32.02]** It would be a mistake, however, to think that the law relating to intentional interference with business relationships has the same conceptual coherence as the contemporary law of negligence. On this subject there has yet to be a seminal decision of the structure of *Donoghue v Stevenson*. It may well be that we are on the brink of such a restatement, presaged by developments in some other common law jurisdictions. As we await this change, we must deal with the law as we find it, carrying as it does the echoes of mediaeval master-servant relationships, supplemented by nineteenth century contractual norms. Having examined the law under conventional headings, we will go on to consider its possible restatement in terms of a single tort of intentional unlawful interference with economic interests.

## II. THE ACTION *PER QUOD SERVITIUM AMISIT*[3]

**[32.03]** The action *per quod servitium amisit* traces its origins to mediaeval times.[4] It is founded on the concept of the servant falling within the proprietorship of his master. The

1. [1932] AC 562 at 580 (HL (Sc)).
2. *British and Irish Steampacket Co Ltd v Branigan* [1958] IR 128 at 133 (HC). Internal citation is to *Quinn v Leatham* [1901] AC 495 at 510. See also *Sheriff v McMullen* [1952] IR 236 at 256 (SC).
3. See generally Cowen 'The Action *Per Quod Servitium Amisit* and the Police'(1953) 2 UW Australia Ann LR 263; Brett 'Consortium and Servitium' (1955) 29 Austr LJ 321 389 at 428; Jones '*Per Quod Servitium Amisit'* (1958) 74 LQR 39; Hansen & Mullan, 'Private Corporations in Canada - Principles of Recovery for the Tortious Disablement of Shareholder Employees: Part II: The Action *Per Quod Servitium Amisit'*, *Studies in Canadian Tort Law* (Klar ed, 1977), Ch 8.
4. Jones '*Per Quod Servitium Amisit'* (1958) 74 LQR 39.

courts have little sympathy with this concept today and have on that account tended to regard the action as anomalous and to restrict its scope as much as possible. Whether this is desirable is questionable; however dubious the origins of the tort, it may be regarded as performing a useful role in the light of the economic realities of today when:

> "it can be persuasively argued that the situation of the employer who has sustained loss by an injury to his servant may be of serious economic importance ... for the first time since the years following the Black Death".[5]

**[32.04]** Where a person commits a tort against a servant by taking the servant away from his or her master, imprisoning or injuring the servant, and the master is thereby deprived of this services, the action *per quod servitium amisit* is available to the master, except where the servant is killed.[6]

## Who is a Servant?

**[32.05]** The concept of "servant" is broadly interpreted so far as the *parameters of the service relationship* are concerned. The action does not depend on any contract of service[7] but rather on the fact of service or even - as the cases on seduction show - the right to service. On the other hand, an attempt has been made by the Courts in a number of jurisdictions to narrow the categories of servant in respect of whom an action may lie. In the area of public service, such as that performed by soldiers, police officers and civil servants, courts in England,[8] Scotland,[9] Australia,[10] and the United States of America[11] (but not Canada[12]) have taken the view that the action should not lie.

**[32.06]** A different view was formerly taken in this country,[13] but in *AG v Ryan's Car Hire Ltd*,[14] the Supreme Court reversed a former decision of its own[15] on the subject. Kingsmill Moore J referred in detail to the decisions in other common law jurisdictions and stated:

---

5. SALMOND (14th ed), p 349 referring to the fact that many employers pay their employees sick pay and medical expenses in the event of injury, and that it may be very difficult to replace a skilled man on whose training much money may have been spent. No action for unjust enrichment will lie in such a case: *AG v Ryan's Car Hire Ltd* [1965] IR 642 (SC). See also *D'Amato v Badger* [1996] 2 Can SCR 1071 where an action sounding in negligence failed for lack of proximity of relationship and on policy grounds, the action *per quod servitium amisit* having been abolished by statute in British Columbia. *Cf Genereux v Peterson Howell & Heather (Canada) Ltd* [1973] OR 558, 34 DLR (3d) 614 (CA); *Vaccaro v Giruzzi* (1992) 93 DLR (4th) 180 (Ont Court (Gen Div)); *Cosford v Cornwall* (1992) 93 DLR (4th) 123 (Ont, CA); *Scott v Bowyer* 1997 Vic LEXIS 28 (SC, Victoria, CA).
6. *Admiralty Commissioners v SS Amerika* [1917] AC 38. *Pilford v Skog Estate* (1989) 64 DLR (4th) 186 (BCCA).
7. *AG for NSW v Perpetual Trustee Co (Ltd)* [1955] AC 457 at 483 (PC).
8. *Inland Revenue Commissioners v Hambrook* [1956] 2 QB 641 (CA).
9. *Reavis v Clan Line Steamers Ltd* [1925] SC 725. So also in South Africa: *Union Government v Ocean & Accident* 1956 (1) SA 577.
10. *Commonwealth v Quince* (1944) 68 CLR 227 (HC, Aust); *AG (NSW) v Perpetual Trustee Co* (1952) 85 CLR 237 (HC, Aust), affd [1955] AC 457 (PC).
11. *US v Standard Oil Co* (1946) 322 US 301.
12. *McArthur v R* [1943] 3 DLR 225; *R v Buchinsky* 24 CCLT 266 (SC); *Schittone v George Minkensky Ltd* 1997 Ont CJ LEXIS 2074 (Ont Court Gen Div).
13. *AG v Dublin United Tramways Co* [1939] IR 590; *Minister for Finance v O'Brien* [1949] IR 91; *AG v CIE* (1956) 90 ILTR 139 (SC).
14. [1965] IR 642 (SC).
15. *Minister for Finance v O'Brien* [1949] IR 91.

> "This mass of high authority, though not binding, to my mind is persuasive to the point of conclusiveness that servants of the king, or, as I would prefer to say, public servants, be they in the armed forces, the police or the civil service, do not fall within the class of servants in respect of whom the action, *per quad servitium amisit,* lies."[16]

**[32.07]** In the *Ryan's Car Hire*[17] case, the servant was a soldier. The constitutional differences between Ireland and England respecting the structure and command of the armed forces did "not seem ... to affect in any way the nature of the services performed by the soldier",[18] stated Kingsmill Moore J. The important distinctive aspects of military life - the subjection to military law, the obligation to obey lawful orders even at the risk to one's life, the limitations on the right to strike or to terminate employment, for example - meant that military service was:

> "different in kind from that required or existing in the ordinary master and servant relationship and that, in the absence of long established precedent, the action *per quod servitium amisit* should not be held applicable to it."[19]

**[32.08]** Whilst military service approximated in may ways to villein service out of which the action *per quod servitium amisit* emerged, the precedents did not recognise an action in respect of such persons, and Kingsmill Moore J stated that he:

> "would certainly be averse to any attempt to extend the scope of an action which, together with the action *per quod consortium amisit,* appears to me to be anomalous and one to be restricted rather than extended."[20]

**[32.09]** Whether the action should be limited more radically so as to deny the right to sue to all masters save those of "menial" servants,[21] is as yet an unresolved question in this country. In England (prior to the abolition of the action in 1982), such a limitation was recognised[22] but on dubious historical authority;[23] it has been rejected in Australia,[24] New Zealand,[25] and the majority of Canadian provinces.[26] The tenor of Kingsmill Moore J's judgment in *Ryan's Car Hire Case*,[27] which includes a discussion of the relevant English decisions, would appear to support[28] the English approach. This was certainly how Finlay CJ interpreted it in *Ryan v Ireland*.[29] Referring to the decision of *Ryan's Car Hire,* the

16. [1965] IR 642 at 663.
17. [1965] IR 642 (SC).
18. [1965] IR 642 at 663.
19. [1965] IR 642 at 664.
20. [1965] IR 642 at 664.
21. That is, servants living as part of their master's households.
22. *Inland Revenue Commissioners v Hambrook* [1956] 2 QB 641 (CA).
23. Jones '*Per Quod Servitium Amisit*' (1958) 74 LQR 39 at 53-58.
24. *Commissioner for Railways (NSW) v Scott* (1959) 102 CLR 392 (HC, Austr); *Marinovski v Zutti* [1984] 2 NSWLR 571 (CA). See also *GIO Australia Ltd v Robson* (1997) NSW LEXIS 1129 (SC, NSW, CA, Common Law Div).
25. *AG v Wilson & Horton Ltd* [1973] 2 NZLR 238 (CA).
26. *Cf* Irvine 'The Action *Per Quod Servitium Amisit* in Canada' (1980) 11 CCLT 241.
27. See also *Chapman v McDonald* [1969] IR 188 at 192 (HC).
28. See however FLEMING, p 753, fn 22 who notes in this context that *Ryan's Car Hire* "did not go beyond 'all public servants'".
29. [1989] IR 177 (SC).

Chief Justice volunteered that "[t]he foundation of the legal claim *per quod servitum amisit* necessarily involves the concept of menial or villein service".[30] It should be noted that since the issues of *Ryan* were unconnected with this tort, Finlay CJ's remarks were clearly *obiter*, with no argument having been presented to the Court as to the proper scope of the action. In the light of modern reconsideration of the utility of the action because of new developments in tort law,[31] the question may still be regarded as an open one.

### Contributory Negligence of a Servant

**[32.10]** The contributory negligence of the servant is attributed to the master so as to reduce the award proportionately.[32]

### Damages

**[32.11]** It appears that some damage must be shown to ground the action.[33] Recovery may be permitted for pecuniary loss actually sustained through the loss of services and other expenses necessarily incurred in consequence of the servant's injury.[34] Thus, the master may normally recover for the extra cost of obtaining and training a substitute for the servant or in paying overtime rates to existing staff. Whether the foreseeability limitation applicable to negligence actions applies to actions *per quod servitium amisit* has not been determined.[35]

## III. Action for Enticement or Harbouring of a Servant

**[32.12]** It is a tort to intentionally entice a servant away from his employment or to harbour a servant who has previously left the master's employment. The action for enticement has developed into the wider tort of intentional interference with contractual relations, which is discussed below.[36] The action for harbouring has become virtually obsolete; it will arise only where the defendant takes into his or her employment or continues to employ a servant who has wrongfully left his or her master's service,[37] where the defendant is aware of this fact,[38] and the plaintiff is able to establish that the former employee wishes to return to the master, being prevented from doing so only by the defendant's action.[39]

---

30. [1989] IR 177 (SC). See also *Byrne v Ireland* [1972] IR 241 at 286 (SC).
31. *Cf* FLEMING, p 754 who observes that to limit the action to menial servants would have "the paradoxical result that the protection for an employer should stand in inverse ratio to his loss ..."
32. Civil Liability Act 1961, ss 35(1) and 35(2) as amended by the Civil Liability Act 1964, s 4. *Cf* Dail Debates Vol 211, Col 585.
33. *Cf Hall v Hollander* (1825) 4 B & C 660, 107 ER 1206.
34. *Chapman v McDonald* [1969] IR 188.
35. *Cf Jones v Fabbi* (1973) 37 DLR (3d) 27.
36. See para **[32.13]** below.
37. *Forbes v Cochrane* (1824) 2 B & C 448, 107 ER 450.
38. *Thomson (DC) & Co Ltd v Deakin* [1952] Ch 646 at 694; *Blake v Lanyon* 6 TR 221. *Wilkins v Weaver* [1915] 2 Ch 322.
39. *Jones Bros (Hunstanton) Ltd v Stevens* [1955] 1 QB 275 (CA).

## IV. Interference with Contractual Relations

### Historical Background

**[32.13]** The tort of interference with contractual relations[40] has developed greatly from its origins in the Black Death in England in 1348, which produced a scarcity of labour. The Statute of Labourers made it an offence for a third party to receive or retain in his service a servant who had left his previous service prematurely.[41]

### Types of Contract Affected

**[32.14]** In the famous decision of *Lumley v Gye*[42] it was held that any malicious[43] interference with a contractual relationship was tortious, and that it was not necessary that the party prevailed upon to break his contract should be a "servant". Since then the courts have repeatedly recognised that not only contracts of personal service but also those of a purely commercial nature[44] may be the subject of this action.

### Persuasion Distinguished from mere Information or Advice

**[32.15]** It has been said many times that a distinction must be drawn between "pressure, persuasion or procuration",[45] on the one hand and mere information or advice, on the other. In *Hynes v Conlon*,[46] union officials informed employers that a certain individual was not a member of the union and that accordingly he should be dismissed, in accordance

---

40. See generally see Kerr & Whyte, *Irish Trade Union Law* (1985), pp 230-239; Weir, *Economic Torts* (1997); Elias & Ewing, *Tort Law and Economic Interests* (2nd ed, 1996); Forde, *Industrial Relations Law* (1991), Ch 6; Carty 'International Violation of Economic Interests: The Limits of Common Law Liability' (1988) 104 LQR 250; Carty 'Unlawful Interference with Trade' (1983) 3 Legal Studies 193; Fridman 'Interference with Trade or Business' (1993) 1 Tort LR 19-99; Dietrich 'Lawful Coercive Threats and the Infliction of Harm' (2000) 8 Torts LJ 187; Elias & Ewing 'Economic Torts and Labour Law: Old Principles and New Liabilities' [1982] Camb LJ 321; Starke 'Unlawful Interference with Contractual Relations' (1956) 7 Res Jud 136; Payne 'Interference with Contract' (1954) 7 CLP 94; Sayre 'Inducing Breach of Contract' (1923) 36 Harv LR 663; Carpenter 'Interference with Contract Relations' (1928) 41 Harv LR 728; Harper 'Interference With Contractual Relations' (1953) 47 NW ULR 873; Stevens 'Interference with Economic Relations - Some Aspects of the Turmoil in the Intentional Torts' (1974) 12 OH LJ 595; Grunfield 'Inducing or Procuring Breach of Contract' (1953) 16 MLR 86; Owen 'Interference with Trade: The Illegitimate Offspring of an Illegitimate Tort' (1976) 3 Monash ULR 41; Danforth 'Note: Tortious Interference with Contract: A Reassertion of Society's Interest in Commercial Stability and Contractual Integrity' (1981) 81 Col LR 1491.
41. *Cf* Jones 'Per Quod Servitium Amisit' (1958) 74 LQR 39; Dobbs 'Tortious Interference with Contractual Relationships' (1980) 34 Ark LR 335, 336-339.
42. (1853) 2 E and B 216, 118 ER 749. See Hughes 'Liability for Loss Caused by Industrial Action' (1970) 86 LQR 181.
43. Malice is no longer an ingredient of the tort: see para **[32.41]** below.
44. Eg *Sherriff v McMullen* [1952] IR 236 (SC); *Stratford v Lindley* [1965] AC 260; *Torquay Hotel v Cousins* [1969] 2 Ch 106; *James McMahon Ltd v Dunne* (1965) 99 ILTR 45 (HC); *Reno Engrais et Produits Chemiques SA v Irish Agricultural Wholesale Society Ltd* High Court, unrep 8 September 1976 (Hamilton J); *Talbot (Ireland) Ltd v ATGWU* Supreme Court, 30 April 1981.
45. *Thomson (DC) & Co Ltd v Deakin* [1952] Ch 646 at 686 (CA). See Grunfield 16 MLR 86 (1953).
46. [1939] Ir Jur 49 (HC).

with current agreements between the employers and the union. Hanna J, of the High Court, held that no tort had been committed. He was:

> "satisfied that there was nothing improper in anything these gentlemen did and that they were all well within the law. There was nothing in the nature of a threat to the employer or in the nature of a severe warning that might be construed into a threat, and the view I take of what took place was no more than telling the employer the attitude which the union was taking up. If union officials could not do what was done in this case, they would be of little use ... So far as I can see in this case there were no threats, no warnings and no violence."[47]

**[32.16]** Similarly, in *McGowan v Murphy*,[48] Walsh J in the Supreme Court stated of members of the resident executive committee of a trade union that:

> "There can be no doubt that in law the[y] ... would have been quite entitled to advise the trade union to terminate the membership of the plaintiff where the matter did not go beyond advice and did not amount to inducing it or procuring it."

**[32.17]** In *Cotter v Ahern*,[49] Finlay J held that members of the INTO had gone beyond merely offering advice to the manager of a national school in respect of an appointment he had just made. If their intention had merely been to convey information or advice, this could have been done by letter rather than by calling on the manager:

> "The purpose of what might be described as a solemn deputation by three of these four defendants clearly was to exert the maximum pressure upon the [manager]."[50]

**[32.18]** So also in *Talbot (Ireland) Ltd v ATGWU*,[51] where the divisional secretary of the defendant union issued a circular in which he sought the support of the other unions for an embargo on the plaintiff's products, the Supreme Court held that:

> "the effect of the embargo as circulated had been no mere empty request, but had been an implemented circular which in effect had procured the breach of many contracts between the company and third parties".[52]

**[32.19]** In certain cases, it may be a matter of some difficulty to determine the precise meaning of words used by the defendant in order to decide whether they amounted to an inducement to break a contract. Thus, in *British & Irish Steampacket Co Ltd v Branigan*,[53] the Court had to determine whether a direction in a telegram made by a union official to the union members to "please give necessary notification to master" of a ship that the ship

---

47. [1939] Ir Jur 49 (HC).
48. Supreme Court, 10 April 1967 at p 4.
49. High Court, 25 February 1977 (Finlay P).
50. P 24. See also *McCobb v Doyle* [1938] IR 444 (HC) - liability imposed on trade union official who requested the plaintiff's dismissal from his employment without notice; *per* Murnaghan J at 449:

    > "I think that the real object of the defendant's visit to [the employer's] factory was to convey, not by way of any threat of violence or intimidation, but by what has been called 'pressure'- by the knowledge that a strike would probably result - that the plaintiffs service should be dispensed with."

51. Supreme Court, 30 April 1981.
52. *Per* Henchy J as reported in the Irish Times, 1 May 1981. Of course, a court should exercise caution in attempting to determine whether a particular communication is a request or a procuration by looking only to its "effects". The Thomas à Beckett affair immediately comes to mind.
53. [1958] IR 128 (HC).

would not sail, amounted to a direction to give the requisite notice of termination. Viewing the telegram as a whole, and having regard to the circumstances in which it was sent, Dixon J of the High Court was satisfied that this portion of the telegram "meant nothing of the kind".[54] The official could not be permitted "to maintain the impossibly contradictory position" that, while the telegram meant that the crew were to refuse to sail the ship and break their contracts in this respect, at the same time they were to give the requisite notice of termination.

## Is a Breach of Contract Necessary?

**[32.20]** Although the tort is frequently referred to as "procuring a breach of contract", forms of interference that do not have this effect may suffice. Thus, where a breach was excused on the account of a *force majeure* clause or on the ground of frustration,[55] the tort was none the less held to have been committed. Where, however, no breach occurs because the contract is void,[56] the traditional view is that no tort is committed. Similarly, the traditional view is that where a contract is determinable, it is not a tort to induce (other than by lawful means) one of the parties to determine it lawfully,[57] but it will not avail a defendant who has induced a party to break a contract, to argue that the contract could have been terminated lawfully by that party.[58]

**[32.21]** It is well here to note[59] that, according to a more radical line of thought, the intentional interference with economic interests should be regarded as a generic tort; on this approach, it would not be necessary to show the actual breach of a contract, provided the interference could be established in other respects.[60] We shall examine the elements of this generic tort presently.

## Degree of Knowledge and Intention Required

**[32.22]** The negligent interference with contractual relationships raises separate issues which are discussed elsewhere.[61] In the present context it is necessary to establish

54. [1958] IR 128 at 130.

55. *Cf Torquay Hotel v Cousins* [1969] 2 Ch 106; *James McMahon Ltd v Dunne* (1965) 99 ILTR 45 at 55 (HC).

56. Eg *De Francesco v Barnum* (1890) 45 Ch D 430; *Said v Butt* [1920] 3 KB 497; *Keane v Boycott* (1795) 2 H Bl 511, 126 ER 676; *Krupp v Bell* (1968) 67 DLR (2d) 256.

57. *McManus v Bowes* [1938] 1 KB 98 at 127. Generally in contracts of employment there is an implied term that strike notice of the length required to terminate the contract will be sufficient to make the strike not amount to a breach of contract: *Becton Dickinson Ltd v Lee* [1973] IR 1 at 35-36 (SC). *A fortiori*, where the contract has not yet come into existence, no liability will attach in respect to this tort for inducing a prospective party not to enter the contract: *Tru-Value Ltd v Switzer & Co* High Court, 10 March 1972 (Kenny J). *Midland Cold Storage Ltd v Steer* [1972] Ch 630. See further Kerr & Whyte, *Irish Trade Union Law* (1985), pp 233-234; Elias & Ewing 'Economic Torts and Labour Law: Old Principles and New Liabilities' [1982] Camb LJ 321 at 329.

58. *Emerald Construction Co Ltd v Lowthian* [1966] 1 WLR 691; *Square Grip Reinforcement Ltd v Macdonald (No 2)* (1968) SLT 65.

59. *Cf* see para **[32.83]** below.

60. *Cf* see para **[32.86]** below.

61. See Ch 10.

knowledge and intention on the part of the defendant regarding the existence and breach of the contract, respectively.

### *(a) Knowledge*

**[32.23]** As regards knowledge, it appears that either actual or constructive knowledge of the existence of the contract will be sufficient[62] and that the defendant need not "know with exactitude all the terms"[63] of the contract. The issue arose in *James McMahon Ltd v Dunne*,[64] where Budd J, of the High Court, did not determine the issue, since the proceedings were of an interlocutory nature.[65] He did, however, consider that there was "strong support" for the proposition that constructive knowledge is sufficient. He continued:

> "Just what type of constructive knowledge is sufficient is a new point yet to be decided here. If we have moved to the stage where constructive knowledge is sufficient is there any reason for confining the ingredient of knowledge to knowledge of a specific contract between specific parties or actual knowledge of any particular contract. In many instances in modern life it must be obvious to the ordinary onlooker that some transaction is taking place on foot of some contract, particularly where matters of payment and delivery are concerned. This applies *a fortiori* where the intervener has special knowledge of the course of dealing, the customs prevailing and the surrounding circumstances.
>
> Where a contract is obvious there must also be many instances in which the terms or at least some of the terms of the contract are likewise obvious. If some term, such as one requiring delivery to someone, clearly a party to the contract, is itself clearly discernible in the particular circumstances to a person to whom the existence of the contract is obvious, and that person procures a breach of that particular term of the contract, to the detriment of one of the parties is there any valid reason in principle for exempting him from liability for what he has done, merely because he did not know who the other party was or of the existence of any particular form of contract or its exact conditions[?] I would think that, *prima facie,* a reasonable argument could be made for fixing such a person with liability on the basis of his constructive knowledge."[66]

**[32.24]** In *Cotter v Ahern*,[67] a deputation of members of the INTO brought pressure on a school manager not to appoint a person as principal who was not a member of their union. In fact, the manager had just made the appointment. In proceedings against the members for having induced the breach of contract, they contended that they had not been aware that a binding agreement had been made, but this contention was rejected. Finlay P noted that "[g]reat care"[68] had been taken by the defendants not to enquire as to whether the plaintiff had been short-listed. Their knowledge of the usual procedures must have meant that the defendants "were aware or ought to have known of the existence of a contractual

---

62. *Cf JT Stratford & Son Ltd v Lindley* [1965] AC 269 (HL (Eng)). *McMahon v Dunne* (1965) 99 ILTR 45.
63. *JT Stratford & Son Ltd v Lindley* [1965] AC 269 at 332. See also *Emerald Construction Co Ltd v Lowthian* [1966] 1 All ER 1013 at 1017 (CA).
64. (1965) 99 ILTR 45 (HC).
65. (1965) 99 ILTR 45 at 54.
66. (1965) 99 ILTR 45 at 54.
67. High Court, 25 February 1977 (Finlay P).
68. High Court, 25 February 1977 (Finlay P) at p 25.

arrangement"[69] between the manager and the appointee. The defendants could not escape liability by what Finlay P deemed to be:

> "an overscrupulous avoidance of ascertaining the true facts lest they should be imputed to have knowledge which would be inconvenient to their purpose".[70]

*(i) Knowledge acquired after interference has commenced*

**[32.25]** The "inconsistent dealing" between the third party and the contract breaker may sometimes be commenced without knowledge by the third party that the contract is being broken. In such a case, of course, the third party sustains no liability:

> "but, if it is continued after the third party has notice of the contract an actionable interference has been committed by him."[71]

***(b) Intention***

**[32.26]** It will be a good defence to show that one intended not to induce any breach of contract,[72] but the general rule is that intention or recklessness will suffice to ground liability.[73]

**[32.27]** As regards the task of proving the necessary intention, Budd J stated, in *James McMahon Ltd v Dunne*,[74] that:

> "a person is presumed to intend the ordinary and necessary consequences of his acts. If the ordinary and probable consequences of the action of [the] defendant would be such as to cause a breach of contract then the intent would ordinarily be presumed."

## The Wrongful Procurement

**[32.28]** There are three possible forms of wrongful interference with contractual relations:[75] (1) direct inducement; (2) direct intervention of another type; and (3) indirect procurement.

---

69. High Court, 25 February 1977 (Finlay P) at p 26.
70. High Court, 25 February 1977 (Finlay P) at p 26.
71. *Thomson (DC) & Co Ltd v Deakin* [1952] Ch 646 at 694, quoted by Hamilton J in *Reno Engrais et Produits Chemiques SA v Irish Agricultural Wholesale Society Ltd* High Court, 8 September 1976 at p 8. (Hamilton J was not called on to discuss the merits of this statement, as the proceedings were of an interlocutory nature.)
72. *White v Riley* [1921] 1 Ch 1 (CA).
73. *Cf Emerald Construction Co Ltd v Lowthian* [1966] 1 All ER 1013 at 1017. See also *Torquay Hotel Co Ltd v Cousins* [1969] 2 Ch 106.
74. (1965) 99 ILTR 45 at 56 (HC). See also *Southern Milling Ltd v Kantoher Food Products and Carton Brothers Ltd* High Court, 26 April 1996, where Geoghegan J considered that the Supreme Court decision in *Taylor v Smyth* [1991] IR 142 did:

    > "not lend any support to the sumission ... that if a manager of one company in which he has a beneficial interest, direct or indirect, makes a decision to breach a contract entered into by that company to the benefit in whole or in part of another company in which he also has a beneficial interest, an inference must be drawn by a court that the other company has induced the breach of contract."

    See also *Montgomery v Shepperton Investment Co Ltd* High Court, 11 July 1995.
75. This division derives from *Thomson (DC) & Co Ltd v Deakin* [1952] Ch 646 especially at 681-682.

### *(a) Direct inducement*

**[32.29]** Active persuasion or enticement of the contracting party constitutes a clear example of direct inducement.[76] In such a case it is not important who spoke the first word.[77] Conversely, a direct threat or ultimatum also falls within this category.[78]

**[32.30]** As we have seen, it has been held to be tortious, as "inconsistent dealings",[79] to have dealings with a party bound by a contract where one is aware that those dealings are inconsistent with the terms of that contract.[80]

### *(b) Direct intervention of another type*

**[32.31]** A wrongful act other than inducement designed to prevent the performance of a contract by another may be tortious. Thus, for example, to kidnap the contracting party or to interfere with the only means of performing the contract - such as removing the only available tools - will be sufficient. It should be stressed that the act must be a wrongful one: thus, a person may buy up all the goods on the market which he knows another party has contracted to supply to the plaintiff.

### *(c) Indirect procurement*

**[32.32]** Indirect procurement is tortious where the defendant induces a third party to do an act in itself wrongful so as to prevent performance of a contract by a fourth party with the plaintiff. The most obvious case is where a person encourages an employee to break his contract of employment, so that his employer cannot perform his contract with the plaintiff.[81] The defendant must have been aware of the fourth party's contract with the plaintiff and intended to have brought about its breach.[82] Moreover, the third party must have broken his contract with the fourth party.[83]

**[32.33]** Finally, the breach of contract by the fourth party must have ensued as a necessary consequence[84] of the third party's breach of contract. Thus, general exhortations, such as

---

76. As in *Lumley v Gye* (1853) 2 E & B 216, 118 ER 749. See also *Cattle Express Shipping Corporation of Liberia v Cheasty* High Court, 19 April 1983 (Barrington J) an *ex tempore* judgment noted by Kerr (1983) 2 J of Ir Soc for Lab Law at 62-63, and *Donohue v Bus Éireann* High Court, 30 July 1999 (Macken J).

77. *British Motor Trade Association v Salvadori* [1949] Ch 556.

78. Eg *Emerald Construction Co Ltd v Lowthian* [1966] 1 All ER 1013.

79. *Thomson (DC) & Co Ltd v Deakin* [1952] Ch 646 at 694.

80. See eg *Sefton v Topham's Ltd* [1964] 1 WLR 1408.

81. *Cf Thomson (DC) & Co Ltd v Deakin* [1952] Ch 646 at 682. See also *Stratford v Lindley* [1965] AC 260; *Sherriff v McMullen* [1952] IR 236 (SC); *James McMahon Ltd v Dunne* (1965) 99 ILTR 45 (HC); *Talbot (Ireland) Ltd v ATGWU* Supreme Court, 30 April 1981. As to the right of the plaintiff to sue where the plaintiff can not perform its contract with others as a result of indirect procurement the courts are divided. The better view appears to be that no action lies: *cf* Grunfeld, *Modern Trade Union Law* (1966), p 394; *Camden Exhibition & Display Ltd v Lynott* [1956] 3 All ER 28 at 35 (CA). See also *Sherriff v McMullen* [1952] IR 236 at 262-263 (SC). But there are possible suggestions in the *Talbot* case that an action lies in such circumstances.

82. *Cf James McMahon Ltd v Dunne* (1965) 99 ILTR 45 at 56.

83. *James McMahon Ltd v Dunne* (1965) 99 ILTR 45.

84. *James McMahon Ltd v Dunne* (1965) 99 ILTR 45 at 49, 56-57.

"Black A" or "Stop supplies to B" will not normally be tortious as the objects proposed by the defendant might have been achieved by lawful means, such as proper notice to terminate employment.[85]

**[32.34]** The question of indirect procurement arose in the Supreme Court decision of *Talbot (Ireland) Ltd v ATGWU*, given on 30 April 1981. The judgments were not subsequently reported. This is unfortunate. Reliance on newspaper accounts, however full they may be, is clearly unsatisfactory having regard to the practical importance of the decision.

**[32.35]** The facts concerned an embargo placed on the plaintiff company's products by the defendant union, endorsed by the Irish Congress of Trade Unions, as a result of a dispute about reduction in employment levels in the plaintiff's car assembly operation. In practice the embargo meant that other unions were asked not to permit the importation of the plaintiff company's cars, spare parts or other components, not to handle them within the country and not to permit services to be carried out in connection with the company's activities. The general secretary of the defendant union had issued two documents the purpose of which was that all members of the unions affiliated to the Congress would lend their support to the embargo. The effect of the embargo was that there were breaches of a number of contracts between the company and those with whom it did business, particularly dealers and customers who had bought vehicles within the guarantee period. Other effects included the non-delivery of post, the refusal of petrol and oil firms to supply the company and the non-collection of refuse.

**[32.36]** The Supreme Court was of the view that a tort had been committed. Henchy J stated that it was:

> "well-established that where a defendant, knowing of a contract between the plaintiff and a third party, intentionally induced a third party to break the contract and thereby cause loss to the plaintiff, a tort was committed unless there was justification for the defendant's action."[86]
>
> The defendants, knowing of the existence of a wide range of contracts between the plaintiff company and other parties, had nevertheless chosen to extend the effect of the industrial action to the stage where they had induced breaches of contract with these parties.

**[32.37]** How far does this decision go in limiting the power of unions and employees to exert pressure on employers through the medium of pressure on persons not directly concerned with the dispute? Some commentators have expressed alarm about the possible scope of the decision in this regard. Concern has centred on the question of the legitimacy of the "all out" strike,[87] so let us examine this question.

---

85. *Cf Thomson (DC) & Co Ltd v Deakin* [1952] Ch 646 at 697-698. *Cf British & Irish Steampacket Co Ltd v Branigan* [1958] IR 128 (HC) discussed at para **[32.19]**. See also *Talbot (Ireland) Ltd v ATGWU* Supreme Court, 30 April 1981.

86. Irish Times, 1 May 1981.

87. See the helpful analyses by Von Prondzynski 'Why the Trade Unions Face an Explosive Issue Today' Irish Independent, 1 May 1981 and Von Prondzynski & McCarthy 'Is the Law Above the Trade Unions?' Irish Times, 18 May 1981.

**[32.38]** In 1970, the Irish Congress of Trade Unions initiated an "All-Out Strike Policy". Its purpose was to strengthen union solidarity and bring about greater discipline in picketing. Under the policy, in the ordinary event, where a union pickets a company, only the members of the union concerned are supposed to observe the picket. However, in certain cases, a union seeking the co-operation of other unions may apply to the Congress for an all-out strike. After consultation with unions likely to be affected, Congress may order an all-out strike. When this happens no member of any union affiliated to Congress may cross the picket. The effect of an all-out strike may well be that the company's business is brought to a standstill. Inevitably, commercial contracts will be broken in the process or as a result of this action. Thus, "[I]f it is illegal to induce breaches of commercial contracts, then it is difficult to see how most all-out strikes can still be effectively pursued".[88]

**[32.39]** Yet in the *Talbot* decision itself, the Court appeared to distinguish between an embargo and a strike (whether an "all-out" one or otherwise)' implying that in the former, but not the latter, case liability would be imposed. Henchy J is reported as stating that:

> "[i]t had been suggested that what had happened was an embargo only in name and that the effect was no more than an all-out strike. But what happened had gone far beyond that - far beyond any picket; far beyond any strike; far beyond any legitimate industrial action. He had no doubt that the ICTU, which was a reputable body, acted inadvertently in placing this total embargo, and no doubt once this matter had been determined by the court, they would abide by the decision given."[89]

**[32.40]** The tenor of this passage certainly clearly suggests that the Court would not look with automatic disfavour on an all-out strike. Where the line is to be drawn - and more particularly, on what conceptual basis it is to be drawn - are questions that defy confident analysis. Possible approaches that have been tentatively proposed[90] are to distinguish between primary and secondary motive or between direct and indirect effect. An alternative approach (suggested by the *Talbot* decision itself) would be to eschew the minefield of motive and instead ask the simple (if not simplistic) question: was the defendant's conduct calculated to procure the breach of commercial contracts? Whatever semantic formula is adopted, the practical reality of the problem cannot be disguised. The courts recognise that it would make the law of industrial relations impossible to operate unless they halt at some point down a path which logic leads them.

## Justification and Malice

**[32.41]** It is now clear that malice is not a necessary ingredient in the tort.[91] Thus, it need not be shown that the defendant acted from an improper motive. The defence of

88. Von Prondzynski, 'Why the Trade Unions Face an Explosive Issue Today' Irish Independent, 1 May 1981.

89. Irish Times, 1 May 1981.

90. Von Prondzynski & McCarthy, 'Is the Law Above the Trade Unions?' Irish Times, 18 May 1981. *Cf* Forde, *Industrial Relations Law* (1991), p 166.

91. *Quinn v Leatham* [1901] AC 495; *South Wales Miners' Federation v Glamorgan Coal Co* [1905] AC 239. See Kerr & Whyte, *Irish Trade Union Law* (1985), pp 231-232.

justification[92] is, however, still somewhat underdeveloped in our law.[93] It may for convenience be divided into three classes: personal relationship, public interest, and self-interest.

***Personal Relationship***

**[32.42]** The relationship between the defendant and the third party may be sufficiently close as to justify an intervention on his part. Thus, a father may with impunity persuade his daughter not to marry an undesirable suitor,[94] and a doctor may advise a patient to give up employment for health reasons.[95]

***Public Interest***

**[32.43]** The public interest may justify interference in a contract, as where a licensing authority bans the showing of an objectionable film,[96] or where an actors' protection society persuaded a theatre proprietor to break an engagement with the manager of a troupe who paid the chorus-girls so poor a wage that they were driven to prostitution.[97] The law does not, however allow a *carte blanche* to associations undertaking a duty to their members to protect their interests:[98] only where the public interest is served by their actions will they be protected.

---

92. See Haydon 'The Defence of Justification in Cases of Intentionally Caused Economic Loss' (1970) 20 U Toronto LJ 139. In *Donohue v Bus Éireann* High Court, 30 July 1999, Macken J granted an interlocutory injunction against the defendant, who had a contract with the Department of Education for the transport of children to and from school, where it induced a sub-contractor to dispense with the services of the plaintiff, who was a bus driver, after it had received an allegation that she had struck pupils. It has conducted an inadequate investigation of the allegation, which was strongly denied by the plaintiff, and had not been fair to her in this procedure. The judgment contains no discussion of the scope of the defence of justification.
93. In contrast to the USA, see Sayre 'Inducing Breach of Contract' (1923) 36 Harv LR 663. In *Talbot (Ireland) Ltd v ATGWU* Supreme Court, 30 April 1981, counsel for one of the defendants argued that the predominant purpose of the defendants was to protect the employment of union members rather than to cause injury to the plaintiffs or others. This argument was rejected by the Court on the basis that, although it would be relevant to the tort of conspiracy, it could not avail persons alleged to have committed the tort of wrongfully inducing a breach of contract. Henchy J noted that the defence of justification, according to Grunfeld, *Modern Trade Union Law* (1966), p 404, was "limited to moral necessity". A close reading of that work, however, suggests that the author is careful not to close the door on other possible cases where justification might be successfully pleaded.
94. *Crofter Handwoven Harris Tweed v Veitch* [1942] AC 435 at 442-443; *Findlay v Blaylock* 1937 SC 21; *Gunn v Barr* [1926] 1 DLR 855.
95. FLEMING, p 763.
96. *Stott v Gamble* [1916] 2 KB 504.
97. *Brimelow v Casson* [1924] 1 Ch 302, criticised in *Camden Nominees v Forcey* [1940] Ch 352 at 366.
98. *Cf SW Miners' Federation v Glamorgan Coal Co* [1905] AC 239; *Read v Friendly Society of Operative Stonemasons* [1902] 2 KB 88; *Pete's Towing Service Ltd v Northern Drivers' Industrial Union* [1970] NZLR 32. See further Forde, *Industrial Relations Law* (1991), pp 153-155, 159-161; *Cf* Kerr & Whyte, *Irish Trade Union Law* (1985), p 239, fn 71 pointing out that the law might well in time have taken a different view had the power to develop a defence of justification in this context not been taken out of the judiciary's hands by s 3 of the Trade Disputes Act 1906.

### *Private interest*

**[32.44]** Private interest is recognised as a justification within very limited confines. Where a person has entered into two inconsistent contracts, one with the plaintiff, the other with the defendant, the defendant may insist on his contractual rights, although he knows that performance of this contract must necessarily interfere with the performance of the other contract.[99] Where, however, a person breaks his contract with the defendant, the defendant has no right to retaliate by inducing another person to break a contract with the first contract-breaker.[100]

### Damages

**[32.45]** Persons liable for inducing a breach of contract are liable in damages "for the natural and probable consequences of that tort".[101] The duty to mitigate will be regarded in a common sense fashion by the court. Where employees have wrongfully walked out on the job at the defendant's bidding, he can scarcely contend that new employees should have been immediately recruited by the employer where, having regard to the labour relations existing at the time, "any attempt to recruit a new crew would inevitabl[y] have led to an increasingly wide extension of the trouble and to a far more serious and possibly crippling loss".[102]

## V. Intimidation

### The Nature of Intimidation[103]

**[32.46]** The tort of intimidation consists of a threat delivered by the defendant to a person, whereby the defendant intentionally causes that person to act or refrain from acting in a manner in which he is entitled to act, either to his own detriment or to the detriment of another.[104] It is only relatively recently that the tort has, in all its manifestations, been described commonly as "intimidation".[105]

---

99. *Read v Friendly Society of Operative Stonemasons* [1902] 2 KB 88 at 95; *Smithies v Operative Plasterers* [1909] 1 KB 210 at 337.

100. *Cf Camden Nominees v Forcey* [1940] Ch 352.

101. *Cotter v Ahern* High Court, unrep 25 February 1977, Finlay P at p 34.

102. *British & Irish Steampacket Co Ltd v Branigan* [1958] IR 128 at 136 (HC).

103. See Kerr & Whyte, *Irish Trade Union Law* (1985), pp 239-242; Forde, *Industrial Relations Law* (1991), pp 155-157; Dietrich 'Lawful Coercive Threats and the Infliction of Harm' (2000) 8 Torts LJ 187; Hughes 'Liability for Loss Caused by Industrial Action' (1970) 86 LQR 181; Heydon 'The Future of the Economic Torts' (1975) 12 UW Austr LR 1; Wedderburn 'Intimidation and the Right to Strike' (1964) 27 MLR 257.

104. WINFIELD & JOLOWICZ, p 635. In *Pete's Towing Services Ltd v Northern Industrial Union of Workers* [1970] NZLR 32 at 41, Speight J defined the tort somewhat more narrowly as "procuring economic harm to another by the use of unlawful threats to curtail that other's freedom of action". It is possible for a person to suffer detriment other than economic harm. Whether an action for such loss would lie under this tort may be doubted, especially if intimidation is to be viewed merely as a species of a wider tort of wrongful interference with economic relations. The torts of assault and the intentional infliction of emotional suffering go some way towards filling this gap but even with an extended view of assault (as in *Barton v Armstrong* [1969] 2 NSWLR 451), it would not be closed completely.

105. The term appears first to have been used by Salmond. For an account of the various descriptions of the tort see Wedderburn 'The Right to Threaten Strikes' (1961) 24 MLR 572 at 575-576.

**[32.47]** There have been cases[106] where the courts have given a remedy for what would today be categorised as intimidation, although the courts themselves expressly declined to use that term. It is indicative of the relatively recent emergence of the tort that, only twenty five years ago, counsel in a House of Lords decision[107] contended that there was no such tort. Indeed, with the probable development of the generic tort of interference with economic interests, it may well be that the courts will eventually lose interest in preserving well-defined conceptual boundaries for the tort of intimidation.

## The Threat

**[32.48]** A threat is an "intimation by one to another that unless the latter does or does not do something the former will do something which the latter will not like".[108] The threat must be "of a coercive nature"[109] "of the 'or else' kind".[110] There is, thus, a distinction between a threat (which is tortious)[111] and a mere warning (which is not).[112]

## Illegal Act or Means

**[32.49]** It is now clear that, to constitute intimidation, the threat must be to do an unlawful act. Where a person would not be liable for *doing* the act, he will not be liable for *threatening* to do it, the courts taking the view that to impose liability for such a threat but not the consummated act would be "absurd".[113]

**[32.50]** What, therefore, is an "unlawful" act for present purposes? Clearly, a threat of violence will be unlawful.[114] Similarly, it appears that a threat to commit any tortious or criminal act[115] will be unlawful. Moreover, a threat to infringe a constitutional right[116] or breach a duty imposed on the defendant by law[117] will also be unlawful.

---

106. *Cf* eg *Riordan v Butler* [1940] IR 347 at 353 (HC).
107. *Rookes v Barnard* [1964] AC 1129 at 1134 (HL (Eng)).
108. *Hodges v Webb* [1920] 2 Ch 70 at 89.
109. *Becton Dickinson Ltd v Lee* [1973] IR 1 at 31 (SC).
110. *Huljich v Hall* [1973] 2 NZLR 279 at 288 (CA).
111. *Cf Rookes v Barnard* [1964] AC 1129 at 1208-1209.
112. *Cf Stratford v Lindley* [1965] AC 260 at 283-284 (*per* Lord Denning MR) and 292 (*per* Pearson LJ); *Rookes v Barnard* [1964] AC 1173 at 1166; *Conway v Wade* [1909] AC 506 at 510 (*per* Lord Loreburn) and 514 (*per* Lord Jones); *Quinn v Leatham* [1901] AC 495 at 538; *Allen v Flood* [1898] AC 1 at 129.
113. *Rookes v Barnard* [1964] AC 1129 at 1168.
114. Eg *Tarleton v McGawley* (1793) 1 Peake 270, 170 ER 153.
115. *Rookes v Barnard* [1964] AC 1129 at 1182 (*per* Lord Evershed) and 1206 (*per* Lord Devlin). In this context it should be noted that picketing which is not protected by the State may at least in some cases constitute either the crime of watching and besetting or the tort of intimidation of customers or of nuisance: *Educational Company of Ireland Ltd v Fitzpatrick (No 2)* [1961] IR 345 at 390-391 398 (SC).
116. *Cf Educational Company of Ireland Ltd v Fitzpatrick (No 2)* [1961] IR 345 (SC) (especially at 396 *per* Kingsmill Moore J). See also *Meskell v CIE* [1973] IR 121 (SC); *Crowley v Cleary* [1968] IR 261 (HC).
117. For example the duty of a common carrier to carry or the duty of an innkeeper to receive guests (*Constantine v Imperial Hotels* [1944] KB 693; *cf* the Hotel Proprietors Act 1963). Whether a threat to breach an equitable obligation is unlawful is not clear but it "may be sufficient": WINFIELD & JOLOWICZ, p 159.

**[32.51]** As regards contractual obligations, it is now clear that a threat to breach a contract may be unlawful. The law was unsettled before the decision of Gavan Duffy J in *Cooper v Millea.*[118] There, the defendants, trade union officials, who were also employees of the GSR, threatened an immediate strike if the plaintiff, a fellow-employee and former member of the union, was allowed to work with them in Waterford. The company accordingly offered the plaintiff unsuitable alternative employment which he refused, whereupon he was dismissed.

**[32.52]** The plaintiff's action for damages against the defendants was successful. Gavan Duffy J stated:

> "This civil bill belongs to the elusive category of actions for intentional interference with a man's employment by illegal means ... It is incontestable that the defendants interfered with the plaintiff's employment by illegal means: for a strike in breach of contract is unlawful and a threat or preintimation of unlawful action constitutes illegal means; the right of action is then established: see Lord Dunedin's speech in *Sorrell v Smith.*[119],[120]

Whether Lord Dunedin's speech went so far is indeed doubtful,[121] but, at all events, Gavan Duffy J's statement of principle in *Cooper v Millea*[122] has prevailed.

**[32.53]** Two years later, *Cooper v Millea*[123] was followed by O'Byrne J in *Riordan v Butler.*[124] The plaintiff, who had just begun to work for an employer, was dismissed without notice by him, in breach of the contract of employment. The employer took this step as a result of a threat by other employees that they would strike in breach of their contracts if the plaintiff was employed. The plaintiff's action against these employees was successful. O'Byrne J stated:

> "Did the defendants adopt illegal means for the purpose of effecting their purpose? This was not a case in which there was anything in the nature of intimidation,[125] or a threat of violence.

---

118. [1938] IR 749 (HC) discussed briefly by McCartney 'Strike Law and the Constitution of Éire: A Note on the Case-Law' in *Labour Relations and the Law: a Comparative Study*, (Kahn-Freund ed 1965), Ch 11 at 157-158; see also *McCobb v Doyle* [1938] IR 444 (HC). *Cf* the doubts as to the correction of *Cooper v Millea* on its facts expressed by Walsh J in *Becton Dickinson Ltd v Lee* [1973] IR 1 at 29-30 (SC) and Murnaghan J's response in *Fire Manufacturing Co v O'Leary* High Court, 29 April 1974.

119. [1925] AC 700 at 730.

120. [1938] IR 758.

121. Lord Dunedin had stated:

> "Expressing the matter in my own words, I would say that a threat is a pre-intimation of proposed action of some sort. That action must be either *per se* a legal action or an illegal, ie, a tortious action. If the threat used to effect some purpose is of the first kind it gives no ground for legal proceedings; if of the second, it falls within the description of illegal means and the right to sue of the person injured is established."

In *Rookes v Barnard* [1964] AC 1129 at 1185 (HL Eng) Lord Evershed stated that he was "aware that in *Cooper v Millea* the learned judge erred in attributing a dictum in support of his view to Lord Dunedin in *Sorrell v Smith*". Lord Evershed added: "I can not however think that by his use of the formula '*id est*' Lord Dunedin was intending to lay it down that only threats of tortious actions would constitute the wrong of intimidation."

122. [1938] IR 749 (HC).

123. [1938] IR 749 (HC).

124. [1940] IR 347 (HC).

> But there was, as it seems to me, the clearest intimation that their defendants would break their contracts with [their employer]. They were employed by the week, and they were bound to give one week's notice for the purpose of terminating their employment. They could, as it seems to me, have arrived at substantially the same result, at which they did arrive, in a perfectly lawful way. Any individual there was entitled to give notice to his employer - a week's notice terminating his employment. The three defendants could have adopted that course, and, if they did so, it seems to me that the plaintiff would not have any right of action against them. But they did not. Their threat, and I use the work in its broadest sense, was that they would walk off the job, that they would cease work immediately in breach of their contract. Was that an unlawful means? It seems to me, having regard to the decision of Mr Justice Gavan Duffy in the case of *Cooper v Millea*[126] that I am bound to hold that it was. The case of *Cooper v Millea* seems to cover this case entirely, and I follow it."[127]

**[32.54]** Some curious results follow from holding it tortious for A to threaten to break a contract with B to the detriment of C. The *actual* breach by A of that contract, however intentional, will not normally *ipso facto* give C a right of action against A.[128] It may seem strange that the mere threat by A to do so will give C a right of action.[129] Other surprising implications in relation to the law of contract have also been identified.[130]

**[32.55]** In England, in the controversial decision of *Rookes v Barnard*[131] in 1964, the House of Lords came to the same view as our High Court had favoured in *Cooper v Millea*[132] and *Riordan v Butler*.[133] In *Rookes v Barnard*,[134] the defendants, union officials, threatened employers that if the plaintiff employee was not removed, a strike of all the employees would take place, in breach of a specific term in the collective agreement. The threat was successful. The House of Lords held that the defendants were guilty of conspiracy to commit the tort of intimidation against the plaintiff.

## Submission to the Threat Essential

**[32.56]** The plaintiff must prove that the person threatened (whether this was himself or another) complied with the demand.[135] If the threatened party resists the demand or has not

125. O'Byrne J would appear here to be referring to intimidation in the narrow sense, as used in ordinary speech; he was not referring it seems to the tort of intimidation.

126. [1938] IR 749 (HC).

127. [1940] IR at 353.

128. *Dunlop v Selindge* [1915] AC 847.

129. *Cf* Wedderburn 'The Right to Threaten Strikes' (1961) 24 MLR 572 at 577-578. But *cf* Hoffman *Rookes v Barnard* (1965) 81 LQR 116 at 124-128 and Davidson, *The Judiciary and the Development of Employment Law* (1984), p 173.

130. See Wedderburn 'Intimidation and the Right to Strike' 27 MLR 257 at 261-267 and Wedderburn 24 MLR at 577-578.

131. [1964] AC 1129 (HL) analysed by Hanson in [1964] Camb LJ 159; Wedderburn in (1964) 27 MLR 257; Hoffman in (1965) 81 LQR 116; Weir in [1964] Camb LJ 225; Christie in (1964) 42 Can BR 464; Smith in (1966-1967) 40 Austr LJ 81, 112 and by Anon in (1964) 98 ILT & Sol J 431 437; revd [1963] 1 QB 623 (CA) analysed by Wedderburn in (1962) 25 MLR 513 and by Anon in (1963) 97 ILT & Sol J 151; restoring Sachs J [1961] 2 All ER 825, analysed by Wedderburn (1961) 24 MLR 572.

132. [1938] IR 749.

133. [1940] IR 347.

134. [1964] ILRM 136.

135. *Cf Morgan v Fry* [1968] 2 QB 710 at 724 (CA); *Stratford (JT) & Son Ltd v Lindley* [1965] AC 269 (HL (Eng)); *Becton Dickinson Ltd v Lee* [1973] IR 1 at 30-31 (SC).

yet complied with it the tort will not have been completed - although, in the latter case, an injunction may be forthcoming in appropriate circumstances. Thus, in *Whelan v Madigan*,[136] where a landlord resorted to outrageous behaviour[137] towards his tenant's including telephoning one of them (a woman) and breathing but not saying anything when she answered, Kenny J held that (although guilty of other torts) he was not guilty of intimidation, since the intimidation had not been successful. Far from leaving the property, the tenants had united to take legal proceedings against their landlord.

### Justification

**[32.57]** The extent to which justification may constitute a defence to the tort of intimidation - if it can do so at all - is uncertain.[138]

## VI. CONSPIRACY[139]

**[32.58]** In Britain uncertainty[140] prevailed for some time as to whether there was any such tort as conspiracy. The position was settled apparently finally by the House of Lords in 1941,[141] but in 1981,[142] the scope of the tort was significantly restricted. In Ireland, the existence of conspiracy as a separate tort was also initially doubted,[143] but has by now gained acceptance.[144] It may be that if the tort of intentional interference with economic interests is recognised here and allowed to develop, the tort of conspiracy will gradually wither, since it is a cumbersome and in some respects arbitrary judicial remedy.

---

136. [1978] ILRM 136 (HC).

137. [1978] ILRM 136 at 142. *Cf Royal Dublin Society v Yates* High Court, 31 July 1997 (Shanley J), where the plaintiff society contended that the defendant had intimidated a male and female employee of the Society. The defendant counterclaimed that certain employees and members of the Society had intimidated him. The Society's claim failed on two grounds: any "threats" the defendant may have made, and Shanley J did not hold that they had in fact been made, had not been complied with by the employees, and even if they had been it was clear that the Society had not succumbed to any threats. The defendants' claim did not succeed on the evidence, Shanley J being satisfied that none of the actions by the members or employees of the Society, of which the defendant complained, "could colourably constitute the tort of intimidation ...". The actions taken by the Society against the defendant on certain of his visits to their premises had, in Shanley J's view, been "no more than consistent with the discharge of th[e] duty of care owed by it to its employees".

138. See Kerr & Whyte *Irish Trade Union Law* (1985), p 242; SALMOND & HEUSTON, p 363.

139. See generally, Charlesworth 'Conspiracy as a Ground of Liability in Tort' (1920) 36 LQR 38; Hughes 'The Tort of Conspiracy' (1952) 15 MLR 209; Fridman '*Mens Rea* in Conspiracy' (1956) 19 MLR 276; Mathews 'The Tort of Conspiracy in Irish Labour Law' (1973) 8 Ir Jur (ns) 252; Whitson 'Note: Civil Conspiracy: A Substantive Tort?' (1979) 59 Boston ULR 920; Burns 'Civil Conspiracy: An Unwieldy Vessel Rides a Judicial Tempest' (1982) 16 UBC LR 229.

140. *Cf* SALMOND (6th ed), pp 576-578.

141. *Crofter Hand Woven Harris Tweed Co Ltd v Veitch* [1942] AC 435 (HL (Sc)). See also *Sorrell v Smith* [1925] AC 700 at 719 (HL).

142. *Lonrho Ltd v Shell Petroleum Co Ltd (No 2)* [1982] AC 173 (HL). A still more restrictive interpretation by the Court of Appeal in *Metall and Rohstoff AG v Donaldson Lufkin and Jenrette* [1990] 1 QB 391, was rejected by the House of Lords in *Lonrho plc v Fayed* [1992] 1 AC 448.

143. *Sweeney v Cooke* [1906] 1 IR 51 at 100-101 (CA). *Cf Kearney v Lloyd* (1890) 26 LR Ir 268 at 287-288 (Ex Div).

144. *Cf Dillon v Dunne's Stores (George's Street) Ltd* Supreme Court, 20 December 1968.

**[32.59]** When analysing the subject, it seems best first to set out the legal principles that our courts have traditionally endorsed, before going on to consider the implications for our law of the British modifications in 1981 which in turn have been followed there by a futher *volte face*.

## The Traditional View

**[32.60]** The traditional view is that the tort consists of "the agreement of two or more to do an unlawful act, or to do a lawful act by unlawful means".[145] In *Connolly v Loughney*,[146] Dixon J stated that:

> "A conspiracy, that is the agreement or combination of two or more people ... was actionable if its object was unlawful or, even though its object was lawful, unlawful means were contemplated or used to attain it."

**[32.61]** Regarding the requirement that there be an agreement of two or more persons to injure the plaintiff, special difficulties attach to the question of conspiracy between husband and wife. Historically, a husband and wife were held incapable of conspiring together,[147] being deemed to be one person by the law, although they were held liable for conspiracies begun before marriage[148] or undertaken with other persons.[149] An English decision[150] in 1981, however, abrogated this exemption and Irish constitutional considerations point in the same direction.[151]

**[32.62]** The parties to a conspiracy need not all act at the same time. Neither need they be of one aim, provided they are agreed on acting together. For the plaintiff to succeed, it is necessary to show not merely that a conspiracy was in existence but also that it resulted in damage to him.[152]

---

145. *Mulcahy v R* (1868) LR 3 HL 306 at 317. There must be a concluded agreement: in *Crofter Properties Ltd v Genport Ltd* High Court, 15 March 1996, Costello J observed that:

> "there is no such tort or wrong as attempting to conspire with somebody. The essence of conspiracy is that there was an agreement or concentrated action."

146. (1953) 87 ILTR 49 at 51 (HC).
147. *DPP v Blady* [1912] 2 KB 89 at 92 (*per* Lush J, dissenting on other matters); *Mawji v R* [1957] AC 126 - rule applied although marriage potentially polygamous.
148. *R v Robinson* (1746) 1 Leach 37 168 ER 121.
149. *R v Robinson* (1746) 1 Leach 37 168 ER 121.
150. *Midland Bank Trust Co Ltd v Green (No 3)* [1979] 2 All ER 193, affd [1981] 3 All ER 744. See Glover 'Conspiracy as between Husband and Wife' (1979) 9 Fam L 181. In *Taylor v Smyth* [1991] IR 142, the Supreme Court held that an actionable conspiracy can occur where there is an agreement between a person and a limited liability company under his or her control on two or more companies under the control of a single person. In *Southern Milling Ltd v Kantoher Food Products and Carton Brothers Ltd* High Court, 26 April 1996, Geoghegan J commenting on this holding observed:

> "In other words, for the purposes of considering whether there was in a given situation an actionable conspiracy, the corporate veil cannot be lifted so as to allege that there was only one person involved."

151. *Cf State (DPP) v Walsh* [1981] IR 412 (SC); *W v W* [1993] 2 IR 476 (SC).
152. *Molloy v Gallagher* [1933] IR 1 (SC) (especially at 13). See further, Burns 'Civil Conspiracy: An Unwieldy Vessel Rides a Judicial Tempest' (1982) 16 UBC LR 229 at 242-243.

## Forms of Conspiracy

**[32.63]** There are two forms of conspiracy: *simple conspiracy* and *unlawful means conspiracy*.[153] The former occurs where two or more persons combine with the predominant purpose of damaging the economic interests of another, without justification. The latter occurs where two or more combine to engage in an unlawful act, such as a crime or tort,[154] and damage to the plaintiff results. This latter category also includes a combination that infringes the plaintiff's constitutional right. The courts have sought to make a distinction here between an "unlawful act" and "unlawful means" but this is scarcely helpful. An infringement of a person's constitutional right is no less an unlawful act than the commission of a tort. Indeed, there is a huge overlap between these two juridical wrongs.[155] Conversely, it may be said that to injure a person by committing a tort is to do so by unlawful means, just as is the infringement of a constitutional right.

**[32.64]** In *Meskell v CIE*,[156] the defendant company was subjected to pressure from trade unions who were dissatisfied with the level of union membership among the company's employees and who were seeking to reduce the number of employees who were in arrears with their union dues. The unions had tried to compel the company to withhold certain benefits from some of the employees: this the company resisted, but instead agreed with the unions to terminate the contracts of employment of all employees and to offer each employee immediate re-employment on the same terms as before save for the additional condition that he be "at all times" a member of one of the four unions. The plaintiff, a bus driver, who had 25 years' service with the company, was one of the employees discharged by the company. He was not re-employed as he failed to accept the special condition regarding union membership.

**[32.65]** The plaintiff sued the defendant for damages for conspiracy coupled with a declaration that his dismissal was a violation of his rights under the Constitution.

**[32.66]** The plaintiff's action was dismissed by Teevan J in the High Court, on the basis that the object or purpose of the defendant's agreement with the union had not been to injure the plaintiff and that accordingly it was not guilty of conspiracy.

**[32.67]** The Supreme Court reversed. The Court held that the agreement with the union infringed the plaintiff's constitutional right of freedom of association.[157]

**[32.68]** Walsh J explained that the defendant was also guilty of the tort of conspiracy. He stated:

> "In the present case one may assume for the purpose of the decision that the object of the agreement between the defendants and the trade unions was the well-being of the defendants and of the unions, and even of the members of the unions. The complaint made here is that

153. See STREET, p 144.

154. *Crofter Handwoven Harris Tweed v Veitch* [1942] AC 435 at 462 (*per* Lord Wright); *Sorrell v Smith* [1925] AC 700 at 723, 729-730 (*per* Lord Dunedin); *Meskell v CIE* [1973] IR 121; *Cf Kearney v Lloyd* (1890) 26 LR Ir 268; *Connolly v Loughney* (1953) 87 ILTR 49.

155. *Hanrahan v Merck Sharp & Dohme (Ireland) Ltd* [1988] ILRM 629 (SC).

156. [1973] IR 121 (SC).

157. *Cf* Hogan & Whyte, *Kelly: The Irish Constitution* (3rd ed, 1994), pp 979-981.

the means adopted to achieve this end were unlawful. If that is so, then there was a conspiracy. To infringe another's constitutional rights or to coerce him into abandoning them or waiving them (in so far as that may be possible), is unlawful as constituting a violation of the fundamental law of the State, in so far as such conduct constitutes the means towards an end which is not in itself unlawful, the means are unlawful and an agreement to employ such means constitutes a conspiracy ... The decision in the *Crofter Case*[158] does not in any way indicate that, because the predominant purpose of an agreement is not unlawful, the agreement cannot amount to a conspiracy even if unlawful means are used."[159]

**[32.69]** *Meskell* forces us to address the question of the parameters of the concept of infringement of a person's constitutional right in this context. Our courts have yet to provide clear guidance on this matter, so the resolution of the question is necessarily tentative. The infringement of a right could conceivably range from conscious and deliberate conduct, with the specific intention of infringing the right, on the one hand, to entirely undeliberate conduct, with no such intention, on the other. To the extent that the courts require conduct leaning towards the former end of the spectrum, the scope of a *Meskell*-type conspiracy contracts. If the courts were to insist on proof of an intention to infringe the right in question, they would in this context be going very close to, if not actually merging with, the approach favoured by the House of Lords in *Lonrho*,[160] considered below,

### *Simple Conspiracy*

**[32.70]** As has been mentioned, simple conspiracy occurs where two or more persons continue with the predominant purpose of damaging the economic interests of another, without justification. In *Sorrell v Smith*,[161] Lord Cave stated:

"(1) A combination of two or more persons wilfully to injure a man in his trade is unlawful and, if it results in damage to him, is actionable.

---

158. *Crofter Hand Woven Harris Tweed Co Ltd v Veitch* [1942] AC 435 (HC).

159. [1973] IR 121 at 134. See further, Mathews 'The Tort of Conspiracy in Irish Labour Law' (1973) 8 Ir Jur (ns) 252 at 264ff; de Blaghd (1974) 108 ILT & Sol J 71. *Meskell's* case was applied by Finlay P in *Cotter v Ahern* High Court, 25 February 1977, where officials of the Irish National Teacher's Organisation sought to frustrate the appointment as principal teacher of a person who was not a member of their union. The conspiracy extended beyond inducement to the manager of one school to break his contract with the plaintiff (as to which see para **[32.17]** above), to preventing the appointment of the plaintiff the following year "at least to one principal teacher's post in the City of Cork". Finlay P was satisfied that:

"an agreement by two or more persons to prevent the appointment or promotion of a national teacher as part of a general campaign or objective to try and ensure that he and all other national teachers in any particular area or in the whole country will become and remain a member of a trade union, is to seek to coerce or penalise that person into waiving his constitutional right to dissociate, and as such is an actionable conspiracy". *Id. p* 34.

See also *Crowley v Ireland* [1980] IR 102; *Hayes v Ireland* [1987] ILRM 651. In *Hayes*, Carroll J held that the protection afforded trade unions against actions for tort by s 4 of the Trade Disputes Act 1906 (as amended), did not extend to claims for damages for unlawful infringement of a constitutional right, which were "in a category of [their] own": [1987] ILRM at 655. See further para **[32.128]-[32.131]** below.

160. [1982] AC 173 (HL). See further para **[32.74]** below.

161. *Sorrell v Smith* [1925] AC 70 at 712 (HL (Eng)). See also *Connolly v Loughney* (1953) 87 ILTR 49 at 55 (HC); *McGowan v Murphy* Supreme Court, 10 April 1967, *per* Walsh J at p 4.

(2) If the real purpose of the combination is, not to injury another, but to forward or defend the trade of those who enter into it, no wrong is committed and no action will lie, although damage to another ensues.

The distinction between the two classes of case is sometimes expressed by saying that in cases of the former class there is not, while in cases of the latter class there is, just cause or excuse for the action taken."

**[32.71]** In the *Crofter* case, Viscount Simon LC pointed out[162] that Lord Cave's two propositions were not necessarily exhaustive. He counselled that:

"it is to be borne in mind that there may be cases where the combination has more than one 'object' or 'purpose'. The combiners may feel that they are killing two birds with one stone, and even though their main purpose may be to protect their own legitimate interests notwithstanding that this involves damage to the plaintiffs, they may also find a further inducement to do what they are doing by feeling that it serves the plaintiffs right. The analysis of human impulses soon leads us into the quagmire of mixed motives, and even if we avoid the word 'motive', there may be more than a simple 'purpose' or 'object'. It is enough to say that if there is more than one purpose actuating a combination, liability must depend on ascertaining the predominant purpose. If that predominant purpose is to damage another person and damage results, that is tortious conspiracy. If the predominant purpose is the lawful protection or promotion of any lawful interest of the combiners (no illegal means being employed), it is not a tortious conspiracy, even though it causes damage to another person."

**[32.72]** In *McGowan v Murphy*,[163] the plaintiff, who had been expelled from his trade union, sought damages for conspiracy by the members of the resident executive committee of the union to prevent him from earning his living. Walsh J, in the Supreme Court, stated:

"If the defendants combined to procure the expulsion of the plaintiff from the trade union and in so doing had as their sole or main purpose or object the injuring of the plaintiff and the plaintiff suffered damage by reason of it the defendants would be guilty of the actionable tort of conspiracy, even if the expulsion was not in breach of the rules of the union. To that extent a combination of persons in such circumstances is in a less favoured position than an individual doing the same act. See *Crofter Harris Tweed Co v Veitch* [1942] 1 All ER 142. If, however, the real purpose of the combination was not to injure the plaintiff but to defend the interests of the trade union by maintaining discipline then no wrong was committed and no action will lie even though damage to the plaintiff resulted provided that the means used were not in themselves unlawful. See ... *Sorrell v Smith* [1925] AC 700."

**[32.73]** An interesting example of an action for conspiracy in the area of trade protection arose in *Tru-Value Ltd v Switzer & Co.*[164] The plaintiff, the proprietor of a chemist shop in one of the leading shopping streets of Dublin, sought an injunction against certain department stores on the street coming together to put pressure on the suppliers of a particular perfume not to enter into a contract to supply the plaintiff with that product.

---

162. [1942] AC at 445. *Cf* Mathews 'The Tort of Conspiracy in Irish Labour Law' (1973) 8 Ir Jur (ns) 252 at 258-260.

163. Supreme Court, 10 April 1967 at p 4. See Mathews 'The Tort of Conspiracy in Irish Labour Law' (1973) 8 Ir Jur (ns) 252 at 260-263.

164. High Court, 10 March 1972 (Kenny J).

Kenny J declined to grant an injunction, on the basis, *inter alia*, that "the defendants' motive would seem to be that they want to protect their businesses".

***Unlawful means conspiracy***

**[32.74]** As has already been mentioned, unlawful means conspiracy occurs where two or more persons combine to engage in an unlawful act such as a crime, tort or infringement of a constitutional right and damage to the plaintiff results. In *Lonhro Ltd v Shell Petroleum Co Ltd (No 2)*[165] in 1981, the House of Lords held that conspiracy by unlawful means where there is no predominant intention of injuring the plaintiff's interests should not be actionable. Lord Diplock (for the Court) noted that it had:

> "an unfettered choice whether to confine the civil action of conspiracy to the narrow field to which alone it has an established claim or whether to extend this already anomalous tort beyond those narrow limits that are all that common sense and the application of the legal logic of the decided cases require.
>
> I am against extending the scope of the civil tort of conspiracy beyond acts done in execution of an agreement entered into by two or more persons for the purpose sought of protecting their own interests but of injuring the interests of the plaintiff."[166]

**[32.75]** It was not immediately clear whether our courts would take the same view. As has already been indicated, a vital aspect of Irish law, which of course has no counterpart in Britain, is the notion, recognised in *Meskell v CIE*,[167] of conspiracy in respect of the infringement of constitutional rights.

**[32.76]** The answer came in *Taylor v Smyth*,[168] where the Supreme Court addressed the issue directly. McCarthy J (Finlay CJ and Hederman J concurring) rejected the *Lonrho* modification in holding that:

> "if there be a combination to use unlawful means to achieve a particular aim, that is actionable conspiracy, whether or not such means amount to an infringement of constitutional rights".

He emphasised that it was the very combination itself that strengthened the hands of the wrongdoers. It was "entirely logical" that what was actionable when done by unlawful means, such as procuring a breach of contract, was actionable against an individual, even though his purpose might be solely one of self interest; it should not cease to be actionable when done in combination by a group with a like purpose.

**[32.77]** McCarthy J endorsed the Supreme Court's analysis in *McGowan v Murphy*.[169] He went on to observe that:

> "[i]f conspiracy be inchoate, it is difficult to see how it can have caused damage, a necessary ingredient of every tort. If it be executed, then the cause of action derives from the execution whether it be because of the unlawful nature of the act done or the unlawful means used.

165. [1982] AC 173 (HL (Eng)).
166. [1982] AC 173 at 189.
167. [1973] IR 121 (SC).
168. [1991] IR 142 analysed by Kerr in (1990) 12 DULJ 166.
169. Supreme Court, 10 April 1967.

Neither of these circumstances, however, would warrant condemning the existence of the tort itself if for no other reason that because of its evidential features."

**[32.78]** This latter consideration featured in a critique by John Eekelaar[170] of Lord Diplock's speech in *Lonrho*. Eekelaar had argued:

> "it would be hard to defend an outcome in which conspirators who have caused injury by unlawful means are allowed to escape liability for conspiracy if they show that they were predominantly motivated by intention to further their own interests, but are caught if each conspirator is sued as an individual tortfeasor under the tort of unlawful interference in trade. It would be a strange reversal of the common perception that combination strengthens the hand of wrongdoers".

He had gone on to identify the evidential advantage as the major one in framing the action in conspiracy when unlawful means are used.

**[32.79]** The Supreme Court's decision in *Taylor v Smyth* provokes a number of observations. First, it should be noted that *Taylor v Smyth* was decided at a time when the English Court of Appeal, in *Metall und Rohstoff AG v Donaldson Lufkin and Jenrette Inc*[171] had interpreted Lord Diplock's approach in *Lonrho Ltd v Shell Petroleum (No 2)*[172] as requiring that the *predominant* intention of the conspirators be to damage the plaintiff. The House of Lords, in *Lonrho plc v Fayed,*[173] decided after *Taylor v Smyth*, made it clear that no such extra qualification is permissible. Some intention to injure is nonetheless required. Is it possible, therefore, that the Supreme Court, when revisiting the issue, would settle for the view favoured in *Lonrho plc v Fayed*? McCarthy J's judgment would seem clearly enough to indicate that he was not sympathetic to such a solution. Until the Supreme Court elaborates further on the nature of infringement of constitutional rights, and, in particular, whether infringement may occur without proof of intention to infringe, the answer to this question will remain uncertain.

**[32.80]** It is interesting to contrast *Taylor v Smyth's* rationale with that which the Supreme Court had adopted in *Dillon v Dunne's Stores (George's Street) Ltd.*[174] There Ó Dálaigh CJ quoted, with apparent approval, Denning LJ's objection, in *Ward v Lewis,*[175] to permitting a plaintiff sue for conspiracy to commit a tort where the defendants are guilty of the substantive tort:

> "It is sometimes sought, by charging conspiracy, to get an added advantage, or instance in proceedings for discovery, or by getting in evidence which would not be admissible in a straight action in tort or to overcome substantive rules of law, such as .... the rules about republication of slander."

**[32.81]** What seemed to be a vice in 1968 is regarded as a virtue in 1990. In this context it is worth recalling that the failure to characterise as tortious conspiracy a consummated

---

170. (1990) 106 LQR 223.

171. [1990] 1 QB 391.

172. [1982] AC 174 (HL, Eng).

173. [1992] 1 AC 448 (HL).

174. Supreme Court, 20 December 1968 extracted in McMahon & Binchy, *Casebook on the Irish Law of Torts* (1st ed, 1983), pp 460-461.

175. [1955] 1 WLR 9 at 11.

conspiracy to commit a tort, breach of contract or breach of trust causing injury to the plaintiff does not prevent the plaintiff from suing the defendants as *concurrent wrongdoers*.[176]

**[32.82]** An interesting provision, which has tended to be overlooked, is s 11(6) of the Civil Liability Act 1961, which provides that:

> [f]or the purpose of any enactment referring to a specific tort, an action for a conspiracy to commit that tort shall be deemed to be an action for that tort.

The meaning of this subsection is clear enough in at least certain respects. Thus, for example, provisions in the Statute of Limitations 1957 prescribing specific periods of limitation for specific torts must be construed as including a reference to actions for conspiracy to commit these torts. This is something different, however, from snuffing out actions for conspiracy to commit these torts, save where the tort is itself a statutory creation. Section 11(6), far from accomplishing the consummation devoutly wished by Denning LJ, seems more consistent with its antithesis since, if there were a general rule preventing an action for conspiracy with respect to a completed tort, s 11(6) would be otiose.

## VII. Intentional Interference with Economic Interests

**[32.83]** We now must consider the possibility that our courts will recognise the existence of a generic economic tort,[177] of which the torts of conspiracy, intimidation and inducing a breach of contract are mere species. In England this development has already taken place. In *Merkur Island Shipping Corporation v Laughton*,[178] the House of Lords accepted that there was just such a generic tort of interfering with the trade or business of another person by doing unlawful acts. In *Bula Ltd v Tara Mines Ltd (No 2)*,[179] in 1987, Murphy J, in interlocutory proceedings,[180] declined to take a position, one way or the other, on this question. His only comment on the merit of the claim for unlawful interference was that:

> "[w]hat can be said is that even by the plaintiffs' own admission in this respect they are seeking to push the law to the limit of its existing frontiers if not indeed to new ones."[181]

**[32.84]** Whether this accurately characterises the generic tort may be debated. The language adopted in some earlier Irish decisions certainly seems harmonious with the generic approach. In *Cooper v Millea*,[182] in 1938, Gavan Duffy J said:

---

176. *Cf* the Civil Liability Act 1961, s 11(2).

177. See Carty 'Intentional Violation of Economic Interests: The Limits of Common Law Liability' (1988) 104 LQR 250; Burns 'Tort Injury to Economic Interests: Some Facets of Legal Response' (1980) 58 Can BR 103; Elias & Ewing 'Economic Torts and Labour Law: Old Principles and New Liabilities' [1982] Camb LJ 321.

178. [1983] 2 AC 570 at 608 (HL).

179. [1987] IR 95 (HC).

180. As to which see Byrne & Binchy, *Annual Review of Irish Law 1987*, pp 169, 339.

181. Byrne & Binchy, *Annual Review of Irish Law 1987*, p 101.

182 [1938] IR 749 at 758 (HC). See also *Riordan v Butler* [1940] IR 347 at 353 (HC). In *Pine Valley Developments Ltd v Minister for the Environment* [1987] ILRM 747 (SC) Finlay CJ, in view of the plaintiffs' disclaimer of any reliance on *Beaudesert Shire Council v Smith* (1969) 120 CLR 145, declined to express any view as to whether the principle enunciated in *Beaudesert* formed part of the law of the State. In *Beaudesert* it was stated that (at 156):

> "This civil bill belongs to the elusive category of actions for intentional interference with a man's employment by illegal means ... It is incontestable that the defendants interfered with the plaintiff's employment by illegal means; for a strike in breach of contract is unlawful and a threat or pre-intimation of unlawful action constitutes illegal means; the right of action is thus established ...."

**[32.85]** Whether a generic tort would resolve or merely compound the present confused state of the law depends greatly on what substance the courts might choose to give it. Merely providing a new, all-embracing label would do nothing. The real matters of substance are those of principle and policy. What does it *mean* to be guilty of unlawful interference with another's economic interests? Can the question be answered in conceptual terms, equivalent to the "neighbourhood" and "proximity" lexicon of the tort of negligence, or are the courts to proceed on an incremental, intuitive basis? Unless these questions are seriously addressed by the courts, there is a danger of creating a tort with insecure foundations.

**[32.86]** One approach would be to define the tort in terms of interference with another's economic interests "by doing an unlawful act",[183] and leave to future judicial exegesis the task of defining what constitutes an unlawful act. The problem with this approach is that inevitably courts will be driven to enquire whether the breach of a statutory duty or of a contract, or the commission of a particular tort, or the breach of trust or other equitable obligation is an "unlawful act". This may well not be the most appropriate type of question to ask. There is no reason to believe that these several legal categories have any necessary connection with the issues at stake in determining whether or not an interference with another's economic interests should be actionable. The range of conduct falling within the scope of the generic tort could well be defined in terms of such factors as the purpose and effect of the defendant's conduct rather than of legal categories designed to serve other functions.

## VIII. TRADE DISPUTES[184]

### Introduction

**[32.87]** In *Roundabout Ltd v Beirne*,[185] Dixon J was surely guilty of serious understatement when he described the subject of trade disputes as "rather technical". In fact it is a

182. (contd)

> "... it appears that the authorities cited do justify a proposition that, independently of trespass negligence or nuisance but by an action for damages upon the case a person who suffers harm or loss as the inevitable consequence of the unlawful, intentional and positive acts of another, is entitled to recover damages from that other."

183. As Lord Diplock has done in *Merkur Island* [1983] 2 AC 570 at 608.

184. See Kerr & Whyte, *Irish Trade Union Law* (1985), Ch 9; Forde, *Industrial Relations Law* (1991), Ch 6; Ahern 'The Industrial Relations Act 1990' (1990-93) 9 JISLL 25; Byrne 'Industrial Relations and Trade Disputes' Lecture 5 of the Law Society of Ireland's Continuing Legal Education Series of Seminars on Employment Law, 16 February 1999; Meehan, *Working Within the Law* (1994), Ch 8; Shillman, *Trade Unionism and Trade Disputes in Ireland* (1960); Delany (1955) 18 MLR 338 and (1956) 19 MLR 310.

185. [1959] IR 423 at 426 (HC).

minefield, through which the lawyer can tread with great caution and very little assurance of safety.

**[32.88]** The principal legislation affecting trade disputes until the enactment of the Industrial Relations Act 1990, was the Trade Disputes Act 1906.[186] In *Goulding Chemicals Ltd v Bolger*,[187] Parke J described the 1906 legislation as "a child of political expediency, hastily conceived and prematurely delivered". The 1990 Act has done much to improve the position but inevitably the 1906 Act, as it was interpreted in the courts, continues to cast its shadow.

## The Industrial Relations Act 1990

**[32.89]** The Industrial Relations Act 1990,[188] represents a pragmatic compromise on the issues that had plagued industrial relations until the relatively tranquil years before its enactment. It concedes ground to both employers and employees and trade unions on matters such as strikes, ballots, picketing and injunctions. On some issues, the employers' position is improved; on others the employees and trade unions are given greater scope.

**[32.90]** Let us examine the main features of Part II of the 1990 Act, which contains the crucial provisions relevant to the law of tort. Certain immunities are conferred by the act, but to appreciate those we must first understand some basic definitions.

### *Definition of "trade dispute"*

**[32.91]** A "trade dispute" means any dispute between employers[189] and workers which is connected with the employment or non-employment, or the terms or conditions of or affecting the employment, of any person.[190] It is clear that the dispute need not be one concerning the legal rights of the parties: indeed, "ordinarily [such disputes] are concerned with other matters."[191]

**[32.92]** An "employer" means a person for whom one or more workers work or have worked or normally work or seek to work, having previously worked[192] for that person.[193] The device of separate incorporation so as to break the employer-employee nexus, which succeeded in *Roundabout Ltd v Beirne*[194] under the 1906 Act (which contained no definition of "employer"), has not been expressly killed off by the new statutory definition.

---

186. 6 Edw 7 c 47.

187. [1977] IR 211 at 242. See also [1977] IR 211 at 235-236 (*per* Kenny J).

188. See Kerr, *The Trade Union and Industrial Relations Acts of Ireland* (1991), p 179ff; Wilkinson 'The Irish Industrial Relations Act 1990 - Corporatism and Conflict Control' (1991) 20 Ind LJ 21; Byrne & Binchy *Annual Review of Irish Law 1990*, pp 347-356.

189. A dispute between workers thus no longer falls within the scope of the definition of a "trade dispute".

190. Section 8.

191. *Quigley v Byrne* [1955] IR 62 at 76 (SC).

192. *Cf McHenry Brothers Ltd v Carey* High Court, 19 November 1976 (Hamilton J); *Bradbury Ltd v Duffy* High Court, 26 March 1979 (McWilliam J). *Cf* para **[32.101]** below.

193. Section 8.

194. [1959] IR 423 (HC).

The Minister for Labour, Mr Ahern, doubted whether it continued to have vitality[195] and commentators[196] believe that the courts today would "lift the corporate veil".

**[32.93]** A "worker" means any person who is or was employed whether or not in the employment of the employer with whom a trade dispute arises, but does not include a member of the Defence Forces or of the Garda Síochána.[197]

**[32.94]** In *Nolan Transport (Oaklands) Ltd v Halligan*[198] the Supreme Court addressed the question of the extent to which ulterior motives might compromise the characterisation of a dispute as a "trade dispute", for the purposes of the 1990 Act. A number of employees had been involved in a couple of altercations, which could be construed as dismissalable which had been followed by a stance adopted by the employer which was consistent with this construction. The union has been pressing for the right to represent the entire workforce. Barron J held that the protection afforded by the 1990 Act to those involved in a "trade dispute" could not be availed of, stating that he did not:

> "believe that the union ever regarded this issue of dismissals as more than an event of use to its advantage. Counsel for the plaintiff says that these dismissals were contrived. I do hold, however, that this aspect of the dismal was not pursued *bona fide* to get the two men back to work but as part of the policy to take all drivers into membership."[199]

**[32.95]** The Supreme Court reversed. Murphy J[200] found himself in disagreement with Barron J as to the motivation and purpose of the union and the legal principles applicable where industrial action was undertaken with a view to achieve more than one objective. Murphy J considered that Barron J had been misled by a passage in O'Daly J's judgment in *Silver Tassie Co Ltd v Cleary*,[201] to the effect that:

> "[t]he dispute must be genuine and not merely colourable. It is quite clear that the genuineness of a dispute does not depend upon what are at the time facts of the dispute, but rather it depends on the *bona fide* of the parties."

**[32.96]** In fact O'Daly J had been dealing with two different concepts in those sentences. The first, relating to the genuineness of the dispute, sought to draw a distinction with "a mere personal quarrel or grumbling or an agitation",[202] which would not suffice. The second concerned the relationship between the *bona fides* of the parties and the objective facts. O'Daly J had been seeking to affirm Dixon J's view, in the High Court in *Silver*

---

195. 398 Dáil Debates, col 329.

196. See Kerr, *The Trade Union and Industrial Relations Acts of Ireland* (1991), p 184; Byrne & Binchy *Annual Review of Irish Law 1990*, p 14; *cf* Wilkson 'The Irish Industrial Relations Act 1990 - Corporatism and Conflict Control' (1991) 20 Ind LJ 21 at 25 fn 26.

197. Section 8. As to continuity of employment under the European Communities (Safeguarding of Employees on the Transfer of Undertakings) Regulations 1980, see *Westman Holidays Ltd v McCormack* [1991] ILRM 833 (SC); Meehan, *Working Within the Law* (1994), p 93; Byrne & Binchy *Annual Review of Irish Law 1991*.

198. [1998] ELR 177 (SC) revg [1995] ELR 1.

199. [1995] ELR 1.

200. O'Flaherty, Denham, Barrington and Lynch JJ concurring.

201. (1958) ILTR 27 at 31 (SC).

202. (1958) ILTR 27, citing *Conway v Wade* [1909] AC 506, in support.

*Tassie*, that a *bona fide* belief that a dispute was a well founded one sufficed and that it was not the courts' functions to decide whether that belief was correct.

**[32.97]** Murphy J was satisfied that the dispute between the appellants and the company was *bona fide*:

> "in the sense that Mr Halligan[203] had an honest belief for which there were reasonable grounds and further that the dispute was genuine in the sense that it represented the immediate quarrel between the parties".[204]

Even if the union had had the ultimate goal of compelling the company's employees to join the union, this goal "did not represent the current dispute".[205]

**[32.98]** Murphy J went on to observe:

> "Part of the difficulty arises from the fact that lawyers and judges have used the words '*bona fide* trade dispute' with different meanings and in different contexts. If employers and workers both acknowledge themselves to be engaged in a trade dispute there is no difficulty in describing it as a *bona fide* trade dispute. But a *bona fide* trade dispute may also exist where one party denies that there is any dispute and the other believes that he has been wronged and is in dispute as a result. On the other hand an outside party or 'meddler' who had no legitimate interest of his own to protect but who stirred up trouble in a business for reasons of malice or spite could not claim to be engaged in a *bona fide* trade dispute ... If, however, a *bona fide* trade dispute does exist between an employer and workers, some of whom happen to be members of a trade union, the trade union is entitled within the Constitution and the law, to support its members who are in dispute. That, in doing this, it may be partly motivated by the aim of impressing its members and other workers and enhancing its own reputation and membership appears to me to be quite irrelevant as long as it acts within the law and does not attempt to infringe the constitutional right to each worker to join or not to join a trade union as he himself thinks best."[206]

**[32.99]** If one reads Murphy J's judgment carefully, one finds that he does not, in fact, contest Barron J's statement of principle that an ostensible trade dispute should not be characterised as a "trade dispute" for the purposes of the Act, where an alleged disputant is "picking a fight" without there being any true issue of contention between the parties. The concept of a dispute is ambiguous since it may relate either to the empirical or rational order. A dispute may be considered to involve the empirically observable phenomenon of conflict - fists flying, harsh words loudly expressed or, in the industrial relations context, such actions as strikes and pickets. But there is the quite different concept of a dispute, which operates in the rational order: parties are in disagreement as to a fact, a moral or other evaluative judgment or an agenda for future action. The definition of "trade dispute" in s 8 of the 1990 Act appears to fall within the latter category, since it requires that the dispute be "connected with" one or more of certain specific facts.

**[32.100]** It seems, therefore, that it is not sufficient for a disputant to point to an empirical phenomena of disputation - a picket, for example - and to one of the specific facts

---

203. An employee whose dismissal was in issue.
204. [1998] ELR 177 at 193.
205. [1998] ELR 177 at 194.
206. [1998] ELR 177.

mentioned in the definition of a "trade dispute". The connection between the two has to be in the rational order. If there is no such connection - for example, because the disputant is seizing on the particular fact to engage in the picket, without any genuine difference of opinion with the other party - then there is no genuine trade dispute, for the purposes of s 8. A pretext is not enough. The court has to raise its eyes above the picket line to see whether there is an issue that truly divides the parties. Of course, it will be a rare case in forthcoming to establish the absence of a *bona fide* dispute but that does not affect the point of principle, which is that, as Barron J stated but the Supreme Court by implication appeared to deny, the protection afforded by the 1990 Act extends only to *bona fide* trade disputes.

***"Employment or non-employment"***[207]

**[32.101]** This phrase has been parsed in several decisions. It is now clear that it is not necessary that the dispute relate to persons who are at the time in employment. Indeed, disputes about dismissals are a frequent phenomenon.[208]

**[32.102]** Formerly, there was some confusion on this question. In *Doran v Lennon*,[209] Overend J held in the High Court that where employees on the instructions of their union had gone on strike after giving shorter notice than their contracts of employment required, their employer was entitled to regard this as repudiation of their contracts of employment. Thereafter,[210] there was no trade dispute in existence. Overend J stated:

> "If it were otherwise, then every employee of a commercial firm, who broke his contract and was dismissed for cause, would be entitled to picket his late master's premises and yet claim the protection of the statute."[211]

**[32.103]** This view was expressly repudiated in the Supreme Court decision of *Goulding Chemicals Ltd v Bolger*,[212] where O'Higgins CJ stated:

> "The definition of 'trade dispute' ... permits of no such limitation and, indeed, is sufficiently wide and general to include any dispute between employers and workmen provided only it is connected with the employment or non-employment, or the terms of employment or the conditions of labour, of any person. Such a definition can comprehend a dispute as to whether an employer ought to have exercised his contractual right to terminate a particular employment or employments. Such dispute would clearly be 'connected with' the employment of the persons in question or with their non-employment. The fact that the

---

207. See Kerr, *The Trade Union and Industrial Relations Acts of Ireland* (1991), p 184; Kerr 'Trade Disputes Act 1906 – "Employment or Non-Employment" (1980) 74 Incorp L Soc of Ireland Gazette 191.

208. *Cf Goulding Chemicals Ltd v Bolger* [1977] IR 211 (SC); *Quigley v Beirne* [1955] IR 62 (SC); *Myerscough & Co Ltd v Kenny* High Court, 18 April 1974 (Gannon J); *Ferguson v O'Gorman* [1937] IR 620 - *Aliter* expulsions from unions: *McGowan v Murphy* Supreme Court, 10 April 1967 *per* Walsh J at p 12.

209. [1945] IR 315 (HC).

210. Some hesitancy was apparent as regards when precisely the trade dispute ended: *cf* [1945] IR 315 at 326.

211. [1945] IR 315. For the contrary view (before *Goulding*), see *Ferguson v O'Gorman* [1937] IR 620; *McHenry Bros. Ltd v Cary* High Court, 19 November 1976 (Hamilton J).

212. [1977] IR 211 at 230 (SC). See also [1977] IR 211 at 230 at 236 (*per* Kenny J).

termination of the employment or employments in question was lawful and for good and substantial reasons appears to me to be completely irrelevant once such termination led to a dispute as to whether the employer should have acted as he did. It is true that the definition of 'workmen' who may engage in a trade dispute is 'all persons employed in trade or industry'. In my view 'employed' here does not mean in actual present employment but rather refers to the occupation or way of life of those who are to be regarded as 'workmen'. Any other meaning could have the effect of withdrawing the protection of the Act from workmen by the simple device of dismissing them and this would have its maximum effect at a time of general unemployment. "

**[32.104]** Disputes may concern not only dismissals but the effects of dismissals such as the question of redundancy payments. It has been held[213] that the statutory enactments relating to redundancy entitlement have not impliedly withdrawn employees so benefitting from the protection of the 1906 Act.

**[32.105]** Just as disputes about dismissals and their effects may fall within the scope of the protection of the Act, so also may disputes about refusals to employ a person seeking employment. This was expressly recognised by Hamilton J in *McHenry Bros Ltd v Carey*,[214] but in *J Bradbury Ltd v Duffy*,[215] McWilliam J expressed the view that "there must be some restriction on the universality of the application of the term 'non-employment'". He gave the "extreme case" of a man starting a new business for which he required ten workmen, fifty applicants applying for these positions: in such circumstances McWilliam J could not accept that the forty unsuccessful applicants would be entitled to take any sort of action solely because they had not been given jobs. So also, where a workman had voluntarily left his job which had been filled, it could hardly be said that he was entitled to take industrial action because his former employer was unable to re-employ him at a job which was no longer available.

**[32.106]** In this regard it is worth noting that O'Higgins CJ, in *Goulding Chemicals Ltd v Bolger*,[216] expressed "considerable sympathy" with the contention that:

> "for a trade dispute to exist there must be some reality in the question of possible employment in the sense that there must be an employer having employment available".

It may be argued, however, that the mere non-availability of employment should not always suffice to place the dispute outside the protection of the section. An arbitrary or

---

213. By Kenny J in *Cunningham Bros Ltd v Kelly* High Court, 18 November 1974 and in *Newbridge Industries v Bateson* High Court, 7 July 1975. In *Goulding Chemicals Ltd v Bolger* [1977] IR 211 (SC), Kenny J expressed the same view (at 238) but the issue had been abandoned by counsel (*cf* at 231 *per* O'Higgins CJ) so Kenny J's remarks on the part in that decision must be regarded as *obiter.*

214. High Court, 19 November 1976.

215. High Court, 26 March 1979 at p 6. See also *Michael McNamara & Co Ltd v Lacken* High Court, 31 May 1991 (Costello J) (*ex temp*) cited by Kerr, *The Trade Union and Industrial Relations Acts of Ireland* (1991), p 184. *Cf Barton v Harten* [1925] 2 IR 37 (KBD) - no trade dispute where union sought reinstatement of a former employee who had been detained by security forces for a year; *per* Moloney CJ (at 4):

> "... there is in reality no dispute at all but only an attempt on the part of an organisation to compel an employer to give employment to one who has been out of his employment for a long time and whose position has been filled in the ordinary course".

216. [1977] IR 211 at 228.

malevolent manipulation of the range of available employment by an employer should make the dispute one about the "non-employment" of those whose legitimate expectations of employment had thus been thwarted. It should, however, be stressed that the courts have not yet been called on to address such a case, and that the express language of the judgments of McWilliams J and O'Higgins CJ does not give great encouragement for the argument here put forward.

***Can there be "a trade dispute" with a trade union?*[217]**

**[32.107]** The 1990 Act leaves unresolved the status of a dispute between an employer and a trade union.

**[32.108]** It seems that the courts have no objection to holding that there may be a "trade dispute" with a trade union. What they insist upon, however, is that a union cannot come in "to raise a trade dispute as a mere intermeddler without authority".[218] As Johnston J stated in *Ryan v Cooke*:[219]

> "A trade union cannot create a trade dispute simply by declaring that a trade dispute exists, thereby giving themselves the right to adopt 'the drastic action', as they themselves call it, of putting a picket on any business premises that their eyes alight upon."

**[32.109]** However, if the union is acting on behalf of its members who are employees of the employer, the courts are quite willing to find that a trade dispute exists, even though the union is active for other employees also. Thus, in *Esplanade Pharmacy Ltd v Larkin*,[220] Ó Dálaigh J stated:

> "Here the real disputant is Mrs O'Neill [an employee of the pharmacy picketed by the union] and the union has been acting on her behalf as well as on behalf of other pharmacy workers. The hand was the hand of the Union but the voice was the voice of Mrs O'Neill."

**[32.110]** Moreover, in the Supreme Court decision of *Sherriff v McMullen*,[221] Murnaghan J[222] recognised that, even where none of the employer's employees is a member of the trade union, there may be occasions in which members of the union may have a "trade dispute" with the employer, but he went on to stress that "it is not every dispute with a trade union which is a trade dispute".[223]

---

217. See Kerr, *The Trade Union and Industrial Relations Acts of Ireland* (1991), pp 185-186; Kerr 'In Contemplation or Furtherance of a Trade Dispute ...' [1979-1980] DULJ 59 at 74 for a detailed analysis. See also Kerr & Whyte *Irish Trade Union Law* (1985), pp 264-267.
218. *Smith v Beirne* (1954) 89 ILTR 24 at 38 (SC). *Cf Ardmore Studios (Ireland) Ltd v Lynch* [1965] IR 1 (HC).
219. The decisions of *McCobb v Doyle* [1938] IR 444 (HC) and *O'Connor v Martin* [1949] Ir Jur Rep 9 (CC) recognise that a union may be a party to a trade dispute.
220. [1957] IR 285 at 298 (SC). See also *Brendan Dunne Ltd v Fitzpatrick* [1958] for some of its members, the union "voiced their objections and acted at their request and on their behalf in what it did".
221. [1952] IR 236 at 262 (SC).
222. With whom Maguire CJ agreed.
223. [1952] IR 262.

### *Constitutional limitation*

**[32.111]** The constitutional right of "free dissociation"[224] limits the scope of the operation of the 1990 Act. In *Educational Co of Ireland v Fitzpatrick (No 2)*,[225] the Supreme Court held that picketing by employees could not be justified where its purpose was to induce employers to force other employees to join the union to which the picketers belonged. Kingsmill Moore J (with whom Ó Dálaigh agreed) stated:

> "The Trade Disputes Act 1906, can no longer be relied upon to justify picketing in aid of a trade dispute, where that dispute is concerned with an attempt to deprive persons of the right of free association or free dissociation guaranteed by the Constitution. The definition of trade dispute must be read as if there were attached thereto the words, 'Provided that a dispute between employers and workmen or between workmen and workmen as to whether a person shall or shall not become or remain a member of a trade union or having as its object a frustration of the right of any person to choose with whom he will or will not be associated in any form of union or association shall not be deemed to be a trade dispute for the purposes of this Act'."[226]

### *"Industrial action" and "strike"*

**[32.112]** Section 8 of the 1990 Act defines "industrial action" and "strike". This is an innovation, the 1906 Act contained no equivalents. The term "industrial action" means any action which affects, or is likely to affect, the terms or conditions, whether express or implied, of a contract and which is taken by any number or body of workers acting in combination or under a common understanding as a means of compelling their employer, or to aid other workers in compelling their employer, to accept or not to accept terms or conditions of or affecting employment. This definition is broad enough to capture such practices as a "go-slow" or "work to rule".[227]

**[32.113]** The term "strike" means a cessation of work by any number or body of workers acting in combination or a concerted refusal or a refusal under a common understanding of any number of workers to continue to work for their employer done as a means of compelling their employer, or to aid other workers in compelling their employer, to accept or not to accept terms or conditions of or affecting employment.

### *Immunities: introduction*

**[32.114]** Sections 10 to 13 of the 1990 Act contain significant immunities: s 10 protects certain acts done in contemplation or furtherance of a trade dispute from criminal or civil liability; s 11 gives similar protection to peaceful picketing; s 12 gives immunities to those who would otherwise be liable for the torts of inducing a breach of contract, intimidation or conspiracy, provided their acts are done in contemplation or furtherance of a trade dispute; and s 13 contains restrictions on actions of tort against trade unions.

**[32.115]** Section 9 specifies the range of application of these immunities. Those conferred by ss 11 to 13 apply only in relation to authorised trade unions which for the time being are

---

224. See Casey 'Some Implications of Freedom of Association in Labour Law: A Comparative Survey with Special Reference to Ireland' (1972) 21 ICLQ 699; Kerr & Whyte *Irish Trade Union Law* (1985), p 242.
225. [1961] IR 345 (SC).
226. [1961] IR 345 at 398.
227. Meehan, *Working Within the Law* (1994), p 94.

holders of negotiation licenses under the Trade Union Act 1941, and the members and officials of these trade unions.[228] Moreover, where, in relation to the employment or non-employment or the terms or conditions of or affecting the employment of *one* individual worker, there are agreed procedures availed of by custom or practice in the employment concerned, or provided for in a collective agreement, for the resolution of individual grievances, including dismissals, ss 10 to 12 apply only where those procedures have been resorted to and exhausted.[229]

***Immunity from liability for conspiracy***

**[32.116]** Section 10 re-enacts the immunity from criminal or civil liability for conspiracy which was formerly contained in s 3 of the Conspiracy and Protection of Property Act 1875 and s 1 of the 1906 Act. So far as civil conspiracy is concerned, sub-s (2) provides that:

> [a]n act done in pursuance of an agreement or combination by two or more persons, if done in contemplation or furtherance of a trade dispute, shall not be actionable unless the act, if done without any such agreement or combination, would be actionable.

**[32.117]** A number of points should be noted about s 10. First, it should be read in conjunction with s 17(1), which provides that s 10 is not to apply in respect of proceedings arising out of or relation to a strike or other industrial action by a trade union or a group of workers in disregard of, or contrary to, the outcome of a secret ballot relating to the issue (or issues) involved in the dispute. Secondly, in contrast to the immunities prescribed in by s 11 and 12, the immunities prescribed in s 10 are not restricted to members or officials of authorised trade unions.[230] Thirdly, as one commentator points out, "an agreement by workers to break their conspiracy despite s 10, as breach of contract is actionable if done by one person alone."[231]

**[32.118]** The phrase, "in contemplation or furtherance of a trade dispute", is of course vital in setting the parameters of the immunity conferred by s 10 (as well as ss 11 to 13). It seems clear that the contemplation must be directed towards the present or the imminent future rather than some contingent and hypothetical chain of circumstances.

**[32.119]** In *Esplanade Pharmacy Ltd v Larkin*,[232] Lavery J endorsed the Supreme Court decision of Lord Shaw's statement in *Conway v Wade*[233] that:

> "the contemplation of such a dispute must be the contemplation of something impending or likely to occur, and that [the words] do not cover the case of coercive interference in which the intervener may have in his own mind that if he does not get his own way he will

228. Section 9(1). See Kerr, *The Trade Union and Industrial Relations Acts of Ireland* (1991), p 187.

229. Section 9(2). Procedures here include, resort to a rights commissioner, the Labour Relations Commission, the Labour Court, an equality officer and the Employment Appeals Tribunal but *not* an appeal to a court: s 9(4). Procedures are declared exhausted if at any stage an employer fails or refuses to comply with them: s 9(3). Kerr, *The Trade Union and Industrial Relations Acts of Ireland* (1991), p 187 cites *Iarnród Éireann v Darby and O'Connor* Irish Times, 23 March 1991 where Morris J was satisfied that the second named defendant was the only worker who had a dispute with the plaintiff and that he had not gone through the agreed procedures; consequently the picket did not enjoy immunity.

230. Kerr, *The Trade Union and Industrial Relations Acts of Ireland* (1991), p 188.

231. Kerr, *The Trade Union and Industrial Relations Acts of Ireland* (1991), p 188.

232. [1957] IR 285 at 295 (SC).

233. [1909] AC 506 at 522.

thereupon create ways and means to bring a trade dispute into existence. To 'contemplate a trade dispute' is to have before the mind some objective event or situation, with those elements or fact or probability to which I have adverted, but does not mean a contemplation, meditation or resolve in regard to something as yet wholly within the mind and of a subjective character."

**[32.120]** In Lavery J's opinion, to accept the submission that, because someone else might do something which would create a trade dispute on account of the exercise by the plaintiffs of their ordinary rights, a trade dispute was imminent "would certainly lead to 'strange and mischievous' results."[234] Such a future dispute which might or might not arise could not, as a contemplated event, fall within the phrase upon which immunity was conditional.[235]

**[32.121]** The question whether acts "in ... furtherance of a trade dispute" should connote acts intended by the actor to further the dispute or merely those which, objectively assessed, actually have that effect, has led to a judicial debate in England.[236] In *Express Newspapers Ltd v MacShane*,[237] the majority of the House of Lords favoured the former interpretation, expressing distaste about the judiciary's involvement in having to assess the efficacy of tactics in industrial relations.

***Immunity from liability for inducing, or threatening to break, or breach of, contract of employment***

**[32.122]** Section 12 provides as follows:

> An act done by a person in contemplation or furtherance of a trade dispute shall not be actionable on the ground only that -
>
> (a) it induces some other person to break a contract of employment, or
>
> (b) it consists of a threat by a person to induce some other person to break a contract of employment or a threat by a person to break his own contract of employment, or
>
> (c) it is an interference with the trade, business or employment of some other person, or with the right of some other person to dispose of his capital or his labour as he wills.

**[32.123]** Section 12 goes further than s 3 of the 1906 Act in granting immunity to those who threaten to induce a breach of contract of employment (for instance, by organising a strike) or who threaten to break their own contracts of employment (for example, by going on strike).

**[32.124]** It remains the position that the breach of contract itself may be actionable. Moreover, s 12 confers no immunity from liability for the tort of unlawful interference with trade or business.[238] It would seem that the Supreme Court decision in *Talbot (Ireland) Ltd v Merrigan*[239] is unaffected by s 12 and that indirect inducements of breaches of commercial contracts continue to be actionable.

---

234. [1957] IR 285 at 295 (internal citation to *Conway v Wade* [1909] AC 506 at 522).

235. *Conway v Wade* [1909] AC 506 at 512 and 522.

236. See Kerr, *The Trade Union and Industrial Relations Acts of Ireland* (1991), p 189.

237. [1980] AC 672.

238. Kerr, *The Trade Union and Industrial Relations Acts of Ireland* (1991), p 194.

239. Supreme Court, 30 April 1981 extracted in McMahon & Binchy, *Casebook on the Irish Law Of Torts* (2nd ed, 1991).

**[32.125]** It is true that the Minister for Labour, during the passage of the legislation, expressed the view that the phrase "shall not be actionable" meant "shall not be actionable by any person ..."[240] The context in which he made this observation, however, was a narrow and specific one[241] which makes it hard to reconcile with the idea that s 12 was, in his opinion, reversing *Talbot*.

## Limited Immunity from Liability in Tort for Trade Unions

**[32.126]** We now must engage in a jurisprudential excursion on what looks like a simple provision in the 1990 Act. Section 13 prescribes a limited immunity for trade unions from liability in tort. It provides as follows:

> (1) An action against a trade union, whether of workers or employers, or its trustees or against any members or officials thereof on behalf of themselves and all other members of the trade union in respect of any tortious act committed by or on behalf of the trade union in contemplation or furtherance of a trade dispute, shall not be entertained by any court.
>
> (2) In an action against any trade union or person referred to in subsection (1) in respect of any tortious act alleged or found to have been committed by or on behalf of a trade union it shall be a defence that the act was done in the reasonable belief that it was done in contemplation or furtherance of a trade dispute.

**[32.127]** A number of features about s 13 may be noted. First, it does not prohibit actions against trade union officials in relation to their personal tortious liability. Second, its protection from suit is limited to *tortious* acts committed[242] in contemplation or furtherance of a trade dispute. If the tortuous acts were committed for any other reason, s 13 affords no protection. Thirdly, the section confers no immunity in respect of actions for breach of contract[243] or restitution,[244] for example, or for unlawful interference with a constitutional right.[245]

---

240. 400 Dáil Debates, Col 1978. *Cf* Kerr, *The Trade Union and Industrial Relations Acts of Ireland* (1991), p 194.

241. The Minister was seeking to oppose the addition of the words "by any person" which Deputy Jim Mitchell had proposed, to deal with a situation where someone *acting in concert with an employer* might take action. The Minister stated that the legal advice which he had received was to the effect that the subsection as framed already covered the point addressed by Deputy Mitchell. In *River Valley Products Ltd v Strutt* High Court, 6 February 1991 cited by Kerr, *The Trade Union and Industrial Relations Acts of Ireland* (1991), p 194, Costello J declined to determine the scope of the section in this context since the proceedings were interlocutory.

242. Or done in the *reasonable belief* that it was in contemplation or furtherance of a trade dispute: s 11(2) - placing onus on defendant to establish such belief and its reasonableness.

243. *O'Neill v Transport & General Workers Union* [1934] IR 633.

244. *Universe Tankships Inc of Monrovia v International Transport Workers Federation* [1980] IRLR 363. The development of the doctrine of "economic duress" carries with it important implications in relation to s 13: see *Atiyah* (1982) 98 LQR 197 and (1983) 99 LQR 353; *Tiplady* (1983) 99 LQR 188. This renders unlawful a wide range of economic pressures, extending more broadly than conduct that would constitute the torts of intimidation or inducing a breach of contract for example. If the doctrine were to be applied without limitation it "would rampage at the whim of the judiciary across the face of the industrial relations": Wedderburn, (1982) 45 MLR 556 at 563. See further Wedderburn, 'Labour Law: From Here to Autonomy?' (1987) 16 Ind LJ 1 at 19-20.

245. *Hayes v Ireland* [1987] ILRM 651 (HC).

**[32.128]** The relationship between s 13 and actions for interference with constitutional rights is more complex than might at first appear. In *Hayes v Ireland*,[246] Carroll J awarded compensation in favour of a pupil whose right to free primary education under Article 42.4 of the Constitution had been infringed by the defendant union (the Irish National Teachers Organisation) in involving itself in a strike at certain schools in the area where the plaintiff lived and in issuing a directive to its members in adjoining schools not to enroll pupils from these schools. This conduct had in earlier litigation[247] been held to amount to the use of unlawful means to deprive children in the area of their constitutional right.

**[32.129]** Awarding damages for the infringement, Carroll J observed:

> "This is not an action based on tort and therefore the defendants cannot rely on the proposition against actions of tort against trade unions or their members contained in section 4 of the Trade Disputes Act 1906 (as amended by section 11 of the Trade Unions Act 1941). This claim is in a category of its own being a claim for damages for unlawful interference with a constitutional right, a concept which was accepted by the Supreme Court in *Meskell v Córas Iompair Éireann*.[248]"[249]

**[32.130]** It should be noted that *Meskell* and *Hayes* concerned wrongdoing which did not constitute a recognisable tort. It was, perhaps, easy for Carroll J to conclude that therefore the statutory immunity from liability for tortious acts did not extend as far as the impugned conduct in the case before her.

**[32.131]** The thrust of judicial analysis of the *Meskell* principle in the years following *Hayes* has been to narrow its potential remit.[250]

**[32.132]** In *Merck Sharp & Dohme (Ireland) Ltd*,[251] Henchy J noted that the implementation of constitutional rights was primarily a matter for the State and that the courts were entitled to intervene only when there had been a failure to implement, or a plainly inadequate effectuation of, the constitutional guarantee in question:

> "A person may of course, in the absence of a common law or statutory cause of action, sue directly for breach of a constitutional right;[252] but when he founds his action on an existing tort he is normally confined to the limitations of that tort. It might be different if it could be shown that the tort in question is basically ineffective to protect his constitutional right."[253]

**[32.133]** How should the court respond to a claim for damages against a trade union for the infringement of a constitutional right where the alleged misconduct falls clearly within the established parameters of a particular tort? Let us take the case where a trade union, in contemplation or furtherance of a trade dispute, engages in an act of trespass on the plaintiff's premises, and the plaintiff, instead of engaging in the futile exercise of suing for the tort of trespass to land, which would inevitably be defeated by s 13, frames the action

246. [1987] ILRM 651 (HC).
247. *Crowley v Ireland* [1980] IR 102 (SC affg HC).
248. [1973] IR 121 at 135-136 (SC).
249. [1987] ILRM 651.
250. See Byrne & Binchy *Annual Review of Irish Law 1997*.
251. [1988] ILRM 629 (SC).
252. Citing *Meskell v CIE* [1973] IR 121.
253. [1988] ILRM 629 at 647.

for damages in terms of an infringement of his or her constitutional entitlements to privacy and freedom of association.

**[32.134]** The trade union would no doubt respond that, under Henchy J's approach, this action should really have been framed in tort, since the tort of trespass to land represents the State's due implementation of a system of protection for the relevant constitutional rights. The trade union would go on to argue that the case does not fall within Henchy J's proviso because the tort in question is *not* "basically ineffective" to protect the plaintiff's constitutional rights. There is nothing wrong with the tort itself; the plaintiff's problem is that, by virtue of s 13, he or she is unable to obtain compensation for *any* tort in the circumstances prescribed by the section. The explanation for the plaintiff's inability to sue lies with the Oireachtas and is not attributable to any inherent "ineffectiveness" of the tort in question.

**[32.135]** The plaintiff might reply that if, for whatever reason, a tort action fails to protect his or her constitutional right, there should be an entitlement to fall back on the inherent guarantee, recognised in *Meskell*, that an infringement of a constitutional right will generate the entitlement to redress.

**[32.136]** Is the proper response that the Oireachtas is entitled to have some role in determining the extent to which the vindication of constitutional rights will be subject to qualification? If the Oireachtas exercises this role in a rational, non-arbitrary and non-discriminatory way, can it be said that a legislative circumscription of the entitlement to sue for damages in respect of a particular tort, or torts in general, does not entitle the putative plaintiff to invoke the Henchy proviso so as to launch a *Meskell*-based action for damages for infringement of constitutional rights? It is clear from Costello P's analysis in *W v Ireland (No 2)*[254] that the mere fact that a plaintiff does not recover damages under the law of torts does not mean that the law of torts applicable to the case must be stigmatised as ineffective in protecting constitutionally guaranteed rights: "[i]t is necessary to consider why the plaintiff's claim has failed."[255]

**[32.137]** In *W v Ireland (No 2)*, Costello P considered that the policy reasons militating against the imposition of a duty of care in negligence on the Attorney General in processing extradition warrants, applied with equal vigour in the constitutional context to deny the plaintiff a claim based on the *Meskell* principle. Earlier in his judgment, Costello P observed that:

> "[l]aws may limit the exercise of protected rights and in each case when the claim is raised it is a question for the court to decide where, in the interests of the common good, the balance should be."[256]

---

254. [1997] 2 IR 141 (HC).

255. [1997] 2 IR 141 (HC).

256. [1997] 2 IR 141 (HC). *Cf* Hogan & Morgan, *Administrative Law in Ireland* (3rd ed, 1998), p 810: "This ... sentence echoes the potential future application of the proportionality doctrine in this area of immunity and quasi-immunity [citing *Daly v Revenue Commissioners* [1995] 3 IR 1 and *Heaney v Ireland* [1997] 1 ILRM 117]. If such a doctrine were to be so applied, one possible compromise might be for the courts to hold that not all special rules of immunity or quasi-immunity are *per se* unconstitutional where such quasi-immunities were objectively justified, but a complete immunity (such that contained in ss 64 and 88 of the Postal and Telecommunications Services Act 1983) would nonetheless seem susceptible to a successful constitutional challenge."

**[32.138]** Clearly the Oireachtas has some considerable leeway in making its own assessment of where the interests of the common good lie. This is plain from *Tuohy v Courtney*[257] where Finlay CJ stated that the Supreme Court was satisfied that, in a challenge to the constitutional validity of any statute in the enactment of which the Oireachtas has been engaged in a balancing of constitutional rights and duties, the role of the courts was:

> "not to impose their view of the correct or desirable balance in substitution for the view of the legislature as displayed in their legislation but rather to determine from an objective stance whether the balance contained in the impugned legislation is so contrary to reason and fairness as to constitute an unjust attack on some individual's constitutional rights."[258]

**[32.139]** It is, of course, always possible that an attack on the constitutional validity of s 13 may be made, at some future point, on the basis that it denies the victims of wrongs the constitutional entitlement to litigate claims, fails to vindicate their rights to property (and bodily integrity in some instances) and violates the principle of equality contained in Article 40.1 We need not seek to predict the outcome of such a challenge other than to observe that, as a matter of "practical politics",[259] a statutory immunity of almost a century's vintage, which has been re-enacted within the past decade, will not be easy to dislodge, especially when one takes into account the inevitably strong political dimension to industrial relations legislation. What is important in the present context is the question whether s 13, assuming that it *is* constitutionally valid, renders the entire system of delictual reparation so "ineffective" under Henchy J's test as to entitle victims to recharacterise their tort claims as claims for damages for interference with constitutional rights.

**[32.140]** It is suggested that the courts will answer this question in the negative, for two reasons. The first, and somewhat formalistic, one is that Henchy J was clearly referring to *particular* torts which are basically ineffective in protecting constitutional rights. He was not referring to a total barrier on the right to sue. The second reason is that, if s 13 is indeed constitutional, then the consequential ineffectiveness of the law of tort is not something that calls for redress through a *Meskell*-based claim.

**[32.141]** There is one remaining difficulty with this answer. It seems arbitrary that a claim for interference with a constitutional right which happens not to be capable of being

---

257. [1994] 3 IR 1 (SC).

258. [1994] 3 IR 1. A similar and surprising willingness to give the Oireachtas a broad margin of appreciation in statutory enactments, impacting on constitutional rights, is apparent in Henchy J's statement in *Hynes-O'Sullivan v O'Driscoll* [1988] IR 436 at (SC) that:

> "[t]he public policy which a new formulation of the law would represent, should more properly be found by the Law Reform Commission or by those others who are in a position to take a broad perspective, as distinct from what is discernible in the tunnelled vision imposed by the facts of a single case. That is particularly so in a case such as this, where the law as to qualified privilege must reflect a due balancing of the constitutional right to freedom of expression and the constitutional protection of every citizen's good name. The articulation of public policy on a matter such as this would seem to be primarily a matter for the legislature.

259. Andrews J's phrase in *Palsgraf v Long Island Railroad Co* (1928) 248 NY 339, 162 NE 99.

characterised also as a claim in tort should, *on that account*, still be maintainable, in spite of s 13.

**[32.142]** It is a matter of historical contingency, rather than of legal principle, where this line has been drawn,[260] or will be drawn in the future.[261]

**[32.143]** Finally, we should consider a more radical argument in relation to the scope of the immunity conferred by s 13. This is that, in the light of the Supreme Court decision of *McDonnell v Ireland*,[262] Carroll J's decision in *Hayes v Ireland*[263] must be considered as having been impliedly reversed. In *McDonnell*, Keane J (Hamilton CJ and O'Flaherty J concurring) characterised claims for damages for interference with constitutional rights as tort actions, at all events for the purposes of the Statute of Limitations 1957. If such claims were to be considered as torts for other purposes also, such as under the Civil Liability Act 1961 (as amended), then the argument that s 13 extends to them would of course be greatly strengthened.

**[32.144]** As against this, it must be acknowledged that no judgment in *McDonnell* goes so far. Keane J, who provided the deepest analysis of the issue, conceded that "significant differences" might arise between torts and claims for damages for infringements of constitutional rights "in some contexts"; it was "unnecessary to embark on those uncharted seas". Barrington J did not even consider it necessary to decide, for the purposes of the case, whether all breaches of constitutional rights were torts within the meaning of the 1957 Act.

### *Picketing*[264]

**[32.145]** Section 11 of the 1990 Act sets out new entitlements in relation to picketing. This section is generally regarded as the most important one of the Act.

**[32.146]** Picketing is "an immensely powerful weapon which closes the businesses of those against whom it is used."[265] The Irish Courts have taken the view that, until it was legalised by the Trade Disputes Act 1906, picketing when pursued in contemplation or

260. For criticism of Costello P's attempt to find a principled basis for the dysjunction in *W v Ireland* (No 2) [1997] 2 IR 141, see Byrne & Binchy, *Annual Review of Irish Law 1997*.

261. It can hardly be the case that courts are obliged, when they come across a tort that is "basically ineffective" under Henchy J's test, to proceed down the avenue of infringement of constitutional rights rather than reformulate the tort on more effective principles. The *stare decisis* principle was never so imprisoning and cases such as *Purtill v Athlone UDC* [1968] IR 205 prove the contrary.

262. Supreme Court, 23 July 1997.

263. [1987] ILRM 651 (HC).

264. See Kerr, *The Trade Union and Industrial Relations Acts of Ireland* (1991), pp 190-193; Kerr & Whyte *Irish Trade Union Law* (1985), Ch 10; Hogan & Whyte, *Kelly: The Irish Constitution* (3rd ed, 1994), pp 964-966; *RWDSU Local 558 v Pepsi-Cola Canada Beverages (West) Ltd* (1998) 167 DLR (4th) 220 (Sask CA); Anon 'How Far Can a "Picket" Go?' (1966) 100 ILT & Sol J 265.

265. *Goulding Chemicals Ltd v Bolger* [1977] IR 211 at 239 (SC). In *Educational Co of Ireland Ltd v Fitzpatrick (No 2)* [1961] IR 345 at 390 (SC) Kingsmill Moore J stated that "... picketing is in the words of counsel in this case 'a murderous weapon'" ... See also *Ryan v Cooke* [1938] IR 512 (HC); *Brendan Dunne Ltd v Fitzpatrick* [1958] IR 29 at 43 (HC).

furtherance of a trade dispute was "an illegal activity".[266] In *Educational Company of Ireland Ltd v Fitzpatrick (No 2)*,[267] Kingsmill Moore J was willing to admit that it might perhaps be possible to picket a premises so discreetly and unobtrusively as not to cause any intimidation or interference with the proper and convenient use of the premises but it did not seem to him that picketing "as ordinarily conducted" fell within this category.

**[32.147]** It may be useful to set out in full the terms of s 11 of the 1990 Act (which replaces, with modification, s 2 of the 1906 Act):

> (1) It shall be lawful for one or more persons, acting on their own behalf or on behalf of a trade union in contemplation or furtherance of a trade dispute, to attend at, or where that is not practicable, at the approaches to, a place where their employer works or carries on business, if they so attend merely for the purpose of peacefully obtaining or communicating information or of peacefully persuading any person to work or abstain from working.
>
> (2) It shall be lawful for one or more persons acting on their own behalf or on behalf of a trade union in contemplation or furtherance of a trade dispute, to attend at, or where that is not practicable, at the approaches to, a place where an employer who is not a party to the trade dispute works or carries on business if, but only if, it is reasonable for those who are so attending to believe at the commencement of their attendance and throughout the continuance of their attendance that that employer has directly assisted their employer who is a party to the trade dispute for the purpose of frustrating the strike or other industrial action, provided that such attendance is merely for the purpose of peacefully obtaining or communicating information or of peacefully persuading any person to work or abstain from working.
>
> (3) For the avoidance of doubt any action taken by an employer in the health services to maintain life-preserving services during a strike or other industrial action shall not constitute assistance for the purposes of subs (2).
>
> (4) It shall be lawful for a trade union official to accompany any member of his union whom he represents provided that the member is acting in accordance with the provisions of subs (1) or (2) and provided that such official is attending merely for the purpose of peacefully obtaining or communicating information or of peacefully persuading any person to work or abstain from work.
>
> (5) For the purpose of this section 'trade union official' means any paid official of a trade union or any officer of a union or branch of a union elected or appointed in accordance with the rules of a union.

**[32.148]** Before we examine the substance of these immunities it may be helpful to note how the courts have interpreted two key phrases which appear in s 11 and which were also a feature of s 2 of the 1906 Act. Section 11 has not so far generated any judicial analysis so we refer to decisions dealing with s 2 of the 1906 legislation.

---

266. *Educational Co of Ireland Ltd v Fitzpatrick (No 2)* [1961] IR 345 at 398 (SC). See also *Esplande Pharmacy Ltd v Larkin* [1957] IR 285 at 291 and 298 (SC). Not all English decisions have taken this view: *cf Hubbard v Pitt* [1976] QB 142 at 176 (CA) - and the cases therein cited; see also Kerr, *The Trade Union and Industrial Relations Acts of Ireland* (1991); Kerr & Whyte *Irish Trade Union Law* (1985), pp 283-288.

267. [1961] IR 345 at 391 (SC).

*(i) "Peacefully obtaining or communicating information"*

**[32.149]** It is clear that fairly strict limits have been set on what constitutes "peacefully obtaining or communicating information". In *Ryan v Cooke*,[268] Johnson J stated that:

> "it cannot be described as a 'peaceful' way of 'communicating information', to disseminate a falsehood."

**[32.150]** Thus an injunction was granted against picketers who carried placards which stated (incorrectly) that "This firm refuses to employ trade union labour." Nevertheless the Courts do not require that all statements be strictly accurate, provided they do not mislead those whom they are designed to influence. In *Quigley v Beirne*,[269] the picketers called out "strike on here" -which was inaccurate since there was (at best) a trade dispute rather than a strike in progress. Dixon J in the High Court stated:

> "This is probably strictly correct but I doubt if the general public would make any practical difference between the phrases 'trade dispute on here' and 'strike on here'; and I would not have been disposed to grant an injunction solely by reason of this matter."[270]

**[32.151]** Dixon J found that no trade dispute was in existence. The Supreme Court reversed him on that question. In regard to the picketing, Maguire CJ noted that, while Dixon J considered that the inscription on the placards[271] referring to a "strike on here" did not make any practical difference "care should be taken in future to avoid such mis-statements".[272]

**[32.152]** In *Esplanade Pharmacy Ltd v Larkin*,[273] something more than technical inaccuracy was involved. A placard contained "a definitely misleading statement",[274] namely, a reference to "maintaining trade union conditions", which "would convey to any member of the public that, in some way, trade union conditions were being broken on the premises".[275] In fact the breach of agreement related to the separate matter of hours of *opening* of a pharmacy as opposed to hours of *employment* of any employee therein. Dixon J said of the misstatement:

> "I think that would mislead any member of the public, and should, itself, be restrained."[276]

**[32.153]** However, since picketing in any shape or form was being restrained, no specific order in this regard was necessary.[277]

---

268. [1938] IR 512 at 522 (HC).
269. [1955] IR 62 (HC revd by SC).
270. [1955] IR 62 at 69.
271. In fact Dixon J had referred not to placards but to "the calling out of 'strike on here' by the picket ..." (p. 69).
272. [l955] IR 73.
273. [1957] IR 285 (HC affd by SC).
274. [1957] IR 285 at 289.
275. [1957] IR 285 at 289.
276. [1957] IR 285 at 289.
277. In the appeal to the Supreme Court, wherein Dixon J was affirmed, this question did not arise.

**[32.154]** It would appear that recommending persons to trade elsewhere does not fall within the protection afforded by s 11 of the 1990 Act. In *Ryan v Cooke*,[278] a case decided under the 1906 legislation, Johnson J stated:

> "Furthermore, the trade union had no right in the course of carrying out a picketing of a business firm to recommend the public to go to a rival shop. Section 2 of the Act does not suggest any such procedure."

**[32.155]** Abusive or threatening language will not fall within the protection afforded to peaceful communication of information (nor, as we shall see, to that afforded to peaceful persuasion).

**[32.156]** In *El Co v Kennedy*,[279] Walsh J stated:

> "The use of words such as 'scab' or 'blackleg' [is] historically so associated with social ostracism and physical violence as to be far beyond anything which might be described as mere rudeness or impoliteness and goes] beyond what is permitted by law.

**[32.157]** In the present context the references made to the race or nationality of the employers[280] could produce the same disorderly response and also go beyond what is permitted by law."

*(ii) "Peaceful persuasion"*

**[32.158]** As we have seen s 11 of the 1990 Act protects picketing where the purpose is that of "peacefully persuading any person to work or abstain from working". Thus, no protection will be afforded to those who picket in order to frighten or intimidate.[281] Such a purpose may be established "by the manner of picketing or the numbers involved".[282]

**[32.159]** In *Brendan Dunne Ltd v Fitzpatrick*,[283] Budd J gave some guidance on the practical application of this criterion:

> "The use of menaces, threats or the use of force are [*sic*] clearly not permissible ... But it seems to me that picketing is not lawful also if the methods adopted are such as to overawe those who happen to be on the premises being picketed or the members of the public who might be minded to have business dealings with them, to the extent that people of ordinary nerve and courage may be prevented from doing what they have a lawful right to do. The method of picketing must be reasonable having regard to all the circumstances. It would not be justifiable I feel to place a picket consisting of a hundred or so persons on a small suburban business premises with one or two of a staff. On the other hand, it might be quite reasonable to place several quite large pickets on a large factory with several entrances. It is

278. [1938] IR 512 at 522 (HC). This statement was followed in *Brendan Dunne Ltd v Fitzpatrick* [1958] IR 29 (HC), being interpreted as clearly part of the *ratio decidendi* of *Ryan v Cooke*. See also *Toppin v Feron* (1909) 43 ILTR 190 (KBD); Anon 'Pickets in Trade Dispute: "Communicating information"' [1932] LJ Ir 8.

279. [1968] IR 69 at 91 (SC). The emotive resonances of the expression "scab" can still cause difficulties: see *Sheriff v Corrigan* Supreme Court, 15 February 2000.

280. The company was an industrial enterprise in Shannon airport: some of the placards read: "Yankee you can't dictate" and an employee of the company was addressed verbally by persons using the same word.

281. *Goulding Chemicals Ltd v Bolger* [1977] IR 211 at 232 (SC).

282. Industrial Relations Act 1990, s 11. See also *EI Co Ltd v Kennedy* [1968] IR 69 at 91 (SC).

283. [1958] IR 29 at 43-44 (HC).

a matter of degree according to the circumstances, and the number of the pickets should bear reasonable relations to the nature of the premises and the number of persons with whom the dispute arises."

**[32.160]** In *EI Co v Kennedy*,[284] Walsh J made it clear that excessive numbers in pickets, when going beyond what is reasonably permissible for the communication or obtaining of information "may amount to obstruction or nuisance .. ." This would suggest that, even where no question of intimidation or undue pressure were involved, resort to excessive numbers could place the picketers outside the scope of s 2 of the 1906 Act.

**[32.161]** In this context it is worth noting the English decision of *News Group Newspapers Ltd v SOGAT*.[285] There Stuart-Smith J held that a person continues to organise events which, in the light of experience amount to nuisance or other tort and in the knowledge or presumed knowledge that such nuisance or other tort is being committed by those whom he organises, he may be taken to have authorised the commission of the tort, particularly where he can control the event and conduct of those taking part, but fails to take any adequate steps to do so. Liability would attach even where the defendant may not encourage the tortious conduct and indeed condemns it. On this basis, those who organise picketing where previous events have shown that this is likely to result in a nuisance by obstruction may be held liable, by analogy with the *Sedleigh-Denfield*[286] principle of private nuisance.

***Primary and secondary picketing***

**[32.162]** Under the 1906 Act, the courts found considerable difficulty with the legal distinctions attaching to "primary" and "secondary" picketing.[287] Section 11 now clarifies the position: sub-s (1) deals with primary picketing; sub-s (2) with secondary picketing.

*(i) Primary picketing*

**[32.163]** Primary picketing involves attendance "at or where that is not practicable, at the approaches to, a place where th[e] employer[288] [of the picketer] works or carries on business". It is not enacted that the picketer actually work at this place himself or herself.

**[32.164]** In *Westman Holidays Ltd v McCormack*,[289] the Supreme Court accepted that the defendant picketers had raised a fair *bona fide* question on the issue when they argued that the words "their employer" must be construed as including an "alleged employer", in the

284. [1968] IR 69 at 91 (SC).

285. [1986] IRLR 337 (HC) critically analysed by Auerbach 'Legal Restraint of Picketing: New Trends New Tensions' (1987) 16 Ind LJ 227 at 237-239.

286. *Sedleigh-Denfield v O'Callaghan* [1940] AC 880.

287. See the second edition of this work pages 590-591. See also Kerr & Whyte *Irish Trade Union Law* (1985), pp 305-308; Kerr 'In Contemplation or Furtherance of a Trade Dispute' [1979-80] Dublin ULJ 59 at 82-87; *Ellis v Wright* [1976] IR 8 (HC); *AH Masser Ltd v 12 Un-named members of AGEMOU* High Court, 23 October 1979 (McWilliam J); *Cleary v Coffey* High Court, 30 October 1979 (McWilliam J). *Cf RWDSU Local 558 v Pepsi-Cola Canada Beverages West Ltd* (1998) 167 DLR (4th) 220 (Sask CA).

288. Section 11(1). Under s 2(1) of the 1906 Act was broader in scope permitting picketing "at or near a house or place where a person resides or works or carries on business or happens to be".

289. [1992] 1 IR 151 (SC).

sense of a person claimed by a worker to have a contract of employment with the worker or an obligation to employ him or her, as otherwise s 11(1) would lose its obvious purpose of protecting picketing in support of a dispute covering non-employment. In this case the picketers had been employed as bar staff at a licensed premises. Their employer had sold the premises, fixtures and fittings and the benefit of the licence to the plaintiff; before his sale was completed, he had dismissed the defendants. The defendants sought employment, unsuccessfully, from the plaintiff and later placed a picket on the premises when it re-opened. The plaintiff argued that it was not "their employer", as it had never employed them. The defendants replied that, by virtue of European Community Law on safeguarding employees' rights on the transfer of undertakings,[290] a notation of their contract with their former employer had been furnished and that accordingly their demand for the enforcement of this notated contract of employment fell within the scope of s 11(1). The Supreme Court accepted that a fair question had been raised on both sides of this argument.

**[32.165]** It may be noted that s 11(1) authorises picketing, not only *at* a place where the employer works or carries on business, but also *at the approaches* to such a place where it is *not practicable* to picket at the place. The legislation does not seek to define the phrase "at the approaches". It leaves this to common-sense judicial interpretation. The question of the practicability of picketing at the place where the employer works or carries on business should, on the basis of the language, be an objective test, no doubt taking into account that strategic decisions in industrial relations have to be made on the basis of information that is less than ideal.

**[32.166]** As regards the potential application of the tort of trespass to land, there is authority relating to s 2(1) of the 1906 Act which supports the lawfulness of picketing on the highway close to the premises identified as a legitimate target by the legislation. In *Ferguson v O'Gorman*,[291] the Supreme Court held that picketing on the highway beside the relevant premises was authorised, O'Sullivan J stating:

> "When legislation declared it lawful for persons to attend at or near a house or place where a person resides or works, or carries on 'business', it cannot reasonably have been contemplated that such a house or place would be situated in a waste or no man's land. The usual approach to a residence or place of business is by a public highway and unless the right to attend at or near a residence or place of business is a right to attend on a public highway, I do not see how such a right can be exercised at all, consistently with the decisions in *Larkin's* Case[292] and *McCusker's* Case[293] that private property may not be invaded."[294]

**[32.167]** We should note here the (remote) possibility that a constitutionally-derived argument[295] may override or modify the scope of the protection afforded by s 11(1), especially where the premises subjected to a picket have some "public" dimension as in the

---

290. European Communities (Safeguarding of Employees; Rights on Transfer of Undertakings) Regulations 1980, (SI 306/1980) implementing Council Directive 77/187/EEC of 14 January 1977.

291. [1937] IR 620 (SC). See also *Ryan v Cooke* [1938] IR (HC).

292. *Larkin v Belfast Harbour Commissioners* [1908] 2 IR 214.

293. *McCusker v Smith* [1918] 2 IR 432.

294. [1937] IR 620 at 648.

295. The argument relies on a robust interpretation of speech rights.

case of a shopping centre. An argument on these basis received the support of Laskin CJ, dissenting, in the Supreme Court of Canada decision of *Harrison v Carswell*.[296] First Amendment rights under the United States Constitution have been interpreted as affording some degree of protection to striking workers in this type of case.[297]

*(ii) Secondary picketing*

**[32.168]** Section 11(2) restricts the right to engage in secondary picketing which had been permitted under the 1906 Act.[298] Attendance at a place[299] where an employer who is *not* a party to the trade dispute works or carries on business is permitted only if it is *reasonable* for those who are so attending to believe from the start and throughout the period of their attendance that that employer has *directly* assisted their employer who is a party to the trade dispute *for the purpose of frustrating the strike or other industrial action.*

**[32.169]** In this context any action taken by an employer in the health services to maintain life-preserving services during a strike or other industrial action does *not* constitute assistance of the employer of the picketers.[300]

**[32.170]** A few points should be noted about the subsection. First, it is not necessary that the picketed employer should *actually* have directly assisted the picketers' employer: it is sufficient if the picketers *reasonably believe* that this was so. Secondly, the belief must be that the picketed employers *directly assisted* the picketers' employer for the purpose of frustrating the strike or other industrial action. The legislation offers no guidance as to the scope of these expressions. It would seem that merely acting for one's own benefit as a result of the gap created by the strike or other industrial action will not suffice. The picketed employer must in the reasonable belief of the picketers have known of the picketers' employers difficulties and have acted with the actual purpose of frustrating the employees' actions, such action being sufficiently potent as to the amount to direct assistance to the picketed employer in respect of frustrating the strike of other industrial action.

*(iii) Role of trade union officials*

**[32.171]** Trade union officials may accompany union members on either a primary or secondary picketing provided the members act in accordance with the provisions of s 11(1) and (2) provided the officials attend merely for the purpose of peacefully obtaining

---

296. [1976] SCR 200 analysed by Ulmer 'Picketing in Shopping Centres' (1979) 13 Os HLJ 879. *Cf Rosso v Ontario Jockey Club* (1987) 46 DLR (4th) 359 at 363 (Ont HC). In Australia, the claim by tresspassing trade unionists to immunity by virtue of Articles 19 and 22 of the International Convenant on Civil and Political Rights was given short shrift by Norling J in *Concrete Constructions (NSW) Pty Ltd v Australian Building Construction Employees and Builders Labourers' Federation* (1988) 86 ALR 385 (Fed Court of Austr Gen Div).

297. See Stein (1998) 73 NY ULR 2029; Goss John, (1996) 57 La LR 361; Zuiga (1994) 12 Hofstra Lab LJ 65.

298. See the second edition of this work pages 590-591.

299. Or where that is not practicable, the approaches to that place. The test on this issue is expressed in the same terms for both primary and secondary picketing.

300. Section 11(3).

communicating information or of peacefully persuading any person to work or abstain from working.[301]

*The requirement of secret ballots*

**[32.172]** Section 14 - "[p]erhaps the most revolutionary provision of ... Part II [of the Act]"[302] - prescribes significant requirements as to the holding of secret ballots. These requirements, important in their own right, have certain crucial consequences in relation to the law of tort. The mere fact that there has been a breach of these requirements does not of itself render a strike or other industrial action unlawful.[303] The sanctions nonetheless are awesome. Trade unions that do not submit to the Registrar of Friendly Societies a copy of their rules as to the statutory ballots will lose their recognition licence (and thus, thereafter, the protection of ss 11 to 13).[304] Moreover, in proceedings relating to a strike or other industrial action by a trade union or group of workers in disregard of or contrary to the outcome of a secret ballot relating to the issues involved in the dispute, the defendants are prohibited from calling ss 10, 11 or 12 in aid.[305] Finally, compliance with the statutory requirements as to secret ballots gives those engaging in a strike or other industrial action extra entitlements to resist the granting of an *ex parte* injunction on behalf of the employers as well as interlocutory injunctions in many cases.[306]

*Restriction of right to an injunction*

**[32.173]** Section 19 provides that, where a secret ballot held in accordance with the requirements of s 14 favours a strike or industrial action and the trade union has given the employer at least a week's notice of its intention to engage in the strike or other industrial action, the employer may not apply *ex parte* for an injunction.[307] Nor may the court grant an injunction restraining the strike or other industrial action where the respondent establishes a fair case that he or she was acting in contemplation or furtherance of a trade dispute.[308] Neither of these restrictions applies in respect of proceedings arising out of or relating to:

(a) unlawfully entering into or remaining upon any property belonging to another, or unlawfully causing damage or causing or permitting damage to be caused to the property of another, or

(b) any action resulting or likely to result in death or personal injury.[309]

---

301. Section 11(4). The term "trade union official" embraces any paid official of a trade union or any officer of a union, or branch of a union elected, or appointed in accordance with the rules of a union: s 11(5).

302. *Nolan Transport (Oaklands) Ltd v Halligan* [1998] ELR 177 at 195 (SC).

303. *Cf* [1998] ELR 177 at 195 at 196.

304. Sections 9(1) and 16.

305. Section 17(1). It is clear, however, that a union engaging in a strike or other individual action, in disregard of the wishes of its members expressed in a secret ballot does not forfeit the immunity conferred on it by s 13: See *Nolan Transport (Oaklands) Ltd v Halligan* [1998] ELR 177 at 197.

306. Section 19.

307. Section 19(1).

308. Section 11(2).

309. Section 11(3).

**[32.174]** Thus malicious damage, violence, threats and even hunger-strikes do not render a respondent immune from an injunction on the basis that he or she has established a fair case that he was acting in contemplation or furtherance of a trade dispute.

**[32.175]** In one important respect, s 19 gives rise to constitutional difficulties. Subsection (2) is drafted in such a way as to prevent the court from granting an injunction, even at the suit of a third party, simply on account of the existence of a fair case that the respondent was acting in contemplation or furtherance of a trade dispute. As we have seen, in many instances, it will be no defence in a tort action for the respondent to establish the fact that he or she was so acting. If, for example, the strike was having the effect of inducing a breach of a commercial contract (as in *Talbot*)[310] or interfering with a school pupils' constitutional right to education (as in *Conway v INTO*),[311] s 19(2) would require the court to stand idly by while the innocent third party's economic or educational interests, constitutional and legal, were being damaged by a tortfeasor who has no statable defense and where the balance of convenience was strongly in favour of granting an injunction. Strikes can last a long time. This frustration of the administration of justice may be considered to infringe the victim's constitutional rights; it may also offend against the separation of the powers. It is of course a worthwhile legislative policy to use "carrots" such as s 19(2) to encourage adherence by trade unions to the statutory requirements on ballots; but this is hardly so pressing a *desideratum* at to warrant such overreach. The qualification in sub-s (4) goes some way, but arguably not sufficiently far, to preserve the constitutional validity of the section as a whole. As to the likelihood of s 19(2)'s being struck down on constitutional grounds, it must be said that this is unlikely, if the judicial attitude towards the 1990 Act which was manifested in *Nolan*[312] continues to hold sway.

**[32.176]** It may be useful at this point to quote s 19(2) in its entirety because the courts have found difficulty in interpreting precisely where the onus of proof lies on the question of the secret ballot. It provides as follows:

> Where a secret ballot has been held in accordance with the rules of a trade union as provided for in section 14, the outcome of which or, in the case of an aggregation of ballots, the outcome of the aggregate ballots, favours a strike or other industrial action and the trade union before engaging in the strike or other industrial actions gives notice of not less than one week to the employer concerned of its intention to do so, a court shall not grant an injunction restraining the strike or other industrial action where the respondent establishes a fair case that he was acting in contemplation or furtherance of a trade dispute.

**[32.177]** In *G & Crampton Ltd v Building & Allied Trade Union*,[313] the Supreme Court, in an *ex tempore* judgment, grappled with the meaning of this provision.

**[32.178]** In *Crampton*, the defendants had placed a picket on the plaintiff's premises. Laffoy J granted an interlocutory injunction. She held that a fair case had been made out

---

310. *Talbot (Ireland) Ltd v ATGWU* Supreme Court, 1981, Irish Times, 1 May 1981 extracted in McMahon & Binchy, *Casebook on the Irish Law of Torts* (2nd ed ,1991).
311. [1991] 2 IR 305 (SC). See also *Crowley v Ireland* [1980] IR 102 (SC); *Hayes v Ireland* [1987] ILRM 651 (HC).
312. *Nolan Transport (Oaklands) Ltd v Halligan* [1998] ELR 177 (SC).
313. [1998] 1 ILRM 420 (SC).

by the defendants that they had been acting in contemplation or furtherance of a trade dispute. She concluded that there was "no evidence whatever before the court" as to the outcome of the secret ballot conducted by the union and in particular that there was no evidence that its outcome favoured picketing the site. On this ground alone she was satisfied that there was no evidence before the court that one of the preconditions stipulated in s 19(2) had been complied with.

**[32.179]** On appeal to the Supreme Court, the defendants argued that this issue had not been raised in the affidavit filed on behalf of the plaintiff and that they had not the opportunity of dealing satisfactorily with the point in view of the shortness of time and the manner in which the case was dealt with.

**[32.180]** Hamilton CJ[314] noted that a question arose by way of interpretation of the legislation as to whether a notice relating to a "strike or other industrial action", without purporting to particularise the nature of the industrial action sought to be taken, had sufficient specificity to comply with terms of ss 14 and 19. On this issue alone there was a fair question to be tried. There was also a fair question to be tried as to the need in all circumstances for the ballot to be investigated for the purpose of ascertaining whether or not the members, whom it was reasonable to expect at the time would be called on to engage in the strike or other industrial action, had been give a fair opportunity of voting. The ballot papers had not contained the proposal on which the members were being called to ballot. Whether the ballot paper was adequate to comply with the requirements of s 14 or the rules of that trade union was also a relevant issue that arose in the case.

**[32.181]** Hamilton CJ invoked Finlay CJ's judgment in *Westman Holidays Ltd v McCormack*,[315] to the effect that, once the court was satisfied that the plaintiff had raised a fair question to be tried, the court should not express any view on the strength of the contending submissions on that question but should proceed to consider the other matters then arising in regard to the granting of an interlocutory injunction.

**[32.182]** Hamilton CJ was satisfied that the affidavits disclosed a fair question to be tried on the issue of whether the provisions of s 11(1) applied to the defendants and also that "a number of questions" stood to be determined with regard to the interpretation of ss 14 and 19 regarding the specificity of the terms of the notice and the absence of an actual proposal on the ballot paper. That being so, Laffoy J had been entitled to come to the conclusion that the condition precedent to the implementation of s 19 had not been complied with. Accordingly the appeal was dismissed.

**[32.183]** The outcome of the appeal seems well justified but the basis on which the Chief Justice came to his decision can be questioned. Section 19(2) requires the court to refuse an injunction where (a) the respondent establishes a fair case that he was acting in contemplation of or furtherance of a trade dispute and (b) a secret ballot has been held in accordance with the rules of the trade union which favours the strike or other industrial action and (c) the requisite period of one week's notice has been given. It says nothing about the court having to concern itself as to whether there is a fair question to be tried. In

314. O'Flaherty and Barrington JJ concurring.

315. [1992] 1 IR 151 at 157 (SC).

the instant case, Laffoy J had come to the firm conclusion to the contrary: that there was "no evidence whatever" before the court as to the outcome of the secret ballot; there was thus "no evidence before the court that one of the preconditions stipulated in s 19(2) ha[d] been complied with". It was mistaken for the Supreme Court to try to read into requirements (b) and (c) the "fair case" test appropriate to requirement (a). Laffoy J's finding should have been let stand undiluted by a "fair case" modification which finds no basis in the provisions of s 19(2).

**[32.184]** The Supreme Court in *Crampton* made no reference to Keane J's earlier analysis of s 19(2) in proceedings for an interlocutory injunction in *Nolan Transport (Oaklands) Ltd v Halligan*.[316] What he had to say is worthy of quotation *in extenso*:

> "[W]hilst there appears to be no authority on the section, it seems to me as a matter of first impression that the onus must be on the person resisting an injunction to establish that the provision of section 14 have been completed with, which seems to me to be crucial to the operation of the section. If the section has been complied with, then the Oireachtas goes on to provide for this unusual and special situation where the court must apply particular consideration to the granting of an interlocutory injunction, considerations which otherwise would not apply. Before a trade union is afforded the protection of section 19 and conversely, an employer is deprived of the protection that he would normally have at common law in relation to the obtaining of an interlocutory injunction in circumstances where his business is or could be affected, I would take the view that the court must be satisfied on the evidence before it that section 14 has been complied with."[317]

**[32.185]** When the case came to the Supreme Court[318] after plenary hearing, Murphy J gave an analysis of the issue of the onus of proof. Discretely distancing himself from what the Supreme Court had held in *Crampton*, on the basis that "there has not been a definitive interpretation of s 19(2)",[319] Murphy J said that he "would find it difficult to escape the conclusion reached by Keane J and accepted by Laffoy J,[320] that the onus lay on the party resisting the application for an interlocutory injunction to show that a secret ballot as envisaged by s 14 had been held. It could "hardly be sufficient"[321] to establish the existence of a stateable case on compliance with the rules that s 14 required a union to adopt. Murphy J acknowledged the practical problems that followed from placing the onus of proof in regard to this issue on the union:

> "The decision of a court on an interlocutory application as to whether or not the particular injunction is granted by section 19(2) is available is itself a final decision and determines finally whether that statutory benefit is available to the trade union. Concern must exist as to how decisions of that nature could be made in practice. There may be serious difficulty, and even a degree of inequality, in requiring the court to make an actual determination on the balance of probabilities as to whether all of the requirements of the secret ballot have been complied with when the substantive issue itself is dealt with at that stage on the basis of 'a serious question to be tried'."[322]

---

316. 10 JISLL 105 (HC).
317. 10 JISLL 105 at 108.
318. *Nolan Transport (Oaklands) Ltd v Halligan* [1998] ELR 177 (SC).
319. *Nolan Transport (Oaklands) Ltd v Halligan* [1998] ELR 177 at 199-200.
320. *Nolan Transport (Oaklands) Ltd v Halligan* [1998] ELR 177 at 200.
321. *Nolan Transport (Oaklands) Ltd v Halligan* [1998] ELR 177.
322. *Nolan Transport (Oaklands) Ltd v Halligan* [1998] ELR 177.

# Chapter 33

# Torts Affecting Family Relations


I. Introduction ........ 867
II. Damages for Loss of Consortium ........ 868
III. Seduction ........ 875
IV. Enticement and Harbouring of a Child ........ 875
V. Action for the Loss of a Child's Services ........ 878


## I. INTRODUCTION

**[33.01]** Tort law, through a variety of actions, affords members of a family some protection against intentional and negligent interference in their relationships with each other.[1] The structure of these actions is antiquated, being based on fictions which have been regarded with increasing distaste in the community in recent times. The Family Law Act 1981 abolished a number of the actions.[2]

**[33.02]** It is worth noting, at the outset of our analysis, that, if these old actions had never existed, courts today would have had to confront the issues they deal with through other mechanisms, notably the tort of negligence[3] or, more speculatively, the constitutional protection of family and personal rights.[4] The fact that the old actions are, to a greater or lesser extent, in decline (some having been extinguished) seems to have discouraged a number of courts from propounding bold applications of the duty of care. Perhaps judicial thinking on these matters will become more innovative in future years.

**[33.03]** One should also be sensitive to the broader social, legal and philosophical contexts. There have been significant changes in the structure of families in Ireland and

1. See Bailey 'A Married Woman's Right of Action for Loss of Consortium in Alberta' (1979) 17 Alta LR 513.
2. The Family Law Act 1981 abolished the torts of criminal conversation, enticement and harbouring of spouses. For a detailed treatment of these torts see the first edition of this work pp 407-412. In England the trend towards statutory abolition has been more marked: *cf* the Law Reform (Miscellaneous Provisions) Act 1970, ss 4 and 5 and the Administration of Justice Act 1982, s 2 based on the Law Reform Committee's *Eleventh Report (Loss of Services etc)* (1963), Cmnd 2017 and the English Law Commission's WP 19 *The Actions for Loss of Services Loss of Consortium, Seduction and Entitlement* (1968). The same trend towards abolition of the common law actions (especially those with a sexual component) is apparent in Australia, Canada and the United States: see Kutner *Law Reform in Tort: Abolition of Liability for "Intentional" Interference with Family Relationships* (1987) 6 Can J of Family L 287; FLEMING, pp 746-750.
3. *Cf* eg *Marx v AG* [1974] 1 NZLR 164 (SC), criticised by Binchy 'Note: Duty and Foresight in Negligence: The 'Control Devices' Out of Control' (1975) 38 MLR 468; *Mulholland v Murphy & Co Ltd* (1943) 77 ILTR 212 (CC); *Jones v Jones* [1985] QB 704; *Pritchard v JH Cobden Ltd* [1987] 1 All ER 300 (CA); Juss, 'Comment' [1987] Camb LJ 210; Hepple 'Tort' [1987] All ER Ann Rev at 299-300.
4. See *Hosford v John Murphy & Sons* [1988] ILRM 300 (HC) discussed para **[33.19]-[33.23]**.

internationally in the past couple of decades. Article 41 of the Constitution was amended in 1995 to provide for divorce.[5] The Status of Children Act 1987 removed many of the legal distinctions based on the marital status of a child's parents.[6] The courts in recent years have tended to place a growing emphasis on privacy[7] and autonomy[8] as constitutional values. Married women's participation in the workplace outside the home has increased radically in the past decade. The rights of children as individual persons rather than simply as members of a family have also been stressed.[9]

## II. Damages for Loss of Consortium

**[33.04]** For many centuries the courts recognised the right of a husband to sue for damages for the tortious interference with his wife's *consortium.*[10] The right was originally based on the husband's position as master of the household, but gradually the element of *consortium* was stressed more than that of *servitium.*[11]

**[33.05]** The question whether a wife might be entitled to sue for the loss of *consortium* of her husband proved controversial.[12] In England, in *Best v Samuel Fox & Co Ltd,*[13] the

5. By the Fifteenth Amendment of the Constitution on 24 November 1995. The proposal was supported by 818,842 (50.28%) and opposed by 809,728 (49.72%). The legislative framework is contained in the Family Law (Divorce) Act 1996. For analysis see Shatter, *Family Law* (4th ed, 1997), Ch 9.

6. For analysis see Shatter's, *Family Law* (4th ed, 1997), Ch 19; Byrne & Binchy, *Annual Review of Irish Law 1987.* The 1987 legislation fell short of complete abolition of the legal distinctions contrary to the recommendations of the Law Reform Commission in its *Report on Illegitimacy* (LRC 4-1982). This has led to conflict with the European Convention on Human Rights: *Keegan v Ireland* (1994) 18 EHRR 342.

7. *Cf Re a Ward of Court* [1995] 2 ILRM 401 (SC) analysed by Byrne & Binchy, *Annual Review of Irish Law 1995.* See further Ch 37 below.

8. *Re a Ward of Court* [1995] 2 ILRM 401 (SC).

9. See eg *Re Article 26 and the Adoption (No 2) Bill 1987* [1989] IR 334; *Southern Health Board v CH* [1996] 2 ILRM 142 (SC).

10. See Note 'Judicial Treatment of Negligent Invasion of Consortium' (1961) 61 Col LR 1341; Payne 'Tortious Invasion of the Right of Marital Consortium' (1968) 8 J of Family L 41 at 50-54, 56-57. Anon 'Loss of Consortium in Admiralty: A Yet Unsettled Question' [1977] Brigham Young ULR 133 at 134-136; Thorton 'Loss of Consortium: Inequality Before the Law' (1984) 10 Sydney LR 259; Harris 'Note' (1964) 8 St Louis ULJ 142; Hesse 'Comment: Wife's Cause of Action for Loss of Consortium Due to a Negligent Injury to Her Husband' (1966) 10 St Louis ULJ 276; Handford 'Relatives' Rights and *Best v Samuel Fox*' (1979) 14 UW Austr LR 79; Little 'Consortium: A Survey of the Present Law' (1981) 19 J of Family L 707; Lindsey 'Note: A More Equitable Approach to Loss of Spiusal Consortium' (199) 75 Iowa LR 713. The wife may of course be compensated by the wrongdoer for the injuries sustained by her by reason of the tort committed against her: *cf W v CIE* [1967] IR 137 (SC).

11. A Canadian decision *Jones v Taylor* (1983) 27 CCLT 84 (Sask QB) holds that no compensation should be allowed to a husband for loss of commercial advantages by reason of the injury of his wife: the husband who was blind, ran a modest family beekeeping operation with the extensive assistance of his wife. This business was significantly interfered with when his wife was injured. The decision may be compared with *Chapman v McDonald* [1969] IR 188 (HC) para **[33.37]**.

12. See Leaphart & McCann 'Consortium: An Action for the Wife'(1970) 34 Montana LR 75; Peterson 'A Wife's Right to Recover for the Loss of Consortium' (1971) 2 Cumb-Sanf LR 189; Taylor 'Note' (1952) 1 Clev-Mar LR No 1 173; Weisman 'Wife's Action for Loss of Consortium' (1971) 20 Clev St LR 315; Oberhellmann & Comeau 'Loss of Consortium: Damages Available to a Wife in Missouri' (1984) 40 J of Mo Bar 99.

13. [1952] AC 716 (HL (Eng)).

House of Lords rejected the wife's claim, considering that the action was anomalous and unworthy of extension to both sexes.

**[33.06]** The matter came before the Irish Supreme Court in *McKinley v Minister for Defence*,[14] in 1992. The plaintiff's husband, a member of the Defence Forces, had been severely injured in an explosion caused by the negligence of the defendant, which resulted in a condition of sterility and impotence. By a majority of three to two,[15] the Supreme Court held that the plaintiff had stated a good cause of action. The majority discerned in the old action for loss of *consortium* elements which were of contemporary significance and value. Both O'Flaherty and Hederman JJ stressed the fact that the Constitution (at that time[16]) gave marriage a special recognition and prescribed that no law was to be enacted providing for the dissolution of marriage. This highlighted the need to afford equal rights to both spouses.[17]

## Extent of Recovery

**[33.07]** The extent of recovery is a matter of uncertainty. In England, the House of Lords in *Best v Samuel Fox & Co Ltd*[18] was divided on the question whether the plaintiff had to prove a *total loss of consortium,* but since then the position has been resolved there in favour of recovery even in cases of partial loss.[19] In this country, the Supreme Court, in *Spaight v Dundon*[20] in 1960, held that:

> "There is no doubt that the husband can recover for the medical and surgical expenses which he has been put to by the injury of his wife and for extra domestic expenses in which he has been involved . . . These are pecuniary losses easily ascertained where already incurred and capable of fair estimation for the future. In addition he is entitled to damages for the total deprivation of his wife's company, even if such deprivation is for a limited period or periods. Such damages should not be too generous ... [No] further grounds for awarding damages can be entertained."[21]

---

14. [1992] 2 IR 333 (SC) analysed by Hogan (1992) 14 Dublin ULJ 115; Byrne & Binchy *Annual Review of Irish Law 1992*, pp 613-618.
15. Hederman, McCarthy and O'Flaherty JJ (Finlay CJ and Egan J dissenting).
16. The Fifteenth Amendment to the Constitution introduced a provision for divorce on 24 November 1995. See Shatter, *Family Law* Ch 9, fn 1.
17. McCarthy J's attempt to develop a theory of equality based on "positive rather than negative [judicial] action" is subjected to incisive criticism by Hogan (1992) 14 Dublin ULJ 115 at 117-120.
18. [1952] AC 716 (HL, Eng).
19. *Hare v BTC* [1956] 1 WLR 250; *Lawrence v Biddle* [1966] I QB 504; *Cutts v Chumley* [1967] I WLR 742 (QBD).
20. [1961] IR 201 (SC), analysed by Delany 'Damages for the Impairment of Consortium' (1961) 27 Ir Jur 44; Hudson 'Note: Impairment of Consortium' (1962) 25 MLR 580. See also O'Donovan 'Legal Recognition of the Value of Housework' (1978) 8 Family L 215 at 217-218. *Cf Collier v Dublin Wicklow & Wexford Ry Co* (1873) IR 8 CL 21 (Com Pleas) - railway company was held liable for only nominal damages where a husband sued for breach of contract, alleging the loss of "the service and society" of his wife; an incident at a railway station had resulted in his wife's being locked up there for the night; *per* Lawson J at 23: "... I cannot see that a deprivation of services has taken place, as the [husband] was not at home that night. He cannot therefore recover damages for the exclusion of the wife from the home that night".
21. [1961] IR 201 at 215.

**[33.08]** Four years later, however, in *O'Haran v Divine*,[22] the Supreme Court appeared to qualify this position somewhat. The facts in both cases were similar, involving the separation of the plaintiff and his wife for a long period, during which time she received medical treatment in hospital. In *Spaight v Dundon*,[23] recovery for the damage to the *consortium* was denied on the basis that there had not been a total loss of *consortium* even for a limited period or periods. Yet in *O'Haran v Divine*,[24] recovery was allowed, Kingsmill Moore J stating:

> "It seems to me that the question must be looked at somewhat broadly. A healthy companion and helper was reduced to a condition where she had to be separated from her husband for restoration of her health. All the immunerable advantages, pleasures and consolations of married life were brought to an end - save a limited measure of communication. I hold that such deprivation may and should be regarded as sufficient to give a claim for damages."[25]

**[33.09]** Whilst this finding could possibly be construed as a liberal application of the concept of "total deprivation of [the plaintiff's] wife's company ... for a limited period or periods",[26] the decision of *O'Haran v Divine*[27] may be interpreted more reasonably as a relaxation of the previous requirement that the loss of *consortium* be total, in favour of a more flexible standard.[28]

**[33.10]** In the Supreme Court decision of *McKinley v Minister for Defence*,[29] O'Flaherty J delivered the following *obiter dictum*, by way of guidance to the High Court judge who would be called on to decide the question of quantum of damages:

> "Kingsmill Moore J, in *Spaight v Dundon*,[30] was of opinion that such damages should not be 'too generous'. That precept, of course, applies to any award for damages. However, I think a benchmark might be sought and found in the level of damages that are awarded for mental distress under the Civil Liability Acts in the case of the death of a spouse. It would seem clear in principle that damages for loss of *consortium should be related to those recoverable for the death of a spouse*."[31]

The maximum amount that could be awarded for mental distress in fatal accident cases at that time was £7,500. It was originally £1,000 but had been raised to £7,500 by legislation in 1981. At present it stands at £20,000.[32]

**[33.11]** In the later High Court decision of *Coppinger v Waterford County Council*,[33] where Geoghegan J was called on to assess the import of these observations, it was

---

22. (1964) 100 ILTR 53 (SC).
23. [1961] IR 201.
24. (1964) 100 ILTR 53.
25. (1964) 100 ILTR 53 at 56.
26. *Spaight v Dundon* [1961] IR 201 at 215.
27. (1964) 100 ILTR 53. See also *Toohey v Hollier* (1955) 92 CLR 618.
28. Another judicial strategy adopted in England is to enable an *injured wife* to sue for the loss of her "housekeeping capacity": *Daly v General Steam Navigation Co Ltd* [1980] 3 All ER 696.
29. [1992] 2 IR 333 (SC).
30. [1961] IR 201.
31. [1992] 2 IR 201 at 215. Emphasis added.
32. Courts Act 1981 and now by Civil Liability (Amendment) Act 1996.
33. [1996] 2 ILRM 427 (HC).

apparent that fidelity to the hierarchical principle rather than conviction as to the merits of O'Flaherty J's analysis guided his determination. Geoghegan J thought it necessary, in particular, to note what O'Flaherty J had not said. He had not been suggesting that mental distress for which damages were recoverable was "in any way a similar kind of injury to loss of *consortium*".[34] O'Flaherty J's use of the word "benchmark" indicated to Geoghegan J that he had not been "in anyway suggesting that because there was a particular ceiling under the Civil Liability Acts for damages for mental distress, the same ceiling should also apply to damages for loss of *consortium*".[35]

**[33.12]** Geoghegan J went on to make two further observations. The first was that the court, in actions for loss of *consortium*, should allow for the devaluation of money values in the fifteen years since the Oireachtas in 1981 had fixed the ceiling at £7,500 for mental distress in wrongful death actions. He considered it "illogical"[36] that a wife such as Mrs Coppinger who took her action in 1981 should be awarded the same as Mrs Coppinger fifteen years later, "simply because of the fact that the Oireachtas has never brought that figure up to date".[37]

**[33.13]** Geoghegan J found *O'Haran v Devine*[38] "extremely helpful"[39] on the question of assessment of damages. The figure of £350 awarded in that case would translate into £4,000 on 1996 values. Geoghegan J noted that Mrs Coppinger had already suffered total loss of consortium for ten years and would probably do so for a further sixteen or seventeen years. Her loss was "infinitely worse"[40] than the mental distress which she would have suffered if her husband had died in the accident. Had he done so:

> "she would have been very upset but I think it likely that she would have rebuilt her life. She was and still is an attractive, intelligent woman and there is no reason to believe that she would not have found another husband if she had wished to remarry. Although account must be taken of the fact that she is still able to communicate with her husband, he is not the man she married and I think that she has suffered real agony in her loss of *consortium*"[41].

Accordingly he awarded the plaintiff £60,000.

---

34. [1996] 2 ILRM 427 at 430-431.
35. [1996] 2 ILRM 427 at 431. *Cf* Byrne & Binchy, *Annual Review of Irish Law 1996*, p 615.
36. [1996] 2 ILRM 427 at 431.
37. [1996] 2 ILRM 427 at 431. As noted above fn 32, the limit now has been revised in 1996 to £20,000.
38. (1964) 100 ILTR 53.
39. [1996] 2 ILRM 427 at 431.
40. [1996] 2 ILRM 427 at 432.
41. [1996] 2 ILRM 427 at 432. Geoghegan J's reference to the attractiveness and hypothetical remarital prospects of the plaintiff, raises wider issues in relation to the criteria for awarding damages. In *Reid v Minister for Finance* High Court 29 July 1996 in an application under the Garda Síochána Compensation Acts 1941 and 1945, Budd J quoted at length from Geoghegan J's judgment in *Coppinger*. He observed that:

    > "[i]n assessing compensation in respect of the death of a policeman, judges over the recent years have frequently glanced over the fence at comparatives in the area of loss of *consortium*. Accordingly, I bear in mind Geoghegan J's remarks with regard to loss of *consortium*, at times being infinitely worse than the mental distress suffered by reasons of a husband's death".

**[33.14]** In *McKinley v Minister for Defence (No 2)*,[42] Carney J had to deal with the reference back to the High Court from the Supreme Court[43] on the question of damages. Echoing the veiw's of Maguire CJ (dissenting) in *Spaight v Dundon*[44] and McCarthy J in the Supreme Court in Mc*Kinley*,[45] Carney J held that the common law action for loss of *consortium* extended to a wife's claim for partial as well as total loss or impairment of *consortium*.

**[33.15]** Carney J was assisted by O'Flaherty J's observations[46] that "a benchmark" might be found in the level of damages awarded for mental distress in fatal accident cases. Carney J noted that "[i]t so happen[ed]"[47] that the sum of £7,500 had just been updated by Ministerial Order to £20,000.[48] He accepted O'Flaherty J's guidance by assessing damages "in this updated sum".[49] He noted that in contrast to *Coppinger*, the case before him had not involved the claim that the injuries to the plaintiff were infinitely worse than the mental distress which she would have suffered if her husband had died in the accident.

## Effect of Victim's Contributory Negligence or Other Default

**[33.16]** Section 35(2) of the Civil Liability Act 1961 (as amended) provides that the contributory negligence of "a wife,[50] child or servant" is not to affect the right of the plaintiff in an action brought "for the loss of *consortium* or services of a wife or for the loss of the services of a child or servant".[51] This provision was, of course, clearly premised on the assumption[52] that wives had no right of action for loss of *consortium*. In *Coppinger v Waterford County Council*,[53] in 1996, in the wake of the Supreme Court decision in *McKinley v Minister for Defence*,[54] Geoghegan J reasoned that s 35(2) should apply with equal force to the contributory negligence of a husband in a claim for loss of *consortium* by a wife, on the basis that the statutory provision had done no more than reflect the common law position in most jurisdictions, including England,[55] that a reduction should not be made for a spouse's contributory negligence, and that:

> "it would be completely contrary to th[e] principle [of equality] if a wife was to suffer reduction by reason of her husband's contributory negligence when, in the reverse situation, that would not happen"[56].

---

42. [1997] 2 IR 176 (HC) noted by Byrne & Binchy, *Annual Review of Irish Law 1997*, pp 795-796.
43. [1992] 2 IR 333 (SC).
44. See para **[33.07]**.
45. [1992] 2 IR 333 (SC).
46. [1992] 2 IR 333 at 358.
47. [1997] 2 IR 176 (HC).
48. Under the Civil Liability (Amendment) Act 1996.
49. [1997] 2 IR 176 (HC).
50. See Kerr, *The Civil Liability Acts* (1999), p 46.
51. For a comprehensive defence of this line of approach see Verge 'Note: Loss of Consortium, Contributory Negligence and Contribution: An Old Problem and a New Solution' (1983) 24 Boston College LR 403.
52. Reinforced by *Best v Samuel Fox & Co* [1952] AC 716 (HL, Eng).
53. [1996] 2 ILRM 427 (HC) analysed by Byrne & Binchy, *Annual Review of Irish Law 1996*, pp 614-617.
54. [1992] 2 IR 333.
55. *Cf Mallett v Dunn* [1949] 2 KB 180.
56. [1996] 2 ILRM 427 at 430.

## Reform of the Law Relating to Loss of Consortium

**[33.17]** The Law Reform Commission, in Working Paper No 7-1979, *The Law Relating to Loss of Consortium and Loss of Services of a Child,* proposed that the action should be retained, but that the "service" basis should be abolished in favour of the right of action being extended to all members of the family of the victim residing together.[57] Recovery should be allowed for all reasonable expenses and other financial losses incurred by the family, as well as for mental distress (without any maximum limit), in contrast to the fatal accident provisions of the Civil Liability Act 1961 (as amended which have provided a benchmark for the courts in recent cases dealing with the loss of *consortium*), and for the less tangible damage to "the continuity, stability and quality of the relationships between members of the family". The Commission also proposed the abrogation of the present rule whereby the contributory negligence of the victim is not taken into account in proceedings for loss of *consortium*.

**[33.18]** In its *First Report on Family Law,* published in 1981, the Commission endorsed the proposals on the subject made in Working Paper No 7-1979. Nothing has yet come of these proposals.

**[33.19]** In *Hosford v John Murphy & Sons Ltd,*[58] Costello J rejected a claim for loss of parental *consortium* brought by the children of a man who had received brain injuries as a result of the defendant's alleged negligence. The essence of the children's case was that they had been denied the benefits of a normal relationship with their father. Costello J held that the existing common law principles had never been extended to a case such as this. He also stated that the Law Reform Commission's proposals would allow for a remedy. Perhaps it could be argued, against Costello J's rejection of the claim, that it was a novel one requiring consideration on its merits rather than being rejected merely on the ground that it had no precedent. The fact that the Supreme Court in *McKinley v Minister for Defence*[59] was able to remodel and extend the tort belies the argument that the only forum for reform is the Oireachtas. Of course, in *McKinley* there was a glaring anomaly - sex discrimination - which required resolution, either by extension or abolition, if the tort was to retain harmony with constitutional norms. Nonetheless, the judgements of the majority

---

57. In the United States some courts have extended recovery in claims for loss of *consortium* to children: see eg *Ferriter v Daniel O'Connell's Sons Inc* (1980) 413 ALE 2d 690; *Weitel v Moes* 311 NW 2d 259 (Iowa 1980); *Berger v Weber* (1981) 411 Mich 1, 303 NW 2d 424; *Hibpshman v Prudhoe Bay Supply* 734 P 2d 991 (Alaska 1987). See Gehle 'Note: Loss of Consortium: Kentucky Should No Longer Prohibit a Child's Claim for Loss of Parental Consortium Due to the Negligent Act of a Third Party' (1995) 84 Ky LJ 173. The Supreme Court of Canada in *Hagarth v Hall* (1998) 166 DLR (45) 193 held that the dependants of a person, negligently injured or killed should have a right of action against the person whose negligence caused the injury or death, for loss of guidance care and companionship. The Court did so by way of judicial reform to reflect a "contemporary conceptions" of loss.

58. [1988] ILRM 300 (HC). In Ch 1 we consider Costello J's analysis of the plaintiffs' claim based on Article 41 of the Constitution. In *Buckley v Farrow* Court Appeal (Civil Div) 4 February 1997 (Lexis transcript) the English Court of Appeal rejected a similar claim based on negligence. The fact that the action for loss of *consortium* had been abolished by the Administration of Justice Act 1982, s 2, weighed against the "sudde[n] recogni[tion of] an action along these very same lines at the suit of a child not previously apparent and thus not abolished by the 1982 Act": *per* Simon Brown LJ (Saville and Millett JJ, concurring).

59. [1992] 2 IR 333 (SC).

in *McKinley* made it clear that the tort could be refashioned in order to give contemporary effect to its underlying values and not merely to correct a defect that was in conflict with the Constitution.

**[33.20]** A more radical argument is that the action for loss of *consortium* should be extended by the courts to include interference in relationships of unmarried couples living together. The Civil Liability Act 1996, which raised the statutory cap on damages for mental distress in fatal accident litigation to £20,000 also brought within the definition of "dependant" a person who, "until the date of the deceased's death, had been living with the deceased as husband or wife for a continuous period of not less than three years."[60] If fatal accidents legislation can provide a "benchmark"[61] for determining the *quantum* of damages in actions for loss of *consortium*, should it not also provide inspiration for the range of claimants in these actions?

**[33.21]** It seems unlikely that the courts will accept this line of argument.[62] The question whether cohabitees should be compensated for relational injury of this kind raises important issues of social policy which the courts may consider should better be left to the Oireachtas to resolve. Certainly the experience in other common law jurisdictions is that the courts have generally showed scant enthusiasm for proceeding down this road.[63]

**[33.22]** As regards a parent's right to sue for damages for wrongful interference with his or her relationship with his or her child, it should be noted that, whilst the action for loss of *consortium* traditionally has not extended so far and *Hosford v Murphy & Sons*[64] would seem to represent a barrier to its contemporary recognition,[65] another avenue maybe pursued. This is the action for breach of parent's statutory right to guardianship, based on Article 41 of the Constitution. Such an action succeeded in *Cosgrove v Ireland*,[66] where the wrongful issuance by the Department of Foreign Affairs of passports for the plaintiff's children to their mother, contrary to the opposition of the plaintiff, their father, led to their departure from Ireland to the Netherlands and the breakdown of his relationship with them.

**[33.23]** Whether an interference falling short of the complete destruction of the exercise of custody or access rights is actionable under the *Cosgrove* principle remains to be seen. Since guardianship represents a compendium of rights, large and small, general and specific, there would seem to be the same difficulty about awarding compensation for

60. The Civil Liability Act 1996, s 47(1)(c).

61. *McKinley v Minister for Defence* [1992] 2 IR 333 (SC). See also *Coppinger v Waterford County Council* [1996] 2 ILRM 427 (HC); *McKinley v Minister for Defence (No 2)* [1997] 2 IR 176 (HC).

62. It should be noted that in *Hosford v John Murphy & Sons Ltd* [1988] ILRM 300, Costello J rejected the claim of plaintiffs who fell within the definition of "dependant" under the fatal accidents legislation.

63. See eg *Strausser v Dow Chemical Co* 1997 US Dist LEXIS 22136 (US Dist So Dist of NY 26 November 1997); *Consorti v Owens v Coring Fiberglass Corp* (1995) 86 NY 2d 449, 634 NYS 2d 18, 657 NE 2d 1301; *Gurliacci v Nayer* (1991) 218 Com 531 590 A 2d 914.

64. See para **[33.19]**.

65. In England the Court of Appeal rejected such an action framed in negligence in *F v Wirral Metropolitan Borough Council* [1991] Fam 69 (CA (Civil Div)). See also *Schwarz v Hill House International Junior School* Court Appeal Civ Div, 25 May 1994, Lexis transcript.

66. [1982] ILRM 48 (HC).

interference with one aspect of guardianship as there has been for a partial infringement of the matrimonial consortium.

## III. Seduction

**[33.24]** The tort of seduction in essence enables the family of an unmarried woman or girl who has a child outside marriage to obtain compensation in the form of damages from the father of the child. The action proceeds on the fiction of a master-servant relationship existing between the woman or girl and her father or mother. It is not necessary to show any undue influence or pressure by the defendant. Nor is the tort limited to cases of pregnancy; indeed quite apart from these cases any sexual conduct with an unmarried male or female whether of a heterosexual or homosexual nature, would seem to be capable of giving rise to liability for seduction, provided some physical or psychological damage can be shown.[67]

**[33.25]** The Law Reform Commission[68] in 1981 recommended that the action for seduction be abolished. In its place, the Commission recommended that there should be created a single family action for seduction, available for the benefit of all members of the family unit. It should no longer be necessary to prove a service relationship between the parents and the seduced girl. The action would be limited to cases such as (a) where the seduced girl was under the age of 18 years at the time of the seduction and was not married at that time and at the time of the hearing,[69] and (b) the seduction resulted in pregnancy. No legislative response to this recommendation was forthcoming and it may confidently be predicted, two decades later, that more will be done on these lines.

**[33.26]** A shadow of unconstitutionality must fall over the action of seduction. It gives a remedy to a person who is not in any real sense a victim of wrongdoing. It interferes with rights of association and privacy. So far as it achieves the goal of protecting young and vulnerable children from sexual exploitation, it does so at a price of serious overbreadth.

## IV. Enticement and Harbouring of a Child

**[33.27]** Where a person entices a child away from his or her parent, or harbours a child who has left or has been removed from his or her parent's control, the parent has a right to sue that person for damages.[70] The actions, like seduction, are based on the fiction of loss of services.

**[33.28]** The case law on these actions is meagre: only two decisions have been reported in England and none in this country.

**[33.29]** In *Evans v Walton*,[71] the English Court of Common Pleas held that, to sustain the action for enticement, it was not necessary for the parent to establish a binding contract of

---

67. For an extended treatment of the present law of seduction, see the first edition of this work, pp 415-417.
68. In Working Paper No 6-1979, *The Law Relating to Seduction and the Enticement and Harbouring of a Child* and in the *First Report on Family Law* (1981).
69. This proposed statutory penalty on marriage may raise some difficulties.
70. See the LRC's Working Paper No 6-1979 *The Law Relating to Seduction and the Enticement and Harbouring of a Child*, Ch 2.
71. (1867) LR 2 CP 615.

service between his child and himself. In *Lough v Ward*,[72] the plaintiff's daughter, aged 16, left her home and entered a somewhat unconventional religious communal establishment of which the defendants, a man and his wife, were heads. The plaintiff's action for damages for enticement and harbouring was successful. Cassels J considered that:

> "the real question is: Would this girl have left her home if the defendants had not induced her? I am satisfied that she would not. She left her home as the result of a state of mind induced by the defendants."

**[33.30]** The fact that the girl might have intended never to return to her home would "only aggravate the loss of service",[73] since:

> "It would certainly be a curious position if the extent of the liability of the defendants should have to be reduced by their successful persuasion of the girl."[74]

**[33.31]** Regarding the girl's wishes to remain with the defendants, Cassells J thought that "there is every ground for disregarding them".[75] He observed that:

> "A religious influence is very dangerous and very powerful, and never so dangerous and never so powerful as when it is exercised by superior minds and older minds over an inferior and younger mind."[76]

**[33.32]** Since *Lough v Ward* was decided over fifty years ago, the law in this country has changed radically, so that, whatever strength the decision may have had in 1945, it would need to be regarded with a good deal of caution today.

**[33.33]** Some differences particularly worthy of note are that the father no longer has the exclusive right to determine the religion of his child,[77] the position in custody proceedings of parents relative to third parties has weakened,[78] and vastly more attention is now likely to be paid by the Court to the wishes[79] and the welfare[80] of a child, as well as his or her rights of association and privacy.

---

72. [1945] 2 All ER 338 (KBD).
73. [1945] 2 All ER 338 at 347.
74. [1945] 2 All ER 338.
75. [1945] 2 All ER 338 at 347-348.
76. [1945] 2 All ER 338 at 349.
77. *Cf In re Tilson Infants* [1951] IR 1 (SC); Shatter's *Family Law* (4th ed, 1997), pp 551-554.
78. See, however, *KC and AC v An Bord Uchtála* [1985] ILRM 302 (SC). *Cf Southern Health Board v CH* [1996] 2 ILRM 142 (SC). See generally Shatter's *Family Law* (4th ed, 1997), pp 43-49, 570-593.
79. See Shatter's *Family Law* (4th ed, 1997), pp 565-566. The constitutional guarantee of freedom of conscience, and the free profession and practice of religion, might be invoked by or on behalf of a child, whose return from an unconventional religious sect is sought by its parents. As to this subject generally see Siegel 'Comment: Deprogamming Religious Cultists' (1978) 11 Loyola of LALR 807; Bates 'Child Law and Religious Extremists: Some Recent Developments' (1978) 10 Ottawa LR 299; Bates 'Child Law and Religious Extremists Signs of a Changing Judicial Policy' (1979) 11 Ottawa LR 681; Le Moult 'Deprogramming Members of Religious Sects' (1978) 46 Fordham LR 599. More generally see Heins '"Other Peoples' Faiths": The Scientology Litigation and the Justifiability of Religious Fraud' (1981) 9 Hastings Constit LQ 153; Wiesen 'Note: Following the Lead of Defamation: A Definitional Balancing Approach to Religious Torts' (1995) 105 Yale LJ 291; Hayden 'Religiously Motivated "Outrageous" Conduct: Intentional Infliction of Emotional Distress as a Weapon against Other People's Faiths' (1993) 34 Wm & Mary LR 580.
80. *Cf* the Guardianship of Infants Act 1964, s 3; Shatter's *Family Law* (4th ed, 1997), p 545 ff.

**[33.34]** The following would, therefore, appear to be the present position (assuming for the moment that the actions are no inconsistent with contemporary constitutional values). The actions may be brought by a parent[81] in respect of the enticement or harbouring of his or her child under the age of majority irrespective of the wishes of the child in question. However, in determining liability, the court will have regard to the child's mental capacity and condition at the time of the alleged enticement or harbouring, in determining whether undue pressure was imposed. Whilst the Constitution protects the freedom of belief, this does not mean that it should afford any protection to coercive or exploitative acts; since the tort of enticement (though not of harbouring) premises liability on such constriction of choice it may be that, even in the case of adult victims, the action lies at the suit of parents. Of course the whole requirement of a service relationship is a nonsense in this context; perhaps it can best be understood (though scarcely supported) as a crude determinant of *locus standi*. It appears reasonable to assume that the same principles regarding the good faith belief of the defendant as to the reason for the child's absence from the home, apply to the harbouring of a child as formerly applied in regard to the harbouring of a spouse.[82] Damages appear to be a matter for the Court's discretion.

## Reform of the Law

**[33.35]** The Law Reform Commission examined[83] the law relating to the enticement and harbouring of children. In its *First Report on Family Law,* published in 1981, the Commission recommended that the actions should be retained with certain changes. Principal among these were that the requirement of a service relationship should be abolished, that the actions should be in the nature of single family actions, as in the case of actions for seduction, that the actions be limited to cases of children under the age of eighteen years who are not married, and that the Court should be required to have regard to the welfare of the child as "the paramount consideration" in assessing damages or granting discretionary relief. As with the Commission's recommendations in regard to the tort of

81. The question as to which parent may sue is generally considered by the commentators to be determined on the same principles as in the action for seduction. But this would create some unfortunate consequences. It would mean that where the service element was missing no action for enticement could be brought. Conversely, persons *in loco parentis* might be given undue powers over the autonomy of children in their care. Although, on analogy with seduction, such persons should have a right of action based on the fiction of a service relationship, the emphasis upon parental rights in *Lough v Ward* [1945] 2 All ER 338 suggests that the courts would be reluctant to recognise the right of action of such persons. Moreover, the constitutional requirement of equality as between married parents in relation to the guardianship of their children (*Re Tilson Infants; Tilson v Tilson* [1951] IR 1 (SC)) makes it almost certain that the courts today would not limit the right of action to the father. *Cf McKinley v Minister for Defence* [1992] 2 IR 333 (SC). It is worth noting that, in the context of the law of domicile, the Supreme Court has made it clear that on the grounds of gender equality (*inter alia*) the doctrine of dependency of married women did not survive the enactment of the Constitution: *W v W* [1993] 2 IR 476. The court said nothing, however, about the gender inequality that underlies the statutory rules relating to the domicile of minors in s 4 of the Domicile and Recognition of Foreign Divorces Act 1986. See further Byrne & Binchy, *Annual Review of Irish Law 1992*.

82. *Cf* the 1st edition of this work p 412.

83. In Working Paper No 6-1979; *The Law Relating to Seduction and the Enticement and Harbouring of a Child* and in its *First Report on Family Law* (1981).

seduction it seems highly unlikely that the legislature will regard favourably to these recommendations. It is worth bearing in mind that an action for infringement of the statutory right to guardianship, under the *Cosgrove* principle, would in any event appear available.

## V. Action for the Loss of a Child's Services[84]

**[33.36]** Where a person causes injury to a child by the commission of a tort in relation to him, the parent of that child may sue the author of the injury for losses sustained by him as a result of the tort. The action is based on the same principles regarding the requirement of a service relationship as apply in relation to the seduction and enticement of a child. Since a service relationship must be established, it has been held[85] that if the child is too young to perform any services, no action will lie.

**[33.37]** In the High Court decision of *Chapman v McDonald*[86] O'Keeffe P held that, in an action for loss of services of a child, only damages for loss of domestic services could be claimed. In this case, a daughter who helped her elderly bedridden mother on a farm was injured as a result of the defendant's negligence. Damages were awarded to the mother for the loss of her daughter's nursing services, which were categorised as domestic, but not for the loss of her help in running the farm, which was held not to be of a domestic nature. O'Keeffe P explained his approach as follows:

> "I do not think that the rendering of some non-domestic services should be taken to deprive the plaintiff of all redress in a case where the services are predominantly domestic, even though including many services of a non-domestic nature."

**[33.38]** The contributory negligence of the child will not reduce the damages to be awarded in an action for loss of services of a child, save in cases where the parent who is suing is vicariously responsible for the child's torts. This is established by s 35(2) of the Civil Liability Act 1961, as amended by s 4 of the Civil Liability Act 1964. Section 4 of the 1964 Act was designed to clarify the position regarding cases where the parent is vicariously responsible for the child. A clear case would be where the child is actually employed by the parent - as a secretary, for example. In such a case, the contributory negligence of the child *will* be taken into account. Where the line is to be drawn regarding parental vicarious liability is today somewhat more difficult to determine than in 1964: the trend of Irish law[87] has been to extend the scope of such liability further than in most other jurisdictions.

**[33.39]** The Law Reform Commission in Working Paper No 7-1979, and in its *First Report on Family Law* published in 1981 proposed that the existing action for loss of services of a child should be transformed into a family action similar in scope to the proposed reformulated action for loss of *consortium* which has already been described.

---

84. See Anon 'Damages Recoverable by Parent for Tort Done to Child' (1939) 73 ILT & Sol J 321.
85. *Hall v Hollander* (1825) 4 B & C 660, 107 ER 1206.
86. [1969] IR 188 (HC).
87. *Cf Moynihan v Moynihan* [1975] IR 192 (SC). *Cf Duffy v Rooney and Dunnes Stores (Dundalk) Ltd* High Court 1997, affd by Supreme Court 1998.

# Chapter 34

# Defamation[1]


I. Introduction .... 879
II. The Tort of Defamation .... 882
III. What is Defamatory? .... 894
IV. Defences .... 917
V. Damages .... 951
VI. Reform of the Law .... 961


## I. INTRODUCTION

**[34.01]** In recent years it is not an exaggeration to say that Irish society has been shaken by various scandals which had remained hidden for decades. These scandals affected the Catholic Church, financial institutions and politicians. They involved alleged sexual abuses, alleged political corruption and cosy cartels among the business circles. Tribunals of enquiry were established to investigate allegations of planning abuses, payments to politicians and off-shore accounts. Inspectors were appointed to investigate irregularities under the companies legislation.

**[34.02]** Many of these exposures were the result of painstaking investigative reporting by sometimes courageous journalists. Not surprisingly, these exposures attracted a fair share of defamation writs and the natural tension between the competing concepts of freedom of speech and the individual's right to his or her reputation has been vigorously revisited by the affected parties in the ensuing litigation. The newspaper industry has canvassed energetically for reforms in the law of defamation which it says unduly inhibits legitimate reporting and comment.[2] The Law Reform Commission has recommended[3] far-reaching reform. A private member's bill (adopting the Law Reform Commission's recommendations) has been tabled by Mr Michael McDowell SC, who has since become

1. See generally McDonald, *Irish Law of Defamation* (2nd ed, 1989); Boyle, & McGonagle, *A Report on Press Freedom and Libel* (National Newspapers of Ireland, Dec 1988). McGonagle, *A Textbook on Media Law* (1996) Ch 4; Gatley, *Libel and Slander* (9th ed, 1998). See also Carter-Ruck, *Libel & Slander* (5th ed, 1997); O'Dell 'When Two Tribes Go to War: Privacy Interests and Media Speech' in *Law and the Media* McGonagle ed (1996); O'Dell 'Does Defamation Value Free Expression? The Possible Influence of *New York Times v Sullivan* on Irish Law' 12 DULJ 50 (1990); Docherty 'Defamation Law: Positive Jurisprudence' (2000) 13 Harv Human Rts J 263; Frazier 'Liberty of Expression in Ireland and the Need for a Constitutional Law of Defamation', (1999) 32 Vand Transnat l L 391; Heuston 'Recent Developments in the Law of Defamation' (1966) 1 Ir Jur (ns) 247; the LRC's, *Consultation Paper on the Civil Law of Defamation* (1991) and its *Report on the Civil Law of Defamation* (LRC 38-1991); McDonald 'Defamation Reform: A Response to the Law Reform Commission' (1992) 10 ILT 270.
2. See also Boyle and McGonagle *A Report on Press Freedom and Libel* (1998, National Newspapers of Ireland).
3. Irish LRC's *Report on the Civil Law of Defamation* (LRC 38-1991).

Attorney General, but it has not been given priority by the Government which has announced that it is preparing its own bill for introduction in the near future.

**[34.03]** The media, for the most part, and in spite of their many spectacular successes, argue that the present law is inhibiting journalists from doing their jobs properly. The "chilling effect" which the law has on editors and reporters is not, they contend, in the interest of a free democratic society. Moreover, some of the awards made by juries in recent times have been very high (in comparison to personal injury awards) and it is alleged, threaten the very survival of some of the smaller newspapers.[4] Awards of £300,000,[5] £250,000[6] and £90,000[7] have recently been made in three well publicised cases.

**[34.04]** As the debate intensifies, those favouring reform have broadened the discussion and have enlisted constitutional arguments, as well as arguments based on the European Convention on Human Rights, to support their cause. The Convention is not, as yet, part of Irish domestic law (although plans to incorporate it are well advanced), but it, and the jurisprudence emerging from it, have been cited in arguments before the Irish courts in an effort to press on them a more liberal approach.

**[34.05]** It is worth noting, however, that the Irish courts have been slow to embrace the constitutional arguments to override the common law on defamation. The position, maintained up to now by the courts in the defamation area, has been that the constitutional protection of the citizen's "good name", is being adequately protected by the common law of torts, and that the common law principles do not require to be modified in the light of the Constitution. Academic arguments[8] suggesting such a modification (and urging greater attention to the right to free speech and the right to communicate) have by and large been ignored by the Irish courts up to very recently. In *Foley v Independent Newspapers*[9] Geogehan J typifies the judicial reluctance to venture unnecessarily from tort dry-land to the uncharted waters of constitutional augmentation law:

> "Counsel for the defendants ... apart from relying on the ordinary common law defence of fair comment calls in aid also Article 40.6.1°i of the Constitution. He has referred me to authorities indicating that the traditional law of contempt of court has been affected by that constitutional provision and he argues that the law of libel may also be affected by it. Even if that submission as a general proposition is correct any consideration of that particular constitutional provision would have to be balanced by consideration of Article 40.3.2° which requires that the State shall by its laws protect as best it may from unjust attack and in the case of injustice done vindicate the good name of every citizen. As far as this particular case

4. See McGonagle, *A Textbook on Media Law* (1996), p 110, fn 116.
5. *De Rossa v Independent Newspapers plc* Supreme Court, 30 July 1999.
6. *O'Brien v Irish Mirror* High Court, 11 November 1999, overturned on appeal to the Supreme Court, 25 October 2000.
7. *McDaid v The Examiner* Irish Times, 18 November 1999, p 4. The majority of plaintiffs are male businessmen or professionals. "The next largest category are State employees, followed by lawyers and politicians". See McGongle, *A Textbook on Media Law* p 78 fn 188.
8. McDonald, *Irish Law of Defamation* (2nd ed, 1989); McGonagle, *A Textbook on Media Law*, (1996) 109, fn 13; O'Dell, 'Does Defamation Value Free Expression? The Possible Influence of *New York Times v Sullivan on Irish Law*' (1990) 12 DULJ 50. See also O'Dell 'When Two Tribes Go to War: Privacy Interests and Media Speech' in *Law and the Media* (McGonagle ed, 1996).
9. [1994] 2 ILRM 61.

> is concerned, I am satisfied that once that balancing is done the plaintiff's entitlement to succeed under the ordinary laws of libel is unaffected."[10]

**[34.06]** The courts' reluctance to draw on constitutional provisions to augment the common law of defamation is a particular reflection of a similar and more general attitude, which the courts have adopted when requested by litigants to supplement existing tort law in this fashion. This general reticence, at least where common law or statute law already exists, has already been noted,[11] and one quotation, from Costello J in 1997, will suffice to illustrate the point:

> "There is therefore no need to constitute the Constitution as conferring a new and discrete cause of action for damages in those cases in which the acts or omissions which constitute the alleged infringement also constitute an actionable wrong at law for which damages are recoverable."[12]

**[34.07]** One of the more interesting and potentially significant decisions handed down in recent years by the House of Lords on these and other matters involved the former Taoiseach, Mr Albert Reynolds.[13] There Mr Reynolds sued the defendant newspaper for an alleged libel published in England. The case was brought before the English Courts and, although it is of persuasive force only in this jurisdiction and is primarily concerned with the specific question of qualified privilege, it contains a wide ranging discussion in the House of Lords of the fundamental issues involved in the tension between free speech and the right to reputation in what is described by Lord Steyn as "The New Landscape". It indicates too the pressures in that jurisdiction to revisit the principles and policies underlying the whole law of defamation. It is interesting that the Law Lords also refer to the European Convention of Human Rights which has now been incorporated into English law. The Human Rights Act 1998, is clearly agitating legal practitioners, and its impact on the English legal system is sure to be significant. English lawyers will therefore also have to consider how the tort of defamation, and established tort law generally, will interface with these new constitutional and human rights developments. Although lawyers in Ireland have addressed these problems to some extent already, we can gain much insight from these developments in that jurisdiction.

**[34.08]** The tort of defamation represents the law's considered response to two competing interests, namely, the right of free speech and the right of the individual to preserve his reputation from unjust attack. In attempting to strike a balance between these interests, however, the law has not always been as sensitive as it might have been to modern social values. Consequently, partly due to historical accident and partly due to the unremitting nature of judicial precedent, the present law on this topic in some respects does not reflect accurately what might be said to be a fair balance in the matter. For example, one might question nowadays, in an age of ruthless investigative reporting, whether the truth of a statement should always be a defence in an action for defamation. Will the quality of political leadership suffer in society if the peccadilloes of adolescence can be raked up and produced some 20 or 30 years later to damage a political opponent? Whether the

---

10. [1994] 2 ILRM 61 at 67.
11. See Ch 1 above.
12. *W v Ireland (No 2)* [1999] 2 IR 141.
13. *Reynolds v Times Newspaper Ltd* [1999] 1 All ER 609. See also para **[34.182]**.

Constitution will play a greater role in this area than it has done heretofore remains in doubt. There are certain indications that it will do so in the future, but as yet this aspect of the subject is virtually a *tabula rasa*. Recent studies[14] suggest that some of the deficiencies in the present law of defamation might be eliminated if the courts properly appreciated the constitutional guarantees of the right to communicate[15] and the right to freedom of expression (which includes press freedom). In this context the courts' task is to formulate more precisely the balance between the competing interests of freedom of expression and the citizen's rights to a good name and to privacy.[16] To discharge the function, however, the courts must have cases brought before it by lawyers who are prepared to argue defamation issues in the constitutional context. Up to recently the judicial indicators did not suggest a major constitutional supplement in this matter. In the past couple of years, the assault on the traditional rules has been led more under the flag of the European Convention on Human Rights, where the issues have already been clarified, than under the Constitution, whose provisions relating to free speech, reputation and privacy are still largely undeveloped in terms of judicial analysis.

**[34.09]** A striking feature of the law of defamation is that it is beset by nice variations and fine distinctions. In this respect it should, however, be mentioned that the Defamation Act 1961, did in part successfully eliminate some of these distinctions.[17] The changes brought about by this legislation, and the proposals for reform, will be dealt with in due course. But first it is necessary to outline the general contours of the tort itself.

## II. The Tort of Defamation

**[34.10]** Defamation is committed by the wrongful publication[18] of a false statement about a person, which tends to lower that person in the eyes of right-thinking members of society or tends to hold that person up to hatred, ridicule or contempt, or causes that person to be shunned or avoided by right-thinking members of society.[19]

---

14. McDonald, *Irish Law of Defamation* (2nd ed, 1989); Boyle, & McGonagle, *A Report on Press Freedom and Libel* (National Newspapers of Ireland, Dec 1988).

15. As recognised by Costello J in *AG v Paperlink* [1984] ILRM 373. Reaffirmed in *Kearney v Ireland* [1986] IR 116. See also *AG for England and Wales v Brandon Book Publishers* [1987] ILRM 135 (HC), noted by Hogan, [1987] Pub L 509. In *Hynes-O'Sullivan v O'Driscoll* [1989] ILRM 349 (SC), the analysis of the constitutional aspects of defamation by Henchy and McCarthy JJ gives no cause for assuming that on this subject our law is likely to develop on lines closely similar to what has taken place in the United States.

16. Boyle, & McGonagle, *A Report on Press Freedom and Libel* (National Newspapers of Ireland, Dec 1988), fn 113. The study by Boyle & McGonagle, critically examines the inhibiting effects of the present law of libel for newspapers in particular and suggests reforms which they claim are required if Irish society is to have a healthy and critical press. See p 59 *et seq*. The study also includes a range of interesting statistics in relation to defamation actions against national newspapers, as to kind of plaintiffs, nature of defamation alleged, legal points raised, defences pleaded and ultimate outcome. See pp 41-47.

17. See Delany 'Proceedings for Defamation Act 1961' (1962-63) 28-29 Ir Jur 1.

18. *Cf M'Loughlin v Doey* (1893) 32 LR Ir 518 (Ex D).

19. *Quigley v Creation Ltd* [1971] IR 269; *Berry v Irish Times* [1973] IR 368.

**[34.11]** Several points in this definition require elaboration. A word of caution is necessary, however. It must be remembered that the above definition derives its authority from judicial pronouncements: it is not a statutory definition. Consequently, it must be approached with some flexibility, and not in the rigid severe way that one might approach a definition drafted by a parliamentary draftsman.

## Publication

**[34.12]** Publication in the present context means communication to a third party.[20] Anyone who makes a statement, who distributes or disseminates a statement, or who repeats a statement to a third person, publishes that statement for the purpose of the law of defamation. In *Berry v Irish Times*[21] the Irish Times was sued for reproducing a photograph of a placard containing a false statement, clearly legible in the photograph, relating to the plaintiff. The defence did not contest that the Irish Times was the publisher on that occasion although it was not the author of the matter on the placard. The word "publisher" here, therefore, has a much wider meaning than that given to it by literary people in the world of books and letters. It may in the present context include printers, book-sellers and newspaper vendors, as well as the ordinary individual who at a social gathering makes a statement about the plaintiff to a third party.

**[34.13]** Communication to a person other than the plaintiff, however, is essential for publication to take place. It is not publication, and consequently no action in defamation will lie, to call a person aside from company and out of earshot of others, to accuse him or her falsely of being a thief or an adulterer. Nor would it be publication, similarly to accuse that person in a private letter addressed to him or her, where one had no reason to believe that the correspondence would be seen by a third party before coming to the plaintiff's attention. Since the gist of the action for defamation is that the false statement tends to lower the plaintiff in the eyes of right-thinking members of society, such loss of face cannot occur if the statement does not travel beyond the plaintiff alone. The plaintiff, in such circumstances, generally does not think less of himself or herself if the statement is false. Consequently, the law considers in such circumstances, that there is no wrong to be remedied.[22] The plaintiff's pride may be hurt, but that is not what the tort of defamation is about.

**[34.14]** The rule which requires the statement to be made to a third party also means, in normal circumstances, that no action will lie if the statement is communicated by private letter[23] or by telephone to the plaintiff only. But if the method of communication would

---

20. With regard to a claim by the plaintiff which is not confined to damage within the jurisdiction, see *Murray v Times Newspapers Ltd* [1997] 3 IR 97 where the European Convention on Jurisdiction and the Enforcement of Judgments 1968, Article 5, para 3 is discussed. See also *Ewins v Carlton UK Television* [1997] 2 ILRM 223.

21. [1973] IR 368. On publication generally, see Anon 'Publication of a Libel' [1932] LJ, IFS 176, Anon 'Publication of Libel by Dissemination of Defamatory Newspaper' (1886) 20 ILT & Sol J 13.

22. It is for this reason too that no action will lie where a person word processes a document and then hands back the defamatory material in word processed form to its author, the defendant. Since the defendant is the original author he or she cannot be made to think less of the plaintiff by the handing back.

23. See *Keogh v Incorporated Dental Hospital of Ireland* [1910] 2 IR 577; Anon 'Publication Through the Post' (1915) 49 ILT & Sol J 259. *Cf Ahern v Maguire* (1840) Arm Mac & Og 39.

normally involve communication to a person other than the addressee (for example, by telegram) then this must be considered sufficient to amount to publication. In this connection it must be noted that the courts take cognisance of human beings' natural curiosity in assuming that messages written on post cards will be read by third parties and, therefore are published.[24] This presumption may be rebutted by the defendant, however.[25]

**[34.15]** In *Paul v Holt*[26] a letter addressed to "Mr Paul, Adavoyle, Meigh, Newry" was delivered to the plaintiff's brother who also lived at that address. The plaintiff's brother read it and showed it to the plaintiff's wife who in turn handed it to the brother's wife. At the trial an application for a direction for want of publication was granted, but in the Court of Appeal it was held that there was no want of publication and a new trial was ordered. There was evidence that the defendant knew there was another Mr Paul at the same address and the civil bill issued by Holt for arrears of rent, and which was the subject matter of the letter, was against two persons, William Paul and James Paul; this being so, the defendant should have proved that he did not know of the existence of the plaintiff's brother. The implication of this decision is that if there is accidental publication in the communication process the defendant will not be liable, but if communication to the third person is due to the negligence or want of care of the defendant, then the defendant is liable for the publication. There is ample authority for this proposition.[27]

**[34.16]** A question that frequently arises in relation to publication is whether a communication between husband and wife is sufficient publication for the purposes of defamation. The question arises primarily because, for some purposes at least, the law traditionally has treated husband and wife as a single unit. The question becomes relevant in two cases. First, if the publication complained of is the communication of a statement by the defendant to the plaintiff's spouse or, second, if the communication complained of is to

---

24. *Robinson v Jones* (1979) 4 LR Ir 39. But otherwise in the case of correspondence in an unsealed envelope: *Huth v Huth* [1915] 3 KB 32. See also *McCann v Edinburgh Roperie & Sailcloth Co* (1891) 28 LR Ir 24. In *Theaker v Richardson* [1962] 1 All ER 229, where the defamatory letter addressed to the plaintiff was placed in "a cheap, flimsy, manilla envelope", which was sealed and sellotaped, the defendant was nonetheless held to have published it to the plaintiff's husband, who opened the envelope, believing it to be election literature. *Per* Harmon LJ (at ):

> "It ... appears to me that the answer to the question of publication of a libel contained in a letter will depend on the state of the defendant's knowledge, either proved or inferred, of the conditions likely to prevail in the place to whereby the libel is destined".

In *Theaker*, the letter was hand-delivered. Harmon LJ declined to take judicial notice of the fact that husbands read wives' letters, but it seemed to him that

> "the master of the house, when confronted with an unstamped document on the door-mat looking like a circular, is not unlikely to pick it up and read it."

The concept of "the master of the house" seems to come from another age. (It is surprising that *Theaker* was decided less than forty years ago). Perhaps it would be reasonable for a court today to assume that either spouse, confronted by a letter of the type that was on the door-mat in that case, would be likely to open it without much thought. *Theaker* is not an authority for the proposition that there is publication where one spouse deliberately opens an envelope which he or she knows is intended for the other spouse only.

25. See SALMOND & HEUSTON (18th ed), p 155.

26. (1935) 69 ILTR 157 (NICA).

27. See *White v Stone Ltd* [1939] 2 KB 827.

the defendant's own spouse. Authorities have now settled that in the first case there is publication[28] but that there is no publication in the second case.[29]

**[34.17]** At first glance there appears to be a contradiction in the attitude of the law here in that it is prepared to treat the defendant and his or her spouse in the second case as a unit, but it is not so prepared to treat the plaintiff and his or her spouse, in the first case. This apparent contradiction can perhaps be justified. To say to a man's wife that her husband is a lecher or a robber may cause the defamed person serious damage within his domestic environment, and indeed it may have much more serious consequences than if the words were spoken to an unrelated third party. To treat the husband and wife as one in those circumstances would not recognise the potential mischief of the communication. But communications between spouses are another matter. Here the marriage relationship is promoted and supported by encouraging full, free and frank discussion.

**[34.18]** A somewhat similar problem arises where the only proof of publication offered by the plaintiff in a defamation action is that he or she bought the offending newspaper or book himself or herself or procured the communication through an agent. In *The Irish People's Assurance Society v The City of Dublin Assurance Co Ltd*[30] the Supreme Court of the Irish Free State held that there was sufficient proof of publication where the communication complained of was made to the plaintiff's agent who had to indulge in some deception to get the information. The Court held (Murnaghan J dissenting) that the practice was notorious and universal as a method by which publication can be proved. The Court approved and followed *Duke of Brunswick v Harmer*.[31] Murnaghan J, dissenting, was unwilling to admit that there was any publication or that the publication, having been procured by the deceit of the plaintiff's agent, was such that the court should recognise. He did not think that the instant case was comparable with the *Duke of Brunswick's* case, which related to the free circulation of newspapers.

### *Innocent dissemination*

**[34.19]** Persons who are in the final stage of the distribution process of a libel, however, such as newspaper vendors, booksellers and others, may avail themselves of a more lenient rule regarding publication. Provided that, as persons carrying on their business properly, they neither knew nor ought to have known that the paper or book contained a libel, they are not deemed to be publishers at all.[32] The onus is on the defendant, however, to establish that he or she is innocent and comes within the exception.[33]

---

28. *Wenman v Ash* (1853) 13 CB 836, 148 ER 1432.
29. *Wennhak v Morgan* (1888) 20 QBD 635. This exemption can more convincingly be explained in terms of privilege: see para **[34.159]** below.
30. [1929] IR 25. This approach would now be re-inforced by the Civil Liability Act 1961, s 34 which greatly restricts the defence of *volenti non fit injuria*. See *O'Hanlon v ESB* [1969] IR 75.
31. (1849) 14 QB 185, 117 ER 75. On proof of publication generally, see McDonald, *Irish Law of Defamation*, p 69.
32. *Cf Fitzgibbon v Eason & Son Ltd* (1910) 45 ILTR 91; *Ross v Eason & Son Ltd* [1911] 2 IR 459 (CA); *O'Brien v Eason & Son* (1913) 47 ILTR 266 (CA); *McDermott v Eason & Son* (1913) 48 ILTR 1 (CA); *Vizetelly v Mudies' Select Library Ltd* [1900] 2 QB 170 (CA); *Bottomley v Woolworth & Co* (1932) 48 TLR 52. See para **[34.111]** below. The exception, however, is not applied generally by the Courts: See McDonald, *Irish Law of Defamation*, p 66.
33. *Ross v Eason & Ltd* [1911] 2 IR 459; *McDermott v Eason & Son* (1913) 48 ILTR 1. A particular author or magazine might be so notorious that a book vendor ought to examine or investigate the publication closely before selling it. *Weldon v Times Book* (1911) 28 TLR 143.

### *Method of publication*

**[34.20]** A word should be said about the method of publication at this juncture. The normal vehicle of communication is language. Consequently most defamatory publications are made by words, spoken or written. But it would be wrong to assume that this is the only possible way by which a defamatory statement can be made. Any method by which meaning can be communicated will suffice.[34] Section 14(2) of the Defamation Act 1961, explicitly recognises this fact where it provides that:

> [a]ny reference in this Part to words shall be construed as including a reference to visual images, gestures and other methods of signifying meaning.

### *Forms of publication: libel and slander*[35]

**[34.21]** Defamation houses within its walls two operable torts: libel and slander. From a definitional point of view the difference between these two forms of defamation lies in the method or form in which the defamatory statement is made. The position in Ireland nowadays seems to be that if the defamatory statement is made in a permanent form it is libel, but if it is made in an impermanent or transient form it is slander.[36] Various other tests have been suggested from time to time as to how one distinguishes between libel and slander. Sometimes it used to be said that written statements amounted to libel whereas oral statements amounted to slander. Again it was suggested that slander was addressed to the sense of hearing whereas libel was addressed to the sense of seeing, or touching (in the case of a blind person). Still again it has been suggested that the difference between libel and slander is to be found in the audience's understanding of the publication. If it realises that the statement being made is in fact being read from a written document or from a script, this in fact makes the matter libel, even if members of the audience never have the opportunity of reading the statement itself.[37] The rationale for the distinction is that intemperate, unconsiderated statements are dealt with more leniently than those which have some degree of planning and deliberation. Moreover, the writers words or other

---

34. In *Corless and Diggin v Ireland* High Court, 23 July 1984, it was held that *the fact* that the plaintiff was transferred from one section of the Garda force in somewhat controversial circumstances, could amount to defamation. In a wrongful dismissal case Costello J was willing to hold that a wrongful dismissal could constitute a defamation.

    > "The claim is founded on the fact that there was a wrongful termination of an office ... But the termination of such an appointment could in itself give rise to a claim for damages for defamation. If wrongful, the consequence may well result in the disparagement of the office holder in the eyes of reasonable people who learn of the termination".

    *O'Callaghan v Meath Vocational Education Committee* High Court, 20 November 1990, at p 16. Security staff in supermarkets when challenging customers suspected of shoplifting may frequently commit the tort of defamation also. See *McEntee v Quinnsworth & Keane* Supreme Court, 7 December 1993.

35. See Day, 'A Note on the Distinction Between Oral and Written Defamation' (1954) 3 Clev-Mar LR 85.

36. Thus far, the decisions have involved cases where permanence was associated with sight as a means of communication: see, eg *Youssoupoff v Metro-Goldwyn Mayer Pictures Ltd* (1934) 50 Times LR 581; *Monson v Tussauds Ltd* [1894] 1 QB 671 (CA). Academic authorities tend to favour the view that, even in cases where the communication in permanent form does not involve sight (such as compact discs, for example), the communication should be characterised as one of libel rather than slander: see, eg WINFIELD & JOLOWICZ, p 392; MARKESINIS & DEAKIN, p 605. *Cf* STREET, p 451; FLEMING, p 603.

37. See FLEMING, p 603.

communications in permanent form can do more damage because of the wider audience that is attached to communications of this character.[38] The importance of the criterion used to distinguish between libel and slander from each other becomes crucial when one has to determine whether a script read out loud, or formerly whether a radio broadcast, is libel or slander. In *Forrester v Tyrrell*[39] the court held that the reading aloud of a defamatory script was itself a libel even though the message to the audience came by way of its hearing faculty. Once a libel was made in a permanent form, it remained a libel even if it was only read out to a new audience. One might say, once a libel always a libel. *Forrester v Tyrrell* was followed in the Northern Ireland case of *Robinson v Chambers*.[40] The defendant, a rector in the Church of Ireland at a meeting of Diocesan Synodsmen read out a letter addressed to the Secretary of the Diocesan Council in which the defendant recommended the removal from office of the plaintiff, the defendant's churchwarden. McDermott J, having noted the artificial and technical nature of the division between slander and libel, went on to hold that the publication must be considered a libel.[41]

**[34.22]** The problem of defamatory statements made on radio and television has now been statutorily solved in Ireland by s 15 of the Defamation Act 1961 which provides: "For the purposes of the law of libel and slander the broadcasting of words by means of wireless telegraphy shall be treated as publication in permanent form."[42]

**[34.23]** Apart from statutorily settling the position about broadcast statements, this provision, implicitly at least, confirms the assumption that the criterion to be used in distinguishing between libel and slander is the permanence or impermanence of the mode of publication. The assumption behind s 15 is undoubtedly that once something is published in a permanent form it is libel.

**[34.24]** The importance of the distinction between libel and slander is primarily twofold. First, a libel may be a crime as well as a tort, and as such can be the subject of criminal proceedings. Part II of the Defamation Act 1961 contains the principal rules relating to such proceedings now. Second, and more important from the tort point of view, libel is actionable *per se*, whereas, save in exceptional circumstances to be mentioned below, the plaintiff in a slander action must prove special damages.

## The Historical Origins of the Libel Slander Distinction[43]

**[34.25]** Slander was early recognised by the ecclesiastical courts as a wrong for which they would in appropriate cases impose penance. From the early part of the 16th century,

38. Yet it is easy enough to envisage cases where a particular spoken communication can involve a high degree of deliberation and a potential for serious damage that well exceeds the generality of communications in written or otherwise permanent form.

39. (1893) 9 TLR 257.

40. [1946] NI 148.

41. See also *Pope v Coates* (1863) 16 ICLR 156. In this case the plaintiff recovered damages against the defendant for writing a libellous letter which was read to the poor law guardians. It was also held that a subsequent reading by the clerk at the request of a guardian absent from the earlier meeting at which the letter was first read, was not a publication of a libel by the defendant.

42. Defamatory statements found in similar modern technology (VDUs, videos, fax printouts, etc) are also likely to be treated as libel. See Scott, *Computer Law*, p 724.

43. This section is based on FLEMING (9th ed), pp 601-602 and 7th ed, pp 518-519 and PROSSER, pp 769 *et seq*. See also Veeder 'History and Theory of the Law of Defamation' (1903) 3 Col LR 546, (1904) 4 Col LR 33;

however, the common law Courts, keen to compete for this business, began to allow actions on the case for slanders. Although originally they confined their jurisdiction to those slanders which imputed a common law offence, and for which no damage had to be shown, they later extended their jurisdiction to all slanders causing "temporal" damage. This presumably was an attempt to justify encroachment on ecclesiastical jurisdiction which was primarily concerned with "spiritual" damage:

> "Although in origin the requirement of 'special damage' was, therefore, nothing more than a ruse in the struggle for jurisdictional supremacy, it was subsequently retained for the wholly different purpose of reducing the volume of litigation unleashed by the popularity of the action for damages. Unfortunately, this temporary expedient justified by the riotous temper of the times, had the result of crippling further development in the law of slander and of foisting on the law of defamation a feature which has been a source of irritation and injustice ever since."[44]

**[34.26]** The Star Chamber at the same time was providing remedies for political and non-political libels. Its face was set against political libels in an effort to suppress the seditious libels that increased in the wake of the invention of the printing press, while in suppressing non-political libels it was endeavouring to provide legal support for the policy that had recently outlawed duelling.

**[34.27]** It is important to note that, at this stage, the distinction between libel and slander related not to the form of the defamatory statement, but rather to the Court in which the matter was heard. It was a jurisdictional distinction, as both libels in Star Chamber and slanders in the common law Courts could be either written or oral.

**[34.28]** With the fall of Star Chamber its jurisdiction in libel was absorbed by the common law Courts (in particular by the King's Bench), and over the succeeding decades the principal contours of the modern tort were worked out. The distinction between libel as a crime (where truth was not a full defence) and libel as a tort began to emerge. Probably because of its association with criminal law, libel also became actionable without proof of special damage. Gradually and for no apparently justifiable reason a line of demarcation came to be drawn between defamation in the written form (libel) and defamation in the oral form (slander), with no special damage being required to be proved for libel. This new development, however, was not accompanied by a rationalisation of the position in slander, where some features of the old common law tort remained, including the distinction between words actionable *per se* and words actionable on proof of special damage only.

**[34.29]** The distinction between libel and slander, and between slander actionable *per se* and slander actionable on proof of special damage only, were, therefore, largely the products of historical accident rather than of rational development. Subsequently, rationalisations for the libel-slander distinction were put forward to maintain the distinction, but it is important to note that these were *ex post facto* justifications for the maintenance of the distinction rather than explanations of its origin. Among the modern

---

43. (contd) Holdsworth 'Defamation in the Sixteenth and Seventeenth Centuries' (1924) 40 LQR 302, 397, (1925) 41 LQR 13; Zeiger 'Note: Alienation of Affections and Defamation: Similar intents -Dissimilar Treatment' (1981) 30 Clev St LR 331 at 341-344. O'Dell 'Reflections on a Revolution in Libel' (1991) 9 ILT (ns) 181, 214.

44. FLEMING (7th ed), p 518.

justifications put forward for the maintenance of the distinction are the following. The permanence of the written word means that libel is a more serious wrong in the sense that it is more likely to cause damage than defamation in an oral or transient form: it lasts longer. Libel, especially where it is made in publications enjoying mass circulation, is more likely to cause damage by virtue of the fact that it reaches such a wide audience, whereas slander is usually made to a limited audience in the immediate vicinity of the defendant. Libel is not capable of being easily recalled or corrected.[45]

## Slander Actionable Per Se

**[34.30]** The general rule is that slander is actionable only where the plaintiff pleads[46] and proves special damage (ie actual damage), but like all general rules there are exceptions. The following types of slander are actionable *per se*.

1. Slanders which impute unchastity or adultery to any woman or girl.[47]
2. Slanders affecting a person's official, professional or business reputation.[48]
3. Slanders imputing a criminal offence punishable by death or imprisonment.
4. Slanders imputing a contagious disease which tends to exclude the sufferer from society.

A further word should be said on each of these cases.

### *Section 16 of the Defamation Act 1961*

**[34.31]** Section 16 provides:

> Words spoken and published which impute unchastity or adultery to any woman or girl shall not require special damage to render them actionable.

**[34.32]** Words include "visual images, gestures and other methods of signifying meaning".[49] These slanders were not actionable *per se* at common law,[50] but were made so by the Slander of Women Act 1891.[51] The 1961 Act repealed this earlier Act, but re-enacted this provision for the benefit of women and girls. In an age of sexual equality a strong case can be made for making this exception extend to imputations of unchastity to

---

45. The distinction between libel and slander has been severely criticised: see Faulks *Report* (1975) para 80 (Cmnd 5909), and the distinction has been abolished in several countries: see Australian Law Reform Commission, *Unfair Publication* (1979), para 76. McDonald, *Irish Law of Defamation*, pp 93-96, suggests that the distinction (and many of the peculiar rules in this area) could well be attacked on the grounds that they infringe the Constitution. The Law Reform Commission in Ireland recommends that the distinction be abolished. See para **[34.263]** below.
46. *Symons v Toronto Dominion Bank* (1997) 38 CCLT (2d) 305.
47. Defamation Act 1961, s 16.
48. Defamation Act 1961, s 19.
49. Defamation Act 1961, s 14(2). "Words" are not given this extended meaning in the English Defamation Act 1952.
50. *Cf Spright v Gosney* (1891) 60 LJ (QB) 231. Thus women whose chastity was impugned had to attempt to bring their action (in the absence of special damage) under another exception usually that of disparagement of office: *Cf Connors v Justice* (1862) 13 ICLR 451; *Dwyer v Meehan* (1886) 18 LR Ir 138.
51. *Cf Tait v Beggs*, 525 (CA affg KBD). See also *Farrelly v Lynch* [1945] Ir Jur Rep 49.

males, as has been done in Newfoundland, for example. Indeed, in the light of our constitutional jurisprudence the present position could well be attacked on this ground.

**[34.33]** The section specifically covers adultery which, in view of the express reference to unchastity, appears to be no more than surplusage.[52] Moreover, there is authority[53] for saying that it also covers lesbian acts.

***Section 19 of the Defamation Act 1961***

**[34.34]** Section 19 provides:

> In an action for slander in respect of words calculated to disparage the plaintiff in any office, profession, calling, trade or business held or carried on by him at the time of the publication,[54] it shall not be necessary to allege or prove special damage, whether or not the words are spoken of the plaintiff in the way of his office, profession, calling, trade or business.

This section brings about a change in the common law position which prevailed before 1961 in this matter. Before 1961 for the slander to be actionable *per se* it had first to disparage the plaintiff in his office, etc, and secondly, the words had to be spoken about his office. Accordingly, to say of a school master that he committed adultery with the school-cleaner was not actionable *per se*, because, although the words might disparage him in his office and might clearly indicate he was unsuitable to be a teacher, nevertheless, the words were not spoken about his office or about his ability to teach.[55] The Act now requires the words only to disparage the plaintiff in his office (they need not be about his office) and earlier precedents are still relevant to this enquiry.

**[34.35]** In *Bennett v Quane*[56] the defendant, a medical doctor, said of the plaintiff (a solicitor): "He brought an action in the Circuit Court instead of the District Court to get more costs for himself." The judge found that the words were defamatory and that, as they were spoken of him "touching" or "in the way" of his calling or profession, they were actionable *per se*:

> "On this point it is my view that to say of a solicitor that his conduct was lacking in that propriety which the best and highest canons of his profession would require is to defame him by words touching him in his profession".[57]

---

52. *Cf Kerr v Kennedy* [1942] 1 KB 409 at 412 (KBD).
53. *Kerr v Kennedy* [1942] 1 KB 409 at 413.
54. It appears that this restriction that the plaintiff be carrying on the business etc *at the time of the publication* is a general precondition to the entitlement to sue for slander without proof of special damage under this heading: see *Hicks v Stephens* (1997) 40 CCLT (2d) 223.
55. *Jones v Jones* [1916] 2 AC 481. *Cf Devine v Keane* (1926) 61 ILTR 118 (HC), where a similar charge against a civic guard was actionable as being spoken about his occupation. *Sayers v Bachelor* (1855) 7 IJ OS 257 - cabinet maker did not have to be honest. *Connors v Justice* (1862) 13 ICLR 451 - chastity essential requisite for female domestic servant.
56. [1948] Ir Jur Rep 28. See Anon 'Slanders on Solicitors' (1947) 81 ILT & Sol J 163. See also *Curneen v Sweeney* (1969) 103 ILTR 29.
57. [1948] Ir Jur Rep 28 at 30. Also see misleading discussion on this issue in the libel suit in *The Irish People's Assurance Society v The City of Dublin Assurance Co Ltd* [1929] IR 25 at 34.

**[34.36]** In contrast in *McMullen v Mulhall and Farrell*[58] where two union officials said to an employer: "McMullen [a house painter] is not a member of any society [ie union] and you must sack him today. You can't employ him", the Supreme Court of the Irish Free State held that these words did not touch him in his vocation, nor were they spoken of him in the way of his calling.[59]

**[34.37]** A distinction which the common law made, however, between offices for profit and offices of honour has seemingly survived s 19 of the 1961 Act. If the words complained of suggest incompetence rather than dishonesty the rule is that they are only actionable *per se* in respect of offices of profit. In other words, it would be actionable *per se* to say of a surgeon or a solicitor or a teacher that he or she was incompetent, but not of an alderman whose position is honorary only. But even in the case of the holder of an honorary office it is actionable *per se* to say that he or she is dishonest or lacks integrity or is so incompetent that his or her removal would be justified.[60] Such a fine distinction should hardly have survived the reformer's hand in 1961.

***Slanders imputing a criminal offence punishable by death or imprisonment***

**[34.38]** Slanders under this heading were actionable *per se* at common law.[61] Whether the policy behind this exception is that such slanders tend to ostracise the plaintiff or put his or her liberty in jeopardy is not clear. That the exception is confined to offences which carry the penalty of imprisonment at least, and does not extend to crimes which are punishable by fine only[62] (this is so even though imprisonment may follow indirectly through the non-payment of the fine), seems to suggest that the policy being promoted relates to the plaintiff's liberty. In *Lemon v Simmons*,[63] where the defendant stated that a husband stole from his wife before they separated, it was held that it was not actionable *per se*, because such appropriation by a husband was normally not punishable in law for somewhat technical reasons. Although the statement suggested dishonesty, the husband's liberty was never threatened. In contrast, however, the argument which suggests that social ostracism is the policy being promoted can be supported by cases like *Gray v Jones*,[64] where the statement that the plaintiff was "a convicted person" was held to be within the rule because, although it did not threaten the plaintiff's liberty, it tended to ostracise the plaintiff socially. Even here there is doubt as to whether the ostracism in question would extend to trade ostracism as well as social ostracism where, for example, a trading company was wrongly accused of a crime punishable by imprisonment.[65]

---

58. [1929] IR 470.
59. Professor Heuston doubted whether this view would still hold. See SALMOND & HEUSTON, (18th ed), p 179.
60. *Robinson v Ward* (1958) 108 L Jo 491; *Alexander v Jenkins* [1892] 1 QB 797.
61. *Cf Ruckley v Kiernan* (1857) 7 ICLR 75; *McCabe v Foot* (1866) 11 Ir Jur (ns) 287; *Dempsey v Wall & Co and Ryan* (1943) 78 ILTR 73 (CC); *Coleman v Keanes Ltd* [1946] Ir Jur Rep 5 (HC); *Corcoran v W & R Jacob* [1945] IR 446. To call a person "a swindler" is not an actionable slander under this head if special damage is not shown. It does not impute a crime. *Black v Hunt* (1978) 2 LR Ir 10, distinguishing *Kinahan v McCullagh* (1877) Ir R 11 CL 1.
62. *McCabe v Foot* (1865) 11 IJNS 287 - statutory fishing offence punishable by fine only.
63. (1888) 57 LJ QB 260.
64. [1939] 1 All ER 798.
65. *Cf D & L Caterers Ltd v D'Ajou* [1945] KB 364 (CA).

**[34.39]** Apart from this policy problem, however, it is clear that in such an action a court exercising civil jurisdiction might in some cases be obliged to examine in depth the criminal question whether a particular crime is punishable by imprisonment or not.

***Imputation that plaintiff suffers from an infectious or contagious disease***

**[34.40]** As the policy here seems to be that such a slander would tend to socially ostracise the plaintiff the exception is confined to existing diseases rather than past ones which no longer pose a social threat.[66]

**[34.41]** There is some doubt, however, as to what diseases are covered. To accuse a person wrongly of having a contagious venereal disease is sufficient to make the defamation actionable *per se*.[67] There is also weaker authority for a similar conclusion in relation to leprosy[68] and plague.[69] In England it has been suggested[70] that it would extend to any contagious skin disease caused by personal uncleanliness. But there is more doubt, and little authority, in respect of tuberculosis, scarlet fever and the like.[71] It is submitted that to suggest that a person has AIDS would nowadays be actionable *per se*.

## Special Damages required in all other Slanders

**[34.42]** Apart from the above exceptions, the plaintiff in a slander action must show special damage. Curiously enough, however, it is not sufficient for the plaintiff to show loss of reputation, although this primarily is the interest which the tort is designed to protect.[72] The plaintiff must show proof of some real or actual damage such as the loss of the material benefits of friends' hospitality[73] or the loss of consortium[74] or the loss of a contractual or other tangible business advantage.[75] Loss of company or expulsion from a religious community, without any material loss, is not enough.[76] Neither is apprehended loss, however likely, sufficient.[77] It should be noted, however, that once some actual damage is shown by the plaintiff, the Court may award aggravated damages in respect of the general loss of reputation.

**[34.43]** The defendant must be shown to have caused the damage to the plaintiff and, in spite of old authorities to the contrary, it seems that the general rules on causation and remoteness in the law of torts should equally apply in defamation nowadays. If the damage is the natural and reasonable consequence of the defamation then the defendant ought to be

---

66. *Taylor v Hall* (1743) 2 Stra 1189, 93 ER 1118; *Carslake v Mapledoram* (1788) 2 TR 473,100 ER 255. There is no Irish authority on this matter.
67. *Bloodsworth v Gray* (1844) 7 Man & G 334, 135 ER 140, *Milner v Reeves* (1617) 1 Roll Abr 43.
68. *Taylor v Perkins* (1607) Cro Jac 144; 79 ER 126. It is likely that AIDS would be included in the category now.
69. *Cf Villers v Monsley* (1769) 2 Wits KB 403, 95 ER 886.
70. *Report of the Porter Committee on the Law of Defamation* (1948), para 45 (Cmd 9305).
71. See STREET, p 453.
72. *Roberts v Roberts* (1864) 5 B & S 384, 122 ER 874.
73. *Davies v Solomon* (1871) LR 7 QB 112.
74. See *Lynch v Knight* (1861) 9 HL Cas 577, 11 ER 854. But, however serious the special damage, if the statement is not defamatory, no action will lie: *Sheahan v Ahearne* (1875) IR 9 CL 412 (QB).
75. *Storey v Challands* (1837) 8 C & P 234, 173 ER 475.
76. *Dwyer v Meehan* (1886) 18 LR Ir 138 (CP Div).
77. *Jones v Jones* [1916] 2 AC 481.

liable for it. Accordingly, if the plaintiff is dismissed (even wrongfully) by the person to whom the defamation is published, in spite of old authorities, the defendant ought to be liable if this was a reasonable consequence of the publication. Professor Heuston was also of the view that:

> "although it was once held that illness resulting from mental trouble produced by slander was too remote, now the decision is questionable in view of modern developments in the law relating to nervous shock".[78]

**[34.44]** The above statement of the position would seem to be based on principle and general trends rather than on pure legal authority, and would seem to admit of one well acknowledged exception in any event: a person is not liable for the special damage caused by the repetition of slanders rather than by the original slander itself except where the person who repeats the slander is under a legal or moral duty to repeat it,[79] or where the repetition is intended, authorised or perhaps foreseen by the person who made the original defamation.[80] On closer analysis, however, the statements made in this paragraph may be no more than a traditional way of saying that, without special knowledge, the person who makes a defamatory statement need not anticipate that others will repeat the defamation; but if he or she should so anticipate he or she will be liable. And what could be more foreseeable than that a person who has a legal or moral duty, or who is intended or authorised or indeed likely to repeat, will in fact so repeat the slanderous statements?

**[34.45]** The Law Reform Commission recommended in 1991 that the distinction between libel and slander should be abolished on the grounds that the distinction is purely historical and has made the law unnecessarily complex. The Commission, however, recommended that a new cause of action should be introduced in which proof of special damage (ie specific pecuniary loss) would not be necessary.[81]

## Foreign Publications

### *Where to sue and for what damages*

**[34.46]** Irish citizens are increasingly exposed to foreign publications (especially English newspapers) and broadcasts (both radio, TV and internet) and if a libel appears in one of these, the question arises as to where the plaintiff can bring his action. This is essentially a matter for resolution by rules relating to the conflicts of laws and a full treatment of the problem can be found in the relevant texts in this area. Because of the increasing flow of international comment in the modern world, however, and the peculiar relevance it has for the tort of defamation a brief word on the topic is necessary.

---

78. SALMOND & HEUSTON, p 189, citing *Allsop v Allsop* (1860) 5 H & N 534, 157 ER 1292 and *Rigby v Mirror Newspapers Ltd* [1964] SR (NSW) 34.
79. *Derry v Handley* (1867) 16 LT 263.
80. *Ward v Lewis* [1955] 1 WLR 9; *Cellactite and British Uralite v HH Robertson C* [1957] CLY 1980; *Speight v Gosnay* (1891) 60 LJQB 231. Same rule applied in libel: see *Weld-Blundell v Stephens* [1920] AC 956 at 987 (*per* Lord Sumner) and 999 (*per* Lord Wrenbury); *Ewins v Carlton Television Ltd* [1997] 2 ILRM 223.
81. LRC Report, 3.3, December 1991.

**[34.47]** In *Ewins v Carlton UK Television Ltd*[82] the plaintiff sued for libel arising out of two documentary programmes on IRA activities, made and published by Carlton and disseminated to the public by ITN, including Carlton and Ulster TV, in 1995. Each of the defendants was a British Company and entered a conditional appearance challenging the jurisdiction of the Irish High Court.

**[34.48]** Barr J, applying the rules of the Brussels Convention, stated that the plaintiff was entitled to sue either where the damage occurred or where the event causing the damage occurred. The programme was broadcast in the Britain but was watched by various means in this jurisdiction by an estimated 111,000 viewers. Holding that there was no legal distinction between publication and distribution, in TV or radio programming, where both happened simultaneously, Barr J concluded that a libel was committed on every occasion and in every place where the words were published. Moreover, the original publisher was liable for the repetition and republication by another where such republication was the natural and probable cause of the original publication. Since it was a natural and probable cause of Carlton's providing the programme to Ulster TV that it would be seen by a significant number of viewers in this jurisdiction, the judge went on to hold that the harm was done in the State within the meaning of Article 5(3) of the Convention. In these circumstances the plaintiff is entitled to sue the publisher either in the place where the tort is committed or where the defendant is domiciled. Where the plaintiff chooses to proceed in the jurisdiction where the defendant is domiciled then the plaintiff will be able to recover for all damages which he or she has suffered within the jurisdiction of the signatory states of the Convention; if however, the plaintiff chooses to sue in Ireland then the damages will be limited to the damage which the publication caused in Ireland.

**[34.49]** It is also worth noting that once the plaintiff has established jurisdiction under the Convention, the Court has no power to refuse jurisdiction on the ground of *forum non conveniens*, except in an extreme case and to prevent injustice (for example, where the plaintiff is abusing process or is guilty of unconscionable conduct), when it might exercise its inherent jurisdiction to refuse to hear the matter.[83]

## III. What is Defamatory?

**[34.50]** As we have seen, in the law of defamation the courts will protect a person's reputation if the false statement, in the phrases favoured by the judiciary, tends to lower the plaintiff in the eyes of right-thinking members of society or if it tends to hold the plaintiff up to hatred, ridicule[84] or contempt, or causes him or her to be shunned or avoided in

---

82. [1997] 2 ILRM 223.

83. See also *Murray v Times Newspapers Ltd* High Court, 12 December 1995 (Barron J); Buttimore 'Recent Discussion on the Brussels Convention on Jurisdiction and Enforcement of Judgments' 4(1) Br Rev 1998, pp 46-50; Kaczorowska 'Foreign Torts in the UK and Ireland – A New European Perspective' 5 Ir EL 20. The jurisdictional basis is now the Jurisdiction of Courts and Enforcemnt of Judgments Act 1988.

84. It was held to be defamatory for a local newspaper to say of two barmen that: "One of the barmen looked like Lazarus before he came out of retirement. The other fellow was the reverse: he looked like him when he went back again", Irish Times, 23 November 1997, (CC) cited by McDonald, *Irish Law of Defamation* (1st ed).

society.[85] Although these judicial criteria may clearly indicate that to call a person a murderer,[86] a thief,[87] a forger,[88] a swindler,[89] a person who would give or receive a bribe[90] or a prostitute would be defamatory, they are not terribly helpful in many cases where the accusation against the plaintiff falls short of criminal conduct. For example, on the above criteria is it defamatory to accuse a Republican of being a Unionist, or to say of a woman that she has been raped?[91]

**[34.51]** In cases such as these one may of course have resort to precedent and such a source may undoubtedly be of assistance. Precedents, however, in this area must be looked at more suspiciously than precedents in other areas of tort law, because the criterion being used by the courts in determining what is defamatory is much more rooted to the date of the statement and to the location of the particular society in question, than the standards used by the courts in other areas of tort. Social values change from time to time and from society to society. To call an Irish person in Ireland a "land-grabber" or an "informer" might well be defamatory, but might well be otherwise construed by an English court. Similarly, the time element is important. To call a person "a red-hot Socialist" in the 1930s might have defamed him or her, whereas today it would not be held to have any derogatory connotation. Because the criterion used by the courts in Ireland, therefore, is rooted to Irish society at the present time, precedents from earlier times, and indeed, precedents from other jurisdictions today, must be suitably interpreted and modified before they can be confidently relied on as authority before Irish courts. "The opinions of juries - and of judges - are notoriously subjective and unpredictable in deciding what is defamatory."[92]

**[34.52]** It should also be noted in this general context that whether a statement is defamatory or not is an objective matter and is not determined by the fact that the speaker meant or intended no harm. On the question of whether there is a defamation or not, the speaker's intent, although possibly relevant to the issue of qualified privilege or damages, is by and large irrelevant.[93]

**[34.53]** One can, of course, get some guidance as to judicial attitudes from previous cases; bearing in mind what has just been said it is worth looking at some of these now.[94]

**[34.54]** A suggestion made by an auctioneer that the plaintiff had not acted in accordance with the highest traditions of his profession as a solicitor was accepted as being

85. See *Quigley v Creation Ltd* [1971] IR 269; *Berry v Irish Times* [1973] IR 368.
86. *A fortiori*, an accusation of genocide. *Cf Daishowa Inc v Friends of the Lubicon* (1998) 41 CCLT (2d) 193 - where, although the word was intended to connote cultural genocide in an environmental context, it had not actually been used with such qualification.
87. *Cf White v Store Security Ltd* Circuit Court, 21 February 1985 (Judge Martin); Evening Herald, 21 February 1985, p 5, cols 1-2; *Boland v Tara Mines Ltd* Irish Times, 3 March 1984, p 8.
88. *Cf McCarthey v Maguire* [1899] 2 IR 802 (CA affg KBD).
89. *Cf Hewson v Cleeve* [1904] 2 IR 536 (CA revg KBD).
90. *Davis v Reeves* (1855) 45 ICLR 79.
91. See *Yousoupoff v Metro Goldwin Mayer Pictures* (1934) 50 TLR 581.
92. *Barrett v Independent Newspapers*, [1986] IR 13 at 32 (SC).
93. *White v Tyrell* (1856) 5 ICLR 477.
94. See McDonald, *Irish Law of Defamation* for a long list of examples.

defamatory in *Curneen v Sweeney*[95] and in *Bennett v Quane*[96] where a medical doctor said of the plaintiff, a solicitor, that "He brought an action in the Circuit Court instead of the District Court to get more costs for himself", it was held that these words were defamatory on the face of them. With some doubt, Judge Ó Briain came to the conclusion that:

> "the words used have a natural tendency to injure the plaintiff in his reputation as a solicitor by implying that he had not acted in this instance in accordance with the highest and strictest traditions of his profession."[97]

**[34.55]** Moreover, in *Fullam v Associated Newspapers Ltd*[98] the former Supreme Court held that to say of a well known professional footballer that he never used his right foot in kicking the ball because he was unable to do so, was capable of being defamatory if it was not true.[99] Indeed, in general it may be said that wrongfully to impute lack of competence, skill or qualification to a businessman, trader or professional man is defamatory.[100]

**[34.56]** In *Doyle v The Economist Newspaper Ltd*[101] the defendant published an article on judicial appointments in Northern Ireland which contained the following statement:

> "When three new county court judges were finally appointed last month, one of them was in fact a Catholic. But his appointment has come in for criticism in the bar library in Belfast, particularly among Catholic QCs who consider that he was appointed as a token, and that some of their Protestant colleagues would have been better fitted for the job."

Doyle J, the Catholic appointee in question, was awarded £50,000 in damages in the Northern Ireland Court of Appeal. Before the appeal was heard, however, the action was settled for (it appears) substantially less.[102]

---

95. (1969) 103 ILTR 29 (SC).
96. [1948] Ir Jur Rep 28.
97. [1948] Ir Jur Rep 28 at 29. See also *McCarthy v Maguire* [1899] 2 IR 802.
98. [1955-56] Ir Jur Rep 45.
99. Cited with apparent approval by Walsh J in *Quigley v Creation Ltd* [1971] IR 269 at 272-273.
100. See *McKeogh v O'Brien Moran* [1927] IR 348 (HC); *Drummond-Jackson v British Medical Association* [1970] 1 All ER 1094 (CA) *Atkinson v Congreve* (1857) 7 ICLR 109; *Thompson and Thompson v Gill and Macmillan et al*, Irish Times, 3 November 1987 - architects wrongly associated with badly designed building. *Cf O'Hea v Guardians of the Cork Union* (1892) 32 LR (Ir) 629 (QBD), where, in the absence of a plea of innuendo, it was held that an advertisement stating that the defendants would appoint a solicitor, "other than the late solicitors", to do all their legal business was not defamatory. *Per* Harrison J at 638-639:

    > "No one can say that the words of the notice ... bear on the face of them any but an innocent meaning ... It is obvious that they can bear a harmless meaning. I could mention several. For instance, the Board may have come to the conclusion and desired to express merely that they wanted one solicitor only, and wished for a new one. They may have felt that other candidates might be slow to apply for an office which others in the same profession had been holding. Perhaps, without any desire to disparage the conduct of these gentlemen, they may have considered that the business had not been done as well as they should have liked, or that their former solicitor had not sufficient time at their disposal, or that there might have been some unpleasantness ..., if the Board had to receive and consider applications as well from their former solicitors as from others. Perhaps they wished simply to make lighter their labour in their choice of candidates."

    To accuse a person of religious bigotry - a Protestant refusing to hire a hearse for a Catholic funeral - was sufficiently derogatory to go to trial: *Treacy v McKenna* (1869) IR 4 CL 374.
101. [1981] NI 171 (HC).
102. Irish Times, 9 December 1980, p 11. For critical comment on the case see article by Young, The Sunday Times, 7 September 1980, p 16.

**[34.57]** In *Sinclair v Gogarty*[103] imputations of sexual impropriety made against the plaintiffs in a book (including the charge that one of them, the proprietor of an antique shop, "sought new mistresses more highly than old masters") were held to be so clearly defamatory that a temporary injunction was granted to prevent the continuing sale of the celebrated novel "As I was Walking Down Sackville Street".[104]

**[34.58]** To accuse a person wrongly of trickery in racing activities would appear to be defamatory. In *Green v Blake*[105] an owner/rider at Killeagh point-to-point was accused of deceitfully carrying under weight. The plaintiff was "warned off", after a hearing which did not comply with the principles of natural justice, and notices to this effect were published in the Racing Calendar. Although the Supreme Court declared the trial to be unsatisfactory for various reasons and ordered a new trial, there was no dispute as to the defamatory nature of the statements. Again, a letter of the Turf Club wrongfully requesting the plaintiff's name to be placed on Defaulters' List was defamatory.[106]

**[34.59]** It was also held to be defamatory to impute that the plaintiff made deliberately false statements to a local corporation for the purposes of deceiving the corporation, and that the plaintiff was unfit for public office.[107] Similarly to suggest jobbery and to accuse members of a local corporation of voting to maintain opportunities for patronage or privileges is defamatory.[108] To say of a politician that he would not pay tax on betting was also held to be defamatory.[109]

**[34.60]** In *De Rossa v Independent Newspapers plc*[110] the plaintiff recovered damages of £300,000 for an article which appeared in the defendant's publication concerning the plaintiff who was leader of the Democratic Left political party. The article made certain allegations as to the sources of support which Mr De Rossa accepted when he was a leading member of the Worker's Party. The jury found that the words complained of meant that the plaintiff was involved in or tolerated serious crime and that he personally supported anti-Semitism and violent Communist oppression, and were libellous. This was not appealed. The measure of damages awarded was appealed as being excessive, but the Supreme Court did not reduce them.

**[34.61]** To accuse a person wrongfully of theft[111] is defamatory. Many of the cases on this are defended on the grounds of privilege, the defamatory nature of the accusation being

---

103. [1937] IR 377. *Cf M'Cullough v Munn* [1908] 2 IR 194 (CA).

104. The details of the libel are not set out in the Report, but are discussed by O'Connor, *Oliver St John Gogarty* (1981), pp 299-308. Other cases where suggestions of immorality were held to be defamatory were, *Tait v Beggs* [1905] 2 IR 525; *Corcoran v Corcoran* (1956) 7 ICLR 272. See also *Cassidy v Kincaid* (1865) 10 IJ NS 176.

105. [1948] IR 242.

106. *Reilly v Gill* 85 ILTR 165 (SC). *Cf Doyle v Griffin* Supreme Court, 21 December 1936 - plaintiff disclaimed a cause of action based on libel and instead brought claim for injurious falsehood; Supreme Court rejected this approach; see, however, Murnaghan J's judgment at pp 12-13.

107. *Nevin v Roddy and Carty* [1935] IR 397 (SC).

108. *Black & Others v Northern Whig Ltd* (1942) 77 ILTR 5 (KBD, NI); *McDonnell v Preece*, Irish Times, 21 November 1985, p 10.

109. *MacSharry v McCormack and Ocline Associates Ltd* Irish Times, 1 May 1985.

110. Supreme Court, 30 July 1999.

111. *Cf Smith v Carr* [1937] IR 248 (HC); *Coleman v Keanes Ltd* [1946] Ir Jur Rep 5 (HC); *Dempsey v Wall and Co Ltd and Ryan* (1943) 78 ILTR 73 (CC). See also Skeffington (1996) ILT 14(1), pp 22-23.

rarely disputed.[112] To make a statement which imputes unnatural offences to the plaintiff is defamatory.[113] Likewise it is defamatory to accuse a person wrongfully of impersonation at elections[114] or to say of the plaintiff that he received money by false pretences[115] or to say that the plaintiff was blackmailing,[116] or gave[117] or received[118] a bribe, or perjured himself.[119] To say of a female model that when she was not working she could be seen at her favourite bar drinking Guinness was held to be defamatory.[120]

**[34.62]** Three more difficult cases deserve a further word. In *Pyke v Hibernian Bank*,[121] three of the plaintiff's cheques drawn by him within permitted overdraft limits, were returned to payees by the bank marked: "Refer to Drawer - Present Again", and "Return to Drawer". Although the plaintiff pleaded innuendoes the trial judge withdrew any question of innuendo from the jury and awarded £400 for libel. (He also awarded £1 for breach of contract). On appeal to the Supreme Court, a four man court split and the High Court decision stood. On the plain meaning of the words O'Byrne J (with whom Geoghegan J agreed) said:

> "It seems to me that one or other of two alternative views at once emerges: either (a) that there are no funds to meet the cheque or (b) that the order for payment contained in the cheque has been countermanded since the cheque was given to the payee and, presumably, consideration was obtained therefor. Either of those views seems to me to be reasonably capable of a defamatory meaning quoad the drawer of the cheque as implying (a) that he is insolvent or (b) that he is guilty of a want of good faith towards the payee of the cheque."[122]

---

112. *Coleman v Keanes Ltd* [1946] Ir Jur Rep 5 - defendant-shopkeeper; *Sevenoakes v Latimer* (1919) 54 ILTR 11 (KBD) - defendant postmaster; *Corcoran v W & R Jacob & Co* [1945] IR 446 - defendant-employer; *Dempsey v Wall & Co Ltd & Philip Ryan* 78 ILTR 73 (CC) - defendant-ex-employer.
113. *Bolton v O'Brien* (1885) 16 LR Ir 483 (CA), affg (1885) 16 LR Ir 97 (KBD).
114. *Higgins v Monaghan & Reilly* (1939) 74 ILTR 56.
115. See *Kirkwood Hackett v Tierney* [1952] IR 185 (SC).
116. *Hartery v Welltrade (Middle East) Ltd & Hurley* [1978] ILRM 38 (HC). To accuse Gardaí of assault and brutality is defamatory. See also *Nestor v O'Brien*, Irish Times, 21 May 1998 (SC) - false accusation of use of heavy handed debt-collectig techniques. *Hogan and O'Neill v Sunday World* High Court 20 March, 1981 (Hamilton J). For example of words not defamatory on their face see *Keogh v Incorporated Dental Hospital of Ireland* [1910] *2* IR 577 (KBD).
117. *Moor v Foster* (1696) Cro Jac 65, ER; *Bendish v Lindsay* (1709) 11 Mod 194; *O'Brien v Mirror Group Newspapers Ltd* Supreme Court, 25 October 2000.
118. *Cf Crawford v Vance* [1908] 2 IR 521 (CA affg KBD).
119. *Costello v Orange* High Court, Irish Times, 21 June 1986, p 20.
120. *Sodden v Image Magazine*, Irish Times, 5 October 1983, p 1.

    "What could be more defamatory of any young or old, single or married woman than to portray her as sitting up drinking at a bar in this fashion. Who would like to think of their daughter or wife, mother or grandmother doing this?" *per* Roe J.
121. [1950] IR 195.
122. [1950] IR 195 at 204. But see *Ross Meats v Bank of Ireland* Irish Times, 10 May 1986, where plaintiff failed. *Cf Lewis v Daily Telegraph Ltd* [1964] AC 234. See also *Grealy v Bank of Nova Scotia*, Supreme Court, 11 April 1975. There a High Court award to a plaintiff whose cheques had been marked by the bank "Refer to drawer", was appealed only on the grounds of there being no evidence of malice on the part of the bank which would destroy a privileged occasion. It was conceded that the words were libellous.

**[34.63]** Maguire CJ was of the opinion that the words "Refer to Drawer" were not capable of defamatory meaning in the absence of innuendo while Black J preferred to find for the defendant on the ground that the occasion was privileged even though the occasion for the communication was brought about by the bank's own mistake.

**[34.64]** In *Quigley v Creation Ltd*[123] the defendant published in a women's weekly magazine an article purporting to be based on an interview with the plaintiff who was a well known Irish actor. No such interview took place and the plaintiff's name appeared immediately below the title of the article 'They've left this Isle". The plaintiff claimed that the words used in the article, in their ordinary meaning, implied that he had left Ireland not for any proper reason such as furthering his art, but solely for love of money and "that in so far as he was seeking employment in Ireland he was doing so dishonestly on a false basis since he had decided to make his career overseas".[124] It was not claimed that the statement would be defamatory in the case of every person, but that it was defamatory in the case of an artist who was primarily interested in giving his art to the people of his own country, as opposed to an artist who held himself out as being interested in giving his art to the highest bidder, irrespective of his origins or from where he drew his inspiration.

**[34.65]** Walsh J delivering the judgment of the Supreme Court made the following statement of the law:

> "Basically, the question of libel or no libel is a matter of opinion and opinions may vary reasonably within very wide limits. When a jury has found that there has been a libel, this Court would be more slow to set aside such a verdict than in other types of actions and it would only do so if it was of opinion that the conclusion reached by the jury was one to which reasonable men could not or ought not have come. It is true that if words only tend to lower a person in the minds of a particular class or section of society, particularly if the standard of that particular section of society is one which the Court cannot recognise or approve, the words will not be held to be defamatory. On the other hand, words are defamatory if they impute conduct which would tend to lower that person in the eyes of a considerable and respectable class of the community, though not in the eyes of the community as a whole. The test is whether it will lower him in the eyes of the average right-thinking man. If it will, then it is defamatory if untrue. It follows naturally that in an action in this country the standard would be that of the average right-thinking person in this community. The law recognises the right of the plaintiff to have the estimation in which he stands in the opinion of the right-minded people in this community unaffected by false statements to his discredit."[125]

The Supreme Court refused to set aside the High Court's verdict in favour of the plaintiff.

**[34.66]** What emerges from this case and others, therefore, is that in determining what is defamatory the Courts will judge the matter in the eyes of right-thinking members of the community or a respectable class of the community.[126] But while this indicates that the court will not consider a statement defamatory if it only tends to lower the plaintiff in the eyes of a non-respectable section of the community (and the court decides which sections

123. [1971] IR 269.
124. [1971] IR 269 at 271.
125. [1971] IR 269 at 272.
126. See *Mawe v Piggott* (1869) IR 4 CL 54 (Com Pleas).

are respectable or non-respectable),[127] it does not tell us directly whether a matter is to be considered defamatory because of what right-thinking members of society in fact think, or because of what they ought to think. In the *Quigley* judgment, Walsh J acknowledges that to state of a woman that she has been raped might well amount to defamation, even though no right-thinking member of society ought to think less of the plaintiff because of her misfortune. He observed:

> "In determining this matter, the judge will construe the words in accordance with a fair and natural meaning such as would be given to them by reasonable persons of ordinary intelligence in our own community; and that necessarily involves a consideration of the standards of the community and the position of the plaintiff in that community. In a community which places a high value on female chastity, to say untruthfully of a woman that she was a victim of a rape may well lower her in the eyes of the community by creating an undesirable interest in her or by leaving her exposed to the risk of being shunned or avoided - however irrational it may appear that a person who has been the victim of a criminal assault should as a result, through no fault of her own, be lowered in the eyes of ordinary reasonable persons in the community:[128] see the remarks of Scrutton LJ in *Youssoupoff v Metro-Goldwyn-Mayer Pictures Ltd*."[129]

This suggests that the court must follow community norms rather than apply its value judgment as to how right-thinking members of society ought to regard the plaintiff.[130] The objection to this approach, of course, is that the courts, in compensating victims of social prejudice whose complaint is that the prejudice is mistakenly focused on them, are taking a tacit, if not compliant, attitude.

**[34.67]** Thus, to impute insanity[131] or insolvency[132] is defamatory even though either of these misfortunes ought not to cause right-thinking members of society to think less of the unfortunates visited by these difficulties. Similarly, the Court of Appeal in England refused to withdraw from the jury the issue whether the words that the plaintiff was "hideously ugly" were capable of being defamatory.[133]

---

127. To say of a bridge player that he or she uses prohibited hand signals, might not shock the general population, but would evoke condemnation from genuine members of the bridge playing community, and accordingly, could well be defamatory. Similarly, to say of a golfer that he "kicked his ball out of the rough" might scandalise genuine golfers, although it might be a matter of little concern to the public at large. On the assumption that bridge players and golfers constitute a "respectable class" of the community, such accusations would be defamatory.

128. *Cf* Weidner & Griffitt 'Rape: A Sexual Stigma?' (1983) 51 J of Personality 153.

129. [1971 ] IR at 272. *Youssoupoff v Metro-Goldwyn Mayer Pictures Ltd* (1934) 50 Times LR 581, fn 66.

130. In other cases, however, the judge, when postulating what the reasonable person would think, will substitute what he (the judge) thinks the reasonable person would think. *Cf* McDonald, *Irish Law of Defamation* (1st ed), p 15. In *Grassi v WIC Radio Ltd* (2000) 49 CCLT (2d) 65 at 79 (BC, SC), Lysyk J spoke of lowering the plaintiff's reputation in the estimation of "reasonable persons in the community".

131. *Morgan v Lingen* (1863) 6 LT 800.

132. *Pyke v Hibernian Bank* [1950] IR 195 at 204. See also *Flynn v Hibernian Bank Ltd* [1938] Ir Jur Rep 34 (HC); *Security Pak Strapping v Evening Press*, Cork Examiner, 20 June 1987, p 11 - defendant suggested plaintiff had gone into liquidation.

133. *Berkoff v Burdhill and Times Newspapers Ltd* [1996] 4 All ER 1008. Noted Hall, (1998) 92 Incorp L Soc of Ireland Gaz, p 7.

**[34.68]** The question as to what is defamatory came before the Supreme Court some decades ago in *Berry v Irish Times Ltd.*[134] The Irish Times in this case published a report of a Sinn Fein picket outside BOAC offices in Dublin. Accompanying the report, a photograph of one of the picketers carrying a placard was reproduced. The placard in question carried the following words which were clearly legible in the newspaper photograph: "Peter Berry - 20th Century Felon Setter - Helped Jail Republicans in England". Mr Berry, who was then Secretary of the Department of Justice, claimed the words were defamatory. No innuendo was pleaded. The jury found that the words were not defamatory and the Supreme Court, on a three to two verdict, refused to set aside the jury's verdict on the basis that no reasonable jury could have made such a finding.

**[34.69]** The implication of the words, according to the plaintiff, was that the plaintiff had furnished the English authorities with information which helped to secure the conviction in England of two Irishmen for criminal, though politically inspired, offences. Ó Dálaigh CJ, delivering the decision of the majority of the Court, put the matter in the following language:

> "It is perhaps surprising that the Supreme Court should be asked to hold, as a matter of law, that it is necessarily defamatory to say of one of the citizens of this country that he assisted in the bringing to justice in another country of a fellow countryman who broke the laws of that country and who was tried and convicted for that offence in the ordinary course of the administration of criminal justice. This Court is bound to uphold the rule of law and its decisions must be conditioned by this duty. Is the matter to be considered differently because the person or persons so convicted were motivated by a desire to resolve, by force of arms, a dispute existing between their own country and the country in which the offence was committed when there is not a state of war between the two countries? To say, in those circumstances, that such an allegation must be defamatory would be to hold that ordinary right-thinking people in this country could not condemn such militant activities- to the extent that one could not but think that a person who assisted in curbing or putting down such militant activities was guilty of disgraceful conduct. That, in effect, is what was alleged against the plaintiff."[135]

**[34.70]** In the absence of an innuendo (such as that the words meant that Mr Berry had improperly misused information or had been in breach of trust so as to render him unfit for office) a jury would not be compelled to hold the words defamatory.[136]

**[34.71]** The vigour of the dissents, however, show clearly how difficult it is to anticipate in such cases how the Courts will interpret the attitude of right-thinking members of society. Fitzgerald J put it his way:

> "It appears to me, and I think it would appear to any Irishman of normal experience and intelligence, that the words complained of were clearly a libel. 'Felon-setter' and 'Helped jail republicans in England' were not words in respect of which one has to have recourse to a

134. [1973] IR 368.

135. [1973] IR 368 at 375-376.

136. Ó Dálaigh CJ suggests at p 376 that if Mr Berry had been called an "informer" he might have succeeded. See *McInerney v Clareman Printing and Publishing Co* [1903] 2 IR 347 (CA affg KBD), where plaintiff was referred to as a "land grabber". Case decided on different point. See also *Mawe v Piggott* (1869) IR 4 CL 54. See also Post, 74 Calif LR 691 at 714-5 referred to in LRC Consultation Paper, p 9.

dictionary to know what they meant to an Irishman; they were equivalent to calling him a traitor."[137]

**[34.72]** McLoughlin J said:

> "It is my view that there must be many right-thinking persons who, although they do not approve of or positively disapprove of the acts of militant republicans in England, would regard the plaintiff with contempt if they believed that he had gone out of his way to supply information to the British police so as to have such persons jailed in England. It may be that one's views on matters of this sort are conditioned by one's up-bringing and education. The school sneak who, however justified, 'splits to the head' was regarded with contempt by all his fellows."[138]

**[34.73]** Earlier in his judgment in the *Berry* case McLoughlin J expressed his opinion in the following way:

> "Put in other words, the suggestion is that this Irishman, the plaintiff, has acted as a spy and informer for the British police concerning republicans in England, thus putting the plaintiff into the same category as the spies and informers of earlier centuries who were regarded with loathing and abomination by all decent people."[139]

**[34.74]** In *Egan v BBC*[140] in a programme on the kidnapping of Dr Herrema, the plaintiff, a Detective Sergeant who lost a finger as a result of a shooting during the siege, was described by the actor portraying Eddie Gallagher, one of the kidnappers, in the following language "Egan - Egan is the bastard that tortured the boys in Mayo when the RUC man was shot, remember?" The BBC admitted that the words in their ordinary and natural meaning were defamatory.

**[34.75]** Two more recent cases, *McDonagh v News Group Newspapers Ltd*[141] and *Reynolds v Molocco t/a "Patrick" and others*[142] illustrate how defamations can arise in modern Ireland and how political contexts and moral values impact on judicial deliberations in determining what is and what is not defamatory.

**[34.76]** In *McDonagh v News Group Newspapers Ltd* the plaintiff was a barrister appointed by the Irish Government to represent Ireland at the inquest held in Gibraltar into the shooting dead of Mairéad Farrell, Seán Savage and Daniel McCann, members of the provisional IRA by members of the SAS regiment of the British army. The Sun newspaper published an article under the headline "Leftie Spies pack Gib Inquest" which the jury held to mean that the plaintiff was a left-wing spy, was a sympathiser with terrorist causes, was biased, lacking in integrity, and incapable of exercising sound judgment, all of which allegations were defamatory and untrue. In refusing to upset the jury's findings (and its award of £90,000), Finlay CJ in reference to the suggestion that the plaintiff was "a sympathiser with terrorist causes", speaking for the Supreme Court said:

---

137. [1973] IR at 378.

138. [1973] IR at 378 at 382. But see *Byrne v Deane* [1937]1 KB 818 and McDonald, *Irish Law of Defamation*, p 18.

139. [1973] IR at 379-380.

140. Irish Times, 10 December 1980, p 13.

141. Supreme Court, 23 November 1993.

142. High Court, 11 December 1998 (Kelly J).

> "I am satisfied that there are not very many general classifications of defamatory accusation which at present in Ireland, in the minds of right-minded people, would be considered significantly more serious. To an extent the seriousness may be somewhat aggravated by the fact that it is an accusation which has been made against a person who has a role, by reason of his standing as a member of the Bar, in the administration of justice"[143]

**[34.77]** In *Reynolds v Malocco t/a "Patrick"*[144] the plaintiff was a company director involved in running two Dublin nightclubs called "Pod" and "Red Box". He sought an interlocutory injunction restraining the defendants from publishing an article entitled "Operation Night-cap Causes John Reynolds Sleepless Nights As Cops Raid Club", in the first issue of a new magazine called "Patrick". The plaintiff claimed that the article defamed him in two respects. He said the words in their natural or ordinary meaning or by innuendo alleged (i) that he has been charged with permitting the sale of drugs in his nightclubs and that he permitted the sale of goods on his premises and was benefiting therefrom and (ii) that he was a homosexual. In relation to the latter allegation the plaintiff was referred to in the article as a "gay bachelor". The defendants accepted that the plaintiff was not a homosexual and disclaimed any intention of pleading justification. In addition they said that they never alleged he was a homosexual. They claimed that the word "gay" in its ordinary meaning is an adjective used to describe a persons demeanour of being "lively, cheerful, vivacious, light-hearted, fond of pleasure and gaiety". Kelly J said that if this argument had been advanced thirty years before this case it would probably have succeeded, "but it is an absurd proposition to put to the Court in 1998". He then went on to say:

> "Language is a living thing and words can change their meaning over the years. Sometimes the primary meaning of a word will undergo subtle or even profound changes. On other occasions the word may acquire a secondary meaning which it did not formerly have. The word 'gay' falls into the second category. Over the last thirty years or so it has come to be synonymous with homosexuals and homosexual activity. One would have to be a resident on the moon not to be aware of this. Not merely has it acquired this secondary meaning but it has in fact eclipsed the primary meaning so that nowadays one rarely hears the term used other than a[s] denoting homosexuals or homosexual activity."[145]

**[34.78]** Kelly J also rejected the argument put forward by the defendant that the word "gay" (as an adjective) qualifying the noun "bachelor", was a term in common use to refer to men who are happily unmarried. The judge was of the view that the term "gay bachelor" in that sense had practically fallen out of use largely because of the secondary meaning of the word "gay".[146] Finally, the defendants squarely confronted the main issue: they said that to say a person is a homosexual nowadays in Ireland is not harmful to his reputation: homosexuality, it was argued, is an accepted part of Irish life and homosexuals are now accepted and integrated into the fabric of Irish life. The plaintiff argued that the allegation of being gay is an allegation of deviant sexual practice which many people in Irish society find repellant. Kelly J found for the plaintiff in this matter, relying on the *obitur dictum* of

143. At p 15 of judgment.
144. High Court, 11 December 1998 (Kelly J).
145. At p 15 of judgment.
146. To say a woman who lost her husband, that she was "A Merry Widow" might not be obviously defamatory.

Stephenson LJ in *Regina v Bishop*.[147] That was a case where the Court of Appeal held that the character of a witness was damaged by an allegation of homosexual conduct made against him and an implication of homosexual immorality against a witness might reflect on his reliability. Stephenson LJ in delivering the judgment of the Court said:

> "[Counsel for the defendant] submitted that in these progressive (or permissive) days is was no longer an imputation on a man's character to say of him that he was a homosexual or that he practised homosexuality. Since 1967, when s 1 of the Sexual Offences Act, 1967 became law, it was no longer an offence to commit a homosexual act with another man of full age in private. No reasonable person would now think the worse of a man who committed such acts: he might not wish to associate with him but he would not condemn him. We think that this argument goes too far and that the gap between what is declared by Parliament to be illegal and punishable and what the common man or woman still regards as immoral or wrong is not wide enough to support it. We respectfully agree with the opinion of Lord Reid in *Regina v Knuller (Publishing Printing and Promotions) Limited* [1973] AC 435 at 457 that 'there is a material difference between merely exempting certain conduct from criminal penalties and making it lawful in the full sense' and with him we read the Act of 1967 as saying that even though homosexual acts between consenting adults in private may be corrupting, if people choose to corrupt themselves in this way that is their affair and the law will not interfere. If Mr Price were to sue the Defendant in respect of his allegation if repeated outside a Court of law, we venture to think that a submission that the words were incapable of a defamatory meaning would be bound to fail and a jury would generally be likely to find them defamatory."[148]

**[34.79]** Acknowledging that the statement was *obiter*, Kelly J said it appeared to be the law in England and in his view "it also represents the legal position in Ireland". Moreover, Kelly J was of the view that merely because homosexuality was no longer a criminal offence, did not necessarily mean that the statement could not be defamatory:

> "The commission of adultery is not a criminal offence but nobody could seriously suggest that an allegation of adultery could not be defamatory. Similarly, to lie is not a criminal offence, but again can it be seriously suggested that to call a person a liar is not defamatory?"[149]

**[34.80]** It might be concluded from this decision that to allege that a woman is a lesbian would also be defamatory in Ireland at this time.

**[34.81]** Kelly J's judgment does not involve a differentiation between homosexual acts and homosexual orientation. There is an important legal difference since clearly being of homosexual orientation does not expose one to the prospect of criminal prosecution[150] whereas engaging in homosexual acts, even in private,[151] formerly did so and continues do to so where the conduct is in public.[152] If the allegation is restricted to one of orientation, such as the assertion that the plaintiff has never translated his homosexual urges into

---

147. (1975) 1 QB 274 (CA).

148. High Court, 11 December 1998 (Kelly J), pp 17-18.

149. High Court, 11 December 1998, p 18.

150. Homosexual orientation is of certain legal significance, however. It is a ground for annulment of a marriage: see *UF (otherwise UC) v JC* [1991] 2 IR 445 (SC); Shatter, *Family Law* (4th ed, 1997); Byrne & Binchy, *Annual Review of Irish Law 1990*.

151. Offences Against the Person Act 1861, ss 61 and 62 and the Criminal Law (Amendment) Act 1885, s 11.

152. Criminal Law (Sexual Offences) Act 1993, s 14.

action, is that defamatory under Kelly J's reasoning? The answer appears to be that it is not necessarily so, since Kelly J's holding seems strongly focused on conduct. Nevertheless, if Irish defamation law responds to the prejudices of society by granting a remedy where a false allegation triggers such a prejudiced response (such as that a woman has been raped, for example, or that a person has a mental illness), it seems that a false allegation of homosexual orientation should on this controversial bias[153] be actionable in defamation.

**[34.82]** In *Reynolds v Times Newspapers Ltd*,[154] the former Taoiseach was libelled by an article in the British edition of the Sunday Times. The article was written days after Mr Albert Reynolds had resigned as Taoiseach and leader of the Fianna Fail party, and was headed "Goodbye gombeen man" and was sub-headed "Why a fib too far proved fatal for the political career of Ireland's peacemaker and Mr Fixit". The matter is discussed later in connection with the defence of qualified privilege, but it appears that Mr Reynolds's claim that the words meant that he deliberately and dishonestly misled the Dáil was considered to be defamatory.

**[34.83]** The recommendations of the Law Reform Commission favoured a new statutory definition of defamation and its proposal in this regard is set out here so that it might suggest to the reader where the present law, as outlined here, might be criticised by some reformers.

**[34.84]** The Commission recommended that defamation be defined as follows:

> (1) Defamation is the publication by any means of defamatory matter concerning the plaintiff.
>
> (2) Defamatory matter defined: defamatory matter is matter which (a) is untrue and (b) tends to injure the plaintiff's reputation.
>
> (3) Publication defined: publication is the intentional or negligent communication of defamatory matter to at least one person other than the plaintiff.
>
> (4) Standard by which injury is measured: matter shall be considered injurious to the plaintiff's reputation if it injures his reputation in the eyes of reasonable members of the community.
>
> (5) "Concerning" defined: defamatory matter concerns the plaintiff if it would correctly or reasonably be understood to refer to the plaintiff.
>
> (6) Burden of Proof: the burden of proof is on the plaintiff to show that there was publication, that the matter contained in the publication was defamatory and that the defamatory matter concerned the plaintiff.[155]

## Vulgar Abuse not Defamatory

**[34.85]** It has often been said that mere vulgar abuse does not amount to defamation and this is largely true. Accordingly, to address a person in terms which the matriarchs of an earlier age would have described as "soldiers' language" might not qualify as defamation nowadays. Many of the vulgar words which at one time were attributed to the vocabulary of army personnel are now so widely adopted as not used in a descriptive sense at all, but

153. See our criticism of this approach, see para **[34.66]** above.

154. [1999] 4 All ER 609.

155. LRC, Report, para 3.13, December 1991. The effect of this recommendation would be that a prejudiced social response would not be considered "reasonable".

rather for colloquial emphasis. Thus, without resorting to more colourful examples, to call a person a "thunderin' whore" or "an old bastard" may not necessarily amount to defamation.[156] The gist of the action in defamation is injury to reputation and if the remarks are made in an abusive way or in anger so that they injure only the pride of the plaintiff rather than his reputation no action lies at common law. Of course, it may not be always easy to draw the line between words which cause injury to a person's reputation and vulgar abuse.[157]

**[34.86]** Moreover, an apparently defamatory statement can be rendered totally innocuous, of course, by the context in which it is uttered. To call a person a thief or a horse-thief might normally be defamatory but to say to an acquaintance in backslapping banter "How are you, you old horse-thief?" would not be defamatory.[158] And a lady in a West End drawing room who says "Lord X, you are a thief, you have stolen my heart" would obviously not be liable in defamation.[159]

**[34.87]** The context and the circumstances of the remark become much more important in the case of a slander than in the case of a written statement. In the latter case, one may assume that a certain amount of care and deliberation was taken in making the statement whereas, with an oral statement, the tone, the gestures and the surrounding circumstances can quite easily give a different slant to what appears to be defamatory on the face of it, and consequently these factors can rarely be ignored.

**[34.88]** In this context it should be emphasised that it is for the plaintiff to prove that the statement is defamatory. He does not, however, have to prove its falsity: the law presumes that defamatory statements are false. If the defendant wishes to assert that the statements are not false, he must undertake the onus of proving their truth, through the defence of justification.[160] The onus on the plaintiff to prove the defamatory nature of the statement becomes particularly important when the plaintiff pleads an innuendo.

## The Innuendo

**[34.89]** Just as a seemingly obvious defamation may be rendered innocent by reference to the circumstances in which the statement was made, so also a seemingly innocent remark may be shown to be defamatory because of a hidden significance which the uttered words bear. It is said that all statements are either prima facie defamatory or prima facie innocent and that secondary meanings can be shown in either case by the person who alleges such a hidden meaning. Where the statement is prima facie defamatory the defendant can, and indeed must, prove the circumstances that extract the barb from the apparently defamatory

156. See, eg *Harberagen v Koppens* [1974] 2 NZLR 597 ("Dutch bastard"). See also Hall, 'Hideously Ugly: Defamation or Mere Ridicule?' (1998) 92 GILSI 7. See also *Fisher v Nation Newspaper and Rooney* [1901] 2 IR 465.

157. Words accompanied by threats of physical violence may of course amount to assault, and abusive language which is intended to cause a person to act so that he suffers nervous shock may be actionable under the rule in *Wilkinson v Downton* [1897] 2 QB 57.

158. *Cf* The American Restatement Torts, Second, 563.

159. See *Broome v Agar* (1928) 138 LT 698, 702 (*per* Sankey LJ); *Gwynne v Wairarapa Times-Age* [1972] NZLR 586 - "Hitler's fascist people" in the context of a labour dispute not defamatory.

160. [1973] IR 368. See para **[34.123]** below.

words if he wishes to escape liability. In contrast, where the statement is prima facie innocent the plaintiff must prove that the words have a secondary meaning which makes them defamatory. In *Berry v The Irish Times*[161] the Supreme Court held that to say of the plaintiff that he was a "20th Century Felon-Setter" and "Helped Jail Republican Prisoners in England" was not defamatory on the face of it and since the plaintiff had not pleaded or proved the innuendo he must fail. Ó Dálaigh CJ, giving the majority's decision, stated:

> "If the allegation was that the plaintiff did it as Secretary of the Department of Justice, then he would do so only on the authority of his Minister or of the Government. Alternatively, the allegation might convey that he did so independently of such authority; but unless it were claimed that in doing so he improperly and in breach of his trust as Secretary of the Department used information which came into his possession as such officer, for example, without the authority of his Minister or of the Government, the allegation must not necessarily be held to be defamatory. No such construction was attempted to be put upon these words. If it had been so, the action would have been of quite a different nature as such an accusation would really have been a reflection on the plaintiff's fitness for his position."[162]

**[34.90]** The secondary meaning may be derived either from the words themselves, such as by "reading between the lines", or by proof of extrinsic and additional facts. To say that the police are investigating X's affairs, might imply that X is under suspicion of having committed a crime.[163] This implication might be deduced from the words themselves. No amount of deduction, however, could make the statement that "X entered No 10 Church Street" defamatory without additional facts being proved, as for example, that No 10 Church Street is a brothel. These situations are known in law as innuendoes. The former type of innuendo, where the defamatory meaning can be implied from the words themselves, is known as a false innuendo (popular innuendo), whereas the latter, where extrinsic or additional information must be produced, is known as a true innuendo (legal innuendo).

**[34.91]** Where the plaintiff relies on a true innuendo he must plead it and he must prove at the trial the extrinsic facts which make the innocent statement defamatory.[164] If he does not plead it he will not be allowed to raise it at the trial.[165] Furthermore, each true innuendo, establishes a separate cause of action.[166] After a close examination of the earlier precedents and earlier legislation, the Law Reform Commission summarised the rules on pleading the innuendo in the following way:

---

161. See para **[34.68]** above.

162. [1973] IR 368 at 376.

163. See eg *Bell v Northern Constitution Ltd* [1943] NI 108 (KBD).

164. See *McCann v Edinburgh Roperie & Sailcloth Co* (1889) 28 LR Ir 24 (ExD); *O'Hea v Guardian of Cork Union* (1892) 32 LR Ir 629 (QBD); *M'Manus v M'Enroe* (1851) 1 ICLR 332 (Com Pleas). See also *Bell v Northern Constitution* [1943] NI 108. With regard to pleading the innuendo and the facts on which it is based, see McDonald, *Irish Law of Defamation*, pp 47-48.

165. For criticisms of the rule see McDonald, *Irish Law of Defamation*, p 50.

166. For the case where the jury found against the innuendo but found that the words were a libel, and where, even though the plaintiff did not claim that the words were actionable *per se*, the trial judge's decision to award damages to the plaintiff was upheld on appeal, see *Fisher v Nation Newspaper Co Ltd and Rooney* [1901] 2 IR 465.

"Where a legal innuendo is relied on, the extrinsic facts supporting it must be proved at a trial if the plaintiff is to succeed upon the innuendo. However, it would appear that it is not necessary in Ireland to plead the extrinsic facts in the Statement of Claim, although this appears to be the normal practice.

Where one or more legal innuendoes are successfully pleaded, each gives rise to a separate cause of action, entitling the plaintiff to a separate verdict and award of damages in respect of each innuendo.

Where a plaintiff pleads a defamatory meaning in the legal innuendo sense only and fails, he may fall back on the ordinary and natural meaning of the words.

Where it is contended that words are defamatory in their ordinary and natural meaning, it is not necessary for the plaintiff to plead any more than the words themselves. Hence where the plaintiff relies on a popular innuendo, it is not probably necessary to plead such an innuendo where there is any doubt as to the meaning; there is a need to crystallise the meaning of a long article.

A defamatory meaning may be conveyed by publishing true and accurate matter in a misleading way or context."[167]

**[34.92]** Examples of false innuendoes, in the Irish law occur in the following cases. In *Campbell v Irish Press Ltd*,[168] the plaintiff, who was in the business of providing billiards and snooker equipment, organised a snooker exhibition at which the well-known snooker player Joe Davis, was the attraction. In a review article published the next day after the exhibition the author was critical of the exhibition and said that Davis failed to make a century break because "the table told lies" (ie was uneven). The jury held that the statement implied that the plaintiff was incompetent in organising such exhibitions. A new trial was ordered on other issues by the Supreme Court, but the fact that the statement was capable of a defamatory meaning was not disputed by the Court.[169] In *Fullam v Associated Newspapers Ltd*[170] a newspaper article claimed that the plaintiff, a successful and well-known professional footballer, never used his right foot except for balancing on. The plaintiff claimed successfully that the statement implied that he was not a competent footballer and that he should not have been picked as an international player.[171] In *The Irish People's Assurance Society v The City of Dublin Assurance Co Ltd*[172] the defendant company reproduced extracts from the plaintiff society's balance sheet relating to amounts due to their banks. The plaintiff claimed successfully that these words were intended to

167. LRC Report, 1991, pp 16-17.

168. (1955) 90 ILTR 105.

169. See also *McMullan v Mulhall & Farrell* [1929] IR 470; *Pyke v Hibernian Bank* [1950] IR 195; *Keogh v Incorporated Dental Hospital* [1910] 2 IR 166, 577; *Eilisword and Berni Ni Fhlatharta v Irish Independent*, Irish Times, 7 July 1988, p 10; *Keating v Stephen's Green Publications Ltd and Browne*, Irish Times, 15 December 1985; *Maxwell v Gorman* Cork Examiner, 12 December 1981, p 11 - defendant sent a postcard to plaintiff's husband saying that the plaintiff "was lucky to get rid of the black baby from Santie". Plaintiff pleaded that words were calculated to mean that the plaintiff was unchaste, had given birth to an illegitimate child and had disposed of the child and that she was of criminal character. Plaintiff was awarded £400.

170. [1953-54] Ir Jur Rep 79 (HC), affd by [1955-56] Ir Jur Rep 45 (SC).

171. See also *Bennett v Quane* [1948] Ir Jur Rep 28.

172. [1929] IR 25.

represent that the plaintiff company was insolvent and financially unsafe.[173] In *Robinson v Chambers*[174] the plaintiff was a churchwarden and a synodsman of Glenavy Parish Church (Church of Ireland) where the defendant was the rector. Differences arose between the two and the defendant published a letter recommending the removal from office of the plaintiff for the following reasons (among others):

> "...
>
> (c) Making collections in the name of the parish without reference to the vestry, and giving no account of same.
>
> (d) Assuming the powers of the Courts of the Synods ..."

**[34.93]** The plaintiff claimed successfully that the words meant and were understood to mean that the plaintiff obtained money by false pretences, that he had committed an offence under the Larceny Act 1916, and that he was a dishonest and untrustworthy person.

**[34.94]** Two further celebrated cases which illustrate well the nature of the true innuendo should be mentioned. In *Tolley v Fry & Sons Ltd*[175] the plaintiff, an amateur golfer, sued the well-known chocolate manufacturers for a libel which arose in the following circumstances: the defendants published a caricature of the plaintiff which represented him in golfing costume having just completed a drive, with a packet of the defendant's chocolate protruding from his pocket, in the company of a caddie who was holding up packets of the defendant's chocolate, and below the caricature was a limerick in the following terms:

> "The caddie to Tolley said: 'Oh, Sir!
>
> Good shot, Sir! That ball, see it go, Sir.
>
> My word, how it flies,
>
> Like a cartet of Fry's.
>
> They're handy, they're good, and priced low, Sir"[176]

---

173. See also *Irish Toys and Utilities Ltd v "The Irish Times" Ltd* [1937] IR 298. In *Maxwell v Gavin Low Ltd* Supreme Court, 11 January 1967, auctioneer who accused plaintiff (wrongly it seems) in the words "You bought the bull", had made a defamatory statement. The occasion was privileged, however, and no malice was shown.

174. [1946] NI 148.

175. [1931] AC 333.

176. [1931] AC 333 at 336-337 (*per* Viscount Hailsham). See also *Gibbings v O'Dea & Co Ltd* [1948-49] MacGillivray & Le Quesne's Copyright Cases p 31 (HC), where the facts closely resembled those in *Tolley v Fry & Sons Ltd.* In this case, however, the jury found for the defendant. The drafting of the plaintiff's claim suggests a close acquaintance with *Tolley v Fry & Sons Ltd.* Today a plaintiff might possibly succeed on a broader ground of appropriation of personality: *Cf* Pannam (1966) 40 Aust LJ 4. See also Weeks 'Comparative Law of Privacy' (1963) 12 Clev-Mar LR 484 at 489-490 and Ch 37 below. *Cf Hollinsworth v BCTV* (1998) 44 CCLT (2d) 83 - broadcasting of videotape of surgery treatment of plaintiff's baldness on provincial television without plaintiff's consent, held not defamatory as the film "was true" and without a false statement or false innuendo the cause of action in defamation had to fail; those who gave the videotape to the television station breached the plaintiff's privacy but television station did not, as it honestly and reasonably believed that it was entitled to broadcast it.

**[34.95]** The plaintiff sued for libel and successfully pleaded the innuendo that the advertisement, which was published without his consent, meant and was understood to mean that he had prostituted his reputation as an amateur golfer for advertising purposes.

**[34.96]** In *Cassidy v Daily Mirror Newspapers Ltd*[177] the defendant company published a photograph of a Mr Cassidy (otherwise known as Corrigan) with a Miss X, and innocently stated that their engagement had been announced. Mr Cassidy was at the time in fact married to, although only occasionally living with, the plaintiff. The plaintiff claimed that several people understood from the newspaper report that Mr Cassidy was not her husband but was living with her in immoral cohabitation. The English Court of Appeal upheld a jury verdict of £500 in favour of the plaintiff. Apart from providing a good example of the true innuendo, this case also shows that liability in libel does not depend on the intention of the defamer, a matter that will be discussed in more detail below.

## Functions of Judge and Jury

**[34.97]** At this juncture a word should be said about the respective functions of the judge and jury in defamation cases. The division of function in the initial stages of the trial is not an unfamiliar division in the law of torts in Ireland. It is for the judge to say at the outset whether the words uttered are capable of a defamatory meaning in law.[178] If the judge decides that the words are capable of such a defamatory meaning, then it is for the jury to decide whether the words in fact have a defamatory meaning in the present circumstances before the Court.[179]

> "In defamation, as perhaps no other form of civil proceedings, the position of the jury is so uniquely important that, while it is for the judge to determine whether the words complained of are capable of a defamatory meaning, the judge should not withhold the matter from the jury unless he is satisfied that it would be wholly unreasonable to attribute a libellous meaning to the words complained of."[180]

**[34.98]** From this it should be clear that most doubtful cases are, therefore, left by the trial judge to the jury, but there are examples where the trial judge at the end of the plaintiff's

---

177. [1929] 2 KB 331. See also *The Nation Newspaper Ltd v Cheshire* (1984) 2 Ken App Rep 17 (CA Nairobi).

178. *Duffy v NewsGroup Newspapers Ltd* [1994] 1 ILRM 364; *Quigley v Creation Ltd* [1971] IR 269, esp Walsh J at 272.

179. *Pyke v The Hibernian Bank Ltd* [1950] IR 195; *Quigley v Creation Ltd* [1971] IR 269. See also *Treacy v McKenna* (1869) IR 4 CL 374 (Exch). At a motion stage where the defendant applies to have the plaintiff's case struck out as being unsustainable the question to be decided is not whether the words are "capable" of being defamatory, but whether it is "arguable" that they are capable of such a meaning. If arguably they are capable of a defamatory meaning they will not be struck out at the preliminary stage. See *Conlon v Times Newspapers Ltd* [1995] 2 ILRM 76.

180. *Quigley v Creation Ltd* [1971] IR 269 at 272 (*per* Walsh J). See also *Paul v Holt* (1935) 69 ILTR 157 (NICA). The judge must leave the statement for the jury to consider if there is a possible defamatory meaning, notwithstanding the possibility of innocent meanings. See McDonald, *Irish Law of Defamation*, p 41. The judge cannot withdraw from jury where he or she considers that the statement is incapable of an innocent meaning. The majority of the Supreme Court forcibly so held in *Barrett v Independent Newspapers Ltd* [1986] IR 45. See also *McDonough v News Group Newspapers Ltd* Supreme Court, 23 November 1993; *Duffy v News Group Newspapers Ltd* [1994] 1 ILRM 364, esp at 371 (*per* O'Flaherty J).

case has given a verdict by direction on the grounds that the words were not capable of bearing a defamatory meaning. In *Irish Toys and Utilities Ltd v "The Irish Times" Ltd*[181] the defendant published an announcement that a new factory was being opened in Belmullet and that it was "proposed to transfer the machinery from the disused toy factory at Tralee". The trial judge refused to let the matter go to the jury on the grounds that the words suggesting that the plaintiffs had gone out of business were not capable of a defamatory meaning.[182]

**[34.99]** In relation to the converse situation, ie, whether the judge can withdraw the case from the jury when he thinks that the words spoken are incapable of an innocent meaning, the better opinion would seem to be that he cannot. To do so would be to usurp the jury's function.[183]

**[34.100]** Once the matter goes to the jury, an appellate court would be most reluctant to upset a jury finding of defamation.[184] Circumstances, however, may occasionally arise where the appellate court will set aside a jury verdict on such a matter.[185] In *McMullan v Mulhall and Farrell*,[186] where the defendants, union officials, wrongfully said to the plaintiff's employer that he must dismiss the plaintiff because he was not a member of a trade union, the jury found that the plaintiff had been slandered. The Supreme Court held, however, that the words were not defamatory and set aside the judgment for the plaintiff and entered a judgment for the defendants.

---

181. [1937] IR 298.

182. In *Kavanagh v Leader Ltd* Supreme Court, 4 March 1955, the well known literary figure Patrick Kavanagh sued the defendant for libel. The Supreme Court upset a jury finding principally on the grounds that the questions put to the jury by the trial judge could have confused it. A new trial was ordered. Because of the notoriety of the case the following extract from the judgment of Kingsmill Moore J, is worth quoting. The article in question was published in a journal called The Leader and was entitled "Profile: Mr Patrick Kavanagh".

> "Brilliantly written, in places sardonic, in places sympathetic, it dealt with Mr Kavanagh's poetry and journalism, and his virtues and character as manifested in his output. It contained also a description of Mr Kavanagh's presiding in a public bar over a coterie of submissive acolytes and, by contrast, an imaginary picture of Mr Kavanagh's land of heart's desire, a London Literary Salon ...
>
> Mr Kavanagh's poetry was given unstinted praise -'The Great Hunger' being described as probably the best poem written in Ireland since 'The Deserted Village' - but his prose writings were criticised unfavourably and his views and character were certainly not held up to admiration. The impression conveyed by the article to me, and which would, I think, have been conveyed to most people, was that Mr Kavanagh was somewhat of a poseur, unsubtle, opinionated and overbearing. For myself I find it difficult to see how anyone could come to a conclusion other than that Mr Kavanagh was held up to ridicule, though perhaps mild ridicule, and to contempt, though perhaps gentle contempt. In fairness, however, it should be said that the object of the article would seem to be, in part at least, to adjure Mr Kavanagh to develop his genius in the fields most suited for it, and that the criticism of his less successful ventures is used, with literary artifice, to focus a spotlight of appreciation on his poetic vision and craftsmanship."

183. *Barrett v Independent Newspapers* [1986] ILRM 601.

184. See *Quigley v Creation Ltd* [1971] IR 269.

185. *Kavanagh v Leader Ltd* Supreme Court, 4 March 1955; *Mclnerney v The "Clareman" Co Ltd* [1903] 2 IR 375.

186. [1929] IR 470.

**[34.101]** Where there is an innuendo a perceptive judicial *dictum* on the respective roles of judge and jury is to be found in Black J's judgment in *Pyke v Hibernian Bank.*[187] Although the Supreme Court in this case was split (2:2), Black J's comments on this matter were not apparently disputed.

> "Finally, there remains the class of case in which, upon principles stated, and so far as the interpretation of the words *per se* is concerned, the judge would have to withdraw the case from the jury, but in which an innuendo is pleaded ascribing a special meaning to the words complained of. In that case, after hearing all the evidence, the judge must consider two questions: (a) Could the words, if used in the special sense alleged, reasonably be regarded as defamatory? and, if they could, (b) Could those to whom the words were published have concluded by reasonable inference, as distinct from conjecture, that the words were used in that special sense? If the judge is satisfied that the answer to both (a) and (b) is 'Yes', he must leave the case to the jury; but if he is satisfied that the answer to either (a) or (b) is 'No', then he must direct for the defendant."[188]

## Reference must be to the Plaintiff

**[34.102]** For the plaintiff to succeed in an action for defamation he must show that the statement in question referred to him. It goes without saying that he cannot complain if the statement strikes at a third party, but in no way refers to the plaintiff. In many cases where the plaintiff is named, and clearly described, no problem will arise. Thus, in *Berry v Irish Times*,[189] although the offending placard carried no greater description than the plaintiff's name, the defendant did not contest that it clearly referred to the plaintiff who was the then Secretary of the Department of Justice. It must be admitted, however, that the plaintiff's name in this case was not a very common one in Ireland, and had it been John Murphy, for example, one wonders whether defence counsel would have been so conciliatory. In most cases, however, the offending defamation, especially if it is a written libel, whether it is made in an article or a book, will carry a more extensive description than the plaintiff's name. It may refer to his address, his occupation and it may even reproduce a photograph of the plaintiff, which will make proof of reference to the plaintiff a relatively simple task.[190]

**[34.103]** Where the reference is not so specific, however, evidence may be introduced to show that the statement in question referred to, or was capable of referring to, the plaintiff.[191] In *Fullam v Associated Newspapers Ltd*,[192] the Court allowed evidence of the

187. [1950] IR 195.

188. [1950] IR 195 at 215. This interpretation of the law differed, according to Black J, from the English position as stated in *Odgers on Libel* (5th ed), p 116 which said that if words are capable of the meaning ascribed to them, however improbable it may appear that such was the meaning conveyed, it must be left to the jury to say whether or not they were in fact so understood.

189. See para **[34.68]** above.

190. *Cf Cooney v Sunday Newspapers Ltd and Terenure Printers Ltd and Computerset Ltd* High Court, 7 November 1978 (Butler J).

191. The author of literary fiction is faced with a real problem in many cases here especially in the form of literary effort sometimes called "faction". Even before this genre, however, authors (and their publishers) always ran a risk here since all fiction writers to a greater or lesser extent use real life models as bases for their literary characters. See Kaufman 'The Creative Process and Libel' New York Times Magazine, 5 April 1987, p 28. See also Wilson 'The Law of Libel and the Art of Fiction' (1981) 44 Law & Contemp Problems 27; Kirby 'Books, Bookselling and the Law' [1982] NZLJ 222.

192. [1953-54] Ir Jur Rep 79 (HC) affd [1955-56] Ir Jur Rep 45 (SC).

jeering of a crowd at a football stadium and of some of his neighbours[193] to show that the article in question referred to the plaintiff. In *Sinclair v Gogarty*[194] where an application for an interlocutory injunction was made, the plaintiffs were not named in the offending book. Reference was, however, made to "Two Jews in Sackville Street" and the affidavit of Mr Samuel Beckett that he understood the reference to be to the plaintiffs was sufficient evidence that the plaintiffs were the persons in question.[195] In *Gallagher and Shatter v Independent Newspapers Ltd*[196] the plaintiffs were solicitors who represented some clients in an action against the Censorship of Publications Board regarding the banning of a booklet on family planning. The plaintiffs complained that the defendant published a letter in the Evening Herald letter column under the heading "The Ultimate in Corruption" and which contained the following statement:

> "The *McGee* 'test' case, and now the *Crummey* case, are scandalous examples of behind the scenes plotting and scheming against the Constitution of the people, against Catholic parents and against Catholic family life by a handful of solicitors and judges, who in each other's company have conspired to adopt the sub-human norms of the foreign Irish Family Planning Association against the laws of Christ's vicar on earth."

**[34.104]** The jury found that the words complained of did not refer to the plaintiff and would not be understood by readers of the article to refer to them. It seems that no evidence (except the plaintiffs' own impressions) was produced by the plaintiffs to show that any person actually understood the words to refer to them.

**[34.105]** It should be noted that the intention of the author is largely irrelevant in deciding whether the words referred to the plaintiff. The test is whether reasonable people knowing some of the circumstances would think it referred to the plaintiff. In this sense the tort of defamation is strict.[197]

## Reference to a Class[198]

**[34.106]** If a defamatory statement is made about a class of persons, then whether one of the class can sue depends on the size of the class and whether the plaintiff can point to facts which show that he or she was particularly referred to. In some cases of course, this may oblige the plaintiff to plead an innuendo.

**[34.107]** If the class is small it may be easy to show that the defamatory statement referred to each member of the class. "My employees have been pilfering tea and I have dismissed some of them" was a statement made by an employer to a Ministry official in Northern Ireland during the last war. Although the case related to another point of law, it would appear that the plaintiff, one of the dismissed employees, would have had little difficulty

---

193. Sections of the crowd used to shout "carpet slipper", a phrase mentioned in the disputed article where it was said that the plaintiff, a professional footballer, was obliged to wear a carpet slipper on his shooting-foot during his training sessions, in an effort to get him to develop his weaker foot.

194. [1937] IR 377.

195. See for another eg of successful application for interim injunction *Scott v Eason & Son Ltd and Batsford Ltd* Irish Times, 9 August 1980, p 8.

196. Irish Times, 10 May 1980, p 10.

197. See para **[34.111]** below.

198. See the *Symposium on Group Defamation* (1964) 13 Clev-Mar LR 1, including Fryer, 'Group Defamation in England', p 26, which contains discussion of the Irish cases on the subject.

proving that in such circumstances the statement referred to him.[199] In *Le Fanu v Malcolmson*[200] an article was published by the defendants suggesting that cruelties were practised upon employees in some Irish factories. Certain other statements in the article, including a reference to Waterford, amounted to sufficient evidence to enable the jury to identify the plaintiff's Waterford factory as the factory primarily attacked. The plaintiff succeeded. Similarly an allegation, against 17 persons who were the subject of a prosecution that all "these defendants helped to murder HF", referred with sufficient particularity to each to enable one to sue the person who made the allegation.[201] It would appear from this that a defamation on the directors of a company or the trustees of a trust would in normal circumstances enable each of the directors or trustees to maintain an action in defamation.[202]

**[34.108]** In contrast to these cases, such general attacks, as "all lawyers are liars" or "all parsons are hypocrites" would normally be too general to permit any individual lawyer or parson to sue. Unless the statement was limited in some way (eg "All lawyers in this town are liars", where there are only three lawyers in question) it would be too general to be taken to refer to any individual.[203]

**[34.109]** In truth, whether an individual in the group can successfully sue in such a case depends on whether a reasonable member of the public would, taking all the facts into account, conclude that the plaintiff himself, was guilty of the alleged conduct or, by innuendo, would be thought of as supporting or endorsing the alleged acts.

## Corporate and Personal plaintiffs

**[34.110]** A personal plaintiff who has been defamed may sue for defamation, regardless of the position that he or she holds. Thus a member of the Judiciary or a politician – even the Taoiseach – may take proceedings for defamation. Similarly a corporate plaintiff may sue for defamation where the defamation affects its corporate reputation. By way of qualification to this entitlement, the House of Lords, in *Derbyshire County Council v Times Newspapers Ltd*,[204] held that a local authority should not be able to maintain an action for defamation, Lord Keith observed that it was:

> "of the highest public importance that a democratically elected governmental body, or indeed any governmental body, should be open to uninhibited public criticism. The threat of a civil action for defamation must inevitably have an inhibiting effect on freedom of speech."[205]

---

199. See *McSorley v Masterson* (1945) 79 ILTR 45 (KBD, NI). *Cf Grassi v WIC Radio Ltd* (2000) 49 CCLT (2d) 65 at 90 (BC, SC).

200. (1848) 1 HL Cas 637, 9 ER 910.

201. *Foxcroft v Lacy* (1613) Hob 89, 80 ER 239.

202. STREET, p 398.

203. *Cf O'Brien v Eason & Son* (1913) 47 ILTR 266 (CA), an unsuccessful action by one member, for attack on an association called the Ancient Order of Hibernians, a political organisation with probably 100,000 members (*per* Holmes, J at 267). See also *Knupfer v London Express Ltd* [1944] AC 116. For analysis of the constitutional dimensions of group defamation, from the standpoint of the United States Constitution, see Campisano 'Note: Group Vilification Reconsidered' (1979) 89 Yale LJ 307.

204. [1993] AC 534 (HL)

205. [1993] AC 534 at 547. The logic of this analysis has been applied to debar a political party from suing for defamation: *Goldsmith v Bhoyrul* [1997] 4 All ER 268 (QBD).

## Unintentional References to the Plaintiff

**[34.111]** A more interesting question arises when the defendant makes a statement wherein he intends to refer to one person but the statement is understood to refer to another person. Can that other person sue the defendant even if the latter did not know it applied to the plaintiff, or was ignorant of the plaintiff's existence? The answer at common law was yes. The tort is strict to the extent and he who makes statements is obliged at common law to see that they do not injure, even unintentionally, innocent persons.[206] In *Hulton v Jones* the defendants published a fictional article about the double existence led by one "Artemus Jones". Among other things it was suggested that Jones, a churchwarden at home in England, was, while on the French side of the Channel, "the life and soul of a gay little band that haunts the Casino and turns night into day, besides betraying a most unholy delight in the society of female butterflies". The plaintiff, a barrister of the same name, recovered £1,750 damages for libel, other reasonable persons considering that the piece referred to him. Although there was some evidence that the defendants were reckless - the plaintiff Jones had been employed by the newspaper previously and was known to some at least of the newspaper's staff if not the author - the Court was willing to hold the defendants liable even in the absence of such recklessness.[207] In the *Newstead* case the Daily Express published a report of a bigamy trial of "Harold Newstead, thirty-year old Camberwell man". Unfortunately for the defendants there were two Harold Newsteads from Camberwell, one a barman of whom the report was true, the other a barber of whom it was not. The English Court of Appeal held that the jury were justified in finding that reasonable persons could have understood the words to apply to the plaintiff.[208] The fact, therefore, that the statement made is true of one person does not mean that it cannot be defamatory of another.

**[34.112]** The rule established by these cases imposed a high duty of vigilence on newspaper editors. When there was knowledge of special facts, or when the statement was *ex facie* defamatory, then it might be suggested that to impose such a high degree of vigilance was not unjust. Where the editor was ignorant of any special facts, however, or the statement was not defamatory on the face of it, the rule imposed an unacceptable onus on him; consequently, the hardship in the case of unintentional defamation was mitigated by s 21 of the Defamation Act 1961.

**[34.113]** This section, like s 4 of the English Defamation Act 1952, provides the person who innocently publishes defamatory matter about another with an opportunity to make an offer of amends. A person is deemed to be an innocent publisher if, and only if, either of the following conditions is satisfied regarding the defamatory words in question:

---

206. *Hulton v Jones* [1910] AC 20 (HL) and *Newstead v London Express Newspaper Ltd* [1940] 1 KB 377. See also *Morgan v Odhams Press Ltd* [1971] 1 WLR 1239; Symmons 'Proof of Reference to the Plaintiff' (1974) 3 Anglo-Am LR 98.

207. See also SALMOND & HEUSTON, p 144, fn 63. More generally see Warner-Fredman 'Comment: Defamation in Fiction: With Malice Toward None and Punitive Damages for All' (1983) 16 Loyola LR 99.

208. The jury, however, assessed damages at one farthing only.

> "(a) that the publisher did not intend to publish them of and concerning that other person, and did not know of circumstances by virtue of which they might be understood to refer to him; or
>
> (b) that the words were not defamatory on the face of them, and the publisher did not know of circumstances by virtue of which they might be understood to be defamatory of that other person, and in either case that the publisher exercised all reasonable care in relation to the publication; ..."[209]

**[34.114]** The requirement of reasonable care is of vital importance, because it emphasises that an offer of amends under s 21 is not available to the defendant where the publisher (or his servant or agent concerned with the contents of the publication) does not exercise reasonable care in relation to the publication. Accordingly if the facts of *Hulton v Jones* came before the Irish courts to-day, the defendant might not have the option of making an offer of amends under s 21, because he did not exercise reasonable care in that case.

**[34.115]** A word should be said in this context about mechanical distributors, such as booksellers and newsvendors. As we have seen they may be liable for defamation, but they will escape liability if they can show that they were not aware that the offending publication contained defamatory matter and that they had no ground for supposing that it might.[210] This is the position under common law, but there is no reason why such distributors should not also fall back on the protection of s 21 of the Defamation Act 1961 if the common law is not sufficient to relieve them from liability.

**[34.116]** The legal effect of an offer of amends varies according to whether it is accepted by the aggrieved party or not. If the offer is accepted, and it is duly performed, then no proceedings for libel or slander may be taken. If it is not accepted, then it is a defence for the defendant to prove that (a) the words were published innocently in relation to the plaintiff, (b) the offer was made as soon as practicable after the defendant received notice of the reference to the plaintiff and (c) the offer has not been withdrawn.

**[34.117]** Under the section the offer must be expressed to be made for the purposes of the section and must be accompanied by an affidavit of the facts relied upon to show the defendant's innocence. If the offer is rejected and the defendant relies upon it as a defence under the section, he will be limited in proving innocence, etc, to the facts set out in the affidavit. Consequently, the drafting of such an affidavit is of some importance.

**[34.118]** An offer of amends will, according to the section, include the correction of the words complained of, an apology to the aggrieved party and, where copies of a document have been distributed, the taking of such steps as are practicable for notifying persons to whom copies have been distributed.

**[34.119]** Where the aggrieved party accepts the offer of amends any dispute between the parties relating to steps to be taken in fulfilment of the offer will be determined by the High Court (or if the proceedings have been commenced in the Circuit Court, by the Circuit Court). Such an order may include an order for costs and expenses.

**[34.120]** It should also be noted that if the aggrieved party has refused the offer of amends it will not amount to a defence where he can prove that he has suffered special damage.[211]

---

209. Section 21(5).

210. *Cf* para **[34.112]** above and supporting text.

211. Section 21(6).

**[34.121]** Finally, s 21(7) provides that a refusal of the offer of amends will not amount to a defence, in relation to the publication by any person of words of which he is not the author, unless the defendant proves that the words were written by the author without malice. According to *Salmond & Heuston,* this:

> "preserves (and indeed extends) the common law rule that the malice of one defendant infects his co-defendants. It seems that if the editor of a newspaper publishes an anonymous letter containing statements *ex facie* innocent, but in fact not so by reason of the fact that the writer is secretly actuated by malice, the editor cannot make use of this statutory defence."[212]

## IV. Defences

**[34.122]** The following are the principal defences available to the defendant in a defamation action:

1. Justification
2. Privilege (Absolute and Qualified)
3. Fair Comment
4. Consent
5. Apology
6. Offer of Amends

Each of these will be dealt with in turn.

### Justification

**[34.123]** The defence of justification obliges the defendant to prove the truth of the alleged defamatory statement. It is felt that if the statement is true then there is no wrong done to the plaintiff because, even if people do think less of him after the statement has been made, it is because the plaintiff had a false reputation at the outset; and the law will not protect a false reputation.[213] In recognising the totality of the defence of justification, the law gives precedence to the interest of freedom of speech over the interest of the individual's reputation. Truth is not a defence in relation to the crime of libel (save in cases of "public benefit"[214]) because of different policy considerations, and some jurisdictions have seen fit to limit it as a defence in civil actions also by a similar insistence that the true statements must have been made in the public interest.[215]

---

212. SALMOND & HEUSTON, p 152 referring to an identical provision in the English Defamation Act 1952. On constitutional issues relating to s 21 see McDonald, *Irish Law of Defamation*, p 233.

213. See *McPherson v Daniels* (1829) 10 B & C 263 at 272 (*per* Littledale J). It is possible that the Constitution affords protection against defamatory, true statements where there is no genuine public interest in knowing the truth: *Cf* the Walsh J's observation, extra-judicially, in 'The Judicial Power and the Protection of the Right of Privacy' [1977] DULJ 3 at 8. Other possible avenues of recovery are the torts of intentional and negligent infliction of emotional suffering. For consideration of developments in the United States, see Mead 'Suing Media for Emotional Distress: A Multi-Method Analysis of Tort Law Evolution', (1983) 23 Washburn LJ 24. On law of privacy see Ch 37 below.

214. Defamation Act 1961, s 6.

215. Some states in USA require good motives and justifiable ends to make truth a defence. For Australian position see FLEMING, pp 613-614. See also England's Rehabilitation of Offenders Act 1974, s 8.

**[34.124]** Where the defence is available it is a total defence and cannot be destroyed either by showing malice on the part of the defendant or that the defendant believed that statement to be false when he made it. It is, however, for the defendant to plead and prove the truth of the statement and not for the plaintiff to show that the defamation was false.[216] Once the plaintiff shows the statement to be defamatory the presumption arises that it is false and the onus is then on the defendant to justify.[217] It should also be mentioned that the defence is a dangerous one, for if the defendant fails he or she may well have to pay aggravated damages for having persisted in the lie.

**[34.125]** The defence is established by the defendant if he or she can prove that the defamatory statement is substantially true, even if it is not true in every detail.[218] So where the defendant stated that the plaintiff was convicted for travelling in a train without a ticket and was fined £1 and three weeks imprisonment in default, the court held there was sufficient justification when the defendant showed that the fine imposed was £1 and two weeks imprisonment in default.[219] The error was not sufficiently great to distort the original statement.

**[34.126]** The defendant's proof, however, must extract the sting of defamation in a substantial way and, where the defendant makes false charges relating to two independent matters, he must generally be prepared to prove both. In *Crawford v Todd*,[220] where the defendant alleged that the plaintiff kept "a Hell's gambling den" and sold intoxicating liquor without a licence, the Court held that the failure by the defendant to prove the second allegation caused the defendant's whole defence of justification to fail. In other words the justification had to be as wide as the defamation.[221]

**[34.127]** The common law position has been qualified to a small extent by statute. Section 22 of the Defamation Act 1961 provides as follows:

> In an action for libel or slander in respect of words containing two or more distinct charges against the plaintiff, a defence of justification shall not fail by reason only that the truth of every charge is not proved, if the words not proved to be true do not materially injure the plaintiff's reputation having regard to the truth of the remaining charges.

---

216. See *Bolton v O'Brien* (1885) 16 LR Ir 483 (CA), affg (1885) 16 LR Ir 97 (QBD); *O'Shaughnessy v Hayden* (1824) 2 Fox & Smi 329. On necessity to plead justification see *Campbell v Irish Press Ltd* (1955) 90 ILTR 105 (SC).

217. *Campbell v Irish Press* (1955) 90 ILTR 105 at 109.

218. If the defendant alleges that the plaintiff is a thief can he prove this by showing that the plaintiff was convicted by a Court of this offence? The better opinion would suggest a positive answer to this question. See McDonald, *Irish Law of Defamation*, p 106 *et seq*. But see *Hollington v Hewthorn* [1943] KB 587.

219. *Alexander v North Eastern Ry Co* (1865) 6 B & S 340, 122 ER 1221. See also *O'Connor v Wallen* (1856) 6 ICLR 378.

220. (1941) 75 ILTR 233 (CA NI). *Cf Morrow v M'Gaver* (1851) 1 Ir CLR 579 (Comm Pi).

221. When the defendant has made more than one statement about the plaintiff, can the plaintiff select the statement he wishes to object to and sever it from the other less objectionable statements? There is little Irish authority on this question but the better opinion suggests that severence is allowable at least when the statements are very different and so severable from each other. See McDonald, *Irish Law of Defamation*, p 102 *et seq*.

**[34.128]** The task for the jury (and more particularly for the judge) in balancing the respective degrees of injury resulting from different charges is an unenviable one.

**[34.129]** Where the defendant makes two independent allegations about the plaintiff, for example, the defendant is a thief and an adulterer, he may be able to justify the first allegation but not the second, in which event he may succeed in establishing a partial justification. He will then be liable only for the defamation contained in the second allegation.[222]

**[34.130]** In relation to proof, the question has arisen as to whether a defendant who stated that the plaintiff has committed a crime (eg murder) can succeed in establishing the defence, when he shows that the plaintiff was convicted by a criminal court of the charge. The better view must undoubtedly be that this should suffice. The alternative would be unacceptable as it would lead to re-trying the criminal in a civil court, with the possibility that the civil court could come to a different conclusion on the balance of probabilities when the first court determined liability on the basis that it was beyond all reasonable doubt.[223]

**[34.131]** Where the statement complained of involves an innuendo the defendant must prove the truth of the statement in both its primary and secondary senses. Thus, if the defendant makes the statement that "X is helping the police with their enquires" in a criminal investigation and the context would also support the innuendo that X is under suspicion, then the defendant must, to succeed in the defence of justification be prepared not only to show that the police interviewed X, but that they suspected him also. In *The Irish People's Assurance Society v The City of Dublin Assurance Co Ltd*,[224] the defendant company published and printed a document wherein it reproduced the following extracts from the plaintiff society's balance sheet:

| | |
|---|---|
| Due to Bank at end of year | £2,618/2/11 |
| Bank Interest | £150/14/9 |

**[34.132]** In rejecting a defence of justification, the Supreme Court held that to prove the literal accuracy of these extracts would not succeed in establishing the defence of justification. The defendant should also prove the truth of the innuendo that the plaintiff society was insolvent or insecure. Fitzgibbon J said:

> "The figures and words may be correctly printed, but in my opinion if they are so arranged or excerpted as to convey an untrue impression of the financial condition of the company, and it is for a jury to decide whether they do so or not, the company is entitled to recover damages for the injury to its credit. It would be possible by judicious extraction to make almost any document convey the contrary of its real purport, and I hold that in such a case a jury is entitled to decide whether the statement of the extracts is true or not, and that mere accuracy of extraction is not *per se* conclusive to the truth of the statement made by the collected

222. See *Sutherland v Stopes* [1925] AC 47; *Goody v Odhams Press Ltd* [1967] 1 QB 333.

223. See *Goody v Odhams Press* [1967] 1 QB 333 and LRC Working Paper 1991, paras 65-66.

224. [1929] IR 25.

extracts. In such a case an innuendo may lawfully be pleaded just as it may where words are written or spoken ironically or in a non-natural sense."[225]

**[34.133]** Finally, it should be noted that to preface a defamatory statement with the clause "It is rumoured that ..." or "It is suspected that ..." (or some equivalent phrase) will not protect the defendant who can only prove that such a rumour or suspicion existed. The law will also oblige him to prove the content of the rumour before it allows him a defence. Were the law otherwise, reporters and the like could easily insulate themselves from legal attack by resorting to such prefaces on all occasions.[226]

## Privilege

**[34.134]** In some circumstances a person who makes a statement on a particular occasion is given exceptional latitude: in such a case the law considers that the public interest in the freedom of speech is best served by guaranteeing uninhibited expression. Such an occasion is said to be privileged in law. Privilege is either absolute or qualified: when it is absolute, the defendant is totally protected in respect of any statements which he may make, irrespective of spite, ill-will or knowledge; when it is qualified, the defendant is protected, except for statements made maliciously. In other words, malice will destroy qualified privilege, but not absolute privilege.

### *Absolute privilege*

**[34.135]** As might be expected, in view of the total immunity which they confer, the occasions recognised as being absolutely privileged in law are not numerous. The principal instances are as follows.

*(i) Presidential privilege*

**[34.136]** Article 13.8.1° of the Constitution provides that the President is not to be answerable to any Court for the exercise and performance of the powers and functions of his office or for any act done or purporting to be done by him in the exercise and performance of these powers and functions. This immunity would appear without question to embrace defamatory statements made by the President, though not, of course, those made by the President outside the contexts specified by Article 13.8.1°.[227]

*(ii) Parliamentary privilege*[228]

**[34.137]** The privilege here extends not only to statements made by members of the Oireachtas in either House, but also to official reports and publications of either House. This privilege, formerly based on s 1 of the Bill of Rights 1688, is now provided for in Article 15.12 and 15.13 of the Irish Constitution which read as follows:

> 12. All official reports and publications of the Oireachtas or of either House thereof and utterances made in either House wherever published shall be privileged.
>
> 13. The members of each House of the Oireachtas shall, except in case of treason as defined in this Constitution, felony or breach of the peace, be privileged from arrest in going to and

225. [1929] IR 25 at 36.

226. See McDonald, *Irish Law of Defamation*, p 117.

227. See also *O'Shaughnessy v Hayden* (1825) Sm & Bat 208.

228. See Heuston, *Essays on Constitutional Law*, (2nd ed, 1964), Ch 4; McDonald, *Irish Law of Defamation*, p 119-126.

returning from, and shall not, in respect of any utterance in either House, be amenable to any court or any authority other than the House itself.

**[34.138]** It would seem that the privilege is an absolute one,[229] and it is probably safe to assume that it protects from examination proceedings in the House for the purpose of finding malice for a statement made outside the House.[230]

**[34.139]** The privilege also extends to all legal proceedings and is not confined to claims for defamation.[231] Further the protection extends to the repetitions and publications of utterances originally made in either House of the Oireachtas. In 1991 statements made in the Dáil alleging irregularities in the beef industry resulted in the establishment by both Houses of a tribunal of enquiry. The nature of parliamentary privilege was explored in *AG v Hamilton (No 2)*[232] when some of the Chairman's holdings were challenged. An argument that the parliamentary privilege should extend to statements made to the Tribunal on the basis that the Tribunal was an agent of the Oireachtas was rejected by the Supreme Court. The Court confined the privilege to utterances in the Houses. The Court held further that the effect of the constitutional provisions was to oust the jurisdiction of the courts and also the jurisdiction of the Tribunal, and although such ouster could be waived it would be so only in the clearest of cases.

**[34.140]** After a period of uncertainty, it is now provided by statute[233] that this privilege extends to utterances made before committees of the Oireachtas by members of either house, to utterances of members, advisers, officials and agents of such committees and to documents and reports of such committees.[234]

*(iii) Newspaper and broadcast reports of court proceedings*

**[34.141]** Section 18(1) of the Defamation Act 1961 provides that:

> A fair and accurate report published in any newspaper or broadcast by means of wireless telegraphy as part of any programme or service provided by means of a broadcasting station within the State or in Northern Ireland of proceedings publicly heard before any court established by law and exercising judicial authority within the State or in Northern Ireland shall, if published or broadcast contemporaneously with such proceedings, be privileged.

**[34.142]** The principal points of note in this section (which replaces s 3 of the Law of Libel Amendment Act 1888), are that the protection extends only to contemporaneous reports, it

229. See *Dillon v Balfour* (1887) 20 LR Ir 600.

230. *Church of Scientology v Johnson-Smith* [1972] 1 QB 522. See Morgan, *Constitutional Law of Ireland*, p 162, fn 15; *Cf* McDonald, *Irish Law of Defamation*, p 121-122.

231. *AG v Hamilton* [1993] 3 IR 227.

232. *AG v Hamilton* [1993] 3 IR 227.

233. Committees of the Houses of the Oireachtas (Privilege and Procedure) Act 1976, s 2. Of course, this statute has merely the presumption of constitutionality, in contrast to Articles 15.12 and 15.13 which are part of the Constitution itself.

234. See also Committee of Public Accounts of Dáil Éireann (Privilege and Procedure) Act 1970. *Cf* the Report of the Committee on the Constitution, December 1967, p 14. Note that no privilege is conferred on witnesses who appear before these committees. In 1984, the then Government expressed its intention to introduce legislation on this matter, but none was forthcoming: McDonald, *Irish Law of Defamation*, pp 125-126, fn. 38. McDonald also suggests that witnesses' statements are absolutely protected at common law; 124-125. See para **[34.150]** below.

extends only to newspapers printed for sale and published in the State or in Northern Ireland[235] and lastly, the privilege does not authorise the publication or broadcasting of any blasphemous or obscene matter.[236] Provided the report is "fair and accurate" it need not be a verbatim one.[237] Reports in daily newspapers are not expected to read like professional law reports[238] and trifling slips do not defeat the privilege.[239] Reports, however, should not be garbled so as to give a false impression of what occurred during the proceedings: thus, other evidence and the argument of both sides should fairly be represented.[240] In *Kane v Mulvaney*,[241] Monahan CJ observed that, although newspapers were free to report the speeches of counsel as part of the proceedings:

> "we cannot hold that publication giving a libellous speech [by counsel] without evidence, and given without any object towards the prosecution of a cause, is a report of proceedings in a court of justice within the meaning of the rule".

**[34.143]** More generally, it is essential that the reported statement should have formed part of the proceedings. Thus, in *Lynam v Gowing*,[242] where a bystander in open court accused a witness of perjury, a report of this accusation was not protected. Dowse B. observed that the words used by the bystander formed:

> "no part of the proceedings of the ... Court. In any well-regulated Court the person using these words would have been turned out of Court, or at the least remanded by the Judge. It is an abuse of terms to call a slanderous observation of this description, volunteered by a bystander, a part of the proceedings ..."

**[34.144]** Although the matter is not unambiguous in s 18, the better opinion is that the privilege here is absolute.[243] This view is also supported by the provision in s 24 of the Act which, in contrast to s 18, is clearly an instance of qualified privilege.

**[34.145]** It should also be noted that the statutory privilege contained in s 18(1) of the 1961 Act is in addition to the Common Law privilege on the same matter. At common law fair and accurate reports of judicial proceedings were privileged. Such reporting was encouraged to promote the policy that justice must be "seen to be done not only by the few members of the public who can spare the time to come to court, but by the whole, vast public which is reached by our press."[244] Sections 18 and 24 of the Defamation Act 1961

---

235. See Defamation Act 1961, s 2.

236. Defamation Act 1961, s 18(2). Besides this statutory privilege, reports of Court proceedings may still be protected at common law: see McDonald, *Irish Law of Defamation*, p 174.

237. McDonald, *Irish Law of Defamation*, pp, 176-177; *Kimber v Press Association* [1893] 1 QB 65.

238. *Cf Hope v Leng Ltd* (1907) 23 Times LR 243 at 244 (CA).

239. *M'Wade v Goodlake* The Times, 23 June 1881, *per* Bramwell LJ

240. *M'Wade v Goodlake* The Times, 23 June 1881.

241. (1866) IR 2 CL 402 at 420 (Com Pleas). *Cf Burnett & Hallamshire Fuel Ltd v Sheffield Telegraph & Star Ltd* [1960] 2 All ER 157 (Sheffield Assizes, Salmon J with jury).

242. (1880) 6 LR Ir 259 at 268 (Ex D). *Cf Hope v Leng Ltd* (1907) 23 Times LR 243.

243. The intention of the framers of the 1888 provision had in fact been to make the privilege a qualified one (*Cf* McDonald, *Irish Law of Defamation*, p 172), but the intention of the framers of section 18(1) itself had been to make it absolute. McDonald, *Irish Law of Defamation*, p 173, this strengthens the argument that section 18(1) should so be interpreted.

244. *Burnett & Hallamshire Fuel Ltd v Sheffield Telegraph and Star Ltd* [1960] 1 WLR 502 at 504 (*per* Salmon, LJ).

gives statutory recognition to those privileged occasions so that in the vast majority of cases there will be no need to go beyond the statute to determine whether the publication is privileged or not. But the statutory provisions are in addition to the Common Law privilege and sometimes there may be a difference. For example, the statutory privileges are confined to the media, whereas the Common Law is not. Secondly, s 18 privilege is applicable only to "contemporaueous reports" whereas no such restriction applies at common law. Finally, the s 18 privilege extends to contemporaueous reports of court proceedings in the Northern Ireland as well as to proceedings in the Republic. Normally, the common law privilege only extends to reports of domestic courts.

*(iv) Judicial proceedings*

**[34.146]** Statements made during judicial proceedings whether by judges, counsel, witnesses, solicitors or parties, are absolutely privileged.[245] The privilege also extends to statements made in preparation of the trial and to documents and pleadings connected with the proceedings.[246] The principle of immunity conceded to the lawmaking body (the Oireachtas) is also conceded here to the bodies concerned with the administration of justice. In *Kennedy v Hilliard*,[247] Pigot CB noted that this immunity was:

> "founded on public policy, which requires that a Judge, in dealing with the matter before him, a party in preferring or resisting a legal proceeding, and a witness in giving evidence, oral or written in a Court of Justice, shall do so with his mind uninfluenced by the fear of an action for defamation ... [I]f parties and their witnesses (and if these were not protected it would be difficult to apply a different rule for the immunity of Judges and jurors) were exposed to actions of this nature, not only would the cases be innumerable in which such actions would be brought (at least against parties and witnesses), but, in every case, the party and the witness would be fettered in seeking or in aiding justice, by his own fears more or less influencing him, according to the strength or the weakness of his individual character, his position and circumstances in life, and the known wealth, obstinacy or malevolence of the party offended."

**[34.147]** The extent of the protection afforded by the privilege can be seen from *Macaulay & Co v Wyse-Power*,[248] where it was held that no action lay for the following statement made by a Circuit Court Judge:

---

245. See *Royal Aquarium and Summer and Winter Garden Society Ltd v Parkinson* [1892] 1 QB 431, especially at 451 (*per* Lopes LJ). See also Anon 'Privileged Reports of Judicial Proceedings', (1878) 12 ILT & Sol J 467; Anon 'Libelling by Report of Judicial Proceedings' (1890) 24 ILT & Sol J 485; Anon 'Defamation in the Course of Judicial Proceedings' (1891) 25 ILT & Sol J 677. As to the broader question of the exemption from legal liability of judges, *Cf Ward v Freeman* (1852) 2 Ir CLR 460 (Exch Ch).

246. *McCabe v Joynt* [1901] 2 IR 115 (QBD) - libel action for irregular registration of a Chancery order as judgment; *Kennedy v Hilliard* (1859) 10 ICLR 195. See also *M'Laughlin v Doey* (1893) 32 LR Ir 518 at 529-531 especially (registration of a judgment later set aside for irregularity. The privilege extends to all acts "in the course of justice," *per* Palles CB at 530). See also *Hasselblad (GB) Ltd v Orbinson* [1985] 2 WLR 1 where a letter of complaint to the Commission of the EEC could not be used as the basis for a libel action.

247. 10 ICLR 195 at 209-210. This passage was quoted with approval by Palles CB *McCabe v Joynt* [1901] 2 IR 115.

248. (1943) 77 ILTR 61.

"In my considered opinion the firm of Messrs Macaulay & Co Ltd of 15 Haymarket, Dublin, is an utterly dishonest and disreputable firm. It is one with which no decent man who has regard for his honour should be associated, and its members are men with whom no decent man should socially have resort ... No person in Connacht should ever again have anything to do with any person even remotely connected with this disreputable firm which earns its profits by battening on the lack of legal knowledge of the simple people of the West."[249]

**[34.148]** The absolute immunity afforded to the judiciary, it would seem, may not protect judges of inferior courts when they act outside their jurisdiction. In such cases it could be said that they are not acting judicially at all and accordingly lose the protection. In *Desmond and MCD Management Services Ltd v Riordan*,[250] Morris P addressed this question and said he was willing to follow the Court of Appeal in England in *Sirros v Moore and Ors*.[251]

"I am satisfied that this must be so because the granting of an immunity to the judiciary of necessity imposes a limitation upon the constitution[al]... rights of the citizen to vindicate his good name and so the limitations ... must be strictly limited .. to achieve its objectives namely to enable the Judge to administer the law freed of the concern that he will be made answerable for his actions. Once the immunity is extended beyond what is necessary for that purpose a conflict with the constitutional rights of the citizen exists. In my view the essential ingredient in the consideration of this matter is the state of knowledge of the Judge. Once he is aware of the fact that he is exceeding his jurisdiction and continues to act then in my view he automatically ceases to be administering the law and the need for the immunity ceases."[252]

In the *Desmond* case, Morris P was concerned with the immunity of a Coroner where he adopted the same rule. From this it would seem that the rule is that a judge of an inferior court, and a Coroner, under the Coroners Act 1962, has absolute immunity in all cases except where he is acting without jurisdiction and he is aware of it.[253]

**[34.149]** It would appear that advocates (which includes not only barristers and solicitors, but also people representing themselves) enjoy absolute privilege at least in relation to relevant statements.[254]

**[34.150]** There is some uncertainty as to whether parties and witnesses enjoy quite so wide-ranging an immunity. In the Supreme Court case of *In re Haughey* in 1971, Ó Dálaigh CJ observed:

"The immunity of witnesses in the High Court does not exist for the benefit of witnesses, but for that of the public and the advancement of the administration of justice and to prevent

---

249. (1943) 77 ILTR 61 at 61. The plaintiff was probably not unduly dismayed at the outcome of the case. In holding that no action was maintainable, Maguire J stressed that he could not find that the proceedings were frivolous or vexatious, and in the absence of a plea of justification the law "presumed that the words and statements were untrue". See also *Tughan v Craig* [1918] 1 IR 245 (Dodd J). It seems that the privilege might have been lost if the offending statement was made *after* judgment in the Court was delivered: *Cf Keenan v Wallace* (1916) 51 ILTR 19.

250. High Court, 14 July 1999.

251. [1975] QB 118.

252. High Court, 14 July 1999, pp 5-6.

253. See also the LRC, *Consultation Paper on the Civil Law of Defamation* (1991), March 1991, para 99.

254. See LRC Consultation Paper 1991, paras 103-103.

witnesses from being deterred, by the fear of having actions brought against them, from coming forward and testifying to the truth. The interest of the individual is subordinated by the law to the higher interest, viz, that of public justice, for the administration of which it is necessary that witnesses should be free to give their evidence without fear of consequences. It is salutary to bear in mind that even in the High Court, if a witness were to take advantage of his position to utter something defamatory having no reference to the cause of matter of inquiry but introduced maliciously for his own purpose, no privilege or immunity would attach and he might find himself sued in an action for defamation."[255]

**[34.151]** Walsh and Budd JJ concurred with the Chief Justice's judgment. The Court made no reference to earlier decisions in which some considerable (though less than unanimous) support for a wide-ranging immunity for witnesses had been voiced. The most important of these is *Kennedy v Hilliard*,[256] where Pigot CB had articulated strong objections in policy to restricting immunity, so far as parties or witnesses were concerned, to material statements:

> "the difficulty is often great, even to one well skilled in the law, of determining upon the questions of the irrelevancy or immateriality of statements or of evidence ... If a party, in making in person (as he may) a pleading or a statement of his own case in a Court of Justice, or in making any affidavit to sustain it, or if a witness (whether a party to the proceeding or not) shall be bound to determine, first, what is the exact line at which a statement or evidence shall be material, and to determine this at the peril of an action for defamation if he be wrong, and if his words be defamatory, the protection which the law professes to give him would be nearly nugatory for its purpose. That purpose is, to give him the courage to resort as party to the legal tribunals for justice, or, as a witness, to give his evidence before those tribunals, undeterred by the fear of a prosecution or an action. It is impossible that he can be free from that fear, if his immunity must depend on his not mistaking what is not material for what is, and upon his rightly distinguishing what *is* from what *is not* libel or actionable slander."

**[34.152]** Greene B was of the same opinion. He stressed the fact that parties and witnesses, who were not lawyers, could scarcely be expected at their peril to assess the relevance of their statements; he observed that "[a] counsel, being *legis peritus,* and retained for a client and being at liberty to exercise his own discretion, may possibly be differently circumstanced".[257] Fitzgerald B felt bound by authority[258] to concur with his colleagues, but disagreed[259] with their perception of the policy merits of the issue.[260]

**[34.153]** Perhaps Ó Dálaigh CJ's remarks can be harmonised with those of Pigot CB and Greene B. The Chief Justice did not suggest that every irrelevant statement by a witness is outside the range of privilege; on the contrary, privilege would protect statements, though admittedly irrelevant, providing only that the witness did not introduce them "maliciously

255. [1917] IR 217 at 264-265 (SC). See McDonald, *Irish Law of Defamation*, p 134.

256. 10 ICLR 195 at 211.

257. 10 ICLR 195 at 225.

258. *Gildea v Brien* (1821) 10 ICLR 230 (Com Pleas). See McDonald, *Irish Law of Defamation*, pp 133-134.

259. 10 1 CLR 195 at 229.

260. See also *M'Loughlin v Doey* (1893) 32 LR Ir 518 at 530 (Ex D); *McCabe v Joynt* [1901] 2 IR 115 at 128-129 (QBD).

for his own purpose". In other words, qualified privilege should be extended to irrelevant statements by a witness made without malice.

**[34.154]** The matter of witness's privilege came before the Court again in 1996 in the High Court case of *Looney v Governor and Company of Bank of Ireland and Morly*.[261] In that case the plaintiff claimed he had been libelled in an affidavit made by the second defendant (an employee of the Bank) in different proceedings. When he sued for libel the defendant issued a motion for dismiss. In ordering the dismiss, Murphy J held that the witness's privilege is absolute and is a very wide privilege. He cited *Kennedy*. He further held that the privilege is not derived from a royal prerogative, but is based on the Constitution and on the independence of the judiciary. Murphy J favoured the widest interpretation in these circumstances saying that by denying an offended party whose reputation is damaged by the irrelevant outbursts in the witness box one was not saying that the witness was not amenable to any legal control. He could, for example, be subject to contempt proceedings. Moreover, where the allegations were made in an affidavit the offended person could be given the opportunity of filing an affidavit contradicting the original allegations.

> "If a witness was to take advantage of his position and of the absolute privilege which he enjoyed, to digress from the proceedings in hand and make a wholly irrelevant and completely unwarranted attack on the good name or reputation of another citizen who did not have a chance of defending himself, this is a matter which could and should be dealt with by the trial judge. In my view such an abuse of legal process would constitute a contempt of court and be punishable accordingly. In that way at least to that extent the rights of an outsider could be protected. To say, as the plaintiff does, that the right to pursue an action for defamation subsists notwithstanding the privilege conferred on witnesses is to my mind mistaken. That privilege derives form the necessity of affording witnesses the opportunity of giving their evidence freely and fearlessly. It does not derive from the royal prerogative. It derives from the very nature of the judicial process and the independent judiciary created by our Court.
>
> As I say, I do not believe that innocent parties are wholly without remedy, but the remedy is not one of civil process for defamation. It has reliance upon the experience of the judges and their duty in general to protect parties who are unfairly, unjustly and unnecessarily attacked in the course of judicial process."[262]

**[34.155]** "Judicial proceedings" is given a wide definition in the rule: as well as exending to superior and inferior courts, the phrase also covers tribunals established by law whenever such tribunals are "exercising functions equivalent to those of an established court of justice".[263] So absolute privilege has been applied to an enquiry before an Inn of Court into the conduct of a barrister,[264] to proceedings before the Disciplinary Committee of the Law Society,[265] and to courts-martial.[266] The privilege does not extend, however, to

261. [1996] 1 IR 157.
262. [1996] 1 IR 157 at 161-2.
263. *O'Connor v Waldron* [1935] AC 76 at 81. It would also extend to the Court of Justice of the European Communities.
264. *Lincoln v Daniels* [1962] 1 QB 237.
265. *Addis v Crocker* [1961] 1 QB 11.
266. *Dawkins v Lord Rokeby* (1873) LR 8 QB 255, affd on appeal (1875) LR 7 HL 744.

bodies that are merely administrative (as opposed to judicial) in character, such as licensing bodies which do not determine rights of parties or the innocence or guilt of persons,[267] although, if the tribunal is recognised by law, and follows judicial procedure, it is not essential that it should have the power to finally determine the issue before it.[268]

**[34.156]** It would seem that the privilege extends to superior courts in any event, and that it should extend to other courts and tribunals when they are not acting manifestly in excess of their jurisdiction.[269]

**[34.157]** Communcations between solicitor and client for the purpose of getting or giving legal advice are sometimes said to attract absolute privilege,[270] although in England the House of Lords has reserved its opinion on this point[271] and the better authorities now suggest that the interests of solicitor and client are adequately catered for by treating such communications as deserving qualified privilege only.[272] If the communications are made in the course of a trial, however, or in the shadow of judicial proceedings, it may be that they would benefit from the absolute privilege which is given to such proceedings. The same rationale adopted by Murphy J in *Looney*,[273] which gives witnesses absolute privilege, it is submitted should also protect from defamation proceedings a complaint to the Gardai in relation to a suspected crime. Other remedies might be available if the complainant is vexatious, such as malicious prosecution, abuse of process, etc, but the chilling threat of a defamation writ, should not discourage complainants from doing their civic duty in such cases.

*(v) State communications*

**[34.158]** Just as absolute privilege is conferred to a large extent on the judicial and legislative branches of government, so too a degree of absolute privilege is conferred on the executive branch of government. On analogy with common law precedents it would seem that communications between the government and the President, and between the members of the Government *inter se* on business pertaining to their offices[274] are absolutely privileged. There are precedents which indicate that such absolute privilege also extends to a communication by a Minister to a subordinate official[275] and by a military officer to his superior.[276] The protection of absolute privilege may also extend to statements made by Secretaries of Government Departments, but communications by civil

267. *Royal Aquarium Society v Parkinson* [1892] 1 QB 431.

268. *Trapp v Mackie* [1979] 1 WLR 377 (tribunal whose function was to report to Minister whose decision was final). See also LRC Constitution Paper 1991, para 104.

269. See further McDonald, *Irish Law of Defamation*, pp 131-132; *Sirros v Moore* [1975] QB 118. But *cf Re McC* [1985] AC 258.

270. *More v Water* [1928] 2 KB 520.

271. *Minter v Priest* [1930] AC 558.

272. See WINFIELD & JOLOWICZ, p 432.

273. See para **[34.154]** above.

274. See *Chatterton v Secretary of State for India* [1895] 2 QB 189.

275. *Peerless Bakery Ltd v Watt* [1955] NZLR 339. See also *M Isaacs & Sons Ltd v Cook* [1925] 2 KB 391 - communication by High Commissioner for Australia to his Prime Minister on commerce matter.

276. *Dawkins v Lord Paulet* (1869) LR 5 QB 94.

servants of lesser rank are probably accorded to the protection of qualified privilege only.[277]

*(vi) Communications between husband and wife*

**[34.159]** Although, as we have seen, it is sometimes said that communications between husband and wife are not actionable in defamation because there is no publication since the husband and wife are one unit in law, a more realistic view of this immunity nowadays is that, in promoting the marriage relationship, the law confers immunity on the ground that communications made between husband and wife are absolutely privileged.[278]

***Qualified privilege***

**[34.160]** In some circumstances the law recognises the right of a person to communicate freely provided it is not done maliciously: such occasions are considered to be occasions of qualified privilege. Generally speaking, the person who makes the statement on such occasions is protected, provided he or she was not motivated by malice in making the statement.

**[34.161]** Moreover, where an occasion is held to be privileged, the mantle of protection which it affords the author is not destroyed because it is read by a secretary, typist, etc. Nor does the author render himself or herself liable because it is read by the secretary or clerk of the person to whom it is communicated.[279] Such a rule is certainly necessary for the efficient conduct of modern-day business; whether it would apply in a non-business context is less certain, but would, in any event, depend on all the circumstances of the case. The original rationale for such rule was that the privilege that existed between the author and the recipient was extended in such cases to cover such incidental publications which were considered "ancillary" to the main privilege. More recently, however, Lord Denning MR, suggested, rightly it seems, that such publication could be defended on grounds that there is an "original" privilege between the author and his or the author's staff in the matter.

**[34.162]** A secretary has a sufficient interest and duty in learning what his or her employer has to say on such occasions, to support an independent privilege between himself or herself and his her employer.[280] Statements made by the defendant's solicitors in preliminary correspondence do not give rise to an independent cause of action and are written on an occasion of qualified privilege.[281]

**[34.163]** It is impossible to enumerate fully the occasions recognised by law as attracting qualified privilege. Nor would it be desirable to do so, as such a list might give the wrong impression that the list is closed. This is not the case and new occasions will undoubtedly arise in the future to which the law will be willing to attach privilege.

**[34.164]** Before examining some of the particular occasions which the law considers to be privileged it is sufficient to say, by way of generalisation, that situations where the maker of the statement has a duty to speak or is obliged to protect an interest are normally

277. See McDonald, *Irish Law of Defamation*, p 141; See also *Richards v Naum* [1967] 1 QB 620.

278. The view expressed in the text is supported by PROSSER & KEETON, p 824.

279. *Boxins v Goblet Freres* [1894] 1 QB 842; *Osborn v Thomas Boulter & Sons* [1930] 2 KB 266; *Riddick v Thames Board Mills Ltd* [1977] QB 881 (CA).

280. *Bryanston Finance Ltd v de Fries* [1975] QB 703.

281. *Hennessy v K TEL Ireland Ltd* Supreme Court, 12 June 1997, Irish Times, 28 July 1997, p 16.

considered to be privileged. In such circumstances, the speaker may speak without fear from the tort of defamation, provided he or she does not speak out of malice.

**[34.165]** In *Reilly v Gill*[282] Geoghegan J quoted with approval Lord Campbell's *dictum* in *Harrison v Bush*[283] as explaining the principle underlying this branch of the law:

> "A communication made *bona fide* upon any subject-matter in which the party communication has an interest, or in reference to which he has a duty, is privileged, if made to a person having a corresponding interest or duty. And the word 'duty' cannot be confined to legal duties which may be enforced by indictment, action or mandamus but must include moral and social duties of imperfect obligation."

**[34.166]** It has been stated that such communications are protected "for the common convenience and welfare of society".[284]

**[34.167]** Certain reports are also privileged in a qualified way, and these are now given statutory recognition in s 24 of the Defamation Act 1961.

**[34.168]** It will be convenient now to deal with each occasion of qualified privilege in turn:

*(i) Duty*

**[34.169]** Where the maker has a legal duty to speak, then it is considered that the law should support this duty by enabling the speaker to communicate in a free and frank manner. In *Kirkwood Hackett v Tierney*[285] the President of University College Dublin, was held to have a duty to make a full enquiry in respect of a money draft alleged to have been paid out wrongly to a student. A statement alleged to have been made by the President to the student in question in the presence of the College Secretary was held to be a privileged communication and was protected in the absence of malice. Again, one employee might have a duty to communicate his or her suspicions about another employee whom he or she suspects of theft, to the employer, and even to the suspected employee.[286] In *Hartery v Welltrade (Middle Fast) Ltd and Hurley*[287] a complaint to the Garda Síochána (police) and a request that a criminal offence (blackmail) should be investigated were held to have been made on a privileged occasion, since they were made, it seems, in the performance of a legal duty.[288]

---

282. (1946) 85 ILTR 165 at 186 (SC).

283. (1855) 5 El & Bl 344 at 348, 119 ER 509 at 512. It should be noted that the quotation in *Reilly v Gill* 85 ILTR 165 is not verbatim, although the key passages are identical. Also cited with approval in *Hamerton v Green* (1863) 16 ICLR 77.

284. *Toogood v Spyring* (1834) 1 CM & R 181 at 193 (*per* Parke B).

285. [1952] IR 185. See generally Stevens 'The Reputation Rights of Students' (1975) 4 J of L & Educ 623 at 627-631.

286. *Corcoran v W & R Jacob & Co* [1945] IR 446; *Dempsey v Wall & Co Ltd & Philip Ryan* 78 ILTR 73 (directors communication to dismissed employee). See also *Denvir v Taylor* [1936] Ir Jur Rep 4 (NICA) - statement by a supervising engineering expert to employer, about an electrician employee.

287. See para **[34.157]** above. *Sevenoaks v Latimer* (1919) 54 ILTR 11 at 14 (KBD): "You can ... go to a solicitor, to a policeman or to a person in authority, but not to a man in the street for the purpose of communicating your conviction of a man's guilt."

288. On whether this should be absolute privilege or not see para **[34.150]** above.

**[34.170]** The duty which renders the occasion privileged need not be a legal duty,[289] however. As has been mentioned, it is sufficient if it is of a moral or social nature.[290] Accordingly, the social or moral duty which impels an employer to write a character reference in respect of an employee or a former employee,[291] or impels parents to warn his child about the person he or she intends to marry[292] or an employer to warn employees about their associates,[293] has been held to be sufficient to make the occasion privileged. It would also undoubtedly extend to cases where a member of the public complained to the proper authorities of the conduct of a public servant, where an aggrieved member of the public[294] or a solicitor complains to the Incorporated Law Society about the conduct of another solicitor,[295] where a person in publishing an apology to one person defames another[296] and where a public representative speaks on a matter of community concern.[297]

**[34.171]** In discharging one's duty in such circumstances, however, the privilege will attach to the occasion only if the person to whom the statement is made has either a reciprocal duty or a reciprocal interest in receiving it.[298]

**[34.172]** Moreover, it is clear that a privileged occasion may not be used for irrelevant defamation. This was stressed in *McKeogh v O'Brien Moran*,[299] where a solicitor overstepped the mark by repeating an irrelevant charge of negligence against a doctor

---

289. The legal duty may be statutory or contractual. In *Corless and Diggin v Ireland* High Court, 23 July 1984 (Hamilton J) the Garda Commissioner was held to have acted on a privileged occasion when, in fulfilling the duties of his office he transferred two officers in controversial circumstances.

290. *Willis v Irish Press* (1938) 72 ILTR 238; *Redmond v Kelly* (1894) 28 ILT & Sol J 555 (Ex). Thus, whereas it is not legally mandatory to report suspected child abuse to the authorities, the Protections for Persons Reporting Child Abuse Act 1998 gives statutory protection to certain specified categories of people who report child abuse in good faith. See Byrne and Binchy, *Annual Review of Irish Law 1998*; Feldman 'Whistleblower Protection: Comparative Legal Developments' (1999) 17 ILR (ns) 264 at 265.

291. *Jackson v Hopperton* (1864) 16 CB (ns) 829 143 ER 1352; *Hopkins v Sadlier* (1893) 28 ILTR 137.

292. *Todd v Hawkins* (1837) 8 C & P 88, 173 ER 411.

293. *Somerville v Hawkins* (1851) 10 CB 583, 138 ER 231.

294. *Hamerton v Green* (1863) 16 ICLR 77.

295. *Hartery v Welltrade (Middle East) Ltd and Hurley* [1978] ILRM 38.

296. See *Willis v Irish Press* (1938) 72 ILTR 238.

297. *McCarthy v Morrissey* [1939] Ir Jur Rep 82. See also *Little v Pomeroy* (1873) IR 7 CL 50 (Exch) - slander by a grand juror imputing to the plaintiff who was tendering for county works want of means in his business as road contractor; held to be privileged. *Cf Swords Community Council v Dunne*, *Ir* Times, 20 March 1981. "Anything a public representative says in good faith without malice related to the business of the Council is privileged." (CC).

298. *Kirkwood Hackett v Tierney* [1952] IR 185; *Corcoran v W & R Jacob & Co* [1945] IR 446; *Hynes-O'Sullivan v O'Driscoll* [1989] ILRM 349. In England it appears that where a person responds to an enquiry concerning the credit of a trader this will be considered an occasion of qualified privilege provided he bona fide believes in the answer and also believes the enquirer has an interest in making the enquiry. It would seem that by analogy with the former employer's privilege relating to references in respect of former employees, this should be followed in Ireland should it arise

299. [1927] IR 348 at 357-359 (HC), citing (*inter alia*) *Murphy v Halpin* (1874) IR 8 CL 127 (Exch). Privilege will be denied *a fortiori* where the solicitor introduces into a letter written on behalf of his client any defamatory and irrelevant statement of his own: *Slipper v Braisby* [1930] NZLR 953 (SC). See further Gatley, p 242.

made by his client, a nurse, whose own conduct had been criticised by the doctor. Hanna J stated that it was settled that:

> "the fact that a charge has been made against a defendant to which there is a duty to reply does not include within the protection of the privilege thereby occasioned, a right to make a counter-charge of a defamatory character irrelevant thereto. The law is, therefore, clear. The solicitor, in corresponding with third parties, is in no better position than his client. He is not free to write everything his client may suggest or state. He cannot be made the conduit pipe for every allegation of a chagrined or malignant litigant. He is bound to apply a plain and simple test, based on fair-play, and exclude from his letter anything defamatory that is not relevant to the occasion. This is, in no sense that I can imagine, a restriction upon a solicitor in the conduct of his business for his clients. It has been acted upon by generations of the profession. It is true that at times 'the best parry is the thrust', but the thrust must be according to the rules of the game."

**[34.173]** A distinction has been made by the courts also in respect of communications volunteered on the one hand and those given in response to a request on the other. In the latter case where a person makes a statement in response to a social or moral duty, the court is more likely to treat the occasion as privileged than the case where the statement is volunteered.[300] The courts do not like to encourage intermeddlers, and the person who before making a statement prefaces his or her opinion with the question, "Are you asking me for my opinion?" may be strengthening his or her legal position with regard to qualified privilege.[301]

*(ii) Interest*

**[34.174]** Statements made in protection of a recognised interest are also privileged in a qualified way. The analogy frequently made here likens this privilege to the right people have to defend themselves or their property from unjust attack. The interests recognised by the courts are varied and numerous and all one can hope to do in a limited space is to indicate some interests which the courts have recognised in the past, while remembering there can be no exhaustive list.

**[34.175]** The owner of property has such an interest in his or her property that a communication made to a suspected shoplifter is conditionally privileged.[302] The following interests were also deemed sufficient to confer privilege on the communication: an accusation by an employer to a dismissed employee even though overheard by other employees;[303] a communication by one solicitor about another to the Incorporated Law Society;[304] a rebuttal in a newspaper by a person criticised at a public meeting;[305] a rebuttal in a newspaper interview by a Member of the European Parliament, who claimed to represent a farming constituency, of an attack on farmers generally, made by the Master of

300. *Gillis v M'Donnell* (1869) LR 4 CL 342 (Com Pl).

301. See STREET (8th ed), pp 420-422.

302. *Coleman v Keanes Ltd* [1946] Ir Jur Rep 5; for an accusation of theft by employer against employee, see *Hyland v Cleary Ltd* Supreme Court 9 April 1964.

303. *Dempsey v Wall & Co Ltd & Ryan* 78 ILTR 73 (1943).

304. *Hartery v Welltrade (Middle East) Ltd and Hurley* [1978] ILRM 38 (HC); *Cf Hamerton v Green* (1863) 16 ICLR 77. See also Anon 'Solicitors' Privilege in Actions for Libel' (1894) 28 ILT & Sol J 331.

305. *Nevin v Roddy & Carty* [1935] IR 397; *O'Donoghue v Hussey* (1871) IR 5 CL 124 (Exch).

the High Court;[306] a communication by trade union representatives to an employer regarding the non-union status of an employee;[307] comments by one party to a dispute about the unsuitability of an arbitrator,[308] a communication by a bank to the payee of a cheque that the drawer has no funds;[309] a criticism by one tailor of another tailor's work to a potential customer,[310] a communication by a client to his solicitor,[311] comments by a public representative on public affairs germane to his community,[312] a communication by a former employee to a collecting agency stating that the delay in paying was due to the departure of the plaintiff from the employment with the relevant files[313] and statements made by an auctioneer at a livestock sale.[314] In *Magrath v Finn*,[315] however, it was held that an address from the altar by a parish priest warning parishioners about the plaintiff was not privileged. As Morris CJ observed, no privilege attached to a clergyman "rebuking sin". Moreover, statements made by trade protection societies, carrying on the business of supplying information, for reward, about the financial standing of businesses or persons engaged in business have been held not to be privileged.[316]

**[34.176]** Whether there should be a recognition of a general public interest which would give rise to qualified privilege is a matter for debate. At present the law recognises such a privilege for the media when a public representative is performing his or her duties and during election campaigns. The House of Lords, however, in England in *Reynolds v The Sunday Times*[317] has rejected the notion that a newspaper has a general qualified privilege whenever it comments on matters of public interest. This action arose out of a newspaper article which suggested that the Taoiseach, Albert Reynolds, had misled the Houses of the Oireachtas. An English jury (the case was taken in England), found that the plaintiff had been defamed, but awarded no damages. Later the trial judge altered this verdict by awarding nominal damages. The defendant appealed up to the House of Lords on the issue of qualified privilege, but as noted above, failed to establish an occasion to which qualified

306. *Lindsey v Maher*, High Court The Irish Times, 4 February 1984.

307. *McMullan v Mulhall & Farrell* [1929] IR 470.

308. *Hobbs v Bayers* (1878) 2 LR Ir 496 (Ex Div).

309. *Pyke v The Hibernian Bank* [1950] IR 195.

310. *Towell v Fallon* (1912) 47 ILTR 176 (KBD).

311. *Minter v Priest* [1930] AC 557 at 581 (*per* Lord Atkin). As to a communication by a litigant regarding the opposing solicitor's conduct, see *McCarthy v Maguire* [1899] 2 IR 802 (CA affg QBD).

312. *McCarthy v Morrissey* [1939] Ir Jur Rep 82.

313. *Hennessy v K-TEL Ireland Ltd* Supreme Court, 12 June 1997. An attempt by the plaintiff to argue that the secretary who typed the letter was tainted with malice, while her boss who dictated the letter was not, was rejected by the Court as being contrary to ordinary commonsense.

314. *Maxwell v Gavin Low Ltd* Supreme Court, 11 January 1967.

315. (1877) IR 11 CL 152 (Com Pl). More generally, see Shelley 'Defamation Privilege in Internal Affairs of Religious Societies' (1966) 15 Clev-Mar LR 356.

316. *Macintosh v Dunn* [1908] AC 390 (PC). *Cf Fitzsimmons v Duncan & Kemp & Co* [1908] 2 IR 482 at 508, 513-514 (CA, *per* Fitzgibbon LJ). In the United States, "the great majority" of courts confer qualified privilege to such statements: PROSSER & KEETON, p 829. And see *London Associates for Protection of Trade v Greenlands Ltd* [1916] 2 AC 15, which appeared to emerge unscathed from the Supreme Court's scrutiny in *Hynes-O'Sullivan v O'Driscoll* [1989] ILRM 349 (SC). This must cast a shadow over *Fitzsimmons*.

317. [1999] 4 All ER 609.

privilege for newspapers commenting on matters of public interest. This would seem to be the better view and one which should be followed by the Irish courts should the matter come up for determination.[318] We examine the decision in greater detail below.[319]

**[34.177]** It would also seem that persons involved in the organisation of horse racing have sufficient interest to make privileged communications regarding members of the racing fraternity in the appropriate racing journals, although in such cases the plaintiff may also fail because he or she consented to the publication. If, however, it can be shown that the publication did not comply with the terms of the consent then this defence will fail. In *Green v Blake*[320] it was held that the plaintiff's consent to the publication of the result of an inquiry must be taken as consent only if the principles of natural justice were observed at the inquiry which was not so in the case before the court. Similarly, in *Reilly v Gill*[321] it was held that the plaintiff's consent to have his name published in the Defaulter's List only created a privilege when it was proved that the plaintiff had, in fact, defaulted. Since no such fact had been proved the defendants did not have a right to publish.[322] These cases illustrate to some extent the difference between consent and qualified privilege: where an occasion is protected by qualified privilege then the defendant is safe except where it is motivated by malice; that the statement is untrue is not fatal. With regard to consent, however, the plaintiff usually consents only to the publication of established facts, and in such cases this does not extend to the publication of untrue statements.

**[34.178]** In all cases where qualified privilege is based on the protection of an interest, however, the interest of the defendant must be balanced by a reciprocal interest or duty on the part of the audience to whom the remarks are addressed.[323] Furthermore, it should be stressed, that in all occasions that attract qualified privilege, the person who makes the statement may communicate only matters relevant to the occasion;[324] and normally such

---

318. See LRC Consultation Paper, 1991, para 111. And LRC Report, 1991, paras 4.26, 7.17ff.

319. See para **[34.182]** below.

320. [1948] IR 242.

321. 85 ILTR 165 (SC). See also *Dawson (t/a AE Dawson & Sons) v Irish Brokers Association* Supreme Court, 6 November 1998 (no qualified privilege where defendant was "in breach of its rules. When it in effect, expelled the plaintiff from membership of the Association").

322. See also *Pyke v The Hibernian Bank* [1950] IR 195 where O'Byrne J (Geoghegan J concurring) considered that the defendant's mistake in respect of the plaintiff's account caused a loss of the privileged occasion. In a penetrating analysis, Black J, took the opposite view.

323. *McCarthy v Morrissey* [1939] Ir Jur Rep 82; *Lynam v Gowing* (1880) 6 LR Ir 259 (Ex Div); *Waring v McCaldin* IR 7 CL *282*. A mistaken belief that the recipient has a duty or interest in the matters referred to by the defendant will not suffice, certainly where, as in *Hynes-O'Sullivan v O'Driscoll* [1989] ILRM 349 (SC), that belief was unreasonable, and perhaps even where it was reasonable. In this case the Court engaged in the rare exercise of analysing the constitutional parameters of defamation. Henchy J (Hederman J concurring) considered that the guarantee in Article 40.3.1° would not be effectuated if a mere subjective, unreasonable belief gave the speaker the defence of privilege. Henchy J did not venture any opinion as to the constitutional implications of such a defence resting on an honest and reasonable belief. McCarthy J, however, expressed the view that such a belief should not give the speaker the defence of privilege. Interestingly, McCarthy J characterised this defence as "an impairment, *in the interests of the common good*, of the right to vindication of one's good name" (emphasis added).

324. *Nevin v Roddy and Carty* [1935] IR 397; See also *Simmonds v Dunne* (1871) IR 5 CL 358 (Exch); *Dwyer v Esmonde* (1878) 2 LR Ir 243 (CA).

communications are permitted only to a restricted class.[325] It is true in some circumstances, however, that publication to the world at large may be justified on the grounds that the public have a sufficient interest in the matter in hand, or, for example, where the defendant is merely responding to an accusation through the same medium in which the initial attack was made (eg newspaper, TV, etc).[326] Moreover, accidental or incidental publication to persons who would not normally have sufficient interest to attract qualified privilege, will not destroy the defendant's privilege. Thus an accusation on a privileged occasion, against a suspected shoplifter, or employee, for example, will not involve the defendant in liability merely because it is incidentally overheard by others who do not have an interest in learning of the accusation.[327]

*(iii)Politics, public figures and the media*

**[34.179]** Over the past few decades and particularly in the last five years, there has been a major international debate as to the proper scope of defamation where the subject matter is political or, more broadly, involves public figures and where the media are involved. There is no necessary connection between these themes but it is striking how they coalesce in discussion. The debate has taken place against a background of rights-language, contained in constitutions, international conventions and human rights legislative initiates. Those (including the media) who advocate the freedom of speech have wrested the high ground from the champions of a person's good name.

**[34.180]** The landmark decision was that of the United States Supreme Court in *New York Times v Sullivan*,[328] holding, on First Amendment grounds, that those who criticise public figures, basing their charges on false factual assertions, are exempt from liability in defamation save where the particular defamed public figure can prove actual malice.

**[34.181]** The New Zealand Court of Appeal, in *Lange v Atkinson and Australian Consolidated Press NZ Ltd*,[329] have taken a somewhat similar approach: protection is afforded to false statements regarding political matters, even in the absence of reasonable care, provided the defendant is not motivated by ill-will and is not seeking to take improper

325. *Robinson v Jones* (1879) 4 LR Ir 391 (Ex D); *Murphy v Halpin* (1874) IR 8 CL 127 (Exch); *Williamson v Freer* (1874) LR 9 CP 393.

326. *O'Donoghue v Hussey* LR 5 CL 124; *Dwyer v Esmonde* (1878) 2 LR Ir 243; *Williamson v Freer* (1874) LR 9 CP 393 at 415.

327. *Corcoran v W & R Jacob & Co* [1945] IR 446; *Dempsey v Wall & Co and Ryan* (1943) 78 ILTR 73. See also *Hartery v Welltrade (Middle East) Ltd & Hurley* [1978] ILRM 38.

328. (1964) 376 US 254.

329. [1998] 3 NZLR 424 (CA), analysed by Tobin 'Political Discussion, Freedom of Expression and Qualified Privilege: *Lange & Atkinson*' (1999) 7 Torts LJ 32. The Privy Council has, however, since asked the New Zealand Court of Appeal to reconsider its decision in the light of the House of Lord's decision in *Reynolds v Times Newspapers* [1999] 4 All ER 609 and the decision of the High Court of Australia in *Lange v Australian Newspapers Ltd* (1992) 189 CLR 520; *New York Times v Sullivan* and its progeny have influenced courts in other Commonwealth jurisdictions: see *Rajogopal v State of TN* [1994] 6 SCC 632 (Indian Supreme Court, applying "reckless disregard for truth" test in respect of defamation of public officials); *National Media Ltd v Bogoshi* 1998 (4) SA 1196 (SA SC, applying "reasonableness" test). See further Docherty 'Defamation Law: Positive Jurisprudence' (2000) 13 Harv Human Rts J 263 at 276-278; Tobin 'Public Interest and the Defamation of Political Figures: The English Approach' (2000) 8 Torts LJ 152.

advantage of the occasion of publication. The High Court of Australia has been more circumspect: it requires the defendant to establish reasonable care on its part in order to avail itself of the privilege.[330]

**[34.182]** The House of Lords made a subtle contribution to the debate on the matter in *Reynolds v Times Newspapers Ltd.*[331]

**[34.183]** In November 1994, Mr Reynolds resigned as Taoiseach and leader of Fianna Fail following a political crisis. The Fianna Fail - Labour Coalition Government came under pressure as a result of the Brendan Smyth affair where delay had occurred in the processing of the extradition from the Republic to the North of a priest charged with paedophile offences there. Tensions had developed between the Taoiseach and the Tainiste, Mr Spring, where Mr Spring felt that he was not kept fully informed as to what was happening. The Sunday after Mr Reynolds' resignation, the defendants published an article on the matter in which it failed to give Mr Reynolds's version of the events. Mr Reynolds sued the publishers, the editor and the author for libel alleging that the sting in the article was that he deliberately and dishonestly misled the Dail, the Cabinet and especially Mr Spring. At trial the jury rejected the defence of justification, but found that there was no malice on the part of author and, extraordinarily, awarded no damages. The judge substituted an award of a penny, and in a subsequent dispute over costs he held that the defendants were not entitled to rely on the defence of qualified privilege. Mr Reynolds appealed, alleging misdirections to the jury, and the defendants cross-appealed on the question of qualified privilege. The Court of Appeal allowed Mr Reynolds's appeal and ordered a retrial. On the issue of the qualified privilege, it ruled that the defendants would not be entitled to rely on the qualified privilege defence in the view of the circumstances of the publication. The defendants appealed, claiming that libellous statements made in the course of political discussion should automatically attract qualified privilege. The question also arose as to whether the Court of Appeal was correct in introducing, in addition to the traditional "duty-interest" test, a "circumstantial test", to determine whether qualified privilege exists.

**[34.184]** The House of Lords rejected the argument that the common law should develop "political information" as a generic category of information which would always attract qualified privilege irrespective of the circumstances. To do so would fail adequately to protect the individual's reputation to the level necessary for the well being of a democratic society. Moreover, it was not possible rationally to distinguish between "political information", which the defendants argued should attract qualified privilege, and other serious matters of public concern where no automatic privilege was to apply. In determining whether a privileged occasion exists, the House of Lords gave a vote of confidence for the common law approach which approached the question of qualified privilege in a flexible way taking all the circumstances of the case into account. The Court of Appeal was wrong, according to the House of Lords, in elevating these factors into a separate and additional test in determining whether the occasion was privileged. The circumstances must be weighed up when the duty/interest is being considered; there is not an additional "circumstantial test" one has to address after the duty/interest criteria is considered.

---

330. *Cf Lange v Australian Newspapers Ltd* (1992) 189 CLR 520 (HC, Austr).

331. [1999] 4 All ER 609.

**[34.185]** To recognise "political information" as automatically attracting qualified privilege would not give due recognition to the individual's reputation in balancing this interest against the right to freedom of expression. If such a privilege existed, said Lord Nichools, then the onus would be on the plaintiff to show malice, a task that would be very difficult, if not impossible, especially when it was recognised that the common law protected the media's right to protect its sources. In the absence of discovery, the individual plaintiff would be at an unacceptable disadvantage, nor would altering the onus of proof assist matters:

> "I have been more troubled by Lord Lester's suggested shift in the burden of proof. Placing the burden of proof on the plaintiff would be a reminder that the starting point today is freedom of expression and limitations of this freedom are exceptions. That has attraction. But if this shift of the onus were applied generally, it would turn the law of qualified privilege upside down. The repercussions of such a far-reaching change were not canvassed before your Lordships. If this change were applied only to political information, the distinction would lack a coherent rationale. There are other subjects of serious public concern. On balance I favour leaving the onus in its traditional place, on him who asserts the privilege, for two practical reasons. A newspaper will know much more of the facts leading up to publication. The burden of proof will seldom, if ever, be decisive on this issue."[332]

**[34.186]** What then are the circumstances which a court ought to take into consideration when applying the duty/interest test to determine whether a privileged occasion exists? Lord Nicholls sought to clarify the position with the following non-exhaustive list of factors to which the court should have regard:

> "Depending on the circumstances, the matters to be taking into account include the following. The comments are illustrative only. (1) The seriousness of the allegation. The more serious the charge, the more the public is misinformed and the individual harmed, if the allegation is not true. (2) The nature of the information, and the extent to which the subject matter is a matter of public of public concern. (3) The source of the information. Some informants have no direct knowledge of the events. Some have their own axes to grind, or are being paid for their stories. (4) The steps taken to verify the information. (5) The status of the information. The allegation may have already been the subject of an investigation which commands respect. (6) The urgency of the matter. News is often a perishable commodity. (7) Whether comment was sought from the plaintiff. He may have information others do not possess or have not disclosed. An approach to the plaintiff will not always be necessary. (8) Whether the article contained the gist of the plaintiff's side of the story. (9) The tone of the article. A newspaper can raise queries or call for an investigation. It need not adopt allegations as statements of fact. (10) The circumstances of the publication, including the timing.
>
> This list is not exhaustive. The weight to be given to these and any other relevant factors will vary from case to case."[333]

---

332. *Reynolds v Times Newspaper Ltd* [1999] 1 All ER 609 at 624. In the USA, where *Sullivan* prevails, extensive discovery is available to the plaintiff which helps to balance the interests more fairly. See Lord Nicholls in *Reynolds* at 622-3.

333. *Reynolds v Times Newspaper Ltd* [1999] 1 All ER 609 at 626. In *Grassi v WIC Radio Ltd* (2000) 49 CCLT (2d) 65 at 93 (BC, SC), Lysyk J quoted this passage from Lord Nicholl's speech. While not specifically endorsing it, he sought to distinguish the facts of the case before him from those specified by Lord Nicholls.

**[34.187]** In the *Reynolds* case itself, the Lords were very much influenced by the fact that in such a hard-hitting article which made serious allegations against Mr Reynolds by name, no mention was made of Mr Reynolds' own explanation to the Dáil. This left the impression on English readers that Mr Reynolds gave no explanation. "An article which fails to do so (ie give the gist of plaintiff's explanation) faces an uphill task in claiming privilege if the allegation proves to be false and the unreported explanation proves to be true".[334] In the absence of this information, the serious allegations presented as statements of facts were not information which the public had a right to know and was not a publication which should in the public interest be protected by privilege. Essentially, in determining whether the occasion was privileged, the courts should consider whether both sides of the story were presented to the public. Failure to give the plaintiff's version of the facts could easily result in a decision which denied privilege to the occasion.

**[34.188]** Although the House of Lords decision is merely persuasive it is submitted that it strikes a balance in the matter which would probably be followed in Ireland. It is submitted that to recognise "political information" as a generic category of information attracting qualified privilege automatically could be taking a step too far and would be tipping the scales too far against the individual's right to his reputation. Having said that, however, the court did suggest that in general there should be a reluctance to stiffle unduly the freedom of the press.

> "In general, a newspaper's unwillingness to disclose the identity of its sources should not weigh against it. Further, it should always be remembered that journalists act without the benefit of the clear light of hindsight. Matters which are obvious in retrospect may have been far from clear in the heat of the moment. Above all, the court should have particular regard to the importance of freedom of expression. The press discharges vital functions as a bloodhound as well as a watchdog. The court should be slow to conclude that a publication was not in the public interest and, therefore, the public had no right to know, especially when the information is in the field of political discussion. Any lingering doubts should be resolved in favour of publication."[335]

**[34.189]** Clearly, after *Reynolds*, although the lines have been drawn, the battle between the competing interests has not been fought. Indeed, it would seem that in so far as each case will be determined on its own facts, guided of course by the criteria set down, every case will be a battle, the elasticity of the common law being preferred to the rigidity and predictability of a hard rule of law. It has to be said, that when one examines the ten factors identified by Lord Nicholls, they give the media a reasonably generous latitude. If they receive credible, though not completely proven, information from a reliable source and take reasonable steps to verify it, including asking the plaintiff for his or her own version of the story and publishing that version fairly and in temperate language, it seems that they have an excellent chance of establishing the defence of qualified privilege. This may not, in express terms be a defence of "reasonable care" but it is surely its close relation.

*(iv)Reports*

**[34.190]** Certain newspaper[336] and broadcasting reports are given qualified privilege by s 24 of the Defamation Act 1961. The reports so protected are mentioned in the Second

334. *Reynolds v Times Newspaper Ltd* [1999] 1 All ER 609 at 627, *per* Lord Nicholls.

335. *Reynolds v Times Newspaper Ltd* [1999] 1 All ER 609 at 626, *per* Lord Nicholls.

336. Publications which are published at greater intervals than once every thirty-six days are not newspapers and do not benefit from the protection offered by the section. See Defamation Act 1961, s 2.

Schedule of the Act and are two kinds: (1) statements privileged without explanation or contradiction, and (2) statements privileged subject to explanation or contradiction. Statements of the second kind are given the protection of qualified privilege except where:

> "it is proved that the defendant has been requested by the plaintiff to publish ... a reasonable statement by way of explanation or contradiction, and has refused or neglected to do so, or had done so in a manner not adequate or not reasonable having regard to all the circumstances".[337]

In other words, in respect of reports of the second kind, the defendant will be protected only if, having been requested by the plaintiff, he publishes a satisfactory explanation or contradiction. The protection does not extend to a publication which is prohibited by law, or is not of public concern or not for the public benefit.[338] The following is a summary[339] of the two kinds of reports:

*(v) Statements privileged without explanation or contradiction*

**[34.191]** A fair and accurate report[340] of any proceedings in public of:

(i) a house of the legislature of any foreign state;

(ii) an international organisation (or conference) of which Ireland is a member (or to which Ireland sends a representative);

(iii) the International Court of Justice or other tribunal deciding matters in dispute between states;

(iv) court proceedings in foreign courts (even if not public).

Also covered are:

(v) fair and accurate copies or extracts from a public register;[341] and

(vi) notices or advertisements of courts in the State or in Northern Ireland.

*(v) Statements privileged subject to explanation or contradiction*

(i) Fair and accurate reports of the findings or decisions of any of the following associations (or their committees)

   (a) associations promoting art, science, religion or learning;

   (b) trade, business, industrial or professional associations;

   (c) sporting associations,

   when the findings or decisions relate to a member (or a person subject by virtue of contract to the control of the association) of the association.

---

337. Defamation Act 1961, s 24(2).

338. Defamation Act 1961, s 24(3).

339. The exact wording of the Act should be consulted for more specific information.

340. Whether the report is fair and accurate is a question of fact for the jury. See *Murphy v Dow Jones Publishing Co (Europe) Inc* High Court, 11 January 1995 (Flood J).

341. Extended even before 1961 to judgments properly recorded, *Cosgrave v Trade Auxiliary Company* IR 8 CL 349 (QB, 1874). Publication had, however, to be correct, and without inference or comment, *McNally v Oldham* (1863) 16 ICLR 298 (QB). In *Annaly v Trade Auxiliary Co* (1890) 26 LR Ir 394 (CA) the defendants published particulars in Stubbs Gazette of a judgment registered in error against the plaintiff personally when it should have been registered against him as executor. Held, as there was no evidence of notice of the error or of malice the defendants were entitled to the verdict.

(ii) Fair and accurate reports of lawful public meetings whether in the State or Northern Ireland.[342]

(iii) Fair and accurate reports of the proceedings at any meeting or sitting of

(a) a local authority;

(b) a judge, acting otherwise than as a court exercising judicial authority;

(c) any commission, tribunal or person appointed for the purpose of any inquiry under statutory authority;[343]

(d) any person appointed by a local authority to hold a local inquiry in pursuance of statute;

(e) any other tribunal, board, committee or body constituted or exercising functions under statutory authority,

whether in the State or Northern Ireland. This privilege applies only to meetings and sittings open to the press and the public.

(iv) Fair and accurate reports of the general meetings of companies or associations (other than private companies) formed in the State or in Northern Ireland.

(v) Copies or fair and accurate reports or summaries of notices issued by a Government Department, a local authority or the Commissioner of the Garda Síochána, or the equivalent in Northern Ireland.

**[34.192]** Finally, it should be noted that while the above provisions replace some privileges found at common law, s 24(4) specifically preserves any other privileges subsisting (otherwise than by virtue of s 4 of Law of Libel Amendment Act 1888) immediately before the commencement of the Act. So, for example, the rule that fair and accurate reports of parliamentary debates are accorded qualified privilege at common law[344] survives the Act. Moreover, s 24 only protects newspaper and broadcasted reports, as defined in the Act; other reports, if privileged, must find support in the common law.

### *Malice*

**[34.193]** The malice which may destroy the defence of qualified privilege has been defined by Brett LJ, in *Clarke v Molyneaux*[345] in the following language:

> "If the occasion is privileged it is so for some reason, and the defendant is only entitled to the protection of the privilege if he uses the occasion for that reason. He is not entitled to the protection if he uses the occasion for some indirect and wrong motive. If he uses the occasion to gratify his anger or his malice, he uses the occasion not for the reason which makes the occasion privileged, but for an indirect and wrong motive ... Malice does not mean malice in law ... but actual malice, that which is popularly called malice. If a man is proved to have stated that which he knew to be false, no one need inquire further ... So if it be proved that out of anger, or for some other wrong motive, the defendant has stated as true that which he does not know to be true ... recklessly, by reason of his anger or other motive, the jury may

342. *Cf Daly v Cork Herald Co* (1897) 31 ILT & Sol J 165 (CC). *McInerney v Clareman Printing & Publishing Co* [1903] 2 IR 347 (CA, affg KBD).

343. For example of this see *Lynam v Gowing* 6 LR Ir 259.

344. *Wason v Walter* (1868) LR 4 QB 73.

345. (1877) 3 QBD 237 at 246-247.

> infer that he used the occasion, not for the reason which justifies it, but for gratification of his anger or other indirect motive."[346]

**[34.194]** In *Coleman v Keanes Ltd*[347] the defendant's servant, suspecting the plaintiff of having taken some bacon from the defendant's shop without having paid for it, followed the plaintiff onto the street, accosted her and asked her to return. In evidence the defendant's servant admitted that when he addressed the plaintiff he spoke for the purpose of either recovering the article or of obtaining payment. The Court held that the words were spoken maliciously since the privilege only protected the servant in the performance of his civic duty of procuring the arrest and prosecution of a suspected thief.[348] It is clear, therefore, that:

> "[i]f the communication is made, not at all for the purpose of protecting interests legally recognised, nor in the performance of a duty which the law encourages, 'the pretence under which it is made, instead of furnishing a defence will aggravate the case'. It is thus seen that 'actual malice' really does not exclusively mean ill-will. It is better described as an improper purpose ie a purpose inconsistent with the social policy which it is the purpose of the law to secure by the technical device of privilege."[349]

**[34.195]** The decision in *Coleman v Keanes Ltd*, while correct in its statement of the law, seems a bit harsh in its result. Clearly, the defendant's servant was concerned when he thought the plaintiff was taking his employer's properly without paying for it. As a responsible employee he challenged the plaintiff. To say he has lost the privilege because he cannot articulate the legal justification with the exactitude required of the law, is too demanding. The employee, broadly speaking, merely wanted to stop the wrongful taking of his employer's property. He should not be expected to be able to justify his actions in refined legal terminology at the risk of being condemned of malice.

---

346. Whether the plaintiff has shown malice to destroy the defence of qualified privilege is a matter for the jury. At the end of the plaintiff's case on application from the defendant "it is for the judge to decide whether the evidence is such as would reasonably entitle the jury to hold as a matter of probability that the publication was actuated by malice ...". Henchy J in *Hynes-O'Sullivan v O'Driscoll* [1988] IR 436 at 451; McCarthy J in the same case said that "the learned trial Judge had to determine whether or not it was open to the jury to conclude that the evidence was more consistent with the existence of an improper or ulterior motive than otherwise" (at 455). Morris J in *Bell v Pederson* High Court, 14 May 1996, relying on the above statements from the Supreme Court, as well as on Finlay CJ's more ambiguous pronouncement, stated that the rule was that "the onus being on the plaintiff to establish malice, if the case is to go to the jury, I must be satisfied that on the balance of probabilities a jury would find malice" (at p 6 of his unreported judgment). It may perhaps be suggested that the judgments in *Hynes-O'Sullivan v O'Driscoll* are somewhat more indulgent to the plaintiff on this issue: see Byrne & Binchy, *Annual Review of Irish Law 1996*, 612-613.

347. [1946] Ir Jur Rep 5.

348. The High Court's decision on this has been criticised, rightly it seems, on the basis that the interest which the owner has in recovering his property is also a sufficient interest to support qualified privilege. See McDonald, *Irish Law of Defamation* (2nd ed, 1989), pp 149-150. See also *Fisher v Nation Newspaper Co Ltd* [1901] 2 IR 465 (CA).

349. HARPER & JAMES (1956 ed), p 452. Internal quotation cited to *Fairman v Ives* (1822) 5 B & Aid 642 at 648, 106 ER 1325 at 1328 (*per* Best J). Described as "want of good faith" by Byrne J in *Kirkwood-Hackett v Tierney* [1952] IR 185 at 199. See also Diplock LJ in *Horrocks v Lowe* [1974] 1 All ER 662.

**[34.196]** The presence of personal spite and ill-will on the part of the author may clearly indicate wrong motive in some cases, and, as we have seen one of the clearest ways malice can be shown is by proving that the defendant did not believe in the truth of his statement or was recklessly careless whether the statement was true or false.[350] The incidental presence, however, of an improper motive will not always be fatal; provided the author was primarily and honestly interested in protecting the recognised interest, the incidental presence of disgust, indignation or annoyance will not destroy the privilege:

> "The motives with which human beings act are mixed. ... It is only where his desire to comply with the relevant duty or to protect the relevant interest plays no significant part in his motives for publishing what he believes to be true that 'express malice' can properly be found".[351]

Put positively, to establish malice the plaintiff must show that the improper motive was the dominant factor operating in the defendant's mind at the relevant time.

**[34.197]** Furthermore, malice will not necessarily be proved merely because the defendant's thought process was flawed or inconsistent. In this regard the law is somewhat indulgent of the defendant. It does not demand that he be "right"; it only demands that he be honest.

> "The freedom of speech protected by the law of qualified privilege may be availed of by all sorts and conditions of men ... In affording to them immunity from suit if they have acted in good faith ... the law must take them as it finds them ... In greater or lesser degree according to their temperaments, their training, their intelligence, they are swayed by prejudice, rely on intuition instead of reasoning, leap to conclusions on inadequate evidence and fail to recognise the cogency of material which might cast doubt on the validity of the conclusions they reach. But despite the imperfections of the mental process by which the belief is arrived at it may still be 'honest' ie a positive belief that the conclusions they have reached are true. The law demands no more."[352]

**[34.198]** As has been already mentioned, belief in the truth of the statement will not necessarily establish privilege. Conversely, however, a belief in the falsity of the statement will normally succeed in destroying the privilege when such belief can be proved. It has been said judicially, however, that there are circumstances where the making of a statement by a person, even when he does not believe in its truth, may not destroy the privilege. For example, a person giving a character reference would be justified in drawing attention to the fact that the subject of the reference was suspected of pilfering, even though the referee himself did not believe it.[353] The better - certainly the fairer - view is that in such cases a duty should fall on the speaker to make it plain that he did not share this suspicion.

**[34.199]** Proof of malice may be found intrinsically from the tone of the communication or extrinsically from evidence of the circumstances under which the statement was made.

---

350. *Clarke v Molyneaux* (1877) 3 QBD 237. See also para **[34.193]** above.
351. *Horrocks v Lowe* [1974] 1 All ER 662 at 150-151.
352. *Horrocks v Lowe* [1974] 1 All ER 662 at 150. This *dictum*, if followed in *Coleman v Keanes Ltd* [1946] Ir Jur Rep 5, might have yielded a different result. See also *MacArthur v Meuser* (1997) 35 CCLT (2d) 197 (Ont Court of Justice).
353. *Cf Clarke v Molyneaux* (1877) 3 QBD 237 at 244 (*per* Bramwell LJ), criticised McDonald, *Irish Law of Defamation* (2nd ed, 1989), p 206.

Scales are not used, however, in examining whether the language used indicates malice; if the occasion is privileged the law will not insist on measured expressions of unnecessary restraint. Violent, excessive or prejudiced language[354] will not defeat the defendant's privilege where the defendant honestly and reasonably believed the truth of his statement.[355] The onus of establishing malice whether from intrinsic or extrinsic sources, lies on the plaintiff and is not a light one to discharge as can be clearly seen from various decisions of the Irish courts.[356]

**[34.200]** It is clear since the Civil Liability Act 1961[357] that the malice of one party in a joint libel will not destroy the privilege or the defence of fair comment of others not so actuated by malice except in the case of *respondeat superior* where the malice of a servant acting in the course of his employment will be attributed to his master.[358] Accordingly, malice on the part of one director, or one trustee will not normally destroy a privileged occasion for other directors or trustees.[359]

---

354. *Hynes-O'Sullivan v O'Driscoll* [1989] ILRM 349 at 366 (SC). *Horrocks v Lowe* [1975] AC 138. In *McCarthy v Maguire* [1899] 2 IR 802 at 808 (QBD affd CA), O'Brien LCJ observed that:

> "it is always right, in considering the question whether there was absence or presence of malice, to pay attention to the character of the information upon which a [defendant] has acted ... A charge of forgery, made without foundation ... against a respectable professional man, [is], in itself, to my mind, strong evidence of malice."

Irrelevant statements, by the defendant may cause the occasion of qualified privilege to be lost. See *McKeogh v O'Brien Moran* [1927] IR 348; LRC Consultation Paper, 1991 at para 115. Even if the irrelevancy does not cause the privileged occasion to be lost, it may be taken as evidence of malice in appropriate cases: *Horrocks v Lowe* [1974] 1 All ER 662 Diplock LJ's judgments, Duncan & Neill, *Defamation*, para 17.09.

355. *Adam v Ward* [1917] AC 309 at 339; *Maxwell v Gavin Low Ltd* Supreme Court, 11 January 1967.

356. See *Kirkwood Hackett v Tierney* [1952] IR 185 (SC); *Corcoran v W & R Jacob & Co* [1945] IR 446; *Maxwell v Gavin Low Ltd* Supreme Court, 11 January 1967; *Hyland v Cleary Ltd* Supreme Court, 9 April 1964; *Hartery v Welltrade (Middle East) Ltd and Hurley* [1978] ILRM 38; *Hennessy v K-TEL Ireland Ltd* Supreme Court, 12 June 1997, Irish Times Law Report, 28 July 1997, p 16. "The onus is a heavy one and is not discharged by showing circumstances which could possibly be construed as showing malice but equally as not so showing," *per* Lynch J in *Hennessy*. For admissibility of other statements made by the defendant to show malice, see *Curneen v Sweeney* (1969) 103 ILTR 29 (SC). As to the respective roles of judge and jury. *Cf Little v Clements* (1851) 1 Ir CLR 194 (QB) and para **[34.97]** above. It seems that a plaintiff cannot establish malice by pointing to a series of instances no single one of which amounts to malice and inviting an inference of malice from their aggregation: *Hynes-O'Sullivan v O'Driscoll* [1989] ILRM 349 ( SC). However, Finlay, CJ accepted (at 357) that the individual instances might be so interrelated as to warrant such an inference, and McCarthy J reserved his position.

357. Civil Liability Act 1961, s 11(4).

358. See also *Webb v Bloch* (1928) 41 CLR 331. So also the malice of an agent will be attributed to his principal: *Fitzsimmons v Duncan and Kemp & Co* [1908] 2 IR 483. Conversely, however, if a principal is entitled to qualified privilege, it is contrary to common sense to say that a secretary who types and sends off a letter dictated by her principal is not entitled to the same privilege, simply because she has no knowledge of the matter. See Lynch, J in *Hennessy*, para **[34.199]** above.

359. *Egger v Chelmsford (Viscount)* [1965] 1 QB 248 (CA); *Sun Life Assurance v Daryample* [1965] SCR 302. For earlier cases to the contrary, see *Smith v Streatfield* [1913] 3 KB 764 (printer); *Adam v Ward* [1917] AC 309, (Secretary).

## Fair Comment on Matters of Public Interest

**[34.201]** To establish this defence the defendant must show:

(i) that the comment was made on a matter of public interest,

(ii) that what he said was comment as opposed to fact, and finally

(iii) that the comment was fair in the sense of being honest.

### *Public interest*

**[34.202]** Generally speaking the matters which may be fairly commented on are of two kinds: first, public matters relating to the Government and the administration of the State whether at a central or local level; and second, matters of a literary, artistic or similar nature submitted to the public for approval. Under the former category the acts and policies of politicians,[360] legislators and public servants may be criticised and commented on, provided the comment is fair. Proceedings in a public court of justice, whether evidence given by witness upon oath, counsel's address or judicial comment, are also all proper subjects for fair comment.[361] Indeed any body which occupies a position of prominence in community or State affairs (the Catholic Church, the GAA, or CIE, for example) would also be a subject of public interest for the purpose of the rule. Under the latter category, the work of artists, whether literary or visual, and printed works which do not claim any artistic pretensions, but which are submitted to the public, can also be fairly criticised. In relation to such matters it is felt that the watch-dog role of the political commentator or the literary critic should not be minimised in a democratic society, and the commentator or critic must not be unduly inhibited by fine distinctions or nice refinements. In this connection it has been well said that:

> "In the case of criticism in matters of art, whether music, painting, literature or drama, where the private character of a person criticised is not involved, the freer the criticism is, the better it will be for the aesthetic welfare of the public."[362]

**[34.203]** It must be recognised, however, that it is the public aspect of the work or the performance that deserves the protection of the law. Consequently, a review or commentary which goes behind the public aspect of the work and ascribes corrupt motives to the author or accuses the author of private immorality is not normally protected by the defence of fair comment.[363] Accusations of such a nature would normally have to be justified in the technical sense of the word (ie proven to be true), or privileged.

---

360. Matters of public interest include the death penalty, the Offices Against the State Acts, and the Special Criminal Court: Kenny J, in *In re Hibernia National Review* [1976] IR 388 at 391.

361. *Kane v Mulvaney* (1866) IR 2 CL 402 (Com Pl). But a report of a defamatory speech of counsel, unsupported by evidence and not given for the proper prosecution of the case, is not a report of court proceedings within the meaning of privilege.

362. *Lyon v Daily Telegraph* [1963] KB 746 at 752 (Scott LJ). *Cf* Anon 'The Limits of Literary Criticism' (1941) 75 ILT & Sol J 47; Anon 'Fair Comment. *Joynt v Cycle Trade Publishing Co*'(1904) 37 ILT & Sol J 437.

363. *Campbell v Spottiswode* (1863) 3 B & S 769, 122 ER 288. *Aliter* perhaps where the private immorality (eg dishonesty, cruelty etc) would have a direct bearing on his public office: *Lyle-Samuel v Odhams Ltd* [1920] 1 KB 135 at 146 (*per* Scrutton LJ). On the general distinction between public and private life, see Anon '"Fair Comment", "Public Interest" and Acquiscence' [1933] LJ IFS 42, discussing the unreported decision of *Casement v London Daily Express Newspapers Ltd* High Court, (1933) (Hanna J, with jury).

**[34.204]** In determining what is of public interest, however, it should be borne in mind that the examples given here do not comprise an exhaustive list and indeed the phrase "of public interest" should be given a wide meaning in the interest of free speech. Denning MR, in 1969, gave a wide definition which commends itself in this regard. "Whether a matter is such as it will affect people at large, so that they may be legitimately interested in, or concerned at, what is going on; or what may happen to them or others; then it is a matter of public interest on which everyone is entitled to make fair comment."[364]

*(i) Comment versus fact*

**[34.205]** The second aspect of the defence is that it is confined to comment or opinion and in this context it is important to distinguish comment from fact. This is not always an easy task,[365] however, but it is important, since facts must be proved to be true (or privileged), while comment need only be shown to be fair or honest. The comment must also be based on facts truly stated.

**[34.206]** The problem of distinguishing fact from comment in law is frequently made more difficult because the comment is usually mingled with facts in the review or criticism in question. The usual form this will take will be a recital of some facts followed by a comment or opinion. An example will illustrate the point. Suppose a political commentator writes the following: "X said at the Council's meeting that he would not be misled by Communists, and he voted against the proposed nationalisation programme. In my opinion, X is not fit to be a public representative." It is clear from this that the opinion in the second sentence is based on the given facts in the first sentence. In such a situation, the facts given and on which the opinion is based must be true for the defence of fair comment to succeed.[366] A similar rule would apply if the facts, although not given in the review, were known to the public. If, however, the facts were not given in the article in question or not known to the public, then the comment or opinion carries with it the implication that it is based on facts which will justify the comment and in such a case the defence of fair comment will not be available, unless the facts are readily accessible to the public. So a person who says, "In my opinion X is a charlatan and a fraud", without giving supporting facts, cannot plead fair comment. The only defences available to him in this case would be justification and privilege. In contrast, however, a literary criticism of a book need not cite all the facts on which the reviewer's judgment is based. Because the book is readily available to the public, and any member of the public may check the facts for himself, fair comment is available as a defence. A rule to the contrary would make the reviewer's or commentator's task an impossible one.

364. *London Artists v Littler* [1969] 2 QB 375 at 391.

365. *Cf* Hogben 'Defamation: A Journalist's Viewpoint' (1984) 589 Law Institute J 383 at 385.

366. It is important to distinguish this from the independent defence of Justification where the defendant must show that matters stated as facts are true. See *Campbell v Irish Press Ltd* (1955) 90 ILTR 105 (SC) where a new trial was ordered partly because the defendant, although he only pleaded the rolled up plea was given an opportunity by the trial judge of making the defence of justification. *Cf Lefroy v Burnside (No 2)* (1879) 4 LR Ir 556 (Ex D). Section 23 of the Defamation Act 1961, discussed below, is also of present relevance since its effect is that in some circumstances not all the facts need be true in order for the defence of fair comment to succeed.

**[34.207]** In brief, therefore, the facts if given or accessible must be shown to be true if they are to support the comment;[367] if the facts on which the comment is based are not given and not available to the public, then the defence of fair comment is not available and the defendant must justify the comment or show that the occasion was privileged. In *Foley v Independent Newspapers (Ireland) Ltd*,[368] an inspector appointed to investigate certain matters under the Companies Acts, was criticised by the defendants in respect of the fees he charged for conducting the investigation. The defence of fair comment failed as the defendants had in their commentary omitted the important fact that the plaintiff's fees had been negotiated in advance with the State.

**[34.208]** At common law it was essential for the defendant to prove that all the facts on which the comment was based were true, and accordingly if the defendant failed to prove the truth of one fact out of several stated, his whole defence would fail.[369] Section 23 of the Defamation Act 1961 has modified the harshness of the rule now by providing that:

> "In an action for libel or slander in respect of words consisting partly of allegations of fact and partly of expression of opinion, a defence of fair comment shall not fail by reason only that the truth of every allegation of fact is not proved, if the expression of opinion is fair comment having regard to such of the facts alleged or referred to in the words complained of as are proved."[370]

*(ii) Comments, facts and value-judgments*

**[34.209]** It may be useful at this point to engage in some broader reflections. A severe weakness of the law in relation to fair comment is the lack of philosophical rigour in its analysis and articulation of the nature of comment and the basis of distinguishing comment from factual assertions. The problem can perhaps be traced to the definition of defamation itself. Defamation involves a communication causing others to avoid or shun the plaintiff or which lowers the plaintiff in the estimation of right-thinking members of society. This can be done by the communication of a factually untrue assertion but it can also be achieved more indirectly, by the use of derogatory language. The object of such derogatory language may well find himself or herself shunned but those who do the shunning may be unclear as to precisely what fact is being alleged against the stigmatised person.

**[34.210]** Philosophers will insist that there is a gulf between factual assertions and the expression of value judgments.[371] The former, being in the empirical order, are capable in

---

367. A suggestion was made in *Mangena v Wright* [1909] 2 KB 958, that, where the alleged facts on which the comments are based are contained in a privileged document, such as a parliamentary publication, then even if "the facts" prove to be untrue, the defence will not fall. For comment see, McDonald, *Irish Law of Defamation* (2nd ed, 1989), p 215. It should also be noted that, as in the case of Justification, if the defendant in attempting to prove the defence of fair comment attempts to prove, but fails, underlying facts, the jury may award aggravated damages. See *Campbell v Irish Press Ltd* (1955) 90 ILTR 105, *per* Kingsmill Moore J.

368. [1994] 2 ILRM 61.

369. *Black & Ors v Northern Whig Ltd* (1942) 77 ILTR 5 (HC).

370. See the LRC's *Consultation Paper on the Civil Law of Defamation* (1991), para 82 for a detailed analysis of this section.

371. For a sophisticated analysis, see Hare, *Essays in Ethical Theory* (1989).

principle of being validated or refuted and thus may be characterised as true or false. The latter, however, operating in the realm of norms rather than facts, are simply incapable of such empirical process of validation or refutation. If I claim that particular conduct was morally wrong, no scientific experiment or inquiry will prove or refute that claim.

**[34.211]** It was on this basis that the European Court of Human Rights, in *Lingens v Austria*,[372] held that a criminal law which afforded only a defence of truth to statements that consisted of value-judgments infringed freedom of opinion under Article 10 of the Convention. The Court noted that:

> "[a] careful distinction needs to be made between facts and value-judgments. The existence of facts can be demonstrated, whereas the truth of value-judgments is not suseptible of proof."[373]

**[34.212]** Ordinary language, moral adjudication and social attitudes are not as pure as the disembodied reflections of the philosopher. They represent a subtle social accretion of generations of intermingling moral codes, the effects of differing religions, educational policies and hierarchies of power. A statement that is professedly a simple value-judgment very often is premised on the assumption by the speaker of a largely shared community of values with his or her listeners. There is, moreover, a strong relationship between the language of values and that of facts. The combined effect of the existence of a community of values and a strong association between the language of values and facts is that an apparently non-factual statement, such as "He is disgraceful", will not be regarded by the listener as the mere expression of a value-judgment by the speaker which is incapable of proof or refutation. Instead it will conjure up in the mind of listener the possibility that the person about whom the remark is made has been involved in conduct which warrants his or her being lowered in the estimation of the community. The fact that the particular conduct alleged of that person has not been specified will not necessarily weaken the listener's inferential process. Since defamation is all about damaging the plaintiff in the moral estimation of the community, the fact that the speaker used the language of value-judgment rather than of facts does not deprive the communication of its damaging potential. In a community of largely shared values, the listener is not likely to respond by thinking: "That is only the speaker's view and it carries no weight because it is merely an unverifiable value-judgment". Instead, the listener may reflect: "Those words of moral criticism indicate that the person about whom they are made is not worthy of the moral esteem of the community".

**[34.213]** It should also be noted how much language straddles the factual and the normative. If I say that a particular primary school teacher was "unfair", I am appealing to a moral concept that is easy to understand, whose contours are widely regarded as non-controversial, at all events in that particular context. With no further specification on my part, the listener will apply the remark to a range of hypothetical conduct and draw a derogatory influence.

---

372. (1986) 8 EHRR 407.

373. (1986) 8 EHRR 407 at 420. See the challenging analysis by Young, 'Fact, Opinion, and the Human Rights Act 1998: Does English Law Need to Modify its Definition of "Statements of Opinion" to Ensure Compliance with Article 10 of the European Convention on Human Rights?' (2000) 20 Oxford J of Legal Studies 89.

**[34.214]** These considerations go some way towards explaining why the law requires that a comment be grounded in specific facts. Otherwise the comment, although seemingly in the realm of values, and thus incapable of proof or refutation, can nonetheless be capable of carrying with it a substratum of factual accusation, based on the listener's understanding of the kinds of facts that tend to generate a normative response of the kind represented in the speaker's utterance.

*(iii) Rolled-Up Plea*

**[34.215]** Because of the difficulty of distinguishing between facts and comment defendant's lawyers adopted at common law a form of pleading known as the rolled-up plea. The plea usually took the following form:

> "in so far as the words complained of contained statements of fact, the said statements were true in substance and in fact, and in so far as the said words consisted of comment, such comments were fair comment published contemporaneously as a matter of public interest."

**[34.216]** It should be noted that this is a plea of fair comment and not a plea of justification. The truth of the facts is pleaded incidentally and only to support the fairness of the comment based on them. Where the defendant seeks to justify the comment, then the truth of the facts and the fairness of the comment must be shown as independent factors. In relation to the rolled-up plea the defendant may be obliged now to give further and better particulars stating which of the words complained of are fact, the truth of which will be proved, and which are comment; and also what facts are to be relied on as supporting the factual statements made.[374]

**[34.217]** The Law Reform Commission in its Consultation Paper[375] quotes Duncan & Neill's useful guidelines for distinguishing statements of fact from comment:

(a) A bare statement of fact without reference to any other fact on which it is based cannot be defended as a comment.

(b) If the defendant sets out or refers to other facts, and makes it clear that the statement complained of is his inference from these facts, the statement may be defended as comment.

(c) The use of phrases such as "in my opinion" or "in other words" is not decisive. However, they are an indication that the succeeding words are comment.

(d) The defendant must separate comment from statements of fact. If the comment is so inextricably mixed up with statements of fact that the reader will be unable to distinguish the two, it cannot be defended by a defence of fair comment.

(e) Newspaper headlines will rarely be treated as comment.

---

374. See *Cooney v Browne and Others* [1985] IR 185 (HC), affd [1985] IR 190 (SC). See also *Osborne v Irish Times Ltd* Supreme Court, 27 January 1954. O'Flaherty J in *Burke v Central Independent Television plc* [1994] 2 IR 61 at 85 (SC), supports Viscount Finlay's distinction between justification and fair comment in *Sutherland v Stopes* [1925] AC 47. In *McDonnell v Sunday Business Post Ltd* High Court, 2 February 2000, O'Sullivan J held that the absence of an affidavit setting out the evidence on which the defendant seeks to rely in establishing the facts grounding a plea of fair comment should not disentitle the defendant to an order for discovery, "[s]ubject, of course, to such plea not amounting to a 'fishing expedition' or otherwise offending the principles applicable to discovery."

375. Para 76.

### *Comment must be fair*

**[34.218]** Finally the comment must be fair in the sense that it must be honestly made. Here the law also favours the critic in that the fairness of the comment is judged more from the subjective viewpoint of the critic than from the objective standpoint. That the defendant honestly believed in the comment made is sufficient to establish the defence. That it was unreasonable in the objective sense will not cause the defence to fail.[376]

**[34.219]** It is sometimes felt that the comment must to some extent be objectively supported by the facts on which it is based if the defence is to succeed, but this is not so. The use of exaggerated, extravagant language, or an illogical or unreasonable comment totally unwarranted by the facts, may be evidence of dishonesty, but that is all it is, and it would not be inconceivable to imagine a commentator maintaining an unreasonable or illogical position in all honesty and good faith, in which case he might still successfully plead fair comment.

**[34.220]** The absence of an honest belief in the truth of the comment will, of course, normally be fatal to the defence of fair comment.[377] Moreover, if the comment is inspired by a wrong motive then the defence may also fail. The presence of such a wrong motive will at least allow the matter of the defendant's honesty to be left to the jury. The defendant is protected if he makes the comment for the benefit of the public, but not if his primary object is to injure the plaintiff. This last rule means that the same comment made by two different people may be both fair and unfair comment if, for example, one person makes the comment for an improper motive. Whether the existence of malice (ie improper motive, spite, ill-will etc) *ipso jure* destroys the defence of fair comment or merely allows evidence to go to the jury from which it may decide that the defendant was not honest seems to be open to some doubt.

**[34.221]** There is one important exception to the general rule that honesty is sufficient to establish the defence of fair comment. If the defendant attributes base, corrupt or dishonest motives to the plaintiff then as well as honesty the defendant must show that the comment was such that it could reasonably be inferred from the facts truly stated.[378]

**[34.222]** An examination of the case law and academic comment show how truly elusive the concept of fairness is in the present context. One might be reasonably happy in accepting what the Courts have held to be unfair in given circumstances. To positively define "fairness", however, in the abstract is difficult, and perhaps the concept can only be addressed meaningfully in the context of a given set of facts.

---

376. See *Turner v Metro-Goldwyn-Mayer* [1950] 1 All ER 449 at 461.

377. The English courts have denied the absoluteness of this rule: *Telnikoff v Matusevitvh* [1991] 4 All ER 817 (HL). One could imagine one instance, where a newspaper editor publishes a letter containing opinions with which he or she does not concur: *cf Cherneskey v Armadale Publishers Ltd* [1979] ISCR 1067 (SCC). See further STREET, pp 482-483; WINFIELD & JOLOWICZ, pp 423-425

378. *Campbell v Spottiswode* (1863) 3 B & S 769; 122 ER 288. The rule has been criticised see Faulks Committee Report (Cmnd 5909, 1975), para 169. See further LRC Consultation Paper, 1991, para 87. Some of the difficulties *Spottiswoode* throws up, might be resolved if attention is paid to whether what the defendant says is fact or opinion. It is only in the latter case that honesty or "reasonably inferred" arises. If it is fact, it must be justified.

*(i) Functions of judge and jury*

**[34.223]** The judge determines whether a matter is capable of being a statement of fact, but having done this he must leave to the jury the task of determining what is fact and what is comment. The judge must also determine as a question of law whether the matter commented on is of public interest and whether there is reasonable evidence of the fairness of the comment. If the judge decides that there is sufficient evidence of fairness to go the jury, then it is for the jury to decide whether the comment was in fact fair or not in the particular circumstances.

## Consent

**[34.224]** The general tortious defence of *volenti non fit iniuria* is available to the defendant in a defamation action to the same extent as it is available in other torts. In view of s 34(1)(b) of the Civil Liability Act 1961, as interpreted in *O'Hanlon v ESB*,[379] this would mean at least that the plaintiff cannot complain if he has consented to the publication under contract or if he has "agreed to waive his legal rights in respect of it, whether or not for value". Short of this, however, is the defence of *volenti* available where the plaintiff invites the defendant to "Repeat that outside the House" or "Repeat that in front of witnesses"? It is submitted that a proper interpretation of s 34(1) of the Civil Liability Act 1961 would not amount to the defence of *volenti* in such circumstances. In making the initation the plaintiff is clearly not waiving his legal rights; on the contrary, he is implying that, but for the priviledged occasion, he would sue. Consent on the part of the plaintiff may have a twofold effect in defamation. It may provide the defendant with a complete defence (consent) or it may provide a foundation for privileged communication. In both cases, however, the consent of the plaintiff must be real.

**[34.225]** Where the plaintiff expressly agreed to such a waiver the legal position is clear. In many cases, however, the defendant may argue that although the consent was not expressly made by the plaintiff, it can be implied from the circumstances of the case. It will take strong evidence, however, to convince the court that the plaintiff intended, in the absence of express words, to waive his legal rights. In *Reilly v Gill*[380] a dispute arose between the plaintiff and a bookmaker as to how much the plaintiff had placed on "Happy Larry" at Tramore Race Meeting. The plaintiff admitted placing a bet of £90 on the horse, but the bookmaker claimed that the plaintiff placed such a bet twice. The Committee of Conyngham Club having heard the dispute decided that the plaintiff should pay £45 to the bookmaker as a compromise to settle the dispute. When the plaintiff refused to pay the Committee wrote to the Turf Club requesting that the plaintiff's name be placed on the Defaulters' List. It was held that in the absence of a finding that the plaintiff had in fact bet on the horse twice, the Committee had no privilege. Accordingly, the plaintiff could not

---

379. [1969] IR 75. Civil Liability Act 1961, s 34(1) provides for apportionment of liability in the case of contributory negligence on the part of the plaintiff. The provision operates, however, subject to s 34(1)(b) which provides as follows:

> "This subsection shall not operate to defeat any defence under a contract or the defence that the plaintiff before the act complained of agreed to waive his legal rights in respect of it, whether or not for value; but, subject as aforesaid, the provisions of this subsection shall apply notwithstanding that the defendant might, apart from this subsection, have the defence of voluntary assumption of risk."

380. (1946) 85 ILTR 165 (SC).

have been said to have consented to having his name put on the Defaulters' List when it had never been established that he was in fact a defaulter. In *Green v Blake*,[381] another case relating to the racing fraternity, it was held by the Supreme Court that the consent of the plaintiff to the publication of the result of an inquiry (by accepting National Hunt Championship rules) must be taken as consent only if the principles of natural justice were observed at the inquiry. As it was found, however, that the principles of natural justice were not observed at the inquiry the absence of real consent destroyed the privileged occasion which the National Hunt Committee may have had. In this case one of the judges was also willing to say that the publication in the Racing Calendar of independent statements by the Turf Club had never been consented to by the plaintiff at all.[382]

## Apology

**[34.226]** It is not a defence to a defamation suit for the defendant to claim that he made or offered to make an apology to the plaintiff. Section 17 of the Defamation Act 1961, however, provides that an offer by the defendant of an apology made before the commencement of the action, or as soon afterwards as he had an opportunity of doing so,[383] if the action was commenced before the defendant had an opportunity of apologising, shall be admissible as evidence in mitigation of damages.[384] An apology, however, must be genuinely given in an appropriate form. If it is not to the plaintiff's satisfaction[385] if it really compounds the original defamation and smarts of insincerity,[386] or if it is "half hearted" or "mean-spirited",[387] it may be rejected by the Court.

**[34.227]** In *McDaid v The Examiner*[388] the defendant newspaper published an article on the front page of its newspaper which alleged in its headline that the plaintiff, then Minister for Tourism, Sport and Recreation, knew "who the sex monsters are, but he won't tell the gardaí". Next day the defendant published a full apology admitting that the article was inaccurate and acknowledging that the Murphy Report into alleged sexual abuse of young children by two swimming coaches which was sent to the Minister did not in fact identify the coaches in question. The trial judge instructed the jury that the only issue they had to try was how much the plaintiff should get. The plaintiff gave evidence that as a

---

381. [1948] IR 242.

382. [1948] IR 242 at 272.

383. See *Egan v Hibernia National Review Ltd, Mulcahy and Irish Times Ltd* High Court 17 July 1980.

384. Section 26 of the Act also admits evidence, in mitigation of damages, of other damages recovered by the plaintiff in respect of words to the same effect as those published by the defendant. Where one concurrent tortfeasor, in an action for libel or slander would have been entitled to a mitigation of damages had he been a single tortfeasor (as, for example, where he has apologised), but another concurrent tortfeasor would not have been (as, for example, where he persists in a plea of justification), the first may not be compelled to make contribution except in respect of the amount of damages payable to him: Civil Liability Act 1961, s 14(6). On an analogous question relating to punitive damages against one concurrent tortfeasor, see Civil Liability Act 1961, s 14(4) and (5).

385. *Campbell-Sharp v Magill* High Court, 29 June 1985.

386. *McSharry v Waterford Post* High Court, 1 May 1985. See also *McConville v Kennelly* High Court, 27 January 1984.

387. *Agnew v Independent Newspapers* High Court, 29 June 1985.

388. High Court, unrep 18 November 1999.

result of the article he was jostled in Grafton Street, and was threatened at Leopardstown Races. The jury awarded £90,000 damages.

### Offer of Amends in Unintentional Defamation

**[34.228]** Section 21 of the Defamation Act 1961 makes provision for an offer of amends in the case of unintentional defamation. The provisions of this section have already been examined and need not be dealt with separately here.[389]

## V. Damages

**[34.229]** The question of damages in defamation litigation has proved highly controversial in recent years.[390] The traditional approach has been to give the jury substantial leeway in making an award. The reason – which has perhaps become somewhat occluded in much contemporary discussion – is that defamation is rooted in community values. The trial judge's role is to ensure that the jury adjudicates only on communications that are capable of being characterised as defamatory but, within that broad limitation, the jury, as representative of the community, makes the decision as to liability.[391] Equally, the jury has the task of quantifying the damage to the plaintiff's reputation in monetary terms[392] with some guidance from the trial judge but not to the extent of having specific figures mentioned in the judge's direction.

**[34.230]** Over the past decade, there has been a veritable assault on this approach. Several factors are involved. Some particularly high awards against media defendants by British juries provoked a strong media campaign to rein in the damages for defamation. This campaign extends well beyond the alleged frailty of jury decision-making, however, since it encompasses the broader argument that the media are unduly restrained by the basic principles of defamation law, on such matters as the onus of proof, strict liability and the limits of the defence of qualified privilege. In combination, all these elements, including the possibility of a high jury award, can have a chilling effect on those in the media who want to expose corruption and other wrongdoing.

**[34.231]** Apart from these broader concerns, there is a discernable patrician disdain among the British judiciary for the capacity of members of juries to understand the value of

---

389. See paras **[34.112]-[34.121]** above.

390. See QUILL, pp 490-491.

391. Thus, in *Quigley v Creation Ltd* [1971] IR 269 at 272, Walsh J observed:

> "Basically, the question of libel or no libel is a matter of opinion and opinions may vary reasonably within very wide limits. When a jury has found that there has been a libel, this court would be more slow to set aside such a verdict than in other types of actions and it would only do so if it was of the opinion that the conclusion reached by the jury was one to which reasonable men could not or ought not have come …
>
> In defamation, as in perhaps no other form of civil proceedings, the position of the jury is so uniquely important that, while it is for the judge to determine whether the words complained of are capable of a defamatory meaning, the judge should not withhold the matter from the jury unless he is satisfied that it would be wholly unreasonable to attribute a libellous meaning to the words complained of."

392. *Cf Barrett v Independent Newspapers Ltd* [1986] IR 13 at 35 (per McCarthy J) (SC):

> "The law reports abound with judicial tributes to the particular respect [for] a jury in libel actions … Walsh J['s] … observations [in *Quigley v Creation Ltd*, [1971] IR 269 at 272] apply no less to the assessment of damages than they do to the issue of libel or no libel."

money once the sums involved are beyond their day-to-day experience:[393] This has led to greater specificity in directions by trial judges in defamation cases[394] and the increasing willingness to include references to amounts of awards in earlier cases that have received the blessing of the appellate courts.[395]

**[34.232]** A third factor should be noted. This is the European dimension. Speaking broadly, there is no tradition in continental European jurisdictions of awarding high sums in defamation cases. Defamation is treated differently in civil law countries, with less emphasis on damages and much more on other processes, including the criminal law and remedies involving retraction.[396] Juries play only a limited role in civil litigation in these countries. Moreover, compensation for personal injuries is also far less extensive in these countries than it is in common law jurisdictions, particularly Ireland where damages levels are high. Bearing these substantial differences in mind, it was relatively easy to predict that the European Court of Human Rights might not look with complete favour on high awards in defamation cases by juries acting with little specific guidance from the trial judge as to what would be an appropriate amount.

**[34.233]** The Irish courts have made it plain that juries are not given a completely free hand when deciding the quantum of damages in defamation cases. On the contrary, they have insisted that juries act on the principle of proportionality, taking into account (*inter alia*) the relative gravity of the charge made against the plaintiff.

**[34.234]** The *locus classicus* is contained in Henchy J's judgment in *Barrett v Independent Newspapers Ltd*,[397] where, it will be recalled, the Supreme Court struck down as excessive a jury award of £65,000 damages in favour of a politician about whom a journalist had written that, in the immediate aftermath of an unsuccessful "push" against Taoiseach Charles Haughey at Leinster House the politician had "leaned over and pulled at my beard and said 'You thought you'd dance on his grave'."

---

393. Thus, in *Sutcliffe v Pressdam Ltd* [1991] 1 QB 153, where the jury made an award £600,000 general damages, Donaldson MR observed that he could:

> "not believe that the jury appreciated the true size of the award which they were making. This is understandable. Despite the inflation which has occurred in the post-war years, sums of money of £100,000 or more, and in many cases less, still lack the reality of the £1 coin or the £5 note. In the lives of ordinary people they are unlikely ever to intrude except in the form of the nominal sale or purchase price of a house … What is, I think, required is some guidance to juries in terms which will assist them to appreciate the real value of large sums."

In *Rantzen v Mirror Group Newspapers (1986) Ltd* [1994] QB 670, the Court of Appeal upheld the trial judge's direction to the jury which advised the jury to relate the amount awarded in damages to "what [money] can buy – a house, a car or a holiday".

394. *Cf Rantzen v Mirror Group Newspapers (1986) Ltd* [1994] QB 670; *John v MGN Ltd* [1996] 2 All ER 35.

395. *John v MGN Ltd* [1996] 2 All ER 35. See also Denham J in *De Rossa v Independent Newspaper plc* Supreme Court, 30 July 1999.

396. See Vick & Macpherson 'Anglicising Defamation Law in the European Union' (1996) 36 Va J of Int L 933 at 952ff; Arnold Nicholson 'Re Libel: A Case Study in English Defamation Law' (2000) 18 Wisconsin Int'l L J 1 at 6-8.

397. [1986] IR 13 (SC).

**[34.235]** Henchy J stated:

> "In a case such as this in which there is no question of punitive, exemplary or aggravated damages, it is the duty of the judge to direct the jury that the damages must be confined to such sum of money as will fairly and reasonably compensate the plaintiff for his injured feelings and for any diminution in his standing among right-thinking people as a result of the words complained. The jury have to be told that they must make their assessment entirely on the facts as found by them, and they must be given such direction on the law as will enable them to reach a proper assessment on the basis of those facts. Among the relevant considerations proper to be taken into account are the nature of the libel, the standing of the plaintiff, the extent of the publication, the conduct of the defendant at all stages of the case, and any other matter which bears on the extent of the damages ... The fact remains... that the jury were not given any real help as to how to assess compensatory damages in this case. A helpful guide for a jury in a case such as this would have been to ask them to reduce to actuality the allegation complained of, namely, that in an excess of triumphalism at this leader's success the plaintiff attempted to tweak the beard of an unfriendly journalist. The jury might then have been asked to fit that allegation into its appropriate place in the scale of defamatory remarks to which the plaintiff might have been subjected. Had they approached the matter in this way, I venture to think that having regard to the various kinds of allegations of criminal, immoral or otherwise contemptible conduct that might have been made against a politician, the allegation actually complained of would have to come fairly low in the scale of damaging accusations. The sum awarded, however, is so high as to convince me that the jury erred in their approach. To put it another way, if £65,000 were to be held to be appropriate damages for an accusation of a minor unpremeditated assault in a moment of exhaltation, the damages proper for an accusation of some heinous or premeditated criminal conduct would be astronomically high. Yet, a fundamental principle of the law of compensatory damages in that the award must always be reasonable and fair and bear a due correspondence with the injury suffered. In my view, the sum awarded in this case went far beyond what a reasonable jury applying the law to all the relevant considerations could reasonably have awarded."[398]

**[34.236]** These observations made it clear that there is no judicial surrender to the vagaries of perverse juries. A criterion of objective proportionality must be applied by juries and failure by a trial judge to apprise them of this obligation may well render his or her change to the jury legally defective. Moreover, the jury's tariff must be such as to keep the maximum sum for damages for the most serious libels within reason: if it is "astronomically high" that will not pass the scrutiny of the Supreme Court.

**[34.237]** In *McDonagh v News Group Newspapers Ltd*,[399] the Supreme Court again favoured an approach based on objective proportionality. Here the jury had awarded £90,000 to the plaintiff, a practising barrister, who had represented the Irish Government at an inquest held in Gibraltar into the death of Mairead Farrell, Sean Savage and Daniel McCann, members of the provisional IRA, by members of the Special Air Service regiment of the British Army. The Sun newspaper had published an article under the headline "Leftie Spies pack SAS Gib Inquest", which, the jury found defamed the plaintiff in several respects, including allegations that he was a left-wing spy, that, his report to the Irish Government on the inquest would be biased, that he was a sympathetic with terrorist

398. [1986] IR 13.

399. Supreme Court, 23 November 1993.

gangs and that he was incapable of performing the duties for which he had been appointed by the Irish Government.

**[34.238]** The Supreme Court dismissed an appeal against the quantum of damages. It seemed to Finlay CJ that, though the figure was "probably at the top of the appropriate range",[400] it was not so great that the Court should interfere. With regard to the allegation that the plaintiff was a sympathiser with terrorists causes the Chief Justice was satisfied that "there are not very many general classifications of defamatory accusation which at present in Ireland, in the minds of right-minded people, would be considered more serious."[401] To an extent the seriousness might be somewhat aggravated by the fact that it was an accusation that had been made against a person who had a professional role in the administration of justice. The other allegations, in their combined effect, constituted an extremely grave accusation of professional misconduct by the plaintiff.

**[34.239]** The Supreme Court gave an extended treatment of the issue in *De Rossa v Independent Newspapers plc*.[402] In that case, the plaintiff, the leader of the Democratic Left Party, had formerly been a leading member of the Workers' Party. The defendant published an article about the plaintiff's role in the Workers' Party which the jury found to be defamatory of him in suggesting that he had been involved in, or tolerated, serious crime and had personally supported anti-semitism and violent communist oppression. The jury awarded £300,000 damages. On appeal to the Supreme Court by the defendant against the quantum of damages the appellant argued existing practice of allowing juries unguided discretion in their assessment of damages in defamation cases led to exercise and disproportionate awards and was contrary to the Constitution and that instead guidelines should be given to juries, including reference to the purchasing power of any contemplated award, comparison with personal injury damages awards and awards in previous libel cases, and the estimates of the trial judge and counsel, respectively of the appropriate level of damages in the case before them. The appellant further argued that the Supreme Court was obliged, under common law and the Constitution, to subject large awards to a more searching scrutiny than formerly.

**[34.240]** The new test proposed by the appellant was that favoured by the English Court of Appeal in *Rantzen v Mirror Group Newspapers Ltd*,[403] namely, whether a reasonable jury could have thought that the particular award it that was made was necessary to compensate the plaintiff and to re-establish his or her reputation.

**[34.241]** The Supreme Court, by a four-to-one majority,[404] rejected this argument and dismissed the appeal. Hamilton CJ, for the majority, expressed the view that "[t]here does not appear to be any conflict between Article 10 [of the European Convention on Human Rights] and the common law or the Constitution".[405] Proportionality was the key principle

400. Supreme Court, 23 November 1993.

401. Supreme Court, 23 November 1993.

402. Supreme Court, 30 July 1999, analysed by Browne 'A judgment that chills media's zeal' Irish Times, 4 August 1999.

403. [1994] QB 670 (CA).

404. Hamilton CJ, Barrington, Murphy and Lynch JJ concurring, Denham J dissenting.

405. Page 32 of Hamilton CJ's judgment.

and this was already well established in Irish case-law on the subject of damages for defamation, notably in Henchy J's judgment in *Barrett*.[406]

**[34.242]** The Chief Justice went on to state that neither the Constitution nor the Convention required that the guidelines to be given to juries should be changed in the manner argued for by the appellant:

> "If the practice as outlined in *Rantzen* case and extended as outlined in *John's* case were to be followed, the jury would be buried in figures, figures suggested by counsel for both parties as to the appropriate level of damages, a figure from the judge representing his opinion as to the appropriate level of damages, figures with regard to damages made or approved by the Court of Appeal in previous libel actions and figures with regard to damages in personal injuries actions and at the same time be subject to the direction of the trial judge and that it is not bound by such figures and must make up its own mind as to the appropriate level of damages.
>
> It is accepted by all that, even if the giving of such guidelines and figures were permissible, the jury would not be bound by such figures and was under an obligation to make up its own mind to the appropriate level of damages.
>
> I am satisfied that the giving of such figures, even though only by way of guideline, would constitute an unjustifiable invasion of the province or domain of the jury."

**[34.243]** Hamilton CJ was equally opposed to having the trial judge refer to awards in personal injuries when directing the jury in defamation proceedings. The high subjective element in assessing the damage to reputation made this comparison unhelpful, in his view.[407]

---

406. See para **[34.235]** above.

407. The relationship between damages for personal injuries and damage for loss of reputation is complex and controversial. It might at first be considered odd that loss of reputation should warrant greater maximum compensation than the worst physical injury imaginable but there is no necessary logical connection between the two. Who is to say that to be falsely accused of being a child molester or a traitor or a racist is more or less serious in its impact than a broken spine? If the intuition is that the broken spine should warrant greater damages, is that an argument for bringing defamation damages down to the artificial level prescribed by the Supreme Court in *Sinnott v Quinnsworth Ltd* [1984] ILRM 523 or for reviewing the adequacy of personal injury awards? The (somewhat crude) rationale for the *Sinnott* tariff surely has no necessary application to defamation cases. In *O'Brien v Mirror Group Newspapers Ltd* Supreme Court, 25 October 2000, Geoghegan J, dissenting on the issue of whether the amount awarded was excessive on the basis that *De Rossa v Independent Newspapers plc* Supreme Court, 30 July 1999 governed its assessment, made the interesting and attractive argument that defamation cases should be treated differently from personal injury awards, with greater deference to the tribunal of fact, because:

> "[i]n the case of personal injuries an appeal court can determine with some confidence what would be the range of awards which a reasonable jury (or nowadays a reasonable judge) might make. This the appeal court can do because although every personal injury case is different from every other personal injury case there are also great similarities. A broken hip case relates to some extent at least to every other broken hip case. A loss of an eye case relates to some extent at least to every other case of loss of an eye etc. Members of the court from their experience at the Bar and/experience as trial judges and indeed experience of previous similar appeals may with some confidence form a view as to what the legitimate spectrum of awards could be. In the case of a libel appeal however, the appeal court although it has to engage in the same exercise, it can only do so with diffidence rather than confidence."

**[34.244]** The Chief Justice stressed the individual character of each defamation case as a further reason why reference to awards in other defamation cases would not assist the jury's task:

> "Each defamation action has its own unique features and a jury in assessing damages must have regard to same: these include the nature of the libel, the standing of the plaintiff, the extent of the publication, the conduct of the defendant at all stages and many other matters. These will vary from case to case. Figures awarded in other cases based on different facts are not matters which the jury is or should be entitled to take into account."[408]

**[34.245]** To retain the traditional guidelines for juries unaltered would not mean that their discretion was limitless:

> "[T]he damages awarded by a jury must be fair and reasonable having regard to all the relevant circumstances and must not be disproportionate to the injury suffered by the injured party and the necessity to vindicate such party in the eyes of the public. Awards made by a jury are subject to a right of appeal and, on the hearing of such appeal, the award made by a jury is scrutinised to ensure that the award complies with these principles."[409]

**[34.246]** Hamilton CJ rejected the *Rantzen*[410] test for appellate tribunals on the basis that it would remove from the jury award its "very unusual and emphatic sanctity."[411] The correct test was that the appellate court could set aside an award only when satisfied that it was so disproportionate to the injury suffered and the wrong done that no reasonable jury would have made it.

**[34.247]** Applying that test to the facts of the case, the Chief Justice was satisfied that the award should stand:

> "To publish of any person words meaning that he or she was involved in or tolerated serious crime and personally supported anti-Semitisum and violent Communist oppression would, if untrue, constitute the gravest and most serious libel: it is hard to imagine a more serious one.
>
> To publish such words in relation to the respondent, a politician dependant on the support of his constituents and his colleagues and at a time when he was engaged in negotiations, as was well known to the appellant at the time of publication, which might lead to his participation in Government, renders such publication more serious and grave, particularly when they might have interfered with his chances of participation in such Government. The words published clearly affected the respondent's personal integrity and professional reputation."[412]

**[34.248]** Moreover, one of the most important facts in the assessment of damages was the effect of the libel on the plaintiff's feelings. It was easy to imagine the hurt and distress which allegations of the kind made by the appellant would cause. The extent of the publication was very wide: the newspaper – *The Sunday Independent* – had a readership of over a million. No apology, retraction or withdrawal of the allegation had been made at any time. During the course of the proceedings, the respondent had been subjected to immensely long and hostile cross-examination by counsel for the appellant. Right to the

---

408. Page 60 of Hamilton CJ's judgment.
409. *Sinnott v Quinnsworth Ltd* [1984] ILRM 523.
410. *Rantzen v Mirror Group Newspapers* [1994] QB 620 (CA).
411. *Barrett v Independent Newspapers Ltd* [1986] IR 13 at 19 (SC).
412. Page 65-66 of Hamilton CJ's judgment

very end of the trial the appellant had contested the right of the respondent to damages and had challenged his motives in bringing the action and his honesty and credibility.

**[34.249]** Having regard to all these considerations, it appeared to Hamilton CJ that the jury "would have been justified in going to the top of the bracket and awarding as damages the largest sum that could fairly be regarded as compensation".[413]

**[34.250]** Denham J, dissenting, favoured giving guidelines to the jury on the level of damages in defamation cases. They "would assist in accessing consistent and comparable decisions, which would enhance public confidence in the administration of justice".[414] Information should be given to the jury of previous awards in libel cases made or affirmed by the Supreme Court. The jury should also be able to compare the value of what courts usually awarded to people in personal injury actions:

> "Compensation is a remedy in both instances. The lame do not walk after an award of compensation. The defamed do not cease to have been defamed after an award of damages. An order of damages is an artificial form by which a court gives a remedy to an injured person.
>
> It is quite reasonable to have proportionality in the wider scheme of damages. Thus, a reference to a case which imposes a cap on general damages might be useful. However, rather than reference to general damages in catastrophic injury cases, where there may be issues of consciousness etc, the tariff for injures such as an eye, a leg or an arm may be helpful. It is entirely reasonable that there be a degree of uniformity, consistency, a sense of compatibility, of rationality, in the wider scheme of damages."[415]

**[34.251]** Denham J considered that the appellate tribunal, in determining whether the jury's award was reasonable and proportionate, could also have resort to some guidelines on damage levels that had been given to the jury.

**[34.252]** As to the amount of damages awarded in the instant case, Denham J referred to *McDonagh v News Group Newspapers Ltd*,[416] whose facts involved "strong similarities"[417] in the seriousness of the defamation allegations and the standing of importance in the community which both plaintiffs shared. The award of £90,000 in *McDonagh* had been considered by the Supreme Court to be at the top of the permissible range. Even making allowance for the further aggravating elements in the instant case, Denham J considered the award of £300,000 to be so large as to be unsustainable.

**[34.253]** In *O'Brien v Mirror Group Newspapers Ltd*[418] the Supreme Court again considered damages awarded by a High Court jury. In that case, a prominent and successful businessman claimed that articles published about him meant that he had paid a bribe to a former Minister to get a radio broadcasting licence and that his business was based on corruption. The jury awarded damages in the amount of £250,000. Although the

413. Page 77 of Hamilton's judgment.

414. Page 10 of Denham J's judgment. Denham J expressed her position in similar terms in *O'Brien v Mirror Group Newspapers Ltd* Supreme Court, Irish Times, 26 October 2000. Again she was the sole dissenting voice on this point in a Court of fire.

415. Page 11 of Denham J's judgment.

416. Supreme Court, 23 November 1993.

417. Page 17 of Denham J's judgment.

418. Supreme Court, 25 October 2000.

Supreme Court ordered that there should be a retrial on the amount of damages, Keane CJ, with whom the other judges agreed, confirmed the Court's approach in *de Rossa*, that specific guidelines should not be given to the jury in defamation cases. Nonetheless, comparing the very serious allegations made against Mr de Rossa with the allegations made against Mr O'Brien, the Court held that an award of £250,000 to Mr O'Brien was disproportionately high, especially when £250,000 was the Court's cap on general damages awarded in the most serious personal injuries cases of paraplegic or quadriplegic injuries. It is interesting to note that while Keane CJ did not in express terms reject Hamilton CJ's repudiation of a comparison between awards in personal injury litigation and in defamation cases, he proceeded on the basis that such a comparison was valid. This is an important departure, for practical purposes, from the approach adopted in *De Rossa*.

**[34.254]** Denham J, dissenting, again argued, as she had done in *de Rossa*, the guidelines and information of other courts should be furnished to juries in these type of cases. She suggested that the Supreme Court should review its decision in *de Rossa*, there were compelling reasons to do so and the issue was of public interest and importance. In the absence of legislation, the Court should use its common law jurisprudence to assist the jury in this regard.

**[34.255]** The Supreme Court decisions in *De Rossa* and *O'Brien* is surely not the last word on the subject of damages in defamation proceedings. The defendants in *De Rossa* have sought to have the case determined by the European Court of Human Rights. The outcome of that case is hard to predict and the Supreme Court's analysis of the Convention in *De Rossa* is disappointingly summary. Hamilton CJ offers no explanation for his bald assertion that "[t]here does not appear to be any conflict between Article 10 [of the Convention] and the common law or the Constitution".[419] Nor does he explain how the exclusion of guidance for juries as to the purchasing power of awards or as to what appellate courts have authorised and the present somewhat deferential appellate approach towards jury awards can be reconciled with what the European Court of Human Rights said in *Tolstoy Miloslavsky v United Kingdom*:[420]

> "The jury had been directed not to punish the appellant but only to award an amount that would compensate the non-pecuniary damage to [the plaintiff]. The sum awarded was three times the size of the highest libel award previously made in England and no comparable award has been made since. An award of the present size must be particularly open to question where the substantive national law applicable at the time fails itself to provide a requirement of proportionality.
>
> In this regard it should be noted that, at the material time, the national law allowed a great latitude to the jury. The Court of Appeal could not set aside an award simply on the grounds that it was excessive but only if the award was so unreasonable that it could not have been made by sensible people and must have been arrived at capriciously, unconscionably or irrationally. In a more recent case, *Rantzan v Mirror Group Newspapers Ltd.* the Court of Appeal itself observed that to grant an almost limitless discretion to a jury failed to provide a satisfactory measurement for lending what was 'necessary in a democratic society' the purposes of Article 10 of the Convention. It noted that the common law – if properly

419. Page 32 of Hamilton J's judgment.
420. (1995) 20 EHRR 442.

understood – required the courts to subject large awards of damages to a more searching scrutiny than had been customary. As to what guideline the judge should give to the jury, the Court of Appeal stated that it was to be hoped that in the course of time a series of decisions of the Court of Appeal, taken under s 8 of the Courts and Legal Services Act 1990, would establish some standards as to what would be proper awards. In the meantime the jury should be invited to consider the purchasing power of any award which they might make and to ensure that any award they made was proportionate to the damage which the plaintiff had suffered and was a sum which it was necessary to award him to provide adequate compensation and to re-establish his reputation.

The Court cannot but endorse the above observations by the Court of Appeal to the effect that the scope of judicial control, at the trial and on appeal, at the time of the applicant's case did not offer adequate and effective safeguards against a disproportionately large award.

Accordingly, having regard to the size of the award in the applicant's case in conjunction with the lack of adequate and effective safeguards at the relevant time against a disproportionately large award, the Court finds that there has been a violation of the applicant's rights under Article 10 of the Convention."[421]

**[34.256]** It is very hard to interpret this passage as offering support for a system that does not contain provision for guiding juries on the lines indicated in *Rantzen*.[422] Whilst the Irish system can be defended on the basis that the jury's discretion is not untrammeled and that the principle of proportionality must underline its award and the appellate assessment of it, the fact remains that the trial judge's hands are tied in being prevented from translating an invocation to be sensitive to requirements of proportionality into offering practical examples of what has been held to be proportionate.

**[34.257]** We now must consider an important issue that did not arise in *De Rossa*, where the award was one of compensatory damages. In what circumstances may an award of exemplary damages be made?[423]

**[34.258]** Prior to *Rookes v Barnard*[424] there was no dispute that exemplary damages might be awarded in defamation cases where the defendant's conduct was particularly oppressive or high-handed. In *Rookes v Barnard*, the House of Lords held that the entitlement to award exemplary damages should be restricted to these instances, only one of which, for practical purposes,[425] is relevant to defamation: this is where the defendant has sought to

---

421. (1995) 20 EHRR 442 at 472-473.

422. See para **[34.240]** above. There is surely merit in Denham J's observation in her dissenting judgment in *O'Brien v Mirror Group Newspapers Ltd* that:

> "[i]n analysing *Tolstoy* it appears that the earlier common law of England and Wales was considered by the European Court of Human Rights to be contrary to the European Convention. It appears to me that there is considerable similarity to Irish law now and the Law of England and Wales prior to the decision in *Rantzen* and *John*. Consequently there is a real issue as to whether the scope of judicial control at the trial and on appeal offers adequate and effective safeguards against disproportionately large awards of damages. It thus raises the issue as to whether there is a breach of the Convention. In all the circumstances it is appropriate that the matter be reopened, reanalysed and reassessed."

423. See FLEMING, p 659-660.

424. [1964] AC 1129 (HL, Eng).

425. It is true that the first category – unconstitutional action by servants of the State – could consist of defamation. A liberal application of this category could bring more cases of defamation within its scope: *Cf Dawson t/a AE Dawson & Sons v Irish Brokers Association* Supreme Court, 6 November 1998, discussed at paras **[34.260]-[34.262]** below.

invest in the commission of the tort, hoping that the profit will exceed the damages award.[426]

**[34.259]** In Ireland there is still a regrettable uncertainty as to whether the *Rookes v Barnard* restrictions have been accepted by the courts. They appear to have been clearly rejected in proceedings for damages for infringements of constitutional rights:[427] for the generality of torts litigation, however, the judicial response has been ambiguous.

**[34.260]** So far as defamation actions are concerned, the Supreme Court addressed the issue in *Dawson (t/a AE Dawson & Sons) v Irish Brokers Association*[428] in 1998. In earlier proceedings between the parties,[429] the Supreme Court had overturned a jury award of £515,000 on the basis that it was excessive. When the case was retried in the High Court, the trial judge interpreted the earlier Supreme Court judgment as holding that neither aggravated nor exemplary damages would be open in the case on retrial. The Supreme Court, on appeal, held that this was a misconstruction of what it had held. It had intended only to refer to the earlier High Court proceedings: a retrial might "take a completely different complexion".[430]

**[34.261]** O'Flaherty J made important observations on the subject, which must be quoted in full:

> "There is often confusion about the proper description of damages and I attempted to unravel it to a degree in my judgment in *McIntyre v Lewis*. To recapitulate: while aggravated damages are distinct, they are still meant to compensate the plaintiff and so they should be regarded as a sub-head of compensatory damages awarded to the plaintiff. On the other hand, exemplary (or punitive) damages are a separate category. They are not compensatory at all. Though the question of exemplary damages was not in issue at the first trial, seemingly, the plaintiff's were anxious to put them in issue at the second trial. In this jurisdiction it is not necessary to plead in regard to exemplary damages in the statement of claim (and it was not done in this case) though it is a requirement in England under that country's rules of court.
>
> So the plaintiffs were entitled at least to advance a case that they were entitled to exemplary damages though, in due course, it would be for the trial judge to decide whether they brought themselves within any category that would entitle them to exemplary damages. Before us the plaintiff relied on a passage from *Gatley on Libel and Slander*[431] that in the case of 'oppressive, arbitrary or unconstitutional action by servants of the government', the latter phrase, it seems, being taken to include all persons purporting to exercise powers of government, central or local, conferred upon them by statute or at common law by virtue of the official status or employment which they hold, exemplary damages might be awarded. The plaintiffs argued before us that, since the defendant body derived its powers from statute, then it could be liable for exemplary damages. I emphasise that I make no judgment as to

426. *Cf* paras **[44.10]-[44.15]** below.

427. *Conway v Irish National Teachers Organisation* [1991] 1 ILRM 497 (SC).

428. Supreme Court, 6 November 1998.

429. Supreme Court, 27 February 1997.

430. Supreme Court, 27 February 1997, p 7 of O'Flaherty J's judgment (Hamilton CJ and Barrington J concurring).

431. 8th ed, para 1454.

whether this submission is right or wrong but it clearly is one that they were entitled to advance."[432]

Gatley's statement of law is derived, of course, from the first of the three instances in which the House of Lords in *Rookes v Barnard*[433] permitted an award of exemplary damages. The tenor of O'Flaherty J's observations seems to be that he saw no difficulty with this restrictive approach: the plaintiffs would succeed if they fell within this category but not, it seems, if their submission to this effect failed. It would, however, be rash to read such an implication into the express language of O'Flaherty J's judgment. He was anxious to take a neutral position on the issue, and his remarks should not be interpreted as representing a considered acceptance of the *Rookes v Barnard* limitations.

**[34.262]** Further light was thrown on the matter in *O'Brien v Mirror Group Newspapers Ltd.*[434] Here, as we have seen, the Supreme Court held that a jury award of £25,000 to a business man who had been accused of bribery and corruption was excessive. In the Supreme Court the plaintiff had cross-appealed, arguing that the issue of exemplary damages ought to have been left to the jury. The Supreme held that, where it was undoubtedly the case "that exemplary damages might be awarded in a action for defamation, and that such an award did not have to fall within one of the three limited categories prescribed in *Rookes v Barnard*, the instant case would not warrant such an award as there was no evidence that the defendants had published the offending article intending to defame the plaintiff and in the knowledge that it was true. Keane CJ specifically observed that *Rookes v Barnard* had not been followed in Ireland, citing *Conway v Irish National Teachers*[435] on authority. This is an important point as the Chief Justice did not seek to restrict *Conway* to cases where damages were being awarded for infringement of constitutional rights.

## VI. Reform of the Law

**[34.263]** The Law Reform Commission has in its 1991 Report recommended many reforms in this area. A Private Member's Bill, based on the Law Reform Commission's proposals, has been introduced by Mr Michael McDowell who has since become Attorney-General, but it is not being given priority at present, as the government is pursuing its own draft. It is anticipated, however, that a new reforming measure will be introduced by the Government in the not too distant future.

**[34.264]** Many of the Law Reform Commission's proposals attempt to reduce the common law position to statutory form and, with slight clarifications and modifications where some of the common law provisions were seen to be anomalous or unfair. It is not appropriate to discuss all these reforms in detail in this work, but some brief comment is warranted on the major recommendations put forward in the report.

432. Page 8-9 of O'Flaherty J's judgment.

433. See para **[44.10]** below.

434. Supreme Court, 25 October 2000.

435. [1991] ILRM 497 (SC).

## Abolition of the distinction between Libel and Slander

**[34.265]** The Law Reform Commission's report proposes the abolition of the distinction between libel and slander and this is to be welcomed. The distinction as we have seen, is largely an historical one and nowadays is hard to defend. To cover those existing cases of slander where at common law special damage need not be proved, it is proposed that a new cause of action in defamation should be created where proof of special damage is not required. In so far as this would shift the focus on to the interest to be protected, that is the plaintiff's reputation, rather than on the means used to tarnish a person's reputation, it is a sensible proposal. Some historical anomalies and distinctions in this area are no more than dead-wood which needs to be cut away, and the distinction between libel and slander is one such piece of dead-wood which will not be missed in any new formulation of the law of defamation.

## Defaming the Dead

**[34.266]** Another proposal put forward by the Law Reform Commission is that there should be a new cause of action in respect of defamatory statements made about a person who was dead at the time of publication. The rule at common law was that one could not defame a dead person, but in an age of sensationalist journalism it seems somewhat unfair that wild allegations which would attract libel proceedings if made during a person's life-time can be unleashed with impunity as soon as the death notice appears. The new approach recognises that a man's reputation deserves to be protected for some time after his death and that the immediate family should not in their immediate grief, have to cope with the additional pain of unwarranted attacks on the deceased's reputation, at least for some reasonable period of time after his death. Such actions are recognised in the continental countries of Europe and the proposed change is sensible. Two conditions attach to the recommendation: the right of action should be vested in the personal representative of the deceased who should be statutorily obliged to consult the immediate family before commencing proceedings. Second, the period of limitation should be three years from the date of death. This relatively short period means that such a reform would not inhibit genuine historians from giving considered assessments in due course without the "chilling effect" of a defamation writ. Moreover, it is proposed that the only remedy in such action should be a declaratory order (and an injunction where appropriate), but not damages, and this is proper since it is the deceased man's reputation that is the primary concern of the law, not the sensitivities of the family.

## Printers and Innocent Distributors

**[34.267]** With regard to innocent dissemination, it is proposed that the stricter rule that makes printers and distributors liable should be modified. The proposal is that printers as such should not be liable unless they are also the publishers. With regard to distributors, who are not publishers, they should not be liable except where the plaintiff has called upon them to cease distributing and they have failed to respond. If the printer or distributor is called upon by the plaintiff to disclose the identity of the publisher and he fails to do so, then the plaintiff, it is proposed, should also be entitled to sue the printer or the distributor as if they were publishers. This too, seems reasonable, and alleviating the position of printers or other innocent distributors in the dissemination of the libel, would appear to be commendable reform. The primary targets in defamation proceedings should be the author, the publisher and those who actively or culpably assist in the publication process; less central figures should be treated more leniently.

## Proposal to Abandon Strict Liability in Favour of Fault Based Liability

**[34.268]** The Commission refused to recommend that reform should move the basis of liability from strict liability to liability based on fault. To do so, it was felt, would be unfair to the person defamed and would tip the scales too much against plaintiff's right to his good name. The Commission, however, although turning its face against reasonable care as a complete defence, was of the opinion, that if the defendant successfully showed that he took reasonable care, then this should deny the plaintiff a right to general damages, while still entitling him to a declaratory order or to damages for financial loss. It would be unfair in the Commission's view to make the plaintiff's right to recover dependent on his ability to prove a breach of duty of reasonable care. In many cases, especially where the defendant is a media organ, it would be very difficult for the plaintiff to prove such a breach and even if the plaintiff enlisted discovery procedures, which would prolong and complicate the proceedings, there would be no guarantee that the onus on the plaintiff would be lightened in many cases. The cost of the litigation would be increased and this would favour the rich and powerful defendants. It will also be argued, of course that strict liability would ensure greater care from the media and this in itself would be a good thing. The Commission concluded, with one member dissenting, that:

> "it should be a defence to a claim for general damages in respect of a defamatory allegation of fact that the defendants exercised reasonable care prior to publication in attempting to ascertain the truth of the allegation".[436]

The Commission, however, recommended that reasonable care should not be a defence to a claim for financial loss or to a claim for a correction order and/or a declaratory judgment.

## New Definition of Defamation and the Presumption of Falsity

**[34.269]** The definition of defamation proposed by the Law Commission is as follows:

> "(1) Defamation is the publication by any means of defamatory matter concerning the plaintiff.
>
> (2) Defamatory matter defined: defamatory matter is matter which (a) is untrue and (b) tends to injure the plaintiff's reputation.
>
> (6) Burden of proof: the burden of proof is on the plaintiff to show that there was publication, that the matter contained in the publication was defamatory and that the defamatory matter concerned the plaintiff."[437]

**[34.270]** It can be seen from this that to succeed under such a measure the plaintiff would have to prove that the statement complained of was untrue. This would reverse the common law presumption that a defamatory statement is presumed to be false and the onus is on the defendant to prove that this is true.

**[34.271]** In reaching this conclusion the majority of the Commissioners formed a view that it is unsatisfactory that the plaintiff should be relieved of proving all the essential ingredients of the wrong which he has alleged. According to the majority the law should

436. LRC Report on Civil Law of Defamation 1991, para 7.27.
437. LRC Report on Civil Law of Defamation 1991, para 3.13.

adopt a neutral stance as to the truth and falsity of statements made, and if the plaintiff wishes to succeed he should be obliged to prove that the statement is false. Furthermore, it is the majority view that in practice the plaintiff will, in the vast majority of cases, deny the truth of the statement and this in turn will force the defendant to prove its truth.

**[34.272]** Two of the five commissioners, however, argued strongly against such a change in the law. Reversing the onus of proof for them would, in effect, result in a presumption that anything said of the plaintiff no matter how damaging, is true.

> "A situation in which the plaintiff would be required in effect to prove his or her innocence is, in our view, inconsistent with the spirit of the constitutional requirement that the State vindicate the good name of every citizen in the case of injustice done."[438]

**[34.273]** Moreover, adopting a neutral stance on the matter, as the majority suggests, does change the position of the parties. It puts the onus on the plaintiff and, if both parties give evidence, the plaintiff will fail unless he proves the falsity on the balance of probability. In many cases when the plaintiff can do no more than deny the allegation, this may not be enough to discharge the onus of proof. "The court will decide against plaintiff, not because it is satisfied that the allegation made against him or her is true, but because, in a case of doubt its truth is assumed".[439]

**[34.274]** In the view of the minority, which with respect, seems to be the preferable view, this matter is a fundamental one for the law of defamation.

> "Difficult choices about competing social values are involved in the reform of defamation law. At the end of the day it will be for the Oireachtas to determine how the balance should be drawn. Do we wish to live in society in which one person may with impunity publish a hurtful and damaging statement about another as long as it remains impossible or difficult for that other to prove that the statement was untrue? Or would we prefer to live in society in which those who publish defamatory statements know that they may have to offer some kind of redress unless they can in some way substantiate their allegations? The matter goes to the heart of defamation law. We believe that the function of the law of defamation should be to provide redress ie appropriate vindication of a person's good name – in any case where defamatory statements are made which are not capable of being substantiated. The majority's proposal to reverse the onus of proof involves a fundamental shift in underlying policy which in our view has not been justified."[440]

**[34.275]** In a system where journalists do not have to disclose their sources, and where the law of privacy is not as yet developed, some might consider that to adopt the majority suggestion would be tilting the balance too much against the private citizen and in favour of the media.

**[34.276]** Returning to the suggestion that the plaintiff should prove the falsity of the statement made and that the ordinary rules of tort should prevail the following comments are appropriate.

**[34.277]** In ordinary negligence actions the plaintiff commences the proceedings by stating that the defendant, to take a concrete example, "struck me with his car while he was driving negligently and broke my leg". The first statement in this scenario is made by the

438. LRC Report on Civil Law of Defamation 1991, para 7.35.
439. LRC Report on Civil Law of Defamation 1991, para 7.35.
440. LRC Report on Civil Law of Defamation 1991, para 7.35.

plaintiff and on the normal rule, that he who avers must prove, the plaintiff is called on to prove his case. If the plaintiff fails to take this initiative, nothing will happen in the civil courts, and the defendant will not become accountable. In defamation, however, the matter is different: the first statement here is not the plaintiff's, but that of the defendant. The defendant may, for example, say "John Smith is a thief". Applying the ordinary rule that he who avers must prove to this situation, one is entitled to call on the defendant to prove the statement (that is justify) or to show that there is available to him some other defence protecting his speech, in the first instance. All the plaintiff should be obliged to do, to launch his action, is to show that the defendant uttered these words at the outset. Thereafter the onus is on the defendant to prove the truth of what he said, and this it would appear is not unfair in the circumstances. Were the law otherwise, it might well be impossible for the plaintiff to prove the untruth of the defamatory statement uttered by the defendant. How, for example, can the plaintiff be expected to disapprove a libel such as the following: "X committed adultery with Y in 1991"? What if Y is unwilling, or unable, to give evidence in X's favour? Should the untrue, but in practical terms irrebuttable, libel be allowed to hang out there as if it were objectively true, merely because the plaintiff cannot bring forward any more proof other than his or her own denial? It is notoriously difficult to prove a negative. Why should the plaintiff be put in this position by a defamatory statement uttered, perhaps even maliciously, by a defendant who may know full well that the plaintiff would be unable to prove the contrary. It is submitted that the onus in these circumstances should remain on the defendant to prove that the defamatory statement is true.

Chapter 35

# Deceit and Injurious Falsehood


I. Deceit........................................................................................................ 967
II. Injurious Falsehood ................................................................................... 977


## I. DECEIT

**[35.01]** The tort of deceit (or fraud) was of greater significance when there was no liability in law for negligent misstatements.[1] Since *Hedley Byrne & Co Ltd v Heller & Partners Ltd*,[2] however, an injured person can now in many cases recover from persons who negligently misrepresented facts to him or her, thereby causing him or her damage. In such circumstances plaintiffs will normally be satisfied with proving negligence, which is an easier task than having to prove fraud. Nevertheless, in some cases the tort of deceit still has attractions. These advantages may be mentioned briefly. First, *Hedley Byrne* states that the duty of care arises in respect of negligent misstatements only when a "special relationship" exists between the parties. No such formal requirement exists in the case of deceit although, in fact, such a relationship frequently exists. Secondly, in deceit the remoteness criterion still favoured is the generous "direct consequences" rule, whereas under *Hedley Byrne* "reasonable foreseeability" is preferred. Thirdly, the ability of the plaintiff to prove fraud on the part of the defendant, as opposed to mere negligence, may shock the jury (where one is present) into a generous mood when it comes to awarding damages. The jury's expression of displeasure at the defendant's conduct may redound to the plaintiff's advantage.

**[35.02]** In order to establish the tort of deceit the plaintiff must prove the following:

"(i) the making of a representation as to a past or existing fact by the defendant;

(ii) that the representation was made knowingly, or without belief in its truth or recklessly, careless whether it be true or false;

(iii) that it was intended by the defendant that the representation should be acted upon by the plaintiff;

---

1. The leading English case on deceit *Derry v Peek* (1889) 14 AC 337 (HL (Eng), provoked much discussion in the United States, where most courts did not adhere to as severe restrictions as were laid down in that case. See Smith 'Liability for Negligent Language' (1900) 14 Harv LR 184; Williston 'Liability for Honest Misrepresentations' (1911) 24 Harv LR 415; Bohlen 'Misrepresentation as Deceit Negligence or Warranty' (1929) 42 Harv LR 733; 'Innocent Misrepresentation' (1930) 24 Ill LR 749; Weisiger 'Bases of Liability for Misrepresentation' (1930) 24 Ill LR 866. See also Prosser 'Misrepresentation and Third Persons' (1966) 19 Vand LR 231 at 233-235. Consumer legislation affords protection against fraudulent statements made in the course of trade, business or profession, by imposing a criminal sanction with power given to the court to order payment of part or all of the fine to the victim: Consumer Information Act 1978 ss 6 and 17(3) analysed by Clark, *Contract Law in Ireland* (4th ed, 1998), pp 169-170.

2. [1964] AC 465. See para **[10.52]**.

(iv) that the plaintiff did act on foot of the representation; and

(v) suffered damages as a result."[3]

A further word on each of those requirements is called for.

## Representation of Fact

**[35.03]** The representation of fact is usually made by spoken or written word. Thus in *Leyden v Malone*,[4] where the defendant and his wife falsely stated that the turnover figure for the business he was selling was much greater than it was in fact, the plaintiff was entitled to damages for deceit when he purchased the business at an inflated price.[5]

**[35.04]** In *Delany v Keogh*[6] an auctioneer selling a public house stated correctly that a rent of £18 had been accepted by the landlord for many years although the lease specified £25. He omitted, however, to mention that the landlord had intimated that he would in future be looking for the higher amount. The auctioneer, before the auction, had received legal advice that such a claim would not be sustainable on the grounds of estoppel. After the property was sold the landlord successfully sued the purchaser for the higher sum. The purchaser's action for deceit against the auctioneer was successful in the Court of Appeal. Holmes LJ stated:

> "It is not necessary that the misrepresentation which will sustain an action of deceit should be made in actual terms. Words may be used in such circumstances, and in such a connexion, as to convey to the person to whom they are addressed a meaning or inference beyond what is expressed, and if it appears that the person employing them knew this, and also knew that such meaning or inference was false, there is sufficient proof of fraud".[7]

**[35.05]** Although the representation is normally made through written or spoken words this is not the only way, of course, in which it can be made. Thus a nod or a wink might, in appropriate circumstances, amount to a representation, and a person who in a university town wears an academic gown may be making a statement that he is a member of the local university.[8] Similarly, to turn back the milometer of a second-hand car would be to make a representation that the car had only done the mileage eventually displayed.

---

3. *Forshall and Fine Arts Collections Ltd v Walsh* High Court, 18 June 1997, (p 64 of Shanley J's judgment). See also *Ennis v Butterly* [1997] 1 ILRM 28 (HC). *Superwood Holdings plc v Sun Alliance and London Assurance plc* Supreme Court, 27 June 1995 (at p 27-28 of Denham J's judgment). *Cf O'Callaghan v Meath Vocational Education Committee* High Court, 20 November 1990 at p 19 of Costello J's judgment. WINFIELD & JOLOWICZ, p 354; SALMOND & HEUSTON, p 369; Sheridan, *Fraud in Equity: A Study in English and Irish Law* (1957), Ch 1; Wylie, *Irish Conveyancing Law* (1978), pp 220-221; 'Symposium on Fraud and Deceit' (1964) 13 Clev-MLR, Pt 23; Green 'Deceit' (1930) 16 Va LR 749; Keeton 'Fraud - Concealment and Non-Disclosure' (1936) 15 Tex LR 1; Keeton 'Fraud -Statements of Intention' (1936) 15 Tex LR 185; Keeton 'Fraud Misrepresentations of Law' (1936) 15 Tex LR 409; James & Gray 'Misrepresentation' (1977-78) 37 MLR 286, 488.
4. Supreme Court, 13 May 1968.
5. *Cf Hindle v O'Dwyer* Supreme Court, 14 February 1955; *O'Donoghue v Nolan and Kelly* High Court, 29 July 1993; *Fenton v Schofield* (1964) 100 ILTR 69 (HC) varied as to damages (SC); *Jury v Stoker* (1882) 9 LR Ir 385 and *Pasley v Freeman* (1789) 3 Term Rep 51, 100 ER 450, the first case where deceit emerged as a separate tort. Defendant falsely misrepresented third party's creditworthiness.
6. [1905] 2 IR 267 (CA revg KBD).
7. [1905] 2 IR 267 at 286-287.
8. *R v Barnard* (1837) 7 C & P 784; 173 ER 342. See also *People v Finkel & Levine* (1951) 1 Frewen 123. *Cf Harland v Fancsali* (1993) 102 DLR (4th) 577 (Ont Court (Gen Div) DS) - bid by married woman for property in her original surname not actionable as deceit.

**[35.06]** Normally silence and inaction will not involve the defendant in liability.[9] There is no general obligation to enlighten the fool or to prevent the business opportunist from taking advantage of the person who labours under a mistake.[10] To the rule that silence will not amount to misrepresentation, however, there are a few well known exceptions. First, if a statement is true when it is made but becomes false during the continuation of negotiations, there is an obligation for the representor to make the correction.[11] Second, a half-truth, which may be true insofar as it goes, may amount to a misrepresentation because what it omits to say suggests something else: *suppressio veri est suggestio falsi*.[12] In *Gill v McDowell*,[13] it was held that there was evidence of misrepresentation sufficient to sustain an action for deceit where the defendant sold a cattle dealer at a fair a hermaphrodite ox, which on account of its abnormal condition, died shortly afterwards. The dealer believed that the animal was either a bullock or a heifer. Considerable reliance was placed by the Court on the fact that the animal was sold together with a heifer and a bullock. This, in the view of Lord O'Brien LCJ, amounted to "a tacit representation" that the animal was itself either a heifer or a bullock. There is, however, much to be said for Madden J's dissenting rejection of this approach. He observed that:

> "there is not a special stand provided for hermaphrodites at a fair, and if the seller had treated the animal as one that could not be sold with bullocks or heifers this would practically amount to a representation or admission that the animal suffered from something that rendered it not ordinarily saleable. I do not think that the seller was bound to do this. In my opinion the maxim *caveat emptor* would apply"[14]

---

9. See WINFIELD & JOLOWICZ, p 355 Keeton 'Fraud - Concealment and Non-Disclosure' (1936) 15 Tex LR 1. *Cf Neville (William) & Sons Ltd v Guardian Builders Ltd* [1990] ILRM 601 (HC); *Reen v Bank of Ireland Finance Ltd* [1983] ILRM 507 at 510 (HC). In equity the position is different: *cf* Sheridan, *Fraud in Equity: A Study in English and Irish Law* (1957), Ch 1; Wylie, *Irish Conveyancing Law* (1978), pp 40-41.
10. *Smith v Hughes* (1871) LR 6 QB 597; *Galbraith v Mitchenall Estates* [1965] 2 QB 473.
11. *Bradford Third Equitable Building Society v Borders* [1941] 2 All ER 205 at 220; *With v O'Flanagan* [1936] Ch 575 at 584. WINFIELD & JOLOWICZ, p 358. See also *Northern Bank Finance Corporation Ltd v Chariton* [1979] IR 149 (SC affg Finlay P 1977). Conversely if a statement is false when made but true when the plaintiff acted upon it there is no misrepresentation. *Briess v Woolley* [1954] AC 333 at 353 (HL (Eng)).
12. See eg *Nottingham Patent Brick and Tile Co Ltd v Butler* (1866) 16 QBD 778; *Peek v Gurney* (1873) LR 6 HL 377 at 403; *Delany v Keogh* [1905] 2 IR 267 (CA revg KBD) *Kelly v Doyle* [1907] 2 IR 355 (CA affg KBD); *Barber v Houston* (1885) 18 LR Ir 475 (CA); *cf Healy v Nolan* (1946) 80 ILTR 78 (SC). Where a husband who is under an obligation to pay his wife half his income sends her £3,000 he is committing deceit if his income is £8,000. See WINFIELD & JOLOWICZ, p 357. *Cf Preston v Shannon Caravans Ltd* High Court, Teevan J, 1967, allegation that defendant fraudulently represented used caravans as new rejected on the evidence. In *Components Tube Co v Naylor* [1900] 2 IR 1 at 59-60 (QBD), Palles CB observed that:

    > "omissions may, upon the construction of the entire document, render false a statement which would have been true had the omitted statement been contained in the document ... where the omission is of this character the deceived party ... can treat it as an active misrepresentation, as distinguished from mere concealment, and therefore make it the ground of an action for damages for deceit."

13. [1903] 2 IR 463 (KBD).
14. [1903] 2 IR 463 at 471. It should be noted that the purchaser was in any event held entitled to relief under the doctrine of mistake.

**[35.07]** Third, where the defendant is under a legal obligation to volunteer information, then of course his silence will not protect him. This might arise for example in insurance contracts (and other contracts *uberrimae fidei*), where a fiduciary relationship exists between the parties, or where there is a statutory obligation on the defendant to volunteer information. In such circumstances the defendant will not be entitled to shelter behind his silence.

**[35.08]** A distinction is made between representations of a factual nature and mere expressions of opinion. Liability does not attach to the latter. Thus, in *Smyth v Lynn*,[15] where an auctioneer's advertisement which stated that the premises were "in excellent structural and decorative repair and ready for immediate owner occupation" this was held to involve the communication of an opinion. Curran J observed:

> "It is not my view that the words used in the advertisement were apt to describe the actual condition of the premises. The law gives no special sanctity to statements contained in an advertisement for the sale of property ... Such advertisements, however, must be looked at in their true perspective. They do not purport to be detailed reports by experts as to the condition of the property to be sold. It is common knowledge that the purpose of such advertisements is to draw attention to the good points of the property, and that one usually finds in such advertisements rather flourishing statements."[16]

It is important to remember that a statement of belief or a statement of opinion may also amount to a statement of fact. If I say "I believe John is an honest man", I am stating a fact about my present frame of mind. If I am lying when I make that statement I am making a misrepresentation about the present state of my mind, and this "is as much a fact as the state of [my] digestion".[17] Moreover, statements of opinion may harbour assertions of fact or may imply knowledge of facts.[18]

**[35.09]** Misrepresentations of law give rise to some uncertainty.[19] The general rule is that the misrepresentation must be one of the fact rather than law.[20] Clearly the boundaries

---

15. (1950) 85 ILTR 57 (NI Ch D).

16. (1950) 85 ILTR 57 at 59. It is clear from Curran J's later observations in the case that he did not intend to confer some blanket immunity on advertisements. He considered that the purchaser had not been the type of person to rely on 'auctioneers' encomiums' and had not in fact relied on what the advertisement had stated. Had the purchaser been a more gullible or defenceless person it seems that the outcome might have been different. From a conceptual standpoint it is hard to see how liability for an expression of opinion should depend on the particular person to whom it is addressed, if the basis for non-liability is that an expression of opinion is not a representation of fact. Perhaps the justification for Curran J's approach is that liability can be imposed where the person giving the opinion realises that, on account of the gullibility or other particular circumstances of the person addressed, the opinion will be understood as an assertion of fact. As to television advertisements see *UL Canada Ltd v ProCourter & Gamble Inc* (1996) 65 CPR 3d 534 (Ont Court (Gen Div)). Liability for misleading advertisements may arise under the European Communities (Misleading Advertising) Regulations 1988: see *O'Connor Nenagh Ltd v Powers Supermarkets Ltd* High Court, 15 March 1993.

17. *Edgington v Fitzmaurice* (1885) 29 Ch D 459 at 483. *Cf O'Callaghan v Meath Vocational Education Committee* High Court, 20 November 1990. See generally Keeton 'Fraud -Statements of Intention' (1937) 15 Tex LR 185; Keeton 'Fraud: Misrepresentations of Opinion' (1937) 21 Minn LR 643.

18. See *Smith v Land and House Property Corporation* (1884) 28 Ch D 7 at 15 and *Brown v Raphael* [1958] 2 All ER 79.

19. *Cf Doolan v Murray* High Court, 21 December 1993 in context of innocent misrepresentation.

20. See Keeton 'Fraud-Misrepresentation of Law' (1937) 15 Texas LR 409.

between fact and law cannot easily be drawn in some cases. If a man represents that he is legally entitled to marry and fails to mention that he is already in a valid subsisting marriage, he may be sued for deceit by the woman he dupes[21] (as well as being prosecuted for bigamy). If directors of a company, knowing that the private Act of Parliament incorporating the company does not give legal power to accept bills of exchange, represent that such power exists, this will equally be characterised as a fraudulent misrepresentation of fact.[22] Where the misrepresentation is one of a purely legal character, there is scant judicial authority for bringing it within the remit of the tort of deceit, but the textbook writers[23] generally advocate its inclusion, at all events where the parties are not on an equal footing with respect to knowledge of the law, intellectual capacity or educational achievement.[24]

## Knowledge of Falsity

**[35.10]** In *Ennis v Butterly*,[25] Kelly J observed that "[t]he essence of the action [for deceit] is dishonesty". It is essential for the plaintiff to prove that the defendant knew of the falsity of his or her representation, or was reckless as to its truth or falsity. A person who makes an honest mistake or who makes a careless statement will not be liable in deceit although nowadays there may be liability for negligent misstatement under *Hedley Byrne*. In the leading case of *Derry v Peek*[26] Lord Herschell put the matter this way:

> "I think the authorities establish the following propositions: First, in order to sustain an action of deceit, there must be proof of fraud, and nothing short of that will suffice. Secondly, fraud is proved when it is shown that a false representation has been made (1) knowingly, or (2) without belief in its truth, or (3) recklessly, careless whether it be true or false."[27]

**[35.11]** In *Derry v Peek*, the directors of a company issued a prospectus wherein they intimated that they were authorised by statute to use steam or mechanical power, instead of horses, to run their tramways. In fact this right existed only if authorised by the Board of Trade. The plaintiff who applied for shares sued subsequently when the Board of Trade

21. *Cf Garnaut v Rowse* (1941) 43 WALR 29.

22. *West London Commercial Bank Ltd v Kitson* (1884) 13 QBD 360. See also *National Conversion Corporation v Cedar Building Corporation* (1969) 23 NY 2d 621, 246 NE 2d 351, 298 NYS 2d 499.

23. *Cf* SALMOND & HEUSTON, p 371; FLEMING, p 698; WINFIELD & JOLOWICZ, p 356.

24. *Cf* FLEMING, p 698 WINFIELD & JOLOWICZ, p 356.

25. [1997] 1 ILRM 28 at 40 (HC).

26. (1889) 14 AC 337 at 374 (HL (Eng)).

27. See also *Forshall and Fine Arts Collections Ltd v Walsh* High Court, 18 June 1997; *Pearson & Son Ltd v Dublin Corporation* [1907] AC 351 (HL (Ir)); *Phelps v White* (1881) 7 LR Ir 160 (CA), affg 5 LR Ir 318. See Forde, *Company Law in Ireland* (3 rd ed, 1999), pp 254-256. The decision in *Derry v Peek* led to the enactment of the Directors' Liability Act 1890, s 2 of which imposed liability on directors and promoters for untrue statements in prospectuses unless they proved that they had "reasonable ground to believe" that the statements were true. See now the Companies Act 1963, s 49; Ussher, *Company Law in Ireland* (1986), pp 399-402. Section 297(1) of the Companies Act 1963, enables the court on the winding up of a company to impose personal liability on those who were knowingly parties to the carrying on of the business with interest to defraud creditors, "or for any fraudulent purpose". In *O'Keefe v Ferris* [1993] 3 IR 165, Murphy J held that this provision should be characterised as a civil remedy other than a criminal offence. See also the Companies Act 1990, s 39.

refused permission. It was held that no action lay for deceit against the defendants because, although the statement made was inaccurate, it had not been made knowingly or recklessly. The directors honestly believed what they stated as true, and so could not be liable in deceit.[28]

**[35.12]** *Derry v Peek* was distinguished by the Irish Court of Appeal in *Delany v Keogh*,[29] the facts of which have already been outlined. Holmes LJ argued that if (on analogy with the facts in *Delany v Keogh*) the directors of the company had known, before they issued the prospectus, that the Board of Trade had refused to consent, or had announced its intention to refuse, then liability would have been imposed, and their position would not have been improved if their solicitor has assured them that there would be no difficulty in obtaining from Parliament an amending act removing the condition.[30] It seems, however, legitimate to express some doubt as to whether in fact the House of Lords would have imposed liability in such circumstances. In the last analysis, *Derry v Peek* was indulgent to the defendants on the facts: *Delany v Keogh* emphatically was not.

## Intention of Defendant

**[35.13]** In making the false misrepresentation the defendant must have intended the plaintiff to act upon it.[31] This requirement is satisfied, however, if it is addressed to a class of persons to which the plaintiff belongs with the intention that the class, or some members of it, should act upon the misrepresentation.[32] If the plaintiff is not intended to act upon the misrepresentation or does not belong to a class to whom it is addressed he cannot sue in deceit. Therefore in *Peek v Gurney*[33] a person who, in reliance on statements made in a company prospectus, bought shares on the market could not sue the directors as the

---

28. "... conscious knowledge of falsity must always amount to wickedness and dishonesty", *Armstrong v Strain* [1951] 1 TLR 856 at 871. See also *Jury v Stoker* (1882) 9 LR Ir 385 (CA); *Components Tube Co Ltd v Naylor* [1900] 2 IR 1 (QB Div). *Cf Doolan v Murray* High Court, unrep 21 December 1993.
29. [1905] 2 IR 267 (CA revg KBD) discussed above at para **[35.04]**.
30. The analogy drawn by Holmes LJ does not appear to be as close as it should have been. If the directors had believed that the Board of Trade's refusal was not legally binding (rather than capable of being circumvented by amending legislation), would Holmes LJ have been so certain that liability would attach?
31. What the defendant intended must be gleaned from his acts however. Moreover, if the plaintiff acts as people usually do, in reliance upon a statement such as the defendant has made it seems that he need not adduce any further evidence as to the defendant's intention that he should so act: *cf* Sheridan, *Fraud in Equity: A Study in English and Irish Law* (1957), Ch 14. *S Pearson & Son Ltd v Dublin Corporation* [1907] AC 351 (HL (Ir)). It is, however, essential for the plaintiff to allege that the representation was made with the intention that the plaintiff should rely on it. Failure to do so can not be remedied by a notice for particulars. Murphy J so held in *Countyglen plc v Carway* High Court, 10 April 1995 observing that:

    "[t]he Notice for Particulars may require flesh to be put on the bones of the pleadings, but the Statement of Claim itself must provide an adequate skeleton containing all of the ingredients of the wrong alleged."

    See also the Rules of the Superior Courts 1986, O 19 r 5(2) and the decisions cited by Ó Floinn, *Practice and Procedure in the Superior Courts* (1996), p 165.
32. *Bradford Third Equitable Benefit Building Society v Borders* [1941] 2 All ER 205 at 211.
33. (1873) LR 6 HL 377.

prospectus is not normally designed to induce persons to buy shares on the market but rather to encourage persons to apply to and buy from the company itself. Further, the company prospectus is usually confined to the original shareholders.[34]

**[35.14]** Provided the intention of the defendant is that the plaintiff should act on the representation, it is not necessary for the plaintiff to show that the representation was made directly to him by the defendant. So where a father bought a gun stating to the vendor that he intended his sons to use it, the vendor was held liable in deceit for falsely representing the condition of the gun in an action by the purchaser's son who was injured while using the gun.[35] Likewise false statements made by the vendor of property to an intending purchaser and passed on to another interested purchaser (but not by the vendor) can form the basis of an action in deceit by the second interested party who thereafter purchases the property.[36] The ultimate motives of the defendant are irrelevant here and all that is required is that the defendant intended the plaintiff to act on the representation. This corresponds to the general rule of tort. Accordingly it is no defence for the defendant to say that he genuinely thought, for example, that investment in the company would be advantageous to the plaintiff or that he did not intend the plaintiff to suffer damage.

## The Plaintiff's Reliance is Essential

**[35.15]** There is no liability in deceit if the plaintiff does not rely on the defendant's misrepresentation. If therefore, the plaintiff ignores the representation and does not allow it to influence his decision, as where, for example, he carries out his own investigation and bases his action on his own survey, the defendant will not be liable.[37] Similarly, if the plaintiff is not influenced by the representation because he is unaware of it[38] or because he is not deceived by it[39] or because, in the case of goods, a patent defect exists, the defendant will not be liable in deceit.[40] However, provided the representation influenced the plaintiff in some measure it need not be the sole factor in causing him to act as he did.

> "It does not have to be the only inducement so far as the success of the plaintiff's claim is concerned if in itself it is a causative inducement and the fact that there may have been others does not affect the issue."[41]

Furthermore, the defendant cannot deny liability by declaring that, in spite of the misrepresentation, the plaintiff caused his own injury because he foolishly failed to check

---

34. See further Forde, *Company Law* (3rd ed, 1999), pp 274-276.
35. *Langridge v Levy* (1837) 2 M & W 519; 150 ER 863.
36. *Pilmore v Hood* (1838) 5 Bing NC 97; 132 ER 1042; *cf Gross v Lewis Hillman Ltd* [1970] Ch 445.
37. *Attwood v Small* (1836) 6 Cl & Fin 232 7 ER 684. See also *Barber v Houston* (1885) 18 LR Ir 475 at 477 (CA). *Cf Kreglinger and Fernau Ltd v Irish National Insurance Co Ltd* [1956] IR 116 (HC).
38. See *Re Northumberland and Durham District Banking Co ex parte Bigge* (1859) 28 LJ Ch 50.
39. See *Horsfall v Thomas* (1862) 1 H & C 90; 158 ER 813. *Cf Nader v Allegheny Airlines Inc* (1980) 626 F 2D 1031 (DC Cir).
40. *Horsfall v Thomas* (1862) 1 H & C 90; 158 ER 813. *Cf Nader v Allegheny Airlines Inc* (1980) 626 F 2D 1031 (DC Cir).
41. *Leyden v Malone* Supreme Court, 13 May 1968 (*per* Walsh J). See also *Paul & Vincent Ltd v O'Reilly* 49 ILTR 89 (CA 1914 affg KBD 1913); *Edgington v Fitzmaurice* (1885) 29 Ch D 459.

out the representation.[42] This is so even if the defendants positively state that facilities are made available to check the truth of the defendant's statements, because "such a clause might in some cases be part of a fraud, and might advance and disguise the fraud".[43]

**[35.16]** In the case of ambiguous statements made by the defendant, liability will attach only if the plaintiff shows:

> "(1) the sense in which he understood the statement; (2) that in that sense it was false; and (3) that the defendant intended him to understand it in that sense or deliberately made use of the ambiguity with the express purpose of deceiving him".[44]

If, therefore, the defendant uses ambiguous phraseology in the sense that the statement is capable of two interpretations, one of which is true and one of which is false, he will be liable only if it is shown that he intended the words to be interpreted in the false sense.[45] If he honestly intended to convey the true meaning to the plaintiff then, even though he awkwardly phrased his expression, resulting in ambiguity, he is not liable in deceit.

**[35.17]** The Supreme Court decision of *Northern Bank Finance Corporation Ltd v Charlton*[46] illustrates some of the above rules and can be discussed with profit at this juncture.

**[35.18]** The facts of this case were as follows. The three defendants and two others, Patrick Quinn and Vincent Deignan, formulated a plan to take over the public company of JE

---

42. *Central Ry of Venezuela v Kirch* (1867) LR 2 HL 99; *Jury v Stoker* (1882) 9 LR Ir 385 at 399 affd by CA (1882); *Gill v McDowell* [1903] 2 IR 463 (KBD 1902). See also *Phelps v White* (1881) 7 LR Ir 160 at 164 (CA *per* Palles CB): "A person who has been unfortunate enough to make, with intent to its being acted upon, a statement false in fact cannot, when that statement has been acted upon, allege that he ought not to have been believed." Although this is entirely true in relation to the question of the defendant's liability, a separate question arises as to whether the contributory negligence of the plaintiff should reduce damages. In view of the manner in which the Civil Liability Act 1961 is drafted (*cf* Ch 4), it seems that contributory negligence is not excluded as a defence in the present context; but that does not mean that the change is likely to afford the defendant any real prospect of relief. Normally his or her fault would be likely to be considered far greater than that of a gullible plaintiff. Indeed the courts might very well with good reason hold that on the grounds of public policy a defendant should (in most cases at least), be prevented from raising the defence of contributory negligence. English authorities interpreting differently-drafted statutory provisions have held that contributory defence may not be pleaded in an action for deceit: *Alliance & Leicester Building Society v Edgestop Ltd* [1994] 2 All ER 38 (Ch D); *Corporation National del Cobre de Chile v Sogemin Metals Ltd* [1997] 2 All ER 917 (Ch D); *Nationwide Building Society v Thimbleby & Co* Ch D, 26 February 1999 (LEXIS transcript). In this context the policy considerations that underlay the decision of the House of Lords in *Smith New Court Securities Ltd v Scrimgeour Vickers (Asset Management) Ltd* [1997] AC 254 have had an effect. See further Kerr, *The Civil Liability Acts* (1999), 42.
43. *S Pearson & Son Ltd v Dublin Corporation* [1907] AC 351 at 360 (HL (Ir)). See WILLIAMS, para 55.
44. WINFIELD & JOLOWICZ, p 361 citing *Smith v Chadwick* (1884) 9 AC 187 at 201 and *Arkwright v Newbold* (1881) 17 Ch D 301 at 324.
45. *Smith v Chadwick* (1884) 9 AC 187 at 201.
46. [1979] IR 149. See also *Greyhill Property Company Ltd v Whitechap Inn Ltd* High Court, unrep 5 October 1993; *East v Maurer* [1991] 2 All ER 733 at 736 (CA); *Royscot Trust Ltd v Rogerson* [1991] 2 QB 297 at 305 309 (CA); *Smith New Court Securities Ltd v Scrimgeour Vickers (Asset Management) Ltd* [1997] AC 254 (HL(Eng)).

Mooney and Co Ltd. The plan was to be assisted by the plaintiff bank by way of loan facilities and by the plaintiff bank's agreeing to act as agents of the promoters in executing the payments. The defendants, when sued on certain guarantees, etc, by the plaintiff bank, counterclaimed for deceit, claiming that they had been induced to enter into the transaction by a number of fraudulent misrepresentations made by the servants of the plaintiff bank. In particular, they claimed that the managing director of the bank had told them, before the deal was completed, that Pat Quinn had already deposited with the bank £200,000, being his share of the purchase price, and that another employee of the bank had assured the defendants at a critical stage of the negotiations that "all the money was in"; they also claimed that, at a later stage, they had been induced to purchase Pat Quinn's shares in Pat Quinn's Holdings Ltd (the company formed to be the vehicle of the takeover) on the basis of a representation that Pat Quinn at that time was in no way indebted to the bank. All of these statements were found to be false and to have been fraudulently made. In addition there was also, in the course of the negotiations, a failure by the bank officials to disclose that Pat Quinn's deposit with the bank had been reduced to some £25,000.

**[35.19]** Because these representations were fraudulent and made by the plaintiff bank to induce the defendants to enter into the takeover and because the defendants did in fact rely on the representations and acted on them to their detriment, they were entitled to damages. The Supreme Court refused to upset the findings of the President of the High Court to the effect that a fraud had been committed by the bank.[47]

## Damage

**[35.20]** To recover in deceit the plaintiff must prove damage. Normally this will be pecuniary loss[48] but it also covers personal injuries[49] and injury to property.[50]

**[35.21]** With regard to remoteness of consequences *Northern Bank Finance Corporation Ltd v Charlton*[51] is the most recent confirmation that direct consequences rather than reasonable foreseeability is the test to be preferred. Henchy J in that case cited with approval *Doyle v Olby (Ironmongers) Ltd*[52] and declared:

47. The decision is particularly interesting also for its discussion of the functions and powers of the Supreme Court as an appellate court rehearing an appeal from the High Court. For a consideration of subsequent decisions on this theme see Byrne & Binchy, *Annual Review of Irish Law 1987*, pp 208-209, 274-275.

48. See, for example, *Northern Bank Finance Corporation Ltd v Chariton* [1979] IR 149; *Leydon v Malone* Supreme Court, 13 May 1968; *Hindle v O'Dwyer* Supreme Court, 14 February 1955; *Phelps v White* (1881) 7 LR Ir 160 (CA). *Fenton v Schofield* 100 ILTR 69 (SC). *Ennis v Butterly* [1997] 1 ILRM 28. *Cf O'Callaghan v Meath Vocational Education Committee* High Court, 20 November 1990 critically analysed by Byrne & Binchy, *Annual Review of Irish Law 1990*, pp 365-367.

49. *Langridge v Levy* (1837) 2 M&W 519, 150 ER 863; *cf Wilkinson v Downton* [1897] 2 QB 57. See also the decisions of the United States of America involving injurious consequences from sexual intercourse where consent was fraudulently obtained, cited by Quill, p 254.

50. *Mullett v Mason* (1866) LR 1 CP 559. *Cf Burrows v Rhodes* [1899] 1 QB 816 cited with approval in *Duffy v Sutton* [1955] IR 248 (SC).

51. See para **[35.18]** above.

52. [1969] 2 QB 158.

> "As far as the tort of fraud or deceit is concerned it is well settled that the measure of damages is based on the actual damage directly flowing from the fraudulent inducement, and that the award may, in an appropriate case (of which this may not be an example), include consequential damages representing what was reasonably and necessarily expended as a result of acting on the inducement ...."[53]

Where the plaintiff was induced to buy property the measure of damage is usually calculated by subtracting the actual value of the property at the time of the purchase from the price paid by the plaintiff on foot of the misrepresentation.[54]

**[35.22]** The *Charlton* decision is also interesting for its examination of the appropriateness of rescission as a remedy in an action for deceit. In the *Charlton* case itself, the President of the High Court ordered rescission, but the Supreme Court, by a three-to-two majority, decided that, since rescission involved *restitutio in integrum*, and since this was not possible in the present case, damages should be awarded to the defendants and the case remitted for assessment of damages.

**[35.23]** Henchy J, for the majority, stated:

> "Where a person has been induced by a fraudulent misrepresentation made collaterally by the other party to a contract to alter his position to his disadvantage, there are two alternative courses open to him: he may claim damages in tort for deceit or he may sue for rescission of the contract which was induced by the misrepresentation. The latter relief, which is an equitable one, will be granted when the court considers that it would be just and equitable to do so, in order to restore the parties, at least substantially, to their respective positions before the fraudulent misrepresentation was acted on ... In this case the defendants sought and were granted rescission of the contract between the defendants and the bank but, in an effort to restore the *status quo ante*, the court went further. By requiring the bank to take the place of the defendants in each of the many instances of the purchase of shares, the court purported to rescind and amend executed contracts which had been made between the defendants and third-party vendors of shares who were not before the court. In my opinion, that is something which the court had no jurisdiction to do."[55]

Damages, therefore, calculated on the basis already outlined are the more appropriate remedy where the *status quo ante* cannot readily be achieved.

## Lord Tenterden's Act

**[35.24]** Since the Statute of Frauds Amendment Act 1828, a fraudulent misrepresentation designed to obtain credit for another person is unenforceable unless the representation is made in writing signed by the party to be charged. Section 6 of the 1828 Act provides as follows:

> No action shall be brought whereby to charge any person upon or by reason of any representation or assurance made or given concerning or relating to the character, conduct, credit, ability, trade or dealings of any other person, to the intent or purpose that such other

---

53. This rule had been previously applied by the court in *Leyden v Malone* Supreme Court, 13 May 1968 and *Hindle v O'Dwyer* Supreme Court, 14 February 1955.

54. *Northern Bank Finance Corporation Ltd v Chariton* [1979] IR 149; *Leydon v Malone* Supreme Court, 13 May 1968; *Hindle v O'Dwyer* Supreme Court, 14 February 1955.

55. [1979] IR 197. See also *Jackson Soanes v Leisure Corp International Ltd* High Court, 18 December 1992.

person may obtain credit, money, or goods upon, unless such representation or assurance be made in writing signed by the party to be charged therewith.

**[35.25]** This section is designed to prevent the plaintiff from suing in tort for deceit when he could not sue on the basis of a guarantee which was not in writing, as required by s 2 of the Statute of Frauds (Ireland) 1695.[56] Section 6 applies only to tort actions based on fraudulent misrepresentation, however; it did not and still does not prevent an action for breach of contract or for negligent misrepresentation.[57] Strange as it may seem, therefore, an injured plaintiff may sue on a negligent misrepresentation relating to a third party's credit-worthiness even if made orally, whereas if the misrepresentation is fraudulent he cannot sue unless there is writing. Finally it should be noted that it is not sufficient under s 6 for the agent of the person to be charged to sign as would be sufficient under the Statute of Frauds itself. This rule applies even where the defendant is a corporation which of necessity must act through an agent. Thus an incorporated bank is not liable for the fraudulent misrepresentation as to credit signed by one of its managers.[58]

## II. Injurious Falsehood[59]

**[35.26]** The tort of injurious falsehood, somewhat similar in a number of respects to defamation (and in other respects to deceit), grew out of an action on the case for injury resulting from impugning the plaintiff's title to land.[60] It now encompasses not only "slander of title" or "slander of goods",[61] but also false statements calculated to injure a person in his trade or, more broadly, even damaging falsehoods of a non-commercial nature.[62] The essence of the tort is that the falsehood deceives others about the plaintiff[63] so as to cause loss to the plaintiff. This distinguishes it from deceit, where it is the plaintiff himself who is deceived. The tort differs from defamation[64] in that the falsehood may

56. *Cf Barrett v Hyndman* (1840) Arm Mac & Og 1 (QB); *Fennell v Mulcahy* (1845) 8 ILR 434 (Exch of Pleas).

57. *Banbury v Bank of Montreal* [1918] AC 626; *Anderson (WB) & Sons Ltd v Rhodes (Liverpool) Ltd* [1967] 2 All ER 850. See Stollery 'Statute of Frauds' (1976) 14 Alta LR 222 at 249; Law Reform Commission of Tasmania's Report No 50; *Suretyship and Guarantee* (1987), pp 13-14 and the Ontario Law Reform Commission's *Report on Amendment of the Law of Contract* (1987), pp 84-85. Legislation in British Columbia, the Law Reform Amendment Act 1985, SBC 1985, C10 s 8, has repealed the statutory equivalent there of our s 6. For a more judicial consideration of s 6 see *Forshall and Fine Arts Collections Ltd v Walsh* High Court, 18 June 1997 at p 69 Shanley J's judgment.

58. *Hirst v West Riding Union Banking Co Ltd* [1901] 2 KB 560.

59. The term is Salmond's; it has gained widespread acceptance in preference to "slander of title", "slander of goods" or "malicious falsehood". See Prosser 'Injurious Falsehood: The Basis of Liability' (1959) 39 Col LR 425; Smith 'Disparagement of Property' (Pts 1-2) (1913) 13 Col LR 13 at 121; McDonald, *Irish Law of Defamation* (1987), pp 23-26; Clark & Smyth *Intellectual Property Law in Ireland* (1997), pp 476-477.

60. *Bliss v Stafford* (1573) Owen 37 74 ER 882; *Banister v Banister* cited in 4 Co Rep 17a; *cf Roche v Meyler* [1896] 2 IR 35 (QBD); *Cooke v McGuigan* (1926) 61 ILTR 45 (HC).

61. In *Kent Adhesive Products Co v Ryan* High Court, 5 November 1993, Costello J characterised as a claim for slander of goods what was in fact one for defamation.

62. Eg *Sheperd v Wakeman* (1662) 1 Sid 79, 82 ER 982 - loss of marriage. *Cf Irish Transport & General Workers Union v Transport & General Workers Union* [1936] IR 471 (HC).

63. *Cf Schulke & Mayr UK Ltd v Alkpharm UK Ltd* Chy Div, 31 July 1997.

64 Sometimes the difference between the two torts is a narrow one; *cf Griffins v Benn* (1911) 27 Times LR 346. See also *Foster v Hood* (1873) 7 ILTR 92 (CP);

reflect perfectly well on the plaintiff whilst nonetheless causing loss to him. If I say of an opera singer that he is planning to retire in order to go into missionary work, most people would think more rather than less of him, but they may be deceived into not engaging him in the belief that he will not be available.[65] The tort differs from that of negligent misstatement in that the statement must have been made maliciously.

**[35.27]** In *Royal Baking Powder Co v Wright Crossley & Co*,[66] Lord Davey stated:

> "To support such an action it is necessary for the plaintiff to prove (1) that the statements complained of were untrue; (2) that they were made maliciously - ie without just cause or excuse; (3) that the plaintiffs have suffered special damage thereby."

**[35.28]** The precise scope of malice[67] is not clear, however. There is some support[68] for the view that, as Lord Davey stated, it means "without just cause or excuse". Other courts have required that some indirect, dishonest or improper motive be established.[69] Clearly, an honest belief in an unfounded claim will not make a defendant liable.[70] Nor will carelessness be sufficient to attract liability under this heading, although the defendant may in such a case be liable for negligent misstatement. Recklessness, in the sense of gross negligence, may perhaps afford a sound basis for liability of injurious falsehood.[71]

**[35.29]** At common law, the action being one on the case, actual damage has to be proved and in this regard the damage must be of a monetary nature: such non-financial damage as injured feelings may not be compensated. Where a trader's goods have been disparaged,

---

64. (contd) *Towell v Fallon* (1912) 47 ILTR 176 (KB Div). *Irish Toys & Utilities Ltd v "The Irish Times" Ltd* [1937] IR 298. See further McDonald, *Irish Law of Defamation* (1987), pp 24-25. *Cf Doyle v Griffin* Supreme Court, 21 December 1936 per Murnaghan J at p 13: "The plaintiff cannot disclaim a cause of action based on libel and by ingenuity turn an action for libel into an action on the case based on *Ratcliffe v Evans* [1892] 2 QB 524". See, however, *Joyce v Sengupta* [1993] 1 All ER 897 (CA), and constrast *Quigley v Creation* [1971] IR 269 with *Kaye v Robertson* [1991] FSR 62.

65. *Cf* the example given in the *Report of the Younger Committee on Privacy* (1972 Cmnd 5012), Appendix 1, para 8. See also *Jones v McGovern* IR 1 CL 100 at 103-104 (QB); and *cf Irish Toys & Utilities Ltd v "The Irish Times" Ltd* [1937] IR 298 (HC). In *Kent Adhesive Products Co v Ryan* High Court, 5 November 1993. In *O'Callaghan v Meath Vocational Education Committee* High Court, 20 November 1990 Costello J observed that "[t]he act of wrongful dismissal does not in itself involve the tort of ... injurious falsehood."

66. 18 RPC 95 at 99 (1901). See also *Glen Ban Ltd v Lefroy* Supreme Court, 18 May 1944.

67. *Cf* Newark 'Malice in Actions on the Case for Words' (1944) 60 LQR 366. *Cf Malone v McQuaid and Registrar of Titles* High Court, 28 May 1998, counsel for the plaintiff conceded that an honest belief in an unfounded claim is not sufficient evidence of malice; recklessness was not established on the evidence. The precise relationship between the requirement of malice and the possible defence of privilege akin to the privilege in the action for defamation has not been discussed in detail by an Irish court. In *Murphy v Dow Jones Publishing Co (Europe) Inc* High Court, 11 January 1995 an action for defamation and injurious falsehood was defeated by the qualified privilege defence prescribed by Defamation Act 1961, s 24 (as to which see para **[34.190]** below.

68. Eg *Joyce v Motor Surveys* [1948] Ch 252.

69. *London Ferro-Concrete Co v Justicz* (1951) 68 RPC 261. *Serville v Constance* [1954] 1 WLR 487.

70. *Loudon v Ryder* (No 2) [1953] Ch 423; *Spring v Guardian Assurance plc* [1995] 2 AC 296; *Greers Ltd v Pearman & Corder Ltd* (1922) 39 RPC 406; *Cooke v McGuigan* (1926) 61 ILTR 45 (HC); *Malone v McQuaid and Registrar of Titles* High Court, 28 May 1998.

71. *Malone v McQuaid and Registrar of Titles* High Court, 28 May 1998. *Cf Sherriff v McMullen* [1952] IR 236 (SC).

however, proof of a general loss of business, rather than loss of identifiable customers, is sufficient.[72]

**[35.30]** The common law position has been altered in some respects by statute. Section 20(1) of the Defamation Act 1961 provides that is it not necessary to allege or prove special damage (a) if the words on which the action is founded are calculated to cause pecuniary damage to the plaintiff and are published in writing or other permanent form,[73] or (b) if the words are calculated to cause pecuniary damage to the plaintiff in respect of any office, profession, calling, trade or business carried on by him at the time of the publication.[74]

72. *Ratcliffe v Evans* [1892] 2 QB 524.
73. Radio and television broadcasts come within the scope of this term: Defamation Act 1961, s 20(2).
74. See *Joyce v Sengupta* [1993] 1 All ER 897 (CA), plaintiff relying on English statutory equivalent of s 20(1) not limited to claiming merely nominal damages.

# Chapter 36

# Misuse of Process


I. Introduction ........ 981
II. Malicious Prosecution ........ 981
III. Malicious Abuse of the Civil Process ........ 986


## I. Introduction

**[36.01]** In this chapter we examine the various kinds of misuse of the criminal and civil process that can give rise to liability in tort. We shall first consider the tort of malicious prosecution; then we shall discuss the liability that arises for malicious abuse of the civil process.

## II. Malicious Prosecution[1]

**[36.02]** In attempting to protect individuals against being wrongfully exposed to criminal proceedings, whilst at the same time encouraging persons to bring criminals to justice, the law has faced some difficulties. If, the moment a person was acquitted, he could turn around and bring an action against those who prosecuted him, "[t]here would, indeed, be an end of the criminal justice of the country ..."[2] The courts have tried to strike a balance between these competing interests in the action for malicious prosecution.

### Ingredients of the Tort

**[36.03]** The tort consists of the institution of unsuccessful criminal proceedings by the defendant, maliciously and without reasonable and probable cause, as a result of which the plaintiff has suffered damage.[3]

#### *(a) Institution of proceedings[4]*

**[36.04]** The defendant must have instituted the proceedings, that is to say, he must have been "actively instrumental in putting the law in force".[5] This does not mean that the

1. See Winfield, *History of Conspiracy and Abuse of Legal Procedure* (1921); Winfield, *The Present Law of Abuse of Legal Procedure* (1921); Stephen, *Malicious Prosecution* (1921); Fridman 'Compensation of the Innocent' (1963) 26 MLR 481; Harper 'Malicious Prosecution False Imprisonment and Defamation' (1937) 15 Texas LR 157; Anon 'Malicious Prosecution' (1900) 34 ILT & Sol J 1.
2. *Kelly v Midland GW Ry of Ireland Co* (1872) IR 7 CL 8 at 16 (QB); *Runham v Wakefield* (1863) 16 ICLR 507 at 518 (QB).
3. *Cf Dullaghan v Hillen* [1957] Ir Jur 10 at 16-17 (CC); *Kelly v Midland Gt Western Ry of Ireland Co* (1872) IR 7 CL 8 at 15 (QB); *McIntyre v Lewis* [1991] IR 121 (SC). Prosecutorial authorities are not immune from actions for malicious prosecution: *Nelles v Ontario* 60 DLR (4th) 609 (SC, Can) cited with apparent approval by Costello P in *W v Ireland (No 2)* [1997] 2 IR 141 at 159.
4. For a comprehensive analysis see Kodilinye 'Setting in Motion Malicious Prosecutions: The Commonwealth Experience' (1987) 36 Int & Comp LQ 157.
5. *Davidson v Smyth* 1887 20 LR Ir 326 at 330 (CP Div). See also *Danby v Beardsley* (1880) 43 LT 603 at 604; *McLoughlin v Doey* (1893) 32 LR Ir 518 at 528-529 (Ex Div). *Cf Evans v London Hospital Medical College* [1981] 1 All ER 715 (QBD) - pathologist producing post-mortem report for police held not to have instituted proceedings.

defendant must himself have conducted the prosecution. It is sufficient if he signed the charges and indicated that he was willing to attend Court and testify against the accused.[6] Moreover, if he positively asserts to a District Justice or Peace Commissioner that he suspects the plaintiff of having committed an offence, and a warrant for the plaintiff's arrest follows, he will be regarded as having instituted the prosecution,[7] but not if he merely gives his account of what happened without formulating any charge.[8] In Scotland,[9] the United States[10] and Canada,[11] public prosecutors have been held immune, by virtue of their office, from proceedings for malicious prosecution. In the light of our Constitution it is not certain that our Courts would favour this approach.

***(b) Proceedings must not have been successful***

**[36.05]**

> "What the plaintiff requires in his action is not a judicial determination of his innocence but merely the absence of any judicial determination of his guilt."[12]

The plaintiff can succeed in this by showing that the proceedings were unsuccessful,[13] whether by reason of acquittal, discontinuance, nonsuit or quashing on appeal. The question whether a *nolle prosequi* is sufficient is a matter of some uncertainty. An old decision[14] indicates that it is not, but modern authority[15] in a number of jurisdictions takes the view that it is. What is clear, however, is that a conviction bars the right of action, even where it is obtained by fraud or perjury.[16] Various rationales have been put forward[17] in

---

6. *Malz v Rosen* [1966] 1 WLR 1008; *Casey v Automobiles Renault Canada Ltd* (1965) 54 DLR (2d) 600 (SC Can).
7. *Clarke v Postan* (1834) 6 C & P 423; 172 ER 1304.
8. *Leigh v Webb* (1800) Esp 165; 170 ER 574. See also *Danby v Beardsley* (1880) 43 LT 603 at 604 (CP Div): "Now what stone has been set rolling? It is simply the stone of suspicion." It seems that the honesty of the belief of the defendant in the plaintiff's guilt has been taken into consideration in determining whether he instituted the proceedings: *Lowe v Collum* (1877) 2 LR Ir 15 (QB). It might, however, be argued that the issue of the defendant's honesty should best be limited to the contexts of reasonable and probable cause and of malice rather than the threshold question regarding institution of proceedings.
9. *Hester v MacDonald* 1961 SC 370.
10. *Imber v Pachtman* (1975) 424 US 409; *Yaselli v Goff* (1926) 12 F 2d 396.
11. *Richman v McMurty* (1983) 25 CC LT 152 (Vet HC). English Courts are not in accord: *cf Rickes v DPP* [1973] 2 AII ER 935 at 941 (CA).
12. SALMOND & HEUSTON, p 398.
13. *Cf Parker v Langley* (1713) 10 Mod 145; 88 ER 667; *Watkins v Lee* (1839) 5 M & W 270; 151 ER 115; *Jones v Gwynn* (1712) 10 Mod 214, 88 ER 699. *Cf Donnelly v Moloney* (1826) Batty's Irish Reports 1825-26 498 (KB) *Molloy v Gallagher* [1933] IR 1 at 13-14 (SC).
14. *Goddard v Smith* (1704) 3 Salk 245, 91 ER 803.
15. For a comparative study see Scott *Criminal Procedure and Tort: The Effect of "Nolle Prosequi" on Action for Malicious Prosecution* (1973) 2 Anglo-Amer LR 288. See also the Law Reform Committee of South Australia's *Eighty-Third Report Relating to Civil Actions for Perjury Committed in Criminal Proceedings and to the Tort of Malicious Prosecutions* (1984), p 8.
16. *Cf Basebe v Matthews* (1867) LR 2 CP 684; *Bouvy v Count de Courte* (1901) 20 NZLR 312; *Everett v Ribbands* [1952] 2 QB 198. See *also Power v Commercial Banking Co Ltd* High Court, 3 February 1975.
17. *Cf* FLEMING, p 678.

justification of this rule: to allow an action would, it is said, unsettle the criminal process; the conviction of the plaintiff is a strong ground for inferring that he was guilty and that the defendant had reasonable and probable cause. Verdicts should not be subjected to collateral attack. These reasons are scarcely convincing.[18] There is an obvious injustice in permitting an action where the malicious prosecutor failed in his design but denying it where he succeeded. Perhaps our courts might be willing to look again at this question at some time in the future.[19]

### *(c) Lack of reasonable and probable cause*

**[36.06]** In some instances, the plaintiff has the somewhat daunting task of proving a negative - that the defendant lacked a reasonable cause for initiating the prosecution. Moreover, he must prove this to the satisfaction of the judge rather than the jury,[20] since it is probable that the jury's sympathies would lie with the plaintiff too strongly to entrust them with this question.[21] Exceptionally, the onus of disproof may be shifted. In *McIntyre v Lewis*[22] the plaintiff alleged that members of the Garda Síochána had assaulted him and, to cover their tracks, had charged him with assault. The criminal proceedings against him had been thrown out. In his later action for assault, false imprisonment and malicious prosecution, the jury awarded him damages for, *inter alia*, malicious prosecution. The Supreme Court rejected the argument that the plaintiff had failed to comply with the requirement of establishing an absence of reasonable and probable cause for bringing the prosecution. Hederman J was of opinion that, once the jury accepted that the assault had been committed by the defendants on the plaintiff rather than the other way round:

> "they could not on the evidence before them have brought in a verdict in favour of the defendants, either in respect of false imprisonment or malicious prosecution, because to do so would have rendered their verdicts inconsistent."[23]

While there might be cases where the trial judge should decide the issue of reasonable and probable cause, this was not one of them. Here the plaintiff did not have the task of proving a negative:

> "There was a single, solitary stark fact to be determined: who had committed the assault. Those with the obligation to determine the facts of this case were the jury and once they had made a finding that the assault had been committed by the gardaí and not the reverse then everything else inevitably followed."[24]

"Reasonable and probable cause" has been defined as:

---

18. *Commonwealth Life Assurance Society Ltd v Smith* (1938) 59 CLR 527 at 539.
19. An action for violation of Constitutional rights might well also be available in such a case. A court might take the view, however, following Costello P's analysis in *W v Ireland (No 2)* [1997] 2 IR 141, that, since the restricted side of tort is based on considered reasons, resort to a constitutional remedy should not be unthinkingly permitted. That said in the wake of *Osman v United Kingdom* [1999] 1 FLR 193, any blanket immunity must now be ?availed of with caution.
20. *Cf Davidson v Smyth* (1887) 20 LR Ir 326 at 330-331 (CP Div); *Cruise v Burke* [1919] 2 IR 182 (KBD).
21. *Cf Leibo v Buckman Ltd* [1952] 2 All ER 1057 at 1062.
22. [1991] 1 IR 121 (SC).
23. [1991] 1 IR 121 at 133
24. [1991] 1 IR 121 at 133. See also [1991] 1 IR 121 at 136.

> "an honest belief in the guilt of the accused based upon a full conviction, founded upon reasonable grounds, of the existence of a state of circumstances which, assuming them to be true, would lead an ordinary, prudent cautious man, placed in the position of the accuser, to the conclusion that the person charged was probably guilty of the crime against him."[25]

**[36.07]** In *Kelly v Midland Great Western Railway of Ireland Co*,[26] Whiteside CJ considered the test to be:

> "whether the circumstances warranted a discreet man in instituting and following up the proceedings - not what impression the circumstances would make on the mind of a lawyer, but what effect they ought to have on the mind of another person, possibly not a lawyer."

**[36.08]** Applying this test, the Queen's Bench in this case held that the defendant railway company had acted reasonably in bringing about the prosecution of the plaintiff, employed by it as foreman porter, where the company had received a complaint from a passenger that the plaintiff had given him a receipt for luggage in an amount half of what he had paid. The company, through its solicitor, had "carefully examined"[27] the evidence, interviewing the passenger and taking down his complaint in writing.

**[36.09]** It is clear that even where the defendant's belief was honest, the plaintiff will nonetheless succeed where the defendant acted without *reasonable cause*.[28]

**[36.10]** In *Davidson v Smyth*[29] the facts were as follows. A house owned by the defendant's brother was set on fire. Some time afterwards the defendant was told by the plaintiff's sister that the plaintiff had been responsible. The defendant spoke to a police constable and encouraged the plaintiff's sister to make a statement before a magistrate. The prosecution against the plaintiff was dismissed.

**[36.11]** In an action for malicious prosecution, the defendant contended that the plaintiff had not discharged the onus of proving that the defendant had acted without reasonable and probable cause. The evidence of the plaintiff's sister had turned out to be contradictory and unconvincing, but the Common Pleas Division (overturning a jury verdict in favour of the plaintiff) held that the plaintiff had not discharged the necessary onus of proof. Murphy J stated:

---

25. *Dullaghan v Hillen* [1957] Ir Jur 10 at 17 (CC) quoting from *Hicks v Faulkner* (1878) 8 QBD 167 at 171affd (1882) 46 LT 130. This definition was approved by the House of Lords in *Herniman v Smith* [1938] AC 305. *Cf Glinski v McIver* [1962] AC 726. See also *Dorene Ltd v Suedes (Ireland) Ltd* [1981] IR 312 at 318-319 (HC).

26. (1872) IR 7 CL 8 at 16 (QB), following the test set out by Lords Chelmsford and Colonsay in *Lister v Perryman* (1870) LR 4 HL 521. (But in *Kelly's* case the relevant mind *was* that of a lawyer!)

27. (1872) IR 7 CL 8 *(per* Whiteside CJ).

28. *Cf Cruise v Burke* [1919] 2 IR 182 (KBD) where the distinction is correctly perceived. In the converse case - where the defendant had reasonable cause to believe in the plaintiff's guilt but did not in fact do so - the action may succeed: the issue of the defendant's belief being one for the jury to determine: *Dallison v Caffery* [1965] 1 QB 348 at 368 and 372; *Cf Moore v Trulock* (1899) 33 ILTR 62 (QBD). Where a defendant has reasonable grounds for, and does in fact believe in, the defendant's guilt before committal for trial but after committal, without learning of any new facts, changes his mind he is under no duty to inform the public prosecutor of this change of mind: *Duane v Barry* (1879) 4 LR Ir 742 (Ex Div).

29. (1887) 20 LR Ir 326 (CP Div).

> "What evidence did the plaintiff give to prove that the defendant did not take reasonable care to inform himself of the true state of the case, and did not honestly believe the case placed before the magistrate? Where, or from whom, was he to make inquiry to test the truth of the story told by plaintiff's sister? What is there to show that the belief he swears he entertained was not an honest one? The person to whom he gave evidence, for which he is to be punished to an extent likely to be ruinous, is the witness to whose testimony plaintiff appeals as truthful, and establishing her case."[30]

**[36.12]** The plaintiff's sister was "the person most likely to know something about the transaction" and, where she came forward as she did, the course the defendant adopted was reasonable and natural. Accordingly:

> "th[e] plaintiff's complaint should be against her own sister, whom she could prosecute for perjury, and not against the defendant for having believed her."[31]

**[36.13]** Some difficulty arises in cases where the prosecution resulted in a conviction which is quashed on appeal. It has been stated[32] that the conviction should be regarded as *prima facie* evidence of probable cause, but the better view today[33] seems to be to regard it as no more than a factor in determining this issue.

***(d) Malice***

**[36.14]** As well as proving absence of reasonable and probable cause the plaintiff must prove malice on the part of the defendant.[34] The courts have evinced some difficulty in defining malice with any degree of precision, which suggests that there are inherent difficulties in investigating the motives of a prosecutor. His or her motives may be mixed,[35] a desire to bring the offender to justice mingling with anger and the thirst for revenge.

**[36.15]** In the Circuit Court decision of *Dullaghan v Hillen*,[36] Fawsitt J stated:

> "The word 'maliciously' implies the doing of that which a person has no legal right to do and the doing of it in order to secure some object by means which are improper. An evil motive is required to complete an actionable wrong."

**[36.16]** Examples of an "evil motive" include punishing a person for having given what the defendant believes to have been perjured evidence against the police on a previous occasion[37] or attempted extortion.[38] The issue of malice is one for the jury subject to two provisos: the Court must decide whether any particular motive is a proper or improper

---

30. (1887) 20 LR Ir 326 at 331.
31. (1887) 20 LR Ir 326 at 331-332.
32. *Hall v Graham* (1795) Ridg Lapp & Schoales 469 at 478.
33. *Cf* WINFIELD & JOLOWICZ, p 382.
34. *McLoughlin v Doey* (1893) 32 LR (Ir) 518 (Ex Div); see also *Dorene Ltd v Suedes (Ireland) Ltd* [1981] IR 312 at 319 (HC).
35. WINFIELD & JOLOWICZ, pp 686-687.
36. [1957] Ir Jur 10 at 16 (CC).
37. *Glinski v McIver* [1962] AC 726.
38. *Cf* FLEMING, p 685. See also *Moore v Trulock* (1899) 33 ILTR 62 at 63 (QBD); *Cf Cruise v Burke* [1919] 2 IR 182.

purpose for the proceeding in question,[39] and it determines whether there is reasonable evidence of malice to go to the jury.[40]

### *(e) Damage*

**[36.17]** The plaintiff must prove some damage in order to succeed in the action.[41] There is some uncertainty regarding the definition of damage in this context, but three types of damage have been certainly recognised: damage to the plaintiff's fame, the safety of his or her person or the security of the plaintiff's property as a result of expense in resisting the charge.[42]

**[36.18]** A plaintiff's "fame" will be damaged "if the matter whereof he [is] accused is scandalous",[43] that term here meaning defamatory. Offences involving imprisonment fulfil this requirement, as do offences implying fraud, but beyond this the line is difficult to draw. An accusation of failure to pay a train fare has been held sufficient to ground the action[44] but not the charge of wrongly pulling the communication cord in a train.[45]

## III. Malicious Abuse of the Civil Process

**[36.19]** It has for long been accepted that certain malicious abuses of the civil process, such as malicious arrest[46] or malicious execution against property,[47] are tortious. Not so clear has been the general principle that the malicious institution or maintenance of an ordinary civil action should constitute a tort. In spite of some clear statements of the principle, especially in *Saville v Roberts*,[48] this issue was, for a long time confused by the unconvincing suggestion preferred by Bowen LJ, in *Quartz Hill Gold Mining Co v Eyre*[49] that, so far as the requirement of proof of damage is concerned:

> "the only costs which the law recognises ... are [those] properly incurred in the action itself. For these the successful defendant has already been compensated."

As *Winfield & Jolowicz*[50] point out:

---

39. *Mitchell v Jenkins* (1833) 5 B & Ad 558; 110 ER 908.
40. *Brown v Hawkes* [1981] 2 QB 718.
41. *McLoughlin v Doey* (1893) 32 LR Ir 518 (Ex Div).
42. *Saville v Roberts* (1698) 12 Mod 208; 88 ER 1267; *Lunham v Wakefield* (1863) 16 ICLR 507 at 518 (QB).
43. *Saville v Roberts* (1698) 12 Mod 208; 88 ER 1267 at 208 and 1267 respectively.
44. *Rayson v South London Tramways Co* [1893] 2 QB 304.
45. *Berry v British Transport Commission* [1962] 1 QB 306.
46. *Cf Roy v Prior* [1970] AC 470; *Delancy v Dale* (1959) 20 DLR (2d) 12; *Foth v O'Hara* (1959) 15 DLR (2d) 332 at 336; *Varawa v Howard Smith* (1911) 13 Comm LR 35. As to the malicious arrest of a ship see *The Walter D Wallet* [1893] P 202. Maliciously procuring a search warrant is also actionable: *Everett v Ribbands* [1952] 2 QB 198 at 205.
47. *Clissold v Crotchley* [1910] 2 KB 244; *Homer v Irwin & Son Ltd* [1972] NI 202.
48. (1698) 1 Ld Raym 374. In accord *Churchill v Siggers* (1854) 3 E & B 929; 118 ER 1389. See also *Grainger v Hill* (1838) 4 Bing NC 212 132 ER 769.
49. (1883) 11 QBD 674 at 690 (CA).
50. WINFIELD & JOLOWICZ, p 689 (footnote references omitted).

"this is, of course, simply untrue, for the taxed costs will hardly ever amount to the total costs of the defence, and it is noteworthy that any deficiency in costs awarded to the accused in a criminal case does amount to damage."

**[36.20]** The matter has now been clearly resolved in Irish law, in *Dorene Ltd v Suedes (Ireland) Ltd*.[51] There Costello, J had "no doubt"[52] that at common law an action of "ancient lineage"[53] lay for maliciously abusing the courts' processes and that this action was not limited to claims arising from the institution of a criminal prosecution and to bankruptcy and winding-up proceedings.[54]

**[36.21]** It seemed to Costello J that authorities established that:

"a claim for damages at common law will lie for the institution or maintenance of a civil action if it can be shown that the action was instituted or maintained (a) without reasonable or probable cause, (b) maliciously, and (c) that the claimant has suffered actual damage or that the impugned action was one which the law presumes will have caused the claimant damage."[55]

**[36.22]** Malice was defined as the presence of "some improper and wrongful motive".[56] An intent to use the legal process in question for a purpose other than its "legally appointed and appropriate purpose"[57] could amount to malice in this connection. Where a plaintiff had obtained legal advice before instituting or pending legal proceedings, the nature of that advice could be "a highly material factor"[58] in considering whether he was motivated by an indirect or improper motive, as it might assist in showing whether the plaintiff was using the proceedings for some legally inappropriate purpose. As to proof of damage, once a claimant could show that he had suffered, "some actual damage as a result of a civil action,"[59] this would suffice. In the absence of actual damage, a claimant would have to show that the impugned action was "one which the law regards as causing damage".[60]

**[36.23]** In the proceedings before the court, Dorene had taken proceedings for specific performance[61] against Suedes for the lease of premises owned by Suedes. Dorene had also registered a *lis pendens*. Two months later, Dorene's senior counsel, "one of the leading counsel at the Irish bar,"[62] had advised that the action could not succeed. Nevertheless, Dorene persisted with it for several further months, during which period they continued to negotiate with Suedes for the acquisition of the premises.

51. [1981] IR 312 (HC).
52. [1981] IR 312 at 314.
53. [1981] IR 312.
54. *Cf Brown v Chapman* (1762) 1 W Bl 427.
55. [1981] IR 312 at 316.
56. [1981] IR 312 at 319.
57. [1981] IR 312 at 319.
58. [1981] IR 312 at 319.
59. [1981] IR 312 at 320.
60. [1981] IR 312 at 320.
61. Dorene also claimed damages for misrepresentation. The two claims were treated identically by Costello J in the absence of any suggestion to the contrary by counsel for either party.
62. [1981] IR 312 at 328.

**[36.24]** Costello J concluded from the evidence that, after receiving this advice some of the directors had nonetheless decided to keep the proceedings going to assist their bargaining position and that they had never intended that the action would go to a hearing. The company was using the proceedings not for their appropriate purpose - to obtain on order for specific performance -but for the different purpose of assisting it in its negotiations. The directors' motives in continuing the action "were wrongful; they were actuated by malice in the legal sense of that term".[63] The proceedings had, in addition been maintained without reasonable and probable cause.[64]

**[36.25]** The instituting by Dorene of the action was not actionable, since it had been made on *bona fide* legal advice from its solicitor at the time. If liability was to attach it could rest only on damage sustained by the maintenance of the action after senior counsel had advised against proceeding further. The evidence established that, had the action been discontinued at that time, Suedes could have sold the premises to another party. In principle, therefore, Suedes were entitled to damages, though the question whether they had in fact sufficient financial loss as a result of this failed sale was an issue which the parties had deferred for a later hearing.[65] Costello J noted that if loss had not occurred it would be necessary for him to consider whether, in its absence, the law would presume that Suedes must have suffered some damage by being deprived of their ability to deal with their property as they had wished.

**[36.26]** Subsequent decisions have endorsed Costello J's approach and have given further detail to the applicable principles.

**[36.27]** As regards the claim which is alleged to have been wrongfully instituted or maintained, it must have either "failed in its entirety or [be] bound to do so".[66] Where the claim has failed, the failure must not have resulted from the resolution by the trial court to a conflict of evidence with regard to primary facts not having arisen from a special legal defence raised by the defendant.[67]

**[36.28]** There is no requirement that a litigant justify the institution or maintenance of the proceedings on economic grounds, though "the manifest absence of such grounds might, in certain circumstances, constitute evidence of malice".[68] The mere fact that the litigation caused inconvenience to others "could not of itself constitute a wrongdoing"[69] this outcome is inevitable in virtually every case.

---

63. [1981] IR 312 at 331.
64. [1981] IR 312.
65. The claim for damages was ultimately satisfied in a compromise: *cf* [1981] IR 312 at 334.
66. *Murphy v Kirwan* [1993] 3 IR 501 at 511 (SC).
67. *Murphy v Kirwan* [1993] 3 IR 501. *Cf Crofter Properties Ltd v Genport* High Court, 15 March 1996.
68. *Bank of Ireland Finance Ltd v McSorley* High Court, 24 June 1994 (Murphy J at p 10 of his judgment).
69. *Bank of Ireland Finance Ltd v McSorley* High Court, 24 June 1994 (Murphy J at p 11 of his judgment). In *Gregory v Protsmouth City Council* [2000] 2 WLR 30, the House of Lords declined to extend the tort of malicious prosecution to disciplinary proceedings: see Cane 'The Scope of Malicious Prosecution' (2000) 116 LQR 346.

**[36.29]** Most common law jurisdictions hold that the victim of perjury is not entitled on that account of civil redress.[70] In *Fagan v Burgess*,[71] O'Higgins J struck out proceedings seeking compensation on this basis as disclosing no reasonable cause of action and as frivolous and vexatious. He considered that the policy reasons for conferring an absolute privilege on judge, jury, counsel, parties and witnesses so far as defamation is concerned were sufficiently strong to extend for actions seeking compensation for damage caused by perjury. O'Flaherty J had said as much, albeit *obiter*, in *Looney v Bank of Ireland*.[72] In *McMullen v Clancy*,[73] McGuinness J reiterated this view, accepting on the authority of the cases opened to her that there was "an overwhelming public policy argument for maintaining the common law rule that a witness is immune from suit in regard to the evidence which he gives in court".

**[36.30]** Brief reference may be made here to the torts of maintenance and champerty. The essence of maintenance is officious intermeddling in civil proceedings, generally by giving financial support.[74] Champerty consists in:

> "unlawfully maintaining a suit in consideration of a bargain to receive, by way of reward, part of anything that may be gained as a result of the proceedings, or some other profit."[75]

**[36.31]** Finally, we should note another possible basis of liability in this general area. In *O'Rourke v An Post and the Commissioner of An Garda Síochána*[76], Judge McMahon awarded damges to the plaintiff for negligence in the investigation by his employer, An Post, and for conveying the results of the negligent internal investigation to the gardaí, thereby leading to the plaintiff's arrest. The plaintiff, with several other employees, was suspected by An Post of stealing. The employer initiated an investigation within its own Investigation Department and because of the incomplete and flawed nature of the investigation, the results of which were conveyed to the gardaí, the plaintiff was arrested. Shortly afterwards, two other employees, who were questioned, confessed. Judge McMahon held that once An Post commenced its investigation, it owed a duty to its employee to carry it out carefully and in a reasonably professional manner. In failing to do so it was in breach of its duty to its employee. Moreover, Judge McMahon held that this was a causative factor in the garda decision to arrest the plaintiff and was a foreseeable consequence of the employer's negligence. Damages of £25,000 were awarded. Since the

---

70. *Hargreaves v Bretherton* [1959] 1 QB 45; *Marrinan v Vibart* [1963] 1 QB 528; *cf Taylor v Director of the Serious Fraud Office* [1998] 4 All ER 801 (HL (Eng)). For detailed analysis of the policy considerations underlying witness immunity going well beyond the issue of perjury see *Carnahan v Coates* 71 DLR (4th) 464 (BC, SC).
71. High Court, unrep 25 March 1998.
72. Supreme Court, 9 May 1997 (*ex temp*).
73. High Court, 3 September 1999.
74. See QUILL, p 344.
75. FLEMING, p 690. See also QUILL, p 345; *Fraser v Buckle* [1996] 2 ILRM 34 (SC), affg [1994] 1 IR 1 (HC); *McElroy v Flynn* [1991] ILRM 294; *O'Keeffe v Scales* [1998] 1 ILRM 393; Byrne & Binchy, *Annual Review of Irish Law 1992*, pp 114-118; O'Dell in Byrne & Binchy, *Annual Review of Irish Law 1993*, pp 184-188; Byrne & Binchy, *Annual Review of Irish Law 1997*, pp 783-785 and O'Dell in the *1997 Review*, pp 208-209.
76. Circuit Court, 27 July 2000 (Judge McMahon).

gardaí had acted reasonably on the information supplied to them by An Post, they did nothing wrong. They were entitled to assume that a State-sponsored body which had expertise in, and experience of, investigation such suspected frauds and thefts and which had a dedicated Investigation Department, would carry out the investigation with care.

**[36.32]** This case illustrates that within the employer/employee relationship breach of the employer's duty of care may provide an alternative legal basis for an injured employee, other than the abuse of legal process already referred to above.

# Chapter 37

# The Right to Privacy


| | | |
|---|---|---|
| I. | Introduction | 991 |
| II. | Torts relating to Privacy | 992 |
| III. | Breach of Confidence | 998 |
| IV. | Criminal Law | 1012 |
| V. | Constitutional Aspects of Privacy | 1012 |


## I. Introduction

**[37.01]** The law has been slow to recognise a general "right to privacy",[1] interference with which constitutes a tort. Two principal reasons for this lucuna have been suggested: historically tort law has tended[2] to be framed in terms of imposing liability in terms of wrongful conduct rather than in respect of the protection of rights. Moreover, there are strong competing interests - freedom of speech[3] being perhaps the most prominent - which make the right to privacy" something less than an incontrovertible *desideratum*.

1. See generally O'Dell 'When Two Tribes Go to War: Privacy Interests and Media Speech' (1997); *Law and Media* McGonagle ed Ch 9; McGonagle, *A Textbook on Media Law* (1996), Ch 5, Warren & Brandies 'The Right to Privacy' (1890) 4 Harv LR 193; Clark, *Data Protection Law in Ireland* (1990), Ch 1; Clark & Smyth, *Intellectual Property Law in Ireland* (1997), Ch 23; Hogan & Whyte, *Kelly: The Irish Constitution* (3rd ed, 1994), pp 767-770, 923, Casey, *Constitutional Law in Ireland* (3rd ed, 2000), pp 317-320; LRC, *Consultation Paper on the Civil Law of Defamation* (1991) Appendix A; LRC, *Consultation Paper on Privacy: Surveillance and the Interception of Communications* (1996); Law Reform Commission, *Report on Privacy: Surveillance and the Interception of Communications* (LRC-1998); WINFIELD & JOLOWICZ, pp 464-471; Todd, 'Protection of Privacy' (1997) in ed, *Torts in the Nineties*; Markesinis 'Our Patchy Law of Privacy - Time to do Something About It' (1990) 53 MLR 802; Seipp 'English Judicial Recognition of a Right to Privacy' (1983) 3 Oxford J of Legal Stud 325; Winfield 'The Right to Privacy' (1931) 47 LQR 23; Taylor 'Privacy and the Law' (1971) 34 MLR 288; Burns 'Law & Privacy: The Canadian Experience' (1976) 54 CBR 1; Dworkin 'Common Law Protection of Privacy' (1967) 2 U Tasmania LR 418; Prosser 'Privacy' (1960) 48 Cal LR 383; Yang 'Privacy: A Comparative Study of English and Russian Law' (1966) 15 ICLQ 175; Walsh 'The Judicial Power and the Protection of the Right of Privacy' [1977] Dublin ULJ 3; Weeks 'Comparative Law of Privacy' (1963) 12 Clev Mar LR 484; Gibson 'Common Law Protection of Privacy' Ch 12 of, *Studies in Canadian Law* Klar ed (1977); Byrne & Binchy, *Annual Survey of Irish Law 1987*, pp 99-101, 343-344; Phillipson & Fenwick 'Breach of Confidence on a Privacy Remedy in the Human Rights Act Era' (2000) 63 MLR 660.
2. There are, however, exceptions: see *Cosgrove v Ireland* [1982] ILRM 48 (HC), and see para **[1.09]** *et seq* above. The grand experiment of the action for damages for infringement of constitutional rights, launched by *Meskell v Coras Iompair Éireann* [1973] IR 121 (SC), has languished in recent years.
3. *Cf* Wright 'Defamation, Privacy and the Publics Right to Know' (1968) 46 Texas LR 630; Bloustein 'First Amendment and Privacy' (1974) 28 Rutgers LR 41.

**[37.02]** In other countries, the courts have shown differing approaches to the question whether a general right of privacy should be recognised at common law. In Australia, such a right has been explicitly denied.[4] In the United States, the right has been recognised and developed in a most sophisticated manner by the courts for over a century.[5] New Zealand courts have also accepted that the invasion of privacy is an actionable tort.[6] In neither England[7] nor Canada[8] has the position been determined conclusively. Legislation in some Canadian provinces has, however, filled this gap in the common law.[9]

**[37.03]** In this country, the courts have developed a constitutional right to privacy,[10] rather than an action in tort for interference with the right to privacy. This does not mean that privacy interests are ignored in tort law. In fact, quite substantial protection is already afforded by a wide range of torts. These torts shall be examined from the standpoint of privacy.

## II. Torts relating to Privacy

### Trespass to Land

**[37.04]** As we have seen,[11] the tort of trespass to land affords generous protection of privacy interests (provided that the plaintiff has the requisite possession in the land). Any wrongful entry onto property is actionable without proof of damage. Moreover, flagrant trespass may provoke awards of substantial damages.[12] The potential of this tort in the protection of privacy has not yet been fully determined. If the courts were to hold[13] that a secret purpose on the part of the entrant, unknown to the person who has invited him or her onto the property, vitiates permission to be there, many invasions of privacy by

4. *Cf Victoria Park Racecourse v Taylor* (1937) 58 Comm LR 479 at 494 (*per* Latham CJ).

5. *Cf* PROSSER & KEETON, Ch 20.

6. *Tucker v News Media Ownership Ltd* [1986] 2 NZLR 716; *Marris v TV3 Network Ltd*, NZ High Court, 14 October 1991 (Neazor J).

7. *Cf Re X (A Minor)* [1975] Fam 47 at 58. See also *Malone v Commissioner of Police (No 2)* [1979] Ch 344 at 357. *Cf Malone v United Kingdom* (1984) 7 EHRR 4, finding that English law's failure to regulate government interception of private communications violated Article 8 of the European Convention: See further Krotoszynski 'Autonomy, Community and Traditions of Liberty: The Contrast of British and American Privacy Law' [1990] Duke LJ 1398 at 1410-1411. In *Kaye v Robertson* [1991] FSR 62 (CA), Glidewell, LJ observed:

> "It is well-known that in English law there is no right to privacy and accordingly there is no right to action for breach of privacy."

See also *Khorasandjian v Bush* [1993] QB 727 (CA), overruled (but not on this point) by *Hunter v Canary Wharf Ltd* [1997] AC 655 (HL, Eng).

8. *Cf* Burns 'Law & Privacy: The Canadian Experience' (1976) 54 CBR 1; *Burnett v The Queen in Right of Canada* (1979) 23 OR (2d) 109; *R v Lewis* (1996) 39 CRR (2d) 26 (BC SC).

9. *Cf* Seipp 'English Judicial Recognition of a Right to Privacy' (1983) 3 Oxford J of Legal Stud 325 at 367-368.

10. The essence and dimensions of this right are quite uncertain. *Cf* para **[37.60]** below.

11. See Ch 23.

12. *Cf Loudon v Ryder* [1953] 2 QB 202. As to the possible limitations on the right to award punitive damages, *cf* para **[44.09]** below; see also *Whelan v Madigan* [1978] ILRM 136 (HC); *Etchingham v Acres & Co Ltd* High Court, 24 July 1975 (Butler J).

13. *Cf* para **[23.14]** above.

surreptitious means[14] would clearly be recognised as tortious. The scope of operation for private investigators, for example, would be greatly reduced.

**[37.05]** One should, however, recognise the limitation of the tort of trespass to land in this context. As the Law Reform Commission points out,[15] the protection afforded by the tort does not extend to surveillance activities which are conducted *outside* the boundaries of the property.[16] So, camera lenses or sophisticated listening devices that penetrate the boundaries would appear to fall outside the scope of the tort, unless an adventurous court were to apply the values underlying the tort to capture these novel incursions. There is no reason why the law should lag behind technological innovation.

**[37.06]** Where the invasion of privacy comes from the skies, there is English authority *Lord Bernstein of Leigh v Skyviews & General Ltd*[17] to the effect that a trespass to air space should be actionable only where the incursion is under the maximum height "necessary for the ordinary use and enjoyment of [the occupiers] land and the structures upon it". In that case, the purpose of the incursion, at a height well above the limit for actionability, was relatively benign: to take aerial photographs of substantial properties in the hope of selling the photographs to the owners. Where, however, the purpose is grossly violative of the privacy of the occupants of the property, the fact that the incursion took place at a great height in surely *nihil ad rem*. If our courts cleave to the *Bernstein* formula, they could nonetheless afford protection against such gross violations holding that the "ordinary use and enjoyment of [ones] land" embraces such protection. There is nothing wrong with having a variable height which is sensitive to the nature and purpose of the particular incursion. One can agree in general with Griffin J that the idea that a satellite commits trespass every time it passes over a suburban garden is an absurdity,[18] while acknowledging that this may be far from the case if, as it does so, the satellite is directing a lethal missile towards the premises or taking an intrusive photograph of those living there.

## Torts Affecting Interests in Goods

**[37.07]** The torts of trespass to goods, conversion and detinue may afford a limited protection against invasion of privacy. Such torts are actionable *per se*, and this assists a plaintiff whose real claim is the invasion of his privacy rather than actual damage to his or her property. Thus, if a person takes another's diary and reads it, the victim will be able to sue the wrongdoer for trespass[19] and obtain damages, in spite of the fact that no harm has

---

14. As where a false identity was adopted or entry to the premises was gained on a false pretext.
15. The Law Reform Commission *Consultation Paper on Privacy: Surveillance and the Interception of Communications* (1996) para 4.4.
16. Subject to the strictures relating to abuse by a member of the public of his or her right to be on the highway, laid down in *Hickman v Maisey* [1900] 1 QB 752 (CA). The occupiers of premises near to a path where there is a public right of way cannot complain where members of the public "peer into the [front] room, thus interfering with their privacy": *Browne v Dowie* (1959) 93 ILTR 179 at 181 (Recorders Court, Belfast).
17. [1978] 1 QB 479 at 488. *Cf Keating & Co Ltd v Jervis Shopping Centre Ltd* High Court, 1 March 1996 (Keane J) noted by Byrne & Binchy *Annual Review of Irish Law 1996*, pp 609-610.
18. *Bernstein of Leigh (Baron) v Skyviews & General Ltd* [1978] 1 QB 479 at 487.
19 *Cf The People (DPP) v Morgan* (1980) 114 ILTR 60 at 62 (CC), where three surreptitious searches of an employees handbag were made by her employers, who suspected her of dishonesty. Sheridan J excluded the evidence deriving from these searches in a criminal prosecution against the employee for embezzlement. He observed that:

come to the diary; but, if the same information is obtained merely by looking over the shoulder of the person as he or she writes in a diary, this will not constitute a trespass.[20]

**[37.08]** The tort of trespass to goods may afford partial, and cumbersomely focused, protection from telephone tapping and the placing of listening devices on telephone receivers to bug calls. The drawback here is that very often the claimant - the owner of the tapped line or the telephone receiver - will not be the person whose privacy has been violated.[21]

## Trespass to the Person

**[37.09]** Torts falling under this head afford some protection of privacy interests but only to a limited extent. The requirement of physical contact[22] or an apprehension[23] of physical contact with the person reduces the effectiveness of the tort in this context.[24] Nevertheless, there are cases where a remedy under this heading will be appropriate. Intentional trespass into a persons home will frequently lead to an apprehension on the part of the occupant that force may be used against him or her. Conversely, false imprisonment may be committed even where the invasion of a person's liberty of movement is entirely surreptitious.[25]

## Intentional Infliction of Mental Suffering

**[37.10]** The tort of intentional infliction of mental suffering affords limited protection for privacy interests.[26] As we have seen,[27] it can control improper techniques of investigation[28] as well as such other invasions of privacy such as intimidatory debt collection[29] and harassment of tenants by landlords.[30]

---

19. (contd)

> "… an examination of the private effects of another person is clearly an act of trespass. In the case of a ladies handbag which is very often a receptacle for the most private documents and effects apart from money, I cannot think of many better examples of gross trespass …"

20. *Cf* Burns 'Law & Privacy: The Canadian Experience' (1976) 54 CBR 1 at 16-17.
21. Law Reform Commission, *Consultation Paper on Privacy: Surveillance and the Interception of Communications*, para 4.18.
22. In *Kaye v Robertson* [1991] FSR 62 (CA) Glidewell CJ accepted that taking flashlight photographs of a patient in hospital could be characterised as a battery (though not on the facts of that case). He observed that:

> "[counsel for the plaintiff] could not refer us to any authority in which the taking of a photograph or indeed the flashing of a light had been held to be a battery. Nevertheless I am prepared to accept that it may well be the case that if shone into another persons eyes and injures his sight, or damages him, in some other way, this may be in law a battery."

SALMOND & HEUSTON, p 64, fn. 40, accepts that "[t]his is a practical approach, but [it] is difficult to reconcile with the fact that trespass is actionable *per se*".

23. The decision of *R v Ireland* [1998] AC 147 opens up new possibilities.
24. *Cf* Younger Committee Report, p 291.
25. *Cf* para **[22.45]** above.
26. *Cf* Gibson 'Common Law Protection of Privacy' (1977) Ch 12 of *Studies in Canadian Tort Law* Klar ed at 348-351.
27. See para **[22.28]** above.
28. *Cf Janvier v Sweeney* [1919] 2 KB 316.
29. *Cf* Borda, (1939) 28 Geo L Forum 55.
30. *Cf* PROSSER & KEETON, pp 61-64.

## Private Nuisance

**[37.11]** The tort of private nuisance has traditionally been considered to have only a relatively modest role in the protection of privacy. It will, of course, afford a remedy against a wide variety of intrusions on the ability of a person to live peaceably in his or her home, but it cannot be availed of to preserve residents from being overlooked by neighbouring properties.[31] But if the ordinary use of property gives way to improper intrusiveness, the tort may come into its own. In *Lord Bernstein of Leigh v Skyview & General Ltd*,[32] where an aerial photograph was taken of the plaintiff's substantial residence, the defendant was held not to be liable in trespass since the plane had not flown at an unreasonably low height above the property.[33] Griffiths J stressed, however, that he did not:

> "wish the judgement to be understood as deciding that in no circumstances could a successful action be brought against an aerial photographer to restrain his activities. The present action is not founded in nuisance for no court would regard the taking of a single photograph as an actionable nuisance. But if the circumstances were such that a plaintiff was subjected to the harassment of constant surveillance of his home from the air, accompanied by the photographing of his every activity, I am far from saying that the courts would not regard such a monstrous invasion of his privacy as an actionable nuisance for which they would give relief. However, that question does not fall for decision in this case and will be decided if and when it arises."[34]

**[37.12]** Whilst generally the case,[35] that the surveillance must have an element continuity, one should hesitate before completely excluding the possibility of a "once-off" intrusion of privacy as being capable of being characterised as actionable nuisance. If the plaintiff can show that the single intrusion was attributable to a prior "state of affairs",[36] he or she should succeed in the action. Thus, where photographers staked out a neighbouring premises, waiting for an opportune moment to violate the occupants privacy, the fact that the consummation of their endeavours was momentary should not deprive the occupant of the right to sue for nuisance.

**[37.13]** A further, significant, limitation is that there is a question mark over who precisely may sue for private nuisance. In England, in *Hunter v Canary Wharf Ltd*,[37] the House of Lords severely restricted the entitlement to those who have "a right to the land affected",

---

31. In *Fleming v Rathdown School Trust*, High Court, 6 April 1993, Denham J quoted a passage from *Halsbury's Laws of England* 4th ed, Vol 34, para 327, to the effect that, "[w]here there is no infringement of a right to light, and where the act complained of is otherwise lawful, no action lies for the invasion of privacy by the opening of windows or for the destruction of a view or prospect, even though the value of a house or premises may be diminished thereby."
32. [1978] QB 479.
33. *Cf* para **[23.39]** above.
34. [1978] QB 479 at 489. See also *Motherwell v Motherwell* (1976) 3 DLR (3d) 62 (Alta SC App Div); *Burkholder v Superior Court* (1979) 96 Cal App 3d 421 at 426, 158 Cal Rptr 86 at 89. In the United States, aerial surveillance has come under constitutional scrutiny: see Higgins 'Note: Aerial Surveillance: Overlooking the Fourth Amendment' (1981) 50 Fordham LR 27.
35. In *Cunard v Antifyre Ltd* [1933] 1 KB 551 at 557, Talbot J observed that "nuisances at least in the vast majority of cases, are influences for a substantial length of time." See also *Hanrahan v Merck, Sharp & Dohme (Ireland) Ltd* [1988] ILRM 629 at 633 (SC) *Cf* para**[24.58]** above.
36. See para**[24.58]** above.
37. [1997] AC 655 (HL, Eng).

who will ordinarily be persons with the right to exclusive possession. As we have seen,[38] the Irish position is not so clearly restrictive: the Supreme Court decision in *Hanrahan v Merck Sharp & Dohme (Ireland) Ltd*[39] proceeded on the unchallenged basis that family members, regardless of legal title should be entitled to sue. In *Molumby v Kearns*,[40] in 1999, O'Sullivan J preferred to limit the entitlement to those "in occupation" of the premises. That term was intended to be more extensive than the *Hunter* test. It includes spouses, at least.[41] One may hope that the Irish courts will also recognise the claim of other family members. The idea that the law must deny a remedy to a child who has been subjected to a violation of his or her privacy is an unattractive one. Our courts are not compelled to take such a reactionary stance; courts in other common law jurisdiction have not done so.[42] When one takes into account the constitutional dimensions, which include protection from intrusion[43] and the guarantee that a remedy will be forthcoming where it can "be shown that the tort in question is basically ineffective to protect [the plaintiff's] constitutional right",[44] there is a strong argument that the *Hunter* limitations should be repudiated.

**[37.14]** The location from which the defendants intrusion is launched must also be considered. It is clear that, if the defendant engages in a violation of privacy from a neighbouring property this falls within the traditional requirements of the tort of private nuisance. The plaintiff need not establish that the defendant was in occupation of the neighbouring property.[45] Watching and besetting premises from the pavement may also amount to this tort.[46] In *Royal Dublin Society v Yates*,[47] Shanley J defined the tort of private nuisance so broadly as to be capable of being committed by a person when actually on the premises of the *plaintiff*. This is a novel, and doubtful, extension of the law. If it were to find further judicial support, the implications for the legal protection of privacy would be immense.

## Injurious Falsehood

**[37.15]** The publication of intrusive personal information may in some circumstances constitute the tort of injurious (or "malicious") falsehood.[48] The essence of this tort is that

38. See para **[24.59]** above.
39. [1988] ILRM 629.
40. High Court, unrep January 1999 (O'Sullivan J).
41. *Cf* para **[24.67]** above.
42. *Motherwell v Motherwell* (1976) 73 DLR (3d) 62.
43. *Cf Kennedy and Arnold v Ireland* [1987] IR 587 (HC); *Maguire v Drury* [1995] 1 ILRM 108 (HC); *X v Flynn* High Court, 19 May 1994 (Costello J); *Kearney v Ireland* [1986] IR 116 (HC); *Murphy v PMPA Insurance* [1978] ILRM 25 (HC).
44. *Hanrahan v Merck Sharp & Dohme (Ireland) Ltd* [1988] ILRM at 629.
45. See para **[24.72]** above. In *Southport Corporation v Esso Petroleum Co Ltd* [1956] AC 218 at 225 Devlin J stated *obiter*: "I can see no reason why ... if the defendant as a licensee or trespasser misuses someone else's land, he should not be liable for a nuisance in the same way as an adjoining occupier would be."
46. *Cf Hubbard v Pitt* [1976] 1 QB 142 (CA); Law Reform Commission, *Consultation Paper on Privacy: Surveillance and the Interception of Communications* (1996) para 4.11.
47. High Court, July 1997 (Shanley J). *Cf* para **[24.73]** above.
48. See para **[35.26]** above, the Law Reform Commissions *Consultation Paper on Privacy in Surveillance and the Interception of Communication* (1996) paras 4.22-4.24; *Kaye v Robertson* [1991] FSR 62 (CA).

the assertions be false, that they have caused[49] or are likely to cause[50] the plaintiff damage of a monetary character, and that they were published maliciously.[51] Thus, truthful disclosures or false allegations that have no such potential to damage the plaintiff financially fall outside the scope of the tort, which plays only a minor role in the protection of privacy interests.

### Negligence

**[37.16]** The action for negligence has considerable potential for the protection of privacy.[52] Interference with a privacy interest may result in economic loss, physical injury or psychiatric disturbance. Of course negligence can consist of inadvertent behaviour where there was no interest to bring about the outcome; but it seems that liability can also attach where the defendant acted recklessly or even intentionally.[53]

**[37.17]** The crucial questions facing the court in a negligence action involving a privacy issue will often concern the existence or scope of the duty of care. Negligence is well able to accommodate competing interests and values. It may find the answers difficult but it has no objection in principle to addressing such an issue as the extent to which the constitutionally protected rights of bodily integrity and health and, more starkly, the right to life itself should be capable of "trumping" privacy interests of people with AIDS.[54] Equally, courts in negligence proceedings can resolve the question of how to reconcile a psychiatrist's duty of confidentiality to his or her patient with the need to protect others from the prospect of murderous assault.[55]

**[37.18]** *Hanahoe v Judge Hussey*,[56] is a recent Irish privacy case sounding in negligence. Kinlen J there awarded damages of £100,000 to a firm of solicitors where, because of the

---

49. *Cf* para **[35.26]** above.
50. *Cf* the Defamation Act 1961, s 20.
51. *Cf* para **[35.28]** above.
52. See Clark, *Data Protection Law in Ireland* (1990).
53. *Cf* WINFIELD & JOLOWICZ, pp 51-52.
54. See Logan 'Who's Afraid of Whom? Courts Require HIV Doctors to Obtain Informed Consent of Patients' (1995) 44 De Paul LR 483; Gostin & Hodge 'Piercing the Veil of Secrecy in HIV/AIDS and other Sexually Transmitted Diseases: Theories of Privacy and Disclosure in Partner Notification' (1998) 5 Duke J of Gender L & Policy 9; Gabel 'Liability for "Knowing" Transmission of HIV: The Evolution of a Duty to Disclose' (1994) 21 Fla St ULR 981; Piorkowski *Note, Between a Rock and a Hard Place: AIDS and the Conflicting Physicians Duties of Preventing Disease Transmission and Safeguarding Confidentiality* (1984) 73 Georgetown LJ 403; Sundbeck 'Note, It Takes Two to Tango: Negligence Liability for the Sexual Transmission of AIDS' (1995) 5 Health Matrix 397; Schalman 'Note: Sleeping with the Enemy: Combating the Sexual Spread of HIV-AIDS Through a Heightened Legal Duty' (1996) 29 J Marshall LR 957; Walter 'Secrets Revealed: The Limits of Medical Confidence' (1993) 9 J Contemporary Health L & Policy 183; McIntosh 'When the Surgeon has HIV: What to Tell Patients About the Risk of Exposure and the Risk of Transmission' (1996) 44 Kansas LR 315.
55. *Cf Tarasoff v Regents of University of California* (1976) 551 P 2d 334 (Cal); Milno, '"Bless Me Father, For I am About to Sin ...." Should the Clergy Counsellors House a Duty to Protect Third Parties?' (1986) 22 Tulsa LJ 139; Perlin 'Tarasoff and the Dilemma of the Dangerous Patient: New Directions for the 1990s' (1992) 16 L & Psychol Rev 29; Lake 'Revisiting Tarasoff' (1994) 58 Albany LR 97.
56. [1998] 3 IR 69, analysed by Byrne & Binchy, *Annual Review of Irish Law 1997*.

negligence of a member (or members) of the Garda Síochána, the fact that the office of the firm was shortly to be subjected to a search under the provisions of s 64 of the Criminal Justice Act 1994 was leaked to the media, which resulted in a "media circus" and damaging publicity for the firm.

**[37.19]** Kinlen J stated:

> "This was a deliberate leaking to the media which caused considerable embarrassment to [the plaintiff firm]. It was intended to embarrass and distress [the plaintiff firm] and it most certainly did. It was an outrageous interference with their privacy and their constitutional rights."[57]

### Breach of Statutory Duty[58]

**[37.20]** Several statutes provide that disclosure of confidential information without due authorisation by members or employees of particular semi-state agencies is an offence.[59] Whether a civil action for breach of statutory duty by a victim of such wrongful disclosure would succeed is not clear; the court might possibly construe the particular provision as having been enacted for the benefit of the public rather than those persons likely to suffer from a wrongful disclosure. As against this, a statutory provision can afford a civil remedy where, as well as serving public interests, it seeks to protect a particular group.[60] On this basis, the court might well afford the victims of such wrongful disclosure a remedy for breach of statutory duty. Section 7 of the Data Protection Act 1988 imposes a statutory duty of care on data controllers and data processors as regards the collection of personal data and in their dealing with that data. The constitutional right to privacy in one's communications[61] would also be applicable, since wrongful disclosure would clearly be unjustifiable according to Hamilton P's test.

## III. Breach of Confidence[62]

**[37.21]** The law affords protection against the misuse of confidential information. The precise juridical basis of this protection is not easy to identify. One finds elements of contract, equity, property law, tort and constitutional law in the leading cases on the

---

57. [1998] 3 IR 69 at 108.

58. See the LRC *Consultation Paper on Privacy: Surveillance and the Interception of Communications* (1996) paras 4.29-4.32; Clark, *Data Protection in Ireland* (1990).

59. *Cf* eg the Postal and Telecommunications Services Act 1983, s 37; the Transport (Re-organisation of Coras lompair Éireann) Act 1986, s 22; the Dublin Transport Authority Act 1986, s 18; the Garda Siochana (Complaints) Act 1986, s 12; and the Labour Services Act 1987, s 13.

60. *Waterford Harbour Commissioners v British Railways Board* [1979] ILRM 296 at 339 (SC).

61. *Kennedy & Arnold v Ireland* [1988] ILRM 472 (HC). See also *Kearney v Ireland* [1986] IR 116 (HC).

62. The subject is comprehensively analysed by Lavery, *Commercial Secrets: The Action For Breach of Confidence in Ireland* (1996). See further Toulson & Phipps, *Confidentiality* (1996); Gurry, *Breach of Confidence* (1984); Keane, *Equity And The Law of Trusts in the Republic Of Ireland* (1988), Ch 30; Clark & Smyth, *Intellectual Property Law in Ireland,* (1997) Ch 23; Lavery 'Breach of Confidence' (1997) 33 Ir Intellectual Prop Rev 15; McDonagh 'Developments in the Action for Breach of Confidence' (1979) 14 Ir Jur (ns) 229; Hammond 'Is Breach of Confidence Properly Analysed in Fiduciary Terms?' (1979) 25 McGill LJ 244; Jones 'Restitution of Benefits Obtained in Breach of Another's Confidence' (1970) 86 LQR 463; Jones 'Breach of Confidence – After Spycatcher' (1990) 42 CLP 48; North 'Breach of Confidence: Is There a New Tort?' (1972) 12 JSPTL 149;

subject.[63] The emphasis has been on equitable principles. Thus in the leading Irish decision of *House of Spring Gardens v Point Blank Ltd*,[64] Costello J, in the High Court, observed that the court was being "asked to enforce what is essentially a moral obligation"[65] and O'Higgins CJ echoed this language in the Supreme Court.[66] Similarly, in *Oblique Financial Services Ltd v The Promise Production Co*,[67] Keane J used the expression "... moral obligation" when describing the basis of judicial intervention.

**[37.22]** The fact that equity plays such a central role in fashioning the remedy makes the courts generally reluctant to characterise it as a tort. *Dicta* of Lord Denning MR and Winn LJ in *Seager v Copydex (No 2)*[68] give some support for the argument that an analogy can be made with the tort of conversion of a property interest[69] but there are formidable difficulties with this approach.[70] Whereas confidential information of a commercial kind might plausibly be regarded as property, this is hardly the case with most[71] personal intimate confidences. Moreover, there are conceptual problems with rationalising the public interest defence to a breach of confidence claim on the basis that no property interest has been interfered with because no obligation of confidence arose.[72]

**[37.23]** In *Coco v AN Clark (Engineers) Ltd*[73] Megarry J stated succinctly the elements of breach of confidence:

---

62. (contd) Stuckey 'The Equitable Action for Breach of Confidence: Is Information Ever Property?' (1981) 9 Sydney LR 402; English Law Commission WP No 58 'Breach of Confidence' (1974); English Law Commission Report, 'Breach of Confidence' (110, 1981). For consideration of the impact of the European Convention of Human Right in this area of the law. see Phillipson & Fenwick 'Breach of Condifence on a Privacy Remedy in the Human Rights Era' (2000) 63 MLR 660.

63. See Lavery, *Commercial Secrets: The Action For Breach of Confidence in Ireland* (1996), Ch 2; Toulson & Phipps, *Confidentiality* (1996), Ch 2; Hammond 'The Origins of the Equitable Duty of Confidence' (1979) 8 Anglo-Amer LR 71.

64. [1984] IR 611 (SC).

65. [1984] IR 611 at 663.

66. [1984] IR 611 at 697. McCarthy J expressed the view that "the obligation of secrecy, whilst enforced by equitable principles, depends more upon commercial necessity than moral duty". This approach is hard to reconcile with the basis on legal intervention which clearly is not reducible to pragmatic considerations. Moreover, intervention is not limited to cases with a commercial dimension. See, eg, *Stephens v Avery* [1988] 2 All ER 477. In *AG for England and Wales v Brandon Book Publishers Ltd* [1987] ILRM 135 at 136 (HC), Carroll J certainly considered that McCarthy J's remark reinforced the view that the *House of Spring Gardens* principles applied only to private individuals in a commercial context. She regarded the latter type of case, however, as a "completely separate category ...".

67. [1994] 1 ILRM 74 at 77.

68. [1969] RPC 250.

69. *Cf* North 'Breach of Confidence: Is There a New Tort?' (1972) 12 JSPTL 149.

70. See Lavery, *Commercial Secrets: The Action For Breach of Confidence in Ireland* (1996), Ch 2. As to whether breach of confidence may be considered a category of "unlawful means" for the purposes of the tort of unlawful interference with economic interests, see the discussion in *Indata Equipment Supplies (t/a AutoFit) v ACL Ltd* [1998] 1 BCLC 412 (CA).

71. Of course in some rare occasions intimate confidences – to the media, for example – will have a cash value.

72. See Cripps, *The Legal Implications of Disclosure in the Public Interest* (2nd ed, 1994), p 31.

73. [1969] FSR 415 at 419-420.

> "In my judgment, three elements are normally required if, apart from contract,[74] a case of breach of confidence is to succeed. First, the information itself ... must have the necessary quality of confidence about it.[75] Secondly, that information must have been imparted in circumstances importing an obligation of confidence. Thirdly, there must be an unauthorised use of that information to the detriment of the party communicating it."[76]

Three elements thus are crucial: (a) the *confidential nature* of the information sought to be protected, (b) the communication of that information importing an *obligation of confidence* and (c) the *unauthorised use* of it.[77] The first two of these elements have given rise to particular difficulty and warrant specific discussion. Let us consider each of them briefly in turn.

## The Confidential Nature of the Information

**[37.24]** In order to have the necessary quality of confidence about it, the information "must not be something which is public property and public knowledge."[78] The "public" here does not mean the public at large: it will suffice to defeat a claim that people in the particular discipline or mode of business or profession have already become aware of the information.[79]

**[37.25]** Conversely, the fact that the information is accessible to the public only after the expenditure of time and effort will not prevent it from having a confidential character. In *House of Spring Gardens v Point Blank Ltd*,[80] Costello J stated:

> "In considering ... the nature of the information, it is relevant to take into account the degree of skill, time and labour involved in compiling the information ... [I]f the information has been compiled by the expenditure of skill, time and labour by the informant, then, although he has obtained it from sources which are public (in the sense that any member of the public with the same skills could obtain it had he acted like the compiler of the information) the information may still, because of its value, be regarded as confidential information and subject to an obligation of confidence. Furthermore, the court will readily decide that the informant correctly regarded the information he was imparting as confidential information if, although based on material which is accessible to the public, it is of a unique nature which has resulted from the skill and labour of the informant."[81]

---

74. Megarry J noted that, "[I]n cases of contract, the primary question is no doubt that of construing the contract and any terms implied in it": [1969] FSR 415 at 419.
75. *Saltman Engineering Co Ltd v Campbell Engineering Co Ltd* 65 RPC 203 at 215 (*per* Lord Greene MR).
76. It should be noted that Megarry J made it clear that his definition arose in a case where he found himself "in the realms of commerce [where] there is no question of any marital relationship such as arose in *Argyll v Argyll* [1967] Ch 302, [1969] FSR 415 at 419.
77. *Cf Private Research Ltd v Brosnan* [1996] 1 ILRM 27 at 31 (HC), quoting with approval from *Coppinger & Skone James on Copyright* (11th ed) para 90.
78. *Saltman Engineering Co Ltd v Campbell Engineering Co Ltd* 65 RPC 203 at 215 (*per* Lord Greene MR).
79. Lavery, *Commercial Secrets: The Action For Breach of Confidence in Ireland* (1996), Ch 2.
80. [1984] IR 611.
81. [1984] IR 611 at 663-664.

On appeal to the Supreme Court, O'Higgins CJ quoted this passage from Costello J's judgment and expressed his agreement with it.[82]

**[37.26]** It is now clear therefore that the persons who obtain information in confidence should not be permitted to use the information obtained in confidence "as a springboard for activities detrimental to the person who made the confidential communication, ... even when all the features have been published or can be ascertained by actual inspection by any member of the public."[83] In *House of Spring Gardens*,[84] the plaintiffs, who had developed a particular kind of bullet-proof vest, entered into an agreement for its commercial exploitation by the defendants, after giving full technical details regarding vests to the defendants. After various difficulties, culminating in litigation by the plaintiffs against the defendants, followed by settlement and a new agreement, the plaintiffs claimed that the defendants subsequently had misused the information they had obtained about the vests, in a manner contrary to the agreement. The plaintiffs claimed (*inter alia*) damages for breach of confidence.

**[37.27]** The defendants unsuccessfully invoked the decision of *Mustad v Dosen*[85] in which the House of Lords had held (in 1928) that a plaintiff could not claim that information contained in the specification for a patent application should be regarded as confidential. In the instant case "a great deal of confidential information"[86] had been given to the defendants which was not covered in the plaintiff's two patent applications. Moreover, *Mustad*, which appeared to have been decided on principles of contract rather than equity, had antedated by many years the development of the equitable principles relating to breach of confidence to which Costello J had referred.[87] Costello J held in favour of the plaintiffs and his judgment was affirmed by the Supreme Court.

**[37.28]** In *Private Research Ltd v Brosnan*,[88] the plaintiff published a monthly analysis of two hundred companies' performance, based on analysis from data contained in the Companies Office files. This publication was sold to six hundred subscribers and was not available to the general public. The first defendant, who had been employed as the plaintiff's marketing manager, set up a company (the second defendant), with the intent of producing a similar publication aimed at the same market but supplemented by on-line computer services. This company circulated some of the plaintiff's subscribers seeking subscriptions to the new product. The plaintiff sought an interlocutory injunction in respect of breach of confidence, *inter alia*. The Circuit Court judge granted the injunction restraining the first defendant from disclosing or using the plaintiff's confidential list, but on appeal to the High Court, McCracken J reversed.

---

82. [1984] IR 611 at 696.
83. *Terrapin Ltd v Builders Supply Co (Hayes) Ltd* [1967] RPC 375 at 391. *Cf* Lavery, *Commercial Secrets: The Action For Breach of Confidence in Ireland* (1996), Ch 2. Keane, *Equity and the Law of Trusts in the Republic of Ireland* (1988), Ch 30.
84. [1984] IR 611.
85. [1963] RPC 41 (HL, Eng).
86. [1984] IR 611 at 664 (*per* Costello J).
87. Keane, *Equity and the Law of Trusts in the Republic of Ireland* (1988), para 30.04 observes that this is "presumably a reference to the spring-board rule which was not articulated until 1960".
88. [1996] 1 ILRM 27 (HC) (Circuit Court appeal).

**[37.29]** McCracken J considered that there was "certainly"[89] a serious issue to be tried on the question whether the identity of the plaintiff's customers was information of a confidential nature; there was "no doubt that that is so in principle in many cases".[90] Equally, "certainly" there was an arguable case that the circumstances under which the first defendant had come to know the identity of the plaintiff's customers had imported an obligation of confidence. The balance of convenience, however, lay against granting the injunction.

**[37.30]** McCracken J was concerned that the effect of the injunction was "to prevent the defendants from carrying on business at all",[91] even though they were perfectly entitled to compete with the plaintiff:

> "The defendants are restrained from soliciting almost six hundred firms, who happen to be customers of the plaintiff. These appear to include all the major banks, a number of the major accountants and a number of the major trading companies in the State. If the defendants solicit these firms, it will not be due to any confidential information imparted to the first named defendant, but will simply be because they are obvious potential customers. It is also alleged by the first named defendant that he has sourced may of the firms he has approached through Dun & Bradstreet Marketing Guide to Ireland, and therefore did not use any confidential information which he may have obtained as a springboard to setting up his business. It would be most unjust to confirm the principle that the defendants are entitled to trade in competition with the plaintiff, and then to prevent them from approaching the most obvious potential customers, whose names as customers of the plaintiff would certainly not be confidential. It may well be that a number of the plaintiff's customers are firms which one might not expect to be a market for a publication of this nature, and therefore information concerning them is confidential, but I think that the injustice of preventing the defendants from approaching the larger customers when the only relief to which the plaintiff would be entitled would be to prevent the defendants from approaching small customers would be very serious."[92]

**[37.31]** Since McCracken J could see no way in practice in which he could make an order differentiating between the different customers and since a general injunction of the kind granted by the Circuit Court judge appeared to cause far greater inconvenience to the defendants than the inconvenience that would flow to the plaintiff from not obtaining an injunction, McCracken J refused to grant the injunction and allowed the appeal.

## Obligation of Confidence

**[37.32]** An obligation of confidence can arise as a term of a contract, express or implied, or "by imposition of law".[93] The circumstances that generate this obligation range widely, capturing such relationships as those between employer and employee,[94] doctor and

89. [1996] 1 ILRM 27.
90. [1996] 1 ILRM 27.
91. [1996] 1 ILRM 27.
92. [1996] 1 ILRM 27.
93. Toulson & Phipps, *Confidentiality* (1996); Gurry, *Breach of Confidence* (1984), para 2-24. See further Lavery, *Commercial Secrets: The Action For Breach of Confidence in Ireland* (1996), Ch 4.
94. See the comprehensive discussion in Lavery, *Commercial Secrets: The Action For Breach of Confidence in Ireland* (1996), Ch 7.

patient,[95] accountants,[96] lawyers,[97] bankers[98] and their clients, intimate personal relationships[99] and other situations where confidences have been reposed for a particular limited purpose.[100]

**[37.33]** In *Coco v AN Clark (Engineers) Ltd*,[101] Megarry J suggested that "that hard-worked creature, the reasonable man" should be pressed into service in this context, adding:

> "It seems to me that, if the circumstances are such that any reasonable man standing in the shoes of the recipient of the information would have realised upon reasonable grounds the information was being given to them in confidence, then this should suffice to impose upon him the equitable obligation of confidence."[102]

**[37.34]** The remedy for breach of confidence extends beyond the confidant to third parties who come into possession of the confidential information.[103] In *Oblique Financial Services Ltd v The Promise Production Co*,[104] Keane J observed:

> "In this case a similar obligation arises, whether by breach of some contractual obligation or some moral obligation. It is obvious from the cases and indeed it is a matter of common sense that the right to confidentiality, which the law recognises in these cases, would be of little value if the third parties to whom this information has been communicated were at liberty to publish it to the general public, without the court being in a position to intervene."

Even third parties who are innocent of knowledge of any wrongdoing when they receive the information may be restrained from disseminating it after notice of the impropriety.[105]

**[37.35]** A fundamental issue of principle, yet to be decided by the Irish courts, is whether the obligation of confidence extends beyond cases where a confider has reposed confidence in a confidant, to cases where, without any such reposition, a person surreptitiously acquires information from another (by surveillance techniques or telephone tapping, for example) which he or she ought to be aware the other regards as confidential.[106] In *Malone v Metropolitan Police Commissioner*,[107] Megarry VC rejected

---

95. See para **[37.40]** below.
96. *Cf Parry-Jones v Law Society* [1969] 1 Ch 1 at 9 (CA).
97. See Toulson & Phipps, *Confidentiality* (1996); Gurry, *Breach of Confidence* (1984), Ch 18. *Cf McMullen v Clancy* High Court, 3 September 1999 where McGuinness J stated at p 31:

    "In general I would not accept the relationship between a barrister instructed by a solicitor and the client as a fiduciary relationship in the sense used by the Canadian Supreme Court [in *Hodgkinson v Simms* (1994) 117 DLR (4th) 161]."
98. See Donnelly, *The Law of Banks and Credit Institutions*, pp 147-166; *Tournier v National Provincial and Union Bank of England* [1924] 1 KB 461.
99. *Argyll v Argyll* [1967] Ch 302; *Stephens v Avery* [1988] 2 All ER 477.
100. See Lavery, *Commercial Secrets: The Action For Breach of Confidence in Ireland* (1996); *House of Spring Gardens Ltd v Point Blank Ltd* [1984] IR 611.
101. [1969] RPC 41 at 48. See further Lavery, *Commercial Secrets: The Action For Breach of Confidence in Ireland* (1996).
102. [1969] RPC 41 at 48.
103. See Lavery, *Commercial Secrets: The Action For Breach of Confidence in Ireland* (1996), Ch 6.
104. [1994] ILRM 74 (HC).
105. See Lavery, *Commercial Secrets: The Action For Breach of Confidence in Ireland* (1996), pp 127ff; *Malone v Commissioner of Police of the Metropolis* [1979] 2 All ER 620 at 634.
106. See Lavery, *Commercial Secrets: The Action For Breach of Confidence in Ireland* (1996), pp 104-109.
107. [1979] 1 Ch 344 at 376.

such a basis of liability, but other decisions in England[108] and in other common law jurisdictions[109] are receptive to it. Of course, extending breach of confidence in this way will permit a remedy in egregious cases where no other remedy exists outside the constitutional context, but that is not necessarily an argument for changing the traditional contours of breach of confidence but rather for ensuring that *some* remedy exists in the legal system. In Ireland, the courts might be better advised to develop the substance and contours of the constitutional remedy for infringement of privacy. Extending breach of confidence so as to embrace surreptitious acquisitions of information has three main difficulties. First, it compromises the normative basis of breach of confidence, which concentrates on the violation of a secret trust that one has reposed in another. Stealing information breaches privacy (and in some cases property) entitlements but does not involve any violation of trust reposed.

**[37.36]** Secondly, the requirement that the information be confidential has to be modified radically to accommodate surreptitious acquisition, where I have a right to seek vindication regardless of the confidential quality of what information has been acquired. To give a remedy under the flag of breach of confidence, the courts have to engage in the dubious process of characterising the information derived from the surreptitious invasion of privacy as confidential when in truth it may lack that quality.

**[37.37]** The third difficulty with treating surreptitious acquisition of information as an aspect of breach of confidence relates to the remedy. In many cases the most appropriate remedy is one for damages to compensate for the invasion of privacy. Courts still are hesitant about ordering a straightforward compensatory award for damages for breach of confidence modelled on tort since breach of confidence is not regarded as a tort. The argument in favour of disconnecting surreptitious acquisitions from breach of confidence and instead simply, treating them as infringements of the constitutional right to privacy must therefore be an attractive one for the courts to consider. Was not *Kennedy v Ireland*[110] a classic instances of an invasion of privacy, rather than breach of confidence?

## Remedies

**[37.38]** The courts have a wide range of remedies for breach of confidence.[111] These include injunctions,[112] Anton Piller orders,[113]

---

108. See, eg, *Ashburton v Pape* [1913] 2 Ch 419 at 475 (*per* Swinfen Eady J) and the other decisions discussed by Lavery, *Commercial Secrets: The Action For Breach of Confidence in Ireland* (1996), 105-106.

109. See, eg, *Smith Kline & French Laboratories (Australia) Ltd v Department of Community Health Services* [1990] FSR 617 and the other decision discussed by Lavery, *Commercial Secrets: The Action For Breach of Confidence in Ireland* (1996), pp 106-107.

110. [1987] IR 587 (HC).

111. See Lavery, *Commercial Secrets: The Action For Breach of Confidence in Ireland* (1996),. Ch 9; Toulson & Phipps, *Confidentiality* (1996), Ch 10.

112. See Lavery, *Commercial Secrets: The Action For Breach of Confidence in Ireland* (1996), pp 221ff, discussing, *inter alia, Aksjeselsckapet Jotul v Waterford Iron Founders Ltd*, High Court, 8 November 1977 (McWilliam J); *Oblique Financial Services Ltd v The Promise Production Co Ltd* [1994] 1 ILRM 74 and *Private Research Ltd v Brosnan* [1996] 1 ILRM 27. See also *Irish National Bank v RTE* [1998] 2 ILRM 196 (SC) (injunction not ordered).

113. *House of Spring Gardens Ltd v Point Blank Ltd* [1984] IR 611. See further Lavery, *Commercial Secrets: The Action For Breach of Confidence in Ireland* (1996), pp 238-240, Toulson & Phipps, *Confidentiality* (1996), see para [10-15].

orders for delivery up or destruction,[114] an account for profits,[115] restitutionary[116] or declaratory[117] relief and damages.[118]

**[37.39]** It has been observed that "[n]o other remedy for breach of confidence had provoked as much academic debate and criticism as the award of damages".[119] It is beyond the scope of the present work to enter into that debate. Suffice it to note that the traditional characterisation of the remedy as one savouring of contract, property and equity made it difficult for the courts to award damages outside cases where Lord Cairns Act afforded an entitlement to do so. Gradually the courts have come to accept that "equitable damages"[120] may be awarded in any appropriate instance.

## Medical Confidences[121]

**[37.40]** This may be an opportune point to discuss the particular matter of medical confidences as they involve a complex intermingling of the legal principles relating to breach of confidence, negligence and the rules of evidence.

**[37.41]** Confidentiality is "a time-honoured principle of medical ethics".[122] It features in the Hippocratic Oath[123] and has the general support of the profession today. It is considered

114. See, eg, *Franklin v Giddins* [1978] Qd R 72; *Robb v Green* [1895] 2 QB 315; *Peter Pan Manufacturing Corporation v Corsets Silhouette Ltd* [1964] 1 WLR 96.

115. See, eg, *House of Spring Gardens Ltd v Point Blank Ltd* [1984] IR 611; *Peter Pan Manufacturing Corporation v Corsets Silhouette Ltd* [1964] 1 WLR 96; *AG v Guardian Newspapers Ltd (No 2)* [1990] 1 AC 109. See further Lavery, *Commercial Secrets: The Action For Breach of Confidence in Ireland* (1996), pp 241-244; Toulson & Phipps, *Confidentiality* (1996), paras 10.04-10.05.

116. See *Pre-Can Exploration & Development Ltd v McTarish* (1966) 57 DLR (2d) 557 (SC, Can); *LAC Minerals Ltd v International Corona Resources Ltd* (1989) 61 DLR (4th) 14 (SC, Can), discussed by Lavery, *Commercial Secrets: The Action For Breach of Confidence in Ireland* (1996), pp 253-254. See further Toulson & Phipps, *Confidentiality* (1996), paras 10.06-10.08.

117. See, eg *Malone v Metropolitan Police Commissioner* [1979] 1 Ch 344. See further Toulson & Phipps, *Confidentiality* (1996), paras 10-14.

118. See Lavery, *Commercial Secrets: The Action For Breach of Confidence in Ireland* (1996), pp 244-252; Toulson & Phipps, *Confidentiality* (1996), paras 2.06-2.11, 10.09-10.13.

119. Lavery, *Commercial Secrets: The Action For Breach of Confidence in Ireland* (1996), p 244.

120. Toulson & Phipps, *Confidentiality* (1996), para 10.10; Lavery, *Commercial Secrets: The Action For Breach of Confidence in Ireland* (1996), p 247 is supportive of this trend. He submits that "equity can award damages under this jurisdiction and that such inherent powers serve to fill any lacunae which would otherwise be apparent if damages could only be awarded under Lord Cairns Act."

121. See Tomkin & Hanafin, *Irish Medical Law*, (1995) Ch 4; Mason & McCall Smith, *Law and Medical Ethics* (4th ed, 1994), Ch 8; Casey & Craven, *Psychiatry and the Law* (1999), Ch 20; O'Kelly & Ronan, *Nursing Law* (199 ), Ch 10; The Medical Council, Ireland, *A Guide to Ethical Conduct and Behaviour* (5th ed, 1998), para 18; Toulson & Phipps, *Confidentiality* (1996), Ch 13; O'Neill 'Matters of Discretion – The Parameters of Doctor/Patient Confidentiality' (1995) 1 Medico-Legal J of Ir 94; Doran, 'Medical Confidentiality: The Role of the Doctrine of Confidentiality in the Doctor-Patient Relationship' (1997) 3 Medico-Legal J of Ir 21; Boyle 'Medical Confidence – Civil Liability for Breach' (1973) 24 NILQ 19; Phelan & Cusack 'The Doctor's Duty of Confidentiality and the Prosecution of Criminal Offences' (1996) 2 Medico-Legal J of Ir 52. In *Hynes v Garvey* [1978] IR 174 at 187 (SC), Henchy J referred to "... the fetters of confidentiality which characterise a doctor-patient relationship".

122. Medical Council, Ireland, *A Guide to Ethical Conduct and Behaviour* (5th ed, 1998), para 18.1.

123. "Whatsoever things I see or hear concerning the life of men, in my attendance on the sick or even apart therefrom, which ought not to be spoken of abroad, I will keep silence thereon, counting such things to be as sacred secrets." [Quoted by Casey & Craven, *Psychiatry and the Law* (1999), Ch 20].

to be "fundamental to the doctor/patient relationship".[124] The principle has never been regarded as an absolute one and some qualifications are clearly necessary in the interests of the patient, of others and of the welfare of society.[125]

**[37.42]** The law has approached the subject from a number of angles. One is to characterise the doctor's obligation in terms of the duty of care in *negligence*.[126] On this approach, the doctor may in some circumstances be required to *respect* the principle of confidentiality and in other circumstances to *breach* confidentiality. In *Furniss v Fitchett*,[127] a general practitioner who gave the plaintiff's husband a letter which in effect certified his belief that the plaintiff exhibited symptoms of paranoia for which she should be given treatment was held guilty of negligence in causing the plaintiff nervous shock when her husband revealed the letter in separation proceedings taken by her against him. Barrowclough CJ, rejecting a motion to set aside the jury verdict against the defendant, stated that the defendant could reasonably foresee that his conduct would result in physical[128] harm to the plaintiff, since he had placed no restriction on the use of the certificate:

> "In these circumstances, I am of opinion that, on the principle of *Donoghue v Stevenson*,[129] there arose a duty of care on his part. I have not forgotten that the certificate was true and accurate, but I see no reason for limiting the duty of care to seeing that it is accurate. The duty must extend also to the exercise of care in deciding whether it should be put into circulation in such a way that it is likely to cause harm to another."[130]

---

124. Medical Council, Ireland, *A Guide to Ethical Conduct and Behaviour* (5th ed, 1998), para 18.1.

125. Medical Council, Ireland, *A Guide to Ethical Conduct and Behaviour* (5th ed, 1998), para 18.3 lists four circumstances where exception may be made in the absence of permission from the patient:

    "1. When ordered by a Judge in a Court of Law, or by a Tribunal established by an Act of the Oireachtas.

    2. When necessary to protect the interest of the patient.

    3. When necessary to protect the welfare of Society.

    4. When necessary to safeguard the welfare of another individual or patient."

126. See the very clear analysis by Boyle 'Medical Confidence – Civil Liability for Breach' (1973) 24 NILQ 19.

127. [1958] NZLR 396 (SC).

128. Barrowclough CJ, influenced by the view of the majority in *Candler v Crane, Christmas & Co* [1951] 2 KB 164 (CA), made it clear that his holding extended only to physical and not economic damage. After *Hedley Byrne*, of course, it is arguable that a doctor's duty in this context is capable of embracing the patient's financial as well as physical welfare.

129. [1932] AC 562 at 580 (HL (SC), *per* Lord Atkin).

130. [1958] NZLR 396. Barrowclough CJ made it clear that he regarded the British Medical Associations Code of Ethics on the issue of confidentiality as "evidence of the general profession standards to which a reasonably careful, skilled and informed practitioner would conform" but not decisive on the issue of the duty of care in negligence. This approach is similar to that which the Irish Supreme Court appears to favour, albeit with some judges wishing to set a more onerous test, in respect of a doctor's duty of disclosure in the context of informed consent to treatment: see *Walsh v Family Planning Services Ltd* [1992] 1 IR 496; *Bolton v Blackrock Clinic*, Supreme Court, 23 January 1997.

**[37.43]** Barrowclough CJ made it plain that he did not regard the doctor's duty of confidentiality as subject to no exception:

> "Take the case of a doctor who discovers that his patient entertains delusions in respect of another, and in his disordered state of mind is liable at any moment to cause death or grievous bodily harm to that other. Can it be doubted for one moment that the public interest requires him to report that finding to some one?"[131]

**[37.44]** The answer given by the courts throughout the common law jurisdictions is that the doctor may well be under an obligation to act inconsistently with the demands of patient confidentiality either by reporting the patient's plans to the intended victim or the appropriate authorities (such as the police) or by removing the danger by other means, such as compulsorily admitting the patient to a mental hospital. The precise scope of this duty of protection to others[132] is a matter of much debate.[133] Some have argued that imposing enforceable legal obligations on doctors to take positive steps to mitigate dangers of this kind leads to excessive incarceration of patients with a violent disposition. It seems that the risk of harm must have a high level of credibility and that the identity of those in danger must be clear before the courts will stigmatise a doctor who has reacted passively to the patient's communication of his or her intentions.

---

130. See further Boyle 'Medical Confidence – Civil Liability for Breach' (1973) 24 NILQ 19. See also *G v Attorney General* [1994] 1 NZLR 714 (HC), where Heron J, invoking *Furniss v Fitchett*, held that the availability of the action for breach of confidence should not count decisively against recognising a duty of care on the part of those placed under a statutory obligation not to reveal certain personal information about a mother to her son, whom she had placed for adoption many years previously. He observed (at 721):

> "The existence of the tort of breach of confidence has some disputed ancestry and background but I think it is essentially narrower in concept and application than the tort of negligence and possibly less efficacious."

131. [1958] NZLR at 405-406.

132. Or, of course, to the protection of the patient himself or herself. *Cf* Craven 'Litigation Against Psychiatrists 1997-1999' (1999) 5 Medico-Legal LJ of Ir 70; Casey & Craven, *Psychiatry and the Law* (1999), p 109; *Healy v North Western Health Board* High Court, 31 January 1996 (Flood J); *Kelly v St Laurence's Hospital* [1989] ILRM 437; *Armstrong v Eastern Health Board* High Court, 5 October 1990 (Barr J), analysed by Byrne & Binchy, *Annual Review of Irish Law, 1990*, pp 523-526.

133. The decision of the Supreme Court of California in *Tarasoff v Regents of the University of California* (1974) 529 P 2d 553, vacated after rehearing (1976) 551 P 2d 334, caused great controversy. Courts in the United States of America are still divided on what is the appropriate scope of the duty resting on doctors who learn confidentially of their patients' harmful disposition. Some decisions (eg *Thompson v County of Almeda* (1980) 614 P 2d 728 (Cal); *Brady v Hopper* (1983) 570 F Supp 1333 (D Colo)) require that the threat relate to a specific, identifiable victim. Others (eg *Lipari v Sears, Roebuck & Co* (1980) 497 F Supp 185 (D Neb)), extend the duty to protect foreseeable (not necessarily identifiable) prospective victims. Still others (eg *Almonte v New York Medical College* (1994) 851 F Supp 34 (D Conn)) take an intermediate position, requiring that there be a specific threat against a specific victim or group. Courts in Florida (*Boynton v Burglass* (1991) 590 So 2d 446), Iowa (*Leonard v State* (1992) 491 NW 2d 508) and Texas (*Thapar v Zezulka* (1999) 994 SW 2d 635) have held that there is no duty to warn prospective victims. See Cantu & Jones Hopson, 'Bitter Medicine: A Critical Look at the Mental Health Care Providers Duty to Warn in Texas' (2000) 31 St Marys LJ 359; Lake 'Revisiting Tarasoff' (1994) 58 Albany LR 97. *Tarasoff* was discussed in the decision of the English Court of Appeal in *Palmer v Tees Health Authority* [1999] Lloyds Rep Med 351, where the identifiability of the prospective victims was considered by Stuart Smith LJ (and, more tentatively, Pill LJ) to be a necessary, though possibly not sufficient, condition of establishing proximity of relationship.

**[37.45]** Another avenue of potential liability is that of breach of confidence. *W v Egdell*[134] is the leading decision. There, the defendant was a psychiatrist who was asked to examine and report on the mental state of the plaintiff who was in a mental hospital having ten years previously been convicted of the manslaughter of five people. The plaintiff was seeking discharge from the hospital. The defendant's report was to the effect that the plaintiff had a psychopathic personality, with a worrying interest in firearms and explosives. On receipt of this report, the plaintiff's solicitor withdrew his application for a discharge. The defendant, who was concerned that the medical personnel in the hospital should be apprised of his opinion of the plaintiff's condition, since it differed significantly from theirs, sent a copy of his report to the hospital which, at his prompting, forwarded it to the Secretary of the State, who in due course sent it to the tribunal that was examining the plaintiff's application. When the plaintiff discovered this, he sought a number of remedies, including damages from the defendant for breach of confidence.

**[37.46]** Scott J dismissed the claim on the basis that the plaintiff's entitlement to confidentiality was a private interest which was trumped by overriding public interest considerations. The English Court of Appeal affirmed, but considered it preferable to characterise the entitlement to confidentiality as a public rather than private interest.

**[37.47]** Bingham LJ stated:

> "The decided cases very clearly establish (1) that the law recognises an important public interest in maintaining professional duties of confidence but (2) that the law treats such duties not as absolute but as liable to be overridden where there is held to be a stronger public interest in disclosure. Thus the public interest in the administration of justice may require … a medical man … to breach his professional duty of confidence … A doctor's duty of confidence to his patient may be overridden by clear statutory language …"[135]

**[37.48]** Bingham LJ acknowledged the force of the argument that a patient making an application for discharge should feel free to bare his or her soul to the psychiatrist who is commissioned to carry out an examination and that this candour would be frustrated if the psychiatrist could give his or her report to those empowered to prevent the patient's release from hospital. Only the most compelling circumstances could justify such conduct. One consideration, however, weighed the balance of public interest decisively in favour of disclosure:

> "Where a man has committed multiple killings under the disability of serious mental illness, decisions which may lead directly or indirectly to his release from hospital should not be made unless a responsible authority is properly able to make an informed judgment that the risk of repetition is so small as to be acceptable. A consultant psychiatrist who becomes aware, even in the course of a confidential relationship, of information which leads him, in the exercise of what the court considers a sound professional judgment, to fear that such decisions may be made on the basis of inadequate information and with a real risk of consequent danger to the public is entitled to take such steps as are reasonable in all the circumstances to communicate the grounds of his concern to the responsible authorities."[136]

---

134. [1990] Ch 359.
135. [1990] Ch 359.
136. [1990] Ch 359.

In the light of what has already been noted about the contours of negligence liability in this context, it seems clear that a doctor may find himself in a position, not simply where a breach of confidence is *excusable* but also where such a breach is *required* in the exercise of his or her professional responsibilities.

**[37.49]** Probably that point was not reached on the facts of *Egdell* but one can envisage other situations – as, for example, where a patient indicates a propensity to kill a fellow patient – where the psychiatrist commissioned to carry out the examination would be obliged, rather than merely entitled, to pass on the report to the appropriate authorities.

**[37.50]** A separate dilemma can arise for a doctor who becomes aware that his or her patient has a communicable disease. Is the doctor in these circumstances entitled to breach the confidence relationship with the patient in order to protect others – such as members of the patient's family or a sexual partner of the patient? Statutory provisions impose the obligation on doctors to notify the public health authorities of persons known or suspected to be suffering from certain specific infectious diseases.[137] There is no statutory obligation, however, to notify the authorities about HIV or AIDS.

**[37.51]** In the absence of direct judicial guidance, Irish commentators have generally tended to view that, while the doctor is not under a common law obligation in negligence to take steps to protect the public at large, or unidentified prospective parties of a person with HIV or AIDS, such an obligation may well arise in respect of a spouse or other sexual partner.[138]

---

137. *Cf* the Health Care Act 1947 and the Infectious Disease Regulations; the Public Health (Control of Disease) Act 1984.

138. *Cf* Casey & Craven, *Psychiatry and the Law* (1999), p 109; O'Neill 'Matters of Discretion – The Parameters of Doctor/Patient Confidentiality' (1995) 1 Medico-Legal J of Ir 94; Doran, 'Medical Confidentiality: The Role of the Doctrine of Confidentiality in the Doctor-Patient Relationship' (1997) 3 Medico-Legal J of Ir 21 appear to take a neutral position. The Medical Council Ireland, in its *Guide to Ethical Conduct and Behaviour*, paras 18.12-18.14, encourages the doctor, in cases where the patient has a communicable disease and others may be at risk, to do his or her best to obtain permission from the patient to let them know. If the patient refuses consent, the Council considers that those who might be at risk of infection while treating the patient should be informed. (It notes that they in turn would be bound by general rules of confidentiality). If a spouse or partner is at risk and the patient refuses consent, the Council states that, "depending on the circumstances of the illness, the doctor is justified in informing the spouse or partner." In England, confidentiality trumped newspapers' entitlement to disclose the identity of two doctors with AIDS who were continuing to practice: *X v Y* [1988] 2 All ER 648 (QBD, Rose J, 1987). It would seem mistaken to regard this case as offering significant support to the argument that a doctor need not warn those at risk of contracting AIDS from a patient. The contest was essentially one between the freedom of the press and confidentiality. On the level of risk of contracting AIDS in the health care context, see ABA AIDS Co-ordinating Committee, (eds Richardson & Russol 'Calming the AIDS Phobia: Legal Implications of the Low Risk of Transmitting HIV in the Health Care Setting' (1995) 28 U Mich JL Reform 733.
In the United States of America, there is a persistent judicial reluctance to impose a duty on doctors to warn those at risk of contracting AIDS from a patient. See generally Carmody 'Mandatory HIV Partner Notification: Efficacy, Legality and Notions of Traditional Public Health' (1999) 4 Texas Forum of Civ Lib & Civ Rts 107; Stenger, 'Comment: Taking *Tarasoff* Where No One Has Gone Before: Looking at Duty to Warn Under the AIDS Crisis' (1996) 15 St Louis U Pub LR 471.

**[37.52]** Our courts have yet to address the complex constitutional issues that arise in relation to the conflict between a doctor's obligation of confidentiality to his or her patient and the doctor's obligation, as a citizen, to report suspected criminal wrongdoing. It is the nature of medical practice that doctors treating patients will discover guilty secrets; if the guilt relates to the committing of a crime, what is the doctor to do?

**[37.53]** We have seen that, if the doctor should reasonably apprehend that others may be at risk of future injury, the doctor may fall under a duty to protect them, either by warning them or the appropriate authorities or by removing the danger by other means (such as, in suitable cases, by seeking to have the patient committed to a mental hospital). Not all cases of past criminality, however, will have such consequences. In some circumstances, the old common law offence of misprision of felony[139] might be considered to apply, though, in *Sykes v DPP*[140] Lord Denning expressed the view that the offence was:

> "subject to just limitations. Non-disclosure may be due to a claim of right made in good faith. For instance, if a lawyer is told by his client that he has committed a felony, it would be no misprision in the lawyer not to report it to the police, for he might in good faith claim that he was under a duty to keep it confidential. Likewise with doctor and patient, and clergyman and parishioner ..."

**[37.54]** A related issue concerns the rules of evidence in regard to privilege and public interest immunity. The traditional view expressed by the courts is that the relationship between doctors and patients does not generate either a privilege or public interest immunity.[141] As a consequence, discovery of documents may be ordered even where they include confidential medical records.

**[37.55]** In *W v B*,[142] where the 22-year-old plaintiff claimed that his former headmaster had sexually assaulted him ten years previously, Barr J held that he was obliged to make discovery of all medical and psychiatric reports and records for the period between the date he became a pupil at the school and the time he first consulted his solicitor about his complaints against the headmaster. Barr J did not accept the argument that the possibility of having to disclose documentation of their character in civil proceedings contributed to the reluctance of many children to complain about sexual abuse caused by adult persons in positions of dominance over them.

**[37.56]** Courts in other common law jurisdictions have addressed aspects of the issue. The United States Supreme Court, in *Jaffee v Redmond*,[143] held that a privilege attaching to the

---

139. It appears that, as a result of the abolition of the distinction between felonies and misdemeanours, effected by s 3 of the Criminal Law Act 1997, this offence has ceased to exist.

140. [1962] AC 528.

141. See, eg *Wheeler v Le Merchant* (1881) 17 ChD 675 at 681 (CA, *per* Jessel MR). *Cf Cook v Carroll* [1945] IR 515 at 519 (HC).

142. High Court, 18 March 1999.

143. (1996) 518 US 1. See Bowen Poulin 'The Psychotherapist – Patient Privilege after Jaffee v Redmond: Where Do We Go From Here?' (1998) 76 Wash ULQ 1341; Peddy Courville, Comment: Rationales for the Confidentiality of Psychotherapist – Patient Communications: Testimonial Privilege and the Construction (1998) 35 Houston LR 187; Mueller, 'Truth and Privacy in the Aftermath of Jaffee v Redmond' (1998) 49 Hastings LJ 945; Maynard 'The Psychotherapist – Patient Privilege: A Rational Approach to Defining Psychotherapist' (1997) 45 Clev St LR 405.

psychotherapist - patient relationship should extend to licensed social workers. The majority of the Court took a different view from that of Barr J on the impact of the possibility of disclosure of medical records on the victim of child sexual abuse. Stevens J, delivering the opinion of the Court, said:

> "Effective psychotherapy … depends upon an atmosphere of confidence and trust in which the patient is willing to make a frank and complete disclosure of facts, emotions, memories and fears. Because of the sensitive nature of the problems for which individuals consult psychotherapists, disclosure of confidential communications made during counselling sessions may cause embarrassment or disgrace. For this reason, the mere possibility of disclosure may impede development of the confidential relationship necessary for successful treatment."[144]

**[37.57]** The Supreme Court of Canada took a similar view in *M v Ryan*.[145] Rather than recognise a privilege that would apply in all cases – as the United States Supreme Court did in *Jaffee* – the Supreme Court of Canada preferred a more individuated approach. McLachlin J, for the majority, stated that:

> "… if the court considering a claim for privilege determines that a particular document or class of documents must be produced to get at the truth and prevent an unjust verdict, it must permit production to the extent required to avoid that result. On the other hand, the need to get at the truth and avoid injustice does not automatically negate the possibility of protection from full disclosure. In some cases, the court may well decide that the truth permits of nothing less than full production. This said, I would venture to say that an order for partial privilege will more often be appropriate in civil cases where …. the privacy interest is compelling. Disclosure of a limited number of documents, edited by the court to remove non-essential material, and the imposition of conditions on who may see and copy the documents and techniques which may be used to ensure, the highest degree of confidentiality and the least damage to the protected relationship, while guarding against the injustice of cloaking the truth."[146]

**[37.58]** Clearly, our courts have yet to address in detail the issue of whether there should be some modification of the rule that recognises no privilege or public interest immunity for doctor-patient relationships,[147] and, if so, whether the privilege or immunity should attach

---

144. (1996) 518 US at 10. The majority sought empirical support for its view from the "studies and authorities" cited in *amicus* briefs of the American Psychiatric Association and the American Psychological Association. For criticism, see Imwinkelreid 'The Rivalry Between Truth and Privilege: The Weakness of the Supreme Court's Instrumental Reasoning in *Jaffee v Redmond*' (1998) 49 Hastings LJ 969.

145. (1997) 143 DLR (4th) 1, (SC, Can). See Ross 'Comment: Partial Privilege and Full Disclosure in Civil Actions' (1997) 35 Alta LR 1067.

146. 143 DLR (4th) 1 at 12-13.

147. The Supreme Court, following the lead of Lord Hailshan in *D v NSPCC* [1978] AC 71 at 230, has recognised that the categories of public interest are not closed and may alter as social conditions develop: *Skeffington v Rooney* [1997] 1 IR 22 (SC) (Keane J's judgment, with which Murphy & Lynch JJ concurred). See further Declan McGrath, Evidence Chapter in Byrne and Binchy eds, *Annual Review of Irish Law 1995*, pp 436-438 As to whether Lord Hailsbury's *dictum* should lead to the establishment of a public interest immunity in the context of communications with a psychiatrist working in a sexual assault unit in a hospital, see *R v Young*, 1999 NSW Lexis 470, BC 9903755 (NSW CCA). *Cf M v L* [1999] 1 NZLR 747 (CA).

to all of these relationships or only some of them (such as that between a psychiatrist and a patient). If the courts recognise a privilege or immunity, they will have to determine whether it should apply without discrimination in both criminal and civil cases[148] and whether it is to be absolute or dependant on the particular circumstances of each case. More fundamentally, our courts will have to harmonise the rules of evidence, the principle of confidentiality and the need to protect those at risk of possible future harm.[149]

## IV. Criminal Law

**[37.59]** Although beyond the scope of this work, it should be noted that the criminal law protects the privacy of individuals against intrusion. In a prosecution[150] of a person for "peeping tom" activities, where the defendant, at nightfall, trespassed on private property in order to look through a window at three girls Gleeson J stated:

> "A man looking at young girls like this is invading their privacy when part of their bodies might be exposed. It is strange if the law cannot control this sort of nastiness."

It is also worth noting that harassment is an offence under s 10 of the Non-Fatal Offences Against the Person Act 1997. Serious interference with a person's "peace and privacy" or causing alarm, distress or harm to that person are necessary ingredients of the offence.

## V. Constitutional Aspects of Privacy

**[37.60]** After this short review of the existing protection of privacy interests under tort law, let us turn to examine the position in constitutional law. The development of the constitutional jurisprudence on this subject has so far lacked a comprehensive analysis of the notion of privacy. What we find are segmented judicial analyses which generally concentrate on a specific contextually defined entitlement to privacy. Thus we can say with certainty that there is a right to privacy in one's telephone communications[151] and that married couples have a right to marital privacy in relation to their access to contraceptive facilities,[152] for example. As to the existence, source and character of a generic right to privacy, uncertainty continues to rule. The judges seem to accept, or at least assume, that there is such a right, yet, in the crucial Supreme Court case of *Norris v Attorney General*,[153] where this right was asserted, neither the majority nor the dissenting judges gave any clear analysis of its provenance or contours. Indeed so fleeting is the discussion in the judgment of O'Higgins CJ for the majority that it is hard to know whether the majority judgment is premised on recognition of such a right. In later decisions, judicial acknowledgment of the right seems to have occurred by osmosis rather than through a threshold confrontation of what the right may involve or imply.

---

148. *Cf* Dawson 'Compelled Production of Medical Records' (1998) 43 McGill LJ 25 at 33ff. *Cf R v O'Connor* (1995) 130 DLR 4th 235 (SC, Can).

149. See Harris 'The Dangerous Patient Exception to Psychotherapist – Patient Privilege: The *Tarasoff* Duty and the *Jaffee* Footnote' (1999) 74 Washington LR 33.

150. See *Irish Times*, 10 April 1981, p 13, col 2. The case was adjourned for six months so that the defendant could pay £100 each to the three girls.

151. *Kennedy and Arnold v Ireland* [1987] IR 587.

152. *McGee v AG* [1974] IR 284.

153. [1984] IR 36.

**[37.61]** Let us refer briefly to some of the milestones in the developing case law, though we would hesitate to suggest that there is a discernible orderly progression of judicial thought on the subject. In truth, it is a concept that is intensely responsive to intuitive, cultural and normative shifts. The courts have yet to construct an elaborate philosophical theory of privacy as a crucial aspect of the relationship between the individual, the State and the law.

## Privacy in Marriage, Intimate Conduct (Sexual and Otherwise) and the Termination of Life

**[37.62]** In *McGee v AG*,[154] the Supreme Court recognised that married couples have a constitutional right to marital privacy, which entitles them to have access to contraceptives. Whilst three of the judges of the majority evinced some caution in expressing the scope of the right which was recognised for the first time in this decision, Budd J was not so circumspect. He stated:

> "Whilst the personal rights [of Article 40.3 of the Constitution] are not described specifically, it is scarcely to be doubted in our society that the right to privacy is universally recognised and accepted with possibly the rarest of exceptions ..."[155]

**[37.63]** It is significant that, in contrast to Budd J and the other members of the majority, who identified the right of marital privacy as a personal right protected under Article 40.3, Walsh J[156] located the right under Article 41.[157]

---

154. [1974] IR 284 (SC), analysed by O'Reilly (1977) 65 Studies 8; Binchy, (1977) 65 Studies 330; Binchy, *Ethical issues in Reproductive Medicine: A Legal Perspective,* Ch 9 of *Ethical Issues in Reproductive Medicine* Reidy ed, (1982) at 95-98; Dooley, (1974) 3 Social Studies 186; McMahon, 'The Law Relating to Contraception in Ireland', Ch 2 of Clarke, *Morality and the Law* (1982); Robinson, *The Protection of Human Rights in the Republic of Ireland*, Ch 60f; Campbell *Do We Need a Bill of Rights?* (1980), pp 71-73; von Prondzynski 'Natural Law and the Constitution' (1977) 1 DULJ 32. More generally, see Stephen & Kellogg *The Worlds Laws on Contraceptives* (1974) 22 Amer J of Comp L 615; Clarke, 'The Role of Natural Law in Irish Constitutional Law' (1982) 17 Ir Jur 187; Walsh 'The Judicial Power and the Protection of the Right to Privacy' [1977] DULJ 3. Prior to *McGee*, the courts had touched on privacy issues in a constitutional context in *The People (Attorney General) v O'Brien* [1965] IR 142 (SC) - privacy of the dwelling. *McMahon v AG* [1972] IR 69 (SC) - secrecy of the ballot.
155. [1974] IR at 322.
156. *Cf* The Hon Mr Justice Hamilton 'Matters of Life and Death' 65 Fordham LR 543 at 546, observing that Walsh J was "generally recognised as the intellectual leader of the Court at that time."
157. Walsh J considered that if (contrary to his view) a prohibition on the availability of contraceptives for use in marriage generally could be justified on the grounds of the exigencies of the common good, Article 40.3 could permit the State to make special exemptions in favour of married persons for whom conception could more than ordinarily endanger their lives: [1984] IR at 315. In *Maher v Collins* [1975] IR 232 (SC), a decision on the assessment of damages in proceedings for criminal conversation handed down by the Supreme Court a year after *McGee*, O'Higgins CJ (Walsh, Budd, Henchy and Griffin JJ concurring) observed that "... the wrong done to the plaintiff was largely concerned with the invasion of the privacy of his marriage ...". Although he made no reference to the constitutional dimension, it seems reasonable to hypothesise that the language of the Court's judgments in *McGee* had some influence on the Chief Justice's choice of phrase. It is interesting to note that O'Higgins CJ considered that "the wrong done to the plaintiff" - the defendant's consensual sexual intercourse with the plaintiff's wife – "was largely concerned with the invasion of the privacy of his marriage and with the insult thereby caused to his honour as a husband ...". Marital privacy here has a curiously unilateral quality: it relates to the *husband's* marriage and his honour.

**[37.64]** In *Murphy v Attorney General*,[158] where the plaintiffs successfully attacked the constitutional validity of legislative provisions imposing greater tax obligations on married couples than those who cohabited outside marriage, one of the arguments made – and rejected – in the High Court and not pursued in the Supreme Court was that the legislative provisions infringed the constitutional right of each spouse to the privacy of his or her income by obliging him or her to disclose to the other spouse particulars of his or her income.

**[37.65]** Hamilton J was of opinion that the Constitution did not guarantee any such privacy to either the husband or the wife. He observed:

> "Though *McGee v The Attorney General*[159] was cited in support of this submission, it is clear that the right of privacy therein referred to was the right to the privacy of the relationships which did not impinge upon the common good or destroy or endanger human life. When a man and a woman marry, they form a family which is a unit of society regarded by the Constitution as the natural primary and fundamental unit group of that society which has rights as such which the State cannot control. As members of that unit and that society, they acquire under the Constitution a special status in that society but must respect the common good of that society.
>
> The common good of that society require that revenue be raised for the purposes of that society by taxation and that information be made available for the purposes of determining the amount payable by any individual. The Constitution does not guarantee the right to either spouse not to disclose to his or her spouse the source or amount of his or her income for the purpose of making such returns."[160]

**[37.66]** This analysis throws little light on the nature of the right to marital privacy recognised in *McGee* - a scarcely surprising consequence of the decidedly curious contention on behalf of the plaintiffs that this right implied a right of one spouse to have secrets from the other. It would perhaps have been sufficient for Hamilton J to have rejected the argument on the basis that marital privacy is concerned with the intimate relationship between spouses rather than the construction of barriers to intimacy.[161]

**[37.67]** The first attempt to convince a court that it should interpret *McGee* as recognising, an individual,[162] rather than simply a marital, right to privacy occurred in *The State*

158. [1982] IR 241 (SC).

159. [1982] IR 241.

160. [1982] IR 241.

161. This is not, of course, to suggest that personal privacy has *no* place in even the most intimate and committed relationship which marriage constitutes: spouses are entitled not to hare *some* secrets with each other. The point of present relevance is that keeping details of ones income from one's spouse is scarcely such an instance. It is worth noting that, in *Madigan v Attorney General* [1986] ILRM 136 (HC), OHanlon J observed that he "doubt[ed] very much" whether a statutory provision compelling the disclosure of information about one's income where this was relevant to determine another's tax liability would infringe any constitutional guarantee.

162. It is, of course, true that the right of marital privacy, recognised in *McGee*, was characterised as a *personal* right by three judges of the majority. One can, however, draw a meaningful distinction between a personal and an individual right. A personal right may be one grounded in relationship and inter-connectedness, as is the right to marital privacy. An individual right (which of course is another instance of a personal right) lacks this relational grounding.

*(Richardson) v Govenor of Mounjoy Prison*,[163] where a female prisoner argued that the absence of a lock on the toilet door violated her right to privacy. Barrington J stated:

> "I would be prepared to accept that such a right exists but it is a right circulated and limited by the institutional environment in which a prisoner must live, and by consideration of security and good order in the prison."[164]

On this basis the claim failed.

**[37.68]** *Richardson* is scarcely an authority of any significant weight on the juridical source and character of the asserted constitutional right to privacy. The facts clearly related to an aspect of personal privacy where – security considerations aside – one might expect the law to come to the aid of those exposed to unnecessary or prurient intrusion. To say this does not commit one to the far broader proposition that the Constitution recognises a generic right to privacy: nor can it follow that such a generic right to privacy is necessarily implied by the judicial recognition of a right to martial privacy.

**[37.69]** In *Norris v AG*[165] the two dissenting members of the Supreme Court went considerably further than the holding in *McGee* by recognising a right of privacy not limited to one arising out of marriage. The plaintiff, who stated in evidence that he was exclusively, congenitally and irreversibly homosexual, contended that statutory prohibitions on buggery[166] and acts of gross indecency between males[167] were inconsistent with his personal rights, guaranteed under Article 40.3 of the Constitution.[168] By a majority, the Supreme Court affirmed McWilliam J in rejecting his challenge.

**[37.70]** The case raises several issues of considerable legal interest. Our discussion must be focused on the question of the plaintiff's asserted right of privacy. It may be useful to quote *in extenso* the disposition by the majority of this aspect of the plaintiff's claim. O'Higgins CJ (with whom Finlay P and Griffin J concurred) said:

> "[T]he plaintiff says that the continued operation of such laws was inconsistent with a right of privacy which he enjoys. Here, in so far as the law and the State are concerned, he asserts a no go area in the field of private morality. I do not accept this view either as a general philosophical proposition concerning the purpose of law or as having particular reference to a right of privacy under the Constitution. I regard the State as having an interest in the general moral well-being of the community and as being entitled, where it is practicable to

163. [1980] ILRM 82 (HC).

164. [1980] ILRM 82.

165. [1984] IR 36 (SC 1983 affg HC, 1980).For critical analysis, see Gearty, (1983) 5 DULJ (ns) 264. A wide-ranging analysis of *Norris*, placing the decision in a broad cultural context, is provided by Quinn, 'The Lost Language of the Irish Gay Male: Textualization in Ireland's Law and Literature (or The Most Hidden Ireland)' (1995) 26 Columbia Human Rights LR 553.

166. Offences Against the Person Act 1861, s 61; also s 62, penalising attempted buggery and assault with intent to commit buggery, and any indecent assault on a male person.

167. Criminal Law Amendment Act 1935, s 11.

168. The plaintiff also based an argument on Article 40.1, not of present relevance. As regards Article 40.3, the plaintiff asserted a right of privacy:

> "identified by the Supreme Court in *McGee v AG*, and not confined to the right of marital privacy but one of the personal rights of the citizen which encompasses but is not exhausted by the right of a husband and wife to privacy in their sexual relations within marriage":

[1984] IR 36 at 96.

> do so, to discourage conduct which is morally wrong and harmful to a way of life and to values which the State wishes to protect.
>
> A right of privacy or, as it has been put, a right to be let alone can never be absolute. There are many acts done in private which the State is entitled to condemn, whether such be done by an individual on his own or with another. The law has always condemned abortion, incest, suicide attempts, suicide pacts, euthanasia or mercy killing. These are prohibited simply because they are morally wrong and regardless of the fact, which may exist in some instances,, that no harm or injury to others is involved. With homosexual conduct, the matter is not so simple or clear. Such conduct is, of course, morally wrong, and has been so regarded by mankind through the centuries. It cannot be said of it, however, as the plaintiff seeks to say, that no harm is done if it is conducted in private by consenting males. Very serious harm may in fact be involved. Such conduct, although carried on with full consent, may lead a mildly homosexually orientated person into a way of life from which he may never recover. As already indicated, known consequences are frustration, loneliness and even suicide. In addition, it is clearly established that an increase in the practice of homosexuality amongst males increases the incidence of all forms of venereal disease, including the incapacitating and often fatal disease of syphilis. Surely, in the light of such possible consequences, no one could regard with equanimity the freeing of such conduct from all legal restraints with the certain result that it would increase and its known devotees multiply. These, however, are not the only considerations.[169]
>
> There is the effect of homosexuality on marriage. As long ago as 1957 the Wolfenden Committee acknowledged, in relation to Great Britain, the serious harm such conduct caused to marriage not only in turning men away from it as a partnership in life but also in breaking up existing marriages. That was the conclusion reached as to the state of facts before the criminal sanctions were removed. One can only suspect that, with the removal of such sanctions and with encouragement thereby given to homosexual conduct, considerably more harm must have been caused in Great Britain to marriage as an institution. In Ireland, in this respect, the State has a particular duty. Article 41, s 3, sub-s 1, of the Constitution provides: 'The State pledges itself to guard with special care the institution of Marriage, on which the Family is founded, and to protect it against attack'. Surely, a law which prohibits acts and conduct by male citizens of a kind known to be particularly harmful to the institution of marriage cannot be regarded as inconsistent with a Constitution containing such a provision.
>
> On the ground of the Christian nature of our State and on the grounds that the deliberate practice of homosexuality is morally wrong, that it is damaging to the health both of individuals and the public and, finally that it is potentially harmful to the institution of marriage, I can find no inconsistency with the Constitution in the laws which make such conduct criminal. It follows, in my view, that no right of privacy, as claimed by the plaintiff, can prevail against the operation of such criminal sanctions."[170]

**[37.71]** This passage requires close analysis, in view of the fact that the European Court of Human Rights held[171] in favour of the plaintiff under the European Convention on Human Rights. It seems that at no point did the majority expressly concede that the plaintiff's asserted right of privacy had any constitutional status. The last paragraph might at first suggest some rather tentative recognition but a closer analysis appears consistent with the rejection of any such status. O'Higgins CJ, states that the four factors mentioned in this

169. O'Higgins CJ, Finlay P and Griffin J; McCarthy and Henchy JJ dissenting.

170. [1984] IR 36 at 64-65.

171. *Norris v Ireland* (1988) 13 EHRR 186. See further fn 179 below.

paragraph were "the grounds" for finding no inconsistency with the Constitution; it followed that the "no right of privacy, as claimed by the plaintiff", could prevail against the operation of the criminal sanctions. If this asserted right of privacy had *any* significant constitutional status, it could scarcely have been dismissed in this fashion. It would have been necessary to weigh it against the four factors identified by the Chief Justice. No such weighing of competing interests was made; reference to the four factors was apparently sufficient to warrant a finding of consistency of the statutory provisions with the Constitution.

**[37.72]** Since O'Higgins CJ did not exclude in express terms the possibility of there being *some* constitutionally-based right to privacy, it is worth considering what type of right this may be if it is to be consistent with the judgment of the majority in *Norris*. It seems that the only type of right capable of recognition in accordance with that judgment would be one not impinging improperly on the four factors identified by the Chief Justice. Thus, for example a constitutionally-protected right to privacy in relation to communications by telephone or letter would seem perfectly reconcilable with the majority judgement, provided, of course, no other constitutionally-protected right of another was improperly interfered with, and provided none of the four factors was improperly frustrated. It should, however, be noted that O'Higgins CJ did not make it clear whether it was the *combination* of the grounds he mentioned which made them sufficient to withstand the challenge of an asserted right of privacy or whether each on its own had this force.

**[37.73]** The dissenting judges took a different view. Henchy J said:

> "That a right of privacy inheres in each citizen by virtue of his human personality, and that such right is constitutionally guaranteed as one of the unspecified personal rights comprehended by Article 40, s 3 are propositions that are well attested by previous decisions of this Court."[172]

**[37.74]** What required to be decided was whether that right of privacy, construed in the context of the Constitution as a whole and given its true evaluation or standing in the hierarchy of constitutional priorities, excluded the impugned statutory provisions as being inconsistent with the Constitution.

**[37.75]** Amongst the citizen's personal rights, Henchy J discerned:

> "a complex of rights which vary in nature, purpose and range (each necessarily being a facet of the citizen's core of individuality within the constitutional order) and which may be compendiously referred to as the right of privacy".[173]

Henchy J noted that a constitutional right to marital privacy had been recognized and implemented by the Court in *McGee*. He observed:

> "There are many other aspects of the right of privacy, some yet to be given judicial recognition. It is unnecessary for the purpose of this case to explore them. It is sufficient to say that they would all appear to fall within a secluded area of activity or non-activity which may be claimed as necessary for the expression of an individual personality, for purposes not always necessarily moral or commendable but meriting recognition in circumstances which

172. [1984] IR 36 at 71.

173. [1984] IR 36 at 71-72.

> do not engender considerations such as State security, public order or morality, or other essential components of the common good."[174]

**[37.76]** Henchy J's discussion of the privacy issue provokes a number of comments. First, it is difficult to identify which "previous decisions" of the Supreme Court had recognised that a constitutionally guaranteed "right of privacy inheres in each citizen by virtue of his human personality". *McGee* was the only case in which the Court had addressed the issue and there it had recognised a right, not of privacy, but of marital privacy. At a stroke, Henchy J sought to transform that distinctive right, premised on an irrevocable interpersonal commitment, into a right lacking any such distinctive attributes.[175]

**[37.77]** Secondly, it is worth considering the possible limits of a right of privacy which would embrace "a secluded area" of conduct which "may be claimed as necessary for the expression of an individual personality", even though this is "for purposes not always necessarily moral or commendable", provided its recognition would not endanger the common good. The tenor of Henchy J's judgment is that he envisaged that the right did not extend beyond "the expression of those primal urges, functions and aspirations which are integral to the human condition of certain kinds of homosexuals"[176] It is far from clear that he would be willing to confer constitutional status on conduct lacking the quality of a "primal urge".

**[37.78]** McCarthy J, also dissenting, accepted that the right to privacy could be defined as "the right to be let alone". As far as he was concerned:

> "[t]he right to privacy is not in issue; the issue is the extent of that right or the extent of the right to be left alone".[177]

**[37.79]** McCarthy J sought to resolve that question exclusively in terms of an examination of the circumstances that would justify the State in interfering with "a claim to the right to perform sexual acts or to give expression to sexual desires or needs in private between consenting adults, male or female."[178] The picture that emerges is of a right of the broadest

---

174. [1984] IR 36 at 72.

175. In the United States, the transformation, in *Eisenstadt v Baird* (1972) 405 US 438, of the right to marital privacy recognised in *Griswold v Connecticut* (1965) 381 US 479 into a right of individual privacy gave rise to much discussion: *Cf*, eg, Smith 'The Constitution and Autonomy', (1982) 60 Tex LR 175 at 189-190, 197; Jones 'Comment', (1973) 3 NYULRL & Soc Charge 56 at 69; Noonan 'The Family and the Supreme Court' (1973) 23 Cath ULR 255 at 266; Rehnquist 'Is an Expanded Right to Privacy Consistent with Fair and Effective Law Enforcement? Or: Privacy, You've Come a Long Way, Baby' (1074) 23 Kan LR 1. The Court in *Eisenstadt* unconvincingly disguised a radical change of values as a matter of logical deduction:

> "It is true that in *Griswold* the right of privacy in question inhered in the marital relationship. Yet the marital couple is not an independent entity with a mind and heart of its own, but an association of two individuals each with a separate intellectual and emotional makeup."

This attempt to individualise the marital relationship seems inconsistent with the appraoch of the Irish Supreme Court in *In re the Matrimonial Home Bill 1993* [1994] IR 305, which regarded the right of spouses to make decisions within the authority of the marital family as "superior to all positive law". clearly these decisions cannot simply be broken down into the decisions cannot simply be broken down into the decisions of two individuals with regard to their marital relationship.

176. [1984] IR 36 at 79.

177. [1984] IR 36 at 101.

178. [1984] IR 36 at 102.

generality with no clearly distinctive features. In contrast to Henchy J, McCarthy J appeared to envisage the concept extending to conduct freely chosen as well as acts springing from "primal urges".

**[37.80]** *Norris* left the law in an unsettled state. As has been noted, the majority did not expressly accept that the plaintiff's asserted right of privacy had a constitutional status; in stark contrast, the dissenting judges warmly embraced it.[179]

**[37.81]** After *McGee*[180] and *Norris*,[181] it might have been expected that analysis of the constitutional aspects of privacy might in time gravitate to the context of abortion, since this is very much the international trend.[182] That did not happen, however, because the Eighth Amendment to the Constitution forestalled such a development.[183]

**[37.82]** A separate life-and-death issue has been addressed by the Supreme Court. This arose in *Re a Ward of Court*,[184] where a family sought permission for the withdrawal of nutrition through a tube from the ward, a member of the family who had for many years

---

179. As a result of the Supreme Court decision, Mr Norris took successful proceedings against Ireland in the European Court of Human Rights: *Norris v Ireland* (1988) 13 EHRR 186. The Court, by eight votes to six, held that the statutory provisions criminalising homosexual conduct, even by consenting adults in private, were an unjustifiable interference with Mr Norris's right to respect for his private life, in breach of Article 8 of the European Convention. The case fell squarely within the Courts earlier holding in *Dudgeon v United Kingdom* (1983) 5 EHRR 373. The Criminal Law (Sexual Offences) Amendment Act 1993 removed the criminal provisions found to offend Article 8. In the United States of America, the Supreme Court, in a plurality decision, upheld a Georgia statute criminalising homosexual conduct: *Bowers v Hardwick* (1986) 478 US 186, analysed by Rich, (1988) 22 Ga LR 773. It specifically rejected the argument that earlier cases stood for the proposition that "the conduct between consenting adults is constitutionally insulated from state proscription". For analysis of the issue from the standpoints of comparative and international law, see Wintemute, *Sexual Orientation and Human Rights: The United States Constitution, The European Convention and the Canadian Charter* (1995); Helfer & Miller 'Sexual Orientation and Human Rights: Towards a United States and Transnational Jurisprudence' (1996) 9 Harv Human Rights J 61; Thornton 'The New International Jurisprudence on the Right to Privacy: A Head-On Collision with Bowers v Hardwick' (1995) 58 Albany LR 725; Catania 'The Unusual Declaration of Human Rights and Sodomy Laws: A Federal Common Law Right to Privacy for Homosexuals Based on Customary International Law', (1994) 31 Amer Crim LR 289; Wilets 'International Human Rights Law and Sexual Orientation' (1994) 18 Hastings International & Comp LR 1; Dubber 'Note: Homosexual Privacy Rights Before the United States Supreme Court and the European Court of Human Rights: A Comparison of Methodologies' (1990) 27 Stan JIL 189.

180. *McGee v AG* [1974] IR 284.

181. *Norris v Ireland* (1988) 13 EHRR 186.

182. The most important decisions include *Roe v Wade* (1973) 410 US 113; *R v Morgantaler* (1988) 44 DLR (4th) 385 (SC, Can). See further Thompson 'International Protection of Womens Rights: An Analysis of *Open Door Counselling Ltd and Dublin Well Woman Centre v Ireland*' (1994) 12 Boston U Intl LJ 371.

183. The Amendment (Article 40.3.3° in its original formulation) provided as follows:

> "The State acknowledges the right to life of the unborn and, with due regard to the equal right to life of the mother, guarantees in its laws to respect and, so far as practicable, by its laws to defend and vindicate that right."

The interpretation of Article 40.3.3° by the Supreme Court in the tragic case of *Attorney General v X* [1992] 1 IR 1 was highly controversial and provoked much international discussion.

184. [1995] 2 ILRM 401 (SC), analysed by Byrne & Binchy, *Annual Review of Irish Law 1995*, pp 156-181. Whyte 'The Right to Die under the Irish Constitution' (1997) 3 Eur Public L 235;

been very nearly in a fully persistent or permanent vegetative state but who nonetheless retained a minimal cognitive capacity. Lynch J granted the requested approval and the Supreme Court, by a majority,[185] affirmed.

**[37.83]** Lynch J referred to privacy a couple of times in his judgment. He expressed the view that, where a person who was being tortured, the torture might reach such a degree of cruelty, with no prospect of relief, that "there must come a time when in the interests of privacy, dignity or autonomy, the victim would be within his rights in ending his own life if he had the means of doing so even before the enactment of the Criminal Law (Suicide) Act 1993",[186] which removed the criminal sanction from suicide and attempted suicide.[187] Later in his judgment Lynch J observed that:

> "it has long been accepted that a competent terminally ill patient may elect not to allow or accept treatment which may prolong his life and, if incompetent, that the medical carers, in agreement with the patients family, may adopt the same course. This illustrates that, despite the fact that the right to life ranks first in the hierarchy of personal rights, it may nevertheless be subjected to the citizen's right of autonomy or self-determination or privacy or dignity, call it what you will, whether exercised by himself, if competent, or on his behalf by agreement between carers and family all acting *bona fide* in the patients best interests."[188]

**[37.84]** On appeal, a number of judges of the Supreme Court echoed this language. Hamilton CJ stated that "[T]he right to privacy is one of the unenumerated personal rights recognised by Article 40.3 which the courts have identified."[189] He reasoned as follows. A terminally ill person's right to privacy justifies him or her in foregoing or discontinuing life-saving treatment.[190] The ward should be regarded as terminally ill because she would die within a short period of time if she were denied the benefit of the nourishment provided by the treatment that was being afforded her - the provision of food through the nasogastric tube constituting medical treatment rather than medical care. Article 40.1 of the Constitution required that the ward should not be deprived of "the opportunity to exercise or have exercised on her behalf, a right enjoyed by other citizens of the State"[191] to the autonomous decision to decline medical treatment:

> "The loss by an individual of his or her mental capacity does not result in any diminution of his or her personal rights recognised by the Constitution, including the right to life, the right to bodily integrity, the right to privacy, including self-determination, and the right to refuse medical care or treatment.
>
> The ward is entitled to have all these rights respected, defended, vindicated and protected from unjust attack and they are in no way lessened or diminished by reason of her incapacity.

---

184. (contd) O'Carroll 'The Right to Die: A Critique of the Supreme Court Judgment in "the *Ward* Case' (1995) 84 Studies 375; Tomkin & McAuley '*Re a Ward of Court*: Legal Analysis' (1995) 2 Medico-Legal J of IR 45; Feenan 'Death, dying and the Law' (1996) 14 Ir LT (ns) 90.
185. Hamilton CJ, O'Flaherty, Blayney and Denham JJ, Egan J dissenting.
186. High Court, 10 May 1995.
187. High Court, 10 May 1995.
188. High Court, 10 May 1995.
189. [1995] 2 ILRM 401 at 427.
190. [1995] 2 ILRM 401 at 427.
191. [1995] 2 ILRM 401 at 428.

> In the circumstances of this ward there is no conflict between the exercise of these rights and the right to life, which the State is by the Constitution obliged to respect, defend, vindicate and protect from unjust attack. Her right to life necessarily implies the right to die a natural death ...
>
> In the exercise of [wardship] jurisdiction, the first and paramount consideration is the well-being, welfare or interests of the ward."[192]

Hamilton CJ was satisfied that there was ample evidence to support Lynch J's authorisation to withdraw nutrition on the basis of the welfare test.

**[37.85]** O'Flaherty J also identified the right of a competent person to refuse medical treatment "even if it leads to death"[193] as "founded both on common law as well as the constitutional rights of bodily integrity and privacy."[194] He too considered that, in the case of an incompetent person, the court in wardship proceedings should apply a welfare test.

**[37.86]** Neither Hamilton CJ nor O'Flaherty J developed the analysis of the nature of the constitutional right to privacy beyond a formal recognition of its existence. They both referred to judicial precedent[195] that was far removed from the stark context of authorising a course of action that was intended to have the result of terminating a person's life.

**[37.87]** Denham J's discussion of privacy is far more radical. She observed that:

> "[p]art of the right to privacy is the giving or refusing of consent to medical treatment. Merely because medical treatment becomes necessary to sustain life does not mean that the right to privacy is lost, neither is the right lost by a person becoming insentient. Nor is the right lost if a person becomes insentient and needs medical treatment to sustain life and is cared for by people who can and wish to continue taking care of the person. Simply it means that the right may be exercised by a different process. The individual retains their personal rights.
>
> The right to privacy is not absolute. It has balanced against the State's duty to protect and vindicate life. However, ... the individual's right to privacy grows as the degree of bodily invasion increases.[196]
>
> The increasing personal right to privacy is in such a situation inconsistent with the defence and vindication of life being as far as practicable[197] and the protection being as best it may.[198]
>
> A constituent of the right of privacy is the right to die naturally, with dignity and with minimum suffering. This right is not lost to a person if they become incapacitated or insentient."[199]

**[37.88]** Denham J made it clear that, in applying the "best interests" test, the totality of the ward's situation, including constitutional right to privacy, autonomy, "dignity in life"[200] and "dignity in death"[201] had to be considered.

---

192. [1995] 2 ILRM 401 at 428-429.
193. [1995] 2 ILRM 401 at 431.
194. [1995] 2 ILRM 401 at 431.
195. *Ryan v Attorney General* [1965] IR 294; *Kennedy v Ireland* [1987] IR 587.
196. Citing *In re Quinlan* (1976) 70 NJ 10 at 41.
197. Article 40.3.1 of the Constitution.
198. Article 40.3.2 of the Constitution.
199. [1995] 2 ILRM 401 at 460.
200. [1995] 2 ILRM 401 at 464. See Feldman 'Human Dingnity as a Legal Value' [1999] Pub L 682, [2000] Pub L 61.
201. [1995] 2 ILRM 401 at 464.

**[37.89]** Denham J's analysis of the character of the constitutional right to privacy is fuller than that of her judicial colleagues. What emerges is a strongly individualist norm in which choices affecting oneself must be respected by others even where this has damaging, or even lethal, consequences. The influence of Mill[202] and Hart on this philosophy is easy to discern.

**[37.90]** On this approach, the actions of the medical and nursing staff in seeking to provide nourishment to the ward by means of the tube are to be regarded as a highly invasive intrusion on the ward's bodily integrity. The ward's dignity – an aspect of privacy on Denham J's analysis – was compromised by her becoming "a passive prisoner of medical technology."[203]

**[37.91]** Outside the areas of sexual conduct and procreation our courts have yet to consider a full range of arguments relating to an asserted constitutional right to privacy. In *Murphy v PMPA Insurance Co*[204] the central question was whether legislation requiring vehicle insurers to give information to the Gardaí could oblige an insurance company to disclose confidential information about an insured person, a Garda, contained on his proposal form. Doyle J construed the statutory provisions in such a way as to protect this confidential information from disclosure. He noted that counsel for the insurers had "not prayed in aid the Constitution or the provisions which it makes for personal rights".[205] In the view of the Judge, the matter was properly dealt with "by applying what appear to be the applicable rules of natural justice".[206] To give effect to the regulation in the circumstances of the case "would entail an encroachment on the natural rights of the insured ... and also ... conflict with the obligation springing from a natural right which lies upon the insurers".[207] This is certainly the language at least of breach of confidence;[208] surely this also anticipates later constitutional developments.

**[37.92]** In *Kennedy and Arnold v Ireland*,[209] Hamilton P held that the tapping by the State of the plaintiffs' telephones infringed their right of privacy, and awarded them damages totalling £50,000. The matter attained a high public profile in January 1983 when the then Minister for Justice gave a press conference outlining the circumstances of the case. A press release of that time was accepted in evidence in the proceedings. This stated that the

---

202. See Kelly *A Short History of Western Legal Theory* (1992), pp 339-340, 443-447

203. [1995] 2 ILRM 401 at 461, citing Brennan J, in dissent, in *Cruzan v Director, Missouri; Department of Health* (1990) 110 S Ct 2841 at 2864.

204. [1978] ILRM 25 (HC).

205. [1978] ILRM 25 (HC).

206. [1978] ILRM 25 at 30.

207. [1978] ILRM 25.

208. [1978] ILRM 25 at 31.

209. *Cf* McDonald 'Some Aspects of the Law on Disclosure of Information' (1979) 14 Ir Jur. (ns) 229 at 240. As regards protection of minors from the glare of media publicity, Costello J, in *X v Flynn* High Court, 19 May 1996 took a paternalistic approach, while O'Hanlon H, in *M v Drury* [1994] 2 IR 8 adopted a much more robust attitude towards freedom of expression. The stark differences in the facts of the respective cases may go some way towards explaining this dissonance. See further Casey *Constitutional Law in Ireland* (3rd ed, 2000), pp 400-402 and O'Dell's magesterial analysis in 'when Two Tribes Go to War: Privacy Interests and Media Speech', Ch o9 of McGonagle ed, *Law and the Media* (1997).

normal precautions operated by Ministers for Justice had not been complied with in relation to the tapping of the plaintiffs' telephones. These normal requirements were that the tapping be for the investigation of serious criminal or subversive activity which could not be investigated by any other means. The fact that these criteria had not been observed in relation to the plaintiffs weighed heavily in the case against the State. Two of the plaintiffs were at the time of the tapping political correspondents with Irish national newspapers. The third was the wife of the second plaintiff.

**[37.93]** Hamilton P was not prepared to accept the argument of the State that the action of the Minister for Justice in ordering the warrants for tapping was merely improper, but not illegal. The President accepted the description of the right of privacy elaborated in the judgments of Henchy and McCarthy JJ in *Norris v Attorney General.*[210] He clearly felt that these statements were not affected by the fact that those judges were in a minority in holding that the plaintiff's asserted right to privacy had a constitutional status.

**[37.94]** Hamilton P elaborated on the right in the particular context of the instant case by stating that:

> "... the right to privacy includes the right to privacy in respect of telephonic conversations and the right to hold such conversations without deliberate, conscious and unjustified interference with, and intrusion thereon by servants of the State who listened to such conversations, recorded them, transcribed them and made the transcriptions thereof available to other persons."[211]

**[37.95]** The President placed great emphasis on the deliberate nature of the tapping in this case, and this emphasis bears close similarities to the approach taken by Costello J in *Hosford v J Murphy & Sons.*[212] It was because of the deliberate nature of the interference that the President awarded damages to the plaintiffs.

**[37.96]** Another question raised by the decision is the juridical nature of the right of action recognised by Hamilton P. It seems plain beyond argument that this was an infringement of the plaintiffs' constitutional right to privacy, rather than a new tort of invasion of privacy.

**[37.97]** On a wider level, the issue of telephone tapping of necessity always involves interference with the right of privacy. Hamilton P made clear his view that such interference could be justified either on the basis that it might have occurred accidentally, or by reference to "the exigencies of the common good". The matter is now subject to a legislative framework, commenced in the Interception of Postal Packets and Telcommunication Messages (Regulation) Act 1993.[213]

---

210. [1988] ILRM 472.

211. [1988] ILRM 472. *Kearney v Ireland* [1986] IR 116 (HC), it was held that the unauthorised interference with the right to communicate, by intercepting postal communications, amounted to an infringement of the plaintiffs constitutional right, under Article 40.3.1 (first recognised in *AG v Paperlink* [1984] ILRM 373 (HC)). In *Kearney,* the plaintiff was a prisoner. Costello J upheld the constitutionality of prison regulations, permitting prison personnel to read and censor letters sent from and to prisoners. Considerations of security and the need to protect the right of privacy of other prisoners justified these powers, in his view. Moreover, he was of opinion that if the power to read letters was not unconstitutional, the power to inspect for contraband could not be invalid.

212. [1988] ILRM 300 (HC).

213. The subject is dealt with comprehensively by Dr Eamonn Hall in Chapter 28 of his work, *The electronic Age: Telecommunication in Ireland* (1993). See further Casey, *Constitutional Law in Ireland* (1987) 311-312.

**[37.98]** A related problem derives from the storage of information on individuals. The Data Protection Act 1988 introduces safeguards in relation to information held on computer only, and does not apply in relation to "manually" held data.[214] The introduction of this legislation was attributable to economic and practical considerations, rather than the protection of privacy rights. The advent of the Financial Services Centre at the Custom House Docks site was a key factor. Whatever protection arises from this legislation, it might well be that, in the light of the *Kennedy* case, the Courts would view with favour an argument that the Constitution posits a right to accuracy in relation to information held on an individual, whether held on computer or otherwise. This would allow a person who claimed to be adversely affected by the holding of inaccurate information on a "manual" system to claim damages, even though falling outside the scope of the legislation.

214. See Byrne & Walsh (1986) 3 ILT (ns) 26. The Act is analysed by Byrne & Binchy, *Annual Survey of Irish Law 1988,* Telecommunications Chapter (1989). For a comprehensive analysis of the subject see Clark, *Data Protection Law in Ireland* (1990).

# Chapter 38

## Liability of the State[1]


I. Introduction ........ 1025
II. Act of State ........ 1030
III. Diplomatic Immunity ........ 1030
IV. Foreign Sovereigns ........ 1031
V. European Communities ........ 1033


### I. INTRODUCTION

**[38.01]** Until the Supreme Court decision in *Byrne v Ireland*[2] in 1969 the common view in Ireland was that the State was immune from tortious liability. This view was based on the assumption that the common law rule which granted immunity to the crown in England was carried over into Irish law in 1922. That the King can do no wrong became, in the Irish context, that the State can do no wrong. The harshness of this rule was mitigated somewhat in non-tortious actions against the State, as in such cases the citizen could be permitted to proceed against the State on a petition of right. This procedure, however, was not available in tort actions.[3] In concrete terms this meant that if a person was negligently run over by a State vehicle the injured party could have no action against the State for his injuries. Moreover, the injured party could not sue the appropriate minister on principles of vicarious liability, because it had been held that the relationship of master and servant did not exist between a State minister and other state servants: they were fellow employees of the State.[4] The injured person's only remedy, therefore, lay against the driver of the vehicle, who frequently presented a poor target for litigation.

**[38.02]** With the rise of the welfare state concept and the increasing tendency for the State to become concerned with the business of the nation and to become a large-scale employer

---

1. See generally Hogan & Morgan, *Administrative Law in Ireland* (3rd ed, 1998), Ch 17; Hogan & Whyte, *Kelly: The Irish Constitution* (3rd ed, 1994), pp 24-36, 1132-1155; Casey, *Constitutional Law in Ireland* (1987), pp 44-48, 61-62; Forde, *Constitutional Law of Ireland* (1987), pp 27-34; Hogan & Kerr 'Report paper presented to Colloquium at Birmingham University' 12-14 September 1985; O'Reilly & Collins *Civil Procedures and the State in Ireland: A Practitioner's Guide* (1990); *Government Liability Compensation and the Law of Civil Wrongs: Aspects of the Law of Ireland*; Osborough 'The Demise of the State's Immunity in Tort' (1973) 8 Ir Jur (ns) 275; Osborough 'The State's Tortious Liability: Further Reflections on *Byrne v Ireland*' (1976) 11 Ir Jur (ns) 11, 279 See also Kelly, *Fundamental Rights in the Irish Law and Constitution* 344 (2nd ed, 1967), p 344. Blachly & Oatman 'Approaches to Government Liability in Tort: A Comparative Survey' (1942) 9 L & CP 191.
2. [1972] IR 241.
3. Kelly, *Fundamental Rights in the Irish Law and Constitution* (2nd ed, 1967), p 345; *Byrne v Ireland* [1972] IR 241 at 266.
4. *Carolan v Minister for Defence* [1972] IR 62; *Nolan v Gilheaney* (1924) 58 ILTSJ 61; see also *Howard v Boner* (1943) 78 ILTR 3; *O'Connell v Kavanagh* (1958) 92 ILTR 10; *O'Hanlon v Minister for Posts and Telegraphs* [1960] Ir Jur Rep 25.

itself, the State's immunity in tort actions became noticeably anomalous. Moreover, the rationale of the common law rule, based as it was on a concept that the monarchy was the personification of the State, did not fit in well with the republican ideals that seemed to inspire both the 1922 and 1937 Irish Constitutions.

**[38.03]** Isolated legislative acts acknowledged the irregularity of the situation in some instances by making specific ministers liable in defined cases. Thus, s 170 of the Road Traffic Act 1933, provided that where injury was caused by negligent driving of a mechanically propelled vehicle belonging to the State, the injured person could sue the Minister for Finance. This section was replaced by s 116 of the Road Traffic Act 1961, and later by s 59 of the Civil Liability Act 1961, a provision which is still in force.[5] These isolated legislative provisions, although alleviating hardship in some cases, merely underlined the incongruity of the immunity in modern Ireland. The anachronistic nature of the immunity had been highlighted by the abandonment of state immunity in England in 1947.[6] *Ex gratia* awards could, it is true, be recommended by the Attorney General but these payments were in general unsatisfactory, both in practice and in principle.[7] By the 1960's legal opinion and some judicial dicta[8] seemed to suggest that the time was right for the immunity to be challenged. The accident which occurred to Mrs Kathleen Byrne when she fell into a trench excavated by post office workers in Bray, Co Wicklow, in 1965, provided a suitable fact situation from which the immunity could be squarely challenged. In her action for damages, Mrs Byrne named Ireland and the Attorney General as defendants.

**[38.04]** The Supreme Court in a four to one decision held that the former prerogative of immunity from suit[9] had ceased to exist in Ireland after the enactment of the 1922 Constitution (the Irish Free State Constitution) and was therefore not carried forward by Articles 49 and 50 of Bunreacht na hÉireann, 1937 (Constitution of Ireland, 1937). Furthermore, it held that the State was a juristic person[10] and vicariously liable for the torts of servants of the State committed in the course of their employment and that there was nothing to prevent the courts from entertaining such an action against the State in respect

5. For other examples see Workmans's Compensation Act 1934, s 64(1); Conditions of Employment Act 1936, s 6; Factories Act 1955, ss 3, 100 and 118.

6. Crown Proceedings Act 1947. The tendency in other countries too was to abandon the immunity. See Osborough (1976) 11 Ir Jur (ns) 284.

7. Osborough (1973) 8 Ir Jur (ns) 279.

8. See Kenny J in *Macauley v Minister for Posts and Telegraphs* [1966] IR 345 at 353.

9. See also *Comyn v Attorney General* [1950] IR 142; *Commissioners of Public Works v Kavanagh* [1962] IR 216.

10. On the prerogative of Treasure trove see *Webb v Ireland* [1988] 353 (SC), critically analysed by Kelly 'Hidden Treasure and the Constitution' (1988) 10 DULJ (ns) 5; Gwynn Morgan 'Constitutional Interpretation' (1988) 10 DULJ (ns) 24; Lenihan 'Royal Prerogatives and the Constitution' (1989) 24 Ir Jur (ns) 1; Costello 'The Expulsion of Prerogative Doctrine from Irish Law: Quantifying and Remedying the Loss of Royal Prerogative' (1997) 32 Ir Jur (ns) 145; Hogan & Morgan, *Administrative Law in Ireland* (3rd ed, 1998), pp 908-909. In *Geoghegan v Institute of Chartered Accountants* [1995] 3 IR 86 at 118 (SC), O'Flaherty J invoked Professor Kelly's article in support of his view that the parameters of *Byrne* and *Webb* "might need to be delineated" in some future case, raising a wider question concerning the royal prerogative. See Hogan & Morgan, *Administrative Law in Ireland* (3rd ed, 1998), pp 910-912; Byrne & Binchy, *Annual Review of Irish Law 1987*, pp 104-107.

of such tortious activities. Procedurely, it also held that the Attorney General was the proper person to represent the State in such proceedings.[11]

**[38.05]** The reasons given for abandoning the State's immunity were largely based on a reading of the Constitution itself. It was clear, for example, on a close reading of the Constitution that sovereignty in Ireland resides with the people and not with State. Moreover, there are several instances in the Constitution where limitations are placed on the State and which indicate that the State is not sovereign in the absolute sense of the word. In particular, the fundamental rights provisions in Articles 40-44 impose limits on the power of the State. Moreover, Article 5 which describes Ireland as a sovereign State must not be interpreted, according to the Supreme Court, as giving the State internal sovereignty (this rests with the people), but rather as giving the State external sovereignty in the limited sense that the State is not subject to the political power of other nations.

**[38.06]** The sweeping reform brought about by the *Byrne* decision, however, like many instances of judicial law reform, is not without problems. Professor Osborough in his thorough analyses[12] lists several difficulties that arise in the wake of the *Byrne* decision. First, the holding in *Byrne*, while clearly making the State vicariously liable for wrongs of its servants, did not, *expressis verbis* hold that the State is liable in other capacities, for example, as an occupier or as an employer. Legal developments since *Byrne*, however, make it plain beyond argument that the State is indeed liable in other capacities.[13] In *Byrne's* case the State's liability was vicarious, but, as Professor Casey observes:

> "presumably in an appropriate case a direct liability could attach so that, for example, the State could be held liable in the rule in *Rylands v Fletcher*. It may be anticipated that the State will be liable where a private individual or company would be; but its liability may well extend beyond this. For the State may injure persons in ways not open to private individuals or companies."[14]

The State may injure persons, for example, through its army or its police force or through the management of its schools or in the discharge of its many regulatory functions under the factories or health legislation,[15] and in some other ways which are not available to individuals as opportunities for wrongdoing.

---

11. The United States still retains the defence of sovereign immunity for tortious liability. The defence was, it is true, abrogated by the Federal Tort Claims Act 1946, but it still survives in certain cases, the most important of which are assault, battery and false imprisonment. See Berman 'Integrating Governmental and Officer Tort Liability' (1977) 77 Col LR 1175. As to the position of executive officials guilty of constitutional violations, see Freed (1977) 732; Northwestern ULR 526; Gregory (1980) 20 Santa Clara LR 453.
12. Osborough 8 Ir Jur (ns) 279 esp 11 Ir Jur (ns) at 12 *et seq*.
13. Eg *Ryan v Ireland* [1989] IR 177 (SC); *Healy v Minister for Defence* High Court, 7 July 1994.
14. Casey, *Constitutional Law in Ireland* (3rd ed, 2000), p 45. The distinction between direct and vicarious liability in this context is clearly analysed by Hogan & Morgan, *Administrative Law in Ireland* (3rd ed, 1998), p 918. See *Sinnott v Ireland and the AG* High Court, September 2000 (Barr J) and para **[1.09]** above.
15. Casey, *Constitutional Law in Ireland* (1987), p 45 citing Hogg, *The Liability of the Crown* (1971), p 77. For infringement of constitutional rights, see Ch 1 above. For negligent exercise of statutory powers, see Chs 13 and 19. For misfeasance of public office, see Ch 19 and Hogan & Morgan, *Administrative Law in Ireland* (3rd ed, 1998), pp 812-816.

**[38.07]** In this context it is worth examining the Supreme Court decision of *Ryan v Ireland*.[16] The plaintiff, a soldier, was injured by a mortar which hit the portacabin where he was billetted. He was serving as a volunteer with the United Nations International Force in the Lebanon and he claimed that he was negligently exposed to unnecessary risk by being placed in an unprotected billet close to a target area when an imminent attack was apprehended. Keane J withdrew the case from the jury and an appeal was taken to the Supreme Court. The defendants' initial submission that a member of the Defence Forces could not sue the State for any injury or damage caused to him in armed conflict, even if it were established that it was caused by the negligence of his superior officers, was later narrowed down to a submission that the State enjoyed immunity from suit at least in respect of negligence alleged during armed conflict, or "in a theatre of war". The Supreme Court held that no such immunity existed in the common law applicable in Ireland, and even if it did such an immunity would not be consistent with Articles 40.3.1°, 40.3.2° or Article 23 of the Constitution. Article 23 of the Constitution provides extensive powers to the Oireachtas to legislate in time of war and armed rebellion. In the light of this express provision it was difficult to sustain an alternative common law doctrine arising from the necessity to ensure the safety of the State. Moreover, serving with the United Nations Peacekeeping Force could not be considered as defending the State in time of war such as to trigger Constitutional protection under Article 23 of the Constitution. The Court also held that the plaintiff's superior officers owed him a duty:

> "to take such care for the safety of the plaintiff as is reasonable in all the circumstances of their relationship and the activity in which they were engaged."[17]

**[38.08]** Neither was the Court, in view of *O'Hanlon v ESB*,[18] willing to accept that the plaintiff consented to the risk of being unnecessarily exposed to injury by negligence. There was sufficient evidence, according to the Supreme Court, to go to the jury and accordingly a new trial was ordered.

**[38.09]** Of course the fact that the State has lost its immunity does not mean that it or its servants are invariably liable for damage it causes. In *Pine Valley Developments Ltd v Minister for the Environment*,[19] for example, the Supreme Court refused to award damages to the plaintiff who suffered loss when planning permission in respect of land was held to have been given *ultra vires* the Minister's power. No liability would be imposed where the Minister had acted in good faith and without negligence on the legal advice of his permanent legal advisers.

**[38.10]** The second point raised by Professor Osborough, that there may be some difficulty in identifying servants of the State for the purposes of rendering the State liable, is perhaps inevitable. All legal rules possess what has been termed a "penumbra of uncertainty", and judicial rules have, perhaps from the nature of things, a greater penumbra than legislative rules. For many years, in the ordinary rule of vicarious liability, the courts have had to cope with the twin concepts of "who is a servant?" and what is meant by the phrase "in the

16. *Ryan v Ireland* [1989] IR 177 and *Healy v Minister for Defence* High Court, 7 July 1994.

17. [1989] IR at 177 at 183.

18. [1969] IR 75 (SC).

19. [1987] IR 23 (SC) analysed by Hogan & Morgan, *Administrative Law in Ireland* (3rd ed, 1998), pp 919-920.

course of employment". In connection with State liability, although these problems may be more acute (for example, are judges[20], gardaí,[21] members of the defence forces, etc, servants of the State?), they hardly represent for the courts insoluble problems incapable of solution on an ad hoc basis.

**[38.11]** It would seem that the general liability imposed by *Byrne* on the State does not repeal the more limited statutory rights given under specific legislation against specified ministers. For example, the liability imposed on the Minister for Finance for the negligent use in the course of a person's duty or employment of a mechanically propelled vehicle belonging to the State, by s 59 of the Civil Liability Act 1961, still survives the *Byrne* decision. In such a case, therefore, the injured person can sue the State under the principle laid down in Byrne, and the Minister for Finance under s 59 of the Civil Liability Act 1961. Both rights coexist.[22]

**[38.12]** The question may be raised as to whether the State can by subsequent legislative act limit its liability for its torts? Would such a legislative limitation be constitutional? A definite answer to this question cannot be given at this stage. Suffice to say that the suggestion has been made that if the right to sue is a property right guaranteed by the Constitution[23] then an attempt by the State to limit its tortious liability by legislation might be unconstitutional.[24] Dr Hogan and Professor Morgan consider that legislation requiring

---

20. See now *Murray v Minister for Finance, Ireland & AG* Irish Times, 22 April 1983 (SC), p 11 reproduced in McMahon & Binchy, *A Casebook on the Irish Law of Torts* (2nd ed, 1991), p 667. *Dowman v Ireland* [1986] ILRM 111; *McIntyre v Lewis* [1991] 1 IR 121; *McHugh v Garda Commissioner* [1986] IR 228; *Walsh v Ireland* Supreme Court, 30 November 1994 analysed by Byrne & Binchy, *Annual Review of Irish Law 1994*, pp 461-462.
21. See *Ryan v Ireland* [1989] IR 177.
22. Osborough 11 Ir Jur (ns) at 300. Double recovery will not, of course, be allowed. See *Parkes v Minister for Finance* (1979) 113 ILTR 118 (CC). Driver during employment drove outside area to attend his sick wife. Minister not liable. In *Murray v Minister for Finance Ireland & AG* Irish Times 22 April 1983 (SC) a garda crashed a squad car in the following circumstances. He had been on duty at Blarney coursing meeting where there was evidence that he had consumed a lot of alcohol. He was to go off duty at 6 pm and the collision occurred at 6.20 pm when he was driving the squad car in the direction of Cork away from his station. The Supreme Court held the High Court was wrong in letting the case go to the jury At this time the Garda was not acting "in the course of his duty or employment".
23. But see on this *Moynihan v Greensmyth* [1977] IR 55.
24. Osborough 11 Ir Jur (ns) at 304 *et seq*. The Postal and Telecommunications Act 1983, ss 64 and 88 confer a wide-ranging immunity on An Post and Bord Telecom Éireann in respect of injury caused by the failure and delay in operating postal services and telecommunications. See also Fire Services Act 1981, s 36 discussed para **[26.26]** above. Section 61 of the Safety Health and Welfare at Work Act 1989 confers absolute immunity on the Safety Authority and enforcing agencies for failure to perform or comply with any of the functions imposed by the legislation on them. For analysis of the constitutional validity of this section see Byrne 'Annotation to the Act' [1989] ICLSA. A similar absolute immunity is conferred by the Environment Protection Agency Act 1992, s 15 on the Agency. Qualified statutory immunity on regulatory authorities was favoured in the Investment Intermediaries Act 1995, s 53; the Stock Exchange Act 1995, s 53(1) and the Irish Takeover Panel Act 1997, s 17. Hogan & Morgan, *Administrative Law in Ireland* (3rd ed, 1998), p 808 consider that this strategy "is more likely to be in accordance with the (qualified) guarantee of rights conferred by the Constitution than is the absolute immunity contained in the 1989 Act"

injured parties to sue the Minister for Finance, and not the State, or imposing a special limitation period on actions against the State "would not unfairly impinge on a person's right to litigate a justiciable controversy".[25] They doubt, however, whether legislation placing an upper limit on the *quantum* of damages recoverable actions against the State or preceding recovery in respect of certain types of economic loss which were otherwise recoverable, would survive constitutional challenge.[26] In *The State (Sheehan) v The Government of Ireland*,[27] an attempt to challenge the immunity conferred on road authorities for damages caused as a result of the failure of adequately maintaining public roads (ie non-feasance) failed in the Supreme Court. This common law immunity had been removed by s 60 of the Civil Liability Act 1961, but the provision was not to come into operation until a date was fixed by government order. The prosecutor maintained that there was an obligation to bring in the order within a reasonable time and that a delay of more than 25 years was unreasonable. The High Court (Costello J) agreed with the prosecutor but the Supreme Court reversed, largely on the basis that the wording of the section could be interpreted as giving the Government a wide discretion as to when the order had to be introduced.

## II. Act of State

**[38.13]** There is one case where the State's actions although apparently tortious are, however, not justicable by the courts, that is, where the act complained of is an "Act of State". An "Act of State" here has been defined as:

> "as an act of the executive as a matter of policy performed in the course of its relation with another State including its relations with the subjects of the State, unless they are temporarily within the allegiance of the [State]."[28]

**[38.14]** At common law executive policy actions of this nature could not be reviewed by the courts. It should be noted, however, that the immunity extended only to dealings with another State or its subjects, and then, only when they were not within the jurisdiction, and it did not apply to the State's actions against its own citizens wherever committed.[29]

## III. Diplomatic Immunity[30]

**[38.15]** The Diplomatic Relations and Immunities Act 1967 contains the present law relating to diplomatic immunities and privileges. Generally speaking the Act gives force of law in the State to certain international conventions including the Vienna Convention on Diplomatic Relations 1961, and the Vienna Convention on Consular Relations 1963 which

---

25. Hogan & Morgan, *Administrative Law in Ireland* (3rd ed, 1998), p 918. Perhaps the special limitation period would be regarded as unacceptable since it would substantively diminish the plaintiff's right to litigate.
26. Hogan & Morgan, *Administrative Law in Ireland* (3rd ed, 1998), p 918.
27. [1987] IR 550.
28. 7 Halsbury's Laws of England (3rd ed), p 279.
29. See generally *Johnstone v Pedlar* [1921] 2 AC 262; *AG v Nissan* [1970] AC 179; see further Binchy, *Irish Conflicts of Law* (1988), pp 171-172.
30. See Binchy, *Irish Conflicts of Law* (1988), pp 178-181.

are reproduced in schedules to the Act. The Act also deals with the immunities and privileges of various international organisations and their officers.

**[38.16]** The common law immunities, which were very comprehensive in the privileges and immunities they conferred and in the class of person to whom they extended, are now contracted to more realistic dimensions. Full personal immunity (civil and criminal) will now be accorded only to members of the diplomatic staff. There are three exceptions to this rule and they relate to (i) real actions relating to private immoveable property, (ii) private succession actions, whether the diplomatic agent is involved as executor, administrator, heir, etc, and (iii) actions relating to a professional or commercial activity exercised outside the official's functions. In these cases even a diplomat cannot plead immunity. Technical and administrative staff attached to the mission have full immunity (civil and criminal) except for acts performed outside the course of their duties; for these they are civilly liable. Lastly, service staff are immune for official acts, but are liable both criminally and civilly for acts performed outside the course of their duties. Generally speaking one may say that total immunity is now confined to the important members of the mission, and as one moves away from the central staff to the peripheral staff the immunities weaken, especially in respect of civil accountability for acts committed outside the course of their duties.

**[38.17]** In *Norton v General Accident, Fire and Life Assurance Co*[31] Maguire J accepted the proposition, already established in English cases[32] that diplomatic privilege was an exemption from local jurisdiction only and not from legal responsibility. The action arose out of an accident involving a diplomat who had left the country.[33] Section 78, sub-s 1(d) of the Road Traffic Act 1933 provided that in certain circumstances an injured person might apply to the court to proceed directly against the insurers or guarantors. The court might allow such proceedings where:

> "the court is satisfied that such owner or driver is not in Saorstát Éireann, or cannot be found, or cannot be served with the process of such court, or that it10.6 is for any other reason just and equitable ..."

The court allowed the proceedings on the ground that it would be "just and equitable" in the circumstances.[34] The diplomatic privilege did not exempt the diplomat from legal responsibility; the privilege was essentially a procedural or jurisdictional one and the statutory provision enabled the court to get around this. Since the privilege existed for the benefit of diplomats there was no reason why it should benefit insurers.

## IV. Foreign Sovereigns

**[38.18]** At common law foreign states and heads of foreign states have traditionally enjoyed immunity for their actions,[35] and since this immunity was based on a generally

31. (1940) 74 ILTR 123.
32. *Dickinson v Del Solar*; *In re Mobile and General Insurance Company Ltd* [1930] 1 KB 376.
33. The action was originally taken while the diplomat was in the country but was discontinued. It was recommenced later when the diplomat had left.
34. See now s 76(1)(d) of the Road Traffic Act 1961 for a similar provision.
35. See generally Binchy, *Irish Conflicts of Law* (1988), pp 173-178; Fitzmaurice 'State Immunity from Proceedings in Foreign Courts' (1933) 14 BYIL; Sinclair 'The Law of Sovereign Immunity: Recent Developments' [1980] 1 Recueil des cours 113 and the Australian Law Reform Commission's Report No 24, *Foreign State Immunity* (1984).

accepted principle of international law, it seems clear that this is the present law in Ireland too. Any suggestion that this immunity might not have survived the adoption of the 1937 Constitution was clarified in favour of the immunity by dicta in *Zarine v Owners of SS "Ramava"*.[36] The more recent jurisprudence, however, suggests that the immunity which foreign States enjoy does not extend to commercial or trading activities conducted by a sovereign State.[37] The immunity, where it exists, may be waived.[38]

**[38.19]** The possibility that the doctrine of sovereign immunity is subject to broad qualification has been raised by the *Pinochet* extradition case,[39] which held that in criminal proceedings for torture, the doctrine should not stand in the way of extradition. If one changes the context to civil proceedings for damages for battery, assault and intentional infliction of emotional suffering taken by a plaintiff who has been tortured, the *Pinochet* case is a clear precedent for an Irish court to revisit the absoluteness of the immunity. In this context it may be called on to consider the argument that sovereign immunity should not be unthinkingly conceded where the plaintiff claims compensation for the violation of a constitutionally protected right, such as the right to bodily integrity, which is recognised in international conventions as a human right inherent in persons by reason of their humanity.[40]

**[38.20]** It is worth noting that the immunity accorded to foreign sovereigns is greater than that allowed to Ireland itself[41] or to the President under the Constitution. Article 13.8.1° of the Constitution provides that:

> "The President shall not be answerable to either House of the Oireachtas or to any court for the exercise and performance of the powers and functions of his office or for any act done or purporting to be done by him in the exercise and performance of these powers and functions."

**[38.21]** It can be seen from this that the immunity is confined to official functions and does not extend to private acts or wrongs committed by the President. The President is also subject to the impeachment process described in Article 12.10 of the Constitution.

---

36. [1942] IR 148.

37. See Binchy, *Irish Conflicts of Law* (1988), pp 174-175. *Government of Canada v Employment Appeals Tribunal* [1992] 2 IR 489 (SC) analysed by Byrne & Binchy, *Annual Review of Irish Law 1991*, pp 90-92; *McEllhinney v Williams* [1996] 1 ILRM 276 (SC); *Fusco v O'Dea* [1994] 2 IR 93 (SC); *Schmidt v Home Secretary of UK* Supreme Court, 24 April 1997; *Herron v Ireland* Supreme Court, 5 December 1997.

38. *Saorstát & Continental Steamship Co De las Morenas* [1945] IR 291 at 299 (SC).

39. *R v Bow Street Metropolitan Stipendiary Megistrate ex parte Pinochet Ugarte (No 3)* [1999] 2 All ER 97 (HL).

40. In *McElhinney v Williams* [1996] 1 ILRM 276 (SC), the plaintiff alleged that a British soldier, while within the State, had attempted to fire a loaded gun at him. Hamilton CJ, (O'Flaherty and Blayney JJ concurring), responded as follows to his argument that the doctrine of sovereign immunity should not apply to a claim for interference with his constitutional right to bodily integrity: "I am satisfied that the principle of sovereign immunity does not contravene any constitutional rights of the appellant." The breadth of and lack of supporting analysis for this proposition suggest that it was based on the view that no violation of a person's constitutional rights, however egregious, could prevent the application of the immunity.

41. *Byrne v Ireland* [1972] IR 241.

## V. European Communities[42]

**[38.22]** The European Communities and employees thereof enjoy in the territories of the Member States such privileges and immunities as are necessary for the performance of their tasks. These immunities, which in the main part are the customary privileges and immunities, are set out for the most part in the Protocol on Privileges and Immunities of the European Communities. Apart from conferring immunity on Members of the Assembly in respect of opinions expressed by them in performance of their duties,[43] the Protocol provides that officials and other servants of the Communities shall:

> "... Subject to the provisions of the Treaties relating, on the one hand, to the rules on the liability of officials and other servants towards the Communities and, on the other hand, to the jurisdiction of the Court in disputes between the Communities and their officials and other servants, be immune from legal proceedings in respect of acts performed by them in their official capacity including their words spoken or written. They shall continue to enjoy this immunity after they have ceased to hold office."[44]

42. For a detailed analysis see McMahon & Murphy, *European Community Law in Ireland* (1989), pp 58-65.
43. Article 9.
44. Article 12. For an example of how such a case might arise and how it will be dealt with in national courts or Court of Justice of the European Communities, see *Sayag* case. Case 5/68 [1968] ECR 395 and Case 9/69 [1969] ECR 336. On immunity of Members of Parliament from libel suit, see *Wagner v Fohrmann et al* Case 10/63 recueil Vol X 381. As to their position in relation to national criminal law systems see *R v Crown Court at Manchester ex parte Director of Public Prosecutions* [1993] 1 All ER 801 (QB).

Chapter 39

# Corporations, Partnerships, Unincorporated Bodies and Trade Unions


| | | |
|---|---|---|
| I. | Corporations | 1035 |
| II. | Partnerships | 1038 |
| III. | Unincorporated Associations | 1038 |
| IV. | Trade Unions | 1042 |


## I. CORPORATIONS[1]

**[39.01]** A corporation is an artificial legal person which may be established by the common law, by royal charter or by statutory authority. The statutory authority may be special, in the sense of being contained in a particular Act of the legislature,[2] or general where a company is formed under the Companies Act 1963. Whatever its legal basis, and irrespective of whether it is a corporation sole or aggregate, whether it is a private or public company, or whether it is a trading or non-trading company, a corporation has normally speaking full legal capacity to sue or be sued in its own name:

> "A corporation is a distinct legal person, separate from its members. This commonplace of corporation law runs as a vital thread through all the branches of the subject. A legal person is capable of being the subject of legal rights and the object of legal duties."[3]

### Corporation as Plaintiff

**[39.02]** A corporation has the same capacity as an individual to sue for torts committed against it. Accordingly a company can sue in negligence, in nuisance, in trespass, etc, when appropriate facts present themselves. It goes without saying, however, that certain torts (eg assault and battery) cannot by their nature be committed against a corporation and cannot, therefore, be the basis of an action by a corporation. This is to be explained not because of a legal disability, but rather because of the nature of the artificial legal personality of the corporation itself: a corporation cannot sue for assault simply because an assault cannot be committed on a corporation.

---

1. See Forde, *Company Law* (3rd ed, 1999), paras 3.41-.3.42; Courtney, *The Law of Private Companies* (1994), para 3.045-3.048; Ellis, *Irish Company Law for Business* (1998), para 4.5; Keane, *Company Law* (3rd ed, 2000), Ch 13; Atiyah, *Vicarious Liability in the Law of Torts* (1967), Ch 34; Goodhart 'Corporate Liability in Tort' (1926) 2 Camb LJ 350; Ussher, *Company Law in Ireland* (1986), pp 159-160.
2. Eg the Electricity Supply Board established by the Electricity (Supply) Act 1927; Córas Iompair Éireann, established by the Transport Act 1950; Bord Gais Éireann, established by the Gas Act 1976 and An Post and Bord Telecom Éireann, established by the Postal and Telecommunications Services Act 1983.
3. Ussher, *Company Law in Ireland* (1986), p 16.

**[39.03]** In defamation it seems that a corporation can certainly sue in respect of statements which tend to cause actual damage to its property or business where it is a trading corporation,[4] and the better opinion nowadays seems to be that any corporation can sue in respect of any defamatory statement about the conduct of its affairs.[5] In England, it was formerly considered that a local authority should be entitled to sue if defamatory statements (eg allegations of corruption, etc) were made in respect of its governing activity.[6] Contemporary emphasis on the value of promoting free speech in the democratic political forum has resulted in the abandonment of this approach, in *Derbyshire County Council v Times Newspapers*.[7] The Lord Keith observed that:

> "[t]here are ... features of a local authority which may be regarded as distinguishing it from other types of corporation, whether trading or non-trading. The most important of these features is that it is a governmental body. Further, it is a democratically elected body, the electoral process nowadays being conducted almost exclusively on party political lines. It is of the highest public importance that a democratically elected government body, or indeed any governmental body, should be open to uninhibited public criticism. The threat of a civil action for defamation must inevitably have an inhibiting effect on freedom of speech ..."[8]

**[39.04]** The House of Lords in the *Derbyshire* case made it plain that, whilst the local authority itself might not sue for defamation, individual councilors would be permitted to do so. It also held that no similar inhibitions, springing from free speech concerns, affected a local authority's right to sue for injurious falsehood.

**[39.05]** In *Council of the Shire of Ballina v Ringland*,[9] the Court of Appeal of the Supreme Court of New South Wales, by a majority,[10] came to the same conclusion as the House of Lords. The judicial concern to keep national law in line with the requirements of international norms is apparent in both decisions.[11] Although in neither instance did international conventions or covenants dictate the outcome, there was clear relief that the holding was in harmony with them. Mahoney JA's dissenting judgment in *Ballina* is nonetheless a powerful antidote to an unthinking genuflection before the altar of free speech, without reflecting on why precisely free speech is valued and the practical implications of giving extra power to those exercising control over the media to influence the decisions and actions of local authorities.[12]

---

4. *Irish People's Assurance Soc v Dublin City Assurance Co* [1929] IR 25. *Cf* Forde, *Company Law* (3rd ed, 1999), paras 3.39.
5. *Cf* WINFIELD & JOLOWICZ, p 835; *D & L Caterers Ltd v D'Ajou* [1945] KB 364; *Willis v Brooks* [1947] 1 All ER 191.
6. *Bognor Regis UDC v Campion* [1972] 2 QB 169, blisteringly criticised by Weir [1972A] Camb LJ 238.
7. [1993] AC 534 (HL).
8. [1993] AC 534, (Lords Griffiths, Goff, Browne-Wilkinson and Woolf concurring).
9. (1994) 33 NSWLR 680 (CA), analysed by Mullany 'Governing Reputation and Local Government Corporations' (1995) 111 LQR 206. See further QUILL, p 294.
10. Gleeson CJ and Kirby P, Mahoney JA, dissenting.
11. Article 10 of the European Convention for the Protection of Human Rights and Fundamental Freedoms and Article 19 of the International Covenant on Civil and Political Rights.
12. "In considering whether criticism of public authorities should be released from the restraints of defamation, the nature and extent of [media] power is relevant. In the great majority of cases ... that criticism is made by or through the media.

## Corporation as Defendant

**[39.06]** Since a corporation is an artificial legal person it must unavoidably act through agents. Consequently the liability of a corporation is usually vicarious liability for the acts of its servants, and in this, corporate liability is no different from the liability of any employer for the tortious acts of its servants. The general principles relating to vicarious liability apply, and in determining whether a person is a servant or whether a servant was acting during and in the course of his or her employment the general case law on this topic is fully relevant.[13] Procedural technicalities which once made suing a corporation somewhat difficult have long since disappeared and now there is no difficulty in suing a corporation even for torts that require malicious intent. In this latter type of case the malice of the servant can readily be ascribed to the corporation.[14]

**[39.07]** Although, therefore, the corporation will normally become liable on vicarious principles only through the acts of its agents and servants, there may be circumstances when the tortious acts may be properly said to be that of the corporation itself. Such will be the case when, for example, the act is done or authorised under the direction of the shareholders in general meeting or under the direction of the board of directors itself.

> "A corporation is an abstraction. It has no mind of its own any more than it has a body of its own; its active and directing will must consequently be sought in the person of somebody who for some purposes may be called an agent, but who is really the directing mind and will of the corporation, the very ego and centre of the personality of the corporation."[15]

In such a case, where the act is that of the central governing authority, liability attaches to the corporation, not because of *respondeat superior*, but because the wrong may be properly said to be that of the corporation itself.[16]

---

12. (contd) Media power is in the relevant sense arbitrary: it is not subject to publicly enforceable rules which control what may be published, nor are those who publish accountable for what is published other than through the law of defamation ... In the Middle Ages all public power was not subject to legal or enforceable rules and those who exercised it could not be made to account legally for the consequence of [its] exercise. The democratic development of constitutional law has been increasingly to require public power to be exercised according to rules or conventions. The legislative power initially exercised by the Sovereign is now exercised effectively by a Parliament, the members of which are directly accountable through periodic election. The executive power is now controlled almost entirely by law ... And judicial power is controlled by rules accountable through appeal and subject to reversal by the legislature. It is the power of the media which alone remains in the relevant sense arbitrary. I do not use the term pejoratively, or by way of criticism: I use it to describe the nature of the power ... The law of defamation is the only - or the only substantial - legal control over what they may say in order to achieve this purpose. Nor do I suggest that those who can publish do not act in the public interest. They can and often do. But the capacity to exercise power otherwise than for good is obvious: the existence of *inter alia* a Hearst or a Maxwell must be recognised and provided for."
13. See Ch 43 below; Ussher, *Company Law in Ireland* (1986), pp 159-160.
14. *Cornford v Carlton Bank Ltd* [1899] 1 QB 392, [1900] 1 QB 22; SALMOND & HEUSTON, p 480.
15. *Lennard's Carrying Co v Asiatic Petroleum Co* [1915] AC 705 at 713 (*per* Lord Haldane). See also MacCann, *A Casebook on Company Law* (1991), pp 187-189.
16. SALMOND & HEUSTON, p 407.

**[39.08]** A theoretical difficulty arises where the tort complained of and committed by the corporation's servant is *ultra vires* the corporation's powers. In such circumstances can the corporation be made liable? Although it is not possible to give a confident answer to this question as "there is no firm precedent for or against a rule relieving the corporation from liability for a tort committed in the course of an *ultra vires* activity",[17] the better opinion nowadays seems to favour the view that, whatever the academic or theoretical objections, the practical answer is that a corporation will be liable in such circumstances. So in *Campbell v Paddington Corporation*[18] the council of the defendant corporation authorised by formal resolution the erection of a stand on a highway. Although the council had no legal right to act as it did, and the stand constituted a public nuisance, the corporation was nevertheless held liable. Moreover, in spite of earlier authorities to the contrary[19] it seems that a corporation will also be liable for the acts of its servants which, although within the scope of their authority or employment, are *ultra vires* the company.[20]

## II. PARTNERSHIPS

**[39.09]** Persons who have entered into a partnership with each other (although the firm so established does not amount to a legal person) may sue and be sued in the firm's name by virtue of Order 14 of the Rules of the Superior Courts 1986.[21] Partners are jointly and severally liable for the tortious actions of any one of their number committed against outsiders during the ordinary course of the firm's business or with the authority of the other partners.[22]

## III. UNINCORPORATED ASSOCIATIONS[23]

**[39.10]** Unincorporated associations cannot sue or be sued in their own names at common law. Normally,[24] therefore, an action against such an association will not be launched against the association by name; rather will it be taken against all the members of the association although such a course of action will have obvious practical difficulties. The Rules of the Superior Courts 1986,[25] however, provide that:

---

17. Jenkins 'Corporate Liability in Tort and the Doctrine of *Ultra Vires*' (1970) 5 Ir Jur (ns) 11 at 28.
18. [1911] 1 KB 869.
19. *Poulton v L & SW Ry* (1867) LR 2 QB 534.
20. SALMOND & HEUSTON, p 407.
21. See Ó Floinn, *Practice and Procedure in the Superior Courts* (1996), pp 116-121.
22. Partnership Act 1890, ss 10 and 12. See generally, Twomey, *Partnership Law* (2000), paras [3.04]-[3.13] and Chs 10-12 for a most comprehensive analysis.
23. See Capper 'Negligence Actions Against Unincorporated Associations' (1993) 44 NILQ 388; Flannigan 'The Liability Structure of Non-Profit Associations: Tort and Fiduciary Liability Assignments' (1998) 77 Can BR 73, (esp at 75-93); Lloyd 'Actions Instituted by or against Unincorporated Bodies' (1949) 12 MLR 409, also (1953) Lloyd 16 MLR 359; Garfinkle 'Liability of Members and Officers of Non-Profit Unincorporated Associations for Contracts or Torts' (1954) 42 Calif LR 812. For trade unions see para **[39.26]** below.
24. For friendly societies, see Friendly Societies Act 1896, as amended by Friendly Societies (Amendment) Act 1953 and Credit Union Act 1966; *Longdon-Griffiths v Smith* [1951] 1 KB 295.
25. Order 15, rule 9. See Ó Floinn, *Practice and Procedure in the Superior Courts* (1996), p 127.

> [w]here there are numerous persons having the same interest in one cause or matter, one or more of such persons may sue or be sued, or may be authorised by the Court to defend, in such cause or matter, on behalf, or for the benefit, of all persons so interested.

The insistence, however, that there be the same common interest weakens the efficacy of such a representative procedure and may mean that such a rule cannot frequently be used in tort actions.[26]

**[39.11]** Apart from the procedural problems just outlined in the preceding paragraph it goes without saying that, to succeed in an action against members or officers of an unincorporated association or club, the defendant must be shown to have committed a tort. This is a substantive matter and the liability or non-liability of the defendants will depend on the particular circumstances of each case.[27] In the absence of statutory basis, such an unincorporated body has no legal personality distinct from its members, and association of itself does not render all the members liable for the acts of individual members. All the members might, however, be vicariously liable in appropriate cases to third parties[28] if the individual member was acting as an agent of the club or "in furtherance of a common interest". In *Crean v Nolan and Others*[29] the defendants who constituted the organising committee of a drag hunt were held not to be liable in a *scienter* action for the killing of sheep by some beagles. It was held that the hunt was long over when the killings took place and the committee did not own the dogs. It was suggested, however, that the defendants might have been liable if the killings occurred during the hunt.

**[39.12]** The question of whether a member may sue the unincorporated club of which he or she was a member was decided in *Murphy v Roche et al*[30] against the plaintiff. Murphy, who was a member of Wolfe Tone Na Sionna GAA Club, paid to attend a dance held in the club's premises. He fell and was injured, allegedly because of negligence on the part of those organising the function. The defendants were named as representatives of the club. The Supreme Court ordered the preliminary issue as to whether the plaintiff could sue his club to be heard first.[31] Gannon J held that the plaintiff could not sue the club because, in effect, he would be suing himself, and the fact that he paid an admission fee like other members of the public did not give him a cause of action distinct from his claim as a

26. *Mercantile Marine Service Association v Toms* [1916] 2 KB 243 (CA); Lloyd 'Actions Instituted By or Against Unincorporated Bodies' (1949) 12 MLR 409, esp at 414; Kerr & Whyte, *Irish Trade Union Law*, pp 62-63; *Mare and Ors v AG for Saorstát Éireann* [1930] IR 471 at 499. Also note that in the Circuit Court Rules provision is made for representative actions "save in actions founded in tort". It appears however that a representative action will lie for wrongful expulsion (or other *ultra vires* acts) because this is not a tort. See *Bruce v Donaldson and Ors* (1918) 53 ILTR 24; *McQuaile v Heeney and O'Connor* [1959] Ir Jur 32. For example of representative defendants, see *Egan v Dublin Health Authority and Ors* Supreme Court, 30 July 1965 - Legion of Mary.

27. *Prole v Allen* [1950] 1 All ER 476; *Crean v Nolan and Ors* (1963) 97 ILTR 125.

28. *Murphy v Roche et al* High Court, 15 May 1987, Gannon J analysed by Byrne & Binchy, *Annual Review of Irish Law 1988*, pp 337.

29. (1963) 97 ILTR 125.

30. High Court, 15 May 1987 (Gannon J).

31. [1987] IR 106 (SC).

member. By paying for admission the plaintiff did not lose or avoid his share of responsibility in relation to such matters.

**[39.13]** The plaintiff argued that the club was a legal entity which was distinct from the individual members. He claimed that the analogy with the legal capacity of the State recognised in *Byrne v Ireland*[32] was appropriate. The Court rejected the comparison and also rejected the argument that the unincorporated association should be treated in the same way as a trade union. To this latter argument the Court obviously accepted the defendant's point that the trade union's capacity was based on statute and would not exist in the absence of such a statutory basis.

**[39.14]** Gannon J, in giving his judgement, quoted from a note of an earlier judgment[33] of his own to the effect that:

> "[b]y reason of the legal identification of the plaintiff with the defendants by virtue of their mutual membership of the Club the plaintiff cannot maintain the present proceedings against the members of their Club or these particular members being the Defendants as trustees."

**[39.15]** In *Kirwan v Mackey*,[34] Carney J invoked the *Murphy* decision when holding, as a preliminary issue, that the plaintiff's claim for negligence against the officer board of a gun club of which he was a member was not maintainable in law against it. The plaintiff, a member of the club, had been injured in the eye by a pellet fired by a former member. He sued the officers, committee and trustees of the gun club, alleging that the former member's membership had lapsed and that accordingly he was not insured or indemnified by the game hunting compensation fund of the National Association of Regional Game Councils.

**[39.16]** In holding that the proceedings were not maintainable against the officer board of the club, Carney J ventured to state that he did not accept that there had been a duty resting on it to notify the plaintiff as to whose membership was live and whose had lapsed "and that a failure to so notify him could make the officer board of the club liable to the plaintiff in damages".

**[39.17]** In *Walsh v Butler*,[35] Morris J confronted the rule that members of a club are not entitled to sue each other in tort. The plaintiff had been injured while playing rugby for Bandon Rugby Football Club. It had been founded around a hundred and fifty years ago. Before 1979, it had no constitution or rules. In that year, when the club acquired a premises, it was decided to apply for a club licence for the sale of intoxicating liquour. Another rugby club provided a copy of its rules for use as a precedent. In due course the appropriate order was made for the granting of the certificate under the Registration of Clubs (Ireland) Act 1904.

**[39.18]** The club continued to operate successfully, but its members "paid virtually no regard to the rules", save for the creation of "various" committees and the holding of an annual general meeting. The procedure prescribed by Rule 9 for the election of members

32. [1972] IR 241.

33. *Nolan v Fagan* High Court, 8 May 1985. See also *Prole v Allen* [1950] 1 All ER 476; *Robertson v Ridley* [1989] 2 All ER 474 (CA).

34. High Court, 18 January 1995.

35. [1997] 2 ILRM 81 (HC).

was never followed. Instead, the club operated on an informal basis by attracting young people directly onto the pitch, training them and absorbing them into one of the teams. Although as team members, they were required to pay an annual subscription, no sanction resulted from failure to do so.

**[39.19]** The plaintiff, born in 1968 had started to play rugby with the club in 1982. In 1989 he was elected vice-captain of the first team; he later took over as team captain shortly afterwards. He had paid his subscription in the 1987-88 season and again in 1988-9 but not, it seemed, for the 1989-90 season. The accident took place in early 1990.

**[39.20]** The defendants sought to avoid liability, as a preliminary issue, on the basis that the plaintiff was a member of the club. They argued that it was within the capacity of all the members of the club to accept a member into the club without having to follow the formal procedure provided for by the rules. They further contended that the plaintiff was estopped by his conduct from seeking to establish that he was not a member of the club as he had held himself out to be such a member for a number of years.

**[39.21]** Morris J held in favour of the plaintiff. It had not been possible for him to acquire membership of the club in defiance of Rule 9 of the rules which required the names and addresses of the persons proposed as ordinary members to be displayed in the club premises for at least two weeks before election and provided that "[a]ll members shall be elected by the general committee".

**[39.22]** Morris, J considered it:

> "clear beyond doubt that the only route by which one may join the club is by election to the general committee. To hold otherwise would give rise to a situation where the committee of the club would have lost all control over affairs of the club. Members could be assumed into the club and shed from the club without the knowledge of the general committee. The contractual relationship as between members regulated by their acceptance of the general committee as the regulating authority would be varied without their approval and consent."

**[39.23]** Even if it was within the capacity of the universal membership of the club to set aside the formal election provision and assume a candidate into the club as a member, there was no evidence that this had occurred. No question of estoppel could arise as the mere act of holding oneself out as a member without adverse consequence to a third party, cannot give rise to estoppel.

**[39.24]** Morris J identified "a further fundamental point": even if the plaintiff had been a member of the club, his membership would have lapsed when his subscription remained unpaid on the date of the annual general meeting in May 1989, under Rule 8 of the club's rules.

**[39.25]** It is not hard to sense in Morris J's judgment an underlying dissatisfaction with the implications of an immunity from suit in this area. In England there has been an increasing judicial willingness[36] to revisit the immunity and there is a strong argument that the Irish courts should embark on the same journey. Indeed there has to be a shadow of

---

36. *Jones v Northampton Borough Council* English Court of Appeal (CD), 15 May 1990; The Times 21 May 1990; *cf McKinley v Montgomery* [1993] NI 93; Flannigan 'The Liability Structure of Non-Profit Associations: Tort and Fiduciary Liability Assignments' (1998) 77 Can BR 73 at 85-86; Capper 'Negligence Action Against Unincorporated Associations' (1993) 44 NILQ 388.

doubt as to the consistency of this immunity with either the Constitution[37] or the European Convention on Human Rights and Fundamental Freedoms.[38] To suggest that the immunity should be abandoned does not, of course, lead to the conclusion that club members who injure club members will necessarily have owed, or breached, a duty of care. All will depend on the circumstances of the particular case.[39]

## IV. TRADE UNIONS[40]

**[39.26]** Although a trade union is not an incorporated body it has long been established that a registered trade union can both sue and be sued in its own name.[41] Unregistered unions are in a weaker position, however, so that from the point of view of legal capacity a distinction exists in law between registered and unregistered trade unions.[42] An unregistered trade union is equated to an unincorporated association of individuals similar to a social club. Its capacity to sue and be sued is restricted and is equated with that of an unincorporated association.[43]

**[39.27]** A registered trade union, however, although not a corporate entity, has long since been recognised in this jurisdiction as being a separate legal entity distinct from its individual members. As far back as 1928 it was stated in the Supreme Court that:

> "... a trade union which has been registered with a name, an address, a constitution and rules is a legal person, at least analogous to a statutory corporation, having an existence apart from its individuals aggregated in the combination ... [It] is as such capable of suing in its registered name in pursuance of its defined objects."[44]

---

37. Arguments based on inequality under Article 40.1 or the arbitrary denial of the right to litigate would appear particularly relevant.
38. *Cf Osman v United Kingdom* [1999] 1 FLR 193 (ECHR, 1998).
39. By way of comparison it will be recalled that the removal of the former immunity of occupiers from a duty of care to trespassers brought about in *Purtill v Athlone UDC* [1968] IR 205 (SC) and *McNamara v ESB* [1975] IR 226 (SC) did not by any means translate into the imposition of a duty of care on all occupiers to all trespassers. See, eg, *Smith v CIE* [1991] IR 314.
40. See Kerr & Whyte, *Irish Trade Union Law* (1985), pp 62-69; Forde, *Industrial Relations Law* (1991), pp 188-191; Fennell & Lynch *Labour Law in Ireland* (1993), pp 70-75, 87; Heuston 'Trade Unions and the Law' (1969) 14 Ir Jur (ns) 10; Shillman, *Trade Unionism and Trade Disputes In Ireland* (1960); Casey 'Some Implications of Freedom of Association in Labour Law: A Comparative Survey with Special Reference to Ireland' (1972) 21 ICLQ 699. A most comprehensive assembly of the literature is contained in Hepple, Neeson & O'Higgins, *A Bibliography of the Literature On British And Irish Labour Law* (1975) esp at 231. On this general subject see above Ch 32.
41. See Trade Union Acts 1871 and 1876; *Taff Vale Railway v Amalgamated Society of Railway Servants* [1901] AC 426 "The pragmatic common law tended to say that although a union was not a legal person it would be treated as if it were one." Heuston 'Trade Unions and the Law' (1969) 14 Ir Jur (ns) 10. *Cf R(IUDWC) v Rathmines UDC* [1928] IR 260.
42. A union although not obliged to do so may register under the Trade Union Act 1871. Certain advantages are accorded to unions which register. See Kerr & Whyte, *Irish Trade Union Law* (1985), pp 48 50.
43. Kerr & Whyte, *Irish Trade Union Law* (1985), p 62.
44. *R (IUDWC) v Rathmines UDC* [1928] IR 260 at 300.

**[39.28]** When, therefore, a registered trade union sues it does not, like an unregistered trade union, sue in a representative capacity. The further consequences of such recognition were referred to by Murnaghan J, in the same case:

> "Once a trade union is recognised as a legal entity, distinct from the personalities of its individuals who happen to be members, it must be considered quite as distinct from these individuals as is an incorporated company from its shareholders."[45]

**[39.29]** Although this position has never been explicitly recognised by the Oireachtas, implicit recognition has been given in the Trade Union Act 1941, where, in the case of registered trade unions, the Act imposed penalties not only on the officers of its union but also on the union itself, whereas in the case of unregistered unions the penalties were imposed only on the union's officers.[46]

**[39.30]** This recognition of separate legal personality also means that a registered union, in addition to being able to sue for the torts of nuisance, negligence, and so on, can also maintain an action for defamation in its own name since it has a reputation of its own apart from that of its members.[47]

**[39.31]** Whether or not a trade union will be liable as a defendant is a very different matter, however. Generally speaking, since 1906, trade unions are not liable in tort. This immunity was conferred by s 4 of the Trade Disputes Act 1906.

**[39.32]** The present law on the matter is contained in s 13 of the Industrial Relations Act 1990, which provides as follows:

> (1) An action against a trade union, whether of workers or employers, or its trustees or against any members or officials thereof on behalf of themselves and all other members of the trade union in respect of any tortious act committed by or on behalf of the trade union in contemplation or furtherance of a trade dispute, shall not be entertained by any court.
>
> (2) In an action against any trade union or person referred to in subsection (1) in respect of any tortious act alleged or found to have been committed by or on behalf of a trade union it shall be a defence that the act was done in the reasonable belief that it was done in contemplation or furtherance of a trade dispute.

In Chapter 32, we examine in detail[48] the scope of the immunity conferred in s 13.

---

45. *R (IUDWC) v Rathmines UDC* [1928] IR 260 at 306. For application of company rules to unions see Kerr & Whyte, *Irish Trade Union Law* (1985), pp 66-69.
46. Sections 12 and 13.
47. *National Union of General and Municipal Workers v Gillian* [1946] KB 81; *BMTA v Salvadori* [1949] Ch 556. No longer the position in England because of Trade Union and Labour Relations Act 1974, s 24. See *Electrical and Plumbing Union v Times Newspapers* [1980] QB 585.
48. See para **[32.126]** and QUILL, pp 428-429.

# Chapter 40

# Minors and Mentally Ill Persons


I. Minors .......... 1045
II. Mentally Ill Persons .......... 1056


## I. Minors

### General Liability in Tort

**[40.01]** The question of the general liability of a minor in tort[1] is one which involves some difficult aspects, but the main features of the law are clear.

**[40.02]** The leading decision on the subject is *O'Brien v McNamee*.[2] The facts briefly were as follows. The defendant, aged seven years and one month, brought a lighted paper into the plaintiff's barn. He placed the paper in the middle of the floor but the flame spread to the hay in the barn and the barn was burnt down. Liability was imposed on the child, based on trespass. In giving judgment, Davitt P stated:

> "Strange as it may seem, the defendant is liable. A child over seven years of age is liable for the torts he commits, provided there is no question of intention involved in the tort and provided that it does not arise out of contract. When the act may or may not be a malicious act, intent may be material. It is then a question whether he wills the consequences."[3]

Since, in an action for trespass "all that is necessary to establish ... is that the act should be voluntary",[4] the defendant was liable.

**[40.03]** Thus, intent is the key. Where capacity to have an intention is not an element of the tort, the minor will be liable in the same way as an adult; where, however, intent is an ingredient in a tort, the minor may escape liability where he was incapable of forming the requisite intent.

**[40.04]** Davitt P's statement above, however, where he says that a "child over seven years of age is liable for the torts he commits ...", is misleading in that it might suggest that a child under that age is exempt from responsibility. Although this is the position in criminal

1. See Bohlen 'Liability in Tort of Infants and Insane Persons' (1924) 23 Mich LR 9; Dunlop 'Torts Relating to Infants' (1966) 5 West LR 116; Black 'The Tort Liability of Children Under the Laws of England and France' (1973) 6 CILJSA 364; Alexander 'Tort Liability of Children and their Parents' Ch 14 of *Studies in Canadian Family Law* Mendes da Costa ed, (1972), p 850ff; Sharpe 'Mental State as Affecting Liability in Tort' (1975) 23 Chitty's LJ 46.
2. [1953] IR 86 (HC).
3. [1953] IR 86 at 87-88.
4. [1953] IR 86 at 88. *Cf* Alexander 'Tort Liability of Children and their Parents' Ch 14 of *Studies in Canadian Tort Law* Mendes da Costa ed, (1972), p 853-854.

law,[5] it is not the position in tort law.[6] Apart from what has already been said about intent, there is no rule of law that automatically exempts from liability children under seven, or indeed under any other fixed age.

## Negligence and Contributory Negligence[7]

**[40.05]** Specific rules have been developed relating to the negligence and contributory negligence of minors. The position relating to contributory negligence has been discussed in a number of decisions, but the position regarding negligence has not yet come before the Irish courts. This may be explained perhaps by the fact that it is in the nature of children to get into situations of danger, frequently resulting in injuries to themselves, but it is less often that a person injured by a child will contemplate legal proceedings, since the child will normally have no assets.

## Contributory Negligence

**[40.06]** The classic statement of the relevant legal principles regarding the contributory negligence of children was made by O'Byrne J in *Fleming v Kerry County Council*:

> "In the case of a child of tender years there must be some age up to which the child cannot be guilty of contributory negligence. In other words, there is some age up to which a child cannot be expected to take any precautions for his own safety. In cases where contributory negligence is alleged against a child, it is the duty of the trial Judge to rule, in each particular case, whether the plaintiff, having regard to his age and mental development, may properly be expected to take some precautions for his own safety and consequently be capable of being guilty of contributory negligence. Having ruled in the affirmative, it becomes a question of fact for the jury, on the evidence, to determine whether he has fallen short of the standard which might reasonably be expected from him having regard to his age and development. In the case of an ordinary adult person the standard is what should be expected from a reasonable person. In the case of a child, the standard is what may reasonably be expected, having regard to the age and mental development of the child and the other circumstances of the case."[8]

A number of aspects of this statement of the law require further consideration.

---

5. The Children Bill 1999, s 52, proposes to raise the age minimum for criminal responsibility to twelve. For a general discussion of this subject, see Hanly 'Child Offenders: The Changing Response of Irish Law' (1997) 19 DULJ 113.

6. The commentators in all common law jurisdictions are in general agreement on this point, *cf*, eg Skolrood 'Rip van Winkle and the Infant's Torts' (1960) 48 Ill Bar J 746. See, however, *Kingston v Kingston* (1968) 102 ILTR 65 at 67 (SC). See also Cross 'Comment' (1975) 9 Akron LR 368; *Decker v Itasca Paper Co* (1910) 111 Minn 439 at 445, 127 NW 183; *cf Cotton v Commr for Road Transport & Tramways* (19424) 3 SR (NSW) 66 at 69 (SC). And see *Re a Debtor* (1950) 66 Times LR (Pt 1) 313 at 321 (CA).

7. See the Law Reform Commission's *Report on the Liability in Tort of Minors and the Liability of Parents for Damage Caused by Minors* (LRC 17-1985), p 4ff. Anon, 'Children and Contributory Negligence' (1966) 100 ILT & Sol J 425; Anon 'Motorists, Children and Contributory Negligence' (1938) 72 ILT & Sol J 119; Anon 'Children and Negligence' (1941) 75 ILT & Sol J 89; Scott 'Children and Negligence' (1966) 116 New LJ 1394; Fridman 'Children and Negligence' (1967) 117 New LJ 35; Shulman 'The Standard of Care Required of Children' (1927) 37 Yale LJ 618; Binchy 'A Minor Confusion: Children and the Law of Negligence' (1980) 74 Incorp L Soc of Ireland Gazette 7; Binchy 'The Adult Activities Doctrine in Negligence Law' (1985) 11 Wm Mitchell LR 733 at 736-741; Fray 'The Standard of Care for Children Revisited' (1980) 45 Missouri LR 597; Keet 'Contributory Negligence of Children' (1963) 12 Clev-Mar LR 395.

8. [1955-1956] Ir Jur Rep 71 at 72 (SC).

### *(a) Minimum age*

**[40.07]** O'Byrne J is clearly correct in stating that "there must be some age up to which the child cannot be guilty of contributory negligence". As Palles CB observed in *Cooke v Midland GW Ry of Ireland*:

> "... The doctrine of contributory negligence is entirely grounded upon the fact that man is a reasoning animal, and has no application to the case of a child of such an age as to be incapable of appreciating the danger, and reasoning in reference to it, any more than if he had been a brute animal."[9]

**[40.08]** A number of decisions have clearly recognised the true function of the Courts on this question. Thus, in the Canadian decision of *Gargotch v Cohen*,[10] Hogg J said:

> "Some of the cases have stated the age at which a child cannot be said to come within the principle of contributory negligence, but apparently the more modern decisions do not attempt to fix an arbitrary limit as to age. It has been held that intelligence and not age is the test to apply in deciding whether a child has been, or can be, guilty of contributory negligence."

**[40.09]** The courts have nonetheless persisted in trying to discover an objective minimum age, applicable to all children, regardless of their particular mental capacity and experience, below which it is impossible to be guilty of contributory negligence. This approach does no great harm where the child is extremely young - an infant in arms, for example - but, once the child is a little older, the question becomes progressively more confusing.

**[40.10]** Bearing this difficulty in mind, let us examine what the courts have had to say on the issue. The age of three years appears to be the youngest at which the Courts have seriously canvassed the possibility of a child having the requisite capacity for contributory negligence. In *Macken v Devine*,[11] Judge Gleeson of the Circuit Court, held that a 3½-year-old plaintiff who had fallen down unguarded steps was not guilty of contributory negligence since he "had not sufficient sense to understand the risk and was incapable of appreciating the danger". In the Canadian decision of *Kaplan v Canada Safeway Ltd*,[12] Disbery J, of the Saskatchewan Queen's Bench, expressed the opinion that it would be "absurd" to regard a child of that age as being capable of contributory negligence. In the

---

9. [1908] IR 242 at 268 (KB).
10. [1940] OWN 479 at 480. In accord in *Sheasgreen v Morgan* [1952] DLR 48 at 61-62 (BC SC). See also *Farrall v Stokes* (1954) 54 SR (NSW) 294 at 298; *Toetshinger v lhnot* (1977) 312 Minn 59, 250 NW 2d 204, noted in (1979) 5 Wm Mitchell LR 213. Charlesworth & Percy, *On Negligence*, para 3-31 (footnote references omitted) argue that:

    "[t]here is no age below which, as a matter of law, it can be said that a child is incapable of contributory negligence. Expressions can be found referring to children 'too young to be capable of contributory negligence' or 'of such a tender age as to be regarded in law as incapable of contributory negligence'. However, these must be taken to be referring to children found, on the facts of a particular case, to have been so young that contributory negligence could not be attributed to them."
11. (1946) 80 ILTR 121 (CC).
12. (1969) 68 DLR (2d) 627 at 630 (Sask QB). See also *Tillander v Gosselin* (1966) 60 DLR (2d) 18 at 20 (Ont HC) affd (1967) 61 DLR (2d) 192n (CA) - speaking of child aged one week less than 3 years: "It is clear that a child of such tender years could not be guilty of negligence". *Cf McEllistrum v Etches* [1956] SCR 787 at 793.

old English decision of *Gardner v Grace*,[13] where the plaintiff was 3½ years old, Channell B stated that "[t]he doctrine of contributory negligence does not apply to an infant of tender age". Cases in the United States of America[14] are also overwhelmingly opposed to holding three-year-olds capable of contributory negligence.

**[40.11]** As the child moves towards four[15] and five,[16] the Courts become increasingly doubtful that he or she is incapable of contributory negligence. By the time the child reaches six, he or she is likely to be held to have the requisite capacity, at all events where the child is regarded as bright.[17] Cases have been reported,[18] however, where the Courts have held children above this age incapable of contributory negligence.

---

13. (1858) 1 F & F 359, 174 ER 763. This statement has been criticised as being "scarcely satisfactory, because it is difficult to say what is or is not a tender age": Smith, *A Treatise on the Law of Negligence* (2nd ed, 1884), p 243. It should be noted that Channell B proposed that the parties settle the action, which might suggest that he did not regard the issue of the child's contributory negligence as a closed one. In *Thomas v British Rys Bd* [1976] QB 912 (CA), the defence of contributory negligence appears not to have been raised where the plaintiff, aged two years, was injured by a train when she sat on the railway line.

14. See the decisions cited by Heinselman 'Annotation: Contributory Negligence of Children' (1937) 107 ALR 4 at 98-101 and by Shipley 'Annotation: Modern Trends as to Contributory Negligence of Children' 77 ALR 2d 917 at 923; Wilkens 'Contributory Negligence of Very Young Children' (1971) 20 Clev St LR 65 at 66-68. See, however, *United Rys & Electric Co of Baltimore v Carneal* (1909) 110 Md 211, 72 A 771 (CA); *Fontaine v Devonis* (1975) 14 RI 541, 336 A 2d 847.

15. *Cf Brown v Foley* [1932] LJ, IFS 205 (HC); *Cullen v Heagney* [1931] LJIFS 149. In *Lipschitz v Caulfields Ltd*, Supreme Court, 20 December 1960; Maguire CJ stated of a four-year-old child that "he could not be guilty of contributory negligence ..." (p 4 of judgment). See also, to similar effect, *Carmarthenshire Co Co v Lewis* [1955] AC 549 at 563 (HL).

16. *Cf Curran v Lapedus* (1938) 72 ILTR 246 (CC), revd (1939) 73 ILTR 89 (HC); *Finnegan v The Irish Shell Co* (1937) 71 ILTR 200 (CC); *Plantza v Glasgow Corporation* (1910) 47 Sc LR 688; *Ryan v Madden* [1944] IR 154. See, however, *Doherty v McKelvey* DPIJ: Trinity and Michaelmas Terms 1994, p 91 at p 92 (HC): "[I]n this particular instance I am quite satisfied that [the five-year-old plaintiff] was far too young to be guilty of contributory negligence". In *Squizzoni v McEntaggart* DPIJ: Hilary and Easter Terms 1994, p 56 (HC), it was conceded that a child of five years "and a couple of days" was "of an age .... where it cannot be guilty of contributory negligence": p 68.

17. *Cf Donovan v Landy's Ltd* [1963] IR 441 (SC); *Curran v Lapedus* (1938) 72 ILTR 246; but see *Brien v McGarry* (1928) 62 ILTR 166 (CC); *Coffee v McEvoy* [1912] 2 IR 290 at 308 (CA). See also *Bye v Bates* (1989) 51 SASR 67.

18. *Cf O'Rourke v Cavan UDC* (1942) 77 ILTR 16 (CC). See also *Brown v Foley* [1932] LJ, IFS 205 (*per* O'Byrne J, during argument): "I thought the dividing line was between seven and nine." In *Murphy v Shields*, DPIJ: Hilary and Easter Terms 1994, p 89 (HC) where a seven-year-old girl was injured by a stray nail in a plank which she was using as a makeshift slide, Barr J observed (at p 91):

    > "Having regard to her age, she could not reasonably be held to have been aware [of] or to have appreciated the danger which the planks presented and I am not satisfied there is sufficient evidence of contributory negligence on her part to justify a finding in that regard."

    The case can perhaps best be interpreted as not one in which a seven-year-old child, by reason of her age, was held incapable of being guilty of contributory negligence but rather as involving a holding that the particular plaintiff, who might well be capable of acting in a way that could be stigmatised as involving contributory negligence on her part, had not done so in the circumstances of the case by virtue of an age-related incapacity to appreciate the particular danger that resulted in her injury.

**[40.12]** The Irish authorities are strongly of the view that nine-year-olds are capable of contributory negligence. In *Behan v Thornhill*[19] The Supreme Court upheld the verdict of Davitt P, dismissing an action for negligence brought by a nine-year-old plaintiff arising out of a collision with the defendant's car. The plaintiff was undoubtedly a bright child - Davitt P stated that he had "seldom seen a brighter boy in the witness box" - but the case did not proceed on this finding alone. Davitt P stated:

> "... I think that a boy of nine years is capable of contributory negligence. It has been held in some cases that younger boys could not be capable of contributory negligence but I am satisfied that a boy of nine years can be capable of contributory negligence."

**[40.13]** In *Menton v CIE*,[20] however, Lavery J, in the Supreme Court, expressed the view that a nine-year-old girl "by reason of her age probably could not have negligence imputed to her". In *Courtney v Masterson*,[21] Black J, in the High Court, stated that he was "not prepared to accept the contention that a boy of ten years is incapable of contributory negligence".

**[40.14]** Whilst the courts have tended to ask whether a child of a certain age may be regarded as having the capacity for contributory negligence, it is clear, as we have noted,[22] that this is not the best approach. As anyone who has had any experience of dealing with young children will appreciate, children develop at different speeds: one six-year-old may be fully aware of the dangers of a particular situation, whilst his or her friend of the same age may have no such appreciation. This subjective element is recognised where the child has been found to be capable of contributory negligence; it should also be taken into account, where the threshold issue of capacity for contributory negligence is being determined.

***(b) Standard to be applied in determining whether a child was guilty of contributory negligence***

**[40.15]** There is a surprising degree of confusion in this country as to the standard to be applied to a child, admittedly capable of contributory negligence, in determining whether he was in the circumstances of the case guilty of contributory negligence. O'Byrne J, in *Fleming v Kerry County Council*,[23] favoured the subjective approach. The standard was:

> "what may reasonably be expected, having regard to the age and mental development of the child and the other circumstances of the case."

**[40.16]** Yet, in the subsequent Supreme Court decision of *Duffy v Fahy*,[24] Lavery J expressed uncertainty as to the meaning of O'Byrne J's statement, considering it to be:

---

19. (1928) 62 ILTR 65 (SC affg HC).
20. Supreme Court, 27 July 1966 at p 2.
21. [1949] Ir Jur Rep 6 at 7 (HC). See also *O'Gorman v Crotty* [1946] Ir Jur Rep 34 (HC) - 10½-year-old boy held capable of contributory negligence; *Hosty v McDonagh* Supreme Court, unrep 29 May, 1973 - child aged 10 years and three months capable of contributory negligence to extent of 30%.
22. See para **[40.09]** above. See also LUNNEY & OLIPHANT, p 252.
23. [1955-1956] Ir Jur Rep 71.
24. [1960] Ir Jur Rep 69 at 74 (SC). The Court in *Duffy* was composed of Lavery, Kingsmill Moore and Maguire JJ. In *Fleming*, it was composed of Maguire CJ, O'Byrne, Lavery, Kingsmill Moore and O'Daly JJ.

> "susceptible of meaning either the mental development of the individual concerned or the mental development of the normal or average child of that age."

**[40.17]** He regarded it as "unnecessary to consider the matter further or to express an opinion thereon".[25] In *Kingston v Kingston*,[26] Walsh J, in an obiter statement, favoured the objective approach, referring only to the age, and not the mental development, of the child.

**[40.18]** Other decisions over the years have been divided on this matter: Some[27] have clearly endorsed the subjective approach, but others[28] have professed to favour the objective standard.

**[40.19]** The Supreme Court has addressed the issue in two cases over the past eighteen years. The first, *McNamara v Electricity Supply Board*,[29] is, of course, a leading one on the subject of occupiers' liability,[30] but in the present context it is the treatment of the plaintiff's contributory negligence that must be considered. In this case the plaintiff, an eleven-year-old boy, was injured when climbing on the defendant's electricity sub-station. He had been warned by his father not to go there. He was aware of the existence of a number of notices around the sub-station warning persons of the dangers but claimed that, although he was able to read, he had never read them. The jury found that he had not been guilty of any contributory negligence and the defendant appealed against this finding (among others).

**[40.20]** In relation to the standard of care appropriate to the plaintiff, Walsh J stated that:

> "The test to be applied is that stated by O'Byrne J in *Fleming v Kerry County Council*,[31] which is that it is for the jury to determine whether the boy fell short of the standard which might be reasonably expected from him having regard to his age and his development."[32]

In this passage and in the passage immediately following,[33] Walsh J appears clearly to favour the subjective standard (whilst considering that, on the facts of the case, a more

---

25. [1960] Ir Jur Rep 69 at 74.
26. (1968) 102 ILTR 65 at 67 (SC).
27. *Tiernan v O'Callaghan* (1944) 78 ILTR 36 (CC); *Byrne v Corporation of Dun Laoghaire* [1940] Ir Jur Rep 40 (HC); *McLoughlin v Antrim Electricity Supply Co* [1941] NI 23 (CA). *Cf* the dictum by Haugh J in *O'Hanlon v Electricity Supply Board* [1969] IR 75 at 83 (SC). In *Preston v Higgins*, Supreme Court, 13 July 1962, where the contributory negligence of a 13½-year old cyclist was in question, reference was made to the child's experience as a cyclist, as an apparently relevant factor. *Cf Hanley v Randles* (1962) 96 ILTR 10 (SC).
28. *O'Gorman v Crotty* [1946] Ir Jur Rep 34; *Finnegan v The Irish Shell Co* (1937) 71 ILTR 200 (*semble*), but the subjective test was not there in issue). See also *Byrne v McDonald*, Supreme Court, 7 February 1957 (Kingsmill Moore J) at p 10 of his judgment. In *Clancy v Commissioners of Public Works in Ireland* [1988] ILRM 268 (HC) Barr J referred only to the plaintiff child's age: *cf* Byrne & Binchy, *Annual Review of Irish Law 1987*, pp. 334-335.
29. [1975] IR 1 (SC), analysed by McMahon 'Note: Herrington and Trespassers in Ireland' (1975) 91 LQR 323.
30. *Cf* para **[12.44]** above.
31. [1955-56] Ir Jur Rep 71.
32. [1975] IR 1 at 17-18
33. [1975] IR 1 at 27

objective standard (of age and experience, but not mental development) would have yielded the same result).

**[40.21]** Henchy J considered that the relevant standard was that "to be expected from a boy aged 11 years of the plaintiff's education and general background ..."[34]

**[40.22]** Griffin J did not refer to the standard in express terms, but he appeared to favour the subjective approach to the extent that he considered[35] the plaintiffs capacity to read - rather than that of the ordinary eleven-year-old - to be of major significance.

**[40.23]** Budd J concurred[36] with the judgment of Walsh J, the brief treatment[37] of the issue by FitzGerald CJ does not indicate a clear leaning towards either the objective or subjective approach. The better view would appear to be that *McNamara* represents a clear preference on the part of the Supreme Court for the subjective approach.

**[40.24]** In *Brennan v Savage Smith & Co*,[38] in 1982, the Supreme Court again considered the question of a child's contributory negligence. There, a 7½-year-old child was injured when he was crushed by a reversing van. The child had been "scutting" on the rear bumper. He had pretended to run away from the van, to make the driver think that he was not "scutting". The driver was unable to see the child when he was reversing. The accident occurred on a service road near a large complex of corporation flats. The Supreme Court held on the evidence that the driver had been negligent. As regards the question of the child's contributory negligence, the Supreme Court unanimously altered the jury finding of 5% to 25%. O'Higgins CJ said:

> "In my view, the finding of 5% against a plaintiff found guilty of contributory negligence is almost an assertion by the jury that such a plaintiff was really blameless. I think that the circumstances would require to be really special to justify such a finding. I do not think that they are so in this particular case. While the plaintiff was only 7½ at the time of the accident, there was no question raised as to his intelligence nor as to his knowledge of what he was doing. He was a child of the environment, well used to vans, lorries and cars and, since he deliberately sought to deceive the driver lest he be stopped, fully aware that 'scutting' was dangerous and wrong. On his own evidence he tried it twice with the defendant's van and it was as the result of the second attempt that he found himself in danger. At this stage I do not think that he realised the danger but he was there because of his own fault and his persistence in doing something which he knew was wrong."[39]

In this passage, O'Higgins CJ appears clearly to endorse the subjective formula of a child's age, intelligence and experience.

**[40.25]** The other judgements do not consider this question in any detail. It is worth noting Henchy J's observation that the plaintiff, in spite of his age, had:

34. [1975] IR 1 at 36.
35. [1975] IR 1 at 21.
36. [1975] IR 1 at 8.
37. [1975] IR 1.
38. [1982] ILRM 223 (SC).
39. [1982] ILRM 223 at 227. It may be argued that the subjective test is socially discriminatory. The fact that the plaintiff was "a child of the environment" served to reduce his compensation. Is it fair that experience flowing from social deprivation should be invoked against children?

"furtively, wilfully and in a way that he knew to be prohibited and to be fraught with the risk of injury, put himself in the position of danger which resulted in the accident".[40]

The general tenor of this statement suggests a subjective rather than an objective approach.

**[40.26]** The subjective approach has widespread support in the common law provinces of Canada,[41] the United States of America[42] and Hong Kong.[43] In England[44] and New Zealand[45] the objective approach appears to command general support. In Australia considerable uncertainty has followed in the wake of the decision of the High Court in *McHale v Watson*.[46]

## Negligence

**[40.27]** As has been mentioned, there have been very few decisions on the question of the negligence of children. There have been statements[47] to the effect that minority will not afford a defence to an action for negligence, but the better view[48] appears to be that the

40. [1982] ILRM 223 at 232.

41. *Cf McEllistrum v Etches* [1956] SCR 787; *Paskiviski v Canadian Pacific Ltd* [1976] 1 SCR 687; *Wade v Canadian National Ry* (1977) 80 DLR (3d) 214 (SC, Can) (*per* Laskin CJ dissenting, but dissent not affecting this issue; Spence and Dickson JJ, concurring with the Chief Justice); *Strehlke v Camenzind* (1977) 111 DLR (3d) 319 (Alta QB); *Sgro v Verbeck* (1980) 111 DLR (3d) 479 (Ont HC); *Wessell v Kinsmen Club of Sault Ste Marie Ontario Inc* (1982) 137 DLR (3d) 96 (Ont HC); *McErlean v Sarel* (1987) 61 OR (2d) 396, 42DLR (4th) 577 (CCA); *Nespolon v Alford* (Ont CA, 1998). A few decisions have flirted with a more objective test: see Edwards, Hopkins & White 'Annual Survey of Canadian Law: Torts: Part 1' (1982) 14 Ott LR 152 at 187, fn 194.

42. See PROSSER & KEETON, p 179ff; Shulman 'The Standard of Care Required of Children' (1927) 37 Yale LJ 618; Ireland 'Comment' (1976) 37 Montana LR 257 at 261-262; Katz 'Note: The Standard of Care Required of Infants' (1952) 25 Temp LQ 478, Irvin 'Comment' (1959) 38 Ore LR 268.

43. *Ho Kwai Loy v Leung Tin Hong* [1978] HKLR 72 (CA); *May Ngai Gloves Factory Ltd v Nam Kam Lan* [1980] HKC 175, (1980) HKC LEXIS 214 (CA).

44. *Cf Lynch v Nurdin* (1841) 1 QB 29, 133 ER 1041; *Hughes v Maciie* (1863) 2 H & C 744, 159 ER 308; *Mangan v Atterson* (1866) LR 1 Ex 239; *Lay v Midland Ry Co* (1875) 34 LT 30 (Exch Div); *Clark v Chambers* (1878) 3 QBD 327; *Gough v Thorne* [ 1966] 1 WLR 1387 (CA); *Jones v Lawrence* [1969] 3 All ER 267; *Culkin v Mcfie & Sons Ltd* [1939] 3 All ER 613; *Mullin v Richards* [1998] 1 WLR 1304 (CA). See further LRC 17-1985, pp 83-84, fn. 61.

45. *Cf Ralph v Henderson & Pollard Ltd* [1968] NZLR 759 esp at 763.

46. (1966) 115 CLR 199 (HC, Austr), noted in (1967) 3 Adelaide LR 118. See further Binchy 'The Adult Activities Doctrine in Negligence Law' (1985) 11 Wm Mitchell LR 733. Applying the objective test are *Mye v Peters* (1967) 68 SR (NSW) 298 (CA); *Broadhurst v Millman* [1976] VR 208; *Charles v Zadow* (1981) 28 SASR 492 (SC) and (more tentatively) *Beasley v Marshall* (1977) 17 SASR 456 (SC). Other decisions have articulated a hybrid test: see *Chan v Fong* (1973) 5 SASR 1 (SC); *Cameron v Commissioner of Rys* [1964] QR 480 (SC). Still others have applied the subjective test: see *Westmoreland v Schultz* (1972) 2 SASR 286n; *Wiech v Amato* (1973) 6 SASR 442 (SC). TRINDADE & CANE, pp 449 refer to Australian decisions that appear to apply a subjective test in respect of a child's contributory negligence, though the authors do not envince much enthusiasm for this approach.

47. Eg *McHale v Watson* (1966) 115 CLR 199 at 224-226 (*per* Menzies J, dissenting), *Halsbury's Laws*, 28(10) (3rd ed, 1957) - referring to decisions that do not appear to support the proposition for which they are cited. But see now 4th ed, 1980, para 10.

48 *Cf* SALMOND & HEUSTON, p 408; see, however, *Kingston v Kingston* (1968) 102 ILTR 65 at 67 . In *Dunn v Teti* (1980) 280 Pa Super 399 at 403-404, 421, A 2d 782 at 784-785,

negligence of a child should be judged by the same standard as that regarding his or her contributory negligence.

**[40.28]** Despite strong pressure from certain academic commentators, the Courts in the United States have maintained the same approach.[49].

## Children Performing Adult Activities[50]

**[40.29]** Reference should be made to a development in the law in a number of countries overseas - including the United States of America,[51] Canada,[52] Australia[53] and New Zealand[54] - which has not so far taken place in Irish law. Courts in these countries have imposed the adult standard of negligence on children performing what are considered to be "adult activities", such as driving a car,[55] motorcycle[56] and tractor[57] (though not usually a bicycle[58] in spite of the dangers associated with this activity for young and old alike).[59]

---

48. (contd) the Superior Court of Pennsylvania rejected as "completely speculative in nature" the argument that contributory negligence usually involves a child's comprehension of the acts or neglect of people around him, and that it takes greater maturity and judgment to comprehend and avoid danger created by others than to avoid danger created by one's own acts. Contrast *Roberts v Ring* (1919) 143 Minn 151, 173 NW 437 and see Shulman 'The Standard of Care Required of Children' (1928) 37 Yale LJ 618 at 619; James 'Accident Liability Reconsidered: The Impact of Liability Insurance' (1948) 57 Yale LJ 549 at 554-556.
49. See eg, *Dunn v Teti* (1980) 280 Pa Super 399, 421 A 2d 782.
50. See Binchy 'The Adult Activities Doctrine in Negligence Law' (1985) 11 Wm Mitchell LR 733.
51. *Cf Dellwo v Pearson* (1961) 258 Minn 452, 107 NW 2d 859 (SC); *Goss v Allen* (1976) 70 NJ 442, 360 A 2d 388 (SC); see further PROSSER & KEETON, pp 181-182, Galiher 'Degree of Care Required on Minors While Performing Adult Tasks' (1968) 17 Defense LJ 657; Longeteig 'The Minor Motorist - A Double Standard of Care?' (1965) 2 Idaho LR 103; see also notes by Rosenberg in (1969) 20 Syracuse LR 823; Stobbs in (1969) 71 W Virg LR 439 and Anon in [1962] Duke LJ 138.
52. *Cf Ryan v Hickson* (1974) 7 OR (2d) 352, 55 DLR (3d) 196 (HC), strongly influenced by the argument of Professor Allen Linden in *Canadian Negligence Law* (1972), pp 33-34. See also *McErlean v Sarel* (1987) 61 OR (2d) 396, 42 DLR (4th) 577 (CA); *Rice v Chan Estate* (1998) 84 ACWS (SC); *Parrill v Genge* (1994) 52 ACWS 3d 229; (1994) ACW 5 LEXIS 9480 (Newfoundland SC); *cf Nespolon v Alford* (1998) 161 DLR (4th) 646 (Ont CA); *R v Creighton* [1993] 3 SCR 3.
53. *Cf Tucker v Tucker* [1956] SASR 297 (SC).
54. *Cf Taurunga Electric Power Board v Karon* [1939] NZLR 104 (CA), analysed by Anon, 'Comment' (1940) 18 Can BR 67. *Cf Ralph v Henderson & Pollard Ltd* [1968] NZLR 759 (SC). See further Binchy 'The Adult Activities Doctrine in Negligence Law' (1985) 11 Wm Mitchell LR 733 at 757-759.
55. *Cf*, eg *Nielsen v Brown* (1962) 232 Or 426, 374 P 2d 896; *Betzold v Erickson* (1962) 35 Ill Appeal 2d 203, 182 NE 2d 342; *Woolaston v Burlington N Inc* (1980) 612 P 2d 1277; *Tucker v Tucker* [1956] SASR 297; *Ralph v Henderson & Pollard Ltd* [1968] NZLR 759 at 763; *Rice v Chan Estate* (1998) 84 ACWS; *Nespolon v Alford* (1998) 161 DLR (4th) 646 - where Abella JA sought to limit the scope of operation of the doctrine.
56. *Cf* eg, *Tipton v Mullinix* (1973) 508 P 2d 1072; *McNall v Farmersins Group* (1979) 181 Ind Appeal 501, 392 NE 2d 520.
57. *Cf*, eg, *Goodfellow v Coggburn* (1977) 98 Idaho 202, 560 P 2d 873.
58. *Cf*, eg, *Williams v Gilbert* (1966) 239Ark 935 SW 2d 333; *Conway v Tambonni* (1966) 68 Ill Appeal 2d 190, 215 NE 2d 303; *Broadhurst v Millman* [1976] Vict R 208 (SC); *Tauranga Electric Power Board v Karon* [1939] NZLR 104 (CA); *Sagor v Joseph Burnett Co* (1937) 122 Conn 447, 190 A 258. See also *McErlean v Sarel* (1987) 61 OR (2d) 396, 42 DLR (4th) 577 - trail bike.
59. *Cf Goss v Allen* (1976) 70 NJ 442 at 453, fn 2, 360 A 2d 388 at 394, fn 2 (*per* Schreider J, dissenting).

**[40.30]** Concern for the plight of the victim seems to be at the base of this development. Yet if one accepts this reason in this limited context, it is difficult to see why allowance should be made for youthfulness in any other case. Moreover, once the "adult activities" doctrine is extended to conduct off the highway, its conceptual inadequacy becomes apparent. It is not hard to accept that driving a power boat[60] should come within the scope of the doctrine, but what about such activities as playing golf,[61] skiing,[62] or deerhunting?[63] Possibly the notion of an "inherently dangerous activity" may explain the Courts' resolution of these questions,[64] but it would scarcely justify the imposition of an objective adult standard on a child engaging in such an activity while applying the subjective standard of care to a child engaged in an activity which, though not inherently dangerous, is on the particular occasion extremely dangerous.

## Tort and Contract

**[40.31]** Under the Infants' Relief Act 1874, many minors' contract are unenforceable, and the courts have been astute to prevent the subverting of the policy of this statute by parties to such contracts seeking to bring their actions in tort instead. Hence, where a cause of action is really founded on the wrongful mode of performance of a contract, the injured party may not proceed by framing the action in tort: as we have seen, in the leading Irish case of *O'Brien v McNamee*, Davitt P, in imposing liability in tort on the infant defendant, held that a child can be liable in tort "provided that it does not arise out of contract". Indeed, this policy has been extended to preclude liability in tort for deceit for a minor who has procured a contract by a fraudulent misrepresentation that he or she of full age.[65]

**[40.32]** However, a minor will be liable for a tort where, although the injury occurs in a contractual setting, the tort is nevertheless independent of the contract. This is merely an application in the context of minors' contracts of the more general problem of concurrent liability between tort and contract. At what point an act ceases to be merely a misperformance of a contract and becomes instead conduct altogether outside the contract

60. *Cf Dellwo v Pearson* (1961) 258 Minn 452, 107 NW 2d 859.

61. *Cf Neumann v Shlansky* (1971) 36 A 2d 540, 318 NYS 2d 925.

62. *Cf Goss v Allen* (1976) 70 NJ 442.

63. *Cf Purtle v Shelton* (1971) 251 Ark 519, 474 SW 2d 123.

64. *Cf Robinson v Lindsay* (1979) 92 Wash 2d 410 at 413, 598 P 2d 392 at 393-394 (SC).

65. *Johnson v Pye* (1966) 1 Sid 258, 82 ER 1091. See generally Atiyah 'The Liability of Infants in Fraud and Restitution' (1959) 22 MLR 273; Payne 'The Contractual Liability of Infants (1966) 5 Western LR 136 at 150-152; Pearse 'Fraudulent Infant Contractors' (1968) 42 Austr LJ 294; Percy 'The Present Law of Infants contracts' (1975) 53 Can BR 1. Indeed, the policy against indriect enforcement of the contract has precluded restitution of money paid pursuant to such fraudulently induced contracts: *R Leslie Ltd v Sheill* [1914] 3 KB 607 (CA), though it is questionable whether the policy is nowadays as strong (see Burrows *The Law of Restitution* (1993), pp 451-453). The Law Reform Commission, in its *Report on Minors' Contracts* (LRC 15-1985) pp 152-153, recommended the continuation of the rule that a minor should not be exposed to an action in tort where this would amount to an indirect enforcement of an unenforceable contract. It was satisfied that the broad restitutionary principle it proposed in relation to minors' contracts in general would afford the adult party adequate protection in such circumstances, including cases of misrepresentation as to age.

is a difficult question and clearly will depend greatly on the Court's assessment of the facts in question.[66]

## Proposals for Reform

**[40.33]** In 1985, the Law Reform Commission made detailed proposals for reform of the law in its *Report on the Liability in Tort of Minors and the Liability of Parents for Damage Caused by Minors*.[67]

**[40.34]** As regards the torts of trespass to the person, goods or land, the Commission was of the view that the attribution of responsibility to a child based on intention or negligence was too simplistic an approach:

> "A very young child may be aware of the probable consequences of his or her actions and may actively desire to bring them about but it may be argued that this species of 'intent' should not be regarded as the same, psychologically or morally, as that of an older person. The young child's lack of maturity, lack of full appreciation of the consequences of his or her action and incompletely developed sense of moral responsibility will all serve to differentiate his or her conduct from that of an older person."[68]

**[40.35]** Accordingly, the Commission recommended that in proceedings against a child under sixteen for trespass, where it has been established that the child's action was voluntary and intentional, liability should be imposed:

> "unless the child can show, to the satisfaction of the Court, that, having regard to his or her age, mental development and experience, he or she had not such personal responsibility for the action that it would be just to impose liability on the child for the action".[69]

This approach echoes the subjective test applied to the question of a child's negligence or contributory negligence.

**[40.36]** Whether it will be as helpful in relation to the issue of moral responsibility for intentional conduct may be debated. In effect, it remits to the court the task of addressing this difficult subject unhampered by legislative limitations.

**[40.37]** As regards negligence and contributory negligence, the Commission was satisfied to retain the subjective test of referring to the particular child's age, intelligence and experience; but it recommended that courts should no longer address the misconceived and misleading question of whether the child was of a sufficient age to be capable of negligence or contributory negligence. The Commission proposed that, at the age of sixteen, the subjective standard should no longer apply; but the Commission had no desire to introduce the "inherent injustice and uncertainty" of the "adult activities" doctrine.[70] To compensate the victims of child drivers who escaped liability by reason only of the

---

66. There appears to be no reported modern Irish decision in point. Two of the leading early decisions *Jennings v Rundall* (1799) 8 TR 335, 101 ER 1419, and *Burnard v Haggis* (1863) 14 CB (NS) 45, 143 ER 360, are concerned with the same general default, the wrongful riding of a hired mare, but come to different conclusions on the facts. See also *Ballett v Mingay* [1943] KB 281 (CA).

67. LRC 17-1985.

68. LRC 17-1985, p 63.

69. LRC 17-1985, p 64

70. LRC 17-1985, at 64

application of the subjective test, the Commission proposed the establishment of a State fund. The fund would apply only to personal injuries; moreover, if a party to the proceedings other than the child were held liable for the injury, that party would compensate the victim with no recourse to the State compensation fund.

## II. Mentally Ill Persons[71]

**[40.38]** The liability of mentally ill persons in tort is a matter of considerable uncertainty. Formerly, it appears that no concession would be made to insanity.[72] Today, that position has been qualified somewhat and the rules on the matter may be summarised as follows.

### Torts of Strict Liability

**[40.39]** In torts of strict liability, it appears that mental illness will not afford a defence unless the defendant could not be regarded as having "acted" voluntarily - where his behaviour was that of an automaton, for example.

### Torts Involving a Specific Mental Ingredient

**[40.40]** Certain torts, such as malicious prosecution or libel on a privileged occasion, require a specific mental ingredient - malice - on the part of the defendant. Where the defendant's mental condition prevents him from having this ingredient, the defendant will not be liable.[73]

### Trespass to the Person, Goods or Land

**[40.41]** So far as the torts of trespass to the person, goods or land are concerned, it seems that once the defendant acted voluntarily[74] he or she will be liable if aware of the nature

---

71. See generally, the Law Reform Commission's *Report on the Liability in Tort of Mentally Disordered Persons* (LRC 18-1985); Fridman 'Mental Incompetency, Part II, (1964) 80 LQR 84 at 84-96; Todd 'The Liability of Lunatics in the Law of Tort' (1952) 26 ALJ 299; Bohlen 'Liability in Tort of Infants and Insane Persons' (1924) 23 Mich LR 9; Picher 'The Tortious Liability of the insane in Canada' (1975) 13 OHLJ 193; Curran 'Tort Liability of the Mentally Ill and Mentally Deficient' (1960) 21 Ohio St LJ 54; Ague 'The Liability of Insane Persons in Tort Action' (1956) 60 Dick LR 211; Wilkinson 'Mental Incompetency as a Defense to Tort Liability' (1944) 17 Rocky Mt LR 38; Robins 'Liability in Tort of Mental Incompetents' [1963] Lectures of the Law Soc of Upper Can 77; Primeau 'Insanity and the Law of Torts' Ch 5 of *Law Reform Reconnaissance Programme, Part II* (1974, Legal Research Institute of the University of Manitoba); Korrell 'The Liability of Mentally Disabled Tort Defendants' (1995) 19 L & Psychol Rev 1.

72. *Cf Weaver v Ward* (1616) Hob 134, 80 ER 284; *Borradaile v Hunter* (1843) 5 Man & G 639 at 669, 134 ER 715 at 728; *Taggart v Innes* (1862) 12 UCCP 77.

73. *Cf Donaghy v Brennan* (1900) 19 NZLR 289, briefly noted by Pollock, (1902) 18 LQR 30.

74. *Cf Beals v Hayward* [1960] NZLR 131 (SC); *White v Pile* (1950) 68 WN (NSW) 176 at 178; *Wilson v Zeron* [1941] OWN 353 at 354, affd [1942] OWN 195 (CA); *Lawson v Wellesley Hospital* (1975) 61 DLR (3d) 445 at 450 (Ont CA), affd (1982) 76 DLR (3d) 688 (SC, Can); *Squittieri v de Santis* (1976) 15 OR (2d) 416, 75 DLR 3d 629 (HC); *Gerigs v Rose* 9 CCLT 222 (Ont HC, affd Ont CA, 28 February 1998); *Whaley v Cartusiano* (1990) 68 DLR (4th) 58 (Ont CA). In *Adamson v Motor Vehicle Insurance Trust* (1957) 58 WALR 56 at 67 (WA SC); Wolfe SPJ expressed the view, obiter that "[if] the law is to be logical, it ought to fix the actor with liability" even in cases where his or her act was not voluntary. *Cf Attorney General of Canada v Connolly* (1989) 64 DLR (4th) 84 (BC, SC).

and quality of the tortious act, even though the defendant does not know that what he or she is doing is wrong.

**[40.42]** The leading English decision on the subject is *Morriss v Marsden*.[75] There, liability for battery was imposed on a catatonic schizophrenic who knew the nature and quality of his act but whose incapacity of reason arising from the disease of his mind was of so grave a character that he did not know that what he was doing was wrong.[76] Stable J accepted that a condition of complete automatism would relieve a defendant of liability, but that:

> "Where there is the capacity to know the nature and quality of the act, that is sufficient although the mind directing the hand that did the wrong was diseased."[77]

**[40.43]** In the Circuit Court decision of *Donohue v Coyle*,[78] an insane person was found liable for battery. In a two-sentence judgment Judge Sheehy stated that in the circumstances he felt he "must follow"[79] the English decision of *Morriss v Marsden*.[80]

**[40.44]** This laconic judgment throws no light on how the Judge came to the conclusion that he "must follow" a decision of a trial judge in another jurisdiction.[81] Possibly he considered Stable J's approach to have a compelling attraction from the standpoint of policy. It is unfortunate that authorities from other common law jurisdictions were not cited to the Court. In fact decisions before and subsequent to *Donohue v Coyle* have favoured widely differing approaches to the question. Some[82] in effect exclude the defence

---

75. [1952] 1 All ER 925 (QB), critically analysed by Todd 'Note' (1952) 15 MLR 486; Todd 'The Liability of Lunatics in the Law of Torts' (1952) 26 Austr LJ 299. Anon 'Note' (1952) 68 LQR. 300, and Fridman 'Mental Incompetency, Part II', (1964) 80 LQR 84 at 87-88, Picher 'The Tortious Liability of the insane in Canada' (1975) 13 OHLJ 193 at 212-213; Robins 'Liability in Tort of Mental Incompetents' [1963] Sp Lectures of the Law Soc of Upper Can 77 at 83-84. The practical problems of granting non-molestation injunctions against mentally disabled defendants are discussed in *Wookey vWookey* [1991] Fam 121 (CA); *P v P* [1999] 3 FCR 547 (CA).

76. [1952] 1 All ER 925 at 926-927.

77. [1952] 1 All ER 925 at 928.

78. [1953-1954] Ir Jur Rep 30 (CC).

79. [1953-1954] Ir Jur Rep 30 at 31.

80. [1952] 1 All ER 925. The same approach was favoured in the Canadian decision of *Phillips v Soloway* (1956) 6 DLR (2d) 570 (Man QB), where Williams CJ followed *Morriss v Marsden*. See Robins 'Tort Liability of the Mentally Disabled' Ch 4 of *Studies in Canadian Tort Law* (1968) Linden ed; Picher 'The Tortious Liability of the insane in Canada' (1975) 13 OHLJ 193 at 210-214. See also *Squittieri v de Santis* (1976) 15 OR (2d) 416 (HC); *Lawson v Wellesley Hospital* (1975) 61 DLR (3d) 445 at 450 (Ont CA), aff'd (1982) 76 DLR (3d) 688 (SC, Can); *Gerigs v Rose* 9 CCLT 222 (Ont HC, affd Ont CA, 28 February 1998); *Whaley v Cartusiano* (1990) 68 DLR (4th) 58 (Ont CA); *Beale v Beale* (1982) 52 NSR (2d) 550 (SC).

81. In this general context Walsh J's observations in his Foreword to McMahon & Binchy, *A Casebook on the Irish Law of Torts* (1st ed, 1983), are of interest.

82. *Cf Adamson v Motor Vehicle Insurance Trust* (1957) 58 WALR 56 (WA, SC); *Taggart v Innes* (1862) 12 UCCP 77.

of insanity; others[83] have taken much the same view as in *Morriss v Marsden*; still others[84] have applied the M'Naghten Rules.

## Proposals for Reform

**[40.45]** In its *Report on the Liability in Tort of Mentally Disabled Persons*,[85] published in 1985, the Law Reform Commission made detailed proposals for the reform of the law. In relation to the torts of trespass to the person, to goods and to land, the Commission recommended that where it is shown (a) that the defendant was so affected by mental disability as substantially to lack the capacity to act freely, and (b) that as a result of this substantial lack of capacity the defendant did the act complained of, the defendant should be relieved of liability for a trespass on the ground that his or her act was not voluntary. Moreover, where the defendant's conduct was voluntary, the defendant should nonetheless be relieved of liability if his or her mental disability was "such as to prevent the defendant from acting with the purpose of bringing about the effect in question".[86] The Commission also considered that where, under present law, a reasonable mistake relieves a defendant from liability for trespass, it should also be an effective defence to establish that the defendant did the act complained of as a result of a mistake brought about by mental disability. As regards other torts in which questions of voluntariness and intention can arise, the Commission recommended that the changes it proposed in relation to trespass should also apply to these other torts.

**[40.46]** The Commission recommended that, when determining a person's negligence or contributory negligence, the law should apply an objective test, unless that person established (a) that at the time of the act in question, he or she was suffering from a serious mental disability which affected him or her in the performance of the act, and (b) that this disability made him or her unable to behave according to the standard of care appropriate to the reasonable person. In such circumstances, the person should be held not to have been guilty of negligence or contributory negligence.

**[40.47]** A few points about this recommendation may be noted. It would dispense with the objective test only where the mental disability was both serious and such as to have made the affected person unable to behave according to the objective test. As the Commission noted:

> "It is not every disability, even a serious one, that would have this effect. It is possible, for example, that a paranoid or seriously depressed person could, in spite of his or her condition, retain the ability to act according to the standard of care appropriate to the reasonable person when performing certain acts, such as driving a car or holding an expensive antique."[87]

---

83. *Cf Wilson v Zeron* [1941] OWN 353, affd on another ground [1942] OWN 195 (CA); *Phillips v Soloway* (1956) 6 DLR (2d) 570 (Man, QB); *Squittieri v de Santis* (1976) 15 OR (2d) 416 (HC); *Beale v Beale* (1928) 24 CCLT 101 (NS SC) (*semble*).

84. Eg *White v Pile* (1950) 68 WN (NSW) 176 criticised by Todd 'The Liability of Lunatics in the Law of Tort' (1952) 26 Austr LJ 299 at 301. See, however, Picher 'The Tortious Liability of the insane in Canada' (1975) 13 OHLJ 193 at 212. See also *Tindale v Tindale* [1950] 4 DLR 363 (BC SC).

85. LRC 18-1985.

86. LRC 18-1985, p 59.

87. LRC 18-1985, p 71.

**[40.48]** The Commission was not, however, disposed to apply this subjective test to cases where a mentally disabled person drives a motor vehicle. Here the objective test should prevail,[88] moderated only by the Commission's general recommendation as to voluntariness, which it considered would "afford sufficient flexibility to deal with cases involving the sudden onset of insanity".[89]

**[40.49]** Finally, the Commission proposed[90] that, in cases where a defendant was not liable in tort by reason of his or her mental disability, an employer or principal who would otherwise be vicariously[91] liable for the tort should be liable in spite of the mental incapacity. Before such liability could attach, the general principle of respondeat superior required that the tort should have been committed in the course of the employee's employment:

> "Thus, for example, if a mentally ill barman attacked a patron whom (on account of the illness) he believed to be a robber, then the employer could be vicariously liable, but if the same barman attacked a patron because (on account of the illness) he thought that the patron was having an affair with his wife, then the employer would not be liable."[92]

88. LRC 18-1985.
89. LRC 18-1985.
90. LRC 18-1985, p 72.
91. Personal liability would, of course attach for lack of due care in the selection of a mentally disabled employee whose condition ought to have excluded him from that particular assignment.
92. LRC 18-1985, p 72.

# Chapter 41

# Survival of Actions on Death

I. Historical Introduction ........ 1061
II. The Present Law ........ 1062

## I. Historical Introduction

**[41.01]** Death can affect recovery in tort in a number of ways, raising three principal questions. First, where one of the parties to an existing tort dispute dies before the case is heard does the right to sue or be sued survive for, or against, the estate of the deceased (as the case may be)? Second, if the act of one person causes the death of another, may the estate of the deceased sue in respect of that injury? Third, may the relatives of a person wrongfully killed sue for loss of benefits incurred by them as a result of the death? In the first case, the death of one of the parties is irrelevant to the commission of the alleged tort; in the second and third cases, however, death is the very act complained of. These questions will be dealt with in this chapter and in Chapter 42.

**[41.02]** The common law answer to the first question was contained in the Latin maxim *actio personalis moritur cum persona*. Death ended all actions in personal torts. The exact reasons for this rule are rather obscure and the rule is difficult to justify when it is appreciated that contract actions (except in relation to personal contracts) survived for or against the estate of the deceased. It has been suggested that the late development of the tort remedy as an incident to criminal punishment in the old appeal of felony and trespass which followed it meant that, when the deceased died, criminal punishment on his or her person being no longer possible, the criminal action fell and the tort action abated with it.[1]

**[41.03]** In any event, whatever its origins and its rationale, some major statutory exceptions were made to the rule, the principal ones being contained in old statutes of 1285 and 1330 (applied to Ireland by Poynings' Law (1495)), and in s 31 of the Debtors' (Ireland) Act 1840. These enactments provided the personal representatives of the deceased with an action in respect of the trespass to real or personal property of the deceased committed during the deceased's lifetime. Other more recent statutory exceptions were to be found in s 117 of the Road Traffic Act 1961 (in relation to personal liability for negligent driving), in s 23 of Air Navigation and Transport Act 1936 (in respect of damage caused by aircraft to persons or property) and in s 6 of the Fatal Injuries Act 1956 (discussed in Chapter 42).

1. See Winfield 'Death as Affecting Liability in Tort' (1929) 29 Col LR 239; White, *Irish Law of Damages for Personal Injuries and Death* (1989), para 14.1.01; Kerr, *The Civil Liability Acts* (1999), pp 7-11.

## II. The Present Law

**[41.04]** The law on this matter was amended and consolidated in the Civil Liability Act 1961 (ss 6-10). The general rule now is that all causes of action[2] (other than "excepted causes of action" within the meaning of the 1961 Act) vested in a deceased person or subsisting against him or her, survive for the benefit of, or against, the deceased person's estate as the case may be. The characteristic feature of the "excepted causes of action" which continue to abate with the death of the plaintiff or the defendant is their heavy personal element. An "excepted cause of action" is defined in s 6 of the Act (as amended by subsequent legislation) as one for defamation or seduction or any claim for compensation under the Workman's Compensation Act 1934.[3]

**[41.05]** Where a person dies, however, and a cause of action vested in that person survives for the benefit of his or her estate, the damages recoverable in such an action cannot include damages for purely "personal" loss. Accordingly, exemplary damages, damages for any pain and suffering or personal injury or for loss or diminution of expectation of life or happiness are irrecoverable in any such action.[4] In other words, while the law is willing to allow an action in such circumstances it is unwilling to allow recovery in respect of those items of damage which are intimately connected with the deceased's person.

---

2. Including a claim under the Unfair Dismissals Act 1977 (as amended): *Williams v Tom Duffy & Co* UD 687/1986, extracted in Madden & Kerr, *Unfair Dismissal: Cases and Commentary* (2nd ed), p 60. It has been pointed out by Kerr, *The Civil Liability Acts* (1999), p 8 that s 1(1) of the 1977 Act defines "employee" as including, "in the case of the death of the employee concerned at any time following the dismissal, his personal representative".

3. Formerly the list of "excepted causes of action" was more extensive. The Family Law Act 1981 declared that after the passing of the Act no action should lie for criminal conversation, for inducing one spouse to leave or remain apart from the other spouse, or for harbouring a spouse (s 1(1)).It also abolished the action for breach of promise of marriage. All of these actions had been "excepted causes of action" under s 6 of the 1961 Act. The Workman's Compensation Acts 1934-1955 were repealed by s 40 of the Social Welfare (Occupational Injuries) Act 1966, as amended by the Social Welfare (Consolidation) Act 1981, "thus rendering s 6(6) [of the 1961 Act] redundant for all practical purposes": Kerr, *The Civil Liability Acts* (1999), p 19; FLEMING, p 743, fn 242, has criticised the manner in which the philosophy underlying "excepted causes of action" has been implemented in survival legislation in most jurisdictions:

> "The common link appears to be injury to dignitary interests but, by identifying torts rather than the nature of the harm, some claims are invidiously excluded from the list (eg false imprisonment and malicious prosecution ...), while others are unjustifiably included (eg 'special damages' for defamation). Besides, it would have been more sensible to distinguish ... between the wrongdoer's death and the victim's. The first does not mitigate the plaintiff's damages at all and should accordingly be ignored."

4. Section 7(2). This reverses *Rose v Ford* [1937] AC 826 on recovery for loss of expectation of life. Note that the death of the defendant would not prevent an award for exemplary damages against his or her estate. This distinction has been criticised: Anon (1935) 48 Harv LR 1008 at 1011. For a critical analysis of the survival of loss of expectation of life claims in some jurisdictions in the United States of America, see Nicholson 'Hedonic Damages in Wrongful Death and Survival of Actions: The Impact of Alzheimer's Disease' (1994) 2 Elder LJ 249. In *Monahan v Nelson* (2000) 186 DLR (4th) 193, the British Columbia Court of Appeal held that, where the plaintiff dies after the final and before judgment has been delivered, the court should back date the judgment to the last day of the trial so as to permit the plaintiff's estate to review non-pecuniary damages to the time of plaintiff's death.

**[41.06]** Where the circumstances which occasioned the death of the deceased also vested in the deceased a cause of action against the defendant, such cause of action survives and may be prosecuted for the benefit of his or her estate. The damages in any such action recoverable must be calculated without reference to any loss or gain consequent on the death of the plaintiff, except that a sum covering funeral expenses may be allowed.[5] This means that if X is killed through Y's negligence, in the action by X's estate against Y, gains which X's estate has made by virtue of insurance policies, etc, or losses such as the termination of a life interest in property, must not be taken into account.

**[41.07]** In *Gammell v Wilson*[6] a 15-year-old traveller was wrongfully killed by the defendant. His father sued as a dependant and also on behalf of the estate. The dependency was valued at £2,000 but the loss to the estate was calculated as being £6,656. The House of Lords held that, where a person is wrongfully killed and his working-life cut short, his estate may recover in respect of the earnings (less cost of maintaining himself) which he would have made during the working-years lost as a result of the accident. As beneficiaries to the deceased's estate, the parents recovered substantially more (£4,656) than they would have as dependants. The High Court of Australia[7] also allowed recovery by the estate of the deceased in respect of loss of earnings in the "lost years". Because of the possibility of double liability to different plaintiffs, legislation has reversed *Gammell* in Britain and in most jurisdictions in Australia.[8] Since *Gammell* is based on statutory provisions and a previous precedent both of which have Irish counterparts,[9] Dr White argues convincingly that it is difficult to see how its effect can be avoided in Ireland.[10]

**[41.08]** The rights conferred under s 7 are in addition to the rights of dependants under the fatal injuries provisions of the Civil Liability Act 1961 (ss 47-51) and under the Air Navigation and Transport Act 1936 (s 7(4)), but in actions under these provisions it seems that damages awarded to dependants will have to take into account damages awarded to the estate under s 7.[11]

---

5. Section 7(3).
6. [1982] AC 27. See also *Furness v B & S Massey Ltd* an appeal heard with *Gammell*. The nature of the dependency action is explained in Ch 42. See further Kerr, *The Civil Liablity Acts* (1999), p 8.
7. *Fitch v Hyde-Cates* (1982) 150 Comm LR 482; *Loo v Harbord Administration Pty Ltd* (1994) NSW LEXIS 13463 BC 9403236 (NSW); *Commonwealth of Australia v McLean* (1996) NSW LEXIS 3697, BC 9606-432 (NSW, CA); *Semenoff v Kokan* (1991) 84 DLR (4th) 76 (BC CA). Canadian decisions, based on differing provincial legislative provisions, are conflicting: see *Lamey v Wentworth Valley Developments Ltd* (1998) 165 DLR (4th) 758 (NS SC); *Duncan Estate v Baddeley* (1997) 1450 DLR 4th 708 (Alta CA). For an economic analysis, see Brown, (1997) 35 Alta LR 1108.
8. As to Britain, see the Administration of Justice Act 1982, s 4. As to Australian statutory changes, see TRINDADE & CANE, p 549.
9. Section 7 of Civil Liability Act 1961 and *Doherty v Bowaters Irish Wallboard Mills Ltd* [1968] IR 277. The English provision is s 1(2)(c) of Law Reform Act 1934 and the case is *Pickett v British Rail Engineering Ltd* [1980] 1 AC 136, [1979] 1 All ER 774. *Gammell*'s effect will be most dramatic where the dependency is small.
10. See White, *Irish Law of Damages for Personal Injuries and Death* (1989), paras 14.3.03-14.3.04; White 'Insurers at Bay - Repercussions of *Gammell v Wilson*' (1981) 75 Incorp L Soc of Ireland Gaz 77; Pigot, '*Gammell v Wilson and Ors* - A Further Commentary' (1982) 76 Inc Law Soc of Ireland Gaz, 65, and White 'Damages for the Lost Earnings of the Lost Years' (1985) 20 Ir Jur (ns) 295. See further para **[41.12]** below.
11. See Explanatory Memorandum to Civil Liability Bill 1960, p 3, White, *Irish Law of Damages for Personal Injuries and Death* (1989), para 14.4.02.

**[41.09]** Since no special limitation period is provided where the plaintiff dies, such actions are subject to the ordinary limitation period set out in the Statute of Limitations 1957, as amended by s 4 of the Statute of Limitations Act 1961.[12]

**[41.10]** Section 8 establishes the rule that causes of action (save for "excepted causes of action") also survive against the deceased person's estate.[13] Section 8(2), moreover, provides for the survival of an action where the proposed defendant dies at the same time as the act which causes the injury, or between the act and the damage necessary to make the act actionable. For example, if D withdraws support from P's property and D dies before damage is caused to P's property, it could be argued that, since there was no damage at the time of D's death, no tort existed then, and no action could lie against D's estate.[14] Section 8(2) provides that an action will lie against D's estate in these circumstances.

**[41.11]** The 1961 Act recognises the legitimate interest of the personal representative of the defendant's estate to wind up the estate within a reasonable time by providing special (shortened) limitation periods during which such actions must be brought. If the action was commenced before the defendant's death, and the action was pending at the date of death, the ordinary period of limitation provided for in the Statute of Limitations 1957 applies. In all other cases the action must be commenced within the ordinary period or within two years of death, whichever is the shorter.[15] In *Moynihan v Greensmyth*[16] an argument was made that s 9 was unconstitutional in so far as the right to sue was a property right protected by Article 40.3.2° of the Constitution. The Supreme Court rejected this argument, declaring that, on the assumption that the plaintiff's right to sue was a property right, it had not been shown that the State had failed to protect it from unjust attack and, in the case of injustice done, had failed to vindicate the property right of the plaintiff, having regard to the competing interest of other citizens to have an early completion of the administration of estates of deceased persons.

**[41.12]** By way of summary, therefore, one may say that on the death of a party to a tortious dispute the right to sue or the liability to be sued normally survives for the benefit of, or against, the estate of the deceased. The kinds of damages recoverable where the

---

12. See para **[46.90]** below.

13. An action commenced by an employee under the Unfair Dismissals Act 1977 is not defeated by the death of the employer: *Hutton v Philippi* [1982] ILRM 578 (Employment Appeals Tribunal UD 1980/291). It is worth noting that s 8, while excluding "excepted causes of action", does not contain an equivalent to s 7 regarding the categories of damages that may be recovered: see Kerr, *The Civil Liablity Acts* (1999), p 9.

14. See *Backhouse v Bonomi* (1861) 9 HLC 503, 11 ER 825.

15. Section 9. This section does not apply to an action for the recovery of damages under the Liability for Defective Products Act 1991: see s 7(3) of the 1991 Act. Kerr, *The Civil Liability Acts* (1999), p 10, notes that s 281(3A) of the Social Welfare (Consolidation) Act 1993, inserted by s 41 of the Social Welfare Act 1996, provides that s 9 shall not apply to an action for the recovery of a debt due to the Minister for Social Community and Family Affairs or to the State under that Act. Section 10 of the 1961 Act provides that such a claim against an insolvent estate, in spite of the fact that it is a demand in the nature of unliquidated damages otherwise than by contract, will be provable in the administration of the defendant's estate.

16. [1977] IR 55; Hogan & Whyte, *Kelly: The Irish Constitution* (3rd ed, 1994), pp 1071-1072. *Cf McCullough v Ireland* [1989] IR 484 (HC).

would-be plaintiff dies are limited, however and, where the death itself is the wrong complained of, then in such an action no account will be taken of gains (eg insurance payments) or losses (eg termination of life interests) consequent on death, but damages to the estate for the "the lost years" might be claimed.[17]

17. It should be repeated, however, that there has as yet been no judicial pronouncement in our courts on the issue raised in *Gammell v Wilson*, discussed at para **[41.07]** above. *Cf Mahon v Burke and Mid-Western Health Board* [1991] ILRM 59 (HC) (approving dictum of Lord Diplock in *Gammell v Wilson* on a narrower issue).

# Chapter 42

# Fatal Injuries


I. Introduction ........ 1067
II. The Statutory Right of the Dependants ........ 1069


## I. Introduction

**[42.01]** Besides the common law rule that no actions survived on the death of one of the parties, another common law rule existed which declared that "the death of a human being could not be complained of as an injury".[1] This meant that while the law recognised other injuries, eg physical injuries, injuries to property, etc, as deserving of protection, no such recognition was given to death. Consequently, at common law the dead man's estate had no right to sue in respect of his death, nor had the relatives or dependants of the deceased any right to sue in respect of the death. In this regard it was true to say that "it was cheaper to kill than to maim". This harsh rule was mitigated by statute, however, as early as 1846 (Lord Campbell's Act) where a statutory right to sue was given to the dependants of the deceased in respect of their dependency. This Act was amended and extended several times since that date and the dependants' right to sue is now to be found in ss 47-51 of the Civil Liability Act 1961[2] (as amended by the Civil Liability (Amendment) Act 1996). Section 48(1) of the Civil Liability Act 1961 now provides as follows:

> "Where the death of a person is caused by the wrongful act of another such as would have entitled the party injured, but for his death, to maintain an action and recover damages in respect thereof, the person who would have been so liable shall be liable to an action for damages for the benefit of the dependants of the deceased."

**[42.02]** Only one such action may be brought in respect of the death[3] and the proper party to initiate proceedings is the personal representative of the deceased; if the personal

---

1. *Baker v Bolton* (1808) 1 Camp 493 at 493, 170 ER 1033 at 1033. For an excellent historical treatment of the subject, leading to a comprehensive comparative analysis see Speiser, *Recovery for Wrongful Death* (2nd ed, 1975). A comprehensive analysis of Irish law is provided by White *Irish Law of Damages for Personal Injuries and Death* (1989) and by Kerr, *The Civil Liability Acts* (1999), pp 57-65. For other detailed treatments, see Knight 'Some Aspects of Damages under the Civil Liability Acts, 1961 and 1964' (1966) 1 Ir Jur (ns) 35. Shatter, *Family Law* (4th ed, 1997), pp 266-270; Delany 'Assessment of Damages in Fatal Injuries Cases' (1962-63) 28-29 Ir Jur 30; de Blaghd 'Ten Years of the Civil Liability Act Parts 10-12' (1972) 106 ILT & Sol J 205, 211 at 217 and the Law Reform Commission's *Report on Personal Injuries: Periodic Payments and Structured Settlements* (LRC 54-1996), Ch 3. For recent English analysis of the subject see Munkman, *Damages for Personal Injuries and Death* (6th ed, 1980) Ch 5; the English Law Commission's Consultation Paper No 148, *Claims for Wrongful Death* (1997), Appendix (A10-A18).
2. This Act re-enacts and amends the Fatal Injuries Act 1956 which consolidated and amended the Fatal Accident Acts 1846-1908. Because of the consolidating nature of the 1961 Act much of the case law on the early legislation remains relevant.
3. Section 48(2).

representative does not take action within six months of the death or if there is no personal representative, then the action may be commenced by any or all of the dependants.[4] Such an action, however, whoever takes it, is in the nature of a class action for the benefit of all the dependants.[5] Moreover, a special period of limitation, of three years from the death, applies to such actions. Section 6(1) of the Statute of Limitations (Amendment) Act 1991 provides that an action under s 48 shall not be brought after the expiration of three years from (a) the date of death or (b) the "date of knowledge" of the person for whose benefit the action is brought, whichever is the later.[6]

**[42.03]** Dr White, in his comprehensive treatment of the subject,[7] contends that the Irish courts are not precluded by the statutory provision from recognising a *common law* right to sue for wrongful death. He bases his argument on the fact that the English authorities,[8] which deny a common law right in England, if closely analysed, are badly reasoned and do not support the conclusion frequently ascribed to them. Moreover, such an action by the dependants at common law can be supported on principle: it conforms with legitimate public expectations, and with the elementary considerations of fairness which have been partially recognised by legislation since 1846. Furthermore, the imposition of a common law duty in such circumstances in favour of the dependants would not be open-ended and would, it is submitted by Dr White, be confined to those who enjoy a *de facto* dependency upon the deceased arising out of a family-type relationship. Finally, there is no Irish decision where such a duty was canvassed and denied: the English authorities are merely persuasive and the US authorities[9] which rejected *Baker v Bolton*[10] are very convincing from the point of view of principle.

**[42.04]** As against this, the fact remains that legislation has dealt with the matter for a hundred and fifty years. The courts might well take the view that any possible common law right of action has long since been subsumed under these legislative provisions which, on a literal interpretation, appear to exclude any such common law gloss.

**[42.05]** If such a right to sue in respect of wrongful death were recognised in the common law of Ireland, depending on how it is eventually formulated by the courts, it might have the advantage as far as plaintiffs are concerned of (i) expanding the class of dependants who are entitled to sue beyond those recognised by statute, and (ii) expanding the kind of damages for which the dependants might claim, beyond the statutory entitlements, to include, perhaps, damages for loss of society and, in the case of children, loss of parental education. The common law might also take a different attitude to the situation where the deceased had compromised his or her claim before dying or where the claim has become statute-barred. The likelihood of this latter heading of damage (loss of parental education) must be somewhat doubtful now in view of the High Court decision in *Hosford v John*

---

4. Section 48(3).
5. Section 48(4). See *Mulholland v McCrea & Anor* [1961] NI 135.
6. See s 2 of the 1991 Act for what is meant by "date of knowledge". See on limitation period *Swords v Saint Patrick's Copper Mines Ltd* [1965] Ir Jur Rep 63 (SC); *Healy v Nolan* (1946) 80 ILTR 78 (SC).
7. White *Irish Law of Damages for Personal Injuries and Death* (1989), Ch 7.
8. Including *Baker v Bolton* (1808) 1 Camp 493.
9. See, for example, *Moragne v States Marine Lines Inc* (1970) 398 US 375.
10. *Baker v Bolton* (1808) 1 Camp 493, 170 ER 1033.

*Murphy & Sons*,[11] where Costello J refused to recognise that the defendant, who injured the plaintiff's father (and for which damages were already paid), also owed an independant duty of care in respect of the consequent damage to the children's relationship with their father. Costello J stated that neither the Constitution nor the common law recognised the heading of damage which deprived the children of moral intellectual, religious and educational benefits which normally flow from the presence of a healthy father in a normal family situation.

## II. The Statutory Right of the Dependants

**[42.06]** As already mentioned, the statutory right of the dependants has now been recognised in Part IV of the Civil Liability Act 1961, as amended by the Civil Liability (Amendment) Act 1996. A discussion of the statutory right to sue involves consideration of three issues: (i) who is entitled to sue? (ii) when and in what circumstances will liability arise? and (iii) for what injury can the statutory beneficiaries sue and how are damages calculated in the statutory action? A further word on each of these is now required.

### Who is Entitled to Sue?

**[42.07]** Before a person can sue under Part IV of the Civil Liability Act 1961 for wrongful death, he or she must show, first of all, financial dependency (or mental distress) and, secondly, a family-type relationship. The statutory provision is open to "dependants" only, which embraces the double concept of financial dependency or mental distress *and* family relationship. This is clearly borne out in the 1961 Act, (as amended) where "dependant" is defined to include only a person in a family-type relationship who has suffered injury or mental distress as a result of the wrongful death.

> Dependant is defined under the legislation to include the following:
>
> (a) a spouse, parent, grandparent, step-parent, child, grandchild, step-child, brother, sister, half-brother or half-sister of the deceased,
>
> (b) a person whose marriage to the deceased has been dissolved by a degree of divorce that was granted under the Family Law (Divorce) Act 1996 or under the law of a country or jurisdiction other than the State and is recognised in the State, or
>
> (c) a person who was not married to the deceased but who, until the date of the deceased's death, had been living with the deceased as husband or wife for a continuous period of not less than three years,
>
> who has suffered injury or mental distress as a result of the death.[12]

**[42.08]** A number of points about this definition may be noted. First, though clearly broad in its scope, it does not extend to persons whose marriage with the deceased is void or, if voidable, has been annulled or to uncles or aunts or nephews and nieces or to relations by affinity other than step-parents and step-children. So far as children are concerned, s 47(2) of the 1961 Act provides that in deducing any relationship for the purposes of Part IV of the Act:

> (a) a person adopted under the Adoption Act 1952 shall be considered the legitimate offspring of the adopter or adopters;
>
> (b) subject to paragraph (a) of this subsection, an illegitimate person shall be considered the legitimate offspring of his mother and reputed father;
>
> (c) a person in *loco parentis* to another shall be considered the parent of that other.

---

11. [1988] ILRM 300 (HC). See further Ch 33.
12. Civil Liability (Amendment) Act 1996, s 1(1), substituting a new sub-s (1) in s 47 of the 1961 Act.

**[42.09]** The references to "legitimate offspring" and "illegitimate person" may be contrasted with the language of the Status of Children Act 1987, which seeks to encourage the abandonment of terms such as these. Nonetheless, the 1987 Act did not actually amend s 47(2), so the claim of a child whose parents were not married to one another, where the father dies, will be determined on the basis that proof that the father was "the reputed father" is the appropriate test. A child living with the deceased, who was not the child's parent, while the deceased was engaged in a *de facto* relationship with the child's parent, will have no claim,[13] unless the deceased was *in loco parentis* to the child.

**[42.10]** The second point worth noting about the definition of "dependant" is that since 1996,[14] it includes cohabitees (or "cohabitants", as legislation internationally tends to refer them in recent years, contrary to customary usage). In order to be a dependant, the surviving cohabitee must have been living with the deceased "as husband or wife" for a continuous period of at least three years prior to the deceased's death. It seems therefore that there must be a sexual component in this relationship[15] and that homosexual partners do not fall within the scope of this definition.[16]

---

13. Kerr, *The Civil Liability Acts* (1999), p 58.

14. The Civil Liability (Amendment) Act 1996, s 1(2) provides that the amendment to s 47(1) applies only in respect of causes of action accruing on or after 25 December 1996. See Shatter, *Family Law* (4th ed, 1997), para 6.28.

15. In changing times, the genteel phrase "living with the deceased as husband or wife" will present difficult issues. The old assumptions about marriage - that it represented the only socially acceptable model for a sexual relationship and that it involved the spouses assuming fairly stereotypical gender roles - have given way to uncertainty about the intensity of commitment necessary to ground sexual relationships and a complete revision of views on gender roles. The judicial precedents (of some years ago) interpreting the phrase held the relationship to be established where the woman did domestic chores for the man. The idea that these decisions should represent the appropriate test today will be anathema to many people. Nevertheless, in cases where the parties have a somewhat "semi-detatched" relationship, possibly avoiding exclusivity or serious commitment, retaining separate control over their finances, a genuine question could arise as to whether, in spite of the fact that they cohabited for the requisite duration, they were living together "as husband and wife". Whether it is, legally speaking, possible to live together as husband and wife without a sexual dimension to the relationship, for the purposes of s 47(1), is not entirely clear. Undoubtedly some husbands and wives do so, where one of them suffers from impotence. There are judicial authorities supporting the proposition that it is possible for spouses to "live together" without a sexual relationship. One suspects that the courts today would long hesitate before transposing these authorities into the context of unmarried cohabitation.
    It should be noted that the claim of a cohabitee does not exclude that of the spouse of the deceased, who need not have been living with the deceased as his or her wife or husband at the time of the deceased's death. The definition is silent on the question whether it is possible for two (or more) persons to have lived as husband and wife with the deceased spouse for the requisite period. As mentioned, where a spouse is concerned, the spouse need not establish this requirement and the definition does not require the court to hold, as a condition of finding that the cohabitee complied with the requirement, that the spouse did not. Where two cohabitees make a claim, must the court make a choice between them? It seems not. Exclusivity is not required. Just as a bigamous spouse may be living as husband or wife with two (or more) partners, so it seems possible for a person (whether married or not) to live as husband and wife with more partners, for the purposes of the definition. As to the minimum three-year requirement for cohabitation, it does not seem that O'Hanlon J's approach in *Hollywood v Cork Harbour Commissioners* [1992] 1 IR 457 could be successfully invoked by constraints for a shorter duration: see Byrne & Binchy *Annual Review of Irish Law 1996*, pp 600-601.

16. *Cf* Kerr, *The Civil Liability Acts* (1999) p 56. Contrast the Domestic Violence Act 1996, which extended the entitlement to apply for a safety order (but not a barring order) to homosexual cohabitees (and others in a relationship with the respondent "the basis of which is not primarily contractual"). See Byrne & Binchy, *Annual Review of Irish Law 1996*, pp 362-363.

**[42.11]** A third feature worthy of note is that a person whose marriage to the deceased has been dissolved by divorce here or abroad is also deemed a "dependant". There is, however, a restriction on the scope of compensation for a divorced spouse: in no circumstance may he or she be awarded compensation for mental distress.[17]

## When and in What Circumstances Will Liability Arise?

**[42.12]** The basis of liability is set out in s 48(1) of the Civil Liability Act 1961. From this it is clear at the outset that a dependant's action will arise only if the deceased (had he or she lived) would have been entitled to sue the wrongdoer. The definition section of the 1961 Act indicates that the wrongdoer's act can be "a default or omission" and that the wrong includes:

> a tort, breach of contract or breach of trust, whether the act is committed by the person to whom the wrong is attributed or by one for whose acts he is responsible, and whether or not the act is also a crime, and whether or not the wrong is intentional.

Accordingly, if the deceased could not have sued the wrongdoer because of consent,[18] then the dependants will have no action either. If, however, as a result of the injuries, the deceased becomes depressed and takes his or her own life, this will not defeat the dependants' action.[19]

**[42.13]** A question which has not been decided in the Irish courts as yet is whether the dependants' action is lost if the deceased's action has been settled or lost through becoming statute barred when he or she dies.[20] For example, suppose D is injured by W and D settles his or her claim within six months of the accident. A year later D dies because of injuries received by virtue of W's original wrongdoing. Can the dependants in such circumstances sue under Part IV of the Civil Liability Act? Is it necessary, in other words, that the deceased could have maintained his or her action at the time of death, or is it sufficient for the dependants to succeed in their action, to show that D had an action *at one time* against W in respect of the wrongful act? Section 48(1) does not address the problem explicitly and the matter would appear to be open under the legislation. The English authorities suggest that if the deceased could not have brought an action at the time of death (because of the Statute of Limitations or because of a prior settlement) then neither can the dependants.[21] But if the deceased by contract limited his or her recovery to a fixed amount (eg £5,000) this would not prevent the dependants from suing for their full

---

17. Section 49A of the Civil Liability Act 1961, inserted by s 3(2) of the Civil Liability (Amendment) Act 1996. The conclusive presumption which the statute forces the court to make about the distress suffered by a divorced spouse may be inspired more by ideology than by a sensitive understanding of human feeling. Spouses who have divorced, or been divorced by, their partners may still be close to them and in some cases continue to love them.
18. Within the meaning of s 34(1)(b) of the Civil Liability Act 1961. See *O'Hanlon v ESB* [1969] IR 75.
19. *Pigney v Pointer Transport Services Ltd* [1957] 2 All ER 807; *Reeves v Commissioner of Police of the Metropolis* [1999] 3 All ER 897. See de Prez 'Liability for Failure to Prevent Acts of Self-Destruction: The House of Lords' Decision in *Reeves v Commissioner of Police of the Metropolis*' (2000) 16 Prof Neg 113.
20. In *Gawley v Belfast Corporation* [1908] 2 IR 34 and *Appelbe v The West Cork Board of Health* [1929] IR 107 the deceaseds' personal injury actions were not statute barred when they died.
21. See *Nunan v Southern Rly Co* [1924] 1 KB 223.

loss.[22] There are authorities in the USA on both sides. The majority appears to support the English approach, but a substantial minority takes a different view. The classic statement of the minority view is to be found in *Rowe v Richards*,[23] where the Supreme Court of South Dakota said:

> "We must confess our inability to grasp the logic of any course of so-called reasoning through which a conclusion is drawn that the husband simply because he may live to suffer from a physical injury and thus become vested with a cause of action for the violation of his own personal right, has an implied power to release a cause of action; one which has not then accrued; one which may never accrue; and one which from its very nature cannot accrue until his death; and one which, if it ever does accrue, will accrue in favour of his wife and be based solely upon a violation of a right vested solely in the wife."

**[42.14]** Although the issue is not free from debate,[24] Lavan J, in *Mahon v Burke and Mid-Western Health Board*,[25] followed the English authorities and the majority position in the United States of America in holding that, where the deceased had settled his personal injuries action arising out of the same incident, this precluded his dependants from bringing a wrongful death action. To hold otherwise would permit double recovery, exposing the defendant to two actions arising from one cause of action.[26]

**[42.15]** With regard to the contributory negligence of the deceased, s 35(1)(b) of the Civil Liability Act 1961 provides that a plaintiff suing on behalf of the dependants in such circumstances is deemed responsible for the acts of the deceased.[27] When the operation of this is taken in conjunction with s 34(1) of the Civil Liability Act 1961, an apportionment can occur in the dependants' action because of the deceased's contributory negligence.

**[42.16]** More interestingly, one may ask what is the effect of the contributory negligence of a dependant in such circumstances? Suppose D is killed as a result of a collision between a car being driven by S, his son, and another car being driven by W. If S is partly to blame, what effect will this have on the action taken on behalf of the dependants of which S is one? Section 35(1)(d) of the Civil Liability Act 1961 provides that the plaintiff in a dependant action is identified with the negligence of the dependants (or any one of them) in his or her action against the wrongdoer. In the example given, if the personal representative of the deceased takes an action against W on behalf of the dependants (say the widow and children, S and E, of the deceased), then the damages awarded to S in this action will be reduced in accordance with s 34(1). Moreover, W may also have a

---

22. *Nunan v Southern Rly Co* [1924] 1 KB 223. The decision was based on an interpretation of s 1 of the Fatal Accidents Act 1846, the relevant part of which has been re-enacted in s 48(1) of the Irish Civil Liability Act 1961. See also *Read v GE Rly* (1868) LR 3 QB 555 and *Williams v Mersey Docks and Harbour Board* [1905] 1 KB 804.
23. 35 SD 201 at 215-216, 151 NW 1001 at 1006. See also PROSSER & KEETON, pp 955-956; *Sea-land Services Inc v Gaudet* (1974) 414 US 573.
24. See White *Irish Law of Damages for Personal Injuries and Death* (1989), Vol 1, para 8.3.06.
25. [1991] 2 IR 495 (HC).
26. See further Kerr, *The Civil Liability Acts* (1999), p 59; *Cf* the argument to the contrary advanced by White *Irish Law of Damages for Personal Injuries and Death* (1989), Vol 1, para 8.3.06.
27. See para **[42.24]** above.

contribution action against S in this example, in respect of damages payable by W to the widow and E.[28]

**[42.17]** One may ask what happens if the deceased was a hardened criminal and the pecuniary benefits which the dependants received were derived from a life of crime. The better opinion in this case would appear to be that public policy should prevent a burglar's family from obtaining compensation for the loss of such illegal income, but that the law should look a good deal more leniently on losses referable to avocations which, although in breach of some licensing or regulatory rule, lack the anti-social dimensions of burglary or usury.[29]

**[42.18]** Finally, in this connection, it is important to note also that to be recoverable the loss to the dependant must arise out of the family-type relationship between the parties. If the loss to the dependant arises because of a business or contractual arrangement between the dependant and the deceased, and not because of the relationship which gives title to sue, this is not recoverable under the statutory action. Accordingly, where the deceased was the wife and professional dancing partner of the dependant, and as a result of her death the husband's earning capacity was greatly diminished, the court refused to give damages to the husband for this loss. The loss was due to the death of a business associate and not due to the death of his wife as such.[30] It should be pointed out, however, that the mere fact that a contract exists between the deceased and the claimant does not always prevent recovery; if the deceased provides services in excess of the contractual value, because of the family relationship, the excess can be claimed by the claimant.[31]

## The Injuries Compensatable and the Method of Calculating Damages

**[42.19]** The damages payable to the dependants in respect of a fatal injuries claim are set out in s 49 of the Civil Liability Act 1961. Generally speaking, they can be grouped under three headings:

(i) Damages in respect of funeral and other expenses actually incurred by reason of the wrongful act: s 49(2).

(ii) The total of such amounts (subject to a maximum award of £20,000), as the judge shall consider reasonable compensation for mental distress resulting from the death to each of such dependants.[32] This was a new heading of allowable damages and is sometimes referred to as *solatium*.

---

28. Civil Liability Act 1961, s 21.

29. See *Burns v Edman* [1970] 2 QB 541; *Le Bagge v Buses Ltd.* [1958] NZLR 630; *Mills v Baitis* [1968] VR 583; *Brownbill v Kenworth Sales* (1982) 39 ALR 191. On exaggerated claim by dependants see *McKenna v McElvaney & MIBI* 24 July 1998 (Johnston J).

30. *Burgess v Florence Nightingale Hospital for Gentlewomen* [1955] 1 QB 349; see also *Sykes v NE Rly Co* (1875) 44 LJCP 191; *Hall v GN Rly Co of Ireland* (1890) 26 LR Ir 289:

> "the pecuniary loss which was necessary to sustain the action must be the loss of pecuniary benefit or advantage arising out of the relationship between the plaintiff and her mother, and not the loss of benefit or advantage derived from any contract between them; ..." at 291 (*per* Andrews J).

31. *Malyon v Plummer* [1964] 1 QB 330.

32. Sections 49(1)(a)(ii) and 49(1)(b), as amended by the Civil Liability (Amendment) Act 1996.

(iii) The total of such amounts as the jury or judge, as the case may be, shall consider proportioned to the injury resulting from the death to each of the dependants.[33] This includes the loss of all pecuniary benefits and the loss of benefits (eg services or kind) reducible to monetary terms. "Accordingly, the damages are to be based on the reasonable expectation of pecuniary benefit or other benefit which can be reduced to a monetary value."[34] This is the principal heading for damages and it will be dealt with more fully hereunder.

A further word about each of these is necessary.

***(a) Funeral expenses***

**[42.20]** In respect of funeral expenses there is usually little problem as the sum paid can be easily proved. The cost of a normal tombstone and the cost of embalming have been allowed but not the cost of an extravagant monument.[35] In England, where a narrower definition has meant a more restrictive interpretation of what is covered by funeral expenses, a headstone costing £595 was allowed in respect of a Traveller boy who was buried in Ireland.[36] In determining the reasonableness the Court took into account the deceased's station in life, his creed and his racial origin. Funeral expenses would also include expenses connected with the burial operation (or with cremation), and also with religious services for the deceased. The "other expenses" which can be claimed here, it seems, as well as having to be reasonable and necessary must also be immediately related to the obsequies, or perhaps the medical expenses,[37] caused by the wrongful act. Apart from these, the most important expenses here would relate to the travelling costs incurred by the dependants visiting the deceased before he died and attending the funeral, but they would also extend to acknowledgement cards to sympathisers, a wake and the cost of mourning clothes. The phrase does not include expenses incurred by a widower for extra domestic help or for extra tuition for his children.[38]

---

33. Section 49(1)(a)(i). See *Gallagher v ESB* [1933] IR 558. See generally Kemp and Kemp, *The Quantum of Damages* Vol 2, Pt 13.

34. *O'Sullivan v CIE,* [1978] IR 407 at 421 (SC). See also Murnaghan J's approach in High Court at 414-415. Under this heading, loss of personal services of a non-monetary kind are, it appears, not recoverable. So damages would not be awarded for loss of deceased's society, protection, and spousal, or parental or filial care. White *Irish Law of Damages for Personal Injuries and Death* (1989), p 397 argues that neither principle nor authority denies recovery for such losses.

35. *O'Brien v Higgins* Supreme Court, 13 March 1967; *Stanton v Ewart F Youlden Ltd* [1960] 1 All ER 429; *Hart v Griffith-Jones,* [1948] 2 All ER 729.

36. *Gammell v Wilson* [1982] AC 27.

37. *Byrne v Houlihan and de Courcy* [1966] IR 274 at 283.

38. *Byrne v Houlihan and de Courcy* [1966] IR 274. Such sums may, of course, be claimed, in appropriate cases, under the general heading (i) above. See further, Maclsaac 'How to Establish Damages on the Death of a Mother' (1977) 1 L Med Q 267. See also *Mulholland v McCrea and Anor* [1961] NI 135 (CA). This case also holds that where a dependant contributed to deceased's injury the amount recoverable by that dependant may be reduced. *Aliter*, in case of action by deceased's estate for loss of expectation of life. The Law Reform Commission has recommended that s 49 of the Civil Liability Act 1961 should be amended to allow for recovery of exemplary, aggravated and restitutionary damages in wrongful death actions. See LRC Report on *Agravated Exemplary and Restitutionary Damages* (LRC 60-2000), paras 2.110, 5.35, 6.54.

### *(b) Mental distress*

**[42.21]** The introduction of damages in respect of mental distress is a novel aspect of the Civil Liability Act 1961.[39] The courage required to introduce such a heading was tempered, however, by confining the award in respect of mental distress to the judge alone,[40] and by limiting the total of such award to £1,000, a sum which was raised in 1981 to £7,500[41] and to £20,000 in 1996.[42] Two further points should be mentioned. In *Cubbard v Rederij Viribus Unitis and Galway Stevedores Ltd*,[43] Lavery J made the following statement on this matter:

> "The view I take of the section is that it is not intended to provide monetary compensation for every member of the family. If it were there would be no end to it. It would mean that there would be damages recovered by a group of people that ordinarily would be very large. I think the section must be considered in the light of some real intense feeling of being grievously affected by the death. I know perfectly well that every member of the family feels the loss of a brother, especially those who are living with him."[44]

In the case before him Lavery J refused to award any sum to the deceased's brother, one of whom was also a member of the same household, on the ground that to award a trivial sum would be an affront to them.

**[42.22]** Lavery J's insistence that some real and intense grief must be felt before *solatium* becomes payable is hardly supported by subsequent cases decided by the Supreme Court.[45]

---

39. See White, *Irish Law of Damages for Personal Injuries and Death* (1989), Ch 10; Knight 'Some Aspects of Damages under the Civil Liability Acts 1961 and 1964' (1966) 1 Ir Jur (ns) 50ff, Veitch 'Solatium -A Debt Repaid?' (1966) 1 Ir Jur (ns) 35. See in Scotland, the Damages (Scotland) Act 1976, which abolishes common law right to *solatium* and replaces it with a right by deceased's "immediate family" to damages for loss of society.
40. Contrast the provision relating to general damages which, until abolition of the juries in personal injuries litigation, were awarded by judge or jury, as the case might be, s 49(l)(a)(i).
41. Courts Act 1981.
42. Civil Liability (Amendment) Act 1996. This sum may be altered in the future by order of the Minister for Justice, Equality and Law Reform: s 2.
43. (1966) 100 ILTR 40 (HC).
44. (1966) 100 ILTR 40. In *O'Brien v Higgins* Supreme Court, 13 March 1967 an elderly man had a High Court award of £100 increased to £300 under this heading.
45. See *O'Brien v Higgins* Supreme Court, March 1967 and *Foley v Spain* High Court, unrep June 1970, both unreported cases, noted by Veitch, (1972) 7 Ir Jur (ns) 77 at 93. See also White, 'The Shocked and the Bereaved: An Historical and Contemporary Study of their Remedies in Tort', unpublished LLM Thesis, Harvard 1980 at 122 *et seq*. White, *Irish Law of Damages for Personal Injuries and Death* (1989), paras 10.301 *et seq*. It should be stressed that what is envisaged in this context, is the mental distress that flows from the death of the deceased, not some physical injury or "nervous shock" suffered by a dependant. Such latter losses may be compensated, though it is not yet clear in Irish law whether the requirement that they be reasonably foreseeable should be supplemented, in the case of "nervous shock" claims, by the baneful "policy" limitations which have plagued British judicial analysis in recent years. In *Heaney v Dublin Corporation*, High Court, 16 May 1991, (Barron J), damages of £7,500 (then the maximum for mental distress) where awarded to the widow of a fireman who died when fighting a fire. Barron J noted that the circumstances of the deceased's death had been "traumatic". If in fact the widow had suffered trauma capable of compensation as "nervous shock", the statutory maximum would have had no application.

In *McCarthy v Walsh*[46] it was held that infant brothers and sisters of the deceased, whose ages ranged from 18 down to 4, were entitled to compensation for mental distress, the two youngest receiving the smallest shares. Thus, in *McDonagh v McDonagh*,[47] in 1991, Costello J concluded that a girl whose mother was killed in a traffic accident when the girl was one-and-a-half was too young to have suffered distress, "whatever about emotional depression", as a result of their mother's death. Costello J considered, however, that the girls sister, aged four at the time of the fatal accident, must have suffered greatly and he divided the maximum statutory amount between her and the parents of the deceased woman.

**[42.23]** In the Supreme Court decision of *Dowling v Jedos Ltd*, on 30 March 1977, Walsh J, delivering the judgment of the Court, explained the principle of assessment of damages for mental distress in the following language:

> "It has, however, already been pointed out in this Court in *McCarthy v Walsh*,[48] that this figure of £1,000 is not to be regarded as being available only for the worst possible case and accordingly it would be incorrect to approach all cases less serious than the worst possible case on the assumption that £1,000[49] could never be awarded. In my view, the correct approach is for the judge to make a notional award in the sum which he would on the evidence be justified in giving to each of the persons who suffered mental distress without taking into account at that stage that the maximum possible total is £1,000. When the notional figures have been arrived at and if their total exceeds £1,000 then as the ratio between them is already known they should be scaled down proportionately so that the total is reduced to £1,000."[50]

The relevant maximum figure for mental distress , it should be recalled, is now £20,000.

**[42.24]** The method of calculation becomes important when one considers the effect of contributory negligence on the part of the deceased. The plaintiff is identified with the deceased's contributory negligence (s 35(1)(b)) in claims under Part IV of the Act including the claim for mental distress. If, therefore, the deceased was 50% responsible for the accident that caused his death the proper way this is to be taken into account, according to *Dowling v Jedos Ltd*, is to calculate the sum to be awarded to the claimants in respect of their mental distress (say, it is £48,000) and then to reduce this sum by the amount of the claimant's contributory negligence (ie 50%) to get the sum which the claimants would be entitled to (£24,000 in the example). Since this exceeds the statutory maximum, all the claimants will get in respect of this damage will be £20,000. In the case where one of the dependants is guilty of contributory negligence then his award for mental distress is calculated separately before being added to the claims of the other dependants in respect of this injury. This then gives one the total figure which should be awarded and the fraction

46. [1965] IR 246.
47. [1992] 1 IR 119 (HC).
48. [1965] IR 246.
49. Now £20,000: Civil Liability (Amendment) Act 1996, s 2(1)(a).
50. This was the approach favoured by Ó Dálaigh CJ [1965] IR at 261-262. Lavery J, at 263, while in general agreement that "this would normally be the proper course", could nonetheless "visualise exceptional cases where a different course might be appropriate" so far as apportionment was concerned.

due to each claimant. If this exceeds £20,000 then the awards will have to be scaled down accordingly.

***(c) Loss of pecuniary benefits: the dependency***

**[42.25]** The principal heading under which dependants may claim damages under the fatal injuries provisions relates to the loss of pecuniary benefits which could have reasonably been expected but for the wrongful act of the defendant.[51] Valuation of the dependency raises difficult problems for the Courts, and not all the difficulties associated with the problem have been definitively or satisfactorily answered. The principle, however, may be stated generally in the following terms. To ascertain the value of the dependency one must first establish the dependants' annual average loss.

**[42.26]** This figure is then multiplied by the number of years during which the loss is likely to continue and is discounted to give the present value of the dependency. Benefits accruing to the dependants as a consequence of the death are deducted to provide the amount recoverable under this heading.

**[42.27]** In trying to determine the dependants' annual average loss, the court will be impressed of course by the deceased's actual income, his prospects for advancement in his job or profession, the fringe benefits to which he was entitled (eg company car, free heat and light, bonuses, pension rights, etc) and the proportion of his income that was directed towards the dependants. Moreover, the pecuniary benefits which the dependants claim to have lost, while obviously covering financial contributions directly made by the deceased and likely to have continued but for his death, also cover loss of services, or acts in kind which can be reduced to financial terms. If, for example, the deceased's contributions in the instruction of his children or in the management of the family garden require the employment of a tutor and gardener after his death, the expenses associated with such replacements would properly be considered as the loss of a pecuniary benefit. So in *O'Sullivan v CIE*[52] the dependants were entitled to have taken into account not only the £30 a week which the deceased contributed to the household expenses, but also a sum of £3 a week which covered vegetables and turf also provided by the deceased.[53] Similarly, if after the deceased's death a carpenter or painter has to be engaged to do routine maintenance work in the home which the deceased did before his death, these costs could also be claimed as a pecuniary loss.

**[42.28]** If the dependants' claim is exaggerated or does not appear to represent the real loss, the Court may decline to follow the dependants' suggested calculations and instead substitute its own form of calculation of the dependants' loss. In *McKenna v McElvaney*,[54] where the deceased had been "a small-time builder" at times an employee and at other times a sub-contractor "who kept absolutely no realistic records of his business",[55]

51. For developments at common law see *Gallagher v ESB* [1933] IR 558 and Kingsmill Moore J in *Byrne v Houlihan* [1966] IR 274 at 277 *et seq*.

52. [1978] IR 407 (SC).

53. See also *Waters v Cruikshank* [1967] IR 378 (loss of services under Fatal Injuries Act 1956, ss 2, 3). For losses in respect of wife and mother see *Berry v Humm & Co* [1915] 1 KB 627.

54. High Court, 24 July 1998 (Johnson J).

55. Page 2 of Johnson J's judgment.

Johnson J substituted his own calculations of the dependants' loss, castigating the claimant's accountants and forwarding the papers to the Revenue Commissioners.

**[42.29]** In *Fitzpatrick v Furey*,[56] the dependants' claim was based on actual income received by the deceased's widow which was between five and six thousand pounds more than had been declared to the Revenue Commissioners in the years before his death. Laffoy J refused to base her calculations on the total income of the deceased for the accounting year prior to his death. Noting that the deceased's widow had made a false declaration to the tax authorities after his death, Laffoy J said:

> "I have found it very difficult to resolve the situation. I can see the merit of the approach advocated by Mr Whelehan [the plaintiff's counsel]. On the other hand, I am faced with the fact that the plaintiff, who herself is entitled to the 'lion's share' of the dependency claim, has made a declaration to the Revenue Commissioners which she now says is false. I accept that the plaintiff, when making the declaration, did the best she could in the circumstances then prevailing ... Nonetheless, I have come to the conclusion that public policy considerations preclude me from quantifying the dependency claim on the basis of [the deceased]'s declared and undeclared income for the accounting year prior to his untimely death."[57]

Laffoy J accordingly calculated the dependency on the returned income, adding a sum for future developments.

**[42.30]** It must be remembered that the plaintiff's dependants can only recover damages in respect of pecuniary benefits that could, in the eyes of the court, be reasonably expected to be made by the deceased *in the future*. Past payments by the deceased, especially if of a periodic and continuing nature, may provide strong evidence of what the dependant would have continued to receive had the deceased lived, but the action is intended to compensate the dependants for what they will not get *in the future*, and for this reason an award may be made in respect of a child's death if it can be shown that in respect of the dependants it would be reasonable to expect a pecuniary benefit at some future date.[58] In *Horgan v Buckley*[59] the Court recognised the expectancy of dependants (the wife and children) where the deceased had returned from America with a stake and married the local schoolteacher. There was evidence that the deceased planned to buy a farm and, even though no farm had been purchased at the date of death, the court accepted evidence that the deceased had been actively enquiring about a farm some days before his death, and this created a sufficient pecuniary expectation on the part of the dependants. It was reasonable to assume that had he lived he would have bought a farm and would have contributed to the support of his wife and children. The rule that is applied in this context is that the dependants' claim, must be based on some facts which reasonably support the inferences which the

56. High Court, 12 June 1998 (Laffoy J).

57. Page 23 of Laffoy J's judgment.

58. See *Hamilton v O'Reilly* [1951] IR 200; *cf Malynn v Farrell* (1956) 90 ILTR 137.

> "Such pecuniary loss is established if it be shown that the plaintiff had a reasonable expectation of pecuniary benefit from the continuance of the life in question, and it is not a condition precedent to the maintenance of the action that the deceased should have been actually earning money or money's worth or contributing to the support of the plaintiff at or before the date of death."

*Horgan v Buckley* [1938] IR 115 at 123 (SC).

59. [1938] IR 115 (SC); [1938] IR 675 (No 2) (SC).

Court is invited to make, otherwise the dependants' claim will fail as being based on pure speculation.[60]

**[42.31]** In attempting to work out the *period of the loss* the Court will take note of the working life expectancy of the deceased and the life expectancy of the relevant dependants. The duration of the dependency in the case of the child dependants, will be related to whether the education of the child was to continue to third level or that the child was likely to move away if the child took up employment.

**[42.32]** Whether the courts will take into account, in calculating the value of the dependency, the impact of taxation and the haunting prospect of inflation are questions which have only recently been answered by Irish courts and then only with some hesitation. In Ireland we may conclude now that the courts will properly take into account both of these factors in calculating the value of the dependency. Accordingly, the fact that the deceased's income would have been taxable when he would have received it will be considered in calculating what disposable income he would have had and the estimated payments he would have made to the dependants. Likewise inflation and the likely increase in real income that would have accrued to the deceased had he continued to earn, are factors which the courts will attempt to accommodate in their computations.

**[42.33]** The tax question was decided in England in 1955 by the House of Lords in *British Transport Commission v Gourley*.[61] This case concerned damages for personal injuries and held that had the plaintiff earned the sum awarded in the ordinary course of affairs it would have been subject to income tax and that this fact should lead to a corresponding reduction in the award. The principle has been applied in England to other awards including actions under the Fatal Accidents Acts.[62]

**[42.34]** In *Glover v BLN Ltd and Others (No* 2)[63] the High Court in a wrongful dismissal action held that the plaintiff's damages should be reduced to take account of the incidence of taxation to which it would have been subjected had such a sum been paid in the course of his employment. Kenny J followed *Gourley* and was not impressed by the arguments put forward to the effect that the practice in the Irish Courts since *Gourley* had been different, that there would be difficulties in ascertaining what the impact of future taxation would be, or that *Gourley* should not be applied to cases of wrongful dismissal. It would seem from this that the *Gourley* principle would be equally applicable to fatal injuries claims in Ireland.

**[42.35]** The principle in all these cases suggests that the sum which the plaintiff receives ought to be capable of yielding a sum equal to the amount of the dependency. If, however, the income which such a sum yields is itself liable to tax then an allowance must also be

60. [1938] IR 115 at 139. See also *Good v Callaghan* Supreme Court, 25 April 1967, for an example of a case where evidence did not establish that the dependants (widow and son) had suffered any financial loss.

61. [1956] AC 185.

62. See SALMOND & HEUSTON, [ 547, (17th ed), pp 586 and 574.

63. [1973] IR 432. Kenny J's approach was subsequently endorsed by the Supreme Court in *Tooke v Walsh* [1984] ILRM 208.

made for this in assessing the amount to be given to the dependants. This principle (referred to as "*Gourley* in reverse") has also been recognised in the English courts[64] and would presumably also be accepted by the Irish courts.[65]

**[42.36]** In *Griffiths v Van Raaj*[66] the Supreme Courts made such an allowance in a personal injury action and it is clear that a similar approch would be appropriate in a fatal injuries award.

**[42.37]** Allowance is also made for the effect of future inflation on the value of money and for the anticipated growth in real earnings of the plaintiff.[67] The Courts make such allowances in personal injuries cases and the same principle applies in fatal injuries actions.[68]

**[42.38]** Since the action is, under this heading, concerned with what would have happened had the deceased lived, it is inevitable that serious problems of evidence can arise in attempting hypothetically to assess what would have happened had the deceased continued to live.[69] All that can be said is that under the conventional method the court will make reasonable assumptions, on the evidence, and will attempt to capitalise these with actuarial assistance.[70] For example, if the deceased was a happily married man of 55 who had always contributed 80% of his pay packet to the household, then the court may say that the loss to the household in the event of his death would be 80% of his salary for 10 years. If it was shown that he had a life expectancy of 70 years then the court may also add 80% of his pension for five years.[71] In some cases the court's task may not be so easy, as, for example, where the deceased was a housewife or a self-employed person or a child who was not earning at all. Quantifying the loss to the dependants in these cases poses an initial problem, which having been solved leads on to the capitalisation problem. In *O'Sullivan v CIE*,[72] where the deceased was a farmer, in addition to the conventional method of assessing loss, two other methods of assessing the dependants' loss were examined: the

64. *Taylor v O'Connor* [1971] AC 115.

65. For a full discussion on this and related problems, and an account of the practical problems associated with this, see White 'Damages for Personal Injury and Wrongful Death' (1981), unpublished LLB Thesis, University College, Cork. White, *Irish Law of Damages for Personal Injuries and Death* (1989), paras 4.6.01-4.6.07.

66. [1985] ILRM 582 (SC) "... and there is no doubt but that the same principle applies in the context of the assessment of pecuniary loss in wrongful death actions" White *Irish Law of Damages for Personal Injuries and Death* (1989), p 381.

67. *McNamara v ESB* [1975] 1 IR 1; *Sexton v O'Keeffe* [1966] IR 204; *Doherty v Bowaters Irish Wallboard Mills Ltd* [1968] IR 277. See Ch 44.

68. White, *Irish Law of Damages for Personal Injuries and Death* (1989), p 341.

69. See *Dowling v Jedos Ltd* Supreme Court, 30 March 1977. This can be particularly difficult if the deceased is a young child. Such cases are not impossible to prove: see *Mulrennan v Connolly* (1939) 73 ILTR 94 (8½-year-old boy); *Gammell v Wilson* [1982] AC 27; *Hamilton v O'Reilly* [1951] IR 200 (3½-year-old girl).

70. *Brennan v Gale* [1949] NI 178.

71. See *O'Sullivan v CIE,* [1978] IR 407; *Tubridy v White* High Court, 31 January 1974; *Hamilton v O'Reilly* [1951] IR 200. See also *Mallett v McMonagle* [1969] NI 91 where a jury award was upset as being over-generous; *cf Brennan v Gale* [1949] NI 178.

72. [1978] IR 409.

differential basis and the capitalised value of the services of the deceased. On the differential basis it was claimed by the deceased's widow that as a result of her husband's death the farm switched from carrying dairy cattle (which was labour intensive) to dry stock. Dry stock activities were less lucrative and so it was suggested that the loss to the dependants should be the capitalised value of the difference in farm income. The third method suggested was to estimate the cost of replacing the deceased's services (the cost of employing a man to do deceased's work) and to capitalise this sum. In the event Griffin J, delivering the decision of the court, proceeded on the conventional method and having arrived at a figure he checked it against the other two methods of calculation. He failed to find a sufficiently large discrepancy between the three methods to justify departure from the conventional method and he affirmed the trial judge's calculation.

**[42.39]** Death may, of course, bring pecuniary benefits as well as losses to the deceased's dependants and the question arises whether these benefits must be taken into account in calculating the dependants' loss. The general answer is that all such gains which the dependants receive must be offset against any loss suffered, and an award will only be made in respect of overall loss suffered, if any.[73] Accordingly, the dependants may benefit under the deceased's will, or on intestacy, and even though such inheritance may have been expected eventually, the *accelerated* nature of the inheritance is a benefit and must be taken into account in estimating the dependants' loss.[74] The Court will also take into account here, however, by way of a balancing factor, the fact that had the deceased lived his savings might also have increased and the dependants might rightly be entitled to anticipate a share of these.[75]

**[42.40]** In general, therefore, one may say that all the pecuniary gains which the dependants derive from the deceased's death are deducted from all the pecuniary losses and an action for the net loss may be maintained. To this general proposition there are a couple of exceptions. First, property, eg a car or a picture or the family home[76] of which a widow claimant had the shared use during the deceased's lifetime, need not be counted as a gain in reduction of her claim. Second, s 50 of the Civil Liability Act 1961 provides that no account is to be taken in a fatal injuries action of:

---

73. See *Byrne v Houlihan and de Courcey* [1966] IR 274; *Murphy v Cronin* [1966] IR 699 at 708. Benefits which the dependants get by way of "voluntary charity" should, it seems, not be taken into account in reducing the dependants' claims. So where a grandmother provided a home for her grandchildren after their mother died, this was not allowed to reduce their claim as dependants. *Hay v Hughes* [1975] 1 All ER 257. See also *Redpath v Belfast and County Ry* [1947] ELI 167; *Peacock v Amusement Equipment Ltd* [1954] 2 QB 347, discussed in *Byrne v Houlihan* [1966] IR 274 at 279 *et seq*.

74. *Tubridy v White* High Court, 31 January 1974; *O'Sullivan v CIE* [1978] IR 407; *Davies v Powell Duffryn Associated Collieries Ltd (No 2),* [1942] AC 601, esp at 611.

75. *Murphy v Cronin* [1966] IR 699 at 710; *O'Sullivan v CIE* [1978] IR 407; *Taylor v O'Connor* [1971] AC 115.

76. *O'Sullivan v CIE* [1978] IR 407; *Murphy v Cronin* [1966] IR 699 at 710.

(a) Any sum payable on the death of the deceased under any contract of insurance,

(b) Any pension, gratuity or other like benefit payable under statute or otherwise in consequence of the death of the deceased.[77]

**[42.41]** The difficulties associated with this topic cannot be dispelled by rigid logic or mathematical principles. Even when some more or less accepted formulae of assessment are applied an element of uncertainty remains. As Kingsmill Moore J observed in *Waters v Cruickshank*: "In truth, damages, in a case such as this, are not a matter of any exact accountancy."[78] Lord Wright in *Davies v Powell Duffryn Associated Collieries Ltd*[79] put the matter this way:

> "It is a hard matter of pounds, shillings and pence, subject to the element of reasonable future probabilities. The starting point is the amount of wages which the deceased was earning, the ascertainment of which to some extent may depend upon the regularity of his employment. Then there is an estimate of how much was required or expended for his own personal and living expenses. The balance will give a datum or basic figure which will generally be turned into a lump sum by taking a certain number of years' purchase. The sum, however, has to be taxed down by having due regard to uncertainties.''[80]

**[42.42]** In citing the above with approval *Salmond & Heuston* comments:

> "In making the assessment the court can look at events since the accident to see whether contingencies have become certainties. 'The court should never speculate where it knows.' But at the end of the day arithmetic may have to be mitigated by common sense, for it is an assessment and not a calculation which is being made."[81]

---

77. See Kerr *The Civil Liability Act* (1999), pp 64-65; the Law Reform Commission's Consultation Paper, *Section 2 of the Civil Liability (Amendment) Act 1964: The Deductibility of Collateral Benefits from Awards or Damages* (1999), paras 7.05-7.06. For a discussion of "gratuity" and "like benefit" see *Murphy v Cronin* [1966] IR 699; *Murray v Shuter* [1976] QB 972. *Cf* Social Welfare (Consolidation) Act 1993, s 236(1) which expressly excludes from assessment of damages any child benefit, survivor's pension, orphan's (contributory) allowance, lone parent's allowance, or widow's or orphan's (non-contributory) pension. However, s 75(3) of the 1993 Act which provides that, notwithstanding s 50 of the 1961 Act, in assessing damages in respect of funeral expenses, resulting from a person's death, account may be taken of any death benefit by way of grant under s 22 of the 1966 Act in respect of funeral expenses, resulting from that person's death. In *Feeney v Ging and Co Council for Laois* High Court, 17 December 1982 (Ellis J), it was held that the fact that deceased's children, the claimants, would be entitled to university grants because of reduced circumstances caused by father's death should be taken into account in reducing the award. It was not a "pension, gratuity or other like benefit payable under statute ...". See also *Hayes v Criminal Injury Comp Tribunal* [1982] ILRM 210 (HC) where social welfare payments may be deducted in a claim under the Scheme. See *McLoughlin v Minister for Public Service* [1986] ILRM 28 - pension payable to widow of garda not to be deducted from compensation awarded under Garda Compensation Act 1941.

78. [1967] IR 378 at 389 (SC).

79. [1942] AC 601.

80. [1942] AC 601 at 617.

81. SALMOND & HEUSTON (19th ed), pp 545-546. Internal quotation footnoted to *Curwen v James* [1963] 1 WLR 748 at 753. It need scarcely be stressed, however, that this does not constitute a licence to award damages "merely on a basis of guesswork or speculation": *Gallagher v ESB* [1933] IR 558 at 566 (SC). See also *Hull v GN Ry Co of Ireland* (1890) 26 LR Ir 289 (Ex); *Horgan v Buckley (No 1)* [1938] IR 115 (SC).

*(d) Changing mores relating to gender roles*

**[42.43]** Courts in fatal injuries litigation cases find themselves confronting troubling issues which require them to adjudicate on matters that are distasteful or controversial. These difficulties spring from the fact that the tasks or functions undertaken by a deceased spouse have an economic value, the loss of which impacts financially on the dependants. A thirty-five-year-old businessman is negligently killed; his widow sues for compensation for the financial loss she sustained resulting from his death. By the time the case comes to trial, she has re-married. Her second husband is as wealthy and as generous as her deceased partner. In truth, she will not suffer anything like the financial loss she would have suffered had she not re-married. Her compensation under the heading of loss of pensionary benefits will accordingly be diminished.

**[42.44]** However, what should be the situation where the widow has *not* re-married at the time of trial? Should the court take into account the *likelihood* that she will do so, either because of evidence that she has formed an actual emotional attachment to a new partner or because she is of an age and disposition and of such attractive qualities that remarriage may be predicted? Even to frame the question is disturbing today because of the cultural assumptions and prejudices that it brings to the surface.

**[42.45]** The court is in something of a dilemma when it confronts the possibility of a widow's remarrying. As Fleming observed, to take it into account "invites an embarrassing inquiry into nubility, although to ignore it in all cases may condone blatant windfalls".[82] Distaste at this type of adjudication led the English legislature in 1971 to require the courts to ignore the remarriage prospects of a widow,[83] but not of a widower, thus solving one problem by creating certain new anomalies.

**[42.46]** When one considers the position of a family where there are three children under the age of six and the wife is killed, one can appreciate that different, but related, unpalatable issues may arise about the husband's actual remarriage or his remarriage prospects. If the husband has not remarried and, for some reason, it is clear that he will not do so, there may well be a significant financial implication. Someone (or perhaps more than one person) will in most cases have to be employed to provide for the children's domestic needs. This will not always be the case, of course. Thus, in *McDonagh v McDonagh*,[84] where the mother of two young children was killed, Costello J, on the evidence, rejected the suggestion that the services she had provided for the children would be replaced by a live-in nanny/housekeeper. On the balance of probabilities, he did not think that this would occur. It had not been shown that such a person was available for this type of employment in the Sligo area, where the family lived.[85] Moreover, Costello J thought it probable that the deceased's husband would continue to avail himself of the help

82. FLEMING, p 736.

83. Law Reform (Miscellaneous Provisions) Act 1971; English law is now consolidated in the Fatal Accidents Act 1976. See WINFIELD AND JOLOWICZ, p 805.

84. [1992] 1 IR 119 (HC)

85. This conclusion may perhaps be debated. A sufficiently attractive salary would surely be all that was necessary to encourage applications for the position, from Sligo or from further afield.

that his sister had most generously given since his wife's death, and who was entitled to be remunerated for her work.[86]

**[42.47]** If a man whose wife has died *does* need to employ a person to look after the children, should the court take into account, when assessing the damages, the fact that he has remarried or the prospects (based on his age and other personal circumstances) that he will do so?

**[42.48]** These general issues came before the Irish courts in two cases in 1990. They are worth examining closely, though one should bear in mind that social attitudes and work patterns of married women have changed over the past decade. The first of these decisions, *Fitzsimons v Bord Telecom Éireann and ESB*[87] is important for another reason: it examines the troublesome question, to which reference has already briefly been made of when is the appropriate time for assessment of the damages suffered. This latter question is particularly relevant to cases where remarriage has occurred or is likely to do so.

**[42.49]** In *Fitzsimons* the deceased, whose death in 1979 was caused by the defendants' negligence, left a widow aged 34 and five children whose ages ranged from two to eleven. The widow remarried in 1985 and had another child. No evidence was adduced in the case in relation to damages: the parties sought judicial guidance on the question whether the benefits arising from the widow's remarriage should be taken into account in assessing damages and, if so, on what basis.

**[42.50]** The nearest Irish authority to the issue is the Supreme Court case of *Byrne v Houlihan*.[88] There, the deceased's substantial estate passed to her husband on her death intestate. Their children claimed compensation for the loss of the reasonable expectation of sharing in the income of her estate during her lifetime and of succeeding to it on her death testate in the course of time. The defendant accepted this claim, but contended that there should be off-set against this reasonable expectation the reasonable expectation that they would benefit to a similar, if not greater, extent from their *father* out of the same funds. At the date of the trial, the father had remarried. Kingsmill Moore J accepted that there was a reasonable expectation, at the date of the mother's death, that the father would provide for the children out of the income and eventually bequeath them a considerable proportion and perhaps all of the capital. Noting that the husband had remarried and might have further children, he added:

> "This would go to reducing the expectation of the children of the first marriage and may be taken into account by the jury in their estimation of damages. But that a reasonable expectation still exists I cannot doubt."[89]

---

86. Costello J thought that the amount should be reduced gradually over the years. The young children - both girls - would not require someone to take them to school when they were older; nor, when they were teenagers, would they need someone to be attendance every afternoon when they returned from school. This approach is somewhat similar to that adopted in English decisions: see Denyer 'What's A Carer Worth?' (1992) 22 Fam L 119.

87. [1991] ILRM 276 (HC).

88. [1966] IR 274 (SC).

89. [1966] IR 274 at 281.

**[42.51]** In *Fitzsimons*, Barron J interpreted this passage as supporting the proposition that "for a benefit to be taken into account there must be a reasonable expectation of it at the date of death, but the actual amount to be taken into account will depend upon the circumstances existing at the date of assessment".[90] Kingsmill Moore J's remarks may perhaps be best interpreted as requiring that there be a reasonable expectation of benefit at the date of death and at the time of trial. He envinced caution as to whether *Peacock v Amusement Equipment Co Ltd*[91] had been "in all respects correctly decided";[92] it conflicted with the later decision of the English Court of Appeal in *Mead v Clarke Chapman & Co Ltd*.[93] *Peacock* had concentrated on the question of reasonable expectation at the time of death; *Mead* had referred to the time of trial, without requiring that a similar expectation should have existed at the time of death.

**[42.52]** At all events, Barron J in *Fitzsimons* saw:

> "no reason why there should not be a recognised principle under which benefits received should or should not be taken into account. The basis of the assessment of damages for fatal injuries is the balancing of losses and benefits. Like any other balance sheet, it seems appropriate to determine first what items can appear on the balance sheet and then secondly the amount of such items. There can be little doubt but that the amount of the items must be determined as of the date of assessment. Perhaps also whether the item can appear should be determined as of the same date. But it seems more logical that if you are establishing a balance sheet required by reason of death that the items to appear on it should be determined as of that date. There is nothing unusual in this two tier approach. There are many cases in our law where a judge must decide as a matter of law whether or not there is sufficient evidence to support a particular allegation and then it must be decided as a matter of fact whether that allegation has been established. A decision whether or not there was a reasonable expectation of a particular benefit accruing is no different from a decision whether or not a head of damages is too remote. The latter is determined as of the date the cause of action accrues. In my view, the former should also be determined as of that date, ie the date of death."[94]

**[42.53]** Barron J considered that there was no reason in principle why remarriage of a widow should be treated any differently from any other circumstance giving rise to a benefit to be set-off against losses sustained. It had been suggested that the reason for taking the possibility, or fact, of remarriage into account was that otherwise the widow would be receiving support from two husbands at the same time; but the same could be said of children taken in by relatives, whose damages were not reduced, or of any other case where a benefit was disregarded other than by reason of a statutory provision.

**[42.54]** So far as the children were concerned, he thought it reasonable to assume that, if their mother remarried, they would go to live with her and their stepfather. If the benefits to them from a stepfather fell to be assessed, they could not be disregarded on the basis that they were voluntary:

---

90. [1991] ILRM 276 at 291.
91. [1954] 2 QB 347 (CA).
92. [1966] IR 274 at 282.
93. [1956] 1 All ER 44 (CA).
94. [1991] ILRM 276 at 292.

> "Voluntary benefits are disregarded not because they are voluntary, but because at the date of the death there was no reasonable expectation that they would occur. This is so equally in respect of losses. Many of the items in respect of which damages are awarded relate to voluntary payments or voluntary services made or provided by the deceased to one or more of the dependants. Such items are allowed when there is a reasonable expectation that the payments or services would have continued but for the death."[95]

**[42.55]** In the light of his analysis, Barron J concluded that the proper approach to adopt in relation to the assessment of damages in the case was that the evidence relating to remarriage should be directed in the first instance to establish whether or not there was a reasonable expectation at the date of the death that this would occur. On the basis that this was established, the evidence should then be directed to determining the then value of the benefits accruing to each of the dependants by reason of that remarriage. The onus of proof in each case lay on the defendants. The standard of proof of reasonable expectation was that of reasonable probability.

**[42.56]** Barron J's approach has much to recommend it since it offers a useful accommodation between the time of death and the time of the hearing. It is, however, capable of yielding results that are not entirely satisfactory. Whereas most people will accept that a child's *good* fortune should not tell against it if the surviving parent unforeseeably remarries and the stepparent lavishes care and financial assistance on the child, it is not so clear that the court should similarly ignore a child's *bad* fortune which has come to pass before the hearing through an unforeseeable remarriage resulting in diversion of expected benefit (such a share in the surviving spouse's estate) away from the child.

**[42.57]** A question of characterisation arises here. If the court were to treat in an identical fashion unforeseeably good and bad outcomes which have occurred by the time of the hearing, it would have to award the child in the case of a bad outcome a low sum of money by reason of the fact that the remarriage to a spouse who is now likely to scoop most of the pool could not have been reasonably expected at the date of the death. This event not having been reasonably probable, it must (on Barron J's formula) be put out of consideration. However, if on the same facts the court were to characterise as the central question *the foreseeability of the surviving spouse's benefiting the child on the surviving spouse's death*, rather than the *foreseeability of remarriage*, then the court would seem entitled to apply the two stage process envisaged by Barron J to yield a quite different result. The court would first hold that it was foreseeable that the child would thus benefit on the death of the surviving spouse; this element in the computation of damage now having passed the first stage, the court would go on to examine it in the light of present realities and would discover that by virtue of the remarriage and of the surviving spouse's (and child's) relationship with the new spouse, it is unlikely that the child will benefit substantially under the surviving spouse's estate. The amount of compensation would accordingly be increased. Whether such a devise of recharacterising the issue is harmonious with the *ipsissima verba* of Barron J's judgment is, however, doubtful.

**[42.58]** Barron J's rationale for disregarding voluntary benefits in general, on the basis of their lack of foreseeability, raises interesting policy issues. It could perhaps be argued that

95. [1991] ILRM 276 at 293.

this rationale underlies s 50 of the Civil Liability Act 1961, which requires the court when assessing fatal injuries damages not to take account of sums payable on the death of the deceased under any contract of insurance or by way of pension. If a statutory exclusion is required, does this not suggest that otherwise the court would have subtracted these benefits (subject to a foreseeability test)? It can, however, be replied that the statutory exclusion encapsulates a social policy that certain benefits, regardless of the question of their foreseeability, should not be deducted, because to do so would penalise the prudent forward-planners for their virtue, as well as generally discouraging the taking of such socially beneficial steps, and giving an unjustified windfall to wrongdoers.[96] In the light of these policy factors, it may be wise to modify Barron J's general principle by the qualification that, while foreseeability of a benefit is a necessary condition of its subtraction from the total amount of compensation, it may not be a sufficient justification to make that subtraction if there are good policy reasons for not doing so.

**[42.59]** In *Cooper v Egan*,[97] Barr J had to deal with the reverse question, of compensating a man for the death of his wife. The plaintiff was aged 27 at the time of the accident caused by the defendants' negligence. His wife was aged 20. At the time of her death, the wife was looking after the couple's baby, then aged four months old, and "also performed a normal wifely role in caring for her husband and in assisting her mother-in-law with household chores". As a result of the accident, the plaintiff and his mother suffered serious personal injuries, so the baby was immediately taken care of by the deceased wife's parents who were still doing so at the time of the trial. The child, now five, regarded his grandparents as his actual parents, though he had regular contact with his father.

**[42.60]** The plaintiff wished to provide a home for his son, who he felt was tending to grow apart from him as time went by. Barr J did not think it his function to consider the wisdom or otherwise of this plan: as a parent the plaintiff was entitled to provide a home for his child. Accordingly the plaintiff and his son were entitled to compensation for the loss of the deceased wife's services as a mother and a housewife.

**[42.61]** Barr J accepted the plaintiff's evidence that he had no intention of marrying in the foreseeable future. In these circumstances the plaintiff was entitled to compensation for the loss of his wife's services for life; with a modest deduction in the capital value of that loss to take account of his possible re-marriage at some future dates as well as the contingency that, had she lived, his wife might not have provided these services for the life of the plaintiff.

**[42.62]** Barr J considered that what the plaintiff needed was a local woman who would work in his home five days a week from about 1 pm to 2 pm, her function being to collect the boy from school or the school bus; to make lunch for him and the plaintiff; to perform housework in the afternoon; and to prepare the evening meal for the family. On the basis that this would cost £100, including PRSI, and taking into account the contingencies to

---

96. Similar social policy issues affect the issue of the deductibility of social welfare payments to victims of personal injury: see *O'Loughlin v Teeling* [1988] ILRM 617 (HC).

97. High Court, 20 December 1990 (Barr J).

which he had referred, Barr J assessed the capital value of this loss at £90,000. To this he added £1,000 for "occasional weekend babysitting" over the following eight years.

**[42.63]** Let us now confront the issues that are lurking under the surface of judicial analysis. Dr White has put forward the challenging thesis[98] that it is not possible to distinguish the benefits obtained by a surviving spouse and children, upon the remarriage of the surviving spouse, from other voluntary benefits, and that accordingly, since the benefits deriving from remarriage do not accrue "in consequence of the death", the occurrence or prospect of remarriage should be regarded as irrelevant in the damages calculation. He relies on the English decision of *Hay v Hughes*,[99] where the Court of Appeal held that the services given by a grandmother to her orphaned grandchildren should not be taken into account by way of reduction since it was more realistic to say that they "resulted from a decision made by her on her initiative after the accident than that they had resulted from the ... deaths [of the children's parents] in the accident ... [G]enerosity does not result from death".[100]

**[42.64]** Whether *Hay v Hughes* compels this conclusion may be debated. Not all English courts have appeared to think so,[101] though it is only fair to record that they have not had to confront the issue directly. Dr White is surely right in sounding a warning note to courts that it would be wrong to assume automatically that a widower's remarriage automatically will involve the assumption of domestic responsibilities by a second wife. Although the second wife will be marrying in the knowledge that her prospective husband has children who need care, there should be no unthinking assumption that she will necessarily opt for work within rather than outside the home.

**[42.65]** At the heart of this issue is the question whether a court should adopt any normative position on whether a second wife should work within the home. It will not be forgotten that, in *L v L*,[102] Barr J considered it:

> "evident that the Constitution envisages that, ideally, a mother should devote all her time and attention to her duties in the home and that it is desirable that she ought not to engage in gainful occupation elsewhere unless compelled to do so by economic necessity".[103]

Of course, he was speaking in the context of the State's obligation to women rather than the responsibilities of married women relative to their family. Nevertheless, the defendant in a fatal accident case, with a view to reducing damages, may assert that a second wife who marries the plaintiff widower, knowing of his children's need for care, is not to be treated in the same way as the grandmother in *Hay v Hughes*. If she decides to work in the home, the defendant may say, she should not be regarded as generous but rather merely as doing what might be expected of her.

---

98. White *Irish Law of Damages for Personal Injuries and Death* (1989), Vol 1, para 9.4.21.
99. [1975] 1 QB 790 (CA).
100. [1975] 1 QB 790 at 816.
101. *Cf Regan v Williamson*, [1976] 2 All ER 244.
102. [1989] ILRM 528 (HC) revd by [1992] ILRM 115 (SC). *Cf* Byrne & Binchy, *Annual Review of Irish Law 1991*, pp 216-222.
103. [1989] ILRM at 542, referring to Article 41 of the Constitution.

**[42.66]** We suspect that the courts will be very hesitant to commit themselves to a normative position on this issue. They may well prefer to achieve substantially the same result by addressing the issue in terms of the objective *likelihood* of a second wife's engaging in activities within the home. How the courts can give any convincing answer, based on such a test, in cases where the prospective second wife has not yet come on the scene, is hard to know. Resort to empirical data on work patterns of married women in reconstructed families would be helpful but would not, in itself, provide the answer. In cases where the husband has *already* remarried, however, the second wife has a flesh and blood existence and can give evidence to assist the court. If the second wife prefers to work outside the home, the courts are likely to take no normative position and hold that the care costs must continue to be attributable to the defendant's default. It is noted that Barr J in *Cooper v Egan* did not think it his function to consider the wisdom or otherwise of the plaintiff's plan to provide a home for his son rather than leave him in the care of his grandparents. This is perhaps an indication that the court would prefer to stand back from taking a particular position on the question of the choice of spousal roles in relation to a situation after a widower remarries.

***(e) Cohabitants claims: calculation of financial loss***

**[42.67]** Finally one should note s 49(5) of the Civil Liability Act 1961, inserted by s 2(1)(c) of Civil Liability (Amendment) Act 1996. It provides as follows:

> Where a person referred to in paragraph (c) of the definition of 'dependent' in s 47(1) had no enforceable right to financial maintenance by the deceased, the court shall take that fact into account, together with any other relevant matter, in determining the damages to be awarded to the person by virtue of subparagraph (i) of paragraph (a) of subsection (i)of the section."

The person in question is a cohabitant of three years' standing. Under present law, such a person has no enforceable right to maintenance[104] by virtue of this fact alone though in some particular circumstances a claim of an essentially alimentary character may arise.[105] Other than instructing the court to take the absence of a legal claim into account, s 2(1)(c) gives no guidance as to how the court is to proceed. Since assessments of financial loss are essentially factual, it seems that the absence of a legal basis for the support that the cohabitant was receiving and would in the future have been likely to have received from the deceased should not, in short, be any reason for reducing the award.

---

104. See Shatter *Family Law* (4th ed, 1997), paras 19.34, 19.79.

105. See *Re JR* [1993] ILRM 657, analysed by Delany, *Equity and The Law of Trusts in Ireland* (2nd ed, 1999), pp 625-627.

## Chapter 43

# Vicarious Liability[1]


| | | |
|---|---|---|
| I. | Introduction | 1091 |
| II. | The Employer/Employee Relationship | 1095 |
| III. | Liability of Firm for Partner's Wrongs | 1112 |
| IV. | Liability of the Owners of Mechanically Propelled Vehicles | 1114 |
| V. | Vicarious Liability for Members of One's Family | 1116 |
| VI. | Doctrine of Common Employment | 1117 |


## I. Introduction

**[43.01]** The law is sometimes prepared to hold one person liable for the wrong committed by another person even though the person held liable is not at fault in the accepted sense of the word. Thus the law may hold the employer liable for the wrongs of an employee, the principal liable for the wrongs of an agent[2] or the firm liable for the wrongs of its partner, in spite of the fact that the employer, the principal or the firm may not have been at fault in any way. When the law imposes liability in these circumstances we speak of the employer, principal or firm being "vicariously liable".[3]

---

1. See Atiyah, *Vicarious Liability in the Law of Torts* (1967); White, *Civil Liability for Industrial Accidents* (1993), Vol 1, p 120ff; Seavey 'Speculations as to "Respondeat Superior"' in *Harvard Legal Essays* (1934, reprinted 1967), p 432; James 'Vicarious Liability' (1954) 28 Tulane LR 161; Laski 'The Basis of Vicarious Liability' (1916) 26 Yale LJ 105; Douglas 'Vicarious Liability and Administration of Risk' (1929) 38 Yale LJ 584 at 720; Williams 'Vicarious Liability and Its Master's Indemnity' (1957) 20 MLR 220 at 437; Williams 'Vicarious Liability: Tort of the Master or the Servant?' (1956) 72 LQR 522; Barak 'Mixed and Vicarious Liability - Suggested Distinction (1966) 29 MLR 160.
2. *Cf* Conant 'Liability of Principals for Torts of Agents: A Comparative View' (1968) 47 Neb LR 42. See also *Higgins v O'Reilly* [1940] Ir Jur Rep 15 (HC) - Parliamentary candidate liable for torts of personation agents. As to ostensible authority see *Allied Irish Banks v Murnane*, High Court, 21 December 1988 (Barron J), noted by Byrne & Binchy, *Annual Review of Irish Law 1988*, pp 425-426; *Irish Permanent Building Society v O'Sullivan*, [1990] ILRM 598 (HC), analysed by Byrne & Binchy, *Annual Review of Irish Law 1990*, pp 562-563.
3. In these circumstances, both the employer and the employee are concurrent wrongdoers and are liable to the injured plaintiff: Civil Liability Act 1961, s 11. In appropriate circumstances, the innocent employer may claim an indemnity from the employee. See also s 21 of the 1961 Act; *Lister v Romford Ice and Cold Storage Co Ltd* [1957] AC 555 (HL), criticised by White, *Civil Liability for Industrial Accidents* (1993), Vol 1, p 123; Williams 'Vicarious Liability and Its Master's Indemnity' (1957) 20 MLR 220 at 437; Williams 'Vicarious Liability: Tort of the Master or the Servant?' (1956) 72 LQR 522; Jolowicz 'The Right to Indemnity between Master and Servant' [1956] Camb LJ 101; Parsons 'Individual Responsibility Versus Enterprise Liability' (1956) 29 Austr LJ 714. *Cf Sinnott v Quinnsworth Ltd* [1984] ILRM 523 (SC).

**[43.02]** Historically speaking this example of strict liability can be traced to earliest times[4] although its modern form in England dates from the end of the seventeenth century.[5] It survived the "no liability without fault" era, to some extent as an anomaly, but nowadays with the trend towards no-fault concepts it can be sustained by more modern justifications such as risk creation and enterprise liability. In other words, the concept of vicarious liability has dovetailed nicely with the more modern ideas that the person who creates the risk, or the enterprise which benefits from the activity causing the damage, should bear the loss. Such persons or enterprises are in a good position to absorb and distribute the loss by price controls and through proper liability insurance. Liability in these cases should, it is felt, follow "the deep pocket".[6]

**[43.03]** Even at this early juncture, however, it may be well to note that the law does not impose liability on the employer for all the wrongs committed by the employee, but only for those which arise out of or are within the scope of the employee's employment. Much of the litigation in this area is concerned with this limitation and it will have to be dealt with more fully at a later point.

**[43.04]** The instances given above where vicarious liability can arise - between employer and employee, principal and agents, and firm and partner - do not constitute an exhaustive list. Other instances of vicarious liability can arise, where the law will hold one person liable for the wrongs of another even though no formal legal relationship exists between the parties in question. Indeed, it seems that in Ireland a person may be vicariously liable whenever he or she has sufficient control over the actions of another.

**[43.05]** This was strikingly illustrated in the Supreme Court decision in *Moynihan v Moynihan*.[7] The plaintiff, who was at the time of the accident two years old, was injured when she pulled a pot of tea on herself in her grandmother's house. The plaintiff had been invited with her parents to a meal by her grandmother (the defendant); when the meal was over the defendant's daughter (the plaintiff's aunt) had left the freshly made tea under a brightly coloured tea-cosy on the breakfast-room table. The plaintiff's father had left the house and her mother was assisting the defendant with the dishes in the kitchen. The defendant's daughter who made the tea left the room hurriedly to answer the telephone, so that the plaintiff was alone and unattended in the breakfast-room when the accident occurred. The trial judge withdrew the case from the jury on the grounds that the defendant could not be responsible for the negligence of her daughter. The plaintiff's appeal to the Supreme Court was successful. The Court held that there was sufficient evidence on which a jury could have found that the defendant's daughter was negligent.

---

4. See Holmes 'Agency' (1891) 4 Harv LR 345, 5 Harv LR 1 (1892); Wigmore 'Responsibility for Tortious Acts: Its History' (1894), p 315.
5. Holdsworth, *History of English Law* (4th ed, 1936), p 46.
6. *Cf Moynihan v Moynihan* [1975] IR 192 at 198 (SC). See also Laski 'The Basis of Vicarious Liability' (1916) 26 Yale LJ 105, and *cf* the policy considerations discussed by Lord O'Brien LCJ in *Heiton and Co v McSweeney* [1905] 2 IR 47 at 55-56 (KBD) - conviction of employers for breach of by-laws through quasi-criminal omission of servant. "[The doctrine of *respondeat superior*] rests not on the notion of the principal's wrong but on the duty of the principal to make good the damage done by his servants or agents in carrying on the principal's affairs." *Byrne v Ireland* [1972] IR 241 at 280 (SC).
7. [1975] IR 192.

Walsh J (with whose judgment O'Higgins CJ agreed) put the question of the defendant's liability this way:

> "The question to be decided therefore is whether, in the circumstances of the case, the relationship between the mother and her daughter Marie was sufficient to make the defendant vicariously liable for the negligence alleged against Marie."[8]

**[43.06]** In Walsh J's opinion the answer to this question was undoubtedly in the affirmative.

> "The nature and limits of this hospitality were completely under the control of the mother and to that extent it may be said that the daughter Marie in her actions on this occasion was standing in the shoes of her mother and carrying out for her mother a task which would primarily have been that of the mother but was in this case assigned to the daughter Marie. As the mother was the person providing the hospitality, the delegation of some of that task to the daughter Marie may be regarded as casual delegation. Marie's performance of it was a gratuitous service for her mother. It was within the control of the mother to decide when the tea would be served and where it would be served and indeed if it was to be served at all. It was also within the control of the mother to decide how it would be served. This power of control was not in any way dependent upon the relationship of mother and daughter but rather upon the relationship of the head of a household with a person to whom some of the duties of the head of the household had been delegated by that head. The position would be no different therefore from that of a case where the head of a household had requested a neighbour to come in and assist in the giving of a dinner-party where she had not any, or only insufficient, hired domestic help. It would produce a strange situation if in such a case the "inviter" should be vicariously liable for the hired domestic help who negligently poured hot sauce over the head of a guest, but should not be equally liable for similar negligence on the part of the co-helper who was the neighbour and not hired. In my view, in the latter case the person requested to assist in the service but who was not hired for that purpose is in the de facto service of the person who makes the request and for whom the duty is being performed."[9]

**[43.07]** In Walsh J's view:

> "on the evidence so far adduced in the present case, the necessary element of control was vested in the defendant and the daughter Marie was in the *de facto* service of her mother for the purpose of the act in which she was alleged to be negligent."[10]

---

8. [1975] IR 192 at 196. The "mother" referred to here was the grandmother of the plaintiff.
9. [1975] IR 192 at 197.
10. [1975] IR 192 at 198. See also Henchy J's strong dissent. It is interesting to note that both the majority judgment and Henchy J's dissent specifically refer, albeit in general terms, to the insurance aspect of such liability: [1975] IR 192 at 198 and 202-203. Walsh J (p 198) specifically reserved his position where evidence might show that the giving of hospitality was a joint enterprise. *Moynihan v Moynihan* laid down defensible rules for determining vicarious liability, but the application of these rules to the facts of the case was hardly convincing. Ascribing the status of a *de facto* service relationship to a relationship between an adult woman and her mother was scarcely consonant with the values of the late twentieth century. It is noteworthy that in *Duffy v Rooney and Dunne's Stores (Dundalk) Ltd* High Court, 23 June 1997 (Laffoy J), affd Supreme Court, 3 November 1998, Laffoy J had little difficulty in distinguishing *Moynihan v Moynihan* in another domestic accident case where an attempt was made to hold a grandparent vicariously liable for the alleged wrong of a daughter living in the house. In *Duffy*, the two-year-old plaintiff was serverely burnt when she went too close to an open fire when visiting her grandparents' home.

**[43.08]** The decision is important because it clearly indicates that the control concept is used, not as a justification for vicarious liability, but rather as a test to determine the persons for whose actions liability will be imposed on the defendant.[11] In other words, if the control element is high, then even in the absence of other features the subordinate may be considered a *de facto* employee, and provided the "controlled person's" acts relate to the "controller's" business the latter will be vicariously liable for injury caused to third persons by such acts.[12]

**[43.9]** A classic instance of a relationship that lacks the requiste element of control is that between a solicitor and counsel in respect of the performance of advocacy functions. In *Fallon v Gannon*,[13] the plaintiff claimed that counsel representing him in earlier litigation in which he was involved had failed to cross-examine the witnesses adequately. The Supreme Court, affirming McMahon J, held that there was not substance in the complaint, but that, in any event, the plaintiff's solicitor could not be vicariously responsible for counsel's conduct in this respect. Finlay CJ stated:

---

10. (contd) At the time her grandfather had her under his care. The grandfather had a fireguard on the fire but it appeared that his daughter possibly removed it some minutes before the accident. Laffoy J imposed personal liability in negligence on the grandfather for having failed in his duty of care to his granddaughter in allowing her enter and cross a room in which there was an unguarded open fire, having failed to notice that the fireguard had been removed. Laffoy J, however, rejected the claim that the grandfather was vicariously liable for his daughter's alleged default. Even if she had removed the fireguard, the evidence had not established that she had been in *de facto* service of her father, in relation to her actions:

> "in the sense that the daughter of the first defendant in *Moynihan v Moynihan* was in the *de facto* service of that defendant doing the task of making the tea and putting the teapot on the table. Even if [the daughter in the instant case] did remove the fireguard, on the evidence, in doing so she acted totally independently of [her father] and not in any sense in pursuance of the performance of a gratuitous service for [him] and, accordingly, the purpose of vicarious liability is not applicable."

One may hope that this sounds the death knell for artificial ascriptions of vicarious liabiliy in the domestic environment.

11. See also *Davey v CIE* (1968) 103 ILT SJ 164 (HC). In *Holohan v Minister for Defence* High Court, 30 July 1998, an employers' liability case involving a member of the Defence Forces who was accidentally struck by a pick used by a sergeant when digging a trench, Kinlen J imposed vicarious liability on the Minister for Defence (and Ireland), observing that "[i]t would be difficult to imagine a more perfect example of a system of control than that which exists within the Defence Forces."

12. With regard to the possibility that the proprietor of a company, as opposed to the company itself, might be vicariously liable for the torts of the company's ostensible employees, White argues that there is no reason why the proprietors should not be liable in appropriate circumstances. If the control element is strong and rests with the proprietors of a company, policy reasons such as deterrence, fairness and efficient loss distribution, which lie behind the modern doctrine of vicarious liability, would argue for the imposition of liability in these cases: See White, *Civil Liability for Industrial Accidents* (1993), Vol 1, pp 144-147. Making the proprietors who control such workers vicariously liable in appropriate cases in no way threatens the commercial usefulness of the limited liability concept, which in any event is more relevant in the case of obligations based on contract rather than obligations based on tort. According to White, the same argument might impose liability on the proprietors of a company where an employee is lent and control moves to the hirer and the employee is injured because of the failure to provide proper plant and equipment.

13. [1988] ILRM 193 (SC).

"The duty of a solicitor with regard to the conduct of a case in court where he has briefed counsel is firstly, to brief appropriate and competent counsel and secondly, to instruct them properly with regard to the facts of the case which he has obtained from his client, and to make provision for the attendance of appropriate witnesses and their proofs. A solicitor has not got any vicarious responsibility for the individual conduct of counsel."[14]

## II. The Employer/Employee Relationship

### Hired Employees: Who is the Employer?

**[43.10]** The control test is also used to solve the problem that frequently arises when a general employer hires out an employee and a machine to a temporary employer. Who is the employer for the purposes of vicarious liability if the hired employee injures someone through his or her negligence? The law on this matter seems to be fairly well settled now in Ireland and may be stated in the following propositions. The presumption is that the hired employee remains in the employment of the general employer and a plaintiff who asserts the contrary has the heavy onus of proving it. Generally speaking, the employee is the employee of the employer who controls not only the task to be performed but also the method of performing it. In each case this is a question of fact. In practice this means that the hired or lent employee remains the employee of the general employer, because in most cases he or she is a skilled operator hired in connection with a machine, the method of operation of which would be entirely a matter for the employee. A transfer of control may sometimes take place, however, when an unskilled person is lent for help with labouring work.[15]

**[43.11]** These principles were clearly stated in *Lynch v Palgrave Murphy Ltd.*[16] In that case Palgrave Murphy Ltd were stevedores who hired out from Crosbie a fork-lift and operator (Byrne) at the rate of £1 an hour. While operating the fork-lift Byrne injured the plaintiff, a casual dock labourer employed by Palgrave Murphy Ltd. The plaintiff sued Palgrave Murphy Ltd, claiming that it was vicariously liable for the tort of the operator. Byrne was employed, paid and subject to dismissal by Crosbie, but was subject to the general directions of Palgrave Murphy Ltd, for example, in determining what load to take, where to put it, etc. The Supreme Court held that the solution to the problem as to who was the employer for the purpose of vicarious liability was to be found by ascertaining, as a matter

14. [1988] ILRM 193 at 197. It may be that Irish courts will follow the lead of the House of Lords and abolish the traditional immunity of an advocate from a duty of care. If there is no actionable negligence on the part of the advocate that would be a reason *a fortiori*, why no vicarious liability should attach to the briefing solicitor. *Cf Deighan v Ireland* [1995] 1 ILRM 88 (HC): "Vicarious liability cannot arise unless there is a primary liability" at 94. If there is a duty of care, however, it is possible to envisage a case where a solicitor might conceivably be vicariously liable. This would be where a junior member of a solicitor's firm acted as advocate. An issue of control might possibly arise in such an instance.

15. *Lynch v Palgrave Murphy Ltd* [1964] IR 150 at 163; see also *Garrard v AE Southey & Co* [1952] 2 QB 174. *Cf* Anon. 'Note: Borrowed Servants and the Theory of Enterprise Liability' (1967) 76 Yale LJ 807; Anon 'Loan of Services' (1952) 86 ILT & Sol J 247; Anon 'Whose Responsibility?' (1955) 89 ILT & Sol J 297. It might be wondered why both the permanent and the temporary employer should not be considered masters for the purposes of vicarious liability. Has the biblical injunction that one cannot serve two masters affected judicial attitudes here? See also *McDonagh v O'Connell and Ors*, High Court, unrep 24 October 1996 (Barr J).

16. [1964] IR 150.

of fact, the degree of control which the defendants were entitled to exercise in relation to the act which was performed negligently. The mere fact that they could assign the task to be done by the operator was not sufficient control to make them liable.[17] For them to be liable it would have to be shown that they had the power to control the way or the method in which the negligent act of the operator was done. In the present case the Court held that the plaintiff had failed to show that the required amount of control had passed to the temporary employers (the defendants). In allowing Palgrave Murphy's Ltd's appeal the Court declared that the case at trial should have been withdrawn from the jury.[18]

## Personal Liability of Employer

**[43.12]** Before going on to examine the most important example of vicarious liability - the liability of a employer for the torts of an employee - an important distinction should be made between the personal liability of the employer for the acts of the employee and the vicarious liability of the employer for the torts of the employee. If the injured person complains that the employer authorised the employee to commit the action complained of, or that the employer was at fault, in selecting or in supervising the employee, he or she is alleging that the employer is personally liable. In this case the attack is made directly on the employer and not on the employer through the employee. This is not vicarious liability. It may be true that the employee was the immediate instrument through which the employer commits the injury, but it is the employer's negligence that is the basis of the complaint. True vicarious liability arises when the law attaches liability to the employer for the employee's torts even when the employer is not at fault. In such cases, of course, before

17. [1964] IR 150 at 155. See also *McGowan v Wicklow County Council and O'Toole* High Court, 27 May 1993 (Morris J). In this case, the first named defendant hired a JCB and a driver from the second named defendant, an independent contractor. The first named defendant was not liable vicariously for an injury caused by the driver: there was evidence that the JCB driver would never be given instructions as to how the job was to be done or how the driver was to manage the machine. A similar approach is taken by the courts, in answering, in these types of cases, who is the operative's employer for the purpose of employer's liability. If the hired driver is injured while working, who owes him or her the employer's duty of care? The courts once more answer this question by focusing on who has control over the employee though, in contrast to vicarious liability they do not exclude the possibility that more than one employeer may have the requisite degree of control to incur liability. In *McDonagh v O'Connell and Ors*, High Court, unrep 24 October 1996, the plaintiff was employed as a labourer by a contractor engaged in restoration work at King John's Castle, Limerick. Limerick Corporation simultaneously decided that a major archeological investigation should be carried out, and the plaintiff was lent to the corporation. He worked under supervision of the Corporation archeologists and was injured when a trench collapsed. It was held that archeological excavation was a specialised activity which had to be supervised by archeologists and that they controlled his work at the time exclusively. The Corporation was therefore the proper defendant. See also Ch 18 and *Mulligan v Holland Dredging (Ireland) Ltd* High Court, 23 January 1995.

18. The Court approved *McCartan v Belfast Harbour Commissioners* [1911] 2 IR 143 and *Mersey Docks & Harbour Board v Coggins & Griffith (Liverpool) Ltd* [1947] AC 1; *Donovan v Laing, Wharton & Down Construction Syndicate* [1893] 1 QB 629 was explained. In that case the temporary employer was held liable because sufficient control had passed to him. See [1964] IR at 156 and 162. See also *Maguire v Lagan (Contractors) Ltd* [1976] NI 49; *Treacy v Robinson and others*; *McGovern v Same* [1937] IR 255; *McManamon v CIE* [1961] IR 30 (SC revsg (HC)).

the law will impose liability on the employer the employee himself or herself must be liable to the injured party.[19]

**[43.13]** An example of the employer being personally liable for injuries caused to a third person occurred in *Dowling v Moore*,[20] where the defendant's employee who was in charge of a pony and van left the van unattended while he was delivering parcels. The unattended pony got frightened and injured the plaintiff's horse. The Court held that the defendant was liable because the two-fold duty imposed on the driver of tending and delivering would prevent even the most attentive man from looking after the pony.[21] The defendant employer, was liable because the system of work he devised was defective.

**[43.14]** A more striking illustration occurs in *Curley v Mannion*.[22] Here the defendant's daughter while closing the back door of the defendant's parked vehicle struck and injured the plaintiff who was cycling on the road. The trial judge refused to let the case go to the jury, but an appeal to the Supreme Court was successful. Walsh J put the matter this way:

> "The learned trial Judge was quite correct in holding that the relationship of parent and child could not of itself impose upon the defendant any vicarious liability for the act of the girl. That, however, did not dispose of the matter.
>
> In my view the defendant, as the owner and driver of the motor car in question, owed a duty to other persons using the highway not merely not to use or drive the car negligently but to take reasonable precautions to ensure that the car, while under his control and supervision, was not used in a negligent fashion."[23]

This was a personal duty and might involve the owner in liability even if, because of her age, the girl in question was not negligent.[24]

## Employer's Liability for the Torts of his or her Employees

**[43.15]** The employer's liability for the torts of the employee is the most important instance of vicarious liability and must be examined in some detail. Generally speaking the law imposes liability on the employer for the torts of the employee if they are committed within the scope of his or her employment.[25] This statement raises three questions:

(i) Who are the employees for the purpose of the rule and how does one distinguish an employee from an independent contractor?

---

19. *Cromer v Sullivan* (1897) 31 ILT & Sol J 439 (CC). *Cf Kennedy v Taltech Engineering Co* High Court, 10 February 1989 (Barr J). "Vicarious liability cannot arise unless there is primary liability", *per* Flood J In *Deighan v Ireland Attorney General* [1995] 2 IR 56 at 63 (HC).
20. (1897) 31 ILT 367 & Sol J (CC).
21. See also *Greene v Lyons & Co* (1897) 31 ILT & Sol J 256 (CC).
22. [1965] IR 543.
23. [1965] IR 543 at 549.
24. See also Ó Dálaigh CJ's judgment to same effect at 546. *Cf Schuster v Whitehead* [1960] OR 125, 21 DLR (2d) 609 (CA), *Russell v Pope* NSSCTD, 26 May 1975, discussed by Hertz, (1976) 2 Dalhousie LJ at 741-743.
25. *Cf Health Board v BC* High Court, 19 January 1994 (Costello P) at p 10 of his judgment:

    "In the absence of express statutory provision, the law in this country, in relation to the liability of an employee for the tortious acts (including statutory torts) of his employee, is perfectly clear - an employer is vicariously liable where the act is committed by his employee within the scope of his employment."

(ii) What does the limitation "within the scope of his or her employment" mean?

(iii) Is a person ever liable for the torts of an independent contractor?

***(a) Who are employees and how are they distinguished from independent contractors?***

**[43.16]** When the courts have considered the question of who is an employee (or in the language of the older cases "servant"[26]), as opposed to an independent contractor, they have included within the term not only, for example, the ordinary employee but also others doing work of a casual nature and even gratuitous volunteers. For the purpose of establishing vicarious liability, the important feature is the "control" element which the principal can exercise over the subordinate. It is true of course that other features of the relationship between the principal and the person doing the work, such as the method of pay (salary or fee), the tax treatment of its "employee", the right to select or dismiss, whether the person provides his or her own equipment or not, the degree of skill which a person possesses (professional skilled person or unskilled worker), whether the contract is "of service" or "for services" in the ordinary person's opinion, whether there is a right to sub-contract[27] or whether the person doing the work is integrated into the business, will also on occasion assist the court in determining whether the relationship of employer and employee exists. Thus, in *Walshe v Baileboro' Co-op Agricultural and Dairy Society and Gargan*,[28] where the plaintiff was injured when struck by Gargan's horse and cart, the Court held that Baileboro' Co-op was vicariously liable for Gargan's negligence even though the horse and cart which Gargan used to collect milk for the Co-op belonged to Gargan himself and even though Gargan was paid a "piecework" rate of 1d per gallon for milk carried. These factors, though important, were not critical and were outweighed by the fact that, the hours of collection were fixed by the Co-op, the type of work left little discretion to the operator and the work was mostly done by Gargan himself (rather than being delegated by him). Gargan was thus an employee in the eyes of the Court.

**[43.17]** Although further efforts at defining more exactly who is an employee for the purpose of the rule constitute an exercise which yields diminishing returns, the continued elaboration of a more specific definition is important, in a positive way, because it enables the court to say for whose liability the employer is liable, and in a negative way to indicate the persons whose torts will not be attributed to the employer. The most important class here are independent contractors. Generally speaking an independent contractor is a person who undertakes to carry out a specific task for another. Normally the independent contractor will undertake to deliver a result, will be paid a fixed sum on completion of the task and reserves control over the means which he or she will use to achieve this end. In contrast an employee normally is employed on a continuous basis to do a series of recurring tasks, is paid on a regular basis and is subject to the employer's instructions as to how the job is to be done. The independent contractor is told what to do, while the employee is not only told what to do but also how he or she must do it.[29] The distinction is

26. It has recently been acknowledged in the House of Lords that this term is no longer appropriate: *Malik v Bank of Credit and Commerce International SA* [1998] AC 20 at 45-46 (*per* Lord Steyn).

27. See *Roche v Kelly & Co Ltd* [1969] IR 100 (SC).

28. [1939] Ir Jur Rep 77 (HC). *Cf McKeon v Bolton* (1851) 1 Ir CLR 377 (QB).

29. See *Roche v Kelly & Co Ltd* [1969] IR 100 (SC).

important because, while the employer is liable for the torts of an employee, no liability attaches normally to the principal for the torts of independent contractors. Thus, if I hire a taxi and the driver negligently injures a third person I am not liable to the third person, whereas if my chauffeur negligently does the same thing I am liable.

**[43.18]** Since the Supreme Court decision in *Moynihan v Moynihan*,[30] however, the degree of control which the principal exercises seems to be emerging as the single most important, if not the crucial factor, in establishing liability, in Ireland at least.

**[43.19]** *Phelan v Coilte Teoranta*[31] illustrates the point. There the operative, Mr Carwood, was a welder/fitter who was engaged nearly full time by Coilte. He travelled all over the state tending to forestry machinery which needed attention. Coilte paid him an hourly rate, negotiated annually, and a mileage allowance in respect of his own car. He provided his own tools and equipment and was entitled to no holiday pay or pension entitlements. Coilte did not deduct PAYE tax or PRSI contributions. In most instances the operative was merely dispatched to a forest and told that the particular machine required repair or attention. Rarely, a Coilte engineering might give him instructions and occasionally a Coilte employee might be directed to assist him as happened in the present case. Barr J, in holding Coilte vicariously liable, stated:

> "I am satisfied that if it is held, as I have done, that in practical terms the degree of control that was exercisable by Coilte over Mr Carwood was the same as one would expect a master to have over a tradesman servant, then the employer is vicariously liable to the plaintiff for Mr Carwood's negligence, even if the relationship between the latter and Coilte is found to be that of independent contractor and employer."[32]

**[43.20]** In Barr J's view the element of control is overriding even if the operative is an independent contractor.

**[43.21]** Phelan's case may be contrasted with *Carroll v Post National Lottery Co*,[33] where Costello P rejected the plaintiff's argument that Lotto agents of the defendant company (or the agents' employees) should be regarded as the company's "servants" so as to implicate the company in vicarious liability for any negligent acts they did in the course of their employmen. Lotto agents (and their employees) were admittedly subject to training and direction by the company in the operation of terminals, the handling of playslips and the generating of tickets but, as Costello P pointed out, the Lotto agents were sales agents selling tickets on commission:

> "Their's is not a contract of employment. Whilst it is true that they are instructed and trained in the operation of the computer terminal it seems to me that they are not in any way subject to the control and direction of the defendant company when they are selling tickets as to the manner in which the sales are to be effected or otherwise. To describe the relationship between the Lotto agent and the defendant company as one of master and servant would be to do violence to the well established characteristics of that relationship as well as the plain

30. [1975] IR 192.
31. [1993] 1 IR 18 (HC), analysed by Byrne & Binchy, *Annual Review of Irish Law 1992*, pp 606-608.
32. [1993] 1 IR at 25. See also *McAuliffe v Minister for Social Welfare* [1995] 1 ILRM 189 (HC), analysed by Byrne & Binchy, *Annual Review of Irish Law 1994*, pp 408-410; *Kelly v Michael McNamara & Co* High Court, Budd J, 5 June 1996; *Deegan v Wholey*, DPIJ: Hilary and Easter Terms 1997, p 121 (HC) (McCracken J).
33. High Court, 17 April 1996 (Costello P).

meaning of the agent's authorisation. *A fortiori*, it cannot be said that a member of the staff of the Lotto agent whilst selling tickets is in a master-and-servant relationship with the defendant company."[34]

**[43.22]** The control test, however, while useful in many cases does not seem to be determinative in all instances, for example, in what have become known as "the hospital cases".[35] Is the health authority or the hospital authority vicariously liable for the negligence of resident surgeons, anaesthetists, nurses, etc? In these cases there is no question of the employer controlling the way in which the surgeon operates, and if the control test is doggedly adhered to the plaintiff may be denied access to "the deep pocket". After much uncertainty[36] the rule seems to be well accepted that medical staff in the full-time service of hospitals are employees for the purposes of vicarious liability.[37] That this has been accepted in Ireland can be seen from such cases as *O'Donovan v Cork County Council*.[38] Here in an action against the defendant council for the alleged negligence of a surgeon and an anaesthetist the defendant council while denying negligence, did not even contest the proposition that it would be vicariously liable if negligence were proved on the part of the surgeon or the anaesthetist. The remnants of the *ancien regime* have not disappeared completely, however, since Irish health services still retain distinctions between public and private patients, which impact on the issue of vicarious liability. In *Bolton v Blackrock Clinic Ltd*,[39] the plaintiff unsuccessfully sued a cardio-thoracic surgeon and a consultant thoracic physician for negligence in her treatment. She also sued the hospital where these specialists worked, on the basis of direct[40] and vicarious liability. Having dismissed the plaintiff's claim against the specialists, Geoghegan J observed:

34. High Court, 17 April 1996 at page 24-25 of Costello, P's judgment. See also *Smyth (S) & Co Ltd v Aer Turas Teo* Supreme Court, 3 February 1997.

35. *Cf* Fridman 'Hospital Liability for Professional Negligence' (1980) 4 LMQ 80.

36. See the decisions cited by Hanna J in *Dennehy v Kildare Co Board of Health* [1936] IR 384 at 399 (HC). See also Kennedy & Grubb eds *Principles of Medical Law* (1998), Ch 8.

37. *Gold v Essex County Council* [1942] 2 KB 293 (CA) - radiographers; *Cassidy v Ministry of Health* [1951] 2 KB 343 (CA) - house-surgeon and assistant medical officers; *Roe v Ministry of Health* [1954] 2 QB 66 (CA) - part-time anaesthetist; *Mooney v Terrett* [1939] Ir Jur Rep 56 (HC) - nursing home liable for nursing negligence.

38. [1967] IR 173. Similarly in *Lindsay v Mid-Western Health Board* [1993] 2 IR 147 at 167 (SC rev (HC) - on grounds not affecting this issue - Morris J noted that the defendant Health Board had accepted that the medical personnel involved in the case were its servants or agents for the purposes of vicarious liability. See also *Morgan v Galway Board of Health* [1943] IR 255 (SC); *Best v Wellcome Foundation Ltd* [1993] 3 IR 421 (SC); *DK v King* [1994] 1 IR 166 (HC); *O'Keeffe v Cody* High Court, 11 March 1994 (Lynch J); *O'Dowd v North Western Health Board* [1983] ILRM 186 at 197 (SC) *per* Henchy J, dissenting, but dissent not affecting this issue - in (unsuccessful) s 260 proceedings taken under the Mental Act 1945, the Health Board that administrated the hospital and not its chief executive officer, could be liable for negligence of its servants or agents (which was not established in the case); vicarious liability was capable of extending to torts of the resident medical superintendant of the hospital but not of a general practitioner who signed the form (again no wrongful conduct being established).

39. High Court, 20 December 1994 (Geoghean J) affd Supreme Court, 23 January 1997.

40. The notion of a direct, non-delegable duty of care on the part of hospitals found favour with Denning LJ, in *Cassidy v Ministry of Health,* [1951] 2 KB 343 at 362-363. It is not yet completely noted in English law: *cf* STREET, pp 511-513 and has been rejected by the Ontario Court of Appeal in *Yepremian v Scarborough General Hospital* (1980) 110 DLR (3d) 513.

"That being so there cannot be any question of vicarious liability on the part of the [hospital] for medical negligence. Indeed, at any rate as the plaintiff was a private patient of the doctors in a private hospital, the question of vicarious liability may not arise."

**[43.23]** There being no evidence of negligence by the hospital itself or its staff, Geoghegan J dismissed the claim for direct negligence also.

***(b) The scope of employee's employment***

**[43.24]** It must be realised that the nature of the employer/employee relationship, when it exists, has definitional limitations. These limitations may be temporal or spatial. There will, of course, also be limitations imposed by the nature of the employment and these we may call functional limitations.

**[43.25]** The temporal limitation could mean, for example, that an employer would not normally be liable for the torts of a nine-to-five employee committed at 10.00 pm or at week-ends. The spatial limitation could mean that the employer would not normally be liable for torts committed by the employee away from the place of work. Such limitations can be easily appreciated and accepted in the typical relationship that exists between, say, a factory owner and his employees. In other less formal types of employment, however, as for example between an employer and a sales representative or between a farmer and a farm labourer, the temporal and spatial limitations of the employment contract may be less well defined. So, in *Boyle v Ferguson*[41] a car salesman who, in the company of two women, was out for "a spin" at 7 pm on a Saturday evening was nevertheless held to be acting within the scope of his employment. The court was obviously impressed by the evidence which showed that the employer was paying for the petrol at the time, that the salesman had been given great latitude in his hours and methods of work and, lastly, that, while on the road "in the company of ladies who were interested in motors, and would be useful as patrons or supporters," the salesman was creating a good impression appropriate to a car salesman. This can be contrasted with *Kiely v McCrea & Sons Ltd*[42] where the High Court held that a commercial traveller, whose terms of employment provided that he should "use his best endeavours to effect the sale of the goods of the company" but prohibited him from using the company's motor car for his private purposes, was acting outside the scope

40. (contd) The acceptance by the Supreme Court of a similar, non-delegable duty on the part of employers, in *Connolly v Dundalk Urban District Council* [1990] 2 IR 1 (HC) may encourage a future Irish court to consider the issue afresh in the context of hospitals. It is, however, one thing for a hospital to have a direct, non-delegable duty in relation to administrative, nursing and general medical services; it is quite another that a patient who contracts for the specialist expertise of a particular doctor, where the hospital is organised merely to provide a supportive environment for a number of such individual doctors, should be able to sue the hospital for the doctor's negligence. see further paras **[18.33]-[18.55]** above.

41. [1911] 2 IR 489.

42. [1940] Ir Jur Rep 1. An employer will not usually be held vicariously responsible for a tort committed by an employee on the way to or from work. "One must not confuse the duty to turn up for one's work with the concept of already being 'on duty' while travelling to it". *Smith v Stages* [1989] 1 All ER 833 at 851 (HL), *per* Lord Lowry. Special circumstances may, however, bring such "travelling time" within the ambit of an employee's duty. Thus, in *Smith v Stages*, the fact that the employee received wages, rather than an allowance, for travelling to a job in his employer's time was crucial to bringing the period of travel within the course of his employment.

of his employment when he negligently drove the car so as to cause an accident while coming home from a dance. Although he had as passengers, at the time of the accident, some employees of firms with which he dealt, this was not sufficient on the occasion to render his employer liable.

**[43.26]** A more difficult question arises in the case of the employee's functions. Where the employee is doing what he or she is employed to do, even if he or she is doing it badly, the employer is liable for the employee's torts. If, however, the employee is doing something he or she is not employed to do, then the employer is not liable. Moreover, there is good authority for saying that "within the scope of authority" is a phrase which must be interpreted liberally in favour of the injured plaintiff.[43] Thus, the employer may be liable even if the employee has acted negligently or criminally and even if the employee has been prohibited from doing the very act which is the subject of the action. In determining the employer's liability the test favoured nowadays is, whether the act in question was within the scope of the employee's duties, not, whether the act was permitted by the employer. If the latter were the criterion, the employer could always protect himself or herself against the employee's carelessness by stipulating in the contract of employment that the employee shall not in the course of his or her duties act negligently.

**[43.27]** In this matter, therefore, the real difficulty lies, not in stating the law, but in applying it to particular cases,[44] and while illustrations may help to provide guidelines, they cannot be expected to do more.

**[43.28]** In *Farry v GN Rly Co*,[45] a station employee detained the plaintiff to force him to give up his ticket after a dispute had arisen as to whether the plaintiff had "broken" his journey. In holding the company responsible for the false imprisonment, Palles CB[46] provided a clear analysis of the issue:

> "In actions of this class, two separate things are to be considered: first, the act done; secondly, the purpose for which it is done ... If the act is outside the scope of the servant's employment, the master is not responsible, and in such a case it is unnecessary to consider the purpose ... But, when the act ... is one within the ordinary scope of the servant's employment then arises the question whether the act complained of was done for the employer; as, if the act, although of a class within the scope of the employment, was done by the servant, for his own purposes, such, for instance, as wreaking his own vengeance or spite upon a particular person, the act, although capable of being done within the scope of employment, is not in fact done within such scope; it is not done *for* the employer."[47]

**[43.29]** The case before the Court was clearly of a class within the scope of the employee's employment and, since the station master had been acting bona fide in protecting the company's rights and not for any purpose of his own, the company was held vicariously liable.

---

43. See eg *Doyle v Fleming's Coal Mines* Supreme Court, 29 July 1955.
44. See *Wilson v Owens* (1885) 16 LR Ir 225 at 234.
45. [1898] 2 IR 352 (QB). See also *Van Den Eynde v Ulster Ry Co* (1871) IR 5 CL 328 (Exch). *Cf Cullimore v Savage South Africa* [1903] 2 IR 589 (CA revsg KB).
46. With whom Boyd and Murphy JJ concurred.
47. [1898] 2 IR at 355-356.

### *(c) Conduct within the scope of employment*

**[43.30]** In *Williams v Morrissey*[48] the defendant was held liable when the employee, who was driving the defendant's cow, threw a stone at the cow to divert the animal, and hit the plaintiff. Similarly, in *Gracey v Belfast Tramway Co*[49] where two employees of the defendant, while taking the defendant's horses to the forge to be shod, raced the horses furiously, thereby causing the plaintiff to be thrown from her trap, the Court held the employer liable. Although the racing of the horses was for their own amusement, the primary purpose of the employees (ie, to take the horses to the forge) was within the scope of their employment.[50] Again a petrol-lorry driver who lit a cigarette during the transfer of petrol from his lorry to a storage tank and caused an explosion was acting within the scope of his employment.[51] In *Murphy v Ross*[52] the Court held that when a boy, who was asked by a foreman to point out a route to a new driver, was injured by the negligence of the driver, there was sufficient evidence that the foreman was acting within the scope of his employment for the matter to go to the jury.

**[43.31]** In *McIntyre v Lewis*,[53] where the plaintiff was beaten up by two members of the Garda Síochána, and then arrested and charged with assaulting one of his assistants, the State was held vicariously liable in assault, false imprisonment and malious prosecution. McCarthy J observed:

> "It was not suggested that the original assault was other than in the course of duty; everything else flowed directly from it, including the bringing and prosecution of the charges against the plaintiff."[54]

**[43.32]** Although there is some authority for saying that the employer's prohibition forbidding the employee from acting as he or she did does not automatically exonerate the employer from liability,[55] the majority of Irish cases where the employer's prohibition was

---

48. (1903) 37 ILTR 65 (KBD).
49. [1901] 2 IR 322. See also *Forshall and Fine Arts Collections Ltd v Walsh* Supreme Court, 31 July 1998 - bank held vicariously liable for negligent representations made by bank manager to purchaser of "classic cars" for Japenese clients as to financial strength of parties with whom purchaser was dong business.
50. See also *Page v The GN Rly Co* (1868) IR 2 CL 228; *Van den Eynde v Ulster Ry Co* (1871) IR 5 CL 328. In *General Engineering Services Ltd v Kingston and St Andrew Corp* [1988] 2 All ER 867 (PC), firemen operating a "go-slow" policy as part of industrial action in support of a pay claim which resulted in the destruction of the plaintiff's property, were held to be acting outside the scope of their employment. Their conduct "was the very negation of carrying out some act authorised by the employer, albeit in a wrongful and unauthorised mode". The special requirement of urgency involved in fire fighting suggests that "go-slows" in less pressing contexts could be capable of involving vicarious liability on the part of an employer. Whether this would be perceived as desirable on policy grounds may, however, be doubted.
51. *Northern Ireland Road Transport Board v Century Ins Co Ltd* [1941] NI 77 (CA); 75 ILTR 44; [1942] NI 47 (HL).
52. [1920] 2 IR 199.
53. [1991] 1 IR 121 (SC).
54. [1991] 1 IR 121 at 137.
55. *Strong v McAuley, McRroy & Co Ltd* (1929) 63 ILTR 39; see also *Hosford v Macken* [1897] 1 IR 292. See also *Kooragang Invests Ply Ltd v Richardson and Wrench* [1981] 3 WLR 493, noted by Murdoch in (1982) 98 LQR 21.

a factor have resulted in the Court holding that the employee acted outside the scope of his or her authority.[56] In truth, however, the employer's prohibition, is, like many other circumstances, just one factor to be taken into account.

**[43.33]** More difficult are the cases where the employee injures another employee because of some tricking or horseplay at the place of work. Again, the criterion should be that if the horseplay is merely a funny or dangerous way of doing what the employee is engaged to do then the employer should be liable for the wrong. Thus, where an employee was employed to push a truck along a passageway and for fun suddenly diverted the truck against a fellow employee, the employer was held vicariously liable.[57] In contrast, where an employee pushed a washbasin, known to be unsteady, against another employee in order to frighten her, it was held that the act was a deliberate act having nothing to do with anything the employee was employed to do, and accordingly it was wholly outside the scope of her employment and the employers were not vicariously liable.[58] Similarly, in *Hough v Irish Base Metals Ltd*,[59] an employer was held not to be vicariously liable for an employee's "larking", when the plaintiff was injured when trying to escape from a gas fire mischievously placed beside him by the employee. If however, the joker employee is in a position of authority, *vis-à-vis* the plaintiff employee, and he uses his position of authority to carry out his "light-hearted prank", then the joker having "used his authority to put his intention in train", may be held to be acting within the scope of his employment as supervisor, and the employer will be vicariously liable. This was decided in *Kennedy v Taltech Engineering*[60] where the supervisor called the plaintiff so that he could snatch an apple out the plaintiff's pocket. In trying to resist, the plaintiff hit his hand off a metal sheet.

### *(d) Conduct outside the scope of employment*

**[43.34]** If the employee acts outside the scope of his or her employment the employer will not be liable. Sometimes it is said that, provided the employee is doing the kind of thing he is employed to do, then the employer remains liable even if the employee does it improperly, but that the employer is not liable if the employee is doing something different in kind from that which he or she is employed to do.

**[43.35]** In *Irving & Irving v Post Office*,[61] a postman-sorter wrote an offensive racist remark on a letter addressed to a couple of Jamaican origin. It was held that since the substance and purpose of what was written was unconnected with the performance of his

---

56. *Byrne v Londonderry Tramway* [1902] 2 IR 457 - permitting passenger to stand on driver's platform; *Cogan v Dublin Motor Co* (1914) 49 ILTR 24 - chauffeur allowing third person to drive car; *Rose v Plenty and Co-operative Retail Services Ltd* [1976] 1 All ER 97 - milkman permitted 13-year-old boy to ride on milk-float contrary to orders, and paid him for his assistance. Employers held vicariously liable for injuries to boy. Permission to carry passengers may sometimes be based on implied authority: see *Kearney v Clare Lime Co Ltd* [1966] IR 338 esp at 343.

57. *Harrison v Michelin Tyre Co Ltd* [1985] 1 All ER 918.

58. *Aldred v Nacanco* [1987] IRLR 292 (CA)

59. Supreme Court, 8 December 1967. See also *Walker v McCormack* Supreme Court, 4 March 1968.

60. High Court, 10 Febuary 1989 (Barr J), noted by Byrne & Binchy, *Annual Review of Irish Law 1989*, pp 437-438.

61. [1987] IRLR 289 (CA).

duties, the Post Office was not vicariously liable. That decision would surely not be followed today, since respect for racial and ethnic diversity of those with whom one conducts business or for whom one provides a service may be regarded as so essential and integral to the work as to come within the scope of the employee's employment.

**[43.36]** In *Lawlor v O'Connor*[62] the defendant's employee, while driving a truck in the course of his employment stopped at the plaintiff's residence and asked her to accompany him in the truck. When the plaintiff refused, the employee grabbed her by the arm onto the running board of the truck and drove off. After about 70 yards, and while the truck was still moving, the employee released the girl without stopping. Not surprisingly, the Court was not willing to hold that this act was done in the course of the employee's employment. The bizarre facts in this case may not make it very useful as a precedent, but it may indicate a reluctance on the part of the Irish Courts to saddle the employer with liability where the employee commits an intentional tort (or a crime) against the person of the plaintiff.[63] Thus, where the employee takes it upon himself or herself to arrest the plaintiff or cause the plaintiff to be arrested, the Courts have frequently, though not invariably,[64] held that the employee, especially if not a senior employee, is no longer acting within the scope of his employment.[65]

**[43.37]** In *McNamara v Brown*,[66] the defendant's employee was employed as a "watcher to prevent poaching in the river". While attempting to apprehend some poachers the employee shot and killed the son of one of the poachers. The employer in this case did not provide the employee with a gun or with an allowance for ammunition, nor was the employee in any real danger at the time of the shooting. The court held that the employee was acting outside the scope of his employment. In this case, and indeed in many of the older cases, the court proceeded on the assumption that an employer was not liable for the acts of his or her employee if the employer could not lawfully do it himself or herself. The thinking was that, if the employer could not lawfully do it, then the employer could not authorise an employee to do it and so the employee could not be acting within the scope of his or her employment[67] The fallacy involved in this reasoning stems from the assumption

62. (1929) 63 ILTR 103. See also *O'Brien v Bergin* Supreme Court, 3 June 1965.

63. *Cf* Burns 'Comment: Employer Liability for Assaults by Employees' (1983) 48 Missouri LR 655. See further para **[18.81]** above.

64. *Van den Eynde v Ulster Ry Co* (1871) IR 5 CL 328 - ticket clerk and station master committing trespass and false imprisonment.

65. *Barry v Dublin United Tramways Co* (1889) 26 LR Ir 150 - company employee excluding and causing to be arrested a member of the public from part of street; *Coleman v Cork Electric Tramways Co Ltd* (1897) 31 ILTR 81 - conductor arresting plaintiff; *Cullimore v Savage South Africa Co* [1903] 2 IR 589 (CA) - ticket seller causing patron to be arrested; *Ibbotson v McAlevy* (1933) 67 ILTR 115. As to the position of the police, see Goode 'The Imposition of Vicarious Liability to the Torts of Police Officers: Considerations of Policy' (1975) 10 Melb ULR 47. More generally see Rose, (1977) 40 MLR 420; Burns 'Comment: Employer Liability for Assaults by Employees' (1983) 48 Missouri LR 655. In *Heaphy v O'Sullivan, the Commissioner of Garda Síochána, Ireland and the AG* High Court, 14 July 1983, Irish Times 15 July 1983, p 11 - an award of £7,000 was made against the defendants for assault (by gardaí on plaintiff while he was in custody).

66. [1918] 1 IR 215. *Cf Kinsella v Hamilton* (1890) 26 LR Ir 671.

67. *Kinsella v Hamilton* (1890) 26 LR Ir 671.

that vicarious liability is based on some form of implied authority (or command) from the employer. The better opinion nowadays has abandoned this line of thought and the courts now simply prefer to hold the employer liable whenever they consider that the employee's action was closely connected with his or her functions, rather than on the basis of some fictitious implied authority.

**[43.38]** Similar criticism can be levelled at the High Court decision in *Reilly v Ryan*.[68] In that case the manager of a bar grabbed the plaintiff customer and used him as a human shield when a man wearing a balaclava entered the bar with a knife and shouted "Give me £40 out of the till." While in this position the plaintiff was stabbed. Blayney J held that the manager was not acting in the course of his employment. He stated that the manager's behaviour could not be said to be impliedly authorised by the employer. "It was a wholly unreasonable and excessive means of dealing with the emergency."[69] For reasons stated above this would seem to be open to criticism. Blayney J appears to argue that ostensible authority, in addition to acting "in the course of his employment", is required when an employee's act is intentional. Such a conclusion would not be fair to the injured person and would run counter to the policy underlying this rule of strict liability.

**[43.39]** *Reilly v Ryan*[70] raises a wider issue concerning the test to be applied when deciding whether a violent act by an employee generates vicarious liability. There is an obvious difference between a case where a bar employee uses too much force when evicting an intoxicated customer (resulting in vicarious liability for the employer) and similar force used by a bar employee on a customer with whose political views he happens to disagree (where the employer will not be held vicariously liable).

**[43.40]** In *Reilly v Ryan*, the employee's instinctive action, if capable of being characterised as intentional[71] surely bore no relation to cases where the employee, for reasons of anger, retribution or the desire to dominate, engaged in violent conduct. The situation was surely akin to that of the "agony of the moment" in negligence.[72] One would imagine that a bus passenger would be able to sue a bus company whose driver, in an act of self-preservation, leapt from the cab when the bus was in the path of rapidly advancing juggernaut.

**[43.41]** Let us take the analysis a stage further and enquire whether an act of self-defence by an employee in a raid on his employer's premises falls within the scope of his employment. In *Kinsella v Hamilton*,[73] Palles CB appeared to think not, but it is interesting

---

68. [1991] ILRM 449.

69. [1991] ILRM 449 at 454.

70. See *Pettersson v Royal Oak Hotel Ltd* [1948] NZLR 136; *Deatons Pty Ltd v Flew* (1949) 79 Comm LR 370; *Rutherford v Hawke's Bay Hospital Board* [1949] NZLR 400; *Griggs v Southside Hotel Ltd*, [1947] 4 DLR 49; *Bigcharles v Merkel* (1972) 32 DLR (3d) 511; *Lakatosh v Ross* (1974) 48 DLR (3d) 694; *Keppel Bus Co Ltd v Ahmad* [1974] 2 All ER 700; *Q v Minto Management Ltd* (1985) 15 DLR (4th) 581 affd (1986) 34 DLR (4th) 767 and *Auckland Workingmen's Club v Rennie* [1976] 1 NZLR 278 (Mahon J).

71. *Cf Larin v Goshen* (1974) 56 DLR (3d) 719.

72. *Cf* para **[20.18]** above.

73. 26 LR Ir at 689.

to note that in *McNamara v Brown*,[74] Campbell CJ confessed that he was "not altogether convinced by this reasoning". We suggest that the Chief Justice's doubts were well-based and that an excessive non-retributive act of self-defence against an assailant or one who threatens an attack should fall within the scope of vicarious liability. If this is so, it is not difficult to accept that a cowardly act of self defence, involving an innocent victim, should also be capable of falling within the net.

**[43.42]** The rule established by the House of Lords in *Lloyd v Grace, Smith & Co*,[75] that the employers of a fraudulent clerk who in the course of his employment misappropriated clients' funds were liable for their clerk's fraud, even though they never authorised the fraud and derived no benefit from it, seems to be the general rule now rather than an exceptional liability, as it was viewed in *McNamara v Brown*.[76] An employer may, therefore, be liable for the torts and crimes of an employee provided they can be seen as being connected within the course of the employee's employment.

**[43.43]** A more recent example of the courts' willingness to impose liability for the crimes of an employee occurred in *Johnson and Johnson v CP Security*.[77] There, a security firm which undertook to protect the plaintiffs' property was held vicariously liable for the theft of the plaintiffs' property by one of the security officers. Having looked at some of the English authorities, and having quoted Lord Denning in *Morris v CW Martin & Sons Ltd*,[78] Egan J said:

> "Lord Denning, it will be seen, stated that some of the cases were baffling and I would be cautious in committing myself to a completely general proposition that an employer would in every conceivable circumstance be held vicariously liable for the tort or criminal act of the employee committed in the course of his employment. I have no hesitation, however, in accepting that the principle of vicarious liability must apply in the present case where the employers were specifically engaged to safeguard the plaintiff's property."[79]

**[43.44]** Clearly, therefore, the employer cannot insulate himself or herself from attack under the principle of vicarious liability by merely saying that they prohibited the employee's activity. A bus company which prohibits its drivers from drinking alcohol while on duty will nevertheless be liable when one of its drivers crashes the bus while under the influence of alcohol. The relevant question in those circumstances is still whether the employee acted in the course of his employment or not. Similarly, this would seem to be the proper way to approach the situation where the driver injures, through his negligence, an unauthorised passenger to whom the driver is giving a lift. In these circumstances since the driver is doing what is clearly part of his job (ie driving), the

---

74. [1918] 1 IR 215 at 224.
75. [1912] AC 716.
76. [1918] 1 IR 215.
77. [1986] ILRM 559 (HC).
78. [1965] 2 All ER 725.
79. [1986] ILRM at 562. *Cf Armagas Ltd v Mundogas SA* [1986] 2 All ER 385 (HL), where the House of Lords held that, in cases where an employee, by fraudulent misrepresentation, caused a plaintiff loss, the employer should be liable only where the employee was acting within his actual or ostensible authority. This was because in such cases the central basis of the employer's liability was the reliance by the injured party on actual or ostensible authority.

employer should be liable for his negligence. It does not alter the position to say that the employer told the driver not to take passengers.[80]

### *(e) Detour and frolic*

**[43.45]** If the policy is to impose liability on the employer not because of his or her own fault, but rather because the risks created are broadly related to the enterprise undertaken, then it would seem that vicarious liability should be imposed whenever the employee's acts could be reasonably foreseen, from the broad view of the enterprise rather than from the employer's view, as being related to the employee's employment.[81] There are, however, some acts which the employee may commit which are, even on a broad view, so totally unconnected with the enterprise or with his functions in the enterprise, that they should not be attributed to the employer. In such cases where the employee is "on a frolic of his own" the employer ought not to be liable. The "detour cases" provide a good illustration of the rule.

**[43.46]** In *O'Connell v Bateman*[82] where the employee borrowed his employer's lorry after work to visit his parents, the Court held that the employer was not liable when the lorry was involved in an accident. Similarly, where the defendant's employee (a taxi driver) took the taxi to his own home without the defendant's permission, parked it and left the switch key available, the employer was held not liable when the vehicle was taken by an unknown person and the plaintiff's premises were damaged.[83] In contrast, however, in *Jameson v Byrne and Maguire*[84] where the employee having completed a petrol delivery, made a detour on his return journey for a reason unconnected with his employment and was involved in an accident, the High Court held that there was evidence from which a jury might infer that the employee was acting within the scope of his employment.

**[43.47]** The difference between the cases seems to be that slight deviations will not relieve the employer of his or her liability whereas a major departure ("a frolic") will mean that the employee is no longer acting within the scope of his or her employment. In each case it is a question of degree and the circumstances of the particular case are vital. It may be

---

80. See White, *Civil Liability for Industrial Accidents* (1993), Vol 1, p 184 esp p 187. His arguments, based on the fact that the passenger is a trespasser, have to be read in the light of the subsequent passing of the Occupiers' Liability Act 1995. See also *Kearney v Ireland* [1986] IR 116 (HC) - plaintiff prisoner's mail interfered with by prison staff contrary to their employer's instructions; plaintiff entitled to damages against the State for infringement of his rights to communicate under Article 40.3 of the Constitution; vicarious liability imposed on the State as liability would have attached to it if the wrong had been a tort. *Per* Costello J (at 122):

> "The wrongful act in this case was obviously connected with the functions for which the prison officer or officers who committed it were employed, and even through the act was not authorised, I cannot hold that it was performed outside the scope of his or their employment."

81. See Douglas 'Vicarious Liability and Administration of Risk' (1929) 38 Yale LJ 584, 720.

82. [1932] LJ Ir 160. See also *Treacy v Robinson and Others; McGovern v Same* [1937] IR 255 (SC); *Brady v Igoe* [1939] Ir Jur Rep 1 (HC). *Cf* Smith 'Frolic and Detour' (1923) 23 Col LR 444, 716.

83. *Quilligan v Long* (1952) 87 ILTR 129 (CC).

84. (1926) 60 ILTR 11. See also *Doyle v Flemings Coal Mines Ltd* Supreme Court, 29 July 1955; *Murray v Minister for Finance et al*, High Court, Irish Times, 28 May 1981; *Parkes v Minister for Finance* (1979) 113 ILTR 118 (CC).

difficult in some cases to determine whether the employee's departure is a slight deviation or a major departure, but a sensible common sense approach may assist in providing the answer. In the driving cases, Salmond & Heuston's comment may be worth consideration:

> "If the deviation constitutes an unauthorised journey, then the servant is 'on a frolic of his own'. But if the deviation is no more than an unauthorised route, then it is a question of fact and degree whether the deviation is sufficiently substantial to put it outside the course of employment."[85]

**[43.48]** By way of summary, therefore, and realising that each case must turn on its own facts, one can say that anything which the employee does in furtherance of his or her task and to further the employer's business and which may fairly and reasonably be regarded as incidental to the task is likely to be within the scope of his or her employment. Matters which are done by the employee not in furtherance of his or her task and not in the interest and which cannot objectively be said to be incidental to the task are likely to be outside the scope of his or her employment.

***(f) Is a person ever liable for the torts of an independent contractor?***

**[43.49]** Although the general rule is that a person is not vicariously liable for the torts of his or her independent contractors,[86] this does not mean that a person is never liable for torts committed by independent contractors. The employer can always be liable where he or she has been personally negligent, for example, in selecting an incompetent contractor. Furthermore, in the torts of nuisance,[87] *Rylands v Fletcher*,[88] breach of statutory duty, liability for wild animals, for example, where liability may be imposed irrespective of fault on the defendant's part, the defendant will be responsible even when the acts complained of are committed by his or her independent contractors. Hence the law recognises that some duties imposed on the employer are of such a nature that they are non-delegable in the sense that the employer cannot escape liability by delegating their performance to an independent contractor. In respect of such a duty, the employer is bound not merely to take reasonable care himself or herself but also to see that reasonable care is taken by anyone to whom the task is delegated.

**[43.50]** Not surprisingly the category of non-delegable duties includes all cases of torts of strict liability. However, liability has also been extended to situations where the duty is normally said to be to take reasonable care, raising the duty in such cases to one of

---

85. SALMOND & HEUSTON, p 447. Internal citation to *Joel v Morison* (1834) 6 C & P 501 at 503. An employee, acting outside the scope of his employment when driving his employer's vehicle, may conceivably be driving with his employer's consent for the purpose of s 118 of the Road Traffic Act 1961. See White, *Civil Liability for Industrial Accidents* (1993), Vol 1, p 183 *et seq*. With regard to whether employees driving to and from work are acting in the course of employment, see Lord Lowry's guiding principle in *Smith v Stages* [1989] 1 All ER 833 (HL) at 851, and see para **[43.25]** above.

86. See *McGowan v Masterson* [1953] IR 101 at 106 (SC). *Cf M'Keon v Bolton* (1851) 1 ICLR 377 (QB). But where the control element is strong the employer may be liable even for the independent contractor's tort. See *Phelan v Coilte Teoranta (Irl) and Ors* [1998] 1 IR 18.

87. *Rivers v Cutting* [1982] 1 WLR 1146 at 1149-50. *Cf O'Donnell v Begley and Bord Telecom Éireann* [1987] ILRM 105.

88. (1868) LR 3 HL 330.

ensuring that reasonable care is taken.[89] So employers are said to have such a duty in respect of providing their employees,[90] and in respect of observing statutory safety standards[91] and in respect of extra-hazardous activities.[92] The list, however, is not closed[93] and liability for the acts of independent contractors will, it seems, be imposed whenever the risk created by the activity is inherently dangerous or would involve special precautions if injury is to be avoided.

**[43.51]** Some examples will illustrate the principles. In *Boylan v Northern Bank Ltd & James Corcoran Ltd*,[94] Costello J held that the demolition of a masonry gable wall measuring about 22 feet by 55 feet and standing within two inches of the plaintiff's premises was an inherently dangerous operation. Accordingly, he imposed liability on the bank for the negligence of the independent contractor engaged to demolish it. In contrast, Blayney J, in *Power v Crowley and Reddy Enterprises Ltd*,[95] came to the opposite conclusion. A labourer working with the defendant in a demolishing operation, removed some blocks form the middle of the wall being demolished thereby rendering it dangerous. The wall collapsed on the plaintiff, a carpenter, who was also engaged in the demolition work. Blayney J did not think that demolishing the wall was an extra hazardous activity and could have been performed perfectly safely if carried out with reasonable care. If scaffolding had been used, as it had earlier in the day, the job could have been carried out without incident. The fact that the activity could cause damage to others if reasonable precautions are not taken is not sufficient to make it extra hazardous. Something more is required, although the courts have not been very helpful or consistent in articulating what this extra something is.

**[43.52]** In *Clements v Tyrone County Council*,[96] in 1904, the defendant was held liable when an independent contractor who was rebuilding the guard wall of a public road left a heap of debris on the road at night with no lighting or fencing, and the plaintiff was injured when thrown from a cart which collided with it. Palles CB distinguished between the position of a person bound to repair, on the one hand, and that of an ordinary member of the public, on the other:

---

89. FLEMING, p 434: "From a practical standpoint, its most perplexing feature is the apparent absence of any coherent theory to explain when, and why a particular duty should be so classified; and it has been questioned whether the resulting uncertainty and complexity of the law is matched by any corresponding advantages." FLEMING, pp 362-363. See also Williams 'Liability for Independent Contractors' [1956] Cam LJ 180; Chapman 'Liability for the Negligence of Independent Contractors' (1934) 50 LQR 71 and the legal argument in *M'Keon v Bolton* (1851) 1 ICLR 377.

90. *Connolly v Dundalk UDC* [1990] 2 IR 1 (SC) analysed in Byrne & Binchy in *Annual Review of Irish Law 1992*, pp 568-9. *Wilson v Tyneside Window Cleaning* [1958] 2 QB 110. See further paras **[18.33]-[18.55]** above.

91. *Groves v Wimborne* [1898] 2 QB 402.

92. See also for carriers' duty to passengers: *Burns v Cork and Bandon Ry Co* 13 Ir CLR 543; *Ryan v Clarkin* [1935] IR 1.

93. As to hospitals, see para **[43.22]** above.

94. High Court, 21 July 1977 (Costello J).

95. High Court, 29 October 1992 (Blayney J), analysed by Byrne & Binchy, *Annual Review of Irish Law 1992*, pp 609-610.

96. [1905] 1 IR 415 (KBD).

"A member of the public has not, without statutory authority, any right to place any obstruction upon a public road. If he does so, he is guilty of an illegal - indeed of a criminal - act. On the other hand, a person under an obligation to repair is entitled to place obstructions upon the road for the purposes of repair, but subject to the essential condition that due care is used that such obstructions shall not be a source of public danger. This duty appears to me to be due by everyone who places an obstruction on a public road, whether the person who so places it does it under an obligation to repair, or other statutory authority to do it, as incidental to some other work. Such a duty is one peculiarly that of the person who lawfully places or authorises the placing of the obstruction, because the preservation of the public from danger is paramount to the right of placing obstructions upon the public road, and consequently is a condition upon which the persons entrusted by the common law or by statute with the right of interfering with the public right of passage obtain that right of interference. It follows that they cannot excuse the non-performance of this duty, by delegating its performance to another who has neglected it."[97]

### *(g) Collateral negligence*[98]

**[43.53]** The employer is never liable for the collateral negligence of his or her independent contractors. Therefore, if I employ a contractor to fix my windows I am not liable if the independent contractor injures someone by dropping a hammer on the unfortunate person's head.[99] Similarly, I am not liable if the garage proprietor, to whom I have given a wheel to repair, injures a third party by causing the tyre to burst by pumping too much pressure into

97. [1905] 2 IR at 423-424. See also *R (Westropp) v Clare County Council* [1904] 2 IR 569; *Penny v Wimbledon UDC* [1899] 2 QB 72 (CA). A more recent and more extreme example of the willingness of the Irish courts to impose liability in similar circumstances can be seen in *Weir v Dun Laoghaire Corporation* [1983] IR 242. There, an elderly lady who had tripped on an uneven part of the road near a bus stop sued the Corporation. The Corporation, which as planning authority had insisted on the building of the bus stop by a developer as a condition to developing a shopping centre, was held liable for the negligence of a sub-contractor employed by the developer to build the bus shelter. The Supreme Court by a majority (O'Higgins CJ and Hederman J, Griffin J dissenting) held that the defendant, as planning authority, knew of the work to be done, and that this knowledge must be attributed to them as a road authority. The Corporation's obligations as a highway authority under the Local Government Act 1925 imposed a responsibility on it to look to the safety of those using a roadway. This the majority held, was a strict liability which could not be delegated. *Weir* was overruled by the Supreme Court in *Convery v Dublin County Council* [1996] 3 IR 153. Keane J (O'Flaherty and Barrington JJ concurring) noted that it appeared that the attention of the court in *Weir* had not been drawn to s 26(11) of the Local Government (Planning and Development) Act 1963, which provides that a person is not entitled solely by reason of a permission or approval under the section to carry out any development. It was clear from this provision that a planning authority (or An Bord Pleanála on appeal) which was confined in reaching its decision to considering the matters referred to in the preceeding subs-s of s 26, could not be said to have authorised the developer by the grant of a permission to commit an act which would be otherwise unlawful, because, for example, it created an unacceptable hazard for people such as the plaintiff in *Weir*. While *Weir* had been cited in *Sunderland v Louth County Council* [1990] ILRM 658, it had not been referred to in the judgment of McCarthy J. The decision in Weir was "clearly irreconcilable" with that in *Sunderland* and had to be regarded as having been reversed *sub silentio*. For a coruscating criticism of *Weir*, see Hogan & Morgan, *Administrative Law in Ireland* (3rd ed, 1998), p 836.

98. See STREET, pp 514-515, SALMOND & HEUSTON, pp 465-466, *Weir v Dun Laoghaire Corporation* [1983] IR 242 at 247, *per* Griffith J.

99. *Cf Padbury v Holliday & Greenwood Ltd* (1912) 28 Times LR 494 (CA).

the wheel. It may be difficult to decide in particular cases what is collateral (or casual) negligence[100] and it is difficult to resist Salmond & Heuston's conclusion on this:

> "Probably the rule as to collateral negligence means nothing more than that the negligence required to impose liability upon the employer of an independent contractor must be negligence committed in the doing of the act itself which he is employed to do, and that negligence in other operations which, though connected with that work, are not themselves part of the work which he has contracted to do is not sufficient. The negligence is central, not casual or collateral. The employer is exempt from liability, not so much because the act done cannot be foreseen or guarded against, but because it is outside the scope of the duty imposed on the employer. If this is all that 'collateral negligence' means, it is only an obscure way of saying that an employer is only liable for acts which are within the scope of the contractor's authority - which is obvious, but unhelpful in any particular case."[101]

## III. Liability of Firm for Partner's Wrongs

**[43.54]** The liability of a firm for the torts of individual partners is largely analogous to the liability of a employer for the torts of an employee. This liability is to be found in ss 10 and 11 of the Partnership Act 1890. A full treatment of this liability is beyond the scope of this work. Readers should consult the monumental treatise of the subject in Twomey *Partnership Law* (2000). Section 10 deals with any wrongful act or omission, whereas s 11 deals with fraudulent misappropriation by one partner of money received. Section 10 provides that:

> Where, by any wrongful act or omission of any partner *acting in the ordinary course of the business of the firm, or with the authority of his co-partners*, loss or injury is caused to any person not being a partner in the firm, or any penalty is incurred, the firm is liable therefore to the same extent as the partner so acting or omitting to act.[102]

**[43.55]** Section 11 provides that in the following cases, namely:

(a) where one partner acting within the scope of his apparent authority receives the money or property of a third person and misapplies it; and

(b) where a firm in the course of its business receives money or property of a third person, and the money or property so received is misapplied by one or more of the partners while it is in the custody of the firm; the firm is liable to make good the loss.

Liability under these sections is joint and several.[103]

---

100. Compare *Padbury v Holliday and Greenwood Ltd* (1912) 28 TLR 494 with *Holliday v National Telephone Co* [1899] 2 QB 392.

101. SALMOND & HEUSTON, p 466 (citation omitted.)

102. Emphasis added. *United Bank of Kuwait v Hammond* (1987) 137 NLJ 921 (QB) - firm not liable for undertaking given to bank by solicitor in the firm knowing that there were no funds to back up undertaking. Undertaking not given in ordinary course of business.

103. Partnership Act 1890, s 12. See *Allied Pharmaceutical Distributors Ltd and All-Phar Services Ltd v Walsh* High Court, 14 December 1990 (Barron J), where partners were held liable for investment advice given by another partner in somewhat unusual circumstances, Barron J being of the view that the partner was carrying out the ordinary business of the partnership. *Cf* Byrne & Binchy in *Annual Review of Irish Law 1990*, p 561.

**[43.56]** *Allied Pharmaceutical Distributors Ltd and All-Phar Services Ltd v Walsh*[104] is of interest in that it involved the imposition of liability on partners for the breach of duty of care of one of them towards the plaintiff company where the conduct in which the partner engaged was not such as would necessarily have bound the partnership on general *Hedley Byrne*[105] principles. The complicated and unusual factual situation may be summarised briefly. The defendant accountancy partnership did work (including auditing) for the plaintiff company. One of the partners acted as a personal executive for the plaintiff company, taking crucial decisions as to its financial investments. Over the years, he invested some of the plaintiff company's money in his family company which eventually became insolvent, resulting in loss to the plaintiff company.

**[43.57]** The relationship between the family company and the partnership was described as Barron J as "a somewhat unusual one". The partnership provided a secretary for the company; all its books were kept in the financial executive's office in the partnership offices. Other partners had for a time been the company's Secretary and a director and at that time several members of the partnership had borrowed small loans from it. Its accounts were audited for a period by employees of the partnership and its tax affairs were dealt with by the tax division of the partnership.

**[43.58]** The partners unsuccessfully argued that, since their ordinary business did not include giving investment advice, they should thus not be liable for the financial executive's advice and actions in that regard. Barron J considered that this was not the true issue; that was, whether in doing what he had done the financial executive was carrying out the ordinary business of the partnership. It was "clearly" the ordinary business of the partnership to allow one of its number to be a director and even chairman of a board of directors of a client company. It was its ordinary business to allow a partner in that position to take deposits from client companies for his own private company. It was moreover its ordinary business that, in those positions, the partner should make decisions in regard to how client companies should apply their monies. In these circumstances what the financial executive had done was within the ordinary business of the partnership.

**[43.59]** It was, however, essential that there should have been a representation by the partnership to the plaintiff that such conduct had its approval. This could be done by conduct, which was the normal way in which an ostensible authority was established. Since the partnership had acted as auditor of the plaintiff and thus was aware of the transactions with the investment company, its failure to suggest that there was anything unusual or improper in making the deposits amounted to a sufficient representation by conduct that the financial executive had their authority to direct the making of these deposits. Barron J considered that:

> "the position is stronger [than a case of principal and agent] when the alleged agency arises between partners. The basis of partnership is mutual trust between the partners. When one partner is put into a position of trust with a client in my view that alone is a representation that the partnership trusts the partner and will stand over whatever he does."[106]

---

104. High Court, 14 December 1990 (Barron J).
105. *Hedley Byrne & Co v Heller & Partners* [1964] AC 465 (HL).
106. High Court, 14 December 1990, at p 17 of judgement.

**[43.60]** The effect of the decision was that the partnership was liable, in the unusual circumstances of the case, when it would not normally have been liable under ordinary *Hedley Byrne* principle.

## IV. Liability of the Owners of Mechanically Propelled Vehicles

### Road Traffic Act 1961, s 118[107]

**[43.61]** In one important case the law openly facilitates, through an extended fiction within the vicarious liability rule, the access of an injured party to "the deep pocket". Under s 118 of the Road Traffic Act 1961 a person who uses a mechanically propelled vehicle with the consent of the owner is treated as the owner's employee for the purpose of determining the owner's liability. This means that if a person lends his or her car to another and that other person negligently injures a third person, the latter can sue the owner as being vicariously liable for the user's negligence. As liability insurance is compulsory in Ireland the injured person's chances of having an insurance company as the real defendant in such cases are increased by the provisions of the section.

**[43.62]** The full section reads as follows:

> Where a person (in this section referred to as the user) uses a mechanically propelled vehicle with the consent of the owner of the vehicle, the user shall, for the purposes of determining the liability or non-liability of the owner for injury caused by the negligent use of the vehicle by the user, and for the purposes of determining the liability or non-liability of any other person for injury to the vehicle or persons or property therein caused by negligence occurring while the vehicle is being used by the user, be deemed to use the vehicle as the employee of the owner, but only in so far as the user acts in accordance with the terms of such consent.[108]

**[43.63]** At common law the owner of a motor car was liable for the negligence of the employee or of his agent if the agent was driving with the owner's consent and on the owner's business or for the owner's purposes. However, mere consent by the owner did not constitute the driver, the employee or agent of the owner, and so the owner would not be liable at common law for the negligence of a person merely permitted to drive the owner's

---

107. See Osborough 'The Vicarious Liability of the Vehicle Owner' (1971) 6 Ir Jur (ns) 77, providing a comprehensive analysis of the relevant Irish decisions. See also, more generally, Osborough 'The Regime of Protection for Road Accident Vicoms' (1970) 5 Ir Jur (ns) 217 and Osborough 'Consensual User in the Vicarious Liability of the Vehicle Owner' (1971) 65 Incorp Soc of Ireland Gaz 7. See analogous provision in s 59 of Civil Liability Act 1961. Discussed Ch 38 above.

108. This section replaced a similar section (s 172) in the Road Traffic Act 1933. For differences see Osborough 'The Vicarious Liability of the Vehicle Owner' (1971) 6 Ir Jur (ns) 77 at 78. This statutory provision avoided the necessity for the Courts to adopt the "family automobile doctrine" which the absence of such a provision forced on the American Courts. See Lattin 'Vicarious Liability and the Family Automobile' (1928) 26 Mich LR 846; Treanor 'Comment: The Family Automobile and the Family Purpose Doctrine (1926) 1 Indiana LJ 89; Earle 'Note' (1961) 49 Ky LJ 573; Annotation (1966) 8 ALR 3rd 1191. See, for evidentiary aspects of this doctrine, *McCormick on Evidence* (2nd ed), S 243 at 808.

car.[109] The 1961 Act changes this position by regarding, for the purposes of vicarious liability, such a permitted user as the owner's employee.

**[43.64]** Of course, the owner will be liable under the 1961 Act only where he or she has given consent to the user, and if the consent is not real no liability will attach to the owner. Thus, in *Kelly v Lombard Motor Co Ltd*[110] the defendant car hire firm was held not liable under the section for the negligence of the hirer of the car because in obtaining the car the user, Patrick O'Donnell, who did not have a driving licence, produced the driving licence of a friend Michael Kelly, and assumed his friend's name. Kenny J stated:

> "It seems to me that the consent in this case by the defendants to the driving of the car was given to a person who held a driving licence. There was never a consent to a person driving the car who did not have a licence and the defendants did not, therefore, consent to Patrick O'Donnell driving the car. They gave their consent to a Michael Kelly, the holder of a driving licence, driving the car."[111]

**[43.65]** Moreover, where a person borrows a vehicle, on the understanding that it will only be used for a particular purpose, the borrower does not have the consent of the owner if the borrower fails to comply with the limitation as to time, place or purpose.[112] It is suspected, however, that the Irish courts would not be ungenerous in construing the word "consent" so as to give effect to the statutory policy that lies behind s 118. In *O'Fiachann v Kiernan, Kiernan and Ors*,[113] a car was leased from Mercantile Credit by a business. This business reorganised itself and the car was then transferred to the new business without the knowledge of Mercantile Credit. It was involved in a collision while being driven by the son of an employee of the new business. Keane J, in the High Court, held that there was

---

109. *Kelly v Lombard Motor Co Ltd* [1974] IR 142 (HC); *Hewitt v Bonvin* [1940] 1 KB 188; *Ormrod v Crosville Motor Services Ltd* [1953] 2 All ER 753 and *Rambarran v Gurrucharran* [1970] 1 All ER 749.

110. [1974] IR 142, analysed by Osborough 'Consensual Driving and Vicarious Liability' (1973) 8 Ir Jur (ns) 88.

111. [1974] IR at 146. See also *Buckley v Musgrave Brook Bond Ltd* [1969] IR 440. *Beechinor v O'Connor* [1939] Ir Jur Rep 5; *O'Connell v Minister for Finance* [1945] Ir Jur Rep 18 (CC); *Thompson v Reynolds* [1926] NI 131. It might also be noted that where M is vicariously liable for the tort of S at common law, both M and S are concurrent wrongdoers, and now, under s 21 of the Civil Liability Act 1961, M will have a right to contribution (generally amounting to indemnity). In the context of s 118 of the Road Traffic Act 1961, however, it has been suggested that no claim for contribution exists in favour of M against S. See White 'Selected Aspects of the Civil Liability Acts 1961 and 1964' (unpublished LLB thesis, University College Cork) p 155 *et seq*. See also *Maher v GN Ry Co* (Ir) *and Warren* [1942] IR 206, discussed by Osborough 'The Vicarious Liability of the Vehicle Owner' (1971) 6 Ir Jur (ns) 77 at 78-79. For interesting fact situation as to what constitutes "driving" see *Stack v Roberts* Supreme Court, 24 July 1958 - man behind the wheel, operating accelerator and brakes; man in the passenger seat, instructing, and operating clutch pedal and gearstick. See also *Neill v Minister for Finance* [1948] IR 88 (SC).

112. *Singh v Raltour* (1987) The Times, 20 October (CA). In *Wright v O'Neill* High Court, 31 October 1991, Flood J held that in the case of a son driving his father's car, the onus was on the father to prove that the son was driving without his consent. See also *Ambrose v O'Regan* Supreme Court, 20 December 1991.

113. High Court, 11 January 1985 (Keane J).

consent for the purpose of s 118.[114] Again in *Buckley v Johnson and Perrott and Woods*[115] the second defendant, Woods, injured the plaintiff while driving the first named defendant's hired car. Woods's hire period was over when the accident occurred and he had not phoned for extended permission. Lavan J, nevertheless, held the hire company liable. In the course of his judgment he said:

> "The provisions of section 118 are unambiguous and intended to affect a radical extension of the principles of vicarious liability in order to ensure that the victim of a road traffic accident was not confined by common law principles in his remedy for damage in an action against a driver who might be uninsured".[116]

**[43.66]** Likewise in *Guerin v Guerin and McGrath*[117] the first named defendant emigrated to England leaving his car at home. Before going, he arranged that a neighbour would use the car to drive his parents to mass since no member of his family could drive. On the day of the accident his father asked another person to drive the car to the post office. The plaintiff, a brother of the owner, was injured when the car was being driven to the post office. Costello J found on the evidence that the owner had given his consent that the car could be used for the convenience of the family, in the absence of specific restriction Costello J considered that there had been an implied consent that the car could be used for family purposes by persons allowed to drive by the father.[118]

## V. Vicarious Liability for Members of One's Family

**[43.67]** Although at common law the husband was liable for the torts of his wife, this example of vicarious liability has been abolished by the Married Women's Status Act 1957. Since that Act a husband may not be sued in respect of his wife's torts irrespective of whether they were committed before or after marriage.[119]

**[43.68]** Parents were never vicariously liable for the torts of their children at common law,[120] and liability would attach to the parents in such circumstances only if it could be shown that there was some personal fault on the part of the parents.[121] Of course, if it can be shown that the child was also the parents' agent or employee then the blood relationship will not prevent liability from arising. This is clearly illustrated in *Moynihan v Moynihan*[122] where the defendant's daughter was held to be the *de facto* employee of the defendant, but liability would also arise if the parent authorised or ratified the act of the child.

---

114. The "owner" under a hire-purchase agreement is the person in possession: Road Traffic Act 1961, s 3(1). *Cf Curley v Collins* [1938] Ir Jur Rep 69 (HC).
115. High Court, 29 July 1992 (Lavan J).
116. Page 8 of Lavan J's judgment.
117. [1992] 2 IR 287 (HC).
118. [1992] 2 IR 287 at 292. See also *Ambrose v O'Regan* Supreme Court, 20 December 1991, revsg High Court, 14 November 1990 (MacKenzie J), analysed by Byrne & Binchy, *Annual Review of Irish Law 1991*, pp 435-436.
119. Section 11. On common law, *cf* Kahn-Freund 'Inconsistencies and Injustices - the Law of husband and Wife' (1952) 15 MLR 133.
120. *Cf Laughan v Wellingborough School* (1932) 101 LJ KB 513 at 515 (CA).
121. *Curley v Mannion* [1965] IR 543.
122. [1975] IR 192.

## VI. DOCTRINE OF COMMON EMPLOYMENT

**[43.69]** One exception to the rule that an employer was liable to third parties for injuries caused by his or her employees occurred at common law where the injured party happened also to be a employee of the employer and was engaged in common employment at the time of the accident. This meant that if one employee was injured by the negligence of a fellow employee he could not sue the common employer on principles of vicarious liability.[123] The reason given in justification for this harsh rule was that the employee in taking up his or her employment impliedly accepted the risks of fellow employees' negligence. It was a typical Victorian doctrine that came to be partially eroded by successive judicial decisions and eventually by legislative enactments in favour of the injured employee.[124] It seems, however, from the wording of the enactments, that the defence might still be available in respect of injuries other than personal injuries. One suspects that the courts would have no sympathy for such an argument. They could well invoke s 34(2)(b) of the Civil Liability Act 1961 as requiring proof of actual communication between co-workers from which a waiver of action might be inferred. Since such communication will almost never have occurred it seems reasonable to predict that the defence of common employment, in all its manifestations, has effectively ceased to be part of Irish law.

---

123. See eg, *Carlos v Congested Districts Board* [1908] 2 IR 91 (KB).

124. See, for example, *Lancaster v LPTB* [1948] 2 All ER 796 - both employees must at times of accident have been engaged in common work; *Groves v Wimborne* (Lord) [1898] 2 QB 402 - defence was not available when the action was based on personal duty imposed on employer. The defence was finally abolished, in respect of personal injuries at least, in Ireland by the Law Reform (Personal Injuries) Act 1958. (In England it had been abolished ten years previously by the Law Reform (Personal Injuries) Act 1948.) For a good examination of the doctrine in operation see Kingsmill Moore J's judgment in *Doyle v Flemings Coal Mines Ltd* Supreme Court, 29 July 1955. In this case Kingsmill Moore J was not willing to extend the doctrine of common employment to include volunteer helpers. How the dictates of underlying policy fashion doctrinal development may be seen by contrasting *Doyle v Fleming Coal Mines Ltd* with *Moynihan v Moynihan*, [1975] IR 192.

# Chapter 44

# Damages[1]

## I. Introduction

**[44.01]** Although in some cases, in preference to monetary compensation, the plaintiff may seek an injunction to stop the defendant committing a tort, in most cases the plaintiff will seek damages as compensation for the wrong committed. Indeed it is fair to say that in the vast majority of cases damages are the essence of the tort claim.

**[44.02]** The topic of damages is a large one and before examining the rules relating to it a word should first be said about the types of damages that may be awarded in a tort action.

## II. Types of Damages Awarded

### Nominal Damages

**[44.03]** Where the plaintiff's legal right has been infringed but he or she has suffered no actual damage, nominal damages may be awarded.[2] This will occur in relation to torts that are actionable *per se*, such as trespass and libel and certain cases of slander. An award of nominal damages does not imply any moral obloquy regarding the plaintiff, whose purpose in bringing the action may have been to vindicate a right[3] rather than to seek substantial compensation.

### Contemptuous Damages

**[44.04]** Contemptuous damages are awarded where the court is of the view that the plaintiff, although technically entitled to a verdict, has no moral claim to damages.[4] Such awards are frequently made in defamation actions. An award of contemptuous damages

---

1. The subject is comprehensively analysed in White, *Irish Law of Damages for Personal Injuries and Death* (1989). See also Kemp & Kemp, *The Quantum of Damages*; Ogus, *The Law Of Damages* (1973); Luntz 'Damages in a Nutshell' (1979) 53 Law Institute J 639.
2. *Cf O'Keeffe v Kilcullen*, High Court, 24 June 1998 (O'Sullivan J):

   > "Nominal damages means a sum of money that may be spoken of but has no existence in point of quantity, the purposes of such damages being twofold, namely, either to assert a right or as a 'peg' on which to hang an order for costs."

   A measurable amount of compensation - as low as a pound, *cf Campbell v Irish Press Ltd* (1955) 90 ILTR 105 (SC), or even less.
3. *Cf* eg *Hanna v Pollock* [1898] 2 IR 532 (QBD); *Kearney v Minister for Justice* [1986] IR 116 (HC) - £25 nominal damages for infringement of constitutional right to communicate; *Murdoch v Workman & Co* (1894) 28 ILTR 39 (QBD); *C & A Modes v C & A Waterford Ltd* [1976] IR 198 (SC); *Irish Land Commission v Walsh* (1963) 97 ILTR 91 (HC).
4. See, eg *Grealey v Casey* (1901) 1 NIJR 121 (CA) - farthing damages in action for battery; *Ahern v Maguire* (1840) Arm Mac & Og 39 - 6d damages in libel action; *Dawson v M'Clelland (No 2)* [1899] 2 IR 503, fn 1 - farthing damages in libel action.

generally penalises the plaintiff since in such cases (contrary to the normal rule that costs follow the verdict) the court will not usually award the plaintiff his costs.

## Special and General Damages[5]

**[44.05]** This aspect of the subject had given rise to much confusion largely because the phrases are given more than one meaning. Sometimes damage of a type that the law will presume to flow from the wrong complained of is referred to as "general damage" and need not be specially pleaded. "Special damage" means:

> "that particular damage (beyond the general damage) which results from the particular circumstances of the case, and of the plaintiff's claim to be compensated, for which he ought to give warning in his pleadings in order that there may be no surprise at the trial."[6]

A somewhat different distinction has also gained widespread approval. The out-of-pocket expenses and loss of earnings that have accrued before a trial for personal injuries have frequently been referred to as "special damages" and damages that are not capable of such calculation, which are known as "general damages".

**[44.06]** Finally, mention should be made of the use of "special damage" as meaning actual damage which a plaintiff must establish in order to show a cause of action in relation to a tort not actionable *per se*,[7] in contrast to torts which *are* actionable *per se* where "general damage" is presumed.[8]

## Restitutio in Integrum and Compensatory Damages

**[44.07]** Subject to the qualification that damages should not be too remote, the general purpose in awarding damages is to place the plaintiff in the same position as he or she had been before the commission of the tort.[9] This principle, of *restitutio in integrum*, provides an effective criterion where the plaintiff has sustained pecuniary loss (in many cases of deceit, negligent misstatement or the wrongful obstruction of ancient lights,[10] for example). But in cases incapable of reasonably precise pecuniary assessment, this principle is not totally effective.[11] A person who has lost a leg in an accident caused by the defendant's negligence will never be capable of being placed in the position he or she was in before the accident. An award of money is, however, regarded by the law as better than nothing. The approach favoured by the courts is that "fair" compensation should be given in such cases,[12] but it is readily conceded that all that can be given is "notional or theoretical compensation to take the place of that which is not possible, namely, actual compensation".[13]

---

5. See Jolowicz 'The Changing Use of "Special Damage" and its Effect on the Law' [1960] Camb LJ 214.
6. *Ratcliffe v Evans* [1892] 2 QB 524 at 528. As to particulars of personal injuries which must be alleged, *cf MacNaughton v Murphy* [1961] Ir Jur Rep 41 (SC).
7. Eg *Iveson v Moore* (1699) 1 Ld Raym 486 at 489, 91 ER 1224 at 1226.
8. Eg *Ashby v White* (1703) 2 Ld Raym 938 at 955, 92 ER 126 at 137 (*per* Holt CJ).
9. *Cf Foley v Thermocement Products Ltd* (1954) 90 ILTR 92 at 98 (SC) - referring to *restitutio in integrum* as "the underlying principle by which courts are guided in awarding damages".
10. *Scott v Goulding Properties Ltd* [1973] IR 200 (SC).
11. See Kelly 'The Inner Nature of the Tort Action' (1967) 2 Ir Jur (ns) 279.
12. *Cf Warren v King* [1964] 1 WLR 1 (CA), criticised by Edmond Davies LJ in *Fowler v Grace* Times, 20 February 1970.
13. *Rushton v National Coal Board* [1953] 1 QB 495 at 502; *cf H West & Son Ltd v Shephard* [1964] AC 326 at 346.

**[44.08]** As we shall see,[14] aggravated damages are a species of compensatory damages. They take account of the manner in which the wrong was committed, the conduct of the wrongdoer afterwards (including how he or she conducts the defence to the claim) and the consequent added hurt or insult to the plaintiff.[15]

## Exemplary Damages[16]

### *(a) Historical Origins*

**[44.09]** In the early development of tort law the distinction between the principles of compensation and punishment was not clearly drawn.[17] It gradually came to be accepted that the dominant principle in awarding damages was that of compensation, but that in cases of unconstitutional[18] or wanton[19] interference with the plaintiff's rights "punitive" (or "exemplary") damages could also be awarded. This seems to have clearly been the position in this country at the early part of the twentieth century.[20] As the years went by, however, doubts began to be expressed as to the propriety of awarding exemplary damages in tort. It was argued that the punitive function had no part of tort law, that it involved double jeopardy for the defendant, compounded by the fact that the burden of proof was less stringent than in criminal cases and that there were no controls on the amount that could be awarded (again in contrast to the criminal law).[21] Moreover, it was contended that a sensitive application of the compensation criterion would ensure that the damages would take account of the aggravating circumstances in which the tort was committed.

### *(b) Rookes v Barnard*

**[44.10]** This new line of argument was adopted in the English decision of *Rookes v Barnard*[22] in 1963. The House of Lords accepted that, applying the compensatory principle, an award might:

> "take into account the motives and conduct of the defendant where they aggravate the injury done to the plaintiff. There may be malevolence or spite or the manner of committing the wrong may be such as to injure the plaintiff's proper feelings of dignity and pride".[23]

---

14. See para **[44.31]** below.
15. *Cf Conway v Irish National Teacher's Organisation* [1991] 2 IR 305 (SC).
16. See generally the LRC's *Report on Aggravated, Explemary and Restitutionary Damages* (LRC 60-2000); Fridman 'Punitive Damages in Tort' (1970) 48 Can BR 373; Hodgin & Vietch 'Punitive Damages-Reassessed' (1972) 21 ICLQ 119; McGregor 'In Defence of Lord Devlin' (1971) 34 MLR 520; Morris 'Punitive Damages in Torts Cases' 44 Harv LR 1173 (1931); Broman 'Comment: Punitive Damages: An Appeal for Deterrence' (1982) 61 Neb LR 651; White 'Exemplary Damages in Irish Tort Law' (1987) 5 Ir LT (ns) 60.
17. *Cf* Ogus *The Law Of Damages* (1973), pp 4-5, 28; McGregor 'Compensation versus Punishment in Damages Awards' (1965) 28 MLR 629. For a stimulating dissent from the contemporary accepted doctrine, see Kelly 'The Inner Nature of the Tort Action' (1967) 2 Ir Jur (ns) 279.
18. *Cf Huckle v Money* (1763) 2 Wils 205, 95 ER 768.
19. *Cf* eg, *Loudon v Ryder* [1953] 2 QB 202; *Tullidge v Wade* (1769) 3 Wils 18, 95 ER 909.
20. *Cf Noblett v Leitrim County Council* [1920] 2 IR (CA); *Worthington v Tipperary County Council* [1920] 21R 233 (CA); *Sligo Corporation v Gilbride* [1929] IR 351 (SC). See also *Melling v Ó Mathgamhna* [1962] IR 1 at 40 (SC).
21. *Cf* Willis 'Measure of Damages When Property is Wrongfully Taken by a Private Individual' (1909) 22 Harv LR 419 at 420-423.
22. [1964] AC 1129 (HL, Eng).
23. [1964] AC 1129 at 1221.

This notion of aggravated damages as a species of compensatory damages has proved controversial. Its reference to the defendant's malevolence or spite, unaccompanied by the requirement of proof that it actually enhanced the plaintiff's injury, looks suspiciously like a punitive criterion under the guise of compensation.[24] What, however, makes *Rookes v Barnard* so important is the decision by the House of Lords to "impose limits not hitherto expressed"[25] on the power to award exemplary damages. In future exemplary damages might be awarded in only three categories of cases:

(1) The "oppressive, arbitrary or unconstitutional action by the servants of government".[26]

(2) Where "the defendant's conduct has been calculated by him to make a profit for himself which may well exceed the compensation payable to the plaintiff".[27]

(3) Where exemplary damages were "expressly authorised"[28] by statute.

**[44.11]** Moreover, three considerations applied to an award of exemplary damages:

(1) A plaintiff should not be able to recover exemplary damages unless *he* had been the victim of the punishable behaviour. No one should be permitted to obtain "a windfall"[29] in consequence of oppressive conduct towards another which did not affect him, although it constituted a tort in respect of him.

(2) Since the power to award exemplary damages constituted a weapon that could be used against liberty as well as in defence of liberty, it should be "used with restraint".[30]

(3) The means of the parties, which are irrelevant in assessing damages under the compensatory criterion, should be material in the assessment of exemplary

---

24. For a thorough analysis of the present law on aggravated damages see the LRC's *Report on Aggravated, Exemplary and Restitutionary Damages* (LRC 60-2000), Ch 5. See also *FW v British Broadcasting Corporation* High Court, 25 March 1999 (Barr J) and *Todd v Cincelli* High Court, 5 March 1998 (Kelly J), cited by the Law Reform commission in its Report, p 19.
25. [1964] AC 1129 at 1226.
26. [1964] AC 1129 at 1226.
27. [1964] AC 1129 at 1226.
28. [1964] AC 1129 at 1227. *Cf* the Reserve and Auxiliary Forces (Protection of Civil Interests) Act 1951, s 13(2) (14 & 15 Geo 6, c 65). There is doubt in Britain as to whether the Copyright Act 1956, s 17(3) (4 & 5 Eliz 2, c 74) permits the awarding of punitive damages: see *Williams v Settle* [1960] 2 All ER 806 (CA); *Rookes v Barnard* [1964] AC 1129 at 1225 (HL, Eng); *Cassell & Co Ltd v Broome* [1972] AC 1027 at 1080-1081 (HL, Eng). In the Supreme Court decision of *Folens v O Dubhghaill* [1973] IR 255 at 266 (SC), Ó Dalaigh, CJ (with whom Walsh and Fitzgerald, JJ concurred) expressed the view that it was "plain enough" that the "additional damages" referred to in s 22(4) of the Copyright Act 1956, s 17(3)) "are to be penal damages". In *Byrne v Houlihan* [1966] IR 274 at 278 (SC), Kingsmill Moore J referred to the Long Title of the Fatal Injuries Act 1956, which states that it is "[a]n Act to make better provision for compensating members of the family of any person killed by the wrongful act or default of another". He observed: "From the wording of the Act itself certain deduction may be made. There is to be no punitive element in the damages - they are by way of 'compensation'."
29. [1964] AC 1129 at 1227.
30. [1964] AC 1129 at 1227

damages, since "[e]verything which aggravates or mitigates the defendant's conduct is relevant".[31]

**[44.12]** Lord Devlin stressed that, without departing from the compensatory principle, due allowance could be made for the circumstances in which the tort was committed.[32] Eight years later, in *Cassell & Co Ltd v Broome*[33] an attempt by the Court of Appeal in 1971[34] to hold that *Rookes v Barnard*[35] had been decided *per incuriam* was unceremoniously disposed of by the House of Lords.[36] Subsequent decisions in England, building on *dicta* of Lords Hailsham, Diplock, Reid and (less clearly) Wilberforce in *Cassell*, have insisted that the cause of action must be one for which prior to *Rookes v Barnard*, an award for exemplary damages had been made. In *AB v South West Water Services Ltd*,[37] the English Court of Appeal, on this basis, ruled out the possibility of awarding exemplary damages for the tort of public nuisance. A similar fate befell the tort of misfeasance of public office in *Kuddus v Chief Constable of Leicestershire*,[38] but with a blistering dissent by Auld LJ.

**[44.13]** *Rookes v Barnard*[39] has not been favourably received in many other jurisdictions. In Australia,[40] New Zealand[41] and Canada,[42] for example, the case does not command support. Moreover, in the United States,[43] exemplary damages may be awarded without the limitations specified in *Rookes v Barnard.*[44]

**[44.14]** If a blanket entitlement on punitive damages has led to criticisms,[45] so also has the limitation of punitive damages effected by *Rookes v Barnard.*[46] The first two categories have been criticised on the basis that they are "arbitrary anomalous *and* unworkable".[47] It

---

31. [1964] AC 1129 at 1228.
32. [1964] AC 1129 at 1229.
33. [1972] AC 1027 (HL).
34. [1971] 2 QB 354 (CA, 1971), criticised by McGregor 'In Defence of Lord Devlin' (1971) 34 MLR 520.
35. See para **[44.10]** above.
36. See fn 28 above.
37. [1993] QB 507 (CA). See also *R v Secretary of State for Transport, ex parte Factortame* [1997] Eu LR 475, 530.
38. [2000] 2 All ER (CA).
39. See para **[44.10]** above.
40. *Cf Uren v John Fairfax & Sons Pty Ltd* (1966) 117 Comm LR 118 (HC); *Associated Consolidated Press Ltd v Uren* (1966) 117 Comm LR 185 (HC, Aust) affd, [1969] 1 AC 590 (PC, 1967); *XL Petroleum (NSW) Pty Ltd v Caltex Oil (Australia) Pty Ltd* (1985) 155 Comm LR 448 (HC, Aust); *Lamb v Cotongo* (1987) 164 Comm LR 1 (HC Aust); *Coloca v BP Australia* [1992] 2 VR 441. See the Law Reform *Consultation Paper on Aggravated Exemplary and Restitutionary Damages*, paras 4.06-4.12 (April 1998), see *Samuels, Comment* (1967) 30 Mod LR 214; *Taylor v Beere* [1982] 1 NZLR 81 (CA); *Donselaar v Donselaar* [1982] 1 NZLR 97 (CA).
41. *Cf Fogg v McKnight* [1968] NZLR 330 (SC).
42. *Cf Vorvis v Insurance Corporation of British Columbia* (1989) 58 DLR (4th) 193 (SC, Can); Law Reform *Consultation Paper on Aggravated Exemplary and Restitutionary Damages*, paras 4.02-4.05.
43. *Cf* Hartnett (1976) 7 Loyola ULJ 811.
44. See para **[44.10]** above.
45. See Willis (1909) 22 Harv LR 419.
46. See para **[44.10]** above.
47. Samuels, Comment (1967) 30 Mod LR 213 at 214.

*has* been contended in respect of the first category, that is, oppressive, arbitrary or unconstitutional action by the servants of Government, that:

> "there is much to be said for the view that today power may be abused by 'the overmighty subject', whether ICI or British Railways, more than by the Crown."[48]

Moreover, the expression "servants of government" is vague and possesses an unusually wide penumbra of uncertainty.[49] The reference to "unconstitutional" action takes on a new significance in this country where a remedy in damages for unconstitutional interferences with the plaintiff's rights has now been recognised.[50]

**[44.15]** Regarding the second category, the concept of "calculating to make a profit" has given rise to concern, especially in the context of defamation in the media,[51] whose proprietors are generally in the business of communication for the purpose of making money.

### *(c) Rookes v Barnard and Irish Law*[52]

**[44.16]** Nearly four decades after *Rookes v Barnard* was decided, it is less than clear whether the principles expressed in that decision have been accepted into Irish law. The Supreme Court has addressed the issue a number of times but its analysis has been confined by the fact that one of the decisions was concerned with exemplary damages for infringements of constitutional rights. The precise relationship between claims of this character and conventional tort claims involves complex jurisprudential questions. Matters are made still more difficult by reason of the failure of the Supreme Court to clarify whether statements made in that decision which are capable of extending to tort claims in fact do so.

**[44.17]** Let us examine the Irish cases in their chronological sequence and then attempt to state the principles that emerge from them.

**[44.18]** In *Dillon v Dunnes' Stores Ltd*,[53] decided in 1968, the Supreme Court gave no indication that it regarded punitive damages as being subject to the *Rookes v Barnard* limitations. In a case that did not obviously fall within any of the three exceptions specified in *Rookes v Barnard*, the Court showed no sign of discomfort. Ó Dálaigh CJ, speaking for the Court, stated:

> "It is, in our opinion, not open to question that in an action for false imprisonment a jury may award punitive damages. The existence of the category of damages known as punitive damages has received statutory recognition: see Civil Liability Act 1961, s 14(4)."[54]

---

48. Heuston 'Tort' Ch 5 of *Annual Survey of Commonwealth Law* (Wade ed, 1966), at 235.
49. *Cf Uren v John Fairfax & Sons Pty Ltd* (1966) 117 Comm LR 118 at 132 (HC, Austr).
50. *Cf* Ch 1 above.
51. *Cf* Heuston 'Tort' Ch 5 of *Annual Survey of Commonwealth Law* (Wade ed, 1966), at 234.
52. See the LRC's *Report on Aggravated, Exemplary and Restitutionary Damages* (LRC 60-2000), Appendix 1; White 'Exemplary Damages in Irish Tort Law' (1987) 5 Ir LT (ns) 60.
53. Supreme Court, 20 December 1968.
54. Supreme Court, 20 December 1968, at p 13. *Cf Maher v Collins* [1975] IR 232 (SC), where O'Higgins CJ appeared to concede (at 238) that the compensatory principle generally applicable to actions for criminal conversation might give way to "other considerations" where the defendant's conduct had been calculated by him to make a profit for himself that might well exceed any compensation likely to be payable to the plaintiff.

**[44.19]** *McDonald v Galvin*[55] is a High Court decision that appears to reject the *Rookes v Barnard* limitations. The case raised a procedural issue: namely, whether, in proceedings for assault and battery where no injuries (other than "pain, shock and humiliation") were alleged, the case should be remitted from the High Court to the District Court or Circuit Court.

**[44.20]** McWilliam J remitted the case to the Circuit Court, stating:

> "I accept the submissions on behalf of the plaintiff that exemplary damages could well be given in certain circumstances in this case and without any evidence other than the statement of claim, I must consider such circumstances as the possibility of the defendant being a wealthy man and in a dominant position as regards the plaintiff and that the incident was most humiliating. At the same time, there were no injuries and I cannot conceive of the episode having taken place in the presence of any person whose presence would have increased the humiliation of the plaintiff and such fact not being mentioned in the Pleading."[56]

This statement would seem to suggest that McWilliam J did not consider that punitive damages were available only when the case fell within the limited categories specified in *Rookes v Barnard*.[57]

**[44.21]** *Whelan v Madigan*,[58] a High Court decision, appears to support the limitations imposed by *Rookes v Barnard*,[59] but the decision is not clear on this question. The case concerned acts of trespass of an intimidatory nature by a landlord designed to induce his tenants to leave their flats, where they were paying low rents. Kenny J considered that the case was one for aggravated rather than exemplary damages. There is nothing in his judgment explicitly holding that punitive damages could not have been awarded, but Kenny J's quotation[60] from *Rookes v Barnard*[61] might suggest at least tacit support for that

---

54. (contd) This exception bears a striking resemblance to the second category specified in *Rookes v Barnard*, and it might be argued that O'Higgins, CJ was tacitly adopting the approach favoured in that decision. Yet the words "punitive damages" were not mentioned, and the Chief Justice appears to have been concentrating his attention on the narrow question of damages for the particular tort of criminal conversation.

    See also the interesting decision of *Hickey & Co Ltd v Roches Stores (Dublin) Ltd* High Court, 14 July 1976 (Finlay P) where, in a contract case, Finlay P held that where a wrongdoer makes a profit or gains unjustly from either a tort or a breach of contract, damages should be assessed so as to deprive him of that profit. This is scarcely an application of the exemplary damages criterion (although Finlay P made a brief, and apparently approving, reference to *Rookes v Barnard*); at all events the decision would permit an award of damages extending well beyond the ordinary compensatory criterion in certain cases. Another aspect of Finlay P's analysis in this decision, which impacts only tangentally on the issue of exemplary damages, did not survive the scrutiny of the Supreme Court in *Allen v Ó Súilleabháin* Supreme Court, 11 March 1997.

55. High Court, 23 February 1976 (McWilliam J).
56. High Court, 23 February 1976, p 6.
57. [1964] AC 1129, McWilliam J was referred to *Rookes v Barnard* during argument at p 2.
58. [1978] ILRM 136 (HC). *Cf Parkes v Howard Johnson Restaurants Ltd* (1970) 74 WWR 255 - punitive damages of $4,000 awarded for harassment of tenant by landlord.
59. [1964] AC 1129.
60. At p 14 of Kenny J's judgment.
61. [1964] AC 1129.

decision. It is interesting to note that, even if the limitations of *Rookes v Barnard*[62] were to apply, punitive damages could still have been awarded, under the second category,[63] for the tortious exclusion of tenants paying a low rent with the aim of obtaining higher rents.

**[44.22]** In *Garvey v Ireland*,[64] where the plaintiff, who had been Garda Commissioner, claimed damages for wrongful removal from office, McWilliam J held that he was entitled to exemplary damages. He referred to the first category in *Rookes v Barnard*[65] of "oppressive, arbitrary or unconstitutional action by the servants of government", and noted that since that decision had not been dealing with the first category type of case Lord Devlin's statement had not been elaborated. In *Broome v Cassell & Co*,[66] however, it had been very fully discussed and McWilliam J was "satisfied from the judgments in [*Broome's*] case that I should award what I have described as exemplary damages".[67]

**[44.23]** McWilliam J considered that these damages had to be related to the injury which the plaintiff had suffered by reason of the arbitrary and oppressive conduct of the government. Having regard to the fact, that in his view, similar injury would, to a large extent, have been sustained by the plaintiff had he been lawfully removed from office, McWilliam J awarded only £500 as exemplary damages.

**[44.24]** This approach is unusual in its emphasis on what appears to be a compensatory rather than punitive criterion, albeit described as exemplary damages by the judge.

**[44.25]** In *Kearney v Minister for Justice*,[68] Costello J appeared to rely on *Rookes v Barnard*[69] in declining to award exemplary damages for infringement of the plaintiff's constitutional right to communicate. The plaintiff was a prisoner; some letters which had been written to him had been intercepted by prison officers and had not reached him for many months. Costello J said:

> "Although quite clearly the court has jurisdiction to award exemplary damages in a case of this sort even at common law,[70] (apart altogether from considerations arising from Irish constitutional law), I do not think that there is sufficient evidence available to show that the wrongful actions were so oppressive or vindictive to justify such an award."[71]

**[44.26]** In the "phone-tapping" case of *Kennedy v Ireland*[72] in 1987, Hamilton P addressed the issue. His general analysis merits some comment. He stated that "[d]amages may be compensatory aggravated, exemplary or punitive", and went on to comment that it was:

---

62. See para **[44.10]** above.
63. *Cf Drane v Evangelou* [1978] 2 All ER 437 (CA), discussed briefly in *Whelan v Madigan*, which holds that punitive damages may be awarded, under the second category, in respect of conduct not entirely dissimilar to that in *Whelan v Madigan*.
64. [1981] ILRM 266 (HC).
65. See para **[44.10]** above.
66. See fn 28 above.
67. [1981] ILRM 266 at 268.
68. [1986] IR 116 (HC).
69. See para **[44.10]** above.
70. Citing *Rookes v Barnard* [1964] AC 1129 at 1226 (the key passage from Lord Devlin's speech).
71. [1986] ILRM 116 at 122.
72. [1988] ILRM 472 (HC). See para **[1.16]** above and Byrne & Binchy, *Annual Review of Irish Law 1987*, pp 99-100, 343-344.

"quite clear from a consideration of the Civil Liability Act 1961 and in particular ss 7(2) and 14(4) thereof that Irish law recognises a distinction as between 'punitive damages' and 'exemplary damages'."

**[44.27]** This view[73] gives rise to difficulty. It is, of course, odd that the 1961 Act should have used separate expressions if it envisaged a single category of damages. Nevertheless, if the expressions are not identical a problem arises as to wherein lies the difference. In other common law jurisdictions it is accepted that the words "punitive" and "exemplary" are interchangeable. Moreover, as we have seen, in the Irish cases before *Kennedy v Ireland* no attempt had been made to distinguish between these two terms.

**[44.28]** There is in fact a somewhat mundane explanation for the language used in the 1961 Act. Section 7(2) traces its origins to s 1(2) of England's Law Reform (Miscellaneous Provisions) Act 1934. Section 14(4), however, derives from s 4(4) of Glanville William's model legislation.[74] The inconsistency in terminology in the 1961 Act may thus be traced, not to nuances of meaning between the concepts of "punitive" and "exemplary" damages, but to the promiscuity of our borrowings from British legislation.[75]

**[44.29]** Hamilton P gave no indication of how the concepts of punitive and exemplary damages should be distinguished from each other. He stated that the plaintiffs were not entitled to punitive damages because the Minister for Justice in his statement in January 1983 had acknowledged that the plaintiffs' phones had been tapped without justification by a predecessor (of an opposing political party). In so doing, said the President, "he, though belatedly, vindicated the good names of the plaintiffs ...". Referring to Lord Devlin's speech in *Rookes v Barnard*, Hamilton P said that he considered that the plaintiffs were entitled to "substantial damages" and that, in the circumstances of the case, it was irrelevant whether they should be described as aggravated or exemplary.

**[44.30]** Though the plaintiffs had not suffered any economic loss, Hamilton P was satisfied that "the injury done to [their] right to privacy was serious, the distress suffered by them as a result thereof significant and in the case of [Ms Kennedy and Mr Arnold] was done consciously, deliberately, but incidentally". He awarded £20,000 each to the first two plaintiffs and £10,000 to Mr Arnold.

**[44.31]** It is not easy to see how *Rookes v Barnard* (and, in particular, Lord Devlin's speech) can be an authority for merging the notions of aggravated and exemplary damages. Assuming that the plaintiffs in *Kennedy v Ireland* were entitled to exemplary damages as

---

73. Though similar to that expressed by White 'Exemplary Damages in Irish Tort Law' (1987) 5 ILT (ns) 60 at 65.

74. Williams, *Joint Torts and Contributory Negligence* (1951) 501. See also White 'Exemplary Damages in Irish Tort Law' (1987) 5 Ir LT (ns) 60 at 76, para 23.

75. *Cf McIntyre v Lewis* [1991] 1 IR 121 (SC), where McCarthy J saw "no real difference" between exemplary and punitive damages. Hederman & O'Flaherty JJ came to the same conclusion on the issue. See Byrne & Binchy, *Annual Review of Irish Law 1990*, pp 576-586. It is regrettable that, as late as 1994, confusion at Supreme Court level could still be discerned. In *Walsh v Ireland* Supreme Court, 30 November 1994, the jury had been invited to assess damages under three headings: general, punitive and exemplary. As matters transpired, the jury made an award under the first heading only. The plaintiff did not appeal against this and Hamilton CJ volunteered the view, on appeal that "[t]his [was] not a case for the award of punitive or exemplary damages". He gave no indication that he saw anything wrong with the disjunction between punitive and exemplary damages at trial.

that term was understood by Hamilton P, the question arises as to whether damages of this type may be awarded in cases falling outside the three mentioned in *Rookes v Barnard*. Hamilton P, did not expressly address this question. On the facts and holding in *Kennedy v Ireland*, the defendant's conduct may be considered to fall within the first of these cases. Whether phonetapping by a private citizen could also warrant exemplary damages was not considered in *Kennedy*. After the Supreme Court's clarification of the circumstances in which exemplary damages may be awarded for infringement of constitutional rights, in *Conway v Irish National Teachers Organisation*[76] (considered in detail below),[77] it now seems clear that exemplary damages may indeed be awarded for infringements by private citizens.

**[44.32]** In *McIntyre v Lewis*,[78] the Court was divided as to the desirability of the *Rookes v Barnard* limitations [brief statement of facts of McIntyre]. Of course the factual circumstances demonstrably fell within the first of *Rookes v Barnard's* three categories; this made it unnecessary for the Court to address the position arising in a case falling outside any of the categories. Nevertheless, what the judges had to say is of considerable interest.

**[44.33]** Hederman J observed merely that:

> "[i]n cases, like this, where there is an abuse of power by employees of the State, the jury are entitled to award exemplary damages. One of the ways in which the rights of the citizen are vindicated, when subjected to oppressive conduct by the employees of the State, is by an award of exemplary damages."[79]

For two reasons, it would seem wrong to interpret this passage as endorsing *Rookes v Barnard*. First, Hederman J made no express statement that he was taking *any* position on the issue; nor did he have to, since the outcome of the case in no way depended on whether the eligibility, of "oppressive conduct by the employees of the State" is less than fully faithful to the first criterion of *Rookes v Barnard* which seems to speak of *unconstitutional* rather than *oppressive* conduct. The range of unconstitutional conduct is clearly far wider than that of oppressive conduct. Even if our courts favoured a wider interpretation of oppression than did the English Court of Appeal in *R v Fulling*[80] (a case dealing with the law of evidence which should not, perhaps, be considered to have any real bearing in the present context), it seems obvious that many unconstitutional acts, even if inflicted on citizens by employees of the State lack the element of oppression. Conversely, it seems reasonable to accept that the mere fact that oppressive conduct relative to a citizen, engaged in by a State employee, even if it is tortious or otherwise contrary to the law, is not *necessarily* unconstitutional.

76. [1991] 2 IR 305.
77. See paras **[44.36-44.54]** below.
78. [1991] 1 IR 121.
79. [1991] 1 IR 121. The phrase "oppresive, arbitrary or unconstitutional" is capable of two constructions, depending on whether it is read disjunctively or conjunctively. If it is conjunctive, then the conduct must be both oppressive *and* either arbitrary or unconstitutional. If disjunctive, the conduct must be oppressive or arbitrary or unconstitutional.
80. [1987] QB 426.

**[44.34]** O'Flaherty J reserved his position on the question whether exemplary damages may be awarded only along the lines of *Rookes v Barnard's* three categories; this was "obviously not the case to decide", this issue (presumably because it fell within the first of these categories). He did, however, adopt the three considerations which Lord Devlin said should always be borne in mind when awards of exemplary damages are being considered. These are:

(1) that the plaintiff many not recover exemplary damages unless he is the victim of the punishable behaviour;

(2) that there is a need for restraint in awarding exemplary damages, and

(3) that the means of both plaintiff and defendant are material in the assessment of exemplary damages.

**[44.35]** McCarthy J, in contrast had no hesitation in exorcising the spectre of the *Rookes v Barnard* categories from Irish law. That decision, he noted, had been the subject of significant adverse comment in other common law jurisdictions. In his view, it was inconsistent with the dynamism that characterises the common law to delimit in any restrictive way the nature of its development.

---

81 *McIntyre v Lewis* [1991] 1 IR 121 involved some judicial consideration of the issue of proportionality as between awards for compensatory damages and awards for exemplary damages. Hederman J considered the amount awarded for exemplary damages "should bear some relation to the amount that would be proper for general damages". O'Flaherty J, in his concurring judgment, stated:

> "The award of exemplary damages is anomalous and where such damages are awarded - which should be very rarely in my judgment - the judge or jury must keep them on a tight rein. If the compensatory amount awarded includes aggravated damages then I believe if any award is made by way of exemplary damages it should properly be a fraction rather than a multiple of the amount awarded by way of compensatory damages (including aggravated damages)."

These observations give pause for thought. Of course juries should not be too quick to award exemplary damages nor too unrestrained in those cases where exemplary damages are appropriate; but the idea of some necessary relationship of proportionality seems unattractive. It is the essence of exemplary damages that their quantum is not determined by reference to a compensatory function. It is a matter of contingency whether the quantum appropriate to fulfil the compensatory function will be high or low; it is just as much a matter of contingency as to whether in any particular case the defendant's conduct warrants high or low exemplary damages. Whether the respective amounts bear a close relationship or are hugely different cannot be preordained by a rule requiring that the exemplary damages not exceed a specific ration relative to what is awarded by way of compensatory damages. If is, of course, true that the seriousness of the injury inflicted by the defendant may be reflected in the quantum of the award of punitive damages, but the extent to which it does so depends on other factors, such as the outrageousness of the defendant's conduct.

As to O'Flaherty J's suggestion that aggravated damages should, in effect, carry most of the load, to the extent that exemplary damages should be merely a fraction rather than a multiple of the amount awarded by way of compensation, two comments seem appropriate.

First, there is perhaps a danger of overloading the process of compensation with too many closely related concepts. Exemplary and aggravated damages, while quite distinct conceptually, are nonetheless very closely related. The truth of the matter is that the category of aggravated damages is a judicial device, conceived with the purpose of facilitating the award of what are, to all intents and purposes, exemplary damages. If this reality is accepted, then there would seem little attraction to the idea that, in a case where the defendant has behaved outrageously, the judge or jury (as the case may be) if disposed to award aggravated damages, should make sure to divide the global award so that the quantum of aggravated damages is *more than* that of exemplary damages.

**[44.36]** *Conway v Irish National Teachers Organisation*[82] involved an action for damages for conspiracy to interfere with the constitutional right to primary education of several school pupils whose education was disrupted by the Drimoleague National School dispute. The defendant Union had forbidden other teachers from teaching in a school where a dispute was ongoing with the Management and one of the members of the defendant Union. As a result the school was closed for a very long time and the education of the pupils suffered badly. The issue of liability had been determined by the High Court in *Crowley v Ireland*.[83] The instant proceedings were accordingly heard in relation to an assessment of damages only. Barron J awarded the plaintiff £10,000 for general loss and the loss of career prospects; to this he added the sum of £1,500 for exemplary damages. The Supreme Court affirmed.

**[44.37]** Finlay CJ set out the following analysis of the relevant principles:

> "In respect of damages for tort or for breach of constitutional right, three headings of damage in Irish law are, in my view, potentially relevant to any particular case. They are:
>
> (1) Ordinary compensatory damages being sums calculated to recompense a wronged plaintiff for physical injury, mental distress, anxiety, deprivation of convenience, or other harmful effects of a wrongful act and/or for monies lost or to be lost and/or expenses incurred or to be incurred by reason of the commission of the wrongful act.
>
> (2) Aggravated damages, being compensatory damages increased by reason of:
>
> (a) the manner in which the wrong was committed, involving such elements as oppressiveness, arrogance or outrage, or
>
> (b) the conduct of the wrongdoer after the commission of the wrong, such as a refusal to apologise or to ameliorate the harm done or the making of threats to repeat the wrong, or
>
> (c) conduct of the wrongdoer and/or his representative in the defence of the claim of the wronged plaintiff, up to and including the trial of the action.
>
> Such a list of the circumstances which may aggravate compensatory damages until they can properly be classified as aggravated damages is not intended to be in any way finite or complete. Furthermore, the circumstances which may properly form an aggravating feature in the measurement of compensatory damages must, in many instances, be in part a recognition of the added hurt or insult to a plaintiff who has been wronged, and in part also a recognition of the cavalier or outrageous conduct of the defendant.
>
> (3) Punitive or exemplary damages arising from the nature of the wrong which has been committed and/or the manner of its commission which are intended to mark the court's particular disapproval of the defendant's conduct in all the circumstances of the case

81. (contd) Nothing would be gained by this elaboration and the practical difficulties in directing a jury on these lines can easily be appreciated. If, on the other hand, the court proceeds on the basis that the conceptual difference between aggravated and exemplary damages should be taken at face value, then there is a separate difficulty with the proposition that the quantum of aggravated damages, if these are awarded, should exceed that of exemplary damages. It is possible to conceive of cases where the appropriate amount of exemplary damages is well in excess of that which should be awarded by way of aggravated damages. See further Byrne & Binchy, *Annual Review of Irish Law 1990*, pp 583-584.

82. [1991] 2 IR 305.

83. [1980] IR 102.

> and its decision that it should publicly be seen to have punished the defendant for such conduct by awarding such damages, quite apart from its obligation, where it may exist in the same case, to compensate the plaintiff for the damage which he or she has suffered."[84]

The Chief Justice went on to address the question whether it is open to a judge in assessing damages for a wrong consisting of a deprivation of a constitutional right, such as the right to free primary education, to assess exemplary damages. For an answer to this question he thought it only necessary to refer to the famous passage from Ó Dálaigh CJ's judgment in *The State (Quinn) v Ryan*,[85] where he stated:

> "It was not the intention of the Constitution in guaranteeing the fundamental rights of the citizen that these rights should be set at nought or circumvented. The intention was that rights of substance were being assured to the individual and that the Courts were the custodians of these rights. As a necessary corollary it follows that no one can with impunity set these rights at nought or circumvent them, and that the Courts' powers in this regard are as ample as the defence of the Constitution requires."

**[44.38]** It seemed clear to Finlay CJ that the court could not be availing itself of powers as ample as the defence of the Constitution and of constitutional rights required unless, in the case of breach of those rights, it held itself entitled to avail itself of one of the most effective deterrent powers that a civil court had: the awarding of exemplary or punitive damages. In an important passage, the Chief Justice added:

> "This does not mean that every wrong which constitutes the breach of a constitutional right in any sense automatically attracts exemplary damages. It does not, in my view, even mean that in every such case, irrespective of the facts or circumstances surrounding it, the court should specifically concern itself with the question of exemplary damages. Many torts, such as assault and defamation, constitute of necessity a breach of constitutional rights, but there are many types of assault and many types of defamation as well in which no conceivable question of awarding … exemplary damages could arise."[86]

**[44.39]** In the particular case the intended consequence of the defendants' acts had been the direct deprivation of the plaintiff of her constitutional right to free primary education, coupled with the special relationship which the defendants bore to the general right of children of free primary education. These circumstances clearly made it a case in which the court should feel obliged to mark its disapproval of the defendants' conduct to the extent of awarding exemplary damages, for four reasons:

(a) The right which was breached on this occasion was one expressly vested in a child by the Constitution;

(b) The right which was breached was one which, having regard to the education and training of a child, was of supreme and fundamental importance;

(c) It must be presumed that the defendants were aware of that importance;

(d) The breach of the constitutional right involved was an intended, as distinct from inadvertent, consequence of the defendants' conduct.

---

84. [1991] 2 IR 305 at 316-317.
85. [1965] IR 70 at 122.
86. [1991] 2 IR 305 at 320.

Finlay CJ found it impossible to ignore the fact that the defendants were persons who, in the form of a trade union, constituted an organisation dealing with all the primary teachers in Ireland. It seemed particularly important that, if such a body acted as it had done, the courts "should, with particular severity, mark their disapproval".[87] Barron J's assessment of exemplary damages had not been excessive.

**[44.40]** Griffin J, concurring, observed that exemplary damages might be awarded where there had been on the part of the defendant wilful and conscious wrongdoing in contumelious disregard of another rights:

> "The object of awarding exemplary damage is to punish the wrongdoer for his outrageous conduct, to deter him and others from such conduct in the future, and to mark the court's (or the jury's ...) detestation and disapproval of that conduct. Such damages are to be awarded even though the plaintiff who recovers them obtains the benefit of what has been described in the case law as a fortunate windfall."[88]

What may be noticed about this analysis is that it makes no attempt to distinguish between torts and infringements of constitutional rights. The restraint against awarding exemplary damage for such infringements, which Ó Dálaigh CJ's statement in *The State (Quinn) v Ryan* represents, is not evident in Griffin J's criteria. Nowhere does he state expressly that an award of exemplary damages for such infringements is permissible only where the defence of the Constitution and of constitutional rights *requires* the court to take such a step.

**[44.41]** Griffin J went on to reject in the clearest of terms the limitation of the award of exemplary damages to cases involving "oppressive, arbitrary or unconstitutional action by the servants of Government", the first category which Lord Devlin prescribed in *Rookes v Barnard*. Griffin J could see "no valid reason, in logic or common sense"[89] for this restriction. He thought it unnecessary to discuss the other categories.

**[44.42]** Finally Griffin J endorsed the approach that O'Flaherty J had taken in *McIntyre v Lewis*,[90] in adopting the three considerations which Lord Devlin in *Rookes v Barnard* had said should always be borne in mind when considering awards of exemplary damages. One may perhaps wonder about what possible rationale could justify the third consideration, regarding the means of both parties, in cases involving infringements of constitutional rights. Why should it make any difference to the exemplary element of an award for damages for interference with the right to a free primary education that a particular child came from a well-off family? If a servant of the State violates the bodily integrity of a citizen, why should the means of the citizen play any part in determining the quantum of exemplary damages?

**[44.43]** McCarthy J, also concurring, drew inspiration from the analogy with the exclusion of evidence generated by a breach of the constitutional rights of the citizen. It may perhaps be debated whether the analogy with the exclusionary rule in evidence holds up. Only at the most general level would there seem to be a conjunction between this rule and the

87. [1991] 2 IR 305 at 322.
88. [1991] 2 IR 305 at 323.
89. [1991] 2 IR 305 at 324.
90. See para **[44.32]** above.

power of the courts to award exemplary damages for infringement of constitutional rights. When one moves from the general to the specific, it may be argued that the exclusionary rule in evidence operates quite differently from the power of the courts to award exemplary damages. The exclusionary rule applies regardless of its consequences; it is justified not on the basis of the circumstances of the individual case but for reasons having no necessary significance in the particular instance. The power to award exemplary damages is quite different: it depends entirely on the requirements of the particular case.

**[44.44]** In *Cooper v O'Connell*,[91] some further light was thrown on the circumstances in which awards of exemplary or aggravated damages are appropriate in tort litigation. The case concerned a course of dental treatment carried out by the defendant dentist on the plaintiff between 1988 and 1991. In spite of having over a hundred and eighty appointments with the plaintiff during this period, the defendant finally accepted that he had failed the plaintiff and indicated that he would send him to another dentist, it transpired that he had not been told about the case. The plaintiff went back to the defendant, who told him that he had made a mistake and that "everybody was entitled to one mistake". He also advised the plaintiff that he could not afford to pay for the remedial treatment and that, as the plaintiff had a good case against him, he should go to see his solicitor.

**[44.45]** The plaintiff received treatment from another dentist and in due course sued the defendant for negligence. Barron J imposed liability and awarded damages of £105,000 for pain and suffering and £50,000 for loss of earnings.

**[44.46]** He declined, however, to award the plaintiff exemplary or aggravated damages. The plaintiff appealed against this refusal, arguing that the defendant had abused a relationship of trust and that, in initially admitting his responsibility and then withdrawing that admission when a defence was delivered on his behalf denying liability, he, or those standing in his shoes, had been guilty of conduct which merited an award of exemplary or aggravated damages.

**[44.47]** Keane J having quoted from Finlay CJ's judgment in *Conway v Irish National Teachers Organisation*,[92] considered that in the instant case no grounds existed for the award of exemplary damages. While the Supreme Court in *Conway* had rejected the view of Lord Devlin in *Rookes v Barnard*, that awards of such damages should be confined to the three categories referred to in his speech, it was also clear from the judgments of Finlay CJ and Griffin and McCarthy JJ that (in the words of McCarthy J):

> "[t]he purpose of awarding such damages is truly to make an example of the wrongdoer so as to show others that such wrongdoing will not be tolerated and, more to the point, will not be relieved on payment of merely compensatory damages."[93]

**[44.48]** Thus, such damages might be awarded in some, but not all, cases where there was an invasion of the plaintiff's constitutional rights, as in *Conway*. It was unnecessary to explore the precise limitations of the circumstances in which such awards might be made; in the context of the instant case it was sufficient to say that the conduct of the defendant and those standing in his shoes did not come within any of the categories which the courts regarded as of such seriousness as to justify an award of exemplary damages:

---

91. Supreme Court, 5 June 1997.
92. See para **[44.36]** above.
93. [1991] 2 IR 305 at 326.

> "In developing the law as to such damages, the courts in this jurisdiction, as in other common law jurisdictions, have essentially been concerned with the principles of public policy which demand that, in a literal sense, an example should be made of the defendant. The fact that a medical practitioner has been admittedly guilty of negligence and that his defence society or insurers have initially put the plaintiff on proof of liability could not conceivably be regarded as circumstances justifying the invocation of this drastic, although essential, rule grounded on public policy."[94]

After this detailed review of the Irish decisions on exemplary damages, let us try to summarise the present position.

**[44.49]** The first, and most practically important, point to make is that the Irish courts have not in any definitive way endorsed the policy of *Rookes v Barnard* to restrict the award of exemplary damages to three limited categories. While it is possible to point to expressions of support from individual judges, even at Supreme Court level, there are many opposing judicial voices and many others in which judges have hesitated to take a final position on the issue. In no case has the Supreme Court given its clear approval to the *Rookes v Barnard* approach.

**[44.50]** The second point, again of considerable practical significance, is that the Supreme Court in *Conway v Irish National Teachers Organisation* made it plain that *Rookes v Barnard* restrictions have no place in actions for damages for infringements of constitutional rights. In failing to clarify the position for tort actions, the Court left open the possibility that *Rookes v Barnard* could still be considered potentially applicable to tort claims.

**[44.51]** If *Rookes v Barnard* were eventually to be acknowledged unambiguously by the Supreme Court as representing the appropriate test for tort claims, there would be an incentive to plaintiffs to characterise the proceedings as claims for damages for infringement of constitutional right, since *Conway* makes it clear that *Rookes v Barnard* has no application to such latter claims. It will be recalled that, in *Hanrahan v Merck Sharpe and Dohme*,[95] Henchy J stated that:

---

94. See also *Kellagher v Walsh* DPIJ: Hilary and Easter Terms 1998, p 74 (HC), where, in addition to £100,000 for general damages, there was an award of £50,000 for punitive damages to the 13-year-old victim of "assault and abuse of the most profound and grave nature on a series of occasions" by a person exercising authority over him, in whom he had placed his trust as a father figure. Quirke J stressed the reprehensible character of the defendant's actions, observing (at p 77):

> "The community will not tolerate his gross abuse of trust and the exploitation of children … I want to say that, if I believed for a moment that his man had resources and had means, then the award of exemplary damages would be commensurate with whatever property or resources that he had."

Quirke J made no reference to any of the limitations prescribed in *Rookes v Barnard*.

95. [1988] ILRM 629 at 636 (SC). See paras **[1.16]** above. In *Sinnott v Minister for Education* High Court, 4 October 2000, where the State was in breach of the constitutional right to education of an adult person with sever autism, with consequent injury to his mother, Barr J did not award punitive damages as the point had not been argued. He added, however, that it was:

> "proper to lay down a marker that the issue of punitive damages will arise if it transipes in future litigation that this warning is not heeded and decision-makers persist in failing to meet the constitutional obligations of the State to the grieviously afflicted and deprived in our society with the urgency which is their right."

"[a] person may of course, in the absence of a common law or statutory cause of action, sue directly for breach of a constitutional right but when he founds his action on an existing tort he is normally confined to the limitations of that tort. It might be different if it could be shown that the tort in question is basically ineffective to protect his constitutional right."

**[44.52]** Let us take the case of a horrendous rape where the victim sues for the tort of battery and it would not be permissible to award her exemplary damages under the *Rookes v Barnard* test as the case did not involve unconstitutional action by the servants of the State, the defendant was not seeking to make a profit from the tort and no relevant statutory provision authorises the award exemplary damages. In such circumstances, the victim would surely argue that she is nonetheless entitled to exemplary damages because "the tort in question is basically ineffective to protect [her] constitutional right[s]" – of bodily integrity, privacy, dignity, autonomy and non-association. In truth there is nothing ineffective about the tort itself: the "basic ineffectiveness" attaches to the *scope of the remedy*, which an application of the *Rookes v Barnard* test inevitably involves for *all* torts where the case does not fall within one of the three exceptions.

**[44.53]** The lesson appears to be clear: if the holding in *Conway v Irish National Teachers Organisation* is that the *Rookes v Barnard* limitations are not to apply in claims for infringement of constitutional rights, it would be futile for the Supreme Court in some future decision to apply the *Rookes v Barnard* limitations to tort claims. To do so would force plaintiffs to recharacterise traditional tort claims in constitutional terms – a process that *Hanrahan* sought to prevent rather than encourage. Indeed, it is far from clear that a court would accept such an attempted recharacterisation in view of the *Hanrahan* strictures.

**[44.54]** The alternative – of applying the *Rookes v Barnard* limitations to claims seeking the vindication of constitutional rights through traditional torts but of not applying these limitations to claims seeking vindication of constitutional rights that do not fall within the traditional tort repertoire – would involve the Court in an anomalous (and arguably unconstitutional) process based on no coherent principle.[96]

***(d) Once and for all award***

**[44.55]** The only form of compensation permitted by the law at present is a lump sum award, in contrast to payments made under the social insurance system or by the law in certain continental countries.[97] Thus, the plaintiff must sue in one action for all loss, past, present and prospective. Whatever happens after the award has been made will not affect the position. Thus, even where the medical evidence given in a case is entirely refuted by subsequent events, nothing can be done to undo the error. This approach has been criticised on the basis that to appraise the value of a chance in the future[98] - the prospect of

---

96. For analysis of the Law Reform Commission's tentative proposals for reform, contained in its *Consultation Paper on Aggravated, Exemplary and Restitutionary Damages*, published in April 1998, see Byrne & Binchy, *Annual Review of Irish Law 1998*, pp 666-669.

97. *Cf* Ch 1, above.

98. As was the case in *McKay v O'Hare* DPIJ: Trinity & Michaelmas Terms 1996, p 196 (HC) where there was a risk of under 1% that the plaintiff would develop overwhelming post-splenectomy infection which carried a 50% risk of mortality. Carney J "having regard, in particular, to the pall of fear which must inevitably hang over the plaintiff for the rest of his life", awarded general damages for the future of £75,000.

an early death or remarriage, for example - is "bound to result either in a windfall or in a denial of adequate redress to the plaintiff".[99]

**[44.56]** On the other hand, the principal parties to litigation appear to prefer the present system. Insurance companies like to be able to close their books on claims at some point, rather than to have to make provision in their reserves for future payments extending indefinitely into the future. For plaintiffs, "a bird in the hand appears to be more satisfying than one in the bush",[100] even, it seems, in countries where a choice between lump sum payments and periodical award is possible.[101]

**[44.57]** The Law Reform Commission, in its *Report on Personal Injuries: Periodic Payments and Structured Settlements*,[102] published in 1996, has recommended wide-ranging reforms in this area of the law. In a comprehensive analysis, it has proposed that there should be a provision in law for the interim award of a facility for provisional awards in cases where a chance of serious deterioration in the plaintiff's health exists as a result of the wrong. It also recommends that provision be made for the use of structured settlements,[103] to which the tax relief under s 5 of the Finance Act 1990 should be extended. This new dispensation would be consensual: the courts would not have power to authorise a structured settlement against the wishes of any party to the litigation. The facility would apply in all cases, including fatal injury litigation.

## III. Appellate Functions Regarding Awards

**[44.58]** The appellate court may overturn an award of damages where no reasonable proportion exists between what was awarded and what the appellate court would have awarded.

---

99. FLEMING, p 256. But see *Danaher v Roscommon County Council* Supreme Court, 21 December 1973 - new trial as to damages ordered by Supreme Court because plaintiff adduced uncontroverted evidence of a deterioration in his medical condition "which would suggest that the prognosis on which the jury acted was incorrect" *per* Henchy J at p 11. And *cf Adderley v GN Ry Co* [1905] 2 IR 378 (CA).

100. Charles, *Justice in Personal Injury Awards: The Continuing Search for Guidelines*, Ch (1977) 2 of KLAR ed *Studies in Canadian Tort Law*, at 42

101. *Cf* Fleming 'Damages: Capital or Rent?' (1969) 19 U Toronto LJ 295 at 296.

102. (1996) LRC 54. See Byrne & Binchy, *Annual Review of Irish Law 1996.*

103. A structured settlement involves a guaranteed income or pension in favour of the plaintiff derived from an annuity bought by the insurer and held for the benefit of the injured person. The income payments can be varied ("structured") over a period of time. See paras 7.40ff of the Law Reform Commission's Report. Structural settlements are now a feature of the law in several other common law jurisdictions. See Lewis, *Structured Settlements: the Law and Practice* (1993). The English Law Commission, in its Report, *Structured Settlements and Interim and Provisional Damages* (1994) LC 224, made proposals broadly similar to those in the Law Reform Commission's Report. The Damages Act 1996, s 2 implements these recommendations in English law. See further *Atiyah's Accidents, Compensation and the Law* (6th ed, 1999 by Cane), pp 118-119. As to the Australian position, see TRINDADE & CANE, pp 510-511.

The principles on which the courts act were articulated in two decisions, *McGrath v Bourne*[104] and *Foley v Thermocement Products Ltd*,[105] both of which have been followed on numerous occasions.[106]

**[44.59]** Having regard to the importance of these expressions of the law, it seems desirable to quote them in full.

**[44.60]** In *McGrath v Bourne*[107] in 1876, Palles CB gave a clear description of how the appellate court should proceed:

> "It is true ... that we cannot set aside a verdict merely because the damages are more than we - were we the tribunal to decide the amount - should be disposed to give; but it is equally true that there is some amount of damages which will be sufficient to induce the Court to interfere. This amount is variously described in different cases. In some cases the epithet applied to it is 'scandalous', in some 'outrageous', in others 'grossly extravagant'. None of these expressions conveys any accurate idea to the mind ... A more clear, legal, and accurate definition was given by my brother Fitzgerald during the argument, when he stated that the amount should be such that no reasonable proportion existed between it and the

---

104. (1876) IR 10 CL 160 (Exch).

105. (1954) 90 ILTR 92 (SC).

106. *McGrath v Bourne* was followed by *Foley* itself: it was also cited with approval in *Harris v Arnott* (1889) 26 LR Ir 55 at 64-65 (Ex Div); *M'Adorney v Huston* (1905) 39 ILTR 148 at 149 (KBD); *McCarthy v Maguire* [1899] 2 IR 802 at 809 (QBD); *Blanchfield v Murphy* (1913) 47 ILTR 24 at 26 (CA); *Donnelly v Cash* Supreme Court, 19 June 1956 *per* Maguire CJ at p 2; *Brabazon v Morgan* Supreme Court, 21 February 1958, *per* Maguire J at p 5; *Boughton v Bray UDC* [1964] Ir Jur Rep 57 at 60 (SC); *Finucane v Thorton* Supreme Court, 31 July 1957, *per* Ó Dalaigh J (p 4) and Maguire J (p 2); *Thompson v Coyle Ltd* Supreme Court, 30 June 1969 *per* Ó Dálaigh CJ at p 3; *Forsyth v Roe Quarry Ltd* Supreme Court, 2 December 1958, *per* Lavery J at p 1 and per Maguire CJ at pp 1-2; *Connell v Fahy* Supreme Court, 24 June 1959, *per* Ó Dálaigh J at p 6; *O'Connor v Russell* Supreme Court, 23 October 1959, *per* Maguire CJ at p 2; *Reddlington v Thos Heiton Ltd* Supreme Court, 27 February 1959, *per* Lavery J at p 2 and *per* Maguire J at p 1; *Hindle v O'Dwyer* Supreme Court, 14 February 1955, *per* Lavery J, p 1; *O'Shaughnessy v Independent Newspapers Ltd* 21 April 1955 *per* Maguire CJ, p 5; *Murphy v Filgate* Supreme Court, 5 July 1968, *per* FitzGerald J at p 1; *Kinsella v Roofing Contractors Ltd* Supreme Court, 8 February 1966 *per* Ó Dálaigh CJ at p 1; *Mulvihill v Limerick County Council* (1952) 87 ILTR 63 (SC); *Harris v Arnott* (1889) 26 LR Ir 55 (Ex D) (affd by CA 1889); *Delahunty v Croke*, Supreme Court, 25 February 1971, *per* Ó Dalaigh CJ at p 1 and *Greene v Boyle* [1934] Ir Jur Rep 3 at 6 (NICA). In the English decision of *Praed v Graham* (1889) 74 QBD 53 at 55, Lord Esher supported the approach favoured in *McGrath v Bourne*; *Foley v Thermocement Products Ltd* has been cited with approval in *Hanley v Randles* (1962) 96 ILTR 10 (SC); *Boughton v Bray UDC* [1964] Ir Jur Rep 57 (SC); *Teeling v Ryan* Supreme Court, 2 May 1967; *Thompson v Coyle Ltd* Supreme Court, 30 June 1967; *Kinsella v Roofing Contractors Ltd* Supreme Court, 8 February 1966; *Lee v Joyce* Supreme Court, 3 December 1964; *Murphy v Filgate* Supreme Court, 5 July 1968; *O'Shaughnessy v Independent Newspapers Ltd* Supreme Court, 21 April 1955; *Reddlington v Thos Heiton & Co* Supreme Court, 27 February 1959; *Ellard v Cade & Son Ltd* Supreme Court, 4 November 1959; *Connell v Fahy* Supreme Court, 24 June 1959; *McMorrow v Knott* Supreme Court, 21 December 1959; *Stewart v JJ Smith & Co (Dublin) Ltd* Supreme Court, 31 July 1957; *Donnelly v Cash* Supreme Court, 21 February 1958; *Forsyth v Roe Quarry Ltd* Supreme Court, 2 December 1958; *Delahunty v Croke* Supreme Court, unrep 25 February 1971. These principles apply to the recipients of damages awards in all proceedings for tort, including libel actions: *Harris v Arnott* (1889) 26 LR Ir 55; *McCarthy v Maguire* [18991 2 IR 802.

107. (1876) IR 10 CL 160 at 164-165 (Exch).

> circumstances of the case. In determining whether or not this amount has been exceeded, we should remember that the jury are the constitutional tribunal[108] to determine the amount of damages, and we should not on light grounds review the decision at which they have arrived. But if, of the various views of the facts which are capable of being taken by reasonable men, we adopt that which is most favourable to the plaintiff, and if adopting this view we arrive at the conclusion that no reasonable proportion exists between the damages which we should be inclined to give and the amount awarded by the jury, then the verdict ought not to stand."

In *Foley v Thermocement Products Ltd*,[109] Lavery J stated that the task of a judge in an appellate court was:

> "to make his own estimate of the damages he would award and then compare this estimate with the verdict and say whether there is any reasonable proportion between the sums or whether the verdict is an entirely erroneous estimate of the damage or is plainly unreasonable. In making his estimate the judge must adopt all points most favourable to the plaintiff and must keep in mind that the jury had the advantage, which he has not had, of hearing the evidence and of seeing the witnesses and in particular hearing and seeing the plaintiff.
>
> No one will deny that this is a most difficult task. It is especially difficult in a case where personal injuries are the subject of the claim. There is no standard by which pain and suffering, facial disfigurement or indeed any continuing disability can be measured in terms of money. All that can be said is that the estimate must be reasonable and different minds will inevitably arrive at widely differing conclusions as to what is reasonable. The task must, however, be undertaken."

In *O'Sullivan v Mellerick*,[110] Ó Dálaigh CJ stated that:

> "In holding an award of damages to be excessive the criterion to be applied is, in part, subjective. The basic factor is one's own estimate of the damages; and, then, comparing this estimate with the jury's assessment, one has to say whether the jury's figure is so disproportionate to the circumstances of the case as to admit of no other view than that the damages are excessive."

**[44.61]** With the abolition of juries in personal injuries litigation, the trial judge's award of damages are scrutinised by the Supreme Court in the same way, and on the same principles, as formerly applied to the jury award. The Supreme Court has emphasised the fact that the trial judge had the opportunity of seeing and hearing the witnesses and has proferred itself cautious about second guessing the trial judge's determination of the damages issue. Thus, in *Murphy v Cork County Council*,[111] the Supreme Court upheld an award of £55,000 for general damages where the plaintiff suffered soft tissue injuries to her neck, leg, arm and lower back. O'Flaherty J (Barrington and Keane JJ concurring) observed that:

---

108. This description of the jury was repeated by Lavery J in *Foley's* case (at 93) but Lavery J subsequently took the view that having regard to the provisions of the 1937 Constitution, it was no longer an accurate one: *Daly v T & J Macken Ltd* Supreme Court, unreported, 6 February 1957 *per* Lavery J at p 1; *Ebbs v Forkin & Co Ltd* Supreme Court, 6 May 1963, *per* Lavery J at p 1.

109. (1954) 90 ILTR 92 at 94 (SC).

110. (1970) 104 ILTR 8 at 10 (SC). See also *Kerr v Ulster Fireclay Works Ltd* [1964] Ir Jur Rep 23 at 24 (NICA); *Murray v John Sisk & Son Ltd* [1965] Ir Jur Rep 41 at 42 (SC); *Maycock v Legg Bros Ltd* Supreme Court, 10 March 1972, *per* FitzGerald J; *O'Toole v Kearns* Supreme Court, 31 July 1957, *per* Kingsmill Moore J; *Brabazon v Morgan* Supreme Court, 21 February 1958, *per* Maguire J at p 5, and *Doherty v Bowaters Irish Wallboard Mills Ltd* [1968] IR 277 (SC) at 283-284 at 291, 293 (*per* Lavery J).

111. Supreme Court, 18 November 1996.

"... the impression that a plaintiff and his or her witnesses make on the trial judge is critical. In those cases where there is not something palpable such as a loss of limb or loss of the sight of an eye and so forth, when one is dealing with subjective matters, then one must rely on the trial judge and the cold pages of the transcript, not to speak of the medical reports, are often a very poor substitute for what the trial judge has before him in the way of oral testimony."[112]

**[44.62]** What degree of variation between the respective assessments of trial judge and Supreme Court should prompt the appellate tribunal to hold that the trial judge's figure is unacceptably high or low? In *Reddy v Bates*[113] McCarthy J suggested a difference of 25%. This solution also found favour in the later Supreme Court decision of *Sheriff v Dowling*.[114]

**[44.63]** An appeal may be taken against an award either on the basis that it was too high or too low. In *Lee v Joyce*,[115] Lavery J noted that an appellate court which held that damages awarded were too generous would be "open to a charge of lack of sympathy and indifference". He added that "[a] judge must bear this odium however unjust the charge".

**[44.64]** A striking example of an award that was too *low* arose in *Blanchfield v Murphy*[116] in 1912. The plaintiff was knocked down by the defendant's horse and cart. His injuries were so severe that his life was in danger for fourteen days; he was confined to bed for six weeks and incapacitated for a long time thereafter; his ribs were broken and he received fifty visits from his doctor. The jury awarded £5 damages.

**[44.65]** Not surprisingly this award was overturned by the King's Bench Division, but the defendant appealed to the Court of Appeal, which affirmed the King's Bench Division. Why the jury had acted in such a miserly fashion puzzled the judges, who speculated as to whether the jury had ignored the right to compensation for pecuniary loss[117] or whether it had considered that the defence of contributory negligence (which issue had not been left to them) was applicable.[118]

---

112. See also *Hay v O'Grady* [1992] 1 IR 210 (SC).
113. [1984] ILRM 197 at 205 (SC).
114. Supreme Court, 26 May 1993.
115. Supreme Court, 3 December 1964, *per* Lavery J dissenting, dissent not affecting *this* point at p 8. See also *Boles v O'Connor* Supreme Court, 10 February 1966, *per* Lavery J, dissenting, dissent not affecting this point at p 2.
Some interesting statistics concerning the incidence of jury awards of damages being set aside by the Supreme Court are provided in the 3rd Interim Report of the Committee on Court Practice and Procedure: *Jury Trial in Civil Actions*, para 39 of Majority Report (1965).
116. 47 ILTR 24 (CA, 1913, affg KBD, 1912). See also *Kerr v Ulster Fireclay Works Ltd* [1964] Ir Jur Rep 23 (NLCA); *Cooney v Thomas Dockrell & Sons Ltd* [1965] Ir Jur Rep 31 (SC); *McArdle v McCaughey Bros Ltd* [1968] IR 47 (SC). In *Higgins v O'Reilly* [1940] Ir Jur Rep 15 (HC), the High Court increased to £20 a Circuit Court jury award of £2 for libel, slander, unlawful arrest malicious prosecution, false imprisonment and trespass to the person. Johnston J said: "I think that a terrible blunder must have taken place somewhere in the awarding of such a sum".
117. [1940] Ir Jur Rep 15 at 25 (*per* Madden J, KBD).
118. [1940] Ir Jur Rep 15 at 26 (*per* Holmes LJ, CA). See also *Horgan v Buckley (No 1)* [1938] IR 115 at 140 (SC): "A jury may be anything but perverse, may in fact be eminently reasonable, and, with every desire to be fair, yet assess damages on the wrong basis." Examples of an award by a judge being increased on the basis that it was too low are *Forde v Forde* Supreme Court, 20 May 1996, *Forde v Iarnród Éireann - Irish Rail* Supreme Court, 4 November 1997 (*ex temp*); *Gillick v Rotunda Hospital*, Supreme Court, 15 May 1998 (*ex temp*) and *Sheriff v Dowling* Supreme Court, 26 May 1993.

**[44.66]** Section 96 of the Courts of Justice Act 1924[119] empowers the appellate tribunal, in lieu of ordering a new trial, to set aside the jury verdict and "enter such judgement as the court thinks proper". The effect of the Court's intervention should be "to lighten the net burden for each of the parties".[120] This power was formerly exercised sparingly, though there are reported instances from some time ago where the Supreme Court took this course. Thus, for example, in *Gahan v Engineering Products Ltd*,[121] in 1971, where the Supreme Court substituted a verdict of £2,000 for £3,200 awarded for pain and suffering resulting from injury to the plaintiff's eye. The Court took this step because it considered that the costs of a retrial of this issue would be disproportionate to the amount involved.

**[44.67]** In more recent years the appellate courts have been far more inclined to substitute their own assessment of the damages for that of the trial judge and thereby save the parties the expense, inconvenience and the delay of a retrial."[122] They cannot take what has by now become "the normal course",[123] however, where the assessment of damages by the trial judge has been attended by a lack of clarity that renders it impossible for them to stand over the actual reasons given by the trial judge for assessing the damages as he or she did.[124]

## Uniformity of Awards

**[44.68]** There is some merit to a legal system where awards for damages are uniform. Such a practice promotes justice between parties in different cases as well as helping legal advisers to predict the quantum of awards.[125] As against this, to introduce too great a degree of uniformity would inhibit the utility of the jury system[126] (as well, incidentally, as probably having a generally deflationary effect on awards).

**[44.69]** When juries were available in personal injuries litigation, the Supreme Court tended towards a middle position on this question, allowing sufficient leeway to juries, whilst at the same time facilitating the task of legal advisers by introducing a degree of

---

119. In *Holohan v Donohue* [1986] IR (SC) the section was held to be consistent with the Constitution.

120. *Crowley v Muskerry Co-Operative Society Ltd* Supreme Court, 11 December 1972, *per* Ó Dálaigh CJ at p 1. When juries decided the award in personal injury litigation, s 96 also had the benefit of preventing the embarrassment to the appellate court of a jury in a second trial awarding damages of the same order as in the first: cf. *M'Greene v Hibernian Taxi Co (No 2)* [1931] IR 319 (SC); *Horgan v Buckley (No 2)* [1938] IR 675 (SC).

121. [1971] IR 30 (SC). See also *Hosty v McDonagh* Supreme Court, 29 May 1973 where, notwithstanding the plaintiff's objection, the Court substituted its own verdict as to damages because "to order a retrial on all issues ... would result in the case being smothered in costs" (*per* Fitzgerald CJ at p 5).

122. *O'Donoghue v W Deecan & Sons Ltd* Supreme Court (*ex temp*), 19 July 1999, Keane J's judgment (Murphy and Lynch JJ concurring) at page 9.

123. *O'Donoghue v W Deecan & Sons Ltd* Supreme Court (*ex temp*), 19 July 1999.

124. *O'Donoghue v W Deecan & Sons Ltd* Supreme Court (*ex temp*), 19 July 1999.

125. *Cf* the English Law Commission's Working Paper No 41 (1971), paras 209-216.

126. *Cf* the 3rd Interim Report of the Committee on Court Practice and Procedure: *Jury Trial in Civil Actions*, para 35 of Majority Report (1965). With the abolition of juries on a personal injury litigation in 1988, the main area where juries continue to function in civil litigation is defamation. The trend of public discussion and of recent judicial utterances is to restrict the remit of juries in this context.

predictability, if not quite an inflexible tariff. In *Kennedy v Limerick County Council*,[127] Ó Dálaigh J stated:

> "It is not possible to compare one case with another in damages but [it] is possible and also desirable to see that particular awards in cases of injury, not presenting special features, are kept within certain outer limits so that some general relationship is maintained between the several categories or degrees of seriousness of injury."

**[44.70]** And in *Forsyth v Roe Quarry Ltd*,[128] Lavery J stated:

> "Within very wide boundaries the Courts should seek some uniformity in the assessment of damages. When this assessment is done by juries whose members appear on the panel for a brief session and then disappear to be succeeded by another panel probably without any previous experience it is difficult to attain this but it must be attempted and this Court has the task of doing so."

It remains to be seen whether the Supreme Court will modify its approach in the wake of the recent abolition of juries for personal injuries litigation.

## IV. Computation of Damages Under Separate Headings

**[44.71]** We now must consider an issue characterised by judicial convolutions over the years. Formerly the courts did not favour the view that each element of damages should be separately computed and stated by the jury under particular headings. Thus, for example, Ó Dálaigh J stated in *McMorrow v Knott* that:

> "Damages in a case of personal injuries are not to be assessed by pricing each element of damage separately and taking the total. A figure thus arrived at does not present a true picture. The several elements of damage instead of being just totalled have to be fused, because the final assessment should be informed by a view of the case not seen in segregation but as a whole." [129]

**[44.72]** Similarly in *Lee v Joyce*,[130] Lavery J stated:

> "A judge and more particularly an appellate judge is expected to explain his decision but I have doubts as to whether in these cases he is required to or should state the estimates of the several heads of damages he has made."

**[44.73]** By the 1960s the view was changing. In *Sexton v O'Keeffe*,[131] Kingsmill Moore J stated that separation into different heads of compensation of special damages and general damages:

> "... in many cases ... would greatly facilitate the Court in arriving at satisfactory conclusions in the event of an appeal, and would help to concentrate the attention of the jury on the matters to be taken into consideration. I am of opinion that it is practice which could with advantage be adopted in all cases where special damages are likely to form a considerable proportion of the award."

127. Supreme Court, 21 December 1959, pp 12-13.
128. Supreme Court, 2 December 1958, p 2.
129. Supreme Court, 21 December 1959, p 4.
130. Supreme Court, 3 December 1964, p 4 (dissenting, dissent not affecting this point).
131. [1966] IR 204 at 210 (SC).

**[44.74]** Similarly, in *McArdle v McCaughey Bros Ltd*,[132] Walsh J expressed "unqualified approval" for this approach, which was helpful in enabling the appellate court to "read the jury's mind" on the various issues of fact that arose for decision in the computation of the damages. It was, he said, a practice to be commended in all claims for damages for personal injury save, perhaps, in the most simple and uncomplicated cases.

**[44.75]** In the Supreme Court decision of *Howell v O'Regan*,[133] Walsh J, speaking for the Court, stressed that it was in the interests of the parties themselves that this approach should be followed:

> "Otherwise every verdict for damages in global form must be construed as amounting to a finding of the maximum which is reasonably open under each of the headings though in fact the jury may have had a different approach. This must now be the approach for the purpose of his appeal."

**[44.76]** The Supreme Court has since revised the practice again. In *Reddy v Bates*,[134] Griffin J (within whom Hederman J concurred) stated that:

> "[i]n a case such as this, where damages are to be assessed under several headings, where the jury has added the various sums awarded and arrived at a total for damages, they should then consider this total sum, as should this court on any appeal, for the purpose of ascertaining whether the total sum awarded is, in the circumstances of the case, fair compensation for the plaintiff for the injury suffered, or whether it is out of all proportion to such circumstances."

By the way of contrast, McCarthy J considered that the fact that the total amount awarded, as to losses, past and future, might appear to be a high figure was:

> "no ground for interference, where each individual figure making up the total is reasonably supportable on the evidence."[135]

**[44.77]** The approach favoured by the majority in *Reddy v Bates* provokes some comment. An immediate response is that it appears to defy the mathematical principle that the whole is neither greater nor smaller than its parts. For how can it be that the total amount of compensation due should be more or less than the sum of its ingredients? To this criticism it may perhaps be replied that it misunderstands the thrust of the Supreme Court's revised approach. The Court is seeking to prevent over-compensation which may result from computation under specific heads. If that computation process were infallible, then there would be no need for the "second look", by way of global estimation, commended by the Court. But there is a real risk that computation under specific headings may lead to

---

132. [1968] IR 47 at 53 (SC). See also *Hanley v Morrissey* Supreme Court, 20 December 1974, *per* Budd J at pp 1-2; *O'Leary v O'Connell* [1968] IR 149 at 155 (SC). Canadian decisions have favoured the same approach: *Andrews v Grand & Toy Alberta Ltd* 83 DLR (3d) 452 (SC Can, 1978); *Guy v Trizec Equities Ltd* (1979) 99 DLR (3d) 243 (SC, Can). See further the Manitoba Law Reform Commission's *Report on Periodic Payment of Damages for Personal Injury and Death* (1987) 12-13. Australian decisions take the view that this approach is permissible but not essential: TRINDADE & CANE, p 531.

133. Supreme Court, 14 May 1970, p 6. See also *Murphy v Rucon Ltd* Supreme Court, 31 January 1969, *per* Ó Dálaigh CJ, p 4.

134. [1984] ILRM 197 at 202 (SC). See the LRC's *Report on Personal Injuries: Periodic Payments and Structured Settlements*, paras 2.28-2.31 (1996) LRC 54.

135. [1984] ILRM at 205.

unintended duplication of compensation. A global estimation should go some way towards protecting the defendant from having to pay for this error.

**[44.78]** But, in proposing the global estimate as the ultimate yardstick, the Supreme Court is opting for the supremacy of an intuitive resolution of the issue of compensation. Is this a sound approach? While admittedly the more controlled approach of computation under specific headings is ultimately reducible, at least in part, to a matter of intuitive judgment, there may be some risk in elevating intuition into such a dominant role.

**[44.79]** It is worth noting that Griffin J did not limit the application of this revised approach to the jury alone: he was satisfied that the Supreme Court should also adopt it. It would seem, therefore, that in non-jury cases the trial judge should be governed by the same rule. The argument against this would, of course, be that, in contrast to a jury, a professional judge should not have to resort to such a crude means of defence against the risk of unintended overcompensation. If this is so, why did Griffin J consider that the Supreme Court should adopt the revised approach? Certainly there is evidence from the judgments that trial judges are to engage in the process of reassessment prescribed by Griffin J in *Reddy v Bates*, though it is rare enough for the judges to make express reference to this fact[136] and rarer still for them to alter the global award in the light of this reassessment.

**[44.80]** An instance where just such alteration was made is *Sturdy v Dublin Corporation*.[137] The plaintiff was tortiously injured when he was 59 years old. At the time of the judgment he was just under 65 years old. His injuries were serious: he lost the sight of one eye and suffered brain damage resulting in a change of personality. Lynch J was disposed to award £100,000 for general damages: £35,000 for the brain damage up to trial, £20,000 for future brain damage, £30,000 for the loss of sight and other injuries to date and £15,000 for the loss of sight and other injuries in the future. He observed, however, that:

> "[t]he Supreme Court … indicated that judges should tell juries, when juries decided these cases, that they should look at the total of their damages after they ha[d] assessed them and if the total did not appear to be in accord with common sense then they should vary it so as to make it accord with common sense. I think that £100,000 for general damages is excessive in the case of a plaintiff almost 65 years of age and I think that the common sense and proper overall figure for general damages past and future is £80,000."[138]

**[44.81]** This is a somewhat alarming process of thought. It is one thing for a judge to reduce the cumulative total because of an intuition that it is too large; it is quite another for the judge to reduce the sum because of an articulated norm. In this case the norm is itself controversial. It appears to be that an old person, by virtue of being old is entitled to less compensation than is his or her due under the specific headings. It is noteworthy that Lynch J made no attempt to cast doubt on the specific sums that he considered appropriate for future general damages. The import of his observations seems to be that old people should have their general damages cut where the cumulative sum is a large one. The basis

136. See, eg *Troute v Brassil* High Court, 19 November 1999 (O'Neill J); *Thornton v Murphy Brewery (Irl) Ltd* DPIJ: Hilary & Easter Terms 1993, p 1 at p 8 (HC); *Power v Crowley* High Court, 29 October 1992 (Blayney J).

137. DPIJ: Michaelmas Term 1991, p 21 (HC).

138. DPIJ: Michaelmas Term 1991, p 21 at 23

of this approach is not clarified: it could perhaps be that old people are less deserving of substantial compensation or that they have less to spend their money on[139] or that there is a futility in the award of high damages where the likely outcome is that, with a relatively short time, the bulk of the sum awarded will pass, though the death of the plaintiff, to the beneficiaries of his or her estate.

## V. Proof of Loss of Earning Capacity[140]

**[44.82]** One of the principal heads of damage in negligence litigation is loss of earnings. Usually there is little problem with lost earnings up to the time of trial, but in assessing future loss the position may be less clear. An excellent summary of the approach of the courts to this subject is presented by Walsh J, in the Supreme Court decision of *Long v O'Brien & Cronin Ltd*:[141]

> "It has been laid down several times[142] in this Court that it is the duty of the plaintiff to adduce evidence sufficient to go to the jury when he sets out to establish that the result of his injuries will be to cause him pecuniary loss in the future as in this case loss of future earning capacity. It has been pointed out in this Court that this may be done in a variety of ways depending on the circumstances of the case. Not merely is the former earning capacity of the plaintiff relevant but so also is the present physical condition, his prospective physical condition, the state of the labour market, the particular trade or skill which he has and the prospects for exercising it in the future having regard to the diminution of his capacity to do so resulting from the injuries he has sustained."

Some of the principal points raised in this passage require further discussion.

### The Physical Condition of the Plaintiff

**[44.83]** The plaintiff's physical condition (actual and prospective) will obviously affect his or her earning capacity.[143] For example, the plaintiff physical condition may make it impossible to be employed in certain occupations.[144] A clear case would be where the plaintiff's condition prevents the plaintiff from performing the tasks which the job involves

---

139. *Cf Sinnott v Quinnsworth Ltd* [1984] ILRM 523 at 532. See further paras **[44.150]** below.

140. See Atiyah 'Loss of Earnings or Earning Capacity' (1971) 45 Austr LJ 228; Peck & Hopkins 'Economics and Impaired Earning Capacity in Personal Injury Cases' (1961) 44 Wash LR 351. See also *McDermott v Gargan* High Court, 24 January 1997 (Flood J).

141. Supreme Court, 24 March 1972, p 6.

142. *Cf* eg *Roche v P Kelly & Co Ltd* [1969] IR 100 (SC); *Sweeney v Crowley* Supreme Court, 30 May 1968; *McKenna v Meighan* [1966] IR 288 (SC); *Murphy v Rucon* Supreme Court, 31 January 1969; *Garry v John Sisk & Son (Dublin) Ltd* Supreme Court, 1973; *Cunningham v Joe Malone Car Hire Services Ltd* Supreme Court, 16 March 1967; *Deegan v Langan* [1966] IR 373 (SC); *Kelly v McCarron & Co Ltd* Supreme Court, 30 May 1968; *O'Donnell v Spicer* Supreme Court, 8 December 1967; *Delaney v Ainsworth* Supreme Court, 23 November 1966.

143. *Cf Cunningham v Joe Malone Car Hire Services Ltd* Supreme Court, 16 March 1967, *per* Budd J, pp 4-5. Medical evidence is naturally essential on the question, though this may be supplemented by that of others, such as career counsellors: *cf O'Donoghue v Deecan & Sons Ltd* Supreme Court, 19 July 1999.

144. Alternatively, if the plaintiff is an employer, his or her physical condition may necessitate the employment of extra staff to do work that the plaintiff used to do before the accident; *cf Byrne v Johns* Supreme Court, 10 March 1972.

- lifting a heavy weight, for instance. However, employment may also be ruled out on less direct grounds.

**[44.84]** Thus, a labourer who loses an eye in an accident may take into account the particular risk of blindness resulting from losing the remaining eye and accordingly not seek employment carrying such risk, such as work on ladders and on heights, or work such as cement mixing, spreading lime and cutting hedges.[145] However, this is far from saying that a plaintiff with a serious disability is automatically free to regard himself or herself as unemployable for the remainder of his or her life.[146] In *Forsyth v Roe Quarry Ltd*[147] Lavery J stated:

> "The loss of an eye is a terrible affliction but its effect on ability to work is not - outside certain classes of work - so very great."

Therefore, a solicitor, or even a carpenter,[148] who loses an eye may be perfectly able to continue working despite his affliction. In such a case, he will, of course, be entitled to compensation for this injury, but not under the heading of loss of earning capacity.

**[44.85]** So also, the loss of a leg is a serious injury, entitling the victim to substantial damages, but it may in some cases not involve a diminution in earning capacity. As Lavery J stated in *Forsyth v Roe Quarry Ltd*:

> "It seems to me impossible to say that a one legged man cannot do any kind of work. Everyone knows many such men living useful and active lives."[149]

**[44.86]** This statement might suggest some lack of appreciation on the part of the Courts of the plight of disabled persons, but in fact they are well aware of the difficulties facing them in seeking employment. In *Ebbs v Forkin & Co Ltd*,[150] Walsh J stated:

> "The fact that a partially disabled workman is able to do a considerable amount of work at his trade is not necessarily a reason for assuming that he will be able to get that work even if it is available. Employers generally are reluctant to employ workmen suffering from physical disabilities, partly because of the restricted scope of their ability to work and partly because of the possible danger of a further accident to the workman himself or to a fellow worker which might be attributable to the disability."

---

145. See *Dwyer v Ascon Ltd* Supreme Court, 16 March 1967. *Cf Gahan v Engineering Products Ltd* [1971] IR 30 (SC).

146. *Cf McKenna v Meighan* [1966] IR 288 at 293 (SC):

> "It may well be that what can be described as a partial disability may from an economic point of view be equal to total if it prevents him from doing the only type of work available to him or may be the cause of no economic loss at all if it does not interfere with the work available to him."

147. Supreme Court, 2 December 1958, p 2. See also *Mulvihill v Limerick County Council* (1952) 87 ILTR 63. But see *Purtill v Athlone UDC* [1968] IR 205 at 214 (SC). *Cf Adderley v GN Ry Co* [1905] 2 IR 378 at 408 (CA):

> "If we judge by our own experience, it is remarkable what a number of people have shared the misfortune of Hannibal, Nelson and Gambetta; how many have but one eye, and how many have only one useful eye? In how many cases has injury to one eye afterwards caused the loss of the other?"

148. *Cf Deegan v Langan* [1966] IR 373 at 377 (SC).

149. Supreme Court, 2 December 1958, p 2.

150. Supreme Court, 6 May 1963, p 1.

## Claims for "Lost Years" of Earnings

**[44.87]** Closely associated with this problem is the question whether a plaintiff whose working life expectancy has been cut short may be compensated for the earnings of the "lost years". If, for example, as a result of the injury, the plaintiff's working life is cut from twenty years to twelve years, is the plaintiff to be entitled to the wages he would have earned for the eight lost years, less, of course, expenses? The better opinion appears to be that he is. This was the view favoured by Walsh J in the Supreme Court decision of *Doherty v Bowaters Irish Wallboard Mills Ltd*[151] where he stated:

> "In my opinion the period or the length of time by which the expectation of life has been reduced must also be taken into account though of course for that particular period the sum to be considered would not be the gross loss of wages for the period but the surplus, if any, after providing for what it would have cost him to live during those years if he had not had the accident."

As is mentioned[152] in Chapters 41 and 42 in the context of fatal injuries, the same approach has been favoured in England.

## The State of the Labour Market

**[44.88]** As Walsh J pointed out in *Long v O'Brien & Cronin Ltd*,[153] the state of the labour market must be taken into consideration in determining prospective loss of earnings, and in this regard the evidence of officials of the local labour exchange or trade union officials familiar with the type of work which the plaintiff used to do may be appropriate.

**[44.89]** In *Murphy v Rucon*,[154] the Supreme Court ordered a retrial on the issue of damages where the only relevant evidence tendered by the plaintiff had been of his unsuccessful attempts to obtain employment after the accident. A union official who was to give evidence on his behalf had not done so as, by some error, he was not qualified to speak of the employment conditions prevailing in the area where the plaintiff resided. Moreover, the evidence on behalf of the plaintiff did not exclude the possibility that he might make his way as a self-employed person.

---

151. [1968] IR 277 at 285. The issue of how many more years the plaintiff would have worked had the accident not happened can give rise to debate: see, eg, *Forde v Pfizer Chemical Corporation Ltd* DPIJ: Hilary and Easter Terms 1991, p 57 (HC). In *Sheriff v Dowling* Supreme Court, 26 May 1993, the Supreme Court held that the trial judge had been mistaken in calculating damages on the assumption that the plaintiff, an executive working at Maynooth University, would have retired at the age of 46 if she had not been injured in the accident which gave rise to the claim. She was a married woman with four children. Egan J (O'Flaherty and Blayney JJ concurring) acknowledged that it was impossible to say with any degree of certainty how long the plaintiff would have worked, the assumption that a married woman would retire from gainful employment at such an early age seemed to him to be "somewhat unfair and not justified by the evidence in th[e] case." *Cf Murnaghan v Gilhooley*, DPIJ: Trinity & Michaelmas Terms 1993, p 60 (HC).

152. See also Mesher & Todd 'Damages for "Lost years" - Recent Developments in the United Kingdom' 29 ICLQ 719 (1980) 114-115, Weir [1981] CLJ 20.

153. See para **[44.82]** above. The defendant will not be permitted to argue that the plaintiff should emigrate to seek more renumerative employment. *Cf Sweeney v Crowley* Supreme Court, 30 May 1968, *per* Ó Dálaigh CJ at p 5 (dissenting, but dissent not affecting this point).

154. Supreme Court, 31 January 1969.

**[44.90]** In 1984, the Supreme Court stressed that the high rate of unemployment and redundancies "must inevitably lead to the conclusion that there is no longer any safe, much less guaranteed, employment".[155] In *Reddy v Bates*,[156] Griffin J expressed the view that this is a factor which juries "should be required to take into account in assessing future loss of earnings in any given case". In *Cooke v Walsh*[157] he reiterated this view, noting that in the eight months which had elapsed since *Reddy v Bates* had been decided, unemployment had considerably increased and "all the forecasts"[158] were that there would be further deterioration in the future. He considered that there should be "a substantial discount from the multiplier for the risk factor where employment is concerned".[159] McCarthy J, in contrast, prophetically "decline[d] to assume"[160] that the existing state of high unemployment would necessarily exist over the following forty years.

155. *Reddy v Bates* [1984] ILRM 197 at 201 (SC).
156. *Reddy v Bates* [1984] ILRM 197 at 201.
157. [1984] ILRM 208 at 217 (SC). O'Higgins CJ, Henchy and Hederman JJ concurred with Griffin J's judgment. McCarthy J dissented.
158. [1984] ILRM 208 at 217.
159. [1984] ILRM 208 at 217.
160 [1984] ILRM 208 at 221. Judges of the High Court have (somewhat fitfully) applied the *Reddy v Bates* reduction rule with varying emphasis. See, eg, *McEvoy v Maringe* DPIJ: Trinity & Michaelmas Terms 1993, p 42 (HC) - 30% discount; *Kirby v South Eastern Health Board* DPIJ: Trinity & Michaelmas Terms 1993, p 234 (HC) - 10% discount where plaintiff was a permanent nurse employed by the Health Board "with a secure job", which Morris J believed she would have continued to hold until retirement; *Mullin v Naughton*, DPIJ: Trinity & Michaelmas Terms 1996, p 161 (HC) - 15% discount where plaintiff had been employed as a farm labourer with the defendant for twelve years and no evidence had been adduced "to suggest that there was any likelihood of that employment being lost because of redundancy or cessation of business"; *Kiely v Carrig*, DPIJ: Trinity & Michaelmas Terms p 209 (HC) - 17% discount for *Reddy v Bates*, "taking into account the plaintiff's excellent pre-accident work record" as an employed butcher, followed by an unsuccessful period running his own business, Barr J being satisfied that the plaintiff would probably have found employment shortly afterwards; *Kelly v Donoghue* DPIJ: Trinity Term 1991, p 3 (HC) - 21% discount, "bearing in mind the relative security of the plaintiff's pre-accident employment" as a skilled motor mechanic; *Slattery v O'Brien*, DPIJ: Hilary and Easter Terms 1993, p 98 (HC) - 9.5% discount where lounge waitress, aged 38 at the time of the accident, was injured in road accident; *Barden v Waterford County Council*, DPIJ: Trinity & Michaelmas Terms 1998, p 6 (HC) - 15% discount in relation to a qualified carer of mentally and physically handicapped persons who was "highly gifted" and would have continued in gainful employment had she not been injured; *Shinwin v Quin - Con Ltd* DPIJ: Trinity & Michaelmas Terms 1998, p 46 (HC) - 5% discount - described by Smith J at p 53 as "a modest reduction" - in relation to factory worker aged 17 on his first job at time of injury; *Brennan v Lissadell Towels Ltd*, DPIJ: Trinity & Michaelmas Terms 1998, P 272 (HC) - 15% discount in relation to designer, aged 40 at time of accident, employed by towel manufacturer, *per* McGuinness J at p 278: "… I don't think that this kind of trade is absolutely secure by any means."; *Coppinger v Waterford County Council* DPIJ: Hilary and Easter Terms 1996, p 1 (HC) - 12% discount where the plaintiff was "a highly thought of engineer rapidly rising to responsible positions"; *Power v Crowley* High Court, 29 October 1992 (Blayney J) - discount of 35% of future loss of earnings having regard to *Reddy v Bates* direction regarding uncertainty of employment and to the requirement that the overall figure of damages should not be excessive; *O'Connor v Northeastern Health Board*, DPIJ: Trinity & Michaelmas Terms 1999, p 150 (HC) - 9% discount for *Reddy v Bates* considerations in relation to permanently appointed porter working as a medical attendant in defendant's hospital;

**[44.91]** It can hardly be in every case that a substantial deduction - or indeed any deduction - would be warranted. The plaintiff's particular talents before the accident may have been so distinctive and attractive to potential employers as to render moot a consideration of the rate of unemployment in the population as a whole.[161] Moreover, the reduction in unemployment over the past several years and the growth in the economy have surely weakened the force of the argument that a *substantial* discount should be made.[162]

## Other Possibilities Affecting Earning Capacity

**[44.92]** As a general rule, the courts take a view that, where there is an issue of the possibility or probability of some disability or illness arising or developing in the future,

---

160. (contd) *Wallace v Fahy*, DPIJ: Hilary & Easter Terms 1996, p 162 (HC) - no discount under *Reddy v Bates* as plaintiff's employment was protected under the Postal and Telecommunications Services Act 1983; *Bedford v Minister for Defence*, DPIJ: Hilary & Easter Terms 1998, p 1 (HC) - 2% discount "for *Reddy v Bates* considerations" in relation to private in Defence Forces. In *Darcy v The Minister for Defence*, DPIJ: Hilary & Easter Terms 1999, p 12 (HC), where a member of the defence forces with prospects of promotion was injured, Macken J declined to make any deduction on the basis of *Reddy v Bates*, stating (at p 16):

> "I don't actually think that in a case of this nature there is any requirement, or indeed justification, for discounting the figure which I am granting in respect of his loss of earnings, which is based on the higher earnings he will likely earn and on the lowest promotional level he would achieve … [b]ecause I think, given the evidence, that it is unlikely, in the absence of his injury, that this gentleman would have been in any way caught by the so-called vicissitudes or the difficulties involved in ordinary employment, there being some considerable degree of security in relation to the Army."

161. Conversely, some kinds of employment - such as the theatre or sporting activities - are notoriously precarious. In *O'Sullivan v Telecom Éireann*, DPIJ: Trinity & Michaelmas Terms 1998, p 265 (HC), where the plaintiff before the accident had "shown at junior and later at senior level, a consistent, outstanding talent as a [football] player with … exceptional qualities of leadership" and was destined at least for a career as a semi-professional player for a club in the FAI premiership, Barr J awarded only £30,000 for future loss of earnings, observing (at p 269):

> "… I recognise that the principle of *Reddy v Bates* looms particularly large in the assessment of future loss of earnings in the area of professional sport. I accept that a soccer player may continue at the level required for the FAI premiership perhaps until aged 35. However, in a given case, youthful enthusiasm may wane and there is the continuing significant risk of serious injury which may cut short a player's career at senior level at any time."

162. One finds in *Murphy v The Minister for Defence* Supreme Court, 19 July 1999 a somewhat watered down interpretation of Griffin J's observations in *Reddy v Bates*. Barron J (Hamilton CJ and Lynch J concurring) observed at pages 2-3 of his judgment: "What *Reddy v Bates* did was to draw attention to the uncertainties of life. The plaintiff might have been prevented from earning in any event by such mishaps as ill-health or an economic downturn." The very real "economic downturn" of the 1980's has now been reduced to hypothetical status, not to be ignored but equally not to result inevitably in a significant automatic reduction in the award. Thus, in *O'Mahony v Buckley*, DPIJ: Trinity & Michaelmas Terms 1999, p 5 (HC), no discount for *Reddy v Bates* was made because the plaintiff had been "secure in full employment with a significant demand in the building trade". In *Ecock v MF Kent & Co* DPIJ, Hilary and Easter Terms 1994, p 178 (HC), Kinlen J applied the *Reddy v Bates* principle of reduction in relation to the particular financial circumstances of the plaintiff's employer. In *Smith v Rhone Poulenc Ireland Ltd* High Court, 11 January 1995 (Flood J), where a 27-year-old sole operator of a beautician's salon, injured in a traffic accident, was totally disabled from gainful employment, Flood J took account of the principles articulated in *Reddy v Bates* when discounting the sum awarded by 25%. He identified the variables that could affect her future income as: "ill health, changes of fashion, competition from more luxurious establishments, cyclical depression in the economy and other factors which affect luxury trades such as beauticians."

the damages to be awarded "should be commensurate with, and proportionate to, the degree of that possibility or probability as the case may be".[163] This rule has, however, been qualified in a manner favourable to the plaintiff. In the Supreme Court decision of *Dunlop v Kenny*,[164] Ó Dálaigh CJ, for the Court, stated that:

> "If the degree of probability is so high as to satisfy a jury that it remains only possible that the condition will not occur, a jury would be justified in acting upon the assumption that it will occur, and should measure the damages accordingly. On the other hand, if the probability that no such event will occur is so great that it is only barely possible that it would occur, damages should nevertheless be awarded, but should be proportionate to the degree of risk, small though it may be."[165]

## Restriction of Employment Options

**[44.93]** Sometimes, the effect of an injury is to reduce the plaintiff's options regarding employment. This will not necessarily have a negative financial impact since the remaining options may be just as potentially lucrative as those that have been sacrificed. The courts are willing to award some compensation for this narrowing of options. Thus, in *Feeney v John Sisk & Sons Ltd*,[166] where a construction worker was rendered permanently unfit for heavy labouring, Barr J noted that he was:

> "an intelligent young man who would appear to the well capable of being re-trained for other employment, which might turn out to be more lucrative than that of builder's labourer. He is, however, entitled to compensation for the reduction in the spectrum of employment which would have been ope[n] to him if uninjured."

In cases of this type, the basis of compensation is (in part at least) loss of amenity rather than truly of economic character.[167]

## Moral Obligation to Pay over Earnings to a Third Party Ignored

**[44.94]** The fact that the plaintiff is under a moral obligation to pay over his earnings to another person may not be invoked by the defendant as a reason for holding that the plaintiff suffered no loss under this head of damages. An argument to this effect was rejected in one sentence by Hanna J in *Dowling v Great Southern Railways Co*,[168] where

163. *Dunlop v Kenny* Supreme Court, 29 July 1969, *per* Ó Dálaigh CJ at p 11. See also *Mernagh v Bell* Supreme Court, 19 January 1956, *per* Kingsmill Moore J at p 2.

164. *Dunlop v Kenny* Supreme Court, 29 July 1969, pp 11 and 12.

165. The second proposition was again propounded in *Ahearne v Thompson* Supreme Court, 26 October 1971, *per* Walsh J, for the Court at p 2.

166. DPIJ: Hilary & Easter Terms 1993, p 254 at p 258 (HC).

167. See also *Balentine v McAleavey*, DPIJ: Michaelmas 1991, p 114 (HC). In *Mulligan v Hewitt*, DPIJ: Hilary & Easter Terms 1991, p 38 (HC); *O'Sullivan v Telecom Éireann*, DPIJ: Trinity & Michaelmas Terms 1998, p 265 (HC), Barr J, as well as awarding damages for loss of earnings to a footballer whose career was ruined as a result of the injury, awarded him £25,000 on the basis that he was "entitled to be compensated for the shattering of his long-held ambition to succeed in professional soccer and for the loss of achievement, satisfaction and pleasure which such a career would have provided." The courts have very frequently awarded compensation for restriction of loss of the capacity to engage in sporting activities, even where there is no financial dimension. See, eg, *Ramsey v Northern Ireland Electricity plc*, DPIJ: Hilary & Easter Terms, 1997 (HC) - plaintiff "suffered a very serious loss of amenity in that she was a very keen sportswoman".

168. [1943] Ir Jur Rep 7 (HC).

the plaintiff was a Jesuit priest bound by a vow of poverty to pay over earnings to the Society of Jesus.

## Actuarial Evidence[169]

**[44.95]** The Irish courts enthusiastically support the use of actuarial evidence[170] in determining future loss of earnings. The Supreme Court in several cases has indicated that:

> "the evidence of an actuary is not only desirable but necessary to enable a jury to arrive at anything like a reasonably accurate figure under this heading."[171]

As Walsh J observed in *Sexton v O'Keeffe*:

> "It is very undesirable in such cases that a jury should be left at large to form their own impression as to expectation of life and the computing of loss dependent upon it without the expert assistance of an actuary who can inform the jury of the precise mathematical calculations involved and to be applied according to the jury's findings on the relevant facts."[172]

To encourage the use of actuarial evidence does not mean, however, that the evidence is in some way qualitatively different from other evidence in the case. It is not better and no worse that what it purports to be - namely, evidence of average life expectancy and of mathematical calculations based on certain assumptions.

**[44.96]** In *Swords v St Patrick's Copper Mines*,[173] Walsh J warned that it:

> "must be emphasised that the actuary is not the judge of the case and that his real value is to act as a guide on the mathematical calculations which must be made to arrive at a figure. It is, therefore, quite open to a jury to give a figure differing from his, whether it be higher or

169. See Prevett 'Actuarial Assessment of Damages' (1972) 35 MLR 140; Wickens, 'Actuarial Assistance in Assessing Damages' (1974) 48 Austr LJ 286. See also the 3rd Interim Report of the Committee on Court Practice and Procedure, *Jury Trial in Civil Actions*, para 36 of Majority Report (1965), and LC 56, para 230 (1973), both strongly recommending the use of actuarial evidence.

170. Actuarial evidence is widely availed of in personal injury litigation. In *Cooke v Walsh* [1984] ILRM 208 at 216 (SC) Griffin J said:

> "In cases of this kind, the function of an actuary is to ascertain what is the capital sum, payable at the time of the hearing of the action, which is equivalent to a loss of each £1 per week for a specified period, taking into account that the capital sum can be invested and earn interest, the probabilities of the plaintiff surviving that period, and inflation. In taking interest rates into his calculations, he considers the relationship between the rates of interest available and the rate of inflation, ie the rate per cent by which the interest that can be earned exceeds the rate of inflation, or, as it is often called, the real rate of return. His calculations are based on the assumption that both capital and interest will be exhausted at the end of the specified period."

171. *Long v O'Brien & Cronin Ltd* Supreme Court, 24 March 1972, per Walsh J at p 5. See also *Kennedy v East Cork Foods Ltd* [1973] IR 244 at 254 (SC); *Donnelly v Browne* Supreme Court, 15 May 1972, *per* Ó Dálaigh CJ at pp 6-7; *Deegan v Langan* [1966] IR 373 at 378 (SC).

172. [1966] IR 204 at 213 (SC). Lavery J's dissenting judgment is worthy of note. Actuarial evidence may also be addressed in relation to the purchase and use of items of property which the plaintiff will need as a result of his or her injury. See, eg *Hassett v The Minister for Defence*, Supreme Court, 7 December 1999 (hearing aids). An attempt to adduce actuarial evidence from an occupational therapist in relation to the longevity of a lounge chair for a 59-year-old plaintiff was given short shrift by Lavan J in *Walsh v Brown*, DPIJ: Hilary & Easter Terms 1997, p 91 (HC).

173. Supreme Court, 30 July 1963 at pp 6-7. Cited with approval by Kingsmill Moore J, in *Sexton v O'Keeffe* [1966] IR 204 at 212 (SC).

> lower, if the evidence or the inferences to be drawn from the evidence warrant that course: that is to say, the jury may postulate a different set of assumptions and calculate accordingly, guided, of course, by the method or system which has been explained or elaborated by the actuary."

Similarly, Ó Dálaigh J, in *McMorrow v Knott*,[174] stated:

> "Actuarial evidence can furnish guidance to a jury in its deliberations, but it must, as a basis for ascertaining loss, be acted upon with caution. Such evidence has to be re-orientated by reference to the special problems raised by the evidence in the case and other countervailing circumstances, such as the ups and down of life in health and business, have to be allowed for."

In the same case, Maguire CJ, stated that, when considering the actuaral evidence:

> "the jury should have been instructed that while it was open to them to consider these figures they should realise that the figure of expectation of life was an artificial one based on statistics and that they were not bound to accept the figure as unalterable in an individual case. They were, of course, entitled to consider the plaintiff's physical condition at the time of the accident but must take into account the ordinary recognised hazards of life to which he would be subject.
>
> Moreover, they were bound to consider the obvious risks in connection with his practice as a solicitor. It might expand as was suggested but as with any calling depending upon individual effort it might diminish. This was not made as clear to the jury as it should have been."[175]

**[44.97]** The courts have recognised[176] that some allowance should be made in actuarial computations for the fact of inflation. The Supreme Court has, however, frowned[177] on suggestions by trial judges in directions to juries that plaintiffs might be able to safeguard themselves against the drop in the value of money in the future by sound investment in business or property.

**[44.98]** With the abolition of juries in personal injuries litigation, actuarial evidence is availed of by trial judges in the same way as juries used it in these cases. Of course it can be used - by judge or jury - in cases not involving personal injury.

**[44.99]** The recent Supreme Court decision of *Murphy v The Minister for Defence*[178] has sought to give guidance to trial judges as to how they should use actuarial evidence in the context of a deduction that they may be disposed to make in the award for loss of earnings based on the principles stated by Griffin J in *Reddy v Bates.*[179] Barron J (Hamilton CJ and Barron J concurring) explained that *Reddy v Bates* had "sought to deal with a situation whereby it was perceived that juries were not carrying out their function properly in relation to loss of future earnings".[180] This had been particularly so in cases where the

---

174. Supreme Court, 21 December 1959, pp 3-4.

175. Page 2. See also *Meegan v Monaghan County Council*, DPIJ: Hilary & Easter Terms 1998, p 95 at 97 (HC).

176. Eg in *Long v O'Brien* Supreme Court, 24 March 1972; *Donnelly v Browne* Supreme Court, 15 May 1972; *Cook v Walsh* [1984] ILRM 208 (SC). See Fleming (1977) 26 AmJCL 51.

177. *Cf Donnelly v Browne* Supreme Court, 15 May 1972.

178. Supreme Court, 19 July 1999.

179. [1984] ILRM 197 (SC).

180. *Reddy v Bates* [1984] ILRM 197, p 1 of Barron J's judgment.

evidence established that the plaintiff would not work again. What it had been sought to award was that the jury should simply multiply the weekly loss of earnings by the appropriate actuarial figure without at the same time taking into account that the plaintiff might *not* have earned them week by week for the rest of his working life. He or she might have been prevented from doing so by such mishaps as ill-health or an economic downturn.

**[44.100]** Barron J observed:

> "There is nothing novel in this. A plaintiff must prove his case which includes establishing his loss. Of course, the defendant might admit that he would have earned his pre-accident weekly wage together with inflationary increases week-in-week-out for the rest of his working life. However, this might be contested. When it is, then the actual loss must be established by evidence in the ordinary way and the Tribunal of Fact – now usually a judge sitting on his own – must determine the issue…
>
> It is not until these determinations have been made that the application of actuarial evidence becomes appropriate. Such evidence merely enables the Court to determine the value at the date of judgment of losses which will only arise in the future and to which discount must be applied because the loss is made good at the date of the judgment rather than as is arises from week to week or at any other time in the future. There is no relationship between the implementation of the principles of *Reddy v Bates* and the admission of actuarial evidence. It might even be suggested that having regard to the manner in which such evidence is usually given that the trial judge having decided the loss and to what date might then ask to be told the appropriate actuarial figure. This would also avoid misconceived objections to an actuary giving evidence, since it highlights that such evidence is dependent upon findings of fact rather than the reverse."[181]

## Taxation[182]

**[44.101]** Where an injured plaintiff is awarded damages for loss of earnings, should the award take into account the fact that, had he or she actually earned the money, he or she would have had to pay tax on it? Whichever way this simple question is resolved, difficulties arise. In favour of taking into account the tax liability, it has been argued that to fail to do so would overcompensate the plaintiff.[183] Against taking it into account, reference has been made to the enormous difficulties in computing damages[184] which would be created for judges or juries: there is, moreover, a feeling that to permit deduction will give the defendant an unjustifiable windfall.[185]

**[44.102]** The question has led to various judicial responses. In England, the House of Lords in *British Transport Commission v Gourley*[186] has held that allowance should be

---

181. *Reddy v Bates* [1984] ILRM 197, pp 3-4

182. See Hall 'Taxation of Compensation for Loss of Income' (1957) 73 LQR 212; Baxter, 'British Transport Commission v Grouley' (1956) 19 MLR 365; Jolowicz 'Damages and Income Tax' [1959] Camb LJ 86; Lown 'Damages and the Incidence of Tax' (1968) 33 Sask LR 253; Goodhart, Note (1956) 72 LQR 153.

183. *Cf British Transport Commission v Gourley* [1956] AC 185 at 202 (HL Eng), *per* Earl Jowitt.

184. *Cf British Transport Commission v Gourley* [1956] AC 185 at 217-218 (*per* Lord Keith, dissenting).

185. Hall 'Taxation of Compensation for Loss of Income' (1957) 73 LQR 212 at 221. But *cf* SALMOND & HEUSTON, p 534, arguing that the defendant "can hardly be supposed to have selected on purpose a plaintiff who was a large taxpayer".

186. [1956] AC 185 (HL, Eng).

made for liability to taxation. The Supreme Court of Canada, however, has favoured the opposite approach, in *The Queen in Right of Ontario v Jennings*.[187] In Australia, the "allowance" approach ultimately prevailed[188] over the view that no account should be taken of the plaintiff's liability to tax.

**[44.103]** In *Glover v BLN Ltd (No 2)*,[189] Kenny J, in the High Court, was called on to decide what the approach of Irish law should be. Until *Glover's* case, decided in 1968, it had never been the practice of the Irish courts to make a deduction from damages in respect of income tax.[190] *Glover's* case was concerned with an action for wrongful dismissal in respect of which the law provided that awards in excess of £3,000 should be taxable;[191] awards for personal injury, however, were not, and are not, taxable[192] - although, if the proceeds of the award are invested, the interest is subject to tax.[193]

---

187. 57 DLR (2d) 644 (SC, Can 1966).

188. *Cullen v Trappell* (1980) 29 ALRI, not following (*Atlas Tiles v Briers* (1978) 52 ALJR 707. For analysis of *Atlas Tiles*, see LWM 'Damages for Loss of Earnings no Longer Discounted for Tax- The High Court Demolishes Edifice- Gourley's Case' 52 Law Institute J 639 (1978)

189. [1973] IR 432 (HC).

190. *Cf* [1973] IR 432 at 437. See also *Sexton v O'Keeffe* [1966] IR 204 at 211 (SC).

191. Finance Act 1964, ss 8 and 9, and 1st Sch, para 13 (No 15). Where the award is taxable, the problem does not arise: *cf Morahan v Archer* [1957] NI 61 (QB).

192. *Cf* the Law Reform Commission *Report on Personal Injuries: Periodic Payments and Structured Settlements* (1996) LRC 54, para 2.41:

> "For tax purposes compensation awards in personal injuries cases are treated as capital, rather than income, receipts. However, s 24(1)(c) of the Capital Gains Act 1975 expressly excludes damages for loss of earnings recovered in a personal injury award from capital gains tax. Consequently the actual lump sum award itself is not taxed in the hands of the recipient."

193 It should be noted, however, that the Finance Act 1990, s 5 provides that where a plaintiff is permanently and totally incapacitated by reason of physical infirmity from maintaining himself or herself and the income from an investment of a lump sum for personal injuries is the sole or main income of the plaintiff, the income will be exempt from income tax. The inspiration for this provision was the public disquiet regarding taxations of income from the settlement entered into in *Dunne v National Maternity Hospital*. See Byrne & Binchy, *Annual Review of Irish Law 1990*, p 458. In *Allen v Ó Suilleabhain* Supreme Court, 11 March 1997, Murphy J identified a fatal weakness in s 5:

> "clearly this was a very substantial benefit for th[e] particular plaintiff [in *Dunne's* case] but ironically, perhaps, the section confers no benefit on the person whose actions are or were heard after the enactment of the 1990 Act as any award made or compromise negotiated after that date in relation to the type of case to which s 5 applies would take into account the fact that the income to be derived from the award would be exempt from tax and accordingly that the payment of a lesser sum would be sufficient to compensate the plaintiff for the loss which he suffered. One may suspect that the legislature had not fully appreciated that s 5 confers such a substantial benefit on the defendants - assurance companies - without conferring any corresponding benefit on unfortunate plaintiffs other than those whose cases had been disposed of before the enactment of the 1990 Act."

A curious and disturbing dissonance has developed between the approach of the courts towards estimating possible future changes in income tax legislation for the purposes of the *Gourley* deduction, on the one hand, and the judicial attitude towards prospective longevity of taxation policy in relation to income produced by an investment of a damages award on the other. No clear position has emerged as to the former (*cf* the LRC's *Report on Personal Injuries: Periodic Payments and Structured Settlements* (1996) LRC 54, paras 2.43-2.45) but in *Griffiths v Van Raaj* [1985] ILRM 582, the majority of the Supreme Court considered that it was wrong to award compensation on the basis of the existing levels of taxation of investment of damages in Britain, where the plaintiff was living, since these were likely to be reduced.

**[44.104]** After a detailed review of *Gourley*,[194] Kenny J stated:

> "An award of damages by a court is intended to compensate the plaintiff for the loss which he has suffered: in some cases the damages may be punitive but compensation or restoration (so far as money can do it) to the position before the accident is the main element. Therefore, it is irrelevant that the defendant will profit by an allowance being made for tax against the loss. If the damages under £3,000 are not chargeable to tax while the lost remuneration would have been, the plaintiff would be getting an award which would exceed the loss which he had suffered by being deprived of the remuneration. Income tax enters into the economic lives of so many of our citizens that the law cannot ignore it when assessing damages. The estimate of the taxation which the plaintiff would have had to pay on the earnings which he would have got if he had not been injured or if his contract had not been broken must necessarily be inaccurate but in a period of inflation and increasing taxation it will, in most cases, be less than the tax which would have been payable. In personal injury cases the medical witnesses cannot be precise in their prophecies about the effects of the accident but despite this the courts have to give awards to compensate for what are scientific and medical uncertainties. In some cases the calculation of the tax which would have been payable may be difficult and may present great problems to juries, but these are no greater than those created by the daily disagreements between eminent medical witnessesd,"[195]

In Kenny J's opinion, the rule adopted by the majority in *Gourley's* case "accords with reason and principle"[196] and he applied it in the case before him.

**[44.105]** Although *Glover (No 2)* purported to determine the position for personal injuries litigation, the former practice continued for many years and there was a marked tendency among practitioners and the judiciary to make no deduction for income tax.

**[44.106]** The issue was addressed, somewhat summarily, by the Supreme Court in *Cooke v Walsh.*[197] There, the majority reiterated the approach that Kenny J had favoured in *Glover (No 2).* The trial judge had multiplied the entirety of the rate of wages lost by the plaintiff by the full multiplier, without any deductions for tax. Griffin J[198] considered this approach to be incorrect:

> "as it is the 'take home pay' and not the gross pay that should have been used as the multiplicand. Had the plaintiff been uninjured, he would have to pay income tax on the wages he would earn, and PRSI and other deductions would be made from his wages, and therefore the sum that would be available to him to spend would be considerably less than [the gross amount]."[199]

---

193. (contd) McCarthy J dissented on this issue, being of the view that it would be wrong for the court to come to such a consideration in the absence of specific evidence. See further the LRC *Report on Personal Injuries: Periodic Payments and Structured Settlements* (LRC 54-1996), paras 2.47ff.
194. [1956] AC 185 (HL, Eng).
195. [1973] IR at 441-442.
196. [1973] IR at 441 at 442. See also *Irish Leisure Industries Ltd v Gaiety Theatre Enterprises Ltd* High Court, 12 February 1975 (O'Higgins CJ).
197. [1984] ILRM 208 (SC).
198. O'Higgins CJ, Henchy and Hederman JJ concurring; McCarthy J dissenting.
199. [1984] ILRM 208 at 217.

McCarthy J, while "recognis[ing] the force of these comments",[200] was not disposed to address an argument on this issue, since it had been raised neither at trial, nor in the grounds of appeal, nor in the argument before the Court.[201]

## Hospital Expenses and "Carer" Costs

**[44.107]** An injured plaintiff is entitled to recover all expenses reasonably incurred (or to be incurred) in respect of his or her medical care.[202] These will include hospital expenses.[203] The better view appears to be that a plaintiff who is eligible to receive free treatment and care under the Health Act 1970 is not obliged to avail himself or herself of free services under pain of being held otherwise to have unreasonably failed to mitigate damages.[204] As Dr White observes:

> "Compelling the victims of accidents wrongfully occasioned to take advantage of such eligibility would result in unfair discrimination between plaintiffs and constitute an unwarranted restriction on individual freedom of choice." [205]

**[44.108]** Section 2 of the Health (Amendment) Act 1986, in essence, shifts onto defendants the cost of medical treatment in respect of road accident injuries, by requiring Health Boards to charge the victims for services they would otherwise have recovered free of charge, enabling the victims to recover from the defendants – in reality, their insurers – the cost of these services.[206]

---

200. [1984] ILRM 208 at 221.

201. In appropriate cases, discovery of all documents in respect of the plaintiff's income tax returns for relevant years may be ordered on application by the defendant. In *Fields v Woodland Products Ltd* Supreme Court, 16 July 1999 (*ex temp*), Keane J (Murphy and Barron JJ concurring) stated at p 5 of his judgment:

> "I understand and I am sure everyone perfectly understands that income tax matters are undoubtedly confidential to the tax payer and the Revenue. But when the parties come to litigate, the situation changes to that extent. The other party, if the tax returns relate to an issue in the proceedings and are in that sense relevant to the proceedings, is clearly entitled to inspect them and make what use is appropriate from his point of view in his defence of the proceedings but for no other purpose."

In computing damages questions can arise as to how to deal with situations where the injured (or deceased) party's tax returns may not have been accurate: see *Fitzpatrick v Furey*, High Court, 12 June 1998 (Laffoy J), discussed at paras **[42.29]** above.

202. The precise dividing line between expense to meet the physical consequences of disability and expenses incurred in attempting to mitigate the loss of enjoyment to life may be difficult to draw in some instances: see, eg *Jeffers v Cahill* High Court, 21 May 1996; *Hassett v The Minister for Defence* Supreme Court, 7 December 1999.

203. See White, *Irish Law of Damages for Personal Injuries and Death* (1989) paras 5.3.02ff; English Law Commission, Consultation Paper 144, *Damages for Personal Injury: Medical, Nursing and Other Expenses* (1996) Appendix A17-A21

204. Civil Liability Act 1961, s 34(2)(b).

205. White, *Irish Law of Damages for Personal Injuries And Death* (1989), para 5.2.01. *Cf Ward v Walsh* Supreme Court, 31 July 1991, critically analysed by Byrne & Binchy, *Annual Review of Irish Law 1991*, pp 443-444.

206. See in White, *Irish Law of Damages for Personal Injuries And Death* (1989), para 5.6.07. Section 2(1) provides laconically that the health board shall "make a charge" upon the person who received or is entitled to receive the damages "in respect of the said in-patient services or out-patient services". In *Crilly v T & J Farrington Ltd* [2000] 1 ILRM 548 (HC), Geoghegan J interpreted the subsection as envisaging "a reasonable charge in the *quantum meriut* sense. "In so far as a plaintiff might receive treatment within a particular speciality (such as orthopaedic services, for example), some averaging within that speciality would be acceptable in arriving at the charge.

**[44.109]** The spouse or parents of an injured victim of a tort can claim compensation for loss of consortium[207] or loss of services[208] as the case may be, in respect of, *inter alia*, the medical expenses that they incur in relation to the victim.

**[44.110]** Very often the spouse, parents or other close relations or friends will take on the task of caring for the injured plaintiff on an ongoing basis. If they do so, will the defendant be able to argue that, since the plaintiff is not in fact out of pocket for these gratuitous services, he or she should not be compensated for a loss that has not been sustained? In *Doherty v Bowaters Irish Wallboard Mills Ltd*,[209] the Supreme Court answered robustly in the negative. Walsh J noted that the jury had been told that they should give consideration to the fact that the plaintiff's parents, for much of the remainder of their lives, were likely to continue to perform tasks of personal attention for the plaintiff if he continued to live with them. In Walsh J's view, this was:

> "a factor which should not affect compensation. It is certain that the plaintiff will require attention. If he continues to live with his parents, the fact that his parents, even if able to provide the attention by their own efforts, might be willing to do so is entirely a chance, though it may well be a happy chance for the plaintiff; but even if such a contingency is in the realms of probability for the limited period of the lifetimes of the parents, it does not follow that the plaintiff ought not to, or might not, reimburse them or remunerate them to the same extent as he would in the case of other attendants. Furthermore, while it might appear that the prospects of going through with the contemplated marriage is no longer a practical possibility in the case of the plaintiff, it cannot be entirely ruled out and in that event also it would not be proper to give any weight to the consideration that a wife might add to her burdens by undertaking the type of attention which is required, even if she was able to do so."[210]

---

207. See paras **[33.04]-[33.23]** above. The most recent decision in which the issue of damages was analysed in an action for loss of consortium is *McKinley v The Minister for Defence (No 2)* [1997] 2 IR 176 (HC).

208. See paras **[33.36]-[33.39]** above.

209. [1968] IR 277.

210. [1968] IR 277 at 286. See also *Cooke v Walsh* [1984] ILRM 208 (SC), where, as White, *Irish Law of Damages for Personal Injuries And Death* (1989), (para 5.6.05) notes, the majority did not deny the propriety of the trial judge's making an award to the plaintiff to compensate the plaintiff's mother for the care and attention she would give him in her home. In *Coppinger v Waterford County Council*, DPIJ: Hilary & Easter Terms 1996, p 1 (HC), Geoghegan J awarded £10,000 to the plaintiff for "care costs" sustained before trial, "being considered a reasonable sum to attribute to the therapeutic as distinct from merely social effect of Mrs Coppinger's visits to the hospital." In *Shields v Boyle* DPIJ: Michaelmas Term 1991, p 88 (HC), where the plaintiff at the time of the accident was a 34-year-old mother of nine children, O'Hanlon J stated (at p 93):

    > "Although no formal agreement was established for payment to her mother for her constant help in keeping the plaintiff's household going since the accident, I take the view that it is permissible to award a sum for services rendered in mitigation of the loss and damage caused by the accident and I allow a sum of £40 per week for 167 weeks..."

    In his statement of the overall figures awarded, O'Hanlon J (at p 94) itemised this particular amount as "Payment to plaintiff's mother". Since he also itemised "Future payment for domestic help", it seems clear that he intended that the award should be made to the plaintiff herself. As to the mother's possible legal entitlement to the sum thus awarded, the judgment is silent. In *Noonan v O'Leary* DPIJ: Hilary & Easter Terms 1991, p 127 (HC), no award was made for baby-sitting services provided by the plaintiff's sister for the plaintiff. Morris J stated (at pp 131-132):

    > "I do not accept that the baby-sitting expenses claimed by [the plaintiff] were something which the plaintiff was required to pay. I believe that her sister, insofar as she helped, did so on a voluntary basis, not as a contract..."

Clearly, wider issues are at stake. If the plaintiff is awarded compensation for "carer" costs gratuitously given, is he or she free to do with it what he or she wishes or does some form of trust[211] or restitutionary[212] claim arise in favour of the gratuitous care-giver? This matter has been much debated in other common law jurisdictions.

**[44.111]** In Ireland, some judges[213] in recent years have been willing to make an award *directly* in favour of the carer-spouse (or other caring relations or friends) rather than

211. In England, in *Cunningham v Harrison* [1973] QB 942 the Court of Appeal held that the injured plaintiff held the compensation in trust for the carer. One day later, in *Donnelly v Joyce* [1974] QB 454, the same court, differently constituted, held that the money was not impressed with such a trust. In *Hunt v Severs* [1994] 2 AC 350, in a highly controversial decision, the House of Lords revived *Cunningham's* trust-based rationale when holding that no compensation should be awarded where the defendant provided the gratuitous services for the plaintiff. To allow such compensation would involve the defendant paying the plaintiff compensation for what was the defendant's own loss. Their Lordships showed no interest in recognising the reality that (in road traffic accidents at least) the defendant's insurance company would be paying the bill. Lord Bridge considered that acceptance of the argument that this factor justified the making of an award in such circumstances:

> "would represent a novel and radical departure in the law of a kind which only the legislative may properly effect. At common law the circumstance that a defendant is contractually indemnified by a third party against a particular liability can have no relevance whatever to the measure of that liability..."

*Hunt v Severs* has provoked a wealth of (largely critical) commentary. See Matthews and Lunney, 'A Tortfeasor's Lot is not a Happy One' (1995) 58 MLR 395; Kemp, 'Voluntary Services Provided by Tortfeasor to his Victim' (1994) 110 LQR 524; Reed, 'A Commentary on *Hunt v Severs*' (1995) 15 Oxford J of Legal Studies 133. The High Court of Australia has rejected the approach favoured in *Hunt v Severs*: see *Kars v Kars* (1996) 141 ALR 37; TRINDADE & CANE, p 523

212. In *Hughes v O'Flaherty* High Court, 19 January 1996, where the plaintiff sustained devastating injuries in a car accident, his wife, a professionally qualified nurse, cared for him. Carney J awarded the plaintiff £35,000 to compensate him for this service, even though he was satisfied that payment was not in the wife's mind when she devoted herself to nursing the plaintiff. Carney J "balanced" her role as a professional in respect of which she was "in the absence of any express contractual agreement entitled to payment on a *quantum meruit* basis" and "her role as a loving and devoted wife in respect of which she is not under our social and legal system entitled to payment". Carney J rejected a similar claim by the plaintiff's son, who took a year off work to mind his father because he was "acting primarily as a devoted son", without the professional qualification that his mother had. See also *Fahy v Dwan* DPIJ: Hilary & Easter Terms 1997, p 71 (HC), where McCracken J awarded, as damages payable to the plaintiff, "an element for what undoubtedly was a lot of assistance which she got from relatives which would have had to be paid for if it came f[rom] anyone else..." at p 74. McCracken J noted that the plaintiff in evidence had said that she would give presents to those who had helped her; nothing in his judgment expressly required the plaintiff to give them the money awarded to her under this heading, however.

213. Eg *Smith v Ireland* High Court, 16 August 1996 (Flood J). In *Conroy v McCormack*, DPIJ: Trinity Term 1991, p 14 (HC), where a bachelor farmer who lived alone on an eight-acre farm in a remote part of Connemara was injured, Barr J awarded £1,500 for a family (who appear to have been neighbours) who were "entitled to be compensated for the work they have done for the plaintiff", as well as £500 for expenses incurred by the plaintiff's sister in coming home from abroad to nurse him. Barr J noted that "she was due to return home on holidays in any event that year so she is not entitled to the entire costs of her visit". Barr J characterised these sums as special damages, consisting of "compensation" for the family and the sister. The total amount of damages awarded to the plaintiff was reduced by $33^{1}/3$% to take account of his contributory negligence. While clearly the award of these sums was to the plaintiff rather than the family or the sister, there was no reference to the legal basis on which the plaintiff received them nor was it clarified whether the amount to which they were entitled (if, indeed any legal entitlement was created by the award) was proportionately reduced by one-third.

resorting to a trust or restitutionary characterisation. How such a strategy can be rationalised judicially is not entirely clear though it obviously harmonises with common-sense intuitions of what is fair. The claim could perhaps be characterised as one sounding in negligence; if it is regarded as involving pure economic loss, that should not be particularly problematic since the levels of proximity and foreseeability are high.[214] A more convincing rationalisation is that what is involved is a judicial extension of the old actions for damage to the family in accordance with the recommendations of the Law Reform Commission[215] two decades ago. Whatever explanation may be preferred, the mystery remains as to how an award may be made in favour of a person who is not a party to the litigation.

## Collateral Benefits[216]

**[44.112]** Since the purpose of awarding damages is to compensate the plaintiff for the loss that he or she has sustained, it might be thought that the courts would have no difficulty in declining to award damages for a part of the claim in respect of which the plaintiff is not in fact out of pocket. Matters are not that easy, however. The plaintiff may, for example, have had the foresight to insure against the loss in question. Why, it may be asked, should the plaintiff's financial responsibility reduce the amount that the tortfeasor has to pay? Similarly, the plaintiff may have been in receipt of the proceeds of a charitable collection after some tragedy, such as a house fire, attributable to the defendant's wrong. Again, there may be some degree of revulsion at the defendant's benefiting from the public's generosity.

**[44.113]** It is possible, however, to envisage cases where the degree of revulsion is less intense. The insurance may have been taken out by the plaintiff's employer rather than the plaintiff himself or herself. Although the plaintiff may be considered to have indirectly purchased this entitlement in the sense that his or her salary level will reflect the costs of such "perk" to the employer, the argument for non-deduction based on the plaintiff's thrift

---

214. *Cf McShane Wholesale Fruit and Vegetables Ltd v Johnston Haulage Co Ltd* [1997] 1 ILRM 86 (HC).

215. *Cf* the LRC's *First Report on Family Law* (LRC 1-1981).

216. This subject is comprehensively analysed by the Law Reform Commission in its *Consultation Paper on Section 2 of the Civil Liability (Amendment) Act 1964: The Deductibility of Collateral Benefits from Awards of Damages* (1999). See also the English Law Commission's Consultation Paper No 147: *Damages for Personal Injury: Collateral Benefits* (1997) and its report *Damages for Personal Injury: Collateral Benefits* (1997) and also its report *Damages for Personal Injury Medical, Nursing and Other Expenses; Collateral Benefits* (1999) LC 262). See also Kerr, *The Civil Liability Acts* (1999), pp 64-65, 79-83; Fleming 'Collateral Source Rule and Loss Allocation in Tort Law' (1966) 54 Calif LR 1478; Atiyah, *Collateral Benefits Again* (1969) 32 MLR 397; Luntz 'The Collateral Source Rule Thirty Years On', Ch 15 of Cane & Stapleton eds, *The Law of Obligations: Essays in Celebration of John Fleming* (1998); Sedler 'The Collateral Source Rule and Personal Injury Damages: The Irrelevant Principle and the Functional Approach' (1961) 58 Ky LJ 36; Lambert 'The Case for the Collateral Source Rule' [1966] Ins LJ 531; Auerbach, *The Collateral Source Rule* (1960) 21 Ohio St LJ 231; West 'The Collateral Source Rule Sans Subrogation: A Plaintiff's Windfall' (1963) 16 Okla LR 395; Anon 'Note: The Mitigating Effect of Damages on Social Welfare Programs' (1949) 63 Harv LR 330; Anon 'Note: Unreason in the Law of Damages: The Collateral Source Rule' [1966] Ins LJ 545; Maxwell 'The Collateral Source Rule in American Law of Damages' (1961) 46 Minn LR 669; Schwartz 'The Collateral Source Rule' (1961) 41 Boston ULR 348; Clark 'Damages and the Social Welfare "Overlap"', (1984) 19 Ir Jur (ns) 40.

is not so strong. Similarly, where the plaintiff is the recipient of a social welfare payment rather than a charitable benefaction, concerns about chilling philanthropy are eased; moreover, since the payment is the plaintiff's legal entitlement, it is hard to see how he or she can argue that he or she has suffered a financial loss to the extent of its value.

**[44.114]** This aspect of the law of damages is generally characterised as that of collateral benefits. While courts in common law jurisdictions have proceeded largely on judicial intuitions of when it is fair to ignore a benefit in calculating damages, some attempts at rationalisation have been offered.[217] One approach is to adopt a causal analysis and characterise the accident as the occasion rather than the cause of the payment.[218] This has an air of artificiality, however, and has largely been abandoned in recent years.[219] Another, more convincing, line of thought is to concentrate on the *source* of the benefit. As the Law Reform Commission notes:

> "[t]he essence of this rationale is that, as the plaintiff has either financed, or earned, the collateral payment, he should not be deprived of the fruits of his own thrift and foresight. Furthermore, it could be argued that the plaintiff had a reasonable expectation of receiving the collateral payment in addition to his damages."[220]

The approach also has its limitations.[221] It does not explain why there should be no deduction of charitable payments received from a third party. Moreover, thrift on the part of the plaintiff may be entirely lacking: the insurance policy may have been financed by a third party or may have been effectively imposed on the plaintiff as the price of a particular commercial transaction, such as a holiday package.

**[44.115]** A third rationale concentrates on the *purpose* of the benefit:[222] if that purpose, express or implied, was to provide the plaintiff with assistance *in addition* to any claim that he or she may have had against the tortfeasor, then it should not be deducted. This approach explains fairly convincingly why payments under insurance policies or charitable contributions should not be deducted. There can, however, be difficulties in ascertaining the intention of the collateral benefit provider and some critics have argued that the crucial question is the effect of the benefit rather than the purpose of the provider.

**[44.116]** In Ireland, the position has largely been dealt with by statute but there remains some aspects of the subject that are dealt with exclusively under common law principles.

**[44.117]** The starting point of our analysis has to be s 2 of the Civil Liability (Amendment) Act 1964, which provides as follows:

> In assessing damages in an action to recover damages in respect of a wrongful act (including a crime) resulting in personal injury not causing death, account shall not be taken of –

---

217. For a penetrating critical analysis of the several competing rationales, see the LRC's *Consultation Paper on Section 2 of the Civil Liability (Amendment) Act 1964: The Deductibility of Collateral Benefits from Awards of Damages*, Ch 3 (August 1999)

218. *National Insurance Co of New Zealand Ltd v Espagne* 105 Comm LR 569 at 580 (HC, Austr). See also *Payne v Railway Executive* [1952] 1 KB 26 at 36 (CA).

219. *Cf Parry v Cleaver* [1970] AC 1 (HL, Eng).

220. White, *Irish Law of Damages for Personal Injuries and Death* (1989), para 3.21.

221. *Cf* White, *Irish Law of Damages for Personal Injuries and Death* (1989), paras 3.22-3.27.

222. *Cf* White, *Irish Law of Damages for Personal Injuries and Death* (1989), 3.28-3.31; *National Insurance Co of New Zealand Ltd v Espagne* 105 Comm LR 569.

(a) any sum payable in respect of the injury under any contract or insurance,

(b) any pension, gratuity or other like benefit payable under statute or otherwise in consequence of the injury.[223]

**[44.118]** A similar provision applies to wrongful death actions, this was provided for in s 50 of the Civil Liability Act 1961[224] which had not extended to actions for personal injury because it was believed that already under the common law there was an established principle of non-deduction for non-fatal cases.[225] A dark shadow of uncertainty was shortly afterwards cast on this assumption by a couple of English decisions[226] so the opportunity was taken in the amending legislation of 1964 to clarify expressly what had been the original intent.

**[44.119]** A number of questions regarding s 2 must be considered. The first concerns the relationship between the section and the earlier position at common law. Is the section to be construed as an exhaustive replacement of the common law rules or does it merely address certain particular kinds of benefits, leaving unchanged the earlier common law rules regarding other kinds of benefits? Dr White favours the latter interpretation[227] of the rule of non-deduction prescribed by s 2 as being probably only applicable to money payments, leaving the question of the deductibility of benefits in kind to continue to be determined by common law. Another possible interpretation is that the section provides an exhaustive list of instances on non-deductibility and that, albeit somewhat infelicitously,[228] embraces non-monetary benefits as well as money payments. It is hardly the case under the identically – drafted s 50 of the 1961 Act that a non-monetary benefit – let us say a house given by way of charitable benefaction to the widow and children of a man who died in a fire – should have to be deducted from the defendants' claim by reason of the fact that the benefaction does not consist of a monetary payment. The courts, when interpreting s 50, clearly have no common law to fall back on since fatal accident claims are the creature of legislation.[229] If s 50 represents an exhaustive list of non-deductible benefits, there is a strong argument that s 2 of the 1964 Act should similarly be interpreted. The fact that s 2 was enacted to resolve the confusion as to the common law position is a further reason for adopting this interpretation. The idea that s 2 requires the court to address and resolve this confusion with respect to benefits not specifically mentioned in the section is one that understandably may not prove attractive to the court.

223. See White, *Irish Law of Damages for Personal Injuries And Death* (1989), paras 4.10.05ff; Kerr, *The Civil Liability Acts* (1999), pp 79-83

224. See para **[42.40]** above. White, *Irish Law of Damages for Personal Injuries and Death* (1989), paras 9.4.03ff; Kerr, *The Civil Liability Acts* (1999), pp 64-65.

225. See the LRC's *Consultation Paper on Section 2 of the Civil Liability (Amendment) Act 1964: The Deductibility of Collateral Benefits from Awards of Damages* (1999) LRC, para 7.08.

226. *Browning v The War Office* [1963] 1 QB 750; *Parsons v BNB Laboratories Ltd* [1964] 1 QB 95. *Cf Greene v Hughes Haulage Ltd* [1998] 1 ILRM 34 (HC).

227. *Cf* White, *Irish Law of Damages for Personal Injuries And Death* (1989), paras 4.10.04, 4.10.14.

228. White, *Irish Law of Damages for Personal Injuries And Death* (1989), para 4.10.05.

229. Whilst the most convincing interpretation is that "payable" qualifies *all* benefits envisaged by the section perhaps the words "payable under statute" could be isolated from "otherwise" so as not to have the word "otherwise" qualify "payable". On that basis a benefit not involving payment could be regarded as an "other like benefit … otherwise in consequence of the injury".

**[44.120]** A second feature of s 2 is that the court is required not to take account of any sum "payable in respect of the injury under any contract of insurance".[230] Thus, clearly, if the sum is paid for some reason other than in respect of the injury, though happening to coincide with its occurrence, it does not come within the scope of the section.[231]

**[44.121]** In *Greene v Hughes Haulage Ltd*,[232] the question arose as to whether the fact that the injured plaintiff was not himself or herself a party to the insurance contract should render the section inapplicable, thus leading to the deduction of the payment made under the contract. Geoghegan J was satisfied that it should not. It was well established[233] in respect of fatal accident claims that the principle of non-deductibility applied in such circumstances. Since it appeared that the purpose of s 2 was to harmonise the law in fatal accidents and personal injuries litigation in this context, Geoghegan J saw no reason why the broad interpretation which had always been given to the expression "under any contract of insurance" in the fatal accident cases should not also be applied to personal injury accidents. He stressed, however, that this did not mean that a simple indemnity policy identifying an employer against some contractual undertaking by it to continue making salary payments to an employee would had become uncaputated would come within s 2. Hamilton P's ruling in *Dennehy v Nordic Cold Storage*[234] could be distinguished on this ground.

**[44.122]** Geoghegan J went on to make it clear that, whilst it was arguably "an anomalous injustice"[235] that no deduction should be made from insurance payments where the defendant was himself the employer since in this case there is no third party claiming advantage from the plaintiff's own insurance benefits, the interpretation of the words of the section could not be governed by such considerations:

> "In most cases the benefit policy will form part of the total remuneration and the employee will therefore be indirectly contributing to the premiums. In other cases it may be possible to imply a term permitting deductibility in the context of employment."[236]

The next point worth noting about s 2 is that its reference to "gratuities" embraces voluntary payments, even where these are repayable in the event of the litigation proving successful, and charitable donations.

---

230. *Cf Fitzpatrick v Modular Cold Stores Manufacturing Co Ltd* DPIJ: Trinity & Michaelmas Terms 1996, p 240 (HC) - payment on foot of income continuance policy which plaintiff had with Lloyd's not deducted.
231. *Cf Fortune v AT Cross Ltd* DPIJ: Trinity & Michaelmas Terms 1996, p 78 (HC) - *ex gratia* payment in consequence of company rationalisation of plaintiff's employment not deductible, as her entitlement to such payment did not in any sense accrue in consequence of her injury.
232. [1998] 1 ILRM 34 (HC). See further LRC's *Consultation Paper on Section 2 of the Civil Liability (Amendment) Act 1964: The Deductibility of Collateral Benefits from Awards of Damages* (1999) LRC, paras 7.17-7.32.
233. Kerr, *The Civil Liability Acts* (1999), pp 79-80.
234. High Court, 8 May 1991.
235. [1998] 1 ILRM 34 at 44.
236. [1998] 1 ILRM 34 at 44.

**[44.123]** In *McElroy v Aldritt*,[237] the plaintiff gave evidence that his employers had continued to pay his wages after the accident on an arrangement that, if he succeeded in the proceedings against the defendant, he would repay the amount paid. The trial judge refused to direct that, on this account, the plaintiff had suffered no loss of earnings.

**[44.124]** The Supreme Court held that the trial judge had acted correctly. Lavery J, speaking for the Court, stated:

> "It is impossible for the defendant as the wrongdoer to mitigate the damages for which he is responsible by relying on voluntary payments made by a third person to provide for the support of the plaintiff on an arrangement that he should be recouped if and when the plaintiff was in a position to do so and it can make no difference that that person was the employer of the plaintiff."

**[44.125]** The principles articulated in *McElroy v Aldritt* have been reiterated in subsequent decisions, the most recent of which is *Hogan v Steele & Co Ltd.*[238] In that case the plaintiff, an employee of the Electricity Supply Board, had received payments from his employer, on a discretionary basis, as a person absent on sick leave due to an accident in which a third party was involved. He had undertaken to refund to his employers the amount so advanced out of any damages he might receive in compensation from the third party. The arrangement followed from a "Comprehensive Agreement" negotiated between the employers and the employees' trade unions. Macken J, holding that the sums advanced should not be deducted from the damages awarded against the defendant, stressed the fact that he had no automatic entitlement to the payments, which was:

> "no more than the sum which, absent the notice party exercising a discretion to pay, and paying, would or could have been borrowed by the plaintiff from a local bank or his credit union. Such borrowings, so long as they were reasonably incurred, would undoubtedly be payable by the defendant to the plaintiff as part of the plaintiff's special damages."[239]

It has to be acknowledged that the difference between an arrangement such as this and the simple provision of sick-pay by an employer is one, not of substance, but of relative levels of prudence and legal sophistication on the part of employers.

**[44.126]** Where the public voluntarily subscribe to a fund for the relief of distress following upon an accident, payments made under the fund will not be deducted from the damages awarded. This was held by the Kings' Bench Division in Northern Ireland, in

---

237. Supreme Court, 11 June 1955. In *Murphy v Cronin* [1966] IR 699 (SC), a fatal injuries case, the deceased had not reached superannuation age but, by the rules of the superannuation fund of which he was a member, a sum equal to his accumulated contributions to the fund, with interest, was payable to his personal representative and a sum equal to 25% of these contributions was payable to his widow (the plaintiff). The Supreme Court held that the latter sum was a "gratuity" within the meaning of s 50 and that the sum payable to the personal representative was a "like benefit", and that accordingly neither sum should be taken into account in assessing damages.

238. [2000] 1 ILRM 330 (HC). See also *Honan v Syntex (Ireland) Ltd* DPIJ: Michaelmas Term 1990, p 272 (HC); *Boyce v Cawley* DPIJ: Michaelmas Term 1991, p 144 (HC) and *McGuinness v O'Reilly* High Court, 30 November 1992 (Morris J), all discussed by Macken J in *Hogan v Steele & Co Ltd* [2000] 1 ILRM 330.

239. [2000] 1 ILRM 330 at 343.

*Redpath v Belfast & County Down Railway*,[240] where a fund had been established in Bangor after a train collision in which several passengers had been killed.

**[44.127]** Section 2(b) requires the court to ignore "any pension" that is payable in consequence of the injury when assessing the plaintiff's damages.[241] The Law Reform Commission explains some of the practical implications clearly:

> "Where an injured plaintiff had contracted to receive a retirement pension at the age of 65 years and because of injuries sustained he take ill health early retirement at the age of 55 years, only the payments over the ten years are in consequence of the injury and thus fall within s 2. After age 65 of the pension payments are no longer collateral benefits, as a person would have been payable even if the accident had not occurred. However, if those payments are less due to the accumulation of less years of service, then a loss is also suffered in the amount of the difference."[242]

**[44.128]** Social welfare payments of all kinds appear capable of being characterised as "benefits" for the purposes of s 2.[243] Of course, before s 2 applies to them they must have been payable in consequence of the injury. Thus payments that are payable in consequence, other, possibly broader causes, such as indigenecy that is not attributable to the injury, will not come within the scope of s 2.[244]

**[44.129]** Where an employee receives "sick-pay", pursuant to the terms of his or her employment contract it seems that this should be regarded as, in essence, part of the employee's earnings. In computing the plaintiff's damages, the court therefore should not treat the plaintiff as having suffered a loss to the extent of the sick-pay and should not treat this sum as a "benefit payable … in consequence of the injury" for the purposes of s 2 of

---

240. [1947] NI 167 (KBD).

241. *Sturdy v Dublin Corporation*, DPIJ: Michaelmas Term 1991, p 21 (HC); *cf Murphy v Cronin* [1966] IR 699 (SC).

242. See the LRC's *Consultation Paper on Section 2 of the Civil Liability (Amendment) Act 1964: The Deductibility of Collateral Benefits from Awards of Damages*, (1999) LRC, para 7.40.

243. See *State (Hayes) v The Criminal Injuries Compensation Tribunal* [1982] ILRM 210 (HC); the LRC's *Consultation Paper on Section 2 of the Civil Liability (Amendment) Act 1964: The Deductibility of Collateral Benefits from Awards of Damages*, (1999) LRC, paras 7.57ff.

244. *Cf* the Law Reform Commission's *Consultation Paper on Section 2 of the Civil Liability (Amendment) Act 1964: The Deductibility of Collateral Benefits from Awards of Damages*, paras 7.61-7.62; Clark 'Damages and the Social Welfare 'Overlap'', (1984) 19 Ir Jur (ns) 40; *Ryan v Compensation Tribunal* [1997] 1 ILRM 194 (HC). In *Kiely v Carrig* DPIJ: Trinity & Michaelmas Terms 1996, p 209 (HC), the plaintiff received unemployment assistance as opposed to the normal unemployment benefit as, during a period of self-employment before the accident, he had ceased to pay PRSI contributions and therefore lost his entitlement to that benefit. Barr J was satisfied that, if the accident had not happened, the plaintiff would probably have found employment shortly afterwards and the question of claiming any social welfare benefit would not have arisen. Barr J observed (at p 212):

> "It follows therefore that, within the meaning of section 2(b) of the 1964 Act, the weekly unemployment assistance received by the plaintiff was a benefit 'payable in consequence of the injury' sustained by him in the accident and accordingly ought not to be taken into account in assessing his loss of earnings to date".

The import of this analysis is that, where a plaintiff, because of the injury, *continues* to receive a benefit payable otherwise than in consequence of the injury, that payment should be recharacterised as being consequential upon the injury at all events from the time the continuance of the payment is attributable to the injury.

the 1964 Act.[245] In *Hogan v Steele & Co Ltd*,[246] Macken J noted that the policy underlying this analysis appeared to be that:

> "where, by the contract of employment, the employee is legally entitled to pay without any agreement to reimburse his employer, no loss could arise to him at all, and therefore, no recoverable loss could exist against the wrongdoer. The payment is, in reality, an unconditional payment, contractually earned and legally vesting in the employee."

**[44.130]** Let us now turn to consider two important statutory provisions which have the effect of reducing significantly some of the advantages that s 2 of the 1964 Act gives to plaintiffs.

**[44.131]** The first of these provisions is s 75(1) of the Social Welfare (Consolidation) Act 1993, which states that, not withstanding s 2 of the 1964 Act (or s 236 of the 1993 Act), in an action for personal injuries[247] there shall in assessing damages be taken into account, against any loss of earnings or profits that has accrued or probably will accrue to the injured person from the injuries, the value of any rights that have accrued or will probably accrue to the injured person therefrom in respect of injury benefit[248] or disablement benefit[249] for the five years beginning with the time when the cause of action accrued. Injury benefit is a weekly benefit payable where a person is unfit for work on account of an accident at work or an occupational disease.[250] Disablement benefit is payable to a person who suffers a loss of physical or mental faculty as a result of an occupational injury or disease while in insurable employment.[251]

**[44.132]** In *O'Sullivan v Iarnród Éireann*,[252] where the plaintiff had received serious personal injuries to his back, the defendant submitted that deductions fell to be made under s 75(1). Counsel for the plaintiff argued that there was no evidence before the court as to what might happen to disablement benefit into the future, on the conclusion of the litigation, and therefore the most that should be taken into account was the amount of benefits that had accrued to date. Morris J rejected this approach. He noted that the plaintiff was then in receipt of disablement benefits and had been so since his occupational injury benefit had run out four years previously. He was not aware of an indication of any intention of the part of the Department of Social Welfare to alter this status. During the course of the evidence, reference had been made to the rule of the Department as to the

---

245. See *Sturdy v Dublin Corporation*, DPIJ: Michaelmas Term 1991, p 21 (HC), explaining *Honan v Syntex Ireland Ltd* DPIJ: Michaelmas Term 1990, p 272 (HC). See further the LRC's *Consultation Paper on Section 2 of the Civil Liability (Amendment) Act 1964: The Deductibility of Collateral Benefits from Awards of Damages*, paras 4.10.09 -4.10.11.

246. [2000] 1 ILRM 330 at 337-338 (HC).

247. Including any such action arising out of a contract.

248. Disregarding any right in respect of injury benefit payable by virtue of Social Welfare (Consolidation) Act 1993, s 210, after the death of the injured person.

249. Disregarding any increase of it under s 57 in respect of constant attendance.

250. LRC's *Consultation Paper on Section 2 of the Civil Liability (Amendment) Act 1964: The Deductibility of Collateral Benefits from Awards of Damages* (1999), p 97, citing the *Guide to Social Welfare Services*, S W 4 (1998), p 124.

251. LRC's *Consultation Paper on Section 2 of the Civil Liability (Amendment) Act 1964: The Deductibility of Collateral Benefits from Awards of Damages* citing the *Guide*, p 126.

252. High Court, 14 March 1994 (Morris J).

plaintiff's disability and incapacity to work. In Morris J's view, the onus, in the circumstances of the case, lay on the plaintiff to show that there was in the Department's contemplation an intention to alter the *status quo*.

**[44.133]** Section 237(1) of the 1993 Act provides that, notwithstanding s 2 of the 1964 Act, and s 236 of the 1993 Act itself, in assessing damages in any action in respect of liability for personal injuries not causing death relating to the use of a mechanically propelled vehicle, there shall be taken into account:

> the value of any rights arising from such injuries which have accrued, or are likely to accrue, to the injured person in respect of disability benefit[253] … or invalidity pension under Part II [of the Act] for the period of five years beginning with the time when the cause of action accrued.[254]

**[44.134]** In *O'Loughlin v Teeling*,[255] McKenzie J expressed strong disapproval of this legislative policy. Referring to the Act whose provisions were repeated in the 1993 consolidating Act, he said that it appeared to him to be:

> "such a dramatic and unfair piece of legislation as to be contrary to natural justice ... [I]t ... appear[s] to me basically unfair that a man getting damages for pain and suffering he underwent should have those damages reduced substantially if not entirely eliminated by reason of benefits paid to him, which partly he was entitled to because of the money he himself ... paid into the Social Welfare Department, and his employer's money. Why should the insurance company take advantage of those payments. A man who gets disability or disablement is in fact getting his own money back; it strikes me as grossly unfair and to a degree contrary to natural justice to attach the money he is getting for suffering in that manner".

**[44.135]** In the case before him, the plaintiff had conceded that the disability payment which he had *already* received ought to be taken into account. The only question therefore said McKenzie J was whether the sum of £5,000 he had been awarded by the jury for future loss of earnings should be attached by reason of the fact that, if he continued to receive Social Welfare benefits of a disability character, he would accumulate from the Department a sum well in excess of that amount so as to eliminate it altogether. In fact, as McKenzie J recognised earlier in his judgment, the deduction could attach not merely to the part of the jury award for loss of earnings but also the part for pain and suffering, which in this case amounted to £7,500 for pain and suffering to date and £6,000 for future pain and suffering.

**[44.136]** Taking what appears to be a benevolent view of the jury award, McKenzie J considered it plain that they had accepted the consensus of medical evidence in the case to the effect that the plaintiff was fit for light work and that if motivated in a certain way he would resume his pre-accident work. In those circumstances it appeared to McKenzie J that the Social Welfare Department could, if confronted with the evidence, cut off the disability benefit. Thus, he could not say with any probability that "beyond a couple of

---

253. See Byrne and Binchy, *Annual Review of Irish Law 1994*.

254. See *O'Brien v Creaton*, DPIJ: Trinity and Michaelmas Terms 1996, p 92 (HC) for an application of s 237(1) that was "Byzantine in … its complexity".

255. [1988] ILRM 617 (HC) (*ex temp*). For a penetrating analysis of the policy issues, see Clark 'Damages and the Social Welfare 'Overlap'', (1984) 19 Ir Jur (ns) 40.

weeks" from then he would be in receipt of this benefit. Accordingly he made no order for deduction. It is somewhat difficult to understand how the jury could have awarded the plaintiff £5,000 for future loss of earnings if they considered that the plaintiff was likely to obtain work (after over two and a half years of unemployment) within a fortnight. It is possible, however, that this sum might have been based on the view that the plaintiff would immediately return to work but at a reduced level of income.

**[44.137]** It should also be noted that s 17(3) of the Consumer Information Act 1978 gives a discretion to the Court in imposing (or varying) a fine for an offence under the Merchandise Marks Acts 1887 to 1970 involving a trade description or for any offence under the Consumer Information Act 1978 to order part or all of the fine to be paid as compensation to any prosecution witness who has suffered personal injury, loss or damage resulting, wholly or partly, from the offence. This discretion is contingent on the witness's making application to the Court for such an order. The witness may not make this application if proceedings claiming damages for the injury, loss or damage have already been instituted. Where such an order is made and subsequently paid to the witness, and the damages are awarded to the witness in later proceedings, the payment made under the order is deemed to be in satisfaction of so much of the damages as is equal to the amount of payment.

**[44.138]** The courts have had difficulty in this context in dealing with cases involving collateral benefits with an international dimension. If the plaintiff (who may, of course, in some cases be a foreign national, domiciliary or resident) has received an insurance or social welfare benefit under foreign law, does s 2 of the 1964 Act apply to it?

**[44.139]** In *Van Keep v Surface Dressing Contractors Ltd*,[256] Budd J held that it showed the plaintiff from the Netherlands received benefits from a mutual insurance system in the Netherlands to which both employers and employees contributed. Budd J stated:

> "It seems to me that this was an insurance scheme and the payments were based on a contractual liability within s 2(a). If I am incorrect in this, then I think that it was 'other like benefit payable in consequence of the injury'."[257]

**[44.140]** In *McKenna v Best Travel Ltd t/a Cypriana Holidays*[258] an Irish plaintiff who was injured when visiting Jerusalem received payments under Iraqi law from the National Insurance Institute under two headings: reimbursement of her medical and dental fees and a monthly payment based on assessment of continuing disability.

**[44.141]** Lavan J was disposed to regard the second of these payments as falling within the scope of s 2 of the 1964 Act. Even if it did not, he considered that:

> "it may be argued that the section merely recognises the general policy considerations favouring non-deductibility of compensating benefits in personal injury actions as

---

256. High Court, 11 June 1993 (Budd J). See Kerr, *The Civil Liability Acts* (1991), p 83.

257. As regards concerns that the defendant might be exposed to a claim from the Dutch institution that had paid the benefit to the plaintiff for part of the sum paid, Budd J observed that it seemed to him that the words of s 2 were "clear", he was sure that if a problem of double payment arose, there was some way in which the defendant and the insurance companies involved w[ould] be able to remedy this perceived mischief."

258. High Court, 17 December 1996 (Lavan J) reversed on other grounds by the Supreme Court, 18 November 1997.

depending on ... 'justice, reasonableness and public policy' ... Arising therefrom the position will be that the second payment should not be deducted."[259]

**[44.142]** Lavan J recognised that the case presented an issue of private international law rather than merely one of statutory interpretation under domestic law. He referred to the approach favoured by the Supreme Court in *Grehan v Medical Incorporated*,[260] which gives a court the flexibility to adopt a choice-of-law rule that is sensitive to the social and economic dimensions. It seemed to Lavan J that in the instant case the court might:

> "decide to consider whether the second payment should be treated as if it were a Social Welfare payment in Ireland or to use the words of the statute, 'other like benefit under statute' on the one hand or apply the Israeli treatment to the payment which, according to [expert legal] opinion, would be to deduct the value of payment from any damages awarded under any Israeli court".[261]

With regard to the first payments, Lavan J considered that the Supreme Court in *Reddy v Bates*[262] seemed "to favour an approach of non-duplication or overlap of damages".[263] Notwithstanding this, Lavan J took the view that the proper test to be applied was that enunciated by Walsh J in *Grehan*,[264] in the "unusual circumstances"[265] of the instant case and applying the *Grehan* test, Lavan J determined both payments to be non-deductible.[266]

## VI. Non-Pecuniary Loss[267]

**[44.143]** As a matter of practice, non-pecuniary loss is broken down into a number of elements. These may, for convenience, be listed as follows:

(1) pain and suffering;

(2) loss of expectation of life.

### Pain and Suffering

**[44.144]** A plaintiff may recover damages not only for the pain and suffering he experiences as a direct result of the injury but also for the pain and suffering that may accompany or result from a medical operation which reasonably necessary to perform. Compensation must be given for future as well as for present and past suffering.[268]

259. Page 10-11 of Lavan J's judgment.
260. [1986] IR 528.
261. Page 11 of Lavan J's judgment.
262. [1984] ILRM 197.
263. Page 11 of Lavan J's judgment.
264. [1986] IR 528.
265. Page 12 of Lavan J's judgment.
266. It is not entirely clear why, if *Reddy v Bates* suggested the non-duplication of damages, the first payment should not have been deducted, since neither Irish nor Israeli law would support such an outcome.
267. The subject is comprehensively analysed in White, *Irish Law of Damages for Personal Injuries and Death* (1989). See also *Butterworths Personal Injury Litigation Service* (eds Gold Rein & de Haas); Munkman, *Damages for Personal Injuries And Death* (10th ed, 1996); *Atiyah's Accidents Compensation and the Law* (6th ed), Ch 6 the English Law Commission's Consultation Paper No 140; *Damages for Personal Injury: Non-Pecuniary Loss*, paras 3.9-3.19 (1995).
268. As to what particulars of injuries must be pleaded, see *MacNaughton v Murphy* [1961] Ir Jur Rep 41 (SC).

**[44.145]** Since pain is subjective, it raises particular difficulties of proof and of computation of damage where obviously "there can be no exact measurement".[269] In *Sexton v O'Keeffe*,[270] Lavery J, in the Supreme Court, was driven to refer to "the really impossible task" of translating suffering into terms of money. In *Lee v Joyce*,[271] referring again to this difficulty, he admitted that it was impossible to explain such a translation "on any logical or mathematical basis". A judge or a jury, he said could only express a personal view as to what was fair compensation, the task for an appellate tribunal being ever more difficult.[272]

### *(a) The rough tariff of £150,000*

**[44.146]** In *Sinnott v Quinnsworth Ltd*[273] in 1984, the Supreme Court introduced a rough tariff in relation to damages for pain and suffering. The plaintiff was a young man who, as a result of a motor accident, became "quadriplegic, with paralysis and sensory loss and loss of control of bladder and bowel and totally dependent on others".[274] The Supreme Court reduced a jury award of £800,000 to £150,000. O'Higgins CJ, in a passage with which the other members of the Court agreed, expressed the view that:

> "unless there are particular circumstances which suggest otherwise, general damages, in a case of this nature, should not exceed a sum in the region of contemporary standards and money values and I am conscious that there may be changes and alterations in the future, as there have been in the past."[275]

**[44.147]** Several comments and questions arise about this approach. First, it should be noted that the case before the Court, though indeed a very distressing and serious one, was not the most severe that could be imagined. There are unfortunately cases where the degree of pain and suffering may be more severe. Perhaps the worst aspect of Mr Sinnott's injuries was the fact that they had:

> "changed him from being an active, healthy young man on the threshold of adult life, into a helpless, dependent, paralysed being conscious of what he ha[d] lost and facing a bleak, uncertain and limited future".

This profound change in expectations was not accompanied by the degree of intense physical pain which some accident victims must confront. Thus it would be quite wrong to conclude that £150,000 is the absolute maximum for general damages in tort actions.

---

269. *Ebbs v Forkin* Supreme Court, 6 May 1963, *per* Lavery J (dissenting but dissent not affecting this point). See further Cantor, *Psychosomatic Injury, Traumatic Psychoneurosis, and Law* (1957) 6 Clev Mar LR 428; Wasmuth, *Psychosomatic Disease and the Law* (1958) 7 Clev Mar LR 34.

270. [1966] IR 204 at 207 (SC). See also *Sinnott v Quinnsworth Ltd* [1984] ILRM 523 at 532 (SC).

271. Supreme Court, 3 December 1964, pp 3-4 (Lavery J was dissenting but the dissent did not affect this issue). See also *Forsyth v Roe Quarry Ltd* Supreme Court, 2 December 1958, *per* Lavery JPI; *Foley v Thermocement Products Ltd* (1954) 90 ILTR 92 at 94 (SC); *McCarthy v Walsh* [1965] IR 246 at 262 (SC).

272. Experience with juries prior to their abolition was that while they awarded generous damages for pain and suffering to the date of trial, the damages for future pain and suffering tend to be somewhat low. *Cf Whelan v Bower* Supreme Court, 13 April 1973; *Casserly v CLE* Supreme Court, 21 July 1978.

273. [1984] ILRM 523 (SC).

274. [1984] ILRM 523 at 529.

275. [1984] ILRM 523 at 532.

**[44.148]** The second point worth considering about the £150,000 guideline is whether it represents merely a "lid on the cauldron", or whether it has implications for setting the quantum of general damages in *all* cases, big or small. On one view, the figure of £150,000 may be seen as a sum beyond which juries should not normally venture, just as the statutory maximum amount for mental distress prescribed by the Civil Liability Act 1961 was interpreted (in *McCarthy v Walsh*[276]) as merely setting a maximum limit with no implications of proportional adjustment downwards for all less serious cases. On another view, £150,000 should be seen, not as an artificial limit, but as a yardstick by which all other cases are judged, thus, if facts somewhat less serious than those in *Sinnott v Quinnsworth Ltd* presented themselves to a Court, a verdict of £150,000 would not be defensible.

**[44.149]** This latter interpretation appears to have found favour with the Supreme Court. In *Griffiths v Van Raj*,[277] the Supreme Court reduced from £160,000 to £100,000 an award for general damages by the trial judge where a girl suffered "severe and permanent intellectual and emotional impairment" as well as some degree of physical handicap, including a lack of balance and intermittent tremors. Griffin J (with whom Hederman J concurred) said:

> "While the plaintiff's injuries are very serious, they cannot be regarded as comparable with, for example, a case of quadriplegia. Although each case must be considered on its own facts, the level of damages awarded in somewhat similar cases, and in much more serious cases than the particular case under consideration, should be kept in mind."[278]

This passage seems consistent only with the view that the £150,000 figure represents a standard for all cases involving general damages rather than a lid above which juries may not generally proceed but up to which they are free to go, even in cases less serious than *Sinnott v Quinnsworth Ltd.*

**[44.150]** In *Sinnott v Quinnsworth Ltd* O'Higgins CJ arrived at the figure of £150,000 by a slow and somewhat controversial route. He stressed the danger that, in "assaying the impossible"[279] in attempting to provide compensation for very serious injuries, juries were in danger of losing "all sense of reality".[280] Two policy factors made it important that this should not happen.

---

276. [1965] IR 246.
277. [1985] ILRM 582 (SC).
278. [1985] ILRM 582 at 588. See *Scannell v O'Keefe t/a George O'Keefe & Sons* DPIJ: Trinity and Michaelmas Terms 1998, p 17 (HC). *Cf Ryan v O'Connor* DPIJ: Michaelmas Term, p 1 (HC), where there was an award of £140,000 to a 21-year-old who received serious injuries to his right arm and hand. Since the judgment contains no discussion of *Sinnott v Quinnsworth Ltd* [1984] ILRM 523, it is hard to know whether the award of this sum was based on the view (a) that the injuries were almost equivalent in seriousness to those in *Sinnott*, (b) that *Sinnott* represented a "lid on the cauldron" rather than a proportionate measure for less serious injuries or (c) that some escalation of the £150,000 figure should be made to take account of inflation. Similar uncertainty attaches to the precise basis of the award of £125,000 general damages for the loss of a hand in *O'Mahony v O'Mahony* DPIJ: Hilary and Easter Terms 1991, p 17 (HC) and the award of £155,000 general damages to a 22-year-old plaintiff who suffered a range of injuries, including major facial scarring and a permanent 30% loss of mobility in her knee, in *Orme v Orme* DPIJ: Trinity & Michaelmas Terms 1992, p 233 (HC).
279. [1984] ILRM 523 at 532.
280. [1984] ILRM 523 at 532.

**[44.151]** First, the defendant or his indemnifiers could legitimately complain if the sum awarded was "so high as to constitute a punishment for the infliction of the injury rather than a reasonable, if imperfect, attempt to compensate the injured".[281] (There is nothing new to this.) Secondly, it mattered to contemporary society "if, by reason of the amount decided upon and the example which it sets for other determinations of damages by juries, the operation of public policy would be thereby endangered''.[282] This is an important reminder that jury awards are not made in a social vacuum: there is a social price, and there comes a point where the price is simply too high.

**[44.152]** The Chief Justice expressed the view that "a limit must exist, and should be sought and recognised, having regard to the facts of each case and the social conditions which obtain in our society". He stressed that "every single penny" of monetary loss or expense to which the plaintiff had been, and would be, put had been provided for under other heads of damages. In assessing general damages, the objective had to be to determine a figure that was fair and reasonable, and to this end it seemed to O'Higgins CJ that:

> "some regard should be had to the ordinary living standards in the country, to the general level of incomes, and to the things upon which the plaintiff might reasonably be expected to spend money.''[283]

This is an important passage. We may enquire as to the nature of the relationship between these three factors - all of them relating to economic income or expenditure - and pain and suffering. Of what possible relevance to the pain of a person in a wheelchair is the fact that the average industrial wage is £10,000?

**[44.153]** The answer is perhaps that there must be some bridge between the experience of pain and an award for general damages. If the award is to take a monetary form, then it must have regard to monetary values in a particular society at a particular time. If I am injured in a traffic accident in Japan, for example, and am offered 10,000 yen in settlement, I simply will have no way of knowing whether this is an attractive settlement unless I can have some medium of translating that sum into monetary terms that I can understand. The exchange rate between the yen and the pound is all that I need to consult to solve my problem. Similarly, reference to the specific factors - relating to income and expenditure - mentioned by O'Higgins CJ may be useful in encouraging those trying personal injury cases to have regard to the actual purchasing power of a pound when they are provisionally disposed to award several hundred thousand of them to an injured party. In other words, if reference to these factors is no more than a reminder of the value of money in our society at a particular time, this is scarcely a matter for complaint.

**[44.154]** However, if the suggestion is that there is some discernible mathematical relationship between pain and "the general level of incomes in the country", for example, then we may ask what is the nature of that relationship. Certainly there is no factual relationship between the two phenomena. If we assume that "the general level of incomes" is £15,000, who is to say that a person who suffers from the same injuries as befell Mr Sinnott should be awarded damages of five times that sum, rather than ten times or, equally, a half? There is, it seems, a missing link in the argument as expressed. There is no

281. [1984] ILRM 523 at 532.

282. [1984] ILRM 523 at 532.

283. [1984] ILRM 523 at 532.

guidance as to what is the relevance of the three economic factors mentioned in the determination of the quantum of compensation for the non-economic phenomenon of pain and suffering.

**[44.155]** One may suspect that a somewhat crude equation is at the base of this relationship. An award of £3 million for quadriplegia would be instinctively condemned by some as "too much", because (it may be argued, from the Chief Justice's standpoint) victims, even of very serious injuries, should not receive such compensation as would place them in an economic position more powerful than almost anyone else in our society. In other words, more sharply expressed, the value-judgment here seems to be that victims of very serious physical injury should not be elevated to greater economic heights than most other members of society. We may accept or reject this value-judgement - and there is much to be said in opposition to it - but it is as well to be aware of it as underlying O'Higgins CJ's approach.

**[44.156]** The other possible interpretation of the Chief Justice's remarks is that society simply cannot afford to compensate victims of serious injuries to an extent beyond the general level of incomes and the ordinary living standards in the country. This may be so, but perhaps it would have been more convincing if the Chief Justice had approached the question by referring to medical and economic data, including the number of cases of serious injury each year, the total amount of compensation awarded in these cases and, more broadly, in personal injuries litigation in general, and the relationship between these sums and other factors such as the cost of motor insurance, social welfare and hospital and other medical expenses. Only in the light of this type of evidence could one form even a tentative judgment as to whether our community is obliged to limit compensation for personal injuries in general. The data would need to be still more detailed before one could make an educated estimate as to whether the community cannot afford more than £150,000 for pain and suffering in cases such as *Sinnott v Quinnsworth Ltd*.

**[44.157]** To summarise if the quantum of damages in torts proceedings prior to *Sinnott v Quinnsworth Ltd* was such as to damage the efficacy of the compensation system or to "endanger the operation of public policy", then indeed there would be good grounds for a more moderate approach in the future, but the reference to ordinary living standards and the general level of incomes appears to be no more than a rough and ready pragmatic way of encouraging this approach.

**[44.158]** The third of the economic factors specified by O'Higgins CJ also merits attention. The jury must have some regard "to the things upon which the plaintiff might reasonably be expected to spend money". In other words, if the plaintiff is unable to spend money - because he is immobilised or mentally injured, for example - he should get less than if he did not suffer from these incapacitates. Under this approach to damages, money is seen as providing no more than a solace, rather than constituting compensation for the objective wrong that has actually been inflicted.[284] It may seem to some people to be unjust

284. The striking similarity between the Irish Supreme Court's approach and that of the Supreme Court of Canada is worth noting. The figure of $100.000 (1978 values) is the upper limit for non-pecuniary awards in personal injury litigation save in exceptional cases: *Andrews v Grand & Toy Alberta Ltd* 83 DLR (3d) 452 (SC, Can); *Thornton v Board of School Trustees of School District No 57 (Prince George)* 83 DLR (3d) 480 (SC, Can); *Arnold v Teno* 83 DLR (3d) 609 (SC, Can); *Lindal v Lindal* 129 DLR (3d) 263 (SC, Can); see also *Fenn v City of Peterborough* 104 DLR (3d) 174 (Ont CA).

and discriminatory to restrict the quantum of damages on account of the lack of plaintiff's capacity to spend.

**[44.159]** A further element in O'Higgins CJ's analysis has been identified in later decisions,[285] though, to be fair to the Chief Justice, it is hard to identify any specific passage of his judgment that actually contains what has been attributed to it. This is the proposition that the amount to be awarded as damages for pain and suffering should be reduced if the particular plaintiff is receiving a very high award under other headings.

**[44.160]** The first of these later decisions is *Burke v Blanch*.[286] The plaintiff, aged 24, had suffered what Costello J described as "devastating injuries"[287] in a car accident caused by the defendant's negligence. He had fractured his thoraco-lumbar spine, which resulted in paraplegia.

**[44.161]** Costello J awarded the plaintiff around half a million pounds under several heads, including special damages and loss of earnings. His disposition of the issue of general damages must be quoted in full:

> "It requires little imagination to fill in the details of the pain and suffering (physical and mental) which … this young [man] … must have suffered and will suffer in the future and is not difficult to comprehend how his life has been shattered by what has happened to him. The Court can compensate him for the pecuniary loss which has followed as a result of the accident (and that I have endeavoured to do) but no award of money can remotely compensate him for his physical and mental suffering, past and future. There are clear legal guidelines laid down by the Supreme Court as to how the assessment of general damages in a case of this sort should be approached …[288] and applying these and in particular bearing in mind that the plaintiff, apart from general damages, will be receiving half a million pounds approximately, I think a fair and reasonable sum for general damages is an additional sum of £100,000."[289]

This passage indicates that, in determining the amount to be awarded for pain and suffering, the Court took into consideration the fact that the plaintiff was receiving around half a million pounds under *other* heads of damages.

**[44.162]** There appears to be a difficulty with this approach. A plaintiff is entitled to compensation under the other heads of damages in their own right. The damages awarded represent an attempt to neutralise an economic deficiency inflicted on him or her: if they achieve this goal, the plaintiff should not be expected to feel grateful, or even happy, but rather relieved that he or she will not have to pay for an economic loss caused by the

---

285. *Burke v Blanch*, High Court, 28 July 1989 (Costello J); *Kealy v Minister for Health*, High Court, 19 April 1999 (Morris P).

286. High Court, 28 July 1989 (Costello J).

287. *Burke v Blanch*, High Court, 28 July 1989.

288. Citing *Reddy v Bates* [1984] ILRM 197; *Cooke v Walsh* [1984] ILRM 208; *Sinnott v Quinnsworth Ltd* [1984] ILRM 523 and *Griffiths v Van Raaj* [1985] ILRM 582. See also *Connolly v Dundalk UDC* [1990] 2 IR 1, where O'Hanlon J, adopting a somewhat similar approach to that favoured by Costello J in *Burke v Blanch*, also had regard to the fact that no award of damages, however large, was likely to enhance the plaintiff's enjoyment of life. See further Byrne & Binchy, *Annual Review of Irish Law 1990*, pp 565-566.

289. *Burke v Blanch*, High Court, 28 July 1989.

defendant's wrong. It is a matter of contingency whether the amount of compensation under these other headings is high or low. The fact that an award under these headings gives the plaintiff money for economic losses which he or she has not yet sustained may encourage the impression that the plaintiff is receiving a windfall or profit, but this is not so. The largeness of the amount merely reflects the economic damage which the plaintiff will sustain.

**[44.163]** An issue of equality under Article 40.1 of the Constitution may well arise in this context. It is hard to see why two plaintiffs who have suffered identical devastating injuries should receive different amounts of compensation for the pain and suffering caused by these injuries simply because the quantum of the economic loss that each suffers – and for which full compensation is due – is not identical.

**[44.164]** The approach favoured by Costello J in *Burke v Blanch* has, however, also received the support of Morris P in *Kealy v Minister for Health*.[290] In this case Morris P distinguished *Sinnott* on the basis, *inter alia*, that the instant case was not one involving an award of very large sums for loss of earnings, medical care, house renovation etc, where on the basis of *Sinnott* (following Griffin J's judgment in *Reddy v Bates*), the court should have regard to the total of the sums when considering whether the award was reasonable. Perhaps the best way of understanding both *Burke v Blanch* and *Kealy v Minister for Health* is not that they require a court to reduce the quantum of an award for pain and suffering simply on account of the largeness of the award under other headings but rather that the court should adopt the intuitive approach, recommended in *Reddy v Bates*, of looking at the total figure and reassessing it in the light of an instinctive "feel" for what is fair and proportionate compensation for the plaintiff.

***(b) The tariff is raised to £250,000***

**[44.165]** As time passed, the *Sinnott* tariff of £150,000 came to be reconsidered by the courts. Two rather obvious reasons account for this: the fall in the value of money after 1984 – initially at a rapid pace but much less in recent years – and the gradual, ultimately radical, improvement in social and economic conditions.

**[44.166]** In *Connolly v Bus Éireann*,[291] in 1996, Barr J referred to the first of these reasons when he stated:

> "It is now over eleven years since the *Sinnott* cap was fixed at £150,000. It seems to me that its true value now is £200,000."

**[44.167]** Geoghegan J, in *Coppinger v Waterford County Council*,[292] decided two months after *Connolly*, thought it "reasonable to follow [Barr J's] view…." In *Connolly*, the

---

290. High Court, 19 April 1999 (Morris P).

291. High Court, 29 January 1996 (Barr J). See also *O'Brien v Creaton*, DPIJ: Trinity and Michaelmas Terms 1996, p 92 (HC) - award of £180,000 for general damages. Three years earlier in *Kenny v Doran*, DPIJ: Hilary and Easter Terms 1993, p 214 (HC), where the plaintiff, aged 36 at the time of the accident, received "appalling damages and injury", including paralysis down his right side, inability to communicate and an awareness of his disability, Johnson J, referring indirectly to *Sinnott v Quinnsworth*, awarded £180,000 for general damages. In *Ecock v MF Kent & Co* DPIJ: Hilary & Easter Terms 1994, p 178 (HC), Kinlen J awarded £200,000 general damages for a serious arm injury.

292. DPIJ: Hilary & Easter Terms 1996, p 1 (HC).

plaintiff, aged fifteen, had suffered a severe neurological deficit, rendering her dependent in most activities, including dressing and toileting; she had visual field defect in one eye and her ability to read books was at the level of a twelve-year-old. In *Coppinger*, an adult plaintiff suffered complete paralysis of his right limbs and of his speech functions. He had no bladder or bowel control and had to be fed through a gastrostomy tube.

**[44.168]** In *Allen v Ó Suilleabháin*,[293] in 1997, the Supreme Court distinguished *Connolly* and *Coppinger* when reducing an award for general damages of £205,000 in favour of the plaintiff to £125,000. The plaintiff sustained a severe, chronic, back injury. The Court accepted as correct the submission of counsel for the first-named defendant as to the appropriate level of general damages to compensate the plaintiff. Part of that submission was that the top figure awarded for general damages in the most severe personal injury cases was £200,000.

**[44.169]** In *Brady v Doherty*,[294] in 1998, where the plaintiff retained a substantial degree of inability but suffered continuous pain which was likely to haunt him for the rest of his life, with resulting on-going depression, Barr J awarded £280,000 for general damages, commenting laconically that he had taken into account *Sinnott* "and subsequent authorities which amplify the principle therein laid down". In *Cody v Hurley*[295] in 1999, McCracken J distinguished *Allen v Ó Suilleabháin* when awarding £190,000 to a plaintiff who had sustained severe back injury had a severe limp and had been required to undergo several traumatic operations, with the "effectiv[e] los[s] of her childhood".[296] McCracken J proceeded "on the basis that the maximum figure referred to by the Supreme Court should now be in the region of £250,000 ...".[297]

**[44.170]** Three months later, in *Kealy v Minister for Health*,[298] on appeal from an award of £165,000 made in favour of the appellant by the Hepatitis C Compensation Tribunal, Morris P took matters still further. The appellant, aged forty-four, had received an injection of contaminated anti-D in 1977. She was eventually diagnosed in 1992 as suffering from hepatitis. In the meantime she had been suffering from a variety of complaints, including depression, insomnia, devastating itchiness and rash, joint pains and loss of energy. She had to undergo physiotherapy constantly. Her probable prognosis was that she would have established cirrhosis in ten years' time and would need to undergo a

293. Supreme Court, 11 March 1997.

294. High Court, 31 July 1998 (Barr J).

295. High Court, 20 January 1999 (McCracken J).

296. High Court, 20 January 1999.

297. High Court, 20 January 1999. See also *Cronin v Cronin* DPIJ: Trinity and Michaelmas Terms 1998, p 150 (HC) - award of £230,000 for general damages for very serious facial and head injuries; *Troute v Brassil* High Court, 19 November 1999 (O'Neill J) - award of £225,000 for general damages for serious injuries including brain damage; *O'N v The Minister for Health and Children* High Court, 19 October 1999 (O'Neill J) - £250,000 general damages award for being infected with Hepatitis C virus; *O'Mahony v Buckley*, DPIJ: Trinity & Michaelmas Terms 1999, p 5 (HC) - £205,000 general damages for post-traumatic stress disorder, depression and serious hip fracture, probably requiring an artificial hip within ten years and a replacement ten or fifteen years later, leaving plaintiff with a limp; *Fitzgerald v Treacy*, DPIJ: Trinity & Michaelmas Terms 1999, p 85 (HC) - £180,000 general damages where plaintiff suffered severe back injury, acute coccydinia and thrombosis in leg.

298. High Court, 19 April 1999 (Morris P).

liver transplant five years thereafter, with a 15-20% prospect of cirrhosis developing in the transplant.

**[44.171]** Morris P considered that the cap on general damages to which the Supreme Court referred in *Sinnott* had "only limited relevance to an award of this type". One point of distinction was that the instant case was not one involving an award of very large sums for loss of earnings, medical care, house renovation, etc. Moreover, *Sinnott* had been decided at a time of depression when interest rates were high and incomes, relative to the present day, were small. Morris P noted that the rate of interest currently available on investments bore no relationship to that of 1987 and the cost of property had multiplied since that time. He went on to say:

> "In my view it would work a genuine injustice to an applicant such as [the appellant] in this case to hold that the cap of £150,000 plus whatever consumer price index increase would be appropriate, was the limit of the damages which she could recover.
>
> My own day to day experience in the Courts ruling in infant settlements is the clearest possible test for me that the cap of £150,000 is no longer regarded as applicable by practitioners in the Courts both on the plaintiff and defendant side.
>
> Accordingly, I approach the assessment of damages without the constraints herein before referred to.
>
> In my view the correct measure of damages for the [appellant] for general damages for a lady whose life has been effectively ruined is £250,000."[299]

***(c) Pain, subjectivity and proof***

**[44.172]** One person's pain cannot be scientifically demonstrated to another.[300] In some cases, of course, a person's behaviour will convince even the most sceptical that he or she is in pain, but however real the subjective experience of pain, and however manifest it may seem from the victim's conduct, in the last analysis the presence or absence of pain must remain a matter of inference.

**[44.173]** Where a plaintiff claims to feel a pain for which his or her doctor cannot account, a jury is entitled to accept the plaintiff's evidence, but, as was said in *Burke v Burke*,[301] where the plaintiff has a series of complaints indicating a serious permanent incapacity but his doctor fails to support this evidence:

> "The jury is not entitled to proceed on the basis that the plaintiff is right and [his] doctor is wrong. They must ... have some regard to the medical evidence called for the plaintiff to support [his] case. They are certainly not entitled to ignore it.[302]

***(d) If the victim responds with fortitude and good spirits to his or her injury the damages may be reduced***

**[44.174]** In Chapter 3, we noted that the plaintiff with the "egg-shell skull", will be entitled to enhanced damages. The converse of increasing the damages where such a plaintiff has

---

299. High Court, 19 April 1999, pp 7-8 of Morris P's judgment.

300. *Cf* Witt Genstein, *Philosophical Investigations*, paras 384-393 (Anscombe trans, 3rd ed, 1967).

301. Supreme Court, 27 July 1971.

302. Supreme Court, 27 July 1971, *per* Fitzgerald J for the majority at p 3.

suffered an unusually serious response to his injury is that a plaintiff who accommodates himself particularly well to his plight will have his damages reduced. This happened in *Prendergast v Joe Malone Self Drive Ltd*,[303] where a girl who received serious facial injuries did not let them get her down.

**[44.175]** Ó Dálaigh CJ stated:

> "It is the plaintiff's personal good fortune but legal ill luck that in meeting a grave ordeal she has shown herself to be a young woman of great character. Her experience might well have daunted even the most courageous. We find, however, that she has achieved a very remarkable rehabilitation: she has fitted herself into a congenial occupation, and in recreational and social activities gone far towards achieving a full life. She bears the scars of a terrible injury, but as members of the Court have been able to observe for themselves she has so mastered this handicap as to remain an attractive and charming young woman."[304]

***(e) Depression, post-traumatic stress disorder and other psychiatric conditions***

**[44.176]** The judgments over the past decade record a striking incidence of depression,[305]

---

303. Supreme Court, 21 June 1967. *Cf O'Toole v Kearns* Supreme Court, 31 July 1957.

304. Supreme Court, 27 July 1971, pp 6-7. See also *Kennedy v Dublin Corporation* DPIJ: Trinity & Michaelmas Terms 1992, p 134 (HC), where the plaintiff recovered sooner than might have been expected from his injuries, the sum awarded took account of this fact. Lavan J observed (at p 134):

> "One principle of damage is known as the [eggshell skull rule], which says that the defendant must take the plaintiff as he finds him, particularly if the circumstances are such that he has a weak constitution. It seems to me that there is a converse and that this defendant in this case is entitled to the benefit of an early recovery by a plaintiff."

305. See, eg *Cassidy v Clarke* DPIJ: Trinity & Michaelmas Terms 1999, p 183 (HC); *Nevin v Johnson & Perrott Ltd* DPIJ: Hilary & Easter Terms 1997, p 46 (HC); *McCarthy v ESB* DPIJ: Hilary & Easter Terms 1997, p 26 (HC); *Shields v Boyle* DPIJ: Michaelmas Term 1991, p 88 (HC); *Forde v Pfizer Chemical Corporation Ltd*, DPIJ: Hilary & Easter Terms 1991, p 57 (HC); *Noonan v O'Leary*, DPIJ: Hilary and Easter Terms 1991, p 127 (HC); *Nason v Cork Corporation* DPIJ: Hilary & Easter Terms 1991, p 170 (HC) - depression partly attributable to accident; *Fox v Bord na Mona* DPIJ: Hilary & Easter Terms 1991, p 266 (HC); *O'Connell v Hynes* DPIJ: Hilary & Easter Terms 1991, p 257 (HC); *Garvey v Walsh* DPIJ: Trinity & Michaelmas Terms 1992, p 52 (HC); *O'Donoghue v Egan* DPIJ: Trinity & Michaelmas Terms 1992, p 90 (HC) - accident aggravated depression; *Tuohy v March* DPIJ: Trinity & Michaelmas Terms 1992, p 109 (HC); *Donoghue v Morgan* DPIJ: Michaelmas Term 1990, p 228 (HC) - depression brought only pain; *Kelly v Kelly* DPIJ: Michaelmas Term 1990, p 321 (HC) - depression and phobia involving fear of developing cancer; *McKenna v Longford Lifestyles* DPIJ: Hilary & Easter Terms 1991, p 20 (HC) - depression resulting from back pain; *Kennedy v Fulflex Manufacturing Ltd* DPIJ: Michaelmas Term 1991, p 140 (HC); *O'Donovan v Southern Health Board* DPIJ: Michaelmas Term 1991, p 175 (HC) - plaintiff suffered from such acute pain in her eyes, neck, shoulders and arm that she attempted unsuccessfully to drown herself; she was diagnosed as suffering from a severe post-traumatic depression; *Quigley v Byrne*, DPIJ: Hilary & Easter Terms 1994, p 32 (HC) - severe depression following "terrifying" traffic accident in which plaintiff, eight months pregnant, feared for the life of her baby; *O'Sullivan v Connolly*, DPIJ: Hilary & Easter Terms 1996, p 96 (HC); *Gillick v Rotunda Hospital* Supreme Court, 15 May 1998 (*ex temp*) - serious reactive depression following negligently performed hysterectomy against wishes of plaintiff; *O'Mahony v Buckley*, DPIJ: Trinity & Michaelmas Terms 1999, p 5 (HC) - depression and post-traumatic stress disorder.

post-traumatic stress disorder[306] and other psychiatric conditions.[307] Very often these various considerations accompany physical injury. In these cases, there is no difficulty in principle in awarding compensation in contrast to cases involving what might be called "pure nervous shock", unaccompanied by physical injury.[308] Here the courts internationally have been cautious about recognising the claims, though it has to be acknowledged that so far the Irish courts have evinced far less concern than their counterparts in other jurisdictions.

**[44.177]** It should be noted that in cases where a physically injured plaintiff suffers an unforeseeable psychiatric response or a psychiatric response that is more severe than might

306. See, eg, *Kelly v Dublin Corporation*, DPIJ: Michaelmas 1991, p 195 (HC) - post-traumatic neurosis resulting from accident was "an overlay of a deeper depressive illness which was not caused by the accident", £15,000 general damages awarded for this condition and some other slight physical injuries; *Mullally v Bus Éireann* [1992] ILRM 722 (HC); *Kelly v Hennessy* [1996] 1 ILRM 321, affg [1993] ILRM 530; *Curran v Cadbury Ireland Ltd* Circuit Court, 17 December 1999 (McMahon J) [1993] ILRM 530; *McDonnell v Sweeney* DPIJ: Hilary & Easter Terms 1999 (HC); *McGowan v Wicklow County Council* High Court, 27 May 1993 (Morris J); *Coffey v Huntenburg* DPIJ: Hilary & Easter Terms 1996, p 57 (HC); *Clancy v Micro Bio (Irl) Ltd* DPIJ: Hilary & Easter Terms 1996, p 67 (HC) - plaintiff developed a post-traumatic stress disorder coupled with generalised anxiety after three work-related accidents in less than three years: a life-threatening explosion, the release of untreated chlorine and the release of chlorine gas; *Varian v Kerr* DPIJ: Trinity & Michaelmas Terms 1992, p 239 (HC) - 10-year-old plaintiff suffered post-traumatic stress disorder following accident in which he was injured and his mother died; *Ryan v Toal* DPIJ: Hilary & Easter Terms 1991, p 208 (HC) - plaintiff suffered post-traumatic stress disorder having been forced to be a passenger in her own car by a person escaping from Garda custody who then drove the car at speeds in excess of 80 mph in dark foggy conditions until it overturned; following gunshots in the direction of the car, plaintiff was used as a human shield until captor was arrested; on basis of expert psychiatric evidence, Morris J ascribed 70% of damages to the period when plaintiff had been exposed to the "furious driving"); *Hogan v Electricity Supply Board* High Court, 17 December 1999 (O'Higgins J) - plaintiff developed symptoms of depression, exacerbation of alcoholism and post-traumatic stress disorder after accident.

307. See, eg, *Dunne v Lawter Products Ltd*, DPIJ: Hilary & Easter Terms 1997, p 66 (HC) - anxiety state, phobia and "irrational fear" in relation to factory where explosion occurred in 1993, followed by second explosion in the factory in 1996, resulting in a general anxiety state; *McGuinness v Fastmac Express Delivery Services Ltd*, DPIJ: Michaelmas Term 1991, p 150 (HC) - plaintiff whose foot and thumb were injured, also received psychiatric treatment "which, while successful, was also highly unpleasant and embarrassing"; *McSweeney v Cork Corporation*, DPIJ: Hilary & Easter Terms 1994, p 37 (HC) - plaintiff, who sustained minor injury to his knee in an accident suffered pains in his back, neck and arms which were "wholly unrelated [to] and by no stretch of the imagination explicable in organic terms as arising from any possible injury to the knee" but were attributable to a heightened anxiety state which was the product of a prior vulnerable condition; awarding damages, Murphy J referred to the "eggshell-skull" principle of law which he considered was "very harsh in its application, that a person who has a problem and who therefore, as a result of that problem responds particularly badly to somebody else's wrongdoing, then the wrongdoer must compensate [him or her] for those unusual consequences of the wrongdoing"; *O'Leary v Hanlon Off Shore Supply Co Ltd*, DPIJ: Hilary & Easter Terms 1994, p 140 (HC) - panic attacks; *O'Connell v ESB*, DPIJ: Hilary & Easter Terms 1996, p 176 (HC) - plaintiff, who sustained injury when the lift in which she was travelling crashed to the ground, developed phobias in relation to lifts, planes and crowds.

308. *Cf* Ch 17 above.

reasonably have been anticipated, the "egg-shell skull" rule[309] ensures that the defendant will have to compensate him or her for the full extent of that response.

**[44.178]** An unusual instance of mental distress occurred in *Broomfield v The Midland Health Board*.[310] The first named plaintiff gave birth to her third child in the defendant's hospital. Shortly afterwards the child was taken away from her to give her a brief rest. Through error, the baby that was returned to her was not her child. After nine days, during which period she had breast-fed the substituted baby and developed a strong attachment for him, the mistake was rectified and her own baby was restored to her. She suffered serious agitation and stress ("aggravated by undue publicity and the attention of journalists"), made worse by the "refusal or … neglect of the hospital to give her the necessary documents, which would have reassured her, about her own child",[311] until a year after the event. Liability was conceded by the Health Board and MacKenzie J awarded her £25,000 and £10,000 to her husband. The husband waived his award and McKenzie J ordered that £35,000 be paid to the mother.

### *(f) Facial injuries*

**[44.179]** The Courts have tended to regard facial injuries as being of more importance for women than for men. In *Prendergast v Joe Malone Self Drive Ltd*,[312] Budd J said:

> "Facial injuries involving the disfigurement of a young woman are admittedly in the category of injuries that must be regarded as serious."

**[44.180]** So also, in *Foley v Thermocement Products Ltd*,[313] Lavery J stated:

> "Facial disfigurement is a very serious matter no matter what a person's age or condition in life may be. While fully recognising this, it is surely the case that a scar on the face of a young woman might reasonably be considered a more serious matter than on the face of a middle aged man."

---

309. *Cf* paras **[3.32]-[3.41]** above; *McSweeney v Cork Corporation* DPIJ: Hilary & Easter Terms 1994, p 37. In some cases the court may find that a post-traumatic stress disorder, even though occurring (or continuing to occur) after the commission of the tort, in attributable exclusively to events other than the trauma of the accident: *cf Hamilton v The Office of Public Works* High Court, 22 December 1993 (Morris J).

310. DPIJ: Michaelmas Term 1990, p 218 (HC).

311. DPIJ: Michaelmas Term 1990.

312. DPIJ: Michaelmas Term 1990, p 6. See also *Crowley v Muskery, Lissarda & Balinhassig Co-op Ltd* Supreme Court, 11 February 1972 *per* Ó Dálaigh CJ at p 5.

313. (1954) 90 ILTR 92 at 94 (SC). See also *Lee v Joyce* Supreme Court, 3 December 1964 *per* Walsh J at p 7; *Roote v Irish Box Print and Packaging Ltd*, DPIJ: Hilary and Easter Terms 1991, p 10 at 14 (HC); *Basmajian v Haire* High Court, 2 April 1993 (Barr J); *Delaney v Dunnes Stores*, DPIJ: Hilary & Easter Terms, 1992, p 1 (HC); *Kilgarriff v Kilgarriff*, DPIJ: Trinity Term 1991, p 37 (HC); *Whelley v Falbey*, DPIJ: Hilary & Easter Terms 1996, p 35 (HC). In *Kennevan v Limerick Corporation* DPIJ: Trinity and Michaelmas Terms 1993, p 277 at 280 (HC), Geoghegan J broadened the differentiation between the sexes to scars that are not on the face. Speaking in the context of a man who had received an unsightly scar on his arm. Geoghegan J observed that:

> "obviously it is trite to say that …. the same scar may be worth very different money, depending on the person who has it - obviously a young unmarried girl would be the highest and an elder person, male would be less …"

**[44.181]** In *Ronayne v Ronayne*,[314] Ó Dálaigh CJ went so far as to observe that a jury might reasonably consider that:

> "nothing can satisfactorily exorcise or tranquillise the insecurity which can affect a young woman conscious of the existence of a facial blemish."

Of course, damages for facial disfigurement should bear some reasonable relation to damages for other disabling physical injuries.[315] Moreover, as we have seen from the *Prendergast case*,[316] the psychological effect of the injury on the particular plaintiff must be the test.

**[44.182]** The social standing of the plaintiff has also been considered relevant. In *Ronayne v Ronayne*,[317] where it was contended by the defendant that cosmetics would camouflage the plaintiff's facial disfigurement. Ó Dálaigh CJ responded that:

> "A jury might also reasonably consider that, while thickly-pasted cosmetics are acceptable in certain ranges of society the plaintiff in more lowly rank of life could not, if I may use the phrase, 'get away with it'."

It may confidently be predicted that no Irish judge would speak in these terms today.[318]

***(g) The unaware plaintiff***[319]

**[44.183]** We now come to a difficult issue which goes to the heart of the philosophy of compensation. If, in addition to causing the plaintiff severe physical injuries,[320] the defendant also renders the plaintiff incapable of appreciating his or her plight (whether on account of unconsciousness or mental incapacity), what effect should this have on the amount of damages? If, for example, the physical injuries would have warranted £100,000 had the plaintiff been aware of his or her plight, should the plaintiff's incapacity to appreciate the position (a) enhance the damages, (b) have no effect on the award; or (c) reduce the damages? And what principle of compensation should dictate the answer to this question?

**[44.184]** This serious issue has led to differing responses in common law jurisdictions at different times. In England, in *H West & Son Ltd v Shephard*,[321] the House of Lords, by a majority, held that one should concentrate on the objective fact of the plaintiff's loss of amenity rather than on the quality of the plaintiff's subjective response to that fact. Lords

314. [1970] IR 15 at 22 (SC).

315. *Prendergast v Joe Malone Self Drive Ltd* Supreme Court, 21 June 1967, *per* Ó Dálaigh, CJ at p 6.

316. *Prendergast v Joe Malone Self Drive Ltd* Supreme Court, 21 June 1967.

317. Supreme Court, 16 July 1970 at p 9.

318. In *Dunphy v T Carroll & Sons Ltd* High Court, 28 June 1984 (Hamilton J with jury) damages were awarded to a 26-year-old male plaintiff who claimed that, as a result of a road accident his lips had been scarred, leaving him with no sensation when he kissed a girl.

319. See Ogus, 'Damage for Lost Amenities. for a Foot, a Feeling or a Function' (1972) 35 MLR 1; Delany, 'Non-Pecuniary Loss in Personal injuries Claims: The Measure of Damages' (1963) 28-29 Ir Jur 27 at 28-29.

320. Cases involving the loss of an amenity include *Quinn v W & T Avery Ltd* (1967) 103 ILTR 142 (SC) and *Kidney' v Castlemore Quarries Ltd* Supreme Court, 13 April 1973; see also *Roche v Kelly & Co Ltd* [1969] IR 100 at 114 (SC); *O'Sullivan v Millerick* (1970) 104 ILTR 8 at 10 (SC).

321. [1964] AC 326.

Reid and Devlin, dissenting, considered that considerably less weight, relatively speaking, should be attached to the objective fact of the plaintiff's injury.

**[44.185]** In Australia, in *Skelton v Collins*,[322] the High Court endorsed the subjective approach. The Supreme Court of Canada for some years favoured the majority approach in *H West & Son Ltd v Shephard*. In *R v Jennings*,[323] in 1966, Cartwright J, speaking for the Court, expressed "full agreement" with the view that:

> "damages for loss of the amenities of life are not to be reduced by reason of the fact that the injured person is unconscious and unaware of his condition."[324]

**[44.186]** Twelve years later, however, in *Andrews v Grand & Toy Albert Ltd*[325] the Supreme Court of Canada adopted a general approach to compensation which no longer stresses the objective injury sustained by the plaintiff. Instead, the emphasis is on solace. Dickson J explained that:

> "'Solace' in this sense is taken in to mean physical arrangements which can make [the plaintiff's] life more endurable rather then 'solace' in the sense of sympathy."[326]

**[44.187]** In Ireland, in *Cooke v Walsh*,[327] the issue of the unaware plaintiff was considered by the Supreme Court. There, the plaintiff, in addition to suffering very serious physical injuries, also sustained brain injuries of such degree that, at the time of the trial (when he was aged eleven), "both doctors estimated his mentality as being that of a child of one and that his mental age would in adult life be hardly more than about two years".[328] Counsel for the defendant submitted that the amount to be awarded for general damages should be moderate on account of the plaintiff's lack of awareness or appreciation of his condition.

**[44.188]** The majority of the court agreed. Griffin J (O'Higgins CJ, Henchy and Hederman JJ concurring) said:

> "The greatest suffering endured by, say, a quadriplegic, is mental suffering. Just as in the instant case, a quadriplegic has been deprived of the amenities of life and has lost the enjoyment of life. But the difference between the two cases is that, in the case of a quadriplegic, unless he has brain damage, he is fully aware of his condition and of what it means to him - he sees himself as a prisoner for life in his wheelchair. In the present case, the plaintiff has, at best, only a mild awareness of appreciation of his condition due to the severe brain damage he sustained in the accident. He has, therefore, been spared the considerable mental suffering which would follow from knowledge or appreciation of the virtual destruction of his life. The plaintiff must still be compensated for his injuries, but in the

---

322. (1966) 115 Comm LR 94.
323. (1966) 57 DLR (2d) 644.
324. (1966) 57 DLR (2d) 644.
325. (1978) 83 DLR (3d) 452.
326. (1978) 83 DLR (3d) 452 at 476. Commenting on this decision, two Canadian writers consider that its effect is that:

> "logically no damages should be awarded to an unaware plaintiff for any non-pecuniary loss whatsoever, whether pain and suffering, loss of amenities or loss of expectation of life. Damages for intangible loss are intended to provide solace for mental distress. Absent awareness, there is no mental distress. Absent mental distress, there is no need for solace and thus no need for compensation."

Cooper-Stephenson & Saunders, *Personal Injury Damages in Canada* (1981), p 378.

327. [1984] ILRM 208 (SC).
328. [1984] ILRM 208 at 218.

> circumstances outlined I agree with [the] submission [of counsel for the defence] that the compensation should be moderate.[329]

**[44.189]** McCarthy J did not concur with this approach. He noted that the matter had not been fully debated on the hearing of the appeal and he preferred to reserve for further consideration:

> "the very wide question which has been the subject of considerable debate, both in the courts and academically, in the United Kingdom, in Canada and in Australia, and, in doubt, in the United States, bearing upon the question as to whether or not an individual who has no real appreciation of his plight should be awarded other than a relatively nominal sum for general damages."[330]

**[44.190]** It is perhaps unfortunate that this important issue should have been determined without full debate. In the absence of any clear analysis, we can only infer the principles grounding the Court's conclusion that compensation should be "moderate". It would appear that the majority had little enthusiasm for basing compensation on the extent of objective injury done to the plaintiff. The stress on the presence or absence of suffering on the part of the plaintiff suggests a strong preference for the subjective approach whereby damages are gauged by evaluating the difference between the happiness and mental tranquillity which the victim would have enjoyed had the accident not occurred and the degree of unhappiness and mental turmoil which he has in fact sustained. However, another point should not be overlooked. In *Sinnott v Quinnsworth Ltd*,[331] as we have seen, one of the three factors mentioned by the Court as affecting the quantum of general damages is that relating to "the things upon which the plaintiff might reasonably be expected to spend money".[332] Applying this factor to cases where the plaintiff is unconscious or suffers serious brain damage, the effect would be further to reduce the amount of compensation to which the plaintiff is entitled.

**[44.191]** This outcome has its defenders, but we may at least raise the question whether it is just to make the quantum of compensation depend so greatly on the psychological capacity and the spending capacity of the particular plaintiff. There is of course a certain futility in awarding large sums to unconscious plaintiffs; but the law can be reformed to deal with this problem without having to adopt a pragmatic philosophy which may be considered by some to reduce rather than fully respect the human stature of the victim.

**[44.192]** The Supreme Court returned to the theme, again in a somewhat unsatisfactory manner in *Dunne v National Maternity Hospital*.[333] The plaintiff had been born "a spastic quadriplegic with major mental handicap, incapable of any understanding". His sight was damaged. He was incontinent and could "perform no useful or intended function for himself, having to be fed, dressed and washed."[334] The jury awarded general damages of £476,000. The defendants, invoking *Cook v Walsh*,[335] argued that, in view of the plaintiff's

329. [1984] ILRM 208 at 219.
330. [1984] ILRM 208 at 223.
331. [1984] ILRM 523 (SC).
332. [1984] ILRM 523 at 532.
333. [1989] IR 91 (SC).
334. [1989] IR 91 at 118 (*per* Finlay CJ)
335. See para **[44.106]** above.

almost complete lack of awareness of his position and his incapacity to derive pleasure or comfort from anything except bodily care and attention and the presence of his family, the amount of general damages should be reduced to a "moderate figure". The Supreme Court agreed and ordered a retrial on this issue (as well as on that of liability).

**[44.193]** Finlay CJ noted that no submission had apparently been made at trial and no argument had been presented on appeal to the effect that as a matter of principle, a person who as a result of injuries tortuously inflicted had no awareness of his or her condition should be entitled "to nil or nominal damages only"[336] for general damages. The Chief Justice "therefore, express[ed] no view on any such proposition".[337] What emerges from *Dunne* is that the Supreme Court was apparently quite content to proceed on the basis that damages for restricted awareness of one's plight should be no more than "moderate". The only question – to be answered in an appropriate case – was whether this should be reduced to zero where the plaintiff had no awareness of his or her position. One might perhaps regard this as a subtle accretion of the subjectivist philosophy but this is not how Morris J saw it in *Lindsay v Mid-Western Health Board*.[338]

**[44.194]** It is interesting to note that the English Law Commission, after widespread consultation, has recommended[339] that no change should be made in English law in this context which, as we have seen, regards the unconscious victim as entitled to generous rather than moderate damages. In its Report, *Damages for Personal Injury: Non-Pecuniary Loss*, published in 1999, it records that:

> "[m]any consultees expressed concern that the allegedly unconscious claimant may have some awareness or may recover a degree of consciousness. The point was also made that permanent unconsciousness may be difficult to define or diagnose,[340] and that, since medical knowledge is developing, now is not the moment to change the law."[341]

## Loss of Expectation of Life[342]

**[44.195]** Compensation for loss of expectation of life raises formidable legal and philosophical problems: the topic "might seem more suitable for discussion in an essay on

---

336. [1989] IR 91 at 119.

337. [1989] IR 91 at 119 (*per* Finlay CJ).

338. [1993] 2 IR 147 (HC). In *Hughes v O'Flaherty* High Court, 19 January 1996, a case involving tragic facts, Carney J had to determine whether the plaintiff's lack of awareness of his injuries was such as to require the court to make a radical reduction of compensation for general damages. The plaintiff had suffered devastating injuries in a traffic accident, including very severe damage to the brain. Carney J, who visited the plaintiff at the National Rehabilitation Centre, found that he had a general apprehension of his situation because he volunteered the words that he was prepared to suffer if that was God's will for him. Accordingly the diminution principle did not apply. Carney J awarded £225,000 for general damages.

339. English Law Commission, *Damages for Personal Injury: Non-Pecuniary Loss* (LC-257), para 2.19.

340. The Commission referred to a British study in which, of 40 patients diagnosed by the referring clinician as being in a vegetative state, only 10 remained vegetative state, 13 slowly emerged from that state during a rehabilitation programme and 17 were considered to have been misdiagnosed as vegetative: Andrews, Murphy, Munday & Littlewood, *Misdiagnosis of the Vegetative State: Retrospective Study in a Rehabilitation Unit* (1996) 313 Br Med J 13.

341. English Law Commission, *Damages for Personal Injury: Non-Pecuniary Loss*, (LC-257), para 2.14.

342. See Delany, 'Non-Pecuniary Loss in Personal Injury Claims: The Measure of Damages' (1963) 28-29 Ir Jur 27 at 27-28.

Aristotelian ethics than in the judgment in a court of law".[343] The existence of the right not to have one's life span reduced by the tortious act of another was first recognised in England in 1935[344] and approved by the House of Lords[345] two years later. Lord Wright stated:

> "A man has a legal right to his own life. I think he has a legal interest entitling him to complain if the integrity of his life is impaired by tortious acts, not only in regard to pain, suffering and disability, but also in regard to the continuance of life or its normal expectancy. A man has a legal right that his life should not be shortened by the tortious act of another. His normal expectancy of life is a thing of temporal value, so that its impairment is something for which damages should be given."[346]

It soon became clear that, unless compensation for loss of expectation of life were to be restricted, it could lead to extensive compensation. Accordingly, in *Benham v Gambling*,[347] the House of Lords set a moderate norm of compensation, reducing an award of £12,000 in respect of a child of two-and-a-half years to £200. (The child had survived the accident for only a few hours.)

**[44.196]** In this jurisdiction, where a cause of action survives for the benefit of the estate of a deceased person, the damages recoverable for the benefit of his estate are not to include damages "for loss or diminution of expectation of life or happiness".[348] Thus, the problem here is limited to cases where the victim is still alive but his or her expectation of life has been reduced.

**[44.197]** It seems that the position today is that damages *may* be recovered under this head, but that they should be moderate.[349]

**[44.198]** In *McMorrow v Knott*,[350] the Supreme Court considered the question. The trial judge had directed the jury that if they found that there had been a loss of expectation of life, the amount of damages might not be different from that which would be awarded on the basis of no loss of expectation of life, because the damages in respect of such loss might be equated to saving in the cost of nursing, the one balancing the other. The Supreme Court held that this was an improper direction.

**[44.199]** Ó Dálaigh J stated:

> "Compensation for shortening of life is a difficult question; but it will now suffice to observe that the Courts have been consistent in declining to allow in respect of this head of damages other than moderate sums of compensation, in no way comparable with the amount which a

343. *Benham v Gambling* [1941] AC 157 at 166 (*per* Lord Simon).

344. *Flint v Lovell* [1935] 1 KB 354 (CA)

345. [1937] AC 826.

346. [1937] AC 826 at 847-848.

347. [1941] AC 157.

348. Civil Liability Act 1961, s 7(2). Note that "loss of expectation of life", being a heading of *non-pecuniary loss*, differs from the *pecuniary* loss which flows from "the lost years" of earnings; the latter loss, it seems, should still be recoverable in proceedings for the benefit of the estate of the deceased: *cf* Chs 41-42 above.

349. The same applies in Northern Ireland: *Williamson v Honeford* [1956] NI 31 (CA); *cf Doherty v Jas Murland Ltd* [1956] NI 34 (CA).

350. Supreme Court, 21 December 1959.

saving of nursing expenses in this case would be likely to represent. Here then, . . . a wrong principle has been imported into the jury's calculations.[351]

**[44.200]** Maguire CJ was somewhat more circumspect. He stated:

> "The head of damage for the shortening of life should not in my opinion be considered on an actuarial basis. It is a difficult matter to lay down a precise method for estimating a figure."[352]

The Chief Justice added:

> "It has been suggested with a good deal of reason that this head of damages might properly be considered as an element of pain and suffering. In considering it and the other heads of damages ... the jury should have been told that it is quite impossible in a case such as this to give perfect compensation. In one sense nothing would compensate the plaintiff for the dreadful consequences of an accident for which admittedly he had no blame. A jury must, however, be just and towards this end must be reasonable in arriving at a figure."[353]

**[44.201]** The Supreme Court records also tantalisingly contain the text of a judgment of Lavery J, which was not actually delivered. Writing to the Registrar of the Supreme Court six years later, Lavery J, stated that he could not recall why the judgment had not been delivered. It is worth looking at this draft judgment since, although technically valueless as a precedent, it affords an interesting insight into the approach of a leading Irish jurist to the question.

**[44.202]** Lavery J discussed the question in some detail. At the outset he noted that:

> "To lay down any rule with reference to this head of damage is undoubtedly a matter of considerable difficulty. Whether the plaintiff could reasonably look forward to a happy life or a miserable one, the loss to him is, in one sense, inestimable."[354]

Lavery J referred to Lord Wright's statement in *Rose v Ford*[355] to the effect that, whilst it was true that no money would adequately compensate a person for the shortening of his life, it would be paradoxical if the law refused to give any compensation at all because none would be adequate.

**[44.203]** Lavery J added:

> "This decision is said to have caused chaos 'not much relieved' according to Mr Heuston in a number of judgments in the Court of Appeal. The present tendency is to give very moderate amounts. It seems to me that a jury should understand that perfect compensation could not be given - they must be reasonable and add what they think appropriate to the damages for pain and suffering."[356]

---

351. Supreme Court, 21 December 1959, p 2.
352. Supreme Court, 21 December 1959, p 3.
353. Supreme Court, 21 December 1959, p 3-4.
354. Supreme Court, 21 December 1959, p 3. See also *Murray v John Sisk & Son (Dublin) Ltd* [1965] Ir Jur Rep 41 at 42 (SC).
355. [1937] AC 826 at 848.
356. Supreme Court, 21 December 1959, p 3.

**[44.204]** In *O'Sullivan v Dwyer*,[357] the Supreme Court held that an award of about £10,000 in 1969 for the loss of expectation of between sixteen and twenty years of life was excessive, and a new trial on the issue of general damages was ordered. Walsh J stated that:

> "When one has already made allowance for the mental distress which may be attributable to the knowledge of the loss of expectation of life, it is difficult to assess in terms of money what might reasonably be given as compensation for the actual loss of expectation of life."[358]

In Walsh J's view, the sum of about £10,000 for loss of expectation of life was not sustainable:

> "That may appear to be a somewhat unsympathetic approach but, however it may appear, the fact is that the loss of 16 to 20 years of life is considerably less in value than having to endure 21 years as a paraplegic."[359]

## VII. Property Damage

**[44.205]** Compensation for damage to property[360] raises problems that are generally less complex than those arising in respect of personal injuries. It is true that the question of recovery for pure economic loss resulting from negligence has given rise to much controversy.[361] but where physical damage is involved, the computation of loss is usually relatively straightforward.

**[44.206]** Problems may arise, however, in attempting to apply the principle of *restitutio in integrum* in cases where premises have been severely damaged or destroyed. The plaintiff may claim that he is entitled to the cost of reinstatement; the defendant may reply that compensation should be limited to the diminution in value of property. Where a gross disproportion exists between these two figures, which is to prevail? Our courts have not taken a doctrinaire position on this question, preferring instead to adopt a pragmatic, discretionary approach, which investigates the reasonableness of the plaintiff's desire for reinstatement. In this regard they will give consideration, with emphasis varying from case to case, to matters such as:

> "the nature of the property, the plaintiff's relation to it, the nature of the wrongful act causing the damage, the conduct of the parties subsequent to the wrongful act, and the pecuniary, economic or other relevant implications or consequences of reinstatement damages as compared with diminished-value damages."[362]

In determining this question it has been said that:

---

357. [1971] IR 275 (SC). The question had been left open in *McArdle v McCaughey Bros Ltd* [1968] IR 47 at 53 (SC).

358. [1971] IR 275 at 290. In this context the old legal adage that it is cheaper to kill than to maim, still holds good.

359. [1971] IR 275. *Cf Brennan v Savage Smyth & Co* [1982] ILRM 223 (SC) which may perhaps indicate willingness to support a higher level of award under this heading, though it is impossible to be clear on what weight the Court gave to the loss of expectation of life, *in itself*, as opposed to the consequential *awareness* of such loss.

360. The subject is dealt with in detail by Ogus, *The Law Of Damages* (1973), Ch 5. See also Downing 'Measuring Damages for Tort Harms to Realty' (1962) 51 Ky L 366.

361. *Cf* Ch 10 above.

362. *Munnelly v Falcon Ltd* [1978] IR 387 at 400 (SC).

> "There may be some cases in which damages equal to the cost of restoration are the only way to put the plaintiff back into the same position as he was before the accident, but they are special cases and the onus lies on the plaintiff to establish that his is one of them."[363]

**[44.207]** Such special cases would include the destruction of long-established businesses in important thoroughfares and commercial centres, buildings with an historical value, and churches or chapels.[364] But an auctioneer who had been carrying on business for only two years at the premises which were destroyed was held[365] not to be entitled to reinstatement damages, in view of the short duration in which he had occupied the premises and in the light of evidence to the effect that many other auctioneers had changed their premises without damage to the volume of their businesses. The same applied to the purchasers of a modern suburban house, where other houses of the same type were available in the same area,[366] there was "no question"[367] of reinstatement damages being awarded.

**[44.208]** Where reinstatement damages are awarded, should there be a discount for the fact that the plaintiff will have a new structure more valuable than the one that has been destroyed? The balance of authority[368] appears to be against ordering a discount, on the basis that the plaintiff should not be compelled to invest capital in his property against his will.

**[44.209]** The problems of collateral benefits can arise in relation to property injuries just as it can in relation to personal injuries. In the High Court decision of *Woodman Matheson & Co Ltd v Brennan*[369] Maguire P held that a sum paid by the plaintiff' insurers for the repair of the property damaged by the defendant's negligence should not be taken into account in assessing damages.

---

363. *Munnelly v Falcon Ltd* [1978] IR 387 at 405 (*per* Kenny J).

364. *Munnelly v Falcon Ltd* [1978] IR 387 at 405-406, (*per* Kenny J), referring to *Murphy v Wexford County Council* [1921] 2 IR 230 at 235 (CA) - malicious injury claim. See also *Harbutt's Plasticine v Wayne Tank Co* [1970] 1 QB 447 and *Hutchinson v Davidson* 1945 SC 395.

365. *Munnelly v Falcon Ltd* [1978] IR 387.

366. *Quinn v Quality Homes Ltd* High Court, 21 November 1977 (Finlay P).

367. *Quinn v Quality Homes Ltd* High Court, 21 November 1977, p 22. In *Murphy v De Braam* Supreme Court, 12 December 1997 (*ex temp*), where the plaintiff's helicopter had been damaged, Barron J (O'Flaherty and Keane JJ concurring) said:

> "Damages in tort are intended to place the plaintiff back in the position in which he would have been but for the wrong committed against him. That does not mean that he should be put in the position of the owner of the chattel with a particular value. That does not restore him to the position in which he was before the tort was committed. He was the owner of such chattel and in a position to use it.
>
> He had no intention to dispose of it. To be put back into the position in which he was at the date of tort it is necessary to replace his chattel for him by the cost likely to be incurred in the purchase of a similar chattel. This figure would not be the same as the value of the chattel lost since there is always a significant difference between buying and selling prices."

368. *Cf Harbutt's Plasticine v Wayne Tank Co* [1970] 1 QB 447; *Badham v Williams* [1968] NZLR 728. But see *Wexford County Council* [1921] 2 IR 230 at 240 (*per* O'Connor LJ). Decisions in the United States also favour the imposition of a discount: *cf* Ogus, *The Law Of Damages* (1973), p 134.

369. (1941) 75 ILTR 34 (HC). *Cf McCailum v G Madill & Sons Ltd* [1965] NI 187 (CA).

# Chapter 45

# Injunctions[1]

## I. Introduction

**[45.01]** In some cases the plaintiff will not regard damages as an appropriate remedy. His or her real concern will be that a wrongful act may be committed or continued in the future or that it will recur; the plaintiff may much prefer that the defendant be ordered to cease doing the wrongful act than merely required to pay a "licence fee" in the form of damages. If I know that I am about to be the victim of a serious libel in tomorrow's newspaper, I may prefer to obtain an injunction prohibiting its appearance than to seek compensation later in the form of damages for my ruined reputation.

## II. Prohibitory, Mandatory and *Quia Timet* Injunctions

**[45.02]** The High Court [the Circuit Court also] has power to issue an injunction wherever it appears "just or convenient" to do so.[2] The injunction may be (a) prohibitory, that is, one restraining the defendant from continuing or repeating a wrongful act; (b) mandatory, that is, one ordering the defendant to do some positive act to end a wrongful state of affairs that has been created by him;[3] or (c) *quia timet*, that is, one restraining wrongful conduct that has not yet been committed but is merely apprehended.

---

1. See Delany *Equity and the Law of Trusts in Ireland* (2nd ed, 1999), Ch 13; Keane *Equity and the Law of Trusts in the Republic of Ireland* (1988), Ch 15; Casey 'The Injunction in Labour Disputes in Éire' (1969) 18 ICLQ 347, and the articles in (1946) 80 ILT Sol J 63-69, (1924) 58 ILT & SJ 189, 303, (1916) 50 ILT & SJ 225, 231, 241, 257. See also the excellent, wide-ranging, lecture by Tyrrell 'Injunctions' Incorporated Law Society of Ireland, Continuing Legal Education, 1 June 1989.

2. Courts (Supplemental Provisions) Act 1961 (No 39), s 8; Supreme Court of Judicature (Ireland) Act 1877 (40 & 41 Vict c 57), s 28(8). See further Delany, *Equity and the Law of Trusts in Ireland* (1996), pp 370-371; Casey 'The Injunction in Labour Disputes in Éire' (1969) 18 ICLQ 347, and the articles in (1946) 80 ILT Sol J 63, 69, (1924) 58 ILT & SJ 189, 303; (1916) 50 ILT & SJ 225, 231, 241, 257. In *Moore v AG* [1927] IR 569 at 580 (SC) Murnaghan J stated that the 1877 provision:

   > "extends the principles upon which jurisdiction was formerly exercised by the Court of Chancery, although no doubt these principles may still be a guide in many cases."

3. See Delany *Equity and the Law of Trusts in Ireland* (2nd ed, 1999), pp 460-464. *Cf AG v Mayo Co Co* [1902] 1 IR 13 - mandatory injunction to remove huts from highway; *O'Connor v Walsh* (1907) 42 ILTR 20 (CA affg HC) - removal of privy blocking light to plaintiff's premises; *Sligo Corporation v Gilbride* [1929] IR 351 (SC) - restoration of wall; *Woodhouse v Newry Navigation Co* [1898] 1 IR 161 (CA) - mandatory injunction to remove stones, ballast and rubbish from plaintiff's oyster beds; *Gibbings v Hungerford* [1904] 1 IR 211 (CA) - mandatory injunction to disconnect houses from drain which, when overloaded with sewerage, caused a nuisance; *Crowley v Ireland* High Court, 1 December 1977 (McWilliam J) - provision of transport for school attendance. As to the circumstances in which a mandatory injunction at the interlocutory stage will be ordered, see *Campus Oil v Minister for Industry and Energy (No 2)* [1983] IR 88 at 107 (SC);

**[45.03]** The Courts will not act precipitously in ordering a *quia timet* injunction:

> "the law requires proof by the plaintiff of a well-founded apprehension of injury - proof of actual and real danger - a strong probability, almost amounting to moral certainty, that [an actionable] tort will be committed."[4]

A *quia timet* injunction was ordered by Kenny J in *Whelan v Madigan*,[5] where the defendant landlord was likely to continue a campaign of intimidation to force his tenants to leave the premises.

**[45.04]** In *McCrane v Louth County Council*,[6] in 1983, O'Hanlon J declined to grant a *quia timet* injunction restraining the defendant from developing a rubbish dump on a site it had acquired, not far from the plaintiffs' houses and places of recreation. He accepted that conditions at existing dumps in the county had been "very unpleasant for people living in their vicinity",[7] and that these dumps had in the past been "malodorous, unsightly and unhygienic".[8] Nevertheless, he was impressed by the fact that the Council's choice of the site had been "based on a responsible scientific appraisal of the problem in line with the most modern research".[9] Although the council could have acquired a far less expensive

---

3. (contd) *Bula Ltd v Tara Mines Ltd* [1988] ILRM 157 (HC), analysed in Byrne & Binchy, *Annual Review of Irish Law 1987* at 167-169; *Boyhan v Tribunal of Inquiry into the Beef Industry* [1992] ILRM 545 (HC); *O'Dea v Ó Briain* [1992] ILRM 364; *Boyle v An Post*, [1992] 2 IR 437 (HC); *A & N Pharmacy Ltd v United Drug Wholesale Ltd*, [1996] 2 ILRM 42 (HC); *ICC Banl plc v Verling* [1995] 1 ILRM 123 (HC); *De Burca v Wicklow County Council* High Court, 24 May 2000; *Tobin v Cashell (Chairman of the Board of Management of Mayfield Community School)* High Court, 21 March 2000 (Kearns J); Delany 'Equity'in Byrne & Binchy, *Annual Review of Irish Law 1996*, pp 294-295. In *O'Reilly v Limerick Corporation* [1989] 4 ILRM 181 (HC), Costello J considered it inappropriate to grant a mandatory injunction requiring the defendant to review its building programme and vary it in relation to the provision of serviced sites for travellers since he could not assume that the defendant would neglect to perform its statutory duty or that, if it was guilty of such negligence, the Minister for the Environment would not exercise his powers under s 111 of the Housing Act 1966 in the light of the Court's order.

4. *AG (Boswell) v Rathmines & Pembroke Joint Hospital Board* [1904] 1 IR 161 at 171 (CA). The passage was quoted with approval by Henchy J in *C & A Modes v C & A (Waterford) Ltd* [1976] IR 198 at 213 (SC); by Meredith J, in *Independent Newspapers Ltd v Irish Press Ltd* [1932] IR 615 at 631 (HC); and by Fawsitt J, in *Radford v Wexford Corporation* (1955) 89 ILTR 184 at 186 (CC). The passage has also been quoted with approval in England: *AG v Nottingham Corporation* [1904] 1 Ch 673 at 677 (*per* Farwell J). See also *Szabo v Esat Digiphone Ltd* [1998] 2 ILRM 102 (HC). See further Delany *Equity and the Law of Trusts in Ireland* (2nd ed, 1999), pp 488-491; Keane *Equity and the Law of Trusts in the Republic of Ireland* (1988), para 15-32.
   Some differences in emphasis in the expression of what circumstances must be shown to obtain *a quia timet* injunction are apparent. In *Radford v Wexford Corporation* (1955) 89 ILTR 184 at 186, Fawsitt J stated that the plaintiff must show "imminent danger of a substantial kind for which damages will be no adequate redress". In the *Independent Newspapers Ltd v Irish Press Ltd* [1932] IR 615 at 631. Meredith J (in a passing-off action) required merely that the Court be satisfied that:
   > "there is a reasonable probability that what is threatened to be done is calculated in the ordinary course of events, or according to the ordinary course of business, to cause damage to the plaintiff."

5. [1978] ILRM 136 (HC).
6. High Court, unrep 9 December 1983 (O'Hanlon J).
7. High Court, unrep 9 December 1983, pp 9-10.
8. High Court, unrep 9 December 1983, p 10.
9. High Court, unrep 9 December 1983, p 11.

site well away from houses, it had decided not to do so for good hydrogeological reasons, in keeping with modern thinking on the proper location and management of waste disposal sites. Instead of resorting to the "haphazard dumping"[10] which had taken place in so many parts of Ireland, the Council had commissioned a report from consultants with very considerable experience, to confirm the suitability of the site and to advise on its development and management.

## When Will an Injunction be Ordered?

**[45.05]** Injunctions may be sought and, when appropriate, obtained in respect of a wide range of torts,[11] including public[12] and private[13] nuisance, trespass to land,[14] passing off,[15]

10. High Court, unrep 9 December 1983, p 12.

11. See Delany *Equity and the Law of Trusts in Ireland* (2nd ed, 1999), pp 500-501.

12. *AG v Mayo Co Co* [1902] 1 IR 13; *AG (Boswell) v Rathmines & Pembroke Joint Hospital Board* [1904] 1 IR 161 (CA). See further Keane, *Equity and the Law of Trusts in the Republic of Ireland* (1988), paras 15.10, 15.17-15.21.

13. *McGrath v Munster & Leinster Bank Ltd* [1959] IR 313 (HC); *Bellew v Cement Ltd* [1948] IR 61 (SC); *Dewar v City & Suburban Racecourse Co* [1899] IR 345; *Radford v Wexford Corporation* (1955) 89 ILTR 184 (CC); *Mangan v McCarthy* (1965) 99 ILTR 91 (HC); *Mullin v Hynes* Supreme Court, 13 November 1972; *Gibbings v Hungerford* [1904] 1 IR 211 (CA); *Sheehan v College of Dance* [1996] Ir L Log W 288 (CC). *Cf Kingstown Township Commissioners v Blackrock Township Commissioners* (1876) IR 10 Eq 160 (Chy); *Rabbette v Mayo County Council* [1984] ILRM 156 (HC); *Stafford v Roadstone Ltd* [1980] ILRM 1 (HC); *McGrane v Lough County Council* High Court, 9 December 1983 (O'Hanlon J).

14. *Kenny Homes & Co Ltd v Leonard* Supreme Court, 18 June 1998; *Pasture Properties Ltd v Evans* High Court, 5 February 1999 (Laffoy J); *Tisdall v McArthur & Co (Steel and Metal) Ltd* [1951] IR 228 (SC affg HC); *Carson v Jeffers* [1961] IR 44 (HC); *Flanagan v Mulhall* [1985] ILRM 134 (HC); *Irish Shell and BP Ltd v John Costello Ltd,* [1984] IR 511 (SC); *Dwyer Nolan Developments Ltd v Dublin County Council*, [1986] IR 130 (HC); *Cullen v Cullen* [1962] IR 268 (HC); *Moore v AG (No 3)* [1930] IR 471 (SC); *Gibbings v Hungerford* [1904] 1 IR 211 (CA); *St John v Ossory* Supreme Court, 23 July 1930; *Dundalk Urban District Council v Conway* High Court, 18 July 1983 (Blayney J); *British Home Stores Ltd v Mitchell* High Court, 18 April 1984 (Lynch J); *Tower Homes Ltd v Brien et al* High Court, 16 July 1984 (Hamilton J). *Cf Sandys v Murray* (1838) 1 Ir Eq Rep 29; *Wrixon v Condran* (1839) 1 Ir Eq Rep 380. See also *Little v Cooper (No 1)* [1937] IR 1 (HC); *Little v Cooper (No 2)* [1937] IR 510 (HC) - trespass on fishery, *Patel v WH Smith (Eziot) Ltd* [1987] 2 All ER 569 (CA); *O'Gara v Murray* High Court, 10 November 1988 (McCarthy J). In cases where a trespasser disobeys an injunction, the court may prefer not to imprison the trespasser, but to leave it to the Gardaí to enforce the provisions of the Prevention of Forceable Entry and Occupation Act 1971: *Ross Co Ltd v Swan* [1981] ILRM 416 (HC).

15 Cases in which an injunction was sought on this ground (though not always successfully) include *Smithkline Beecham plc v Antigen Pharmaceuticals Ltd* [1999] 2 ILRM 190 (HC); *Guinness Ireland Group v Kilkenny Brewing Co Ltd* [1999] 1 ILRM 531 (HC); *DSG Retail Ltd v PC World Ltd* High Court, 13 January 1998 (Laffoy J); *Radio Limerick One Ltd v Treaty Radio Ltd* High Court, 13 November 1997 (Costello P); *O'Neill's Irish International Sports Company v O'Neill's Footwear Dryer Co Ltd*, High Court, 30 April 1997 (Barron J); *Symonds Cider & English Wine Co Ltd v Showerings (Ireland) Ltd* [1997] 1 ILRM 481 (HC); *R Griggs Group Ltd v Dunnes Stores Ireland Co* High Court, 4 October 1996 (McCracken J); *Private Research Ltd v Brosnan* [1996] 1 ILRM 27 (HC); *B & S Ltd v Irish Auto Trader Ltd,* [1995] 2 ILRM 152 (HC); *An Post v Irish Permanent plc* [1995] 1 ILRM 336 (HC); *Kent Adhesive Products Co t/a, Kapco v Ryan* High Court, 5 November 1993 (Costello J);

defamation,[16] malicious prosecution,[17] and trespass to the person[18] or goods,[19] injurious falsehood[20] and breach of statutory duty.[21] Torts relating to industrial relations[22] (such as

---

15. *(contd) An Bord Trachtála v Waterford Foods plc* [1994] FSR 316 (Keane J); *Curust Financial Services Ltd v Loewe-Lack-Werk Otto Loewe GmbH*, [1994] 1 IR 458 (SC); *Gabicci v Dunnes Stores Ltd* High Court, 31 July 1991 (Carroll J); *Mantruck Services Ltd v Ballinlough Electrical Refrigeration Co Ltd* [1992] 1 IR 351 (SC); *Falcon Travel Ltd v Owners Abroad Group plc, t/a Falcon Leisure Group*, [1991] 1 IR 175 (HC); *Adidas Sportsschuhfabriken Adi Dassler KA v Charles O'Neill & Co Ltd*, [1983] ILRM 112 (SC); *Polycell Products Ltd v O'Carroll* [1959] Ir Jur Rep 34 (HC); *Independent Newspapers Ltd v Irish Press Ltd* [1932] IR 615 (HC); *JUR Modes v JUR (Waterford) Ltd* [1976] IR 198 (SC); *"The Derry Journal" Ltd v Rialto Theatres Ltd* (1930) 64 ILTR 87 (NI Ch D); *Griffin v Kelly's Strand Hotel* High Court, 24 January 1980 (McWilliam J); *Jameson v Dublin Distillers Co* [1900] 1 IR 43. *Cf Hennessy (James) & Co v Keating* [1908] 1 IR 466 (HL); *Beecham Group Ltd v Eirat Pharmaceuticals Ltd* High Court, 27 March 1985 (Barron J), Irish Times, 28 March 1985, p 10, col 1, *Woodhouse v Newry Navigation Co* [1898] 1 IR 161 (CA); *Player & Wills (Ireland) Ltd v Gallagher (Dublin) Ltd* High Court, 26 September 1983 (Barron J); *Mitchelstown Co-operative Agricultural Society Ltd v Goldenvale Food Products Ltd* High Court, 12 December 1985 (Costello J). *Three Stripe International v Charles O'Neill & Co* [1989] ILRM 124 (HC); *Benckiser Gmbh v Fibrisol Service Ltd* High Court, 13 May 1988 (Costello J). *Cf Valentine v Valentine* (1892) 31 LR Ir 488, where an injunction was denied because the plaintiff had refused to state what were the specific acts complained of. As to injunctions restraining infringement of copyright, see *Universal City Studios Ltd v Mulligan* High Court, 25 March 1998 (Laffoy J). As to injunctions restraining use of trade marks see *Montex Holdings Ltd v The Controller of Patents, Designs and Trade Marks* High Court, 14 January 2000 (O'Sullivan J).
16. See Delany, *Equity and the Law of Trusts in Ireland* (2nd ed, 1999), pp 476-480; *Reynolds v Malocco* [1999] 1 ILRM 289 (HC); *Connolly v RTE* [1991] 2 IR 446; *Sinclair v Gogarty* [1937] IR 377 (SC); *Dunlop v Dunlop Rubber Co* [1920] 1 IR 280; *Gallagher v Tuohy* (1924) 58 ILTR 134 (HC); *Cullen v Stanley* [1926] IR 73 (SC); *"The Derry Journal" Ltd v Rialto Theatres Ltd* (1930) 64 ILTR 87 (NI Chy D); *Fitzgerald v Clancy* [1902] 1 IR 207; *Scott v Eason & Sons and Batsford Ltd* Irish Times. 9 August 1980, p 8; *Dickson (Alex) & Sons Ltd v Dickson (Alexander) & Sons* [1909] 1 IR 185 (CA); *Hammersmith Skating Rink Co v Dublin Skating Rink Co* (1876) IR 10 Eq 235 (VC). As to injunctions restraining breach of confidence see *National Irish Bank Ltd v Radio Telefís Éireann* [1998] 2 ILRM 196 (SC).
17. *Good v Collins and Kenna* High Court, 4 February 1983 (Finlay P), Irish Times, 5 February 1983, p 8.
18. *O'Boyle v AG* [1929] IR 558 (HC) - arrest; *Egan v Egan* [1975] Ch 218 (Oliver J) - injunction against apprehended acts of violence by 19-year-old son of mother.
19. *Sligo Corporation v Gilbride* [1929] IR 351 (SC). *Cf Magee v D'arcy*, 4 LR Ir 312 (Ex D) - trover and detinue. See also *Jennings v Quinn* [1968] IR 305 (SC). *Mahoney v Neenan (No 2)* (1966) 100 ILTR 205 (HC). A plaintiff seeking the return of goods, where the action for detinue or injunction against trespass is considered inappropriate or insufficient, sometimes resorts to an application for a mandatory injunction for their return, either in the alternative or in addition to the other action. *Cf Hanley v ICC Finance Ltd* [1996] 1 ILRM 463 (HC); *Wymes v Tehan* [1988] IR 717 (HC); *Keenan Brothers Ltd v CIE* (1963) 97 ILTR 54 (HC).
20. *Glen Ban Ltd v Lefroy* Supreme Court, 18 May 1944; *Kent Adhesive Products Co t/a Kapco v Ryan* High Court, 5 November 1993 (Costello J).
21. *Wall v Feeley* High Court, 26 October 1983 (Costello J). *Cf McDonald v Feely* Supreme Court, 23 July 1980; *Stelzer v Wexford North Slob Commissioners* [1988] ILRM 279 (HC); *Mourneview Estate Ltd v Dundalk UDC* (1967) 101 ILTR 189 (HC).
22. Eg *O'Neill v Transport & General Workers Union* [1934] IR 633 (HC).

inducement of breach of contract, intimidation and conspiracy) have also, of course, been fertile ground for injunction proceedings.[23]

**[45.06]** The better view[24] appears to be that an injunction may be sought against the commission or continuance of any tort, but, since the remedy is equitable, the Court has a discretion as to whether in the circumstances of any case an injunction should issue. It will take into account such factors as the absence of any need for granting an injunction in the light of assurances given by the defendant,[25] or of the lack of likelihood of any recurrence of the wrongful conduct[26] whether by virtue of steps already taken by the defendant[27] or for any other reason.

## III. Perpetual, Interlocutory and Interim Injunctions

**[45.07]** Injunctions (whether prohibitory, mandatory or *quia timet*) are of these kinds: perpetual, interlocutory or interim.

**[45.08]** A perpetual injunction is issued at the end of the trial of the action on its merits.[28] An interlocutory or interim[29] injunction is merely provisional,[30] being designed to preserve matters *in statu quo* until the complete hearing of the case. The Court, in granting an interlocutory injunction, does not attempt to anticipate the outcome of the proceedings, but rather confirms that there is a substantial question to be tried.

**[45.09]** To secure an interlocutory injunction, the plaintiff must pass three tests; he or she must show, first, "a serious question to be tried";[31] secondly, that the balance of convenience lies in favour of granting an interlocutory injunction;[32] and, thirdly, that irreparable damage would follow if the injunction were refused.[33]

---

23. See Casey 'The Injunction in Labour Disputes in Éire' (1969) 18 ICLQ 347; von Prondzynski 'Trade Disputes and the Courts: The Problem of the Labour Injunction' (1981) 16 Ir J (ns) 228; Kerr 'The Problem of the Labour Injunction Revisited' (1983) 16 Ir Jur (ns) 34. The changes brought about by the Industrial Relations Act 1990 have reduced the force and scope of the injunction weapon in this context. Delany *Equity and the Law of Trusts in Ireland* (2nd ed, 1999), pp 473-476.
24. WINFIELD & JOLOWICZ, p 794.
25. *Corry v National Union of Vintners, Grocers & Allied Trades Assistants* [1950] IR 315 (SC); *Cullen v Cullen* [1962] IR 268 (HC).
26. *Maher v Beirne* (1959) 93 ILTR 101 (HC).
27. *Halpin v Tara Mines Ltd,* High Court, 16 February 1976 (Gannon J), as explained in *Patterson v Murphy* [1978] ILRM 85 (HC). See also *McDonald v Feely* Supreme Court, 23 July 1980.
28. *Cf Mackey v Scottish Widows Fund Life Assurance Society* (1877) IR 11 Eq 541. See further Delany, *Equity and the Law of Trusts in Ireland* (2nd ed, 1999), p 443; Keane, *Equity and the Law of Trusts in the Republic of Ireland* (1988), paras 15.08-15.09.
29. An interim injunction is an injunction of an interlocutory nature granted by the Court on application to it ex parte by the plaintiff. It is very much an emergency "holding operation" until proceedings with both parties appearing can take place.
30. *Campus Oil Ltd v Minister for Industry and Energy (No 2)* [1983] IR 88 at 106 (SC), adopting the statement of law appearing in *Kerr On Injunctions* (6th ed, 1927), p 2 which had been quoted by Lavery J, in *Educational Company of Ireland Ltd v Fitzpatrick* [1961] IR 323 at 336 (SC).
31. *American Cyanamid v Ethicon* [1975] AC 396 at 407 (HL, per Lord Diplock).
32. *Cf Polycell Products Ltd v O'Carroll* [1959] Ir Jur Rep 34 at 39 (HC); *Cork Corporation v Rooney* (1881) 7 LR Ir 191 at 206; *Educational Company v Fitzpatrick* [1961] IR 323 at pp 337-338 (*per* Lavery J), 342 (*per* Kingsmill Moore J) and 344 (*per* Ó Dálaigh J). See further Coghlan 'Impecunious Litigants, Damages and Interlocutory Remedies: Time for Reform' (2000) 1 Hibernian LJ 45.
33. *Cf Polycell Products Ltd v O'Carroll* [1959] Ir Jur Rep 34 at 39.

## A "Serious Question" to be Tried

**[45.10]** In Ireland until 1983, the precise requirement for the strength of the plaintiff's case necessary to pass the first hurdle was not clear. Courts oscillated between such formulae as "a probability" of success, "a prima facie case" and "a strong prima facie case". Even within the same judgments different formulae could be found.[34] In the English decision of *American Cyanamid v Ethicon*,[35] the House of Lords grasped the nettle. Lord Diplock admitted that the use of such expressions led to confusion. He added:

> "The court no doubt must be satisfied that the claim is not frivolous or vexatious; in other words, that there is a serious question to be tried."[36]

**[45.11]** In *Campus Oil Ltd. v Minister for Indusry and Energy (No 2)*,[37] the Supreme Court endorsed this test. O'Higgins CJ (Hederman J concurring) expressed the view that "the test to be applied is whether a fair bona fide question has been raised by the person seeking relief".[38] He expressed "entire agree[ment]"[39] with what Lord Diplock had said on this matter in *American Cyanamid*. Griffin J (Hederman J adopting his comments), considered that any differences between the tests applied in *American Cyanamid* and in the leading Irish decisions were "more apparent than real".[40] He adopted Lord Diplock's test as being "a correct statement of the law to be applied in cases of this kind".[41]

### *(a) Interlocutory injunction in defamation proceedings*

**[45.12]** The requirement, of establishing a serious question to be tried, is subject to some qualification in cases of alleged defamation.[42] The matter has been dealt with in several decisions, most recently in the important judgment of Kelly J in *Reynolds v Malocco t/a "Patrick"*.[43]

**[45.13]** Two issues in particular need to be considered: the strength of the plaintiff's case, taken in conjunction with the balance of convenience question, and the effect of justification.

#### *(i) Strength of plaintiff's case*

**[45.14]** In the Supreme Court decision of *Sinclair v Gogarty*,[44] Sullivan CJ stated:

---

34. *Cf* the different formulations in *Educational Company of Ireland Ltd v Fitzpatrick* [1961] IR 323 and *Esso Petroleum Company (Ireland) Ltd v Fogarty* [1965] IR 531.
35. [1975] AC 396.
36. [1975] AC 396 at 407.
37. [1983] IR 88 (SC affg HC).
38. [1983] IR 88 at 107.
39. [1983] IR 88.
40. [1983] IR 88 at 111. Griffin J noted that in *Rex Pet Foods Ltd v Lamb Bros (Dublin) Ltd*, High Court, 26 August 1982, Finlay P had said that the statements of principles contained in *Educational Company, Esso Petroleum Company* and *American Cyanamid* "do not differ but to some extent each complements the other in certain aspects of the questions raised".
41. [1983] IR at 111.
42. See Delany *Equity and the Law of Trusts in Ireland* (2nd ed, 1999), pp 476-480; McDonald, *Irish Law of Defamation* (1987), pp 258-263; Gatley, Ch 35, Carter-Ruck, pp 163-166. Canadian decisions are analysed by Martin 'Interlocutory Injunction in Libel Actions' (1982) 20 UW Ont LR 129.
43. [1999] 1 ILRM (HC).
44. [1937] IR 377 (SC).

> "I realise that in granting an interlocutory injunction to restrain the publication of a libel the Court is exercising a jurisdiction which has been described as a jurisdiction of a delicate nature. The principle upon which the Court should act in considering such application ... is this, that an interlocutory injunction should only be granted in the clearest cases where any jury would say that the matter complained of was libellous, and where if the jury did not so find the Court would set aside the verdict as unreasonable. It is unnecessary for me to decide whether that principle is applicable in all cases. I accept it as applicable in the present case".[45]

**[45.15]** In *X v RTE*,[46] the plaintiff sought an injunction restraining RTE from naming him as a person who had been involved in the Birmingham bombings of 1974, in a television programme due to be broadcast that evening. His affidavit stated that he had been informed and believed it to be true that his name was to be thus mentioned in the programme. He stated that such assertion was completely untrue and added:

> "Such publication would not only defame me but also expose me to the risk of personal violence by persons excited by animosity against me. I do not believe that damages would be a sufficient remedy if the programme were broadcast."

**[45.16]** The plaintiff's solicitor, in an affidavit, stated that she had received instructions from the plaintiff the previous evening, that she had telephoned RTE and that there was nobody there who could deal with the particular matter. At 9.50 on the morning of the hearing she had sent a letter by fax to RTE in which she indicated her belief that her client was going to be named as one of the bombers in the forthcoming programme. She had asked for an undertaking that the programme broadcast would not include any such reference and said that in the absence of an undertaking she must assume that RTE intended to show the programme with defamatory matter and that she would be forced to act accordingly. She also asked for permission to look at the programme.

**[45.17]** Permission was not granted. She received a letter, before 11 am, in which RTE stated that it found it "impossible to give the undertaking in her letter."

**[45.18]** Costello J refused the plaintiff's application on two grounds. First, he was not satisfied, having regard to the plaintiff's failure to name the person who had informed him that his name was going to be used as suggested in the programme, that there was sufficient proof of an apprehension of defamation; secondly, that the plaintiff's delay in moving with regard to an ex parte application disentitled him to relief.

**[45.19]** The Supreme Court affirmed. Finlay, CJ stated that he understood the general principle applicable to injunction applications in regard to the publication of defamatory matter to be that, if a defendant indicated an intention in the proceedings to justify the matter complained of and provided some substantial grounds to satisfy the Court that he had a reasonable chance of doing so, then, ordinarily, the publication would not be restrained. That general principle seemed to him to make it absolutely essential that if, in regard to a publication, the precise time and date of which had been publicly notified more

---

45. [1937] IR 377 at 384. *Cf Dunlop v Dunlop Rubber Co* [1920] 1 IR 280. See also *"The Derry Journal" Ltd v The Rialto Theatres Ltd* (1930) 64 ILTR 87 (NI Ch D).
46. Supreme Court, 27 March 1990, affg High Court, 27 March 1990 (Costello J) Irish Times, 28 March 1990.

than a week in advance, a plaintiff seeking ex parte an injunction against publication should have compelling reasons indicated to the Court why he had not moved earlier than on a time scale which made it impossible for the defendant to be heard.

**[45.20]** In this concurring judgment, McCarthy J expressed the opinion that the constitutional guarantee of the vindication of the good name of every citizen had to be read in the context of the constitutional guarantee of freedom of expression. That good name might be vindicated in damages but a restraint on freedom of expression could not be similarly remedied. (It might in parentesis be added, however, that it might be subsequently remedied by removal of the injunction).

**[45.21]** The Court's approach and holding in this decision are controversial. Of course there should be stringent judicial controls on "gagging writs", and a close security on the plaintiff's case before an injunction is granted. However, there are surely some limits to this approach. If a plaintiff can credibly assert that the publication of the allegedly defamatory material is likely to expose him to the risk of being murdered, this must be a factor of such significance as to be afforded great weight. The idea that it should be swept aside by his delay in taking the proceedings seems bizarre. Being penalised in costs is one thing; being subjected to the risk of death another. Of course it may be that, in some cases, the circumstances of the delay will be so striking as to warrant the inference that the asserted risk of being killed is fanciful: if a plaintiff was slow in seeking the court's protection it may suggest that he did not himself believe that the publication would be likely to provoke violence against him. If this was the basis of the Court's holding, it would perhaps have been desirable for the Court to have said so clearly.

**[45.22]** A more difficult aspect of the problem relates to the question of the defamatory character of a statement made about a plaintiff who produces credible evidence that its publication will expose him to the serious risk of being killed. How is a court to weigh the competing interests of the parties if the plaintiff passes the *Campus Oil* threshold on the issues of the defamatory quality of the statement and the risk to free speech? Does the answer in any way depend on the strength of the plaintiff's case as to the defamatory quality of the statement, or is that aspect to be treated as a constant rather than variable factor once it is shown that there is a serious question to be tried on that issue? These are troublesome questions to which courts may be reluctant to provide frank answers in their judgments. Here it is often a case of having to infer these principles from the orders actually made in the case, with the judgments offering only limited assistance in this task.

**[45.23]** Whatever about a general rule in this area, the courts should surely be sensitive to the differences between cases. It is one thing to permit a defendant to cause the plaintiff financial injury, since that can (in principle at least) be remedied by an award of damages. It is quite another thing to permit a defendant by indirect means to occasion the destruction of a person's life, or of his or her family relationships (as might be the case with the publication of a false allegation of child sexual abuse, for example). From the constitutional standpoint, apart from the right to one's good name (under Article 40.3.2°), other rights also need to be considered, such as the rights to life, health and bodily integrity.

**[45.24]** In *Connolly v Radio Telefís Éireann*[47], the plaintiff sought an interlocutory injunction in July 1991 to prevent RTE from using film taken at a garda checkpoint during its Christmas campaign against drunken driving. It had been broadcast a number of times in December 1990. The portion to which the plaintiff objected showed her car stopped and a garda talking to her as the driver although she could not be seen. This was intercut with another shot of a woman driver being breathalysed and a voice-over saying that this woman was just below the limit. Such a sequence had been broadcast twice. A variant, also broadcast twice, showed a driver handing out a breathalyser from the car followed by a shot of the plaintiff standing at the rear of the car talking to a garda. The plaintiff stated in her affidavit that she recalled having been stopped by a garda on the road in question and asked to show him the contents of the boot of her car; there had been no question of drink consumption at all throughout the conversation with the garda. There were only three models of the same color as the particular brand of car that she was driving in the jurisdiction.

**[45.25]** The gravamen of the plaintiff's case was that the film sequences, in conjunction with the commentary about drunken driving, defamed her. She had sought an undertaking from RTE that it would not use the film again; its reply was that, whilst it had no intention at present of using the film, it had the right to do so if it wanted to. The plaintiff was not identified on the film, her face did not appear and the registration number of her car did not appear. The film had been shot at night and was relatively indistinct. Nevertheless, as Carroll J noted, it was sufficiently clear for the plaintiff (who had not seen the original transaction) to have been told by others that they had identified her.

**[45.26]** Carroll J refused to grant the interlocutory injunction. She saw no reason why she should not apply, in conjunction, the *Campus Oil* principles and the principle that in defamation cases injunctions are very rarely granted and never if the defendant claims justification as a defence:

> "So that in considering the balance of convenience, the court must take into account the right to freedom of expression balanced against the plaintiff's right to a good name and reputation in the light of the law on injunctive relief in defamation cases."[48]

**[45.27]** Given that there was an issue to be tried and "the fact that damages are not an adequate remedy for defamation", it came down to a consideration of the balance of convenience judged in the light of case law. In Carroll J's view, that balance lay against granting an injunction. In spite of the plaintiff's fears, there was no immediate danger of the footage being used and RTE had promised to co-operate in bringing the matter to an early trial. It was preferable in the circumstances of the case that the alleged libel, which was contested, should be tried by a jury rather than that an injunction should issue.

**[45.28]** Carroll J's approach is consistent with earlier precedents leaning against prior restraint in defamation cases. If, as *X v RTE*[49] appears to establish, an asserted risk of being killed is not sufficient to override the defendant's stance of a willingness to plead

47. [1991] 2 IR 446 (HC).
48. [1991] 2 IR 446 at 448.
49. Supreme Court, 27 March 1990.

justification, then, *a fortiori*, the plaintiff in the instant case would seem to have a forlorn hope of success at the interlocutory stage. Carroll J's reference "to the right of freedom of expression" seems clearly to connote a right of constitutional dimensions.

**[45.29]** In *Reynolds v Molocco t/a "Patrick"*,[50] the plaintiff, in interlocutory proceedings for an injunction, claimed that material published in the defendant's magazine defamed him by stating or implying that he had permitted the sale of drugs, or had at least turned a blind eye to this sale, in his nightclubs. The defendant contended that the word used did not bear the meanings ascribed to them but that, if they did, he would plead justification at the trial of the action.

**[45.30]** Kelly J referred to *Sinclair v Gogarty*[51] and to Lord Coleridge's sentiments regarding the public interest underlying free speech, which he had expressed in *Bonnard v Perryman*,[52] a decision cited with approval in *Sinclair v Gogarty*. Kelly J observed that these sentiments:

> "have been heeded by the courts and nowadays are fortified by the provision of Article 10 of the European Convention for the Protection of Human Rights and Fundamental Freedom."[53]

Kelly J considered it "therefore clear"[54] that he had to determine whether or not the plaintiff's complaints had been made out with the degree of clarity required to enable him to conclude that the words complained of were "undoubtedly defamatory."[55]

**[45.31]** So far as the allegations relating to durgs were concerned Kelly J considered that the words used could not, in their natural and ordinary meaning, be stigmatised as being "without doubt"[56] defamatory of the plaintiff. Looking at the impugned parts of the article as a whole, however, Kelly J concluded that it contained an innuendo so clear that, in the absence of a successful plea of justification,[57] a jury verdict that the piece was not defamatory would be likely to be set aside by the Supreme Court. Kelly J granted the injunction.

*(ii) Effect of a plea of justification*

**[45.32]** If the plaintiff passes the formidable hurdle in defamation proceedings of establishing a sufficiently strong case, but the defendant pleads justification, what is the court to do? Decline to grant an interlocutory injunction simply by reason of the existence of the plea or investigate its merits?

**[45.33]** In *Gallagher v Tuohy*,[58] Murnaghan J favoured the former option. The plaintiff sought an interlocutory injunction to restrain the dissemination of material charging him

---

50. [1999] 1 ILRM 289 (HC).
51. [1937] IR 377.
52. [1891] 2 Ch 269.
53. [1999] 1 ILRM 289 at 295.
54. [1999] 1 ILRM 289 at 295.
55. [1999] 1 ILRM 289 at 295.
56. [1999] 1 ILRM 289 at 298.
57. See para **[43.35]** below.
58. (1924) 58 ILTR 134 (HC).

with gross professional incompetence. Murnaghan J declined to make such an order on the basis that, since the defendants pleaded justification, he could not prejudge the issue and decide that the plea of justification was erroneous.

**[45.34]** In, *Cullen v Stanley*,[59] however, the Supreme Court favoured the latter option. The plaintiff, a parliamentary candidate for the Irish Labour Party, sought an interim injunction against the publication of an accusation that he had acted as a "scab" some years previously. The Supreme Court held that he was entitled to an interim injunction by virtue of statutory provisions[60] designed to curb electoral abuses. O'Connor J, alone among the judges, held that the plaintiff would be entitled to an injunction at common law. He noted that the alleged libel involved the "most improbable"[61] accusation that the plaintiff had been released from an industrial school in order to act the part of a strike-breaker. He added:

> "Let us see, then, what is the evidence which the defendant has presented to the Court to enable it to see whether there is any foundation for the allegation complained of. He gives us nothing but the baldest affidavit, in which he merely states that the whole of the allegations complained of are true in substance and in fact, and that he shall be able to prove the same at the trial by subpoenaing witnesses and by cross-examination of the plaintiff. There is no statement that at the time he published the defamatory matter he had any information to go upon, or has even now any such information. In fact the affidavit is consistent with this - that having made the statement the defendant is now looking round for materials for justification. That is not the way to satisfy the Court that the defendant is in a position to sustain a plea of justification, or has reasonable grounds for pleading it."[62]

**[45.35]** In *Reynolds v Malocco t/a "Patrick"*[63] Kelly J referred to *Gallagher v Tuohy* and *Cullen v Stanley*. He stated:

> "Of these two approaches I prefer the latter. I do not think that a rule which permits a defendant to in effect oust the ability of this court to intervene by way of injunction in an appropriate case by the simple expedient of expressing an intention to plead justification at the trial of the action is consistent with the obligations imposed on the Court under the Constitution. Furthermore, the application of such a rigid rule, without an ability on the part of the Court to ascertain whether the plea of justification had any substance or not, would provide a happy ground for unscrupulous defamers. I am therefore satisfied that it is open to the Court to examine the evidence addressed by the defendant in support of the justification plea so as to ascertain whether it has any substance or prospect of success."[64]

---

59. [1926] IR 73 (SC).
60. Prevention of Electoral Abuses Act 1923 (No 38), s 11(5). *Cf In the Matter of Thomas M Kettle* (1906) 40 ILTR 234 (HC, KB).
61. [1926] IR 73 at 85.
62. [1926] IR 73 at 85, O'Connor J did:

> "not think that the [English] Court of Appeal [in *Bonnard v Perryman* [1891] 2 Ch 269] intended to lay down a rule which should be rigidly applied to every case because the judgment of Coleridge CJ wound up with the observation that, on the whole, the Court thought it was wiser in that case, as in generally, and in all but exceptional cases, must be, to abstain from interference until the trial of the plea of justification."

63. [1999] 1 ILRM 289 (HC).
64. [1999] 1 ILRM 289 at 297.

**[45.36]** Having examined the admissible evidence contained in the defendants' affidavit, Kelly J stated that he did not think it went "anywhere near demonstrating the existence of an arguable prospect of making out the defence of justification".[65] Accordingly he granted the interlocutory injunction.

## The Balance of Convenience

**[45.37]** In determining the "balance of convenience" the Court will have regard to the probable implications for both parties which granting or refusing an injunction would involve. Usually,[66] the question involves balancing the probable financial consequences.[67] A good example is afforded by *Murtagh Properties Ltd v Cleary*,[68] where an interlocutory injunction was granted by Kenny J against picketing of the plaintiff's public house by the defendant trade union, the picket being designed to compel the plaintiffs to dismiss bar waitresses because the union objected to the employment of women. Kenny J noted that if an injunction were not granted:

> "the plaintiffs might well find themselves with no choice except either to close down their businesses or to act unconstitutionally by dismissing the bar waitresses whom they have employed ...[69]

**[45.38]** A decision of the former Supreme Court in 1946 was to the effect that, in determining the balance of convenience, the Court should not take into account the public convenience as a relevant consideration. In *Bellew v Cement Ltd*,[70] the Court, by a majority,[71] upheld the granting of an interlocutory injunction against blasting operations being carried out by the defendants in their quarry, which were alleged to constitute a nuisance. The defendants had contended that the injunction would result in the cessation of the production of cement at a time - shortly after the war - when building was an urgent public necessity.

**[45.39]** Maguire CJ could not "attach very much importance to the effect of this injunction upon the public convenience".[72] In his opinion, the Court was:

> "not entitled to take the public convenience into consideration when dealing with the rights of private parties. This matter is a dispute between private parties, and I think that the Court should be concerned, only, to see that the rights of the parties are safeguarded."[73]

---

65. [1999] 1 ILRM 289 at 299.
66. The risk of personal injury is sometimes a factor: *McDonald v Feely* Supreme Court, 23 July 1980; *Topping v Warne Surgical Products Ltd* [1986] NILR Bull No 9, p 14 (Ch D). As to the problem of violence, or apprehended violence, within the family, see *Egan v Egan* [1975] Ch 218; more generally, see Horgan 'Legal Protection for the Victim of Marital Violence' (1978) 13 Ir Jur (ns) 233. Shatter, *Family Law* (4th ed, 1997), Ch 16 and the Domestic Violence Act 1996. See further para **[22.27]** above.
67. The cases dealing with this issue in relation to the tort of passing off are dealt with above, Ch 31. Costello J's distinctive approach is analysed in detail in Byrne & Binchy, *Annual Review of Irish Law 1988*.
68. [1972] IR 330 (HC).
69. [1972] IR 330 at 334.
70. [1948] IR 61 (SC). See also *Gibbings v Hungerford* [1904] 1 IR 211 (CA).
71. Maguire CJ, Murnaghan & Geoghegan JJ; O Byrne and Black JJ. dissenting
72. [1948] IR 64 at 64.
73. [1948] IR 64 at 64.

Similarly, Murnaghan J did not:

> "think that we are entitled to deprive [the plaintiff] of his legal rights on some idea of public convenience."[74]

**[45.40]** Black J dissenting, however, declared that "public convenience" is not totally irrelevant and stated that:

> "it must be plain that the inconvenience to the [defendant] company entailed by an injunction would transcend, perhaps a hundred-fold, the inconvenience that would result to the plaintiff from its refusal pending the trial. Nor is it the defendants alone that would suffer. To stop their work, must have grave consequences for the public at a time when . . . more than four-fifths of the entire cement used in this country is produced by the defendants, and at a time when houses are badly wanted, and when the building trade is expected to be about to awake from its long torpor. No doubt, as has often been laid down, public convenience cannot justify refusal to a remedy for a nuisance. It is another matter to say that it cannot, or ought not to, affect the way in which a nuisance should be dealt with."[75]

**[45.41]** *Bellew v Cement Ltd*, may be contrasted with the decision of Costello J, in *Wall v Feely*,[76] in 1983. There, the judge ordered an interlocutory injunction in favour of five families of travellers, restraining Dublin Country Council from evicting them from the Tallaght by-pass, where, they said, they had been permitted to remain for many months. On the question of the balance of convenience, Costello J envisaged that "very great hardship indeed"[77] would be caused to the plaintiffs if they were to be then evicted from the by-pass. In considering this question, he thought that he was entitled to have regard to the public inconvenience, to the defendants as a local authority. However, even taking this factor into account, he did not think that eviction pending the trial of the issues was appropriate.

**[45.42]** In *Clifford v Drug Treatment Centre Board*,[78] McCracken J declined to grant an interlocutory injunction requiring an out-patient drug treatment centre in Pearse Street, Dublin to restrict the number of patients attending it on the basis of nuisance to adjoining commercial premises, though he did require the centre not to increase the numbers. Although he was satisfied that the plaintiffs had made out a prima facie case on the nuisance issue, he considered that the balance of convenience lay against granting the injunction requiring a reduction of numbers.

---

74. [1948] IR 64 at 65.
75. [1948] IR 64 at 70. The convenience of the public is a matter to which the court may have regard in proceedings brought by a private citizen under the Local Government (Planning and Development) Act 1976, s 27. In *Stafford v Roadstone Ltd* [1980] ILRM 1 at 20 (HC), Barrington J considered that the Oireachtas:

    > "could hardly have intended that the High Court would be obliged, on the application of a private citizen with no interest in the lands, automatically to close down eg an important factory, because of some technical breach of the planning law irrespective of the inconvenience to workers and the public generally."
76. High Court, 26 October 1983 (Costello J).
77. High Court, 26 October 1983. *Cf An Post v Irish Permanent plc* [1995] 1 ILRM 336 (HC), where Kinlen J left the issue unresolved at interlocutory stage, considering that it would "more properly be determined by the trial judge."
78. High Court, 7 November 1997 (McCracken J).

**[45.43]** McCracken J stated:

> "It is urged on me on behalf of the defendant, and I think rightly urged, that I must take into account, not only the convenience of the defendant, but also the convenience or damage to the persons attending the Centre, and indeed the public at large. The plaintiffs are seeking to reduce the numbers at present attending the Centre to the 1992 level. The immediate result of this would be that less drug addicts would be treated, which is clearly against the public interest, besides depriving possibly hundreds of individuals to badly needed treatment. I certainly do not think that I would be justified in taking such a step at interlocutory stage on possibly a temporary basis."[79]

**[45.44]** The truth of the matter is that, although *Bellew* was a decision of the (former) Supreme Court, its approach to the public interest dimension is completely out of harmony with contemporary values. *Clifford* represents a far surer compass for the future.

## Irreparable Damage

**[45.45]** In *Moore v AG*,[80] where an interlocutory injunction was sought against persons who were fishing salmon in large quantities from the plaintiff's[81] fishery, the question of "irreparable damage" was discussed by the Supreme Court. Kennedy CJ stated:

> "The injunction is asked for on the ground that the operations of the defendants are causing irreparable injury to the fishery. The damage was said to be irreparable in the first place because damages could not be recovered from the defendants, owing to their poverty. In my opinion, however, that is not the meaning of 'irreparable injury' in the sense in which it is used in relation to interlocutory injunctions.[82] The damage which will be restrained is injury for which adequate compensation cannot be made by means of pecuniary damages,[83] such as the destruction of the subject-matter of the dispute. I think, therefore, the real question of substance on this application is whether the acts alleged against the defendant are destructive of, or likely to cause permanent injury to, the fishery.[84]

**[45.46]** Thus, in *Brennan v Glennon*,[85] an interlocutory injunction was granted where, as a result of picketing by the defendants, a factory was likely to close down in a matter of days and the plaintiffs would have lost their jobs. As O'Higgins CJ noted:

> "This litigation would then have become a dead letter for their purposes. If they were successful in the action they could not be properly compensated by damages. The loss would be irreparable."[86]

---

79. High Court, 7 November 1997 at pp 5-6 of McCracken J's judgment.
80. [1927] IR 569 (SC). See also *Brennan v Glennon* Supreme Court, 26 November 1975.
81. The plaintiff's title to the fishery was in dispute.
82. *Cf* Casey 'The Injunction in Labour Disputes in Éire' (1969) 18 ICLQ 347 at 351.
83. A mere difficulty in computing the damages is not in itself. a reason for granting an injunction: *Reno Engrais et Produits Chemiques SA v Irish Agricultural Wholesale Society Ltd* High Court, unrep 8 September 1976 (Hamilton J), at p 9.
84. [1927] IR at 575-576. *Cf Magee v D'Arcy* (1879) 4 LR Ir 312 (Ex D), where an interlocutory injunction against the sale of ten Connemara ponies was refused; *per* Dowse B at 315: "... I am convinced any other ponies, or a sum representing their value would do [the plaintiff] just as well as the interesting group of animals on whose wrongs [his counsel] was so eloquent."
85. Supreme Court, 26 November 1975.
86 Supreme Court, 26 November 1975, pp 4-5 *Cf Elliott v Alpine Investments Ltd* High Court, 11 July 1975 (Kenny J), where, in granting an interlocutory injunction against an obstruction to the plaintiffs' right of way, Kenny J stated (at p 6):

## IV. Damages in Lieu of an Injunction

**[45.47]** Since Lord Cairns's Act 1858,[87] the Court has been empowered to award damages either in addition to or in lieu of an injunction. The discretion conferred on the Court is untramelled, but attempts have been made in some of the decisions to articulate general guidelines. In *Patterson v Murphy*,[88] Costello J summarised these guidelines as follows:

> "1. When an infringement of the plaintiff's right and a threatened further infringement to a material extent has been established the plaintiff is prima facie entitled to an injunction. There may be circumstances, however, depriving the plaintiff of this prima facie right but generally speaking the plaintiff will only be deprived of an injunction in very exceptional circumstances.
>
> 2. If the injury to the plaintiff's right is small, and is one capable of being estimated in money, and is one which can be adequately compensated by a small money payment, and if the case is one in which it would be oppressive to the defendant to grant an injunction, then these are circumstances in which damages in lieu of an injunction may be granted.
>
> 3. The conduct of the plaintiff may be such as to disentitle him to an injunction. The conduct of the defendant may be such as to disentitle him from seeking the substitution of damages for an injunction.
>
> 4. The mere fact that a wrongdoer is able and willing to pay for the injury he has inflicted is not a ground for substituting damages."

**[45.48]** Another attempt to express general principles had been made in *Coll v Home & Colonial Stores Ltd*[89] by Lord Macnaghten:

> "In some cases, of course, an injunction is necessary - if, for instance, the injury cannot fairly be compensated by money - if the defendant has acted in a high-handed manner - if he has endeavoured to steal a march upon the plaintiff or to evade the jurisdiction of the Court. In all these cases an injunction is necessary, in order to do justice to the plaintiff and as a warning to others. But if there is really a question as to whether the obstruction is legal or not, and if the defendant has acted fairly and not in an unneighbourly spirit, I am disposed to think that the Court ought to incline to damages rather than an injunction."

**[45.49]** This passage was adopted by Dixon J in *McGrath v Munster & Leinster Bank Ltd*,[90] where he awarded damages rather than an injunction in respect of nuisance resulting from a diminution of the light entering the premises which the plaintiff occupied as a solicitor. The Court referred to two additional circumstances for taking this course: the

---

86. (contd) "if their right is clear and undisputed, they are entitled to an injunction now even if they could not prove irreparable damage". See also *Yeates v Minister for Posts and Telegraphs* High Court, 21 February 1978 (Kenny J).

87. 21 & 72 Vict c 27, s 2. See Delany, *Equity and the Law of Trusts in Ireland* (2nd ed, 1999), pp 454-460; Jolowicz 'Damages in Equity - A Study of Lord Cairns' Act' [1975] Camb LJ 224.

88. [1978] ILRM 85 at 99-100 (HC). See generally Burrows 'Nuisance. The Law and Economics' (1970) 2 Kingston LR 20. *Cf Curust Financial Services Ltd v Loewe-Lack-Werk Otto Loewe GmbH* [1994] 1 IR 458 (SC).

89. [1904] AC 179 at 193 (HL).

90. [1959] IR 313 at 328 (HC). See also *Cullen v Cullen* [1962] IR 268 at 287 (HC). *Belled v Clement Ltd* [1948] IR 61 at 67 (SC).

plaintiff had only a limited interest (as tenant) in the premises and she had not pressed her original claim for an injunction.[91]

**[45.50]** It is scarcely "acting in a neighbourly spirit" to drive a neighbour out of the best business room of his house. Thus, in *Mackey v Scottish Widows Fund Life Assurance Society*,[92] an injunction was granted to a seed merchant against the defendant Society which had erected a building of such proportions as to diminish the light and thus prevent the plaintiff from using a room in his premises for selecting and sampling seeds.[93]

**[45.51]** An interesting example of the exercise of judicial discretion under Lord Cairn's Act arose in *Cullen v Cullen*.[94] There, the plaintiff, a businessman and farmer, sought damages and an injunction against his adult sons restraining them from trespassing on the family farm. The plaintiff had a history of periodic mental illness and was suspicious of his sons' intentions. Two English decisions[95] had been reported on the question but, although an injunction was granted in one of them,[96] the Court had stressed that the circumstances of the case were "very grave".[97]

**[45.52]** Kenny J held that the case was one for damages rather than an injunction. In his view, an injunction would hinder the possibility of reconciliation and would prejudice the mother's position on the farm. Relations between fathers and sons:

> "should not be governed by the heavy artillery of Court orders, injunctions or the threat of commital to prison, but by respect, affection, honour and the feeling of moral obligation."[98]

---

91. *Cf Woodhouse v Newry Navigation Co* [1898] 1 IR 161 (CA) - mandatory injunction ordered; plea for damages in lieu rejected: plaintiff held not to have acquiesced in defendant's trespass. Difficulty in complying with an injunction should not of itself, be a ground for awarding damages in lieu: *cf* Keane, *Equity and the Law of Trusts in the Republic of Ireland* (1988), para 15.08, commenting on a passage from Gannon J's judgment in *Halpin v Tara Mines Ltd* High Court, 16 February 1976.
92. (1877) IR 11 Eq 541.
93. See also *O'Connor v Walsh* 42 ILTR 20 (HC affd CA). Other cases where an injunction was claimed in respect of nuisance resulting from diminution of light include *Smith v Dublin Theatre Co Ltd* [1936] IR 692 (HC) - claim not pressed and held (at 696) to be "clear that, under all the circumstances of the case, damages would be the appropriate remedy ..."; *Gannon v Hughes* [1937] IR 284 (HC) - the Court was apparently willing to grant an injunction, but a compromise between the parties was announced at the conclusion of the judgment; and *Walsh v Goulding* High Court, 31 July 1968 (Teevan J) - damages awarded in lieu of an injunction. See also *Scott v Goulding Properties Ltd* [1973] IR 200. Some of the Irish decisions are discussed by Hudson 'Fight for Inadequate Windows' [1984] Conv 408. More generally see Bland *The Law of Easements and Profits à Prendre* (1997).
94. [1962] IR 268 (HC).
95. *Waterhouse v Waterhouse* (1905) 94 LT 133 (Ch D); *Stevens v Stevens* (1907) 24 TLR 20 (KBD)
96. *Stevens v Stevens* (1907) 24 TLR 20.
97. *Stevens v Stevens* (1907) 24 TLR 20 at 21.
98. [1962] IR 290.

# Chapter 46

# Limitations[1]


I. Introduction .......... 1203
II. The General Rule .......... 1204
III. When Does the Cause of Action Accrue? .......... 1204
IV. Personal Injuries .......... 1209
V. Date of Knowledge .......... 1210
VI. Undue Delay As a Basis for Dismissal of Proceedings .......... 1217
VII. Persons Under a Disability .......... 1220
VIII. Fraud .......... 1224
IX. Extinction of Title in Conversion and Detinue .......... 1225
X. Special Periods of Limitation .......... 1225


## I. Introduction

**[46.01]** Tort actions are subject to periods of limitation within which proceedings must be commented. The reasons are fairly clear: it would be unfair for a person to be subjected to litigation many years after he or she is alleged to have committed a tort, where the plaintiff has been dilatory in launching the proceedings. Moreover, fresh evidence is more likely than stale to yield a just and accurate determination of the case. As against this, it can be appreciated that there are sometimes good reasons for delay in taking proceedings. Our law attempts to steer a middle course between, on the one hand, allowing the court a broad discretion to extend the periods of limitation in cases that appear desirable,[2] and, on the other, paying no regard to reasons that might justify delay.

**[46.02]** The law on the subject is principally contained in the Statute of Limitations 1957,[3] which consolidated and amended the previous law, and the Statute of Limitations (Amendment) Act 1991 which introduced a "discoverability" requirement in personal injury litigation. Overseeing all limitation issues is the Constitution, which some years ago proved to have a potent effect on the development of the law. More recently, the Supreme Court has shown a marked reluctance to invoke the Constitution in opposition to legislative

1. See generally Brady & Kerr, *The Limitation Of Actions In The Republic of Ireland* (2nd ed, 1994), Ch 3; Woolf, *The Time Barrier in Personal Injury Claims*; Preston & Newsom, *Limitation of Actions* (3rd ed); Franks, *Limitation of Actions* (1959); Fifth Interim Report of the Law Revision Committee: *Statutes of Limitations* (Cmd 5334, 1936); Law Reform Committee's Twentieth Report: *Interim Report on Limitation of Actions In Personal Injury Claims* (Cmnd 5630, 1974); the Law Reform Commission's *Report on the Statute of Limitation: Claims in Respect of Latent Personal Injuries* (LRC) the LRC's Consultation Paper on the *Statutes of Limitations: Claims in Contract and Tort in Respect of Latent Damage (Other than Personal Injury)* (November 1998).
2. *Cf* the attempt to do this in English law: Latent Damage Act 1986.
3. See Brady & Kerr, *The Limitation Of Actions In The Republic Of Ireland* (2nd ed, 1994), Chs 1, 3.

policy choices as to where it draws the line in hard cases.[4] The combination of judicial activism and patchy legislative initiatives has forced the courts to develop a discretionary gloss on the Statute of Limitations, in aid of defendants, so that we now have the unhappy position that uncertainty attaches both to the possible duration of a prospective defendant's liability and to the circumstances in which a plaintiff, within this period, will be prevented from proceeding with his or her action.

## II. The General Rule

**[46.03]** The general period of limitation for an action founded on tort is six years from the date on which the cause of action accrued.[5] The appropriate period, however, for an action claiming damages for negligence, nuisance or breach of duty[6] or if the plaintiff claims damages for personal injuries[7] to any person is three years from the date of accrual or the "date of knowledge", if later than the date of accrual.[8] Other special periods of limitation will be considered below.

## III. When Does the Cause of Action Accrue?

**[46.04]** The period of limitation, as has been mentioned, runs from "the date on which the cause of action accrued".[9] Where, therefore, a wrongful act is actionable *per se*, without proof of actual damage - as in libel,[10] slander that is actionable *per se*, assault or other trespass to the person, trespass to lands or goods[11] - the statute begins to run from the time when the act is committed.

**[46.05]** Where there is continuing trespass or nuisance, as where a heap of stones is placed and left upon the plaintiff's land, or where the plaintiff is falsely imprisoned for a number of days,[12] a fresh cause of action arises *de die in diem*.

---

4. *Hegarty v O'Loughran* [1990] 1 IR 148; *Tuohy v Courtney (No 2)* [1994] 2 ILRM 503. Also in the constitutional context, it is worth noting that claims for infringement of constitutional rights have been characterised as torts for the purposes of limitation of actions: *McDonnell v Ireland* [1998] 1 IR 134 (SC), analysed by Byrne and Binchy, *Annual Review of Irish Law 1998*, pp 543 –549. As to limitation in the context of claims for failure to implement a European Community law Directive, see *Tate v Minister for Social Welfare* [1995] 1 ILRM 507 (HC), analysed by Byrne and Binchy, *Annual Review of Irish Law 1995*, pp 363-365.
5. Section 11(2)(a) of the Statute.
6. Whether the duty exists by virtue of a contract or statutory provision or otherwise: s 11(2)(b).
7. "Personal injuries" include any disease and any impairment of a persons physical or mental condition: s 2(1).
8. Statute of Limitations (Amendment) Act 1991.
9. Section 2(2)(a) and (b) of the 1957 Act. As to problems of computation, see *McGuinness v Vauxhall Motors Ltd* High Court, 31 July 1980 (McMahon J). *Cf Somers v Erskine (No 2)* [1944] IR 368 (SC); *Freeney v Bray UDC* [1982] ILRM 29, noted by Kerr, 4 Dublin ULJ (ns) 135; *Poole v O'Sullivan* [1993] ILRM 55 (HC)..
10. *Brunswick (Duke of) v Harmer* (1849) 14 QB 185, 117 ER 75.
11. *Cf Wilchkin v Gahan* (1795) Ridg Lap & Scho 591.
12. *Bailey v Warden* (1815) 4 M & S 400, 105 ER 882; *Hardy v Ryle* (1829) 9 B & C 603, 109 ER 224.

**[46.06]** When the tort is actionable only on proof of damage,[13] all courts are agreed that time does not begin to run before some damage actually occurs. Thus, a person injured by a negligently manufactured product may sue the manufacturer in certain cases many years after the product left the manufacturer's factory. Damage, however, may occur before it is discovered. At this point the law becomes complex and uncertain.[14] The issue has confronted the courts in several common law jurisdictions in the past quarter century. By and large the trend (save in Britain) has been towards "stopping the clock" until the plaintiff has had a reasonable opportunity to discover the injury. In default of judicial activism, the legislature has usually stepped in to grant such an extension. In the United States, however, the thrust of the legislation[15] has been in aid of the defendant, with "statutes of repose" introducing an absolute cut-off point after which no action may be taken, even where the victim could not have discovered the injury within the specified period. It will be recalled that Article 11 of the EEC Products Liability Directive reflects the American approach.

**[46.07]** It is as well to separate two types of injury in this context: injury to the *person* and injury to *property*. The policy considerations regarding the discoverability issue are not identical so far as these are concerned, although one might perhaps have expected the courts to be more anxious to extend the range of protection where personal injury was involved. This is not in fact what happened and the legislature was obliged to step in, with the passage of the Statute of Limitations (Amendment) Act 1991.

**[46.08]** The saga is a long and complicated one. We shall first set out the important judicial decisions on the subject and then seek to state the existing legal principles in the light of their holdings and *dicta*. The issue was raised, but not resolved, in the Supreme Court decision of *Cahill v Sutton*[16] in 1980. There the plaintiff's constitutional challenge to s 11(2)(b), on the grounds that it killed an action before an injured person might reasonably have become aware of his or her right to sue, failed on the basis of her lack of *locus standi*.

13. Negligence is, of course, the most obvious example. In Northern Ireland, it has been held that a claim based on negligence is a separate claim from one based on statutory duty, so that a claim made within the limitation period, in which negligence only has been alleged, cannot be supplemented outside the limitation period for actions for breach of statutory duty by a claim for breach of statutory duty: *Scampton v Colhoun* [1959] NI 106 (QBD).

14. See Byrne & Binchy, *Annual Review of Irish Law 1987*, pp 246-255.

15. See Turner 'The Counter-Attack to Retake the Citadel Continues: An Analysis of the Constitutionality of Statutes of Repose in Products Liability' (1981) 46 J of Air L & Commerce 449; Randell 'Comment: Due Process Challenges to Statutes of Repose' (1986) 40 Sw LJ 997; Green 'The Paradox of Statutes of Limitations in Toxic Substances Litigation' (1988) 76 Calif LR 965 at 979-980.

16. [1980] IR 269. Henchy J noted (at 287) that the fact that it was not possible for the Court to hold that the impugned provision was unconstitutional was "due solely" to the plaintiff's lack of *locus standi*. He thought it "proper" to point out (at 288) that the justice and fairness of attaching a saver as to discoverability, such as had been inserted by the British Limitation Act 1963, s 1, were so obvious that the enactment by our parliament of a similar provision would merit urgent consideration. In *Norris v AG* [1984] IR 36 at 89 (SC). McCarthy J, dissenting, thought it "fair to infer" from *Cahill v Sutton* that the Supreme Court inclined to the view that s 11(2)(b) was constitutionally invalid.

**[46.09]** In *Morgan v Park Developments Ltd*,[17] Carroll J expressed the view that the "discoverability" rule should apply to the interpretation of s 11(2) of the Statute in an action for negligence in the building of a house; the argument that a plaintiff could have his action barred before he knew he had one appeared to Carroll J "indefensible in the light of the Constitution". She was of the view that:

> "no law which could be described as harsh and absurd or which the courts say was unreasonable and unjustifiable in principle. . . could also be constitutional."[18]

**[46.10]** In favouring the "discoverability" test, Carroll J rejected the approach that the House of Lords had adopted in *Pirelli General Cable Works Ltd v Oscar Faber & Partners*.[19] The following year, the majority of the Supreme Court of Canada[20] also rejected the *Pirelli* approach.[21]

**[46.11]** *Hegarty v O'Loughran*[22] is a crucial decision. The case involved a claim for damages for injuries to the plaintiff's nose, alleged to have resulted from medical treatment. The defendants contended that the action was statute-barred under s 11(2)(b) of the Statute of Limitations 1957. The resolution of the defendant's argument depended on the time at which the cause of action should be considered to arise. The plaintiff did not claim that s 11(2)(b) was constitutionally invalid.

**[46.12]** Barron J held in favour of the defendants. During argument before the Supreme Court, three possible constructions of s 11(2)(b) were canvassed. According to the first, the cause of action should be deemed to have accrued when the wrongful act was committed. According to the second, it accrued only when personal injury manifested itself. On the third, which the plaintiff championed, the cause of action accrued only when the injured party could, by the exercise of reasonable diligence, have discovered that the injury had been caused by the wrongful act complained of.

**[46.13]** In his judgment (with which Griffin J concurred) Finlay CJ favoured the second of these constructions. He disagreed with Carroll J's approach in *Morgan v Park Developments Ltd*[23] which had proceeded on the basis that, if two or more possible constructions for s 11(2)(a) were open, the one in harmony with the Constitution should be preferred. In the view of the Chief Justice, whilst the general approach to statutory construction was correctly stated by Carroll J, no ambiguity araose in s 11(2)(a) or (b), since these provisions did not lend themselves to more than one construction.

---

17. [1983] ILRM 156 (HC).
18. [1983] ILRM 156 at 160.
19. [1983] 2 AC 1 (HL, Eng).
20. In *City of Kamloops v Nielson* (1984) 10 DLR (4th) 641.
21. The New Zealand Court of Appeal, in *Askin v Knox* [1989] 1 NZLR 248, evinced no enthusiasm for *Pirelli*, though it took no final position on the discoverability issue, making it plain that it considered it a matter for legislation: see the New Zealand Law Commission's Report No 6 *Limitation Defences in Civil Proceedings* (1988) paras 77, 99. The Commission recommended a "discoverability" approach, subject to a 15 year long-stop period. It should be recalled that in New Zealand personal injuries are subject to an Accident Compensation scheme, thus "remov[ing] a factor which complicates statutes of limitation - and their reform -elsewhere": para 294. See further TRINDADE & CANE, pp 767-768.
22. [1990] 1 IR 148, affg [1987] ILRM 603.
23. [1983] ILRM 156.

**[46.14]** The inclusion within the legislation of s 71(1), which prevented time from running in the event of fraudulent concealment, would have been entirely redundant if s 11(2)(a) or (b) were to be construed as preventing the cause of action from accruing until the time the plaintiff discovered or ought to have discovered that he or she had a cause of action. Similar considerations appeared to apply to s 48, dealing with disability, at least in so far as that disability consisted of unsoundness of mind.

**[46.15]** The extent and nature of the provisions of England's Limitation Act 1963, which introduced the discovery test into English law, and the recommendations of the Irish Law Reform Commission with a like objective, strongly supported the conclusion that "to interpret this subsection as being based on discoverability, though possibly very desirable, would be to legislate".[24]

**[46.16]** Noting that no challenge to the constitutional validity of the subsection had been made in the proceedings, Finlay CJ went on to say that he did not accept that to construe it as meaning that "the time limit commenced when provable personal injury, capable of attracting monetary compensation occurred"[25] was necessarily to construe it as a constitutionally flawed provision.

**[46.17]** In a crucial passage, the Chief Justice said:

> "In legislation creating a time limit for the commencement of actions, the time provided for any particular type of action; the absolute or qualified nature of the limit; whether the court is vested with a discretion in certain cases in the interests of justice; and the special instances, if any, in which exceptions from the general time limit are provided are with others all matters in the formulation of which the legislature must seek to balance between, on the one hand, the desirability of enabling persons with causes of action to litigate them, and on the other hand, the desirability of finality and certainty in the potential liability which citizens may incur into the future.
>
> It is quite clear that what is sometimes classified as the harshness and injustice of a person failing to bring a cause of action to trial by reason of exceeding a time limit not due to his or her own particular fault, may well be counterbalanced by the harshness and injustice of a defendant called upon to defend himself at a time when by the passage of years his recollection, the availability of his witnesses and even documentary evidence relevant to a claim in tort or contract have disappeared.
>
> If and when a challenge is made to the constitutional validity of this subsection by a person adversely affected by it, and the matter is fully argued on the facts established in a particular case, it will be necessary for the courts to make a decision upon it. Until that time, however, I would reserve my view on the question of its constitutional validity other than to presume it constitutional, as I must do."[26]

**[46.18]** Finlay CJ therefore concluded that the proper construction of the subsection was that contended for on behalf of the defendant and that time began to run:

> "when a provable personal injury, capable of attracting compensation, occurred to the plaintiff which was the completion of the tort alleged to be committed against her".[27]

---

24. [1990] 1 IR 148.
25. [1990] 1 IR 148.
26. [1990] 1 IR 148.
27. [1990] 1 IR 148.

Applying this test to the facts of the case, the Chief Justice held that the time limit had well expired when the proceedings were commenced. The plaintiff, on Barron J's finding, "was dissatisfied with the operation by … 1976". This referred to the plaintiff's dissatisfaction with the results of the second operation, which it had been performed in 1974. Since proceedings were not begun until 1982, it appeared that this was "upwards of five to six years" after the time limit has expired.

**[46.19]** In his concurring judgment, Griffin J clearly adhered to the Chief Justice's construction. He did not address the merits of the third construction that had been posited during argument.

McCarthy J, who also held in favour of the defendants, did so on a more radical basis. Time begins to run from the date at which the wrongful act "has caused personal injury beyond what can be regarded as negligible, even when that injury is unknown to and cannot be discovered by the sufferer". This is the test stated by Lord Reid in *Cartledge v E Jopling & Sons Ltd.* McCarthy J found Lord Reid's reasoning "wholly convincing". In his opinion, the words of s 11(2)(b) were "so clear as not to admit of any interpretation save that expressed in *Cartledge*".

**[46.20]** In *Irish Equine Foundation v Robinson*,[28] Geoghegan J provided an incisive interpretation of *Hegarty v O'Loughran*. He was dealing with a claim for alleged negligence in respect of the design and construction of a building. Laying particular emphasis on what Griffin J said in *Hegarty v O'Loughran*, Geoghegan J concluded that the decision:

> "Must be taken as authority for the view that, prior to the Statute of Limitations (Amendment) Act 1991, the cause of action for personal injury did not arise until the injury was manifest but it did then arise irrespective of whether it ever occurred to the party injured or could ever have reasonably occurred to the party injured that it resulted from the negligence of somebody else."

The effect of *Hegarty v O'Loughran*, as thus interpreted, is that the clock starts ticking when the injury is manifest in the sense of being capable of being discovered by the plaintiff. It does not have to be the case that the plaintiff ought reasonably be capable of attributing the injury to the negligence (or other tortious conduct) of the defendant. Indeed, nothing said in *Hegarty v O'Loughran* would stop the clock, even where the plaintiff could not reasonably make a causal connection between the defendant's conduct and the injury, without any question of his or her being also able to appreciate that that conduct was tortious. Thus the 'discoverability' test prescribed in *Hegarty v O'Loughran* is considerably less indulgent to plaintiffs' interests than that specified in the Statute of Limitations (Amendment) Act 1991. Once the physical injury is manifest, time starts to run.

The point is of very great practical significance, in spite of the 1991 legislation, since practitioners must address the limitation issue in respect of cases falling outside the scope of that legislation, which deals with personal injuries and death. The crucial question is whether the requirement specified in *Hegarty v O'Loughran* in respect of a personal injury

28. [1999] 2 ILRM 289 (HC).

claim that the injury be 'manifest' should be extended to claims for damage to property or for pure economic loss. In *Irish Equine Foundation v Robinson*, Geoghegan J stated:

> "In my view, it is at least arguable that the nature of personal injury damage is no different from the nature of damage resulting from defects in a building that the concept of an injury becoming manifest as being relevant to the commencement of the limitation period may only be applicable in personal injury cases but I accept that the opposite can also be argued. I find it quite unnecessary to decide this point and, that being so, I don't think that I should decide it."[29]

The tenor of these observations is not very receptive to the suggestion that *Hegarty* can be transposed into the environment of claims for damage to property or for pure economic loss. The Supreme Court decision in *Tuohy v Courtney*[30] might also appear hostile to such a transposition. A close reading of that decision, however, and of the judgement of Lynch J in the High Court which the Supreme Court affirmed, will show that the topic for discussion was the constitutional validity of the statutory provision rather than a debate as to its precise breadth of application. It was agreed on all sides that it did not provide a discoverability criterion as broad as that specified in the 1991 legislation. What was not addressed in any definitive way was the question whether the requirement in *Hegarty* that the injury be manifest should be transposed to claims for property damage and pure economic loss. That question still remains unresolved. We suggest that there is merit in making such a transposition. There are no obviously pressing social reasons for interpreting the legislation in such a way as to deprive plaintiffs of the right to sue when they could not even have been aware that their property had been damaged or they had sustained economic loss. It is true that these claims have a six-year rather than a three-year limitation period but insidious property damage and economic loss can devastate lives just as much as some personal injuries can do. Having said this, it should be acknowledged that the *Hegarty* wording does not logically compel such a transposition and that the question ultimately is still open for resolution.

## IV. PERSONAL INJURIES

**[46.21]** The Statute of Limitations (Amendment) Act 1991[31] has introduced a special limitation period for actions for personal injuries. Section 3(1) provides as follows:

> "An action other than one to which section 6 of this Act[32] applies, claiming damages in respect of personal injuries to a person caused by negligence, nuisance or breach of duty (whether the duty exists by virtue of a contract or of a provision made by or under a statute or independently of any contract or any such provision) shall not be brought after the expiration

29. [1999] 2 ILRM 289 at 294.
30. [1994] 3 IR 1 (SC).
31. See Brady & Kerr, *The Limitation Of Actions In The Republic of Ireland* (2nd ed, 1994), pp 74-79. The Act is based on the recommendations of the Law Reform Commission in its *Report on the Statute of Limitations: Claims in Respect of Latent Personal Injuries* (1987) (LRC-21), analysed by McGann, (1988) 6 ILT (ns) 15. See also the second edition of this work, pp 332-334.
32. This is a claim for fatal injuries: see para **[42.02]** above.

of three years from the date on which the cause of action accrued or the date of knowledge (if later) of the person injured."[33]

**[46.22]** The phrase "(if later)" is ambiguous. It could mean either later than three years from the date on which the cause of action accrued or later than the date on which the cause of action accrued. In *Boylan v Motor Distributors Ltd*,[34] Lynch J favoured the latter interpretation. This is surely correct. It harmonises with the clear policy of the legislation, which is to ensure that plaintiffs are not prejudiced by the delay in their capacity to discover personal injuries that they have suffered or, where they are aware that they have suffered an injury, there is delay in their ability to appreciate that it is a significant one. As counsel for the plaintiff in *Boylan* pointed out, the former interpretation, rejected by Lynch J, would mean that the limitation sword would descend on a plaintiff who discovered a day or even a few hours before the three years post-accrual period expired, that he or she had suffered a significant injury attributable to the defendant's conduct. In such a case on the former interpretation, the plaintiff would have to initiate the proceedings within this tiny period.

## V. Date of Knowledge

**[46.23]** A person's date of knowledge is the date on which he or she had knowledge of the following facts:

(a) that the person alleged to have been injured has been injured,

(b) that the injury in question was significant,

(c) that the injury was attributable in whole or in part to the act or omission which is alleged to contribute negligence, nuisance or breach of duty,

(d) the identity of the defendant, and

(e) if it is alleged that the act or omission was that of a person other than the defendant, the identity of that person and the additional facts supporting the bringing of an action against the defendant.[35]

**[46.24]** Knowledge that any acts or omission did or did not, as a matter of law, involve negligence, nuisance or breach of duty is irrelevant.[36] Thus, for example, if an employee is perfectly aware that he or she has a significant injury and is equally aware that the injury is attributable to his or her work environment, but does not appreciate that the employer is liable to be sued for negligence for permitting employees work in this unsafe environment, the clock will nonetheless start ticking against the employee's claim. This will be so even in cases where the employee could not reasonably have been aware of the legal dimension – as, for example, where an asylum seeker with no knowledge of the Irish legal regime is employed in circumstances where the employer is negligent.

---

33. Section 3(3) and (4) introduce a similar law change to actions for damages under s 13(7) of the Sale of Goods and Supply of Services Act 1980 in respect of the implied condition on the sale of a motor vehicle that it is free from any defect that would render it a danger to the public, the relevant period being two rather than three years, and under s 21 of the Control of Dogs Act 1986.

34. High Court, 9 June 1993 (Lynch J).

35. Section 2(1).

36. Section 2(1).

**[46.25]** While the legislation refers to the date on which a person "had knowledge" of the five specified facts, it does not refer simply to the actual content of that person's mind. It also includes knowledge which he or she might reasonably have been expected to acquire:

(a) from facts observable or ascertainable by him or her,[37] or

(b) from facts ascertainable by him or her with the help of medical or other appropriate expert advice which it is reasonable for him or her to seek.[38]

**[46.26]** A person is not, however, fixed under s 2 with knowledge of a fact ascertainable with the help of expert advice so long as he or she has taken all reasonable steps to obtain (and, where appropriate to act on) that advice.[39] Moreover, a person who has been injured is not fixed under s 2 with knowledge of a fact relevant to the injury which he or she has failed to acquire as a result of that injury.[40]

**[46.27]** Thus, a plaintiff who sits back culpably ignoring symptoms, will not be able to prevent the clock from starting to tick if he or she would have discovered reasonably ascertainable facts relevant to his or her condition if he or she investigated the symptoms. So far as seeking medical or other expert advice is concerned, the effect of the legislation is that a person who does not take reasonable steps to acquire such advice will be considered to know the facts that would have been ascertainable with the help of that advice. However, if the person does take all reasonable steps to obtain and, where appropriate, act on that advice, and the advice falls short of making that person aware of certain facts that the advice of this character might be expected to unearth – because the expert was negligent, for example – these particular facts will not be deemed to be known by the injured person. So, if the expert proves to be a poor detective, the injured person will not be prejudiced. It should, however, be noted that if the expert proves to be incompetent in other ways – as, for example, where a lawyer gives bad legal advice[41] – this will not prevent the clock from starting to tick.

---

37. On general principles of agency, "knowledge which [a client's solicitor] might reasonably have been expected to acquire in their capacity as agents must be imputed to the [client] himself by virtue of paragraph (a)": *O'Driscoll v Dublin Corporation* [1999] 1 ILRM 106 (HC).

38. Section 2(2).

39. Section 2(3)(a).

40. Section 2(3)(b).

41. In such circumstances, the injured person may have a claim for negligence against the lawyer. In *O'Driscoll v Dublin Corporation* [1999] 1 ILRM 106 (HC), Geoghegan J, expressed agreement with the view, canvassed in *Fowell v National Coal Board*, The Times, 21 May 1986 (CA) and *Halford v Brookes* [1991] 1 WLR 428 that the reference in s 2(2)(6) to "other appropriate expert advice" was a reference to the advice of an expert witness rather than to the parties own lawyers. *Cf Nash v Eli Lilly & Co* [1993] 4 All ER 383 and *Henderson v Temple Pier Co Ltd* [1998] 3 All ER 324 (distinguishing between a lawyer's factual knowledge and legal advice). See also STREET, p 573; *WINFIELD & JOLOWICZ*, p 898, fn 8. In *Boylan v Motor Distributors Ltd* High Court, 9 June 1993, Lynch J accepted that the plaintiff would be fixed with knowledge that her solicitor had or ought to have had, which knowledge in turn depended on the information he might reasonably be expected to have gleamed from her instructions.

**[46.28]** Finally. if the result of the injury is such as to render the injured person unable to gain knowledge of a fact relevant to the injury, he or she will not be fixed with knowledge under s 2(2). This provision is arguably otiose. If the injury had such a result, it is hard to see how, in the first place, the injured person "might reasonably have been expected to acquire" the knowledge in question.

**[46.29]** Each of the five factual elements necessary, in combination, to trigger the "date of knowledge" needs to be considered briefly.

## That the Person alleged to have been Injured had been Injured

**[46.30]** It is, of course, quite possible for a person to be injured without being aware of that fact. This is the very reason why the 1991 Act was passed.

**[46.31]** In *Maitland v Swan and Sligo County Council*[42] the defendant surgeon operated on the plaintiff in 1969, removing her right ovary. The plaintiff learned of the removal by 1971 at the latest. It was not until 1983 that she found out that she did not have a normal left ovary. She sued the surgeon in negligence. Her plenary summons was issued in 1985.

**[46.32]** On behalf of the surgeon, it was contended that the limitation period had expired. Counsel for the defendant argued that the alleged injury was the removal of the plaintiff's right ovary, of which fact the plaintiff, as has been stated, became aware no later than 1971. Even if she believed that she had a viable left ovary, she must have known that the removal of her right ovary was a significant injury in that it deprived her of the benefit of an alternative gonad should any harm happen subsequently to her left ovary.

**[46.33]** Barr J rejected this argument. He noted that s 2 of the 1991 Act did not define "injured" in the context of the Act, he considered it to be synonymous with the word "harmed". In his view, a person undergoing necessary surgery, skilfully and successfully performed, did not suffer an injury in the context of the Act. Such an operation was a curative, beneficial process and had no element of harmfulness in it, even if the procedure involved the removal of an important organ with in consequence a degree of permanent disablement for the patient. The removal of the plaintiff's right ovary was not, in itself, evidence of negligence and would not suggest negligence to a lay person.[43] It was only in 1983 that the plaintiff could reasonably have known that the 1969 operation, apparently curative and beneficial, was in fact harmful to her.

---

42. High Court, 6 April 1992 (Barr J). See also *Kerwick v Minister for Defence* High Court, 19 March 1999 (O'Donovan J) on the troublesome issues that can arise where a plaintiff suffers separate, though, related, kinds of injury. For analysis, see Byrne and Binchy, *Annual Review of Irish Law 1999*, pp 288-289.

43. In noting this, Barr J was not mistakenly using a test – specifically repudiated by s 2(1) – of determining the "date of knowledge" by reference to whether the plaintiff knew (or ought to have known) that the defendant's conduct, "as a matter of law, involve[d] negligence ..." It was only in the specific context of a physical intervention, ostensibly beneficial, that the question of awareness of the defendant's allegedly negligent conduct came to be considered, since it would throw light on whether the plaintiff was aware, as a matter of fact rather than law, that the intervention had an injurious character.

**[46.34]** Barr J's analysis is surely correct. It would seem clearly mistaken to characterise the immediate aftermath of a well-conducted medical operation as an injury, undoubtedly its therapeutic intent and effect would have to be taken into account.[44]

**[46.35]** A somewhat subtle issue regarding ascription of causal responsibility arose in *Behan v Bank of Ireland*.[45] The plaintiff, a farmer, claimed that he had been negligently advised by his bank manager in 1981 against selling a large portion of his lands at a time where Irish agriculture was going through a period of difficulty. The manager had allegedly advised him that he would be able to "farm his way out of his problems" and allegedly assured him that the bank would give him the necessary financial facilities to enable him to overcome his difficulties.

**[46.36]** The plaintiff issued proceedings in 1990. Morris J dismissed the action for the economic consequences allegedly flowing from the bank manager's allegedly negligent advice on the basis that the evidence was to the effect that, by 1983 at the latest, "the plaintiff must have known, assuming that his case was correct", that the advice he received in May 1981 had been bad advice and accordingly his cause of action accrued as at that date. Since more than six years has elapsed subsequent to 1983, before the proceedings were issued, the plaintiff's claim for negligence was statute barred.

**[46.37]** The plaintiff further claimed that the financial pressures resulted in his excessive consumption of alcohol "in December 1981/1982"[46] and to his suffering a nervous breakdown in March 1982. The Supreme Court, affirming Morris J, held that this claim for personal injuries for negligent advice was statute barred. Keane J (Barron and O'Flaherty JJ concurring) said:

> "The cause of action in this instance accrued in 1982 when the nervous breakdown occurred and, accordingly, the claim was ... statute barred at the time the plenary summons was issued."[47]

**[46.38]** When one examines the requirement in s 2(1) of the 1991 Act of knowledge that the injury was attributable to the allegedly negligent conduct one encounters a difficulty. As we have seen, the plaintiff was not aware until 1983 that the advice he had received from the bank manager in 1981 (assuming that his case was correct) had been bad. The plaintiff was of course aware of his injury and of the fact that it could be attributable to his financial concerns. It is less clear that he could be said to have been aware that his injury

---

44. *Cf Forbes v Wandsworth Health Authority* [1997] QB 402 (CA); *French v East London & City Health Authority* [2000] Lloyds Rep Med 35 (CA). The case raises wider issues of definition. If a person consents to have his or her ear pierced and the person carrying out the piercing does so negligently in a way that insidiously damages the ear, the injurious effects not manifesting themselves until four years later, it would seem wrong to dismiss the case on the basis that the plaintiff was aware that the ear had been mutilated to a small degree. Context is important. The ear-piercing example shows that it is not only the therapeutic context of medicine that can render non-injurious a particular physical state that would otherwise be so characterised. In *Gallagher v Minister for Defence* High Court, 25 February 1998 (O'Higgins J), an "army deafness" case, one reason for holding the plaintiff's claim not to be statute-barred was the fact that the plaintiff had only a suspicion that his hearing problem was attributable to his work environment.
45. [1998] 2 ILRM 507 (SC), affg High Court, 2 July 1997 (Morris J).
46. [1998] 2 ILRM 507.
47. [1998] 2 ILRM 507.

was attributable to the advice that he had received from the bank manager. In 1982, he believed that that advice was sound. It was only in 1983 (on the case he was advancing) that he came to realise that the advice was not good. Until he reached that conclusion, he could hardly have ascribed *factual* causal responsibility for his injury to the act of the bank manager. As long as he had continued to regard the advice as sound, he would be expected to have ascribed factual causal responsibility for his condition to the general financial state of agriculture at the time.

**[46.39]** The process of ascribing causal responsibility to human conduct (whether act or omission) is inextricably conjoined with ascribing moral responsibility. This is not, of course, to suggest that there is no logical difference between the two modes of ascription. Undoubtedly there is such a cleavage; but in many cases where an injury occurs in the context of a broad tapestry of facts, a morally blameless factual component will blend into the background to such an extent that it could not reasonably be considered to put the injured person on notice that the injury was "attributable in whole or in part" to it. Unless and until the finger of blame points towards the particular act of this seemingly colourless character, it should not be considered to start the limitation clock ticking.

**[46.40]** In the instant proceedings, of course, the question whether 1982 or 1983 was the date at which the clock started ticking was irrelevant to the plaintiffs claim for personal injuries since the three-year period had long elapsed by the time he issued the proceedings in 1990.

### That the Injury was Significant

**[46.41]** The limitation clock does not start to tick against the plaintiff from the time that he or she first becomes aware that he or she has sustained an injury: there must also be an awareness that the injury is "significant". So, if a plaintiff receives an injury that seems quite trivial – a small bruise on the knee, but the injury festers and gradually turns into something far more serious, the clock will not start until the injury moves from one of trivial character to become a more significant injury. There can also be cases where the injury was indeed of significant character from the start but the plaintiff could not initially have appreciated this fact.

**[46.42]** The courts have had to confront the difficult questions of determining what constitutes a significant injury in this context. The matter has been addressed in the particularly complex context of the army deafness litigation, where the gradual deterioration of the capacity to hear is often a function of ageing. The courts have had to sever the loss of hearing capacity attributable to the ageing process from that attributable to the army's negligence in exposing its soldiers unreasonably to high levels of noise. Complied with this different causal dissection, the courts have to work out when the plaintiff, with a gradual loss of hearing capacity, became (or ought to have become) aware that this loss represented an "injury" and – a more challenging task – when he or she became (or ought to have become) aware that this injury was significant.

**[46.43]** The issue arose in *Whitely v Minister for Defence*.[48] The plaintiff had enlisted in the army in 1957 and served until 1978. During this period of twenty one years he was

48. [1997] 2 ILRM 416. See also *Bolger v O'Brien* Supreme Court, 16 March 1999, analysed by Byrne and Bincy, *Annual Review of Irish Law 1999*, pp 285-288.

exposed to excessive noise without adequate protection. The crucial question was whether the plaintiffs claim, initiated in 1995, fell foul of the limitation period of three years after his "date of knowledge".

**[46.44]** The plaintiff's evidence was to the effect that, while he was in the army, he noticed that he was encountering a problem with his hearing and a ringing in his ears immediately after he had been exposed to high levels of noise. After he was voluntarily discharged from the army in 1978, he suffered from tinnitus and difficulty with speech discrimination in the presence of background noise.

**[46.45]** Quirke J dismissed the plaintiff's claim on the basis that is was statute-barred. He was of the view that as early as 1978 or 1980 the plaintiff would have considered his hearing loss and his tinnitus sufficiently serious to justify his instituting proceedings for damages against "a defendant who did not dispute liability and was able to satisfy judgment."[49] This was the criterion for determining whether the plaintiff regarded the injury as significant which is prescribed by English legislation and which, not commanding the support of the Law Reform Commission, had been omitted from the 1991 Act. Quirke J accepted that, in these circumstances, the English criterion was not the appropriate one. A "broader and more subjective test"[50] had to be applied. In the light of the evidence, he concluded that there was no particular circumstances existing between 1978 and 1993 which would have interfered with the plaintiff's capacity to understand the nature and extent of his injury. The "more objective dimension"[51] of the test was contained in s 2(2) of the 1991 Act. Quirke J was of the view that the plaintiff knew or ought reasonably to have known, from facts which were known or ascertainable by him alone that he had sustained an injury which was significant.

**[46.46]** In *Gallagher v Minister for Defence*,[52] the plaintiff, an Army bandsman, sued his employer for negligence in exposing him to excessive noise levels in the band-hall over a 38-year career. He had an audiogram in November 1989, "the result or real significance of [which] was not explained to him".[53] A month later, a Lieutenant Colonel explained to him that his hearing was not good and that, as a precaution, he would not be allowed play or practice in the band-room until he was referred to a specialist. The plaintiff understood that his superior officer, in saying this, "was deferring to the specialist view which had not been yet obtained."[54] Having talked to the Lieutenant Colonel, the plaintiff was aware that there was something wrong with his hearing. The plaintiff issued proceedings in February 1993.

**[46.47]** On the question of what constitutes "knowledge" for the purpose of s 2 of the 1991 Act, O'Higgins J regarded as "a most reasonable approach"[55] that which Lord Donaldson had adopted in *Halford v Brookes*[56] when he had observed that:

---

49. England's Limitation Act 1980, s 14(2).
50. [1997] 2 ILRM 416.
51. [1997] 2 ILRM at 416.
52. High Court, 25 February 1998 (O'Higgins J).
53. High Court, 25 February 1998.
54. High Court, 25 February 1998.
55. High Court, 25 February 1998.
56. [1991] 1 WLR 428 at 443

> "In this context knowledge clearly does not mean I know for certain and beyond possibility of contradiction. It does, however, mean know with sufficient confidence to justify embarking on the preliminaries to the issue of a writ, such as submitting a claim to the proposed defendant, taking legal or other advice and collecting evidence. Suspicion, particularly if it is vague and unsupported, will indeed not be enough, but reasonable belief will normally suffice."

**[46.48]** Applying this test to the facts of the instant case, O'Higgins J concluded that, while the plaintiff knew he had been injured, as of November 1989, he had not had at that time an awareness that his injury was "significant" for the purposes of s 2(1). O'Higgins J was guided in this context by Quirke J's interpretation of the test, in *Whitely v Minister for Defence*,[57] as primarily a subjective one, though, in O'Higgins J's view, the evidence was such that the plaintiff was not shown to have knowledge that his injury was significant even under the more restrictive British legislative test.

### That the Injury was attributable to the Conduct alleged to constitute Negligence, Nuisance or Breach of Duty

**[46.49]** We have already noted that the clock does not start to operate against the claim until the injured person knows that the injury "was attributable in whole or part to the act or omission which is alleged to constitute negligence, nuisance or breach of duty".[58] We have also observed that it is not necessary for the injured party to have any suspicion that this act or omission can be stigmatised as negligent, a nuisance or breach of duty. The test is entirely factual.

**[46.50]** In *Gallagher v Minister for Defence*,[59] O'Higgins J followed English authority[60] in holding that, whilst "knowledge" does not mean absolute certainty, it involves something considerably more than vague and unsupported suspicion.

### The Identity of the Defendant

**[46.51]** The identity of the defendant may in some cases not be known to the injured person. The victims of an environmental tort or a product defect,[61] for example, may have

---

57. [1997] 2 ILRM 416.

58. This is a claim for fatal injuries: see para **[42.02]** above.

59. High Court, 25 February 1998, snslydrf by Byrne and Binchy, *Annual Review of Irish Law 1998*, p 480.

60. *Halford v Brookes* [1991] 1 WLR 428 at 443. See also *Wilkinson v Ancliffe (BLT) Ltd* [1986] 3 All ER 427 at 438 (CA, *per* Slade LJ). See also *Jones v Liverpool Health Authority* (1995) 30 BMLR 1 (CA); *Forbes v Wandsworth Health Authority* [1997] QB 402. *Cf Stephen v Riversdale Health Authority* [1990] 1 Med LR 261. See further Kennedy & Grubbeds, *Medical Law* (1998), p 425.

61. *Cf Sindell v Abbott Laboratories* (1980) 607 P 2d 924 (Cal). An interesting question arises in relation to s 11(3) of the Civil Liability Act 1961, which provides as follows:

> "Where two or more persons are at fault and one or more of them is or are responsible for damage while the other or others is or are free from casual responsibility, but it is not possible to establish which is the case, such two or more persons shall be deemed concurrent wrongdoers in respect of the damage."

In a case where this rule applies, liability may be imposed even though the plaintiff does not have knowledge that the injury is attributable (as a factual rather than legal matter), to the act or omission of any particular defendant. Does this mean that there is, in effect, no limitation period covering this case? Or should the court interpret "attributable" in the manner favoured by the English courts, but only in this context *ex necessitate*?

difficulty in finding the true source of their injuries. Similarly corporate complexities may make it difficult to know which of several companies forming part of a group is responsible for an injury.[62]

### The Identity of a Person other than the Defendant (where Appropriate)

**[46.52]** As we have already noted, one of the requirements necessary to activate the "date of knowledge" is that the person know the identity of a person other than the defendant, in cases where it is alleged that the injurious act or omission was that of such person, as well as the additional facts supporting the bringing of an action against the defendant. This will arise in cases of vicarious liability. So, for example, if a person is injured by another who is acting in the course of his or her employment, the clock does not start, in relation to the victim's claim against the employer, until the victim knows the identity of the employer, the nature of the employment relationship with the employee and the other circumstances that support the bringing of an action against the employer – which, in this case, would include the fact that the employee was acting in the course of his or her employment.

## VI. Undue Delay As a Basis for Dismissal of Proceedings

**[46.53]** We must now consider an aspect of the law which, as has been mentioned, is not concerned specifically with the discoverability rule but which none the less in practice qualifies it greatly. This concerns the general discretion inhering in the Court to dismiss proceedings on the basis of inordinate or inexcusable delay in their prosecution.

**[46.54]** The principle was invoked by the Supreme Court in *O'Domhnaill v Merrick*,[63] where proceedings initiated long after an accident, but within the statutory limitation period by virtue of the long extension for minors, were dismissed after the progress of the case had slowed down once the writ was out. Thus, delay in prosecuting the case which would not have been sufficient to warrant dismissal became so when the long extension for minors was taken into account. (The reason for this long extension for minors will be examined presently.)

**[46.55]** In *Toal v Duignan*[64] the Supreme Court developed the principle, so as to limit still further the plaintiff's entitlements. Though disclaiming any intent to extend the range of judicial exemption of liability for defendants, the Court in fact went much further than its earlier decision in *O'Domhnaill v Merrick*,[65] which it professed to follow.

**[46.56]** Very briefly, the facts were as follows. The plaintiff, who was born in 1961, claimed that he learned in the summer of 1983 that he suffered from a condition of sterility as a result of an undiagnosed undescended testicle at the time of his birth. He sued an array of defendants, including the doctors who attended his mother and himself at the time of his birth, as well as the maternity hospital, and a general practitioner who attended him for mumps when he was ten years old. The gravamen of his case against the doctors attending

---

62. *Cf Simpson v Norwest Holst Southern Ltd* [1980] 2 All ER 471 (CA).
63. [1984] IR 151.
64. [1991] ILRM 135.
65. [1984] IR 151.

his mother and himself in 1961 was that they should either have prescribed remedial treatment or warned his parents of the need to obtain remedial treatment subsequently.

**[46.57]** This case looks very like a straightforward "discoverability" one, rather that involving any reference to the suspension of the clock from running against a plaintiff during his minority. The plaintiff's claim was that he first learned of the position in 1983: by then he was twenty-two years old.

**[46.58]** The Supreme Court, affirming Keane J, held that the proceedings should be struck out. Although there had been delay subsequent to the time the proceedings were instituted in October 1984, the Court dealt with the appeal on the basis that the plaintiff was not personally responsible for any delay in the prosecution of the proceedings after that date.

**[46.59]** So why did the plaintiff, who had instituted his proceedings within fifteen months of discovering his condition, find that the proceedings were struck out? The answer appears to be because of the hardship that the defendants would experience if the case were allowed to continue. Finlay CJ, for the Court, addressed the position of the defendants alleged to have been negligent at the time of the plaintiffs birth:

> "It would be impossible for either the hospital authorities or the consultants engaged, in the absence of the most detailed clinical notes and records, to defend themselves twenty-six years on from attendance at a birth in 1961. It is wholly impossible, the death having occurred of both the gynaecologist and paediatrician concerned either for the hospital or for the widow sued as a personal representative of the paediatrician to defend themselves in any way against the allegations which are being made against them.
>
> Even though, therefore, the plaintiff may be blameless in regard to the date at which these proceedings have been instituted and with regard to the period of twenty-five to twenty-six years since the events out of which they arose, as far as these defendants are concerned there would be an absolute and obvious injustice in permitting the case to continue against them. One cannot but be moved with sympathy for the plaintiff who obviously feels deeply about the medical condition which he is advised he presently suffers from, but that sympathy could not be permitted to justify what would be an unjust proceeding against these defendants."[66]

**[46.60]** The Chief Justice considered that the case was governed by *O Domhnaill v Merrick*; the principles of that decision might be summarised in their application to the instant case as being that:

> "where there is a clear and patent unfairness in asking a defendant to defend a case after a very long lapse of time between the acts complained of and the trial, then if that defendant has not himself contributed to the delay, irrespective of whether the plaintiff has contributed to it or not, the court may as matter of justice have to dismiss the action."[67]

**[46.61]** The Court also struck out the plaintiff's claim against the general practitioner who had treated him in 1971, though it involved a shorter lapse of time between the acts or omissions complained of and the trial. The Chief Justice noted that what the general practitioner was being asked to do was "to recollect detailed conversations and advice

---

66. [1991] ILRM 135.
67. [1991] ILRM 135

given or not given sixteen years ago". The same legal considerations applied to her case as to that of the other defendants. Thus, Finlay CJ was satisfied that:

> "even if the claims being made ... represented a statable case against her ... it would be unjust and unfair after this lapse of time to expect her to be able properly to defend herself."[68]

**[46.62]** *Toal v Duignan* is a watershed decision, with profoundly disturbing implications for the victims of "sleeping" torts. Henceforth a plaintiff, even where his or her conduct in relation to the proceedings has been unimpeachable, may find that his or her action is struck out by reason only of the difficulties for defendants caused by the effluxion of time. This is not a direct application of the *O Domhnaill v Merrick* principle, for that case involved inordinate and inexcusable delay in the prosecution of the proceedings.

**[46.63]** The effect of *Toal v Duignan* is to bring in a judicial "long stop", operating as an important qualification to the discoverability principle. That long stop kills a plaintiff's claim, regardless of the fact that he could not reasonably have learned of his right of action any earlier than he did, or of the fact that he took all reasonable steps to expedite proceedings once he learned of his entitlement to sue.

**[46.64]** In *Primor plc v Stokes Kennedy Crowley*[69] the Supreme Court returned to the theme and brought about greater certainty in the Law. Hamilton CJ set out the relevant principles in a passage that has become the *locus classicus*:

> "a the courts have an inherent jurisdiction to control their own procedure and to dismiss a claim when the interests of justice require them to do so;
>
> (b) it must, in the first instance, be established by the party seeking a dismissal of proceedings for want of prosecution on the ground of delay in the prosecution thereof, that the delay was inordinate and inexcusable;
>
> (c) even where the delay has been both inordinate and inexcusable the court must exercise a judgment on whether, in its discretion, on the facts balance of justice is in favour of or against the proceeding of the case;
>
> (d) in considering this latter obligation the court is entitled to take into consideration and have regard to:
>
> (i) the implied constitutional principles of basic fairness of procedures,
>
> (ii) whether the delay and consequent prejudice in the special facts of the case are such as to make it unfair to the defendant to allow the action to proceed,
>
> (iii) any delay on the part of the defendant because litigation is a two party operation the conduct of both parties should be looked at,
>
> (iv) whether any delay or conduct of the defendant amount to acquiescence on the part of the defendant in the plaintiff's delay,
>
> (v) the fact that conduct by the defendant which induces the plaintiff to incur further expense in pursuing the action does not, in law, constitute an absolute bar preventing the defendant from obtaining a striking out order but is a relevant factor to be taken into account by the judge in exercising his discretion whether

68. [1991] ILRM 135.

69. [1996] 2 IR 459 (SC).

or not to strike out the claim, the weight to be attached to such conduct depending upon all the circumstances'

(vi) whether the delay gives rise to a substantial risk that it is not possible to have a fair trial or is likely to cause or have caused serious prejudice to the defendant,

(vii) the fact that the prejudice to the defendant referred to in (vi) may arise in many ways and be other than that merely caused by the delay, including damage to a defendant's reputation and business."[70]

**[46.65]** As Hamilton CJ made clear in *Primor*, even where the delay has been both inordinate and inexcusable the court must exercise a judgment on whether, in its discretion, on the facts the balance of justice is in favour of or against the proceeding of the case. Amongst the issues which may affect where this balance of justice lies in a particular case is prejudice eg in the form of non-availability of an essential witness, as was the case in *Byrne v ITGWU*.[71] The plaintiff has been dismissed from his employment in 1981 and claimed that he had instructed a representative of the defendant union to proceed with his appeal to the Employment Appeals Tribunal but no appeal was lodged within the six week limitation period. The tribunal found that it had no jurisdiction to hear the appeal and the plaintiff claimed that the failure to lodge the appeal amounted to negligence on the part of the union. The first two firms of solicitors which the plaintiff approached did little to further the case and in 1992 he consulted a third firm which proceeded with the claim. The defendant brought a motion to have the claim dismissed for want of prosecution and claimed that it had been prejudiced by the delay as the person who had been handling the case had died in the meantime. Morris J dismissed the claim for want of prosecution finding that the delay had been inordinate, and as no excuse had been offered, also inexcusable, and as a result of the delay the defendant had been prejudiced in that an essential witness had died.

## VII. Persons Under a Disability

**[46.66]** Special provisions as to limitation apply to persons under a disability, the law taking a broad view that such persons are, as a class, in need of special protection. Who, then, is a person "under a disability"? The law allows for four categories:

---

70. [1996] 2 IR 459 at 475-476

71. High Court, 30 November 1995. Other decision applying the *Primor* test include *Carroll Shipping Ltd v Mathews Mulcahy Sutherland* High Court, 18 December 1996 (noted in Byrne and Binchy, *Annual Review of Irish Law 1996*, pp 439-441); *Private Motorists Protection Association (in liquidation) V Private Motorists Provident Society (in liquidation)* High Court, 20 February 1997 (Costello P), analysed by Byrne and Binchy, *Annual Review of Irish Law 1997*, pp 549-551; *Reidy v National Maternity Hospital* High Court, 31 July 1997 (Barr J); *McGregor (Robert) and Sons (Ireland) Ltd v The Mining Board* High Court, 5 October 1998 (Carroll J); *Truck & Machinery Sales Ltd v General Accident Fire and Life Assurance Co plc* High Court, 12 November 1999 (Geoghegan J) - an important case, discussing delay from external causes, analysed Byrne and Binchy, *Annual Review of Irish Law 1999*, pp 290-292; *Hughes v Moy Contractors* High Court, 29 July 1999 (Carroll J); *Collins v Bus Atha Cliath/Dublin Bus* Supreme Court, 22 October 1999; *Martin v Moy Contractors* Supreme Court, 9 February 1999; *Dunne v Electricity Board* High Court, 19 October 1999 (Laffoy J), all noted in Byrne and Binchy, *Annual Review of Irish Law 1999*, pp 292-299.

(a) an infant, that is, a person under the age of twenty-one years;

(b) a person of unsound mind;

(c) a convict subject to the operation of the Forfeiture Act 1870, in whose case no administrator or curator has been appointed under that Act.[72]

(d) a victim of sexual abuse who is suffering from consequent pshchological injury.[73]

**[46.67]** A person who is detained "in pursuance of any enactment authorising the detention of persons of unsound mind or criminal lunatics" is conclusively presumed to be of unsound mind, the presumption being without prejudice to the generality of the term.[74] In an English decision,[75] Lord Denning MR interpreted the term, "person of unsound mind", as meaning a person who:

> "is by reason of mental illness, incapable of managing his affairs in relation to the accident as a reasonable man would do."

**[46.68]** Winn LJ was understandably concerned lest the period of limitation be suspended where an injured person is "unconscious or ill or in a state of delirium without more being shown".[76] The borderline between physical and mental injury is extremely difficult to determine and there would be dangers in too liberal an interpretation of unsoundness of mind in this context.

**[46.69]** A number of somewhat complex provisions apply to persons under a disability. The general rule is that if, on the date when a right of action accrued, the person to whom it accrued was under a disability, the action may be brought at any time before the expiration of six years from the date when the person ceases to be under a disability or dies, whichever event first occurs, notwithstanding that the period of limitation has expired.[77] Thus, for example, where a person of unsound mind has a right of action, the appropriate period will not begin to run until he regains his sanity or until he dies, whichever is the sooner.

**[46.70]** To this rule there are exceptions. First, where the right of action originally accrued to some person not under a disability through whom the person under a disability claims, no extension will be permitted.[78] It may be presumed that the legislature considered that an inherited claim is in the nature of a windfall and that the person under a disability should not therefore be permitted to impose his condition, as it were, on a defendant with whom he had no direct contact. Secondly, where a right of action which has accrued to a person under a disability accrues, on his death while still under a disability, to another person under a disability, no further extension of time is allowed by reason of the disability of the second person.[79] Again the defendants interests are regarded as outweighing those of the

---

72. Section 48(1) of the Statute of Limitations 1957.
73. Statute of Limitations (Amendment) Act 2000 discussed in para **[46.96]** below
74. Section 48(2) of the Statute of Limitations 1957.
75. *Kirby v Leather* [1965] 2 QB 367 (CA).
76. *Kirby v Leather* [1965] 2 QB 367 at 383. See also at 385 (*per* Danckwerts LJ). See also *Rohan v Bord na Móna* [1991] ILRM 123 (HC).
77. Statute of Limitations 1957, *s* 49(1)(a).
78. Statute of Limitations 1957, *s* 49(1)(b).
79. Statute of Limitations 1957, s 49(1)(c).

person who inherits a right of action. Both of these exceptions raise a constitutional issue. The goal of protecting a dependent against undue delay in litigation against him is no doubt a valid one, but the means of execution may be considered too crude, especially where, as here, the persons on whom the axe falls are under a disability.

**[46.71]** A provision that has given rise to some controversy and constitutional litigation is s 49(2) of the Statute of Limitations 1957, which is to the following effect:

> (a) In the case of actions for damages for negligence, nuisance or breach of duty (whether the duty exists by virtue of a contract or of a provision made by or under a statute or independently of any contract or of any such provision) where the damages claimed by the plaintiff for the negligence, nuisance or breach of duty consist of or include damages in respect of personal injuries to any person -
>
> (i) subsection (1) of this section shall have effect as if for the words six years there were substituted the words three years, and
>
> (ii) this section shall not apply unless the plaintiff proves that the person under the disability was not, at the time when the right of action accrued to him, in the custody of a parent.
>
> (b) For the purposes of paragraph (a) of this subsection, parent in relation to a person under a disability means his father, mother, grandfather, grandmother, stepfather or stepmother, notwithstanding that the relationship is illegitimate or in consequence of adoption under the Adoption Act, 1952.[80]

**[46.72]** The twofold purpose of this provision is relatively clear: it was to reduce the general limitation period to three years in the case of personal injury litigation, and to make the special extensions in respect of persons under a disability not apply to cases where the person under the disability was in the custody of a parent when the right of action accrued to him.

**[46.73]** The legislature was apparently of the view that:

> "where the disability was that of infancy, it was not reasonable to extend the period of limitation beyond that afforded to a person of full age in those particular cases in which the infant was in such a position that, by virtue of the natural relationship that existed between it and a parent, the parent would normally and reasonably be expected to look after the child's legal interests and see that such action was taken as would protect those interests."[81]

The first purpose was achieved without difficulty; the second has given rise to some difficulty.

**[46.74]** In *O'Brien v Keogh*,[82] the constitutionality of the provision was challenged by a minor who had failed to take proceedings within the period allowed for a person under a disability in the custody of a parent but who would still have been within the permissable period had he not been in the custody of a parent.

**[46.75]** The Supreme Court held that he was entitled to succeed. It rejected the plaintiff's argument that the legislation involved invidious discrimination based on the physical

---

80. No 25 of 1952.

81. *Currie v Fairy Hill Ltd* [1968] IR 232 at 237-238 (SC).

82. [1972] IR 144 (SC).

location of the particular minor. On the Court's analysis the essential difference was between being in the custody of a person who is either a parent or is, in effect, in *loco parentis* on the one hand and not being in such custody on the other hand.[83] Ó Dálaigh CJ considered that:

> "Far from effecting inequality, the purpose of the provision would appear to attempt to establish equality between the two groups ...
>
> Article 40 does not require identical treatment of all persons without recognition of differences in relevant circumstances. It only forbids invidious discrimination."[84]

**[46.76]** The Court accepted, however, the plaintiff's contention that the right to sue for personal injuries is a chose in action and a property right, and that it is one of the personal rights of a citizen which the State, under s 3 of Article 40 of the Constitution, has the duty to respect, defend, protect and vindicate. The Chief Justice considered that s 49(2)(a)(ii) of the Statute of Limitations 1957 had "patently failed to do this"[85] in the case of infants who are under the custody of parents.

**[46.77]** In the Court's opinion, counsel for the Attorney General "was right"[86] to concede that the right to litigate claims was a personal right of the citizen within Article 40 of the Constitution.[87] The Court instanced cases where the provision could work hardship and injustice. For example, a family party in a car might be involved in a collision in which parents and children were injured, the parents dying shortly afterwards. The statute would then start running against the children who might be "inmates of a public-welfare institution".[88] A child who was a passenger in his father's car might be injured as a result of his parent's negligent driving, and the parent might raise the statute against proceedings not taken within three years of the accrual of the right of action.

**[46.78]** Since the provision had "no purpose" without the words that established the date of the running of the statute, the impugned paragraph had to fail in its entirety on account of its "constitutional frailty".[89]

**[46.79]** The effect of the decision is that all persons under a disability - not just infants - no longer have the period of extension provided by the statute curtailed in any way by reason of their being in the custody of a parent.

**[46.80]** Whether *O'Brien v Keogh*[90] is good law in the light of the subsequent Supreme Court decision of *Moynihan v Greensmyth*[91] is uncertain. In *Moynihan's* case, the Supreme Court pointed out that in two earlier decisions, *Foley v Irish Land Commission*[92] and *AG* v

---

83. [1972] IR 144 at 156.
84. [1972] IR 144 at 156.
85. [1972] IR 144 at 154.
86. [1972] IR 144 at 155.
87. *Cf Macauley v Minister for Posts & Telegraphs* [1966] IR 345.
88. [1972] IR 144 at 157.
89. [1972] IR 144 at 157.
90. [1972] IR 144 (SC).
91. [1977] IR 55 (SC), affg High Court, 1976 (Murnaghan J).
92. [1952] IR 118 (SC).

*Southern Industrial Trust Ltd*,[93] (neither of which had been cited to the Court in *O'Brien v Keogh)*,[94] it had held, in effect, that the property rights guaranteed by Article 40, s 3, sub-s 2 were not rights over particular items of property but were property rights guaranteed under Article 43, under which it might in certain circumstances be permissable to divest a citizen of the ownership of a particular item of property. O'Higgins CJ stated that, in order to give a comprehensive answer to the question, it would be necessary for the Court to give a considerable ruling", after reviewing its previous decisions, "not all of which ... are reconcilable with each other". He went so far as specifically to reserve[95] on whether *O'Brien v Keogh* had been correctly decided.[96]

## VIII. Fraud

**[46.81]** Fraud can also affect the limitation periods. Where either:

(a) an action is based on the fraud of the defendant or his agent or of any person through whom he claims or his agent, or

(b) the right of action is concealed by the fraud of any such person,

then the period of limitation does not begin to run until the plaintiff has discovered the fraud or could with reasonable diligence have discovered it.[97]

**[46.82]** The word "fraud" as used in paragraphs (a) and (b) has two different meanings. In paragraph (a) it means such fraud as will itself give rise to a right of action - in other words the tort of deceit;[98] in paragraph (b), on the other hand, it has "the same meaning as fraud in the Real Property Limitation Act 1833[99] and in the general equitable principles on which this section of the Acts is based and which it extends.[100] Thus, no degree of moral turpitude is required, and the term here includes conduct "which, having regard to some special relationship between the two parties concerned is an unconscionable thing for the one to do towards the other".[101]

---

93. (1957) 94 ILTR 161 (SC).

94. *Wilkinson v Ancliffe (BLT) Ltd* [1986] 3 All ER 427 at 438 (CA, *per* Slade LJ). See also *Jones v Liverpool Health Authority* (1995) 30 BMLR 1 (CA); *Forbes v Wandsworth Health Authority* [1997] QB 402.

95. [1977] IR at 71. *Cf Campbell v Ward* [1981] ILRM 60 (HC), where, in spite of O'Higgins CJ's doubts, Carroll J considered herself bound by *O'Brien v Keogh* until such time as the Supreme Court reviewed that decision.

96. For consideration of the subsequent complicated jurisprudence on the relationship between Articles 40.3 and 43, see Casey, *Constitutional Law in Ireland*, (1987), Ch 18; Forde, *Constitutional Law of Ireland* (1987) Part XXII.

97. Statute of Limitations 1957, *s* 71(1). See *Behan v Bank of Ireland* [1998] 2 ILRM 507 (SC) and *Heffernan v O'Herlihy* High Court, 3 April 1998, both of which are noted in Byrne and Binchy *Annual Law Review 1998*, pp 482-483.

98. *Cf* Barber v Houston (1885) 18 LR Ir 475 (Ex Div).

99. 3 & 4 Will 4, c 27.

100. *Beaman v ARTS Ltd* [1949] 1 KB 550 at 567 (CA, *per* Somervell LJ).

101. *Kitchen v RAF Association* [1958] 1 WLR 563 at 573(CA *per* Lord Evershed MR).

**[46.83]** The extension of the limitation period in the case of fraud will not permit the recovery of property that has been purchased for valuable consideration by a person not party to the fraud.[102]

## IX. Extinction of Title in Conversion and Detinue

**[46.84]** Prior to 1957, the expiration of the limitation period merely barred a right of action for conversion and detinue, and did not divest the owner of the chattel or his title to it. Thus, if he could recover it otherwise than by action, he was entitled to do so. Furthermore, any further conversion or wrongful detention of the chattel by a third person entitled the owner to sue in respect of it, his action running from the time of the subsequent wrongful act.

**[46.85]** Section 12 of the Statute of Limitations 1957 has changed the position on both these points. Now, the owner's title to the chattel is extinguished after the expiry of the relevant limitation period, unless he has in the meantime recovered possession of it.[103] Moreover, where a chattel has been converted or wrongfully detained, and before the owner recovers possession of it a further conversion or wrongful detention takes place, no action may be brought in respect of this subsequent tort after the expiration of six years from the accrual of the cause of action in respect of the original conversion or detention.[104]

## X. Special Periods of Limitation

**[46.86]** Some special periods of limitation may be noted.

### Actions for Contribution under the Civil Liability Act 1961

**[46.87]** An action for contribution under Chapter II of the Civil Liability Act 1961 may be brought within the same period as the injured person is allowed in law for bringing an action against the contributor,[105] or within two years after the liability of the claimant[106] is ascertained, or the injured person's damages are paid, whichever is the greater.[107] It was held by Finlay P, in *Buckley v Lynch*,[108] that:

> "the entire right to recover contribution, and any legal procedure created for the enforcement of that right by the Act of 1961, must be deemed to be an action for contribution ..."

within the meaning of the limitation provision.

---

102. Section 71(2) of the Statute of Limitations 1957.
103. Statute of Limitations 1957, s 12(2). The provision is subject to s 26, which deals with chattels held in trust.
104. Statute of Limitations 1957, s 12(1) (also subject to s 26).
105. That is, any wrongdoer (other than the claimant in relation to contribution), who "is, or would if sued at the time of wrong have been, liable in respect of the same damage" as the claimant: s 21(1) of the 1961 Act.
106. Civil Liability Act 1961, s 31.
107. Civil Liability Act 1961, s 31. In *Neville v Margan Ltd* High Court, 1 December 1988 Blayney J expressed the tentative view that s 31 provides for two rather than three:

> "alternative periods, the first being the period the injured person has for bringing an action against the contributor, and the second being whichever of two periods of two years is appropriate on the facts."

108. [1978] IR 6 at 11 (HC).

## Admiralty Actions[109]

**[46.88]** Section 46(2) of the Civil Liability Act 1961 prescribes a general limitation period of two years from the date of damage, death or injury in actions to enforce a claim for damages or lien in respect of damage[110] to a vessel, cargo or property or the loss of life or personal injury suffered by a person on board a vessel, caused by the sole or concurrent fault of the defendant vessel; an action for contribution in respect of any overpaid proportion of any of these damages must be commenced within a year from the date of payment. The Court is given a discretion by s 46(3), exercisable subject to the Rules of Court, to extend the period, subject to such conditions as it thinks fit; moreover, if satisfied that there has not during this period been any reasonable opportunity of arresting the defendant vessel within the jurisdiction of the Court or within the territorial waters of the country to which the plaintiffs vessel belongs or in which the plaintiff resides or has his principal place of business, it must extend this period to an extent sufficient to give the plaintiff this reasonable opportunity.

## Causes of Action that Survive Against Estate of Deceased Person

**[46.89]** No proceedings are maintainable in respect of any cause of action[111] which has survived against the estate of a deceased person[112] unless:

(a) the proceedings were commenced against him within the period of limitation prescribed for that action and were pending at the date of his death, or

(b) were commenced within the prescribed period or within two years after his death, whichever period first expires.[113]

Thus, for example, where a negligent motorist dies shortly after an accident in which he injures a cyclist, the cyclist has no more than two years after the motorist's death in which to take proceedings.

**[46.90]** In *Moynihan v Greensmyth*,[114] the constitutional validity of this two-year limitation period was unsuccessfully challenged by a minor on the basis that it offended against s 3 of Article 40 of the Constitution, wherein the State guarantees, by its laws, to:

> "... protect as best it may from unjust attack and, in the case of injustice done, [to] vindicate the ... property rights of every citizen."[115]

**[46.91]** On the one hand, the plaintiff conceded that the limitation period was not unconstitutional in relation to those not suffering from incapacity and that, "in such

109. See Brady & Kerr, *The Limitation Of Actions In The Republic of Ireland* (2nd ed, 1994), pp 87-88.

110. "Damage" here includes salvage or other expenses, consequent on the fault of the vessel, recoverable at law by way of damages; these expenses are deemed to be a damage caused when they are incurred: s 46(4) of the Act. See *Lawless Dublin Port and Docks Board* [1998] 1 ILRM 514 (HC) (Barr J), analysed by Byrne and Binchy, *Annual Review of Irish Law 1998*, pp 483-486. In *Carleton v O'Regan* [1997] 1 ILRM 370 (HC) Barr J declined to exercise his discretion to extend the period under s 46(2).

111. Including the right to contribution under Chapter II of the Civil Liability Act 1961: see s 30 of that Act.

112. *Cf* Civil Liability Act 1961, s 8.

113. Civil Liability Act 1961, s 9.

114. [1977] IR 55 (SC), affg High Court, 1976 (Murnaghan J).

115. Article 40(3)(2).

circumstances, the period was reasonable and fair".[116] On the other hand, counsel for the defendant and counsel for the Attorney-General conceded that the right claimed by the plaintiff was a "property right", which they did not assert to be outside the scope of Article 40.[117]

**[46.92]** The gravamen of the plaintiff's case was that it was improper and unjust to impose on a person under a disability the task of initiating proceedings within two years after the death of the defendant.

**[46.93]** The Supreme Court, affirming Murnaghan J in the High Court, rejected the plaintiffs claim. O'Higgins CJ, delivering the judgment of the Court, stated:

> "Bearing in mind the State's duty to others - in particular those who represent the estate of the deceased, and beneficiaries - some reasonable limitation on actions against the estate was obviously required. If the period of infancy were to form part of the period of limitation ... then the danger of stale claims being brought would be very real and could constitute a serious threat to the rights of beneficiaries of the estate of a deceased. The alternative was to apply a period of limitation which would have general application. It had to be either one or the other, and it does not appear that any compromise was possible."[118]

## Defective Products

**[46.94]** The Liability of Defective Products Act 1991, which supplements the existing common law of negligence by providing a remedy for injury or damage caused by defective products stops the clock until three years after the date that the cause of action occurred or the date (if later) on which the plaintiff became aware, or should reasonably have become aware, of the damage, the defect and the identity of the producer.[119]

**[46.95]** This, of course, is similar to the approach towards discoverability adopted by the Statute of Limitations (Amendment) Act 1991, but it is not identical. It does not, for example, contain any requirement of actual or constructive awareness of the significance of the damage; nor does it require any causal attribution of responsibility for the damage to the producer. A further important difference is the the Liability for Defective Products Act 1991 includes damage to property as well as injury and death, in contrast to the Statute of Limitations (Amendment) Act 1991.

**[46.96]** The drawback, from the standpoint of prospective plaintiffs, is contained in s 7(2)(9), which extinguishes a right of action, regardless of any question of discoverability, on the expiration of ten years from the date on which the producer puts into

---

116. [1977] IR 55 at 72. (See also *McCullough v Ireland*, High Court, 16 March 1989 (Barron J)).
117. The Supreme Court evinced much concern regarding this issue, warning that it wished to make it clear that "... it does not necessarily accept that those concessions ... are well founded": [1977] IR 55 at 71 (*per* O'Higgins CJ).
118. [1977] IR 55 at 72. On the role of estoppel, see *O'Keeffe v Commissioners of Public Works*, Supreme Court, 24 March 1980. *Cf O'Reilly v Cranville* [1971] IR 90; *Traynor v Fegan* [1985] IR 586 (HC); *Doran v Thompson & Sons Lid* [1978] IR 223 (SC); *Smith v Ireland* [1983] ILRM 300 (HC).
119. Liability for Defective Products Act 1991, s 7(1). See further Brady and Kerr, *The Limitation of Actions in the Republic of Ireland* (2nd ed, 1994) pp 85 – 86.

circulation the product that caused the damage (unless, of course, the injured person has in the meantime instituted preceedings against the producer).

## Claims Relating to Child Abuse

**[46.97]** Over the past few decades there has been a growing international awakening to the facts of child abuse. Medical research four decades ago revealed that children were being subjected to a range of violence and neglect in their domestic environments which had not previously been known, though perhaps it was often suspected. Over the past twenty years, evidence as to child sexual abuse has become widespread. In the Irish context, there is now some understanding of the abuse that occurred in some State-administered institutions. A Commission to Enquire into Child Abuse, chaired by Hon Miss Justice Laffoy, has been established.[120]

**[46.98]** One of the great difficulties about civil claims for compensation for child abuse is that victims are slow to come forward and initiate litigation. The reasons are complex. They may have suppressed their memory of the traumatic events, they may be suffering from post-traumatic stress disorder, the prospect of suing may simply be too daunting or they may not have made the causal connection between their psychological distress and the abuse.

**[46.99]** Internationally, the courts and legislatures have adopted widely ranging strategies to deal with the phenomenon of child abuse, sexual or non-sexual, in the context of limitation of actions. One approach is to apply the 'discoverability' test. This has resulted in extension of time in Canada[121] but not in a recent decision of the New Zealand Court of Appeal.[122]

**[46.100]** Another approach, now favoured in Ireland in the context of sexual abuse, is the disability model. This concentrates, not on the victim's a awareness of the abuse, but on his or her capacity to initiate litigation in response to it. If the abuse had weighed so heavily on the victim as to render him or her incapable of doing so for same time, the clock stops during that period and the general limitations rules as to disability apply.

**[46.101]** The Statute of Limitations (Amendment) Act 2000, in s 2, inserts a new s 48A into the Statute of Limitations 1957. In simple terms, it provides that a person bringing an action founded on tort in respect of an act of sexual abuse committed against him or her during minority is to be treated as being under a disability while he or she is suffering from any psychological injury caused by that act or any other act of the transgressor and the psychological injury is of such significance that his or her will, or his or her ability to make a reasoned decision, to living that action is substantially impaired. The legislation does not define 'psychological injury'. The concept would appear to range wider than mental illness. Whether it goes so far as including any inhibition of freedom of choice or capacity to act remains to be seen.

---

120. Commission to Enquire into Child Abuse Act 2000.

121. *M(K) v M(H)* (1992) 96 DLR (4th) 289 (SCC).

122. *T v H* [1995] 3 NZLR 37 (CA). *Cf S v G* [1995] 3 NZLR 681 and *H v R* [1996] 1 NZLR 299. These decisions are discussed by the Law Reform Commission in its Consultation Paper, *The Law of Limitation of Actions arising from the Non-Sexual Abuse of Children* (CP 16-2000), para 2.099 – 2.101.

**[46.102]** An "act of sexual abuse" is defined as including:

(a) any act of causing, inducing or coercing a person to participate in any sexual activity,

(b) any act of causing, inducing or coercing a person to observe any other person engaging in any sexual activity, or

(c) any act committed against, or in the presence of, a person would, in all circumstances, regard as misconduct of a sexual nature,

provided that the commission of the act concerned is recognised by law as giving rise to a cause of action. Thus the conduct must constitute a tort. Since certain kinds of sexual abuse may not actually involve physical contact, as the definition makes clear, it may well that our courts will be called on, and probably disposed to, extend the existing repertoire of torts, such as those of assault and intentional infliction of emotional suffering, interpret them broadly and have resort to the strategy of compensating for infringements of constitutional rights. It seems very likely, in the light of *McDonnell v Ireland*,[123] that such claims would be characterised as being 'founded on tort', as the legislation requires.

**[46.103]** It should be noted that the legislation applies, not just to claims against the alleged transgressors themselves,[124] but also against those alleged to have been guilty of negligence or breach of duty in respect of the personal injuries caused by the act of sexual abuse. So, for example, if a victim takes a claim against a school or other institution, or indeed the State itself, arguing that the defendant negligently facilitated or failed to prevent the abuse, the Statute of Limitations (Amendment) Act 2000 applies to that claim.

**[46.104]** Section 3 of the Act contains a saver in relation to the court's power to dismiss an action on the ground of delay where this would be in the interests of justice. The section gives no guidance to the court as to what weight it should attach to the fact that legislative policy supports the taking of actions, even after a long time, where disability as defined in the legislation exists. The Law Reform Commission has recently published a Consultation Paper on the question of limitations in regard to non-sexual abuse.[125] The policy issues here are considerably more complex as the parameters of non-sexual abuse in contrast to sexual abuse, and not so easy to define, What is sound discipline in the eyes of one person may be a violent assault on a defenceless child in the eyes of another.

---

123. [1998] 1 IR 134 (SC).

124. Two small points of controversy may be noted about the claim against the alleged transgressor. In order to fall within the scope of s 48A the plaintiff must be suffering from any psychological injury that:

> "is caused, in whole or in part by th[e] act [of sexual abuse], or by any other act, of the person who committed the first mentioned act ..."

It would appear from this language that, in order to obtain the benefit of the legislation, the plaintiff must actually establish the defendant did what the claim alleges he or she did (unless the plaintiff is relying on a causal connection between the psychological injury and some *other* act of the defendant, about which we shall have some observations below). How is the court to determine whether the case falls within s 48A without addressing the merits of the Claim? Is it to adopt a strategy of leaving the claim in its entirety, without prejudice to dismissing it on the limitations issue at the termination of the proceedings. So far as the reference to "some other act" of the defendant is concerned, it should be noted that (cin ontrast to "an act of sexual abuse"), this other act need not give rise to a cause of action.

125. LRC Consultation Paper, *The Law of Limitations of Actions arising from Non-Sexual Abuse of Children* (CP 16-2000).

**[46.105]** The Commission is not keen on the disability model since it sees difficulties surrounding resort to psychological evidence. It provisionally recommends a fixed period of time after a victim of non-sexual abuse reached majority, It is divided on whether this period should be fifteen years or twelve years with a supplementary judicial discretion to extend the period for up to three years. In cases involving claims for both sexual and non-sexual abuse, the limitations regime is more favourable to the plaintiff should apply. In contrast to the legislation of 2000, the defendant would have to be in a relationship of trust and dependency with the plaintiff or fall under a supervisory duty or vicarious liability; claims for non-sexual abuse against strangers would thus not fall within the extended limitations period provisionally recommended by the Commission.

# Index

**ab initio**
doctrine of, trespass to land 23.23-23.26
**abnormal contingency**
legal causation 2.19
**abortion**
right to privacy 37.81
**absolute privilege**
defamation 34.133-34.157, 34.136, 34.142
**abuse of possession**
conversion 30.04-30.18
**abuse of public office**
public authorities 19.62
**abuse of rights**
trespass to land 23.14-23.21
**accidents**
breach of statutory duty 21.34
fire, liability for 26.06-26.10
inevitable, nuisance 24.102
motor vehicles 1.121, 1.128-1.154, 7.15-7.19
physically disabled 7.13-7.20
probability of 7.24, 7.27-7.34
professional negligence 14.182-14.193
psychiatric damage 17.54, 17.60
*res ipsa loquitur* 9.20-9.38
*Rylands v Fletcher* 25.22-25.24
state liability 38.17
statistical unlikliehood of 9.37
work accidents 20.62
*see also* **fatal injury**; **injury**; **personal injury**; **physical injury**; **psychiatric damage**
**accord, and release**
concurrent wrongdoers 4.17-4.18
**accumulations**
*Rylands v Fletcher* 25.17
**act of a stranger**
liability for fire 26.12
*Rylands v Fletcher* 25.35-25.37
**act of God**
*Rylands v Fletcher* 25.38-25.42
**act of others**
nuisance 24.110-24.112
***actio personalis moritur cum persona***
survival actions on death 40.02
**actionable**
on/without proof of special damage, and slander 34.28-34.29
*per se*
damages 44.03, 44.06
libel 34.24, 34.28
limitations 46.04
privacy of communication 1.65
slander 34.28-34.29, 34.30-34.49
torts affecting interest in goods 37.07
trespass 22.04
trespass to goods 28.07-28.09
trespass to land 23.33
*sina damno*, constitutional rights 1.61-1.65
**actions**
business relations 32.3-32.11
concurrent wrongdoers 4.14
fatal injuries 42.13
infringement of constitutional rights 1.75, 1.76
limitations 46.07-46.20, 46.88, 46.89, 46.90-46.93
survival actions on death 41.01-41.12
**activity duties**
fitness of premises 13.17
injuries caused by animals 27.13-27.14
**actual damage** 44.06
constitutional infringements 1.61
**actual knowledge**
business relations 32.23
**actual loss or damage**
negligence 5.02, 5.05, 44.06
**actual malice**
defamation 34.194
**acturial evidence**
damages 44.95-44.100
**admiralty actions**
limitations 46.89
**admissible claims**
psychiatric damage 17.28

**adult activities**
minors 40.29-40.30, 40.37
**adultery**
defamation 34.33
**adverse possession**
detinue 29.02-29.08
**advice**
professional negligence 14.176-14.180
**aerial photography**
right to privacy 37.11
**affirmative duties**
introduction 8.01-8.05
bar-room assaults 8.26-8.31
children 8.19
common law 8.01-8.02, 8.31
duty to control others 8.17-8.44
employers' liability 18.127
failure to perform an act 8.04, 8.05
failure to warn 8.05
fraudulent non-disclosure 8.05
incapacitated persons and their potential victims 8.06-8.16
injury, protection from 8.06-8.16
intentional wrongdoing 8.23-8.25
intoxicated persons 8.07-8.16
medical negligence 8.25
motor vehicles 8.19-8.22
negligent non-disclosure 8.05
neighbour test 8.09
non-disclosure 8.05
nonfeasance 8.04, 8.05
*novus actus interveniens* 8.07
occupiers' liability 8.31
potential victims 8.06-8.16
prisoners 8.31-8.44
psychiatric patients 8.25
third parties 8.07
visitors 8.31
**age**
children 16.12, 16.37-16.39, 16.62
consent and trespass to the person 22.74-22.85
mental development of children 40.06-40.14
**aggravated damages**
*Rookes v Barnard* 44.08, 44.10, 44.31, 44.37
**agony of the moment**
defences 20.18-20.22, 20.23
fire, liability for 26.33
**agricultural community**
occupiers' liability 12.61-12.62
**agricultural products**
(primary), manufacturers' and producers' liability 11.174-11.175
**airspace**
right to privacy 37.06
**alternative danger cases**
novus actus interveniens 2.47
**ambiguous statements**
deceit 35.16
**animals**
conversion 30.19
**animals, liability for injuries caused by**
introduction 27.01-27.02
activity duties 27.13
defences 27.26, 27.48
dogs 16.58-16.60, 27.27-27.41, 27.66
duty of care of occupier 27.10
general principles of tort 27.03-27.14
Law Reform Commission proposals 27.66
negligence 27.03-27.04
nuisance 27.05-27.06
occupiers' liability 27.09-27.14, 27.33-27.47
*Rylands v Fletcher* 27.08
trespass 27.07, 27.10, 27.32, 27.42-27.48
special rules, liability under 27.15-27.65
cattle trespass 27.42-27.48
damage 27.37-27.41, 27.54
defences 27.26, 27.48
dogs 27.27-27.41
domestic animals 27.16, 27.23, 27.42-27.47
extent of liability 27.47
highways 27.49-27.60
horses 27.61-27.65
immunity from liability 27.50-27.55
incidence of liability 27.24-27.25

*animals, liability for injuries caused by (contd)*
injury to lifestock 27.37-27.38
possession and ownership 27.45
*scienter* principle 27.15-27.26, 27.29, 27.51
wild animals 27.16, 27.23
***Anns* formula**
economic loss and negligence 10.09
**annual average loss**
fatal injuries 42.25-42.27
**apology**
defamation 34.226-34.227
**appeals**
defences 20.55
**appellate functions**
damages
**award too high or too low** 44.63-44.67
overturn of award 44.58
procedure of court 44.60
trial judge and Supreme Court, damages 44.61-44.62
uniformity of awards 44.68-44.70
**apportionment, of damages**
defences 20.43-20.45, 20.55
**architects**
fitness of premises 13.81-13.82
**army deafness**
compensation 1.190
duty of knowledge 46.42-46.48
**arrest**
trespass to the person 22.105-22.110
**assault**
affirmative duties 8.26-8.31
and battery, medical negligence 14.89, 14.92, 14.94
trespass against the person 22.20-22.27
**assessment**
negligent conduct and standard of care 7.25-7.54
**assuming the relationship**
care of children 16.52
**assumption of responsibility**
*Hedley Byrne* principle 10.09, 10.116-10.141
**Australia**
business relations 32.05, 32.09
character merchandising 31.79-31.81
damages 44.13, 44.101-44.106, 44.185
medical negligence 14.79, 14.85, 14.144
privilege and defamation 34.181
psychiatric damage 17.34
public authorities 19.03
right to privacy 37.02
schools 16.49-16.52, 16.54-16.55
survival actions on death 41.07
**award for pain and suffering**
manufacturers' and producers' liability 11.123

**bailees and bailment**
conversion 30.22, 30.24
detinue 29.09-29.19
occupiers' liability 12.142
**balance of convenience**
injunctions 45.37-45.44
passing off 31.62
**banks**
conversion 30.13-30.18
deceit 35.24-35.25
**bar-room assaults**
affirmative duties 8.26-8.31
**barristers**
duty of care 14.164, 14.167
immunity 14.161-14.168
non-litigious work 14.167-14.168
present legal position 14.167
professional negligence 14.161-14.168
*see also* **professional negligence**
**battery**
medical negligence 14.77-14.81
trespass against the person 22.03, 22.11-22.19
**behaviour of medical practitioner**
medical negligence 14.08, 14.09
behaviour on the highway 3.30, 15.16-15.57
**benefit of the public or a class of persons**
breach of statutory duty 21.10-21.18

**benefits**
fatal injuries 42.19, 42.24-42.42
**best interests test**
right to privacy 37.88
**big bangs**
remoteness of damage 3.43
**blameworthiness**
defences 20.46-20.48, 20.54
*Rylands v Fletcher* 25.53
**blanket immunities**
duty of care 6.86
**Blood Transfusion Service Board (BTSB)**
state compensation 1.182
**Blood Tribunal**
state compensation 1.189
***Bolam* test**
medical negligence 14.82
***bona fide* acts**
constitutional rights 1.32
***bona fides* of defendant**
conversion 30.12-30.18
**branches (tree)**
private nuisance 24.29-24.32
**breach of confidence**
communicable diseases 37.50-37.51
communication of information 37.23
conversion of a property interest 37.22
criminal wrongdoing, suspected 37.52-37.53
damages 37.39
elements of 37.23
equitable principles 37.21-37.22
medical confidences 37.40-37.58
private and public interest 37.46-37.47
right to privacy 37.23, 37.38-37.58
*see also* **right to privacy**
**breach of contract**
business relations 32.20-32.21
economic loss 10.30-10.39
trade disputes 32.122-32.126
v. tort 1.109-1.116
**breach of statutory duty** 21.05-21.61
accident, type of 21.34
benefit of the public or a class of persons 21.10-21.18
breach of statute required 21.22-21.24
civil actions 21.08
contributory negligence 21.52-21.61
damages 21.12
data protection 21.08
defences 20.50
delegation of duty 21.49
duty of care 6.58-6.59
employee 21.56-21.57, 21.61
employers' liability 18.23-18.32, 18.111, 18.146, 18.150, 21.61
fire, liability for 26.32
housing 21.11-21.18
licensing requirements 21.33
limitations
injury attributable to conduct 46.49-46.50
on recovery 21.21-21.45
loss or injury established by plaintiff 21.25
negligence 21.47-21.51
*novus actus interveniens* 21.25
offending conduct must cause loss 21.25
penalties and remedies 21.19
plaintiff protected by statute 21.35-21.45
plaintiff's breach not a bar 21.46-21.51
public authorities 19.05, 19.29, 19.51
public duty 21.12
respective degrees of fault 21.61
right to privacy 37.20
scope of statutory obligation 21.23
statutory interpretation, other techniques of 21.10
**breach of trust, and restitution** 1.117
**Britain**
conspiracy 32.58-32.59, 32.75
duty of care 6.02, 6.03, 6.10-6.24, 6.28, 6.32, 6.35
pure economic loss 6.36, 6.51
economic loss 10.45, 10.161
*Hedley Byrne* principle 10.77, 10.141, 11.86-11.87
manufacturers' and producers' liability 11.08-11.09, 11.75, 11.84-11.88

*Britain (contd)*
public authorities 19.07-19.14
survival actions on death 41.07
**broadcast reports of court proceedings**
defamation 34.141-34.145
**Brussels Convention**
defamation 34.48-34.49
**BTSB (Blood Transfusion Service Board)**
state compensation 1.182
**builder/vendor and builder/lessor** 13.57-13.82, 19.22-19.34
architects 13.81-13.82
defects discovered before injury or damage 13.71-13.76
engineers 13.81-13.82
fitness of premises 13.57-13.82, 13.71-13.76
reform, proposals for 13.80
surveyors 13.81-13.82
voluntary schemes 13.77-13.79
*see also* **builders**; **fitness of premises**
**builders**
contract builders 13.49-13.56, 14.226
dangerous defects 13.50-13.56
defective products 11.81-11.83, 11.100
defects of quality 13.49
defects, qualitative non-dangerous, duty of care 6.49
fitness of premises 13.01, 13.48-13.82, 19.22-19.34
professional negligence 14.226
*see also* **buildings**; **fitness of premises**; **premises**
**building societies**
professional negligence 14.219-14.223
**building standards**
fitness of premises 13.77
**buildings**
structural dangers 16.70-16.84
occupiers' liability 12.115-12.122
*see also* **builders**; **fitness of premises**; **premises**; **property**
**bullying**
employers' liability 18.80
**burden of proof**
*see* **proof**
**buses, school, and road negligence** 15.08-15.15, 15.52
**business relations, torts affecting**
introduction 32.01-32.02
action *per quod servirum amisit* 32.3-32.11
actual knowledge 32.23
conspiracy 32.58-32.82
constitutional rights 32.50, 32.69, 32.74-32.76
contractual relations 32.13-32.45
interference with another's interests, generic tort of 32.83-32.86
intimidation 32.46-32.57
knowledge, actual/constructive 32.23
servant 32.10, 32.12
strikes 32.51
threat 32.48, 32.56
trade disputes 32.87-32.185
trade unions 32.16-32.18, 32.24, 32.34-32.40, 32.64-32.69
*see also* **businesses**; **conspiracy**; **contractual relations**; **trade disputes**
**businesses**
expertise, *Hedley Byrne* principle 10.147
insurance costs 1.166-1.168
passing off 31.42, 31.57-31.60, 31.76
reputation misappropriated 31.76
vicarious liability 43.54-43.60
*see also* **business relations**, **torts affecting**
**'but for' test**
causation 2.10-2.15, 2.17

**calculation of damages**
conversion 30.40-30.44
fatal injuries 42.19, 42.44, 42.45-42.66 *passim*
***Campus Oil* principles**
interlocutory injunctions 45.22, 45.26
**Canada**
affirmative duties 8.06
business relations 32.05, 32.09
damages 44.13, 44.101-44.106, 44.186

*Canada (contd)*
manufacturers' and producers' liability 11.09
medical negligence 14.79, 14.85, 14.144, 14.150
minors 40.08-40.10, 40.10, 40.26
professional negligence 14.164
right to privacy 37.57
schools 16.56
**cap on damages**
manufacturers and producers strict liability 1.167, 1.171, 11.170, 11.172-11.173
mental distress in fatal accidents 33.20
**carers**
damages 44.107-44.112
**carriers and bailees**
occupiers' liability 12.142
**castles**
professional negligence 14.217
**cattle**
trespass to land 27.07, 27.42-27.48
**causal analysis**
collateral benefits 44.114
**causal causation/connection**
negligence 5.02, 5.05, 5.07
**causal link**
causation 2.07, 2.25, 2.26, 2.54, 2.61
**causal responsibility**
limitations 46.35-46.40
**causation**
introduction 2.01-2.05
'but for' test 2.10-2.15
causal link 2.07, 2.25, 2.26, 2.54, 2.61
defamation 34.43
defences 20.41-20.42
employers' liability 18.119-18.124, 18.146
factual causation 2.07, 2.61
fire damage 26.16-26.18
intervening act 2.24-2.60
legal causation 2.17-2.23
liability 2.07-2.08, 2.50
manufacturers' and producers' liability 11.62-11.70, 11.127-11.135, 20.41-20.42
material element and substantial factor 2.15
medical negligence 2.20-2.21, 2.61-2.63, 14.55
negligence, causal connection 5.05, 5.07
non-disclosure and medical negligence 14.137-14.149
*novus actus interveniens* 2.24-2.60
proof of negligence 2.10, 9.49
recklessness 2.28, 2.37-2.49
remoteness 2.01, 2.04, 2.23
voluntary human act 2.19, 2.43, 2.47
*see also* ***novus actus interveniens***; **remoteness**; ***res ipsa loquitur***
**causes of action**
death 41.04, 41.10, 46.90-46.93
***caveat emptor***
deceit 35.06
fitness of premises 13.03, 13.04, 13.44, 13.67
*Hedley Byrne* principle 10.123
***caveat lessee***
fitness of premises 13.03, 13.44
**champerty**
tort of 36.30
**chattels**
conversion 30.02-30.10 *passim*, 30.23-30.24, 30.30, 30.32
detinue 29.01-29.19
duty of care, dangerous chattels 6.53
trespass to goods 28.13-28.14
**children**
introduction 16.01
affirmative duties 8.19
age of child 16.12, 16.37-16.39, 16.62
child's services, action for the loss of 33.36-33.39
discipline of 22.93-22.104
family relations 33.27-33.39
fatal injuries 42.30-42.31, 42.46-42.47, 42.49-42.50, 42.54, 42.56
foreseeability of harm 16.03-16.05, 16.16
guardians, statutory duties and rights of 21.62-21.74

*children (contd)*
motor vehicles 15.03-15.15, 16.10-16.11, 16.65-16.67
occupiers' liability 12.27-12.33, 12.93, 16.70, 16.73
paedophiles, *Hanrahan* rationale 1.33
parental negligence 16.02-16.15
persons under a disability 46.67, 46.75-46.77
playground supervision 16.18, 16.26-16.50, 16.52
proximity 16.16
reasonableness of attributing blame 16.03
roads, negligence on 8.19, 15.03-15.15, 15.51-15.52
schools' negligence 16.16-16.84
trespass to the person 22.74, 22.93-22.104
younger children 16.28, 16.33-16.44, 16.46-16.48, 16.62, 16.66-16.67
*see also* **families**; **family relations**; **minors**; **schools**
**Circuit Court judgments**
professional negligence 14.182-14.188
**Circuit Courts**
trial by jury 1.165
**circumstantial test**
defamation 34.183
**civil actions**
breach of statutory duty 21.08
**civil liability**
breach of statutory duty 21.21
fire 26.28, 26.32
limitations, and actions for contributions 46.88
public authorities 19.29, 19.49
**claim for contribution rules 4.23-4.26**
**claims**
concurrent wrongdoers, contributions 4.23-4.24
defences, set-off claims 20.56
employers' liability 18.23-18.32
loss of earnings, professional negligence 14.184-14.187, 14.191-14.192
psychiatric damage, admissible claims 17.28
*see also* **compensation**; **damages**
**class**
defamation 34.106-34.109
**cohabitees (cohabitants)**
consortium, damages for loss of 33.21
fatal injuries 42.10
**collateral benefits**
general 44.112-44.143
causal analysis 44.114
Civil Liability Acts (1961 and 1964) 44.117-44.122
common law principles 44.116, 44.119
disability payments 44.131-44.142
employer's payments 44.123-44.126
fatal accident claims 44.121
hospital expenses and carer cost 44.107-44.112
insurance 44.112-44.113, 44.120
international dimensions 44.138-44.142
non-deduction principle for non-fatal cases 44.118
pensions 44.127
purpose of the benefit 44.115
reduction of advantages 44.130-44.142
sick pay 44.129
social welfare payments 44.113
source of the benefit 44.114
statutory provisions 44.131-44.142
trade description offences 44.137-44.142
voluntary payments 44.122-44.126
**collateral negligence**
vicarious liability 43.53
**collectivist approach**
liability for loss 1.124
**comment**
facts and value judgements 34.209-34.214
versus fact 34.205-34.208
*see also* **fair comment**
**Committee on Court Practice and Procedure**
professional negligence 14.167-14.168
**common duty of care**
*see* **duty of care**
**common employment doctrine**
defences 20.03
employers' liability 18.02, 18.76, 18.105

*common employment doctrine (contd)*
loss distribution 1.124
vicarious liability 43.69
**common law**
affirmative duties 8.01-8.02, 8.31
breach of duty
defences 20.50, 20.108
negligence 21.53-21.59
concurrent wrongdoers 4.02, 4.04, 4.06, 4.09
damages 1.129, 44.116, 44.119, 44.184-44.189
deceit 35.29
defamation 34.05, 34.06, 34.34, 34.37, 34.38, 34.185
employers' liability 18.58, 18.97, 18.111, 18.159
fatal injuries 42.05
fire, liability for 26.03, 26.29
fitness of premises, immunity 13.22-13.24, 13.52, 13.57, 13.63, 13.67
injunctions 45.34
insurance and damages 1.129
joint and several tortfeasors 4.02, 4.05
libel/slander distinction 34.25, 34.28
manufacturers' and producers' liability 11.02, 11.53, 11.56, 11.97
negligence, breach of statutory duty 21.53-21.59
occupiers' liability 12.03-12.15, 12.22-12.23, 12.42
public authorities 19.02, 19.09, 19.11, 19.13
remoteness of damage 3.03
right to privacy 37.53
state liability, immunities 38.14, 38.16
survival actions on death 41.02
trespass to land 23.06
trespass to the person 21.67, 22.74-22.85, 22.105
**common man**
*novus actus interveniens* 2.51
**common sense**
*res ipsa loquitur* 9.38
**communicable diseases**
right to privacy 37.50-37.51
**communications**
defamation 34.12-34.15, 34.16-34.17, 34.159, 34.173
medical negligence 14.61-14.67
right to privacy 37.23, 37.72-37.74, 37.92-37.97
**companies**
*see* **businesses**
**comparative negligence**
manufacturers' and producers' liability 11.159
**compensation**
compensatory damages 44.07-44.08, 44.37
duty of care 6.67
equality of compensation 44.163
fatal injuries 42.19-42.66
inadequate compensation 44.202
motor vehicles 1.138-1.154
personal injury 1.135-1.137, 1.147-1.150, 1.155-1.180
psychiatric damage 17.04-17.08
schemes and insurance 1.107-1.108, 1.126-1.154, 1.166-1.192 *passim*
statutory duties and rights 21.02
*see also* **claims**; **damages**
**component parts**
manufacturers' and producers' liability 11.21-11.22
**computation of damages 44.71-44.81**
**concurrent wrongdoers**
introduction 4.01-4.07
definition 4.08-4.09
action against all, any or one 4.14
Civil Liability Act 1961, 4.03-4.04, 4.05, 4.07, 4.08, 4.10, 4.12, 4.17, 4.26
claims for contribution rule 4.23-4.26
common law principles 4.02, 4.04, 4.06, 4.09
contribution between 4.19-4.26
damages, payment of (satisfaction) 4.17
*damnum* (damage) 4.06
distribution of loss 4.24

*concurrent wrongdoers (contd)*
entitlement to recover fair contributions 4.03
estoppel 4.25
*iniuriae* (wrong) 4.06
joint and several liability 4.05, 4.07, 4.09
joint concurrent tortfeasors 4.05
joint tortfeasors 4.01-4.02
judgments 4.14-4.16
legislation 4.19
litigation in one action 4.03
manufacturers and producers strict liability 11.164-11.166
nuisance 4.13
period of limitation 4.25
plaintiff cannot recover more than total amount of damages 4.03
property restored 4.22
right to contribution 4.26
satisfaction, release and accord 4.17-4.18
several concurrent tortfeasors 4.05
several independent tortfeasors 4.05
several tortfeasors 4.01-4.02
tort v contract 1.109
torts are separate 4.05

**conduct**
occupiers' liability 12.106
of defendant
character 28.13
defences 20.81-20.83
standard of care 7.21, 7.38-7.43
of employee, vicarious liability 43.24-43.44, 43.48
of rescuer, defences 20.84-20.92
offending, and breach of statutory duty 21.25
*see also* **negligent conduct**

**confinement**
trespass against the person 22.37-22.38, 22.58

**consent**
defamation, qualified privilege 34.177
defences, defamation 34.224-34.225
medical negligence 14.76-14.136
of plaintiff 25.30-25.31
trespass to land 23.48
trespass to the person 22.59-22.85

**consequences**
direct (natural) and remoteness 3.05, 35.21

**consortium**
assessment of damages 33.12-33.13
cohabitees 33.21
*Cosgrave* principle 33.23
damages for loss of 33.04-33.16
extent of recovery 33.07-33.15
husbands 33.04, 33.06
law relating to 33.17-33.23
loss of consortium 44.109
medical treatment 33.07, 33.08
mental distress 33.10-33.11, 33.13, 33.15, 33.20
parental consortium 33.19, 33.22
unmarried couples 33.20-33.21
victim's contributory negligence 33.16
wives 33.04-33.05, 33.14-33.15
*see also* **family relations**

**conspiracy**
business relations 32.58-32.82
constitutional rights 32.69, 32.74-32.76
forms of conspiracy 32.63-32.69
simple conspiracy 32.63, 32.70-32.73
trade disputes 32.116-32.121
traditional view 32.60-32.62
unlawful means conspiracy 32.63, 32.74-32.82

**constitutional arguments**
defamation 34.04-34.06

**constitutional law**
trespass to land 23.03-23.05

**constitutional rights**
business relations 32.50, 32.69, 32.74-32.76
freedom of expression 45.20, 45.28
infringements 1.17, 1.36, 1.61-1.65
damages 44.24-44.31, 44.36-44.39, 44.40, 44.48
occurrence of 1.66-1.71
limitation on right to damages 1.22-1.32
of private individuals 1.14-1.16
right of privacy 37.60-37.98

*constitutional rights (contd)*
trade disputes 32.128-32.142
wrongful interference with 1.09-1.83
*see also* **rights**; **statutory duties and rights**
**consumers**
manufacturers' and producers' liability 11.26, 11.122-11.125, 11.174
**contemptuous damages** 44.04-44.57
**continuing obligation**
fitness of premises 13.37-13.40, 13.43
**continuing trespass**
trespass to land 23.34-23.36
**contract builders**
fitness of premises 13.49-13.56
**contracting out**
manufacturers' and producers' liability 11.161-11.163
**contractor**
independent *see* **independent contractor**
**contracts**
contractual entrants, occupiers' liability 12.07, 12.79, 12.131-12.135
contractual liability 1.109-1.116
economic loss
breach of contract 10.30-10.39
concurrent liability 10.17
contractual dimension 10.29
contractual expectancies 10.46
third party 10.40
fitness of premises 12.49-12.51, 13.03-13.11, 13.44-13.45
*Hedley Byrne* principle 10.19-10.20, 10.114-10.115, 10.149-10.154
manufacturers' and producers' liability 11.05-11.07, 11.161-11.163
provision of, duty of care 6.46-6.47
strangers to contracts, occupiers' liability 12.131-12.135
*see also* **contractual relations**
**contractual relations**
all-out strikes 32.37-32.40
breach of contract a necessity 32.20-32.21
business relations 32.13-32.45
damages 32.45
direct inducement 32.29-32.30
direct intervention of another type 32.29-32.30
embargoes 32.34-32.40
fourth party 32.32-32.33
historical background 32.14
indirect procurement 32.32-32.40
intention 32.26-32.27
justification and malice 32.41-32.44
knowledge and intention required 32.22-32.27
malice and justification 32.41-32.44
obligations 32.51, 32.53-32.54
personal relationship 32.42
persuasion, information or advice 32.15-32.19
pickets 32.38
private interest 32.44
public interest 32.43
third party 32.25, 32.32-32.33
wrongful procurement 32.28-32.40
*see also* **contracts**
**contribution**
between, concurrent wrongdoers 4.19-4.26
claims for contribution rule 4.23-4.26
**contributory negligence**
breach of statutory duty 21.52-21.61
business relations 32.10
causation 2.26
conversion 30.39
defences 5.08, 20.02-20.60
employers' liability 18.01, 18.23, 18.150-18.158
family relations 33.16, 33.38
fatal injuries 42.15, 42.15-42.16
fire 26.33
imputed, defences 20.57-20.60
manufacturers and producers 11.158-11.160
minors 40.05-40.26
negligence 5.08
*novus actus interveniens* 2.26, 2.46, 2.52, 2.56
nuisance 24.105
servant, business relations 32.10

**control**
duty to control others 8.17-8.44
employer/employee relationship 43.08-43.09, 43.18-43.23
right to control 9.18-9.19
**conversion**
introduction 30.01
definition 30.01
abusing possession 30.04-30.18
animals 30.19
bailment 30.22, 30.24
banks 30.13-30.18
*bona fides* of defendant 30.12-30.18
chattels 30.02-30.10 *passim*, 30.23-30.24, 30.30, 30.32
contributory negligence 30.39
damages 30.40-30.44
denying title 30.11-30.18
Derrynaflan Hoard 30.25-30.38
and detinue 30.09
extinction of title, limitations 46.85-46.86
finders 30.23-30.38
*jus tertii* 30.21-30.22
negligence 30.13
owner's/occupier's right 30.02, 30.02-30.22, 30.25-30.38
personal property 30.19
possession 30.02-30.03, 30.04-30.18, 30.19-30.22
right to possession of land 30.29, 30.34
right to privacy 37.07, 37.22
scope of the tort 30.19-30.44
taking possession 30.02-30.03
title of plaintiff 30.20-30.38
trespass to goods 28.02
trespass to land 30.25-30.38
value of article 30.41-30.44
**convicts**
limitations 46.67
**copyright**
passing off 31.01
**corporal punishment**
trespass to the person 22.113
**corporations** 39.01-39.08
as defendant 39.06-39.08
as plaintiff 39.02-39.05
defamation 39.03-39.04
free speech 39.05
vicarious liability 39.06-39.08
*see also* **partnerships**; **trade unions**; **unincorporated associations**
***Cosgrave* principle**
family relations 33.23
**cost of care and hospital expenses**
damages 44.107-44.112
**cost of risk elimination**
standard of care 7.25, 7.44-7.54
**counsel, and solicitor**
professional negligence 14.195-14.198
**county registrars**
torts 1.176-1.180
**courts**
choice of, professional negligence 14.181-14.194
**Courts Service**
torts 1.177-1.179
**creditworthiness**
*Hedley Byrne* principle 10.52-10.62
**criminal entrants** 12.66, 12.110-12.114
**criminal law**
right to privacy 37.59
v tort 1.107
**criminal offence**
punishable by death or imprisonment 34.38-34.39
**criminal wrongdoing**
suspected, and right to privacy 37.52-37.53
**cross-examination of witnesses**
professional negligence 14.196
**current operations (activity duty)**
fitness of premises 13.17
**customer**
passing off 31.09, 31.19
**cyclists**
negligence on roads 15.37, 15.44

**damage**
actual, proof of, constitutional infringements 1.61

*damage (contd)*
animals, injuries caused by 27.37-27.41, 27.54
deceit 35.20-35.24
duty of care 6.02, 6.36-6.51
economic loss 10.01, 10.02
irreparable damage, passing off 31.62, 31.73
manufacturers' and producers' liability 11.117-11.126
particular or special 24.05-24.11
property, to and by vehicles 1.101-1.103
remoteness of damage 3.04, 3.20-3.42
*see also* **remoteness of damage**
damages
introduction 44.01-44.02
actual damage 44.06
against the state 1.16
aggravated damages 44.08, 44.10
appellate functions regarding awards 44.58-44.71
breach of statutory duty 21.12
business relations 32.11, 32.45
cap on
manufacturers' and producers' strict liability 1.167, 1.171, 11.170, 11.172-11.173
mental distress in fatal accidents 33.20
causation 2.01
compensatory damages 44.07-44.08, 44.37
computation of damages under separate headings 44.71-44.81
global estimate 44.77-44.78
over-compensation 44.77
reduced awards 44.80-44.81
revised practice 44.76-44.79
concurrent wrongdoers 4.03, 4.17
consortium, loss of 33.04-33.16
contemptuous damages 44.04-44.57
conversion 30.40-30.44
deceit 35.03, 35.19
defamation 34.42-34.45, 34.229-34.262
defences 20.02, 20.09-20.10, 20.28, 20.43-20.45, 20.51-20.54
detinue 29.12-29.19
employment and loss of earnings 44.82-44.142
exemplary damages 44.09-44.57
fair compensation 44.07
fatal accidents 44.121
fatal injuries 42.19, 42.44, 42.45-42.66 *passim*
fitness of premises 13.55
injunctions 45.01, 45.47-45.52
joint tortfeasors 4.17-4.26
limitations and constitutional rights 1.22-1.32
medical negligence 14.40, 14.91
nominal damages 44.03
non-pecuniary loss 44.143-44.204
passing off 31.73-31.74
payment of (satisfaction), concurrent wrongdoers 4.17
personal injuries litigation 44.61-44.62, 44.98, 44.104-44.105, 44.121
plaintiff cannot recover more than the total amount, concurrent wrongdoers 4.03
proof of loss of earning capacity 44.82-44.142, 44.97
property damage 44.205-44.209
psychiatric damage 17.47
public authorities 19.22, 19.76
punitive damages 44.09-44.57
recent analysis, defamation 34.239
remoteness, causation 2.01, 2.04
*restitutio in integrum* 44.07-44.08, 44.206
right to privacy, breach of confidence 37.39
*Rookes v Barnard* 44.10-44.54
special damages 44.05
subjective element, defamation 34.243-34.245
survival actions on death 41.05-41.06, 41.08, 41.12
torts defined 1.118-1.120
types of damages awarded 44.03-44.57
*see also* **collateral benefits**; **exemplary damages**; **non-pecuniary loss**; **property**; ***Rookes v Barnard***
***damnum* (damage)**
concurrent wrongdoers 4.06

**danger**
and children 16.03-16.11
occupiers' liability 12.12, 12.14, 12.50-12.53, 12.72-12.73, 12.109, 12.130
on property, *Rylands v Fletcher* 25.18
public nuisance, highways 24.17-24.18
structural, school buildings 16.70-16.84
**dangerous activities**
vicarious liability 43.50-43.51
**dangerous acts**
duty to control others 8.17-8.22
**dangerous chattels**
duty of care 6.53
**dangerous defects**
fitness of premises 13.12-13.47, 13.50-13.56, 13.71-13.76
**dangerous propensities of child**
parental negligence 16.06-16.08
**dangerous substances**
manufacturers' and producers' liability 11.30
**dangerous things** 11.07, 11.08, 16.03-16.05
**dangerous work environments**
employers' liability 18.07, 18.25-18.27, 18.109-18.127 *passim*, 18.128-18.158
standard of care 7.52
**data protection**
breach of statutory duty 21.08
right to privacy 37.98
**date of knowledge**
limitations 46.03
**date on which cause of action accrues**
limitations 46.04-46.20
***de minimis* principle**
statutory duties 21.72
**deafness**
compensation 1.190
duty of knowledge 46.42-46.48
**death**
defamation of the dead 34.266
family relations 33.10-33.11, 33.15, 33.20
injunctions, risk of 45.21, 45.23, 45.28
limitations 41.09, 41.11, 46.90-46.93
of child 42.30
right to privacy 37.62, 37.82-37.85
risk of, injunctions 45.21, 45.23, 45.28
*see also* **survival actions on death**
**deceased person**
actions 46.90-46.93
non-pecuniary loss 44.196-44.197
**deceit**
tort described 35.01-35.02
ambiguous statements 35.16
banks 35.24-35.25
*caveat emptor* 35.06
damage 35.20-35.24, 35.29
damages 35.03, 35.19
direct consequences rule 35.01
distinguished 35.26
factual representation 35.03-35.09
false statements 35.26
fraudulent misrepresentation 35.09, 35.19, 35.24-35.25
fraudulent non-disclosure 8.05
*Hedley Byrne* principle 10.58-10.62, 10.111, 35.01
injurious falsehood 35.26-35.30
intention of defendant 35.13-35.14
intention to deceive, passing off 31.05-31.07, 31.50-31.53
knowledge of falsity 35.10-35.12
Lord Tenterden's Act 35.24-35.25
malice 35.28
misrepresentation 35.01-35.06, 35.09, 35.18-35.19, 35.25
negligent misrepresentation 10.58, 30.01, 35.01
negligent misstatement 35.26
opinion and factual representation 35.08
plaintiff's reliance 35.15-35.19
proof of fraud 35.10
representation of fact 35.03-35.09, 35.19
rescission 35.23
silence and inaction 35.06-35.07
slander 35.26
special relationship 35.01
**Declined Cases Committee**
motor insurance 1.145

**deep pocket, the**
vicarious liability 43.02, 43.61
**defamation**
introduction 34.01-34.11
what is defamatory 34.50-34.122
objectivity 34.52
precedents 34.51
previous cases 34.53-34.57, 34.68-34.70, 34.74-34.77
absolute privilege 34.135-34.159, 34.138, 34.144
actual malice 34.194
adultery 34.33
apology 34.226-34.227
belief in falsity of a statement 34.198
Brussels Convention 34.48-34.49
causation and remoteness 34.43
class, reference must be to 34.106-34.109
comment 34.205-34.208, 34.209-34.214
common law 34.05, 34.06, 34.34, 34.37, 34.38
communication 34.12-34.15, 34.16-34.17, 34.159, 34.173
consent 34.177, 34.224-34.225
constitutional arguments 34.04-34.06
context of statement 34.86-34.88
court proceedings 34.141-34.145
damages 34.229-34.237, 34.239, 34.240-34.256, 34.257-34.262
defences 34.122-34.133, 34.224-34.225
defendant 34.197-34.198, 34.277
definitions
malice 34.193
new definition 34.269-34.277
of tort 34.10-34.11
statutory 34.84
diseases, infectious or contagious 34.40-34.41
duty 34.169-34.173
effect of the libel 34.246
European Court of Human Rights, defamation 34.232, 34.255
exemplary damages 34.257-34.262
facts and value judgements 34.205-34.208, 34.209-34.214
fair comment 34.200, 34.201-34.223
false innuendo (popular) 34.90, 34.91, 34.93
false statements 34.59-34.60
foreseeability 34.44
forms of publication 34.21-34.24
homosexuality 34.77-34.81
immunity 34.146, 34.146-34.152
imputed lack of competence 34.55
independent privilege 34.162
injunctions 45.12-45.36
innocent dissemination 34.19, 34.267
innuendo 34.70, 34.89-34.96, 34.101, 34.131
interest, and privilege 34.174-34.178
interpretation, difficulty of 34.71
irrelevant defamation 34.172
judge and jury, functions of 34.97-34.101
judicial proceedings 34.146-34.157
juries 34.97-34.101, 34.229-34.231, 34.256
justification 34.122, 34.122-34.133, 34.127
language changes 34.77-34.81
Law Reform Commission 34.02, 34.45, 34.83-34.84, 34.91, 34.217, 34.263-34.264
legislation 34.09, 34.22, 34.31-34.37
lesbianism 34.33, 34.80
level of damages 34.230-34.235, 34.247-34.254
libel 34.07, 34.21-34.24, 34.28, 34.65-34.67
libel/slander distinction 34.25-34.29, 34.265
malice 34.185, 34.193-34.200, 34.220
media 34.02-34.03, 34.08, 34.22-34.23, 34.182-34.189
motive, malice 34.196
newspapers 34.02-34.03, 34.07, 34.112
offer of amends 34.113-34.114, 34.116-34.121, 34.228
original privilege 34.161
partial justification 34.129
passing off 31.82

*defamation (contd)*
plaintiff 34.34-34.37, 34.102-34.105, 34.110, 34.111-34.121, 34.273-34.277
politics 34.179-34.190
preservation of reputation 34.08, 34.185
principle of proportionality 34.233-34.237
printers, reform of the law 34.267
privilege *see* **privilege**
proof of falsity of statement 34.88, 34.269
proof of malice 34.199
proof of truth of statement 34.124-34.126, 34.130-34.132
public figures 34.179-34.190
public interest, general 34.176-34.177
publication 34.12-34.29, 34.46-34.49, 34.113, 34.115
qualified privilege 34.144, 34.160-34.178, 34.183, 34.184-34.188
radio and television 34.22-34.23
Rantzen test 34.240-34.256, 34.246-34.245, 34.256
reciprocal interest or duty 34.178
reform of the law 34.263-34.277
remoteness of damage 34.43
reports 34.190-34.192
right-thinking people 34.50, 34.66-34.72 *passim*, 34.105, 34.109
rights of free speech 34.08, 34.185
rights-language 34.179
rolled-up plea 34.215-34.217
scandals 34.01-34.02
slander 34.21-34.24, 34.28-34.29, 34.30-34.49, 34.87
special damage 34.25, 34.28, 34.30, 34.42-34.45
special facts 34.112
state communications 34.158
statements 34.89, 34.191-34.192
statutory privilege 34.145
suits, where to sue and for what damages 34.46-34.49
television, libel suit 34.47-34.48
trickery 34.61
true innuendo (legal) 34.90-34.91, 34.94-34.96
unintentional defamation 34.112
vulgar abuse 34.85-34.88
witnesses 34.150-34.154
*see also* **privilege**; **qualified privilege**

**default of plaintiff**
*Rylands v Fletcher* 25.32-25.34, 25.47

**defects**
fitness of premises 11.81-11.83, 11.100, 13.12-13.47, 13.49, 13.50-13.56, 13.71-13.76
manufacturers' and producers' strict liability 11.108-11.116
property, professional negligence 14.221-14.225
*see also* **fitness of premises**; **manufacturers' and producers' liability for defective products**

**defence forces**
employers' liability 18.128-18.132

**defence of self**
occupiers' liability 12.140
trespass to the person 22.114-22.122
vicarious liability 43.41

**defences**
introduction 20.01
agony of the moment 20.18-20.22, 20.23
animals, injuries caused by 27.26, 27.48
apportionment of damages 20.43-20.45
breach of duty 20.50, 21.74
causation 20.41-20.42
Civil Liability Act 1961 20.08-20.13, 20.58, 20.63-20.64, 20.99
common employment doctrine 20.03
conduct of the defendant 20.81-20.83
conduct of the rescuer 20.84-20.92
contributory negligence 5.08, 20.02-20.60
damages 20.02, 20.09-20.10, 20.28, 20.43-20.45, 20.51-20.54
defamation 34.122-34.133, 34.224-34.225
degrees of fault 20.46-20.54
dilemma principle 20.23
drunken drivers 20.70
failure to mitigate damage 20.24-20.33, 20.36, 20.53

*defences (contd)*
fatal injuries 20.58
fault, degrees and apportionment of 20.46-20.55
foreseeability 20.92
identification, doctrine of 20.57-20.60
illegality (*ex turpi causa*) 20.01, 20.93-20.108
imputed contributory negligence 20.57-20.60
injuries 20.61-20.92 *passim*
intentional wrongdoing 20.13, 20.49
last clear chance 20.04, 20.12
manufacturers' and producers' liability 11.136-11.146
medical treatment 20.30
morality 20.93, 20.96, 20.108
*novus actus interveniens* 20.25, 20.28
nuisance 20.02, 24.93-24.112
particular risk 20.15-20.17
public conscience test 20.103-20.104
*Re Polemis* 20.92
rescuers 20.78-20.92
risk sports 20.75
*Rylands v Fletcher* 25.29-25.44
seat belt defence 20.34-20.45
self-preservation 20.19
set-off claims 20.56
simpliciter, contributory negligence 20.44
trespass to land 20.61, 23.45-23.46, 23.47-23.51
trespass to the person 22.59-22.122
ultimate negligence 20.04-20.07
volenti non-fit injuria 20.01, 20.03, 20.61-20.92, 20.64-20.65, 20.98-20.100
Wagon Mound 20.92
work accidents 20.62
*see also* **voluntary assumption of risk**

**defendant**
conduct of
and plaintiff's rights 1.70
conversion 30.12-30.18
defences 20.81-20.83
private nuisance 24.37-24.55
standard of care 7.21-7.22, 7.25, 7.38-7.43
trespass to goods 28.13
corporations as 39.06-39.08
deceit, intention of defendant 35.13-35.14
defamation 34.197-34.198, 34.277
duty of care, breach of duty 6.58-6.59
hardship, and limitations 46.59-46.61
identity, duty of knowledge 46.51
interest in freedom of action 1.02
liability of
*novus actus interveniens* 2.50
proof of negligence 9.45, 9.52
management of defendant and *res ipsa loquitur* 9.17-9.19
nuisance, acts of others combined 24.110-24.112
*Rylands v Fletcher* 25.18, 25.28
statutory duties and rights 21.02, 21.61
survival actions on death 41.06, 41.11, 46.51, 46.59-46.61
trespass to land, state of mind 23.37-23.40
trespass to the person 22.02-22.04, 22.15

**definitive approach**
duty of care 6.28

**delegation of duty**
breach of statutory duty 21.49

**deliberate act**
*novus actus interveniens* 2.33, 2.46

**Deloitte and Touche report 1.167-1.175, 1.180**

**Denham Working Group**
personal injury compensation 1.177-1.180

**dental treatment**
medical negligence 14.127

**denying title**
conversion 30.11-30.18

**dependants**
statutory duties and rights, fatal injuries 42.06-42.66

**depression**
non-pecuniary loss 44.176-44.178

**Derrynaflan Hoard**
conversion 30.25-30.38
detinue 29.16, 29.19
*Hedley Byrne* principle 10.142-10.146

**description**
passing off 31.40-31.48
**detinue**
introduction 29.01
adverse possession 29.02-29.08
bailment and finding contrasted 29.09-29.19
chattel, return of and value as assessed 29.04, 29.10, 29.11, 29.12-29.19
conversion 30.09
damages 29.12-29.19
Derrynaflan Hoard 29.16, 29.19
limitations, extinction of title 46.85-46.86
remedies 29.10
right to privacy 37.07
trespass to goods 28.02
**detour and frolic**
vicarious liability 43.45-43.48
**development risks defence**
manufacturers' and producers' strict liability 11.170, 11.171
**diagnosis**
medical negligence 14.43-14.56
**dicoverability rule**
limitations 46.09-46.10, 46.15
**dilemma principle**
defences 20.23
**diplomatic immunity**
state liability 38.15-38.17
**direct evidence**
*res ipsa loquitur* 9.43
**direct (natural) consequences**
remoteness of damage 3.03, 3.05, 3.06
**direct/indirect interference** 28.04, 28.06
**disabilities**
general rule 46.70
collateral benefits 44.131-44.142
controversial litigation 46.72-46.77
convicts 46.67
exceptions 46.71-46.74
infants 46.67, 46.75-46.77
limitations 46.67-46.81
mental disability, and standard of care 7.23-7.24
parental custody 46.75-46.77
persons of unsound mind, limitations 46.67, 46.68-46.69
physical disability, and standard of care 7.12-7.22
property rights 46.81
six-year rule 46.70
*see also* **limitations**
**disability payments**
collateral benefits 44.131-44.142
**discipline, parental**
trespass to the person 22.93-22.104
**disclosure**
medical negligence 14.82-14.135
**discoverability rule**
limitations 46.53, 46.57, 46.63
**diseases, defamation** 34.40-34.41
**dismissals**
trade disputes 32.101-32.105
**distribution and circulation**
manufacturers' and producers' liability 11.136-11.138, 11.169
**distribution of loss** 1.05, 1.121-1.137, 4.24-4.25
divorce, fatal injuries 42.11
**doctor**
reasonable behaviour 14.08
*see also* **medical negligence**
**dogs** 16.58-16.60, 27.27-27.41, 27.66
**domestic animals**
conversion 30.19
liability for 27.16, 27.23, 27.42-27.47
scope of the tort 30.19
**domestic violence**
trespass against the person 22.27
**drivers**
and children 15.03-15.15, 16.10-16.11, 16.65-16.67
driving when blinded 15.23-15.26
employers' liability 18.103
intoxicated, defences 20.70
negligence 15.03-15.15, 15.30, 15.34-15.35, 15.41-15.43
physical capacities 7.12-7.54
uninsured 1.138-1.154
*see also* **highways**; **motor vehicles**; **roads, negligence on**

**duress**
trespass to the person 22.65-22.67
**duties**
statutory *see* **statutory duties and rights**
**duty of care**
introduction 6.01-6.02
animals, injuries caused by 27.13-27.14
blanket immunities 6.86
compensation 6.67
concepts and policy 6.03-6.06, 6.07, 6.12-6.13, 6.14, 6.28
public policy 6.32, 6.80-6.81, 6.89-6.90
scope 6.03, 6.07, 6.12, 6.14
social policy 6.55, 6.67
dangerous chattels 6.53
defendant in breach of duty 6.58-6.59
definitive approach 6.28
economic loss 10.01, 10.02, 10.09, 10.09-10.15, 10.20, 10.39
employers' liability 6.45, 18.03-18.74, 18.75, 18.127
exclusionary rules 6.86
fitness of premises 13.18
for what is duty owed 6.02
foreseeability 6.28, 6.30, 6.40-6.41, 6.83
friendly societies 6.56
*Hedley Byrne* principle 10.72, 10.76, 10.80, 10.128, 10.132-10.139
immunity 6.85, 6.90
incapacitated persons 8.06-8.16
incremental approach 6.22, 6.26
injury or damage 6.36-6.51, 8.06-8.16
judicial development 6.07-6.35
Britain 1932-1999, 6.02, 6.03, 6.10-6.24, 6.28, 6.32, 6.35
Europe 6.68-6.90
Ireland 6.07, 6.25-6.35
limitations 6.84
manufacturers 6.49, 11.08-11.09, 11.76
motor vehicles 6.61-6.64
negative considerations 6.12, 6.14, 6.27
negligence 5.02-5.04, 6.01-6.02, 6.05, 6.26, 6.43-6.47, 6.60-6.63, 6.68-6.90
duty issues 10.01
grave negligence 6.85
neighbour principle *see* **neighbour principle**
objective criteria 6.60-6.67
occupier 12.13-12.14, 12.16, 12.20, 12.45, 12.64-12.65, 12.80-12.144 *passim*
injury or damage 6.38, 6.53, 6.55
particular contexts 6.36-6.51
contractual provision 6.46-6.47
employers' liability 6.45
judgments 6.45-6.48
nervous shock 6.50
privity doctrine 6.48
property damage 6.49
qualitative non-dangerous defect 6.49
third party liability 6.42-6.45
physical injury or damage 6.36, 6.37-6.49, 6.53, 6.55
police immunity 6.85
*prima facie* duty 6.27
professional negligence 14.169-14.174
property 6.49, 6.57
proportionality 6.85
proximity 6.02, 6.12-6.34 *passim*, 6.36, 6.52-6.54, 6.78, 6.85, 6.88
psychiatric damage 6.36, 6.50, 17.50-17.53, 17.62
pure economic loss 6.02, 6.36, 6.51
reasonably foreseeable harm 6.25
right to privacy 37.17
rights of access 6.86
schools 16.50, 16.54-16.55
three step 6.33, 6.87
to whom is duty owed 6.02
trespassers 6.38, 6.53, 6.55
troublesome issues 6.55-6.67
two-step 6.05, 6.15, 6.19, 6.20, 6.23, 6.30, 6.35
negligence 6.78
physical injury 6.40
producers' liability 11.76
unforeseeability 6.29
vicarious benefit 6.55
voluntary assumption of risk 6.67
*Wagon Mound* 6.29
what aspect of duty 6.36
*see also* **employers' liability**; **proximity**; **standard of care**

**duty of disclosure**
medical negligence 14.82-14.135
**duty of knowledge**
army deafness 46.42-46.48
causal responsibility 46.35-46.40
date of knowledge 46.23, 46.29
defendant's identity 46.51
defined 46.47
facts observable/ascertainable 46.25, 46.27
financial advice 46.35-46.40
identity of person other than defendant 46.52
injury attributable to conduct 46.49-46.50
knowledge test 46.47-46.48
moral responsibility 46.39
negligent advice 46.27, 46.38
person alleged to have been injured 46.30-46.40
significance of injury 46.41-46.48
surgery 46.31-46.34
unable to gain knowledge 46.28
*see also* **limitations**
**duty of protection**
right to privacy 37.44
**duty owed**
duty of care 6.49
manufacturers and producers 11.13, 11.17, 11.35-11.60
occupiers' liability 12.13-12.14, 12.17-12.19, 12.43-12.45, 12.64-12.66, 12.80-12.108, 12.123-12.135
by whom 6.02
manufacturers and producers 11.11-11.22
component parts 11.21-11.22
dangerous defects 11.16-11.73 *passim*
installers and assemblers 11.14
repairers 11.13
retailers 11.16-11.20
suppliers 11.15, 11.21-11.22, 11.107
to whom
duty of care 6.02
manufacturers and producers 11.16, 11.23-11.73
dangerous substances 11.30
intermediate examination 11.27-11.29
ultimate consumer 11.26
*see also* **manufacturers' and producers' liability for defective products**
**duty to control others**
affirmative duties 8.17-8.44
**duty to warn**
manufacturers and producers 11.02, 11.19, 11.31-11.60, 11.73, 11.111, 11.128-11.131
do-it-yourself 11.60
inflammability tests 11.55
medical negligence 14.111-14.112, 14.142-14.143, 14.159-14.160
regulatory code 11.52
standard requirements 11.45-11.46, 11.55, 11.70, 11.114
transfer by gift 11.61
vaccines 11.63-11.70
warning labels 11.51
*see also* **manufacturers' and producers' liability for defective products**
**duty/interest test**
defamation 34.164-34.166, 34.169-34.171, 34.183, 34.186

**ear-piercing**
medical negligence 14.73-14.74
**earning capacity**
proof of loss of, and damages 44.82-44.142
**ecclesiastical courts**
libel/slander distinction 34.25
**economic damage**
remoteness of damage 3.20, 3.37-3.41
**economic loss**
introduction 10.01-10.09
*Anns* formula 10.09
assumption of responsibility 10.09
contractual dimension 10.04, 10.16-10.49
duty of care 1.20, 6.36, 6.51, 10.02, 10.09-10.15, 10.18-10.49 *passim*
*Hedley Byrne* principle 10.02, 10.19-10.20, 10.50-10.157

*economic loss (contd)*
intentionally inflicted loss 10.06
Irish approach 10.10-10.15
neighbour principle 10.07
products liability 10.158-10.162
pure economic loss 10.02, 10.09-10.15, 10.158-10.162
recoverability 10.13
*see also* ***Hedley Byrne*** **principle**; **manufacturers' and producers' liability for defective products**; **negligence**
**economics, realities**
*res ipsa loquitur* 9.26
**education**
*see* **children**; **schools**
**EEC Directive on Product Liability 1985** 1.121, 11.03, 11.91-11.175, 21.61, 46.06
**EEC Motor Insurance Directive** 1.147
**egg-shell skull rule**
damages 44.174, 44.177
negligence 5.06
psychiatric damage 17.08
remoteness of damage 3.22, 3.32-3.41, 3.43
**elective treatment**
medical negligence 14.100, 14.105, 14.107-14.110
**electricity**
*Rylands v Fletcher* 25.16
**embargoes**
business relations 32.34-32.40
*see also* **strikes**
**emergency vehicles 15.53-15.57**
**emotional distress**
torts defined 1.119
**emotional suffering**
trespass to the person 22.28-22.34
**employee**
breach of statutory duty 21.25-21.33, 21.56-21.57, 21.61
employers' duty of care to 6.45, 18.03-18.74
trespass to the person 22.35-22.57
vicarious liability 43.10-43.11, 43.69
*see also* **employer**; **employer/employee relationship**; **employers' liability**; **employment**; **vicarious liability**
**employer**
contractual responsibility 10.30-10.39
damages, collateral benefits 44.123-44.126
defined, trade disputes 32.92
duty of care to employee 6.45, 18.03-18.74
occupiers' liability 12.141, 12.144, 18.69-18.70, 18.81
*see also* **employee**; **employer/employee relationship**; **employers' liability**; **employment**; **vicarious liability**
**employer/employee relationship** 43.03-43.09, 43.10-43.53
employers' liability for torts (crimes) of employee 43.03, 43.12, 43.15-43.53
collateral negligence 43.53
control 43.08-43.09, 43.18-43.23
dangerous activities 43.50-43.51
detour and frolic 43.45-43.48
employee identified 43.15, 43.16-43.23
employee liable for other employees 43.69
employee's functions 43.26-43.29
employer's duty of care 6.45, 18.03-18.74
employer's personal liability 43.12-43.14, 43.49
hired employees 43.10-43.11
independent contractor 43.15, 43.16-43.23, 43.49-43.53
non-delegable duties 43.49-43.52
*Rylands v Fletcher* 43.49
scope of employee's employment 43.24-43.44, 43.48
conduct within scope of employment 43.30-43.33
conduct without scope of employment 43.34-43.44
*see also* **employee**; **employer**; **employers' liability**; **employment**; **vicarious liability**
**employers' liability**
introduction 18.01-18.02
affirmative duties 18.127
assessment of 18.75-18.158

*employers' liability (contd)*
causation 18.119-18.124, 18.146
coincidental injuries 18.147-18.149
common employment doctrine 18.02, 18.76, 18.105, 20.03
contributory negligence 18.150-18.158
dangerous work environments 7.52.54, 18.07, 18.25-18.27, 18.109-18.127 *passim*, 18.128-18.158
defence forces 18.128-18.132
duty of care to an employee 6.45, 18.03-18.74
breach of statutory duty 18.23-18.32, 18.111, 18.146, 18.150, 21.61
employee's circumstances 18.01-18.09
guidelines 18.10-18.12
independent contractor 18.33-18.55
non-delegable 18.33-18.55
omissions 18.13-18.22
property damage 18.56, 18.65-18.70
psychiatric injury 18.56, 18.60-18.64
pure economic loss 18.56, 18.67, 18.71-18.74
scope of duty 18.75, 18.127
foreseeability 18.12, 18.18, 18.64, 18.119-18.124, 18.148
insurance 1.112, 18.101
motor vehicles 18.103
negligence and cause of injury 18.146
passive smoking 18.125
physical injuries 18.84, 18.107-18.126, 18.146-18.158
provision of competent staff 18.75, 18.76-18.80
provision of proper equipment 18.75, 18.95-18.103, 18.126, 18.152-18.157
safe place of work 18.55, 18.75, 18.81-18.94, 18.102
safe system of work 18.24, 18.75, 18.78, 18.104-18.158
security firm employees 18.133-18.145
unsafe system of work 18.107-18.110
voluntary assumption of risk 18.02, 18.23, 18.159-18.165
weight and lifting 18.111-18.124
*see also* **employee**; **employer**; **employment**; **vicarious liability**
**employment**
earnings, and damages 44.82-44.142
scope of, vicarious liability 43.24-43.44, 43.30-43.33, 43.34-43.44, 43.48
standard of care 7.51-7.54
trade disputes and non-employment 32.101-32.107
**engineers, fitness of premises** 13.81-13.82
**England**
animals, injuries caused by 27.23
breach of statutory duty 21.06-21.07, 21.23
business relations 32.05, 32.09, 32.55, 32.82
conspiracy, tort of 32.61, 32.79
conversion 30.24
damages 44.10-44.12, 44.101-44.106, 44.184, 44.194, 44.195
defamation 34.07, 34.41, 34.67, 34.96, 34.111, 34.113, 34.176, 34.182-34.189
defences 20.51, 20.105
duty of care 6.57, 6.65
economic loss 10.48-10.49
employers' liability 18.46, 18.66
family relations 33.05, 33.07, 33.28-33.34
fatal injuries 42.03, 42.13, 42.33, 42.45, 42.63
*Hedley Byrne* principle 10.52-10.57
immunity 38.03, 39.25
injunctions 45.09, 45.10-45.36
intentional interference with economic interests 32.83-32.86
limitations 46.15, 46.45, 46.50
manufacturers' and producers' liability 11.02, 11.05, 11.20, 11.107
medical negligence 14.18, 14.20, 14.26, 14.79, 14.84, 14.144
mentally ill persons 40.43
minors 40.10, 40.26
nuisance 24.62, 24.110
passing off 31.65-31.72, 31.79-31.81
professional negligence 14.164
proof of negligence 9.02, 9.05

*England (contd)*
psychiatric damage 17.02, 17.26-17.30
remoteness of damage 3.37, 3.41
*res ipsa loquitur* 9.24
right to privacy 37.06, 37.13, 37.35, 37.45-37.49
*Rylands v Fletcher* 25.26, 25.51-25.54
schools 16.27, 16.67
trade disputes 32.121, 32.161
trespass to land 23.18, 23.26, 23.31
trespass to the person 22.17, 22.32, 22.96-22.100
vicarious liability 43.43

**entrants**
animals, injuries caused by 27.10
contractual entrants 12.07, 12.79, 12.131-12.135
criminal entrants 12.66, 12.110-12.114
occupiers' liability 12.06-12.14, 12.06-12.15, 12.53, 12.123-12.135

**entry**
trespass to land 23.02-23.21

**epilepsy**
standard of care 7.17, 7.22

**equipment**
employers' liability 18.75, 18.95-18.103, 18.126, 18.152-18.157

**equitable principles**
breach of confidence 37.21-37.22

**equivalent to contract**
*Hedley Byrne* principle 10.66, 10.72

**escape**
*Rylands v Fletcher* 25.19-25.24, 25.34, 25.35, 25.38, 25.42, 27.08

**escapees**
schools 16.67

**estoppel**
concurrent wrongdoers 4.25
*Hedley Byrne* principle 10.142-10.146
medical negligence 14.143

**Europe**
European Community
defamation 34.04, 34.07, 34.211
duty of care 6.68-6.90
state liability 38.22
torts 1.84-1.103
European Convention for the Protection of Human Rights and Fundamental Freedom, injunctions 45.30
European Convention on Human Rights
defamation 34.04, 34.07
immunity 14.167, 39.25
right to privacy 37.71
European Court of Human Rights
defamation 34.211
discipline of children 22.96-22.101, 22.104
duty of care 6.68

**evidence**
*res ipsa loquitur* 9.43

**evil motive**
misuse of process 36.15-36.16

***ex gratia* payments**
motor accident compensation 1.149-1.150
whooping cough vaccination 1.187

**exclusionary rules**
duty of care 6.86
*Rookes v Barnard* 44.43

**exemplary damages 44.09-44.57**
aggravated damages 44.31
historical origins 44.09
limited 44.10
punitive damages 44.26-44.29
survival actions on death 40.05
three considerations 44.34, 44.42
*see also* ***Rookes v Barnard***

**explosives**
*Rylands v Fletcher* 25.16

**extent of liability**
animals, injuries caused by 27.47
public nuisance 24.19-24.23

**extinction of liability**
new European regime 11.147-11.157

**extinction of title**
in conversion and detinue 46.85-46.86

**facial injuries**
damages 44.179-44.182

**facts ascertainable/observable**
duty of knowledge 46.25, 46.27

**factual causal responsibility**
duty of knowledge 46.38-46.39
**factual causation 2.07, 2.07-2.16, 2.61**
**factual representation**
deceit 35.03-35.09
**failure to conform**
negligence 5.02, 5.04
**failure to control child**
parental negligence 16.09-16.14
**failure to disclose material risks**
medical negligence 14.103-14.104
**failure to inform patient**
medical negligence 14.155
**failure to keep a proper look out on roads 15.17-15.22**
**failure to mitigate damage**
defences 20.24-20.33, 20.36, 20.53
psychiatric damage 17.47
**failure to obtain informed consent**
medical negligence 14.119-14.124
**failure to perform an act (non-feasance)** 8.04, 8.05
**failure to release**
trespass against the person 22.47-22.57
**failure to warn**
affirmative duties 8.05
**fair comment**
defamation 34.200, 34.201-34.223
honesty 34.218-34.221
public interest 34.202-34.204, 34.220
rolled-up plea 34.216, 34.218-34.222
**false imprisonment**
trespass to the person 22.35-22.57
**false statements**
deceit 35.26-35.30
defamation 34.59-34.60, 34.198, 34.269-34.277
false innuendo (popular) 34.90, 34.91, 34.93
presumption of falsity 34.269-34.277
proof of falsity of statement 34.88, 34.269
**families**
damages in lieu of an injunction 45.51-45.52
fatal injuries 42.07-42.11, 42.18
guardianship of children and statutory rights 21.62-21.74
vicarious liability 43.57, 43.67-43.68
*see also* **children**; **families**; **family relations**; **minors**; **parental negligence**; **parents**
**family relations**
*see also* **children**; **families**; **minors**; **parental negligence**; **parents**
**family relations**
torts affecting
introduction 33.01-33.03
child's rights 33.33-33.34
child's services, action for the loss of 33.36-33.39
consortium 33.04-33.16
contributory negligence of child 33.38
enticing and harbouring of a child 33.27-33.35
father's rights 33.33
loss of services 33.24, 33.27
married couples, loss of consortium 33.04-33.16
parent may sue 33.36
parent's vicarious responsibility 33.38
reform of the law 33.35
seduction 33.24-33.26
service relationship 33.24, 33.36-33.39
*see also* **children**; **consortium**; **families**; **minors**; **parental negligence**; **parents**
**fatal injury**
introduction 42.01-42.05
actions 42.13
annual average loss 42.25-42.27
benefits payable 42.39-42.42
calculation of damages 42.19, 42.44, 42.45-42.66 *passim*
children 42.30, 42.31, 42.46-42.47, 42.49-42.50, 42.54, 42.56
claims, collateral benefits 44.121
cohabitees (cohabitants) 42.10
contributory negligence 42.15-42.16
defences 20.58
dependants, statutory rights 42.06-42.66

*fatal injury (contd)*
divorce 42.11
factual support for claims 42.30-42.38
family relations 33.10-33.11, 33.15, 33.20
family-type relationships 42.07-42.11, 42.18
funeral expenses 42.20
gender roles 42.43-42.66
grandparents 42.59, 42.63, 42.66
husband 42.27-42.29, 42.38-42.45
inflation 42.32, 42.37
inheritances 42.39-42.40
injuries compensatable 42.19-42.66
liability 42.12-42.18
mental distress (*solatium*) 42.19, 42.21-42.24
parents 42.22
pecuniary benefits, loss of 42.19, 42.24-42.42
personal representative of deceased 42.02
reasonable expectation 42.50, 42.55
remarriage 42.43-42.66
suits, who is entitled to sue 42.01, 42.07-42.11
taxation 42.32-42.36
voluntary benefits 42.54, 42.58
widows/widowers 42.43-42.45, 42.53
wives 42.46-42.48, 42.59-42.62, 42.65-42.66
women, working 42.48, 42.64-42.66
*see also* **accidents**; **injury**; **personal injury**; **physical injury**; **psychiatric damage**

**fathers**
rights and family relations 33.33

**fault**
concept of, and negligence 1.122
degrees of, and breach of statutory duties 21.61-21.69
degrees of, and defences 20.46-20.54
fault-based liability compensation 1.126, 1.160, 11.02

**felony and misdemeanor**
trespass to the person 22.106

**fencing, animals**
liability for injuries caused 27.54

**financial advice**
duty of knowledge 46.35-46.40

**finders**
conversion 30.23-30.38

**fire, liability for**
introduction 26.01-26.02
historical background 26.02
accident 26.06-26.10
acts of a stranger 26.12
agony of the moment 26.33
breach of statutory duty 26.32
burden of proof under the act 26.20
causation of damage 26.16-26.18
civil liability 26.28, 26.32
common law 26.03, 26.29
contributory negligence 26.33
negligence 26.11-26.14, 26.23-26.24, 26.33
*novus actus interveniens* 26.34-26.35
occupiers' liability 26.03-26.22
person other than occupier 26.23-26.37
personal injuries and damage 26.19
remedies not defeated 26.21-26.22
rescuers 26.30, 26.34-26.37
safety 26.26
Stardust tragedy 26.26
voluntary assumption of risk 26.35

**firms**
*see* **businesses**

**first party insurance**
motor vehicles 1.142-1.143

**fitness for human habitation of premises** 13.25-13.30, 13.30, 13.35, 13.42-13.43

**fitness of premises**
introduction 13.01-13.02
builder/vendor and builder/lessor 13.57-13.82, 19.22-19.34
builder's liability 13.48-13.56
building standards 13.77
*caveat emptor* 13.03, 13.04, 13.44, 13.67
*caveat lessee* 13.03, 13.44
common duty of care 13.18

*fitness of premises (contd)*
common law immunity 13.22-13.24, 13.52, 13.57, 13.63, 13.67
continuing obligation 13.37-13.40, 13.43
contracts 12.49-12.51, 13.03-13.11, 13.44-13.45
damages 13.55
defects discovered before injury or damage 13.71-13.76
duty of care 13.18
fitness for human habitation 13.25-13.30, 13.30, 13.35, 13.42-13.43
foreseeability 13.44, 13.55, 13.63, 13.81
four corners rule 13.06
implied warranty 13.27-13.29, 13.44
lessee 13.12
lessor and vendor 13.01, 13.03-13.47, 13.57-13.82
owners and builders, defective products 11.81-11.83, 11.100
private vending or letting 13.44
schools, structural dangers 16.70-16.84
self-regulatory measures 13.77-13.79
statutory duties 13.22-13.47, 13.68
tenant 13.28-13.29, 13.32-13.40, 13.43-13.46
vendor and lessor 13.01, 13.03-13.47, 13.57-13.82
visitors 13.18
warranties 13.11, 13.27-13.29, 13.44-13.46
**flammable fabric**
manufacturers' and producers' liability 11.17, 11.35-11.60
**football**
schools' negligence 16.25, 16.80-16.84
**forcible entry**
trespass to land 23.03
**foreign sovereigns**
state liability 38.18-38.21
**foreseeability**
causation 2.30, 2.40
defamation 34.44
defences 20.92
duty of care 6.28, 6.30, 6.40-6.41, 6.83
employers' liability 18.12, 18.18, 18.64, 18.119-18.124, 18.148
fatal injury 42.57-42.58
fitness of premises 13.44, 13.55, 13.63, 13.81
injury 17.08, 17.22-17.23, 17.44, 17.58
*novus actus interveniens* 2.30, 2.34, 2.40
of harm, childcare 16.03-16.05, 16.16
remoteness of damage 3.03-3.05, 3.29-3.31
trespass to the person 22.07
*see also* **reasonable foreseeability**
**former possession**
*res ipsa loquitur* 9.18-9.19
**four corners rule**
fitness of premises 13.06
**fourth party**
business relations 32.32-32.33
**fraud**
affirmative duties 8.05
deceit 35.09, 35.19, 35.24-35.25
definitions 46.83
*Hedley Byrne* principle 10.58-10.61, 10.111
limitations 46.82-46.84
minors 40.32
proof of, deceit 35.10
trespass to the person 22.65-22.67
vicarious liability 43.42
*see also* **deceit**
**fraudulent misrepresentation**
deceit 35.09, 35.19, 35.24-35.25
**fraudulent non-disclosure**
affirmative duties 8.05
**fraudulent representation**
*Hedley Byrne* principle 10.58-10.61, 10.111
minors 40.32
free competition
passing off 31.82
**free speech**
corporations 39.05
defamation 34.08, 34.179, 34.185
**freedom of expression**
interlocutory injunctions 45.20, 45.28

**frequent trespassers** 12.26
**friendly societies**
duty of care 6.56
**frolic**
and detour, vicarious liability 43.45-43.48
**function of the law**
*Torts* 1.01-1.03
**funeral expenses**
fatal injury 42.20

**Garda Síochána**
trespass to land 23.07
trespass to the person 22.105-22.113
*see also* **police immunity**
**gas**
*Rylands v Fletcher* 25.16
**gender roles**
fatal injury 42.43-42.66
**general and approved practice**
medical negligence 14.09, 14.15
**general damages**
non-pecuniary loss 44.148-44.149, 44.153-44.158
**general negligence**
occupiers' liability 12.53-12.54
**general practitioners**
medical negligence 14.31-14.40
**given mark or get up**
passing off 31.59
**goods**
description of goods 31.29
passing off 31.01-31.82
seizure of goods 28.14-28.16
*see also* **trespass to goods**
**goodwill**
passing off 31.28, 31.41, 31.60
**grandparents**
fatal injury 42.59, 42.63, 42.66
**grave negligence**
duty of care 6.85
**gravity of injury**
standard of care 7.25, 7.35-7.37
**Green Book method**
compensation 1.191
**Greenfield option**
personal litigation 1.174
**guardianship, of children**
statutory duties and rights 21.62-21.74, 22.76, 22.83-22.85
**guest's statutory right**
occupiers' liability 12.57
**gymnastic exercise**
schools' negligence 16.19-16.20

***Hanrahan* restatement**
causation 2.58-2.60
damages 44.53
*novus actus interveniens* 2.60
*res ipsa loquitur* 9.49-9.53
tort law and constitutional rights 1.17-1.21, 1.33-1.47, 1.69
**harassment**
trespass against the person 22.32
**health**
public 19.39
***Hedley Byrne* principle**
areas of competence 10.147-10.148
assumption of responsibility 10.09, 10.116-10.141
breakthrough 10.52-10.57
Britain 10.77, 10.141, 11.86-11.87
*caveat emptor* 10.123
contractual setting 10.19-10.20, 10.114-10.115, 10.149-10.154
creditworthiness 10.52-10.62
deceit 10.58-10.62, 10.111, 35.01
Derrynaflan Hoard 10.142-10.146
duty of care 10.72, 10.76, 10.80, 10.128, 10.132-10.139
economic loss 10.02, 10.19-10.20, 10.50-10.157
English approach 10.52-10.57
equivalent to contract 10.66, 10.72
expertise in business 10.147
fraudulent representation 10.58-10.61, 10.111
implied statements 10.109-10.110
innocent misrepresentation 10.156
Ireland 10.64-10.71

*Hedley Byrne principle (contd)*
judicial development of principle 10.72-10.88
negligent misrepresentation 10.80-10.115 *passim*
negligent misstatement 10.50, 10.52-10.88 *passim*, 10.124, 10.137, 10.146
negligent statement, contractual 10.149-10.154
neighbour principle 10.51, 10.73, 10.75, 10.83
non-dangerous defects, and manufacturers' liability 11.78, 11.86-11.87
old approach 10.50-10.51
playground supervision 16.52
promissory estoppel 10.142-10.146
scope of representation 10.89-10.115
shareholders 10.67-10.71
special relationship 10.152
standards of behaviour 10.149
statements in a contractual setting 10.149-10.154
statutory misrepresentation 10.155-10.157
third party 10.58, 10.62, 10.71, 10.132
two-step 10.77
vicarious liability 43.56, 43.60
wills 10.73-10.76
*see also* **economic loss; manufacturers' and producers' liability for defective products**
**Hepatitis C Tribunal** 1.182-1.183, 1.186
**High Court actions** 1.165, 1.169
**highways**
animals, liability for injuries caused 27.27.49-27.27.60
authorities 19.43-19.49, 24.113-24.121
behaviour on 15.16-15.57
nuisance 19.43-19.49, 24.14-24.18, 24.85-24.92
occupiers' liability 12.39-12.41
private nuisance, premises adjoining 24.85-24.92
public nuisance 3.30, 12.39-12.41, 24.13, 34.14-34.19
trespass to land 23.17-23.21
*see also* **roads**

**Hillsborough**
psychiatric damage 17.30
**hired employees**
vicarious liability 43.10-43.11
**homosexuality**
defamation 34.77-34.81
right to privacy 37.69-37.71
**honest difference of opinion**
medical negligence 14.09, 14.13, 14.21-14.22
**honesty**
defamation 34.197-34.198, 34.218-34.221
**horn**
sounding (motor vehicles) 15.49-15.52
**horses**
liability for injuries caused by 27.61-27.65
racing 1.111
**hospital expenses and carer cost**
damages 44.107-44.112
**hotel licences**
professional negligence 14.206-14.212
**housing**
breach of statutory duty 21.11-21.18
**husbands**
consortium 33.04, 33.06
fatal injury 42.27-42.29, 42.38-42.45

**identification**
doctrine of, and defences 20.57-20.60
**illegal acts or means**
business relations 32.49-32.55
**illegality**
defences (*ex turpi causa*) 20.01, 20.93-20.108
trespass to the person 22.65-22.67
**immovables (land)**
manufacturers' and producers' strict liability 11.100
**immunity from liability**
animals 27.50-27.55
barristers and professional negligence 14.161-14.168
defamation 34.146, 34.146-34.152
duty of care 6.85, 6.90

*immunity from liability (contd)*
fitness of premises 13.22-13.24, 13.52, 13.57, 13.63, 13.67
misuse of process 36.04
public authorities 19.05
right to privacy 37.54-37.58
solicitors and professional negligence 14.199
state liability 38.01, 38.07, 38.09, 38.14, 38.21
trade disputes 32.114-32.125, 32.122-32.126, 32.143-32.144
unincorporated associations 39.25
**impecunious plaintiff**
remoteness of damage 3.32-3.41
**implied statements**
*Hedley Byrne* principle 10.109-10.110
**implied terms approach**
employers' liability 18.58
**implied warranty**
fitness of premises 13.27-13.29, 13.44
**imported products**
manufacturers' and producers' liability 11.106
**imposed liability**
occupiers' liability 12.141-12.142
**imprisonment**
continuance of imprisonment 22.39-22.44
criminal offence punishable by death or imprisonment 34.38-34.39
false imprisonment 22.35-22.57
physical and psychological imprisonment 22.40
*see also* **trespass against the person**
**imputed contributory negligence**
defences 20.57-20.60
manufacturers' and producers' liability 11.158
**imputed lack of competence**
defamation 34.55
**incapacitated persons**
affirmative duties 8.06-8.16
**incidence of liability**
injuries caused by animals 27.45
**inclusio unius est exclusio alterius rule**
trespass to the person 22.82
**inconsistencies**
*res ipsa loquitur* 9.42
**incremental approach**
duty of care 6.22, 6.26
**independent contractor**
contract builders 13.49-13.56
employers' liability 18.33-18.55
occupiers' liability 12.136-12.138
*Rylands v Fletcher* 25.36
vicarious liability 43.15, 43.16-43.23, 43.49-43.53
**independent privilege**
and defamation 34.162
*see also* **privilege**
**indirect procurement**
business relations 32.32-32.40
**industrial design**
passing off 31.01
**industrial values**
*Rylands v Fletcher* 25.03
**ineffectual defences**
nuisance 24.103-24.112
**infants**
*see* **children**; **minors**
**inference of negligence**
proof of negligence 9.03-9.10
**inflation**
damages 44.97
fatal injury 42.32, 42.37
**information**
unauthorised use of 37.23, 37.38-37.58
and right to privacy 37.23, 37.24-37.31, 37.38-37.58
breach of confidence, liability for 37.45-37.49
confidentiality, duty of 37.43
doctor's obligation 37.42-37.44
duty of care in negligence 37.42-37.44
misprision of felony 37.53
privilege and public interest immunity 37.54-37.58
protection, duty of 37.44
remedies 37.38-37.39

*information (contd)*
right to privacy 37.23, 37.24-37.31, 37.38-37.58
sexual assualt 37.55-37.56
*see also* **right to privacy**
**informed consent**
and medical negligence 14.76-14.136
**infringement**
constitutional rights 1.36, 1.39, 1.61-1.65, 1.66-1.71
*Meskell* principle 1.14, 1.31, 1.39, 1.48-1.59, 1.61, 1.65, 1.66, 1.69, 1.81-1.82, 21.66
rights and statutory duties 21.71
**inherently dangerous things**
manufacturers' and producers' liability 11.07, 11.08
**inheritances**
fatal injury 42.39-42.40
***iniuriae* (wrong)**
concurrent wrongdoers 4.06
**injunctions**
introduction 45.01
balance of convenience 45.37-45.44
common law 45.34
damages in lieu of an injunction 45.47-45.52
damages not appropriate 45.01
defamation proceedings 45.12-45.36
definitions 45.08
families and damages 45.51-45.52
financial consequences 45.37
interim injunctions 45.07-45.46
interlocutory injunctions 45.07-45.46
irreparable damage 45.45-45.46
local authority 45.41
mandatory injunctions 45.02-45.06, 45.07
nuisance 45.42-45.44
ordering of an injunction 45.05-45.06
perpetual injunctions 45.07-45.46
picketing 45.37
prohibitory injunctions 45.02-45.06, 45.07
public convenience 45.39-45.40, 45.44
*quia timet* injunctions 45.02-45.06, 45.07
serious question test 45.09, 45.10-45.36
travellers 45.41
**injurious falsehood**
deceit 35.26, 35.28
right to privacy 37.15
*see also* **deceit**
**injury**
cause of 9.45-9.48, 9.52
compensation for malicious injuries 1.107, 1.134
defences 20.61-20.92 *passim*
duty of care 6.02, 6.36-6.51, 8.06-8.16
economic 3.20, 3.37-3.41
employers' liability 18.01-18.64 *passim*, 18.84, 18.107-18.126, 18.146-18.158
fire liability 26.19
foreseeable injury 17.08, 17.22-17.23, 17.44, 17.58
gravity of, standard of care 7.25, 7.35-7.37
limitations 46.07, 46.49-46.50
negligence and cause, *res ipsa loquitur* 2.10, 9.45-9.48, 9.52
off school's premises 16.18, 16.65-16.67
physical, trespass to the person, battery 22.11-22.19
premises, defects discovered before injury or damage 13.71-13.76
protection from 8.06-8.16
psychiatric 17.12-17.63
psycho-physical 17.02, 17.15-17.34 *passim*
remoteness of damage 3.17, 3.20-3.23, 3.20-3.24, 3.27-3.28, 3.32-3.36
*Rylands v Fletcher* 25.22-25.24
to land, private nuisance 24.26-24.32
to property 46.07
trespass to the person 22.11-22.19
vicarious liability 43.30-43.33
*see also* **accidents**; **animals, liability for injuries caused by**; **fatal injury**; **psychiatric damage**
**innocent dissemination**
defamation 34.19, 34.267
**innocent misrepresentation**
*Hedley Byrne* principle 10.156

**innominate torts**, 1.83
**innuendo**
defamation 34.70, 34.89-34.96, 34.90, 34.93, 34.101, 34.131
false innuendo (popular), defamation 34.90, 34.91, 34.93
true innuendo (legal), defamation 34.90-34.91, 34.94-34.96
**installers and assemblers**
defective products 11.14
**instruction**
negligence in 16.18, 16.19-16.25, 16.69
**instrumentality**
*res ipsa loquitur* 9.32
**insurance** 1.138-1.152
claims, reform proposals 1.166-1.192
damages 44.112-44.113, 44.120
drivers, torts 1.138-1.154
employers' liability 1.112, 18.101
motor accident compensation 1.138-1.154
no-fault compensation schemes 1.131-1.132
operation of insurance 1.144-1.153
other compensation 1.126-1.137
private insurance 1.127
right to privacy 37.91
state 1.107, 1.128-1.136, 1.144
torts 1.126-1.154, 1.166-1.192 *passim*
uninsured driver 1.153-1.154
vicarious liability 43.61
Voluntary Health Insurance Act 1957 19.75-19.77
**intellectual property**
passing off 31.01
**intention**
business relations and contracts 32.26-32.27
minors 40.03, 40.36
passing off 31.05-31.07, 31.50-31.53
right to privacy and mental suffering 37.10
trespass to the person 22.05-22.09
**intentional damage**
remoteness of damage 3.04, 3.25
**intentional wrong-doing 8.23-8.25, 18.67**
defences 20.13, 20.49
**intentionally inflicted loss** 10.06
**interest**
defamation and privilege 34.174-34.178
in goods and right to privacy 37.07
**interference**
business relations 32.83-32.86
trespass to goods 28.04-28.06, 28.13
trespass to land 23.30-23.32, 23.41-23.46
**interim injunctions** 45.07-45.46
**interlocutory injunctions** 45.07-45.46
passing off 31.21, 31.61-31.82
**intermediate examination**
defective products 11.27-11.29
**international conventions**
state liability 38.15
**internet**
impact of
medical negligence 14.27
**interpersonal approach to tort law 1.123**
**interpersonal conflicts 1.01**
**interpersonal infringement**
constitutional rights 1.79
**interpretations**
defamation 34.71
*res ipsa loquitur* 9.44
statutory, breach of statutory duty 21.10
**intervening act**
causation 2.24-2.60
**intimidation**
business relations 32.46-32.57
constitutional rights 32.50
contractual obligations 32.51, 32.53-32.54
illegal act or means 32.49-32.55
justification 32.57
nature of intimidation 32.46-32.47
strikes 32.51
submission to threat 32.56
threat 32.48
unlawful act 32.49-32.53
**intoxicated persons**
*res ipsa loquitur* 8.07-8.16, 9.29-9.32
**intrusion**
right to privacy 37.14

**invitees**
occupiers' liability 12.08-12.12, 12.50, 12.53, 18.81
**Ireland**
psychiatric damage 17.35-17.63
public authorities 19.56-19.81
*Rylands v Fletcher* 25.45-25.55
torts 1.155-1.165
**irreparable damage**
injunctions 45.45-45.46
passing off 31.62, 31.73
**is and ought, standard of care 7.06**

**joint and several tortfeasors**
contribution rules 4.01-4.02, 4.05, 4.07, 4.09, 4.23-4.26
*see also* **concurrent wrongdoers**
**joint concurrent tortfeasors** 4.05
**joint tortfeasors**
concurrent wrongdoers 4.01-4.02
**judges**
and jury, defamation 34.97-34.101
and jury, proof of negligence 9.03, 9.09-9.10
trial judges and damages 44.61-44.62, 44.98
**judgments**
concurrent wrongdoers 4.14-4.16
duty of care 6.45-6.48
**judicial development**
duty of care 6.07-6.35
**judicial proceedings**
defamation 34.146-34.157
**junctions**
road negligence on 15.38-15.48, 15.55
***Junior Books*** 11.75, 11.81-11.90
**juries**
medical negligence 14.09, 14.14-14.15
standard of care 7.06
trial by jury 1.116, 1.163-1.165
**jus tertii**
conversion 30.21-30.22
private nuisance 24.112
trespass to land 23.45-23.46
**justification**
and malice, business relations 32.41-32.44
defamation 34.122, 34.122-34.133
interlocutory injunctions 45.26, 45.28-45.29, 45.32-45.36

**knowledge**
and intention required, business relations 32.23
date of, limitations 46.03, 46.29
of falsity, deceit 35.10-35.12

**labour market**
state of and damages 44.88-44.92
**laissez-faire**
employers' liability 18.01, 18.165
occupiers' liability 12.04, 12.22, 12.24
**land**
conversion 30.29-30.38
non-natural use 19.52, 27.08
occupiers' liability 12.04
private nuisance
commercial exploitation 24.54
enjoyment of land 24.33-24.36
physical injury 24.26-24.32
proprietary interest in land 24.59-24.60
right to land 24.62-24.71
trespass to land
above and below surface 23.39-23.40
placing things on land 23.29-23.36
remaining on land 23.22-23.28
*see also* **trespass to land**
**landlord**
private nuisance 24.74-24.77
**language changes**
defamation 34.77-34.81
**last clear chance**
defences 20.04, 20.12
**Law Reform Commission**
care of children 16.15
damages 44.57, 44.114, 44.127
defamation 34.02, 34.45, 34.83-34.84, 34.91
reports and proposals 34.263-34.264
statements of fact and comment 34.217

*Law Reform Commission (contd)*
family relations 33.17-33.23, 33.25, 33.39
injuries caused by animals 27.66
minors 40.33
personal injury limitations 46.45
'Report on Non-Fatal Offences Against the Person' 22.94
tort reform 1.126
**lawful authority**
trespass to goods 28.14-28.18
trespass to the person 22.105-22.113
**legal causation**
remoteness of damage 2.17-2.22, 2.23
**legal personality**
unincorporated associations 39.11
**lesbianism**
defamation 34.33, 34.80
**lessee**
fitness of premises 13.12
**lessor**
fitness of premises 13.01, 13.03-13.47, 13.57-13.82, 19.22-19.34
as occupier 13.18-13.19
*see also* **builder/vendor and builder/lessor**; **fitness of premises**
**libel**
alleged 34.07
as a tort 34.28
as crime 34.24, 34.28
defamation 34.21-34.24
effect of the libel 34.246
injunctions 45.14-45.16
opinion 34.65-34.67
proof of special damage 34.28
*see also* **defamation**; **libel/slander distinction**; **slander**
**libel/slander distinction**
abolition of distinction 34.25-34.29, 34.265
common law courts 34.25, 34.28
ecclesiastical courts 34.25
historical origins 34.25-34.29
Star Chamber 34.26-34.28
*see also* **defamation**; **slander**
**licensees**
occupiers' liability 12.13-12.14, 12.50-12.52
**licensing requirements**
breach of statutory duty 21.33
**life-expectation**
loss of and damages 44.195-44.204
**limitation period**
concurrent wrongdoers 4.25
contract and tort actions 1.99, 1.116
infringement of constitutional rights 1.76
manufacturers' and producers' liability 11.147-11.157
*see also* **limitations**
**limitations**
introduction 46.01-46.02
general rule 46.03
actionable *per se* 46.04
actions for contributions under the Civil Liability Act 1961 46.88
admiralty actions 46.89
breach of statutory duty 21.21-21.45
constitutional rights 1.22-1.32, 1.76
date of knowledge 46.03, 46.29
date on which cause of action accrues 46.04-46.20, 46.05
deceased person's estate 46.90-46.93
defendant's hardship 46.59-46.61
discoverability rule 46.09-46.10, 46.15, 46.53, 46.57, 46.63
duty of care 6.84
duty of knowledge 46.23-46.52
EEC Products Liability Directive 46.06
extension of period 46.54, 46.84
extinction of title in conversion and detinue 46.85-46.86
fraud 46.82-46.84
fresh cause of action *de diem in diem* 46.05
injury to person 46.07-46.20
injury to property 46.07
knowledge test 46.47-46.48
legislation 46.02
long stop 46.63-46.65
minors 46.54
personal injuries 46.21-46.22, 46.30-46.40

*limitations (contd)*
persons under a disability 46.67-46.81
plaintiff not responsible 46.58
proceedings struck out 46.59-46.61
proof of damage 46.06
right to privacy 37.05, 37.12-37.13
sleeping torts 46.62
special periods 46.21, 46.87-46.93
Statute of Limitations 1957 11(2)(b) 46.02, 46.11-46.12, 46.12-46.20
Statute of Limitations 1957 s 49(2) 46.72-46.74
stopping the clock 46.06
survival actions on death 41.09, 41.11
three year post-accrual period 46.22, 46.40, 46.43
time limit for commencement of actions 46.16-46.18, 46.20
two year period 46.90-46.93
undue delay as basis for dismissal of proceedings 46.53-46.66
vicarious liability 43.24-43.25
*see also* **disabilities**; **duty of knowledge**; **limitation period**
**limited immunity**
from liability for trade unions, trade disputes 32.126-32.185
**liquor licences**
professional negligence 14.206-14.216
**litigation**
in one action, concurrent wrongdoers 4.03
solicitors and professional negligence 14.180-14.199
**little bangs**
remoteness of damage 3.43
**livestock**
liability for injuries 27.28-27.31, 27.36-27.37
**loans**
public authorities 19.22-19.34
**local authorities**
injunctions 45.41
**logos**
passing off 31.16, 31.65-31.71
**long stop**
manufacturers' and producers' liability 11.149
**Lord Tenterden's Act**
deceit 35.24-35.25
**loss**
distribution of 1.05, 1.121-1.137, 4.24-4.25
of services, family relations 33.24, 33.27
or injury, breach of statutory duty 21.25
personal loss, survival actions on death 41.05

***McDonnell v Ireland*, and *Meskell* principle** 1.48-1.59
**malice** 34.185, 34.193-34.200, 34.220
definitions 34.193, 36.22
abuse of the civil process 36.19-36.29
defined 36.22
principles 36.26-36.29
proof of damage 36.19
business relations 32.41-32.44
compensation 1.107, 1.134
deceit 35.28
defamation and proof of malice 34.199
malicious prosecution 36.02-36.18
damage 36.17-36.18, 36.19-36.22
ingredients of the tort 36.03
motives 36.14-36.16
onus of proof/disproof 36.06, 36.11
proceedings 36.04-36.05
reasonable and probable cause, lack of 36.06-36.16
test for 36.07
public authorities 19.54, 19.62-19.67, 19.71, 19.80-19.81
trespass to the person 22.29
*see also* **misuse of process**
**mandatory injunctions** 45.02-45.06, 45.07
**mandatory regulations**
manufacturers' and producers' liability 11.136, 11.141
**manufacturers' and producers' liability for defective products**
introduction 11.01-11.07

*manufacturers' and producers' liability for defective products (contd)*
historical background 11.04-11.07
abolition of the privity requirement 11.08-11.10
Britain 11.08, 11.75, 11.86-11.87
causation 11.62-11.70, 11.127-11.135
common law 11.02, 11.53, 11.56, 11.97
contracts, contract law 11.05-11.07, 11.161-11.163
duty owed 6.49, 11.13, 11.17, 11.35-11.60
by whom 11.11-11.22, 11.107
to whom 11.16, 11.23-11.73
duty to warn 11.02, 11.19, 11.31-11.60, 11.73, 11.111, 11.128-11.131
England 11.02, 11.05, 11.20, 11.107
fault-based liability 11.02
inherently dangerous things 11.07, 11.08
*Junior Books* 11.75, 11.81-11.90
Liability for Defective Products Act 1991, 11.02, 11.56, 11.91-11.175
neighbour formula 11.09
non-commercial producer, builders 11.81-11.83
non-dangerous defects 6.49, 11.74-11.90, 11.109
owner/builder/vendor 11.81-11.83, 11.100, 19.22-19.34
privity requirement 11.06-11.07, 11.08-11.10
pure economic loss 10.158-10.161
reasonable foreseeability 11.81
*res ipsa loquitur* 11.71-11.73, 11.129
scientific authority 11.68-11.69, 11.136, 11.142-11.143
strict liability new European regime 11.02, 11.91-11.175
*see also* **duty to warn**; **economic loss**; **strict liability**; **strict liability, new European regime**
**market research surveys**
passing off 31.19-31.27
**marriage**
right to privacy 37.62, 37.67-37.68, 37.75-37.76
**married couples**
loss of consortium 33.04-33.16
**material disclosure test**
medical negligence 14.134-14.135
**material element and substantial factor**
causation 2.15
**mechanics**
professional negligence 14.02
**media** 34.02-34.03, 34.22-34.23
broadcast reports of court proceedings 34.141-34.145
press freedom 34.08
privilege 34.179-34.190
**medical evidence**
professional negligence 14.186, 14.188, 14.190, 14.193-14.194
**medical negligence**
statement of principles 14.09-14.16, 14.231
abnormalities at birth 14.44-14.47
adequacy of treatment 14.61-14.66
affirmative duties 8.25
battery 14.77-14.81, 14.88, 14.92
being wise after the event 14.17-14.18
*Bolam* test 14.82
*Bolitho* test 14.84
bronchial and lung surgery 14.119-14.121
causation 2.20-2.21, 2.61-2.63, 14.55
causation, and non-disclosure 14.137-14.149
communication between medical staff 14.61-14.67
customary practice 14.130
damages awarded 14.40, 14.91
dental treatment 14.127
diagnosis 14.43-14.56
*Dunne* test 14.09, 14.12, 14.16, 14.23, 14.35, 14.51, 14.67
and disclosure 14.95-14.104, 14.124, 14.128
Dupuytren's contracture 14.107-14.114
duty of disclosure 14.15-14.51, 14.82-14.135
ear-piercing 14.73-14.74
elective treatment 14.100, 14.105, 14.107-14.110

*medical negligence (contd)*
error of judgment 14.10-14.20
estoppel 14.143
explanations to patients 14.100, 14.105-14.114
failure to disclose material risks 14.103-14.104, 14.127
failure to inform 14.155
failure to obtain informed consent 14.119-14.124
general and approved practice 14.09, 14.15
general practitioners 14.31-14.40
hand-surgery 14.107-14.114
honest difference of opinion 14.09, 14.13, 14.21-14.22
house-calls 14.32-14.40
inconclusive diagnosis 14.48-14.49
informed choice 14.102, 14.109-14.114
informed consent 14.76-14.136, 14.147, 14.150-14.151
internet, impact of 14.27
issue of consent 14.117-14.124
jury decisions 14.09, 14.14-14.15
keeping up-to-date 14.24-14.27
known complications 14.134
material disclosure test 14.134-14.135, 14.139
medical practitioner of equal specialisation and skill 14.09, 14.12
medical research 14.150-14.151
mothers and pregnancy 14.33-14.40, 14.153-14.158
negligence 14.77-14.81
non-disclosure 14.137-14.149, 14.153-14.160
*novus actus interveniens* 2.57
O'Flaherty/Hederman view 14.122-14.123, 14.126-14.127
other medical personnel 14.42
patient would not have undergone treatment 14.138
patient's frankness and diagnosis 14.52-14.55
patient's frankness, and diagnosis 14.52-14.55
patient's right of self-determination 14.82
post-operative treatment 14.108
professional disclosure standard 14.151
professional standard test 14.129-14.130
prudent patient (objective) test 14.139, 14.144-14.147
reasonable behaviour of medical practitioner 14.08, 14.09
reasonable patient 14.134, 14.148
reflex sympathetic dystrophy syndrome 14.107-14.110
remoteness of damage 3.22-3.23
*res ipsa loquitur* 9.28
risk, disclosure of 14.111-14.114, 14.130-14.133, 14.130-14.134, 14.137, 14.148-14.149
*Scarman* test 14.139
schools of thought 14.21-14.23, 14.24
*Sidaway* case 14.84, 14.105, 14.114, 14.116, 14.118
specialists 14.30
standard of care required 14.09-14.16
subjective plaintiff-centred test 14.144
surgery, elective 14.100, 14.105, 14.107-14.110
technical assault and battery 14.89, 14.92, 14.94
tests for establishing negligence 14.09, 14.82, 14.95-14.104
therapeutic privilege 14.136
treatment 14.28-14.29, 14.56-14.72, 14.152-14.160
trespass to the person 14.88
unqualified persons 14.73-14.75
urology 14.68-14.72
vasectomy 14.86-14.92
*Walsh* 14.85, 14.115, 14.118, 14.122-14.125, 14.128, 14.134, 14.139-14.142
warning 14.111-14.112, 14.142-14.143, 14.159-14.160
*see also* **professional negligence**

**medical negligence treatment**
innovative 14.28-14.29

**medical practitioner**
of equal specialisation and skill and medical negligence 14.09, 14.12
**medical research**
medical negligence 14.150-14.151
**medical treatment**
damages 44.108
defences 20.30
family relations, loss of consortium 33.07, 33.08
right to privacy 37.40-37.58, 37.84-37.85, 37.89-37.90
trespass to the person 22.68-22.73
***mens rea* of defendant**
passing off 31.51
**mental disability**
*see* **mental distress**; **mentally ill persons**; **psychiatric damage**
**mental distress**
family relations 33.10-33.11, 33.13, 33.15, 33.20
(*solatium*), fatal injury 42.19, 42.21-42.24
*see also* **mentally ill persons**; **psychiatric damage**
**mental injury**
*see* **psychiatric damage**
**mentally ill persons** 40.38-40.49
reform proposals 40.45-40.49
standard of care 7.23-7.25
torts involving a specific mental ingredient 40.40
torts of strict liability 40.38
trespass to the person, goods or land 40.41-40.44
voluntary acts 40.42
*see also* mental distress; psychiatric damage
**merchandise**
passing off 31.01-31.82
***Meskell* principle**
infringement of constitutional rights 1.14, 1.31, 1.39, 1.48-1.59, 1.61, 1.65, 1.66, 1.69, 1.81-1.82, 21.66
trade disputes 32.130-32.140
**MIBI (Motor Insurers Bureau of Ireland) 1.146-1.152**
**military service**
business relations 32.07-32.08
**minors** 40.01-40.37
adult activities 40.29-40.30, 40.37
age and mental development of child 40.06-40.14
contributory negligence 40.05-40.26
minimum age 40.07-40.14
standards applied 40.15-40.26
fraudulent representation 40.32
general liability in tort 40.01-40.04
intention 40.03, 40.36
limitations, extension of period 46.54
minimum age 40.07-40.14
objective approach 40.09, 40.17-40.18, 40.23, 40.26
subjective approach 40.14, 40.15-40.18, 40.20-40.26, 40.37
negligence 40.05, 40.27-40.28
nine-year olds 40.12-40.13
reform proposals 40.33-40.37
tort and contract 40.31-40.32
trespass 40.02, 40.35
trespass to the person 22.74-22.85
*see also* **children**; **families**; **family relations**
**mischievous propensity**
injuries caused by animals 27.15-27.17
**misdemeanor and felony**
trespass to the person 22.106
**misfeasance**
liability imposed 1.116
of public office 19.53-19.81
trespass to land 23.24
**misprision of felony**
right to privacy 37.53
**misrepresentation**
*see* **fraudulent misrepresentation**; **innocent misrepresentation**; **negligent misrepresentation**; **statutory misrepresentation**

**misuse of process**
introduction 36.01
champerty, tort of 36.30
evil motive 36.15-36.16
immunity 36.04
maintenance, tort of 36.30
malicious abuse of the civil process 36.19-36.29
malicious prosecution 36.02-36.18
*see also* **malice**
**moderate damages**
non-pecuniary loss 44.192-44.194
**morality**
damages and obligations 44.94
defences 20.93, 20.96, 20.108
duty of knowledge and responsibility 46.39
**mothers**
and pregnancy, medical negligence 14.33-14.40, 14.153-14.158
**motive**
defamation 34.196
misuse of process 36.14-36.16
trespass to the person 22.05-22.09
**Motor Insurers Bureau of Ireland (MIBI)** 1.146-1.152
**motor vehicles**
accidents
and compensation 1.138-1.154
and psychiatric damage 17.35-17.63
personal injury, compensation 1.147-1.150
standard of care 7.15-7.19
state interest 1.144-1.154
affirmative duties 8.19-8.22
behaviour on the highway 3.30, 15.16-15.57
children 15.03-15.15, 16.09-16.11, 16.65-16.67
drivers 15.03-15.57 *passim*, 16.09-16.11, 16.65-16.66, 18.103, 20.69-20.70
duty of care 6.61-6.64
emergency vehicles 15.53-15.57
employers' liability 18.69, 18.103
insurance 1.144-1.154
manufacturers' liability 11.24-11.25
nuisance 19.43-19.49, 24.117
occupiers' liability 12.38, 18.69-18.70
owner/employer's liability 18.69-18.70, 43.13-43.14, 43.61-43.66
property damage 1.101-1.103
school buses 15.08-15.15
seat belts 15.56, 20.34-20.45
*see also* **drivers**; **highways**; **roads, negligence on**
**movables**
manufacturers' and producers' liability 11.100
**multiple causes**
causation 2.19
*novus actus interveniens* 2.51

**name**
passing off 31.49-31.56, 31.60
registration of business names 31.42
trade marks/names 31.01, 31.10-31.18, 31.30-31.35, 31.41
**National Crime Forum** 1.136
**natural law philosophy**
constitutional rights, 1.77
**natural phenomena**
*Rylands v Fletcher* 25.38-25.42
**necessity**
trespass to land 23.50-23.51
trespass to the person 22.92
**negative causal connection**
*novus actus interveniens* 2.34, 2.41, 2.43
**negative considerations**
duty of care 6.12, 6.14, 6.27
**negligence**
introduction 5.01
elements of the tort 5.02-5.09
actual loss or damage 5.02, 5.05
animals, injuries caused by 27.03-27.04
breach of statutory duty 21.47-21.51
causal causation/connection 5.02, 5.05, 5.07
cause of injury 9.45-9.48, 9.52
contributory negligence 5.08
conversion 30.13

*negligence (contd)*
defective products 11.21-11.26, 11.31-11.33, 11.158-11.160
defences
contributory negligence 5.08
failure to mitigate damage 20.24-20.33
drivers 15.03-15.15, 15.23-15.26, 15.30, 15.34-15.35, 15.41-15.43
duty of care 5.02-5.04, 6.01-6.02, 6.05, 6.26, 6.43-6.47, 6.60-6.63, 6.68-6.90
duty of knowledge 46.27, 46.38, 46.49-46.50
economic contractual dimension 10.16-10.48
economic loss *see* economic loss
egg-shell skull rule 5.06
employers' liability, cause of injury 18.82, 18.146
failure to conform 5.02, 5.04
fault concept 1.122
fire 26.11-26.14, 26.23-26.24, 26.33
fitness of premises 13.22-13.47, 13.82
foreseeability and remoteness of damage 3.29
*Hedley Byrne* principle 10.50-10.157
inference of 9.03-9.10
instruction in schools 16.18, 16.19-16.25, 16.69
medical negligence 14.77-14.81
minors 40.05, 40.27-40.28
nervous shock 5.03
*novus actus interveniens* 2.59
occupiers' liability 12.53-12.54
one-sided secret determination 5.09
proof of 9.01-9.53
psychiatric damage 5.03, 17.01-17.63
public authorities 13.22-13.47, 13.82, 19.05-19.49
pure economic loss 10.02, 10.09-10.15
remoteness of damage 3.05-3.19, 3.29, 5.06
*res ipsa loquitur* 9.15, 9.45-9.48, 9.52
right to privacy 37.16-37.19, 37.42-37.44
schools, structural dangers 16.70-16.84
standard of care 5.04, 7.31-7.37
strict liability 1.121-1.137
trespass to the person 22.01-22.04
voluntary assumption of risk 5.09
see *also* **affirmative duties; children; contributory negligence; duty of care; economic loss; manufacturers' and producers' liability for defective products; medical negligence; motor vehicles; negligence; negligent conduct; proof of negligence; psychiatric damage; *res ipsa loquitur*; roads, negligence on; standard of care; voluntary assumption of risk**

**negligent conduct**
cost of risk elimination 7.25, 7.44-7.54
gravity of injury 7.25, 7.35-7.37
probability of an accident 7.24, 7.27-7.34
social utility of defendant's conduct 7.25, 7.38-7.43
*see also* **standard of care**

**negligent misrepresentation**
deceit 30.01
fitness of premises 13.05
*Hedley Byrne* principle 10.58, 10.80-10.115 *passim*

**negligent misstatement**
deceit 35.26
*Hedley Byrne* principle 10.50, 10.52-10.88 *passim*, 10.124, 10.137, 10.146

**negligent non-disclosure**
affirmative duties 8.05

**negligent statement**
*Hedley Byrne* principle 10.149-10.154

**neighbour principle**
affirmative duties 8.09
duty of care 6.02, 6.05-6.21 *passim*, 6.34, 8.12
economic loss 10.07
*Hedley Byrne* 10.51, 10.73, 10.75, 10.83
manufacturers' liability 11.09
professional negligence 14.169
psychiatric damage 6.36, 6.50, 17.63

**nervous shock**
*see* **psychiatric damage**

**New South Wales**
schools 16.54
**New Zealand**
damages 44.13
injuries and insurance 1.132
minors 40.26
privilege and defamation 34.181
professional negligence 14.164
right to privacy 37.02
**newspapers**
and defamation 34.141-34.145
*see also* **media**; **publication**
**no foal, no fee**
compensation 1.172
**no-fault compensation schemes**
insurance 1.131-1.132
**nominal damages** 44.03
**non-commercial producer**
manufacturers' and producers' liability 11.81-11.83, 11.136, 11.140
**non-dangerous defects** 6.49, 11.74-11.90, 11.109
contractually prescribed criterion 11.80
defective goods (as opposed to defective advice) 11.78
defendants 11.76
*Hedley Byrne* principle 11.78, 11.86-11.87
*Junior Books* 11.81-11.90
liability insurance 1.116
qualitative defects, duty of care 6.49
two-step approach 11.76
vendor 11.78, 11.79
*see also* **manufacturers' and producers' liability for defective products**
**non-deduction principle for non-fatal cases**
damages 44.118
**non-delegable duties**
employers' liability 43.49-43.52
occupiers' liability 12.144
public nuisance 24.19
*Rylands v Fletcher* 25.49-25.51
vicarious liability 43.49-43.52
**non-disclosure**
medical negligence 14.137-14.149, 14.153-14.160
**non-fatal offences**
trespass against the person 22.32, 22.74, 22.80, 22.94, 22.104
**non-natural use**
of land, and animals 27.08
property, and road use 19.52
*Rylands v Fletcher* 25.05-25.06, 25.07-25.17
**non-occupier/occupier**
*Rylands v Fletcher* 25.26-25.27, 25.36, 25.48-25.49
**non-pecuniary loss** 44.143-44.204
damages 44.143-44.204
deceased person 44.196-44.197
depression 44.176-44.178
differing responses 44.184-44.189
egg-shell skull 44.174, 44.177
equality of compensation 44.163
facial injuries 44.179-44.182
general damages 44.148-44.149, 44.153-44.158
inadequate compensation 44.202
life-expectation, loss of 44.195-44.204
moderate damages 44.192-44.194
pain and suffering 44.144-44.194
policy factors 44.150-44.152
psychiatric conditions 44.176-44.178
psychological effect test 44.181
pure nervous shock 44.176-44.178
reductions possible 44.159-44.163, 44.164, 44.174-44.175, 44.192-44.194
shortening of life 44.198-44.202
subjective approach 44.164, 44.172-44.173, 44.190-44.191
tariff raised to £250, 000 44.165-44.171
tariff (rough) of £150.000 44.146-44.164
unaware plaintiff 44.183-44.194
victim's response 44.174-44.175
**nonfeasance**
affirmative duties 8.04, 8.05
liability imposed 1.116

**North America**
breach of statutory duty 21.05-21.06
road injuries and insurance 1.131
*see also* **United States**
***novus actus interveniens***
summary 2.50-2.53
affirmative duties 8.07
alternative danger cases 2.47
breach of statutory duty 21.25
causation 2.24-2.60, 2.60
common man 2.51
contributory negligence 2.26, 2.46, 2.52, 2.56
defences 20.25, 20.28
defendant is liable 2.50
deliberate act 2.33, 2.46
fire, liability for 26.34-26.35
foreseeability 2.28-2.36, 2.40
intervenor/intervening act 2, 27, 2.28-2.36, 2.50
medical negligence 2.57
multiple cause liability 2.51
negative causal connection 2.34, 2.41, 2.43
negligence 2.59
policy grounds liability 2.51
private nuisance 2.58, 2.59
proof 2.54-2.60
recklessness 2.28-2.36, 2.37-2.49
*res ipsa loquitur* rule 2.59
roads, negligence on 15.46
supervening event 2.48
third party 2.27, 2.43, 2.50
voluntary act 2.43, 2.47
**nuisance**
introduction 24.01-24.02
acts of others combined with defendants 24.110-24.112
causation 2.57-2.60
coming to the nuisance 24.104-24.109
concurrent wrongdoers 4.13
contributory negligence 24.105
defences 24.93-24.112
duty of knowledge 46.49-46.50
fitness of premises 13.20-13.21
*Hanrahan* resolution 1.18
highway authorities 24.113-24.121
highways 19.43-19.49, 24.14-24.18
ineffectual defences 24.103-24.112
inevitable accident 24.102
injunctions 45.42-45.44
*jus tertii* 24.112
legislative authority 24.93-24.96
*novus actus interveniens* 2.58, 2.59
prescription 24.97-24.102
private nuisance 24.14-24.121
public authorities 19.50, 24.113-24.121
public nuisance 24.03-24.23
remoteness of damage 3.30
*see also* **private nuisance**; **public nuisance**
**nuisance, public**
*see* **public nuisance**
**nursing/nurses**
professional negligence 14.02, 14.42

**objective criteria**
duty of care 6.60-6.67
**obligation of confidence**
reasonable man test 37.33
remedies 37.34, 37.35, 37.37
right to privacy 37.32-37.37
surreptitious acquisition of information 37.35-37.37
third parties 37.34
*see also* **right to privacy**
**occupancy duties**
injuries caused by animals 27.10
**occupier**
duty of care 12.13-12.14, 12.16, 12.20, 12.45, 12.64-12.65, 12.80-12.144 *passim*
animals 27.10
injury or damage 6.38, 6.53, 6.55
fitness of premises 13.18-13.19
non-occupier *Rylands v Fletcher* 25.26-25.27, 25.36, 25.48-25.49
person other than occupier, liability for fire 26.23-26.37
private nuisance 24.69-24.71, 24.78-24.84, 24.92
rights and conversion 30.25-30.38
*see also* **occupiers' liability**

**occupiers' liability**
introduction 12.01-12.02
definition 12.74-12.76
affirmative duties 8.31
agricultural community 12.61-12.62
animals 27.09-27.14, 27.33-27.47
carriers and bailees 12.142
categories of entrants 12.06-12.14
children 12.27-12.33, 12.93, 16.70, 16.73
common law 12.03-12.15, 12.08-12.12, 12.22-12.23, 12.42, 12.50, 12.53
conduct 12.106
contractual entrants 12.07, 12.79, 12.131-12.135
criminal entrants 12.66, 12.110-12.114
dangers 12.12, 12.14, 12.50-12.53, 12.72-12.73, 12.109, 12.130
defence, of self, others, property 12.140
duty owed, by occupiers 12.13-12.14, 12.17-12.19, 12.43-12.45, 12.64-12.66, 12.80-12.108, 12.123-12.135
employers 12.141, 12.144, 18.69-18.70, 18.81
entrants 12.06-12.14, 12.53, 12.123-12.135
financial dimension 12.08
fire 26.03-26.22
frequent trespassers 12.26
general negligence 12.53-12.54
guest's statutory right 12.57
highways 12.39-12.41
Hotel Proprietors Act 1963 12.56-12.58
imposed liability 12.141-12.142
independent contractors' negligence 12.136-12.138
laissez-faire theory 12.04, 12.22, 12.24
land occupier 12.04
licensees 12.13-12.14, 12.50-12.52
motor vehicles 12.38, 18.69-18.70
new approach to trespassers 1974-1995 12.42-12.55
non-delegable duties 12.144
nuisance, near a highway 12.39-12.41
occupier as lessor 13.18-13.19
occupier defined 12.74-12.76
occupier/non-occupier, *Rylands v Fletcher* 25.26-25.27, 25.36, 25.48-25.49
Occupiers' Liability Act 1995 12.01, 12.16, 12.59-12.144, 12.101
premises, structure on 12.115-12.122
preservation of higher duties 12.139-12.144
recklessness 12.33, 12.34-12.38, 12.109
recreational activities 12.83-12.85
recreational users 12.63-12.65, 12.69, 12.79, 12.86-12.95, 12.95-12.122 *passim*
schools 16.70-16.84
scope of liability 12.67-12.73
standard of care 7.30, 12.49
strangers to contracts 12.131-12.135
structures 12.115-12.122
trespassers 12.01, 12.06, 12.16-12.58, 12.60, 12.63, 12.96, 12.97-12.108, 12.126, 16.83-16.84
visitors 12.63, 12.78-12.82, 12.94, 12.123-12.130, 16.73-16.84
*see also* **occupier**

**offer of amends**
defamation 34.113-34.114, 34.116-34.121, 34.228

**official day**
schools 16.60

**omission**
by negligence
employers' liability 18.13-18.22

**once and for all award**
damages 44.55-44.57

**one-sided secret determination**
negligence 5.09

**onus of proof**
malicious prosecution 36.06, 36.11
manufacturers' and producers' liability 11.02, 11.73, 11.128-11.131
*res ipsa loquitur* 9.33, 9.41, 9.45
trade disputes 32.176-32.185
trespass to goods 28.12
*see also* **proof; proof of loss of earning capacity; proof of negligence**

**operational duties**
public authorities 19.08-19.10
**opinion and factual representation**
deceit 35.08
**opt-ins and opt-outs**
manufacturers' and producers' liability 11.170-11.175
**original privilege and defamation** 34.161
*see also* **privilege**
**owners**
of animals 27.28-27.30, 27.34
and builders
and vendor 19.22-19.34
defective products 11.100
fitness of premises 11.81-11.83, 11.100
non-commercial producers 11.81-11.83
conversion 30.02-30.22, 30.25-30.38
private nuisance 24.62-24.71, 24.92
vicarious liability, mechanically propelled vehicles 43.61-43.66

**packaged products**
passing off 31.30-31.35
**paedophiles**
*Hanrahan* rationale 1.33
**pain and suffering**
damages 44.144-44.194
**parental negligence**
age of child 16.12, 16.37-16.39, 16.62
dangerous propensities of child 16.06-16.08
dangerous things 16.03-16.05
failure to control child 16.09-16.14
Law Reform Commission's seventeenth report 16.15
which parent is liable 16.13-16.14
*see also* **children**; **families**; **family relations**; **minors**; **parents**
**parents**
custody 46.75-46.77
discipline 22.93-22.104
family relations 33.19, 33.22, 33.36, 33.38
fatal injury 42.22
guardianship 21.62-21.74, 22.76, 22.83-22.85
negligence 16.02-16.15
of injured victim and damages 44.109-44.111
and schools 16.64
*see also* **children**; **families**; **family relations**; **minors**; **parental negligence**
**parliamentary privilege and defamation** 34.137-34.140
*see also* **privilege**
**particular or special damage**
public nuisance 24.05-24.11
**particular risk**
defences 20.15-20.17
**partnerships** 39.09, 43.57-43.60
*see also* **businesses**; **corporations**; **trade unions**; **unincorporated associations**
**passing off**
introduction 31.01-31.04
actual name, use of 31.49-31.56
balance of convenience 31.62
business names 31.42
character merchandising 31.79-31.81
confusion 31.19, 31.75
damages 31.73-31.74
deceit 31.02
defamation 31.82
essence of the tort 31.02
given mark or get up 31.59
intellectual property 31.01
intention to deceive not essential 31.05-31.07, 31.53
interlocutory injunction proceedings 31.21, 31.54, 31.61-31.82, 31.76-31.82
international context 31.16-31.18
irreparable damage 31.62, 31.73
logos 31.16, 31.65-31.71
*mens rea* of defendant 31.51
misappropriation of business reputation 31.76
name, use of 31.49-31.56, 31.60
*prima facie* case 31.40, 31.44
scope of the tort 31.05-31.60
actual name, use of 31.49-31.56

*passing off (contd)*
businesses not trading in the state 31.57-31.60
clothes 31.11-31.13, 31.36-31.39
description of goods 31.29
descriptive expressions 31.40-31.48
packaged products 31.30-31.35
risk of confusion 31.08-31.18
survey evidence 31.19-31.27
shared goodwill 31.28, 31.41, 31.60
trade marks 31.01, 31.35
trade names 31.10-31.18, 31.30-31.35, 31.41, 31.42
**passive smoking**
employers' liability 18.125
**patients**
diagnosis 14.52-14.55
explanations to patients 14.100, 14.105-14.114
psychiatric damage 8.25
right of self-determination 14.82
**Pearson Commission Report 1.121**
**pedestrians**
negligence on roads 15.17, 15.27-15.36
**penalties and remedies**
breach of statutory duty 21.19
**pensions**
damages 44.127
***per incuriam* decision**
damages 44.12
***per quod servirum amisit***
business relations 32.3-32.11
**period of limitation**
concurrent wrongdoers 4.25
**period of loss**
fatal injury 42.31
**perpetual injunctions 45.07-45.46**
**personal injury**
compensation 1.135-1.137, 1.147-1.149, 1.147-1.150, 1.155-1.180, 1.156-1.192
damages 44.61-44.62, 44.98, 44.104-44.105, 44.121
fire liability 26.19
limitations 46.07-46.22, 46.30-46.40
*Rylands v Fletcher* 25.22-25.24
trespass to the person 22.11-22.19
*see also* **accidents**; **injury**; **physical injury**
**personal liability**
of employer 43.12-43.14, 43.49
**personal property**
conversion 30.19
**personal relationship**
business relations 32.42
**persons of unsound mind**
limitations 46.67, 46.68-46.69
**phone-tapping**
damages 44.26-44.31
**physical capacities**
standard of care 7.12-7.54
**physical injury**
employers' liability 18.01-18.64 *passim*, 18.84, 18.107-18.126, 18.146-18.158
to land, private nuisance 24.26-24.32
trespass to the person, battery 22.11-22.19
*see also* **accidents**; **fatal injury**; **injury**; **personal injury**; **psychiatric damage**
**physically disabled**
accidents and standard of care, accidents 7.12-7.20
**picketing**
abusive or threatening language 32.155
business relations 32.38
definitely misleading statement 32.152-32.153
employer 32.162-32.165
immunity from injunction 32.174-32.175
Industrial Relations Act 1990 32.145-32.147
injunctions 32.173-32.185, 45.37
legality of pickets 32.146
peaceful persuasion 32.158-32.161
peacefully obtaining or communicating information 32.149-32.157
place, approaches to 32.165
primary picketing 32.162-32.167
race or nationality of employers 32.157
recommendation to trade elsewhere 32.154
secondary picketing 32.162, 32.168-32.170
secret ballot 32.172, 32.176-32.185

*picketing (contd)*
trade union officials, role of 32.171
trespass to land 23.19-23.21, 32.166
*see also* **trade disputes**
**placing things on land**
trespass to land 23.29-23.36
**plaintiff**
concurrent wrongdoers 4.03
consent/default of plaintiff, *Rylands v Fletcher* 25.30-25.34, 25.47
conversion 30.20-30.38
corporations as 39.02-39.05
damages 44.183-44.194
deceit 35.15-35.19
defamation 34.34-34.37, 34.102-34.105, 34.110, 34.111-34.121, 34.273-34.277
interest in security 1.01
limitations 46.58
remoteness of damage 3.32-3.41
rights of, and defendant's conduct 1.70
statutory duties and rights 21.02, 21.25-21.33, 21.35-21.45, 21.46-21.51, 21.61
trespass to goods 28.10
trespass to the person 22.02-22.04
**planning legislation**
public authorities 19.35-19.42, 19.43-19.49
**playground supervision**
schools' negligence 16.18, 16.26-16.45, 16.45-16.50, 16.52
**pleas**
expertise and pleading, *res ipsa loquitur*, 9.04, 9.39
**police immunity**
duty of care 6.85
*see also* **Garda Síochána**
**policy grounds liability**
*novus actus interveniens* 2.51
**politics and political information**
defamation 34.179-34.190
**positive misfeasance**
trespass to land 23.24
**possession**
adverse possession 29.02-29.08
and ownership, animals 27.45-27.46
conversion 30.02-30.03, 30.04-30.18, 30.19, 30.19-30.22
former possession 9.18-9.19
trespass to goods 28.10
trespass to land 23.41-23.46
**post-traumatic stress disorder** 17.03, 17.41, 17.47, 18.60-18.61
damages 44.176-44.178
**potential victims**
affirmative duties 8.06-8.16
**powers**
*see* **statutory duties and rights**
**premises**
adjoining highway, private nuisance 24.85-24.92
defective, public authorities 13.22-13.46
professional negligence 14.201-14.204, 14.216-14.225, 14.226-14.230
structure on, occupiers' liability 12.115-12.122
*see also* **fitness of premises**
**prescription**
nuisance 24.97-24.102
**presidential privilege**
defamation 34.136
**press freedom**
defamation 34.08
**presumption of negligence**
*res ipsa loquitur* 9.13
***prima facie* case**
duty of care 6.27
passing off 31.40, 31.44
**primary agricultural products**
manufacturers' and producers' liability 11.174-11.175
**primary schools** 16.61-16.63
**printers and innocent distributors**
defamation 34.267
**prisoners**
affirmative duties 8.31-8.44
constitutional rights 1.15
**privacy**
constitutional aspects
abortion 37.81
communications 37.72-37.74

*privacy (contd)*
computer and manually held data 37.98
data protection 37.98
homosexuality 37.69-37.71
insurance companies 37.91
interests, constitutional infringements 1.65
interpretations 37.76-37.98
intimate conduct (sexual and otherwise) 37.62, 37.67-37.68
limitations 37.77
marriage 37.62, 37.67-37.68, 37.75-37.76
medical treatment 37.84-37.85, 37.89-37.90
protection of, trespass to goods 28.09
suicide 37.83
tax obligations 37.64
telephone tapping 37.92-37.97
termination of life 37.62, 37.82-37.85
*see also* **right to privacy**
**private individuals**
constitutional rights of 1.14-1.16, 1.77
**private interest**
business relations 32.44
**private nuisance**
introduction 24.24-24.25
animals, liability for injuries caused 27.05-27.06
causation 2.57-2.60
commercial exploitation of land 24.54
creator of the nuisance 24.72-24.73
damage 24.25-24.32
harm, gravity of 24.56-24.57
highway, premises adjoining 24.85-24.92
intention of causing annoyance 24.48
landlord 24.74-24.77
occupier 24.69-24.71, 24.78-24.84, 24.92
physical injury to land 24.26-24.32
premises 24.76-24.77, 24.85-24.92
prescription 24.97-24.102
proprietary interest in land 24.59-24.60
reasonable user 24.54
repairs 24.77
residential areas 24.42-24.46, 24.56
right to land 24.62-24.71
right to privacy 37.11-37.14
social and economic contexts 24.37
as a state of affairs 24.58
substantial interference in enjoyment of land 24.33-24.36
travellers 24.80-24.84
trees 24.26-24.32, 24.87-24.88
urban areas 24.37-24.48
utility of defendant's conduct 24.37-24.55
water on property 24.51-24.53
who may be sued 24.72-24.73
who may sue 24.59-24.72
*see also* **nuisance**; **public nuisance**
**private vending or letting**
fitness of premises 13.44
**privilege**
broadcast reports of court proceedings 34.141-34.145
defamation 34.134-34.178
duty/interest test 34.164-34.166, 34.169-34.171
interest 34.174-34.178
media 34.179-34.190
original privilege 34.161
parliamentary privilege 34.137-34.140
presidential privilege 34.136
right to privacy and public interest immunity 37.54-37.58
*see also* **defamation**; **qualified privilege**
**privity doctrine**
duty of care 6.48
**privity requirement**
manufacturers' and producers' liability 11.06-11.07
**procedural effect**
*res ipsa loquitur* 9.41-9.48
**producer**
defined 11.102-11.107
strict liability 11.96-11.98
*see also* **manufacturers' and producers liability for defective products**

**product, meaning of**
manufacturers' and producers' strict liability 11.99-11.101, 11.99-11.102-116, 11.136-11.146
**products liability**
pure economic loss 10.158-10.161
**professional negligence**
introduction 14.01-14.07
definitions of 'profession' 14.01-14.04
main principles 14.04-14.07
accidents 14.182-14.193
advice 14.176-14.180
barristers 14.161-14.168
building societies 14.219-14.223
change of use of premises 14.217
Circuit Court judgments 14.182-14.188
claims for loss of earnings 14.184-14.187, 14.191-14.192
Committee on Court Practice and Procedure 14.167-14.168
conflict of interest 14.226-14.231
counsel, liaising with 14.195-14.198
counsel, selection of 14.197-14.198
court, choice of 14.181-14.194
cross-examination of witnesses 14.196
defects of property 14.221-14.225
duty of care 14.164, 14.167, 14.169-14.174
hotels 14.206-14.212
immunity of barrister/solicitor 14.161-14.168, 14.199
liquor licences 14.206-14.216
litigiation, solicitor's negligence 14.180-14.199
mechanics 14.02
medical evidence 14.186, 14.188, 14.190, 14.193-14.194
neighbour principle 14.169
non-litigious work 14.167-14.168
nursing/nurses 14.02, 14.42
premises/property 14.201-14.204, 14.216-14.225, 14.226-14.230
present legal position 14.167
property, buying and selling 14.200-14.231
proximity 14.174
public houses 14.206-14.212
requisitions 14.201-14.205
rights of way 14.226-14.230
solicitor, as advocate 14.199
solicitors 14.169-14.231
solicitor's negligence and medical negligence 14.231
standard of care 14.174-14.231
surveys 14.220-14.225
tortious right of action 14.169-14.174
*see also* **medical negligence**
**professional standard test**
medical negligence 14.129-14.130
**prohibitory injunctions** 45.02-45.06, 45.07
**proof**
and causation, manufacturers' and producers' liability 11.127-11.135, 20.41-20.42
*novus actus interveniens* 2.54-2.60
of causation, defences 20.41-20.42
of damage, limitations 46.06
of falsity of statement, defamation 34.88, 34.269
of fraud 35.10
of intent to deceive 31.05-31.07, 31.50-31.53
*see also* **onus of proof**; **proof of loss of earning capacity**; **proof of negligence**
**proof of loss of earning capacity** 44.82-44.142
acturial evidence 44.95-44.100
carers of injured victim 44.109-44.111
claims for lost years of earnings 44.87
collateral benefits 44.112-44.143
consortium (services), loss of 44.109
employment options restricted 44.93
hospital expenses and carer cost 44.107-44.112
inflation 44.97
labour market, state of 44.88-44.92
medical treatment 44.108
moral obligations to pay over earnings 44.94
other possibilities 44.92
parents of injured victim 44.109-44.111

*proof of loss of earning capacity (contd)*
physical condition of plaintiff 44.83-44.87
road accident injuries 44.108
spouse of injured victim 44.109-44.111
taxation 44.101-44.106
trial judges 44.98
*see also* **damages**; **onus of proof**; **proof**; **proof of negligence**

**proof of negligence**
introduction 9.01-9.10
causation 2.10, 2.54-2.60, 9.49, 11.127-11.135, 20.41-20.42
fire 26.20
*Hanrahan* restatement 9.49-9.53
inference of negligence 9.03-9.10
*res ipsa loquitur* 9.03, 9.11-9.53
*see also* **damages**; **negligence**; **onus of proof**; **proof**; **proof of loss of earning capacity**; ***res ipsa loquitur***

**property**
conversion 30.02-30.22
damage 44.205-44.209
collateral benefits 44.112-44.143, 44.209
defence of and trespass to the person 22.114-22.122
duty of care 6.49, 6.57
employers' liability 18.56, 18.65-18.70
injury to, limitations 46.07
motor insurance 1.147
occupiers' liability 12.140
owners, duty of care 6.57
professional negligence 14.200-14.231, 14.201-14.204, 14.216-14.225, 14.226-14.230
*restitutio in integrum* principle 44.206-44.208
restored, concurrent wrongdoers 4.22
right to privacy 37.22
rights, limitations 46.81, 46.92
roads and non-natural use of property 19.52
source of danger on, *Rylands v Fletcher* 25.18
special cases of damage 44.206-44.207
*see also* **buildings**; **premises**

**proportionality**
duty of care 6.85

**protection from injury**
duty of care 8.06-8.16

**proximity**
children, care of 16.16
duty of care 6.02, 6.12-6.34 *passim*, 6.36, 6.78, 6.85, 6.88
levels of generality 6.52-6.54
economic loss 10.09, 10.75, 10.83
professional negligence 14.174
proximity/policy approach, public authorities 19.08, 19.16, 19.21-19.49
psychiatric damage 17.27-17.30, 17.32, 17.58-17.61

**prudent patient test**
medical negligence 14.139, 14.144-14.147

**psychiatric damage**
introduction 17.01-17.34
admissible claims 17.28
aftermath of accident 17.54, 17.60
Australia 17.34
compensation 17.04-17.08
cultural context 17.07
damages 44.176-44.178
duty of care 6.36, 6.50, 17.50-17.53, 17.62
egg-shell skull rule 17.08
employers' liability 18.56, 18.60-18.64
England 17.02, 17.26-17.30
family relations 33.10-33.11, 33.13, 33.15, 33.20
foreseeability 17.08, 17.23, 17.27, 17.31, 17.41, 17.44, 17.58
Hillsborough 17.30
Irish law, developments in 17.35-17.63
limitations 46.67, 46.68-46.69
mental injury, defined 17.02-17.03
negligence 5.03
neighbour principle 6.36, 6.50, 17.63
nervous shock 6.02, 17.06, 17.12, 17.21, 17.35-17.63
patients and affirmative duties 8.25
physical injury 17.15-17.35 *passim*
post-traumatic stress disorder 17.03, 17.41, 17.47, 18.60-18.61

*psychiatric damage (contd)*
proximity 17.27-17.30, 17.32, 17.58-17.61
psycho-physical injury 17.02, 17.15-17.34 *passim*
pure nervous shock 44.176-44.178
relationship of injured persons 17.28, 17.59
remoteness of damage 3.20, 3.32
secondary victims 17.08
standard of care 7.23-7.25
unforeseeable psychiatric damage 17.08
*see also* **accidents**; **fatal injury**; **injury**; **personal injury**; **physical injury**
**psychiatric illness**
*see* **psychiatric damage**
**psychological effect test**
damages 44.181
**psychological injury**
*see* **psychiatric damage**
**public authorities**
introduction 19.01-19.04
abuse of public office 19.62
breach of statutory duty 19.05, 19.29, 19.51
Britain 19.07-19.10-14
builder-vendors 19.22-19.25
civil liability/rights 19.29, 19.49
common law 19.02, 19.09, 19.11, 19.13
damages 19.22, 19.76
defective premises 13.22-13.47
discretion 19.08-19.15
fitness of premises 13.22-13.47, 13.82
immunity from liability 19.05
loans 19.23-19.34
malice 19.54, 19.62-19.67, 19.71, 19.80-19.81
misfeasance of public office 19.53-19.81
negligence 19.05-19.49
nuisance 19.50
planning legislation 19.35-19.42, 19.43-19.49
proximity/policy approach 19.08, 19.16, 19.21-19.49
public health 19.39
public nuisance 19.43-19.49, 19.50
*Rylands v Fletcher* 19.52
standard of care, test 19.17-19.20
statutory duties and rights 19.02-19.03, 19.28-19.29, 19.51
*Sunderland v Louth County Council* 19.21, 19.35-19.42
third parties 19.05
traffic 19.43-19.49
urban/suburban areas 19.43-19.49
VHI (Voluntary Health Insurance Act 1957) 19.75-19.77
*Ward v McMaster* 19.21-19.34
**public benefit**
breach of statutory duty 21.10-21.18
plea, private nuisance 24.38
**public conscience test**
defences 20.103, 20.103-20.104
**public convenience**
injunctions 45.39-45.40, 45.44
**public duty**
breach of statutory duty 21.12
**public figures**
defamation 34.179-34.190
**public health**
public authorities 19.39
**public houses**
professional negligence 14.206-14.212
**public interest**
business relations 32.43
defamation 34.176-34.177, 34.202-34.204, 34.220
right to privacy 37.46-37.47, 37.54-37.58
**public nuisance**
introduction 24.03-24.04
dangers on highway 24.17-24.18
defences 20.02
extent of liability 24.19-24.23
highways 3.30, 12.39-12.41, 24.13, 34.14-34.19
non-delegable duties 24.19
occupiers' liability 12.39-12.41
particular or special damage 24.05-24.11
personal injury 24.09
planning law 24.10
pollution 24.10-24.11
prescription 24.97-24.102

*public nuisance (contd)*
traffic 19.43-19.49
types of nuisance 24.12-24.13
unreasonableness 24.09
*see also* **nuisance**; **private nuisance**
**public office**
abuse of 19.62
**public policy**
duty of care 6.32, 6.80-6.81, 6.89-6.90
**publicans' licences**
professional negligence 14.206-14.212
**publication**
defamation 34.12-34.29
foreign publications 34.46-34.49
forms of defamation 34.21-34.24
innocent publication 34.113
mechanical distributors 34.115
proof of publication 34.18
**punitive damages**
and exemplary damages 44.26-44.29
*Rookes v Barnard* 44.14, 44.18, 44.26-44.29, 44.37-44.38
*see also* **exemplary damages**
**pupil-teacher**
ratio 16.45
relationship 16.55
trespass to the person 22.102-22.103
**purchaser**
tenant, fitness of premises 13.40, 13.45-13.46
**pure economic loss**
damages 1.116
duty of care 6.02, 6.36, 6.51
economic loss 10.02, 10.10-10.15, 10.158-10.162
employers' liability 18.56, 18.67, 18.71-18.74
products liability 10.158-10.161
**pure nervous shock**
*see* **psychiatric damage**

**qualified privilege** 34.144, 34.160-34.178
circumstantial test 34.183
consent 34.177
duty/interest test 34.183, 34.186
political information 34.184-34.188
privileged occasion 34.186
*see also* **defamation**; **privilege**
**qualitative non-dangerous defect**
manufacturers and producers 6.49
**quantum (or measure)**
causation 2.01, 2.05
***quia timet* injunctions 45.02-45.06, 45.07**

**radio, and defamation 34.22-34.23**
see also **media**
**Rantzen test**
defamation 34.240-34.256, 34.246-34.247, 34.256
**Re Polemis**
defences 20.92
remoteness of damage 3.05, 3.13, 3.16, 3.18, 3.32, 3.42
**reasonable and probable cause**
misuse of process 36.06-36.16
**reasonable care**
employers' liability 18.12, 18.20, 18.71
**reasonable evidence**
*res ipsa loquitur* 9.15
**reasonable foreseeability**
*Hedley Byrne* 35.01
manufacturers' and producers' liability 11.81
*novus actus interveniens* 2.28-2.36
psychiatric damage 17.27, 17.31, 17.41
reasonably foreseeable harm, duty of care 6.25
reasonably unforeseen harm, duty of care 6.29
remoteness of damage 3.03, 3.06-3.19
see also **foreseeability**
**reasonable inference**
proof of negligence 9.03-9.10
**reasonable man test**
medical negligence 14.134, 14.148
right to privacy 37.33
**reasonable person**
standard of care 7.02, 7.03-7.11
**reasonable user**
private nuisance 24.54

**reasonableness of attributing blame**
children 16.03
**recklessness**
*novus actus interveniens* 2.37-2.49
intervenor 2.28-2.36
occupiers' liability 12.33, 12.34-12.38, 12.109
**recoverability**
economic loss 10.13
**recovery**
new torts 1.06
**recreational activities**
occupiers' liability 12.83-12.85
**recreational users**
animals, injuries caused by 27.10
occupiers' liability 12.63-12.65, 12.69, 12.79, 12.86-12.95, 12.95-12.122 *passim*, 16.73-16.84
schools 16.77-16.84
**reflex sympathetic dystrophy syndrome**
medical negligence 14.107-14.110
**reform**
defamation 34.263-34.277
fitness of premises 13.80
insurance claims 1.166-1.192
standard of care 7.24
**Registrar of Friendly Societies**
duty of care 6.56
**registration of business names**
passing off 31.42
**reinstatement damages**
property damage 44.206-44.208
**relationship of injured persons**
psychiatric damage 17.28, 17.59
**release and accord**
concurrent wrongdoers 4.17-4.18
**remarriage**
and fatal injury 42.42-42.66
**remedies**
detinue 29.10
not defeated, liability for fire 26.21-26.22
**remoteness of damage**
introduction 3.01-3.04
big bangs 3.43
causation 2.01, 2.04, 2.23
common law approach 3.03
damages 2.01, 2.04
defamation 34.43
defences 20.92
direct (natural) consequences 3.03, 3.05, 3.06
foreseeability 3.03-3.05
intentional damage 3.04, 3.25
little bangs 3.43
negligence 3.05-3.19, 3.29, 5.06
physical injury 3.17, 3.20-3.23, 3.32-3.36
plaintiffs' impecuniosity 3.32-3.41
psychological injury 3.20, 3.32
*Re Polemis* 3.05, 3.13, 3.16, 3.18, 3.32, 3.42
reasonable foreseeability 3.03, 3.06-3.19
strict torts 3.42
in tort 1.116
trespass 22.04
types of damage 3.20-3.42
  economic 3.20, 3.37-3.41
  egg-shell principle 3.22, 3.32-3.41, 3.43
  foreseeability and remoteness of damages 3.29-3.31
  impecunious plaintiff 3.32-3.41
  intentional damage 3.25
  medical causes 3.22-3.23
  nuisance 3.30
  physical injury 3.17, 3.20-3.23, 3.32-3.36
  psychiatric injury 3.20, 3.32
  unintentional and unforeseeable 3.26-3.28
*Wagon Mound (No 1)* 3.03, 3.06-3.19, 3.25, 3.26, 3.29-3.31, 3.32, 3.35, 3.42, 3.43
**repairers**
liability for defective products 11.13
**replevin**
trespass to goods 28.02
representation of fact
deceit 35.03-35.09
**reputation**
preservation or loss of and defamation 34.08, 34.42, 34.179, 34.185

**requisitions**
professional negligence 14.201-14.205
***res ipsa loquitur***
accidents 9.20-9.38
animals on highways 27.57-27.58
application of the principle 9.15-9.40
causation 2.10, 2.58-2.60, 2.59, 9.49
common sense 9.38
direct evidence 9.43
distribution of loss 1.124
does not apply 9.40
due care, excercise of 9.20
economic realities 9.26
explanations not forthcoming 9.40
former possession 9.18-9.19
*Hanrahan* restatement 9.49-9.53
inconsistencies 9.42
injury, cause of 9.45-9.48, 9.52
instrumentality 9.32
interpretations 9.44
intoxicated persons 9.29-9.32
liability of defendant 9.45, 9.48
management of the defendant 9.17-9.19
medical negligence 9.28
need not be expertly pleaded 9.28, 9.39
negligence 2.57-2.60
and cause of injury 2.10, 9.45-9.48, 9.52
inference of 9.03-9.10
presumption of 9.13
proof of 9.03, 9.11-9.48
*novus actus interveniens* 2.59
nuisance 9.50
onus of proof 9.33, 9.41, 9.45
ordinary circumstances 9.20
origins 9.12-9.14
procedural effect 9.41-9.48
products liability 11.71-11.73, 11.128-11.131
proof 9.03, 9.11-9.48, 9.33, 9.36, 9.41, 9.45
reasonable evidence 9.15
right to control 9.18-9.19
*Rylands v Fletcher* 25.09
social realities 9.26
statistical unlikliehood of accident 9.37
technological changes 9.25
the 'thing' 9.20-9.38
*see also* **negligence**; **proof of negligence**
**rescission**
deceit 35.23
**rescuers**
defences 20.78-20.92
fire, liability for 26.30, 26.34-26.37
**residential areas**
private nuisance 24.42-24.46, 24.56
**restitutio in integrum principle**
damages 44.07-44.08, 44.206
**restitution**
and breach of trust, torts defined 1.117
**retailers**
manufacturers' and producers' liability 11.16-11.20
**retrospection**
manufacturers' and producers' strict liability 11.167-11.169
**right to privacy**
introduction 37.01-37.03
best interests test 37.88
breach of confidence 37.21-37.58
breach of statutory duty 37.20
confidential nature of information 37.23-37.31
criminal law 37.59
death, right to die naturally 37.87-37.88
definition 37.78
immunity 37.54-37.58
injurious falsehood 37.15
intentional infliction of mental suffering 37.10
interest in goods 37.07, 37.07-37.08
limitations 37.77
negligence 37.16-37.19
not absolute 37.87
obligation of confidence 37.32-37.37
private nuisance 37.11-37.14
privilege 37.54-37.58
public interest 37.46-37.47, 37.54
torts relating to privacy 37.04-37.19
trespass to land 37.04-37.06

*right to privacy (contd)*
trespass to the person 37.09
unauthorised use of information 37.23, 37.38-37.58
*see also* **privacy**; **rights**
**right-thinking people**
defamation 34.50, 34.66-34.72 *passim*, 34.105, 34.109
**rights**
and statutory duties 21.01-21.04
civil liability/rights, public authorities 19.29, 19.49
conferred, survival actions on death 41.09
of access, duty of care 6.86
of bodily integrity, constitutional rights 1.38
of entry, trespass to land 23.03-23.21
of free speech, defamation 34.08, 34.179, 34.185
of self-determination, medical negligence 14.82
of way, roads 15.42
to communicate, damages 44.25-44.31
to contribution, concurrent wrongdoers 4.26
to control, *res ipsa loquitur* 9.18-9.19
to possession, conversion 30.20-30.38
to primary education, damages 44.36-44.39
to trial by jury 1.163-1.165
*see also* **right to privacy**; **statutory duties and rights**
**rights of way**
professional negligence 14.226-14.230
**rights-language**
defamation 34.179
**risk**
cost of risk elimination, and standard of care 7.25, 7.44-7.54
defences 20.75, 20.77
economic loss 10.29
employers' liability 18.10-18.11, 18.18, 18.149
medical negligence 14.103-14.104, 14.111-14.114, 14.130-14.134, 14.137, 14.148-14.149
of confusion, passing off 31.08-31.18
**roads, negligence on**
introduction 15.01-15.02
accidents 1.121, 7.12-7.54
behaviour on the highway 15.16-15.57
children 8.19, 15.04-15.15, 15.51-15.52
cyclists 15.37, 15.44
drivers 15.03-15.57 *passim*
driving when blinded 15.23-15.26
duty of the driver 15.03-15.15
emergency vehicles 15.53-15.57
failure to keep a proper look out 15.17-15.22
horn, sounding 15.49-15.52
insurance 1.131
junctions 15.38-15.48, 15.55
loss distribution 1.121
negligence per se 15.23-15.26
non-natural use of property 19.52
*novus actus interveniens* 15.46
nuisance on the highway 24.14-24.18, 24.85-24.92, 24.113-24.121
pedestrians 15.17, 15.27-15.36
planning legislation 19.43-19.49
right of way 15.42
school buses 15.08-15.15, 15.52
seat belt defence 20.34-20.45
traffic accidents 1.121, 44.108
traffic lights 15.47-15.48, 15.55
trespass 23.17-23.21
vicarious liability 43.52, 43.61-43.66
*see also* **drivers**; **highways**; **motor vehicles**
**rolled-up plea**
defamation 34.215-34.217
***Rookes v Barnard***
Irish law 44.16-44.54
appropriate circumstances 44.44-44.48
basic ineffectiveness 44.52
calculating to make a profit 44.10, 44.14
compensatory criterion 44.24, 44.37
constitutional rights 44.24-44.31, 44.36-44.39, 44.40, 44.48
current position 44.49-44.54
damages 44.10-44.54
exclusionary rule 44.43

*Rookes v Barnard (contd)*
exemplary damages 44.10-44.54
aggravated damages 44.31
limited 44.10
punitive damages 44.26-44.29
three considerations 44.34, 44.42
express authorisation 44.10
*Hanrahan* strictures 44.53
limitations 44.19-44.21, 44.41
once and for all award 44.55-44.57
*per incuriam* decision 44.12
phone-tapping 44.26-44.31
reforms recommended 44.57
right to communicate 44.25-44.31
right to primary education 44.36-44.39
scope of the remedy 44.52
servants of the government 44.10, 44.14, 44.33
*see also* **damages**
**roots (tree)**
private nuisance 24.27-24.28
**rural values**
*Rylands v Fletcher* 25.03
***Rylands v Fletcher***
introduction 25.01-25.06
scope 25.07-25.28
accidents 25.22-25.24
act of a stranger 25.35-25.37
act of God 25.38-25.42
animals, injuries caused by 27.08
blameworthiness 25.53
consent of plaintiff 25.30-25.31
default of plaintiff 25.32-25.34, 25.47
defences 25.29-25.44
defendant 25.18, 25.28
electricity 25.16
English decisions 25.26, 25.51-25.54
entitlement to sue 25.25-25.27
escape 25.19-25.24, 25.34, 25.35, 25.38, 25.42
explosives 25.16
gas 25.16
independent contractor 25.36
industrial values 25.03
international developments 25.02
Irish law, future in 25.45-25.55
*Mullan v Forrester* 25.15
natural phenomena 25.38-25.42
non-delegable duty 25.49-25.51
non-natural use 25.05-25.06, 25.07-25.17
occupier/non-occupier 25.26-25.27, 25.36, 25.48-25.49
other accumulations 25.17
personal injury 25.22-25.24
public authorities 19.52
*res ipsa loquitur* 25.09
responsibility 25.49-25.50
rural values 25.03
source of danger on property 25.18
statutory authority 25.43-25.44
strict liability 25.20-25.21, 25.31, 25.34, 25.37, 25.47-25.48
supermarket accidents 25.22-25.24
trees 25.13-25.14
ultra-hazardous activities 25.28
vicarious liability 43.49
walls 25.15
water 25.11-25.12

**safety**
employers' liability 18.24, 18.55, 18.75, 18.78, 18.81-18.94, 18.102, 18.104-18.158
fire, liability for 26.26
manufacturers' and producers liability 11.110-11.114
**safety equipment**
*see* **equipment**
**satisfaction**
concurrent wrongdoers 4.17-4.18
**scandals**
defamation 34.01-34.02
**school buses**
negligence on roads 15.08-15.15, 15.52
**schools**
age of children 16.37-16.39, 16.62
assuming the relationship 16.52
Australia 16.49-16.52, 16.54-16.55
buildings, structural dangers 16.70-16.84
Canada 16.56

*schools (contd)*
dogs 16.58-16.60
duty of care 16.50, 16.54-16.55
escapees 16.67
fitness of premises 16.70-16.84
football 16.25, 16.80-16.84
gymnastic exercise 16.19-16.20
*Hedley Byrne* principle 16.52
motor vehicles 16.65-16.67
negligence
child care 16.16-16.84
in instruction 16.18, 16.19-16.25, 16.69
injuries off school's premises 16.18, 16.65-16.67
other acts of negligence 16.18, 16.68-16.69
supervision in school playgrounds 16.18, 16.26-16.45, 16.45-16.50, 16.52
supervision outside school hours 16.46-16.64
nursery schools 16.66-16.67
occupiers' liability 16.70-16.84
official day 16.60
parents 16.64
primary schools 16.61-16.63
recreational users 16.77-16.84
student-teacher ratio 16.45
teacher-pupil relationship 16.55
teachers, trespass to the person 22.102-22.103
trespassers 16.83-16.84
visitors 16.73-16.84
younger children 16.28, 16.33-16.44, 16.46-16.48, 16.62, 16.66-16.67
*see also* **children**; **families**; **family relations**; **minors**
***scienter* principle**
animals 27.15-27.26, 27.29, 27.51
**scientific authority**
manufacturers' and producers' liability 11.68-11.69, 11.136, 11.142-11.143
technological change and innovation 9.25, 37.05
**Scotland**
business relations 32.05, 32.09
manufacturers' and producers' liability 11.156
**search**
trespass to land 23.04-23.06, 23.12-23.13
**seat belts**
motor vehicles 15.56, 20.34-20.45
**secondary meaning of name**
passing off 31.53
**secondary victims**
psychiatric damage 17.08
**secret ballot**
picketing 32.172, 32.176-32.185
**security firm employees**
employers' liability 18.133-18.145
**seduction**
family relations 33.24-33.26
**seizure of goods**
trespass to goods 28.14-28.16
**self-defence**
occupiers' liability 12.140
trespass to the person 22.86-22.89
vicarious liability 43.41
**self-insurers**
compensation schemes 1.128
**self-preservation**
defences 20.19
**self-regulatory measures**
fitness of premises 13.77-13.79
**serious question test 45.09, 45.10-45.36**
*Campus Oil* principles 45.22, 45.26
defamation proceedings 45.12-45.36
ex parte injunction 45.19
freedom of expression 45.20, 45.28
injunctions 45.09, 45.10-45.36
interlocutory injunctions not granted 45.32-45.34
justification, plea of 45.26, 45.28-45.29, 45.32-45.36
libel 45.14-45.16
merits investigated 45.32-45.34
prima facie case 45.10
probability of success 45.10
risk of death 45.21, 45.23, 45.28
strength of plaintiff's case 45.14-45.31
strong prima facie case 45.10
without doubt defamatory 45.30-45.31
*see also* **injunctions**

**servants**
business relations 32.3-32.12
of the government, damages 44.10, 44.14, 44.33
**service relationship**
family relations 33.24, 33.36-33.39
**services**
passing off 31.01
**set-off claims**
defences 20.56
**several concurrent tortfeasors**
concurrent wrongdoers 4.05
**several independent tortfeasors**
concurrent wrongdoers 4.05
**several tortfeasors**
concurrent wrongdoers 4.01, 4.01-4.02
**sexual assault**
right to privacy 37.55-37.56
**sexual harassment**
employers' liability 18.80
**shareholders**
*Hedley Byrne* principle 10.67-10.71
**sick pay**
damages 44.129
**simple conspiracy**
business relations 32.63, 32.70-32.73
**slander**
actionable *per se* 34.28-34.29, 34.30-34.49
criminal offence punishable by death or imprisonment 34.38-34.39
libel/slander distinction
abolition of distinction 34.265
common law courts 34.25, 34.28
ecclesiastical courts 34.25
historical origins 34.25-34.29
Star Chamber 34.26-34.28
of title, and deceit 35.26
of women 34.32
proof of special damage 34.28-34.29
repetition of 34.44
special damage 34.30, 34.42-34.45
vulgar abuse 34.87
*see also* **deceit**; **defamation**; **libel**
**sleeping torts**
limitations 46.62
**social contexts and policies**
duty of care 6.55, 6.67
economy and private nuisance 24.37
employers' liability 18.24, 18.57, 18.165
*res ipsa loquitur* 9.26
standard of care 7.07-7.11, 7.25, 7.38-7.43
torts 1.02-1.03
**social welfare payments**
damages 44.113
**solicitors**
accidents 14.182-14.193
advice 14.176-14.180
as advocate 14.199
building societies 14.219-14.223
buying and selling property 14.200-14.231
change of use of premises 14.217
choice of court 14.181-14.194
Circuit Court judgments 14.182-14.188
claims for loss of earnings 14.184-14.187, 14.191-14.192
conflict of interest 14.226-14.231
cross-examination of witnesses 14.196
defects of property 14.221-14.225
duty of care 14.169-14.174
immunity 14.199
liaising with counsel 14.195-14.198
liquor licences 14.206-14.216
medical evidence 14.186, 14.188, 14.190, 14.193-14.194
negligence in litigation 14.180-14.199
neighbour principle 14.169
professional negligence 14.169-14.231
property/premises 14.201-14.204, 14.216-14.225, 14.226-14.230
proximity 14.174
requisitions 14.201-14.205
rights of way 14.226-14.230
selection of counsel 14.197-14.198
solicitors' negligence and medical negligence 14.231
standard of care 14.174-14.231
surveys 14.220-14.225
tortious right of action 14.169-14.174
*see also* **professional negligence**

**source of danger on property**
*Rylands v Fletcher* 25.18
**special damage**
defamation 34.25, 34.28, 34.30, 34.42-34.45
**special damages 44.05**
**special facts**
defamation 34.112
**special relationship**
deceit 35.01
**specialists**
medical negligence 14.30
**specific factors**
in assessing standard of care 7.25-7.54
**sports garments**
passing off 31.11-31.13, 31.36-31.39, 31.54
**spouses**
communication between, and defamation 34.16-34.17, 34.159
of injured victim, and damages 44.109-44.111
**staff**
*see* **employee**; **employers' liability**
**standard of care**
introduction 7.01-7.02
accidents 7.13-7.20, 7.24, 7.27-7.34
conduct of defendant 7.21, 7.38-7.43
dangerous avocations 7.52
employment 7.51-7.54
epilepsy 7.17, 7.22
forgetfulness 7.09-7.10
is and ought 7.06
juries 7.06
knowledge 7.07-7.11
medical negligence 14.09-14.16
mentally disabled persons 7.23-7.25
negligence 5.04, 7.31-7.37
negligent conduct, specific factors in assessing 7.25-7.54
occupiers' liability 7.30, 12.49
physical capacities 7.12-7.54
physically disabled persons 7.12-7.14
professional negligence 14.174-14.231
public authorities, tests 19.17-19.20
reasonable person 7.02, 7.03-7.11
reform of liability 7.24
social policy 7.05-7.11, 7.43
specific factors in assessing 7.25-7.54
tests 7.24, 19.17-19.20
unreasonable conduct 7.26
*see also* **duty of care**
**standard requirements**
manufacturers' and producers' liability 11.45-11.46, 11.55, 11.70, 11.114
**standards of behaviour**
*Hedley Byrne* principle 10.149
**Star Chamber**
libel/slander distinction 34.26-34.28
**Stardust tragedy**
liability for fire 1.181, 1.183, 1.186, 26.26
**state**
businesses not trading in, and passing off 31.57-31.60
communications and defamation 34.158
compensation 1.107-1.108, 1.181-1.192
damages against, 1.16
insurance 1.107, 1.128-1.136, 1.144
status and constitutional rights, 1.77
*see also* **state, liability of**
**state, liability of**
introduction 38.01-38.12
accidents 38.17
act of state 38.13-38.14
*Byrne* decision 38.03-38.06, 38.11
diplomatic immunity 38.15-38.17
European communities 38.22
foreign sovereigns 38.18-38.21
immunity 38.01, 38.03, 38.07, 38.09, 38.14, 38.21
international conventions 38.15
legislative limitation 38.12
limitations on 38.18-38.21
ministers liable 38.03-38.06
not always liable 38.09-38.10
*Pinochet* case 38.19
servants of the state identified 38.11
welfare state 38.02
*see also* **state**

**statements**
context of statement 34.86-34.88
prima facie defamatory or innocent 34.89
privileged, subject to, or without, explanation or contradiction 34.191-34.192
proof of truth of statement 34.124-34.126, 34.130-34.132
*see also* **defamation**; **privilege**
**statistical unlikliehood of accident**
*res ipsa loquitur* 9.37
**statutory authority**
*Rylands v Fletcher* 25.43-25.44
**statutory duties and rights**
introduction 21.02
breach of statutory duty 21.05-21.61
defamation 34.169-34.173
defences 20.50, 21.74
dependants and fatal injury 42.06-42.66
duties, and corresponding rights 1.14
fitness of premises 13.22-13.46, 13.22-13.47, 13.68
guardianship of children 21.62-21.74
interference with statutory rights 21.62-21.74
occupiers' liability 12.57
public authorities 19.02-19.03, 19.28-19.29, 19.51
ranges of conduct 21.70-21.74
trespass to land 23.07-23.21
*see also* **breach of statutory duty**; **rights**
**statutory interpretation**
breach of statutory duty 21.20
**statutory misrepresentation**
*Hedley Byrne* principle 10.155-10.157
**statutory privilege**
defamation 34.145
**statutory rights**
*see* **statutory duties and rights**
**strangers to contracts**
occupiers' liability 12.131-12.135
**strict liability, new European regime** 11.02, 11.91-11.175
preparation of directive 11.92-11.93
award for pain and suffering 11.123
cap on damages 11.170, 11.172-11.173
circulation of product 11.136-11.138, 11.143-11.144, 11.169
concurrent wrongdoers 11.164-11.166
consumer 11.122-11.125, 11.174
contracting out prohibited 11.161-11.163
contributory negligence 11.158-11.160
damage, scope of 11.127-11.135
defective products 11.108-11.116, 11.133, 11.139
defences 11.136-11.146
design of products 11.145-11.146
development risks defence 11.142, 11.170, 11.171
EEC Directive on Product Liability 1985 1.121, 11.02-11.03, 11.91-11.175
extinction of liability 11.147-11.157
immovables (land) 11.100
imported products 11.106
limitation period and extinction of liability 11.147-11.157
long stop provision 11.149
mandatory regulations 11.136, 11.141
misuse 11.112
movables 11.100
non-commercial producer 11.136, 11.140
opt-ins and opt-outs 11.170-11.175
primary agricultural products 11.174-11.175
producer liable 11.96-11.98
producer, who is a producer 11.102-11.116
products and producers 11.99-11.101, 11.102-11.116, 11.136-11.146
proof and causation 11.127-11.135
property damage 11.124
raw material 11.146
retrospection 11.167-11.169
safety 11.110-11.114, 21.61
scope of damage 11.117-11.126
ten-year cut-off 11.149-11.155
third party 11.98, 11.164-11.165
time factor 11.112-11.115
tort law reforms 1.121-1.137
*see also* **manufacturers' and producers' liability for defective products**

**strict liability**
*Rylands v Fletcher* 25.20-25.21, 25.31, 25.34, 25.37, 25.47-25.48
**strict liability safety standards**
breach of statutory duty 21.61
**strict torts**
remoteness of damage 3.42
**strikes**
business relations 32.37-32.40, 32.51
**structural dangers**
school buildings 16.70-16.84
**structures**
*see* **buildings**
**student-teacher**
ratio 16.45
relationships 16.55
trespass to the person 22.102-22.103
**subjective test**
standard of care 7.24
**substantial certainty**
trespass to the person 22.07
**suburban/urban areas** 19.43-19.49, 24.37-24.48
**suicide**
right to privacy 37.83
**suits**
corporations, partnership, unincorporated bodies and trade unions 39.01-39.32
where to sue and for what damages, defamation 34.46-34.49
who may be sued
private nuisance 24.72-24.73
survival actions on death 41.12
who may sue
fatal injury 42.01, 42.07-42.11
joint and several tortfeasors 4.06
private nuisance 24.59-24.72, 37.13
*Rylands v Fletcher* 25.25-25.27
survival actions on death 41.12
**supermarkets**
accidents in, *Rylands v Fletcher* 25.22-25.24
**supervening event**
*novus actus interveniens* 2.48
**supervision**
in school playgrounds 16.18, 16.26-16.45, 16.45-16.50, 16.52
outside school hours 16.46-16.64
**suppliers**
defective products 11.15, 11.21-11.26, 11.108-11.117
**surgery**
limitations 46.31-46.34
medical negligence 14.100, 14.105, 14.107-14.114, 14.119-14.121
**surveyors**
fitness of premises 13.81-13.82
**surveys**
passing off 31.19-31.27
professional negligence 14.220-14.225
**survival actions on death** 41.01-41.12
introduction 41.01-41.12
action against the defendant 41.06
amendments to law 41.04
causes of action 41.04, 41.10
common law 41.02
damages 41.05-41.06, 41.08, 41.12
exemplary damages 40.05
limitations 41.09, 41.11
personal loss 41.05
personal representative of defendant's estate 41.11
right to privacy 41.05-41.06, 41.08, 41.12
right to sue or be sued 41.12
rights conferred 41.09
statutory exceptions 41.03
trespass to real or personal property 41.03
wrongful killing 41.07

**taking possession**
conversion 30.02-30.03
**tariff**
of £150.000, damages 44.146-44.164
raised to £250, damages 44.165-44.171
**taxation**
damages 44.101-44.106
fatal injury 42.32-42.36
right to privacy 37.64

**teacher-student**
ratio 16.45
relationship 16.55
trespass to the person 22.102-22.103
**teaching**
negligence in instruction 16.18, 16.19-16.25, 16.69
**technological change and innovation**
*res ipsa loquitur* 9.25
right to privacy 37.05
scientific authority 11.68-11.69, 11.136, 11.142-11.143
**telephone tapping**
right to privacy 37.92-37.97
**television and defamation** 32.22-32.23, 34.47-34.48
*see also* **defamation**; **media**
**temporary employer**
employers' liability 18.35
**ten-year cut-off**
manufacturers' and producers' liability 11.149-11.155
**tenants**
breach of statutory duty 21.12
fitness of premises 13.28-13.29, 13.32-13.40, 13.43-13.46
tenant purchaser 13.40, 13.45-13.46
**therapeutic privilege**
medical negligence 14.136
**'thing', the, *res ipsa loquitur* 9.20-9.38**
**third party**
affirmative duties 8.07
business relations 32.25, 32.32-32.33
causation 2.47
communication to and defamation 34.12-34.15
contracts 1.111
contractual relations 32.25, 32.32-32.33
damages 44.94
economic loss, claims for 10.40
*Hedley Byrne* principle 10.58, 10.62, 10.71, 10.132
insurance 1.127, 1.142, 1.148
liability, duty of care 6.42-6.45
manufacturers' and producers' strict liability 11.98, 11.164-11.165
*novus actus interveniens* 2.27, 2.43, 2.50
premises, employers' liability 18.91
public authorities 19.05
right to privacy 37.34
trespass to the person 22.90-22.91
**threat**
business relations 32.48, 32.56
**three step test**
duty of care 6.33, 6.87
**three year post-accrual period**
limitations 46.22, 46.40, 46.43
**time factor**
manufacturers' and producers' liability 11.113-11.115
**title**
extinction of, conversion and detinue 46.85-46.86
of the plaintiff, trespass to goods 28.10
**tortious liability 1.109-1.116**
**torts**
overview of law 1.01-1.192
definitions of tort 1.02, 1.104-1.120
function of the law of tort 1.01-1.03
animals, injuries caused by 27.03-27.14
basic effectiveness 1.72-1.76
battery 22.11-22.14
breach of contract v tort 1.109-1.116
business relations, interference with another's interests 32.83-32.86
compensation schemes and insurance 1.126-1.137
concurrent wrongdoers, torts are separate 4.05
constitutional rights 1.14-1.16, 1.36, 1.61-1.65, 1.66-1.71, 1.77-1.79
conversion 37.07, 37.22
criminal law 1.107
dangerous defects, fitness of premises 13.12-13.47
defamation 34.10-34.11
defendant, freedom of action 1.02
detinue 20.01

*torts (contd)*
employee, crimes of 43.03, 43.12, 43.15-43.53
European Community 1.84-1.103
independent contractor 43.49-43.53
innominate torts 1.83
insurance, and other schemes of compensation 1.126-1.154, 1.166-1.192 *passim*
interest in goods, right of privacy 37.07-37.08
interpersonal conflicts 1.01
intimidation 32.46-32.57
Irish litigation 1.155-1.165
joint and several liability 4.07
limitation on right to damages 1.22-1.32, 1.99
*McDonnell v Ireland*, 1.48-1.59
mentally ill persons 40.38, 40.40
*Meskell* principle 1.14, 1.31, 1.39, 1.48-1.59, 1.61, 1.65, 1.66, 1.81-1.82
negligence to strict liability 1.121-1.125
passing off, scope of the tort 31.05-31.60
plaintiff's interest in security 1.02
products liability 11.96, 11.98
public authorities 19.01
recognised interests 1.04-1.08
reform proposals 1.166-1.192
restitution, and breach of trust 1.117
tortious liability 1.109-1.116
tortious right of action, and professional negligence 14.169-14.174
trespass to goods 23.03-23.18
uninsured drivers 1.138-1.154
unintentional torts 3.04
unliquidated damages 1.118-1.120
*W v Ireland* 1.33-1.47
wrongful interference with constitutional rights 1.09-1.83

**trade description offences**
damages 44.137-44.142

**trade disputes**
introduction 32.87-32.88
*bona fide* trade dispute 32.96-32.98
breach of contract of employment 32.122-32.126
concept of a dispute 32.99-32.100
conspiracy, immunity from liability 32.116-32.121
constitutional aspects 32.111, 32.128-32.142
contract of employment 32.122-32.126
definitions 32.91-32.100, 32.112-32.113
dismissals 32.101-32.105
empirical or rational order 32.99-32.100
employer defined 32.92
employment or non-employment 32.101-32.107
fair case test 32.183
genuineness of the dispute 32.96
immunities 32.114-32.125, 32.122-32.126, 32.143-32.144
inducing 32.122-32.126
industrial action and strike, defined 32.112-32.113
Industrial Relations Act 1990 32.89-32.125, 32.147
limited immunity from liability for trade unions 32.126-32.185
*Meskell* principle 32.130-32.140
no immunity for certain actions 32.127
no recognisable tort 32.130
non-employment 32.101-32.107
peaceful persuasion 32.158-32.161
peacefully obtaining or communicating information 32.149-32.157
picketing 32.145-32.165, 32.168-32.170
place, approaches to 32.165
primary picketing 32.162-32.167
protection from suit limited 32.127
race or nationality of employers 32.157
recommendation to trade elsewhere 32.154
redundancy payments 32.104
refusal to employ 32.105, 32.183
secondary picketing 32.162, 32.168-32.170
secret ballot 32.172, 32.176-32.185
status of dispute between employer and trade union 32.107-32.110
strike and industrial action 32.112-32.113

*trade disputes (contd)*
threatening to break 32.122-32.126
torts, particular torts, damages claims 32.133-32.136
trade dispute with a trade union 32.107-32.110
trade union officials 32.127, 32.171
trespass to land 32.166
worker defined 32.93
*see also* **business relations, torts affecting**; **immunity**; **picketing**; **trade unions**
**trade marks/names**
passing off 31.01, 31.10-31.18, 31.30-31.35, 31.41
**trade unions 39.26-39.32**
business relations 32.16-32.18, 32.24, 32.34-32.40, 32.64-32.69
defamation 39.30
immunity 39.31, 39.32
registered and unregistered 39.26
separate legal personality 39.27-39.30
*see also* **corporations**; **partnerships**; **trade disputes**; **unincorporated associations**
**traders**
passing off 31.01-31.82
**traffic**
public authorities 19.43-19.49
**traffic lights**
negligence on roads 15.47-15.48, 15.55
**transfer by gift**
manufacturers' and producers' liability 11.61
**transferred intent**
trespass to the person 22.05-22.09
**travellers**
injunctions 45.41
private nuisance 24.80-24.84
**treatment**
medical negligence 14.28-14.29, 14.56-14.72, 14.73-14.75
problems arising from 14.152-14.160
without informed consent 14.77-14.81
**trees**
private nuisance 24.16-24.32, 24.87-24.88
*Rylands v Fletcher* 25.13-25.14
**trespass**
animals, liability for injuries caused by 27.07, 27.10, 27.32
minors 22.74-22.85, 40.02, 40.35
to real or personal property 41.03
to the person 22.74-22.85
**trespass against the person 22.10-22.58**
apprehension 22.22, 22.24
assault 22.20-22.27
battery 22.03, 22.11-22.19
confinement 22.37-22.38, 22.58
contact results from defendant's act 22.15
continuance of imprisonment 22.39-22.44
disposition of defendant 22.16-22.19
failure to release 22.47-22.57
false imprisonment 22.35-22.57
harrassment 22.23
infliction of emotional suffering 22.28-22.34
non-fatal offences against the person 22.32, 22.74, 22.80, 22.104
physical and psychological imprisonment 22.40
*Wilkinson v Downton* principle 22.33-22.34
**trespass to goods**
introduction 28.01-28.02
actionable *per se* 28.07-28.09
character of defendant's conduct 28.13
chattels 28.13-28.14
conversion 28.02
*de bonis asportasis* 28.02
defence of property 22.114
detinue 28.02
direct/indirect interference 28.04, 28.06
interference 28.04-28.06, 28.13
lawful authority 28.14-28.18
mentally ill persons 40.41-40.44
occupier's liability and motor vehicles 12.38
onus of proof 28.12
possession 28.10
protection of privacy 28.09

*trespass to goods (contd)*
replevin 28.02
right to privacy 37.07
seizure of goods 28.14-28.16
survival actions on death 41.03
title of the plaintiff 28.10
tort, elements of 23.03-23.18
trespass to land 28.10
trover 28.02

**trespass to land**
introduction 23.01
*ab initio*, doctrine of 23.23-23.26
above and below surface of land 23.39-23.40
abuse of rights of 23.14-23.21
actionable *per se* 23.33
animals 27.07, 27.10, 27.32, 27.42-27.48
common law 23.06
consent 23.48
constitutional law 23.03-23.05
continuing trespass 23.34-23.36
conversion 30.25-30.38
defences 20.61, 23.47-23.51
defendant's state of mind 23.37-23.40
Derrynaflan Hoard 30.25-30.38
entry 23.02-23.21
forcible entry 23.03
Garda Síochána, powers of 23.07
highway 23.17-23.21
interference 23.30-23.32, 23.41-23.46
mentally ill persons 40.41-40.44
misfeasance, positive 23.24
necessity 23.50-23.51
picketing 23.19-23.21
placing things on land 23.29-23.36
remaining on land 23.22-23.28
right of entry 23.04-23.21
right to privacy 37.04-37.06
rights, constitutional, common law, statutory 23.03-23.13
search 23.04-23.06, 23.12-23.13
statutory rights 23.07-23.21
trespass to goods 28.10

**trespass to the person**
introduction 22.01-22.09
defences 22.59-22.122
arrest without warrant 22.106
compulsory protective custody 22.112
consent to physical contact 22.59-22.87
consent vitiated by fraud, duress or illegality 22.65-22.67
corporal punishment 22.113
defence of property 22.114-22.122
discipline of children 22.93-22.104
excess of consent 22.64
failure to obtain consent 22.71
felony and misdemeanor 22.106
Garda Síochána, powers of 22.105-22.113
guardianship 22.76, 22.83-22.85
illegality 22.65-22.67
*inclusio unius est exclusio alterius* rule 22.82
lawful authority 22.105-22.113
medical negligence 14.88
medical procedures 22.68-22.73
mentally ill persons 40.41-40.44
minors 22.74-22.85
necessity 22.92
powers of arrest 22.105-22.110
property 22.114
right to privacy 37.09
schoolteachers 22.102-22.103
self defence 22.86-22.89
third person 22.90-22.91
voluntariness, intention and motive 22.05-22.09
wardship proceedings 22.84

**trespassers**
animals, liability for injuries caused by 27.07, 27.10, 27.32
conversion 30.25-30.38
duty of care 6.38, 6.53, 6.55
frequent trespassers 12.26
new approach to trespassers 1974-1995 12.42-12.55
occupiers' liability 12.01, 12.06, 12.16-12.58, 12.26, 12.60, 12.63, 12.96, 12.97-12.108, 12.126, 16.83-16.84
schools 16.83-16.84
trespassers identified 12.96
*see also* **occupiers' liability**

**tribunals**
personal injury 1.174, 1.181-1.192
**trover**
trespass to goods 28.02
**trust**
breach of, and restitution 1.117
**two-step**
duty of care 6.05, 6.15, 6.19, 6.20, 6.23, 6.30, 6.35, 6.40, 6.78
*Hedley Byrne* principle 10.77
manufacturers' and producers' liability 11.76
negligence 6.78
physical injury 6.40
producers liability 11.76

***ubi jus, ibi remedium*** **principle**
statutory duties 21.67
**ultimate negligence**
defences 20.04-20.07
**ultra vires**
misfeasance of public office 19.56, 19.67
**ultra-hazardous activities**
*Rylands v Fletcher* 25.28
**unauthorised use of information**
*see* **information, unauthorised use of**
**undue delay**
limitations 46.53-46.66
**unfair competition**
passing off 31.77
**unforeseeability**
duty of care 6.29
psychiatric response 17.08
*see also* **foreseeability**
**unincorporated associations** 39.10-39.25
immunity from suit 39.25
legal personality 39.11
procedural problems 39.10
suits 39.12-39.25
*see also* **corporations**; **partnerships**; **trade unions**
**unintended injuries**
trespass to the person 22.01
**unintentional and unforeseeable damage** 3.25, 3.26-3.28
**unintentional torts**
remoteness of damage 3.04
**United States**
affirmative duties 8.06
breach of statutory duty 21.24
business relations 32.05, 32.09
constitution 1.14
fatal injury 42.03, 42.13
limitations 46.06
manufacturers' and producers' liability 11.09, 11.159
medical negligence 14.144, 14.159
mentally disabled persons and standard of care 7.24
minors 40.10, 40.26
privilege and defamation 34.180
professional negligence 14.164
right to privacy 37.02, 37.56
trespass to the person 22.17, 22.23
unfair competition, passing off 31.77
*see also* **North America**
**unlawful act**
business relations 32.49-32.53
**unlawful means conspiracy**
business relations 32.63, 32.74-32.82
**unliquidated damages**
torts defined 1.118-1.120
**unmarried couples**
family relations 33.20-33.21
**unreasonable conduct**
standard of care 7.26
**unreasonableness**
public nuisance 24.09
**urban/suburban areas 19.43-19.49, 24.37-24.48**
**urology**
medical negligence 14.68-14.72

**vaccines**
compensation payments 1.187-1.188
manufacturers' and producers' liability 11.63-11.70

**value as assessed**
detinue 29.10, 29.11, 29.12-29.17
**value of article**
conversion 30.41-30.44
**vasectomy**
medical negligence 14.86-14.92
**vehicles**
*see* **motor vehicles**
**vendor**
and lessor
activity duty 13.17
dangerous defects 13.12-13.47
defects created after demise 13.17
defects of quality 13.03-13.11
lessor's liability as occupier 13.18-13.19
liability in negligence 13.05, 13.22-13.47
liability in nuisance 13.20-13.21
public authority's liability in negligence 13.22-13.47
fitness of premises 13.01, 13.03-13.47, 13.57-13.82
manufacturers' and producers' liability 11.78, 11.79, 11.82, 11.100
public authorities 19.22-19.34
*see also* **builder/vendor and builder/lessor**; **fitness of premises**
**VHI (Voluntary Health Insurance Act 1957)** 19.75-19.77
**vicarious benefit**
duty of care 6.55
**vicarious liability**
introduction 43.01-43.09
common employment doctrine 18.02, 43.69
corporations 39.06-39.08
the deep pocket 43.02, 43.61
employers' liability for employees torts 43.03, 43.12, 43.15-43.53
families 43.57, 43.67-43.68
firm's liability for partner's wrongs 43.54-43.60
*Hedley Byrne* principle 43.56, 43.60
mechanically propelled vehicles 43.61-43.66
partnerships 43.57-43.60
personal liability 43.12-43.14, 43.49
roads 43.52, 43.61-43.66
*see also* **employee**; **employer**; **employer/employee relationship**; **employers' liability**
**vicarious responsibility**
family relations 33.38
**victim**
carers of injured victim and damages 44.109-44.111
consortium and family relations 33.16
rights of, compensation 1.136-1.137
secondary, psychiatric damage 17.08
victim's response and damages 44.174-44.175
**Vienna conventions**
diplomatic immunity 38.15
**violent acts**
by employee, vicarious liability 43.39-43.41
**violent crimes**
state compensation for 1.107
**visitors**
affirmative duties 8.31
fitness of premises 13.18
injuries caused by animals 27.10
occupiers' liability 12.63, 12.78-12.82, 12.94, 12.123-12.130, 16.73-16.84
**volenti non fit injuria**
*see* **voluntary assumption of risk**
**voluntariness**
intention and motive, trespass to the person 22.05-22.09
**voluntary acts**
causation 2.19, 2.43, 2.47
mentally ill persons 40.42
**voluntary assumption of risk**
defences 20.01, 20.03, 20.61-20.92, 20.64-20.65, 20.98-20.100
duty of care 6.67
employers' liability 18.02, 18.23, 18.159-18.165
fire, liability for 26.35
negligence 5.09

**voluntary benefits**
fatal injury 42.54, 42.58
**voluntary human act**
causation 2.19, 2.43, 2.47
**voluntary payments**
damages 44.122-44.126
**voluntary schemes**
fitness of premises 13.77-13.79
**vulgar abuse**
defamation 34.85-34.88, 34.87

***W v Ireland***
torts 1.33-1.47
***Wagon Mound (No 1)***
duty of care 6.29
employers' liability 18.148
remoteness of damage 3.03, 3.06-3.19, 3.25, 3.26, 3.29-3.31, 3.32, 3.35, 3.42, 3.43
defences 20.92
**walls**
*Rylands v Fletcher* 25.15
**wardship proceedings**
trespass to the person 22.84
**warning**
failure to warn, affirmative duties 8.05
*see also* **duty to warn**
warrant
arrest without, and trespass to the person 22.106
**warranties**
fitness of premises 13.11, 13.27-13.29, 13.44-13.46
**water**
on property, private nuisance 24.51-24.53
*Rylands v Fletcher* 25.11-25.12
**weights**
lifting and employers' liability 18.111-18.124
**welfare payments**
state compensation 1.126
**welfare state**
state liability 38.02
**whooping cough vaccines**
compensation payments 1.187-1.188
manufacturers' duty to warn 11.63-11.67
**widows/widowers**
fatal injury 42.43-42.47, 42.53
**wild animals**
liability for injuries caused by 27.16, 27.23
**Wilkinson v. Downton principle**
trespass against the person 22.33-22.34
**wills**
*Hedley Byrne* principle 10.73-10.76
**witnesses**
defamation 34.150-34.154
professional negligence 14.196
**wives**
family relations 33.04-33.05, 33.14-33.15
fatal injury 42.46-42.48, 42.59-42.62, 42.65-42.66
**women**
defamation 34.32
fatal injury 42.46-42.48, 42.59-42.62, 42.64-42.66
**work accidents**
defences 20.62
women, fatal injury 42.48, 42.64-42.66
**wrongful interference with constitutional rights** 1.09-1.83
**wrongful invasion**
passing off 31.76
**wrongful killing**
survival actions on death 41.07
**wrongful procurement**
business relations 32.28-32.40